CODE OF VIRGINIA
1950

With Provision for Subsequent Pocket Parts

ANNOTATED

Prepared under the Supervision of
The Virginia Code Commission

BY

The Editorial Staff of the Publishers

VOLUME 2

2000 REPLACEMENT VOLUME

(Including Acts of the 2000 Regular Session and annotations taken from South Eastern Reporter, 2d series, through Volume 525, page 77.)

LEXIS Publishing™

LEXIS®·NEXIS® · MARTINDALE-HUBBELL®
MATTHEW BENDER® · MICHIE™ · SHEPARD'S®

LEXIS, NEXIS, *Shepard's* and Martindale-Hubbell are registered trademarks, LEXIS Publishing and MICHIE are trademarks, and *lexis.com* is a service mark of Reed Elsevier Properties Inc., used under license. Matthew Bender is a registered trademark of Matthew Bender Properties Inc.

© 2000 by Matthew Bender & Company, Inc.,
one of the LEXIS Publishing™ companies.
All rights reserved.

P.O. Box 7587, Charlottesville, VA 22906-7587

4902111

ISBN 0-327-13074-1

www.lexis.com

Customer Service: 1-800-446-3410

Scope of Annotations

The annotations of this 2000 Replacement Volume 2 include decisions reported through:

South Eastern Reporter, 2nd Series, through Volume 525, p. 77.
Supreme Court Reporter, through Volume 120, p. 1290.
Federal Reporter, 3rd Series, through Volume 203, p. 842.
Federal Supplement, 2nd Series, through Volume 82, p. 1386.
Federal Rules Decisions, through Volume 190, p. 637.
Bankruptcy Reporter, through Volume 244, p. 884.
Virginia Law Review, through Volume 86, p. 162.
Washington and Lee Law Review, through Volume 56, p. 1124.
William and Mary Law Review, through Volume 41, p. 384.
University of Richmond Law Review, through Volume 33, p. 1272.
George Mason University Law Review, through Volume 8, p. 429.

Unpublished Opinions of Court of Appeals

Some of the annotations contained in this supplement are derived from unpublished opinions of the Court of Appeals of Virginia. These opinions will not appear in the Court of Appeals Reports or any other court reporter. The unpublished opinions can be identified by their citation, which gives the parties' names, a case number, "Ct. of Appeals," and a date.

The Court of Appeals has placed the following footnote on all unpublished opinions: "Pursuant to Code § 17.1-413, recodifying § 17-116.010, this opinion is not designated for publication."

"Although an unpublished opinion of the Court has no precedential value, a court or commission does not err by considering the rationale and adopting it to the extent it is persuasive." Fairfax County School Board v. Rose, 29 Va. 32, 509 S.E.2d 525 (Va. App. 1999).

A copy of the full text of any unpublished opinion can be obtained by contacting: Court of Appeals of Virginia, Attention: Clerk's Assistant (Opinions), 109 North Eighth Street, Richmond, Virginia 23219.

User's Guide

In order to assist both the legal profession and the lay person in obtaining the maximum benefit from the Code of Virginia, a User's Guide has been included in Volume 1. This guide contains comments and information on the many features found within the Code of Virginia intended to increase the usefulness of this set of laws to the user. See Volume 1 for the complete User's Guide.

Suggestions, comments, or questions about the Code of Virginia or this Cumulative Supplement are welcome. You may call us toll free at (800) 446-3410, fax us toll free at (800) 643-1280, email us at LLP.Customer.Support@Lexis-Nexis.com, or write Code of Virginia Editor, Lexis Publishing, P.O. Box 7587, Charlottesville, Virginia 22906-7587.

For an online bookstore, technical and customer support, and other company information, visit Lexis Publishing's Internet home page at **http://www.lexis.com.**

Table of Titles

TITLE
1. General Provisions.
2. Administration of the Government Generally [Repealed].
2.1. Administration of the Government Generally.
3. Agriculture, Horticulture and Food [Repealed].
3.1. Agriculture, Horticulture and Food.
4. Alcoholic Beverages and Industrial Alcohol [Repealed].
4.1. Alcoholic Beverage Control Act.
5. Aviation [Repealed].
5.1. Aviation.
6. Banking and Finance [Repealed].
6.1. Banking and Finance.
7. Boundaries, Jurisdiction and Emblems of the Commonwealth [Repealed].
7.1. Boundaries, Jurisdiction and Emblems of the Commonwealth.
8. Civil Remedies and Procedure; Evidence Generally [Repealed].
8.01. Civil Remedies and Procedure.
8.1. Commercial Code — General Provisions.
8.2. Commercial Code — Sales.
8.2A. Commercial Code — Leases.
8.3. Commercial Code — Commercial Paper [Repealed].
8.3A. Commercial Code — Negotiable Instruments.
8.4. Commercial Code — Bank Deposits and Collections.
8.4A. Commercial Code — Funds Transfers.
8.5. Commercial Code — Letters of Credit [Repealed].
8.5A. Commercial Code — Letters of Credit.
8.6. Commercial Code — Bulk Transfers [Repealed].
8.6A. Commercial Code — Bulk Transfers.
8.7. Commercial Code — Warehouse Receipts, Bills of Lading and Other Documents of Title.
8.8. Commercial Code — Investment Securities [Repealed].
8.8A. Commercial Code — Investment Securities.
8.9. Commercial Code — Secured Transactions; Sales of Accounts, Contract Rights and Chattel Paper [Repealed].
8.9A. Secured Transactions.
8.10. Commercial Code — Effective Date — Transitional Provisions.
8.11. 1973 Amendatory Act — Effective Date and Transition Provisions.
9. Commissions, Boards and Institutions Generally.
10. Conservation Generally [Repealed].
10.1. Conservation.
11. Contracts.
12. Corporation Commission [Repealed].
12.1. State Corporation Commission.
13. Corporations Generally [Repealed].
13.1. Corporations.
14. Costs, Fees, Salaries and Allowances [Repealed].
14.1. Costs, Fees, Salaries and Allowances [Repealed].
15. Counties, Cities and Towns [Repealed].
15.1. Counties, Cities and Towns [Repealed].
15.2. Counties, Cities and Towns.
16. Courts Not of Record [Repealed].
16.1. Courts Not of Record.
17. Courts of Record [Repealed].

TITLE
17.1. COURTS OF RECORD.
18. CRIMES AND OFFENSES GENERALLY [Repealed].
18.1. CRIMES AND OFFENSES GENERALLY [Repealed].
18.2. CRIMES AND OFFENSES GENERALLY.
19. CRIMINAL PROCEDURE [Repealed].
19.1. CRIMINAL PROCEDURE [Repealed].
19.2. CRIMINAL PROCEDURE.
20. DOMESTIC RELATIONS.
21. DRAINAGE, SOIL CONSERVATION, SANITATION AND PUBLIC FACILITIES DISTRICTS.
22. EDUCATION [Repealed].
22.1. EDUCATION.
23. EDUCATIONAL INSTITUTIONS.
24. ELECTIONS [Repealed].
24.1. ELECTIONS [Repealed].
24.2. ELECTIONS.
25. EMINENT DOMAIN.
26. FIDUCIARIES GENERALLY.
27. FIRE PROTECTION.
28. FISH, OYSTERS AND SHELLFISH [Repealed].
28.1. FISH, OYSTERS, SHELLFISH AND OTHER MARINE LIFE [Repealed].
28.2. FISHERIES AND HABITAT OF THE TIDAL WATERS.
29. GAME, INLAND FISHERIES AND DOGS [Repealed].
29.1. GAME, INLAND FISHERIES AND BOATING.
30. GENERAL ASSEMBLY.
31. GUARDIAN AND WARD.
32. HEALTH [Repealed].
32.1. HEALTH.
33. HIGHWAYS, BRIDGES AND FERRIES [Repealed].
33.1. HIGHWAYS, BRIDGES AND FERRIES.
34. HOMESTEAD AND OTHER EXEMPTIONS.
35. HOTELS, RESTAURANTS AND CAMPS [Repealed].
35.1. HOTELS, RESTAURANTS, SUMMER CAMPS, AND CAMPGROUNDS.
36. HOUSING.
37. INSANE, EPILEPTIC, FEEBLE-MINDED AND INEBRIATE PERSONS [Repealed].
37.1. INSTITUTIONS FOR THE MENTALLY ILL; MENTAL HEALTH GENERALLY.
38. INSURANCE [Repealed].
38.1. INSURANCE [Repealed].
38.2. INSURANCE.
39. JUSTICES OF THE PEACE [Repealed].
39.1. JUSTICES OF THE PEACE [Repealed].
40. LABOR AND EMPLOYMENT [Repealed].
40.1. LABOR AND EMPLOYMENT.
41. LAND OFFICE [Repealed].
41.1. LAND OFFICE.
42. LIBRARIES [Repealed].
42.1. LIBRARIES.
43. MECHANICS' AND CERTAIN OTHER LIENS.
44. MILITARY AND EMERGENCY LAWS.
45. MINES AND MINING [Repealed].
45.1. MINES AND MINING.
46. MOTOR VEHICLES [Repealed].
46.1. MOTOR VEHICLES [Repealed].
46.2. MOTOR VEHICLES.
47. NOTARIES AND OUT-OF-STATE COMMISSIONERS [Repealed].
47.1. NOTARIES AND OUT-OF-STATE COMMISSIONERS.
48. NUISANCES.
49. OATHS, AFFIRMATIONS AND BONDS.
50. PARTNERSHIPS.

TITLE
51. Pensions and Retirement [Repealed].
51.01. Persons With Disabilities [Recodified].
51.1. Pensions, Benefits, and Retirement.
51.5. Persons With Disabilities.
52. Police (State).
53. Prisons and Other Methods of Correction [Repealed].
53.1. Prisons and Other Methods of Correction.
54. Professions and Occupations [Repealed].
54.1. Professions and Occupations.
55. Property and Conveyances.
56. Public Service Companies.
57. Religious and Charitable Matters; Cemeteries.
58. Taxation [Repealed].
58.1. Taxation.
59. Trade and Commerce [Repealed].
59.1. Trade and Commerce.
60. Unemployment Compensation [Repealed].
60.1. Unemployment Compensation [Repealed].
60.2. Unemployment Compensation.
61. Warehouses, Cold Storage and Refrigerated Locker Plants [Repealed].
61.1. Warehouses, Cold Storage and Refrigerated Locker Plants.
62. Waters of the State, Ports and Harbors [Repealed].
62.1. Waters of the State, Ports and Harbors.
63. Welfare [Repealed].
63.1. Welfare (Social Services).
64. Wills and Decedents' Estates [Repealed].
64.1. Wills and Decedents' Estates.
65. Workmen's Compensation [Repealed].
65.1. Workers' Compensation [Repealed].
65.2. Workers' Compensation.
66. Juvenile Justice.

In addition, this publication contains

Constitution of the United States of America.
Constitution of Virginia.
Rules of Supreme Court of Virginia.
Legal Ethics Opinions.
Unauthorized Practice of Law Opinions.
Table of Comparative Sections.
Table of Tax Code Sections.
Table of Reorganization Provisions of 1948.
Table of Acts Through 1948 Not Previously Codified.
Table of Acts Codified Subsequent to 1948.
Table of Sections Amended or Repealed.
Tables of Comparable Sections for Certain Repealed and Revised Titles.

Table of Contents

VOLUME 2

Title 8.

Civil Remedies and Procedure; Evidence Generally.

[Repealed.]

Title 8.01.

Civil Remedies and Procedure.

CHAPTER	PAGE
1. General Provisions as to Civil Cases, §§ 8.01-1 through 8.01-4.2	3
2. Parties, §§ 8.01-5 through 8.01-24	8
3. Actions, §§ 8.01-25 through 8.01-227.3	30
4. Limitations of Actions, §§ 8.01-228 through 8.01-256	239
5. Venue, §§ 8.01-257 through 8.01-267	334
5.1. Multiple Claimant Litigation Act, §§ 8.01-267.1 through 8.01-267.9	351
6. Notice of Lis Pendens or Attachment, §§ 8.01-268, 8.01-269	353
7. Civil Actions; Commencement, Pleadings, and Motions, §§ 8.01-270 through 8.01-284	356
8. Process, §§ 8.01-285 through 8.01-327.2	380
9. Personal Jurisdiction in Certain Actions, §§ 8.01-328 through 8.01-330	419
10. Dockets, §§ 8.01-331 through 8.01-335	441
11. Juries, §§ 8.01-336 through 8.01-363	445
12. Interpleader; Claims of Third Parties to Property Distrained or Levied on, etc., §§ 8.01-364 through 8.01-373	476
13. Certain Incidents of Trial, §§ 8.01-374 through 8.01-384.2	484
14. Evidence, §§ 8.01-385 through 8.01-420.5	513
15. Payment and Setoff, §§ 8.01-421 through 8.01-423	577
16. Compromises, §§ 8.01-424 through 8.01-425.1	585
17. Judgments and Decrees Generally, §§ 8.01-426 through 8.01-465	588
17.1. Uniform Enforcement of Foreign Judgments Acts, §§ 8.01-465.1 through 8.01-465.5	634
17.2. Uniform Foreign Country Money-Judgments Recognition Act, §§ 8.01-465.6 through 8.01-465.13	636
17.3. Uniform Foreign-Money Claims Act, §§ 8.01-465.14 through 8.01-465.25	638
18. Executions and Other Means of Recovery, §§ 8.01-466 through 8.01-525	641
19. Forthcoming Bonds, §§ 8.01-526 through 8.01-532	683
20. Attachments and Bail in Civil Cases, §§ 8.01-533 through 8.01-576	686
20.1. Summary Jury Trial, §§ 8.01-576.1 through 8.01-576.3	718
20.2. Dispute Resolution Proceedings, §§ 8.01-576.4 through 8.01-576.12	719
21. Arbitration and Award, §§ 8.01-577 through 8.01-581.016	722
21.1. Medical Malpractice, §§ 8.01-581.1 through 8.01-581.20	736
21.2. Mediation, §§ 8.01-581.21 through 8.01-581.23	761
22. Receivers, General and Special, §§ 8.01-582 through 8.01-606	762

CHAPTER	PAGE
23. Commissioners in Chancery, §§ 8.01-607 through 8.01-619	773
24. Injunctions, §§ 8.01-620 through 8.01-634	782
25. Extraordinary Writs, §§ 8.01-635 through 8.01-668	794
26. Appeals to the Supreme Court, §§ 8.01-669 through 8.01-675.2	821
26.1. Appeals to the Court of Appeals, §§ 8.01-675.3, 8.01-675.4	844
26.2. Appeals Generally, §§ 8.01-676 through 8.01-688	846

CODE OF VIRGINIA

Title 8.

Civil Remedies and Procedure; Evidence Generally.

[Repealed.]

§§ 8-1 through 8-924: Repealed by Acts 1977, c. 617.

Cross references. — See Editor's note under § 8.01-1.

CODE OF VIRGINIA

Title 8.01.

Civil Remedies and Procedure.

Chap. 1. General Provisions as to Civil Cases, §§ 8.01-1 through 8.01-4.2.
2. Parties, §§ 8.01-5 through 8.01-24.
3. Actions, §§ 8.01-25 through 8.01-227.3.
4. Limitations of Actions, §§ 8.01-228 through 8.01-256.
5. Venue, §§ 8.01-257 through 8.01-267.
5.1. Multiple Claimant Litigation Act, §§ 8.01-267.1 through 8.01-267.9.
6. Notice of Lis Pendens or Attachment, §§ 8.01-268, 8.01-269.
7. Civil Actions; Commencement, Pleadings, and Motions, §§ 8.01-270 through 8.01-284.
8. Process, §§ 8.01-285 through 8.01-327.2.
9. Personal Jurisdiction in Certain Actions, §§ 8.01-328 through 8.01-330.
10. Dockets, §§ 8.01-331 through 8.01-335.
11. Juries, §§ 8.01-336 through 8.01-363.
12. Interpleader; Claims of Third Parties to Property Distrained or Levied on, etc, §§ 8.01-364 through 8.01-373.
13. Certain Incidents of Trial, §§ 8.01-374 through 8.01-384.2.
14. Evidence, §§ 8.01-385 through 8.01-420.5.
15. Payment and Setoff, §§ 8.01-421 through 8.01-423.
16. Compromises, §§ 8.01-424 through 8.01-425.1.
17. Judgments and Decrees Generally, §§ 8.01-426 through 8.01-465.
17.1. Uniform Enforcement of Foreign Judgments Act, §§ 8.01-465.1 through 8.01-465.5.
17.2. Uniform Foreign Country Money-Judgments Recognition Act, §§ 8.01-465.6 through 8.01-465.13.
17.3. Uniform Foreign-Money Claims Act, §§ 8.01-465.14 through 8.01-465.25.
18. Executions and Other Means of Recovery, §§ 8.01-466 through 8.01-525.
19. Forthcoming Bonds, §§ 8.01-526 through 8.01-532.
20. Attachments and Bail in Civil Cases, §§ 8.01-533 through 8.01-576.
20.1. Summary Jury Trial, §§ 8.01-576.1 through 8.01-576.3.
20.2. Dispute Resolution Proceedings, §§ 8.01-576.4 through 8.01-576.12.
21. Arbitration and Award, §§ 8.01-577 through 8.01-581.016.
21.1. Medical Malpractice, §§ 8.01-581.1 through 8.01-581.20.
21.2. Mediation, §§ 8.01-581.21 through 8.01-581.23.
22. Receivers, General and Special, §§ 8.01-582 through 8.01-606.
23. Commissioners in Chancery, §§ 8.01-607 through 8.01-619.
24. Injunctions, §§ 8.01-620 through 8.01-634.
25. Extraordinary Writs, §§ 8.01-635 through 8.01-668.
26. Appeals to the Supreme Court, §§ 8.01-669 through 8.01-675.2.
26.1. Appeals to the Court of Appeals, §§ 8.01-675.3, 8.01-675.4.
26.2. Appeals Generally, §§ 8.01-676 through 8.01-688.

CHAPTER 1.

GENERAL PROVISIONS AS TO CIVIL CASES.

Sec.
8.01-1. How proceedings may be in actions pending when title takes effect.
8.01-1.1. References to former sections, articles and chapters of Title 8 and other titles.
8.01-2. General definitions for this title.
8.01-3. Supreme Court may prescribe rules; effective date thereof; rules to be printed and distributed; rules to

Sec.
    be published, indexed, and annotated; effect of subsequent enactments of General Assembly.
8.01-4. District courts and circuit courts may prescribe certain rules.
8.01-4.1. How jurisdiction determined when proceeding is on penal bond.
8.01-4.2. Who may execute bond for obtaining writ or order.

§ 8.01-1. How proceedings may be in actions pending when title takes effect. — Except as may be otherwise provided in § 8.01-256 of Chapter 4 (§ 8.01-228 et seq.) (Limitations of Actions), all provisions of this title shall apply to causes of action which arose prior to the effective date of any such provisions; provided, however, that the applicable law in effect on the day before the effective date of the particular provisions shall apply if in the opinion of the court any particular provision (i) may materially change the substantive rights of a party (as distinguished from the procedural aspects of the remedy) or (ii) may cause the miscarriage of justice. (Code 1950, § 8-2; 1977, c. 617.)

REVISERS' NOTE

This section provides some latitude to the court in applying the provisions of Title 8.01 to causes of action arising prior to October 1, 1977, the effective date of the title. However, Title 8 statutes of limitations continue to apply to such causes of action.

Cross references. — For text of rules of court, see Volume 11.

Editor's note. — The General Assembly at its regular session of 1972 directed the Virginia Code Commission, by House Joint Resolution No. 31, to make a study of Title 8 of the Code of Virginia and to report its findings in the form of a recodification of that title. In November of 1976, the Commission sent to the Governor and General Assembly its report containing a proposed revision of Title 8, along with revisers' notes and other explanatory matter, which was published as House Document No. 14 of the 1977 session. The Commission's draft of the revision of Title 8, as amended by the General Assembly, became c. 617 of the Acts of 1977. Effective October 1, 1977, it repealed Title 8 of the Code and enacted in lieu thereof a new Title 8.01.

In addition to its revision by c. 617, former Title 8 was also amended by certain other acts passed at the 1977 session, which acts took effect July 1, 1977, or earlier. As required by § 9-77.11 and also by Acts 1977, c. 617, cl. 4, the Code Commission incorporated most of these amendments into new Title 8.01. One such 1977 act, Acts 1977, c. 224, amended § 8-313, dealing with the circumstances under which a deposition may be read in a case at law. Section 8-313, along with other sections relating to depositions, was not carried over into the new Title 8.01, since it was contemplated that the entire subject would be covered by the revision of Part Four of the Rules of the Supreme Court. Therefore, the amendment to § 8-313 was not codified by the Code Commission in new Title 8.01; however, the substance of the amendment was incorporated by the Supreme Court in revised Rule 4:7. Another 1977 act, Acts 1977, c. 621, added a new § 8.01-66.1, which, although enacted as a part of new Title 8.01, contained no effective date provision, and so took effect July 1, 1977.

A companion bill to c. 617, making conforming changes in various sections of titles of the Code other than Title 8, and transferring certain sections of Title 8 to other titles, was enacted as Acts 1977, c. 624.

The revisers' notes from the Code Commission report, House Document No. 14 of the 1977 session of the General Assembly, have been reviewed, in some instances condensed, and re-edited by the original consultants to the Code Commission in the preparation of Title 8.01, and appear under the appropriate sections herein. However, the revisers' notes have not been edited to reflect subsequent amendments to the sections under which they appear or any other provisions.

Law Review. — For note highlighting major changes in Virginia civil procedure under Title 8.01, see 12 U. Rich. L. Rev. 245 (1977). For article reviewing recent developments and changes in legislation, case law, and Virginia Supreme Court Rules affecting civil litigation, see "Civil Practice and Procedure," 26 U. Rich. L. Rev. 679 (1992).

I. DECISIONS UNDER CURRENT LAW.

"Substantive" rights, as well as "vested" **rights, are included within those interests protected from retroactive application of statutes.** Shiflet v. Eller, 228 Va. 115, 319 S.E.2d 750 (1984).

Retroactivity. — The code provisions in this title apply retroactively unless they affect substantive rights. Gaynor v. OG/GYN Specialists, Ltd., 51 F. Supp. 2d 718 (W.D. Va. 1999).

Applied in Goodstein v. Weinberg, Buffenstein, Hirschler & Fleischer, 219 Va. 105, 245 S.E.2d 140 (1978); Strickland v. Simpkins, 221 Va. 730, 273 S.E.2d 539 (1981); Board of Supvrs. v. Safeco Ins. Co. of Am., 226 Va. 329, 310 S.E.2d 445 (1983); Potomac Hosp. Corp. v. Dillon, 229 Va. 355, 329 S.E.2d 41 (1985); Harris v. DiMattina, 250 Va. 306, 462 S.E.2d 338 (1995).

§ 8.01-1.1. References to former sections, articles and chapters of Title 8 and other titles. — Whenever in this title any of the conditions, requirements, provisions or contents of any section, article or chapter of Title 8 or any other title of this Code as such titles existed prior to October 2, 1977, are transferred in the same or in modified form to a new section, article or chapter of this title or any other title of this Code and whenever any such former section, article or chapter is given a new number in this or any other title, all references to any such former section, article or chapter of Title 8 or such other title appearing elsewhere in this Code than in this title shall be construed to apply to the new or renumbered section, article or chapter containing such conditions, requirements, provisions or contents or portions thereof. (1978, c. 422.)

§ 8.01-2. General definitions for this title. — As used in this title, unless the context otherwise requires, the term:

1. *"Action"* and *"suit"* may be used interchangeably and shall include all civil proceedings whether at law, in equity, or statutory in nature and whether in circuit courts or district courts;

2. *"Decree"* and *"judgment"* may be used interchangeably and shall include orders or awards;

3. *"Fiduciary"* shall include any one or more of the following:
   a. guardian,
   b. committee,
   c. trustee,
   d. executor,
   e. administrator, and administrator with the will annexed,
   f. curator of the will of any decedent, or
   g. conservator;

4. *"Rendition of a judgment"* means the time at which the judgment is signed and dated;

5. *"Person"* shall include individuals, a trust, an estate, a partnership, an association, an order, a corporation, or any other legal or commercial entity;

6. *"Person under a disability"* shall include:
   a. a person convicted of a felony during the period he is confined;
   b. an infant;
   c. a drug addict or an alcoholic as defined in § 37.1-1;
   d. an incapacitated person as defined in § 37.1-134.6;
   e. an incapacitated ex-service person under § 37.1-134.20; or

f. any other person who, upon motion to the court by any party to an action or suit or by any person in interest, is determined to be (i) incapable of taking proper care of his person, or (ii) incapable of properly handling and managing his estate, or (iii) otherwise unable to defend his property or legal rights either because of age or temporary or permanent impairment, whether physical, mental, or both;

7. *"Sheriff"* shall include deputy sheriffs and such other persons designated in § 15.2-1603;

8. *"Summons"* and *"subpoena"* may be used interchangeably and shall include a subpoena duces tecum for the production of documents and tangible things. (1977, c. 617; 1988, c. 37; 1997, c. 921.)

REVISERS' NOTE

This provision defines several terms appearing throughout Title 8.01. Some of these are based on definitions utilized for specific provisions in Title 8; e.g., "person"—see former § 8-81.1. Others, such as a "person under a disability," are specially created generic terms. Some terms have definitions for a particular chapter; e.g., see § 8.01-581.1.

Law Review. — For comment on rights of the convicted felon on parole, see 13 U. Rich. L. Rev. 367 (1979). For survey of Virginia law on wills, trusts, and estates for year 1979-80, see 67 Va. L. Rev. 369 (1981).

I. DECISIONS UNDER CURRENT LAW.

An "action" and a "cause of action" are quite different: "action" is defined by this section, and "cause of action" is defined as a set of operative facts which, under the substantive law, may give rise to a right of action. Because of that difference, there are no express terms in the nonsuit statute, § 8.01-380, making it specifically applicable to condemnation proceedings. Trout v. Commonwealth Transp. Comm'r, 241 Va. 69, 400 S.E.2d 172 (1991).

The statutory definition of fiduciary is not an exclusive one. Rather, it simply specifies that certain kinds of fiduciaries are included in the term. Moreover, there is no indication in the statute or in Virginia decisional law that the General Assembly intended this section to supplant the well-settled common law pursuant to which an accounting is available to redress a breach of the fiduciary responsibility inherent in an agency relationship or in the special relationship shown to have existed between husband and wife in the instant case. McClung v. Smith, 870 F. Supp. 1384 (E.D. Va. 1994), modified, 89 F.3d 829 (4th Cir. 1996).

Son as fiduciary to father's estate. — A son clearly stands in a fiduciary relationship to his father's estate when he is appointed as his father's committee. Aetna Ins. Co. v. Byrd, 15 Bankr. 154 (Bankr. E.D. Va. 1981).

Absent showing of actual incapacity, judgment against alcoholic only voidable. — Where defendant contended that at the time of his habitual offender adjudication he was an alcoholic and a person under disability, the court's failure to appoint a guardian ad litem to represent him did not render the adjudication void and subject to collateral attack. Absent a showing of actual incapacity, a judgment against an alcoholic is voidable only, not subject to collateral attack. The record supported the trial court's determination that, at the time of his habitual offender adjudication, defendant's condition did not require the appointment of a guardian ad litem. Eagleston v. Commonwealth, 18 Va. App. 469, 445 S.E.2d 161 (1994).

§ 8.01-3. Supreme Court may prescribe rules; effective date thereof; rules to be printed and distributed; rules to be published, indexed, and annotated; effect of subsequent enactments of General Assembly. — A. *Supreme Court to prescribe rules.* — The Supreme Court, subject to §§ 17.1-503 and 16.1-69.32, may, from time to time, prescribe the forms of writs and make general regulations for the practice in all courts of the Commonwealth; and may prepare a system of rules of practice and a system of pleading and the forms of process and may prepare rules of evidence to be used in all such courts. This section shall be liberally construed so as to eliminate unnecessary delays and expenses.

B. *Effective date; printing and distribution; maintenance by clerks of courts.* — New rules and amendments to rules shall not become effective until sixty days from adoption by the Supreme Court, and shall be printed and distributed as public documents pursuant to § 17.1-318. Such rules and amendments shall be maintained in a special book kept for such purpose by the clerks of court to which they are distributed.

C. *Rules to be published.* — The Virginia Code Commission shall publish and cause to be properly indexed and annotated the rules adopted by the Supreme Court, and all amendments thereof by the Court, and all changes made therein pursuant to subsection D hereof.

D. *Effect of subsequent enactments of the General Assembly on rules of court.* — The General Assembly may, from time to time, by the enactment of a general law, modify, or annul any rules adopted or amended pursuant to this section. In the case of any variance between a rule and an enactment of the General Assembly such variance shall be construed so as to give effect to such enactment.

E. The rules of evidence prepared by the Supreme Court shall be submitted to the Virginia Code Commission for approval as provided in § 9-77.11:01 and shall be codified upon enactment by the General Assembly. (Code 1950, §§ 8-1, 8-1.1, 8-1.2, 8-86.1; 1950, p. 3; 1952, c. 234; 1954, c. 333; 1971, Ex. Sess., c. 2; 1972, c. 856; 1977, c. 617; 1979, c. 658; 1984, c. 524.)

REVISERS' NOTE

Section 8.01-3 combines former law on rules promulgated by the Supreme Court.

Subsection A combines former §§ 8-1, 8-1.1, 8-1.2, and the first paragraph of former § 8-86.1 pertaining to the rule-making authority of the Supreme Court. Sections 17-116.4 and 16.1-69.32 impose on the Supreme Court the duty to consult with the chairmen of the House and Senate Courts of Justice Committees and with the executive committees of the judicial conferences of Virginia for the circuit and district courts.

Since Title 8 deals with civil procedure, the authority in former § 8-1.1 regarding criminal practice was deleted.

The second paragraph of former § 8-86.1 is changed in subsection B and reference is made to new § 2.1-543.1 which requires printing and distribution of rules as public documents. Clerks of courts are directed to maintain the rules in a special book. New rules and amendments are not effective until sixty days after adoption; however, to permit advance familiarization they are to be distributed upon adoption.

Former § 8-1.2 is amplified in subsection C to require that the Virginia Code Commission publish, index and annotate the Rules of the Supreme Court and all amendments thereto. Subsection D restates the power granted the General Assembly by Va. Const., Art. VI, § 5.

Cross references. — For text of rules of court adopted by the Supreme Court, see Volume 11.

Law Review. — For survey of the Virginia law on pleading and practice for the year 1961-1962, see 48 Va. L. Rev. 1523. For survey of Virginia law on evidence for the year 1969-1970, see 56 Va. L. Rev. 1325 (1970). For article on the abolition of the forms of action in Virginia, see 17 U. Rich. L. Rev. 273 (1983). For survey on civil procedure and practice in Virginia for 1989, see 23 U. Rich. L. Rev. 511 (1989).

I. Decisions Under Current Law.
II. Decisions Under Prior Law.

I. DECISIONS UNDER CURRENT LAW.

Applied in Pulliam v. Coastal Emergency Servs. of Richmond, Inc., 257 Va. 1, 509 S.E.2d 307 (1999).

II. DECISIONS UNDER PRIOR LAW.

Editor's note. — The case cited below was decided under corresponding provisions of former law. The term "this section," as used below, refers to former provisions. This section confirms an inherent power of the courts. Smith v. Commonwealth, 161 Va. 1112, 172 S.E. 286 (1934).

§ 8.01-4. District courts and circuit courts may prescribe certain rules.

— The district courts and circuit courts may, from time to time, prescribe rules for their respective districts and circuits. Such rules shall be limited to those rules necessary to promote proper order and decorum and the efficient and safe use of courthouse facilities and clerks' offices. No rule of any such court shall be prescribed or enforced which is inconsistent with this statute or any other statutory provision, or the Rules of Supreme Court or contrary to the decided cases, or which has the effect of abridging substantive rights of persons before such court. Any rule of court which violates the provisions of this section shall be invalid.

The courts may prescribe certain docket control procedures which shall not abridge the substantive rights of the parties nor deprive any party the opportunity to present its position as to the merits of a case solely due to the unfamiliarity of counsel of record with any such docket control procedures. (Code 1950, § 8-1.3; 1970, c. 366; 1977, c. 617; 1999, c. 839; 2000, c. 803.)

REVISERS' NOTE

Section 8.01-4 comports former § 8-1.3 with the 1973 district and circuit court reorganization acts. The phrase in former § 8-1.3 "the orderly management of court dockets" was omitted because it might lead to promulgation of local rules which would create lack of uniformity in procedure.

Former § 8-4.3 (Order for medical examination...) has been deleted since in substance it has been incorporated in Rule 4:10.

Editor's note. — Acts 1999, c. 839, cl. 2, provides: "That the provisions of this act shall take effect July 1, 2000. The Courts of Justice Committee of the Senate and the Courts of Justice Committee of the House of Delegates along with the Supreme Court of Virginia shall review and make recommendations to the General Assembly by December 1, 1999, as to which matters are docket control procedures and which matters are local rules. It is the clear intent of the General Assembly that there be no local rules and that any docket control procedures not affect the substantive rights of the litigants."

The 1999 amendment, effective July 1, 2000, rewrote this section, which formerly read: "The district courts and circuit courts may, from time to time, prescribe for their respective districts and circuits such rules as may be reasonably appropriate to promote proper order and decorum, and the convenient and efficient use of courthouses and clerks' offices. No rule of any such court shall be prescribed or enforced which is inconsistent with any statutory provision, or the Rules of the Supreme Court, or contrary to the decided cases, or which has the effect of abridging substantive rights of persons before such Court."

The 2000 amendments. — The 2000 amendment by c. 803, in the first paragraph, substituted "limited to those rules necessary" for "strictly limited to only those rules absolutely necessary" in the second sentence and inserted "or the Rules of Supreme Court" in the third sentence; and added the second paragraph.

Law Review. — For survey of Virginia law on practice and pleading for the year 1969-1970, see 56 Va. L. Rev. 1500 (1970). For survey of Virginia law on practice and pleading for the year 1970-1971, see 57 Va. L. Rev. 1561 (1971).

I. DECISIONS UNDER PRIOR LAW.

Editor's note. — The case cited below was decided under corresponding provisions of former law.

Rule may not add to statutes regulating practice of law by judges. — The General Assembly expressly limited its grant of rule-making power by excluding rules "inconsistent with any statutory provision." The General Assembly has seen fit to adopt statutes regulating the practice of law by judges of courts not of record. If rule adopted by judge adds to these regulations, the rule does not fall within his statutory rule-making power. Davis v. Sexton, 211 Va. 410, 177 S.E.2d 524 (1970).

§ 8.01-4.1. How jurisdiction determined when proceeding is on penal bond. — When a proceeding before a court is on a penal bond, with condition for the payment of money, the jurisdiction shall be determined as if the undertaking to pay such money had been without a penalty. And when jurisdiction depends on the amount of a judgment, if it be on such a bond, the jurisdiction shall be determined by the sum, payment whereof will discharge the judgment. (Code 1950, § 8-3; 1977, c. 617.)

I. DECISIONS UNDER PRIOR LAW.

Editor's note. — The case cited below was decided under corresponding provisions of former law.

The claim that a bond sued on does not constitute a contract, but simply provides for a penalty, is unavailing to oust a court of equity of jurisdiction. Kabler v. Spencer, 114 Va. 589, 77 S.E. 504 (1913).

§ 8.01-4.2. Who may execute bond for obtaining writ or order. — A bond for obtaining any writ or order may be executed by any person with sufficient surety, though neither be a party to the case. (Code 1950, § 8-4; 1977, c. 617.)

Cross references. — As to the giving of bond under Chapter 20 (§ 8.01-533 et seq.) of this title, see § 8.01-556.

CHAPTER 2.
Parties.

Article 1.
General Provisions.

Sec.
8.01-5. Effect of nonjoinder or misjoinder; limitation on joinder of insurance company.
8.01-6. Amending pleading; relation back to original pleading.
8.01-6.1. Amendment of pleading changing or adding a claim or defense; relation back.
8.01-6.2. Amendment of pleading; relation back to original pleading; confusion in trade name.
8.01-7. When court may add new parties to suit.

Article 2.
Special Provisions.

8.01-8. How minors may sue.
8.01-9. Guardian ad litem for persons under disability; when guardian ad litem need not be appointed for person under disability.
8.01-10. Joinder of tenants in common.
8.01-11. Proceedings on writing binding deceased person.
8.01-12. Suit by beneficial owner when legal title in another.

Sec.
8.01-13. Assignee or beneficial owner may sue in own name; certain discounts allowed.
8.01-14. Suit against assignor.
8.01-15. Suits by and against unincorporated associations or orders.

Article 3.
Death or Change of Parties.

8.01-16. New parties may have continuance.
8.01-17. When party whose powers cease is defendant.
8.01-18. When suit discontinued unless revived.
8.01-19. Effect of marriage or change of name of party.
8.01-20. Effect of marriage, change of name or death on appeal.
8.01-21. Judgment when death or disability occurs after verdict but before judgment.
8.01-22. When death or disability occurs as to any of several plaintiffs or defendants.
8.01-23. Decree in suit when number of parties exceeds thirty and one of them dies.

Article 4.

Writ of Scire Facias Abolished.

Sec.
8.01-24. Writ of scire facias abolished; substitutes therefor.

Article 1.

General Provisions.

§ 8.01-5. Effect of nonjoinder or misjoinder; limitation on joinder of insurance company. — A. No action or suit shall abate or be defeated by the nonjoinder or misjoinder of parties, plaintiff or defendant, but whenever such nonjoinder or misjoinder shall be made to appear by affidavit or otherwise, new parties may be added and parties misjoined may be dropped by order of the court at any time as the ends of justice may require.

B. Nothing in this section shall be construed to permit the joinder of any insurance company on account of the issuance to any party to a cause of any policy or contract of liability insurance, or on account of the issuance by any such company of any policy or contract of liability insurance for the benefit of or that will inure to the benefit of any party to any cause. (Code 1950, § 8-96; 1954, c. 333; 1977, c. 617.)

REVISERS' NOTE

Section 8.01-5 carries forward the policy of former § 8-96 by providing that parties may be added to or dropped from an action without prejudice until all parties necessary for the just disposition of the case are before the court. See also Rules 2:15, 3:9A and 3:14 which provide for the addition of parties to an action.

Omitted from § 8.01-5 are those parts of former § 8-96 which exempt a party from being added if the action could not be maintained against him for specified reasons — i.e. a new party who was neither a resident of the Commonwealth nor subject to service of process therein, or where the action was barred by the statute of limitation or under the provisions of Chapter 1 of Title 11 (Contracts — General Provisions). The substance of these provisions is better implemented under Rule 3:9A.

Cross references. — For rules of court generally, see Volume 11. For rule of court as to cross bills against new parties in equity suits, see Rule 2:14. For rules of court as to intervention and substitution of parties in suits in equity, see Rules 2:15, 2:16. For rule of court permitting a defendant in an action at law to plead a cross claim against one or more other defendants, see Rule 3:9. For rule of court as to joinder of parties in actions at law, see Rule 3:9A. For rule of court as to third party practice in an action at law, see Rule 3:10. As to joining joint obligors upon contract, see § 8.01-30.

I. Decisions Under Current Law.
II. Decisions Under Prior Law.

I. DECISIONS UNDER CURRENT LAW.

Nonjoinder not grounds for dismissal. — The alleged nonjoinder of parties plaintiff was not a proper ground for dismissing action. Indeed, if the defendants had desired to pursue the matter, they and the trial court should have followed the procedures set forth in the statute and the rule for determining whether the purported partners were necessary parties. Fox v. Deese, 234 Va. 412, 362 S.E.2d 699 (1987).

Misjoinder of parties should be raised by a motion to drop the improperly joined parties, not by a demurrer. Powers v. Cherin, 249 Va. 33, 452 S.E.2d 666 (1995).

Applied in Travelers Ins. Co. v. Riggs, 671 F.2d 810 (4th Cir. 1982).

II. DECISIONS UNDER PRIOR LAW.

Editor's note. — The cases cited below were decided under corresponding provisions of

former law. The term "this section," as used below, refers to former provisions.

The Virginia statutes are liberal in their provisions for adding new parties in cases of nonjoinder. McDaniel v. North Carolina Pulp Co., 198 Va. 612, 95 S.E.2d 201 (1956).

The purpose of this section was to extend the power of the court by further providing that in any suit or action when it appeared there was a nonjoinder of necessary parties, then the court, in the exercise of its discretion, could compel the joinder of such parties, and not to end in one suit or action the rights of a plaintiff and the liabilities of those who otherwise might be defendants in future litigation. Hogan v. Miller, 156 Va. 166, 157 S.E. 540 (1931).

Nonjoinder defined. — Nonjoinder means that a party has been omitted who ought to be joined with an existing party, not substituted for an existing party. Bardach Iron & Steel Co. v. Tenenbaum, 136 Va. 163, 118 S.E. 502 (1923).

This section relates to nonjoinder and misjoinder, and not to substitution of one sole plaintiff for another sole plaintiff. Bardach Iron & Steel Co. v. Tenenbaum, 136 Va. 163, 118 S.E. 502 (1923).

The word "may" means the same as "shall" in a statute of this kind which is in furtherance of justice. Lee v. Mutual Reserve Fund Life Ass'n, 97 Va. 160, 33 S.E. 556 (1899).

This is purely a procedural statute and in no wise changes the nature of tort liability. The effect of the statute as to nonjoinder is that the omission of a defendant necessary for the maintenance of the plaintiff's action can be corrected by the method provided. Hogan v. Miller, 156 Va. 166, 157 S.E. 540 (1931).

Rule that cotrespassers jointly and severally liable not changed. — The settled rule in Virginia, which has not been disturbed by the enactment of this section, is that cotrespassers are jointly and severally liable, and the party injured may sue all of them jointly, or two or more of them jointly or one of them severally, as he may see proper; and § 8.01-443 fortifies this conclusion. Hogan v. Miller, 156 Va. 166, 157 S.E. 540 (1931).

Insurer may be added as party defendant at its own request. — This section is undoubtedly for the benefit of the insurer and does not foreclose the right to be added as a party defendant at its request where it is clear that the insurer has a definite interest in the action. Matthews v. Allstate Ins. Co., 194 F. Supp. 459 (E.D. Va. 1961).

Action of plaintiffs in making insurer a party defendant was premature where liability of the insured had not been determined. Laws v. Spain, 51 F.R.D. 307 (E.D. Va. 1970).

Section inapplicable to insurer prosecuting contribution suit between tort-feasors. — This section has no application to a situation where the sole real party in interest is an insurance company prosecuting a contribution suit between tort-feasors. Laws v. Spain, 51 F.R.D. 307 (E.D. Va. 1970).

Election of cause of action. — In an action for malicious prosecution against a corporation and a special officer employed by it, when it developed that plaintiff's causes of action were not the same as to both defendants, and that they could not properly be sued jointly as to two torts alleged to have been committed against plaintiff, plaintiff should have been required to elect which cause of action he would pursue. Norfolk Union Bus Term., Inc. v. Sheldon, 188 Va. 288, 49 S.E.2d 338 (1948).

§ 8.01-6. Amending pleading; relation back to original pleading. — A misnomer in any pleading may, on the motion of any party, and on affidavit of the right name, be amended by inserting the right name. An amendment changing the party against whom a claim is asserted, whether to correct a misnomer or otherwise, relates back to the date of the original pleading if (i) the claim asserted in the amended pleading arose out of the conduct, transaction, or occurrence set forth in the original pleading and (ii) within the limitations period prescribed for commencing the action against the party to be brought in by the amendment, that party received such notice of the institution of the action that he will not be prejudiced in maintaining a defense on the merits and he knew or should have known that but for a mistake concerning the identity of the proper party, the action would have been brought against him. (Code 1950, § 8-97; 1954, c. 333; 1977, c. 617; 1990, c. 80; 1996, c. 693.)

REVISERS' NOTE

Section 8.01-276 obviates the need for reference to the former use of pleas in abatement for misnomer. Otherwise, § 8.01-6 does not change the substance of former § 8-97.

Cross references. — As to "railroad" or "railway," see § 1-13.24. As to indictments, see §§ 19.2-216 through 19.2-238.

I. Decisions Under Current Law.
II. Decisions Under Prior Law.

I. DECISIONS UNDER CURRENT LAW.

Misnomer arises when the right person is incorrectly named, not where the wrong defendant is named. Swann v. Marks, 252 Va. 181, 476 S.E.2d 170 (1996).

The personal representative of a decedent and the decedent's "estate" are two separate entities; the personal representative is a living individual while the "estate" is a collection of property. Thus, one cannot be substituted for another under the concept of correcting a misnomer. Swann v. Marks, 252 Va. 181, 476 S.E.2d 170 (1996).

II. DECISIONS UNDER PRIOR LAW.

Editor's note. — The cases cited below were decided under corresponding provisions of former law. The term "this section," as used below, refers to former provisions.

A misnomer is a mistake in name but not person. Rockwell v. Allman, 211 Va. 560, 179 S.E.2d 471 (1971).

An amendment is permitted where right party is before court, although under a wrong name. Rockwell v. Allman, 211 Va. 560, 179 S.E.2d 471 (1971).

But where the wrong person is named, it cannot be corrected by labelling it a misnomer. Rockwell v. Allman, 211 Va. 560, 179 S.E.2d 471 (1971).

No correction allowed for material error. — When the mistake in the name of a corporation, whether plaintiff or defendant, is slight, and it clearly appears what corporation is meant — or as it is sometimes expressed, where the pleading incorrectly names a corporation, but correctly describes it — the mistake is amendable. But where the error is so material (especially in the name of the defendant) that no such corporation exists, it is fatal at the trial; and this section does not obviate the result stated. Leckie v. Seal, 161 Va. 215, 170 S.E. 844 (1933); Baldwin v. Norton Hotel, Inc., 163 Va. 76, 175 S.E. 751 (1934).

When amendment to cure misnomer allowed notwithstanding statute of limitations. — If the right party is before the court although under a wrong name, an amendment to cure a misnomer will be allowed, notwithstanding the running of the statute of limitations, provided there is no change in the cause of action originally stated. Jacobson v. Southern Biscuit Co., 198 Va. 813, 97 S.E.2d 1 (1957).

Omission of "incorporated". — Where a corporation defendant is misdescribed simply by the omission of the word incorporated, and there is no other corporation of the name stated, the plaintiff should be permitted to insert the omitted word in the proper place in his declaration. Arminius Chem. Co. v. White's Adm'x, 112 Va. 250, 71 S.E. 637 (1911).

An action against a corporation in its former name cannot be defeated by showing that it had changed its name without any change of its membership. Welfley v. Shenandoah Iron, Lumber, Mining & Mfg. Co., 83 Va. 768, 3 S.E. 376 (1887).

§ 8.01-6.1. Amendment of pleading changing or adding a claim or defense; relation back.

— Subject to any other applicable provisions of law, an amendment of a pleading changing or adding a claim or defense against a party relates back to the date of the original pleadings for purposes of the statute of limitations if the court finds (i) the claim or defense asserted in the amended pleading arose out of the conduct, transaction or occurrence set forth in the original pleading, (ii) the amending party was reasonably diligent in asserting the amended claim or defense, and (iii) parties opposing the amendment will not be substantially prejudiced in litigating on the merits as a result of the timing of the amendment. In connection with such an amendment, the trial court may grant a continuance or other relief to protect the parties. This section shall not apply to eminent domain or mechanics' lien claims or defenses. (1996, c. 693.)

§ 8.01-6.2. Amendment of pleading; relation back to original pleading; confusion in trade name.

— A. A pleading which states a claim against a party whose trade name or corporate name is substantially similar to the trade name or corporate name of another entity may be amended at any time by inserting the correct party's name, if such party or its agent had actual notice of the claim prior to the expiration of the statute of limitations for filing the claim.

B. In the event that suit is filed against the estate of a decedent, and filed within the applicable statute of limitations, naming the proper name of estate of the deceased and service is effected or attempted on an individual or individuals as executor, administrator or other officers of the estate, such filing tolls the statute of limitations for said claim in the event the executor, administrator or other officers of the estate are unable to legally receive service at the time service was attempted, or defend suit because their authority as executor, administrator or other officer of the estate excludes defending said actions, or their duties as executor, administrator or other officer of the estate had expired at the time of service or during the time of defending said action. (1999, c. 686.)

§ 8.01-7. When court may add new parties to suit. — In any case in which full justice cannot be done, or the whole controversy ended, without the presence of new parties to the suit, the court, by order, may direct the clerk to issue the proper process against such new parties, and, upon the maturing of the case as to them, proceed to make such orders or decrees as would have been proper if the new parties had been made parties at the commencement of the suit. (Code 1950, § 8-129; 1977, c. 617.)

REVISERS' NOTE

Section 8.01-7 expands former § 8-129 to encompass actions at law as well as suits in equity. The provision gives the court power to add new parties sua sponte, while a motion is required to initiate other joinder of party provisions.

ARTICLE 2.

Special Provisions.

§ 8.01-8. How minors may sue. — Any minor entitled to sue may do so by his next friend. Either or both parents may sue on behalf of a minor as his next friend. (Code 1950, § 8-87; 1977, c. 617; 1998, c. 402.)

Cross references. — As to appointment of guardian ad litem for person under a disability, see § 8.01-9. As to appointment of guardian ad litem in suit for sale of lands of a person under a disability, see § 8.01-73.

Law Review. — For note discussing a state-incarcerated felon's capacity to sue under 42 U.S.C. § 1983 in federal courts despite prohibitive state statutes, see 30 Wash. & Lee L. Rev. 329 (1973). For an article, "Legal Issues Involving Children," see 32 U. Rich. L. Rev. 1345 (1998).

I. DECISIONS UNDER PRIOR LAW.

Editor's note. — The cases cited below were decided under corresponding provisions of former law. The term "this section," as used below, refers to former provisions.

Next friend need not be formally appointed. — Any person may bring a suit in the name of an infant as its next friend and ordinarily the court will recognize him as such next friend, and take cognizance of the case as properly brought and prosecuted. If it appears to the court that the suit is not for the benefit of the infant or that the person named as next friend is not a suitable person for the purpose, the court may dismiss the suit without prejudice, or assign another person to prosecute it as next friend of the infant, and the court may, if it think fit, direct an inquiry by a commissioner to ascertain whether the person prosecuting it as next friend is a fit person for the purpose. Wilson v. Smith, 63 Va. (22 Gratt.) 493 (1872).

According to the procedure in this jurisdiction, suits may be commenced and prosecuted by the next friend of an infant without previous appointment or formal order of admission. In such case the admission and approval by the court of the person acting as next friend is implied unless expressly disallowed. The courts are disposed to regard convenience and substance rather than form in mere matters of procedure. Jackson v. Counts, 106 Va. 7, 54 S.E. 870 (1906).

The practice in Virginia is for such suits to be instituted in the name of the infant by one of the parents or other near relative without formal appointment. If the suit or action proceeds without objection, it is a recognition by the court that the infant is a party to the proceeding. Womble v. Gunter, 198 Va. 522, 95 S.E.2d 213 (1956), commented on in 14 Wash. & Lee L. Rev. 338 (1957).

The suit of an infant by his next friend must be brought in the infant's name and not in that of the next friend, that is, the infant and not the next friend must be the real party plaintiff. And a suit in the name of the next friend "on behalf of the infant" cannot be maintained. Kirby v. Gilliam, 182 Va. 111, 28 S.E.2d 40 (1943).

This section requires that the suit be brought in the infant's name and not that of the next friend when the infant is the real party plaintiff. Bolen v. Bolen, 409 F. Supp. 1371 (W.D. Va. 1975).

And the consent of the infant is not necessary to authorize a suit on his behalf by a next friend, but any person may file a bill on behalf of an infant and even against the latter's will. Upon objection, the court will order an inquiry by a master to ascertain whether the suit is for the infant's benefit and whether some other person is best entitled to act as prochein ami, and will make such order as seems best for the interests of the infant. Kirby v. Gilliam, 182 Va. 111, 28 S.E.2d 40 (1943).

Consent of the infant was not necessary for a suit to be maintained in her name by her next friend. Womble v. Gunter, 198 Va. 522, 95 S.E.2d 213 (1956), commented on in 14 Wash. & Lee L. Rev. 338 (1957).

But infant must be real party plaintiff. — The mother of an infant consort cannot maintain in her own name an action to annul the marriage of her daughter. Kirby v. Gilliam, 182 Va. 111, 28 S.E.2d 40 (1943).

Infant is bound by suit. — An infant, having sued under this section, is bound to the same degree, and the same extent as an adult. Gimbert v. Norfolk S.R.R., 152 Va. 684, 148 S.E. 680 (1929).

In the absence of fraud an infant is as much bound by a decree or judgment of a court as is an adult. The law recognizes no distinction between a decree against an infant and a decree against an adult, and, therefore, an infant can impeach it only upon grounds which would invalidate it in case of an adult party. Womble v. Gunter, 198 Va. 522, 95 S.E.2d 213 (1956), commented on in 14 Wash. & Lee L. Rev. 338 (1957).

But decree may be vacated if section not followed. — In a suit by an infant seeking to annul her marriage, relief was denied because of the insufficiency of the evidence. The cause was instituted and prosecuted to final decree in the name of the infant instead of by her next friend, in spite of the provisions of this section. Because the failure to institute and prosecute the suit by a next friend cast substantial doubt on the validity of the decree, the Supreme Court remanded the cause with direction that the decree be vacated and the cause proceeded in by the next friend of the infant complainant. Kilbourne v. Kilbourne, 165 Va. 87, 181 S.E. 351 (1935).

And next friend cannot waive infant's rights. — It is not competent for the next friend of infant plaintiffs to waive the rights of the latter, and it is error to decree on such waiver. Hite v. Hite, 23 Va. (2 Rand.) 409 (1824); Armstrong's Heirs v. Walkup, 50 Va. (9 Gratt.) 372 (1852).

Dismissal without prejudice. — If a suit be brought in the name of the next friend and not in the infant's name, the suit must be dismissed without prejudice to the right of the next friend to refile the suit in the name of the infant. Bolen v. Bolen, 409 F. Supp. 1371 (W.D. Va. 1975).

A child can maintain a suit for negligently inflicted prenatal injuries. Bolen v. Bolen, 409 F. Supp. 1371 (W.D. Va. 1975).

Next friend should bring suit to annul marriage. — In this State an infant wife cannot bring suit in her own name to annul her marriage, but under this section must sue for this purpose by her next friend. Kirby v. Gilliam, 182 Va. 111, 28 S.E.2d 40 (1943).

Suits for personal injuries. — An action for an assault and battery committed upon an infant, ought not to be brought in the name of the guardian of such infant, but in the name of such infant by his or her next friend. Stewart v. Crabbin's Guardian, 20 Va. (6 Munf.) 280 (1819).

Infants held bound by no contest provision in will. — Infant beneficiaries who joined in the contest of a will by their parents as next friends were bound by a no contest provision in the will equally with the adult contestants, where it was the testator's clearly expressed intention to restrain all beneficiaries from a contest. Womble v. Gunter, 198 Va. 522, 95 S.E.2d 213 (1956), commented on in 14 Wash. & Lee L. Rev. 338 (1957).

Suits by guardian for protection of ward's property. — An infant should sue by his next friend; not by his guardian. The rule of this section, of course, is not applicable when it is incumbent on the guardian to sue for the protection of his ward's property, nor is it applicable when it would be in derogation of the statutory right of the guardian to institute a suit. Garland v. Norfolk Nat'l Bank of Commerce & Trusts, 156 Va. 653, 158 S.E. 888 (1931).

Suits against guardian of infant. — A second guardian of an infant has no authority to file a bill in his own name, against a former guardian, for an account of his transaction in relation to the ward's estate. An infant may by his next friend, call the acting guardian, or any preceding guardian, to account by a bill in chancery. But the bill must be in his own name by his next friend. Lemon v. Hansbarger, 47 Va. (6 Gratt.) 301 (1849).

Next friend as a witness. — One who is made next friend to an infant without his knowledge or consent is not disqualified from being a witness. Burwell v. Corbin, 22 Va. (1 Rand.) 131 (1822).

Removal of next friend. — The next friend is to be removed if he is treacherous or negligent of the interests of the infant. Burwell v. Corbin, 22 Va. (1 Rand.) 131 (1822).

Cost of suit. — The prochein ami is liable for the costs of the suit. Burwell v. Corbin, 22 Va. (1 Rand.) 131 (1822).

§ 8.01-9. Guardian ad litem for persons under disability; when guardian ad litem need not be appointed for person under disability. — A. A suit wherein a person under a disability is a party defendant shall not be stayed because of such disability, but the court in which the suit is pending, or the clerk thereof, shall appoint a discreet and competent attorney-at-law as guardian ad litem to such defendant, whether the defendant has been served with process or not. If no such attorney is found willing to act, the court shall appoint some other discreet and proper person as guardian ad litem. Any guardian ad litem so appointed shall not be liable for costs. Every guardian ad litem shall faithfully represent the estate or other interest of the person under a disability for whom he is appointed, and it shall be the duty of the court to see that the interest of the defendant is so represented and protected. Whenever the court is of the opinion that the interest of the defendant so requires, it shall remove any guardian ad litem and appoint another in his stead. When, in any case, the court is satisfied that the guardian ad litem has rendered substantial service in representing the interest of the person under a disability, it may allow the guardian reasonable compensation therefor, and his actual expenses, if any, to be paid out of the estate of the defendant. However, if the defendant's estate is inadequate for the purpose of paying compensation and expenses, all, or any part thereof, may be taxed as costs in the proceeding or, in the case of proceedings to adjudicate a person under a disability as an habitual offender pursuant to former § 46.2-351.2 or former § 46.2-352, shall be paid by the Commonwealth out of the state treasury from the appropriation for criminal charges. In a civil action against an incarcerated felon for damages arising out of a criminal act, the compensation and expenses of the guardian ad litem shall be paid by the Commonwealth out of the state treasury from the appropriation for criminal charges. If judgment is against the incarcerated felon, the amount allowed by the court to the guardian ad litem shall be taxed against the incarcerated felon as part of the costs of the proceeding, and if collected, the same shall be paid to the Commonwealth.

B. Notwithstanding the provisions of subsection A or the provisions of any other law to the contrary, in any suit wherein a person under a disability is a party defendant and is represented by an attorney-at-law duly licensed to practice in this Commonwealth, who shall have entered of record an appearance for such person, no guardian ad litem need be appointed for such person unless the court determines that the interests of justice require such appointment; or unless a statute applicable to such suit expressly requires an answer to be filed by a guardian ad litem. The court may, in its discretion, appoint the attorney of record for the person under a disability as his guardian ad litem, in which event the attorney shall perform all the duties and functions of guardian ad litem.

Any judgment or decree rendered by any court against a person under a disability without a guardian ad litem, but in compliance with the provisions of this subsection B, shall be as valid as if the guardian ad litem had been

§ 8.01-9

appointed. (Code 1950, §§ 8-88, 8-88.1; 1972, c. 720; 1977, c. 617; 1996, c. 887; 1999, cc. 945, 955, 987.)

REVISERS' NOTE

Section 8.01-9 combines former §§ 8-88 and 8-88.1.

Former § 8-88 has been expanded to include all persons under a disability (as defined in § 8.01-2) whenever such persons are party defendants to a suit. Otherwise this subsection is substantially the same as former § 8-88 except that unnecessary references to the judge in vacation have been eliminated, and it has been made clear that an attorney appointed as guardian ad litem is not liable for costs. Compensation and expenses of the guardian ad litem may be taxed as costs in the proceeding if the estate of the person under a disability is inadequate.

Two principal changes have been made to former § 8-88.1. First, the provision permitting the court to dispense with the appointment of a guardian ad litem has been amended; if a statute requires in a particular suit that the guardian ad litem file an answer, see e.g. § 8.01-73, then one must be appointed under this section. Where a guardian ad litem is to be appointed, the second change permits the court to appoint the attorney of record for the person under a disability. The attorney must be licensed to practice in Virginia.

Former § 8-89 (When fact of defendant's nonresidence to be returned, and suit abated) has been deleted as obsolete and unnecessary.

Cross references. — As to guardian ad litem in suits for sale or encumbrance of lands of persons under certain disabilities, see §§ 8.01-73, 8.01-75. For special provisions as to guardians ad litem in certain proceedings, see § 8.01-261 (venue to recover dower and curtesy of spouse under disability); § 8.01-73 (sale of land); § 8.01-297 (suit against convict); § 8.01-394 (lost records); § 21-310 (drainage districts); § 26-50 (to appoint trustee). As to powers of guardian of a minor's estate, see § 31-14.1. As to probate, see § 64.1-75 et seq.

The 1999 amendments. — The 1999 amendments by cc. 945 and 987, which are identical, inserted "former" preceding "§ 46.2-351.2" and preceding "§ 46.2-352" in the sixth sentence of subsection A.

The 1999 amendments by c. 955, in subsection A, inserted "the" preceding "opinion that" in the fifth sentence and added the last two sentences.

Law Review. — For survey of Virginia law on practice and pleading in the year 1971-1972, see 58 Va. L. Rev. 1309 (1972). For note discussing a state-incarcerated felon's capacity to sue under 42 U.S.C. § 1983 in federal courts despite prohibitive state statutes, see 30 Wash. & Lee L. Rev. 329 (1973).

I. Decisions Under Current Law.
II. Decisions Under Prior Law.

I. DECISIONS UNDER CURRENT LAW.

Legislative intent. — The General Assembly did not intend to require a circuit court to appoint a guardian ad item whenever the court issues a subpoena to compel a juvenile's testimony or where the circuit court initiates criminal contempt proceedings against the juvenile where juvenile is represented by counsel. Wilson v. Commonwealth, 23 Va. App. 318, 477 S.E.2d 7 (1996).

Best interest of child is paramount concern. — The strong public policy of this Commonwealth posits that the paramount concern where children are concerned is their best interests and this public policy would be thwarted if a child were bound by a paternity determination in which the child's independent rights and interests were not adequately protected. Commonwealth ex rel. Gray v. Johnson, 7 Va. App. 614, 376 S.E.2d 787 (1989).

A guardian ad litem has standing to file a petition for termination of residual parental rights. Stanley v. Fairfax, 242 Va. 60, 405 S.E.2d 621 (1991).

Appointment criteria in custody disputes. — While a guardian ad litem appointment is not required in every contested custody case, a finding that the appointment of a guardian ad litem is necessary and would be in the child's best interest is an essential prerequisite. Verrocchio v. Verrocchio, 16 Va. App. 314, 429 S.E.2d 482 (1993).

Power to file petition seeking termination of residual parental rights implicit. — No specific statutory provision either grants or denies the guardian ad litem the power to file a petition seeking the termination of residual parental rights, but such action is implicit in the general charge of authority given the guardian ad litem in this section to represent faithfully the interests of the individual under disability for whom he or she is appointed. Stanley v. Fairfax County Dep't of Social Servs., 10 Va. App. 596, 395 S.E.2d 199 (1990), aff'd, Stanley v. Fairfax, 242 Va. 60, 405 S.E.2d 621 (1991).

Appointment permissible in custody hearing ancillary to divorce proceeding. — Circuit courts conducting a custody hearing as part of divorce proceedings are not constrained by the absence of a specific provision within this section providing for appointment of a guardian ad litem. Accordingly, in those contested custody cases where the trial judge finds that the best interests of the child are not adequately protected by the parties, appointment of a guardian ad litem for the child is appropriate. Verrocchio v. Verrocchio, 16 Va. App. 314, 429 S.E.2d 482 (1993).

Failure to appoint guardian ad litem for alcoholic does not render judgment void. — Where defendant contended that at the time of his habitual offender adjudication he was an alcoholic and a person under disability, the court's failure to appoint a guardian ad litem to represent him did not render the adjudication void and subject to collateral attack. Absent a showing of actual incapacity, a judgment against an alcoholic is voidable only, not subject to collateral attack. The record supported the trial court's determination that, at the time of his habitual offender adjudication, defendant's condition did not require the appointment of a guardian ad litem. Eagleston v. Commonwealth, 18 Va. App. 469, 445 S.E.2d 161 (1994).

Actual selection left solely in hands of court. — The actual selection of a guardian ad litem, is left solely in the hands of the court. The court is not bound by the defendant's demands or requests. Ruffin v. Commonwealth, 10 Va. App. 488, 393 S.E.2d 425 (1990), overruled on other grounds, Pigg v. Commonwealth, 17 Va. App. 756, 441 S.E.2d 216 (1994).

Limited fact-finding role. — Under Virginia law, the role of a guardian ad litem appointed under subsection A is to investigate thoroughly the facts and carefully examine the facts surrounding the case. The recommendation of infant's court-appointed guardian ad litem was thus irrelevant to the disposition of the case as it was inconsistent with the limited role of the guardian as an independent fact finder and not a surrogate decision maker when family members are involved. In re Baby "K", 832 F. Supp. 1022 (E.D. Va. 1993), aff'd, 16 F.3d 590 (4th Cir.), cert. denied, 513 U.S. 825, 115 S. Ct. 91, 130 L. Ed. 2d 42 (1994).

Weight given guardian's custody recommendation. — The recommendation of the guardian ad litem in instant child custody case, while not binding or controlling, should not be disregarded. The duty of a guardian ad litem in a child custody dispute is to see that the interest of the child is represented and protected. The child had no other independent participant in the proceeding, aside from the trial court, to protect his interests. Thus, this diligent guardian ad litem's recommendation that custody be awarded to the grandmother was entitled to be considered by the court in reaching a decision on the issue. Bottoms v. Bottoms, 249 Va. 410, 457 S.E.2d 102 (1995).

Guardian must, at minimum, discuss matter with person under disability. — A person who has been appointed guardian ad litem must, if possible, at a minimum discuss the matter with the person under disability. Ruffin v. Commonwealth, 10 Va. App. 488, 393 S.E.2d 425 (1990), overruled on other grounds, Pigg v. Commonwealth, 17 Va. App. 756, 441 S.E.2d 216 (1994).

Duty to make bona fide examination of facts. — A guardian has a duty to make a bona fide examination of the facts in order to properly represent the person under a disability. Ruffin v. Commonwealth, 10 Va. App. 488, 393 S.E.2d 425 (1990), overruled on other grounds, Pigg v. Commonwealth, 17 Va. App. 756, 441 S.E.2d 216 (1994).

Displeasure with guardian's services. — A guardian ad litem has no duty to report to the court every instance in which a client expresses displeasure with his services. In the event that a defendant is unhappy with his guardian ad litem, it is his burden to show that the guardian is unfit to fulfill satisfactorily his obligations. Ruffin v. Commonwealth, 10 Va. App. 488, 393 S.E.2d 425 (1990), overruled on other grounds, Pigg v. Commonwealth, 17 Va. App. 756, 441 S.E.2d 216 (1994).

In proceedings involving custody of child of unwed minor, guardian ad litem for the unknown father had standing to appeal the entrustment agreement decision by the juvenile and domestic relations district court. Norfolk Div. of Social Servs. v. Unknown Father, 2 Va. App. 420, 345 S.E.2d 533 (1986).

Habitual offender adjudication not subject to collateral attack. — Because defendant failed to prove that his alcoholism rendered him incapable of defending his interest, the failure to appoint a guardian ad litem did not create a jurisdictional defect, consequently, the habitual offender adjudication was not subject to a collateral attack on the grounds that a guardian ad litem should have been appointed. Hall v. Commonwealth, No. 0347-92-3 (Ct. of Appeals May 17, 1994).

Necessity of guardian ad litem appointment. — By stipulating that defendant was an alcoholic at the time of his habitual offender hearing, the Commonwealth placed defendant within the class of persons entitled to the appointment of a guardian ad litem, if not otherwise represented by counsel, during an habitual offender adjudication. England v.

Commonwealth, 18 Va. App. 121, 442 S.E.2d 402 (1994).

II. DECISIONS UNDER PRIOR LAW.

Editor's note. — The cases cited below were decided under corresponding provisions of former law. The term "this section," as used below, refers to former provisions.

Guardian ad litem must be appointed for infant. — In every action or suit against an infant defendant, it is the duty of the court wherein the same is pending, or of the judge or clerk thereof in vacation, to appoint a guardian ad litem to represent the interest or estate of the infant. Turner v. Barraud, 102 Va. 324, 46 S.E. 318 (1904); Kanter v. Holland, 154 Va. 120, 152 S.E. 328 (1930).

An infant can only appear and defend by a guardian ad litem, and proceedings against him are generally fatally defective unless the record shows that such guardian was assigned him. Langston v. Bassette, 104 Va. 47, 51 S.E. 218 (1905); Weaver v. Glenn, 104 Va. 443, 51 S.E. 835 (1905); Kavanaugh v. Shackett, 111 Va. 423, 69 S.E. 335 (1910).

Or else judgment void. — The law in Virginia is that a personal judgment rendered against an infant for whom no guardian ad litem has been appointed is void. Kanter v. Holland, 154 Va. 120, 152 S.E. 328 (1930).

It is the settled law of this Commonwealth that a personal judgment rendered against an infant for whom it does not affirmatively appear of record that a guardian ad litem has been appointed is void. Hence, when on appeal from such a judgment it does not appear that a guardian was appointed below, the judgment obtained will have to be set aside and the action remanded for a new trial. Moses v. Akers, 203 Va. 130, 122 S.E.2d 864 (1961).

But failure is not reversible error when decree in infant's favor. — If it clearly appears that the decree is beneficial to the infant, failure to appoint a guardian ad litem will not be reversible error. Langston v. Bassette, 104 Va. 47, 51 S.E. 218 (1905).

Necessity for guardian ad litem for insane person. — It is only where there is no committee, or where there is a conflict of interest between the committee and the insane person, that it becomes necessary to appoint a guardian ad litem for the insane defendant. Hinton v. Bland, 81 Va. 588 (1886); Howard v. Landsberg's Comm., 108 Va. 161, 60 S.E. 769 (1908).

Where the amended bill in a partition suit suggested that one of the parties was non compos mentis, and prayed for the appointment of a guardian ad litem, but the party and her husband and the appellant were all strenuously denying her insanity, and the issue was undetermined when she died, the fact that no guardian ad litem was appointed for her under this section is no ground for reversing the decree. Cottrell v. Mathews, 120 Va. 847, 92 S.E. 808 (1917).

When lunatic not a necessary party. — A lunatic having a regular appointed committee is not a necessary party to suit concerning his estate. Howard v. Landsberg's Comm., 108 Va. 161, 60 S.E. 769 (1908).

Appointment when infants and insane persons unknown parties. — The preliminary report of a commissioner showed that several interested persons were infants, and the court appointed a guardian ad litem who filed his answer in that capacity, and also an answer for the infants by himself as guardian. It was alleged that this was error because the infants had not been made parties to the suit. It was held that this position was not tenable, as the infants were among the "unknown heirs" named as defendants in the amended bill in the suit and served by publication, and the action of the court was, therefore, entirely regular and proper. Goins v. Garber, 131 Va. 59, 108 S.E. 868 (1921).

There is no legislative intent that this section should apply to § 53.1-221 et seq., pertaining to the appointment of committees for convict defendants. Dunn v. Terry, 216 Va. 234, 217 S.E.2d 849 (1975).

Appointment of committee waiverable. — There is a significant difference between the status of an infant or insane person and that of a convict and such difference is persuasive that appointment of a committee for a convict was a procedural requirement that could be waived. Dunn v. Terry, 216 Va. 234, 217 S.E.2d 849 (1975).

Convicts are not civilly dead in Virginia. Dunn v. Terry, 216 Va. 234, 217 S.E.2d 849 (1975).

And are not legally incompetent to transact business. — Unlike an infant or insane person, a convict was not legally incompetent to transact business either before or after his conviction in a criminal case. Dunn v. Terry, 216 Va. 234, 217 S.E.2d 849 (1975).

Appointment not presumed. — Where the interests of infants are concerned it must affirmatively appear from the record that a guardian ad litem was duly appointed. Where the record is silent on the subject it will not be presumed. Brown v. M'Rea, 18 Va. (4 Munf.) 439 (1815); Catron v. Bostic, 123 Va. 355, 96 S.E. 845 (1918).

Any court may appoint. — It is a power incident to every court to appoint a guardian ad litem, and he may be appointed, although the infant has not been served with notice. Word v. Commonwealth, 30 Va. (3 Leigh) 743 (1827); Strayer v. Long, 83 Va. 715, 3 S.E. 372 (1887).

Guardian ad litem not required to accept appointment. — A guardian ad litem appointed to prosecute an appeal on an infant's behalf is not obliged to accept the appointment. A reasonable time ought therefore to be given him to consider whether he will accept and to prepare for trial. Wells v. Winfree, 16 Va. (2 Munf.) 342 (1811). But as to power of court of equity to compel acceptance, see Strayer v. Long, 83 Va. 715, 3 S.E. 372 (1887).

Insufficient evidence of acceptance. — Where an order appointing counsel for one of the defendants' guardian ad litem for an infant interested in the suit, was indorsed "seen" and signed but no answer filed, it was held that this was not sufficient evidence of acceptance. Jeffries v. Jeffries, 123 Va. 147, 96 S.E. 197 (1918).

The infant is never to be prejudiced by the act, default or admission of his guardian ad litem. Daingerfield v. Smith, 83 Va. 81, 1 S.E. 599 (1887); Morris v. Virginia Ins. Co., 85 Va. 588, 8 S.E. 383 (1888).

Power to consent to sale. — Infant defendants are incompetent to consent to decree of sale, and their guardian ad litem cannot consent for them. Daingerfield v. Smith, 83 Va. 81, 1 S.E. 599 (1887).

It is not competent for guardians of infant parties, to waive any benefit to which the infants are entitled in a decree; and it is error to decree on such consent. Hite v. Hite, 23 Va. (2 Rand.) 409 (1824).

A guardian ad litem may consent, for his wards, to the removal of the suit from one circuit to another. Lemmon v. Herbert, 92 Va. 653, 24 S.E. 249 (1896).

Presumption as to answer. — When it appears of record that the infant defendants appeared and answered by their guardian ad litem, and that there was a general replication thereto, it will be presumed in the appellate court that the answer was regularly filed, though the answer itself is not found among the papers in the record. Smith v. Henkel, 81 Va. 524 (1886).

But record must show answer filed. — The heirs being infants, though their guardian was a party and answered, they were entitled to be defended by a guardian ad litem, and although one was appointed for them, and there was a paper purporting to be an answer found among the papers of the cause, yet as it did not appear that it had been filed, it was error to decree the sale of the infant's land, without an answer filed by the guardian ad litem. Ewing v. Ferguson, 74 Va. (33 Gratt.) 548 (1880).

Effect of answer. — No rule is better settled, than that an answer of an infant by guardian ad litem cannot be read against him at all, for any purpose. Bank of Alexandria v. Patton, 40 Va. (1 Rob.) 499 (1843).

Fees of guardian. — In the absence of peculiar facts, such as the creation of a fund which enures to the common benefit of all concerned, the allowance of guardian ad litem fees is regulated by this section. An estate of an infant contingent remainderman was such an estate as that contemplated by this section, and, therefore, it was error for the court to decree the payment of the guardian ad litem's fee out of the corpus of the trust estate, and in view of the fact that the fee was based on the theory that it should be paid out of the corpus and not fall upon the infant, the infant should be given an opportunity, if so advised, to question the reasonableness of the fee finally allowed. Patterson v. Old Dominion Trust Co., 156 Va. 763, 159 S.E. 168 (1931).

Guardian's fee in partition proceeding held payable from proceeds of sale. — In a partition proceeding in which a guardian ad litem, through his own efforts, had increased the amount offered for the property in question by at least $15,000, a $2,000 fee awarded to the guardian had to be paid from the proceeds of the judicial sale, rather than from the infants' shares of the proceeds. Austin v. Dobbins, 219 Va. 930, 252 S.E.2d 588 (1979).

§ 8.01-10. Joinder of tenants in common. — Tenants in common may join or be joined as plaintiffs or defendants. (Code 1950, § 8-90; 1977, c. 617.)

§ 8.01-11. Proceedings on writing binding deceased person. — A. A bond, note, or other written obligation to a person or persons who, or some of whom, are dead at the time of its execution may be proceeded on in the name of the personal representative of such person, or the survivors or survivor, or of the representative of the last survivor of such persons.

B. If one person bound either jointly or as a partner with another by a judgment, bond, note, or otherwise for the payment of a debt, or the performance or forbearance of an act, or for any other thing, die in the lifetime of such other, the representative of the decedent may be charged in the same manner as the decedent might have been charged, if those bound jointly or as partners, had been bound severally as well as jointly, otherwise than as partners. (Code 1950, §§ 8-92, 8-93; 1977, c. 617.)

REVISERS' NOTE

Section 8.01-11 combines former §§ 8-92 and 8-93 without substantive change.

Former § 8-91 (Suing in the names of persons who are dead) has been deleted as obsolete. Cf. § 55-22.

Cross references. — As to effect of death after verdict, see §§ 8.01-20, 8.01-21. As to effect of death during pendency of suit, see § 8.01-22. As to validity of bond, note or other writing payable to deceased person, see § 11-9. As to compromise as affecting liability, see §§ 11-10, 11-11. As to right of contribution, see § 11-13. As to order of liability of decedent's estate for debts, see §§ 64.1-181 through 64.1-187. As to substitution of parties, see Rules 2:16, 3:15.

I. DECISIONS UNDER PRIOR LAW.

Editor's note. — The cases cited below were decided under corresponding provisions of former law. The term "this section," as used below, refers to former provisions.

Bond payable to administrator. — An administrator may declare in the debet and detinet on a bond executed to himself as such, and his executor or administrator has the right to bring an action upon it. Bowden v. Taggart, 17 Va. (3 Munf.) 513 (1811).

Where an administrator is one of the obligors in a bond for the payment of a sum of money to the decedent he cannot maintain an action against his co-obligors to enforce the payment of the money. Rodes v. Rodes, 65 Va. (24 Gratt.) 256 (1874).

Where executor died before forthcoming bond taken. — An executor recovered judgment against a debtor of his testator, and sued out execution thereon. Before the execution was delivered to the sheriff, the executor died. The execution being then delivered to the sheriff, he levied it on property of defendant, and took a forthcoming bond payable to the executor in his official capacity. It was held that the execution was properly levied, though the executor was dead before it was delivered, and the forthcoming bond was rightly taken to the executor in his official capacity, and was good. Thereupon, a motion for award of execution on the forthcoming bond was made by the executor of aforesaid execution. It was held that the forthcoming bond belonged to the original testator's estate, and the second executor was entitled to the motion, and to award of execution on the bond, as the representative of the original testator, not as the representative of the first executor. Turnbull v. Claibornes, 30 Va. (3 Leigh) 392 (1831).

Contribution and subrogation between partners not affected. — This section does not affect the rules as to contribution between partners and subrogation of a partner to the rights of partnership creditors whose debts he has paid. Sands v. Durham, 99 Va. 263, 38 S.E. 145 (1901).

Order of priority as to partners. — The social assets are applicable first to the social debts, and if insufficient, the social creditors come in as general creditors pari passu, with separate creditors of the same class upon the separate estate of the deceased partner. This principle has the sanction of the deliberate and unanimous decision of this court in Ashby v. Porter, 67 Va. (26 Gratt.) 455, 465 (1875), and an implicit legislative adoption of this section taken word for word, from section 13, chapter 144, Code of 1849, with the construction which it had received by this court, and that construction has been followed and reaffirmed by the court in the case of Robinson v. Allen, 85 Va. 721, 8 S.E. 835 (1889); Pettyjohn v. Woodruff, 86 Va. 478, 10 S.E. 715 (1890).

Section does not affect marshaling of assets. — This section does not change or affect the order in which the assets of the decedent are to be applied in the payment of debts as prescribed by § 64.1-157. Robinson v. Allen, 85 Va. 721, 8 S.E. 835 (1889).

Nor principle as to loss of remedy upon grounds not personal. — The statute in relation to joint obligations, though it gives an action against the personal representative of a deceased joint obligor, does not affect the principle that the defeat of the remedy against one joint obligor upon a ground not personal to himself, defeats it as to all obligors. Brown v. Johnson, 54 Va. (13 Gratt.) 644 (1857).

Pendency of two suits. — Where two suits having same object are pending, a decree in one for account, suspends the other. A suit to administer a deceased partner's separate property for his separate creditors, and a suit to administer partnership property for the partnership creditors, not having the same object, this rule does not apply. Robinson v. Allen, 85 Va. 721, 8 S.E. 835 (1889).

§ 8.01-12. Suit by beneficial owner when legal title in another. —

When the legal title to any claim or chose in action, for the enforcement of the

§ 8.01-13

collection of which a court of equity has jurisdiction, is in one person and the beneficial equitable title thereto is in another, the latter may either maintain a suit in the name of the holder of the legal title for his use and benefit or in his own name to enforce collection of the same. In either case the beneficial equitable owner shall be deemed the real plaintiff and shall be liable for costs. (Code 1950, § 8-93.1; 1977, c. 617.)

Cross references. — See § 8.01-13 and note thereto. As to liability for costs where suit is brought by one person for the benefit of another, see § 17.1-603. As to when a person not a party may take or sue under instrument, see § 55-22.

Law Review. — For survey of Virginia law on practice and pleading for the year 1974-1975, see 61 Va. L. Rev. 1799 (1975).

I. DECISIONS UNDER PRIOR LAW.

Editor's note. — The cases cited below were decided under corresponding provisions of former law. The term "this section," as used below, refers to former provisions.

Equity rule modified. — The equitable rule that a suit in equity must invariably be brought in the name of the real party in interest and not in the name of another has been modified and changed in Virginia by this section. Stuart Court Realty Corp. v. Gillespie, 150 Va. 515, 143 S.E. 741 (1928).

Suit by assignee/real estate broker. — A real estate broker brought his action for commissions against the administrator of a landowner. The landowner had placed his property in the hands of another broker for sale, who had asked plaintiff to assist him in making a sale and agreed to share commissions with him. It was held that the contract between the brokers was in effect an equitable assignment by the original broker to plaintiff of a one-half interest in the contract with the landowners, and that the plaintiff, under this section, had the right to maintain an action in his own name to enforce the collection of his commission against the landowner's administrator. Arwood v. Hill's Adm'r, 135 Va. 235, 117 S.E. 603 (1923).

Assignment of judgment does not carry right to sue sheriff. — The assignment of a judgment does not carry with it, as an incident, the right to sue the sheriff and the sureties on his official bond for a breach of the condition thereof occurring prior to the assignment. Commonwealth v. Wampler, 104 Va. 337, 51 S.E. 737 (1905).

Pleading and practice. — In an action in the name of one for the use of another, it is usual to state the fact in the declaration, or on it, or on the writ. But this is not necessary. The indorsement may be made at any time during the progress of the suit. It is sometimes not made until after execution is issued, which is then indorsed for the benefit of the party for whose benefit the suit was brought. Hayes v. Virginia Mut. Protection Ass'n, 76 Va. 225 (1882). See also, Clarksons v. Doddridge, 55 Va. (14 Gratt.) 42 (1857); Fadeley v. Williams, 96 Va. 397, 31 S.E. 515 (1899); Consumers Ice Co. v. Jennings, 100 Va. 719, 42 S.E. 879 (1902).

§ 8.01-13. Assignee or beneficial owner may sue in own name; certain discounts allowed. — The assignee or beneficial owner of any bond, note, writing or other chose in action, not negotiable may maintain thereon in his own name any action which the original obligee, payee, or contracting party might have brought, but, except as provided in § 8.9-206, shall allow all just discounts, not only against himself, but against such obligee, payee, or contracting party, before the defendant had notice of the assignment or transfer by such obligee, payee, or contracting party, and shall also allow all such discounts against any intermediate assignor or transferor, the right to which was acquired on the faith of the assignment or transfer to him and before the defendant had notice of the assignment or transfer by such assignor or transferor to another. (Code 1950, § 8-94; 1964, c. 219; 1966, c. 396; 1977, c. 617.)

Cross references. — As to rights of assignee against assignor, see § 8.01-14 and note. As to equitable jurisdiction, see § 8.01-33. As to survival of causes of action, see § 8.01-56. As to payment and set-offs as defenses, see §§ 8.01-422, 8.01-423. As to assignment of various types of interest, see § 38.2-3111 (life insurance policies); §§ 55-217, 55-221 (leases). As to when person not a party may take and sue under an instrument, see § 55-22.

Law Review. — For survey of Virginia law on torts for the year 1972-1973, see 59 Va. L. Rev. 1590 (1973).

§ 8.01-13 CIVIL REMEDIES AND PROCEDURE § 8.01-13

I. Decisions Under Current Law.
   A. General Consideration.
   B. What Constitutes an Assignment.
II. Decisions Under Prior Law.
   A. General Consideration.
   B. What May Be Assigned.
   C. What Constitutes an Assignment.
      1. In General.
      2. Necessity for Consideration.
      3. Notice.
   D. Effect of Assignment.
      1. Assignee Takes Subject to Equities and Set-Offs.
      2. Right to Sue.

I. DECISIONS UNDER CURRENT LAW.

A. General Consideration.

Effect of misnomer in corporate name. — A misnomer in a corporate name does not invalidate an assignment when it is clear what corporation the parties intended, and such a mistake may be shown in evidence, upon the general issue. Lataif v. Commercial Indus. Constr., Inc., 223 Va. 59, 286 S.E.2d 159 (1982).

B. What Constitutes an Assignment.

Appointment of an agent or the grant of a power of attorney cannot qualify as an assignment. Both are revocable, and the latter expires at the grantor's death. Kelly Health Care, Inc. v. Prudential Ins. Co. of Am., 226 Va. 376, 309 S.E.2d 305 (1983).

Assignment of benefits payable to an insured under a health insurance policy is a contingent entitlement to certain benefits, i.e., an entitlement which may or may not vest sometime in the future. That entitlement, however, is one coupled with an interest, an interest derived from contract. As such, it is a proper subject of assignment. Kelly Health Care, Inc. v. Prudential Ins. Co. of Am., 226 Va. 376, 309 S.E.2d 305 (1983).

Health care provider was held not to be an assignee of an insured's benefits under a health insurance policy where one of the documents on which it relied did no more than appoint the health care provider as the insured's special agent with entitlement to collect payments from the insurer as the insured's entitlements fell due and the other document granted the insurer authority in the nature of a power of attorney to make such payments. Kelly Health Care, Inc. v. Prudential Ins. Co. of Am., 226 Va. 376, 309 S.E.2d 305 (1983).

Applied in Sunsport, Inc. v. Barclay Leisure Ltd., 984 F. Supp. 418 (E.D. Va. 1997).

II. DECISIONS UNDER PRIOR LAW.

A. General Consideration.

Editor's note. — The cases cited below were decided under corresponding provisions of former law. The term "this section," as used below, refers to former provisions.

This section does not create any new cause of action, and has no application to cases in which there is no assignment. Commonwealth v. Wampler, 104 Va. 337, 51 S.E. 737 (1905).

Applicable to law, not equity, actions. — The terminology of this section connotes its applicability to actions at law rather than to suits in equity. Moreover, there is a valid distinction between the accrual of the equitable, inchoate right to contribution that arises at the time of jointly negligent acts and the maturation of the right to recover contribution that arises only after payment of an equally large share of the common obligation. Nationwide Mut. Ins. Co. v. Minnifield, 213 Va. 797, 196 S.E.2d 75 (1973).

It is limited in its application to nonnegotiable instruments, and cannot be construed to apply to negotiable instruments negotiated after maturity, because an instrument negotiable in its origin continues to be negotiable until it has been restrictively indorsed or discharged by payment or otherwise. Stegal v. Union Bank & Fed. Trust Co., 163 Va. 417, 176 S.E. 438 (1934).

This section does not apply to negotiable paper, though such paper has been transferred after due. Davis v. Miller, 55 Va. (14 Gratt.) 1 (1857).

It imposes no conditions on the assignee's right to sue, but allows the assignee to bring in his own name any suit which the assignor may have brought. United States ex rel. Shade Shop, Inc. v. R.B. McDanel Co., 16 F. Supp. 905 (E.D. Va. 1936).

Section enacted primarily for benefit of plaintiff. — The history of this section shows that it was enacted primarily for the benefit, convenience and protection of the plaintiff or an assignee of the plaintiff, and not for the benefit or protection of the defendant whose rights are amply safeguarded. Miller v. Tomlinson, 194 Va. 367, 73 S.E.2d 378 (1952).

Rules of evidence not changed. — This section cannot be construed to change the rules of evidence applicable. Noland Co. v. Wagner, 153 Va. 254, 149 S.E. 478 (1929).

As to history of former law, see Carozza v. Boxley, 203 F. 673 (4th Cir. 1913).

B. What May Be Assigned.

Assignable rights of action. — A right of action for mere personal torts, such as assault and battery, false imprisonment, malicious prosecution, defamation and deceit, which die with the party and do not survive, cannot be assigned, but a right of action to recover damages for an injury to property, real or personal, may be assigned. Dillard v. Collins, 66 Va. (25 Gratt.) 343 (1874); Norfolk & W.R.R. v. Read, 87 Va. 185, 12 S.E. 395 (1890).

A right of action in pending suit against railroad company for negligently setting fire to plaintiff's property may be assigned in whole or in part. Tyler v. Ricamore, 87 Va. 466, 12 S.E. 799 (1891).

When a lower proprietor of land is damaged by the permanent diversion of water from a stream by a city, and after the diversion such proprietor sells and conveys his property thus damaged to a third person and assigns to him all the assignor's rights which belonged to the owner of the property at the time of the diversion, the purchaser is thus clothed with all rights which belonged to the owner at the time of diversion, and has the right to recover the damages resulting from such diversion. Such damages are a legitimate subject of assignment, and it is immaterial that the assignee was also the grantee of the land who purchased it at a reduced price in consequence of the diversion. City of Lynchburg v. Mitchell, 114 Va. 229, 76 S.E. 286 (1912).

A right of action against a common carrier for injury to goods while in course of transportation is assignable. Norfolk & W.R.R. v. Read, 87 Va. 185, 12 S.E. 395 (1890).

Indemnitors as assignees of right of contribution against joint tort-feasors. — Under this section and § 55-22, an action was properly brought by a transit company to secure contribution from other joint tort-feasors for the benefit of insurance companies that had indemnified the transit company for a settlement made with a passenger injured in one of its busses. The indemnitors were assignees and the beneficial owners of the right of the transit company to enforce contribution against such tort-feasors, and they had the right to proceed in the name of the transit company for their own use and benefit. McKay v. Citizens Rapid Transit Co., 190 Va. 851, 59 S.E.2d 121 (1950).

A contingent or future interest may be assigned. Prince v. Barham, 127 Va. 462, 103 S.E. 626 (1920).

Leases. — It is settled law that in the absence of express prohibition all leases are assignable. Wainwright v. Bankers' Loan & Inv. Co., 112 Va. 630, 72 S.E. 129 (1911).

Mechanic's lien. — The contract and mechanic's lien under the statute may be assigned, and the assignee may enforce the lien in the same mode that the mechanic might do it. Iaege v. Bossieux, 56 Va. (15 Gratt.) 83 (1859).

Open accounts. — A debt due from another, though evidenced by an open account, is a chose in action, and the beneficial owner thereof may maintain an action therefor in his own name under this section. Phillips v. City of Portsmouth, 115 Va. 180, 78 S.E. 651 (1913).

Under this section an ordinary running account between parties, showing an alleged indebtedness from the one to the other, is assignable. Porter v. Young, 85 Va. 49, 6 S.E. 803 (1888).

Personal service contracts. — Where the personal services of another are expressly contracted for, or are necessarily involved in the subject matter of the contract, the contract is founded on personal trust and confidence, and is not assignable until the services have been performed. Epperson v. Epperson, 108 Va. 471, 62 S.E. 344 (1908); McGuire v. Brown, 114 Va. 235, 76 S.E. 295 (1912).

C. What Constitutes an Assignment.

1. In General.

No particular form necessary. — To constitute an assignment of a debt or other chose in action in equity no particular form is necessary. Any order, writing, or act, which makes an appropriation of a fund, will amount to an equitable assignment of the fund, and taking all the surrounding circumstances into consideration, if it appears that the assignor intended to assign a particular fund to the assignee, and the assignee so understood and accepted it, then it is sufficient to pass to the assignee the debt so secured. Cunningham v. Herndon, 6 Va. (2 Call) 530 (1801); Atwell v. Towles, 15 Va. (1 Munf.) 175 (1810); Switzer v. Noffsinger, 82 Va. 518 (1886). See also S.H. Hawes & Co. v. William R. Trigg Co., 110 Va. 165, 65 S.E. 538 (1909), modified, 218 U.S. 452, 31 S. Ct. 49, 54 L. Ed. 1107 (1910); Hughes v. Burwell, 113 Va. 598, 75 S.E. 230 (1912); Rinehart & Dennis Co. v. McArthur, 123 Va. 556, 96 S.E. 829 (1918); Poff v. Poff, 128 Va. 62, 104 S.E. 719 (1920).

But section only applies to assignee or beneficial owner. — A debtor sold and conveyed property to a purchaser, who, as part of the consideration, covenanted that he would pay certain debts of his grantor. The purchaser conveyed to a second purchaser, who, likewise, as a part of consideration for the conveyance to him, covenanted that he would pay the said debts of the original grantor. A motion for a joint judgment at law in favor of the creditor against the original debtor and each of the purchasers, who had successively covenanted to pay the debts, cannot be maintained under this section. For the creditor is neither assignee nor beneficial owner of the debts which the successive purchasers had promised to pay, but the true owner of the debt of the original debtor. McIlvane v. Big Stoney Lumber Co., 105 Va. 613, 54 S.E. 473 (1906).

Subrogation is not the same as assignment. Nationwide Mut. Ins. Co. v. Minnifield, 213 Va. 797, 196 S.E.2d 75 (1973).

But distinction between assignment and subrogation not determinative in construing section. — As the term "beneficial owner" in this section is broad enough to include a subrogee, the distinction between assignment and subrogation is not determinative in construing this section. Nationwide Mut. Ins. Co. v. Minnifield, 213 Va. 797, 196 S.E.2d 75 (1973).

2. Necessity for Consideration.

A written assignment of a claim does not necessarily import a valuable consideration; and if it be fairly inferable, from the circumstances, that the assignment was a gift, the assignor cannot be held responsible to make good the claim, to the immediate assignee or to his assignees for value. Wood v. Duval, 36 Va. (9 Leigh) 6 (1837).

Presumption as to amount. — In absence of proof of consideration for assignment, it must be presumed to have been the value of the thing assigned, and such value measures the recovery on recourse. Barley v. Layman, 79 Va. 518 (1884).

3. Notice.

Effect of notice. — The debtor, before notice of the assignment may, by contract with his creditors, thoroughly modify the legal relation subsisting between them, or may enter into a new and different contract, which shall by express words constitute an extinguishment of the subsisting contract. The assignee should be diligent in giving notice to the debtor, that he might know his real creditor. Without such notice, the debtor has every reason to consider the payee still his creditor, and any payment made to the payee, or new contract expressly entered into between them in extinguishment of the note, before notice of the assignment, is in contemplation of law a payment of the note, and the assignee cannot recover upon it as against the payee, if the defendant pleads payment, and files with his plea an account showing the nature of the payment relied on. Huffman v. Walker, 67 Va. (26 Gratt.) 314 (1875); Switzer v. Noffsinger, 82 Va. 518 (1886).

Recordation. — Assignments of choses in action need not be recorded in Virginia. Hence, such recordation if made would not constitute constructive notice to third persons. Kirkland v. Brune, 72 Va. (31 Gratt.) 126 (1878); Gregg v. Sloan, 76 Va. 497 (1881); Bickle v. Chrisman, 76 Va. 678 (1882); Gordon v. Rixey, 76 Va. 694 (1882); Daily v. Warren, 80 Va. 512 (1885); Ginter v. Breeden, 90 Va. 565, 19 S.E. 656 (1894).

Legal effect of notice of assignment is not to make the debtor disclose his defenses, but to preclude him from setting up after-acquired defenses against assignor. Norton v. Rose, 2 Va. (2 Wash.) 233 (1796); Garland v. Richeson, 25 Va. (4 Rand.) 266 (1826); Feazle v. Dillard, 32 Va. (5 Leigh) 30 (1834); Gordon v. Rixey, 76 Va. 694 (1882); Stebbins v. Bruce, 80 Va. 389 (1885).

D. Effect of Assignment.

1. Assignee Takes Subject to Equities and Set-Offs.

Assignee takes same rights and is subject to same liabilities as assignor. — It is settled law in this State that assignee of nonnegotiable paper stands in the shoes of his assignor, and takes subject to all defenses of the debtor against the assignor existing before notice of assignment. Davis v. Miller, 55 Va. (14 Gratt.) 1 (1857); Etheridge v. Parker, 76 Va. 247 (1882); Stebbins v. Bruce, 80 Va. 389 (1885).

It has been settled by many decisions that the effect of the statute is not to give the assignee of nonnegotiable paper a legal title, so that equities are cut off against him, but only to permit him to enforce in his own name an equitable title at law, subject to all prior equities, just as when he sued in the assignor's name. Davis v. Miller, 55 Va. (14 Gratt.) 1 (1857); Clarksons v. Doddridge, 55 Va. (14 Gratt.) 42 (1857); Iaege v. Bossieux, 56 Va. (15 Gratt.) 83 (1859); Tyler v. Ricamore, 87 Va. 466, 12 S.E. 799 (1891).

Under this section an assignee is clothed with just such capacity to sue as existed at common law in his assignor. He is vested with power to institute such actions, and such actions only, as his assignor could have maintained. Aylett v. Walker, 92 Va. 540, 24 S.E. 226 (1896).

In an action by an assignee the defendant may avail himself of all defenses he had against the assignor before he received notice of the assignment. Hartford Fire Ins. Co. v. Mutual Sav. & Loan Co., 193 Va. 269, 68 S.E.2d 541 (1952).

Breaches of contract occurring after assignment. — Where the right asserted by the debtor against the assignee was not the right of set-off, growing out of an extrinsic transaction, but rather the right of recoupment, allowing diminution of the claim made for failure of the claimant to live up to the terms of the agreement out of which the claim arose, breaches by the assignor of its contract could be properly urged against its assignee though occurring after the assignment. National Bank & Trust Co. v. Castle, 196 Va. 686, 85 S.E.2d 228 (1955).

Effect when debtor and creditor firms have common partners. — The assignee of a nonnegotiable chose in action may, under this section, maintain thereon in his own name any action which his assignor might have maintained. But where the debtor and the creditor are firms in which there are one or more common partners, no action at law can be maintained in the name of the assignee of the chose, as none could have been maintained by his assignors. Aylett v. Walker, 92 Va. 540, 24 S.E. 226 (1896).

Set-off may be waived. — In accordance with the well settled principle that an individual may waive any statutory or constitutional provision intended for his benefit, one having the right of set-off may waive it. But where an agreement is relied on in justification of a departure from the general rules governing set-off, it must appear that the proposed set-off is embraced therein. Armour & Co. v. Whitney & Kemmerer, Inc., 164 Va. 12, 178 S.E. 889 (1935).

2. Right to Sue.

In name of assignee. — The assignee or beneficial owner of a contract may, under the express provisions of this section, maintain an action thereon in his own name. Oliver Ref. Co. v. Portsmouth Cotton Oil Ref. Corp., 109 Va. 513, 64 S.E. 56 (1909).

Under this section a trustee and assignee of a joint stock company may sue in his own name for unpaid subscriptions to the capital stock of the company. Glenn v. Scott, 28 F. 804 (C.C.W.D. Va. 1886).

In name of either party. — Where money due a subcontractor was assigned by him to creditors pursuant to an order to pay which was accepted by the contractors, the only effect of this section was to enable the assignee to sue in the name of the assignor taking the assigned claim subject to all equities of the assignor in whom the legal title still remained, and it was therefore error to refuse to permit the assignor to sue thereon for his own benefit and for the use of his assignees to the extent of their interest. Carozza v. Boxley, 203 F. 673 (4th Cir. 1913).

Under this section suit may be brought on an assigned chose in action either in the name of the original obligee or payee, in his name for the use of the assignee or in the name of the assignee alone. Carozza v. Boxley, 203 F. 673 (4th Cir. 1913).

Under this section an action on a fire insurance policy, which contained a standard mortgage clause, could be maintained by the owner of the realty and did not have to be brought by the mortgagee. Glens Falls Ins. Co. v. Sherritt, 95 F.2d 823 (4th Cir. 1938).

The assignee of a bond under our statute does not acquire the legal title to the debt, but an equitable right, which, by virtue of the statute, he may assert at law in his own name, and he has his election to sue, at law, in his own name, or in that of the original obligee, for his benefit. Garland v. Richeson, 25 Va. (4 Rand.) 266 (1826).

Under this section the assignee of an insurance policy could have sued in his own name, but not having done so, a recovery for his benefit is not thereby barred. The indorsement of the fact is sometimes not made until after the execution is issued. Aetna Ins. Co. v. Aston, 123 Va. 327, 96 S.E. 772 (1918).

A deed of trust on a chose in action is an assignment pro tanto of the chose and an action thereon in the name of the assignor for the benefit of himself and the creditor secured is properly brought. Newton v. White, 115 Va. 844, 80 S.E. 561 (1914).

Right to sue accruing prior to assignment of judgment not included. — This section does not authorize an assignee of a judgment to maintain an action against an officer and the sureties on his official bond for a breach occurring prior to the assignment, by reason of the officer's failure to return a forthcoming bond taken on the judgment as prescribed by statute to give the bond the force of a judgment against the obligors. The section does not invest in assignees as an incident to assignment a litigious right against a third person for an injury which accrued prior to the assignment. Commonwealth v. Wampler, 104 Va. 337, 51 S.E. 737 (1905).

Legatee has no right to collect debts under this section. — This section was not intended to overthrow the well-established principle and the rule of law that, in case of death, the personal estate of the decedent passes "to the personal representatives, and that he alone has title in law to them," and to afford to a legatee the right to bring an action at law to collect a debt belonging to the estate of the testator, without first deriving title from the personal representative. Strader v. Metropolitan Life Ins. Co., 128 Va. 238, 105 S.E. 74 (1920).

§ 8.01-14. Suit against assignor. — Any assignee or beneficial owner may recover from any assignor of a writing; but only joint assignors shall be joined as defendants in one action. A remote assignor shall have the benefit of the same defense as if the suit had been instituted by his immediate assignee. (Code 1950, § 8-95; 1977, c. 617.)

I. DECISIONS UNDER PRIOR LAW.

Editor's note. — The cases cited below were decided under corresponding provisions of former law. The term "this section," as used below, refers to former provisions.

Action may be by motion against remote assignor. — Under the provisions of this section an action may be maintained by motion by an assignee of a chose in action against a remote assignor thereof to recover money upon the contract implied by the assignment that he will repay the consideration received by him for the chose, if by the use of due diligence it cannot be made out of the obligor or maker. Long v. Pence, 93 Va. 584, 25 S.E. 593 (1896).

Note necessary as evidence. — In a proceeding by an assignee of a note against a remote assignor to recover on the contract implied by the assignment, the note is a necessary piece of evidence for the plaintiff in order to prove the assignment, and also to show the measure of plaintiff's recovery. Long v. Pence, 93 Va. 584, 25 S.E. 593 (1896).

§ 8.01-15. Suits by and against unincorporated associations or orders. — All unincorporated associations or orders may sue and be sued under the name by which they are commonly known and called, or under which they do business, and judgments and executions against any such association or order shall bind its real and personal property in like manner as if it were incorporated. (Code 1950, § 8-66; 1962, c. 250; 1977, c. 617.)

REVISERS' NOTE

Section 8.01-15 is the first sentence of former § 8-66; the second sentence of which regarding process was deleted as unnecessary in light of § 8.01-305.

Law Review. — For survey of Virginia law on business associations for the year 1974-1975, see 61 Va. L. Rev. 1650 (1975). For article on condominium association liability for failure to provide adequate security or maintenance in the common areas, see 22 U. Rich. L. Rev. 127 (1988).

I. DECISIONS UNDER PRIOR LAW.

Editor's note. — The cases cited below were decided under corresponding provisions of former law. The term "this section," as used below, refers to former provisions.

This section may be viewed as merely procedural. Hawthorne v. Austin Organ Co., 71 F.2d 945 (4th Cir.), cert. denied, 293 U.S. 623, 55 S. Ct. 237, 79 L. Ed. 710 (1934).

"Unincorporated association" defined. — The words "unincorporated association," as employed in this section, denote a voluntary group of persons joined together by mutual consent for the purpose of promoting some stated objective. Such an association suggests an organized group made up of persons who become members of the association voluntarily, but subject to certain rules or bylaws; the members are customarily subject to discipline for violations or non-compliance with the rules of the association. Yonce v. Miners Mem. Hosp. Ass'n, 161 F. Supp. 178 (W.D. Va. 1958).

The word "association" as here used refers to associations such as trade unions, fraternal organizations, business organizations, and the like. Yonce v. Miners Mem. Hosp. Ass'n, 161 F. Supp. 178 (W.D. Va. 1958).

Capacity to sue or be sued does not necessarily imply standing. — This section specifically confers upon an unincorporated association the capacity to sue or be sued, but the fact that an association has capacity to sue does not necessarily imply that it also has standing to maintain a particular action. Richmond Black Police Officers Ass'n v. City of Richmond, 386 F. Supp. 151 (E.D. Va. 1974).

Name of organization should be used in actions. — An action to compel railway to recognize a labor organization as bargaining agent, in view of this section, should be prosecuted in the name of the organization. Railway Employees' Dep't of Am. Fed'n of Labor v. Virginian Ry., 39 F. Supp. 354 (E.D. Va. 1941).

Authority to proceed with litigation. — This section contemplates that litigation brought pursuant thereto will be instituted by the officers of such unincorporated association or order who have charge of its affairs or by members of the association or order who have been legally authorized to proceed with the litigation. Brown v. Virginia Advent Christian

Conference, 194 Va. 909, 76 S.E.2d 240 (1953).

Real estate investment trust created under Chapter 9 of Title 6.1 is an "unincorporated association" within the meaning of this section, entitled to sue in its own name. Grenco Real Estate Inv. Trust v. Brooker, 215 Va. 413, 211 S.E.2d 33 (1975).

The United Mine Workers of America Welfare and Retirement Fund is a trust and is not an unincorporated association in the sense contemplated by this section. Yonce v. Miners Mem. Hosp. Ass'n, 161 F. Supp. 178 (W.D. Va. 1958).

ARTICLE 3.

Death or Change of Parties.

§ 8.01-16. New parties may have continuance. — Except in the Supreme Court any new party to a case, whether he be joined or substituted, may in the discretion of the court have a continuance; and the court may allow him to plead anew or amend the pleadings so far as it deems reasonable, but in other respects the case shall proceed to final judgment or decree for or against him, in like manner as if he had been an original party to the case. (Code 1950, § 8-150; 1977, c. 617.)

REVISERS' NOTE

The substantive effect of the section remains the same as former § 8-150 whereby a continuance is discretionary with the trial court in any case where a new party is joined or substituted. With the abolition of the writ of scire facias, § 8.01-24, the procedure will be by motion.

I. DECISIONS UNDER PRIOR LAW.

Editor's note. — The case cited below was decided under corresponding provisions of former law. The term "this section," as used below, refers to former provisions.

This section refers to such cases as are revived by an order entered in term. Stearns v. Richmond Paper Mfg. Co., 86 Va. 1034, 11 S.E. 1057 (1890).

§ 8.01-17. When party whose powers cease is defendant. — When the party whose powers cease is defendant, the plaintiff may continue his suit against him to final judgment or decree; provided that a successor in interest may be substituted in accordance with the Rules of Court; and provided further that upon motion the court may order that the suit proceed against the former party as well as the successor. (Code 1950, § 8-152; 1954, c. 333; 1977, c. 617.)

REVISERS' NOTE

Section 8.01-17 follows former § 8-152 by giving a plaintiff the right to continue his action against a defendant whose powers have ceased, e.g., an executor who has died. The first proviso permits the appointment of a successor for such a defendant. See Rules 2:16 and 3:15.

The second proviso permits the plaintiff, upon court order, to proceed against such defendant as well as his successor; former § 8-152 is expanded to permit this in law as well as equity.

Cross references. — For rules of court as to substitution of parties, see Rules 2:16, 3:15.

§ 8.01-18. When suit discontinued unless revived. — If the committee, personal representative, heir, or devisee of the plaintiff or appellant who was a party, or of the decedent whose personal representative was plaintiff or appellant, shall not make a motion for substitution of parties under the applicable Rules of Court within a reasonable time after there may have been a suggestion on the record of the fact making such motion proper, the suit of such plaintiff or appellant shall be discontinued, unless good cause be shown to the contrary. (Code 1950, § 8-153; 1954, c. 333; 1977, c. 617.)

REVISERS' NOTE

A "reasonable time" has been inserted for the substitution of parties under the Rules of Court. Otherwise minor language changes are made in the proposal without material change to former § 8-153.

Cross references. — For rules of court governing substitution of parties, see Rules 2:16, 3:15.

§ 8.01-19. Effect of marriage or change of name of party.

The marriage of a party shall not cause a suit or action to abate. If a party changes his name, upon affidavit or other proof of the fact, the suit or action shall proceed in the new name, but if the change of name be not suggested before judgment, the judgment shall be as valid, and may be enforced in like manner, as if no such change of name had taken place. (Code 1950, § 8-147; 1973, c. 401; 1977, c. 617.)

§ 8.01-20. Effect of marriage, change of name or death on appeal.

If at any time after verdict or judgment in the trial court during the pendency of an appeal or before the appeal is granted, the marriage, change of name or death of a party, or any other fact which might otherwise be relied on in abatement occurs, and such fact is suggested or relied on in abatement in the Court of Appeals or the Supreme Court, the court may, in its discretion, take or retain jurisdiction and enter judgment or decree in the case as if such event had not occurred. (Code 1950, § 8-148; 1973, c. 401; 1977, c. 617; 1984, c. 703.)

I. Decisions Under Current Law.
II. Decisions Under Prior Law.

I. DECISIONS UNDER CURRENT LAW.

Death after notice of appeal. — Where plaintiff's death occurred after the trial court lost jurisdiction of his action and after the notice of appeal had been filed, the appeal was ordered to proceed in the decedent's name as if the death had not occurred. Locke v. Johns-Manville Corp., 221 Va. 951, 275 S.E.2d 900 (1981).

Applied in Norfolk & P. Belt Line R.R. v. Barker, 221 Va. 924, 275 S.E.2d 613 (1981); Lawrence v. Wirth, 226 Va. 408, 309 S.E.2d 315 (1983); Hogan v. Carter, 226 Va. 361, 310 S.E.2d 666 (1983); Morris v. Mosby, 227 Va. 517, 317 S.E.2d 493 (1984).

II. DECISIONS UNDER PRIOR LAW.

Editor's note. — The cases cited below were decided under corresponding provisions of former law. The term "this section," as used below, refers to former provisions.

Death after appeal allowed. — Where an appeal is allowed or writ of error awarded before the death of a party to a suit or action, the case is from that moment a case pending in the appellate court, and under this section there is no abatement in the appellate court because of the death. The same was very nearly true at common law. The statute effected no other change in the procedure than that it expressly leaves it to the discretion of the appellate court, where the death is made known to such court and is suggested on its record, to proceed with the case and enter judgment or decree as if such death had not occurred; whereas prior to the statute, a practice had grown up requiring, in case of death of either party, if made known to the appellate court and suggested on its record, a revival of the appeal or writ of error by consent. Poff v. Poff, 128 Va. 62, 104 S.E. 719 (1920).

Death before appeal allowed. — Where the death of a party to a suit or action occurs before an appeal is allowed or writ of error is awarded, the suit or action abates as to the deceased party. If an appeal or writ of error is sought in behalf of the estate of such deceased party, the application must be made by petition of his representative. Poff v. Poff, 128 Va. 62, 104 S.E. 719 (1920).

An appeal or writ of error cannot be granted to one who is dead and the appellate court is without authority under this section to enter judgment in a case in which the appellate proceedings were begun after the death of the alleged plaintiff in error. Booth v. Dotson, 93 Va. 233, 24 S.E. 935 (1896).

Divorce suit. — In a suit for divorce by a wife against her husband, the trial court decreed a divorce to the husband on his cross-bill. The husband died pending appeal by his wife after the case was argued and submitted to the Supreme Court. By virtue of this section the appellate court may, in its discretion, enter its decree dealing with the adjudications of the original decree as if no death of any party to the cause had occurred. Cumming v. Cumming, 127 Va. 16, 102 S.E. 572 (1920).

Suggestion of bankruptcy. — In a proceeding for refund of taxes a District of Columbia corporation obtained a decree declaring an Arlington County license tax invalid and a refund was paid by the county. Pending the county's appeal counsel for the corporation filed a suggestion of bankruptcy and made a motion for dismissal. The rules of court being inapplicable to actions for refund of taxes, it was held under this section that the mere suggestion of bankruptcy when no motion had been made to substitute the trustee and no formal proof of bankruptcy or any stay order by the bankruptcy court had been offered did not justify dismissal of the appeal. County Bd. v. Kent Stores of Wash., Inc., 196 Va. 929, 86 S.E.2d 44 (1955).

§ 8.01-21. Judgment when death or disability occurs after verdict but before judgment.

— When a party dies, or becomes convicted of a felony or insane, or the powers of a party who is a personal representative or committee cease, if such fact occurs after verdict, judgment may be entered as if it had not occurred. (Code 1950, § 8-145; 1977, c. 617.)

Cross references. — For rules of court as to substitution of parties, see Rules 2:16, 3:15.

I. Decisions Under Current Law.
II. Decisions Under Prior Law.

I. DECISIONS UNDER CURRENT LAW.

Purpose. — The clear purpose of this section is to eliminate the wastefulness of retrying an action which has been completely litigated. Boyd v. Bulala, 647 F. Supp. 781 (W.D. Va. 1986), aff'd in part, rev'd in part, 877 F.2d 1191 (4th Cir. 1989); Bulala v. Boyd, 239 Va. 218, 389 S.E.2d 670 (1990).

Sections 8.01-21, 8.01-25, 8.01-50, and 8.01-56 compared. — The requirements of the survival and wrongful death statutes, §§ 8.01-25, 8.01-50 and 8.01-56, apply when the death occurs before a final verdict, whereas this section applies where the death occurs after the verdict. Boyd v. Bulala, 647 F. Supp. 781 (W.D. Va. 1986), aff'd in part, rev'd in part, 877 F.2d 1191 (4th Cir. 1989); Bulala v. Boyd, 239 Va. 218, 389 S.E.2d 670 (1990).

Sections 8.01-25 and 8.01-56 are not in conflict with this section. They were enacted to extend the application of § 8.01-50, the wrongful death statute, those situations not covered by the original Lord Campbell's Act, in which a plaintiff who has filed an action for personal injuries, dies of those injuries before a verdict is returned. It was unnecessary at common law to amend, revive, or convert the action of the party who survived the return of a verdict, and it is equally unnecessary under the present statutory scheme. Bulala v. Boyd, 239 Va. 218, 389 S.E.2d 670 (1990).

Death of child after medical malpractice verdict. — Death of a child born with birth defects after a medical malpractice verdict did not require converting her claim into one for wrongful death. This section directly so provides, by directing that in such cases, "judgment may be entered as if [death] had not occurred." Sections 8.01-25 and 8.01-56 are not in conflict. They deal with the situation where death occurs before verdict. Boyd v. Bulala, 905 F.2d 764 (4th Cir. 1990).

Death of plaintiff after trial not grounds for new trial or admission of new evidence. — Motion by defendant in medical malpractice action either to grant a new trial or to open the record to admit new evidence, which motion was prompted by the death of the infant plaintiff some six weeks after the trial, on grounds that had she died before trial, the parents could not have recovered certain elements of damages, including her future medical costs, was denied. Under Federal Rules of Civil Procedure 59 and 60(b)(2), newly discovered evidence must pertain to facts which existed at the time of trial. Were the rule otherwise, litigation would never end. Moreover, this section specifically provides for the entry of judgment when a party dies after the verdict. Boyd v. Bulala, 672 F. Supp. 915 (W.D. Va. 1987).

II. DECISIONS UNDER PRIOR LAW.

Editor's note. — The case cited below was decided under corresponding provisions of former law.

Convict's privilege to waive appointment of committee. — There are no statutes or rules to deny a convict, already within the civil jurisdiction of the court at the time of his felony conviction and incarceration, the privilege of waiving the appointment of a committee and proceeding to trial and judgment in a law action in which he is represented by counsel of his own choosing. Dunn v. Terry, 216 Va. 234, 217 S.E.2d 849 (1975).

§ 8.01-22. When death or disability occurs as to any of several plaintiffs or defendants. — If a party plaintiff or defendant becomes incapable of prosecuting or defending because of death, insanity, conviction of felony, removal from office, or other reason and there are one or more co-plaintiffs or co-defendants, the court on motion may in its discretion either (i) suspend the case until a successor in interest is appointed in accordance with the Rules of Court, or (ii) sever the action or suit so that the case shall proceed against the remaining parties without delay, with the case as to the former party being continued and tried separately against the successor in interest when he is substituted as provided by the Rules of Court. (Code 1950, § 8-146; 1977, c. 617.)

REVISERS' NOTE

Since Rules 2:16 and 3:15 provide an adequate procedure for substitution of a party if he dies, etc., former § 8-146 is altered to give the court discretion to halt the entire proceedings pending the appointment of a successor or to permit the action to proceed against the living parties severing the decedent and preserving a separate action as to him.

Since § 8.01-25 provides that all actions survive, the provision in former § 8-146 regarding the question of survivability has been deleted.

Cross references. — For rules of court as to substitution of parties, see Rules 2:16, 3:15.

I. DECISIONS UNDER PRIOR LAW.

Editor's note. — The cases cited below were decided under corresponding provisions of former law.

Before appeal is allowed. — Where the death of a party to a suit or action occurs before an appeal is allowed or writ of error is awarded, the suit or action abates as to the deceased party. If an appeal or writ of error is sought in behalf of the estate of such deceased party, the application must be made by petition of his representative. Poff v. Poff, 128 Va. 62, 104 S.E. 719 (1920).

Convict's privilege to waive appointment of committee. — There are no statutes or rules to deny a convict, already within the civil jurisdiction of the court at the time of his felony conviction and incarceration, the privilege of waiving the appointment of a committee and proceeding to trial and judgment in a law action in which he is represented by counsel of his own choosing. Dunn v. Terry, 216 Va. 234, 217 S.E.2d 849 (1975).

Ejectment. — Husband and wife brought an action of ejectment to recover land. It did not abate when the husband died, but upon his death the cause of action survived to his wife. McMurray v. Dixon, 105 Va. 605, 54 S.E. 481 (1906).

§ 8.01-23. Decree in suit when number of parties exceeds thirty and one of them dies. — When, in any suit in equity, the number of parties exceeds thirty, and any one of the parties jointly interested with others in any question arising therein, shall die, the court may, notwithstanding, if in its opinion all classes of interests are represented and no one will be prejudiced thereby, proceed to render a decree in such suit as if such party were alive; decreeing to the heirs, devisees, legatees, distributees, or personal representatives, as the case may be, such interest as the deceased person, if alive, would be entitled to. The provisions of § 8.01-322 shall apply to decrees entered hereunder. (Code 1950, §§ 8-155, 8-156; 1977, c. 617.)

REVISERS' NOTE

Section 8.01-23 combines former §§ 8-155 and 8-156.

Article 4.

Writ of Scire Facias Abolished.

§ 8.01-24. Writ of scire facias abolished; substitutes therefor. — The writ of scire facias is hereby abolished. Relief heretofore available by scire facias may be obtained by appropriate action or motion pursuant to applicable statutes and Rules of Court. (1977, c. 617.)

REVISERS' NOTE

Scire facias is a cumbersome, obsolete writ which is little understood and whose objectives can be better served by a more direct form of pleading. Thus the writ is abolished and replaced by the motion.

CHAPTER 3.

Actions.

Article 1.

Survival and Assignment of Causes of Actions.

Sec.
8.01-25. Survival of causes of action.
8.01-26. Assignment of causes of action.

Article 2.

Actions on Contracts Generally.

8.01-27. Civil action on note or writing promising to pay money.
8.01-27.1. Additional recovery in certain civil actions concerning checks.
8.01-27.2. Civil recovery for giving bad check.
8.01-28. When judgment to be given in action upon contract or note unless defendant appears and denies claim under oath.
8.01-29. Procedure in actions on annuity and instalment bonds, and other actions for penalties for nonperformance.
8.01-30. Procedure in actions on contracts made by several persons.

Sec.
8.01-31. Accounting in equity.
8.01-32. Action on lost evidences of debt; indemnifying bond.
8.01-33. When equity has jurisdiction.

Article 3.

Injury to Person or Property.

8.01-34. When contribution among wrongdoers enforced.
8.01-35. Damages for loss of income not diminished by reimbursement.
8.01-35.1. Effect of release or covenant not to sue in respect to liability and contribution.
8.01-36. Joinder of action of tort to infant with action for recovery of expenses incurred thereby.
8.01-37. Recovery of lost wages in action for injuries to emancipated infant.
8.01-37.1. Claims for medical services provided by United States; proof of reasonable value.
8.01-38. Tort liability of hospitals.
8.01-38.1. Limitation on recovery of punitive damages.

CIVIL REMEDIES AND PROCEDURE

Sec.
8.01-39. Completion or acceptance of work not bar to action against independent contractor for personal injury, wrongful death or damage to property.
8.01-40. Unauthorized use of name or picture of any person; exemplary damages; statute of limitations.
8.01-40.1. Action for injury resulting from violation of Computer Crimes Act; limitations.
8.01-40.2. Unsolicited transmission of advertising materials by facsimile machine.
8.01-41. Wrongful distraint, attachment.
8.01-42. Loss or injury to clothing in dyeing, dry cleaning, or laundering.
8.01-42.1. Civil action for racial, religious, or ethnic harassment, violence or vandalism.
8.01-42.2. Liability of guest for hotel damage.
8.01-43. Action against parent for damage to public property by minor.
8.01-44. Action against parent for damage to private property by minor.
8.01-44.1. Immunity from civil liability of members of certain committees, etc.
8.01-44.2. Action against physician for vaccine-related injury or death.
8.01-44.3. Divulgence of communications by qualified interpreters and communications assistants.
8.01-44.4. Action for shoplifting and employee theft.
8.01-44.5. Exemplary damages for persons injured by intoxicated drivers.

Article 4.

Defamation.

8.01-45. Action for insulting words.
8.01-46. Justification and mitigation of damages.
8.01-46.1. Disclosure of employment-related information; presumptions; causes of action; definitions.
8.01-47. Immunity of school personnel investigating or reporting certain incidents.
8.01-48. Mitigation in actions against newspapers, etc.
8.01-49. Defamatory statements in radio and television broadcasts.
8.01-49.1. Liability for defamatory material on the Internet.

Article 5.

Death by Wrongful Act.

8.01-50. Action for death by wrongful act; how and when to be brought.

Sec.
8.01-51. No action when deceased has compromised claim.
8.01-52. Amount of damages.
8.01-53. Class and beneficiaries; when determined.
8.01-54. Judgment to distribute recovery when verdict fails to do so.
8.01-55. Compromise of claim for death by wrongful act.
8.01-56. When right of action not to determine nor action to abate.

Article 6.

Injuries to Railroad Employees.

8.01-57. Liability of railroads for injury to certain employees.
8.01-58. Contributory negligence no bar to recovery; violation of safety appliance acts.
8.01-59. Assumption of risk; violation of safety appliance acts.
8.01-60. Contracts exempting from liability void; set-off of insurance.
8.01-61. Definition of "common carrier" as used in article.
8.01-62. Action may embrace liability under both State and federal acts.

Article 7.

Motor Vehicle Accidents.

8.01-63. Liability for death or injury to guest in motor vehicle.
8.01-64. Liability for negligence of minor.
8.01-65. Defense of lack of consent of owner.
8.01-66. Recovery of damages for loss of use of vehicle.
8.01-66.1. Remedy for arbitrary refusal of motor vehicle insurance claim.

Article 7.1.

Lien for Hospital, Medical and Nursing Services.

8.01-66.2. Lien against person whose negligence causes injury.
8.01-66.3. Lien inferior to claim of attorney or personal representative.
8.01-66.4. Subrogation.
8.01-66.5. Written notice required.
8.01-66.6. Liability for reasonable charges for services.
8.01-66.7. Hearing and disposal of claim of unreasonableness.
8.01-66.8. Petition to enforce lien.
8.01-66.9. Lien in favor of Commonwealth, its programs, institutions or departments on claim for personal injuries.
8.01-66.9:1. Lien against recovery for medical treatment provided to prisoner.

Sec.
8.01-66.10. Death claims settled by compromise or suit.
8.01-66.11. Necessity for settlement or judgment.
8.01-66.12. Term physician to include chiropractor.

Article 8.

Actions for the Sale, Lease, Exchange, Redemption and Other Disposition of Lands of Persons Under a Disability.

8.01-67. Definitions; persons under a disability; fiduciary.
8.01-68. Jurisdiction.
8.01-69. Commencement of suit; parties.
8.01-70, 8.01-71. [Repealed.]
8.01-72. When death to abate such suit.
8.01-73. Guardian ad litem to be appointed.
8.01-74. Leases on behalf of persons under disability; new leases.
8.01-75. Who not to be purchaser.
8.01-76. How proceeds from disposition to be secured and applied; when same may be paid over.
8.01-77. What proceeds of sale to pass as real estate.
8.01-78. Alternate procedure for sale of real estate of person under disability.
8.01-79. Same; reference of petition to commissioner.
8.01-80. Same; action of court on report; application of proceeds of transaction.

Article 9.

Partition.

8.01-81. Who may compel partition of land; jurisdiction; validation of certain partitions of mineral rights.
8.01-82. When shares of two or more laid off together.
8.01-83. Allotment to one or more parties, or sale, in lieu of partition.
8.01-84. Application of proceeds of sale to payment of lien.
8.01-85. Disposition of share in proceeds of person under disability.
8.01-86. [Repealed.]
8.01-87. Validation of certain partitions prior to act of 1922.
8.01-88. Decree of partition to vest legal title.
8.01-89. When proceeds of sale deemed personal estate.
8.01-90. When name or share of parties unknown.
8.01-91. Effect of partition or sale on lessee's rights.
8.01-92. Allowance of attorneys' fees out of unrepresented shares.

Sec.
8.01-93. Partition of goods, etc., by sale, if necessary.

Article 10.

Sale, Lease, or Exchange of Certain Estates in Property.

8.01-94. When sold, leased or exchanged.
8.01-95. Procedure in such case.

Article 11.

General Provisions for Judicial Sales.

8.01-96. Decree for sale; how made; bond of commissioner.
8.01-97. Delinquent taxes to be ascertained.
8.01-98. Sales of land when purchase price insufficient to pay taxes, etc.
8.01-99. Bond required of special commissioner for sale.
8.01-100. Liability of clerk for false certificate or failure to give bond.
8.01-101. Purchasers relieved of liability for purchase money paid to such commissioner.
8.01-102. Purchasers not required to see to application of purchase money.
8.01-103. Special commissioner or other person appointed to do so to receive purchase money, etc.; liability of clerk for failure to give notice of appointment.
8.01-104. [Repealed.]
8.01-105. Rule against special commissioner, purchaser, etc., for judgment for amounts due.
8.01-106. How cause heard upon rule and judgment rendered.
8.01-107. Trial by jury of issues made upon rule.
8.01-108. When sureties of commissioner, purchaser, etc., proceeded against by rule.
8.01-109. Commission for selling, collecting, etc.; each piece of property to constitute separate sale.
8.01-110. Appointment of special commissioner to execute deed, etc.; effect of deed.
8.01-111. What such deed to show.
8.01-112. Reinstatement of cause to appoint special commissioner to make deed.
8.01-113. When title of purchaser at judicial sale not to be disturbed.

Article 12.

Detinue.

8.01-114. When property to be taken by officer; summary of evidence, affidavits and report to be filed.

CIVIL REMEDIES AND PROCEDURE

Sec.	
8.01-115.	Bond required as prerequisite.
8.01-116.	Return of property to defendant or other claimant.
8.01-117.	Exceptions to sufficiency of bonds.
8.01-118.	[Repealed.]
8.01-119.	Hearing to review issuance of order or process under § 8.01-114 or to consider request for such order or process.
8.01-120.	No verdict as to some items; omission of price or value.
8.01-121.	Final judgment.
8.01-122.	Charges for keeping property.
8.01-123.	Recovery of damages sustained for property withheld during appeal.

Article 13.

Unlawful Entry and Detainer.

8.01-124.	Motion for judgment in circuit court for unlawful entry or detainer.
8.01-125.	When summons returnable to circuit court; jury.
8.01-126.	Summons for unlawful detainer issued by magistrate, clerk or judge of a general district court.
8.01-127.	Removal of action.
8.01-127.1.	Removal of residential unlawful detainer actions.
8.01-128.	Verdict and judgment; damages.
8.01-129.	Appeal from judgment of general district court.
8.01-130.	Judgment not to bar action of trespass or ejectment.

Article 14.

Ejectment.

8.01-131.	Action of ejectment retained; when and by whom brought.
8.01-132.	What interest and right plaintiff must have.
8.01-133.	Who shall be defendants; when and how landlord may defend.
8.01-134.	How action commenced and prosecuted.
8.01-135.	What is to be stated in motion for judgment.
8.01-136.	How premises described.
8.01-137.	Plaintiff to state how he claims.
8.01-138.	There may be several counts and several plaintiffs.
8.01-139.	What proof by plaintiff is sufficient.
8.01-140.	Effect of reservation in deed; burden of proof.
8.01-141.	When action by cotenants, etc., against cotenants, what plaintiff to prove.
8.01-142.	Verdict when action against several defendants.
8.01-143.	When there may be several judgments against defendants.

Sec.	
8.01-144.	Recovery of part of premises claimed.
8.01-145.	When possession of part not possession of whole.
8.01-146.	When vendee, etc., entitled to conveyance of legal title, vendor cannot recover.
8.01-147.	When mortgagee or trustee not to recover.
8.01-148.	Right of defendant to resort to equity not affected.
8.01-149.	Verdict when jury finds for plaintiffs or any of them.
8.01-150.	Verdict when any plaintiff has no right.
8.01-151.	How verdict to specify premises recovered.
8.01-152.	How verdict to specify undivided interest or share.
8.01-153.	Verdict to specify estate of plaintiff.
8.01-154.	When right of plaintiff expires before trial, what judgment entered.
8.01-155.	How judgment for plaintiff entered.
8.01-156.	Authority of sheriffs, etc., to store and sell personal property removed from premises; recovery of possession by owner; disposition or sale.
8.01-157.	[Repealed.]
8.01-158.	How claim of plaintiff for profits and damages assessed.
8.01-159.	When court to assess damages.
8.01-160.	Defendant to give notice of claim for improvements.
8.01-161.	How allowed.
8.01-162.	Postponement of assessment and allowance.
8.01-163.	Judgment to be conclusive.
8.01-164.	Recovery of mesne profits, etc., not affected.
8.01-165.	Writ of right, etc., abolished.

Article 15.

Improvements.

8.01-166.	How defendant may apply therefor, and have judgment suspended.
8.01-167.	How damages of plaintiff assessed.
8.01-168.	For what time.
8.01-169.	How value of improvements determined in favor of defendant.
8.01-170.	If allowance for improvements exceed damages, what to be done.
8.01-171.	Verdict for balance, after offsetting damages against improvements.
8.01-172.	Balance for defendant a lien on the land.
8.01-173.	How tenant for life, paying for improvements, reimbursed.
8.01-174.	Exception as to mortgagees and trustees.
8.01-175.	When plaintiff may require his es-

CODE OF VIRGINIA

Sec.
- tate only to be valued; how determined; how he may elect to relinquish his title to defendant.
- 8.01-176. How payment of such value to be made by defendant; when land sold therefor.
- 8.01-177. When such value to be deemed real estate.
- 8.01-178. When and how defendant, if evicted, may recover from plaintiff amount paid.

Article 16.

Establishing Boundaries to Land.

- 8.01-179. Motion for judgment to establish boundary lines.
- 8.01-180. Parties defendant; pleadings.
- 8.01-181. Surveys.
- 8.01-182. Claims to rents, etc., not considered.
- 8.01-183. Recordation and effect of judgment.

Article 17.

Declaratory Judgments.

- 8.01-184. Power to issue declaratory judgments.
- 8.01-185. Venue.
- 8.01-186. Further relief.
- 8.01-187. Commissioners to determine compensation for property taken or damaged.
- 8.01-188. Jury trial.
- 8.01-189. Injunction.
- 8.01-190. Costs.
- 8.01-191. Construction of article.

Article 18.

Recovery of Claims Against the Commonwealth of Virginia.

- 8.01-192. How claims to be prosecuted.
- 8.01-193. Defense and hearing.
- 8.01-194. Jury may be impaneled; judgment.
- 8.01-195. No judgment to be paid without special appropriation.

Article 18.1.

Tort Claims Against the Commonwealth of Virginia.

- 8.01-195.1. Short title.
- 8.01-195.2. Definitions.
- 8.01-195.3. Commonwealth, transportation district or locality liable for damages in certain cases.
- 8.01-195.4. Jurisdiction of claims under this article; right to jury trial; service on Commonwealth or locality.
- 8.01-195.5. Settlement of certain cases.
- 8.01-195.6. Notice of claim.
- 8.01-195.7. Statute of limitations.

Sec.
- 8.01-195.8. Release of further claims.
- 8.01-195.9. Claims evaluation program.

Article 19.

Actions by the Commonwealth.

- 8.01-196. Comptroller to institute proceedings.
- 8.01-197. In what name; when not to abate.
- 8.01-198. Action, against whom instituted.
- 8.01-199. Judgment, nature of.
- 8.01-200. Mistakes against State corrected.
- 8.01-201. Execution; real estate to be sold.
- 8.01-202. Execution, to whom issued.
- 8.01-203. Goods and chattels liable before real estate.
- 8.01-204. Notice of sale of real estate; when sale to be made.
- 8.01-205. How sale made.
- 8.01-206. Terms of sale.
- 8.01-207. Who to collect purchase money and make deed; disposition of proceeds of sale.
- 8.01-208. When successor of officer to make deed.
- 8.01-209. Bond for purchase money to have force of judgment.
- 8.01-210. Judgment against deceased obligors.
- 8.01-211. When venditioni exponas issued to sheriff of adjacent county; what to contain.
- 8.01-212. Officer to deliver to sheriff goods and chattels levied on.
- 8.01-213. Where same to be sold.
- 8.01-214. Where real estate to be sold.
- 8.01-215. Return of officer when sale not made because of prior encumbrance.
- 8.01-216. Comptroller's power to adjust old claims.

Article 20.

Change of Name.

- 8.01-217. How name of person may be changed.

Article 21.

Miscellaneous Provisions.

- 8.01-218. Replevin abolished.
- 8.01-219. Effect of judgment in trover.
- 8.01-220. Action for alienation of affection, breach of promise, criminal conversation and seduction abolished.
- 8.01-220.1. Defense of interspousal immunity abolished as to certain causes of action arising on or after July 1, 1981.
- 8.01-220.1:1. Civil immunity for officers, trust-

Sec.		Sec.	
	ees and directors of certain tax exempt organizations.		ing in certain Bar Association activities.
8.01-220.1:2.	Civil immunity for teachers under certain circumstances.	8.01-226.2.	Civil immunity for licensed professional engineers and licensed architects participating in rescue or relief assistance.
8.01-220.1:3.	Immunity for members of church, synagogue or religious body.		
8.01-220.1:4.	Civil immunity for officers and directors of certain nonprofit organizations.	8.01-226.3.	Civil immunity for officers, directors and members of certain crime information-gathering organizations.
8.01-220.2.	Spousal liability for emergency medical care.	8.01-226.4.	Civil immunity for hospice volunteers.
8.01-221.	Damages from violation of statute, remedy therefor and penalty.	8.01-226.5.	Immunity for installers and inspectors of child restraint devices.
8.01-222.	Notice to be given cities and towns of claims for damages for negligence.	8.01-226.5:1.	Civil immunity for school board employees supervising self-administration of asthma medication.
8.01-223.	Lack of privity no defense in certain cases.		
8.01-223.1.	Use of constitutional rights.	8.01-226.6.	"Year 2000" civil immunity for certain governmental officers and employees.
8.01-224.	Defense of governmental immunity not available to certain persons in actions for damages from blasting, etc.		
		8.01-226.7.	Owner and agent compliance with residential lead-based paint notification; maintenance immunity.
8.01-225.	Persons rendering emergency care, obstetrical services exempt from liability.	8.01-227.	Remedy by motion on certain bonds given or taken by officers; notice.
8.01-225.1.	Immunity for team physicians.		**Article 22.**
8.01-225.2.	Immunity for those rendering emergency care to animals.		**Year 2000 Liability and Damages.**
8.01-226.	Duty of care to law-enforcement officers and firefighters, etc.	8.01-227.1.	Purpose.
		8.01-227.2.	Definitions.
8.01-226.1.	Civil immunity when participat-	8.01-227.3.	Liability and damages limited.

ARTICLE 1.

Survival and Assignment of Causes of Actions.

§ 8.01-25. Survival of causes of action. — Every cause of action whether legal or equitable, which is cognizable in the Commonwealth of Virginia, shall survive either the death of the person against whom the cause of action is or may be asserted, or the death of the person in whose favor the cause of action existed, or the death of both such persons. Provided that in such an action punitive damages shall not be awarded after the death of the party liable for the injury. Provided, further, that if the cause of action asserted by the decedent in his lifetime was for a personal injury and such decedent dies as a result of the injury complained of with a timely action for damages arising from such injury pending, the action shall be amended in accordance with the provisions of § 8.01-56.

As used in this section, the term "death" shall include the death of an individual or the termination or dissolution of any other entity. (Code 1950, § 8-628; 1950, p. 948; 1952, c. 378; 1954, c. 607; 1964, c. 34; 1977, c. 617.)

REVISERS' NOTE

The section removes various limitations imposed by case and statutory law and provides that all causes of action survive the death of the plaintiff or defendant. Cf. § 64.1-145. Thus the former problem of determining what was indirect and direct injury to property has been eliminated and with it the question of determining whether there was a statute of limita-

§ 8.01-25   CODE OF VIRGINIA   § 8.01-25

tions of one or five years. Compare, e.g., Cover v. Critcher, 143 Va. 357, 130 S.E. 238 (1925), with Trust Co. v. Fletcher, 152 Va. 868, 148 S.E. 785 (1929), and Worrie v. Boze, 198 Va. 533, 95 S.E.2d 192, aff'd on rehearing, 198 Va. 891, 96 S.E.2d 799 (1957). See Herndon v. Wickham, 198 Va. 824, 97 S.E.2d 5 (1957) and annotations under former §§ 8-628.1 and 8-24.

The first proviso pertaining to the award of punitive damages codifies case law. See Dalton v. Johnson, 204 Va. 102, 129 S.E.2d 647 (1963).

The second proviso codifies case law that the Virginia wrongful death statute is not a "survival" statute but creates a new right in the personal representative of the decedent who dies as a result of a previous tortious injury. Grady v. Irvine, 254 F.2d 224 (4th Cir.), cert. denied, 358 U.S. 819, 79 S. Ct. 30, 3 L. Ed. 2d 60 (1958); Wilson v. Whittacker, 207 Va. 1032, 154 S.E.2d 124 (1967).

Formerly, in the absence of statute, only causes of action which survive may be assigned. Winston v. Gordon, 115 Va. 899, 80 S.E. 756 (1914); City of Richmond v. Hanes, 203 Va. 102, 122 S.E.2d 895 (1961). Assignability has been separated from survivability. See § 8.01-26.

Law Review. — For discussion of wrongful death action and special damages, see 47 Va. L. Rev. 354 (1961). For survey of Virginia law on torts for the year 1969-1970, see 56 Va. L. Rev. 1419 (1970). For survey of Virginia commercial law for the year 1972-1973, see 59 Va. L. Rev. 1426 (1973). For survey of Virginia law on practice and pleading for the year 1976-77, see 63 Va. L. Rev. 1459 (1977). For article, "Civil Rights and 'Personal Injuries': Virginia's Statute of Limitations for Section 1983 Suits," see 26 Wm. & Mary L. Rev. 199 (1985).

I. Decisions Under Current Law.
II. Decisions Under Prior Law.

I. DECISIONS UNDER CURRENT LAW.

Legislative intent. — It was the obvious intent of the legislature to give to survivors of decedents the cause of action set forth in this section rather than have it expire upon the death of the party having same. In re Musgrove, 7 Bankr. 892 (Bankr. W.D. Va. 1981).

The sweeping language of the opening sentence of this section manifests an intent to preserve a right of recovery after the death of either or both of the parties in interest, while the subsequent limiting language has the effect of confining wrongful death relief to that allowable under the wrongful death statutes. Miltier v. Beorn, 696 F. Supp. 1086 (E.D. Va. 1988).

Sections 8.01-21, 8.01-50, 8.01-56 and this section compared. — The requirements of the survival and wrongful death statutes, §§ 8.01-50, 8.01-56 and this section, apply when the death occurs before a final verdict, whereas § 8.01-21 applies where the death occurs after the verdict. Boyd v. Bulala, 647 F. Supp. 781 (W.D. Va. 1986), rev'd on other grounds, 877 F.2d 1191 (4th Cir. 1989).

This section and § 8.01-56 are not in conflict with § 8.01-21. They were enacted to extend the application of § 8.01-50, the wrongful death statute, those situations not covered by the original Lord Campbell's Act, in which a plaintiff who has filed an action for personal injuries, dies of those injuries before a verdict is returned. It was unnecessary at common law to amend, revive, or convert the action of the party who survived the return of a verdict, and it is equally unnecessary under the present statutory scheme. Bulala v. Boyd, 239 Va. 218, 389 S.E.2d 670 (1990).

Death of a child born with birth defects after a medical malpractice verdict did not require converting her claim into one for wrongful death. Section 8.01-21 directly so provides, by directing that in such cases, "judgment may be entered as if [death] had not occurred." This section and § 8.01-56 are not in conflict. They deal with the situation where death occurs before verdict. Boyd v. Bulala, 905 F.2d 764 (4th Cir. 1990).

Choice of recovery theory in malpractice action. — The plain language contained in this section and § 8.01-56 unequivocally mandates that a person may not recover for the same injury under the survival statute and the wrongful death statute. There can be but one recovery. Hence, the plaintiffs, as a matter of law, could not have recovered in the underlying tort action against defendants on both theories of wrongful death and survival. Therefore, in malpractice action, at an appropriate time after discovery has been completed, the plaintiffs must be required to elect whether they will proceed against the defendant attorneys on the theory that the attorneys breached a duty owed to the plaintiffs in the prosecution of the wrongful death action or breached a duty owed to the plaintiffs in the prosecution of the survival action. Hendrix v. Daugherty, 249 Va. 540, 457 S.E.2d 71 (1995).

Coexistence of wrongful death and 42 U.S.C. § 1983 claims. — The structural relationship between this section and § 8.01-50 shows that under Virginia law, a wrongful death claim can peaceably coexist with a 42 U.S.C. § 1983 claim. Miltier v. Beorn, 696 F. Supp. 1086 (E.D. Va. 1988).

This section defers to the wrongful death statute as the exclusive statement of the grievances that Virginia will recognize when a tort victim dies of her injuries. El-Meswari v. Washington Gas Light Co., 785 F.2d 483 (4th Cir. 1986).

Under the new statutory scheme, survivability no longer is germane in determining which statute of limitations applies. This section provides that all causes of action survive the death of the plaintiff or defendant. Moreover, the problem of determining direct or indirect injury has been eliminated. Section 64.1-145 now provides, in part, that: "Any action at law for damages for the . . . destruction of, or damage to any estate of or by the decedent, whether such damage be direct or indirect, may be maintained by or against the decedent's personal representative. Any such action shall survive pursuant to § 8.01-25." Now, under the straightforward provisions of § 8.01-243(B), "[e]very" action for "injury to property" is governed by a five-year statute of limitations. Pigott v. Moran, 231 Va. 76, 341 S.E.2d 179 (1986).

Where two witnesses vary in their statements of fact. — Where administratrix brought action for personal injuries based on nursing homes treatment of decedent, dismissal of the action prior to completion of administratrix's evidence deprived her of opportunity to prove damages for personal injury and, therefore, constituted reversible error; although one doctor testified that nursing home's treatment hastened decedent's death, the testimony did not leave administratrix with only a wrongful death action; court should have allowed administratrix to proceed with testimony of another doctor that the cause of death was pneumonia since when two or more witnesses introduced by a party litigant vary in their statements of fact, such party has the right to ask the court or jury to accept as true the statements most favorable to him. Lucas v. HCMF Corp., 238 Va. 446, 384 S.E.2d 92 (1989).

II. DECISIONS UNDER PRIOR LAW.

Editor's note. — The cases cited below were decided under corresponding provisions of former law. The term "this section, "as used below, refers to former provisions.

Section changes common law. — Prior to this section, no action for personal injuries not resulting in death could be maintained against the wrongdoer unless such action was brought by the injured party prior to his death. This section changed this rule of common law. Sherley v. Lotz, 200 Va. 173, 104 S.E.2d 795 (1958).

Statute of limitations not changed. — There was no intent on the part of the legislature when it enacted this section to change the statute of limitations from one to five years on causes of action for personal injury. Herndon v. Wickham, 198 Va. 824, 97 S.E.2d 5 (1957); Sherley v. Lotz, 200 Va. 173, 104 S.E.2d 795 (1958).

The cause of action which this section provides shall not be lost is not a new cause. Bagley v. Weaver, 211 Va. 779, 180 S.E.2d 686 (1971).

It is the same cause of action which an injured person was prosecuting or could have prosecuted prior to his death from an unrelated cause. Bagley v. Weaver, 211 Va. 779, 180 S.E.2d 686 (1971).

Recovery for mental anguish, pain, and suffering permitted. — It was the intent of the General Assembly to permit a recovery for mental anguish, pain, and suffering in causes of action preserved by this section. Bagley v. Weaver, 211 Va. 779, 180 S.E.2d 686 (1971).

Evidence to support action for such recovery. — In view of the express elimination of the language which before 1964 excluded a recovery for mental anguish, pain and suffering, the same kind of evidence would be necessary and admissible to support the action that would be proper if the injured person himself were suing. There would be the same elements of damage for the consideration of the jury in assessing the damages, and the evidence would mainly relate to, and the damages be for, the physical and mental suffering of the deceased and the injuries and loss generally sustained by him and his estate. Bagley v. Weaver, 211 Va. 779, 180 S.E.2d 686 (1971).

Recoveries under this section and § 8.01-50 et seq. distinguished. — The limit of recovery in an action under § 8.01-50 et seq. is different from that in the action preserved by this section. In one, the amount of the recovery is limited by statute, is for the benefit of certain designated beneficiaries, and is free from debts and liabilities. In the other, the limit is the amount of damages that can be proved, is an asset of the decedent's estate, and is subject to the payment of his debts. Bagley v. Weaver, 211 Va. 779, 180 S.E.2d 686 (1971).

§ 8.01-26. Assignment of causes of action. — Only those causes of action for damage to real or personal property, whether such damage be direct or indirect, and causes of action ex contractu are assignable. The provisions of this section shall not prohibit any injured party or his estate from making a

§ 8.01-26

voluntary assignment of the proceeds or anticipated proceeds of any court award or settlement as security for new value given in consideration of such voluntary assignment. (1977, c. 617; 1991, c. 256.)

REVISERS' NOTE

Formerly, the test of assignability was survival, and only those causes of action which would survive to the personal representative were assignable; actions which survived and therefore were assignable were those which grew out of breach of contract or were for direct injury to real or personal property. See Winston v. Gordon, 115 Va. 899, 80 S.E. 756 (1914); Richmond Redevelopment & Hous. Auth. v. Laburnum Constr. Corp., 195 Va. 827, 80 S.E.2d 574 (1954).

Section 8.01-25 allows all causes of actions to survive. Section 8.01-26 separates the issue of assignability from that of survival — i.e. no longer will an action be assignable simply because it survives. Instead, unless the action falls within § 8.01-26, it is not assignable even though it is an action which survives under § 8.01-25. However, with the exception of the elimination of the illogical distinction between direct and indirect damage to property, the section codifies existing case law on the assignment of actions. See Birmingham v. Chesapeake & O.R.R., 98 Va. 548, 37 S.E. 17 (1900) also cited in Maynard v. General Elec. Co., 486 F.2d 538 at 540 (5th Cir. 1973); Friedman v. People's Serv. Drug Store, 208 Va. 700, 160 S.E.2d 563 (1968).

Law Review. — For note, "Assignability of a Tort Cause of Action in Virginia," see 41 Va. L. Rev. 687 (1955). For survey of Virginia law on practice and pleading for the year 1976-77, see 63 Va. L. Rev. 1459 (1977).

I. Decisions Under Current Law.
II. Decisions Under Prior Law.

I. DECISIONS UNDER CURRENT LAW.

Tort claims for interference with business are assignable, since the right to do business is a valuable property right. Grey Line Auto Parts, Inc. v. Snead, 1 Bankr. 551 (Bankr. E.D. Va. 1979).

Claim under Federal Employers Liability Act. — The language of this section makes it clear that an unliquidated and contingent claim such as a Federal Employers Liability Act claim is neither assignable nor subject to the reach of creditor process under Virginia law and is therefore exempt property pursuant to 11 U.S.C. § 522(b)(2)(A). In re Musgrove, 7 Bankr. 892 (Bankr. W.D. Va. 1981).

Legal malpractice claims not assignable. — Section specifying which causes of action are assignable does not abrogate the common law rule which prohibits the assignment of legal malpractice claims. MNC Credit Corp. v. Sickels, 255 Va. 314, 497 S.E.2d 331 (1998).

Assignment of settlement proceeds or insurance benefits distinguished. — Although this section prohibits the assignment of a cause of action for personal injuries, there is a legally significant distinction between an assignment of a personal injury cause of action and an assignment of the settlement proceeds or insurance benefits thereof. Community Hosp. v. Musser, 24 Bankr. 913 (W.D. Va. 1982).

Assignment of proceeds of personal injury cause of action sub judice is permissible. In re Duty, 78 Bankr. 111 (Bankr. E.D. Va. 1987).

Applicability to hospitals seeking recovery limited to value of services actually rendered. — The reasons underlying the common-law rule against assignment of tort claims (now codified in this section), namely, the prevention of champerty and maintenance, do not support its application to hospitals seeking recoveries limited to the value of services actually supplied to the debtors, where the debtors retained complete control over their personal injury cases, the hospitals' rights exist only in the proceeds, not in the debtors' causes of action, and the hospitals had no right to proceed against the third-party tort-feasors even if the debtors decided not to pursue their tort claims. Community Hosp. v. Musser, 24 Bankr. 913 (W.D. Va. 1982).

Equitable assignment to hospital of sums to be recovered from tort-feasor. — The prohibition against assignments of causes of action for personal injury does not proscribe a hospital from obtaining an equitable assignment of the sums to be recovered by an individual from a tort-feasor to the extent of the value of the services provided by the hospital in treatment of the individual's personal injuries.

Community Hosp. v. Musser, 24 Bankr. 913 (W.D. Va. 1982).

Assignment of personal injury claim invalid where import of act not understood. — Purported assignment of a personal injury claim executed by a native of the Philippines with a halting grasp of English at the direction of the hospital which was treating him for his extensive injuries, the import of which was not understood by the assignor, was invalid under this section. Roanoke Mem. Hosp. Ass'n v. Baylon, 21 Bankr. 54 (Bankr. W.D. Va.), aff'd, 24 Bankr. 913 (Bankr. W.D. Va. 1982).

A cause of action for wrongful death is an asset of the bankruptcy estate and may not be assigned. In re Tidwell, 19 Bankr. 846 (Bankr. E.D. Va. 1982).

II. DECISIONS UNDER PRIOR LAW.

Editor's note. — The case cited below was decided under corresponding provisions of prior law.

There is a sound distinction between assignment of a tort claim and subrogation of hospital and medical payments by contract. Collins v. Blue Cross & Blue Shield, 213 Va. 540, 193 S.E.2d 782 (1973).

ARTICLE 2.

Actions on Contracts Generally.

§ 8.01-27. Civil action on note or writing promising to pay money. — A civil action may be maintained upon any note or writing by which there is a promise, undertaking, or obligation to pay money, if the same be signed by the party who is to be charged thereby, or his agent. The action may also be maintained on any such note or writing for any past due installment on a debt payable in installments, although other installments thereof be not due. (Code 1950, § 8-509; 1954, c. 333; 1977, c. 617.)

Cross references. — For rule of court that procedure shall be by notice of motion, for judgment, see Rule 3:3.

Law Review. — For article, "Reconsidering Inducement," see 76 Va. L. Rev. 877 (1990).

§ 8.01-27.1. Additional recovery in certain civil actions concerning checks. — A. In any civil claim or action made or brought against the drawer of a check, draft or order, payment of which has been refused by the drawee depository because of lack of funds in or credit with such drawee depository, the holder or his agent shall be entitled to claim, in addition to the face amount of the check (i) legal interest from the date of the check, (ii) the protest or bad check return fee, if any, charged to the holder by his bank or other depository, and (iii) a processing charge of twenty-five dollars.

B. Any holder of a check, draft or order, payment of which has been refused by the drawee for insufficient funds or credit, who charges the drawer amounts in excess of those authorized in subsection A on account of payment being so refused shall, upon demand, be liable to the drawer for the lesser of (i) twenty-five dollars plus the excess of the authorized amount or (ii) twice the amount charged in excess of the authorized amount. (1981, c. 230; 1992, c. 238; 1996, c. 334.)

Cross references. — As to criminal penalty for issuing bad checks, see § 18.2-181.

Law Review. — For article reviewing recent developments and changes in legislation, case law, and Virginia Supreme Court Rules affecting civil litigation, see "Civil Practice and Procedure," 26 U. Rich. L. Rev. 679 (1992).

§ 8.01-27.2. Civil recovery for giving bad check. — In the event a check, draft or order, the payment of which has been refused by the drawee because of lack of funds in or credit with such drawee, is not paid in full within thirty days after receipt by the drawer of written notice by registered, certified, or regular mail with the sender retaining sufficient proof of mailing, which may be a U.S. Postal Certificate of Mailing, from the payee that the check,

§ 8.01-28   CODE OF VIRGINIA   § 8.01-28

draft or order has been returned unpaid, the payee may recover from the drawer in a civil action brought by the filing of a warrant in debt, the lesser of $250 or three times the amount of the check, draft or order. The amount recovered as authorized by this section shall be in addition to the amounts authorized for recovery under § 8.01-27.1. No action may be initiated under this section if any action has been initiated under § 18.2-181. The drawer shall be obligated to pay the cost of service and the cost of mailing, as applicable. (1985, c. 579; 1988, c. 433; 1992, c. 501.)

§ 8.01-28. When judgment to be given in action upon contract or note unless defendant appears and denies claim under oath. — In any action at law on a note or contract, express or implied, for the payment of money, or unlawful detainer pursuant to § 55-225 or § 55-248.31 for the payment of money or possession of the premises, or both, if (i) the plaintiff files with his motion for judgment or civil warrant an affidavit made by himself or his agent, stating therein to the best of the affiant's belief the amount of the plaintiff's claim, that such amount is justly due, and the time from which plaintiff claims interest, and (ii) a copy of the affidavit together with a copy of any account filed with the motion for judgment or warrant and, in actions pursuant to § 55-225 or § 55-248.31, proof of required notices is served on the defendant as provided in § 8.01-296 at the time a copy of the motion for judgment or warrant is so served, the plaintiff shall be entitled to a judgment on the affidavit and statement of account without further evidence unless the defendant either appears and pleads under oath or files with the court before the return date an affidavit or responsive pleading denying that the plaintiff is entitled to recover from the defendant on the claim. A denial by the defendant in general district court need not be in writing. The plaintiff or defendant shall, on motion, be granted a continuance whenever the defendant appears and pleads. If the defendant's pleading or affidavit admits that the plaintiff is entitled to recover from the defendant a sum certain less than that stated in the affidavit filed by the plaintiff, judgment may be taken by the plaintiff for the sum so admitted to be due, and the case will be tried as to the residue. (Code 1950, § 8-511; 1954, c. 610; 1960, c. 426; 1977, c. 617; 1983, c. 136; 1991, cc. 56, 503.)

REVISERS' NOTE

"Plea" in former § 8-511 has been changed to "pleading" since the former word might be interpreted to require the defendant to file a "plea" rather than to use an answer or grounds of defense.

Cross references. — As to judgment for defendant in circuit court when plaintiff is entitled to less than $100, see § 17.1-514. For rule of court that procedure shall be by notice of motion, for judgment, see Rule 3:3. For rule that pleas of the general issue are abolished, see Rule 3:5. For rules as to grounds of defense, see Rules 3:5 and 3:7. For rule of court on judgment by default, and inquiry as to damages, see Rule 3:17.

I. Decisions Under Current Law.
II. Decisions Under Prior Law.

I. DECISIONS UNDER CURRENT LAW.

Defendant must file written pleading denying indebtedness. — The final sentence of the statute and the appended revisers' note make it evident that the legislative purpose is to place upon the defendant the burden of filing a written pleading under oath, denying his

§ 8.01-28

indebtedness, if he wishes to preclude the entry of judgment on the affidavit without further evidence. Snead v. Bendigo, 240 Va. 399, 397 S.E.2d 849 (1990).

II. DECISIONS UNDER PRIOR LAW.

Editor's note. — The cases cited below were decided under corresponding provisions of former law. The term "this section," as used below, refers to former provisions.

The purpose of this section, like that of its ancestors, is to expedite the adjudication of certain claims for the payment of money by preventing the delay that results from the dilatory assertion of sham defenses. Sheets v. Ragsdale, 220 Va. 322, 257 S.E.2d 858 (1979).

This section was intended to prevent delay caused to plaintiffs by continuances upon dilatory pleadings when no real defenses exist, and to simplify and shorten the proceedings. Grigg v. Dalsheimer, 88 Va. 508, 13 S.E. 993 (1891); L.E. Mumford Banking Co. v. Farmers & Merchants Bank, 116 Va. 449, 82 S.E. 112 (1914); Gehl v. Baker, 121 Va. 23, 92 S.E. 852 (1917).

Section and Rule 1:10 construed together. — This section, relating to when a plaintiff is to be granted judgment in an action for payment of money in which the defendant fails to deny plaintiff's claim under oath, and Rule 1:10, providing that the statutory benefit provided a plaintiff will be waived unless the plaintiff timely claims it, read together in light of their respective histories and prevailing case law, are fully compatible and complementary. This section creates only an optional benefit; Rule 1:10 simply defines one mode of waiver. Sheets v. Ragsdale, 220 Va. 322, 257 S.E.2d 858 (1979).

Substantial compliance is sufficient. — This section was enacted to prevent the filing of sham pleadings merely for delay, and a substantial compliance with its provisions is all that is required. Carpenter v. Gray, 113 Va. 518, 75 S.E. 300 (1912); Paris v. Brown, 143 Va. 896, 129 S.E. 678 (1925); see also, Levitin v. Norfolk Nat'l Bank, 163 Va. 694, 177 S.E. 205 (1934).

And strict rule as to affidavits is not to be applied. — The strict rule applied in construing affidavits in attachment cases in equity, where the jurisdiction of the court is involved, is not to be applied to the affidavit allowed by this section. Carpenter v. Gray, 113 Va. 518, 75 S.E. 300 (1912).

The affidavit need not in express terms state that the affiant is the plaintiff in the action, but is sufficient if the language plainly shows that fact. Carpenter v. Gray, 113 Va. 518, 75 S.E. 300 (1912).

It should state time from which interest is claimed. — The affidavit filed with a motion under this section should state the time from which the plaintiff claims interest. Merriman Co. v. Thomas & Co., 103 Va. 24, 48 S.E. 490 (1904).

And time stated in affidavit is controlling. — The fact that an account filed with a motion claimed interest from January 1, 1910, did not affect the validity of the affidavit filed under this section, which claimed interest from March 1, 1910, since the date fixed by the latter was in favor of the defendant, and would control in entering up judgment if no defense was made. Carpenter v. Gray, 113 Va. 518, 75 S.E. 300 (1912).

Affidavit of bookkeeper is insufficient. — This section requires the affidavit of the plaintiff or his agent, and, in the absence of evidence on the subject, a "bookkeeper" will not be held to be such agent. Merriman Co. v. Thomas & Co., 103 Va. 24, 48 S.E. 490 (1904); Taylor v. Sutherlin-Meade Tobacco Co., 107 Va. 787, 60 S.E. 132 (1908).

An affidavit "that the matters stated in the annexed pleadings are true" is a substantial compliance with the provisions of this section. Jackson v. Dotson, 110 Va. 46, 65 S.E. 484 (1909).

Section may be waived. — A plaintiff in an action may waive, or be estopped from asserting, his right to have judgment entered in his favor for the amount claimed by him in the affidavit filed with his motion, although the defendant has failed to comply with the provisions of this section entitling him to make defense to the claim asserted, and such waiver may be express or implied. Carpenter v. Gray, 113 Va. 518, 75 S.E. 300 (1912).

The benefit this section bestows is not self-executing; it becomes available to the plaintiff only if he elects to claim it and does so in the manner the section prescribes. Even then, the statutory benefit is not an indefeasible right, but the verification requirement may be waived by the plaintiff either expressly or by implication, or he may by his conduct be estopped to take advantage of it. Sheets v. Ragsdale, 220 Va. 322, 257 S.E.2d 858 (1979).

Failure to move to strike unverified pleading within seven days held waiver. — Where plaintiff failed, under Rule 1:10, to move to strike defendants' pleading for want of verification within seven days after it was filed, plaintiff waived the verification requirement and the trial court erred in granting default judgment. Sheets v. Ragsdale, 220 Va. 322, 257 S.E.2d 858 (1979).

Plaintiff may be estopped from claiming benefits of this section. L.E. Mumford Banking Co. v. Farmers & Merchants Bank, 116 Va. 449, 82 S.E. 112 (1914).

Consenting to or accepting continuance is waiver. — A plaintiff may, either expressly or by implication, waive compliance on the part of the defendant with the requirements of this section, or may by his conduct be estopped from taking advantage of its terms. Consenting to, or accepting without objection, a continuance of the case, are familiar methods of waiving the provisions of the section. Gehl v. Baker, 121 Va. 23, 92 S.E. 852 (1917).

Failure to object to unsworn pleadings. — This section is for the benefit of the plaintiff, and may be waived by him, and it will be deemed to have been waived where he not only makes no objection when the pleading is tendered without a sufficient affidavit, but accepts without objection a continuance of the case until the next term of the court, "with leave to the defendant to file within fifteen days his grounds of defense." Jackson v. Dotson, 110 Va. 46, 65 S.E. 484 (1909).

Where pleadings withdrawn and new pleadings tendered. — If a plaintiff files with his declaration the affidavit prescribed by this section, no pleadings can be filed by the defendant which are not accompanied by the affidavit required of him by this section, unless the affidavit has been waived, and although pleadings have been filed unaccompanied by such an affidavit without objection on the part of the plaintiff, yet if they are withdrawn and new pleadings are tendered by the defendant, the plaintiff may insist on the lack of an affidavit as a valid objection to the new pleadings. Spencer v. Field, 97 Va. 38, 33 S.E. 380 (1899).

Plaintiff has no duty to inform defendant of affidavit filed nor of errors. — In opposing a motion for a continuance made by a defendant who has not complied with the provisions of this section, it is not necessary for the plaintiff's counsel to call defendant's attention to the fact, which a casual observance of the plaintiff's pleading would have disclosed, that there was an account and affidavit filed with the declaration; neither is it his duty to ask the court to correct an error of the clerk, either in taking the rules or in placing the case on the wrong docket. The plaintiff is not responsible for such errors, and cannot be prejudiced by them. Carpenter v. Gray, 113 Va. 518, 75 S.E. 300 (1912).

Judgment entered for plaintiff after unsworn pleadings stricken is valid. — Where a plaintiff files with his declaration the affidavit prescribed by this section, and the defendant files his pleadings without affidavit, and the pleadings are stricken out, and a subsequent pleading with affidavit is rejected and final judgment given for the plaintiff, the judgment is not void. Whether it is erroneous or not, quaere. Grigg v. Dalsheimer, 88 Va. 508, 13 S.E. 993 (1891).

There is no presumption that defendant filed affidavit. — Where, on appeal, the record is silent as to an affidavit by defendant, there is no presumption that any such was filed. Spencer v. Field, 97 Va. 38, 33 S.E. 380 (1899).

§ 8.01-29. Procedure in actions on annuity and instalment bonds, and other actions for penalties for nonperformance. — In an action on an annuity bond, or a bond for money payable by instalments, when there are further payments of the annuity, or further instalments to become due after the commencement of the action, or in any other action for a penalty for the nonperformance of any condition, covenant, or agreement, the plaintiff may assign as many breaches as he may think fit, and shall, in his motion for judgment assign the specific breaches for which the action is brought. The jury impaneled in any such action shall ascertain the damages sustained, or the sum due, by reason of the breaches assigned, and judgment shall be entered for the penalty, to be discharged by the payment of what is so ascertained, and such further sums as may be afterwards assessed. Motion may be made by any person injured against the defendant and, for what may be assessed or found due upon the new breach or breaches assigned, execution may be awarded. (Code 1950, § 8-513; 1954, c. 333; 1977, c. 617.)

REVISERS' NOTE

The only significant change to former § 8-513 is the elimination of the reference to the writ of scire facias; § 8.01-24 has replaced it with a simple motion. Other language of former § 8-513 has been deleted as unnecessary.

Cross references. — For rule of court that procedure shall be by notice of motion for judgement, see Rule 3:3.

I. DECISIONS UNDER PRIOR LAW.

Editor's note. — The cases cited below were decided under corresponding provisions of former law. The term "this section," as used below, refers to former provisions.

It is at least doubtful whether this section was intended to apply to actions on official bonds, although, in regard to such bonds, it has been held that the judgment ought to be entered in the form provided in this section. Sangster v. Commonwealth, 58 Va. (17 Gratt.) 124 (1866).

And judgment does not preclude other actions on such bond. — In no case has it been decided that where a judgment on an official bond has been so entered, it is a bar to any other action on the bond, and precludes any other recovery upon it than by motion for judgment. Sangster v. Commonwealth, 58 Va. (17 Gratt.) 124 (1866).

Form of judgment. — In an action upon a sheriff's bond in the name of the Commonwealth, for the benefit of a person aggrieved by the misconduct of the sheriff, the judgment should be entered for the penalty, to be discharged by the payment of the damages assessed and costs, "and such other damages as may be hereafter assessed upon suing out a scire facias, and assigning new breaches, by the said [person aggrieved], or any other person or persons injured." Bibb v. Cauthorne, 1 Va. (1 Wash.) 91 (1792).

§ 8.01-30. Procedure in actions on contracts made by several persons.

— Upon all contracts hereafter made by more than one person, whether joint only or joint and several, an action may be maintained and judgment rendered against all liable thereon, or any one or any intermediate number, and if, in an action on any contract heretofore or hereafter made, more than one person be sued and process be served on only a part of them, the plaintiff may dismiss or proceed to judgment as to any so served, and either discontinue as to the others, or from time to time as the process is served, proceed to judgment against them until judgment be obtained against all. Such dismissal or discontinuance of the action as to any defendant shall not operate as a bar to any subsequent action which may be brought against him for the same cause. (Code 1950, § 8-514; 1954, c. 333; 1977, c. 617.)

Cross references. — As to judgment in joint action on contract, where plaintiff is barred as to one or more but not all defendants, see § 8.01-442. For rule of court that procedure shall be by notice of motion for judgment, see Rule 3:3.

I. DECISIONS UNDER PRIOR LAW.

Editor's note. — The cases cited below were decided under corresponding provisions of former law. The term "this section," as used below, refers to former provisions.

Section changes the common law. — In an action ex contractu against several defendants, the common-law rule was that all should be summoned actually, or constructively by prosecution to outlawry, before judgment could be had against any. This section changes this for another rule, whereby judgment may be had against one defendant served with process, and a discontinuance as to the others, or at the plaintiff's election, subsequent service of process and judgment, in the same suit, against the other defendants. Bush v. Campbell, 67 Va. (26 Gratt.) 403 (1875).

Judgment may be rendered against defendant served with process. — Where only one of several defendants has been served with process, judgment may be rendered against him. Norfolk & W.R.R. v. Shippers Compress Co., 83 Va. 272, 2 S.E. 139 (1887).

Where in an action against seven joint obligors, summons was returned executed as to four, and "No inhabitants" as to two, and as to the other, "I understand he is dead," and at rules the six pleaded for misjoinder of surviving obligors with a dead obligor, and the clerk abated the action as to those returned "No inhabitants," and the "dead" one, the court committed no error in rejecting the pleadings and entering judgment against the four who had been summoned. Dillard v. Turner, 87 Va. 669, 14 S.E. 123 (1891).

And case discontinued as to those not served. — The discontinuance provided for by this section is a discontinuance as against any one or more defendants upon whom process had not been served. Corbin v. Planters Nat'l Bank, 87 Va. 661, 13 S.E. 98 (1891).

One of several persons jointly liable may be sued alone. — In view of § 8.01-5 and this section, there is no merit in an objection by a defendant in an action upon a contract that his liability is joint with another, that such person was a necessary party and that defendant could not be sued alone. Reed & Rice Co. v. Wood, 138 Va. 187, 120 S.E. 874 (1924).

Judgment may be had against sureties though principal not served. — Judgment on a forthcoming bond may be had against the

§ 8.01-31

sureties under this section, though the principal has never been served with notice of a motion for an award of execution on the bond. Newberry v. Sheffey, 89 Va. 286, 15 S.E. 548 (1892).

And against some of stockholders jointly liable on subscription. — Since the obligation of a subscriber to stock to contribute to the amount of his subscription for the purpose of the payment of debts is contractual, and arises from the subscription to the stock, there can be no doubt of the right of a plaintiff under this section to proceed to judgment against a part of the defendants jointly liable for a subscription without proceeding against the others. Chisholm v. Gilmer, 81 F.2d 120 (4th Cir.), aff'd, 299 U.S. 99, 57 S. Ct. 65, 81 L. Ed. 63 (1936).

And plaintiff may recover entire claim from one obligor. — Where two clients jointly accept services rendered by an attorney, it is proper to charge that the attorney may recover the entire amount of the fee from either of the two clients, under this section, if he elects to sue one of them only. Culbert v. Hutton, 138 Va. 677, 123 S.E. 367 (1924).

§ 8.01-31. Accounting in equity. — An accounting in equity may be had against any fiduciary or by one joint tenant, tenant in common, or coparcener for receiving more than comes to his just share or proportion, or against the personal representative of any such party. (Code 1950, § 8-514.1; 1956, c. 160; 1977, c. 617.)

REVISERS' NOTE

Former § 8-514.1 has been modified by deleting "bailiff" and other such terms which contemplate a fiduciary and the word "fiduciary" substituted in the place of those terms. See § 8.01-2.

Cross references. — As to liability of fiduciary for losses by negligence or failure to make defense, see § 26-5.

I. Decisions Under Current Law.
II. Decisions Under Prior Law.

I. DECISIONS UNDER CURRENT LAW.

Applicability. — This statute does not apply only to commercial or income-producing property. Gaynor v. Hird, 15 Va. App. 379, 424 S.E.2d 240 (1992).

Availability. — There is no indication in the statute or in Virginia decisional law that the General Assembly intended § 8.01-2 to supplant the well-settled common law pursuant to which an accounting is available to redress a breach of the fiduciary responsibility inherent in an agency relationship or in the special relationship shown to have existed between husband and wife in the instant case. McClung v. Smith, 870 F. Supp. 1384 (E.D. Va. 1994), modified, 89 F.3d 829 (4th Cir. 1996).

Upon divorce, marital home fell within scope of section. — Upon parties' divorce, their marital home, which they had owned as tenants by the entirety, became their property as tenants in common, and thus fell within the scope of this section. Gaynor v. Hird, 15 Va. App. 379, 424 S.E.2d 240 (1992).

Reach of *Gaynor*. — Gaynor v. Hird, 15 Va. App. 379, 424 S.E.2d 240 (1992), which involved an accounting in equity pursuant to this section, after the parties' property was converted from ownership as tenants by the entirety to ownership as tenants in common, does not require an accounting of rental value pre-divorce when the parties own the property as tenants by the entirety. Longmyer v. Longmyer, No. 1543-94-4 (Ct. of Appeals April 11, 1995).

Rental value award to non-occupying ex-spouse permissible. — Where upon their divorce, the parties owned marital residence as tenants in common, and husband was required to bear his share of the financial burden of owning the property, the trial court did not abuse its discretion in awarding husband one-half of the reasonable rental value of the marital home for the period it was occupied exclusively by wife following their divorce. Ashley v. Ashley, No. 0851-93-1 (Ct. of Appeals Nov. 30, 1993).

When, instead of renting it out, the co-tenant in possession occupies and uses the whole property to the exclusion of his co-tenants, and thus, in effect, becomes himself the renter, the just and true rule is to charge him with a reasonable rent for the use and occupation of the property in the condition in which it was when he received it, and to hold him accountable to his co-tenants for their just shares of such rent. Gaynor v. Hird, 15 Va. App. 379, 424 S.E.2d 240 (1992).

It is not the purpose of the equitable distribution scheme to deprive an aggrieved spouse of a generally recognized remedy for the misapplication or misappropriation of separate funds entrusted to the other spouse pursuant to a special relationship. McClung v. Smith, 870 F. Supp. 1384 (E.D. Va. 1994), modified, 89 F.3d 829 (4th Cir. 1996).

Spouse not exempted. — There is no authority which, in the name of furthering marital harmony, would exempt from the remedy of an accounting a spouse who has been entrusted with the separate funds of another for a limited purpose and misapplied them. McClung v. Smith, 870 F. Supp. 1384 (E.D. Va. 1994), modified, 89 F.3d 829 (4th Cir. 1996).

II. DECISIONS UNDER PRIOR LAW.

Editor's note. — The cases cited below were decided under corresponding provisions of former law.

Responsibility of cotenants for taxes and other liens. — Unless something more can be shown than the mere fact that one cotenant is in possession of the premises, each cotenant should be ratably responsible for taxes and other liens against the property. Jenkins v. Jenkins, 211 Va. 797, 180 S.E.2d 516 (1971).

Cotenant who discharges an encumbrance upon common property is entitled to ratable contribution from his cotenant. Jenkins v. Jenkins, 211 Va. 797, 180 S.E.2d 516 (1971).

The central characteristic of a tenancy in common is simply that each tenant is deemed to own by himself, with most of the attributes of individual ownership, a physically undivided part of the entire parcel. Jenkins v. Jenkins, 211 Va. 797, 180 S.E.2d 516 (1971).

§ 8.01-32. Action on lost evidences of debt; indemnifying bond. — A civil action may be maintained on any past due lost bond, note, or other written evidence of debt, and if judgment is rendered for the plaintiff, there shall be entered as a part of the judgment that the plaintiff is not to have the benefit thereof, nor be allowed to enforce it by execution or otherwise, unless and until he shall have first entered into bond before the court or the clerk therein in such penalty as is prescribed in the judgment, and with condition to indemnify and save harmless the defendant from all loss or damage he may sustain or incur by reason of having to pay in whole or in part such past due lost bond, note, or other written evidence of debt to some other person than the plaintiff. The indemnifying bond hereinbefore required shall be payable to the defendant, and shall be filed in the clerk's office of the court in which the judgment is rendered.

In the event of any inconsistency between this section and any applicable provisions of § 8.3A-309, the provisions of that section shall control. (Code 1950, § 8-517; 1954, c. 333; 1964, c. 219; 1977, c. 617; 2000, c. 245.)

REVISERS' NOTE

The catchline of former § 8-517 has been changed to emphasize the real purpose of this statute which is to permit an action on lost instruments that were evidences of debt. The former words "or defendants" and "order awarding" were deleted as unnecessary. (With respect to the deletion of "or defendants" see § 1-13.15.) The cross reference to the UCC was corrected.

The 2000 amendments. — The 2000 amendment by c. 245 substituted "is" for "be" following "if judgment" in the first sentence of the first paragraph and substituted "§ 8.3A-309" for "§ 8.3-804" in the second paragraph.

I. DECISIONS UNDER PRIOR LAW.

Editor's note. — The cases cited below were decided under corresponding provisions of former law. The term "this section," as used below, refers to former provisions.

Purpose of section. — This section was enacted to authorize the maintenance of an action at law "on any past due lost bond, note, or other written evidence of debt," and to require a proper indemnity for the defendant's protection. Prior to its adoption, an action at law could be maintained on lost bonds and lost choses in action of any kind, provided they were not negotiable. If the paper was negotiable, and there was ample proof that it was destroyed, an action at law could likewise be maintained; but upon negotiable paper which was simply lost or mislaid and not destroyed, no action at law would lie. In such actions as were allowed no indemnifying bond was required. Bickers v. Pinnell, 199 Va. 444, 100 S.E.2d 20 (1957).

Section does not affect jurisdiction of equity. — Courts of equity still have jurisdiction to enforce payment of a lost bond, although courts of law are given jurisdiction over such bonds by this section, for it is well settled that courts of equity having once acquired jurisdiction never lose it because jurisdiction of the same matters is given to courts of law, unless the statute conferring such jurisdiction uses prohibitory or restrictive words. Kabler v. Spencer, 114 Va. 589, 77 S.E. 504 (1913).

Claim against decedent's estate evidenced by lost instrument. — This section does not expressly or impliedly deprive a commissioner of accounts of the express and specific authority conferred on him under §§ 64.1-171, 64.1-172 and 64.1-173 to receive proof of debts and demands against a decedent or his estate in the settlement of the accounts of a personal representative of a decedent. Bickers v. Pinnell, 199 Va. 444, 100 S.E.2d 20 (1957).

There was no merit in the contention that because the note evidencing a debt of a decedent was lost, the creditor was required to bring an action under this section against the executor, and precluded from proving her claim before a commissioner of accounts under §§ 64.1-171 through 64.1-173. Bickers v. Pinnell, 199 Va. 444, 100 S.E.2d 20 (1957).

§ 8.01-33. When equity has jurisdiction. — A court of equity shall not have jurisdiction of a suit upon a bond, note, or writing, by an assignee or holder thereof, unless it appear that the plaintiff had not an adequate remedy thereon at law. (Code 1950, § 8-518; 1977, c. 617.)

Cross references. — As to right of assignee to sue in his own name, see § 8.01-13.

I. DECISIONS UNDER PRIOR LAW.

Editor's note. — The cases cited below were decided under corresponding provisions of former law. The term "this section," as used below, refers to former provisions.

The object of this section was to provide against the abuse of crowding the chancery court with suits by assignees upon plain bonds, but out of abundant caution the provision was extended, and very properly, to a mere transferee or holder of a bond or other writing. Winn v. Bowles, 20 Va. (6 Munf.) 23 (1817); Walters v. Farmers Bank, 76 Va. 12 (1881).

But equity, having taken jurisdiction on other grounds, will retain it. — This section was not intended to affect the principle that when the court has once rightly obtained cognizance of the controversy and of the parties, its power is effectual for complete relief. Walters v. Farmers Bank, 76 Va. 12 (1881).

And equity has jurisdiction of suit by partial assignee. — For the enforcement of payment of a part of a debt assigned by the creditor without the assent or acceptance of the debtor, there is no jurisdiction in a court of law, but such partial recovery may be had in a court of equity. Phillips v. City of Portsmouth, 112 Va. 164, 70 S.E. 502 (1911).

Section is not applicable to promise to assume mortgage debt. — This section has no application to a suit brought upon the promise of defendants to assume the payment of a mortgage debt, which promise was implied by law from their acceptance of a writing not signed by defendants, conveying the property to them subject to the mortgage. Blanton v. Keneipp, 155 Va. 668, 156 S.E. 413 (1931).

ARTICLE 3.

Injury to Person or Property.

§ 8.01-34. When contribution among wrongdoers enforced. — Contribution among wrongdoers may be enforced when the wrong results from negligence and involves no moral turpitude. (Code 1950, § 8-627; 1977, c. 617.)

REVISERS' NOTE

The minor change which deleted "mere act" preceding "negligence" was made merely for clarification and does not materially alter the statute as it has been interpreted by case law.

Law Review. — For survey of Virginia law on torts for the year 1972-1973, see 59 Va. L. Rev. 1590 (1973). For survey of Virginia law on property for the year 1973-1974, see 60 Va. L. Rev. 1583 (1974). For article, "Effect of Virginia Workmen's Compensation Act upon the Right of a Third-Party Tortfeasor to Obtain Contribution from an Employer Whose Concurrent Negligence Causes Employee's Death or Injury," see 13 U. Rich L. Rev. 117 (1978). For comment, "The Covenant Not to Sue: Virginia's Effort to Bury the Common Law Rule Regarding the Release of Joint Tortfeasors," see 14 U. Rich. L. Rev. 809 (1980). For case note on contribution for antitrust contribution, see 66 Va. L. Rev. 797 (1980).

I. Decisions Under Current Law.
II. Decisions Under Prior Law.

I. DECISIONS UNDER CURRENT LAW.

Right to contribution from joint tort-feasors was statutorily created by the Virginia General Assembly in 1919. This right is codified in this section, subject now to the provisions of § 8.01-35.1. Carickhoff v. Badger-Northland, Inc., 562 F. Supp. 160 (W.D. Va. 1983).

Before contribution will be permitted, a right of action by the plaintiff must exist as to the joint tort-feasor against whom contribution is sought. VEPCO v. Wilson, 221 Va. 979, 277 S.E.2d 149 (1981).

A contribution plaintiff cannot recover from a contribution defendant unless the injured party could have recovered against the contribution defendant. Pierce v. Martin, 230 Va. 94, 334 S.E.2d 576 (1985).

The principles of contribution are equally applicable to indemnity, but the distinguishing feature of indemnity is that it must necessarily grow out of a contractual relationship. VEPCO v. Wilson, 221 Va. 979, 277 S.E.2d 149 (1981).

Third-party plaintiff may bring action for contribution, despite the fact that no payment has been made. Rambone v. Critzer, 548 F. Supp. 660 (W.D. Va. 1982).

Applied in Allianz Ins. Co. v. Garrett, 153 F.R.D. 89 (E.D. Va. 1994).

II. DECISIONS UNDER PRIOR LAW.

Editor's note. — The cases cited below were decided under corresponding provisions of former law. The term "this section," as used below, refers to former provisions.

This section changed the common-law rule. — At common law there was no contribution among joint tort-feasors, but that right is now given by this section. Norfolk & P. Belt Line R.R. v. Parker, 152 Va. 484, 147 S.E. 461 (1929). See also McLaughlin v. Siegel, 166 Va. 374, 185 S.E. 873 (1936); American Employers' Ins. Co. v. Maryland Cas. Co., 218 F.2d 335 (4th Cir. 1954).

At common law contribution was not permitted amongst joint tort-feasors. Mahone v. McGraw-Edison Co., 281 F. Supp. 582 (E.D. Va. 1968).

The doctrine of contribution is founded on principles of equity and natural justice. Hudgins v. Jones, 205 Va. 495, 138 S.E.2d 16 (1964).

The right to contribution is based upon the equitable principle that where two or more persons are subject to a common burden it shall be borne equally. Nationwide Mut. Ins. Co. v. Minnifield, 213 Va. 797, 196 S.E.2d 75 (1973).

The right of contribution is controlled by this section. Mahone v. McGraw-Edison Co., 281 F. Supp. 582 (E.D. Va. 1968).

But it gives a right of contribution only where the person injured has a right of action against two persons for the same indivisible injury. Though the concurring negligence of two persons may have resulted in an indivisible injury to a third, if the third person has a cause of action against only one of them, that one cannot enforce contribution from the other. The statute allowing contribution does not create any greater liability than existed before its enactment. Norfolk S.R.R. v. Gretakis, 162 Va. 597, 174 S.E. 841 (1934).

This section gives a right of contribution only where the party damaged has a right of action against two or more parties for the same indivisible damage. In short, if the damaged party has a cause of action against only one of the parties responsible for the damage, that one cannot enforce contribution from the other. American Tobacco Co. v. Transport Corp., 277 F. Supp. 457 (E.D. Va. 1967); Laws v. Spain, 312 F. Supp. 315 (E.D. Va. 1970).

Virginia, while permitting contribution between co-tort-feasors, withholds it as against a joint offender who cannot in law be forced to answer to the plaintiff for his negligence. Drumgoole v. VEPCO, 170 F. Supp. 824 (E.D. Va. 1959).

The right of contribution is withheld against a joint tort-feasor who cannot in law be forced to answer to a plaintiff for his alleged negligence. Mahone v. McGraw-Edison Co., 281 F. Supp. 582 (E.D. Va. 1968).

This section does not create any greater liability than existed before its enactment. Laws v. Spain, 312 F. Supp. 315 (E.D. Va. 1970).

Joint tort-feasor. — Joint tort-feasor means "two or more persons jointly or severally liable in tort for the same injury to person or property." Laws v. Spain, 312 F. Supp. 315 (E.D. Va. 1970).

Recovery amongst joint tort-feasors, absent contract, is limited to contribution. Hartford Accident & Indem. Co. v. Williams, 291 F. Supp. 103 (W.D. Va. 1968).

When contribution permitted. — While no right of contribution among wrongdoers existed at common law, that right is now permitted by this section and may be enforced when the wrong is an act of negligence and involves no moral turpitude. The wrongdoer, of course, must be a joint tort-feasor; that is, the concurring negligence of both parties must have contributed to bring about the injury sustained by a third. North River Ins. Co. v. Davis, 274 F. Supp. 146 (W.D. Va. 1967), aff'd, 392 F.2d 571 (4th Cir. 1968).

When contribution a matter of right. — When parties are bound to bear a burden, and are liable from the same circumstances existing as to both, contribution is a matter of right in equity. Hudgins v. Jones, 205 Va. 495, 138 S.E.2d 16 (1964).

The right of contribution arises only when one tort-feasor has paid or settled a claim for which other wrongdoers are also liable. Nationwide Mut. Ins. Co. v. Minnifield, 213 Va. 797, 196 S.E.2d 75 (1973).

It does not permit contribution among participants in intentional illegal acts. — The affirmative provision of this section permitting contribution is limited to cases in which the wrong is a mere act of negligence, and the added phrase excluding acts of moral turpitude plainly shows that the legislature did not intend to extend the privilege to participants in intentional illegal acts. Carriers Ins. Exch. v. Truck Ins. Exch., 310 F.2d 653 (4th Cir. 1962).

This section did not justify contribution or indemnity between a lessor and lessee of a tractor-trailer carrying gasoline for liability caused by an explosion where the transaction was being conducted in deliberate disregard of the Interstate Commerce Commission's regulations. Carriers Ins. Exch. v. Truck Ins. Exch., 310 F.2d 653 (4th Cir. 1962).

Or where liability arose out of act involving moral turpitude. — The party who otherwise would be entitled to contribution may forfeit his right where the joint liability arose out of an act involving moral turpitude or a voluntary tort. Hudgins v. Jones, 205 Va. 495, 138 S.E.2d 16 (1964).

Contribution allowed where party is only a technical wrongdoer. — Where a party is only a technical wrongdoer, and did not actually participate in the wrongful act, such party, on being compelled to pay damages to the injured party, is entitled to contribution or indemnity from the actual wrongdoer. McLaughlin v. Siegel, 166 Va. 374, 185 S.E. 873 (1936).

Claim must have been paid. — Before contribution may be had it is essential that a cause of action by the person injured lie against the alleged wrongdoer from whom contribution is sought. Further, this right arises only when one tort-feasor has paid or settled a claim for which other wrongdoers are also liable. Bartlett v. Roberts Recapping, Inc., 207 Va. 789, 153 S.E.2d 193 (1967).

The right to contribution arises only when one of the joint tort-feasors has paid a claim for which the other wrongdoer is also liable. The payment need not be the result of a judgment for the right of contribution will lie although no previous judgment determining the issues of negligence and contributory negligence has been obtained. North River Ins. Co. v. Davis, 274 F. Supp. 146 (W.D. Va. 1967), aff'd, 392 F.2d 571 (4th Cir. 1968).

The right to contribution arises only when one tort-feasor has paid or settled a claim for which the other wrongdoer is liable. Laws v. Spain, 312 F. Supp. 315 (E.D. Va. 1970).

The right given by this section arises when, and only when, one tort-feasor has paid a claim for which they are both liable. Laws v. Spain, 312 F. Supp. 315 (E.D. Va. 1970).

Assignment of right to contribution. — The right to enforce contribution granted by this section is a chose in action. And there appears no logical reason why it is not capable of being assigned. McKay v. Citizens Rapid Transit Co., 190 Va. 851, 59 S.E.2d 121, 20 A.L.R.2d 918 (1950).

Insurer's right to contribution. — Under this statute not only a joint tort-feasor but also his insurer, who has paid a judgment against him and another joint tort-feasor, has the right of contribution from the latter. McKay v. Citizens Rapid Transit Co., 190 Va. 851, 59 S.E.2d 121, 20 A.L.R.2d 918 (1950); American Employers' Ins. Co. v. Maryland Cas. Co., 218 F.2d 335 (4th Cir. 1954).

An accident occurred involving two cars in which the drivers of both were at fault, so that each insured became immediately liable and the indemnity provisions of each policy became effective with respect to all the injuries in-

§ 8.01-35 CIVIL REMEDIES AND PROCEDURE § 8.01-35

curred. Thereupon the two insurance companies became subject to a common obligation to the extent of the respective limits of their policies, and when one of them paid the total amount of the debt, the right to contribution from the other arose. American Employers' Ins. Co. v. Maryland Cas. Co., 218 F.2d 335 (4th Cir. 1954).

The right to contribution is not a personal right of the tort-feasor but is a chose in action to which an insurer may be subrogated. Nationwide Mut. Ins. Co. v. Jewel Tea Co., 202 Va. 527, 118 S.E.2d 646 (1961); Hudgins v. Jones, 205 Va. 495, 138 S.E.2d 16 (1964).

An insurer's right to contribution was not barred by a judgment which it had previously obtained against the same defendant involving the same accident but based upon subrogation to a separate cause of action. Nationwide Mut. Ins. Co. v. Jewel Tea Co., 202 Va. 527, 118 S.E.2d 646 (1961).

An insurer making settlement of claims against its insured is subrogated to his right of contribution from joint tort-feasors. Nationwide Mut. Ins. Co. v. Minnifield, 213 Va. 797, 196 S.E.2d 75 (1973).

Jurisdiction of equity. — While the right to enforce contribution originally belonged to courts of equity on general principles of justice, jurisdiction to proceed in courts of law to enforce contribution is well recognized in some cases, but equity retains such original jurisdiction and will take jurisdiction when to do so will avoid a multiplicity of suits, or where the relief at law would be incomplete or inadequate. Hudgins v. Jones, 205 Va. 495, 138 S.E.2d 16 (1964).

Transfer of case to law side. — Though the right to contribution arose in equity and though equity retains concurrent jurisdiction in such matters with courts of law, the court did not abuse its discretion in transferring the case to the law side. No matter was involved that was peculiarly cognizable in equity and the basic issues of negligence that were involved traditionally are tried at law. Hudgins v. Jones, 205 Va. 495, 138 S.E.2d 16 (1964).

Action will lie though no previous judgment has been obtained. — A right of action for contribution will lie though no previous judgment determining the issues of negligence and contributory negligence has been obtained. There is nothing in our statute which requires that the issues of negligence and contributory negligence be adjudicated before an action for contribution may be brought. Nationwide Mut. Ins. Co. v. Jewel Tea Co., 202 Va. 527, 118 S.E.2d 646 (1961).

Action based on compromise settlement. — Where the action for contribution is based upon a compromise settlement rather than a judgment, the alleged joint tort-feasor may challenge the right to contribution on grounds that the compromise settlement is unreasonable, excessive, made in bad faith, or that he was not concurrently negligent, or that his negligence was not a proximate cause of the injuries compromised. Nationwide Mut. Ins. Co. v. Jewel Tea Co., 202 Va. 527, 118 S.E.2d 646 (1961).

The burden is upon the alleged joint tort-feasor to show that compromises upon which the right to contribution is based were unreasonable or excessive. Nationwide Mut. Ins. Co. v. Jewel Tea Co., 202 Va. 527, 118 S.E.2d 646 (1961).

The right to maintain the action for contribution need not be founded upon a judgment determining the issues of negligence. It may be based upon a compromise settlement, rather than a judgment. Laws v. Spain, 312 F. Supp. 315 (E.D. Va. 1970).

Statute of limitations. — The cause of action in cases of this kind arises out of an implied promise to pay, and therefore the three-year statute of limitations would apply. Nationwide Mut. Ins. Co. v. Jewel Tea Co., 202 Va. 527, 118 S.E.2d 646 (1961).

The right of action under this section arises upon payment or discharge of the obligation, and it is then that the statute of limitations begins to run. Nationwide Mut. Ins. Co. v. Jewel Tea Co., 202 Va. 527, 118 S.E.2d 646 (1961).

Exoneration and indemnity comes about when one secondarily liable has to pay and then comes back to the party primarily responsible. Mahone v. McGraw-Edison Co., 281 F. Supp. 582 (E.D. Va. 1968).

Exoneration is the right to be reimbursed by reason of having paid that which another should be compelled to pay, and is generally based upon contract, express or implied. Mahone v. McGraw-Edison Co., 281 F. Supp. 582 (E.D. Va. 1968).

Sufficiency of pleading. — In an action brought under this section, use of the word "proximate" or the phrase "proximately caused" was held not necessary in a pleading that was seeking contribution for tortious injury or death caused by negligent acts of omission or commission. Legal responsibility in that respect can be charged by other language so long as it apprises defendant that he is charged with negligently causing or contributing to the injuries or death. Goode v. Courtney, 200 Va. 804, 108 S.E.2d 396 (1959).

§ 8.01-35. Damages for loss of income not diminished by reimbursement. — In any suit brought for personal injury or death, provable damages for loss of income due to such injury or death shall not be diminished because of reimbursement of income to the plaintiff or decedent from any other source, nor shall the fact of any such reimbursement be admitted into evidence. (Code 1950, § 8-628.3; 1974, c. 155; 1977, c. 617.)

Law Review. — For survey of Virginia law on torts for the year 1973-1974, see 60 Va. L. Rev. 1615 (1974).

I. DECISIONS UNDER CURRENT LAW.

Section does not apply to losses incurred because of medical expenses. — This section is limited by its own terms to damages for "loss of income," and the Virginia Supreme Court and the Virginia legislature view this as separate and distinct from losses incurred because of medical expenses. Therefore, this section does not apply where the plaintiff seeks to introduce medical bills. Karsten v. Kaiser Found. Health Plan, 808 F. Supp. 1253 (E.D. Va. 1992), aff'd, 36 F.3d 8 (4th Cir. 1994).

§ 8.01-35.1. Effect of release or covenant not to sue in respect to liability and contribution. — A. When a release or a covenant not to sue is given in good faith to one of two or more persons liable in tort for the same injury, or the same property damage or the same wrongful death:

1. It shall not discharge any of the other tort-feasors from liability for the injury, property damage or wrongful death unless its terms so provide; but any amount recovered against the other tort-feasors or any one of them shall be reduced by any amount stipulated by the covenant or the release, or in the amount of the consideration paid for it, whichever is the greater. In determining the amount of consideration given for a covenant not to sue or release for a settlement which consists in whole or in part of future payment or payments, the court shall consider expert or other evidence as to the present value of the settlement consisting in whole or in part of future payment or payments. A release or covenant not to sue given pursuant to this section shall not be admitted into evidence in the trial of the matter but shall be considered by the court in determining the amount for which judgment shall be entered; and

2. It shall discharge the tort-feasor to whom it is given from all liability for contribution to any other tort-feasor.

B. A tort-feasor who enters into a release or covenant not to sue with a claimant is not entitled to recover by way of contribution from another tort-feasor whose liability for the injury, property damage or wrongful death is not extinguished by the release or covenant not to sue, nor in respect to any amount paid by the tort-feasor which is in excess of what was reasonable.

C. For the purposes of this section, a covenant not to sue shall include any "high-low" agreement whereby a party seeking damages in tort agrees to accept as full satisfaction for any judgment no more than one sum certain and the party or parties from whom the damages are sought agree to pay no less than another sum certain regardless of whether any judgment rendered at trial is higher or lower than the respective sums certain set forth in the agreement and whereby such party provides notice to all of the other tort-feasors of the terms of such "high-low" agreement immediately after such agreement is reached.

D. A release or covenant not to sue given pursuant to this section shall be subject to the provisions of §§ 8.01-55 and 8.01-424.

E. This section shall apply to all such covenants not to sue executed on or after July 1, 1979, and to all releases executed on or after July 1, 1980. This section shall also apply to all oral covenants not to sue and oral releases agreed to on or after July 1, 1989, provided that any cause of action affected thereby accrues on or after July 1, 1989. A release or covenant not to sue need not be in writing where parties to a pending action state in open court that they have agreed to enter into such release or covenant not to sue and have agreed further to subsequently memorialize the same in writing. (1979, c. 697; 1980, c. 411; 1982, c. 196; 1983, c. 181; 1985, c. 330; 1989, c. 681; 2000, c. 351.)

Cross references. — As to effect of judgment against one joint wrongdoer, see § 8.01-443.

The 2000 amendments. — The 2000 amendment by c. 351 added present subsection C, and redesignated former subsections C and D as present subsections D and E.

Law Review. — For comment, "The Covenant Not to Sue: Virginia's Effort to Bury the Common Law Rule Regarding the Release of Joint Tortfeasors," see 14 U. Rich. L. Rev. 809 (1980). For survey of Virginia law on torts for the year 1978-1979, see 66 Va. L. Rev. 375 (1980). For comment discussing the retroactive application of this section, see 18 U. Rich. L. Rev. 829 (1984). For 1985 survey of Virginia civil procedure and practice, see 19 U. Rich. L. Rev. 679 (1985). For comment on decision, "Jones v. General Motors Corp., 856 F.2d 22 (4th Cir. 1988)," see 47 Wash. & Lee L. Rev. 504 (1990).

I. Decisions Under Current Law.
II. Decisions Under Prior Law.

I. DECISIONS UNDER CURRENT LAW.

Purpose. — The General Assembly intended to change a rule of law which tended to reward a recalcitrant tort-feasor at the expense of a joint tort-feasor who was willing to settle out of court. The legislative intent, as shown by the statutory language, was to promote the use of a covenant not to sue by permitting payment thereunder and discharge of one joint tort-feasor without causing the covenant to effect the release of the other joint tort-feasors. Hayman v. Patio Prods., Inc., 226 Va. 482, 311 S.E.2d 752 (1984).

In 1979, recognizing the potential hardship under the common law, the Virginia legislature enacted this section. The statute provides that a release entered into by one joint tort-feasor does not necessarily discharge the remaining tort-feasors. The legislative purpose is to facilitate settlement and promote the use of releases. State Farm Mut. Auto. Ins. Co. v. Reynolds, 676 F. Supp. 106 (W.D. Va. 1987).

Two policy goals underlie the uniform law from which this section was derived and guide its interpretation; the overarching purpose is to foster settlements in the multiple tortfeasor context and the ancillary goal is to prevent collusion and thereby reasonably ensure a fair distribution of responsibility for a plaintiff's damages among tortfeasors. Dacotah Mktg. & Research v. Versatility, 21 F. Supp. 2d 570 (E.D. Va. 1998).

Section facilitates prompt settlement. — The statute authorizes payment of consideration under the covenant not to sue without discharging nonpaying joint tort-feasors. The statute protects the paying tort-feasor from liability for contribution and prohibits him from exacting contribution from nonpaying joint tort-feasors against whom claims remain outstanding. The statute facilitates prompt settlement, payment, and discharge of paying tort-feasors without releasing those nonpaying joint tort-feasors who prefer to have their liability determined in litigation, with its attendant delays. Hayman v. Patio Prods., Inc., 226 Va. 482, 311 S.E.2d 752 (1984).

Injured party protected from unnecessary delays and loss of claims. — The effect of the statute is to protect the injured party from unnecessary delays and loss of claims. State Farm Mut. Auto. Ins. Co. v. Reynolds, 676 F. Supp. 106 (W.D. Va. 1987).

For history and construction of section, see Carickhoff v. Badger-Northland, Inc., 562 F. Supp. 160 (W.D. Va. 1983).

Effect of subdivision A 1 is to encourage precisely worded releases, while at the same time offer some relief from the harsh common law rule. Although the case concerned a general boiler plate release, the statute did not suggest any reading, other than a literal interpretation, was mandated. State Farm Mut. Auto. Ins. Co. v. Reynolds, 676 F. Supp. 106 (W.D. Va. 1987).

Good faith requirement. — The collusion that will invalidate a release under the good faith standard occurs when the arm's length negotiations between the plaintiff and settling tortfeasors break down; a release is not given in good faith if the plaintiff no longer seeks to gain as much as possible through settlement and the release is given to facilitate a collusive alliance against or to otherwise facilitate intentionally injuring the interests of nonsettling parties. Dacotah Mktg. & Research v. Versatility, 21 F. Supp. 2d 570 (E.D. Va. 1998).

Analysis of whether a release was given in good faith begins with the presumption that the settlement has been made in good faith, and the burden is on the challenging party to show that the settlement is infected with collusion or other tortious or wrongful conduct. Dacotah Mktg. & Research v. Versatility, 21 F. Supp. 2d 570 (E.D. Va. 1998).

When a release given to one of two or more

joint tortfeasors is the result of collusion between the plaintiff and the settling tortfeasor and is not given in good faith, the release does not discharge the colluding tortfeasor and is void and of no effect at all. Dacotah Mktg. & Research v. Versatility, 21 F. Supp. 2d 570 (E.D. Va. 1998).

The words "releases executed" used in subsection D (now subsection E) of this section are not a mandate that a plaintiff sign a written release but merely a collective synonym for the several releases addressed in the preceding paragraphs of the statute, i.e., a release "given in good faith," a release "given pursuant to this section," a release "given," and a release into which a party "enters." Fairfax Hosp. Sys. v. Nevitt, 249 Va. 591, 457 S.E.2d 10 (1995).

At common law in Virginia, there was no right to contribution from joint tort-feasors, but that right was statutorily created by the Virginia General Assembly in 1919. This right is codified in § 8.01-34, subject now to the provisions of this section. Carickhoff v. Badger-Northland, Inc., 562 F. Supp. 160 (W.D. Va. 1983).

Section affects substantive rights of joint tort-feasors, not merely the procedural aspects of their remedy. Shiflet v. Eller, 228 Va. 115, 319 S.E.2d 750 (1984).

Issues affecting the substantive right of contribution are to be determined by the law which existed at the time of the tort giving rise to the cause of action for contribution. Shiflet v. Eller, 228 Va. 115, 319 S.E.2d 750 (1984).

Releasable parties not limited to health care provider. — The settlement credit mandate of this section does not require that a person who has been released be a health care provider. It requires only that such a person and the defendant health care provider at trial be joint tortfeasors mutually liable for the same injury; health care group was such a joint tortfeasor. Fairfax Hosp. Sys. v. Nevitt, 249 Va. 591, 457 S.E.2d 10 (1995).

Applicability to vicariously liable parties. — This section's plain language appears to apply to a party who is vicariously liable, as its coverage extends to one of two or more persons liable in tort for the same injury. And while a master and servant are not technically joint tort-feasors with respect to the servant's tortious act, in Virginia their liability is joint and several and governed by the same principles that are applicable to joint tort-feasors. Harris v. Aluminum Co. of Am., 550 F. Supp. 1024 (W.D. Va. 1982).

There is no evidence that the General Assembly intended to exclude the vicarious liability of masters or principals from the scope of this section. Harris v. Aluminum Co. of Am., 550 F. Supp. 1024 (W.D. Va. 1982).

The inclusion of a reference to "joint tort-feasors" in the title of the several acts affecting this section does not make the decision to apply the statute to those vicariously liable a constitutionally impermissible extension of the bounds of the act. Thurston Metals & Supply Co. v. Taylor, 230 Va. 475, 339 S.E.2d 538 (1986).

The application of this section is not limited to "joint tort-feasors," as that term is narrowly defined, but the statute also applies to those vicariously liable as employers, masters, and principals. Thurston Metals & Supply Co. v. Taylor, 230 Va. 475, 339 S.E.2d 538 (1986).

Application not at odds with Constitution. — Application of the plain words of the substantive language of this section to those vicariously liable, even though they technically are not joint tort-feasors, is not at odds with Va. Const., Art. IV, § 12 because it is in furtherance of the purpose of the enactment, which is to encourage settlements. Thurston Metals & Supply Co. v. Taylor, 230 Va. 475, 339 S.E.2d 538 (1986).

Compliance with insurance provisions. — The public policy in favor of settlement of tort suits contained in this section has no bearing on the question of whether an insured must comply with policy provisions in order to collect insurance money in lieu of damages from a tort-feasor. Virginia Farm Bureau Mut. Ins. Co. v. Gibson, 236 Va. 433, 374 S.E.2d 58 (1988).

Pre-1979 right of contribution among joint tort-feasors included a right to be released when a joint tort-feasor has been released. Bartholomew v. Bartholomew, 233 Va. 86, 353 S.E.2d 752 (1987).

Offset not prohibited by FELA. — Permitting a defendant to offset against the damages awarded the plaintiff the amount received by the plaintiff in a settlement with a third party does not violate the Federal employers' Liability Act, 45 U.S.C. § 51 et seq., provision which proscribes a "device" enabling a defendant "to exempt itself from liability." Downer v. CSX Transp., Inc., 256 Va. 590, 507 S.E.2d 612 (1998).

Recovery against other joint tort-feasors not barred by covenant not to sue. — The effect of this section as first enacted was to prevent a covenant not to sue, drawn in compliance with the statute, from having the effect, upon payment of the agreed consideration, of a release and accord and satisfaction barring recovery from the other joint tort-feasors. Hayman v. Patio Prods., Inc., 226 Va. 482, 311 S.E.2d 752 (1984).

Amounts recovered under release or covenant not to sue. — Pursuant to this section, the amounts recovered under a release or a covenant not to sue shall reduce the plaintiff's judgment against another by the amount stipulated in the covenant or release, irrespective of whether the settling party is in fact a joint tort-feasor. Greenbaum v. Travelers Ins. Co., 705 F. Supp. 1138 (E.D. Va. 1989).

In determining amount of release monies to be credited against recovery, the trial court must identify the amount of consideration paid by a tortfeasor for a release. In determining this amount, the court must look at the injury or damage covered by the release and, if more than a single injury, allocate, if possible, the appropriate amount of compensation for each injury. Tazewell Oil Co. v. United Va. Bank/Crestar Bank, 243 Va. 94, 413 S.E.2d 611 (1992).

Error in credit calculation found. — Where trial court reduced the $2,000,000 jury verdict rendered against the hospital by $600,000 (the amount of the health care group's settlement) and then reduced the remainder ($1,400,000) to the medical malpractice cap ($1,000,000), the plain meaning of this section and § 8.01-581.15, read together, is that where there is a verdict by a jury or a judgment by a court against a health care provider for "injury to ... a patient" and the total amount recovered in that action and in all settlements related to the medical malpractice injury exceeds one million dollars, the total amount the plaintiff can recover for that injury is $1,000,000. Accordingly, the trial court erred when it failed to apply the $600,000 credit for the statutory recovery cap in determining the quantum of plaintiff's judgment. Fairfax Hosp. Sys. v. Nevitt, 249 Va. 591, 457 S.E.2d 10 (1995).

Distinction in subsection D (now subsection E) between covenants not to sue and releases is consistent with a long recognized distinction in Virginia common law. It was long the law of Virginia that a release of one joint tort-feasor amounted to a release of all joint tort-feasors. On the other hand, a covenant not to sue one joint tort-feasor did not necessarily prevent actions against fellow tort-feasors. Perdue v. Sears, Roebuck & Co., 694 F.2d 66 (4th Cir. 1982).

Retroactive application of section, resulting in destruction of substantive right which a party was possessed of prior to enactment of section, is improper. Carickhoff v. Badger-Northland, Inc., 562 F. Supp. 160 (W.D. Va. 1983).

In a medical malpractice case arising out of a surgical operation performed in 1977, where the patient's committee sued the hospital and three physicians, jointly and severally, and in 1983 agreed to settle her claims against the physicians for $475,000, releasing the physicians and purporting to reserve her claims against the hospital, this section could not be applied retroactively to adversely affect hospital's right of contribution from the released tort-feasors. Potomac Hosp. Corp. v. Dillon, 229 Va. 355, 329 S.E.2d 41, cert. denied, 474 U.S. 971, 106 S. Ct. 352, 88 L. Ed. 2d 320 (1985).

Where defendant's substantive right, manifested by her ability to defend successfully the suit by the plaintiff after plaintiff had released joint tort-feasor, would be impaired if the statute was permitted to operate retroactively, the application of the statute would be constitutionally invalid, and issues affecting the substantive right would be determined by the law which existed in 1976, the time of the tort giving rise to the cause of action for contribution. Bartholomew v. Bartholomew, 233 Va. 86, 353 S.E.2d 752 (1987).

When this section, including subsection D, adversely affects a substantive right, it cannot be applied retroactively to impair that right, because such application would violate the nonsettling joint tort-feasor's due process rights. Bartholomew v. Bartholomew, 233 Va. 86, 353 S.E.2d 752 (1987).

Section not retroactively applied so as to adversely affect right of contribution. — Where the cause of action for contribution accruing to a joint tort-feasor arose at the time of the jointly negligent acts in October, 1977, it necessarily followed that this section, enacted in 1979, which adversely affected that substantive right, could not be applied retroactively to impair that right. Such a retroactive application of the enactment would violate his due process rights and would be invalid. Shiflet v. Eller, 228 Va. 115, 319 S.E.2d 750 (1984).

Applicable version of section determined by date release or covenant signed. — The 1982 amendment, which added the second sentence of subdivision A 1 and added subsection D, is a clarification of the July 1, 1980, version of this section. There is no issue of whether this section is retroactive or prospective. Each version of this section applies to covenants not to sue and/or releases signed during the effective dates of each version. Statzer v. King Kutter Corp., 550 F. Supp. 1062 (W.D. Va. 1982).

Not date cause of action arose. — The court must look to the date of the release rather than the date that the cause of action arose in order to determine the applicable version of this section. Statzer v. King Kutter Corp., 550 F. Supp. 1062 (W.D. Va. 1982).

Intent of parties is controlling on effect of release. — A nondischarged tort-feasor may claim a setoff based on any sums paid by another to obtain a release, but the effect of the release itself is controlled by the intent of the parties as expressed in the terms of the writing. Lemke v. Sears, Roebuck & Co., 853 F.2d 253 (4th Cir. 1988).

Written release, issued by an injured motorist to the other motorist involved in an auto accident, failed to bring an action against the auto manufacturer which named other motorist as third party defendant within the scope of this section, where the written release was executed two and one-half years after a similar oral release was given, and after the statute of limitations on injured motorist cause of action against other motorist had expired, and after the action against the manufacturer had commenced. Jones v. GMC, 856 F.2d 22 (4th Cir. 1988).

Approval of releases. — Those portions of a release that are not made part of a wrongful death compromise settlement approved by a circuit court are not binding on the parties to the release. Ramey v. Bobbitt, 250 Va. 474, 463 S.E.2d 437 (1995).

Trial court did not err in utilizing the present value of infant's structured settlement with physician in reducing the infant's verdict against the hospital. Under this section, the hospital was not entitled to a credit equal to the undiscounted sum of payments which the settlement agreement provided for the infant. Fairfax Hosp. Sys. v. McCarty, 244 Va. 28, 419 S.E.2d 621 (1992).

Nonsettling joint tort-feasor is not necessarily freed from liability for damages. Contribution may be recovered if his liability is established. State Farm Mut. Auto. Ins. Co. v. Reynolds, 676 F. Supp. 106 (W.D. Va. 1987).

When settling tort-feasor may seek contribution from nonsettling tort-feasor. — The legislature's purpose in enacting this section supports the inference, that if a release between a claimant and a tort-feasor extinguishes the liability of a second tort-feasor, then the settling tort-feasor may still seek contribution from the nonsettling tort-feasor. State Farm Mut. Auto. Ins. Co. v. Reynolds, 676 F. Supp. 106 (W.D. Va. 1987).

Principal not automatically released by covenant given to agent. — A covenant not to sue given to an alleged agent pursuant to this section does not automatically release the alleged principal from vicarious liability based on the acts of the alleged agent. Harris v. Aluminum Co. of Am., 550 F. Supp. 1024 (W.D. Va. 1982).

Inapplicable to indemnity rights arising from contractual relationship. — This statute governs only those claims for contribution between tort feasors, a relation that is created in law by the commission of the tort. The statute does not purport to speak to indemnity rights which arise from a contractual relationship between contracting parties. Whittle v. Timesavers, Inc., 572 F. Supp. 584 (W.D. Va. 1983), rev'd on other grounds, 749 F.2d 1103 (4th Cir. 1984).

Validity not affected by single document multi-claim release. — There is no requirement of separate documents for the release of contract and tort claims. Consolidation of them in a single document does not defeat an otherwise valid compliance with this section as to the release of tort claims. Tazewell Oil Co. v. United Va. Bank/Crestar Bank, 243 Va. 94, 413 S.E.2d 611 (1992).

Indivisible injuries. — Where there is one indivisible injury for which settlement has been consummated, unconditional release of one allegedly liable for the injury bars recovery against others also allegedly liable, regardless of the theory upon which liability is predicated. Cauthorn v. British Leyland, U.K., Ltd., 233 Va. 202, 355 S.E.2d 306 (1987).

Where the injuries complained of are those for which the compromise settlement provided compensation, and plaintiff sustained injuries which, although they may have had more than a single cause, constituted a single indivisible injury, her settlement with and release of the insurance companies and their insureds constituted an accord and satisfaction of her cause of action for her single indivisible injury, and as such, this release also released all other parties allegedly responsible for her injuries. Cauthorn v. British Leyland, U.K., Ltd., 233 Va. 202, 355 S.E.2d 306 (1987).

Requirements of statute satisfied. — Where hospital argued that, in order to avoid the effect of the common-law rule, plaintiff was required by this section to subscribe a written release before dismissing health care group with prejudice from the case, and where the settlement, consummated by delivery of check and execution of the joint tortfeasor release, was preceded by an agreement in principle memorialized by several writings, namely, the letter addressed by plaintiff's counsel to health care group's counsel, the copy of the written release later executed, unchanged, by plaintiff and the order subscribed by counsel for plaintiff and health care group reciting that claims had been settled, pursuant to this section, plaintiff complied with the requirements of this section and the hospital was not released. Fairfax Hosp. Sys. v. Nevitt, 249 Va. 591, 457 S.E.2d 10 (1995) (decided prior to the 1989 amendment).

Applied in Perdue v. Sears, Roebuck & Co., 523 F. Supp. 203 (W.D. Va. 1981); Farish v. Courion Indus., Inc., 754 F.2d 1111 (4th Cir. 1985); Bell v. Owen Thomas, Inc., 115 F.R.D. 299 (W.D. Va. 1987); Boyd v. Bulala, 678 F. Supp. 612 (W.D. Va. 1988); Allianz Ins. Co. v. Garrett, 47 F.3d 665 (4th Cir. 1995).

II. DECISIONS UNDER PRIOR LAW.

Editor's note. — The case cited below was decided under corresponding provisions of prior law. The term "this section," as used below, refers to former provisions.

Writing required. — While none of the language of this section standing alone might be dispositive, the provision as a whole points to the requirement of a writing. Jones v. GMC, 856 F.2d 22 (4th Cir. 1988) (decided prior to the

1989 amendment, which added the second and third sentences in present subsection E).

The statutory language of this section which speaks of executed releases and covenants appears to contemplate the signing of a written instrument. The drafters of the statute specifically selected the word "executed" in lieu of alternative terms such as "made" or "entered" which might have encompassed an oral agreement. This interpretation is further supported by other language in the statute which suggests that some written document was contemplated. Jones v. GMC, 856 F.2d 22 (4th Cir. 1988) (decided prior to the 1989 amendment, which added the second and third sentences in present subsection E).

Requirement of a writing ensures that the parties thereto understand who is being released in return for what consideration. It serves notice to joint tort-feasors that they remain bound and avoids the need to undertake extensive litigation over questions of the validity and effect of the release, with all the attendant problems of having the parties and their attorneys take the stand to testify about their understanding of the terms, consideration, and conditions of the release. Jones v. GMC, 856 F.2d 22 (4th Cir. 1988) (decided prior to the 1989 amendment, which added the second and third sentences in present subsection E).

§ 8.01-36. Joinder of action of tort to infant with action for recovery of expenses incurred thereby. — Where there is pending any action by an infant plaintiff against a tort-feasor for a personal injury, any parent, or guardian of such infant, who is entitled to recover from the same tort-feasor the expenses of curing or attempting to cure such infant from the result of such personal injury, may bring an action against such tort-feasor for such expenses, in the same court where such infant's case is pending, either in the action filed in behalf of the infant or in a separate action. If the claim for expenses be by separate action, upon motion of any party to either case, made to the court at least one week before the trial, both cases shall be tried together at the same time as parts of the same transaction. But separate verdicts when there is a jury trial shall be rendered, and the judgment shall distinctly separate the decision and judgment in the separate causes of action.

In the event of the cases being carried to the Supreme Court, which may be done if there be the jurisdictional amount in either case, they shall both be carried together as one case and record, but the Supreme Court shall clearly specify the decision in each case, separating them in the decision to the extent necessary to do justice among the parties. (Code 1950, § 8-629; 1954, c. 333; 1973, c. 277.)

Cross references. — For rule of court that procedure shall be by notice of motion for judgment, see Rule 3:3.

I. Decisions Under Current Law.
II. Decisions Under Prior Law.

I. DECISIONS UNDER CURRENT LAW.

Applied in Hutto v. BIC Corp., 800 F. Supp. 1367 (E.D. Va. 1992).

II. DECISIONS UNDER PRIOR LAW.

Editor's note. — The cases cited below were decided under corresponding provisions of former law. The term "this section," as used below, refers to former provisions.

This section recognizes the common law rule that two separate causes of action arise out of an injury to an infant by wrongful act. One cause of action is on behalf of the infant to recover damages for pain and suffering, permanent injury and impairment of earning capacity after attaining majority. The other is on behalf of the parent for loss of services during minority and necessary expenses incurred for the infant's treatment. Moses v. Akers, 203 Va. 130, 122 S.E.2d 864 (1961).

An infant is not entitled to recover the expenses incurred in healing or attempting to be healed of his injuries in an action brought against a tort-feasor to recover damages for personal injuries unless (1) he has paid or agreed to pay the expenses; or (2) he alone is responsible by reason of his emancipation or the death or incompetency of his parents; or (3) the parent has waived the right of recovery in favor of the infant; or (4) recovery therefor is permitted by statute. Moses v. Akers, 203 Va.

130, 122 S.E.2d 864 (1961).

Father's cause of action derivative. — A father's cause of action for medical and incidental expenses was a derivative action, and where there was no verdict in the child's case, there could be none in the father's case. Norfolk S. Ry. v. Fincham, 213 Va. 122, 189 S.E.2d 380 (1972).

§ 8.01-37. Recovery of lost wages in action for injuries to emancipated infant. — In any suit for personal injuries brought on behalf of an emancipated infant, when such infant has sustained lost wages as a result of such injuries, he shall be entitled to recover such lost wages as a part of his damages. Where recovery is made hereunder or where recovery is attempted to be made and a decision on the merits adverse to said infant results, no other person may recover such lost wages. (Code 1950, § 8-629.1; 1970, c. 421; 1977, c. 617.)

§ 8.01-37.1. Claims for medical services provided by United States; proof of reasonable value. — Whenever any person sustains personal injuries caused by the alleged negligence of another, and a claim against any person alleged to be liable is created in favor of the United States under federal law (42 U.S.C. § 2651 et seq.) for the reasonable value of medical, surgical or dental care and treatment provided, the injured party may, on behalf of the United States, claim the reasonable value of the medical services provided as an element of damages in a civil action against the person alleged to be liable. It shall not be required that the United States intervene in the action or be made a party in order to establish its claim. A sworn written statement of the authorized representative of the department or agency providing such services prepared in accordance with the regulations promulgated pursuant to 42 U.S.C. § 2652 shall be admissible as evidence of the reasonable value of the care and treatment provided. (1984, c. 42; 1985, c. 205.)

I. DECISIONS UNDER CURRENT LAW.

No distinguishing between injured infants and injured adults. — This statute does not distinguish between injured infants and injured adults as it uses the term "injured persons." Hutto v. BIC Corp., 800 F. Supp. 1367 (E.D. Va. 1992).

Parents' cause of action for medical expenses accrued at the time they became liable to pay injured minor's medical bills. Hutto v. BIC Corp., 800 F. Supp. 1367 (E.D. Va. 1992).

§ 8.01-38. Tort liability of hospitals. — Hospital as referred to in this section shall include any institution within the definition of hospital in § 32.1-123.

No hospital, as defined in this section, shall be immune from liability for negligence or any other tort on the ground that it is a charitable institution unless (i) such hospital renders exclusively charitable medical services for which service no bill for service is rendered to, nor any charge is ever made to the patient or (ii) the party alleging such negligence or other tort was accepted as a patient by such institution under an express written agreement executed by the hospital and delivered at the time of admission to the patient or the person admitting such patient providing that all medical services furnished such patient are to be supplied on a charitable basis without financial liability to the patient. However, notwithstanding the provisions of § 8.01-581.15 a hospital which is exempt from taxation pursuant to § 501 (c) (3) of Title 26 of the United States Code (Internal Revenue Code of 1954) and which is insured against liability for negligence or other tort in an amount not less than $500,000 for each occurrence shall not be liable for damage in excess of the limits of such insurance, or in actions for medical malpractice pursuant to Chapter 21.1 (§ 8.01-581.1 et seq.) for damages in excess of the amount set forth in § 8.01-581.15. (Code 1950, § 8-629.2; 1974, c. 552; 1976, c. 765; 1977, c. 617; 1983, c. 496; 1986, cc. 389, 454; 2000, c. 464.)

The 2000 amendments. — The 2000 amendment by c. 464 substituted "for damages in excess of the amount set forth in § 8.01-581.15" for "the lesser of the limits of such insurance or $1 million" at the end of the second paragraph.

Law Review. — For survey of Virginia law on torts for the year 1973-1974, see 60 Va. L. Rev. 1615 (1974). For survey of Virginia tort law for the year 1975-1976, see 62 Va. L. Rev. 1489 (1976). For survey of Virginia law on torts for the year 1976-77, see 63 Va. L. Rev. 1491 (1977). For a re-examination of sovereign tort immunity in Virginia, see 15 U. Rich. L. Rev. 247 (1981). For article, "Charitable Immunity: What Price Hath Charity?," see 28 U. Rich. L. Rev. 953 (1994). For a review of damages in medical malpractice in Virginia, see 33 U. Rich. L. Rev. 919 (1999).

I. DECISIONS UNDER CURRENT LAW.

Immunity for hospitals providing medical care free of charge. — The Virginia General Assembly eliminated charitable immunity for most hospitals, essentially limiting its application to hospitals that provide medical care free of charge. Davidson v. Colonial Williamsburg Found., 817 F. Supp. 611 (E.D. Va. 1993).

Under this section, charitable hospitals are immune from liability in Virginia if they do not charge patients for services and 26 U.S.C. § 501(c)(3) tax-exempt hospitals have limited liability. Power v. Arlington Hosp. Ass'n, 42 F.3d 851 (4th Cir. 1994).

College was not entitled to use the defense of charitable immunity from tort liability, where the charter did not specifically restrict operation of the college to charitable or eleemosynary purposes nor was the manner of operation of the college strictly charitable in nature. Radosevic v. Virginia Intermont College, 633 F. Supp. 1084 (W.D. Va. 1986).

The public policy in Virginia favors a more restrictive approach to determining that an institution is immune from tort liability on the grounds of the charitable immunity doctrine. This is evidenced by the legislative abrogation of the doctrine of charitable immunity for hospitals and the judicial reluctance to automatically apply a charitable label to various institutions. Radosevic v. Virginia Intermont College, 633 F. Supp. 1084 (W.D. Va. 1986).

The 1986 amendment to this section merely clarified its application. Etheridge v. Medical Center Hosps., 237 Va. 87, 376 S.E.2d 525 (1989).

§ 8.01-38.1. Limitation on recovery of punitive damages. — In any action accruing on or after July 1, 1988, including an action for medical malpractice under Chapter 21.1 (§ 8.01-581.1 et seq.), the total amount awarded for punitive damages against all defendants found to be liable shall be determined by the trier of fact. In no event shall the total amount awarded for punitive damages exceed $350,000. The jury shall not be advised of the limitation prescribed by this section. However, if a jury returns a verdict for punitive damages in excess of the maximum amount specified in this section, the judge shall reduce the award and enter judgment for such damages in the maximum amount provided by this section. (1987, c. 255.)

Law Review. — For comment, "The Constitutional Attack on Virginia's Medical Malpractice Cap: Equal Protection and the Right to Jury Trial," see 22 U. Rich. L. Rev. 95 (1987). For case note, "Punitive Damage 'Overkill' After TXO Production Corp. v. Alliance Resources: The Need for a Congressional Solution," see 36 Wm. & Mary L. Rev. 751 (1995).

I. DECISIONS UNDER CURRENT LAW.

Constitutionality. — This section does not violate the due process guarantees secured by the Federal and Virginia Constitutions. Wackenhut Applied Technologies Ctr., Inc. v. Sygnetron Protection Sys., 979 F.2d 980 (4th Cir. 1992).

"Any action" not limited to unintentional tort actions. — There is no definitional language indicating that the term "any action" is limited to unintentional tort actions. Wackenhut Applied Technologies Ctr., Inc. v. Sygnetron Protection Sys., 979 F.2d 980 (4th Cir. 1992).

Review of punitive damage awards can no longer be conducted under "excessiveness" standard. — In order to comport with the due process requirements of the Fifth Amendment, post-trial and appellate review of punitive damage awards in the federal courts of the Fourth Circuit, based upon state statutes and common law, can no longer be conducted under Virginia's "excessiveness" standard but must instead proceed under standards similar to those enunciated by the Alabama courts in Hammond v. City of Gadsden, 493 So. 2d 1374 (Ala. 1986), Green Oil Co. v. Hornsby, 539 So. 2d 218 (Ala. 1989), and Central Ala. Elec. Coop. v. Tapley, 546 So. 2d 371 (Ala. 1989), as upheld in Pacific Mut. Life Ins. Co. v. Haslip, 499 U.S. 1, 111 S. Ct. 1032, 113 L. Ed. 2d 1 (1991); Johnson v. Hugo's Skateway, 949 F.2d 1338 (4th Cir. 1991), aff'd in part, rev'd in part, upon reh'g en banc, 974 F.2d 1408 (4th Cir. 1992).

Award of treble damages not subject to this limitation. — Under the plain language of this section, the limitation of $350,000 applies only to an award of "punitive" damages. Advanced Marine Enters., Inc. v. PRC, Inc., 256 Va. 106, 501 S.E.2d 148 (1998).

§ 8.01-39. Completion or acceptance of work not bar to action against independent contractor for personal injury, wrongful death or damage to property.

— In any civil action in which it is alleged that personal injury, death by wrongful act or damage to property has resulted from the negligence of or breach of warranty by an independent contractor, it shall not be a defense by such contractor to such action that such contractor has completed such work or that such work has been accepted as satisfactory by the owner of the property upon which the work was done or by the person hiring such contractor.

Nothing contained herein shall be construed to limit, modify or otherwise affect the provisions of § 8.01-250. (Code 1950, § 8-629.3; 1974, c. 669; 1977, c. 617.)

Law Review. — For survey of Virginia law on torts for the year 1973-1974, see 60 Va. L. Rev. 1615 (1974).

§ 8.01-40. Unauthorized use of name or picture of any person; exemplary damages; statute of limitations.

— A. Any person whose name, portrait, or picture is used without having first obtained the written consent of such person, or if dead, of the surviving consort and if none, of the next of kin, or if a minor, the written consent of his or her parent or guardian, for advertising purposes or for the purposes of trade, such persons may maintain a suit in equity against the person, firm, or corporation so using such person's name, portrait, or picture to prevent and restrain the use thereof; and may also sue and recover damages for any injuries sustained by reason of such use. And if the defendant shall have knowingly used such person's name, portrait or picture in such manner as is forbidden or declared to be unlawful by this chapter, the jury, in its discretion, may award exemplary damages.

B. No action shall be commenced under this section more than twenty years after the death of such person. (Code 1950, § 8-650; 1977, c. 617.)

REVISERS' NOTE

The first sentence of former § 8-650 was transferred to § 18.2-216.1 since its import is purely penal. The civil remedy retained in § 8.01-40 A was expanded by removing the restriction that the unauthorized use must pertain to a Virginia resident. Subsection A was otherwise rewritten without material change in substance.

Subsection B establishes a twenty-year limitation period which begins upon the death of the person whose name is misused.

Cross references. — For rules of court on equity procedure, see Rules 2:1 through 2:21. For rules governing actions in personam for money, see Rules 3:1 through 3:18.

Law Review. — For comment, "The Case for a Broader Right of Privacy in Virginia," see 7 Wm. & Mary L. Rev. 127 (1966). For survey of Virginia law on torts for the year 1976-77, see 63 Va. L. Rev. 1491 (1977). For 1995 survey of civil practice and procedure, see 29 U. Rich. L.

Rev. 897 (1995). For a symposium, 'Aggressive Newsgathering and the First Amendment,' see 33 U. Rich. L. Rev. 1121 (2000). For an essay, 'Privacy and Celebrity: An Essay on the Nationalization of Intimacy,' see 33 U. Rich. L. Rev. 1121 (2000). For an article, 'Protect the Press: A First Amendment Standard for Safeguarding Aggressive Newsgathering,' see 33 U. Rich. L. Rev. 1143 (2000). For an article, 'Ride-alongs, Paparazzi, and Other Media Threats to Privacy,' see 33 U. Rich. L. Rev. 1167 (2000). For an article, 'I Spy: The Newgatherer Under Cover,' see 33 U. Rich. L. Rev. 1185 (2000). For an article, 'Qualified Intimacy, Celebrity, and the Case for a Newgathering Privilege,' see 33 U. Rich. L. Rev. 1233 (2000).

I. Decisions Under Current Law.
II. Decisions Under Prior Law.

I. DECISIONS UNDER CURRENT LAW.

Constitutionality. — Subsection A of this section, as applied to the facts of the instant case—plaintiff's name was prominently featured in real estate flyer—is not constitutionally invalid under either the free-speech provisions of the First Amendment to the federal Constitution or the applicable provisions of Va. Const., Art. I, § 12. Town & Country Properties, Inc. v. Riggins, 249 Va. 387, 457 S.E.2d 356 (1995).

This section is in derogation of the common law. Falwell v. Penthouse Int'l, Ltd., 521 F. Supp. 1204 (W.D. Va. 1981).

And therefore must be strictly construed. Falwell v. Penthouse Int'l, Ltd., 521 F. Supp. 1204 (W.D. Va. 1981).

Virginia recognizes no right of privacy other than that specifically conferred by this section. Falwell v. Penthouse Int'l, Ltd., 521 F. Supp. 1204 (W.D. Va. 1981).

Protective mantle extends to celebrities. — Ordinary citizens are entitled to the protective mantle of this section, and persons in a celebrity status should receive no less coverage in this respect. Town & Country Properties, Inc. v. Riggins, 249 Va. 387, 457 S.E.2d 356 (1995).

Exception for matters that are newsworthy or of public interest. — An exception exists under this section for items that are "newsworthy" or "matters of public interest," which covers articles in newspapers and magazines, as well as pictures used to illustrate the articles, unless the picture bears no real relationship to the article or the article is an advertisement in disguise. Williams v. Newsweek, Inc., 63 F. Supp. 2d 734 (E.D. Va. 1999), aff'd, 202 F.3d 262 (4th Cir. 1999).

Exception for uses that are incidental. — There is an exception to the statute for uses that are incidental to the purpose of the work, and according to this exception, a publisher will be liable for the publication of an unauthorized picture only if there is a direct and substantial connection between the appearance of the plaintiff's name or likeness and the main purpose and subject of the work. Williams v. Newsweek, Inc., 63 F. Supp. 2d 734 (E.D. Va. 1999), aff'd, 202 F.3d 262 (4th Cir. 1999).

Limitation period for actions under subsection A. — Subsection A is aimed at preventing the appropriation, without consent, of an individual's name or likeness while he is alive and for 20 years after he dies. It creates in an individual a species of property right in their name and likeness. Consequently, the limitation period contained in subsection B of § 8.01-243 should be applied. Lavery v. Automation Mgt. Consultants, Inc., 234 Va. 145, 360 S.E.2d 336 (1987).

Subsection B is a cutoff statute, not a statute of limitation. — The legislature intended subsection B to be a cutoff statute, and, as such, to operate as an outside time period in which true statutes of limitations would operate and beyond which no suit based on subsection A could be maintained. The General Assembly in enacting subsection B was not setting a time period within which suit must be brought, instead, it was providing a cutoff point after which suit could not be brought. Lavery v. Automation Mgt. Consultants, Inc., 234 Va. 145, 360 S.E.2d 336 (1987).

Notwithstanding the characterizations of subsection B of this section made by the revisers' notes under §§ 8.01-228 and 8.01-243, subsection B of this section is not the statute of limitations applicable to a cause of action under subsection A. Lavery v. Automation Mgt. Consultants, Inc., 234 Va. 145, 360 S.E.2d 336 (1987).

Use of New York decisions in construing section. — This section is substantially similar to § 51 of the New York Civil Rights Law, and the U.S. Court of Appeals for the Fourth Circuit would look to the New York courts for guidance in construing the Virginia privacy statute. Falwell v. Flynt, 797 F.2d 1270 (4th Cir. 1986), rev'd on other grounds, 485 U.S. 46, 108 S. Ct. 876, 99 L. Ed. 2d 41 (1988).

The General Assembly has fixed the "knowingly used" standard for punitive damages in the type of action under this section. The Virginia Supreme Court shall not engage in judicial legislation by adding ingredients not specified in the statute. Town & Country Properties, Inc. v. Riggins, 249 Va. 387, 457 S.E.2d 356 (1995).

An individual holds a property interest

in his or her reputation, which represents the individual's personal identity in the community and which is the thing of value in the individual's name. Nossen v. Hoy, 750 F. Supp. 740 (E.D. Va. 1990).

Use of candidate's name or picture by political organization. — This section or its common-law counterparts in other states, may not be construed to prohibit political organizations from using a candidate's name or picture in a political campaign without his consent. Such an expansive interpretation of the law of tortious appropriation of name would trench on important freedoms secured by the First Amendment. Friends of Gramm v. Americans for Gramm, 587 F. Supp. 769 (E.D. Va. 1984).

Interview in magazine not for trade or advertising purpose. — Plaintiff minister's allegations that an interview conducted and published by defendant journalists and magazine invaded his privacy by commercializing his personality failed to state a claim upon which relief could be granted, since Virginia recognizes no common-law action for invasion of privacy, and the interview did not, as a matter of law, qualify as being for a trade or advertising purpose under this section. Falwell v. Penthouse Int'l, Ltd., 521 F. Supp. 1204 (W.D. Va. 1981).

"False light" invasion of privacy not actionable. — Allegations that an interview conducted and published by defendant journalists and magazine invaded plaintiff minister's privacy by placing the plaintiff in a "false light" in the public eye failed to state a claim upon which relief could be granted, since Virginia recognizes no common-law action for invasion of privacy, and the acts complained of did not fall within the narrow purview of this section. Falwell v. Penthouse Int'l, Ltd., 521 F. Supp. 1204 (W.D. Va. 1981).

Where advertising parody of plaintiff published in defendants' magazine was not reasonably believable, and contained a disclaimer, publication of the parody did not constitute a use of plaintiff's name and likeness for purposes of trade. Falwell v. Flynt, 797 F.2d 1270 (4th Cir. 1986), rev'd on other grounds, 485 U.S. 46, 108 S. Ct. 876, 99 L. Ed. 2d 41 (1988).

Plaintiff's name was used for advertising purposes in a manner forbidden by this section where plaintiff's ex-wife specifically directed the printer who set the type and distributed the real estate flyer "to make the words John Riggins bigger than the other words" and to make them "stand out." Plaintiff's name, therefore, was an integral part of the flyer and could not be deemed merely incidental to the flyer's clear commercial message. Town & Country Properties, Inc. v. Riggins, 249 Va. 387, 457 S.E.2d 356 (1995).

Applied in Ward v. Connor, 495 F. Supp. 434 (E.D. Va. 1980); Brown v. ABC, 704 F.2d 1296 (4th Cir. 1983).

II. DECISIONS UNDER PRIOR LAW.

Editor's note. — The case cited below was decided under corresponding provisions of former law. The term "this section," as used below, refers to former provisions.

No general right of privacy exists in the law of Virginia. Evans v. Sturgill, 430 F. Supp. 1209 (W.D. Va. 1977).

Except for the limited right conferred by this section. — See Evans v. Sturgill, 430 F. Supp. 1209 (W.D. Va. 1977).

Making sworn statements resulting in arrest warrant. — Plaintiff's actions in making sworn statements to the Commonwealth's attorney, resulting in the issuance of a warrant for the arrest of the defendant for felonious theft of an airplane, did not fall within the narrow purview of the limited right of privacy created by this section. Evans v. Sturgill, 430 F. Supp. 1209 (W.D. Va. 1977).

§ 8.01-40.1. Action for injury resulting from violation of Computer Crimes Act; limitations. — Any person whose property or person is injured by reason of a violation of the provisions of the Virginia Computer Crimes Act (§ 18.2-152.1 et seq.) may sue and recover damages as provided in § 18.2-152.12. An action shall be commenced before the earlier of (i) five years after the last act in the course of conduct constituting a violation of the Computer Crimes Act or (ii) two years after the plaintiff discovers or reasonably should have discovered the last act in the course of conduct constituting a violation of the Computer Crimes Act. (1985, c. 92.)

Law Review. — For article on Virginia's response to computer abuses, see 19 U. Rich. L. Rev. 85 (1984).

§ 8.01-40.2. Unsolicited transmission of advertising materials by facsimile machine. — Any person aggrieved by the intentional electronic or telephonic transmission to a facsimile device of unsolicited advertising material offering goods, real estate, or services for sale or lease may bring an action against the person responsible for the transmission to enjoin further violations and to recover the greater of (i) actual damages sustained, together with costs and reasonable attorneys' fees, or (ii) $200. Carriers or other companies which provide facsimile transmission services shall not be responsible for transmissions of unsolicited advertising materials by their customers. An action brought pursuant to this section shall be commenced within two years of the transmission. (1990, c. 246.)

§ 8.01-41. Wrongful distraint, attachment. — If property be distrained for any rent not due, or attached for any rent not accruing, or taken under any attachment sued out without good cause, the owner of such property may, in an action against the party suing out the warrant of distress or attachment, recover damages for the wrongful distraint, seizure, or sale. (Code 1950, § 8-651; 1977, c. 617.)

REVISERS' NOTE

The former § 8-651 phrase "seizure, and also, if the property be sold, for the sale thereof" has been deleted and the words "distraint, seizure, or sale" substituted to conform with modern practice.

Cross references. — As to recovery for rent, generally, see §§ 55-227 through 55-238. As to procedure when distress has been levied and tenant is unable to give forthcoming bond, see § 55-232. As to recovery for distress not wrongful, but irregular, see § 55-236. For rules of court governing actions in personam for money, see Rules 3:1 through 3:18.

I. DECISIONS UNDER PRIOR LAW.

Editor's note. — The cases cited below were decided under corresponding provisions of former law. The term "this section," as used below, refers to former provisions.

The manifest intention of this section is to prevent the landlord from oppressing his tenant. The right to sue in damages for an illegal distress was recognized at common law and the enactment of the statute was in furtherance of the right so recognized. Gurfein v. Howell, 142 Va. 197, 128 S.E. 644 (1925).

Ignorance no excuse. — The right to distrain or attach for rent has always been regarded by the courts as a most drastic one, and in order to restrain the landlord from a too free use of this power, he must exercise the same at his peril. The law presumes that he knows the amount of his tenant's indebtedness and ignorance on his part will not relieve him for compensatory damages for a mistake committed by him. Gurfein v. Howell, 142 Va. 197, 128 S.E. 644 (1925).

As to reading of section in connection with § 8.01-551 and former § 8.01-552, relating to the giving of attachment bonds, see Harris v. Lipson, 167 Va. 365, 189 S.E. 349 (1937).

Action for trespass available. — Where a distress is made for rent pretended to be due, when in truth there is none due, and the goods distrained are not sold, the remedy is by action at common law, and trespass may be maintained. But the party suing is not obliged to bring trespass, he may waive the trespass and bring case. Olinger v. M'Chesney, 34 Va. (7 Leigh) 660 (1836).

Quashing of attachment does not imply lack of good cause. — Under this section the fact that an attachment is quashed on the ground that it was sued out without sufficient cause does not necessarily imply that there was lack of good cause. Harris v. Lipson, 167 Va. 365, 189 S.E. 349 (1937).

When landlord liable for acts of agent. — A landlord who employs an agent to lease his property and receive the rents is not liable in damages for the act of the agent in unlawfully suing out a distress warrant against the tenant, unless he directed or approved the proceedings had under the distress warrant, or failed to repudiate such proceedings after full knowledge of them. Fishburne v. Engledove, 91 Va. 548, 22 S.E. 354 (1895).

Measure of damages. — In the absence of any charge of fraud, malice, oppression, or other special aggravation, the measure of the plaintiff's damages is compensation for the injury suffered — such damages as are the natural and proximate result of the injury complained of. Fishburne v. Engledove, 91 Va.

§ 8.01-42

548, 22 S.E. 354 (1895).

In an action for illegal distress, instructions which ignore the right of plaintiff to recover nominal damages where an illegal levy has been made are erroneous under this section. Gurfein v. Howell, 142 Va. 197, 128 S.E. 644 (1925).

Damages due for excessive distraint. — While a lien legally attaches to all property as might be on the premises when the lien is asserted or within 30 days prior to distraint, the landlord can distrain goods only to the extent necessary to satisfy the rent justly believed to be due, the tenant possessing an action for damages for excessive distraint. United States v. Melchiorre, 292 F. Supp. 305 (E.D. Va. 1968).

"Fair" damages erroneous. — Where a landlord distrains for an amount in excess of the rent due the tenant is entitled to recover at least nominal damages. But an instruction that in such a case the tenant is entitled to fair damages for wrong suffered is erroneous, as it is more than probable that "fair" means more than "compensation" to the average individual, and when the jury was told to find "fair damages" for the wrong suffered, instead of being told they could only compensate for the injury done, they conceived the idea, no doubt, that they had the right to punish instead of the power to compensate. Gurfein v. Howell, 142 Va. 197, 128 S.E. 644 (1925).

Effect of failing to plead and prove special damages. — Where the notice of motion for illegally suing out a distress warrant did not allege and the proof failed to disclose any special damages suffered by plaintiff, a verdict for plaintiff in a substantial amount should be set aside as excessive. Gurfein v. Howell, 142 Va. 197, 128 S.E. 644 (1925).

Plaintiff has burden of proving substantial damages. — In an action for illegal distress, the defendant was entitled to have the jury instructed that before the plaintiff could recover any except nominal damages, the burden was upon him to prove by a preponderance of the evidence that he had sustained substantial damages. To merely show that an illegal levy has been made is not sufficient to entitle the plaintiff to recover substantial damages. Gurfein v. Howell, 142 Va. 197, 128 S.E. 644 (1925).

Plaintiff has burden of proving exemplary damages. — In order to recover exemplary damages in an action under this section the burden is upon the plaintiff to show not only that the act complained of is illegal, but that it was either malicious or oppressive, or that it was attended by especially aggravating circumstances. Evans v. Schuster, 178 Va. 61, 16 S.E.2d 301 (1941).

When variance in allegations fatal. — In action for a wrongful distress, if the plaintiff allege that he held under a lease for five months, for $20.00 payable in repairs and labor, and at the trial it appear that the lease was for 12 months, for a money rent of $65.00, the variance will be fatal. Olinger v. M'Chesney, 34 Va. (7 Leigh) 660 (1836).

Value of property question of fact. — In an action for illegal distress the price obtained at a forced sale is not the sole criterion as to the value of the goods levied on. The value of the property at the time of the levy is a question of fact to be determined by the court or the jury trying the issue. Gurfein v. Howell, 142 Va. 197, 128 S.E. 644 (1925).

What question for court and what for jury. — In an action under this section it was held that the question of exemplary damages should not have been submitted to the jury, since it was for the court to say whether the evidence tended to establish a proper case for their allowance, and for the jury to determine in such case whether they should be allowed. Evans v. Schuster, 178 Va. 61, 16 S.E.2d 301 (1941).

Judgment in another action not evidence. — Judgment for the tenant in an action of unlawful detainer brought by the landlord is not evidence in a proceeding under this section that no rent was due at the time the distress warrant was sued out. Fishburne v. Engledove, 91 Va. 548, 22 S.E. 354 (1895).

§ 8.01-42. Loss or injury to clothing in dyeing, dry cleaning, or laundering. — No person engaged in the business of dyeing, dry cleaning, or laundering wearing apparel, cloth or other articles, shall be liable, or in any action or suit against him be held liable, for the loss of, or injury to, any wearing apparel, cloth or other articles delivered to him to be dyed, dry cleaned, or laundered, in an amount greater than the purchase price minus depreciation of such wearing apparel, cloth or other articles, unless at the time of the delivery to him of any such wearing apparel, cloth or other articles, the value of the same, and when there is more than one piece or article the value of each piece or article, be agreed upon and evidenced by a writing stating such value, or separate values when there is more than one piece or article, signed by him; provided, however, that:

1. Nothing in this section contained shall be construed as requiring of any such person more than the exercise of such degree of care as is now imposed by existing law;

2. In no event shall any such person be held liable in any suit or action involving any such loss or injury for any sum greater than the damages suffered, and proved, by the plaintiff therein when such damages would not under the rules of law existing prior to June 18, 1920, exceed the purchase price minus depreciation of such wearing apparel, cloth, or other article;

3. Nothing in this section shall be construed as interfering with or inhibiting, or impairing the obligation of, any written contract between any hotel, railroad company, steamboat company or other patron and any person engaged in the business of dyeing, dry cleaning, or laundering of wearing apparel, cloth or other article, in relation to such work;

4. No liability shall rest upon or be borne by any hotel for any loss of or damage to wearing apparel, cloth or other article, the property of any guest of such hotel who shall have delivered, or caused the same to have been delivered, for dyeing, dry cleaning, or laundering to any person engaged in the business of dyeing, dry cleaning, or laundering.

5. [Repealed.] (Code 1950, § 8-654; 1977, cc. 192, 617.)

Editor's note. — Pursuant to § 9-77.11 and Acts 1977, c. 617, cl. 4, the Code Commission has incorporated in § 8.01-42 as set out above the changes made in former § 8-654, corresponding to this section, by amendment in Acts 1977, c. 192. The amendment made the section applicable to dry cleaning as well as dyeing and laundering, substituted "greater than the purchase price minus depreciation of" for "exceeding twenty times the charges made or to be made by him for the work done or contemplated to be done on any" near the middle of the introductory paragraph, substituted "the purchase price minus depreciation of such wearing apparel, cloth, or other article" for "twenty times the amount of such charges" at the end of subdivision 2, and deleted subdivision 5, which required the price to be charged, and a reference to the section, to be printed on laundry slips and similar slips used in the business.

§ 8.01-42.1. Civil action for racial, religious, or ethnic harassment, violence or vandalism.

— A. An action for injunctive relief or civil damages, or both, shall lie for any person who is subjected to acts of (i) intimidation or harassment or (ii) violence directed against his person; or (iii) vandalism directed against his real or personal property, where such acts are motivated by racial, religious, or ethnic animosity.

B. Any aggrieved party who initiates and prevails in an action authorized by this section shall be entitled to damages, including punitive damages, and in the discretion of the court to an award of the cost of the litigation and reasonable attorneys' fees in an amount to be fixed by the court.

C. The provisions of this section shall not apply to any actions between an employee and his employer, or between or among employees of the same employer, for damages arising out of incidents occurring in the workplace or arising out of the employee-employer relationship. (1988, c. 492.)

I. DECISIONS UNDER CURRENT LAW.

Evidence sufficient to support finding of violation of this section. — The jury's finding that plaintiff was racially intimidated or harassed in violation of this section was supported by sufficient evidence where the plaintiff was the only black person in an otherwise totally white skating rink, and without prior warning, within an hour of the rink's closing, the plaintiff was waved off the floor and was told "They want to see you in the back room." Johnson v. Hugo's Skateway, 949 F.2d 1338 (4th Cir. 1991), aff'd in part, rev'd in part, upon reh'g en banc, 974 F.2d 1408 (4th Cir. 1992).

Awards of attorneys' fees under this section are upheld on appeal unless under all the facts and circumstances the award is clearly wrong. Johnson v. Hugo's Skateway, 949 F.2d 1338 (4th Cir. 1991), aff'd in part, rev'd in part, upon reh'g en banc, 974 F.2d 1408 (4th Cir. 1992).

§ **8.01-42.2. Liability of guest for hotel damage.** — Any registered guest in a hotel, motel, inn or other place offering to the public transitory lodging or sleeping accommodations for compensation shall be civilly liable to the innkeeper for all property damage to such accommodation or its furnishings which occurs during the period of such person's occupancy when such damage results (i) from the negligence of the guest or of any person for whom he is legally responsible or (ii) from the failure of the guest to comply with reasonable rules and regulations of which he is given actual notice by the innkeeper. (1989, c. 426.)

§ **8.01-43. Action against parent for damage to public property by minor.** — The Commonwealth, acting through the officers having charge of the public property involved, or the governing body of a county, city, town, or other political subdivision, or a school board may institute an action and recover from the parents or either of them of any minor living with such parents or either of them for damages suffered by reason of the willful or malicious destruction of, or damage to, public property by such minor. No more than $2,500 may be recovered from such parents or either of them as a result of any incident or occurrence on which such action is based. (Code 1950, § 8-654.1; 1960, c. 132; 1972, c. 825; 1977, c. 617; 1983, c. 330; 1987, c. 193; 1994, cc. 508, 552; 1996, c. 698.)

§ **8.01-44. Action against parent for damage to private property by minor.** — The owner of any property may institute an action and recover from the parents, or either of them, of any minor living with such parents, or either of them, for damages suffered by reason of the willful or malicious destruction of, or damage to, such property by such minor. No more than $2,500 may be recovered from such parents, or either of them, as a result of any incident or occurrence on which such action is based. Any recovery from the parent or parents of such minor shall not preclude full recovery from such minor except to the amount of the recovery from such parent or parents. The provisions of this statute shall be in addition to, and not in lieu of, any other law imposing upon a parent liability for the acts of his minor child. (Code 1950, § 8-654.1:1; 1966, c. 532; 1972, c. 825; 1977, c. 617; 1984, c. 48; 1987, c. 193; 1994, cc. 508, 552; 1996, c. 698.)

I. DECISIONS UNDER CURRENT LAW.

This is a vicarious liability statute which imposes liability without a determination of the parents' independent negligence. The "additional" law mentioned in the last sentence refers to existing law based on vicarious liability, such as the liability of a parent based upon a principal-agent relationship. Bell v. Hudgins, 232 Va. 491, 352 S.E.2d 332 (1987).

In the absence of a principal-agent relationship, parents may not be liable for the malicious, intentional acts of their minor child based on the independent negligence of the parents in failing to control the child. Bell v. Hudgins, 232 Va. 491, 352 S.E.2d 332 (1987).

§ **8.01-44.1. Immunity from civil liability of members of certain committees, etc.** — Every member of any committee, board, group, commission, or other entity established pursuant to federal or state law or regulation which functions to authorize, review, evaluate, or make recommendations on the nature, conduct, activities, or procedures involved in or related to programs or research protocols conducted under the supervision of members of the faculty or staff of any hospital, college, or university, including but not limited to the design or conduct of experiments involving human subjects, shall be immune from civil liability for any act, decision, omission, or utterance done or made in performance of such duties as a member of such committee, board, group, commission, or other entity, unless such act, decision, omission, or utterance is done or made in bad faith or with malicious intent or unless the member, when acting to authorize the nature, conduct, activities, or procedures involved in or related to a program or research protocol, knows or reasonably should know that the program or research protocol is being or will be conducted in violation of Chapter 5.1 (§ 32.1-162.16 et seq.) of Title 32.1. However, the immunity created herein shall not apply to those persons engaged in the actual conduct of the programs or research protocols. (1980, c. 479; 1981, c. 40; 1992, c. 603.)

§ 8.01-44.2. Action against physician for vaccine-related injury or death.

— In any case where a person could file or could have filed a petition for compensation pursuant to Subtitle 2 of Title XXI of the Public Health Services Act of the United States (42 U.S.C. § 300aa-10 et seq.) for the vaccine-related injury or death associated with the administration of a vaccine in the Commonwealth by or under the supervision of a physician licensed to practice medicine in Virginia, no civil action shall lie against such physician, or any person administering such vaccine on behalf of such physician for injury or death resulting from an adverse reaction to such vaccine, except where such injury or death was caused by gross negligence of the physician, his agents or employees, in the administration of such vaccine. (1987, c. 664.)

Law Review. — For note, "A One Shot Deal: The National Childhood Vaccine Injury Act," see 41 Wm. & Mary L. Rev. 309 (1999).

§ 8.01-44.3. Divulgence of communications by qualified interpreters and communications assistants.

— If the content of any communication which is facilitated for compensation in the professional capacity of a qualified interpreter, as defined in § 63.1-85.4:1, or in the professional capacity of any communications assistant employed by the statewide dual party relay service established under Article 5 (§ 56-484.4 et seq.) of Chapter 15 of Title 56, is divulged by such interpreter or assistant, any such party to the communication aggrieved by such divulgence may recover from such interpreter or assistant the greater of (i) actual damages sustained, together with costs and reasonable attorneys' fees, or (ii) $100. No such recovery shall be permitted if the interpreter or assistant and the parties to the communication have agreed that the interpreter or assistant may divulge the content of the communication. (1992, c. 614.)

§ 8.01-44.4. Action for shoplifting and employee theft.

— A. A merchant may recover a civil judgment against any adult or emancipated minor who shoplifts from that merchant for two times the actual cost of the merchandise to the merchant, but in no event an amount less than fifty dollars. However, if the merchant recovers the merchandise in merchantable condition, he shall be entitled to liquidated damages of no more than $350.

B. A merchant may recover a civil judgment against any person who commits employee theft for two times the actual cost of the merchandise to the merchant, but in no event an amount less than fifty dollars. However, if the merchant recovers the merchandise in merchantable condition, he shall be entitled to liquidated damages of no more than $350.

C. The prevailing party in any action brought pursuant to this section shall be entitled to reasonable attorneys' fees and costs not to exceed $150.

D. A conviction of or a plea of guilty to a violation of any other statute is not a prerequisite to commencement of a civil action pursuant to this section or enforcement of a judgment. No action may be initiated under this section if any criminal action has been initiated against the perpetrator for the alleged offense under §§ 18.2-95, 18.2-96, 18.2-102.1, or § 18.2-103 or any other criminal offense defined under subsection F. However, nothing herein shall preclude a merchant from nonsuiting the civil action brought pursuant to this section and proceeding criminally under §§ 18.2-95, 18.2-96, 18.2-102.1 or § 18.2-103 or any other criminal offense defined under subsection F.

E. Prior to the commencement of any action under this section, a merchant may demand, in writing, that an individual who may be civilly liable under this section make appropriate payment to the merchant in consideration for the merchant's agreement not to commence any legal action under this section.

F. For purposes of this section:

"Employee theft" means the removal of any merchandise or cash from the premises of the merchant's establishment or the concealment of any merchandise or cash by a person employed by a merchant without the consent of the merchant and with the purpose or intent of appropriating the merchandise or cash to the employee's own use without full payment.

"Shoplift" means any one or more of the following acts committed by a person without the consent of the merchant and with the purpose or intent of appropriating merchandise to that person's own use without payment, obtaining merchandise at less than its stated sales price, or otherwise depriving a merchant of all or any part of the value or use of merchandise: (i) removing any merchandise from the premises of the merchant's establishment; (ii) concealing any merchandise; (iii) substituting, altering, removing, or disfiguring any label or price tag; (iv) transferring any merchandise from a container in which that merchandise is displayed or packaged to any other container; (v) disarming any alarm tag attached to any merchandise; or (vi) obtaining or attempting to obtain possession of any merchandise by charging that merchandise to another person without the authority of that person or by charging that merchandise to a fictitious person. (1992, c. 721.)

The number of this section was assigned by the Virginia Code Commission, the number in the 1992 act having been 8.01-44.3.

§ 8.01-44.5. Exemplary damages for persons injured by intoxicated drivers.

— In any action for personal injury or death arising from the operation of a motor vehicle, engine or train, the finder of fact may, in its discretion, award exemplary damages to the plaintiff if the evidence proves that the defendant acted with malice toward the plaintiff or the defendant's conduct was so willful or wanton as to show a conscious disregard for the rights of others.

A defendant's conduct shall be deemed sufficiently willful or wanton as to show a conscious disregard for the rights of others when the evidence proves that (i) when the incident causing the injury or death occurred, the defendant had a blood alcohol concentration of 0.15 percent or more by weight by volume or 0.15 grams or more per 210 liters of breath; (ii) at the time the defendant began, or during the time he was, drinking alcohol, he knew that he was going to operate a motor vehicle, engine or train; and (iii) the defendant's intoxication was a proximate cause of the injury to or death of the plaintiff.

However, when a defendant has unreasonably refused to submit to a test of his blood alcohol content as required by § 18.2-268.2, a defendant's conduct shall be deemed sufficiently willful or wanton as to show a conscious disregard for the rights of others when the evidence proves that (i) when the incident causing the injury or death occurred the defendant was intoxicated, which may be established by evidence concerning the conduct or condition of the defendant; (ii) at the time the defendant began, or during the time he was, drinking alcohol, he knew that he was going to operate a motor vehicle; and (iii) the defendant's intoxication was a proximate cause of the injury to the plaintiff or death of the plaintiff's decedent. A certified copy of a court's determination of unreasonable refusal pursuant to § 18.2-268.3 shall be prima facie evidence that the defendant unreasonably refused to submit to the test. (1994, c. 570; 1998, c. 722; 1999, c. 324.)

The 1999 amendment inserted "or 0.15 grams or more per 210 liters of breath" in clause (i) of the second paragraph.

I. DECISIONS UNDER CURRENT LAW.

Plaintiff must prove each of elements. — This statute requires that the plaintiff prove each of the statutory elements and, if the plaintiff fails to produce any evidence that at the time the defendant began drinking alcohol, or during the time he or she was drinking alcohol, the defendant knew he or she was going to operate a motor vehicle, a claim for statutory punitive damages may be correctly struck. Webb v. Rivers, 256 Va. 460, 507 S.E.2d 360 (1998).

ARTICLE 4.

Defamation.

§ 8.01-45. Action for insulting words. — All words shall be actionable which from their usual construction and common acceptance are construed as insults and tend to violence and breach of the peace. (Code 1950, § 8-630; 1977, c. 617.)

Cross references. — For criminal provision regarding abusive language, see § 18.2-416. For criminal provision as to slander and libel, see § 18.2-417. For rules of court governing actions in personam for money, see Rules 3:1 through 3:18.

Law Review. — For note, "Qualified Privilege as a Defense to Defamation," see 45 Va. L. Rev. 772 (1959). For note on the merger of libel and slander, see 47 Va. L. Rev. 1116 (1961). For survey of Virginia law on torts for the year 1973-1974, see 60 Va. L. Rev. 1615 (1974). For article on model abusive debt collection statute for Virginia, see 15 Wm. & Mary L. Rev. 567 (1974). For note on the corporate libel plaintiff, see 38 Wash. & Lee L. Rev. 716 (1981). For article on libel and slander in Virginia, see 17 U. Rich. L. Rev. 769 (1983). For article, "Reputation, Compensation, and Proof," see 25 Wm. & Mary L. Rev. 747 (1984). For article, "Defamation and the First Amendment: The End of the Affair," see 25 Wm. & Mary L. Rev. 779 (1984). For article, "First Amendment Limitations on Recovery From the Press — An Extended Comment on 'The Anderson Solution'," see 25 Wm. & Mary L. Rev. 793 (1984). For article, "The Plaintiff's Burden in Defamation: Awareness and Falsity," see 25 Wm. & Mary L. Rev. 825 (1984). For article, "Hard Defamation Cases," see 25 Wm. & Mary L. Rev. 891 (1984). For article on defamation of public figures, see 25 Wm. & Mary L. Rev. 905 (1984). For article, "Of Public Figures and Public Interest — The Libel Law Conundrum," see 25 Wm. & Mary L. Rev. 937 (1984). For article, "Public Figures Revisited," see 25 Wm. & Mary L. Rev. 957 (1984). For article on modern defamation law in Virginia, see 21 U. Rich. L. Rev. 3 (1986). For an article, "Civil Practice and Procedure," see 32 U. Rich. L. Rev. 1009 (1998).

I. Decisions Under Current Law.
   A. General Consideration.
   B. Damages.
   C. Illustrations of Actionable Words.
   D. Evidence.
   E. Pleading and Practice.
II. Decisions Under Prior Law.
   A. General Consideration.
   B. Words Actionable Under Statute.
      1. In General.
      2. Illustrations.
   C. Publication.
   D. Parties Liable.
   E. Malice.
   F. Privileged Communications.
   G. Justification.

H. Damages.
I. Evidence.
J. Pleading and Practice.
  1. In General.
  2. Motion.
  3. Pleas.
  4. Instructions.
  5. Province of Court and Jury.

I. DECISIONS UNDER CURRENT LAW.

A. General Consideration.

Constitutional limitations on "insulting words" claim. — Although application of this provision is no longer confined to its original purpose of preventing duels, it has been interpreted by Virginia courts to be virtually co-extensive with the common-law action for defamation. For this reason any constitutional limitations that apply to the plaintiffs' defamation action must necessarily apply to their "insulting words" claim as well. Potomac Valve & Fitting, Inc. v. Crawford Fitting Co., 829 F.2d 1280 (4th Cir. 1987).

Opinions protected by First Amendment. — Where the defendants' statement is capable of being proved or disproved, but when viewed in context it is clearly an opinion, it is therefore protected by the First Amendment. Potomac Valve & Fitting, Inc. v. Crawford Fitting Co., 829 F.2d 1280 (4th Cir. 1987).

Action for insulting words assimilated to common-law action for libel and slander. — Where the plaintiff's motion for judgment was unclear as to whether the proceeding was under this section or involved common-law libel, no distinction was required to be made, since the trial of an action for insulting words is completely assimilated to the common-law action for libel or slander, and from the standpoint of the law of this state is an action for libel or slander. Mills v. Kingsport Times-News, 475 F. Supp. 1005 (W.D. Va. 1979).

The trial of an action for insulting words is completely assimilated to the common-law action for libel and slander, and from the standpoint of the Virginia law it is an action for libel and slander. Welch v. Kennedy Piggly Wiggly Stores, Inc., 63 Bankr. 888 (W.D. Va. 1986).

In many cases defamation claims and claims brought under this section "must ineluctably 'rise or fall together.'" Dwyer v. Smith, 867 F.2d 184 (4th Cir. 1989).

This section plainly requires that the words used must not only be insults, but they must also "tend to violence and breach of the peace". Allen & Rocks, Inc. v. Dowell, 252 Va. 439, 477 S.E.2d 741 (1996).

In Virginia, a libel plaintiff must show that the alleged libel was published "of or concerning" him. He need not show that he was mentioned by name in the publication. Instead, the plaintiff satisfies the "of or concerning" test if he shows that the publication was intended to refer to him and would be so understood by persons reading it who knew him. In other words, the test is met if the plaintiff shows that the publication was "in its description or identification such as to lead those who knew or knew of the plaintiff to believe that the article was intended to refer to [him]." But if the publication on its face does not show that it applies to the plaintiff, the publication is not actionable, unless the allegations and supporting contemporaneous facts connect the libelous words to the plaintiff. If the rule were otherwise, any plaintiff could adopt and apply to himself any libelous matter and obtain a recovery. Gazette, Inc. v. Harris, 229 Va. 1, 325 S.E.2d 713, cert. denied sub nom., Fleming v. Moore, 472 U.S. 1032, 105 S. Ct. 3513, 87 L. Ed. 2d 643, cert. denied sub nom. Port Packet Corp. v. Lewis, 473 U.S. 905, 105 S. Ct. 3528, 87 L. Ed. 2d 653 (1985).

In order to establish prima facie evidence of publication, a plaintiff is not required to present testimony from a third party regarding what that person heard and understood, or to identify the person to whom the defamatory words were published. Instead, a plaintiff may prove publication of defamatory remarks by either direct or circumstantial evidence that the remarks were heard by a third party who understood these remarks as referring to the plaintiff in a defamatory sense. Food Lion, Inc. v. Melton, 250 Va. 144, 458 S.E.2d 580 (1995).

As a matter of state law the negligence standard should be applicable to media and nonmedia defendants alike. Gazette, Inc. v. Harris, 229 Va. 1, 325 S.E.2d 713, cert. denied sub nom., Fleming v. Moore, 472 U.S. 1032, 105 S. Ct. 3513, 87 L. Ed. 2d 643, cert. denied sub nom Port Packet Corp. v. Lewis, 473 U.S. 905, 105 S. Ct. 3528, 87 L. Ed. 2d 653 (1985).

The application of this negligence standard is expressly limited, however, to circumstances where the defamatory statement makes substantial danger to reputation apparent. The trial judge shall make such determination as a matter of law. If, on the other hand, no substantial danger to reputation is apparent from the statement in issue, New York Times malice must be established to recover compensatory damages. Gazette, Inc. v. Harris, 229 Va. 1, 325 S.E.2d 713, cert. denied sub nom., Fleming v. Moore, 472 U.S. 1032, 105 S. Ct. 3513, 87 L. Ed. 2d 643, cert. denied sub nom. Port Packet Corp. v. Lewis, 473 U.S. 905, 105 S. Ct. 3528, 87 L. Ed. 2d 653 (1985).

Plaintiff must prove falsity. — In an action brought by a private individual to recover actual, compensatory damages for a defamatory publication, the plaintiff may recover upon proof by a preponderance of the evidence that the publication was false, and that the defendant either knew it to be false, or believing it to be true, lacked reasonable grounds for such belief, or acted negligently in failing to ascertain the facts on which the publication was based. Under this standard, truth no longer is an affirmative defense to be established by the defendant. Instead, the plaintiff must prove falsity, because he is required to establish negligence with respect to such falsity. Such liability may be based upon negligence, whether or not the publication in question relates to a matter of public or general concern. Gazette, Inc. v. Harris, 229 Va. 1, 325 S.E.2d 713, cert. denied sub nom., Fleming v. Moore, 472 U.S. 1032, 105 S. Ct. 3513, 87 L. Ed. 2d 643, cert. denied sub nom. Port Packet Corp. v. Lewis, 473 U.S. 905, 105 S. Ct. 3528, 87 L. Ed. 2d 653 (1985).

The threshold determination to be made by trial judge on the question of whether there is substantial danger to reputation apparent from the content of a publication resembles the determination traditionally made by the court on the question whether a statement is libelous per se. A trial judge must decide, viewing the circumstances objectively, whether a reasonable and prudent editor should have anticipated that the words used contained an imputation necessarily harmful to reputation. The harmful potential of the words used here, i.e., that plaintiffs were accused of crimes, should have been apparent to the paper's editor, if he had exercised ordinary care. Gazette, Inc. v. Harris, 229 Va. 1, 325 S.E.2d 713, cert. denied sub nom., Fleming v. Moore, 472 U.S. 1032, 105 S. Ct. 3513, 87 L. Ed. 2d 643, cert. denied sub nom. Port Packet Corp. v. Lewis, 473 U.S. 905, 105 S. Ct. 3528, 87 L. Ed. 2d 653 (1985).

Defamatory words need not be sufficient within themselves to establish all the elements of the offense imputed. Such simplicity is not required. Schnupp v. Smith, 249 Va. 353, 457 S.E.2d 42 (1995).

In determining whether or not language does impute a criminal offense the words must be construed in the plain and popular sense in which the rest of the world would naturally understand them. It is not necessary that they should make the charge in express terms. It is sufficient if they consist of a statement of matters which would naturally and presumably be understood by those who heard them as charging a crime. Schnupp v. Smith, 249 Va. 353, 457 S.E.2d 42 (1995).

It is general rule that allegedly defamatory words are to be taken in their plain and natural meaning and to be understood by courts and juries as other people would understand them, and according to the sense in which they appear to have been used. In order to render words defamatory and actionable it is not necessary that the defamatory charge be in direct terms but it may be made indirectly, and it matters not how artful or disguised the modes in which the meaning is concealed if it is in fact defamatory. Accordingly, a defamatory charge may be made by inference, implication or insinuation. Gazette, Inc. v. Harris, 229 Va. 1, 325 S.E.2d 713, cert. denied sub nom., Fleming v. Moore, 472 U.S. 1032, 105 S. Ct. 3513, 87 L. Ed. 2d 643, cert. denied sub nom. Port Packet Corp. v. Lewis, 473 U.S. 905, 105 S. Ct. 3528, 87 L. Ed. 2d 653 (1985).

When a qualified privilege is established and not defeated by a plaintiff's evidence of common-law malice, the negligence standard is subsumed in the higher standard and it is of no consequence that the plaintiff might have met the lower standard of negligence. Gazette, Inc. v. Harris, 229 Va. 1, 325 S.E.2d 713, cert. denied sub nom., Fleming v. Moore, 472 U.S. 1032, 105 S. Ct. 3513, 87 L. Ed. 2d 643, cert. denied sub nom. Port Packet Corp. v. Lewis, 473 U.S. 905, 105 S. Ct. 3528, 87 L. Ed. 2d 653 (1985).

Failure of newspaper reporter to verify accusations made against plaintiff. — In a defamation action brought by a school teacher against newspaper reporter and his employer, where a number of supervisors, a fellow teacher, and students, including some classmates of the complaining students, testified as to plaintiff's good qualities as a teacher and contradicted virtually all the negative statements made by the persons the reporter interviewed, the students who contradicted the negative testimony were all shown to have been readily available for interview in the Richmond area, while the school authorities would not furnish the reporter with the names or addresses of other students in plaintiff's classes, the jury could have inferred from the evidence that the reporter could have obtained this information from the students he interviewed but negligently failed to do so, and, in fact, one student gave the reporter the names of some of the other students, but the reporter apparently did nothing with the information, the jury had ample evidence from which to conclude that a reasonably prudent news reporter writing the article could readily have contacted a number of other students to verify (or contradict) these accusations and should have done so. Richmond Newspapers, Inc. v. Lipscomb, 234 Va. 277, 362 S.E.2d 32 (1987), cert. denied, 486 U.S. 1023, 108 S. Ct. 1997, 100 L. Ed. 2d 228 (1988).

Private plaintiff's burden of proof in libel action against nonmedia defendant. — In a case involving a private plaintiff in a libel action against a nonmedia defendant, it is not necessary to show actual out-of-pocket damage in a nonlibel per se action and a showing of loss of reputation and standing in the community, embarrassment, humiliation, and mental suffering will be sufficient for the award of damages. Sateren v. Montgomery Ward & Co., 234 Va. 303, 362 S.E.2d 324 (1987).

Adoption of a "journalistic malpractice test" would be inappropriate for a number of reasons: (a) While responsible newspapers serve many worthwhile objectives, profit is an important consideration. Startling, sensational stories tend to sell more newspapers than dull, factual stories. Thus, there is an inherent conflict of interest when a journalist is required to draw inferences from news items. It seems imprudent to permit media experts to set a standard under these circumstances. (b) The evidence does not establish that journalists are required to have special education for their profession, as engineers, doctors, lawyers, or certified public accountants must, nor have they acquired knowledge, training, and experience unique to certain trades focusing upon scientific matters, such as electricity, blasting and the like, which a jury could not understand without expert assistance. (c) The adoption of such a standard might mean that there could be no recovery unless a media expert testified that the conduct did not meet the standard of care in the journalistic community. Richmond Newspapers, Inc. v. Lipscomb, 234 Va. 277, 362 S.E.2d 32 (1987), cert. denied, 486 U.S. 1023, 108 S. Ct. 1997, 100 L. Ed. 2d 228 (1988).

Profane language used during labor dispute held not to support liability under this section. See Crawford v. United Steel Workers, 230 Va. 217, 335 S.E.2d 828 (1985), cert. denied, 475 U.S. 1095, 106 S. Ct. 1490, 89 L. Ed. 2d 892 (1986).

Erroneous report of commitment for psychiatric evaluation. — An erroneous newspaper report that the plaintiff had been committed to a state hospital for psychiatric evaluation as the result of a preliminary hearing on a homicide charge was not libelous per se; however, a libel per quod action did lie in that the plaintiff's allegations of humiliation, embarrassment, and permanent stigma, occasioned by inquiries about her commitment, would give rise to special damages if proven. Mills v. Kingsport Times-News, 475 F. Supp. 1005 (W.D. Va. 1979).

B. Damages.

Precision hard to obtain in damages calculation. — It is difficult, if not impossible, to prove with mathematical precision the quantum of damages for injury to reputation, humiliation, and embarrassment which may flow from a defamation. Schnupp v. Smith, 249 Va. 353, 457 S.E.2d 42 (1995).

On the issue of compensatory damages in libel cases when New York Times malice need not be proven, Virginia will continue to follow the established standard of review mandated by § 8.01-680, that is, "the judgment of the trial court shall not be set aside unless it appears from the evidence that such judgment is plainly wrong or without evidence to support it." Gazette, Inc. v. Harris, 229 Va. 1, 325 S.E.2d 713, cert. denied sub nom., Fleming v. Moore, 472 U.S. 1032, 105 S. Ct. 3513, 87 L. Ed. 2d 643, cert. denied sub nom. Port Packet Corp. v. Lewis, 473 U.S. 905, 105 S. Ct. 3528, 87 L. Ed. 2d 653 (1985).

Punitive damages. — An appellate court in Virginia, on the issue of punitive damages or where "New York Times malice" must be proven, must independently decide whether the evidence in the record on appeal is sufficient to support a finding of New York Times "actual malice" by clear and convincing proof. This does not mean that the reviewing court may disregard the determinations made on credibility of witnesses by the trier of fact or that the presumption of correctness that attaches to factual findings is to be discounted. The rule simply means that appellate judges in such a case must examine the facts pertinent to the punitive damage award and exercise independent judgment to "determine whether the record establishes actual malice with convincing clarity." Gazette, Inc. v. Harris, 229 Va. 1, 325 S.E.2d 713, cert. denied sub nom., Fleming v. Moore, 472 U.S. 1032, 105 S. Ct. 3513, 87 L. Ed. 2d 643, cert. denied sub nom. Port Packet Corp. v. Lewis, 473 U.S. 905, 105 S. Ct. 3528, 87 L. Ed. 2d 653 (1985).

Public school teacher not a public official. — Public school teacher was not in that class of public officials which can only recover compensatory damages for defamation by establishing the constitutional malice described in New York Times Co. v. Sullivan, 376 U.S. 254, 84 S. Ct. 710, 11 L. Ed. 2d 686 (1964); Richmond Newspapers, Inc. v. Lipscomb, 234 Va. 277, 362 S.E.2d 32 (1987), cert. denied, 486 U.S. 1023, 108 S. Ct. 1997, 100 L. Ed. 2d 228 (1988).

Appellate review of proof of malice. — To sustain an award of punitive damages, plaintiff, as a private person, is required to establish New York Times malice by clear and convincing proof. To decide if that requirement has been met, the Supreme Court conducts an "independent examination of the whole record," resolving disputed factual issues and inferences favorably to the plaintiff. Richmond Newspapers, Inc. v. Lipscomb, 234 Va. 277, 362 S.E.2d 32 (1987), cert. denied, 486 U.S. 1023, 108 S. Ct. 1997, 100 L. Ed. 2d 228 (1988).

C. Illustrations of Actionable Words.

Words that impute the commission of a crime which is punishable by imprisonment in a state or federal institution are actionable per se. Schnupp v. Smith, 249 Va. 353, 457 S.E.2d 42 (1995).

Content of a news item which states that an unmarried woman is pregnant creates a substantial danger to reputation and should warn a reasonably prudent editor of the item's defamatory potential. Gazette, Inc. v. Harris, 229 Va. 1, 325 S.E.2d 713, cert. denied sub nom., Fleming v. Moore, 472 U.S. 1032, 105 S. Ct. 3513, 87 L. Ed. 2d 643, cert. denied sub nom. Port Packet Corp. v. Lewis, 473 U.S. 905, 105 S. Ct. 3528, 87 L. Ed. 2d 653 (1985).

Comments on work performance. — The defendants correctly contended that the language used by board chairman explaining former employee's work performance was not such as to provoke violence or breach of the peace, as required by this section, and accordingly, that the trial court should not have submitted the insulting words issue to the jury. Allen & Rocks, Inc. v. Dowell, 252 Va. 439, 477 S.E.2d 741 (1996).

D. Evidence.

Expert testimony as to standards for investigative reporting properly excluded. — The trial court did not err in excluding evidence from an expert witness, a nationally known journalist, proffered on the standards for investigative reporting. A jury in this state is as competent as any expert to form an intelligent and accurate opinion as to whether a reporter should have conducted additional investigations. Richmond Newspapers, Inc. v. Lipscomb, 234 Va. 277, 362 S.E.2d 32 (1987), cert. denied, 486 U.S. 1023, 108 S. Ct. 1997, 100 L. Ed. 2d 228 (1988).

E. Pleading and Practice.

No duty to segregate defamatory and non-defamatory material in jury instructions. — There is no duty upon a trial court to segregate potentially defamatory from non-defamatory material in granting instructions to the jury. Richmond Newspapers, Inc. v. Lipscomb, 234 Va. 277, 362 S.E.2d 32 (1987), cert. denied, 486 U.S. 1023, 108 S. Ct. 1997, 100 L. Ed. 2d 228 (1988).

It was jury's function to determine which statements in newspaper article were defamatory statements of fact about the plaintiff, taking into consideration the entire background of the case and the context in which those statements were made. Richmond Newspapers, Inc. v. Lipscomb, 234 Va. 277, 362 S.E.2d 32 (1987), cert. denied, 486 U.S. 1023, 108 S. Ct. 1997, 100 L. Ed. 2d 228 (1988).

II. DECISIONS UNDER PRIOR LAW.

A. General Consideration.

Editor's note. — The cases cited below were decided under corresponding provisions of former law. The term "this section," as used below, refers to former provisions.

Original purpose now of no importance. — Since the amendment of the original statute in 1849, in dealing with the statute against insulting words, no weight or importance has been attached to the purpose for which it was originally enacted. The original object of the statute, in the matter of preventing dueling, is no longer entitled to consideration in considering the statute. W.T. Grant Co. v. Owens, 149 Va. 906, 141 S.E. 860 (1928).

The purpose now is to prevent breaches of peace. — The purpose of this section was to extend the common law so as to give a right of action for insulting words, even though containing no imputation which was actionable at common law. The design of the statute is to prevent breaches of the peace, to discourage offensive and excessive freedom in the use of that unruly member, the tongue, to inflict punishment therefor, and by subjecting those who are so hasty of temper and inconsiderate of the feelings of others as to insult them to such actual and punitive damages as may be awarded by a jury. Hines v. Gravins, 136 Va. 313, 112 S.E. 869 (1922), cert. denied, 265 U.S. 583, 44 S. Ct. 458, 68 L. Ed. 1191 (1924). See also, Weatherford v. Birchett, 158 Va. 741, 164 S.E. 535 (1932).

The gravamen of an action under this section is the insult to the feelings of the offended party, not the intention of the party using the words. Cook v. Patterson Drug Co., 185 Va. 516, 39 S.E.2d 304 (1946).

In an action for insulting words the insult is the basis of the action and where such insults are given, the jury are to pass upon them regardless of whether the words spoken are true or false. Brooks v. Calloway, 39 Va. (12 Leigh) 466 (1841).

Action for libel and slander. — An action for insulting words under this section has been treated since the amendment of the original statute in 1849 entirely as an action for libel or slander, for words actionable per se, with two exceptions: "No demurrer shall preclude a jury from passing thereon," (eliminated by 1940 amendment) and no publication of the words is necessary. In all other respects an action under the statute is placed on all fours with an action for defamation at common law. In fact, from the standpoint of the Virginia law, the action for insulting words is an action for libel or slander. W.T. Grant Co. v. Owens, 149 Va. 906, 141 S.E. 860 (1928).

All actions for libel and insulting words under this section are to be treated as slander, even though the language used is defamatory on its face, and the common-law rules of slander are to be applied. Shupe v. Rose's Stores, Inc., 213 Va. 374, 192 S.E.2d 766 (1972), cert. denied, Port Packet Corp. v. Lewis, 473 U.S. 905, 105 S. Ct. 3528, 87 L. Ed. 2d 653 (1985).

An action under the insulting words statute is either an action for libel or slander and in an action for libel or slander the common-law rules of slander are to be applied. Shupe v. Rose's Stores, Inc., 213 Va. 374, 192 S.E.2d 766 (1972), cert. denied, Port Packet Corp. v. Lewis, 473 U.S. 905, 105 S. Ct. 3528, 87 L. Ed. 2d 653 (1985).

As at common law. — The 1940 amendment to this section, eliminating the words "and no demurrer shall preclude a jury from passing thereon," gave the court the same power and control over actions brought under this section that it exercised over common-law actions for libel and slander. Darnell v. Davis, 190 Va. 701, 58 S.E.2d 68 (1950).

Statute does not affect common-law remedy. — The legislature did not intend by passing the statute of insulting words to interfere with the common-law action for defamation and a party aggrieved may still proceed at common law as if the statute had never been passed. Brooks v. Calloway, 39 Va. (12 Leigh) 466 (1841); Moseley v. Moss, 47 Va. (6 Gratt.) 534 (1850); Hogan v. Wilmoth, 57 Va. (16 Gratt.) 80 (1860).

Publication is difference. — An action for insulting words under this section is treated precisely as an action for slander or libel, for words actionable per se, with one exception, namely, no publication is necessary. The trial of an action for insulting words is completely assimilated to the common-law action for libel or slander, and from the standpoint of the Virginia law it is an action for libel or slander. Carwile v. Richmond Newspapers, Inc., 196 Va. 1, 82 S.E.2d 588 (1954); O'Neil v. Edmonds, 157 F. Supp. 649 (E.D. Va. 1958); Marsh v. Commercial & Sav. Bank, 265 F. Supp. 614 (W.D. Va. 1967).

B. Words Actionable Under Statute.

1. In General.

Words actionable at common law may be actionable under statute. — All common-law defamations are insults, and many of them something more. Actions for insulting words, spoken or written, may be brought under this section, though the words are actionable at common law. Payne v. Tancil, 98 Va. 262, 35 S.E. 725 (1900).

This statute applies to words written as well as to words spoken. Chaffin v. Lynch, 83 Va. 106, 1 S.E. 803 (1887).

At common law defamatory words which are actionable per se are: (1) Those which impute to a person the commission of some criminal offense involving moral turpitude, for which the party, if the charge is true, may be indicted and punished; (2) those which impute that a person is infected with some contagious disease, where if the charge is true, it would exclude the party from society; (3) those which impute to a person unfitness to perform the duties of an office or employment of profit, or want of integrity in the discharge of the duties of such an office or employment; (4) those which prejudice such person in his or her profession or trade. All other defamatory words which, though not in themselves actionable, occasion a person special damages are actionable. Shupe v. Rose's Stores, Inc., 213 Va. 374, 192 S.E.2d 766 (1972), cert. denied, Port Packet Corp. v. Lewis, 473 U.S. 905, 105 S. Ct. 3528, 87 L. Ed. 2d 653 (1985).

Meaning of language cannot be extended beyond its ordinary and common acceptation. — While ordinarily the gravamen of the action is the insult to the feelings of the offended party, and not the intention of the party using the words, the nature of the words used must from their usual construction and common acceptation be construed as insults and tend to violence and breach of the peace. The meaning of the alleged defamatory language cannot, by innuendo, be extended beyond its ordinary and common acceptation. O'Neil v. Edmonds, 157 F. Supp. 649 (E.D. Va. 1958).

In determining whether or not the language imputes a criminal offense, the words must be construed in the plain and popular sense in which the rest of the world would naturally understand them. It is not necessary that they should make the charge in express terms. It is sufficient if they consist of a statement of matters which would naturally and presumably be understood by those who heard them as charging a crime. Zayre of Va., Inc. v. Gowdy, 207 Va. 47, 147 S.E.2d 710 (1966).

Manner and occasion of speaking or writing words. — Insults by words spoken to or concerning another, depend so much upon the manner, the occasion, the allusions, and peculiar circumstances, as to defy all rules of technical precision and import, and must of necessity be regarded as questions of fact, to be submitted to the experience, observation and the common sense of a jury. Moseley v. Moss, 47 Va. (6 Gratt.) 534 (1850); Corr v. Lewis, 94 Va. 24, 26 S.E. 385 (1896).

Whether the words are or are not insulting

depends on the place, the manner and circumstances in which they are uttered. The literal meaning of the words may import praise; but, if spoken ironically and with intent to wound, they may amount to the keenest insult. It is equally true that the literal meaning of words may import insult, and yet the manner of their utterance, and the circumstances under which they are said, would satisfy anyone that no insult was intended. Brooks v. Calloway, 39 Va. (12 Leigh) 466 (1841); Corr v. Lewis, 94 Va. 24, 26 S.E. 385 (1896).

In order to determine whether words are insulting, all the surrounding facts and circumstances must be taken into consideration, and the whole case must be looked at in the light of its own particular facts. Zayre of Va., Inc. v. Gowdy, 207 Va. 47, 147 S.E.2d 710 (1966).

2. Illustrations.

Improper letter to married woman. — A letter written by a man to a married woman falsely asserting that the writer has received a letter from her and that he will meet her at the designated place is within the statute. Rolland v. Batchelder, 84 Va. 664, 5 S.E. 695 (1888).

An accusation of robbery is actionable under the statute. Lightner v. Osborn, 142 Va. 19, 127 S.E. 314 (1925).

The publication of the false report of a person's death is not actionable when unaccompanied by special circumstances. O'Neil v. Edmonds, 157 F. Supp. 649 (E.D. Va. 1958).

A letter to plaintiff's employer, stating that plaintiff was in default in repayment of a loan and refused to answer correspondence or respond to personal calls, was not libelous per se, where the letter did not suggest dishonesty, insolvency or bankruptcy, and plaintiff was not a merchant or trader or engaged in a vocation where credit was necessary, and since no special damages were alleged or proved, the letter was not actionable. Weaver v. Beneficial Fin. Co., 200 Va. 572, 106 S.E.2d 620 (1959).

Statement that police chief failed to account for fines not actionable. — To publish of the chief of police, who is chargeable with the collection from his subordinates of fines imposed by the police justice, that he has within the past twelve months collected certain fines of a certain officer, which fines do not appear by the records of the police court to have been reported, is not actionable under this section in the absence of an averment in the declaration that the words used from their usual construction and common acceptance are construed as insults and tend to violence and breach of the peace. Moss v. Harwood, 102 Va. 386, 46 S.E. 385 (1904).

C. Publication.

Publication is not necessary. — Under this section against insulting words, publication is not necessary in order to entitle a plaintiff to recover for insulting words. Davis v. Heflin, 130 Va. 169, 107 S.E. 673 (1921); Hines v. Gravins, 136 Va. 313, 112 S.E. 869 (1922), cert. denied, 265 U.S. 583, 44 S. Ct. 458, 68 L. Ed. 1191 (1924).

Words only have to be conveyed to person libelled. — It is a sufficient publication under this section to send a writing containing the insulting words to the person libelled. Rolland v. Batchelder, 84 Va. 664, 5 S.E. 695 (1888).

The mailing of a slanderous letter to a third party amounts to a publication, provided the letter reaches its destination and is read by the addressee, or any third party. Davis v. Heflin, 130 Va. 169, 107 S.E. 673 (1921).

Place of publication and circulation is where cause of action arises. — It is not the place where the libelous article is printed, but the place where it is published and circulated, that makes the words actionable under this section. Haskell v. Bailey, 63 F. 873 (4th Cir. 1894).

Defendant, in Virginia, wrote a letter to a third party in Washington, D. C., containing defamatory statements about the plaintiff. Plaintiff questioned defendant in Virginia in regard to the letter and defendant substantially repeated and assumed responsibility for the contents of the letter when he admitted its authorship and said to defendant that the letter spoke for itself. The defendant was liable in Virginia under this statute as he reiterated the insulting words to plaintiff in Virginia. Davis v. Heflin, 130 Va. 169, 107 S.E. 673 (1921).

D. Parties Liable.

A corporation, as any other master, is liable in damages under this section for insulting words uttered by its agent while engaged in the ordinary course of his employment, and in connection therewith. W.T. Grant Co. v. Owens, 149 Va. 906, 141 S.E. 860 (1928); Jordan v. Melville Shoe Corp., 150 Va. 101, 142 S.E. 387 (1928).

Director General of Railroads not liable. — Assuming, for the purposes of this case, that a principal is liable for compensatory damages under this section for insulting words uttered by his agent in the course of his employment, when such words are neither authorized nor ratified by the principal, there is a difference in this respect between the Director General of Railroads and other employers, and an action for compensatory damages in such case cannot be maintained against the Director General. Hines v. Gravins, 136 Va. 313, 112 S.E. 869 (1922), cert. denied, 265 U.S. 583, 44 S. Ct. 458, 68 L. Ed. 1191 (1924).

Judges are not liable to civil action for their judicial acts, even when such acts are in

§ 8.01-45   CODE OF VIRGINIA   § 8.01-45

excess of their jurisdiction, and are alleged to have been done maliciously or corruptly. Fletcher v. Bryan, 175 F.2d 716 (4th Cir. 1949).

E. Malice.

Constitutional malice standard required. — The trial court committed reversible error when in a punitive damage instruction to the jury it incorporated the common-law definition of malice rather than the constitutional malice standard. Newspaper Publishing Corp. v. Burke, 216 Va. 800, 224 S.E.2d 132 (1976).

Malicious libel enjoys no constitutional protection in any context. Old Dominion Branch 496 v. Austin, 213 Va. 377, 192 S.E.2d 737 (1972), rev'd on other grounds, 418 U.S. 264, 94 S. Ct. 2770, 41 L. Ed. 2d 745 (1974).

Legal malice is presumed from the utterance of insulting words. It may be found in the negligence or recklessness of the defamer's acts. An injury to a defamed person may be as grievous whether or not his defamer had an honest belief in the truth of his words. Cook v. Patterson Drug Co., 185 Va. 516, 39 S.E.2d 304 (1946).

In an action under the statute the law infers malice from the publication of matter which is insulting or defamatory. Chaffin v. Lynch, 83 Va. 106, 1 S.E. 803 (1887).

The motive which actuated the person using the words is not material, except upon the questions of malice and the measure of damages. Cook v. Patterson Drug Co., 185 Va. 516, 39 S.E.2d 304 (1946).

Actual malice is necessary in order to abuse a qualified privilege. Marsh v. Commercial & Sav. Bank, 265 F. Supp. 614 (W.D. Va. 1967).

Actual malice is indispensable for punitive damages. — Under this section, malice, either express or implied, is essential to a recovery for slander or for insulting words, but actual or express malice need not be proved except as a basis for punitive damages. For the latter purpose it is indispensable. Windsor v. Carlton, 136 Va. 652, 118 S.E. 222 (1923).

Statements and conduct of a defendant after the utterance of a slander are admissible to show malice. Kroger Grocery & Baking Co. v. Rosenbaum, 171 Va. 158, 198 S.E. 461 (1938).

Burden of proof. — Ordinarily, the law implies malice from the use of words defamatory or insulting. But the presumption is the other way where the occasion of the publication is privileged, and the onus is then upon the plaintiff to prove malice in fact. Marsh v. Commercial & Sav. Bank, 265 F. Supp. 614 (W.D. Va. 1967).

F. Privileged Communications.

Privileged communication defined. — A privileged communication is one made in good faith upon any subject matter in which the party communicating has an interest or in reference to which he has, or honestly believes he has, a duty, to a person having a corresponding interest or duty, and which contains matter which, without the occasion upon which it is made, would be defamatory and actionable. Marsh v. Commercial & Sav. Bank, 265 F. Supp. 614 (W.D. Va. 1967).

Where the defendant acts in performance of a duty, legal or social, or in defense of his own interest, the occasion is privileged. Marsh v. Commercial & Sav. Bank, 265 F. Supp. 614 (W.D. Va. 1967).

Privilege is a bar to the action unless the plaintiff proves by a preponderance of the evidence an abuse of the privilege. Guide Publishing Co. v. Futrell, 175 Va. 77, 7 S.E.2d 133 (1940); Massey v. Jones, 182 Va. 200, 28 S.E.2d 623 (1944).

Where public interest in free expression and communication of ideas is sufficient to outweigh the interest of the State in protecting the individual plaintiff from damage to his reputation and social relationships, the law does not allow recovery of damages, compensatory or punitive, occasioned by defamatory speech or publication, unless there has been an abuse of the privilege by showing that the defamatory language, either written or spoken, was made with actual malice. Old Dominion Branch 496 v. Austin, 213 Va. 377, 192 S.E.2d 737 (1972), rev'd on other grounds, 418 U.S. 264, 94 S. Ct. 2770, 41 L. Ed. 2d 745 (1974).

Must be made in good faith to be privileged. — Where the occasion of the publication declared on was privileged, the jury should have been instructed to find whether it was used in good faith by the defendant. Chaffin v. Lynch, 83 Va. 106, 1 S.E. 803 (1887).

Circumstances of publication may confer privilege. — A libelous statement, otherwise actionable, may not be so for the reason that the circumstances under which it was published confer upon the publisher a privilege to publish it. Old Dominion Branch 496 v. Austin, 213 Va. 377, 192 S.E.2d 737 (1972), rev'd on other grounds, 418 U.S. 264, 94 S. Ct. 2770, 41 L. Ed. 2d 745 (1974).

Privileged when communication to person having a corresponding interest or duty. — A communication, made in good faith on a subject matter in which the person communicating has an interest, or owes a duty, legal, moral or social, is qualifiedly privileged if made to a person having a corresponding interest or duty. Taylor v. Grace, 166 Va. 138, 184 S.E. 211 (1936).

Qualified privilege. — The rule is well settled that when the communication upon which the action is based is one of qualified privilege, the question is not whether the charge was true or false, but only whether the privilege was abused or the language employed was uttered or published with malice, and unless there is evidence from which a jury may fairly conclude there was malice, there can be no recovery. Marsh v. Commercial & Sav. Bank, 265 F. Supp. 614 (W.D. Va. 1967).

When the words complained of are uttered upon an occasion of qualified privilege, then in order to recover, it must appear from the evidence that the language used was disproportioned in strength and violence to the occasion, or went beyond the exigency of the occasion, or that the occasion was abused to gratify the ill will of the defendant; in other words, that the defendant was acting from actual malice. Marsh v. Commercial & Sav. Bank, 265 F. Supp. 614 (W.D. Va. 1967).

One insult cannot be set off against another. Yet if a man is attacked by another in a newspaper, he may reply. If his reply is not unnecessarily defamatory of his assailant, and is honestly made in self-defense, it will be privileged. Chaffin v. Lynch, 83 Va. 106, 1 S.E. 803 (1887); Haycox v. Dunn, 200 Va. 212, 104 S.E.2d 800 (1958).

Criticism of public official. — When a person is in a public capacity he may be criticized by the newspapers in the public interest; and that rebuts the presumption of malice in law which the court might otherwise make, and leaves malice in fact to be proved, and malice in fact to be found, either in the special language of the article or in circumstances proved which point to some motive of enmity to the particular individual. Story v. Norfolk-Portsmouth Newspapers, Inc., 202 Va. 588, 118 S.E.2d 668 (1961).

Language uttered in judicial proceeding is privileged. — See Massey v. Jones, 182 Va. 200, 28 S.E.2d 623 (1944).

But the privilege of a party or counsel in judicial proceedings is limited. — A party or counsel shall not avail himself of his situation to gratify private malice by uttering slanderous expressions, either against a party, witness or third person, which have no relation to the cause or subject matter of the inquiry. Lightner v. Osborn, 142 Va. 19, 127 S.E. 314 (1925).

When order dismissing employee is privileged. — A statement by a corporation in an order dismissing an employee that he was dismissed because of untrue statement made by him concerning reflection cast by one officer of the company, where there was no evidence of malice on the part of the company or its agents, was held to be a privileged communication and was not actionable. Brown v. Norfolk & W. Ry., 100 Va. 619, 42 S.E. 664 (1902).

A State Police officer is not afforded an absolute privilege for words spoken in a departmental hearing before the superintendent of State Police. Elder v. Holland, 208 Va. 15, 155 S.E.2d 369 (1967) commented on in 3 U. Rich. L. Rev. 202 (1968).

A State Police officer is not immune from liability for defamatory words spoken while performing his duties. Elder v. Holland, 208 Va. 15, 155 S.E.2d 369 (1967) commented on in 3 U. Rich. L. Rev. 202 (1968).

Illustration of conditional privilege. — For illustration of occasion held to be one of conditional privilege, see Luhring v. Carter, 193 Va. 529, 69 S.E.2d 416 (1952).

G. Justification.

In Virginia both the truth and privilege are complete defenses in bar of any action for defamation, whether it be for common-law slander or libel, or for insulting words. The same rules of law with reference to the pleading and proof of these defenses apply in an action under this section as in an action for common-law slander or libel since the enactment of § 8.01-46. Rosenberg v. Mason, 157 Va. 215, 160 S.E. 190 (1931). See Guide Publishing Co. v. Futrell, 175 Va. 77, 7 S.E.2d 133 (1940); Massey v. Jones, 182 Va. 200, 28 S.E.2d 623 (1944).

H. Damages.

Punitive damages may be awarded without actual or compensatory damages if a plaintiff shows per se defamation by the media and meets by clear and convincing evidence the standard of actual malice. Newspaper Publishing Corp. v. Burke, 216 Va. 800, 224 S.E.2d 132 (1976).

In actions under this section, damages are presumed from proof of the utterance of insulting words made actionable by the statute, and in order to recover it is not necessary to prove actual or pecuniary loss. Weatherford v. Birchett, 158 Va. 741, 164 S.E. 535 (1932).

The law presumes that damages result from the utterance of insulting words, made actionable by the statute, just as it does where the words uttered are actionable per se. It is not necessary in either case in order to recover, to prove actual or pecuniary loss. Boyd v. Boyd, 116 Va. 326, 82 S.E. 110 (1914); W.T. Grant Co. v. Owens, 149 Va. 906, 141 S.E. 860 (1928). See also, Jordan v. Melville Shoe Corp., 150 Va. 101, 142 S.E. 387 (1928).

No rule for measure of damages. — In an action, under this section, there is no rule of law fixing the measure of damages, nor can it be reached by any process of computation. Boyd v. Boyd, 116 Va. 326, 82 S.E. 110 (1914).

The amount of the damages is to be measured by the prejudice sustained by the plaintiff. Moseley v. Moss, 47 Va. (6 Gratt.) 534 (1850).

There is no fixed standard for measuring exemplary or punitive damages, and the amount of the award is largely a matter of discretion with the jury. Old Dominion Branch 496 v. Austin, 213 Va. 377, 192 S.E.2d 737 (1972), rev'd on other grounds, 418 U.S. 264, 94 S. Ct. 2770, 41 L. Ed. 2d 745 (1974).

Written communication to justice of peace under former § 19.1-18. — Where a person is charged with criminal trespass, arrested, and let to bail, and the injured private individual causing the arrest asserts in a written communication to a justice of the peace under former § 19.1-18 that he has received satisfaction for the injury, such written communication is one made in a judicial proceeding and is relevant to the matter under inquiry, and no recovery upon such writing can be had under this section. Darnell v. Davis, 190 Va. 701, 58 S.E.2d 68 (1950).

If express malice on the part of the defendant is shown, exemplary damages are presumed and need not be proved. It is not improper to instruct the jury that if from the evidence they believe defendant uttered the slander from malice, they may find exemplary damages. Lightner v. Osborn, 142 Va. 19, 127 S.E. 314 (1925).

When corporation liable for punitive damages. — In such case the person who has suffered injury may recover compensatory damages from the corporation as principal, and may recover punitive damages if the principal has authorized the act or has subsequently ratified it. Jordan v. Melville Shoe Corp., 150 Va. 101, 142 S.E. 387 (1928).

Actual damages must be proved for judgment against principal on unauthorized insult of agent. — In an action for insulting words against the Director General of Railroads, no actual damages were proved, and the only damages which could be recovered were punitive damages, and this only because of this section. It was held that plaintiff had failed in his proof to show that he was entitled to any damages, as punitive damages could not be recovered against the Director General. Hines v. Gravins, 136 Va. 313, 112 S.E. 869 (1922), cert. denied, 265 U.S. 583, 44 S. Ct. 458, 68 L. Ed. 2d 1191 (1924).

Authorization or ratification by principal necessary to sustain punitive damages against him. — In an action for damages for insulting words under this section against the Director General of Railroads, there being no evidence that the federal agent or the Director General ever at any time authorized, ratified, or approved the offensive charge made by a carrier's agent, instructions authorizing the recovery of punitive damages were erroneous. Hines v. Gravins, 136 Va. 313, 112 S.E. 869 (1922), cert. denied, 265 U.S. 583, 44 S. Ct. 458, 68 L. Ed. 2d 1191 (1924).

In an action for insulting words, defendant corporation was liable for compensatory damages for the utterance of insulting words by its agent, in the course of his employment in the business of the corporation, but not for punitive damages, because the corporation neither authorized the use of such words nor had it since ratified their use. The trial court, therefore, was right in setting aside the verdict as the damages awarded, or part thereof, were clearly punitive, but it erred in entering judgment for the defendant corporation. It should have awarded a new trial on the question of the amount of compensatory damages. Jordan v. Melville Shoe Corp., 150 Va. 101, 142 S.E. 387 (1928).

Effect of bad reputation of plaintiff. — While there is no rule fixing the quantum of compensation for insult, mental suffering, and injury to the reputation of the plaintiff or for punishment of the offender, one of unblemished reputation is entitled to greater damages than one whose reputation is such that he is little hurt from the action of which complaint is made. The effect of bad reputation is to reduce the damage inflicted. Stubbs v. Cowden, 179 Va. 190, 18 S.E.2d 275 (1942).

Effect of motive of defendant. — The motive which actuated the person using the words is not material, except upon the questions of malice and the measure of damages. Cook v. Patterson Drug Co., 185 Va. 516, 39 S.E.2d 304 (1946).

Questions for jury. — In cases under this section, the jury is regarded as the best and safest tribunal to determine not only the character of the alleged insulting words, but also the measure of damages. Its verdict will not be set aside in this State, unless it is so grossly excessive, or inadequate, as to indicate that the jury, in rendering it were actuated by prejudice, or corruption, or that they were misled by some mistaken view of the case. Boyd v. Boyd, 116 Va. 326, 82 S.E. 110 (1914); Weatherford v. Birchett, 158 Va. 741, 164 S.E. 535 (1932); Kroger Grocery & Baking Co. v. Rosenbaum, 171 Va. 158, 198 S.E. 461 (1938).

The determination of the amount of damages in an action under this section is primarily the province of the jury under proper instructions of the court, and the courts are generally reluctant to interfere with their verdict. Nevertheless, each case must be considered on its own facts and circumstances, and whether the award is inadequate or excessive is a legal question addressed to the sound discretion of the court in the exercise of its supervisory power over verdicts to prevent a miscarriage of justice. Stubbs v. Cowden, 179 Va. 190, 18 S.E.2d 275 (1942).

Instruction as to mitigation. — In a proceeding for damages under the statute, instructing jury that if plaintiff was entitled to recover anything, then in assessing damages they could take into consideration her improper relations with the husband of defendant, if proven in the case, in mitigation of damages, was not error. Stubbs v. Cowden, 179 Va. 190, 18 S.E.2d 275 (1942).

I. Evidence.

Proof of insulting words. — In an action under the statute, the plaintiff makes out a prima facie case simply by proving the insulting words whether written or spoken as laid in the motion. Chaffin v. Lynch, 83 Va. 106, 1 S.E. 803 (1887).

Proof of truth and privilege as defense. — The truth and privilege are complete defenses, and the same rules of law with reference to the proof of these defenses apply in an action under this section as in an action for common-law slander or libel. Massey v. Jones, 182 Va. 200, 28 S.E.2d 623 (1944).

Burden on plaintiff of proving circumstances and meaning of words. — In an action under this section plaintiff, treasurer of a quasi-religious organization, contended that defendant, founder and head of the organization, by the use of certain language to the congregation, meant that plaintiff had made a false report of the financial affairs of the organization entrusted to him and had misapplied money. It was held that a literal meaning of the words used did not import misapplication of funds and, this being true, it was encumbent on plaintiff to prove that the manner and circumstances in which the words were uttered conveyed the meaning placed upon them by him. Taylor v. Grace, 166 Va. 138, 184 S.E. 211 (1936).

Where the occasion is one of qualified privilege the burden is cast upon plaintiff to prove malice in fact. In such cases proof might be accomplished by the language itself if it is capable of affording evidence of express malice, or by extrinsic evidence. Story v. Norfolk-Portsmouth Newspapers, Inc., 202 Va. 588, 118 S.E.2d 668 (1961).

Evidence of malice. — In an action for libel the court did not err in permitting a witness to testify that plaintiff gave her, as a representative of a newspaper, a writing to be inserted conditionally as an advertisement which reflected on defendant's honor, and indicated that he had not been straight in his accounts while in defendant's employ. This evidence was admissible to show malice. Lightner v. Osborn, 142 Va. 19, 127 S.E. 314 (1925).

In an action for libel it was not error for the court to permit a witness to testify to a conversation which he overheard between defendant and a third party in which defendant said plaintiff was "one of the grandest rascals that ever was and if he wanted a man to do the darkest, dirtiest deed he would recommend" plaintiff. The court instructed the jury to consider this evidence for the purpose of ascertaining the state of mind of the defendant. Lightner v. Osborn, 142 Va. 19, 127 S.E. 314 (1925).

Where the jury found in favor of the alleged utterer of defamatory statements and where the editor failed and neglected to recheck the facts after plaintiff told him the statements were untrue, there was evidence from which the jury could find that the defamatory publication complained of was made with constitutional malice. Newspaper Publishing Corp. v. Burke, 216 Va. 800, 224 S.E.2d 132 (1976).

Inference of malice from use of violent and disproportionate language. — The inference of actual malice which may arise from the use of violent and disproportionate language is evidentiary and rebuttable. Story v. Norfolk-Portsmouth Newspapers, Inc., 202 Va. 588, 118 S.E.2d 668 (1961).

Evidence of falsity of statements. — In an action for libel it was not error to permit plaintiff to testify that certain statements alleged to have been made in a letter sent by defendant's corporation to another corporation were false. Lightner v. Osborn, 142 Va. 19, 127 S.E. 314 (1925).

Evidence of character of plaintiff in mitigation of damages. — In an action on the statute as well as at common law the general bad character of the plaintiff is admissible in mitigation of damages. Moseley v. Moss, 47 Va. (6 Gratt.) 534 (1850).

The man of unblemished reputation is entitled to greater damage than is one whose reputation is already so bad as to receive little or no detriment from the action of which complaint is made. The purpose of admitting evidence of bad reputation is to diminish the damage, not to bar the action. Injury to the reputation is not the only element for which compensatory damages are allowed, but the pain, the mortification, the insult is usually in proportion to a person's good or bad reputation. Weatherford v. Birchett, 158 Va. 741, 164 S.E. 535 (1932).

Newspaper articles admissible. — In an action under this section for procuring the publication of libelous words in newspaper articles, such articles are admissible in evidence after the use of the actionable words has been established, not only on the question of damages, but in connection with the use of the words sued on as tending to show that the language was employed by defendant prior to the publication. Haskell v. Bailey, 63 F. 873 (4th Cir. 1894).

Oral statement prior to publication. — A verdict that defendant caused the publication of libelous articles under this section will be sustained when it appears from his testimony as a witness for plaintiff that he used the words set out in the declaration in a conversation with one of the editors of the paper prior to their publication. Haskell v. Bailey, 63 F. 873 (4th Cir. 1894).

And like words spoken on another occasion. — When the words laid in the declaration have been proved, and not before, proof of the speaking of like words as those laid, either before or after they were spoken, is admissible to affect the measure of damages. Hansbrough v. Stinnett, 66 Va. (25 Gratt.) 495 (1874).

As tending to show malice, it is always competent for the plaintiff to prove that the defendant has repeated the slander charged, or has used the same, or similar words, upon other occasions. And where statements other than the one upon which the action is based tend to show actual malice in the utterance of the slander sued on, such statements may also be shown in evidence. Lightner v. Osborn, 142 Va. 19, 127 S.E. 314 (1925).

Other slanderous words, spoken or written of plaintiff, whether before or after those laid in the declaration, may be given in evidence, to show malice on the part of the defendant when that is an issue in the case. Kroger Grocery & Baking Co. v. Rosenbaum, 171 Va. 158, 198 S.E. 461 (1938).

Admission of general manager of corporation weeks after publication not admissible. — In an action under the statute, admissions by the general manager of the defendant corporation made weeks after the publication of the alleged libel are not a part of the res gestae and cannot be introduced as evidence for the plaintiff. M. Reusch v. Roanoke Cold Storage Co., 91 Va. 534, 22 S.E. 358 (1895), overruled on other point, Rosenberg & Sons v. Craft, 182 Va. 512, 29 S.E.2d 375 (1944).

Character of witnesses no evidence as to damages. — In an action for defamation, where the speaking of the insulting words is admitted, the character of the witnesses who testified only as to the language used and the circumstances attending its utterance, and not as to the damages sustained, is of no value in determining the damages sustained. Boyd v. Boyd, 116 Va. 326, 82 S.E. 110 (1914).

When repetition may be shown in evidence against original slanderer. — When a repetition is authorized and is the direct and natural result of the original slander, it may be shown in evidence against the original defamer, and this is especially true where it was intended and contemplated that the slander be repeated. Luhring v. Carter, 193 Va. 529, 69 S.E.2d 416 (1952).

Evidence held insufficient to sustain verdict for plaintiff under count for insulting words. M. Rosenberg & Sons v. Craft, 182 Va. 512, 29 S.E.2d 375 (1944).

J. Pleading and Practice.

1. In General.

Election of remedies. — A person aggrieved by the insulting words of another may elect whether he will proceed as at common law or under the statute. Moseley v. Moss, 47 Va. (6 Gratt.) 534 (1850); Hogan v. Wilmoth, 57 Va. (16 Gratt.) 80 (1860); Chaffin v. Lynch, 83 Va. 106, 1 S.E. 803 (1887); Payne v. Tancil, 98 Va. 262, 35 S.E. 725 (1900); Sun Life Assurance Co. of Can. v. Bailey, 101 Va. 443, 44 S.E. 692 (1903).

A person aggrieved by the insulting words of another must declare either for a common-law slander or for insulting words under the statute; he cannot declare for both unless he does so separately in distinct counts of the declaration. Moseley v. Moss, 47 Va. (6 Gratt.) 534 (1850); Bourland v. Eidson, 49 Va. (8 Gratt.) 27 (1851); Hogan v. Wilmoth, 57 Va. (16 Gratt.) 80 (1860); Chaffin v. Lynch, 83 Va. 106, 1 S.E. 803 (1887).

Jurisdiction and venue. — Words actionable at common law may be sued on in a common-law action in any jurisdiction where the defendant may be found. But where the action rests upon a statute and the words were spoken or published exclusively in a state other than that in which the action was brought, the plaintiff must prove as a fact that a like statute was in force in such other state. Davis v. Heflin, 130 Va. 169, 107 S.E. 673 (1921). See also, Haskell v. Bailey, 63 F. 873 (4th Cir. 1894).

Effect of elimination of provision as to demurrer. — The 1940 amendment of this section which eliminated the sentence that no demurrer shall preclude a jury from passing thereon, revealed that it was the intent of the legislature that the court should exercise the same power and authority over actions for insulting words that it exercises over actions of libel and slander. M. Rosenberg & Sons v. Craft, 182 Va. 512, 29 S.E.2d 375 (1944).

Bill of particulars held not to state new cause of action. — Bill of particulars filed in action for slander more than one year after the alleged tort did not state a new and distinct cause of action against the defendants which would be barred by the statutes of limitations and was not an amendment to the original notice of motion where the bill of particulars only particularized, specified, and pointed out the intended and accomplished result of the original statements and the damages directly caused thereby. Luhring v. Carter, 193 Va. 529, 69 S.E.2d 416 (1952).

2. Motion.

What must be stated in motion. — In an action of slander, if the plaintiff proceeds under the statute, he must in his motion aver that the words from their usual construction and common acceptation are construed as insults, and tend to violence and breach of the peace, or else employ some other equivalent averment to denote that the words are actionable under the statute. Hogan v. Wilmoth, 57 Va. (16 Gratt.) 80 (1860).

A motion alleged in each count that the words used are, "from their usual construction and common acceptance, construed as insults, and tend to violence and breach of the peace." Such are the terms of the statute, which makes the motion one under the statute, though the words used are objectionable at common law. Haskell v. Bailey, 63 F. 873 (4th Cir. 1894).

If plaintiff does not move under the statute, his motion must set out a common-law slander, and if the words charged do not amount to slander they cannot be helped by the innuendo. Moseley v. Moss, 47 Va. (6 Gratt.) 534 (1850).

Where the motion does not show by the proper averments that the action is under the statute, it may be demurred to as defective, unless it sets out properly, and in substantial compliance with the rules of pleading, such a charge as constitutes defamation at the common law. Hogan v. Wilmoth, 57 Va. (16 Gratt.) 80 (1860).

3. Pleas.

Pleading the truth and privilege. — The same rules of law with reference to pleading the defenses of the truth and privilege apply in an action under this section as in an action at law for common-law slander or libel. Massey v. Jones, 182 Va. 200, 28 S.E.2d 623 (1944).

When plea of special damages required. — Where alleged defamatory language was not actionable per se, and there were no allegations or proof of special damages, the trial court did not err in striking out plaintiff's evidence and dismissing the action. Shupe v. Rose's Stores, Inc., 213 Va. 374, 192 S.E.2d 766 (1972), cert. denied, Port Packet Corp. v. Lewis, 473 U.S. 905, 105 S. Ct. 3528, 87 L. Ed. 2d 653 (1985).

Plea of bankruptcy of plaintiff. — In an action of slander, a plea that since the commencement of the action the plaintiff has been adjudicated a bankrupt, is not a good plea. Dillard v. Collins, 66 Va. (25 Gratt.) 343 (1874).

4. Instructions.

Instruction as to malice. — In an action for libel an instruction that if from the evidence the jury believe that the charges contained in the letter were untrue, and if they further believe from the evidence that the defendant has reiterated the charges therein, this is a circumstance tending to show malice on the part of the defendant, was not erroneous. Lightner v. Osborn, 142 Va. 19, 127 S.E. 314 (1925).

Instruction as to privilege. — In an action under this section, instruction that if a newspaper's account of a court proceeding was a fair, impartial and substantially accurate report the privilege of the newspaper to publish it was a complete defense, was fair to the plaintiff and correctly stated the law. Vaughan v. News Leader Co., 105 F.2d 360 (4th Cir. 1939).

Privilege and abuse thereof. — Where allegedly libelous publications were made in response to attacks on certain of defendants made by plaintiff in his newspaper, the court was held to have instructed correctly that the occasion was privileged, but the instructions were held faulty in that they did not sufficiently define for the jury what constitutes an abuse of privilege. Haycox v. Dunn, 200 Va. 212, 104 S.E.2d 800 (1958).

Instructions as to truth of statements. — In an action for libel defendant requested the court to instruct the jury that if they believe from the evidence that the alleged libelous statements contained in the letter from defendant were substantially true, they must find for the defendant. The court refused to give this instruction as offered, but amended the same by inserting after the words "substantially true" the words "in the ordinary and usually accepted meaning thereof." Vaughan v. Lytton, 126 Va. 671, 101 S.E. 865 (1920).

Instructions as to damages. — Where the court had properly instructed the jury as to the rights of plaintiff to recover exemplary damages, it was not error for the court to modify an instruction for defendant limiting the plaintiff to actual damages by adding: "But this instruction must be considered in connection with instructions" in regard to exemplary damages. Lightner v. Osborn, 142 Va. 19, 127 S.E. 314 (1925).

Instruction as to burden of proof. — In an action under this section, an instruction that the burden was upon each plaintiff to prove by a preponderance of the evidence that the defendant circulated defamatory statements with actual malice correctly stated the law. Old Dominion Branch 496 v. Austin, 213 Va. 377, 192 S.E.2d 737 (1972), rev'd on other grounds, 418 U.S. 264, 94 S. Ct. 2770, 41 L. Ed. 2d 745 (1974).

Instruction held erroneous. — Where the publication complained of depicted the plaintiff as the "operator" of a club which was being run illegally, it was error to instruct the jury to find for defendant if they found plaintiff owned the club and consented to its illegal operation. Saleeby v. Free Press, Inc., 197 Va. 761, 91 S.E.2d 405 (1956).

5. Province of Court and Jury.

It is the duty of the court to define what constitutes insulting words, and it is for the jury to say whether the particular words come within the definition. Cook v. Patterson Drug Co., 185 Va. 516, 39 S.E.2d 304 (1946).

It is for the jury to determine whether or

not the words were insulting. Moseley v. Moss, 47 Va. (6 Gratt.) 534 (1850).

In an action under this section whether or not the words used are insulting is a jury question, depending on whether from "their usual construction and common acceptation" they may be "construed as insults, and tend to violence and breach of the peace." Cook v. Patterson Drug Co., 185 Va. 516, 39 S.E.2d 304 (1946).

When question of law or of fact. — To justify publication of defamatory matter, the occasion must be privileged, and must be used bona fide, without malice. Whether the occasion be privileged, is a question of law for the court. Whether it has been used bona fide, is a question of fact for the jury. Chaffin v. Lynch, 83 Va. 106, 1 S.E. 803 (1887).

Determination of whether or not the occasion is one of qualified privilege is ordinarily a matter to be decided by the court. Yet if the evidence upon which the asserted privilege is based is in substantial conflict, whether or not the occasion is one of privilege becomes a mixed question of law and fact to be determined by the jury under appropriate instructions from the court. Luhring v. Carter, 193 Va. 529, 69 S.E.2d 416 (1952).

Though the occasion be qualifiedly privileged, if the language used be clearly disproportionate, extraneous and impertinent to the occasion and subject at hand, and thus beyond the scope and protection of the privilege, then there is no factual issue on the abuse of privilege to submit to the jury. Luhring v. Carter, 193 Va. 529, 69 S.E.2d 416 (1952).

The question of privilege was one for the court, and the question of the use which the defendants made of their privilege, that is, whether they acted maliciously or not, was a question for the jury to decide. Haycox v. Dunn, 200 Va. 212, 104 S.E.2d 800 (1958).

The existence of a privileged (either absolute or qualified) occasion is a question of law to be decided by the court. Marsh v. Commercial & Sav. Bank, 265 F. Supp. 614 (W.D. Va. 1967).

It is for the jury to determine what damage was occasioned to the plaintiff by the insulting words. Moseley v. Moss, 47 Va. (6 Gratt.) 534 (1850).

In action under this section, the question whether a published report of a court proceeding was a "fair, impartial and accurate report" was one for the jury. Whether the plaintiff suffered any damages from an inaccurate report was also a question for the jury. Vaughan v. News Leader Co., 105 F.2d 360 (4th Cir. 1939).

Malice is question for jury. — Notwithstanding that the occasion was privileged, there was evidence upon which the jury might properly have found that the privilege was abused. The language itself, italicized by the defendant, taken in connection with the previous correspondence and dispute between the parties, would warrant the court in upholding the action of the jury upon the question of malice. Vaughan v. Lytton, 126 Va. 671, 101 S.E. 865 (1920).

The words used, under the circumstances recited, were sufficient to submit to the jury the question whether or not defendants were actuated by actual malice. Haycox v. Dunn, 200 Va. 212, 104 S.E.2d 800 (1958).

Ordinarily, the question of whether the defendant acted with malice is a question of fact to be presented to the jury. But where the communication is privileged, unless there is evidence from which a jury may fairly conclude that there was malice, there can be no recovery. Marsh v. Commercial & Sav. Bank, 265 F. Supp. 614 (W.D. Va. 1967).

Setting aside verdict. — While as a general rule the jury is regarded as the best and safest tribunal to determine whether the words are or are not actionable, the court has inherent power to set aside the verdict, "in order to correct any manifest departure from right and justice." Guide Publishing Co. v. Futrell, 175 Va. 77, 7 S.E.2d 133 (1940).

In an action under the statute the court would have the power to correct any manifest departure from right and justice on the part of the jury. Corr v. Lewis, 94 Va. 24, 26 S.E. 385 (1896).

§ 8.01-46. Justification and mitigation of damages. — In any action for defamation, the defendant may justify by alleging and proving that the words spoken or written were true, and, after notice in writing of his intention to do so, given to the plaintiff at the time of, or for, pleading to such action, may give in evidence, in mitigation of damages, that he made or offered an apology to the plaintiff for such defamation before the commencement of the action, or as soon afterwards as he had an opportunity of doing so in case the action shall have been commenced before there was an opportunity of making or offering such apology. (Code 1950, § 8-631; 1977, c. 617.)

Law Review. — For survey of Virginia tort law for the year 1975-1976, see 62 Va. L. Rev. 1489 (1976).

I. Decisions Under Current Law.
II. Decisions Under Prior Law.

I. DECISIONS UNDER CURRENT LAW.

As a matter of state law the negligence standard should be applicable to media and nonmedia defendants alike. Gazette, Inc. v. Harris, 229 Va. 1, 325 S.E.2d 713, cert. denied sub nom., Fleming v. Moore, 472 U.S. 1032, 105 S. Ct. 3513, 87 L. Ed. 2d 643, cert. denied sub nom. Port Packet Corp. v. Lewis, 473 U.S. 905, 105 S. Ct. 3528, 87 L. Ed. 2d 653 (1985).

The application of this negligence standard is expressly limited, however, to circumstances where the defamatory statement makes substantial danger to reputation apparent. The trial judge shall make such determination as a matter of law. If, on the other hand, no substantial danger to reputation is apparent from the statement in issue, New York Times malice must be established to recover compensatory damages. Gazette, Inc. v. Harris, 229 Va. 1, 325 S.E.2d 713, cert. denied sub nom., Fleming v. Moore, 472 U.S. 1032, 105 S. Ct. 3513, 87 L. Ed. 2d 643, cert. denied sub nom. Port Packet Corp. v. Lewis, 473 U.S. 905, 105 S. Ct. 3528, 87 L. Ed. 2d 653 (1985).

Plaintiff must prove falsity. — In an action brought by a private individual to recover actual, compensatory damages for a defamatory publication, the plaintiff may recover upon proof by a preponderance of the evidence that the publication was false, and that the defendant either knew it to be false, or believing it to be true, lacked reasonable grounds for such belief, or acted negligently in failing to ascertain the facts on which the publication was based. Under this standard, truth no longer is an affirmative defense to be established by the defendant. Instead, the plaintiff must prove falsity, because he is required to establish negligence with respect to such falsity. Such liability may be based upon negligence, whether or not the publication in question relates to a matter of public or general concern. Gazette, Inc. v. Harris, 229 Va. 1, 325 S.E.2d 713, cert. denied sub nom., Fleming v. Moore, 472 U.S. 1032, 105 S. Ct. 3513, 87 L. Ed. 2d 643, cert. denied sub nom. Port Packet Corp. v. Lewis, 473 U.S. 905, 105 S. Ct. 3528, 87 L. Ed. 2d 653 (1985).

II. DECISIONS UNDER PRIOR LAW.

Editor's note. — The cases cited below were decided under corresponding provisions of former law. The term "this section," as used below, refers to former provisions.

It is not necessary to prove the literal truth of statements made. Alexandria Gazette Corp. v. West, 198 Va. 154, 93 S.E.2d 274 (1956).

And slight inaccuracies of expression are immaterial, provided the defamatory charge is true in substance, and it is sufficient to show that the imputation is "substantially" true. Saleeby v. Free Press, Inc., 197 Va. 761, 91 S.E.2d 405 (1956); Alexandria Gazette Corp. v. West, 198 Va. 154, 93 S.E.2d 274 (1956).

Truth only shown by plea of justification. — The truth of defamatory words, written or spoken, cannot in this State be shown under the plea of not guilty, either in bar or in mitigation of damages, but can only be shown under a plea of justification. Williams Printing Co. v. Saunders, 113 Va. 156, 73 S.E. 472 (1912).

The language used in this section that "the defendant may justify by alleging and proving that the words spoken or written were true," plainly intends that the truth shall be specially pleaded, for if the legislature had intended that the proof should be given in under the plea of not guilty, there was no occasion to require that it should be alleged. Williams Printing Co. v. Saunders, 113 Va. 156, 73 S.E. 472 (1912).

An apology under this section goes only to mitigate damages, and if the plaintiff agrees to accept it in complete satisfaction it is an agreement without consideration. James v. Powell, 154 Va. 96, 152 S.E. 539 (1930).

An apology published after an action for libel has been instituted would be of no avail. James v. Powell, 154 Va. 96, 152 S.E. 539 (1930).

§ 8.01-46.1. Disclosure of employment-related information; presumptions; causes of action; definitions.

— A. Any employer who, upon request by a person's prospective or current employer, furnishes information about that person's professional conduct, reasons for separation or job performance, including, but not limited to, information contained in any written performance evaluations, shall be immune from civil liability for furnishing such information, provided that the employer is not acting in bad faith. An employer shall be presumed to be acting in good faith. The presumption of good faith shall be rebutted if it is shown by clear and convincing evidence that the employer disclosed such information with knowledge that it was false, or with reckless disregard for whether it is false or not, or with the intent to deliberately mislead.

B. In a civil action brought against an employer for disclosing the information described in subsection A, if the trier of fact determines the employer acted in bad faith, punitive damages may be awarded, as provided by § 8.01-38.1.

C. As used in this section, the following words and phrases shall have the following meanings:

"Employee" means any person, paid or unpaid, in the service of an employer.

"Employer" means any person, firm or corporation, including the Commonwealth of Virginia and its political subdivisions, and their agents, who has one or more employees or individuals performing services under any contract of hire or service, express or implied, oral or written.

"Information" includes, but is not limited to, facts, data and opinions.

"Job performance" includes, but is not limited to, ability, attendance, awards, demotions, duties, effort, evaluations, knowledge, skills, promotions, productivity and disciplinary actions.

"Professional conduct" includes, but is not limited to, the ethical standards which govern the employee's profession, or lawful conduct which is expected of the employee by the employer.

"Prospective employer" means any employer who is considering a person for employment. (2000, c. 1005.)

Editor's note. — Acts 2000, c. 1005, cl. 2 provides that the provisions of the act shall apply to any cause of action occuring on or after July 1, 2000.

§ 8.01-47. Immunity of school personnel investigating or reporting certain incidents.

— In addition to any other immunity he may have, any teacher, instructor, principal, school administrator, school coordinator, guidance counselor or any other professional, administrative or clerical staff member or other personnel of any elementary or secondary school, or institution of higher learning who, in good faith with reasonable cause and without malice, acts to report, investigate or cause any investigation to be made into the activities of any student or students or any other person or persons as they relate to conduct involving bomb threats, firebombs, explosive materials or other similar devices as described in clauses (v) and (vi) of § 22.1-280.1 A, or alcohol or drug use or abuse in or related to the school or institution or in connection with any school or institution activity, shall be immune from all civil liability that might otherwise be incurred or imposed as the result of the making of such a report, investigation or disclosure. (Code 1950, § 8-631.1; 1972, c. 762; 1977, c. 617; 1982, c. 259; 1988, c. 159; 1995, c. 759; 2000, c. 79.)

Editor's note. — At the direction of the Code Commission, the amendment to this section by Acts 1995, c. 759, was not implemented in light of the decision not to implement the amendment by Acts 1995, c. 759, to § 22.1-280.1 because of a conflict with the amendment to § 22.1-280.1 by Acts 1995, c. 773.

The 1995 amendment would have inserted "or, in the case of principals or their designees, makes reports to local law-enforcement officials as required by § 22.1-280.1" following "any school or institution activity" near the end of this section.

The 2000 amendments. — The 2000 amendment by c. 79 inserted "conduct involving bomb threats, firebombs, explosive materials or other similar devices as described in clauses (v) and (vi) of § 22.1-280.1 A, or."

Law Review. — For 1995 survey of civil practice and procedure, see 29 U. Rich. L. Rev. 897 (1995).

§ 8.01-48. Mitigation in actions against newspapers, etc.

— In any civil action against the publisher, owner, editor, reporter or employee of any newspaper, magazine or periodical under § 8.01-45, or for libel or defamation, because of any article, statement or other matter contained in any such

§ 8.01-48 CIVIL REMEDIES AND PROCEDURE § 8.01-48

newspaper, magazine or periodical, the defendant, whether punitive damages be sought or not, may introduce in evidence in mitigation of general and punitive damages, or either, but not of actual pecuniary damages, all the circumstances of the publication, including the source of the information, its character as affording reasonable ground of reliance, any prior publication elsewhere of similar purport, the lack of negligence or malice on the part of the defendant, the good faith of the defendant in such publication, or that apology or retraction, if any, was made with reasonable promptness and fairness; provided that the defendant may introduce in evidence only such circumstances and to the extent set forth in his or its grounds of defense. (Code 1950, § 8-632; 1954, c. 333; 1977, c. 617.)

Law Review. — For comment on the constitutional privileges of publishers, see 11 U. Rich. L. Rev. 177 (1976). For survey of Virginia tort law for the year 1975-1976, see 62 Va. L. Rev. 1489 (1976).

I. Decisions Under Current Law.
II. Decisions Under Prior Law.

I. DECISIONS UNDER CURRENT LAW.

As a matter of state law the negligence standard should be applicable to media and nonmedia defendants alike. Gazette, Inc. v. Harris, 229 Va. 1, 325 S.E.2d 713, cert. denied sub nom., Fleming v. Moore, 472 U.S. 1032, 105 S. Ct. 3513, 87 L. Ed. 2d 643, cert. denied sub nom. Port Packet Corp. v. Lewis, 473 U.S. 905, 105 S. Ct. 3528, 87 L. Ed. 2d 653 (1985).

The application of this negligence standard is expressly limited, however, to circumstances where the defamatory statement makes substantial danger to reputation apparent. The trial judge shall make such determination as a matter of law. If, on the other hand, no substantial danger to reputation is apparent from the statement in issue, New York Times malice must be established to recover compensatory damages. Gazette, Inc. v. Harris, 229 Va. 1, 325 S.E.2d 713, cert. denied sub nom., Fleming v. Moore, 472 U.S. 1032, 105 S. Ct. 3513, 87 L. Ed. 2d 643, cert. denied sub nom. Port Packet Corp. v. Lewis, 473 U.S. 905, 105 S. Ct. 3528, 87 L. Ed. 2d 653 (1985).

Plaintiff must prove falsity. — In an action brought by a private individual to recover actual, compensatory damages for a defamatory publication, the plaintiff may recover upon proof by a preponderance of the evidence that the publication was false, and that the defendant either knew it to be false, or believing it to be true, lacked reasonable grounds for such belief, or acted negligently in failing to ascertain the facts on which the publication was based. Under this standard, truth no longer is an affirmative defense to be established by the defendant. Instead, the plaintiff must prove falsity, because he is required to establish negligence with respect to such falsity. Such liability may be based upon negligence, whether or not the publication in question relates to a matter of public or general concern. Gazette, Inc. v. Harris, 229 Va. 1, 325 S.E.2d 713, cert. denied sub nom., Fleming v. Moore, 472 U.S. 1032, 105 S. Ct. 3513, 87 L. Ed. 2d 643, cert. denied sub nom. Port Packet Corp. v. Lewis, 473 U.S. 905, 105 S. Ct. 3528, 87 L. Ed. 2d 653 (1985).

II. DECISIONS UNDER PRIOR LAW.

Editor's note. — The case cited below was decided under corresponding provisions of former law. The term "this section," as used below, refers to former provisions.

Purpose of section. — By the express mandate of this section certain evidence in mitigation, not admissible prior to this section where punitive damages were not claimed, was made admissible, and was designed to mitigate general damages to which a plaintiff theretofore had been entitled. News Leader Co. v. Kocen, 173 Va. 95, 3 S.E.2d 385 (1939).

Province of jury. — The jury might determine that the evidence introduced under the provisions of this section eliminated all general or compensatory damages not "actual pecuniary," and thus allow plaintiff only nominal damages. The weight to be given the evidence introduced in mitigation is peculiarly the province of the jury, and not of the court. News Leader Co. v. Kocen, 173 Va. 95, 3 S.E.2d 385 (1939).

Instruction on damages. — Obviously it would be error to use the expression "slight actual damages" or "substantial actual damages." As compensatory damages include all damages other than punitive or exemplary, the use of the word "substantial" in an instruction unduly emphasizes the amount of damages which may be awarded. Any modifying word or phrase of the term "actual or compensatory damages" does not clarify the meaning intended to be conveyed and should be avoided.

News Leader Co. v. Kocen, 173 Va. 95, 3 S.E.2d 385 (1939).

§ **8.01-49. Defamatory statements in radio and television broadcasts.** — The owner, licensee or operator of a radio and television broadcasting station or network of stations, and the agents or employees of any such owner, licensee or operator, shall not be liable for any damages for any defamatory statement published or uttered in or as a part of any such broadcast, by one other than such owner, licensee or operator, or agent or employee thereof, unless it shall be alleged and proved by the complaining party, that such owner, licensee, operator, such agent or employee, failed to exercise due care to prevent the publication or utterance of such statement in such broadcast; provided, however, that in no event shall any owner, licensee or operator, or the agents or employees of any such owner, licensee or operator of such a station or network of stations be held liable for damages for any defamatory statement broadcast over the facilities of such station or network by or on behalf of any candidate for public office. (Code 1950, § 8-632.1; 1977, c. 617.)

REVISERS' NOTE

The former § 8-632.1 phrase "visual or sound radio" modifying "broadcasts" has been changed to "radio and television" so as to clearly indicate the section's applicability to all such broadcasts.

Law Review. — For comment on the constitutional privileges of publishers, see 11 U. Rich. L. Rev. 177 (1976). For note on defamation of public figures, see 39 Wash. & Lee L. Rev. 1327 (1982). For article on libel and slander in Virginia, see 17 U. Rich. L. Rev. 769 (1983).

§ **8.01-49.1. Liability for defamatory material on the Internet.** — A. No provider or user of an interactive computer service on the Internet shall be treated as the publisher or speaker of any information provided to it by another information content provider. No provider or user of an interactive computer service shall be liable for (i) any action voluntarily taken by it in good faith to restrict access to, or availability of, material that the provider or user considers to be obscene, lewd, lascivious, excessively violent, harassing, or intended to incite hatred on the basis of race, religious conviction, color, or national origin, whether or not such material is constitutionally protected, or (ii) any action taken to enable, or make available to information content providers or others, the technical means to restrict access to information provided by another information content provider.

B. Definitions. As used in this section:

"Information content provider" means any person or entity that is responsible, in whole or in part, for the creation or development of information provided through the Internet or any other interactive computer service.

"Interactive computer service" means any information service, system, or access software provider that provides or enables computer access by multiple users to a computer server, including specifically a service or system that provides access to the Internet and such systems operated or services offered by libraries or educational institutions.

"Internet" means the international computer network of interoperable packet-switched data networks. (2000, c. 930.)

Article 5.

Death by Wrongful Act.

§ 8.01-50. Action for death by wrongful act; how and when to be brought. — A. Whenever the death of a person shall be caused by the wrongful act, neglect, or default of any person or corporation, or of any ship or vessel, and the act, neglect, or default is such as would, if death had not ensued, have entitled the party injured to maintain an action, or to proceed in rem against such ship or vessel or in personam against the owners thereof or those having control of her, and to recover damages in respect thereof, then, and in every such case, the person who, or corporation or ship or vessel which, would have been liable, if death had not ensued, shall be liable to an action for damages, or, if a ship or vessel, to a libel in rem, and her owners or those responsible for her acts or defaults or negligence to a libel in personam, notwithstanding the death of the person injured, and although the death shall have been caused under such circumstances, as amount in law to a felony.

B. Every such action under this section shall be brought by and in the name of the personal representative of such deceased person within the time limits specified in § 8.01-244.

C. If the deceased person was an infant who was in the custody of a parent pursuant to an order of court or written agreement with the other parent, administration shall be granted first to the parent having custody; however, that parent may waive his right to qualify in favor of any other person designated by him. If no such parent or his designee applies for administration within thirty days from the death of the infant, administration shall be granted as in other cases. (Code 1950, § 8-633; 1958, c. 470; 1977, c. 617; 1981, c. 115.)

REVISERS' NOTE

This proposal combines former §§ 8-633 and 8-634 with the former being subsection (a), and the latter subsection (b). Changes include:

(1) The survival provisions in former § 8-633 have been deleted as unnecessary. See § 8.01-25.

(2) The statute of limitations provisions in former §§ 8-633 and 8-634 have been removed and placed in § 8.01-244.

(3) The last paragraph of former §§ 8-633 and 8-634 regarding the statute of limitations in pre-July 1, 1958 actions have been deleted as no longer having any significance.

Cross references. — For rules of court governing actions in personam for money, see Rules 3:1 through 3:18. For rule on substitution of parties, see Rule 3:15.

Law Review. — For article, "Basic Protection and Future of Negligence Law," see 3 U. Rich. L. Rev. 1 (1968). For survey of Virginia law on torts for the year 1967-1968, see 54 Va. L. Rev. 1649 (1968); for the year 1968-1969, see 55 Va. L. Rev. 1395 (1969). For comment, "Wrongful Death: Assignment of Right to Potential Proceeds," see 26 Wash. & Lee L. Rev. 384 (1969). For survey of Virginia law on torts for the year 1969-1970, see 56 Va. L. Rev. 1419 (1970). For articles on damages recoverable for wrongful death, see 5 U. Rich. L. Rev. 213 (1971) and 12 Wm. & Mary L. Rev. 396 (1970). For survey of Virginia law on torts for the year 1972-1973, see 59 Va. L. Rev. 1590 (1973). For note discussing diversity jurisdiction and wrongful death actions brought by nonresident administrators, see 30 Wash. & Lee L. Rev. 282 (1973). For article, "Telling the Time of Human Death by Statute: An Essential and Progressive Trend," see 31 Wash. & Lee L. Rev. 521 (1974). For note, "Tort Law — Interspousal Immunity — Action for Wrongful Death Against Surviving Spouse Held Maintainable When Such Act Terminates Marriage and Neither Child Nor Grandchild Survives Decedent — Korman v. Carpenter, 216 Va. 86, 216 S.E.2d 195 (1975)," see 10 U. Rich. L. Rev. 434 (1976). For comment, "The Covenant Not to Sue: Virginia's Effort to Bury the Common Law Rule Regarding the Release of Joint Tortfeasors," see 14 U. Rich. L. Rev. 809 (1980). For survey of Virginia law on practice and pleading for the year 1978-1979, see 66 Va. L. Rev. 343 (1980). For note discussing wrongful death of child conceived by in vitro fertilization, see 17 U. Rich. L. Rev. 311 (1983). For article, "Civil Rights and 'Personal Injuries': Virginia's Statute of Limitations for Section 1983 Suits," see 26 Wm. & Mary L. Rev. 199 (1985). For 1987 survey of Virginia civil procedure and practice, see 21 U. Rich. L. Rev. 667 (1987). For note, "Recovery for the Wrongful Death of a Fetus," see 25 U. Rich. L. Rev. 391 (1991). For a review of damages in medical malpractice in Virginia, see 33 U. Rich. L. Rev. 919 (1999).

I. Decisions Under Current Law.
  A. General Consideration.
  B. Right of Action.
  C. Action by Personal Representative.
II. Decisions Under Prior Law.
  A. General Consideration.
  B. Right of Action.
    1. In General.
    2. Conflict of Laws.
    3. Who May Sue; Defenses.
    4. Who May Be Sued.
    5. Evidence.
  C. Actions Against Ships.
  D. Action by Personal Representative.

I. DECISIONS UNDER CURRENT LAW.

A. General Consideration.

Purpose of statute. — The intent of the wrongful death statute is not to accumulate an estate for the decedent but to compensate for a loss suffered by those entitled to recover. Cassady v. Martin, 220 Va. 1093, 266 S.E.2d 104 (1980).

The object of the wrongful death statute is to compensate these beneficiaries for their loss occasioned by the decedent's death. The words "damage" and "loss" clearly indicate a damage and loss sustained by someone, and the loss means the loss to the statutory beneficiary in this case. Cassady v. Martin, 220 Va. 1093, 266 S.E.2d 104 (1980).

This section is not penal or exemplary but remedial. Hewitt v. Firestone Tire & Rubber Co., 490 F. Supp. 1358 (E.D. Va. 1980).

And being remedial, this statute is construed broadly. Hewitt v. Firestone Tire & Rubber Co., 490 F. Supp. 1358 (E.D. Va. 1980).

Punitive damages not awarded if offender is dead. — Where the offender is dead at the time of trial, punitive or exemplary damages may not be awarded. The purpose of punitive damages is to punish the offender, not to compensate the victim. Tarbrake v. Sharp, 894 F. Supp. 270 (E.D. Va. 1995).

Where the alleged offender and the plaintiff were both killed in an automobile accident, an award of punitive damages will not serve its intended purpose of punishing the tortfeasor. Tarbrake v. Sharp, 894 F. Supp. 270 (E.D. Va. 1995).

Sections 8.01-21, 8.01-25, 8.01-50, and 8.01-56 compared. — The requirements of the survival and wrongful death statutes, §§ 8.01-25, 8.01-50 and 8.01-56, apply when the death occurs before a final verdict, whereas § 8.01-21 applies where the death occurs after the verdict. Boyd v. Bulala, 647 F. Supp. 781 (W.D. Va. 1986), aff'd in part, rev'd in part, 877 F.2d 1191 (4th Cir. 1989); Bulala v. Boyd, 239 Va. 218, 389 S.E.2d 670 (1990).

Sections were enacted to extend application of this section. — Sections 8.01-25 and 8.01-56 are not in conflict with § 8.01-21. They were enacted to extend the application of this section, the wrongful death statute, those situations not covered by the original Lord Campbell's Act, in which a plaintiff who has filed an action for personal injuries, dies of those injuries before a verdict is returned. It was unnecessary at common law to amend, revive, or convert the action of the party who survived the return of a verdict, and it is equally unnecessary under the present statutory scheme. Bulala v. Boyd, 239 Va. 218, 389 S.E.2d 670 (1990).

Unborn child is not a "person" within the meaning of the wrongful death statute. Modaber v. Kelley, 232 Va. 60, 348 S.E.2d 233 (1986).

Negligence in womb when child born alive and later dies. — An action for a child's wrongful death could be maintained against a tortfeasor whose negligence occurred when the decedent was in the mother's womb, where the child was born alive but died the same evening, and its premature delivery and death were proximately caused by the tortfeasor's negligence. Kalafut v. Gruver, 239 Va. 278, 389 S.E.2d 681 (1990).

Debtor's right to proceeds of wrongful death action is a property right; as a property right, it is subject to creditor process, and is not exemptable from the debtor's estate. In re Tignor, 21 Bankr. 219 (Bankr. E.D. Va. 1982), rev'd on other grounds sub nom. Tignor v. Parkinson, 729 F.2d 977 (4th Cir. 1984).

Decedent's suicide barred recovery for wrongful death action by personal representative. — That the decedent did not have a full appreciation of the injury she would incur from her actions was of no consequence; decedent's participation in an unlawful and immoral act by committing suicide barred recovery for wrongful death by her personal representative. Hill v. Nicodemus, 755 F. Supp. 692 (W.D. Va. 1991), aff'd, 979 F.2d 987 (4th Cir. 1992).

Tolling provision of the Virginia Medical Malpractice Act, former § 8.01-581.9, which tolled the statute of limitations for 120 days from the giving of notice of 60 days following issuance of an opinion by the medical review panel, applied to the two year limitations contained in the Virginia Wrongful Death Act, this section and § 8.01-244(B). Wertz v. Grubbs, 245 Va. 67, 425 S.E.2d 500 (1993).

Accrual when injury known and not when injury would cause death. — Deceased's claim for the personal injury that allegedly caused her death accrued April 8, 1984, when she wrote in her notes that "on June 1 '83, I had a physical .... In retrospect, a mammogram should have been ordered because of previous breast biopsies, family history, and post-menopausal age 59," even though she did not know at that time she was going to die; when she died on April 9, 1986, the two-year statute of limitations of Federal Tort Claims Act had run on any claim based on negligence in failing to make a timely diagnosis, and thus, wrongful death action was properly dismissed as time-barred. Miller v. United States, 932 F.2d 301 (4th Cir. 1991).

Statute of limitations was not tolled by continuous treatment theory. — In action for wrongful death due to medical malpractice by government doctors in failing to order a mammogram under Federal Tort Claims Act, 28 U.S.C. § 1346, statute of limitation on action was not tolled by under continuous treatment theory since treatment received after deceased discovered that she should have been ordered to have a mammogram had nothing to do with the ordering of a mammogram, and the doctors who administered such treatment were not acting under the advice or direction of the doctor who failed to order the mammogram. Miller v. United States, 932 F.2d 301 (4th Cir. 1991).

Applicability of other jurisdiction's wrongful death statute. — Doctrine of lex loci delicti was applicable to substantive issues in action filed in Virginia as a result of an airplane crash in Maryland and because there was a dispute regarding wrongful death statutes which was a substantive issue because Maryland's wrongful death statute limits the recovery of parents for the death of an adult child to pecuniary loss, while Virginia's wrongful death statute contains no such limitation, Maryland law was therefore applicable. Spring v. United States, 833 F. Supp. 575 (E.D. Va. 1993).

Applied in Vicars v. Mullins, 227 Va. 432, 318 S.E.2d 377 (1984); Lucas v. HCMF Corp., 238 Va. 446, 384 S.E.2d 92 (1989); Riddle v. Shell Oil Co., 764 F. Supp. 418 (W.D. Va. 1990).

B. Right of Action.

A claim under this section is not extinguished by simultaneous assertion of a claim under 42 U.S.C. § 1983. Miltier v. Beorn, 696 F. Supp. 1086 (E.D. Va. 1988).

The structural relationship between § 8.01-25 and this section shows that under Virginia law, a wrongful death claim can peaceably coexist with a 42 U.S.C. § 1983 claim. Miltier v. Beorn, 696 F. Supp. 1086 (E.D. Va. 1988).

Uninsured motorist recovery barred by exclusive remedy clause of workmen's compensation law. — Virginia law does not permit recovery by an insured's estate under the uninsured motorist provision of the insured's policy (paid for by the insured), where the insured was killed in a work-related motor vehicle accident and where the employer/vehicle owner and co-employee/vehicle operator both had insurance, but where the exclusive remedy clause of the Virginia Workmen's Compensation Act bars recovery under those other policies. Aetna Cas. & Sur. Co. v. Dodson, 235 Va. 346, 367 S.E.2d 505 (1988).

A wrongful death action is a right of action to enforce a cause of action, both created by statute in derogation of the common law. Horn v. Abernathy, 231 Va. 228, 343 S.E.2d 318 (1986).

Section does not create new cause of action. — This section does not create a new cause of action, but only a right of action in a personal representative to enforce the decedent's claim for any personal injury that caused death; for this reason, a wrongful death action is necessarily time-barred, if at the time of the decedent's death, her personal injury claim based on the tortious conduct that ultimately caused death is already time-barred. Miller v. United States, 932 F.2d 301 (4th Cir. 1991).

This section confers on the decedent's personal representative a new and original right of action the object of which is to compensate the beneficiaries for their loss. In re Tignor, 21 Bankr. 219 (Bankr. E.D. Va. 1982), rev'd on other grounds sub nom. Tignor v. Parkinson, 729 F.2d 977 (4th Cir. 1984).

Subsection B vests the right of action in

the decedent's personal representative.
The right of action, however, is not a right to enforce a cause of action personal to the personal representative. As the party-plaintiff, he is merely a surrogate for the beneficiaries of the cause of action named in § 8.01-53. Horn v. Abernathy, 231 Va. 228, 343 S.E.2d 318 (1986).

No action for death of stillborn infant. — A stillborn infant is not a person within the meaning of the wrongful death statute. No action will lie for the death of a stillborn infant. Myrick v. United States, 723 F.2d 1158 (4th Cir. 1983).

Injury to an unborn child constitutes injury to the mother and she may recover for such physical injury and mental suffering associated with a stillbirth. She is not entitled, however, to damages ordinarily recoverable in a wrongful death action. For example, the mother may not recover for anticipated loss of the child's society, companionship, comfort, or guidance. She may not be compensated for an expected loss of income of the child or for services, protection, care, or assistance expected to be provided by the child had he lived. Modaber v. Kelley, 232 Va. 60, 348 S.E.2d 233 (1986).

Intoxication, voluntarily induced, is not the type of physical incapacity which will excuse contributory negligence via application of the last clear chance doctrine, when such conduct does not otherwise excuse fault; therefore, plaintiff, whose decedent was guilty of contributory negligence as a matter of law in lying unconscious or asleep in the middle of interstate due to his voluntary intoxication, was not entitled to rely on the last clear chance doctrine as a basis for recovery against defendant truck driver. Pack v. Doe, 236 Va. 323, 374 S.E.2d 22 (1988).

C. Action by Personal Representative.

Administratrix may bring action under 42 U.S.C. § 1983. — A cause of action under 42 U.S.C. § 1983, alleging that actions by defendants which resulted in decedent's death violated the decedent's civil rights, survived decedent's death, such that a duly qualified administratrix was entitled to pursue the decedent's claims against defendants. O'Connor v. Several Unknown Correctional Officers, 523 F. Supp. 1345 (E.D. Va. 1981).

And damages are recoverable for deprivation of decedent's civil rights. — A decedent's claims under 42 U.S.C. § 1983, based on violations of his civil rights which caused his death, survive him, and his duly qualified administratrix may be awarded compensatory and punitive damages for the deprivation if she succeeds on the merits of the case, since allowing the administratrix to obtain compensation only for whatever loss was suffered by statutory beneficiaries under the Virginia wrongful death statute and excluding any punitive award would be inconsistent with the compensatory and deterrent policies behind 42 U.S.C. § 1983. O'Connor v. Several Unknown Correctional Officers, 523 F. Supp. 1345 (E.D. Va. 1981).

II. DECISIONS UNDER PRIOR LAW.

A. General Consideration.

Editor's note. — The cases cited below were decided under corresponding provisions of former law. The term "this section," as used below, refers to former provisions.

Legislative history. — At common law the right of action to recover damages for "wrongful death" was unknown. This situation existed in Virginia until January 14, 1871, when the original act giving such a right to a personal representative was enacted. The prototype of this act is the English statute known as "Lord Campbell's Act," which was passed in 1846. VEPCO v. Decatur, 173 Va. 153, 3 S.E.2d 172 (1939).

The wrongful death statutes were originally adopted by the General Assembly in 1871 and modeled after Lord Campbell's Act passed by the English Parliament in 1846. Lawrence v. Craven Tire Co., 210 Va. 138, 169 S.E.2d 440 (1969), commented on in 4 U. Rich. L. Rev. 322 (1970).

At common law no civil action was maintainable against a person for the wrongful death of another. Lawrence v. Craven Tire Co., 210 Va. 138, 169 S.E.2d 440 (1969), commented on in 4 U. Rich. L. Rev. 322 (1970).

Purpose of statute. — This section and § 8.01-55 intend to withdraw from the wrongdoer the immunity from civil liability which the rule of the common law afforded him, and to provide for the recovery of such damages notwithstanding the death of the injured person. In so doing, however, it was plainly not the intention to continue or cause to survive his right of action for the injury, but to substitute for it and confer upon his personal representative a new and original right of action. Anderson v. Hygeia Hotel Co., 92 Va. 687, 24 S.E. 269 (1896); Grady v. Irvine, 254 F.2d 224 (4th Cir.), cert. denied, 358 U.S. 819, 79 S. Ct. 30, 3 L. Ed. 2d 60 (1958); Wilson v. Whittaker, 207 Va. 1032, 154 S.E.2d 124 (1967).

The object of the statute was to give a right of action where none existed at common law, and to prevent an action from abating which would otherwise have abated, but not to allow two actions against the same defendant for the same injury. Brammer's Adm'r v. Norfolk & W. Ry., 107 Va. 206, 57 S.E. 593 (1907).

The primary object of this section and §§ 8.01-53 and 8.01-54 is to compensate the family of deceased and not to benefit his creditors. Withrow v. Edwards, 181 Va. 344, 25 S.E.2d 343, rev'd on other grounds, 181 Va. 592,

25 S.E.2d 899, cert. denied, 320 U.S. 761, 64 S. Ct. 70, 88 L. Ed. 453 (1943).

Rules of statutory construction are not applicable to this section and §§ 8.01-51 through 8.01-56 as they are so plain and free from doubt. Porter v. VEPCO, 183 Va. 108, 31 S.E.2d 337 (1944).

This section and §§ 8.01-51 through 8.01-56 have no extraterritorial effect. Withrow v. Edwards, 181 Va. 344, 25 S.E.2d 343, rev'd on other grounds, 181 Va. 592, 25 S.E.2d 899, cert. denied, 320 U.S. 761, 64 S. Ct. 70, 88 L. Ed. 453 (1943); Sherley v. Lotz, 200 Va. 173, 104 S.E.2d 795 (1958).

Recoveries under this article and § 8.01-25 distinguished. — The limit of recovery in an action under this article is different from that in the action preserved by § 8.01-25. In one, the amount of the recovery is limited by statute, is for the benefit of certain designated beneficiaries, and is free from debts and liabilities. In the other, the limit is the amount of damages that can be proved, is an asset of the decedent's estate, and is subject to the payment of his debts. Bagley v. Weaver, 211 Va. 779, 180 S.E.2d 686 (1971).

For Fourth Circuit case, arising under North Carolina law, holding that the citizenship of the beneficiaries, rather than that of the administrator, is controlling for diversity purposes, see Miller v. Perry, 456 F.2d 63 (4th Cir. 1972).

B. Right of Action.

1. In General.

Requirements for maintenance of wrongful death action. — Since the wrongful death act was adopted in Virginia nearly a century ago, it has required for maintenance of a wrongful death action (1) the death of a "person" caused by a wrongful act, neglect, or default, etc., and (2) that the act, neglect or default be "such as would, if death had not ensued, have entitled the party injured to maintain an action" for personal injuries. Lawrence v. Craven Tire Co., 210 Va. 138, 169 S.E.2d 440 (1969), commented on in 4 U. Rich. L. Rev. 322 (1970).

The right of action for damages for personal injuries, including punitive damages, if any, expires upon the death of the injured person. The death by wrongful act statute does not cause to survive this right of action, but it creates in the decedent's personal representative a new right of action to compensate decedent's statutory beneficiaries for their loss. Its purpose was not to punish the wrongdoer. Wilson v. Whittaker, 207 Va. 1032, 154 S.E.2d 124 (1967).

"Cause of action" and "right of action" distinguished. — The Supreme Court of Virginia construes its wrongful death statute as creating no new "cause of action" but a "right of action" where no right before existed. The "cause of action" is said to be complete and accrued the moment the tort is committed, but the "right of action" for wrongful death does not arise during the continued life of the injured person, nor does the injured person's "right of action" for personal injury survive his death, if death results from the injury. Grady v. Irvine, 254 F.2d 224 (4th Cir.), cert. denied, 358 U.S. 819, 79 S. Ct. 30, 3 L. Ed. 2d 60 (1958).

Cause of action the same regardless of nature of right. — Whether the right of action given the personal representative be regarded as a survival of the right of action of his decedent, as a revival of the right, as a substituted right, or as a new right, the cause of action is the same, that is, the wrongful injury to the decedent, the wrong which entitled him to maintain an action, if death had not ensued. Payne v. Piedmont Aviation, Inc., 294 F. Supp. 216 (E.D. Va. 1968).

But the right of action is dependent upon right of deceased. — Under the statute the cause of action of the injured party, while alive, is the same cause of action that passes to the personal representative, and the right of the personal representative to recover for the death of his decedent stands upon no higher ground than that occupied by the injured party while living. The statute authorizes an action for wrongful death upon the condition that the facts are such that the deceased might have maintained the action had he lived, for the injury resulting from the same act or omission. VEPCO v. Decatur, 173 Va. 153, 3 S.E.2d 172 (1939).

And the right of action must exist at decedent's death. — Where a statute in effect gives a remedy to recover damages where the death of a person is caused by the negligent or wrongful act of another, such remedy depends upon the existence in the decedent, at the time of death, of a right of action to recover damages for such injury. Payne v. Piedmont Aviation, Inc., 294 F. Supp. 216 (E.D. Va. 1968).

Where the action for death is under a survival statute or is dependent on the existence of a cause of action in favor of decedent at the time of his death, the action is barred if at the time of death the applicable statute had run against decedent's right of action. Payne v. Piedmont Aviation, Inc., 294 F. Supp. 216 (E.D. Va. 1968).

If the right of action of the injured person has expired at the date of his death, there is no right of action left which the personal representative can exercise. Payne v. Piedmont Aviation, Inc., 294 F. Supp. 216 (E.D. Va. 1968).

Section continues, transmits or substitutes right of action of deceased. — While this section, strictly speaking, may not create a new cause of action, it continues, transmits or substitutes the right, with certain limitations stated in the cognate statutes, to bring the action which decedent had at the time of his death. Sherley v. Lotz, 200 Va. 173, 104 S.E.2d 795 (1958); Lawrence v. Craven Tire Co., 210 Va. 138, 169 S.E.2d 440 (1969), commented on in 4 U. Rich. L. Rev. 322 (1970).

This section creates no new cause of action, but simply continues, transmits, or substitutes the right to sue which the decedent had until his death, the effect of which is to permit the personal representative to pick up the abated right of the deceased and prosecute it for the benefit of decedent's beneficiary. Payne v. Piedmont Aviation, Inc., 294 F. Supp. 216 (E.D. Va. 1968).

Only one recovery can be had. — Whether an action be brought by the injured party in his lifetime and revived after his death, or a new action be brought by the personal representative within the statutory period, as provided in the statute, only one recovery can be had, and that for the benefit of the next of kin named in the statute, where any such exists. Brammer's Adm'r v. Norfolk & W. Ry., 107 Va. 206, 57 S.E. 593 (1907).

This is true when action brought by decedent is revived. — If an action brought by the injured party in his lifetime be revived in the name of his personal representative after his death, and proceed to final judgment, it is a bar to any other action to recover damages for the same injury. Brammer's Adm'r v. Norfolk & W. Ry., 107 Va. 206, 57 S.E. 593 (1907).

Section has no effect on rule as to loss of minor's services. — The common-law right of a personal representative or parent to recover for losses between the time of injury and the resulting death of a minor, including medical expenses and losses occasioned by his inability to attend to business during that time, is not affected by this section. Stevenson v. Ritter Lumber Co., 108 Va. 575, 62 S.E. 351 (1908).

Action does not abate upon death of class beneficiaries. — Under the wrongful death statute the cause of action is conferred upon decedent's personal representative and does not abate upon the death of class beneficiaries. Johns v. Blue Ridge Transf. Co., 199 Va. 63, 97 S.E.2d 723 (1957).

Infancy of beneficiary of action does not toll limitation period. — The statute of limitations for wrongful death actions was not tolled by reason of infancy of the beneficiary of the wrongful death action, since the infant's disability could not prevent the timely institution of the action in view of the fact that wrongful death actions may be brought only by and in the name of the personal representative of the deceased. Beverage v. Harvey, 602 F.2d 657 (4th Cir. 1979).

Judgment binding in subsequent action in federal court. — A final judgment for defendant in a state wrongful death action is binding on the beneficiaries as to their individual claims for personal injuries asserted in a subsequent action against the same defendant in a federal court. Taylor v. Anderson, 303 F.2d 546 (4th Cir. 1962).

2. Conflict of Laws.

Law of state where injury occurred governs rights under section. — All matters pertaining to the substantive right of recovery under this section, including the right to recover, the nature of the right, and the party in whom it is vested, are governed by the law of the state where the injury resulting in death occurred. Betts v. Southern Ry., 71 F.2d 787 (4th Cir. 1934).

Where an injury has been inflicted in a sister state the laws of that state govern as to the extent of the remedy. Dowell v. Cox, 108 Va. 460, 62 S.E. 272 (1908).

Where the accident occurred in Maryland, any right of action for the resulting death arises out of the law of Maryland and not out of that of Virginia. Maryland ex rel. Joynes v. Coard, 175 Va. 571, 9 S.E.2d 454 (1940).

But the acceptance of compensation under the law of one state cannot affect the right to pursue a remedy against a third person under the wrongful death statute of another, unless there is something in the law of the latter which so provides. Betts v. Southern Ry., 71 F.2d 787 (4th Cir. 1934).

3. Who May Sue; Defenses.

Negligent plaintiff cannot recover if he would benefit. — Plaintiff could not recover in an action under this section for the negligent killing of his infant son, if he proximately contributed to the accident and would benefit from a recovery. Ratcliffe v. McDonald's Adm'r, 123 Va. 781, 97 S.E. 307 (1918). See; Richmond, F. & P.R.R. v. Martin, 102 Va. 201, 45 S.E. 894 (1903).

But contributory negligence of one party does not bar whole recovery. City of Danville v. Howard, 156 Va. 32, 157 S.E. 733 (1931).

A child en ventre sa mere cannot maintain a common-law action for personal injuries. Lawrence v. Craven Tire Co., 210 Va. 138, 169 S.E.2d 440 (1969), commented on in 4 U. Rich. L. Rev. 322 (1970).

No action for death of stillborn child. — The Virginia wrongful death statute as written does not provide an action for the wrongful death of a stillborn child. Lawrence v. Craven Tire Co., 210 Va. 138, 169 S.E.2d 440 (1969), commented on in 4 U. Rich. L. Rev. 322 (1970).

Interspousal immunity lost at death. — Reason for interspousal immunity is to foster a harmonious and conjugal relationship. Obviously, the reason for the rule is lost upon the death of one of the parties for there is no longer a marriage to be saved or a union to be preserved. Korman v. Carpenter, 216 Va. 86, 216 S.E.2d 195 (1975), commented on in 4 U. Rich. L. Rev. 322 (1976).

Action against surviving spouse. — An action for wrongful death may be maintained, predicated upon injuries to one spouse during marriage arising out of a wrongful act by the other spouse, when such an act results in the termination of the marriage by death, and when the deceased spouse is survived by no living child or grandchild. Korman v. Carpenter, 216 Va. 86, 216 S.E.2d 195 (1975), commented on in 4 U. Rich. L. Rev. 322 (1976).

This section affords a deceased wife's personal representative no right of action unless the right existed immediately before her death. Surratt v. Thompson, 212 Va. 191, 183 S.E.2d 200 (1971).

Resident alien friends are entitled to the benefits and remedies afforded by this section. Hence, a resident alien widow, residing in another state, may maintain on behalf of herself and children an action for the wrongful death of her husband. Pocahontas Collieries Co. v. Rukas, 104 Va. 278, 51 S.E. 449 (1905).

The action for death by the wrongful act or neglect of another given by this section may be maintained for the benefit of alien relatives resident in a foreign country, although they are not expressly named in the statute. Lowmoor Iron Co. v. La Bianca, 106 Va. 83, 55 S.E. 532 (1906).

Consent which would bar recovery by decedent bars recovery under this section. — If the consent of decedent to the commission of an immoral or illegal act would have been a bar to decedent's right to recover had she survived, such consent bars recovery in an action by her administrator for her wrongful death under the provisions of this section. Miller v. Bennett, 190 Va. 162, 56 S.E.2d 217 (1949).

Consent of decedent to illegal abortion. — Consent of a mature married woman to an attempt to produce an illegal abortion, resulting in death, bars recovery under this section in an action by her administrator against the party attempting to procure the abortion. Miller v. Bennett, 190 Va. 162, 56 S.E.2d 217 (1949).

Spouse who deserted decedent and lived in adultery is not barred. — There is no provision in our statutes barring the right of a spouse who has deserted the decedent and lived in adultery from sharing in a recovery for wrongful death; therefore he or she is not so barred. Matthews v. Hicks, 197 Va. 112, 87 S.E.2d 629 (1955).

4. Who May Be Sued.

Committee of convict can be sued. — A right of action, conferred by this section, may be brought against the committee of a convict. Merchant's Adm'r v. Shry, 116 Va. 437, 82 S.E. 106 (1914).

5. Evidence.

Measure of damages. — In an action for death by wrongful act, the measure of damages is the pecuniary loss, if any, sustained by the beneficiaries; compensation for their loss of the decedent's care, attention and society, and for their solace and comfort for the sorrow and suffering occasioned by the death of a decedent. Evidence regarding the magnitude and seriousness of the injuries of a decedent, the extent of the mutilation of his body, and other circumstances likely to inflame or prejudice a jury, or invite its sympathy, should not be admitted. Where, as in this case, evidence of this type is admissible here for the reason that it has relevancy in establishing the identity of the driver, in the accident resulting in death, it should be restricted to a showing that the decedent's injuries were such as could have resulted in the deposit of hair, blood and flesh found in the vehicle and testified to by witnesses. Breeding v. Johnson, 208 Va. 652, 159 S.E.2d 836 (1968).

Evidence as to widow and children of deceased. — In an action under the statute by the administrator of a party killed upon a railroad track against the company, the plaintiff may upon the trial, and before the jury has rendered a verdict, introduce evidence to prove that the deceased left a widow and children, and the number and ages of the children. B & O R.R. v. Sherman's Adm'r, 71 Va. (30 Gratt.) 602 (1878).

Evidence of the physical condition of one or more of the beneficiaries is immaterial to the question of liability or the quantum of the damages. Crawford v. Hite, 176 Va. 69, 10 S.E.2d 561 (1940).

Evidence that deceased was heavy drinker and that family relations were troubled. — Evidence having been placed before the jury by counsel for the administratrix tending to show deceased to have been a man of sober habits and a devoted and hardworking father, it was error to refuse cross-examination to show he was a heavy drinker and that the family relations were troubled. Basham v. Terry, 199 Va. 817, 102 S.E.2d 285 (1958), commented on in 4 U. Rich. L. Rev. 322 (1959).

Warrants sworn out against deceased by wife and daughter. — Copies of warrants of arrest sworn out against decedent by his wife and daughter four and five years before his death would have been admissible in mitigation of damages allowable for loss of "care, attention and society" by reason of his death. Such evidence would not have been too remote if so offered in proper form. But the offer of testimony as to the warrants was properly excluded, this not being the best evidence. Basham v. Terry, 199 Va. 817, 102 S.E.2d 285 (1958), commented on in 4 U. Rich. L. Rev. 322 (1959).

Moral delinquencies. — Evidence offered by the defendants of young girl's moral delinquencies held not relevant on the amount of damages which the jury might award to her parents and other members of her family for the loss of her society and for the sorrow, suffering and mental anguish occasioned to them by her death. Gamble v. Hill, 208 Va. 171, 156 S.E.2d 888 (1967).

C. Actions Against Ships.

Right enforced in jurisdiction where injury occurred. — The lien created by this section, which provides that a ship or vessel, which would have been liable if death had not ensued, shall be liable to an action for damages or to a libel in rem, may be enforced by a suit in rem in a court of admiralty, where the injury occurred at a place within the maritime jurisdiction. The Anglo-Patagonian, 235 F. 92 (4th Cir.), cert. denied, 242 U.S. 636, 37 S. Ct. 19, 61 L. Ed. 539 (1916).

Fact that pilot is in charge does not absolve ship for liability. — At the time of the collision for which she was in fault, the fact that a ship was in charge of a compulsory pilot does not absolve her from liability for the death of persons caused by the collision under this section. Indra Line, Ltd. v. Palmetto Phosphate Co., 239 F. 94 (4th Cir. 1916).

The remedy in rem is in the nature of an admiralty lien and can be enforced in a federal court which has admiralty jurisdiction, and only in a federal court. Continental Cas. Co. v. The Benny Skou, 200 F.2d 246 (4th Cir. 1952), cert. denied, 345 U.S. 992, 73 S. Ct. 1129, 97 L. Ed. 1400 (1953).

The Virginia statute creates a lien on the ship in a case of wrongful death. Lewis v. Jones, 27 F.2d 72 (4th Cir.), cert. denied, 278 U.S. 634, 49 S. Ct. 32, 73 L. Ed. 551 (1928).

This section authorizes recovery for the death of a longshoreman under the substantive principles of the maritime law. Rederi A/B Dalen v. Maher, 303 F.2d 565 (4th Cir. 1962).

Lien can be enforced in federal courts. — This section, giving a right of suit in rem against a vessel wrongfully or negligently causing the death of any person, creates a lien, and may be enforced by a libel in rem in the federal courts, when the accident occurs in their maritime jurisdiction. The Glendale v. Evich, 81 F. 633 (4th Cir. 1897).

Once the conclusion is reached that a state statute gives a lien on the ship for wrongful death, such a lien can unquestionably be enforced in a suit in admiralty. Lewis v. Jones, 27 F.2d 72 (4th Cir.), cert. denied, 278 U.S. 634, 49 S. Ct. 32, 73 L. Ed. 551 (1928).

In this section Virginia has bestowed upon admiralty a right to grant a recovery not previously possessed by admiralty. The endowment must be taken cum onere. Rights and liabilities under this section must be the same on the water as on the land. Continental Cas. Co. v. The Benny Skou, 101 F. Supp. 15 (E.D. Va. 1951), aff'd, 200 F.2d 246 (4th Cir. 1952), cert. denied, 345 U.S. 992, 73 S. Ct. 1129, 97 L. Ed. 1400 (1953).

Contributory negligence is not absolute defense. — Contributory negligence is not an absolute bar to a right of recovery in an action against ships under this section. Holley v. The S.S. Manfred Stansfield, 269 F.2d 317 (4th Cir.), cert. denied, 361 U.S. 883, 80 S. Ct. 154, 4 L. Ed. 2d 119 (1959), commented on in 45 Va. L. Rev. 1222 (1959).

And maritime rule of comparative negligence will be applied. — A federal court sitting in admiralty in an action against a vessel and its owners for death of employee of a stevedore will apply the rule that contributory negligence mitigates damages. Holley v. The S.S. Manfred Stansfield, 269 F.2d 317 (4th Cir.), cert. denied, 361 U.S. 883, 80 S. Ct. 154, 4 L. Ed. 2d 119 (1959), commented on in 45 Va. L. Rev. 1222 (1959).

The maritime rule of comparative negligence where the injury resulting in death occurs on navigable waters of the State is unmistakably indicated in the language of this section. Holley v. The S.S. Manfred Stansfield, 269 F.2d 317 (4th Cir.), cert. denied, 361 U.S. 883, 80 S. Ct. 154, 4 L. Ed. 2d 119 (1959), commented on in 45 Va. L. Rev. 1222 (1959).

Recovery may not be used to reimburse employer or compensation carrier. — The provisions of the Longshoremen's and Harbor Workers' Compensation Act, 33 U.S.C.A., § 901 et seq., do not amend the wrongful death statute of Virginia to the extent that the share of a beneficiary under the death statute may be used to reimburse the employer or compensation carrier for death benefits paid to a beneficiary under the Longshoremen's and Harbor Workers' Compensation Act who is not a recipient beneficiary under the death statute. Holley v. The Manfred Stansfield, 186 F. Supp. 805 (E.D. Va. 1960).

Jones Act and Death on the High Seas Act. — A state wrongful death statute would not be applicable to a situation where the right to maintain an action has been expressly granted under the Jones Act and the Death on the High Seas Act. McPherson v. Steamship S. African Pioneer, 321 F. Supp. 42 (E.D. Va. 1971).

D. Action by Personal Representative.

The personal representative is the only party that can maintain an action under this section. Goff v. Norfolk & W.R.R., 36 F. 299 (W.D. Va. 1888).

The administrator sues, not for the benefit of the estate, but primarily and substantially as trustee for certain particular kindred of the deceased. Patterson v. Anderson, 194 Va. 557, 74 S.E.2d 195, cert. denied, 345 U.S. 965, 73 S. Ct. 952, 97 L. Ed. 1384 (1953).

The personal representative of the deceased sues primarily as trustee for certain statutory beneficiaries and not for the general benefit of the decedent's estate. Conrad v. Thompson, 195 Va. 714, 80 S.E.2d 561 (1954); Wilson v. Whittaker, 207 Va. 1032, 154 S.E.2d 124 (1967).

Foreign personal representative cannot maintain action in Virginia. — Since the 1950 amendment of § 26-59 a personal representative, who is not a resident of Virginia and who has not qualified or been appointed as such in the State, cannot maintain an action in a United States district court sitting in Virginia, under the Virginia Statute of Death by Wrongful Act. Holt v. Middlebrook, 214 F.2d 187 (4th Cir. 1954).

Virginia requires that the personal representative who prosecutes an action under its wrongful death act must be a resident of that State. This requirement has been held to be binding in the federal courts. Grady v. Irvine, 254 F.2d 224 (4th Cir.), cert. denied, 358 U.S. 819, 79 S. Ct. 30, 3 L. Ed. 2d 60 (1958).

This section and § 26-59 prohibit an Ohio administrator from instituting an action for wrongful death in Virginia. Goranson v. Capital Airlines, 221 F. Supp. 820 (E.D. Va. 1963), cert. denied, 382 U.S. 984, 86 S. Ct. 560, 15 L. Ed. 2d 473 (1966).

Thus action against citizen of Virginia may be maintained only in state courts. — At present an action for wrongful death against a citizen of Virginia may be maintained only in the state courts, and this situation will continue unless the General Assembly of Virginia should choose to modify the effect of the 1950 amendment to § 26-59. Rodgers v. Irvine, 161 F. Supp. 784 (W.D. Va. 1957), aff'd sub nom. Grady v. Irvine, 254 F.2d 224 (4th Cir.), cert. denied, 358 U.S. 819, 79 S. Ct. 30, 3 L. Ed. 2d 60 (1958).

But out-of-state administrator can maintain action in another state. — See Kaufmann v. Service Trucking Co., 139 F. Supp. 1 (D. Md. 1956), holding that a domiciliary administrator appointed in Illinois could maintain an action in Maryland under the Virginia statute without qualifying in Virginia.

If administrator and defendant of different states sufficient for federal jurisdiction. — Where the administrator and defendant are citizens of different states, the action may be brought in the federal courts, though the deceased was a citizen of the same state with defendant, where his widow and children still reside. In such action the real beneficiaries need not be named in the declaration. Harper v. Norfolk & W.R.R., 36 F. 102 (W.D. Va. 1887).

The fact that a citizen of another state is selected as administrator for the purpose of conferring on the United States circuit court jurisdiction of an action to be brought by him, does not defeat that jurisdiction. Goff v. Norfolk & W.R.R., 36 F. 299 (W.D. Va. 1888).

§ 8.01-51. No action when deceased has compromised claim.

— No action shall be maintained by the personal representative of one who, after injury, has compromised for such injury and accepted satisfaction therefor previous to his death. (Code 1950, § 8-635; 1977, c. 617.)

I. DECISIONS UNDER PRIOR LAW.

Editor's note. — The case cited below was decided under corresponding provisions of former law. The term "this section," as used below, refers to former provisions.

Compromise bars action. — If a man, having suffered a personal injury, compromises for such injury and accepts full satisfaction therefor, and afterwards dies from the effects of the injury, a question arises as to the right of his personal representative to maintain an action for death by wrongful act, neglect, or default. This section settles the question by providing that such action cannot be maintained. This is the weight of authority and is supported by the better reasoning. Brammer's Adm'r v. Norfolk & W. Ry., 107 Va. 206, 57 S.E. 593 (1907).

§ 8.01-52. Amount of damages.

— The jury or the court, as the case may be, in any such action under § 8.01-50 may award such damages as to it may seem fair and just. The verdict or judgment of the court trying the case without a jury shall include, but may not be limited to, damages for the following:

1. Sorrow, mental anguish, and solace which may include society, companionship, comfort, guidance, kindly offices and advice of the decedent;

2. Compensation for reasonably expected loss of (i) income of the decedent and (ii) services, protection, care and assistance provided by the decedent;

3. Expenses for the care, treatment and hospitalization of the decedent incident to the injury resulting in death;

4. Reasonable funeral expenses; and

5. Punitive damages may be recovered for willful or wanton conduct, or such recklessness as evinces a conscious disregard for the safety of others.

Damages recoverable under 3, 4 and 5 above shall be specifically stated by the jury or the court, as the case may be. Damages recoverable under 3 and 4 above shall be apportioned among the creditors who rendered such services, as their respective interests may appear. Competent expert testimony shall be admissible in proving damages recoverable under 2 above.

The court shall apportion the costs of the action as it shall deem proper. (Code 1950, § 8-636.1; 1974, c. 444; 1977, cc. 460, 617; 1982, c. 441.)

REVISERS' NOTE

Former §§ 8-636.1 and 8-638 contain, inter alia, duplicate provisions as to beneficiaries, fail to denote when these beneficiaries are to be determined, and are unclear as to the specification of the damages. Sections 8.01-52, 8.01-53, and 8.01-54 amend and reorder the provisions of the former sections to present them more logically and to clarify the procedures.

Section 8.01-52 adopts former § 8-636.1 with several changes. The section expressly recognizes that the amount of damages may be awarded by the jury or by the court if the case is tried without a jury, and damages for medical and funeral expenses are required to be specifically stated. Provisions in former § 8-636.1 defining the class and beneficiaries have been deleted and incorporated into § 8.01-53. A provision has been added providing that competent expert testimony is admissible regarding the proof of damages for loss of income, services, etc. of the decedent.

Editor's note. — Pursuant to § 9-77.11 and Acts 1977, c. 617, cl. 4, the Code Commission has given effect, in § 8.01-52 as set out above, to the amendment to former § 8-636.1, corresponding to this section, in Acts 1977, c. 460. The amendment added the second sentence of the next-to-last paragraph.

Law Review. — For discussion of punitive damages and their possible application in automobile accident litigation, see 46 Va. L. Rev. 1036 (1960). For case note on the measure of damages for wrongful death of a minor child, see 18 Wash. & Lee L. Rev. 277 (1961). For note, "Wrongful Death Damages in Virginia," see 12 Wm. & Mary L. Rev. 396 (1970). For article on damages recoverable for wrongful death, see 5 U. Rich. L. Rev. 213 (1971). For survey of Virginia law on domestic relations for the year 1970-1971, see 57 Va. L. Rev. 1487 (1971). For survey of Virginia law on torts for the year 1971-1972, see 58 Va. L. Rev. 1349 (1972). For survey of Virginia law on torts for the year 1973-1974, see 60 Va. L. Rev. 1615 (1974). For survey of Virginia law on evidence for the year 1976-77, see 63 Va. L. Rev. 1428 (1977). For an overview of Virginia Supreme Court decisions on domestic relations, see 15 U. Rich. L. Rev. 321 (1981).

I. Decisions Under Current Law.
  A. General Consideration.
  B. Reasonably Expected Loss.
II. Decisions Under Prior Law.

I. DECISIONS UNDER CURRENT LAW.

A. General Consideration.

Construction of "fair" and "just". — As used in this section, the terms "fair" and "just" are to be given broad and liberal construction. Sawyer v. United States, 465 F. Supp. 282 (E.D. Va. 1978); Miltier v. Beorn, 696 F. Supp. 1086 (E.D. Va. 1988).

Purpose of damages specified. — The damages specified in this section as recoverable are designed to compensate the beneficiaries for the losses they suffer as a result of the decedent's death, and not to accumulate an estate for the decedent. O'Connor v. Several Unknown Correctional Officers, 523 F. Supp. 1345 (E.D. Va. 1981).

The only limit imposed on the amount of

wrongful death damages is what may seem fair and just. Miltier v. Beorn, 696 F. Supp. 1086 (E.D. Va. 1988).

Section 8.01-25 defers to the wrongful death statute as the exclusive statement of the grievances that Virginia will recognize when a tort victim dies of her injuries. El-Meswari v. Washington Gas Light Co., 785 F.2d 483 (4th Cir. 1986).

Punitive damages provision not retroactive. — Allowing punitive damages in a wrongful death action constitutes a major change in both the effect and purpose of the Virginia Death by Wrongful Act statute. To retroactively apply such a significant change in the law without an explicit legislative directive would be to ignore an established rule of statutory construction as well as tampering with parties' vested rights and incurred obligations as they existed under the then existing law. Accordingly, the 1982 amendment to this section will not be given retroactive effect. Estate of Armentrout v. International Harvester Co., 547 F. Supp. 136 (W.D. Va. 1982).

Notwithstanding remedial aspects of such provision. — While a statute which alters procedures or supplies remedies for enforcing an existing right may be given retrospective effect, there must still be some indication that the legislature enacting the statutory change intends it be given such operation. The 1982 General Assembly has not indicated that it intended the amendment to operate retrospectively. Therefore, even if the amendment is considered remedial, the court will not apply it in cases arising prior to its effective date. Estate of Armentrout v. International Harvester Co., 547 F. Supp. 136 (W.D. Va. 1982).

1974 amendment did not allow punitive damages. — The 1974 amendment to former § 8-636.1 could only be interpreted to indicate the legislature's intent that the enumerated elements listed as recoverable damages were not meant to exclude other factors a jury could consider in arriving at compensation for the beneficiary's loss. It did not allow punitive damages. Estate of Armentrout v. International Harvester Co., 547 F. Supp. 136 (W.D. Va. 1982).

Dependency not prerequisite. — The damage provision of this statute requires proof of loss by the statutory beneficiary or beneficiaries. Dependency is not a prerequisite. Marshall v. Goughnour, 221 Va. 265, 269 S.E.2d 801 (1980).

Beneficiary under the Virginia Wrongful Death Act need not be a dependent, nor a minor child. Wilson v. United States, 637 F. Supp. 669 (E.D. Va. 1986).

Award not intended to be replacement for loss sustained. — Under the broad language of this section, "any 'pecuniary loss' suffered by the statutory beneficiaries is clearly a proper element of damage," but loss of comfort, guidance and society, like sorrow, mental anguish and solace, are virtually incalculable except in a rough and gross manner. Money is no substitute, and under the statute the amount which may be awarded is what "may seem fair and just." Such an award is not suggested or intended to be replacement of the loss sustained. It is the means provided by which the damaging party may make some amends for the wrong done. Sawyer v. United States, 465 F. Supp. 282 (E.D. Va. 1978).

Damages determined from facts and circumstances. — Damages in a death case where the measure is what is fair and just, as in personal injury actions, are to be determined from all of the facts and circumstances. Sawyer v. United States, 465 F. Supp. 282 (E.D. Va. 1978).

Determination of damages for loss of society. — Damages for loss of society can be left to turn mainly upon the good sense and deliberate judgment of the trier, as insistence on mathematical precision would be illusory, and the judge or jury must be allowed to make a reasonable approximation, guided by judgment and practical experience. It is enough if the evidence shows the extent of damages as a matter of a just and reasonable inference, although the result be only an approximation. Sawyer v. United States, 465 F. Supp. 282 (E.D. Va. 1978).

Damages recoverable for deprivation of decedent's civil rights. — A decedent's claims under 42 U.S.C. § 1983, based on violations of his civil rights which caused his death, survive him, and his duly qualified administratrix may be awarded compensatory and punitive damages for the deprivation if she succeeds on the merits of the case, since allowing the administratrix to obtain compensation only for whatever loss was suffered by statutory beneficiaries under the Virginia wrongful death statute and excluding a punitive award would be inconsistent with the compensatory and deterrent policies behind 42 U.S.C. § 1983. O'Connor v. Several Unknown Correctional Officers, 523 F. Supp. 1345 (E.D. Va. 1981).

Speculative nature of decedents' income. — The evidence as to reasonably expected loss of decedent's income was inadmissible as a matter of law as being too speculative where decedent had a mental age of nine and was a functional illiterate who could only write his name and decedent's only employment noted in the record continued for only eight weeks, during which time he lost six or seven days. Cassady v. Martin, 220 Va. 1093, 266 S.E.2d 104 (1980).

No recovery by mother under this section for stillbirth. — Injury to an unborn child constitutes injury to the mother and she may recover for such physical injury and mental suffering associated with a stillbirth. She is not entitled, however, to damages ordinarily recoverable in a wrongful death action. For example, the mother may not recover for anticipated loss of the child's society, companionship, comfort, or guidance. She may not be compensated for an expected loss of income of the child or for services, protection, care, or assistance expected to be provided by the child had he lived. Modaber v. Kelley, 232 Va. 60, 348 S.E.2d 233 (1986).

Expert testimony of grief excluded. — In a wrongful death action, the district court's decision to exclude a doctor's expert testimony, concluding that the jury could assess the mother's inner grief without expert guidance, represented a reasonable exercise of the trial judge's broad discretion under Federal Rule of Evidence 702 to determine that a proposed expert will not significantly assist the arbiter of fact. El-Meswari v. Washington Gas Light Co., 785 F.2d 483 (4th Cir. 1986).

Indirect physical injuries as illustration of mental anguish. — Although indirect physical injuries allegedly suffered by the mother as a result of her child's death are not compensable in themselves, the court might nevertheless admit the mother's proffered information to illustrate her claim of direct mental anguish. El-Meswari v. Washington Gas Light Co., 785 F.2d 483 (4th Cir. 1986).

Subdivision 1 does not authorize recovery for injury to the decedent's mother's heart or her miscarriage. The legislation addresses the decedent's death as an independent event in the mother's life and attempts to compensate the mother for the disruption of that single relationship. It claims no competence to trace or to relieve the indirect, although no doubt powerful, influence of the decedent's death as it touches all of her mother's future life. El-Meswari v. Washington Gas Light Co., 785 F.2d 483 (4th Cir. 1986).

Foreign burial. — The statutory guarantee of "reasonable funeral expenses" includes recovery for the foreign burial of a foreign citizen. El-Meswari v. Washington Gas Light Co., 785 F.2d 483 (4th Cir. 1986).

Admissibility of expectancy table in § 8.01-419. — The expectancy of continued life of the decedent is relevant and necessary to establish the extent of loss for the decedent's society, companionship, comfort, guidance, advice, services, protection, care, and assistance set out in this section. The expectancy table in § 8.01-419, therefore, is admissible if such items of loss are supported by the evidence. Graddy v. Hatchett, 233 Va. 65, 353 S.E.2d 741 (1987).

Loss of society, companionship, etc. — This section now permits recovery for the beneficiaries' loss of society, companionship, comfort, guidance, advice, services, protection, care, and assistance provided by the decedent. These statutory elements contemplate assignment of a dollar value to these losses and recovery therefor whether or not the beneficiaries can establish their dependency on the decedent. Graddy v. Hatchett, 233 Va. 65, 353 S.E.2d 741 (1987).

Special verdict relating to damages for solace, lost income, lost services, etc. — This section provides no authority for a special verdict relating to damages for solace, lost income, and lost services and protection. Johnson v. Smith, 241 Va. 396, 403 S.E.2d 685 (1991).

Error in refusal to set aside verdict where no award for sorrow, mental anguish, etc. — In a wrongful death action where the decedent's widow and children were awarded nothing for sorrow, mental anguish and solace, and the children were awarded nothing for lost services and protection, the award by the jury rendered the entire verdict suspect and lead to the conclusion that the jury must have misconceived or misunderstood the facts or the law; hence, the trial court erred in refusing to set aside the verdict. Johnson v. Smith, 241 Va. 396, 403 S.E.2d 685 (1991).

Evidence held to support recovery for society, companionship, comfort, guidance, advice, services, protection, care, and assistance of 17-year-old decedent who was survived by his parents, a younger brother, two older half-sisters, and two older half-brothers. Graddy v. Hatchett, 233 Va. 65, 353 S.E.2d 741 (1987).

Burden for proving punitive damages. — Virginia law views skeptically the utility of punitive damages as a deterrent to anything less than willful misconduct. The resulting interpretation of subdivision 5 places two burdens upon a plaintiff who seeks to prove that a defendant acted "with such recklessness as evinces a conscious disregard for the safety of others." First, the plaintiff must show that the defendant intended all of the acts or omissions that created an extraordinary risk and that the defendant appreciated or had sufficient information to recognize the magnitude of the risk. Second, the plaintiff must show that the defendant responsible for such a risk responded to it with purposeful carelessness, deliberate inattention to known danger, or any intended violation or disregard of the rights of others. Punitive damages are available under this standard only if the plaintiff satisfies both requirements. El-Meswari v. Washington Gas Light Co., 785 F.2d 483 (4th Cir. 1986).

Negligence not amounting to conscious disregard precluded punitive damages. — Virginia law precluded an award of punitive damages in a claim, arising from a fatal traffic accident, against a lessee of a stalled truck on a highway, whose actions and omissions, while negligent and unlawful, did not amount to a conscious disregard of the rights of others. Peacock v. J.C. Penney Co., 764 F.2d 1012 (4th Cir. 1985).

Applied in Hewitt v. Firestone Tire & Rubber Co., 490 F. Supp. 1358 (E.D. Va. 1980); Minnick v. United States, 767 F. Supp. 115 (E.D. Va. 1990).

B. Reasonably Expected Loss.

"Reasonably expected" loss of decedent's income in subdivision 2 means such loss as the beneficiaries have suffered, or may suffer. Wilson v. United States, 637 F. Supp. 669 (E.D. Va. 1986).

The words "reasonably expected" in subdivision 2 of this section must clearly refer to the beneficiaries; assuredly, a decedent cannot "reasonably" expect the loss of earnings after she has passed away. Wilson v. United States, 637 F. Supp. 669 (E.D. Va. 1986).

Subdivision 2 makes no distinction between income lost prior to death and that which decedent would have probably earned over a normal work-life expectancy period. Wilson v. United States, 637 F. Supp. 669 (E.D. Va. 1986).

Decedent's son, who had dropped out of college and left the family home, showed no evidence of reasonable expectancy of pecuniary loss occasioned by his mother's death. Wilson v. United States, 637 F. Supp. 669 (E.D. Va. 1986).

Loss of daughter's earning capacity due to illness of parents and grandmother. — Where decedent was living when the daughter graduated from college in December, 1983, and the evidence showed that all expenses for the daughter's education had been paid by the parents, the loss due to defendants' negligence to the daughter between February, 1983, when she dropped out of college, until the mother's death in January, 1985, was essentially a loss of the daughter's earning capacity due to the fact that she could have secured employment but for the illness of her mother, father and grandmother. Adopting the "fair and just" rule as being entitled to a broad and liberal construction, the court would fix this figure at $5,000 confined to the mother's illness and the daughter's reasonable expectancy that, had her mother been in reasonably good health, the mother would have cared for her father and grandmother. Wilson v. United States, 637 F. Supp. 669 (E.D. Va. 1986).

Plans of recent graduate. — In a wrongful death suit, evidence of declarations made by the deceased, an 18-year-old high school graduate, which indicated that he planned to become an architect and thereafter to send his younger, fatherless brother to medical school and to provide his widowed mother a new home, was rejected on the ground that it was too speculative. Howell v. Cahoon, 236 Va. 3, 372 S.E.2d 363 (1988).

II. DECISIONS UNDER PRIOR LAW.

Editor's note. — The cases cited below were decided under corresponding provisions of former law. The term "this section," as used below, refers to former provisions.

The Supreme Court has given the phrase "fair and just" a broad and liberal construction. This section contains no words of limitation confining the jury to merely pecuniary damages. Matthews v. Hicks, 197 Va. 112, 87 S.E.2d 629 (1955); Gough v. Shaner, 197 Va. 572, 90 S.E.2d 171 (1955).

The phrase "fair and just" in this section, relating to the amount and distribution of damages in a case of an award for wrongful death, should be given a broad and liberal construction. Eisenhower v. Jeter, 205 Va. 159, 135 S.E.2d 786 (1964).

What losses to be considered. — Among the losses to be considered under this section are the loss of services, nurture and care, and other advantages and benefits of a pecuniary nature which probably will be lost in the future. Vandergrift v. United States, 500 F. Supp. 229 (E.D. Va. 1978).

Damages which to the jury "may seem fair and just" are the damages suffered by the statutory beneficiaries. Wilson v. Whittaker, 207 Va. 1032, 154 S.E.2d 124 (1967).

Damages are not confined to pecuniary loss. — In an action the jury, in assessing the damages, are not confined to the mere pecuniary loss and injury, but may give such damages as to them "may seem fair and just." Matthews v. Warner, 70 Va. (29 Gratt.) 570 (1877); Ratcliffe v. McDonald's Adm'r, 123 Va. 781, 97 S.E. 307 (1918); Matthews v. Hicks, 197 Va. 112, 87 S.E.2d 629 (1955).

Under this section, the measure of damages in case of a man's death is not limited to the pecuniary value of his life to his estate, but may be exemplary, punitive, and given as a solatium. Harris v. Royer, 165 Va. 461, 182 S.E. 276 (1935).

In an action under this section, the evidence would primarily relate to and the damages be not only for the pecuniary loss the wife, husband, parent, or child has sustained, but it would be proper for the jury, in computing damages, to take also into consideration the grief and mental anguish of such relatives, and their loss in being deprived of the care, attention, and society of deceased, and to include in the verdict such sum as the jury deem fair and just. Anderson v. Hygeia Hotel Co., 92 Va. 687, 24 S.E. 269 (1896).

But it is a proper element. — This section allows the jury to award within the statutory limit such damages "as to it may seem fair and just." Under this broad and permissive language, any "pecuniary loss" suffered by the statutory beneficiaries is clearly a proper element of damage. Gough v. Shaner, 197 Va. 572, 90 S.E.2d 171 (1955).

No pecuniary loss necessary. — It is not necessary that a child have earned money or have a present earning capacity for his statutory beneficiaries to suffer pecuniary loss because of his death. Gough v. Shaner, 197 Va. 572, 90 S.E.2d 171 (1955).

Recovery of pecuniary loss. — Any pecuniary loss suffered by the statutory beneficiaries is clearly a proper element of damage. See Vandergrift v. United States, 500 F. Supp. 229 (E.D. Va. 1978).

Recovery for mental anguish of beneficiaries, but not of decedent. — In this action given by the statute, the plaintiff cannot recover for the physical pain and mental anguish of the decedent. The mental anguish of the beneficiaries may be increased by the mental and physical suffering of the decedent and they may recover damages therefor, but it is their mental anguish and not the physical pain and mental anguish of the decedent for which recovery is allowed. Virginia Iron, Coal & Coke Co. v. Odle's Adm'r, 128 Va. 280, 105 S.E. 107 (1920).

Evidence of the pecuniary condition of the deceased and the members of his family is inadmissible for the purpose of proving the liability of the defendant or the quantum of the damages because this section gives a right of recovery regardless of whether the deceased or the members of his family are rich or poor. Crawford v. Hite, 176 Va. 69, 10 S.E.2d 561 (1940); Matthews v. Hicks, 197 Va. 112, 87 S.E.2d 629 (1955).

Absent evidence of contribution or the monetary value of services rendered a dependent, there can be no award for loss of services. Vandergrift v. United States, 500 F. Supp. 229 (E.D. Va. 1978).

The amount of recovery is left entirely to the discretion of the jury. Ratcliffe v. McDonald's Adm'r, 123 Va. 781, 97 S.E. 307 (1918); Harris v. Royer, 165 Va. 461, 182 S.E. 276 (1935); Chick Transit Corp. v. Edenton, 170 Va. 361, 196 S.E. 648 (1938).

The amount of damages is solely within the discretion of the jury and may not be set aside as inadequate or excessive, unless it is clearly shown that the verdict was a result of passion, prejudice, or corruption. Matthews v. Hicks, 197 Va. 112, 87 S.E.2d 629 (1955).

Where evidence showed that when decedent was killed, he was a normal, well developed, thirteen year old school boy, enjoying good health and of average intelligence, those proved facts were sufficient to justify an instruction allowing the jury to find that "pecuniary loss" was suffered by his statutory beneficiaries. In doing so the jurors had the right on that evidence to form their own conclusion as to what was decedent's probable life expectancy and consider what they, in their sound judgment, thought would be his probable earnings in the future. Gough v. Shaner, 197 Va. 572, 90 S.E.2d 171 (1955).

Measure of damages. — Damages may be for loss of deceased's care, attention and society, as well as such sum as the jury may deem fair and just as a solatium to the beneficiaries for their sorrow and mental anguish caused by the death. Wilson v. Whittaker, 207 Va. 1032, 154 S.E.2d 124 (1967).

Facts and circumstances are to be considered. — Fixing damages in a death case where the measure is what is fair and just is to be determined from all of the facts and circumstances. Vandergrift v. United States, 500 F. Supp. 229 (E.D. Va. 1978).

Determination of damages for loss of society. — Damages for loss of society can be left to turn mainly upon the good sense and deliberate judgment of the trier, as insistence on mathematical precision would be illusory, and the judge or jury must be allowed to make a reasonable approximation, guided by judgment and practical experience. It is enough if the evidence shows the extent of damages as a matter of a just and reasonable inference, although the result be only an approximation. Vandergrift v. United States, 500 F. Supp. 229 (E.D. Va. 1978).

Award not reduced by amounts otherwise paid. — The theory that the award under this section, being for the full amount of damages, should be reduced by any amounts otherwise paid by the government to the injured parties, simply has no application in Virginia when the damages are found to exceed the former statutory maximum awardable. Harris v. United States, 218 F. Supp. 785 (E.D. Va. 1963).

It is not necessary to prove life expectancy of decedent by mortality tables. — In an action for wrongful death in this jurisdiction, it is not essential to prove the expectation of the life of the decedent by mortality tables. Eisenhower v. Jeter, 205 Va. 159, 135 S.E.2d 786 (1964).

Daughter's work-life earning capacity. — Only in compelling circumstances is it likely that earnings of a daughter may be expected to be applied substantially to the maintenance and support of her brothers and of her mother. Mullins v. Seals, 562 F.2d 326 (4th Cir. 1977).

Evidence regarding a daughter's work-life earning capacity was irrelevant in an action for wrongful death where there was no basis for a finding that the daughter would have made any substantial financial contribution to her family if she had lived. Mullins v. Seals, 562 F.2d 326 (4th Cir. 1977).

Loss of services not recoverable as solace. — Loss of a decedent wife's services, which were pecuniary losses, were not recoverable as solace. Pugh v. Yearout, 212 Va. 591, 186 S.E.2d 58 (1972).

Record should show nature of services. — Where the record does not show the nature of the services rendered by the decedent the jury has no basis for awarding damages for loss of services. Claar v. Culpepper, 212 Va. 771, 188 S.E.2d 86 (1972).

A jury verdict assessing damages for wrongful death is final and the Supreme Court has no authority to disturb it. Highway Express Lines v. Fleming, 185 Va. 666, 40 S.E.2d 294 (1946). See also Cooke v. Griggs, 183 Va. 851, 33 S.E.2d 764 (1944).

Instruction as to elements and quantum of damages. — In instructing on the elements and quantum of damages allowable under the broad and liberal language of this section, the court rightly told the jury that they might find in a sum not exceeding $25,000, and in ascertaining damages, take into consideration (among other enumerated things) the loss of decedent's "care, attention and society to his wife and to each of his five children," and also take into consideration and award such additional sum as they might "deem fair and just by way of solace and comfort to his wife and five children for the sorrow, suffering and mental anguish occasioned to each of them by his death." Basham v. Terry, 199 Va. 817, 102 S.E.2d 285 (1958), commented on in 16 Wash. & Lee L. Rev. 97 (1959).

There was no error in an instruction which told the jury that in the event they found for plaintiff they could assess such damages as they deemed fair and just under all the circumstances of the case. Norfolk S. Ry. v. Wood, 182 Va. 30, 28 S.E.2d 15 (1943).

Evidence that deceased was receiving social security payments. — In an action for death by wrongful act there was no error in admitting evidence that decedent at the time of his death was receiving stated monthly social security payments. Jessee v. Slate, 196 Va. 1074, 86 S.E.2d 821 (1955).

§ 8.01-53. Class and beneficiaries; when determined. — A. The damages awarded pursuant to § 8.01-52 shall be distributed as specified under § 8.01-54 to (i) the surviving spouse, children of the deceased and children of any deceased child of the deceased or (ii) if there be none such, then to the parents, brothers and sisters of the deceased, and to any other relative who is primarily dependent on the decedent for support or services and is also a member of the same household as the decedent or (iii) if the decedent has left both surviving spouse and parent or parents, but no child or grandchild, the award shall be distributed to the surviving spouse and such parent or parents or (iv) if there are survivors under clause (i) or clause (iii), the award shall be distributed to those beneficiaries and to any other relative who is primarily dependent on the decedent for support or services and is also a member of the same household as the decedent. Provided, however, no parent whose parental rights and responsibilities have been terminated by a court of competent jurisdiction or pursuant to a permanent entrustment agreement with a child welfare agency shall be eligible as a beneficiary under this section. For purposes of this section, a relative is any person related to the decedent by blood, marriage, or adoption and also includes a stepchild of the decedent.

B. The class and beneficiaries thereof eligible to receive such distribution shall be fixed (i) at the time the verdict is entered if the jury makes the specification, or (ii) at the time the judgment is rendered if the court specifies the distribution.

C. A beneficiary may renounce his interest in any claim brought pursuant to § 8.01-50 and, in such event, the damages shall be distributed to the beneficiaries in the same class as the renouncing beneficiary or, if there are none, to the beneficiaries in any subsequent class in the order of priority set forth in subsection A. (Code 1950, §§ 8-636.1, 8-638; 1954, c. 333; 1973, c. 401; 1974, c. 444; 1977, cc. 460, 617; 1979, c. 356; 1992, c. 74; 1994, c. 515.)

REVISERS' NOTE

Subsection 8.01-53 A (i) and (ii), similar to former §§ 8-636.1 and 8-638, defines the class and beneficiaries to receive the damages awarded and states when they are to be determined.

Subsection A (iii) is the final proviso of former

§ 8-638 with one exception. By referring to "parent," the former section included as beneficiaries within the third class only the mother or father of the decedent and not both. By referring to "parent or parents," the third class now includes as beneficiaries both living parents or either surviving one.

Subsection B sets the time when the class and beneficiaries who may receive the awarded damages will be fixed. This proposal codifies case law. See e.g., Baltimore & O.R.R. v. Wightman's Adm'r, 70 Va. (29 Gratt.) 431 (1877), rev'd on other grounds, 104 U.S. 5, 26 L. Ed. 643 (1881); Johns v. Blue Ridge Transf. Co., 199 Va. 63, 97 S.E.2d 723 (1957).

Law Review. — For survey of Virginia law on evidence for the year 1976-77, see 63 Va. L. Rev. 1428 (1977). For an overview of Virginia Supreme Court decisions on domestic relations, see 15 U. Rich. L. Rev. 321 (1981). For article reviewing recent developments and changes in legislation, case law, and Virginia Supreme Court Rules affecting civil litigation, see "Civil Practice and Procedure," 26 U. Rich. L. Rev. 679 (1992).

I. Decisions Under Current Law.
II. Decisions Under Prior Law.

I. DECISIONS UNDER CURRENT LAW.

The classes of beneficiaries named in the statute are exclusive; a court is not at liberty to consider additional or alternative beneficiaries. Hewitt v. Firestone Tire & Rubber Co., 490 F. Supp. 1358 (E.D. Va. 1980).

Determination of eligible beneficiary. — Under subsection B of this section, any person included among the pertinent categories of beneficiaries specified in subsection A at the time the jury's verdict is entered is a beneficiary eligible to receive a distribution. Mann v. Hinton, 249 Va. 555, 457 S.E.2d 22 (1995).

Beneficiaries under this section distinguished from general beneficiaries. — Virginia makes a careful distinction between beneficiaries under this section and the general beneficiaries of the decedent's estate. Miltier v. Beorn, 696 F. Supp. 1086 (E.D. Va. 1988).

Personal representative merely surrogate for beneficiaries. — Section 8.01-50(B) vests the right of action in the decedent's personal representative. The right of action, however, is not a right to enforce a cause of action personal to the personal representative. As the party-plaintiff, he is merely a surrogate for the beneficiaries of the cause of action named in this section. Horn v. Abernathy, 231 Va. 228, 343 S.E.2d 318 (1986).

Issue of paternity of beneficiary in a wrongful death suit was one for resolution by the jury. Cassady v. Martin, 220 Va. 1093, 266 S.E.2d 104 (1980).

Standard of proof of paternity. — Absent the presumption of legitimacy which attaches to a child born in wedlock, the standard of proof of paternity in a wrongful death case is proof by a preponderance of the evidence. Smith v. Givens, 223 Va. 455, 290 S.E.2d 844 (1982).

When hearsay evidence of paternity admissible. — For purposes of the pedigree exception to the hearsay rule, the decedent in a wrongful death action is a member of the family or related to the family, whose history the decedent's declaration of paternity concerns, viz., the family composed of those named as beneficiaries in this section; thus, hearsay evidence of the decedent's declarations is admissible in such a case, provided no other better evidence can be obtained. Smith v. Givens, 223 Va. 455, 290 S.E.2d 844 (1982).

Hearsay evidence of paternity precluded where mother's testimony available. — In wrongful death case, where alleged illegitimate child of decedent, under the provisions of § 8.01-411 et seq. and Indiana law, could have taken his mother's deposition in Indiana and, in compliance with Supreme Court Rule 4:7(a)(4), introduced her testimony as direct evidence in support of his claim, the pedigree exception did not apply and the trial court erred in admitting hearsay evidence of decedent's paternity. Smith v. Givens, 223 Va. 455, 290 S.E.2d 844 (1982).

Where the first wife fails to rebut the presumption favoring the last marriage because the evidence does not show that divorce records were searched in other places where the deceased had resided, or could have resided, the second spouse will be held to be the surviving spouse, and thus a beneficiary pursuant to this section. Hewitt v. Firestone Tire & Rubber Co., 490 F. Supp. 1358 (E.D. Va. 1980).

The term "children," as used in this section, does not include unadopted stepchildren. Brown v. Brown, 226 Va. 320, 309 S.E.2d 586 (1983), cert. denied, 467 U.S. 1242, 104 S. Ct. 3513, 82 L. Ed. 2d 821 (1984).

Adopted child as beneficiary. — Where an infant is adopted by the parents of the deceased after the death of the deceased but before damages were awarded for wrongful death of decedent, the adopted infant falls within the class of beneficiaries delineated in this section. Knodel v. Dickerman, 246 Va. 124, 431 S.E.2d 323 (1993).

Administratrix may recover for deprivation of decedent's civil rights. — A decedent's claims under 42 U.S.C. § 1983, based on violations of his civil rights which caused his death, survive him, and his duly qualified administratrix may be awarded compensatory and punitive damages for the deprivation if she succeeds on the merits of the case, since allowing the administratrix to obtain compensation only for whatever loss was suffered by statutory beneficiaries under the Virginia wrongful death statute and excluding a punitive award would be inconsistent with the compensatory and deterrent policies behind 42 U.S.C. § 1983. O'Connor v. Several Unknown Correctional Officers, 523 F. Supp. 1345 (E.D. Va. 1981).

Distributees of shipyard worker determined under this section, not federal admiralty law. — Virginia's wrongful death statute, not federal admiralty law, was applicable in determining who was entitled to share in distribution of a settlement award, where the decedent was a shipyard worker killed while engaged in the repair of a barge in Norfolk. There is no federal cause of action for the death of nonseamen in state territorial waters occasioned by negligence. Therefore, the cause of action was cognizable only under Virginia law, and admiralty law could not be relied on to establish who was a distributee. Brown v. Brown, 226 Va. 320, 309 S.E.2d 586 (1983), cert. denied, 467 U.S. 1242, 104 S. Ct. 3513, 82 L. Ed. 2d 821 (1984).

Matter of law determination of relative status. — Only when the facts and circumstances are such that reasonable persons could not differ should the trial court decide as a matter of law whether a decedent's relative is a "dependent" or "member of the same household." Mann v. Hinton, 249 Va. 555, 457 S.E.2d 22 (1995).

Applied in Alderman v. Chrysler Corp., 480 F. Supp. 600 (E.D. Va. 1979); In re Tignor, 21 Bankr. 219 (Bankr. E.D. Va. 1982).

II. DECISIONS UNDER PRIOR LAW.

Editor's note. — The cases cited below were decided under corresponding provisions of former law. The term "this section," as used below, refers to former provisions.

Object of statute. — The primary object of this statute is to compensate the family of the deceased. Richmond, F. & P.R.R. v. Martin's Adm'r, 102 Va. 201, 45 S.E. 894 (1903).

An action for wrongful death is not for the benefit of the decedent's estate, but for certain near relatives. Conrad v. Thompson, 195 Va. 714, 80 S.E.2d 561 (1954).

The purpose of the wrongful death statute is not to allow damages solely to those who might look to decedent for support. Statutory beneficiaries who may have had no reasonable expectance of support from the decedent may recover for loss of care, attention and society, as well as for suffering and mental anguish caused them by his death. Wolfe v. Lockhart, 195 Va. 479, 78 S.E.2d 654 (1953); Wilson v. Whittaker, 207 Va. 1032, 154 S.E.2d 124 (1967).

In a wrongful death action the suit was prosecuted on behalf of the siblings of the decedent and was not for the benefit of the minor decedent's general estate. Taylor v. Anderson, 303 F.2d 546 (4th Cir. 1962).

The primary object of the wrongful death statute, like its prototype, Lord Campbell's Act, is to compensate the family of the deceased and not to benefit his creditors. Carroll v. Sneed, 211 Va. 640, 179 S.E.2d 620 (1971).

Object of article and Federal Death Act the same. — While the persons who were designated as beneficiaries under the Federal Death Act and the Virginia Wrongful Death Act are not described in identical language, the primary object of the two legislative acts is the same. Carroll v. Sneed, 211 Va. 640, 179 S.E.2d 620 (1971).

The classes of beneficiaries described in the statute are exclusive, and other classes or persons cannot be added by judicial construction. Porter v. VEPCO, 183 Va. 108, 31 S.E.2d 337 (1944); Matthews v. Hicks, 197 Va. 112, 87 S.E.2d 629 (1955).

This section controls over statute of descents and distribution. — If the distributees named in the statute of descents and distribution are different from the persons entitled to the proceeds named in this section, the provisions of the latter control. Withrow v. Edwards, 181 Va. 344, 25 S.E.2d 343, rev'd on other grounds, 181 Va. 592, 25 S.E.2d 899, cert. denied, 320 U.S. 761, 64 S. Ct. 70, 88 L. Ed. 453 (1943); Carroll v. Sneed, 211 Va. 640, 179 S.E.2d 620 (1971).

Punishment of wrongdoer not intended. — The right of action for damages for personal injuries expires upon the death of the injured person. The death by wrongful act statute does not cause to survive this right of action, but it creates in the decedent's personal representative a new right of action to compensate decedent's statutory beneficiaries for their loss. Its purpose was not to punish the wrongdoer. Wilson v. Whittaker, 207 Va. 1032, 154 S.E.2d 124 (1967).

Manner of awarding damages. — Unlike a personal estate passing under the intestate law, which is a fund to be distributed equally among members of the same class, damages in wrongful death actions should be awarded individually and separately to the statutory beneficiaries according to their respective damages. Carroll v. Sneed, 211 Va. 640, 179 S.E.2d 620 (1971).

Beneficiaries within designated class may receive whole or any part of recovery. — Even though a minor son has certain rights of possible participation under the death statute, it remained within the discretion of the jury or the court hearing the case without a jury to direct in what proportion the damages should be distributed to the surviving widow and/or child, and it is clear from this section that beneficiaries within the designated class may receive the whole or any part of the recovery. Holley v. The Manfred Stansfield, 186 F. Supp. 805 (E.D. Va. 1960).

Death of class beneficiaries does not terminate cause of action. — The death of class beneficiaries before recovery does not terminate the cause of action. Johns v. Blue Ridge Transf. Co., 199 Va. 63, 97 S.E.2d 723 (1957).

Under this section brothers and sisters of the half blood fall within the same class as parents of a decedent and may participate in the damages awarded if the jury or court, as the case may be, shall elect to so specify. Wolfe v. Lockhart, 195 Va. 479, 78 S.E.2d 654 (1953).

The right of the "widowed mother" of the decedent is not based on dependence. Waters v. Harrell, 183 Va. 764, 33 S.E.2d 194 (1945).

And the widowed mother's remarriage is no bar. — The "widowed mother's" remarriage has nothing to do with the rights of persons whom the statute undertakes to benefit, in the absence of an express provision of law affecting such rights. If the legislature had intended the right which they have to the "widowed mother" to abate upon remarriage, it could easily have said so by adding appropriate words. Waters v. Harrell, 183 Va. 764, 33 S.E.2d 194 (1945).

A surviving spouse, who has deserted the decedent and lived in adultery, is not barred from sharing in damages for wrongful death. Matthews v. Hicks, 197 Va. 112, 87 S.E.2d 629 (1955).

A person who claims to be a decedent's child has the burden of proving that the decedent was his parent. Carroll v. Sneed, 211 Va. 640, 179 S.E.2d 620 (1971).

A child of a bigamous marriage was entitled to participate under the Wrongful Death Act by virtue of former § 64.1-7. Grove v. United States, 170 F. Supp. 176 (E.D. Va.), aff'd sub nom. Grove v. Metropolitan Life Ins. Co., 271 F.2d 918 (4th Cir. 1959).

"Children" includes illegitimate children. — The term "children," as used in this section, and irrespective of any constitutional consideration, includes illegitimate children. Carroll v. Sneed, 211 Va. 640, 179 S.E.2d 620 (1971).

The word "children" as used in this section includes the illegitimate child of a father whose death gives rise to a wrongful death action. Carroll v. Sneed, 211 Va. 640, 179 S.E.2d 620 (1971).

An illegitimate child is made a beneficiary and entitled to share in the recovery under the Virginia wrongful death statute. Carroll v. Sneed, 211 Va. 640, 179 S.E.2d 620 (1971).

But damages awarded such child should not reduce award to wife or other children. — Except as limited by the maximum amount of recovery, an award of damages to an illegitimate child should not reduce the damages awarded to a wife or other children of the decedent. Carroll v. Sneed, 211 Va. 640, 179 S.E.2d 620 (1971).

An illegitimate child who has had little or no connection with his father cannot prove damage from the loss of his father's care, attention and society, or any sorrow and mental anguish. Carroll v. Sneed, 211 Va. 640, 179 S.E.2d 620 (1971).

Nature of recovery. — An illegitimate child who had been a member of decedent's family since birth suffered a substantial loss in the death of her father. He had bestowed upon her a father's love, care and affection, and he had maintained and supported her. The recovery obtained was in compensation for these losses. Carroll v. Sneed, 211 Va. 640, 179 S.E.2d 620 (1971).

Illegitimate child as sole member of first class. — Since illegitimate children are included under the Wrongful Death Act, an illegitimate child who is the sole member of the first class of beneficiaries, but who has sustained no damage, will unjustly preclude any award to a decedent's parents and more remote kindred who have sustained damages. But the existence of an unworthy legitimate child who has sustained no damage likewise precludes any award to a decedent's parents or more remote kindred who have sustained damages. Carroll v. Sneed, 211 Va. 640, 179 S.E.2d 620 (1971).

A resident alien widow, residing in another state, may maintain on behalf of herself and children an action for the wrongful death of her husband. Pocahontas Collieries Co. v. Rukas, 104 Va. 278, 51 S.E. 449 (1905).

Unrelated woman living with decedent. — In an action for the wrongful death of a ship repair yard worker, a woman who was unrelated to the decedent through blood or marriage, but who had lived with the decedent for several years and had received some support from the decedent, was not entitled to any recovery under this section. Ford v. American Original Corp., 475 F. Supp. 10 (E.D. Va. 1979), cert. denied, 467 U.S. 1242, 104 S. Ct. 3513, 82 L. Ed. 2d 821 (1984).

Contributory negligence of one benefi-

ciary does not bar whole recovery. — The contributory negligence of a beneficiary bars his recovery. However, under this section it is the duty of the jury to specify the amount, or proportion, of the recovery to be received by each of the beneficiaries and the contributory negligence of one party only defeats recovery so far as he is concerned. City of Danville v. Howard, 156 Va. 32, 157 S.E. 733 (1931).

Distribution of fund recovered for tortious killing. — Any distribution of the fund recovered for a tortious killing committed in this State must be in accordance with the wrongful death statute creating the right of action. Carroll v. Sneed, 211 Va. 640, 179 S.E.2d 620 (1971).

Jury entitled to know age and physical condition of beneficiaries. — This section places upon the jury the duty of apportioning the damages among the designated beneficiaries. In order that such apportionment may be intelligently made the jury is entitled to know the physical condition, the health, and the ages of the respective persons who may under the statute share in the proceeds of the recovery. Crawford v. Hite, 176 Va. 69, 10 S.E.2d 561 (1940). See Matthews v. Hicks, 197 Va. 112, 87 S.E.2d 629 (1955).

Disclaimer of right to participate in award does not prevent estoppel by judgment. — The father of the decedent in a wrongful death action could not, by disclaiming his statutory right under this section to participate in the unlawful death award, effectively avoid the estoppel created by a final determination for the defendant in a state court which would otherwise bar his subsequent personal action against the same defendant. Taylor v. Anderson, 303 F.2d 546 (4th Cir. 1962).

§ 8.01-54. Judgment to distribute recovery when verdict fails to do so. — A. The verdict may and the judgment of the court shall in all cases specify the amount or the proportion to be received by each of the beneficiaries, if there be any. No verdict shall be set aside for failure to make such specification.

B. If either party shall so request the case shall be submitted to the jury with instructions to specify the distribution of the award, if any. If the jury be unable to agree upon or fail to make such distribution, the court shall specify the distribution and enter judgment accordingly. For the purpose of distribution the court may hear additional evidence.

C. The amount recovered in any such action shall be paid to the personal representative who shall first pay the costs and reasonable attorney's fees and then distribute the amount specifically allocated to the payment of hospital, medical, and funeral expenses. The remainder of the amount recovered shall thereafter be distributed by the personal representative, as specified in subsections A and B above, to the beneficiaries set forth in § 8.01-53; provided that any distribution made to any such beneficiaries shall be free from all debts and liabilities of the decedent. If there be no such beneficiaries, the amount so recovered shall be assets in the hands of the personal representative to be disposed of according to law. (Code 1950, § 8-638; 1954, c. 333; 1973, c. 401; 1977, c. 617.)

REVISERS' NOTE

Section 8.01-54 is based on former § 8-638 and clarifies the procedure for the specification of the damages awarded under § 8.01-52 and distribution to those beneficiaries determined under § 8.01-53.

Subsection A is the substance of the first two sentences of former § 8-638. Subsection B requires the court, upon request of either party, to instruct the jury to specify the distribution of the award among the beneficiaries and clarifies the court's authority to apportion the award.

Subsection C provides that the damages awarded are to be paid to the decedent's personal representative. After payment of costs and reasonable attorney's fees, the representative is to distribute the medical and funeral expenses as specifically allocated under § 8.01-52. The remainder of the awarded damages are to be distributed as specified in subsections A and B to the beneficiaries as determined under § 8.01-53. If there are no beneficiaries under § 8.01-53, the personal representative is to dispose of the remaining awarded damages according to law; then, and only then, can the remainder of the awarded damages be subjected to claims by creditors of the decedent.

Law Review. — For articles on damages recoverable for wrongful death, see 12 Wm. & Mary L. Rev. 396 (1970) and 5 U. Rich. L. Rev. 213 (1971).

I. Decisions Under Current Law.
II. Decisions Under Prior Law.

I. DECISIONS UNDER CURRENT LAW.

The use of special verdicts in negligence cases is unknown in Virginia, and, unless the parties agree otherwise, there is no reason to require such a verdict where negligence results in death and causes sorrow, mental anguish, lost income, and lost services and protection. Rather, damages for these elements should be awarded in a lump sum and distributed to the beneficiaries according to this section. Johnson v. Smith, 241 Va. 396, 403 S.E.2d 685 (1991).

Trial court has authority to question attorney's fees. — Legislature intended issue of reasonableness of attorney's fees to issue in settlement of any wrongful death case; thus, trial court erred in stating that it had no authority to question attorney's fees. Lovelace v. Lovelace, 237 Va. 174, 375 S.E.2d 750 (1989).

Applied in Hewitt v. Firestone Tire & Rubber Co., 490 F. Supp. 1358 (E.D. Va. 1980).

II. DECISIONS UNDER PRIOR LAW.

Editor's note. — The cases cited below were decided under corresponding provisions of former law. The term "this section," as used below, refers to former provisions.

Any distribution of the fund recovered for a tortious killing committed in this State must be in accordance with the death by wrongful act statutes. Withrow v. Edwards, 181 Va. 344, 25 S.E.2d 343, rev'd on other grounds, 181 Va. 592, 25 S.E.2d 899, cert. denied, 320 U.S. 761, 64 S. Ct. 70, 88 L. Ed. 453 (1943); Matthews v. Hicks, 197 Va. 112, 87 S.E.2d 629 (1955).

The death by wrongful act statutes create the right of action for tortious death, limit the recovery, and name the classes of beneficiaries who may share in the recovery. Such recovery can be distributed only in accordance with the express terms of the statute. Porter v. VEPCO, 183 Va. 108, 31 S.E.2d 337 (1944).

Damages are not part of decedent's estate. — Damages recovered in an action for wrongful death are not part of the estate of the decedent, and the recovery can be distributed only in accordance with the express terms of this statute. Porter v. VEPCO, 183 Va. 108, 31 S.E.2d 337 (1944).

And are not subject to dower or curtesy. — The damages recovered in an action for wrongful death are not subject to the dower or curtesy of the surviving consort. Porter v. VEPCO, 183 Va. 108, 31 S.E.2d 337 (1944).

Evidence of debts of decedent inadmissible. — As the wrongful death action recovery is exclusively for the benefit of certain class beneficiaries, and free from all debts of the decedent, evidence of such items would not be admissible in such action. Holley v. The Manfred Stansfield, 186 F. Supp. 805 (E.D. Va. 1960).

§ 8.01-55. Compromise of claim for death by wrongful act. — The personal representative of the deceased may compromise any claim to damages arising under or by virtue of § 8.01-50, including claims under the provision of a liability insurance policy, before or after an action is brought, with the approval of the court in which the action was brought, or if an action has not been brought, with the consent of any circuit court. Such approval may be applied for on petition to such court, by the personal representative, or by any potential defendant, or by any interested insurance carrier. If a potential defendant or any insurance carrier petitions the court for approval, the personal representative shall be made a party to the proceeding. The petition shall state the compromise, its terms and the reason therefor. The court shall require the convening of the parties in interest in person or by their authorized representative, but it shall not be necessary to convene grandchildren whose living parents are made parties to the proceeding. The parties in interest shall be deemed to be convened if each such party (i) endorses the order by which the court approves the compromise or (ii) is given notice of the hearing and proposed compromise as provided in § 8.01-296 if a resident of the Commonwealth or as provided in § 8.01-320 if a nonresident, or is otherwise given reasonable notice of the hearing and proposed compromise as may be required by the court.

If the court approves the compromise, and the parties in interest do not agree upon the distribution to be made of what has been or may be received by the personal representative under such compromise, or if any of them are incapable of making a valid agreement, the court shall direct such distribution as a jury might direct under § 8.01-52 as to damages awarded by them. In other respects, what is received by the personal representative under the compromise shall be treated as if recovered by him in an action under § 8.01-52. (Code 1950, § 8-639; 1960, cc. 35, 587; 1977, c. 617; 1981, c. 286; 1991, c. 97; 1995, c. 366.)

REVISERS' NOTE

Besides changes to conform former § 8-639 with modern practice, reference to "an automobile" insurance policy has been deleted and "a liability" policy substituted. This change recognizes that there are many types of liability insurance policies issued besides auto policies.

Law Review. — For survey of Virginia law on trusts and estates for the year 1976-77, see 63 Va. L. Rev. 1503 (1977). For comment, "The Covenant Not to Sue: Virginia's Effort to Bury the Common Law Rule Regarding the Release of Joint Tortfeasors," see 14 U. Rich. L. Rev. 809 (1980).

I. Decisions Under Current Law.
II. Decisions Under Prior Law.

I. DECISIONS UNDER CURRENT LAW.

Parties in interest have general grant of standing. — Legislature meant for parties in interest to be heard once they were convened; thus, this section provides general grant of standing to parties in interest to be heard in proceeding to approve compromise. Lovelace v. Lovelace, 237 Va. 174, 375 S.E.2d 750 (1989).

Trial court has authority to question attorney's fees. — Legislature intended issue of reasonableness of attorney's fees to issue in settlement of any wrongful death case; thus, trial court erred in stating that it had no authority to question attorney's fees. Lovelace v. Lovelace, 237 Va. 174, 375 S.E.2d 750 (1989).

Beneficiaries have standing to challenge attorney's fees. — Statutory beneficiaries in wrongful death case have standing to challenge reasonableness of attorney's fees. Lovelace v. Lovelace, 237 Va. 174, 375 S.E.2d 750 (1989).

Settlements of wrongful death claims open to public. — The judicial records in issue were accumulated in a wrongful death action. Settlements of wrongful death claims must be approved by the courts, and the public has a societal interest in learning whether compromise settlements are equitable and whether the courts are administering properly the powers conferred upon them, therefore, the trial court erred in sealing that class of data. Shenandoah Publishing House, Inc. v. Fanning, 235 Va. 253, 368 S.E.2d 253 (1988).

Release absent court approval not binding. — When a circuit court approves a compromise settlement under this section, the terms of the release on which it is based likewise are subject to the court's approval. Ramey v. Bobbitt, 250 Va. 474, 463 S.E.2d 437 (1995).

Those portions of a release that are not made part of a wrongful death compromise settlement approved by a circuit court are not binding on the parties to the release. Ramey v. Bobbitt, 250 Va. 474, 463 S.E.2d 437 (1995).

Applied in Hewitt v. Firestone Tire & Rubber Co., 490 F. Supp. 1358 (E.D. Va. 1980); Potomac Hosp. Corp. v. Dillon, 229 Va. 355, 329 S.E.2d 41 (1985); Kelly v. R.S. Jones & Assocs., 242 Va. 79, 406 S.E.2d 34 (1991).

II. DECISIONS UNDER PRIOR LAW.

Editor's note. — The cases cited below were decided under corresponding provisions of former law. The term "this section," as used below, refers to former provisions.

"May" mandatory. — The legislative purpose in changing the old law was to require court approval of all compromises in order better to protect those the legislature had selected as beneficiaries. In light of that purpose, the word "may" as used in the second sentence of this section is mandatory. Under that construction, the first sentence grants the authority to compromise, and the second specifies the condition of that authority. Caputo v. Holt, 217 Va. 302, 228 S.E.2d 134 (1976).

Release absent court approval not binding. — Absent court approval acquired in the manner provided by this section, the release executed by an unqualified administrator was not binding upon the statutory beneficiaries, and the plea of release was properly denied. Caputo v. Holt, 217 Va. 302, 228 S.E.2d 134 (1976).

This section does not apply in action by infant for personal injuries. — Sections 8.01-424 and 8.01-425 and this section relating to compromises by fiduciaries and on behalf of parties incapable of making binding contracts, have no application to a settlement effected involving the payment of the whole demand asserted by a motion in an action by an infant for personal injuries. The case stands upon the same footing as an adult's case. Hinton v. Norfolk & W. Ry., 137 Va. 605, 120 S.E. 135 (1923).

§ 8.01-56. When right of action not to determine nor action to abate.

— The right of action under § 8.01-50 shall not determine, nor the action, when brought, abate by the death, dissolution, or other termination of a defendant; and when a person who has brought an action for personal injury dies pending the action, such action may be revived in the name of his personal representative. If death resulted from the injury for which the action was originally brought, a motion for judgment and other pleadings shall be amended so as to conform to an action under § 8.01-50, and the case proceeded with as if the action had been brought under such section. In such cases, however, there shall be but one recovery for the same injury. (Code 1950, § 8-640; 1954, c. 333; 1977, c. 617.)

REVISERS' NOTE

The second clause of former § 8-640 has been changed to eliminate certain procedural stipulations which are covered by § 8.01-50 and the rules. The former section provided for the dissolution of a corporate defendant. The addition of "or other termination" of a defendant expands this provision to encompass other organizations such as associations and trusts.

Cross references. — As to judgment when death occurs after verdict, see § 8.01-21. For rule of court on substitution of parties, see Rule 3:15.

Law Review. — For note, "Assignability of a Tort Cause of Action in Virginia," see 41 Va. L. Rev. 687 (1955). For discussion of wrongful death action and special damages, see 47 Va. L. Rev. 354 (1961). For article, "Civil Rights and 'Personal Injuries': Virginia's Statute of Limitations for Section 1983 Suits," see 26 Wm. & Mary L. Rev. 199 (1985).

I. Decisions Under Current Law.
II. Decisions Under Prior Law.

I. DECISIONS UNDER CURRENT LAW.

Sections 8.01-21, 8.01-25, 8.01-50, and 8.01-56 compared. — The requirements of the survival and wrongful death statutes, §§ 8.01-25, 8.01-50 and 8.01-56, apply when the death occurs before a final verdict, whereas § 8.01-21 applies where the death occurs after the verdict. Boyd v. Bulala, 647 F. Supp. 781 (W.D. Va. 1986), aff'd in part, rev'd in part, 877 F.2d 1191 (4th Cir. 1989); Bulala v. Boyd, 239 Va. 218, 389 S.E.2d 670 (1990).

Section 8.01-25 and this section are not in conflict with § 8.01-21. They were enacted to extend the application of § 8.01-50, the wrongful death statute, those situations not covered by the original Lord Campbell's Act, in which a plaintiff who has filed an action for personal injuries, dies of those injuries before a verdict is returned. It was unnecessary at common law to amend, revive, or convert the action of the party who survived the return of a verdict, and it is equally unnecessary under the present statutory scheme. Bulala v. Boyd, 239 Va. 218, 389 S.E.2d 670 (1990).

Death of a child born with birth defects after a medical malpractice verdict did not require converting her claim into one for wrongful death. Section 8.01-21 directly so provides, by directing that in such cases, "judgment may be entered as if [death] had not occurred." Section 8.01-25 and this section are not in conflict. They deal with the situation where death occurs before verdict. Boyd v. Bulala, 905 F.2d 764 (4th Cir. 1990).

This section modifies the "every cause of action" language of § 8.01-25 to place all personal injury actions in which death occurred as a result of the injury under the wrongful death rubric. Miltier v. Beorn, 696 F. Supp. 1086 (E.D. Va. 1988).

Conversion of foreign action to Virginia action. — A valid foreign personal injury action may be converted to a Virginia wrongful death action, even though the foreign action was not filed within Virginia's two-year limitations period. Riddle v. Shell Oil Co., 764 F. Supp. 418 (W.D. Va. 1990).

Choice of recovery theory in malpractice action. — The plain language contained in § 8.01-25 and this section unequivocally mandates that a person may not recover for the same injury under the survival statute and the wrongful death statute. There can be but one recovery. Hence, the plaintiffs in instant case, as a matter of law, could not have recovered in the underlying tort action against defendants on both theories of wrongful death and survival. Therefore, it necessarily follows that in the present malpractice action, at an appropriate time after discovery has been completed, the plaintiffs must be required to elect whether they will proceed against the defendant attorneys on the theory that the attorneys breached a duty owed to the plaintiffs in the prosecution of the wrongful death action or breached a duty owed to the plaintiffs in the prosecution of the survival action. Hendrix v. Daugherty, 249 Va. 540, 457 S.E.2d 71 (1995).

Where two witnesses vary in their statements of facts. — Where administratrix brought action for personal injuries based on nursing homes treatment of decedent, dismissal of the action prior to completion of administratrix's evidence deprived her of opportunity to prove damages for personal injury and, therefore, constituted reversible error; although one doctor testified that nursing home's treatment hastened decedent's death, the testimony did not leave administratrix with only a wrongful death action; court should have allowed administratrix to proceed with testimony of another doctor that the cause of death was pneumonia since when two or more witnesses introduced by a party litigant vary in their statements of fact, such party has the right to ask the court or jury to accept as true the statements most favorable to him. Lucas v. HCMF Corp., 238 Va. 446, 384 S.E.2d 92 (1989).

II. DECISIONS UNDER PRIOR LAW.

Editor's note. — The cases cited below were decided under corresponding provisions of former law. The term "this section," as used below, refers to former provisions.

Purpose of statute. — This section was designed to give the right of revival in cases where the plaintiff in actions for personal injuries died pending the action, without regard to the cause of death, and not to make all actions for personal injuries revivable. Birmingham v. C & O Ry., 98 Va. 548, 37 S.E. 17 (1900).

Right given is not strictly a survival of the right of action. — While this section gives a statutory right in case of the death of the plaintiff that right given is not, properly speaking, a survival of the right of action as interpreted by the Supreme Court. Ruebush v. Funk, 63 F.2d 170 (4th Cir. 1933). But see Tignor v. Parkinson, 729 F.2d 977 (4th Cir. 1984).

The statutes of Virginia do not, in any real sense, provide for the survival of a right of action for personal injury if the injured person dies as a result of the injury. Grady v. Irvine, 254 F.2d 224 (4th Cir.), cert. denied, 358 U.S. 819, 79 S. Ct. 30, 3 L. Ed. 2d 60 (1958).

Meaning of "action". — The Supreme Court of Virginia interprets the terms "cause of action" and "action," as used in this section and § 8.01-25, as encompassing only such rights of action as are otherwise granted or contemplated by statute. They do not include every right of action which, at any time, may have existed as a result of the tortious conduct. Grady v. Irvine, 254 F.2d 224 (4th Cir.), cert. denied, 358 U.S. 819, 79 S. Ct. 30, 3 L. Ed. 2d 60 (1958).

No recovery for mental anguish, etc. — This section gives a right of revival in cases where the plaintiff dies pending the action, without regard to the cause of death. In such case if death resulted from the injury, the pleadings are required to be amended, and the case proceeded with as if brought under the death by wrongful act statutes. In that event there could be no recovery for the mental anguish, pain or suffering of the decedent. Seymour v. Richardson, 194 Va. 709, 75 S.E.2d 77 (1953).

Federal court loses jurisdiction where resident administrator is substituted for nonresident plaintiff. — Where a nonresident plaintiff brings an action for personal injuries against a citizen of Virginia in the federal district court in Virginia, and while the action is pending dies of his injuries, and his administrator moves to be substituted as plaintiff and to amend the complaint so as to conform to an action for death by wrongful act, the federal court upon granting the motion loses jurisdiction of the action, since under § 26-59 the administrator must be a citizen of Virginia, and thus there is no diversity of citizenship between the parties. Grady v. Irvine, 254 F.2d 224 (4th Cir.), cert. denied, 358 U.S. 819, 79 S. Ct. 30, 3 L. Ed. 2d 60 (1958).

ARTICLE 6.

Injuries to Railroad Employees.

§ 8.01-57. Liability of railroads for injury to certain employees. — Every common carrier by railroad engaged in intrastate commerce shall be liable in damages to any of its employees suffering injury while employed by such carrier or, in the case of the death of any such employee, to his personal representative, for such injury or death, resulting in whole or in part from the wrongful act or neglect of any of its officers, agents, servants, or employees, or by reason of any defect, or insufficiency due to its neglect in its cars, engines, appliances, machinery, track, roadbed, works, boats, wharves or other equipment, except when such employee is injured while engaged in interstate commerce, and except when such employee is injured in the course of his regular employment and such regular employment does not expose such employee to the hazards incident to the maintenance, use and operation of such railroad. If the action be for the death of an employee, §§ 8.01-50 through 8.01-56 shall apply thereto. (Code 1950, § 8-641; 1954, c. 614; 1977, c. 617.)

REVISERS' NOTE

The reference to former "§§ 8-634 to 8-640" has been changed to "§§ 8.01-50 through 8.01-56" so as to include the entire wrongful death article. The former language "so far as applicable and when not in conflict herewith" has been deleted to avoid any possibility of a conflict with §§ 8.01-50 through 8.01-56.

Cross references. — As to limitation of action for personal injury, see §§ 8.01-243 and 8.01-244. For rules of court governing actions in personam for money, see Rules 3:1 through 3:18.

I. DECISIONS UNDER PRIOR LAW.

Editor's note. — The cases cited below were decided under corresponding provisions of former law. The term "this section," as used below, refers to former provisions.

For history of Virginia Employers' Liability Act, see Karabalis v. E.I. Du Pont De Nemours & Co., 129 Va. 151, 105 S.E. 755 (1921).

Power of legislature to classify railroads. — It is within the constitutional authority of the legislature in enactments such as the Virginia Employers' Liability Act, which are in the exercise of the police power of the State, to adopt a classification which would embrace every corporation operating every kind of road or way on which rails of iron are laid for the wheels of cars to run on, without regard to the character of the railroad as fixed by the business in which it is engaged, e.g., whether the corporation is engaged in the business of a common carrier or of manufacturing. Karabalis v. E.I. Du Pont De Nemours & Co., 129 Va. 151, 105 S.E. 755 (1921).

This section is not applicable to railroads engaged in interstate commerce. Norfolk & W. Ry. v. Hall, 49 F.2d 692 (4th Cir. 1931).

But no allegation as to intrastate commerce is necessary. — Where an injured railroad employee is suing the employer for injuries sustained in employment, it is unnecessary to allege that the employee was engaged in intrastate commerce which is allegation for surplusage, because this and the following sections, covering intrastate commerce, are almost word for word like the federal act. Norfolk & P. Belt Line R.R. v. White, 143 Va. 875, 129 S.E. 339 (1925).

Construction of similar acts adopted. — This section closely follows the language of the Federal Employers' Liability Act, and the Supreme Court will adopt the construction placed upon apposite language by the Supreme Court of the United States. C & O Ry. v. Mizelle, 136 Va. 237, 118 S.E. 241 (1923).

The general rule is that when the General Assembly adopts a statute which has been previously enacted by another sovereignty and construed by the courts of that sovereignty, then such previous construction of the statute is held to be also adopted. C & O Ry. v. Mizelle, 136 Va. 237, 118 S.E. 241 (1923).

Statute is considered in light of kindred legislation. — Whatever may be the specific words used in an employers' liability act, or in kindred legislation to classify the objects of the statute, the legislative meaning of the words must be found by considering them in the light of other legislation in the particular state on

§ 8.01-58 CIVIL REMEDIES AND PROCEDURE § 8.01-59

the same subject, and of the meaning which is given to the same words in other existing general legislation of such state. Karabalis v. E.I. Du Pont De Nemours & Co., 129 Va. 151, 105 S.E. 755 (1921).

Private railroad operated by manufacturing company not within act. — The Virginia Employers' Liability Act, as contained in this article, does not apply to the class of employees therein specified of a manufacturing corporation operating in the State a private railroad, merely incidental to and in connection with its manufacturing business. The act only applies to employees of corporations operating in this State railroads used or authorized by law to be used as common carriers engaged in intrastate commerce. Karabalis v. E.I. Du Pont De Nemours & Co., 129 Va. 151, 105 S.E. 755 (1921).

Machinist repairing engine in shop cannot invoke act. — The plaintiff, a machinist, who was working on the repair of an engine in the shops of defendant railway, was not engaged in intrastate commerce, or transportation service, within the meaning of the Virginia statute, and hence cannot invoke either this section or § 8.01-59, which applies to actions brought under this section. Plaintiff was not engaged in either interstate or intrastate commerce. C & O Ry. v. Mizelle, 136 Va. 237, 118 S.E. 241 (1923).

§ 8.01-58. Contributory negligence no bar to recovery; violation of safety appliance acts. — In all actions brought against any such common carrier to recover damages for personal injuries to any employee or when such injuries have resulted in his death, the fact that such employee may have been guilty of contributory negligence shall not bar a recovery, but the damages shall be diminished by the jury in proportion to the amount of negligence attributable to such employee; and no such employee, who may be injured or killed, shall be held to have been guilty of contributory negligence in any case when the violation by such common carrier of any statute enacted for the safety of employees contributed to the injury or death of such employee. (Code 1950, § 8-642; 1954, c. 614; 1977, c. 617.)

I. DECISIONS UNDER PRIOR LAW.

Editor's note. — The cases cited below were decided under corresponding provisions of former law. The term "this section," as used below, refers to former provisions.

Employment need not be intrastate commerce as in §§ 8.01-57 and 8.01-59. — It was argued that this section both in the Code and in the original act (Acts 1916, p. 763), should be construed together with the preceding § 8.01-57 and the following § 8.01-59, and that so construed all three refer to injuries suffered while the employees are engaged in intrastate commerce. But it was held that such a construction would do violence to the language of the section. C & O Ry. v. Mizelle, 136 Va. 237, 118 S.E. 241 (1923).

Test is whether carrier is engaged in intrastate commerce. — Under this section, contributory negligence is no longer an absolute bar to an action by an injured employee of any common carrier by railroad whose motive power is steam engaged in intrastate commerce, whether such employee is injured while engaged in such commerce or not. The test under this section is not whether at the time of his injury the employee was engaged in intrastate commerce, but merely whether the defendant carrier is engaged in such commerce. C & O Ry. v. Mizelle, 136 Va. 237, 118 S.E. 241 (1923).

Negligence of defendant must be established. — Until the negligence of defendant is established, no question of contributory negligence of plaintiff can arise. It is essential, therefore, first to establish the negligence of the defendant. In the instant case, negligence of defendant was not established, as the failure of plaintiff's intestate to put up the blue flag for his protection, as required by a rule of the railroad company, was the sole proximate cause of his death. Shumaker's Adm'r v. Atlantic C.L.R.R., 125 Va. 393, 99 S.E. 739 (1919).

There is nothing in this section which denies the defense of assumed risk, though to a limited extent it is denied by § 8.01-59 in actions brought under § 8.01-57. C & O Ry. v. Mizelle, 136 Va. 237, 118 S.E. 241 (1923).

§ 8.01-59. Assumption of risk; violation of safety appliance acts. — In any action brought against any common carrier, under or by virtue of § 8.01-57, to recover damages for injuries to, or death of, any of its employees, the knowledge of any employee injured or killed of the defective or unsafe character or condition of any machinery, ways, appliances, or structures of such carrier shall not of itself be a bar to recovery for an injury or death caused thereby, nor shall such employee be held to have assumed the risk of his employment in any case in which the violation by such common carrier of any statute enacted for the safety of employees contributed to the injury, or death of such employee. (Code 1950, § 8-643; 1977, c. 617.)

I. DECISIONS UNDER PRIOR LAW.

Editor's note. — The cases cited below were decided under corresponding provisions of former law. The term "this section," as used below, refers to former provisions.

Purpose of section. — This section was intended to conform the law of assumption of risk in intrastate commerce to the rule applied by the federal decisions to the similar statute applicable to interstate commerce. Roberts v. Southern Ry., 151 Va. 815, 144 S.E. 863 (1928).

No effect on interstate carriers when Congress has acted. — Where Congress has spoken upon the question of the liability of interstate carriers to their employees, this section, as to assumption of risk and the violation of the Safety Appliance Act, cannot be looked to for guidance as to the liability of such carriers to their employees. Southern Ry. v. Wilmouth, 154 Va. 582, 153 S.E. 874, cert. denied, 282 U.S. 878, 51 S. Ct. 81, 75 L. Ed. 775 (1930).

§ **8.01-60. Contracts exempting from liability void; set-off of insurance.** — Any contract, rule, regulation or device whatsoever the purpose or intent of which shall be to enable any common carrier to exempt itself from any liability created by § 8.01-57, shall to that extent be void; but in any action brought against any such common carrier under or by virtue of such section, such common carrier may set off therein any sum it has contributed or paid to any insurance, relief, benefit or indemnity company that may have been paid to the injured employee or the person entitled thereto on account of the injury or death for which such action was brought. (Code 1950, § 8-644; 1977, c. 617.)

§ **8.01-61. Definition of "common carrier" as used in article.** — The term "common carrier" as used in §§ 8.01-57 to 8.01-60 shall include the receivers or other persons or corporations charged with the duty of the management or operation of the business of a common carrier by railroad; but shall not include persons, firms or corporations owning or operating railroads when such railroads are primarily and chiefly used as incidental to the operation of coal, gypsum or iron mines or saw mills, nor shall it apply to any railroad owned or operated by any county. (Code 1950, § 8-645; 1954, c. 614; 1977, c. 617.)

§ **8.01-62. Action may embrace liability under both State and federal acts.** — The motion for judgment or other pleading in any such action may embrace a cause of action growing out of any statute of the United States or this Commonwealth for such injury or death, without being demurrable on this account, and without the plaintiff being required to elect under which statute he claims. Sections 8.01-57 through 8.01-61 shall not apply to electric railways operated wholly within this Commonwealth. (Code 1950, § 8-646; 1954, c. 614; 1977, c. 617.)

REVISERS' NOTE

The reference in former § 8-646 to any "act of Congress of the United States of America" has been deleted and "statute of the United States or this Commonwealth" has been substituted. This change does not broaden the scope of former § 8-646 but is made to reflect case law that it is not necessary for the plaintiff to specify whether the action is brought under the United States or the Virginia statute; i.e., it is sufficient if the facts alleged bring the action within either statute since the Virginia court has jurisdiction under both the federal and State laws. Shumaker's Adm'x v. Atlantic Coast Line R.R., 125 Va. 393, 99 S.E. 739 (1919).

§ 8.01-63   CIVIL REMEDIES AND PROCEDURE   § 8.01-63

I. DECISIONS UNDER PRIOR LAW.

Editor's note. — The case cited below was decided under corresponding provisions of former law.

State and federal statutes exclusive in their jurisdiction. — Whenever the acts of Congress relative to the liability of common carriers engaged in interstate commerce to their employees are applicable, they are exclusive, but if not applicable and the state statute is, the latter will be applied. No case can arise where both statutes are applicable. Shumaker's Adm'r v. Atlantic C.L.R.R., 125 Va. 393, 99 S.E. 739 (1919).

But state court has jurisdiction of both. — It is often extremely difficult to determine whether the injured servant was engaged in interstate commerce or not. The advantage of suing in the state court is that that court has jurisdiction under both acts, and if necessary facts are stated, jurisdiction will be maintained under the appropriate statute. Shumaker's Adm'r v. Atlantic C.L.R.R., 125 Va. 393, 99 S.E. 739 (1919).

ARTICLE 7.

Motor Vehicle Accidents.

§ 8.01-63. Liability for death or injury to guest in motor vehicle. — Any person transported by the owner or operator of any motor vehicle as a guest without payment for such transportation and any personal representative of any such guest so transported shall be entitled to recover damages against such owner or operator for death or injuries to the person or property of such guest resulting from the negligent operation of such motor vehicle. However, this statute does not limit any defense otherwise available to the owner or operator. (Code 1950, § 8-646.1; 1974, c. 551; 1977, c. 617.)

Cross references. — For rules of court governing procedure in actions in personam for money, see Rules 3:1 through 3:18.

Law Review. — For discussion of punitive damages and their possible application in automobile accident litigation, see 46 Va. L. Rev. 1036 (1960). For case note on assumptions of risk as a limitation of liability in guest-host relationships, see 18 Wash. & Lee L. Rev. 316 (1961). For comment, "The Case Against the Guest Statute," see 7 Wm. & Mary L. Rev. 321 (1966). For comment on guest statute applicability to motor-driven golf carts, see 25 Wash. & Lee L. Rev. 293 (1968). For survey of Virginia law on torts for the year 1968-1969, see 55 Va. L. Rev. 1395 (1969); for the year 1970-1971, see 57 Va. L. Rev. 1501 (1971); for the year 1971-1972, see 58 Va. L. Rev. 1349 (1972); for the year 1973-1974, see 60 Va. L. Rev. 1615 (1974); for the year 1974-1975, see 61 Va. L. Rev. 1856 (1975).

I. Decisions Under Current Law.
II. Decisions Under Prior Law.

I. DECISIONS UNDER CURRENT LAW.

Simple negligence is the failure to exercise that degree of care which an ordinary prudent person would exercise under the same or similar circumstances to avoid injury to another. Gossett v. Jackson, 249 Va. 549, 457 S.E.2d 97 (1995).

Sufficient evidence of driver's conduct as proximate cause of negligence. — Plaintiff's presented evidence from which the jury could have inferred that defendant's negligence was a proximate cause of the accident. For example, defendant had previously stopped the car at intersections minutes before the accident occurred and the jury could have found that but for defendant's excessive speed of 60 m.p.h., he would have been able to use the brakes to stop the car and, thus, prevent the accident. The jury could have also found that the car's mechanical condition was not a proximate cause of the accident because police officer testified that the condition of the car did not affect its speed. Furthermore, the jury could have found that defendant was negligent in his operation of the car because he took his hands off the steering wheel of the car as it was "weaving" and traveling at a speed of 60 m.p.h. immediately before the collision. Gossett v. Jackson, 249 Va. 549, 457 S.E.2d 97 (1995).

Applied in Creasy v. United States, 645 F. Supp. 853 (W.D. Va. 1986); Community Motor Bus Co. v. Windley, 224 Va. 687, 299 S.E.2d 367 (1983).

II. DECISIONS UNDER PRIOR LAW.

Editor's note. — The cases cited below were decided under corresponding provisions of

former law. The term "this section," as used below, refers to former provisions.

Statute does not apply to transportation by airplane. — Transportation by airplane is markedly different from transportation by automobile, and neither this section nor the policy behind it should be applied to airplane travel without legislative action. Walthew v. Davis, 201 Va. 557, 111 S.E.2d 784 (1960).

"Guest" defined. — The word "guest" is used to denote one whom the owner or possessor of a motor car or other vehicle invites or permits to ride with him as a gratuity, that is, without any financial return, except such slight benefits as it is customary to extend as a part of the ordinary courtesies of the road. Thus the mere benefit resulting from companionship, or the advantage resulting from a promise to assist in the driving, is not of a legal value sufficient in itself to transfer a gratuitous undertaking into an undertaking for payment. Mayer v. Puryear, 115 F.2d 675 (4th Cir. 1940).

Even though he may be driving his host's car, a person is still considered a guest as far as his host is concerned. Mayer v. Puryear, 115 F.2d 675 (4th Cir. 1940); Leonard v. Helms, 269 F.2d 48 (4th Cir. 1959).

There was no business relationship between plaintiff and defendant where plaintiff undertook to assist defendant and another friend in helping move material in a truck and the offer to help was a nature of rendition of neighborly assistance without expectation of personal benefit or compensation. The plaintiff was riding as a mere guest. Miller v. Ellis, 188 Va. 207, 49 S.E.2d 273 (1948).

To raise the status of a passenger from that of guest to paying passenger there must be shown more than incidental benefit conferred on, or social amenities extended to, the owner or operator of the vehicle; the benefit must be a consideration for the transportation. Davis v. Williams, 194 Va. 541, 74 S.E.2d 58 (1953); Dickerson v. Miller, 196 Va. 659, 85 S.E.2d 275 (1955).

Where plaintiff upon defendant's invitation rode to work with him and voluntarily paid the defendant, without request, the equivalent of bus fare regularly for a period of more than one year, it was held that plaintiff was a paying passenger and not a "guest" within the meaning of this section. Davis v. Williams, 194 Va. 541, 74 S.E.2d 58 (1953).

Payments made or services performed for transportation, to be sufficient to elevate one from a guest to a paying passenger, must be more than gratuitous gestures of reciprocal hospitality, or social amenities, extended without thought of bargaining for the transportation. Groome v. Birkhead, 214 Va. 429, 201 S.E.2d 789 (1974).

It is not necessary that driver receive actual cash in return for transportation. — With respect to "payment" it is not necessary that the operator of the vehicle receive actual cash in return for the transportation supplied, since services or other benefits given by the occupant, if regarded by the parties as consideration inducing the offer of transportation, may be sufficient to entitle the occupant to the status of a paying passenger, as distinguished from a guest passenger. Dickerson v. Miller, 196 Va. 659, 85 S.E.2d 275 (1955); Hill Hdwe. Corp. v. Hesson, 198 Va. 425, 94 S.E.2d 256 (1956), commented on in 13 Wash. & Lee L. Rev. 84 (1956); Richardson v. Charles, 201 Va. 426, 111 S.E.2d 401 (1959); Parker v. Leavitt, 201 Va. 919, 114 S.E.2d 732 (1960); Gilliland v. Singleton, 204 Va. 115, 129 S.E.2d 641 (1963).

The payment referred to in this section does not, of course, have to be in cash in order to make the occupant a paying passenger rather than a guest. If a person bargains for services and the transportation is given in consideration thereof, the person performing the services is a paying passenger and not a guest passenger, but the services performed must be more than gratuitous gestures of reciprocal hospitality, or social amenities extended without thought of bargaining for the transportation. Smith v. Tatum, 199 Va. 85, 97 S.E.2d 820 (1957).

And one who performs services in return for transportation is paying passenger. — If a person bargains for services and as consideration therefor offers transportation, the person performing or agreeing to perform the services and accepting such transportation is a paying passenger and not a guest passenger. Dickerson v. Miller, 196 Va. 659, 85 S.E.2d 275 (1955), commented on in 13 Wash. & Lee L. Rev. 84 (1956).

Defendant, who was manager of a restaurant, by promising her transportation home, induced decedent to stay beyond her usual hours to clean up. Decedent was therefore a paying passenger. Dickerson v. Miller, 196 Va. 659, 85 S.E.2d 275 (1955).

It is not necessary to prove that there was an express enforceable contract between the operator and the occupant of a motor vehicle resulting from considerations moving from one to the other to raise the status of the occupant from that of a guest to that of a paying passenger. However, mere giving and receiving of friendly and reciprocal benefits and amenities between the driver and occupant without any thought of creating a business or contractual relation is insufficient to change the status of a guest to that of a paying passenger within the meaning of this section. Hill Hdwe. Corp. v. Hesson, 198 Va. 425, 94 S.E.2d 256 (1956).

But mere incidental benefit is not sufficient. — An incidental benefit resulting to the defendant from transportation is not sufficient to enlarge the liability from guest to passenger. The benefit to the defendant must be a consideration for the transportation. More than an incidental benefit must have induced the defendant to extend the ride. The benefits, in short, must be more than gratuitous gestures of reciprocal hospitality, or social amenities, extended without thought of bargaining for the transportation. Richardson v. Charles, 201 Va. 426, 111 S.E.2d 401 (1959).

Owner does not become guest of one whom he allows to drive. — The owner of a car did not lose his character of host and become the guest of his companion when he permitted her to drive the car for her own pleasure. The change of places in the vehicle did not alter the relationship of host and guest, where the guest asked for and was granted the privilege of driving the car. There was no gratuitous undertaking on her part for the benefit of the owner but, rather, the acceptance of a favor from him, which was tendered because it gave her pleasure. Leonard v. Helms, 269 F.2d 48 (4th Cir. 1959).

Where the owner permitted another to operate his automobile but only on condition that the owner accompany the other, the owner did not become a "guest without payment" and thus could recover against the other upon proof of simple negligence in the operation of the automobile. Parker v. Leavitt, 201 Va. 919, 114 S.E.2d 732 (1960).

A father-in-law who was riding with his daughter-in-law for the purpose of giving her a driver's lesson, where she was driving under a learner's permit, was not a paying passenger but a guest in the vehicle; and his administratrix could recover for his death. Smith v. Tatum, 199 Va. 85, 97 S.E.2d 820 (1957).

The transportation of a mother by her daughter and the mother's undertaking to purchase gasoline are mere gratuitous gestures of reciprocal hospitality extended in a family relationship; thence the mother is not a paying passenger in her daughter's vehicle, within the meaning of this section. Groome v. Birkhead, 214 Va. 429, 201 S.E.2d 789 (1974).

Fact that driver and passenger drank and dined together. — Where the purpose of a trip was purely business, the fact that the automobile driver and his passenger had a social drink and dined together during the course of the trip did not change the complexion of it. Richardson v. Charles, 201 Va. 426, 111 S.E.2d 401 (1959).

"Car pool" arrangement. — Where plaintiff was one of three women who had entered into a "car pool" arrangement whereby each would furnish transportation alternately for a week at a time, and there was no dispute as to the business relationship between the parties nor doubt that by the arrangement they were thus compensated in a substantial business sense, plaintiff was not a "guest without payment" within the meaning of the statute. Gilliland v. Singleton, 204 Va. 115, 129 S.E.2d 641 (1963).

Plaintiff held a paying passenger. — Under the circumstances, the plaintiff was not "a guest without payment" for her transportation within the meaning of this statute, but was a paying passenger. Gammon v. Hyde, 199 Va. 918, 103 S.E.2d 221 (1958).

Defendant was a salesman of used cars and had sold one to plaintiff for delivery on a certain day. When delivery was delayed defendant offered to drive plaintiff in another car to a neighboring town where plaintiff had business. On the return trip the accident occurred. On these facts it was properly ruled as a matter of law that plaintiff was a passenger rather than a guest. The trip was clearly motivated by the business transaction between the parties, and it was of substantial benefit to defendant and his employer to furnish the transportation. Richardson v. Charles, 201 Va. 426, 111 S.E.2d 401 (1959).

Where plaintiff gave defendant $.20 each day after riding home from work with defendant, and defendant accepted this payment as "bus fare to help cover the expenses," plaintiff was clearly a paying passenger. Thoms v. Dowdy, 201 Va. 581, 112 S.E.2d 868 (1959).

Plaintiff was held to be a paying passenger where she and defendant, friends of long standing, entered into an arrangement to defray in equal shares the cost of operating defendant's automobile during the course of a planned excursion. Bernard v. Bohanan, 203 Va. 372, 124 S.E.2d 191 (1962).

If the parties, by pre-trip arrangement, provided that the infant plaintiff would compensate the defendant for one half the expenses of operating the car on the trip, this would have been more than a mere social or incidental benefit to the defendant; it would have constituted a substantial pecuniary contribution to help defray such expenses, placing the infant plaintiff in the status of a paying passenger. Sturman v. Johnson, 209 Va. 227, 163 S.E.2d 170 (1968).

Plaintiff held guest. — Where the evidence proved that the service to be rendered by the defendant in teaching plaintiff to park was a gratuity and a friendly act, plaintiff was a guest passenger and had no right to recover except upon proof of gross negligence. Jenkins v. Womack, 201 Va. 68, 109 S.E.2d 97 (1959).

Where passenger is child. — The degree of care owed a child is proportionate to the apparent ability of the child in view of his age, maturity and intelligence to foresee and avoid the perils which may be encountered, if those perils are such as have become apparent to or should have been discovered by the operator of a motor vehicle in the exercise of ordinary care under all the circumstances. The younger the child and the less able to look out for himself the greater the care which may reasonably be expected of the motorist. This degree of care required of the operator of a motor vehicle to his guest who is a minor, however, does not relieve the injured minor from the necessity of proving gross negligence in order to recover for his injuries. Ruett v. Nottingham, 200 Va. 722, 107 S.E.2d 402 (1959).

A child can become a guest in a motor vehicle and subject himself to the gross negligence rule only if he can knowingly and voluntarily accept an invitation to become a guest. Smith v. Kauffman, 212 Va. 181, 183 S.E.2d 190 (1971).

A child under the age of 14 years is incapable of knowingly and voluntarily accepting an invitation to become a guest in an automobile so as to subject himself to this negligence rule. Smith v. Kauffman, 212 Va. 181, 183 S.E.2d 190 (1971).

Must show cause of accident. — In order for plaintiff to prevail the evidence must show something more than that the accident may have resulted from one of two causes, for one of which the defendant is responsible, and for the other of which he is not. Grasty v. Tanner, 206 Va. 723, 146 S.E.2d 252 (1966).

Testimony of witness who did not see accident. — A witness who did not actually see the motor vehicle in movement is incompetent to give testimony based on sound alone as to the speed at which it was moving. Meade v. Meade, 206 Va. 823, 147 S.E.2d 171 (1966).

Assumption of risk. — A passenger in an automobile does not assume the risk of injury from the driver's negligent operation of the vehicle merely because he knows that the driver has been drinking ardent spirits, where there is no evidence that the driver's ability to drive was impaired thereby. Meade v. Meade, 206 Va. 823, 147 S.E.2d 171 (1966).

A guest may be guilty of contributory negligence if he knows or reasonably should know that his driver had been drinking intoxicating liquor to an extent likely to affect the manner of his driving and voluntarily continues as a passenger after a reasonable opportunity to leave the automobile. Meade v. Meade, 206 Va. 823, 147 S.E.2d 171 (1966).

Questions for court or for jury. — If the evidence is such that reasonable men should not differ as to the conclusions drawn from what has been proved, the question is one of law for the court; and conversely, if reasonable men may differ, then the question is one of fact for determination by a jury. Barham v. Virginia Nat'l Bank, 206 Va. 153, 142 S.E.2d 569 (1965).

If reasonable men should not differ as to the conclusion to be drawn from the facts proved, the question becomes one of law for the court. Bond v. Joyner, 205 Va. 292, 136 S.E.2d 903 (1964); Scott v. Foley, 205 Va. 382, 136 S.E.2d 849 (1964).

Burden of proof. — The burden is on the plaintiffs in an action by guest to establish how and why the accident occurred. Crabtree v. Dingus, 194 Va. 615, 74 S.E.2d 54 (1953); Hailey v. Johnson, 201 Va. 775, 113 S.E.2d 664 (1960).

The burden is on plaintiff to prove by a preponderance of the evidence that the defendant's negligent operation of the automobile proximately caused the accident and the resulting injuries. Smith v. Prater, 206 Va. 693, 146 S.E.2d 179 (1966).

§ 8.01-64. Liability for negligence of minor. — Every owner of a motor vehicle causing or knowingly permitting a minor under the age of sixteen years who is not permitted under the provisions of § 46.2-335 to drive such a vehicle upon a highway, and any person who gives or furnishes a motor vehicle to such minor, shall be jointly or severally liable with such minor for any damages caused by the negligence of such minor in driving such vehicle. (Code 1950, § 8-646.2; 1977, c. 617.)

I. DECISIONS UNDER PRIOR LAW.

Editor's note. — The case cited below was decided under corresponding provisions of former law. The term "this section," as used below, refers to former provisions.

Section must be strictly construed. — This section, while remedial, is in derogation of the common law and, therefore must be strictly construed. It must be presumed that the legislature acted with full knowledge of the strict interpretation that must be placed upon a statute of the nature of this section. Hannabass v. Ryan, 164 Va. 519, 180 S.E. 416 (1935).

The language "who is not permitted under the provisions of § 46.1-357 [§ 46.2-335]... to drive" deals solely with those not licensed by the State to operate a motor vehicle upon the streets and highways. Had the legislature intended to extend the liability of the owner of a motor vehicle to embrace those who may be prohibited from the operation of such a vehicle by a city ordinance it would have so expressed that intention in the statute. Hannabass v. Ryan, 164 Va. 519, 180 S.E. 416 (1935) (decided prior to repeal of Title 46.1).

§ 8.01-65. Defense of lack of consent of owner. — It shall be a valid defense to any action brought for the negligent operation of a motor vehicle for the owner of such vehicle to prove that the same was being driven or used without his knowledge or consent, express or implied, but the burden of proof thereof shall be on such owner. (Code 1950, § 8-646.8; 1977, c. 617.)

REVISERS' NOTE

For clarification, the word "such" which preceded the word "action" in the second line of former § 8-646.8 has been deleted and the language "brought for the negligent operation of a motor vehicle" has been inserted following "action."

§ 8.01-66. Recovery of damages for loss of use of vehicle. — A. Whenever any person is entitled to recover for damage to or destruction of a motor vehicle, he shall, in addition to any other damages to which he may be legally entitled, be entitled to recover the reasonable cost which was actually incurred in hiring a comparable substitute vehicle for the period of time during which such person is deprived of the use of his motor vehicle. However, such rental period shall not exceed a reasonable period of time for such repairs to be made or if the original vehicle is a total loss, a reasonable time to purchase a new vehicle. Nothing herein contained shall relieve the claimant of the duty to mitigate damages.

B. Whenever any insurance company licensed in this Commonwealth to write insurance as defined in § 38.2-124 or any self-insured company refuses or fails to provide a comparable temporary substitute vehicle to any person entitled to recover the actual cost of hiring a substitute vehicle as set forth in subsection A, and if the trial judge of a court of proper jurisdiction subsequently finds that such refusal or failure was not made in good faith, such company shall be liable to that person in the amount of $500 or double the amount of the rental cost he is entitled to recover under subsection A of this section, whichever amount is greater. If the trial court finds that an action brought against an insurance company or any self-insured company under subsection B of this section is frivolous, or not to have been brought in good faith, the court may in its discretion require the plaintiff to pay the reasonable attorney's fees, not to exceed $200, incurred by the defendant in defending the action. This section shall in no way preclude any party from seeking such additional common law remedies as might otherwise be available. (Code 1950, § 8-646.9; 1975, c. 478; 1977, c. 617; 1979, c. 499; 1986, c. 296; 1987, c. 116; 1989, c. 348.)

Law Review. — For survey of Virginia law on insurance for the year 1974-1975, see 61 Va. L. Rev. 1759 (1975).

§ 8.01-66.1. Remedy for arbitrary refusal of motor vehicle insurance claim. — A. Whenever any insurance company licensed in this Commonwealth to write insurance as defined in § 38.2-124 denies, refuses or fails to pay to its insured a claim of $2,500 or less in excess of the deductible, if any, under the provisions of a policy of motor vehicle insurance issued by such company to the insured and it is subsequently found by the judge of a court of proper jurisdiction that such denial, refusal or failure to pay was not made in good faith, the company shall be liable to the insured in an amount double the amount otherwise due and payable under the provisions of the insured's policy of motor vehicle insurance, together with reasonable attorney's fees and expenses.

The provisions of this subsection shall be construed to include an insurance company's refusal or failure to pay medical expenses to persons covered under the terms of any medical payments coverage extended under a policy of motor vehicle insurance, when the amount of the claim therefor is $2,500 or less and the refusal was not made in good faith.

B. Notwithstanding the provisions of subsection A, whenever any insurance company licensed in this Commonwealth to write insurance as defined in § 38.2-124 denies, refuses or fails to pay to a third party claimant, on behalf of an insured to whom such company has issued a policy of motor vehicle liability insurance, a claim of $2,500 or less made by such third party claimant and if the judge of a court of proper jurisdiction finds that the insured is liable for the claim, the third party claimant shall have a cause of action against the insurance company. If the judge finds that such denial, refusal or failure to pay was not made in good faith, the company, in addition to the liability assumed by the company under the provisions of the insured's policy of motor vehicle liability insurance, shall be liable to the third party claimant in an amount double the amount of the judgment awarded the third party claimant, together with reasonable attorney's fees and expenses.

C. Notwithstanding the provisions of subsections A and B whenever any person who has paid a fee to the Department of Motor Vehicles to register an uninsured motor vehicle pursuant to § 46.2-706 or any person who has furnished proof of financial responsibility in lieu of obtaining a policy or policies of motor vehicle liability insurance pursuant to the provisions of Title 46.2 or any person who is required and has failed either to pay such fee or to furnish such proof pursuant to the provisions of Title 46.2 denies, refuses or fails to pay to a claimant a claim of $2,500 or less made by such claimant as a result of a motor vehicle accident; and if the trial judge of a court of proper jurisdiction finds that such denial, refusal or failure to pay was not made in good faith, such person shall be liable to the claimant in an amount double the amount otherwise due and payable together with reasonable attorney's fees and expenses.

For the purposes of this subsection C "person" shall mean and include any natural person, firm, partnership, association or corporation.

D. 1. Whenever a court of proper jurisdiction finds that an insurance company licensed in this Commonwealth to write insurance as defined in § 38.2-124 denies, refuses or fails to pay to its insured a claim of more than $2,500 in excess of the deductible, if any, under the provisions of a policy of motor vehicle insurance issued by such company to the insured and it is subsequently found by the judge of a court of proper jurisdiction that such denial, refusal or failure to pay was not made in good faith, the company shall be liable to the insured in the amount otherwise due and payable under the provisions of the insured's policy of motor vehicle insurance, plus interest on the amount due at double the rate provided in § 6.1-330.53 from the date that the claim was submitted to the insurer or its authorized agent, together with reasonable attorney's fees and expenses.

2. The provisions of this subsection shall be construed to include an insurance company's refusal or failure to pay medical expenses to persons covered under the terms of any medical payments coverage extended under a policy of motor vehicle insurance when the refusal was not made in good faith. (1977, c. 621; 1979, c. 521; 1980, c. 437; 1989, c. 698; 1991, c. 155; 1997, c. 401.)

REVISERS' NOTE

The generic terms "fiduciary" and "person under a disability" have been substituted for various individuals specified in former sections of the predecessor Title 8 article.

Law Review. — For survey of Virginia law on insurance for the year 1976-77, see 63 Va. L. Rev. 1448 (1977).

I. DECISIONS UNDER CURRENT LAW.

Standard of reasonableness. — This is a remedial statute and operates as a punitive statute in the same manner as Va. Code § 38.2-209 and the standard of reasonableness applied in using that statute should be used when applying this statute. Nationwide Mut. Ins. Co. v. St. John, 259 Va. 71, 524 S.E.2d 649 (2000).

An insured's evidentiary burden under this remedial standard is the preponderance of the evidence standard. Nationwide Mut. Ins. Co. v. St. John, 259 Va. 71, 524 S.E.2d 649 (2000).

For discussion of this section and how it relates to tort of bad faith failure to settle an insurance claim, see A & E Supply Co. v. Nationwide Mut. Fire Ins. Co., 612 F. Supp. 760 (W.D. Va. 1985), rev'd on other grounds, 798 F.2d 669 (4th Cir. 1986), cert. denied, 479 U.S. 1091, 107 S. Ct. 1302, 94 L. Ed. 2d 158 (1987).

ARTICLE 7.1.

Lien for Hospital, Medical and Nursing Services.

§ 8.01-66.2. Lien against person whose negligence causes injury. — Whenever any person sustains personal injuries caused by the alleged negligence of another and receives treatment in any hospital, public or private, or receives medical attention or treatment from any physician, or receives nursing service or care from any registered nurse, or receives physical therapy treatment from any registered physical therapist in this Commonwealth, or receives medicine from a pharmacy, such hospital, physician, nurse, physical therapist or pharmacy shall each have a lien for the amount of a just and reasonable charge for the service rendered, but not exceeding $2,000 in the case of a hospital, and $500 for each physician, nurse, physical therapist, or pharmacy on the claim of such injured person or of his personal representative against the person, firm or corporation whose negligence is alleged to have caused such injuries. (Code 1950, § 32-138; 1979, c. 722; 1981, c. 313; 1988, cc. 505, 544; 1995, cc. 470, 550, 669.)

Law Review. — For article, "How Bankruptcy Exemptions Work: Virginia as an Illustration of Why the 'Opt Out' Clause Was a Bad Idea," see 8 Geo. Mason L. Rev. 1 (1985).

I. Decisions Under Current Law.
II. Decisions Under Prior Law.

I. DECISIONS UNDER CURRENT LAW.

Debtor's exemption considered in creating lien. — The General Assembly was mindful of the debtor's exemption when it prescribed and fixed in favor of hospitals and doctors the lien rights against personal injury proceeds set forth in this section. Johnston Mem. Hosp. v. Hess, 21 Bankr. 465 (Bankr. W.D. Va. 1982), rev'd on other grounds, 44 Bankr. 598 (Bankr. W.D. Va. 1984).

Applied in Community Hosp. v. Musser, 24 Bankr. 913 (W.D. Va. 1982).

II. DECISIONS UNDER PRIOR LAW.

Editor's note. — The case cited below was decided under corresponding provisions of former law. The terms "this article" and "these sections," as used below, refer to former provisions.

This article merely creates a method of payment to hospitals, physicians and nurses which, in effect, makes any recovery in a death action subject to the limitations set forth in these sections. The only effect of this article is to protect pro tanto the rights of those who have rendered services to the injured person pending his demise. In other words, it in effect adds their particular condition to the extent specified in the statute, to those other beneficiaries mentioned in the statutes creating the cause of action and regulating the distribution of the recovery. Holley v. The Manfred Stansfield, 186 F. Supp. 805 (E.D. Va. 1960).

§ 8.01-66.3. Lien inferior to claim of attorney or personal representative. — The lien provided for in § 8.01-66.2 shall be of inferior dignity to the

§ 8.01-66.4   CODE OF VIRGINIA   § 8.01-66.7

claim or lien of the attorney of such injured person or of his personal representative for professional services for representing such injured person or his personal representative in his claim or suit for damages for such personal injuries. (Code 1950, § 32-139; 1979, c. 722.)

§ 8.01-66.4. Subrogation. — Any municipal corporation or any person, firm or corporation who may pay the charges for which a lien is provided in § 8.01-66.2 shall be subrogated to such lien. (Code 1950, § 32-140; 1979, c. 722.)

I. DECISIONS UNDER PRIOR LAW.

Editor's note. — The case cited below was decided under corresponding provisions of former law. The term "this section," as used below, refers to former provisions.

For case holding invalid a municipal personnel rule allowing the municipality to obtain greater rights of subrogation than permitted by this section, see City of Richmond v. Hanes, 203 Va. 102, 122 S.E.2d 895 (1961).

§ 8.01-66.5. Written notice required. — No lien provided for in § 8.01-66.2 or § 8.01-66.9 shall be created or become effective in favor of the Commonwealth, an institution thereof, or a hospital, physician, nurse or physical therapist unless and until a written notice of lien setting forth the name of the Commonwealth, or the institution, hospital, physician, nurse or physical therapist and the name of the injured person, has been served upon or given to the person, firm or corporation whose negligence is alleged to have caused such injuries, or to the attorney for the injured party, or to the injured party. Such written notice of lien shall not be required if the attorney for the injured party knew that medical services were either provided or paid for by the Commonwealth. (Code 1950, § 32-142; 1979, c. 722; 1980, c. 623; 1983, c. 263; 1988, c. 544; 1998, c. 183.)

I. DECISIONS UNDER CURRENT LAW.

Lien may be perfected by giving written notice. — This section provides that the lien may be perfected by giving written notice to the injured person or his attorney; there is no requirement that suit must be pending against the alleged tort-feasor when the lien is perfected. Commonwealth v. Lee, 239 Va. 114, 387 S.E.2d 770 (1990).

§ 8.01-66.6. Liability for reasonable charges for services. — The notice set forth in § 8.01-66.5, when served upon or given to the person, firm or corporation whose negligence is alleged to have caused injuries or to the attorney for the injured party, shall have the effect of making such person, firm, corporation or attorney liable for the reasonable charges for the services rendered the injured person to the extent of the amount paid to or received by such injured party or his personal representative exclusive of attorney's fees, but, except in liens created under § 8.01-66.9, not in excess of the maximum amounts prescribed in § 8.01-66.2. (Code 1950, § 32-143; 1979, c. 722; 1980, c. 623.)

§ 8.01-66.7. Hearing and disposal of claim of unreasonableness. — If the injured person questions the reasonableness of the charges made by a hospital, nurse or physician claiming a lien pursuant to § 8.01-66.2, the injured person or the hospital, physician or nurse may file, in the court that would have jurisdiction of such claim if such claim were asserted against the injured person by such hospital, physician or nurse, a petition setting forth the facts. The court shall hear and dispose of the matter in a summary way after five days' notice to the other party in interest. (Code 1950, § 32-145; 1979, c. 722.)

§ 8.01-66.8. Petition to enforce lien. — If suit is instituted by an injured person or his personal representative against the person, firm or corporation allegedly causing the person's injuries, a hospital, physician or nurse, in lieu of proceeding according to §§ 8.01-66.5 to 8.01-66.7, may file in the court wherein such suit is pending a petition to enforce the lien provided for in § 8.01-66.2 or § 8.01-66.9. Such petition shall be heard and disposed of in a summary way. (Code 1950, § 32-146; 1979, c. 722; 1980, c. 623.)

§ 8.01-66.9. Lien in favor of Commonwealth, its programs, institutions or departments on claim for personal injuries. — Whenever any person sustains personal injuries and receives treatment in any hospital, public or private, or receives medical attention or treatment from any physician, or receives nursing services or care from any registered nurse in this Commonwealth, or receives pharmaceutical goods or any type of medical or rehabilitative device, apparatus, or treatment which is paid for pursuant to the Virginia Medical Assistance Program, the State/Local Hospitalization Program and other programs of the Department of Medical Assistance Services, the Maternal and Child Health Program, or the Children's Specialty Services Program, or provided at or paid for by any hospital or rehabilitation center operated by the Commonwealth, the Department of Rehabilitative Services or any state institution of higher education, the Commonwealth shall have a lien for the total amount paid pursuant to such program, and the Commonwealth or such Department or institution shall have a lien for the total amount due for the services, equipment or devices provided at or paid for by such hospital or center operated by the Commonwealth or such Department or institution, or any portion thereof compromised pursuant to the authority granted under § 2.1-127, on the claim of such injured person or of his personal representative against the person, firm, or corporation who is alleged to have caused such injuries.

The Commonwealth or such Department or institution shall also have a lien on the claim of the injured person or his personal representative for any funds which may be due him from insurance moneys received for such medical services under the injured party's own insurance coverage or through an uninsured or underinsured motorist insurance coverage endorsement. The lien granted to the Commonwealth for the total amounts paid pursuant to the Virginia Medical Assistance Program, the State/Local Hospitalization Program and other programs of the Department of Medical Assistance Services, the Maternal and Child Health Program, or the Children's Specialty Services Program shall have priority over the lien for the amounts due for services, equipment or devices provided at a hospital or center operated by the Commonwealth. The Commonwealth's or such Department's or institution's lien shall be inferior to any lien for payment of reasonable attorney's fees and costs, but shall be superior to all other liens created by the provisions of this chapter and otherwise. Expenses for reasonable legal fees and costs shall be deducted from the total amount recovered. The amount of the lien may be compromised pursuant to § 2.1-127.

The court in which a suit by an injured person or his personal representative has been filed against the person, firm or corporation alleged to have caused such injuries or in which such suit may properly be filed, may, upon motion or petition by the injured person, his personal representative or his attorney, and after written notice is given to all those holding liens attaching to the recovery, reduce the amount of the liens and apportion the recovery, whether by verdict or negotiated settlement, between the plaintiff, the plaintiff's attorney, and the

Commonwealth or such Department or institution as the equities of the case may appear, provided that the injured person, his personal representative or attorney has made a good faith effort to negotiate a compromise pursuant to § 2.1-127. The court shall set forth the basis for any such reduction in a written order. (Code 1950, § 32-139.1; 1972, c. 481; 1974, c. 518; 1979, c. 722; 1981, c. 562; 1982, c. 491; 1983, c. 263; 1984, c. 767; 1985, c. 580; 1986, c. 238; 1988, c. 544; 1989, c. 624; 1992, c. 104.)

I. DECISIONS UNDER CURRENT LAW.

Purpose. — The legislative purpose of this section was to secure to the public treasury such recompense as could be found, where public funds had been expended for the treatment of tortious injuries. Commonwealth v. Lee, 239 Va. 114, 387 S.E.2d 770 (1990).

Terms "any person" and "claim of such injured person." — The term "any person" in this section is not limited in scope to person sui juris and includes infants within its plain meaning. Likewise, the phrase "claim of such injured person" means precisely what it purports to say; therefore, this section imposes the Commonwealth's lien upon the injured person's claim against the alleged tort-feasor, regardless of the nature of the claim. Commonwealth v. Lee, 239 Va. 114, 387 S.E.2d 770 (1990).

Court does not have authority to discharge lienholder's underlying debt. — The final sentence of this section does not give the court authority to discharge the lienholder's underlying debt, except to subject it to a credit for the amount apportioned to it in the settlement. Rector & Visitors of UVA v. Harris, 239 Va. 119, 387 S.E.2d 772 (1990) (decided under version of section prior to 1989 amendment).

Shares of recovery apportioned immune from claims of other parties. — When a court, acting pursuant to the final sentence of this section, apportions a recovery between a plaintiff, the plaintiff's attorney, and the Commonwealth or its institutions, that apportionment is binding upon the parties whose claims were adjudicated in the apportionment proceeding, provided such parties had proper notice. The shares of the recovery thus apportioned are thereafter immune from the claims of the other parties to the apportionment, although such claims, subject to credits resulting from the apportionment, may be enforced against other property. Rector & Visitors of UVA v. Harris, 239 Va. 119, 387 S.E.2d 772 (1990).

Amendment vested judge authority to compromise and reduce Commonwealth's lien. — The effect of the 1981 amendment of this section was to vest in the trial judge, in the circumstances specified by the statute, the authority, otherwise vested in the Attorney General, the Governor, and the appropriate department head by § 2.1-127, to compromise and reduce the Commonwealth's lien. The purpose of the amendment was to reduce expense and delay, to avoid litigation, and to promote settlements. Commonwealth v. Smith, 239 Va. 108, 387 S.E.2d 767 (1990).

Purpose of amendment met only if statute construed to promote settlements. — The legislative purpose of the 1981 amendment of this section is met only if the statute is construed to promote, not to frustrate, settlements. Commonwealth v. Smith, 239 Va. 108, 387 S.E.2d 767 (1990).

Decision to reduce lien affirmed despite prior accepted offer of settlement. — Supreme Court affirmed trial court's decision to reduce Commonwealth's lien for plaintiff's medical care expenses, despite fact that the accepted offer of settlement had been proposed several years prior to the date for trial, where the lower court found that the offer was not acceptable until the court had reduced the amount of the Commonwealth's lien pursuant to the provisions of this section. Commonwealth v. Smith, 239 Va. 108, 387 S.E.2d 767 (1990) (decided under version of section prior to 1989 amendment).

§ 8.01-66.9:1. Lien against recovery for medical treatment provided to prisoner. — In any civil action brought for injuries or death suffered by any person while confined in a state or local correctional facility, the Commonwealth or the locality, as the case may be, shall have a lien against any recovery by settlement or verdict for all actual expenses incurred by the Commonwealth or the locality for medical, surgical and hospital treatment and supplies for the prisoner, whether provided by public or private health care providers, as a result of the injury. Such lien shall be subject to the payment of reasonable attorneys' fees and costs. (1984, c. 519.)

§ **8.01-66.10. Death claims settled by compromise or suit.** — In case of personal injuries resulting in death and settlement therefor by compromise or suit under the provisions of §§ 8.01-50 to 8.01-56, the liens provided for in this article may be asserted against the recovery, or against the estate of the decedent, but not both. If asserted against the recovery and paid, such liens shall attach pro rata to the amounts received respectively by such beneficiaries as are designated to receive the moneys distributed and in their respective amounts; and such beneficiaries, or the personal representative for their benefit, shall be subrogated to the liens against the estate of such decedent provided for by § 64.1-157. (Code 1950, § 32-141; 1979, c. 722.)

§ **8.01-66.11. Necessity for settlement or judgment.** — Nothing contained in this article shall be construed as imposing liability on any person, firm or corporation whose negligence is alleged to have caused injuries or on the attorney for the injured party where no settlement is made, or, in case of an attorney, where no funds come into his hands, or where no judgment is obtained in favor of such injured party or his personal representative. (Code 1950, § 32-144; 1979, c. 722.)

§ **8.01-66.12. Term physician to include chiropractor.** — Wherever the term physician is used in this article, it shall include chiropractor. (1993, c. 702.)

ARTICLE 8.

Actions for the Sale, Lease, Exchange, Redemption and Other Disposition of Lands of Persons Under a Disability.

§ **8.01-67. Definitions; persons under a disability; fiduciary.** — The terms *"fiduciary"* and *"person under a disability"* as used in this article shall have the meanings ascribed to them in § 8.01-2. (1977, c. 617.)

I. DECISIONS UNDER CURRENT LAW.

Applied in Upton v. Hall, 225 Va. 168, 300 S.E.2d 777 (1983).

§ **8.01-68. Jurisdiction.** — Circuit courts in the exercise of their equity jurisdiction, upon being satisfied by competent evidence independent of the admissions in the pleadings or elsewhere in the proceedings, that one or more of the types of relief hereinafter specified will promote the interest of an owner of land, or any interest therein, who is a person under a disability as defined in this chapter for whom a conservator has not been appointed pursuant to Article 1.1 (§ 37.1-134.6 et seq.) of Chapter 4 of Title 37.1, and taking into consideration the rights of any other party interested in such land, may order the sale, exchange, lease, encumbrance, redemption, or other disposition of such real estate as to the court may seem just and equitable.

In the case of the sales of such lands or interest therein, the court shall be governed by the established practices for judicial sales generally except as they may be specifically modified by provisions of this article. (Code 1950, §§ 8-675, 8-677, 8-681, 8-682, 8-683; 1952, c. 360; 1977, c. 617; 1997, c. 921.)

REVISERS' NOTE

The section combines and simplifies former §§ 8-675, 8-677, 8-681, 8-682, and 8-683 while retaining the thrust of these sections. Thus, § 8.01-68 promotes the interest of the person under a disability without injuriously affecting the rights of the persons who may also have an interest in the land.

Cross references. — As to leases on behalf of person under a disability, see § 8.01-74. As to petition by fiduciary for sale of real estate of person under a disability, see §§ 8.01-78 through 8.01-80. As to disposition of proceeds of partition of person under a disability, see § 8.01-85. As to sale of contingent estate, see §§ 8.01-94, 8.01-95. As to protection of purchaser at judicial sale, see § 8.01-113. As to commutation of life estate of person under disability, see § 55-276. For rules of court governing suits in equity, see Rules 2:1 through 2:21. For rule relating to intervenors, see Rule 2:15.

Law Review. — For article, "Updating Virginia's Probate Law," see 4 U. Rich. L. Rev. 223 (1970). For an article, "Reform of Adult Guardianship Law," see 32 U. Rich. L. Rev. 1273 (1998).

I. Decisions Under Current Law.
II. Decisions Under Prior Law.
  A. General Consideration.
  B. Jurisdiction.
  C. When Sale Proper.
  D. Interests That May Be Sold.
  E. Confirmation of Sale Already Made.
  F. Procedure.
  G. Setting Aside Decree.

I. DECISIONS UNDER CURRENT LAW.

Recovery for improvements against one who was not party to lease. — White v. Pleasants, 227 Va. 508, 317 S.E.2d 489 (1984).

Applied in Commonwealth v. Taylor, 256 Va. 514, 506 S.E.2d 312 (1998).

II. DECISIONS UNDER PRIOR LAW.

A. General Consideration.

Editor's note. — The cases cited below were decided under corresponding provisions of former law. The terms "this chapter" and "this section," as used below, refer to former provisions.

Infants' lands can be sold only as provided in this chapter. — Infants' lands can be sold only under the authority and for the purpose contained in this and the following sections of this chapter. Clark v. George, 161 Va. 104, 170 S.E. 713 (1933).

Section is to be liberally construed. — This section is highly remedial, and upon familiar principles must receive a liberal construction, to give effect to the intention of the legislature and enhance the remedy. Faulkner v. Davis, 59 Va. (18 Gratt.) 651 (1868); Rhea v. Shields, 103 Va. 305, 49 S.E. 70 (1904).

As to subjects to be sold. — The rule requiring a liberal construction to be placed upon statutes for the sale of lands of persons under disability has reference rather to the subjects sought to be sold in which such persons are interested than to the procedure by which such sales are effected. It does not authorize a mode of procedure not in substantial compliance with the statute authorizing the sale. Coleman v. Virginia Stave & Heading Co., 112 Va. 61, 70 S.E. 545 (1911). See also, Parker v. Stephenson, 127 Va. 431, 104 S.E. 39 (1920).

But substantial compliance with provisions of this chapter is required. — When a suit is instituted to confirm the sale of infants' lands, there must be not only a substantial compliance with this section but a substantial compliance with the other provisions of this chapter. Clark v. George, 161 Va. 104, 170 S.E. 713 (1933).

If a suit for the sale of lands of an insane person be brought under this section, there must be a substantial compliance with the other sections of this chapter. Wheeler v. Thomas, 116 Va. 259, 81 S.E. 51 (1914).

Character of property not changed except to extent required. — The legislative intent expressed in the statutes concerning the sale of lands owned by infants and incompetents is that the character and nature of an incompetent's land is not to be changed except to the extent required, and the proceeds of sale shall be impressed with the character of the land. Bryson v. Turnbull, 194 Va. 528, 74 S.E.2d 180 (1953).

Consent decree in partition proceedings void for noncompliance with article. — A consent decree in partition proceedings, to the effect that respondents' share of the land be set off to them in bulk as joint tenants with the right of survivorship, was void as to an incompetent respondent where the requirements of the statutes providing for the sale of lands belonging to persons under disability were not complied with, although the incompetent's committee was a party to the suit and the incompetent was represented by a guardian ad litem. Leonard v. Boswell, 197 Va. 713, 90 S.E.2d 872 (1956).

B. Jurisdiction.

Jurisdiction is not inherent. — In this State a court of equity has no authority under its general jurisdiction as guardian of infants to sell their real estate whenever it is to the advantage of the infants to do so, whether for reinvestment or for their maintenance and education. Faulkner v. Davis, 59 Va. (18 Gratt.) 651 (1868); Kavanaugh v. Shacklett, 111 Va. 423, 69 S.E. 335 (1910); Coleman v. Virginia Stave & Heading Co., 112 Va. 61, 70 S.E. 545 (1911).

This section grants such jurisdiction. — The doctrine in this State is well settled that courts of equity possess no inherent power, as guardians of infants, to sell their real estate for the purpose of reinvestment, and the obvious purpose of this section is to invest those courts with that jurisdiction in respect to estates of all persons under disability. Rhea v. Shields, 103 Va. 305, 49 S.E. 70 (1904). See also, Faulkner v. Davis, 59 Va. (18 Gratt.) 651 (1868); Rinker v. Streit, 73 Va. (33 Gratt.) 663 (1880); Kavanaugh v. Shacklett, 111 Va. 423, 69 S.E. 335 (1910); Coleman v. Virginia Stave & Heading Co., 112 Va. 61, 70 S.E. 545 (1911).

The jurisdiction of the circuit courts of the Commonwealth to authorize the application of the proceeds of the corpus of infants' real estate to their maintenance and education is altogether statutory. Whitehead v. Bradley, 87 Va. 676, 13 S.E. 195 (1891); Hess v. Hess, 108 Va. 483, 62 S.E. 273 (1908).

But it is special and limited. — In a suit under this section for the sale of an infant's lands, the court does not exercise a general, but only a special, statutory and limited, jurisdiction. Therefore, the conditions of fact, under which this section confers jurisdiction upon the court to enter a decree of sale, must affirmatively appear on the face of the proceedings in the suit in order that the decree may be valid. Farant Inv. Corp. v. Francis, 138 Va. 417, 122 S.E. 141 (1924).

And court may exercise only powers expressly granted. — Possessing no inherent power to sell the land of an infant, courts of equity are limited by the powers expressly granted by this chapter. Newman v. Light, 152 Va. 760, 148 S.E. 818 (1929).

C. When Sale Proper.

Sale to pay debts of decedent is not authorized. — Nowhere in this chapter is there any authority for the sale of infant's lands or a confirmation of such a sale for the purpose of paying the debts of a testator or intestate by or from whom the title to the lands has been devised or inherited by the infants. Clark v. George, 161 Va. 104, 170 S.E. 713 (1933).

Unless testator expressly prohibits sale. — It was not the purpose of the legislature to overrule an imperative prohibition of the testator, applicable to all circumstances that might occur or exist; and, therefore, the power to sell is withheld from the courts where the will expressly directs that the property shall not be sold. Where there is no such absolute prohibition, the testator must be regarded as having left the matter subject to the general authority conferred by the law. Talley v. Starke, 47 Va. (6 Gratt.) 339 (1849).

In Talley v. Starke, 47 Va. (6 Gratt.) 339 (1849), a testator directed his estate, after payment of his debts, to be kept together until his youngest child should come of age, to be controlled and managed by his executor and his wife with their best discretion, so as to make it productive of the greatest amount of profits for the support of his wife and children. It was held that a court of equity might direct a sale of the real estate under the statute if it was for the benefit of the infant children, and those who were of age consented. The direction of the testator that his estate should be kept together did not amount to an absolute prohibition of a sale, which would have made it incompetent for the court to decree such a sale. Faulkner v. Davis, 59 Va. (18 Gratt.) 651 (1868).

And construction of will is not prerequisite to sale. — This section does not require as a prerequisite that the will under which infants hold land shall be construed before a sale is ordered. Lancaster v. Barton, 92 Va. 615, 24 S.E. 251 (1896).

D. Interests That May Be Sold.

Land in which infant has any interest may be sold. — Courts of equity have authority to sell land in which infants have an interest, whether in possession or remainder, vested or contingent, if the proper parties can be brought before the courts. Faulkner v. Davis, 59 Va. (18 Gratt.) 651 (1868).

Fee may be sold though infant has only life estate. — Under this section, a court of equity at the suit of the trustee of a life estate in land may sell not only the life estate, but also the remainder limited on that estate, over which the trust does not extend, the proceeds of the sale or the subject in which they are invested being held upon the same trusts and subject to the same limitations as the original estate. Rhea v. Shields, 103 Va. 305, 49 S.E. 70 (1904).

Or remainder. — A father as guardian of his infant children files a bill for the sale of real estate held by himself for life and by his children in remainder, and it is sold accordingly. This is authorized by this section. Cooper v. Hepburn, 56 Va. (15 Gratt.) 551 (1860).

But mere contingent interest alone should not be sold. — Under no circumstances would a court of equity decree the sale of a mere contingent interest of infants alone. Faulkner v. Davis, 59 Va. (18 Gratt.) 651 (1868).

E. Confirmation of Sale Already Made.

Court may confirm sale made before suit is brought. — The former section has been generally construed as authorizing the court which has jurisdiction to order a sale to approve and confirm a sale made by the fiduciary before suit is brought, subject to the court's approval and confirmation, provided it be clearly shown, independently of any admissions in the answers, that the interests of the infant, insane person or beneficiaries in the trust, as the case may be, will be promoted, and the court is of opinion that the right of no person will be violated thereby. Smith v. White, 107 Va. 616, 59 S.E. 480 (1907).

If it appears advantageous. — A bill by the guardians of infant children to have a contract for the sale of real estate confirmed, or the real estate resold, is properly maintainable under this section. It is competent for the court to confirm the sale already made, if it appears advantageous, instead of ordering a resale. Garland v. Loving, 22 Va. (1 Rand.) 396 (1823).

Court should not confirm sale when necessity therefor has ceased. — When the court is called upon to confirm a sale had under this section, and the necessity therefor, which seemed to exist when the sale was ordered, shall have ceased, it is proper that the court should refuse to confirm the sale. Harkrader v. Bonham, 88 Va. 247, 16 S.E. 159 (1891).

Subsequent approval does not validate unauthorized expenditure. — Where a sale commissioner paid the purchase money of an infant's realty sold under decree of court to the infant's guardian, and the latter expended the principal thereof for the ward's maintenance and education, without previous authority from the court, subsequent approval by the court was too late to give validity either to the expenditure or the payment. Whitehead v. Bradley, 87 Va. 676, 13 S.E. 195 (1891).

F. Procedure.

Petition may be filed in appropriate pending suit. — This section is construed not as requiring an independent bill for the purpose of selling an infant's lands but as permitting such a sale on petition filed in any appropriate suit already pending. Carter Coal Co. v. Litz, 54 F. Supp. 115 (W.D. Va. 1943), aff'd, 140 F.2d 934 (4th Cir. 1944).

Infant is treated as hostile party. — In proceedings to sell their land, infants stand in the position of hostile parties, and are treated as objecting to every step taken therein. Coleman v. Virginia Stave & Heading Co., 112 Va. 61, 70 S.E. 545 (1911).

And need not demur. — In a suit to sell or mortgage the lands of an infant, he is considered as objecting at every point, and no demurrer is needed on his part. Parker v. Stephenson, 127 Va. 431, 104 S.E. 39 (1920).

Omission of averment that plaintiff sues as guardian is not fatal. — The omission of a formal averment that a bill is brought by the plaintiff as guardian does not violate the proceedings, where the bill states that the plaintiff is the guardian, and the whole frame of the bill is in pursuance of what is required to be set out in such a case, and the infants are made defendants. Cooper v. Hepburn, 56 Va. (15 Gratt.) 551 (1860).

Petition should set forth all infant's property. — A bill did not contain an express allegation that the real estate which was set forth therein constituted all of the estate, real or personal, belonging to the infant, but it appeared from the evidence that the real estate set forth did, as a matter of fact, constitute all of the infant's estate. It was held that this ultimate fact was all that was required to be stated, and that if the court found that the plaintiff alleged and proved this fact, and there was nothing on the face of the proceedings to negative the finding, then it was adequate. Farant Inv. Corp. v. Francis, 138 Va. 417, 122 S.E. 141 (1924).

It is immaterial that the bill in a suit for the sale of the infant's lands, in addition to setting out all of the real and personal estate belonging to the infant does not add the statement that this is all the real and personal estate belonging to the infant. Farant Inv. Corp. v. Francis, 138 Va. 417, 122 S.E. 141 (1924).

And plaintiff should adduce proof of propriety of sale. — A failure to aver what property the infant owns besides that sought to be sold, and to adduce any proof of the propriety of the sale, is not adequate and a sale based thereon is a nullity. Coleman v. Virginia Stave & Heading Co., 112 Va. 61, 70 S.E. 545 (1911).

Propriety cannot be determined on ex parte affidavits. — The propriety of making a sale under this section, or of confirming a conditional sale, made before suit brought under this section, cannot be determined upon ex parte affidavits. Smith v. White, 107 Va. 616, 59 S.E. 480 (1907). See also, Coleman v. Virginia Stave & Heading Co., 112 Va. 61, 70 S.E. 545 (1911).

Validity of appointment of guardian cannot be attacked. — The fact that the guardian was appointed by a court having no power to do so cannot be raised as an objection to the validity of a sale of an infant's lands, since such appointment cannot be attacked collaterally. Durrett v. Davis, 65 Va. (24 Gratt.) 302 (1874).

G. Setting Aside Decree.

Where court has jurisdiction, decree is conclusive. — Where a court has jurisdiction pursuant to this section, both of the parties and of the subject matter in litigation, its decree, though erroneous, is conclusive until reversed or set aside. Rhea v. Shields, 103 Va. 305, 49 S.E. 70 (1904).

And cannot be attacked collaterally. — The court having had jurisdiction of the case under this section, the validity and propriety of a decree for the sale of infant's land cannot be questioned in a collateral proceeding. Quesenberry v. Barbour, 75 Va. (31 Gratt.) 491 (1879).

Adjudicated fact cannot be inquired into in collateral proceeding. — Where a decree for the sale of an infant's land is assailed, and nothing appears on the face of the record of the proceedings which tends to negative the adjudicated fact that the bill plainly set out all of the real and personal estate belonging to the infant, it must be assumed that there was evidence sufficient to support this adjudication, so that the fact is not open for further inquiry in a collateral proceeding. Farant Inv. Corp. v. Francis, 138 Va. 417, 122 S.E. 141 (1924).

But if jurisdiction is lacking, sale is void. — Where proceedings are wholly wanting in some of the jurisdictional requirements of this section, a sale is void and subject to collateral attack. Robert v. Hagan, 121 Va. 573, 93 S.E. 619 (1917).

And noncompliance with chapter invalidates decree. — In suit for the sale of infants' lands under this chapter, where it appears that the bill was not verified and no answer was filed by the guardian ad litem, in proper person of the infants, nor by the infants over the age of fourteen years, and there were other vital defects in the proceedings, the court was without jurisdiction to decree a sale of the lands, and the decree, the sale, and all proceedings thereunder were utterly void and without effect, and might be assailed directly or collaterally. Substantial compliance with this chapter is essential to the validity of the proceedings. Brenham v. Smith, 120 Va. 30, 90 S.E. 657 (1916).

But sales beneficial to infants will not be set aside on the ground of irregularities therein. Cooper v. Hepburn, 56 Va. (15 Gratt.) 551 (1860). See also, Brown v. Armistead, 27 Va. (6 Rand.) 594 (1828).

And § 8.01-113 applies to sales of lands, under this section, of infants made in suits properly brought for that purpose. Cooper v. Hepburn, 56 Va. (15 Gratt.) 551 (1860); Dixon v. McCue, 62 Va. (21 Gratt.) 373 (1871); Quesenberry v. Barbour, 72 Va. (31 Gratt.) 491 (1879); Lancaster v. Barton, 92 Va. 615, 24 S.E. 251 (1896).

§ 8.01-69. Commencement of suit; parties. — Any of the relief specified in this article may be sought by bill in equity filed by a fiduciary, as defined in this article, or by any other person having an interest in the subject matter of the proceedings. A person under a disability, fiduciary, all those who would be the heirs or distributees of the defendant person under disability if he had died at the time of the commencement of this proceeding, except as provided in § 8.01-78, and all other persons interested in the subject matter of the proceeding, shall be made parties defendant when not parties plaintiff. (Code 1950, § 8-676; 1952, c. 360; 1972, c. 361; 1973, c. 338; 1977, c. 617; 1983, c. 459.)

REVISERS' NOTE

This is a simplification of the first paragraph of former § 8-676, the second paragraph of which was former § 8.01-70.

Cross references. — For rule as to issuance and service of process on a defendant who is a person under a disability, see Rule 2:4.

I. Decisions Under Current Law.
II. Decisions Under Prior Law.
   A. General Consideration.
   B. Persons Who Would Be Heirs of Person Under Disability.

I. DECISIONS UNDER CURRENT LAW.

Representative capacity. — An individual or entity does not acquire standing to sue in a representative capacity by asserting the rights of another unless authorized by the statute to do so. W.S. Carnes, Inc. v. Board of Supvrs., 252 Va. 377, 478 S.E.2d 295 (1996).

II. DECISIONS UNDER PRIOR LAW.

A. General Consideration.

Editor's note. — The cases cited below were decided under corresponding provisions of former law. The term "this section," as used below, refers to former provisions.

Presence of necessary parties is jurisdictional. — The presence of the necessary parties required by this section in a suit for the sale of infants' lands is jurisdictional, and a decree rendered in their absence is void as to infants whose interests are affected thereby. Gee v. McCormick, 142 Va. 173, 128 S.E. 541 (1925); Newman v. Light, 152 Va. 760, 148 S.E. 818 (1929).

And want of proper parties invalidates mortgage and sale. — Where, in a suit for the sale or mortgage of an infant's lands, it was the purpose of the parties to proceed under this and the preceding section, and they endeavored to conform thereto, but the proceedings were substantially defective for want of proper parties, a mortgage made in pursuance thereof and a sale thereunder were void. Parker v. Stephenson, 127 Va. 431, 104 S.E. 39 (1920).

Lack of substantial compliance with section voids proceedings. — Where the state court failed to substantially comply with former § 8-676, which set forth jurisdictional requirements for an action to sell, encumber or lease infants' land, the lack of substantial compliance made the proceeding void ab initio and in toto because the court lacked jurisdiction. Payne v. Consolidation Coal Co., 607 F. Supp. 378 (D. Va. 1985) (decided under former § 8-676).

The infants must be made parties defendant by guardian ad litem. Snavely v. Harkrader, 70 Va. (29 Gratt.) 112 (1877).

Or they may be plaintiffs with their guardian. — The fact that infants were plaintiffs with their mother, instead of being made defendants, is no objection to the proceedings in a suit for the sale of land. Quesenberry v. Barbour, 72 Va. (31 Gratt.) 491 (1879).

Purchaser at sale to be confirmed is necessary party. — Where the petition asks that a contract previously entered into by the guardian for the sale of the infant's land be confirmed by the court, the purchaser under the contract is a necessary party. Hughes v. Johnston, 53 Va. (12 Gratt.) 479 (1855).

B. Persons Who Would Be Heirs of Person Under Disability.

"Distributees" and "heirs" refer to natural persons only. — The words "distributees" and "heirs," as used in this section, have reference to natural persons only, and not to the Commonwealth, as the Commonwealth takes property not as an heir but by title paramount. Farant Inv. Corp. v. Francis, 138 Va. 417, 122 S.E. 141 (1924).

Presumptive heirs of infant must be parties defendant. — All persons who would be the heirs of the infant if he were dead must, under this section, be made parties defendant. Snavely v. Harkrader, 70 Va. (29 Gratt.) 112 (1877).

Unless they are plaintiffs. — Where a bill is filed by a father and mother, who are trustees of certain lands for their infant children, to sell these lands, it is a sufficient compliance with this section that the infants should be made parties defendant, their parents, who are the persons who would be the heirs of each infant if he were dead, being already plaintiffs. Lancaster v. Barton, 92 Va. 615, 24 S.E. 251 (1896).

Where a bill is filed by a guardian, it is not necessary to make him a party defendant on the ground that he would be an heir of the infant if the infant were dead. Durrett v. Davis, 65 Va. (24 Gratt.) 302 (1874).

The reason for the requirement that the heirs of the infants be made parties is twofold: First, the presumed affection of such heirs for the infants; and, second, their personal contingent interest in the land sought to be sold. It is a natural conclusion that those who may become the owners of the land or its proceeds will see that the same is not sacrificed by a guardian who is recreant of the trust imposed upon him. Gee v. McCormick, 142 Va. 173, 128 S.E. 541 (1925); Newman v. Light, 152 Va. 760, 148 S.E. 818 (1929). See Bryson v. Turnbull, 194 Va. 528, 74 S.E.2d 180 (1953).

Doctrine of representation applies. — Land was conveyed in trust for a husband and wife and the survivor of them for life, and at the death of the survivor to their children who would be living at the death of the survivor, and the descendants of such of the children as should then be dead leaving descendants. After the death of the husband, a bill was filed by the wife against the children and trustees for a sale of the land. It was held that a sale decreed upon the bill would bind the descendants of any child dying within the lifetime of the wife, under the doctrine of representation. Faulkner v. Davis, 59 Va. (18 Gratt.) 651 (1868).

But not where interests are hostile. — When the interests of the life tenant and the remaindermen are hostile, infant remaindermen cannot be considered as being before the

§ 8.01-70   CIVIL REMEDIES AND PROCEDURE   § 8.01-72

court by representation by the life tenant. Turner v. Barraud, 102 Va. 324, 46 S.E. 318 (1904).

Questions of who would be heirs is one of fact. — In order to effectuate the title of a purchaser at a judicial sale of an infant's lands, it must appear from the proceedings that the provisions of this chapter have been substantially complied with. However, the question as to who would be the heirs of an infant if he were dead is one of fact. Newman v. Light, 152 Va. 760, 148 S.E. 818 (1929).

Finding that infant had no kin cannot be assailed collaterally. — In an action of ejectment, a decree in a suit for the sale of an infant's land was assailed because those who would have been the infant's heirs or distributees, if he had been dead, had not been made defendants to the suit, as required by this section. The bill alleges that the infant had no kin or relations. The commissioner reported that all necessary parties were before the court, and that it was proved that the infant had no relations whatever. And the court, upon the hearing on the report and the evidence returned therewith, confirmed the commissioner's report, and by so doing adjudicated its finding of fact that the infant, if he had been dead, would have had no heirs or distributees at the time of the suit. Nothing appeared on the face of the proceedings sufficient to negative this adjudicated fact. It was held that this finding of fact was final and conclusive, no appeal having been taken, and it could not be assailed collaterally, or affected by any extrinsic evidence. Farant Inv. Corp. v. Francis, 138 Va. 417, 122 S.E. 141 (1924).

Effect of failure to make presumptive heirs defendants. — In a suit to sell or mortgage an infant's lands, brought by the infant's mother in her own right and as guardian of the infant, there was a failure to comply with this section by making the heirs of an infant parties to the suit. It was insisted that if the court had jurisdiction on any ground, its decree was not void, but at most only voidable, and that the mother had the right to sue as creditor of her husband's estate, having paid his debts and legacies. But as the bill made no charge that the mother was a creditor, and did not show that at the time it was filed she had paid any debt or legacy of her husband, there was nothing in it to show jurisdiction on this ground. Parker v. Stephenson, 127 Va. 431, 104 S.E. 39 (1920).

Contingent remainderman is not necessary party after failure of contingency. — Where land is devised to a certain person during his natural life, and to his children if he should have lawful issue, and if not, to the testator's grandchildren and their heirs forever, and the life tenant marries and has children, the remainder vests in the children, and the alternative remainder to the grandchildren is defeated; hence the grandchildren are not necessary parties to a proceeding to sell the real estate after the birth of the children of the life tenant. Cooper v. Hepburn, 56 Va. (15 Gratt.) 551 (1860) (decided under former § 8-676).

§§ 8.01-70, 8.01-71: Repealed by Acts 1990, c. 831, effective January 1, 1991.

Cross references. — As to the abolition of dower and curtesy, effective Jan. 1, 1991, see § 64.1-19.2.

§ 8.01-72. When death to abate such suit. — A suit instituted under this article shall abate by reason of the death of the person under a disability unless a sale, exchange, lease, encumbrance, redemption, or other disposition of real estate has been confirmed by a decree in such suit. (Code 1950, § 8-678; 1952, c. 360; 1977, c. 617.)

REVISERS' NOTE

This section has been rewritten but there has been no change to the substance of the former law that confirmation by the court of its action will allow the court to proceed to a conclusion of the transaction even though the defendant party under a disability may have died subsequent to such confirmation.

Cross references. — For rule of court on substitution of parties, see Rule 2:16.

§ 8.01-73. Guardian ad litem to be appointed.

— In every suit brought under this article, a guardian ad litem shall be appointed for any person under a disability not otherwise represented by a guardian or committee, or trustee appointed pursuant to § 37.1-134, and for all persons proceeded against by an order or publication under the designation of "parties unknown" as provided for in § 8.01-316. The guardian ad litem shall file an answer as such. (Code 1950, § 8-679; 1952, c. 360; 1972, c. 361; 1977, c. 617; 1997, c. 540.)

REVISERS' NOTE

Former § 8-679 has been changed by the elimination of useless provisions regarding an answer by infants over the age of fourteen. Since the infant must be made a party, he may presumably answer regardless of age if he wishes to do so.

The guardian ad litem shall also represent the interest of "unknown parties," if any, who are proceeded against by order of publication.

Former § 8-680 (Failure to answer ...) has been deleted as unnecessary.

Cross references. — As to appointment of guardian ad litem in other suits, see § 8.01-9. As to appointment of guardian ad litem in proceedings for the sale or leasing of certain contingent and other estates, see § 8.01-94. For rule as to issuance and service of process on a defendant who is a person under a disability, see Rule 2:4.

I. DECISIONS UNDER PRIOR LAW.

Editor's note. — The cases cited below were decided under corresponding provisions of former law. The term "this section," as used below, refers to former provisions.

The failure of a guardian ad litem to answer in his own proper person is error. Gee v. McCormick, 142 Va. 173, 128 S.E. 541 (1925).

Mere formal defects in the answer of the guardian ad litem do not vitiate the proceedings. Coleman v. Virginia Stave & Heading Co., 112 Va. 61, 70 S.E. 545 (1911).

This section does not apply to partition suits. Cottrell v. Mathews, 120 Va. 847, 92 S.E. 808 (1917).

§ 8.01-74. Leases on behalf of persons under disability; new leases.

— A. *Leases on behalf of persons under a disability.* — When a person under a disability is entitled to or bound to renew any lease, any fiduciary on behalf of such person under a disability or any other interested person may apply by motion after reasonable notice to parties having a present interest in the property to be leased, to the circuit court as prescribed in subdivision 3 of § 8.01-261, and by the order of the court any person appointed by it may, from time to time, surrender or accept a surrender of such lease, or take or make a new lease of the same premises for such term and with such provisions as the court directs. Such reasonable sums as are incurred to renew any such lease shall, with interest thereon, be paid out of the profits of the leasehold premises, and be a charge thereon until payment.

B. *New leases.* — When it shall appear to a circuit court that the interests of a person under a disability will be promoted by the execution of a new lease, where no prior lease exists, any fiduciary or any other person interested in the subject matter may apply in like summary fashion as stated in subsection A of this section and upon showing to the satisfaction of the court that the provisions therein were complied with, including reasonable notice to parties having a present interest to the property to be leased, the circuit court upon the consideration of the probable length of the disability and the duration of the proposed lease, may order such lease to be executed. Such lease may be renewed or surrendered at any time pursuant to subsection A of this section and under such conditions as the court may direct. (Code 1950, § 8-674; 1952, c. 360; 1977, c. 617.)

REVISERS' NOTE

Former § 8-674 has been extended to permit the summary proceedings thereof to apply also to the renewal of leases as well as to new leases.

Law Review. — For note on sale, lease and encumbrance of infants' lands in Virginia, see 47 Va. L. Rev. 534. For note on the need for legislation in the area of the sale of infants' lands, see 51 Va. L. Rev. 355 (1965).

I. DECISIONS UNDER PRIOR LAW.

Editor's note. — The case cited below was decided under corresponding provisions of former law. The terms "this chapter" and "this section," as used below, refer to former provisions.

This chapter recognizes the inviolability of trust estates. — This and the following sections in this chapter recognize the inviolability of trust estates from lease, or sale, unless the interests of the cestuis que trustent will be promoted thereby, and unless the rights of no person will be violated. Schroeder v. Woodward, 116 Va. 506, 82 S.E. 192 (1914).

§ 8.01-75. Who not to be purchaser.

— At any sale under this article neither a fiduciary for a person under a disability, as defined under this article, nor the guardian ad litem shall be a purchaser directly or indirectly; provided, however, such fiduciary may be a purchaser if the court finds that such a purchase by the fiduciary is in the best interests of the person under a disability. (Code 1950, § 8-684; 1977, c. 617; 1980, c. 346.)

REVISERS' NOTE

This section changed former § 8-684 to remove the disqualification of a lessee as a purchaser of the land.

Cross references. — As to application of this section in suits to sell certain contingent and other estates, see § 8.01-95.

Law Review. — For survey of Virginia law on wills, trusts, and estates for year 1979-80, see 67 Va. L. Rev. 369 (1981).

I. DECISIONS UNDER PRIOR LAW.

Editor's note. — The cases cited below were decided under corresponding provisions of former law. The term "this section," as used below, refers to former provisions.

This section was enacted for the benefit and protection of the persons under disability, and not of their guardians, committees or trustees. Redd v. Jones, 71 Va. (30 Gratt.) 123 (1878).

Sale is not void but voidable. — Where land is sold under a decree of court in pursuance of a bill filed by the committee of an insane person and purchased by the committee contrary to this section, the sale is voidable and not void. It is in force until set aside, and this cannot be done collaterally. Cline v. Catron, 63 Va. (22 Gratt.) 378 (1872).

And in some cases might be sustained. — There may be a case in which a purchase made by a guardian or other fiduciary, of the land of his ward or other beneficiary, sold under this chapter, would and ought to be sustained and enforced. Redd v. Jones, 71 Va. (30 Gratt.) 123 (1878).

Bona fide purchaser will be protected. — A sale could not be set aside at the instance of an heir at law of a lunatic on the ground that the committee was himself the real purchaser, where the land had been conveyed to a trustee to secure a bona fide debt, and the party seeking to set aside the sale failed to allege notice to the trustee or the beneficiary of the fact relied on to set aside the sale, especially when the party seeking to set aside the sale herself joined in the deed of trust. Carter v. Allen, 62 Va. (21 Gratt.) 241 (1871).

§ 8.01-76. How proceeds from disposition to be secured and applied; when same may be paid over. — The proceeds of sale, or rents, income, or royalties, arising from the sale or lease, or other disposition, of lands of persons under a disability, whether in a suit for sale or lease thereof, or in a suit for partition, or in condemnation proceedings, shall be invested under the direction of the court for the use and benefit of the persons entitled to the estate; and in case of a trust estate subject to the uses, limitations, and conditions, contained in the writing creating the trust. The court shall take ample security for all investments so made, and from time to time require additional security, if necessary, and make any proper order for the faithful application and safe investment of the fund, and for the management and preservation of any properties or securities in which the same has been invested, and for the protection of the rights of all persons interested therein, whether such rights be vested or contingent, but nothing hereinbefore contained shall prevent the court having charge thereof from directing such funds to be paid over to the legally appointed and qualified fiduciary (as defined in § 8.01-67) of the person under a disability, whenever the court is satisfied that such fiduciary has executed sufficient bond; or from applying at any time all or any portion thereof to the proper needs and requirements of the person under a disability. Provided, however, that if such funds do not exceed $4,000, the court, in its discretion and without the intervention of a fiduciary, may pay such funds to any person deemed appropriate by the court for the use and benefit of a person under a disability, whether such person resides within or without the Commonwealth. Such funds not in excess of $4,000 shall, when paid over to such person deemed appropriate, be treated as personal property. (Code 1950, § 8-685; 1952, c. 360; 1968, c. 380; 1970, c. 355; 1972, c. 159; 1974, c. 139; 1977, c. 617; 1978, c. 419; 1981, c. 129.)

REVISERS' NOTE

Former § 8-685 has been changed to permit the court to order payment of up to $2500 to "any person deemed appropriate" rather than only to "parents." This does not change the court's consideration that such lesser amount is to be used only for the use and benefit of a person under a disability, whether such person resides within or without the Commonwealth.

Cross references. — As to application of proceeds under alternative procedure for sale of lands of person under a disability, see § 8.01-80. As to applicability of this section in proceedings to sell or lease certain contingent and other estates, see § 8.01-95. As to transfer by court to foreign guardian of proceeds of sale of real estate of nonresident infant, incapacitated person, or cestui que trust, see § 26-61.

Law Review. — For article, "Updating Virginia's Probate Law," see 4 U. Rich. L. Rev. 223 (1970).

I. DECISIONS UNDER PRIOR LAW.

Editor's note. — The case cited below was decided under corresponding provisions of former law. The term "this section," as used below, refers to former provisions.

Proceeds can be paid only as provided in this section. — After sale of an infant's lands, the court can only have the proceeds paid, for purposes of investment, into the hands of some person, who may or may not be the infant's guardian, upon special bonds being given for the care of the same, as prescribed by this section. Pope v. Prince, 105 Va. 209, 52 S.E. 1009 (1906).

§ 8.01-77. What proceeds of sale to pass as real estate. — The proceeds received under the preceding provisions of this article or under Article 9 (§ 8.01-81 et seq.) of this chapter, from the sale or division of real estate of a person under a disability or so much thereof as may remain at such person's

§ 8.01-78. CIVIL REMEDIES AND PROCEDURE § 8.01-78

death, if such person continue until death incapable from any cause of making a will, shall pass to those who would have been entitled to the land if it had not been sold or divided. (Code 1950, § 8-689; 1952, c. 360; 1968, c. 66; 1977, c. 617.)

I. DECISIONS UNDER PRIOR LAW.

Editor's note. — The cases cited below were decided under corresponding provisions of former law. The term "this section," as used below, refers to former provisions.

Purpose of section. — It is evident that while the legislature designed to authorize courts of chancery to sell infant's real estate, without which they had no authority to sell, it was at the same time its design that such sale should be made without affecting the infant's rights incident to an ownership of real estate, and without violating the rights of those who would be entitled to the estate, if the infant were dead. Indeed, it would not have been proper, if competent to the legislature, to have authorized a court to deprive the infant of a vested beneficial right incident to his ownership of real estate, he being incapable of assenting thereto, or to have diverted or "violated" the rights of those who would be entitled to the estate at the death of an infant under disability. Vaughan v. Jones, 64 Va. (23 Gratt.) 444 (1873).

Character of land is not to be changed except to extent required. — The legislative intent is made clear; viz., the character and nature of an incompetent's land is not to be changed except to the extent required. Bryson v. Turnbull, 194 Va. 528, 74 S.E.2d 180 (1953).

And proceeds are impressed with character of land sold. — Upon the involuntary sale, under a judicial decree, of the land of an incompetent person, incapable of dealing with the real estate, the proceeds should be impressed with the character of the land sold and should pass as such at death if the disabilities have not been removed. Bryson v. Turnbull, 194 Va. 528, 74 S.E.2d 180 (1953).

Where an infant's lands are sold under a decree of court, the proceeds retain the character of realty and pass as real estate. Thus, on the death of a female infant leaving a child, the proceeds will go to the child, and on its death during infancy, the husband surviving, the property will go to the child's heirs on the part of his mother, subject to the life estate of the husband, the impress of realty never having been removed. Vaughan v. Jones, 64 Va. (23 Gratt.) 444 (1873).

The conversion of an infant's real estate into money does not change its character as realty, and the proceeds of the sale retain the impress of real estate until the infant attains the age of 21 (now 18) years. Rinker v. Streit, 73 Va. (33 Gratt.) 663 (1873).

Section applies in suits for partition. — Where a suit for the sale of real property under a will, although not in the usual form and procedure, was more or less, in effect, a suit for the partition of real estate in which all parties joined and consented, the proceeds passed as real estate. Rinker v. Trout, 171 Va. 327, 198 S.E. 913 (1938).

§ **8.01-78. Alternate procedure for sale of real estate of person under disability.** — If the personal estate of any person under a disability for whom a fiduciary has been appointed under any of the provisions of Title 37.1, be insufficient for the discharge of his debts or if the personal estate or residue thereof after payment of debts and the rents and profits of his real estate be insufficient for his maintenance and that of his family, if any, the fiduciary of his estate may petition a circuit court for authority to mortgage, lease or sell so much of the real estate of such person as may be necessary for the purposes aforesaid, or any of them, setting forth in the petition the particulars and amount of the estate, real and personal, and a statement of the application of any personal estate, and debts and demands existing against the estate. Those persons who would be heirs or distributees of the person under a disability if he had died at the time of commencement of the proceeding need not be made parties defendant to a proceeding pursuant to this section. (Code 1950, § 8-689.1; 1952, c. 360; 1977, c. 617; 1983, c. 459.)

Cross references. — As to sale of contingent estates, see §§ 8.01-94, 8.01-95.

I. DECISIONS UNDER PRIOR LAW.

Editor's note. — The cases cited below were decided under corresponding provisions of former law. The term "this section," as used below, refers to former provisions.

Power to sell lunatic's realty depends on statute. — The committee of a lunatic has no power except as prescribed by statute to dispose of the real estate of a lunatic. Lake v.

Hope, 116 Va. 687, 82 S.E. 738 (1914).

No statute authorizes purchase of realty by committee. — While this section provides when and where a committee may petition for the sale, lease, or mortgage of the real estate of his ward, there is no specific statute authorizing a committee to purchase real estate, but Boisseau v. Boisseau, 79 Va. 73, 52 Am. R. 616 (1884), approves the rule that, with the sanction of a court, the property of an infant may be converted by his guardian from personalty into real estate when the conversion appears to be for the ward's benefit. Somers v. Godwin, 182 Va. 144, 27 S.E.2d 909 (1943).

§ 8.01-79. Same; reference of petition to commissioner. — On the presenting of such petition it may be referred to a commissioner in chancery or to a special commissioner appointed by the court, to inquire into and report upon the matters therein contained, whose duty it shall be to make such inquiry, to give notice to and hear all parties interested in such real estate and to report thereon with all convenient speed. (Code 1950, § 8-689.2; 1977, c. 617.)

§ 8.01-80. Same; action of court on report; application of proceeds of transaction. — If upon the filing of the report and examination of the matter it shall appear to the court to be proper, an order shall be entered for the mortgaging, leasing, or sale, on such terms and conditions as the court may deem proper, of so much of such real estate as may be necessary; but no conveyance shall be executed until such shall have been confirmed by the court. The proceeds of such transactions shall be secured and applied under the order of the court. (Code 1950, § 8-689.3; 1977, c. 617.)

REVISERS' NOTE

The last sentence of former § 8-689.3, which was limited to sales, has been expanded to include mortgaging and leasing.

ARTICLE 9.

Partition.

§ 8.01-81. Who may compel partition of land; jurisdiction; validation of certain partitions of mineral rights. — Tenants in common, joint tenants, executors with the power to sell, and coparceners of real property, including mineral rights east and south of the Clinch River, shall be compellable to make partition and may compel partition, but in the case of an executor only if the power of sale is properly exercisable at that time under the circumstances; and a lien creditor or any owner of undivided estate in real estate may also compel partition for the purpose of subjecting the estate of his debtor or the rents and profits thereof to the satisfaction of his lien. Any court having general equity jurisdiction shall have jurisdiction in cases of partition; and in the exercise of such jurisdiction may take cognizance of all questions of law affecting the legal title that may arise in any proceedings, between such tenants in common, joint tenants, executors with the power to sell, coparceners and lien creditors.

All partitions of mineral rights heretofore had, are hereby validated. (Code 1950, § 8-690; 1964, c. 167; 1968, c. 412; 1977, c. 617; 1984, c. 226.)

REVISERS' NOTE

The term "person under a disability" has been substituted for various individuals specified in former sections of the predecessor Title 8 article.

§ 8.01-81

Cross references. — As to venue of suit for partition, see § 8.01-261, subdivision 3. As to partition of estate in which homestead exemption is claimed, see § 34-8. As to necessity for deed in voluntary partition by coparceners, see § 55-2. For rules of court governing equity practice and procedure, see Rules 2:1 through 2:21.

Law Review. — For note on sale, lease and encumbrance of infants' lands in Virginia, see 47 Va. L. Rev. 534 (1961). For note on creditors' rights and cotenancies, see 48 Va. L. Rev. 405 (1962). For comment on extension of entireties doctrine, see 20 Wash. & Lee L. Rev. 260 (1963). For article, "The Virginia Land Trust — An Overlooked Title Holding Device for Investment, Business and Estate Planning Purposes," see 30 Wash. & Lee L. Rev. 73 (1973).

I. Decisions Under Current Law.
   A. General Consideration.
   B. What May Be Partitioned.
   C. Who May Be Compelled to Make Partition.
   D. Improvements.
II. Decisions Under Prior Law.
   A. General Consideration.
   B. Jurisdiction.
      1. In General.
      2. Questions of Law Affecting Legal Title.
   C. What May Be Partitioned.
   D. Who May Compel Partition.
   E. Who May Be Compelled to Make Partition.
   F. Improvements.
   G. Pleading and Practice.

I. DECISIONS UNDER CURRENT LAW.

A. General Consideration.

Wife held entitled to half of proceeds although not named in deed to land sold. — In an action brought by a divorced wife to partition a parcel of land where an examination of the record, the various exhibits filed, and the testimony of the witnesses established clearly and satisfactorily that throughout the period of their marriage and thereafter until the wife filed her bill of complaint seeking partition of the parties, both parties were under the impression that the land had been conveyed to them jointly and as tenants by the entirety, but where, because the wife was under the age of 21, the deed to the property of husband and wife was taken in name of the husband alone, the divorced wife still had an undivided one-half interest in the real property and, the property having been sold by agreement, the trial court properly decreed that each party was entitled to one half of the proceeds. Pleasants v. Pleasants, 221 Va. 1017, 277 S.E.2d 170 (1981).

Divorce proceeding. — The method of accomplishing partition in a divorce proceeding differs from the method of arriving at a monetary award. The amount of a monetary award is determined after considering 11 specific factors, § 20-107.3 E, and is based on the equities and the rights and interests of each party in the marital property. On the other hand, partition, an entirely statutory procedure, is governed by this article since no directions for its implementation are contained in § 20-107.3. Morris v. Morris, 3 Va. App. 303, 349 S.E.2d 661 (1986).

Partition of real property in a divorce proceeding is governed by this section. Mains v. Mains, No. 1362-89-4 (Ct. of Appeals Oct. 23, 1990).

Partition under subsection C of § 20-107.3 is governed by this article. Clayberg v. Clayberg, 4 Va. App. 218, 355 S.E.2d 902 (1987).

Partition as now permitted in the equitable distribution statute is no different from that permitted prior to the adoption of § 20-107.3, except that it may now be done in the divorce case rather than as a separate proceeding. However, when it is done, it must conform to the mandate of this article. Clayberg v. Clayberg, 4 Va. App. 218, 355 S.E.2d 902 (1987).

Trial court did not err in ordering the sale of jointly owned property when the parties were unable to agree on the value of the properties for purposes of an allotment. Mains v. Mains, No. 1362-89-4 (Ct. of Appeals Oct. 23, 1990).

Partition procedures for § 20-107.3. — Section 20-107.3 does not contain provisions directing how partition shall be conducted; therefore the procedures for distribution of the property and/or the proceeds of its sale, as disclosed by the partition statutes, and court decisions interpreting those statutes, must be followed. Fitchett v. Fitchett, 6 Va. App. 562, 370 S.E.2d 318 (1988).

Partition must be conducted in ordinary course of docket. — Where trial court is empowered to order partition, the court has no right to defer such action but must conduct the procedure in the ordinary course of managing its docket. Fitchett v. Fitchett, 6 Va. App. 562, 370 S.E.2d 318 (1988).

B. What May Be Partitioned.

A joint tenancy with right of survivorship, as at common law, is subject to partition by a judgment lien creditor of one of the several joint tenants. Jones v. Conwell, 227 Va. 176, 314 S.E.2d 61 (1984).

This section prohibits the partitioning of mineral rights west and north of the Clinch River; therefore, if a court has no authority to partition mineral rights west and north of the Clinch River, a fortiori, such mineral rights cannot be partitioned without the consent of all cotenants. Chosar Corp. v. Owens, 235 Va. 660, 370 S.E.2d 305 (1988).

Tenant's conduct of mining operations was such an appropriation of a specific portion of the Splashdam seam, located west and north of the Clinch River, which was in effect, a unilateral partitioning of the mineral estate, and the trial court correctly ruled that tenant's mining excluded the nonconsenting cotenants from their interests in the property. Chosar Corp. v. Owens, 235 Va. 660, 370 S.E.2d 305 (1988).

C. Who May Be Compelled to Make Partition.

Joint tenants with right of survivorship. — The words "joint tenants" as used in this section were intended by the legislature to include joint tenants with right of survivorship and, pursuant to this section, such tenant shall be compellable to make partition at the instance of a judgment lien creditor. Jones v. Conwell, 227 Va. 176, 314 S.E.2d 61 (1984).

Where the life tenant is not a tenant in common with the remaindermen, it follows that he has no right to compel partition of the property against the owners of the remainder interest. Whitby v. Overton, 243 Va. 20, 413 S.E.2d 42 (1992).

D. Improvements.

Compensation of joint tenant. — In a partition suit, a joint tenant is usually entitled to compensation for permanent improvements he has made to the property. White v. Pleasants, 227 Va. 508, 317 S.E.2d 489 (1984).

II. DECISIONS UNDER PRIOR LAW.

A. General Consideration.

Editor's note. — The cases cited below were decided under corresponding provisions of former law. The term "this section," as used below, refers to former provisions.

Partition defined. — Partition is the division between two or more persons of lands which they jointly own as coparceners, joint tenants or tenants in common. Martin v. Martin, 112 Va. 731, 72 S.E. 680 (1911).

A partition proceeding is entirely statutory, and finds its authority in this section.

Phillips v. Wells, 147 Va. 1030, 133 S.E. 581 (1926); Price v. Simpson, 182 Va. 530, 29 S.E.2d 394 (1944).

B. Jurisdiction.

1. In General.

Section confers jurisdiction on courts of equity. — The jurisdiction of equity to decree partition of lands and take cognizance of all questions of law arising therein affecting title is settled by this section. Effinger v. Hall, 81 Va. 94 (1885); Davis v. Tebbs, 81 Va. 600 (1886).

This section simply confers upon the courts of equity the same powers exercised by the common-law courts in the partition of land and, in addition, authorizes courts of equity to settle all questions of law affecting legal title to the land involved. Cauthorn v. Cauthorn, 196 Va. 614, 85 S.E.2d 256 (1955); Nickels v. Nickels, 197 Va. 498, 90 S.E.2d 116 (1955).

Jurisdiction is not inherent. — This section and § 8.01-83 create and confer special statutory jurisdiction upon courts of equity for the partition and sale of land. Failure to substantially comply with the provisions of the statutes is fatal to the proceedings. Equity has no inherent jurisdiction to order a sale of land for the purpose of partition. Cauthorn v. Cauthorn, 196 Va. 614, 85 S.E.2d 256 (1955); Nickels v. Nickels, 197 Va. 498, 90 S.E.2d 116 (1955).

Jurisdiction may be invoked as a matter of right. — Courts of equity have jurisdiction of suits for the partition of real estate, and the application for the exercise of that jurisdiction is not now addressed to the sound discretion of the court, but may be made as a matter of right. Grove v. Grove, 100 Va. 556, 42 S.E. 312 (1902).

No jurisdiction to partition lands in other states. — The courts of this State have no jurisdiction to decree a partition of lands lying in another state, although all the parties are before the court. Poindexter v. Burwell, 82 Va. 507 (1886); Wimer v. Wimer, 82 Va. 890, 5 S.E. 536 (1886); Pillow v. Southwest Va. Imp. Co., 92 Va. 144, 23 S.E. 32 (1895).

Partition of real property in kind was an ancient heritage of equity jurisdiction, existing at common law independently of statute. To such extent the statutes are only declaratory of the common law. Leonard v. Boswell, 197 Va. 713, 90 S.E.2d 872 (1956).

But jurisdiction has been materially enlarged by statute. — The Virginia statutes materially enlarge equity jurisdiction in suits for partition; new powers are conferred which were theretofore nonexistent. Thus, the right of a cotenant to an enforced sale where partition in kind is impracticable, is a right created by statute. Leonard v. Boswell, 197 Va. 713, 90 S.E.2d 872 (1956).

This section does not authorize a court

of equity to sell or allot any undivided interest in land. This power is conferred upon courts of equity by § 8.01-83. Cauthorn v. Cauthorn, 196 Va. 614, 85 S.E.2d 256 (1955); Nickels v. Nickels, 197 Va. 498, 90 S.E.2d 116 (1955).

Court may do all necessary to afford complete relief. — While this section defines the procedure to be followed in a suit for partition, there is no inhibition restricting the powers of a court of equity to do all that is necessary to be done in order that complete relief may be afforded the parties. Price v. Simpson, 182 Va. 530, 29 S.E.2d 394 (1944).

It is now settled law that if a suit be properly one for partition, the court, having jurisdiction of the parties and the subject matter, may proceed to give complete relief. Even in matters of purely legal right the equitable as well as the legal rights of the parties may be determined. Leonard v. Boswell, 197 Va. 713, 90 S.E.2d 872 (1956).

It may pass upon accounts of liens and priorities. — In suits for partition courts of equity have authority to pass upon all questions necessary to justice between the parties, such as accounts of liens and priorities on the lands to be partitioned. Hinton v. Bland, 81 Va. 588 (1886).

Court does not act merely in a ministerial capacity. — In partition suits a court of equity, acting under authority conferred by statute, does not act merely in a ministerial character and in obedience to the call of the parties who have a right to the partition, but its action is founded upon its general jurisdiction, and its relief is granted and administered ex aequo et bono according to its own notions of justice and equity. Leonard v. Boswell, 197 Va. 713, 90 S.E.2d 872 (1956).

Consent decree pursuant to request for partition. — Since the competent parties to a partition suit could have created among themselves a joint tenancy with the right of survivorship as at common law, the court having jurisdiction of the parties and the subject matter, could, at their request, appoint commissioners to act in their behalf and thus accomplish the same result through the entry of a consent decree. Leonard v. Boswell, 197 Va. 713, 90 S.E.2d 872 (1956).

Compensation for improvements. — As a general rule a joint tenant who at his own expense places permanent improvements upon common property is entitled in a partition suit to compensation for the improvements. This is so, whether his cotenant agreed thereto or not. Compensation of this kind is allowable not as a matter of legal right but purely as a desire of a court of equity to do justice and to prevent one tenant from becoming enriched at the expense of another. Shotwell v. Shotwell, 202 Va. 613, 119 S.E.2d 251 (1961).

In the absence of consent on the part of the cotenant the amount of compensation for permanent improvements is limited to the amount by which the value of the common property has been enhanced. Shotwell v. Shotwell, 202 Va. 613, 119 S.E.2d 251 (1961).

2. Questions of Law Affecting Legal Title.

Court may take cognizance of all questions affecting legal title. — In this State the rule is well established that when a court of equity acquires jurisdiction of a cause for any purpose, it will retain it, and do complete justice between the parties, enforcing, if necessary, legal rights and applying legal remedies to accomplish that end. This is especially true of suits for partition, where, by express provision of this section, a court of equity may take cognizance of all questions of law affecting the legal title that may arise in any proceeding. Laurel Creek Coal & Coke Co. v. Browning, 99 Va. 528, 39 S.E. 156 (1901). See Bradley v. Zehmer, 82 Va. 685 (1886); Fry v. Payne, 82 Va. 759, 1 S.E. 197 (1887); Price v. Simpson, 182 Va. 530, 29 S.E.2d 394 (1944).

Power is confined to claims of parties who may compel or be compelled to make partition. — By the terms of this section the power of courts of equity to adjudicate questions of law affecting the legal title in partition suits is confined to the conflicting claims of parties who may compel or be compelled to make partition. Miller v. Armentrout, 196 Va. 32, 82 S.E.2d 491 (1954).

Purpose of this provision is to prevent delay. — The object of the provision in this section that the court may take cognizance of all questions of law affecting the legal title to the property was to obviate the delays and difficulties which frequently arose in partition suits where questions of title were involved. Adkins v. Adkins, 117 Va. 445, 85 S.E. 490 (1915).

It is constitutional. — The provision of this section authorizing a court of equity in a partition suit to settle all questions of law that may arise in the case does not violate the constitutional provision guaranteeing the right to trial by jury. Pillow v. Southwest Va. Imp. Co., 92 Va. 144, 23 S.E. 32 (1895).

It extends jurisdiction of courts in partition suits. — In the enactment of this section, the legislature intended to broaden and extend the jurisdiction of the courts in partition suits. Seefried v. Clarke, 113 Va. 365, 74 S.E. 204 (1912).

But question must arise as incident to partition. — In order to give the court jurisdiction in a partition suit under this section of a question affecting the legal title, the question must arise as an incident to a partition, and must be such as to require a decision before the partition can be satisfactorily made as between the persons at whose instance or in whose behalf the partition is to be made. Bailey v. Johnson, 118 Va. 505, 88 S.E. 62 (1916).

Independent hostile claim cannot be considered. — An independent hostile claim going to the whole property involved, and denying in toto and ab initio the title of the parties claiming the joint ownership of land, cannot be set up and adjudicated in a partition suit brought by the latter. The provision in giving courts of equity jurisdiction to pass upon "all questions of law affecting the legal title" was never intended to make a proceeding under this section a substitute for an action of ejectment. Bailey v. Johnson, 118 Va. 505, 88 S.E. 62 (1916).

Thus, jurisdiction does not extend to matters of general indebtedness. — The provision that a court of equity "may take cognizance of all questions of law affecting the legal title that may arise," is applicable only to questions affecting the legal title to the subject of partition, and not to matters of general indebtedness between the parties. Adkins v. Adkins, 117 Va. 445, 85 S.E. 490 (1915).

Having no relation to subject of partition. — There is no provision for the settlement in partition suits of all controversies that may arise between tenants in common, growing out of their general indebtedness to each other, which have no relation to or bearing upon the title to the subject of partition. Adkins v. Adkins, 117 Va. 445, 85 S.E. 490 (1915).

A claim of adverse possession does not prevent the operation of this section. Fry v. Payne, 82 Va. 759, 1 S.E. 197 (1886).

And defendant cannot defeat jurisdiction by adverse claim. — A suit for partition cannot be made a substitute for an action of ejectment; but a defendant to a bill which states a good case for partition cannot defeat the jurisdiction in equity merely by denying in toto and ab initio the complainant's title, and asserting in himself a title independent of and hostile to that under which the complainant claims. Goodman v. Goodman, 124 Va. 579, 98 S.E. 625 (1919).

Where he claims under one who held jointly with complainant. — While a suit for partition cannot be made a substitute for an action of ejectment, yet if the defendant in such a suit claims under one who was a joint owner with the complainant, or those under whom he claims, the defendant cannot defeat the right of the complainant to have his legal rights settled in a suit for partition by merely alleging and proving that he denies the rights of the complainant and holds adversely to him. Pillow v. Southwest Va. Imp. Co., 92 Va. 144, 23 S.E. 32 (1895). See also, Morgan v. Hailey, 107 Va. 331, 58 S.E. 564 (1907).

Decree settling adverse claim cannot be assailed collaterally. — When a court of equity has taken jurisdiction to partition land to the whole of which the defendant claims legal title, the decree of the court, even if erroneous, cannot be collaterally assailed in another suit. Morgan v. Hailey, 107 Va. 331, 58 S.E. 564 (1907).

Court may set aside deed to part of land. — In the exercise of its jurisdiction to take cognizance of all questions of law affecting the legal title to the property to be partitioned, a court may set aside a deed to one of the parties of a part of the land to be divided, either because the grantor had no power to make the deed, or because of his mental incapacity. Seefried v. Clarke, 113 Va. 365, 74 S.E. 204 (1912).

Decision upholding deed is res adjudicata in subsequent suit. — In a suit for partition of land, one of the co-owners, being a nonresident, was served with process by publication. A deed from the nonresident co-owner was put in evidence and held sufficient to transfer the grantor's interest in the land to be partitioned. In a subsequent suit brought by the grantor for partition of the same land, it was held that, the court in the first suit having had jurisdiction of the parties and the subject matter, and the authority, pursuant to this section, to take cognizance of all questions of law affecting the legal title that might arise in the proceedings, its decision as to the sufficiency of the deed was res adjudicata, and could not be collaterally attacked, though the grantor was not personally served with process in the first suit. Beattie v. Wilkinson, 36 F. 646 (W.D. Va. 1888).

C. What May Be Partitioned.

Equitable estates are subject to partition. — Under the provisions of this section, a court of equity has jurisdiction to partition equitable estates in land. So where a decedent was the complete equitable owner of a lot at the time of his death, equity may decree that the lot be sold for partition among his heirs at law, upon a bill filed by some of the heirs against the remaining heirs for partition. Stewart v. Stewart, 122 Va. 642, 95 S.E. 388 (1918).

The fact that land is under lease for a term of years is no objection to a partition thereof in this State, by virtue of § 8.01-91. Lucy v. Kelly, 117 Va. 318, 84 S.E. 661 (1915).

Property subject to liens may be partitioned. — Where some of the cotenants have sold their undivided interest in lands and reserved liens for the unpaid purchase money, the existence of these liens on the undivided shares does not, per se, prevent the division of the common property among the owners. The liens will be considered as attaching to the parcels under the partition in severalty. Wright v.

Strother, 76 Va. 857 (1882).

Right of lien creditor to have partition set aside. — Where partition has been made among cotenants, it will not be disturbed at the instance of the lien creditors, unless they show that it is unequal and unfair as respects the security for their debts. Wright v. Strother, 76 Va. 857 (1882).

All lands of original cotenancy need not be included. — The rule that all the lands of the original cotenancy should be included does not prevail in Virginia. Thus, where a decedent left several tracts of land susceptible of partition among his heirs at law, there might be partition of a single tract without the others. Price v. Simpson, 182 Va. 530, 29 S.E.2d 394 (1944).

D. Who May Compel Partition.

Claimants under common ancestor. — Where, although the allegations of a bill for partition are meager, yet upon a natural and reasonable interpretation it makes out a case in which the complainant and defendant claim under a common ancestor, the complainant claiming an undivided one fourth of the land by inheritance, and the defendant an undivided three fourths, partly by inheritance and partly by purchase, the complainant and defendant are coparceners as to a part and tenants in common as to the residue of the land, the parties are clearly within the express terms of this section, and, no objection to the form or sufficiency of the bill being interposed, it is a good bill for partition. Goodman v. Goodman, 124 Va. 579, 98 S.E. 625 (1919).

Life tenants. — Pursuant to this section and § 8.01-94, a tenant for life in an undivided moiety of property may maintain a suit against those who own the estate in remainder of that moiety, whether they are in esse or not, and the fee simple owners of the other moiety, and compel partition of the property, and, if the property is not susceptible of partition in kind, the life tenant may have a sale and division of the proceeds. Carneal v. Lynch, 91 Va. 114, 20 S.E. 959 (1895).

The fact that one owns a life estate in the whole of a tract and the remainder in fee in only one half thereof does not bar his right to maintain a suit for partition of the land. Lucy v. Kelly, 117 Va. 318, 84 S.E. 661 (1915).

Reversioners and remaindermen. — A reversioner or remainderman cannot compel partition during the continuance of the particular estate. Seibel v. Rapp, 85 Va. 28, 6 S.E. 478 (1888).

Under this section one of several remaindermen cannot compel a partition of the land during the continuance of the life estate, unless, perhaps, he has acquired the life estate. Powell v. Tilson, 161 Va. 318, 170 S.E. 750 (1933). See Lucy v. Kelly, 117 Va. 318, 84 S.E. 661 (1915).

Holder of legal title to entire property. — A party holding the legal title to the whole of a tract of land in an undivided two thirds of which others own the complete equitable estate, with the right to call for the legal title, may, under the liberal provisions of this section, file a bill against such others for a partition of the whole. Hagan v. Taylor, 110 Va. 9, 65 S.E. 487 (1909).

Guardians. — A guardian of infants may maintain a suit for partition of real estate held jointly by the infants and other adult persons. Cooper v. Hepburn, 56 Va. (15 Gratt.) 551 (1860); Zirkle v. McCue, 67 Va. (26 Gratt.) 517 (1875).

Lien creditors. — A lien creditor may compel partition of land, or a sale thereof when partition cannot conveniently be made. Peatross v. Gray, 181 Va. 847, 27 S.E.2d 203 (1943).

Suit by widow for partition of husband's estate. — A widow filed her bill, in which she asked to have her interests and those of her children, whose guardian she was, in her husband's estate ascertained and laid off, to have her dower allotted in kind or commuted in money, and the interests of her children ascertained and placed under her control as their guardian, and for a settlement of the rights of all the parties. The administrator and children of the husband were made defendants, and the case regularly proceeded in. It was held that this was a suit for partition, and the widow might properly bring it. Zirkle v. McCue, 67 Va. (26 Gratt.) 517 (1875).

Tenants in common. — A bill may be filed by one tenant in common against another for the purpose of having partition of the property held in common, and to subject the interest of the defendant to a deed of trust thereon for the benefit of the complainant. Price v. Crozier, 101 Va. 644, 44 S.E. 890 (1903).

Tenants by entirety. — Under this section partition is not compellable between tenants by entirety, but that end is reached through § 55-20, which makes tenants by entirety tenants in common, in turn modified by § 55-21 where it is declared that this conversion shall not take place when it is manifestly not intended. Allen v. Parkey, 154 Va. 739, 149 S.E. 615 (1929).

Persons without interest. — Persons claiming under a party whose interest in land has been extinguished have no standing in court as complainants in a partition suit. Stevens v. McCormick, 90 Va. 735, 19 S.E. 742 (1894).

E. Who May Be Compelled to Make Partition.

Infants as well as adults are included within the provision of this section that tenants in common, joint tenants, and coparceners shall be compellable to make partition. Payne v. Payne, 179 Va. 562, 19 S.E.2d 690 (1942).

F. Improvements.

Compensation for improvements. — As a general rule a joint tenant who at his own expense places permanent improvements upon common property is entitled in a partition suit to compensation for the improvements. This is so, whether his cotenant agreed thereto or not. Compensation of this kind is allowable not as a matter of legal right but purely as a desire of a court of equity to do justice and to prevent one tenant from becoming enriched at the expense of another. Shotwell v. Shotwell, 202 Va. 613, 119 S.E.2d 251 (1961).

In the absence of consent on the part of the cotenant the amount of compensation for permanent improvements is limited to the amount by which the value of the common property has been enhanced. Shotwell v. Shotwell, 202 Va. 613, 119 S.E.2d 251 (1961).

Burden is on the person claiming reimbursement for improvements to prove the actual construction of the improvements, and second, to show the amount by which the value of the common property is enhanced. Shotwell v. Shotwell, 202 Va. 613, 119 S.E.2d 251 (1961).

Generally, a tenant in common, joint tenant, or coparcener who places permanent improvements upon common property at his own expense is entitled to compensation in the event of partition, but before an allowance can be considered he must prove what improvements were made and show the amount by which the value of the property has been enhanced. Rutledge v. Rutledge, 204 Va. 522, 132 S.E.2d 469 (1963).

G. Pleading and Practice.

Section does not restrict courts as to procedure. — No restrictions or limitations are placed upon courts of equity by this section in the matter of procedure; they are left free to adopt such method as may be best suited to meet the exigencies of the particular case. Any instrumentality that the court may call to its assistance, whether it be a master in chancery or a special board of commissioners, is advisory merely. The question must at last be left to the determination of the court upon the law and the evidence. Phillips v. Dulaney, 114 Va. 681, 77 S.E. 449 (1913).

All original parties in interest need not be convened. — Where a decedent dies intestate, leaving several tracts or parcels of land susceptible of partition among his heirs at law, it is not essential that all original parties in interest and their alienees, if any, be convened and all the real estate left by the decedent be included in a suit for partition. Price v. Simpson, 182 Va. 530, 29 S.E.2d 394 (1944).

Bill need not make formal deraignment of title. — It is not necessary in a bill for partition to make a formal deraignment of title, or any deraignment further than is necessary to show how the parties became coparceners and entitled to partition. Goodman v. Goodman, 124 Va. 579, 98 S.E. 625 (1919).

But it must show relationship entitling plaintiff to partition. — The complainant in a partition suit must aver and prove that he occupies such a relationship to the defendant as entitles him to invoke the equity jurisdiction. If his bill fails to show this, it is bad on demurrer. If it does show this, and the answer denies it, then upon a hearing on bill and answer, either with or without a replication, the bill will be dismissed. Goodman v. Goodman, 124 Va. 579, 98 S.E. 625 (1919).

Residuary legatee under cotenant's will not necessary party. — A residuary legatee under a will was not a necessary party to a partition suit directed at certain land in which the testator owned a fractional interest. Salvation Army v. Campbell, 202 Va. 223, 116 S.E.2d 334 (1960).

The burden is on the person claiming reimbursement for improvements to prove the actual construction of the improvements, and second, to show the amount by which the value of the common property is enhanced. Shotwell v. Shotwell, 202 Va. 613, 119 S.E.2d 251 (1961).

Generally, a tenant in common, joint tenant, or coparcener who places permanent improvements upon common property at his own expense is entitled to compensation in the event of partition, but before an allowance can be considered he must prove what improvements were made and show the amount by which the value of the property has been enhanced. Rutledge v. Rutledge, 204 Va. 522, 132 S.E.2d 469 (1963).

Bill held sufficient. — A bill averring that plaintiff is entitled, under a duly probated will, to part of a tract of land held by defendant, who owns the other part under the same will, and praying for partition, is sufficient, though it fails to aver that defendant purchased his part with notice of plaintiff's claim, where it sufficiently appears that defendant was put on inquiry, and thus was affected with knowledge of all he might have discovered had he done his duty. Davis v. Tebbs, 81 Va. 600 (1886).

§ 8.01-82. When shares of two or more laid off together. — Any two or more of the parties, if they so elect, may have their shares laid off together

§ 8.01-83   CIVIL REMEDIES AND PROCEDURE   § 8.01-83

when partition can be conveniently made in that way. (Code 1950, § 8-691; 1977, c. 617.)

I. DECISIONS UNDER PRIOR LAW.

Editor's note. — The cases cited below were decided under corresponding provisions of former law. The term "this section," as used below, refers to former provisions.

This section does not forbid the assignment of the shares of two cotenants together. Phillips v. Dulaney, 114 Va. 681, 77 S.E. 449 (1913).

Objection to manner of partition. — An objection by defendants to a partition that the commissioner laid off their shares together, without their consent, is without merit, where they refused the court's offer to have the allotment subdivided. Phillips v. Dulaney, 114 Va. 681, 77 S.E. 449 (1913).

Creation of joint tenancy with right of survivorship. — This section expressly provides that the shares of two or more of the cotenants may be laid off together if they so desire, and it would seem that regardless of the tenancy in which parties hold title to land they may contract for the right of survivorship. Leonard v. Boswell, 197 Va. 713, 90 S.E.2d 872 (1956).

§ 8.01-83. Allotment to one or more parties, or sale, in lieu of partition. — When partition cannot be conveniently made, the entire subject may be allotted to any one or more of the parties who will accept it and pay therefor to the other parties such sums of money as their interest therein may entitle them to; or in any case in which partition cannot be conveniently made, if the interest of those who are entitled to the subject, or its proceeds, will be promoted by a sale of the entire subject, or allotment of part and sale of the residue, the court, notwithstanding any of those entitled may be a person under a disability, may order such sale, or an allotment of a part thereof to any one or more of the parties who will accept it and pay therefor to the other parties such sums of money as their interest therein may entitle them to, and a sale of the residue, and make distribution of the proceeds of sale, according to the respective rights of those entitled, taking care, when there are creditors of any deceased person who was a tenant in common, joint tenant, or coparcener, to have the proceeds of such deceased person's part applied according to the rights of such creditors. (Code 1950, § 8-692; 1950, p. 467; 1977, c. 617.)

Cross references. — As to compensation for improvements, see notes to § 8.01-81. As to partition or sale of real estate in which homestead exemption is claimed, see § 34-8.

I. Decisions Under Current Law.
  A. General Consideration.
  B. Sale.
II. Decisions Under Prior Law.
  A. General Consideration.
  B. Allotment of Entire Subject to One Party.
  C. Allotment of Part and Sale of Part.
  D. Sale of Entire Subject.

I. DECISIONS UNDER CURRENT LAW.

A. General Consideration.

Primary question in suits for partition is whether or not a division in kind is convenient, practicable and for the best interest of the parties; the secondary question is whether their interest will be promoted by a sale in whole or in part. Sensabaugh v. Sensabaugh, 232 Va. 250, 349 S.E.2d 141 (1986).

Discretion of court. — Whether an allotment should be decreed is a matter resting within the sound discretion of a trial court. White v. Pleasants, 227 Va. 508, 317 S.E.2d 489 (1984).

Allotment in kind jointly to cotenants. — While two cotenants may, by agreement, have their joint interests allotted in kind to them jointly, they cannot be compelled to do so against their wishes, or the wishes of either. White v. Pleasants, 227 Va. 508, 317 S.E.2d 489 (1984).

The 1988 amendment to subsection C of § 20-107.3 gave the trial judge discretion to order a transfer of the property to one of the parties without first determining whether partition in kind could be conveniently made; thus, under the amended statute, a transferor could be deprived of real property susceptible to partition in kind to which he or she would have been absolutely entitled under this section. Such a fundamental change in the law affects substantive rights and thus the 1988 statutory amendment to § 20-107.3 C was not merely procedural. Marion v. Marion, 11 Va. App. 659, 401 S.E.2d 432 (1991).

Section 20-107.3, as amended in 1988, gave the trial judge discretion in a divorce proceeding to order a transfer of property to one of the parties without first determining whether partition in kind could be conveniently made. Thus, under the amended statute, one spouse in the divorce proceeding could be deprived of ownership of real property susceptible to partition to which that spouse would have been absolutely entitled under this section. Gaynor v. Hird, 11 Va. App. 588, 400 S.E.2d 788 (1991).

Applied in Upton v. Hall, 225 Va. 168, 300 S.E.2d 777 (1983); Quillen v. Tull, 226 Va. 498, 312 S.E.2d 278 (1984).

B. Sale.

Prerequisites to sale. — First the court must conclude that the property cannot be conveniently partitioned. Next, the court must decide whether sale is in the best interest of the parties. If the first step is not reached the second step cannot be taken. Sensabaugh v. Sensabaugh, 232 Va. 250, 349 S.E.2d 141 (1986).

A court has no power to order the sale of property without first determining that partition in kind cannot be conveniently made and then determining that sale will be in the best interest of all the parties. Sensabaugh v. Sensabaugh, 232 Va. 250, 349 S.E.2d 141 (1986).

Method. — Chancellor was required to order such method of sale as would obtain the highest price for the property, unless the evidence showed that the parties' conduct or other circumstances made use of that method unachievable. Orgain v. Butler, 255 Va. 129, 496 S.E.2d 433 (1998).

Failure to substantially comply with provisions of statutes is fatal to proceedings. Equity has no inherent jurisdiction to order a sale of land for the purpose of partition. Sensabaugh v. Sensabaugh, 232 Va. 250, 349 S.E.2d 141 (1986).

Burden of proof. — The burden is on the proponent of sale to prove all the prerequisites to sale. Sensabaugh v. Sensabaugh, 232 Va. 250, 349 S.E.2d 141 (1986).

Co-owners urging partition by sale or allotment must first prove partition in kind not conveniently made. Without such proof, a court of equity has no authority to order any such sale. Smith v. Woodlawn Constr. Co., 235 Va. 424, 368 S.E.2d 699 (1988).

Order of sale is error absent proof that land cannot be conveniently partitioned. — Where a party seeking sale of property in lieu of partition fails to prove that the land cannot be conveniently partitioned then it is error for the trial court to order the sale of the subject property. Sensabaugh v. Sensabaugh, 232 Va. 250, 349 S.E.2d 141 (1986).

And sale is rendered void. — The failure to make the threshold finding that partition could not be conveniently made renders an order of sale void. Sensabaugh v. Sensabaugh, 232 Va. 250, 349 S.E.2d 141 (1986).

Proof of prerequisites to sale must affirmatively appear in record. Sensabaugh v. Sensabaugh, 232 Va. 250, 349 S.E.2d 141 (1986).

Conclusory statement that land would bring "more money" if sold. — Even if the value with partition and without partition is relevant to the convenience of the partition, a decision in that regard cannot be made on the basis of a conclusory statement that land if sold as a whole would bring "more money." Sensabaugh v. Sensabaugh, 232 Va. 250, 349 S.E.2d 141 (1986).

II. DECISIONS UNDER PRIOR LAW.

A. General Consideration.

Editor's note. — The cases cited below were decided under corresponding provisions of former law. The term "this section," as used below, refers to former provisions.

Section abrogates common-law rule. — In Virginia, the common-law rule that in a partition suit the shares should be allotted in severalty is abrogated, and the rule that the court is clothed with ample power to resort to the most advantageous devices which the nature of the case may admit is substituted. Price v. Simpson, 182 Va. 530, 29 S.E.2d 394 (1944).

It provides additional methods of partition. — Under this section, a court has jurisdiction to decree a partition of lands by allotment, by metes and bounds, or by a sale of the lands and division of the proceeds. Beattie v. Wilkinson, 36 F. 646 (W.D. Va. 1888).

In a partition suit, a court of chancery may allot the whole of the property to any party who will take it and pay their respective shares to the others in money, it may sell the whole and divide the proceeds, or it may sell a part and divide the rest. Price v. Simpson, 182 Va. 530, 29 S.E.2d 394 (1944).

The power to sell or allot an undivided interest in land is conferred upon courts of equity by this section. Cauthorn v. Cauthorn, 196 Va. 614, 85 S.E.2d 256 (1955); Nickels v. Nickels, 197 Va. 498, 90 S.E.2d 116 (1955).

The court is by this section given broad authority to deal with the subject as the interest of the parties and the circumstances of the case may require. Its conclusion is, of course, subject to review upon appeal. Stamps v. Williamson, 190 Va. 145, 56 S.E.2d 71 (1949).

If the court determines from competent evidence in the record before it that the land is not susceptible of division in kind, the court is given broad powers to deal with the subject as the interest of the parties and the circumstances of the case may require. Cauthorn v. Cauthorn, 196 Va. 614, 85 S.E.2d 256 (1955).

But authority is predicated on determination that partition cannot be conveniently made. — The authority of the court to allot or to sell land in a partition suit is predicated upon its being judicially determined from the record that "partition cannot be conveniently made." The existence of this fact must be determined by the court before ordering the sale or allotment. Cauthorn v. Cauthorn, 196 Va. 614, 85 S.E.2d 256 (1955).

The power of the court to allot all or a part of the land or to sell all or a part thereof is in all cases dependent upon a judicial determination from the record that "partition cannot be conveniently made." Nickels v. Nickels, 197 Va. 498, 90 S.E.2d 116 (1955).

And that interests of those entitled to subject or proceeds are served. — In addition to the finding that partition cannot be conveniently made, the power of the court to allot part of the land and sell the residue or to sell the entire subject and distribute the proceeds is dependent upon the further judicial determination from the record that "the interest of those who are entitled to the subject or its proceeds will be promoted" by such disposition. Nickels v. Nickels, 197 Va. 498, 90 S.E.2d 116 (1955).

Convenience of division in kind. — If the property is found to be divisible in kind, any co-owner has the right to insist that partition be so made, and therefore the primary question in every suit for partition is whether a division in kind may be conveniently made. Nickels v. Nickels, 197 Va. 498, 90 S.E.2d 116 (1955).

The circumstances which should guide the court in its disposition of the matter will depend not merely on the allegations in the pleadings, but on the evidence or lack of evidence adduced to support such allegations. Stamps v. Williamson, 190 Va. 145, 56 S.E.2d 71 (1949).

Courts may adopt methods of procedure. — The procedure for determining whether a division in kind can or cannot be conveniently made is not provided for and therefore the courts are left free to adopt such methods of procedure as may be best suited to meet the exigencies of the particular case. Thus, the court may in its sound discretion determine this issue from the evidence before it or it may call to its assistance a master in chancery or a special board of commissioners. But in its final analysis the question must be left to the determination of the court upon the evidence as disclosed by the record. Nickels v. Nickels, 197 Va. 498, 90 S.E.2d 116 (1955).

Noncompliance with statute is fatal to proceeding. — This section created and conferred a special statutory jurisdiction upon the court. A failure to comply with its provisions is fatal to the proceedings. Equity has no inherent jurisdiction to order a sale of land for the purpose of partition. Roberts v. Hagan, 121 Va. 573, 93 S.E. 619 (1917).

Under this section creditors may come into a partition suit and their rights will be protected. Those who do come in are bound by what was done and cannot sue again. But creditors who are not parties are not bound by anything done in the suit. Lowry v. Noell, 177 Va. 238, 13 S.E.2d 312 (1941).

Acceptance of highest bid does not create judicial sale. — Even when the property is auctioned under court decree, the acceptance of the highest bid does not create a judicial sale. A judicial sale is not consummated until the proceeding is confirmed by the court. Until then, the proceeding is in fieri, the accepted bidder is merely a preferred proposer, and the court retains the power to set the proceeding aside and order a new sale. Austin v. Dobbins, 219 Va. 930, 252 S.E.2d 588 (1979).

Failure of court to show opinion accepting bid to counsel. — Proceedings conducted in regard to a petition for partition did not comply with the rules and standards governing judicial sales where, notwithstanding the continuing competition between two active bidders, the expressed interest of other potential buyers, and the possibility that a sale by parcels would yield a greater return, the chancellor wrote a memorandum opinion accepting the latest bid in gross, which opinion was written less than two weeks after that bid was tendered, and was never circulated among counsel. Austin v. Dobbins, 219 Va. 930, 252 S.E.2d 588 (1979).

Purchase by co-owner. — The fact that the purchaser at a judicial sale for the purpose of partitioning real estate was a co-owner of the property to be partitioned did not render the sale improper. Austin v. Dobbins, 219 Va. 930, 252 S.E.2d 588 (1979).

B. Allotment of Entire Subject to One Party.

The language of the allotment provision is permissive and its exercise rests in the sound discretion of the court. Thrasher v. Thrasher, 202 Va. 594, 118 S.E.2d 820 (1961); Shotwell v. Shotwell, 202 Va. 613, 119 S.E.2d 251 (1961).

Whether allotment is justified is question for court. — The court under this section is given power under certain conditions in partition proceedings to assign the whole tract at a valuation to any party who will accept it and pay therefor to other parties such sums of money as their interest therein may entitle them to. Whether or not the conditions exist is for the court to decide, but a wrong conclusion on that question would not render its decree void. Johnson v. Merrit, 125 Va. 162, 99 S.E. 785 (1919). See Roberts v. Hagan, 121 Va. 573, 93 S.E. 619 (1917).

Where more than one of the persons entitled to partition sought allotment of the entire property to himself the lower court did not abuse its discretion in refusing allotment to either. Thrasher v. Thrasher, 202 Va. 594, 118 S.E.2d 820 (1961); Shotwell v. Shotwell, 202 Va. 613, 119 S.E.2d 251 (1961).

C. Allotment of Part and Sale of Part.

Section does not authorize sale to pay costs of partition. — In a suit for partition, where no sale is necessary and none is made for the purpose of partition, the court is without jurisdiction to sell the land assigned to one of the partners to satisfy his share of the costs of partition. The judgment for such costs would probably be a preferred lien on the land, but would have to be enforced like other judgment liens by a bill in equity. Virginia Iron, Coal & Coke Co. v. Roberts, 103 Va. 661, 49 S.E. 984 (1905).

Allotment to co-owner who is also life tenant. — In a suit for partition by one who owned one half of the land in fee and a life estate in the other half, it was not error to allot to her part of the land and compensate her in money out of the proceeds of the sale of the residue for inequality resulting to her in the partition. Lucy v. Kelly, 117 Va. 318, 84 S.E. 661 (1915).

Owelty to be paid out of proceeds of sale. — Where commissioners in partition assign one tract of land to a party, and fix a value on another tract and ascertain how much thereof shall be paid to the party receiving the other tract for owelty of partition, and the tract valued sells for a less sum than that fixed by the commissioners, the sum to be paid of owelty of partition should be fixed with reference to the price brought at the sale thereof and not to the valuation ascertained by the commissioners. Lucy v. Kelly, 117 Va. 318, 84 S.E. 661 (1915).

D. Sale of Entire Subject.

Necessity for sale and interests of parties control. — Under this section, to justify the sale of land in a partition suit, it must appear that the land is not conveniently susceptible of partition in kind, and that the interests of the parties will be promoted by a sale. Custis v. Snead, 53 Va. (12 Gratt.) 260 (1855); Howery v. Helms, 61 Va. (20 Gratt.) 1 (1870); Zirkle v. McCue, 67 Va. (26 Gratt.) 517 (1875).

While a lien creditor may compel partition of land, or a sale thereof when partition cannot conveniently be made, the court has no authority to order such a sale unless it is made to appear by an inquiry before a commissioner or otherwise that partition cannot be made in some of the modes provided by statute. Peatross v. Gray, 181 Va. 847, 27 S.E.2d 203 (1943).

Sale is void if land can be divided in kind. — If it conclusively appears from the record in the partition suit that the land can be divided in kind and that, notwithstanding this fact, the court orders a sale without the consent of competent parties such decree ordering the sale is void and not merely voidable. Cauthorn v. Cauthorn, 196 Va. 614, 85 S.E.2d 256 (1955).

Facts justifying sale should be disclosed. — Upon a bill for partition of land, as a general rule, the share of each parcener should be assigned to him in severalty. And if from the condition of the subject or the parties, it is proper to pursue a different course, the facts justifying a departure from the rules should, at least where infants are concerned, be disclosed by the report or otherwise appear, to enable the court to judge whether or not their interest will be injuriously affected. Custis v. Snead, 53 Va. (12 Gratt.) 260 (1855).

And should appear in record. — It is not necessary that the facts necessary to warrant a decree for sale should appear from the reports of commissioners or by the depositions of witnesses. It is sufficient if the facts appearing in the record reasonably warrant the decree of sale. This is especially true when the proceeding is to defeat the title of an innocent purchaser. Zirkle v. McCue, 67 Va. (26 Gratt.) 517 (1875).

Otherwise, court has no authority to decree sale. — Where there was no evidence before the court on which to base a decree for the sale of the land, as the report of the commissioners was discredited by the circumstances under which it was made, it was held that no sale could be had, for a court has no authority to decree a sale of land for partition unless it is made to appear by an inquiry before a commissioner in chancery, or in some other way, that partition in kind cannot be made. Cunningham v. Johnson, 116 Va. 610, 82 S.E. 690 (1914).

Court should direct inquiry. — It is the duty of the court, before making a decree for a sale, to ascertain by an inquiry, by a commissioner or otherwise, that partition cannot be made in some of the modes provided by this and the preceding section, without a sale. Howery v.

Helms, 61 Va. (20 Gratt.) 1 (1870).

But party must object in trial court to failure to do so. — In a suit for partition, the court has no authority to order a sale of the land unless it is made to appear by an inquiry before a commissioner, or otherwise, that partition cannot be made in some of the other modes provided by this article. But when it did not so appear, and no inquiry was asked in the court below, a party who promoted the suit and at whose instance the decree was made, will not be allowed to raise the objection for the first time in the appellate court. Howery v. Helms, 61 Va. (20 Gratt.) 1 (1870).

Interests of parties should be ascertained before ordering sale. — An order for sale of land in partition before ascertaining the interests of the several parties is premature and erroneous, as they are entitled to know how they stand in order that they may bid intelligently, if they desire to bid at the sale. Stevens v. McCormick, 90 Va. 735, 19 S.E. 742 (1894).

Unless there is no dispute as to title or interest. — Where there is no dispute as to the title or interest of any party to the suit, the shares of the parties need not be ascertained before ordering the sale. Lucy v. Kelly, 117 Va. 318, 84 S.E. 661 (1915).

Private sales are permitted. — In ordering a sale of land for partition, the court may, in its discretion, authorize a private sale, subject to its approval. Conrad v. Fuller, 98 Va. 16, 34 S.E. 893 (1900).

Court's decision as to desirability of sale is conclusive. — In a suit for partition, whether the interests of those who are entitled to the subject or its proceeds will be promoted by a sale of the entire subject or not are questions for the court in which the suit is pending to decide, and its decision cannot be questioned in any collateral suit, except on the ground of fraud or surprise. Wilson v. Smith, 63 Va. (22 Gratt.) 493 (1872); Hurt v. Jones, 75 Va. 341 (1881).

Facts not justifying setting aside sale. — The fact that the parties owned another tract of land in another county, and that it did not appear that partition in kind of the two tracts could not be made, is not ground for setting aside as sale, where the parties did not wish to sell the other tract. Frazier v. Frazier, 67 Va. (26 Gratt.) 500 (1875).

§ 8.01-84. Application of proceeds of sale to payment of lien. — When there are liens on the interest of any party in the subject so sold, the court may, on the petition of any person holding a lien, ascertain the liens, and apply the dividend of such party in the proceeds of sale to the discharge thereof, so far as the same may be necessary. (Code 1950, § 8-693; 1977, c. 617.)

I. DECISIONS UNDER PRIOR LAW.

Editor's note. — The cases cited below were decided under corresponding provisions of former law. The term "this section," as used below, refers to former provisions.

Court may apply proceeds of sale to discharge of lien. — Courts of equity have jurisdiction of suits for partition, and have power, where there are liens by judgment or otherwise on the interests of any party, to apply the dividends of such party in the proceeds of sale to the discharge of such lien. Grove v. Grove, 100 Va. 556, 42 S.E. 312 (1902).

Defendant may assert claim or lien. — Under this section defendants in a partition suit may assert any claim or lien they may have upon the land, and if the claim or lien is established, the proceeds of the sale for partition may be applied thereto. Reynolds v. Adams, 125 Va. 295, 99 S.E. 695 (1919).

Failure to assert charge or lien. — Where defendants in a partition suit made no assertion of any charge or lien in their favor on the real estate in question in their pleadings in the cause, it is not error for the decree to ignore the rights of defendants in this respect. Reynolds v. Adams, 125 Va. 295, 99 S.E. 695 (1919).

Right of cotenant who has discharged more than his share of encumbrance. — In decreeing partition, a court of equity will adjust all the equitable rights of the parties interested in the property, and if one of the cotenants has paid more than his just share of an encumbrance on the common property, or advanced more than his proportion of the purchase money, the court may decree that payment of the excess be made to him, and that, in default of such payment, the share of the tenant in default may be sold to satisfy the amount equitably due from it. Grove v. Grove, 100 Va. 556, 42 S.E. 312 (1902).

§ 8.01-85. Disposition of share in proceeds of person under disability. — The court making an order for sale shall, when the dividend of a party exceeds $2500, if such party be a person under a disability, order the same to be disposed as the proceeds of a sale under the provisions of § 8.01-76 are required to be invested. (Code 1950, § 8-694; 1952, c. 249; 1968, c. 381; 1977, c. 617.)

REVISERS' NOTE

Former §§ 8-685 and 8-694 were difficult to reconcile. By deleting certain language in former § 8-694 and making reference to § 8.01-76, the proper disposition of proceeds from a sale of the land of a person under a disability is clarified.

§ 8.01-86: Repealed by Acts 1990, c. 831, effective January 1, 1991.

Cross references. — As to the abolition of dower and curtesy, effective Jan. 1, 1991, see § 64.1-19.2.

§ 8.01-87. Validation of certain partitions prior to act of 1922. — All partitions heretofore had, when the proceedings conformed to the law as it existed prior to the amendment of § 5281 of the Code of 1919 by an act approved March 27, 1922, although they did not conform to such section as it read under the amendment of 1922, as aforesaid, are hereby validated; but nothing in this validating section shall be construed as intended to affect vested rights. (Code 1950, § 8-696; 1977, c. 617.)

REVISERS' NOTE

Former § 8-697 (Validation of sales when stock has been taken instead of cash) had no modern utility and was deleted.

§ 8.01-88. Decree of partition to vest legal title. — A decree heretofore or hereafter made, confirming any partition or allotment in a suit for partition, shall vest in the respective co-owners, between or to whom the partition or allotment is made, the title to their shares under the partition or allotment, in like manner and to the same extent, as if such decree direct such title be conveyed to them and the conveyance was made accordingly. (Code 1950, § 8-698; 1977, c. 617.)

Cross references. — As to necessity of deed for voluntary partition by coparceners, see § 55-2. As to recordation of judgments and decrees in partition suits, see § 55-138.

I. DECISIONS UNDER PRIOR LAW.

Editor's note. — The case cited below was decided under corresponding provisions of former law. The term "this section," as used below, refers to former provisions.

The object of this section was to do away with the necessity for conveyances between the parties, or by a commissioner of the court, in partition suits, in order to invest the several co-owners with the legal title to the land allotted to each in the suit. Wright v. Johnson, 108 Va. 855, 62 S.E. 948 (1908).

§ 8.01-89. When proceeds of sale deemed personal estate. — The proceeds of any sale made under § 8.01-83 shall, except as provided in § 8.01-77, be deemed personal estate from the time of the confirmation of such sale by the court. (Code 1950, § 8-699; 1977, c. 617.)

§ 8.01-90. When name or share of parties unknown. — If the name or share of any person interested in the subject of the partition be unknown, so much as is known in relation thereto shall be stated in the bill. (Code 1950, § 8-700; 1977, c. 617.)

§ 8.01-91   CIVIL REMEDIES AND PROCEDURE   § 8.01-94

Cross references. — As to order of publication against unknown parties, see § 8.01-316. For provision as to reopening of suit by unknown parties, see § 8.01-322.

§ 8.01-91. Effect of partition or sale on lessee's rights.

— Any person who, before the partition or sale, was lessee of any of the lands divided or sold, shall hold the same of him to whom such land is allotted or sold on the same term on which by his lease he held it before the partition. (Code 1950, § 8-701; 1977, c. 617.)

I. DECISIONS UNDER PRIOR LAW.

Editor's note. — The cases cited below were decided under corresponding provisions of former law. The term "this section," as used below, refers to former provisions.

The fact that land is under lease for a term of years is no objection to a partition thereof in this State, by virtue of this section. Lucy v. Kelly, 117 Va. 318, 84 S.E. 661 (1915).

But tenant must claim under valid lease. — This section applies only when the lessee claims under a valid lease against all of the joint owners; it does not apply where only a part of the tenants in common undertook to lease a particular portion of the joint property. Phillips v. Dulaney, 114 Va. 681, 77 S.E. 449 (1913).

Rights of tenant who is owner of undivided portion. — The fact that a tenant or lessee of land was the owner of an undivided portion therein did not deprive him of the rights given a tenant or lessee under this section. Mitchell v. Weaver, 116 F. Supp. 707 (E.D. Va. 1953).

§ 8.01-92. Allowance of attorneys' fees out of unrepresented shares.

— In any partition suit when there are unrepresented shares, the court shall allow reasonable fees to the attorney or attorneys bringing the action on account of the services rendered to the parceners unrepresented by counsel. (Code 1950, § 8-701.1; 1950, p. 96; 1977, c. 617.)

§ 8.01-93. Partition of goods, etc., by sale, if necessary.

— When an equal division of goods or chattels cannot be made in kind among those entitled, a court of equity may direct the sale of the same, and the distribution of the proceeds according to the rights of the parties. (Code 1950, § 8-702; 1977, c. 617.)

I. Decisions Under Current Law.
II. Decisions Under Prior Law.

I. DECISIONS UNDER CURRENT LAW.

Trial courts not permitted to defer suits for partition. — If the trial courts were permitted to defer suits for partition, rights granted in this section requesting immediate partition would be denied to the party. Fitchett v. Fitchett, 6 Va. App. 562, 370 S.E.2d 318 (1988).

II. DECISIONS UNDER PRIOR LAW.

Editor's note. — The case cited below was decided under corresponding provisions of former law. The term "this section," as used below, refers to former provisions.

Choses in action are not "goods and chattels". — The words "goods and chattels," as used in this section, do not apply to choses in action, but only to visible and tangible property. First Nat'l Bank v. Holland, 99 Va. 495, 39 S.E. 126 (1901).

ARTICLE 10.

Sale, Lease, or Exchange of Certain Estates in Property.

§ 8.01-94. When sold, leased or exchanged.

— Whenever an interest in property, real or personal, is held by a person, natural or artificial, with remainder or limitation over contingent upon any event, or for his life or for the life of another, and there is limited thereon any other estate, vested or contingent, to any other such person, whether in being or to be thereafter born or created in any manner whatsoever, such person holding an interest in the property so subject to remainder or limitation over or for his own life, or his committee, guardian, if a minor, or conservator, or, if the estate so held be for the life of another, then his heir or personal representative, as the case may be, may for the purpose of obtaining a sale or leasing or exchange of the fee simple interest or absolute estate in such property, if the sale or leasing or exchange thereof is not prohibited by the instrument creating the estate, and the remaindermen, or any of them, whether in being or hereafter to be born or created, are from any cause incapable at the time of filing the bill as herein provided or of giving their assent, or the remainder or limitation over is contingent or defeasible, file a bill in equity in the circuit court stating plainly the property to be sold or leased or exchanged and all facts calculated to show the propriety of such sale or lease or exchange. A like bill may be filed for the sale or leasing or exchange of the remainder in such estate by a remainderman, his guardian, conservator or committee. All persons interested in the property presently or contingently, other than the plaintiff, shall be made defendants, and if such remaindermen be not born or created at such time of filing such bill, such suit shall not for such cause abate, but such unborn person or uncreated artificial person shall be made defendant and subject to the decree of the court by the name of "person unknown or person yet to be born or created," and the court shall upon the filing of such bill appoint a guardian ad litem to defend the interest of such unborn person or uncreated artificial person. If it be clearly shown independently of any admissions in the pleadings that the interest of the plaintiff will be promoted and the rights of no other person will be violated thereby, the court may decree a sale or lease or exchange of the property or any part thereof, or of the remainder therein. In case of a sale on credit, the court shall take ample security. If such sale on credit be of real estate, a lien thereon shall be reserved. The title to any land acquired in any exchange herein provided for shall be held and owned by the same persons in the same way, to the same extent and subject to the same conditions that they owned the land given in such exchange. (Code 1950, § 8-703.1; 1958, c. 271; 1977, c. 617; 1997, c. 801.)

REVISERS' NOTE

References in former § 8-703.1 to venue or jurisdiction have been deleted. See chapter 5 (Venue). The requirement of verification of the bill has been eliminated and the last sentence of former § 8-703.1 has been deleted as misleading.

Cross references. — For general provisions as to sale or lease of lands of persons under disabilities, see §§ 8.01-67 through 8.01-80.

I. DECISIONS UNDER CURRENT LAW.

Applied in Weddle v. Nunley, 43 Bankr. 415 (Bankr. W.D. Va. 1984).

§ 8.01-95. Procedure in such case. — The procedure in such suit and the investment of the proceeds of sale shall be in accordance with §§ 8.01-73, 8.01-75 and 8.01-76, so far as the same can be made applicable, and the court may, in its discretion, commute the life estate according to § 55-269.1. In the case of a lease, however, the rents may be made payable direct to the person or persons entitled thereto, for the time being. (Code 1950, § 8-703.2; 1977, c. 617.)

Cross references. — For rules of court governing equity practice and procedure, see Rules 2:1 through 2:21.

I. DECISIONS UNDER CURRENT LAW.

Applied in Weddle v. Nunley, 43 Bankr. 415 (Bankr. W.D. Va. 1984).

ARTICLE 11.

General Provisions for Judicial Sales.

§ 8.01-96. Decree for sale; how made; bond of commissioner. — In decreeing a sale under any provisions of law, the court may provide for the sale of property in any part of the Commonwealth, and may direct the sale to be for cash, or on such credit and terms as it may deem best, and it may appoint one or more special commissioners to make such sale. No special commissioner, appointed by a court, shall receive money under a decree, until he gives bond, with approved security, before such court or its clerk, in a penalty to be prescribed by the court, conditioned upon the faithful discharge of his duties as such commissioner and to account for and pay over as the court may direct all money that may come into his hands as such commissioner. (Code 1950, § 8-655; 1977, c. 617.)

Cross references. — As to sale of property of persons under disabilities, see §§ 8.01-67 through 8.01-80 and § 8.01-85. As to payment of small amounts to certain persons without the intervention of a fiduciary, see § 8.01-606.

I. Decisions Under Prior Law.
  A. General Consideration.
  B. Terms of Sale.
  C. Confirmation of Sale.
  D. Bond of Commissioner.

I. DECISIONS UNDER PRIOR LAW.

A. General Consideration.

Editor's note. — The cases cited below were decided under corresponding provisions of former law. The term "this section," as used below, refers to former provisions.

B. Terms of Sale.

Sale may be private. — A direction to a commissioner, in a decree for the sale of real estate, to receive private offers and report them to the court to be acted upon in vacation is within the discretion of the trial court, in order to obtain the best price for the land. Conrad v. Fuller, 98 Va. 16, 34 S.E. 893 (1900).

Contract of parties governs sales under mortgages and other instruments. — A court may direct the sale of property to be for cash, or on such credit and terms as it may deem best, but this rule does not apply to mortgages, deeds of trust, and other instruments, in which the terms of sale are agreed upon. In such cases the contract of the parties governs. Pairo v. Bethell, 75 Va. 825 (1881); Stimpson v. Bishop, 82 Va. 190 (1886).

Realty of value should be sold on reasonable credit. — The general rule to be deduced from the decisions is that real property of value should be sold on a reasonable credit, unless under peculiar circumstances, and the circumstances to take the case out of general rule should appear by the record. Pairo v. Bethell, 75 Va. 825 (1881).

Court may change terms of sale before confirmation. — So long as the sale is unconfirmed, and the property and the sale remain under the power of the court, it has the power to change the terms of the sale. Tebbs v. Lee, 76 Va. 744 (1882).

Resale of land on default of purchaser. — Before there can be a decree of resale, it is proper and necessary that the purchaser have notice of the proceeding. The practice is to proceed by the service of a rule on the purchaser to show cause why the lands should not be resold. And upon the filing of a petition for a resale and a report showing that the purchase money has not all been paid, the court may direct such a rule. Thornton v. Fairfax, 70 Va. (29 Gratt.) 669 (1878). See also Clarkson v. Read, 56 Va. (15 Gratt.) 288 (1858); Long v. Weller, 70 Va. (29 Gratt.) 347 (1877); Berlin v. Melhorn, 75 Va. 639 (1881); Boyce v. Strother, 76 Va. 862 (1882); Ogden v. Davidson, 81 Va. 757 (1885).

Terms of resale held proper. — Where a

judgment debtor bought his own land at a sale under a decree in a creditors' suit against him, and failed to pay the purchase money, a resale on terms of one-fourth cash and the balance in one, two and three years was not inequitable under this section. Dickinson v. Clement, 87 Va. 41, 12 S.E. 105 (1890).

C. Confirmation of Sale.

Discretion of court. — It lies within the discretion of the court ordering the sale to determine whether it will accept the bid and confirm the sale, or set it aside. Terry v. Coles, 80 Va. 695 (1885); Moore v. Triplett, 96 Va. 603, 32 S.E. 50 (1899).

Discretion is not arbitrary. — The court, in acting upon a report of a sale, does not exercise an arbitrary discretion, but a sound legal discretion in view of all the circumstances. It is to be exercised in the interest of fairness, prudence, and a just regard to the rights of all concerned. Berlin v. Melhorn, 75 Va. 639 (1881).

Sale should be sustained if possible. — Sound policy requires that judicial sales should be sustained as far as possible, where it is consistent with the rights of others and the rule that innocent purchasers are favorites of the law. Coleman v. Virginia Stave & Heading Co., 112 Va. 61, 70 S.E. 545 (1911).

Before confirmation, lesser grounds are sufficient. — Where a sale has not been confirmed, the reasons for setting it aside need not be so strong as they should be after confirmation. Todd v. Gallego Mills Mfg. Co., 84 Va. 586, 5 S.E. 676 (1888).

Confirmation may be set aside during term. — It is within the discretion of the court at any time during the term to set aside the decree of confirmation and rescind the sale, upon proper motion and notice to the purchaser and the parties concerned, for good cause shown. Langyher v. Patterson, 77 Va. 470 (1883).

Confirmation cures defects. — Subsequent confirmation is equivalent to previous authority, cures departures from the terms prescribed, and cures all defects in the execution of the decree, except those founded in lack of jurisdiction or in fraud. It makes the sale the court's own act, and renders it no longer executory, but executed. Langyher v. Patterson, 77 Va. 470 (1883).

Any party may appeal from refusal to confirm sale. — From the refusal to confirm a sale and order for resale, any party may appeal, and to refuse suspension of the decree is error, but the Supreme Court will not reverse the decree for that error when it is right on its merits. Todd v. Gallego Mills Mfg. Co., 84 Va. 586, 5 S.E. 676 (1888).

Sale set aside for mistake, misrepresentation or fraud. — In a judicial sale, if it should be made to appear, either before or after the sale has been ratified, that there has been any injurious mistake, misrepresentation or fraud, the biddings will be reopened, the reported sale rejected or the order of ratification rescinded, and the property again sent into the market and resold. Merchants Bank v. Campbell, 75 Va. 455 (1881).

Grounds for setting aside sale. — The following have been held to be grounds for setting aside sales: breach of duty by officer, Brock v. Rice, 68 Va. (27 Gratt.) 812 (1876), fraud or mistake, Carr v. Carr, 88 Va. 735, 14 S.E. 368 (1892), conduct preventing fair completion, Teel v. Yancey, 64 Va. (33 Gratt.) 691 (1880), sale on inclement day, Roberts v. Roberts, 54 Va. (13 Gratt.) 639 (1857), defect of title, Daniel v. Leitch, 54 Va. (13 Gratt.) 195 (1856), gross inadequacy of price, Coles v. Coles, 83 Va. 525, 5 S.E. 673 (1887).

Ordinarily, a commissioner to sell is not allowed to purchase the subject, either directly or indirectly. Such a purchase, however, is not absolutely void, but voidable only at the election of any party interested in the land. Hurt v. Jones, 75 Va. 341 (1881).

Purchase by commissioner at resale. — Upon the failure of the purchaser at a judicial sale to pay the purchase money, there was a decree appointing a commissioner to resell the land. The commissioner himself purchased the land at the resale. No objection or exception to the commissioner's purchase was made or taken by any party, the purchase money was paid, and the sale was approved and ratified. It was held that the sale was good, inasmuch as the full amount of the purchase money, for the payment of which the resale was ordered, was assured and paid to the parties entitled, and they could have received nothing more on a resale to another, for the surplus, if any, would have belonged to the purchaser at the original sale. Hurt v. Jones, 75 Va. 341 (1881).

Advance bids. — In a proper case, where it would be just to all the parties concerned, the court may, in the exercise of a sound discretion, set aside a sale made by commissioners under a decree, and reopen the biddings upon the offer of an advance bid of a sufficient amount deposited or well secured. But it has never been held imperative upon the courts to set aside the sale and reopen the bids. It is a question addressed to the sound discretion of the courts, subject to review by the appellate tribunal, and the propriety of its exercise depends upon the circumstances of each case, and can only be rightfully exercised when it can be done with a due regard to the rights of all concerned, the purchaser included. Roudabush v. Miller, 73 Va. (32 Gratt.) 454 (1879). See also Effinger v. Ralston, 62 Va. (21 Gratt.) 430 (1871); Hudgins v. Lanier, 64 Va. (23 Gratt.) 494 (1873); Brock v. Rice, 68 Va. (27 Gratt.) 812 (1876); Curtis v. Thompson,

70 Va. (29 Gratt.) 474 (1877); Merchants Bank v. Campbell, 75 Va. 455 (1881); Berlin v. Melhorn, 75 Va. 639 (1881); Hansucker v. Walker, 76 Va. 753 (1882); Langyher v. Patterson, 77 Va. 470 (1883); Effinger v. Kenney, 79 Va. 551 (1884); Terry v. Coles, 80 Va. 695 (1885); Yost v. Porter, 80 Va. 855 (1885).

It is error to set aside a judicial sale solely because after the sale an advance bid of 10% has been made. Lillard v. Graves, 123 Va. 193, 96 S.E. 169 (1918).

D. Bond of Commissioner.

Bond must be given before commissioner receives money. — This section requires a bond of commissioners of sale, and the bond must be given before the commissioners receive any money under the decree, whether it is directed therein or not. McAllister v. Bodkin, 76 Va. 809 (1882).

Waiver of bond requirement. — The bond with security required of a commissioner is for the benefit of those entitled to the proceeds of the sale. If he collects without giving bond, and they ratify his act and look to him for payment, no one else can complain or claim that any equity is raised in his favor. Lee v. Swepson, 76 Va. 173 (1882).

Decree not requiring bond is not erroneous. — It is not error that the decree does not require the commissioner of sale to give bond and security; this section requires that he shall, before he collects any money. McAllister v. Bodkin, 76 Va. 809 (1882); Cooper v. Daugherty, 85 Va. 343, 7 S.E. 387 (1888).

Commissioners cannot execute bonds with each other as sureties. — Two commissioners were appointed to sell land, and were required before proceeding to act to execute a bond with security conditioned according to law. Each executed a separate bond with the other as his surety. It was held that this was not a compliance with the decree, and that though the bonds were given in court. Tyler v. Toms, 75 Va. 116 (1880).

Purchaser must see that bond has been given. — This section is imperative, that a bond shall be given, and it is the duty of a purchaser at a judicial sale to see that the bond has been given before he pays his money to the commissioner, or he does it at his own risk. Hess v. Rader, 67 Va. (26 Gratt.) 746 (1875).

Payment to commissioner who has not given bond is invalid. — Where the purchaser at a sale made under decree of court pays the purchase money to a commissioner who has not given the bond required by law, the payment is invalid, unless a certificate of the clerk that a bond was given was published with the advertisement of the sale. Whitehead v. Bradley, 87 Va. 676, 13 S.E. 195 (1891).

And purchaser is liable for loss sustained thereby. — A commissioner who has not given bond as required has no authority to receive the purchase money, and the purchaser at the unauthorized private sale is responsible to the party who is entitled to the proceeds, for so much as has not been properly invested by the commissioner and cannot be made out of his estate. Hess v. Rader, 67 Va. (26 Gratt.) 746 (1875).

The sale of the land was to be on credit, with bonds to be taken for the several deferred payments, and the title to be retained. As the bonds fell due, the purchaser paid the money to one of the commissioners, who had not given bond as required by this section, and who was not authorized by the decree to collect the purchase money. The commissioner deposited the money as collected in a bank to his credit as commissioner, not using it or mingling it with his own, and it was lost by the failure of the bank. It was held that the purchaser was bound to pay the purchase money of the land again, and that the commissioner, having received the money without authority, was liable to the purchaser for the amount so paid. Tyler v. Toms, 75 Va. 116 (1880).

But commissioner is liable to purchaser. — Where a commissioner who had not executed the required bond receives the purchase money of a sale, he is liable to the purchaser for any loss sustained thereby. Hess v. Rader, 67 Va. (26 Gratt.) 746 (1875).

And purchaser is subrogated to rights of creditor against commissioner. — If a purchaser should have to pay the purchase money a second time, he would be subrogated to the creditor's rights under a decree requiring the commissioner to pay it. Lee v. Swepson, 76 Va. 173 (1882).

Land is liable for purchase money received and misapplied. — Where a purchaser at a judicial sale of land pays the purchase money to the commissioner, but the commissioner has not executed the bond required by the decree, or the bond executed by him is disapproved by the clerk, the purchaser has paid in his own wrong, and the land is liable for the purchase money received by the commissioner and misapplied, though the land has been conveyed by the commissioner to the purchaser, as the decree directed to be done when the purchase money was paid. Lloyd v. Erwin, 70 Va. (29 Gratt.) 598 (1877).

And person entitled is not required to proceed first against commissioner. — The parties entitled to the fund are not bound to proceed against the commissioner and his sureties in the bond he executed, but which the clerk disapproved, before proceeding against the land to have it subjected to the judgment of the purchase money misapplied by the commissioner. Lloyd v. Erwin, 70 Va. (29 Gratt.) 598 (1877).

§ 8.01-97. Delinquent taxes to be ascertained.

— In every suit brought in this Commonwealth for the sale of lands for the payment of debts or to subject lands to the payment of liens binding thereon, it shall be the duty of the court, or any commissioner to whom the cause is referred, to ascertain all delinquent taxes on such land together with interest and penalties if any. (Code 1950, § 8-656; 1977, c. 617.)

REVISERS' NOTE

Former § 8-656 has been simplified and language pertaining to the sale of land for delinquent taxes has been deleted since such a sale is provided for in § 58.1-3965.

I. DECISIONS UNDER PRIOR LAW.

Editor's note. — The cases cited below were decided under corresponding provisions of former law. The term "this section," as used below, refers to former provisions.

This section was not written for the benefit of the delinquent landowner. Woodhouse v. Burke & Herbert Bank & Trust Co., 166 Va. 706, 185 S.E. 876 (1936).

It is error to decree sale before ascertaining liens. — Where there are various liens on the land of a debtor, it is premature and erroneous to decree a sale of the land to satisfy the liens, without first ascertaining all the liens existing against the land and determining and definitely fixing their respective amounts and priorities. Strayer v. Long, 83 Va. 715, 3 S.E. 372 (1887); Bristol Iron, Coal & Coke Co. v. Caldwell, 95 Va. 47, 27 S.E. 838 (1897); Artrip v. Rasnake & Son, 96 Va. 277, 31 S.E. 4 (1898); Rush v. Dickenson County Bank, 128 Va. 114, 104 S.E. 700 (1920); Tackett v. Bolling, 172 Va. 326, 1 S.E.2d 285 (1939).

§ 8.01-98. Sales of land when purchase price insufficient to pay taxes, etc.

— In any proceedings for the sale of real estate or to subject real estate to the payment of debts, it appears to the court that the real estate cannot be sold for enough to pay off the liens of taxes, levies, and assessments returned delinquent against it, and it further appears that the purchase price offered is adequate and reasonable, such sale shall be confirmed, and the court shall decree the payment and distribution of the proceeds of such sale pro rata to the taxes, levies, and assessments due the Commonwealth or any political subdivision thereof, after having first deducted the cost of such proceedings in court. Such decree shall be certified to the clerk of the appropriate court who has charge of the delinquent tax books, and such clerk shall cause the lien of such taxes, levies, and assessments to be marked satisfied upon the list of delinquent lands regardless of whether the same shall have been paid in full. (Code 1950, § 8-657; 1977, c. 617.)

§ 8.01-99. Bond required of special commissioner for sale.

— Except as hereinafter provided, no special commissioner shall advertise the property for sale or renting, or sell or rent the same, until he shall have given bond in a penalty to be prescribed by the court sufficient to cover at least the probable amount of the whole purchase money or such portion of the rent the court deems appropriate, and shall have obtained from such clerk a certificate that such bond has been given. The certificate or a copy thereof shall be appended to the advertisement; provided, however, that in any case of such sale or rental, the court may direct all the cash proceeds thereof to be deposited by the purchaser or lessee to the credit of such court in some bank to be designated by it, and may direct that all evidences of indebtedness arising from such transaction or rent be deposited for safekeeping with such bank or the clerk of such court and the court may in its discretion thereafter dispense with the bond.

The clerk shall make the certificate whenever the bond has been given and note the same in the proceedings in the cause. The certificate or a copy thereof shall be returned with the report of the sale or renting. (Code 1950, § 8-658; 1977, c. 617.)

REVISERS' NOTE

Former § 8-658 has been simplified and expanded. The court may consider "such portion" of the rent which it deems appropriate in determining the amount of the penalty bond for the rental of real estate. This flexibility may permit a reduction in cost of the bond.

The provision for a clerk's fee in former § 8-658 has been deleted as obsolete.

Cross references. — As to liability of purchaser who pays money to a commissioner who has not executed the required bond, see note to § 8.01-96. See also § 8.01-101.

I. DECISIONS UNDER PRIOR LAW.

Editor's note. — The case cited below was decided under corresponding provisions of former law. The term "this section," as used below, refers to former provisions.

Bond must be given before court requiring it, or judge or clerk thereof. — The bond required by this section to be given by commissioners to sell lands can only be given before the court which requires the bond to be given, or before the judge thereof, or the clerk of the court in his office, and it is error to direct the clerk of any other court to take it. Southwest Va. Mining Co. v. Chase, 95 Va. 50, 27 S.E. 826 (1897).

§ 8.01-100. Liability of clerk for false certificate or failure to give bond. — If any clerk make a certificate as to the bond, which is untrue, he and the sureties on his official bond shall be liable to any person injured thereby. (Code 1950, § 8-661; 1977, c. 617; 1978, c. 718.)

REVISERS' NOTE

The criminal violation of former § 8-661 has been classified as a Class 3 misdemeanor.

Cross references. — As to penalties for false certificate or failure to give bond, see § 18.2-209.1.

§ 8.01-101. Purchasers relieved of liability for purchase money paid to such commissioner. — When the certificate pursuant to the provisions in § 8.01-99 shall have been published with an advertisement of the sale or renting of property, or when such bond shall have been given prior to a sale or renting not publicly advertised, any person purchasing or renting such property in pursuance of such advertisement or in pursuance of the decree or order of sale or renting, shall be relieved of all liability for the purchase money or rent, or any part thereof, which he may pay to any special commissioner, as to whom the proper certificate shall have been appended to such advertisement, or who shall have given the bond aforesaid. (Code 1950, § 8-659; 1977, c. 617.)

I. DECISIONS UNDER PRIOR LAW.

Editor's note. — The cases cited below were decided under corresponding provisions of former law. The term "this section," as used below, refers to former provisions.

This section applies to all judicial sales, whether original or resales, and a purchaser who seeks to avail himself of the protection afforded by it must show either that the commissioner to whom payments were made actually gave the bond required of him, or that the clerk's certificate that such bond had been given was appended to the advertisement. The fact that a bond was required of and given by the same commissioner before making the original sale, and that the surety of the purchaser at the original sale became the purchaser at the resale, cannot change the result. Tompkins v. Dyerle, 102 Va. 219, 46 S.E. 300 (1904).

When payment invalid. — Where the purchaser at a sale made under decree of court pays the purchase money to a commissioner who has not given the bond required by law, the payment is invalid, unless a certificate of the clerk that bond has been given was published with the advertisement of sale. Whitehead v. Bradley, 87 Va. 676, 13 S.E. 195 (1891). See also, Pulliman v. Thompkins, 99 Va. 602, 39 S.E. 221 (1901).

§ 8.01-102. Purchasers not required to see to application of purchase money. — No purchaser or renter at a duly authorized sale or renting made by a receiver, personal representative, trustee, or other fiduciary shall be required to see to the application of the purchase money. (Code 1950, § 8-660; 1977, c. 617.)

I. DECISIONS UNDER PRIOR LAW.

Editor's note. — The cases cited below were decided under corresponding provisions of former law. The term "this section," as used below, refers to former provisions.

Purchaser takes title free of equities. — Under this section, if the purchaser pays the purchase money and conveyance is made to him, he takes the legal title free from the equities that attached to it in the hands of the trustee. Broun v. City of Roanoke, 172 Va. 227, 1 S.E.2d 279 (1939).

Except where he does not pay purchase money. — It is true that under this section the purchaser from a trustee is not required to see to the application of purchase money; but, if he does not pay the purchase money, and legal title is conveyed to him, he takes it subject to the same equities as attached to it in the hands of the trustee. Ballard Bros. Fish Co. v. Stephenson, 49 F.2d 581 (4th Cir.), cert. denied, 283 U.S. 864, 51 S. Ct. 656, 75 L. Ed. 1468 (1931). See Burke v. Sweeley, 177 Va. 47, 12 S.E.2d 763 (1941).

§ 8.01-103. Special commissioner or other person appointed to do so to receive purchase money, etc.; liability of clerk for failure to give notice of appointment. — The special commissioner, who makes the sale or renting, shall receive and collect all the purchase money or rent, unless some other person be appointed to collect the same and in such case the court shall require of such person bond with surety in such penalty as to it may seem fit. When such appointment is made, it shall be the duty of the clerk to give notice thereof, in writing, to the purchaser or lessee, to be served as other notices are required by law to be served; but no payment shall be made to the person so appointed, until he shall have given the bond required by the decree or order; provided, however, that if, before the purchaser or lessee has received notice of such appointment, he shall have made any payment on account of the purchase money or rent to the special commissioner, or any person appointed for the purpose, who made the sale or renting, such special commissioner, or other person, who made the sale or renting, and the sureties on his bond, shall be responsible for the money so paid, and the purchaser or lessee, who made the payment, shall not be responsible therefor.

If any clerk fail to give the notice hereinbefore required to be given by him, he and the sureties on his official bond shall be liable to any person injured by such failure. (Code 1950, § 8-662; 1977, c. 617; 1978, c. 718.)

REVISERS' NOTE

The criminal violation of former § 8-662 has been classified as a Class 4 misdemeanor.

Cross references. — As to failure of clerk to give notice of appointment of special commissioner to collect purchase money or rent, see § 18.2-209.2.

I. DECISIONS UNDER PRIOR LAW.

Editor's note. — The case cited below was decided under corresponding provisions of former law. The term "this section," as used below, refers to former provisions.

The court and not the commissioner is the real seller at a judicial sale, and the commissioner is merely the ministerial agent of the court and the medium through which the purchaser makes an offer to the court. The proceeds of the sale are funds in the custody of the court and subject to its orders. French v. Pobst, 203 Va. 704, 127 S.E.2d 137 (1962).

§ 8.01-104: Repealed by Acts 1978, c. 718.

Cross references. — For present provisions covering the subject matter of the repealed section, see § 18.2-114.1.

§ 8.01-105. Rule against special commissioner, purchaser, etc., for judgment for amounts due.

— Any court of this Commonwealth, may, at the instance of any party in interest, award a rule against any special commissioner or receiver appointed by or acting under the authority of such court, and against the surety of such commissioner or receiver, or against a purchaser at a judicial sale under a decree of such court, and against the surety or sureties of such purchaser, returnable to such date as the court may fix, to show cause why judgment shall not be entered against them for any amount which the court may ascertain to be due from such commissioner, receiver, or purchaser. A rule issued under this section shall be executed at least fifteen days before the return day thereof. (Code 1950, § 8-664; 1977, c. 617.)

I. DECISIONS UNDER PRIOR LAW.

Editor's note. — The cases cited below were decided under corresponding provisions of former law. The term "this section," as used below, refers to former provisions.

Purpose. — This section was evidently intended to provide a simple and easy method of taking personal judgment against a defaulting purchaser and his sureties. Rush v. Dickenson County Bank, 128 Va. 114, 104 S.E. 700 (1920).

Section is not exclusive. — While a rule may be issued against a commissioner under this section such method of procedure is not exclusive; and a reference to another commissioner to ascertain the amount due served the function of a rule to give notice and an opportunity to defend. French v. Pobst, 203 Va. 704, 127 S.E.2d 137 (1962).

§ 8.01-106. How cause heard upon rule and judgment rendered.

— Upon the return of a rule executed under § 8.01-105 upon any of the parties thereto, the court may if neither party demand a jury, proceed to hear and determine all questions raised by such rule, and shall enter a judgment against such special commissioner, receiver, or purchaser, as the case may be, and his surety or sureties, for the amount appearing to be due by such commissioner, receiver or purchaser, or may enter judgment against such of them as have been summoned to answer such rule. If it appears in such proceeding that such commissioner, receiver, purchaser, or any of them, or their sureties is dead, or under a disability, then such rule shall be awarded against the personal representative of those dead, and the fiduciary of those who are under a disability, and judgment may be rendered jointly and severally against such personal representative, fiduciary and those laboring under no disability in the same proceeding. (Code 1950, § 8-665; 1977, c. 617.)

§ 8.01-107. Trial by jury of issues made upon rule.

— If, upon the return of such rule, any party thereto demand a trial by jury, the court shall order a trial by jury to ascertain what liability, if any, exists against any such special commissioner, receiver, or purchaser, and their sureties; and the court shall enter judgment on the verdict awarded by the jury. New trials may be granted as in other cases; and notwithstanding such rules be awarded and judgment be rendered against part only of the persons liable thereto, the court may award new rules and proceed to judgment against all the parties who are liable thereto. The provisions of this section, and §§ 8.01-105 and 8.01-106, shall apply to any officers and their sureties, acting under the decree of the court. (Code 1950, § 8-666; 1977, c. 617.)

§ 8.01-108. **When sureties of commissioner, purchaser, etc., proceeded against by rule.** — Whenever a special commissioner, a receiver, purchaser at a judicial sale, or his personal representative, or any of them, can be proceeded against by rule for the recovery of money under §§ 8.01-105, 8.01-106 and 8.01-107, the surety of such commissioner, receiver, or purchaser, and the personal representatives of such sureties, may also be proceeded against under such sections. (Code 1950, § 8-667; 1977, c. 617.)

§ 8.01-109. **Commission for selling, collecting, etc.; each piece of property to constitute separate sale.** — For the services of commissioners or officers under any decree for a sale, including the collection and paying over of the proceeds, there may be allowed a commission of five percent on amounts up to and including $100,000, and two percent on all amounts above $100,000. If the sale is made by one commissioner or officer and the proceeds collected by another, the court under whose decree they acted shall apportion the commission between them as may be just.

For the purposes of this section, each piece of property so sold shall constitute a separate sale, even though more than one piece of property is sold under the same decree. (Code 1950, § 8-669; 1950, p. 459; 1966, c. 416; 1974, c. 197; 1977, c. 617; 1993, c. 311.)

I. DECISIONS UNDER CURRENT LAW.

Applied in Austin v. Dobbins, 219 Va. 930, 252 S.E.2d 588 (1979).

§ 8.01-110. **Appointment of special commissioner to execute deed, etc.; effect of deed.** — A court in a suit wherein it is proper to decree the execution of any deed or writing may appoint a special commissioner to execute the same on behalf of any party in interest and such instrument shall be as valid as if executed by the party on whose behalf it is so executed. (Code 1950, § 8-670; 1977, c. 617.)

I. DECISIONS UNDER PRIOR LAW.

Editor's note. — The cases cited below were decided under corresponding provisions of former law. The term "this section," as used below, refers to former provisions.

Deed passes title of all parties. — A deed by a special commissioner appointed and empowered by the court to convey under this section will pass the title of all the parties to the suit. Hurt v. Jones, 75 Va. 341 (1881).

Commissioner cannot convey land in another state. — A person within the Commonwealth may be decreed to execute a conveyance for lands lying in another state, or to cancel a deed for such lands obtained by fraud; but the courts of this State are without jurisdiction to sell and convey land situated beyond the limits of the State. Poindexter v. Burwell, 82 Va. 507 (1886); Gibson v. Burgess, 82 Va. 650 (1886); Wimer v. Wimer, 82 Va. 890, 5 S.E. 536 (1886).

Relief should be of an in rem nature. — In a suit for specific performance of a contract to sell land, where personal service was had outside the State, the language of the decree directing the defendant to perform the contract and convey the property to the complainant made it an in personam decree, and hence it went beyond permissible limits. If the complainant was entitled to any relief, it should be of an in rem nature and accomplished by the appointment of a commissioner as provided by this section. Cranford v. Hubbard, 208 Va. 689, 160 S.E.2d 760 (1968).

§ 8.01-111. What such deed to show. — Every deed executed by any such commissioner pursuant to the provisions of § 8.01-110 shall specifically set out as nearly as practicable the name of the person on whose behalf the same is executed; provided, that when such deed conveys the right, title or interest of the heirs of a person who is dead it shall be sufficient for such deed to set out that the same is executed on behalf of the heirs of such decedent. But a failure to comply with the provisions of this section shall not affect or invalidate any such deed; and all deeds heretofore executed by any such commissioner in which such persons or heirs are not specifically set out are hereby validated. (Code 1950, § 8-671; 1977, c. 617.)

§ 8.01-112. Reinstatement of cause to appoint special commissioner to make deed. — Any ended cause may be reinstated for the purpose of entering a decree directing a deed to be made to any party clearly shown by the record to be entitled thereto, or for the purpose of substituting a new commissioner to make a deed in the place of one previously appointed for that purpose, but who has died or become incapacitated to act before making such deed. (Code 1950, § 8-672; 1977, c. 617.)

§ 8.01-113. When title of purchaser at judicial sale not to be disturbed. — If a sale of property is made under a decree of a court, and such sale is confirmed, the title of the purchaser at such sale shall not be disturbed unless within twelve months from such confirmation the sale is set aside by the trial court or an appeal is taken to the Court of Appeals or allowed by the Supreme Court, and a decree is therein afterwards entered requiring such sale to be set aside. This limitation shall not affect any right of restitution of the proceeds of sale. (Code 1950, § 8-673; 1977, c. 617; 1984, c. 703.)

I. Decisions Under Current Law.
II. Decisions Under Prior Law.

I. DECISIONS UNDER CURRENT LAW.

When mistake merits setting aside sale. — Not every mistake merits the setting aside of a previously confirmed judicial sale. The mistake must be mutual unless it was induced by the fraud or culpable negligence of the other. Branton v. Jones, 222 Va. 305, 281 S.E.2d 799 (1981).

Unilateral mistake as to property sold in gross. — Vendors were not entitled to have a sale of property, sold in gross, set aside where the vendors were unilaterally mistaken as to the acreage of the property sold, since the buyer's mere silence concerning the correct boundaries and acreage of the property did not constitute fraud. Branton v. Jones, 222 Va. 305, 281 S.E.2d 799 (1981).

Mistake irrelevant where sale is in gross. — Where a contract for the sale of land is in gross, such contract is a contract of hazard. The parties to such a sale assume the risk of a deficiency or excess in the number of acres in the property. Where the parties intend a contract of hazard regarding a property's acreage, it is immaterial whether or not the sellers or the buyer, or both, were mistaken as to the number of acres in the tract. Branton v. Jones, 222 Va. 305, 281 S.E.2d 799 (1981).

Discretion of court in deciding whether to confirm sale. — Prior to confirmation, a court can exercise considerable discretion in deciding whether to confirm a sale, but after confirmation the purchaser at a judicial sale is as much entitled to the benefit of his purchase as a purchaser in pais, and the sale in the one case can be set aside only on such grounds as would be sufficient in the other. Branton v. Jones, 222 Va. 305, 281 S.E.2d 799 (1981).

Grounds for setting aside sale after confirmation. — After confirmation, a judicial sale cannot be set aside except for fraud, mistake, surprise, or other cause for which equity would give like relief, if the sale had been made by the parties in interest, instead of by the court. Branton v. Jones, 222 Va. 305, 281 S.E.2d 799 (1981).

II. DECISIONS UNDER PRIOR LAW.

Editor's note. — The cases cited below were decided under corresponding provisions of former law. The term "this section," as used below, refers to former provisions.

This section is to be liberally construed. Brenham v. Smith, 120 Va. 30, 90 S.E. 657 (1916).

This section cannot serve to breathe life into a void decree of sale. Forrer v. Brown, 221 Va. 1098, 277 S.E.2d 483 (1981).

One not a party may not be divested of ownership. — This section cannot authorize a court by judicial sale to divest one not a party to the suit of his ownership of property. Forrer v. Brown, 221 Va. 1098, 277 S.E.2d 483 (1981).

Section applies to sales of lands of infants made in suits properly brought for that purpose. Lancaster v. Barton, 92 Va. 615, 24 S.E. 251 (1896). See also, Cooper v. Hepburn, 56 Va. (15 Gratt.) 551 (1858).

But it is not to be construed to contravene statutes protecting infants. — So far as the statutes for the sale of infants' lands are concerned, it will not be questioned that the primary and controlling consideration underlying their enactment was the welfare of the infants whose lands are to be sold, and in construing this section the purpose to ignore or contravene this consideration may not be imputed to the legislature. Brenham v. Smith, 120 Va. 30, 90 S.E. 657 (1916).

It does not apply to a proceeding to compel purchasers to comply with their contracts by paying the purchase money to the persons legally entitled to receive it. Whitehead v. Bradley, 87 Va. 676, 13 S.E. 195 (1891).

Sale is not complete until confirmation and conveyance. — Whether the sale be by a master, commissioner, or other functionary authorized by the court to conduct the sale, the bargain is not ordinarily considered as complete until the sale is confirmed and the conveyance is made. Brock v. Rice, 68 Va. (27 Gratt.) 812 (1876); Terry v. Coles, 80 Va. 695 (1885).

Section does not protect sales under void decrees. — In no case has this section been applied where the relief sought was based on a void decree. So where the court was without jurisdiction to issue the decree, this section cannot be applied. Gee v. McCormick, 142 Va. 173, 128 S.E. 541 (1925). See also, Brenham v. Smith, 120 Va. 30, 90 S.E. 657 (1916).

Since the decree of sale was void as to complainants, the purchasers under it could take no benefit from the provision of this section. Finkel Outdoor Prods., Inc. v. Bell, 205 Va. 927, 140 S.E.2d 695 (1965).

Title is not to be disturbed although decree is erroneous or voidable. — It appears from the history and the language of this section that the title of a purchaser at a judicial sale shall not be disturbed after 12 months from the date of the decree of confirmation, even though the decree is erroneous or voidable. Robertson v. Stone, 199 Va. 41, 97 S.E.2d 739 (1957).

Confirmation relates back to sale. — After the sale is confirmed, the confirmation relates back to the sale, and the purchaser is entitled to everything he would have been entitled to had the confirmation and conveyance been contemporaneous with the sale. Taylor v. Cooper, 37 Va. (10 Leigh) 317 (1839).

Limitation is suspended by bill of review. — Where the decree setting aside the proceedings under the original bill and dismissing the same was entered 12 months after the confirmation of the sale, but the bill of review was filed before the expiration of the 12 months, the period of limitation was suspended until the entry of the decree complained of. Gee v. McCormick, 142 Va. 173, 128 S.E. 541 (1925). See Anderson v. Biazzi, 166 Va. 309, 186 S.E. 7 (1936).

This section limits § 8.01-322, which allows a person not served with process to have a rehearing of the case within two years from the date of judgment or decree and any injustice corrected. Robertson v. Stone, 199 Va. 41, 97 S.E.2d 739 (1957).

Section does not defeat title of one not party to suit. — It was clearly not the purpose of the legislature by the enactment of this section to authorize a court by judicial sale to divest one of his ownership of property, who is not a party to the suit. Such a procedure would be without due process of law. Mountain Mission School, Inc. v. Buchanan Realty Corp., 207 Va. 518, 151 S.E.2d 403 (1966).

ARTICLE 12.

Detinue.

§ 8.01-114. When property to be taken by officer; summary of evidence, affidavits and report to be filed. — A. A proceeding in detinue to recover personal property unlawfully withheld from the plaintiff may be brought on a warrant or motion for judgment if pretrial seizure is not sought at the time of filing.

A petition in detinue for pretrial seizure pursuant to this article may be filed either to commence the detinue proceeding or may be filed during the pendency of a detinue proceeding which commenced on a warrant or motion for judgment. If a petition is filed, it shall:

1. Describe the kind, quantity and estimated fair market value of the specific personal property as to which plaintiff seeks possession;

2. Describe the basis of the plaintiff's claim of entitlement to recover the property, with such certainty as will give the adverse party reasonable notice of the true nature of the claim and the particulars thereof and, if based on a contract to secure the payment of money, the amount due on such contract; and

3. Allege one or more of the grounds mentioned in § 8.01-534 and set forth specific facts in support of such allegation. Further, if a petition is filed, a judge, or a magistrate appointed pursuant to Article 3 (§ 19.2-33 et seq.) of Chapter 3 of Title 19.2, may issue an order or other process directed to the sheriff or other proper officer, as the case may be, commanding him to seize the property for the recovery of which such action or warrant is brought, or a specified portion thereof, and deliver same to the plaintiff pendente lite under the circumstances hereinafter set forth.

B. The judge or the magistrate may issue such an order or other process in accordance with the prayer of the petition after an ex parte review of the petition only upon a determination that: (i) the petition conforms with subsection A and (ii) there is reasonable cause to believe that the grounds for detinue seizure described in the petition exist. The plaintiff praying for an order shall, at the time that he files his petition, pay the proper costs, fees and taxes, and in the event of his failure to do so, the order shall not be issued.

C. The judge or magistrate, as the case may be, may receive evidence only in the form of a sworn petition which shall be filed with the papers in the cause.

D. The order commanding the seizure of property shall be issued and served together with the form for requesting a hearing on a claim of exemption from seizure as provided in § 8.01-546.1. The order shall be issued and returned as provided in § 8.01-541 and may be issued or executed on any day, including a Saturday, Sunday or other legal holiday. Service shall be in accordance with the methods described in § 8.01-487.1. The provisions of § 8.01-546.2 shall govern claims for exemption. (Code 1950, § 8-586; 1973, c. 408; 1974, c. 122; 1977, c. 617; 1978, c. 403; 1986, c. 341; 1993, c. 841.)

REVISERS' NOTE

This section, former § 8-586, and others in this article were amended in 1974 to make the procedure comply with the requirements set out in Fuentes v. Shevin, 407 U.S. 67 (1972) and Sniadach v. Family Finance Corporation, 395 U.S. 337, 89 S. Ct. 1820, 23 L. Ed. 2d 349 (1969). These two cases were further discussed in Mitchell v. W. T. Grant, 416 U.S. 600 (1974) in which the Supreme Court restricted the scope of the two former cases. In general, no substantive changes have been made to former § 8-586 ff.

Cross references. — As to hearing on order or process issued under this section, see § 8.01-119. For rules of court relating to actions in detinue, see Rules 3:1 through 3:18.

Law Review. — For comment on cumulative remedies under article 9 of the U.C.C., see 14 Wm. & Mary L. Rev. 213 (1972). For article discussing the constitutionality of Virginia's detinue and attachment statutes, see 12 U. Rich. L. Rev. 157 (1977). For article on the abolition of the forms of action in Virginia, see 17 U. Rich. L. Rev. 273 (1983).

I. Decisions Under Current Law.
II. Decisions Under Prior Law.

I. DECISIONS UNDER CURRENT LAW.

Fixing damages on basis of affidavit held error where not supported by evidence. — The trial court erred in relying exclusively on an affidavit filed by the plaintiff in fixing the amount of the judgment when it was clear that the evidence at the hearing did not support the amount awarded. Before fixing the amount of the final judgment, the court should have held a further hearing on the damage issue. At that hearing, additional relevant evidence on the issue of damages should have been received from all parties and the respective parties should have been allowed to prove with reasonable certainty the worth of the property seized by the plaintiff. J.I. Case Co. v. United Va. Bank, 232 Va. 210, 349 S.E.2d 120 (1986).

Judgment against plaintiff where property seized and placed beyond court's jurisdiction. — Where the plaintiff, after seizing the property under authority of statute and placing it beyond the jurisdiction of the court, decides to manipulate the statutory scheme by exercising the privilege of nonsuit, the detinue statutes contemplate entry of a specific judgment in the detinue proceedings against the plaintiff for the value of the property. J.I. Case Co. v. United Va. Bank, 232 Va. 210, 349 S.E.2d 120 (1986).

Mandamus for forced entry error. — Where under the common law, it was unlawful for a sheriff to break the doors of a person's house to arrest that person in a civil suit in debt or trespass, where this venerable principle underlies the whole law dealing with the right to break and enter a dwelling house for civil recovery of property, and where the General Assembly has not plainly manifested an intent to abrogate this common law principle, the trial court erred in issuing writ of mandamus directing the sheriff to use due diligence and reasonable means to execute all validly issued detinue seizure orders and to take all appropriate action necessary to seize personal property including forced entry into the premises where such property was located or believed to be located. Williams v. Matthews, 248 Va. 277, 448 S.E.2d 625 (1994).

II. DECISIONS UNDER PRIOR LAW.

Editor's note. — The cases cited below were decided under corresponding provisions of former law. The terms "this article" and "this section," as used below, refer to former provisions.

The writ of seizure under the provisions of this section is intended to be only ancillary to the action of detinue, and can only be issued in a pending suit. Preston v. Legard, 160 Va. 364, 168 S.E. 445 (1933).

Jurisdiction of equity to decree delivery of papers not affected. — This article does not affect the jurisdiction of a court of equity to decree the specific delivery of title papers to heirs at law, devisees and other persons properly entitled thereto where such papers are wrongfully withheld. Kelly v. Lehigh Mining & Mfg. Co., 98 Va. 405, 36 S.E. 511 (1900).

Insolvency of defendant no ground for injunction. — The insolvency of a defendant in detinue is no ground for an injunction to prevent the removal or disposition of the subject of litigation. An ample remedy is afforded the plaintiff by this section. Langford & Bro. v. Taylor, 99 Va. 577, 39 S.E. 223 (1901).

§ 8.01-115. Bond required as prerequisite.

— No such order or process, however, shall be issued until a bond, conforming with the requirements of § 8.01-537.1, is posted with the judge or magistrate, in a penalty at least double the estimated fair market value of the property claimed, payable to the defendant, with the additional condition to redeliver the property so seized to the defendant, or to the person from whose possession it was taken, if the right to the possession shall be adjudged against the plaintiff. (Code 1950, § 8-587; 1977, cc. 230, 617; 1986, c. 341; 1993, c. 841.)

Editor's note. — Acts 1977, c. 230, amended former § 8-587, corresponding to this section. In the section as it stood prior to the amendment, the bond was "to be approved by and filed with the clerk or trial justice." The amendment substituted "judge, substitute judge or magistrate" for "or trial justices" in the quoted phrase. Pursuant to § 9-77.11 and Acts 1977, c. 617, cl. 4, the Code Commission has substituted "clerk, judge, substitute judge or magistrate" for "court" near the beginning of § 8.01-115 as enacted by Acts 1977, c. 617, in the section as set out above.

I. Decisions Under Current Law.
II. Decisions Under Prior Law.

I. DECISIONS UNDER CURRENT LAW.

Court retains jurisdiction over property until parties' rights determined. — The right of possession given to a detinue plaintiff under Virginia's statutory scheme contemplates retention of the seized property within the jurisdiction of the trial court until the substantive rights of the parties are finally determined. J.I. Case Co. v. United Va. Bank, 232 Va. 210, 349 S.E.2d 120 (1986).

II. DECISIONS UNDER PRIOR LAW.

Editor's note. — The case cited below was decided under corresponding provisions of former law. The term "this section," as used below, refers to former provisions.

Omission of condition as to payment of damages does not vitiate bond. — A bond providing for payment of costs as provided by this section, but omitting all reference to payment of damages, also prescribed, is not totally vitiated by such omission, but may be sued on as a statutory bond for the one good condition expressed therein. Jackson v. Hopkins, 92 Va. 601, 24 S.E. 234 (1896).

§ 8.01-116. Return of property to defendant or other claimant. — A. Subject to the provisions of subsection B below, the defendant in any such proceeding, or any other person claiming title to the property so seized and taken possession of by the officer, may have such property returned to him at any time after such seizure upon executing a bond, with sufficient surety, to be approved by the officer, payable to the plaintiff, in a penalty at least double the estimated value of the property. The bond shall contain a condition to (i) pay all costs and damages which may be awarded against the defendant in the proceeding and all damages which may accrue to any person by reason of the return of the property to the defendant or the claimant and (ii) have the property forthcoming to answer any judgment or order of the court or judge respecting the same. The bond shall be delivered to the officer and returned by him to the office of the clerk. The officer, on receiving the bond, shall forthwith return the property taken by him to the defendant or any other person claiming title thereto or from whose possession it was taken.

B. In any such proceeding, upon application of the defendant after reasonable notice to the plaintiff or his attorney, the judge of the court in which the proceeding is pending may order the property returned to the defendant upon such lesser security and upon such terms as in the nature of the case may be just and reasonable.

C. If no bond or security is delivered to the officer after his seizing and taking possession of such property, the property, if in the hands of the officer, shall be kept by him. However, if the property is perishable or expensive to keep, it may be sold by order of the court in the same manner as if it were a sale under execution. (Code 1950, § 8-588; 1973, c. 408; 1977, c. 617; 1993, c. 841.)

I. DECISIONS UNDER CURRENT LAW.

Court retains jurisdiction over property until parties' rights determined. — The right of possession given to a detinue plaintiff under Virginia's statutory scheme contemplates retention of the seized property within the jurisdiction of the trial court until the substantive rights of the parties are finally determined. J.I. Case Co. v. United Va. Bank, 232 Va. 210, 349 S.E.2d 120 (1986).

§ 8.01-117. Exceptions to sufficiency of bonds. — Either party may file exceptions to the sufficiency of the bond of the other or of the claimant of the property, if he has given bond, or such claimant may file exceptions to the sufficiency of the bond of either party. The court before whom the proceeding is pending, may, on the motion of either party or of the claimant, after reasonable notice to the others, pass upon such exceptions and make such order thereupon as may be just and reasonable. (Code 1950, § 8-589; 1977, c. 617; 1993, c. 841.)

I. DECISIONS UNDER PRIOR LAW.

Editor's note. — The case cited below was decided under corresponding provisions of former law. The term "this section," as used below, refers to former provisions.

Exceptions of claimant to bond do not alter status of parties. — It was contended that the corporation court had jurisdiction to issue an alias summons against a defendant because his wife, as a claimant, by an indorsement under this section of her exceptions to the sufficiency of the seizure bond filed in the papers, made herself a party to the action. There was no merit in this contention. The plaintiff in no wise made the wife a party to the suit, or contemplated that she should be a party, and the fact that she took exception to the sufficiency of the bond under this section did not alter the status of the contemplated defendant. Preston v. Legard, 160 Va. 364, 168 S.E. 445 (1933).

§ **8.01-118:** Repealed by Acts 1986, c. 341.

§ **8.01-119. Hearing to review issuance of order or process under § 8.01-114 or to consider request for such order or process.** — A. Within thirty days after the issuance of any ex parte order or process pursuant to § 8.01-114, or promptly upon application of either party, and in either event after reasonable notice, the court in which such proceeding is pending shall conduct a hearing to review the decision to issue the order or other process described in § 8.01-114, or to consider the request of the plaintiff for issuance of such order or other process, whether or not the plaintiff has attempted to previously obtain an order pursuant to § 8.01-114. The hearing may be combined with a prompt hearing held pursuant to § 8.01-546.2 on an exemption claimed or a trial on the merits or both. If combined with a hearing on an exemption claim, the hearing shall be conducted within ten business days of the filing of the request for a hearing. If the plaintiff gives reasonable notice of his intention to apply for such an order or process before the court, such hearing may be on the return day of the warrant. Evidence may be presented in the same manner as in subsection B of § 8.01-114.

B. At the conclusion of the hearing, if the evidence establishes the facts set forth in subdivision 1 of subsection A of § 8.01-114, and the court is satisfied from the evidence that (i) one or more of the grounds set forth in § 8.01-534 exist, (ii) there is good reason to believe that the defendant is insolvent, so that any recovery against him for the alternate value of the property and for damages and costs will probably prove unavailing, or (iii) the plaintiff may suffer other irreparable harm if his request is denied, and if it further appears to the court that there is a substantial likelihood that the plaintiff's allegations will be sustained at the trial, then the court shall issue the order or other process requested by the plaintiff, or let stand an order issued in the cause pursuant to § 8.01-114.

If the decision of the court is in favor of the defendant, the former order or process issued in the cause shall be abated and the property returned to the possession of the person from whom it was taken to abide the final trial of the action or warrant. Proof of insolvency as grounds for possession of goods by the plaintiff shall not be introduced for purposes of affirming a prior ex parte order, but only upon an initial application for possession after reasonable notice.

C. Issuance of any order or process pursuant to this section shall be subject to the provisions of §§ 8.01-115 and 8.01-116. (Code 1950, § 8-591; 1973, c. 408; 1977, c. 617; 1986, c. 341; 1993, c. 841.)

§ **8.01-120. No verdict as to some items; omission of price or value.** — If in such detinue action, on an issue concerning several things, in one or more counts, no verdict be found for part of them, it shall not be error, but the plaintiff shall be barred of his title to the things omitted; and if the verdict omit the price or value, the court may at any time have a jury impaneled to ascertain the same. (Code 1950, § 8-592; 1977, c. 617.)

§ **8.01-121. Final judgment.** — When final judgment is rendered on the trial of such detinue proceeding, the court shall dispose of the property or proceeds according to the rights of those entitled. When, in any such proceeding, the plaintiff prevails under a contract which, regardless of its form or express terms, was in fact made to secure the payment of money to the plaintiff or his assignor, judgment shall be for the recovery of the amount due the plaintiff thereunder or for the specific property, and costs. The defendant shall have the election of paying the amount of such judgment or surrendering the specific property. The court may grant the defendant a reasonable time not exceeding thirty days, within which to make the election upon such security being given as the court may deem sufficient. When the property involves an animal as defined in § 3.1-796.66, the court may order the return of the animal to the prevailing plaintiff without regard to any alternative method of recovery.

If the defendant elects to surrender the property as aforesaid, upon delivery of the property to the plaintiff or repossession thereof by him, the plaintiff may proceed to sell the property in accordance with the applicable provisions of the Uniform Commercial Code (§§ 8.9-501 through 8.9-507) with all the rights and responsibilities therein provided. (Code 1950, § 8-593; 1964, c. 219; 1977, c. 617; 1987, c. 1; 1993, c. 841.)

REVISERS' NOTE

Former § 8-593 has been modified to allow the plaintiff to recover a deficiency judgment.

Cross references. — As to affirmation of judgment for specific personal property, see § 8.01-123. As to what writs may issue on judgments for personal property, see § 8.01-472.

Law Review. — For note, "Effect of the Uniform Commercial Code on Virginia Law," see 20 Wash. & Lee L. Rev. 267 (1963).

I. Decisions Under Current Law.
II. Decisions Under Prior Law.

I. DECISIONS UNDER CURRENT LAW.

Effect of bankruptcy provision. — Bankruptcy law controls all property interests of a debtor and his/her relationships with creditors; therefore, to the extent that any state law conflicts with a Bankruptcy Code provision, it is of no force and effect, especially when such a law would have an adverse impact on a debtor's financial rehabilitation and fresh start by permitting creditors to obtain personal judgments in violation of the discharge injunctive order under the premise that it is in lieu of property when it is nothing more than an unsecured personal liability deficiency of its secured claim. Martin v. AVCO Fin. Servs., 157 Bankr. 268 (Bankr. W.D. Va. 1993).

Court retains jurisdiction over property until parties' rights determined. — The right of possession given to a detinue plaintiff under Virginia's statutory scheme contemplates retention of the seized property within the jurisdiction of the trial court until the substantive rights of the parties are finally determined. J.I. Case Co. v. United Va. Bank, 232 Va. 210, 349 S.E.2d 120 (1986).

Sanctions not imposed for creditor's apparent good faith but impermissible use of judgment proceedings. — Creditor who sought a warrant of detinue for recovery of collateral after debtor was discharged in bankruptcy appeared to have acted in the good-faith, albeit mistaken, belief that its actions in getting judgment against debtor, garnishing the debtor's wages, and threatening criminal action for disposal of collateral were permissible; therefore, sanctions would not be imposed on the creditor. Martin v. AVCO Fin. Servs., 157 Bankr. 268 (Bankr. W.D. Va. 1993).

II. DECISIONS UNDER PRIOR LAW.

Editor's note. — The cases cited below were decided under corresponding provisions of former law. The term "this section," as used below, refers to former provisions.

This section was enacted for the benefit of the vendee and gives him and not the vendor the right of election. Ashworth v. Fleenor, 178 Va. 104, 16 S.E.2d 309 (1941).

Judgment for price or property. — In an action for detinue it was held that judgment should be for the unpaid purchase price or, in the alternative, the property as required by this section. Osmond-Barringer Co. v. Hey, 7 Va. L. Reg. (n.s.) 175 (1921).

Debt extinguished upon surrender of property. — While this section does not in terms provide for the extinguishment of the debt upon the surrender of the property by the defendant, the conclusion is inescapable that such was the legislative intent, "regardless of the form of the contract or its express terms." Lloyd v. Federal Motor Truck Co., 168 Va. 72, 190 S.E. 257 (1937).

Under this section defendant cannot by election merely abide the judgment. He must, in order to avail himself of the benefit conferred by the statute in this regard, elect to pay the judgment, and, if necessary, the court will require the execution of a security bond to insure payment. Lloyd v. Federal Motor Truck Co., 168 Va. 72, 190 S.E. 257 (1937).

§ **8.01-122. Charges for keeping property.** — The legal charges, if any, for keeping any such property, while in the possession of the officer, shall be paid by the plaintiff and certified by the officer to the court who, in case such order or process be not abated and final judgment be rendered for the plaintiff, shall tax the same along with the other costs of the suit. (Code 1950, § 8-594; 1977, c. 617.)

§ **8.01-123. Recovery of damages sustained for property withheld during appeal.** — When a judgment for specific personal property is affirmed by an appellate court, or an injunction to such judgment is dissolved, the person who is entitled to execution of such judgment, or who would be entitled if execution had not been had, may, on motion to the court from which such execution has issued, or might issue, after fifteen days' notice to the defendant or his personal representative, have a jury impaneled to ascertain the damages sustained by reason of the detention of such property, subsequent to such judgment, or if it was on a verdict, subsequent to such verdict; and judgment shall be rendered for the damages, if any, so ascertained. (Code 1950, § 8-595; 1977, c. 617.)

ARTICLE 13.

Unlawful Entry and Detainer.

§ **8.01-124. Motion for judgment in circuit court for unlawful entry or detainer.** — If any forcible or unlawful entry be made upon lands, or if, when the entry is lawful and peaceable, the tenant shall detain the possession of land after the right has expired, without the consent of him who is entitled to the possession, the party so turned out of possession, no matter what right of title he had thereto, or the party against whom such possession is unlawfully detained may file a motion for judgment in the circuit court alleging that the defendant is in possession and unlawfully withholds from the plaintiff the premises in question. (Code 1950, § 8-789; 1954, c. 549; 1975, c. 235; 1977, c. 617.)

REVISERS' NOTE

This is a clarification of former § 8-789 rewritten also to be consistent with other sections.

Cross references. — For limitation of action for unlawful entry or detainer, see § 8.01-236. As to venue, see § 8.01-261, subdivision 3.
Law Review. — For survey of Virginia law on property for the year 1974-1975, see 61 Va. L. Rev. 1834 (1975). For article discussing the constitutionality of Virginia's detinue and attachment statutes, see 12 U. Rich. L. Rev. 157 (1977).

I. Decisions Under Current Law.
II. Decisions Under Prior Law.
   A. General Consideration.
   B. Elements.
      1. Possession.
      2. Right of Possession.
      3. The Force Required.
   C. By and Against Whom Action Lies.
      1. In General.
      2. Landlord and Tenant.
   D. Notice to Quit and Demand of Possession.
   E. Defenses.
   F. Pleading and Practice.

I. DECISIONS UNDER CURRENT LAW.

Applied in Kennedy v. Block, 784 F.2d 1220 (4th Cir. 1986); Sentara Enters., Inc. v. CCP Assocs., 243 Va. 39, 413 S.E.2d 595 (1992).

II. DECISIONS UNDER PRIOR LAW.

A. General Consideration.

Editor's note. — The cases cited below were decided under corresponding provisions of former law. The terms "this statute," "this act," and "this section," as used below, refer to former provisions.

Statute liberally construed. — As the defendant can in no case be turned out of possession, unless it is apparent that he ought to surrender the possession on the demand of the plaintiff, and to retain it would be unjust, this statute, being remedial, should be given a liberal construction. Allen v. Gibson, 25 Va. (4 Rand.) 468 (1826).

Purpose of action. — The remedy of unlawful entry and detainer was designed to protect the actual possession, whether rightful or wrongful, and to afford summary redress and restitution. Olinger v. Shepherd, 53 Va. (12 Gratt.) 462 (1855); Davis v. Mayo, 82 Va. 97 (1886); Fore v. Campbell, 82 Va. 808, 1 S.E. 180 (1887); Mears v. Dexter, 86 Va. 828, 11 S.E. 538 (1890); Tayloe v. Rose, 10 Va. L. Reg. 1002 (1904).

While the purpose of this and the following sections is to prevent violence and disturbances which are likely to follow when one entitled to the lawful possession of premises undertakes to assert his rights by force, the right of action is civil in character and the result, if the plaintiff prevails, is merely to restore the possession to one from whom it has been forcibly taken, or to give possession to one from whom it is being unlawfully withheld. The judgment has only the effect of placing the parties in status quo. Shorter v. Shelton, 183 Va. 819, 33 S.E.2d 643 (1945).

In order to maintain cause of action for unlawful detainer, plaintiff must prove that defendant forcibly or unlawfully entered the land, maintained possession of the land without a right to do so, without plaintiff's consent and withheld possession from plaintiff. Cherokee Corp. of Linden, Inc. v. Capital Skiing Corp., 222 Bankr. 281 (Bankr. E.D. Va. 1998), aff'd, 191 F.3d 447 (4th Cir. 1999).

A warrant for unlawful entry and detainer is a civil action. Kincheloe v. Tracewells, 52 Va. (11 Gratt.) 587 (1854).

Unlawful detainer and ejectment distinguished. — In ejectment, title or right of possession is always involved. The design of unlawful detainer is to protect the actual possession whether rightful or wrongful, and to afford summary redress and restitution. Forcible entry of the owner is unlawful. Entry of stranger is unlawful, whether forcible or not. Judgment only restores the status quo, but settles nothing as to the title or right of possession. Davis v. Mayo, 82 Va. 97 (1886). See also, Olinger v. Shepherd, 53 Va. (12 Gratt.) 462 (1855).

Title is not involved in the action of unlawful detainer, and evidence of title is often inadmissible. Allen v. Gibson, 25 Va. (4 Rand.) 468 (1826); Emerick v. Tavener, 50 Va. (9 Gratt.) 220 (1852); Olinger v. Shepherd, 53 Va. (12 Gratt.) 462 (1855). But see, Corbett v. Nutt, 59 Va. (18 Gratt.) 624 (1868), aff'd, 77 U.S. 464, 19 L. Ed. 976 (1870); Tayloe v. Rose, 10 Va. L. Reg. 1002 (1904).

Use of reasonable force by owner. — This section does not in express terms deprive the owner of the common-law right to take possession by reasonable force of premises to which he may be entitled. The real owner of the premises, having a right of entry, will not commit a trespass by entering, though with force, unless he also commit a breach of the peace, but he may be turned out in an action of forcible entry. Shorter v. Shelton, 183 Va. 819, 33 S.E.2d 643 (1945).

B. Elements.

1. Possession.

It is necessary to show that the defendant unlawfully withholds the possession. Power v. Tazewells, 66 Va. (25 Gratt.) 786 (1875).

Possession under claim of title is sufficient to sustain an action of forcible entry and detainer against one entering without title. Fore v. Campbell, 82 Va. 808, 1 S.E. 180 (1887).

Actual occupancy of whole tract not required. — The possession to which the proceeding for unlawful entry will apply, is not confined to actual occupancy or enclosure, but it is any possession which is sufficient to sustain an action of trespass. And thus actual possession of a part of a tract of land under a bona fide claim and color of title to the whole is such a possession of the whole or so much thereof as is not in the adverse possession of others, as will sustain this proceeding. Olinger v. Shepherd, 53 Va. (12 Gratt.) 462 (1855).

Proper title is irrelevant to claim of unlawful detainer because lawful possession of property is the only issue to be determined in a claim for unlawful detainer. Cherokee Corp. of Linden, Inc. v. Capital Skiing Corp., 222 Bankr. 281 (Bankr. E.D. Va. 1998), aff'd, 191 F.3d 447 (4th Cir. 1999).

Color of title without possession, actual or constructive, is not sufficient to support an action of unlawful detainer. Hot Springs Lumber & Mfg. Co. v. Sterrett, 108 Va. 710, 62 S.E. 797 (1908).

Inference of possession at time action brought. — Where the proof shows that a defendant in an action of unlawful detainer had been in possession of the premises claimed in the declaration for five years before the action was brought and always refused to give up possession, the jury might and should infer that he was in possession at the time of action brought. Hence, the court must so find on a demurrer to the evidence by the defendant. Hobday v. Kane, 114 Va. 398, 76 S.E. 902 (1913). See also, Kincheloe v. Tracewells, 52 Va. (11 Gratt.) 587 (1854).

2. Right of Possession.

Not necessary in order to recover. — If the defendant enters upon lands of the plaintiff unlawfully, the plaintiff is entitled to recover possession without any regard to the right of possession, the actual possession giving the plaintiff the right of possession against any party not having the right of entry. Tayloe v. Rose, 10 Va. L. Reg. 1002 (1904); Olinger v. Shepherd, 53 Va. (12 Gratt.) 462 (1855).

May recover for ouster from lands of State. — In a proceeding for an unlawful entry or detainer, if the defendant has entered unlawfully, the plaintiff is entitled to recover without any regard to the question of his right of possession. This though the land from which he is ousted is the land of the State. Olinger v. Shepherd, 53 Va. (12 Gratt.) 462 (1855).

One with right of immediate possession may be liable. — A person may render himself liable to an action of forcible entry and detainer by entering on his own premises, even when he has the right of immediate possession. Tayloe v. Rose, 10 Va. L. Reg. 1002 (1904); Olinger v. Shepherd, 53 Va. (12 Gratt.) 462 (1855).

3. The Force Required.

To sustain a complaint for forcible entry, the force must be actual, not constructive. Otherwise, the remedy given for an unlawful entry would be unnecessary. Pauley v. Chapman, 41 Va. (2 Rob.) 235 (1843).

But entry of a stranger is unlawful whether forcible or not. Davis v. Mayo, 82 Va. 97 (1886).

If an entry on land, though peaceable, be unlawful, the owner may recover the possession from the intruder in an action of unlawful entry and detainer. Allen v. Gibson, 25 Va. (4 Rand.) 468 (1826).

C. By and Against Whom Action Lies.

1. In General.

One in possession under agreement to purchase cannot be ousted before his lawful possession is terminated by demand or otherwise. Williamson v. Paxton, 59 Va. (18 Gratt.) 475 (1868).

But such possession may be terminated by the acceptance of a lease. Locke v. Frasher, 79 Va. 409 (1884).

Under this act, a mortgagee may obtain possession of the mortgaged premises after forfeiture, by the mode of proceeding therein pointed out. Allen v. Gibson, 25 Va. (4 Rand.) 468 (1826).

One tenant in common may have an action of unlawful entry and detainer for the whole land, against any party having no legal right whatever, without joining his cotenant. Allen v. Gibson, 25 Va. (4 Rand.) 468 (1826).

A remainderman may recover in an action of unlawful detainer land conveyed by the life tenant to a third party, provided he himself did not join in the grant. Such action may be brought within three years from the death of the life tenant. Hope v. Norfolk & W.R.R., 79 Va. 283 (1884).

As may trustees. — It is immaterial to the support of the action of unlawful detainer whether the plaintiffs acquired any personal ownership in the property by the deeds. Allen v. Paul, 65 Va. (24 Gratt.) 332 (1874). See also, Davis v. Mayo, 82 Va. 97 (1886).

And occupant of public lands for oyster beds. — A person who has obtained an assignment of certain oyster beds for the planting and sowing of oysters, has paid the tax and had the beds staked off as required, has such an exclusive interest in them, that he may maintain an action of unlawful detainer against a party who enters upon said beds and holds them against him. Power v. Tazewells, 66 Va. (25 Gratt.) 786 (1875).

And city. — A city which was the owner of the ground which it had not disposed of, covered by water, both as riparian proprietor and as having had long possession thereof, could maintain an action of unlawful entry and detainer against any intruder upon said water lots. Norfolk City v. Cooke, 68 Va. (27 Gratt.) 430 (1876).

Vendor cannot maintain action after sale. — One who has sold to another a tract of land on condition and has afterwards conveyed such tract to a third party cannot, on failure to perform the condition, maintain an action of unlawful detainer for possession of that tract in his own name. Dobson v. Culpepper, 64 Va. (23 Gratt.) 352 (1873).

2. Landlord and Tenant.

The general rule is that the possession of the tenant is the possession of the landlord, and is not adverse to him, and the tenant will not be allowed to deny his landlord's title. Dobson v. Culpepper, 64 Va. (23 Gratt.) 352 (1873); Jordan v. Katz, 89 Va. 628, 16 S.E. 866 (1893); Reusens v. Lawson, 91 Va. 226, 21 S.E. 347 (1895).

The operation of this rule is not affected by the fact that the tenant is in actual possession at the time he accepts the lease. By such acceptance he as effectually recognizes the title and possession of the lessor as if he had entered and taken possession under and by virtue of the lease itself. Emerick v. Tavener, 50 Va. (9 Gratt.) 220 (1852); Locke v. Frasher, 79 Va. 409 (1884); Jordan v. Katz, 89 Va. 628, 16 S.E. 866 (1893).

Grantee from landlord must sue tenant. — Where a landlord sells and conveys to a purchaser land in the possession of a tenant of the landlord, and the tenant refuses to surrender possession, the grantee is the proper person to bring unlawful detainer to recover possession of the tenant. Harrison v. Middleton, 52 Va. (11 Gratt.) 527 (1854); Hobday v. Kane, 114 Va. 398, 76 S.E. 902 (1913).

Tenant alienating part or all of premises remains liable to his lessor in an action to recover possession of the whole premises, if possession be withheld after termination of the tenancy, whether such alienation be by sublease or conveyance in fee with warranty, and whether the action be ejectment or unlawful detainer. Emerick v. Tavener, 50 Va. (9 Gratt.) 220 (1852).

Section provides adequate remedy to tenant not put in possession. — A tenant sued his landlord for damages alleged to be due by reason of the failure of the landlord to put the tenant in possession of the property which was being held by a former tenant. In the absence of express contract the landlord owed no duty to put the tenant into actual possession of the property but only to put him into legal possession, because this section, providing a summary remedy for unlawful entry or detainer, gives the tenant an adequate, simple and summary remedy for such a wrong. This section specifically provides that unlawful detainer shall lie for one entitled to possession in any case in which a tenant shall detain the possession of land after his right has expired without the consent of him who is entitled to possession. Hannan v. Dusch, 154 Va. 356, 153 S.E. 824 (1930).

Unlawful detainer is the proper action to be brought by the lessee of a ferry and the wharfs, docks, landings and other property used for the purposes of the ferry against a third person who is in the possession of, and unlawfully withholds from him, a part of the land leased by him. The action is not to recover a mere franchise, but land leased to the plaintiff. Consolvo v. Ferries Co., 112 Va. 318, 71 S.E. 634 (1911).

D. Notice to Quit and Demand of Possession.

Notice necessary if defendant did not obtain possession adversely. — If defendant holds land not adversely but under the plaintiff, notice to quit or demand of possession must be shown before the action of unlawful detainer can be maintained. Williamson v. Paxton, 59 Va. (18 Gratt.) 475 (1868); Pettit v. Cowherd, 83 Va. 20, 1 S.E. 392 (1887); Johnson v. Goldberg, 207 Va. 487, 151 S.E.2d 368 (1966).

But where the defendant, in his answer, denies that he is a tenant of the plaintiff, he holds the land adversely, and is not entitled to a notice to vacate. Johnson v. Goldberg, 207 Va. 487, 151 S.E.2d 368 (1966).

E. Defenses.

When equitable defenses available. — In unlawful detainer, as well as in ejectment, under plea of not guilty, defendant can avail himself of equitable defenses, but only when "there is a writing stating the purchase and the terms thereof, signed by the vendor or his agent." Dobson v. Culpepper, 64 Va. (23 Gratt.) 352 (1872); Locke v. Frasher, 79 Va. 409 (1884).

Requisites when defendants put in possession by plaintiffs. — In an action of unlawful detainer, where the defendants have been put into possession of the premises by the plaintiffs, the defendants cannot set up a plea of adverse possession unless they prove that they disclaimed to hold of the plaintiffs or bona fide abandoned possession of the premises or asserted and claimed an adverse right to the premises, with notice thereof to the plaintiffs three years before the institution of the action. Allen v. Paul, 65 Va. (24 Gratt.) 332 (1874). See also, Buchanan v. Norfolk S.R.R., 150 Va. 17, 142 S.E. 405 (1928).

Lessee estopped to deny lessor's title. — The lease being for a certain quantity of land, situate as therein described, and lessee having executed it under his hand and seal, and thereby recognized the description and boundaries therein specified, and that he then held the same in possession, and the warrant being for the precise tenement described in the lease, neither lessee, nor one claiming under him, can be entertained to deny that the tenement had its boundaries, or that they were within them. Emerick v. Tavener, 50 Va. (9 Gratt.) 220 (1852).

Except when obtained by fraud. — A person, possessing and claiming title to land, supposing another to have better title, took a lease from him. In an action by the lessor to recover possession, the tenant may set up such mistake and show he had good title to the land, provided such mistake was induced by the lessor through misrepresentations amounting to fraud. Alderson v. Miller, 56 Va. (15 Gratt.) 279 (1858); Locke v. Frasher, 79 Va. 409 (1884).

Compliance with contract of sale good defense. — When a conveyance is not made to purchaser who fails to fulfill his contract, and the vendor conveys to another and brings unlawful detainer against the original purchaser, compliance with the contract is a good defense. Dobson v. Culpepper, 64 Va. (23 Gratt.) 352 (1873).

Plaintiff's failure to pay required rent to State no bar to recovery. — In unlawful entry and detainer to recover oyster beds assigned to plaintiff by the county oyster inspector, his failure to pay rent to the State does not affect his right to recover from defendants, unlawfully in possession. Mears v. Dexter, 86 Va. 828, 11 S.E. 538 (1890).

F. Pleading and Practice.

A wife is not a necessary party to an action of unlawful entry and detainer against her husband, trustee for her, in possession of land, which he contracted to purchase for her. Williamson v. Paxton, 59 Va. (18 Gratt.) 475 (1868).

Statement may supplement warrant. — To entitle the plaintiff to recover upon a warrant of unlawful detainer, he must prove that the defendant withheld the possession at the date of the warrant. But if the warrant does not state the withholding of the possession by the defendant, that may be aided by the complaint which states the fact. Kincheloe v. Tracewells, 52 Va. (11 Gratt.) 587 (1854).

Description of premises. — In a writ of unlawful detainer, under the statute, the omission to state in the complaint the estimated quantity of the land in dispute, is not fatal, if the complaint contains a reasonably certain description. Allen v. Gibson, 25 Va. (4 Rand.) 468 (1826).

Purchase of property at trustee's auction. — See Cherokee Corp. of Linden, Inc. v. Capital Skiing Corp., 222 Bankr. 281 (Bankr. E.D. Va. 1998), aff'd, 191 F.3d 447 (4th Cir. 1999).

Evidence of title inadmissible. — Title is not involved in an action of forcible entry and detainer, and therefore, as a general rule, evidence of title is inadmissible. Emerick v. Tavener, 50 Va. (9 Gratt.) 220 (1852).

But deed may be offered to show extent of possession. — A deed, though it may be invalid to pass the title it purports to convey, may be admissible evidence as a link in plaintiff's chain of title to show the bounds of the land claimed by him, and the extent of his possession. Harrison v. Middleton, 52 Va. (11 Gratt.) 527 (1854); Olinger v. Shepherd, 53 Va. (12 Gratt.) 462 (1855).

Records are admissible to show right of possession. — In unlawful detainer by a corporation against its ex-treasurer for possession of a house and lot allowed him as a residence while in office as part of his emoluments, the records of the corporation are admissible as evidence to show the arrangements made between the parties. Frazier v. VMI, 81 Va. 59 (1885).

And oral lease for more than year is admissible to show how defendant obtained possession. — Upon the trial of a writ of unlawful detainer, defendant sets up title in himself. Plaintiff may prove that the defendant entered on the premises under a parol lease from himself, though the lease proved was to continue more than one year. Adams v. Martin, 49 Va. (8 Gratt.) 107 (1851).

Recordation of power of attorney not necessary for admission in evidence. — It is unnecessary to record a power of attorney under seal appointing an agent to take charge of real estate and to bring suit for its protection in order for it to be admitted in evidence in an action of unlawful detainer to recover possession of the land. Hobday v. Kane, 114 Va. 398, 76 S.E. 902 (1913).

Burden on plaintiff to show that possession not withheld for three years. — An action of unlawful detainer is purely a statutory action. The burden of proof is upon the plaintiff to show by a preponderance of the evidence that possession has not been withheld over three years, but there is no requirement in the statute that the summons should allege that possession has not been withheld over three years, and the practice in Virginia uniformly pursued for a great length of time has been to the contrary and ought to be regarded as showing what the law is on the subject. Allen v. Paul, 65 Va. (24 Gratt.) 332 (1874); Fore v. Campbell, 82 Va. 808, 1 S.E. 180 (1887); Pettit v. Cowherd, 83 Va. 20, 1 S.E. 392 (1887); Daily v. Rucker, 151 Va. 72, 144 S.E. 466 (1928), decided before 1978 amendment to § 8.01-236, which now provides period of limitations for this action.

§ 8.01-125. When summons returnable to circuit court; jury.

— When the action is commenced in the circuit court, the summons is returnable thereto and, upon application of either party trial by jury shall be had. (Code 1950, § 8-792; 1954, c. 333; 1970, c. 272; 1977, c. 617.)

REVISERS' NOTE

Former § 8-792 has been altered so that it applies only to actions commenced in a circuit court. Also, actions of unlawful entry and detainer no longer will have precedence on the civil docket. See also Revisers' note to § 8.01-331.

§ 8.01-126. Summons for unlawful detainer issued by magistrate, clerk or judge of a general district court.

— In any case when possession of any house, land or tenement is unlawfully detained by the person in possession thereof, the landlord, his agent, attorney, or other person, entitled to the possession may present to a magistrate, clerk or judge of a general district court a statement under oath of the facts which authorize the removal of the tenant or other person in possession, describing such premises; and thereupon such magistrate, clerk or judge of a general district court shall issue his summons against the person or persons named in such affidavit. The process issued upon any such summons issued by a magistrate, clerk or judge may be served as provided in §§ 8.01-293 and 8.01-296 or § 8.01-299. When issued by a magistrate it may be returned to and the case heard and determined by the judge of a general district court. If the summons for unlawful detainer is filed to terminate a tenancy pursuant to the Virginia Residential Landlord Tenant Act (§ 55-248.2 et seq.), the initial hearing on such summons shall occur as soon as practicable, but not more than twenty-one days from the date of filing. If the case cannot be heard within twenty-one days from the date of filing, the initial hearing shall be held as soon as practicable. If the plaintiff requests that the initial hearing be set on a date later than twenty-one days from the date of filing, the initial hearing shall be set on a date the plaintiff is available that is also available for the court. Such summons shall be served at least ten days before the return day thereof. (Code 1950, § 8-791; 1954, c. 333; 1966, c. 436; 1968, c. 639; 1972, c. 397; 1975, c. 235; 1977, c. 617; 1978, c. 344; 1980, c. 502; 2000, c. 1055.)

The 2000 amendments. — The 2000 amendment by c. 1055 added the fourth, fifth and sixth sentences and substituted "ten" for "five" in the last sentence.

Law Review. — For survey of Virginia law on property for the year 1974-1975, see 61 Va. L. Rev. 1834 (1975).

I. Decisions Under Current Law.
II. Decisions Under Prior Law.

I. DECISIONS UNDER CURRENT LAW.

Where federal housing laws and regulations established a reviewing process outside the courts and the tenant did not receive a hearing meeting the standards of that process, an unlawful detainer action was not an adequate remedy at law to protect the statutory and regulatory procedures afforded the tenant. Cooper v. Tazewell Square Apts., Ltd., 577 F. Supp. 1483 (W.D. Va. 1984).

Applied in Kennedy v. Block, 784 F.2d 1220 (4th Cir. 1986).

II. DECISIONS UNDER PRIOR LAW.

Editor's note. — The case cited below was decided under corresponding provisions of former law.

Protection for tenants in federally assisted housing. — The substantive right not to be arbitrarily evicted from federally assisted housing on the mere expiration of a lease in turn requires that a tenant be afforded the following protections: (1) timely notice specifying the reasons for the eviction; (2) an opportunity to confront and cross-examine adverse witnesses and present his own evidence; (3) the right to retain an attorney; and (4) the right to an impartial decision based solely on the evidence adduced at the hearing. Anderson v. Denny, 365 F. Supp. 1254 (W.D. Va. 1973).

Tenants residing in federally assisted housing are entitled to a declaratory judgment that they cannot be evicted from their tenancies until they receive notice alleging good cause, and such allegations are to be proved in a hearing in the state courts, under the procedural and substantive law of Virginia. Anderson v. Denny, 365 F. Supp. 1254 (W.D. Va. 1973).

§ 8.01-127. Removal of action. — Notwithstanding the provisions of § 16.1-92, in any case where the amount in controversy exceeds the sum of $500, in which an action has been commenced or a summons has been issued pursuant to § 8.01-126, in or returnable to a general district court, removal of the action to the circuit court shall be conditional upon the tenant giving security for all rent which has accrued and may accrue upon the premises, but for not more than one year's rent in all, whether it accrues before or accrues after the removal, and also for all damages that have accrued or may accrue from an unlawful use and occupation of the premises. (Code 1950, § 8-791.1; 1975, c. 235; 1977, c. 617.)

REVISERS' NOTE

The former phrase "with sufficient corporate or cash surety" has been deleted. It is up to the court to determine the type and adequacy of the security to be required. The security shall not be for more than one year's rent.

§ 8.01-127.1. Removal of residential unlawful detainer actions. — A. In any case involving a residential tenancy not involving a default in rent in which an action has been commenced or a summons has been issued pursuant to § 8.01-126, in or returnable to a general district court, removal of the action to the circuit court shall be conditioned upon the defendant (i) filing an affidavit of substantial defense pursuant to the requirements of § 16.1-92 and (ii) paying the costs accrued to the time of removal, the writ tax as fixed by law, and in the court to which it is removed, the costs as fixed by subdivision A 13 of § 17.1-275.

B. The affidavit of substantial defense described in subsection A and any representation by the landlord that there has been a default in rent shall be subject to the requirements of § 8.01-271.1.

C. If the defendant fails to pay rent at such time and in such manner as required by the terms of the rental agreement and applicable law, the landlord may file with the circuit court, and serve upon the defendant, or his attorney, an affidavit made by himself, his agent, or his attorney, stating that the rent is delinquent. If within three business days of service of such notice, the defendant or his attorney fails to file, and the court does not receive an affidavit stating that the rent has been paid timely, the circuit court shall enter an order of possession granting the landlord immediate possession of the premises.

If an affidavit is filed on behalf of the defendant stating that payment has been made, the matter shall come before the circuit court forthwith to resolve the issue of payment.

D. Unlawful detainer actions removed to the circuit court shall be accorded priority on the civil docket. (1995, c. 599.)

Law Review. — For 1995 survey of civil practice and procedure, see 29 U. Rich. L. Rev. 897 (1995).

§ 8.01-128. Verdict and judgment; damages. — If it appear that the plaintiff was forcibly or unlawfully turned out of possession, or that it was unlawfully detained from him, the verdict or judgment shall be for the plaintiff for the premises, or such part thereof as may be found to have been so held or detained. The verdict or judgment shall also be for such damages as the plaintiff may prove to have been sustained by him by reason of such forcible or unlawful entry, or unlawful detention, of such premises, and such rent as he may prove to have been owing to him, provided such damages and rent claimed shall not exceed the jurisdictional amount of the court in which the action is tried. No such verdict or judgment shall bar any separate concurrent or future action for any such damages or rent as may not be so claimed. (Code 1950, § 8-793; 1954, c. 609; 1977, c. 617.)

REVISERS' NOTE

The restriction in former § 8-793 as to rent being claimed only up to the time of the institution of the action has been removed. Other unnecessary language has been deleted; but no change in substance is intended.

I. Decisions Under Current Law.
II. Decisions Under Prior Law.

I. DECISIONS UNDER CURRENT LAW.

Lessor may evict lessee without losing right to recover deficiency later. — In creating an exemption to the rules of claim-splitting, this section provides the lessor with an opportunity to evict the lessee without losing its right to recover any later deficiency in rent after making an effort to minimize the lessee's damages by renting to another tenant. Virginia Dynamics Co. v. Payne, 244 Va. 314, 421 S.E.2d 421 (1992).

Right to file subsequent action after eviction must be expressly waived. — The lessor's statutorily created right to file a subsequent action for rent would have to be expressly waived in order for such a right to be considered contracted away. Virginia Dynamics Co. v. Payne, 244 Va. 314, 421 S.E.2d 421 (1992).

Applied in Seoane v. Drug Emporium, Inc., 249 Va. 469, 457 S.E.2d 93 (1995).

II. DECISIONS UNDER PRIOR LAW.

Editor's note. — The cases cited below were decided under corresponding provisions of former law. The term "this article," as used below, refers to former provisions.

The judgment restores only the status quo and settles nothing as to the title or right of possession. Davis v. Mayo, 82 Va. 97 (1886).

No independent action for damages for forcible dispossession. — This article does not undertake to give a party forcibly dispossessed any right to institute a separate and independent action for damages therefor. Shorter v. Shelton, 183 Va. 819, 33 S.E.2d 643 (1945).

Removal of encroachment. — Where the evidence showed that removal of an encroachment was essential to appellants' full enjoyment of their land, the trial court erred in refusing to issue the injunction sought. Appellants had no adequate remedy at law by way of ejectment or unlawful detainer, for by neither action could they accomplish their object to obtain quiet possession of their land. Benoit v. Baxter, 196 Va. 360, 83 S.E.2d 442 (1954).

§ 8.01-129. Appeal from judgment of general district court. — An appeal shall lie from the judgment of a general district court, in any proceeding under this article, to the circuit court in the same manner and with like effect and upon like security as appeals taken under the provisions of § 16.1-106 et seq. except as specifically provided in this section. The appeal shall be taken within ten days and the security approved by the court from which the appeal is taken. Notwithstanding the provisions of § 16.1-106 et seq. the bond shall be posted and the writ tax paid within ten days of the date of the judgment. Unless otherwise specifically provided in the court's order, no writ of execution shall issue on a judgment for possession until the expiration of this ten-day period, except in cases of judgment of default for the nonpayment of rent where the writ of execution shall issue immediately upon entry of judgment for possession, if requested by the plaintiff. When the appeal is taken by the defendant, he shall be required to give security also for all rent which has accrued and may accrue upon the premises, but for not more than one year's rent, and also for all damages that have accrued or may accrue from the unlawful use and occupation of the premises for a period not exceeding three months. Trial by jury shall be had upon application of any party. (Code 1950, § 8-794; 1950, p. 68; 1977, c. 617; 1984, c. 565; 1998, c. 750.)

REVISERS' NOTE

The sentence in former § 8-794 stating what type of security may be taken has been deleted. The type and adequacy of the security is left up to the court.

Cross references. — As to appeals generally, see § 8.01-669 et seq.

I. DECISIONS UNDER CURRENT LAW.

This section did not permit an appeal from denial of motion for new trial. — This section was inapplicable where tenant in unlawful detainer action did not appeal district court's judgment awarding possession to landlord but appealed only from the court's denial of motion for a new trial. Ragan v. Woodcroft Village Apts., 255 Va. 322, 497 S.E.2d 740 (1998).

Applied in Letendre v. Fugate, 701 F.2d 1093 (4th Cir. 1983); Kennedy v. Block, 606 F. Supp. 1397 (W.D. Va. 1985).

§ 8.01-130. Judgment not to bar action of trespass or ejectment. — No judgment in an action brought under the provisions of this article shall bar any action of trespass or ejectment between the same parties, nor shall any such judgment or verdict be conclusive, in any such future action, of the facts therein found. (Code 1950, § 8-795; 1977, c. 617.)

I. DECISIONS UNDER PRIOR LAW.

Editor's note. — The cases cited below were decided under corresponding provisions of former law.

Judgment settles nothing as to title or right of possession. — In an action of forcible entry and detainer the judgment has only the effect of placing the parties in status quo. It settles nothing even between them in regard to the title or right of possession. It is no bar to an action of trespass or ejectment between the same parties. Olinger v. Shepherd, 53 Va. (12 Gratt.) 462 (1855); Davis v. Mayo, 82 Va. 97 (1886).

ARTICLE 14.

Ejectment.

§ 8.01-131. Action of ejectment retained; when and by whom brought. — A. The action of ejectment is retained, subject to the provisions hereinafter contained, and to the applicable Rules of Court.

B. Such action may be brought in the same cases in which a writ of right might have been brought prior to the first day of July, 1850, and by any person claiming real estate in fee or for life or for years, either as heir, devisee or purchaser, or otherwise. (Code 1950, §§ 8-796, 8-797; 1954, c. 333; 1977, c. 617.)

Cross references. — For section abolishing writ of right, see § 8.01-165. For rules of court governing procedure in actions of ejectment, see Rules 3:1 through 3:18.

Law Review. — For article on the abolition of the forms of action in Virginia, see 17 U. Rich. L. Rev. 273 (1983).

I. Decisions Under Current Law.
II. Decisions Under Prior Law.

I. DECISIONS UNDER CURRENT LAW.

Ejectment is an action to determine the title and right of possession to real property. Sheffield v. Department of Hwys. & Transp., 240 Va. 332, 397 S.E.2d 802 (1990).

The landowner's constitutional right is a right to just compensation, not a right to recover possession of the property. Sheffield v. Department of Hwys. & Transp., 240 Va. 332, 397 S.E.2d 802 (1990).

Form of action. — Ejectment was a common law action designed to try title to land and by statute it continues to be a law action. Seoane v. Drug Emporium, Inc., 249 Va. 469, 457 S.E.2d 93 (1995).

Ejectment remedy inappropriate to prosecute inverse condemnation claim against Commonwealth. — Given the nature of the action of ejectment, and the entitlement of the successful claimant to be put into possession of the disputed land, the remedy is inappropriate and unsuitable as a vehicle to prosecute an inverse condemnation claim against the Commonwealth. Sheffield v. Department of Hwys. & Transp., 240 Va. 332, 397 S.E.2d 802 (1990).

II. DECISIONS UNDER PRIOR LAW.

Editor's note. — The cases cited below were decided under corresponding provisions of former law. The terms "this article," and "this section," as used below, refer to former provisions.

English law compared. — An action of ejectment brought under this article affects the title to land more than the action of ejectment in England. United States v. Lee, 106 U.S. 196, 1 S. Ct. 240, 27 L. Ed. 171 (1882).

Ejectment does not lie where entry cannot be made. — Ejectment lies for the recovery of corporeal hereditaments. It does not lie for anything where an entry cannot be made, as for example, easements, licenses, rights of user. Steinman v. Vicars, 99 Va. 595, 39 S.E. 227 (1901); King v. Norfolk & W. Ry., 99 Va. 625, 39 S.E. 701 (1901). But see, Reynolds v. Cook, 83 Va. 817, 3 S.E. 710 (1887).

Ejectment is the proper action for one having legal title, who is not in possession, in order to recover possession and establish his title. Jennings v. Gravely, 92 Va. 377, 23 S.E. 763 (1895).

Distinguished from forcible or unlawful entry. — The action of forcible or unlawful entry is materially different from the action of ejectment. In the latter action, title is involved, while in the former only the right to possession is tried. In the action of forcible entry the plaintiff need only show the right of immediate possession, while in ejectment the plaintiff must always recover on the strength of his title. Power v. Tazewells, 66 Va. (25 Gratt.) 786 (1875); Davis v. Mayo, 82 Va. 97 (1886).

Trustee as plaintiff. — A trustee, holding the legal title, may maintain ejectment, even after the trust is satisfied. Although a cestui que trust, after the trust is satisfied, may maintain ejectment, that does not deprive the trustee, holding the legal title, of his right to maintain such an action. Hopkins v. Stephens, 23 Va. (2 Rand.) 422 (1824).

Effect of statute on existing rights. — If the plaintiff in ejectment would have been entitled at the time the Code of 1849 went into effect and at the time of the institution of his suit, to recover in a writ of right, he is entitled to recover in the present action of ejectment, under the provisions of this section. Mitchell v. Baratta, 58 Va. (17 Gratt.) 445 (1867).

§ 8.01-132. What interest and right plaintiff must have. — No person shall bring such ejectment action unless he has, at the time of commencing it, a subsisting interest in the premises claimed and a right to recover the same, or to recover the possession thereof, or some share, interest or portion thereof. (Code 1950, § 8-799; 1977, c. 617.)

Cross references. — As to proceedings to establish right of reentry, see § 55-239.

I. Decisions Under Current Law.
   A. General Consideration.
   B. Requirement of Recovery on Strength of Own Title.
II. Decisions Under Prior Law.
   A. General Consideration.
   B. Requirement of Recovery on Strength of Own Title.
   C. When Title Must Exist.
   D. Evidence of Title.

I. DECISIONS UNDER CURRENT LAW.

A. General Consideration.

The landowner's constitutional right is a right to just compensation, not a right to recover possession of the property. Sheffield v. Department of Hwys. & Transp., 240 Va. 332, 397 S.E.2d 802 (1990).

Grantor of deed of trust may maintain action in own name. — In an action of ejectment a deed of trust should be construed as a mere lien on the property, and the grantor may maintain an action in ejectment in his own name. Providence Properties, Inc. v. United Va. Bank/Seaboard Nat'l, 219 Va. 735, 251 S.E.2d 474 (1979).

Grantee of property that has a public easement was not entitled to maintain an action in ejectment, since in Virginia, no person shall bring such ejectment action unless he has, at the time of commencing it, a subsisting interest in the premises claimed and a right to recover the same, or to recover the possession thereof. Laughlin v. Morauer, 849 F.2d 122 (4th Cir. 1988).

Contingent or expectant interest. — Under this section even if grantee was conveyed some kind of contingent or expectant interest by the deed, he had no right to recover the same because the record does not indicate any kind of abandonment of the park or vacation of the plat, or cessation of use, or the like, to give him any right to assert any future interest he may have in the property. Laughlin v. Morauer, 849 F.2d 122 (4th Cir. 1988).

B. Requirement of Recovery on Strength of Own Title.

Plaintiff must recover on strength of own title. — In actions for ejectment, the plaintiff has the burden of proving that he has good title and the right to possession, and he must recover upon the strength of his own title rather than upon the weakness of the defendant's title. Providence Properties, Inc. v. United Va. Bank/Seaboard Nat'l, 219 Va. 735, 251 S.E.2d 474 (1979).

II. DECISIONS UNDER PRIOR LAW.

A. General Consideration.

Editor's note. — The cases cited below were decided under corresponding provisions of former law. The terms "this article," and "this section," as used below, refer to former provisions.

The plaintiff in an action of ejectment must have legal title and a present right of possession under it at the time of the commencement of the action. Nelson v. Triplett, 81 Va. 236 (1885); Jennings v. Gravely, 92 Va. 377, 23 S.E. 763 (1895).

Presumed where title clear. — As a general rule, a plaintiff in ejectment must show a legal title in himself, and a present right to possession under such title. In the absence, however, of evidence to the contrary, the law presumes that the right of possession is incident to and follows the legal title. Casselman v. Bialas, 112 Va. 57, 70 S.E. 479 (1911).

Plaintiff must trace title from Commonwealth. — As a general rule a plaintiff to recover in an action of ejectment must trace unbroken chain of title to the Commonwealth or established title by adverse possession. Bugg v. Leay, 107 Va. 648, 60 S.E. 89 (1908); Spriggs v. Jamerson, 115 Va. 250, 78 S.E. 571 (1913). See also Sulphur Mines Co. v. Thompson, 93 Va. 293, 25 S.E. 232 (1896).

But this is not necessary when title of parties is from a common source. — It is not necessary for plaintiff to trace title to the Commonwealth where both he and the defendant claim title from a common source. In such a case the defendant is estopped to go back of the common source in order to question the plaintiff's title and it is sufficient for the plaintiff to show that he has better title from that source. Hurley v. Charles, 110 Va. 27, 65 S.E. 468 (1909); Jennings v. Marston, 121 Va. 79, 92 S.E. 821 (1917).

However, the plaintiff cannot connect the defendant with the common source of title by proof of a parol purchase of the land. Hurley v. Charles, 110 Va. 27, 65 S.E. 468 (1909).

Present, operative, outstanding legal

title in another will defeat a recovery by the plaintiff although the defendant does not connect himself therewith. Holladay v. Moore, 115 Va. 66, 78 S.E. 551 (1913).

Effect of prior possession. — Prior peaceful possession by the plaintiff is prima facie evidence of ownership and seisin, and is sufficient to authorize recovery unless the defendant shows a better title in himself or another. McMurray v. Dixon, 105 Va. 605, 54 S.E. 481 (1906); Holladay v. Moore, 115 Va. 66, 78 S.E. 551 (1913).

The principle that possession under color of title constitutes a prima facie title is under the great weight of authority restricted to those factual situations where the defendant is a mere intruder or trespasser without color of title. Bull Run Dev. Corp. v. Jackson, 201 Va. 95, 109 S.E.2d 400 (1959).

Demand and notice necessary before action against tenant at will. — Before bringing an action of ejectment against a tenant at will, demand and notice to quit are necessary, and a vendee, who is put in possession without conveyance being made, is a tenant at will and entitled to notice. Pettit v. Cowherd, 83 Va. 20, 1 S.E. 392 (1887); Jones v. Temple, 87 Va. 210, 12 S.E. 404 (1890).

B. Requirement of Recovery on Strength of Own Title.

The plaintiff in ejectment must recover on the strength of his own title and cannot rely on the weakness of the defendant's claim. McKinney v. Daniel, 90 Va. 702, 19 S.E. 880 (1894); Merryman v. Hoover, 107 Va. 485, 59 S.E. 483 (1907); Davis v. Bostic, 125 Va. 698, 100 S.E. 463 (1919).

Exceptions. — To the general rule that a plaintiff in ejectment must recover on the strength of his own title there are several well defined exceptions resting for the most part on the principle of estoppel. Tapscott v. Cobbs, 52 Va. (11 Gratt.) 172 (1854); Rhule v. Seaboard Air Line Ry., 102 Va. 343, 46 S.E. 331 (1904).

As when landlord sues tenant. — A tenant is estopped to deny his landlord's title, and, hence, in an action of ejectment by a landlord he is not required to establish title as against the tenant. Miller v. Williams, 56 Va. (15 Gratt.) 213 (1858); Suttle v. Richmond, F. & P.R.R., 76 Va. 284 (1882).

Also, when one is in possession against an intruder. — Although, in general, legal title in the plaintiff must be shown in order to sustain a recovery in ejectment, as against mere intruders without semblance of right, prior peaceable possession is sufficient. Rhule v. Seaboard Air Line Ry., 102 Va. 343, 46 S.E. 331 (1904); McMurray v. Dixon, 105 Va. 605, 54 S.E. 481 (1906).

And when grantor enforces forfeiture for breach of condition. — Where there is a breach of condition subsequent, the legal title to the land remains in the grantee until the forfeiture is consummated, but the practice in Virginia, under § 55-239, is to bring ejectment in such case although the plaintiff has not the legal title. Pence v. Tidewater Townsite Corp., 127 Va. 447, 103 S.E. 694 (1905).

C. When Title Must Exist.

A plaintiff in ejectment must have title at the time of the commencement of his action and cannot acquire it afterwards. Merryman v. Hoover, 107 Va. 485, 59 S.E. 483 (1907).

But where a plaintiff, after suit brought, aliens the land he may recover for the benefit of the alienee. Right to recover at the commencement of the action is all that is required by the statute. Bolling v. Teel, 76 Va. 487 (1882).

D. Evidence of Title.

The documentary evidence relied on must identify the land in dispute. Blakey v. Morris, 89 Va. 717, 17 S.E. 126 (1893); Craig-Giles Iron Co. v. Wickline, 126 Va. 223, 101 S.E. 225 (1919).

A grant from the Commonwealth confers constructive seisin sufficient to support an action of ejectment. Actual seisin is not necessary. Howdashell v. Krenning, 103 Va. 30, 48 S.E. 491 (1904).

When grant may be presumed. — The plaintiff in an action of ejectment may show title in himself either by showing a grant from the crown or the Commonwealth and connecting himself therewith by a regular chain of title, or by showing such a chain of facts as will warrant the jury in presuming a grant. Sulphur Mines Co. v. Thompson, 93 Va. 293, 25 S.E. 232 (1896); Spriggs v. Jamerson, 115 Va. 250, 78 S.E. 571 (1913); Brunswick Land Corp. v. Perkinson, 146 Va. 695, 132 S.E. 853 (1926); Prettyman v. M.J. Duer & Co., 189 Va. 122, 52 S.E.2d 156 (1949); Bull Run Dev. Corp. v. Jackson, 201 Va. 95, 109 S.E.2d 400 (1959).

A plaintiff claiming title under a lost deed must show strong and conclusive evidence of the contents of the deed. Carter v. Wood, 103 Va. 68, 48 S.E. 553 (1904).

Decree requiring execution of conveyance does not give plaintiff title. — A decree requiring the execution of a conveyance does not of itself vest title in the complainant, and should not be received as evidence of legal title in an action of ejectment. Nelson v. Triplett, 81 Va. 236 (1885).

Title to land may be acquired by adverse possession, and such title is sufficient to support an action of ejectment. Norfolk v. Cooke, 68 Va. (27 Gratt.) 430 (1876); Thomas v. Jones, 69

Va. (28 Gratt.) 383 (1877).

Plaintiff has burden of proving boundaries. — A plaintiff in ejectment claiming under an inclusive grant, embracing excepted lands, has the burden of establishing his boundaries and locating the excepted lands, and of showing that the land claimed by the defendants is within the grant and not in the excepted portions. Reusens v. Lawson, 91 Va. 226, 21 S.E. 347 (1895); Virginia Coal & Iron Co. v. Keystone Coal & Iron Co., 101 Va. 723, 45 S.E. 291 (1903); Sutherland v. Gent, 116 Va. 783, 82 S.E. 713 (1914).

Proper boundary evidence. — Calls and descriptions of a survey made of a coterminous tract, by the same surveyor about the same time, is proper evidence upon question of boundary unless plainly irrelevant, although the grant issued thereon was to a stranger. Reusens v. Lawson, 91 Va. 226, 21 S.E. 347 (1895). See also Overton v. Davisson, 42 Va. (1 Gratt.) 211 (1844).

The record of a former proceeding may be given in evidence to show the authority of a commissioner to execute a deed. Smith v. Chapman, 51 Va. (10 Gratt.) 445 (1853); Hitchcox v. Rawson, 55 Va. (14 Gratt.) 526 (1858).

Record of another action between different parties is not admissible. — The record of another action of ejectment between other parties not in privity with either party to the present suit, is not admissible as evidence of the boundaries or location of the land in controversy. Stinchcomb v. Marsh, 56 Va. (15 Gratt.) 202 (1858); Reusens v. Lawson, 100 Va. 143, 40 S.E. 616 (1902).

Equitable title is not sufficient to support an action of ejectment. Dillard v. Jeffries, 118 Va. 81, 86 S.E. 844 (1915); Davis v. Bostic, 125 Va. 698, 100 S.E. 463 (1919).

§ 8.01-133. Who shall be defendants; when and how landlord may defend.

— The person actually occupying the premises and any person claiming title thereto or claiming any interest therein adversely to the plaintiff may also, at the discretion of the plaintiff, be named defendants in the action. If there be no person actually occupying the premises adversely to the plaintiff, then the action must be against some person exercising ownership thereon or claiming title thereto or some interest therein at the commencement of suit. If a lessee be made defendant at the suit of a party claiming against the title of his landlord such landlord may appear and be made a defendant with or in place of his lessee. (Code 1950, § 8-800; 1954, c. 333; 1977, c. 617.)

I. Decisions Under Current Law.
II. Decisions Under Prior Law.

I. DECISIONS UNDER CURRENT LAW.

Defendants where no person actually occupying premises. — Where there is no person actually occupying the disputed property when an action for ejectment was initiated, the action must be brought against "some person," but not every person, exercising ownership or claiming title to or an interest in the property. Providence Properties, Inc. v. United Va. Bank/Seaboard Nat'l, 219 Va. 735, 251 S.E.2d 474 (1979).

Ejectment remedy inappropriate to prosecute inverse condemnation claim against Commonwealth. — Given the nature of the action of ejectment, and the entitlement of the successful claimant to be put into possession of the disputed land, the remedy is inappropriate and unsuitable as a vehicle to prosecute an inverse condemnation claim against the Commonwealth. Sheffield v. Department of Hwys. & Transp., 240 Va. 332, 397 S.E.2d 802 (1990).

II. DECISIONS UNDER PRIOR LAW.

Editor's note. — The cases cited below were decided under corresponding provisions of former law. The term "this section," as used below, refers to former provisions.

Effect of section. — This section does not alter the rule that ejectment cannot be maintained by a plaintiff in possession of the land. The object of the action is to try the possessory title to corporeal hereditaments, and to recover the possession thereof. The effect of the section is simply to permit a plaintiff in his discretion, to join as defendants with the occupant any person claiming title thereto or an interest therein adversely to the plaintiff. Steinman v. Vicars, 99 Va. 595, 39 S.E. 227 (1901).

Proper remedy when neither party in possession. — The proper remedy is by an action of ejectment, when the owner holds the legal title, but has not actual possession, and another asserts an adverse claim to the land, but has not actual possession of it. Stearns v.

Harman, 80 Va. 48 (1885).

Ejectment may be properly brought against persons who have made entries and surveys of any part of the land in controversy, and are setting up claims to it, though not in occupation of it at the time suit is brought. Harvey v. Tyler, 69 U.S. (2 Wall.) 328, 17 L. Ed. 871 (1864).

One who has had land surveyed and regularly paid taxes on it and claims to own it may be made defendant to an action of ejectment when no one is in actual occupation. Lynchburg Cotton Mill v. Rives, 112 Va. 137, 70 S.E. 542 (1911).

When occupant is necessary defendant. — This section permits the plaintiff to join with the occupant as defendants any other persons claiming title to the land. It may be conceded that the actual occupant is always a necessary party defendant to an action of ejectment in the sense that another defendant may by timely and proper procedure compel the plaintiff to bring the occupant before the court. The presence of the occupant, however, is not essential to the jurisdiction of the court, and if the claimant of the premises who is sued does not appropriately raise the point, and defends the action upon the merits, he is bound by the judgment. Matoaka Coal Corp. v. Clinch Valley Mining Corp., 121 Va. 522, 93 S.E. 799 (1917).

Who is an occupant of premises. — One operating mines under a contract with a lessee which gave him exclusive possession thereof for the time being, but whose possession was not exclusive of and was subordinate to the possession of the entire tract by the lessee, is not the party actually occupying the premises, as those terms are used in this section. Matoaka Coal Corp. v. Clinch Valley Mining Corp., 121 Va. 522, 93 S.E. 799 (1917).

Meaning of "lessee". — The term "lessee," is used, not so much to define an estate as to express the relation existing where one person holds under and in subordination to the title of another. Hanks v. Price, 73 Va. (32 Gratt.) 107 (1879).

Right of landlord to defend. — In an action of ejectment, brought against the person in possession, the landlord of such person may come in and be allowed to defend the action under the statute whether the actual relation of lessor and lessee exists between them or not. This will be permitted even where the plaintiff and the defendant in possession have submitted the matters between them to arbitration, an award made in favor of the plaintiff, and a rule awarded against the defendant in possession to show cause why the award should not be entered as the judgment of the court against him. Hanks v. Price, 73 Va. (32 Gratt.) 107 (1879).

Effect when husband sued and legal title in wife. — Where a husband who was in possession merely by sufferance, his wife holding the legal title, was sued in ejectment, the wife not being a party to the suit, it was held that her rights were not affected and that she could convey them to a purchaser, innocent or otherwise. The husband also could acquire a life estate by her death and would not be estopped and was entitled to have the judgment by default against him opened. But where the wife's deed was not filed for recordation until long after such judgment, she is not entitled to an order restraining execution of the judgment, although she is entitled to have the judgment opened and be allowed to defend. King v. Davis, 137 F. 222 (C.C.W.D. Va. 1905), aff'd sub nom., Blankenship v. King, 157 F. 676 (4th Cir. 1906).

§ 8.01-134. How action commenced and prosecuted.

— The action shall be commenced and prosecuted as other actions at law. The name of the real claimant shall be inserted as plaintiff, and all the provisions of law concerning a lessor of a plaintiff shall apply to such plaintiff. (Code 1950, § 8-801; 1977, c. 617.)

I. DECISIONS UNDER CURRENT LAW.

Form of action. — Ejectment was a common law action designed to try title to land and by statute it continues to be a law action. Seoane v. Drug Emporium, Inc., 249 Va. 469, 457 S.E.2d 93 (1995).

§ 8.01-135. What is to be stated in motion for judgment.

— It shall be sufficient for the plaintiff to aver in his motion for judgment that on some day specified therein, which shall be after his title accrued, he was possessed of the premises claimed, and, being so possessed thereof, the defendant afterwards, on some day likewise specified, entered into such premises or exercised acts of ownership thereon or claimed title thereto or some interest therein, to the damage of the plaintiff in such sum as he shall state in his motion for judgment. (Code 1950, § 8-802; 1954, c. 333; 1977, c. 617.)

§ **8.01-136. How premises described.** — The premises claimed shall be described in the motion for judgment with convenient certainty, so that, from such description, with the aid of information derived from the plaintiff, possession thereof may be delivered. (Code 1950, § 8-803; 1954, c. 333; 1977, c. 617.)

I. DECISIONS UNDER PRIOR LAW.

Editor's note. — The cases cited below were decided under corresponding provisions of former law. The terms "this article," and "this section," as used below, refer to former provisions.

The object of the description of lands in a motion is to so identify them that the sheriff may give possession. It is not necessary that the sheriff should be able to tell from an inspection of the record of what lands he is to give possession. Howdashell v. Krenning, 103 Va. 30, 48 S.E. 491 (1904).

Defective description. — A motion in ejectment, which describes the land as a part of a larger tract owned by plaintiff, near certain creeks which have no public notoriety, is defective, and may be demurred to. Hitchcox v. Rawson, 55 Va. (14 Gratt.) 526 (1858).

Effect of verdict for plaintiff for land insufficiently described in motion. — A verdict which finds for the plaintiff the land insufficiently described in the motion is too vague. There is no more certainty and precision in the verdict than there is in the motion, and the defect in the latter is not cured by the former. Hitchcox v. Rawson, 55 Va. (14 Gratt.) 526 (1858).

Where the motion sufficiently describes the premises, a general finding for the plaintiff of the lands described is sufficiently certain. Messick v. Thomas, 84 Va. 891, 6 S.E. 482 (1887).

Effect of verdict for whole of land when defendant claims only part. — Where the defendant claimed only part of the land, a verdict for the plaintiff for the whole of the land described in the motion is sufficiently certain and does not injure the defendant. Messick v. Thomas, 84 Va. 891, 6 S.E. 482 (1887).

Verdict held correct when a variance between the verdict and motion. — The quantity and boundaries of the land described in a motion and in the verdict varied from each other. But the verdict found that the land therein described was the tenement mentioned in the declaration. It was to be presumed that the description given in a motion was a mistaken description, and that the land recovered by the verdict was the land demanded. Koiner v. Rankin, 52 Va. (11 Gratt.) 420 (1854).

Where a motion described the land in controversy as lying north of a road, and the verdict as south of that road, the description in other particulars being the same, the variance was held immaterial and the description in the motion must be presumed to be mistaken. Benn v. Hatcher, 81 Va. 25 (1885).

§ **8.01-137. Plaintiff to state how he claims.** — The plaintiff shall also state whether he claims in fee or for his life, or the life of another, or for years, specifying such lives or the duration of such term, and when he claims an undivided share or interest he shall state the same. (Code 1950, § 8-804; 1977, c. 617.)

I. Decisions Under Current Law.
II. Decisions Under Prior Law.

I. DECISIONS UNDER CURRENT LAW.

Standing to maintain action. — The action of ejectment may be maintained by one who has an interest in and a right to recover possession of the premises, or a share, interest, or portion thereof. Brown v. Haley, 233 Va. 210, 355 S.E.2d 563 (1987).

Proof. — The action of ejectment is concerned only with the ownership rights of the plaintiff, and the proof necessary to support the action consists of the documents which vest title in the owner and any other evidence related to the issue of title. Brown v. Haley, 233 Va. 210, 355 S.E.2d 563 (1987).

Verdict must specify plaintiff's share or interest. — A verdict for the plaintiff in an action for ejectment must specify the share or interest of the plaintiff, whether in the whole or a part of the premises claimed, and the estate of the plaintiff, whether in fee, for life, or for a term of years. Brown v. Haley, 233 Va. 210, 355 S.E.2d 563 (1987).

II. DECISIONS UNDER PRIOR LAW.

Editor's note. — The case cited below was decided under corresponding provisions of former law. The term "this section," as used below, refers to former provisions.

Sufficient allegation of joint tenancy. —

Where a motion alleges that, on a day certain before bringing the action, plaintiffs were possessed, "each in fee simple absolute, of an undivided share or interest in" the land, and the action "is for the whole land so claimed, and not for any part or parcel" thereof, the motion is sufficient, under this section. Roach v. Blakey, 89 Va. 767, 17 S.E. 228 (1893).

§ 8.01-138. There may be several counts and several plaintiffs. — The motion for judgment may contain several counts, and several parties may be named as plaintiffs jointly in one count and separately in others. (Code 1950, § 8-805; 1954, c. 333; 1977, c. 617.)

I. DECISIONS UNDER PRIOR LAW.

Editor's note. — The case cited below was decided under corresponding provisions of former law. The term "this statute," as used below, refers to former provisions.

Amendment in pursuance of this section is not a new action. — When joint plaintiffs amended their motion so that in some counts they were joint and in some counts separate, it was not considered the commencement of a new cause of action. Holmes v. Grabeel, 81 F. 145 (W.D. Va. 1896).

§ 8.01-139. What proof by plaintiff is sufficient. — The consent rule, formerly used, remains abolished. The plaintiff need not prove an actual entry on, or possession of, the premises demanded, or receipt of any profits thereof, or any lease, entry, or ouster, except as hereinafter provided. But it shall be sufficient for him to show a right to the possession of the premises at the time of the commencement of the suit. (Code 1950, § 8-809; 1977, c. 617.)

Cross references. — As to what interest and right plaintiff must have to bring action, see § 8.01-132.

I. DECISIONS UNDER PRIOR LAW.

Editor's note. — The case cited below was decided under corresponding provisions of former law. The term "this statute," as used below, refers to former provisions.

Defendant's possession presumed lawful. — Since the plaintiff must recover on the strength of his own title the defendant's possession will be presumed lawful until the contrary is shown. Virginia Coal & Iron Co. v. Keystone Coal & Iron Co., 101 Va. 723, 45 S.E. 291 (1903).

§ 8.01-140. Effect of reservation in deed; burden of proof. — In any action, suit or other judicial proceeding involving the title to land embraced in the exterior boundaries of any patent, deed or other writing, which reserves one or more parcels of land from the operation of such patent, deed or other writing, if there be no claim made by a party to the proceedings that the land in controversy, or any part thereof, lies within such reservation, such patent, deed or other writing shall be construed, and shall have the same effect, as if it contained no such reservation; and if any party to such proceeding claims that the land in controversy, or any part thereof, lies within such reservation, the burden shall be upon him to prove the fact, and all land not shown by a preponderance of the evidence to lie within such reservation shall be deemed to lie without the same.

This section shall apply in cases involving the right to the proceeds of any such land when condemned or sold, as well as in cases where the title to land is directly involved, and shall apply in any case in which the title to any part of the land, or its proceeds, but for this section, would or might be in this Commonwealth. (Code 1950, § 8-810; 1977, c. 617.)

I. DECISIONS UNDER PRIOR LAW.

Editor's note. — The cases cited below were decided under corresponding provisions of former law. The term "this section," as used below, refers to former provisions.

When section applicable. — This section does not apply in favor of a claimant in condemnation proceedings. It is clear from the wording of the statute that it was not intended to apply in all controversies over the title to land, but only in the cases expressly mentioned. United States v. Grogg, 9 F.2d 424 (W.D. Va. 1925).

Liberal construction. — Although this section is a remedial statute and entitled to a liberal construction, such a construction should stop far short of carrying the statute to purposes and objects entirely beyond those mentioned in it. United States v. Grogg, 9 F.2d 424 (W.D. Va. 1925).

Burden on defendant of proving land within reservation. — The practical effect of this section is to place upon the defendant the burden of proving that the land in controversy lies within the limits of the reservation. Radford Veneer Corp. v. Jones, 143 Va. 124, 129 S.E. 260 (1925); Sutherland v. Gent, 116 Va. 783, 82 S.E. 713 (1914).

§ 8.01-141. When action by cotenants, etc., against cotenants, what plaintiff to prove.
— If the action be by one or more tenants in common, joint tenants or coparceners against their cotenants, the plaintiff shall be bound to prove actual ouster or some other act amounting to total denial of the plaintiff's right as cotenant. (Code 1950, § 8-811; 1977, c. 617.)

I. DECISIONS UNDER PRIOR LAW.

Editor's note. — The cases cited below were decided under corresponding provisions of former law. The term "this section," as used below, refers to former provisions.

Nature of possession needed to constitute adverse possession. — The possession of one joint tenant, tenant in common, or coparcener is prima facie the possession of all the other cotenants, and the mere possession of the one will not be taken to be adverse to the title and possession of the other. Yet if the defendant prove actual ouster or other notorious act or acts, amounting to a total denial of the plaintiff's rights as cotenant, and of such a character as to afford direct or presumptive proof that the other cotenants or plaintiffs had had knowledge of the claim of exclusive ownership thus set up and held by the defendants, or those under whom they claim, such possession of the land is held continuously and uninterruptedly under such circumstances under color of title for the length of time prescribed by law, constitutes adverse possession, and will ripen into a good and sufficient title in the defendants. Stonestreet v. Doyle, 75 Va. 356 (1881).

Silent possession insufficient. — A silent possession by a cotenant, unaccompanied by acts amounting to an ouster, or giving notice of an adverse claim cannot be construed into adverse possession. Saunders v. Terry, 116 Va. 495, 82 S.E. 68 (1914).

§ 8.01-142. Verdict when action against several defendants.
— If the action be against several defendants, and a joint possession of all be proved, and the plaintiff be entitled to a verdict, it shall be against all, whether they pleaded separately or jointly. (Code 1950, § 8-812; 1977, c. 617.)

§ 8.01-143. When there may be several judgments against defendants.
— If the action be against several defendants, and it appear on the trial that any of them occupy distinct parcels in severalty or jointly, and that other defendants possess other parcels in severalty or jointly, the plaintiff may recover several judgments against them, for the parcels so held by one or more of the defendants, separately from others. (Code 1950, § 8-813; 1977, c. 617.)

§ 8.01-144. Recovery of part of premises claimed.
— The plaintiff may recover any specific or any undivided part or share of the premises, though it be less than he claimed in the motion for judgment. (Code 1950, § 8-814; 1954, c. 333; 1977, c. 617.)

§ 8.01-145. When possession of part not possession of whole.
— In a controversy affecting real estate, possession of part shall not be construed as possession of the whole when an actual adverse possession can be proved. (Code 1950, § 8-815; 1977, c. 617.)

I. DECISIONS UNDER PRIOR LAW.

Editor's note. — The cases cited below were decided under corresponding provisions of former law. The term "this statute," as used below, refers to former provisions.

This statute was not passed merely for the protection of squatters, and must have been intended to embrace the case of an actual possession of the rightful owners beyond, and to the adverse claimant within, the limits of the part in controversy. Taylor v. Burnsides, 42 Va. (1 Gratt.) 165 (1844). See Stull v. Rich Patch Iron Co., 92 Va. 253, 23 S.E. 293 (1895).

§ 8.01-146. When vendee, etc., entitled to conveyance of legal title, vendor cannot recover.

— A vendor, or any claiming under him, shall not, at law any more than in equity, recover against a vendee, or those claiming under him, lands sold by such vendor to such vendee, when there is a writing, stating the purchase and the terms thereof, signed by the vendor or his agent and there has been such payment or performance of what was contracted to be paid or performed on the part of the vendee, as would in equity entitle him, or those claiming under him, to a conveyance of the legal title of such land from the vendor, or those claiming under him, without condition. (Code 1950, § 8-816; 1977, c. 617.)

Cross references. — As to right of defendant to resort to equity, see § 8.01-148.

I. DECISIONS UNDER PRIOR LAW.

Editor's note. — The cases cited below were decided under corresponding provisions of former law. The term "this section," as used below, refers to former provisions.

The purpose of the section was to prevent oppression by one having mere legal title and to obviate the necessity for a jury in equity to establish a perfect defense. Until a statute was passed to remedy the evil, a vendee in possession, who had paid every dollar of his purchase money, and had written evidence of his contract, was liable to be turned out of possession at any time by his vendor upon the mere legal title, and was at least compelled to make his defense in a court of equity. And the same rule prevailed to a great extent with respect to mortgages and deeds of trust, which had been satisfied. Suttle v. Richmond, F. & P.R.R., 76 Va. 284 (1882).

This section is dictated by a restrictive and not by a general policy. Virginia Iron, Coal & Coke Co. v. Cranes' Nest Coal & Coke Co., 102 Va. 405, 46 S.E. 393 (1904).

This section applies to the action of unlawful detainer as well as ejectment. Dobson v. Culpepper, 64 Va. (23 Gratt.) 352 (1873).

Written contract prerequisite. — Although a defendant in ejectment may be clothed with a perfect equitable title, he cannot avail himself thereof in ejectment unless he can bring himself within the terms of the section, requiring a contract in writing. Jennings v. Gravely, 92 Va. 377, 23 S.E. 763 (1895).

Writing need not be produced in all cases. — The section does not admit of the construction that the writing must be produced in all cases, but that, although evidence of a parol contract is inadmissible, the best possible evidence of the required writing may be admitted. The writing must have been executed, but it may be established by pleadings in a court of record, and by reference in the record to a contract as a document filed in the court. Clinchfield Coal Corp. v. Steinman, 223 F. 743 (4th Cir. 1915).

Contract must also be performed. — In order to rely on this section, the defendant must show not only the written contract of sale setting out the terms but also his own performance of the contract. Dobson v. Culpepper, 64 Va. (23 Gratt.) 352 (1873).

Defendant may resort to equity to enjoin the enforcement of a judgment rendered against him in an action of ejectment even though the equitable defense might, under this section, have been proved in the action of ejectment. Withrow v. Porter, 131 Va. 623, 109 S.E. 441 (1921).

Equitable estoppel cannot be set up as a defense to an action of ejectment. Casselman v. Bialas, 112 Va. 57, 70 S.E. 479 (1911); Suttle v. Richmond, F. & P.R.R., 76 Va. 284 (1882).

The equitable defense under this section is limited to mortgages and deeds of trust, where the mortgage money has been fully paid, or the trust completely performed; or to sales, where the vendee has paid all the purchase money and performed everything incumbent on him, so as to entitle him to a specific execution on the contract in equity, and a conveyance of the legal title, without any condition proper in equity to be on him imposed. It must be a sale, and not a partnership in the acquisition of the land, and the terms of the contract must be plain. Davis v. Teays, 44 Va. (3 Gratt.) 283 (1846).

§ 8.01-147. When mortgagee or trustee not to recover.

— The payment of the whole sum, or the performance of the whole duty, or the accomplishment of the whole purpose, which any mortgage or deed of trust may have been made to secure or effect, shall prevent the grantee, or his heirs, from recovering at law, by virtue of such mortgage or deed of trust, property thereby conveyed, whenever the defendant would in equity be entitled to a decree, revesting the legal title in him without condition. (Code 1950, § 8-817; 1977, c. 617.)

I. DECISIONS UNDER PRIOR LAW.

Editor's note. — The cases cited below were decided under corresponding provisions of former law. The term "this section," as used below, refers to former provisions.

Grantor may bring action. — Where a deed of trust by a wife was satisfied and reconveyance made to the husband, it was held under this section that neither the trustee nor the husband should bring ejectment but that the wife was the proper party. The effect of the section is to prevent the trustee from bringing ejectment and to authorize the grantor to maintain such an action. Lynchburg Cotton Mill v. Rives, 112 Va. 137, 70 S.E. 542 (1911).

Purchaser from trust. — Where land was conveyed in trust to secure specific debts and afterwards conveyed outright, the purchaser takes good title subject to the trust, and when that is satisfied is entitled to the benefit of this section, though the trustee has not conveyed it to him. Hale v. Horne, 62 Va. (21 Gratt.) 112 (1871).

§ 8.01-148. Right of defendant to resort to equity not affected.

— Whether the defendant shall or shall not make or attempt a defense under §§ 8.01-146 and 8.01-147, he shall not be precluded from resorting to equity for any relief to which he would have been entitled if such sections had not been enacted. (Code 1950, § 8-818; 1954, c. 333; 1977, c. 617.)

I. Decisions Under Current Law.
II. Decisions Under Prior Law.

I. DECISIONS UNDER CURRENT LAW.

Applied in Brown v. Haley, 233 Va. 210, 355 S.E.2d 563 (1987).

II. DECISIONS UNDER PRIOR LAW.

Editor's note. — The case cited below was decided under corresponding provisions of former law. The term "this section," as used below, refers to former provisions.

Effect of this section. — If the equitable matter on which a party relies to obtain an injunction against the enforcement of a judgment in ejectment against him could not have been shown in that action under §§ 8.01-146 and 8.01-147, to offer it as a defense in that action would have been futile. If, on the other hand, it was such a defense, then under the express terms of this section, whether defendant does or does not attempt such equitable defense, he is not precluded from resorting to equity. Withrow v. Porter, 131 Va. 623, 109 S.E. 441 (1921).

§ 8.01-149. Verdict when jury finds for plaintiffs or any of them.

— If the jury be of opinion for the plaintiffs, or any of them, the verdict shall be for the plaintiffs, or such of them as appear to have right to the possession of the premises, or any part thereof, and against such of the defendants as were in possession thereof or claimed title thereto at the commencement of the action. (Code 1950, § 8-819; 1977, c. 617.)

Cross references. — As to recovery of part of premises claimed, see § 8.01-144.

I. DECISIONS UNDER PRIOR LAW.

Editor's note. — The case cited below was decided under corresponding provisions of former law. The term "this section," as used below, refers to former provisions.

Sufficient compliance. — A finding for the plaintiff on the "remaining one third of the several tracts of land claimed as aforesaid by the defendants, and of which two thirds have been found for them," was held a sufficient compliance with this section. Collins v. Riley, 104 U.S. 322, 26 L. Ed. 752 (1881).

§ 8.01-150. Verdict when any plaintiff has no right. — When any plaintiff appears to have no such right, the verdict as to such plaintiff shall be for the defendants. (Code 1950, § 8-820; 1977, c. 617.)

§ 8.01-151. How verdict to specify premises recovered. — When the right of the plaintiff is proved to all the premises claimed, the verdict shall be for the premises generally as specified in the motion for judgment, but if it be proved to only a part or share of the premises, the verdict shall specify such part particularly as the same is proved, and with the same certainty of description as is required in the motion for judgment. (Code 1950, § 8-821; 1954, c. 333; 1977, c. 617.)

I. DECISIONS UNDER PRIOR LAW.

Editor's note. — The cases cited below were decided under corresponding provisions of former law. The term "this section," as used below, refers to former provisions.

This section is mandatory and it is reversible error to render judgment on a verdict that fails to comply with its requirements. Grizzle v. Davis, 119 Va. 567, 89 S.E. 870 (1916). See Smith v. Bailey, 141 Va. 757, 127 S.E. 89 (1925).

Plaintiff put on terms or new trial granted if verdict excessive. — If the verdict of the jury, in an action of ejectment, finds for the plaintiff more land than he is entitled to recover the courts shall put him on terms to release the excess by proper description, or else grant a new trial. Fry v. Stowers, 98 Va. 417, 36 S.E. 482 (1900).

§ 8.01-152. How verdict to specify undivided interest or share. — If the verdict be for an undivided share or interest in the premises claimed, it shall specify the same, and if for an undivided share or interest of a part of the premises, it shall specify such share or interest, and describe such part as before required. (Code 1950, § 8-822; 1977, c. 617.)

I. DECISIONS UNDER PRIOR LAW.

Editor's note. — The case cited below was decided under corresponding provisions of former law. The term "the statute," as used below, refers to former provisions.

One joint tenant cannot recover the interest of all as sole plaintiff. Therefore his undivided interest must be clearly designated. Marshall v. Palmer, 91 Va. 344, 21 S.E. 672 (1895). See also, Nye v. Lovitt, 92 Va. 710, 24 S.E. 345 (1896).

§ 8.01-153. Verdict to specify estate of plaintiff. — The verdict shall also specify the estate found in the plaintiff, whether it be in fee or for life, stating for whose life, or whether it be a term of years, and specifying the duration of such term. (Code 1950, § 8-823; 1977, c. 617.)

I. DECISIONS UNDER PRIOR LAW.

Editor's note. — The cases cited below were decided under corresponding provisions of former law. The term "this section," as used below, refers to former provisions.

Sufficient verdict. — Where the motion stated that plaintiff held title in fee simple to lands, a verdict finding the defendant guilty "in manner and form as stated in the motion," was held a sufficient description of the estate to which the plaintiff was entitled. Hawley v. Twyman, 65 Va. (24 Gratt.) 516 (1874).

Defective verdict. — A verdict: "We, the jury, find for the plaintiff," is fatally defective in that it fails to specify the estate found in the plaintiff as required by this section. White v. Lee, 144 Va. 523, 132 S.E. 307 (1926).

Action for use of lands for uncertain and indefinite period. An action of ejectment does not lie to recover the mere use of unemployed lands for an uncertain and indefinite period under this section. King v. Norfolk & W. Ry., 99 Va. 625, 39 S.E. 701 (1901).

§ 8.01-154. **When right of plaintiff expires before trial, what judgment entered.** — If the right or title of a plaintiff in ejectment expire after the commencement of the suit, but before trial, the verdict shall be according to the fact, and judgment shall be entered for his damages sustained from the withholding of the premises by the defendant, and as to the premises claimed, the judgment shall be for the defendant. (Code 1950, § 8-824; 1977, c. 617.)

I. DECISIONS UNDER PRIOR LAW.

Editor's note. — The case cited below was decided under corresponding provisions of former law. The term "the statute," as used below, refers to former provisions.

Right to recover at commencement of suit is all required by the statute. When several plaintiffs after suit brought aliened their interest in the land, it was held that such alienation cannot prevent their recovery for benefit of the alienee. Bolling v. Teel, 76 Va. 487 (1882).

§ 8.01-155. **How judgment for plaintiff entered.** — The judgment for the plaintiff shall be, that he recover the possession of the premises, according to the verdict of the jury, if there be a verdict, or if the judgment be by default, or on demurrer, according to the description thereof in the motion for judgment. (Code 1950, § 8-825; 1954, c. 333; 1977, c. 617.)

§ 8.01-156. **Authority of sheriffs, etc., to store and sell personal property removed from premises; recovery of possession by owner; disposition or sale.** — In any county or city, when personal property is removed from premises pursuant to an action of unlawful detainer or ejectment, or pursuant to any other action in which personal property is removed from premises in order to restore such premises to the person entitled thereto, the sheriff shall cause such personal property to be placed in a storage area designated by the governing body of the county or city if such an area has been so designated, or, in the case of a manufactured home and with the consent of the lot owner, upon the manufactured home lot, unless the owner of such personal property then and there removes it from the public way.

The owner, before obtaining possession of such personal property so placed in a storage area by the sheriff shall pay to the parties entitled thereto the reasonable and necessary costs incidental to such removal and storage. Should such owner fail or refuse to pay such costs within thirty days from the date of placing the property in storage, the sheriff shall, after due notice to the owner and holders of liens of record, dispose of the property by publicly advertised public sale. The proceeds from such sale shall be used to pay all costs of removal, storage, and sale, all fees and liens, and the balance of such funds shall be paid to the person entitled thereto. Should the cost of removal and storage exceed the proceeds realized from such sale the county or city shall reimburse the sheriff for such excess. (Code 1950, § 8-825.1; 1964, c. 387; 1977, c. 617; 1992, c. 454; 1993, c. 16.)

§ 8.01-157: Repealed by Acts 1990, c. 831, effective January 1, 1991.

Cross references. — As to the abolition of dower and curtesy, effective January 1, 1991, see § 64.1-19.2.

§ 8.01-158. **How claim of plaintiff for profits and damages assessed.** — If the plaintiff file with his motion for judgment a statement of the profits and other damages which he means to demand, and the jury find in his favor, they shall, at the same time, unless the court otherwise order, assess the damages for mesne profits of the land for any period not exceeding five years previously to the commencement of the suit until the verdict, and also the damages for any destruction or waste of the buildings or other property during the same time for which the defendant is chargeable. (Code 1950, § 8-827; 1954, c. 333; 1977, c. 617.)

Cross references. — For assessment of damages for improvements, see §§ 8.01-166 through 8.01-178.

I. DECISIONS UNDER PRIOR LAW.

Editor's note. — The cases cited below were decided under corresponding provisions of former law. The term "this section," as used below, refers to former provisions.

When jury to ascertain damages. — Where the statements of profits and damages are filed with the motion, the jury sworn to try the issue in ejectment may at the same time make the required inquiries; or the inquiries may, if the court so order, be made by the same jury after verdict or by a new jury. Goodwyn v. Myers, 57 Va. (16 Gratt.) 336 (1862).

It is proper to charge interest upon rents and profits. Bolling v. Lersner, 67 Va. (26 Gratt.) 36, appeal dismissed, 91 U.S. 594, 23 L. Ed. 366 (1875).

§ **8.01-159. When court to assess damages.** — If there be no issue of fact tried in the cause, and judgment is to be rendered for the plaintiff on demurrer, or otherwise, such damages shall be assessed by the court, unless either party shall move to have them assessed by a jury, or the court shall think proper to have them so assessed, in which case a jury shall be impaneled to assess them. If the defendant is in default the court shall proceed to render judgment and assess damages as provided in Rule of Court 3:17. (Code 1950, § 8-828; 1954, c. 333; 1977, c. 617.)

I. DECISIONS UNDER PRIOR LAW.

Editor's note. — The cases cited below were decided under corresponding provisions of former law. The term "this section," as used below, refers to former provisions.

When inquiry of damages proper. — An office judgment in an action of ejectment does not become final without the intervention of the court or a jury; but there ought, in every such case, to be an order for an inquiry of damages. James River & Kanawha Co. v. Lee, 57 Va. (16 Gratt.) 424 (1863); Smithson v. Briggs, 74 Va. (33 Gratt.) 180 (1880).

When inquiry unnecessary. — When the plaintiff did not file a statement of damages in ejectment and the defendant was in default, the court was authorized, under this section, at the term following the office judgment after default, or at any subsequent term, to enter judgment that plaintiff recover possession of the land sued for, and make such office judgment final, without setting the cause for inquiry at the next term. King v. Davis, 137 F. 222 (C.C.W.D. Va. 1905), aff'd sub nom., Blankenship v. King, 157 F. 676 (4th Cir. 1906).

§ **8.01-160. Defendant to give notice of claim for improvements.** — If the defendant intends to claim allowance for improvements made upon the premises by himself or those under whom he claims, he shall file with his pleading a statement of his claim therefor, in case judgment be rendered for the plaintiff. (Code 1950, § 8-829; 1954, c. 333; 1977, c. 617.)

I. DECISIONS UNDER PRIOR LAW.

Editor's note. — The cases cited below were decided under corresponding provisions of former law. The term "this section," as used below, refers to former provisions.

Section only applies when decree or judgment against defendant. — In interpreting this section and § 8.01-166, it is held that they apply only to actions of ejectment or to cases in which a judgment or decree is entered against the defendant for land. Wood v. Krebbs, 74 Va. (33 Gratt.) 685 (1880); Effinger v. Hall, 81 Va. 94 (1885); Truslow v. Ball, 166 Va. 608, 186 S.E. 71 (1936).

Section does not apply in suits to enforce parol contracts to convey real estate. Truslow v. Ball, 166 Va. 608, 186 S.E. 71 (1936).

Nor to action by judgment creditor. — The provisions of this section have no application to a judgment creditor seeking to enforce his lien upon the land upon which the improvements have been made. Flanary v. Kane, 102 Va. 547, 46 S.E. 312, rehearing denied, 46 S.E. 681 (1904).

§ 8.01-161. **How allowed.** — In such case, the damages of the plaintiff, and the allowance to the defendant for improvements, shall be estimated, and the balance ascertained, and judgment therefor rendered, as prescribed in Article 15 (§ 8.01-166 et seq.) of this chapter. (Code 1950, § 8-830; 1977, c. 617.)

I. DECISIONS UNDER PRIOR LAW.

Editor's note. — The case cited below was decided under corresponding provisions of former law. The term "this statute," as used below, refers to former provisions.

Same jury passes on claims for mesne profits, waste, and improvements. — In actions of ejectment if there is a claim by the plaintiff for mesne profits and damages for waste, and by defendant for improvements, both claims must be passed upon by the same jury. Goodwyn v. Myers, 57 Va. (16 Gratt.) 336 (1862).

§ 8.01-162. **Postponement of assessment and allowance.** — On the motion of either party, the court may order the assessment of such damages and allowance to be postponed until after the verdict on the title is recorded. (Code 1950, § 8-831; 1977, c. 617.)

§ 8.01-163. **Judgment to be conclusive.** — Any such judgment in an action of ejectment shall be conclusive as to the title or right of possession established in such action, upon the party against whom it is rendered, and against all persons claiming from, through, or under such party, by title accruing after the commencement of such action, except as hereinafter mentioned. (Code 1950, § 8-832; 1977, c. 617.)

I. Decisions Under Current Law.
II. Decisions Under Prior Law.

I. DECISIONS UNDER CURRENT LAW.

Applied in Providence Properties, Inc. v. United Va. Bank/Seaboard Nat'l, 219 Va. 735, 251 S.E.2d 474 (1979).

II. DECISIONS UNDER PRIOR LAW.

Editor's note. — The cases cited below were decided under corresponding provisions of former law. The term "this section," as used below, refers to former provisions.

The judgment referred to in this section is one on the merits. Payne v. Buena Vista Extract Co., 124 Va. 296, 98 S.E. 34 (1919).

Holding did not purport to, and could not, affect the rights of persons who were not parties or their successors in interest. See Page v. Luhring, 211 Va. 503, 178 S.E.2d 527 (1971).

Landlord not bound by judgment against tenant. — When the tenant alone was sued in ejectment to recover land on which the tenant was in possession, and, before execution, the tenant removed and the landlord entered, neither the landlord nor a subsequent tenant could be considered as claiming through or under the former tenant who was sued. The landlord was therefore not bound by the judgment as an estoppel. King v. Davis, 137 F. 198 (C.C.W.D. Va. 1903), aff'd, Blankenship v. King, 157 F. 676 (4th Cir. 1906).

§ 8.01-164. **Recovery of mesne profits, etc., not affected.** — Nothing in this chapter shall prevent the plaintiff from recovering mesne profits, or damages done to the premises, from any person other than the defendant, who may be liable to such action. (Code 1950, § 8-834; 1977, c. 617.)

§ 8.01-165. **Writ of right, etc., abolished.** — No writ of right, writ of entry, or writ of formedon, shall be hereafter brought. (Code 1950, § 8-835; 1977, c. 617.)

Article 15.

Improvements.

§ 8.01-166. How defendant may apply therefor, and have judgment suspended. — Any defendant against whom a decree or judgment shall be rendered for land, when no assessment of damages has been made under Article 14 (§ 8.01-131 et seq.) of this chapter, may, at any time before the execution of the decree or judgment, present a pleading to the court rendering such decree or judgment, stating that he, or those under whom he claims while holding the premises under a title believed by him or them to have been good, have made permanent improvements thereon, and moving that he should have an allowance for the same which are over and above the value of the use and occupation of such land; and thereupon the court may, if satisfied of the probable truth of the allegation, suspend the execution of the judgment or decree, and impanel a jury to assess the damages of the plaintiff, and the allowances to the defendant for such improvements. (Code 1950, § 8-842; 1977, c. 617.)

Cross references. — As to defendant's claim for improvements in action of ejectment, see § 8.01-160.

I. Decisions Under Current Law.
II. Decisions Under Prior Law.

I. DECISIONS UNDER CURRENT LAW.

Whenever there is a duty to inquiry, the party bound to inquire is affected with knowledge of all that would have been discovered had the party performed the duty. Richardson v. Parris, 246 Va. 203, 435 S.E.2d 389 (1993).

Inapplicable to one with notice of infirmity in his title. — Although this section permits a recovery for improvements when the one who made them mistakenly held the land "under a title believed by him . . . to have been good," this section has no application to one who is not a bona fide purchaser, and a person with notice, actual or constructive, of infirmity in his title cannot recover for improvements. White v. Pleasants, 227 Va. 508, 317 S.E.2d 489 (1984).

In order to be a bona fide purchaser and therefore qualify for protection under this section, the belief in the validity of the title must be founded on ignorance of fact, not ignorance of law. Richardson v. Parris, 246 Va. 203, 435 S.E.2d 389 (1993).

Recovery for improvements unavailable. — Where the insufficiency of the affidavit for the order of publication was apparent on the face of the record to be discovered by the subsequent purchaser or their agent before entry of the decree confirming the sale, the failure to recognize the facial insufficiency of the affidavit was ignorance of law, not ignorance of fact. Thus, because the subsequent purchaser had constructive notice of the title infirmity, they were not bona fide purchasers and were precluded from recovering for improvements. Richardson v. Parris, 246 Va. 203, 435 S.E.2d 389 (1993).

Applied in Richmond v. Hall, 251 Va. 151, 466 S.E.2d 103 (1996).

II. DECISIONS UNDER PRIOR LAW.

Editor's note. — The cases cited below were decided under corresponding provisions of former law. The term "this section," as used below, refers to former provisions.

This section alters the common-law rule and allows, as a set-off to the plaintiff's claim for rent and damages, compensation for permanent improvements made by defendant at a time when there was reason to believe the title good under which he was holding the premises, not exceeding, however, the increase of value to the same. Hollingsworth v. Funkhouser, 85 Va. 448, 8 S.E. 592 (1888).

It applies only to actions of ejectment or to cases in which a decree or judgment is rendered against a defendant for land. It does not apply to a suit for the specific enforcement of an alleged parol contract to convey land. Graeme v. Cullen, 64 Va. (23 Gratt.) 266 (1873); Branham v. Artrip, 115 Va. 314, 79 S.E. 390 (1913).

It has no application to the case of a purchaser at a judicial sale, against whom a claim for the purchase money is asserted, and in whose favor there has been no decree of confirmation. Tyler v. Toms, 75 Va. 116 (1880).

Nor to a judgment creditor seeking to enforce his lien upon the land upon which the improvements have been made. Flanary v. Kane, 102 Va. 547, 46 S.E. 312, rehearing denied, 46 S.E. 681 (1904).

No allowance is made for improvements erected by one who is not a bona fide purchaser. Burton v. Mill, 78 Va. 468 (1884); Smith v. Woodward, 122 Va. 356, 94 S.E. 916 (1918).

Effect of being life tenant. — A party cannot be said to be acting in good faith in putting improvements on land when he knows that at best he has only a life estate in the land. Wright v. Johnson, 108 Va. 855, 62 S.E. 948 (1908).

Effect of actual or constructive notice. — Under this section a person with notice, actual or constructive, of a defect in his title is not entitled, upon being dispossessed by the rightful owner, to recover compensation for permanent improvements made on the premises. Kian v. Kefalogiannis, 158 Va. 129, 163 S.E. 535 (1932). See Keister v. Cubine, 101 Va. 768, 45 S.E. 285 (1903); Truslow v. Ball, 166 Va. 608, 186 S.E. 71 (1936).

This section restricts recovery for improvements to one "holding the premises under a title believed by him ... to be good." This section has no application to one who is not a bona fide purchaser, and a person with notice, actual or constructive, of infirmity in his title cannot recover for improvements. Graeme v. Cullen, 64 Va. (23 Gratt.) 266 (1873); Hurn v. Keller, 79 Va. 415 (1884); Smith v. Woodward, 122 Va. 356, 94 S.E. 916 (1918).

Means of notice with the duty of using those means, is equivalent to actual notice. Effinger v. Hall, 81 Va. 94 (1885).

Effect of laches on part of plaintiff. — If the owner is guilty of gross laches in asserting his claim, after he is apprised of it, he will not be permitted to recover, except upon compensation. Walker v. Beauchler, 68 Va. (27 Gratt.) 511 (1876); Wood v. Krebbs, 74 Va. (33 Gratt.) 685 (1880).

What constitutes permanent improvement. — Whether the work was done and the money expended with reference to the future betterment of the premises, or for future immediate advantage of the occupant is the consideration which should control. Cullop v. Leonard, 97 Va. 256, 33 S.E. 611 (1899).

Commercial fertilizers cannot be regarded as permanent improvements. Effinger v. Kenney, 92 Va. 245, 23 S.E. 742 (1895). See also, Wright v. Johnson, 108 Va. 855, 62 S.E. 948 (1908).

§ 8.01-167. How damages of plaintiff assessed. — The jury, in assessing such damages, either under this article or under Article 14 (§ 8.01-131 et seq.) of this chapter, shall determine the annual value of the premises during the time the defendant was in possession thereof, exclusive of the use by the tenant of the improvements thereon made by himself or those under whom he claims, and also the damages for waste or other injury to the premises committed by the defendant. (Code 1950, § 8-843; 1977, c. 617.)

Cross references. — As to nonconsideration of plaintiffs' claims for damages in proceeding to establish boundaries to land, see § 8.01-182.

I. DECISIONS UNDER PRIOR LAW.

Editor's note. — The cases cited below were decided under corresponding provisions of former law. The terms "this chapter" and "this section," as used below, refer to former provisions.

What to be offset. — The clear annual value, exclusive of the improvements, of the premises during the time he was in possession, is estimated by the jury against the defendant. This value, and other damages, if any, in behalf of the plaintiff, and the allowance to the defendant for improvements, shall be offsets, one against the other. Wood v. Krebbs, 74 Va. (33 Gratt.) 685 (1880); Hollingsworth v. Funkhouser, 85 Va. 448, 8 S.E. 592 (1888).

Plaintiff's remedy to recover damages in proceeding to establish boundaries to land. — For discussion of the remedy of plaintiff in a proceeding to establish boundaries to land under Article 16 of this chapter to recover damages under this section, see Brunswick Land Corp. v. Perkinson, 153 Va. 603, 151 S.E. 138 (1928).

§ 8.01-168. For what time. — The defendant shall not be liable for such annual value for any longer time than five years before the suit, or for damages for any such waste or other injury done before such five years, except when he claims for improvements as aforesaid. (Code 1950, § 8-844; 1977, c. 617.)

§ 8.01-169. How value of improvements determined in favor of defendant. — If the jury shall be satisfied that the defendant, or those under whom he claims, made on the premises, at a time when there was reason to believe the title good under which he or they were holding the same, permanent and valuable improvements, they shall determine the value of such improvements as were so made before receipt by the person making the same of notice in writing of the title under which the plaintiff claims, not exceeding the amount actually expended in making them, and not exceeding the amount to which the value of the premises is actually increased thereby at the time of such determination. (Code 1950, § 8-845; 1977, c. 617.)

I. DECISIONS UNDER PRIOR LAW.

Editor's note. — The cases cited below were decided under corresponding provisions of former law. The term "this section," as used below, refers to former provisions.

Proof of value. — Compensation can only be allowed upon clear and full proof of the amount to which the value of the premises is actually increased thereby at the time of the assessment. Hollingsworth v. Funkhouser, 85 Va. 448, 8 S.E. 592 (1888).

Purchaser cannot close eyes to record title. — To hold that a purchaser can close his eyes to his record title and recover for improvements on the theory that "there was reason to believe the title good" would be to set a premium on negligence and nullify our registry statutes. McDonald v. Rothgib, 112 Va. 749, 72 S.E. 692 (1911).

§ 8.01-170. If allowance for improvements exceed damages, what to be done.

— If the sum determined for the improvements exceed the damages determined by the jury against the defendant as aforesaid, they shall then determine against him, for any time before such five years, the rents and profits accrued against, or damage for waste or other injury done by him, or those under whom he claims, so far as may be necessary to balance his claim for improvements, but in such case he shall not be liable for the excess, if any, of such rents and profits, or damages, beyond the value of the improvements. (Code 1950, § 8-846; 1977, c. 617.)

I. DECISIONS UNDER PRIOR LAW.

Editor's note. — The cases cited below were decided under corresponding provisions of former law. The term "this section," as used below, refers to former provisions.

The defendant, as tenant in possession, is entitled to compensation for improvements made in excess of the benefits derived from the use and occupation of the land. Wood v. Krebbs, 74 Va. (33 Gratt.) 685 (1880).

Defendant was to be charged for the rents and profits of the land exclusive of his improvements, while he held it, and to be allowed a reasonable compensation for the permanent improvements he had made upon it, though this shall be in excess of the rents and profits. Walker v. Beauchler, 68 Va. (27 Gratt.) 511 (1876).

§ 8.01-171. Verdict for balance, after offsetting damages against improvements.

— After offsetting the damages assessed for the plaintiff and the allowances to the defendant for improvements, if any, the jury shall find a verdict for the balance for the plaintiff or defendant, as the case may be, and judgment or decree shall be entered therefor according to the verdict. (Code 1950, § 8-847; 1977, c. 617.)

§ 8.01-172. Balance for defendant a lien on the land.

— Any such balance due to the defendant shall constitute a lien upon the land recovered by the plaintiff, until the same shall be paid. (Code 1950, § 8-848; 1977, c. 617.)

§ 8.01-173. How tenant for life, paying for improvements, reimbursed.

— If the plaintiff claim only an estate for life in the land recovered, and pay any sum allowed to the defendant for improvements, he, or his personal representative at the determination of his estate, may recover from the remainderman or reversioner, the value of such improvements as they then exist, not exceeding the amount so paid by him, and shall have a lien therefor on the premises, in like manner as if they had been mortgaged for the payment thereof, and may keep possession of such premises until the same be paid. (Code 1950, § 8-849; 1977, c. 617.)

I. DECISIONS UNDER PRIOR LAW.

Editor's note. — The case cited below was decided under corresponding provisions of former law. The term "this statute," as used below, refers to former provisions.

When a life tenant makes improvements himself, they constitute no charge upon the land when it passes to the reversioner or remainderman, according to the general rule. Effinger v. Hall, 81 Va. 94 (1885).

§ 8.01-174. Exception as to mortgagees and trustees. — Nothing in this article, nor anything concerning rents, profits, and improvements, in Article 14 (§ 8.01-131 et seq.) of this chapter, shall extend or apply to any suit brought by a mortgagee, or trustee in a deed of trust to secure creditors, his heirs, or assigns, against a mortgagor or grantor in such deed of trust, his heirs, or assigns, for the recovery of the mortgaged premises or of the land conveyed by such deed of trust. (Code 1950, § 8-850; 1977, c. 617.)

§ 8.01-175. When plaintiff may require his estate only to be valued; how determined; how he may elect to relinquish his title to defendant. — A. When the defendant shall claim allowance for improvements, the plaintiff may, by an entry on the record, require that the value of his estate in the premises, without the improvements, shall also be ascertained.

B. The value of the premises in such case shall be determined as it would have been at the time of the inquiry, if no such improvements had been made, and shall be ascertained in the manner hereinbefore provided for determining the value of improvements.

C. The plaintiff in such case, if judgment is rendered for him, may at any time, enter on the record his election to relinquish his estate in the premises to the defendant at the value so ascertained under this section, and the defendant shall thenceforth hold all the estate that the plaintiff had therein at the commencement of the suit, provided he pay therefor such value, with interest, in the manner in which the court may direct. (Code 1950, §§ 8-851, 8-852, 8-853; 1977, c. 617.)

I. DECISIONS UNDER PRIOR LAW.

Editor's note. — The cases cited below were decided under corresponding provisions of former law. The term "this section," as used below, refers to former provisions.

Value of plaintiff's estate ascertained as of same time as the improvement. — The value of the plaintiff's estate in the premises without the improvements, is to be ascertained as at the time when the assessment of the value of the improvements was made. Goodwyn v. Myers, 57 Va. (16 Gratt.) 336 (1862). See also, Corr v. Porter, 74 Va. (33 Gratt.) 278 (1880).

Estate to be valued by a different jury. — If defendant claims for improvements on the land, the plaintiff may at any time before a judgment is rendered on the assessment of the value of the improvements, though after the jury which tried the issue or passed upon the defendant's claim for improvement has been discharged, require that the value of his estate in the premises, without the improvements, shall also be ascertained. This inquiry is to be made by another jury. Goodwyn v. Myers, 57 Va. (16 Gratt.) 336 (1862).

Where the plaintiff in the ejectment suit requires the value of his estate in the premises in controversy to be ascertained, the inquiry must be made by a different jury from that which tried the cause on its merits. Goodwyn v. Myers, 57 Va. (16 Gratt.) 336 (1862); Corr v. Porter, 74 Va. (33 Gratt.) 278 (1880).

No objection to use of same jury can be made after verdict. — The same jury which tried the case on its merits was allowed, without objection from either side, to fix the value of the land, the rents and profits thereof, and the value of the improvements claimed by the defendant. It is too late after verdict to object to this action of the court. Corr v. Porter, 74 Va. (33 Gratt.) 278 (1880).

§ 8.01-176. **How payment of such value to be made by defendant; when land sold therefor.** — The payments shall be made to the plaintiff, or into court for his use, and the land shall be bound therefor, and if the defendant fail to make such payments within or at the times limited therefor respectively, the court may order the land to be sold and the proceeds applied to the payment of such value and interest, and the surplus, if any, to be paid to the defendant; but if the net proceeds be insufficient to satisfy such value and interest, the defendant shall not be bound for the deficiency. (Code 1950, § 8-854; 1977, c. 617.)

§ 8.01-177. **When such value to be deemed real estate.** — If the party by or for whom the land is claimed in the suit be a person under a disability, such value shall be deemed to be real estate, and be disposed of as the court may consider proper for the benefit of the persons interested therein. (Code 1950, § 8-855; 1977, c. 617.)

§ 8.01-178. **When and how defendant, if evicted, may recover from plaintiff amount paid.** — If the defendant or his heirs or assigns shall, after the premises are so relinquished to him, be evicted thereof by force of any better title than that of the original plaintiff, the person so evicted may recover from such plaintiff or his representative the amount so paid for the premises, as so much money had and received by such plaintiff in his lifetime for the use of such person, with lawful interest thereon from the time of such payment. (Code 1950, § 8-856; 1977, c. 617.)

ARTICLE 16.

Establishing Boundaries to Land.

§ 8.01-179. **Motion for judgment to establish boundary lines.** — Any person having a subsisting interest in real estate and a right to its possession, or to the possession of some share, interest or portion thereof, may file a motion for judgment to ascertain and designate the true boundary line or lines to such real estate as to one or more of the coterminous landowners. Plaintiff in stating his interest shall conform to the requirements of § 8.01-137, and shall describe with reasonable certainty such real estate and the boundary line or lines thereof which he seeks to establish. (Code 1950, § 8-836; 1954, c. 606; 1977, c. 617.)

Cross references. — As to what interest or right plaintiff must have to bring action of ejectment, see § 8.01-132. As to where action of ejectment must be brought, see § 8.01-261. For rules of court governing actions for establishment of boundaries, see Rules 3:1 through 3:18.

Law Review. — For discussion of boundary proceedings, see 45 Va. L. Rev. 1455 (1959).

I. Decisions Under Prior Law.
  A. General Consideration.
  B. Nature of Action.
  C. Comparable to Ejectment.
  D. Title of Plaintiff.
  E. Parties.

I. DECISIONS UNDER PRIOR LAW.

A. General Consideration.

Editor's note. — The cases cited below were decided under corresponding provisions of former law. The terms "this statute" and "this section," as used below, refer to former provisions.

B. Nature of Action.

The proceeding to settle and determine boundaries under this section is an action

for the recovery of property. Bradshaw v. Booth, 129 Va. 19, 105 S.E. 555 (1921).

A summary proceeding at law. — The remedy given by this section for ascertaining and determining "the boundary lines of real estate" is a summary proceeding at law, and not in equity. Wright v. Rabey, 117 Va. 884, 86 S.E. 71 (1915).

Matters which may be settled. — In a proceeding under this section, the court will settle the line between plaintiff and defendants so far as their lands are coterminous, but the plaintiff cannot in such proceeding contest the rights of the defendants to the use of a river in which the plaintiff has no title, nor the title of defendants to land which in no way fixes the location of the line in question. James River Kanawha Power Co. v. Old Dominion Iron & Steel Corp., 138 Va. 461, 122 S.E. 344 (1924).

Proceeding not incompatible with action for trespass. — Plaintiff's action to try the right of possession by means of its petition (now motion for judgment) under this section, is not incompatible with the concomitant action by it for the defendant's trespass. But plaintiff's claim to the right of possession, to the land in dispute, while related to a claim for damages for defendant's trespass upon the land, constitutes a distinct and independent subject of action. Brunswick Land Corp. v. Perkinson, 153 Va. 603, 151 S.E. 138 (1930).

But proceeding did not toll statute of limitation against action of trespass. — Defendant, in an action for trespass, pleaded the statute of limitations. But plaintiff claimed that the statute of limitations had been tolled by a proceeding under this section instituted after the alleged trespass by the plaintiff in the instant case against defendant to determine the boundary between plaintiff and defendant and establish title to the land upon which the trespass was alleged to have been committed. It was held that the statute was not tolled. Brunswick Land Corp. v. Perkinson, 153 Va. 603, 151 S.E. 138 (1930).

Proceeding not a substitute for partition. — The proceeding to determine boundaries under this section was not intended as a substitute for a suit for partition, nor does it afford the same relief. The former proceeding is governed by the same principles as obtained in an action of ejectment. The court has no jurisdiction therein to establish lines which have never been designated with proper certainty by the source of title of the plaintiff. Whereas that is precisely the relief which a suit for partition in kind affords to those who own several freeholds in the same land, which have never been divided in severalty with respect to the right of possession, by definite designation, in the source of title, of the dividing line or lines. Hodges v. Thornton, 138 Va. 112, 120 S.E. 865 (1924).

But proceeding may determine dividing line under partition agreement. — In a proceeding under this section, if a partition deed from grantors to their cotenant did not include all the lands which, according to the agreed line, were the property of the cotenant and now belong to his successor in title, it was proper for the jury to so fix the dividing line as to give to the cotenant's successor in title the land which was the cotenant's under the terms of the partition agreement. Vanover v. Hollyfield, 151 Va. 287, 144 S.E. 450 (1928).

Must designate boundaries in motion. — This section is a statutory remedy to have ascertained and designated the true boundary line or lines of coterminous landowners, and the plaintiff is required to designate with reasonable certainty in his motion the boundary line or lines which he seeks to establish. James River Kanawha Power Co. v. Old Dominion Iron & Steel Corp., 138 Va. 461, 122 S.E. 344 (1924).

Burden of proving common grantor. — Where the parties to a boundary-line proceeding purport to trace their title to a common grantor, the burden is upon the plaintiff to prove perfect legal title by showing an unbroken chain running back to the common source. Bulifant v. Slosjarik, 221 Va. 983, 277 S.E.2d 151 (1981).

Effect of deed recorded years after execution. — In a boundary-line proceeding in which plaintiffs and defendant both claimed to trace their title to the disputed strip to a common grantor, there was evidence that the deed was recorded, but where the deed is recorded many years after its execution and no satisfactory explanation accounts for its whereabouts during the intervening period, no presumption of delivery arises from the mere fact of recordation; therefore, the plaintiffs failed to establish title to the disputed strip because they did not prove proper delivery of the deed. Bulifant v. Slosjarik, 221 Va. 983, 277 S.E.2d 151 (1981).

C. Comparable to Ejectment.

Proceeding as a substitute for action of ejectment. — This statute, which was presumably enacted with knowledge of the long established right of joinder in actions of ejectment, was intended, and has been used, as a frequently available and convenient substitute for ejectment. This is shown by the language of the statute, by its location in the Code of 1919 in the chapter on ejectment, and inferentially at least by the reported decisions. Fray v. Pollock, 7 Va. L. Reg. (n.s.) 95 (1921).

While the judgment of the court under this section may not in terms be a judgment rendered for land, yet in substance and effect it is for land to the same extent as in a judgment entered in an action of ejectment. Pickeral v.

Federal Land Bank, 177 Va. 743, 15 S.E.2d 82 (1941).

Same principles applicable. — Where in a proceeding under the section to establish a boundary line the title and right of possession of the coterminous owners is brought into dispute by the pleadings, the same principles of law are applicable as would be applicable to the same subject in an action of ejectment. Brunswick Land Corp. v. Perkinson, 146 Va. 695, 132 S.E. 853 (1926). See Prettyman v. M.J. Duer & Co., 189 Va. 122, 52 S.E.2d 156 (1949); Wade v. Ford, 193 Va. 279, 68 S.E.2d 528 (1952); Allen v. Powers, 194 Va. 662, 74 S.E.2d 688 (1953); Bull Run Dev. Corp. v. Jackson, 201 Va. 95, 109 S.E.2d 400 (1959); Custis Fishing & Hunting Club, Inc. v. Johnson, 214 Va. 388, 200 S.E.2d 542 (1973).

In a proceeding under this section, to determine boundaries, the same principles are inevitably involved as are involved on the same subject in actions of ejectment. Where the plaintiff to recover relies on title to land up to a certain location of its boundary on the ground, although the defendant may in general terms admit by the pleadings that the plaintiff has title to some land claimed by the latter, yet when the defendant denies that the plaintiff's title extends to such location, the plaintiff is inescapably put to his proof of such a title by evidence of title which the defendant cannot be heard to dispute. Such evidence must trace the title either from the Commonwealth or other common grantor. Bradshaw v. Booth, 129 Va. 19, 105 S.E. 555 (1921).

Where in a proceeding under the section to establish a boundary line the title and right of possession of the coterminous owners is brought into dispute by the pleadings, the same principles of law are applicable as would be applicable to the same subject in an action of ejectment. Bulifant v. Slosjarik, 221 Va. 983, 277 S.E.2d 151 (1981).

But section not coextensive with ejectment. — This section is not in every respect coextensive with the action of ejectment. The statute is coextensive with the action of ejectment only in cases of coterminous ownership, and, in such cases, only to the extent that the lands of the parties are shown to be coterminous. James River Kanawha Power Co. v. Old Dominion Iron & Steel Corp., 138 Va. 461, 122 S.E. 344 (1924).

The proceeding to establish boundary lines under this section may be used as a substitute for the action of ejectment where there is a dispute between coterminous landowners over the true boundary line or lines, and much of the law relating to ejectment applies to this proceeding. Pickeral v. Federal Land Bank, 177 Va. 743, 15 S.E.2d 82 (1941).

Distinguished from ejectment. — An important distinction exists between a proceeding to establish a boundary line and an action of ejectment, in that an action of ejectment will not lie when the plaintiff is in possession, whereas a proceeding to establish a boundary line may be brought whether the plaintiff is in possession or not. They are, therefore, not coextensive in that respect. Brunswick Land Corp. v. Perkinson, 146 Va. 695, 132 S.E. 853 (1926).

No intent to grant advantage. — There is little or no difference except as to procedure between an action in ejectment and a proceeding under this section, and there is nothing in this section which would suggest that the legislature intended to give parties litigating their rights under the statute any advantage over parties who had proceeded by ejectment. Choate v. Calhoun, 153 Va. 52, 149 S.E. 470 (1929).

An equitable estoppel cannot be pleaded or proven in ejectment or in an action under this section. Allen v. Powers, 194 Va. 662, 74 S.E.2d 688 (1953).

D. Title of Plaintiff.

Fee owner entitled to proceed under section. — The title of the plaintiff being a fee, and the controversy being with the owners of "coterminous real estate" as to the true location of boundary lines between the plaintiff and the defendants, the plaintiff had the right to proceed under this section and was not driven to an action of ejectment. Christian v. Bulbeck, 120 Va. 74, 90 S.E. 661 (1916).

Plaintiff must recover on the strength of his own title. — In a proceeding under this section to determine the boundary line or lines between certain coterminous land of the parties, as well as in ejectment, a plaintiff who cannot rely on actual possession, must recover, if at all, upon the strength of his own title. Griggs v. Brown, 126 Va. 556, 102 S.E. 212 (1920). See also, Christian v. Bulbeck, 120 Va. 74, 90 S.E. 661 (1916).

As a general rule a plaintiff must recover on the strength of his own title, and, when he relies solely on his own paper title, must trace it either from the Commonwealth or other common grantor, but it is well settled that he is not required to do this when he shows such a state of facts as will warrant the jury in presuming a grant. Brunswick Land Corp. v. Perkinson, 146 Va. 695, 132 S.E. 853 (1926); Prettyman v. M.J. Duer & Co., 189 Va. 122, 52 S.E.2d 156 (1949); Bull Run Dev. Corp. v. Jackson, 201 Va. 95, 109 S.E.2d 400 (1959).

As a general rule, in an action in ejectment as well as in a proceeding under this section to establish a boundary line of coterminous lands, in order for a plaintiff to prevail he must do so on the strength of his own title, and when he relies on his own paper title he must trace an unbroken chain of title back to the Commonwealth or to a common grantor or prove such a state of facts as will warrant the presumption of a grant. Page v. Luhring, 208 Va. 643, 159 S.E.2d 642 (1968).

Plaintiff said that his prior peaceful possession of the disputed land under color of title constituted prima facie evidence of ownership and seisin sufficient to warrant a judgment of ownership unless defendant showed a better title, which he had not done. The principle relied on is a recognized exception to the general rule that a plaintiff must win on the strength of his own title. However the exception is restricted to those situations where the defendant is an intruder or trespasser without color of title. Page v. Luhring, 208 Va. 643, 159 S.E.2d 642 (1968).

Generally, a plaintiff must prevail, if at all, on the strength of his own title. Custis Fishing & Hunting Club, Inc. v. Johnson, 214 Va. 388, 200 S.E.2d 542 (1973).

How title proved. — In order for plaintiff to prevail in a proceeding under this section he must prove (1) that he has a perfect legal title to the land in dispute by showing an unbroken chain of title either to the Commonwealth or to a common grantor; or (2) that he has title to the land by adverse possession; or (3) such a state of facts as will warrant the court in presuming a grant. Bull Run Dev. Corp. v. Jackson, 201 Va. 95, 109 S.E.2d 400 (1959).

Plaintiffs bear burden of proof. — In boundary proceedings, those who initiate the proceedings bear the burden of proof by a preponderance of the evidence. When plaintiffs in such proceedings fail to prove paper title or title by adverse possession, they must bear that burden by proving a state of facts that will warrant the court in presuming a grant. Ferris v. Snellings, 213 Va. 452, 192 S.E.2d 804 (1972).

Having initiated the proceedings, plaintiffs had the burden of establishing the boundaries of their property by a preponderance of the evidence. Central Nat'l Bank v. Florence, 215 Va. 463, 211 S.E.2d 564 (1975).

If the plaintiff is unable to trace his title from the Commonwealth or other common grantor, he has the burden of proving facts that will warrant a jury in presuming a grant. Custis Fishing & Hunting Club, Inc. v. Johnson, 214 Va. 388, 200 S.E.2d 542 (1973).

Parol evidence not an independent source of title. — The extent of boundaries of land, and thus the title to land, cannot be established wholly by parol evidence, unsupported by written evidence of title, where title by adverse possession is not involved and where the case is one in which the title claimed is by deed and must have been derived by deed, if derived at all; for to hold otherwise would be to permit parol evidence to become an independent source of title, which is not permissible. Ferris v. Snellings, 213 Va. 452, 192 S.E.2d 804 (1972).

Deed must specifically define boundaries. — If plaintiffs claim title by deed, their deed must specifically define the boundaries of their claim. Ferris v. Snellings, 213 Va. 452, 192 S.E.2d 804 (1972); Central Nat'l Bank v. Florence, 215 Va. 463, 211 S.E.2d 564 (1975).

Effect of prior possession. — When plaintiff has never had actual or constructive possession of any part of the land in controversy in a proceeding under this section to determine boundaries, he must show a complete legal title to the premises in order to recover. If plaintiff had had a prior possession to that of the defendant and the possession of the latter had been obtained by intrusion and trespass without color of title, such prior possession would have raised a presumption of title in the plaintiff which would have been sufficient to show a complete legal title to the premises in him. Bradshaw v. Booth, 129 Va. 19, 105 S.E. 555 (1921).

The principle that possession under color of title constitutes a prima facie title is under the great weight of authority restricted to those factual situations where the defendant is a mere intruder or trespasser without color of title. Bull Run Dev. Corp. v. Jackson, 201 Va. 95, 109 S.E.2d 400 (1959).

An exception to the rule that, generally, a plaintiff must prevail, if at all, on the strength of his own title permits the plaintiff to establish a prima facie case of ownership by showing that he has taken prior peaceful possession under color of title, but this exception is limited to cases in which the defendant is a mere intruder or trespasser without color of title. Custis Fishing & Hunting Club, Inc. v. Johnson, 214 Va. 388, 200 S.E.2d 542 (1973).

Possession necessary to afford presumption of grant. — Courts will presume a grant where one has for a long period of time held an uninterrupted possession of land while exercising proprietary rights. The possession necessary to afford a presumption of a grant must be actual, open, adverse, exclusive and uninterrupted, as well as inconsistent with the existence of title in another. Ferris v. Snellings, 213 Va. 452, 192 S.E.2d 804 (1972).

Plaintiff's presumption of grant theory failed where the defendants were not mere intruders or trespassers, but owners of property adjoining the mill pond, who had acquired a colorable claim, asserted in their grounds of defense, to riparian interests extending to the center of the pond. Custis Fishing & Hunting Club, Inc. v. Johnson, 214 Va. 388, 200 S.E.2d 542 (1973).

In the absence of express exclusion by deed or contract, an owner adjoining a fresh water pond acquires whatever interest in the pond his grantor had, regardless of the use of descriptive boundary terms such as "along" or "with" the pond. Custis Fishing & Hunting Club, Inc. v. Johnson, 214 Va. 388, 200 S.E.2d 542 (1973).

E. Parties.

Relation of parties as owners of mineral and surface rights is not that of coterminous landowners and hence the remedy for settling disputed boundary lines, provided in this section, is not available to either side. Buchanan Coal Co. v. Street, 175 Va. 531, 9 S.E.2d 339 (1940).

§ 8.01-180. Parties defendant; pleadings.

— The plaintiff shall make defendants to such motion for judgment all persons having a present interest in the boundary line or lines sought to be ascertained and designated. (Code 1950, § 8-837; 1954, c. 606; 1977, c. 617.)

I. DECISIONS UNDER PRIOR LAW.

Editor's note. — The cases cited below were decided under corresponding provisions of former law. The term "this section," as used below, refers to former provisions.

Adverse possession may be set up as a defense to a petition (now motion for judgment) under this section. Christian v. Bulbeck, 120 Va. 74, 90 S.E. 661 (1916); Bradshaw v. Booth, 129 Va. 19, 105 S.E. 555 (1921).

The burden of establishing adverse possession is upon the defendant. Westland Realty Corp. v. Griffin, 151 Va. 1005, 145 S.E. 718 (1928).

Plaintiff's acquiescence in defendant's survey did not work estoppel. — The mere acquiescence of plaintiff in a survey by defendant of the land in controversy in a proceeding under this section, to determine boundaries, at the time of the purchase of the real estate by defendant, does not estop plaintiff from afterwards asserting an adverse claim of title inconsistent with the validity of the survey in the accuracy of which he had acquiesced. Such mere acquiescence alone will not work an estoppel. In order to do so the acquiescence must have influenced the subsequent conduct of the defendant to his prejudice. Bradshaw v. Booth, 129 Va. 19, 105 S.E. 555 (1921).

Defendant receives no benefit from compromise not accepted. — Where a defendant in a proceeding to ascertain a boundary between him and the plaintiff has refused to accept an offer of a compromise line made in the petition (now motion for judgment), and has denied the right of the plaintiff to the line both in his pleadings and proof, he has no right to claim any benefit from such offer. Hamman v. Miller, 116 Va. 873, 83 S.E. 382 (1914).

§ 8.01-181. Surveys.

— The court may appoint a surveyor and direct such surveys to be made as it deems necessary, and the costs thereof shall be assessed as the court may direct. (Code 1950, § 8-838; 1954, c. 606; 1977, c. 617.)

REVISERS' NOTE

Provisions regarding trial in former § 8-838 were deleted as unnecessary. Added is the provision that the court may assess the cost of any survey ordered.

Former § 8-841 (Writ of error to judgment) was deleted as unnecessary.

I. DECISIONS UNDER PRIOR LAW.

Editor's note. — The cases cited below were decided under corresponding provisions of former law. The term "this section," as used below, refers to former provisions.

Statutory duty as to surveys. — The provisions of this section are not intended to prevent the court of its own motion from ordering such survey or surveys as it might deem necessary to give effect to its judgment as to what constitutes the boundary between the parties by locating and marking the line on the ground. It is not only the right, but the duty, of the court to have such survey or surveys made whenever deemed proper. This holding is made statutory by the present form of the section. Hamman v. Miller, 116 Va. 873, 83 S.E. 382 (1914).

A private survey is admissible as evidence of a boundary line between those who are parties to it or who claim under it, but it is not admissible as independent evidence against others. Robinson v. Peterson, 200 Va. 186, 104 S.E.2d 788 (1958).

Opinion testimony of surveyor of no probative value. — The testimony of the surveyor in a boundary line case giving his opinion about the lines is of no probative value. Hargrove v. Harris, 167 Va. 320, 189 S.E. 307 (1937). See also, Griggs v. Brown, 126 Va. 556, 102 S.E. 212 (1920).

§ 8.01-182. Claims to rents, etc., not considered.

— In a proceeding under this article, no claim of the plaintiff for rents, profits or damages shall be considered. (Code 1950, § 8-839; 1977, c. 617.)

§ 8.01-183. Recordation and effect of judgment.

— The judgment of the court shall be recorded in the current deed book of the court. The judgment shall forever settle, determine, and designate the true boundary line or lines in question, between the parties, their heirs, devisees, and assigns. The judgment may be enforced in the same manner as a judgment in an action of ejectment. (Code 1950, § 8-840; 1977, c. 617.)

I. DECISIONS UNDER PRIOR LAW.

Editor's note. — The case cited below was decided under corresponding provisions of former law. The term "this statute," as used below, refers to former provisions.

Holding did not purport to, and could not, affect the rights of persons who were not parties or their successors in interest. Page v. Luhring, 211 Va. 503, 178 S.E.2d 527 (1971).

ARTICLE 17.

Declaratory Judgments.

§ 8.01-184. Power to issue declaratory judgments.

— In cases of actual controversy, circuit courts within the scope of their respective jurisdictions shall have power to make binding adjudications of right, whether or not consequential relief is, or at the time could be, claimed and no action or proceeding shall be open to objection on the ground that a judgment order or decree merely declaratory of right is prayed for. Controversies involving the interpretation of deeds, wills, and other instruments of writing, statutes, municipal ordinances and other governmental regulations, may be so determined, and this enumeration does not exclude other instances of actual antagonistic assertion and denial of right. (Code 1950, § 8-578; 1977, c. 617.)

Cross references. — For method of securing construction of act requiring payment of money out of state treasury, see § 8.01-653.

Law Review. — For comment on challenging rezoning in Virginia, see 15 U. Rich. L. Rev. 423 (1981). For note, "Desuetude and Declaratory Judgment: A New Challenge to Obsolete Laws," see 76 Va. L. Rev. 1057 (1990).

I. Decisions Under Current Law.
  A. General Consideration.
  B. Actual Controversy.
II. Decisions Under Prior Law.
  A. General Consideration.
  B. Actual Controversy.

I. DECISIONS UNDER CURRENT LAW.

A. General Consideration.

This section and § 8.01-191 are to be liberally interpreted and administered with a view to making the courts more serviceable to the people. Board of Supvrs. v. Southland Corp., 224 Va. 514, 297 S.E.2d 718 (1982).

The controversy must be one that is justiciable, that is, where specific adverse claims, based upon present rather than future or speculative facts, are ripe for judicial adjustment. Reisen v. Aetna Life & Cas. Co., 225 Va. 327, 302 S.E.2d 529 (1983).

Court not to render advisory opinions.
— Enactment of the declaratory judgment statutes did not vest the courts with authority to render advisory opinions, decide moot questions, or answer merely speculative inquiries. Reisen v. Aetna Life & Cas. Co., 225 Va. 327, 302 S.E.2d 529 (1983).

When a state provides an adequate procedure for obtaining just compensation, a property owner cannot claim a violation of the federal provision until it has used the state procedure and been denied just compensation. Pasquotank Action Council, Inc. v. City of Va. Beach, 909 F. Supp. 376 (E.D. Va. 1995).

Standing generally. — A plaintiff has standing to bring a declaratory judgment proceeding if he has "a justiciable interest" in the subject matter of the litigation, either in his own right or in a representative capacity. Cupp v. Board of Supvrs., 227 Va. 580, 318 S.E.2d 407 (1984).

A justiciable controversy involves specific adverse claims based on present facts that are ripe for adjudication. Mosher Steel-Virginia v. Teig, 229 Va. 95, 327 S.E.2d 87 (1985).

A hypothetical or abstract interest is insufficient to confer standing to bring a declaratory judgment action. Mosher Steel-Virginia v. Teig, 229 Va. 95, 327 S.E.2d 87 (1985).

Where there is no administrative remedy equal to the relief sought, a complainant in a declaratory judgment proceeding, having no adequate legal remedy by judicial review, properly states a justiciable cause of action. Mosher Steel-Virginia v. Teig, 229 Va. 95, 327 S.E.2d 87 (1985).

The binding adjudications of right made under this section must resolve issues specifically pled in the petition for declaratory judgment, and the court is not empowered to make binding adjudications of right which are not specifically pled. Scottsdale Ins. Co. v. Glick, 240 Va. 283, 397 S.E.2d 105 (1990).

Controversy held ripe for adjudication.
— A justiciable controversy ripe for adjudication exists where plaintiff has brought an action for damages resulting from personal injuries and defendant's insurer seeks a declaratory judgment as to obligation to pay if defendant is subsequently found liable for plaintiff's injuries and the circumstances give rise to a real probability that the insurer owed no coverage to the defendant. Reisen v. Aetna Life & Cas. Co., 225 Va. 327, 302 S.E.2d 529 (1983).

Standing of owner of options to buy land subject to zoning. — Where a developer owned options to buy real estate that was subject to piecemeal downzoning by the local government, the developer had standing to bring a declaratory judgment proceeding since it had a justiciable interest in the subject matter of the litigation and, further, the developer's interest by virtue of the options was not hypothetical or abstract because, as an optionee, it had an exclusive, irrevocable, binding contractual right to purchase the real estate according to the terms of the several option agreements. Board of Supvrs. v. Fralin & Waldron, Inc., 222 Va. 218, 278 S.E.2d 859 (1981).

Unauthorized practice of law by title insurance company. — Whether a title insurance company is engaging in the unauthorized practice of law by its participation in real estate closings may be resolved by declaratory judgment. Blodinger v. Broker's Title, Inc., 224 Va. 201, 294 S.E.2d 876 (1982).

The fact that unauthorized practice of law is a misdemeanor does not preclude declaratory relief to attorneys who sought determination as to whether a title insurance company's activities constituted the unauthorized practice of law, where their goal was not solely to stop the illegal conduct of others, but to ensure that their own conduct conformed to the law and the tenets of the legal profession. Blodinger v. Broker's Title, Inc., 224 Va. 201, 294 S.E.2d 876 (1982).

Trial court incorrectly held that declaratory judgment was not available to construe provision of written lease to determine whether continued occupancy of certain premises would subject lessee to liability for continuing damages, and his employees and customers to criminal liability for trespass; lessee was entitled to declaratory judgment action given unavailability of any remedy by customary processes and liberal construction of § 8.01-191. Hop-In Food Stores, Inc. v. Serv-N-Save, Inc., 237 Va. 206, 375 S.E.2d 753 (1989).

Applied in Adams v. Board of Supvrs., 569 F. Supp. 20 (W.D. Va. 1983).

B. Actual Controversy.

Legality of an ordinance is tested not only by what has been done under its provisions but what may be done thereunder. Although the board of supervisors had not yet imposed the restrictions and conditions on the plaintiffs, it claimed it had the power to do so and this claim of power threatened the plaintiffs. Thus, a controversy, within the contemplation of the Declaratory Judgment Act, existed. Cupp v. Board of Supvrs., 227 Va. 580, 318 S.E.2d 407 (1984).

Employer may challenge, in declaratory judgment proceeding the constitutionality of warrant authorizing inspection of the employer's manufacturing facility to determine whether the facility is being operated in compliance with the occupational safety and health laws (§ 40.1-1 et seq.). Mosher Steel-Virginia v. Teig, 229 Va. 95, 327 S.E.2d 87 (1985).

No justiciable controversy existed where parties not named as defendants. — In an action for declaratory judgment by a motorist against her automobile insurer and the automobile insurer for owner of another automobile involved in an accident, no justiciable controversy existed because the motorist did not name the owner and driver of the other automobile as defendants. Erie Ins. Group v. Hughes, 240 Va. 165, 393 S.E.2d 210 (1990).

Declaratory judgment proceeding may not be maintained against a party with whom there is no controversy in order to resolve a controversy existing with one not a party to the proceeding. Treacy v. Smithfield Foods, Inc., 256 Va. 97, 500 S.E.2d 503 (1998).

Declaratory judgment inappropriate where disputed issue could be determined in future litigation. — Declaratory judgment was inappropriate in case of worker injured by actions of co-worker, because case did not involve a determination of rights but only a disputed issue to be determined in future litigation between the parties, namely, whether the injuries arose out of and in the course of the injured worker's employment. USAA Cas. Ins. Co. v. Randolph, 255 Va. 342, 497 S.E.2d 744 (1998).

II. DECISIONS UNDER PRIOR LAW.

A. General Consideration.

Editor's note. — The cases cited below were decided under corresponding provisions of former law. The terms "this article" and "this section," as used below, refer to former provisions.

Constitutionality. — The declaratory judgments law, as embraced in this chapter, is constitutional. Patterson v. Patterson, 144 Va. 113, 131 S.E. 217 (1926); Carr v. Union Church, 186 Va. 411, 42 S.E.2d 840 (1947).

Declaratory judgments are creatures of statutes. D.D. Jones Transf. & Whse. Co. v. Commonwealth ex rel. SCC, 174 Va. 184, 5 S.E.2d 628 (1939).

An action for declaratory judgment is statutory. Sood v. Advanced Computer Techniques Corp., 308 F. Supp. 239 (E.D. Va. 1969).

The Supreme Court has no original jurisdiction of a proceeding for a declaratory judgment. D.D. Jones Transf. & Whse. Co. v. Commonwealth ex rel. SCC, 174 Va. 184, 5 S.E.2d 628 (1939); Portsmouth Restaurant Ass'n v. Hotel & Restaurant Employees Alliance, Local 807, 183 Va. 757, 33 S.E.2d 218 (1945).

Purpose of the declaratory judgment act is to afford relief from the uncertainty and insecurity attendant upon controversies over legal rights, without requiring one of the parties interested so to invade the rights asserted by the other as to entitle him to maintain an ordinary action therefor. Criterion Ins. Co. v. Grange Mut. Cas. Co., 210 Va. 446, 171 S.E.2d 669 (1970).

The intent of the declaratory judgment statutes is not to give parties greater rights than those which they previously possessed, but to permit the declaration of those rights before they mature. In other words, the intent of the act is to have courts render declaratory judgments which may guide parties in their future conduct in relation to each other, thereby relieving them from the risk of taking undirected action incident to their rights, which action, without direction, would jeopardize their interests. This is with a view rather to avoid litigation than in aid of it. Liberty Mut. Ins. Co. v. Bishop, 211 Va. 414, 177 S.E.2d 519 (1970).

Preventive relief is moving purpose. — The act does not require one to wait until a right has been violated to seek judicial relief. Preventive relief is the moving purpose. Portsmouth Restaurant Ass'n v. Hotel & Restaurant Employees Alliance, Local 807, 183 Va. 757, 33 S.E.2d 218 (1945).

Declaratory judgments are intended to supplement rather than to supersede ordinary causes of action and to relieve litigants of the common-law rule that no declaration of rights may be judicially adjudged until a right has been violated. American Nat'l Bank & Trust Co. v. Kushner, 162 Va. 378, 174 S.E. 777 (1934).

Declaratory judgments are intended to supplement rather than to supersede ordinary causes of action. Preventive relief is the moving purpose. Liberty Mut. Ins. Co. v. Bishop, 211 Va. 414, 177 S.E.2d 519 (1970).

Effect of the declaratory judgment act, as embraced in this and the succeeding sections of this article, is to increase the usefulness of the courts and remove doubt or uncertainty as to the final result of legal controversies, by empowering the courts to enter declaratory judgments and decrees touching the rights of the parties in such cases. Patterson v. Patterson, 144 Va. 113, 131 S.E. 217 (1926); Winborne v. Doyle, 190 Va. 867, 59 S.E.2d 90 (1950).

Customary processes of court are preferred. — In common cases where a right has matured or a wrong has been suffered, customary processes of the court, where they are ample and adequate, should be adopted, rather than a petition for a declaratory judgment. American Nat'l Bank & Trust Co. v. Kushner, 162 Va. 378, 174 S.E. 777 (1934); Williams v. Southern Bank, 203 Va. 657, 125 S.E.2d 803 (1962).

The declaratory judgment act is remedial and is to be liberally interpreted and administered. Yukon Pocahontas Coal Co. v. Ratliff, 175 Va. 366, 8 S.E.2d 303 (1940); Portsmouth Restaurant Ass'n v. Hotel & Restaurant Employees Alliance, Local 807, 183 Va. 757, 33

S.E.2d 218 (1945); Dean v. Paolicelli, 194 Va. 219, 72 S.E.2d 506 (1952).

Justiciable interest must be present. — In order to entitle any person to maintain an action in court it must be shown that he has a justiciable interest in the subject matter in litigation; either in his own right or in a representative capacity. Lynchburg Traffic Bureau v. Norfolk & W. Ry., 207 Va. 107, 147 S.E.2d 744 (1966).

Preventing multiplicity of suits. — The fact that multiplicity of actions may be avoided if a declaratory judgment be granted is not always a ground for assuming jurisdiction. There must be some real necessity for the exercise of jurisdiction on such ground. It must be made to appear that there is no adequate remedy at law as practical and effective to attain the ends of justice as may be accomplished in a court of equity and that the questions of law and fact involved are common to each of the several actions. Williams v. Southern Bank, 203 Va. 657, 125 S.E.2d 803 (1962); Liberty Mut. Ins. Co. v. Bishop, 211 Va. 414, 177 S.E.2d 519 (1970).

It makes no difference on which side of the court a case proceeds if it is brought properly under the declaratory judgments statutes. Carr v. Union Church, 186 Va. 411, 42 S.E.2d 840 (1947).

An action for declaratory judgment may proceed on law or chancery side of the court. Sood v. Advanced Computer Techniques Corp., 308 F. Supp. 239 (E.D. Va. 1969).

Exercise of jurisdiction is within discretion of trial court. — Upon a petition for a declaratory judgment, whether or not jurisdiction shall be taken is within the sound discretion of the trial court. Something more than an "actual controversy" is necessary. American Nat'l Bank & Trust Co. v. Kushner, 162 Va. 378, 174 S.E. 777 (1934); D.D. Jones Transf. & Whse. Co. v. Commonwealth ex rel. SCC, 174 Va. 184, 5 S.E.2d 628 (1939); Andrews v. Universal Moulded Prods. Corp., 189 Va. 527, 53 S.E.2d 837 (1949).

Whether or not jurisdiction shall be taken is within the sound discretion of the trial court. Something more than an "actual controversy" is necessary. In common cases where a right has matured or a wrong has been suffered, customary processes of the court, where they are ample and adequate, should be adopted. Liberty Mut. Ins. Co. v. Bishop, 211 Va. 414, 177 S.E.2d 519 (1970).

The power to make a declaratory judgment is a discretionary one and must be exercised with care and caution. It will not, as a rule, be exercised where some other mode of proceeding is provided. Liberty Mut. Ins. Co. v. Bishop, 211 Va. 414, 177 S.E.2d 519 (1970).

Rule is permissive, not mandatory. Commonwealth ex rel. Art Comm'n v. Silvette, 215 Va. 596, 212 S.E.2d 261 (1975).

Courts not to render advisory opinions. — The act providing for declaratory judgments, contemplates that the parties to the proceeding shall be adversely interested in the matter as to which the declaratory judgment is sought and their relation thereto such that a judgment or decree will operate as res judicata as to them. It authorizes the entry of such judgment before the right is violated, and even though no consequential relief is or could be asked for or granted. It does not, however, confer upon the courts the power to render judicial decisions which are advisory only. Chick v. McBain, 157 Va. 60, 160 S.E. 214 (1931).

The courts are not constituted, and the declaratory judgment statute was not intended to vest them with authority, to render advisory opinions, to decide moot questions or to answer inquiries which are merely speculative. City of Fairfax v. Shanklin, 205 Va. 227, 135 S.E.2d 773 (1964); Virginia Historic Landmarks Comm'n v. Board of Supvrs., 217 Va. 468, 230 S.E.2d 449 (1976).

Consequential or incidental relief may be obtained in an action in which a declaratory judgment is sought. Winborne v. Doyle, 190 Va. 867, 59 S.E.2d 90 (1950); Dean v. Paolicelli, 194 Va. 219, 72 S.E.2d 506 (1952).

But failure to seek incidental relief does not bar enforcement of rights in other proceedings. — The failure to seek incidental relief in a suit for a declaratory judgment does not constitute a bar to other proceedings to enforce the rights determined by the judgment, whether such other proceeding is by petition filed in that cause or in a separate and independent action. Winborne v. Doyle, 190 Va. 867, 59 S.E.2d 90 (1950).

Question determinable in either declaratory judgment proceeding or another pending proceeding. — Where a declaratory judgment proceeding and another pending proceeding in which relief is sought involve the identical question, the court may decide the issue in either proceeding, and is under no compulsion to do so in the declaratory judgment proceeding rather than in the other. And it having been determined that the matter can be decided in the other proceeding, the declaratory judgment proceeding serves no further purpose, and may be dismissed. Andrews v. Universal Moulded Prods. Corp., 189 Va. 527, 53 S.E.2d 837 (1949).

Exhaustion of administrative remedies required. — When a landowner claims a zoning ordinance is invalid as applied to his specific property, he must exhaust adequate and available administrative remedies before proceeding by declaratory judgment to make a direct judicial attack on the applied constitutionality of the ordinance. Gayton Triangle

Land Co. v. Board of Supvrs., 216 Va. 764, 222 S.E.2d 570 (1976).

But not where useless. — Landowner challenging the validity of a zoning ordinance as applied to his property need not apply for a variance before bringing his declaratory judgment action if the challenged restrictions or obligations could not be remedied by variance. Gayton Triangle Land Co. v. Board of Supvrs., 216 Va. 764, 222 S.E.2d 570 (1976).

Not proper where judgment as to disputed fact is determinative of issues. — Where a declaratory judgment as to a disputed fact would be determinative of issues, rather than a construction of definite stated rights, status, and other relations, commonly expressed in written instruments, the case is not one for declaratory judgment. Williams v. Southern Bank, 203 Va. 657, 125 S.E.2d 803 (1962); Liberty Mut. Ins. Co. v. Bishop, 211 Va. 414, 177 S.E.2d 519 (1970).

Determining ownership of land claimed by State. — A declaratory judgment proceeding is an adequate means for determining the ownership of land which the State Highway Commissioner (now Commonwealth Transportation Commissioner) believes to be land of the State. Gilliam v. Harris, 203 Va. 316, 124 S.E.2d 188 (1962).

Res judicata. — Under this section and § 8.01-186, where a prior action was instituted to construe a will and to have the court determine who was entitled to the rents, issues, and profits from a particular house after a particular event, no other issue being presented, the question of the rental value of the house was not barred from consideration in a subsequent action under the doctrine of res judicata. Winborne v. Doyle, 190 Va. 867, 59 S.E.2d 90 (1950).

Particular instances. — For case determining rights under conflicting licenses for brush blinds, see Brumley v. Grimstead, 170 Va. 340, 196 S.E. 668 (1938).

For case as to sufficiency of the bill to state a case for a declaratory judgment concerning the right to an interpretation of an arbitration award and order of the War Labor Board, see Portsmouth Restaurant Ass'n v. Hotel & Restaurant Employees Alliance, Local 807, 183 Va. 757, 33 S.E.2d 218 (1945).

A proceeding to determine whether the petitioners had the right to employ in their mercantile establishment a registered optometrist under the provisions of former Title 54, Chapter 14, of the Code presented an "antagonistic assertion and denial of right" and was proper case for a declaratory judgment. Cowardin v. Burrage, 195 Va. 54, 77 S.E.2d 428 (1953).

Petitioners as users of a district sewerage system, had no such proprietary interest in the system under the Sanitary District Law, §§ 21-112.22 through 21-140.3, as to entitle them to challenge the action of the county board of supervisors in increasing rates in order to secure funds to build a treatment plant. Abbott v. Board of Supvrs., 200 Va. 820, 108 S.E.2d 243 (1959).

It may well be that after a decision is made by the board of zoning appeals which aggrieves a taxpayer, the elements would then exist to support a declaratory judgment action in which the authority of the board could be challenged. But that is not to say that such elements exist where the board has not made any decision. City of Fairfax v. Shanklin, 205 Va. 227, 135 S.E.2d 773 (1964).

Since there was no specific case regarding apartment usage within the city involved, plaintiff's case had to depend, of necessity, upon future or speculative facts, that is to say, that a special use permit might, someday, be granted by the board which might aggrieve the plaintiff. Under these circumstances, the motion for declaratory judgment, upon its face, merely sought an advisory opinion, or a decision upon a moot question, or an answer to a speculative inquiry. City of Fairfax v. Shanklin, 205 Va. 227, 135 S.E.2d 773 (1964).

When a justiciable controversy exists between two insurance companies as to their obligations under the terms of their respective policies, a declaratory judgment proceeding may be maintained by one of the companies against the other. Criterion Ins. Co. v. Grange Mut. Cas. Co., 210 Va. 446, 171 S.E.2d 669 (1970); Liberty Mut. Ins. Co. v. Bishop, 211 Va. 414, 177 S.E.2d 519 (1970).

Where the plaintiffs sought, in essence, the recovery of a money judgment, a sum certain, and various claims and rights asserted had all accrued and matured, and the wrongs had been suffered, when their petition for a declaratory judgment was filed, the trial court erred in hearing the action pursuant to the declaratory judgment statutes. Liberty Mut. Ins. Co. v. Bishop, 211 Va. 414, 177 S.E.2d 519 (1970).

If an ordinance is unreasonable and unconstitutional in its entirety and the result of such unreasonableness is to confiscate plaintiff's property or to discriminate against it, then an action for a declaratory judgment lies. Board of Supvrs. v. Rowe, 216 Va. 128, 216 S.E.2d 199 (1975).

Officer may mandamus himself. — Under this article the Auditor of Public Accounts, as an individual, may prosecute a writ of mandamus against himself as Auditor. Moore v. Moore, 147 Va. 460, 137 S.E. 488 (1927).

B. Actual Controversy.

Purpose of words "actual controversy" and "actual antagonistic assertion and denial of right." — In this and the following sections of this chapter the words "actual controversy" and "actual antagonistic assertion and denial of right" were intended to prevent the consideration of moot questions by the court, and not to deprive the courts of jurisdiction to enter a declaratory decree where there is actual antagonistic assertion and denial of right. Patterson v. Patterson, 144 Va. 113, 131 S.E. 217 (1921).

Actual controversy test. — The test of the applicability of this article is the determination of the existence of an actual controversy. The manifest intention of the legislature was to provide for a speedy determination of actual controversies between citizens, and to prune, as far as is consonant with right and justice, the dead wood attached to the common-law rule of "injury before action" and a multitude of suits to establish a single right. Neal v. State-Planters Bank & Trust Co., 166 Va. 158, 184 S.E. 203 (1936). See Yukon Pocahontas Coal Co. v. Ratliff, 175 Va. 366, 8 S.E.2d 303 (1940); Liberty Mut. Ins. Co. v. Bishop, 211 Va. 414, 177 S.E.2d 519 (1970).

There must be "actual controversy" based on "actual antagonistic assertion and denial of right." — It must appear that there is an "actual controversy" existing between the parties, based upon an "actual antagonistic assertion and denial of right," before the application for declaratory judgment can be entertained and an adjudication made. City of Fairfax v. Shanklin, 205 Va. 227, 135 S.E.2d 773 (1964); Lynchburg Traffic Bureau v. Norfolk & W. Ry., 207 Va. 107, 147 S.E.2d 744 (1966); Virginia Historic Landmarks Comm'n v. Board of Supvrs., 217 Va. 468, 230 S.E.2d 449 (1976).

Controversy is not created by taking a position and then challenging the government to dispute it. City of Fairfax v. Shanklin, 205 Va. 227, 135 S.E.2d 773 (1964).

Controversy must be one that is justiciable, that is, where specific adverse claims, based upon present rather than future or speculative facts, are ripe for judicial adjustment. City of Fairfax v. Shanklin, 205 Va. 227, 135 S.E.2d 773 (1964); Virginia Historic Landmarks Comm'n v. Board of Supvrs., 217 Va. 468, 230 S.E.2d 449 (1976).

To invoke the jurisdiction of the court under this section, the controversy must be one that is justiciable; that is, where specific adverse claims based upon present rather than future or speculative facts are ripe for judicial adjustment. Board of Supvrs. v. Rowe, 216 Va. 128, 216 S.E.2d 199 (1975).

Before an action may be maintained under the act there must be a justiciable controversy, for the rendering of advisory opinions is not a part of the function of the judiciary in Virginia. Criterion Ins. Co. v. Grange Mut. Cas. Co., 210 Va. 446, 171 S.E.2d 669 (1970); Liberty Mut. Ins. Co. v. Bishop, 211 Va. 414, 177 S.E.2d 519 (1970).

Controversy may be shown by pleading or evidence. — Whether or not there is a controversy is a question of fact, which may be shown by the pleadings or by the evidence. Yukon Pocahontas Coal Co. v. Ratliff, 175 Va. 366, 8 S.E.2d 303 (1940).

Allegations showing actual controversy. — Where complaints alleged that defendants were dividing the surface of a portion of the land claimed under the deed, erecting and permitting the erection of buildings and other improvements thereon that were inconsistent with mining purposes, and destroying the rights, privileges and easements of complainants, and excluding them from the use of the surface of the land, in violation of the rights, privileges and easements expressly and impliedly conveyed to them by the deed, and that they had no plain, adequate and complete relief at law, such allegations showed that there was an actual controversy and an actual antagonistic assertion or denial of rights between the parties. Yukon Pocahontas Coal Co. v. Ratliff, 175 Va. 366, 8 S.E.2d 303 (1940).

When a property owner alleges that a zoning ordinance creates discriminatory, arbitrary and capricious classifications bearing no substantial relation to the public health, safety or welfare, or that a zoning ordinance imposes land use restrictions or affirmative land use obligations so unreasonable as to constitute a "taking" of property without compensation or due process of law or that a zoning ordinance is otherwise unconstitutional and that he has suffered damage to his property located in a district affected by such ordinance, he has stated a case of actual controversy within the meaning of this section and one that is ripe for judicial adjustment. Board of Supvrs. v. Rowe, 216 Va. 128, 216 S.E.2d 199 (1975).

§ 8.01-185. Venue. — The venue of actions seeking declarations of right with or without consequential relief shall be determined in accordance with provisions of Chapter 5 (§ 8.01-257 et seq.) of this title. (Code 1950, § 8-579; 1954, c. 333; 1977, c. 617.)

REVISERS' NOTE

The special venue provision of former § 8-579 has been changed and venue will be determined in accordance with the general venue provisions of chapter 5, §§ 8.01-257 ff.

Former § 8-580 (Procedure) has been deleted as unnecessary.

---

§ 8.01-186. Further relief. — Further relief based on a declaratory judgment order or decree may be granted whenever necessary or proper. The application shall be by motion to a court having jurisdiction to grant the relief. If the application is deemed sufficient the court shall, on reasonable notice, require an adverse party whose rights have been adjudicated by the declaration of right to show cause why further relief should not be granted forthwith. (Code 1950, § 8-581; 1977, c. 617.)

I. Decisions Under Current Law.
II. Decisions Under Prior Law.

I. DECISIONS UNDER CURRENT LAW.

The phrase "further relief" in this section does not authorize a court to award attorney's fees to a litigant. Russell County Dep't of Social Servs. v. Quinn, 259 Va. 139, 523 S.E.2d 492 (2000).

II. DECISIONS UNDER PRIOR LAW.

Editor's note. — The cases cited below were decided under corresponding provisions of former law. The term "this section," as used below, refers to former provisions.

The provisions of this section clearly contemplate further action to enforce the rights determined by a declaratory judgment. Winborne v. Doyle, 190 Va. 867, 59 S.E.2d 90 (1950).

The relief contemplated and provided for by § 8.01-184 is not limited to a bare declaration of rights. In a proper case under that section and this section, such consequential, other, and additional relief as is justified by the pleadings, and by the private or public rights and interests involved, may be awarded. Dean v. Paolicelli, 194 Va. 219, 72 S.E.2d 506 (1952).

Remedy not exclusive. — The remedy for enforcement of the rights determined by the declaratory judgment prescribed by this section is not exclusive. Such a proceeding is intended to supplement rather than supersede ordinary causes of action. Winborne v. Doyle, 190 Va. 867, 59 S.E.2d 90 (1950).

Illustrative case. — For case as to the sufficiency of a bill for declaratory judgment and further relief where the plaintiff sought the cancellation or annulment of an easement, see First Nat'l Trust & Sav. Bank v. Raphael, 201 Va. 718, 113 S.E.2d 683 (1960).

§ 8.01-187. Commissioners to determine compensation for property taken or damaged. — Whenever it is determined in a declaratory judgment proceeding that a person's property has been taken or damaged within the meaning of Article I, Section 11 of the Constitution of Virginia and compensation has not been paid or any action taken to determine the compensation within sixty days following the entry of such judgment order or decree, the court which entered the order or decree may, upon motion of such person after reasonable notice to the adverse party, enter a further order appointing commissioners to determine the compensation. The appointment of commissioners and all proceedings thereafter shall be governed by the procedure prescribed for the condemning authority. (Code 1950, § 8-581.1; 1968, c. 782; 1971, Ex. Sess., c. 1; 1977, c. 617.)

Cross references. — As to reimbursement of the plaintiff for costs, expenses, etc., incurred in a proceeding under this section, see § 25-251.

I. Decisions Under Current Law.
  A. General Consideration.
  B. Sovereign Immunity.
II. Decisions Under Prior Law.

I. DECISIONS UNDER CURRENT LAW.

A. General Consideration.

This section is a remedial statute. It disturbs no vested rights and creates no new obligation. It merely supplies another remedy to enforce existing rights. See Chaffinch v. C & P Tel. Co., 227 Va. 68, 313 S.E.2d 376 (1984).

Statutory remedy does not preempt common-law remedies against a nonsovereign entity vested with the power of eminent domain unless the statute, expressly or by necessary implication, so provides. Chaffinch v. C & P Tel. Co., 227 Va. 68, 313 S.E.2d 376 (1984).

When a state provides an adequate procedure for obtaining just compensation, a property owner cannot claim a violation of the federal provision until it has used the state procedure and been denied just compensation. Pasquotank Action Council, Inc. v. City of Va. Beach, 909 F. Supp. 376 (E.D. Va. 1995).

Applied in Northern Va. Law Sch., Inc. v. City of Alexandria, 680 F. Supp. 222 (E.D. Va. 1988).

B. Sovereign Immunity.

Waiver of sovereign immunity from inverse condemnation claims. — The just-compensation clause of Va. Const., Art. I, § 11, constitutes a waiver of sovereign immunity from inverse condemnation claims, and this section creates a statutory mechanism for the enforcement of such claims. Chaffinch v. C & P Tel. Co., 227 Va. 68, 313 S.E.2d 376 (1984).

Public service companies have never enjoyed immunity from liability for damaging private property, the power of eminent domain entrusted to them by § 56-464 confers none, and there is nothing in the language of this section or the annals of legislative history which reflects legislative intent to immunize them from actions at common law. Chaffinch v. C & P Tel. Co., 227 Va. 68, 313 S.E.2d 376 (1984).

II. DECISIONS UNDER PRIOR LAW.

Editor's note. — The cases cited below were decided under corresponding provisions of former law. The term "this section," as used below, refers to former provisions.

This section is a remedial statute. It disturbs no vested rights and creates no new obligation. It merely supplies another remedy to enforce existing rights. Stroobants v. Fugate, 209 Va. 275, 163 S.E.2d 192 (1968).

Mandamus will not lie to compel the Highway Commissioner (now Commonwealth Transportation Commissioner) to institute condemnation proceedings in the proper court to ascertain what compensation is due petitioners for the damages which, they allege, have been done to their property by the acts of the respondent, since, under this section, the cause of action asserted by the petitioners can be resolved in a declaratory judgment proceeding in a lower court. Stroobants v. Fugate, 209 Va. 275, 163 S.E.2d 192 (1968).

Section applicable though not in force when cause of action arose. — While this section was not in force when petitioners' cause of action arose, it became effective on June 28, 1968, and they are entitled to avail themselves of the procedure outlined therein. Stroobants v. Fugate, 209 Va. 275, 163 S.E.2d 192 (1968).

§ 8.01-188. Jury trial. — When a declaration of right or the granting of further relief based thereon shall involve the determination of issues of fact triable by a jury, such issues may be submitted to a jury in the form of interrogatories, with proper instructions by the court, whether a general verdict be required or not. (Code 1950, § 8-582; 1977, c. 617.)

Law Review. — For an article, "Civil Practice and Procedure," see 32 U. Rich. L. Rev. 1009 (1998).

I. DECISIONS UNDER CURRENT LAW.

This section addresses only the form in which an issue of fact may be submitted to a jury, and does not provide a party in a declaratory judgment suit a separate right to a binding jury verdict. Angstadt v. Atlantic Mut. Ins. Co., 254 Va. 286, 492 S.E.2d 118 (1997).

§ 8.01-189. Injunction. — The pendency of any action at law or suit in equity brought merely to obtain a declaration of rights or a determination of a question of construction shall not be sufficient grounds for the granting of any injunction. (Code 1950, § 8-583; 1977, c. 617.)

I. DECISIONS UNDER PRIOR LAW.

Editor's note. — The cases cited below were decided under corresponding provisions of former law. The term "this section," as used below, refers to former provisions.

Suit held pure bill for injunction. — A suit for declaratory judgment and injunction against threatened actions at law was really a pure bill for an injunction. It asked the chancellor to try a disputed question of fact as a determinative issue, and to substitute a suit in equity for several actions at law, although it alleged that there was an absolute defense in each action, pleadable at law. A court of equity will not enjoin the prosecution of an action at law when the defendant can make a full and adequate defense in such action. A suit at law cannot be enjoined and the litigation transferred to the equity forum merely on the assertion of defenses that are pleadable at law. An action at law will not be enjoined except where a court of chancery may afford a more adequate and perfect remedy. Williams v. Southern Bank, 203 Va. 657, 125 S.E.2d 803 (1962).

Demurrer on ground that prayer for injunction violated section not good. — A bill for divorce, by a husband against his wife, asked for a construction of a separation contract between the husband and wife and a deed of trust executed in pursuance of the contract, and also asked for an injunction against the enforcement of the contract and the deed of trust. The wife demurred on the ground that the prayer for the injunction was in violation of this section, which provides that the pendency of an action or suit to obtain a declaration of rights or a determination of a question of construction should not be sufficient grounds for the granting of an injunction. It was held that this was not a good ground of demurrer. Gloth v. Gloth, 154 Va. 511, 153 S.E. 879 (1930).

§ 8.01-190. Costs. — The costs, or such part thereof as the court may deem proper and just in view of the particular circumstances of the case, may be awarded to any party. (Code 1950, § 8-584; 1977, c. 617.)

§ 8.01-191. Construction of article. — This article is declared to be remedial. Its purpose is to afford relief from the uncertainty and insecurity attendant upon controversies over legal rights, without requiring one of the parties interested so to invade the rights asserted by the other as to entitle him to maintain an ordinary action therefor. It is to be liberally interpreted and administered with a view to making the courts more serviceable to the people. (Code 1950, § 8-585; 1977, c. 617.)

Law Review. — For comment on challenging rezoning in Virginia, see 15 U. Rich. L. Rev. 423 (1981).

I. Decisions Under Current Law.
II. Decisions Under Prior Law.

I. DECISIONS UNDER CURRENT LAW.

This section and § 8.01-184 are to be liberally interpreted and administered with a view to making the courts more serviceable to the people. Board of Supvrs. v. Southland Corp., 224 Va. 514, 297 S.E.2d 718 (1982).

Trial court incorrectly held that declaratory judgment was not available to construe provision of written lease to determine whether continued occupancy of certain premises would subject lessee to liability for continuing damages, and his employees and customers to criminal liability for trespass; lessee was entitled to declaratory judgment action given unavailability of any remedy by customary processes and liberal construction of this section. Hop-In Food Stores, Inc. v. Serv-N-Save, Inc., 237 Va. 206, 375 S.E.2d 753 (1989).

No justiciable controversy existed where parties not named as defendants. — In an action for declaratory judgment by a motorist against her automobile insurer and the automobile insurer for owner of another automobile involved in an accident, no justiciable controversy existed because the motorist did not name the owner and driver of the other automobile as defendants. Erie Ins. Group v. Hughes, 240 Va. 165, 393 S.E.2d 210 (1990).

Award of attorney's fees not authorized. — Although the plain language in this section requires that the courts interpret and administer the Declaratory Judgment Act with a view to making the courts more serviceable to the people, this does not authorize a court to make an award of attorney's fees. Russell County Dep't of Social Servs. v. Quinn, 259 Va. 139, 523 S.E.2d 492 (2000).

Applied in Board of Supvrs. v. Fralin &

Waldron, Inc., 222 Va. 218, 278 S.E.2d 859 (1981); Blodinger v. Broker's Title, Inc., 224 Va. 201, 294 S.E.2d 876 (1982); Reisen v. Aetna Life & Cas. Co., 225 Va. 327, 302 S.E.2d 529 (1983); Cupp v. Board of Supvrs., 227 Va. 580, 318 S.E.2d 407 (1984).

II. DECISIONS UNDER PRIOR LAW.

Editor's note. — The cases cited below were decided under corresponding provisions of former law. The terms "this section" and "this article," as used below, refer to former provisions.

Intent of this article is not to give parties greater rights than those which they previously possessed, but to permit the declaration of those rights before they mature. Fairfield Dev. Corp. v. City of Virginia Beach, 211 Va. 715, 180 S.E.2d 533 (1971).

The intent of this article is to have courts render declaratory judgments which may guide parties in their future conduct in relation to each other, thereby relieving them from the risk of taking undirected action incident to their rights, which action, without direction, would jeopardize their interests. This is with a view rather to avoid litigation than in aid of it. Fairfield Dev. Corp. v. City of Virginia Beach, 211 Va. 715, 180 S.E.2d 533 (1971).

This article is remedial and is to be liberally construed and administered. Criterion Ins. Co. v. Grange Mut. Cas. Co., 210 Va. 446, 171 S.E.2d 669 (1970).

The construction of this article, while liberal, must be reasonable and confined within definite limits. Declaratory judgments are not to be used as instruments of procedural fencing, either to secure delay or to choose a forum. Williams v. Southern Bank, 203 Va. 657, 125 S.E.2d 803 (1962).

The declaratory judgment acts do not create or change any substantive rights, or bring into being or modify any relationships, or alter the character of controversies, which are the subject of judicial power. Their construction, while liberal, must be reasonable and confined within definite limits. They are not to be used as instruments of procedural fencing, either to secure delay or to choose a forum. Liberty Mut. Ins. Co. v. Bishop, 211 Va. 414, 177 S.E.2d 519 (1970).

Power to make declaratory judgment is discretionary. — While the courts have, in obedience to this section, given a liberal interpretation to the Declaratory Judgment Act, they have nevertheless recognized that the power to make a declaratory judgment is a discretionary one and must be exercised with care and caution. Fairfield Dev. Corp. v. City of Virginia Beach, 211 Va. 715, 180 S.E.2d 533 (1971).

And it will not be exercised where some other mode of proceeding is provided. Hence, where the petitioners, in essence, were seeking a money judgment for a sum certain, and the court had nothing to determine that would guide the parties in their future conduct in relation to each other, but each petitioner had paid the fee, and the only issue to be determined was whether it was entitled to have the fees refunded, their remedy was by motion for judgment and not by petition for declaratory judgment. Fairfield Dev. Corp. v. City of Virginia Beach, 211 Va. 715, 180 S.E.2d 533 (1971).

ARTICLE 18.

Recovery of Claims Against the Commonwealth of Virginia.

§ 8.01-192. How claims to be prosecuted. — When the Comptroller or other authorized person shall disallow, either in whole or in part, any such claim against the Commonwealth as is provided for by §§ 2.1-223.1, 2.1-223.3 or 8.01-605 at which time a right of action under this section shall be deemed to accrue, the person presenting such claim may petition an appropriate circuit court for redress. (Code 1950, § 8-752; 1966, c. 452; 1977, c. 617.)

REVISERS' NOTE

The requirement of former § 8-752 that a claim against the State be brought only in the Circuit Court of the city of Richmond has been changed. Section 8.01-192 permits such a claim to be brought in "an appropriate circuit court." The sentence beginning with "and when a person has any other claim..." in former § 8-752 has been deleted. The intent of the statute is confined to only "pecuniary claims" and thus would not include "any other claims" against the Commonwealth.

Law Review. — For survey of Virginia law on torts for the year 1972-1973, see 59 Va. L. Rev. 1590 (1973). For survey of Virginia administrative law for the year 1973-1974, see 60 Va. L. Rev. 1446 (1974). For a re-examination of sovereign tort immunity in Virginia, see 15 U. Rich. L. Rev. 247 (1981). For note on the abrogation of sovereign immunity in Virginia: The Virginia Tort Claims Act, see 7 Geo. Mason L. Rev. 291 (1984).

I. Decisions Under Current Law.
II. Decisions Under Prior Law.
   A. General Consideration.
   B. Actions Based Upon Exercise of Eminent Domain Power.

I. DECISIONS UNDER CURRENT LAW.

There is no reason to vitiate the right of the state not to be subject to suit in her own courts by a broad and unwarranted interpretation of the legislative intent behind the limited waiver of sovereign immunity in this section. Commonwealth v. Luzik, 259 Va. 198, 524 S.E.2d 871 (2000).

For discussion of doctrine of sovereign immunity, see Hinchey v. Ogden, 226 Va. 234, 307 S.E.2d 891 (1983).

Immunity from suit in federal court. — The Commonwealth, never having waived her immunity under U.S. Const., Amend. XI, is not amenable to a suit for damages in federal court, even when the basis for such suit is a claimed violation of 42 U.S.C. § 1983. Only officials of the Commonwealth may be enjoined from acts that violate the Constitution. Croatan Books, Inc. v. Virginia, 574 F. Supp. 880 (E.D. Va. 1983).

Eleventh Amendment immunity not waived. — Virginia has not waived its Eleventh Amendment immunity. This section, which generally governs recovery of claims against the State, waives sovereign immunity in actions brought in Virginia courts. But it does not express the clear legislative intent necessary to constitute a waiver of Eleventh Amendment immunity. McConnell v. Adams, 829 F.2d 1319 (4th Cir. 1987), cert. denied, 486 U.S. 1006, 108 S. Ct. 1731, 100 L. Ed. 2d 195 (1988).

Nothing in Virginia cases interpreting this section suggests that it should be applied in circumstances other than in claims properly instituted under this section and the scheme provided for pursuing such claims in §§ 8.01-193 to 8.01-195. Commonwealth v. Luzik, 259 Va. 198, 524 S.E.2d 871 (2000).

Even if employee's claim for back wages was subject to sovereign immunity under this section, complainant's suit would still not satisfy the requirements for seeking payment of a contract debt from the state as prescribed by this section, where the suit was not brought in the style of a contract claim or in the manner prescribed for such claims by the statutory scheme. Commonwealth v. Luzik, 259 Va. 198, 524 S.E.2d 871 (2000).

Waiver of immunity in state court does not necessarily operate as a consent to be sued in federal court. Jacobs v. College of William & Mary, 495 F. Supp. 183 (E.D. Va. 1980), aff'd, 661 F.2d 922 (4th Cir.), cert. denied, 454 U.S. 1033, 102 S. Ct. 572, 70 L. Ed. 2d 477 (1981).

Clear legislative intent to waive immunity in federal courts not expressed in section. — In order for a waiver of sovereign immunity to be found effective as to actions brought in a federal court, as well as to actions brought in the state's own courts, a clear legislative intent to that effect must be found. A "clear legislative intent" has not been expressed to extend the provisions of this section, effectively waiving the bar of sovereign immunity, to actions brought in federal court. Jacobs v. College of William & Mary, 495 F. Supp. 183 (E.D. Va. 1980), aff'd, 661 F.2d 922 (4th Cir.), cert. denied, 454 U.S. 1033, 102 S. Ct. 572, 70 L. Ed. 2d 477 (1981).

Immunity from suit for unlawful application of former § 13.1-93. — In deciding whether a state has waived its constitutional protection under U.S. Const., Amend. XI, waiver will be found only where stated by the most express language or by such overwhelming implications from the text as will leave no room for any other reasonable construction. Because there has been no such clear manifestation, indeed, because there has been no manifestation at all, of intent to waive this immunity on the part of the Commonwealth, her immunity prevents her being haled into federal court to answer a claim it conspired to shut down a business by unlawfully applying former § 13.1-93 to revoke its corporate charter. Croatan Books, Inc. v. Virginia, 574 F. Supp. 880 (E.D. Va. 1983).

Sovereign immunity has no application to valid contract actions. — The doctrine of sovereign immunity has no application in actions based upon valid contracts entered into by duly authorized agents of the government. The sovereign is as liable for its contractual debt as any citizen would be, and that liability may be enforced by suit in the "appropriate circuit court" if proper and timely proceedings are taken. Wiecking v. Allied Medical Supply Corp., 239 Va. 548, 391 S.E.2d 258 (1990).

Injunctive relief as to future conduct of state officials. — The State's Eleventh Amendment immunity does not protect it from suits for injunctive relief governing its officials' future conduct. McConnell v. Adams, 829 F.2d 1319 (4th Cir. 1987), cert. denied, 486 U.S. 1006, 108 S. Ct. 1731, 100 L. Ed. 2d 195 (1988).

II. DECISIONS UNDER PRIOR LAW.

A. General Consideration.

Editor's note. — The cases cited below were decided under corresponding provisions of former law. The terms "this article" and "this section," as used below, refer to former provisions.

The State cannot be sued without its consent. Stuart v. Smith-Courtney Co., 123 Va. 231, 96 S.E. 241 (1918).

Even if a suit in form be against the state's officers and agents, yet if in effect it be against the State, it is not maintainable except by the state's permission. Sayers v. Bullar, 180 Va. 222, 22 S.E.2d 9 (1942); Eriksen v. Anderson, 195 Va. 655, 79 S.E.2d 597 (1954); Davis v. Marr, 200 Va. 479, 106 S.E.2d 722 (1959).

This section expressly gives such consent for suits upon certain claims. Stuart v. Smith-Courtney Co., 123 Va. 231, 96 S.E. 241 (1918).

Ever since 1778 all persons have enjoyed, by express statute, this right to sue the State. Parsons v. Commonwealth, 80 Va. 163 (1885).

The statute will be liberally construed. Green v. Marye, 112 Va. 352, 71 S.E. 555 (1911); Stuart v. Smith-Courtney Co., 123 Va. 231, 96 S.E. 241 (1918); Commonwealth v. Chilton Malting Co., 154 Va. 28, 152 S.E. 336 (1930).

When doctrine of sovereign immunity applies. — Where judgment would act directly against the state, and the state is the real party in interest, the doctrine of sovereign immunity applies regardless of the status of the named defendant. Medicenters of Am., Inc. v. Virginia, 373 F. Supp. 305 (E.D. Va. 1974).

Exclusivity of provisions. — This chapter provides the only cases and procedure in which actions may be maintained against the State. Sayers v. Bullar, 180 Va. 222, 22 S.E.2d 9 (1942); Eriksen v. Anderson, 195 Va. 655, 79 S.E.2d 597 (1954).

Procedure under this article is provided for in the three sections immediately following. Stuart v. Smith-Courtney Co., 123 Va. 231, 96 S.E. 241 (1918).

Applicable to pecuniary obligations based upon contracts. — If it is alleged that out of the exercise of governmental discretion there arises a pecuniary obligation of the State, based upon a contract, the Circuit Court of the City of Richmond is open for the determination of that issue. Stuart v. Smith-Courtney Co., 123 Va. 231, 96 S.E. 241 (1918).

The State will not be astute to escape inquiry into its liability for its alleged contracts, or to take advantage of technical defenses which are permissible to other litigants. Stuart v. Smith-Courtney Co., 123 Va. 231, 96 S.E. 241 (1918); Western State Hosp. v. Mackey, 151 Va. 495, 145 S.E. 419 (1928); Commonwealth v. Chilton Malting Co., 154 Va. 28, 152 S.E. 336 (1930).

Waiver of immunity in state courts does not necessarily operate as a consent to be sued in federal court. Medicenters of Am., Inc. v. Virginia, 373 F. Supp. 305 (E.D. Va. 1974).

A state has the power to waive sovereign immunity in state courts without affecting sovereign immunity in federal courts. Medicenters of Am., Inc. v. Virginia, 373 F. Supp. 305 (E.D. Va. 1974).

Clear legislative intent to waive immunity in federal courts not expressed in section. — In order for a waiver of sovereign immunity to be found effective as to actions brought in a federal court, as well as to actions brought in the state's own courts, a clear legislative intent to that effect must be found. A "clear legislative intent" has not been expressed to extend the provisions of this section, effectively waiving the bar of sovereign immunity, to actions brought in federal court. Medicenters of Am., Inc. v. Virginia, 373 F. Supp. 305 (E.D. Va. 1974).

The claims dealt with by this section are those which are payable out of the state treasury in pursuance of appropriations made by law. Hence jurisdiction over an action against a state-created tunnel district and commission to recover compensation for damage to property was not limited to the Circuit Court of the City of Richmond. Morris v. Elizabeth River Tunnel Dist., 203 Va. 196, 123 S.E.2d 398 (1962).

Proceedings based upon contracts will lie against the State and its agencies by authority of this statute. Stuart v. Smith-Courtney Co., 123 Va. 231, 96 S.E. 241 (1918); Commonwealth v. Chilton Malting Co., 154 Va. 28, 152 S.E. 336 (1930); Davis v. Marr, 200 Va. 479, 106 S.E.2d 722 (1959).

Whether the claims be liquidated or unliquidated. — Under this section the State may be sued for any debt or claim due, whether liquidated or unliquidated. Higginbotham v. Commonwealth, 66 Va. (25 Gratt.) 627 (1874), cited in Parsons v. Commonwealth, 80 Va. 163 (1885).

But actions based upon torts are not authorized against the State, or its governmental agencies, by this section. Stuart v. Smith-Courtney Co., 123 Va. 231, 96 S.E. 241 (1918); Commonwealth v. Chilton Malting Co.,

154 Va. 28, 152 S.E. 336 (1930); Sayers v. Bullar, 180 Va. 222, 22 S.E.2d 9 (1942); Eriksen v. Anderson, 195 Va. 655, 79 S.E.2d 597 (1954).

There is no statute in Virginia granting a right to sue the State for torts. The power to consent to suit for torts rests in the legislature and not in the judiciary. Elizabeth River Tunnel Dist. v. Beecher, 202 Va. 452, 117 S.E.2d 685 (1961).

The fact that the Elizabeth River Tunnel District Act provides that it may sue and be sued cannot be advanced as an assertion of state waiver of immunity or state consent to suit for torts. Waiver of immunity cannot be implied from general statutory language or by implication. Elizabeth River Tunnel Dist. v. Beecher, 202 Va. 452, 117 S.E.2d 685 (1961).

Damages may be recovered only from state officers personally, as a judgment against them in their official capacity would in essence be a judgment against the State of Virginia. Landman v. Royster, 354 F. Supp. 1302 (E.D. Va. 1973).

An action against state officers in their official capacity generally does not lie under 42 U.S.C. § 1983, since the State is not a "person" within the meaning of that statute. Landman v. Royster, 354 F. Supp. 1302 (E.D. Va. 1973).

Moreover, such a recovery is barred by the Eleventh Amendment, which prohibits suits against a state without its consent. Landman v. Royster, 354 F. Supp. 1302 (E.D. Va. 1973).

Action upon failure of Commonwealth to maintain highway crossover. — Where the owner of land abutting a limited access highway brought suit against the State Highway Commission (now Commonwealth Transportation Board) and the Commissioner to enjoin them from maintaining a "no left turn" sign at an opening in the median strip dividing the highway opposite complainant's property, and to recover damages, and complainant alleged that as part of the consideration for a strip of land conveyed by him for the highway the Commonwealth had agreed to construct and maintain permanently a crossover opposite his property so as to allow access to businesses located on his property from the far lane of the highway, the suit was essentially one against the Commonwealth asserting a claim for damages for breach of contract and as such cognizable only in the Circuit Court of the City of Richmond. Davis v. Marr, 200 Va. 479, 106 S.E.2d 722 (1959).

Suit to enjoin clerk of court. — This section has no application to a suit to enjoin a clerk of court from receiving the money on an insufficient application to purchase delinquent lands, and from making a deed to the purchaser. Baker v. Briggs, 99 Va. 360, 38 S.E. 277 (1901).

B. Actions Based Upon Exercise of Eminent Domain Power.

Action may be brought under Va. Const., Art. I, § 11, against agency having power of eminent domain. — A common-law action may be successfully maintained under Va. Const., Art. I, § 11, against an agency of the State clothed with the power of eminent domain to recover compensation for damage done to property by such agency in effecting a public improvement. Heldt v. Elizabeth River Tunnel Dist., 196 Va. 477, 84 S.E.2d 511 (1954); Morris v. Elizabeth River Tunnel Dist., 203 Va. 196, 123 S.E.2d 398 (1962).

Such action is not based on tort liability. — An action against an agency of the State to recover compensation for property taken or damaged for public uses is not an action predicated on tort liability or negligence. Rather it is based on Va. Const., Art. I, § 11. Morris v. Elizabeth River Tunnel Dist., 203 Va. 196, 123 S.E.2d 398 (1962).

Va. Const., Art. I, § 11 and eminent domain statutes inapplicable to tortious or unlawful acts. — Where petitioners sought to mandamus to compel Highway Commissioner (now Commonwealth Transportation Commissioner) to institute condemnation proceedings to fix damages caused by negligent operation of stone quarry by commissioner's agents contending that the proceeding was not one for a tort but one under the eminent domain statutes to compel compensation for property damage as required by Va. Const., Art. I, § 11, mandamus was refused since neither the Constitution nor the eminent domain statutes have application to tortious or unlawful acts. Eriksen v. Anderson, 195 Va. 655, 79 S.E.2d 597 (1954).

§ 8.01-193. Defense and hearing. — In every such case, the Comptroller shall be a defendant. He shall file an answer stating the objections to the claim. The cause shall be heard upon the petition, answer, and the evidence. (Code 1950, § 8-753; 1977, c. 617.)

I. DECISIONS UNDER PRIOR LAW.

Editor's note. — The case cited below was decided under corresponding provisions of former law. The term "this statute," as used below, refers to former provisions.

Dismissing petition as to State held not reversible error. — After a creditor filed his petition against the State and the Auditor of Public Accounts, praying judgment against the State for the amount of his debt, the court ex mero motu dismissed the petition against the State, but retained it against the Auditor and summoned him to answer and show cause why judgment should not be entered against the State for the amount claimed. It was held that, though the order dismissing the petition against the State may have been unnecessary, yet as it did not affect the petitioner's right or remedy, it was not reversible error. Parsons v. Commonwealth, 80 Va. 163 (1885).

§ 8.01-194. Jury may be impaneled; judgment.

— The court may, and on the motion of any party shall, cause a jury to be impaneled to ascertain any facts which are disputed, or the amount of any claim which is unliquidated. (Code 1950, § 8-754; 1977, c. 617.)

REVISERS' NOTE

Added to former § 8-754 is the language "on motion of either party the Court shall"; the last sentence has been deleted as unnecessary.

Former § 8-755 (Facts to be certified) has been deleted as unnecessary.

§ 8.01-195. No judgment to be paid without special appropriation.

— No judgment against the Commonwealth, unless otherwise expressly provided, shall be paid without a special appropriation therefor by law. (Code 1950, § 8-756; 1977, c. 617.)

REVISERS' NOTE

Former § 8-757 (When suits may not be brought) has been deleted. For statute of limitations, see § 8.01-255.

Former § 8-759 (In what court brought) has been deleted. For venue, see § 8.01-257 ff.

Law Review. — For a review of damages in medical malpractice in Virginia, see 33 U. Rich. L. Rev. 919 (1999).

I. DECISIONS UNDER PRIOR LAW.

Editor's note. — The cases cited below were decided under corresponding provisions of former law. The terms "this article" and "this section," as used below, refer to former provisions.

This section limits the effect of judgments or decrees which may be rendered against the Commonwealth in proceedings under this article. Stuart v. Smith-Courtney Co., 123 Va. 231, 96 S.E. 241 (1918); Davis v. Marr, 200 Va. 479, 106 S.E.2d 722 (1959).

Which merely establish the claims sued on. — Proceedings under this article, if they result in a judgment, simply establish the claim sued on. No execution can be levied thereunder to subject either the property of the State, its governmental agencies, or that of persons constituting such governmental agency. Stuart v. Smith-Courtney Co., 123 Va. 231, 96 S.E. 241 (1918).

And a special appropriation is necessary before payment of the demand established by a judgment or decree under this article. Stuart v. Smith-Courtney Co., 123 Va. 231, 96 S.E. 241 (1918).

But the legislature cannot be required to make the appropriation referred to in this section. Smith v. State Hwy. Comm'n, 131 Va. 571, 109 S.E. 312 (1921).

ARTICLE 18.1.

Tort Claims Against the Commonwealth of Virginia.

§ 8.01-195.1. Short title.

— This article shall be known and may be cited as the "Virginia Tort Claims Act." (1981, c. 449.)

Law Review. — For a re-examination of sovereign tort immunity in Virginia, see 15 U. Rich. L. Rev. 247 (1981). For note on the abrogation of sovereign immunity in Virginia: The Virginia Tort Claims Act, see 7 Geo. Mason L. Rev. 291 (1984). For comment on local liability for negligent inspection of buildings and equipment, see 18 U. Rich. L. Rev. 809 (1984).

I. DECISIONS UNDER CURRENT LAW.

For discussion of doctrine of sovereign immunity, see Hinchey v. Ogden, 226 Va. 234, 307 S.E.2d 891 (1983).

Article essentially waives state's sovereign immunity to the extent of $25,000 per claim. Al-Mustafa Irshad v. Spann, 543 F. Supp. 922 (E.D. Va. 1982).

Not a waiver of immunity under Eleventh Amendment. — This section waives sovereign immunity in some cases for tort liability provided the suit is filed in state court. Such waiver may not properly be construed as a waiver of immunity under the U.S. Const., Amend. XI to the same or similar suits in federal court. Reynolds v. Sheriff, City of Richmond, 574 F. Supp. 90 (E.D. Va. 1983).

The Virginia Tort Claims Act, while generally waiving sovereign immunity for tort claims filed in state courts, does not waive the state's Eleventh Amendment immunity. McConnell v. Adams, 829 F.2d 1319 (4th Cir. 1987), cert. denied, 486 U.S. 1006, 108 S. Ct. 1731, 100 L. Ed. 2d 195 (1988).

Doctrine of sovereign immunity has largely disappeared for tort claims accruing on or after July 1, 1982, since on that date, this article went into effect. Al-Mustafa Irshad v. Spann, 543 F. Supp. 922 (E.D. Va. 1982).

Doctrine of sovereign immunity is "alive and well" in Virginia. Though the Supreme Court has, over the years, discussed the doctrine in a variety of contexts and refined it for application to constantly shifting facts and circumstances, it has never seen fit to abolish it. Nor does the General Assembly want the doctrine abolished. Messina v. Burden, 228 Va. 301, 321 S.E.2d 657 (1984).

Not a waiver of immunity under Eleventh Amendment. — This section waives sovereign immunity in some cases for tort liability provided the suit is filed in state court. Such waiver may not properly be construed as a waiver of immunity under the U.S. Const., Amend. XI to the same or similar suits in federal court. Reynolds v. Sheriff, City of Richmond, 574 F. Supp. 90 (E.D. Va. 1983).

Not a waiver of immunity under Eleventh Amendment. — The Virginia Tort Claims Act, while generally waiving sovereign immunity for tort claims filed in state courts, does not waive the state's Eleventh Amendment immunity. McConnell v. Adams, 829 F.2d 1319 (4th Cir. 1987), cert. denied, 486 U.S. 1006, 108 S. Ct. 1731, 100 L. Ed. 2d 195 (1988).

Injunctive relief as to future conduct of state officials. — The state's Eleventh Amendment immunity does not protect it from suits for injunctive relief governing its officials' future conduct. McConnell v. Adams, 829 F.2d 1319 (4th Cir. 1987), cert. denied, 486 U.S. 1006, 108 S. Ct. 1731, 100 L. Ed. 2d 195 (1988).

Postdeprivation remedy to prison inmates. — This article clearly provides a meaningful postdeprivation remedy to prison inmates for tort claims of $25,000 or less accruing after July 1, 1982. Al-Mustafa Irshad v. Spann, 543 F. Supp. 922 (E.D. Va. 1982).

Act provides remedy to prison inmate not given credit for time in jail in another state. — A former inmate in Virginia's prison system could not bring action under 42 U.S.C. § 1983 for compensatory and punitive damages for having been held seven days longer than he would have been if he had been given credit for seven days spent in a jail in Florida, before Virginia authorities obtained custody of him, because the Tort Claims Act provided adequate tort remedies for post-deprivation compensation. Wadhams v. Procunier, 772 F.2d 75 (4th Cir. 1985).

Assault on inmate by prison guard. — The Tort Claims Act provided an adequate remedy where a prison guard allegedly assaulted an inmate. Accordingly, plaintiff stated no procedural due process claim. Perry v. Walker, 586 F. Supp. 1264 (E.D. Va. 1984).

Negligent injury of inmate not deprivation of liberty. — An inmate at the city jail in Richmond who was injured when he slipped on a pillow negligently left on the stairs by respondent, a correctional deputy stationed at the jail, was not "deprived" of his "liberty" interest under the Fourteenth Amendment in freedom from bodily injury. The due process clause of the Fourteenth Amendment is simply not implicated by a negligent act of an official causing unintended loss of or injury to life, liberty or property. Daniels v. Williams, 474 U.S. 327, 106 S. Ct. 662, 88 L. Ed. 2d 662 (1986) (decision as to action accruing before effective date of this article).

Applied in Groves v. Cox, 559 F. Supp. 772 (E.D. Va. 1983); Wohlford v. Virginia, 699 F. Supp. 572 (W.D. Va. 1988).

§ 8.01-195.2. Definitions. — As used in this article:

"Agency" means any department, institution, authority, instrumentality, board or other administrative agency of the government of the Commonwealth of Virginia and any transportation district created pursuant to Chapter 45

(§ 15.2-4500 et seq.) of Title 15.2 and Chapter 630 of the 1964 Acts of Assembly.

"Employee" means any officer, employee or agent of any agency, or any person acting on behalf of an agency in an official capacity, temporarily or permanently in the service of the Commonwealth, or any transportation district, whether with or without compensation.

"School boards" as defined in § 22.1-1 are not state agencies nor are employees of school boards state employees.

"Transportation district" shall be limited to any transportation district or districts which have entered into an agreement in which the Northern Virginia Transportation District is a party with any firm or corporation as an agent to provide passenger rail services for such district or districts while such firm or corporation is performing in accordance with such agreement. (1981, c. 449; 1986, cc. 534, 584; 1991, c. 23.)

Editor's note. — Acts 1986, c. 584, cl. 2, as amended by Acts 1988, c. 801, cl. 2, provided that the provisions of the 1986 act shall have no force and effect after July 1, 1990, unless reenacted by the General Assembly prior to such date. Since the General Assembly did not reenact the amendatory provisions of Acts 1986, c. 584, as amended, prior to July 1, 1990, the provisions expired.

Law Review. — For comment on local liability for negligent inspection of buildings and equipment, see 18 U. Rich. L. Rev. 809 (1984).

§ 8.01-195.3. Commonwealth, transportation district or locality liable for damages in certain cases.

— Subject to the provisions of this article, the Commonwealth shall be liable for claims for money only accruing on or after July 1, 1982, and any transportation district shall be liable for claims for money only accruing on or after July 1, 1986, on account of damage to or loss of property or personal injury or death caused by the negligent or wrongful act or omission of any employee while acting within the scope of his employment under circumstances where the Commonwealth or transportation district, if a private person, would be liable to the claimant for such damage, loss, injury or death. However, except to the extent that a transportation district contracts to do so pursuant to § 15.2-4518, neither the Commonwealth nor any transportation district shall be liable for interest prior to judgment or for punitive damages. The amount recoverable by any claimant shall not exceed (i) $25,000 for causes of action accruing prior to July 1, 1988, $75,000 for causes of action accruing on or after July 1, 1988, or $100,000 for causes of action accruing on or after July 1, 1993, or (ii) the maximum limits of any liability policy maintained to insure against such negligence or other tort, if such policy is in force at the time of the act or omission complained of, whichever is greater, exclusive of interest and costs.

Notwithstanding any provision hereof, the individual immunity of judges, the Attorney General, attorneys for the Commonwealth, and other public officers, their agents and employees from tort claims for damages is hereby preserved to the extent and degree that such persons presently are immunized. Any recovery based on the following claims are hereby excluded from the provisions of this article:

1. Any claim against the Commonwealth based upon an act or omission which occurred prior to July 1, 1982.

1a. Any claim against a transportation district based upon an act or omission which occurred prior to July 1, 1986.

2. Any claim based upon an act or omission of the General Assembly or district commission of any transportation district, or any member or staff thereof acting in his official capacity, or to the legislative function of any agency subject to the provisions of this article.

3. Any claim based upon an act or omission of any court of the Commonwealth, or any member thereof acting in his official capacity, or to the judicial functions of any agency subject to the provisions of this article.

4. Any claim based upon an act or omission of an officer, agent or employee of any agency of government in the execution of a lawful order of any court.

5. Any claim arising in connection with the assessment or collection of taxes.

6. Any claim arising out of the institution or prosecution of any judicial or administrative proceeding, even if without probable cause.

7. Any claim by an inmate of a state correctional facility, as defined in § 53.1-1, unless the claimant verifies under oath, by affidavit, that he has exhausted his remedies under the adult institutional inmate grievance procedures promulgated by the Department of Corrections. The time for filing the notice of tort claim shall be tolled during the pendency of the grievance procedure.

8. Any claim arising from the failure of a computer, software program, database, network, information system, firmware or any other device, whether operated by or on behalf of the Commonwealth of Virginia or one of its agencies, to interpret, produce, calculate, generate, or account for a date which is compatible with the "Year 2000" date change.

Nothing contained herein shall operate to reduce or limit the extent to which the Commonwealth or any transportation district, agency or employee was deemed liable for negligence as of July 1, 1982, nor shall any provision of this article be applicable to any county, city or town in the Commonwealth or be so construed as to remove or in any way diminish the sovereign immunity of any county, city or town in the Commonwealth. (1981, c. 449; 1982, c. 397; 1986, c. 584; 1988, c. 884; 1989, c. 446; 1993, c. 481; 1998, cc. 203, 820.)

Editor's note. — Acts 1986, c. 584, which amended this section, as amended by Acts 1988, c. 801, purported to provide for expiration of the provisions of the 1986 act on July 1, 1990. However, in light of the amendment and reenactment of this section by Acts 1988, c. 884 and Acts 1989, c. 446, at the direction of the Code Commission, the expiration provisions of Acts 1986, c. 584, as amended in 1988, have been given no further effect.

Law Review. — For comment on local liability for negligent inspection of buildings and equipment, see 18 U. Rich. L. Rev. 809 (1984). For note on the abrogation of sovereign immunity in Virginia: The Virginia Tort Claims Act, see 7 Geo. Mason L. Rev. 291 (1984). For comment, "Obstacles to Holding a Parole Official in Virginia Liable for the Negligent Release or Supervision of a Parolee," see 22 U. Rich. L. Rev. 83 (1987).

I. DECISIONS UNDER CURRENT LAW.

This section is a limited waiver of governmental immunity from tort claims and not a legislative definition of the Commonwealth's duty of care to those with claims against it. Commonwealth v. Coolidge, 237 Va. 621, 379 S.E.2d 338 (1989).

Only negligent conduct is protected by the statute; acts constituting gross negligence or intentional torts are not immunized. Coppage v. Mann, 906 F. Supp. 1025 (E.D. Va. 1995).

Section fails to provide adequate postdeprivation remedy for loss of right to appeal. Hutchins v. Carrillo, 27 Va. App. 595, 500 S.E.2d 277 (1998).

Test in determining governmental employee's claims of immunity. — In determining government employees' claims of immunity, the court examines the function employee was performing and the extent of the state's interest and involvement in that function. Whether the act performed involves the use of judgment and discretion is a consideration, but it is not always determinative. Of equal importance is the degree of control and direction exercised by the state over the employee whose negligence is involved. Lohr v. Larsen, 246 Va. 81, 431 S.E.2d 642 (1993).

Broad discretion weighs in favor of immunity claim. — If a broad discretion is vested in a government employee in performing the function complained of, it will weigh heavily in favor of a government employee's claim of immunity. The court has not limited the element of discretion in determining governmental immunity to governmental policymakers; it has been extended to a state-employed physician. Resolution of the issue of sovereign immunity goes beyond determining whether the act constitutes the formulation or execution of policy. Lohr v. Larsen, 246 Va. 81, 431 S.E.2d 642 (1993).

Subdivision 4 does not exclude discretionary acts from its scope; instead, it specifically encompasses any claim that is based upon acts or omissions occurring in the execution of a lawful court order. Baumgardner v. Southwestern Va. Mental Health Inst., 247 Va. 486, 442 S.E.2d 400 (1994).

Commonwealth's interest and involvement in employee's function. — If the function that a government employee was negligently performing was essential to a governmental objective and the government had a great interest and involvement in that function, those factors would weigh in favor of the employee's claim of sovereign immunity. On the other hand, if that function has only a marginal influence upon a governmental objective, and the government's interest and involvement in that function are "slight," these factors weigh against granting governmental immunity to a government employee. Lohr v. Larsen, 246 Va. 81, 431 S.E.2d 642 (1993).

Extent of government control influences consideration of immunity claim. — The extent of a government's control and direction of its employee also influences consideration of that employee's claim of immunity. A high level of control weighs in favor of immunity; a low level of such control weighs against immunity. Lohr v. Larsen, 246 Va. 81, 431 S.E.2d 642 (1993).

Section does not limit damages recoverable from transit authority nor exempt transit authority from requirements of Tort Claims Act. — Limits on recoverable damage stated in Virginia Tort Claims Act were not applicable to Washington Metropolitan Transit Authority, even though considered part of state government; language of compact creating Transit Authority amounted to waiver of right of sovereign immunity, does not contain any limitation on the amount of compensatory damages that a plaintiff may recover, and does not mention or refer to the Virginia Tort Claims Act. Washington Metro. Area Transit Auth. v. Briggs, 255 Va. 309, 497 S.E.2d 139 (1998).

Wide discretion and higher level of governmental control. — The issue of wide discretion that influences consideration of the grant of governmental immunity appears to be at odds with consideration of a higher level of governmental control. However, when a government employee is specially trained to make discretionary decisions, the government's control must necessarily be limited in order to make maximum use of the employee's special training and subsequent experience. Lohr v. Larsen, 246 Va. 81, 431 S.E.2d 642 (1993).

Sovereign immunity not limited to when employees follow "state established rules." — Doctrine of sovereign immunity is not limited to those instances in which specially trained state employees follow "state-established rules," "state-prescribed methods," or "state-standardized procedures." These factors were considerations in concluding that the necessary control element was present, but such constraints are not required to establish the necessary governmental control over a state employee who is a professional. Lohr v. Larsen, 246 Va. 81, 431 S.E.2d 642 (1993).

Commonwealth's immunity from liability for mental health and mental retardation board's acts and omissions. — The plain meaning of this section preserves the Commonwealth's immunity from liability for the acts and omissions alleged in administrator's motion for judgment against state mental health and mental retardation board. Baumgardner v. Southwestern Va. Mental Health Inst., 247 Va. 486, 442 S.E.2d 400 (1994).

State-employed physician was entitled to sovereign immunity. — Where the Commonwealth controlled absolutely the equipment doctor used, the procedures he could perform and even the brand names of the medication he could prescribe, further, the doctor could not decline to accept a particular person as a patient, the state-employed public health physician was entitled to the protection of the doctrine of sovereign immunity in a medical malpractice case from liability for his alleged acts of ordinary negligence. Lohr v. Larsen, 246 Va. 81, 431 S.E.2d 642 (1993).

Applied in Messina v. Burden, 228 Va. 301, 321 S.E.2d 657 (1984).

§ 8.01-195.4. Jurisdiction of claims under this article; right to jury trial; service on Commonwealth or locality.

— The general district courts shall have exclusive original jurisdiction to hear, determine, and render judgment on any claim against the Commonwealth or any transportation district cognizable under this article when the amount of the claim does not exceed $1,000, exclusive of interest and any attorneys' fees. Jurisdiction shall be concurrent with the circuit courts when the amount of the claim exceeds $1,000 but does not exceed $10,000, exclusive of interest and such attorneys' fees. Jurisdiction of claims when the amount exceeds $10,000 shall be limited to the circuit courts of the Commonwealth. The parties to any such action in the circuit courts shall be entitled to a trial by jury.

In all actions against the Commonwealth commenced pursuant to this article, the Commonwealth shall be a proper party defendant, and service of process shall be made on the Attorney General. The notice of claim shall be filed pursuant to § 8.01-195.6 on the Director of the Division of Risk Management or the Attorney General. In all such actions against a transportation district, the district shall be a proper party and service of process and notices shall be made on the chairman of the commission of the transportation district. (1981, c. 449; 1984, c. 698; 1986, c. 584; 1987, cc. 567, 674; 1989, cc. 121, 337; 1991, c. 23; 1992, cc. 111, 796.)

Cross references. — As to venue in actions under the Virginia Tort Claims Act, see now subdivision 18 of § 8.01-261.

Editor's note. — Acts 1986, c. 584, cl. 2, as amended by Acts 1988, c. 801, cl. 2, provided that the provisions of the 1986 act shall have no force and effect after July 1, 1990, unless reenacted by the General Assembly prior to such date. Since the General Assembly did not reenact the amendatory provisions of Acts 1986, c. 584, as amended, prior to July 1, 1990, the provisions expired.

Law Review. — For note on the abrogation of sovereign immunity in Virginia: The Virginia Tort Claims Act, see 7 Geo. Mason L. Rev. 291 (1984). For survey on civil procedure and practice in Virginia for 1989, see 23 U. Rich. L. Rev. 511 (1989). For article reviewing recent developments and changes in legislation, case law, and Virginia Supreme Court Rules affecting civil litigation, see "Civil Practice and Procedure," 26 U. Rich. L. Rev. 679 (1992).

§ 8.01-195.5. Settlement of certain cases. — The Attorney General shall have authority in accordance with § 2.1-127 to compromise and settle claims against the Commonwealth cognizable under this article.

The chairman of the commission for a transportation district against which a claim was filed pursuant to this article, or such other person as may be designated by the commission, shall have the authority to compromise, settle and discharge the claim provided (i) the proposed settlement and reasons therefor are submitted to the commission in writing and approved by its members or (ii) the settlement is made in accordance with a written policy approved by the transportation district commission for such settlements. The Director of the Division of Risk Management may adjust, compromise and settle claims against the Commonwealth cognizable under this article prior to the commencement of suit unless otherwise directed by the Attorney General. (1981, c. 449; 1986, c. 584; 1991, c. 23; 1992, c. 796.)

Editor's note. — Acts 1986, c. 584, cl. 2, as amended by Acts 1988, c. 801, cl. 2, provided that the provisions of the 1986 act shall have no force and effect after July 1, 1990, unless reenacted by the General Assembly prior to such date. Since the General Assembly did not reenact the amendatory provisions of Acts 1986, c. 584, as amended, prior to July 1, 1990, the provisions expired.

§ 8.01-195.6. Notice of claim. — Every claim cognizable against the Commonwealth or a transportation district shall be forever barred unless the claimant or his agent, attorney or representative has filed a written statement of the nature of the claim, which includes the time and place at which the injury is alleged to have occurred and the agency or agencies alleged to be liable. The statement shall be filed with the Director of the Division of Risk Management or the Attorney General within one year after such cause of action accrued if the claim is against the Commonwealth. If the claim is against a transportation district the statement shall be filed with the chairman of the commission of the transportation district within one year after the cause of action accrued. However, if the claimant was under a disability at the time the cause of action accrued, the tolling provisions of § 8.01-229 shall apply. The claimant or his agent, attorney or representative shall, in a claim cognizable against the Commonwealth, mail the notice of claim via the United States Postal Service by certified mail, return receipt requested, addressed to the Director of the Division of Risk Management or the Attorney General in Richmond. The notice, in a claim cognizable against a transportation district, shall be mailed via the United States Postal Service by certified mail, return receipt requested, addressed to the chairman of the commission of the transportation district.

In any action contesting the filing of the notice of claim, the burden of proof shall be on the claimant to establish mailing and receipt of the notice in conformity with this section. The signed return receipt indicating delivery to the Director of the Division of Risk Management, the Attorney General, or the chairman of the commission of the transportation district, when admitted into evidence, shall be prima facie evidence of filing of the notice under this section. The date on which the return receipt is signed by the Director, the Attorney General, or the chairman shall be prima facie evidence of the date of filing for purposes of compliance with this section.

Claims against the Commonwealth involving medical malpractice shall be subject to the provisions of this article and to the provisions of Chapter 21.1 (§ 8.01-581.1 et seq.) of this title. However, the recovery in such a claim involving medical malpractice shall not exceed the limits imposed by § 8.01-195.3. (1981, c. 449; 1984, cc. 638, 698; 1986, c. 584; 1991, c. 23; 1992, c. 796.)

Editor's note. — Acts 1986, c. 584, cl. 2, as amended by Acts 1988, c. 801, cl. 2, provides that the provisions of the act shall have no force and effect after July 1, 1990, unless reenacted by the General Assembly prior to such date. Since the General Assembly did not reenact the provisions of the act prior to July 1, 1990, the provisions expired.

Law Review. — For note on the abrogation of sovereign immunity in Virginia: The Virginia Tort Claims Act, see 7 Geo. Mason L. Rev. 291 (1984).

I. DECISIONS UNDER CURRENT LAW.

Requirements. — The plaintiff's notice did not meet the statutory requirements because it did not specify the location of her injury with sufficient particularity. Halberstam v. Commonwealth, 251 Va. 248, 467 S.E.2d 783 (1996).

Applied in McGuire v. Commonwealth, 988 F. Supp. 980 (E.D. Va. 1997).

§ 8.01-195.7. Statute of limitations. — Every claim cognizable against the Commonwealth or a transportation district under this article shall be forever barred, unless within one year after the cause of action accrues to the claimant the notice of claim required by § 8.01-195.6 is properly filed. An action may be commenced pursuant to § 8.01-195.4 (i) upon denial of the claim by the Attorney General or the Director of the Division of Risk Management or, in the case of a transportation district, by the chairman of the commission of that district or (ii) after the expiration of six months from the date of filing the notice of claim unless, within that period, the claim has been compromised and discharged pursuant to § 8.01-195.5. All claims against the Commonwealth or a transportation district under this article shall be forever barred unless such action is commenced within eighteen months of the filing of the notice of claim.

The limitations periods prescribed by this section and § 8.01-195.6 shall be subject to the tolling provision of § 8.01-229 and the pleading provision of § 8.01-235. Additionally, claims involving medical malpractice in which the notice required by this section and § 8.01-195.6 has been given shall be subject to the provisions of § 8.01-581.9. Notwithstanding the provisions of this section, if notice of claim against the Commonwealth was filed prior to July 1, 1984, any claimant so filing shall have two years from the date such notice was filed within which to commence an action pursuant to § 8.01-195.4. (1981, c.

449; 1984, cc. 638, 698; 1985, c. 514; 1986, c. 584; 1988, cc. 778, 801; 1992, c. 796.)

Editor's note. — Acts 1986, c. 584, which amended this section, as amended by Acts 1988, c. 801, purported to provide for expiration of the provisions of the 1986 act on July 1, 1990. However, in light of the amendment and reenactment of this section by Acts 1988, cc. 778, 801, at the direction of the Code Commission, the expiration provisions of Acts 1986, c. 584, as amended in 1988, have been given no further effect.

Section 8.01-581.9, which is referred to in the second sentence of the second paragraph, was repealed by Acts 1993, c. 928.

Law Review. — For article, "Civil Rights and 'Personal Injuries': Virginia's Statute of Limitations for Section 1983 Suits," see 26 Wm. & Mary L. Rev. 199 (1985).

§ 8.01-195.8. **Release of further claims.** — Notwithstanding any provision of this article, the liability for any claim or judgment cognizable under this article shall be conditioned upon the execution by the claimant of a release of all claims against the Commonwealth, its political subdivisions, agencies, and instrumentalities or against the transportation district, and against any officer or employee of the Commonwealth or the transportation district in connection with, or arising out of, the occurrence complained of. (1981, c. 449; 1986, c. 584; 1991, c. 23.)

Editor's note. — Acts 1986, c. 584, cl. 2, as amended by Acts 1988, c. 801, cl. 2, provided that the provisions of the 1986 act shall have no force and effect after July 1, 1990, unless reenacted by the General Assembly prior to such date. Since the General Assembly did not reenact the amendatory provisions of Acts 1986, c. 584, as amended, prior to July 1, 1990, the provisions expired.

§ 8.01-195.9. **Claims evaluation program.** — The Division of Risk Management of the Department of the Treasury and the Attorney General shall develop cooperatively an actuarially sound program for identifying, evaluating and setting reserves for the payment of claims cognizable under this article. (1988, c. 644; 2000, cc. 618, 632.)

The 2000 amendments. — The 2000 amendments by cc. 618 and 632 are identical, and substituted "the Treasury" for "General Services."

ARTICLE 19.

Actions by the Commonwealth.

§ 8.01-196. **Comptroller to institute proceedings.** — The Comptroller shall institute and prosecute all proceedings proper to enforce payment of money to the Commonwealth. (Code 1950, § 8-758; 1977, c. 617.)

I. Decisions Under Current Law.
II. Decisions Under Prior Law.

I. DECISIONS UNDER CURRENT LAW.

Applied in Commonwealth ex rel. Pross v. Board of Supvrs., 225 Va. 492, 303 S.E.2d 887 (1983).

II. DECISIONS UNDER PRIOR LAW.

Editor's note. — The case cited below was decided under corresponding provisions of former law. The term "this section," as used below, refers to former provisions.

Collection of money payable under former § 15.1-73. — The Comptroller was granted exclusive authority under this section and § 8-761 (see now § 8.01-198) to institute proceedings to collect money payable under former § 15.1-73 which prohibited city and town officials from having an interest in contracts with or claims against the city or town. Commonwealth v. Holland, 211 Va. 530, 178 S.E.2d 506 (1971).

§ 8.01-197. In what name; when not to abate. — Any such action shall be in the name of the Commonwealth of Virginia except when it is on a bond payable to, or a contract made with, the Governor or some other person. And then it may be in the name of such Governor or other person for the use of the Commonwealth, notwithstanding such Governor or other person may have died, resigned, or been removed from office before the commencement of the action. And there shall be no abatement thereof, by reason of the death, resignation, or removal from office of any such plaintiff pending the action. (Code 1950, § 8-760; 1977, c. 617.)

Cross references. — For rule of court on substitution of parties, see Rule 3:15.

I. DECISIONS UNDER CURRENT LAW.

Applied in Commonwealth v. Millsaps, 232 Va. 502, 352 S.E.2d 311 (1987).

§ 8.01-198. Action, against whom instituted. — Any such action may be instituted against any person indebted or liable to the Commonwealth in any way whatever, and against his sureties, and against his and their personal representatives. And it may be made when the debt or liability is created or secured by a bond or other instrument, whether the same be payable to the Commonwealth or to any person acting in a public character on behalf of the Commonwealth, or be for the payment of money or the performance of other duties. Every judgment on any such motion shall be in the name of the Commonwealth. (Code 1950, § 8-761; 1954, c. 550; 1977, c. 617.)

Cross references. — For rules of court relating to notice of motion for judgment and defendant's response, see Rules 3:3, 3:5.

I. DECISIONS UNDER PRIOR LAW.

Editor's note. — The case cited below was decided under corresponding provisions of former law. The term "this section," as used below, refers to former provisions.

Collection of money payable under former § 15.1-73. — The Comptroller was granted exclusive authority under § 8-758 (see now § 8.01-196) and this section to institute proceedings to collect money payable under former § 15.1-73 which prohibited city and town officials from having an interest in contracts with or claims against the city or town. Commonwealth v. Holland, 211 Va. 530, 178 S.E.2d 506 (1971).

§ 8.01-199. Judgment, nature of. — On any such motion, the judgment shall be for so much principal and interest as would be recoverable by action. It may be also for fifteen per centum damages in addition thereto when the proceeding is against a treasurer, sheriff, or other collector, or his sureties, or his or their personal representatives, for taxes or other public money which ought to have been paid into the state treasury. In such proceeding, the court, in pronouncing judgment, may consider all the circumstances, and give judgment for the damages or not, or for such part of the damages, as it may deem proper. (Code 1950, § 8-762; 1977, c. 617.)

§ 8.01-200. Mistakes against State corrected. — After a debt to the Commonwealth shall have been paid, if it appear that an error or mistake has been committed to its prejudice, whether before or after the issuing of execution, a motion may be made on ten days' notice against any person liable for the debt, for the amount of such error or mistake, and judgment may be given therefor, without interest or damages thereon. (Code 1950, § 8-763; 1977, c. 617.)

§ 8.01-201. **Execution; real estate to be sold.** — In a writ of fieri facias upon a judgment or decree against any person indebted or liable to the Commonwealth, or against any surety of his, after the words "we command you that of the," the clerk shall insert the words "goods, chattels, and real estate," and conform the subsequent part of such writ thereto. And under any writ so issued, real estate may be taken and sold. (Code 1950, § 8-764; 1977, c. 617.)

§ 8.01-202. **Execution, to whom issued.** — An execution on behalf of the Commonwealth from the Circuit Court of the City of Richmond may, if the Comptroller see fit, be directed to any sheriff, of any political subdivision, and shall be served by any of such officers in whose hands the Comptroller may cause it to be placed. (Code 1950, § 8-765; 1977, c. 617.)

§ 8.01-203. **Goods and chattels liable before real estate.** — Every writ of fieri facias, issued according to § 8.01-201, shall be levied first on the goods and chattels of the person against whose estate such writ issued. If, in the political subdivision, the residence of such person, there are no goods and chattels liable thereto, or not a sufficiency thereof, then the officer having such writ shall levy it on the real estate of such person. (Code 1950, § 8-766; 1977, c. 617.)

I. DECISIONS UNDER CURRENT LAW.

Lack of notice. — Although lack of notice is not a prerequisite to the operation of § 8.9-312(5), this section provides that "every contract or duty within this act imposes an obligation of good faith in its performance or enforcement." Accordingly, allegations and proof of a leading on, bad faith or inequitable conduct on the part of a secured party may affect the priorities established under § 8.9-312(5) by estopping the assertion of a priority. Grossmann v. Saunders, 237 Va. 113, 376 S.E.2d 66 (1989).

§ 8.01-204. **Notice of sale of real estate; when sale to be made.** — When a levy is so made upon real estate, the officer making it shall post notice thereof, and of the time and place of sale, at such public places as may seem to him expedient, and at the front door of the courthouse of the political subdivision in which the real estate is, on a court day. The time of selling real estate shall be not less than sixty nor more than ninety days from the time of posting the notice at the courthouse door. And the sale shall take place at the premises or at the door of the courthouse, as the officer may deem most advisable. (Code 1950, § 8-767; 1977, c. 617.)

§ 8.01-205. **How sale made.** — If the amount of the execution be not sooner paid, such officer shall proceed, on the day mentioned in the notice, to sell at public auction the interest of the party against whom the execution issued in the real estate or so much thereof as the officer may deem sufficient; and if a part only be sold it shall be laid off in one parcel in such place and manner as the debtor or his agent may direct or, if he give no direction, as the officer may deem best. (Code 1950, § 8-768; 1977, c. 617.)

§ 8.01-206. **Terms of sale.** — The sale shall be upon six months' credit; and if the land be not purchased for the Commonwealth, the officer shall take bond of the purchaser, with sureties, for the payment of the purchase money to the Commonwealth. Every such bond shall mention on what occasion the same was taken, and be returned to the office of the court from which the execution issued, and the clerk shall endorse thereon the date of its return. (Code 1950, § 8-769; 1977, c. 617.)

Cross references. — As to effect of bonds given under this section, see §§ 8.01-209, 8.01-210.

§ 8.01-207. Who to collect purchase money and make deed; disposition of proceeds of sale. — On or before the maturity of such bond the sheriff or other officer who made the sale shall withdraw the bond from the clerk's office, leaving his receipt therefor and an attested copy thereof, and collect the same. So soon as the purchase money has been paid, the sheriff or other principal officer, or the deputy who acted in making the sale, shall, as commissioner, and in the name of the Commonwealth, convey the land to the purchaser by deed executed at his costs, reciting the execution, the sale and the price of the land. Such deed shall pass to the purchaser all the interest which the party against whom the execution issued had in the land at the date of the judgment or decree. Out of the money so collected the sheriff or officer who made the sale shall pay all costs attending such execution and sale, the costs of a survey, if there was one, all delinquent and unpaid taxes and levies on such land and the debt due the Commonwealth, and the residue, if any, he shall pay to the judgment debtor. (Code 1950, § 8-770; 1977, c. 617.)

§ 8.01-208. When successor of officer to make deed. — When the officer and his deputy who acted in making the sale have both died or removed from the Commonwealth before making such deed, the same may be executed by any successor of such officer. (Code 1950, § 8-771; 1977, c. 617.)

§ 8.01-209. Bond for purchase money to have force of judgment. — When any bond taken under § 8.01-206 becomes payable and is returned to the office of the court from which the execution issued, it shall have the force of a judgment against such of the obligors therein as may be then alive. Execution may be issued thereon against them. And the same shall be proceeded under in like manner as an execution issued on such a judgment or decree as is mentioned in § 8.01-201, save only that the clerk shall endorse "no security is to be taken," and the officer shall govern himself accordingly and sell for ready money any real estate which he may levy on under the same. (Code 1950, § 8-772; 1977, c. 617.)

§ 8.01-210. Judgment against deceased obligors. — A judgment may be obtained against the survivors of a deceased obligor of a bond taken under the provisions of § 8.01-206 by an action at law against the personal representative of such obligor. (Code 1950, § 8-773; 1954, c. 550; 1977, c. 617.)

§ 8.01-211. When venditioni exponas issued to sheriff of adjacent county; what to contain. — When return is made on any execution on behalf of the Commonwealth that goods, chattels or real estate remain unsold for want of bidders, or to that effect, the clerk of the court from which such execution issued shall, when required by the Comptroller, issue a writ of venditioni exponas, directed to the sheriff of any county adjacent to that in which the levy was made that the Comptroller may designate. Such writ shall recite the execution under which the levy was made, the nature of such levy and return that the property remains unsold for the want of bidders and shall command the sheriff of such adjacent county, if the property remaining unsold be goods or chattels, to go into the county in which the levy was made and receive the same from the officer that made the levy and, whether the property be goods, chattels, or real estate, to sell the same. (Code 1950, § 8-774; 1977, c. 617.)

§ 8.01-212   CODE OF VIRGINIA   § 8.01-216

I. DECISIONS UNDER PRIOR LAW.

Editor's note. — The case cited below was decided under corresponding provisions of former law. The term "this statute," as used below, refers to former provisions.

Liability of purchaser who gets no land. — Where a sale was made of judgment debtor's interest in land under writ of venditioni exponas in behalf of the Commonwealth, which interest was absorbed by liens paramount to the writ, the purchaser must pay the price though he may get no land. Spotts v. Commonwealth, 85 Va. 531, 8 S.E. 375 (1888).

§ 8.01-212. Officer to deliver to sheriff goods and chattels levied on. — The officer who made the levy shall deliver the goods and chattels to the sheriff to whom such writ of venditioni exponas may be directed, upon such sheriff's producing to him such writ and executing a receipt for such goods and chattels. If the officer shall fail to deliver the same and return be made on such writ to that effect, the court from which it issued, upon motion, may give judgment against him and his sureties for the whole sum that the execution amounted to at the time of such failure, with interest thereon from that time. (Code 1950, § 8-775; 1977, c. 617.)

§ 8.01-213. Where same to be sold. — The sheriff to whom such writ of venditioni exponas is directed, shall sell the goods and chattels in the county where received, if they can be sold therein, and if not he shall cause them to be removed to the courthouse of his own county and there sold. The removal shall be at the costs of the party against whom the execution issued, and the sale under the execution shall be to raise the cost of removal, in addition to the amount which it would otherwise have been necessary to raise. (Code 1950, § 8-776; 1977, c. 617.)

§ 8.01-214. Where real estate to be sold. — Such sheriff shall also sell the real estate levied on in the county wherein the levy was made, if it can be done, and if it cannot he shall make the sale at the courthouse of his own county. (Code 1950, § 8-777; 1977, c. 617.)

§ 8.01-215. Return of officer when sale not made because of prior encumbrance. — In any case in which an officer, having an execution on behalf of the Commonwealth, shall decline levying it because of any previous conveyance, execution, or encumbrance, a return shall be made setting forth the nature of such conveyance, execution or encumbrance, in whose favor, and for what amount, and the court in which the conveyance or encumbrance is recorded, or from which the execution issued. (Code 1950, § 8-778; 1977, c. 617.)

I. DECISIONS UNDER PRIOR LAW.

Editor's note. — The case cited below was decided under corresponding provisions of former law. The term "this section," as used below, refers to former provisions.

State's right to resort to court of equity. — The failure of an officer to comply with the provisions of this section did not affect the right of the State to pursue its remedy in a court of equity. Moreover, the right to sell the real estate of the defendants under execution did not deprive the State of the right, if it elected to exercise it, to resort to a court of equity to subject such real estate to the lien of its judgment. Commonwealth v. Ford, 70 Va. (29 Gratt.) 683 (1878).

§ 8.01-216. Comptroller's power to adjust old claims. — The Comptroller, with the advice of the Attorney General, may adjust and settle upon equitable principles, without regard to strict legal rules, any doubtful or disputed account or claim in favor of the Commonwealth which may have been standing on the books of his office not less than two years, and may, with the like advice, dismiss any proceedings instituted by him; but before such adjustment or settlement can in any wise affect the rights of the Commonwealth it shall be approved and endorsed by the Attorney General and shall then be submitted to the supervision of the judge of the Circuit Court of the City of Richmond, accompanied by a written statement signed by the Comptroller of the facts and reasons which, in his opinion, render such adjustment or settlement just and proper. When such judge endorses the same with his written approval, signed in his official character, it shall be considered and treated as valid and binding. (Code 1950, § 8-779; 1977, c. 617.)

I. DECISIONS UNDER PRIOR LAW.

Editor's note. — The case cited below was decided under corresponding provisions of former law. The term "this statute," as used below, refers to former provisions.

This section has no application to the submission by the Auditor (now Comptroller) to the judgment of a court of competent jurisdiction, and a settlement made in good faith, by and with the advice and consent of the Attorney General, who represented and conducted the litigation on behalf of the Commonwealth, is binding on both litigants. Commonwealth v. Schmelz, 116 Va. 62, 81 S.E. 45 (1914).

ARTICLE 20.

Change of Name.

§ 8.01-217. How name of person may be changed. — Any person desiring to change his own name, or that of his child or ward, may apply therefor to the circuit court of the county or city in which the person whose name is to be changed resides, or if no place of abode exists, such person may apply to any circuit court which shall consider such application if it finds that good cause exists therefor under the circumstances alleged. Applications of probationers and incarcerated persons may be accepted if the court finds that good cause exists for such application. An incarcerated person may apply to the circuit court of the county or city in which such person is incarcerated. In case of a minor who has no living parent or guardian, the application may be made by his next friend. In case of a minor who has both parents living, the parent who does not join in the application shall be served with reasonable notice of the application and, should such parent object to the change of name, a hearing shall be held to determine whether the change of name is in the best interest of the minor. If, after application is made on behalf of a minor and an ex parte hearing is held thereon, the court finds by clear and convincing evidence that such notice would present a serious threat to the health and safety of the applicant, the court may waive such notice.

Every application shall be under oath and shall include the place of residence of the applicant, the names of both parents, including the maiden name of his mother, the date and place of birth of the applicant, the applicant's felony conviction record, if any, whether the applicant is presently incarcerated or a probationer with any court, and if the applicant has previously changed his name, his former name or names. On any such application and hearing, if such be demanded, the court, shall, unless the evidence shows that the change of name is sought for a fraudulent purpose or would otherwise infringe upon the rights of others or, in case of a minor, that the change of name is not in the best interest of the minor, order a change of name and the clerk of the court shall spread the order upon the current deed book in his office, index it in both the old and new names, and transmit a certified copy to the State Registrar of Vital Records and the Central Criminal Records Exchange. Transmittal of a copy to the State Registrar of Vital Records and the Central Criminal Records Exchange shall not be required of a person who changed his or her former name by reason of marriage and who makes application to resume a former name pursuant to § 20-121.4. If the applicant shall show cause to believe that in the event his change of name should become a public record, a serious threat to the health or safety of the applicant or his immediate family would exist, the chief judge of the circuit court may waive the requirement that the application be under oath or the court may order the record sealed and direct the clerk not to spread and index any orders entered in the cause, and shall not transmit a certified copy to the State Registrar of Vital Records or the Central Criminal Records Exchange. Upon receipt of such order by the State Registrar of Vital Records, for a person born in this Commonwealth, together with a proper request and payment of required fees, the Registrar shall issue certifications of the amended birth record which do not reveal the former name or names of the applicant unless so ordered by a court of competent jurisdiction. Such certifications shall not be marked "amended" and show the effective date as provided in § 32.1-272. Such order shall set forth the date and place of birth of the person whose name is changed, the full names of his parents, including the maiden name of the mother and, if such person has previously changed his name, his former name or names. (Code 1950, § 8-577.1; 1956, c. 402; 1973, c. 401; 1976, c. 115; 1977, cc. 457, 617; 1979, cc. 599, 603, 612; 1980, cc. 448, 455; 1981, c. 297; 1983, c. 335; 1985, c. 483; 1991, c. 144.)

REVISERS' NOTE

Changes to former § 8-577.1 include: (1) notice to the parent not joining in the application shall be served rather than mailed and (2) the penal provision has been transferred to Title 18.2.

Cross references. — As to constitutional authority of General Assembly to confer on courts power to change names, see Va. Const., Art. IV, § 14. As to penalty for unlawful change of name, see § 18.2-504.1. As to change of name of adopted minor, see § 63.1-226.

Editor's note. — Pursuant to § 9-77.11 and Acts 1977, c. 617, cl. 4, the Code Commission has given effect, in § 8.01-217 as set out above, to the amendment to former § 8-577.1, corresponding to this section, in Acts 1977, c. 457. The amendment inserted "without regard to sex" in the second sentence of the second paragraph and added the present third and fourth sentences of the second paragraph.

Acts 1993, c. 929, cl. 3, as amended by Acts 1994, c. 564, cl. 1, and Acts 1996, c. 616, cl. 3, provides that the amendment to this section by Acts 1993, c. 929, cl. 1, shall become effective June 1, 1998, "only if state funds are provided by the General Assembly sufficient to provide adequate resources, including all local costs, for the court to carry out the purposes of this act and to fulfill its mission to serve children and families of the Commonwealth." The funding was not provided.

Law Review. — For comment on married women's names, see 11 U. Rich. L. Rev. 121 (1976). For survey of Virginia law on domestic relations for the year 1975-1976, see 62 Va. L. Rev. 1431 (1976). For survey of Virginia domestic relations law for the year 1977-1978, see 64 Va. L. Rev. 1439 (1978). For survey of Virginia law on domestic relations for the year 1978-1979, see 66 Va. L. Rev. 281 (1980). For an overview of Virginia Supreme Court decisions on domestic relations, see 15 U. Rich. L. Rev. 321 (1981). For note on the rights of parents in their children's surnames, see 70 Va. L. Rev. 1303 (1984).

I. Decisions Under Current Law.
II. Decisions Under Prior Law.
  A. General Consideration.
  B. Minors.
  C. Married Women.

I. DECISIONS UNDER CURRENT LAW.

An unwed parent, as well as a married parent, has standing to object to a minor child's change of name. Beyah v. Shelton, 231 Va. 432, 344 S.E.2d 909 (1986).

Change from name of father to that of stepfather held not in child's best interest. — Evidence failed to support the trial court's finding that the change of name of four-year-old child from that of her father, who had never married her mother, to that of her stepfather was in the child's best interest, where the father visited his daughter on a regular basis, made regular support payments, and had a close parental relationship with her, and where there was no evidence that the father had engaged in any misconduct that would embarrass or otherwise harm his daughter if she continued using his name. Beyah v. Shelton, 231 Va. 432, 344 S.E.2d 909 (1986).

II. DECISIONS UNDER PRIOR LAW.

A. General Consideration.

Editor's note. — The cases cited below were decided under corresponding provisions of former law. The term "this section," as used below, refers to former provisions.

Provisions as to incarcerated persons violate First Amendment. — This section violated U.S. Const., Amend. 1, insofar as it withheld legal recognition of a prisoner's religiously motivated change of name. Barrett v. Virginia, 689 F.2d 498 (4th Cir. 1982).

And are not justified by considerations of prison discipline. — The categorical refusal, embodied in this section, to accord legal recognition to religious names adopted by incarcerated persons was not reasonably and substantially justified by considerations of prison discipline and order. In this respect, therefore, this section offended against the free exercise of religion guaranteed by U.S. Const., Amend. 1. Barrett v. Virginia, 689 F.2d 498 (4th Cir. 1982).

Common law. — Under the common law, a person is free to adopt any name if it is not done for a fraudulent purpose or in infringement upon the rights of others. In re Strikwerda, 216 Va. 470, 220 S.E.2d 245 (1975); In re Miller, 218 Va. 939, 243 S.E.2d 464 (1978).

Section implements constitutional mandate. — Virginia Const., Art. IV, § 14 provides that "the General Assembly shall confer on the courts power to ... change the names of persons." The General Assembly has carried out its constitutional mandate by the enactment of this section. In re Strikwerda, 216 Va. 470, 220 S.E.2d 245 (1975).

There is nothing in this section, or in the common law, requiring a showing of a compelling need to justify a change of name. Such a requirement would be inconsistent with the common-law principle that names may be changed in the absence of a fraudulent purpose. In re Miller, 218 Va. 939, 243 S.E.2d 464 (1978).

Notice to creditors is not an express requirement under this section. In re Miller, 218 Va. 939, 243 S.E.2d 464 (1978).

Relief under § 59.1-69 et seq., not co-extensive with that under this section. — The relief afforded by § 59.1-69 et seq., relating to transacting business under an assumed name, is not co-extensive with that afforded by this section. In re Miller, 218 Va. 939, 243 S.E.2d 464 (1978).

Section provides no effective procedure for challenging petitioner's evidence that the petition was not filed for an unlawful purpose. This is a statutory omission that may deserve consideration by the General Assembly. In re Strikwerda, 216 Va. 470, 220 S.E.2d 245 (1975).

Inclusion in this section of criminal penalties for one who unlawfully "changes his name or assumes another name" suggests that, in the absence of an illegal purpose, a change of name petition should be granted. In re Strikwerda, 216 Va. 470, 220 S.E.2d 245 (1975).

B. Minors.

Continued use of divorced father's name. — Where the mother offered only slight evidence showing nothing more than "minor inconvenience or embarrassment," to support her application for change of names of her children, and, on the other hand, the evidence was overwhelming that the father had not abandoned the natural ties with his children, that he had not engaged in misconduct which would embarrass the children in the continued use of his name, and that otherwise it would not be detrimental to the children to continue to bear the father's name, in these circumstances, the finding is not warranted that a change of names would serve the children's best interest. Flowers v. Cain, 218 Va. 234, 237 S.E.2d 111 (1977).

Change of child's name where divorced father objects. — When a divorce occurs and the mother is awarded custody, usually it is in the child's best interest to maintain and encourage rather than weaken the relationship between father and child. Generally, a name change of a child will not be ordered over the father's objection unless: (a) The father has abandoned the natural ties ordinarily existing between parent and child; (b) he has engaged in misconduct sufficient to embarrass the child; (c) the child will suffer substantial detriment in continued use of father's name; or (d) the child is of sufficient age and discretion to make an intelligent choice and desires to change the name. Flowers v. Cain, 218 Va. 234, 237 S.E.2d 111 (1977).

In the face of an objection by the natural father to the changing of his children's names and the absence of substantial reasons, the change should not be ordered. Flowers v. Cain, 218 Va. 234, 237 S.E.2d 111 (1977).

Burden of proving change in children's best interest. — In a hearing on the objection by a natural father to the changing of his children's names, the burden was upon the mother to prove by satisfactory evidence that a change in the children's names would be in their best interest. Flowers v. Cain, 218 Va. 234, 237 S.E.2d 111 (1977) (decided prior to 1979 amendments).

Six and seven-year old children held too young to make intelligent choice. — Where one child was only six years old and the other only seven at the time of the hearing on the objection of their natural father to changing their names, neither child was capable of making an intelligent choice in the matter of his name. Flowers v. Cain, 218 Va. 234, 237 S.E.2d 111 (1977).

C. Married Women.

Although a married woman customarily assumes her husband's surname, there is no statute requiring her to do so. In re Miller, 218 Va. 939, 243 S.E.2d 464 (1978).

Married woman not prohibited from resuming maiden name. — There is no conflict or inconsistency between this section and former § 20-107. Nothing in the wording of this section purports to exclude from its provisions a married woman who desires to change her name back to her maiden name. Nothing in the wording of former § 20-107 indicates that this is intended to be the exclusive statutory authority for such a change of name. There is no statute that prohibits a married woman from resuming her maiden name. In re Strikwerda, 216 Va. 470, 220 S.E.2d 245 (1975).

This section did not change the common-law principles to be considered in petitions filed by married women seeking to resume their maiden names. In re Miller, 218 Va. 939, 243 S.E.2d 464 (1978).

When a married woman resumes her maiden name, the possibility of damage to a creditor to whom she and her husband are jointly obligated is no greater than when a single woman marries and takes the surname of her husband, or when a divorced woman or a widow remarries and takes the surname of the husband. This inevitable confusion is not sufficient reason for denying an application for a change of name not sought for a fraudulent purpose. In re Miller, 218 Va. 939, 243 S.E.2d 464 (1978).

A change in the name would not have a disruptive effect on family life. To reason that a name change of the mother would have an embarrassing effect on her children is pure speculation. In re Miller, 218 Va. 939, 243 S.E.2d 464 (1978).

ARTICLE 21.

Miscellaneous Provisions.

§ 8.01-218. Replevin abolished. — No action of replevin shall be hereafter brought. (Code 1950, § 8-647; 1977, c. 617.)

Cross references. — For the statutory provisions relating to detinue, see §§ 8.01-114 through 8.01-123.

§ 8.01-219. Effect of judgment in trover. — A judgment for the plaintiff in an action of trover shall not operate to transfer the title to the property converted unless and until such judgment has been satisfied. (Code 1950, § 8-648; 1977, c. 617.)

Cross references. — For rules of court governing procedure in actions in personam for money, see Rules 3:1 through 3:18.

Law Review. — For article on the abolition of the forms of action in Virginia, see 17 U. Rich. L. Rev. 273 (1983).

§ 8.01-220. Action for alienation of affection, breach of promise, criminal conversation and seduction abolished. — A. Notwithstanding any other provision of law to the contrary, no civil action shall lie or be maintained in this Commonwealth for alienation of affection, breach of promise to marry, or criminal conversation upon which a cause of action arose or occurred on or after June 28, 1968.

B. No civil action for seduction shall lie or be maintained where the cause of action arose or accrued on or after July 1, 1974. (Code 1950, § 20-37.2; 1968, c. 716; 1974, c. 606; 1977, c. 617.)

§ 8.01-220.1 CIVIL REMEDIES AND PROCEDURE § 8.01-220.1:1

REVISERS' NOTE

Former § 8-649 (Seduction) has been deleted. See § 8.01-220 B.

I. DECISIONS UNDER CURRENT LAW.

Action for alienation of affection of son brought by father. — For case assuming, for purposes of the case, that an action for alienation of the affection of a son brought by a father has been abrogated by the statute, or never existed in the first place, see Raftery v. Scott, 756 F.2d 335 (4th Cir. 1985).

As to distinctions between intentional infliction of emotional distress and alienation of affection, see Raftery v. Scott, 756 F.2d 335 (4th Cir. 1985).

§ 8.01-220.1. Defense of interspousal immunity abolished as to certain causes of action arising on or after July 1, 1981. — The common-law defense of interspousal immunity in tort is abolished and shall not constitute a valid defense to any such cause of action arising on or after July 1, 1981. (1981, c. 451.)

Law Review. — For a re-examination of sovereign tort immunity in Virginia, see 15 U. Rich. L. Rev. 247 (1981). For an overview of Virginia Supreme Court decisions on domestic relations, see 15 U. Rich. L. Rev. 321 (1981). For a comment on the legislative abrogation of interspousal immunity in Virginia, see 15 U. Rich. L. Rev. 939 (1981).

I. DECISIONS UNDER CURRENT LAW.

Action brought within federal admiralty jurisdiction. — Virginia law with respect to interspousal immunity in tort held inapplicable in action brought within federal admiralty jurisdiction for wife's injuries sustained allegedly as result of husband's negligent maintenance of pleasure boat. See Byrd v. Byrd, 657 F.2d 615 (4th Cir. 1981).

Applied in Raftery v. Scott, 756 F.2d 335 (4th Cir. 1985).

§ 8.01-220.1:1. Civil immunity for officers, trustees and directors of certain tax exempt organizations. — A. Directors, trustees and officers of organizations exempt from income taxation under § 501 (c) or § 528 of the Internal Revenue Code who serve without compensation shall be immune from civil liability for acts taken in their capacities as officers, trustees or directors of such organizations.

B. In any proceeding against a director, trustee or officer of an organization exempt from income taxation under § 501 (c) or § 528 of the Internal Revenue Code who receives compensation, the damages assessed for acts taken in his capacity as an officer, trustee or director and arising out of a single transaction, occurrence or course of conduct shall not exceed the amount of compensation received by the officer, trustee or director during the twelve months immediately preceding the act or omission for which liability was imposed. As used herein "compensation" shall mean payment for services over and above per diem and expenses.

C. The liability of an officer, trustee or director shall not be limited as provided in this section if the officer, trustee or director engaged in willful misconduct or a knowing violation of the criminal law or if liability derives from the operation of a motor vehicle, or from the violation of a fiduciary obligation imposed during the period of declarant control by § 55-79.74. (1987, c. 637; 1988, c. 566.)

Law Review. — For 1987 survey of Virginia business and corporate law, see 21 U. Rich. L. Rev. 645 (1987).

§ 8.01-220.1:2. Civil immunity for teachers under certain circumstances. — A. Any teacher employed by a local school board in this Commonwealth shall not be liable for any civil damages for any acts or omissions resulting from the supervision, care or discipline of students when such acts or omissions are within such teacher's scope of employment and are taken in good faith in the course of supervision, care or discipline of students, unless such acts or omissions were the result of gross negligence or willful misconduct.

B. This section shall not be construed to limit, withdraw or overturn any defense or immunity already existing in statutory or common law or to affect any claim occurring prior to the effective date of this law. (1997, cc. 349, 879.)

§ 8.01-220.1:3. Immunity for members of church, synagogue or religious body. — No member of any church, synagogue or religious body shall be liable in tort or contract for the actions of any officer, employee, leader, or other member of such church, synagogue or religious body solely because of his membership in such church, synagogue or religious body. Nothing in this section shall prevent any person from being held liable for his own actions. (1997, c. 480.)

The number of this section, § 8.01-220.1:3, was assigned by the Code Commission, the number in the original enactment having been § 8.01-220.1:2.

§ 8.01-220.1:4. Civil immunity for officers and directors of certain nonprofit organizations. — A. Directors and officers of any entity created to ensure the implementation in the Commonwealth of a national tobacco trust established to provide payments to tobacco growers and tobacco quota owners to ameliorate adverse economic consequences resulting from a national settlement of states' claims against tobacco manufacturers shall be immune from civil liability for acts taken in their capacities as officers or directors of such entities.

B. The liability of an officer or director shall not be limited as provided in this section if the officer or director was grossly negligent or engaged in willful misconduct or a knowing violation of the criminal law. (2000, c. 1048.)

Editor's note. — Acts 2000, c. 1048, cl. 2 provides that the immunity provided to officers and directors in subsection A of § 8.01-220.1:4 of the act shall be effective for all acts taken on and after July 1, 1999.

§ 8.01-220.2. Spousal liability for emergency medical care. — On and after July 1, 1984, each spouse shall be jointly and severally liable for all emergency medical care furnished to the other spouse by a physician licensed to practice medicine in the Commonwealth, or by a hospital located in the Commonwealth, including all follow-up inpatient care provided during the initial emergency admission to any such hospital, which is furnished while the spouses are living together. For the purposes of this section, emergency medical care shall mean any care the attending physician or other health care professional deems necessary to preserve the patient's life or health and which, if not rendered timely, can be reasonably anticipated to adversely affect the patient's recovery or imperil his life or health. (1984, c. 482.)

§ 8.01-221. Damages from violation of statute, remedy therefor and penalty. — Any person injured by the violation of any statute may recover

§ 8.01-221   CIVIL REMEDIES AND PROCEDURE   § 8.01-221

from the offender such damages as he may sustain by reason of the violation, even though a penalty or forfeiture for such violation be thereby imposed, unless such penalty or forfeiture be expressly mentioned to be in lieu of such damages. And the damages so sustained together with any penalty or forfeiture imposed for the violation of the statute may be recovered in a single action when the same person is entitled to both damages and penalty; but nothing herein contained shall affect the existing statutes of limitation applicable to the foregoing causes of action respectively. (Code 1950, § 8-652; 1954, c. 333; 1977, c. 617.)

Cross references. — As to the recovery of penalties by the Commonwealth, see § 19.2-341.

Law Review. — For survey of Virginia law on property for the year 1973-1974, see 60 Va. L. Rev. 1583 (1974).

I. Decisions Under Current Law.
II. Decisions Under Prior Law.

I. DECISIONS UNDER CURRENT LAW.

Section confers no new right of action. — This section merely preserves any right of action the injured person may have, and does not give him any new right of action. Ward v. Connor, 495 F. Supp. 434 (E.D. Va. 1980), rev'd on other grounds, 657 F.2d 45 (4th Cir. 1981), cert. denied, 455 U.S. 907, 102 S. Ct. 1253, 71 L. Ed. 2d 445 (1982).

This section creates no new right of action for damages for violation of some other criminal or penalty statute; no civil right of action exists unless such other statute by its terms so provides, or unless proof of the same facts that establish violation of such other statute also constitutes proof of an otherwise existing civil action for damages independent of the criminal statute. Vansant & Gusler, Inc. v. Washington, 245 Va. 356, 429 S.E.2d 31 (1993).

This section permits damages for those injured by a violation of the Virginia Code. However, this section does not create a new right of action where none existed. Instead, it prevents a wrongdoer from avoiding civil liability based on the theory that he has paid his penalty under a penal statute. Pettengill v. United States, 867 F. Supp. 380 (E.D. Va. 1994).

Although this section does not create any new rights of action but instead preserves any existing right of action that an injured person may have against a wrongdoer who has previously been the subject of statutory penalties for his misconduct, it is consistent with the idea that the provision for a statutory penalty does not foreclose a person's right to recover damages for the same statutory violation unless the statute so provides. Morgan v. American Family Life Assurance Co., 559 F. Supp. 477 (W.D. Va. 1983).

Applied in A & E Supply Co. v. Nationwide Mut. Fire Ins. Co., 798 F.2d 669 (4th Cir. 1986).

II. DECISIONS UNDER PRIOR LAW.

Editor's note. — The cases cited below were decided under corresponding provisions of former law. The term "this section," as used below, refers to former provisions.

Purpose. — It is very evident that the purpose of this section was merely to preserve to an injured person the right to maintain his action for the injury he may have received by reason of the wrongdoing of another, and to prevent the wrongdoer from setting up the defense that he had paid the penalty of his wrongdoing under a penal statute. It cannot be supposed that in enacting this section the legislature had the remotest idea of creating any new ground for bringing an action for damages. Tyler v. Western Union Tel. Co., 54 F. 634 (W.D. Va. 1893). See also Connolly v. Western Union Tel. Co., 100 Va. 51, 40 S.E. 618 (1902); Hortenstein v. Virginia-Carolina Ry., 102 Va. 914, 47 S.E. 996 (1904).

Confers no new right of action. — This section merely preserves any right of action the injured person may have, and does not give him any new right of action. Tyler v. Western Union Tel. Co., 54 F. 634 (W.D. Va. 1893).

This section confers no new or enlarged right upon a party injured as a result of the violation of a statute. A party suing for an injury arising from an act of a defendant, in violation of a statute, claiming damages, and not merely the penalty prescribed in the act, must allege and prove the same facts he would have to allege and prove if the act of negligence complained of was not in violation of a statute. Hortenstein v. Virginia-Carolina Ry., 102 Va. 914, 47 S.E. 996 (1904).

Applies to any violation of statutory duty. — This section seems, in terms, to provide for the measure of damages in any case in which there shall be an injury resulting from the violation of any statute in this State. Western Union Tel. Co. v. Reynolds Bros., 77 Va. 173 (1883).

But proximate cause must also be established. — While one who violates a statute or an ordinance may be regarded as a wrongdoer, and the act regarded as negligence, still it may or may not be the proximate cause of the injury complained of according to the facts of the particular case. The element of proximate cause must be established, and it will not necessarily be presumed from the fact that an ordinance or statute has been violated. Wyatt v. C & P Tel. Co., 158 Va. 470, 163 S.E. 370 (1932).

Common-law duty of landlords not enlarged. — In an action against landlords to recover for injuries sustained by a tenant's invitee when some steps at the entrance of defendants' building tilted over and caused him to fall, where it was contended that the steps were being maintained in violation of local ordinances, it was held that neither the ordinances nor this section enlarged the common-law duty of the landlords to their tenant or the tenant's invitee. Oliver v. Cashin, 192 Va. 540, 65 S.E.2d 571 (1951).

§ 8.01-222. Notice to be given cities and towns of claims for damages for negligence. — No action shall be maintained against any city or town for injury to any person or property or for wrongful death alleged to have been sustained by reason of the negligence of the city or town, or of any officer, agent or employee thereof, unless a written statement by the claimant, his agent, attorney or representative of the nature of the claim and of the time and place at which the injury is alleged to have occurred or been received shall have been filed with the city attorney or town attorney, or with the mayor, or chief executive, within six months after such cause of action shall have accrued, except if the complainant during such six-month period is able to establish by clear and convincing evidence that due to the injury sustained for which a claim is asserted that he was physically or mentally unable to give such notice within the six-month period, then the time for giving notice shall be tolled until the claimant sufficiently recovers from said injury so as to be able to give such notice; and statements pursuant to this section shall be valid, notwithstanding any contrary charter provision of any city or town.

This section, on and after June 30, 1954, shall take precedence over the provisions of all charters and amendments thereto of municipal corporations in conflict herewith granted prior to such date. It is further declared that as to any such charter or amendment thereto, granted on and after such date, that any provision therein in conflict with this section shall be deemed to be invalid as being in conflict with Article IV, Section 12 of the Constitution of Virginia unless such conflict be stated in the title to such proposed charter or amendment thereto by the words "conflicting with § 8.01-222 of the Code" or substantially similar language. (Code 1950, § 8-653; 1954, c. 427; 1962, c. 483; 1971, Ex. Sess., c. 1; 1973, c. 6; 1977, c. 617.)

Law Review. — For survey of Virginia law on torts for the year 1971-1972, see 58 Va. L. Rev. 1349 (1972). For survey of Virginia law on municipal corporations for the year 1972-1973, see 59 Va. L. Rev. 1548 (1973). For survey of Virginia law on torts for the year 1972-1973, see 59 Va. L. Rev. 1590 (1973). For survey of Virginia law on torts for the year 1976-77, see 63 Va. L. Rev. 1491 (1977). For note on the abrogation of sovereign immunity in Virginia: The Virginia Tort Claims Act, see 7 Geo. Mason L. Rev. 291 (1984).

I. Decisions Under Current Law.
II. Decisions Under Prior Law.

I. DECISIONS UNDER CURRENT LAW.

Purpose of the statute is to enable a city to make a prompt investigation of tort claims, to correct dangerous or defective conditions, and, where justified, to avoid the expense and delay of litigation by making voluntary settlements with claimants. Town of Crewe v. Marler, 228 Va. 109, 319 S.E.2d 748 (1984).

Provisions of this section are mandatory, but not jurisdictional. Town of Crewe v. Marler, 228 Va. 109, 319 S.E.2d 748 (1984); Miles v. City of Richmond, 236 Va. 341, 373 S.E.2d 715 (1988).

Notice provision applies to nuisance claims. — The notice of injury provisions of

§ 8.01-222　　　　　　　CIVIL REMEDIES AND PROCEDURE　　　　　　　§ 8.01-222

this section apply to nuisance claims in which negligence is an essential element. Breeding v. Hensley, 258 Va. 207, 519 S.E.2d 369 (1999).

Notice insufficient absent description of precise location. — The purported notice contained in letters from the claimant's attorney to the town manager failed to comply substantially with the statute where the letters did not describe the precise location of the accident, even though the city had actual notice of the time and place of the accident. Town of Crewe v. Marler, 228 Va. 109, 319 S.E.2d 748 (1984).

No exception for failure to state place of injury even if "everyone" knows of it. — The General Assembly has not made an exception in the statute in favor of those claimants who fail to state the place at which an injury occurs, even though "everyone" may know the location of injury. The arbitrary and peremptory provisions of the statute are necessary to accomplish the purposes of the enactment. Town of Crewe v. Marler, 228 Va. 109, 319 S.E.2d 748 (1984).

This section is to be construed liberally, and substantial compliance with its terms is sufficient. Miles v. City of Richmond, 236 Va. 341, 373 S.E.2d 715 (1988).

Liberal construction does not remedy failure to state location. — The statute should be construed liberally and substantial compliance with its terms is sufficient. Nevertheless, construction can never supply the total absence of a necessary allegation and when a notice wholly fails to state where an accident occurred, such an omission cannot be remedied by statutory construction. Town of Crewe v. Marler, 228 Va. 109, 319 S.E.2d 748 (1984).

Section not applicable to municipal employees. — The terms of this section do not extend by implication to apply to claims against municipal employees. Breeding v. Hensley, 258 Va. 207, 519 S.E.2d 369 (1999).

Agent of injured party. — A building superintendent who prepared, signed, and forwarded to the city attorney a statement concerning the injury of a woman on a public elevator was her agent or representative in compliance with this section. Miles v. City of Richmond, 236 Va. 341, 373 S.E.2d 715 (1988).

II. DECISIONS UNDER PRIOR LAW.

Editor's note. — The cases cited below were decided under corresponding provisions of former law. The term "this section," as used below, refers to former provisions.

The purpose of this section is to afford the city authorities the opportunity to investigate the circumstances, examine the locality in which the injury is alleged to have occurred, and to discover the witnesses promptly so as to ascertain the facts while their recollections are fresh. Such provisions tend to discourage and avoid the expense of litigation because a prompt settlement may be made in a proper case. They also tend to prevent perjury and fraud. City of South Norfolk v. Dail, 187 Va. 495, 47 S.E.2d 405 (1948).

The purpose of this section is to enable a city to make a prompt investigation of tort claims, to correct dangerous or defective conditions, and, where justified, to avoid the expense and delay of litigation by making voluntary settlements with claimants. A written report of accident filed by police officers upon notice from claimant fulfilled that purpose. Heller v. City of Virginia Beach, 213 Va. 683, 194 S.E.2d 696 (1973).

Giving of notice is mandatory and essential. — The present rule in Virginia is that the giving of the required notice is mandatory and is an essential element of plaintiff's case, which he must allege and prove. But failure to make the allegation or to prove that the notice had been given, like any other allegation and proof of an essential element of plaintiff's case, must be raised in the same manner as any other nonjurisdictional defense to the action. Daniel v. City of Richmond, 199 Va. 490, 100 S.E.2d 763 (1957).

Time prescribed is arbitrary and peremptory. — The time in which to give the notice prescribed by this section is arbitrary and peremptory. The legislature may make any exception it chooses, or refuse to make any at all, and, whether or not an exception exists, for instance in favor of infants, insane persons or others, is to be determined from the statutory law. If exceptions are made by statute, they exist; if not, they do not exist. Daniel v. City of Richmond, 199 Va. 490, 100 S.E.2d 763 (1957).

Failure to give notice merely gives preferential benefit to city. — In reality, the failure to give notice to the city within the prescribed time does no more than confer upon the city the preferential benefit of a statute of limitations. City of South Norfolk v. Dail, 187 Va. 495, 47 S.E.2d 405 (1948).

It is a matter of defense. — The failure to make the allegation of notice should be taken advantage of by the city as a matter of defense to the action. City of South Norfolk v. Dail, 187 Va. 495, 47 S.E.2d 405 (1948).

And is not jurisdictional or a bar to an action. — While the provisions of this section are mandatory and a compliance with them is necessary, they are not jurisdictional to the institution of an action against a city. Therefore, failure to allege compliance with this section in the declaration should not be held to be a complete bar to the institution of an action against a city, nor a condition precedent to the right to institute such an action. City of South Norfolk v. Dail, 187 Va. 495, 47 S.E.2d 405 (1948).

The passage of time has no legal effect

on a city's omission of performance of the governmental function of collecting garbage, for which the city is immune from liability, and does not make the omission one relating to the city's proprietary function. Taylor v. City of Newport News, 214 Va. 9, 197 S.E.2d 209 (1973).

Sufficiency of notice. — A notice was adequate which told the city of the nature of the plaintiff's claim when the injury occurred and the place at which the injury was suffered. City of Portsmouth v. Cilumbrello, 204 Va. 11, 129 S.E.2d 31 (1963).

A written statement made in the claimant's presence with his approval as he furnished the necessary information to police officers is sufficient "notice." Heller v. City of Virginia Beach, 213 Va. 683, 194 S.E.2d 696 (1973).

An oral report by telephone did not sufficiently comply with the notice requirement and actual knowledge by the city of the details of the accident could not be substituted for the notice required by statute or charter. Heller v. City of Virginia Beach, 213 Va. 683, 194 S.E.2d 696 (1973).

The notice required in this section was held not necessary in a suit in admiralty. The West Point, 71 F. Supp. 206 (E.D. Va. 1947).

Objection that notice not given must be made in trial court. — A city cannot raise the matter of a plaintiff's failure to give notice as required by this section for the first time in the Supreme Court. City of South Norfolk v. Dail, 187 Va. 495, 47 S.E.2d 405 (1948).

A city employee may act in a dual capacity to the extent of giving routine mechanical assistance to those desiring to file tort claims against the city. A police officer who wrote out, signed and arranged for delivery to the city attorney of the statement of claim did so as the claimant's agent or representative in substantial compliance with the provisions of this section. Heller v. City of Virginia Beach, 213 Va. 683, 194 S.E.2d 696 (1973).

§ 8.01-223. Lack of privity no defense in certain cases. — In cases not provided for in § 8.2-318 where recovery of damages for injury to person, including death, or to property resulting from negligence is sought, lack of privity between the parties shall be no defense. (Code 1950, § 8-654.4; 1966, c. 439; 1977, c. 617.)

Law Review. — For note discussing Virginia's disavowal of privity of contract in commercial transactions as a basis for extended liability, see 14 Wm. & Mary L. Rev. 409 (1972). For article, "The Collision of Tort and Contract in the Construction Industry," see 21 U. Rich. L. Rev. 457 (1987). For survey on construction law in Virginia for 1989, see 23 U. Rich. L. Rev. 541 (1989).

I. Decisions Under Current Law.
II. Decisions Under Prior Law.

I. DECISIONS UNDER CURRENT LAW.

The legislature intended that this section apply only from the date of its enactment. Farish v. Courion Indus., Inc., 722 F.2d 74 (4th Cir. 1983), aff'd on reh'g en banc, 754 F.2d 1111 (4th Cir. 1988).

The legislature intended this section and § 8.2-318 to apply prospectively only from the dates of their enactments. Farish v. Courion Indus., Inc., 754 F.2d 1111 (4th Cir. 1985).

This section is a companion statute to § 8.2-318. Bryant Elec. Co. v. City of Fredericksburg, 762 F.2d 1192 (4th Cir. 1985).

This section is in derogation of the common-law privity requirement. — Under Virginia's rules of statutory construction, it is not to be extended beyond its express terms. Farish v. Courion Indus., Inc., 722 F.2d 74 (4th Cir. 1983), aff'd on reh'g en banc, 754 F.2d 1111 (4th Cir. 1985); Bryant Elec. Co. v. City of Fredericksburg, 762 F.2d 1192 (4th Cir. 1985), aff'd on reh'g en banc, 754 F.2d 1111 (4th Cir. 1988).

Privity not abolished where only economic loss suffered. — This section does not appear to abolish the common-law requirement of privity for negligence suits in which the plaintiff has suffered only economic loss. Bryant Elec. Co. v. City of Fredericksburg, 762 F.2d 1192 (4th Cir. 1985).

This section does not eliminate the privity requirement in a negligence action for economic loss alone. Blake Constr. Co. v. Alley, 233 Va. 31, 353 S.E.2d 724 (1987).

Where there is no duty alleged between plaintiff and defendants, and because seemingly the loss or damage is purely economic where no privity exists, there is no cause of action for negligence. John C. Holland Enters., Inc. v. J.P. Mascaro & Sons, 653 F. Supp. 1242 (E.D. Va.), aff'd, 829 F.2d 1120 (4th Cir. 1987).

This section does not eliminate the privity requirement in a negligence action for economic loss alone because it is in derogation of the common law and is not to be enlarged beyond its express terms. Beard Plumbing & Heating v. Thompson Plastics, 152 F.3d 313 (4th Cir. 1998).

Lack of privity held bar to recovery. — Virginia law does not permit recovery by a home purchaser against the pool installer and the architect for damages to an indoor swimming pool and the foundation of a house caused by a leaking pool, where the pool installer and the architect were not in privity of contract with the home purchaser; the damages were injuries to property and not economic losses, and even if the indoor swimming pool and its separate room enclosure were built against the house but outside its foundation, that fact would not affect the result. Sensenbrenner v. Rust, Orling & Neale, Architects, Inc., 236 Va. 419, 374 S.E.2d 55 (1988).

Where the stockholder's reliance upon alleged substandard professional services rendered by accounting firm induced him to make the warranties and to execute the escrow indemnity covenant that became the foundation of his liability to corporation, and his liability was measured by the diminution in the value of the whole stock package, i.e., the difference between the sale price of his stock fixed in reliance upon the bargained-for services and the value determined by a correct accounting formula, in effect, stockholder alleged nothing more than disappointed economic expectations, and his loss, then, was a purely economic loss. Therefore, because stockholder lacking privity of contract with accounting firm and sought to recover damages for economic loss under negligence principles, the trial court did not err in granting the accounting firm's demurrer to the original motion for judgment. Ward v. Ernst & Young, 246 Va. 317, 435 S.E.2d 628 (1993).

Applied in Hayward v. Holiday Inns, Inc., 459 F. Supp. 634 (E.D. Va. 1978); Obenshain v. Halliday, 504 F. Supp. 946 (E.D. Va. 1980); Copenhaver v. Rogers, 238 Va. 361, 384 S.E.2d 593 (1989); Redman v. John D. Brush & Co., 111 F.3d 1174 (W.D. Va. 1997); Doe v. Irvine Scientific Sales Co., 7 F. Supp. 2d 737 (E.D. Va. 1998).

II. DECISIONS UNDER PRIOR LAW.

Editor's note. — The case cited below was decided under corresponding provisions of former law. The term "this section," as used below, refers to former provisions.

Neither this section nor § 8.2-318 alters the rule demanding privity of contract in warranty actions against architects. Gravely v. Providence Partnership, 549 F.2d 958 (4th Cir. 1977).

§ 8.01-223.1. Use of constitutional rights. — In any civil action the exercise by a party of any constitutional protection shall not be used against him. (1985, c. 192.)

§ 8.01-224. Defense of governmental immunity not available to certain persons in actions for damages from blasting, etc. — The defense of governmental immunity shall not be available to any person, firm or corporation in any cause of action for damages to the property of others proximately or directly resulting from blasting or the use of explosives in the performance of work for or on behalf of any governmental agency. (Code 1950, § 8-654.5; 1970, c. 642; 1977, c. 617.)

Law Review. — For survey of recent legislation on torts — blasting and governmental immunity, see 5 U. Rich. L. Rev. 201 (1970). For note on the abrogation of sovereign immunity in Virginia: The Virginia Tort Claims Act, see 7 Geo. Mason L. Rev. 291 (1984).

I. DECISIONS UNDER CURRENT LAW.

Applied in Laughon & Johnson, Inc. v. Burch, 222 Va. 200, 278 S.E.2d 856 (1981).

§ 8.01-225. Persons rendering emergency care, obstetrical services exempt from liability. — A. Any person who:

1. In good faith, renders emergency care or assistance, without compensation, to any ill or injured person at the scene of an accident, fire, or any life-threatening emergency, or en route therefrom to any hospital, medical clinic or doctor's office, shall not be liable for any civil damages for acts or omissions resulting from the rendering of such care or assistance.

2. In the absence of gross negligence, renders emergency obstetrical care or assistance to a female in active labor who has not previously been cared for in

connection with the pregnancy by such person or by another professionally associated with such person and whose medical records are not reasonably available to such person shall not be liable for any civil damages for acts or omissions resulting from the rendering of such emergency care or assistance. The immunity herein granted shall apply only to the emergency medical care provided.

3. In good faith and without compensation, administers epinephrine to an individual for whom an insect sting treatment kit has been prescribed shall not be liable for any civil damages for ordinary negligence in acts or omissions resulting from the rendering of such treatment if he has reason to believe that the individual receiving the injection is suffering or is about to suffer a life-threatening anaphylactic reaction.

4. Provides assistance upon request of any police agency, fire department, rescue or emergency squad, or any governmental agency in the event of an accident or other emergency involving the use, handling, transportation, transmission or storage of liquefied petroleum gas, liquefied natural gas, hazardous material or hazardous waste as defined in § 18.2-278.1 or regulations of the Virginia Waste Management Board shall not be liable for any civil damages resulting from any act of commission or omission on his part in the course of his rendering such assistance in good faith.

5. Is an emergency medical care attendant or technician possessing a valid certificate issued by authority of the State Board of Health who in good faith renders emergency care or assistance whether in person or by telephone or other means of communication, without compensation, to any injured or ill person, whether at the scene of an accident, fire or any other place, or while transporting such injured or ill person to, from or between any hospital, medical facility, medical clinic, doctor's office or other similar or related medical facility, shall not be liable for any civil damages for acts or omissions resulting from the rendering of such emergency care, treatment or assistance, including but in no way limited to acts or omissions which involve violations of State Department of Health regulations or any other state regulations in the rendering of such emergency care or assistance.

6. Has attended and successfully completed a course in cardiopulmonary resuscitation which has been approved by the State Board of Health who, in good faith and without compensation, renders or administers emergency cardiopulmonary resuscitation, cardiac defibrillation, including, but not limited to, the use of an automated external defibrillator, or other emergency life-sustaining or resuscitative treatments or procedures which have been approved by the State Board of Health to any sick or injured person, whether at the scene of a fire, an accident or any other place, or while transporting such person to or from any hospital, clinic, doctor's office or other medical facility, shall be deemed qualified to administer such emergency treatments and procedures and shall not be liable for acts or omissions resulting from the rendering of such emergency resuscitative treatments or procedures.

7. In compliance with § 32.1-111.14:1 registers an automated external defibrillator for use at the scene of an emergency, operates a registered automated external defibrillator at the scene of an emergency, trains individuals to be operators of registered automated external defibrillators, or orders automated external defibrillators which are subsequently registered, shall be immune from civil liability for any personal injury that results from any act or omission in the use of a registered automated external defibrillator in an emergency where the person performing the defibrillation acts as an ordinary, reasonably prudent person would have acted under the same or similar circumstances, unless such personal injury results from gross negligence or willful or wanton misconduct of the person rendering such emergency care.

8. Is a volunteer in good standing and certified to render emergency care by the National Ski Patrol System, Inc., who, in good faith and without compen-

sation, renders emergency care or assistance to any injured or ill person, whether at the scene of a ski resort rescue, outdoor emergency rescue or any other place or while transporting such injured or ill person to a place accessible for transfer to any available emergency medical system unit, or any resort owner voluntarily providing a ski patroller employed by him to engage in rescue or recovery work at a resort not owned or operated by him, shall not be liable for any civil damages for acts or omissions resulting from the rendering of such emergency care, treatment or assistance, including but not limited to acts or omissions which involve violations of any state regulation or any standard of the National Ski Patrol System, Inc., in the rendering of such emergency care or assistance, unless such act or omission was the result of gross negligence or willful misconduct.

9. Is an employee of a school board, authorized by a prescriber and trained in the administration of insulin and glucagon, who, upon the written request of the parents as defined in § 22.1-1, assists with the administration of insulin or administers glucagon to a student diagnosed as having diabetes who requires insulin injections during the school day or for whom glucagon has been prescribed for the emergency treatment of hypoglycemia shall not be liable for any civil damages for ordinary negligence in acts or omissions resulting from the rendering of such treatment if the insulin is administered according to the child's medication schedule or such employee has reason to believe that the individual receiving the glucagon is suffering or is about to suffer life-threatening hypoglycemia. Whenever any employee of a school board is covered by the immunity granted herein, the school board employing him shall not be liable for any civil damages for ordinary negligence in acts or omissions resulting from the rendering of such insulin or glucagon treatment.

B. Any licensed physician serving without compensation as the operational medical director for a licensed emergency medical services agency in this Commonwealth shall not be liable for any civil damages for any act or omission resulting from the rendering of emergency medical services in good faith by the personnel of such licensed agency unless such act or omission was the result of such physician's gross negligence or willful misconduct.

Any person serving without compensation as a dispatcher for any licensed public or nonprofit emergency services agency in this Commonwealth shall not be liable for any civil damages for any act or omission resulting from the rendering of emergency services in good faith by the personnel of such licensed agency unless such act or omission was the result of such dispatcher's gross negligence or willful misconduct.

Any individual, certified by the State Office of Emergency Medical Services as an emergency medical services instructor and pursuant to a written agreement with such office, who, in good faith and in the performance of his duties, provides instruction to persons for certification or recertification as a certified basic life support or advanced life support emergency medical services technician shall not be liable for any civil damages for acts or omissions on his part directly relating to his activities on behalf of such office unless such act or omission was the result of such emergency medical services instructor's gross negligence or willful misconduct.

Any licensed physician serving without compensation as a medical advisor to an E-911 system in this Commonwealth shall not be liable for any civil damages for any act or omission resulting from rendering medical advice in good faith to establish protocols to be used by the personnel of the E-911 service, as defined in § 58.1-3813.1, when answering emergency calls unless such act or omission was the result of such physician's gross negligence or willful misconduct.

Any licensed physician who directs the provision of emergency medical services, as authorized by the State Board of Health, through a communications device shall not be liable for any civil damages for any act or omission resulting from the rendering of such emergency medical services unless such act or omission was the result of such physician's gross negligence or willful misconduct.

Any licensed physician serving without compensation as a supervisor of a registered automated external defibrillator in this Commonwealth shall not be liable for any civil damages for any act or omission resulting from rendering medical advice in good faith to the registrant of the automated external defibrillator relating to personnel training, local emergency medical services coordination, protocol approval, automated external defibrillator deployment strategies, and equipment maintenance plans and records unless such act or omission was the result of such physician's gross negligence or willful misconduct.

C. Any provider of telecommunication service, as defined in § 58.1-3812, including mobile service, in this Commonwealth shall not be liable for any civil damages for any act or omission resulting from rendering such service with or without charge related to emergency calls unless such act or omission was the result of such service provider's gross negligence or willful misconduct.

Any volunteer engaging in rescue or recovery work at a mine or any mine operator voluntarily providing personnel to engage in rescue or recovery work at a mine not owned or operated by such operator, shall not be liable for civil damages for acts or omissions resulting from the rendering of such rescue or recovery work in good faith unless such act or omission was the result of gross negligence or willful misconduct.

D. Nothing contained in this section shall be construed to provide immunity from liability arising out of the operation of a motor vehicle.

For the purposes of this section, the term "compensation" shall not be construed to include (i) the salaries of police, fire or other public officials or personnel who render such emergency assistance, (ii) the salaries or wages of employees of a coal producer engaging in emergency medical technician service or first aid service pursuant to the provisions of §§ 45.1-161.38, 45.1-161.101, 45.1-161.199 or § 45.1-161.263, (iii) complimentary lift tickets, food, lodging or other gifts provided as a gratuity to volunteer members of the National Ski Patrol System, Inc., by any resort, group or agency, or (iv) the salary of any person who, in compliance with § 32.1-111.14:1, (a) registers an automated external defibrillator for the use at the scene of an emergency, (b) trains individuals, in courses approved by the Board of Health, to operate registered automated external defibrillators at the scene of emergencies, (c) orders automated external defibrillators for subsequent registration and use at the scene of emergencies, or (d) operates, in accordance with the training required by § 32.1-111.14:1, a registered automated external defibrillator at the scene of an emergency.

For the purposes of this section, an emergency medical care attendant or technician shall be deemed to include a person licensed or certified as such or its equivalent by any other state when he is performing services which he is licensed or certified to perform by such other state in caring for a patient in transit in this Commonwealth, which care originated in such other state. (Code 1950, § 54-276.9; 1962, c. 449; 1964, c. 568; 1968, c. 796; 1972, c. 578; 1975, c. 508; 1977, c. 441; 1978, cc. 94, 707; 1979, cc. 713, 729; 1980, c. 419; 1983, c. 72; 1984, cc. 493, 577; 1987, cc. 260, 382; 1990, c. 898; 1996, c. 899; 1997, cc. 334, 809; 1998, cc. 493, 500; 1999, cc. 570, 1000; 2000, cc. 928, 1064.)

Editor's note. — This section was enacted, and a substantially identical section, § 54-276.9, was repealed, by Acts 1979, c. 713, effective Oct. 1, 1979, a companion act to Acts 1979, c. 711, which rewrote Title 32 as Title 32.1. Acts 1979, c. 729, amended former § 54-276.9 by adding a new subsection (a1). The Code Commission codified subsection (a1), added to § 54-276.9 by Acts 1979, c. 729, as a subsection in this § 8.01-225 as set out above. See § 9-77.11.

The 1999 amendments. — The 1999 amendment by c. 570, in subsection A, deleted "and" preceding "such individual" in subdivision 6, and added subdivision 9.

The 1999 amendment by c. 1000, divided former subsection A into present subsection A and subdivision A 1 by inserting the 1 designation preceding "In good faith"; inserted the 2 through 6 designations at the beginning of the former first through fifth paragraphs; deleted "Any person who" at the beginning of the present subdivisions A 2 through A 4; substituted "Is an" for "Any" in subdivision A 5, in present subdivision A 6, substituted "Has" for "Any person having," and inserted "including, but not limited to, the use of an automated external defibrillator", added present subdivision A 7, inserted the 8 designation at the beginning of the former sixth paragraph, and substituted "Is a" for "Any" preceding "volunteer"; deleted the subsection B1 designation preceding "Any licensed physician," and added the last paragraph of subsection B; redesignated former subsection B2 as present subsection C, and added the present second paragraph; redesignated former subsection C as present subsection D; in present subsection D, deleted the former second paragraph, which read: "Any licensed physician who directs the provision of emergency medical services, as authorized by the State Board of Health, through a communications device shall not be liable for any civil damages for any act or omission resulting from the rendering of such emergency medical services unless such act or omission was the result of such physician's gross negligence or willful misconduct," and deleted the former last paragraph which read: "Any volunteer engaging in rescue or recovery work at a mine or any mine operator voluntarily providing personnel to engage in rescue or recovery work at a mine not owned or operated by such operator, shall not be liable for civil damages for acts or omissions resulting from the rendering of such rescue or recovery work in good faith unless such act or omission was the result of gross negligence or willful misconduct."

The 2000 amendments. — The 2000 amendment by c. 928 rewrote subdivision A 7; substituted "Is an" for "Any" at the beginning of present subdivision A 9; added the fifth undesignated paragraph in present subsection B; in the second undesignated paragraph of present subsection D, deleted "or" preceding "(iii)", and added "or" and clause (iv) at the end of the paragraph.

The 2000 amendment by c. 1064 substituted "service" for "system," and substituted "§ 58.1-3813.1" for "§ 58.1-3813" in the next-to-last paragraph of subsection C.

Law Review. — For survey of Virginia law on torts for the year 1978-1979, see 66 Va. L. Rev. 375 (1980). For article, "A Duty to Rescue: Some Thoughts on Criminal Liability," see 69 Va. L. Rev. 1273 (1983). For comment on Virginia's Birth-Related Neurological Injury Compensation Act, see 22 U. Rich. L. Rev. 431 (1988).

I. DECISIONS UNDER CURRENT LAW.

Common law Good Samaritan doctrine has been accepted in Virginia and therefore applies to the federal government under the Federal Tort Claims Act. Creasy v. United States, 645 F. Supp. 853 (W.D. Va. 1986).

Volunteers are normally liable for negligence. — The enactment of this section, which exempts from civil liability any person who renders emergency care or assistance in good faith without compensation, indicates that volunteers are normally liable for negligence in Virginia. Creasy v. United States, 645 F. Supp. 853 (W.D. Va. 1986).

§ 8.01-225.1. Immunity for team physicians. — Any physician, surgeon or chiropractor licensed to practice by the Board of Medicine in this Commonwealth who, in the absence of gross negligence or willful misconduct, renders emergency medical care or emergency treatment to a participant in an athletic event sponsored by a public, private or parochial elementary, middle or high school while acting without compensation as a team physician, shall not be liable for civil damages resulting from any act or omission related to such care or treatment. (1989, c. 436; 1993, c. 702.)

§ 8.01-225.2. Immunity for those rendering emergency care to animals. — Any person, including a person licensed to practice veterinary medicine, who in good faith and without compensation renders emergency care or treatment to an injured animal at the scene of an emergency or accident shall not be liable for any injuries to such animals resulting from the rendering of such care or treatment. (1998, c. 669.)

§ 8.01-226. Duty of care to law-enforcement officers and firefighters, etc. — An owner or occupant of real property containing premises normally open to the public shall, with respect to such premises, owe to firefighters, Department of Emergency Management hazardous materials officers, nonfirefighter regional hazardous materials emergency response team members, and law-enforcement officers who in the performance of their duties come upon that portion of the premises normally open to the public the duty to maintain the same in a reasonably safe condition or to warn of dangers thereon of which he knows or has reason to know, whether or not such premises are at the time open to the public.

An owner or occupant of real property containing premises not normally open to the public shall, with respect to such premises, owe the same duty to firefighters, Department of Emergency Management hazardous materials officers, nonfirefighter regional hazardous materials emergency response team members, and law-enforcement officers who he knows or has reason to know are upon, about to come upon or imminently likely to come upon that portion of the premises not normally open to the public.

While otherwise engaged in the performance of his duties, a law-enforcement officer, Department of Emergency Management hazardous materials officer, nonfirefighter regional hazardous materials emergency response team member, or firefighter shall be owed a duty of ordinary care.

For purposes of this section, the term "law-enforcement officers" shall mean only police officers, sheriffs and deputy sheriffs and the term "firefighter" includes (i) emergency medical personnel and (ii) special forest wardens designated pursuant to § 10.1-1135. (1987, c. 442; 1992, c. 731; 1996, cc. 646, 660; 2000, c. 962.)

The 2000 amendments. — The 2000 amendment by c. 962, in the last paragraph, inserted the clause (i) designator, added "and" at the end of clause (i) and added clause (ii).

I. DECISIONS UNDER CURRENT LAW.

The fireman's rule. — This statute does not abrogate the common law fireman's rule, but rather, clarifies the duty of care owed to firemen and police officers while performing their duties. The 1992 amendment was not intended to create liability where there is none or to change the assumption of risk factor. Greene v. Consolidated Freightways Corp., 74 F. Supp. 2d 616 (E.D. Va. 1999).

§ 8.01-226.1. Civil immunity when participating in certain Bar Association activities. — Any person shall be immune from civil liability for, or resulting from, any act, decision, omission, communication, finding, opinion or conclusion done or made in connection with the investigation and counseling of a lawyer for possible substance abuse pursuant to the guidelines of the Virginia Bar Association plan of "Lawyers Helping Lawyers," or in the performance of his duties as a member or agent of the Virginia Bar Association's Committee on Substance Abuse, which Committee functions primarily to provide assistance in the form of counseling to any lawyer having an impaired ability to practice law because of abuse of the use of alcohol or other drug if such act, decision, omission, communication, finding, opinion or conclusion is done or made in good faith and without malicious intent. The Virginia Bar Association and its officers, directors, employees, servants and agents shall also be immune from civil liability for any acts or omissions made or done in good faith and without malicious intent for, or resulting from, (i) the Virginia Bar Association plan of "Lawyers Helping Lawyers," (ii) any act, decision, omission, communication, finding, opinion or conclusion of the Committee on Substance Abuse or any of its members or agents, or (iii) the establishment of programs or the activities of such Committee.

Nothing in this section shall be construed to grant immunity to any claim by a client against a person licensed to practice law. (1987, c. 527; 1992, c. 534.)

The number of this section was assigned by the Virginia Code Commission, the number in the 1987 act having been 8.01-226.

§ **8.01-226.2. Civil immunity for licensed professional engineers and licensed architects participating in rescue or relief assistance.** — Any licensed professional engineer or licensed architect who, in good faith and without charge or compensation, utilizes his professional skills in providing rescue or relief assistance at the scene of or in connection with a natural or manmade disaster or other life-threatening emergency, shall not be liable for any civil damages for acts or omissions on his part resulting from the rendering of such assistance or professional services in the absence of gross negligence or willful misconduct. (1992, c. 702; 1997, c. 866.)

§ **8.01-226.3. Civil immunity for officers, directors and members of certain crime information-gathering organizations.** — Any officer, director or member of a nonprofit organization which, pursuant to a written agreement with a local government or a law-enforcement agency, regularly assists law-enforcement agencies by (i) publicly soliciting information from anonymous informants concerning criminal activity; (ii) gathering such information from informants; (iii) offering and paying rewards to informants for such information; and (iv) communicating such information to law-enforcement agencies, shall not be liable for any civil damages for acts or omissions on his part directly relating to his activities on behalf of such organization but only in the absence of gross negligence or willful misconduct. (1993, c. 769.)

§ **8.01-226.4. Civil immunity for hospice volunteers.** — Any individual who, in good faith, without compensation, and in the absence of gross negligence or willful misconduct, renders care to a terminally ill patient pursuant to a hospice program whose sole purpose is to provide care and treatment to terminally ill patients and whose services are equally available to all members of the community, shall not be liable for any civil damages for acts or omissions resulting from the rendering of such care. (1994, c. 738.)

§ **8.01-226.5. Immunity for installers and inspectors of child restraint devices.** — Any person who has successfully met the minimum required training standards for installation of child restraint devices established by the National Highway Traffic Safety Administration of the United States Department of Transportation, who in good faith and without compensation installs, or inspects the installation of, a child restraint device shall not be liable for any damages resulting from an act or omission related to such installation or inspection, unless such act or omission was the result of the person's gross negligence or willful misconduct. (1999, c. 293.)

§ **8.01-226.5:1. Civil immunity for school board employees supervising self-administration of asthma medication.** — A. Any school principal or other employee of a school board who, in good faith, without compensation, and in the absence of gross negligence or willful misconduct, supervises the self-administration of inhaled asthma medications by a student, pursuant to § 22.1-274.2, shall not be liable for any civil damages for acts or omissions resulting from the supervision of self-administration of inhaled asthma medications by such student.

B. For the purposes of this section, "employee" shall include any person employed by a local health department who is assigned to a public school pursuant to an agreement between a local health department and a school board. (2000, c. 871.)

Editor's note. — Acts 2000, c. 871, cl. 2 provides that the Superintendent of Public Instruction shall notify local school boards of the passage of the act by a Superintendent's Administrative Memorandum within 30 days of its enactment.

§ 8.01-226.6. "Year 2000" civil immunity for certain governmental officers and employees. — No officer or employee of the Commonwealth or any of its political subdivisions, agencies and instrumentalities, including without limitation any officer described in Article VII, Section 4 of the Constitution of Virginia, any director of finance described in §§ 15.2-519, 15.2-617 or § 15.2-826, or any regional jail superintendent described in § 53.1-109, shall be held liable for any claim arising from, or in any way relating to, the failure of a computer, software program, database, network information system, firmware or any other device to interpret, produce, calculate, generate or account for a date which is compatible with the "Year 2000" date change. The immunity conferred by this section shall not apply if the act or omission at issue was the result of the officer's or employee's gross negligence or willful misconduct. (1999, c. 1002.)

The number of this section was assigned by the Virginia Code Commission, the number in the 1999 act having been 8.01-226.5.

Cross references. — For other Y2K provisions enacted in 1999, see §§ 8.01-227.1 through 8.01-227.3 and § 8.01-418.3.

§ 8.01-226.7. Owner and agent compliance with residential lead-based paint notification; maintenance immunity. — A. As used in this section, the following definitions apply:

"Agent" means any party who enters into a contract with a seller or lessor, including any party who enters into a contract with a representative of the seller or lessor, for the purpose of selling or leasing a residential dwelling. This term includes all persons licensed under Chapter 21 (§ 54.1-2100 et seq.) of Title 54.1. This term does not apply to purchasers or any purchaser's representative who receives compensation from the purchaser.

"Lead-based paint" means paint or other surface coatings that contain lead equal to or in excess of 1.0 milligram per square centimeter or 0.5 percent by weight.

"Lead-based paint hazard" means any condition that causes exposure to lead from lead-contaminated dust, lead-contaminated soil, or lead-contaminated paint that is deteriorated or present in accessible surfaces, friction surfaces, or impact surfaces that would result in adverse human health effects as established by the appropriate federal or state agency.

"Residential dwelling" means a structure or part of a structure that is used as a home or residence by one or more persons who maintain a household, whether single family or multifamily.

B. Any agent who has complied with the requirements of the United States Residential Lead-Based Paint Hazard Reduction Act of 1992 (42 U.S.C. 4851 et seq.) shall not be liable for civil damages in any personal injury or wrongful death action for lead poisoning arising from the condition of a residential dwelling, provided that before the purchaser or tenant signs any contract to purchase or lease the residential dwelling:

1. An EPA-approved lead hazard information pamphlet was provided to the purchaser or lessee;

2. Any known lead-based paint and lead-based paint hazard on the property and any additional information or reports available to the owner concerning the same were provided to the purchaser or lessee;

3. The purchaser or tenant signed a written statement acknowledging the disclosure and receipt of the literature; and

4. If the agent is a public housing authority, it has complied with all applicable federal laws and regulations.

However, if the agent performs or agrees to perform lead-based paint maintenance on the residential dwelling or if the party, a purchaser or a lessee is instructed to contract for lead-based paint repairs, the agent shall not be entitled to immunity unless the agent has also met the requirements of subsection C of this section.

C. An owner of a residential dwelling, or agent responsible for the maintenance of a residential dwelling, who has complied with the requirements of the United States Residential Lead-Based Paint Hazard Reduction Act of 1992 (42 U.S.C. 4851 et seq.) shall not be liable for civil damages in a personal injury or wrongful death action for lead poisoning arising from the condition of the residential dwelling, provided that before the purchaser or tenant signs any contract to purchase or lease the residential dwelling:

1. An EPA-approved lead hazard information pamphlet was provided to the purchaser or lessee;
2. Any known lead-based paint and lead-based paint hazard on the property and any additional information or reports available to the owner concerning same were provided to the purchaser or lessee;
3. The purchaser or tenant signed a written statement acknowledging the disclosure and receipt of the literature; and
4. With regards to lead-based paint and lead-based paint hazards, the residential dwelling was maintained in a fit and habitable condition and in compliance with the state laws and regulations, including but not limited to the Uniform Statewide Building Code, and applicable federal laws and regulations. (2000, c. 1071.)

§ 8.01-227. Remedy by motion on certain bonds given or taken by officers; notice. — The court in which any bond given or taken by an officer is required to be returned, filed or recorded, may, on motion of any person protected by such bond, give judgment in favor of such person for such amount as he would be entitled by virtue of the bond to recover in an action at law. Any such motion shall be made after reasonable notice, not less than ten days, to the obligors on the bond. Service may be in any manner sufficient to support a judgment in personam. (Code 1950, §§ 8-140.1, 8-140.2; 1954, c. 546; 1977, c. 617.)

REVISERS' NOTE

Former §§ 8-140.1 and 8-140.2 have been simplified and combined herein.

Cross references. — For rules of court relating to notice of motion for judgment and defendant's response, see Rules 3:3 and 3:5.

I. DECISIONS UNDER PRIOR LAW.

Editor's note. — The cases cited below were decided under corresponding provisions of former law. The term "this section," as used below, refers to former provisions.

Alternative remedy. — The statutory remedy provided by this section did not supersede the long established action for breach of a condition of a bond by common-law writ and declaration. Such action continued as a concurrent alternative remedy. Commonwealth ex rel. Duvall v. Hall, 194 Va. 914, 76 S.E.2d 208 (1953).

Sufficiency of notice. — To sustain a motion on bond of sheriff, any notice, however informal, which informs the defendants of the nature and objects of the motion, is sufficient. Carr v. Meade, 77 Va. 142 (1883).

Failure of deputy to pay over tax ticket proceeds. — A county treasurer may proceed by motion under former §§ 15.1-86 and 15.1-88, (see now §§ 15.2-1623 and 15.2-1625) upon 10 days' notice as required by this section, against his deputies and his sureties, for the failure of the deputy to pay over the proceeds of or to account for tax tickets placed in his hands for collection. Hall v. Ratliff, 93 Va. 327, 24 S.E. 1011 (1896).

Article 22.
Year 2000 Liability and Damages.

§ 8.01-227.1. Purpose. — The General Assembly finds that maintaining the health and stability of the various business enterprises located in the Commonwealth is in the public interest in order to insure the uninterrupted delivery of goods and services to the Commonwealth's citizenry. The General Assembly further finds that the Year 2000 problem is a one-time occurrence for which no one person is accountable and, therefore, the business enterprises of the Commonwealth should not have their ability to continue to deliver goods and services impaired by having to contest lawsuits arising from Year 2000 problems over which such business enterprises have no control. This act is intended to place prudential limitations on the potential liability of the Commonwealth's business enterprises, while preserving the appropriate right of recovery by persons suffering economic losses as a result of another's fault or negligence. This act shall not limit enforcement of laws, regulations, or permits by state or local governmental bodies or agencies. (1999, c. 954.)

Cross references. — For other Y2K provisions enacted in 1999, see § 8.01-226.6 and § 8.01-418.3.

§ 8.01-227.2. Definitions. — For purposes of this article:
"Person" means the same as defined in § 1-13.19.
"Regulated entity" means any insured financial institution or public utility.
"Third party" means, with respect to a person against whom a claim for damages is made based upon a Year 2000 problem, any (i) person having no contractual or affiliate relationship with the person against whom a claim is made, (ii) state or federal governmental or quasi-governmental agency or entity, or (iii) regulated entity other than the person against whom a claim is made.
"Year 2000 problem" means any computing, physical, enterprise, or distribution system complication that has occurred or may occur as a result of the change of the year from 1999 to 2000 in any person's technology system, including, without limitation, computer hardware, programs, software, or systems; embedded chip calculations or embedded systems; firmware; microprocessors; or management systems, business processes, or computing applications that govern, utilize, drive, or depend on the Year 2000 processing capabilities of the person's technology systems. Such complications may include the common computer programming practice of using a two-digit field to represent a year, resulting in erroneous date calculations; an ambiguous interpretation of the term or field "00"; the failure to recognize 2000 as a leap year; algorithms that use "99" or "00" to activate another function; or the use of any other applications, software, or hardware that are date-sensitive.
"Year 2000 processing" means the processing, calculating, comparing, sequencing, displaying, storing, transmitting, or receiving of date or date-sensitive data from, into, or between the twentieth and twenty-first centuries, during the years 1999 and 2000, and leap year calculations. (1999, c. 954.)

§ 8.01-227.3. Liability and damages limited. — Notwithstanding any other provision of law to the contrary, the following provisions shall apply in connection with any civil action against a person in which the claim for damages is based upon a Year 2000 problem:

1. No person shall be liable to any person who is (i) not in privity of contract with such person, (ii) not a person to whom an express warranty has been extended by such person, or (iii) in the case of a trust, not the beneficiary of a trust administered by such person.

2. No person shall be liable for damages caused by a delay or interruption in performance, or in the delivery of goods or services, resulting from or in connection with (i) a Year 2000 problem to the extent such Year 2000 problem was caused by a third party or (ii) a third party's Year 2000 problem.

3. No employee, officer, or director shall be liable in his capacity as such to any person.

4. No person shall be liable for consequential or punitive damages.

5. Total damages shall not exceed actual direct damages.

6. This section shall not affect the right of recovery for damages in connection with wrongful death, personal injury or property damage. (1999, c. 954.)

CHAPTER 4.

Limitations of Actions.

Article 1.

In General.

Sec.
8.01-228. Scope of limitations; "personal action" defined.
8.01-229. Suspension or tolling of statute of limitations; effect of disabilities; death; injunction; prevention of service by defendant; dismissal, nonsuit or abatement; devise for payment of debts; new promises; debts proved in creditors' suits.
8.01-230. Accrual of right of action.
8.01-231. Commonwealth not within statute of limitations.
8.01-232. Effect of promises not to plead statute.
8.01-233. When action deemed brought on counterclaim or cross-claim; when statute of limitations tolled; defendant's consent required for dismissal.
8.01-234. Repeal of limitation not to remove bar of statute.
8.01-235. Bar of expiration of limitation period raised only as affirmative defense in responsive pleading.

Article 2.

Limitations on Recovery of Realty and Enforcement of Certain Liens Relating to Realty.

8.01-236. Limitation of entry on or action for land.
8.01-237. Effect of disabilities upon right of entry on, or action for, land.

Sec.
8.01-238. To repeal grant.
8.01-239. Ground rents.
8.01-240. Liens for water, sewer, or sidewalk assessments.
8.01-241. Limitation of enforcement of deeds of trust, mortgages and liens for unpaid purchase money.
8.01-241.1. Permissible form for certificate.
8.01-242. Same; when no maturity date is given; credit line deeds of trust.

Article 3.

Personal Actions Generally.

8.01-243. Personal action for injury to person or property generally; extension in actions for malpractice against health care provider.
8.01-243.1. Actions for medical malpractice; minors.
8.01-243.2. Limitations of actions by confined persons; exhaustion.
8.01-244. Actions for wrongful death; limitation.
8.01-245. Limitation on actions upon the bond of any fiduciaries or as to suits against fiduciaries themselves; accrual of cause of action where execution sustained.
8.01-246. Personal actions based on contracts.
8.01-247. When action on contract governed by the law of another state or country barred in Virginia.
8.01-247.1. Limitation on action for defamation, etc.
8.01-248. Personal actions for which no other limitation is specified.
8.01-249. When cause of action shall be

Sec.			Article 5.	
	deemed to accrue in certain personal actions.		Miscellaneous Limitations Provisions.	
8.01-250.	Limitation on certain actions for damages arising out of defective or unsafe condition of improvements to real property.	Sec.		
		8.01-253.	Limitation of suits to avoid voluntary conveyances, etc.	
		8.01-254.	Limitation on enforcement of bequests and legacies.	
8.01-250.1.	Limitation on actions involving removal of asbestos.	8.01-255.	Time for presenting claim against Commonwealth.	
	Article 4.	8.01-255.1.	Limitation of action for breach of condition subsequent or termination of determinable fee simple estate.	
	Limitations on Enforcement of Judgments and Decrees.			
8.01-251.	Limitations on enforcement of judgments.	8.01-255.2.	Limitation on motion for new execution after loss of property sold under indemnity bond.	
8.01-252.	Actions on judgments of another state.	8.01-256.	As to rights and remedies existing when this chapter takes effect.	

Article 1.

In General.

§ 8.01-228. Scope of limitations; "personal action" defined. — Every action for which a limitation period is prescribed by law must be commenced within the period prescribed in this chapter unless otherwise specifically provided in this Code. As used in this chapter, the term "personal action" shall include an action wherein a judgment for money is sought, whether for damages to person or property. (1977, c. 617.)

REVISERS' NOTE

Section 8.01-228 is new and recognizes that most of the statutory limitations for civil actions scattered throughout former Title 8 and elsewhere in the Code have been collected in this Title 8.01 chapter. Some are not found herein. E.g., see § 8.01-40 B.

While statutes of limitations may apply in some instances to equity suits, § 8.01-228 does not change the established rule that laches are generally applicable to purely equitable claims.

Law Review. — For survey of Virginia law on practice and pleading for the year 1976-77, see 63 Va. L. Rev. 1459 (1977).

I. DECISIONS UNDER CURRENT LAW.

Applied in Horn v. Abernathy, 231 Va. 228, 343 S.E.2d 318 (1986); Lavery v. Automation Mgt. Consultants, Inc., 234 Va. 145, 360 S.E.2d 336 (1987); Glens Falls Ins. Co. v. Stephenson, 235 Va. 420, 367 S.E.2d 722 (1988).

§ 8.01-229. Suspension or tolling of statute of limitations; effect of disabilities; death; injunction; prevention of service by defendant; dismissal, nonsuit or abatement; devise for payment of debts; new promises; debts proved in creditors' suits. — A. *Disabilities which toll the statute of limitations.* — Except as otherwise specifically provided in §§ 8.01-237, 8.01-241, 8.01-242, 8.01-243, 8.01-243.1 and other provisions of this Code,

1. If a person entitled to bring any action is at the time the cause of action accrues an infant, except if such infant has been emancipated pursuant to Article 15 (§ 16.1-331 et seq.) of Chapter 11 of Title 16.1, or incapacitated, such person may bring it within the prescribed limitation period after such disability is removed; or

2. After a cause of action accrues,

a. If an infant becomes entitled to bring such action, the time during which he is within the age of minority shall not be counted as any part of the period within which the action must be brought except as to any such period during which the infant has been judicially declared emancipated; or

b. If a person entitled to bring such action becomes incapacitated, the time during which he is incapacitated shall not be computed as any part of the period within which the action must be brought, except where a conservator, guardian or committee is appointed for such person in which case an action may be commenced by such conservator, committee or guardian before the expiration of the applicable period of limitation or within one year after his qualification as such, whichever occurs later.

For the purposes of subdivisions 1 and 2 of this subsection, a person shall be deemed incapacitated if he is so adjudged by a court of competent jurisdiction, or if it shall otherwise appear to the court or jury determining the issue that such person is or was incapacitated within the prescribed limitation period.

3. If a convict is or becomes entitled to bring an action against his committee, the time during which he is incarcerated shall not be counted as any part of the period within which the action must be brought.

B. *Effect of death of a party.* — The death of a person entitled to bring an action or of a person against whom an action may be brought shall toll the statute of limitations as follows:

1. Death of person entitled to bring a personal action. — If a person entitled to bring a personal action dies with no such action pending before the expiration of the limitation period for commencement thereof, then an action may be commenced by the decedent's personal representative before the expiration of the limitation period including the limitation period as provided by subdivision E 3 or within one year after his qualification as personal representative, whichever occurs later.

2. Death of person against whom personal action may be brought. — a. If a person against whom a personal action may be brought dies before the commencement of such action and before the expiration of the limitation period for commencement thereof then a claim may be filed against the decedent's estate or an action may be commenced against the decedent's personal representative before the expiration of the applicable limitation period or within one year after the qualification of such personal representative, whichever occurs later.

b. If a person against whom a personal action may be brought dies before suit papers naming such person as defendant have been filed with the court, then such suit papers may be amended to substitute the decedent's personal representative as party defendant before the expiration of the applicable limitation period or within two years after the date such suit papers were filed with the court, whichever occurs later, and such suit papers shall be taken as properly filed.

3. Effect of death on actions for recovery of realty, or a proceeding for enforcement of certain liens relating to realty. — Upon the death of any person in whose favor or against whom an action for recovery of realty, or a proceeding for enforcement of certain liens relating to realty, may be brought, such right of action shall accrue to or against his successors in interest as provided in Article 2 (§ 8.01-236 et seq.) of this chapter.

4. Accrual of a personal cause of action against the estate of any person subsequent to such person's death. — If a personal cause of action against a decedent accrues subsequent to his death, an action may be brought against the decedent's personal representative or a claim thereon may be filed against the estate of such decedent before the expiration of the applicable limitation period or within two years after the qualification of the decedent's personal representative, whichever occurs later.

5. *Accrual of a personal cause of action in favor of decedent.* — If a person dies before a personal cause of action which survives would have accrued to him, if he had continued to live, then an action may be commenced by such decedent's personal representative before the expiration of the applicable limitation period or within one year after the qualification of such personal representative, whichever occurs later.

6. *Delayed qualification of personal representative.* — If there is an interval of more than two years between the death of any person in whose favor or against whom a cause of action has accrued or shall subsequently accrue and the qualification of such person's personal representative, such personal representative shall, for the purposes of this chapter, be deemed to have qualified on the last day of such two-year period.

C. *Suspension during injunctions.* — When the commencement of any action is stayed by injunction, the time of the continuance of the injunction shall not be computed as any part of the period within which the action must be brought.

D. *Obstruction of filing by defendant.* — When the filing of an action is obstructed by a defendant's (i) filing a petition in bankruptcy or filing a petition for an extension or arrangement under the United States Bankruptcy Act or (ii) using any other direct or indirect means to obstruct the filing of an action, then the time that such obstruction has continued shall not be counted as any part of the period within which the action must be brought.

E. *Dismissal, abatement, or nonsuit.*

1. Except as provided in subdivision 3 of this subsection, if any action is commenced within the prescribed limitation period and for any cause abates or is dismissed without determining the merits, the time such action is pending shall not be computed as part of the period within which such action may be brought, and another action may be brought within the remaining period.

2. If a judgment or decree is rendered for the plaintiff in any action commenced within the prescribed limitation period and such judgment or decree is arrested or reversed upon a ground which does not preclude a new action for the same cause, or if there is occasion to bring a new action by reason of the loss or destruction of any of the papers or records in a former action which was commenced within the prescribed limitation period, then a new action may be brought within one year after such arrest or reversal or such loss or destruction, but not after.

3. If a plaintiff suffers a voluntary nonsuit as prescribed in § 8.01-380, the statute of limitations with respect to such action shall be tolled by the commencement of the nonsuited action, and the plaintiff may recommence his action within six months from the date of the order entered by the court, or within the original period of limitation, or within the limitation period as provided by subdivision B 1, whichever period is longer. This tolling provision shall apply irrespective of whether the action is originally filed in a federal or a state court and recommenced in any other court, and shall apply to all actions irrespective of whether they arise under common law or statute.

F. *Effect of devise for payment of debts.* — No provision in the will of any testator devising his real estate, or any part thereof, subject to the payment of his debts or charging the same therewith, or containing any other provision for the payment of debts, shall prevent this chapter from operating against such debts, unless it plainly appears to be the testator's intent that it shall not so operate.

G. *Effect of new promise in writing.*

1. If any person against whom a right of action has accrued on any contract, other than a judgment or recognizance, promises, by writing signed by him or his agent, payment of money on such contract, the person to whom the right has accrued may maintain an action for the money so promised, within such

number of years after such promise as it might be maintained if such promise were the original cause of action. An acknowledgment in writing, from which a promise of payment may be implied, shall be deemed to be such promise within the meaning of this subsection.

2. The plaintiff may sue on the new promise described in subdivision 1 of this subsection or on the original cause of action, except that when the new promise is of such a nature as to merge the original cause of action then the action shall be only on the new promise.

H. *Suspension of limitations in creditors' suits.* — When an action is commenced as a general creditors' action, or as a general lien creditors' action, or as an action to enforce a mechanics' lien, the running of the statute of limitations shall be suspended as to debts provable in such action from the commencement of the action, provided they are brought in before the commissioner in chancery under the first reference for an account of debts; but as to claims not so brought in the statute shall continue to run, without interruption by reason either of the commencement of the action or of the order for an account, until a later order for an account, under which they do come in, or they are asserted by petition or independent action.

In actions not instituted originally either as general creditors' actions, or as general lien creditors' actions, but which become such by subsequent proceedings, the statute of limitations shall be suspended by an order of reference for an account of debts or of liens only as to those creditors who come in and prove their claims under the order. As to creditors who come in afterwards by petition or under an order of recommittal, or a later order of reference for an account, the statute shall continue to run without interruption by reason of previous orders until filing of the petition, or until the date of the reference under which they prove their claims, as the case may be.

I. When an action is commenced within a period of thirty days prior to the expiration of the limitation period for commencement thereof and the defending party or parties desire to institute an action as third-party plaintiff against one or more persons not party to the original action, the running of the period of limitation against such action shall be suspended as to such new party for a period of sixty days from the expiration of the applicable limitation period.

J. If any award of compensation by the Workers' Compensation Commission pursuant to Chapter 5 (§ 65.2-500 et seq.) of Title 65.2 is subsequently found void ab initio, other than an award voided for fraudulent procurement of the award by the claimant, the statute of limitations applicable to any civil action upon the same claim or cause of action in a court of this Commonwealth shall be tolled for that period of time during which compensation payments were made. (Code 1950, §§ 8-8, 8-13, 8-15, 8-20, 8-21, 8-25, 8-26, 8-29 through 8-34; 1964, c. 219; 1966, c. 118; 1972, c. 825; 1977, c. 617; 1978, cc. 65, 767; 1983, cc. 404, 437; 1986, c. 506; 1987, cc. 294, 645; 1988, c. 711; 1989, c. 588; 1990, c. 280; 1991, cc. 693, 722; 1993, c. 844; 1997, c. 801; 2000, c. 531.)

REVISERS' NOTE

Section 8.01-229 consolidates in one section various situations which have the general effect of tolling or suspending the running of the statutes of limitation (there are other tolling provisions; see, e.g. § 8.01-581.9[repealed in 1993]).

Subsection A incorporates the major thrust of former §§ 8-8 and 8-30 by tolling statutes of limitation when the person entitled to bring an action is disabled by infancy or "unsound mind" at the time when his cause of action accrues. In addition, the provision changes prior law and provides that disabilities which arise after the cause of action accrues also suspend the running of the limitation period.

The tolling of the running of the statute where a convict has a cause of action against his committee comports with the revision of former § 8-15. See § 8.01-245.

Subsection B 1 replaces former § 8-31 as to the tolling of the statute of limitations by the death of a party entitled to bring a personal action. Former § 8-31 adds an extra year from the death of the person entitled to bring a personal action to the applicable limitation period. Subsection 8.01-229 B 1 makes the date of qualification of the decedent's personal representative the commencement date and extends the statute of limitation for an extra year only when the action would otherwise be barred within that year.

Subsection B 2 modifies and simplifies former § 8-31 and a portion of § 8-13. When a cause of action accrues but no action is commenced before the decedent's death, if the applicable statute of limitations has not expired before death, the action may be commenced against the decedent's personal representative within two years from its accrual or within one year of his qualification, whichever is later. The final sentence specifies which subsection, § 8.01-229 B 1 or B 2, is to apply should both the potential plaintiff and defendant die before the action is commenced.

Subsection B 3 references §§ 8.01-236 through 8.01-242 indicating that the effect of death on actions for recovery of land and proceedings for enforcement of certain liens relating to realty will be governed thereby instead of by § 8.01-229 B 1 and B 2. See, e.g., §§ 8.01-236 and 8.01-237 whereby the tolling of the limitation period by death in adverse possession actions and lien enforcement proceedings cannot extend the statute of limitation beyond the outside maximum set by such statutes.

Subsection B 4 concerns the accrual of a cause of action against a person's estate after his death and authorizes the bringing of an action or the filing of a claim against such decedent's estate within one year after the cause of action accrues or within two years after the qualification of the decedent's personal representative, whichever occurs last. The provision replaces that portion of former § 8-13 which allowed five years to sue on such actions. See also § 8.01-229 B 2.

Subsection B 5 supplements former §§ 8-21 and 8-32 with regard to the appropriate limitation for causes of action accruing after the death of a prospective plaintiff. Formerly, no provision addressed the application of the statute of limitations where the cause of action accrued to a decedent's estate under §§ 64.1-144 and 64.1-145 and there was no delay in the qualification of the decedent's personal representative. Section 8.01-229 B 5 fills this gap and gives the decedent's personal representative at least a year after his qualification, or such longer time as provided by the applicable statute of limitations, in which to bring suit.

Subsection B 6 changes the last sentence of former § 8-32 and provides that if the qualification of a decedent's personal representative is delayed beyond one year after the decedent's death such personal representative will be deemed to have qualified on the last day of such period for the purpose of measuring the applicable statute of limitation [and extensions thereof by §§ 8.01-229 B 1, 2, 4 and 5, for example]. This reduces the former delay period from two to one year.

Subsection C tolls the statute of limitations when commencement of the action is stayed by injunction. The rationale is basically the same as that for former §§ 8-33 and 8-34 and for §§ 8.01-229 D and E (i.e., when the plaintiff seeks to commence an action within the prescribed limitation period, the plaintiff should not be precluded from recovery by subsequent expiration of the statute of limitations before the merits of the case have been finally adjudicated).

Subsection D is basically a revision of former § 8-33 except that the former limitation to defendants "who had before resided in the Commonwealth" has been deleted. No change has been made to case law that the limitation period is not tolled if process can be served despite the defendant's absence — e.g. service of process under the "long-arm" statute. See Bergman v. Turpin, 206 Va. 539, 145 S.E.2d 135 (1965).

Subsection E 1 provides for tolling the statute of limitations when an action brought in due time abates or is dismissed without a determination of the merits. The provision is analogous to the treatment of wrongful death actions. See § 8.01-244 B; Norwood v. Buffey, 196 Va. 1051, 86 S.E.2d 809 (1955).

Subsection E 2 preserves two provisions of former § 8-34 which are not within the ambit of subsection E 1. The same reasoning underlies both proposals, namely that the plaintiff who brings his action within due time should not be denied a decision on the merits because of subsequent procedural developments or fortuities which have no bearing upon the purpose of statutes of limitation.

Subsection E 3 qualifies the application of subsection E 1, and requires a plaintiff who takes a nonsuit to renew his suit within six months or the running of the statute of limitations will not be affected by the commencement of the original action.

Subsections F, G and H are former §§ 8-29, 8-25 and 8-26, and 8-20, respectively. Besides clarifying these sections generally, in subsection F the phrase: "or containing any other provision for the payment of debts" has been grafted on the language of former § 8-29 to make it clear that customary testamentary language such as "I direct the payment of my just debts" should not operate to waive the statute of limitations. The last sentence of former § 8-26 has been omitted from subsection G 2 because of Rule 3:12. Thus, unless a defendant pleading the statute of limitations expressly calls for a reply, the plaintiff need not give notice to the defendant that he intends to rely upon a new promise in writing.

Cross references. — As to death or change of parties, generally, see § 8.01-16 et seq. As to death by wrongful act, see § 8.01-50 et seq. As to accrual of cause of action, see § 8.01-230. As to promise not to plead statute, see § 8.01-232. As to effect of disability in action on land, etc., see § 8.01-237. As to limitation of enforcement of deeds of trust, mortgages and purchase-money liens, see § 8.01-241. As to limitations in actions for wrongful death, including exception to subsection B of this section, see § 8.01-244. As to attachment of absconding debtors, see § 8.01-534.

Editor's note. — Acts 1991, c. 722, cl. 2 provides "That the provisions of this act are declaratory of the original intent of the General Assembly in enacting Chapter 617 of the 1977 Acts of Assembly" (Title 8.01).

Acts 1997, c. 801, cl. 2, provides: "That the provisions of this act shall become effective on January 1, 1998. The powers granted and duties imposed pursuant to this act shall apply prospectively to guardians and conservators appointed by court order entered on or after that date, or modified on or after that date if the court so directs, without regard to when the petition was filed. The procedures specified in this act governing proceedings for appointment of a guardian or conservator or termination or other modification of a guardianship shall apply on and after that date without regard to when the petition therefor was filed or the guardianship or conservatorship created."

The 2000 amendments. — The 2000 amendment by c. 531 added subsection J.

Law Review. — For survey of Virginia law on torts for the year 1972-1973, see 59 Va. L. Rev. 1590 (1973). For note discussing a state incarcerated felon's capacity to sue under 42 U.S.C. § 1983 in federal courts despite prohibitive state statutes, see 30 Wash. & Lee L. Rev. 329 (1973). For survey of Virginia law on practice and pleading for the year 1978-1979, see 66 Va. L. Rev. 343 (1980). For 1985 survey of Virginia civil procedure and practice, see 19 U. Rich. L. Rev. 679 (1985). For article, "Civil Rights and 'Personal Injuries': Virginia's Statute of Limitations for Section 1983 Suits," see 26 Wm. & Mary L. Rev. 199 (1985). For 1987 survey of Virginia civil procedure and practice, see 21 U. Rich. L. Rev. 667 (1987). For survey on civil procedure and practice in Virginia for 1989, see 23 U. Rich. L. Rev. 511 (1989). For 1991 survey of civil practice and procedure, see 25 U. Rich. L. Rev. 663 (1991). For a review of civil practice and procedure in Virginia for year 1999, see 33 U. Rich. L. Rev. 801 (1999).

I. Decisions Under Current Law.
   A. General Consideration.
   B. Dismissal, Abatement or Nonsuit.
   C. Effect of New Promise in Writing.
   D. Third-party Claims Where Original Action Commenced Within 30 Days of Expiration of Period.
II. Decisions Under Prior Law.
   A. General Consideration.
   B. Effect of Disability.
   C. Effect of Death of a Party.
   D. Prevention of Service by Defendant.
   E. Dismissal, Abatement or Nonsuit.
   F. Effect of Devise for Payment.
   G. Effect of New Promise in Writing.
   H. Suspension of Limitations in Creditors' Suits.

I. DECISIONS UNDER CURRENT LAW.

A. General Consideration.

The two paragraphs of § 8.01-244 are inextricably interrelated; one is the predicate for the other, and the tolling provisions of subsection B of this section do not apply to the time limitation imposed by § 8.01-244. Horn v. Abernathy, 231 Va. 228, 343 S.E.2d 318 (1986).

The term "personal action" is defined as any action wherein a judgment for money is sought, whether for damages to person or property. The term was never intended to apply to a right of action for death by wrongful act, and such a right of action is not within the purview of subsection B. Horn v. Abernathy, 231 Va. 228, 343 S.E.2d 318 (1986).

Tolling provision amendment not retroactive. — Lower court correctly ruled that plaintiff's wrongful death action was time-barred because plaintiff failed to refile after nonsuit within the time prescribed by wrongful death statute of limitations in effect when original cause of action accrued; tolling provision amendment to wrongful death statute was substantive, not procedural, and therefore did not apply retroactively. Riddett v. Virginia Elec. and Power Co., 255 Va. 23, 495 S.E.2d 819 (1998).

Since amendments affecting statutes of limitations generally affect substantive, rather than procedural, rights and such substantive rights are typically protected from retroactive application of laws, the amendment to this section allowing tolling of the statute of limitations while plaintiff is "incapacitated," which plaintiff argued should include incarceration, did not apply to preserve plaintiff's cause of action where the statute of limitations had already passed when the amendment took effect. Lewis v. Gupta, 54 F. Supp. 2d 611 (E.D. Va. 1999) (decided under this section prior to the amendment effective January 1, 1998, allowing tolling while plaintiff is "incapacitated").

Statute not tolled during period of imprisonment. — The Virginia tolling statute as it read prior to January 1, 1998, does not toll statute of limitations during a potential plaintiff's period of incarceration. Lewis v. Gupta, 54 F. Supp. 2d 611 (E.D. Va. 1999) (decided under this section prior to the amendment effective January 1, 1998, allowing tolling while plaintiff is "incapacitated").

Third-party plaintiff actions. — Because of the bar of the statute of limitations, the injured person did not have an enforceable cause of action against the party from whom contribution was sought and, therefore, third-party plaintiff was similarly barred in his claim against third-party defendant. Smith-Moore Body Co. v. Heil Co., 603 F. Supp. 354 (E.D. Va. 1985).

Subsection I was introduced in direct response to the Rambone v. Critzer, 548 F. Supp. 660 (W.D. Va. 1982) decision. It was introduced in an effort to remove perceived inequities which would arise when an original plaintiff, delayed to the last days of the limits applicable to his claim to file suit. Smith-Moore Body Co. v. Heil Co., 603 F. Supp. 354 (E.D. Va. 1985).

Applicability in federal court. — When a federal statute of limitations is applicable, a court must look to federal law for any appropriate tolling provisions. Where there are no such provisions, it would be inappropriate for the court to look to this section to toll the running of the limitations period. Hewlett v. Russo, 649 F. Supp. 457 (E.D. Va. 1986).

Applicability to action under 42 U.S.C. § 1983. — In an action brought pursuant to 42 U.S.C. § 1983 against three former employees of the United States Bureau of Prisons at Petersburg Federal Correctional Institute alleging that they failed to provide plaintiff with a secure and safe place of confinement while he was incarcerated, Virginia law applied to toll the running of statute of limitations where the plaintiff's action would have been barred but for the fact that the plaintiff previously had filed a pro se action. Clymer v. Grzegorek, 515 F. Supp. 938 (E.D. Va. 1981).

Applicability to insurance claims. — General tolling statutes do not apply to required contractual limitations periods for insurance suits. Bilicki v. Windsor-Mount Joy Mut. Ins. Co., 954 F. Supp. 129 (E.D. Va. 1996).

Request for appointment of umpire for insurance arbitration did not toll contractual limitations period. Bilicki v. Windsor-Mount Joy Mut. Ins. Co., 954 F. Supp. 129 (E.D. Va. 1996).

Claim for medical expenses under § 8.01-243 B not tolled by subsection A. — A parent's claim for medical expenses under § 8.01-243 B is not tolled by the provisions of subsection A. Hutto v. BIC Corp., 800 F. Supp. 1367 (E.D. Va. 1992).

Applied in Cramer v. Crutchfield, 648 F.2d 943 (4th Cir. 1981); Ford v. Sweet, 224 Va. 374, 297 S.E.2d 657 (1982); Williams v. City of Portsmouth, 538 F. Supp. 74 (E.D. Va. 1982); Baker v. Zirkle, 226 Va. 7, 307 S.E.2d 234 (1983); Gemco-Ware, Inc. v. Rongene Mold & Plastics Corp., 234 Va. 54, 360 S.E.2d 342 (1987); Alessio v. Adkins, 102 Bankr. 485 (Bankr. E.D. Va. 1989); Price v. Food Lion, Inc., 768 F. Supp. 181 (E.D. Va. 1991); Wertz v. Grubbs, 245 Va. 67, 425 S.E.2d 500 (1993); McManama v. Plunk, 250 Va. 27, 458 S.E.2d 759 (1995). See also, Lewin v. Medical College, 931 F. Supp. 443 (E.D. Va. 1996); Douglas v. Chesterfield County Police Dep't, 251 Va. 363, 467 S.E.2d 474 (1996); Neal v. Xerox Corp., 991 F. Supp. 494 (E.D. Va. 1998).

B. Dismissal, Abatement or Nonsuit.

A federal court sitting in diversity must honor Virginia law restricting the court within which a nonsuited plaintiff may recommence in order to invoke the saving provision, as the Virginia restriction is an integral part of the several policies served by Virginia's statutes of limitations and must be applied in consolidated federal diversity actions. Yarber v. Allstate Ins. Co., 674 F.2d 232 (4th Cir. 1982).

The effect of an application of the tolling provision of subdivision E 1 of this section is to grant an extended period during which a claim arising after October 1, 1977, might be prosecuted. This provision is not merely procedural or remedial. Strickland v. Simpkins, 221 Va. 730, 273 S.E.2d 539 (1981).

For purposes of subdivision E 1 a dismissal with prejudice is a determination on the merits. Gilbreath v. Brewster, 250 Va. 436, 463 S.E.2d 836 (1995).

Subdivision E 3 applies only where plaintiff voluntarily dismissed action. — Section 8.01-380 pertains exclusively to limitations on the plaintiff's ability to obtain a nonsuit and the organization of subsection E supports the conclusion that subdivision E 3 applies only where the plaintiff has voluntarily dismissed an action. Ambrose Branch Coal Co. v. Tankersley, 106 Bankr. 462 (W.D. Va. 1989).

Subsection E does not apply to claims for workers' compensation. Hammond v. Madison Decorating Corp., No. 0884-85 (Ct. of Appeals Mar. 19, 1986).

Subdivision E 3 of this section is inapplicable to wrongful death actions because § 8.01-244 B controls. Dodson v. Potomac Mack Sales & Serv., Inc., 241 Va. 89, 400 S.E.2d 178 (1991); Flanagan v. Virginia Beach Gen. Hosp., 12 Va. App. 760, 406 S.E.2d 914 (1991).

Because subdivision E 3 of this section deals generally with the subject of tolling statutes of limitations and conflicts with § 8.01-244 B, which deals specifically with the tolling of wrongful death actions, the latter section controls for two reasons: First, § 8.01-228 provides in pertinent part that every action for which a limitation period is prescribed by law must be commenced within the period prescribed in this chapter unless otherwise specifically provided in the Code. Section 8.01-244 B provides for the limitation of wrongful death actions and a tolling period in a specific way, and thus "otherwise specifically provides" its own requirements. Second, in construing conflicting statutes, when one statute speaks to a subject in a general way and another deals with a part of the same subject in a more specific manner, where they conflict, the latter prevails. Dodson v. Potomac Mack Sales & Serv., Inc., 241 Va. 89, 400 S.E.2d 178 (1991).

The 1983 version of subdivision E 3 should apply prospectively, and not retroactively. Sherman v. Hercules, Inc., 636 F. Supp. 305 (W.D. Va. 1986).

Procedure under 1978 version of subdivision E 3. — Under subdivision E 3 of this section (1978 version) and § 8.01-380 (1977 version) if a plaintiff took a nonsuit, the statute of limitations would be tolled provided that the plaintiff recommenced the action in the same court in which the nonsuit was taken within six months. Thus, where plaintiffs filed their actions in federal court in 1980, took voluntary dismissals in 1985, and recommenced their actions within six months, they were entitled to invoke the tolling provision of the 1978 version of subdivision E 3 of this section to save their cases from the personal injury statute of limitations. Sherman v. Hercules, Inc., 636 F. Supp. 305 (W.D. Va. 1986).

The Virginia Code quite clearly requires the state courts to give effect to FRCP 41 dismissals as nonsuits, for subdivision E 3 provides in terms that it "... shall apply irrespective of whether the action is originally filed in a federal or state court and recommenced in any court." Scoggins v. Douglas, 760 F.2d 535 (4th Cir. 1985).

The district court was correct when it equated dismissal pursuant to FRCP 41(a)(1) to a dismissal under subdivision E 3 of this section rather than to a dismissal under subdivision E 1. Scoggins v. Douglas, 760 F.2d 535 (4th Cir. 1985).

The difference in a FRCP Rule 41 dismissal and a Virginia nonsuit under § 8.01-380 goes more to matters of form than substance. While the Virginia statute does not require the consent of the defendant and can be taken at later stages in the proceeding, both the federal rule and the Virginia statute have as their purpose the voluntary dismissal of an action by a plaintiff without prejudice at some stage of a proceeding. Scoggins v. Douglas, 760 F.2d 535 (4th Cir. 1985).

Requiring compliance with the tolling provisions of subsection E is consistent with federal law, and the mere placing of a time constraint on the filing of a § 1983 action is not a consideration sufficient to find an inconsistency. Scoggins v. Douglas, 760 F.2d 535 (4th Cir. 1985).

Cause of action under 42 U.S.C. § 1983, which accrued on Dec. 17, 1980, was barred by Virginia's two-year statute of limitations for personal injury actions, where the action was voluntarily dismissed by the plaintiff without prejudice on Jan. 26, 1982, pursuant to FRCP 41(a)(1), and was not refiled until Dec. 27, 1982. Scoggins v. Douglas, 760 F.2d 535 (4th Cir. 1985).

Tolling provision not retroactive. — The tolling provision of subdivision E 3 of this section is not to be applied retroactively to an action which arose and was pending prior to October 1, 1977. Wood v. Holcombe, 221 Va. 691, 273 S.E.2d 541 (1981).

The tolling provision of subdivision E 3 of this section applies only to causes or rights of action accruing on or after October 1, 1977. Fidelity & Deposit Co. v. Celotex Corp., 221 Va. 698, 273 S.E.2d 542 (1981).

A claim under the Workers' Compensation Act is not an "action" within the meaning of this title; therefore, subdivision E 1 of this section does not toll the running of the statute of limitations on claims made under the Workers' Compensation Act. Musick v. Codell Constr. Co., 4 Va. App. 471, 358 S.E.2d 739 (1987).

Subdivision E 3 tolled the statute of limitations upon plaintiff's commencement of the original action but, because defendant was not served with process until more than one year after such commencement, Rule 3:3 forbade entry of any judgment against defendant in that action, and the action ended with entry of the order allowing a nonsuit pursuant to § 8.01-380, however, subdivision E 3 intervened to give plaintiff a six-month period after entry of the nonsuit order in which to recommence his action and by recommencing the action within the allowed period plaintiff insulated his claim against a plea of the statute limitations. Clark v. Butler Aviation-Washington Nat'l, Inc., 238 Va. 506, 385 S.E.2d 847 (1989).

Tolling provision does not apply to contractual period of limitations. — The plain meaning of the phrase in subdivision E 3 "the statute of limitations with respect to such action shall be tolled by the commencement of the nonsuited action," is that, after a voluntary nonsuit, the statute of limitations, not a contractual period of limitations, is tolled, and the plaintiff may recommence the suit within six months or within the original period of limitations, whichever is longer. Massie v. Blue Cross & Blue Shield, 256 Va. 161, 500 S.E.2d 509 (1998).

Once trial court has decided particular claim, that portion of action has been submitted for decision and the plaintiff may no longer suffer a nonsuit of that claim as a matter of right. Therefore, when the trial court has reached a final determination in a proceeding regarding any claims or parties to claims, those claims and parties are excluded by operation of law from any nonsuit request. Smith v. Consolidation Coal Co., 7 F. Supp. 2d 751 (W.D. Va. 1998).

Plaintiff could still file her motion for judgment recommencing her action on the following Monday, where six months from her voluntary nonsuit fell on a Saturday. Ward v. Insurance Co. of N. Am., 253 Va. 232, 482 S.E.2d 795 (1997).

C. Effect of New Promise in Writing.

Effect of new promise in writing is to begin the running of a new statute of limitations permitting suit within such number of years after such promise as it might be maintained if such promise were the original cause of action. Nevertheless, consistent with the foregoing rule, the new promise may be governed by a shorter, private contractual period in lieu of the statutory period of limitations. Board of Supvrs. v. Sampson, 235 Va. 516, 369 S.E.2d 178 (1988).

Part payment of the principal or payment of interest, standing alone, does not toll or remove the bar of the statute of limitations. Guth v. Hamlet Assocs., 230 Va. 64, 334 S.E.2d 558 (1985).

When payment by check is involved, the rule is based on the requirement that a writing, to be an acknowledgment under the statute, must be an unqualified admission of a subsisting debt which the party is liable for and willing to pay. Guth v. Hamlet Assocs., 230 Va. 64, 334 S.E.2d 558 (1985).

Reports on interest and balance and tax forms were acknowledgments although otherwise required. — The fact that status reports showing monthly interest earned and the balance of principal and interest due and tax forms to pay the debts because the documents had to be prepared under the contracts and the law did not make the reports insufficient as acknowledgments. Subsection G does not distinguish between "necessary" and "gratuitous" writings. Guth v. Hamlet Assocs., 230 Va. 64, 334 S.E.2d 558 (1985).

And were attributable to guarantor. — Status reports showing monthly interest earned and the balance of principal and interest due and tax forms were attributable to the guarantor on promissory notes, for purposes of determining whether the reports constituted acknowledgment of the debt. Guth v. Hamlet Assocs., 230 Va. 64, 334 S.E.2d 558 (1985).

D. Third-party Claims Where Original Action Commenced Within 30 Days of Expiration of Period.

Time for defendant to bring action against third-party defendant. — The 1983 amendment to this section makes clear that at any time a plaintiff waits to the eleventh hour to file a lawsuit against a defendant who has a claim (whether it be contribution, indemnity, or otherwise) against a third-party defendant, then the original defendant shall have 60 days in which to bring his action, notwithstanding the fact that the statute of limitations may have run against the original plaintiff. Wingo v. Norfolk & W. Ry., 638 F. Supp. 107 (W.D. Va. 1986), rev'd on other grounds, 834 F.2d 375 (4th Cir. 1987).

Tolling provision for minor's claim inapplicable to parent's claim. — The statute of limitations tolling provision for a minor's claim does not apply to a parent's claim for medical expenses and emotional distress stemming from the same incident of alleged malpractice; the parent's claims are subject to the limitation period of § 8.01-243 (B). Perez ex rel. Perez v. Espinola, 749 F. Supp. 732 (E.D. Va. 1990).

II. DECISIONS UNDER PRIOR LAW.

A. General Consideration.

Editor's note. — The cases cited below were decided under corresponding provisions of former law. The terms "the statute of limitations" and "this section," as used below, refer to former provisions.

B. Effect of Disability.

Section creates no new right to sue, since its very terms referred to a preexisting right established outside the section and not to any separate and distinct right born within the section itself. Hurdle v. Prinz, 218 Va. 134, 235 S.E.2d 354 (1977).

Application of § 1-13.42, fixing age of majority at 18. — Application of the age of majority statute to the plaintiffs, both of whom were under the age of 21 at the time their causes of action accrued prior to the enactment of the statute, causing the statute of limitations to run from the time plaintiffs reached the age of 18 rather than from the age of 21 as at common law, was not error. Hurdle v. Prinz, 218 Va. 134, 235 S.E.2d 354 (1977).

Section could not properly be read to delay until age 21 the running of the statute of limitations on causes of action for personal injury which accrued while plaintiffs were under 21 years of age, where § 1-13.42, changing the age of majority and therefore changing the status of plaintiffs, was enacted before plaintiffs reached 21. Hurdle v. Prinz, 218 Va. 134, 235 S.E.2d 354 (1977).

Infancy of beneficiary of wrongful death action. — The statute of limitations for wrongful death actions was not tolled by reason of infancy of the beneficiary of the wrongful death action, since the infant's disability could not prevent the timely institution of the action in view of the fact that wrongful death actions may be brought only by and in the name of the personal representative of the deceased. Beverage v. Harvey, 602 F.2d 657 (4th Cir. 1979).

Tacking successive disabilities not allowed. — Where a disability existing at the time the cause of action accrued is removed, another disability arising subsequently cannot be tacked to it, to avoid the bar of the statute. Fitzhugh v. Anderson, 12 Va. (2 Hen. & M.) 289 (1808); Hudson v. Hudson, 20 Va. (6 Munf.) 352 (1819); Parsons v. M'Cracken, 36 Va. (9 Leigh) 495 (1838); Hancock v. Hutcherson, 76 Va. 609 (1882); Blackwell v. Bragg, 78 Va. 529 (1884); McDonald v. Hovey, 110 U.S. 619, 4 S. Ct. 142, 28 L. Ed. 269 (1884).

But in case of coexisting disabilities, last must be removed before statute begins to run. — Where there are two or more disabilities coexisting in the same person when his right of action accrues, he is not obliged to act until the last is removed. Wilson v. Branch, 77 Va. 65 (1883); Blackwell v. Bragg, 78 Va. 529 (1884).

Suits by next friend. — Persons under disability when their rights accrue, may prosecute any remedy in equity they are entitled to, by prochein ami at any time while the disability continues. Hansford v. Elliott, 36 Va. (9 Leigh) 79 (1837).

Statute does not begin to run until infant reaches majority. — If one is an infant when his right accrues, the statute of limitations does not run against the right until he attains the age of 21 (now 18). Baird v. Bland, 17 Va. (3 Munf.) 570 (1812); Brown v. Lambert, 74 Va. (33 Gratt.) 256 (1880); Redford v. Clarke, 100 Va. 115, 40 S.E. 630 (1902).

This applies to claim of infant for legacy. — Where a testator bequeathed property to an infant son, the act of limitations never could begin to run against the claim and title of the son to the property till he attained a full age. Lynch v. Thomas, 30 Va. (3 Leigh) 682 (1832).

"Insane" defined. — The term "insane" as used in statutes extending the time within which to commence an action has been held to mean such a condition of mental derangement as actually to bar the sufferer from comprehending rights which he is otherwise bound to know. Williams v. Westbrook Psychiatric Hosp., 420 F. Supp. 322 (E.D. Va. 1976).

Where sanity is basis of action for wrongful confinement. — A plaintiff may not rely on an adjudication of insanity to toll the statute of limitations and, at the same time, allege wrongfulness of confinement and treatment due to alleged sanity. Williams v. Westbrook Psychiatric Hosp., 420 F. Supp. 322 (E.D. Va. 1976).

Statute not tolled during period of imprisonment. — If a committee for a prisoner does not institute a suit promptly, the prisoner's rights may be lost since the Virginia statute of limitations is not tolled during the period of incarceration, as it is in many states treating a prisoner as incapable of maintaining litigation. Almond v. Kent, 459 F.2d 200 (4th Cir. 1972).

This section has no reference to nonresidents. — See Baber v. Baber, 121 Va. 740, 94 S.E. 209 (1917).

C. Effect of Death of a Party.

Subsection B has no application to appeals and writs of error. Williams v. Dean, 144 Va. 831, 131 S.E. 1 (1925).

Subdivisions B 1 and 2 do not apply to real actions. Steffey v. King, 126 Va. 120, 101 S.E. 62 (1919). See Barley v. Duncan, 177 Va. 192, 13 S.E.2d 294 (1941).

Does not include trustee in deed of trust. — Since the trustee named in a deed of trust is given no authority or right of his own to institute a suit to foreclose a deed of trust, he has no right or remedy to lose or to preserve within the meaning of this section, and this section does not apply to the death of a trustee. Boggs v. Fatherly, 177 Va. 259, 13 S.E.2d 298 (1941).

Cause of action to recover for services rendered decedent in return for oral promise to make will was "capable of coming into existence during the life" of decedent, thus this section applied so as to make the limitation four years from decedent's death instead of three years under § 8.01-246 (4). Archer v. National Bank, 194 Va. 641, 74 S.E.2d 153 (1953).

Subdivision B 4 does not apply to the claim of a residuary legatee. Wilson v. Butt, 168 Va. 259, 190 S.E. 260 (1937).

Debtor cannot revive judgment of deceased creditor. — Upon the death of a judgment creditor, the judgment debtor has no authority to revive the judgment in the name of the personal representative of the judgment creditor. City of Charlottesville v. Stratton's Adm'r, 102 Va. 95, 45 S.E. 737 (1903).

But creditor may sue in equity without first reviving judgment. — A judgment creditor may bring a suit in equity against the personal representative and heirs or devisees of his deceased judgment debtor without first reviving his judgment. James v. Life, 92 Va. 702, 24 S.E. 275 (1896).

D. Prevention of Service by Defendant.

Subsection D does not grant a right and a remedy but merely grants or extends and enlarges a remedy. Duffy v. Hartsock, 187 Va. 406, 46 S.E.2d 570 (1948).

It applies only to persons living when the right of action accrued, its object being to stop the running of the statute of limitations as to the classes of persons therein mentioned, as long as they obstructed the prosecution of any such right of action as is mentioned in this chapter. Templeman v. Pugh, 102 Va. 441, 46 S.E. 474 (1904).

Removal is itself an obstruction. — Where a debtor who resides in the State removes, after contracting the debt, to another state, the removal is itself an obstruction to the prosecution of a suit by the creditor to recover the debt, and the statute of limitations will not run against the debt whilst the debtor resides out of the State. Ficklin v. Carrington, 72 Va. (31 Gratt.) 219 (1878). But see Wilson v. Koontz, 11 U.S. (7 Cranch) 202, 3 L. Ed. 315 (1812); Brown v. Butler, 87 Va. 621, 13 S.E. 71 (1891).

The burden of proving removal of the defendant from the State is on the plaintiff. Pilson v. Bushong, 70 Va. (29 Gratt.) 229 (1877); Lindsay v. Murphy, 76 Va. 428 (1882); Brown v. Butler, 87 Va. 621, 13 S.E. 71 (1891).

Section inapplicable where substituted service provided. — Where, under §§ 8.01-301 through 8.01-312, plaintiff can obtain service of process upon defendant before the expiration of the two-year limitation period prescribed by § 8.01-243 and secure a valid personal judgment if he is so entitled, his remedy is complete and unaffected by the absence of defendant, and subsection D is not applicable. Bergman v. Turpin, 206 Va. 539, 145 S.E.2d 135 (1965).

Temporary absence does not affect running of statute. — A carpenter going from place to place in different states and working at his trade has not left the State within the meaning of this section. Brown v. Butler, 87 Va. 621, 13 S.E. 71 (1891).

Mere silence is not fraudulent concealment of facts. — The concealment of a cause of action which will prevent the running of the statute of limitations must consist of some trick or artifice preventing inquiry, or calculated to hinder a discovery of the cause of action by the use of ordinary diligence. Mere silence is not sufficient. The fraud which will relieve the bar of the statute must be of that character which involves moral turpitude and must have the effect of debarring or deterring the plaintiff from his action. Culpeper Nat'l Bank v. Tidewater Imp. Co., 119 Va. 73, 89 S.E. 118 (1916).

Constructive fraud is not such as will toll the running of the statute of limitations. The character of fraud necessary to toll the statute must be of a variety involving moral turpitude. A defendant must intend to conceal the discovery of the cause of action by trick or artifice and must have thus actually concealed it from the plaintiff in order for the exception to apply. Richmond Redevelopment & Hous. Auth. v. Laburnum Constr. Corp., 195 Va. 827, 80 S.E.2d 574 (1954); Hawks v. DeHart, 206 Va. 810, 146 S.E.2d 187 (1966).

Fraudulent concealment of shortages by depository of public funds. — A bank, which had aided and abetted a county treasurer in a scheme to conceal shortages in his treasurer's account, and had made false certifications as to the treasury balances on deposit with it, was guilty of such obstruction as is contemplated by this section, and an action against the bank by the treasurer's surety, which had settled for the shortages, was not barred by the statute of limitations. Jones v. United States Fid. & Guar. Co., 165 Va. 349, 182 S.E. 560 (1935).

No evidence of fraudulent concealment. — Where the plaintiffs and defendant have similar educational and occupational backgrounds, all parties read the entire deed prior to its execution, the plaintiffs appeared to understand the transaction, there was evidence to the effect that the plaintiffs and the defendant definitely indicated a desire to execute a deed of bargain and sale rather than a deed of trust, and plaintiffs have not established any act by defendant or anyone else, prior or subsequent to execution, which would have prevented the plaintiffs from discovering the true nature of the deed, the facts do not evidence fraudulent concealment. Burton v. Terrell, 368 F. Supp. 553 (W.D. Va. 1973).

Misrepresentations made to obtain money due under contract. — Where plaintiff's pleadings charged merely that defendant made misrepresentations to obtain money due under a contract, it did not show a case for tolling the statute on the ground of fraudulent concealment of a cause of action for damages from an explosion due to defective work done under contract. Richmond Redevelopment & Hous. Auth. v. Laburnum Constr. Corp., 195 Va. 827, 80 S.E.2d 574 (1954).

Removal and concealment of property. — Removal of property to a distant county, thus keeping the owners in ignorance of where it was, was an obstruction to the assertion of their rights by action, precluding the defendant from pleading the statute of limitations. Rankin v. Bradford, 28 Va. (1 Leigh) 163 (1829).

Promise to settle is not obstruction of plaintiff's right. — A promise to settle and pay the balance found due on the settlement will not stop the running of the statute of limitations during the time the settlement is delayed. It is at most only a promise to pay an unascertained balance, and such a promise is not an obstruction of the plaintiff's right within the meaning of this section, nor does the mere failure to comply with such a promise amount to a fraud on the plaintiff, even if fraud could be relied on in a court of law to repel the bar of the statute of limitations. Liskey v. Paul, 100 Va. 764, 42 S.E. 875 (1902).

Agreement not to sue suspends running of statute. — A mutual understanding and agreement between a debtor and creditor, that suit shall not be brought upon an account until the debtor shall have gone to Europe, and returned, is a good bar to the act of limitations during his absence from this country, and may be given in evidence to prevent the court's expunging from an account items appearing to have been due five years before his death. Holladay v. Littlepage, 16 Va. (2 Munf.) 316 (1811).

E. Dismissal, Abatement or Nonsuit.

Liberal construction. — Statutes quite similar to subsection E have their origin in the Act of 1623 (21 James I, c. 16, § 4). Such statutes are highly remedial and should be liberally construed in furtherance of their purposes, and are not to be frittered away by any narrow construction. Woodson v. Commonwealth Util., Inc., 209 Va. 72, 161 S.E.2d 669 (1968).

Purpose. — An analysis of subsection E shows that its purpose is to negate the harsh results flowing from the statute of limitations in certain specific instances. Woodson v. Commonwealth Util., Inc., 209 Va. 72, 161 S.E.2d 669 (1968).

The basic purpose reflected in the tolling rule is to save the right of action for plaintiffs who, without fault, have been unable to obtain an adjudication on the merits. Atkins v. Schmutz Mfg. Co., 435 F.2d 527 (4th Cir. 1970), cert. denied, 402 U.S. 932, 91 S. Ct. 1526, 28 L. Ed. 2d 867 (1971).

As a general rule, if the statute of limitations has once begun to run no subsequent event will interrupt it. Parsons v. M'Cracken, 36 Va. (9 Leigh) 495 (1838); Caperton v. Gregory, 52 Va. (11 Gratt.) 505 (1854).

In only four instances is there a suspension of the statute of limitations by reason of the pendency of a former suit brought in due time. These are: (1) where the suit abates "by the return of no inhabitant," — that is, where the writ is not served for that reason; (2) where the suit abates by reason of the "death or marriage" of a party; (3) where, after the plaintiff has obtained a judgment or decree in his favor, it is "arrested or reversed upon a ground which does not preclude a new action or suit for the same cause"; (4) where "there be occasion to bring a new action or suit by reason of the loss or destruction of any of the papers or records in a former suit or action which was in due time." Jones v. Morris Plan Bank, 170 Va. 88, 195 S.E. 525 (1938); Woodson v. Commonwealth Util., Inc., 209 Va. 72, 161 S.E.2d 669 (1968); Atkins v. Schmutz Mfg. Co., 435 F.2d 527 (4th Cir. 1970), cert. denied, 402 U.S. 932, 91 S. Ct. 1526, 28 L. Ed. 2d 867 (1971).

Ignorance of rights does not suspend statute. — Mere ignorance on the part of a creditor is not sufficient to suspend the operation of the statute of limitations. Foster v. Rison, 58 Va. (17 Gratt.) 321 (1867); Bickle v. Chrisman, 76 Va. 678 (1882); Matthews & Co. v. Progress Distilling Co., 108 Va. 777, 62 S.E. 924 (1908).

Void confessed judgment within subdivision E 2. — A judgment confessed by the president of defendant corporation in favor of a trustee in bankruptcy and later declared void and set aside because of the president's lack of authority is clearly within the letter of the saving provision of this section, which provides that where a plaintiff has obtained a judgment in an action commenced in due time and it is "arrested or reversed upon a ground which does not preclude a new action . . . for the same cause . . ., the same may be brought within one year after such . . . arrest or reversal of judgment . . . ." Hence the statute of limitations does not preclude plaintiff's right to proceed with his motion for judgment in the present case. Woodson v. Commonwealth Util., Inc., 209 Va. 72, 161 S.E.2d 669 (1968).

Statute is not suspended where suit commenced in wrong forum. — Plaintiff argued that the general purpose of subsection E was to save a bona fide litigant from the bar of the statute of limitations where he had brought his action within the time prescribed by law, and such suit failed or was dismissed otherwise than upon the merits, and that such a saving clause was by implication written into the statute. This section in an earlier code contained such a saving clause but it was eliminated on the recommendation of the revisers of the Code of 1919. It was held that the General Assembly had expressly determined to eliminate the saving clause in favor of litigant, such as plaintiff, who had proceeded in the wrong forum, and this was a complete answer to the argument that the saving clause was by implication written into the law. Jones v. Morris Plan Bank, 170 Va. 88, 195 S.E. 525 (1938).

When the two-year period of limitation had run, there was no basis for granting relief to a plaintiff whose prior suit was brought in the wrong forum or was dismissed otherwise than upon the merits. Atkins v. Schmutz Mfg. Co., 435 F.2d 527 (4th Cir. 1970), cert. denied, 402 U.S. 932, 91 S. Ct. 1526, 28 L. Ed. 2d 867 (1971).

Action dismissed for void process. — It is no answer to the bar set up by the plea of the act of limitations, that the plaintiff sued out a writ for the same cause of action within the time prescribed by the act, which writ was executed and returned, and went off the docket for want of formality. Callis v. Waddy, 16 Va. (2 Munf.) 511 (1811).

Agreement of parties deferring liability of debtor. — A covenant was entered into between the maker and the payee of a note, that the note should be held by the maker until his liability as bail for the payee should cease, and that he then should deliver it. The statute did not run upon the note from the time the covenant was executed until the liability of the maker as bail ceased. Bowles v. Elmore, 48 Va. (7 Gratt.) 385 (1851).

Entry of order in creditors' suit. — From the time of the entry of an order of reference in a creditors' suit, the statute of limitations will cease to run against all lien creditors who assert their demands in the suit. Harvey v. Steptoe, 58 Va. (17 Gratt.) 289 (1867); Bank of Old Dominion v. Allen, 76 Va. 200 (1882); Norvell v. Little, 79 Va. 141 (1884); Houck v. Dunham, 92 Va. 211, 23 S.E. 238 (1895); Craufurd v. Smith, 93 Va. 623, 23 S.E. 235, 25 S.E. 657 (1896); Callaway v. Saunders, 99 Va. 350, 38 S.E. 182 (1901); Gunnell v. Dixon, 101 Va. 174, 43 S.E. 340 (1903); Robinett v. Mitchell, 101 Va. 762, 45 S.E. 287 (1903).

Running of statute not tolled by false representations of party. — An agreement by defendant, purporting to act as president of a nonexistent corporation, to erect a gasoline station on property which he did not own and lease it for ten years beginning on a certain date was breached when the defendant failed to do so by such date. And the Virginia five-year statute of limitations began to run from such time. The running of the statute was not tolled by the fact that defendant falsely represented that the corporation was a Virginia corporation and that it owned the property in question. Galumbeck v. Suburban Park Stores Corp., 214 F.2d 660 (4th Cir. 1954).

Tolling effect of prior suit in another federal court. — Since Virginia's tolling statute and state decisions construing it have been so largely influenced by the nature and the structure of Virginia's system of trial courts, and since the question in the instant case arises out of the federal court system and reasonable answers are dependent upon the nature and the structure of that system and its effective functioning, the tolling effect of a prior suit in another federal court is a matter of federal, not state, law. Atkins v. Schmutz Mfg. Co., 435 F.2d 527 (4th Cir. 1970), cert. denied, 402 U.S. 932, 91 S. Ct. 1526, 28 L. Ed. 2d 867 (1971).

Though there was no transfer of the action in the Western District of Kentucky and the question of its transferability was not raised, the commencement of this action in the Western District of Virginia during the pendency of the Kentucky action achieved the same practical result. A determination of the tolling effect of the commencement and prosecution of the federal action in the Western District of Kentucky ought to be had under the same body of law regardless of the procedural means by which prosecution of the substantive cause of action is discontinued in the district court sitting in Kentucky and continued in a district court sitting in Virginia. Atkins v. Schmutz Mfg. Co., 435 F.2d 527 (4th Cir. 1970), cert. denied, 402 U.S. 932, 91 S. Ct. 1526, 28 L. Ed. 2d 867 (1971).

Where the purposes of the statute of limitations have been satisfied, the institutional basis of Virginia's tolling rule becomes critical to a consideration of the applicability of that rule to an action in a federal court. Atkins v. Schmutz Mfg. Co., 435 F.2d 527 (4th Cir. 1970), cert. denied, 402 U.S. 932, 91 S. Ct. 1526, 28 L. Ed. 2d 867 (1971).

Where an action abates by the death of defendant, the statute of limitations is suspended for only one year, in which time plaintiff may commence a new action. Brown v. Putney, 1 Va. (1 Wash.) 302 (1794).

Subdivision E 2 does not affect time for appeals. — The time for taking the appeal from orders of clerks relating to probate of wills or administration of estates, prescribed by § 64.1-78, is not extended by the provisions of this section giving an extension in certain cases "if there be occasion to bring a new suit." Tyson v. Scott, 116 Va. 243, 81 S.E. 57 (1914).

Suspended year does not run from the judgment of the appellate court, but from that of the lower court, excluding from the computation the time during which the action was pending in the appellate court. Bradley Salt Co. v. Norfolk Importing & Exporting Co., 101 F. 681 (4th Cir. 1900).

F. Effect of Devise for Payment.

Section applies whether or not debt barred at testator's death. — A devise of real estate for the payment of debts will not affect the operation of the statute of limitation upon the debts, whether they are barred at the testator's death or not, unless the contrary intention on his part plainly appears. Johnston v. Wilson, 70 Va. (29 Gratt.) 379 (1877).

Devise is not evidence of intent. — Subsection F is a legislative declaration that all the provisions as to the limitation of actions shall apply in favor of a testator's debts, although there is a devise of real estate for their payment, unless it plainly appears that the testator otherwise intended. The devise is not of itself sufficient evidence of the intent. It must appear from some provision or phrase independent of the devise, which indicates the purpose of the testator. Johnston v. Wilson, 70 Va. (29 Gratt.) 379 (1877).

G. Effect of New Promise in Writing.

New promise renders promisor liable to action. — If a person makes a promise that he will pay a debt he justly owes, for the recovery of which all legal and equitable remedies are barred by the statute of limitations, the promise renders him liable to an action. Robinson v. Bass, 100 Va. 190, 40 S.E. 660 (1902).

Promise must be in writing. — This section must be construed in the light of the law as it existed prior to the enactment of any similar statute, and in the light of the history of the section and the statutes in which it had its origin. When so construed, it provides by necessary implication that an oral acknowledgment or new promise to pay a debt, shall not be sufficient to take the debt out of the statutes of limitations and support a recovery thereof after an action on the original promise has become barred; and that any acknowledgment or new promise, to have that effect, must be made by writing, signed by the person to be charged thereby or his agent. Gwinn v. Farrier, 159 Va. 183, 165 S.E. 647 (1932). See Robinson v. Bass, 100 Va. 190, 40 S.E. 660 (1902); Kesterson v. Hill, 101 Va. 739, 45 S.E. 288 (1903); Tucker v. Owen, 94 F.2d 49 (4th Cir. 1938).

And it must be determinate and unequivocal. — A new promise to remove the bar of the statute of limitations must be determinate and unequivocal. Coles v. Martin, 99 Va. 223, 37 S.E. 907 (1901). See also, Aylett v. Robinson, 36 Va. (9 Leigh) 45 (1837); Bell v. Crawford, 49 Va. (8 Gratt.) 110 (1851).

But the new promise may be either express or implied. Rowe v. Marchant, 86 Va. 177, 9 S.E. 995 (1889).

An acknowledgment in writing from which a promise of payment may be implied is sufficient. Dinguid v. Schoolfield, 73 Va. (32 Gratt.) 803 (1880); Rowe v. Marchant, 86 Va. 177, 9 S.E. 995 (1889).

If there is an unequivocal admission that the debt is still due and unpaid, unaccompanied by any expression, declaration or qualification indicative of an intention not to pay, the state of facts out of which the law implies a promise is then present, and the party is bound by it. Nesbit v. Galleher, 174 Va. 143, 5 S.E.2d 501 (1939).

The acknowledgment need not be in any particular form or contain any particular substance. But it ought to be a direct and unqualified admission of a present subsisting debt, from which a promise to pay would naturally and irresistibly be implied. Nesbit v. Galleher, 174 Va. 143, 5 S.E.2d 501 (1939).

But it must be clear and unqualified. — An acknowledgment from which a promise may be implied must be unqualified. Aylett v. Robinson, 36 Va. (9 Leigh) 45 (1837); Bell v. Crawford, 49 Va. (8 Gratt.) 110 (1851); Switzer v. Noffsinger, 82 Va. 518 (1886).

To imply a promise of payment from a subsequent acknowledgment, the acknowledgment must be an unqualified admission of a subsisting debt which the party is liable for and willing to pay. Coles v. Martin, 99 Va. 223, 37 S.E. 907 (1901); Quackenbush v. Isley, 154 Va. 407, 153 S.E. 818 (1930).

It must not consist of equivocal, vague and indeterminate expressions, but ought to contain an unqualified and direct admission of a previous, subsisting debt, which the party is liable for and willing to pay. Nesbit v. Galleher, 174 Va. 143, 5 S.E.2d 501 (1939).

And not a mere attempt at settlement. — An acknowledgment in writing, to operate as a new promise, must be a clear and definite acknowledgment of a precise sum, plainly importing willingness and liability to pay, and not in any wise conditional, nor by way of promise or attempt at settlement. Aylett v. Robinson, 36 Va. (9 Leigh) 45 (1837); Bell v. Crawford, 49 Va. (8 Gratt.) 110 (1851); Coles v. Martin, 99 Va. 223, 37 S.E. 907 (1901); Liskey v. Paul, 100 Va. 764, 42 S.E. 875 (1902); Kesterson v. Hill, 101 Va. 739, 45 S.E. 288 (1903).

Form of new promise does not fix limitation on original contract. — The provision in this section that suit may be brought "within such number of years after such promise, as it might be maintained if such promise were the original cause of action," means "if the date of such promise were the date of the accrual of the original cause of action," and is not intended to mean that the form of the new promise fixes the limitation of an action on the original contract.

Ingram v. Harris, 174 Va. 1, 5 S.E.2d 624 (1939).

Promise to pay one debt does not affect another not referred to. — A letter containing a promise to pay an account asked for, and stating that if the writer could only draw in her means, she could pay every cent she owed, is not sufficient to take an old account not referred to out of the operation of the statute of limitations. Coles v. Martin, 99 Va. 223, 37 S.E. 907 (1901).

But promise to pay ascertainable amount is sufficient. — Where there is a new promise to pay not specifying any amount, but which can be made certain as to the amount, it is sufficient. Coles v. Martin, 99 Va. 223, 37 S.E. 907 (1901).

New promise must be made by debtor. — A new promise, to repel the plea of the statute of limitations, must be made by the person against whom the right to maintain an action has accrued. Bell v. Crawford, 49 Va. (8 Gratt.) 110 (1851); Switzer v. Noffsinger, 82 Va. 518 (1886).

To creditor. — Generally, a promise sufficient to toll statute of limitations should be made directly to the creditor or some person acting for him, and declarations or admissions to strangers are insufficient. Layman v. Layman, 171 Va. 317, 198 S.E. 923 (1938).

A declaration or admission to a third person is deemed insufficient to avoid the bar of the statute of limitations, not so much because the acknowledgment is made to a stranger as because there is no sufficient evidence of an intention to contract. Layman v. Layman, 171 Va. 317, 198 S.E. 923 (1938).

A promise to pay a debt, made to a person not legally or equitably interested in the same, and who does not pretend to have had any authority from the creditor to call upon the debtor in relation to the debt, will not avoid the bar of the statute of limitations. Layman v. Layman, 171 Va. 317, 198 S.E. 923 (1938).

Unless intended to be communicated to creditor. — Where the acknowledgment of a debt is to a stranger, and it appears that it was the intention of the debtor that the acknowledgment made to him should be communicated to and should influence the creditor, it is just as effectual to defeat the statute of limitations as if it had been made directly to the creditor or his authorized agent. Layman v. Layman, 171 Va. 317, 198 S.E. 923 (1938).

Performance of conditions must be shown. — If the acknowledgment or new promise be coupled with any terms or conditions, they must be proven to have been performed, or else no recovery can be had. Farmers Bank v. Clarke, 31 Va. (4 Leigh) 603 (1833).

A promise "to settle" is ineffectual. — It requires a promise to pay, or such an acknowledgment in writing that a promise to pay may be implied from it, to take a debt out of the statute of limitations and it is well settled that a promise merely "to settle" is not sufficient. Aylett v. Robinson, 36 Va. (9 Leigh) 45 (1837); Bell v. Crawford, 49 Va. (8 Gratt.) 110 (1851); Gover v. Chamberlain, 83 Va. 286, 5 S.E. 174 (1887); Liskey v. Paul, 100 Va. 764, 42 S.E. 875 (1902).

On a plea of non assumpsit within five years, it was proved that within five years the defendant acknowledged the items in the plaintiff's account to be just, but said that he had some offsets; and that at a subsequent time, the defendant promised the plaintiff that he would settle all their differences and accounts fairly, and would not avail himself of the act of limitations. It was held that this proof was not sufficient to justify the jury in finding for the plaintiff. Sutton v. Burruss, 36 Va. (9 Leigh) 381 (1838).

An account stated, which is not supported by a writing signed by the debtor or his agent, will not prevent the running of the statute of limitations against previously existing items of indebtedness included therein. Magarity v. Shipman, 93 Va. 64, 24 S.E. 466 (1896). See Tazewell's Ex'r v. Whittle's Adm'r, 54 Va. (13 Gratt.) 329 (1856); Radford v. Fowlkes, 85 Va. 820, 8 S.E. 817 (1889).

Promise by insolvent is not fraudulent as to other creditors. — An insolvent debtor may make a new promise to pay one of his creditors a debt barred by the act of limitations, and may give a specific lien on his property to secure the same, and in the absence of fraud, other creditors cannot object. The new promise is not per se such a fraudulent act as will entitle other creditors to set up the statute of limitations against the debt or the security given for it. The only condition imposed on the creditor by this section is that the new promise shall be in writing and signed by the debtor or his agent. Robinson v. Bass, 100 Va. 190, 40 S.E. 660 (1902).

A clear acknowledgment of a debt coupled with a plea of poverty as a reason for delay in payment, is sufficient to repel the statute of limitations. Nesbit v. Galleher, 174 Va. 143, 5 S.E.2d 501 (1939).

A letter was held to constitute an acknowledgment sufficient to repel the bar of the statute of limitations under this section. Nesbit v. Galleher, 174 Va. 143, 5 S.E.2d 501 (1939).

A letter written by a father to an officer of the bank named as executor in his will constituted an acknowledgment of a debt of the father to his daughter, and was not made to a stranger, but to one charged with the duty to act for his estate and for his daughter, and the acknowledgment was intended to influence her in accepting a settlement of the debt. It was not necessary that the acknowledgment be made directly to her in order to start a new period of limitations, since the debtor, her father, derived an advantage from it. Bickers v. Pinnell, 199 Va. 444, 100 S.E.2d 20 (1957).

Letter and notations on checks given to pay interest. — There was, in a letter written by a father to an officer of the bank which was named as executor under his will, and in his notations on checks given to pay interest on a loan made to the father by his daughter, ample "acknowledgment from which a promise of payment might be implied," which promise under this section started a new period of limitations. Bickers v. Pinnell, 199 Va. 444, 100 S.E.2d 20 (1957).

Financial statement and checks of close corporation. — Where a close corporation as debtor is involved, a financial statement, listing the stale debt, signed by the corporation's accountant who is also one of its directors, and corporate checks, issued in payment of interest on the debt, are sufficient acknowledgment in writing of the indebtedness from which may be implied a promise to pay the obligation, and upon which to fix a new period of limitation. Tyler Gilman Corp. v. Williams, 216 Va. 548, 221 S.E.2d 129 (1976).

Deposition in suit to which creditor was not party may suffice. — A deposition of the maker of a note, given and signed by him, in a case in which the obligee was not a party, for the purpose of obtaining a credit for the note as to be paid by the maker, and for which he was allowed such a credit in that case, is such an acknowledgment of the debt as will defeat the plea of the statute of limitations in an action on the note by the obligee. Dinguid v. Schoolfield, 73 Va. (32 Gratt.) 803 (1880).

If a promise may be inferred therefrom. — A deposition declaring that a statement contained in an inventory of a decedent's estate is not a correct statement of what is owing cannot be considered as an unqualified and direct acknowledgment of a subsisting indebtedness from which a promise to pay could be inferred. Walter v. Whitacre, 113 Va. 150, 73 S.E. 984 (1912).

Implied promise to pay bonds destroyed by obligor. — R. took from plaintiff, while he was sick, certain bonds representing debts due by R., and destroyed them, but, on plaintiff's recovery, gave him a written acknowledgment of their destruction. The bonds were at that time barred by the statute of limitations, but R. wrote under a written statement of the date and amount of the bonds a statement that "the above entries of the amounts of money due by me" to plaintiff were correct, and that the bonds "were never paid by me." This was held to be a sufficient acknowledgment of the debt to take it from under the statute. Rowe v. Marchant, 86 Va. 177, 9 S.E. 995 (1889).

Part payment does not remove the bar of the statute. — This section provides, by necessary implication, that a part payment of a debt, unless evidenced by a writing that in itself amounts to an acknowledgment or a new promise to pay, shall not be sufficient to take the debt out of the statutes of limitation and support a recovery thereof after an action on the original promise has become barred. Gwinn v. Farrier, 159 Va. 183, 165 S.E. 647 (1932).

Part payment of a note after it had become barred was not sufficient to remove the bar of the statute. Gover v. Chamberlain, 83 Va. 286, 5 S.E. 174 (1886).

Nor does payment of interest. — A part payment of the principal or payment of interest does not, at least in Virginia, remove the bar of the statute. Quackenbush v. Isley, 154 Va. 407, 153 S.E. 818 (1930); Layman v. Layman, 171 Va. 317, 198 S.E. 923 (1938).

Or stop the running of time. — The partial payment of debt already due does not affect the running of the statute or operate to create a new cause of action. W.L. Becker & Co. v. Norfolk & W. Ry., 125 Va. 558, 100 S.E. 478 (1919).

Acknowledgment in bill by attorney insufficient. — A bill in chancery filed for the construction of a testator's will and the administration of his estate under the care of the court, which is signed by counsel only, and which lists a debt due by the complainant to the testator, is not such an acknowledgment by the debtor or his agent as will take the debt out of the bar of the statute of limitations, in the absence of any evidence that the counsel was authorized to make an admission of indebtedness. Walter v. Whitacre, 113 Va. 150, 73 S.E. 984 (1912).

Acknowledgment of title to property insufficient. — In an action of detinue, defendant pleaded the statute of limitations and plaintiff replied that within five years defendant acknowledged the article detained to be plaintiff's property. This was held insufficient, for under this section the operation of the statute can be avoided only by showing a written acknowledgment or promise to pay money. Morris v. Lyon, 84 Va. 331, 4 S.E. 734 (1888).

Province of court and jury. — It is the province of court when the facts are undisputed, to decide what acts or declarations amount to a new promise which will take a case out of the operation of the statute of limitations. But where the evidence was conflicting, the evidence to show the promise must be left to the jury. Fisher v. Duncan, 11 Va. (1 Hen. & M.) 563 (1807).

Section not applicable to hearings before commissioner of accounts. — The provisions of this section were not applicable to hearings before a commissioner of accounts under former §§ 64-161 through 64-163 (see now §§ 64.1-171 to 64.1-173). Bickers v. Pinnell, 199 Va. 444, 100 S.E.2d 20 (1957).

H. Suspension of Limitations in Creditors' Suits.

In order to apply this subsection H, it should be clearly established that the suit is of the character and nature specified and that the debt was presented and dealt with as required. Mitchell v. Cox, 189 Va. 236, 52 S.E.2d 105 (1949).

§ **8.01-230. Accrual of right of action.** — In every action for which a limitation period is prescribed, the right of action shall be deemed to accrue and the prescribed limitation period shall begin to run from the date the injury is sustained in the case of injury to the person or damage to property, when the breach of contract occurs in actions ex contractu and not when the resulting damage is discovered, except where the relief sought is solely equitable or where otherwise provided under § 8.01-233, subsection C of § 8.01-245, §§ 8.01-249, 8.01-250 or other statute. (1977, c. 617; 1996, c. 328.)

REVISERS' NOTE

Section 8.01-230 retains the traditional rule of Virginia case law that a cause of action accrues when the wrongful act or breach of duty or contract occurs. In tort cases this has generally been construed to occur when injury or other damage takes place irrespective of when discovered. See e.g., Hawks v. DeHart, 206 Va. 810, 146 S.E.2d 187 (1966); but see § 8.2-725 [cause of action with regard to breach of certain warranties as to future performance does not accrue until latent defect in goods discovered or should have been discovered].

The exceptions follow existing law. See e.g., Revisers' notes to §§ 8.01-223, 8.01-245 C, 8.01-249, and 8.01-250. Equity suits to which statutes of limitations may apply are also excepted. Cf. Revisers' note to § 8.01-228.

Cross references. — As to when right of action on claim against Commonwealth accrues, see § 8.01-192. For provision as to persons under disability, see § 8.01-229.

Law Review. — For comment, "Toward a Uniform State Product Liability Law — Virginia and the Uniform Product Liability Act," see 36 Wash. & Lee L. Rev. 1145 (1979). For comment on this section in light of Farley v. Goode, 219 Va. 969, 252 S.E.2d 594 (1979), see 4 Geo. Mason L. Rev. 285 (1981). For article on Virginia's continuing negligent treatment rule, see 15 U. Rich. L. Rev. 231 (1981). For article, "Products Liability and the Virginia Statute of Limitations — A Call for the Legislative Rescue Squad," see 16 U. Rich. L. Rev. 323 (1982). For comment, "Statutes of Limitations in Occupational Disease Cases: Is Locke v. Johns-Manville a Viable Alternative to the Discovery Rule?," see 39 Wash. & Lee L. Rev. 263 (1982). For 1987 survey of Virginia property law, see 21 U. Rich. L. Rev. 821 (1987). For an article, "Civil Practice and Procedure," see 32 U. Rich. L. Rev. 1009 (1998). For a review of construction law in Virginia for year 1999, see 33 U. Rich. L. Rev. 827 (1999).

I. Decisions Under Current Law.
  A. General Consideration.
  B. Torts.
    1. In General.
    2. Personal Injury.
II. Decisions Under Prior Law.
  A. General Consideration.
  B. Torts.
    1. In General.
    2. Personal Injury.
    3. Property Damage.
  C. Contracts.

I. DECISIONS UNDER CURRENT LAW.

A. General Consideration.

For purposes of statute of limitations, there is but a single, indivisible cause of action for all injuries sustained, whether or not all of the damage is immediately apparent. Joyce v. A.C. & S., Inc., 785 F.2d 1200 (4th Cir. 1986).

The mere fact that most of the damage occurs many years later does not change Virginia law or create a new cause of action. Irvin v. Burton, 635 F. Supp. 366 (W.D. Va. 1986).

"Cause of action" and "right of action" compared. — There is a tendency by some to treat "cause of action" and "right of action" as interchangeable terms. While a cause of action and a right of action may accrue simultaneously, they need not do so. A right of action is a remedial right to presently enforce a cause of action. There can be no right of action until there is a cause of action. Stone v. Ethan Allen, Inc., 232 Va. 365, 350 S.E.2d 629 (1986).

In an action for breach of warranty on common elements of condominium project, any unit owner whose deed was delivered before October 1, 1977, the effective date of this section, was entitled to the benefit of the rule that his right of action did not accrue until his property rights were injured. He had no property rights until he became an owner, and therefore his right of action accrued when his deed was delivered, if within the warranty period. On the other hand, a purchaser whose deed was delivered on or after October 1, 1977, was affected by this section. The statute of limitations began to run as to his claim when the breach of contract or duty occurred. That event took place when the first unit was conveyed to an individual owner. Harbour Gate Owners' Ass'n v. Berg, 232 Va. 98, 348 S.E.2d 252 (1986).

Equitable tolling only applies in Virginia where the defendant has actually concealed his culpability and the fact of the injury. A plaintiff aware of his injury is on "inquiry notice" to discover his cause of action by use of ordinary diligence. Resolution Trust Corp. v. Walde, 856 F. Supp. 281 (E.D. Va. 1994).

Virginia lacks a "cross-jurisdictional" equitable tolling rule. Wade v. Danek Med., Inc., 182 F.3d 281 (4th Cir. 1999).

Applicability of Virginia's tolling rule in diversity action. — In any case in which a state statute of limitations applies — whether because it is "borrowed" in a federal question action or because it applies under *Erie* in a diversity action — the state's accompanying rule regarding equitable tolling should also apply. Hence in a diversity action brought in federal court based on alleged injury arising out of back surgery, Virginia's rule against equitable tolling, rather than federal rule, would apply. Wade v. Danek Med., Inc., 182 F.3d 281 (4th Cir. 1999).

Equitable relief exception to contract action accrues upon breach. — For cases in which the relief sought is solely equitable, Virginia law provides an exception to the rule that a contract action accrues upon breach. Goodell v. Rehrig Int'l, Inc., 683 F. Supp. 1051 (E.D. Va. 1988), aff'd, 865 F.2d 1257 (4th Cir. 1989).

Under this section accrual occurs when the breach of contract or duty occurs and therefore, like copyright infringement claims, unfair competition claims can be comprised of a multitude of separate and distinct claims, where "each occurrence inflicts a new injury and gives rise to a separate cause of action and plaintiff's claim was not barred as to any injury accruing during the five year period preceding the filing of suit. Hoey v. Dexel Sys. Corp., 716 F. Supp. 222 (E.D. Va. 1989). But see Unlimited Screw Prods., Inc. v. Malm, 781 F. Supp. 1121 (E.D. Va. 1991).

Legal malpractice. — When malpractice is claimed to have occurred during the representation of a client by an attorney with respect to a particular undertaking or transaction, the breach of contract or duty occurs and the statute of limitations begins to run when the attorney's services rendered in connection with that particular undertaking or transaction have terminated, notwithstanding the continuation of a general attorney-client relationship, and irrespective of the attorney's work on other undertakings or transactions for the same client. Keller v. Denny, 232 Va. 512, 352 S.E.2d 327 (1987).

Life insurance policy. — With respect to life insurance policies, when a policy requires a demand for payment and proof of death, the statute of limitations begins to run on the date of the demand and proof. Arrington v. Peoples Sec. Life Ins. Co., 250 Va. 52, 458 S.E.2d 289 (1995).

Suit on oral contract must be brought within three years after cause of action accrues, which is at breach, not at discovery of any resulting damage. Goodell v. Rehrig Int'l, Inc., 683 F. Supp. 1051 (E.D. Va. 1988), aff'd, 865 F.2d 1257 (4th Cir. 1989).

Derivative claims accrue when primary claim accrues. — Where the parents' purported claim is derivative of their daughter's claim, it accrued at the same time as the daughter's claim, thus, it did not accrue when the parents first learned of the alleged tort against their child. Mahony v. Becker, 246 Va. 209, 435 S.E.2d 139 (1993).

Where former employee could have demanded issuance of stock certificate on start of employment based on oral contract, the statute of limitations begins to run at that time for breach of contract, not after he has

§ 8.01-230   CODE OF VIRGINIA   § 8.01-230

been fired since to do otherwise would give him the ability to start the statute running at any moment he chooses. Goodell v. Rehrig Int'l, Inc., 683 F. Supp. 1051 (E.D. Va. 1988), aff'd, 865 F.2d 1257 (4th Cir. 1989).

Limitation began to run when divorce case ended by entry of final decree. — It was apparent from the allegations of the bill of complaint that the particular undertaking or transaction, which attorney was engaged to handle for client terminated on Dec. 30, 1980, when the divorce case was ended by the entry of a final decree incorporating the property settlement agreement and the limitation period then began to run and expired three years later; thus, the chancellor correctly held that this suit, filed in Dec. 1984, was time-barred. MacLellan v. Throckmorton, 235 Va. 341, 367 S.E.2d 720 (1988).

Summary judgment was erroneously awarded to defendant in a medical malpractice suit where plaintiff's allegations as to when injury occurred could have been properly construed so as to fall within the two-year statute of limitations. Renner v. Stafford, 245 Va. 351, 429 S.E.2d 218 (1993).

Psychologist's breach of confidence. — Patient's cause of action accrued at the time clinical psychologist revealed his confidences to patient's wife in 1983 and 1984, not after patient learned of the indiscretions, in 1993. Bullion v. Gadaleto, 872 F. Supp. 303 (W.D. Va. 1995).

Applied in First Va. Bank-Colonial v. Baker, 225 Va. 72, 301 S.E.2d 8 (1983); Large v. Bucyrus-Erie Co., 707 F.2d 94 (4th Cir. 1983); Quillen v. International Playtex, Inc., 789 F.2d 1041 (4th Cir. 1986); Westminster Investing Corp. v. Lamps Unlimited, Inc., 237 Va. 543, 379 S.E.2d 316 (1989); C-T of Va., Inc. v. Barrett, 124 Bankr. 689 (W.D. Va. 1990); Stefano v. First Union Nat'l Bank, 981 F. Supp. 417 (E.D. Va. 1997).

B. Torts.

1. In General.

If any injury or damage immediately results from the wrongful or negligent act of another, the party aggrieved has a cause of action, and the statute of limitations begins to run at that time. Stone v. Ethan Allen, Inc., 232 Va. 365, 350 S.E.2d 629 (1986).

The initial degree of damage is immaterial. If any injury or damage immediately results from the wrongful or negligent act of another, the party aggrieved has a cause of action, and the statute of limitations begins to run at that time. Only the slightest injury is required to start the running of the limitations period. It is of no consequence that the amount of damages is not ascertainable until a later date. Resolution Trust Corp. v. Walde, 856 F. Supp. 281 (E.D. Va. 1994).

2. Personal Injury.

"Injury." — Injury, as it is used in this section, means positive, physical or mental hurt to the claimant, not legal wrong to him in the broad sense that his legally protected interests have been invaded. Lo v. Burke, 249 Va. 311, 455 S.E.2d 9 (1995).

"Injury" means "a positive, physical or mental hurt." St. George v. Pariser, 253 Va. 329, 484 S.E.2d 888 (1997).

The statutory word "injury" means positive, physical or mental hurt to the claimant, not legal wrong to him in the broad sense that his legally protected interests have been invaded; thus, the running of the time is tied to the fact of harm to the plaintiff, without which no cause of action would come into existence and is not keyed to the date of the wrongful act, another ingredient of a personal injury cause of action. Locke v. Johns-Manville Corp., 221 Va. 951, 275 S.E.2d 900 (1981).

Limitations period begins to run when the initial injury, even if relatively slight, is sustained, and the manifestation of more substantial injuries at a later date does not extend the limitations period. Large v. Bucyrus-Erie Co., 524 F. Supp. 285 (E.D. Va. 1981), aff'd, 707 F.2d 94 (4th Cir. 1983).

An injury is deemed to occur, and the statute of limitations period begins to run, whenever any injury, however slight, is caused by the negligent act, even though additional or more severe injury or damage may be subsequently sustained as a result of that act. St. George v. Pariser, 253 Va. 329, 484 S.E.2d 888 (1997).

Only slightest injury required to start running of limitation period. — In Virginia, only the slightest injury is required to start the running of the limitations period. International Surplus Lines Ins. Co. v. Marsh & McLennan, Inc., 838 F.2d 124 (4th Cir. 1988).

Statute runs from injury, not later onset of symptoms. — In actions for personal injury the accrual point is when damage occurs, therefore, it is conceivable that when a disease manifests itself by symptoms, such as pain, discomfort or impairment of function, expert medical testimony will demonstrate the injury occurred weeks, months or even years before onset of the symptoms; thus, the cause of action would accrue and the limitations period would run from the earlier and not the later time. Locke v. Johns-Manville Corp., 221 Va. 951, 275 S.E.2d 900 (1981).

Relevance of time of wrongful act or exposure incidental. — The time of a defendant's wrongful or negligent act, or of a plaintiff's exposure to an outstanding wrong committed by the defendant, is not relevant in and of itself. It becomes relevant to the running of the limitations period only incidentally: i.e., only if the wrongful act or exposure to it causes some injury to the plaintiff. Large v. Bucyrus-Erie Co., 524 F. Supp. 285 (E.D. Va. 1981), aff'd, 707 F.2d 94 (4th Cir. 1983).

In the absence of retroactive application of § 8.01-249 (4), the cause of action accrues and the statute of limitations begins to run when an injury is sustained, pursuant to this section. The cause of action accrues when the injury is diagnosable based on medical technology existing at the time of the injury. Moreover, the cause of action is deemed to have accrued whenever the injury, however slight, is complete. Palmer v. Norfolk & W. Ry., 646 F. Supp. 610 (W.D. Va. 1985).

Proof of time plaintiff hurt. — For purposes of this section, the "time plaintiff was hurt" is to be established from available competent evidence, produced by a plaintiff or a defendant, that pinpoints the precise date of injury with a reasonable degree of medical certainty. Locke v. Johns-Manville Corp., 221 Va. 951, 275 S.E.2d 900 (1981).

Dates of acts as indicators of dates of injury. — The actual dates of the defendants' acts or of exposure are reliable indicators of the date of injury only if the act or exposure and the injury occur contemporaneously. Large v. Bucyrus-Erie Co., 524 F. Supp. 285 (E.D. Va. 1981), aff'd, 707 F.2d 94 (4th Cir. 1983).

An injury need not occur contemporaneously with a negligent act, but may arise at some later point. St. George v. Pariser, 253 Va. 329, 484 S.E.2d 888 (1997).

Products liability cases. — Actions under Virginia law grounded in a personal injury-products liability factual pattern are governed by the torts statute, which runs from the time of injury. Bly v. Otis Elevator Co., 713 F.2d 1040 (4th Cir. 1983), modified on reh'g en banc, 754 F.2d 1111 (4th Cir. 1985).

Accrual of action for medical malpractice occurring during course of treatment. — When medical malpractice is claimed to have occurred during a continuous and substantially uninterrupted course of examination and treatment in which a particular illness or condition should have been diagnosed in the exercise of reasonable care, the date of injury occurs, the cause of action for that malpractice accrues, and the statute of limitations commences to run when the improper course of examination, and treatment if any, for the particular malady terminates. Farley v. Goode, 219 Va. 969, 252 S.E.2d 594 (1979).

Rule presupposes proof that treatment was continuous and uninterrupted. — The rule that when medical malpractice is claimed to have occurred during a continuous and substantially uninterrupted course of treatment and examination in which a particular illness or condition should have been diagnosed in the exercise of reasonable care, the statute of limitations commences to run when the course of treatment and examination terminates presupposes that a continuous course of improper examination or treatment which is substantially uninterrupted is proved as a matter of fact. When the malpractice complained of constitutes a single isolated act, however, the statute of limitations commences to run from the date of the injury. Farley v. Goode, 219 Va. 969, 252 S.E.2d 594 (1979).

Wrongful conception. — Even though a legal wrong may have occurred in 1989 when the defendants performed the negligent sterilization procedure on plaintiff, no injury under the Locke v. Johns-Manville Corp, 221 Va. 951, 275 S.E. 2d 900 (1981) accrual rule occurred at that time because plaintiff had suffered no "positive, physical or mental hurt" related to her alleged cause of action, wrongful conception. Nunnally v. Artis, 254 Va. 247, 492 S.E.2d 126 (1997).

An obstetrician's negligent failure to properly execute a laparoscopic tubal cauterization on a patient commences the two-year statute of limitations under § 8.01-243. This statute does not begin anew when the patient later learns that she is pregnant. Irvin v. Burton, 635 F. Supp. 366 (W.D. Va. 1986).

Claim of patient who alleged that her doctor's failure to remove intrauterine device caused her to become infertile was barred. — by the two-year statute of limitations, since the statute of limitations began to run from the moment a plaintiff suffered an injury, as she was injured when the intrauterine device was allowed to remain in her body, and her malpractice claim accrued when her relationship with her doctor ended in 1979, while her malpractice suit was not commenced until Feb. 1984. Granahan v. Pearson, 782 F.2d 30 (4th Cir. 1985).

Two-year period of limitations barred plaintiff's claims that he was injured from each exposure to paint products prior to two years before filing his suit, but plaintiff's claims of injuries, that occcured within two years of the suit, for which he went to the emergency room, were not barred. Williams v. E.I. DuPont de Nemours & Co., 11 F.3d 464 (4th Cir. 1993).

Limitations plea not sustained. — Where there was nothing in the record which would place the date of plaintiff's injury more than two years prior to the filing of the motion for judgment in this case, defendant wholly failed to meet his burden of proof to sustain his statute of limitations plea. St. George v. Pariser, 253 Va. 329, 484 S.E.2d 888 (1997).

II. DECISIONS UNDER PRIOR LAW.

A. General Consideration.

Editor's note. — The cases cited below were decided under corresponding provisions of

former law. The terms "the statute" and "the statute of limitations," as used below, refer to former provisions.

A right of action cannot accrue until there is a cause of action. Sides v. Richard Mach. Works, Inc., 406 F.2d 445 (4th Cir. 1969), commented on in 4 U. Rich. L. Rev. 148 (1969); Caudill v. Wise Rambler, Inc., 210 Va. 11, 168 S.E.2d 257 (1969).

Essential elements of a good cause of action, whether based on an alleged breach of contract or on a tortious act, are a legal obligation of a defendant to the plaintiff, a violation or breach of that right or duty, and a consequential injury or damage to the plaintiff. In the absence of injury or damage to a plaintiff or his property, he has no cause of action and no right of action can accrue to him. Caudill v. Wise Rambler, Inc., 210 Va. 11, 168 S.E.2d 257 (1969).

There may be several rights of action and one cause of action and rights may accrue at different times from the same cause. Caudill v. Wise Rambler, Inc., 210 Va. 11, 168 S.E.2d 257 (1969).

Action accrues at time of wrongful act. — In the absence of special circumstances that are common to various types of cases, particularly disability of the plaintiff or fraudulent concealment by the defendant, the cause of action accrues and the statute commences to run at the time of the wrongful act. Hawks v. DeHart, 206 Va. 810, 146 S.E.2d 187 (1966).

Determining time of accrual. — The statute of limitations begins to run when the right of action accrues. The determination of the precise time at which the cause of action is to be deemed to have accrued not infrequently presents a question of nice discrimination between the event creating, or per se giving rise to, the cause of action and the event which merely recognizes and ascertains the existence of a cause of action previously existing. Brunswick Land Corp. v. Perkinson, 153 Va. 603, 151 S.E. 138 (1930).

Statute begins to run when cause of action accrues. — As a general rule, the statute of limitations commences to run against a cause of action at the time of its accrual. Cookus v. Peyton, 42 Va. (1 Gratt.) 431 (1845); Bowles v. Elmore, 48 Va. (7 Gratt.) 385 (1851); Andrews v. Roanoke Bldg. Ass'n & Inv. Co., 98 Va. 445, 36 S.E. 531 (1900); McCormick v. Romans, 214 Va. 144, 198 S.E.2d 651 (1973).

When this section applies, it begins to run from the date of injury. Tyler v. R.R. St. & Co., 322 F. Supp. 541 (E.D. Va. 1971), commented on in 6 U. Rich. L. Rev. 167 (1971).

Not from when damage ascertained. — The limitation begins to run from the moment the cause of action accrues and not from the time it is ascertained that damage has been sustained. Hawks v. DeHart, 206 Va. 810, 146 S.E.2d 187 (1966); Burton v. Terrell, 368 F. Supp. 553 (W.D. Va. 1973).

The limitation statute is triggered when the harm is done and not when the plaintiff discovers the injury. Smithfield Packing Co. v. Dunham-Bush, Inc., 416 F. Supp. 1156 (E.D. Va. 1976).

It is the occurrence of the offense which marks the beginning of the running of the statute and the date of consequential injuries is immaterial. Sitwell v. Burnette, 349 F. Supp. 83 (W.D. Va. 1972).

Difficulty in ascertainment does not change rule. — The limitation begins to run from the moment the cause of action accrues and not from the time it is ascertained that damage has been sustained. The difficulty in ascertaining the fact that a cause of action exists does not change the general rule. Richmond Redevelopment & Hous. Auth. v. Laburnum Constr. Corp., 195 Va. 827, 80 S.E.2d 574 (1954).

The applicable period of limitation begins to run from the moment the cause of action arises rather than from the time of discovery of injury or damage, and difficulty in ascertaining the existence of a cause of action is irrelevant. Comptroller ex rel. VMI v. King, 217 Va. 751, 232 S.E.2d 895 (1977).

Despite later occurrence of substantial damages. — Where an injury, though slight, is sustained in consequence of the wrongful or negligent act of another and the law affords a remedy therefor the statute of limitations attaches at once. It is not material that all the damages resulting from the act should have been sustained at that time and the running of the statute is not postponed by the fact that the actual or substantial damages do not occur until a later date. Caudill v. Wise Rambler, Inc., 210 Va. 11, 168 S.E.2d 257 (1969).

Where the damage arises from a cause not then immediately effective, the cause of action does not arise until the injury can be shown. The reason and justice of this is perfectly apparent, for a plaintiff who merely feared ultimate damage under such circumstances would invite defeat if he only relied upon his fears and was unable to prove any actual damage. So the courts have formulated the general rule thus: Whenever any injury, however slight it may be, is complete at the time the act or omission is completed, the cause of action then accrues; but, whenever the act or omission is not legally injurious, there is no cause of action until such injurious consequences occur, and it accrues at the time of such consequential injury. Sides v. Richard Mach. Works, Inc., 406 F.2d 445 (4th Cir. 1969), commented on in 4 U. Rich. L. Rev. 148 (1969).

Necessity for demand. — The principle that a cause of action does not accrue until demand has been made is subject to the well-recognized exception that where the only act necessary to perfect the plaintiff's cause of action is one to be performed by the plaintiff and he is under no restraint or disability, he cannot indefinitely suspend the statute of limitations by delaying the performance of that act. This is based upon the principle that it is not the policy of the law to permit a party against whom the statute runs to defeat its operation by neglecting to do an act which devolves upon him in order to perfect his remedy against another. C & O Ry. v. Willis, 200 Va. 299, 105 S.E.2d 833 (1958).

Contribution. — The right to contribution becomes complete and enforceable upon the payment and discharge of the common obligation. Thus, a cause of action for contribution arises at that time. Van Winckel v. Carter, 198 Va. 550, 95 S.E.2d 148 (1956).

Demand and refusal not required as prerequisite to breach of covenant. — Where defendants' remote predecessors in title granted to a railway land for a right of way, covenanting to fence the remainder of their land to keep in cattle and agreeing that they and those claiming under them would not hold the railway responsible if their cattle wandered on the track and were killed, the covenants were broken by failure to erect the fences within a reasonable time after the railroad began to operate along the right of way, and under the facts of the case it was not a prerequisite to breach, that there be proved a demand by the covenantee and refusal by covenantor. C & O Ry. v. Willis, 200 Va. 299, 105 S.E.2d 833 (1958).

Demand payable at death of debtor. — Where a demand is payable at the death of the debtor, the statute only begins to run at his death. Duncan v. Duncan, 117 Va. 487, 85 S.E. 485 (1915). See also, Duncan v. Wright, 38 Va. (11 Leigh) 542 (1841).

Claim of child to compensation for services. — If a child had a valid claim to compensation for her services to her mother, it accrued during the lifetime of the mother, and the statute of limitations then began to run. Harshberger v. Alger, 72 Va. (31 Gratt.) 52 (1878).

Legacy limited on future event. — Where a legacy is limited upon a future event, a cause of action cannot accrue, nor the statute of limitations begins to run, nor laches be imputed, until that event occurs. Effinger v. Hall, 81 Va. 94 (1885).

Recovery of distributive shares upon discovery of will. — Twenty years after distribution of a supposed intestate's estate, his will was discovered. The statute of limitations to recover from a distributee, who was not a legatee, the amount paid to him did not begin to run until the discovery of the will. Craufurd v. Smith, 93 Va. 623, 23 S.E. 235, 25 S.E. 657 (1896).

Action between trustee and cestui que trust. — The statute of limitations does not begin to run in favor of the trustee against a claim of the cestui pertaining to the trust until the termination of the trust. Lomax v. Pendleton, 7 Va. (3 Call) 538 (1790); Redwood v. Riddick, 18 Va. (4 Munf.) 222 (1814).

Running of statute against remainderman. — The statute of limitations does not commence to run against a remainderman in favor of the purchaser of the life estate until the death of the life tenant. Ball v. Johnson, 49 Va. (8 Gratt.) 281 (1851); Hope v. Norfolk & W. Ry., 79 Va. 283 (1884); Effinger v. Hall, 81 Va. 94 (1885); Davis v. Tebbs, 81 Va. 600 (1886); Hannon v. Hounihan, 85 Va. 429, 12 S.E. 157 (1888); Beattie v. Wilkinson, 36 F. 646 (W.D. Va. 1888).

A life tenant of personal property sold her life interest and died. The purchaser continuing to hold the property did not hold under, but adversely to the remainderman, and the statute commenced to run on the death of the life tenant. Layne v. Norris, 57 Va. (16 Gratt.) 236 (1861).

Assessment on unpaid stock by court. — Where the officers of a corporation which has assigned all its property, including the unpaid portion of its capital stock, neglect to levy an assessment on the unpaid stock, and the levy is made by the court in a proceeding instituted by the trustee, limitation begins to run from the date of the assessment by the court. Vanderwerken v. Glenn, 85 Va. 9, 6 S.E. 806 (1888). See also, Lewis' Adm'r v. Glenn, 84 Va. 947, 6 S.E. 866 (1888).

Enforcement of stockholders' double liability. — The statute of limitations did not begin to run against action to enforce bank stockholders' double liability until the date on which the court ascertained the extent of the liability and ordered the receiver to enforce it. Hospelhorn v. Corbin, 179 Va. 348, 19 S.E.2d 72 (1942).

Assessment against stockholder. — As between a company and its stockholders, and as between the company's creditors and its stockholders, the statute of limitations begins to run from the time the assessments become due and payable pursuant to the company's call. Gold v. Paynter, 101 Va. 714, 44 S.E. 920 (1903).

Loan of stock to be returned on demand. — A testator had borrowed five shares of stock, to be transferred back to the lender whenever he demanded it. The testator in his will gave the stock to a legatee. His executrix qualified on February 12, 1917, and delivered the stock to the legatee November 11, 1917. More than a year after the executrix qualified, complainant, the lender, demanded the stock from her. Upon her refusal on June 21, 1922, complainant instituted suit for the recovery of the stock. It was held that the right of action did not accrue on the date of the qualification of the executrix, but accrued only upon a demand and a refusal, or a conversion of the property by someone holding the stock under the original bailee, and therefore the suit was not barred by this section. Stevenson v. Jones, 142 Va. 391, 128 S.E. 568 (1925).

Effect of power of attorney to confess judgment. — The fact that annexed to an obligation to pay a certain sum upon a certain date was a power of attorney, authorizing a designated attorney to confess judgment at any time after the date for the amount of the obligation, did not accelerate the running of the statute of limitations, which did not begin to run until the date of maturity. Although the defendants or their agent might confess judgment "at any time" prior to that date, the creditor could not compel them to do so. Walker v. Temple, 130 Va. 567, 107 S.E. 720 (1921).

Action by carrier for freight charges. — A carrier's cause of action for freight charges against the consignee of goods arises when the carrier delivers the goods to the consignee. W.L. Becker & Co. v. Norfolk & W. Ry., 125 Va. 558, 100 S.E. 478 (1919).

Shipowners' claims for demurrage. — Where bills of lading upon which shipowners' claims for demurrage were predicated, were issued in December, 1940, and January, 1941, but the shipments did not arrive in the United States until April, 1941, and under the terms of the bills of lading it would be impossible to determine the amount due thereon until the vessel arrived in the United States, the right to bring any action thereon first accrued and the five-year statute of limitations began to run when the vessel arrived in April, 1941. Brown & Williamson Tobacco Corp. v. The S.S. Anghyra, 157 F. Supp. 737 (E.D. Va. 1957), rev'd on other grounds, 277 F.2d 9 (4th Cir.), cert. denied, 364 U.S. 879, 81 S. Ct. 168, 5 L. Ed. 2d 102 (1960).

In an action for deceit in the sale of a chattel, it was held that the cause of action accrued at the time of the deceit practiced, and the limitation began to run immediately. Rice v. White, 31 Va. (4 Leigh) 474 (1833).

In an action by a de jure officer to recover emoluments received by a de facto officer during his occupancy of a public office, the statute begins to run in favor of a person who occupied the office under bona fide claim of right from the judgment of the court annulling his pretensions to the office. Brunswick Land Corp. v. Perkinson, 153 Va. 603, 151 S.E. 138 (1930).

B. Torts.

1. In General.

Action accrues when tort committed. — The limitation begins to run from the moment that the right of action occurs; and such right occurs when the tort is committed and a cause of action exists. Sitwell v. Burnette, 349 F. Supp. 83 (W.D. Va. 1972).

Separate causes of action from single wrongful act. — From a single wrongful act of the defendant two separate causes of action may arise: one for property damage and the other for personal injuries. Caudill v. Wise Rambler, Inc., 210 Va. 11, 168 S.E.2d 257 (1969).

A cause of action in property damage actions vis-a-vis personal injury accrues at a different time even though the actions have their genesis in a common product and share the same purchase date. Smithfield Packing Co. v. Dunham-Bush, Inc., 416 F. Supp. 1156 (E.D. Va. 1976).

Accrual of action for property damage and personal injuries from purchase of automobile. — At the time the plaintiff purchased the automobile, when the alleged breach of the implied warranty of fitness occurred, she had a cause of action against the defendants for property damage and a potential cause of action for personal injuries. Her right to recover for property damage accrued at the time of the alleged breach of warranty, that is, when she purchased the automobile. Her right to recover damages for personal injuries accrued at the time she was injured. Caudill v. Wise Rambler, Inc., 210 Va. 11, 168 S.E.2d 257 (1969).

Warranty that can be implied from sale of appliance was breached the day of the sale so as to set statute of limitations running. Insurance Co. of N. Am. v. GE Co., 376 F. Supp. 638 (W.D. Va. 1974).

But action accrues on date of injury in negligence action. — In simple tort actions based solely on negligence theories the cause of action accrues upon the injury and not when the item was purchased. Campbell v. Colt Indus., Inc., 349 F. Supp. 166 (W.D. Va. 1972).

Action for contribution. — Where a transit company, sued along with other joint tort-feasors by a passenger injured on one of its buses, made a settlement with the passenger, to which the other joint tort-feasors refused to contribute, the statute of limitations did not begin to run against an action by the transit company, on behalf of the insurance carriers that indemnified it for such settlement, against the other joint tort-feasors for contribution, until payment to the injured passenger was made by the indemnitors through the transit company. McKay v. Citizens Rapid Transit Co., 190 Va. 851, 59 S.E.2d 121 (1950).

Accrual of action for architectural deficiencies. — In causes of action for tortious breach of implied warranty that architectural drawings and specifications were properly prepared, and for tortious breach of the architects' duty to exercise their reasonable skills, ability and judgment in the preparation of such plans, the cause of action for direct damages from both accrued at the time the defective work was performed, not at the time the damages resulting from the breaches were discovered. Federal Reserve Bank v. Wright, 392 F. Supp. 1126 (E.D. Va. 1975).

A cause of action against architects for allegedly defective design was barred by the statute of limitations which began to run not later than the date of final approval of the working drawings and specifications. However, this ruling was not dispositive where there was evidence that the damage to the building was caused by negligent failure of the architects to perform their duties of supervision during construction. Comptroller ex rel. VMI v. King, 217 Va. 751, 232 S.E.2d 895 (1977).

Action for taking water from stream. — Where a plaintiff was injured for the first time by the increased quantity of water taken from a stream by the defendant, his right of action accrued from that date, although the defendant had long before erected a tank and pumping station on its own land and taken smaller quantities of water from the stream. Norfolk & W. Ry. v. Allen, 118 Va. 428, 87 S.E. 558 (1915).

A **cause of action for the pollution of a stream** by the discharge of sewage therein accrues when the discharge is in sufficient quantities to pollute the stream and create a nuisance. McKinney v. Trustees, 117 Va. 763, 86 S.E. 115 (1915). See also, Virginia Hot Springs Co. v. McCray, 106 Va. 461, 56 S.E. 216 (1907).

Dam flooding land. — Where the injury complained of arose from the flooding of complainant's lands by reason of defendant's dam — a permanent structure — the cause of action arose at the time of the first commencement of the injury following the original erection of the dam. Norfolk & W. Ry. v. Hayden, 121 Va. 118, 93 S.E. 77 (1917).

In an action against bank directors for misconduct and neglect of duties, where fraud is not alleged or proved, and no concealment on the part of the directors is shown, the statute of limitations begins to run from the time the alleged wrongs were committed. Winston v. Gordon, 115 Va. 899, 80 S.E. 756 (1914).

Father's action for seduction of daughter. — Where the daughter lived away from her father's house at the time of the seduction, but returned and was confined there and nursed, the statute of limitations will only begin to run against the father's action for the seduction from the time of the daughter's return. Clem v. Holmes, 74 Va. (33 Gratt.) 722 (1880). See Fry v. Leslie, 87 Va. 269, 12 S.E. 671 (1891).

2. Personal Injury.

Factors making claim for personal injuries actionable. — For a claim for personal injuries to become actionable these factors are indispensable: (1) a legal obligation of the defendant to the claimant; (2) a commission or omission by the defendant breaching that duty; (3) negligence of the defendant occasioning the breach; and (4) harm to the claimant as a proximate consequence of the breach. Only from the happening of all of these ingredients does a cause of action evolve. Until all of them have become executed actualities, no right of action for the harm is constituted. Sides v. Richard Mach. Works, Inc., 406 F.2d 445 (4th Cir. 1969), commented on in 4 U. Rich. L. Rev. 148 (1969); Barnes v. Sears, Roebuck & Co., 406 F.2d 859 (4th Cir. 1969).

Action accrues when plaintiff injured. — A plaintiff's right of action for damages for personal injuries does not accrue until he is hurt. Caudill v. Wise Rambler, Inc., 210 Va. 11, 168 S.E.2d 257 (1969).

Plaintiff's action against defendant accrued when he was injured. Atkins v. Schmutz Mfg. Co., 435 F.2d 527 (4th Cir. 1970), cert. denied, 402 U.S. 932, 91 S. Ct. 1526, 28 L. Ed. 2d 867 (1971).

Right of action accrued not at time of seller's negligence but at time of buyer's injury. Barnes v. Sears, Roebuck & Co., 406 F.2d 859 (4th Cir. 1969).

Statute begins running at time of wrong, not when discovered. — The time for the commencement of the running of personal injury statutes of limitation is that point in time when the wrong is done, and not when the plaintiff discovers the damage. Greeson v. Sherman, 265 F. Supp. 340 (W.D. Va. 1967).

In personal injury actions the limitation on the right to sue begins to run when the wrong is done and not when the plaintiff discovers that he has been damaged. Hawks v. DeHart, 206 Va. 810, 146 S.E.2d 187 (1966); Bolen v. Bolen, 409 F. Supp. 1374 (W.D. Va. 1976).

Nor at time of purchase. — A plaintiff's action for personal injuries, alleged to have been caused by the negligence of the seller in the inspection and sale of a bicycle, accrued at the time of the plaintiff's alleged injuries and not at the time he purchased the bicycle. Barnes v. Sears, Roebuck & Co., 406 F.2d 859 (4th Cir. 1969).

Nor at time of breach of warranty. — Plaintiffs' rights of action for personal injuries accrued at the time they were hurt and not at the time of the alleged breach of warranty.

Caudill v. Wise Rambler, Inc., 210 Va. 11, 168 S.E.2d 257 (1969); Campbell v. Colt Indus., Inc., 349 F. Supp. 166 (W.D. Va. 1972).

The statute of limitations begins to run for breach of warranty actions at the time of injury. Campbell v. Colt Indus., Inc., 349 F. Supp. 166 (W.D. Va. 1972).

Medical malpractice cases. — Virginia is committed to the rule that in personal injury actions the limitation on the right to sue begins to run when the wrong is done and not when the plaintiff discovers that he has been damaged, even in malpractice cases. Morgan v. Schlanger, 374 F.2d 235 (4th Cir. 1967).

The rule in medical malpractice cases is that the right to bring an action for personal injury begins to run when the wrong is done and not when the plaintiff discovers that he has been damaged. Cradle v. Superintendent, Correctional Field Unit #7, 374 F. Supp. 435 (W.D. Va. 1973).

Foreign body left in patient at time of surgery. — Where a foreign body is left in a patient at the time of surgery, the accrual of the cause of action is at the closing of the incision, not at the discovery of the fact some time afterward. Hawks v. DeHart, 206 Va. 810, 146 S.E.2d 187 (1966).

Republication of defamatory statement. — The author of a defamation is liable for its republication by a third party, provided such republication is the natural and probable consequence of his act, or if he has presumptively or actually authorized its republication. Such republication constitutes a new cause of action against the original author, and an action brought within one year from the date of the republication is timely, although more than a year has passed since the first publication. Weaver v. Beneficial Fin. Co., 199 Va. 196, 98 S.E.2d 687 (1957).

3. Property Damage.

Action accrues on purchase date. — In property damage actions, regardless of whether they sound in contract or tort, the accrual time begins on the purchase date. Smithfield Packing Co. v. Dunham-Bush, Inc., 416 F. Supp. 1156 (E.D. Va. 1976).

Statute begins running when action accrues. — In property damage actions the limitation begins to run when cause of action accrues rather than when damage has been sustained. Smithfield Packing Co. v. Dunham-Bush, Inc., 416 F. Supp. 1156 (E.D. Va. 1976).

Accrual of action based on breach of warranty. — The purchaser's cause of action against the dealer and manufacturer for property damage, based on theories of breach of warranty, express or implied, arises at the time of purchase of the product. Eden Corp. v. Utica Mut. Ins. Co., 350 F. Supp. 637 (W.D. Va. 1972).

C. Contracts.

Statute runs from date payment due. — The statute of limitations on a contract begins to run from the time payment is due. Of necessity, the due date depends upon the terms, either expressed or implied, of the contract in issue. Clifton D. Mayhew, Inc. v. Blake Constr. Co., 482 F.2d 1260 (4th Cir. 1973).

Account for goods sold. — The statute of limitations begins to run from the time the account is due. The due date depends upon the terms, express or implied, upon which the articles are sold. Columbia Heights Section 3, Inc. v. Griffith-Consumers Co., 205 Va. 43, 135 S.E.2d 116 (1964).

Contracts in writing not under seal. — As to actions based upon contracts in writing not under seal, under familiar principles of law, the statute begins to run from the time of a violation or breach of a legal duty or obligation owed a plaintiff by a defendant. McCloskey & Co. v. Wright, 363 F. Supp. 223 (E.D. Va. 1973).

On the happening of an anticipatory breach the promisee has the right to await the time for performance and bring suit when that time has arrived, and the statute of limitations on the promisee's right of action does not begin to run until the time for performance fixed by the terms of the contract, unless there has been a repudiation of the entire contract, when the statute would start to run from the repudiation. Simpson v. Scott, 189 Va. 392, 53 S.E.2d 21 (1949).

Where there is an undertaking which requires a continuation of services, the statute of limitations does not begin to run until the termination of the undertaking. McCormick v. Romans, 214 Va. 144, 198 S.E.2d 651 (1973).

Where there is a continuing agreement between attorney and client, the statute of limitations does not begin to run until the termination of the agreement. McCormick v. Romans, 214 Va. 144, 198 S.E.2d 651 (1973).

Contract to execute purchase-money notes. — Where there is a sealed agreement between the plaintiff and defendant that the latter shall execute notes at a specified time, in payment for land, the statute begins to run against the agreement at that time. Davis v. McMullen, 86 Va. 256, 9 S.E. 1095 (1889).

Default in one of several notes. — If a contract provides that on default in the payment of one of several notes the remaining unpaid notes shall become due, the stipulation has the effect of fixing a contingency upon the happening of which the debt is to mature at a time earlier than the dates given in the notes for their maturity, and the statute of limitations begins to run against the entire debt upon such default. Country Club Portsmouth, Inc. v. Wilkins, 166 Va. 325, 186 S.E. 23 (1936).

Instrument guaranteeing payment of note. — Where a loan was made by administrators, at which time a guarantor executed an instrument guaranteeing payment of the note but deferring liability under the guaranty until its determination by advertising and selling the property under and by virtue of the terms of the deed of trust which secured the loan, there was no merit in a contention that the statute of limitations began to run upon the guaranty when the note became due and was not paid; for the administrators had a reasonable time after the maturity of the note, within which to demand a foreclosure, and that reasonable time was measured by the time during which an action could have been maintained on the primary obligation. Thus the statute did not begin to run on the guaranty until the original note was barred by this section. Whitehurst v. Duffy, 181 Va. 637, 26 S.E.2d 101 (1943).

Action on note redelivered to maker as indemnity. — The statute of limitations did not begin to run against a note that had been redelivered to the maker to hold as indemnity against loss as bail for the payee until the liability of the maker as bail ceased. Bowles v. Elmore, 48 Va. (7 Gratt.) 385 (1851).

Contract to give a lien on a contingent estate. — Limitations do not begin to run against an action for the breach of an agreement by contingent beneficiaries to have a claim made a lien on the corpus of the estate, until the death of the life tenant. Brown v. Ford, 120 Va. 233, 91 S.E. 145 (1895).

Accrual of cause of action on employment contract. — If a party elects to treat an employment contract as in force until actual termination of the employment relationship occurs in hopes of negotiating a reconciliation without judicial intervention, and such attempts at settlement fail, the cause of action accrues at the time the employment relationship ceases. Taliaferro v. Willett, 411 F. Supp. 595 (E.D. Va. 1976).

Claim for services rendered under oral contract to devise land. — The cause of action for the reasonable value of services rendered a decedent pursuant to an oral contract to devise land, which contract is unenforceable under the statute of frauds, accrues upon the death of the decedent without making the devise agreed on. Ricks v. Sumler, 179 Va. 571, 19 S.E.2d 889 (1942).

Contract for wages and additional compensation by devise. — The cause of action for breach of a contract under which plaintiff worked for defendant's decedent for nominal wages with the promise of additional compensation by devise did not accrue until the death of decedent. Although the employment has been terminated by decedent, this was not an anticipatory breach of the entire contract. Simpson v. Scott, 189 Va. 392, 53 S.E.2d 21 (1949).

Service in consideration for all or part of estate. — Where a party renders valuable service to another in consideration for such other's promise to leave him all or part of his estate the promisee is not entitled to receive compensation until the death of the promisor. Payment is not due until that time; hence, the statute of limitations does not begin to run until the death of the promisor. Cochran v. Bise, 197 Va. 483, 90 S.E.2d 178 (1955).

Subscription to stock. — The statute of limitations begins to run in favor of stockholders for amounts due upon unpaid stock subscriptions only from the time such assessments are made. Morrow v. Vaughan-Bassett Furn. Co., 173 Va. 417, 4 S.E.2d 399 (1939).

Agreement by one purporting to act as president of a nonexistent corporation to erect a gasoline station on property which he did not own and lease it for 10 years beginning on a certain date was breached when he failed to do so by such date. The statute of limitations began to run from such time. Galumbeck v. Suburban Park Stores Corp., 214 F.2d 660 (4th Cir. 1954).

§ 8.01-231. Commonwealth not within statute of limitations.

— No statute of limitations which shall not in express terms apply to the Commonwealth shall be deemed a bar to any proceeding by or on behalf of the same. (Code 1950, § 8-35; 1958, c. 221; 1977, c. 617; 1988, c. 544.)

I. Decisions Under Current Law.
II. Decisions Under Prior Law.

I. DECISIONS UNDER CURRENT LAW.

Time does not run against the State. — This section is absolute and unqualified. It makes no distinction between so-called "pure" statutes of limitation (those which time-restrict the availability of a remedy) and "special" limitations (those prescribed by statute as an element of a newly created right). Hence, whether the time limitation prescribed in § 15.1-552 is "special" and "jurisdictional" or merely procedural, it does not operate as a bar to any proceeding by or on behalf of the Commonwealth. Commonwealth ex rel. Pross v. Board of

Supvrs., 225 Va. 492, 303 S.E.2d 887 (1983).

Transit authority was instrumentality of Commonwealth and was exempt from statute of limitations. — District court incorrectly determined that the transit authority's action brought pursuant to a written contract against an architectural and engineering firm was barred by Virginia's statute of limitations; as an agency and instrumentality of the Commonwealth of Virginia, transit authority is exempt from application of the statute of limitations. Delon Hampton & Assocs. v. Washington Metro. Area Transit Auth., 943 F.2d 355 (4th Cir. 1991).

Habitual offender proceedings. — This section provides that no statute of limitation which shall not in express terms apply to the Commonwealth shall be deemed a bar to any proceeding by or on behalf of the same. Since the Department of Motor Vehicles is not incorporated for charitable or educational purposes, this section is applicable. The Habitual Offender Act contains no such explicit limitation provision and former § 46.1-387.3 (now § 46.2-352) contemplates habitual offender proceedings taking place "more than five years" after the conviction which triggers the proceeding. Therefore, the proceeding is not time-barred by any statute of limitation. Bouldin v. Commonwealth, 4 Va. App. 166, 355 S.E.2d 352 (1987).

Applied in LaVay Corp. v. Dominion Fed. Sav. & Loan Ass'n, 830 F.2d 522 (4th Cir. 1987).

II. DECISIONS UNDER PRIOR LAW.

Editor's note. — The cases cited below were decided under corresponding provisions of former law. The term "the statute of limitations," as used below, refers to former provisions.

Time does not run against the State. — As against the government the bar of the statute of limitations cannot be set up. Time does not run against the State, nor bar the rights of the public. Norfolk & W. Ry. v. Board of Supvrs., 110 Va. 95, 65 S.E. 531 (1909); Board of Supvrs. v. Norfolk & W. Ry., 119 Va. 763, 91 S.E. 124 (1916). See also, Levasser v. Washburn, 52 Va. (11 Gratt.) 572 (1854); Hurst v. Dulany, 84 Va. 701, 5 S.E. 802 (1888); Reusen v. Lawson, 91 Va. 226, 21 S.E. 347 (1895).

Unless statute expressly so provides. — The statute of limitations does not run against the State unless expressly mentioned. Virginia Hot Springs Co. v. Lowman, 126 Va. 424, 101 S.E. 326 (1919).

Legislative intent to exempt must be clear. — In light of the policy that surrounds statutes of limitation, the bar of such statutes should not be lifted unless the legislature makes unmistakably clear that such is to occur in a given case. Where there exists any doubt, it should be resolved in favor of the operation of the statute of limitations. Burns v. Board of Supvrs., 227 Va. 354, 315 S.E.2d 856 (1984).

Section merely exempts State. — The statute of limitations does not affect the validity of a claim but merely sets up a defense to it. The governmental exception does not preserve a right of action, but merely exempts the sovereign from the general defense established. McCloskey & Co. v. Wright, 363 F. Supp. 223 (E.D. Va. 1973).

Immunity of governmental bodies from the statutes of limitation is strictly limited. Burns v. Board of Supvrs., 227 Va. 354, 315 S.E.2d 856 (1984).

Agencies included under section if not specifically excluded. — Because the legislature specifically excluded two categories of state agencies from the saving grace of this section, it appears that it intended to include other state agencies. Burns v. Board of Supvrs., 227 Va. 354, 315 S.E.2d 856 (1984).

Entity created by county is not exempt from statute. — A county is not one and the same as the sovereign with regard to the applicability of statutes of limitation. If a county is not entitled to ignore a statute of limitations, an entity created by that county can have no greater authority to do so. Burns v. Board of Supvrs., 227 Va. 354, 315 S.E.2d 856 (1984).

County board of supervisors, in its capacity as the governing body of a sanitary district, is not entitled to the benefit of this section. Burns v. Board of Supvrs., 227 Va. 354, 315 S.E.2d 856 (1984).

School boards are subject to statutes of limitation, since they are "incorporated" within the meaning of this section. County School Bd. v. Whitlow, 223 Va. 157, 286 S.E.2d 230 (1982).

No title by adverse possession can be acquired in a public street. Bellenot v. City of Richmond, 108 Va. 314, 61 S.E. 785 (1908). See note to § 8.01-236.

The Richmond Redevelopment and Housing Authority, though a political subdivision of the State, is not one acting for purely governmental purposes, and hence is subject to the bar of the statute of limitations. Richmond Redevelopment & Hous. Auth. v. Laburnum Constr. Corp., 195 Va. 827, 80 S.E.2d 574 (1954).

§ 8.01-232. Effect of promises not to plead statute. — A. Whenever the failure to enforce a promise, written or unwritten, not to plead the statute of limitations would operate as a fraud on the promisee, the promisor shall be estopped to plead the statute. In all other cases, an unwritten promise not to plead the statute shall be void, and a written promise not to plead such statute shall have the effect of a promise to pay the debt or discharge the liability. No provision of this subsection shall operate contrary to subsections B and C of this section.

B. No acknowledgment or promise by any personal representative of a decedent shall charge the estate of the decedent, revive a cause of action otherwise barred, or relieve the personal representative of his duty to defend under § 26-5 in any case in which but for such acknowledgment or promise, the decedent's estate could have been protected under a statute of limitations.

C. No acknowledgment or promise by one of two or more joint contractors shall charge any of such contractors in any case in which but for such acknowledgment another contractor would have been protected under a statute of limitations. (Code 1950, §§ 8-27, 8-28; 1977, c. 617.)

REVISERS' NOTE

Section 8.01-232 combines former §§ 8-27 and 8-28.

Subsection A adds a proviso to former § 8-27 to codify case law and make explicit the interrelationship between former §§ 8-27 and 8-28. See Soble v. Herman, 175 Va. 489, 9 S.E.2d 459 (1940); Gwinn v. Farrier, 159 Va. 183, 165 S.E. 647 (1932). The effect of this subsection is to allow prospective defendants [with the exception of personal representatives and joint contractors who are provided for in subsections B and C] to bind themselves by written promise not to plead the statute of limitations.

Subsection B incorporates the substance of former § 8-28 with regard to personal representatives' incapacity to charge a decedent's estate where the estate could have been protected by pleading the statute of limitations. The language which prohibits the revival of a cause of action otherwise barred is a codification of Brown v. Rice, 76 Va. 629 (1883). The reference to the personal representative's duty to defend relates this subsection to § 26-5 which imposes personal liability for damage resulting from failure of a fiduciary to plead the applicable statute of limitations.

Subsection C represents the remaining portion of former § 8-28 which is incorporated without substantial change.

Cross references. — As to liability of fiduciaries for paying debts barred by the statute of limitations, see § 26-5. As to power of personal representative to renew debts, see § 64.1-143.

I. DECISIONS UNDER PRIOR LAW.

Editor's note. — The cases cited below were decided under corresponding provisions of former law. The terms "the statute of limitations" and "this section," as used below, refer to former provisions.

The word "promise" means the obligation of the person liable. Soble v. Herman, 175 Va. 489, 9 S.E.2d 459 (1940).

And word "promisor" refers to one legally bound to discharge obligation. — The word "promisor" refers to the person making the promise, or to some other person who has become legally bound to discharge the obligation. It does not refer to some third person who ultimately may be benefited by the enforcement of the statute of limitations. Soble v. Herman, 175 Va. 489, 9 S.E.2d 459 (1940).

"Fraud" must relate to present or pre-existing fact. — "Fraud," as used in the phrase "would operate as a fraud on the promisee," must relate to a present or a pre-existing fact and cannot be established by allegation or proof of an unfulfilled, naked, oral promise. This construction of the first sentence is in accord with the clear meaning of the last sentence, and renders entire subsection A reasonably clear. Soble v. Herman, 175 Va. 489, 9 S.E.2d 459 (1940). But see Tucker v. Owen, 94 F.2d 49 (4th Cir. 1938), wherein the federal court stated that the scope of subsection A should not be restricted by a narrow interpretation of the word "fraud."

Necessity for writing. — The second sentence in subsection A, in express terms, places the promise not to plead the statute of limitations on the same plane as a promise to pay the debt; that is, such promises must be in writing to be enforceable. Soble v. Herman, 175 Va. 489, 9 S.E.2d 459 (1940).

Meaning of "could have been protected". — The use of the words "could have been protected" does not imply that the limiting clause in this section relates to the time of the promise by the personal representative. The clause should not be construed as if it read "could have been protected at the time the promise was made." It would appear that the

General Assembly merely loosely used "could have been" for "can be" or "could be," or that they viewed the section as speaking at a time subsequent to that at which a promise in question was made, rather than at the time of the enactment of the section. Gwinn v. Farrier, 159 Va. 183, 165 S.E. 647 (1932).

Subsection A not extended to promises by personal representatives or beneficiaries of decedents' estates. — To extend the words "promise" and "promisor" to include administrators, executors, heirs, distributees, devisees and legatees, would tend to cause delay and create confusion in the speedy and orderly administration of estates and, to some extent, would be in conflict with the construction that has been uniformly placed upon the provisions of §§ 11-2 and 26-5 and subsection A. Soble v. Herman, 175 Va. 489, 9 S.E.2d 459 (1940).

Policy of subsection B is that the estate shall be protected against promises made by a personal representative to pay debts of his decedent, because in most instances he has no personal knowledge of the transaction, and in many instances may make mistaken concessions or agreements which he ought not to make or would not make if he were fully informed with reference to the transaction. St. Joseph's Soc'y v. Virginia Trust Co., 175 Va. 503, 9 S.E.2d 304 (1940).

Promise made after the bar of the statute has fallen, or an oral promise upon which the promisee does not rely, would be covered by the second sentence of subsection A, and therefore be ineffective. Tucker v. Owen, 94 F.2d 49 (4th Cir. 1938).

Debt barred by statute of limitations at death of debtor cannot be revived by the promise of the personal representative to pay it. Brown v. Rice, 67 Va. (26 Gratt.) 467 (1875); Brown v. Rice, 76 Va. 629 (1882); Smith v. Pattie, 81 Va. 654 (1886).

Subsection B applies whether promise made before or after debt is barred. — The true construction of subsection B is this: No acknowledgment of, or promise to pay, or part payment on a debt of a decedent made by his personal representative, either before or after the debt is barred, shall operate to take it out of the statute of limitations. Gwinn v. Farrier, 159 Va. 183, 165 S.E. 647 (1932); St. Joseph's Soc'y v. Virginia Trust Co., 175 Va. 503, 9 S.E.2d 304 (1940).

Application of section to renewal of notes. — In a suit for the purpose of ascertaining debts and liabilities of a testator's estate, appellant alleged that the estate was indebted to it, as evidenced by a negotiable note executed by the executor of the estate. The note in issue was a renewal of a note executed by the testator, which had been renewed at intervals of six months by the executor for a period of five years from the time of his qualification, although § 64.1-143 permits such renewals only for a period of two years from the time of qualification. It was held that the debt was barred by this section. St. Joseph's Soc'y v. Virginia Trust Co., 175 Va. 503, 9 S.E.2d 304 (1940).

Promise by copartner cannot revive debt. — One partner cannot as against his copartner revive an old obligation, which is barred by the statute of limitations. Davis v. Poland, 92 Va. 225, 23 S.E. 292 (1895). See also, Woodson v. Wood, 84 Va. 478, 5 S.E. 277 (1888).

§ 8.01-233. When action deemed brought on counterclaim or cross-claim; when statute of limitations tolled; defendant's consent required for dismissal. — A. A defendant who pleads a counterclaim or cross-claim shall be deemed to have brought an action at the time he files such pleading.

B. If the subject matter of the counterclaim or cross-claim arises out of the same transaction or occurrence upon which the plaintiff's claim is based, the statute of limitations with respect to such pleading shall be tolled by the commencement of the plaintiff's action. (Code 1950, § 8-244; 1954, c. 611; 1977, c. 617.)

REVISERS' NOTE

Section 8.01-233 is substantially former § 8-244. Subsection B provides for relation back to the time when a plaintiff's claim is filed of a cross-claim which arises out of the same transaction upon which the plaintiff's claim is based, thereby giving the same treatment to cross-claims as was given to counterclaims under the former statute.

The final sentence of former § 8-244 prohibited the plaintiff from dismissing his action without defendant's consent after a defendant counterclaimed. This provision has been amended and is relocated in § 8.01-380.

§ 8.01-234   CIVIL REMEDIES AND PROCEDURE   § 8.01-235

Cross references. — For rules of court as to counterclaims and cross-claims, see Rules 3:8, 3:9, and 3:10.

I. DECISIONS UNDER CURRENT LAW.

This section would seem to require some physical injury to plaintiff's property before suit may be maintained in absence of privity. Bryant Elec. Co. v. City of Fredericksburg, 762 F.2d 1192 (4th Cir. 1985).

Appeal from improper dismissal of defendant against whom cross-claim filed. — When an order of nonsuit improperly dismisses a party defendant against whom a valid cross-claim has been duly filed, effectively time-barring the cause of action set forth in the cross-claim, such order is a final, appealable judgment as to the cross-claimant. Iliff v. Richards, 221 Va. 644, 272 S.E.2d 645 (1980).

Defendant's counterclaim did not arise out of the same transaction or occurrence where the issues of fact and law in the complaint and counterclaims were not largely the same; proof of defendant's counterclaims required separate evidence than proof of plaintiff's complaint and principles of res judicata would not bar a subsequent suit on the counterclaims because the proof and issues raised by the counterclaim were unrelated to the proof and issues raised by the complaint. Unlimited Screw Prods., Inc. v. Malm, 781 F. Supp. 1121 (E.D. Va. 1991).

Applied in Unlimited Screw Prods., Inc. v. Malm, 781 F. Supp. 1121 (E.D. Va. 1991).

§ 8.01-234. Repeal of limitation not to remove bar of statute. — If, after a right of action or remedy is barred by a statute of limitations, the statute be repealed, the bar of the statute as to such right or remedy shall not be deemed to be removed by such repeal. (Code 1950, § 8-36; 1977, c. 617.)

Cross references. — As to the effect of repeal of statutes generally, see §§ 1-16, 1-17 and notes.

I. Decisions Under Current Law.
II. Decisions Under Prior Law.

I. DECISIONS UNDER CURRENT LAW.

Virginia's policy favoring prospective application of statutes of limitations is codified both in this section and § 8.01-256. This section provides that an action barred by a statute of limitations is not revived by repeal of that limitation provision. Section 8.01-256 provides that the 1977 amendments to the limitation provisions are inapplicable to any cause of action that accrued prior to the effective date of those amendments. Saunders v. H.K. Porter Co., 643 F. Supp. 198 (E.D. Va. 1986), rev'd on other grounds, 843 F.2d 815 (4th Cir.), cert. denied, 488 U.S. 889, 109 S. Ct. 221, 102 L. Ed. 2d 211 (1988).

II. DECISIONS UNDER PRIOR LAW.

Editor's note. — The case cited below was decided under corresponding provisions of former law. The term "this section," as used below, refers to former provisions.

Section prescribes rule different from that of United States Supreme Court. — By this section it was intended to prescribe a rule different from that declared by the Supreme Court of the United States in Campbell v. Holt, 115 U.S. 620, 6 S. Ct. 209, 29 L. Ed. 483 (1885), that a debtor has no vested right in a bar interposed to the collection of his debt, and that the bar may be removed by repeal of the statute as to debts upon which limitations have already run. Kesterson v. Hill, 101 Va. 739, 45 S.E. 288 (1903).

§ 8.01-235. Bar of expiration of limitation period raised only as affirmative defense in responsive pleading. — The objection that an action is not commenced within the limitation period prescribed by law can only be raised as an affirmative defense specifically set forth in a responsive pleading. No statutory limitation period shall have jurisdictional effects and the defense that the statutory limitation period has expired cannot be set up by demurrer. This section shall apply to all limitation periods, without regard to whether or not the statute prescribing such limitation period shall create a new right. (1977, c. 617.)

REVISERS' NOTE

Section 8.01-235 requires that any statute of limitations must be pleaded as an affirmative defense by the party claiming its benefit. As to statutorily created rights unknown to common law, e.g., wrongful death actions, this changes case law which required the party asserting such a right to plead that he had brought the action within the limitation period. To this extent the section therefore repeals Branch v. Branch, 172 Va. 413, 2 S.E.2d 327 (1939).

I. DECISIONS UNDER CURRENT LAW.

This section is merely a procedural statute governing the manner of pleading statutes of limitation. Harper v. City Council, 220 Va. 727, 261 S.E.2d 560 (1980).

Effect upon prior law. — According to its plain terms, this section deals with the manner in which reliance on limitation periods must be asserted in responsive pleadings. It does not abolish the substantive distinction heretofore recognized between a "pure" and "special" statute of limitation. Prior law has been changed only to the extent that a distinction in pleading had been premised on the theory that "special" statutes of limitation were jurisdictional in effect. Harper v. City Council, 220 Va. 727, 261 S.E.2d 560 (1980).

Applied in Commonwealth ex rel. Pross v. Board of Supvrs., 225 Va. 492, 303 S.E.2d 887 (1983).

ARTICLE 2.

Limitations on Recovery of Realty and Enforcement of Certain Liens Relating to Realty.

§ 8.01-236. Limitation of entry on or action for land. — No person shall make an entry on, or bring an action to recover, any land unless within fifteen years next after the time at which the right to make such entry or bring such action shall have first accrued to such person or to some other person through whom he claims; provided that an action for unlawful entry or detainer under § 8.01-124 shall be brought within three years after such entry or detainer. (Code 1950, § 8-5; 1954, c. 604; 1977, c. 617; 1978, c. 471.)

Cross references. — As to who may bring action of ejectment, see § 8.01-132. As to further time allowed persons under disability, see § 8.01-237. As to effect of copy and certificate of unsigned land grant on adverse possession, see § 41.1-7. For limitation of suit, etc., against person in possession of lands by reentry, see § 55-248. As to the abolition of dower and curtesy, effective January 1, 1991, see § 64.1-19.2.

Law Review. — For survey of Virginia law on torts for the year 1972-1973, see 59 Va. L. Rev. 1590 (1973). For survey of Virginia law on property for the year 1974-1975, see 61 Va. L. Rev. 1834 (1975).

I. Decisions Under Current Law.
  A. General Consideration.
  B. Dower.
  C. Requisites for Adverse Possession.
II. Decisions Under Prior Law.
  A. General Consideration.
  B. Requisites for Adverse Possession.
    1. In General.
    2. Possession for Statutory Period.
    3. Actual Possession.
    4. Notorious and Visible.
    5. Exclusive.
    6. Continuous.

7. Hostile and Under Claim of Right.
C. Color of Title.
D. Conflicting Grants — Interlocks.
E. Possession Originally Consistent with Title of True Owner.
  1. In General.
  2. Cotenants.
  3. Mortgagor and Mortgagee.
  4. Vendor and Purchaser.
  5. Entry Under Parol Gift.
  6. Trust Estates.
  7. Life Tenant and Remainderman.
  8. Landlord and Tenant.
  9. Widow in Possession of Mansion.
F. Property Which May Be Held Adversely.
G. Effect of Adverse Possession.
H. Evidence.
I. How Title by Adverse Possession Lost.

I. DECISIONS UNDER CURRENT LAW.

A. General Consideration.

Elements. — To establish title to land by adverse possession it is necessary to show actual, hostile, exclusive, visible and continuous possession for the statutory period of 15 years. McIntosh v. Chincoteague Volunteer Fire Co., 220 Va. 553, 260 S.E.2d 457 (1979).

Adverse possession of child as against parent. — As a general rule, adverse possession cannot arise from possession of a child as against his parent. In order to establish adverse possession in such a case, the owner must have had some "clear, definite, or unequivocal notice" of the child's intention to assert exclusive ownership, and the character of the possession is a jury question. McIntosh v. Chincoteague Volunteer Fire Co., 220 Va. 553, 260 S.E.2d 457 (1979).

B. Dower.

Dower was an interest in land for which a right of entry exists in favor of a widow under Virginia law. Devers v. Chateau Corp., 748 F.2d 902 (4th Cir. 1984), aff'd in part, rev'd in part, 792 F.2d 1278 (4th Cir. 1986).

Section applicable to action to insure dower rights. — The 15-year statute of limitations applied to an action to insure the dower rights of a widow. Devers v. Chateau Corp., 748 F.2d 902 (4th Cir. 1984), aff'd in part, rev'd in part, 792 F.2d 1278 (4th Cir. 1986).

Existence of equitable remedy for exercise of dower did not affect limitation period. — A widow could exercise her dower rights either at law or in equity. The fact that an equitable remedy exists in addition to a legal remedy did not mean that the statute of limitations for entry to land did not apply. Devers v. Chateau Corp., 748 F.2d 902 (4th Cir. 1984), aff'd in part, rev'd in part, 792 F.2d 1278 (4th Cir. 1986).

C. Requisites for Adverse Possession.

Adverse possession requires that the acts relied upon must have been actual, continuous, exclusive, hostile, open and notorious and accompanied by a claim of right for the statutory period. Payne v. Consolidation Coal Co., 607 F. Supp. 378 (D. Va. 1985).

The terms claim of right, claim of title and claim of ownership mean the intention of an adverse possessor to take the land and use it as his own. The terms do not imply any claim of actual title or right. Payne v. Consolidation Coal Co., 607 F. Supp. 378 (D. Va. 1985).

II. DECISIONS UNDER PRIOR LAW.

A. General Consideration.

Editor's note. — The cases cited below were decided under corresponding provisions of former law. The terms "the statute of limitations," "this statute," and "this section," as used below, refer to former provisions.

The ruling purpose and policy of this statute, which must be looked to in determining its true meaning and effect, is to give stability to land titles. McClanahan's Adm'r v. Norfolk & W. Ry., 122 Va. 705, 96 S.E. 453 (1918).

The statute is a personal defense. — As a general rule the plea of the statute of limitations is a personal defense to be made only by the party against whom the demand is asserted, and can only be waived by him if he desires to do so. Clayton v. Henley, 73 Va. (32 Gratt.) 65 (1879); Smith v. Hutchinson, 78 Va. 683 (1883); McCartney v. Tyrer, 94 Va. 198, 26 S.E. 419 (1897).

It is applied in equity. — This section will be applied in equity when a suit is brought for land, and for an account of the rents and profits. Drumright v. Hite, 2 Va. Dec. 465, 26 S.E. 583 (1897). See also, Preston v. Preston, 95 U.S. 200, 24 L. Ed. 494 (1877).

The effect of this section cannot be avoided by

resorting to a chancery suit. McClanahan's Adm'r v. Norfolk & W. Ry., 122 Va. 705, 96 S.E. 453 (1918).

B. Requisites for Adverse Possession.

1. In General.

Adverse possession must be actual, exclusive, hostile, open and notorious, accompanied by a bona fide claim of title against that of all other persons, and it must be continued for the period of the statutory bar. Williams v. Snidow, 31 Va. (4 Leigh) 14 (1832); Creekmur v. Creekmur, 75 Va. 430 (1881); Hollingsworth v. Sherman, 81 Va. 668 (1885); Chapman v. Chapman, 91 Va. 397, 21 S.E. 813 (1895); Drumright v. Hite, 2 Va. Dec. 465, 26 S.E. 583 (1897); Yellow Poplar Lumber Co. v. Thompson, 108 Va. 612, 62 S.E. 358 (1908); Fleming v. Lockhart, 171 Va. 127, 198 S.E. 489 (1938); Walton v. Rosson, 216 Va. 732, 222 S.E.2d 553 (1976).

The contention that the United States had gained such title by adverse possession under this section as to extinguish an easement of access to a highway was untenable, where the position of the government had not been adverse in the sense that it had been open, notorious, hostile, inconsistent with the easement, and maintained with the intention to hold adversely. Nothing else will give good title by adverse possession under the Virginia decisions. United States v. Belle View Apts., 217 F.2d 636 (4th Cir. 1954).

To work a disseisin or ouster of the owner of land, it is not sufficient to set up a mere claim or color of title. The acts relied on must show actual, hostile, exclusive and continuous possession for the period of the statutory bar; acts of such notoriety that the true owner has actual knowledge, or may be presumed to know, of the adverse claim. Leake v. Richardson, 199 Va. 967, 103 S.E.2d 227 (1958).

The acts relied upon to establish ownership by adverse possession must show actual, hostile, exclusive, visible and continuous possession for the statutory period of 15 years. Peck v. Daniel, 212 Va. 265, 184 S.E.2d 7 (1971).

Holding must be such as to give notice that seisin is molested. — To effect a disseisin the holding must be actual and hostile occupation of the land for the statutory period that is calculated to give notice that the seisin is molested. LaDue v. Currell, 201 Va. 200, 110 S.E.2d 217 (1959).

The character of the acts necessary to vest one with a title by adverse possession varies with the nature of the property involved, the conditions surrounding its use, the use to which the property may be adapted. Leake v. Richardson, 199 Va. 967, 103 S.E.2d 227 (1958); Walton v. Rosson, 216 Va. 732, 222 S.E.2d 553 (1976).

Corporeal and incorporeal rights. — In principle, there is no great difference as to the acquisition of rights whether they be corporeal or incorporeal, except as the statute of limitations introduces the difference. The tests as regards adverse possession are equally applicable to the acquisition of prescriptive rights. The possession of the claimant must be adverse under a claim of right, exclusive, continuous, uninterrupted and with a knowledge and acquiescence of the owner of the estate in, over or out of which the right is claimed. Leake v. Richardson, 199 Va. 967, 103 S.E.2d 227 (1958).

Cutting timber does not constitute adverse possession. — Merely cutting and selling timber from the disputed land, at widely separated intervals, does not constitute adverse possession. Craig-Giles Iron Co. v. Wickline, 126 Va. 223, 101 S.E. 225 (1919). See also, Pasley v. English, 46 Va. (5 Gratt.) 141 (1848); Anderson v. Harvey, 51 Va. (10 Gratt.) 386 (1853).

Nor does grazing cattle. — The mere fact that plaintiff's cattle, and those of plaintiff's predecessor in title had from time to time during many years roamed over the disputed marsh land, when it was not covered by water at high tide, did not call for or warrant the giving of an instruction with respect to adverse possession. Whealton v. Doughty, 112 Va. 649, 72 S.E. 112 (1911).

Nor making surveys. — A junior patentee visited the county where the lands in dispute were situated, and employed an agent to enter upon and survey the tract in question and various other tracts claimed by him in that county. The agent employed a surveyor and chain carriers, who went upon the tract and surveyed and remarked it for the junior patentee. It was held that these facts would not have warranted the jury in finding an ouster of the senior patentee and a seisin in the junior. Dawson v. Watkins, 41 Va. (2 Rob.) 259 (1843).

When no adverse possession of wild and uncultivated land. — While lands remain uncleared, or in a state of nature, they are not susceptible of adverse possession against the older patentee, unless by acts of ownership effecting a change in their condition. To constitute adverse possession there must be occupancy, cultivation, improvement or other open, notorious and habitual acts of ownership. Turpin v. Saunders, 73 Va. (32 Gratt.) 27 (1879); Harmon v. Ratliff, 93 Va. 249, 24 S.E. 1023 (1896); City of Richmond v. Jones, 111 Va. 214, 68 S.E. 181 (1910).

Nor of tidal lands. — If the tide ebbs and flows over property, it is doubtful whether a title by adverse possession can be acquired to it, separate and distinct from the rights of the riparian owner. And the principle that in order to acquire title by adverse possession to wild lands, there must be some change in their physical condition as a visible evidence of occupation and ownership would seem to apply with equal if not greater force to land under water, subject to the ebb and flow of the tide, upon which it is difficult, if not impossible, to erect any visible and permanent evidence of occupation. Austin v. Minor, 107 Va. 101, 57 S.E. 609 (1907).

2. Possession for Statutory Period.

Owner must have right of entry or cause of action. — The statute of limitations does not begin to run against an owner of any real estate or of any interest therein until such owner has the right to "make an entry on, or bring an action to recover" the land. Hubbard v. Davis, 181 Va. 549, 25 S.E.2d 256 (1943).

Possession must give rise to cause of action. — Adverse possession to constitute title must be such an invasion of the rights of another as will give that other a cause of action, and the latter must fail to institute his action within the time prescribed by the statute in order to confer title on the adverse holder. In other words, he must be negligent in the enforcement of his rights. It is only as to such persons that the title so acquired is good, and only when the rights of all persons are thus barred is the title perfect. McClanahan's Adm'r v. Norfolk & W. Ry., 122 Va. 705, 96 S.E. 453 (1918).

Statute begins to run when cause of action accrues. — Statutes of limitations governing actions for land adversely possessed will not begin to run until the claimant takes possession in fact, under color of title or claim of right where such requirements prevail, and a cause of action therefor accrues. Marion Inv. Co. v. Virginia Lincoln Furn. Corp., 171 Va. 170, 198 S.E. 508 (1938).

What statute applies. — The period of time necessary to ripen possession, under claim of right, into complete title, is determined by the limitations provided by law when the plaintiff's right of action first accrued. Hollingsworth v. Sherman, 81 Va. 668 (1886).

Effect of undelivered deed of trust. — In an action of ejectment, the disputed property was sold under a deed of trust. The sale was confirmed, the purchase price paid and possession taken by the purchasers, but no deed was delivered until 10 years later, after which plaintiff acquired title from the purchasers. Plaintiff conceded that defendant had been in actual possession of the land for more than the 10 (now 15) years required by this section, but contended that the statute did not commence to run against the purchasers at the judicial sale until they actually obtained their deed, three years before suit was instituted. It was held that, since the purchasers were in a position, upon confirmation of the sale, to protect their title and interest by appropriate action, the statute of limitations began to run against them from the time they were entitled to the deed. Marion Inv. Co. v. Virginia Lincoln Furn. Corp., 171 Va. 170, 198 S.E. 508 (1938).

Lands acquired pursuant to federal statute. — Where records disclosed (1) that since November 4, 1918, the United States government, pursuant to statute, had been continuously in possession of the lands described in the complaint, claiming fee-simple title thereto, (2) that almost 30 years had elapsed between that date and the institution of an action to recover possession of the lands, and (3) that more than 15 years had elapsed since the decree in a prior suit to quiet title, resulting in favor of the government, the action was barred by this section. Ellis v. Cates, 88 F. Supp. 19 (E.D. Va.), aff'd, 178 F.2d 791 (4th Cir. 1949), cert. denied, 339 U.S. 964, 70 S. Ct. 999, 94 L. Ed. 1373 (1950).

Right of infant to disaffirm conveyance of remainder. — An infant grantor conveyed his estate in remainder, and the grantee took possession of the land and held it adversely to the life tenant for 15 years. The grantor came of age shortly after making the conveyance. It was held that, the grantee having acquired title to the life estate by adverse possession and holding title to the remainder in fee under the infant's conveyance, the life estate merged into the remainder, and the statute began to run against the right of the grantor to disaffirm his conveyance no later than at the time of the merger, and not at the time of the death of the life tenant. McCauley v. Grim, 115 Va. 610, 79 S.E. 1041 (1913).

3. Actual Possession.

The possession of the defendant must be actual. Dawson v. Watkins, 41 Va. (2 Rob.) 259 (1843); Pasley v. English, 46 Va. (5 Gratt.) 141 (1848); Turpin v. Saunders, 73 Va. (32 Gratt.) 27 (1879); Yellow Poplar Lumber Co. v. Thompson, 108 Va. 612, 62 S.E. 358 (1908).

This rule applies to grant from Commonwealth. — A grant from the Commonwealth puts the patentee of the land constructively into possession thereof, and there can be no ouster of that possession except by actual adverse possession — some act or acts palpable to the senses which serve to admonish the patentee that his seisin is molested. Green v. Pennington, 105 Va. 801, 54 S.E. 877 (1906); City of Richmond v. Jones, 111 Va. 214, 68 S.E. 181 (1910).

The usual kind of actual possession relied upon to effect a disseisin is occupancy use or residence upon the premises for the statutory period of time, evidenced by cultivation, enclosure, or erection of improvements, or other plainly visible, continuous and notorious manifestation of exclusive possession in keeping with the character and adaptability of the land. LaDue v. Currell, 201 Va. 200, 110 S.E.2d 217 (1959).

More than sporadic taking of products required. — For disseisin to be effective the entry must be with intent to oust the owner and the possession must be evidenced by some act or acts indicating an actual possession of the land itself, as distinguished from mere sporadic taking of the products thereof. LaDue v. Currell, 201 Va. 200, 110 S.E.2d 217 (1959).

Acts must serve notice of intent to appropriate land itself. — Acts done upon land requisite to constitute adverse possession must be such as to indicate and serve as notice of an intention to appropriate the land itself, and not the mere products of it, to the dominion and ownership of the party entering, such as acts of permanent improvement. Whealton v. Doughty, 112 Va. 649, 72 S.E. 112 (1911). See also, Hollingsworth v. Sherman, 81 Va. 668 (1885); Brock v. Bear, 100 Va. 562, 42 S.E. 307 (1902).

4. Notorious and Visible.

The possession must be open and notorious, in order to confer title to land by adverse possession. Austin v. Minor, 107 Va. 101, 57 S.E. 609 (1907); Yellow Poplar Lumber Co. v. Thompson, 108 Va. 612, 62 S.E. 358 (1908).

The ground upon which an adverse title is established is the supposed laches of the true owner. The possession of the adverse claimant must not only be with claim of title, but must be visible, and of such notoriety that the true owner may be presumed to know of it. Turpin v. Saunders, 73 Va. (32 Gratt.) 27 (1879); Hollingsworth v. Sherman, 81 Va. 668 (1885).

Where the land is uncleared, or in a state of nature, or where it consists of a fresh water pond or stream surrounded by lands of different persons, whose title as riparian owners includes the land under the water to the center of such pond or stream, the acts of ownership must indicate a change of condition, showing a notorious claim of title, accompanied by the essential elements of adverse possession. Leake v. Richardson, 199 Va. 967, 103 S.E.2d 227 (1958).

5. Exclusive.

Adverse possession must be exclusive in order to constitute an ouster of the true owner. Chapman v. Chapman, 91 Va. 397, 21 S.E. 813 (1895); Austin v. Minor, 107 Va. 101, 57 S.E. 609 (1907); Gardner v. Montague, 108 Va. 192, 60 S.E. 870 (1908); Providence Forge Fishing & Hunting Club v. Miller Mfg. Co., 117 Va. 129, 83 S.E. 1047 (1915); Cumbee v. Ritter, 123 Va. 448, 96 S.E. 747 (1918).

When requirement met. — Acts sufficient to apprise everyone of exclusive occupation and use, with unequivocal, emphatic and public assertion of ownership, meet the requirements of the Virginia law governing title by adverse possession. Guaranty Title & Trust Corp. v. United States, 264 U.S. 200, 44 S. Ct. 252, 68 L. Ed. 636 (1924).

6. Continuous.

Possession must be continuous to acquire good title by adverse possession. Taylor v. Burnsides, 42 Va. (1 Gratt.) 165 (1844); Stonestreet v. Doyle, 75 Va. 356 (1881); Austin v. Minor, 107 Va. 101, 57 S.E. 609 (1907); Merryman v. Hoover, 107 Va. 485, 59 S.E. 483 (1907).

The claimants had not sufficiently established that they continuously possessed the property where the evidence is unclear where possession and use took place and whether the acts were connected with use of the disputed or undisputed parcels and where many of the uses of the disputed parcels during the period in question were intermittent and sporadic. Calhoun v. Woods, 246 Va. 41, 431 S.E.2d 285 (1993).

Effect of entry by true owner. — The tenant cannot sustain his defense of continued adverse possession, so as to make the statute a bar, if the demandants, or those under whom they claim, have within the statutory period before bringing the action entered upon the land in controversy and taken actual possession thereof, by residence, improvement, cultivation, or other open, notorious and habitual acts of ownership. Taylor v. Burnsides, 42 Va. (1 Gratt.) 165 (1844).

Once adverse claimant vacates, owner is in constructive possession. — Virginia follows the rule that once the adverse claimant vacates the premises, the owner, by reason of his legal title, will be regarded as in constructive possession and the adverse period of the claimant is at an end. United States v. Tobias, 899 F.2d 1375 (4th Cir. 1990).

Tacking several possessions together. — When several persons enter upon land in succession, the several possessions cannot be tacked so as to preserve the essential continuity unless there is privity of estate between them, or the several estates are connected. And one cannot sustain his defense of adverse possession if, during the period of limitation, the possession has been abandoned by him or those under whom he claims. Hollingsworth v. Sherman, 81 Va. 668 (1885). See Christian v. Bulbeck, 120 Va. 74, 90 S.E. 661 (1916), where tacking of possession of one under whom defendant claimed was permitted.

"Tacking" allows successive adverse users in privity with prior adverse users to aggregate the two adverse periods. However, tacking is prohibited if the prior owner abandons the premises. United States v. Tobias, 899 F.2d 1375 (4th Cir. 1990).

Possession under invalid deed cannot be tacked to possession of true owner. — Claimants of land by adverse possession could not tack their possession obtained by void deed to the possession of the true owners who held under legal title. Harris v. Deal, 189 Va. 675, 54 S.E.2d 161 (1949).

7. Hostile and Under Claim of Right.

Adverse possession presupposes a disseisin. — By "adverse possession" we mean a possession which presupposes a disseisin of the rightful occupant, and not a possession under or through the latter. McClanahan's Adm'r v. Norfolk & W. Ry., 122 Va. 705, 96 S.E. 453 (1918).

Occupancy must be hostile. — The occupancy which is necessary to support a claim of title by adverse possession must be hostile. Cline v. Catron, 63 Va. (22 Gratt.) 378 (1872); Gardner v. Montague, 108 Va. 192, 60 S.E. 870 (1908); Providence Forge Fishing & Hunting Club v. Miller Mfg. Co., 117 Va. 129, 83 S.E. 1047 (1915); Cumbee v. Ritter, 123 Va. 448, 96 S.E. 747 (1918).

And with intention to hold adversely. — An adverse possession depends upon the intention with which the possession was taken and held. Intention, either express or implied, to hold adversely is an indispensable element. Clarke v. McClure, 51 Va. (10 Gratt.) 305 (1853); Haney v. Breeden, 100 Va. 781, 42 S.E. 916 (1902); Stuart v. Meade, 119 Va. 753, 89 S.E. 866 (1916).

A plea of this statute of limitations cannot be sustained where the holding relied on has not been adverse. Cox v. Williams, 183 Va. 152, 31 S.E.2d 312 (1944).

Possession by mistake is not adverse. — Where a person occupies and possesses the land of another through a misapprehension or mistake as to the boundaries of his land, with no intention to claim as his own that which does not belong to him, but only intending to claim to the true line, whatever that may be, he does not hold adversely. Schaubuch v. Dillemuth, 108 Va. 86, 60 S.E. 745 (1908); Clinchfield Coal Co. v. Viers, 111 Va. 261, 68 S.E. 976 (1910). See also, Davis v. Owen, 107 Va. 283, 58 S.E. 581 (1907).

Possession must be under claim of right. — A mere naked possession without claim of right, no matter how long, never ripens into a good title, but is regarded as being held for the benefit of the true owner. Nowlin v. Reynolds, 66 Va. (25 Gratt.) 137 (1874); Yellow Poplar Lumber Co. v. Thompson, 108 Va. 612, 62 S.E. 358 (1908).

But "claim of right" means only intention of disseisor to appropriate land as his own. — The terms "claim of right," "claim of title," and "claim of ownership," when used in connection with adverse possession, mean nothing more than the intention of the disseisor to appropriate and use the land as his own to the exclusion of all others, irrespective of any semblance or shadow of actual title or right. Marion Inv. Co. v. Virginia Lincoln Furn. Corp., 171 Va. 170, 198 S.E. 508 (1938).

Claim of title need not be based on writing. Marion Inv. Co. v. Virginia Lincoln Furn. Corp., 171 Va. 170, 198 S.E. 508 (1938).

Thus, the disseisor need not have a deed or writing giving color of title or furnishing foundation for belief or claim of ownership or legal right to enter and take possession. His intention to appropriate and use the land as his own to the exclusion of all others suffices. Guaranty Title & Trust Corp. v. United States, 264 U.S. 200, 44 S. Ct. 252, 68 L. Ed. 636 (1924).

C. Color of Title.

Definition. — Color of title, for the purposes of the statute of limitations as to land, is that which has the semblance or appearance of title, legal or equitable, but which in fact is not title. Sharp v. Shenandoah Furnace Co., 100 Va. 27, 40 S.E. 103 (1901); Knight v. Grim, 110 Va. 400, 66 S.E. 42 (1909).

The principal office of color of title is to define the boundaries and fix the extent of the adverse holding. Sharp v. Shenandoah Furnace Co., 100 Va. 27, 40 S.E. 103 (1901); Blacksburg Mining & Mfg. Co. v. Bell, 125 Va. 565, 100 S.E. 806 (1919).

It is inherent in color of title that the title claimed thereunder is invalid, is in fact no title, and the writing may indeed be absolutely void; but if the other requisites of adverse possession are complied with by the disseisor, it will constitute color of title. Nowlin v. Reynolds, 66 Va. (25 Gratt.) 137 (1874); Baber v. Baber, 121 Va. 740, 94 S.E. 209 (1917); Blacksburg Mining & Mfg. Co. v. Bell, 125 Va. 565, 100 S.E. 806 (1919).

Title claimed may be good or bad, legal or equitable. — It is immaterial whether an adverse possession under a claim of title be under a good or a bad, a legal or an equitable title. Shanks v. Lancaster, 46 Va. (5 Gratt.) 110 (1848); Interstate Coal & Iron Co. v. Clintwood Coal & Timber Co., 105 Va. 574, 54 S.E. 593 (1906); Baber v. Baber, 121 Va. 740, 94 S.E. 209 (1917); Marion Inv. Co. v. Virginia Lincoln Furn. Corp., 171 Va. 170, 198 S.E. 508 (1938).

Claim of title, as opposed to color of title, is a mere assertion of ownership or right, without paper title. Walton v. Rosson, 216 Va. 732, 222 S.E.2d 553 (1976).

**Existence of color of title does not dispense with the necessity for acts of adverse possession. It is merely evidence tending to support complainants' claim when accompanied by the essential elements of adverse possession. Nor did the recordation of the deeds subsequent to the acquisition of their lands by defendants constitute of itself notice to them of the beginning of the running of the statute. Leake v. Richardson, 199 Va. 967, 103 S.E.2d 227 (1958).

The possession of one tract extends in law to an adjoining tract held under color of title by the same person. Peck v. Daniel, 212 Va. 265, 184 S.E.2d 7 (1971).

D. Conflicting Grants — Interlocks.

Effect of conflicting grants. — Where one grant conflicts in part with another, occasioning an interlock, the elder patentee under his grant acquires constructive seisin in deed of all the land embraced within its boundaries, although he has taken no actual possession of any part thereof. The junior grantee under his grant acquires similar constructive seisin in deed of all the land embraced by its boundaries, except that portion within the interlock, the seisin of which has already vested in the senior grantee. Green v. Pennington, 105 Va. 801, 54 S.E. 877 (1906). See also, Breeden v. Haney, 95 Va. 622, 29 S.E. 328 (1898).

Senior patentee prevails where neither claimant has possession. — If neither party has actual possession of part of the interlock, the elder seisin in law of the senior patentee will prevail. Overton v. Davisson, 42 Va. (1 Gratt.) 211 (1844); Koiner v. Rankin, 52 Va. (11 Gratt.) 420 (1854); Cline v. Catron, 63 Va. (22 Gratt.) 378 (1872).

A senior grant confers constructive possession to the limits of its boundary which would prevail without proof of actual possession, unless there was a disseisin. LaDue v. Currell, 201 Va. 200, 110 S.E.2d 217 (1959).

Effect of possession of part of interlock by senior patentee. — Actual possession by the senior patentee of any part of an interlock will be constructive possession of all not in the actual adverse possession of the junior patentee. Overton v. Davisson, 42 Va. (1 Gratt.) 211 (1844); Koiner v. Rankin, 52 Va. (11 Gratt.) 420 (1854).

Effect of possession of part of interlock by junior patentee. — If the junior patentee has actual possession of part of the interlock, and senior patentee has possession of no part of his grant, the junior has a constructive possession of the interlock, while the senior has a mere seisin in law. The constructive possession of the junior will prevail as to the whole. Taylor v. Burnsides, 42 Va. (1 Gratt.) 165 (1844); Overton v. Davisson, 42 Va. (1 Gratt.) 211 (1844); Turpin v. Saunders, 73 Va. (32 Gratt.) 27 (1879).

To overcome the constructive seisin in deed of the senior patentee and work an ouster there must be an actual invasion of his boundary by some act or acts palpable to the senses and which should serve to admonish him that his seisin was molested. Green v. Pennington, 105 Va. 801, 54 S.E. 877 (1906). See also, Harman v. Ratliff, 93 Va. 249, 24 S.E. 1023 (1896).

Disseisin can be proved only by a taking of actual possession of some part of the interlock. LaDue v. Currell, 201 Va. 200, 110 S.E.2d 217 (1959).

E. Possession Originally Consistent with Title of True Owner.

1. In General.

Law looks at intent with which possession taken. — An adverse possession depends upon the intention with which the possession was taken and held. Wherever the act itself imports that there is a superior title in another, by whose permission and in subordination to whose still continuing and subsisting title, the entry is made, such entry cannot be adverse to the owner of the legal title; and such possession so commencing cannot be converted into an adverse possession, but by disclaimer, the assertion of an adverse title and notice. Clarke v. McClure, 51 Va. (10 Gratt.) 305 (1853); Stuart v. Meade, 119 Va. 753, 89 S.E. 866 (1916).

Holder must disavow owner's title. — Where possession is originally taken and held under the true owner, a clear, positive and continued disclaimer and disavowal of the true owner's title, and the assertion of an adverse one, must be brought home to the true owner before any foundation can be laid for the operation of the statute of limitations. Creekmur v. Creekmur, 75 Va. 430 (1881); Hulvey v. Hulvey, 92 Va. 182, 23 S.E. 233 (1895); Duggins v. Woodson, 117 Va. 299, 84 S.E. 652 (1915); Christian v. Bulbeck, 120 Va. 74, 90 S.E. 661 (1916).

2. Cotenants.

Necessity for disseisin or ouster. — The possession of one coparcener or tenant in common being the possession of all, one in possession of the whole subject cannot avail himself of such possession as a defense under the statute of limitations, against the rest, without an actual disseisin or ouster of his coparceners or cotenants. Purcell v. Wilson, 45 Va. (4 Gratt.) 16 (1847); Emerick v. Tavener, 50 Va. (9 Gratt.) 220 (1852); Stonestreet v. Doyle, 75 Va. 356 (1881); Fry v. Payne, 82 Va. 759, 1 S.E. 197 (1887); Lagorio v. Dozier, 91 Va. 492, 22 S.E. 239 (1895).

Assertion of right must be brought home to cotenant. — Where the possession of property is acquired in privity with another the possession of one is ordinarily deemed the possession of all, and this presumption prevails in favor of all until an assertion of an adverse right is brought home to the actual knowledge of a cotenant out of possession. Rutledge v. Rutledge, 204 Va. 522, 132 S.E.2d 469 (1963).

A purchaser from a cotenant may hold adversely. Johnston v. Virginia Coal & Iron Co., 96 Va. 158, 31 S.E. 85 (1898).

Claimant under will. — A son took possession of the land of his father, claiming title to it under a lost will. Such taking and holding possession was adverse to the other heirs, and the statute of limitations commenced to run from the time of the taking possession. Caperton v. Gregory, 52 Va. (11 Gratt.) 505 (1854).

3. Mortgagor and Mortgagee.

A privity exists which precludes the idea of a hostile, tortious possession which could silently ripen into a title by adverse possession under the statute of limitations where a mortgagee holds under the owner of the legal title. Chapman v. Armistead, 18 Va. (4 Munf.) 382 (1815); Newman v. Chapman, 23 Va. (2 Rand.) 93 (1823); Thompson v. Camper, 106 Va. 315, 55 S.E. 674 (1906).

4. Vendor and Purchaser.

Section inapplicable. — This section generally relates to adverse possession and is not applicable to a situation where a vendee has a valid deed of bargain and sale which the vendor contends he was fraudulently induced to execute. Burton v. Terrell, 368 F. Supp. 553 (W.D. Va. 1973).

Possession of vendor not adverse until disclaimer. — The possession of a vendor of land after conveyance in fee to his grantee is in subserviency to the grantee, and a clear, positive and continued disclaimer and disavowal of such relation, and the assertion of an adverse right, brought home to the knowledge of the true owner, are indispensable to change the character of the grantor's possession and render it adverse to the grantee. Schaubuch v. Dillemuth, 108 Va. 86, 60 S.E. 745 (1908); Gillespie v. Hawks, 206 Va. 705, 146 S.E.2d 211 (1966).

From the time the grantor explicitly disclaims holding under the grantee, and openly asserts his title to the premises, in hostility to the title claimed under his own previous deed, his possession becomes adverse, even though he knew his title to be bad, and from that moment the statute of limitations will begin to run. Creekmur v. Creekmur, 75 Va. 430 (1881).

In order to make the plea of limitation effectual in a case where the grantor remains in possession, using the land as he did before his deed, he must show some notorious act of ownership over the property, distinctly hostile to the claim of the grantee. Gillespie v. Hawks, 206 Va. 705, 146 S.E.2d 211 (1966).

The same is true of possession of original owner after judicial sale. — The possession of the original owner, and of those claiming under him, from the time of the sale by the commissioners until the final decree, is not an adverse possession to the purchaser and those claiming under him. Evans v. Spurgin, 47 Va. (6 Gratt.) 107 (1849). See also, Whitlock v. Johnson, 87 Va. 323, 12 S.E. 614 (1891).

And of possession of vendee under executory contract of sale. — One who enters into possession of land pursuant to a contract of purchase cannot be said to hold adversely to his vendor. And though the purchaser has, by the payment of the entire purchase money, acquired full equitable title, such equitable title is derived from his vendor, who retained the legal title for future conveyance. The purchaser holds in subordination to and under the protection of the title of his vendor, and no length of time is sufficient for such possession to ripen silently into a title by adverse possession. Clarke v. McClure, 51 Va. (10 Gratt.) 305 (1853); Nowlin v. Reynolds, 66 Va. (25 Gratt.) 137 (1874); Chapman v. Chapman, 91 Va. 397, 21 S.E. 813 (1895).

Necessity and sufficiency of disclaimer of vendor's right. — Before adverse possession can arise between a vendor and his vendee, or between the grantee of the vendor and such vendee, where the vendor has retained the title, and the statute of limitations can commence to run, the vendee must have dissevered the privity of title between them by the assertion of an adverse right, and openly and continuously disclaimed the title of his vendor, and such disclaimer must be clearly brought home to the knowledge of the vendor or his grantee. Chapman v. Chapman, 91 Va. 397, 21 S.E. 813 (1895); Alleghany v. Parrish, 93 Va. 615, 25 S.E. 882 (1896). See Allen v. Powers, 194 Va. 662, 74 S.E.2d 688 (1953).

The hostility of the grantor's holding must be brought to the grantee's attention in such a manner as to put the latter on notice of the grantor's intention to occupy the property in his own right. Gillespie v. Hawks, 206 Va. 705, 146 S.E.2d 211 (1966).

The mere fact that the grantor remains in possession, using the property as before conveyance, is not sufficient in itself to bind the grantee with notice that the grantor is holding adversely to him. Gillespie v. Hawks, 206 Va. 705, 146 S.E.2d 211 (1966).

A vendee cannot be said to hold adversely to his vendor where possession remains in privity with and subservient to the legal title of the vendor. In such case a vendee is not permitted to impeach or assail the title of his vendor. Allen v. Powers, 194 Va. 662, 74 S.E.2d 688 (1953).

Presumption. — Where a grantor continues in possession of the land after the execution and delivery of the deed, his possession will be regarded as holding the premises in subserviency to the grantee, as his tenant or as trustee for him; however, this presumption is rebuttable and under proper circumstances a grantor may by adverse possession acquire title to land which he has conveyed. Gillespie v. Hawks, 206 Va. 705, 146 S.E.2d 211 (1966).

Burden. — The burden was on the heirs of the grantor to prove that the possession by the grantor was adverse to his grantee. Gillespie v. Hawks, 206 Va. 705, 146 S.E.2d 211 (1966).

5. Entry Under Parol Gift.

Not adverse until disclaimer. — An entry on land under a parol gift from the owner is, in its nature, a recognition of the continued existence of a subsisting title in the legal owner, and a claim to hold an estate by gift from the legal owner is a claim to hold in subordination of his title. Thus, until there has been a disclaimer, the statute does not commence to run in favor of the tenant. Clarke v. McClure, 51 Va. (10 Gratt.) 305 (1853); Thompson v. Camper, 106 Va. 315, 55 S.E. 674 (1906).

6. Trust Estates.

Possession of grantor in deed of trust not adverse. — The possession of a grantor in a deed of trust after the execution of the deed, is not adverse to the title of the trustee, but is only as his tenant at will or sufferance. The possession so continues after the sale by the trustee until it is determined by the will of the legal owner, or at least until the title of the legal owner is disclaimed with his knowledge. Creigh v. Henson, 51 Va. (10 Gratt.) 231 (1853).

Trustee cannot acquire title against cestui que trust. — No lapse of time, however long, will give a trustee a right to trust property by adverse possession as against the cestui que trust. Thompson v. Camper, 106 Va. 315, 55 S.E. 674 (1906).

Rule applies to constructive trusts. — Land was sold under an order of court, the sale was confirmed and the purchase money paid, but no deed was given, and the former owner's heirs remained in possession. It was held that equity looks upon the heirs as trustees, and in such a case before the statute begins to run in their favor, they must make a clear, positive and continued disclaimer and disavowal of title in the purchaser and his heirs, and the assertion of an adverse right, brought home to the knowledge of the purchaser or his heirs. Whitlock v. Johnson, 87 Va. 323, 12 S.E. 614 (1891).

7. Life Tenant and Remainderman.

The possession of a life tenant as such cannot be adverse to the remainderman or reversioner, because the right of action of the latter does not accrue until the death of the life tenant. Hannon v. Hounihan, 85 Va. 429, 12 S.E. 157 (1888); Duggins v. Woodson, 117 Va. 299, 84 S.E. 652 (1915).

Grantees and devisees of life tenant. — After the termination of a life estate, the possession of a grantee from the life tenant holding under a deed conveying the fee simple is deemed adverse to the remainderman, and if the remainderman permits the devisee of a fee simple interest under the will of the life tenant to take possession of the property under the will, such possession is adverse to the remainderman so as to bar his title after the expiration of the statutory period. Rutledge v. Rutledge, 204 Va. 522, 132 S.E.2d 469 (1963).

Tenant by curtesy. — Where defendants' predecessor acquired possession as a tenant by curtesy, limitations do not begin to run against the remainderman and in favor of defendants until their possession has become notoriously tortious and adverse. Duggins v. Woodson, 117 Va. 299, 84 S.E. 652 (1915).

8. Landlord and Tenant.

Acts of tenant changing nature of possession. — The statute does not begin to run against a landlord until the possession, before in privity with him, becomes tortious and wrongful by the disloyal acts of the occupying tenant, which must be open, continuous and notorious, so as to preclude any doubt of the character of the holding or the fact of knowledge on the part of the landlord. Creigh v. Henson, 51 Va. (10 Gratt.) 231 (1853); Thompson v. Camper, 106 Va. 315, 55 S.E. 674 (1906); Baber v. Baber, 121 Va. 740, 94 S.E. 209 (1917).

Action by heirs of landlord. — If the possession of a tenant was sufficient to bar the action of the landlord, at the time of his death, it is sufficient to bar the action of his heirs. Overton v. Davisson, 42 Va. (1 Gratt.) 211 (1844).

9. Widow in Possession of Mansion.

Widow must publish her adverse claim. — As a widow is entitled to hold the mansion and curtilage until dower is assigned to her, the statute of limitations will not begin to run until her possession ends or she publishes her claim and possession to be adverse by actual and open disseisin. Hannon v. Hounihan, 85 Va. 429, 12 S.E. 157 (1888).

F. Property Which May Be Held Adversely.

Lands of the Commonwealth. — The bar of the statute of limitations has no application as between a private party and the Commonwealth, as to realty of the latter. Seekright v. Lawson, 35 Va. (8 Leigh) 458 (1836); Hurst v. Dulany, 84 Va. 701, 5 S.E. 802 (1888); Eastern State Hosp. v. Graves, 105 Va. 151, 52 S.E. 837 (1906).

Actual possession of a part of a tract of land, under color and claim of title to the whole, is possession of the whole, and this principle applies to lands of the Commonwealth as against persons not lawfully claiming under her. Green v. Pennington, 105 Va. 801, 54 S.E. 877 (1906).

Waste and unappropriated land. — Though waste and unappropriated land is claimed by the patentee of adjoining land as being included within the boundaries of his patent, and actual possession thereof is taken by such patentee, and maintained for 15 years, such possession cannot be adverse to the Commonwealth, and her grantee of the land is consequently entitled to recover it. Seekright v. Lawson, 35 Va. (8 Leigh) 458 (1836). See also, Norfolk City v. Cooke, 68 Va. (27 Gratt.) 430 (1876); Harman v. Ratliff, 93 Va. 249, 24 S.E. 1023 (1897).

Public highways and streets. — No title by adverse possession can be acquired in a public street. Bellenot v. City of Richmond, 108 Va. 314, 61 S.E. 785 (1908); Virginia Hot Springs Co. v. Lowman, 126 Va. 424, 101 S.E. 326 (1919).

Right to obstruct highway. — One cannot acquire by adverse possession the right to shut up or obstruct a public highway. Taylor v. Commonwealth, 70 Va. (29 Gratt.) 780 (1878); Yates v. Town of Warrenton, 84 Va. 337, 4 S.E. 818 (1888); Depriest v. Jones, 2 Va. Dec. 109, 21 S.E. 478 (1895); Norfolk & W. Ry. v. Board of Supvrs., 110 Va. 95, 65 S.E. 531 (1909); Board of Supvrs. v. Norfolk & W. Ry., 119 Va. 763, 91 S.E. 124 (1916).

G. Effect of Adverse Possession.

Adverse possession vests title in disseisor. — Under this section adverse possession for the required period not only bars the owner's right of entry or action but vests title in the disseisor. Guaranty Title & Trust Corp. v. United States, 264 U.S. 200, 44 S. Ct. 252, 68 L. Ed. 636 (1924).

The result of the statute of limitations is so absolute that the adverse possession operates as a transfer of the legal title, hence a disseisin of the holder of the better title. Taylor v. Burnsides, 42 Va. (1 Gratt.) 165 (1844); Middleton v. Johns, 45 Va. (4 Gratt.) 129 (1847); Nowlin v. Reynolds, 66 Va. (25 Gratt.) 137 (1874); Thomas v. Jones, 69 Va. (28 Gratt.) 383 (1877).

And title so acquired is perfect. — A true adverse possession for the statutory period confers upon the occupant a new, independent, unencumbered, indefeasible title, a weapon of defense and offense, good alike at law and in equity in all proceedings which call in question its validity or endanger its security. In short, such a title, though not derived from the former owner, is as good as it would be possible to acquire by deed from a former owner of a perfect title, or by a grant from the Commonwealth. McClanahan's Adm'r v. Norfolk & W. Ry., 122 Va. 705, 96 S.E. 453 (1918).

Defects in title are cured. — Defects in a person's title to land are cured by lapse of time, where he has been in the uninterrupted, honest, and adverse possession of the land under color of title for over 15 years. Bryan v. Augusta Perpetual Bldg. & Loan Co., 104 Va. 611, 52 S.E. 357 (1905).

Right of claimant under equitable title barred. — An equitable title to land asserted against the holder of the legal title, is barred by an adverse possession for the statutory period held by the claimant of the legal title, the claimant of the equity having full knowledge of such possession from its commencement and being under no disability. Straughan v. Wright, 25 Va. (4 Rand.) 493 (1826); Cresap v. M'Lean, 32 Va. (5 Leigh) 381 (1826).

Lien of judgment against former owner barred. — Under §§ 8.01-462 through 8.01-464 the lien of a judgment may be indefinitely continued against the land of the judgment debtor in his possession, or in the possession of others holding titles derived from and in privity with him. But obviously the same rule cannot be applied to strangers who have acquired a perfect legal title not in privity with but adversely to the title of the judgment debtor. In other words, the life of a judgment may be indefinitely prolonged as to any property upon which it can operate, but whenever the right of the judgment debtor to make an entry on or bring an action to recover any land held adversely is tolled by this section, the right of his judgment creditor to subject such land to the satisfaction of his judgment also ceases. The lien is a vested right, but not more so than the title to which the lien attaches, and when the statute destroys the latter it necessarily destroys the former. McClanahan's Adm'r v. Norfolk & W. Ry., 122 Va. 705, 96 S.E. 453 (1918). See Neff's Adm'r v. Newman, 150 Va. 203, 142 S.E. 389 (1928). But see Flanary v. Kane, 102 Va. 547, 46 S.E. 312, rehearing denied, 46 S.E. 681 (1904), in which it was held that this section applies only to the right to make an entry or to bring an action to recover land; it does not apply to the suit of a judgment creditor to enforce his lien against land.

H. Evidence.

Necessity for proof of adverse possession. — Proof of adverse possession is essential as a foundation for a plea of bar arising from statutes of limitation. Lamar v. Hale, 79 Va. 147 (1884). See also, Boatright v. Meggs, 18 Va. (4 Munf.) 145 (1813).

Evidence admissible to show possession. — Evidence tending to show that the defendant's predecessor in title claimed the land in controversy and exercised acts of ownership over it, by cutting timber and clearing and improving portions of it with the knowledge of the plaintiff, is clearly competent as tending to show where he and the plaintiff regarded the line between them, and also as tending to show adverse possession on the part of the defendant's predecessor in title even though the acts mentioned were not in themselves sufficient to show title by adverse possession. Smith v. Stanley, 114 Va. 117, 75 S.E. 742 (1912). See also, Taylor v. Burnsides, 42 Va. (1 Gratt.) 165 (1844).

And to show possession not adverse. — The record of a suit for specific performance brought three years before the commencement of an ejectment action was admissible to show that defendant's possession was not adverse at that time. Marbach v. Holmes, 105 Va. 178, 52 S.E. 828 (1906).

Possession under claim of right. — Where one claims title by open, notorious and adverse possession for a period sufficient to give good title, it is competent for him to prove not only that he had possession, but that the possession was under a claim of right, and that his claim and the character of the possession were such that he was generally reputed in the neighborhood to be the owner. Lusk v. Pelter & Co., 101 Va. 790, 45 S.E. 333 (1903).

Entry and survey under patent are admissible to show color of title. — A tenant in ejectment claiming under a junior patent founded on an inclusive survey may, to show possession under color of title prior to his patent, introduce in evidence the entries for the different tracts embraced in the inclusive survey, the order of court authorizing the survey, and the survey itself. Shanks v. Lancaster, 46 Va. (5 Gratt.) 110 (1848).

But are not proof of disseisin. — Evidence of the making of an inclusive survey, the obtaining of a patent thereon, and probable notice of these proceedings to the demandants' ancestor, did not constitute any proof of such possession as is necessary to work a disseisin. Koiner v. Rankin, 52 Va. (11 Gratt.) 420 (1854).

Proof of notice of adverse possession. — It has been held, in cases involving cotenants or others originally having privity of title with the disseisor, that constructive notice of adverse possession may be presumed from a great lapse of time with circumstances which may warrant such presumption. Such notice, like any other fact involved in a civil case, may be proved by circumstantial evidence, the probative value and sufficiency of the circumstantial evidence to sustain the burden of proof required being entirely with the jury. Leake v. Richardson, 199 Va. 967, 103 S.E.2d 227 (1958).

Burden of proof. — The character of the user being a question of fact, the burden of showing the essential elements of adverse possession is upon the person asserting such ownership. Leake v. Richardson, 199 Va. 967, 103 S.E.2d 227 (1958); Peck v. Daniel, 212 Va. 265, 184 S.E.2d 7 (1971).

Record of condemnation proceedings is admissible to show color of title. Knight v. Grim, 110 Va. 400, 66 S.E. 42 (1909).

Evidence held sufficient to establish title by adverse possession. Mock v. Copenhaver, 184 Va. 744, 36 S.E.2d 542 (1946).

Evidence held insufficient to show adverse possession by complainants who never enclosed disputed area or placed any improvements on it, and showed only sporadic cultivation and mowing. LaDue v. Currell, 201 Va. 200, 110 S.E.2d 217 (1959).

I. How Title by Adverse Possession Lost.

Re-entry of holder of paper title. — Although title by adverse possession is complete, it will be destroyed by the re-entry of the party having the paper title and his holding the land by virtue of the paper title for the statutory period. Marbury v. Jones, 112 Va. 389, 71 S.E. 1124 (1911).

§ 8.01-237. Effect of disabilities upon right of entry on, or action for, land.

— Notwithstanding the provisions of subsection A of § 8.01-229, no disabilities or tacking of disabilities shall preserve to any person or his successors a right to make entry on or bring an action to recover land for more than twenty-five years after such right first accrued, although such person or persons shall have been disabled during the whole of such twenty-five years. (Code 1950, §§ 8-7, 8-8; 1977, c. 617.)

REVISERS' NOTE

Section 8.01-237 qualifies the application of § 8.01-229 A to rights of entry on or actions for land and modifies former §§ 8-7 and 8-8. A 25-year limit is placed on the right to enter on or bring an action for land regardless of the disabilities of persons so entitled.

I. Decisions Under Current Law.
II. Decisions Under Prior Law.

I. DECISIONS UNDER CURRENT LAW.

This section is not a true statute of limitations but a "cutoff" provision that operates to define the maximum period within which an action may be brought, regardless of applicable statutes of limitations. Lavery v. Automation Mgt. Consultants, Inc., 234 Va. 145, 360 S.E.2d 336 (1987).

II. DECISIONS UNDER PRIOR LAW.

Editor's note. — The cases cited below were decided under corresponding provisions of former law. The terms "this statute" and "the act of limitations," as used below, refer to former provisions.

Tacking disabilities not allowed. — Where a disability existing at the time the cause of action accrued is removed, another disability arising subsequently cannot be tacked to it to avoid the bar of the statute. Fitzhugh v. Anderson, 12 Va. (2 Hen. & M.) 289 (1808); Hudson v. Hudson, 20 Va. (6 Munf.) 352 (1819); Parsons v. McCracken, 36 Va. (9 Leigh) 495 (1838).

Disabilities which bring a person within the exceptions of the statute cannot be filed one upon another; a party claiming the benefit of this proviso can only avail himself of the disability existing when the right of action first accrued. Lessee of Mercer v. Selden, 42 U.S. (1 How.) 37, 11 L. Ed. 38 (1843).

Recurring lunacy. — Where after one was adjudged a lunatic and his land was sold in an action by a creditor against his committee, limitations on an action by the lunatic to recover the land commenced to run when he was discharged as restored to sanity, and continued to run notwithstanding a recurrence of insanity nine years later. Howard v. Landsberg's Comm., 108 Va. 161, 60 S.E. 769 (1908).

Infancy of one joint tenant does not affect other tenants. — As ejectment lies in Virginia for an undivided interest in realty, the infancy of one joint tenant will not prevent the running of the act of limitations as to the other joint tenants not under disability. Redford v. Clarke, 100 Va. 115, 40 S.E. 630 (1902).

§ 8.01-238. To repeal grant. — A bill in equity to repeal, in whole or in part, any grant of land by the Commonwealth, shall be brought within ten years next after the date of such grant. (Code 1950, § 8-9; 1977, c. 617.)

Cross references. — As to bill to repeal land grants generally, see § 41.1-13.

I. Decisions Under Current Law.
II. Decisions Under Prior Law.

I. DECISIONS UNDER CURRENT LAW.

Actions by Commonwealth not barred. — Since this section does not, by its express terms, apply to the Commonwealth, it cannot bar an action by it. Bradford v. Nature Conservancy, 224 Va. 181, 294 S.E.2d 866 (1982).

Section is inapplicable to a declaratory judgment action to determine the rights of the parties. Bradford v. Nature Conservancy, 224 Va. 181, 294 S.E.2d 866 (1982).

This section may not be used to defeat a landowner's effort to show that a grant under former § 41-84 (now § 41.1-16) is void and to have a court of equity confirm his title. Johnson v. Buzzard Island Shooting Club, Inc., 232 Va. 32, 348 S.E.2d 220 (1986).

II. DECISIONS UNDER PRIOR LAW.

Editor's note. — The case cited below was decided under corresponding provisions of former law. The term "the statute," as used below, refers to former provisions.

Applies to land grant obtained by false representations. — In a suit to repeal a land grant, it was claimed that the patent had been obtained upon false suggestions, and circumstances were relied on to establish the existence of a trust, to take the case out of the operation of the statute, but it was held that the language was express that no patent could be repealed after the lapse of 10 years. Goodwin v. M'Cluer, 44 Va. (3 Gratt.) 291 (1846).

§ **8.01-239. Ground rents.** — No action shall be brought for the recovery of any ground rent reserved upon real estate after the expiration of ten years from the time such ground rent becomes due and payable. (Code 1950, § 8-10; 1977, c. 617.)

I. DECISIONS UNDER PRIOR LAW.

Editor's note. — The case cited below was decided under corresponding provisions of former law. The term "this statute," as used below, refers to former provisions.

Action for ground rent imposed under authority of statute. — Where ground rent is reserved in land conveyed by trustees, by authority of an act of assembly, which rent is to be paid to the owner of the land when he is ascertained, the statute of limitations does not run on the claim of the proprietor against the purchaser to recover such rents. Mulliday v. Machir, 45 Va. (4 Gratt.) 1 (1846).

§ **8.01-240. Liens for water, sewer, or sidewalk assessments.** — No suit shall be brought to enforce the lien of any water, sewer, or sidewalk assessment, heretofore or hereafter made, against lands which have been conveyed by the person owning them at the time of such assessment to a grantee for value unless the same be brought within ten years from the due recordation of the deed from such person to grantee and within twenty years from the due docketing of such assessment. (Code 1950, §§ 8-10.1, 8-10.2; 1958, c. 516; 1966, c. 434; 1977, c. 617.)

§ **8.01-241. Limitation of enforcement of deeds of trust, mortgages and liens for unpaid purchase money.** — No deed of trust or mortgage heretofore or hereafter given to secure the payment of money, and no lien heretofore or hereafter reserved to secure the payment of unpaid purchase money, shall be enforced after twenty years from the time when the original obligation last maturing thereby secured shall have become due and payable according to its terms and without regard to any provision for the acceleration of such date; provided that the period of one year from the death of any party in interest shall be excluded from the computation of time. The limitations prescribed by this section may be extended by the recordation of a certificate in the form provided in § 8.01-241.1 prior to the expiration of the limitation period prescribed herein in the clerk's office in which such lien is recorded and executed either by the party in whom the beneficial title to the property so encumbered is vested at the time of such recordation or by his duly authorized attorney-in-fact, or agent. Recordation of the certificate shall extend the limitations of the right to enforce the lien for twenty years from the date of the recordation of the certificate. The clerk of the court shall index the certificate in both names in the index of the deed book and give reference to the book and page in which the original writing is recorded. Unless the deed or deeds executed pursuant to the foreclosure of any mortgage or to the execution of or sale under any deed of trust is recorded in the county or city where the land is situated within one year after the time the right to enforce the mortgage or deed of trust shall have expired as hereinabove provided, such deed or deeds shall be void as to all purchasers for valuable consideration without notice and lien creditors who make any purchase of or acquire any lien on the land conveyed by any such deed prior to the time such deed is so recorded. (Code 1950, § 8-11; 1950, p. 19; 1977, c. 617; 1980, c. 499; 1994, c. 547; 1999, c. 788.)

REVISERS' NOTE

The last sentence of former § 8-11 referring to "glebe lands" has been deleted in § 8.01-241 as no longer necessary.

§ 8.01-241

The 1999 amendment rewrote the second sentence, which formerly read: "The limitations prescribed by this section may be extended by an endorsement to that effect, entered prior to the expiration of the limitation period prescribed herein by the party in whom the beneficial title to the property so encumbered is at the time of such endorsement by the beneficial titleholder or his duly authorized attorney-in-fact, or agent, upon a certificate recorded in the clerk's office in which such lien is recorded."

Law Review. — For article on title examination in Virginia, see 17 U. Rich. L. Rev. 229 (1983).

I. Decisions Under Current Law.
II. Decisions Under Prior Law.

I. DECISIONS UNDER CURRENT LAW.

Demand not barred at law by limitations not barred in equity. — Where a legal demand is asserted in equity which is not barred at law by the applicable statute of limitations, neither is it barred in equity. Thus, given that the statute of limitation for enforcing a deed of trust lien is 20 years, the doctrine of laches will not bar the enforcement of a deed of trust prior to the expiration of the time period. United States v. Lomas Mtg., USA, Inc., 742 F. Supp. 936 (W.D. Va. 1990).

II. DECISIONS UNDER PRIOR LAW.

Editor's note. — The cases cited below were decided under corresponding provisions of former law. The terms "the statute" and "this section," as used below, refer to former provisions.

This section creates an absolute bar to any proceeding for the enforcement of a deed of trust or mortgage after 20 years from the time the right to enforce it accrued. Cohen v. Jenkins, 125 Va. 635, 100 S.E. 678 (1919).

But it does not affect the rule of presumption of payment. — The rule of presumption of payment from lapse of time is not affected by the positive bar of the statute of limitations. Turnbull v. Mann, 99 Va. 41, 37 S.E. 288 (1900).

Institution of suit stops running of statute. — If the suit is instituted before the expiration of the 20-year period, the bar of the statute does not become effective. Anderson v. Biazzi, 166 Va. 309, 186 S.E. 7 (1936).

The legislature, in enacting this section, did not intend, from the language, "No deed of trust or mortgage . . . shall be enforced after 20 years . . .," that a final decree, from which there could be no appeal and under which there must be an irrevocable conveyance of the property to the purchaser, must be entered before the expiration of the 20-year period. The legislature meant by the language used that the institution of a suit to subject the land was the enforcement of the deed of trust or mortgage. Anderson v. Biazzi, 166 Va. 309, 186 S.E. 7 (1936).

Party may be estopped by fraud to plead section. — The defendants were precluded and estopped by their own fraud from relying upon the statute of limitations contained in this section as a bar to the enforcement of a deed of trust. Sadler v. Marsden, 160 Va. 392, 168 S.E. 357 (1933).

The lien of the trust deed was not extended in the manner provided for by this section and so went out of being after 20 years. Since it was not extended, it could not as such thereafter be revived, unless possibly some principle of estoppel can be invoked or some fraud has been practiced. Wilson v. Butt, 168 Va. 259, 190 S.E. 260 (1937).

Action for recovery of money and suit to enforce lien distinguished. — Though an action at law to recover purchase money is barred, a suit in equity to enforce a deed of trust or mortgage is not affected by any time short of that provided in this section. Tunstall v. Withers, 86 Va. 892, 11 S.E. 565 (1890).

That the personal liability of the vendee of real estate for the purchase money has been barred by the statute of limitations does not bar a suit in equity to enforce the lien, provided the latter is brought within the time prescribed by this section. Rector v. Tazewell Coal & Iron Co., 179 Va. 803, 20 S.E.2d 504 (1942).

Provision for extension of lien should be sympathetically considered. — The provision in this section providing that the limitation of 20 years could be extended by an endorsement to that effect entered upon the margin of the deed book on which the same was recorded made certain matters which had been uncertain and should receive sympathetic consideration by the courts. Cunningham v. Williams, 178 Va. 542, 17 S.E.2d 355 (1941).

Extended lien is not subject to intervening rights. — Prior to Acts 1897-98, p. 516, it was possible for parties interested to substitute a new lien for an old one, and a deed of trust or mortgage might be placed upon the same land for the old debt, but the new lien would be subject to such rights of others as might have intervened. Under the present statute, however, there can be no such intervention where the statutory marginal extension is made, as distinguished from the substitution of a new lien for the old. Cunningham v. Williams, 178 Va. 542, 17 S.E.2d 355 (1941).

Provision as to death of party is not

§ 8.01-241.1   CODE OF VIRGINIA   § 8.01-242

retroactive. — The provision of this section excluding a year on the death of a party from the computation of time in estimating the period in which a suit to enforce a deed of trust would be barred, did not affect the period of limitation within which a deed of trust might be enforced, where the obligation secured by such deed of trust matured prior to the adoption of this provision. Boggs v. Fatherly, 177 Va. 259, 13 S.E.2d 298 (1941).

This section has no application where the lien is not a deed of trust or mortgage given to secure the payment of money. Harper v. Harper, 159 Va. 210, 165 S.E. 490 (1932).

§ 8.01-241.1. Permissible form for certificate. — Any extension of the limitations of the right to enforce the lien of a deed of trust or mortgage shall conform substantially with the following form:

CERTIFICATE OF EXTENSION OF LIMITATION OF
RIGHT TO ENFORCE DEED OF TRUST OR MORTGAGE

Place of Record ....
Date of Deed of Trust/Mortgage ....
Deed Book .... Book Page ....
Name of Guarantor(s) ....
Name of Trustee(s) ....
Maker(s) of Note ....
Date of Note(s) ....

I/we, the beneficial title holder(s) of the property encumbered by the above mentioned deed of trust/mortgage, do hereby certify that the lien of the same is hereby extended twenty years from the date of my/our endorsement upon this certificate.

....
Beneficial Titleholder/Attorney-in-Fact/Agent
Commonwealth of Virginia
County/City of .... :
    Subscribed, sworn to and acknowledged before me by
    ...., this .... day of ...., 20 ...
    My Commission expires: ....
    Notary Public
(1994, c. 547.)

§ 8.01-242. Same; when no maturity date is given; credit line deeds of trust. — No deed of trust or mortgage given to secure the payment of money, other than credit line deeds of trust described in § 55-58.2, and no lien reserved to secure the payment of unpaid purchase money, in which no date is fixed for the maturity of the debt secured by such deed of trust, mortgage, or lien, shall be enforced after twenty years from the date of the deed of trust, mortgage, or other lien; provided that the period of one year from the death of any party in interest shall be excluded from the computation of time, and provided further that the limitation may be extended by recordation of a certificate within the twenty-year period in the manner set forth in § 8.01-241. No credit line deed of trust described in § 55-58.2 in which no date is fixed for the maturity of the debt secured thereby shall be enforced after forty years from the date of the credit line deed of trust; provided that the period of one year from the death of any party in interest shall be excluded from the computation of time. (Code 1950, § 8-12; 1977, c. 617; 1994, c. 547; 1999, c. 788.)

The 1999 amendment inserted "other than credit line deeds of trust described in § 55-58.2" near the beginning of the first sentence, and added the second sentence.

I. DECISIONS UNDER CURRENT LAW.

Junior lienor was a party in interest. — Junior lienor, who was the mortgagor of the

§ 8.01-243　　　　CIVIL REMEDIES AND PROCEDURE　　　　§ 8.01-243

property which was the subject of the foreclosure and the holder of a second deed of trust which secured his note, was a necessary party, as well as a party in interest to foreclosure suit for the purposes of this section; therefore, his death extended the statute of limitations by one year, as provided in this section. Allen v. Chapman, 242 Va. 94, 406 S.E.2d 186 (1991).

ARTICLE 3.

Personal Actions Generally.

§ 8.01-243. Personal action for injury to person or property generally; extension in actions for malpractice against health care provider. — A. Unless otherwise provided in this section or by other statute, every action for personal injuries, whatever the theory of recovery, and every action for damages resulting from fraud, shall be brought within two years after the cause of action accrues.

B. Every action for injury to property, including actions by a parent or guardian of an infant against a tort-feasor for expenses of curing or attempting to cure such infant from the result of a personal injury or loss of services of such infant, shall be brought within five years after the cause of action accrues.

C. The two-year limitations period specified in subsection A shall be extended in actions for malpractice against a health care provider as follows:

1. In cases arising out of a foreign object having no therapeutic or diagnostic effect being left in a patient's body, for a period of one year from the date the object is discovered or reasonably should have been discovered; and

2. In cases in which fraud, concealment or intentional misrepresentation prevented discovery of the injury within the two-year period, for one year from the date the injury is discovered or, by the exercise of due diligence, reasonably should have been discovered.

However, the provisions of this subsection shall not apply to extend the limitations period beyond ten years from the date the cause of action accrues, except that the provisions of § 8.01-229 A 2 shall apply to toll the statute of limitations in actions brought by or on behalf of a person under a disability. (Code 1950, § 8-24; 1954, c. 589; 1973, c. 385; 1977, c. 617; 1986, cc. 389, 454; 1987, cc. 294, 645, 679.)

REVISERS' NOTE

Subsection A is substantially the first sentence of former § 8-24. Subsection B takes the 5-year limitation of the second sentence of former § 8-24 and applies it to all tort actions for injury to property. This includes a parent's action for expenses or loss of services of an infant. See Moses v. Akers, 203 Va. 130, 122 S.E.2d 864 (1961); Watson v. Daniel, 165 Va. 564, 183 S.E. 183 (1936); Cf. § 8.01-36. The one-year limitation in former § 8-24 for certain tort actions involving injury to property has been eliminated. See Revisers' note to § 8.01-25.

The section does not apply to claims for injuries to property resulting from breach of contract. See, e.g., § 8.01-246.

Cross references. — As to the survival of actions, see §§ 8.01-25 and 8.01-56. As to limitation of action for unauthorized use of name or picture, see § 8.01-40. As to actions for death by wrongful act, see § 8.01-50 et seq. As to tolling or suspension of statute of limitations generally, see § 8.01-229. As to actions for medical malpractice on behalf of a person who was a minor at the time of accrual of the cause of action, see § 8.01-243.1. As to action for carrying away goods, committing waste or damaging an estate of decedents, see § 64.1-145.

Law Review. — For survey of Virginia law on torts for the year 1967-1968, see 54 Va. L. Rev. 1649 (1968). For survey of Virginia law on torts for the year 1970-1971, see 57 Va. L. Rev. 1501 (1971). For survey of Virginia law on insurance for the year 1970-1971, see 57 Va. L. Rev. 1608 (1971). For survey of Virginia law on torts for the year 1972-1973, see 59 Va. L. Rev. 1590 (1973). For note discussing a state-incarcerated felon's capacity to sue under 42 U.S.C.

§ 1983 in federal courts despite prohibitive state statutes, see 30 Wash. & Lee L. Rev. 329 (1973). For survey of Virginia developments in constitutional law for the year 1974-1975, see 61 Va. L. Rev. 1677 (1975). For survey of Virginia law on practice and pleading for the year 1974-1975, see 61 Va. L. Rev. 1799 (1975). For survey of Virginia practice and pleading for the year 1975-1976, see 62 Va. L. Rev. 1460 (1976). For survey of Virginia law on practice and pleading for the year 1976-77, see 63 Va. L. Rev. 1459 (1977). For comment,"Toward a Uniform State Product Liability Law — Virginia and the Uniform Product Liability Act," see 36 Wash. & Lee L. Rev. 1145 (1979). For note, "Virginia Should Adopt Strict Tort Recovery in Products Liability Suits Involving Personal Injury," see 14 U. Rich. L. Rev. 391 (1980). For survey of Virginia law on practice and pleading for the year 1978-1979, see 66 Va. L. Rev. 343 (1980). For article discussing statutes of limitation and repose in toxic substances litigation, see 16 U. Rich. L. Rev. 247 (1982). For article, "Products Liability and the Virginia Statute of Limitations — A Call for the Legislative Rescue Squad," see 16 U. Rich. L. Rev. 323 (1982). For comment on statutes of limitations applicable in legal malpractice actions, see 16 U. Rich. L. Rev. 907 (1982). For comment, "Statutes of Limitations in Occupational Disease Cases: Is Locke v. Johns-Manville a Viable Alternative to the Discovery Rule?," see 39 Wash. & Lee L. Rev. 263 (1982). For article, "Virginia's Statute of Limitations for Section 1983 Claims After Wilson v. Garcia," see 19 U. Rich. L. Rev. 257 (1985). For article, "Civil Rights and 'Personal Injuries': Virginia's Statute of Limitations for Section 1983 Suits," see 26 Wm. & Mary L. Rev. 199 (1985). For note on a suggested remedy for toxic injury: Class actions, epidemiology, and economic efficiency, see 26 Wm. & Mary L. Rev. 497 (1985). For 1987 survey of Virginia civil procedure and practice, see 21 U. Rich. L. Rev. 667 (1987). For survey on medical malpractice in Virginia for 1989, see 23 U. Rich. L. Rev. 731 (1989). For an article, "Civil Practice and Procedure," see 32 U. Rich. L. Rev. 1009 (1998). For an article on federal product liability reform legislation's consistency with Virginia law, see 4 Geo. Mason L. Rev. 279 (1996).

I. Decisions Under Current Law.
   A. General Consideration.
   B. Proceedings to Which Section Applicable.
      1. In General.
      2. Personal Injuries.
      3. Civil Rights Actions.
      4. Wrongs Affecting Property and Property Rights.
   C. Effect of Running of Statute.
   D. Asbestos Injuries.
II. Decisions Under Prior Law.
   A. General Consideration.
   B. Proceedings to Which This Section Applicable.
      1. In General.
      2. Personal Injuries.
      3. Civil Rights Actions.
      4. Wrongs Affecting Property and Property Rights.
         a. Injuries to Property.
         b. Actions to Recover Personal Property.
         c. Breach of Duty.
         d. Liability Imposed by Statute.
   C. Effect of Running of Statute.
   D. Pleading and Practice.

I. DECISIONS UNDER CURRENT LAW.

A. General Consideration.

Purpose. — Statutes of limitation are designed to compel the prompt assertion of an accrued right of action; not to bar such a right before it has accrued. Locke v. Johns-Manville Corp., 221 Va. 951, 275 S.E.2d 900 (1981).

Virginia's statute of limitations for fraud most closely resembles the federal policies reflected in the Lanham Act of prohibiting fraudulent advertising and addressing claims of deception and misrepresentation, constituting trademark infringement and unfair competition. Unlimited Screw Prods., Inc. v. Malm, 781 F. Supp. 1121 (E.D. Va. 1991).

Statute is procedural rather than substantive. — The Virginia two-year personal injury statute of limitations, unlike the two-year wrongful death statute of limitations, is procedural rather than substantive. Riddle v. Shell Oil Co., 764 F. Supp. 418 (W.D. Va. 1990).

Under the new statutory scheme, survivability no longer is germane in determining which statute of limitations applies. Section 8.01-25 provides that all causes of action survive the death of the plaintiff or defendant. Moreover, the problem of determining direct or indirect injury has been eliminated. Section 64.1-145 now provides, in part, that: "Any action at law for damages for the ... destruction of, or damage to any estate of or by the decedent, whether such damage be direct or indirect, may be maintained by or against the decedent's personal representative. Any such action shall survive pursuant to § 8.01-25." Now, under the straightforward provisions of subsection B of this section, "[e]very" action for "injury to property" is governed by a five-year statute of limitations. Pigott v. Moran, 231 Va. 76, 341 S.E.2d 179 (1986).

"Injury." — In applying subsection A of this section, the Virginia Supreme Court interprets "injury" in the same manner as that word is construed to determine when a cause of action for personal injuries accrues: a positive, physical or mental hurt to the claimant. Purcell v. Tidewater Constr. Corp., 250 Va. 93, 458 S.E.2d 291 (1995).

Continuing treatment rule. — The rule of decision in Farley v. Goode, 219 Va. 969, 252 S.E.2d 594 (1979) and Fenton v. Danaceau, 220 Va. 1, 255 S.E.2d 349 (1979) was not that the negligence of the defendant physician extended until the physician-patient relationship ended. Instead, the rule of decision was that if there existed a physician-patient relationship where the patient was treated for the same or related ailments over a continuous and uninterrupted course, then the plaintiff could wait until the end of that treatment to complain of any negligence which occurred during that treatment. Thus, within the confines of Farley, Fenton, and this opinion, Virginia has a true continuing treatment rule. Grubbs v. Rawls, 235 Va. 607, 369 S.E.2d 683 (1988).

Plaintiff substantially interrupted her physician-patient relationship with the defendant when she sought treatment and examination for her condition from another physician and broke the continuity of her treatment by the defendant; thus she could not claim the benefit of the continuous treatment rule, even though she later returned to the defendant for treatment of the same condition. Bennett v. Clark, 69 F. Supp. 2d 809 (E.D. Va. 1999).

Doctrine of equitable estoppel. — Assuming that on the summary judgment record the undisputed evidence reveals no conduct amounting to fraud, this does not entitle defendant to judgment as a matter of law, since under Virginia law, one may be estopped to plead the bar of a statute of limitations by conduct short of fraud, under the general doctrine of equitable estoppel. Under that doctrine, estoppel occurs where the aggrieved party reasonably relied on the words and conduct of the person to be estopped in allowing the limitations period to expire. Barry v. Donnelly, 781 F.2d 1040 (4th Cir. 1986).

With the exception of actions based on federally created rights, the Virginia Supreme Court has not applied subsection A of this section to a cause of action which did not involve either mental or physical injury to the body. Purcell v. Tidewater Constr. Corp., 250 Va. 93, 458 S.E.2d 291 (1995).

Federal court did not create statute of limitations in Oman v. Johns-Manville Corp., 764 F.2d 224 (4th Cir.), cert. denied, 474 U.S. 970, 106 S. Ct. 351, 88 L. Ed. 2d 319 (1985), but narrowed the scope of admiralty jurisdiction such that Virginia's preexisting statute of limitations, this section, now controls. Grimes v. Owens-Corning Fiberglass Corp., 843 F.2d 815 (4th Cir.), cert. denied, 488 U.S. 889, 109 S. Ct. 221, 102 L. Ed. 2d 211 (1988).

Applied in Lykins v. Attorney Gen. of United States, 86 F.R.D. 318 (E.D. Va. 1980); Hupman v. Cook, 640 F.2d 497 (4th Cir. 1981); Cramer v. Crutchfield, 648 F.2d 943 (4th Cir. 1981); West v. ITT Continental Baking Co., 683 F.2d 845 (4th Cir. 1982); Truman v. Spivey, 225 Va. 274, 302 S.E.2d 517 (1983); Baker v. Zirkle, 226 Va. 7, 307 S.E.2d 234 (1983); Dye v. Staley, 226 Va. 15, 307 S.E.2d 237 (1983); Large v. Bucyrus-Erie Co., 707 F.2d 94 (4th Cir. 1983); Blanck v. McKeen, 707 F.2d 817 (4th Cir. 1983); Scoggins v. Douglas, 760 F.2d 535 (4th Cir. 1985); Gwin v. Graves, 230 Va. 34, 334 S.E.2d 294 (1985); Hogan v. Brotherhood of Ry., Airline & S.S. Clerks, 629 F. Supp. 1166 (W.D. Va. 1986); Stone v. Ethan Allen, Inc., 232 Va. 365, 350 S.E.2d 629 (1986); LaVay Corp. v. Dominion Fed. Sav. & Loan Ass'n, 830 F.2d 522 (4th Cir. 1987); Luddeke v. Amana Refrigeration, Inc., 239 Va. 203, 387 S.E.2d 502 (1990); Vines v. Branch, 244 Va. 185, 418 S.E.2d 890 (1992); Starnes v. Cayouette, 244 Va. 202, 419 S.E.2d 669 (1992); Harris v. DiMattina, 250 Va. 306, 462 S.E.2d 338 (1995); Luczkovich v. Melville Corp., 911 F. Supp. 208 (E.D. Va. 1996); Osborne v. Rose, 954 F. Supp. 1142 (W.D. Va. 1997); Douglas v. Dabney S. Lancaster Community College, 990 F. Supp. 447 (W.D. Va. 1997); Byelick v. Vivadelli, 79 F. Supp. 2d 610 (E.D. Va. 1999).

B. Proceedings to Which Section Applicable.

1. In General.

Object of litigation, not form of suit, governs. — It is the object of litigation which determines the applicability of a statute of limitations, not the form in which the suit is instituted. Chesapeake Bay Found., Inc. v. Virginia State Water Control Bd., 501 F. Supp. 821 (E.D. Va. 1980).

For purposes of statute of limitations, there is but a single, indivisible cause of action for all injuries sustained, whether or not all of the damage is immediately apparent. Joyce v. A.C. & S., Inc., 785 F.2d 1200 (4th Cir. 1986).

The statute of limitations does not accrue separately for each set of damages which results from a wrongful act. Once a cause of action is complete and the statute of limitations begins to run, it runs against all damages resulting from the wrongful act, even damages which may not arise until a future date. Brown v. ABC, 704 F.2d 1296 (4th Cir. 1983).

In Virginia, a statute of limitations does not accrue separately for each set of damages resulting from a wrongful act. The statute of limitations runs against all damages, including damages that do not arise until a future date. Granahan v. Pearson, 782 F.2d 30 (4th Cir. 1985).

Third-party plaintiff claim. — "Because of the bar of the statute of limitations, the injured person did not have an enforceable cause of action against the party from whom contribution is sought" and, therefore, third-party plaintiff was similarly barred in his claim against third-party defendant. Smith-Moore Body Co. v. Heil Co., 603 F. Supp. 354 (E.D. Va. 1985).

Tolling provision for minor's claim inapplicable to parent's claim. — The statute of limitations tolling provision for a minor's claim does not apply to a parent's claim for medical expenses and emotional distress stemming from the same incident of alleged malpractice; the parent's claims are subject to the limitation period of subsection (B). Perez ex rel. Perez v. Espinola, 749 F. Supp. 732 (E.D. Va. 1990).

Maritime torts. — When general maritime claims are at issue, the equity rule of laches, rather than any rigid statute of limitations, governs. Moore v. Exxon Transp. Co., 502 F. Supp. 583 (E.D. Va. 1980).

Wrongful discharge. — The one-year statute of limitations under this section applied to plaintiff's wrongful discharge claims, regardless of the fact that plaintiffs alleged in two counts that the wrongful discharge caused damages in the form of emotional and physical harm. Michael v. Sentara Health Sys., 939 F. Supp. 1220 (E.D. Va. 1996).

Where plaintiffs argued that the two-year statute of limitations applied to their claims because the two-year statute of limitations for personal injury suits was applicable for causes of action based on federally created rights, the two counts in question were claims for wrongful discharge, not for breach of contract, personal injury, or violation of any federal statute. Thus, the exception for claims dependent upon "federally created rights" did not help plaintiffs. Michael v. Sentara Health Sys., 939 F. Supp. 1220 (E.D. Va. 1996).

Wrongful termination. — Where suit for wrongful termination was not a suit for a "positive, physical or mental hurt" and plaintiff advanced no other applicable limitation period, cause of action for wrongful termination was subject to the limitation period established in § 8.01-248. Purcell v. Tidewater Constr. Corp., 250 Va. 93, 458 S.E.2d 291 (1995).

Section not applicable to private actions under federal securities law. — The two-year limitations period of the Virginia "blue sky law," rather than the five-year limitation of subsection B of this section, applies to private actions under § 10(b) of the Securities Exchange Act of 1934, § 10(b), 15 U.S.C. § 78j(b) because the "blue sky law" addresses the problem of misinformation in securities transactions, the policy concern of § 10(b). Gurley v. Documation, Inc., 674 F.2d 253 (4th Cir. 1982).

2. Personal Injuries.

Editor's note. — Some of the cases below were decided prior to the 1986 amendment to this section, which added subsection C.

Action for all damages resulting from tortious conduct must be brought within two years of the time in which competent medical evidence can pinpoint when the plaintiff was hurt. Joyce v. A.C. & S., Inc., 591 F. Supp. 449 (W.D. Va. 1984), aff'd, 785 F.2d 1200 (4th Cir. 1986).

Date on which statute of limitations begins to run is the date when the injury is received, notwithstanding that the plaintiff may sustain more substantial injuries at a later date. Wade v. Danek Medical Inc., 5 F. Supp. 2d 379 (E.D. Va. 1998), aff'd, 182 F.3d 281 (4th Cir. 1999).

The limitations period begins to run when the injury, no matter how slight, is sustained and regardless of whether more substantial injuries occur later, it is immaterial that all injuries may not have occurred at the time of the initial negligent act; the running of the statute is not postponed by later additional injury. Smith v. Danek Med., Inc., 47 F. Supp. 2d 698 (W.D. Va. 1998).

Virginia does not follow a discovery rule in applying the statute of limitations; the statute of limitations begins to run at the date of the injury, even if no diagnosis was made or communicated to the plaintiff until later. Smith v. Danek Med., Inc., 47 F. Supp. 2d 698 (W.D. Va. 1998).

Virginia law does not calculate statute of limitations in personal injury from the date of diagnosis. Wade v. Danek Medical Inc., 5 F. Supp. 2d 379 (E.D. Va. 1998), aff'd, 182 F.3d 281 (4th Cir. 1999).

"Completion" of injuries. — Where the plaintiff's injuries are "complete" more than two years before suit, the action is untimely. Large v. Bucyrus-Erie Co., 524 F. Supp. 285

(E.D. Va. 1981), aff'd, 707 F.2d 94 (4th Cir. 1983).

The statute of limitations cannot begin to run against a claim until all the elements of the cause of action exist and that one of the essential elements of a cause of action for personal injury is the injury itself. Brown v. ABC, 704 F.2d 1296 (4th Cir. 1983).

Unlawful searches and seizures. — Under Virginia law, an unlawful search and seizure is characterized as a personal injury, not an injury to property; thus the applicable statute of limitations is two years under this section. Samuel v. Rose's Stores, Inc., 907 F. Supp. 159 (E.D. Va. 1995).

False imprisonment cases. — The applicable statute of limitations for a claim of false imprisonment, recognized as a personal injury, is two years. Samuel v. Rose's Stores, Inc., 907 F. Supp. 159 (E.D. Va. 1995).

False imprisonment is a tort committed against an individual's body because that individual's body is actually confined to an area and deprived of physical liberty; accordingly, an action for false imprisonment is an action for personal injuries and, thus, subject to the two-year statute of limitations. Jordan v. Shands, 255 Va. 492, 500 S.E.2d 215 (1998).

Break of fiduciary duty claims. — The one-year personal, not the five-year property, statute of limitations is most appropriate for a breach of fiduciary duty cause of action. FDIC v. Cocke, 7 F.3d 396 (4th Cir. 1993), cert. denied, 513 U.S. 807, 115 S. Ct. 53, 130 L. Ed. 2d 12 (1994).

Breach of duty of confidentiality. — Since the breach of the duty of confidentiality is a personal injury and no other statute provides an alternate limitations period, such an action must be brought within two years from the date the cause of action accrued. Bullion v. Gadaleto, 872 F. Supp. 303 (W.D. Va. 1995).

Products liability cases. — Actions under state law grounded in a personal injury-products liability factual pattern are governed by the torts statute, which runs from the time of injury. Bly v. Otis Elevator Co., 713 F.2d 1040 (4th Cir. 1983), modified on reh'g en banc, 754 F.2d 1111 (4th Cir. 1985).

Where it was undisputed that plaintiff was "hurt" as early as 1970 with asbestos-related injury, his suit, brought in 1983, for any and all asbestos-related injuries was barred by this section. Joyce v. A.C. & S., Inc., 591 F. Supp. 449 (W.D. Va. 1984), aff'd, 785 F.2d 1200 (4th Cir. 1986).

Medical malpractice. — Summary judgment was erroneously awarded to defendant in a medical malpractice suit where plaintiff's allegations as to when injury occurred could have been properly construed so as to fall within the two-year statute of limitations. Renner v. Stafford, 245 Va. 351, 429 S.E.2d 218 (1993).

Action for medical malpractice occurring during continuous and uninterrupted course of treatment. — When medical malpractice is claimed to have occurred during a continuous and substantially uninterrupted course of examination and treatment in which a particular illness or condition should have been diagnosed in the exercise of reasonable care, the date of injury occurs, the cause of action for that malpractice accrues, and the statute of limitations commences to run when the improper course of examination, and treatment if any, for the particular malady terminates. Farley v. Goode, 219 Va. 969, 252 S.E.2d 594 (1979); Large v. Bucyrus-Erie Co., 524 F. Supp. 285 (E.D. Va. 1981), aff'd, 707 F.2d 94 (4th Cir. 1983).

An obstetrician's negligent failure to properly execute a laparoscopic tubal cauterization on a patient commences the two-year statute of limitations under this section. This statute does not begin anew when the patient later learns that she is pregnant. Irvin v. Burton, 635 F. Supp. 366 (W.D. Va. 1986).

Claim of patient who alleged that her doctor's failure to remove intrauterine device caused her to become infertile was barred by the two-year statute of limitations, since the statute of limitations began to run from the moment a plaintiff suffered an injury, she was injured when the intrauterine device was allowed to remain in her body, her malpractice claim accrued when her relationship with her doctor ended in 1979, and her malpractice suit commenced in Feb. 1984. Granahan v. Pearson, 782 F.2d 30 (4th Cir. 1985).

Wrongful conception. — Even though a legal wrong may have occurred in 1989 when the defendants performed the negligent sterilization procedure on plaintiff, no injury under the Locke v. Johns-Manville Corp, 221 Va. 951, 275 S.E. 2d 900 (1981) accrual rule occurred at that time because plaintiff had suffered no "positive, physical or mental hurt" related to her alleged cause of action, wrongful conception. Nunnally v. Artis, 254 Va. 247, 492 S.E.2d 126 (1997).

Parents' claim to recover medical expenses they incurred as a result of the wrongful birth caused by the physicians' alleged negligent failure to inform them of the fetus' anomalies was governed by the two-year statute of limitations, instead of five-year statute of limitations because they did not plead and did not have an action for injury to property, rather, they pled that as parents, they were deprived of an informed opportunity to terminate the pregnancy, and thus, their cause of action was personal in nature. Glascock v. Laserna, 247 Va. 208, 439 S.E.2d 380 (1994).

Parents could not recover damages for loss of services based upon allegations of wrongful birth because the basis of their claim was that they were deprived of an informed opportunity to terminate the pregnancy instead of allegations that physicians caused "personal injury" to their child. Glascock v. Laserna, 247 Va. 208, 439 S.E.2d 380 (1994).

A parent's claim for medical expenses is not derivative of her child's claim for personal injury for statute of limitations purposes. Kerstetter v. United States, 57 F.3d 362 (4th Cir. 1995).

And the extinction by reason of the statute of limitations of a child's claim for personal injury does not itself extinguish her parent's cause of action for medical expenses. Kerstetter v. United States, 57 F.3d 362 (4th Cir. 1995).

Rule presupposes proof as fact of continuous and uninterrupted treatment. — The rule that when medical malpractice is claimed to have occurred during a continuous and substantially uninterrupted course of treatment and examination in which a particular illness or condition should have been diagnosed in the exercise of reasonable care, the statute of limitations commences to run when the course of treatment and examination terminates, presupposes that a continuous course of improper examination or treatment which is substantially uninterrupted is proved as a matter of fact. When the malpractice complained of constitutes a single isolated act, however, the statute of limitations commences to run from the date of the injury. Farley v. Goode, 219 Va. 969, 252 S.E.2d 594 (1979).

Racial discrimination suits under 42 U.S.C. § 2000a. — The two-year period of limitations for personal injuries applies to a suit alleging racial discrimination in violation of Title II of the Civil Rights Act of 1964, 42 U.S.C. § 2000a. Brown v. Loudoun Golf & Country Club, Inc., 573 F. Supp. 399 (E.D. Va. 1983).

Two-year period of limitations barred plaintiff's claims that he was injured from each exposure to paint products, prior to two years before filing his suit, but plaintiff's claims of injuries, that occcurred within the two years of suit, for which he went to the emergency room, were not barred. Williams v. E.I. DuPont de Nemours & Co., 11 F.3d 464 (4th Cir. 1993).

Unlawful search and seizure is characterized as a personal injury, rather than an injury to property and the applicable statute of limitations provision is contained in subsection A which sets a two-year time limit for filing an action. Cramer v. Crutchfield, 496 F. Supp. 949 (E.D. Va. 1980), aff'd, 648 F.2d 943 (4th Cir. 1981).

Cause of action for emotional distress against a party over its interference with plaintiff's right to collect unemployment compensation, is governed by the two-year statute of limitations governing actions for personal injury. Welch v. Kennedy Piggly Wiggly Stores, Inc., 63 Bankr. 888 (W.D. Va. 1986).

Right of action for contribution arises upon discharge of common obligation. — Before contribution will lie it is essential that a cause of action by the person injured have existed against the third-party defendant. But if such cause of action existed, the right of action to recover contribution arises upon discharge of the common obligation and the statute of limitations begins to run at that time. In order for contribution to lie, the injured party's cause of action against the third-party defendant need not be presently enforceable; it merely is necessary that the plaintiff, at some time in the past, have had an enforceable cause of action against the party from whom contribution is sought. Gemco-Ware, Inc. v. Rongene Mold & Plastics Corp., 234 Va. 54, 360 S.E.2d 342 (1987).

Where plaintiff was treated jointly by two doctors for a stomach ailment and her condition worsened, plaintiff was entitled to wait until the doctors terminated their treatment before the statute of limitation began to run. Grubbs v. Rawls, 235 Va. 607, 369 S.E.2d 683 (1988).

3. Civil Rights Actions.

Applicable to all civil rights actions, etc. — The two-year statute of limitations provided in this section would be applicable to a former railroad brakeman's cause of action brought under the section of the Civil Rights Act providing for civil action for deprivation of rights and providing for equal rights under the law for all persons within the jurisdiction of the United States. Steward v. Norfolk, F. & D. Ry., 486 F. Supp. 744 (E.D. Va. 1980), aff'd, 661 F.2d 927 (4th Cir. 1981).

State statute of limitations for personal injury actions usually determines timeliness. — The Reconstruction Civil Rights Acts create causes of action where there has been injury, under color of state law, to the person or to the constitutional or federal statutory rights which emanate from or are guaranteed to the person. As a consequence, it is the state statute of limitations for personal injuries which is usually looked to in determining when claims are time-barred. United Steelworkers v. Dalton, 544 F. Supp. 291 (E.D. Va. 1982).

This section applies to actions under 42 U.S.C. § 1981. White v. City of Suffolk, 460 F. Supp. 516 (E.D. Va. 1978).

But the local statute of limitations is not applicable when continuous discrimination, rather than a single discriminatory act, is alleged. White v. City of Suffolk, 460 F.

Supp. 516 (E.D. Va. 1978).

In 42 U.S.C. § 1983 actions, statutes of limitations are borrowed from state law. United Steelworkers v. Dalton, 544 F. Supp. 291 (E.D. Va. 1982).

Suits brought pursuant to 42 U.S.C. §§ 1983 and 1985, are governed by this section. Buntin v. Board of Trustees, 548 F. Supp. 657 (W.D. Va. 1982).

Federal law fixes time right of action accrues. — In actions under 42 U.S.C. §§ 1983 and 1985, while the time limitation itself is borrowed from state law, the federal rule fixes the time of accrual of a right of action. Buntin v. Board of Trustees, 548 F. Supp. 657 (W.D. Va. 1982).

Inmate section 1983 actions. — In Virginia § 1983 cases, if an inmate has not delivered his complaint to prison officials for mailing within the two-year period following the time when he knew or had reason to know of his alleged injury, the Virginia statute of limitations bars that inmate from bringing suit about the injury. In this case, since no certificate of mailing accompanied inmate's complaint, the time of filing was the date at which the action was deemed to have commenced for statute of limitation purposes. Garrett v. Angelone, 940 F. Supp. 933 (W.D. Va. 1996), aff'd, 107 F.3d 865 (4th Cir. 1997).

Inmate was barred from obtaining monetary damages or injunctive relief under § 1983 for claims of which he knew or had reason to know before September 14, 1993. Inmate's filing of earlier discrimination action indicated that he knew or should have known the facts necessary to bring a discrimination claim about events occurring in 1991 through 1993. Garrett v. Angelone, 940 F. Supp. 933 (W.D. Va. 1996), aff'd, 107 F.3d 865 (4th Cir. 1997).

Action against prison employees. — In an action brought pursuant to 42 U.S.C. § 1983 against three former employees of the United States Bureau of Prisons at Petersburg Federal Correctional Institute alleging that they failed to provide plaintiff with a secure and safe place of confinement while he was incarcerated, Virginia law applied to toll the running of the statute of limitations where the plaintiff's action would have been barred but for the fact that the plaintiff previously had filed a pro se action. Clymer v. Grzegorek, 515 F. Supp. 938 (E.D. Va. 1981).

Nonrenewal of teaching contract. — A federal civil rights action which claimed that a state medical school violated an employee's due process rights by not renewing her teaching contract, in violation of alleged lifetime tenure property rights, filed some six years after the action accrued, i.e., after the employee learned that her employer retained its faculty exclusively under contracts of various lengths and that there was no lifetime tenure, was time barred, notwithstanding the fact that she did not receive her nonrenewal notice until some two years prior to the filing of her action. Sabet v. Eastern Va. Medical Auth., 611 F. Supp. 388 (E.D. Va.), aff'd, 775 F.2d 1266 (4th Cir. 1985).

Allegedly improper salary differential was continuing conduct. — Action under 42 U.S.C. §§ 1983 and 1985, alleging that salary differential paid to state troopers in Division Seven but not paid to troopers in Division Four was arbitrary and unconstitutional, was not barred by this section, although plaintiffs first became aware of the differential in 1974, since the conduct alleged to be wrongful was continuing in nature. Eldridge v. Bouchard, 620 F. Supp. 678 (W.D. Va. 1985).

As to U.S. Supreme Court decision that the limitations period for civil RICO actions is the four-year federal statute of limitations applicable to Clayton Act actions, see Agency Holding Corp. v. Malley-Duff & Assocs., 483 U.S. 143, 107 S. Ct. 2759, 97 L. Ed. 2d 121 (1987).

4. Wrongs Affecting Property and Property Rights.

Five-year limitation applicable where focus on injury to property. — Where an action seems to have as its focus not relief from injury to the plaintiffs' persons, but to their property, it is thus subject to a five-year limitation under this section. Chesapeake Bay Found., Inc. v. Virginia State Water Control Bd., 501 F. Supp. 821 (E.D. Va. 1980); Adams v. Star Enters., 851 F. Supp. 770 (E.D. Va. 1994), aff'd, 51 F.3d 417 (4th Cir. 1995).

Plaintiff is entitled to the five-year statute of limitations provided for by subsection B for both its common law fraud and fraud under Racketeer-Influenced and Corrupt Organization Act claims for damage to its business property. Bush Dev. Corp. v. Harbour Place Assocs., 632 F. Supp. 1359 (E.D. Va. 1986).

This section is applicable only where injury to property is direct and immediate result of wrongful conduct. Where the injury to property is an indirect or consequential injury resulting from a direct injury to the person, the one or two-year statute of limitations for personal injury applies. Brown v. ABC, 704 F.2d 1296 (4th Cir. 1983).

The Virginia Supreme Court has been extremely technical in its determination of whether the damage for which a plaintiff seeks to recover is a direct injury to property and thereby qualifies for the benefit of the five-year statute of limitations. In order for the five-year statute to apply, the following facts, among other things, must be found: (1) the injury must be against and affect directly the plaintiff's property, (2) the plaintiff must sue only for the direct injury, and (3) the injury, to qualify as a direct injury, must be the very first injury which results from the wrongful act. Brown v. ABC, 704 F.2d 1296 (4th Cir. 1983).

Tortious interference causing breach or termination of relationship. — Claim of tortious interference against an intervening party that induces or causes a breach or termination of a relationship or expectancy between other parties is governed by the five-year statute of limitations for actions for injury to property. Welch v. Kennedy Piggly Wiggly Stores, Inc., 63 Bankr. 888 (W.D. Va. 1986).

Slander of title. — The fact that plaintiff instituted an action for slander of title approximately five and one-half years after the filing of defendants' memorandum of lis pendens was not dispositive of her claim for slander of title, since her cause of action did not fully accrue and the limitations period did not begin to run until the defendants released their claim against her property. Since plaintiff filed her action within one year of this release, she was held not to be barred by application of Virginia's statute of limitations for defamation actions (§ 8.01-248), much less its limitations period of injury to property (this section), the court finding it unnecessary to decide the issue of the applicable limitations period. Warren v. Bank of Marion, 618 F. Supp. 317 (W.D. Va. 1985).

Realtor's fraud not action for injury to property. — The fraud allegedly committed by the realtor had no impact on the real property itself. The purchasers' land was in the same condition and was available for the same use after the alleged fraud as it was before. The defendants' conduct was directed at the plaintiffs personally and not their property, real or personal. Consequently, the trial court correctly decided the one-year limitation governs an action for fraud. Pigott v. Moran, 231 Va. 76, 341 S.E.2d 179 (1986).

A claim for the wrongful act resulting in the alleged diminution in value of the purchasers' property because it abutted land zoned for industrial rather than residential uses, was not an action for "injury to property" within the meaning of subsection B. Pigott v. Moran, 231 Va. 76, 341 S.E.2d 179 (1986).

Fraud is a tort. The wrongful act is aimed at the person and, when sued upon at law, fraud will support a recovery for financial damage personal to the individual. Pigott v. Moran, 231 Va. 76, 341 S.E.2d 179 (1986).

Constructive trusts. — The applicability of this statute to cases asserting a constructive trust is a settled matter of law in Virginia. Brown v. Goldstein (In re Johnson), 80 Bankr. 791 (Bankr. E.D. Va. 1987), aff'd, 960 F.2d 396 (4th Cir. 1992).

Action for conversion against bank. — Five-year limitation period found in subsection B of this section applied to an action for conversion against a bank; two-year period in subsection A of this section was not applicable, nor was the one-year period found in § 8.01-248. Bader v. Central Fid. Bank, 245 Va. 286, 427 S.E.2d 184 (1993).

Action by purchaser against manufacturer of a tank trailer for consequential damages suffered when it overturned, spilling its cargo, was required to be brought within five years of the date of purchase. Burke-Parsons-Bowlby Corp. v. E.D. Etnyre & Co., 585 F. Supp. 620 (W.D. Va. 1984).

Five-year limitation not applicable to RICO action. — Virginia's five-year limitations period, subsection B, for injury to property does not apply to a civil racketeer influenced and corrupt organizations (RICO) action under 18 U.S.C. § 1961 et seq., since such injury is not the distinguishing aspect of RICO. RICO's central feature is not injury to property, but personal liability so to eliminate the effects of organized crime on legitimate business. HMK Corp. v. Walsey, 637 F. Supp. 710 (E.D. Va. 1986), aff'd, 828 F.2d 1071 (4th Cir. 1987), cert. denied, 484 U.S. 1009, 108 S. Ct. 706, 98 L. Ed. 2d 657 (1988).

Landowner was entitled to seek recovery for damage to his property caused by each discharge of sewage. Each discharge was a separate actionable event for which the landowner was entitled to seek recovery during the five years preceding the filing of suit. Cause of action did not accrue when bypasses from the pump station began. Hampton Rds. San. Dist. v. McDonnell, 234 Va. 235, 360 S.E.2d 841 (1987).

Where the original discharge of sewage onto owner's property did not produce all the damage to the property and the discharges were not continuous, instead, they occurred only at intervals, each discharge inflicted a new injury for which the owner had a separate cause of action. Hampton Rds. San. Dist. v. McDonnell, 234 Va. 235, 360 S.E.2d 841 (1987).

Appropriation of individual's name or likeness. — Subsection A of § 8.01-40 is aimed at preventing the appropriation, without consent, of an individual's name or likeness while he is alive and for 20 years after he dies. It creates in an individual a species of property right in their name and likeness. Consequently, the limitation period contained in subsection B of this section should be applied. Lavery v. Automation Mgt. Consultants, Inc., 234 Va. 145, 360 S.E.2d 336 (1987).

Lender's fraud not action for injury to property. — Where plaintiff alleged that they were fraudulently induced to convey to lenders security interest in both corporate and individual assets, which they subsequently lost entirely through foreclosure and repossession, and where plaintiffs, suffered loss of all use, enjoyment and value in their property by reason of alleged fraud, allegedly wrongful acts were aimed at persons of plaintiffs, rather than injuring their property since property had same form, same value, and was adapted to same uses after defendants' actions as before; therefore, statute of limitations for personal injury rather than injury to property was appropriate. J.F. Toner & Son, Inc. v. Staunton Prod. Credit Ass'n, 237 Va. 155, 375 S.E.2d 530 (1989).

Actions for legal malpractice governed by limitation periods applicable to actions for breach of contract, thus, the trial court correctly applied the three-year limitation because the bill of complaint did not allege that the contract between attorney and client was in writing. MacLellan v. Throckmorton, 235 Va. 341, 367 S.E.2d 720 (1988).

Claim for medical expenses not tolled by § 8.01-229(A). — A parent's claim for medical expenses under subsection (B) is not tolled by the provisions of § 8.01-229(A). Hutto v. BIC Corp., 800 F. Supp. 1367 (E.D. Va. 1992).

C. Effect of Running of Statute.

Impleader barred when plaintiff's claim time-barred. — Where the statute of limitations on any claim that a plaintiff may have against a third-party defendant has run, the defendant has no right to implead. Rambone v. Critzer, 548 F. Supp. 660 (W.D. Va. 1982).

A federal court sitting in diversity must honor Virginia law restricting the court within which a nonsuited plaintiff may recommence in order to invoke saving provision as the Virginia restriction is an integral part of the several policies served by Virginia's statutes of limitations and must be applied in consolidated federal diversity actions. Yarber v. Allstate Ins. Co., 674 F.2d 232 (4th Cir. 1982).

Dismissal on statute of limitations grounds is not within intendment of Fed. R. Civ. P. 41(b). — A dismissal on statute of limitations grounds under this section is not within the intendment of Fed. R. Civ. P. 41(b) and, therefore, is not an adjudication on the merits. The only issue on the merits which would be res judicata in a subsequent action in any court is that the action is time-barred in any action that would necessarily apply this section. In all other respects the merits of the claim are unaffected. Burgess v. Cohen, 593 F. Supp. 1122 (E.D. Va. 1984).

Clinical laboratory not agent or employee of doctors and not health care provider. Consequently, the act did not apply to the lab, and filing the Notice of Claim under the act did not toll the statute of limitations as to the claim of negligence against the lab. Richman v. National Health Labs., Inc., 235 Va. 353, 367 S.E.2d 508 (1988).

D. Asbestos Injuries.

Subsection A applicable to asbestos cases filed before ruling in Oman v. Johns-Manville Corp. — Virginia's two-year personal injury statute of limitations, subsection A of this section, applies retroactively to asbestos cases filed prior to the Fourth Circuit's ruling in Oman v. Johns-Manville Corp., 764 F.2d 224 (4th Cir.), cert. denied, 474 U.S. 970, 106 S. Ct. 351, 88 L. Ed. 2d 319 (1985).

II. DECISIONS UNDER PRIOR LAW.

A. General Consideration.

Editor's note. — The cases cited below were decided under corresponding provisions of former law. The term "this section," as used below, refers to former provisions.

It is the object of litigation which determines the applicability of a statute of limitations, not the form in which suit is instituted. Almond v. Kent, 459 F.2d 200 (4th Cir. 1972); Sitwell v. Burnette, 349 F. Supp. 83 (W.D. Va. 1972).

Statutes of limitations are designed to suppress fraudulent and stale claims from being asserted after a great lapse of time, to the surprise of the parties, when the evidence may have been lost, the facts may have become obscure because of defective memory, or the witnesses have died or disappeared. Barnes v. Sears, Roebuck & Co., 406 F.2d 859 (4th Cir. 1969); Atkins v. Schmutz Mfg. Co., 435 F.2d 527 (4th Cir. 1970), cert. denied, 402 U.S. 932, 91 S. Ct. 1526, 28 L. Ed. 2d 867 (1971).

The courts ought to be relieved of the burden of trying stale claims when a plaintiff has slept on his rights. Atkins v. Schmutz Mfg. Co., 435 F.2d 527 (4th Cir. 1970), cert. denied, 402 U.S. 932, 91 S. Ct. 1526, 28 L. Ed. 2d 867 (1971).

And to compel prompt assertion of accrued right of action. — Statutes of limitation are designed to compel the prompt assertion of an accrued right of action; not to bar such a right before it has accrued. Caudill v. Wise Rambler, Inc., 210 Va. 11, 168 S.E.2d 257 (1969).

The oft-stated purpose of statutes of limitation is to compel the assertion of a right of action promptly while the evidence is available and still relatively fresh. Atkins v. Schmutz Mfg. Co., 435 F.2d 527 (4th Cir. 1970), cert. denied, 402 U.S. 932, 91 S. Ct. 1526, 28 L. Ed. 2d 867 (1971).

Statutes of limitation are statutes of repose, the object of which is to compel the exercise of a right of action within a reasonable time. Atkins v. Schmutz Mfg. Co., 435 F.2d 527 (4th Cir. 1970), cert. denied, 402 U.S. 932, 91 S. Ct. 1526, 28 L. Ed. 2d 867 (1971).

Statutes of limitation are statutes of repose. Barnes v. Sears, Roebuck & Co., 406 F.2d 859 (4th Cir. 1969).

And they must be construed strictly to that end under Virginia law. Barnes v. Sears, Roebuck & Co., 406 F.2d 859 (4th Cir. 1969).

But the Supreme Court is reluctant to reach unjust results. — The Supreme Court has indicated its reluctance in deciding statute of limitation questions to reach results which are unjust and inequitable. Atkins v. Schmutz Mfg. Co., 435 F.2d 527 (4th Cir. 1970), cert. denied, 402 U.S. 932, 91 S. Ct. 1526, 28 L. Ed. 2d 867 (1971).

Statutes of limitation are primarily designed to assure fairness to defendants. Such statutes promote justice by preventing surprises through the revival of claims that have been allowed to slumber until evidence has been lost, memories have faded, and witnesses have disappeared. The theory is that even if one has a just claim it is unjust not to put the adversary on notice to defend within the period of limitation and that the right to be free of stale claims in time comes to prevail over the right to prosecute them. Atkins v. Schmutz Mfg. Co., 435 F.2d 527 (4th Cir. 1970), cert. denied, 402 U.S. 932, 91 S. Ct. 1526, 28 L. Ed. 2d 867 (1971).

Historically, periods of limitations have on occasion been described as established to cut off rights, justifiable or not, which might otherwise be asserted, and as requiring strict adherence by the judiciary. In recent years, however, a marked preference has attached to the view that statutory limitations are primarily designed to assure fairness to defendants, and that they promote justice by preventing surprises through the revival of claims that have been allowed to slumber until evidence has been lost, memories have faded and witnesses have disappeared. Taliaferro v. Dykstra, 388 F. Supp. 957 (E.D. Va. 1975).

B. Proceedings to Which This Section Applicable.

1. In General.

This section applies only to personal actions. Harper v. Harper, 159 Va. 210, 165 S.E. 490 (1932).

Maritime torts. — This section should not have been accorded a decisive influence in a maritime tort action. Giddens v. Isbrandtsen Co., 355 F.2d 125 (4th Cir. 1966).

In the enforcement of a maritime claim, admiralty prefers the equity rule of laches as opposed to any rigid limitation. Giddens v. Isbrandtsen Co., 355 F.2d 125 (4th Cir. 1966).

Claims against trustees. — A trustee cannot take advantage of the act of limitations against the claim of the cestui que trust or of persons claiming under him. Redwood v. Riddick, 18 Va. (4 Munf.) 222 (1814).

Free speech rights under federal labor law. — A cause of action asserting free speech rights secured to a member of a labor union under the provisions of the Labor Management Reporting and Disclosure Act of 1959, 29 U.S.C. § 411(a)(2) is controlled by the two-year statute of limitations under this section. Howard v. Aluminum Workers Int'l Union, 418 F. Supp. 1058 (E.D. Va. 1976), aff'd, 589 F.2d 771 (4th Cir. 1978).

Action for unfair union representation. — The two-year Virginia tort limitations set forth in this section controls an action charging union with unfair representations rather than the five-year contract statute of limitations under § 8.01-246. Howard v. Aluminum Workers Int'l Union, 418 F. Supp. 1058 (E.D. Va. 1976), aff'd, 589 F.2d 771 (4th Cir. 1978).

2. Personal Injuries.

Two-year limitation applies. — An action to recover damages for personal injuries caused by the wrongful act, neglect, or default of any person or corporation must be brought within one year (now two years) from the time such injury was inflicted. Anderson v. Hygeia Hotel Co., 92 Va. 687, 24 S.E. 269 (1896); Birmingham v. C & O Ry., 98 Va. 548, 37 S.E. 17 (1900).

This section applies to every action for personal injuries whether based on tort or contract. — This section, and thus the two-year limitation, does not apply only to tort actions, but to every action for personal injuries, whether it is based upon tort or contract. Therefore, the wrong alleged, not the form of the action, is what counts in the measurement and application of the appropriate limitation. Tyler v. R.R. St. & Co., 322 F. Supp. 541 (E.D. Va. 1971), commented on in 6 U. Rich. L. Rev. 167 (1971).

This section applies in an action for personal injuries grounded upon breach of implied warranty. Friedman v. Peoples Serv. Drug Stores, 208 Va. 700, 160 S.E.2d 563 (1968); Tyler v. R.R. St. & Co., 322 F. Supp. 541 (E.D. Va. 1971), commented on in 6 U. Rich. L. Rev. 167 (1971).

Since an action to recover damages for personal injuries based on a breach of warranty is essentially an action for personal injuries, the limitation thereon is governed by this section, and not by this section applicable to an action based on contract. Caudill v. Wise Rambler, Inc., 210 Va. 11, 168 S.E.2d 257 (1969).

The period of limitations in actions for personal injuries was not changed by the passage of § 8.01-25, providing that no cause of action is lost because of the death of the person liable for the injury or of the person in whose favor the cause of action existed. Herndon v. Wickham, 198 Va. 824, 97 S.E.2d 5 (1957); Sherley v. Lotz, 200 Va. 173, 104 S.E.2d 795 (1958).

A medical malpractice complaint, which alleged that the malpractice occurred during a continuous and substantially uninterrupted course of examination and treatment which commenced in October 1971, and terminated in July 1972, and which alleged that a particular condition was improperly treated and diagnosed, set forth a case for application of the continuing treatment rule. The date of injury occurred, the cause of action for that malpractice accrued and the statute of limitations commenced to run when the improper course of examination and treatment for the particular malady terminated in July 1972. Fenton v. Danaceau, 220 Va. 1, 255 S.E.2d 349 (1979).

Claim for personal injuries based on unseaworthiness. — This section places a claim for personal injuries based on unseaworthiness within the field of tort liability. Dawson v. Fernley & Eger, 196 F. Supp. 816 (E.D. Va. 1961).

The warranty of seaworthiness as extended to the longshoreman is not contractual in nature, but is merely an incident of the relationship of the parties, namely, the shipowner with the longshoreman who performs duties traditionally done by the seaman. For this reason it follows that this section would be applicable in Virginia to a claim by a longshoreman against a shipowner for personal injuries as to any action instituted in Virginia. Dawson v. Fernley & Eger, 196 F. Supp. 816 (E.D. Va. 1961).

Action for injuries resulting from sale of unwholesome food must be brought within one year (now two years) after the right to bring the same shall have first accrued. Colonna v. Rosedale Dairy Co., 166 Va. 314, 186 S.E. 94 (1936).

Section does not apply to death by wrongful act. — As an action for death by wrongful act is not a survival of the right of the injured person, but a new right conferred by statute upon the personal representative, the period of limitation is not five (now two) years under this section but is determined by § 8.01-244 and is one (now two) year. Anderson v. Hygeia Hotel Co., 92 Va. 687, 24 S.E. 269 (1896); Manuel v. Norfolk & W. Ry., 99 Va. 188, 37 S.E. 957 (1901).

Nor to action for contribution by joint tort-feasors. — See McKay v. Citizens Rapid Transit Co., 190 Va. 851, 59 S.E.2d 121 (1950).

Nor to action under Federal Tort Claims Act. — This section does not apply to a suit in a federal court under the Federal Tort Claims Act on a cause of action which arose in Virginia. Jefferson v. United States, 77 F. Supp. 706 (D. Md. 1948), aff'd, 178 F.2d 518 (4th Cir. 1949); 340 U.S. 135, 71 S. Ct. 153, 95 L. Ed. 152 (1950).

Free speech rights under federal labor law. — In an action by workers alleging that their unions had abridged their rights to free speech guaranteed by the Labor-Management Reporting and Disclosure Act, 29 U.S.C. § 411, the limitations period applicable to tort actions was properly applied since the speech claims were closely akin to personal injury claims under Virginia law. Howard v. Aluminum Workers Int'l Union & Local 400, 589 F.2d 771 (4th Cir. 1978).

Action for unfair labor representation. — The appropriate limitations period in an action by workers alleging that their unions had broken the duty of fair representation imposed upon them by the Labor Management Relations Act, 29 U.S.C. § 159, is taken from the limitations applicable to tort actions. Howard v. Aluminum Workers Int'l Union & Local 400, 589 F.2d 771 (4th Cir. 1978).

3. Civil Rights Actions.

By its language this section applies a two-year limitation of personal injury claims and by judicial construction, civil rights allegations carry a two-year limitation. Williams v. Westbrook Psychiatric Hosp., 420 F. Supp. 322 (E.D. Va. 1976).

The timeliness of 42 U.S.C. § 1983 "constitutional tort" actions is governed by Virginia's two-year "personal injury" statute. Van Horn v. Lukhard, 392 F. Supp. 384 (E.D. Va. 1975); Bulls v. Holmes, 403 F. Supp. 475 (E.D. Va. 1975).

The first sentence of this section establishes the limitation period of two years applicable to suits brought under 42 U.S.C. § 1981, alleging denial of admission to private schools solely on the basis of race. Runyon v. McCrary, 427 U.S. 160, 96 S. Ct. 2586, 49 L. Ed. 2d 415 (1976).

The two-year statute of limitations applies to actions brought under 42 U.S.C. § 1985. Brady v. Sowers, 453 F. Supp. 52 (W.D. Va. 1978).

Deprivation of property due to alleged racial discrimination. — A case involving only the question of whether defendants deprived plaintiff of his property because he was black was basically a tort, a personal injury issue requiring the two-year statute of limitations under this section. Harris v. Obenshain, 452 F. Supp. 1172 (E.D. Va. 1978).

Effect of filing § 1983 action in another state. — The filing of an action under 42 U.S.C. § 1983 in a federal district court in North Carolina did not toll the running of the applicable two-year statute of limitations in Virginia where the attorney's decision to file the action in North Carolina was legally unsound, the later action in a federal district court in Virginia could not be treated as a transfer, and the only logical reason that could be found for filing in North Carolina was to avoid the Virginia statute of limitations. Brady v. Sowers, 453 F. Supp. 52 (W.D. Va. 1978).

Where plaintiff requested equitable relief as well as monetary damages in a civil rights action he cannot negate the applicability of statute of limitations. Wilkinson v. Hamel, 381 F. Supp. 768 (W.D. Va. 1974).

Second paragraph of former § 8-24 imposing a one-year limitation on suits under 42 U.S.C. § 1983 was unconstitutional because it both burdened the assertion of a federally created right of substantial importance, and because it effected an invidious and unwarranted discrimination against assertion of the "constitutional tort." Van Horn v. Lukhard, 392 F. Supp. 384 (E.D. Va. 1975).

And two-year limitation continued to be applied. — The discrimination toward federal civil rights actions in the 1973 amendment to this section imposing a one-year limitation on 42 U.S.C. § 1983 suits was apparent. Analogous torts arising under Virginia law were not similarly limited. Nor was any attempt made to rationally prescribe a limitation period for federal civil rights suits in terms of the object of the litigation. Rather, Virginia apparently sought to limit all federal civil rights causes of action without regard to the federal statutory and constitutional values at stake. The court therefore decided to continue to apply the two-year limitation period of former § 8-24 incorporated into federal law. Edgerton v. Puckett, 391 F. Supp. 463 (W.D. Va. 1975).

Where plaintiffs brought action based on discrimination in housing under 42 U.S.C. § 1982, the two-year limitation period in this section was applicable so as to avoid an impermissible burden upon and discrimination against the assertion of a federally created right. Brown v. Blake & Bane, Inc., 409 F. Supp. 1246 (E.D. Va. 1976).

Decisions under section as it read prior to 1973 amendment, which was held unconstitutional. — The two-year period of limitations, applying to "every action for personal injuries," applies generally to 42 U.S.C. § 1983 suits for deprivation of civil rights. Almond v. Kent, 459 F.2d 200 (4th Cir. 1972); Sitwell v. Burnette, 349 F. Supp. 83 (W.D. Va. 1972).

The two-year statute of limitations applies to actions in this State for personal damages brought pursuant to 42 U.S.C. § 1983. Landman v. Royster, 354 F. Supp. 1302 (E.D. Va. 1973).

The two-year statute of limitations for personal injuries is applied in all civil rights actions that might be redressed by recovery of damages. Wilkinson v. Hamel, 381 F. Supp. 768 (W.D. Va. 1974).

The two-year period applies to all rights which could be redressed under 42 U.S.C. § 1983 by the recovery of money damages. Sitwell v. Burnette, 349 F. Supp. 83 (W.D. Va. 1972).

While the back-pay claim of a party-plaintiff would have been barred by the two-year statute of limitation in this section in a discrimination suit, the overall suit was not subject to such a bar because of the public interest at stake. In re Plywood Antitrust Litig., 376 F. Supp. 1405 (J.P.M.L. Va. 1974).

Virginia's two-year statute of limitations was declared appropriate for personal injury suits based on racial discrimination in the sale of real estate in violation of 42 U.S.C. § 1982. Allen v. Gifford, 462 F.2d 615 (4th Cir.), cert. denied, 409 U.S. 876, 93 S. Ct. 128, 34 L. Ed. 2d 130 (1972).

The fact that plaintiff had failed to assert a timely claim under the Fair Housing Act, 42 U.S.C. § 3601 et seq., had no effect on the timeliness of the cause of action relating to property rights of citizens, because the statute of limitations applicable to a cause of action brought under 42 U.S.C. § 1982, was the state statute of limitations expressly or most nearly applicable to the type of claim asserted, which in Virginia was contained in this section which provided a two-year limitation for personal injuries. Hampton v. Roberts, 386 F. Supp. 609 (W.D. Va. 1974).

As to U.S. Supreme Court decision that the limitations period for civil RICO actions is the four-year federal statute of limitations applicable to Clayton Act actions, see Agency Holding Corp. v. Malley-Duff & Assocs., 483 U.S. 143, 107 S. Ct. 2759, 97 L. Ed. 2d 121 (1987).

4. Wrongs Affecting Property and Property Rights.

a. Injuries to Property.

The five-year limitation controls actions of trespass to land. — An action of trespass to land, unless continuous, is barred in five years under this section; when the trespass is continuous the recovery is limited to the five years preceding the action. Moore v. Postal Tel. Cable Co., 3 Va. Law Reg. (n.s.), 111 (1917).

Actions for damages to one's property, estate, or business receive the benefit of the five-year period under this section. Almond v. Kent, 321 F. Supp. 1225 (W.D. Va. 1970), rev'd on other grounds, 459 F.2d 200 (4th Cir. 1972); Eden Corp. v. Utica Mut. Ins. Co., 350 F. Supp. 637 (W.D. Va. 1972).

Negligent failure to warn. — As the object of the charge of negligent failure to warn is to recover for the property damage that was done, such action would survive, and is timely brought since it is within the five-year period of limitation that would apply. Insurance Co. of N. Am. v. GE Co., 376 F. Supp. 638 (W.D. Va. 1974).

An action for conspiracy to injure another in his reputation, trade, etc., brought under §§ 18.2-499 and 18.2-500, does survive, and hence, is subject to the five-year limitation in this section. Federated Graphics Cos. v. Napotnik, 424 F. Supp. 291 (E.D. Va. 1976).

Actions for nuisances. — An action to

recover damages, past and future, for a permanent nuisance must be brought within five years from the time the cause of action accrues. Wooley v. Mathieson Alkali Works, 119 Va. 862, 89 S.E. 880 (1916).

For pollution of a stream. — An action for pollution of a stream by the discharge of sewage therein from a permanent sewer system is barred by this section five years from the time of the construction of the sewer. Virginia Hot Springs Co. v. McCray, 106 Va. 461, 56 S.E. 216 (1907).

Or of a well. — The limitation to an action to recover damages for injury to the plaintiff's property by reason of pollution of plaintiff's well by cesspools constructed and maintained by the defendant on his land adjacent to that of the plaintiff is five years. Hawling v. Chapin, 115 Va. 792, 80 S.E. 587 (1914).

Where defendant's alleged negligence was the alleged direct cause of fire leading to property damage, plaintiff has stated a cause of action that alleges a direct, assignable, and survival cause of action to which the five-year period of limitations under this section applies. Insurance Co. of N. Am. v. GE Co., 376 F. Supp. 638 (W.D. Va. 1974).

And for damage caused by smoke from railroad. — Damages to an adjoining landowner caused by cinders and smoke from a railroad track cast upon his land is permanent and continuous, and entire damages are recoverable in a single action, and the limitation in such case is five years under this section. Southern Ry. v. Fitzpatrick, 129 Va. 246, 105 S.E. 663 (1921).

b. Actions to Recover Personal Property.

Uninterrupted possession of personal property for more than five years is a bar to a suit by the former owner thereof to recover the same. Garland v. Enos, 18 Va. (4 Munf.) 504 (1815).

This section applies to a suit to establish a secret trust. — A fraudulent bill of sale, absolute on its face but with a secret trust, was made of property. The beneficiaries on becoming of age set up a claim to the property which the trustee denied to be just. Eight years later they filed a bill to establish the secret trust. It was held that the statute of limitations was a bar to the bill. Owen v. Sharp, 39 Va. (12 Leigh) 427 (1841).

And an action by the receiver of a national bank to recover assets of the bank which were transferred to the directors was governed by this section. White v. FDIC, 122 F.2d 770 (4th Cir. 1941), cert. denied, 316 U.S. 672, 62 S. Ct. 1043, 86 L. Ed. 1747 (1942).

c. Breach of Duty.

Action for compensatory and punitive damages for conspiring to breach contract. — An action for compensatory and punitive damages for malicious acts of defendant in conspiring to breach a contract not to engage in teaching dancing within two years after defendant's employment with plaintiffs ended was within the five-year period prescribed by this section, since the action was one for damages to plaintiffs' estate, which would survive under former § 64.1-145. Worrie v. Boze, 198 Va. 533, 95 S.E.2d 192 (1956), aff'd on rehearing, 198 Va. 891, 96 S.E.2d 799 (1957).

Bank directors may invoke statute. — Directors of a bank which is a going concern are not trustees of an express trust, but are trustees of an implied trust created by operation of law upon their official relation to the bank, and the statute of limitations and the doctrine of laches may be invoked in their defense when they are sued for a breach of such trust. Winston v. Gordon, 115 Va. 899, 80 S.E. 756 (1914).

And five-year limitation controls action for negligence of director. — The cause of action against the directors of a bank for neglect of duty as such directors grows out of their breach of duty, and hence the limitation applicable thereto is five years. Winston v. Gordon, 115 Va. 899, 80 S.E. 756 (1914).

In a suit against bank directors for negligence in the administration of the affairs of the bank, the five-year statute of limitation applies. The two-year limitation in former § 13-207 is not applicable to all acts of directors as such; it refers to the positive duties required of directors by the statute law, and not to negligence. Anderson v. Bundy, 161 Va. 1, 171 S.E. 501 (1933); Marshall v. Fredericksburg Lumber Co., 162 Va. 136, 173 S.E. 553 (1934).

And action for fraudulent embezzlement by carrier. — The act of limitations may be pleaded in bar to an action against a common carrier for fraudulently embezzling goods entrusted to its care. Cook v. Darby, 18 Va. (4 Munf.) 444 (1815).

Suit based on unions' alleged breach of duty and employer's complicity in such breach clearly sounds in tort, and the court therefore will apply the Virginia limitation period governing tort suits. Coleman v. Kroger Co., 399 F. Supp. 724 (W.D. Va. 1975).

d. Liability Imposed by Statute.

Action by automobile dealer for violations of former § 46.1-547. — The five-year statute of limitations applies to an automobile dealer's action against an automobile sales corporation for cancellation of the dealer's franchise and other violations of former § 46.1-547. E.L. Bowen & Co. v. American Motors Sales Corp., 153 F. Supp. 42 (E.D. Va. 1957).

This section applies to suits for copyright infringement under former 17 U.S.C. § 25 (see 17 U.S.C. § 501 et seq.), and, as such suits survive, the five-year limitation controls. Pathe Exch., Inc. v. Dalke, 49 F.2d 161 (4th Cir. 1931).

An action to recover triple damages for violation of Sherman Anti-Trust Act is governed by the five-year limitation prescribed by this section. Barnes Coal Corp. v. Retail Coal Merchants Ass'n, 128 F.2d 645 (4th Cir. 1942).

And the right of action on an assessment on national bank stock is governed by this section. Cable v. Commercial & Sav. Bank, 31 F. Supp. 628 (W.D. Va. 1940). But see Hospelhorn v. Corbin, 179 Va. 348, 19 S.E.2d 72 (1942), wherein it was held that the double liability of stockholders in a bank and trust company, imposed by a Maryland statute, was contractual in nature and therefore controlled by the three-year limitation in § 8.01-246.

But not to claims for compensation under Fair Labor Standards Act. — This section is not applicable to an action to recover compensation under the Fair Labor Standards Act. Reliance Storage & Inspection Co. v. Hubbard, 50 F. Supp. 1012 (W.D. Va. 1943).

C. Effect of Running of Statute.

A complaint filed after the time allowed by this section is subject to the statute of limitations and is time-barred. Davenport v. Deseret Pharmaceutical Co., 321 F. Supp. 659 (E.D. Va. 1971).

New parties brought into suit after running of statute. — When the statute of limitations runs between the time of commencement of a suit and time when new parties are brought into the suit, the new parties may validly plead the statute of limitations, but the original parties may not plead the statute of limitations. Phillip v. Sam Finley, Inc., 270 F. Supp. 292 (W.D. Va. 1967).

Despite the fact that defendant received no notice of the amendment adding her as a party to action until after the statute of limitation period had run, the amendment itself was timely made before the statute of limitations ran and the action was "commenced" by such filing, so motion for summary judgment upon the ground of the running of the statute of limitations before receipt of notice must be denied. Leathers v. Serrell, 376 F. Supp. 983 (W.D. Va. 1974).

Adverse possession of a chattel for five years ripens into title. Newly v. Blakey, 13 Va. (3 Hen. & M.) 57 (1808); Spotswood v. Dandridge, 14 Va. (4 Hen. & M.) 139 (1809); Garland v. Enos, 18 Va. (4 Munf.) 504 (1815); Layne v. Norris, 57 Va. (16 Gratt.) 236 (1861); Morris v. Lyon, 84 Va. 331, 4 S.E. 734 (1881).

And possessor may maintain action for recovery of property. — A plaintiff in detinue, who, after having had five years peaceable possession of property, acquired without force or fraud, lost that possession, may regain it on the mere ground of his previous possession, on the same principle that a defendant may protect himself, on that length of possession, under the act of limitations. Newly v. Blakey, 13 Va. (3 Hen. & M.) 57 (1808). See also, Owen v. Sharp, 39 Va. (12 Leigh) 427 (1841).

Property wrongfully seized under execution. — Property transferred by a deed of trust was taken under execution and sold, and the purchasers remained in peaceable possession thereof for five years, before suit was instituted to recover it. It was held that the statute of limitations was a bar to the recovery. Sheppards v. Turpin, 44 Va. (3 Gratt.) 373 (1847).

Property held contrary to terms of will. — A widow held, by virtue of her husband's will, certain personal property for life, with power to dispose of it afterwards among his children as she should think proper. The widow bequeathed the property to trustees for the benefit of one only of those children. It was held that the child must be considered as holding the property under the widow's will, adversely in relation to the other children, and therefore was protected by the statute of limitations from a claim in their behalf. Hudson v. Hudson, 20 Va. (6 Munf.) 352 (1819).

Property held adversely by administratrix. — A widow qualified as administratrix of her husband, and took possession of and held certain property, in which she claimed a life estate as having been given to her by her father's will. She was afterwards removed from her office of administratrix; but continued to hold the property, claiming it as her own for life; and she held it for more than five years after she ceased to be administratrix. It was held that the statute of limitations would protect her against any claim by the administrator de bonis non and next of kin of her husband. Livesay v. Helms, 55 Va. (14 Gratt.) 441 (1858).

D. Pleading and Practice.

Not necessary to plead statute in action to recover property. — In an action to recover property, if the defendant has been in adverse possession a sufficient length of time to render the statute of limitations a bar to the action, this possession gives title; and it is not necessary to plead the statute. Layne v. Norris, 57 Va. (16 Gratt.) 236 (1861).

A plea of "the act of limitations" in those words only, to which the plaintiff replies generally, is good after verdict. Cook v. Darby, 18 Va. (4 Munf.) 444 (1815).

Time of filing plea is in discretion of trial court. — The time of filing pleas is a matter within the sound discretion of the trial court, and the trial court did not abuse its discretion in allowing the defendants to file a plea of the statute of limitations in this section on the day of the trial. Vance v. Maytag Sales Corp., 159 Va. 373, 165 S.E. 393 (1932).

Instruction as to rights of intervenor. — In an action to recover for the burning of plaintiff's house, in which an insurance company intervened, the court properly refused to instruct the jury that in determining defendant's liability to the insurance company, it might consider the fact that the insurance company made no demand on defendant for more than five years after the fire; for, as the plaintiff, through whom the intervenor claimed, was not barred by the statute of limitations, the time of intervention was immaterial. Norfolk & W. Ry. v. Thomas, 110 Va. 622, 66 S.E. 817 (1910).

Federal courts must adopt the limitation of this section in diversity cases. — In a diversity case tried in Virginia, Guaranty Trust Co. v. York, 326 U.S. 99, 65 S. Ct. 1464, 89 L. Ed. 2079 (1945), compels adoption of the requirement, applicable in the State courts of Virginia, that actions for personal injuries "be brought within two years next after the right to bring the same shall have accrued." Atkins v. Schmutz Mfg. Co., 435 F.2d 527 (4th Cir. 1970), cert. denied, 402 U.S. 932, 91 S. Ct. 1526, 28 L. Ed. 2d 867 (1971).

But five-year limitation governs father's action for medical care of child. — In action by father to recover the pecuniary loss he has sustained by being required to furnish medical treatment to his child and by losing the child's services, it was held that the plaintiff had a separate cause of action, not growing out of a personal injury to himself, but for the pecuniary loss suffered by his estate; that such an action could be brought by a personal representative under § 64.1-145 in the event of plaintiff's death and that the five-year statute of limitation is applicable. Watson v. Daniel, 165 Va. 564, 183 S.E. 183 (1936).

§ 8.01-243.1. Actions for medical malpractice; minors. — Notwithstanding the provisions of § 8.01-229 A and except as provided in subsection C of § 8.01-243, any cause of action accruing on or after July 1, 1987, on behalf of a person who was a minor at the time the cause of action accrued for personal injury or death against a health care provider pursuant to Chapter 21.1 (§ 8.01-581.1 et seq.) shall be commenced within two years of the date of the last act or omission giving rise to the cause of action except that if the minor was less than eight years of age at the time of the occurrence of the malpractice, he shall have until his tenth birthday to commence an action. Any minor who is ten years of age or older on or before July 1, 1987, shall have no less than two years from that date within which to commence such an action. (1987, cc. 294, 645.)

Law Review. — For comment on Virginia's Birth-Related Neurological Injury Compensation Act, § 38.2-5000 et seq., see 22 U. Rich. L. Rev. 431 (1988).

§ 8.01-243.2. Limitations of actions by confined persons; exhaustion. — No person confined in a state or local correctional facility shall bring or have brought on his behalf any personal action relating to the conditions of his confinement until all available administrative remedies are exhausted. Such action shall be brought by or on behalf of such person within one year after cause of action accrues or within six months after all administrative remedies are exhausted, whichever occurs later. (1998, c. 596; 1999, c. 47.)

The 1999 amendment inserted "or local" preceding "correctional facility."

§ 8.01-244. Actions for wrongful death; limitation. — A. Notwithstanding the provisions of § 8.01-229 B, if a person entitled to bring an action for personal injury dies as a result of such injury with no such action pending before the expiration of two years next after the cause of action shall have accrued, then an action under § 8.01-50 may be commenced within the time limits specified in subsection B of this section.

B. Every action under § 8.01-50 shall be brought by the personal representative of the decedent within two years after the death of the injured person.

§ 8.01-244   CODE OF VIRGINIA   § 8.01-244

If any such action is brought within such period of two years after such person's death and for any cause abates or is dismissed without determining the merits of such action, the time such action is pending shall not be counted as any part of such period of two years and another action may be brought within the remaining period of such two years as if such former action had not been instituted. However, if a plaintiff suffers a voluntary nonsuit pursuant to § 8.01-380, the nonsuit shall not be deemed an abatement nor a dismissal pursuant to this subsection, and the provisions of subdivision E 3 of § 8.01-229 shall apply to such a nonsuited action. (Code 1950, §§ 8-633, 8-634; 1958, c. 470; 1977, c. 617; 1991, c. 722.)

REVISERS' NOTE

Section 8.01-244 combines the substance of the limitation provisions of former §§ 8-633 and 8-634; the tolling provision of those sections has been transferred to § 8.01-229 D.

Cross references. — For procedure in actions for wrongful death, see § 8.01-50 et seq.

Editor's note. — Acts 1991, c. 722, cl. 2, provides "That the provisions of this act are declaratory of the original intent of the General Assembly in enacting Chapter 617 of the 1977 Acts of Assembly" (Title 8.01).

Law Review. — For survey of Virginia law on practice and pleading for the year 1978-1979, see 66 Va. L. Rev. 343 (1980). For article discussing statutes of limitation and repose in toxic substances litigation, see 16 U. Rich. L. Rev. 247 (1982). For article, "Civil Rights and 'Personal Injuries': Virginia's Statute of Limitations for Section 1983 Suits," see 26 Wm. & Mary L. Rev. 199 (1985).

I. Decisions Under Current Law.
II. Decisions Under Prior Law.

I. DECISIONS UNDER CURRENT LAW.

The limitations period in the Virginia wrongful death statute is a substantive limitation. Riddle v. Shell Oil Co., 764 F. Supp. 418 (W.D. Va. 1990).

The two paragraphs of this section are inextricably interrelated, one is the predicate for the other, and the tolling provisions of § 8.01-229 B do not apply to the time limitation imposed by this section. Horn v. Abernathy, 231 Va. 228, 343 S.E.2d 318 (1986).

Section 8.01-229 E 3 is inapplicable to wrongful death actions because subsection B of this section controls. Dodson v. Potomac Mack Sales & Serv., Inc., 241 Va. 89, 400 S.E.2d 178 (1991); Flanagan v. Virginia Beach Gen. Hosp., 12 Va. App. 760, 406 S.E.2d 914 (1991).

Because § 8.01-229 E 3 deals generally with the subject of tolling statutes of limitations and conflicts with subsection B of this section, which deals specifically with the tolling of wrongful death actions, the latter section controls for two reasons: First, § 8.01-228 provides in pertinent part that every action for which a limitation period is prescribed by law must be commenced within the period prescribed in this chapter unless otherwise specifically provided in the Code. This section provides for the limitation of wrongful death actions and a tolling period in a specific way, and thus "otherwise specifically provides" its own requirements. Second, in construing conflicting statutes, when one statute speaks to a subject in a general way and another deals with a part of the same subject in a more specific manner, where they conflict the latter prevails. Dodson v. Potomac Mack Sales & Serv., Inc., 241 Va. 89, 400 S.E.2d 178 (1991).

Tolling provision amendment not retroactive. — Lower court correctly ruled that plaintiff's wrongful death action was time-barred because plaintiff failed to refile after nonsuit within the time prescribed by wrongful death statute of limitations in effect when original cause of action accrued; tolling provision amendment to wrongful death statute was substantive, not procedural, and therefore did not apply retroactively. Riddett v. Virginia Elec. and Power Co., 255 Va. 23, 495 S.E.2d 819 (1998).

Tolling provision of the Virginia Medical Malpractice Act, former § 8.01-581.9, which tolled the statute of limitations for 120 days from the giving of notice or 60 days following issuance of an opinion by the medical review panel, applied to the two year limitations contained in the Virginia Wrongful Death Act, § 8.01-50 and subsection (B). Wertz v. Grubbs, 245 Va. 67, 425 S.E.2d 500 (1993).

Action under 42 U.S.C. § 1983. — In determining which state statute of limitations applies to a 42 U.S.C. § 1983 action, a federal court should apply the time bar used by the forum state for similar torts. Under this section, the limitations period for a wrongful death action is two years. Bruce v. Smith, 581 F. Supp. 902 (W.D. Va. 1984).

Conversion of foreign personal injury action to Virginia wrongful death action. — A valid foreign personal injury action may be converted to a Virginia wrongful death action, even though the foreign action was not filed within Virginia's two-year limitations period. Riddle v. Shell Oil Co., 764 F. Supp. 418 (W.D. Va. 1990).

The defendant has the burden of proof to establish facts necessary to prevail on a statute of limitations plea. Lo v. Burke, 249 Va. 311, 455 S.E.2d 9 (1995).

Applied in Rochelle v. Rochelle, 225 Va. 387, 302 S.E.2d 59 (1983); Douglas v. Chesterfield County Police Dep't, 251 Va. 363, 467 S.E.2d 474 (1996); Pulliam v. Coastal Emergency Servs. of Richmond, Inc., 257 Va. 1, 509 S.E.2d 307 (1999).

II. DECISIONS UNDER PRIOR LAW.

Editor's note. — The cases cited below were decided under corresponding provisions of former law. The term "this section," as used below, refers to former provisions.

The object of an action and not its form determines which statute of limitations is applicable. Payne v. Piedmont Aviation, Inc., 294 F. Supp. 216 (E.D. Va. 1968).

When limitation begins to run. — The limitation begins to run from the moment the cause of action accrues and not from the time it is ascertained that damage has actually been sustained. Payne v. Piedmont Aviation, Inc., 294 F. Supp. 216 (E.D. Va. 1968).

The statute of limitations begins to run from the time of the wrongful or negligent act, and not from the time of the injury. Payne v. Piedmont Aviation, Inc., 294 F. Supp. 216 (E.D. Va. 1968).

Right of action for wrongful death does not accrue until the death. It is granted by the statute directly for the benefit of the statutory beneficiaries, and is, in no sense, derived from the fatally injured person. Grady v. Irvine, 254 F.2d 224 (4th Cir.), cert. denied, 358 U.S. 819, 79 S. Ct. 30, 3 L. Ed. 2d 60 (1958).

Time limitation is condition on right to sue. — This section provides that every action hereunder must be brought within one year (now two years) after death of the injured person; and it is settled in such a case that the time within which the suit must be brought operates as a limitation of the liability itself as created, and not of the remedy alone. It is a condition attached to the right to sue at all. Continental Cas. Co. v. Thorden Line, 186 F.2d 992 (4th Cir. 1951).

Right of action must exist at decedent's death. — The last paragraph of this section was not intended to allow a personal representative to bring an action for wrongful death at a time, perhaps, ten, fifteen, or twenty-five years subsequent to the date of the wrong that produced death, where perhaps the decedent did not, in his lifetime, deem it practical or worthwhile to assert any legal right to recover damages, or negligently failed to bring action within the time allowed him. Street v. Consumer Mining Corp., 185 Va. 561, 39 S.E.2d 271 (1946).

Statute tolled during pendency of action brought by foreign administrator. — Where death action brought by a foreign administrator was dismissed under § 26-59 because of the absence of a resident administrator and a subsequent action was brought by the nonresident administrator and a resident administratrix, under the saving provision of this section, which is to be liberally construed, the running of the limitation period was tolled during the time the prior action was pending, since it alleged the same cause of action as the subsequent proceeding and had been dismissed without determining the merits and since the plaintiffs in the two actions were substantially the same parties. McDaniel v. North Carolina Pulp Co., 198 Va. 612, 95 S.E.2d 201 (1956).

Statute not tolled by infancy of beneficiary of action. — The statute of limitations for wrongful death actions was not tolled by reason of infancy of the beneficiary of the wrongful death action, since the infant's disability could not prevent the timely institution of the action in view of the fact that wrongful death actions may be brought only by and in the name of the personal representative of the deceased. Beverage v. Harvey, 602 F.2d 657 (4th Cir. 1979).

Absence of the defendant will not alone defeat the limitation of the death statute. Continental Cas. Co. v. The Benny Skou, 101 F. Supp. 15 (E.D. Va. 1951), aff'd, 200 F.2d 246 (4th Cir. 1952), cert. denied, 345 U.S. 992, 73 S. Ct. 1129, 97 L. Ed. 1400 (1953).

Action against incarcerated convict. — Although a wrongful death action commenced against an incarcerated convict is an abortive proceeding, it is nevertheless an action under Rule 3:3, and therefore tolls the statute of limitations under the provisions of this section. Scott v. Nance, 202 Va. 355, 117 S.E.2d 279 (1960).

When time extended. — For a former action to extend the time for bringing an action for wrongful death under the Virginia statute beyond the one-year period (now two-year), it must have been brought against the same person as is named defendant in the subsequent action. Lindgren v. United States Shipping Bd. Merchant Fleet Corp., 55 F.2d 117 (4th Cir.), cert. denied, 286 U.S. 542, 52 S. Ct. 499, 76 L. Ed. 1280 (1932).

It is not to be assumed, in the absence of an express provision to that effect, that it was the intention of the legislature that the time to bring an action against one person should be extended by reason of the fact that it had been brought against someone else. Lindgren v. United States Shipping Bd. Merchant Fleet Corp., 55 F.2d 117 (4th Cir.), cert. denied, 286 U.S. 542, 52 S. Ct. 499, 76 L. Ed. 1280 (1932).

Applicable to voluntary nonsuit. — The provision of this section excluding the time during which any action brought within the one-year (now two-year) period is pending, where such action "for any cause abates or is dismissed without determining the merits," is remedial in purpose, is to be liberally construed and applies to a case of voluntary nonsuit. Norwood v. Buffey, 196 Va. 1051, 86 S.E.2d 809 (1955).

Two-year limitation in this section does not apply to an action brought in Virginia under the Tennessee wrongful death statute. Sherley v. Lotz, 200 Va. 173, 104 S.E.2d 795 (1958).

§ 8.01-245. Limitation on actions upon the bond of any fiduciaries or as to suits against fiduciaries themselves; accrual of cause of action where execution sustained. — A. No action shall be brought upon the bond of any fiduciary except within ten years next after the right to bring such action shall have first accrued.

B. When any fiduciary has settled an account under the provisions of Title 26, and whether or not he has given bond, a suit to surcharge or falsify such account, or to hold such fiduciary or his sureties liable for any balance stated in such account, to be in his hands, shall be brought within ten years after the account has been confirmed.

C. In actions upon the bond of any personal representative of a decedent or fiduciary of a person under a disability against whom an execution has been obtained or where a court acting upon the account of such representative or committee shall order payment or delivery of estate in the hands of such committee and representative, the cause of action shall be deemed to accrue from the return day of such execution or from the time of the right to require payment or delivery upon such order, whichever shall happen first. (Code 1950, §§ 8-13, 8-15, 8-16; 1964, c. 219; 1966, c. 118; 1972, c. 825; 1977, c. 617.)

REVISERS' NOTE

Section 8.01-245 consolidates limitations applicable to fiduciaries into a single section.

Subsection A preserves the former § 8-13 ten-year limitation period as to actions on fiduciary bonds under seal. Thus, while a seal no longer has impact on the limitations period, actions on fiduciary bonds will have a longer statute of limitations than contract actions. See § 8.01-246 (2).

Subsection B clarifies former § 8-16, without change in substance (like former § 8-16, the introductory proviso of § 8.01-246 makes it clear that contract limitations do not apply to fiduciaries).

Subsection C simplifies former § 8-15. Thus, the cause of action against fiduciaries does not generally accrue until the disability is removed, but where an execution against the fiduciary has already been obtained, the cause of action accrues immediately upon failure to satisfy the execution or order.

Law Review. — For article, "Civil Rights and 'Personal Injuries': Virginia's Statute of Limitations for Section 1983 Suits," see 26 Wm. & Mary L. Rev. 199 (1985).

I. Decisions Under Current Law.
II. Decisions Under Prior Law.

I. DECISIONS UNDER CURRENT LAW.

Applied in First Funding Corp. v. Birge, 220 Va. 326, 257 S.E.2d 861 (1979).

II. DECISIONS UNDER PRIOR LAW.

Editor's note. — The cases cited below were decided under corresponding provisions of former law. The term "this section," as used below, refers to former provisions.

This section is exclusive. — There is no other limitation applicable to the sureties upon the official bonds of executors or administrators, other than that provided by this section. Leake's Ex'r v. Leake, 75 Va. 792 (1881).

When action on fiduciary bond accrues. — Action on a fiduciary's bond is barred only after ten years from the accrual of the cause of action — that is, from the return day of execution against fiduciary, or from the time of the right to require payment or delivery from the fiduciary. Sharpe v. Rockwood, 78 Va. 24 (1883); Morrison v. Lavell, 81 Va. 519 (1886); Robertson v. Gillenwaters, 85 Va. 116, 7 S.E. 371 (1888). But see McCormick v. Wright, 79 Va. 524 (1884).

Bond of surety. — Where suit is brought, not on an open account, but on the surety's bond, the ten-year limitation applies under this section. Fidelity & Cas. Co. v. Lackland, 175 Va. 178, 8 S.E.2d 306 (1940).

Suit to surcharge or falsify account. — In the absence of fraud or mutual mistake, no suit to surcharge and falsify the account of a receiver, or to hold him or his sureties liable for any balance stated in his account to be in his hands, can be brought, except within ten years after the account had been confirmed, as required by the provisions of this section. Senseny v. Boyd, 114 Va. 308, 76 S.E. 280 (1912).

Subsection B does not apply to suit on guardian's bond. — It was not the intention of the legislature that subsection B should override the clear language of subsection C. Subsection B has no application to suits by wards upon the bonds of guardians. Newsom v. Watkins, 168 Va. 370, 191 S.E. 756 (1937).

Subsection C prescribes a plain test for determining when the cause of action is to be deemed to have accrued in suits upon fiduciary bonds. Leake's Ex'r v. Leake, 75 Va. 792 (1881).

Decree in favor of distributee. — The statute of limitations in favor of the sureties of fiduciaries did not begin to run in favor of the surety of an executor until a decree against the executor in favor of the distributees of the estate; and this though the surety was not a party to the suit in equity pursuant to which the decree against the executor was rendered. Franklin v. Depriest, 54 Va. (13 Gratt.) 257 (1856).

Bond for balance due on settlement of accounts. — Where an administrator had finally settled his accounts and given bond for the balance due, the statute began to run in favor of his surety on that bond from the time of its execution. Tilson v. Davis, 73 Va. (32 Gratt.) 92 (1879).

Defense of statute by one surety on joint obligation enures to benefit of all. — When the suit is on the joint obligation of all the sureties of an administrator, the defense of the statute by one of them, not being purely personal to him, enures to the benefit of all. Ashby v. Bell, 80 Va. 811 (1885).

Effect of suspension of suit. — A suit was brought on an executor's bond and decided in 1858, but, because there was no hand to receive the fund, was retained on docket till 1867, when it was dismissed with leave to reinstate it on motion of any person interested. The suit was reinstated in 1878, and a supplementary suit brought. It was held that the supplementary suit should be deemed a continuation of the original suit, quoad questions arising under the statute of limitations. Sharpe v. Rockwood, 78 Va. 24 (1883).

§ 8.01-246. Personal actions based on contracts.

— Subject to the provisions of § 8.01-243 regarding injuries to person and property and of § 8.01-245 regarding the application of limitations to fiduciaries, and their bonds, actions founded upon a contract, other than actions on a judgment or decree, shall be brought within the following number of years next after the cause of action shall have accrued:

1. In actions or upon a recognizance, except recognizance of bail in a civil suit, within ten years; and in actions or motions upon a recognizance of bail in a civil suit, within three years, omitting from the computation of such three years such time as the right to sue out such execution shall have been suspended by injunction, supersedeas or other process;

2. In actions on any contract which is not otherwise specified and which is in writing and signed by the party to be charged thereby, or by his agent, within five years whether such writing be under seal or not;

3. In actions by a partner against another for settlement of the partnership account or in actions upon accounts concerning the trade of merchandise

between merchant and merchant, their factors, or servants, within five years from the cessation of the dealings in which they are interested together;

4. In actions upon any unwritten contract, express or implied, within three years.

Provided that as to any action to which § 8.2-725 of the Uniform Commercial Code is applicable, that section shall be controlling except that in products liability actions for injury to person and for injury to property, other than the property subject to contract, the limitation prescribed in § 8.01-243 shall apply. (Code 1950, §§ 8-13, 8-17, 8-23; 1964, c. 219; 1966, c. 118; 1977, c. 617.)

REVISERS' NOTE

Section 8.01-246 consolidates the limitations of former §§ 8-13, 8-17, and 8-23.

Subdivision 1 incorporates former § 8-17. The term "motion" has replaced "scire facias." See § 8.01-24. With respect to suspension by injunction, cf. § 8.01-229 C.

Subdivision 2 applies a five-year limitation generally to written contracts regardless of whether such contracts be under seal. The elimination of the impact of the seal on the limitation period changes former § 8-13.

Subdivision 3 incorporates provisions of former § 8-13 regarding partnership accounts and accounts between merchants.

Subdivision 4 continues the former § 8-13 three-year limitation for unwritten contracts.

The proviso relating to the application of § 8.2-725, the UCC four-year limitation to contracts for the sale of goods, is the same as that contained in former § 8-13, except for the express stipulation that the UCC limitation, like other contract limitations, has no applicability to an action for injuries to person or to actions for injury to property which is not subject to the contract of sale. The distinctions contained in this proviso regarding the types of injury and the applicable statute of limitations in products liability actions, § 8.01-243, are in accord with Virginia law. Compare Friedman v. Peoples' Serv. Drug Stores, 208 Va. 700, 160 S.E.2d 563 (1968) with Tyler v. R.R. Street & Co., 322 F. Supp. 541 (E.D. Va. 1971).

The meaning of "award" in former § 8-13 is unclear and "award" has been deleted in § 8.01-246.

Cross references. — As to effect of new promise on statute, see § 8.01-229. For provision that statute not to apply to proceedings by State, see § 8.01-231. As to effect of promise not to plead statute, see § 8.01-232. As to limitation of personal actions generally, see § 8.01-243. As to limitation on enforcement of judgments, see § 8.01-251. As to limitation of claims against the State, see §§ 8.01-195.7, 8.01-255. For statute of limitations applying to negotiable and non-negotiable notes, notwithstanding this section, see § 8.3A-118. As to limitation on enforcement of mechanics' lien, see § 43-17. For sufficiency of allegation that action is barred by statute of limitations, where particular statute relied on is not specified, see Rule 3:16(e).

Law Review. — For survey of the Virginia law on contracts and sales for the year 1967-1968, see 54 Va. L. Rev. 1572 (1968). For survey of Virginia law on torts for the year 1967-1968, see 54 Va. L. Rev. 1649 (1968). For survey of Virginia law on practice and pleading for the year 1973-1974, see 60 Va. L. Rev. 1572 (1974). For survey of Virginia law on practice and pleading for the year 1974-1975, see 61 Va. L. Rev. 1799 (1975). For survey of Virginia practice and pleading for the year 1975-1976, see 62 Va. L. Rev. 1460 (1976). For article discussing statutes of limitation and repose in toxic substances litigation, see 16 U. Rich. L. Rev. 247 (1982). For article, "Products Liability and the Virginia Statute of Limitations — A Call for the Legislative Rescue Squad," see 16 U. Rich. L. Rev. 323 (1982). For comment on statutes of limitations applicable in legal malpractice actions, see 16 U. Rich. L. Rev. 907 (1982). For article, "Civil Rights and 'Personal Injuries': Virginia's Statute of Limitations for Section 1983 Suits," see 26 Wm. & Mary L. Rev. 199 (1985). For note, "Virginia's Acquisition of Unclaimed and Abandoned Personal Property," see 27 Wm. & Mary L. Rev. 409 (1986). For 1987 survey of Virginia civil procedure and practice, see 21 U. Rich. L. Rev. 667 (1987). For survey on property law in Virginia for 1989, see 23 U. Rich. L. Rev. 773 (1989). For an article on federal product liability reform legislation's consistency with Virginia law, see 4 Geo. Mason L. Rev. 279 (1996).

§ 8.01-246

I. Decisions Under Current Law.
   A. General Consideration.
   B. Proceedings to Which Section Applicable.
      1. Actions on Written Contracts.
      2. Other Contracts Express or Implied.
   C. Products Liability.
   D. Partnerships and Joint Ventures.
II. Decisions Under Prior Law.
   A. General Consideration.
   B. Proceedings to Which Section Applicable.
      1. Actions on Written Contracts.
      2. Partnership and Merchant Accounts.
      3. Other Contracts Express or Implied.
   C. Pleading and Practice.
      1. Raising Defense.
         a. Who May Raise Defense.
         b. Mode and Sufficiency.
         c. Time of Raising.
      2. Replication.
      3. Evidence.

I. DECISIONS UNDER CURRENT LAW.

A. General Consideration.

Federal courts do not adopt state statutes of limitations in cases involving a federal question, particularly when there is a federal statute of limitations on point. United States v. E & C Coal Co., 647 F. Supp. 268 (W.D. Va. 1986).

To successfully prove a claim of equitable estoppel under Virginia law the party seeking to defeat a plea of the statute of limitations must prove that: (1) a material fact was falsely represented or concealed; (2) the representation or concealment was made with knowledge of the fact; (3) the party to whom the representation was made was ignorant of the truth of the matter; (4) the representation was made with the intention that the other party should act on it; (5) the other party was induced to act on it; and (6) the party claiming the estoppel was misled to his injury. Alessio v. Adkins, 102 Bankr. 485 (Bankr. E.D. Va. 1989).

Only slightest injury required to start running of limitations period. — In Virginia, only the slightest injury is required to start the running of the limitations period. International Surplus Lines Ins. Co. v. Marsh & McLennan, Inc., 838 F.2d 124 (4th Cir. 1988).

Consent to search not a contract. — In action alleging, among other things, that officers to whom plaintiff gave consent to search of home breached agreement by bringing other officers along and searching for items not covered by the agreement, plaintiff could not claim the benefit of the five-year limitation on contract actions, as consent to a search is not a contract. Williams v. City of Portsmouth, 538 F. Supp. 74 (E.D. Va.), aff'd, 692 F.2d 754 (4th Cir. 1982).

Section held inapplicable. — In action under § 301 of the Labor Management Relations Act (29 U.S.C. § 185) to vacate an arbitration award, the most closely analogous statute of limitation under Virginia law was former § 8.01-579 (see now § 8.01-581.010 5), rather than this section or § 8.01-248. Local Union 8181, UMW v. Westmoreland Coal Co., 649 F. Supp. 603 (W.D. Va. 1986).

This dispute did not involve a common law action founded upon an express or implied contract, but rather an employer's duty to pay causally related medical benefits awarded to the claimant by the commission; thus the three year statute of limitations established by this section did not apply. Combustion Eng'g, Inc. v. Lafon, 22 Va. App. 235, 468 S.E.2d 698 (1996).

Limitation began to run when final decree entered in divorce case. — It was apparent from the allegations of the bill of complaint that the particular undertaking or transaction, which attorney was engaged to handle for client terminated on Dec. 30, 1980, then the divorce case was ended by the entry of a final decree incorporating the property settlement agreement. The limitation period then began to run and expired three years later. Thus, the chancellor correctly held that this suit, filed in Dec. 1984, was time-barred. MacLellan v. Throckmorton, 235 Va. 341, 367 S.E.2d 720 (1988).

Applied in APCO v. GE Co., 508 F. Supp. 530 (W.D. Va. 1980); Crosson v. Conlee, 745 F.2d 896 (4th Cir. 1984); Guth v. Hamlet Assocs., 230 Va. 64, 334 S.E.2d 558 (1985); Harris & Harris v. Tabler, 232 Va. 75, 348 S.E.2d 241 (1986); Harbour Gate Owners' Ass'n v. Berg, 232 Va. 98, 348 S.E.2d 252 (1986); Meadows v. Eaton Corp., 642 F. Supp. 284 (W.D. Va. 1986); Boone v. C. Arthur Weaver Co., 235 Va. 157, 365 S.E.2d 764 (1988); Belcher v. Kirkwood, 238 Va. 430, 383 S.E.2d 729 (1989); Delon Hampton &

Assocs. v. Washington Metro. Area Transit Auth., 943 F.2d 355 (4th Cir. 1991); Vines v. Branch, 244 Va. 185, 418 S.E.2d 890 (1992); Koonan v. Blue Cross & Blue Shield, 802 F. Supp. 1424 (E.D. Va. 1992).

B. Proceedings to Which Section Applicable.

1. Actions on Written Contracts.

Section expressly provides that where § 8.2-725 is applicable, that section shall be controlling. Sprague & Henwood v. Johnson, 606 F. Supp. 1564 (W.D. Va. 1985).

Cause of action on notes did not accrue until conditions in notes were satisfied. — Notes which incorporated various conditions which had to be satisfied before the debt evidenced by the notes became due and payable were not negotiable instruments and were simply contracts to pay money subject to certain conditions. As a result, the cause of action on the notes did not accrue and the statute did not begin to run until the conditions were fulfilled. Salomonsky v. Kelly, 232 Va. 261, 349 S.E.2d 358 (1986).

Actions for legal malpractice are governed by the limitations periods etc., thus, the trial court correctly applied the three-year limitation because the bill of complaint did not allege that the contract between attorney and client was in writing. MacLellan v. Throckmorton, 235 Va. 341, 367 S.E.2d 720 (1988).

Either the three- or five-year breach of contract statute of limitations would apply based on a finding as to whether the alleged malpractice was governed by a written or oral contract. To the extent that attorney's alleged wrongdoing stems from his actions as a director, the one-year statute will apply; to the extent the allegations stem from his service as savings and loan attorney, the applicable longer statutory period will apply. FDIC v. Cocke, 7 F.3d 396 (4th Cir. 1993), cert. denied, 513 U.S. 807, 115 S. Ct. 53, 130 L. Ed. 2d 12 (1994).

In Virginia, the applicable statutes of limitations for legal malpractice suits are the statutes of limitations for breaches of contracts. Marley Mouldings, Inc. v. Suyat, 970 F. Supp. 496 (W.D. Va. 1997).

The running of the statute of limitations for legal malpractice begins when the attorney's services in the matter in question have terminated. Marley Mouldings, Inc. v. Suyat, 970 F. Supp. 496 (W.D. Va. 1997).

Evidence did not show a complete and concluded agreement, required to bring malpractice action within the five year statute of limitations for breach of contract actions, but only an oral contract, triggering a three year limitation, which had run. Marley Mouldings, Inc. v. Suyat, 970 F. Supp. 496 (W.D. Va. 1997).

Action by accommodation maker of note against accommodated party. — An accommodation maker of a note was entitled to proceed against the accommodated party on the written instrument, and therefore the five-year limitation on written instruments under subdivision 2 was applicable rather than the three-year limitation under subdivision 4, where the maker made payment of the note to the holder, and the note was marked "paid" by the bank, since this endorsement did not have the effect of discharging the accommodated party's obligation to the maker, and since, under § 49-27, one secondarily liable on a note is substituted to the rights and remedies of the creditor. Payne v. Payne, 219 Va. 12, 245 S.E.2d 133 (1978).

Action on guaranty of demand note. — Under Virginia law, the cause of action on a guaranty of demand note accrues at the same time as does the claim on the note. WAMCO, III, Ltd. v. First Piedmont Mtg. Corp., 856 F. Supp. 1076 (E.D. Va. 1994), But see, Union Recovery Ltd. Partnership v. Horton, 252 Va. 418, 477 S.E.2d 521 (1996).

Life insurance. — With respect to life insurance policies, when a policy requires a demand for payment and proof of death, the statute of limitations begins to run on the date of the demand and proof. Arrington v. Peoples Sec. Life Ins. Co., 250 Va. 52, 458 S.E.2d 289 (1995).

Where plaintiffs filed ordinary bill of complaint instituting suit in equity upon written contracts, seeking alternative relief in the form of rescission on the ground of substantial failure of consideration or damages for breach of contract, a substantial failure of consideration is a well recognized ground for rescission of a contract. For this type of proceeding, the statute of limitations in Virginia is five years. Marriott v. Harris, 235 Va. 199, 368 S.E.2d 225 (1988).

2. Other Contracts Express or Implied.

Limitation period for breach of contract inapplicable to tort action. — Plaintiff cannot rely on the three-year limitation period for breach of contract both as a matter of fact, as well as Virginia law, where its damage award depends on a characterization of defendant's action as tortious. LaVay Corp. v. Dominion Fed. Sav. & Loan Ass'n, 830 F.2d 522 (4th Cir. 1987), cert. denied, 484 U.S. 1065, 108 S. Ct. 1027, 98 L. Ed. 2d 991 (1988).

Action for breach of warranty against supplier not in privity. — In an action for breach of warranty brought by a buyer against the supplier of a component part of the article at issue, the supplier was subject to a three-year statute of limitations for actions founded upon unwritten contracts since it was not privy to the contract of sale between the buyer and a

§ 8.01-246

construction equipment retailer. W.J. Rapp Co. v. Whitlock Equip. Corp., 222 Va. 80, 279 S.E.2d 133 (1981).

Wrongful disharge under conscience clause. — Where plaintiffs questioned whether Virginia's Conscience Clause (§ 18.2-75) imbued their claims with sufficient implied contractual obligations to warrant application of this section's three-year contract limitation period to a wrongful discharge claim based on the Conscience Clause, the court recently rejected a similar argument, holding that wrongful discharge claims fall under Virginia's catchall statute of limitations, § 8.01-248. Michael v. Sentara Health Sys., 939 F. Supp. 1220 (E.D. Va. 1996).

Action for reinstatement as an employee. — In an action for reinstatement as an employee, the relevant statute of limitations is subdivision 4. After an employee's discharge, all of the wrongs alleged relate solely to that event and the employer's refusal to change its decision. Thus the continuing violation doctrine does not apply. Otherwise, the employee could keep his claim of wrongful discharge forever alive by requesting once every three years that the employer reinstate him. This, of course, would destroy the policies of finality and repose underlying the statute of limitations. West v. ITT Continental Baking Co., 683 F.2d 845 (4th Cir. 1982).

An action to enforce an unwritten contract, express or implied, is barred by the statute of limitations if such action is not brought within three years after the cause of action accrues. Brown v. Harms, 251 Va. 301, 467 S.E.2d 805 (1996).

Inverse condemnation action is an action based on an implied contract. It follows that application of the period of limitations contained in subdivision 4 is proper. Prendergast v. Northern Va. Regional Park Auth., 227 Va. 190, 313 S.E.2d 399 (1984).

Attorney and client. — Where there existed a continuation of services in the relationship between attorney and client, the statute did not begin to run from the time plaintiffs had the right to demand payment, although the attorney had a right to require payment for services prior to the termination of their relationship. Wood v. Carwile, 231 Va. 320, 343 S.E.2d 346 (1986).

Right of action for contribution arises upon discharge of common obligation. — Before contribution will lie it is essential that a cause of action by the person injured have existed against the third-party defendant. But if such cause of action existed, the right of action to recover contribution arises upon discharge of the common obligation and the statute of limitations begins to run at that time. In order for contribution to lie, the injured party's cause of action against the third-party defendant need not be presently enforceable; it merely is necessary that the plaintiff, at some time in the past, have had an enforceable cause of action against the party from whom contribution is sought. Gemco-Ware, Inc. v. Rongene Mold & Plastics Corp., 234 Va. 54, 360 S.E.2d 342 (1987).

Oral contract for transfer of stock. — Cause of action on oral contract for transfer of stock accrued, and the statute of limitations began to run, on January 1, 1983, the date on which payment was due, and not on August 1, 1979, when the stock was transferred. Andrews v. Sams, 233 Va. 55, 353 S.E.2d 735 (1987).

C. Products Liability.

Claim based on defective appliance arising prior to October 1, 1977, held governed by § 8.2-725. — Where plaintiffs' home was damaged by fire on July 20, 1977, allegedly due to a defect in a portable refrigerator delivered to their residence on February 8, 1975, the limitation period for the warranty claims was four years and the time began to run from February 8, 1975, when the refrigerator was delivered, pursuant to § 8.2-725. Plaintiff's contention that their causes of action for breach of warranty accrued on July 20, 1977, when the fire occurred and that the limitation period was five years was misplaced, since this section was not effective until October 1, 1977. Stone v. Ethan Allen, Inc., 232 Va. 365, 350 S.E.2d 629 (1986).

D. Partnerships and Joint Ventures.

Period of limitations for joint venturer's right of action inter se. — Because the rules of law governing partnerships generally apply to joint ventures, the statute of limitations applicable to joint venturer's rights of action inter se is the five-year period prescribed by subdivision 3, governing actions between partners, rather than the limitation governing actions on contracts. Roark v. Hicks, 234 Va. 470, 362 S.E.2d 711 (1987).

Like partners, joint venturers have a fiduciary relationship among themselves which begins with the opening of the negotiations for the formation of the syndicate, applies to every phase of the business which is undertaken, and continues until the enterprise has been completely wound up and terminated. For that reason, the statute of limitations does not begin to run on joint venturers' claims inter se at the time of dissolution. Rather, it begins to run at the completion of winding up the affairs of the dissolved enterprise. Roark v. Hicks, 234 Va. 470, 362 S.E.2d 711 (1987).

II. DECISIONS UNDER PRIOR LAW.

A. General Consideration.

Editor's note. — The cases cited below were decided under corresponding provisions of

former law. The terms "the statute" and "this section," as used below, refer to former provisions.

A statute of limitations is a statute of repose. Templeman v. Pugh, 102 Va. 441, 46 S.E. 474 (1903); Virginia Hot Springs Co. v. McCray, 106 Va. 461, 56 S.E. 216 (1907).

To compel exercise of right of action. — Statutes of limitation are statutes of repose, the object of which is to compel the exercise of a right of action within a reasonable time. They are designed to suppress fraudulent and stale claims from being asserted after a great lapse of time, to the surprise of the parties, when the evidence may have been lost, the facts may have become obscure because of defective memory, or the witnesses have died or disappeared. Richmond Redevelopment & Hous. Auth. v. Laburnum Constr. Corp., 195 Va. 827, 80 S.E.2d 574 (1954).

Object of an action, and not its form, determines what act of limitation is applicable. Birmingham v. C & O Ry., 98 Va. 548, 37 S.E. 17 (1900).

Section is available only as a defense and never as a cause of action. Weems v. Carter, 30 F.2d 202 (4th Cir. 1929).

It is to be distinguished from rule presuming payment. — There is a recognized distinction between the statute of limitations and the presumption of payment from lapse of time, the condition of the parties, and their relation towards each other. In the former case the bar is absolute; in the latter it is a rule of evidence, and may be rebutted. Coles v. Ballard, 78 Va. 139 (1883); Clendenning v. Thompson, 91 Va. 518, 22 S.E. 233 (1895).

A limitation fixed by statute is arbitrary and peremptory, admitting of no excuse or delay beyond the period fixed, unless such excuse be recognized by the statute itself. The legislature has full power to make any exception it chooses, or to refuse to make any at all. If the statute makes exceptions, they exist; if not, they do not exist, as there is no limitation of actions at common law. Quackenbush v. Isley, 154 Va. 407, 153 S.E. 818 (1930).

And the legislature may alter limitation on existing contract. — It is within the power of the legislature to shorten the period of limitation on an existing contract, leaving always a reasonable time within which to invoke a remedy for its breach, or to prolong the period of limitation where the right to plead the statute has not accrued. Smith & Marsh v. Northern Neck Mut. Fire Ass'n, 112 Va. 192, 70 S.E. 482 (1911).

Statute applied in equity. — In cases concerning claims of an equitable nature, equity acts by analogy; that is, it applies the same bar to such claims that would be applied at law, under the statute, to legal claims of analogous character. Smith v. Thompson, 48 Va. (7 Gratt.) 112 (1850); Harshberger v. Alger, 72 Va. (31 Gratt.) 52 (1878); De Baun v. De Baun, 119 Va. 85, 89 S.E. 239 (1916).

Courts of equity follow the law as respects the statute of limitations. If a legal claim, barred at law, is asserted in equity, it is equally barred there. Rowe v. Bentley, 70 Va. (29 Gratt.) 756 (1878); Harshberger v. Alger, 72 Va. (31 Gratt.) 52 (1878); Bank of Old Dominion v. Allen, 76 Va. 200 (1882); Coles v. Ballard, 78 Va. 139 (1883); Hutcheson v. Grubbs, 80 Va. 251 (1885); Ayre v. Burke, 82 Va. 338, 4 S.E. 618 (1886); Switzer v. Noffsinger, 82 Va. 518 (1886); McCarty v. Ball, 82 Va. 872, 1 S.E. 189 (1887); Cottrell v. Watkins, 89 Va. 801, 17 S.E. 328 (1893); Redford v. Clarke, 100 Va. 115, 40 S.E. 630 (1902).

This section applies only to personal actions. Harper v. Harper, 159 Va. 210, 165 S.E. 490 (1932).

And to actions on contracts only. — This section applies only to suits arising upon contracts, and does not apply to an action against bank directors for misconduct and neglect of duties. Winston v. Gordon, 115 Va. 899, 80 S.E. 756 (1914).

But the language used in the classifications of contracts is all-inclusive and no obligation based on a contract, whether written, verbal or implied, is omitted. Hospelhorn v. Corbin, 179 Va. 348, 19 S.E.2d 72 (1942).

Section 8.01-243 applies to every action for personal injuries whether based on tort or contract. — Section 8.01-243, and thus the two-year limitation, does not apply only to tort actions, but to every action for personal injuries, whether it is based upon tort or contract. Therefore, the wrong alleged, not the form of the action, is what counts in the measurement and application of the appropriate limitation. Tyler v. R.R. St. & Co., 322 F. Supp. 541 (E.D. Va. 1971), commented on in 6 U. Rich. L. Rev. 167 (1971).

Since both this section and § 8.2-725 refer to actions in contract, it is not difficult to draw an analogy between § 8.01-243 as opposed to this section, and § 8.01-243 as opposed to § 8.2-725. It would appear that the Virginia courts would hold that § 8.01-243 applies in all cases in which a personal injury is involved, regardless of whether § 8.2-725 or this section is in issue, and the federal district court so holds. Tyler v. R.R. St. & Co., 322 F. Supp. 541 (E.D. Va. 1971), commented on in 6 U. Rich. L. Rev. 167 (1971).

Section 8.01-243 applies in an action for personal injuries grounded upon breach of implied warranty. Friedman v. Peoples Serv. Drug Stores, 208 Va. 700, 160 S.E.2d 563 (1968).

Since an action to recover damages for personal injuries based on a breach of warranty is essentially an action for personal injuries, the limitation thereon is governed by § 8.01-243, and not by this section applicable to an action based on contract. Caudill v. Wise Rambler, Inc., 210 Va. 11, 168 S.E.2d 257 (1969).

Debt is not cancelled though action is barred. — The provision is that no action "shall be brought" after a designated date. The debt is not cancelled, and there is no presumption of payment. It remains as an abiding moral obligation. Wilson v. Butt, 168 Va. 259, 190 S.E. 260 (1937).

Conflict of laws. — The statute of limitations of Virginia was held applicable in a suit brought in Virginia on a contract made in Kentucky. Bank of United States v. Donnally, 33 U.S. (8 Peters) 361, 8 L. Ed. 974 (1834).

This section applies in an action brought in a federal court in the State. Weems v. Carter, 30 F.2d 202 (4th Cir. 1929).

An action for negligence of an architect in performing professional services, while sounding in tort, is an action for breach of contract and is thus governed by statute of limitations applicable to contract. Comptroller ex rel. VMI v. King, 217 Va. 751, 232 S.E.2d 895 (1977).

Action for breach by depository of terms of escrow arrangement. — Where, in a suit to recover a sum which the plaintiffs allegedly lost as a result of the defendant attorney's breach of duty in closing a real estate transaction, allegations of the complaint clearly set forth the existence of an escrow arrangement involving the plaintiffs as grantors, defendants as compensated depositories, and a certain company as grantee, in an escrow arrangement, the parties occupy a principal-agent relationship, a relationship which is essentially contractual in nature, and since a breach by a depository of the terms of an escrow arrangement gives rise to a cause of action contractual in nature, the plaintiff's case was governed by the three-year period of limitation applicable to causes of action for contracts not in writing, contained in this section, rather than the one-year limitation for personal causes of action provided by § 8.01-248. Winslow, Inc. v. Scaife, 219 Va. 997, 254 S.E.2d 58 (1979).

B. Proceedings to Which Section Applicable.

1. Actions on Written Contracts.

Notes not under seal. — An action on a promissory note not under seal is barred in five years. Watson v. Hurt, 47 Va. (6 Gratt.) 633 (1850); Johnson v. Anderson, 76 Va. 766 (1882).

The statutory limitation ordinarily applying to a negotiable note or an instrument not under seal is five years. Quackenbush v. Isley, 154 Va. 407, 153 S.E. 818 (1930).

Statement of indebtedness may constitute "contract in writing". — Where a husband sold personal property jointly owned by himself and his wife, and took a note payable to himself, and then rendered his wife a statement in writing over his signature, showing that her share of the sale amounted to a sum stated, "which is due you out of R's note when collected," the statement constituted "a contract in writing, signed by the party to be charged thereby" within the contemplation of this section, and the period of limitation was five years. Lurty v. Lurty, 107 Va. 466, 59 S.E. 405 (1907).

Claim against prior indorser of negotiable note. — The claim of an indorser of a negotiable note to be reimbursed by a prior indorser for the payment of the note was not founded upon any implied promise or contract of the prior indorser growing out of the relations of the parties, but arose by virtue of former § 6-420 and was founded upon the note itself and the indorsement of the prior indorser; therefore the period of limitation was five years, and not three years, after the right of action first accrued. Mann v. Bradshaw, 136 Va. 351, 118 S.E. 326 (1923).

Agreement concerning alimony. — An action to recover money in lieu of alimony, based on writings and stipulations made by the parties during the pendency of an action for divorce, is barred by the five-year limitation. Newman v. McComb, 112 Va. 408, 71 S.E. 624 (1911).

Effect of recital of debt in deed of trust. — The mere recital of a debt in a deed of trust executed as collateral security, without any express covenant or promise therein to pay the debt, does not convert the simple contract debt secured by the trust deed into a specialty for the purposes of the statute of limitations. Wolf v. Violett, 78 Va. 57 (1883).

Architects' contract with government. — This section applies where allegations by builders are premised upon duties alleged to flow from architects' contract with the government. McCloskey & Co. v. Wright, 363 F. Supp. 223 (E.D. Va. 1973).

Action for unfair representation by union. — The two-year tort limitation set forth in § 8.01-243 controls an action charging union with unfair representations rather than the five-year contract statute of limitations under this section. Howard v. Aluminum Workers Int'l Union, 418 F. Supp. 1058 (E.D. Va. 1976), aff'd, 589 F.2d 771 (4th Cir. 1978).

2. Partnership and Merchant Accounts.

Cessation of partnership dealings. — The words "cessation of the dealings in which they are interested together" do not refer to the cessation of the active operations of the partnership, but embrace also any act done after its dissolution in winding it up. Foster v. Rison, 58 Va. (17 Gratt.) 321 (1867). See Hodge v.

Kennedy, 198 Va. 416, 94 S.E.2d 274 (1956).

Subdivision 3 as to accounts between merchant and merchant applies only to current or open accounts and not to accounts stated. Ellison v. Weintrob, 139 Va. 29, 123 S.E. 512 (1924).

But not to account where items all on one side. — The five-year limitation prescribed for accounts between merchants by this section is not applicable where there was never a mutual or current account, never any barter or exchange of goods between merchants, but only a single transaction with the debits all on one side. Ellison v. Weintrob, 139 Va. 29, 123 S.E. 512 (1924).

If the items of the account between merchant and merchant are all on one side, the claim will not be within the reason or principle of subdivision 3, which intends open and current accounts where there were mutual dealings and mutual credits or debits. Watson v. Lyle, 31 Va. (4 Leigh) 236 (1833); Wortham & Co. v. Smith & Sampson, 56 Va. (15 Gratt.) 487 (1860).

Ignorance of rights and fraud of partner. — Where one partner for himself and another settles the partnership accounts with the acting partner, and receives payments of money for himself and the others, the fact that the other was ignorant of the existence of the debt due from the partner who collected the money, until within five years before the institution of a suit, is not sufficient to repel the bar of the statute. To have that effect such ignorance must proceed from the fraud of the partner collecting the money. Foster v. Rison, 58 Va. (17 Gratt.) 321 (1867). See Bickle v. Chrisman, 76 Va. 678 (1882).

Statute had not run where debts outstanding within five years before suit. — Upon a bill filed by a surviving partner against the administratrix of a deceased partner, the plea of the statute of limitations could not be sustained, where it appeared that there were good debts due to the firm outstanding within five years before the suit was brought. Coalter v. Coalter, 40 Va. (1 Rob.) 79 (1842); Marsteller v. Weaver, 42 Va. (1 Gratt.) 391 (1845); Jordan v. Miller, 75 Va. 442 (1881).

3. Other Contracts Express or Implied.

Oral contract. — Where evidence showed that the contract involved was oral and not written, the applicable period of limitation under this section was three years. Stauffer v. Fredericksburg Ramada, Inc., 411 F. Supp. 1136 (E.D. Va. 1976).

Attorney malpractice. — An action for the negligence of an attorney in the performance of professional services, while sounding in tort, is an action for breach of contract and thus governed by the statute of limitations applicable to contracts. Oleyar v. Kerr, 217 Va. 88, 225 S.E.2d 398 (1976).

Action for amount of undercharge in freight shipment rate. — Congress not having prescribed any time within which an action shall be brought to recover the difference between an undercharge and the published rate on an interstate shipment of freight, the limitation on such a contract is that applicable to other implied contracts, which, under the statute of this State is three years. Atlantic C.L.R.R. v. Virginia Mfg. Co., 119 Va. 5, 88 S.E. 103 (1916).

Action for reasonable value of services rendered under unenforceable contract. — An action to recover the reasonable value of services rendered pursuant to a contract that was unenforceable under the statute of frauds is governed by the three-year limitation in this section. Ricks v. Sumler, 179 Va. 571, 19 S.E.2d 889 (1942).

Action to recover taxes illegally exacted. — An action to recover taxes illegally exacted and paid under compulsion is governed by the statute of limitations applicable to a suit to recover money had and received under an implied promise to pay. City of Charlottesville v. Marks' Shows, Inc., 179 Va. 321, 18 S.E.2d 890 (1942).

Action on stock assessment. — On stock assessments, when no written contract has been established, the limitation on the right of recovery is three years from the date of the call on the stock. Liberty Sav. Bank v. Otterview Land Co., 96 Va. 352, 31 S.E. 511 (1898).

The implied contract of assignee of stock to pay unpaid installments is governed by the three-year limitation in this section. Gold v. Paynter, 101 Va. 714, 44 S.E. 920 (1903).

Action to enforce bank stockholder's double liability. — Actions to enforce bank stockholder's double liability created by the laws of another state are governed by this section. Hospelhorn v. Corbin, 179 Va. 348, 19 S.E.2d 72 (1942).

Action for contribution by joint tortfeasors. — Where a transit company brought an action for contribution, on behalf of insurance carriers who had indemnified the company for damages paid to a passenger for personal injuries, against tort-feasors jointly responsible with the transit company for the injuries, the cause of action arose out of an implied promise to pay, and therefore the three-year statute applied. McKay v. Citizens Rapid Transit Co., 190 Va. 851, 59 S.E.2d 121 (1950).

The cause of action in cases of this kind arises out of the implied promise to pay, and therefore the three-year statute of limitations would apply. Nationwide Mut. Ins. Co. v. Jewel Tea Co., 202 Va. 527, 118 S.E.2d 646 (1961).

Implied contract for contribution by co-surety. — The right of action of a surety who calls upon a cosurety for contribution is based upon the implied promise growing out of the equitable relations which the sureties bear to each other, and not upon the written contract by which they become sureties. The statute of limitations applicable to such a case is three years, and not the limitation which applies to the bond, note or other writing which the surety has been compelled to pay. Tate v. Winfree, 99 Va. 255, 37 S.E. 956 (1901).

Parol agreement as to mode of payment of notes. — The maker and the payee of notes secured by a deed of trust entered into a contemporaneous parol agreement under which the payee was to go into possession of the land conveyed by the deed of trust and take the rents and profits of the land and the services of the maker for the term of the loan, at the end of which time the notes were to be discharged and the land released from the lien of the deed of trust. It was held that this agreement was a mere executory oral contract, barred by the three-year limitation in this section, and not a payment of the notes, against which limitation would not run, because it did not appear that there had ever been any acceptance of the possession of the land or the services of the maker as a payment of the notes. Rector v. Hancock, 127 Va. 101, 102 S.E. 663 (1920).

Vendee's obligation to pay purchase money. — Where the vendee's obligation to pay the purchase price of land is not evidenced in any other manner than by his acceptance of the deed, it is a simple contract debt, and the statute of limitations applicable to that class of debts is to be applied. Harris v. Shield, 111 Va. 643, 69 S.E. 933 (1911).

Unsigned agreement by grantee to pay notes for deferred purchase money payments. — The grantee's contract, by reason of his acceptance of a deed without executing it, containing a covenant on his part to pay notes given for deferred payments of purchase money, is a simple contract, and not a specialty, and is subject to the act of limitations applicable to simple contracts, to-wit: three years. Taylor v. Forbes, 101 Va. 658, 44 S.E. 888 (1903).

Assumption by grantee of bonds given for purchase money. — In Virginia it is held that if the grantee of a deed assumes the payment of bonds given by his grantor for purchase money, and does not sign the deed, this creates a simple contract debt which is barred within three years from the time when it is assumed. W.L. Becker & Co. v. Norfolk & W. Ry., 125 Va. 558, 100 S.E. 478 (1919).

Action for double compensation under the Fair Labor Standards Act. — The double compensation provision of the Fair Labor Standards Act for failure to pay the minimum wages is compensation, not a penalty or punishment by the government, and this section is applicable to both the unpaid wages under the act and the double liability. Reliance Storage & Inspection Co. v. Hubbard, 50 F. Supp. 1012 (W.D. Va. 1943).

Suit against devisee to enforce right to support from realty. — Where testator devised a tract of land to his son, and also provided that his daughter was to have her home and support on the tract as long as she remained single, and the daughter was compelled to leave because of the conduct of the son's wife, the son's personal liability to the daughter arose by virtue of an implied or quasi-contract, and the statutory period of limitations applicable to an oral agreement applied and barred the entry of a personal judgment against him as to any sum which accrued more than three years prior to the institution of suit. Davis v. Davis, 190 Va. 468, 57 S.E.2d 137 (1950).

Recovery of money paid under mistake. — Subject to the provision in § 8.01-249, the three-year limitation applies to actions to recover money paid under mistake of fact. Hughes v. Foley, 203 Va. 904, 128 S.E.2d 261 (1962).

Recovery of money paid to county treasurer as compensation. — Money received by a county treasurer in good faith as compensation for his services, and allowed to him in a settlement with the board of supervisors regularly made, is not held by him as a trustee, and the statute of limitations applies to an action against him to recover it back. Board of Supvrs. v. Vaughan, 117 Va. 146, 83 S.E. 1056 (1915).

Suit for settlement of county funds. — Demands arising more than three years before the institution of a suit by the supervisors of a county against the county treasurer for a settlement and adjustment of the county funds received by him are not barred by the statute of limitations. Herrell v. Board of Supvrs., 113 Va. 594, 75 S.E. 87 (1912).

Bond of county treasurer. — The right of the holder of a county warrant drawn on funds in the hands of a county treasurer, and duly registered, to assert his claim against a fund created by the treasurer for the indemnity of his sureties is never barred as to the treasurer, and as to the sureties it is not barred until ten years from the time the right of action accrues. Jennings v. Taylor, 102 Va. 191, 45 S.E. 913 (1903).

C. Pleading and Practice.

1. Raising Defense.

a. Who May Raise Defense.

Statute is a personal defense. — The defense of the statute of limitations is a personal privilege, and to be made availing must be pleaded by defendants. The court has no power to interpose a plea ex mero motu. Clayton v. Henley, 73 Va. (32 Gratt.) 65 (1879);

Smith v. Hutchinson, 78 Va. 683 (1884); McCartney v. Tyrer, 94 Va. 198, 26 S.E. 419 (1897).

Creditors may set it up in equity. — Where equity has taken possession of an estate for the purpose of distributing it among the creditors, any one of them interested in the fund may interpose the defense to the claim of another creditor. Tazewell's Ex'r v. Whittle's Adm'r, 54 Va. (13 Gratt.) 329 (1856); McCartney v. Tyrer, 94 Va. 198, 26 S.E. 419 (1897).

One creditor may set up the statute of limitations in a creditors' suit against the demand of another, although the debtor himself did not rely on it. Callaway v. Saunders, 99 Va. 350, 38 S.E. 182 (1901).

b. Mode and Sufficiency.

Defense may be raised by answer. — Anything in an answer which will apprise the plaintiff that the defendant relies on the statute of limitations is sufficient, if such facts are stated as are necessary to show that the statute is applicable. Tazewell's Ex'r v. Whittle's Adm'r, 54 Va. (13 Gratt.) 329 (1856).

Must be relied on in pleadings. — In order for the statute of limitations to be of avail to a party it must be relied on in the pleadings. Hickman v. Stout, 29 Va. (2 Leigh) 6 (1830); Smith v. Hutchinson, 78 Va. 683 (1884); Gibson v. Green, 89 Va. 524, 16 S.E. 661 (1893).

The statute of limitations cannot be insisted on in equity without being pleaded, or in some form relied on as a defense in the pleadings. Hickman v. Stout, 29 Va. (2 Leigh) 6 (1830); Gibson v. Green, 89 Va. 524, 16 S.E. 661 (1893); Hubble v. Poff, 98 Va. 646, 37 S.E. 277 (1900).

But not where there is no notice of set-off. — Where a defendant does not file the plea of set-off, but files his account and gives notice of set-off, the plaintiff has no opportunity to apply the statute of limitations, and he is therefore at liberty to rely upon it in evidence though it has not been set up in the replication. Trimyer v. Pollard, 46 Va. (5 Gratt.) 460 (1842).

Plea should state act relied on. — A plea of the statute of limitations should state on what act the defendant relies. A plea which merely refers in general terms to "the act of limitations" is irregular. Wortham & Co. v. Smith & Sampson, 56 Va. (15 Gratt.) 487 (1860).

It should refer to time of suit. — The plea of the statute of limitations should refer to the time of the institution of the suit. Smith v. Walker, 1 Va. (1 Wash.) 135 (1792).

When plea to some of several claims applicable to all. — Where a plea of the statute of limitations in form applies to only two out of three claims sued on, but it is clear that both parties and the court treated it as applicable to all the claims sued on, and all were in fact barred by the statute, and the trial court so held, its judgment, though technically erroneous, will not be reversed. Liskey v. Paul, 100 Va. 764, 42 S.E. 875 (1902).

Taking issue on plea constituting no defense. — Where the defendant pleaded that the demand sued for had accrued more than three years before the action was instituted, and the plaintiff took issue on the plea, and it appeared that the right to recover was founded on a contract evidenced by writings, the court did not err in refusing to instruct the jury on the issue raised by the plea of the three-year statute, though the plaintiff should have demurred or objected to the plea instead of taking issue upon it. Newman v. McComb, 112 Va. 408, 71 S.E. 624 (1911).

Answer by legatee to bill against executor and legatee. — In a bill by creditor of testator against executor and legatee, the latter relies upon the statute of limitations in his answer. This is sufficient to protect the estate from a decree against the executor. Tazewell's Ex'r v. Whittle's Adm'r, 54 Va. (13 Gratt.) 329 (1856).

Bar of the statute may be set up in equity by excepting to the report of the commissioner. Johnston v. Wilson, 70 Va. (29 Gratt.) 379 (1877); Smith v. Pattie, 81 Va. 654 (1886); Ayre v. Burke, 82 Va. 338, 4 S.E. 618 (1886); Leith v. Carter, 83 Va. 889, 5 S.E. 584 (1887).

Waiver of statute of limitations as a defense. — In a suit by a board of supervisors against a county treasurer for the settlement of his accounts, the treasurer's answer uniting in the prayer of the bill for an account, and specifically praying for an inquiry into all settlements made by him "from the time he became such treasurer until the present moment," is a waiver of the statute of limitations. Herrell v. Board of Supvrs., 113 Va. 594, 75 S.E. 87 (1912).

c. Time of Raising.

Plea not allowed after joinder of issue on another plea. — A plea of the act of limitations ought not to be received after issue joined on another plea, unless some good reason be assigned why the plea of the act of limitations was not sooner tendered. Martin v. Anderson, 27 Va. (6 Rand.) 19 (1827).

Delay in filing plea in equity. — A plea of the statute of limitations which is not interposed in a chancery suit until after the evidence is closed, may well be rejected, as coming too late, where no excuse is offered for the delay. Herrell v. Board of Supvrs., 113 Va. 594, 75 S.E. 87 (1912).

The transferee was unable to enforce a note where he did not bring his action within the five year limitation following the note's maturity. Yeskolski v. Crosby, 480 S.E.2d 474 (1997).

2. Replication.

Exceptions to statute must be pleaded. — Where the statute is pleaded, plaintiff, to bring himself within its savings, must set forth the facts relied on either by replication or by amending his bill. Lewis v. Bacon, 13 Va. (3 Hen. & M.) 89 (1808); Switzer v. Noffsinger, 82 Va. 518 (1886).

And allegations must be supported by evidence. — Where a replication was filed to the plea of the statute of limitations that the accounts concerned the trade of merchandise between merchant and merchant, but no evidence was adduced to prove that either party was a merchant during the time of their dealings, nor any evidence of the character of the dealings between them, the replication was not supported by the evidence and the demand was therefore barred. Watson v. Lyle, 31 Va. (4 Leigh) 236 (1833).

3. Evidence.

Burden of proof is on the pleader. — The burden is on the pleader to make out a case to which the statute clearly applies. Goodell's Ex'r v. Gibbons, 91 Va. 608, 22 S.E. 504 (1895); Virginia Ry. & Power Co. v. Ferebee, 115 Va. 289, 78 S.E. 556 (1913); Virginia Lumber & Extract Co. v. O.D. McHenry Lumber Co., 122 Va. 111, 94 S.E. 173 (1917).

If the creditor relies upon a charge in a will to prevent the operation of the statute, it is for him to show that the testator died before his debt was barred. Tazewell's Ex'r v. Whittle's Adm'r, 54 Va. (13 Gratt.) 329 (1856).

Where the statute of limitations is pleaded as a defense, the party relying thereon has the burden of showing by a preponderance of the evidence that the cause of action arose more than the statutory period before the action was instituted. Columbia Heights Section 3, Inc. v. Griffith-Consumers Co., 205 Va. 43, 135 S.E.2d 116 (1964).

Where a statement of account specified that it was due "on receipt," the burden was on defendant, who pleaded the statute of limitations, to prove the date of receipt. Columbia Heights Section 3, Inc. v. Griffith-Consumers Co., 205 Va. 43, 135 S.E.2d 116 (1964).

The burden is upon the party pleading the statute of limitations as a defense to show by a preponderance of the evidence that the cause of action arose more than the statutory period before the action was instituted. Clifton D. Mayhew, Inc. v. Blake Constr. Co., 482 F.2d 1260 (4th Cir. 1973).

The course of dealings between the parties may show their intent. Clifton D. Mayhew, Inc. v. Blake Constr. Co., 482 F.2d 1260 (4th Cir. 1973).

§ 8.01-247. When action on contract governed by the law of another state or country barred in Virginia. — No action shall be maintained on any contract which is governed by the law of another state or country if the right of action thereon is barred either by the laws of such state or country or of this Commonwealth. (Code 1950, § 8-23; 1977, c. 617.)

REVISERS' NOTE

Section 8.01-247 restates former § 8-23 relating to foreign contracts. The words "is governed by the law of" are substituted for the former words "was made or was to be performed in," because the former phrase is more in keeping with modern conflicts of laws principles. No change in substance is intended thereby. The section also removes the residency proscription of former § 8-23.

I. DECISIONS UNDER CURRENT LAW.

Repeated defamations do not constitute a continuing tort, such that the statute of limitations runs only from the last statement, as the courts have uniformly recognized that each separate defamatory statement itself constitutes a separate and distinct cause of action. Lewis v. Gupta, 54 F. Supp. 2d 611 (E.D. Va. 1999).

Applied in Zukowski v. Dunton, 650 F.2d 30 (4th Cir. 1981); Blue Cross & Blue Shield Ass'n v. Group Hospitalization & Medical Servs., Inc., 744 F. Supp. 700 (E.D. Va. 1990).

§ 8.01-247.1. Limitation on action for defamation, etc. — Every action for injury resulting from libel, slander, insulting words or defamation shall be brought within one year after the cause of action accrues. (1995, c. 9.)

§ 8.01-248. **Personal actions for which no other limitation is specified.** — Every personal action accruing on or after July 1, 1995, for which no limitation is otherwise prescribed, shall be brought within two years after the right to bring such action has accrued. (Code 1950, § 8-24; 1954, c. 589; 1973, c. 385; 1977, c. 617; 1995, c. 9.)

REVISERS' NOTE

Section 8.01-248 is a catch-all provision for actions not otherwise covered by a statute of limitation; e.g., malicious prosecution and abuse of process. Cf. § 8.01-249 (3).

Law Review. — For survey of Virginia law on torts for the year 1976-77, see 63 Va. L. Rev. 1491 (1977). For survey of Virginia law on practice and pleading for the year 1978-1979, see 66 Va. L. Rev. 343 (1980). For article, "Virginia's Statute of Limitations for Section 1983 Claims After Wilson v. Garcia," see 19 U. Rich. L. Rev. 257 (1985). For article, "Civil Rights and 'Personal Injuries': Virginia's Statute of Limitations for Section 1983 Suits," see 26 Wm. & Mary L. Rev. 199 (1985). For 1987 survey of Virginia civil procedure and practice, see 21 U. Rich. L. Rev. 667 (1987). For 1995 survey of employment law, see 29 U. Rich. L. Rev. 1027 (1995).

I. Decisions Under Current Law.
II. Decisions Under Prior Law.

I. DECISIONS UNDER CURRENT LAW.

Effect of 1995 amendment. — The 1995 amendment to this section, which extended the limitation period on miscellaneous causes of action to two years, did not apply retroactively to cover plaintiff's cases. Nothing in the amended statute suggested that it applied retroactively, and in fact, the inclusion of an effective date, July 1, 1995, suggested just the opposite. Michael v. Sentara Health Sys., 939 F. Supp. 1220 (E.D. Va. 1996).

The statute of limitations cannot begin to run against a claim until all the elements of the cause of action exist and that one of the essential elements of a cause of action for personal injury is the injury itself. Brown v. ABC, 704 F.2d 1296 (4th Cir. 1983).

The statute of limitations does not accrue separately for each set of damages which results from a wrongful act. Once a cause of action is complete and the statute of limitations begins to run, it runs against all damages resulting from the wrongful act, even damages which may not arise until a future date. Brown v. ABC, 704 F.2d 1296 (4th Cir. 1983).

Cause accrues despite lack of quantifiable harm. — Where plaintiff was aware of accountant's report letters and their review by third party absence of quantifiable harm as of that time did not mean that plaintiff's cause of action had not yet accrued. Semida v. Rice, 863 F.2d 1156 (4th Cir. 1988).

Tolling of statute. — A statute of limitations is tolled until a person intentionally misled by a putative defendant could reasonably discover the wrongdoing and bring action to redress it. Under Virginia's doctrine of equitable estoppel, however, the Federal Deposit Insurance Corporation (FDIC) would have to do more than show that all of savings and loan directors were implicated in the wrongdoing, and that it was unable to sue until it became the corporation's receiver. The FDIC also would have to show that the directors concealed their wrongdoing from savings and loan, subsidiary, and their shareholders, the parties from whom the FDIC derived its interest in this lawsuit, during the period after the last act of alleged misconduct until the FDIC became receiver. It would be for the district court, on remand, to determine the extent to which equitable estoppel tolled Virginia's one-year statute of limitations. FDIC v. Cocke, 7 F.3d 396 (4th Cir. 1993), cert. denied, 513 U.S. 807, 115 S. Ct. 53, 130 L. Ed. 2d 12 (1994).

This section held inapplicable. — A claim which sought to pierce the corporate veil of automobile dealership and impose personal liability on the defendant shareholders for the fraudulent conveyance of the dealership's assets was not a fraud claim and thus was subject to limitation period in § 8.01-253 rather than this section. Curley v. Dahlgren Chrysler-Plymouth, Dodge, Inc., 245 Va. 429, 429 S.E.2d 221 (1993).

Defamation. — The Virginia Supreme Court has consistently applied the one-year statute of limitation in this section to defamation actions. Morrissey v. William Morrow & Co., 739 F.2d 962 (4th Cir. 1984), cert. denied,

469 U.S. 1216, 105 S. Ct. 1194, 84 L. Ed. 2d 340 (1985).

This section is applicable to actions for defamation. Welch v. Kennedy Piggly Wiggly Stores, Inc., 63 Bankr. 888 (W.D. Va. 1986).

The statute of limitations under the law of the Commonwealth of Virginia for defamation is one year. Lewin v. Medical College, 910 F. Supp. 1161 (E.D. Va. 1996), See also, 931 F. Supp. 443 (E.D. Va. 1996), aff'd, 120 F.3d 261, 131 F.3d 135 (4th Cir. 1997).

Defamation based on memorandum of lis pendens. — In proceeding on a theory of personal defamation, based on statements made in a memorandum of lis pendens, plaintiff's threshold burden was to prove that defendants' alleged defamatory statements were falsely made. Had defendants prevailed in their action in state court to have fraudulent conveyances set aside, plaintiff would be estopped from pursuing such a claim since defendants' assertions would have been adjudged as valid. Thus, it was only after the court ruled in plaintiff's favor (as defendant) that her action for defamation fully accrued. Since she instituted the suit within one year from the date of the state court's final order her defamation action was timely. Warren v. Bank of Marion, 618 F. Supp. 317 (W.D. Va. 1985).

Transmission of contract file held not republication. — Where employee of company sent contract file with defamatory letter, employee's transmission of contract file did not constitute republication since employee had no reason to know of defamatory contents of file and did nothing to draw particular attention to letter; since letter was republished at time it was first distributed to company, multiple copies within organization were considered part of aggregate communication, and aggregate communication was treated as single publication for which only one action for damages could have been maintained. Semida v. Rice, 863 F.2d 1156 (4th Cir. 1988).

Slander of title. — The fact that plaintiff instituted an action for slander of title approximately five and one-half years after the filing of defendants' memorandum of lis pendens was not dispositive of her claim for slander of title, since her cause of action did not fully accrue and the limitations period did not begin to run until the defendants released their claim against her property. Since plaintiff filed her action within one year of this release, she was held not to be barred by application of Virginia's statute of limitations for defamation actions (this section), much less its limitations period of injury to property (§ 8.01-243), the court finding it unnecessary to decide the issue of the applicable limitations period. Warren v. Bank of Marion, 618 F. Supp. 317 (W.D. Va. 1985).

Maritime claims. — When general maritime claims are at issue, the equity rule of laches, rather than any rigid statute of limitations, governs. Moore v. Exxon Transp. Co., 502 F. Supp. 583 (E.D. Va. 1980).

The most appropriate limitation period for federal Education for All Handicapped Children Act(20 U.S.C. § 1400 et seq.) claims is the one-year period of this section. Kirchgessner ex rel. Kirchgessner v. Davis, 632 F. Supp. 616 (W.D. Va. 1986).

Individuals with Disabilities Education Act. — The appropriate period of limitations for actions brought under the Individuals with Disabilities Education Act, 20 U.S.C. §§ 1400-85, is one year; the one-year statute of limitations was borrowed from this section, which provides the limitations period for all personal actions when a specific time frame is not provided by the statute creating the cause of action. Richards v. Fairfax County Sch. Bd., 798 F. Supp. 338 (E.D. Va. 1992), aff'd, 7 F.3d 225 (4th Cir. 1993).

This section provides the appropriate limitation for judicial review actions brought under the Individuals with Disabilities Education Act (IDEA), 20 U.S.C. § 1471 et seq., as well as administrative IDEA proceedings. Manning ex rel. Manning v. Fairfax School, 176 F.3d 235 (4th Cir. 1999).

Fraud and constructive fraud. — The statute of limitations for fraud and constructive fraud is one year. LaVay Corp. v. Dominion Fed. Sav. & Loan Ass'n, 645 F. Supp. 612 (E.D. Va. 1986), modified on other grounds, 830 F.2d 522 (4th Cir. 1987), cert. denied, 484 U.S. 1065, 108 S. Ct. 1027, 98 L. Ed. 2d 991 (1988).

When action for fraud accrues. — A cause of action based on fraud accrues at the time when the fraud is discovered or by the exercise of due diligence ought to have been discovered. United States v. Daves, 72 Bankr. 943 (Bankr. E.D. Va. 1987).

Limitation period for oral contracts inapplicable to claim of fraud. — The duty to refrain from fraudulent acts is imposed by tort law, not by any contract between the parties. The character of fraud is not changed from tort to contract merely because the parties are also engaged in a contractual relationship. Thus, the three-year period of limitations applicable to actions on oral contracts does not apply to a claim of fraud predicated upon alleged misrepresentations by insurer's agent that caused the insurer to include the wife's car under the husband's policy when the wife, not the husband, was the owner of the car. House v. Kirby, 233 Va. 197, 355 S.E.2d 303 (1987).

Lender's fraud. — Where plaintiff alleged that they were fraudulently induced to convey to lenders security interest in both corporate and individual assets, which they subsequently lost entirely through foreclosure and repossession, and where plaintiffs, suffered loss of all use, enjoyment and value in their property by

§ 8.01-248

reason of alleged fraud, allegedly wrongful acts were aimed at persons of plaintiffs, rather than injuring their property since property had same form, same value, and was adapted to same uses after defendants' actions as before; therefore, statute of limitations for personal injury rather than injury to property was appropriate. J.F. Toner & Son, Inc. v. Staunton Prod. Credit Ass'n, 237 Va. 155, 375 S.E.2d 530 (1989).

Virginia does not recognize adverse domination. Resolution Trust Corp. v. Everhart, 37 F.3d 151 (4th Cir. 1994).

Action for conversion against bank. — Five-year limitation period found in subsection B of § 8.01-243 applied to an action for conversion against a bank; two-year period in subsection A of § 8.01-243 was not applicable, nor was the one-year period found in this section. Bader v. Central Fid. Bank, 245 Va. 286, 427 S.E.2d 184 (1993).

Realtor's fraud. — The fraud allegedly committed by the realtor had no impact on the real property itself. The purchasers' land was in the same condition and was available for the same use after the alleged fraud as it was before. The defendants' conduct was directed at the plaintiffs personally and not their property, real or personal. Consequently, the trial court correctly decided the one-year limitation governs an action for fraud. Pigott v. Moran, 231 Va. 76, 341 S.E.2d 179 (1986).

Fraud is a tort. — The wrongful act is aimed at the person and, when sued upon at law, fraud will support a recovery for financial damage personal to the individual. Pigott v. Moran, 231 Va. 76, 341 S.E.2d 179 (1986).

Unlawful searches and seizures. — Under Virginia law, an unlawful search and seizure is characterized as a personal injury, not an injury to property; thus the applicable statute of limitations is two years under this section. Samuel v. Rose's Stores, Inc., 907 F. Supp. 159 (E.D. Va. 1995).

Actions for legal malpractice are governed by the limitations periods applicable to actions for breach of contract. Either the three- or five-year contract statute of limitations would apply based on a finding as to whether the alleged malpractice was governed by a written or oral contract. To the extent that attorney's alleged wrongdoing stems from his actions as a director, the one-year statute will apply; to the extent the allegations stem from his service as savings and loan attorney, the applicable longer statutory period will apply. FDIC v. Cocke, 7 F.3d 396 (4th Cir. 1993), cert. denied, 513 U.S. 807, 115 S. Ct. 53, 130 L. Ed. 2d 12 (1994).

Actions for wrongful discharge. — This section's one year statute of limitations applies to actions for wrongful discharge. Guiden v. Southeastern Public Serv. Auth., 760 F. Supp. 1171 (E.D. Va. 1991).

The one-year statute of limitations under this section applied to plaintiff's wrongful discharge claims, regardless of the fact that plaintiffs alleged that the wrongful discharge caused damages in the form of emotional and physical harm. Michael v. Sentara Health Sys., 939 F. Supp. 1220 (E.D. Va. 1996).

A common law cause of action for wrongful discharge is most analogous to an action under ERISA. In such a case an employee is claiming that her employer fired her wrongfully, either to prevent her from obtaining retirement benefits or in retaliation for the employee's earlier exercise of her rights under a benefits agreement. Such a proceeding is almost identical to an action for wrongful discharge in violation of public policy, and therefore, the wrongful discharge claims in this case fell under the one year catch-all statute of limitations under this section, and not the five-year statute of limitations for contract claims. Sutter v. First Union Nat'l Bank, 932 F. Supp. 753 (E.D. Va. 1996).

Where plaintiffs questioned whether Virginia's Conscience Clause (§ 18.2-75) imbued their claims with sufficient implied contractual obligations to warrant application of Virginia's three-year contract limitation period set out in § 8.01-246, to a wrongful discharge claim based on the Conscience Clause, the court recently rejected a similar argument, holding that wrongful discharge claims fall under Virginia's catchall statute of limitations, this section. Michael v. Sentara Health Sys., 939 F. Supp. 1220 (E.D. Va. 1996).

Actions for constructive discharge. — Plaintiff argued that the constructive discharge fell within the relevant period in the tolling agreement, thereby making plaintiff's filing timely. Virginia, though, does not recognize a cause of action for constructive wrongful discharge. Thus, the court granted defendants' motion for summary judgment as to the plaintiff's claims for constructive wrongful discharge. Michael v. Sentara Health Sys., 939 F. Supp. 1220 (E.D. Va. 1996).

Wrongful termination. — Where suit for wrongful termination was not a suit for a "positive, physical or mental hurt" and plaintiff advanced no other applicable limitation period, cause of action for wrongful termination was subject to the limitation period established in this section. Purcell v. Tidewater Constr. Corp., 250 Va. 93, 458 S.E.2d 291 (1995) (decision prior to 1995 amendment).

While a wrongful discharge claim is not a perfect mirror for a WARN Act claim, the catchall nature of this section is particularly suited for "borrowing" because it explicitly operates as the default statute under Virginia law; thus where plaintiff filed his claim beyond the applicable one-year limitations period, dismissal was required. Luczkovich v. Melville Corp., 911 F. Supp. 208 (E.D. Va. 1996).

RICO actions. — The four-year federal statute of limitations applicable to Clayton Act (15 U.S.C. § 15b) actions is the appropriate limitations period for civil RICO actions. The one-year "catch-all" limitations period in this section is inapplicable to civil RICO actions. HMK Corp. v. Walsey, 828 F.2d 1071 (4th Cir. 1987), cert. denied, 484 U.S. 1009, 108 S. Ct. 706, 98 L. Ed. 2d 657 (1988).

U.S. Supreme Court has held the four-year federal statute of limitations applicable to Clayton Act(15 U.S.C. § 15b) actions to be the appropriate limitations period. See Agency Holding Corp. v. Malley-Duff & Assocs., 483 U.S. 143, 107 S. Ct. 2759, 97 L. Ed. 2d 121 (1987).

Federal labor action. — In action under § 301 of the Labor Management Relations Act(29 U.S.C. § 185) to vacate an arbitration award, the most closely analogous statute of limitation under Virginia law was former § 8.01-579 (see now § 8.01-581.010 5), rather than § 8.01-246 or this section. Local Union 8181, UMW v. Westmoreland Coal Co., 649 F. Supp. 603 (W.D. Va. 1986).

An action under section 921(d) of the Longshore and Harbor Workers' Compensation Act, 33 U.S.C. § 921(d), was not governed by Virginia's twenty year statute of limitations for the enforcement of judgments, § 8.01-251, although plaintiffs argued that actions to enforce state workers' compensation awards were subject to this limitation period. Rather, this section Virginia's catch - all or general statute of limitations, would be borrowed, and plaintiffs' claims were barred. Kinder v. Coleman & Yates Coal Co., 974 F. Supp. 868 (W.D. Va. 1997).

Actions involving special education programs. — The one-year statute of limitations contained in this section applies to actions involving special education programs brought pursuant to subsection D of § 22.1-214, rather than the 30-day statute of limitations provided by the Virginia Administrative Process Act (§ 9-6.14:1 et seq.) and Supreme Court Rules 2A:2 and 2A:4. School Bd. v. Nicely, 12 Va. App. 1051, 408 S.E.2d 545 (1991).

Refusal of school system to fund placement of handicapped child in out-of-state school. — For case applying the one-year statute of limitations of this section to parents' action in federal district court pursuant to 20 U.S.C. § 1415 challenging school system's refusal to fund handicapped child's placement in a certain out-of-state residential school, rather than the shorter limitations of Supreme Court Rules 2A:2 and 2A:4 applicable under § 22.1-214, see Schimmel ex rel. Schimmel v. Spillane, 819 F.2d 477 (4th Cir. 1987).

Breach of fiduciary duty by corporate officer is tort. — Under Virginia law, a suit alleging breach of fiduciary duty by a corporate officer is a tort, not a contract claim. C-T of Va., Inc. v. Barrett, 124 Bankr. 689 (W.D. Va. 1990).

Breach of fiduciary duty governed by one year statute of limitations. — Suits for breach of fiduciary duty and accompanying negligence are governed by Virginia's one year catch-all statute of limitations. Kline v. Nationsbank, 886 F. Supp. 1285 (E.D. Va. 1995).

The one-year personal, not the five-year property, statute of limitations is most appropriate for a breach of fiduciary duty cause of action. FDIC v. Cocke, 7 F.3d 396 (4th Cir. 1993), cert. denied, 513 U.S. 807, 115 S. Ct. 53, 130 L. Ed. 2d 12 (1994).

One year limitations period applied to the claims asserted by resolution trust corporation against numerous former officers and directors of savings bank including negligence, gross negligence, and breach of fiduciary duties in connection with seven transactions the savings bank entered into between 1981 and 1985. Resolution Trust Corp. v. Everhart, 837 F. Supp. 155 (E.D. Va. 1993), aff'd. 37 F.2d 151 (4th Cir. 1994).

Virginia law was to apply to resolution trust corporation's claims. — The fact that savings bank was a federally chartered institution does not alter the requirement that district court apply Virginia law to determine whether the claims of negligence, gross negligence, and breach of fiduciary duty asserted by resolution trust corporation against the officers and directors of the savings bank were barred by the statute of limitations, thus the savings bank's argument that adverse domination tolled the statute of limitations was moot. Resolution Trust Corp. v. Everhart, 837 F. Supp. 155 (E.D. Va. 1993), aff'd. 37 F.2d 151 (4th Cir. 1994).

Negligence on trustee's part. — Where the true object of the litigation is the trustee and his alleged lack of care in administering assets of the debtor's estate, not the damage to the facility and the land upon which it is located, the proper statute of limitation is contained in this section. Huennekens v. Walker, 165 Bankr. 815 (Bankr. E.D. Va. 1994).

The Resolution Trust Corporation (RTC) may not pursue claims that became time barred under applicable law prior to its appointment as receiver. Each of the RTC's claims in the instant case are governed by Virginia's one year statute of limitations applicable to claims for personal injury other than bodily injury. Resolution Trust Corp. v. Walde, 856 F. Supp. 281 (E.D. Va. 1994).

Applied in Haynes v. Anderson & Strudwick, Inc., 508 F. Supp. 1303 (E.D. Va. 1981); United Steelworkers v. Dalton, 544 F. Supp. 282 (E.D. Va. 1982); Brown v. Loudoun Golf & Country Club, Inc., 573 F. Supp. 399 (E.D. Va. 1983); Devers v. Chateau Corp., 748 F.2d 902 (4th Cir. 1984); Gwin v. Graves, 230 Va. 34, 334 S.E.2d

294 (1985); Bush Dev. Corp. v. Harbour Place Assocs., 632 F. Supp. 1359 (E.D. Va. 1986); Lavery v. Automation Mgt. Consultants, Inc., 234 Va. 145, 360 S.E.2d 336 (1987); LaVay Corp. v. Dominion Fed. Sav. & Loan Ass'n, 830 F.2d 522 (4th Cir. 1987); Oden v. Salch, 237 Va. 525, 379 S.E.2d 346 (1989); Starks v. Albemarle County, 716 F. Supp. 934 (W.D. Va. 1989); Brubaker v. City of Richmond, 943 F.2d 1363 (4th Cir. 1991); Unlimited Screw Prods., Inc. v. Malm, 781 F. Supp. 1121 (E.D. Va. 1991); Vines v. Branch, 244 Va. 185, 418 S.E.2d 890 (1992).

II. DECISIONS UNDER PRIOR LAW.

Editor's note. — The cases cited below were decided under corresponding provisions of former law. The term "this section," as used below, refers to former provisions.

Section does not apply to a suit to enforce a lien on land. — This section has no application to a suit which is purely an equitable one for the enforcement of a charge or lien upon land, and which could not be converted into a judgment in personam against anyone, because in express language the section is limited to every personal action for which no limitation is otherwise prescribed. Gilley v. Nidermaier, 176 Va. 32, 10 S.E.2d 484 (1940).

There has been a split of opinion as to which limitations period applies in fraud actions. Maine v. Leonard, 353 F. Supp. 968 (W.D. Va. 1973).

Limitation of local "blue sky" statutes applied to federal actions involving fraud. — See Maine v. Leonard, 353 F. Supp. 968 (W.D. Va. 1973).

When cause of action for fraud accrues. — In Virginia a cause of action of which the gravamen of same is fraud shall be deemed to accrue, both at law and equity, at the time such fraud is discovered, or by the exercise of due diligence ought to have been discovered.

Stevens v. Abbott, Proctor & Paine, 288 F. Supp. 836 (E.D. Va. 1968).

Malicious prosecution and conspiracy distinguished. — Malicious prosecution involves wrongful conduct directed at a person which may indirectly damage property. The statutory action for conspiracy under §§ 18.2-499 and 18.2-500, on the other hand, focuses upon conduct directed at property, i.e., one's business. Accordingly, the nature of the two actions differ so that the one-year limitation applies to the former and the five-year period to the latter. Federated Graphics Cos. v. Napotnik, 424 F. Supp. 291 (E.D. Va. 1976).

Section not applicable to action for breach by depository of terms of escrow agreement. — Where, in a suit to recover a sum which the plaintiffs allegedly lost as a result of the defendant attorney's breach of duty in closing real estate transaction, allegations of the complaint clearly set forth the existence of an escrow arrangement involving the plaintiffs as grantors, defendants as compensated depositories, and a certain company as grantee, in an escrow arrangement, the parties occupy a principal-agent relationship, a relationship which is essentially contractual in nature, and since a breach by a depository of the terms of an escrow arrangement gives rise to a cause of action contractual in nature, plaintiff's case was governed by the three-year period of limitation applicable to causes of action for contracts not in writing, contained in § 8.01-246, rather than the one-year limitation for personal causes of action provided by this section. Winslow, Inc. v. Scaife, 219 Va. 997, 254 S.E.2d 58 (1979).

The statute of limitations cannot begin to run against a claim until all the elements of the cause of action exist and that one of the essential elements of a cause of action for personal injury is the injury itself. Brown v. ABC, 704 F.2d 1296 (4th Cir. 1983).

§ 8.01-249. When cause of action shall be deemed to accrue in certain personal actions. — The cause of action in the actions herein listed shall be deemed to accrue as follows:

1. In actions for fraud or mistake and in actions for rescission of contract for undue influence, when such fraud, mistake, or undue influence is discovered or by the exercise of due diligence reasonably should have been discovered;

2. In actions or other proceedings for money on deposit with a bank or any person or corporation doing a banking business, when a request in writing be made therefor by check, order, or otherwise;

3. In actions for malicious prosecution or abuse of process, when the relevant criminal or civil action is terminated;

4. In actions for injury to the person resulting from exposure to asbestos or products containing asbestos, when a diagnosis of asbestosis, interstitial fibrosis, mesothelioma, or other disabling asbestos-related injury or disease is first communicated to the person or his agent by a physician. However, no such action may be brought more than two years after the death of such person;

5. In actions for contribution or for indemnification, when the contributee or the indemnitee has paid or discharged the obligation. A third-party claim permitted by subsection A of § 8.01-281 and the Rules of Court may be asserted before such cause of action is deemed to accrue hereunder;

6. In actions for injury to the person, whatever the theory of recovery, resulting from sexual abuse occurring during the infancy or incapacity of the person, upon removal of the disability of infancy or incapacity as provided in § 8.01-229 or, if the fact of the injury and its causal connection to the sexual abuse is not then known, when the fact of the injury and its causal connection to the sexual abuse is first communicated to the person by a licensed physician, psychologist, or clinical psychologist. As used in this subdivision, "sexual abuse" means sexual abuse as defined in subdivision 6 of § 18.2-67.10 and acts constituting rape, sodomy, object sexual penetration or sexual battery as defined in Article 7 (§ 18.2-61 et seq.) of Chapter 4 of Title 18.2;

7. In products liability actions against parties other than health care providers as defined in § 8.01-581.1 for injury to the person resulting from or arising as a result of the implantation of any prosthetic device for breast augmentation or reconstruction, when the fact of the injury and its causal connection to the implantation is first communicated to the person by a physician;

8. In actions on an open account, from the later of the last payment or last charge for goods or services rendered on the account. (Code 1950, §§ 8-13, 8-14; 1964, c. 219; 1966, c. 118; 1977, c. 617; 1985, c. 459; 1986, c. 601; 1991, c. 674; 1992, c. 817; 1993, c. 523; 1995, c. 268; 1997, cc. 565, 801.)

REVISERS' NOTE

Section 8.01-249 provides that certain causes of action should not accrue for the purpose of applying statutes of limitation until the damage or injury is discoverable by the plaintiff. While this represents an exception to the general rule embodied in § 8.01-230 that a cause of action shall be deemed to accrue when the wrong occurs or when the technical breach of contract duty occurs, § 8.01-249 follows Virginia law.

Subsection 1 incorporates former § 8-14 which tolled the statute of limitations in cases of fraud or mistake in the payment of money. The subsection extends the principle to all situations of fraud, mistake or undue influence.

Subsection 2 is an incorporation without substantive change of a proviso from former § 8-13 regarding the necessity for demand in actions for money on deposit before a cause of action shall be deemed to accrue.

Subsection 3 recognizes the common-law action for malicious prosecution, or abuse of process and provides that the statute of limitations, § 8.01-248, does not begin to run until the determination of the associated criminal or civil action (in favor of the defendant who is the plaintiff in the civil action).

Cross references. — For provisions concerning change of venue, with exception for actions arising under subdivision 4 of this section, see § 8.01-265.

Editor's note. — Acts 1991, c. 674, cl. 2 which enacted subdivision 6 of this section, in stated: "That the provisions of subdivision 6 of § 8.01-249 shall apply to all actions filed on or after July 1, 1991, without regard to when the act upon which the claim is based occurred provided that no such claim which accrued prior to July 1, 1991, shall be barred by application of those provisions if it is filed within one year of the effective date of this act."

Acts 1992, c. 817, which enacted subdivision 7 of this section, in cl. 2 provides: "That the provisions of subdivision 7 of § 8.01-249 shall apply to all actions filed on or after July 1, 1992, without regard to when the act upon which the claim is based occurred."

Acts 1996, c. 377, cl. 1, provides: "That as authorized by Section 14 of Article IV of the Constitution of Virginia, Chapter 268 of the 1995 Acts of Assembly [which amended this section] shall apply to all actions accruing on or after July 1, 1991, for injury to the person resulting from sexual abuse occurring during the infancy or incompetency of the person and which were or are filed on or after July 1, 1995."

Acts 1997, c. 801, cl. 2, provides: "That the provisions of this act shall become effective on January 1, 1998. The powers granted and duties imposed pursuant to this act shall apply prospectively to guardians and conservators appointed by court order entered on or after that date, or modified on or after that date if the court so directs, without regard to when the petition was filed. The procedures specified in this act governing proceedings for appointment of a guardian or conservator or termination or other modification of a guardianship shall apply on and after that date without regard to when the petition therefor was filed or the guardianship or conservatorship created."

Acts 1997, c. 565, cl. 2, provides: "That the provisions of this act [which amended this section] are declaratory of existing law."

Law Review. — For article on Virginia's continuing negligent treatment rule, see 15 U. Rich. L. Rev. 231 (1981). For article, "Civil Rights and 'Personal Injuries': Virginia's Statute of Limitations for Section 1983 Suits," see 26 Wm. & Mary L. Rev. 199 (1985). For note, "Admiralty Jurisdiction in Asbestos Litigation: The Fourth Circuit Draws the Line," see 43 Wash. & Lee L. Rev. 454 (1986). For comment, "Recovering Asbestos Abatement Cost," see 10 Geo. Mason L. Rev. 451 (1988). For 1991 survey on legal issues involving children, see 25 U. Rich. L. Rev. 773 (1991). For article, "Redressing Wrongs of the Blamelessly Ignorant Survivor of Incest," see 26 U. Rich. L. Rev. 1 (1991). For an article on federal product liability reform legislation's consistency with Virginia law, see 4 Geo. Mason L. Rev. 279 (1996).

I. Decisions Under Current Law.
  A. General Consideration.
  B. Injury From Asbestos.
II. Decisions Under Prior Law.

I. DECISIONS UNDER CURRENT LAW.

A. General Consideration.

Virginia's statute of limitations for fraud most closely resembles the federal policies reflected in the Lanham Act (15 U.S.C. § 1125) of prohibiting fraudulent advertising and addressing claims of deception and misrepresentation, constituting trademark infringement and unfair competition. Unlimited Screw Prods., Inc. v. Malm, 781 F. Supp. 1121 (E.D. Va. 1991).

Only slightest injury required to start running of limitations period. — In Virginia, only the slightest injury is required to start the running of the limitations period. International Surplus Lines Ins. Co. v. Marsh & McLennan, Inc., 838 F.2d 124 (4th Cir. 1988).

A cause of action can accrue before a malignant tumor manifests itself by symptoms since it is the onset of the disease itself that triggers the running of the limitation period. Lo v. Burke, 249 Va. 311, 455 S.E.2d 9 (1995).

Meaning of phrase. — The language "by the exercise of due diligence reasonably should have been discovered," as used in this section, means such a measure of prudence, activity, or assiduity, as is properly to be expected from, and ordinarily exercised by, a reasonable and prudent man under the particular circumstances, not measured by any absolute standard, but depending on the relative facts of the special case. STB Mktg. Corp. v. Zolfaghari, 240 Va. 140, 393 S.E.2d 394 (1990).

Subdivision 6 deals with claims of only the victim of the abuse, not with derivative claims. Mahony v. Becker, 246 Va. 209, 435 S.E.2d 139 (1993).

Where injury was incurred and damages began to accrue before plaintiff discovered alleged breach, plaintiff's cause of action was complete upon discovery of the existence of the breach. Therefore, the breach of fiduciary duty claim was barred by the tort statute of limitations. This result was consistent with the Virginia statute of limitations scheme, which focuses on when a plaintiff should act, by starting the running of the statute on discovery of the breach. International Surplus Lines Ins. Co. v. Marsh & McLennan, Inc., 838 F.2d 124 (4th Cir. 1988).

Issues of when a fraud should reasonably have been discovered are typically best left to the jury, as with most issues of reasonableness. Pennsylvania Life Ins. Co. v. Bumbrey, 665 F. Supp. 1190 (E.D. Va. 1987).

The determination as to due diligence is a factual one; a two year delay (between 1986 and 1988) in discovering a nearly $200,000 billing error does not constitute due diligence. Liberty Mut. v. Williams Int'l Indus., Inc., 780 F. Supp. 359 (E.D. Va. 1991).

Recordation of fraudulent documents, an examination of which would have led a reasonably prudent person to conclude that first deed of trust was paid in full and second deed of trust partially satisfied by proceeds from the foreclosure sale, was not in and of itself sufficient to impute notice of the fraud to judgment creditor; where creditor did not have any reason to believe that conveyance of second deed of trust and distribution of foreclosure proceeds were fraudulent until it discovered additional information when it interrogated debtor, under these facts and circumstances, creditor exercised due diligence, and its cause of action for fraud did not accrue until that date. STB Mktg. Corp. v. Zolfaghari, 240 Va. 140, 393 S.E.2d 394 (1990).

Indemnification/contribution action. — Section 8.01-281 authorizes a party in a pending action to file a third-party motion for judgment (complaint) seeking indemnification or contribution. Rule 3:10(a) establishes the procedure for filing such a claim. When a claim for indemnity or contribution is filed as a separate cause of action, it does not accrue until the person seeking the relief has paid more than his or her share of the obligation. Virginia Int'l Terms., Inc. v. Ceres Marine Terms., Inc., 879 F. Supp. 31 (E.D. Va. 1995).

The trial court erred in summarily dismissing the fraud count where the record showed that material facts were genuinely in dispute respecting when the plaintiff discovered, or by the exercise of due diligence should have discovered, the alleged fraud. Gilmore v. Basic Indus., Inc., 233 Va. 485, 357 S.E.2d 514 (1987).

Applied in Cramer v. Crutchfield, 496 F. Supp. 949 (E.D. Va. 1980); Pigott v. Moran, 231 Va. 76, 341 S.E.2d 179 (1986); LaVay Corp. v. Dominion Fed. Sav. & Loan Ass'n, 645 F. Supp. 612 (E.D. Va. 1986); Goad v. Celotex Corp., 831 F.2d 508 (4th Cir. 1987); Oden v. Salch, 237 Va. 525, 379 S.E.2d 346 (1989); Byelick v. Vivadelli, 79 F. Supp. 2d 610 (E.D. Va. 1999).

B. Injury From Asbestos.

Subdivision 4 not retroactive. — The 1985 amendment, which added subdivision 4, cannot be applied retroactively because there is no evidence that the Virginia General Assembly intended a retroactive application. Palmer v. Norfolk & W. Ry., 646 F. Supp. 610 (W.D. Va. 1985).

In the absence of retroactive application of subdivision 4, the cause of action accrues and the statute of limitations begins to run when an injury is sustained, pursuant to § 8.01-230. The cause of action accrues when the injury is diagnosable based on medical technology existing at the time of the injury. Moreover, the cause of action is deemed to have accrued whenever the injury, however slight, is complete. Palmer v. Norfolk & W. Ry., 646 F. Supp. 610 (W.D. Va. 1985).

II. DECISIONS UNDER PRIOR LAW.

Editor's note. — The cases cited below were decided under corresponding provisions of former law. The term "this section," as used below, refers to former provisions.

Section contemplates both actual and constructive fraud. — This section makes no distinction between actual fraud and constructive fraud, and it is construed to contemplate both. Excalibur Ins. Co. v. Speller, 220 Va. 304, 257 S.E.2d 848 (1979).

When action for fraud accrues. — An action for fraud accrues when the fraud is discovered, or when, by the exercise of due diligence, it should have been discovered. Eshbaugh v. Amoco Oil Co., 234 Va. 74, 360 S.E.2d 350 (1987).

The burden is on the plaintiff to prove that he acted with due diligence and yet did not discover the fraud or mistake until within the statutory period of limitation immediately preceding the commencement of the action. Hughes v. Foley, 203 Va. 904, 128 S.E.2d 261 (1962).

Facts showing no lack of due diligence. — In an action for fraud, based upon statements made to induce plaintiff to make investments through defendants, the interest on bonds was regularly paid by the defendants from the time they were purchased until shortly before the action was brought, and up to that time plaintiff had no reason to suspect that they were worthless, or to make inquiry in regard to them. The conduct of the defendants concealed the true status of the bonds, and plaintiff had every reason to believe that his money was safely invested, as represented to him by the defendants. It was held that plaintiff's claim was not barred by the statute of limitations because of lack of diligence on his part to discover the fraud. Mears v. Accomac Banking Co., 160 Va. 311, 168 S.E. 740 (1933).

Due diligence was not proved where it appeared from plaintiff's testimony that because of his own carelessness in failing to inspect his canceled checks, he overlooked a duplicate payment which he had made to defendant and failed to discover his mistake for nine years. Hughes v. Foley, 203 Va. 904, 128 S.E.2d 261 (1962).

Inapplicable to action to void deed. — This section is inapplicable to a situation in which the plaintiff seeks to void a valid deed of bargain and sale of real property on allegations of fraud since it is a specific statutory directive pertaining to actions to recover money. See Burton v. Terrell, 368 F. Supp. 553 (W.D. Va. 1973).

Action by insurer for money paid to wrong party in settlement of wrongful death action. — The right of an insurer to recover sums it paid in settlement of a claim for wrongful death did not accrue at the time of settlement, but at the time the court determined that the party paid, who was the administrator of the estate, was not in fact the decedent's son and heir, so that the insurer's motion for judgment for moneys had and received was not time-barred when it was filed within one year after such an adjudication. Excalibur Ins. Co. v. Speller, 220 Va. 304, 257 S.E.2d 848 (1979).

Cancellation of sublease in reliance on sublessor's misrepresentation. — Where sublessee surrendered possession of the service station as a result of the sublease cancellation agreement in reliance upon sublessor's alleged misrepresentation when he signed the cancellation agreement, sublessee suffered damages by agreeing to a shorter leasehold period.

Eshbaugh v. Amoco Oil Co., 234 Va. 74, 360 S.E.2d 350 (1987).

For malicious prosecution action decided under former § 8-24, see Morrison v. Jones, 551 F.2d 939 (4th Cir. 1977).

§ 8.01-250. Limitation on certain actions for damages arising out of defective or unsafe condition of improvements to real property.

— No action to recover for any injury to property, real or personal, or for bodily injury or wrongful death, arising out of the defective and unsafe condition of an improvement to real property, nor any action for contribution or indemnity for damages sustained as a result of such injury, shall be brought against any person performing or furnishing the design, planning, surveying, supervision of construction, or construction of such improvement to real property more than five years after the performance of furnishing of such services and construction.

The limitation prescribed in this section shall not apply to the manufacturer or supplier of any equipment or machinery or other articles installed in a structure upon real property, nor to any person in actual possession and in control of the improvement as owner, tenant or otherwise at the time the defective or unsafe condition of such improvement constitutes the proximate cause of the injury or damage for which the action is brought; rather each such action shall be brought within the time next after such injury occurs as provided in §§ 8.01-243 and 8.01-246. (Code 1950, § 8-24.2; 1964, c. 333; 1968, c. 103; 1973, c. 247; 1977, c. 617.)

REVISERS' NOTE

Section 8.01-250 does not change the substance of former § 8-24.2; the addition of the last sentence makes it clear that actions brought under the section are subject to the limitations of §§ 8.01-243 and 8.01-246.

Law Review. — For survey of Virginia law on practice and pleading in the year 1971-1972, see 58 Va. L. Rev. 1309 (1972). For survey of Virginia law on torts for the year 1972-1973, see 59 Va. L. Rev. 1590 (1973). For survey of Virginia law on torts for the year 1973-1974, see 60 Va. L. Rev. 1615 (1974). For survey of Virginia law on practice and pleading for the year 1974-1975, see 61 Va. L. Rev. 1799 (1975). For survey of Virginia law on practice and pleading for the year 1976-77, see 63 Va. L. Rev. 1459 (1977). For article on Virginia's continuing negligent treatment rule, see 15 U. Rich. L. Rev. 231 (1981). For article discussing statutes of limitation and repose in toxic substances litigation, see 16 U. Rich. L. Rev. 247 (1982). For a review of construction law in Virginia for year 1999, see 33 U. Rich. L. Rev. 827 (1999).

I. Decisions Under Current Law.
  A. General Consideration.
  B. Manufacturers and Suppliers of Equipment and Machinery.
II. Decisions Under Prior Law.

I. DECISIONS UNDER CURRENT LAW.

A. General Consideration.

Section does not violate due process clause. — It is only when a right has accrued or a claim has arisen that it is subject to the protection of the due process clause. This section merely prevents what might otherwise be a cause of action from ever arising and therefore does not violate the due process clause. Hess v. Snyder Hunt Corp., 240 Va. 49, 392 S.E.2d 817 (1990).

Section is not a true statute of limitations but a "cutoff provision" that operates to define the maximum period within which an action may be brought, regardless of applicable statutes of limitations. Lavery v. Automation Mgt. Consultants, Inc., 234 Va. 145, 360 S.E.2d 336 (1987).

This section is not a statute of limitations. School Bd. v. United States Gypsum Co., 234 Va. 32, 360 S.E.2d 325 (1987).

This section is not a statute of limitations, but a statute of repose, something in fact, different in concept, definition, and function. Commonwealth v. Owens-Corning Fiberglas Corp., 238 Va. 595, 385 S.E.2d 865 (1989).

This section is not a procedural statute. School Bd. v. United States Gypsum Co., 234 Va. 32, 360 S.E.2d 325 (1987).

The statute, by its express terms, is restricted in its application to what are in effect tort actions to recover for "injury" to property or persons and not to actions in contract. Fidelity & Deposit Co. v. Bristol Steel & Iron Works, Inc., 722 F.2d 1160 (4th Cir. 1983).

Rights bestowed by this section upon defendants (which arose when statutory period expired) are substantive if not vested and, as such, may not be impaired by retroactive application of § 8.01-250.1. School Bd. v. United States Gypsum Co., 234 Va. 32, 360 S.E.2d 325 (1987).

General Assembly intended this section to be a statute of repose. The time limitation in such a statute begins to run from the occurrence of an event unrelated to the accrual of a cause of action, and the expiration of the time extinguishes not only the legal remedy but also all causes of action, including those which may later accrue as well as those already accrued. School Bd. v. United States Gypsum Co., 234 Va. 32, 360 S.E.2d 325 (1987).

Lapse of statutory period extinguishes all rights, including those arising from later injury. — As a statute of repose, this section is a redefinition of the substantive rights and obligations of the parties to any litigation "arising out of the defective and unsafe condition of an improvement to real property." Specifically, the lapse of the statutory period was meant to extinguish all the rights of a plaintiff, including those which might arise from an injury sustained later, and to grant a defendant immunity from liability for all the torts specified in the statute. School Bd. v. United States Gypsum Co., 234 Va. 32, 360 S.E.2d 325 (1987).

The lapse of the statutory period was meant to extinguish all the rights of a plaintiff, including those which might arise from an injury sustained later, and to grant a defendant immunity from liability for all the torts specified in the statute, which itself is only applicable to those torts specified. Tate v. Colony House Bldrs., Inc., 257 Va. 78, 508 S.E.2d 597 (1998).

Inapplicable to action arising out of contract of indemnity. — An action not sounding in tort, but arising out of a specific written contract of indemnity, is outside the scope of this section. Fidelity & Deposit Co. v. Bristol Steel & Iron Works, Inc., 722 F.2d 1160 (4th Cir. 1983).

Fraud. — Fraud is not a tort specified in this statute because the wrongful act involved in fraud is aimed at the person; because fraud invariably acts upon the person of the victim, rather than upon property, its consequence is personal damage rather than injury to property. Tate v. Colony House Bldrs., Inc., 257 Va. 78, 508 S.E.2d 597 (1998).

Actions against architectural and engineering firm arose out of contract and were outside scope of section. — Where transit authority asserted breach of contract, negligence, and breach of warranties claims against architectural and engineering firm, despite firm's argument that the claims "sounded" in tort because they arose out of alleged negligence, this was a contract action and was outside the scope of this section. Delon Hampton & Assocs. v. Washington Metro. Area Transit Auth., 943 F.2d 355 (4th Cir. 1991).

Inapplicable to products liability action concerning asbestos-containing products. — This section did not apply to a products liability action brought by insulation workers against the manufacturer of asbestos-containing products because the harmful exposure occurred prior to the point at which insulation products were incorporated into realty. Willis v. Raymark Indus., Inc., 905 F.2d 793 (4th Cir. 1990).

Evidence as to asbestos incorporated into structures more than five years before suit inadmissible. — No evidence is admissible as to asbestos products which were incorporated into structures which were part of the real estate more than five years before plaintiffs filed suit. Palmer v. Norfolk & W. Ry., 646 F. Supp. 610 (W.D. Va. 1985).

Applied in Roller v. Basic Constr. Co., 238 Va. 321, 384 S.E.2d 323 (1989); Starks v. Albemarle County, 716 F. Supp. 934 (W.D. Va. 1989); Eagles Court Condominium Unit Owners Ass'n v. Heatilator, Inc., 239 Va. 325, 389 S.E.2d 304 (1990).

B. Manufacturers and Suppliers of Equipment and Machinery.

General words "or any other articles" add no new or further categories to those excluded from the operation of the statute by the specific words of the second paragraph: "the manufacturer or supplier of any equipment or machinery." Cape Henry Towers, Inc. v. National Gypsum Co., 229 Va. 596, 331 S.E.2d 476 (1985); Grice v. Hungerford Mechanical Corp., 236 Va. 305, 374 S.E.2d 17 (1988).

Section distinguishes suppliers of ordinary building materials from suppliers of

machinery or equipment. — The General Assembly intended to perpetuate a distinction between, on the one hand, those who furnish ordinary building materials, which are incorporated into construction work outside the control of their manufacturers or suppliers, at the direction of architects, designers, and contractors, and, on the other hand, those who furnish machinery or equipment. Cape Henry Towers, Inc. v. National Gypsum Co., 229 Va. 596, 331 S.E.2d 476 (1985); Grice v. Hungerford Mechanical Corp., 236 Va. 305, 374 S.E.2d 17 (1988).

It excludes suppliers of machinery or equipment. — Unlike ordinary building materials, machinery and equipment are subject to close quality control at the factory and may be made subject to independent manufacturer's warranties, voidable if the equipment is not installed and used in strict compliance with the manufacturer's instructions. Materialmen in the latter category have means of protecting themselves which are not available to the former. This section covers the former category and excludes the latter. Cape Henry Towers, Inc. v. National Gypsum Co., 229 Va. 596, 331 S.E.2d 476 (1985); Grice v. Hungerford Mechanical Corp., 236 Va. 305, 374 S.E.2d 17 (1988).

An electrical panel box and its component parts were ordinary building materials and not equipment within the contemplation of this section. Grice v. Hungerford Mechanical Corp., 236 Va. 305, 374 S.E.2d 17 (1988).

Items used in swimming pool construction were ordinary building materials and not equipment within the meaning of this section. Luebbers v. Fort Wayne Plastics, Inc., 255 Va. 368, 498 S.E.2d 911 (1998).

Water pipes as equipment. — Where the defendant supplied pipe for a water line, this section did not bar the plaintiff's fraud claim because relatively sophisticated discrete materials such as the pipes used by the defendant are more like equipment and less like ordinary building materials; furthermore, ordinary building materials are incorporated into construction work outside the control of their manufacturers or suppliers and the defendant exercised control over the structural integrity of the pipes, and, therefore, the pipes' incorporation into the overall project was not outside the control of the defendant. City of Richmond v. Madison Mgt. Group, Inc., 918 F.2d 438 (4th Cir. 1990).

II. DECISIONS UNDER PRIOR LAW.

Editor's note. — The cases cited below were decided under corresponding provisions of former law. The term "this section," as used below, refers to former provisions.

Legislative determination of five-year cutoff is rational. — The legislative determination that there should be a five-year cutoff for actions to recover damages arising out of defective improvements to real property is clearly rational, particularly in light of the abolition of lack of privity as a defense to such actions. Smith v. Allen-Bradley Co., 371 F. Supp. 698 (W.D. Va. 1974).

Section does not constitute a statute of limitations in the strict sense. Federal Reserve Bank v. Wright, 392 F. Supp. 1126 (E.D. Va. 1975).

This section by its wording does not require that every action to which it applies shall be brought within the specified period of time provided therein, as is typical of statutes of limitation generally. Federal Reserve Bank v. Wright, 392 F. Supp. 1126 (E.D. Va. 1975).

But merely imposes an "outside limit" within which the customary statutes of limitation continue to operate. Federal Reserve Bank v. Wright, 392 F. Supp. 1126 (E.D. Va. 1975).

This section imposes an outside time limit beyond which an action for damages resulting from improper design, construction or supervision of improvements to realty may not be maintained. Federal Reserve Bank v. Wright, 392 F. Supp. 1126 (E.D. Va. 1975).

This section sets an outside limit within which the applicable statutes of limitation operate. Comptroller ex rel. VMI v. King, 217 Va. 751, 232 S.E.2d 895 (1977).

The purpose of this section is not to extend existing limitation periods, such as the two-year period applicable to personal injury actions, but to establish an arbitrary termination date after which no litigation of the type specified may be initiated. Comptroller ex rel. VMI v. King, 217 Va. 751, 232 S.E.2d 895 (1977).

Reasonable construction of this section would suggest a single limitation period to run from the final completion date of the entire project, whether the claim arises from faulty design or from faulty construction. Federal Reserve Bank v. Wright, 392 F. Supp. 1126 (E.D. Va. 1975).

Legislative intent as to 1973 amendment. — The General Assembly evinced an intent in enacting the 1973 amendment to this section to eradicate every vestige of the section, as fully as it constitutionally could, insofar as installers of machinery and equipment were concerned. Hupman v. Cook, 640 F.2d 497 (4th Cir. 1981).

Action time barred where installation five years old at time of 1973 amendment. — An action may not be instituted against the installer of equipment for any injuries resulting from installation already five years old on the date of the 1973 amendment to this section, since the limitation period would already have run before the amendment was passed.

Hupman v. Cook, 640 F.2d 497 (4th Cir. 1981).

But not where less than five years old. — In an action seeking to hold defendants liable as installers of machinery and equipment alleged to have occasioned an injury to plaintiff where installation occurred 10 years prior to the action, but where injury occurred one year prior to the action and, where installation was less than five years old when the 1973 amendment to this section was passed, the action was not time barred since the General Assembly meant to eliminate altogether the benefit of the five-year limitation accounting period from the date of installation. Hupman v. Cook, 640 F.2d 497 (4th Cir. 1981).

§ 8.01-250.1. Limitation on actions involving removal of asbestos. — Notwithstanding the provisions of § 8.01-234 or any other section in this chapter, every action against a manufacturer or supplier of asbestos or material containing asbestos brought by or on behalf of any agency of the Commonwealth incorporated for charitable or educational purposes; counties, cities or towns; or school boards, to recover for (i) removal of asbestos or materials containing asbestos from any building owned or used by such entity, (ii) other measures taken to correct or ameliorate any problem related to asbestos in such building or (iii) reimbursement for such removal, correction or amelioration which would otherwise be barred prior to July 1, 1990, as a result of expiration of the applicable period of limitation, is hereby revived or extended. Any action thereon may be commenced prior to July 1, 1990. (1985, c. 262; 1986, c. 458.)

I. DECISIONS UNDER CURRENT LAW.

Rights bestowed by § 8.01-250 upon defendants (which arose when statutory period expired) are substantive if not vested and, as such, may not be impaired by retroactive application of this section. School Bd. v. United States Gypsum Co., 234 Va. 32, 360 S.E.2d 325 (1987).

Application of this section where asbestos installed between 1939 and 1971 held unconstitutional. — In an action against manufacturers of asbestos products seeking compensatory and punitive damages allegedly sustained in inspecting, analyzing, containing, removing and replacing asbestos-containing products allegedly placed in certain school buildings between 1939 and 1971, application of this section was unconstitutional under the due process clause of Va. Const., Art. I, § 11, since the revival statute was designed primarily, not to relieve the hazard to public health, but to relieve budgetary concerns. School Bd. v. United States Gypsum Co., 234 Va. 32, 360 S.E.2d 325 (1987).

ARTICLE 4.

Limitations on Enforcement of Judgments and Decrees.

§ 8.01-251. Limitations on enforcement of judgments. — A. No execution shall be issued and no action brought on a judgment including a judgment in favor of the Commonwealth, after twenty years from the date of such judgment, unless the period is extended as provided in this section.

B. The limitation prescribed in subsection A may be extended on motion of the judgment creditor or his assignee with notice to the judgment debtor, and an order of the circuit court of the jurisdiction in which the judgment was entered to show cause why the period for issuance of execution or bringing of an action should not be extended. Any such motion must be filed within the twenty-year period from the date of the original judgment or from the date of the latest extension thereof. If upon the hearing of the motion the court decides that there is no good cause shown for not extending the period of limitation, the order shall so state and the period of limitation mentioned in subsection A shall be extended for an additional twenty years from the date of filing of the motion to extend. Additional extensions may be granted upon the same procedure, subject in each case to the recording provisions prescribed in § 8.01-458. This extension procedure is subject to the exception that if the action is against a personal representative of a decedent, the motion must be within two years from the date of his qualification, the extension may be for only two years from the time of the filing of the motion, and there may be only one such extension.

C. No suit shall be brought to enforce the lien of any judgment, including judgments in favor of the Commonwealth, upon which the right to issue an execution or bring an action is barred by other subsections of this section, nor shall any suit be brought to enforce the lien of any judgment against the lands which have been conveyed by the judgment debtor to a grantee for value, unless the same be brought within ten years from the due recordation of the deed from such judgment debtor to such grantee and unless a notice of lis pendens shall have been recorded in the manner provided by § 8.01-268 before the expiration of such ten-year period.

D. In computing the time, any time during which the right to sue out execution on the judgment is suspended by the terms thereof, or by legal process, shall be omitted. Sections 8.01-230 et seq., 8.01-247 and 8.01-256 shall apply to the right to bring such action in like manner as to any right.

E. The provisions of this section apply to judgments obtained after June 29, 1948, and to judgments obtained prior to such date which are not then barred by the statute of limitations, but nothing herein shall have the effect of reducing the time for enforcement of any judgment the limitation upon which has been extended prior to such date by compliance with the provisions of law theretofore in effect.

F. This section shall not be construed to impair the right of subrogation to which any person may become entitled while the lien is in force, provided he institutes proceedings to enforce such right within five years after the same accrued, nor shall the lien of a judgment be impaired by the recovery of another judgment thereon, or by a forthcoming bond taken on an execution thereon, such bond having the force of a judgment.

G. Limitations on enforcement of judgments entered in the general district courts shall be governed by § 16.1-94.1. (Code 1950, §§ 8-393, 8-394, 8-396, 8-397; 1956, c. 512; 1958, c. 221; 1960, c. 274; 1977, c. 617; 1983, c. 499.)

REVISERS' NOTE

Section 8.01-251 consolidates former §§ 8-393, 8-394, 8-396 and 8-397.

Subsection A relates primarily to § 8-397, subsection B to § 8-396, subsection C to § 8-393, subsection D to § 8-397, subsection E to § 8-396, and subsection F to § 8-394. The essence of the former sections is set forth without substantive change except that the five-year period in former § 8-396 for extending a judgment against a personal representative has been reduced to two years; the penalty bond procedure in former § 8-397 has been deleted, and the reference to former § 8-33 found in former § 8-397 has been deleted. Reference to the writ of scire facias has been deleted. See § 8.01-24.

Cross references. — As to limitations generally, see § 8.01-228 et seq. For statute as to when process shall be returnable, if not otherwise specially provided, see § 8.01-294. As to forthcoming bond, see §§ 8.01-465, 8.01-528, 8.01-532. As to executions on judgements, see §§ 8.01-466 through 8.01-505. As to homestead exemptions, see § 34-24. As to subrogation generally, see § 49-27 and note. As to recordation of deed, see §§ 55-106 through 55-112.

I. Decisions Under Current Law.
II. Decisions Under Prior Law.
  A. General Consideration.
  B. Suspension of Operation of Statute.
  C. Motion on Judgment.
  D. Subrogation.

I. DECISIONS UNDER CURRENT LAW.

Ten-year period does not violate Full Faith and Credit Clause. — A forum state may apply its own statute of limitations to an action on a foreign judgment without violating the Full Faith and Credit Clause. This statute is procedural only; it does not affect the judgment creditor's substantive right unless the period of limitations is so stringent and unreasonable as to deny the right. A 10-year period is neither stringent nor unreasonable and therefore does not offend this portion of the Constitution. Carter v. Carter, 232 Va. 166, 349 S.E.2d 95 (1986).

Section does not violate Equal Protection Clause. — Domestic judgment creditors and foreign judgment creditors are inherently different classes. The domestic judgment creditor has an immediate right to enforcement of his judgment, without further action. The foreign judgment creditor has no right of enforcement in Virginia until he reduces his foreign judgment to a Virginia judgment. As these creditors are not similarly situated, statutory provisions treating them differently may not be successfully challenged under the Equal Protection Clause. Carter v. Carter, 232 Va. 166, 349 S.E.2d 95 (1986).

Disparate treatment of foreign judgment creditors has legitimate state purpose. — If the Equal Protection Clause is even applicable to the dissimilar classes of creditors addressed by this section and § 8.01-252, the disparate treatment of foreign judgment creditors is rationally related to a legitimate state purpose. Therefore, the 10-year limitations period of § 8.01-252 does not violate the Fourteenth Amendment. Carter v. Carter, 232 Va. 166, 349 S.E.2d 95 (1986).

Foreign judgment creditor may have up to 30 years to enforce judgment. — Once the foreign judgment is reduced to a Virginia judgment under § 8.01-252, enforcement of the judgment, like any originating in Virginia, is subject to the 20-year limitations period of this section. Thus, a foreign judgment creditor may actually have as many as 30 years to enforce his judgment. Carter v. Carter, 232 Va. 166, 349 S.E.2d 95 (1986).

Enforcement of foreign support orders in URESA proceedings. — In a Uniform Reciprocal Enforcement of Support Act (URESA) proceeding where a foreign support order merely establishes an ongoing, unliquidated spousal support obligation, the provisions of § 8.01-252 are not applicable. Once a Virginia judgment for a sum certain for accumulated support arrearages is obtained, this section controls the time within which that judgment may be enforced in this Commonwealth. However, in a URESA proceeding where the foreign support order adjudicates a sum certain due and owing, § 8.01-252 acts as a cutoff provision and operates as an outside limit in which the URESA proceeding must be commenced. Bennett v. Commonwealth, Dep't of Social Servs. ex rel. Waters, 15 Va. App. 135, 422 S.E.2d 458 (1992).

An action under section 921(d) of the Longshore and Harbor Workers' Compensation Act, 33 U.S.C. Section 921(d), was not governed by Virginia's twenty year statute of limitations for the enforcement of judgments, although plaintiffs argued that actions to enforce state workers' compensation awards were subject to this limitation period. Section 8.01-248, Virginia's catch-all or general statute of limitations, would be borrowed, and plaintiffs' claims were barred. Kinder v. Coleman & Yates Coal Co., 974 F. Supp. 868 (W.D. Va. 1997).

Applied in Johnston Mem. Hosp. v. Hess, 44 Bankr. 598 (W.D. Va. 1984).

II. DECISIONS UNDER PRIOR LAW.

A. General Consideration.

Editor's note. — The cases cited below were decided under corresponding provisions of former law. The terms "the statute," "the statute of limitations," and "this section," as used below, refer to former provisions.

Lien of judgment ceases when right to execution barred. — The principle is now settled by statute that the lien of a judgment ceases with the life of the judgment. Hutchison v. Grubbs, 80 Va. 251 (1885); Ayre v. Burke, 82 Va. 338, 4 S.E. 618 (1886); Brown v. Butler, 87 Va. 621, 13 S.E. 71 (1891); Ackiss v. Satchell, 104 Va. 700, 52 S.E. 378 (1905).

The lien of a judgment ceases when the right to sue out of execution on the judgment is barred by the statute of limitations. McCarty v. Ball, 82 Va. 872, 1 S.E. 189 (1887); Kennerly v. Swartz, 83 Va. 704, 3 S.E. 348 (1887), overruled on other grounds, 99 Va. 582, 39 S.E. 218 (1901); Serles v. Cromer, 88 Va. 426, 13 S.E. 859 (1891).

Lien is unenforceable in equity when judgment barred at law. — Judgment liens are creatures of statute, and cannot be enforced in equity after they have ceased to be enforceable at law. Hutchison v. Grubbs, 80 Va. 251 (1885); McCarty v. Ball, 82 Va. 872, 1 S.E. 189 (1887).

But where debt is secured by mortgage, lien survives. — Where there is a judgment for a debt secured by a mortgage, deed of trust or vendor's lien, the lien does not grow out of the judgment itself but is collateral thereto and may be enforced in equity although the judgment be barred or annihilated. Paxton v. Rich, 85 Va. 378, 7 S.E. 531 (1888).

This section does not apply to a motion on a forthcoming bond. Lipscomb v. Davis, 31 Va. (4 Leigh) 303 (1833).

Or to a judgment quando acciderint. — A judgment quando acciderint does not come within the operation of this section. Smith v. Charlton, 48 Va. (7 Gratt.) 425 (1851).

Judgment may be good against surety though barred as to principal. — Pursuant to § 8.01-442 and subsection B, where judgment has been recovered against principal and surety, no length of time short of the period prescribed by this section will bar the right of the creditor to enforce his judgment against the surety or his estate, even though the judgment is barred as to the principal. Manson v. Rawlings, 112 Va. 384, 71 S.E. 564 (1911); Fidelity & Cas. Co. v. Lackland, 175 Va. 178, 8 S.E.2d 306 (1940).

B. Suspension of Operation of Statute.

Exceptions to the operation of the statute of limitations must be found in the statute itself. Clarke v. Nave, 116 Va. 838, 83 S.E. 547 (1914).

Exceptions to the limitation of time to institute proceedings to enforce a judgment must be found in this section itself and in cognate sections. Steffey v. King, 126 Va. 120, 101 S.E. 62 (1919); Barley v. Duncan, 177 Va. 202, 13 S.E.2d 298 (1941).

An order of reference for an account of liens stops the running of the statute of limitations as to all judgment creditors who come in under the order and prove their liens or assert them in the suit. Gunnell v. Dixon, 101 Va. 174, 43 S.E. 340 (1903).

Death of party does not suspend running of time. — The extension of one year from the death of a party described in § 8.01-229 is not one of the exceptions expressed in this section. Barley v. Duncan, 177 Va. 202, 13 S.E.2d 298 (1941).

Nor does homestead exemption. — The prohibition of the enforcement of a judgment against property set apart as a homestead does not suspend the running of the statute of limitations as to the judgment. A claim of homestead by the judgment debtor is not one of the exceptions mentioned in the following section nor does the inability to enforce the judgment against the homestead prevent the creditor's keeping the judgment alive. Ackiss v. Satchell, 104 Va. 700, 52 S.E. 378 (1905).

Nor by absence of debtor from State. — The running of the statute of limitations on suits to enforce judgment liens is not tolled by the absence of the judgment debtor from the State, since such suits are expressly excepted from the application of § 8.01-229. Duffy v. Hartsock, 187 Va. 406, 46 S.E.2d 570 (1948).

Nor does creditor's bill except as to creditors who come into suit. — A creditor's bill to subject the lands of his debtor to judgment liens does not suspend the running of the statute of limitations except as to creditors who come into the suit, and, upon the same principle, as to creditors who do not come in, the act is not suspended as to persons and property not brought into the lien creditor's suit while it is a pending suit and before a final decree. Blair v. Rorer's Adm'r, 135 Va. 1, 116 S.E. 767 (1923).

But decree suspending execution suspends running of limitations. — Where the collection of an execution on a judgment is suspended by a decree in chancery, the period during which the decree of suspension remains in force is to be excluded in the computation of time. Davis v. Roller, 106 Va. 46, 55 S.E. 4 (1906).

But not by provision requiring creditor to execute bond. — A provision of a decree in favor of a receiver that he shall execute a bond in a fixed penalty before receiving any money thereunder does not suspend the decree. Serles v. Cromer, 88 Va. 426, 13 S.E. 859 (1891).

Or by agreement of parties not made part of judgment. — An agreement not made a part of a judgment, that no execution shall be placed in the hands of the sheriff for a stated period does not prevent the running of the statute of limitations against the judgment. The agreement is not within the letter or the spirit of this section. Clarke v. Nave, 116 Va. 838, 83 S.E. 547 (1914).

Statute does not run while injunction to judgment is pending. — The statute of limitations does not run while an injunction to the judgment is pending. Hutsonpiller v. Stover, 53 Va. (12 Gratt.) 579 (1855).

Time pending appeal is not excluded. — It would be denying effect to the plain provisions of the statutes to hold that there should be added to the exceptions contained in subsection D another to the effect that the time pending an appeal must be excluded from the time specified by subsection B in which execution may issue. Seal v. Puckett, 159 Va. 297, 165 S.E. 496 (1932).

Nor is time of pending suit when no order suspending execution is made. — A petition filed by a judgment creditor in a chancery suit, upon which no other order of court was ever made except an order of dismissal, seven years after it was filed was not "legal process," which suspended the right to sue out execution on the judgment. Dabney v. Shelton, 82 Va. 349, 4 S.E. 605 (1886).

Where nonresident judgment creditors are summoned by order of publication, and no order is made to suspend the issuing of executions, a suit to enforce a contract for the sale of the judgment debtor's land is no such "legal process" as, under this section, suspends judgment creditors' right to sue out executions and stops the running of the statute of limitations against such judgments. Straus v. Bodeker, 86 Va. 543, 10 S.E. 570 (1889).

War may suspend running of limitations. — The operation of the statute of limitations upon judgments is suspended during a period of war, when the judgment plaintiff is resident in the territory of one of the belligerent parties, and the defendant in the other. Brewis v. Lawson, 76 Va. 36 (1881).

C. Motion on Judgment.

Action lies as soon as judgment recovered. — At the common law an action of debt lies as soon as judgment is recovered, and without regard to the plaintiff's right to take out execution, for the remedy by execution is cumulative only, and the statutes giving this remedy do not impair the common-law right of action on the judgment as a debt of record. American Ry. Express Co. v. F.S. Royster Guano Co., 141 Va. 602, 126 S.E. 678 (1925), aff'd, 273 U.S. 274, 47 S. Ct. 355, 71 L. Ed. 642 (1927).

Judgment sued on does not merge with new judgment obtained thereon. — A judgment upon which action has been brought does not merge with the new judgment in such a manner as to defeat the lien of the old judgment and give the lien of the new judgment priority over other liens only as of the date of its entry. Whatever may be the general doctrine in other jurisdictions as to the merger of one judgment in another, it cannot be so applied in Virginia as to convert the provisions of this section into a delusion and a snare. Hay v. Alexandria & W.R.R., 20 F. 15 (E.D. Va. 1884).

Motion should state facts necessary to authorize relief sought. — It is essential that the writ of scire facias (now motion) which serves the double purpose of a writ (now motion) and declaration should state all the facts necessary to authorize the relief sought. It should follow the judgment to be revived as to the amount, date, and parties. White v. Palmer, 110 Va. 490, 66 S.E. 44 (1909); American Ry. Express Co. v. F.S. Royster Guano Co., 141 Va. 602, 126 S.E. 678 (1925), aff'd, 273 U.S. 274, 47 S. Ct. 355, 71 L. Ed. 642 (1927).

Judgment should be that plaintiff have execution. — The extent of the jurisdiction of the court upon a proper writ of scire facias (now motion) to revive a judgment is to render judgment that the plaintiffs in the writ (now motion) may have execution of the judgment set forth in the writ (now motion). All beyond this is outside of the jurisdiction of the court and a mere nullity, and it may be so treated by any court in any proceeding, direct or collateral. If the judgment on the scire facias (now motion) goes further and besides awarding execution on the original judgment awards the payment of money, the latter is void for want of jurisdiction and may be assailed collaterally. A judgment of revival merely is not a lien on land, though the judgment revived will constitute such lien. White v. Palmer, 110 Va. 490, 66 S.E. 44 (1909).

Irregular or erroneous scire facias (now motion) is voidable only. — An irregular or erroneous scire facias (now motion) to revive a judgment is voidable only, and if the irregularity is not taken advantage of in some appropriate method, the judgment of revivor is valid. It cannot be collaterally assailed, and will support title derived from an execution issued by its authority. White v. Palmer, 110 Va. 490, 66 S.E. 44 (1909).

D. Subrogation.

Subsection F is remedial in its nature and affects only a procedural matter. Aetna Cas. & Sur. Co. v. Whaley, 173 Va. 11, 3 S.E.2d 395 (1939).

It may bar right of subrogation to foreign judgment. — If it be assumed that a surety which has paid a foreign judgment is entitled to enforce subrogation thereto in the courts of this State, though it has no Virginia judgment, the five-year limitation in this section applies to that right. Aetna Cas. & Sur. Co. v. Whaley, 173 Va. 11, 3 S.E.2d 395 (1939).

Failure to ask specifically for subrogation is not ground for a demurrer to a bill filed by a surety against his principal to subject the land of the principal of the lien of a judgment which he has paid as surety, where the bill alleges a state of facts which shows that the complainant is entitled to subrogation, and contains a prayer for general relief. Hawpe v. Bumgardner, 103 Va. 91, 48 S.E. 554 (1904).

§ 8.01-252. Actions on judgments of another state. — Every action upon a judgment rendered in another state or country shall be barred, if such action would there be barred by the laws of such state or country, and in no event shall an action be brought upon any such judgment rendered more than ten years before the commencement of the action. (Code 1950, § 8-22; 1977, c. 617.)

REVISERS' NOTE

Former § 8-22, has been rewritten to render the section coherent. The ten-year residency requirement has been omitted as irrational and, arguably, a denial of due process.

I. DECISIONS UNDER CURRENT LAW.

Section does not violate Equal Protection Clause. — Domestic judgment creditors and foreign judgment creditors are inherently different classes. The domestic judgment creditor has an immediate right to enforcement of his judgment, without further action. The foreign judgment creditor has no right of enforcement in Virginia until he reduces his foreign judgment to a Virginia judgment. As these creditors are not similarly situated, statutory provisions treating them differently may not be successfully challenged under the Equal Protection Clause. Carter v. Carter, 232 Va. 166, 349 S.E.2d 95 (1986).

Purpose. — The original legislative purpose underlying the 10-year statute of limitations was to provide defendants in actions on foreign judgments an opportunity to challenge the personal or subject matter jurisdiction of the foreign court. Carter v. Carter, 232 Va. 166, 349 S.E.2d 95 (1986).

This section is not a true statute of limitations but a "cutoff provision" that operates to define the maximum period within which an action may be brought, regardless of applicable statutes of limitations. Lavery v. Automation Mgt. Consultants, Inc., 234 Va. 145, 360 S.E.2d 336 (1987).

Disparate treatment of foreign judgment creditors has legitimate state purpose. — If the Equal Protection Clause is even applicable to the dissimilar classes of creditors addressed by these sections, the disparate treatment of foreign judgment creditors is rationally related to a legitimate state purpose. Therefore, the 10-year limitations period of this section does not violate the Fourteenth Amendment. Carter v. Carter, 232 Va. 166, 349 S.E.2d 95 (1986).

Foreign judgment creditor may have up to 30 years to enforce judgment. — Once the foreign judgment is reduced to a Virginia judgment under this section, enforcement of the judgment, like any originating in Virginia, is subject to the 20-year limitations period of § 8.01-251. Thus, a foreign judgment creditor may actually have as many as 30 years to enforce his judgment. Carter v. Carter, 232 Va. 166, 349 S.E.2d 95 (1986).

This section embraces an order for a sum certain or liquidated amount for spousal support rendered in another state, as well as other judgments. Bennett v. Commonwealth, Dep't of Social Servs. ex rel. Waters, 15 Va. App. 135, 422 S.E.2d 458 (1992).

The terms "support order," "judgment," and "money judgment" as used in the Uniform Reciprocal Enforcement of Support Act (URESA) sections see (§ 20-88.12 et seq.) and this section are not identical for purposes of the application of these statutes to a particular support order. Bennett v. Commonwealth, Dep't of Social Servs. ex rel. Waters, 15 Va. App. 135, 422 S.E.2d 458 (1992).

Enforcement of foreign support orders in URESA proceedings. — In a Uniform Reciprocal Enforcement of Support Act (URESA) proceeding see (§ 20-88.12 et seq.) where a foreign support order merely establishes an ongoing, unliquidated spousal support obligation, the provisions of this section are not applicable. Once a Virginia judgment for a sum certain for accumulated support arrearages is obtained, § 8.01-251 controls the time within which that judgment may be enforced in this Commonwealth. However, in a URESA proceeding where the foreign support order adjudicates a sum certain due and owing, this section acts as a cutoff provision and operates as an outside limit in which the URESA proceeding must be commenced. Bennett v. Commonwealth, Dep't of Social Servs. ex rel. Waters, 15 Va. App. 135, 422 S.E.2d 458 (1992).

Applied in Taylor v. Taylor, 14 Va. App. 642, 418 S.E.2d 900 (1992).

ARTICLE 5.

Miscellaneous Limitations Provisions.

§ 8.01-253. Limitation of suits to avoid voluntary conveyances, etc.

— No gift, conveyance, assignment, transfer, or charge, which is not on consideration deemed valuable in law, or which is upon consideration of marriage, shall be avoided in whole or in part for that cause only, unless within five years from its recordation, and if not so recorded within five years from the time the same was or should have been discovered, suit be brought for that purpose, or the subject thereof, or some part of it, be distrained or levied on by or at the suit of a creditor, as to whom such gift, conveyance, assignment, transfer, or charge, is declared to be void by § 55-81. (Code 1950, § 8-19; 1977, c. 617.)

I. Decisions Under Current Law.
II. Decisions Under Prior Law.

I. DECISIONS UNDER CURRENT LAW.

Action claiming personal liability of corporate shareholders for fraudulent conveyance not fraud. — A claim which sought to pierce the corporate veil of automobile dealership and impose personal liability on the defendant shareholders for the fraudulent conveyance of the dealership's assets was not a fraud claim and thus was subject to limitation period in this section rather than § 8.01-248. Curley v. Dahlgren Chrysler-Plymouth, Dodge, Inc., 245 Va. 429, 429 S.E.2d 221 (1993).

Applied in Docter, Docter & Salus v. United States (In re Abingdon Realty Corp.), 21 Bankr. 290 (Bankr. E.D. Va. 1982); In re Massey, 225 Bankr. 887 (Bankr. E.D. Va. 1998).

II. DECISIONS UNDER PRIOR LAW.

Editor's note. — The cases cited below were decided under corresponding provisions of former law. The terms "the act of limitations" and "this section," as used below, refer to former provisions.

Section is not applicable to commissioner's suit to vacate deed to debtor. — This section refers to suits by creditors to annul voluntary conveyances by their debtors to third persons in derogation of the creditor's rights, and not to a suit by a commissioner to vacate a deed executed by him to a debtor upon the ground of misrepresentation on the part of the grantee that the purchase price had been paid. Williams v. Blakey, 76 Va. 254 (1882).

Nor is it applicable to fraudulent conveyances. — The limitations prescribed by this section, within which to bring a suit to set aside a voluntary conveyance, has no application to an attack on a conveyance on the ground of actual fraud. Kinney v. Craig, 103 Va. 158, 48 S.E. 864 (1904). See also Atkinson v. Solenberger, 112 Va. 667, 72 S.E. 727 (1911).

Cases of actual fraud are not included under this section. Snoddy v. Haskins, 53 Va. (12 Gratt.) 363 (1855); Flook v. Armentrout, 100 Va. 638, 42 S.E. 686 (1902); Kinney v. Craig, 103 Va. 158, 48 S.E. 864 (1904).

It does not protect property in hands of distributee. — This section does not protect from liability for decedent's debts property which has passed into the hands of distributees. Coles v. Ballard, 78 Va. 139 (1883).

Exceptions to the operation of this section must be found in the statute itself, for "the doctrine of an inherent equity creating an exception where the statute creates none, is now universally exploded." Bickle v. Chrisman, 76 Va. 678 (1882); Matthews & Co. v. Progress Distilling Co., 108 Va. 777, 62 S.E. 924 (1908).

Running of statute is not postponed until settlement is made. — The running of the act of limitation to suits to avoid voluntary conveyances is not postponed simply because no settlement has been had between the parties and the exact amount due has not been ascertained. Vashon v. Barrett, 99 Va. 344, 38 S.E. 200 (1901).

Voluntary conveyance between husband and wife. — In the absence of fraud, a suit by creditors to annul a conveyance to a husband in trust for his wife, on the ground that the consideration was paid by the husband, is barred in five years. Welsh v. Solenberger, 85 Va. 441, 8 S.E. 91 (1888).

Marriage settlement. — Under this section, a marriage settlement cannot be avoided on the ground that it is voluntary after five years from the date of its admission to record, no actual fraud being charged. McCue v. Harris, 86 Va. 687, 10 S.E. 981 (1890).

Burden of proving time of transfer. — The burden of proving that the transfer, alleged to be voluntary, was made more than five years before the institution of the suit to have it set aside is on the party pleading the statute. Vashon v. Barrett, 99 Va. 344, 38 S.E. 200 (1901).

§ 8.01-254. Limitation on enforcement of bequests and legacies. —

Wherever by any will, the testator devises any real estate to some person and requires such person to pay some other person a specified sum of money, or provides a legacy for some person which constitutes a charge against the real estate of the testator, or any part thereof, no suit or action shall be brought to subject such real estate to the payment of such specified sum of money or such legacy, as the case may be, after twenty years from the time when the same shall have been payable, and if the will specifies no time for the payment thereof, it shall be deemed to have been payable immediately upon death of the testator. (Code 1950, § 8-21; 1977, c. 617.)

I. DECISIONS UNDER PRIOR LAW.

Editor's note. — The case cited below was decided under corresponding provisions of former law. The term "this section," as used below, refers to former provisions.

Applicable to devise for support of third person. — Where testator devised a tract of land to his son and also provided that his daughter was to have her home and support on the tract as long as she remained single, it was held that, while the right vested in the daughter by the will is not uniformly regarded as a legacy in the strict sense of that word, it was the legislative intent to make the period of limitation provided by this section applicable to such a provision for support. Davis v. Davis, 190 Va. 468, 57 S.E.2d 137 (1950).

§ 8.01-255. Time for presenting claim against Commonwealth.

— Any pecuniary claim authorized to be presented under §§ 2.1-223.1 and 2.1-223.3 shall be barred unless presented in writing to the comptroller or other authorized person no later than five years after the right to such claim shall arise. If such claim be not thus barred, any action thereon against the Commonwealth must be brought no later than three years after disallowance of such claim in whole or in part. (Code 1950, § 8-752; 1966, c. 452; 1977, c. 617.)

REVISERS' NOTE

The statutes of limitations for claims against the State found in former §§ 8-752 and 8-757, are in conflict with each other. Section 8.01-255 retains the three-year period of limitations in former § 8-752 which will apply to every action brought against the Commonwealth arising from a pecuniary claim after a disallowance thereof, in whole or in part. Any such claim must be presented in writing to the Comptroller or other authorized person no later than five years after the right to the claim arises.

Cross references. — For referral of time-barred claims to Governor for such payment as he directs, see § 2.1-223.6.

Law Review. — For survey of Virginia law on torts for the year 1972-1973, see 59 Va. L. Rev. 1590 (1973). For a re-examination of sovereign tort immunity in Virginia, see 15 U. Rich. L. Rev. 247 (1981). For note on the abrogation of sovereign immunity in Virginia: The Virginia Tort Claims Act, see 7 Geo. Mason L. Rev. 291 (1984).

I. Decisions Under Current Law.
II. Decisions Under Prior Law.

I. DECISIONS UNDER CURRENT LAW.

The limitations period for claims against the State is tolled by the pursuit of administrative remedies. Randall v. Lukhard, 709 F.2d 257 (4th Cir. 1983), adhered to, in part, different results reached on reh'g, in part en banc, 729 F.2d 966 (4th Cir.), cert. denied, 469 U.S. 872, 105 S. Ct. 222, 83 L. Ed. 2d 152 (1984).

II. DECISIONS UNDER PRIOR LAW.

Editor's note. — The case cited below was decided under corresponding provisions of former law. The term "this statute," as used below, refers to former provisions.

Seaman's maintenance and cure claim. — Although contract claims against the Commonwealth of Virginia are governed by a 10 (now three) year statute of limitations, this period is not the appropriate guideline for determining whether a seaman's maintenance and cure claim should be barred by the doctrine of laches. West v. Marine Resources Comm'n, 330 F. Supp. 966 (E.D. Va. 1970).

§ 8.01-255.1. Limitation of action for breach of condition subsequent or termination of determinable fee simple estate.

— No person shall commence an action for the recovery of lands, nor make an entry thereon, by reason of a breach of a condition subsequent, or by reason of the termination

§ 8.01-255.2   CIVIL REMEDIES AND PROCEDURE   § 8.01-256

of an estate of fee simple determinable, unless the action is commenced or entry is made within ten years after breach of the condition or within ten years from the time when the estate of fee simple determinable has been terminated. Where there has been a breach of a condition subsequent or termination of an estate fee simple determinable which occurred prior to July 1, 1965, recovery of the lands, or an entry may be made thereon by the owner of a right of entry or possibility of reverter, by July 1, 1977. Possession of land after breach of a condition subsequent or after termination of an estate of fee simple determinable shall be deemed adverse and hostile from the first breach of a condition subsequent or from the occurrence of the event terminating an estate of fee simple determinable. (Code 1950, § 8-5.1; 1975, c. 136; 1977, c. 617.)

Law Review. — For survey of Virginia law on property for the year 1974-1975, see 61 Va. L. Rev. 1834 (1975). For article on title examination in Virginia, see 17 U. Rich. L. Rev. 229 (1983).

§ 8.01-255.2. Limitation on motion for new execution after loss of property sold under indemnity bond. — A motion made pursuant to § 8.01-476 shall be made within five years after the right to make the same shall have accrued. (Code 1950, § 8-408; 1977, c. 617.)

§ 8.01-256. As to rights and remedies existing when this chapter takes effect. — No action, suit, scire facias, or other proceeding which is pending before October 1, 1977, shall be barred by this chapter, and any action, suit, scire facias or other proceeding so pending shall be subject to the same limitation, if any, which would have been applied if this chapter had not been enacted. If a cause of action, as to which no action, suit, scire facias, or other proceeding is pending, exists before October 1, 1977, then this chapter shall not apply and the limitation as to such cause of action shall be the same, if any, as would apply had this chapter not been enacted. Any new limitation period imposed by this chapter, where no limitation previously existed or which is different from the limitation existing before this chapter was enacted, shall apply only to causes or rights of action accruing on or after October 1, 1977. (Code 1950, § 8-37; 1977, c. 617.)

REVISERS' NOTE

Section 8.01-256 clarifies and updates former § 8-37.

Law Review. — For survey of Virginia law on practice and pleading for the year 1978-1979, see 66 Va. L. Rev. 343 (1980). For article, "Civil Rights and 'Personal Injuries': Virginia's Statute of Limitations for Section 1983 Suits," see 26 Wm. & Mary L. Rev. 199 (1985).

I. Decisions Under Current Law.
II. Decisions Under Prior Law.

I. DECISIONS UNDER CURRENT LAW.

The purpose of this section was to assure that causes of action which existed or were pending prior to October 1, 1977, would be treated as if this chapter had not been enacted. Strickland v. Simpkins, 221 Va. 730, 273 S.E.2d 539 (1981).

The purpose of this section was to maintain the status quo as to an action pending before its enactment and as to causes of action existing then. Sherman v. Hercules, Inc., 636 F. Supp. 305 (W.D. Va. 1986).

Virginia's policy favoring prospective application of statutes of limitations is codified both in § 8.01-234 and this sec-

333

§ 8.01-257 CODE OF VIRGINIA § 8.01-257

tion. Section 8.01-234 provides that an action barred by a statute of limitations is not revived by repeal of that limitation provision. This section provides that the 1977 amendments to the limitation provisions are inapplicable to any cause of action that accrued prior to the effective date of those amendments. Saunders v. H.K. Porter Co., 643 F. Supp. 198 (E.D. Va. 1986), rev'd on other grounds, 843 F.2d 815 (4th Cir.), cert. denied, 488 U.S. 889, 109 S. Ct. 221, 102 L. Ed. 2d 211 (1988).

Applied in First Va. Bank-Colonial v. Baker, 225 Va. 72, 301 S.E.2d 8 (1983); Stone v. Ethan Allen, Inc., 232 Va. 365, 350 S.E.2d 629 (1986); Eshbaugh v. Amoco Oil Co., 234 Va. 74, 360 S.E.2d 350 (1987).

II. DECISIONS UNDER PRIOR LAW.

Editor's note. — The cases cited below were decided under corresponding provisions of former law. The term "this section," as used below, refers to former provisions.

A suit in which there has been a final decree is not a pending suit, in the sense of this section. Yarborough v. Deshazo, 48 Va. (7 Gratt.) 374 (1851).

Section does not save remedy by appeal. — This section does not operate to save to the party a remedy by way of appeal, etc., to the Supreme Court, allowed by previous acts but taken away by the act in question. McGruder v. Lyons, 48 Va. (7 Gratt.) 233 (1851).

Suit under section 8.01-241 to enforce lien. — As § 8.01-241, which prescribes a limit to the enforcement of a deed of trust, mortgage, or lien reserved to secure the payment of unpaid purchase money was enacted long after the creation of the lien sought to be enforced, in consequence of this section the lien was not barred. Jameson v. Rixey, 94 Va. 342, 26 S.E. 861 (1897).

CHAPTER 5.

VENUE.

Sec.
8.01-257. Venue generally.
8.01-258. Venue not jurisdictional.
8.01-259. Application.
8.01-260. Proper venue; preferred forum in certain actions; permissible forums for other actions.
8.01-261. Category A or preferred venue.
8.01-262. Category B or permissible venue.

Sec.
8.01-262.1. Place for bringing action under a contract related to construction.
8.01-263. Multiple parties.
8.01-264. Venue improperly laid; objection.
8.01-265. Change of venue by court.
8.01-266. Costs.
8.01-267. Discretion of judge.

§ 8.01-257. Venue generally. — It is the intent of this chapter that every action shall be commenced and tried in a forum convenient to the parties and witnesses, where justice can be administered without prejudice or delay. Except where specifically provided otherwise, whenever the word "action(s)" is used in this chapter, it shall mean all actions at law, suits in equity, and statutory proceedings, whether in circuit courts or district courts. (1977, c. 617.)

REVISERS' NOTE

There has been confusion as to the relationship of venue to process and to jurisdiction. E.g., County School Board v. Snead, 198 Va. 100, 92 S.E.2d 497 (1956).

Section 8.01-257 is a new provision which restates the common-law concept that venue was merely a convenient place of trial; i.e., is related only to geographical situs of trial. See also § 8.01-258.

Unless otherwise provided, the venue provisions of this chapter are to be applicable to all civil actions regardless of the type of proceeding or in which court the action is brought.

Cross references. — As to venue to award injunction, see § 8.01-261.

Law Review. — For survey of Virginia law on practice and pleading for the year 1976-77, see 63 Va. L. Rev. 1459 (1977).

I. DECISIONS UNDER CURRENT LAW.

Presumption of plaintiff's choice of forum not absolute. — While the presumption of correctness attaches to a plaintiff's choice of forum, it is not absolute. Indeed, the presumption cannot be enhanced simply because the action arises under the Federal Employers' Liability Act. Norfolk & W. Ry. v. Williams, 239 Va. 390, 389 S.E.2d 714 (1990).

Denial of transfer was abuse of discretion. — Denial of defendant railroad's motion to transfer a Federal Employers' Liability Act action was an abuse of discretion, where the trial court was presented with sufficient information to show good cause to transfer, including substantial inconvenience to the parties and witnesses, as well as indications of a forum originally selected for not simply justice, but perhaps justice blended with some harassment. Norfolk & W. Ry. v. Williams, 239 Va. 390, 389 S.E.2d 714 (1990).

Applied in Downs v. VEC, 4 Va. App. 454, 358 S.E.2d 737 (1987).

§ 8.01-258. Venue not jurisdictional.

— The provisions of this chapter relate to venue — the place of trial — and are not jurisdictional. No order, judgment, or decree shall be voidable, avoided, or subject to collateral attack solely on the ground that there was improper venue; however, nothing herein shall affect the right to appeal an error of court concerning venue. (1977, c. 617.)

REVISERS' NOTE

Section 8.01-258 distinguishes between jurisdiction and venue. Historically, the concept of venue has dealt with the place where a suit is commenced and jurisdiction deals with service of process and the power of the court to act. Yet, chapter 3 of former Title 8 made no reference to such a distinction, and confusion arose because of the multiplicity of venue provisions, the employment of "jurisdiction" when "venue" is meant (e.g., former §§ 8-42, 8-133; Lucas v. Biller, 204 Va. 309, 130 S.E.2d 582 (1963)), and limitations on the service of process (e.g., to the county of commencement in many actions; see former §§ 8-39 and 8-47). Moreover, whenever venue was required to be laid in a certain county and the result of improper venue was dismissal or a void judgment, then the effect of venue was jurisdictional. E.g., former § 8-38 (9) as construed by Davis v. Marr, 200 Va. 479, 106 S.E.2d 722 (1959).

Several changes have been made in Title 8.01 to eliminate process and jurisdiction:

(1) Statewide service of process in all civil actions is authorized.

(2) Objections to venue are waived unless raised on or before the day of trial if in a general district court or if in a circuit court within 21 days after service of process commencing the action or within such other time as is fixed for filing of responsive pleadings.

(3) Appropriately filed objection to improper choice of venue results not in dismissal, but rather in transfer of the action to a proper venue with the costs of transfer paid by the party responsible for laying improper venue. See, e.g., §§ 8.01-264, 8.01-266.

(4) A judgment is not subject to collateral attack on the sole ground that the suit was commenced in an improper place. However, the right to appeal a ruling of the court concerning venue is preserved. See §§ 8.01-258 and 8.01-267.

Law Review. — For survey of Virginia law on practice and pleading for the year 1976-77, see 63 Va. L. Rev. 1459 (1977). For survey on civil procedure and practice in Virginia for 1989, see 23 U. Rich. L. Rev. 511 (1989).

I. DECISIONS UNDER CURRENT LAW.

Applied in Decker v. Decker, 12 Va. App. 536, 405 S.E.2d 12 (1991).

§ 8.01-259. Application.

— Nothing in this chapter shall apply to venue in the following proceedings:

(1), (2) [Repealed.]
(3) Habeas corpus;
(4) Tax proceedings, other than those in Title 58.1;
(5) Juvenile and domestic relations district courts proceedings concerning children; or

(6) [Repealed.]
(7) Adoptions.
(8) [Repealed.]
In all other actions, venue shall be in accordance with the provisions of this chapter, and, with respect to such actions, in case of conflict between the provisions of this chapter and other provisions outside this chapter relating to venue, all such other provisions are hereby superseded. (1977, c. 617; 1987, c. 567; 1989, c. 556.)

REVISERS' NOTE

This section identifies unique proceedings which will remain the subject of special venue statutes. Attempting to consolidate such provisions into the general venue chapter would render the chapter cumbersome and complex. Except for these exceptions, the general venue provisions prescribed in §§ 8.01-260 to 8.01-262 will apply to all other actions.

Editor's note. — Acts 1993, c. 929, cl. 3, as amended by Acts 1994, c. 564, cl. 1, and Acts 1996, c. 616, cl. 3, provided that the amendment to this section by Acts 1993, c. 929, cl. 1, would become effective June 1, 1998, "only if state funds are provided by the General Assembly sufficient to provide adequate resources, including all local costs, for the court to carry out the purposes of this act and to fulfill its mission to serve children and families of the Commonwealth." The funding was not provided.

§ 8.01-260. Proper venue; preferred forum in certain actions; permissible forums for other actions.

— Except for those actions expressly excluded from the operation of this chapter, and subject to the provisions of §§ 8.01-264 and 8.01-265, the venue for any action shall be deemed proper only if laid in accordance with the provisions of §§ 8.01-261 and 8.01-262. (1977, c. 617.)

REVISERS' NOTE

Sections 8.01-260 to 8.01-262 can be considered together. They indicate those forums where venue is proper in any action, other than those excluded by § 8.01-259.

Sections 8.01-260 to 8.01-262 are made subject to § 8.01-264 to emphasize that venue not laid in accordance with the provisions of these sections must be objected to before the action will be transferred to a court of proper venue. Also, these three sections are made subject to § 8.01-265 to establish the priority of the forum non conveniens provisions of that section over the more specific venue provisions of §§ 8.01-261 and 8.01-262. Furthermore, while § 8.01-260 states that venue is proper "only" if laid pursuant to §§ 8.01-261 and 8.01-262, it should be understood that §§ 8.01-264 and 8.01-265 prevent any such "preferred" or "permissible" venue from being jurisdictional.

Category A (§ 8.01-261), Preferred Venue, generally lists those actions where so-called "mandatory venue" was applicable under former provisions of the Code. However, Category A (§ 8.01-261), like Category B (§ 8.01-262), does not have jurisdictional effect and improper venue is waived if not affirmatively pleaded.

Category B (§ 8.01-262), Permissible Venue, lists those forums in which venue is proper in actions other than those listed in Category A and other than those excluded by § 8.01-259; thus, Category B will be applicable to most actions.

Law Review. — For survey of Virginia law on practice and pleading for the year 1976-77, see 63 Va. L. Rev. 1459 (1977).

I. DECISIONS UNDER CURRENT LAW.

Applied in Faison v. Hudson, 243 Va. 413, 417 S.E.2d 302 (1992).

§ 8.01-261. Category A or preferred venue. — In the actions listed in this section, the forums enumerated shall be deemed preferred places of venue and may be referred to as "Category A" in this title. Venue laid in any other forum shall be subject to objection; however, if more than one preferred place of venue applies, any such place shall be a proper forum. The following forums are designated as places of preferred venue for the action specified:

1. In actions for review of, appeal from, or enforcement of state administrative regulations, decisions, or other orders:

   a. If the moving or aggrieved party is other than the Commonwealth or an agency thereof, then the county or city wherein such party:
   (1) Resides;
   (2) Regularly or systematically conducts affairs or business activity; or
   (3) Wherein such party's property affected by the administrative action is located.

   b. If the moving or aggrieved party is the Commonwealth or an agency thereof, then the county or city wherein the respondent or a party defendant:
   (1) Resides;
   (2) Regularly or systematically conducts affairs or business activity; or
   (3) Has any property affected by the administrative action.

   c. If subdivisions 1 a and 1 b do not apply, then the county or city wherein the alleged violation of the administrative regulation, decision, or other order occurred.

2. Except as provided in subdivision 1 of this section, where the action is against one or more officers of the Commonwealth in an official capacity, the county or city where any such person has his official office.

3. The county or city wherein the subject land, or a part thereof, is situated in the following actions:
   a. To recover or partition land;
   b. To subject land to a debt;
   c. To sell, lease, or encumber the land of persons under disabilities;
   d. [Repealed.]
   e. To sell wastelands;
   f. To establish boundaries;
   g. For unlawful entry or detainer;
   h. For ejectment; or
   i. To remove clouds on title.

4. [Reserved.]

5. In actions for writs of mandamus, prohibition, or certiorari, except such as may be issued by the Supreme Court, the county or city wherein is the record or proceeding to which the writ relates.

6. In actions on bonds required for public contract, the county or city in which the public project, or any part thereof, is situated.

7. In actions to impeach or establish a will, the county or city wherein the will was probated, or, if not probated at the time of the action, where the will may be properly offered for probate.

8., 9. [Repealed.]

10. In actions on any contract between a transportation district and a component government, any county or city any part of which is within such transportation district.

11. In attachments,
    a. With reference to the principal defendant and those liable with or to him, venue shall be determined as if the principal defendant were the sole defendant; or
    b. In the county or city in which the principal defendant has estate or has debts owing to him.

12. [Repealed.]

13. a. In any action for the collection of state, county, or municipal taxes, any one of the following counties or cities shall be deemed preferred places of venue:

(1) Wherein the taxpayer resides;
(2) Wherein the taxpayer owns real or personal property;
(3) Wherein the taxpayer has a registered office, or regularly or systematically conducts business; or
(4) In case of withdrawal from the Commonwealth by a delinquent taxpayer, wherein venue was proper at the time the taxes in question were assessed or at the time of such withdrawal.

b. In any action for the correction of an erroneous assessment of state taxes and tax refunds, any one of the following counties or cities shall be deemed preferred places of venue:

(1) Wherein the taxpayer resides;
(2) Wherein the taxpayer has a registered office or regularly or systematically conducts business;
(3) Wherein the taxpayer's real or personal property involved in such a proceeding is located; or
(4) The Circuit Court of the City of Richmond.

14. In proceedings by writ of quo warranto:

a. The city or county wherein any of the defendants reside;
b. If the defendant is a corporation, the city or county where its registered office is or where its mayor, rector, president, or other chief officer resides; or
c. If there is no officer or none of the defendants reside in the Commonwealth, venue shall be in the City of Richmond.

15. In proceedings to award an injunction:

a. To any judgment or judicial proceeding of a circuit court, venue shall be in the court in the county or city in which the judgment was rendered or such proceeding is pending;
b. To any judgment or judicial proceeding of a district court, venue shall be in the circuit court of the county or city in which the judgment was rendered or such proceeding is pending; or
c. To any other act or proceeding, venue shall be in the circuit court of the county or city in which the act is to be done, or being done, or is apprehended to be done or the proceeding is pending.

16. [Repealed.]

17. In disbarment or suspension proceedings against any attorney-at-law, in the county or city where the defendant:

a. Resides;
b. Has his principal office or place of practice when the proceeding is commenced;
c. Resided or had such principal office or place of practice when any misconduct complained of occurred; or
d. Has any pending case as to which any misconduct took place.

18. In actions under the Virginia Tort Claims Act, Article 18.1 (§ 8.01-195.1 et seq.) of Chapter 3 of this title:

a. The county or city where the claimant resides;
b. The county or city where the act or omission complained of occurred; or
c. If the claimant resides outside the Commonwealth and the act or omission complained of occurred outside the Commonwealth, the City of Richmond.

19. In suits for annulment, affirmance, or divorce, the county or city in which the parties last cohabited, or at the option of the plaintiff, in the county or city in which the defendant resides, if a resident of this Commonwealth, and in cases in which an order of publication may be issued against the defendant under § 8.01-316, venue may also be in the county or city in which the plaintiff resides.

20. In distress actions, in the county or city when the premises yielding the rent, or some part thereof, may be or where goods liable to distress may be found. (1977, c. 617; 1978, c. 334; 1979, c. 331; 1985, c. 433; 1987, c. 567; 1988, c. 766; 1989, c. 556; 1990, c. 831; 1993, c. 841.)

REVISERS' NOTE

Category A lists certain actions and denominates specific forums as the proper venue for those actions (subject to §§ 8.01-264 and 8.01-265). Under former Virginia statutes and case law, in the situations listed in Category A, venue was generally exclusive or mandatory, and timely objection to venue improperly laid would result in dismissal of the action. Also, if no timely objection were brought and such an action proceeded to judgment, such judgment was void and subject to collateral attack. Thus, mandatory venue related more to jurisdiction than to venue.

To further clarify the distinction between venue and jurisdiction, Category A uses the term "preferred" venue to refer to those situations in which venue had heretofore generally been denominated as "mandatory" or "exclusive." "Preferred" venue is not jurisdictional since, under §§ 8.01-258 and 8.01-264, dismissal is not available as a remedy for improper venue and a judgment rendered cannot be voided or collaterally attacked on such grounds. Instead, upon timely objection, the action shall be transferred to a "preferred" forum under this section, and, if no timely objection is made, the venue defect is waived.

Subsection 1 is § 9-6.14:5 of the Administrative Process Act of 1975. In general, this subsection has eliminated the necessity for citizens being forced to go to Richmond in order to challenge administrative actions or to protect their rights against adverse administrative decisions.

Subsection 2 changes the venue in former §§ 8-38 (9), 8-40 and 8-752 and establishes venue as the county or city where any defendant public officer has his official office. This provision comports with subsection 1.

Subsection 3 collects in a single provision those "local actions" where the situs of realty has traditionally been considered the principal place of venue.

With the exception of subsection 8, subsections 5 through 10 designate preferred venue in certain actions where venue was previously mandatory. Subsection 8 also consolidates venue references of former §§ 64.1-24, 64.1-30 and 64.1-34 (probate of a will is not included; for venue, see § 64.1-75).

Subsection 11 restates the concept of former § 8-522. The language of former § 8-522 pertaining to the principal defendant "and those jointly liable with him" has been changed to "those liable with or to him." This change is made to clarify the concept that potential defendants are not only those primarily liable with the principal debtor but also those who are potentially liable to the principal debtor.

Subsection 12 changes former § 8-703 which required that proceedings involving partition of personal property be brought in the "jurisdiction wherein the property, or the greater part thereof, is located." To avoid having to determine where the greatest share of the property is to be found, the subsection permits venue where any part of the personal property in question is located. This is the same venue criterion applied to the recovery of personal property; see subsection 5 of § 8.01-262.

Because the property to be partitioned may be distinct and separately located from the evidence of that property, (e.g., stock certificate as evidence of corporate ownership), paragraph (b) permits the latter as an additional venue site.

So that the party seeking to partition personal property will be insured of a forum in which to proceed, if venue cannot lie pursuant to paragraphs a and b, paragraph c permits venue where the plaintiff resides.

Subsection 13 amends the provisions of Title 58 concerning the venue of suits for collection of State taxes (see §§ 58.1-3940 through 58.1-3960) and of those relating to the correction of erroneous assessments and tax refunds. (See §§ 58.1-1821, 58.1-1833, and 58.1-3984.) The amendments generally base venue on the location of the taxpayer instead of on the location of the tax assessment.

As to the collection of State taxes, the venue provisions of former § 58-1015 are altered by the deletion of the forum where the taxes were assessed or payable; this provision is replaced with paragraph a which locates venue in the county or city where the delinquent taxpayer is located (or owns property) at the time of the action to collect the taxes. Only if the taxpayer has left the Commonwealth does the time of assessment become pertinent as to venue.

In actions to correct erroneous assessments and tax refunds, the former venue provisions of § 58.1-1825 have been changed; paragraph b makes no reference to the court in which the officer who made the assessment gave bond or makes no distinction as to venue between domestic and foreign corporations. Also, § 58.1-3984 as to venue is amended by the deletion as a proper forum of the county or city wherein the assessment was made.

Cross references. — See note to § 8.01-262. As to venue in criminal prosecutions, see §§ 19.2-244 through 19.2-253 and sections relating to particular offenses.

Editor's note. — Section 58-1015, which is referred to in the Revisers' Note, was repealed by Acts 1984, c. 675. Sections 64.1-24, 64.1-30, and 64.1-34, referred to in the sixth paragraph of the Revisers' Note were repealed by Acts 1990, c. 831.

Acts 1993, c. 929, cl. 3, as amended by Acts 1994, c. 564, cl. 1, provided that the amendment to this section by Acts 1993, c. 929, cl. 1, as amended by Acts 1996, c. 616, cl. 3, would become effective June 1, 1998, "only if state funds are provided by the General Assembly sufficient to provide adequate resources, including all local costs, for the court to carry out the purposes of this act and to fulfill its mission to serve children and families of the Commonwealth." The funding was not provided.

Law Review. — For 1985 survey of Virginia administrative procedure, see 19 U. Rich. L. Rev. 657 (1985). For 1987 survey of Virginia civil procedure and practice, see 21 U. Rich. L. Rev. 667 (1987).

I. Decisions Under Current Law.
II. Decisions Under Prior Law.
   A. General Consideration.
   B. Particular Actions and Proceedings.
   C. Injunctions.
   D. Annulment, Affirmance, or Divorce.

I. DECISIONS UNDER CURRENT LAW.

Applied in Decker v. Decker, 12 Va. App. 536, 405 S.E.2d 12 (1991); City of Danville v. Virginia State Water Control Bd., 18 Va. App. 594, 446 S.E.2d 466 (1994).

II. DECISIONS UNDER PRIOR LAW.

A. General Consideration.

Editor's note. — The cases cited below were decided under corresponding provisions of former law. The term "this section," as used below, refers to former provisions.

Purpose. — An examination of this section makes it clear that the objective sought to be attained by the legislature was to provide an orderly, practical and appropriate method for determining the proper venue of an action or suit, with the purpose in mind to insure to a litigant, insofar as possible, his right to have his case tried in a convenient and familiar jurisdiction. Dowdy v. Franklin, 203 Va. 7, 121 S.E.2d 817 (1961).

Venue of all actions is fixed by statute. — The venue of all actions in this State, whether local or transitory, is fixed by statute, and the statutes declare where actions against corporations as well as individuals may be brought. Virginia & S.W. Ry. v. Hollingsworth, 107 Va. 359, 58 S.E. 572 (1907).

Venue is a privilege that may be waived. — The Code provisions fixing venue confer a privilege upon the defendant to have the action or suit against him heard and determined in the local courts there specified. But it is a privilege which may be waived. Moore v. Norfolk & W. Ry., 124 Va. 628, 98 S.E. 635 (1919).

This section does not confer jurisdiction on a court, but simply fixes the venue by giving the defendant the privilege of having his case heard in a particular county or city; and this privilege may be waived by him. Morgan v. Pennsylvania R.R., 148 Va. 272, 138 S.E. 566 (1927). See Woodhouse v. Burke & Herbert Bank & Trust Co., 166 Va. 706, 185 S.E. 876 (1936).

Rules of Supreme Court do not change law in regard to venue. — While the new Rules of Supreme Court prescribe the practice and procedure for prosecuting actions, they do not change the law as it previously existed in regard to venue. Commonwealth ex rel. Duvall v. Hall, 194 Va. 914, 76 S.E.2d 208 (1953).

B. Particular Actions and Proceedings.

Suits by Commonwealth not specially provided for. — Except in cases where it is otherwise specially provided, the Commonwealth may prosecute her suits in any of the courts in which other parties may prosecute suits of like character. Commonwealth v. Ford, 70 Va. (29 Gratt.) 683 (1878).

State Highway Commission. — The venue of a suit to enjoin the State Highway Commission (now State Highway and Transportation Commission) and its servants from interfering with a draining ditch is properly laid, under former § 8.01-621, in the county where the acts complained of were to be done, and of which one of the defendants was resident. State Hwy. Comm'n v. Nock, 138 Va. 212, 120 S.E. 869 (1924).

Action on sheriff's official bond. — Since former § 8-716, (see now § 8.01-227) which provided a remedy by motion on official bonds but restricted the venue to the court to which the official bond was required to be returned, did not prescribe an exclusive remedy for the breach of the condition of a sheriff's bond, venue of such an action was governed by the provisions of this section and former § 8-716.

Commonwealth ex rel. Duvall v. Hall, 194 Va. 914, 76 S.E.2d 208 (1953).

An action by a lessor to recover rent, or to recover on agreements for royalties in a lease, is not a suit "to recover land" within the meaning of a venue statute such as this section. Cowan v. Zimmerman, 176 Va. 16, 10 S.E.2d 555 (1940).

Subjecting land to payment of debt. — Upon a bill filed by a creditor of the M. Co. against the persons constituting that company, in the circuit court of C. county, to subject to the payment of his debt the land of one of them lying in C. county, and mining interests in land lying in F. county, one of the members of the company resided in C. county, and the others were nonresidents of the State. Held, the court had jurisdiction of the cause, both on the ground that a part of the subject sought to be subjected lay in the county of C., and that one of the defendants resided in that county. Clayton v. Hensley, 73 Va. (32 Gratt.) 65 (1879).

Right to proceeds of sale of land. — An equity suit to determine the right to proceeds from foreclosure sale under a deed of trust held properly brought in county where the land was located even though none of the necessary defendants resided there. Bradley v. Canter, 201 Va. 747, 113 S.E.2d 878 (1960).

Section creates no ground for attachment. — This section relates only to venue of attachments, and creates no ground for attachment. It merely fixes the venue of attachments in those cases in which the issuance of an attachment is authorized under § 8.01-534, or some other section of this chapter. Winfree v. Mann, 154 Va. 683, 153 S.E. 837 (1930).

C. Injunctions.

This section applies only to a pure bill of injunction, not to a bill seeking other relief, to which the injunction sought is merely ancillary. Winston v. Midlothian Coal Mining Co., 61 Va. (20 Gratt.) 686 (1871); Muller v. Bayly, 62 Va. (21 Gratt.) 521 (1871). See also, Hough v. Shreeve, 18 Va. (4 Munf.) 490 (1815); Singleton v. Lewis, 20 Va. (6 Munf.) 397 (1819); Pulliam v. Winston, 32 Va. (5 Leigh) 324 (1834); McKenry v. Staunton Hill Club, 12 Va. L. Reg. (n.s.) 97 (1925).

Where a bill seeks relief, and asks for an injunction to restrain the sale of real estate in another county, as ancillary to the relief sought, the court of the county or city where the defendants, or some of them reside, has jurisdiction of the cause; and the order for the injunction properly proceeds from the court of that county or city. Winston v. Midlothian Coal Mining Co., 61 Va. (20 Gratt.) 686 (1871).

This section is directory as to venue. — As to the venue for suits for injunctions, this section and § 8.01-627 are directory and not mandatory. Southern Sand & Gravel Co. v. Massaponax Sand & Gravel Corp., 145 Va. 317, 133 S.E. 812 (1926).

Effect when cause is not brought in good faith. — If there is any reason to doubt that the chancery cause is brought in good faith for the purposes alleged in the bill, or if the prayer for other relief beyond the injunction is merely colorable and thrown in to give jurisdiction it would not be allowable to take the case out of the provisions of this section. McKenry v. Staunton Hill Club, 12 Va. L. Reg. (n.s.) 97 (1925).

Injunctions against judicial proceedings. — Under this section, the circuit court of a county has jurisdiction of a suit to enjoin the clerk of such county from conveying certain delinquent lands to an applicant for the purchase thereof. Baker v. Briggs, 99 Va. 360, 38 S.E. 277 (1901).

A bill to enjoin levy of execution must be filed in the county in which the judgment was recovered. The circuit court of another county has no jurisdiction of the case. Beckley v. Palmer, 52 Va. (11 Gratt.) 625 (1854).

Injunction against proceedings in other courts. — A circuit court sitting in equity has jurisdiction to issue an injunction against legal proceedings in other courts of equal authority, where the injunction is merely incidental or ancillary to the main relief sought, and such court has the right to return the injunction to its own clerk's office. McKenry v. Staunton Hill Club, 12 Va. L. Reg. (n.s.) 97 (1925).

Injunction against other acts or proceedings maintained where done. — An injunction cannot be maintained in a county other than that in which the act or proceeding is to be done, or is doing, or apprehended. Norfolk & W.R.R. v. Postal Tel. Cable Co., 88 Va. 932, 14 S.E. 689 (1892).

Venue to enjoin Highway and Transportation Commission in county where act done. — The venue under this section of a suit to enjoin the State Highway Commission (now State Highway and Transportation Commission) and another, and their servants, from interfering with a draining ditch is properly laid in the county where the acts which complainant seeks to enjoin were to be done or attempted, and of which one of the defendants was a resident. State Hwy. Comm'n v. Nock, 138 Va. 212, 120 S.E. 869 (1924).

D. Annulment, Affirmance, or Divorce.

Editor's note. — The cases cited below were decided under former subsection B of § 20-96 and former § 20-98.

The venue statutes in divorce proceedings are mandatory and jurisdictional. Netzer v. Reynolds, 231 Va. 444, 345 S.E.2d 291 (1986).

As to mandatory nature of former venue statute (former § 20-98), see Colley v. Colley, 204 Va. 225, 129 S.E.2d 630 (1963).

Filing in wrong venue renders court without jurisdiction. — Where petitioner filed a bill in the county where she was residing, defendant resided in another county, and the last place of cohabitation of the parties was in neither of these two counties, the trial court was without jurisdiction to grant a divorce. White v. White, 181 Va. 162, 24 S.E.2d 448 (1943).

Where the defendant in a divorce suit is a resident of the State, the jurisdiction of a local court over him must arise from one of two facts: residence within the court's jurisdiction, or that the parties last cohabited together within such jurisdiction. Richardson v. Richardson, 8 Va. L. Reg. (n.s.) 257 (1922).

Certain facts are jurisdictional and do not merely concern venue. — The jurisdiction of the courts of Virginia to grant divorces being special statutory and limited jurisdiction, the fact that the plaintiff had been domiciled (now resident also) in Virginia for at least one year (now six months) next preceding the commencement of the suit for divorce, that plaintiff was domiciled in Virginia at the time of bringing the suit, that defendant was not a resident of Virginia, and that the plaintiff was a resident of the city or county in which the suit was instituted were jurisdictional, and did not concern merely venue. Chandler v. Chandler, 132 Va. 418, 112 S.E. 856 (1922).

Bill must show venue, which cannot be waived. — As the jurisdiction of divorce suits is a special statutory and limited one, it would seem that such jurisdiction must be exercised in conformity to the statute bestowing it. In such cases the question of venue becomes jurisdictional; with the result that not only is no plea in abatement necessary to raise the question of venue, but the bill is demurrable unless it shows on its face that the suit is instituted in its proper statutory venue. It follows that the objection cannot be waived, and the court will mero motu dismiss the bill when defective in this respect. Blankenship v. Blankenship, 125 Va. 595, 100 S.E. 538 (1919).

Whether or not the complainant followed the venue fixed by statute was a question of fact, which the verdict of the jury answered in the affirmative upon ample evidence to support it, and that verdict is conclusive. Towson v. Towson, 126 Va. 640, 102 S.E. 48 (1920).

Domicile and cohabitation are distinctly different concepts and should not be equated or confused. Domicile is not determined solely by the location where people reside, while cohabitation is. Cohabitation does not require an intent to remain somewhere indefinitely, while domicile does. Rock v. Rock, 7 Va. App. 198, 372 S.E.2d 211 (1988).

The word "cohabit" means having dwelt together under the same roof with more or less permanency, and does not signify the having of sexual intercourse as it does in some other statutes. Colley v. Colley, 204 Va. 225, 129 S.E.2d 630 (1963).

"Cohabitation" has reference to a continuing condition. — Cohabitation, in its proper meaning in the law of divorce, has reference to a continuing condition and not to an act — the permanent or public living or dwelling together in the marital relation. The fact that plaintiff in a divorce suit had been compelled by the cruelty of her husband to flee to another city, where she was on several occasions visited by him, occupying same bed and room with him through fear and against her volition, did not establish such city as the "last place of cohabitation" for the purpose of giving the city's courts jurisdiction. Rock v. Rock, 7 Va. App. 198, 372 S.E.2d 211 (1988).

Where husband and wife cohabited in both a city and a county, the court held that they last cohabited in the city in which they were intending to live for the winter, and in which they were in fact living when husband took his clothes and left. Rock v. Rock, 7 Va. App. 198, 372 S.E.2d 211 (1988).

Amending decree to show true last place of marital cohabitation. — Where there was ample unrefuted "record evidence" that the last place of marital cohabitation, as properly defined in the context of the divorce venue statute, between parties who were divorced in 1966 was in the City of Alexandria, the trial court had the inherent power to allow an appropriate amendment to the bill of complaint to disregard the erroneous conclusion of law contained in the commissioner's report, stating that the parties last cohabited in Danville, and to amend its final decree of divorce nunc pro tunc, in order to make the record "speak the truth." Netzer v. Reynolds, 231 Va. 444, 345 S.E.2d 291 (1986).

§ 8.01-262. Category B or permissible venue. — In any actions to which this chapter applies except those actions enumerated in Category A where preferred venue is specified, one or more of the following counties or cities shall be permissible forums, such forums being sometimes referred to as "Category B" in this title:

1. Wherein the defendant resides or has his principal place of employment

or, if the defendant is a corporation, wherein its mayor, rector, president or other chief officer resides;

2. Wherein the defendant has a registered office, has appointed an agent to receive process, or such agent has been appointed by operation of the law; or, in case of withdrawal from this Commonwealth by such defendant, wherein venue herein was proper at the time of such withdrawal;

3. Wherein the defendant regularly conducts affairs or business activity, or in the case of withdrawal from this Commonwealth by such defendant, wherein venue herein was proper at the time of such withdrawal;

4. Wherein the cause of action, or any part thereof, arose;

5. In actions to recover or partition personal property, whether tangible or intangible, the county or city:
 (a) Wherein such property is physically located; or
 (b) Wherein the evidence of such property is located;
 (c) And if subdivisions 5 (a) and 5 (b) do not apply, wherein the plaintiff resides.

6. In actions against a fiduciary as defined in § 8.01-2 appointed under court authority, the county or city wherein such fiduciary qualified;

7. In actions for improper message transmission or misdelivery wherein the message was transmitted or delivered or wherein the message was accepted for delivery or was misdelivered;

8. In actions arising based on delivery of goods, wherein the goods were received;

9. If there is no other forum available in subdivisions 1 through 8 of this category, then the county or city where the defendant has property or debts owing to him subject to seizure by any civil process; or

10. Wherein any of the plaintiffs reside if (i) all of the defendants are unknown or are nonresidents of the Commonwealth or if (ii) there is no other forum available under any other provisions of § 8.01-261 or this section. (1977, c. 617; 1978, c. 414; 1979, c. 331; 1985, c. 213; 1999, c. 73.)

REVISERS' NOTE

Category B, permissible venue, is applicable to most actions — specifically to those actions for which no preferred forum is designated in Category A, § 8.01-261, and which are not excluded by § 8.01-259. The provision that "one or more" of the forums listed in subsections 1 through 9 are permissible, gives the plaintiff the choice of the forums enumerated. Subsection 10 is a last resort provision, giving the plaintiff a forum where no forum is available under any other provision of §§ 8.01-260 to 8.01-262.

Together with § 8.01-263, subsection 1 incorporates former § 8-38 (1) (i.e., the residence of any defendant) and adds the defendant's place of employment. Section 16.1-76 provides for venue at the defendant's place of employment in actions in general district courts, and subsection 1 provides the same venue for all courts.

Subsection 2 incorporates the substance of former § 8-38 (2) and (6) and extends these provisions to all defendants, i.e., it provides plaintiffs with at least one forum against partnerships, unincorporated associations, and individuals, as well as corporations, which are engaged in activities requiring registration or appointment of agents for service of process.

The provision for "principal office" in former § 8-38 (2) is deleted as redundant because it is covered in § 8.01-262 (3); similarly, the provision for venue where a corporation's "mayor, rector, president or other chief officer resides" was deleted since subsection 1 of § 8.01-262 and subsections 3 and 10 of § 8.01-262, combine to provide at least one forum for the plaintiff against resident or nonresident defendants generally.

While subsection 3 has no statutory antecedent, it establishes a logical forum when considered in the context of fairness and convenience of the parties.

Subsection 4 incorporates former § 8-39. With the adoption of statewide service of process, § 8.01-292, venue based on where the cause of action arose will no longer be subject to a potential process limitation. Cf. former § 8-47.

Subsection 5 reflects common-law practice in that the most convenient forum for such actions is often the forum wherein such property is located.

Subsection 6 is essentially former § 8-38 (5). [Venue under this subsection is the same as venue based on a fiduciary's "residence" under proposed subsection 1. Dowdy v. Franklin, 203 Va. 7, 121 S.E.2d 817 (1961). Venue based on the fiduciary's place of employment under proposed subsection 1 can, however, be different than that based on the place of qualification or "residence."]

Subsection 7 incorporates § 56-474 by providing forums in actions against telephone and telegraph companies for improper transmission of messages.

Subsection 8 extends § 3.1-720 to make the place of receipt a place of permissible venue in any action based on the delivery of goods.

Subsection 9 is primarily applicable to in personam actions where seizure of property is used as a means of bringing a nonresident defendant before the court. The forums already available to the plaintiff under subsections 1 through 8 will usually encompass the place where the defendant has property or debts subject to seizure. Only when no other forum is available under these subsections will the location of defendant's debts or property become a basis of venue.

Subsection 10 provides the plaintiff with at least one forum, i.e., in the county or city where he resides when all the defendants are nonresidents or are unknown and when there is no other forum available under any other provision of §§ 8.01-260 to 8.01-262. This subsection includes the former venue provisions of the Virginia long-arm statutes, § 8-81.4, and the nonresident and unknown motor vehicle statutes, former §§ 8-38 (6a) and (6b), 38.1-381 (e).

The 1999 amendment, in subdivision 10, substituted "Wherein any plaintiffs reside if" for "In actions in which," inserted the clause (i) and (ii) designations, and deleted "then the county or city where any of the plaintiffs reside" following "or this section."

Law Review. — For 1985 survey of Virginia civil procedure and practice, see 19 U. Rich. L. Rev. 679 (1985). For 1995 survey of civil practice and procedure, see 29 U. Rich. L. Rev. 897 (1995).

I. Decisions Under Current Law.
II. Decisions Under Prior Law.
   A. General Consideration.
   B. Corporations.

I. DECISIONS UNDER CURRENT LAW.

Defendant did not "regularly" conduct affairs or business activity within the City where he only made seven visits per year to insurance brokerage firms and three appearances per year to business seminars. Meyer v. Brown, 256 Va. 53, 500 S.E.2d 807 (1998).

Applied in Faison v. Hudson, 243 Va. 413, 417 S.E.2d 302 (1992).

II. DECISIONS UNDER PRIOR LAW.

A. General Consideration.

Editor's note. — The cases cited below were decided under corresponding provisions of former law. The term "this section," as used below, refers to former provisions.

An action for breach of contract may be brought in the jurisdiction where the contract is made, or in that in which a breach occurs. Big Seam Coal Corp. v. Atlantic C.L.R.R., 196 Va. 590, 85 S.E.2d 239 (1955).

An action against a liability insurer by the injured party under the contract provision required by § 38.1-380 (see now § 38.2-2200) may be brought in the county or city where execution on the judgment against the insured is returned unsatisfied. Virginia Farm Bureau Mut. Ins. Co. v. Saccio, 204 Va. 769, 133 S.E.2d 268 (1963).

Action for breach of collective bargaining agreement. — An individual employee and member of a labor union may sue his employer for a breach of a collective bargaining agreement between the union and the employer in a State court. Pearman v. Industrial Rayon Corp., 207 Va. 854, 153 S.E.2d 227 (1967).

Where cause of action on modified contract arises. — A corporation, at its home office, employed an agent to sell its stock. Subsequently it informed the agent by telegram, in answer to a telegram from him, that it had no more stock for sale, but that he could continue to sell stock in conjunction with another, who had an option on all the stock left, and divide commissions with him. It was held that this was not a new contract, but a modification of the original agreement, and that an action to recover commissions on stock sold before and after the telegram must be brought within the jurisdiction of the home office of the corporation and could not be maintained in the jurisdiction where the telegram was received

§ 8.01-262.1 CIVIL REMEDIES AND PROCEDURE § 8.01-262.1

by the agent. Ferguson & Hutter v. Grottoes Co., 92 Va. 316, 23 S.E. 761 (1895).

Delivery of carrier of goods in bad condition. — Upon a shipment of horses from St. Louis, Mo., to Norfolk, Va., the failure to deliver safely at Norfolk gives rise to a cause of action at that place. Norfolk & W. Ry. v. Crull, 112 Va. 151, 70 S.E. 521 (1911).

Where the principal defendant is a nonresident, suit may be brought in a county where one or more of the other defendants reside, though the attached real estate of the nonresident defendant lies in another county. Porter v. Young, 85 Va. 49, 6 S.E. 803 (1888).

Order of service of resident and nonresident defendants is immaterial. — Where suit was brought in the court of law and chancery in the city of the residence of one defendant, that court had jurisdiction under this section, and the process could be executed upon the other defendants in any county or city in the State, either before or after service of the resident defendant. It was sufficient if process had been properly executed on the resident defendant at the time of the trial. Brame v. Nolen, 139 Va. 413, 124 S.E. 299 (1924).

Suit against husband for separate maintenance. — Where a husband's bill in a divorce suit alleged that he was a resident of Arlington County, the venue of his wife's suit for separate maintenance against him was properly laid in the circuit court of that county. Westfall v. Westfall, 196 Va. 97, 82 S.E.2d 487 (1954).

An action for false arrest and false imprisonment may be brought, under this section, in the county of imprisonment, where defendants were served, although they resided and the arrest was made in another county. Shugart v. Cruise, 260 F. 36 (4th Cir. 1919).

Confinement in penitentiary of another state does not change residence. — The residence of a citizen of this State is not changed by reason of his conviction and confinement in the penitentiary of another state. Guarantee Co. of N. Am. v. First Nat'l Bank, 95 Va. 480, 28 S.E. 909 (1898).

B. Corporations.

Declaration in the certificate of incorporation as to location of the principal office is conclusive on that point, and the motive of the corporation in so declaring is immaterial. Loyd's Executorial Trustees v. City of Lynchburg, 113 Va. 627, 75 S.E. 233 (1912).

A corporation holding land in different counties, if so empowered by its charter, may be proceeded against by attachment in any county wherein such land may be, though its principal office is located or its chief officer resides elsewhere. B & O R.R. v. Gallahue's Adm'rs, 53 Va. (12 Gratt.) 655 (1855).

Foreign corporations. — An action against a foreign corporation may be brought where the statutory agent of the corporation resides. It cannot be brought in another county or city, and have process sent to the county or city in which the statutory agent resides. Deatrick v. State Life Ins. Co., 107 Va. 602, 59 S.E. 489 (1907).

Interstate railroad. — A foreign railroad company engaged in interstate commerce, operating a part of its road in this State and owning permanent real property in the State, is so far a resident in the counties or cities in which it operates its road, that it is within the purview of this section, and may there be sued alone or in conjunction with other persons, natural or artificial, residing elsewhere in the State. Seaboard Air Line Ry. v. J.E. Bowden & Co., 144 Va. 154, 131 S.E. 245 (1926).

Subdivision 4 applies to suits against corporations. — A cause of action growing out of a corporation's contracts, acts, negligences or omissions may arise in a different county or city from the location of its principal office, and suit may be brought where the cause of action arose without reference to the residence of the defendant corporation. B & O R.R. v. Gallahue's Adm'rs, 53 Va. (12 Gratt.) 655 (1855). See Virginia & S.W. Ry. v. Hollingsworth, 107 Va. 359, 58 S.E. 572 (1907).

§ 8.01-262.1. Place for bringing action under a contract related to construction. — A. Where a party whose principal place of business is in the Commonwealth enters into a contract on or after July 1, 1997, to design, manage construction of, construct, alter, repair, maintain, move, demolish, or excavate, or supply goods, equipment, or materials for the construction, alteration, repair, maintenance, movement, demolition, or excavation of a building, structure, appurtenance, road, bridge, or tunnel which is physically located in the Commonwealth, any cause of action arising under such contract may be brought in the jurisdiction where the construction project is located, or such other jurisdiction where the venue is proper under the provisions of this chapter. Any provision in the contract mandating that such action be brought in a location outside the Commonwealth shall be unenforceable.

B. The forum for any arbitration proceedings required in such a contract entered into on or after July 1, 1991, shall be in this Commonwealth. If the contract provides for arbitration proceedings outside the Commonwealth, such provision is unenforceable and arbitration proceedings shall be in the county or city where the work is to be performed, unless the parties agree to conduct the proceedings elsewhere within the Commonwealth. The enforceability of the remaining provisions of the arbitration agreement and the method of selecting a forum for the conduct of the arbitration proceedings are as provided in this Code, the Federal Arbitration Act, and any applicable rules of arbitration. (1991, c. 489; 1997, c. 424; 1999, c. 130.)

Editor's note. — The Federal Arbitration Act, referred to in this section, is codified at 9 U.S.C. § 1, et seq.

The 1999 amendment added the last sentence in subsection A.

§ **8.01-263. Multiple parties.** — In actions involving multiple parties, venue shall not be subject to objection:

1. If one or more of the parties is entitled to preferred venue, and such action is commenced in any such forum; provided that in any action where there are one or more residents and one or more nonresidents or parties unknown, venue shall be proper (preferred or permissible, as the case may be) as to at least one resident defendant;

2. In all other cases, if the venue is proper as to any party. (1977, c. 617.)

REVISERS' NOTE

Section 8.01-263 is necessary in order for the other venue provisions to function effectively in multiple party situations. Thus, by subsection 1, where any party is entitled to a preferred forum under § 8.01-261, venue will not be transferred pursuant to §§ 8.01-264, 8.01-265, if the action is commenced in a preferred forum to which any other party is entitled pursuant to § 8.01-261.

The proviso to subsection 1 reflects former § 8-38 (7), and gives preference to resident defendants when both resident and nonresident defendants are involved in an action.

Where subsection 1 does not apply, subsection 2 simplifies matters by recognizing no priorities. It allows the action to be maintained so long as venue is proper as to any one party.

§ **8.01-264. Venue improperly laid; objection.** — A. Venue laid in forums other than those designated by this chapter shall be subject to objection, but no action shall be dismissed solely on the basis of venue if there be a forum in the Commonwealth where venue is proper. In actions where venue is subject to objection, the action may nevertheless be tried where it is commenced, and the venue irregularity shall be deemed to have been waived unless the defendant objects to venue by motion filed, as to actions in circuit courts, within twenty-one days after service of process commencing the action, or within the period of any extension of time for filing responsive pleadings fixed by order of the court. As to actions in general district courts, a motion objecting to venue, which may be in the form of a letter or other written communication, shall be filed with or received by the court on or before the day of trial. Waiver by any defendant shall not constitute waiver for any other defendant entitled to object to venue. Such motion shall set forth where the defendant believes venue to be proper, may be in writing, and shall be promptly heard by the court upon reasonable notice by any party. The court shall hear the motion only on the basis of the action as commenced against the original defendant and not on the basis of subsequent joinder or intervention of any other party. If such motion is sustained, the court shall order the venue transferred to a proper forum under the appropriate provisions of §§ 8.01-195.4, 8.01-260, 8.01-261 and 8.01-262 and shall so notify each party.

B. In the event a party defendant whose presence created venue is dismissed after the parties are at issue, then the remaining parties defendant

§ 8.01-264   CIVIL REMEDIES AND PROCEDURE   § 8.01-264

may object to venue within ten days after such dismissal if the remaining defendants can demonstrate that the dismissed defendant was not properly joined or was added as a party defendant for the purpose of creating venue. However, nothing in this section shall impair the right of the court under § 8.01-265 to retain the action for trial on motion of a plaintiff and for good cause shown.

C. The initial pleading, in any action brought in a general district court, shall inform the defendant of his right to object to venue if the action is brought in any forum other than that specified in §§ 8.01-261, 8.01-262, or § 8.01-263. The information to the defendant shall be stated in clear, nontechnical language reasonably calculated to accomplish the purpose of this subsection.

D. Where a suit described in subdivision 19 of § 8.01-261 is filed in a venue that is not described therein, the court, on its own motion and upon notice to all parties, may transfer the suit to a venue described in such subdivision provided the transfer is implemented within sixty days after service of process upon all parties. (1977, c. 617; 1982, c. 601; 1985, cc. 433, 492; 1986, cc. 396, 403; 1987, c. 709; 1991, c. 692.)

REVISERS' NOTE

Section 8.01-264 changes former law and requires that where an appropriate objection is made to improperly laid venue, the case shall be transferred to a proper forum rather than be dismissed. The party responsible for improper venue is liable for costs. § 8.01-266.

The section provides that improper venue, whether "preferred" or "permissible," is waived if the defendant does not make timely objection. The result is that improper venue is not a fatal defect.

Objection to venue shall be made by motion setting forth where venue is proper. See also § 8.01-276. It shall be promptly heard by the court. Objection is timely if made on or before the day of trial if the action is commenced in a general district court. Similarly, objection to venue is timely if made within 21 days after service of process commencing an action in a circuit court or within such other time that such court may order for filing responsive pleadings. This changes former law; e.g., this objection is timely even if other pleadings are filed by the defendant prior to the expiration of the time for objection. If a defendant's motion is not timely, the objection shall be waived but in cases of multiple defendants, the waiver shall not be binding on any other defendant whose motion is timely filed.

Law Review. — For survey of Virginia law on practice and pleading for the year 1976-77, see 63 Va. L. Rev. 1459 (1977). For 1985 survey of Virginia civil procedure and practice, see 19 U. Rich. L. Rev. 679 (1985). For survey on domestic relations in Virginia for 1989, see 23 U. Rich. L. Rev. 561 (1989). For article reviewing recent developments and changes in legislation, case law, and Virginia Supreme Court Rules affecting civil litigation, see "Civil Practice and Procedure," 26 U. Rich. L. Rev. 679 (1992).

I. DECISIONS UNDER CURRENT LAW.

Moving party has burden of bringing transfer motion to attention of trial court. — This section, states that a venue objection and transfer motion "shall be promptly heard by the court"; the moving party, has the burden of promptly bringing the matter to the trial court's attention. Faison v. Hudson, 243 Va. 413, 417 S.E.2d 302 (1992).

The court did not err in denying the permit holder's motion to change venue because no defendant filed a timely objection to venue. The original defendant, the Department, failed to object to venue within twenty-one days of residents commencing the appeal as required by this section, and thus waived any venue objection. The permit holder intervened in the case after the twenty-one day period for objecting to venue had passed. Thus no timely objection to venue was filed. Residents Involved in Saving Env't, Inc. v. Commonwealth, Dep't of Envtl. Quality, 22 Va. App. 532, 471 S.E.2d 796 (1996).

Whether to transfer or retain the case is a matter resting within the discretion of the trial court. Faison v. Hudson, 243 Va. 413, 417 S.E.2d 302 (1992).

Trial court's decision to retain case was not an abuse of discretion. — Where the motion to transfer venue was not heard until approximately one month before the scheduled trial, good cause existed for retaining the case, and therefore, the trial court did not abuse its discretion in so ruling. Faison v. Hudson, 243 Va. 413, 417 S.E.2d 302 (1992).

Applied in Downs v. VEC, 4 Va. App. 454, 358 S.E.2d 737 (1987); Decker v. Decker, 12 Va. App. 536, 405 S.E.2d 12 (1991).

§ 8.01-265. Change of venue by court. — In addition to the provisions of § 8.01-264 and notwithstanding the provisions of §§ 8.01-195.4, 8.01-260, 8.01-261 and 8.01-262, the court wherein an action is commenced may, upon motion by any defendant and for good cause shown, (i) dismiss an action brought by a person who is not a resident of the Commonwealth without prejudice under such conditions as the court deems appropriate if the cause of action arose outside of the Commonwealth and if the court determines that a more convenient forum which has jurisdiction over all parties is available in a jurisdiction other than the Commonwealth or (ii) transfer the action to any fair and convenient forum having jurisdiction within the Commonwealth. Such conditions as the court deems appropriate shall include, but not be limited to, a requirement that the defendant agree not to assert the statute of limitations as a defense if the action is brought in a more convenient forum within a time specified by the court. The court, on motion of a plaintiff and for good cause shown, may retain the action for trial. Except by agreement of all parties, no action enumerated in Category A, § 8.01-261, shall be transferred to or retained by a forum not enumerated in such category. Good cause shall be deemed to include, but not be limited to, the agreement of the parties or the avoidance of substantial inconvenience to the parties or the witnesses.

The provisions of (i) of this section shall not apply to causes of action which accrue under § 8.01-249(4). (Code 1950, §§ 8-38, 8-157, 8-158; 1950, p. 78; 1954, c. 660; 1956, c. 432; 1956, Ex. Sess., c. 11; 1960, c. 569; 1964, c. 502; 1968, c. 386; 1979, c. 662; 1982, c. 601; 1991, c. 530.)

REVISERS' NOTE

Section 8.01-265 consolidates the forum non conveniens transfer provisions of former §§ 8-38 (10) and 8-157 (a) and readopts former § 8-158 which was repealed in 1966. Venue may be generally transferred if it is improperly laid under §§ 8.01-260, 8.01-261 and 8.01-262 and objection is made by the defendant pursuant to § 8.01-264. However, if the venue is preferred and is properly laid under § 8.01-261, the court may transfer the case only upon agreement of all parties. If an action is not within § 8.01-261, though the venue may be improperly laid the court may, on motion of the plaintiff and for good cause, retain the action for trial. The definition of good cause encompasses former § 8-38 (10) (provision for transfer where judge is interested in case) as well as the convenience of witnesses and parties and the interest of justice of former § 8-157 (a). The adjectives "fair and convenient" used to describe the transferee forum give more guidance than "any other forum" used in former § 8-157 (a). The words "having jurisdiction" connote jurisdiction over the subject matter of the proceeding; and no court in the Commonwealth is prevented by any provision of this chapter from having such jurisdiction.

Law Review. — For 1985 survey of Virginia civil procedure and practice, see 19 U. Rich. L. Rev. 679 (1985). For 1991 survey of civil practice and procedure, see 25 U. Rich. L. Rev. 663 (1991).

I. Decisions Under Current Law.
II. Decisions Under Prior Law.

I. DECISIONS UNDER CURRENT LAW.

Constitutionality. — This section violates neither the Fourteenth Amendment equal protection clause nor the due process clause of the Va. Const., Art. I, § 11, or its prohibition against special or private laws, under Va. Const., Art. IV, §§ 14 and 15. Caldwell v. Seaboard Sys. R.R., 238 Va. 148, 380 S.E.2d 910 (1989), cert. denied, 493 U.S. 1095, 110 S. Ct. 1169, 107 L. Ed. 2d 1071 (1990) (decided prior to the 1991 amendment).

The attenuating effects, if any, upon interstate commerce inherent in the application of this section are slight, and are clearly overborne by a legitimate state interest in providing maximum access to its courts; thus, interstate commerce is not impermissibly burdened by this section. Caldwell v. Seaboard Sys. R.R., 238 Va. 148, 380 S.E.2d 910 (1989), cert. denied, 493 U.S. 1095, 110 S. Ct. 1169, 107 L. Ed. 2d 1071 (1990) (decided prior to the 1991 amendment).

This section does not provide for the transfer of a case from one forum to another based upon the standard that one forum is fair and substantially more convenient than another forum. City of Danville v. Virginia State Water Control Bd., 18 Va. App. 594, 446 S.E.2d 466 (1994).

Attorney inconvenience not within good cause definition. — This section defines good cause as "the avoidance of substantial inconvenience to the parties or the witnesses." It does not mention the inconvenience of their attorneys. If inconvenience for the attorneys for the parties was sufficient to cause a transfer of venue, the venue statutes could be manipulated because the parties could select an attorney located in the forum of their choice and circumvent the plain intent of the venue statute. Therefore, the inconvenience caused by one or two trips, at most, to Lynchburg from Richmond in the instant case to argue motions and the merits of the case was not adequate good cause to transfer the case under this section. City of Danville v. Virginia State Water Control Bd., 18 Va. App. 594, 446 S.E.2d 466 (1994).

Presumption of plaintiff's choice of forum not absolute. — While the presumption of correctness attaches to a plaintiff's choice of forum, it is not absolute. Indeed, the presumption cannot be enhanced simply because the action arises under the Federal Employers' Liability Act. Norfolk & W. Ry. v. Williams, 239 Va. 390, 389 S.E.2d 714 (1990) (decided prior to the 1991 amendment).

Court lacked authority to transfer divorce action. — Where appellant consented to venue in the one county when she initially filed her bill of complaint there, and because appellee did not object to the selection of venue, he waived his privilege to have the suit transferred to a different county pursuant to this section and effectively agreed to venue in the original county of filing. On these procedural facts, the trial court was not required to act sua sponte to transfer the suit to a different county, and moreover, had no statutory authority to do so. Decker v. Decker, 12 Va. App. 536, 405 S.E.2d 12 (1991) (decided prior to the 1991 amendment).

Denial of transfer was abuse of discretion. — Denial of defendant railroad's motion to transfer a Federal Employers' Liability Act action was an abuse of discretion, where the trial court was presented with sufficient information to show good cause to transfer, including substantial inconvenience to the parties and witnesses, as well as indications of a forum originally selected for not simply justice, but perhaps justice blended with some harassment. Norfolk & W. Ry. v. Williams, 239 Va. 390, 389 S.E.2d 714 (1990) (decided prior to the 1991 amendment).

Applied in Faison v. Hudson, 243 Va. 413, 417 S.E.2d 302 (1992); Virginia Elec. & Power Co. v. Dungee, 258 Va. 235, 520 S.E.2d 164 (1999).

II. DECISIONS UNDER PRIOR LAW.

Editor's note. — The cases cited below were decided under corresponding provisions of former law. The term "this section," as used below, refers to former provisions.

Prejudice as grounds for removal. — This section deals primarily with the transfer of causes from one court to another, where a change of venue is made necessary by local prejudice. Taylor v. Taylor, 185 Va. 126, 37 S.E.2d 886, rehearing denied, 185 Va. 416, 38 S.E.2d 449 (1946).

Local prejudice of such a character as to prevent a fair and impartial trial in the county or district where the action is brought is a well recognized ground for a change of venue. Ramsay v. Harrison, 119 Va. 682, 89 S.E. 977 (1916).

Consent of parties equivalent to motion. — The consent of all parties to the removal of a cause from one court having jurisdiction to another court of like jurisdiction is equivalent to a motion, by such parties for such removal, and guardian ad litem of infant parties may give their consent. Lemmon v. Herbert, 92 Va. 653, 24 S.E. 249 (1896).

Affidavits and evidence in support of motion. — An application by a defendant for a change of venue, on the ground of general prejudices existing against him in the town where the cause is to be tried, should be supported by the affidavits of disinterested individuals. Boswell v. Flockheart, 35 Va. (8 Leigh) 364 (1837).

The affidavits in support of the motion for a change of venue, especially where opposed by counter affidavits of disinterested persons, should state the facts and circumstances tending to show that a fair and impartial trial cannot be had where the case is pending and not the mere belief or opinion of the affiants. Less than this is not sufficient under the statute permitting a change of venue for good cause shown. Ramsay v. Harrison, 119 Va. 682, 89 S.E. 977 (1916).

Mere belief that fair trial cannot be had is insufficient. — Under this section it is error to change venue in a civil proceeding because of the mere belief of a party or his witnesses that he cannot have a fair trial in the jurisdiction where the case is pending. There must be proof that a fair trial cannot be had. MacPherson v. Green, 197 Va. 27, 87 S.E.2d 785 (1955).

A case filed in a court which lacks subject matter jurisdiction over the controversy cannot be transferred to the proper court. Atkins v. Schmutz Mfg. Co., 435 F.2d 527 (4th Cir. 1970), cert. denied, 402 U.S. 932, 91 S. Ct. 1526, 28 L. Ed. 2d 867 (1971).

Laying venue in wrong court. — Although this section permits some transfers of cases from one court to another, a plaintiff who lays venue in the wrong court will have his case dismissed and not transferred. Atkins v. Schmutz Mfg. Co., 435 F.2d 527 (4th Cir. 1970), cert. denied, 402 U.S. 932, 91 S. Ct. 1526, 28 L. Ed. 2d 867 (1971).

Prejudice held insufficient for transfer. — In an action against a railroad for a personal injury, the fact that a prejudice exists against the company in the city in which the action is pending because the company had removed its shops from the city and abandoned the city as a terminal, in violation of a contract with the city, is not sufficient to justify a change of venue of the action, especially when the witnesses by whom the feeling against the company is shown express the opinion that a perfectly fair and impartial jury to try the case can be gotten in the city. Atlantic & D. Ry. v. Reiger, 95 Va. 418, 28 S.E. 590 (1897).

§ 8.01-266. Costs. — In any action which is transferred or retained for trial pursuant to this chapter, the court in which the action is initially brought may award an amount necessary to compensate a party for such inconvenience, expense, and delay as he may have been caused by the commencement of the suit in a forum to which an objection, pursuant to § 8.01-264, is sustained or by the bringing of a frivolous motion to transfer. In addition, the court may award those attorney's fees deemed just and reasonable which are occasioned by such commencement of a suit or by such motion to transfer. The awarding of such costs by the transferor court shall not preclude the assessment of costs by the clerk of the transferee court. (1977, c. 617; 1994, c. 32.)

REVISERS' NOTE

Section 8.01-266 provides sanctions as a remedy for improper venue. By providing that the court "shall award" reasonable actual costs, the section makes the imposition of such costs mandatory (i.e., the court has discretion to transfer, but not as to the imposition of costs). Additionally, the court is granted discretion to award attorney's fees. The costs to be imposed are only those which have been actually incurred up to the point in time of the granting of transfer or denial of such a motion. If transfer of the action is granted, costs should include those fees of the transferor court necessary to implement the order. Thereafter costs are to be awarded in accordance with chapter 3 of Title 14.1.

Law Review. — For survey of Virginia law on practice and pleading for the year 1976-77, see 63 Va. L. Rev. 1459 (1977).

§ 8.01-267. Discretion of judge. — Both the decision of the court transferring or refusing to transfer an action under § 8.01-265 and the decision of the court as to amount of costs awarded under § 8.01-266 shall be within the sound discretion of the trial judge. However, nothing herein shall affect the right to assign as error a court's decision concerning venue. (1977, c. 617.)

REVISERS' NOTE

Section 8.01-267 provides that certain discretionary decisions of the trial judge may be appealable only for abuse of such discretion: (1) whether to transfer a case for reasons of forum non conveniens (§ 8.01-264); and (2) the amount of costs awarded upon transfer (§ 8.01-266).

While neither transfer nor refusal to transfer are immediately appealable, the trial judge's decision is ultimately reviewable on the grounds that he abused his discretion, or that the forum to which the action was transferred or in which the case was allowed to remain was not a proper place of venue under §§ 8.01-260 to 8.01-262.

Law Review. — For survey on property law in Virginia for 1989, see 23 U. Rich. L. Rev. 773 (1989).

CHAPTER 5.1.

Multiple Claimant Litigation Act.

Sec.
8.01-267.1. Standards governing consolidation, etc., and transfer.
8.01-267.2. When actions pending in same court.
8.01-267.3. Consolidation and other combined proceedings.
8.01-267.4. Transfer.

Sec.
8.01-267.5. Joinder and severance.
8.01-267.6. Separate trials; special interrogatories.
8.01-267.7. Later-filed actions.
8.01-267.8. Interlocutory appeal.
8.01-267.9. Effect on other law.

§ 8.01-267.1. Standards governing consolidation, etc., and transfer. — On motion of any party, a circuit court may enter an order joining, coordinating, consolidating or transferring civil actions as provided in this chapter upon finding that:

1. Separate civil actions brought by six or more plaintiffs involve common questions of law or fact and arise out of the same transaction, occurrence or series of transactions or occurrences;

2. The common questions of law or fact predominate and are significant to the actions; and

3. The order (i) will promote the ends of justice and the just and efficient conduct and disposition of the actions, and (ii) is consistent with each party's right to due process of law, and (iii) does not prejudice each individual party's right to a fair and impartial resolution of each action.

Factors to be considered by the court include, but are not limited to, (i) the nature of the common questions of law or fact; (ii) the convenience of the parties, witnesses and counsel; (iii) the relative stages of the actions and the work of counsel; (iv) the efficient utilization of judicial facilities and personnel; (v) the calendar of the courts; (vi) the likelihood and disadvantages of duplicative and inconsistent rulings, orders or judgments; (vii) the likelihood of prompt settlement of the actions without the entry of the order; and (viii) as to joint trials by jury, the likelihood of prejudice or confusion.

The court may organize and manage the combined litigation and enter further orders consistent with the right of each party to a fair trial as may be appropriate to avoid unnecessary costs, duplicative litigation or delay and to assure fair and efficient conduct and resolution of the litigation, including but not limited to orders which organize the parties into groups with like interest; appoint counsel to have lead responsibility for certain matters; allocate costs and fees to separate issues into common questions that require treatment on a consolidated basis and individual cases that do not; and to stay discovery on the issues that are not consolidated. (1995, c. 555.)

§ **8.01-267.2. When actions pending in same court.** — For purposes of this chapter, actions shall be considered pending in the same circuit court when they have been (i) filed in that court, regardless of whether the defendant has been served with process, or (ii) properly transferred to that court. (1995, c. 555.)

§ **8.01-267.3. Consolidation and other combined proceedings.** — On motion of any party, a circuit court in which separate civil actions are pending which were brought by six or more plaintiffs may enter an order coordinating, consolidating or joining any or all of the proceedings in the actions upon making the findings required by § 8.01-267.1. The order may provide for any or all of the following:
1. Coordinated or consolidated pretrial proceedings;
2. A joint hearing or, if requested by any party, trial by jury with respect to any or all common questions at issue in the actions; or
3. Consolidation of the actions. (1995, c. 555.)

§ **8.01-267.4. Transfer.** — A. Whenever there are pending in different circuit courts of the Commonwealth civil actions brought by six or more plaintiffs which involve common issues of law or fact and arise out of the same transaction, occurrence or the same series of transactions or occurrences, any party may apply to a panel of circuit court judges designated by the Supreme Court for an order of transfer. Upon such application and upon making the findings required by § 8.01-267.1, the panel may order some or all of the actions transferred to a circuit court in which one or more of the actions are pending for purposes of coordinated or consolidated pretrial proceedings. The circuit court to which actions are transferred may enter further orders as provided in § 8.01-267.3. Any subsequent application for further transfer shall be made to the circuit court to which the actions were transferred. Upon completion of pretrial proceedings and any joint hearings or trials, the circuit court may remand the actions to the circuit courts in which they were originally filed or may retain them for final disposition.

B. Any party who files an application for transfer shall at the same time give notice of such application to all parties and to the clerk of each circuit court in which an action that is the subject of the application is pending. Upon receipt of the notice, a circuit court shall not enter any further orders under § 8.01-267.3 until after the panel has entered an order granting or denying an application for transfer pursuant to subsection A. (1995, c. 555.)

§ **8.01-267.5. Joinder and severance.** — Six or more parties may be joined initially as plaintiffs in a single action if their claims involve common issues of fact and arise out of the same transaction or occurrence or the same series of transactions or occurrences. On motion of a defendant, the actions so joined shall be severed unless the court finds that the claims of the plaintiffs were ones which, if they had been filed separately, would have met the standards of § 8.01-267.1 and would have been consolidated under § 8.01-267.3. If the court orders severance, the claims may proceed separately upon payment of any appropriate filing fees due in the separate circuit courts within sixty days of entry of the order. The date of the original filing shall be the date of filing for each of the severed actions for purposes of applying the statutes of limitations. (1995, c. 555.)

§ **8.01-267.6. Separate trials; special interrogatories.** — In any combined action under this chapter, the court, on motion of any party, may order separate or bifurcated trials of any one or more claims, cross-claims, counterclaims, third-party claims, or separate issues, always preserving the right of trial by jury.

Additionally, the court may submit special interrogatories to the jury to resolve specific issues of fact. (1995, c. 555.)

§ 8.01-267.7. Later-filed actions. — Later-filed actions may be joined with ongoing litigation in accordance with the procedures of § 8.01-267.3 or § 8.01-267.4 and the standards of § 8.01-267.1. Parties in later-filed actions joined with on-going multiple claimant litigation may, in the discretion of the court, be bound to prior proceedings but only to the extent permitted by law and only to the extent that the court finds that the interests of such parties were adequately and fairly represented. Consistent with the language of this section and the standards of § 8.01-267.1, the parties may utilize all prior discovery taken by any party in on-going multiple party litigation as if the parties in the later-filed actions had been parties at the time the discovery was taken. On motion of any party or by the person from whom discovery is sought, the court may limit or prohibit discovery by parties in later-filed actions if the court finds that the matters on which the discovery is sought have been covered adequately by prior discovery. (1995, c. 555.)

§ 8.01-267.8. Interlocutory appeal. — A. The Supreme Court or the Court of Appeals, in its discretion, may permit an appeal to be taken from an order of a circuit court although the order is not a final order where the circuit court has ordered a consolidated trial of claims joined or consolidated pursuant to this chapter.

B. The Supreme Court or the Court of Appeals, in its discretion, may permit an appeal to be taken from any other order of a circuit court in an action combined pursuant to this chapter although the order is not a final order provided the written order of the circuit court states that the order involves a controlling question of law as to which there is substantial ground for difference of opinion and that an immediate appeal from the order may materially advance the ultimate termination of the litigation.

C. Application for an appeal pursuant to this section shall be made within ten days after the entry of the order and shall not stay proceedings in the circuit court unless the circuit court or the appellate court shall so order. (1995, c. 555.)

§ 8.01-267.9. Effect on other law. — The procedures set out in this chapter are in addition to procedures otherwise available by statute, rule or common law and do not limit in any way the availability of such procedures, but shall not apply to any action against a manufacturer or supplier of asbestos or product for industrial use that contains asbestos to which the provisions of § 8.01-374.1 may apply. (1995, c. 555.)

CHAPTER 6.

Notice of Lis Pendens or Attachment.

Sec.
8.01-268. When and how docketed and indexed.
8.01-269. Dismissal or satisfaction of same.

§ 8.01-268. When and how docketed and indexed. — A. No lis pendens or attachment shall bind or affect a subsequent bona fide purchaser of real or personal estate for valuable consideration and without actual notice of such lis pendens or attachment, until and except from the time a memorandum setting forth the title of the cause or attachment, the general object thereof, the court wherein it is pending, the amount of the claim asserted by the plaintiff, a description of the property, and the name of the person whose estate is intended to be affected thereby, shall be admitted to record in the clerk's office of the circuit court of the county or the city wherein the property is located; or if it be in that part of the City of Richmond lying north of the south bank of the James River and including the islands in such river, in the clerk's office of the Circuit Court, Division I, of such city, or if it be in the part of the City of Richmond lying south of the south bank of the James River, in the clerk's office of the Circuit Court, Division II, of such city. Clerks of circuit courts are authorized and directed to admit to record memoranda of lis pendens or attachment for actions pending in any court of this Commonwealth, or in any other state, federal, or territorial court. The provisions of this section shall not be construed to mean that any such memoranda heretofore recorded are not properly of record. Such memorandum shall not be deemed to have been recorded unless and until indexed as required by law.

B. No memorandum of lis pendens shall be filed unless the action on which the lis pendens is based seeks to establish an interest by the filing party in the real property described in the memorandum. (Code 1950, § 8-142; 1973, c. 544; 1976, c. 178; 1977, c. 617; 1988, c. 503.)

Cross references. — As to lien of attachment, see § 8.01-557. As to what documents recorded in deed books, see § 17.1-227. As to additional documents to be recorded in deed book, see § 17.1-229. As to indexing in general, see § 17.1-249.

Law Review. — For article on fraudulent conveyances and preferences in Virginia, see 36 Wash. & Lee L. Rev. 51 (1979). For article on title examination in Virginia, see 17 U. Rich. L. Rev. 229 (1983). As to recent legislation relating to lis pendens, see 22 U. Rich. L. Rev. 517 (1988).

I. Decisions Under Current Law.
II. Decisions Under Prior Law.

I. DECISIONS UNDER CURRENT LAW.

Section enacted to prevent harshness of former rule. — At one time, if title to real estate were at stake in litigation, the mere pendency of the suit was deemed sufficient to charge a purchaser with notice of the challenge to title and subject his interest in the property to the outcome of the suit. To correct the harshness of this rule, the General Assembly enacted a provision currently codified as this section, requiring any notice of pending litigation or lis pendens to be docketed in the circuit court clerks' office for the jurisdiction in which the land is located before such notice will bind a bona fide purchaser. Hart v. United Va. Bank, 24 Bankr. 821 (Bankr. E.D. Va. 1982).

This section must be read in conjunction with § 8.01-458, which states that "[e]very judgment for money rendered in this Commonwealth by any state or federal court . . . shall be a lien on all the real estate of . . . the defendant . . . ." Thus, any suit in which the defendant is an individual has the potential to affect the title to real estate. Hart v. United Va. Bank, 24 Bankr. 821 (Bankr. E.D. Va. 1982).

Difference between notices of lis pendens and attachment is only formal. — The section speaks of "lis pendens or attachment," so that even if "lis pendens" technically were available only for actions directly involving title to real property, the identical procedure, with identical effect, may be obtained by filing a notice of attachment. The difference is formal rather than substantive. Hart v. United Va. Bank, 24 Bankr. 821 (Bankr. E.D. Va. 1982).

Filing of memorandum lis pendens neither creates nor enforces a lien. Rather, plaintiff's filing of the lis pendens pursuant to this section served merely as notice of the pendency of the suit to any one interested and a warning that he should examine the proceedings therein to ascertain whether the title to the property was affected or not by such proceedings. Green Hill Corp. v. Kim, 842 F.2d 742 (4th Cir. 1988).

Notice of lis pendens is qualified privileged communication. — Judicial proceedings have been recognized in Virginia as constituting one of the principal occasions where communications are absolutely privileged.

However, that when all the interests involved are taken into consideration the filing of a notice of lis pendens is more appropriately characterized as a qualified privileged occasion. Warren v. Bank of Marion, 618 F. Supp. 317 (W.D. Va. 1985).

Section not limited to suits directly involving title to real estate. — This section provides for the filing of memoranda against a defendant's personal as well as his real property, which indicates an intent by the legislature that such filings not be restricted to suits directly involving title to real estate. Hart v. United Va. Bank, 24 Bankr. 821 (Bankr. E.D. Va. 1982).

Procedure available to any party seeking money judgment. — Under this section and § 8.01-458, the recording of a memorandum of lis pendens is open to any litigating party seeking a money judgment against an individual property owner in Virginia. Hart v. United Va. Bank, 24 Bankr. 821 (Bankr. E.D. Va. 1982).

Memorandum of lis pendens is merely a notice to third parties that a claim has been asserted to the property described. Hart v. United Va. Bank, 24 Bankr. 821 (Bankr. E.D. Va. 1982).

II. DECISIONS UNDER PRIOR LAW.

Editor's note. — The cases cited below were decided under corresponding provisions of former law. The term "this section," as used below, refers to former provisions.

This section is remedial, and in construing it, there should be borne in mind the old law, the mischief intended to be remedied, and the remedy. Vicares v. Sayler, 111 Va. 307, 68 S.E. 988 (1910). See also Swetnam v. Antonsanti, 150 Va. 534, 143 S.E. 716 (1928).

What constitutes action lis pendens. — That to constitute an action or suit lis pendens the property involved must be the identical property transferred pendente lite, of a kind subject to the rule and sufficiently described in the pleadings to identify it, and the court must have jurisdiction at the time of the transfer over the subject matter and the party from whom the interest is acquired. French v. Loyal Co., 32 Va. (5 Leigh) 627 (1834); Davis v. Christian, 56 Va. (15 Gratt.) 11 (1859); Briscoe v. Ashby, 65 Va. (24 Gratt.) 454 (1874).

It has no application to the federal courts. — This section has no application to federal courts sitting in Virginia, as such courts have no power to enforce the registration of such memoranda. King v. Davis, 137 F. 198 (C.C.W.D. Va. 1903), aff'd sub nom. Blankenship v. King, 157 F. 676 (4th Cir. 1906).

Notice unnecessary where judgment obtained. — Purchasers of land are conclusively affected with notice of judgment duly obtained and docketed against the owner, and no lis pendens or other notice of a suit to subject the land to such judgment is needed to affect them. Sharitz v. Moyers, 99 Va. 519, 39 S.E. 166 (1901).

Lien is only upon property conveyed. — The lien thus conferred is only upon the property conveyed, and not, like the lien of a judgment, on all of the debtor's estate. Davis v. Bonney, 89 Va. 755, 17 S.E. 229 (1893).

Suit by creditors to subject decedent's lands to payment of debts. — The filing of a notice of lis pendens, in a suit by creditors of a decedent to subject his lands to payment of his debts, is required in order to charge a purchaser of such lands from the heir, without actual notice of the suit, with knowledge thereof. Easley v. Barksdale, 75 Va. 274 (1881). See also Heeke v. Allan, 127 Va. 65, 102 S.E. 655 (1920).

Effect of notice of attachment proceedings. — A lis pendens in attachment proceedings filed in the clerk's office of the proper county, operates to give constructive notice of the lien of the attachment to a subsequent grantee of the defendant, and such grantee stands upon no better footing as to the attaching creditor than his grantor. Breeden v. Peale, 106 Va. 39, 55 S.E. 2 (1906).

Effect of express notice. — A purchaser pendente lite, and with express notice is not an innocent purchaser for value. He is not a purchaser at all in the eyes of the law. Culbertson v. Stevens, 82 Va. 406, 4 S.E. 607 (1886).

What constitutes actual notice. — In the absence of record notice, the statutory actual notice which will affect a purchaser pending a suit must affect the conscience of the purchaser, and the notice may be either actual or circumstantial or presumptive, but it is not sufficient if it merely puts the purchaser on inquiry, but it must be clear and strong and such as to fix on him the imputation of bad faith in making the purchase. Vicars v. Sayler, 111 Va. 307, 68 S.E. 988 (1910).

Actual notice binds the purchaser although lis pendens not recorded. — Where one purchases with actual notice of the lis pendens, although it has not been recorded, he is bound by the decree in the case. Hurn v. Keller, 79 Va. 415 (1884).

But purchaser with neither actual nor record notice protected. — A purchaser without notice of the pendency of the suit takes a good title when the lis pendens is not docketed as provided by these statutes. Cammack v. Soran, 71 Va. (30 Gratt.) 292 (1878); Easley v. Barksdale, 75 Va. 274 (1881).

Voluntary purchaser pendente lite, not protected. — Even though no memorandum was left with the clerk to be recorded and indexed, a voluntary grantee, pendente lite, takes in subordination to the rights of the creditors of his grantor adjudicated in the suit, and cannot impeach the proceedings in that suit by an independent suit brought for that purpose. Davis v. Anderson, 99 Va. 620, 39 S.E. 588 (1901).

Purchaser to be substituted to grantor's position. — A purchaser pendente lite is entitled, on becoming a party to the action to be substituted to his grantor's position and rights. Sharitz v. Moyers, 99 Va. 519, 39 S.E. 166 (1901).

Sufficiency of the memorandum. — A memorandum required by this section that fails to comply with the statutory requirement with respect to setting forth the description of the property intended to be affected by the lis pendens and contain in itself a material misdescription, and is absolutely unaided in its description of the property by the references to the pleading, is fatally defective. Motley v. H. Vicello & Bros., 132 Va. 281, 111 S.E. 295 (1922).

The sufficiency of the description of the property contained in the memorandum must be tested as of the time the memorandum becomes effective. Thus, where the memorandum refers to the bill which was not filed until some days after the memorandum became effective, the description of the property in the memorandum cannot be aided by the description in the bill. Motley v. H. Vicello & Bros., 132 Va. 281, 111 S.E. 295 (1922).

§ 8.01-269. Dismissal or satisfaction of same. — If such attachment or lis pendens is quashed or dismissed or such cause is dismissed, or judgment or final decree in such attachment or cause is for the defendant or defendants, the court shall direct in its order (i) that the names of all interested parties thereto, as found in the recorded attachment or lis pendens be listed for the clerk, and (ii) that the attachment or lis pendens be released and, the court may, in an appropriate case, impose sanctions as provided in § 8.01-271.1. It shall then become the duty of the clerk in whose office such attachment or lis pendens is recorded, to record the order and, unless a microfilm recording process is used, to enter on the margin of the page of the book in which the same is recorded, such fact, together with a reference to the order book and page where such order is recorded. However, in any case in which an appeal or writ of error from such judgment or decree or dismissal would lie, the clerk shall not record the order or make the entry until after the expiration of the time in which such appeal or writ of error may be applied for, or if applied for after refusal thereof, or if granted, after final judgment or decree is entered by the appellate court.

In any case in which the debt for which such attachment is issued, or suit is brought and notice of lis pendens recorded is satisfied by payment, it shall be the duty of the creditor, within ten days after payment of same to mark such notice of lis pendens or attachment satisfied on the margin of the page of the deed book in which the same is recorded, unless a microfilm recording process is used. (Code 1950, § 8-143; 1962, c. 589; 1977, c. 617; 1985, c. 310; 1986, c. 278; 1989, c. 450.)

Law Review. — For survey on civil procedure and practice in Virginia for 1989, see 23 U. Rich. L. Rev. 511 (1989).

CHAPTER 7.

CIVIL ACTIONS; COMMENCEMENT, PLEADINGS, AND MOTIONS.

Article 1.

Civil Actions Generally.

Sec.
8.01-270. Transfer of cases from one side of court to other.

Article 2.

Pleadings Generally.

Sec.
8.01-271. Compliance with Rules of Supreme Court.
8.01-271.1. Signing of pleadings, motions, and

Sec.		Sec.	
	other papers; oral motions; sanctions.	8.01-278.	When plea of infancy not allowed; liability of infants for debts as traders; liability of infants on loans to defray expenses of education.
8.01-272.	Pleading several matters; joining tort and contract claims; separate trial in discretion of court; counterclaims.		
8.01-273.	Demurrer; form; grounds to be stated; amendment.	8.01-279.	When proof is unnecessary unless affidavit filed; handwriting; ownership; partnership or incorporation.
8.01-273.1.	Motion for judgment; motion to refer; Virginia Birth-Related Neurological Injury Compensation Act.	8.01-280.	Pleadings may be sworn to before clerk; affidavit of belief sufficient.
8.01-274.	Motion to strike defensive pleading in equity and at law; exceptions abolished.	8.01-281.	Pleading in alternative; separate trial on motion of party.
8.01-275.	When action or suit not to abate for want of form; what defects not to be regarded.		

Article 3.

Particular Equity Provisions.

8.01-275.1.	When service of process is timely.	8.01-282.	Motion to strike evidence in chancery causes.
8.01-276.	Demurrer to evidence and plea in abatement abolished; motion to strike evidence and written motion, respectively, to be used in lieu thereof.	8.01-283.	Effect of answer as evidence or affidavit; bills of discovery, etc.
8.01-277.	Defective process; motion to quash; amendment.	8.01-284.	Order for interrogatories after bill taken for confessed.

Article 1.

Civil Actions Generally.

§ 8.01-270. Transfer of cases from one side of court to other. — No case shall be dismissed simply because it was brought on the wrong side of the court, but whenever it shall appear that a plaintiff has proceeded at law when he should have proceeded in equity, or in equity when he should have proceeded at law, the court shall direct a transfer to the proper forum, and shall order such change in, or amendment of, the pleadings as may be necessary to conform them to the proper practice; and, without such direction, any party to the suit or action shall have the right at any stage of the cause, to amend his pleadings so as to obviate the objection that his suit or action was not brought on the right side of the court.

After any such amendment has been made, the case shall be placed by the clerk on the proper docket of the court and proceed and be determined upon such amended pleadings.

The defendant shall be allowed a reasonable time after such transfer in which to prepare the case for trial. (Code 1950, § 8-138; 1977, c. 617.)

Law Review. — For survey on property law in Virginia for 1989, see 23 U. Rich. L. Rev. 773 (1989).

I. Decisions Under Current Law.
  A. General Consideration.
  B. Transfer From Law to Equity.
II. Decisions Under Prior Law.
  A. General Consideration.
  B. Transfer From Equity to Law.
  C. Transfer From Law to Equity.

I. DECISIONS UNDER CURRENT LAW.

A. General Consideration.

Applicable only where case brought on wrong side of court. — This statute applies only where a plaintiff has erroneously brought his case on the wrong side of the court. It furnishes no authority for a transfer where the plaintiff has invoked the proper forum. Stanardsville Volunteer Fire Co. v. Berry, 229 Va. 578, 331 S.E.2d 466 (1985).

B. Transfer From Law to Equity.

Where erroneous transfer to equity deprived plaintiff of its right to jury trial, the error was not harmless. Stanardsville Volunteer Fire Co. v. Berry, 229 Va. 578, 331 S.E.2d 466 (1985).

Transfer of action for trespass to equity was error. — Because trespass quare clausum fregit fell within one of the original nine common-law forms of action, such an action was properly brought on the law side of the court, and the court erred in transferring the action to equity over the plaintiff's objection. Stanardsville Volunteer Fire Co. v. Berry, 229 Va. 578, 331 S.E.2d 466 (1985).

Defendant entitled to separate proceeding to test equity claim in action at law. — If defendants in a trespass action had wished to test their claim to an easement across plaintiff's property before undergoing jury trial in the trespass case, they were entitled to bring a chancery suit seeking vindication of their claim to an easement by estoppel, and to enjoin prosecution of the plaintiff's action at law until their property claim could be determined. Their remedy was not a transfer from law to equity. Stanardsville Volunteer Fire Co. v. Berry, 229 Va. 578, 331 S.E.2d 466 (1985).

II. DECISIONS UNDER PRIOR LAW.

A. General Consideration.

Editor's note. — The cases cited below were decided under corresponding provisions of former law. The terms "the statute" and "this section," as used below, refer to former provisions.

Section prevents dismissal of actions brought on wrong side of court. — This section was intended primarily for the benefit of plaintiffs and is mandatory upon the trial courts only to the extent of prohibiting them from dismissing a case "simply because it was brought on the wrong side of the court" — that is, where the only question was as to the forum. French v. Stange Mining Co., 133 Va. 602, 114 S.E. 121 (1922); Conway v. American Nat'l Bank, 146 Va. 357, 131 S.E. 803 (1926); Nash v. Harman, 148 Va. 610, 139 S.E. 273 (1927); C & P Tel. Co. v. City of Newport News, 194 Va. 409, 73 S.E.2d 394 (1952).

If this section had never been enacted, and if complainant had first brought a suit in equity which the court of its own motion erroneously dismissed for want of jurisdiction, an action at law might afterwards have been properly dismissed for the same reason, and he, the complainant, would have been without remedy had he not appealed from the first order in time. It was to prevent such a miscarriage of justice that this section was passed. Colvin v. Butler, 150 Va. 672, 143 S.E. 333 (1928).

Purpose of this section is to protect rights of parties, save cost and prevent delay. Thomas v. Lauterbach, 205 Va. 176, 135 S.E.2d 781 (1964).

This section is remedial and not technical, and was enacted to protect the rights of parties and to save costs and delay. Quick v. Southern Churchman Co., 171 Va. 403, 199 S.E. 489 (1938).

This section is remedial and not technical and therefore harmless infringements of its provisions will be disregarded by the court. Universal C.I.T. Credit Corp. v. Kaplan, 198 Va. 67, 92 S.E.2d 359 (1956); Pennsylvania State Shopping Plazas, Inc. v. Olive, 202 Va. 862, 120 S.E.2d 372 (1961).

This section is remedial and not technical. Thomas v. Lauterbach, 205 Va. 176, 135 S.E.2d 781 (1964).

No authority for arbitrary transfer. — This section authorizes the transfer of cases from one side of the court to another only where the case is brought on the wrong side of the court, and gives no authority for the arbitrary transfer of a case, with or without motion of the parties, except where the question of a proper jurisdiction of the subject matter is involved. Quick v. Southern Churchman Co., 171 Va. 403, 199 S.E. 489 (1938).

Transfer may be waived. — Where after complainants had been offered and had rejected the privilege of amending their pleading, they signified their intention to stand by their bill and not to amend the same, and made no motion to remand the cause to the law side of the court as to any of the parties defendant, it was held that the court need not under such circumstances compel complainants to accept the benefit of the statute. Its provisions may be waived, and the language of the decree justified the inference that it was so waived in this instance. French v. Stange Mining Co., 133 Va. 602, 114 S.E. 121 (1922).

And waiver precludes raising transfer on appeal. — Failure to request in the trial court a transfer from the equity to the law side constituted a waiver of the provisions of this section and precluded appellant from contending on appeal that the case should have been transferred. Pennsylvania State Shopping Plazas, Inc. v. Olive, 202 Va. 862, 120 S.E.2d 372 (1961).

When responsive pleadings in a case change the issue involving the subject matter, and from all the pleadings it appears to the court that complete relief cannot be obtained on the side of the court where the case was originally brought, the court should transfer the case to that side of the court where complete relief may be granted in one proceeding. Thomas v. Lauterbach, 205 Va. 176, 135 S.E.2d 781 (1964).

Chancery court may act as substitute for court of law. — When a court of chancery retains jurisdiction of the cause, and proceeds therein to establish legal rights and administer legal remedies, it acts as a substitute for a court of law, rather than as a court of chancery. Smith v. Smith, 92 Va. 696, 24 S.E. 280 (1896).

Legal defenses then become available. — The fact that the chancery court assumes to substitute for a court of law, instead of transferring it to the law side of the court, constitutes good cause for permitting the defendant to file any defense which he could have filed had the case been transferred to the law side. Iron City Sav. Bank v. Isaacsen, 158 Va. 609, 164 S.E. 520 (1932).

Section not followed where pleading dismissed and same case required to be pleaded on other side. — Where a third amended bill alleged no grounds of equity jurisdiction, but a matter appropriate for decision only on the law side, to have dismissed the amended bill and required plaintiff to file a new motion for judgment on the law side, stating the same case and evoking the same defenses, would have been disobedient to the statute and merely sacrificed substance to form. Commercial & Sav. Bank v. Maher, 202 Va. 286, 117 S.E.2d 120 (1960).

Correction of erroneous transfer. — Such error as was committed when the cause was transferred from equity to law was corrected when it was transferred back from law to equity. Colvin v. Butler, 150 Va. 672, 143 S.E. 333 (1928).

Decree transferring a case not final but appealable. — A decree transferring a case from one side of the court to the other under this section should be treated as appealable and not final. Then it may still be brought under review. Colvin v. Butler, 150 Va. 672, 143 S.E. 333 (1928); Buchanan Coal Co. v. Street, 175 Va. 531, 9 S.E.2d 339 (1940).

Dismissal rather than transfer not reversible error. — Where the trial court dismisses a bill which should have been transferred to the common law docket instead of dismissed, the error is not reversible as it affects a mere question of procedure, and as the substantial rights of the parties can be preserved by an amendment of the decree, by adding thereto the provision that such dismissal is without prejudice to the right of the complainants to institute a motion or action at law, the Supreme Court will so amend the decree. George A. Rucker & Co. v. Glennan, 130 Va. 511, 107 S.E. 725 (1921).

Dismissal not reversible where transfer would provide little or no advantage. — Where, under this section a transfer of the cause to the law side of the court with directions to reframe the pleadings would have little, if any, advantage over dismissing the suit without prejudice, it is not reversible error so as to dismiss the suit. French v. Stange Mining Co., 133 Va. 602, 114 S.E. 121 (1922). See also Hamilton v. Goodridge, 164 Va. 123, 178 S.E. 874 (1935).

Transfer on remand from Supreme Court. — In a suit in equity where it appears that the complainant's remedy is at law, the Supreme Court will remand the cause to the court below, with leave to complainants, if so advised, to have the same, in accordance with this section, transferred to the law side of the court, and to amend their pleadings so as to be entitled to ask for a judgment at law against the defendant. Carle v. Corhan, 127 Va. 223, 103 S.E. 699 (1920).

B. Transfer From Equity to Law.

Transfer not error where no right to equitable relief shown. — Where plaintiff has failed to show any peculiar equity which would entitle it to relief on the chancery side of the court, has not made out a cause for injunctive relief, and has raised little more than a specter that a multiplicity of actions would result from denial of equitable jurisdiction, it was not error to transfer the matter to the law side of the court. Pennsylvania-Little Creek Corp. v. Cobb, 215 Va. 44, 205 S.E.2d 661 (1974).

And when court does not have equitable jurisdiction transfer should be made. — Where a court of chancery failed to acquire actual jurisdiction to grant any of the equitable relief prayed for in a bill, the court should have transferred the cause of action of the complainant against the defendant to the law side of the court in accordance with this section. Iron City Sav. Bank v. Isaacsen, 158 Va. 609, 164 S.E. 520 (1932).

Court may instead award issue out of chancery. — Although this section appears to be mandatory, where the court instead of remanding a suit for trial at law, where complainant sought to enforce a claim for unliquidated damages in equity, as would have been proper, awarded an issue out of chancery to ascertain the damages suffered by the complainant, the error will be regarded as harmless, as the issue out of chancery and trial by jury accorded to the parties every substantial right. Sacks v. Theodore, 136 Va. 466, 118 S.E. 105 (1923).

Transfer to law side is not authorized simply because evidence is conflicting. — Where a decree was required to be reversed for failure to award a judgment for proved damages, the Supreme Court could not transfer the cause to the law side of the court simply because the evidence was conflicting, for this section permits the transfer only when the case is brought on the wrong side of the court. Washington Golf & Country Club, Inc. v. Briggs & Brennan Developers, Inc., 198 Va. 586, 95 S.E.2d 233 (1956).

Demurrer should not be sustained but case transferred. — The instant case was a suit against a corporation and its individual stockholders. Defendant demurred to the bill on the ground that complainants had an adequate remedy at law, and the court sustained the demurrer. If it be conceded that complainants are limited to an assertion of their alleged rights in a court of law, the bill should not have been dismissed, but pursuant to the provisions of this section, the cause should have been transferred to the law side of the court and there disposed of as directed by the statute. J.S. Salyer Co. v. A.J. Doss Coal Co., 157 Va. 144, 160 S.E. 54 (1931).

Transfer where equitable remedy lost through delay. — Where preferred stockholders were not permitted to subscribe to a new issue of stock, and they delayed action until such stock had been issued to the common stockholders, a court of equity was powerless to compel an additional issue. The only available remedy to such stockholders was an action at law, and they could not be heard to say that the remedy was inadequate. Thomas Branch & Co. v. Riverside & Dan River Mills, Inc., 139 Va. 291, 123 S.E. 542 (1924).

Transfer to law side when jury question presented. — Where the court refused to decree specific performance and referred the cause to a master commissioner to ascertain and report what amount, if any, was owing appellee for stone removed by appellant from the premises which were the subject of the alleged contract, this was held error, since, if appellant was indebted to appellee, the amount of such indebtedness should be ascertained by a trial by jury in a court of law, and, under the provision of this section the case should have been transferred to the law court for trial on the merits. C & O Ry. v. Douthat, 176 Va. 244, 10 S.E.2d 881 (1940).

Disputes as to title and boundaries of land. — In the absence of some peculiar equity arising out of the conduct, situation or relation of the parties, a court of equity is without jurisdiction to settle disputes as to title and boundaries of land, and the matter must be transferred. Pennsylvania-Little Creek Corp. v. Cobb, 215 Va. 44, 205 S.E.2d 661 (1974).

Waiver of transfer of eminent domain proceeding. — Where appellants could have moved to transfer an eminent domain proceeding from the equity to the law side, but failed to make such motion, they waived their rights and could not successfully raise the issue on appeal. Brown v. May, 202 Va. 300, 117 S.E.2d 101 (1960).

C. Transfer From Law to Equity.

Permitting transfer to avoid multiple suits. — To require plaintiffs to proceed at law because their initial pleadings set out a case cognizable only in that forum, thus necessitating a second suit in equity for specific performance, when by a transfer of the case the latter forum could dispose of the entire subject matter, would be contrary to the plain purpose of this section, which is to save cost and prevent delay. Thomas v. Lauterbach, 205 Va. 176, 135 S.E.2d 781 (1964).

Transfer for accounting not allowed when no mistake existed. — The filing of a plea of a mistake in accounts by the plaintiff does not entitle the defendant to an accounting in view of the fact that there was no mistake of fact at all, but merely a difference of opinions, estimates and conjectures as to what would be the natural result arising from uncertain future events. Inasmuch as the accounts were admittedly correct as they stood, the court did not err in refusing to transfer the case to the equity side of the court, under this section. Foreman v. Clement, 139 Va. 70, 123 S.E. 336 (1924).

Neither nonresidence nor desire to plead equitable set-off are grounds for transfer. — This section does not authorize the transfer of purely legal action to the chancery side of the court because of the nonresidence of the plaintiff and in order that the defendant may assert a demand as a set-off that is not pleadable in an action at law. Dexter-Portland Cement Co. v. Acme Supply Co., 147 Va. 758, 133 S.E. 788 (1926).

Action against indorser on note. — This section confers no power upon a court to transfer an action at law against the indorser on a note to the equity side of the court, on motion by the indorser in the suit at law. Conway v. American Nat'l Bank, 146 Va. 357, 131 S.E. 803 (1926).

ARTICLE 2.

Pleadings Generally.

§ 8.01-271. Compliance with Rules of Supreme Court. — Subject to the provisions of this title, pleadings shall be in accordance with Rules of the Supreme Court. (1977, c. 617.)

REVISERS' NOTE

Section 8.01-271 merely recognizes established practice. See also § 8.01-3.

The following Title 8 sections are deleted:

§ 8-98. (Plea in abatement to be verified.) The plea in abatement is abolished by § 8.01-276.

§ 8-105. (Unnecessary to aver jurisdiction to make profert.) This section is unnecessary. The portion of the statute that relates to profert and oyer is encompassed by the rules and the procedure for discovery.

§ 8-106. (When place of contract, etc., need not be set forth.) This provision is obsolete and unnecessary.

§ 8-111. (Court may require particulars of claim or defense.) This section is deleted as unnecessary. See Rule 3:16.

§ 8-119. (Amendment of pleadings; immaterial errors or defects.) This section is deleted as unnecessary. See Rule 1:8.

§ 8-133. (Exceptions to jurisdiction; plea in abatement.) The plea in abatement is abolished by § 8.01-276.

§ 8-138.1. (Transfer of cases from courts not having both law and equity jurisdiction to courts having such jurisdiction.)

§ 8-138.2. (Transfer of cases where court is abolished or jurisdiction removed or deprived.)

§ 8-139. (Enforcement of process of contempt.)

The material is either obsolete and unnecessary or covered by other statutes. See, e.g., §§ 18.2-456 and 19.2-11.

§ 8-141. (Control by court over proceedings in office.) References to "the court in vacation" have been deleted throughout Title 8.01.

§ 8.01-271.1. Signing of pleadings, motions, and other papers; oral motions; sanctions. — Every pleading, written motion, and other paper of a party represented by an attorney shall be signed by at least one attorney of record in his individual name, and the attorney's address shall be stated on the first pleading filed by that attorney in the action. A party who is not represented by an attorney, including a person confined in a state or local correctional facility proceeding pro se, shall sign his pleading, motion, or other paper and state his address.

The signature of an attorney or party constitutes a certificate by him that (i) he has read the pleading, motion, or other paper, (ii) to the best of his knowledge, information and belief, formed after reasonable inquiry, it is well grounded in fact and is warranted by existing law or a good faith argument for the extension, modification, or reversal of existing law, and (iii) it is not interposed for any improper purpose, such as to harass or to cause unnecessary delay or needless increase in the cost of litigation. If a pleading, written motion, or other paper is not signed, it shall be stricken unless it is signed promptly after the omission is called to the attention of the pleader or movant.

An oral motion made by an attorney or party in any court of the Commonwealth constitutes a representation by him that (i) to the best of his knowledge, information and belief formed after reasonable inquiry it is well grounded in fact and is warranted by existing law or a good faith argument for the extension, modification or reversal of existing law, and (ii) it is not interposed for any improper purpose, such as to harass or to cause unnecessary delay or needless increase in the cost of litigation.

If a pleading, motion, or other paper is signed or made in violation of this rule, the court, upon motion or upon its own initiative, shall impose upon the person who signed the paper or made the motion, a represented party, or both, an appropriate sanction, which may include an order to pay to the other party or parties the amount of the reasonable expenses incurred because of the filing of the pleading, motion, or other paper or making of the motion, including a reasonable attorney's fee. (1987, cc. 259, 682; 1998, c. 596.)

Law Review. — For 1987 survey of Virginia civil procedure and practice, see 21 U. Rich. L. Rev. 667 (1987). For note, "Will Tort Reform Combat the Medical Malpractice Insurance Availability and Affordability Problems That Virginia's Physicians Are Facing," see 44 Wash. & Lee L. Rev. 1463 (1988). For survey on civil procedure and practice in Virginia for 1989, see 23 U. Rich. L. Rev. 511 (1989). For 1991 survey of civil practice and procedure, see 25 U. Rich. L. Rev. 663 (1991).

I. DECISIONS UNDER CURRENT LAW.

An objective standard of "reasonableness" is applied in determining whether the "warranted by existing law" portion of this section has been violated. Tullidge v. Board of Supvrs., 239 Va. 611, 391 S.E.2d 288 (1990).

In determining whether one's conduct in signing a document violated the statute, the trial court applies an objective standard of reasonableness. Woodruff v. Greene, No. 0114-98-2 (Ct. of Appeals Dec. 22, 1998).

Issues subject to legitimate debate. — Where there were a number of issues which, even though decided against the beneficiaries of a trust, were subject to legitimate debate and some of the remedies they sought could not have been granted without joining the parties moving for sanctions, the trial court did not abuse its discretion in denying the imposition of sanctions and attorney's fees. Ward v. NationsBank, 256 Va. 427, 507 S.E.2d 616 (1998).

Sanctions against father for filing motion to have child examined affirmed. — Imposition of sanctions against a father for filing a motion to have his child examined by an independent psychiatrist was affirmed, where he did not have grounds to support the motion, and where motion was filed as a ploy to prevent the child's mother from leaving the area. Yohay v. Justice, No. 0631-89-4 (Ct. of Appeals Oct. 2, 1990).

Sanctions against husband based on motion to vacate arbitration award held proper. — Where husband's arguments were almost totally based upon false assertions and he made no legal argument that would entitle him to relief, and it was more than a year after the arbitrator had made his findings in the proposed award before husband made any objection to it, trial court did not abuse its discretion by awarding sanctions based on the alleged errors cited by husband in his motion to vacate the arbitration award and the findings of the arbitrator; however, because of the issues, regarding how an arbitration award should be treated by a trial court in domestic relations cases which was raised by husband was of first impression in Virginia and because husband had a facially reasonable argument that the equitable distribution award was excessive, the award of sanctions will be remanded to the trial court for review and for a new award that recognizes that the motion before it was not totally frivolous and without merit. Bandas v. Bandas, 16 Va. App. 427, 430 S.E.2d 706 (1993).

Trial court erred in imposing sanctions under this section against a county board of supervisors in a zoning case, where the board reasonably believed that it was authorized to act on a request for rezoning and was therefore justified in filing its defensive pleadings in the case. County of Prince William v. Rau, 239 Va. 616, 391 S.E.2d 290 (1990).

Sanctions against attorney reversed. — Sanction imposed against an attorney, who filed a pro se action which unsuccessfully challenged a county's relocation of its administrative offices, was reversed, where the attorney's construction of a pertinent Virginia statute was "warranted by existing law." Tullidge v. Board of Supvrs., 239 Va. 611, 391 S.E.2d 288 (1990).

Although Supreme Court upheld the trial court's ruling on defendant's demurrers for failure of plaintiff to state a cause of action, an award of sanctions against plaintiff's attorney was not upheld where the Supreme Court ruled that plaintiff's claims were objectively reasonable under existing law. Nedrich v. Jones, 245 Va. 465, 429 S.E.2d 201 (1993).

The withdrawal of a petition, based on the party's belief that its evidence is insufficient to satisfy the standard of review, does not constitute a concession that the appeal was not warranted by existing law. Woodruff v. Greene, No. 0114-98-2 (Ct. of Appeals Dec. 22, 1998).

Applied in Oxenham v. Johnson, 241 Va. 281, 402 S.E.2d 1 (1991).

§ 8.01-272. Pleading several matters; joining tort and contract claims; separate trial in discretion of court; counterclaims. — In any civil action, a party may plead as many matters, whether of law or fact, as he shall think necessary. A party may join a claim in tort with one in contract provided that all claims so joined arise out of the same transaction or occurrence. The court, in its discretion, may order a separate trial for any claim. Any counterclaim brought in an action under Part Three of the Rules of

§ 8.01-272   CIVIL REMEDIES AND PROCEDURE   § 8.01-272

Court shall be governed by such Rules. (Code 1950, § 8-134; 1954, c. 333; 1977, c. 617; 1979, c. 367.)

REVISERS' NOTE

Section 8.01-272 extends former § 8-134 and overrules the prior prohibition against the joinder of tort and contract claims. See, e.g., Kavanaugh v. Donovan, 186 Va. 85, 93, 41 S.E.2d 489 (1947); Standard Products v. Woolridge, 214 Va. 476, 201 S.E.2d 801 (1974). The term "claim" encompasses any counterclaim, cross-claim, or third-party claim. However, § 8.01-272 does not go as far as FRCP 18 (a) in that § 8.01-272 restricts the joinder to claims arising out of the same transaction or occurrence. The court may, upon motion, sever such claims for separate trial.

Cross references. — For rules of court on filing answers and grounds of defense after pleas and demurrers have been overruled, see Rules 2:12, 3:7. For rule abolishing pleas of the general issue, see Rule 3:5. For rule of court as to including several pleadings in the same paper, see Rule 3:16.

Law Review. — For survey of Virginia law on practice and pleading for the year 1976-77, see 63 Va. L. Rev. 1459 (1977). For a re-examination of sovereign tort immunity in Virginia, see 15 U. Rich. L. Rev. 247 (1981). For comment on tort and contract aspects of legal malpractice in Virginia, see 16 U. Rich. L. Rev. 907 (1982). For article on the abolition of the forms of action in Virginia, see 17 U. Rich. L. Rev. 273 (1983).

I. Decisions Under Current Law.
II. Decisions Under Prior Law.

I. DECISIONS UNDER CURRENT LAW.

This section could not be applied retroactively to allow the joinder of actions in tort and contract where the statute became effective more than 10 months after final judgment in the trial court and almost three months after a writ of error was granted, since application of the statute might materially change the substantive rights of a party, as distinguished from the procedural aspects of the remedy. Goodstein v. Weinberg, Buffenstein, Hirschler & Fleischer, 219 Va. 105, 245 S.E.2d 140 (1978).

This section changed common-law rule applicable to misjoinder and expressly permitted a party to join claims in tort with claims in contract if the claims arose out of the same transaction or occurrence. Thus, the special circumstances which compelled the result in Goodstein v. Weinberg, 219 Va. 105, 245 S.E.2d 140 (1978) are unlikely to recur. MacLellan v. Throckmorton, 235 Va. 341, 367 S.E.2d 720 (1988).

Dismissal for misjoinder of defendants and causes of action held erroneous. — Where a fair reading of the amended motion for judgment showed that plaintiff pleaded alternative theories of recovery against the same group of defendants and that the claims arose out of the same transaction or occurrence; the trial court erred in dismissing plaintiff's action on the ground of misjoinder of parties defendant and causes of action. Fox v. Deese, 234 Va. 412, 362 S.E.2d 699 (1987).

The plaintiff's claim against driver for negligent operation of an automobile does not arise from the same transaction or occurrence as the plaintiff's claim against doctor for medical malpractice where first, there was negligent operation of a motor vehicle by driver resulting in an accident; and, then there was negligent medical treatment of plaintiff at a later date by the doctor resulting in injury. Powers v. Cherin, 249 Va. 33, 452 S.E.2d 666 (1995).

Applied in Kamlar Corp. v. Haley, 224 Va. 699, 299 S.E.2d 514 (1983); C & P Tel. Co. v. Sisson & Ryan, Inc., 234 Va. 492, 362 S.E.2d 723 (1987).

II. DECISIONS UNDER PRIOR LAW.

Editor's note. — The cases cited below were decided under corresponding provisions of former law. The terms "the statute" and "this section," as used below, refer to former provisions.

Demurrer and plea to whole declaration. — It is settled under our statute that a plea and demurrer, at the same time, to the whole declaration, are admissible. Stone & Co. v. Patterson, 10 Va. (6 Call) 71 (1806); Syme v. Griffin, 14 Va. (4 Hen. & M.) 277 (1809). See also, Bassett v. Cunningham, 34 Va. (7 Leigh) 402 (1836); C & O Ry. v. American Exch. Bank, 92 Va. 495, 23 S.E. 935 (1896).

If a defendant plead and demur to the whole

declaration, and the demurrer be overruled, judgment ought not to be entered, without first trying the issues joined on the other pleas. Waller v. Ellis, 16 Va. (2 Munf.) 88 (1809).

Pleading several matters in one plea. — The several matters are intended to be pleaded in several pleas, and if the defendant include several distinct matters of defense in one plea, he has no right to complain of the plaintiff for replying generally to such plea. If the plaintiff in such case can be said to be guilty of a fault in pleading, it is induced by his adversary, who is guilty of the first fault. O'Bannon v. Saunders, 65 Va. (24 Gratt.) 138 (1873).

Inconsistent pleas are allowable, and in trying one, the court cannot look to the existence of the other, hence each branch of the pleading is looked on as totally separate and distinct from every other, and the defenses under one cannot be straightened or curtailed by the existence of the other. Were it otherwise, the liberty of pleading several, and even contradictory, pleas would be defeated. Waller v. Ellis, 16 Va. (2 Munf.) 88 (1809); Norfolk Hosiery & Underwear Mills v. Aetna Hosiery Co., 124 Va. 221, 98 S.E. 43 (1919); Wilroy v. Halbleib, 214 Va. 442, 201 S.E.2d 598 (1974).

Under this section to revive a default judgment in ejectment, denying service of process, declaration, and notices in the manner at the time and places stated in the returns, and alleging service by an unauthorized person, are not objectionable, though repugnant. King v. Davis, 137 F. 198 (C.C.W.D. Va. 1903), aff'd sub nom. Blankenship v. King, 157 F. 676 (4th Cir. 1906).

And alternate defenses may be submitted to jury. — Where the contestant of a will could assert inconsistent defenses and present evidence based on those defenses, it would not constitute error to submit to the jury the alternate defenses of undue influence and forgery if justified by the evidence. Wilroy v. Halbleib, 214 Va. 442, 201 S.E.2d 598 (1974).

But not pleas of matters already pleaded. — Where the matter of a plea is already in issue, the plea is wholly unnecessary, and this is good ground for rejecting it. Reed v. Hanna, 24 Va. (3 Rand.) 56 (1824); Fant v. Miller, 58 Va. (17 Gratt.) 47 (1866).

Although this section gives the defendant the right to plead as many matters of defense as he chooses, yet it does not give him the "absolute right" to his special pleas setting up defenses admissible under pleas already received, and the court may strike out such special pleas though already admitted and issue joined. Virginia Fire & Marine Ins. Co. v. Buck, 88 Va. 517, 13 S.E. 973 (1891).

Demurrer to pleading previously answered. — Though a demurrer, an answer and other defensive pleadings may be filed at the same time, yet after an answer has been properly filed in a chancery cause, and so long as it remains filed, a litigant, adult or infant, should not thereafter be allowed to demur to the pleading that has been previously answered. Whether or not the answer may be withdrawn and the litigant then allowed to demur rests in the court's sound discretion. O'Neill v. Cole, 194 Va. 50, 72 S.E.2d 382 (1952).

Filing of special plea does not waive other defenses. — In a proceeding by notice of motion for judgment on notes, a special plea setting up the breach of a collateral agreement is not a waiver of other grounds of defense, for a defendant may plead as many matters of law or fact as he may think necessary, and he is not required to file all of his pleas in bar at the same time. Duncan v. Carson, 127 Va. 306, 103 S.E. 665 (1920).

Motion to strike. — Special demurrers having been abolished, the motion to strike out or reject can be used to obviate objections to pleadings such as duplicity and the like, which cannot now be raised by demurrer. C & O Ry. v. Rison, 99 Va. 18, 37 S.E. 320 (1900).

Where the objection to a second plea is that the matter of that plea is already put in issue, the party ought not to be put to the hazard of a demurrer, in order to avail himself of the objection; the proper and safe practice being, to try that question on a motion to reject the plea, or to strike it out, if it has been entered on record. Reed v. Hanna, 24 Va. (3 Rand.) 56 (1824).

Objection is the proper remedy when the plea is not appropriate to the action. Skeen v. Belcher, 128 Va. 122, 104 S.E. 582 (1920).

An objection will not take the place of the formal motion to strike out or reject. Bank of Bristol v. Ashworth, 122 Va. 170, 94 S.E. 469 (1917).

Section applies to proceedings in equity. — This section is extended by analogy to proceedings in courts of equity. Elmore v. Maryland & Va. Milk Producers Ass'n, 145 Va. 42, 134 S.E. 472 (1926).

§ 8.01-273. Demurrer; form; grounds to be stated; amendment. — A. In any suit in equity or action at law, the contention that a pleading does not state a cause of action or that such pleading fails to state facts upon which the relief demanded can be granted may be made by demurrer. All demurrers shall be in writing and shall state specifically the grounds on which the demurrant concludes that the pleading is insufficient at law. No grounds other than those stated specifically in the demurrer shall be considered by the court. A demurrer may be amended as other pleadings are amended.

B. Wherever a demurrer to any pleading has been sustained, and as a result thereof the demurree has amended his pleading, he shall not be deemed to have waived his right to stand upon his pleading before the amendment, provided the order of the court shows that he objected to the ruling of the court sustaining the demurrer. On any appeal of such a case the demurree may insist upon his original pleading, and if the same be held to be good, he shall not be prejudiced by having made the amendment. (Code 1950, §§ 8-99, 8-120; 1954, c. 333; 1977, c. 617.)

REVISERS' NOTE

Subsection A modifies former § 8-99. Subsection B incorporates the material provisions of former § 8-120.

Under prior practice the specific grounds of a demurrer did not have to be stated unless a party to the action by motion, or the court, required it. Subsection A changes this and requires the demurrant to state the specific grounds in his demurrer. Only those grounds stated will be considered.

The joinder in demurrer provided for in former § 8-99 has long been in disuse and has been deleted; the reference to demurrers in criminal cases has been deleted as inappropriate for inclusion in the civil procedure title.

No change is made to existing practice of testing a defensive pleading in equity and at law by a motion to strike § 8.01-274.

Cross references. — For rules of court on pleadings in general in equity and at law, see Rules 2:7, 2:12, 3:5, 3:12, 3:16.
Law Review. — For note, "The Specificity of Pleading in Modern Civil Practice: Addressing Common Misconceptions," see 25 U. Rich. L. Rev. 135 (1991).

I. Decisions Under Current Law.
II. Decisions Under Prior Law.

I. DECISIONS UNDER CURRENT LAW.

Facts in bill of complaint considered true. — In reviewing a decree sustaining a demurrer, all facts alleged in or reasonably inferable from a bill of complaint are considered true. West Alexandria Properties, Inc. v. First Va. Mtg. & Real Estate Inv. Trust, 221 Va. 134, 267 S.E.2d 149 (1980).

A demurrer, unlike a motion for summary judgment, does not allow the court to evaluate and decide the merits of a claim; it only tests the sufficiency of factual allegations to determine whether the motion for judgment states a cause of action. Fun v. Virginia Military Inst., 422 S.E.2d 770 (1992).

Applied in Board of Supvrs. v. Southland Corp., 224 Va. 514, 297 S.E.2d 718 (1982); Wingfield v. Franklin Life Ins. Co., 41 F. Supp. 2d 594 (E.D. Va. 1999).

II. DECISIONS UNDER PRIOR LAW.

Editor's note. — The cases cited below were decided under corresponding provisions of former law. The terms "the statute" and "this section," as used below, refer to former provisions.

The object of this section is twofold; that is to prevent reliance being placed upon an undisclosed objection to a mere matter of form, which is capable of amendment, and to prevent the demurrant from presenting, on appeal, grounds for the demurrer not relied upon before the trial court. Morriss v. White, 146 Va. 553, 131 S.E. 835 (1926).

Section eliminates practice of assigning different grounds for demurrer at trial and on appeal. — This section, if taken advantage of by the trial courts, will do away with the practice of assigning one ground of demurrer in the trial court and relying upon a wholly different ground in the appellate court — a practice which frequently results in the reversal of trial courts upon questions never presented to as considered by them. Lane Bros. & Co. v. Bauserman, 103 Va. 146, 48 S.E. 857 (1904).

Court may require specific writing. — While the grounds for demurrer are not required to be in writing, the trial court, on motion of any party thereto, shall, or of its own motion may, require the grounds of demurrer relied on to be stated specifically in the demurrer; and no grounds shall be considered other than those so stated. Klein v. National Toddle House Corp., 210 Va. 641, 172 S.E.2d 782 (1970).

Only grounds stated are considered. — Where grounds for a demurrer were voluntarily stated therein, only the grounds so stated would be considered. Klein v. National Toddle House Corp., 210 Va. 641, 172 S.E.2d 782 (1970).

Where a plaintiff voluntarily stated the grounds of his demurrer under the former statute only the grounds so stated could be considered. The fact that the grounds were stated voluntarily, and were not required by the court, is immaterial. The statute applies as well in one case as the other. Virginia & S.W. Ry. v. Hollingsworth, 107 Va. 359, 58 S.E. 572 (1907).

Effect when error in sustaining demurrer harmless. — Where, under this section, the plaintiff amended his declaration under protest, a demurrer thereto having been sustained, but relied on the amended declaration instead of the original, the question of the propriety of the action of the trial court in sustaining the demurrer becomes moot and will not be considered on appeal, as the error of the trial court, if error there was, was harmless. W.S. Forbes & Co. v. Southern Cotton Oil Co., 130 Va. 245, 108 S.E. 15 (1921). See Mears v. Accomac Banking Co., 160 Va. 311, 168 S.E. 740 (1933).

When statement of grounds not in record on appeal. — When the grounds of demurrer in an action at law have been stated in writing, in accordance with the statute, but they are not copied into the record, the Supreme Court will treat the case as if there had been no demurrer. Lane Bros. & Co. v. Bauserman, 103 Va. 146, 48 S.E. 857 (1904).

Insufficient statement of grounds. — See Newton v. White, 115 Va. 844, 80 S.E. 561 (1914); Richmond College v. Scott-Nuckols Co., 124 Va. 333, 98 S.E. 1 (1919).

Where counsel for defendants merely stated in the grounds of defense that a notice of motion did "not in law sufficiently state a case; hence subject to demurrer," it was held that this did not constitute a demurrer to the notice. Ratcliffe v. McDonald's Adm'r, 123 Va. 781, 97 S.E. 307 (1918).

§ 8.01-273.1. Motion for judgment; motion to refer; Virginia Birth-Related Neurological Injury Compensation Act. — A. In any civil action, where a party, who is a participating hospital or physician as defined in § 38.2-5001, moves to refer a cause of action to the Workers' Compensation Commission for the purposes of determining whether the cause of action satisfies the requirements of the Virginia Birth-Related Neurological Injury Compensation Act (§ 38.2-5000 et seq.), the court shall forward the motion to refer together with a copy of the motion for judgment to the Commission and stay all proceedings on the cause of action pending an award and notification by the Commission of its disposition; provided, however, that the motion to refer the cause of action to the Workers' Compensation Commission shall be filed no later than 120 days after the date of filing a grounds of defense by the party seeking the referral.

B. Upon entry of the order of referral by the court, the clerk of the circuit court shall file with the Workers' Compensation Commission within thirty days a copy of the motion for judgment and the responsive pleadings of all the parties to the action. The clerk shall copy all counsel of record in the civil action on the transmittal letter accompanying the materials being filed with the Workers' Compensation Commission. All parties to the civil action shall be entitled to participate before the Commission upon filing a notice of appearance with the Clerk of the Commission within twenty-one days after receipt of the transmittal letter to the clerk of the circuit court. Notwithstanding the provisions of § 32.1-127.1:03, the moving party shall provide the Commission with an original and five copies of the following: appropriate assessments, evaluations, and prognoses and such other records obtained during discovery and are reasonably necessary for the determination of whether the infant has suffered a birth-related neurological injury. The medical records and the pleadings referenced in this subsection shall constitute a petition as referenced in § 38.2-5004. The moving party shall be reimbursed for all copying costs upon entry of an award of benefits as referenced in § 38.2-5009. (1999, c. 822; 2000, c. 207.)

The 2000 amendments. — The 2000 amendment by c. 207, effective April 1, 2000, added the subsection A designator and near the beginning of subsection A inserted "who is a participating hospital or physician as defined in § 38.2-5001," at the end of subsection A added the language beginning "provided, however, that" and ending with "party seeking the referral," and added subsection B.

§ 8.01-274. Motion to strike defensive pleading in equity and at law; exceptions abolished.

— Exceptions to answers for insufficiency are abolished. The test of the sufficiency of any defensive pleading in any suit in equity or action at law shall be made by a motion to strike; if found insufficient, but amendable, the court may allow amendment on terms. If a second pleading is adjudged insufficient, the court may enter such judgment or decree or take such other action that it deems appropriate. (Code 1950, § 8-122; 1954, c. 605; 1977, c. 617; 1978, c. 336.)

REVISERS' NOTE

Case law indicated that a defensive pleading at law could be tested by a motion to strike. Similarly, former § 8-122 provided that a challenge for insufficiency, either of law or fact, directed to a defensive pleading in equity was made by a "motion to strike out."

Section 8.01-274 in combination with § 8.01-273 provides a uniform procedure for challenging pleadings in a civil action, whether in equity or at law: aggressive pleadings are to be challenged by the demurrer, and defensive pleadings by the motion to strike.

I. DECISIONS UNDER PRIOR LAW.

Editor's note. — The cases cited below were decided under corresponding provisions of former law. The term "this section," as used below, refers to former provisions.

This section has enlarged the function of exceptions to answers and covers every form of insufficiency of answer — whether nonresponsive to the allegations of the bill, evasive, or insufficient as a matter of law. Thomasson v. Walker, 168 Va. 247, 190 S.E. 309 (1937).

Under it the motion to strike now takes the place of exceptions to answers for insufficiency. The effect of the motion to strike is to admit that even if the facts set up in the answer are true, yet they are not sufficient as a matter of law to constitute a bar to the action or proceeding. Casilear v. Casilear, 168 Va. 46, 190 S.E. 314 (1937).

There is no conflict between this section and section 8.01-283, the privilege and manner of testing the answer simply being enlarged. Both sections are available to a litigant. He may exercise his choice, and unless he is willing to stake his whole case upon a hearing on bill and answer only, he may avail himself of the motion to strike, and thereby secure a judicial expression which may guide him in further proceeding. Thomasson v. Walker, 168 Va. 247, 190 S.E. 309 (1937).

§ 8.01-275. When action or suit not to abate for want of form; what defects not to be regarded.

— No action or suit shall abate for want of form where the motion for judgment or bill of complaint sets forth sufficient matter of substance for the court to proceed upon the merits of the cause. The court shall not regard any defect or imperfection in the pleading, whether it has been heretofore deemed mispleading or insufficient pleading or not, unless there be omitted something so essential to the action or defense that judgment, according to law and the very right of the cause, cannot be given. (Code 1950, §§ 8-102, 8-109; 1954, c. 333; 1977, c. 617.)

REVISERS' NOTE

Section 8.01-275 combines former §§ 8-102 and 8-109, and deletes the unnecessary reference to a demurrer. The exception in former § 8-109 for demurrer to a plea in abatement has been abolished. See § 8.01-276.

§ 8.01-275 CODE OF VIRGINIA § 8.01-275

Cross references. — For what a judgment not to be reversed, see § 8.01-678. For rule of court on general provisions as to pleadings, see Rule 3:16.

Law Review. — For comment, "Recovering Asbestos Abatement Cost," see 10 Geo. Mason L. Rev. 451 (1988).

I. Decisions Under Prior Law.
  A. General Consideration.
  B. Illustrative Cases.

I. DECISIONS UNDER PRIOR LAW.

A. General Consideration.

Editor's note. — The cases cited below were decided under corresponding provisions of former law. The term "this section," as used below, refers to former provisions.

Section based upon public policy. — This section and § 8.01-678, requiring the courts to disregard trifling defects in pleadings or procedure, are based upon a sound public policy, and are supported by the unanswerable logic of the progressive exponents of the best legal thought, with which the Supreme Court has been in full accord. Kennedy v. Mullins, 155 Va. 166, 154 S.E. 568 (1930).

Purpose. — The purpose of this section is that demurrers challenging pleadings on grounds that are not substantial or material, and which do not go to the very merits of a cause, are no longer allowed. Griffin v. Griffin, 183 Va. 443, 32 S.E.2d 700 (1945). See Washington v. Garrett, 189 Va. 57, 52 S.E.2d 83 (1949); Turpin v. Lyle, 377 F. Supp. 170 (W.D. Va. 1974).

Formal and substantial defects distinguished. — If the matter pleaded be in itself insufficient without reference to the manner of pleading it, the defect is substantial; but if the only fault is in the form of alleging it, the defect is formal. Norfolk & P. Belt Line R.R. v. Sturgis, 117 Va. 532, 85 S.E. 572 (1915).

A motion is sufficient if it informs the defendant of the nature of the demand made upon him, and states such facts as will enable the court to say that if the facts are proved as alleged they establish a good cause of action. Virginia Portland Cement Co. v. Luck's Adm'r, 103 Va. 427, 49 S.E. 577 (1905); Virginia & N.C. Wheel Co. v. Harris, 103 Va. 708, 49 S.E. 991 (1905); Cosmopolitan Life Ins. Co. v. Koegel, 104 Va. 619, 52 S.E. 166 (1905); Stonegap Colliery Co. v. Hamilton, 119 Va. 271, 89 S.E. 305 (1916).

Where motion, though inartificially commencing statement of cause of action with a quod cum, yet states the essential averments in direct and positive terms, it is sufficient. Roanoke Nat'l Bank v. Hambrick, 82 Va. 135 (1886).

Test as to sufficiency of notice of motion. — The tendency of modern times is to simplify matters of mere procedure, and for this reason the procedure by motion is looked upon with great indulgence, and notices are upheld as sufficient, however informal, where they contain sufficient substance to fairly apprise the defendant of the nature of the demand made upon him, and state sufficient facts to enable the court to say that if the facts stated are proved, the plaintiff is entitled to recover. Mankin v. Aldridge, 127 Va. 761, 105 S.E. 459 (1920).

A motion is sufficient if it informs the defendant of the nature of the demand made upon him, and states such facts as will enable the court to say that if the facts are proved as alleged they establish a good cause of action. Stonegap Colliery Co. v. Hamilton, 119 Va. 271, 89 S.E. 305 (1916).

A motion is sufficient which contains sufficient matter to enable the plaintiff to prove his case and so apprises the defendant of that case as to enable him to make defense. Cosmopolitan Life Ins. Co. v. Koegel, 104 Va. 619, 52 S.E. 166 (1905).

What particularity required in motion. — The motion in a case sets forth minutely the time, the place and the circumstances under which the plaintiff received the injuries complained of. To require more would be to compel the plaintiff to set forth in the motion matters of evidence. This has never been required, even under the strict rule of pleading which formerly prevailed. Kelly v. Schneller, 148 Va. 573, 139 S.E. 275 (1927).

If a pleading to the merits shows sufficient substance for the court to see how to give judgment according to law and the very right of the case it is good, though defective in form, under the provisions of this section. Stonegap Colliery Co. v. Hamilton, 119 Va. 271, 89 S.E. 305 (1916).

That a motion is unnecessarily long is immaterial in view of this section. Norfolk & W. Ry. v. Whitehurst, 125 Va. 260, 99 S.E. 568 (1919).

Demurrer lies only to defects apparent on face of pleading. — A demurrer properly lies for such defects and such only as are apparent upon the face of the pleading. Russell Creek Coal Co. v. Wells, 96 Va. 416, 31 S.E. 614 (1898); Watts v. Commonwealth, 99 Va. 872, 39 S.E. 706 (1901).

Demurrer proper when motion sets out facts insufficient on their face. — Under

368

this section, providing that a demurrer shall not be sustained to a motion alleging negligence of defendant because the particulars of the negligence are not alleged, should the facts relied upon to establish negligence be set out in the motion and are on their face insufficient, then a demurrer may be interposed. Crosswhite v. Shelby Operating Corp., 182 Va. 713, 30 S.E.2d 673 (1944), aff'd on rehearing, 185 Va. 585, 37 S.E.2d 7 (1946).

Duplicity is no ground of demurrer. — Since the effect of this section is to abolish special demurrers, mere duplicity in a count in a declaration is no longer a good ground of demurrer. Norfolk & W.R.R. v. Ampey, 93 Va. 108, 25 S.E. 226 (1896).

Affidavit accompanying pleadings not subject to demurrer. — A demurrer to a plea required by statute to be verified by affidavit does not bring to the attention of the court the lack of the affidavit, which is no part of the plea. Plaintiff should object to the reception of the plea when tendered because not so verified. He cannot make objection after having taken issue, either of law, or fact, on it. Lewis v. Hicks, 96 Va. 91, 30 S.E. 466 (1898).

Decision of an issue of law on a demurrer is a decision on the merits and constitutes res adjudicata as to any other proceedings where the same parties and the same issues are involved. Turpin v. Lyle, 377 F. Supp. 170 (W.D. Va. 1974).

A demurrer must go to the heart of the cause, and if it is sustained it is a decision on the merits of the cause. Griffin v. Griffin, 183 Va. 443, 32 S.E.2d 700 (1945).

A demurrer goes to the heart of the case, and if sustained, it is a decision on the merits. Thus a judgment rendered thereon has the effect of a judgment on the merits where there has been no amendment sought or appeal noted. Turpin v. Lyle, 377 F. Supp. 170 (W.D. Va. 1974).

What defects not cured. — Where there has been a demurrer to any pleading and the same has been overruled, this section cures no defect, imperfection, or omission therein, except such as could have been regarded on demurrer. Southern Ry. v. Willcox, 98 Va. 222, 35 S.E. 355 (1900).

It is defendant's right and duty to call for a bill of particulars if the notice of motion in a wrongful death action failed to particularize the acts of negligence. P.L. Farmer, Inc. v. Cimino, 185 Va. 965, 41 S.E.2d 1 (1947). See Washington v. Garrett, 189 Va. 57, 52 S.E.2d 83 (1949).

B. Illustrative Cases.

Practice when general allegation of negligence insufficient in plaintiff's pleading. — The plaintiff may not, under the provisions of this section, force a defendant into a trial upon the evidence upon a general averment alleging that the defendant has been negligent without alleging any specific act which he charges to have constituted the negligence of the defendant. In such a case, if the defendant calls for a bill of particulars and the bill of particulars filed, when read in conjunction with the notice of motion, fails to set forth with reasonable certainty and particularity any specific act of negligence charged and sufficient facts with reference thereto to enable the court to say that if the facts set forth be proven substantially as alleged, the defendant has been guilty of some specific act of negligence for which the plaintiff is entitled to recover, the defendant may move the court to strike out the bill of particulars and exclude all evidence tendered by the plaintiff. Kaylor v. Quality Bread & Cake Co., 155 Va. 156, 154 S.E. 572 (1930).

Allegation of duty. — An allegation of duty is only a conclusion of law. When the facts alleged show the duty, and are stated with sufficient clearness to prevent surprise and enable the court to proceed upon the merits of the cause, a motion ought to be sustained. Virginia & N.C. Wheel Co. v. Harris, 103 Va. 708, 49 S.E. 991 (1905).

In an action against a city for personal injuries sustained by reason of an alleged defect in a sidewalk, a motion alleged that it was the duty of the city to keep its streets sound, safe, and suitable for public use and travel, and particularly the sidewalk in question. The allegation of duty was mere surplusage, and under the provisions of this section and § 8.01-678, directing the court to disregard formal defects in pleading, it was no ground for a motion in arrest of judgment. City of Richmond v. McCormack, 120 Va. 552, 91 S.E. 767 (1917).

Statement of duty not necessary. — An allegation of duty is only a conclusion of law; and where the facts alleged show the duty, and are stated with sufficient clearness to prevent surprise and enable the court to proceed upon merits of the cause, the motion ought to be sustained. Virginia & N.C. Wheel Co. v. Harris, 103 Va. 708, 49 S.E. 991 (1905).

Averment as to relations of the parties in personal injury action. — A motion in an action for personal injuries is sufficient if such averments are made as to the circumstances under which the injury was inflicted as will show the existence of the duty which it is averred has been neglected by the defendant to the injury of the plaintiff. The relations of the parties need not be otherwise averred, unless there be omitted something essential to the action that judgment cannot be given according to law and the very right of the case. Norfolk & W. Ry. v. Wood, 99 Va. 156, 37 S.E. 846 (1901).

Motion in action by licensee must show intentional or wilful injury, etc. — In an action for personal injuries by a licensee plaintiff, the motion does not state a good cause of action which does not aver that the defendant intentionally or wilfully injured the plaintiff, or that, after the defendant saw or knew of his danger, or by use of ordinary care might have known of his danger could have avoided injuring him, but failed to do so. Norfolk & W. Ry. v. Wood, 99 Va. 156, 37 S.E. 846 (1901).

Sufficient statement of place and date. — In an action for damages for personal injuries sustained at a railroad crossing, where four counts in the motion gave the date and place of the accident, and such particulars thereof as plainly informed the company of every fact relied on by the plaintiff, which was essential to enable it to make its defense, this was sufficient, and the court below properly overruled the demurrer. Norfolk & S. Ry. v. Smith, 122 Va. 302, 94 S.E. 789 (1918).

Omission of date note placed for collection. — In an action against a bank for negligence in failing to protest a note placed with it for collection, it is sufficient if the motion avers it was so placed before its maturity, though the date of the placing is not specified. Roanoke Nat'l Bank v. Hambrick, 82 Va. 135 (1886).

Omission of promise to pay. — Under this section a common count of indebitatus for services rendered, in a motion, is not subject to demurrer because of the omission of the usual allegation of a promise to pay. City of Newport News v. Potter, 122 F. 321 (4th Cir. 1903).

Misuse of "trespass" and "case" not substantial. — If a pleading to the merits shows sufficient substance for the court to see how to give judgment according to law and the very right of the case it is good under the provisions of this section, even though it is defective in form. The mere fact that the declaration designated an action as "trespass" when the facts alleged show that it is "case" is immaterial. Stonegap Colliery Co. v. Hamilton, 119 Va. 271, 89 S.E. 305 (1916).

Contractor's claim for balance due on work done. — Where the motion of a contractor suing for a balance due on work done by him, sufficiently advised the defendant of the nature of the contractor's claim, and although it did not in specific terms charge fraud or bad faith on the part of the architects who were required by the working contracts and specifications to approve the work, did so in substance, the motion is sufficient under this section. Richmond College v. Scott-Nuckols Co., 124 Va. 333, 98 S.E. 1 (1919).

§ 8.01-275.1. When service of process is timely. — Service of process in an action or suit within twelve months of commencement of the action or suit against a defendant shall be timely as to that defendant. Service of process on a defendant more than twelve months after the suit or action was commenced shall be timely upon a finding by the court that the plaintiff exercised due diligence to have timely service made on the defendant. (1994, c. 519.)

I. DECISIONS UNDER CURRENT LAW.

Applied in Gilbreath v. Brewster, 250 Va. 436, 463 S.E.2d 836 (1995).

§ 8.01-276. Demurrer to evidence and plea in abatement abolished; motion to strike evidence and written motion, respectively, to be used in lieu thereof. — Demurrers to the evidence and pleas in abatement are hereby abolished.

Any matter that heretofore could be reached by a demurrer to the evidence may hereafter be subject to a motion to strike the evidence.

Any defense heretofore required or permitted to be made by plea in abatement may be made by written motion stating specifically the relief demanded and the grounds therefor. Except when the ground of such motion is the lack of the court's jurisdiction over the person of an indispensable party, or of the subject matter of the litigation, such motion shall be made within the time prescribed by Rules of the Supreme Court.

If the motion challenges the venue of the action, the movant shall state therein why venue is improperly laid and what place or places within the Commonwealth would constitute proper venue for the action. (1977, c. 617.)

REVISERS' NOTE

Section 8.01-276 abolishes the obsolete demurrer to the evidence of former § 8-140 and, in its place, recognizes the more common motion to strike the evidence, Virginia's analogue to the federal motion for a directed verdict.

The section also abolishes pleas in abatement; instead, a written motion stating specifically the relief demanded and the grounds therefor is required. Former §§ 8-98 and 8-133 have been deleted accordingly.

Cross references. — As to when plaintiff may take a nonsuit, see § 8.01-380.

I. Decisions Under Current Law.
II. Decisions Under Prior Law.

I. DECISIONS UNDER CURRENT LAW.

When motion to strike granted. — When the sufficiency of a plaintiff's evidence is challenged by a motion to strike, the trial court should grant the motion only when it conclusively appears that the plaintiff has proved no cause of action against the defendant, or when it plainly appears that the trial court would be compelled to set aside any verdict found for the plaintiff as being without evidence to support it. Newton v. Veney, 220 Va. 947, 265 S.E.2d 707 (1980).

Doubts as to sufficiency of evidence resolved in plaintiff's favor. — When the sufficiency of a plaintiff's evidence is challenged by a motion to strike, the trial court should resolve any reasonable doubts as to the sufficiency of the evidence in plaintiff's favor. Newton v. Veney, 220 Va. 947, 265 S.E.2d 707 (1980).

Since it may obviate delay and expense of new trial. — When the sufficiency of a plaintiff's evidence is challenged by a motion to strike, the trial court should resolve any reasonable doubt as to the sufficiency of the evidence in plaintiff's favor; this is so because when a judgment based on a granted motion is reversed on appeal, a new trial must be conducted, but, when a plaintiff's verdict follows a denied motion, whether the verdict is set aside or confirmed by judgment below, the appellate court may enter final judgment thereby obviating the delay and expense of a new trial. Trail v. White, 221 Va. 932, 275 S.E.2d 617 (1981).

II. DECISIONS UNDER PRIOR LAW.

Editor's note. — The cases cited below were decided under corresponding provisions of former law. The term "this section," as used below, refers to former provisions.

The object of this section in requiring the grounds of a demurrer to the evidence (now motion to strike) to be stated in writing was at least twofold: First, to require the demurrant (now movant) to give notice in writing of the grounds or causes of demurrer (now motion) which he intended to rely on, and, second, to prevent him from assigning grounds of demurrer (now motion) in the appellate court wholly different from those relied on in the trial court. McMenamin v. Southern Ry., 115 Va. 822, 80 S.E. 596 (1914); Black v. Daughtry, 130 Va. 24, 107 S.E. 694 (1921).

Practice of subsequently reducing to writing not prejudicial. — It is common practice among lawyers, upon the announcement of a demurrer to the evidence (now motion to strike), to agree that it may be subsequently reduced to writing. And it is not perceived that plaintiff was prejudiced by that irregularity in that respect in this instance, especially as defendant's counsel duly delivered the grounds of demurrer (now motion) in writing to counsel for the plaintiff and to the court. Cooper v. Norfolk S.R.R., 125 Va. 73, 99 S.E. 606 (1919).

How evidence considered on motion. — On a demurrer to the evidence (now motion to strike), the court is bound to consider all evidence of the demurrant (now movant) in conflict with that of the demurree (now movee) as withdrawn, the credibility of the latter's witnesses admitted, and all facts admitted which the demurree's (now movee's) evidence, thus considered, proved or conduced to prove, or which might reasonably be inferred from his whole evidence, direct and circumstantial. Newberry v. Watts, 116 Va. 730, 82 S.E. 703 (1914).

Refusal to allow amendment of grounds of motion not prejudicial. — The refusal to permit a demurrant to the evidence (now movant) to amend his grounds of demurrer (now motion) after a verbal joinder in the demurrer (now motion) has been announced by the demurree (now movee) is not prejudicial to the demurrant (now movant) where, under the grounds already assigned he has the right to rely upon, and does in fact argue the same point proposed to be made and relied on by the amendment. Virginia Iron & Coke Co. v. Munsey, 110 Va. 156, 65 S.E. 478 (1909).

§ 8.01-277. Defective process; motion to quash; amendment.

— A person, upon whom process to answer any action has been served, may take advantage of any defect in the issuance, service or return thereof by a motion to quash filed prior to or simultaneously with the filing of any pleading to the merits. Upon sustaining the motion, the court may strike the proof of service or permit amendment of the process or its return as may seem just. (Code 1950, § 8-118; 1954, c. 333; 1977, c. 617; 1994, c. 37.)

REVISERS' NOTE

Former § 8-118 required that the pleaders use a plea in abatement when the process was defective and amendable and a motion to quash when the process was invalid and thus not amendable. Section 8.01-277 adopts the motion to quash as the one form of motion to bring process questions before the court. The court will then decide either that the error in process or the return is curable by amendment and permit correction or that the error is not curable and that the action should therefore be dismissed.

Cross references. — As to service on counsel of copies of pleadings and requests for subpoenas duces tecum, see Rule 1:12. As to subpoenas in chancery and proof of service thereof, see Rules 2:4 and 2:5. As to return of certain writs, see Rule 3:2. As to notice of motion for judgment and proof of service thereof, see Rules 3:3 and 3:4.

I. Decisions Under Current Law.
II. Decisions Under Prior Law.

I. DECISIONS UNDER CURRENT LAW.

Statute inapplicable where process never served. — By its express terms, this statute applies only where process has actually been served on the defendant; it does not permit a defendant to simultaneously make a voluntary general appearance and assert the bar provided by rule because he was not served with process. Gilpin v. Joyce, 257 Va. 579, 515 S.E.2d 124 (1999); Brown v. Burch, 30 Va. App. 670, 519 S.E.2d 403 (1999).

II. DECISIONS UNDER PRIOR LAW.

Editor's note. — The cases cited below were decided under corresponding provisions of former law. The term "this section," as used below, refers to former provisions.

A motion to quash process is not like a former plea in abatement but simply an informal method to raise a question, which ordinarily could have been raised by a plea in abatement. Eure v. Morgan Jones & Co., 195 Va. 678, 79 S.E.2d 862 (1955).

Objection to improperly executed process. — Where the service of process on a defendant is invalid, because it was not legally executed, objection thereto may be made informally by motion, or in case of nonappearance of the defendant, the court will itself raise the objection, if observed, and no formal plea is required. Commonwealth ex rel. Duvall v. Hall, 194 Va. 914, 76 S.E.2d 208 (1953).

Courts are liberal in allowing officers to amend their returns, according to the truth, when a casual and honest mistake has occurred. Amendments may be allowed, even to take away a cause of action on the original return, and though the officer has gone out of office, or is dead. Stotz v. Collins & Co., 83 Va. 423, 2 S.E. 737 (1887); Shenandoah V.R.R. v. Ashby's Trustees, 86 Va. 232, 9 S.E. 1003 (1889).

But allowance not ground for continuance. — The allowance of an amendment to the sheriff's return on a writ of summons is not ground for a continuance, though before the amendment, there was nothing to show a valid service of the writ, especially where the case had been previously set for trial by consent. Atlantic & D.R.R. v. Peake, 87 Va. 130, 12 S.E. 348 (1890).

When sheriff may amend return. — A sheriff may be allowed to amend his return after judgment by default, so as to show proper service. Commercial Union Assurance Co. v. Everhart's Adm'r, 88 Va. 952, 14 S.E. 836 (1892).

Amendments may be allowed after action commenced against sheriff and sureties, but not after judgment. Wardsworth v. Miller, 45 Va. (4 Gratt.) 99 (1847); Carr v. Meade, 77 Va. 142 (1883).

Amendments have been allowed after lapses of seven or thirteen years. Rucker v. Harrison, 20 Va. (6 Munf.) 181 (1818); Shenandoah V.R.R. v. Ashby's Trustees, 86 Va. 232, 9 S.E. 1003 (1889).

Amendments in federal courts. — Returns of substituted service which are defective may be amended in the federal court, and the decisions of the State court are not binding as to such amendment. King v. Davis, 137 F. 198 (C.C.W.D. Va. 1903), aff'd sub nom. Blankenship v. King, 157 F. 676 (4th Cir. 1906).

No amendment without notice. — Where a return of substituted service is fatally defective, and the court has not otherwise acquired jurisdiction of the defendant, application to amend the return will not be granted without notice. King v. Davis, 137 F. 198 (C.C.W.D. Va. 1903), aff'd sub nom. Blankenship v. King, 157 F. 676 (4th Cir. 1906).

§ 8.01-278. When plea of infancy not allowed; liability of infants for debts as traders; liability of infants on loans to defray expenses of education. — A. If any minor now transacting business or who may hereafter transact business as a trader fails to disclose (i) by a sign in letters easy to be read, kept conspicuously posted at the place wherein such business is transacted and (ii) also by a notice published for two weeks in a newspaper meeting the requirements of § 8.01-324, the fact that he is a minor, all property, stock, and choses in action acquired or used in such business shall as to the creditors of any such person be liable for the debts of such person, and no plea of infancy shall be allowed.

B. If any minor shall procure a loan upon the representation in writing that the proceeds thereof are to be expended by such minor to defray any or all expenses incurred by reason of attendance at an institution of higher education, which has been approved by any regional accrediting association which is approved by the United States Office of Education, or by reason of attendance at any school eligible for the guarantee of the State Education Assistance Authority, such minor shall be liable for the repayment thereof as though he were an adult, and no plea of infancy shall be allowed. (Code 1950, §§ 8-135, 8-135.1; 1960, c. 78; 1970, c. 7; 1977, c. 617.)

REVISERS' NOTE

Section 8.01-278 combines former §§ 8-135 and 8-135.1. In that minors under the age of sixteen are now attending institutions of higher education, the reference to age in former § 8-135.1 has been deleted. Otherwise, there is no change in substance.

§ 8.01-279. When proof is unnecessary unless affidavit filed; handwriting; ownership; partnership or incorporation. — A. Except as otherwise provided by § 8.3A-308, when any pleading alleges that any person made, endorsed, assigned, or accepted any writing, no proof of the handwriting shall be required, unless it be denied by an affidavit accompanying the plea putting it in issue.

B. When any pleading alleges that any person, partnership, corporation, or unincorporated association at a stated time, owned, operated, or controlled any property or instrumentality, no proof of the fact alleged shall be required unless an affidavit be filed with the pleading putting it in issue, denying specifically and with particularity that such property or instrumentality was, at the time alleged, so owned, operated, or controlled.

C. When parties sue or are sued as partners, and their names are set forth in the pleading, or when parties sue or are sued as a corporation, it shall not be necessary to prove the fact of the partnership or incorporation unless with the pleading which puts the matter in issue there be filed an affidavit denying such partnership or incorporation. (Code 1950, §§ 8-114 to 8-116; 1954, c. 333; 1958, c. 66; 1964, c. 219; 1977, c. 617.)

REVISERS' NOTE

Section 8.01-279 combines former §§ 8-114 to 8-116 which dispense with the proof of certain facts alleged in pleadings unless the verity of such facts is put in issue by an affidavit. The only substantive change has been to expand subsection B (formerly § 8-115) to include partnerships and unincorporated associations.

I. Decisions Under Current Law.
II. Decisions Under Prior Law.
   A. General Consideration.
   B. Handwriting.
   C. Ownership.
   D. Partnership; Incorporation.

I. DECISIONS UNDER CURRENT LAW.

Photocopy of license agreement held properly admitted. — Where plaintiff questioned at trial the authenticity of the signatures on the license agreement and objected to the fact that the manager for defendant's store who identified the agreement could not authenticate the signatures from personal knowledge, but did not comply with the statutory mandate, and moreover, in conjunction with its motion to dismiss, defendant submitted the affidavit of its manager identifying the document and verifying the signatures, the trial court properly admitted a photocopy of the license agreement. Carmody v. F.W. Woolworth Co., 234 Va. 198, 361 S.E.2d 128 (1987).

Applied in Richman v. National Health Labs., Inc., 235 Va. 353, 367 S.E.2d 508 (1988).

II. DECISIONS UNDER PRIOR LAW.

A. General Consideration.

Editor's note. — The cases cited below were decided under corresponding provisions of former law. The term "this section," as used below, refers to former provisions.

B. Handwriting.

The basis of statutes dispensing with proof of signature, in the absence of an affidavit denying the allegations of such, is that the failure of the defendant to establish, set up or assert his defense, in the manner prescribed by law, raises a presumption that the material facts alleged or pleaded are admitted to be true. Bova v. Roanoke Oil Co., 180 Va. 332, 23 S.E.2d 347 (1942).

When subsection A applicable. — Subsection A only applies where the declaration alleges that the defendant, or the person stated to have made the writing, subscribed his name thereto. Kelley v. Paul, 44 Va. (3 Gratt.) 191 (1846); Shepherd, Hunter & Co. v. Frys, 44 Va. (3 Gratt.) 442 (1847).

Subsection A does not apply to a transfer of paper by mere delivery. Clason v. Parrish, 93 Va. 24, 24 S.E. 471 (1896).

Subsection A applies to instruments signed with the name of the partnership. But the question is still open, whether the persons sought to be charged are members of the partnership. Shepherd, Hunter & Co. v. Frys, 44 Va. (3 Gratt.) 442 (1847).

The defenses contemplated by subsection A involve a denial of the making (the factum) of the writing, indorsement, assignment, acceptance or other writing by the person charged therewith, not of other facts in connection with rights of the holder to recover thereon. Holdsworth v. Anderson Drug Co., 118 Va. 359, 87 S.E. 565 (1916).

A plea under subsection A is equivalent to a plea of non est factum. Holdsworth v. Anderson Drug Co., 118 Va. 359, 87 S.E. 565 (1916); Hillman v. Cornett, 137 Va. 200, 119 S.E. 74 (1923).

Answer under oath sufficient. — Subsection A was substantially complied with by the answer, under oath, filed in the cause, in which the genuineness of the alleged receipt was disputed, and its validity challenged, and the strictest proof of its genuineness called for. Harnsberger v. Cochran, 82 Va. 727, 1 S.E. 120 (1887). See also, Piedmont Bank v. Hatcher, 94 Va. 229, 26 S.E. 505 (1897).

Affidavit may be filed during trial at the discretion of the court. — In an action upon a note the court allowed the plaintiff during the trial to file an affidavit denying the signature of payee to a receipt for a part payment upon the note. Defendants had relied upon subsection A, and objected to any evidence denying the genuineness of the receipt. Their objection was properly sustained. Then, upon motion, the plaintiff was permitted to file an affidavit denying the genuineness of such signature, which was approved on appeal. Keister v. Philips, 124 Va. 585, 98 S.E. 674 (1919).

Objection to the evidence must be made in trial court. — A plaintiff in equity files with his bill, as the ground of his claim, an order on one of the defendants, which has not been accepted. No proof of the execution of the order is given, but its genuineness is not questioned in the court below, and it is made the basis of a decree in favor of the plaintiff. It is too late to make objection in the appellate court, to the want of proof of the order. James River & Kanawha Co. v. Littlejohn, 59 Va. (18 Gratt.) 53 (1867).

Bill dismissed upon default of proof. — Where the answer of the maker of a note denies that the payee indorsed it to the complainant as alleged in the latter's bill, and the denial is supported by affidavit, as required by subsection A, the burden of proof is thrown upon the complainant to show such indorsement, and in default thereof his bill should be dismissed. Harnsberger v. Cochran, 82 Va. 727, 1 S.E. 120 (1887); Piedmont Bank v. Hatcher, 94 Va. 229, 26 S.E. 505 (1897); Hillman v. Cornett, 137 Va. 200, 119 S.E. 74 (1923).

Effect of failure to deny by affidavit. — When any writing whatsoever is relied on in a pleading, unless it is questioned by an affidavit or sworn pleading it cannot be questioned at all and the party relying on it will not be required to introduce any evidence at all to prove it. Chestnut v. Chestnut, 104 Va. 539, 52 S.E. 348 (1905); Taylor v. Carter, 117 Va. 845, 86 S.E. 120 (1915); Hillman v. Cornett, 137 Va. 200, 119 S.E. 74 (1923).

Where notice of motion for judgment alleged that contract was signed by defendant, and there was no affidavit denying such signature, proof thereof was not required. Bova v. Roanoke Oil Co., 180 Va. 332, 23 S.E.2d 347 (1942).

In view of § 8.01-389 providing for the admission of foreign deeds in evidence, and this section, it was proper for the court to admit a deed of trust in evidence which was not filed with the answer, but was subsequently offered, where such deed was relied upon by the defendant in answer to an attachment and not denied by affidavit of plaintiff. F.D. Cummer & Son Co. v. R.M. Hudson Co., 141 Va. 271, 127 S.E. 171 (1925).

Title bond sufficient evidence of title where execution not denied. — Under this statute, prior to the 1919 revision, where an answer set up a title bond as a source of title and the bond was filed as part of the answer, the execution and delivery of the title bond not being denied, no other evidence of its execution was necessary. Robinett v. Taylor, 121 Va. 583, 93 S.E. 616 (1917). See also, Simmons v. Simmons, 74 Va. (33 Gratt.) 451 (1880).

A bill having alleged that the order filed as the ground of plaintiff's claim was drawn by one of the defendants, no proof of the signature was necessary. James River & Kanawha Co. v. Littlejohn, 59 Va. (18 Gratt.) 53 (1867).

Effect of plea denying that plaintiff is holder in due course. — The fact that the defendant swears to a plea denying that the plaintiff is the holder in due course of the negotiable note sued on does not throw upon the plaintiff the burden of showing that he is such holder. Holdsworth v. Anderson Drug Co., 118 Va. 359, 87 S.E. 565 (1916).

C. Ownership.

The purpose of the legislature should not be ignored. That purpose was to make it unnecessary to prove ownership or agency where ownership or agency is alleged, unless an affidavit is filed putting the matter in issue. Subsection B is a wise statute, but it may not be invoked unless proper allegations are made. It was not the purpose of subsection B to catch the unwary, but to obviate the necessity of proving matter which rests peculiarly in the possession of the defendant. Carlton v. Martin, 160 Va. 149, 168 S.E. 348 (1933). See Kirn v. Bembury, 163 Va. 891, 178 S.E. 53 (1935).

The basis of subsection B dispensing with proof of ownership, in the absence of an affidavit denying the allegation of such, is that the failure of the defendant to establish, set up or assert his defense, in the manner prescribed by law, raises a presumption that the material facts alleged or pleaded are admitted to be true. Bova v. Roanoke Oil Co., 180 Va. 332, 23 S.E.2d 347 (1942).

Subsection B is remedial and its purpose is to relieve the plaintiff of proving more or less formal matters, and like subsection A, it is designed to aid plaintiffs to concentrate their proof upon the real merits of the controversy without having to be prepared, at the time of trial, to prove the genuineness of the signature to writings in the one instance, or the ownership or control of instrumentalities in the other, unless such matters are put in issue by a sworn plea. Lough v. Lyon, 168 Va. 136, 190 S.E. 290 (1937).

Subsection B is remedial and its purpose is to relieve the plaintiff of proving more or less formal matters. Breeding v. Johnson, 208 Va. 652, 159 S.E.2d 836 (1968).

And is liberally construed. — Subsection B is highly remedial and is to be liberally construed. Green v. Lum, 147 Va. 392, 137 S.E. 484 (1927); Vandergrift v. Summerall, 158 Va. 725, 164 S.E. 718 (1932); Driver v. Brooks, 176 Va. 317, 10 S.E.2d 887 (1940). See Lough v. Lyon, 168 Va. 136, 190 S.E. 290 (1937).

Subsection B is applicable to either plaintiff or defendant. Hague v. Valentine, 182 Va. 256, 28 S.E.2d 720 (1944).

Allegations making subsection B applicable. — In an action to recover for injuries received in an automobile collision, plaintiff alleged that one of the defendants, a dealer whose license plates were used on the car which collided with plaintiff's, operated and controlled such car, by and through the other defendant, the owner and driver thereof, and that such other defendant was driving the car as the agent of the defendant dealer. No affidavit was filed, under this subsection B, specifically denying the allegations, and therefore the trial court refused to admit any evidence tending to disprove such allegations. It was held, that the allegations made the provisions of this subsection B applicable. Driver v. Brooks, 176 Va. 317, 10 S.E.2d 887 (1940).

Affidavit not required when no allegation of ownership in pleadings. — In an action for injuries arising out of an automobile accident, the notice of motion contained no allegation that one of the defendants owned, operated or controlled the automobile involved. Therefore, it was entirely proper for her counsel to introduce evidence showing that she did not own, operate or control the said automobile. Subsection B required no affidavit in this case. Carlton v. Martin, 160 Va. 149, 168 S.E. 348 (1933).

Subsection B is applicable to a plea of contributory negligence in which the ownership and operation alleged in the notice is denied. Hague v. Valentine, 182 Va. 256, 28 S.E.2d 720 (1944).

But subsection B inapplicable to plea denying existence of relation of master and servant and master's breach of duty. — Subsection B does not require an affidavit to a plea putting in issue averments of the existence of the relation of master and servant and a breach of the master's duty to provide a safe place to work, for subsection B is remedial and its purpose is to relieve the plaintiff of proving more or less formal matters. Lough v. Lyon, 168 Va. 136, 190 S.E. 290 (1937).

It is also inapplicable where defendant is neither owner, operator, nor guest in automobile. — The uncontradicted evidence clearly showed that one of the defendants was not the owner or operator of the automobile. It showed that she had no control of it and that the operators of it were not her agents and it also showed that she was not riding in it at the time. It is inconceivable that the legislature through subsection B intended that such a result would follow. It was never intended that subsection B should have any application to such facts. Carlton v. Martin, 160 Va. 149, 168 S.E. 348 (1933).

Operation of vehicle put in issue. — In an action for death arising from an automobile accident, defendant filed affidavit that he had no memory of the day of the accident and that insofar as he knew, or was able to determine, he did not drive, operate or control the automobile involved in the accident. Plaintiff moved to quash the affidavit upon the ground that it did not comply with this subsection B, which motion was properly overruled. Plaintiff alleged that defendant drove the automobile that was involved in the accident; defendant made an issue of this allegation by the filing of an affidavit, and having no recollection of the accident, necessarily based it on information and belief. This was sufficient to put plaintiff on notice that the operation of the vehicle was to be an issue. Breeding v. Johnson, 208 Va. 652, 159 S.E.2d 836 (1968).

And where defendant is rental agent of house where injury occurred. — Subsection B is highly remedial and is to be liberally construed. But it has no application to an action by a prospective tenant against rental agents, where the motion did not allege, nor the proof show, that the defendants had such control of the premises as comes within the purview of subsection B. Turner v. Carneal, 156 Va. 889, 159 S.E. 72 (1931).

Effect of filing affidavit. — The instant case was an action against an executor for injuries to plaintiff while riding in his decedent's car. The executor filed an affidavit to the effect that plaintiff was riding in the car of deceased without authority from deceased. The affidavit was admissible under and a sufficient compliance with subsection B. If no such affidavit had been filed the plaintiff would have been relieved by subsection B of the necessity of proving that the driver had the authority, express or implied, of his master to suffer, permit, or invite the plaintiff to ride in the car. But when this affidavit was filed it put the driver's authority to do so in issue, and the burden rested upon the plaintiff to prove that the driver had such authority, expressed or implied. Morris v. Dame's Ex'r, 161 Va. 545, 171 S.E. 662 (1933).

Effect of failure to file affidavit. — Where defendants failed to file an affidavit under subsection B, denying under oath the ownership and operation of an automobile as alleged, they were not allowed to question such ownership and operation. It stood as a proven fact. Hague v. Valentine, 182 Va. 256, 28 S.E.2d 720 (1944).

In an action for injuries arising out of an automobile accident, plaintiff alleged that defendant, or his agent or servant, had negligently driven the taxicab into the automobile in which plaintiff was riding. No affidavit was filed by defendant denying that the driver of the taxicab was his agent. It was held that plaintiff had the right to assume that the agency was admitted, and that manifestly it would have been unfair to require her to prove the agency after she had closed her case in chief. Vandergrift v. Summerall, 158 Va. 725, 164 S.E. 718 (1932). See also, Sydnor v. Bonifant, 158 Va. 703, 164 S.E. 403 (1932).

Deposition from former action read by consent does not cure lack of affidavit. —

The instant case was an action on an automobile insurance policy on a fleet of trucks. Defendant, in a special plea, alleged that at the time of the accident the truck was being operated and maintained by a copartnership of which plaintiff was a member, and, therefore, under subsection B, had the plaintiff desired to require proof of this allegation, it was necessary for him to file an affidavit with the pleadings, putting that fact in issue, and, using the language of subsection B, "denying specifically and with particularity that such property or instrumentality was, at the time alleged, so owned, operated, or controlled." No such affidavit has ever been filed in this case. A deposition filed in a former action and read by consent as evidence in this case, in which plaintiff denied the partnership, was insufficient to supply the lack of the affidavit. Maryland Cas. Co. v. Cole, 156 Va. 707, 158 S.E. 873 (1931).

D. Partnership; Incorporation.

The basis of subsection C dispensing with proof of partnership or incorporation in the absence of an affidavit denying the allegation of such, is that the failure of the defendant to establish, set up or assert his defense, in the manner prescribed by law, raises a presumption that the material facts alleged or pleaded are admitted to be true. Bova v. Roanoke Oil Co., 180 Va. 332, 23 S.E.2d 347 (1942).

No express averment of incorporation necessary unless affidavit filed. — In an action against a railroad company, it is not necessary to aver in the motion that it is a corporation, nor is it necessary to prove on the trial that the defendant is a corporation, unless with the plea there is filed an affidavit denying that it is. B & O R.R. v. Sherman's Adm'r, 71 Va. (30 Gratt.) 602 (1878), overruled on other grounds, Hortenstein v. Virginia-Carolina Ry., 102 Va. 914, 47 S.E. 996 (1904).

In an action of assumpsit the writ and declaration was in the name of a plaintiff which indicated that the plaintiff was a corporation, but it was not stated to be a corporation. The defendant pleaded non assumpsit, but did not file an affidavit that the plaintiff was not a corporation. Under this subsection C it was not necessary that the plaintiff should prove it was a corporation. Gillett v. American Stove & Hollow Ware Co., 70 Va. (29 Gratt.) 565 (1877).

Incorporation at time of transaction, not of institution of suit, must be denied. — An affidavit denying the existence of any such corporation as the defendant at the time of the institution of the suit, but not denying the existence of such corporation at the time of the contract sued on, is not sufficient under subsection C to put plaintiff to proof of the existence of such corporation. Richmond Union Passenger Ry. v. New York & Sea Beach Ry., 95 Va. 386, 28 S.E. 573 (1897).

Affidavit not necessary when agreement to form partnership alleged. — Under subsection C where plaintiffs or defendants sue or are sued as partners, it is not necessary to prove the fact of partnership, unless with the pleading which puts the matter in issue there is an affidavit denying such partnership. However, a denial of the partnership must be supported by an affidavit only when a partnership, as such, is a party to the litigation. The requirement does not include a case where one party alleges an agreement to form a partnership and the other party denies any such agreement. Kennedy v. Mullins, 155 Va. 166, 154 S.E. 568 (1930).

Only party filing affidavit gets benefit therefrom. — In the instant case defendants were sued as composing an alleged partnership and an office judgment entered against them. Thereupon, in due time, one of the defendants entered a plea of non assumpsit and an affidavit alleging that no such partnership exists and that he had never been a member of such partnership as alleged in the declaration. It was held that this plea and affidavit did not "put the matter in issue" as to other alleged partners, and could not inure to their benefit. While entirely sufficient to set aside the office judgment as to the defendant making the plea, it could not have that effect as to other defendants. Perkins v. Miners Bank, 126 Va. 66, 101 S.E. 50 (1919).

Affidavit filed by defendant after all evidence introduced. — After all of the evidence had been introduced on behalf of the plaintiff, the greater part of which evidence being for the purpose of proving an alleged partnership, and the plaintiff had announced his case closed, and after the defendant had introduced all of the evidence in his behalf to deny the existence of the alleged partnership, and had announced his case closed, but while both the plaintiff and the defendant, who were only witnesses in the case, were still in the court room, counsel for plaintiff called the attention of the court to the failure of the defendant to file with his plea the proper affidavit under subsection C denying the partnership. Thereupon, on the motion of counsel for the defendant and over the objection and exception of the plaintiff, the court permitted the counsel for the defendant to prepare and file such an affidavit. It was held that under these circumstances, where neither the evidence nor the facts were certified to the Supreme Court so that that court had no facts showing that plaintiff's rights had been injuriously affected, the judgment in favor of the defendant should be affirmed. Dean v. Dean, 122 Va. 513, 95 S.E. 431 (1918).

Sufficient to set aside office judgment. — A plea of non assumpsit, accompanied by affidavit under subsection C, is sufficient to set aside office judgment as to the party filing it. Perkins v. Miners Bank, 126 Va. 66, 101 S.E. 50 (1919).

Plea need not be in writing when affidavit filed. — If an affidavit accompanies a plea of non assumpsit denying incorporation, it is not necessary that the plea should be in writing. Dudley v. Carter Red Ash Collieries Co., 125 Va. 701, 100 S.E. 466 (1919).

When no affidavit filed verdict settles issue. — In an action of unlawful detainer, defendants denied that a partnership existed between them, and claimed that none was alleged or proved. The summons was against defendants, naming them, trading as the Lewis Creek Mercantile Company, and the notice to terminate the lease was against the same concern. The defendants appeared, pleaded not guilty, and issue was joined. There was no affidavit denying partnership under subsection C. It was held that all conflicts between the testimony of plaintiffs and defendants were settled by the verdict of the jury in favor of plaintiffs. Thompson v. Artrip, 131 Va. 347, 108 S.E. 850 (1921).

Defendant may not show partnership dissolved absent affidavit. — Under a former, similar statute pertaining to actions on promissory notes, it was held that where the declaration charged that the defendants by their partnership name subscribed the note, and there was no affidavit by the defendants or any of them putting the execution of the note in issue, the defendants were precluded from showing that the partnership had been dissolved before the note was made, and that the person making it had no authority to execute it for the other parties. Phaup v. Stratton, 50 Va. (9 Gratt.) 615 (1853).

§ 8.01-280. Pleadings may be sworn to before clerk; affidavit of belief sufficient. — Any pleading to be filed in any court may be sworn to before the clerk or any officer authorized to administer oath thereof; and when an affidavit is required in support of any pleading or as a prerequisite to the issuance thereof, it shall be sufficient if the affiant swear that he believes it to be true. (Code 1950, § 8-131; 1977, c. 617.)

I. DECISIONS UNDER PRIOR LAW.

Editor's note. — The case cited below was decided under corresponding provisions of former law. The term "the statute," as used below, refers to former provisions.

Sufficiency of affidavit. — If an affidavit in support of a pleading is sufficient when affiant swears that "he believes it to be true," there is no reason in principle for holding that an affidavit concluding "true to the best of his knowledge and belief" is not a substantial compliance with the statute. Paris v. Brown, 143 Va. 896, 129 S.E. 678 (1925).

§ 8.01-281. Pleading in alternative; separate trial on motion of party. — A. A party asserting either a claim, counterclaim, cross-claim, or third-party claim or a defense may plead alternative facts and theories of recovery against alternative parties, provided that such claims, defenses, or demands for relief so joined arise out of the same transaction or occurrence. Such claim, counterclaim, cross-claim, or third-party claim may be for contribution, indemnity, subrogation, or contract, express or implied; it may be based on future potential liability, and it shall be no defense thereto that the party asserting such claim, counterclaim, cross-claim, or third-party claim has made no payment or otherwise discharged any claim as to him arising out of the transaction or occurrence.

B. The court may, upon motion of any party, order a separate trial of any claim, counterclaim, cross-claim, or third-party claim, and of any separate issue or of any number of such claims; however, in any action wherein a defendant files a third-party motion for judgment alleging that damages to the person or property of the plaintiff were caused by the negligence of the third-party defendant in the operation of a motor vehicle, the court shall, upon motion of the plaintiff made at least five days in advance of trial, order a separate trial of such third-party claim. (Code 1950, § 8-96.1; 1974, c. 355; 1977, c. 617; 1981, c. 426; 1983, c. 183.)

REVISERS' NOTE

Former § 8-96.1 restricted pleading in the alternative to actions arising out of a motor vehicle accident. Section 8.01-281 removes this restriction.

Subsection A grants a party asserting any claim or defense the right to join alternative claims or defenses — i.e. to present alternative statements of the facts or alternative legal theories. Subsection B provides that upon motion of any party the court may sever claims for a separate trial.

NB: This section does not provide for class actions.

Law Review. — For survey of Virginia law on torts for the year 1973-1974, see 60 Va. L. Rev. 1615 (1974).

I. DECISIONS UNDER CURRENT LAW.

Rule 3:10 and this section are mere procedural devices to promote judicial economy by having all claims, actual or potential, arising from the same transaction or occurrence, determined in one proceeding. Virginia Int'l Terms., Inc. v. Ceres Marine Terms., Inc., 879 F. Supp. 31 (E.D. Va. 1995).

The 1981 amendment to this section was a procedural device for the sake of judicial economy. It just allows third-party plaintiffs to make indemnity claims before the actual claim has technically accrued. Wingo v. Norfolk & W. Ry., 638 F. Supp. 107 (W.D. Va. 1986), rev'd on other grounds, 834 F.2d 375 (4th Cir. 1987).

Sufficiency. — Where the allegations of a pleading support two alternative theories of recovery, the pleading of one is not made insufficient by the insufficiency of the other. Balzer & Assocs. v. Lakes on 360, Inc., 250 Va. 527, 463 S.E.2d 453 (1995).

Claim based on future potential liability in contribution. — According to subsection A of this section and Supreme Court Rule 3:10(a), a claim based on future potential liability in contribution may be asserted in a third-party motion for judgment filed in a pending suit even though the third-party claimant has made no payment or otherwise discharged any claim against him. Gemco-Ware, Inc. v. Rongene Mold & Plastics Corp., 234 Va. 54, 360 S.E.2d 342 (1987).

Effect of section. — In the absence of this section and Rule 3:10, a party having a claim for indemnity or contribution against another would be prevented from pursuing the claim until it accrued. Virginia Int'l Terms., Inc. v. Ceres Marine Terms., Inc., 879 F. Supp. 31 (E.D. Va. 1995).

Accrual of indemnification action. — This section authorizes a party in a pending action to file a third-party motion for judgment (complaint) seeking indemnification or contribution. Rule 3:10(a) establishes the procedure for filing such a claim. When a claim for indemnity or contribution is filed as a separate cause of action, it does not accrue until the person seeking the relief has paid more than his or her share of the obligation. Virginia Int'l Terms., Inc. v. Ceres Marine Terms., Inc., 879 F. Supp. 31 (E.D. Va. 1995).

Dismissal for misjoinder of defendants and causes of action held erroneous. — Where a fair reading of the amended motion for judgment showed that plaintiff pleaded alternative theories of recovery against the same group of defendants and that the claims arose out of the same transaction or occurrence; the trial court erred in dismissing plaintiff's action on the ground of misjoinder of parties defendant and causes of action. Fox v. Deese, 234 Va. 412, 362 S.E.2d 699 (1987).

Chancellor correctly determined activities were a nuisance. — Because it was a suit in equity and there was no motion for an issue out of chancery, the chancellor correctly held that he must first determine whether the activities complained of constituted a nuisance. Packett v. Herbert, 237 Va. 422, 377 S.E.2d 438 (1989).

Applied in Rambone v. Critzer, 548 F. Supp. 660 (W.D. Va. 1982); Powers v. Cherin, 249 Va. 33, 452 S.E.2d 666 (1995); Hoar v. Great E. Resort Mgt., 256 Va. 374, 506 S.E.2d 777 (1998).

ARTICLE 3.

Particular Equity Provisions.

§ 8.01-282. Motion to strike evidence in chancery causes. — In any chancery cause when a defendant moves the court to strike out all of the evidence, upon any grounds, and such motion is overruled by the court, such defendant shall not thereafter be precluded from introducing evidence in his behalf, and the procedure thereon shall be the same and shall have the same effect as the motion to strike the evidence in an action at law. (Code 1950, § 8-122.1; 1954, c. 605; 1977, c. 617.)

I. DECISIONS UNDER CURRENT LAW.

When the sufficiency of a plaintiff's evidence is challenged by a motion to strike, a trial court must view the evidence and all reasonable inferences drawn therefrom in the light most favorable to the plaintiff and, moreover, when the challenge is made at the conclusion of the plaintiff's case-in-chief, the trial court should in every case overrule the motion where there is any doubt on the question. Shepherd v. Colton, 237 Va. 537, 378 S.E.2d 828 (1989).

§ 8.01-283. Effect of answer as evidence or affidavit; bills of discovery, etc. — Unless a complainant in a suit in equity shall, in his bill, request an answer or answer under oath to certain specified interrogatories, the answer of the defendant, though under oath, shall not be evidence in his favor, unless the cause be heard upon bill and answer only; but may, nevertheless, be used as an affidavit with the same effect as heretofore upon a motion to grant or dissolve any injunction, or upon any other incidental motion in the cause; but this section shall not apply to either pure bills of discovery or what are known as mixed bills of discovery, and shall not prevent a defendant from testifying in his own behalf, where he would otherwise be a competent witness. (Code 1950, § 8-123; 1977, c. 617.)

§ 8.01-284. Order for interrogatories after bill taken for confessed. — Although a bill be taken for confessed as to any defendant, the plaintiff may have an order for him to be brought in to answer interrogatories. (Code 1950, § 8-130; 1977, c. 617.)

REVISERS' NOTE

Section 8.01-284 is former § 8-130; the last sentence thereof was deleted as unnecessary.

CHAPTER 8.

Process.

Article 1.

In General.

Sec.
8.01-285. Definition of certain terms for purposes of this chapter; process, return, statutory agent.
8.01-286. Forms of writs.
8.01-287. How process to be served.
8.01-288. Process received in time good though neither served nor accepted.
8.01-289. No service of process on Sunday; exceptions.

Article 2.

How Process Is Issued.

Sec.
8.01-290. Plaintiffs required to furnish full name and last known address of defendants, etc.
8.01-291. Copies to be made.
8.01-292. To whom process directed and where executed.

Article 3.

Who and Where to Serve Process.

8.01-293. Who to serve process.

Sec.		Sec.	
8.01-294.	Sheriff to get from clerk's office process and other papers; return of papers.	8.01-311.	Continuance of action where service made on Commissioner or Secretary.
8.01-295.	Territorial limits within which sheriff may serve process in his official capacity; process appearing to be duly served.	8.01-312.	Effect of service on statutory agent; duties of such agent.
		8.01-313.	Specific addresses for mailing by statutory agent.
		8.01-314.	Service on attorney after entry of general appearance by such attorney.

Article 4.
Who to Be Served.

8.01-296.	Manner of serving process upon natural persons.	8.01-315.	Notice to be mailed defendant when service accepted by another.
8.01-297.	Process on convict defendant.	8.01-316.	Service by publication; when available.
8.01-298.	How summons for witness or juror served.	8.01-317.	What order of publication to state; how published; when publication in newspaper dispensed with.
8.01-299.	How process served on domestic corporations generally.		
8.01-300.	How process served on municipal and county governments and on quasi-governmental entities.	8.01-318.	Within what time after publication case tried or heard; no subsequent publication required.
8.01-301.	How process served on foreign corporations generally.	8.01-319.	Publication of interim notice.
		8.01-320.	Personal service outside of Virginia.
8.01-302.	Service of certain process on foreign or domestic corporations.	8.01-321.	Orders of publication in proceedings to enforce liens for taxes assessed upon real estate.
8.01-303.	On whom process served when corporation operated by trustee or receiver.	8.01-322.	Within what time case reheard on petition of party served by publication, and any injustice corrected.
8.01-304.	How process served on copartner or partnership.		
8.01-305.	Process against unincorporated associations or orders, or unincorporated common carriers.	8.01-323.	In what counties city newspapers deemed published for purpose of legal advertisements.
8.01-306.	Process against unincorporated associations or orders, or unincorporated common carriers; principal office outside Virginia and business transactions in Virginia.	8.01-324.	Newspapers which may be used for legal notices and publications.
		8.01-325.	Return by person serving process.
		8.01-326.	Return as proof of service.
		8.01-326.1.	Service of process or notice on statutory agent; copy to be sent to defendant and certificate filed with court; effective date of service.
8.01-307.	Definition of terms "motor vehicle" and "nonresident" in motor vehicle and aircraft accident cases.		
8.01-308.	Service on Commissioner of the Department of Motor Vehicles as agent for nonresident motor vehicle operator.		
		8.01-327.	Acceptance of service of process.

Article 5.
Privilege From Civil Arrest.

8.01-309.	Service on Secretary of Commonwealth as agent of nonresident operator or owner of aircraft.	8.01-327.1.	Definition of "arrest under civil process".
8.01-310.	How service made on Commissioner and Secretary; appointment binding.	8.01-327.2.	Who are privileged from arrest under civil process.

Article 1.

In General.

§ 8.01-285. Definition of certain terms for purposes of this chapter; process, return, statutory agent. — For the purposes of this chapter:
  1. The term *"process"* shall be deemed to include notice;
  2. The term *"return"* shall be deemed to include the term "proof of service";

3. The term *"statutory agent"* means the Commissioner of the Department of Motor Vehicles and the Secretary of the Commonwealth, and the successors of either, when appointed pursuant to law for the purpose of service of process on the nonresident defined in subdivision 2 of § 8.01-307. (1977, c. 617; 1991, c. 672.)

REVISERS' NOTE

In order to avoid undue repetition, § 8.01-285 defines terms that are used repeatedly throughout this chapter.

§ **8.01-286. Forms of writs.** — Subject to the provisions of § 8.01-3, the Supreme Court may prescribe the forms of writs, and where no such prescription is made, the forms of writs shall be the same as heretofore used. (Code 1950, § 8-43; 1977, c. 617.)

REVISERS' NOTE

Section 8.01-286 amends former § 8-43 to reference the controlling provisions of § 8.01-3.

Cross references. — For statute authorizing Supreme Court to prescribe forms of writs, see § 8.01-3. For rule of court prescribing form of subpoena in chancery, see Rule 2:4. For rule of court prescribing form of notice of motion for judgment, see Rule 3:3.

§ **8.01-287. How process to be served.** — Upon commencement of an action, process shall be served in the manner set forth in this chapter and by the Rules of the Supreme Court. (Code 1950, § 8-56; 1952, c. 77; 1954, c. 543; 1977, c. 617.)

REVISERS' NOTE

Section 8.01-287 simplifies former § 8-56.

§ **8.01-288. Process received in time good though neither served nor accepted.** — Except for process commencing actions for divorce or annulment of marriage or other actions wherein service of process is specifically prescribed by statute, process which has reached the person to whom it is directed within the time prescribed by law, if any, shall be sufficient although not served or accepted as provided in this chapter. (Code 1950, § 8-53; 1977, c. 617; 1987, c. 594; 1988, c. 583.)

REVISERS' NOTE

Section 8.01-288 qualifies § 8.01-287 by stating that any process which reaches the person to whom it is directed shall be sufficient even though it has not been served or accepted as specified in this chapter or the Rules of Court. Section 8.01-288 amends former § 8-53 which applied this concept but only to individuals. Section 8.01-288 applies to every type defendant, e.g., a corporation, not just to an individual, who is a defendant. The exception provided for divorce and annulment actions parallels the mandate of Rules 2:4 and 2:9.

Law Review. — For note, "Obtaining Jurisdiction Over Corporations in Virginia," see 12 U. Rich. L. Rev. 369 (1978). For 1985 survey of Virginia civil procedure and practice, see 19 U. Rich. L. Rev. 679 (1985). For 1987 survey of Virginia civil procedure and practice, see 21 U. Rich. L. Rev. 667 (1987). For survey on civil procedure and practice in Virginia for 1989, see 23 U. Rich. L. Rev. 511 (1989).

I. Decisions Under Current Law.
II. Decisions Under Prior Law.

I. DECISIONS UNDER CURRENT LAW.

This section cures defective service when process actually reaches the necessary person within the prescribed time limit. This cure extends to actions unless the particular statute specifically provides it will not apply. Bendele ex rel. Bendele v. Commonwealth, Dep't of Medical Assistance Servs., 29 Va. App. 395, 512 S.E.2d 827 (1999).

Section applicable to petitions for judicial review of decisions of the Virginia Employment Commission. — Petitions for judicial review under § 60.2-500 B must comply with the requirements of Chapter 8 of Title 8.01 (§ 8.01-285 et seq.) and Rule 2A of the Rules of the Supreme Court; the "curing statute" (§ 8.01-288) applies to the service of petitions under § 60.2-500 B because this section does not specifically prescribe a particular method of service. VEC v. Porter-Blaine Corp., 27 Va. App. 153, 497 S.E.2d 889 (1998).

Insufficiency of petition for judicial review of Virginia Employment Commission's decision cured by this section. — Circuit court did not err when it denied Virginia Employment Commission's motion to dismiss petition for judicial review due to insufficient service. Although service of petition upon the Commissioner by overnight mail failed to comply with the requirements for personal service set forth in Chapter 8 of Title 8.01, the commissioner actually received the two copies of the petition by mail within the time limits prescribed by law, making service sufficient under § 8.01-288. VEC v. Porter-Blaine Corp., 27 Va. App. 153, 497 S.E.2d 889 (1998).

Timely service held not shown. — Where the only evidence of the time of receipt of process offered by plaintiffs, other than an undated return receipt, was the testimony of their own counsel that an employee of defendant insurer had telephoned him "two days before the return day," even if counsel's testimony had been admitted into evidence, it would not have proved that the letter was received in the time required by this section and § 16.1-82. Davis v. American Interinsurance Exch., 228 Va. 1, 319 S.E.2d 723 (1984).

Section not applicable to juvenile cases. — This section is not applicable to the service of a summons under § 16.1-264, which provides for service in juvenile cases, since it excepts process commencing actions wherein service of process is specifically prescribed by statute. Garritty v. Virginia Dep't of Social Servs. ex rel. Sinift, 11 Va. App. 39, 396 S.E.2d 150 (1990).

Savings provisions of this section did not apply when party mailed simple copy of the petition for appeal that she had filed to the agency. That was not process. Bendele ex rel. Bendele v. Commonwealth, Dep't of Medical Assistance Servs., 29 Va. App. 395, 512 S.E.2d 827 (1999).

Applied in Karara v. County of Tazewell, 450 F. Supp. 169 (W.D. Va. 1978); Pennington v. McDonnell Douglas Corp., 576 F. Supp. 868 (E.D. Va. 1983); Allied Towing Corp. v. Great E. Petro. Corp., 642 F. Supp. 1339 (E.D. Va. 1986); In re Motorsports Merchandise Antitrust Litig., 186 F.R.D. 344 (W.D. Va. 1999).

II. DECISIONS UNDER PRIOR LAW.

Editor's note. — The case cited below was decided under corresponding provisions of former law. The term "this section," as used below, refers to former provisions.

Delivery of copy to servant held valid. — Where the deputy marshal served the notice of the motion of judgment upon the defendant by leaving a copy thereof at his residence with the servant who answered the door, and made return that he had left a copy at defendant's residence with his wife, more than 15 days before the return day, the attorney for defendant going to the deputy marshal and asking that he change the return to show delivery to the servant, motion to dismiss was denied on the ground that the notice had reached its destination within the time prescribed by law. The fact that the attorney for defendant, more than 15 days before the return day, was requesting that the deputy marshal change his return, was sufficient proof that the notice had reached its destination within the time prescribed by law. This was sufficient service under this section. Eley v. Gamble, 75 F.2d 171 (4th Cir. 1935).

§ 8.01-289. No service of process on Sunday; exceptions. — No civil process shall be served on Sunday, except in cases of persons escaping out of custody, or where it is otherwise expressly provided by law. (Code 1950, § 8-4.2; 1977, c. 617.)

Cross references. — As to issue and execution of attachment on Sunday, see § 8.01-542.

ARTICLE 2.

How Process Is Issued.

§ 8.01-290. Plaintiffs required to furnish full name and last known address of defendants, etc. — Upon the commencement of every action, the plaintiff shall furnish in writing to the clerk or other issuing officer the full name and last known address of each defendant and if unable to furnish such name and address, he shall furnish such salient facts as are calculated to identify with reasonable certainty such defendant. The clerk or other official whose function it is to issue any such process shall note in the record or in the papers the address or other identifying facts furnished. Failure to comply with the requirements of this section shall not affect the validity of any judgment. (Code 1950, § 8-46.1; 1962, c. 10; 1977, c. 617.)

Cross references. — For rules of court concerning how requirements of this section may be met, see Rules 2:2, 3:3.

§ 8.01-291. Copies to be made. — The clerk issuing any such process unless otherwise directed shall deliver or transmit therewith as many copies thereof as there are persons named therein on whom it is to be served. (Code 1950, § 8-57; 1977, c. 617.)

Cross references. — For rule of court requiring the plaintiff in an equity suit to furnish clerk with as many copies of bill of complaint as there are defendants to be served, see Rule 2:3. For rule of court requiring clerk to attach copy of bill of complaint to each subpoena for service on each defendant in an equity suit, see Rule 2:4. For rule of court requiring plaintiff to furnish clerk with as many copies of motion for judgment as there are defendants, and requiring the clerk to attach copy of motion to each notice for service on each defendant, see Rule 3:3.

§ 8.01-292. To whom process directed and where executed. — Process from any court, whether original, mesne, or final, may be directed to the sheriff of, and may be executed in, any county, city, or town in the Commonwealth. (Code 1950, § 8-44; 1954, c. 333; 1977, c. 617.)

REVISERS' NOTE

Section 8.01-292 modifies former law to allow unrestricted statewide service of process. Former § 8-44 permitted such service generally, but where venue was based on where the cause of action arose (former § 8-39), with certain exceptions former § 8-47 restricted process to the bailiwick of the court wherein the action was filed. This restriction is eliminated.

Cross references. — For rule as to issuance of subpoena in chancery, see Rule 2:4. For rules as to time of service of subpoena in chancery and bill of complaint, and return thereof, see Rules 2:4, 2:5. For rule as to issuance of notice of motion for judgment, see Rule 3:3. For rules as to time of service of notice of motion for judgment and return thereof, see Rules 3:3, 3:4.

Law Review. — For survey of Virginia law on practice and pleading for the year 1976-77, see 63 Va. L. Rev. 1459 (1977).

I. DECISIONS UNDER PRIOR LAW.

Editor's note. — The cases cited below were decided under corresponding provisions of former law. The term "this section," as used below, refers to former provisions.

This section is qualified by § 8.01-299, relating to the service of process upon a corporation. Pereira v. Davis Fin. Agency, 146 Va. 215, 135 S.E. 823 (1926).

This section is not applicable to proceedings in the appellate court. It deals with process, rules and pleadings, and is only applicable to proceedings in a trial court. D.F. Tyler Corp. v. Evans, 156 Va. 576, 159 S.E. 393 (1931).

Original mesne and final process are on same footing. Johnston v. Pearson, 121 Va. 453, 93 S.E. 640 (1917).

Process may be served by person other than officer to whom directed. Crosswhite v. Barnes, 139 Va. 471, 124 S.E. 242 (1924); Federal Land Bank v. Birchfield, 173 Va. 200, 3 S.E.2d 405 (1939).

Necessity for issuance before return day. Noell v. Noell, 93 Va. 433, 25 S.E. 242 (1896).

Omission of word "next" held immaterial. — A writ issued November 25, 1908, returnable to the third Monday in January, sufficiently appears to be returnable within 90 days from its date. The omission of the word "next" after January was immaterial. Arminius Chem. Co. v. White's Adm'x, 112 Va. 250, 71 S.E. 637 (1912).

The doctrine of waiver has no application to a void process. Johnston v. Pearson, 121 Va. 453, 93 S.E. 640 (1917).

ARTICLE 3.

Who and Where to Serve Process.

§ 8.01-293. Who to serve process. — A. The following persons are authorized to serve process:

1. The sheriff within such territorial bounds as described in § 8.01-295; or
2. Any person of age eighteen years or older and who is not a party or otherwise interested in the subject matter in controversy.

Whenever in this Code the term "officer" or "sheriff" is used to refer to persons authorized to make, return or do any other act relating to service of process, such term shall be deemed to refer to any person authorized by this section to serve process.

B. Notwithstanding any other provision of law (i) only a sheriff may execute an order or writ of possession for personal, real or mixed property, including an order or writ of possession arising out of an action in unlawful entry and detainer or ejectment; (ii) any sheriff or law-enforcement officer as defined in § 9-169 of the Code of Virginia may serve any capias or criminal show cause order; and (iii) only a sheriff, the high constable for the City of Norfolk or Virginia Beach or a treasurer may levy upon property. (Code 1950, §§ 8-52, 8-54; 1954, c. 543; 1960, c. 16; 1968, c. 484; 1977, c. 617; 1981, c. 110; 1986, c. 275; 1996, cc. 501, 608; 1997, c. 820.)

REVISERS' NOTE

Section 8.01-293 combines portions of former §§ 8-52 and 8-54.

The former proviso of subsection 2, relating to suits for annulment and divorce, retained from former § 8-54 the requirement that service of original process in divorce suits be by the sheriff. Former law was changed to the extent that other service in divorce suits, e.g., notice for the taking of depositions where the other party was not represented by counsel, was not required to be served by the sheriff. The definition of the term "sheriff" in § 8.01-2 eliminates any need for the exception clause of former § 8-54 (i.e., the reference to § 15.1-77).

Cross references. — As to acceptance of service of process generally, see § 8.01-327. As to service in divorce or annulment actions, see § 20-99.1:1. For rules of court relating to returns of subpoenas in chancery and notices of motions for judgment, see Rules 2:5, 3:4.

Law Review. — For 1987 survey of Virginia civil procedure and practice, see 21 U. Rich. L.

Rev. 667 (1987). For survey on civil procedure and practice in Virginia for 1989, see 23 U. Rich. L. Rev. 511 (1989).

§ **8.01-294. Sheriff to get from clerk's office process and other papers; return of papers.** — Every sheriff who attends a court shall, every day when the clerk's office is open for business, go to such office and receive all process, and other papers to be served by him, and give receipts therefor, unless he has received notice from a regular employee of the clerk's office that there are no such papers requiring service and shall return all papers within seventy-two hours of service, except when such returns would be due on a Saturday, Sunday, or legal holiday. In such case, the return is due on the next day following such Saturday, Sunday, or legal holiday. (Code 1950, § 8-49; 1954, c. 545; 1977, c. 617; 1978, c. 831.)

REVISERS' NOTE

The requirement that the sheriff go to the clerk's office to receive process every day that the clerk's office is open modifies the requirement of once per week in former § 8-49.

Cross references. — For rule of court providing clerk shall deliver subpoena in chancery for service, see Rule 2:4. For rule of court providing that clerk shall deliver notice of motion for judgment, see Rule 3:3.

I. DECISIONS UNDER PRIOR LAW.

Editor's note. — The case cited below was decided under corresponding provisions of former law. The term "this section," as used below, refers to former provisions.

This section is not applicable to proceedings in the appellate court, and is only applicable to proceedings in a trial court. D.F. Tyler Corp. v. Evans, 156 Va. 576, 159 S.E. 393 (1931).

§ **8.01-295. Territorial limits within which sheriff may serve process in his official capacity; process appearing to be duly served.** — The sheriff may execute such process throughout the political subdivision in which he serves and in any contiguous county or city. If the process appears to be duly served, and is good in other respects, it shall be deemed valid although not directed to an officer, or if directed to any officer, though executed by some other person. This section shall not be construed to require the sheriff to serve such process in any jurisdiction other than in his own. (Code 1950, § 8-50; 1977, c. 617; 1982, c. 674.)

REVISERS' NOTE

Former § 8-50 only permitted a county sheriff to execute process outside of the political subdivision in which he served and then only in cities contiguous to his county. Section 8.01-295 amends the section such that the territorial limits for service of process by a sheriff of either a county or a city is expanded to include "any contiguous county or city."

ARTICLE 4.

Who to Be Served.

§ **8.01-296. Manner of serving process upon natural persons.** — In any action at law or in equity or any other civil proceeding in any court, process, for which no particular mode of service is prescribed, may be served upon natural persons as follows:
1. By delivering a copy thereof in writing to the party in person; or

2. By substituted service in the following manner:

a. If the party to be served is not found at his usual place of abode, by delivering a copy of such process and giving information of its purport to any person found there, who is a member of his family, other than a temporary sojourner or guest, and who is of the age of sixteen years or older; or

b. If such service cannot be effected under subdivision 2 a, then by posting a copy of such process at the front door or at such other door as appears to be the main entrance of such place of abode, provided that not less than ten days before judgment by default may be entered, the party causing service or his attorney or agent mails to the party served a copy of such process and thereafter files in the office of the clerk of the court a certificate of such mailing. In any civil action brought in a general district court, the mailing of the application for a warrant in debt or affidavit for summons in unlawful detainer or other civil pleading or a copy of such pleading, whether yet issued by the court or not, which contains the date, time and place of the return, prior to or after filing such pleading in the general district court, shall satisfy the mailing requirements of this section. In any civil action brought in a circuit court, the mailing of a copy of the pleadings with a notice that the proceedings are pending in the court indicated and that upon the expiration of ten days after the giving of the notice and the expiration of the statutory period within which to respond, without further notice, the entry of a judgment by default as prayed for in the pleadings may be requested, shall satisfy the mailing requirements of this section and any notice requirement of the Rules of Court. Any judgment by default entered after July 1, 1989, upon posted service in which proceedings a copy of the pleadings was mailed as provided for in this section prior to July 1, 1989, is validated.

c. The person executing such service shall note the manner and the date of such service on the original and the copy of the process so delivered or posted under subdivision 2 and shall effect the return of process as provided in §§ 8.01-294 and 8.01-325.

3. If service cannot be effected under subdivisions 1 and 2 of this section, then by order of publication in appropriate cases under the provisions of §§ 8.01-316 through 8.01-320. (Code 1950, § 8-51; 1954, c. 333; 1977, c. 617; 1989, cc. 518, 524; 1990, cc. 729, 767; 1996, c. 538.)

REVISERS' NOTE

Section 8.01-296 generally incorporates former § 8-51 and makes it clear that the section applies only to service of process on natural persons. Subdivision 3 interrelates the publication provisions of §§ 8.01-316 through 8.01-320 with the provisions of subdivisions 1 and 2 regarding personal and substituted service and stipulates when service by publication is available on natural persons.

To increase the likelihood of actual notice, § 8.01-296 revises former § 8-51 to require that before a default judgment can be entered, process must be mailed not less than ten days prior to the entry of judgment, to the defendant's last known address, in addition to posting at his abode, when personal service or service on a family member cannot be obtained. This changes former § 8-51 which requires only the posting of process on the front door of the defendant's usual place of abode as a means of substituted service.

Law Review. — For note, "Defects in Process or Service in Virginia: Void or Voidable," see 44 Va. L. Rev. 654 (1958).

I. Decisions Under Current Law.
  A. General Consideration.
  B. Service by Posting.

II. Decisions Under Prior Law.
  A. General Consideration.
  B. Service on Family Member.
  C. Service by Posting.

I. DECISIONS UNDER CURRENT LAW.

A. General Consideration.

Terms allowing constructive service must be strictly followed. — Statutes authorizing constructive service of process are to be complied with strictly. National Trust for Historic Preservation v. 1750 K Inv. Partnership, 100 F.R.D. 483 (E.D. Va. 1984), aff'd, 755 F.2d 929 (4th Cir. 1985).

Failure to mail copy of complaint to defendant prior to entry of default. — Where the plaintiff does not mail a copy of the complaint to the defendant prior to the entry of a default judgment, the service is not complete and therefore is invalid; in such instance, the court never has in personam jurisdiction over the defendant and a judgment in plaintiff's favor must be vacated. National Trust for Historic Preservation v. 1750 K Inv. Partnership, 100 F.R.D. 483 (E.D. Va. 1984), aff'd, 755 F.2d 929 (4th Cir. 1985).

Service of process was proper under § 8.01-329(A) of long-arm statute. — Where personal jurisdiction was authorized by the Virginia long-arm statute, § 8.01-328.1, and defendant was served in the manner provided for in Chapter 8 (§ 8.01-285 et seq.) of Title 8.01, namely under subdivision 2 a of this section, service of process was proper under § 8.01-329(A) of the Virginia long-arm statute, and defendant's motion to dismiss for lack of jurisdiction over the person was denied. Frederick v. Koziol, 727 F. Supp. 1019 (E.D. Va. 1990).

Substituted service constituted constructive notice insufficient under § 46.2-357. — Serving the habitual offender order on defendant's father at defendant's usual place of abode, even if such service may have conformed with the requirements of subdivision (2)(a), constituted a form of constructive notice only. Constructive notice does not satisfy the statutory requirement contained in § 46.2-357, the requirement that defendant "knew his license had been suspended," that he had been declared to be an habitual offender and ordered not to drive. Reed v. Commonwealth, 15 Va. App. 467, 424 S.E.2d 718 (1992).

Effect of service by publication. — Where the service upon wife in Oregon of copy of bill of complaint filed by husband seeking divorce in Virginia had the effect of service by publication, and no other, the divorce decree did not deprive wife of the right to seek a determination by the trial court of the property right she may have had in husband's military pension. Toomey v. Toomey, 19 Va. App. 756, 454 S.E.2d 735 (1995).

The record proved that husband was aware of the proceeding against him, a fact made clear by both the duly authenticated certificates of notice and husband's entrance by special appearance to contest the trial court's jurisdiction. Husband did not appeal the court's subsequent finding that it did have personal jurisdiction, and consequently that finding became final 21 days after entry of the order. Such actions are sufficient to constitute waiver. Burd v. Burd, No. 1156-96-4 (Ct. of Appeals Feb. 11, 1997).

Filing of objections to report waived objections to jurisdiction — Where husband made a general appearance by filing objections to commissioner's report and a motion for summary judgment, and while the motion for summary judgment alleged that the "first order entered in this cause ... was without jurisdiction and before husband was properly before the court," the husband's filing of objections to the commissioner's report that did not attack the court's jurisdiction waived his objections to the court's exercise of personal jurisdiction. Davis v. Davis, No. 1125-97-1 (Ct. of Appeals Nov. 18, 1997).

B. Service by Posting.

Mailing of process to place where party may receive mail. — When the party causing service of process mails a copy of the pleading to the party served at a place where that party may receive mail, there has been compliance with the statutory directive of subdivision 2 b that the party "mails to the party served a copy of the pleading." Washington v. Anderson, 236 Va. 316, 373 S.E.2d 712 (1988).

Such as his residence. — Although judgment debtor was mailed service of process to address where he resided and not to his post office address where he received mail, substituted service was sufficient under subdivision 2 b to support a default judgment, since the judgment debtor made no showing that he did not or could not receive delivery of mail at his residence. Washington v. Anderson, 236 Va. 316, 373 S.E.2d 712 (1988).

II. DECISIONS UNDER PRIOR LAW.

A. General Consideration.

Editor's note. — The cases cited below were decided under corresponding provisions of former law. The terms "this statute" and "this section," as used below, refer to former provisions.

The provisions of this section are not modified by § 8.01-299. Pereira v. Davis Fin. Agency, 146 Va. 215, 135 S.E. 823 (1926).

This statute does not apply to a notice of dishonor of negotiable paper. McVeigh v. Bank of Old Dominion, 67 Va. (26 Gratt.) 785 (1875).

Methods of service are not cumulative but successive. — The different methods of service provided by this section are not cumulative but successive. Service cannot be made upon a member of the family if the defendant be found at his place of abode, and there can be no posting if a member of the family above the age of 16 years be found at the place of abode of the defendant. When one method of service is substituted for another, the return must show a right to adopt the inferior method of service by negativing ability to get the better service. Washburn v. Angle Hdwe. Co., 144 Va. 508, 132 S.E. 310 (1926).

Terms allowing constructive service must be strictly followed. — The terms of this section by which constructive service of process is allowed in lieu of personal service, must be strictly followed. Crockett v. Etter, 105 Va. 679, 54 S.E. 864 (1906).

There is no substituted service in case of illness. — The legislature has not provided in this section for a substituted service of process in case of the extreme illness of a defendant. It being the province of the legislature to define the method of service of process, and it having done so, the Supreme Court has no power to add to the statute. Narrows Grocery Co. v. Bailey, 161 Va. 278, 170 S.E. 730 (1933).

Waiver of defect. — Appearing and contesting of service is no waiver of defect of notice. Fowler v. Mosher, 85 Va. 421, 7 S.E. 542 (1888).

B. Service on Family Member.

Purpose of provision as to service on member of family. — The purpose of the provision was to require service upon some person who would feel interested by the ties of consanguinity, and the relation of dependence, to communicate the fact of the service to the party for whom it was designed. Fowler v. Mosher, 85 Va. 421, 7 S.E. 542 (1888).

In order to receive process, wife must be member of family. — This section should be construed as requiring that the wife should be a member of defendant's family in order to be entitled to receive the process, so that a return showing service by leaving a copy with defendant's wife, but not stating that she was a member of defendant's family, is insufficient. King v. Davis, 137 F. 198 (C.C.W.D. Va. 1903), aff'd sub nom. Blankenship v. King, 157 F. 676 (4th Cir. 1906).

Delivery must be at usual place of abode. — A judgment by default rendered upon a notice, the return of service upon which recited that it was executed by delivering it to defendant's wife, "not at his usual place of abode," instead of at his usual place of abode, is void. Crockett v. Etter, 105 Va. 679, 54 S.E. 864 (1906).

There is a presumption that a daughter is a member of the family. Smithson v. Briggs, 74 Va. (33 Gratt.) 180 (1880).

Delivery to a mere boarder is insufficient. Fowler v. Mosher, 85 Va. 421, 7 S.E. 542 (1888).

Service on defendant's son, who was not a member of defendant's family, was not legal service and the judgment was void and invalid. Finney v. Clark, 86 Va. 354, 10 S.E.2d 569 (1889).

"Last home," or "residence," not synonymous with "usual place of abode." — Last home, or residence, or place of abode, are not synonymous with the usual place of abode, etc., and, in making substituted service, under this section the copy of the notice must be left at defendant's usual place of abode and not elsewhere. Washburn v. Angle Hdwe. Co., 144 Va. 508, 132 S.E. 310 (1926), but see Smithson v. Briggs, 74 Va. (33 Gratt.) 180 (1880) and Fowler v. Mosher, 85 Va. 421, 7 S.E. 542 (1888), holding "residence" and "home" synonymous with "usual place of abode."

C. Service by Posting.

Service valid though defendant and his family were absent for two months. — Service by posting was valid notwithstanding that defendant and his family were in Florida for a two-month period at the time of the service. The absence was only temporary. Spiegelman v. Birch, 204 Va. 96, 129 S.E.2d 119 (1963).

Posting copy after house vacated is void. — A notice posted upon a house seven months after it had been vacated by the defendant was not posted upon his "usual place of abode," and a judgment founded on such defective notice was absolutely void. Earle v. McVeigh, 91 U.S. 503, 23 L. Ed. 398 (1875).

Return showing posting on "the door" is invalid. — Under this section authorizing substituted service by posting a copy on the "front door," a return showing service by posting up and leaving on "the door" of defendant's usual dwelling house does not show a valid service. King v. Davis, 137 F. 198 (C.C.W.D. Va. 1903), aff'd sub nom. Blankenship v. King, 157 F. 676 (4th Cir. 1906).

§ **8.01-297. Process on convict defendant.** — In all actions against one who has been convicted of a felony and is confined in a local or regional jail or State correctional institution, process shall be served on such convict and, subject to § 8.01-9, a guardian ad litem shall be appointed for him. Such service may be effected by delivery to the officer in charge of such jail or institution whose duty it shall be to deliver forthwith such process to the convict. (Code 1950, § 8-55; 1954, c. 543; 1977, c. 617.)

REVISERS' NOTE

Section 8.01-297 expands former § 8-55 by providing for service on incarcerated felons in all actions.

Notice to a representative of a convict also is contemplated since the section requires appointment of a guardian ad litem unless the convict is represented by an attorney pursuant to § 8.01-9 who would himself receive notice of the action. This procedure does not require service on the convict's committee and to this extent represents a departure from the requirement of former § 8-55 when alimony was sought from the convict.

§ **8.01-298. How summons for witness or juror served.** — In addition to the manner of service on natural persons prescribed in § 8.01-296, a summons for a witness or for a juror may be served:

1. At his or her usual place of business or employment during business hours, by delivering a copy thereof and giving information of its purport to the person found there in charge of such business or place of employment; or

2. In the case of a juror, by mailing a summons to the person being served, at least seven days prior to the day he is summoned to appear. (Code 1950, § 8-58; 1954, c. 366; 1973, c. 439; 1977, c. 617; 1979, c. 444.)

I. DECISIONS UNDER CURRENT LAW.

This section equally applicable to civil and criminal cases. — The provisions of this title prescribing the modes of service of witness subpoenas, including this section, are equally applicable to criminal and civil cases. Bellis v. Commonwealth, 241 Va. 257, 402 S.E.2d 211 (1991).

Disobedience to "any lawful process" is made subject to summary punishment or contempt by § 18.2-456 (5); "process" includes a subpoena directed to a witness. Bellis v. Commonwealth, 241 Va. 257, 402 S.E.2d 211 (1991).

§ **8.01-299. How process served on domestic corporations generally.** — Except as prescribed in § 8.01-300 as to municipal and quasi-governmental corporations, process may be served on a corporation created by the laws of this State as follows:

1. By personal service on any officer, director, or registered agent of such corporation; or

2. By substituted service on stock corporations in accordance with § 13.1-637 and on nonstock corporations in accordance with § 13.1-836. (Code 1950, § 8-59; 1954, c. 23; 1956, c. 432; 1958, c. 13; 1976, c. 395; 1977, c. 617; 1991, c. 672.)

REVISERS' NOTE

Section 8.01-299 revises former § 8-59. The section, coupled with statewide service under § 8.01-292, provides for personal service upon a corporate officer, director or registered agent anywhere in Virginia.

Law Review. — For survey of Virginia practice and pleading for the year 1975-1976, see 62 Va. L. Rev. 1460 (1976). For note, "Obtaining Jurisdiction Over Corporations in Virginia," see 12 U. Rich. L. Rev. 369 (1978).

I. Decisions Under Current Law.
II. Decisions Under Prior Law.

I. DECISIONS UNDER CURRENT LAW.

Applied in In re Motorsports Merchandise Antitrust Litig., 186 F.R.D. 344 (W.D. Va. 1999).

II. DECISIONS UNDER PRIOR LAW.

Editor's note. — The cases cited below were decided under corresponding provisions of former law. The term "this section," as used below, refers to former provisions.

Service on officers is valid. — Where process is duly served on officers of corporation, such service is valid, though they disclaim the right to answer officially. Lewis' Adm'r v. Glenn, 84 Va. 947, 6 S.E. 866 (1888).

But service is not recognition that officer is legal representative in all proceedings. — The fact that this section (as it formerly read) authorizes service of process against a corporation on its treasurer is not a recognition of the treasurer as the representative of the corporation in all legal proceedings. Taylor v. Sutherlin-Meade Tobacco Co., 107 Va. 787, 60 S.E. 132 (1908).

Service on a director who has been notified of his election, is valid, especially where he makes no disclaimer. The fact that he does not notify the corporation is immaterial. Danville & W.R.R. v. Brown, 90 Va. 340, 18 S.E. 278 (1893).

Service of nonresident president by third party is insufficient. — Where a suit is brought in a county in this State against a corporation domiciled in that county, and process is served upon the president of the corporation resident in Philadelphia, by a third party, who makes affidavit, as required, such service is insufficient to give the court jurisdiction. Dillard v. Central Va. Iron Co., 82 Va. 734, 1 S.E. 124 (1887).

Service on wife of agent is invalid. — Process against a corporation cannot be executed by service on the wife of an agent. Water Front Coal Co. v. Smithfield Marl, Clay & Transp. Co., 114 Va. 482, 76 S.E. 937 (1913). See Shenandoah Valley R.R. v. Griffith, 76 Va. 913 (1882).

Service in case of defunct corporations. — Service of process on the late president of a corporation which has ceased to exist is sufficient. Richmond Union Passenger Ry. v. New York & S.B. Ry., 95 Va. 386, 28 S.E. 573 (1897).

Effect of director's disclaimer on validity of return. — The return of an officer is to be taken as true. This is true irrespective of a disclaimer on the part of a director, who was served, which is stated in the return, for such disclaimer may be treated as surplusage, and at most is a statement made out of court of a fact which might or might not be proved at the hearing. Davis Bakery, Inc. v. Dozier, 139 Va. 628, 124 S.E. 411 (1924).

When president of corporation may be served. — Service of process on the president of a corporation in the county or city wherein the action is brought and in which he resides may be made at any time before or on the return day of such process. Jones & Co. v. C.W. Hancock & Sons, 117 Va. 511, 85 S.E. 460 (1915).

Declaration in the certificate of incorporation as to the location of the principal office, is conclusive, and the motive of the corporation in declaring is immaterial. Loyd's Executorial Trustees v. City of Lynchburg, 113 Va. 627, 75 S.E. 233 (1912).

§ 8.01-300. How process served on municipal and county governments and on quasi-governmental entities. — Notwithstanding the provisions of § 8.01-299 for service of process on other domestic corporations, process shall be served on municipal and county governments and quasi-governmental bodies or agencies in the following manner:

1. If the case be against a city or a town, on its city or town attorney in those cities or towns which have created such a position, otherwise on its mayor, manager or trustee of such town or city; and

2. If the case be against a county, on its county attorney in those counties which have created such a position, otherwise on its attorney for the Commonwealth; and

3. If the case be against any political subdivision, or any other public governmental entity created by the laws of the Commonwealth and subject to suit as an entity separate from the Commonwealth, then on the director,

commissioner, chief administrative officer, attorney, or any member of the governing body of such entity; and

4. If the case be against a supervisor, county officer, employee or agent of the county board, arising out of official actions of such supervisor, officer, employee or agent, then, in addition to the person named defendant in the case, on each supervisor and the county attorney, if the county has a county attorney, and if there be no county attorney, on the clerk of the county board.

Service under this section may be made by leaving a copy with the person in charge of the office of any officer designated in subdivisions 1 through 4. (Code 1950, § 8-59; 1954, c. 23; 1956, c. 432; 1958, c. 13; 1976, c. 395; 1977, c. 617; 1980, c. 732; 1985, c. 416.)

REVISERS' NOTE

Section 8.01-300 supersedes those provisions of former § 8-59 which specified how service should be made in suits against municipalities. The section clarifies the requirements for service in suits against a county or against a public or quasi-governmental corporate body.

Law Review. — For 1985 survey of Virginia civil procedure and practice, see 19 U. Rich. L. Rev. 679 (1985).

I. DECISIONS UNDER PRIOR LAW.

Editor's note. — The cases cited below were decided under corresponding provisions of former law. The term "the statute," as used below, refers to former provisions.

In suit against municipality, notice must be served on some designated officer. — In a proceeding to confiscate debts due from a municipal corporation, the notice to the debtor must be upon the mayor or other officer named in the statute. Fairfax v. City of Alexandria, 69 Va. (28 Gratt.) 16, aff'd, 95 U.S. 774, 24 L. Ed. 583 (1877).

Service on the auditor of Alexandria, without an appearance by the city or the creditor did not give the court jurisdiction of the debt which the city owed the creditor. Alexandria v. Fairfax, 95 U.S. 774, 24 L. Ed. 583 (1877).

§ 8.01-301. How process served on foreign corporations generally. —
Service of process on a foreign corporation may be effected in the following manner:

1. By personal service on any officer, director or on the registered agent of a foreign corporation which is authorized to do business in the Commonwealth, and by personal service on any agent of a foreign corporation transacting business in the Commonwealth without such authorization, wherever any such officer, director, or agents be found within the Commonwealth;

2. By substituted service on a foreign corporation in accordance with §§ 13.1-766 and 13.1-928, if such corporation is authorized to transact business or affairs within the Commonwealth;

3. By substituted service on a foreign corporation in accordance with § 8.01-329 where jurisdiction is authorized under § 8.01-328.1, regardless of whether such foreign corporation is authorized to transact business within the Commonwealth; or

4. By order of publication in accordance with §§ 8.01-316 and 8.01-317 where jurisdiction in rem or quasi in rem is authorized, regardless of whether the foreign corporation so served is authorized to transact business within the Commonwealth. (Code 1950, § 8-60; 1977, c. 617; 1991, c. 672.)

REVISERS' NOTE

Section 8.01-301 clarifies the methods of service on foreign corporations. Generally, the proposal does not change present law; but, by consolidation and cross-reference, it indicates in a single section the interrelationship among process provisions of Title 13.1 (§§ 13.1-111 and 13.1-274), of the Virginia Long-Arm Statute (§§ 8.01-328 ff.), for orders of publication (§§ 8.01-316 and 8.01-317), and for personal service (former § 8-60). Subsection 4 also delineates when service by publication is available on foreign corporations.

Section 8.01-301 effects a substantive change in former law by allowing service in the alternative (i.e., at the option of the plaintiff under Title 13.1 or under the Long-Arm Statute) in cases where the prerequisites are met for long-arm jurisdiction over foreign corporations. This changes former § 8-81.3 whereby substituted service was available only where service could not otherwise be effected under the Code. The result of the former statutory scheme was that where §§ 13.1-111 and 13.1-274 were applicable (i.e., to foreign corporations authorized to transact business within the State), substituted service could always be made thereunder on the clerk of the State Corporation Commission and, thus, service under § 8-81.3 on the Secretary of the Commonwealth was never available in such cases. On the other hand, where the foreign corporation to be served was not authorized to do business within the State, service under §§ 13.1-111 and 13.1-274 was not available, and service on such foreign corporation could be had by service on the Secretary of the Commonwealth under former § 8-81.3. The revision eliminates such unnecessary intricacies in cases where long-arm jurisdiction applies by allowing the plaintiff to choose to effect service under either the Long-Arm Statute or Title 13.1.

Another substantive change comports with the change permitting statewide service under § 8.01-292. Section 8.01-301 allows service on a corporation to be made personally anywhere within the state (1) on an officer, director, or registered agent of a foreign corporation authorized to do business in Virginia and (2) on an officer, director, or any agent of a foreign corporation which is not authorized to do business within Virginia. Thus, although § 8.01-301 retains the distinction between registered and unregistered corporations, the effect of § 8.01-292 is to make all personal service under proposed § 8.01-301 sufficient so long as the officer, director, registered or other agent is served within the State.

Cross references. — As to service by publication, see §§ 8.01-316 through 8.01-324.

Editor's note. — Sections 13.1-111 and 13.1-274, referred to in the Revisers' note, were repealed by Acts 1985, c. 522. See now §§ 13.1-766 and 13.1-928.

Law Review. — For note, "Obtaining Jurisdiction Over Corporations in Virginia," see 12 U. Rich. L. Rev. 369 (1978). For survey of Virginia practice and pleading for the year 1977-1978, see 64 Va. L. Rev. 1501 (1978). For 1985 survey of Virginia civil procedure and practice, see 19 U. Rich. L. Rev. 679 (1985).

I. Decisions Under Current Law.
   A. General Consideration.
   B. Doing Business.
II. Decisions Under Prior Law.
   A. General Consideration.
   B. Persons Who May Be Served.
   C. Doing Business.

I. DECISIONS UNDER CURRENT LAW.

A. General Consideration.

Burden of proof is on the plaintiff to establish jurisdiction through proper service pursuant to this section, and this is true even where the action has been removed to federal court. Consolidated Eng'g Co. v. Southern Steel Co., 88 F.R.D. 233 (E.D. Va. 1980).

B. Doing Business.

Contacts must be extensive if injury did not arise in forum state. — When a plaintiff in a suit against a foreign corporation is a nonresident and its claimed injury does not arise in the forum State, the contacts between the foreign corporation and the forum must be substantial to invoke the exercise of jurisdiction over the corporation, and if the plaintiff's injury does not arise out of something done in the forum State, then other contacts between the corporation and the State must be fairly extensive before the burden of defending a suit there may be imposed upon it without offending traditional notions of fair play and substantial justice. Consolidated Eng'g Co. v. Southern Steel Co., 88 F.R.D. 233 (E.D. Va. 1980).

Mere fact that a wholly owned subsidiary corporation is "present" or "doing business" in the forum State is an insufficient basis for invoking in personam jurisdiction over a nonresident parent corporation, not otherwise present or doing business in the forum since the test is not the degree of control over the subsidiary by the parent but, rather, the factual question is whether the subsidiary and the parent keep their corporate operations distinct and separate; therefore, as long as the two corporations maintain formal corporate separateness in all respects, the de facto control of one by the other does not justify piercing the corporate veil. Consolidated Eng'g Co. v. Southern Steel Co., 88 F.R.D. 233 (E.D. Va. 1980).

II. DECISIONS UNDER PRIOR LAW.

A. General Consideration.

Editor's note. — The cases cited below were decided under corresponding provisions of former law. The term "this section," as used below, refers to former provisions.

Purpose of statute. — The statutes designating or requiring the designation of particular persons upon whom process against corporations might be served were not enacted for the purpose of granting special privileges and advantages to foreign corporations or to restrict the right to sue them. On the contrary, their intention was to give an advantage to domestic plaintiffs by furnishing a sure and simple manner by which the foreign corporation could be held to answer in the courts of the state into which it had entered to do business. Junk v. R.J. Reynolds Tobacco Co., 24 F. Supp. 716 (W.D. Va. 1938).

This section is permissive and for the benefit of the party seeking to obtain service of process. Trueblood v. Grayson Shops of Tenn., Inc., 32 F.R.D. 190 (E.D. Va. 1963).

Failure on the part of a corporation to comply with legal formalities cannot be used as a shield to escape liability. Trueblood v. Grayson Shops of Tenn., Inc., 32 F.R.D. 190 (E.D. Va. 1963).

Statute cannot deprive citizen of right to sue in federal court. — Even if it be true that under the Virginia statute a citizen of Virginia suing a foreign corporation in the state courts must cause process to be served upon the statutory agent if one has been designated, this statute cannot serve to deprive a citizen of a right granted by the federal law, namely, to sue in the federal court, where such right is unquestioned except for the existence of such statute. Junk v. R.J. Reynolds Tobacco Co., 24 F. Supp. 716 (W.D. Va. 1938).

Federal courts are bound by decisions of State court. — In interpreting the language of the process statute of a state, the federal courts are bound by the decisions of the state courts. Iliff v. American Fire Apparatus Co., 277 F.2d 360 (4th Cir. 1960); Alcalde v. The Los Mayas, 184 F. Supp. 873 (E.D. Va. 1960).

Order must designate the newspaper in which publication is to be made. A.S. White & Co. v. Jordan, 124 Va. 465, 98 S.E. 24 (1919).

B. Persons Who May Be Served.

Service may be made on an agent of a foreign corporation failing to comply with the statute requiring the designation of an agent upon whom process might be served. Junk v. R.J. Reynolds Tobacco Co., 24 F. Supp. 716 (W.D. Va. 1938).

Service upon the agent of a foreign corporation in charge of its local business and collecting money which was remitted to it was sufficient. Atlantic Greyhound Lines v. Metz, 70 F.2d 166 (4th Cir.), cert. denied, 293 U.S. 562, 55 S. Ct. 73, 79 L. Ed. 662 (1934).

Service on district sales representative is sufficient. — A district sales representative of a foreign corporation is a representative of the corporation of sufficient rank to justify the service of process upon him under this section. Mas v. Orange-Crush Co., 99 F.2d 675 (4th Cir. 1938).

C. Doing Business.

Corporation must be doing business within the State. — It seems that service upon the statutory agent of a foreign insurance company is valid only so long as such company continues to do business in the State. Deatrick v. State Life Ins. Co., 107 Va. 602, 59 S.E. 489 (1907); Bank of Bristol v. Ashworth, 122 Va. 170, 94 S.E. 469 (1917).

In order for a defendant to be amenable to service of process under this section and § 13.1-111 (see now § 13.1-766), it must have been "doing business" in Virginia. Sikes v. Rexall Drug Co., 176 F. Supp. 33 (W.D. Va. 1959).

It is required both by Virginia and federal law that a corporation be doing business or transacting affairs in Virginia to be subject to service. Goldrick v. D.M. Picton Co., 56 F.R.D. 639 (E.D. Va. 1971).

Whether "doing business" depends on facts. — The phrase "doing business" is ephemeral and not easily defined and each case must turn upon its own particular facts. Sikes v. Rexall Drug Co., 176 F. Supp. 33 (W.D. Va. 1959).

In determining whether a foreign corporation is "doing business" within the State, each case must be decided on its own facts. Moore-McCormack Lines v. Bunge Corp., 307 F.2d 910 (4th Cir. 1962).

The test of traditional notions of fair play and substantial justice should be given great weight in ascertaining in a particular case whether the activities of a foreign corporation within the State are sufficient to subject it to constructive service of process. Moore-McCormack Lines v. Bunge Corp., 307 F.2d 910 (4th Cir. 1962).

What constitutes "doing business." — Whether a corporation is doing business in a state in such a way as to render it subject to the jurisdiction of the courts thereof, depends upon the fact of each particular case. The only general rule deducible from the decisions is that "the business must be of such a nature and character as to warrant the inference that the corporation has subjected itself to the local jurisdiction, and is by its duly authorized officers or agent present within the state or district where service is attempted." Atlantic Greyhound Lines v. Metz, 70 F.2d 166 (4th Cir.), cert. denied, 293 U.S. 562, 55 S. Ct. 73, 79 L. Ed. 662 (1934).

A nonresident corporation entering into a contract with a State corporation for the manufacture of its products, and maintaining an agent in the State where he received mail and spent most of his time, was doing business in the legal sense in the State of Virginia, and the agent was a representative of the corporation of sufficient rank to justify the service of process upon him under the provisions of this section. Certain-Teed Prods. Corp. v. Wallinger, 89 F.2d 427 (4th Cir.), cert. denied, 302 U.S. 707, 58 S. Ct. 26, 82 L. Ed. 546 (1937).

A foreign corporation actually present through its agents and doing business within a state is not, of course, exempted from the jurisdiction because it is acting in behalf of a domestic corporation. Atlantic Greyhound Lines v. Metz, 70 F.2d 166 (4th Cir.), cert. denied, 293 U.S. 562, 55 S. Ct. 73, 79 L. Ed. 662 (1934).

Jurisdiction is not dependent upon the connection of the nonresident defendant with the transaction that gives rise to the suit before the court. What the defendant may have done in the particular case is relevant, but not conclusive, upon the question of jurisdiction. The latter must be decided after considering the sum total of the defendant's intrastate transactions. Moore-McCormack Lines v. Bunge Corp., 307 F.2d 910 (4th Cir. 1962).

But this is a factor. — While jurisdiction is not dependent upon the connection of the nonresident defendant with the transaction giving rise to the suit, yet it is a relevant factor for consideration on the question of jurisdiction. Pappas v. Steamship Aristidis, 249 F. Supp. 692 (E.D. Va. 1965).

If plaintiff's injury does not arise out of something done in the forum state, then other contacts between the corporation and the state must be fairly extensive before the burden of defending a suit there may be imposed upon it without offending "traditional notions of fair play and substantial justice." Goldrick v. D.M. Picton Co., 56 F.R.D. 639 (E.D. Va. 1971).

Where a plaintiff is a stranger to the forum state and his injuries did not occur in the state or arise out of the foreign corporation's activities in the state, the contacts between the corporation and the forum state must be fairly substantial before in personam jurisdiction over the corporation may be imposed without offending the notions of fairness and justice inherent in due process. Grevas v. M/V Olympic Pegasus, 557 F.2d 65 (4th Cir.), cert. denied, 434 U.S. 969, 98 S. Ct. 515, 54 L. Ed. 2d 456 (1977).

Minimal contacts at least are a prerequisite to the exercise of jurisdiction. Pappas v. Steamship Aristidis, 249 F. Supp. 692 (E.D. Va. 1965).

Substituted service upon a nonresident is valid if he has had such minimum contacts within the State that the maintenance of the suit would not offend traditional notions of due process and fair play. Moore-McCormack Lines v. Bunge Corp., 307 F.2d 910 (4th Cir. 1962).

"Regularity test." — The "regularity test" applies only when the commercial contact is insignificant in itself, and the cause of action did not arise therefrom. Pappas v. Steamship Aristidis, 249 F. Supp. 692 (E.D. Va. 1965).

The "regularity test" should be applied where (1) the cause of action arose in another state and is in no way connected with any business ever done in Virginia, and (2) the defendant's commercial contacts with Virginia have been confined to two trips in five years and are insignificant. Pappas v. Steamship Aristidis, 249 F. Supp. 692 (E.D. Va. 1965).

Finding of regular contacts with the forum state is not an indispensable predicate to the assertion of jurisdiction. Pappas v. Steamship Aristidis, 249 F. Supp. 692 (E.D. Va. 1965).

Corporation must do more than maintain soliciting agent in State. — The general rule is that in order to be "doing business" and thus subject to statutory service such as contemplated by this section and § 13.1-111 (see now § 13.1-766) a corporation must maintain more than a mere soliciting agent within a state. Sikes v. Rexall Drug Co., 176 F. Supp. 33 (W.D. Va. 1959).

Recent decisions of the Supreme Court of Virginia generally adhere to the view that mere solicitation of orders by a foreign corporation does not amount to the doing of business in a state within the meaning of this section. That court, however, does not ignore federal decisions on the point but relies in great part on decisions of the Supreme Court of the United States. Iliff v. American Fire Apparatus Co., 277 F.2d 360 (4th Cir. 1960).

But solicitation of business may be taken into consideration. — In the determination of whether there exists such minimum contacts within the State as would not offend traditional notions of due process and fair play by the maintenance of a suit against a foreign corporation, the solicitation of business by the employees of the nonresident within the State may be taken into consideration. Moore-

McCormack Lines v. Bunge Corp., 307 F.2d 910 (4th Cir. 1962).

Doing of business by subsidiary does not confer jurisdiction over parent. — The doing of business of a subsidiary corporation in a state does not without more confer jurisdiction over the nonresident parent corporation. Goldrick v. D.M. Picton Co., 56 F.R.D. 639 (E.D. Va. 1971).

And service on parent does not confer jurisdiction over subsidiary. — The service of process on the parent company does not permit the court to exercise personal jurisdiction over the wholly owned subsidiary, if they are two separate distinct entities and so operate. Goldrick v. D.M. Picton Co., 56 F.R.D. 639 (E.D. Va. 1971).

Activities insufficient to render corporation amenable to service. — Where the only activity of defendant corporation's soliciting agents other than soliciting orders was assisting customers in the use of advertising media and the display of products and the payment of "push money" to customers' employees, this was not enough to meet the "solicitation plus" test indicated by the United States Supreme Court. Sikes v. Rexall Drug Co., 176 F. Supp. 33 (W.D. Va. 1959).

The fact that the parent corporation of the defendant contracted with the International Seaman's Union to furnish crews for its vessels and vessels of its subsidiaries, and crewmen for defendant went from Virginia to serve on vessels of defendant in North Carolina, did not justify assuming jurisdiction. Goldrick v. D.M. Picton Co., 56 F.R.D. 639 (E.D. Va. 1971).

One visit of a vessel to Virginia would not come within the minimal contact requirement where the cause of action arose in another state. Pappas v. Steamship Aristidis, 249 F. Supp. 692 (E.D. Va. 1965).

Activities of ship's husbanding agent. — Service of process upon a husbanding agent while the vessel is in port, and thereafter until the husbanding agent submits an invoice for the many details attended to by the agent occasioned by the vessel's visit to Virginia, constitutes "doing business . . . or . . . transacting affairs" within Virginia. Alcalde v. The Los Mayas, 184 F. Supp. 873 (E.D. Va. 1960).

Where the only affairs transacted in Virginia by a ship's husbanding agent were limited to the duty to see to the welfare of an injured seaman, arrange for his care and cure, and attend to his repatriation, such affairs were isolated instances too remotely associated with the constructive presence of a foreign shipping company to permit the exercise of jurisdiction. Alcalde v. The Los Mayas, 184 F. Supp. 873 (E.D. Va. 1960).

Foreign corporation held not to be doing business in State. — See Iliff v. American Fire Apparatus Co., 277 F.2d 360 (4th Cir. 1960).

§ 8.01-302. Service of certain process on foreign or domestic corporations. — In addition to other provisions of this chapter for service on corporations, process in attachment or garnishment proceedings, and notice by a creditor of judgment obtained and execution thereon issued in his favor, may be served on any agent of a foreign or domestic corporation wherever such agent may be found within the Commonwealth. Service so made shall constitute sufficient service upon such corporation; provided that notice of judgment obtained and execution issued shall comply in all respects to the provisions of §§ 8.01-502, 8.01-503 and 8.01-504. (Code 1950, § 8-63; 1977, c. 617.)

REVISERS' NOTE

Former § 8-63 sought to delineate the reach of process in garnishment (see also §§ 8.01-511 ff.), attachment, and execution proceedings by defining the word "agent" in terms of a list of job titles which were themselves undefined and nonexclusive. Section 8.01-302 provides that service on "any agent" is sufficient thereby leaving to the courts the interpretation of the term "agent."

Law Review. — For note, "Obtaining Jurisdiction Over Corporations in Virginia," see 12 U. Rich. L. Rev. 369 (1978).

§ 8.01-303. On whom process served when corporation operated by trustee or receiver. — When any corporation is operated by a trustee or by a receiver appointed by any court, in any action against such corporation, process may be served on its trustee or receiver; and if there be more than one such trustee or receiver, then service may be on any one of them. In the event that no service of process may be had on any such trustee or receiver, then process may be served by any other mode of service upon corporations authorized by this chapter. (Code 1950, § 8-64; 1977, c. 617.)

REVISERS' NOTE

Section 8.01-303 updates former § 8-64. References to lessees in former § 8-64 are eliminated as no longer appropriate, since lessees should not be agents for the service of process on lessors. Service on the receiver or trustee of the corporation is the primary means of obtaining jurisdiction, but if unavailable then process may be served by any other appropriate method. The only substantive change is the deletion of the last sentence of former § 8-64 which makes service by publication on a receiver or trustee the equivalent of personal service. Such a provision is deemed unnecessary and constitutionally suspect; see i.e., Pennoyer v. Neff, 95 U.S. 714, 24 L. Ed. 565 (1878).

Law Review. — For note, "Obtaining Jurisdiction Over Corporations in Virginia," see 12 U. Rich. L. Rev. 369 (1978).

I. DECISIONS UNDER CURRENT LAW.

Applied in Oliver v. AMC, 616 F. Supp. 714 (E.D. Va. 1985).

§ 8.01-304. How process served on copartner or partnership. — Process against a copartner or partnership may be served upon a general partner, and it shall be deemed service upon the partnership and upon each partner individually named in the action, provided the person served is not a plaintiff in the suit and provided the matter in suit is a partnership matter.

Provided further that process may be served upon a limited partner in any proceeding to enforce a limited partner's liability to the partnership. (Code 1950, § 8-59.1; 1950, p. 455; 1977, c. 617.)

REVISERS' NOTE

Section 8.01-304 draws a distinction between general partnerships and limited partnerships. The section makes no substantive change to former § 8-59.1 but clarifies the manner in which service may be made on a limited partnership as provided by § 50-73.7. Because the general partner controls the business, process must be served on a general rather than a limited partner unless the action is to enforce the limited partner's liability to the partnership.

Note: Former § 8-65 (How served ...) is deleted by this revision because of statewide service under § 8.01-292.

§ 8.01-305. Process against unincorporated associations or orders, or unincorporated common carriers. — Process against an unincorporated (i) association, (ii) order, or (iii) common carrier, may be served on any officer, trustee, director, staff member or other agent. (Code 1950, §§ 8-66, 8-67; 1962, c. 250; 1977, c. 617.)

REVISERS' NOTE

Section 8.01-305 consolidates former §§ 8-66 and 8-67. The first sentence of former § 8-66 is transferred to § 8.01-15. Statewide service, § 8.01-292, and the availability of orders of publication under § 8.01-316 make associated portions of former § 8-67 redundant. The terms listed in § 8.01-305 are substituted for and are inclusive of the job titles specified in former § 8-66.

§ 8.01-306. Process against unincorporated associations or orders, or unincorporated common carriers; principal office outside Virginia and business transactions in Virginia. — If an unincorporated (i) association, (ii) order, or (iii) common carrier has its principal office outside Virginia and transacts business or affairs in the Commonwealth, process may be served on any officer, trustee, director, staff member, or agent of such association, order, or carrier in the city or county in which he may be found or on the clerk of the State Corporation Commission, who shall be deemed by virtue of such transaction of business or affairs in the Commonwealth to have been appointed statutory agent of such association, order, or carrier upon whom may be made service of process in accordance with § 12.1-19.1. Service, when duly made, shall constitute sufficient foundation for a personal judgment against such association, order or carrier. If service may not be had as aforesaid, then on affidavit of that fact an order of publication may be awarded as provided by §§ 8.01-316 and 8.01-317. (Code 1950, § 8-66.1; 1962, c. 250; 1977, c. 617; 1991, c. 672.)

REVISERS' NOTE

While former § 8-66.1 provided that a record be kept, § 8.01-306 keys to § 8.01-312 which requires that an affidavit of compliance must be filed by the clerk of the State Corporation Commission in the office of the clerk of the court in which the action is pending. This change conforms with the procedure for §§ 8.01-307 to 8.01-313.

Editor's note. — A sentence in this section referring to compliance with § 8.01-312, referred to in the Revisers' Note above, was deleted from this section by Acts 1991, c. 672.

§ 8.01-307. Definition of terms "motor vehicle" and "nonresident" in motor vehicle and aircraft accident cases. — For the purpose of §§ 8.01-308 through 8.01-313:

1. The term *"motor vehicle"* shall mean every vehicle which is self-propelled or designed for self-propulsion and every vehicle drawn by or designed to be drawn by a motor vehicle and includes every device in, upon, or by which any person or property is or can be transported or drawn upon a highway, except devices moved by human or animal power and devices used exclusively upon stationary rails or tracks.

2. The term *"nonresident"* includes any person who, though a resident of the Commonwealth when the accident or collision specified in § 8.01-308 or § 8.01-309 occurred, has been continuously outside the Commonwealth for at least sixty days next preceding the date when process is left with the Commissioner of the Department of Motor Vehicles or the Secretary of the Commonwealth and includes any person against whom an order of publication may be issued under the provisions of § 8.01-316. (Code 1950, § 8-67.1; 1950, p. 620; 1952, c. 681; 1956, c. 64; 1966, c. 518; 1977, c. 617.)

REVISERS' NOTE

Sections 8.01-307 through 8.01-313 condense former §§ 8-67.1 through 8-67.4 without altering the substance of the former provisions. Though the revision has significantly altered the working and organization of the former sections, §§ 8.01-307 through 8.01-313 do not change the procedure or substance of former law.

§ 8.01-308

Cross references. — As to registration of motor vehicles by nonresidents, see §§ 46.2-655 through 46.2-661.

Law Review. — For comment on saving statute's effect on limitations of actions with long-arm jurisdiction, see 26 Wash. & Lee L. Rev. 366 (1969).

I. Decisions Under Current Law.
II. Decisions Under Prior Law.

I. DECISIONS UNDER CURRENT LAW.

Applied in Dennis v. Jones, 240 Va. 12, 393 S.E.2d 390 (1990).

II. DECISIONS UNDER PRIOR LAW.

Editor's note. — The cases cited below were decided under corresponding provisions of former law. The term "this section," as used below, refers to former provisions.

This section is in derogation of the common law and must be strictly construed. Warner v. Maddox, 68 F. Supp. 27 (W.D. Va. 1946).

Due process. — In considering whether this section complies with the requirements of due process, the crucial issue is the extent of the defendant's contacts with the jurisdiction. North River Ins. Co. v. Davis, 237 F. Supp. 187 (W.D. Va. 1965), aff'd, 392 F.2d 571 (4th Cir. 1968).

Virginia may provide for substituted service upon former residents of the State in actions arising from acts done in the State during the period of their residence. North River Ins. Co. v. Davis, 237 F. Supp. 187 (W.D. Va. 1965), aff'd, 392 F.2d 571 (4th Cir. 1968).

Section renders § 8.01-229 inapplicable. — Where, under this section and § 8.01-310, plaintiff can obtain service of process upon defendant before the expiration of the two-year limitation period prescribed by § 8.01-243 and secure a valid personal judgment if he is so entitled, his remedy is complete and unaffected by the absence of defendant, and § 8.01-229, the tolling statute, is not applicable. Bergman v. Turpin, 206 Va. 539, 145 S.E.2d 135 (1965), commented on in 7 Wm. & Mary L. Rev. 406 (1966).

Section authorizes service on nonresident joint tort-feasor in action for contribution. — A passenger on a bus operated by plaintiff brought an action against plaintiff and also against the owner and the driver of a truck for injuries received by her as a result of a collision between plaintiff's bus and the truck. Plaintiff effected a settlement in good faith and sued the owner, the driver, and the lessee-operator of the truck for contribution as joint tort-feasors. As nonresidents, defendants were served by service of process upon the Commissioner of the Division of Motor Vehicles under this section. They appeared specially and moved to quash the process as void, alleging that this section had no application. This motion was properly overruled, for this section by express terms covers a situation of this kind and authorizes such process and service thereof. McKay v. Citizens Rapid Transit Co., 190 Va. 851, 59 S.E.2d 121 (1950).

Evidence held sufficient to show agency. — Evidence held to show that driver of car was agent of defendant foreign corporation so that latter could properly be served with process under this and the following section. Barber v. Textile Mach. Works, 178 Va. 435, 17 S.E.2d 359 (1941).

§ 8.01-308. Service on Commissioner of the Department of Motor Vehicles as agent for nonresident motor vehicle operator. — Any operation in the Commonwealth of a motor vehicle by a nonresident, including those nonresidents defined in subdivision 2 of § 8.01-307, either in person or by an agent or employee, shall be deemed equivalent to an appointment by such nonresident of the Commissioner of the Department of Motor Vehicles, and his successors in office, to be the attorney or statutory agent of such nonresident for the purpose of service of process in any action against him growing out of any accident or collision in which such nonresident, his agent, or his employee may be involved while operating motor vehicles in this Commonwealth. Acceptance by a nonresident of the rights and privileges conferred by Article 5 (§ 46.2-655 et seq.) of Chapter 6 of Title 46.2 shall have the same effect under this section as the operation of such motor vehicle, by such nonresident, his agent, or his employee. (Code 1950, § 8-67.1; 1950, p. 620; 1952, c. 681; 1956, c. 64; 1966, c. 518; 1977, c. 617.)

I. DECISIONS UNDER CURRENT LAW.

Applied in Dennis v. Jones, 240 Va. 12, 393 S.E.2d 390 (1990).

§ **8.01-309. Service on Secretary of Commonwealth as agent of nonresident operator or owner of aircraft.** — Any nonresident owner or operator of any aircraft that is operated over and above the land and waters of the Commonwealth or uses aviation facilities within the Commonwealth, shall by such operation and use appoint the Secretary of the Commonwealth as his statutory agent for the service of process in any action against him growing out of any accident or collision occurring within or above the Commonwealth in which such aircraft is involved. (Code 1950, § 8-67.4; 1952, c. 384; 1954, c. 333; 1977, c. 617.)

Law Review. — For article on the law governing airplane accidents, see 39 Wash. & Lee L. Rev. 1303 (1982).

§ **8.01-310. How service made on Commissioner and Secretary; appointment binding.** — A. Service of process on either the Commissioner of the Department of Motor Vehicles as authorized under § 8.01-308 or on the Secretary of the Commonwealth as authorized under § 8.01-309, shall be made by leaving a copy of such process together with the fee for service of process on parties, in the amount prescribed in § 2.1-71.2, for each party to be thus served, in the hands, or in the office, of such Commissioner or such Secretary and such service shall be sufficient upon the nonresident. All fees collected by the Commissioner pursuant to the provisions of this section shall be paid into the state treasury and shall be set aside as a special fund to be used to meet the expenses of the Department of Motor Vehicles.

B. Appointment of the Commissioner or Secretary as attorney or agent for the service of process on a nonresident under § 8.01-308 or § 8.01-309 shall be irrevocable and binding upon the executor or other personal representative of such nonresident:

1. Where a nonresident has died before the commencement of an action against him regarding an accident or collision under § 8.01-308 or § 8.01-309 shall be irrevocable and binding upon the executor or other personal representative of such nonresident; or

2. Where a nonresident dies after the commencement of an action against him regarding an accident or collision under § 8.01-308 or § 8.01-309, the action shall continue and shall be irrevocable and binding upon his executor, administrator, or other personal representative with such additional notice of the pendency of the action as the court deems proper. (Code 1950, §§ 8-67.2, 8-67.4; 1952, c. 384; 1954, c. 333; 1970, c. 680; 1972, c. 408; 1976, c. 26; 1977, c. 617; 1987, c. 696; 1992, c. 459; 2000, c. 579.)

The 2000 amendments. — The 2000 amendment by c. 579, in the first sentence of subsection A, substituted "the fee for service of process on parties, in the amount prescribed in § 2.1-71.2," for "a fee of fifteen dollars".

Law Review. — For survey of recent legislation on civil procedure and service of process on Commissioner of Motor Vehicles, see 5 U. Rich. L. Rev. 186 (1970). For survey of Virginia law on practice and pleading for the year 1969-1970, see 56 Va. L. Rev. 1500 (1970). For article on the law governing airplane accidents, see 39 Wash. & Lee L. Rev. 1303 (1982).

§ **8.01-311. Continuance of action where service made on Commissioner or Secretary.** — The court, in which an action is pending against a nonresident growing out of an accident or collision as specified in §§ 8.01-308 and 8.01-309, may order such continuances as necessary to afford such nonresident reasonable opportunity to defend the action. (Code 1950, § 8-67.3; 1954, c. 547; 1977, c. 617.)

§ 8.01-312. Effect of service on statutory agent; duties of such agent.

— A. Service of process on the statutory agent shall have the same legal force and validity as if served within the Commonwealth personally upon the person for whom it is intended.

Provided that such agent shall forthwith send by registered or certified mail, with return receipt requested, a copy of the process to the person named therein and for whom the statutory agent is receiving the process.

Provided further that the statutory agent shall file an affidavit of compliance with this section with the papers in the action; this filing shall be made in the office of the clerk of the court in which the action is pending.

B. Unless otherwise provided by § 8.01-313 and subject to the provisions of § 8.01-316, the address for the mailing of the process required by this section shall be that as provided by the party seeking service. (Code 1950, § 8-67.2; 1954, c. 333; 1970, c. 680; 1972, c. 408; 1976, c. 26; 1977, c. 617.)

I. Decisions Under Current Law.
II. Decisions Under Prior Law.

I. DECISIONS UNDER CURRENT LAW.

Applied in Dennis v. Jones, 240 Va. 12, 393 S.E.2d 390 (1990).

II. DECISIONS UNDER PRIOR LAW.

Editor's note. — The cases cited below were decided under corresponding provisions of former law. The terms "the statute" and "this section," as used below, refer to former provisions.

This section is constitutional. — This section makes reasonable provision for probable communication and is constitutional. Carroll v. Hutchinson, 172 Va. 43, 200 S.E. 644 (1939).

But it is in derogation of the common law and must be strictly construed. Warner v. Maddox, 68 F. Supp. 27 (W.D. Va. 1946).

Failure to comply prevents valid judgment. — This section definitely requires a copy of the summons or notice to be forthwith sent to the defendant or defendants; therefore, failure to comply with that certain and definite provision of the section cannot result in any valid judgment against the defendant. Weiss v. Magnussen, 13 F. Supp. 948 (E.D. Va. 1936).

Under the provisions of this section, failure on the part of the plaintiff to furnish the correct information to enable him to send the summons or notice to the defendant or defendants will prevent the plaintiff from obtaining any valid judgment against the defendants. Weiss v. Magnussen, 13 F. Supp. 948 (E.D. Va. 1936).

Section does not provide for service upon a personal representative. — See Warner v. Maddox, 68 F. Supp. 27 (W.D. Va. 1946).

Meaning of "forthwith". — It was early settled in Virginia that "forthwith" means with "due diligence, under all the circumstances." Wooddy v. Old Dominion Ins. Co., 72 Va. (31 Gratt.) 362, 31 Am. R. 732 (1879); Omohundro v. Palmer, 158 Va. 693, 164 S.E. 541 (1932).

There is no precise definition, so far as time is concerned, of the word "forthwith." The term does not in all cases mean instanter, but it does have a relative meaning, and has been construed by the courts to mean "within a reasonable time," or with reasonable celerity or reasonable dispatch, depending upon the facts and circumstances of the particular case. Reynolds v. Dorrance, 94 F.2d 184 (4th Cir. 1938).

There is no accurate definition of the term "forthwith" and the mailing within a reasonably prompt time, where the interest of none of the parties has been affected, would seem to be a compliance with the statute. Devier v. George Cole Motor Co., 27 F. Supp. 978 (W.D. Va. 1939).

Prompt correction of error held substantial compliance. — Where the notices were promptly mailed to the defendant at a wrong address the day after they were filed, and when the error in the defendant's address was discovered and his right address ascertained they were again promptly mailed to him by the official, and the notices were received by the defendant 21 days prior to the return day of the notices, it was held that the notices were served in a manner substantially complying with this section. Reynolds v. Dorrance, 94 F.2d 184 (4th Cir. 1938).

The statute does not require delivery or receipt of the notice. It requires that it be sent by registered mail to the defendant. The statute is not violative of the United States

Constitution if it makes reasonable provision for probable communication of notice to the defendant. The court recognizes the intention of the legislature to be that the place to which the notice is sent must be one at which receipt will probably be had by the addressee. Powell v. Knight, 74 F. Supp. 191 (E.D. Va. 1947).

And the return receipt need not be filed as an exhibit. The request for a return receipt was never essential. Powell v. Knight, 74 F. Supp. 191 (E.D. Va. 1947).

Purpose of return receipt. — The only purpose of the return receipt is to verify delivery to the addressee and it would seem to follow that if a return receipt is not mandatory under this section, actual receipt by the addressee of a copy of summons and complaint sent by the official to the residence of the nonresident defendant is not mandatory in order to comply with this section and effect valid process. Powell v. Knight, 74 F. Supp. 191 (E.D. Va. 1947).

Service valid despite court being advised notice returned undelivered. — Trial court had jurisdiction over defendant, who was served in accordance with the statutory requirements of former §§ 46.1-387.5 and 8-67.2, where the trial court was advised that the statutory notice given defendant of the proceedings was returned undelivered; the trial court did have jurisdiction over defendant because service was effectuated in accordance with the applicable statute. Steed v. Commonwealth, 11 Va. App. 175, 397 S.E.2d 281 (1990).

Affidavit of counsel is not necessary. — It was contended that the service of the notices of motion was defective because counsel who left the notices with the Director (now Commissioner) filed no affidavit. It was held that such an affidavit is not necessary. Reynolds v. Dorrance, 94 F.2d 184 (4th Cir. 1938).

§ 8.01-313. Specific addresses for mailing by statutory agent. — A. For the statutory agent appointed pursuant to §§ 8.01-308 and 8.01-309, the address for the mailing of the process as required by § 8.01-312 shall be the last known address of the nonresident or, where appropriate under subdivision 1 or 2 of § 8.01-310 B, of the executor, administrator, or other personal representative of the nonresident. However, upon the filing of an affidavit by the plaintiff that he does not know and is unable with due diligence to ascertain any post-office address of such nonresident, service of process on the statutory agent shall be sufficient without the mailing otherwise required by this section. Provided further that:

1. In the case of a nonresident defendant licensed by the Commonwealth to operate a motor vehicle, the last address reported by such defendant to the Department of Motor Vehicles as his address on an application for or renewal of a driver's license shall be deemed to be the address of the defendant for the purpose of the mailing required by this section if no other address is known, and, in any case in which the affidavit provided for in § 8.01-316 of this chapter is filed, such a defendant, by so notifying the Department of such an address, and by failing to notify the Department of any change therein, shall be deemed to have appointed the Commissioner of the Department of Motor Vehicles his statutory agent for service of process in an action arising out of operation of a motor vehicle by him in the Commonwealth, and to have accepted as valid service such mailing to such address; or

2. In the case of a nonresident defendant not licensed by the Commonwealth to operate a motor vehicle, the address shown on the copy of the report of accident required by § 46.2-372 filed by or for him with the Department, and on file at the office of the Department, or the address reported by such a defendant to any state or local police officer, or sheriff investigating the accident sued on, if no other address is known, shall be conclusively presumed to be a valid address of such defendant for the purpose of the mailing provided for in this section, and his so reporting of an incorrect address, or his moving from the address so reported without making provision for forwarding to him of mail directed thereto, shall be deemed to be a waiver of notice and a consent to and acceptance of service of process served upon the Commissioner of the Department of Motor Vehicles as provided in this section.

B. For the statutory agent appointed pursuant to § 26-59, the address for the mailing of process as required by § 8.01-312 shall be the address of the fiduciary's statutory agent as contained in the written consent most recently filed with the clerk of the circuit court wherein the qualification of such fiduciary was had or, in the event of the death, removal, resignation or absence from the Commonwealth of such statutory agent, or in the event that such statutory agent cannot with due diligence be found at such address, the address of the clerk of such circuit court. (Code 1950, § 8-67.2; 1954, c. 333; 1970, c. 680; 1972, c. 408; 1976, c. 26; 1977, c. 617; 1983, c. 467; 1984, c. 780; 1991, c. 672.)

I. DECISIONS UNDER CURRENT LAW.

Constitutionality. — Subdivision A 2, providing for use of the nonresident defendant's address as reported on the accident report or as reported by the defendant to the investigating officer, is strictly a secondary provision which is triggered only in the event that "no other address is known." Read in its entirety, this section requires that the plaintiff utilize the last-known address of the defendant, and that failing that, the accident report address or address reported to the investigating officer may be used. Consequently, this section requires notice of service that is reasonably probable to result in a nonresident defendant receiving actual notice and is therefore constitutional. Banks v. Leon, 975 F. Supp. 815 (W.D. Va. 1997).

§ 8.01-314. Service on attorney after entry of general appearance by such attorney.

— When an attorney authorized to practice law in this Commonwealth has entered a general appearance for any party, any process, order or other legal papers to be used in the proceeding may be served on such attorney of record. Such service shall have the same effect as if service had been made upon such party personally; provided, however, that in any proceeding in which a final decree or order has been entered, service on an attorney as provided herein shall not be sufficient to constitute personal jurisdiction over a party in any proceeding citing that party for contempt, either civil or criminal, unless personal service is also made on the party.

Provided, further, that if such attorney objects by motion within five days after such legal paper has been so served upon him, the court shall enter an order in the proceeding directing the manner of service of such legal paper. (Code 1950, § 8-69; 1977, c. 617; 1981, c. 495.)

REVISERS' NOTE

The only significant change in former § 8-69 accomplished by § 8.01-314 is the inversion of the present provision requiring five days' notice before entry of an order directing service on the attorney of record so that service on the attorney is good without more unless the attorney objects within five days of receiving such service. The change allows the same amount of time for the attorney served to act, but requires service to be made only once rather than twice as under the former statute. Service would be made in accordance with Rule 1:12.

I. Decisions Under Current Law.
II. Decisions Under Prior Law.

I. DECISIONS UNDER CURRENT LAW.

This section compared with § 8.01-319. — Section 8.01-319 imposes different, not "less," notice requirements for a pro se litigant than one represented by counsel. A pro se litigant is required to advise the clerk of court of his address and any change in it. If a litigant is not pro se, but is represented by counsel, papers may be served on "an attorney authorized to practice law in this Commonwealth" who has entered a general appearance for the litigant pursuant to this section. Both of these provisions serve to ensure that notice of the proceedings may be served on the litigants. Eddine v. Eddine, 12 Va. App. 760, 406 S.E.2d 914 (1991).

Failure of litigant to inform clerk of change of address. — If a litigant wishes to be informed of the proceedings, he or she must either keep the court advised of where service may be accomplished or be represented by counsel upon whom service may be had. In a domestic relations case the husband's failure to receive notice because he moved from his residence without notifying the clerk for his new address did not deprive him of due process of law. Eddine v. Eddine, 12 Va. App. 760, 406 S.E.2d 914 (1991).

Service held valid where subsequent proceeding was continuation of first proceeding. — In a proceeding on a motion to vacate, service of a copy of the motion on the attorney who had been defendant's counsel of record in a prohibition proceeding was not defective, since the two proceedings were continuing stages of a proceeding initiated by the defendant and counsel had never withdrawn by leave of court and notice to defendant, pursuant to Supreme Court Rule 1:5. Virginia Dep't of Cors. v. Crowley, 227 Va. 254, 316 S.E.2d 439 (1984).

Until counsel had effectively withdrawn pursuant to provisions of Rule 1:5 of the Rules of the Virginia Supreme Court, service upon him was proper. Francis v. Francis, 30 Va. App. 584, 518 S.E.2d 842 (1999).

II. DECISIONS UNDER PRIOR LAW.

Editor's note. — The case cited below was decided under corresponding provisions of former law. The term "this section," as used below, refers to former provisions.

This section deals, in broad language, with cases generally. Davis v. Davis, 206 Va. 381, 143 S.E.2d 835 (1965).

§ 8.01-315. Notice to be mailed defendant when service accepted by another. — No judgment shall be rendered upon, or by virtue of, any instrument in writing authorizing the acceptance of service of process by another on behalf of any person who is obligated upon such instrument, when such service is accepted as therein authorized, unless the person accepting service shall have made and filed with the court an affidavit showing that he mailed or caused to be mailed to the defendant at his last known post-office address at least ten days before such judgment is to be rendered a notice stating the time when and place where the entry of such judgment would be requested. (Code 1950, § 8-70; 1977, c. 617.)

§ 8.01-316. Service by publication; when available. — A. Except in condemnation actions, an order of publication may be entered against a defendant in the following manner:

1. An affidavit by a party seeking service stating one or more of the following grounds:

a. That the party to be served is (i) a foreign corporation, (ii) a foreign unincorporated association, order, or a foreign unincorporated common carrier, or (iii) a nonresident individual, other than a nonresident individual fiduciary who has appointed a statutory agent under § 26-59; or

b. That diligence has been used without effect to ascertain the location of the party to be served; or

c. That the last known residence of the party to be served was in the county or city in which service is sought and that a return has been filed by the sheriff that the process has been in his hands for twenty-one days and that he has been unable to make service; or

2. In any action, when (i) a pleading states that there are or may be persons, whose names are unknown, interested in the subject to be divided or disposed of; (ii) briefly describes the nature of such interest; and (iii) makes such persons defendants by the general description of "parties unknown"; or

3. In any action, when (i) the number of defendants upon whom process has been served exceeds ten and (ii) it appears by a pleading, or exhibit filed, that such defendants represent like interests with the parties not served with process.

Under subdivisions 1 and 2 of this section, the order of publication may be entered by the clerk of the court. Under this subdivision such order may be entered only by the court.

Every affidavit for an order of publication shall state the last known post office address of the party against whom publication is asked, or if such address is unknown, the affidavit shall state that fact.

B. The cost of such publication shall be paid initially by the party seeking service; however, such costs ultimately may be recoverable pursuant to § 17.1-601. (Code 1950, § 8-71; 1952, c. 522; 1977, c. 617; 1982, c. 384; 1983, c. 467; 1996, c. 352; 1999, c. 353.)

REVISERS' NOTE

Section 8.01-316 amends former § 8-71: (1) in subsection 1 a, foreign unincorporated associations, orders and common carriers are added to the list of parties which can be served by order of publication; (2) subsection 1 c, which consolidates former § 8-71 and former Rule 2:6 (b), does not substantially change former practice, because the "twice delivered" requirement of former § 8-71 has been eliminated from Rule 2:6. Other minor changes have been made.

Cross references. — As to service by publication on corporations, see §§ 8.01-301 and 8.01-303. As to service by publication on unincorporated associations, see § 8.01-305. As to when order of publication shall be posted and mailed, and time after publication for case to be tried or heard, see § 8.01-317. For statute providing that personal service out of State shall have effect of order of publication, see § 8.01-320. For statutes concerning orders of publication in divorce suits, see §§ 20-104, 20-105, 20-112. As to default where notice is given by publication, see Rule 2:7.

The 1999 amendment rewrote subsection B, which formerly read: "The cost of such publication shall be paid by the petitioner or applicant."

Law Review. — For survey of Virginia law on practice and pleading in the year 1971-1972, see 58 Va. L. Rev. 1309 (1972). For discussion of the question of whether Virginia denies indigents the right to divorce, see 12 U. Rich. L. Rev. 735 (1978).

I. Decisions Under Current Law.
II. Decisions Under Prior Law.

I. DECISIONS UNDER CURRENT LAW.

The purpose of an order of publication, which is in lieu of process, is to bring the defendant into court, to apprise the defendant of the nature of the proceedings, and to notify the party that his or her rights will be affected by the litigation. "Because the notice is constructive only, the order of publication and the statute authorizing it both must be strictly construed." Dennis v. Jones, 240 Va. 12, 393 S.E.2d 390 (1990).

The object of this section and § 8.01-317 is to protect parties by giving them notice and an opportunity to present a defense, and because service by publication constitutes constructive notice only, these sections must be strictly construed. Khanna v. Khanna, 18 Va. App. 356, 443 S.E.2d 924 (1994).

Grounds stated must be true and not idle declarations. — Even though this section provides that the party seeking service shall file an affidavit "stating" one or more of the required grounds, the grounds so stated must, in fact, be true and not merely idle declarations having no factual basis. Dennis v. Jones, 240 Va. 12, 393 S.E.2d 390 (1990).

Grounds stated in the affidavit must in fact be true and not merely idle declarations having no factual basis for purposes of service by publication. Khanna v. Khanna, 18 Va. App. 356, 443 S.E.2d 924 (1994).

The noun "diligence" means "devoted and painstaking application to accomplish an undertaking." The determination whether diligence has been used is a factual question to be decided according to the circumstances of each case. Dennis v. Jones, 240 Va. 12, 393 S.E.2d 390 (1990).

No demonstration of devoted effort to locate defendant. — Mere "informal contacts" with unnamed friends at two governmental agencies, made only prior to the sheriff's effort to serve process, did not demonstrate "devoted and painstaking" efforts to locate defendant, especially where the evidence established without conflict that routine methods were readily available to plaintiff. Dennis v. Jones, 240 Va. 12, 393 S.E.2d 390 (1990).

Husband clearly did not exercise the diligence required in trying to locate wife for purposes of service by publication where it was uncontested that husband knew of and attended the pending criminal proceedings in juvenile and domestic relations court which he initiated by complaint, that he met with wife in court, and that during this same period of time he filed with the circuit court a sworn affidavit stating that he had used due diligence "in attempting to locate [his wife]." Although it was true that he did not know her precise address, he did know of the concurrent proceedings in the juvenile and domestic relations court's office or from the Commonwealth Attorney's office, and in addition, husband's failure to reveal to wife the pending annulment suit prevented her from receiving actual notice by allowing possible acceptance of service. Khanna v. Khanna, 18 Va. App. 356, 443 S.E.2d 924 (1994).

Default judgment void and should have been set aside. — Where, the attempt to serve defendant through the DMV was ineffective, and personal jurisdiction was not obtained over her, the default judgment was void and should have been set aside under the provisions of Code § 8.01-428(A). Dennis v. Jones, 240 Va. 12, 393 S.E.2d 390 (1990).

Insufficient affidavit. — It is necessary under the order of publication method to file an affidavit stating that the party to be served by the order of publication "is" a nonresident individual; a statement that the individual "may not be" a resident of the Commonwealth is insufficient. Richardson v. Parris, 246 Va. 203, 435 S.E.2d 389 (1993).

II. DECISIONS UNDER PRIOR LAW.

Editor's note. — The cases cited below were decided under corresponding provisions of former law. The terms "the statute" and "this section," as used below, refer to former provisions.

The object of this section and § 8.01-317 is to protect the innocent party, provide the defendant with actual notice, and give him an opportunity to make his defense, if he has any. McFarland v. McFarland, 179 Va. 418, 19 S.E.2d 77 (1942).

Section is strictly construed. — Since notice by publication is constructive only, the order of publication, as well as the statute authorizing it must be strictly construed. Steinman v. Jessee, 108 Va. 567, 62 S.E. 275 (1908); Peatross v. Gray, 181 Va. 847, 27 S.E.2d 203 (1943); Forrer v. Brown, 221 Va. 1098, 277 S.E.2d 483 (1981).

The statutes, §§ 8.01-316 and 8.01-317, authorizing an order of publication as a substitute service of process must be strictly construed and applied. Robertson v. Stone, 199 Va. 41, 97 S.E.2d 739 (1957).

And strict compliance is required. — Where constructive service of process is allowed in lieu of personal service, the terms of the statute by which it is authorized and prescribed must be strictly followed, or the service will be invalid. Staunton Perpetual Bldg. & Loan Co. v. Haden, 92 Va. 201, 23 S.E. 285 (1895).

Publication in a proceeding under § 4-56 (now repealed) is entirely different from order of publication which is required under this section. Ives v. Commonwealth, 182 Va. 17, 27 S.E.2d 906 (1943).

Sufficiency of affidavit to authorize proceedings. — The affidavit of the local attorney of a corporation that the names of certain persons to be made defendants to a bill by such corporation are to the affiant unknown is a sufficient compliance with this section to authorize a proceeding by publication against such persons as "parties unknown." Fayette Land Co. v. Louisville & N.R.R., 93 Va. 274, 24 S.E. 1016 (1896).

Affidavit need not be in record nor reduced to writing. — In view of the presumption of regularity, a decree purporting to be against nonresidents, which recited that the order of publication had been duly published and executed, is not open to collateral attack on the ground that the affidavit on which the order was made is not in the record; this section not in terms requiring the affidavit to be reduced to writing. Virginia & W. Va. Coal Co. v. Charles, 251 F. 83 (W.D. Va. 1917), aff'd, 254 F. 379 (4th Cir. 1918), appeal dismissed, 252 U.S. 569, 40 S. Ct. 345, 64 L. Ed. 720 (1920).

Affidavit must be directly attacked. — Infants named as defendants to bill for sale of ancestors' land to pay debts, against whom order for publication is made upon affidavit of their nonresidence, must show falsity of affidavit either then or after they come of full age, in direct proceedings to avoid the decree entered in the suit, and cannot attack it collaterally. Lawson v. Moorman, 85 Va. 880, 9 S.E. 150 (1889).

Service by publication may be made on nonresident executor as defendant. — This section and §§ 8.01-317 to 8.01-320, relating to orders of publication, though general in their character, afford ample authority for a proceeding by publication against a nonresident executor upon a bill for specific execution of a contract to convey real estate contracted to be sold by him, especially where the beneficiaries under the will are residents of the State, are united as defendants, and are before the court on personal service of process. Clem v. Givens, 106 Va. 145, 55 S.E. 567 (1906).

And on unknown heirs. — In a suit for specific performance, a number of persons referred to in the bill as "unknown heirs" were made parties to the proceeding by this general classification and an order of publication was made and published against them as such. No objection was made to the sufficiency of the bill or publication in this respect. It was held that this section expressly authorized this course. Goins v. Garber, 131 Va. 59, 108 S.E. 868 (1921).

§ 8.01-317. **What order of publication to state; how published; when publication in newspaper dispensed with.** — Except in condemnation actions, every order of publication shall give the abbreviated style of the suit, state briefly its object, and require the defendants, or unknown parties, against whom it is entered to appear and protect their interests on or before the date stated in the order which shall be no sooner than fifty days after entry of the order of publication. Such order of publication shall be published once each week for four successive weeks in such newspaper as the court may prescribe, or, if none be so prescribed, as the clerk may direct, and shall be posted at the front door of the courthouse wherein the court is held; also a copy of such order of publication shall be mailed to each of the defendants at the post office address given in the affidavit required by § 8.01-316. The clerk shall cause copies of the order to be so posted, mailed, and transmitted to the designated newspaper within twenty days after the entry of the order of publication. Upon completion of such publication, the clerk shall file a certificate in the papers of the case that the requirements of this section have been complied with. Provided, the court may, in any case where deemed proper, dispense with such publication in a newspaper. The cost of such publication shall be paid by the petitioner or applicant. (Code 1950, § 8-72; 1977, c. 617; 1982, c. 384; 1996, cc. 352, 710.)

REVISERS' NOTE

Section 8.01-317 revises former § 8-72 to mandate that the order of publication contain a specific date by which the party served is required to appear and defend his interests. This clarifies former § 8-72 which required the defendant to appear within 10 days after the last or fourth week of publication and not stipulating when such period was required to commence; instead, under § 8.01-317 publication is required to commence within 10 days of the date the order of publication is entered and the defendant served thereby is required to appear on a date certain specified in the order not less than 50 days after the date of entry of the order.

Cross references. — As to publication of interim notice, see § 8.01-319. As to publication of notice of the taking of an account, see § 8.01-611.

Effect of amendment. — The 1996 amendment by c. 710 substituted "post office address" for "post-office address," in the second sentence and substituted "within twenty days" for "within ten days" in the third sentence.

Law Review. — For discussion of the question of whether Virginia denies indigents the right to divorce, see 12 U. Rich. L. Rev. 735 (1978).

I. Decisions Under Current Law.
II. Decisions Under Prior Law.

I. DECISIONS UNDER CURRENT LAW.

Strict construction of section. — The object of this section and § 8.01-316 is to protect parties by giving them notice and an opportunity to present a defense, and because service by publication constitutes constructive notice only, these sections must be strictly construed. Khanna v. Khanna, 18 Va. App. 356, 443 S.E.2d 924 (1994).

Compliance requires certificate filing. — Compliance with the mailing requirement of this section will not be assumed if certificate attesting to such compliance is absent. Proof that order was posted on a courthouse door and delivered to a newspaper was not proof that the order was also mailed. Instead, the absence of the required certificate plainly suggested the opposite conclusion. Therefore, in the absence of evidence that the clerk's office had filed a certificate of compliance, service of process was defective. Carlton v. Paxton, 14 Va. App. 105, 415 S.E.2d 600, aff'd, 15 Va. App. 265, 422 S.E.2d 423 (1992).

II. DECISIONS UNDER PRIOR LAW.

Editor's note. — The cases cited below were decided under corresponding provisions of former law. The term "this section," as used below, refers to former provisions.

The object of this section and § 8.01-316

is to protect the innocent party, provide the defendant with actual notice, and give him an opportunity to make his defense, if he has any. McFarland v. McFarland, 179 Va. 418, 19 S.E.2d 77 (1942).

Purpose of order of publication. — The order of publication takes the place of process, and its purpose is to bring a party into court, to apprise him of the nature of the proceeding against him, and to notify him that his rights will be affected thereby. Peatross v. Gray, 181 Va. 847, 27 S.E.2d 203 (1943); Jennings v. City of Norfolk, 198 Va. 277, 93 S.E.2d 302 (1956); Robertson v. Stone, 199 Va. 41, 97 S.E.2d 739 (1957).

Section strictly construed. — The statutes, § 8.01-316 and this section, authorizing an order of publication as a substitute service of process must be strictly construed and applied. Robertson v. Stone, 199 Va. 41, 97 S.E.2d 739 (1957).

This section does not require the place of appearance to be stated. If the caption of the order shows the style of the suit and the court in which it is pending, this gives the parties sufficient notice where they must appear, and the words "in the clerk's office of this court" are mere surplusage and may be disregarded. Blalock v. Riddick, 186 Va. 284, 42 S.E.2d 292 (1947).

But the names of parties must be stated. — An order of publication to commence a suit against parties not previously served with process must state their names. Martin v. South Salem Land Co., 94 Va. 28, 26 S.E. 591 (1896).

And stated correctly. — A defendant whose name is "Steinman" is not properly proceeded against by publication where the name is spelled "Stainmau" in the caption of the order which is the notice, and "Stinman" in the part of the publication which is regarded as the warning, although the initials of his Christian name are correctly given in each place. Steinman v. Jessee, 108 Va. 567, 62 S.E. 275 (1908).

Absolute accuracy in identifying party is not required. — Although the person or persons to whom the notice is directed must be identified with reasonable certainty absolute accuracy is not required. Robertson v. Stone, 199 Va. 41, 97 S.E.2d 739 (1957).

A nonresident party to a partition suit was named in the order of publication as Alma E. Robinson whereas her correct name was Alma E. Robertson. The record showed that she took her interest in the land under her father's will which named her Robinson, that she had signed deeds to other lands under this name, and that while the order of publication mailed by the clerk to her correct address was returned marked "unclaimed," she was sent and signed for notice of the hearing before the commissioner. In the light of this evidence the order of publication was a sufficient compliance with the statutes to give the court jurisdiction and its decree ordering the sale was not void. Robertson v. Stone, 199 Va. 41, 97 S.E.2d 739 (1957).

Identification of unknown parties. — When unknown parties are to be proceeded against, it is essential that the order of publication recite some identifying data concerning such parties, such as the class to which the unknown parties belong or the source or origin of any claim they may have; it is not sufficient to merely recite they are not known without specifying how they may be interested in the subject matter of the suit. Forrer v. Brown, 221 Va. 1098, 277 S.E.2d 483 (1981).

Newspaper must be designated. — The newspaper in which the order is to be published must be designated in the order. Forrer v. Brown, 221 Va. 1098, 277 S.E.2d 483 (1981).

The order of publication must show object of suit. — In a suit to set aside a deed made by a special commissioner in a divorce proceeding, process in the wife's suit for divorce being by order of publication, which merely showed that the object of the suit was to obtain a divorce on the ground of desertion, it was held that property rights which in no wise grew out of the marital relation being involved, the order of publication was not sufficient to apprise the defendant of the object of the suit within the meaning of this section. Watson v. Mose, 165 Va. 661, 183 S.E. 428 (1936).

Copy of order must be posted. — Proof that an order of publication has been properly published in a newspaper is not sufficient. It should also be proved that a copy was properly posted. Myrick v. Adams, 18 Va. (4 Munf.) 366 (1815).

Where before an attachment is returned "executed," an order of publication was made, and the order was not posted by the clerk at the front door of the courthouse on the first day of the court after it is entered, the attachment should be abated. Petty v. Frick Co., 86 Va. 501, 10 S.E. 886 (1890).

Decree which recites that the order of publication was duly executed is conclusive as to proper posting. Craig v. Sebrell, 50 Va. (9 Gratt.) 131 (1852).

And where the decree states that publication had been properly made, it will be sufficient, and the court will not look into the record for the evidence of the fact. Moore v. Holt, 51 Va. (10 Gratt.) 284 (1853). See Hunter v. Spotswood, 1 Va. (1 Wash.) 145 (1792); Gibson v. White & Co., 17 Va. (3 Munf.) 94 (1812).

Who may make objection for want of due publication. — Objection for want of due publication against an absent defendant, may be taken, it would seem, by other defendants who may be affected by the decree against him; and if made in the appellate court, will prove fatal, though the absent defendant is not a party in the appeal. Hunter v. Spotswood, 1 Va. (1 Wash.) 145 (1792); Gibson v. White & Co., 17 Va. (3 Munf.) 94 (1812); Craig v. Sebrell, 50 Va. (9 Gratt.) 131 (1852).

Order of publication held insufficient for failure properly to state nonresident parties, or interest of unknown parties, or object of suit. Harris v. Deal, 189 Va. 675, 54 S.E.2d 161 (1949).

§ 8.01-318. Within what time after publication case tried or heard; no subsequent publication required.

— If after an order of publication has been executed, the defendants or unknown parties against whom it is entered shall not appear on or before the date specified in such order, the case may be tried or heard as to them. When the provisions of § 8.01-317, or, if applicable, the provisions of § 8.01-321, have been complied with, no other publication or notice shall thereafter be required in any proceeding in court, or before a commissioner, or for the purpose of taking depositions, unless specifically ordered by the court as to such defendants or unknown parties. (Code 1950, § 8-73; 1968, c. 456; 1977, c. 617.)

REVISERS' NOTE

Section 8.01-318 revises former § 8-73, in part to conform to changes made by § 8.01-317. With regard to notice subsequent to the date specified in the order of publication, the provisions of Rule 2:17 and former § 8-73 are retained, but see § 8.01-427.1 regarding three days notice before a default judgment or decree can be obtained in a circuit court action.

Note: Former § 8-73.1 (Effect of newspaper suspending publication ...) is deleted as superfluous, see § 8.01-317.

Editor's note. — Section 8.01-427.1, referred to in the second sentence of the Revisers' note, was repealed by Acts 1978, c. 426.

I. DECISIONS UNDER PRIOR LAW.

Editor's note. — The cases cited below were decided under corresponding provisions of former law. The term "this section," as used below, refers to former provisions.

Notice of subsequent proceedings. — Where an order of publication has been duly executed against nonresident or unknown defendants, no other notice is required to be given them in any proceeding in court, or before a commissioner, or for the purpose of taking depositions, unless specially ordered by the court. But if they so appear, then they are entitled to notice in all the subsequent proceedings in the suit. Burwell v. Burwell, 78 Va. 574 (1884).

It is entirely competent for the legislature to dispense with more than one publication, and to provide that one publication shall be notice of all proceedings in the cause subsequent to the completion of the order, and the legislature of this State has so provided by this section. Jeffries v. Jeffries, 123 Va. 147, 96 S.E. 197 (1918).

Notice of certification of record not required. — If the original order of publication is found to have been in proper form, it dispenses with the necessity of giving nonresident beneficiaries notice of the application for a certification of the record. Such certification is a "proceeding in court" within the meaning of this section. Blalock v. Riddick, 186 Va. 284, 42 S.E.2d 292 (1947).

Notice of taking of depositions. — Under this section, "the case may be tried or heard" as to the nonresident, but the section does not authorize the taking of the bill for confessed at any time nor the doing of any act before the completion of the order. Depositions taken before that time without other notice than that furnished by the order are not taken pursuant to the statute, and cannot be given in evidence against a nonresident who has not appeared in the case, nor assented thereto. Jeffries v. Jeffries, 123 Va. 147, 96 S.E. 197 (1918).

Decree based on petitions held valid. — Where nonresidents were proceeded against by order of publication, as required by this section, decrees made in the cause are not objectionable because they were based upon a petition filed in the cause of which defendants had no notice, where the petitions were entirely germane to the relief sought by the bill. Johnson v. Merrit, 125 Va. 162, 99 S.E. 785 (1919).

§ 8.01-319. Publication of interim notice.

— A. In any case in which a nonresident party or party originally served by publication has been served as provided by law, and notice of further proceedings in the case is required but no method of service thereof is prescribed either by statute or by order or rule of court, such notice may be served by publication thereof once each week for two successive weeks in a newspaper published or circulated in the city or county in which the original proceedings are pending. If the original proceedings were instituted by order of publication, then the publication of such notice of additional or further proceedings shall be made in the same newspaper. A party, who appears pro se in an action, shall file with the clerk of the court in which the action is pending a written statement of his place of residence and mailing address, and shall inform the clerk in writing of any changes of residence and mailing address during the pendency of the action. The clerk and all parties to the action may rely on the last written statement filed as aforesaid. The court in which the action is pending may dispense with such notice for failure of the party to file the statement herein provided for or may require notice to be given in such manner as the court may determine.

B. Notwithstanding any provision to the contrary in paragraph A hereof, depositions may be taken, testimony heard and orders and decrees entered without an order of publication, when the defendant has been legally served with or has accepted service of process to commence a suit for divorce or for annulling or affirming a marriage, and he or she or the plaintiff:

1. Shall thereafter become a nonresident; or
2. Shall remove from the county or city in which the suit is pending, if a resident thereof, or in which he or she resided at the time of the institution of the suit, or was served with process, without having filed with the clerk of the court where the suit is pending a written statement of his or her intended future place of residence, and a like statement of subsequent changes of residence; or
3. When after such written statement has been filed with the clerk, notice shall have been served upon him or her at the last place of residence given in the written statement as provided by law; or
4. Could not be found by the sheriff of the county or city for the service of the notice, and the party sending the service makes affidavit that he has used due diligence to find the adverse party without success. If such absent party has an attorney of record in such suit, notice shall be served on such attorney, as provided by § 8.01-314.

C. This section shall not apply to orders of publication in condemnation actions. (Code 1950, § 8-76; 1950, p. 68; 1954, c. 333; 1960, c. 16; 1970, cc. 241, 279; 1977, c. 617; 1978, c. 676; 1979, c. 464; 1982, c. 384.)

REVISERS' NOTE

Section 8.01-319 substantially revises former § 8-76 and makes it plain that the publication relates only to interim notices after process has been legally served in the original action. Such interim notice has been principally utilized in divorce actions.

Cross references. — As to service by publication generally, see §§ 8.01-316 through 8.01-318. As to personal service on nonresidents out of State, see § 8.01-320.

Law Review. — For survey of Virginia law on practice and pleading for the year 1969-1970, see 56 Va. L. Rev. 1500 (1970). For survey of Virginia domestic relations law for the year 1977-1978, see 64 Va. L. Rev. 1439 (1978).

I. DECISIONS UNDER CURRENT LAW.

This section compared with § 8.01-314. — This section imposes different, not "less," notice requirements for a pro se litigant than one represented by counsel. A pro se litigant is required to advise the clerk of court of his address and any change in it. If a litigant is not pro se, but is represented by counsel, papers may be served on "an attorney authorized to practice law in this Commonwealth" who has entered a general appearance for the litigant pursuant to § 8.01-314. Both of these provisions serve to ensure that notice of the proceedings may be served on the litigants. Eddine v. Eddine, 12 Va. App. 760, 406 S.E.2d 914 (1991).

Filing of a responsive pleading which contains the pro se party's address is sufficient to satisfy the requirements of subsection A; once this pleading has been filed, if the defendant does not remove from the county, city or state in which the suit is pending, depositions can be taken, oral testimony heard, and orders and decrees entered without publication so long as notice has been served as provided by law. Soliman v. Soliman, 12 Va. App. 234, 402 S.E.2d 922 (1991).

Subsection B inapplicable where service by mail of notice was not proper service. — Since service by mail of the notice of the commissioner's hearing was not proper service pursuant to § 20-99, subsection B was not applicable to the case. Soliman v. Soliman, 12 Va. App. 234, 402 S.E.2d 922 (1991).

Failure to inform clerk of change of address. — If a litigant wishes to be informed of the proceedings, he or she must either keep the court advised of where service may be accomplished or be represented by counsel upon whom service may be had. In a domestic relations case, the husband's failure to receive notice because he moved from his residence without notifying the clerk for his new address did not deprive him of due process of law. Eddine v. Eddine, 12 Va. App. 760, 406 S.E.2d 914 (1991).

In a divorce case, where wife failed to provide a written statement of her address to the clerk of the trial court after her attorney withdrew from the case, and husband mailed the notice and a copy of the decree to the marital residence where wife was served with the bill of complaint, wife's own failure to notify the court and husband of her proper mailing address resulted in her not receiving notice of entry of the final decree. Under these circumstances, the trial court did not err in entering the final decree in wife's absence. Schlieper v. Schlieper, No. 2219-94-4 (Ct. of Appeals Oct. 17, 1995).

§ 8.01-320. Personal service outside of Virginia. — A. Personal service of a process on a nonresident person outside the Commonwealth may be made by: (i) any person authorized to serve process in the jurisdiction where the party to be served is located; or (ii) any person eighteen years of age or older who is not a party or otherwise interested in the subject matter of the controversy and notwithstanding any other provision of law to the contrary, such person need not be authorized by the circuit court to serve process which commences divorce or annulment actions. When the court can exercise jurisdiction over the nonresident pursuant to § 8.01-328.1, such service shall have the same effect as personal service on the nonresident within Virginia. Such service when no jurisdiction can be exercised pursuant to § 8.01-328.1, or service in accordance with the provisions of subdivision 2 a of § 8.01-296 shall have the same effect, and no other, as an order of publication duly executed, or the publication of a copy of process under this chapter, as the case may be; however, depositions may be taken at any time after twenty-one days' notice of the taking of the depositions has been personally served. The person so served shall be in default upon his failure to file a pleading in response to original process within twenty-one days after such service. If no responsive pleading is filed within the time allowed by law, the case may proceed without service of any additional pleadings, including the notice of the taking of depositions.

B. Any personal service of process outside of this Commonwealth executed in such manner as is provided for in this section prior or subsequent to October 1, 1977, in a divorce or annulment action is hereby validated. Personal service of process outside this Commonwealth in a divorce or annulment action may be executed as provided in this section. (Code 1950, § 8-74; 1954, c. 333; 1970, c. 552; 1977, c. 617; 1978, c. 90; 1981, c. 6; 1983, c. 402; 1984, c. 18; 1985, c. 177; 1986, c. 263; 1987, c. 594; 1997, c. 754.)

Editor's note. — Acts 1993, c. 929, cl. 3, as amended by Acts 1994, c. 564, cl. 1, and Acts 1996, c. 616, cl. 3, provided that the amendment to this section by Acts 1993, c. 929, cl. 1, would become effective June 1, 1998, "only if state funds are provided by the General Assembly sufficient to provide adequate resources, including all local costs, for the court to carry out the purposes of this act and to fulfill its mission to serve children and families of the

§ 8.01-321   CODE OF VIRGINIA   § 8.01-321

Commonwealth." The funding was not provided.

Law Review. — For survey of Virginia law on practice and pleading for the year 1969-1970, see 56 Va. L. Rev. 1500 (1970); for the year 1971-1972, see 58 Va. L. Rev. 1309 (1972).

I. Decisions Under Current Law.
II. Decisions Under Prior Law.

I. DECISIONS UNDER CURRENT LAW.

The effect of personal service is to give the trial court no more and no less jurisdiction in the litigation than would have arisen from an order of publication duly posted and published. Mitchell v. Mitchell, 227 Va. 31, 314 S.E.2d 45 (1984).

Effect of decrees and orders. — The meaning of this section is that the trial court can enter decrees and orders affecting a party to the same extent as if the party had been served by publication. Mitchell v. Mitchell, 227 Va. 31, 314 S.E.2d 45 (1984).

Effect of subsection A on manner of service and jurisdiction. — While subsection A limits the effect of service of process on a nonresident outside of Virginia, this section does not pertain to the manner of service or eliminate jurisdiction once conferred. Frederick v. Koziol, 727 F. Supp. 1019 (E.D. Va. 1990).

Limitations of subsection A do not apply to § 8.01-329 A. — As an order of publication confers only in rem jurisdiction, application of subsection A to § 8.01-329 A would destroy the personal jurisdiction conferred by the long-arm statute in § 8.01-328.1; moreover, application of subsection A to § 8.01-329 A would mean that service on the Secretary of the Commonwealth, who need only mail a copy to the person to be served at his last known address, would sustain personal jurisdiction, whereas personal service or substituted service designed to provide actual notice would support only in rem jurisdiction; therefore, the limitations of subsection A do not apply to service of process pursuant to § 8.01-329 A. Frederick v. Koziol, 727 F. Supp. 1019 (E.D. Va. 1990).

Schedule for appearing and filing pleadings. — The party is entitled to the same time schedule for appearing or filing pleadings as such party could have claimed if such party had been served by publication. Mitchell v. Mitchell, 227 Va. 31, 314 S.E.2d 45 (1984).

Applied in Morris v. Morris, 4 Va. App. 539, 359 S.E.2d 104 (1987); Harrel v. Preston, 15 Va. App. 202, 421 S.E.2d 676 (1992).

II. DECISIONS UNDER PRIOR LAW.

Editor's note. — The cases cited below were decided under corresponding provisions of former law. The term "this section," as used below, refers to former provisions.

Personal service is equivalent to order of publication. — The acknowledgment by nonresidents of legal service within the District of Columbia must be treated as equivalent to an order of publication duly posted and published, and does not give the court jurisdiction over the persons of the defendants so as to entitle it to render personal decrees against them. Smith & Winnsatt v. Chilton, 77 Va. 535 (1883).

It is obvious that the personal service of the notice under this section makes such notice not only equivalent to an order of publication duly executed, but gives to the receiver of the notice the advantage and benefit of actual knowledge which he might not otherwise receive. Light v. City of Danville, 168 Va. 181, 190 S.E. 276 (1937).

Personal service outside the State has the same effect as an order of publication duly executed, and upon any trial or hearing under this section such judgment, decree or order shall be entered as may appear just. Cranford v. Hubbard, 208 Va. 689, 160 S.E.2d 760 (1968).

§ 8.01-321. Orders of publication in proceedings to enforce liens for taxes assessed upon real estate. — Whenever an order of publication is entered in any proceeding brought by any county, city or town to enforce a lien for taxes assessed upon real estate, such order need not be published more than once a week for two successive weeks. The party served by publication shall be required to appear and protect his interest by the date stated in the order of publication which shall be not less than twenty-four days after entry of such order. The publication shall in other respects conform to § 8.01-317, and when such publication so conforms, the provisions of § 8.01-318 shall apply. (Code 1950, § 8-77; 1977, c. 617.)

REVISERS' NOTE

Section 8.01-321 revises former § 8-77 to require that the order of publication in tax lien cases contain a specific date by which the party served thereby is required to appear and defend his interests. Cf. § 8.01-317.

§ 8.01-322. Within what time case reheard on petition of party served by publication, and any injustice corrected.

— If a party against whom service by publication is had under this chapter did not appear before the date of judgment against him, then such party or his representative may petition to have the case reheard, may plead or answer, and may have any injustice in the proceeding corrected within the following time and not after:

1. Within two years after the rendition of such judgment, decree or order; but
2. If the party has been served with a copy of such judgment, decree, or order more than a year before the end of such two-year period, then within one year of such service.

For the purpose of subdivision 2 of this section, service may be made in any manner provided in this chapter except by order of publication, but including personal or substituted service on the party to be served, and personal service out of the Commonwealth by any person of eighteen years or older and who is not a party or otherwise interested in the subject matter in controversy. (Code 1950, § 8-78; 1977, c. 617.)

REVISERS' NOTE

Section 8.01-322 makes no substantial change to former § 8-78. The enumeration of the alternative possibilities as to when a rehearing is available clarifies the impact of the present statutory scheme. The revision makes clear that personal service out of State is sufficient.

Law Review. — For 1985 survey of Virginia domestic relations law, see 19 U. Rich. L. Rev. 731 (1985).

I. Decisions Under Current Law.
II. Decisions Under Prior Law.

I. DECISIONS UNDER CURRENT LAW.

Jurisdiction prerequisite to rehearing. — The only case that may be reheard is the one over which the trial court had jurisdiction. Hayes v. Hayes, 3 Va. App. 499, 351 S.E.2d 590 (1986).

A person proceeded against by order of publication is a party not served with process within the meaning of the Code of Virginia. Thus, where service by publication is the method by which personal jurisdiction is sought to be obtained in a divorce proceeding, a jurisdictional question inevitably arises. Hayes v. Hayes, 3 Va. App. 499, 351 S.E.2d 590 (1986).

Defendant who has been served not entitled to two-year period. — The General Assembly has provided that a nonresident defendant who has formal notice of a judgment shall have less time than the usual two-year period to petition for a rehearing. Implicit in this provision is concern that a defendant may not be aware of an adverse judgment or decree until he receives formal notice of it. If a defendant has received personal service at the commencement of the litigation, however, and fails to protect his interests, he accepts the risk of an unfavorable result. Therefore, such a defendant is beyond the intendment of the statute. Mitchell v. Mitchell, 227 Va. 31, 314 S.E.2d 45 (1984).

Section is intended to protect a party who has no knowledge at all of litigation affecting him. Mitchell v. Mitchell, 227 Va. 31, 314 S.E.2d 45 (1984); Stephens v. Stephens, 229 Va. 610, 331 S.E.2d 484 (1985).

Support proceeding not barred. — When the only service upon wife was by publication, and she neither appeared in person nor by

§ 8.01-322 CODE OF VIRGINIA § 8.01-322

counsel, and the court entered a decree dissolving the bonds of matrimony by reason of the separation of the parties for more than two consecutive years immediately preceding the institution of the suit for divorce by husband, this section did not bar wife's statutory right to an award of support against husband when her request was made more than two years after the final decree of divorce was entered. Hayes v. Hayes, 3 Va. App. 499, 351 S.E.2d 590 (1986).

Jurisdiction over equitable distribution application. — The two-year period provided in this section did not vest jurisdiction in the circuit court to reconsider wife's application for equitable distribution. Toomey v. Toomey, 251 Va. 168, 465 S.E.2d 838 (1996).

II. DECISIONS UNDER PRIOR LAW.

Editor's note. — The cases cited below were decided under corresponding provisions of former law. The term "this section," as used below, refers to former provisions.

Section applies alike in equity and at law. — This section is a general statute applicable alike to suits in equity and actions at law. Robertson v. Stone, 199 Va. 41, 97 S.E.2d 739 (1957).

Section is limited by, and must be construed together with, § 8.01-113, which provides that the title of purchasers at judicial sales shall not be disturbed after 12 months from the date of the decree or order confirming the sale, "but there may be restitution of the proceeds to those entitled." Robertson v. Stone, 199 Va. 41, 97 S.E.2d 739 (1957).

This section is not applicable where the defendant was fully cognizant of the proceedings and made several special appearances prior to his general appearance, participated in the proceedings, testified as a witness, and was granted exhaustive hearings. Lawrence v. Lawrence, 212 Va. 44, 181 S.E.2d 640 (1971).

A party who has been proceeded against by order of publication as required is a party "who was not served with process" within the meaning of this statute. Robertson v. Stone, 199 Va. 41, 97 S.E.2d 739 (1957).

This section provides that any defendant who was "not served with process" and who did not appear in a suit may petition for a rehearing within the relevant times prescribed therein. A party proceeded against by an order of publication has not been "served with process" within the meaning of this section. The petitioners, who were so proceeded against and had not appeared in a suit devisavit vel non under § 64.1-88, were therefore entitled under this section to petition the court for a rehearing. Thomas v. Best, 209 Va. 103, 161 S.E.2d 803 (1968).

Effect of acknowledged service. — A defendant in a chancery suit who has acknowledged service of the summons to commence the suit is bound by the decrees and orders entered therein which relate to matters put in issue by the bill, but is not bound by a decree against him founded upon a petition filed in the cause, of which he had no notice, and may, under this section, file a petition in the cause, within the time prescribed therein to have the case made by such petition reheard. Keys Planing Mill Co. v. Kirkbridge, 114 Va. 58, 75 S.E. 778 (1912).

Misrepresentation, fraud, or deceit need not be alleged. — This section, which permits a direct attack, does not require a petitioner to allege or prove misrepresentation, fraud, or deceit as a condition to his right to a rehearing. Thomas v. Best, 209 Va. 103, 161 S.E.2d 803 (1968).

No statute authorizes a court to grant an indefinite time within which to move to reinstate a suit in which a final decree has been rendered, and which has been stricken from the docket, without notice. Hence a decree for divorce a vinculo which gives leave to either party to move the court to reinstate the suit without notice is erroneous. Shelton v. Shelton, 125 Va. 381, 99 S.E. 557 (1919).

Thus, after the prescribed time has expired a bill of review comes too late. Johnson v. Merrit, 125 Va. 162, 99 S.E. 785 (1919).

And leave to file a petition for rehearing does not stop the running of the statute fixing the time within which the petition must actually be filed. Woodson v. Leyburn, 83 Va. 843, 3 S.E. 873 (1887).

But void decree may be attacked after prescribed time. — Failure to file a petition within two years from date of decree is not fatal to that part of a divorce decree which was void, and it could be attacked at any time and in any court in which it was brought into question. Watson v. Mose, 165 Va. 661, 183 S.E. 428 (1936).

Rehearing in partition suit. — One who files a petition under this section for rehearing in a partition suit is entitled to have corrected the injustice created by sale of the property at less than its true value; however, the amount due petitioner is determined by taking the value of the land at the time of the sale rather than at the time of the rehearing. Robertson v. Stone, 199 Va. 41, 97 S.E.2d 739 (1957).

Right to rehearing in divorce suit. — A defendant in a divorce suit who was proceeded against as a nonresident by order of publication, as provided in this section, was not served with process within the meaning of that term as used in this section, and as she did not appear and was not served with a copy of the decree, she was entitled to a rehearing. Sims v. Sims, 140 Va. 435, 126 S.E. 486 (1924).

Unjust compromise agreement. — This section permits a court upon a rehearing to correct "any injustice in the proceedings." An injustice was done to the petitioners and to other heirs and distributees who were not parties to a compromise agreement in a suit under § 64.1-88. By the compromise agreement the parties sought to settle a suit to impeach the decedent's will, which suit, if successful, would have resulted in benefits for all the decedent's heirs and distributees. But the compromise agreement provided that certain heirs and distributees, parties to the agreement, should receive shares of the decedent's estate and that the balance of her estate should be distributed in accordance with the will. The agreement was unjust because it benefited the heirs and distributees who were parties to the agreement, but provided no benefit for the other heirs and distributees. Thomas v. Best, 209 Va. 103, 161 S.E.2d 803 (1968).

Absent defendant may file petition pending appeal. — In a suit in which there is an absent defendant, there is a decree against the home defendant, from which he appeals. Pending the appeal, the absent defendant may file his petition in the court below to be permitted to appear and file his answer in the cause, and may have the decree reheard and set aside, if it is erroneous as to him. If upon such rehearing the decree, or so much of it as is the subject of appeal, is wholly set aside, the appeal will generally be dismissed. But if an appeal is taken from the decree on the rehearing, before the dismissal of the first appeal, the appellate court may refuse to dismiss it. James River & Kanawha Co. v. Littlejohn, 59 Va. (18 Gratt.) 53 (1867).

§ 8.01-323. In what counties city newspapers deemed published for purpose of legal advertisements. — Any newspaper published in a city adjoining or wholly or partly within the geographical limits of any county shall be deemed to be published in such county or counties as well as in such city, for the purpose of legal advertisements. (Code 1950, § 8-80; 1977, c. 617.)

§ 8.01-324. Newspapers which may be used for legal notices and publications. — A. Whenever any ordinance, resolution, notice, or advertisement is required by law to be published in a newspaper, such newspaper, in addition to any qualifications otherwise required by law, shall:

1. Have a bona fide list of paying subscribers;
2. Have been published and circulated at least once a week for twenty-four consecutive weeks without interruption for the dissemination of news of a general or legal character;
3. Have a general circulation in the area in which the notice is required to be published;
4. Be printed in the English language; and
5. Have a second-class mailing permit issued by the United States Postal Service.

B. However, a newspaper which does not have a second-class mailing permit may petition the circuit court for the jurisdiction in which the newspaper is located for authority to publish ordinances, resolutions, notices or advertisements. Prior to filing the petition, the newspaper shall publish a notice of intention to file a petition pursuant to this section in a newspaper published or having general circulation in the jurisdiction in which the petition will be filed. The court shall grant the authority for a period of one year upon finding that the newspaper (i) meets the other requirements of this section; (ii) has been continually published for at least one year, employs a full-time news staff, reports local current events and governmental meetings, has an editorial page, accepts letters to the editor and is, in general, a news forum for the community in which it is circulated; (iii) has a circulation within the community to which the publication is directed and maintains permanent records of the fact and substance of the publication; and (iv) has an audit of circulation certified by an independent auditing firm or a business recognized in the newspaper industry as a circulation auditor. The authority shall be continued for successive one-year periods upon the filing of an affidavit certifying that the newspaper continues to meet the requirements of this subsection.

C. If a county with a population of less than 15,000 had regularly advertised its ordinances, resolutions, notices in a newspaper published in the county

§ 8.01-325   CODE OF VIRGINIA   § 8.01-325

which had a general circulation in the county, a bona fide list of paying subscribers, a second class mailing permit and the newspaper continued to be published in the county and continued to have a general circulation in the county but failed to maintain its bona fide list of paying subscribers and its second class mailing permit, any advertisement of ordinances, resolutions, notices in the newspaper by the county shall be deemed to have been in compliance with this section. (Code 1950, § 8-81; 1977, c. 617; 1983, c. 297; 1989, c. 611; 1992, cc. 392, 537, 719.)

§ 8.01-325. Return by person serving process. — Unless otherwise directed by the court, the person serving process shall make return thereof to the clerk's office within seventy-two hours of service, except when such return would be due on a Saturday, Sunday, or legal holiday. In such case, the return is due on the next day following such Saturday, Sunday, or legal holiday. The process shall state thereon the date and manner of service and the name of the party served.

Proof of service shall be in the following manner:

1. If service by sheriff, the form of the return of such sheriff as provided by the Rules of the Supreme Court; or

2. If service by any other person qualified under § 8.01-293, whether service made in or out of the Commonwealth, his affidavit of such qualifications; the date and manner of service and the name of the party served; and stamped, typed, or printed on the return of process, an annotation that the service was by a private server, and the name, address, and telephone number of the server; or

3. In case of service by publication, the affidavit of the publisher or his agent giving the dates of publication and an accompanying copy of the published order. (Code 1950, §§ 8-52, 8-329; 1977, c. 617; 1996, c. 538.)

REVISERS' NOTE

Section 8.01-325 consolidates in a single section former §§ 8-52 and 8-329 regarding the method of return of service. Though the language of subsections 1 and 2 is more concise than that of former § 8-52, no change in substance is intended. The reference in subsection 1 to the Rules of Court relates to Rules 2:5 and 3:4. Subsection 3 in requiring an affidavit by the publisher or his agent, alters former § 8-329 which, though designating certain publication officials, provides that affidavit of any other person is also sufficient to evidence service by publication.

See also additional service requirements under §§ 8.01-296 and 8.01-427.1 regarding default judgments and decrees.

Editor's note. — Section 8.01-427.1, referred to in the second paragraph of the Revisers' Note, was repealed by Acts 1978, c. 426.

I. Decisions Under Current Law.
II. Decisions Under Prior Law.

I. DECISIONS UNDER CURRENT LAW.

Invalid service of process. — Where nothing in the record established that process server was qualified to serve process under Virginia's procedural requirements, service of process was invalid, and the court did not acquire personal jurisdiction over defendant. Harrel v. Preston, 15 Va. App. 202, 421 S.E.2d 676 (1992).

II. DECISIONS UNDER PRIOR LAW.

Editor's note. — The cases cited below were decided under corresponding provisions of former law. The term "this section," as used below, refers to former provisions.

What constitutes the return. — A return on a writ or process is the short official statement of the officer indorsed thereon of what he has done in obedience to the mandate of the writ, or why he has done nothing. The signature of the officer thereto is no part of the return, but is merely intended to authenticate it. Slingluff v. Collins, 109 Va. 717, 64 S.E. 1055 (1909).

Effect of return "executed in person". — A return "executed in person," signed by the deputy sheriff with his own name and that of his principal shows that the summons was actually served on the defendants. Barksdale v. Neal, 57 Va. (16 Gratt.) 314 (1862).

Return must show time of service. — Upon a return "not found, and copy left, etc.," without showing when the copy was left, it did not appear that the summons was duly served. Wynn v. Wyatt, 38 Va. (11 Leigh) 584 (1841).

Courts will look to dates on return when necessary. — Process to commence a suit is part of the record for the purposes of amendment, and the court will look to the return thereon, when necessary, not only to show the date of the return, but also the date of the execution of the writ. House v. Universal Crusher Corp., 115 Va. 558, 79 S.E. 1049 (1913).

Presumption as to time of return. — In the absence of a date, or other evidence showing when the return of an officer on a writ was made, it is presumed to have been made at a time when he had the right to make it, and in due time, as the prima facie presumption is that the officer has done his duty. Rowe v. Hardy, 97 Va. 674, 34 S.E. 625 (1899).

The court may allow the sheriff to amend his return so as to show a proper service. Stotz v. Collins & Co., 83 Va. 423, 2 S.E. 737 (1887).

When oath required. — The simple statement of an officer as to the manner of service is sufficient, while the statement of another person must be upon oath. This difference under early statutes did not exist, but the statement was required to be on oath, whether made by an officer or another person. Barksdale v. Neal, 57 Va. (16 Gratt.) 314 (1862).

Service by any person is valid if return is verified by affidavit. — This section authorizes service by any person if the return be verified by affidavit. So a plea alleging that the person making the service was the paid agent of the plaintiff, employed to compromise with divers claimants of the land sued for and to aid the plaintiff in recovering the land, etc., is insufficient. King v. Davis, 137 F. 198 (C.C.W.D. Va. 1903), aff'd sub nom. Blankenship v. King, 157 F. 676 (4th Cir. 1906).

§ 8.01-326. Return as proof of service. — No return shall be conclusive proof as to service of process. The return of a sheriff shall be prima facie evidence of the facts therein stated, and the return of a qualified individual under subdivision 2 of § 8.01-293 shall be evidence of the facts stated therein. (1977, c. 627.)

REVISERS' NOTE

Section 8.01-326 alters former case law by abolishing the anachronistic verity rule and providing that a return by any qualified person shall constitute evidence of service and that a sheriff's return shall constitute prima facie evidence of service. The section overrules the line of cases represented by Caskie v. Durham, 152 Va. 345, 147 S.E. 218 (1929).

Law Review. — For survey of Virginia law on practice and pleading for the year 1976-77, see 63 Va. L. Rev. 1459 (1977).

§ 8.01-326.1. Service of process or notice on statutory agent; copy to be sent to defendant and certificate filed with court; effective date of service. — Any statutory agent who has been served with process or notice shall forthwith mail a copy of such process or notice to the person or persons to be served at the last known post office address of such person and file a certificate of compliance with the papers in the action. Service of process or notice on a statutory agent shall be effective as of the date the certificate of compliance is filed with the clerk of the court in which the action or suit is pending. (1990, c. 741.)

§ **8.01-327. Acceptance of service of process.** — Service of process may be accepted by the person for whom it is intended by signing the proof of service and indicating the jurisdiction and state in which it was accepted. However, service of process in divorce or annulment actions may be accepted only as provided in § 20-99.1:1. (1977, c. 617; 1987, c. 594; 1988, cc. 583, 642.)

REVISERS' NOTE

Section 8.01-327 states how service of process may be accepted. The proviso recognizes the specific requirement of § 20-99.1:1 in suits for divorce or annulment (cf. § 20-99).

ARTICLE 5.

Privilege From Civil Arrest.

§ **8.01-327.1. Definition of "arrest under civil process".** — The terms *"arrest under civil process"* and *"civil arrest"* shall be synonymous and shall be the apprehending and detaining of a person pursuant to specific provisions of this title to achieve the following:
  1. A full and proper answer or response to interrogatories under § 8.01-506;
  2. His obedience to the orders, judgments, and decrees of any court. (1977, c. 617; 1984, c. 93.)

REVISERS' NOTE

Section 8.01-327.1 defines, for the first time, "arrest under civil process."

§ **8.01-327.2. Who are privileged from arrest under civil process.** — In addition to the exemptions made by §§ 30-4, 30-6, 30-7, 30-8, 19.2-280, and 44-97, the following persons shall not be arrested, apprehended, or detained under any civil process during the times respectively herein set forth, but shall not otherwise be privileged from service of civil process by this section:
  1. The President of the United States, and the Governor of the Commonwealth at all times during their terms of office;
  2. The Lieutenant Governor of the Commonwealth during attendance at sessions of the General Assembly and while going to and from such sessions;
  3. Members of either house of the Congress of the United States during the session of Congress and for fifteen days next before the beginning and after the ending of any session, and during any time that they are serving on any committee or performing any other service under an order or request of either house of Congress;
  4. A judge, grand juror or witness, required by lawful authority to attend any court or place, during such attendance and while going to and from such court or place;
  5. Members of the national guard or naval militia while going to, attending at, or returning from, any muster or court-martial;
  6. Ministers of the gospel while engaged in performing religious services in a place where a congregation is assembled and while going to and returning from such place; and
  7. Voters going to, attending at, or returning from an election. Such privilege shall only be on the days of such attendance. (1977, c. 617.)

REVISERS' NOTE

The common law is not repudiated by this legislation. Section 8.01-327.2 clarifies former § 8-4.1 by stating that the privilege from arrest under this section does not extend to service of civil process.

Cross references. — As to privilege of members of General Assembly, its clerks and their assistants from arrest, see §§ 30-6, 30-7. As to exemption of members of national guard or naval militia from arrest, see § 44-97.

I. Decisions Under Current Law.
II. Decisions Under Prior Law.

I. DECISIONS UNDER CURRENT LAW.

Judges, grand jurors, and witnesses. — This section does not repudiate the common-law rule, but it does create an exception to the privilege by permitting service of civil process upon a judge, grand juror or witness. Lester v. Bennett, 1 Va. App. 47, 333 S.E.2d 366 (1985).

Attorneys and parties. — Although the common-law privilege was extended to attorneys and parties, this section by its terms does not apply to either attorneys or parties. Therefore, immunity from arrest and service of process is available to a party only if permitted under the common law. Lester v. Bennett, 1 Va. App. 47, 333 S.E.2d 366 (1985).

Person appearing for custody proceeding not immune from process in support action. — The relationship which exists between a suit to enforce support payments and a proceeding to change custody of a minor child is such that to grant immunity to the party who is in Virginia seeking to obtain custody of the minor child from arrest and service of process in connection with an action brought by his former wife to collect delinquent child support payments would obstruct the due administration of justice. Lester v. Bennett, 1 Va. App. 47, 333 S.E.2d 366 (1985).

II. DECISIONS UNDER PRIOR LAW.

Editor's note. — The cases cited below were decided under corresponding provisions of former law. The term "this section," as used below, refers to former provisions.

Judges, attorneys, witnesses, and suitors are exempt from arrest in civil suits during their attendance at court. Commonwealth v. Ronald, 8 Va. (4 Call) 97 (1786).

No civil jurisdiction can be acquired nor civil process served where the criminal process is used as a mere pretense to bring the defendant within the state. Wheeler v. Flintoff, 156 Va. 923, 159 S.E. 112 (1931).

Immunity from civil process should clearly extend to such property of the nonresident witness as is shown to be reasonably necessary to his case while in attendance in court in Virginia. Davis v. Hackney, 196 Va. 651, 85 S.E.2d 245 (1955).

CHAPTER 9.

PERSONAL JURISDICTION IN CERTAIN ACTIONS.

Sec.
8.01-328. Person defined.
8.01-328.1. When personal jurisdiction over person may be exercised.
8.01-329. Service of process or notice; service

Sec.
on Secretary of Commonwealth.
8.01-330. Jurisdiction on any other basis authorized.

§ 8.01-328. Person defined. — As used in this chapter, "person" includes an individual, his executor, administrator, or other personal representative, or a corporation, partnership, association or any other legal or commercial entity, whether or not a citizen or domiciliary of this Commonwealth and whether or not organized under the laws of this Commonwealth. (Code 1950, § 8-81.1; 1964, c. 331; 1977, c. 617.)

Law Review. — For comment, "Personal Jurisdiction over Nonresidents: Some Statutory Developments," see 7 Wm. & Mary L. Rev. 146 (1966). For note, "Obtaining Jurisdiction Over Corporations in Virginia," see 12 U. Rich. L. Rev. 369 (1978). For a note, "Casting the Net: Another Confusing Analysis of Personal Jurisdiction and Internet Contacts in *Telco Communication, Inc. v. An Apple A Day*," see 32 U. Rich. L. Rev. 63 (1998).

I. DECISIONS UNDER CURRENT LAW.

The assertion of in personam jurisdiction by the trial court over the nonresident defendant for a cause of action arising from the consummation of the contract in Virginia between the plaintiff and the nonresident corporation was proper under the provision of the Virginia long-arm statute where the company aggressively reached into Virginia and recruited a Virginia resident for employment elsewhere. Nan Ya Plastics Corp. United States v. DeSantis, 237 Va. 255, 377 S.E.2d 388, cert. denied, 492 U.S. 921, 109 S. Ct. 3248, 106 L. Ed. 2d 594 (1989).

In adopting §§ 8.01-328 to 8.01-330, the legislature evinced a policy of extending the jurisdiction of its courts to the maximum extent permitted by the due process clause of the United States Constitution. Caldwell v. Seaboard Sys. R.R., 238 Va. 148, 380 S.E.2d 910 (1989), cert. denied, 493 U.S. 1095, 110 S. Ct. 1169, 107 L. Ed. 2d 1071 (1990).

Applied in First Charter Land Corp. v. Fitzgerald, 643 F.2d 1011 (4th Cir. 1981); Morris v. Morris, 4 Va. App. 539, 359 S.E.2d 104 (1987).

§ 8.01-328.1. When personal jurisdiction over person may be exercised. — A. A court may exercise personal jurisdiction over a person, who acts directly or by an agent, as to a cause of action arising from the person's:

1. Transacting any business in this Commonwealth;
2. Contracting to supply services or things in this Commonwealth;
3. Causing tortious injury by an act or omission in this Commonwealth;
4. Causing tortious injury in this Commonwealth by an act or omission outside this Commonwealth if he regularly does or solicits business, or engages in any other persistent course of conduct, or derives substantial revenue from goods used or consumed or services rendered, in this Commonwealth;
5. Causing injury in this Commonwealth to any person by breach of warranty expressly or impliedly made in the sale of goods outside this Commonwealth when he might reasonably have expected such person to use, consume, or be affected by the goods in this Commonwealth, provided that he also regularly does or solicits business, or engages in any other persistent course of conduct, or derives substantial revenue from goods used or consumed or services rendered in this Commonwealth;
6. Having an interest in, using, or possessing real property in this Commonwealth;
7. Contracting to insure any person, property, or risk located within this Commonwealth at the time of contracting;
8. Having (i) executed an agreement in this Commonwealth which obligates the person to pay spousal support or child support to a domiciliary of this Commonwealth, or to a person who has satisfied the residency requirements in suits for annulments or divorce for members of the armed forces pursuant to § 20-97 provided proof of service of process on a nonresident party is made by a law-enforcement officer or other person authorized to serve process in the jurisdiction where the nonresident party is located, (ii) been ordered to pay spousal support or child support pursuant to an order entered by any court of competent jurisdiction in this Commonwealth having in personam jurisdiction over such person, or (iii) shown by personal conduct in this Commonwealth, as alleged by affidavit, that the person conceived or fathered a child in this Commonwealth; or
9. Having maintained within this Commonwealth a matrimonial domicile at the time of separation of the parties upon which grounds for divorce or separate maintenance is based, or at the time a cause of action arose for divorce or separate maintenance or at the time of commencement of such suit, if the other party to the matrimonial relationship resides herein.

§ 8.01-328.1 CIVIL REMEDIES AND PROCEDURE § 8.01-328.1

Jurisdiction in subdivision 9 of this subsection is valid only upon proof of service of process pursuant to § 8.01-296 on the nonresident party by a person authorized under the provisions of § 8.01-320. Jurisdiction under subdivision 8 (iii) of this subsection is valid only upon proof of personal service on a nonresident pursuant to § 8.01-320.

B. Using a computer or computer network located in the Commonwealth shall constitute an act in the Commonwealth. For purposes of this subsection, "use" and "computer network" shall have the same meanings as those contained in § 18.2-152.2.

C. When jurisdiction over a person is based solely upon this section, only a cause of action arising from acts enumerated in this section may be asserted against him; however, nothing contained in this chapter shall limit, restrict or otherwise affect the jurisdiction of any court of this Commonwealth over foreign corporations which are subject to service of process pursuant to the provisions of any other statute. (Code 1950, § 8-81.2; 1964, c. 331; 1977, c. 617; 1978, c. 132; 1981, c. 6; 1982, c. 313; 1983, c. 428; 1984, c. 609; 1986, c. 275; 1987, c. 594; 1988, cc. 866, 878; 1992, c. 571; 1999, cc. 886, 904, 905.)

The 1999 amendments. — The 1999 amendments by cc. 886, 904 and 905 are identical, and added subsection B and redesignated former subsection B as subsection C.

Law Review. — For article, "Virginia's 'Long Arm' Statute: An Argument for Constitutionality of Jurisdiction over Nonresident Individuals," see 51 Va. L. Rev. 712 (1965). For note on Virginia's "long arm" statute, see 51 Va. L. Rev. 719 (1965). For comment on jurisdiction over breach of warranty actions, see 22 Wash. & Lee L. Rev. 152 (1965). For survey of Virginia law on torts for the year 1969-1970, see 56 Va. L. Rev. 1419 (1970). For survey of Virginia law on practice and pleading for the year 1970-1971, see 57 Va. L. Rev. 1561 (1971). For survey of Virginia law on practice and pleading for the year 1973-1974, see 60 Va. L. Rev. 1572 (1974). For discussion of fourth circuit developments in the 1973 term, see 31 Wash. & Lee L. Rev. 61 (1974). For note, "Obtaining Jurisdiction Over Corporations in Virginia," see 12 U. Rich. L. Rev. 369 (1978). For survey of Virginia practice and pleading for the year 1977-1978, see 64 Va. L. Rev. 1501 (1978). For note on Shaffer v. Heitner and the establishment by the Supreme Court of a uniform approach to state court jurisdiction, see 35 Wash. & Lee L. Rev. 131 (1978). For article, "Products Liability and the Virginia Statute of Limitations — A Call for the Legislative Rescue Squad," see 16 U. Rich. L. Rev. 323 (1982). For article on recent developments in Virginia domestic relations law, see 68 Va. L. Rev. 507 (1982). For article on personal jurisdiction over domestic and alien defendants, see 69 Va. L. Rev. 85 (1983). For note on minimum contacts and contracts, see 40 Wash. & Lee L. Rev. 1639 (1983). For note on due process aspects of Virginia's domestic relations long-arm legislation, see 24 Wm. & Mary L. Rev. 229 (1983). For article on the single contract as minimum contacts, see 28 Wm. & Mary L. Rev. 89 (1986). For 1987 survey of Virginia civil procedure and practice, see 21 U. Rich. L. Rev. 667 (1987). As to spousal support jurisdiction, see 22 U. Rich. L. Rev. 565 (1988). For note, "Invalidation of Residency Requirements for Admission to the Bar: Opportunities for General Reform," see 23 U. Rich. L. Rev. 231 (1989). For survey on civil procedure and practice in Virginia for 1989, see 23 U. Rich. L. Rev. 511 (1989). For a note, "Casting the Net: Another Confusing Analysis of Personal Jurisdiction and Internet Contacts in *Telco Communication, Inc. v. An Apple A Day,*" see 32 U. Rich. L. Rev. 63 (1998). For an article, "Domestic Relations," see 31 U. Rich. L. Rev. 1069 (1997). For a review of civil practice and procedure in Virginia for year 1999, see 33 U. Rich. L. Rev. 801 (1999).

I. Decisions Under Current Law.
  A. General Consideration.
  B. Transacting Business.
    1. In General.
    2. Minimum Contacts.
    3. What Constitutes Transacting Business.
  C. Tortious Injury.
    1. In General.
    2. Acts or Omissions in Commonwealth.
    3. Breach of Warranty.
    4. Acts or Omissions Outside the Commonwealth.

II. Decisions Under Prior Law.
   A. General Consideration.
   B. Transacting Business.
      1. In General.
      2. Minimum Contacts.
      3. What Constitutes Transacting Business.
   C. Contracting to Supply Services or Things.
   D. Tortious Injury.
      1. Acts or Omissions in Commonwealth.
      2. Acts or Omissions Outside Commonwealth.
      3. Breach of Warranty.
   E. Real Property in Virginia.

I. DECISIONS UNDER CURRENT LAW.

A. General Consideration.

Purpose of Virginia's long-arm statute is to assert jurisdiction over nonresidents who engage in some purposeful activity in this State to the extent permissible under the due process clause. Miller & Rhoads v. West, 442 F. Supp. 341 (E.D. Va. 1977); GE Co. v. Rose Int'l, Inc., 475 F. Supp. 602 (W.D. Va. 1979); August v. HBA Life Ins. Co., 17 Bankr. 628 (Bankr. E.D. Va. 1982), rev'd on other grounds, 734 F.2d 168 (4th Cir. 1984); United Coal Co. v. Land Use Corp., 575 F. Supp. 1148 (W.D. Va. 1983); Bassett Furn. Indus., Inc. v. Sexton, 596 F. Supp. 454 (W.D. Va. 1984).

The purpose of the Virginia long-arm statute is to assert jurisdiction to the extent permissible under the due process clause of the federal Constitution. Brown v. ABC, 704 F.2d 1296 (4th Cir. 1983).

"Person" defined. — The definition of the term "person" in this section is all inclusive, sufficient to bring within the ambit of the statute every natural or fictitious entity, including trustees, capable of performing the acts, such as transacting business, which are made the basis for the exercise of personal jurisdiction over a nonresident. Combs v. Dickenson-Wise Medical Group, 233 Va. 177, 355 S.E.2d 553 (1987).

The plain meaning of the phrase "arising from" is "caused by"; thus, it is evident that Virginia's General Assembly used the phrase "arising from" to require that there be a causal link between the acts relied on for personal jurisdiction and the cause of action asserted. Significantly, courts agree that this causation element requires more than simple "but-for" causation; it requires something akin to legal or proximate causation. Chedid v. Boardwalk Regency Corp., 756 F. Supp. 941 (E.D. Va. 1991).

The plain meaning of the phrase "arising from" is "caused by." Verosol B.V. v. Hunter Douglas, Inc., 806 F. Supp. 582 (E.D. Va. 1992).

Section construed to extend in personam jurisdiction to constitutional limit. — This section, as in the case of other state statutes as well, has been construed to extend in personam jurisdiction to the outmost perimeters of due process. Peanut Corp. of Am. v. Hollywood Brands, Inc., 696 F.2d 311 (4th Cir. 1982).

This section has often been recognized as permitting jurisdiction to the extent due process permits. Sowards v. Switch Energy Co., 744 F. Supp. 1399 (W.D. Va. 1990).

Jurisdiction has been construed to extend as broadly as that permitted by due process. Chisholm v. UHP Projects, Inc., 1 F. Supp. 2d 581 (E.D. Va. 1998).

Jurisdiction exists if due process met. — Where the assertion of personal jurisdiction can withstand due process scrutiny, then such assertion must also be valid under this section. GE Co. v. Rose Int'l, Inc., 475 F. Supp. 602 (W.D. Va. 1979).

Reach of statute and due process inquiries coincide. — While determining whether personal jurisdiction exists typically requires a two-step process, in which the court first assesses whether the particular facts and circumstances of a case fall within the language of the long-arm statute and then considers whether the due process clause would permit such jurisdiction to be asserted, because this section extends personal jurisdiction to the fullest extent permitted by the due process clause the court's inquiry is collapsed into the single question of whether asserting jurisdiction violates the due process clause. Coastal Video Communications Corp. v. Staywell Corp., 59 F. Supp. 2d 562 (E.D. Va. 1999).

Extent of personal jurisdiction. — The Virginia long-arm statute extends personal jurisdiction to the full extent permitted by due process. Reynolds Metals Co. v. FMALI, Inc., 862 F. Supp. 1496 (E.D. Va. 1994).

Jurisdiction of courts over out-of-state defendants. — Except where the General Assembly has placed explicit affirmative limitations on the extent of long-arm jurisdiction in Virginia, as it has in subdivisions A 4 and A 5 of this section, the courts of Virginia, including the United States District Courts sitting in diversity cases, may take personal jurisdiction over out-of-state defendants under each of the

§ 8.01-328.1   CIVIL REMEDIES AND PROCEDURE   § 8.01-328.1

subdivisions of this section to the extent allowed by the due process clause of the Fourteenth Amendment. Darden v. Heck's, Inc., 459 F. Supp. 727 (W.D. Va. 1978).

Placement of website on internet inadequate to justify jurisdiction. — Personal jurisdiction could not be exercised over a defendant where the only conduct alleged by the plaintiff was the defendant's placement of a website on the internet with knowledge of the possibility that the site might be accessed in Virginia; the plaintiff had made no showing of any purposeful availment by the defendant of Virginia, as distinct from any other state, or even any purposeful activity directed at or related to the plaintiff. Rannoch, Inc. v. Rannoch Corp., 52 F. Supp. 2d 681 (E.D. Va. 1999).

Activity must be purposefully targeted. — Although subdivision A 4 of this section is an assertion of specific jurisdiction and thus does not require the "systematic and continuous contacts" needed for the constitutional exercise of general jurisdiction, less than "continuous and systematic" contacts will satisfy the due process clause only when the activity out of which the claim arises is purposefully targeted at the forum state; some element of purposeful direction or availment is constitutionally necessary. Rannoch, Inc. v. Rannoch Corp., 52 F. Supp. 2d 681 (E.D. Va. 1999).

Statute provides additional methods of service on nonresident not exclusive methods. — The long arm statute provides additional methods of service on a nonresident, not the exclusive methods of service, and did not supplant the previously authorized method of personal service provided by law. Ragouzis v. Ragouzis, 10 Va. App. 312, 391 S.E.2d 607 (1990).

Long arm statute intended to facilitate service on nonresident defendants. — The provisions of the long arm statute were clearly intended to facilitate service on nonresident defendants, not to make it more difficult to serve them. Ragouzis v. Ragouzis, 10 Va. App. 312, 391 S.E.2d 607 (1990).

When jurisdiction is sought pursuant to a long-arm statute, a dual analysis is normally required: first, it must be determined whether the statutory language, as a matter of construction, purports to assert personal jurisdiction over a defendant; and second, assuming that the answer to the first question is affirmative, it must be determined whether the statutory assertion of personal jurisdiction is consonant with the due process clause of U.S. Const., amend. 14. Peanut Corp. of Am. v. Hollywood Brands, Inc., 696 F.2d 311 (4th Cir. 1982).

Plaintiff must satisfy two burdens to justify the courts' exercise of jurisdiction over defendant. First it must prove that defendant somehow meets one of the statutory requirements of this section. Second it must prove that the court's exercise of jurisdiction will not overstep the limits of due process. Omega Homes, Inc. v. Citicorp Acceptance Co., 656 F. Supp. 393 (W.D. Va. 1987).

Personal jurisdiction analysis is a two step process. First, each alleged cause of action must be measured for a fit against each alleged part of the Long Arm Statute, this section. If no fit is found, the inquiry is at an end: There is no personal jurisdiction. On the other hand, if any of the Long Arm provisions fit, a further inquiry must be made before jurisdiction can be sustained. This further inquiry is to ascertain whether the Long Arm's reach in that particular instance exceeds its constitutional grasp. Processing Research, Inc. v. Larson, 686 F. Supp. 119 (E.D. Va. 1988).

If long arm statute applies, then due process determination needed. — If the long-arm statute applies, the court must then determine whether asserting personal jurisdiction over defendant thereunder comports with the due process clause of the Fourteenth Amendment. Verosol B.V. v. Hunter Douglas, Inc., 806 F. Supp. 582 (E.D. Va. 1992).

Burden of proof. — Because the plaintiff must prove personal jurisdiction, it bears the burden of proving that its version of the parties' relationship is accurate and that the defendant's version is not. Initiatives, Inc. v. Korea Trading Corp., 991 F. Supp. 476 (E.D. Va. 1997).

Foreseeability. — The foreseeability that is critical to due process analysis is not the mere likelihood that a product will find its way into the forum State. Rather, it is that the defendant's conduct and connection with the forum State are such that he should reasonably anticipate being haled into court there. Gordonsville Indus., Inc. v. American Artos Corp., 549 F. Supp. 200 (W.D. Va. 1982).

When jurisdiction over a person is based solely upon this section, only a cause of action arising from acts enumerated in this section may be asserted against a defendant. Unidyne Corp. v. Aerolineas Argentinas, 590 F. Supp. 391 (E.D. Va. 1984).

The long arm of this section does not extend to a contract formed and performed outside Virginia. Promotions, Ltd. v. Brooklyn Bridge Centennial Comm., 763 F.2d 173 (4th Cir. 1985).

In order for a court to obtain in personam jurisdiction and the respective ability to enforce personal monetary obligations, the nonresident must be personally served by a law-enforcement officer or other official authorized to serve process pursuant to subdivision A 8 (i) of this section. Morris v. Morris, 4 Va. App. 539, 359 S.E.2d 104 (1987).

Where the wife proceeded by an order of publication but did not personally serve the husband with process, the trial court did not obtain personal jurisdiction over the husband and could not direct him to pay spousal support. Morris v. Morris, 4 Va. App. 539, 359 S.E.2d 104 (1987).

Personal jurisdiction absent in divorce decree. — Where record proved that agreement that was incorporated in the decree was signed by the parties in Maryland two years prior to the filing of the divorce, and the agreement referred to Virginia only as the place where the parties were married, the recitations in the divorce pleadings and the final divorce decree were plainly insufficient to enable a Virginia court to obtain personal jurisdiction over the husband, a nonresident, under any provision of this section. Price v. Price, 17 Va. App. 105, 435 S.E.2d 652 (1993).

Lack of personal jurisdiction in divorce decree not automatic bar to effective dissolution. — Although the circuit court did not obtain personal jurisdiction over the husband in the divorce action, the allegations in the divorce pleadings sufficed to provide the trial court with in rem jurisdiction to dissolve the marriage. Price v. Price, 17 Va. App. 105, 435 S.E.2d 652 (1993).

Lack of personal jurisdiction in divorce decree bar to subsequent enforcement of support provisions. — Although the circuit court entered a valid divorce decree it lacked personal jurisdiction over the husband when the divorce decree was entered in 1985 and it had no power to enter an enforceable support order. Consequently, the judge's order ruling the husband in contempt for violating the support provisions of the 1985 divorce decree was reversed and the rule to show cause was dismissed. Price v. Price, 17 Va. App. 105, 435 S.E.2d 652 (1993).

The record proved that husband was aware of the proceeding against him, a fact made clear by both the duly authenticated certificates of notice and husband's entrance by special appearance to contest the trial court's jurisdiction. Husband did not appeal the court's subsequent finding that it did have personal jurisdiction, and consequently that finding became final 21 days after entry of the order. Such actions are sufficient to constitute waiver. Burd v. Burd, No. 1156-96-4 (Ct. of Appeals Feb. 11, 1997).

Limitations of § 8.01-320 A do not apply to § 8.01-329 A. — As an order of publication confers only in rem jurisdiction, application of § 8.01-320 A to § 8.01-329 A would destroy the personal jurisdiction conferred by the long-arm statute in this section; moreover, application of § 8.01-320 A to § 8.01-329 A would mean that service on the Secretary of the Commonwealth, who need only mail a copy to the person to be served at his last known address, would sustain personal jurisdiction, whereas personal service or substituted service designed to provide actual notice would support only in rem jurisdiction; therefore, the limitations of § 8.01-320 A do not apply to service of process pursuant to § 8.01-329 A. Frederick v. Koziol, 727 F. Supp. 1019 (E.D. Va. 1990).

Service of process was proper under § 8.01-329 A. — Where personal jurisdiction was authorized by the Virginia long-arm statute, this section, and defendant was served in the manner provided for in Chapter 8 of the Virginia Code, namely under § 8.01-296(2)(a), service of process was proper under § 8.01-329 A of the Virginia long-arm statute, and defendant's motion to dismiss for lack of jurisdiction over the person was denied. Frederick v. Koziol, 727 F. Supp. 1019 (E.D. Va. 1990).

Choice-of-law provisions not determinative. — While choice-of-law provisions in contracts are relevant in determining whether a defendant purposely availed itself of a particular state's law, they cannot alone establish jurisdiction. Initiatives, Inc. v. Korea Trading Corp., 991 F. Supp. 476 (E.D. Va. 1997).

Foreign executor or administrator. — The enactment of the Virginia long-arm statute has removed the old Virginia common-law rule that an executor or administrator is not subject to suit in a state other than that of his appointment, unless he brings into or collects from the state assets of the decedent's estate. Crosson v. Conlee, 745 F.2d 896 (4th Cir. 1984), cert. denied, 470 U.S. 1054, 105 S. Ct. 1759, 84 L. Ed. 2d 822 (1985).

Illustrative cases. — Aside from the allegations in the amended complaint, the plaintiff had not indicated the factual basis for the court to exercise jurisdiction over the defendants who appeared to reside in Mexico. The allegations did not discharge plaintiff's burden on a motion for summary judgment where there had been ample opportunity for discovery. Dunham v. Hotelera Canco S.A. de C.V., 933 F. Supp. 543 (E.D. Va. 1996).

Where both husband and wife had lived in Virginia but currently neither party lived there, and where Virginia circuit court ruled that it was bound by the 1992 South Carolina order, including that court's finding that it had jurisdiction over husband and the subject matter, the trial court erred by declining to exercise its continued jurisdiction to enforce its original support order. While husband argued that the divorce decree was ex parte, the record demonstrated conclusively that the Virginia circuit court had personal jurisdiction over husband at the time the divorce decree was entered. Commonwealth, Va. Dep't of Social Servs. ex rel. Kenitzer v. Richter, 23 Va. App. 186, 475 S.E.2d 817 (1996).

Where none of foreign defendant's officers, directors, or employees visited Virginia in connection with the contract, and the correspondence, meeting agenda, and the contract itself did not contain any indications that foreign defendant expected plaintiff to conduct business on its behalf in Virginia, the defendant had not purposefully availed itself of the benefits and protection of Virginia law and there was no specific personal jurisdiction over defendant. Initiatives, Inc. v. Korea Trading Corp., 991 F. Supp. 476 (E.D. Va. 1997).

A plaintiff seeking a judgment declaring that its publication did not infringe the copyright on a publication produced by the defendant failed to establish that the court could exercise personal jurisdiction over the defendant where there was no evidence that the defendant's publication, although advertised in Virginia by catalogue and over the internet, had ever been sold in the state and, where, even if there was such evidence, the fact that the defendant's publication had been sold in Virginia would be irrelevant, since, if the plaintiff's activities constituted infringement, this would be true regardless of where the defendant's publication was sold; absent evidence that the plaintiff's action arose from the defendant's sale of the copyrighted material or the defendant's other exploitation of the copyright in Virginia, the court did not have specific, personal jurisdiction over the defendant. Coastal Video Communications Corp. v. Staywell Corp., 59 F. Supp. 2d 562 (E.D. Va. 1999).

Applied in Clymer v. Grzegorek, 515 F. Supp. 938 (E.D. Va. 1981); August v. HBA Life Ins. Co., 734 F.2d 168 (4th Cir. 1984); Unidyne Corp. v. Aerolineas Argentinas, 640 F. Supp. 354 (E.D. Va. 1985); Lomah Elec. Targetry, Inc. v. ATA Training Aids Aust. Pty. Ltd., 828 F.2d 1021 (4th Cir. 1987); Selman v. American Sports Underwriters, Inc., 697 F. Supp. 225 (W.D. Va. 1988); Mock v. Mock, 11 Va. App. 616, 400 S.E.2d 543 (1991); Raymond, Colesar, Glaspy & Huss v. Allied Capital Corp., 761 F. Supp. 423 (E.D. Va. 1991); Harrel v. Preston, 15 Va. App. 202, 421 S.E.2d 676 (1992); African Dev. Co. v. Keene Eng'g, 963 F. Supp. 522 (E.D. Va. 1997); Frontline Test Equip., Inc. v. Greenleaf Software, Inc., 10 F. Supp. 2d 583 (W.D. Va. 1998); Kilmer v. Ryder Integrated Logistics, Inc., 82 F. Supp. 2d 568 (W.D. Va. 1999).

B. Transacting Business.

1. In General.

Real limitation is due process clause. — The real limitation on the exercise of personal jurisdiction under the "transacting business" provision of this section is the Due Process Clause of the Fourteenth Amendment. Industrial Carbon Corp. v. Equity Auto & Equip. Leasing Corp., 737 F. Supp. 925 (W.D. Va. 1990), appeal dismissed, 922 F.2d 835 (4th Cir. 1991).

The "manifest purpose" of subdivision A 1 is to assert jurisdiction over nonresidents who engage in some purposeful activity in Virginia to the extent permissible under the due process clause; the acts conferring jurisdiction under this section must coincide with the acts giving rise to the substantive claim, and no single factor is dispositive; the determination whether the statute permits jurisdiction requires examination of both the quantity and quality of the contacts, and this involves questions such as who benefited from the contacts, who initiated them and why, whether the contacts involved any person's physical presence in the state, and what further conduct in the forum state was contemplated by the parties. Raymond, Colesar, Glaspy & Huss v. Allied Capital Corp., 761 F. Supp. 423 (E.D. Va. 1991).

The purpose of this long-arm statute is to extend jurisdiction to the extent permissible under the Due Process Clause. Affinity Memory & Micro v. K&Q Enterprises, 20 F. Supp. 2d 948 (E.D. Va. 1998).

Subdivision A 1 repudiates "doing business" rationale. — Subdivision A 1 of this section the "transacting business" subdivision of the long-arm statute, is a repudiation of the "doing business" rationale for the assertion of in personam jurisdiction over nonresident defendants. Viers v. Mounts, 466 F. Supp. 187 (W.D. Va. 1979).

The scope of the transacting business requirement of this section is limited only by the parameters of due process. Medeco Sec. Locks, Inc. v. Fichet-Bauche, 568 F. Supp. 405 (W.D. Va. 1983); Bassett Furn. Indus., Inc. v. Sexton, 596 F. Supp. 454 (W.D. Va. 1984).

This section is a single-act statute. — This section is a "single act" statute, requiring only a single act of doing business by a person in the Commonwealth to confer jurisdiction over that person by the courts of this State. Darden v. Heck's, Inc., 459 F. Supp. 727 (W.D. Va. 1978); Williams Crane & Rigging, Inc. v. B & L Sys., 466 F. Supp. 956 (E.D. Va. 1979); Associates Fin. Servs. Co. v. McPeek, 222 Va. 176, 278 S.E.2d 847 (1981).

This section contemplates the extension of personal jurisdiction to encompass all nonresidents who transact any business within the state so long as the cause of action asserted arises from the nonresident's transaction of business. One act of transacting business will suffice. Viers v. Mounts, 466 F. Supp. 187 (W.D. Va. 1979).

Since this section provides "transacting any business in this Commonwealth," it is a single-act statute requiring only one transaction in Virginia to confer jurisdiction on its courts. United Coal Co. v. Land Use Corp., 575 F. Supp. 1148 (W.D. Va. 1983).

A single act may constitute a transaction of business under the Virginia long-arm statute if the asserted action arose from that one transaction. Unidyne Corp. v. Aerolineas Argentinas, 590 F. Supp. 391 (E.D. Va. 1984).

This section is a single-act statute. Therefore, jurisdiction will exist with respect to a cause of action arising from the business transaction if by that one act the nonresident can be said to have engaged in some purposeful activity in Virginia. United States v. Pierre Point Shipping & Inv. Co., 655 F. Supp. 1379 (E.D. Va. 1987).

A single act amounting to "transacting business" and giving rise to a cause of action may be sufficient to confer jurisdiction under this statute. Affinity Memory & Micro v. K&Q Enterprises, 20 F. Supp. 2d 948 (E.D. Va. 1998).

If by that act defendant engaged in purposeful activity. — A single act committed in Virginia by a nonresident is sufficient to invoke the protection of the jurisdictional statute with respect to any cause of action arising therefrom if by that one act the nonresident can be said to have engaged in some purposeful activity in Virginia. Viers v. Mounts, 466 F. Supp. 187 (W.D. Va. 1979).

Single act rule applies only when assertion of jurisdiction meets due process. — Since asserting in personam jurisdiction under the "transacting business" subdivision is limited by the parameters of the due process clause, the inquiries concerning (1) the reach of the statutory authority for the assertion of in personam jurisdiction over nonresidents and (2) the limits due process places on such an assertion of jurisdiction merge and become identical. Thus, the "single act" rule of the long-arm statute is applicable only when the assertion of jurisdiction thereunder comports with due process. Viers v. Mounts, 466 F. Supp. 187 (W.D. Va. 1979).

Jurisdiction must be based on acts within state. — The statute confers no jurisdiction for the assertion of claims that do not arise from the defendant's acts in the state. City of Va. Beach v. Roanoke River Basin Ass'n, 776 F.2d 484 (4th Cir. 1985).

The pertinent factors for assessing whether a defendant has transacted business in the forum are (1) where any contracting occurred, and where negotiations took place, (2) who initiated the contact, (3) the extent of the communications, both telephonic and written, between the parties and (4) where the obligations of the parties under the contract were to be performed. Affinity Memory & Micro v. K&Q Enterprises, 20 F. Supp. 2d 948 (E.D. Va. 1998).

Activities supporting jurisdictional and substantive claims must coincide. — In order for a cause of action to arise from business transacted in Virginia, the activities that support the jurisdictional claim must coincide with those that form the basis of the plaintiff's substantive claim. A single act by a nonresident which amounts to "transacting business" in Virginia and gives rise to a cause of action may be sufficient to confer jurisdiction upon Virginia courts. City of Va. Beach v. Roanoke River Basin Ass'n, 776 F.2d 484 (4th Cir. 1985).

Nonresident successor in interest to the manufacturer. — The absence of continuity of either ownership or management precluded the finding that any de facto corporate reorganization occurred; therefore, the federal court lacked jurisdiction over the nonresident successor in interest to the manufacturer. Crawford Harbor Assocs. v. Blake Constr. Co., 661 F. Supp. 880 (E.D. Va. 1987).

2. Minimum Contacts.

Nonresident must have certain "minimum contacts" with the forum which evince his purposeful availment of the privilege of conducting activities within the forum State, thus invoking the benefits and protections of its laws. Viers v. Mounts, 466 F. Supp. 187 (W.D. Va. 1979).

Due process requires that a nonresident have certain minimum contacts within the territory of the forum so that the maintenance of the action does not offend traditional notions of fair play and substantial justice. Darden v. Heck's, Inc., 459 F. Supp. 727 (W.D. Va. 1978).

To satisfy constitutional due process a defendant must have certain minimum contacts with the forum state such that maintenance of a suit does not offend traditional notions of fair play and substantial justice. Virginia's long-arm statute has been construed to be as broad as the standard of constitutional due process. Weight v. Kawasaki Motors Corp., 604 F. Supp. 968 (E.D. Va. 1985).

A state court may exercise this kind of long-arm jurisdiction only if there also exist minimum contacts between the defendant and the forum so that the exercise of jurisdiction does not exceed the parameters of constitutional guarantees of due process. Omega Homes, Inc. v. Citicorp Acceptance Co., 656 F. Supp. 393 (W.D. Va. 1987).

Even if the requirements of the long-arm statute are satisfied, due process requires that the defendant have sufficient minimum contacts with Virginia so that requiring it to defend its interests in Virginia would not offend traditional notions of fair play and substantial justice. Affinity Memory & Micro v. K&Q Enterprises, 20 F. Supp. 2d 948 (E.D. Va. 1998).

The requirement of purposeful activity in Virginia serves the purpose of ensuring that the constitutional requirements of due process are met, namely, that the defendants have certain "minimum contacts" with the forum state which evince their purposeful availment of the privilege of conducting activities within the forum state. United States v. Douglas, 626 F. Supp. 621 (E.D. Va. 1985).

Defendant must purposefully avail itself

of privilege of conducting activities in forum state. — It is essential in each case that there be some act by which the defendant purposefully avails itself of the privilege of conducting activities within the forum State, thus invoking the benefits and protections of its laws. Darden v. Heck's, Inc., 459 F. Supp. 727 (W.D. Va. 1978).

This section cannot be used to obtain jurisdiction over a nonresident defendant corporation, unless that corporation purposefully avails itself of the privilege of conducting business activities in Virginia. Herman Cantor Corp. v. Cattle King Packing Co., 22 Bankr. 604 (Bankr. E.D. Va. 1982).

Jurisdiction is constitutionally appropriate where the defendant has purposefully directed its activities at the forum and the litigation arises out of or relates to those activities. Affinity Memory & Micro v. K&Q Enterprises, 20 F. Supp. 2d 948 (E.D. Va. 1998).

Jurisdiction may be exercised where defendant so avails itself. — Where a foreign corporation has purposefully availed itself of the privilege of conducting business activities within Virginia and thereby invoked the benefits and protection of the laws of this State, it would not offend traditional notions of fair play and substantial justice to require it to submit to the jurisdiction of the courts of this State. August v. HBA Life Ins. Co., 17 Bankr. 628 (Bankr. E.D. Va. 1982), rev'd on other grounds, August v. HBA Life Ins. Co., 734 F.2d 168 (4th Cir. 1984).

More than simple connection required between state and contract sued upon. — This section exists for the purpose of asserting jurisdiction over nonresidents to the extent permissible under the due process clause; however, there must be more than a simple connection between the contract which is being sued upon and the state asserting jurisdiction. Herman Cantor Corp. v. Cattle King Packing Co., 22 Bankr. 604 (Bankr. E.D. Va. 1982).

Minimum contacts may exist even though no certificate under former § 13.1-102 required. — The contention that a firm was not "doing business" in Virginia in such a manner as to necessitate procurement of a certificate of authority from the State Corporation Commission under former § 13.1-102, and therefore has insufficient "minimum contact" with Virginia to permit in personam jurisdiction must be rejected. Peanut Corp. of Am. v. Hollywood Brands, Inc., 696 F.2d 311 (4th Cir. 1982).

Absent minimum contacts there can be no question of venue. Herman Cantor Corp. v. Cattle King Packing Co., 22 Bankr. 604 (Bankr. E.D. Va. 1982).

Jurisdiction over parent corporation. — For the court to exercise in personam jurisdiction over a defendant parent corporation, the plaintiff should show (1) that the subsidiary's activities in Virginia are sufficient to confer jurisdiction pursuant to this section and (2) that the relationship between the parent and its subsidiary is such that the subsidiary's actions can be imputed to the parent. The plaintiff can fulfill the second requirement by proving either that the parent uses the subsidiary as its alter ego, or that the subsidiary is the implied agent of the parent. Omega Homes, Inc. v. Citicorp Acceptance Co., 656 F. Supp. 393 (W.D. Va. 1987).

Standing alone, the mere existence of a parent-subsidiary relationship does not conclusively indicate that a parent is within a court's jurisdiction by way of the subsidiary's in-state activities. Omega Homes, Inc. v. Citicorp Acceptance Co., 656 F. Supp. 393 (W.D. Va. 1987).

Generally, court can impute behavior of in-state subsidiary to out-of-state parent corporation if the plaintiff proves that the defendant operates in state through an agent. Omega Homes, Inc. v. Citicorp Acceptance Co., 656 F. Supp. 393 (W.D. Va. 1987).

Multiemployer bargaining group without physical presence in the state. — A multiemployer bargaining group had sufficient minimum contacts with Virginia so as to sustain the assertion of personal jurisdiction without offending the traditional notions of fair play and justice, despite lack of physical presence in this state. Doe v. Connors, 796 F. Supp. 214 (W.D. Va. 1992).

Jurisdiction over parent corporation where subsidiary is fictitious shield. — A court can assert jurisdiction over a parent corporation if the plaintiff's evidence demonstrates that the subsidiary is a fictitious shield erected by the parent to protect itself from liability. Omega Homes, Inc. v. Citicorp Acceptance Co., 656 F. Supp. 393 (W.D. Va. 1987).

Out-of-state parent corporation held not subject to jurisdiction. — Court could not exercise long-arm jurisdiction over defendant where there was no evidence that out-of-state defendant parent corporation controlled the services that flowed through its subsidiaries or that the subsidiaries were maintained solely to shield defendant from legal liability despite the facts that defendant supervised the creation of the subsidiaries, undertook to finance them and even contributed management skills and resources. Omega Homes, Inc. v. Citicorp Acceptance Co., 656 F. Supp. 393 (W.D. Va. 1987).

British tour service advertising in Virginia. — Where defendant, a British tour service, did not have a representative in Virginia who solicited business but did solicit business from the public by advertising its services through travel agencies in the state and by sending marketing brochures to travel agencies for the perusal of the public, the defendant doubtless intended to develop its market in

Virginia and to reap the resulting economic benefits; therefore, defendant was subject to Virginia's long-arm statute. Carter v. Trafalgar Tours Ltd., 704 F. Supp. 673 (W.D. Va. 1989). But see Chedid v. Boardwalk Regency Corp., 756 F. Supp. 941 (E.D. Va. 1991).

Advertising and solicitation activities in Virginia. — Plaintiff who slipped and fell at a New Jersey gambling casino could not sue the casino in Virginia on the basis of the casino's advertising and solicitation activities in Virginia; except for remote and inadequate "but-for" linkage, there was no causal relation whatever between the advertising and solicitation activities plaintiff relied on to establish personal jurisdiction and the alleged acts of negligence plaintiff relied on as the cause of his injury. Chedid v. Boardwalk Regency Corp., 756 F. Supp. 941 (E.D. Va. 1991).

Minimum contacts held not present. — Defendant corporation's activities did not constitute minimum contacts necessary for jurisdiction in a patent action where it wrote a letter to plaintiff threatening patent infringement litigation, placed advertisements in national trade magazines which reached subscribers in Virginia, made minimal sales in Virginia, but maintained no sales agent in Virginia. Defendant's failure to prevent sales of its product is of no jurisdictional value. Medeco Sec. Locks, Inc. v. Fichet-Bauche, 568 F. Supp. 405 (W.D. Va. 1983).

Where defendant had on a few occasions exhibited its wares in Virginia and had accepted, in New York, orders submitted by Virginia customers, the total activities of defendant within Virginia cannot be said to have invoked the protection and benefit of the laws of Virginia so as to allow the use of the long-arm statute so to obtain personal jurisdiction. A contract of sale accepted in a foreign state and performed there would not satisfy the minimum contacts rule. Luke v. Dalow Indus., Inc., 566 F. Supp. 1470 (E.D. Va. 1983).

Automobile liability insurer could anticipate the risk that its clients would travel in their automobiles to different states and become involved in accidents and litigation there, particularly where it promised to defend its policyholders from any claim or suit arising from a loss or accident within its policy territory, which included the entire United States; therefore, the insurer's contacts with this Commonwealth were sufficient to establish personal jurisdiction. Rossman v. State Farm Mut. Auto. Ins. Co., 832 F.2d 282 (4th Cir. 1987).

Automobile liability insurer must answer to suit in Virginia if its assured causes injury here. Rossman v. Consolidated Ins. Co., 595 F. Supp. 505 (E.D. Va. 1984), dismissed, 785 F.2d 305 (4th Cir. 1986).

3. What Constitutes Transacting Business.

One act of transacting business committed in Virginia by a nonresident may be sufficient to bring the nonresident within the jurisdictional reach of the court. United States v. Douglas, 626 F. Supp. 621 (E.D. Va. 1985).

Jurisdiction will exist with respect to a cause of action arising from the business transaction if by that one act the nonresident can be said to have engaged in some purposeful activity in Virginia. United States v. Douglas, 626 F. Supp. 621 (E.D. Va. 1985).

A settled principle, to be sure, is that a single act may constitute transaction of business under Virginia's Long Arm, provided the action arose from that one transaction. But this principle simply serves to underscore that it is the nature and quality of acts and not their number that determines whether transaction of business has occurred. It does not mean that any single act suffices. Processing Research, Inc. v. Larson, 686 F. Supp. 119 (E.D. Va. 1988).

Although a single act by a non-resident defendant may qualify as "transacting business," the single act must be significant in order to confer jurisdiction. DeSantis v. Hafner Creations, Inc., 949 F.Supp. 419 (E.D. Va 1996).

In order for a cause of action to arise from any business transacted in Virginia, the activities that support the jurisdictional claim must coincide with those that form the basis of the plaintiff's substantive claim. St. Jarre v. Heidelberger Druckmaschinen, 816 F. Supp. 424 (E.D. Va. 1993), aff'd, 19 F.3d 1430 (4th Cir. 1994).

Advertising, negotiating, mailing, and communicating held to constitute transacting business. — Seller of scuba equipment purposefully availed itself of privileges of transacting business in Virginia and therefore was subject to personal jurisdiction of district court where seller solicited business in Virginia in nationally distributed magazine subsequently negotiated and undertook contractual obligation with Virginia resident, mailed purchase orders to buyer of air compressor in Virginia, accepted payment from Virginia and after sale of air compressor, continued to deal with buyer in Virginia by telephone and through mails. Cancun Adventure Tours, Inc. v. Underwater Designer Co., 862 F.2d 1044 (4th Cir. 1988).

A contract which is accepted and becomes effective in another forum generally will not satisfy minimum contacts. Superfos Invs. Ltd. v. Firstmiss Fertilizer, Inc., 774 F. Supp. 393 (E.D. Va. 1991).

Consummation of contract in Virginia. — The assertion of in personam jurisdiction by the courts of Virginia over a nonresident defendant for causes of action arising from the consummation of a contract in Virginia between the nonresident and a Virginia citizen is contemplated by the "transacting business" subdivision of the long-arm statute, and is also constitutionally sound. Viers v. Mounts, 466 F. Supp. 187 (W.D. Va. 1979).

Where on at least two fairly recent occasions, the defendants sold and shipped to this Commonwealth machines covered by patents upon which the declaratory judgment respecting infringement was sought, those contacts satisfied the statutory requirement that the cause of action arise from the defendants' transacting business within this Commonwealth. Furmanite Am., Inc. v. Durango Assocs., 662 F. Supp. 348 (E.D. Va. 1986).

The assertion of in personam jurisdiction by the trial court over the nonresident defendant for a cause of action arising from the consummation of the contract in Virginia between the plaintiff and the nonresident corporation was proper under the provision of the Virginia long-arm statute where the company aggressively reached into Virginia and recruited a Virginia resident for employment elsewhere. Nan Ya Plastics Corp. United States v. DeSantis, 237 Va. 255, 377 S.E.2d 388, cert. denied, 492 U.S. 921, 109 S. Ct. 3248, 106 L. Ed. 2d 594 (1989).

Contacts with Virginia clearly were sufficient to constitute the transaction of business within the meaning of the long-arm statute where defendant initiated the relationship with plaintiffs inviting them to become subfranchisors, knowing that they were Virginia residents, defendant anticipated that subfranchisors, would establish franchises in Virginia, the contract was sent to plaintiffs in Virginia and signed by them in Virginia, the parties communicated on a daily basis via telephone, mail and fax, defendant sent letters and other communications to plaintiffs in Virginia and received payments from franchises located in Virginia, the corporate defendant contends that the contract was performed in Georgia because that was where payments were received, however, the contract also called for plaintiffs to recruit and set up franchises in Virginia, to oversee those franchises for the franchisor, and to collect payments from franchisees in Virginia for remittance to defendant, and a substantial part, if not all, of the contract was in fact performed in Virginia. Holland v. Hay, 840 F. Supp. 1091 (E.D. Va. 1994).

Negotiation of terms of subsequent contract insufficient. — In an action for breach of contract, negotiation of the essential terms of a subsequent contract was insufficient under the due process clause to satisfy the minimum contacts standard necessary to support an assertion of in personam jurisdiction over nonresidents. Viers v. Mounts, 466 F. Supp. 187 (W.D. Va. 1979).

Mere contract negotiations carried out in Virginia between a state citizen and a nonresident, with execution and performance of the contract in a foreign forum, would not appear to provide the nexus with Virginia necessary for in personam jurisdiction to be asserted under the "transacting business" subdivision for a cause of action arising from that contract's breach, since in such a situation the nonresident doubtfully would have been in a position to purposefully avail (himself) of the privilege of conducting activities within (Virginia), thus invoking the benefits and protections of its laws. Viers v. Mounts, 466 F. Supp. 187 (W.D. Va. 1979).

Mere contract negotiations carried out in Virginia between a state citizen and a nonresident, with execution and performance of the contract in a foreign forum is not a sufficient transaction of business to assert jurisdiction over the defendant. United Coal Co. v. Land Use Corp., 575 F. Supp. 1148 (W.D. Va. 1983).

Activities of nonresident buyer. — While the courts have shown themselves more willing to assume jurisdiction over a nonresident seller than over a nonresident buyer, to the extent the buyer vigorously negotiates, perhaps dictates, contract terms, inspects production facilities and otherwise departs from the passive buyer role it would seem that any unfairness which would normally be associated with the exercise of long-arm jurisdiction over him disappears. GE Co. v. Rose Int'l, Inc., 475 F. Supp. 602 (W.D. Va. 1979).

The mere fact of the defendant's status as a buyer could not function to protect it from the reach of this section where the sum total of the defendant's activities leading to the purchase which was the subject of the action against the defendant served to negate its protestations of passivity. GE Co. v. Rose Int'l, Inc., 475 F. Supp. 602 (W.D. Va. 1979).

Officers and directors held beyond reach of section. — Officers and directors of a foreign corporation which transacted business in this State without a certificate of authority were beyond the reach of the long-arm statute where plaintiff sought under § 13.1-119 (now § 13.1-758) to hold them jointly and severally liable for breach of contract, as the plaintiff neither alleged nor provided evidence that the corporation was an agent of the defendants either by express, incidental or apparent power. Miller & Rhoads v. West, 442 F. Supp. 341 (E.D. Va. 1977).

Airline's contract with second airline to transport property from New York to Virginia does not make the second airline the agent of the first airline for purposes of obtaining in personam jurisdiction over the first airline. Unidyne Corp. v. Aerolineas Argentinas, 590 F. Supp. 391 (E.D. Va. 1984).

One isolated shipment did not establish jurisdiction. — Where defendant appears to have done everything possible to confine its

United States business to its home state of Alaska during this transaction, and never had any dealings with Virginia whatsoever other than when it shipped goods to Virginia on one isolated occasion for the convenience of purchaser, who could not remain in Alaska to take delivery there as originally contemplated by the parties, jurisdiction over defendant was lacking. Chung v. NANA Dev. Corp., 783 F.2d 1124 (4th Cir.), cert. denied, 479 U.S. 948, 107 S. Ct. 431, 93 L. Ed. 2d 381 (1986).

The district court's determination that defendant's failure to insure the goods rendered it the party at fault did not overcome a lack of jurisdiction, where defendant's actions were not sufficiently purposeful. Personal jurisdiction is not to be determined by a peek at the merits, but established on independent grounds. Chung v. NANA Dev. Corp., 783 F.2d 1124 (4th Cir.), cert. denied, 479 U.S. 948, 107 S. Ct. 431, 93 L. Ed. 2d 381 (1986).

Mere phone calls and letters, and arguably fax communications, in furtherance of a transaction, are insufficient to form a basis for personal jurisdiction. Superfos Invs. Ltd. v. Firstmiss Fertilizer, Inc., 774 F. Supp. 393 (E.D. Va. 1991).

Telephonic and written communications. — Where telephonic negotiations occurred with one of the participants located in Virginia, and numerous written communiques between the parties were sent to and received in Virginia, there was sufficient "contracting" in Virginia to amount to the transaction of business from which the cause of action arose. Peanut Corp. of Am. v. Hollywood Brands, Inc., 696 F.2d 311 (4th Cir. 1982).

Mere telephone conversations, telex messages and letters negotiating a transaction are insufficient to form a basis for in personam jurisdiction. Unidyne Corp. v. Aerolineas Argentinas, 590 F. Supp. 391 (E.D. Va. 1984).

Where defendants merely forwarded an unsolicited letter outlining suggestion of plaintiff Virginia corporation that New York City market pieces of the Brooklyn Bridge in commemoration of its centennial to the company that controlled the Brooklyn Bridge logo, district court properly dismissed action brought against them by plaintiff for lack of personal jurisdiction under this section. Promotions, Ltd. v. Brooklyn Bridge Centennial Comm., 763 F.2d 173 (4th Cir. 1985).

Mere telephone conversations, telexes and letters negotiating a transaction do not suffice. Processing Research, Inc. v. Larson, 686 F. Supp. 119 (E.D. Va. 1988).

Payment, delivery, and negotiations constitute transacting business. — The aggregate contacts of paying the purchase price in the forum state, delivering purchased goods in the state, traveling to the state for negotiations or inspections making a contract with an economic impact on the state, and construing the agreement according to the law of the forum, constituted "transacting business" in Virginia. United Coal Co. v. Land Use Corp., 575 F. Supp. 1148 (W.D. Va. 1983).

Communications, negotiations, and appointment of agent held to constitute transacting business. — Where defendant sent several telephonic, telexic, and written communications to Virginia; negotiated the original contract and a contract dispute in the State; received a signed letter-agreement from Virginia and returned it there; authorized a Virginia corporation to be its exclusive sales agent with a third corporation; received payments allegedly drawn on and finally paid by Virginia banks; obtained shipment orders from its agent; and reaped the benefits of having its Virginia agent sell the goods, it transacted business in Virginia, although the goods sold under the contract never passed through the Commonwealth and the formal contract was not executed by the defendant in Virginia. United Coal Co. v. Land Use Corp., 575 F. Supp. 1148 (W.D. Va. 1983).

Corporation was subject to personal jurisdiction in absence of executed contract. — Where a proposed contract between defendant auto leasing company, a Michigan corporation, and plaintiff Virginia corporation, required defendant to lease to plaintiff personal property which defendant owned and which was located in Virginia, where proposed contract if executed would have made defendant subject to suit in Virginia on the contract, and where defendant granted to plaintiff, by sending it the proposal, the power to consummate such a contract with it, and encouraged plaintiff to send a deposit to it as called for in the proposal, defendant could be held liable to suit in Virginia in regard to the proposed contract. Industrial Carbon Corp. v. Equity Auto & Equip. Leasing Corp., 737 F. Supp. 925 (W.D. Va. 1990), appeal dismissed, 922 F.2d 835 (4th Cir. 1991).

Where plaintiffs' claims of fraud and violations of the Virginia Retail Franchising Act stem directly from the ongoing contractual relationship between parties and their status as franchisor and subfranchisor, a status created by the subfranchise contract, ultimately was the basis suit, clearly, the cause of action arose from defendant's transaction of business in Virginia within meaning of long-arm statute. Holland v. Hay, 840 F. Supp. 1091 (E.D. Va. 1994).

Foreign motor vehicle manufacturer. — Recent decisions in which foreign motor vehicle manufacturers had a sales arrangement have held that the fact that a foreign parent conducts its marketing and distribution in the United States through an independent distribution system does not shield it from in personam jurisdiction. Due process is satisfied as long as the foreign manufacturer knew and intended that its vehicles would be sold in Virginia. Weight v. Kawasaki Motors Corp., 604 F. Supp. 968 (E.D. Va. 1985).

Legal representation. — Where one defendant met with attorney in Virginia to discuss the possibility of attorney's firm representing defendants in California, engaged the Virginia law firm to represent them in their California litigation, settled disputes concerning that representation via telephone communications between attorneys in Virginia, and defendants in Oregon, and after attorney had been representing defendant for more than two years in the California case, one defendant traveled to Virginia to meet with the firm and discussed retainer agreement and unpaid fees and costs, and where numerous correspondence was exchanged between law firm, and defendants mailed checks to attorneys in Virginia to cover costs and attorney's fees, these circumstances, when considered together, held to constitute contacts sufficient to satisfy the Virginia long-arm statute. Hirschkop & Grad v. Robinson, 757 F.2d 1499 (4th Cir. 1985).

Decision to associate with law firm on case. — Few examples of transacting business are more classic than California attorney's decision to associate a Virginia law firm on a case and his subsequent dealings with that firm; because California attorney transacted business in Virginia, and because Virginia attorney's cause of action arose directly from those activities, the Virginia long-arm statute was satisfied. English & Smith v. Metzger, 901 F.2d 36 (4th Cir. 1990).

A lawyer who knowingly serves abusive process in a jurisdiction may expect to be haled into court where service was effectuated, since by such action he is purposely availing himself of the privilege of conducting activities within the forum state. Schleit v. Warren, 693 F. Supp. 416 (E.D. Va. 1988).

Gathering financial information and publishing newspaper article. — A Massachusetts corporation which analyzed financial information gathered from the Federal Reserve Board and distributed its analysis to its customers, mostly money market and cash managers, some of whom were in Virginia, which after specifying that credit for the material be spelled out, furnished information to a financial columnist based in New York City who used it to write an article which appeared in the Richmond Times-Dispatch, stating that plaintiff, a Virginia bank, had a $476,000 annualized net loss and would reach zero equity within eleven months, could be subjected to personal jurisdiction under Virginia long-arm statute in a defamation suit brought by the Virginia bank. Blue Ridge Bank v. Veribanc, Inc., 755 F.2d 371 (4th Cir. 1985).

Placing advertisement in national periodical and responding to inquiry not enough to invoke section. — Where an aircraft broker did nothing more than place a classified ad in a national periodical specializing in used aircraft and then respond to an inquiry from a prospective buyer and its bank in Virginia, his actions did not fit the actions necessary to invoke this section. Processing Research, Inc. v. Larson, 686 F. Supp. 119 (E.D. Va. 1988).

The total sale of little more than $300 worth of goods in one year, triggered by advertisement in a national magazine, did not satisfy the "substantial revenue" basis for jurisdiction. DeSantis v. Hafner Creations, Inc., 949 F.Supp. 419 (E.D. Va 1996).

Where the defendant purposefully availed itself of the opportunity to provide ongoing benefit coverage for Commonwealth residents under a health and benefit plan, including the plaintiff's decedent, such activity constitutes the transaction of business within the meaning of subdivision A 1 of this section, particularly in light of the fact that benefit claims under the plan appeared to be handled exclusively through correspondence between the plan and its participants. Skelton v. Lowen, 665 F. Supp. 469 (E.D. Va. 1987).

Sales of equipment to Virginia corporation. — A Minnesota corporation which, over a period of years, sold $120,000 worth of equipment to a Virginia corporation, and solicited business by telephone from this corporation, and sent them a series of letters and bids, and on at least one occasion sent a representative to visit the corporation in Virginia, clearly transacted business in Virginia, for jurisdictional purposes under this section. Eastern Scientific Mktg., Inc. v. Tekna-Seal, Inc., 696 F. Supp. 173 (E.D. Va. 1988).

Employment on commission basis. — In a breach of contract and tort action, where plaintiff received at his Virginia mailing address defendant's letter offering him a position as a manufacturer's representative and a later letter purporting to change the terms of his sales commissions, and finally a letter purporting to terminate his employment with defendant, and in addition, plaintiff regularly received his commission checks in Virginia and discussed the terms and conditions of his employment by phone from Virginia, those exchanges constituted transaction of business within this state. Herbert v. Direct Wire & Cable, Inc., 694 F. Supp. 192 (E.D. Va. 1988).

Claim for sales commissions. — A claim by a Pennsylvania sales representative against a Minnesota corporation for commissions earned on sales to a Virginia customer, seeking damages for potential future sales in the state, where it was sole sales representative, arose out of transactions in Virginia for purposes of this section. Eastern Scientific Mktg., Inc. v. Tekna-Seal, Inc., 696 F. Supp. 173 (E.D. Va. 1988).

Delivery, communications, and repair of boat held to constitute transacting business. — The defendant transacted business within the meaning of this section where, even though the defendant had initially agreed to deliver boat to South Carolina, the defendant was paid additional consideration to deliver purchased vessel to Virginia, the defendant's employees had telephone conversations with the plaintiff, discussed the status of repairs and improvements to the boat, and finally, the repair work was performed in Virginia. Rivera v. Witt, 257 Va. 280, 512 S.E.2d 558 (1999).

C. Tortious Injury.

1. In General.

The exercise of jurisdiction under subdivision A 4 of this section has two requirements: (1) a tortious injury in Virginia caused by an act or omission outside of Virginia; and (2) a relationship between the defendant and the Commonwealth which exists in any one of three ways which are specified in A 4. Blue Ridge Bank v. Veribanc, Inc., 755 F.2d 371 (4th Cir. 1985); Robinson v. Egnor, 699 F. Supp. 1207 (E.D. Va. 1988).

Jurisdiction under subdivision A 4 requires the court to find that the specific statutory requirements are met even in those situations where it could plausibly be argued that a lesser standard would meet due process, inasmuch as insistence that these particulars be satisfied is a course mandated by legislative judgment. Robinson v. Egnor, 699 F. Supp. 1207 (E.D. Va. 1988).

The fact that the qualifier "tortious" is present in subsection A 4 but missing in A 5 need not concern the court. The word "tortious" is something of a misnomer, since whether or not the injury was tortious is generally the fact at issue. Whether the court may assert jurisdiction pursuant to A 4 or A 5, therefore, turns on whether injury has occurred in Virginia. Pennington v. McDonnell Douglas Corp., 576 F. Supp. 868 (E.D. Va. 1983).

Factors considered under "substantial revenue" test. — Certain factors of the "substantial revenue" test have been established: (1) that revenue derived from sales, and not profits, must be substantial, (2) that the revenue may be derived from a single transaction; and (3) that the sale itself need not take place in Virginia so long as the goods are used or consumed in this State. Gordonsville Indus., Inc. v. American Artos Corp., 549 F. Supp. 200 (W.D. Va. 1982).

Percentage of total sales occurring in Virginia. — One fact that may be considered is the percentage of total sales of the nonresident corporation which occur in Virginia. Gordonsville Indus., Inc. v. American Artos Corp., 549 F. Supp. 200 (W.D. Va. 1982).

It is difficult to identify an absolute amount which ipso facto must be deemed substantial. Gordonsville Indus., Inc. v. American Artos Corp., 549 F. Supp. 200 (W.D. Va. 1982).

Tortious injury is the wrongful death of the decedent, not economic consequences thereof. — Wrongful death acts may grant relief for intangible injury to the survivors, but the tortious injury is the death of the decedent, not the economic consequences that flow from his death. Injury to the plaintiff did not occur in Virginia where the decedent was killed in an airplane crash in the Mediterranean Sea, and therefore subsections A 4 and A 5 of this section were not applicable. Pennington v. McDonnell Douglas Corp., 576 F. Supp. 868 (E.D. Va. 1983).

Abuse of civil process. — In determining whether Virginia's long-arm statute purports to confer jurisdiction for abuse of civil process, the court must decide two sub-issues: first, whether the process server acts as the agent of the attorney, thereby coming under the general requirements of the Virginia long-arm statute; and second, whether the tortious "act" occurred in this forum, thereby bringing the facts within the specific requirements of subdivision A 3 of this section. Schleit v. Warren, 693 F. Supp. 416 (E.D. Va. 1988).

An attorney may be held liable for torts arising from a process server's acts done within the scope of the agency relationship. Schleit v. Warren, 693 F. Supp. 416 (E.D. Va. 1988).

Communication with media. — Because all actions of the defendants were performed outside of Virginia, their single respective acts in communicating with the media regarding plaintiff were insufficient to confer jurisdiction unless one of the three relationships described in subdivision (A)(4) existed between the defendant and the Commonwealth even if the plaintiff was injured within the state. Defendants' telephone interviews with the media were too random, fortuitous, and attenuated to support the court's exercise of either specific or general jurisdiction. Barry v. Whalen, 796 F. Supp. 885 (E.D. Va. 1992).

Where defendant was not physically present in Virginia when committing the tort at issue, this section did not apply. DeSantis v. Hafner Creations, Inc., 949 F.Supp. 419 (E.D. Va 1996).

2. Acts or Omissions in Commonwealth.

The due process considerations of the United States Constitution are not a limi-

tation on subdivision A 3 of the Virginia long-arm statute. Navis v. Henry, 456 F. Supp. 99 (E.D. Va. 1978).

But, instead, subdivision A 3 is less inclusive than due process. Navis v. Henry, 456 F. Supp. 99 (E.D. Va. 1978).

Defendant's action constituted "act" in Commonwealth. — Defendant organization's placement of plaintiff's name on a "scab" list, which was posted on various bulletin boards in a computer center electronic switchboard system operated within the state, which subsequently resulted in the termination of his contract negotiations with a potential employer, constituted an "act" in this Commonwealth. Krantz v. Air Line Pilots Ass'n, Int'l, 245 Va. 202, 427 S.E.2d 326 (1993).

Single act is sufficient. — A single act causing tortious injury by a mere sojourner within the State subjects that person to service of process under the Virginia long-arm statute without offending the due process clause. Navis v. Henry, 456 F. Supp. 99 (E.D. Va. 1978).

A single act committed within the Commonwealth resulting in tortious injury confers jurisdiction upon the actor, although a single act committed outside the Commonwealth and resulting in tortious injury within is insufficient to confer jurisdiction unless the defendant has engaged in some persistent course of conduct or derives substantial revenue from goods used or consumed or services rendered within Virginia. Darden v. Heck's, Inc., 459 F. Supp. 727 (W.D. Va. 1978).

A single act of a defendant, committed inside the Commonwealth either personally or through an agent, will be sufficient to invoke the jurisdiction of the courts of the Commonwealth over that defendant with respect to any cause of action arising from that act. Darden v. Heck's, Inc., 459 F. Supp. 727 (W.D. Va. 1978).

It has generally been held that a single act committed within the Commonwealth resulting in tortious injury is sufficient under the due process clause to confer jurisdiction over the actor, even if the actor is a mere sojourner within the states. Humphreys v. Pierce, 512 F. Supp. 1321 (W.D. Va. 1981).

When event meets "single act" test. — An event does not meet the "single act" test and thereby confer jurisdiction if it can only technically be said to have transpired in Virginia. It meets this test if and only if it satisfies the requirements of due process, that by this act defendant has shown a purpose of conducting activities in this State to an extent that it would be fair and just to require him to submit to the jurisdiction of its courts. Darden v. Heck's, Inc., 459 F. Supp. 727 (W.D. Va. 1978).

Injury through negligence of vacationer. — Where the defendant was visiting Virginia on vacation and while attempting to get a fire going in his charcoal grill, allegedly through his negligence, the charcoal lighter fluid exploded and injured plaintiffs, defendant was subject to jurisdiction and service of process under this section and § 8.01-329. Navis v. Henry, 456 F. Supp. 99 (E.D. Va. 1978).

Claim alleging common-law action of deceit. — This statute permitted service of process on the defendant since the plaintiff's misrepresentation claims sufficiently alleged the common-law action of deceit, and since that action arose out of the defendant's misrepresentation in Virginia, resulting in tortious injury in the State. Humphreys v. Pierce, 512 F. Supp. 1321 (W.D. Va. 1981).

Use of Internet as sufficient act. — The use of an AOL account, a Virginia based service, to post allegedly defamatory messages to an interactive newsgroup was a sufficient act to satisfy subdivision A 3 of this section. Bochan v. La Fontaine, 68 F. Supp. 2d 692 (E.D. Va. 1999).

Where defendants used a commercial entity to post press releases on the Internet, subsection (3) applied to defendants. But for the Internet service providers and users present in Virginia, the alleged tort of defamation would not have occurred in Virginia. The conspiracy and tortious interference counts, to some degree, also required contacts in Virginia. Numerous investors and brokers were located in Virginia, and the presence of facilities in Virginia was necessary for those individuals to access the press releases. In addition, because plaintiff company was located in Virginia, the firm absorbed the harm there, which was a necessary element to each of its claims. Telco Communications Group, Inc. v. An Apple a Day, Inc., 977 F. Supp. 404 (E.D. Va. 1997).

3. Breach of Warranty.

Architect's trips to construction site in Virginia. — Defendant architect's acknowledged trips to a construction site in Virginia were sufficient to confer jurisdiction over him in an action alleging breach of an implied warranty as the result of the collapse of a roof. Darden v. Heck's, Inc., 459 F. Supp. 727 (W.D. Va. 1978).

4. Acts or Omissions Outside the Commonwealth.

Where allegedly defamatory letters, through written in and mailed from Illinois and distributed throughout the country, were nevertheless directed in their intended effect at the activities in Virginia of Virginia residents, plaintiff lived and worked in Virginia, his corporate business was incorporated in Virginia and its officers were residents there, and all the operations, activities and services of plaintiff's corporate business were conducted in Virginia by plaintiff and other employees, jurisdiction over defendants existed under subdivision A 4. First Am. First, Inc. v. National Ass'n of Bank Women, 802 F.2d 1511 (4th Cir. 1986).

Where defendant, located outside Virginia, sent communications to plaintiff located within Virginia, and defendant had never been to Virginia and never committed a tortious act while located within the physical boundaries of Virginia, plaintiff failed to allege facts sufficient to justify the exercise of jurisdiction over defendant under subsection (A)(3). Alton v. Wang, 941 F. Supp. 66 (W.D. Va. 1996).

Because defendants conducted their advertising and soliciting over the Internet, which could be accessed by a Virginia resident 24 hours a day, the defendants did so regularly for purpose of the long-arm statute. Accordingly, the court found that posting a Web site advertisement or solicitation constituted a persistent course of conduct, and that the two or three press releases rose to the level of regularly doing or soliciting business, thus satisfying subsection 4. Telco Communications Group, Inc. v. An Apple a Day, Inc., 977 F. Supp. 404 (E.D. Va. 1997).

Company sufficiently advertises and solicits business within Virginia to establish personal jurisdiction under subdivision A 4 of this section where it uses an interactive website that is accessible in Virginia 24 hours a day to promote and advertise its products, even though no sales are concluded through the site, because the site offers product information, company name and telephone numbers, offers no surcharge for credit card use, and places no geographical limits on purchasers. Bochan v. La Fontaine, 68 F. Supp. 2d 692 (E.D. Va. 1999).

Where plaintiff alleged that Chinese defendant contacted plaintiff's Massachusetts publisher, informed the publisher of the dispute between plaintiff and defendant, and threatened to sue the publisher unless he was given a copy of the book to review, although plaintiff may have suffered economic losses as a result of defendant's actions, plaintiff's actual injury — the postponement of the publication of plaintiff's book — occurred in Massachusetts, not Virginia. Accordingly, this court was unable to proceed under subsection (A)(4) because the tortious injury did not occur in Virginia. Alton v. Wang, 941 F. Supp. 66 (W.D. Va. 1996).

II. DECISIONS UNDER PRIOR LAW.

A. General Consideration.

Editor's note. — The cases cited below were decided under corresponding provisions of former law. The terms "long-arm statute," "this chapter," "the statute," and "this section," as used below, refer to former provisions.

Purpose. — This chapter is a deliberate and conscious effort on the part of the General Assembly of Virginia to assert jurisdiction over nonresident defendants to the extent permissible by the due process clause. It is designed to provide redress in Virginia courts against persons who inflict injuries upon, or incur obligations to, those entitled to legitimate protection. However, in making such provision, the statutes must be fair and reasonable, give to the defendant proper notice of the claim against him, and provide him an adequate and realistic opportunity to appear and be heard in his defense. Carmichael v. Snyder, 209 Va. 451, 164 S.E.2d 703 (1968).

The purpose of Virginia's long-arm statute is to assert jurisdiction over nonresidents who engage in some purposeful activity in this State to the extent permissible under the due process clause. John G. Kolbe, Inc. v. Chromodern Chair Co., 211 Va. 736, 180 S.E.2d 664 (1971); Danville Plywood Corp. v. Plain & Fancy Kitchens, Inc., 218 Va. 533, 238 S.E.2d 800 (1977).

Section constitutional. — This section does not contravene due process rights guaranteed an individual by the Fourteenth Amendment and the Constitution of Virginia. Snow v. Clark, 263 F. Supp. 66 (W.D. Va. 1967).

If the exercise of jurisdiction is constitutional, the long-arm statute contemplates it. Ajax Realty Corp. v. J.F. Zook, Inc., 493 F.2d 818 (4th Cir. 1972), cert. denied, 411 U.S. 966, 93 S. Ct. 2148, 36 L. Ed. 2d 687 (1973).

Extension of jurisdiction limited by due process. — The mere fact that the legislature has passed a "long-arm" statute does not permit an extension of jurisdiction beyond due process limits, even if authorized by the legislation. St. Clair v. Righter, 250 F. Supp. 148 (W.D. Va. 1966).

Provisions upon which section modeled. — This section, with the exception of subsection A 5, is modeled upon provisions of the Illinois Civil Practice Act and the Uniform Interstate and International Procedure Act. John G. Kolbe, Inc. v. Chromodern Chair Co., 211 Va. 736, 180 S.E.2d 664 (1971).

This section is clear and specific. Carmichael v. Snyder, 209 Va. 451, 164 S.E.2d 703 (1968).

Liberal interpretation. — This section was drafted to incorporate the liberal interpretation of "presence within the territorial jurisdiction." V & V Mining Supply, Inc. v. Matway, 295 F. Supp. 643 (W.D. Va. 1969).

The Virginia long-arm statutes are remedial only and do not disturb vested rights or create new obligations; they merely supply a remedy to enforce an existing right. Their only purpose and effect were to give to the courts of this Commonwealth jurisdiction to hear and decide a cause of action of the kind described in the statutes against a nonresident defendant. Walke v. Dallas, Inc., 209 Va. 32, 161 S.E.2d 722 (1968).

The State has an interest in providing redress for its citizens, particularly in real estate transactions. Carmichael v. Snyder, 209 Va. 451, 164 S.E.2d 703 (1968).

This section was intended to be procedural in character. Jackson v. National Linen Serv. Corp., 248 F. Supp. 962 (W.D. Va. 1965); Etzler v. Dille & McGuire Mfg. Co., 249 F. Supp. 1 (W.D. Va. 1965).

It was not intended to create a new right but rather provide a means by which existing rights might be secured. Jackson v. National Linen Serv. Corp., 248 F. Supp. 962 (W.D. Va. 1965); Etzler v. Dille & McGuire Mfg. Co., 249 F. Supp. 1 (W.D. Va. 1965).

Hence, it may be applied retroactively. Jackson v. National Linen Serv. Corp., 248 F. Supp. 962 (W.D. Va. 1965); Etzler v. Dille & McGuire Mfg. Co., 249 F. Supp. 1 (W.D. Va. 1965).

The Virginia long-arm statutes, contained in this chapter, are applicable to the causes of action described in this section which arose before as well as those which arise after the enactment of the statute. Walke v. Dallas, Inc., 209 Va. 32, 161 S.E.2d 722 (1968).

The generally accepted rule is that statutes of limitation, or remedial statutes, are not retrospective in their application in the absence of clear legislative intent. But the long-arm statutes are not of the type to which that rule applies. They create no new cause of action and take away no existing right or remedy. They only provide a forum for asserting an existing right, with respect to which the law in force at the time of the trial must prevail. Walke v. Dallas, Inc., 209 Va. 32, 161 S.E.2d 722 (1968).

The application of long-arm statutes involves two steps. It is necessary to determine (1) whether the statute permits service of process on the nonresident defendant, and (2) whether service under the statute violates the due process clause of the federal Constitution. Haynes v. James H. Carr, Inc., 427 F.2d 700 (4th Cir. 1970), cert. denied, 400 U.S. 942, 91 S. Ct. 238, 27 L. Ed. 2d 245 (1970).

The burden of proving jurisdictional facts rests upon the plaintiff. Haynes v. James H. Carr, Inc., 427 F.2d 700 (4th Cir.), cert. denied, 400 U.S. 942, 91 S. Ct. 238, 27 L. Ed. 2d 245 (1970).

Serving process on the Secretary of the Commonwealth is permissible only in the situations outlined by this section. V & V Mining Supply, Inc. v. Matway, 295 F. Supp. 643 (W.D. Va. 1969).

"Long-arm statute." — A "long-arm statute" is merely legislative approval for the exercise by the courts in that state of their inherent jurisdictional power, at least to the limits set out in the statute. St. Clair v. Righter, 250 F. Supp. 148 (W.D. Va. 1966).

Extension of jurisdiction beyond requirement of physical presence. — The development of the doctrine extending jurisdiction in personam over nonresidents beyond the requirement of physical presence to include actions arising out of certain activities within the forum state was set forth by the Supreme Court of the United States in International Shoe Co. v. Washington, 326 U.S. 310, 66 S. Ct. 154, 90 L. Ed. 95 (1945), and McGee v. International Life Ins. Co., 355 U.S. 220, 78 S. Ct. 199, 2 L. Ed. 2d 223 (1957); John G. Kolbe, Inc. v. Chromodern Chair Co., 211 Va. 736, 180 S.E.2d 664 (1971).

Particulars of section must be satisfied. — Since the legislature particularized in this section what it deemed the permissible outer limits for the acquisition of personal jurisdiction consistent with due process, insistence that these particulars be satisfied even in those situations where it could plausibly be argued that a lesser standard would meet due process requirements is a course mandated by legislative judgment. Willis v. Semmes, Bowen & Semmes, 441 F. Supp. 1235 (E.D. Va. 1977).

Federal court will not assume jurisdiction where state courts would not. — A federal court sitting in diversity will not, and in the absence of congressional rule-making cannot, assume in personam jurisdiction where the state courts of the forum state would not. Willis v. Semmes, Bowen & Semmes, 441 F. Supp. 1235 (E.D. Va. 1977).

Although a defendant may be properly before a federal court in this State on one cause of action where personal jurisdiction has been obtained under the long-arm statute, he need not be subject to jurisdiction on causes of action that do not have the statutorily required nexus with forum activities. Willis v. Semmes, Bowen & Semmes, 441 F. Supp. 1235 (E.D. Va. 1977).

A federal district court can use this section to extend its jurisdiction over nonresident defendants. Jackson v. National Linen Serv. Corp., 248 F. Supp. 962 (W.D. Va. 1965); Etzler v. Dille & McGuire Mfg. Co., 249 F. Supp. 1 (W.D. Va. 1965); St. Clair v. Righter, 250 F. Supp. 148 (W.D. Va. 1966).

A federal district court may constitutionally subject a defendant to in personam jurisdiction under subsection A 5 of this section. Etzler v. Dille & McGuire Mfg. Co., 249 F. Supp. 1 (W.D. Va. 1965).

Subsection B purports to limit the exercise of personal jurisdiction solely to the precise causes of action which might be sued on individually under subsection A of this section. Elefteriou v. Tanker Archontissa, 443 F.2d 185 (4th Cir. 1971).

Applied in Haynes v. James H. Carr, Inc., 307 F. Supp. 1228 (E.D. Va. 1969).

B. Transacting Business.

1. In General.

This section is a single-act statute. — Since this section provides "Transacting any business in this Commonwealth," it is a single-act statute requiring only one transaction in Virginia to confer jurisdiction on its courts. John G. Kolbe, Inc. v. Chromodern Chair Co., 211 Va. 736, 180 S.E.2d 664 (1971).

Even a single act may constitute a transaction of business in this State under this section. Willis v. Semmes, Bowen & Semmes, 441 F. Supp. 1235 (E.D. Va. 1977).

A single act by a nonresident which amounts to "transacting business" in Virginia and gives rise to a cause of action may be sufficient to confer jurisdiction upon its courts. Danville Plywood Corp. v. Plain & Fancy Kitchens, Inc., 218 Va. 533, 238 S.E.2d 800 (1977).

The significant difference between Virginia's "long-arm" statute and the "single-act" statutes of other states is that the General Assembly saw fit to separate the causal act from the resulting injury. St. Clair v. Righter, 250 F. Supp. 148 (W.D. Va. 1966).

Subsection A 1 discarded the concept of "doing business" as the exclusive test of jurisdiction and provided instead that personal jurisdiction may be asserted over a nonresident if, in person or through an agent, he transacts any business in this State. John G. Kolbe, Inc. v. Chromodern Chair Co., 211 Va. 736, 180 S.E.2d 664 (1971).

It is not necessary for a defendant to be "doing business" in the technical sense to fall within this section. Jackson v. National Linen Serv. Corp., 248 F. Supp. 962 (W.D. Va. 1965); Etzler v. Dille & McGuire Mfg. Co., 249 F. Supp. 1 (W.D. Va. 1965).

2. Minimum Contacts.

Due process requires minimum contacts. — Due process requires only that in order to subject a defendant to a judgment in personam, if he be not present within the territory of the forum, he have certain minimum contacts with it such that the maintenance of the suit does not offend traditional notions of fair play and substantial justice. Carmichael v. Snyder, 209 Va. 451, 164 S.E.2d 703 (1968); John G. Kolbe, Inc. v. Chromodern Chair Co., 211 Va. 736, 180 S.E.2d 664 (1971).

Due process requires that a nonresident have certain minimum contacts within the territory of the forum so that the maintenance of the action does not offend traditional notions of fair play and substantial justice. Danville Plywood Corp. v. Plain & Fancy Kitchens, Inc., 218 Va. 533, 238 S.E.2d 800 (1977).

Defendant must purposefully avail itself of privilege of conducting activities in forum state. — For long-arm service to come within the limits of the due process clause the defendant must have certain minimum contacts with the forum such that the suit does not offend "traditional notions of fair play and substantial justice." Such contacts are met only when there be some act by which the defendant purposefully avails itself of the privilege of conducting activities within the forum state, thus invoking the benefits and protections of its laws. Marston v. Gant, 351 F. Supp. 1122 (E.D. Va. 1972).

It is essential in each case that there be some act by which the defendant purposefully avails itself of the privilege of conducting activities within the forum state, thus invoking the benefits and protections of its laws. John G. Kolbe, Inc. v. Chromodern Chair Co., 211 Va. 736, 180 S.E.2d 664 (1971).

Jurisdiction may be exercised where defendant so avails itself. — Where a foreign corporation has purposefully availed itself of the privilege of conducting business activities within Virginia and thereby invoked the benefits and protection of the laws of this State, it would not offend traditional notions of fair play and substantial justice to require it to submit to the jurisdiction of the courts of this State. John G. Kolbe, Inc. v. Chromodern Chair Co., 211 Va. 736, 180 S.E.2d 664 (1971).

Whether due process is satisfied must depend rather upon the quality and nature of the activity in relation to the fair and orderly administration of the laws which it was the purpose of the due process clause to insure. That clause does not contemplate that a state may make binding a judgment in personam against an individual or corporate defendant with which the state has no contacts, ties, or relations. Carmichael v. Snyder, 209 Va. 451, 164 S.E.2d 703 (1968).

Application of minimum contacts rule will vary with quality and nature of defendant's activity, but it is essential in each case that there be some act by which the defendant purposefully avails itself of the privileges of conducting activities within the forum State, thus invoking the benefits and protections of its laws. Danville Plywood Corp. v. Plain & Fancy Kitchens, Inc., 218 Va. 533, 238 S.E.2d 800 (1977).

Contact held sufficient to support jurisdiction. — The passing of the risk of loss of goods shipped to the nonresident defendant F.O.B. Danville, and technical acceptance of the goods in Virginia by the plaintiff's delivery to the carrier, were insufficient to establish that the defendant had the necessary minimum contacts to satisfy due process and give jurisdiction to Virginia courts. Danville Plywood Corp. v. Plain & Fancy Kitchens, Inc., 218 Va. 533, 238 S.E.2d 800 (1977).

Contact to support jurisdiction in Vir-

ginia held insufficient. — Where the only connection between a Virginia corporation and an alien corporation was a cancellation agreement which had been entered into in another state, and the alien corporation had no other business in Virginia, there was not sufficient contact to support jurisdiction in Virginia. Davis H. Elliot Co. v. Caribbean Utils. Co., 64 F.R.D. 594 (W.D. Va. 1974).

3. What Constitutes Transacting Business.

Transacting business under subdivision A 1. — An alien corporation transacts business in Virginia within the meaning of subdivision A 1 of this section where it sends its technicians and employees to the State for supervision of the installation and modification of equipment purchased from it, its principal officer visits Virginia from time to time to confer with officials of its wholly owned subsidiary, a New York corporation which does business in Virginia, concerning the sale of machinery, and all seven of the subsidiary's service, plant, and design engineers benefit from previous employment by the alien corporation or other subsidiaries in their present pension plans with the subsidiary corporation. Olin Mathieson Chem. Corp. v. Molins Orgs., Ltd., 261 F. Supp. 436 (E.D. Va. 1966).

Contract made in Virginia but performed elsewhere. — Where a contract is made in the State of Virginia, but substantially all of the performance under the terms of the contract takes place outside the State of Virginia, service of process and jurisdiction lie pursuant to this section for breach of such contract. I.T. Sales, Inc. v. Dry, 222 Va. 6, 278 S.E.2d 789 (1981).

C. Contracting to Supply Services or Things.

Unpaid wage claim. — A plaintiff's claim that he was not paid the full amount of the wages due and owing him when he was removed from a ship may provide a basis for the assertion of personal jurisdiction against the foreign owner of the vessel, since federal law requires that a seaman discharged by a vessel making foreign voyages be paid his wages "within twenty-four hours after the cargo has been discharged, or within four days after the seaman has been discharged, whichever first happens." An employment relationship is a contractual relationship and the failure to make payment in Virginia, as required by statute (if not by the provisions of the contract), would give rise to a cause of action arising from the owner's contracting to supply services or things in Virginia within the meaning of subdivision A 2 of this section. Of course, whether personal jurisdiction lies depends upon whether the unpaid wage claim was asserted in good faith.

Elefteriou v. Tanker Archontissa, 443 F.2d 185 (4th Cir. 1971).

D. Tortious Injury.

1. Acts or Omissions in Commonwealth.

Patent infringement action. — The court cannot hold that an alien company should be required to answer to suit for patent infringement in any district where its goods are resold after it has sold to exporters with knowledge that the goods will be shipped to the United States, within the context of subdivision A 3 of this section, in the absence of affirmative acts tending to induce infringement. Marston v. Gant, 351 F. Supp. 1122 (E.D. Va. 1972).

2. Acts or Omissions Outside Commonwealth.

Codification of due process limits on long-arm jurisdiction. — The "persistent course of conduct" and "substantial revenue" provisions of subdivision A 4 of this section seek to codify in terms what the Virginia legislators took to be the due process limits on long-arm jurisdiction. Marston v. Gant, 351 F. Supp. 1122 (E.D. Va. 1972).

Minimum proof of "persistent course of conduct." — At a minimum, the plaintiff must prove that the defendant maintained some sort of ongoing interactions with the forum state in order to show the defendant is engaged in a "persistent course of conduct" in a particular factual situation. Willis v. Semmes, Bowen & Semmes, 441 F. Supp. 1235 (E.D. Va. 1977).

"Tortious injury" a misnomer. — This section refers to the causing of a "tortious injury," which is something of a misnomer, since whether or not the injury was tortious is generally the fact at issue. St. Clair v. Righter, 250 F. Supp. 148 (W.D. Va. 1966).

Construction of subdivision A 4. — The language of subdivision A 4 of this section must be interpreted with relation to the statute as a whole. St. Clair v. Righter, 250 F. Supp. 148 (W.D. Va. 1966).

Subdivision A 4 of this section must be interpreted with a view toward extending personal jurisdiction, rather than restricting it. Marston v. Gant, 351 F. Supp. 1122 (E.D. Va. 1972).

Subdivision A 4 is considerably more restrictive than subdivision A 3 of this section. St. Clair v. Righter, 250 F. Supp. 148 (W.D. Va. 1966).

And does not include causal act occurring outside State. — Where the alleged tortious injury occurred upon the publication of the alleged libel within Virginia, but was caused by the act of writing and mailing the letters outside Virginia, the acts do not fall within the terms of subsection A 4. St. Clair v. Righter, 250 F. Supp. 148 (W.D. Va. 1966).

Single-act interpretation precluded by

§ 8.01-328.1   CODE OF VIRGINIA   § 8.01-328.1

legislature. — The legislature purposely omitted the adjective "tortious" when referring to the act or omission in subdivision A 4 of this section, and included it with reference to the resulting injury, in order to make certain that a single-act interpretation would be precluded. St. Clair v. Righter, 250 F. Supp. 148 (W.D. Va. 1966).

The sale of goods to exporters in Japan, with knowledge that they would be eventually resold throughout the entire United States, is sufficient for the court to infer that the defendant purposefully availed itself of Virginia's protection under subdivision A 4 of this section if the revenue it derives from the ultimate sales in Virginia is of a sufficient amount as to represent "substantial revenue." Marston v. Gant, 351 F. Supp. 1122 (E.D. Va. 1972).

Employee salaries held not substantial revenue. — Substituted service upon nonresident defendants was not permitted under this section in that the alleged nexus between the defendants' employer's operations in Virginia and the salaries and benefits paid to defendants by the employer was far too tenuous to suggest that the defendants themselves derived substantial revenue from services rendered in Virginia. Causey v. Pan Am. World Airways, Inc., 66 F.R.D. 392 (E.D. Va. 1975).

3. Breach of Warranty.

Subdivision A 5 of this section is constitutional, as the use of the words "regularly," "persistent," and "substantial," places it well within the permissible limits of due process. Jackson v. National Linen Serv. Corp., 248 F. Supp. 962 (W.D. Va. 1965); Etzler v. Dille & McGuire Mfg. Co., 249 F. Supp. 1 (W.D. Va. 1965).

Assertion of jurisdiction under subdivision A 5 does not offend the due process clause of the Fourteenth Amendment. Ajax Realty Corp. v. J.F. Zook, Inc., 493 F.2d 818 (4th Cir. 1972), cert. denied, 411 U.S. 966, 93 S. Ct. 2148, 36 L. Ed. 2d 687 (1973).

It is only necessary that a defendant be engaged in some persistent course of conduct, or derive substantial revenue from goods used in this State, to fall within this section. Jackson v. National Linen Serv. Corp., 248 F. Supp. 962 (W.D. Va. 1965); Etzler v. Dille & McGuire Mfg. Co., 249 F. Supp. 1 (W.D. Va. 1965).

There is a trend toward liberal construction of "substantial revenue" provisions. Ajax Realty Corp. v. J.F. Zook, Inc., 493 F.2d 818 (4th Cir. 1972), cert. denied, 411 U.S. 966, 93 S. Ct. 2148, 36 L. Ed. 2d 687 (1973).

It is difficult to identify an absolute amount which ipso facto must be deemed "substantial." Ajax Realty Corp. v. J.F. Zook, Inc., 493 F.2d 818 (4th Cir. 1972), cert. denied, 411 U.S. 966, 93 S. Ct. 2148, 36 L. Ed. 2d 687 (1973).

Percentage of total sales is only a factor to be considered. — Although percentage of total sales may be a factor to be considered in determining the question of "substantial revenue" under subdivision A 5, it cannot be dispositive, for a small percentage of the sales of a corporate giant may indeed prove substantial in an absolute sense. Ajax Realty Corp. v. J.F. Zook, Inc., 493 F.2d 818 (4th Cir. 1972), cert. denied, 411 U.S. 966, 93 S. Ct. 2148, 36 L. Ed. 2d 687 (1973).

Revenue constituting "substantial revenue." — Although defendant did not regularly do or solicit business, or pursue a persistent course of conduct, in Virginia, the $37,000 which it derived from plaintiff's use of the goods in Virginia constitutes "substantial revenue" for purposes of subdivision A 5. Ajax Realty Corp. v. J.F. Zook, Inc., 493 F.2d 818 (4th Cir. 1972), cert. denied, 411 U.S. 966, 93 S. Ct. 2148, 36 L. Ed. 2d 687 (1973).

Substantial revenue was derived from the sale of lawn movers in Virginia where the defendant manufacturer engaged in a persistent course of conduct by shipping the mowers directly to purchasers in Virginia. Etzler v. Dille & McGuire Mfg. Co., 249 F. Supp. 1 (W.D. Va. 1965).

Although $25,000 was a small amount when compared to defendant's total volume of sales of five million dollars, it was substantial enough to satisfy this section. Jackson v. National Linen Serv. Corp., 248 F. Supp. 962 (W.D. Va. 1965).

Where defendant enjoyed a sufficient financial benefit from the use of its goods in Virginia, it would not be unreasonable to hold that it must account in Virginia for alleged defects, at least where the statute requires, and defendant ultimately had, a reasonable expectation that the goods would be used in Virginia. Ajax Realty Corp. v. J.F. Zook, Inc., 493 F.2d 818 (4th Cir. 1972), cert. denied, 411 U.S. 966, 93 S. Ct. 2148, 36 L. Ed. 2d 687 (1973).

E. Real Property in Virginia.

Scope of jurisdiction generally. — This section gives the court the right to exercise personal jurisdiction over a person who acts directly as to a cause of action arising from that person having an interest in, using, or possessing real property in Virginia. Significantly, the statute refers to a cause of action which arises from a person having an interest in real estate. Carmichael v. Snyder, 209 Va. 451, 164 S.E.2d 703 (1968).

Jurisdiction is grounded on the relationship existing between the defendant and the realty out of which the cause of action arose at the time the cause of action arose.

Carmichael v. Snyder, 209 Va. 451, 164 S.E.2d 703 (1968).

Controversies relating to property. — In controversies relating to property which is within the jurisdiction of the court, where personal service of process within the State is impossible or is for any reason impracticable, a method of constructive or substituted service may be provided for; and with a reasonable exercise of such legislative discretion, the courts will not assume to interfere. Carmichael v. Snyder, 209 Va. 451, 164 S.E.2d 703 (1968).

A contract which involves an interest in land has a substantial connection with the State. Carmichael v. Snyder, 209 Va. 451, 164 S.E.2d 703 (1968).

This section gives jurisdiction at the time of, and because of, the execution of a contract which vested in defendant an interest in land. It was then that defendant "acted directly."

Carmichael v. Snyder, 209 Va. 451, 164 S.E.2d 703 (1968).

Defendant having rendered himself amenable by virtue of acting directly as to a cause of action arising from his having an interest in real estate in Virginia, plaintiffs could maintain an action in personam to collect the amount due them under contract. Carmichael v. Snyder, 209 Va. 451, 164 S.E.2d 703 (1968).

The fact that defendants no longer have an interest in the realty and no longer live in this State is immaterial. Carmichael v. Snyder, 209 Va. 451, 164 S.E.2d 703 (1968).

The fact that plaintiffs sold the property and sued for damages, rather than bringing a suit for specific performance, or a suit for the purchase price of the real estate, did not thereby divest the Virginia court of jurisdiction over defendant. Carmichael v. Snyder, 209 Va. 451, 164 S.E.2d 703 (1968).

§ 8.01-329. Service of process or notice; service on Secretary of Commonwealth. — A. When the exercise of personal jurisdiction is authorized by this chapter, service of process or notice may be made in the same manner as is provided for in Chapter 8 (§ 8.01-285 et seq.) of this title in any other case in which personal jurisdiction is exercised over such a party, or process or notice may be served on any agent of such person in the county or city in this Commonwealth in which that agent resides or on the Secretary of the Commonwealth of Virginia, hereinafter referred to in this section as the "Secretary," who, for this purpose, shall be deemed to be the statutory agent of such person.

B. When service is to be made on the Secretary, the party or his agent or attorney seeking service shall file an affidavit with the court, stating either (i) that the person to be served is a nonresident or (ii) that, after exercising due diligence, the party seeking service has been unable to locate the person to be served. In either case, such affidavit shall set forth the last known address of the person to be served.

When the person to be served is a resident, the signature of an attorney, party or agent of the person seeking service on such affidavit shall constitute a certificate by him that process has been delivered to the sheriff or to a disinterested person as permitted by § 8.01-293 for execution and, if the sheriff or disinterested person was unable to execute such service, that the person seeking service has made a bona fide attempt to determine the actual place of abode or location of the person to be served.

C. Service of such process or notice on the Secretary shall be made by the plaintiff's, his agent's or the sheriff's leaving a copy of the process or notice, together with a copy of the affidavit called for in subsection B hereof and the fee prescribed in § 2.1-71.2 in the office of the Secretary in the City of Richmond, Virginia. Service of process or notice on the Secretary may be made by mail if such service otherwise meets the requirements of this section. Such service shall be sufficient upon the person to be served, provided that notice of such service, a copy of the process or notice, and a copy of the affidavit are forthwith mailed by certified mail, return receipt requested, by the Secretary to the person or persons to be served at the last known post-office address of such person, and a certificate of compliance herewith by the Secretary or someone designated by him for that purpose and having knowledge of such compliance, shall be forthwith filed with the papers in the action. Service of process or notice on the Secretary shall be effective on the date the certificate of compliance is filed with the court in which the action is pending.

D. Service of process in actions brought on a warrant or motion for judgment pursuant to § 16.1-79 or § 16.1-81 shall be void and of no effect when such service of process is received by the Secretary within ten days of any return day set by the warrant. In such cases, the Secretary shall return the process or notice, the copy of the affidavit, and the prescribed fee to the plaintiff or his agent. A copy of the notice of the rejection shall be sent to the clerk of the court in which the action was filed.

E. The Secretary shall maintain a record of each notice of service sent to a person for a period of two years. The record maintained by the Secretary shall include the name of the plaintiff or the person seeking service, the name of the person to be served, the date service was received by the Secretary, the date notice of service was forwarded to the person to be served, and the date the certificate of compliance was sent by the Secretary to the appropriate court. The Secretary shall not be required to maintain any other records pursuant to this section. (Code 1950, § 8-813; 1977, c. 617; 1979, c. 31; 1986, c. 388; 1987, cc. 449, 450, 459; 1990, c. 741; 1998, c. 259.)

REVISERS' NOTE

Section 8.01-329 is former § 8-81.3 changed such that process under the long-arm provision may be served alternatively rather than in the order stated by the former statute.

Former § 8-81.4 has been deleted since venue is incorporated in § 8.01-262, subsection 10.

Law Review. — For note, "Obtaining Jurisdiction Over Corporations in Virginia," see 12 U. Rich. L. Rev. 369 (1978). For survey of Virginia law on practice and pleading for the year 1978-1979, see 66 Va. L. Rev. 343 (1980).

I. Decisions Under Current Law.
II. Decisions Under Prior Law.

I. DECISIONS UNDER CURRENT LAW.

If the requirements of this section are met, service is complete and conclusive. Basile v. American Filter Serv., Inc., 231 Va. 34, 340 S.E.2d 800 (1986).

Limitations of § 8.01-320 A do not apply to subsection A. — As an order of publication confers only in rem jurisdiction, application of § 8.01-320 A to subsection A would destroy the personal jurisdiction conferred by the long-arm statute in § 8.01-328.1; moreover, application of § 8.01-320 A to subsection A would mean that service on the Secretary of the Commonwealth, who need only mail a copy to the person to be served at his last known address, would sustain personal jurisdiction, whereas personal service or substituted service designed to provide actual notice would support only in rem jurisdiction; therefore, the limitations of § 8.01-320 A do not apply to service of process pursuant to subsection A. Frederick v. Koziol, 727 F. Supp. 1019 (E.D. Va. 1990).

Service of process on the Secretary of the Commonwealth. — Where the exercise of personal jurisdiction was authorized under the long-arm statute, the defendants were amenable to service of process on the Secretary of the Commonwealth, and the action did not have to be dismissed for insufficiency of process. Furmanite Am., Inc. v. Durango Assocs., 662 F. Supp. 348 (E.D. Va. 1986).

Plaintiff was not required to serve Secretary of Commonwealth. — Subsection A provides for three modes of service — service in the manner of the provisions of Chapter 8, of Title 8.01 (§ 8.01-285 et seq.), service on an agent within the Commonwealth, and service on the Secretary of the Commonwealth; therefore, plaintiff was not required to serve the Secretary of the Commonwealth as the statutory agent of defendant. Rather, since personal jurisdiction was authorized by the long-arm statute, plaintiff was entitled to serve defendant in the manner provided for in Chapter 8. Frederick v. Koziol, 727 F. Supp. 1019 (E.D. Va. 1990).

Failure to include the corporate defendant's zip code does not invalidate the service where the evidence established that omission of the zip code could not result in delivery to any location other than the corporation's correct address. Basile v. American Filter Serv., Inc., 231 Va. 34, 340 S.E.2d 800 (1986).

Secretary's letter of notice marked "undeliverable." — Insurance company's suggestion that plaintiff could not rely on service pursuant to this section because the Secretary's letter of notice was returned marked "undeliverable" and "not at this address" was without merit. Banks v. Leon, 975 F. Supp. 815 (W.D. Va. 1997).

Injury through negligence of vacationer. — Where the defendant was visiting Virginia on vacation and while attempting to get a fire going in his charcoal grill, allegedly through his negligence, the charcoal lighter fluid exploded and injured plaintiffs, defendant was subject to jurisdiction and service of process under § 8.01-328.1 and this section. Navis v. Henry, 456 F. Supp. 99 (E.D. Va. 1978).

Service of process was proper under subsection A. — Where personal jurisdiction was authorized by § 8.01-328.1, and defendant was served in the manner provided for in Chapter 8 (§ 8.01-285 et seq.) of this title, namely under § 8.01-296 2 a, service of process was proper under subsection A of this section, and defendant's motion to dismiss for lack of jurisdiction over the person was denied. Frederick v. Koziol, 727 F. Supp. 1019 (E.D. Va. 1990).

Affidavit held insufficient. — Affidavit given in support of long-arm service was insufficient where affidavit filed by plaintiff's counsel stated neither of alternatives which former subsection A 1 (see now subsection B) requires, but instead stated that petitioner in cause had been unable to obtain service against above named defendant, and where substantial basis existed for conclusion that plaintiff herself could probably not have given affidavit that she was "unable to locate" person to be served, as required by long-arm statute. Khatchi v. Landmark Restaurant Assocs., 237 Va. 139, 375 S.E.2d 743 (1989).

Applied in United Coal Co. v. Land Use Corp., 575 F. Supp. 1148 (W.D. Va. 1983); Pennington v. McDonnell Douglas Corp., 576 F. Supp. 868 (E.D. Va. 1983); Unidyne Corp. v. Aerolineas Argentinas, 590 F. Supp. 391 (E.D. Va. 1984); Weight v. Kawasaki Heavy Indus., Ltd., 597 F. Supp. 1082 (E.D. Va. 1984); Hirschkop & Grad v. Robinson, 757 F.2d 1499 (4th Cir. 1985); Philipp Bros. v. M/V Ocea, 144 F.R.D. 312 (E.D. Va. 1992).

II. DECISIONS UNDER PRIOR LAW.

Editor's note. — The cases cited below were decided under corresponding provisions of former law. The term "this section," as used below, refers to former provisions.

Serving process on the Secretary of the Commonwealth is permissible only in the situations outlined by § 8.01-328.1. V & V Mining Supply, Inc. v. Matway, 295 F. Supp. 643 (W.D. Va. 1969).

This section authorizes service on the Secretary of the Commonwealth in a suit against a foreign corporation as to any cause of action arising from its transacting any business in this State. John G. Kolbe, Inc. v. Chromodern Chair Co., 211 Va. 736, 180 S.E.2d 664 (1971).

Contact held insufficient to support jurisdiction. — Since the only connection between a Virginia corporation and an alien corporation was a cancellation agreement which had been entered into in another state, and the alien corporation had no other business in Virginia, there was not sufficient contact to support jurisdiction in Virginia. Davis H. Elliot Co. v. Caribbean Utils. Co., 64 F.R.D. 594 (W.D. Va. 1974).

§ 8.01-330. Jurisdiction on any other basis authorized. — A court of this State may exercise jurisdiction on any other basis authorized by law. (Code 1950, § 8-81.5; 1964, c. 331; 1977, c. 617.)

Law Review. — For note, "Obtaining Jurisdiction Over Corporations in Virginia," see 12 U. Rich. L. Rev. 369 (1978).

CHAPTER 10.

DOCKETS.

Sec.
8.01-331. Entry of cases on current dockets.
8.01-332. Calling current docket.
8.01-333. [Reserved.]
8.01-334. [Repealed.]

Sec.
8.01-335. Certain cases struck from dockets after certain period; reinstatement.

§ 8.01-331. **Entry of cases on current dockets.** — When any civil action is commenced in a circuit court, or any such action is removed to such court and the required writ tax and fees thereon paid, the clerk shall enter the same in the civil docket. Law cases shall be entered separately from equity cases on the docket. These dockets may be either (i) a substantial, well-bound loose-leaf book, (ii) a visible card index or (iii) automated data processing media. Each case shall be entered on the civil docket, on which shall be entered:

1. The short style of the suit or action,
2. The names of the attorneys,
3. The nature of the suit or action, and
4. The date filed and case file number.

In addition the docket may contain the following information applicable in an individual case as deemed appropriate:

1. The names of the parties,
2. The date of the issuance of process,
3. A memorandum of the service of process,
4. A memorandum of the orders and proceedings in the case, and
5. The hearing date(s) and type(s) of hearing(s) conducted on such date(s).

The clerk may enter the clerk's fees in the case on such docket instead of in the fee book prescribed by § 14.1-168.

Cases appealed from the juvenile and domestic relations district courts shall be docketed as provided in this section and, to the extent inconsistent with this section, § 16.1-302. (Code 1950, §§ 8-160, 8-165; 1954, c. 333; 1956, c. 307; 1977, c. 617; 1983, c. 293; 1990, c. 258.)

REVISERS' NOTE

Former §§ 8-160 and 8-165 have been combined in § 8.01-331. The term "action" is used collectively to include all proceedings brought or pending in circuit courts. Subsection 5 changes the former sections to require the noting of the date on which the action was filed instead of the date docketed.

Editor's note. — Acts 1993, c. 930, cl. 3, as amended by Acts 1994, c. 564, cl. 2, and Acts 1996, c. 616, cl. 4, provided that the amendment to this section by Acts 1993, c. 930, cl. 1, would become effective June 1, 1998, "if state funds are provided, including all local costs, to carry out the purposes of this bill by the General Assembly." The funding was not provided.

Section 14.1-168, referred to at the end of the next-to-last paragraph, was repealed by Acts 1998, c. 872, effective October 1, 1998.

Cross references. — For rules of court as to setting chancery causes for hearing and docketing same, see Rules 2:7, 2:8. For rule of court as to docketing of cases when parties are at issue, see Rule 3:13.

I. DECISIONS UNDER PRIOR LAW.

Editor's note. — The case cited below was decided under corresponding provisions of former law. The term "this section," as used below, refers to former provisions.

Date of notice of motion for judgment. — Under this section it is necessary for the clerk to keep a record of the date each notice of motion for judgment is returned and filed in his office. Brame v. Nolen, 139 Va. 413, 124 S.E. 299 (1924).

§ 8.01-332. **Calling current docket.** — The current docket may be called for the purpose of fixing cases for trial, on such days or at such intervals as may be directed by order of court. (Code 1950, §§ 8-162, 8-167; 1977, c. 617.)

REVISERS' NOTE

Section 8.01-332 is former § 8-162 with certain changes. The precedence given to actions of forcible or unlawful entry and detainer is abolished. However, the precedence granted proceedings in which the Commonwealth is a party is retained. Section 8.01-332 eliminates the necessity of calling the docket at each term and apparently embraces both law and equity cases. The discretion given the court as to the time of calling its docket made it unnecessary to reenact former § 8-163 relating to certain cities.

Cross references. — For rules of court as to setting chancery causes for hearing and docketing same, see Rules 2:7, 2:8.

§ 8.01-333: Reserved.

§ 8.01-334: Repealed by Acts 1983, c. 293.

§ 8.01-335. Certain cases struck from dockets after certain period; reinstatement. — A. Except as provided in subsection C, any court in which is pending an action, wherein for more than two years there has been no order or proceeding, except to continue it, may, in its discretion, order it to be struck from its docket and the action shall thereby be discontinued. However, no case shall be discontinued if either party requests that it be continued. The court shall thereafter enter a pretrial order pursuant to Rule 4:13 controlling the subsequent course of the case to ensure a timely resolution of that case. If the court thereafter finds that the case has not been timely prosecuted pursuant to its pretrial order, it may strike the case from its docket. The clerk of the court shall notify the parties in interest if known, or their counsel of record at his last known address, at least fifteen days before the entry of such order of discontinuance so that all parties may have an opportunity to be heard on it. Any case discontinued under the provisions of this subsection may be reinstated, on motion, after notice to the parties in interest if known or their counsel of record, within one year from the date of such order but not after.

B. Any court in which is pending a case wherein for more than three years there has been no order or proceeding, except to continue it, may, in its discretion, order it to be struck from its docket and the action shall thereby be discontinued. The court may dismiss cases under this subsection without any notice to the parties. The clerk shall provide the parties with a copy of the final order discontinuing or dismissing the case. Any case discontinued or dismissed under the provisions of this subsection may be reinstated, on motion, after notice to the parties in interest, if known, or their counsel of record within one year from the date of such order but not after.

C. If a civil action is pending in a circuit court on appeal from a general district court and (i) an appeal bond has been furnished by or on behalf of any party against whom judgment has been rendered for money or property and (ii) for more than one year there has been no order or proceeding, except to continue the matter, the action may, upon notice to the parties in accordance with subsection A, be dismissed and struck from the docket of the court. Upon dismissal pursuant to this subsection, the judgment of the general district court shall stand and the appeal bond shall be forfeited after application of any funds needed to satisfy the judgment. (Code 1950, § 8-154; 1954, c. 621; 1977, c. 617; 1990, c. 730; 1992, cc. 532, 792, 803, 835; 1994, c. 517; 1997, c. 680; 1999, c. 652.)

REVISERS' NOTE

The subject matter of former § 8-154 is incorporated in § 8.01-335. The only significant change is one of language to make it clear that the action of the court permitted after the two year period is to *discontinue,* while that permitted after the five year period is to *dismiss.*

§ 8.01-335 CODE OF VIRGINIA § 8.01-335

Cross references. — As to appeals from courts not if record in civil cases, see § 16.1-106 et seq.

Editor's note. — Rule 4:13, referred to in subsection A, is set out in the Rules of the Supreme Court.

The 1999 amendment, in subsection B, inserted the second and third sentences, and deleted "and for cause" following "on motion" in the fourth sentence.

I. Decisions Under Current Law.
II. Decisions Under Prior Law.

I. DECISIONS UNDER CURRENT LAW.

Purpose of subsection A. — Subsection A provides a device designed to benefit the trial courts in setting cases for trial and expediting litigation; it does not provide substantive rights to litigants to have cases dismissed for failure to prosecute within two years. Nash v. Jewell, 227 Va. 230, 315 S.E.2d 825 (1984).

The purpose of subsection A is to enable trial courts to identify cases which litigants or their counsel are not interested in pursuing to a conclusion. Nash v. Jewell, 227 Va. 230, 315 S.E.2d 825 (1984).

Subsection A does not apply to suits in which a final order or decree has been entered. Schoenwetter v. Schoenwetter, 8 Va. App. 601, 383 S.E.2d 28 (1989).

Purpose of subsection B is to enable trial courts to eliminate from their dockets cases for which there is no reasonable prospect of trial. Nash v. Jewell, 227 Va. 230, 315 S.E.2d 825 (1984).

Subsections A and B compared. — Subsection B permits courts to dismiss inactive cases without notice; by contrast, the purpose of subsection A is to enable courts to ascertain from the plaintiffs whether there is a desire and intent to try cases which have been dormant for two or more but less than five years. Nash v. Jewell, 227 Va. 230, 315 S.E.2d 825 (1984).

Proper use of two-year statute in subsection A is to expedite rather than to terminate litigation. Nash v. Jewell, 227 Va. 230, 315 S.E.2d 825 (1984).

Trial court improperly used subsection A to strike a suit in which a final decree had been entered and since the trial court employed a mode of procedure to discontinue a case that clearly did not fall within the authorization of this section the order of discontinuance entered in the case was void. Schoenwetter v. Schoenwetter, 8 Va. App. 601, 383 S.E.2d 28 (1989).

Action should not be discontinued where defendant ready and willing to go to trial. — As a general rule, if a plaintiff who is ready and willing to go to trial is brought before the court under the provisions of this section and demonstrates an intent to proceed with his case, the court should not discontinue his action. Nash v. Jewell, 227 Va. 230, 315 S.E.2d 825 (1984).

Plaintiff not put to terms where he filed praecipe and obtained trial date. — Where the trial court had before it defendant's motion to discontinue, and the plaintiff had filed a praecipe and obtained a trial date, the purpose of subsection A, therefore, was served. The trial court knew that the plaintiff had not abandoned the case, was ready for trial, and had arranged for an early trial date. There was no reason, therefore, for the trial court to put the plaintiff on terms to try the case. Nash v. Jewell, 227 Va. 230, 315 S.E.2d 825 (1984).

Dismissal of action terminated right to pendente lite spousal support. — The authority for the court to provide for spousal support "during the pendency of the suit" is limited to the right to make such award only for the period the action is pending, notwithstanding the wording of the pendente lite decree which provided that the award should continue until "further order of the court." The order of dismissal by operation of law under subsection B of this section terminated the wife's right to further pendente lite support. Smith v. Smith, 4 Va. App. 148, 354 S.E.2d 816 (1987).

But did not retroactively nullify accrued pendente lite support. — There is no persuasive authority or reason to hold that the dismissal of an action pursuant to subsection B of this section, standing alone, retroactively nullifies the right to accrued spousal support under a pendente lite order. To so hold would be in derogation of the well established principle that court-ordered support becomes vested when it accrues and the courts are without authority to make any change with regard to arrearages. Smith v. Smith, 4 Va. App. 148, 354 S.E.2d 816 (1987).

And denial of accrued support would violate due process. — A dismissal under subsection B requires no notice to the parties, and, thus, to hold that the right to the amount of support that had accrued could be taken away by dismissal of the action would be in violation of the due process clause of the Fourteenth Amendment to the United States Constitution. Smith v. Smith, 4 Va. App. 148, 354 S.E.2d 816 (1987).

Termination of mensa decree upon dismissal of divorce suit. — Dismissal of a divorce suit, in which no decree or proceeding has taken place within five years, terminates a mensa decree which may have been entered therein. Crenshaw v. Crenshaw, 12 Va. App. 1129, 408 S.E.2d 556 (1991).

Applied in Brown v. Brown, 240 Va. 376, 397 S.E.2d 837 (1990).

II. DECISIONS UNDER PRIOR LAW.

Editor's note. — The cases cited below were decided under corresponding provisions of former law. The term "this section," as used below, refers to former provisions.

This section is designed to speed litigation, and should, in general, be obeyed. Lowry v. Noell, 177 Va. 238, 13 S.E.2d 312 (1941).

The term "discontinuance" has a well settled meaning in the law and has had from a very ancient time. A discontinuance is "in effect a nonsuit," and the effect of a nonsuit is simply to put an end to the present action, but is no bar to a subsequent action for the same cause. Payne v. Buena Vista Extract Co., 124 Va. 296, 98 S.E. 34 (1919).

Reinstatement after one year. — A cause stricken from the docket under this provision cannot be reinstated after the lapse of one year, except by consent of all parties. A decree striking a cause from the docket is an adjudication that everything has been done in the cause that the court intends to do. The decree may be erroneous, but the error does not render it less final, and the court having by its order put the cause beyond its control, cannot upon a discovery of error recall it in a summary way and resume a jurisdiction which has been exhausted. Snead v. Atkinson, 121 Va. 182, 92 S.E. 835 (1917).

A decree striking a cause from the docket pursuant to this section is an adjudication that everything has been done in the cause which the court intended to do, and is final, and the cause cannot be reinstated on the docket after the lapse of one year without the consent of all parties to be affected thereby. Echols v. Brennan, 99 Va. 150, 37 S.E. 786 (1901).

CHAPTER 11.

JURIES.

Article 1.

When Jury Trial May Be Had.

Sec.
8.01-336. Jury trial of right; waiver of jury trial; court-ordered jury trial; trial by jury of plea in equity; issue out of chancery.

Article 2.

Jurors.

8.01-337. Who liable to serve as jurors.
8.01-338. Who disqualified.
8.01-339. No person eligible for whom request is made.
8.01-340. No person to serve who has case at that term.
8.01-341. Who are exempt from jury service.
8.01-341.1. Exemptions from jury service upon request.
8.01-341.2. Deferral or limitation of jury service for particular occupational inconvenience.
8.01-342. Restrictions on amount of jury service permitted.

Article 3.

Selection of Jurors.

8.01-343. Appointment of jury commissioners.

Sec.
8.01-344. Notification of jury commissioners; their oath.
8.01-345. Lists of qualified persons to be prepared by jury commissioners; random selection process.
8.01-346. Lists to be delivered to clerk and safely kept by him; addition and removal of names.
8.01-347. How names put in jury box.
8.01-348. How names of jurors drawn from box.
8.01-349. Notations on ballots drawn; return to box; when such ballots may be drawn again.
8.01-350. [Repealed.]
8.01-350.1. Selection of jurors by mechanical or electronic techniques for the term of court.
8.01-351. Preparation and disposition of list of jurors drawn.
8.01-352. Objections to irregularities in jury lists or for legal disability; effect thereof.

Article 4.

Jury Service.

8.01-353. Notice to jurors; making copy of jury panel available to counsel; objection to notice.

445

Sec.		Sec.	
8.01-354.	"Writ of venire facias" defined.		cases; how jurors selected from panel.
8.01-355.	Jurors on list to be used for trial of cases during term; discharge or dispensing with attendance of jurors; drawing additional jurors.	8.01-360.	Additional jurors when trial likely to be protracted.
		8.01-361.	New juror may be sworn in place of one disabled; when court may discharge jury.
8.01-356.	Failure of juror to appear.		
8.01-357.	Selection of jury panel.		
8.01-358.	Voir dire examination of persons called as jurors.	8.01-362.	Special juries.
		8.01-363.	When impartial jury cannot be obtained locally.
8.01-359.	Trial; numbers of jurors in civil		

ARTICLE 1.

When Jury Trial May Be Had.

§ 8.01-336. Jury trial of right; waiver of jury trial; court-ordered jury trial; trial by jury of plea in equity; issue out of chancery. — A. The right of trial by jury as declared in Article I, Section 11 of the Constitution of Virginia and by statutes thereof shall be preserved inviolate to the parties.

B. *Waiver of jury trial.* — In any action at law in which the recovery sought is greater than $100, exclusive of interest, unless one of the parties demand that the case or any issue thereof be tried by a jury, or in a criminal action in which trial by jury is dispensed with as provided by law, the whole matter of law and fact may be heard and judgment given by the court.

C. *Court-ordered jury trial.* — Notwithstanding any provision in this Code to the contrary, in any action at law in which there has been no demand for trial by jury by any party, a circuit court may on its own motion direct one or more issues, including an issue of damages, to be tried by a jury.

D. *Trial by jury of plea in equity.* — In any action in which a plea has been filed to an equitable claim, and the allegations of such plea are denied by the plaintiff, either party may have the issue tried by jury.

E. *Issue out of chancery.* — In any suit in equity, the court may, of its own motion or upon motion of any party, supported by such party's affidavit that the case will be rendered doubtful by conflicting evidence of another party, direct an issue to be tried by a jury. (Code 1950, §§ 8-208.21, 8-211, 8-212, 8-213, 8-214; 1954, c. 333; 1973, c. 439; 1974, c. 611; 1975, c. 578; 1977, c. 617.)

REVISERS' NOTE

Subsection A, Jury trial of right, generally adopts the wording of FRCP 38 (a), but substitutes appropriate reference to the "Commonwealth" in lieu of "the United States" and to Va. Const., Art. I, § 11 instead of the Seventh Amendment to the United States Constitution.

Subsection B, Waiver of jury trial, combines former § 8-211 with § 8-208.21. If a civil action or an issue in the action is triable of right by jury under subsection A, unless a party to such action requests that the action or issue be so tried, he waives that right. The $20 amount in former § 8-211 has been increased to $100 in the enacted statute.

Subsection C, Court ordered jury trial, is declaratory of established practice.

Subsection D, Trial by jury of plea in equity, is former § 8-213 without substantial change.

Subsection E, Issue out of chancery, is former § 8-214 without substantial change.

Cross references. — As to applicability of Chapter 11 (§ 8.01-336 et seq.) in criminal cases, see § 19.2-260. As to waiver of jury trial in criminal cases, see § 19.2-262. As to suits to remove cloud from title, see § 55-153. As to trial by jury of escheat cases, see §§ 55-173, 55-174, and 55-177.

Law Review. — For comment, "Jury Trials for Juvenile Delinquents in Virginia," see 28 Wash. & Lee L. Rev. 135 (1971). For article,

"Trial by Jury and Speedy Justice," see 28 Wash. & Lee L. Rev. 309 (1971). For survey of Virginia criminal law for the year 1971-1972, see 58 Va. L. Rev. 1206 (1972). For survey of Virginia law on pleading and practice for the year 1972-1973, see 59 Va. L. Rev. 1559 (1973). For survey of Virginia law on practice and pleading for the year 1973-1974, see 60 Va. L. Rev. 1572 (1974). For article, "Appeal De Novo in Virginia: An Examination of Its Present Utility," see 42 Wash. & Lee L. Rev. 1149 (1985). For article, "A Proposal to Simplify Virginia Burdens of Proof," see 12 Geo. Mason L. Rev. 1 (1989). For a note, "Invaluable Tool vs. Unfair Use of Private Information: Examining Prosecutors' Use of Jurors' Criminal History Records in Voir Dire," see 56 Wash. & Lee L. Rev. 1079 (1999).

I. Decisions Under Current Law.
  A. General Consideration.
  B. Jury Trial of Right.
  C. Issue Out of Chancery.
II. Decisions Under Prior Law.
  A. General Consideration.
  B. Jury Trial of Right.
  C. Trial by Jury of Plea in Equity.
  D. Issue Out of Chancery.

I. DECISIONS UNDER CURRENT LAW.

A. General Consideration.

In equity, a litigant has no constitutional right to trial by jury, and, absent a plea in equity, no statutory right. Wright v. Castles, 232 Va. 218, 349 S.E.2d 125 (1986).

All parties to civil litigation are entitled to a fair and impartial trial by a jury of persons who stand indifferent in the cause. Edlow v. Arnold, 243 Va. 345, 415 S.E.2d 436 (1992).

Right to jury trial not improperly denied where plaintiff did not follow procedure. — Dismissal of suit, which complained only of the denial of a trial by jury and asserted a collusion by defendants to deny him one, was proper, where plaintiff's own actions in bringing suit in the general district court rather than the circuit court deprived him of a trial by jury. He had originally brought his personal injury claim in circuit court, as he was entitled to by § 17-123, he would have received a jury upon request under this section. He also could have received a de novo jury trial by properly perfecting his appeal from general district court under § 16.1-113. His failure to receive a jury trial, therefore, was the result of his own failure to follow valid state procedures rather than the result of any collusion by defendants in violation of 42 U.S.C. § 1983. Beaudett v. City of Hampton, 775 F.2d 1274 (4th Cir. 1985), cert. denied, 475 U.S. 1088, 106 S. Ct. 1475, 89 L. Ed. 2d 729 (1986).

Bankruptcy court's authority to provide jury trial. — The common-law right of trial by jury imbedded in the Constitution of the United States and of Virginia coupled with the statutory enabling statutes eliminates any question as to whether or not the bankruptcy court is vested with the authority to provide a trial by jury where such right otherwise exists in other courts, whatever the forum. Brown v. Frank Meador Buick, Inc., 8 Bankr. 450 (Bankr. W.D. Va. 1981).

What is a plea. — A plea, whether at law or in equity, is a discrete form of defensive pleading; distinguished from an answer or grounds of defense, a plea does not address the merits of the issues raised by the bill of complaint or the motion for judgment; rather, it alleges a single state of facts or circumstances (usually not disclosed or disclosed only in part by the record) which, if proven, constitutes an absolute defense to the claim. Nelms v. Nelms, 236 Va. 281, 374 S.E.2d 4 (1988).

Pleadings in general answers and a cross-bill were not pleas in equity within the intendment of subsection D; consequently, the chancellor could not have relied on this subsection for his decision to submit a question of mental competence to a jury. Nelms v. Nelms, 236 Va. 281, 374 S.E.2d 4 (1988).

Trial court did not err in denying father's request for a jury trial. — Although father maintained that a jury should have been impanelled to determine whether he should have been relieved of his obligation to support his child due to violation of his rights by mother's seduction of him and decision to keep the child, even assuming the allegations were true, they did not constitute a bar to the enforcement of his support obligations; in Virginia, both parents of a child owe that child a duty of support during minority. Hur v. Virginia Dep't of Social Serv. Div. of Child Support Enforcement ex rel. Klopp, 13 Va. App. 54, 409 S.E.2d 454 (1991).

Plaintiff may withdraw consent to three-person special jury before trial has begun. — Given the clearly expressed constitutional purpose and legislative intent to preserve the right to trial by jury in both criminal and civil cases, a consent to a special three-person jury under § 8.01-359 D may be withdrawn before trial under the same conditions as are enunciated in Thomas v. Commonwealth, 218 Va. 553, 238 S.E.2d 834 (1977). Painter v. Fred Whitaker Co., 235 Va. 631, 369 S.E.2d 191 (1988).

Waiver of right to jury trial. — Although pursuant to subsection B a civil litigant that fails to demand a jury waives their right to a trial by jury, nothing in that subsection compels a bench trial in Virginia Circuit Courts upon a party's waiver of trial by jury since the subsection simply establishes waiver of the right to a jury trial; it does not address how, or even whether, the waiver will be enforced by the Circuit Courts of Virginia. Keatley v. Food Lion, Inc., 715 F. Supp. 1335 (E.D. Va. 1989).

Standard of review. — Whether a civil litigant has been denied the right to trial by a fair and impartial jury is a question treated on appeal as one addressed to the sound discretion of the trial court and, unless there has been abuse of that discretion, the judgement below will not be reversed on appeal. Edlow v. Arnold, 243 Va. 345, 415 S.E.2d 436 (1992).

Applied in Malbon v. Pennsylvania Millers Mut. Ins. Co., 636 F.2d 936 (4th Cir. 1980); Travis v. Bulifant, 226 Va. 1, 306 S.E.2d 865 (1983); Helen W. v. Fairfax County Dep't of Human Dev., 12 Va. App. 877, 407 S.E.2d 25 (1991); Mary Moody N., Inc. v. Bailey, 244 Va. 118, 418 S.E.2d 882 (1992); New River Media Group, Inc. v. Knighton, 245 Va. 367, 429 S.E.2d 25 (1993); Gelardi v. Transamerica Occidental Life Ins. Co., 163 F.R.D. 495 (E.D. Va. 1995).

B. Jury Trial of Right.

This section and its predecessors provide for a jury trial as a matter of right on the motion of either party. Stanardsville Volunteer Fire Co. v. Berry, 229 Va. 578, 331 S.E.2d 466 (1985).

C. Issue Out of Chancery.

Trials of issues out of chancery and on plea in equity differ. — There are distinct differences between the trial of an issue out of chancery, now covered by subsection E, and trial of an issue on a plea in equity. Stanardsville Volunteer Fire Co. v. Berry, 229 Va. 578, 331 S.E.2d 466 (1985).

Discretion of chancellor. — Under subsection E of this section, the chancellor may, upon the motion of any party, direct an issue out of chancery whenever the facts stated in the party's affidavit render the resolution of the cause doubtful; alternatively, the chancellor may, of his own motion, submit an issue to a jury even though not requested by either party. In either event, the decision is one within the sound discretion of the chancellor. Nelms v. Nelms, 236 Va. 281, 374 S.E.2d 4 (1988).

Decision to impanel jury left to trial court's sound discretion. — The issue whether to impanel a jury is left to the trial court's sound discretion and will not be reversed absent an abuse of discretion. Hur v. Virginia Dep't of Social Serv. Div. of Child Support Enforcement ex rel. Klopp, 13 Va. App. 54, 409 S.E.2d 454 (1991).

Effect of jury's findings under subsection E. — Unlike a jury's response to an interrogatory submitted under subsection D, a jury's findings under subsection E are not binding and conclusive, but are merely advisory, informing the conscience of the chancellor. Nelms v. Nelms, 236 Va. 281, 374 S.E.2d 4 (1988).

Appellate review where chancellor decides case despite jury verdict. — When the chancellor has decided the case himself, despite the verdict of the jury and contrary to their findings, on appeal the duty devolves upon the appellate court to examine the evidence, and if in its opinion the preponderance thereof is with the verdict, the decree will be reversed and final judgment entered in accordance with the verdict. But where the evidence preponderates in support of the judgment of the chancellor, his judgment will be upheld. Angstadt v. Atlantic Mut. Ins. Co., 254 Va. 286, 492 S.E.2d 118 (1997).

II. DECISIONS UNDER PRIOR LAW.

A. General Consideration.

Editor's note. — The cases cited below were decided under corresponding provisions of former law. The term "this section," as used below, refers to former provisions.

B. Jury Trial of Right.

Subsection A applicable to trials in a court of record. — Subsection A is applicable to all trials in the courts of record, other than the Supreme Court, had on motions (now in actions at law), and is not confined to motions for the recovery of money in an action of debt. Lambert v. Board of Supvrs., 140 Va. 62, 124 S.E. 254 (1924).

C. Trial by Jury of Plea in Equity.

Subsection D mandatory. — The object of this section is not to inform the conscience of the chancellor, but to determine the issue of fact raised by the plea. The chancellor has no discretion about awarding the jury trial. The statute is mandatory that "either party may have such issue tried by a jury," and the verdict when rendered stands like any other verdict of a jury where the right to such trial is given without discretion on the part of the court. The court cannot disregard the verdict nor discharge the jury before verdict, as he may on the trial of an issue out of chancery. Towson v. Towson, 126 Va. 640, 102 S.E. 48 (1920); Elmore v. Maryland & Va. Milk Producers' Ass'n, 145 Va. 42, 134 S.E. 472 (1926); Fitchette v. Cape Charles Bank, 146 Va. 715, 132 S.E. 688 (1926); Phillips v. Wells, 147 Va. 1030, 133 S.E. 581 (1927).

The object of subsection D is to determine the issue of fact raised by the plea, not to inform the conscience of the chancellor. The chancellor has no discretion about awarding the jury trial when the plea has been properly filed. It is a wholly statutory proceeding. Eagle Lodge, Inc. v. Hofmeyer, 193 Va. 864, 71 S.E.2d 195 (1952).

How issue made up. — In a proceeding by motion in order to entitle the defendants to a trial by jury, an issue must be made up. This issue may be tendered by a plea, or by an informal statement in writing of the grounds of defense. A mere oral statement is not sufficient. In cases where the statute requires the plea to be verified by affidavit, that requirement of the statute must be complied with. Preston v. Salem Imp. Co., 91 Va. 583, 22 S.E. 486 (1895); Whitley v. Booker Brick Co., 113 Va. 434, 74 S.E. 160 (1912).

No formal pleas are necessary, except in cases where statutes require them, but the defendant may make his defense by an informal statement in writing of the grounds of his defense. This statement will be treated as a plea or pleas, and the plaintiff may rely thereto with like informality. The defendant, however, may plead formally if he chooses, according to the course of the common law, and this is in all cases the better practice. But in every case an issue must in some way be made up on the record, in order to have a trial by jury. Dickens v. Radford-Willis S. Ry., 121 Va. 353, 93 S.E. 625 (1917).

Pleading must be in form and substance a plea. — Subsection D requires that the pleading filed by a defendant, upon which the plaintiff may take issue and as to which either party may then demand a jury trial, be in form and in substance a plea, and not merely an answer or an answer and cross-claim. Bolling v. GMAC, 204 Va. 4, 129 S.E.2d 54 (1963).

Issue for trial by jury, under this section, is entirely different from an issue out of chancery. Elmore v. Maryland & Va. Milk Producers' Ass'n, 145 Va. 42, 134 S.E. 472 (1926); Phillips v. Wells, 147 Va. 1030, 133 S.E. 581 (1926).

The defense by plea is used where the defendant desires to present a single state of facts (although possibly made up of numerous circumstances) as a defense to the plaintiff's suit. If the plea is sufficient, that is, if it states a matter of fact sufficient, if true, to end the controversy in favor of defendant, then defendant is entitled as a matter of right to have the issue tried by a jury. Campbell v. Johnson, 203 Va. 43, 122 S.E.2d 907 (1961).

The office of a plea is to present a simple issue of fact which operates as a bar to the plaintiff's right of recovery. The fact put in issue by the plea constitutes in itself a complete defense to the bill, or to that part of the bill to which it is pleaded. Bolling v. GMAC, 204 Va. 4, 129 S.E.2d 54 (1963).

Plaintiffs are entitled to trial by jury of their punitive damage claim. O'Brien v. Snow, 215 Va. 403, 210 S.E.2d 165 (1974).

Negligence, contributory negligence, and proximate cause are ordinarily questions for the jury to determine. It is only when reasonable men should not differ as to the reasonable inferences and proper conclusions to be drawn from the evidence that they become questions of law to be decided by the court. Schutt v. Brockwell, 214 Va. 38, 196 S.E.2d 921 (1973).

Pleas to jurisdiction in divorce action. — In a suit for divorce brought by a husband on the ground of desertion, two pleas to the jurisdiction were filed by the wife. Issue was taken on these pleas, and a verdict found by a jury on both pleas in favor of the husband. The jury trial was demanded by the husband. It was held that the trial court committed no error in impaneling a jury to try the issues made on the pleas to the jurisdiction, as this was not a case of an issue out of chancery, and was not controlled by the rules regulating the awarding of such issues, but is a wholly statutory proceeding. Towson v. Towson, 126 Va. 640, 102 S.E. 48 (1920).

Plea denying embezzlement. — Where the bill sought to impose a trust on embezzled property, a plea denying the embezzlement raised no issue as to the amount embezzled. Under the plea the question of the amount taken could not properly have been submitted to the jury. The amount involved in the embezzlement was in no way a bar to the suit. It was merely an issue as to the merits of the suit and therefore properly subject to a general answer in equity and not subject to a special plea. Campbell v. Johnson, 203 Va. 43, 122 S.E.2d 907 (1961).

Plea of misrepresentation and asking "offset". — In a suit to enforce a conditional sales contract defendant's "answer and cross-claim" alleging misrepresentation by the seller and asking damages to be "offset" against the purchase price was not a plea such as is contemplated by this section. Bolling v. GMAC, 204 Va. 4, 129 S.E.2d 54 (1963).

D. Issue Out of Chancery.

The object of an issue is to satisfy the conscience of the chancellor in a doubtful case. An issue is not directed merely because the evidence is contradictory. The propriety of ordering an issue is determined by the application of sound legal discretion to the circumstances of the situation. Crebs v. Jones, 79 Va. 381 (1884); Bunkley v. Commonwealth, 130 Va. 55, 108 S.E. 1 (1921). See also, Catron v. Norton Hdwe. Co., 123 Va. 380, 96 S.E. 853 (1918); Hook v. Hook, 126 Va. 249, 101 S.E. 223 (1919); Elmore v. Maryland & Va. Milk Producers' Ass'n, 145 Va. 42, 134 S.E. 472 (1926).

The chancellor is the keeper of his own conscience and the purpose of an issue out of chancery is to satisfy him. Harris v. Citizens Bank & Trust Co., 172 Va. 111, 200 S.E. 652 (1939).

Judicial discretion. — It was not intended by subsection E to change the firmly established rule of law that the chancellor is to properly exercise his discretion on sound legal principles of reason and justice. Any other interpretation of subsection E would make the whole matter of directing an issue one of right and not of discretion on the part of the court. Stevens v. Duckett, 107 Va. 17, 57 S.E. 601 (1907); Bunkley v. Commonwealth, 130 Va. 55, 108 S.E. 1 (1921); Southgate v. Sanford & Brooks Co., 147 Va. 554, 137 S.E. 485 (1927).

The granting of an issue out of chancery under this section lies not within the arbitrary, but within the sound judicial discretion of the chancellor. Elmore v. Maryland & Va. Milk Producers' Ass'n, 145 Va. 42, 134 S.E. 472 (1926).

Discretion subject to review. — The object of an issue is to satisfy the conscience of the chancellor in a doubtful case. But it is not to be directed merely because the evidence is contradictory. The conflict of evidence must be great and its weight so nearly evenly balanced that the court is unable or with difficulty able to determine where preponderance lies. It is a matter within the sound judicial discretion of the chancellor and is subject to review on appeal. Eastern Fin. Co. v. Gordon, 179 Va. 674, 20 S.E.2d 522 (1942).

Where the chancellor (although not requested to do so) has failed to order an issue out of chancery in a proper case, and the Supreme Court is not satisfied that the ends of justice have been attained, it will reverse and remand the cause, with directions to impanel a jury and determine the issue. Catron v. Norton Hdwe. Co., 123 Va. 380, 96 S.E. 853 (1918); Hook v. Hook, 126 Va. 249, 101 S.E. 223 (1919).

The chancellor may order an issue out of chancery, under subsection E, but it is a matter subject to his sound judicial discretion and is subject to review on appeal. To justify it, the conflict of evidence must be great and its weight so nearly evenly balanced that the court is unable or with difficulty able to determine where preponderance rests. It is not enough that the evidence be contradictory. Harris v. Citizens Bank & Trust Co., 172 Va. 111, 200 S.E. 652 (1939).

When issue should be ordered. — In cases of exceptional difficulty and conflict of testimony it is error for the court to fail to order an issue out of chancery. Bunkley v. Commonwealth, 130 Va. 55, 108 S.E. 1 (1921). See also, Elmore v. Maryland & Va. Milk Producers' Ass'n, 145 Va. 42, 134 S.E. 472 (1926).

What affidavits must show. — The mere allegation in an affidavit by either the plaintiff or defendant that the case would be rendered doubtful by the conflicting evidence of the opposite party, is not sufficient to cause the court to direct an issue out of chancery. In a motion to direct an issue in a chancery cause, the affidavit, or affidavits, must show the reason for such direction and call in question the exercise of the sound discretion of the court. Southgate v. Sanford & Brooks Co., 147 Va. 554, 137 S.E. 485 (1927).

It is difficult to see how the affidavit could have been amplified unless it had set out in detail precisely what the witness would have testified to, and this was not required. Eastern Fin. Co. v. Gordon, 179 Va. 674, 20 S.E.2d 522 (1942).

Affidavits alone held insufficient grounds for order. — It was held that under subsection E, that the mere affidavits of parties and counsel that the case will be rendered doubtful by conflicting evidence, is not sufficient to warrant a chancellor in ordering an issue. Stevens v. Duckett, 107 Va. 17, 57 S.E. 601 (1907).

Where petitioners in their affidavit stated that they would introduce "a large number of witnesses who would contradict the witnesses of the complainant, and that there would result a great conflict in the testimony to be offered by the parties to the suit, presenting issues of fact which are necessary to be determined, out of a mass of conflicting testimony, in order to arrive at a correct decision of the case," and asked the court to direct an issue out of chancery, the court erred in directing an issue upon this affidavit, and the case should be considered on the merits, as if no issue had been awarded. Bunkley v. Commonwealth, 130 Va. 55, 108 S.E. 1 (1921).

Verdict merely persuasive. — The verdict, when an issue out of chancery has been directed, is not binding but is merely persuasive. Harris v. Citizens Bank & Trust Co., 172 Va. 111, 200 S.E. 652 (1939).

But chancellor should generally abide by it. — As a general proposition, when an issue is properly ordered it is the practice, unless good cause appears for the contrary course, for the chancellor to abide by the verdict. Bunkley v. Commonwealth, 130 Va. 55, 108 S.E. 1 (1921).

Where no objection was made in trial

court to action of the court in directing an issue out of chancery on its own motion, objection for the first time in the appellate court came too late and would not be considered. Twohy v. Harris, 194 Va. 69, 72 S.E.2d 329 (1952).

Where parties did not object in trial court, thus in effect agreed to the direction of an issue out of chancery by such court on its own motion, the effect of the verdict on appeal is the same as it would have been had the issue been directed at the instance of one of the parties upon showing of the necessity therefor. Twohy v. Harris, 194 Va. 69, 72 S.E.2d 329 (1952).

Standard of review. — The settled practice is that when a question of fact is referred to a jury in an issue out of chancery, depending upon conflicting testimony, the verdict approved by the trial court will be affirmed on appeal unless it is palpably and obviously erroneous or without evidence to support it. Twohy v. Harris, 194 Va. 69, 72 S.E.2d 329 (1952).

The necessity for an issue out of chancery must plainly appear before the Supreme Court can say that judicial discretion has been abused in not directing it. Harris v. Citizens Bank & Trust Co., 172 Va. 111, 200 S.E. 652 (1939).

ARTICLE 2.

Jurors.

§ 8.01-337. Who liable to serve as jurors. — All citizens over eighteen years of age who have been residents of the Commonwealth one year, and of the county, city or town in which they reside six months next preceding their being summoned to serve as such, and competent in other respects, except as hereinafter provided, shall be liable to serve as jurors. No person shall be deemed incompetent to serve on any jury because of blindness or partial blindness. Military personnel of the United States Army, Air Force or Navy shall not be considered residents of this Commonwealth by reason of their being stationed herein. (Code 1950, § 8-208.2; 1973, c. 439; 1977, c. 617; 1987, c. 189.)

Cross references. — For provisions prohibiting the penalizing of an employee for service on jury panel, see § 18.2-465.1. For provisions relating to trial by jury in criminal cases, see § 19.2-260 et seq.

Law Review. — For comment on the petit jury in Virginia, see 24 Wash. & Lee L. Rev. 366 (1967). For survey of Virginia law on practice and pleading for the year 1969-1970, see 56 Va. L. Rev. 1500 (1970). For article, "Trial by Jury and Speedy Justice," see 28 Wash. & Lee L. Rev. 309 (1971). For survey of Virginia criminal law for the year 1971-1972, see 58 Va. L. Rev. 1206 (1972). For note "The Constitutionality of Excluding Young People From Jury Service," see 29 Wash. & Lee L. Rev. 131 (1972). For survey of Virginia law on pleading and practice for the year 1972-1973, see 59 Va. L. Rev. 1559 (1973). For a note, "Invaluable Tool vs. Unfair Use of Private Information: Examining Prosecutors' Use of Jurors' Criminal History Records in Voir Dire," see 56 Wash. & Lee L. Rev. 1079 (1999).

I. DECISIONS UNDER PRIOR LAW.

Editor's note. — The cases cited below were decided under corresponding provisions of former law. The term "this section," as used below, refers to former provisions.

Disqualification and exemption provisions nondiscriminatory. — Virginia law has many disqualification and exemption provisions for selection to the jury list, none of which are discriminatory. Stephens v. Cox, 449 F.2d 657 (4th Cir. 1971).

Some Virginia disqualifications and exemptions, by an entirely impartial operation, may disqualify more Negroes than whites. Stephens v. Cox, 449 F.2d 657 (4th Cir. 1971).

Duty to learn who is qualified. — Where personal knowledge of the races of persons to be selected for the jury list is a factor, a charge of discrimination may not be avoided by a showing that sufficient qualified Negroes were unknown to the selecting officials. There is a duty to learn who is qualified. The same principle is applicable to the preparation of the list of potential grand jurors. Stephens v. Cox, 449 F.2d 657 (4th Cir. 1971).

Token inclusion of Negroes forbidden. — The Constitution forbids not only the exclusion of Negroes from jury service, but all discrimination by race. A token inclusion of Negroes is also forbidden. Stephens v. Cox, 449 F.2d 657 (4th Cir. 1971).

Prima facie case of racial discrimination. — A showing that a substantial disparity exists between the proportion of presumptively qualified Negroes in the general population and their proportion on juries will establish a prima facie case of racial discrimination, if the disparity is coupled either with additional positive indicia of discrimination or with a showing that the selection procedure provides an opportunity for discrimination. Stephens v. Cox, 449 F.2d 657 (4th Cir. 1971).

Suggestion of circumstances lawfully accounting for disparity insufficient. — Where there are many possible circumstances which, if they exist, might account lawfully for an observed disparity between the number of adult Negroes and the number of Negroes serving on juries in a certain locality, the suggestion of their possible existence is not enough. It must be demonstrated by the Commonwealth when the facts shown prima facie are indicative of discrimination. Stephens v. Cox, 449 F.2d 657 (4th Cir. 1971).

Discrimination against women not proved. — Where the jury list was properly chosen in accord with this section, the mere absence of women did not constitute proof of purposeful and intentional discrimination. Near v. Commonwealth, 202 Va. 20, 116 S.E.2d 85 (1960), cert. denied, 365 U.S. 873, 81 S. Ct. 907, 5 L. Ed. 2d 862 (1961); 369 U.S. 862, 82 S. Ct. 951, 8 L. Ed. 2d 19 (1962).

§ 8.01-338. Who disqualified. — The following persons shall be disqualified from serving as jurors:
1. Persons adjudicated incapacitated;
2. Persons convicted of treason or a felony; or
3. Any other person under a disability as defined in § 8.01-2 and not included in subdivisions 1 or 2 above. (Code 1950, § 8-208.3; 1973, c. 439; 1977, c. 617; 1997, c. 801.)

REVISERS' NOTE

Subsection 3 of former § 8-208.3 has been deleted as no longer applicable. Added is new subsection 3 which disqualifies as jurors all persons under a disability as defined in § 8.01-2, which is obviously broader in coverage than the former disqualification.

Law Review. — For comment on rights of the convicted felon on parole, see 13 U. Rich. L. Rev. 367 (1979).

I. DECISIONS UNDER CURRENT LAW.

No showing of "probable injustice." — Although two convicted felons served on defendant's jury, trial court was not required to set aside verdict and grant him a new trial for no evidence was presented to the court to suggest that the two jurors' legal disability as felons would probably cause injustice to the defendant. Mighty v. Commonwealth, 17 Va. App. 495, 438 S.E.2d 495 (1993).

§ 8.01-339. No person eligible for whom request is made. — No person shall be eligible to serve on any jury when he, or any person for him, solicits or requests a jury commissioner to place his name in a jury box or in any way designate such person as a juror. (Code 1950, § 8-208.4; 1973, c. 439; 1977, c. 617.)

§ 8.01-340. No person to serve who has case at that term. — No person shall be admitted to serve as a juror at a term of a court during which he has any matter of controversy which has been or is expected to be tried by a jury during the same term. (Code 1950, § 8-208.5; 1973, c. 439; 1977, c. 617.)

§ 8.01-341. Who are exempt from jury service. — The following shall be exempt from serving on juries in civil and criminal cases:
1. The President and Vice-President of the United States,
2. The Governor, Lieutenant Governor and Attorney General of the Commonwealth,
3. The members of both houses of Congress,
4. The members of the General Assembly, while in session or during a period when the member would be entitled to a legislative continuance as a matter of right under § 30-5,

5. Licensed practicing attorneys,
6. The judge of any court, members of the State Corporation Commission, members of the Virginia Workers' Compensation Commission, and magistrates,
7. Sheriffs, deputy sheriffs, state police, and police in counties, cities and towns,
8. The superintendent of the penitentiary and his assistants and the persons composing the guard,
9. Superintendents and jail officers, as defined in § 53.1-1, of regional jails. (Code 1950, § 8-208.6; 1973, c. 439; 1977, cc. 458, 617; 1978, cc. 176, 340; 1980, c. 535; 1982, c. 315; 1987, c. 256; 1990, c. 758; 1993, c. 572; 1998, c. 83.)

Editor's note. — Pursuant to § 9-77.11 and Acts 1977, c. 617, cl. 4, the Code Commission has given effect, in this section, to the amendment to former § 8-208.6, corresponding to this section, by Acts 1977, c. 458. The amendment deleted subdivisions 10 through 13, 18, 22, 23, 26 and 27. All of the classes exempted in the deleted subdivisions are included as optional exemptions in § 8.01-341.1, also enacted by Acts 1977, c. 458.

Law Review. — For survey of Virginia constitutional law for the year 1972-1973, see 59 Va. L. Rev. 1445 (1973). For comment, "The Questionable Validity of the Automatic Exemption of Attorneys from Jury Service," see 14 U. Rich. L. Rev. 837 (1980).

I. DECISIONS UNDER PRIOR LAW.

Editor's note. — The case cited below was decided under corresponding provisions of former law. The term "this statute," as used below, refers to former provisions.

Disqualification and exemption provisions nondiscriminatory. — Virginia law has many disqualification and exemption provisions for selection to the jury list, none of which are discriminatory. Stephens v. Cox, 449 F.2d 657 (4th Cir. 1971).

Some of the Virginia disqualifications and exemptions, by an entirely impartial operation, may disqualify more Negroes than whites. Stephens v. Cox, 449 F.2d 657 (4th Cir. 1971).

§ 8.01-341.1. Exemptions from jury service upon request. — Any of the following persons may serve on juries in civil and criminal cases but shall be exempt from jury service upon his request:
1. through 3. [Repealed.]
4. A mariner actually employed in maritime service,
5. through 7. [Repealed.]
8. A person who has legal custody of and is necessarily and personally responsible for a child or children sixteen years of age or younger requiring continuous care by him during normal court hours,
9. A person who is necessarily and personally responsible for a person having a physical or mental impairment requiring continuous care by him during normal court hours,
10. Any person over seventy years of age,
11. Any person whose spouse is summoned to serve on the same jury panel,
12. Any person who is the only person performing services for a business, commercial or agricultural enterprise and whose services are so essential to the operations of the business, commercial or agricultural enterprise that such enterprise must close or cease to function if such person is required to perform jury duty. (Code 1970, § 8-208.6:1; 1977, c. 458; 1987, c. 256; 1997, c. 693; 1999, c. 153.)

The number of this section was assigned by the Virginia Code Commission, the number in the 1977 act having been 8-208.6:1.

The 1999 amendment rewrote the introductory paragraph, which formerly read: "The following may claim exemptions from serving-on juries in civil and criminal cases," and substituted "A mariner" for "Mariners" in subdivision 4.

Law Review. — For comment, "The Questionable Validity of the Automatic Exemption of Attorneys From Jury Service," see 14 U. Rich. L. Rev. 837 (1980).

§ 8.01-341.2. Deferral or limitation of jury service for particular occupational inconvenience.

— The court, on its own motion, may exempt any person from jury service for a particular term of court, or limit that person's service to particular dates of that term, if serving on a jury during that term or certain dates of that term of court would cause such person a particular occupational inconvenience. Any such person who is selected for jury service, and who is exempted under the provisions of this section, shall not be discharged from his obligation to serve on a jury, but such obligation shall only be deferred until the term of court next after such particular occupational inconvenience shall end. (1981, c. 108; 1987, c. 155.)

I. DECISIONS UNDER CURRENT LAW.

Privilege is personal to juror and unrelated to employer's inconvenience. — The privilege afforded by this section, one the statute makes available at the discretion of the trial court, is purely personal to the prospective juror and altogether unrelated to the inconvenience suffered by the person's employer. Mu'Min v. Commonwealth, 239 Va. 433, 389 S.E.2d 886 (1990), aff'd, 500 U.S. 415, 111 S. Ct. 1899, 114 L. Ed. 2d 493, reh'g denied, 501 U.S. 1269, 112 S. Ct. 13, 115 L. Ed. 2d 1097 (1991).

§ 8.01-342. Restrictions on amount of jury service permitted.

— A. The jury commissioners shall not include on the jury list provided for in § 8.01-345 the name of any person who has been called and reported to any state court for jury duty at any time during the period of three years next preceding the date of completion of such jury list.

B. If such person has been called and reported for jury duty in the trial of any case, either civil or criminal, at any one term of a court, he shall not be permitted to serve as a juror in any civil or criminal case, at any other term of that court during the three-year period set forth in subsection A of this section, unless all the persons whose names are in the jury box have been drawn to serve during such three-year period; however, such person shall be permitted to serve on any special jury ordered pursuant to § 8.01-362 and on any grand jury. (Code 1950, §§ 8-208.7, 8-208.10; 1973, c. 439; 1974, c. 369; 1977, cc. 451, 617; 1984, c. 165; 1992, c. 312; 1994, c. 27.)

REVISERS' NOTE

Subsections A and B of § 8.01-342 combine the last paragraph of former § 8-208.10 and the first paragraph of former § 8-208.7, respectively. Minor language changes have been made for clarity and are not intended to alter the substance of the former sections.

ARTICLE 3.

Selection of Jurors.

§ 8.01-343. Appointment of jury commissioners.

— The judge of each circuit court in which juries are impaneled shall, prior to the first day of July in each year, appoint for the next ensuing year ending on the following first day of July not less than two nor more than fifteen persons as jury commissioners, who shall be competent to serve as jurors under the provisions of this chapter, and shall be citizens of intelligence, morality, and integrity. Any one judge of the judicial circuit may make such appointment under this section. No practicing attorney-at-law, however, shall be appointed as a jury commissioner.

Such appointment shall be certified by the judge to the clerk of the court for which the appointment is made, who shall enter the same on the common-law order book of such court. No jury commissioner shall be eligible to reappointment for at least three years after the expiration of the year for which he was appointed. For the purpose of this section, the two divisions of the Circuit Court of the City of Richmond shall be deemed to be separate courts. (Code 1950, § 8-208.8; 1973, c. 439; 1977, c. 617; 1979, c. 269; 1996, c. 332; 1999, c. 221; 2000, c. 251.)

The 1999 amendment substituted "fifteen" for "nine" in the first sentence.
The 2000 amendments. — The 2000 amendment by c. 251 substituted "July" for "October" twice in the first sentence.

§ 8.01-344. Notification of jury commissioners; their oath.

— Such commissioners shall be immediately notified of their appointment by the clerk, and before entering upon the discharge of their duties shall take and subscribe an oath or affirmation before the clerk of such court in the following form: "I do solemnly swear (or affirm) that I will honestly, without favor or prejudice, perform the duties of jury commissioner during the year; that in selecting persons to be drawn as jurors, I will not select any person I believe to be disqualified or exempt from serving as a juror; that I will select none whom I have been requested to select; and that in all my selections I will endeavor to promote only the impartial administration of justice." (Code 1950, § 8-208.9; 1973, c. 439; 1977, c. 617.)

Law Review. — For survey of Virginia law on pleading and practice for the year 1972-1973, see 59 Va. L. Rev. 1559 (1973).

I. DECISIONS UNDER PRIOR LAW.

Editor's note. — The cases cited below were decided under corresponding provisions of former law. The term "this section," as used below, refers to former provisions.

Constitutionality. — The jury selection process under former § 8-181 was not unconstitutional on its face. Archer v. Mayes, 213 Va. 633, 194 S.E.2d 707 (1973).

Section insures selection of truly representative jury. — If the command of this section is obeyed as the solemn oath dictates, it insures selection of a jury truly representative of the community, and constitutional requirements are satisfied. Archer v. Mayes, 213 Va. 633, 194 S.E.2d 707 (1973).

Selection of cross-section required. — Nothing in this section prevents the commissioners from selecting jurors who represent a cross-section of the population of the community suitable in intelligence and honesty for that duty. To the contrary, the commissioners are required, in the performance of their duty, to select prospective jurors who represent a cross-section of the community. Archer v. Mayes, 213 Va. 633, 194 S.E.2d 707 (1973).

Commissioners not permitted to select only persons personally known to them. — There is no language in the jury commissioners' oath which states that the commissioners are required or permitted to select only those persons who are personally known to them. The duty of the commissioners is to select only those persons whom they "believe to be of good repute for intelligence and honesty." This belief may come from any number of reliable sources in the community where prospective jurors reside. Archer v. Mayes, 213 Va. 633, 194 S.E.2d 707 (1973).

§ 8.01-345. Lists of qualified persons to be prepared by jury commissioners; random selection process.

— The commissioners shall, not later than December 1 following their appointment, submit a list showing the names, addresses and, if available, the occupations of such of the inhabitants of their respective counties or cities as are well qualified under § 8.01-337 to serve as jurors and are not excluded or exempt by §§ 8.01-338 to 8.01-341 and 8.01-342. Such master jury list shall be used in selecting jurors for a twelve-month period beginning on the first day of the first term of court in the calendar year next succeeding December 1. The number of persons selected for each court shall be as specified in the order appointing the commissioners.

The jury commissioners shall utilize random selection techniques, either manual, mechanical or electronic, using a current voter registration list and, where feasible, a list of persons issued a driver's license as defined in § 46.2-100 from the Department of Motor Vehicles, city or county directories, telephone books, personal property tax rolls, and other such lists as may be designated and approved by the chief judge of the circuit, to select the jurors representative of the broad community interests, to be placed on the master jury list. The commissioners shall make reasonable effort to exclude the names of deceased persons and unqualified persons from the master jury list. After such random selection, the commissioners shall apply such statutory exceptions and exemptions as may be applicable to the names so selected. The chief judge shall promulgate such procedural rules as are necessary to ensure the integrity of the random selection process and to ensure compliance with other provisions of law with respect to jury selection and service.

Where a city and county adjoin, in whole or in part, the names of the inhabitants of a city shall not be placed upon the county list, nor those of a county upon the city list except in those cases in which the circuit court of the county and the circuit court of the city have concurrent jurisdiction of both civil and criminal cases arising within the territorial limits of such county or city. However, in the case of the City of Franklin and the County of Southampton, the number of jurors selected from Southampton County shall be proportionate to the number of jurors selected from the City of Franklin based upon the respective populations of the county and city. (Code 1950, § 8-208.10; 1973, c. 439; 1974, c. 369; 1977, cc. 451, 617; 1978, c. 209; 1979, c. 665; 1983, c. 107; 1984, c. 50; 1989, cc. 616, 632; 1990, c. 758; 2000, c. 828.)

REVISERS' NOTE

Section 8.01-345 is largely identical with former § 8-208.10 with the following change: The former statute required the prior authorization of the chief judge of the circuit in order for the jury commissioners to use random selection techniques, and then the use of such techniques was merely permissible. Section 8.01-345 dispenses with the prior authority of the chief judge and makes the use of random selection techniques mandatory upon the commissioners. The duty of the chief judge to promulgate procedural rules to ensure the integrity of the random selection process and compliance with other laws with respect to jury selection and service is retained.

The last paragraph of the former statute has been transferred to present § 8.01-342, as it appeared to be more closely related to the subject matter of that section.

Editor's note. — Former § 8-208.10, corresponding to this section, was amended by Acts 1977, c. 451. Pursuant to § 9-77.11 and Acts 1977, c. 617, cl. 4, that amendment was deemed to have amended this section.

The 2000 amendments. — The 2000 amendment by c. 828 added the present second sentence in the second paragraph.

Law Review. — For survey of Virginia constitutional law for the year 1972-1973, see 59 Va. L. Rev. 1445 (1973).

I. Decisions Under Current Law.
II. Decisions Under Prior Law.

I. DECISIONS UNDER CURRENT LAW.

Evidence was insufficient to establish prima facie case of racial discrimination. — Where the evidence adduced showed that jury commissioners never hand-picked jurors, where the jury selection process in county was done by random computer selection from the voter registration list, where the voter registration list did not indicate the race of the prospective jurors and jury commissioners had no way of knowing the race of prospective jury members until they arrived, and where this section sets out the procedure for jury selection and no evidence suggested that this selection process was not followed, based on this evidence, appellant failed to show intentional racial discrimination or that the juror selection process left open this opportunity, and therefore, appellant's evidence was insufficient to establish a prima facie case of racial discrimination. Moats v. Commonwealth, 12 Va. App. 349, 404 S.E.2d 244 (1991).

II. DECISIONS UNDER PRIOR LAW.

Editor's note. — The cases cited below were decided under corresponding provisions of former law. The term "this section," as used below, refer to former provisions.

Statutory provisions with respect to empaneling juries are mandatory and not directory. Harmon v. Commonwealth, 212 Va. 442, 185 S.E.2d 48 (1971).

There is a constitutional right to a jury drawn from a group which represents a cross section of the community. And a cross section of the community includes persons with varying degrees of training and intelligence and with varying economic and social positions. Under the United States Constitution, the jury is not to be made the representative of the most intelligent, the most wealthy or the most successful, nor of the least intelligent, the least wealthy, or the least successful. It is a democratic institution, representative of all qualified classes of people. Witcher v. Peyton, 405 F.2d 725 (4th Cir. 1969).

And selection must accord with this. — Section of jurors must always accord with the fact that the proper functioning of the jury system, and, indeed, our democracy itself, requires that the jury be a body truly representative of the community, and not the organ of any special group or class. If that requirement is observed, the officials charged with choosing jurors may exercise some discretion to that end that competent jurors may be called. But they must not allow the desire for competent jurors to lead them into selections which do not comport with the concept of the jury as a cross section of the community. Tendencies, no matter how slight, toward the selection of jurors by any method other than a process which will insure a trial by a representative group are undetermining processes weakening the institution of jury trial, and should be sturdily resisted. That the motives influencing such tendencies may be of the best must not blind courts to the dangers of allowing any encroachment whatsoever on this essential right. Steps innocently taken may one by one lead to the irretrievable impairment of substantial liberties. Witcher v. Peyton, 405 F.2d 725 (4th Cir. 1969).

In the selection of juries recognition must be given to the fact that those eligible for jury service are to be found in every stratum of society. Jury competence is an individual rather than a group or class matter. That fact lies at the very heart of the jury system. To disregard it is to open the door to class distinctions and discriminations which are abhorrent to the democratic ideals of trial by jury. Witcher v. Peyton, 405 F.2d 725 (4th Cir. 1969).

Admission of discrimination not needed to attack jury selection procedure. — It is not necessary to a successful attack upon a jury selection procedure that petitioner obtain an admission from the judge and jury commissioners that they have discriminated. Witcher v. Peyton, 405 F.2d 725 (4th Cir. 1969).

§ 8.01-346. Lists to be delivered to clerk and safely kept by him; addition and removal of names.

— The list so prepared shall be delivered to the clerk of the court to be safely kept by him. The judge may from time to time order the commissioners to add to the list such additional number of jurors as the court shall direct and to strike therefrom any who have become disqualified or exempt. (Code 1950, § 8-208.11; 1973, c. 439; 1977, c. 617.)

I. DECISIONS UNDER PRIOR LAW.

Editor's note. — The cases cited below were decided under corresponding provisions of former law. The term "this section," as used below, refers to former provisions.

This section is not unconstitutional on its face. Archer v. Mayes, 213 Va. 633, 194 S.E.2d 707 (1973).

The jury list is a secret document which is not open to public inspection. Archer v. Mayes, 213 Va. 633, 194 S.E.2d 707 (1973).

The proper administration of justice requires that the jury list be kept secret until the jurors drawn for service, unless good cause be shown. The jury list is in no sense a public record to be exposed to the general public. Archer v. Mayes, 213 Va. 633, 194 S.E.2d 707 (1973).

And it cannot be examined except for good cause shown. Archer v. Mayes, 213 Va. 633, 194 S.E.2d 707 (1973).

Nothing in this section deprives the judge of the court in the exercise of his discretion, where good cause is shown, to permit an examination of the jury list. But it cannot be inferred that the jury list shall be opened for inspection to members of the bar or private citizens without assigning good and sufficient reasons therefor. Archer v. Mayes, 213 Va. 633, 194 S.E.2d 707 (1973).

Thus, the right of access to official records allowed under the Freedom of Information Act does not include jury

lists. Archer v. Mayes, 213 Va. 633, 194 S.E.2d 707 (1973).

§ 8.01-347. How names put in jury box. — When such list is made out, the commissioners shall cause all the names thereon to be fairly written, each on a separate paper or ballot, and shall so fold or roll up the ballots that they will resemble each other as nearly as may be and the names written thereon will not be visible on the outside, and shall deposit the ballots with the list in a secure box prepared for that purpose. Such box shall be locked and safely kept by the clerk of such court and opened only by the direction of the judge thereof. (Code 1950, § 8-208.12; 1973, c. 439; 1977, c. 617.)

I. DECISIONS UNDER PRIOR LAW.

Editor's note. — The cases cited below were decided under corresponding provisions of former law. The term "this section," as used below, refers to former provisions.

This section is not unconstitutional on its face. Archer v. Mayes, 213 Va. 633, 194 S.E.2d 707 (1973).

The jury list is a secret document which is not open to public inspection. Archer v. Mayes, 213 Va. 633, 194 S.E.2d 707 (1973).

The proper administration of justice requires that the jury list be kept secret until the jurors are drawn for service, unless good cause be shown. The jury list is in no sense a public record to be exposed to the general public. Archer v. Mayes, 213 Va. 633, 194 S.E.2d 707 (1973).

And it cannot be examined except for good cause shown. Archer v. Mayes, 213 Va. 633, 194 S.E.2d 707 (1973).

Nothing in the statutes deprives the judge of the court in the exercise of his discretion, where good cause is shown, to permit an examination of the jury list. But it cannot be inferred that the jury list shall be opened for inspection to members of the bar or private citizens without assigning good and sufficient reasons therefor. Archer v. Mayes, 213 Va. 633, 194 S.E.2d 707 (1973).

Thus, the right of access to official records allowed under the Freedom of Information Act does not include jury lists. Archer v. Mayes, 213 Va. 633, 194 S.E.2d 707 (1973).

§ 8.01-348. How names of jurors drawn from box. — Prior to or during any term of court at which a jury may be necessary, the clerk or deputy clerk, in the presence of the judge or, in his absence, a commissioner in chancery appointed for the purpose by the judge, shall, after thoroughly mixing the ballots in the box, openly draw therefrom such number of ballots as are necessary for the trial of all cases during the term or as the judge shall direct. However, a commissioner shall not be eligible to witness the drawing of a jury to be used in the trial of any case in which he will be interested as attorney or otherwise. (Code 1950, § 8-208.13; 1973, c. 439; 1977, c. 617; 1983, c. 425.)

I. DECISIONS UNDER PRIOR LAW.

Editor's note. — The case cited below was decided under corresponding provisions of former law. The term "this statute," as used below, refers to former provisions.

Statutory provisions with respect to empaneling juries are mandatory and not directory. Harmon v. Commonwealth, 212 Va. 442, 185 S.E.2d 48 (1971).

§ 8.01-349. Notations on ballots drawn; return to box; when such ballots may be drawn again. — If any ballot drawn from the box shall bear the name of a person known by the clerk or other person attending the drawing to be deceased, exempt or disqualified by law, not a resident of the county or city, or physically or mentally incapacitated for jury service, an appropriate notation on the ballot, as well as opposite the name of such person on the jury list, shall be made and the ballot shall be placed by the clerk in an envelope kept for that purpose. The other ballots, marked "drawn," shall be placed in a separate envelope and a notation of the date of the drawing shall be made on the jury list opposite the name of each juror drawn. The envelope shall be kept in the box. After all ballots have been drawn from the box, the ballots marked "drawn" may be again drawn subject to the provisions hereof applying to the original drawing. (Code 1950, § 8-208.14; 1973, c. 439; 1977, c. 617.)

§ 8.01-350: Repealed by Acts 1977, c. 451.

Cross references. — For present statute covering selection of jurors by mechanical or electronic means, see § 8.01-350.1.
Editor's note. — Acts 1977, c. 451, repealed former § 8-208.14:1, corresponding to § 8.01-350 as enacted by Acts 1977, c. 617. Pursuant to § 9-77.11 and Acts 1977, c. 617, cl. 4, the Code Commission has treated Acts 1977, c. 451, as repealing § 8.01-350.

§ 8.01-350.1. Selection of jurors by mechanical or electronic techniques for the term of court. — Notwithstanding the provisions of §§ 8.01-347 through 8.01-349, the chief judge may order that selection of the list of jurors necessary for the trial of all cases during any term of court for that year be made by the use of random selection techniques, either mechanically or electronically, from the list submitted pursuant to § 8.01-345. (1978, c. 400.)

§ 8.01-351. Preparation and disposition of list of jurors drawn. — The clerk shall make and sign a list of the names on the ballots in alphabetical order showing the name, age, address, occupation and employer of each juror, and shall deliver an attested copy of the list to the sheriff. The list shall be signed also by the judge or the commissioner in chancery appointed by the judge. The list shall be available in the clerk's office for inspection by counsel in any case to be tried by a jury during the term. (Code 1950, § 8-208.15; 1973, c. 439; 1977, c. 617; 1988, c. 818.)

§ 8.01-352. Objections to irregularities in jury lists or for legal disability; effect thereof. — A. Prior to the jury being sworn, the following objections may be made without leave of court: (i) an objection specifically pointing out the irregularity in any list or lists of jurors made by the clerk from names drawn from the jury box, or in the drawing, summoning, returning or impaneling of jurors or in copying or signing or failing to sign the list, and (ii) an objection to any juror on account of any legal disability; after the jury is sworn such objection shall be made only with leave of court.

B. Unless objection to such irregularity or disability is made pursuant to subsection A herein and unless it appears that the irregularity was intentional or that the irregularity or disability be such as to probably cause injustice in a criminal case to the Commonwealth or to the accused and in a civil case to the party making the objection, then such irregularity or disability shall not be cause for summoning a new panel or juror or for setting aside a verdict or granting a new trial. (Code 1950, §§ 8-208.7, 8-208.27, 8-208.29; 1973, c. 439; 1977, c. 617.)

REVISERS' NOTE

Section 8.01-352 consolidates certain provisions found in former §§ 8-208.7, 8-208.27, and 8-208.29. Under this section, objections to any irregularity in the jury list, etc., or to any legal disability generally must be made before the jury is sworn. Thereafter, such objections may be made only with leave of court. This alters former § 8-208.27 which permits objection only before the jury is sworn. Furthermore, the present section places an objection to a legal disability under former § 8-208.29 on the same footing as an objection to jury list irregularity under former § 8-208.27. The revisers believe that the term "legal disability" is meant to incorporate all exemptions or disqualifications from jury service found in §§ 8.01-338 through 8.01-342.

The provision in former § 8-208.7 making it reversible error if the court should permit a juror to serve twice during the one-year period mentioned in § 8.01-342 over the objection of a party, has been eliminated.

Law Review. — For survey of Virginia law on practice and pleading for the year 1970-1971, see 57 Va. L. Rev. 1561 (1971).

I. Decisions Under Current Law.
II. Decisions Under Prior Law.

I. DECISIONS UNDER CURRENT LAW.

Erroneous exclusion of all jurors who had served on any felony panel. — Section 8.01-355 permits the trial court to excuse any jurors whose names were drawn for service on a particular panel and, thus, authorizes the trial court's direction to the clerk. The clerk's misunderstanding of the trial court's direction and the subsequent exclusion of all jurors who had served on any felony panel in the then-current term was an irregularity under subsection A of this section, which is cured under subsection B of this section, because the exclusion was not intentional, nor did it operate to cause any prejudice to defendant. Accordingly, held no reversible error in the selection of the venire. O'Dell v. Commonwealth, 234 Va. 672, 364 S.E.2d 491, cert. denied, 488 U.S. 871, 109 S. Ct. 186, 102 L. Ed. 2d 154 (1988).

No showing of "probable injustice." — Although two convicted felons served on defendant's jury, trial court was not required to set aside verdict and grant him a new trial for no evidence was presented to the court to suggest that the two jurors' legal disability as felons would probably cause injustice to the defendant. Mighty v. Commonwealth, 17 Va. App. 495, 438 S.E.2d 495 (1993).

Record failed to demonstrate that a juror who purportedly lacked proficiency in the English language had a disability which was "such as to probably cause injustice" where challenged juror understood all of the trial court's questions and the trial court made a factual finding that she had a sufficient level of understanding of the English language which permitted her to participate fully in the jury deliberations. Mason v. Commonwealth, 255 Va. 505, 498 S.E.2d 921 (1998).

A motion for a new trial on the ground of juror misconduct is addressed to the sound discretion of the trial court and, unless there has been abuse of that discretion, the judgment below will not be reversed on appeal. Commercial Union Ins. Co. v. Moorefield, 231 Va. 260, 343 S.E.2d 329 (1986).

And court has duty to investigate charges of misconduct. — In considering a motion to set aside when juror misconduct is alleged, the trial court has the affirmative duty to investigate the charges and to ascertain whether or not, as a matter of fact, the jury was guilty of such misconduct. Commercial Union Ins. Co. v. Moorefield, 231 Va. 260, 343 S.E.2d 329 (1986).

And trial court may properly summon one or more jurors to testify under oath in open court and to answer relevant questions propounded by the court and counsel about what transpired. This is an exception to the general rule that testimony of jurors is inadmissible to impeach their verdict. Ordinarily, jurors will not be allowed to explain their verdict by stating the reasons upon which their conclusions are based. Commercial Union Ins. Co. v. Moorefield, 231 Va. 260, 343 S.E.2d 329 (1986).

Hearsay affidavits not admissible in support of motion for new trial. — Although juror testimony may be received upon an issue of juror misconduct, hearsay affidavits are not admissible in support of a motion for a new trial. Nevertheless, such an affidavit may be sufficient to require the trial court to investigate the matters recited in the document. Commercial Union Ins. Co. v. Moorefield, 231 Va. 260, 343 S.E.2d 329 (1986).

Waiver of peremptory strikes not ground for seating partial panel. — Under appropriate circumstances, a waiver of peremptory strikes by one or both parties is helpful and useful to the alleviation of an overcrowded docket. However, where a defendant, as here, has alerted the court to the existence of a potential problem and elects to stand on the statutory mandate of a panel of 20 jurors, he is entitled to a full panel of impartial jurors and may not be required to accept a lesser number simply because the Commonwealth agrees to waive one or more of its peremptory strikes. Fuller v. Commonwealth, 14 Va. App. 277, 416 S.E.2d 44 (1992).

Counsel failed to provide a racially neutral reason for removing African-American from the venire. Hill v. Berry, 247 Va. 271, 441 S.E.2d 6 (1994).

The defendant did not waive its right to insist that a juror be examined, where defendant failed to summon the juror, failed to make explicit, timely demand that the court take such action, and failed to arrange for a hearing at which the juror's testimony could be presented, but before entry of the new-trial order defendant reminded the trial judge on three occasions that the court had the power to summon the juror, and on two occasions formally moved the court to summon the juror before finally ruling on the motion. Commercial Union Ins. Co. v. Moorefield, 231 Va. 260, 343 S.E.2d 329 (1986).

Plaintiff's motion not waived. — Where the trial court implicitly granted plaintiff leave of court to make his motion challenging the impaneling of jurors after the jury was sworn, and the court permitted plaintiff to make his motion, which the court subsequently considered on its merits and denied, plaintiff's motion was not waived. Hill v. Berry, 247 Va. 271, 441 S.E.2d 6 (1994).

The trial court abused its discretion in failing to summon and examine a juror who allegedly heard statements before trial which might have improperly influenced deliberations, where the juror may not have fully heard or clearly understood the statement that a third party said the husband intentionally set fire to his own home, she may have discounted it as purely hearsay and rumor, and, even if she accepted the statement, she may have disregarded it in an effort to be a conscientious juror and to give the parties a fair trial. Commercial Union Ins. Co. v. Moorefield, 231 Va. 260, 343 S.E.2d 329 (1986).

An inquiry into the effect of innocent but improper pre-trial statements made to a juror is incomplete when the trial court has not summoned and examined the particular juror to whom the statements were made. Information only from a nonjuror, a person not privy to jury deliberations, is inadequate to form the basis for a conclusion that the jury's deliberative process was probably tainted by extraneous statements. Commercial Union Ins. Co. v. Moorefield, 231 Va. 260, 343 S.E.2d 329 (1986).

Court did not err in denying appellant leave to raise issues. — In addition to leaving the court an incomplete remedy with respect to the jurors improperly excluded, the untimely motion in this case limited the court's ability to weigh the expenditure of additional judicial resources and the ensuing, perhaps substantial, delay in the administration of justice, and therefore, the trial court did not abuse its discretion in denying appellant leave to raise Batson issues after the jury was sworn. Lewis v. Commonwealth, 25 Va. App. 745, 492 S.E.2d 492 (1997).

Applied in Miller v. Commonwealth, 7 Va. App. 367, 373 S.E.2d 721 (1988).

II. DECISIONS UNDER PRIOR LAW.

Editor's note. — The cases cited below were decided under corresponding provisions of former law. The term "this section," as used below, refers to former provisions.

Statutory provisions with respect to impaneling juries are mandatory and not directory. Harmon v. Commonwealth, 212 Va. 442, 185 S.E.2d 48 (1971).

Swearing of jury should preclude subsequent exceptions. — The completion of the process of selection and the subsequent swearing of the jury should preclude the defendant from thereafter advancing exceptions to the jury. Russell v. Peyton, 278 F. Supp. 804 (W.D. Va. 1968).

Where no objection was made before the jury was sworn, it was incumbent upon the party making objection to show that he was injured by the alleged irregularity in impaneling the jury. Oyler v. Ramsey, 211 Va. 564, 179 S.E.2d 904 (1971).

Intentional irregularity not cured. — The issuance of writs of venire facias different from what the law prescribes was an intentional irregularity and not within the curative provisions of former § 19.1-201. Harmon v. Commonwealth, 212 Va. 442, 185 S.E.2d 48 (1971).

Relationship to material witness. — Defendant knowingly permitted, without objection, the brother of a material witness to be sworn as a juror, and his motion to discharge the jury was made only after it developed that the witness's testimony was not in accord with what defendant hoped and thought it would be. Even if the relationship between the juror and the witness were a sufficient reason for disqualifying the juror, defendant's objection to the qualification of the juror and his motion to discharge the jury came too late. Burks v. Webb, 199 Va. 296, 99 S.E.2d 629 (1957).

ARTICLE 4.

Jury Service.

§ 8.01-353. Notice to jurors; making copy of jury panel available to counsel; objection to notice. — A. The sheriff shall notify the jurors on the list, or such number of them as the judge may direct to appear in court on such day as the court may direct. Such notice shall be given a juror as provided by § 8.01-298. Verbal direction given by the judge, or at his direction, to a juror who has been given notice as hereinbefore provided that he appear at a later specified date, shall be a sufficient notice. Any notice given as provided herein shall have the effect of an order of court. No particular time in advance of the required appearance date shall be necessary for verbal notice hereunder, but the court may, in its discretion, excuse from service a juror who claims lack of sufficient notice. Upon request, the clerk or sheriff or other officer responsible for notifying jurors to appear in court for the trial of a case shall make available to all counsel of record in that case, a copy of the jury panel to be used for the trial of the case at least forty-eight hours before the trial. Such copy of the jury panel shall show the name, age, address, occupation and employer of each person on the panel. Any error in the information shown on such copy of the jury panel shall not be grounds for a mistrial or assignable as error on appeal, and the parties in the case shall be responsible for verifying the accuracy of such information.

B. No judgment shall be arrested or reversed for the failure of the record to show that there was service upon a juror of notice to appear in court unless made a ground of exception in the trial before the jury is sworn. (Code 1950, § 8-208.16; 1973, c. 439; 1974, c. 243; 1976, c. 261; 1977, c. 617; 1980, c. 452; 1981, c. 150; 1988, c. 350.)

REVISERS' NOTE

Section 8.01-353 is largely based on former § 8-208.16, but the reference to the term of court is omitted so that the judge may now summon the jurors for the particular day on which their attendance is required. Furthermore, service of the original notice to prospective jurors is to be in accordance with § 8.01-298.

Editor's note. — Acts 1993, c. 929, cl. 3, as amended by Acts 1994, c. 564, cl. 1, and Acts 1996, c. 616, cl. 3, provided that the enactment of § 8.01-353.01 by Acts 1993, c. 929, cl. 1, would become effective June 1, 1998, "only if state funds are provided by the General Assembly sufficient to provide adequate resources, including all local costs, for the court to carry out the purposes of this act and to fulfill its mission to serve children and families of the Commonwealth." The funding was not provided.

Law Review. — For survey of Virginia practice and pleading for the year 1975-1976, see 62 Va. L. Rev. 1460 (1976).

I. DECISIONS UNDER PRIOR LAW.

Editor's note. — The case cited below was decided under corresponding provisions of former law. The term "this statute," as used below, refers to former provisions.

The statutory provisions with respect to empaneling juries are mandatory and not directory. Harmon v. Commonwealth, 212 Va. 442, 185 S.E.2d 48 (1971).

§ 8.01-354. "Writ of venire facias" defined. — The term *"writ of venire facias"* for the purpose of this chapter shall be construed as referring to the list or lists of jurors made by the clerk from names drawn from the jury box and notice to appear in court served or mailed as provided herein shall be equivalent to summoning such juror in execution of a writ of venire facias. (Code 1950, § 8-208.24; 1973, c. 439; 1976, c. 617.)

§ 8.01-355. Jurors on list to be used for trial of cases during term; discharge or dispensing with attendance of jurors; drawing additional jurors. — Jurors whose names appear in the list provided for under §§ 8.01-348 and 8.01-351 shall be used for the trial of cases, civil and criminal, to be tried during the term. The judge shall direct the selection of as many jurors as may be necessary to appear for the trial of any case. Any court shall have power to discharge persons summoned as jurors therein, or to dispense with their attendance on any day of its sitting. When by reason of challenge or otherwise a sufficient number of jurors summoned cannot be obtained for the trial of any case, the judge may select from the names on the jury list provided for by § 8.01-345 the names of as many persons as he deems necessary and cause them to be summoned to appear forthwith for the trial. (Code 1950, § 8-208.17; 1973, c. 439; 1975, c. 359; 1977, c. 617.)

I. DECISIONS UNDER CURRENT LAW.

Erroneous exclusion of all jurors who had served on any felony panel. — This section permits the trial court to excuse any jurors whose names were drawn for service on a particular panel and, thus, authorizes the trial court's direction to the clerk. The clerk's misunderstanding of the trial court's direction and the subsequent exclusion of all jurors who had served on any felony panel in the then-current term was an irregularity under subsection A of § 8.01-352, which is cured under subsection B of § 8.01-352, because the exclusion was not intentional, nor did it operate to cause any prejudice to defendant. Accordingly, held no reversible error in the selection of the venire. O'Dell v. Commonwealth, 234 Va. 672, 364 S.E.2d 491 (1988), cert. denied, 488 U.S. 871, 109 S. Ct. 186, 102 L. Ed. 2d 154 (1988).

§ 8.01-356. Failure of juror to appear. — If any juror who has been given due notice to appear in court shall fail to do so without sufficient excuse, he shall be fined not less than $25 nor more than $100. (Code 1950, § 8-208.18; 1973, c. 439; 1977, c. 617.)

§ 8.01-357. Selection of jury panel. — On the day on which jurors have been notified to appear, jurors not excused by the court shall be called in such manner as the judge may direct to be sworn on their voir dire until a panel free from exceptions shall be obtained. The jurors shall be selected randomly. The remaining jurors may be discharged or excused subject to such orders as the court shall make. (Code 1950, § 8-208.19; 1973, c. 439; 1977, c. 617; 1999, c. 3.)

The 1999 amendment, in the second sentence, deleted "Upon motion of any party" preceding "the jurors shall" and substituted "randomly" for "by lot."

Law Review. — For note, "Criminal Procedure and Criminal Law: Virginia Supreme Court Decisions During the 70's," see 15 U. Rich. L. Rev. 585 (1981).

I. DECISIONS UNDER CURRENT LAW.

The right to a trial by an impartial jury is guaranteed under both the United States and Virginia Constitutions and this guarantee is reinforced by legislative enactment and by the rules of court. Gosling v. Commonwealth, 7 Va. App. 642, 376 S.E.2d 541 (1989).

Deferral of argument on challenge for cause. — A trial judge may have good reason to defer argument on a challenge for cause until after voir dire has been completed. However, argument on a challenge for cause should not be deferred until after the parties have exercised their peremptory challenges and the jury has been sworn. Brooks v. Commonwealth, 24 Va. App. 523, 484 S.E.2d 127 (1997).

Juror properly retained on panel. — The trial court did not erroneously overrule motion on part of defendant, who was convicted by a jury of murder in the first degree, to remove a juror from the panel for cause where juror was a conscientious and perceptive juror, fully cognizant of the duties and responsibilities attendant to that service, her responses during voir dire revealed an impartial mind, untainted by prejudgment and receptive to consideration of the case in accordance with the evidence and instructions of the court, notwithstanding prior knowledge and interest in the offenses, and she, therefore, stood indifferent to the cause and was properly retained on the panel. Swanson v. Commonwealth, 18 Va. App. 182, 442 S.E.2d 702 (1994).

The trial court erred in refusing to strike potential juror for cause where, although she stated that she would attempt not to base her judgment on information she had gained through the news media, she could not assure the court that she would render her verdict based solely on the evidence adduced at trial. Her answers raised a reasonable doubt as to her qualification to serve as a juror, a doubt that should have been resolved by granting defendant's motion to strike her for cause. DeHart v. Commonwealth, 19 Va. App. 139, 449 S.E.2d 59 (1994).

Error to force use of peremptory strike. — This section assures a defendant a right to an impartial jury drawn from a panel of 20 free from exceptions, and it is prejudicial error for the trial court to force a defendant to use the peremptory strike afforded him by § 19.2-262 to exclude a venireman who is not free from exception. Justus v. Commonwealth, 220 Va. 971, 266 S.E.2d 87 (1980).

Putting the defense in a position where it is forced to exercise its peremptory challenges to exclude a biased juror is not harmless error. Gosling v. Commonwealth, 7 Va. App. 642, 376 S.E.2d 541 (1989).

Under Virginia law, compelling defendant to use peremptory challenge to remove juror who should have been removed for cause is prejudicial error. Satcher v. Netherland, 944 F. Supp. 1222 (E.D. Va. 1996), aff'd in part and rev'd in part on other grounds sub nom. Satcher v. Pruett, 126 F.3d 561 (4th Cir.), cert. denied, 522 U.S. 1010, 118 S. Ct. 595, 139 L. Ed. 2d 431 (1997).

The right to a trial by an impartial jury is guaranteed under both the United States and Virginia Constitutions and this guarantee is reinforced by legislative enactment and by the rules of court. Gosling v. Commonwealth, 7 Va. App. 642, 376 S.E.2d 541 (1989).

Applied in Brown v. Commonwealth, 29 Va. App. 199, 510 S.E.2d 751 (1999).

§ 8.01-358. Voir dire examination of persons called as jurors. — The court and counsel for either party shall have the right to examine under oath any person who is called as a juror therein and shall have the right to ask such person or juror directly any relevant question to ascertain whether he is related to either party, or has any interest in the cause, or has expressed or formed any opinion, or is sensible of any bias or prejudice therein; and the party objecting to any juror may introduce any competent evidence in support of the objection; and if it shall appear to the court that the juror does not stand indifferent in the cause, another shall be drawn or called and placed in his stead for the trial of that case.

A juror, knowing anything relative to a fact in issue, shall disclose the same in open court. (Code 1950, §§ 8-208.28, 8-215; 1973, c. 439; 1977, c. 617; 1981, c. 280.)

Cross references. — As to ruin dire examination, see Rule 3A:14.

Law Review. — For 1985 survey of Virginia criminal procedure, see 19 U. Rich. L. Rev. 697 (1985). For a note, "Invaluable Tool vs. Unfair Use of Private Information: Examining Prosecutors' Use of Jurors' Criminal History Records in Voir Dire," see 56 Wash. & Lee L. Rev. 1079 (1999).

I. Decisions Under Current Law.
  A. General Consideration.
  B. Impartiality as to Punishment.
  C. Illustrative Cases.
II. Decisions Under Prior Law.

I. DECISIONS UNDER CURRENT LAW.

A. General Consideration.

An accused is entitled to an impartial jury as a matter of constitutional guarantee, reinforced by legislative mandate and by the rules of court. Martin v. Commonwealth, 221 Va. 436, 271 S.E.2d 123 (1980).

The right to a trial by an impartial jury is guaranteed under both the United States and Virginia Constitutions and this guarantee is reinforced by legislative enactment and by the rules of court. Gosling v. Commonwealth, 7 Va. App. 642, 376 S.E.2d 541 (1989).

All doubt as to juror impartiality must be resolved in accused's favor. — When asked if there was doubt in her mind whether she could sit impartially as a juror, juror responded, "It's possible but not likely." While it is unclear from the record whether juror meant to say that it was possible but not likely that she could be impartial or whether she meant it was possible she was prejudiced but not likely, all doubts as to the impartiality of a juror must be resolved in favor of the accused and the trial court abused its discretion and committed manifest error by refusing to strike juror for cause. Foley v. Commonwealth, 8 Va. App. 149, 379 S.E.2d 915 (1989).

Where the voir dire in this case raised reasonable doubt concerning a juror's ability to stand indifferent in the cause as required by this section, reversal of the conviction was required. Clements v. Commonwealth, 21 Va. App. 386, 464 S.E.2d 534 (1995).

Viewing the venire person's voir dire in its entirety, the record disclosed a series of tentative, equivocal responses to questioning intended to probe and ascertain the venire person's state of mind, leaving reasonable doubt of her partiality as a matter of law and requiring that she be removed for cause. Under such circumstances, it was reversible error to require defendant to exhaust a peremptory strike to remove the juror. Pennington v. Commonwealth, No. 1346-95-3 (Ct. of Appeals Feb. 4, 1997).

Which is a substantive right. — The constitutional and statutory guarantee of an impartial jury is no mere legal technicality, but a substantive right scrupulously to be observed in the day-to-day administration of justice. Martin v. Commonwealth, 221 Va. 436, 271 S.E.2d 123 (1980).

Discretion of court in jury selection. — Generally, whether a prospective juror should be excluded for cause is a matter within the sound discretion of the trial court, and its action in refusing to exclude a particular venireman is entitled to great weight on appeal. Martin v. Commonwealth, 221 Va. 436, 271 S.E.2d 123 (1980).

As long as the selection procedure results in a fair and impartial jury, the manner in which a jury is to be selected is properly within the trial court's sound discretion. Turner v. Commonwealth, 221 Va. 513, 273 S.E.2d 36 (1980), cert. denied, 451 U.S. 1011, 101 S. Ct. 2347, 68 L. Ed. 2d 863 (1981).

Whether a venireman can lay aside a preconceived opinion and render a verdict solely on the evidence is a mixed question of law and fact. Resolution of the question rests within the sound discretion of the trial court. Calhoun v. Commonwealth, 226 Va. 256, 307 S.E.2d 896 (1983).

It is the court's duty to procure an impartial jury. The court's fulfillment of this duty, however, involves the exercise of sound judicial discretion. Scott v. Commonwealth, 1 Va. App. 447, 339 S.E.2d 899 (1986), aff'd, 233 Va. 5, 353 S.E.2d 460 (1987).

The court's duty, in the exercise of its discretion, is to empanel jurors who are free from bias or prejudice against the parties and who stand indifferent in the cause. Scott v. Commonwealth, 1 Va. App. 447, 339 S.E.2d 899 (1986), aff'd, 233 Va. 5, 353 S.E.2d 460 (1987).

Upon review, the appellate court gives deference to the trial court's decision as to whether to retain or exclude prospective jurors, and a trial court's decision on this issue will be affirmed unless there has been manifest error amounting to an abuse of discretion. Cantrell v. Crews, 259 Va. 47, 523 S.E.2d 502 (2000).

Sufficient explanations for peremptory strikes. — Commonwealth's concerns with jurors who were not paying attention, one of whom was seen smiling at appellant, provided sufficient race-neutral explanations for the use of two of its peremptory strikes. Allred v. Commonwealth, No. 0223-94-2 (Ct. of Appeals March 14, 1995).

Trial court is not required to exclude all jurors who have any preconceived opinion of the case. Calhoun v. Commonwealth, 226 Va. 256, 307 S.E.2d 896 (1983).

To hold that the mere existence of any preconceived notion as to the guilt or innocence of an accused, without more, is sufficient to rebut the presumption of a prospective juror's impartiality would be to establish an impossible standard. Calhoun v. Commonwealth, 226 Va. 256, 307 S.E.2d 896 (1983).

It is sufficient if the juror can lay aside impression or opinion and render verdict based on evidence presented in court. Calhoun v. Commonwealth, 226 Va. 256, 307 S.E.2d 896 (1983).

Discretion of court as to voir dire. — Where the court carefully reviewed defendant's refused questions and concluded that he was not prejudiced thereby, and where defendant cannot show that the trial court abused its discretion in refusing to ask the remaining questions, the Supreme Court will not disturb the lower court's ruling. Bassett v. Commonwealth, 222 Va. 844, 284 S.E.2d 844 (1981), cert. denied, 456 U.S. 938, 102 S. Ct. 1996, 72 L. Ed. 2d 458 (1982), cert. denied, 499 U.S. 983, 111 S. Ct. 1639, 113 L. Ed. 2d 734 (1991).

The questions propounded by counsel must be relevant and the trial court must, in its discretion, decide the issue of relevancy, subject to review for abuse. LeVasseur v. Commonwealth, 225 Va. 564, 304 S.E.2d 644 (1983), cert. denied, 464 U.S. 1063, 104 S. Ct. 744, 79 L. Ed. 2d 202 (1984); Henshaw v. Commonwealth, 3 Va. App. 213, 348 S.E.2d 853 (1986).

It is the duty of the court to procure an impartial jury. Consistent with this duty, the trial courts of Virginia conduct the examination of the venire, including the mandatory seven questions set out in Rule 3A:14. The trial court's responsibility in the matter of the venire, however, does not exclude the participation of counsel. Scott v. Commonwealth, 1 Va. App. 447, 339 S.E.2d 899 (1986), aff'd, 233 Va. 5, 353 S.E.2d 460 (1987).

A trial court's error in refusing to allow counsel-conducted voir dire is harmless if it plainly appears that the jury panel remained impartial and that the defendant was not otherwise prejudiced by the jury selection process the court employed. Charity v. Commonwealth, 22 Va. App. 582, 471 S.E.2d 821 (1996).

In conducting voir dire, the court questioned prospective jurors on each of the matters the defendant's counsel raised. Counsel failed to proffer any questions that were not asked, and he failed to interject any follow-up questions to those the court did ask. The defendant's sole objection was that the court had failed to follow the mandate of this section. The court's error

§ 8.01-358 CODE OF VIRGINIA § 8.01-358

did not affect the selection of the jury or its partiality, affect the verdict or otherwise prejudice the defendant. Charity v. Commonwealth, 22 Va. App. 582, 471 S.E.2d 821 (1996).

Court's refusal to ask requested questions. — While the wiser course generally is to propound appropriate questions designed to identify racial prejudice if requested by the defendant, a trial court's refusal to do so is not constitutionally objectionable in the absence of factors similar to those in Ham v. South Carolina, 409 U.S. 524, 93 S. Ct. 848, 35 L. Ed. 2d 46 (1973); Turner v. Commonwealth, 221 Va. 513, 273 S.E.2d 36 (1980), cert. denied, 451 U.S. 1011, 101 S. Ct. 2347, 68 L. Ed. 2d 863 (1981).

Unless the refusal to ask a question amounts to a denial of due process or otherwise impinges upon the right to a fair and impartial jury, the present wording of this section and former Rule 3A:20(a) (see now Rule 3A:14) empowers a trial court to use its discretion in determining whether to ask questions proposed by either the Commonwealth or the defendant. Turner v. Commonwealth, 221 Va. 513, 273 S.E.2d 36 (1980), cert. denied, 451 U.S. 1011, 101 S. Ct. 2347, 68 L. Ed. 2d 863 (1981).

The trial court did not abuse its discretion in refusing to allow the plaintiff to examine the jury panel about the medical malpractice insurance crisis since the requested examination would have injected the subject of insurance into the trial. Speet v. Bacaj, 237 Va. 290, 377 S.E.2d 397 (1989).

Refusal to read preferred statement. — The manner in which jury selection is conducted is within the discretion and control of the trial court, guided by this section and Rule 3A:14, and there is no provision in Virginia law which requires a trial court to read to prospective jurors a statement offered by a defendant. Buchanan v. Commonwealth, 238 Va. 389, 384 S.E.2d 757 (1989), cert. denied, 493 U.S. 1063, 110 S. Ct. 880, 107 L. Ed. 2d 963 (1990).

The test of relevancy is whether the questions relate to any of the four criteria set forth in the statute. If an answer to the question would necessarily disclose, or clearly lead to the disclosure of the statutory factors of relationship, interest, opinion, or prejudice, it must be permitted. Questions which go beyond this standard are entirely within the trial court's discretion. LeVasseur v. Commonwealth, 225 Va. 564, 304 S.E.2d 644 (1983), cert. denied, 464 U.S. 1063, 104 S. Ct. 744, 79 L. Ed. 2d 202 (1984); Henshaw v. Commonwealth, 3 Va. App. 213, 348 S.E.2d 853 (1986).

Party has no right, statutory or otherwise, to propound any question he wishes, or to extend voir dire questioning ad infinitum. LeVasseur v. Commonwealth, 225 Va. 564, 304 S.E.2d 644 (1983), cert. denied, 464 U.S. 1063, 104 S. Ct. 744, 79 L. Ed. 2d 202 (1984).

Former Rule 3A:20(a) resolved ambiguity in this section. — Former Supreme Court Rule 3A:20(a), which clearly made counsel's participation in voir dire contingent upon the trial court's approval, resolved any ambiguity present in the statutory language of this section. Turner v. Commonwealth, 221 Va. 513, 273 S.E.2d 36 (1980), cert. denied, 451 U.S. 1011, 101 S. Ct. 2347, 68 L. Ed. 2d 863 (1981) But see now Rule 3A:14.

Section recognizes advantage to counsel-conducted voir dire. — In amending this section to state that the court and counsel for either party shall have the right to examine under oath persons called as jurors, the legislature implicitly recognized the advantage to counsel-conducted voir dire. Lankford v. Foster, 546 F. Supp. 241 (W.D. Va. 1982), aff'd, 716 F.2d 896 (4th Cir. 1983), cert. denied, 467 U.S. 1214, 104 S. Ct. 2655, 81 L. Ed. 2d 362 (1984).

But no constitutional right to counsel-conducted voir dire. — While the defendant has a constitutional right to a fair and impartial jury, he has no constitutional right to counsel-conducted voir dire. Turner v. Commonwealth, 221 Va. 513, 273 S.E.2d 36 (1980), cert. denied, 451 U.S. 1011, 101 S. Ct. 2347, 68 L. Ed. 2d 863 (1981).

Counsel - conducted voir dire is a statutory, not a constitutional right. Charity v. Commonwealth, 22 Va. App. 582, 471 S.E.2d 821 (1996); Charity v. Commonwealth, 24 Va. App. 258, 482 S.E.2d 59 (1997).

Trial court's failure to allow appellant's counsel to ask voir dire questions of the prospective jurors was a clear deviation from the mandate of this section. That such a deviation is an abuse of discretion is beyond cavil. Charity v. Commonwealth, 24 Va. App. 258, 482 S.E.2d 59 (1997).

Harmless error found in failure to follow statute. — Although court clearly failed to follow the mandate of this section when it refused to allow defense attorney to question jurors himself, it plainly appears from the record that this error did not affect the questions propounded to the prospective jurors, the selection or composition of the jury panel or its partiality. Thus, the record plainly shows that the erroneous, non-constitutional ruling did not deprive appellant of a fair trial or substantial justice and, therefore, plainly did not affect the verdict. Charity v. Commonwealth, 24 Va. App. 258, 482 S.E.2d 59 (1997).

Denial of a motion to permit each venireman to be questioned individually out of the presence of all others on voir dire was within the court's discretion. Fisher v. Commonwealth, 236 Va. 403, 374 S.E.2d 46 (1988), cert. denied, 490 U.S. 1028, 109 S. Ct. 1766, 104 L. Ed. 2d 201 (1989).

Question may not be allowed although question relates to section's criteria. — Even if the question propounded by defense counsel related to any one of the four criteria described in this section, the trial court in its discretion may have declined to allow the question if it were objectionable for other reasons and if defense counsel was given a sufficient opportunity to determine the indifference of the veniremen. Wall v. Commonwealth, No. 0120-89-2 (Ct. of Appeals July 30, 1991).

Question may be denied if counsel given opportunity to determine veniremens' indifference. — Even if a question relates to one of the four criteria described in this section, a trial court may not abuse its discretion in denying defense counsel an opportunity to ask a particular question if trial counsel is given sufficient opportunity to determine whether the veniremen are indifferent to the proceeding. Wall v. Commonwealth, No. 0120-89-2 (Ct. of Appeals July 30, 1991).

Error to force use of peremptory challenge. — It was prejudicial error for the trial court to force the accused to use a peremptory challenge to exclude a venireman who was not free from exception. Martin v. Commonwealth, 221 Va. 436, 271 S.E.2d 123 (1980).

It is prejudicial error to force a defendant to use the peremptory strike to exclude a venireman who is not free from exception. Scott v. Commonwealth, 1 Va. App. 447, 339 S.E.2d 899 (1986), aff'd, 233 Va. 5, 353 S.E.2d 460 (1987).

The removal of a juror by peremptory challenge is irrelevant to the decision on appeal if the court erred in refusing to strike him for cause. Scott v. Commonwealth, 1 Va. App. 447, 339 S.E.2d 899 (1986), aff'd, 233 Va. 5, 353 S.E.2d 460 (1987).

Refusal to remove juror who is not impartial not harmless. — A trial court's refusal to remove a juror who is not impartial does not constitute harmless error even if counsel uses a peremptory strike to exclude the juror. David v. Commonwealth, 26 Va. App. 77, 493 S.E.2d 379 (1997).

Reasonable doubt as to impartiality. — Any reasonable doubt that a venireman does not stand indifferent in the cause must be resolved in favor of the accused. Justus v. Commonwealth, 220 Va. 971, 266 S.E.2d 87 (1980), cert. denied, 455 U.S. 983, 102 S. Ct. 1491, 71 L. Ed. 2d 693 (1982); Barker v. Commonwealth, 230 Va. 370, 337 S.E.2d 729 (1985).

A juror must stand indifferent in the cause, and a venireman must be excluded if the trial court entertains a reasonable doubt as to his qualifications. Calhoun v. Commonwealth, 226 Va. 256, 307 S.E.2d 896 (1983).

Doubts as to the impartiality of a juror must be resolved in favor of the accused. Educational Books, Inc. v. Commonwealth, 3 Va. App. 384, 349 S.E.2d 903 (1986).

Any reasonable doubt whether a juror stands impartial is sufficient to ensure his exclusion, because it is not only important that justice should be impartially administered, but it should also flow through channels as free from suspicion as possible. Mullis v. Commonwealth, 3 Va. App. 564, 351 S.E.2d 919 (1987).

Automatic exclusions not subject to court's discretion. — Ordinarily, a determination whether a juror is qualified rests within the sound discretion of the trial court, and its finding will not be disturbed on appeal absent manifest error. Some veniremen, however, are excluded for cause automatically, irrespective of a showing of impartiality during voir dire. Such automatic exclusions leave no room for judicial discretion. Barker v. Commonwealth, 230 Va. 370, 337 S.E.2d 729 (1985).

Jurors are not required to be totally ignorant of the facts and issues involved in a case on which they sit. Justus v. Commonwealth, 220 Va. 971, 266 S.E.2d 87 (1980), cert. denied, 455 U.S. 983, 102 S. Ct. 1491, 71 L. Ed. 2d 693 (1982).

Mere interest does not per se require venireman to be set aside. — Per se disqualification of veniremen is not favored; mere interest in the subject matter of a prosecution does not, per se, require that a venireman be set aside for cause. Webb v. Commonwealth, 11 Va. App. 220, 397 S.E.2d 539 (1990).

Equivocal responses. — An equivocal response on a collateral matter does not mandate disqualification of a prospective juror. Flint v. Commonwealth, No. 1024-88-4 (Ct. of Appeals Aug. 28, 1990).

Trial judge did not err in denying a motion to exclude jurors for cause on the basis of their equivocal responses to questions which improperly required them to speculate concerning evidence that would be produced at trial. Flint v. Commonwealth, No. 1024-88-4 (Ct. of Appeals Aug. 28, 1990).

Pretrial juror questionnaire. — Where three weeks before trial, defendant submitted to the court a two-page "Juror's Personal Data Questionnaire" and moved the court to order each venireman to complete and return it before trial, the court correctly denied the motion; to the extent a pretrial juror questionnaire would probe a juror's attitudes outside the courtroom, it would detract from the trial judge's "opportunity to observe and evaluate prospective jurors first hand." Strickler v. Commonwealth, 241 Va. 482, 404 S.E.2d 227, cert. denied, 502 U.S. 944, 112 S. Ct. 386, 116 L. Ed. 2d 337 (1991).

Review of entire voir dire. — Whether a prospective juror should have been excluded for cause must be decided upon a review of the entire voir dire, rather than an isolated question and answer. Mullis v. Commonwealth, 3 Va. App. 564, 351 S.E.2d 919 (1987).

Applied in Commercial Union Ins. Co. v. Moorefield, 231 Va. 260, 343 S.E.2d 329 (1986); Mu'Min v. Commonwealth, 239 Va. 433, 389

S.E.2d 886 (1990); Moten v. Commonwealth, 14 Va. App. 956, 420 S.E.2d 250 (1992); Goins v. Commonwealth, 251 Va. 442, 470 S.E.2d 114 (1996); Brown v. Commonwealth, 29 Va. App. 199, 510 S.E.2d 751 (1999).

B. Impartiality as to Punishment.

Impartiality on question of punishment required. — Virginia Const., Art. I, § 8 and this section require jurors to be impartial not only upon the issue of guilt or innocence but also upon the question of punishment. Patterson v. Commonwealth, 222 Va. 653, 283 S.E.2d 212 (1981).

Elimination permitted for bias in favor of death penalty. — The process of selection of an impartial jury permits elimination for cause of those veniremen who are biased in favor of the death penalty under all circumstances as well as those who are biased against its imposition under all circumstances. Patterson v. Commonwealth, 222 Va. 653, 283 S.E.2d 212 (1981).

And failure to question jury on bias invalidates death sentence. — In a prosecution for robbery and capital murder, the refusal by the trial judge to ask the jury whether, if the jury should happen to convict the defendant of capital murder, each juror would be able to consider voting for a sentence less than death, or to ask an equivalent question, was prejudicial error invalidating the sentence to death. Patterson v. Commonwealth, 222 Va. 653, 283 S.E.2d 212 (1981).

Though verdict not necessarily invalidated. — A jury qualified by unconstitutional standards respecting punishment is not necessarily biased with respect to a defendant's guilt. Patterson v. Commonwealth, 222 Va. 653, 283 S.E.2d 212 (1981).

Questions regarding religious scruples about the death penalty. See Justus v. Commonwealth, 222 Va. 667, 283 S.E.2d 905 (1981), cert. denied, 455 U.S. 983, 102 S. Ct. 1491, 71 L. Ed. 2d 693 (1982).

Exclusion of jurors who would not vote for death penalty under any circumstances. — Trial court correctly excluded three prospective jurors for cause where one stated that he would not convict a defendant of a crime which potentially carried the death penalty, despite what the evidence might show, where another said she would not vote to impose the death penalty despite what the evidence would show, and where another reiterated that he would not vote for the death penalty regardless of any instructions the court might give. Strickler v. Commonwealth, 241 Va. 482, 404 S.E.2d 227, cert. denied, 502 U.S. 944, 112 S. Ct. 386, 116 L. Ed. 2d 337 (1991).

C. Illustrative Cases.

Question relating to bias and prejudice. — Where a cashier was murdered in an armed robbery, defendant's proposed question as to whether prospective jurors had family or friends who were cashiers dealt with prospective bias and prejudice and was within the criteria of this section. Mackall v. Commonwealth, 236 Va. 240, 372 S.E.2d 759 (1988), cert. denied, 492 U.S. 925, 109 S. Ct. 3261, 106 L. Ed. 2d 607 (1989).

Questions relating to venireman's opinion of eyewitness testimony. — Questions asking the veniremen's opinions concerning eyewitness testimony did not address interest or partiality of the veniremen or their ability to stand indifferent in the cause. Barrette v. Commonwealth, 11 Va. App. 357, 398 S.E.2d 695 (1990).

Refusal to allow question relating to voice identification. — Trial court did not abuse its discretion in refusing to allow defendant to ask on voir dire if there was "anyone on the jury panel who believe[d] that a person's testimony who identifie[d] a voice [was] always reliable?"; question was designed less to elicit an affirmative response than to suggest to the veniremen the defendant's anticipated argument; furthermore, the question was difficult to understand and the defendant had a sufficient opportunity to determine the objectivity of the veniremen. Wall v. Commonwealth, No. 0120-89-2 (Ct. of Appeals July 30, 1991).

Venireman deemed per se not to be "disinterested." — A venireman who has an interest in the cause or who is related to a party is deemed per se not to be "disinterested" and must be set aside for cause; this rule extends to criminal prosecution. Webb v. Commonwealth, 11 Va. App. 220, 397 S.E.2d 539 (1990).

Refusal to exclude for cause venireman who believes accused must prove his innocence is an abuse of discretion and a denial of a defendant's right to an impartial jury. Martin v. Commonwealth, 221 Va. 436, 271 S.E.2d 123 (1980).

Prospective juror may not as a per se rule be disqualified on ground that Commonwealth's Attorney had formerly represented him. Calhoun v. Commonwealth, 226 Va. 256, 307 S.E.2d 896 (1983).

Where voir dire examination discloses that juror is leaning one way or the other and will not act with entire impartiality, the juror is biased and must be removed. Educational Books, Inc. v. Commonwealth, 3 Va. App. 384, 349 S.E.2d 903 (1986).

A prospective juror employed by the victim of a crime may face overt or subtle influences on his capacity to hear the evidence and render judgment fairly and impartially. However, a prospective juror's employment as a "morning man" in a supermarket, without more, should not lead the court to impute a bias to him which is not disclosed by the record. Such employment does not constitute per se the "interest in the cause" prohibited by this section. Scott v. Commonwealth, 1 Va. App. 447, 339 S.E.2d 899 (1986), aff'd, 233 Va. 5, 353 S.E.2d 460 (1987).

In defendant's jury trial for robbery, venireman was not per se disqualified because he was a retired employee of the corporation whose money was taken in the robbery. Barrette v. Commonwealth, 11 Va. App. 357, 398 S.E.2d 695 (1990).

Representation of juror by plaintiff's attorney's firm in similar matter. — A prospective juror was disqualified from serving on a civil jury where the juror was represented in a similar matter by the same firm as was representing the plaintiff; such disqualification was required even though the juror stated that the circumstances of her representation would have no bearing on her judgment as a juror and that she could be totally fair to both sides, and was also required notwithstanding the fact that the venue was a community where people were going to know each other and have some kind of association. Cantrell v. Crews, 259 Va. 47, 523 S.E.2d 502 (2000).

Venireman who was victim of crime similar to that on trial. — Trial court did not err in refusing to set aside for cause a venireman who acknowledged that, several months before the trial, she had herself been the victim of a crime similar to that on trial. Webb v. Commonwealth, 11 Va. App. 220, 397 S.E.2d 539 (1990).

Knowledge of conviction for offense for which accused being retried. — When a venireman knows of an accused's previous conviction of the same offense for which he is being retried, the venireman cannot qualify as a juror in the new trial. Barker v. Commonwealth, 230 Va. 370, 337 S.E.2d 729 (1985).

Mistrial should have been granted for juror who was no longer impartial. — Juror who, during luncheon recess, expressed to third parties a conviction that an individual who may be instrumental in obtaining the release of a person charged with a crime should "feel guilty" that the accused is "allowed to walk the streets," charged attorneys whose clients are released of having no remorse as long as the lawyers get paid, and opined that defendant either was not going to be "as fortunate" or was "not going to get off," was probably no longer impartial, even though he had promised the court that he could maintain an open mind on the issues until the remainder of the case was completed, and defendant's motion for mistrial should have been granted. Haddad v. Commonwealth, 229 Va. 325, 329 S.E.2d 17 (1985).

Association with law-enforcement personnel. — A prospective juror is not subject to automatic exclusion because of an association with law-enforcement personnel, provided the juror has no knowledge of the facts of the case and demonstrates impartiality toward the parties. Clozza v. Commonwealth, 228 Va. 124, 321 S.E.2d 273 (1984), cert. denied, 469 U.S. 1230, 105 S. Ct. 1233, 84 L. Ed. 2d 370 (1985).

Where prospective juror had served as a chief probation and parole officer for many years, but had retired long before the trial, the court correctly determined that juror would be impartial and there was nothing in the record supporting any challenge to that determination; if a prospective juror has no knowledge of the facts of the case and demonstrates impartiality, he is not subject to a challenge for cause merely because he has had an association with law-enforcement personnel. Strickler v. Commonwealth, 241 Va. 482, 404 S.E.2d 227, cert. denied, 502 U.S. 944, 112 S. Ct. 386, 116 L. Ed. 2d 337 (1991).

Officer was not a "party" within the meaning of this section and Rule 3A:14(a)(1) when his sole role in a criminal prosecution was as a witness, thus, a juror's relationship to such a police officer-witness did not require per se dismissal of that juror from the venire. Such a juror may be retained if the trial court is satisfied that the juror can set aside considerations of the relationship and evaluate all the evidence fairly. Lilly v. Commonwealth, 255 Va. 558, 499 S.E.2d 522 (1998), rev'd on other grounds, 527 U.S. 116, 119 S. Ct. 1887, 144 L. Ed. 2d 117 (1999).

Influence of jurors by another juror who was attorney. — Evidence failed to support a finding of juror misconduct sufficient to warrant setting aside verdict, and the trial court abused its discretion in ruling to the contrary, where viewed as a whole, it disclosed a situation where two jurors were influenced by the opinions of a third, dominant juror who was an attorney, a status which may have rendered him exempt from jury service but which did not make him incompetent to serve. Caterpillar Tractor Co. v. Hulvey, 233 Va. 77, 353 S.E.2d 747 (1987).

The trial court's failure to make inquiries during the voir dire concerning the opinion of jurors, together with the court's refusal of a proposed voir dire question which would have resolved any doubt that the defendant did not have to prove his innocence, created a reasonable doubt as to the impartiality of the jury. Trent v. Commonwealth, No. 0896-85 (Ct. of Appeals Aug. 6, 1987).

Questions as to weight jurors would give to police testimony. — In an appropriate case, counsel may inquire of prospective jurors whether they would give greater or less weight to the testimony of a police officer than to that of another witness simply because of his official status. When it is anticipated that a major part of the prosecution's case will hinge upon a credibility determination between prosecution witnesses who have an official status and other defense witnesses who do not, then not only is such an inquiry of whether jurors would give unqualified credence to those witnesses appropriate, but it may be required. Mullis v. Commonwealth, 3 Va. App. 564, 351 S.E.2d 919 (1987).

It was immaterial that a juror stated that she had a "prejudice" rather than a fixed opinion as to the guilt or innocence of the defendant. Although many of the cases holding a juror disqualified for bias are premised upon the juror's preordained verdict, the constitutional protections do not end there. Educational Books, Inc. v. Commonwealth, 3 Va. App. 384, 349 S.E.2d 903 (1986).

Juror's use of term "great prejudice" was sufficient to warrant her removal from the panel although there was no showing that her "prejudice" was tantamount to the type of prejudice required to exclude a juror for cause. Regardless of the words used by the juror, if she asserts that she is leaning one way or the other and that she would not act with total impartiality, she is biased. Educational Books, Inc. v. Commonwealth, 3 Va. App. 384, 349 S.E.2d 903 (1986).

Circumstances under which juror voiced her concerns clearly revealed a basis necessitating her exclusion, where she withheld her remarks until after the completion of the Commonwealth's opening statement, giving her an extended period of time to reflect on her potential prejudices, the fact that she made her statement at a time when it would disrupt the proceedings, as opposed to a time when it was specifically requested, evinced, her strong belief that she could not function impartially as a juror, and, she expressed a "great prejudice" against the defendant. Additionally, when asked by the court whether she could render a fair and impartial verdict based solely upon the evidence presented at trial, she responded: "I simply feel I have some preconceived ideas." Educational Books, Inc. v. Commonwealth, 3 Va. App. 384, 349 S.E.2d 903 (1986).

Juror who believes it improper to drive after drinking may be unable to evaluate fairly and impartially the evidence of one who drives after drinking but claims nevertheless not to have been intoxicated. Henshaw v. Commonwealth, 3 Va. App. 213, 348 S.E.2d 853 (1986).

In a prosecution for driving under the influence, it was improper for the court not to allow defendant's counsel to ask venire members "whether any of them thought it improper to drive after drinking alcoholic beverages." Any juror who thought it improper to drive after drinking might not have evaluated impartially his defense. Henshaw v. Commonwealth, 3 Va. App. 213, 348 S.E.2d 853 (1986).

Juror's reluctance to serve. — Trial court did not commit manifest error in refusing to strike juror who expressed only her personal discomfort at the prospect of continued service after the Commonwealth had presented its case, not a concern that she could not fairly and impartially consider the evidence. A juror's reluctance to serve is not a basis for disqualification. Meekins v. Commonwealth, No. 0134-94-4 (Ct. of Appeals March 21, 1995).

Effect of failure to timely respond to voir dire question. — Juror's failure to give a timely response to the voir dire question did not prejudice appellant's right of peremptory challenge such that the trial court erred in refusing to grant a mistrial. Notwithstanding the failure to timely respond to the question, there was no dispute at trial that juror stood indifferent to the cause. Because there was no basis for a challenge for cause, juror's presence on jury did not affect the essential fairness of the trial, notwithstanding the impairment to appellant's right of peremptory challenge. Taylor v. Commonwealth, 25 Va. App. 12, 486 S.E.2d 108 (1997), aff'd, 256 Va. 214, 505 S.E.2d 378 (1998).

Rehabilitative evidence based on assent to leading questions. — Where the record showed that after the juror declared her bias in favor of the prosecution, the evidence used to rehabilitate her did not come from her but was based on her mere assent to leading questions, this juror was not per se disqualified because of her declared bias; had her rehabilitative responses come from her in response to non-leading questions, the trial court would not have abused its discretion by refusing to strike her for cause. Because her rehabilitative responses consisted solely of her mere assent to the court's leading questions, she should have been stricken for cause. David v. Commonwealth, 26 Va. App. 77, 493 S.E.2d 379 (1997).

II. DECISIONS UNDER PRIOR LAW.

Editor's note. — The cases cited below were decided under corresponding provisions of former law. The term "this section," as used below, refers to former provisions.

It is the duty of the trial court, through the legal machinery provided for that purpose, to procure an impartial jury to try every case. Salina v. Commonwealth, 217 Va. 92, 225 S.E.2d 199 (1976).

Jurors are not required to be totally ignorant of the facts and issues involved in a case on which they sit. Breeden v. Commonwealth, 217 Va. 297, 227 S.E.2d 734 (1976).

The purpose of the voir dire examination is to ascertain whether any juror has any interest in the case or any bias or prejudice in relation to it, and that he in fact stands "indifferent in the cause." Questioning beyond this scope lies within the sound discretion of the trial court. Davis v. Sykes, 202 Va. 952, 121 S.E.2d 513 (1961); Hope Windows, Inc. v. Snyder, 208 Va. 489, 158 S.E.2d 722 (1968).

Discretion of trial court. — The words added "may ask such person or juror directly any relevant question" do not mean that the court must do so. The language used is not mandatory but permissive and leaves the matter to the discretion of the trial court. Harmon v. Commonwealth, 209 Va. 574, 166 S.E.2d 232 (1969).

The courts must zealously guard the precept that only jurors free from partiality may sit at trials. Durham v. Cox, 328 F. Supp. 1157 (W.D. Va. 1971).

To be impartial, a juror must be indifferent as he stands unsworn. Durham v. Cox, 328 F. Supp. 1157 (W.D. Va. 1971).

Proof of impartiality should come from prospective juror. — In an attempt to rehabilitate an arguably biased venirewoman, the proof that a prospective juror is impartial and fair should come from her and not be based on her mere assent to persuasive suggestions. Breeden v. Commonwealth, 217 Va. 297, 227 S.E.2d 734 (1976).

Ascertaining mental attitude of appropriate indifference. — Impartiality of a juror is not a technical conception. It is a state of mind. For the ascertainment of this mental attitude of appropriate indifference, the federal Constitution lays down no particular tests and procedure is not chained to any ancient and artificial formula. Durham v. Cox, 328 F. Supp. 1157 (W.D. Va. 1971).

There are no settled rules for determining, in a particular case, whether a juror fulfills the requirement of impartiality. Durham v. Cox, 328 F. Supp. 1157 (W.D. Va. 1971).

The disqualifying nature of a juror's impression which would show partiality lies not so much in the particular content of the impression as in its weight upon the juror's mind. The touchstone must be the juror's ability to lay the impression aside, whatever it may be, and to base his verdict upon the law and the evidence alone. The ascertainment of whether and to what extent a particular juror possesses this quality must, of necessity, depend almost entirely upon his own acknowledgments. Durham v. Cox, 328 F. Supp. 1157 (W.D. Va. 1971).

Juror's strong and deep impressions constitute sufficient objection. — Light impressions which may fairly be supposed to yield to the testimony that may be offered, and which may leave the mind open to a fair consideration of that testimony, constitute no sufficient objection to a juror; but those strong and deep impressions which will close the mind against the testimony that may be offered in opposition to them and which will combat that testimony and resist its force, do constitute a sufficient objection to him. Durham v. Cox, 328 F. Supp. 1157 (W.D. Va. 1971).

The juror is the best judge of whether or not his prepossessions amount to a decided opinion. Durham v. Cox, 328 F. Supp. 1157 (W.D. Va. 1971).

Remarks of juror during trial, even if reprehensible, cannot be taken advantage of after verdict. For a juror to say upon hearing a fact testified by a witness, "Yes, sir; I know all about it. That's so," is only in obedience to the mandate of this section. Atlantic & D.R.R. v. Peake, 87 Va. 130, 12 S.E. 348 (1890).

Declaration of impartiality. — If a juror is in a frame of mind which would enable him to render an impartial verdict, uninfluenced by his previous impressions, it is but fair to presume that he will so declare when questioned as to impartiality. The fact that he does not, or is unable to do so, and thus solve the doubt, is sufficient to disqualify him. Durham v. Cox, 328 F. Supp. 1157 (W.D. Va. 1971).

Inability to unequivocally assert impartiality. — A juror who cannot unequivocally state, at the time of the trial, that he can give a defendant a fair and impartial trial, and whose answer, in response to questions concerning his bias, concludes with "Something would be there. I don't know," is not an impartial juror within the meaning of the Sixth Amendment to the federal Constitution and Va. Const., Art. I, § 8. Durham v. Cox, 328 F. Supp. 1157 (W.D. Va. 1971).

The material point for consideration in the answer of a juror as to the juror's impartiality is his inability or unwillingness to state how far his judgment would be affected by his preconceived opinions. Where his response to the inquiry of a court to his impartiality is that he could "not now say that he had such opinion that evidence would not remove it," and where he did not say that the opinion was of such a character that evidence would remove it, indicating that he was in doubt whether the opinion he had formed would yield to the testimony to be adduced on the trial, he has not removed doubt as to his impartiality. Durham v. Cox, 328 F. Supp. 1157 (W.D. Va. 1971).

Reasonable doubt as to impartiality ensures exclusion of juror. — Upon the issue of whether a particular juror is free from partiality, nothing should be left to inference or doubt. If there be a reasonable doubt whether the juror possesses these qualifications, that doubt is sufficient to ensure his exclusion. For, it is not only important that justice should be impartially administered, but it should also flow through channels as free from suspicion as possible. Durham v. Cox, 328 F. Supp. 1157 (W.D. Va. 1971); Breeden v. Commonwealth, 217 Va. 297, 227 S.E.2d 734 (1976).

By ancient rule, any reasonable doubt as to a

juror's qualifications must be resolved in favor of the accused. Breeden v. Commonwealth, 217 Va. 297, 227 S.E.2d 734 (1976).

Where there is a reasonable doubt whether a juror is qualified, that doubt must be resolved in favor of the accused. Salina v. Commonwealth, 217 Va. 92, 225 S.E.2d 199 (1976).

Borderline objections resolved in favor of disqualification. — There is no right to have a particular person on a jury, so borderline objections to the disqualification of jurors for cause should always be resolved in favor of the disqualification. Hope v. Peyton, 340 F. Supp. 197 (W.D. Va. 1972).

Insisting on juror who acknowledges himself to be under influences. — To insist on a juror's sitting on a cause when he acknowledges himself to be under influences, no matter whether they arise from interest, from prejudices, or from religious opinions, which will prevent him from giving a true verdict according to law and evidence, would be to subvert the objects of a trial by jury, and to bring into disgrace and contempt, the proceedings of courts of justice. The courts do not sit to procure the verdicts of partial and prejudiced men; but of men honest and indifferent in causes. This is the administration of justice which the law requires. Durham v. Cox, 328 F. Supp. 1157 (W.D. Va. 1971).

Court's refusal to ask requested questions. — The trial court did not abuse its discretion by refusing to ask whether jurors knew persons expected to testify merely to aid litigants in making peremptory challenges. Davis v. Sykes, 202 Va. 952, 121 S.E.2d 513 (1961).

In a prosecution for larceny of oysters it was not error for the trial court to refuse defendant's request to ask the jury whether any of them owned, leased, or operated assigned oyster grounds. Melvin v. Commonwealth, 202 Va. 511, 118 S.E.2d 679 (1961).

The contention that the voir dire examination of the jury was improperly restricted in an action for personal injuries allegedly suffered by pedestrian struck by car driven by defendant who had been drinking beer at enlisted men's club, by the refusal of the court to allow prospective jurors to be questioned concerning membership in social clubs or awarding damages for pain and suffering was without merit. Jackson v. Prestage, 204 Va. 481, 132 S.E.2d 501 (1963).

In a prosecution for larceny of oysters, the fact that a member of the jury panel might have been the owner, lessee or operator of assigned oyster grounds would not have disqualified him to serve on the jury. Melvin v. Commonwealth, 202 Va. 511, 118 S.E.2d 679 (1961).

Mention of insurance improper. — Deliberate injection of insurance coverage by plaintiff's counsel on voir dire examination was improper and prejudicial to defendants' right to a trial by an impartial jury. Hope Windows, Inc. v. Snyder, 208 Va. 489, 158 S.E.2d 722 (1968).

Stockholders. — That a stockholder in a company which is a party to a lawsuit is incompetent to sit as a juror is well settled. Salina v. Commonwealth, 217 Va. 92, 225 S.E.2d 199 (1976).

A stockholder in a corporation is not only incompetent to act as a juror in a case where the corporation is a party, he is likewise incompetent to serve where the corporation has a direct pecuniary interest in the controversy. Salina v. Commonwealth, 217 Va. 92, 225 S.E.2d 199 (1976).

The trial court committed reversible error when it refused to dismiss four members of the venire who owned stock in one or both of the banks from which defendant was charged with larceny by check. Salina v. Commonwealth, 217 Va. 92, 225 S.E.2d 199 (1976).

Where the criminal act suffered by the corporation has the direct effect of diminishing the assets of the corporation held for the benefit of its stockholders, a stockholder, regardless of the size of his holdings, could not be said to stand indifferent in the cause. Salina v. Commonwealth, 217 Va. 92, 225 S.E.2d 199 (1976).

One related to the victim within the ninth degree by consanguinity or affinity is not competent to serve as a juror. Salina v. Commonwealth, 217 Va. 92, 225 S.E.2d 199 (1976).

§ 8.01-359. Trial; numbers of jurors in civil cases; how jurors selected from panel. — A. Five persons from a panel of eleven shall constitute a jury in a civil case when the amount involved exclusive of interest and costs does not exceed the maximum jurisdictional limits as provided in § 16.1-77 (1). Seven persons from a panel of thirteen shall constitute a jury in all other civil cases except that when a special jury is allowed, twelve persons from a panel of twenty shall constitute the jury.

B. The parties or their counsel, beginning with the plaintiff, shall alternately strike off one name from the panel until the number remaining shall be reduced to the number required for a jury. Where there are more than two parties, all plaintiffs shall share three strikes between them and all defendants and third-party defendants shall share three strikes between them.

C. In any case in which there are two or more parties on the same side, if counsel or the parties are unable to agree on the full number to be stricken, or, if for any other reason a party or his counsel fails or refuses to strike off the full number of jurors allowed such party, the clerk shall place in a box ballots bearing the names of the jurors whose names have not been stricken and shall cause to be drawn from the box such number of ballots as may be necessary to complete the number of strikes allowed the party or parties failing or refusing to strike. Thereafter, if the opposing side is entitled to further strikes, they shall be made in the usual manner.

D. In any civil case in which the consent of the plaintiff and defendant shall be entered of record, it shall be lawful for the plaintiff to select one person who is eligible as a juror and for the defendant to select another, and for the two so selected to select a third of like qualifications, and the three so selected shall constitute a jury in the case. They shall take the oath required of jurors, and hear and determine the issue, and any two concurring shall render a verdict in like manner and with like effect as a jury of seven. (Code 1950, § 8-208.21; 1973, c. 439; 1974, c. 611; 1975, c. 578; 1977, c. 617; 1985, c. 188.)

REVISERS' NOTE

Section 8.01-359 makes no changes in subsections (2), (3), (4) and (5) of former § 8-208.21. The $1000 amount in subsection (2) of the former statute has been changed to the maximum jurisdictional limits as provided in § 16.1-77 (1) in subsection A. Subsection (1) of former § 8-208.21 has been incorporated into § 8.01-336 B and C.

I. DECISIONS UNDER CURRENT LAW.

Trial court may not compel party to agree to special three-member jury because it considers that body a superior trier of fact. Painter v. Fred Whitaker Co., 235 Va. 631, 369 S.E.2d 191 (1988).

Plaintiff may withdraw consent to special three man jury prior to trial. — Given the clearly expressed constitutional purpose and legislative intent to preserve the right to trial by jury in both criminal and civil cases, a consent to a special three-person jury under subsection D may be withdrawn before trial under the same conditions as are enunciated in Thomas v. Commonwealth, 218 Va. 553, 238 S.E.2d 834 (1977). Painter v. Fred Whitaker Co., 235 Va. 631, 369 S.E.2d 191 (1988).

§ 8.01-360. Additional jurors when trial likely to be protracted. — Whenever in the opinion of the court the trial of any criminal or civil case is likely to be a protracted one, the court may direct the selection of additional jurors who shall be drawn from the same source, in the same manner and at the same time as the regular jurors. These additional jurors shall have the same qualifications, and be considered and treated in every respect as regular jurors and be subject to examination and challenge as such jurors. When one additional juror is desired, there shall be drawn three veniremen, and the plaintiff and defendant in a civil case or the Commonwealth and accused in a criminal case shall each be allowed one peremptory challenge. When two or more additional jurors are desired there shall be drawn twice as many venireman as the number of additional jurors desired. The plaintiff and defendant in a civil case or the Commonwealth and accused in a criminal case shall each be allowed one additional peremptory challenge for every two additional jurors. The court shall select, by lot, those jurors to be designated additional jurors. The plaintiff and defendant in a civil case or the Commonwealth and accused in a criminal case shall be advised by the court which jurors are additional jurors at the time the jury is impaneled; however, in no event, shall any juror be made aware of his status as a regular or additional juror until he is excused as a juror. Before final submission of the case, the court shall excuse any additional jurors in order to reduce the number of jurors to that required by §§ 8.01-359 and 19.2-262. (Code 1950, § 8-208.22; 1973, c. 439; 1977, c. 617; 1992, c. 536; 1998, c. 279.)

Law Review. — For article reviewing recent developments and changes in legislation, case law, and Virginia Supreme Court Rules affecting civil litigation, see "Civil Practice and Procedure," 26 U. Rich. L. Rev. 679 (1992).

I. DECISIONS UNDER CURRENT LAW.

Applied in Strickler v. Commonwealth, 241 Va. 482, 404 S.E.2d 227 (1991).

§ 8.01-361. New juror may be sworn in place of one disabled; when court may discharge jury.

— If a juror, after he is sworn, be unable from any cause to perform his duty, the court may, in its discretion, cause another qualified juror to be sworn in his place, and in any case, the court may discharge the jury when it appears that they cannot agree on a verdict or that there is a manifest necessity for such discharge. (Code 1950, § 8-208.23; 1973, c. 439; 1977, c. 617.)

I. Decisions Under Current Law.
II. Decisions Under Prior Law.

I. DECISIONS UNDER CURRENT LAW.

Broad discretion to determine whether manifest necessity exists for discharge. — In determining whether manifest necessity for discharge of the jury exists, a trial court is vested with broad discretion. Smith v. Commonwealth, 239 Va. 243, 389 S.E.2d 871 (1990), cert. denied, 498 U.S. 881, 111 S. Ct. 221, 112 L. Ed. 2d 177 (1990).

A court may discharge the jury when it appears that they cannot agree on a verdict or that there is manifest necessity for such discharge. Tyler v. Commonwealth, 21 Va. App. 702, 467 S.E.2d 294 (1996).

Appearance of defendant in shackles. — The trial court abused its discretion by not discharging the jury when the defendant was brought into the courtroom in shackles in full view of the jury although he had only been charged with a nonviolent crime and the Commonwealth made no assertion that he was violent or dangerous. Miller v. Commonwealth, 7 Va. App. 367, 373 S.E.2d 721 (1988).

Accused's rights in selecting replacement juror. — While this section does not specifically prescribe the procedure for selecting a replacement juror, due process requires that the procedure afford the accused equivalent safeguards of his rights as those furnished when selecting additional jurors before the trial begins. Irving v. Commonwealth, 19 Va. App. 581, 453 S.E.2d 577 (1995).

Applied in Manning v. Commonwealth, 2 Va. App. 352, 344 S.E.2d 197 (1986).

II. DECISIONS UNDER PRIOR LAW.

Editor's note. — The cases cited below were decided under corresponding provisions of former law. The term "this section," as used below, refers to former provisions.

Necessity for discharge is discretionary with trial court. — There is no general rule as to what facts and circumstances constitute such a necessity to discharge a jury, but the trial court is authorized by the section to exercise its discretion in making the determination according to the circumstances of the case. Turnbull v. Commonwealth, 216 Va. 328, 218 S.E.2d 541 (1975).

Discharge where jury agreed to two-thirds verdict. — Where the defendant was denied his right to a unanimous verdict in his first trial when the jury agreed to a two-thirds verdict, there was a manifest necessity as required by this section that the trial court declare a mistrial so that the petitioner would be assured of his right not to be convicted without the unanimous consent of the whole jury. Price v. Slayton, 347 F. Supp. 1269 (W.D. Va. 1972).

No double jeopardy where manifest necessity for mistrial. — Although jeopardy attaches to a criminal defendant when the jury is sworn, the trial court, in its sound discretion, may declare a mistrial where there appears to be a manifest necessity for it or where the ends of justice so require. Where this is the case, the defendant may be retried without a violation of the double jeopardy clause of the Fifth Amendment. Price v. Slayton, 347 F. Supp. 1269 (W.D. Va. 1972).

§ 8.01-362. Special juries. — Any court in a civil case in which a jury is required may allow a special jury, in which event the court shall order such jurors to be summoned as it shall designate, and from those summoned, a jury shall be made in accordance with the provisions of § 8.01-359 A. The court may, in its discretion, cause the entire cost of such jury to be taxed as a part of the cost in such action, and to be paid by the plaintiff or defendant as the court shall direct. (Code 1950, § 8-208.25; 1973, c. 439; 1977, c. 617.)

§ 8.01-363. When impartial jury cannot be obtained locally. — In any case in which qualified jurors who are not exempt from serving and who the judge is satisfied can render a fair and impartial trial cannot be conveniently found in the county or city in which the trial is to be, the court may cause so many jurors as may be necessary to be summoned from any other county or city by the sheriff thereof, or by its own officer, from a list prepared pursuant to Article 3 (§ 8.01-343 et seq.) of this chapter and furnished by the circuit court of the county or city from which the jurors are to be summoned. (Code 1950, § 8-208.26; 1973, c. 439; 1977, c. 617.)

I. Decisions Under Current Law.
II. Decisions Under Prior Law.

I. DECISIONS UNDER CURRENT LAW.

Trial court's decision to import venire from another county was sound decision. — Trial judge's decision to avoid any possible prejudice by importing venire from another county in homicide prosecution due to extensive news coverage of previous trial was a sound exercise of discretion for it clearly eliminated any possibility that defendant would not be tried by a fair and impartial jury. Fisher v. Commonwealth, 16 Va. App. 447, 431 S.E.2d 886 (1993).

Refusal to exclude veniremen who read newspaper article not error. — Trial court did not err in refusing to exclude all of the veniremen who had read a news article about defendant, published two days before her trial for manslaughter, where defendant failed to show that the publicity created a widespread feeling of prejudice within the community that was reasonably certain to prevent a fair and impartial trial. Wilmoth v. Commonwealth, 10 Va. App. 169, 390 S.E.2d 514 (1990).

II. DECISIONS UNDER PRIOR LAW.

Editor's note. — The case cited below was decided under corresponding provisions of former law. The term "this statute," as used below, refers to former provisions.

The court may refuse to summon a jury from another county until an ineffectual effort has been made to obtain an impartial jury from the county where the trial is to take place., Rees v. Commonwealth, 203 Va. 850, 127 S.E.2d 406 (1962), cert. denied, 372 U.S. 964, 83 S. Ct. 1088, 10 L. Ed. 2d 128 (1963).

Defendant was not entitled to a change of venue or venire where there was no evidence of inflammatory newspaper or radio coverage of the case, no evidence of mass prejudice, hostility or threat of mob action, either before the jury was sworn or during the course of the trial, nor unusual difficulty in securing an impartial jury., Rees v. Commonwealth, 203 Va. 850, 127 S.E.2d 406 (1962), cert. denied, 372 U.S. 964, 83 S. Ct. 1088, 10 L. Ed. 2d 128 (1963).

Brevity of jury's deliberations held not to show prejudice. — Defendant's contention that prejudice on the part of the jury was proved by the fact they deliberated only a relatively short time was without merit. Rees v. Commonwealth, 203 Va. 850, 127 S.E.2d 406 (1962), cert. denied, 372 U.S. 964, 83 S. Ct. 1088, 10 L. Ed. 2d 128 (1963).

CHAPTER 12.

INTERPLEADER; CLAIMS OF THIRD PARTIES TO PROPERTY DISTRAINED OR LEVIED ON, ETC.

Article 1.
Interpleader.

Sec.
8.01-364. Interpleader.

Article 2.
Claims of Third Parties to Property Distrained or Levied on.

8.01-365. How claim of third party tried.
8.01-366. Sale of property when no forthcoming bond is given.
8.01-367. Indemnifying bond to officer.

Sec.
8.01-368. Return of such bond to clerk's office.
8.01-369. Effect of such bond.
8.01-370. Claimant may give suspending bond; proceedings to have title settled; action on indemnifying or suspending bond.
8.01-371. How forthcoming bond taken of claimant of property the sale whereof has been suspended.
8.01-372. Sale despite bond when property perishable, etc.
8.01-373. When property sells for more than claim, how surplus paid.

ARTICLE 1.
Interpleader.

§ 8.01-364. Interpleader. — A. Whenever any person is or may be exposed to multiple liability through the existence of claims by others to the same property or fund held by him or on his behalf, such person may file a pleading and require such parties to interplead their claims. It is not ground for objection to the joinder that the claims of the several claimants or the titles on which their claims depend do not have a common origin or are not identical but are adverse to and independent of one another, or that the plaintiff avers that he is not liable in whole or in part to any or all of the claimants. A defendant in an action who is exposed to similar liability may likewise obtain such interpleader. The provisions of this rule supplement and do not in any way limit the joinder of parties permitted in § 8.01-5.

B. The remedy herein provided is in addition to and in no way supersedes or limits the remedy provided by any other section of this Code.

C. In any action of interpleader, the court may enter its order restraining all claimants from instituting or prosecuting any proceeding in any court of the Commonwealth affecting the property involved in the interpleader action until further order of the court.

Such court shall hear and determine the case and may discharge the appropriate party from further liability, make the injunction permanent, and make all appropriate orders to enforce its judgment.

D. A person interpleading may voluntarily pay or tender into court the property claimed, or may be ordered to do so by the court; and the court may thereupon order such party discharged from all or part of any liability as between the claimants of such property. (Code 1950, § 8-226; 1977, c. 617; 1978, c. 415.)

REVISERS' NOTE

Section 8.01-364 is a new section in Title 8.01 and replaces former § 8-226. The purpose of the statute is to provide Virginia with a comprehensive modern statutory method of interpleader comparable to those which exist in most other jurisdictions, including the federal system.

Despite the expression of apprehension to the contrary by some critics when the section was being considered, it is not intended to authorize the bringing of "class actions." Neither its content nor its structure is adaptable to such actions.

Like most modern interpleader statutes, § 8.01-364 is patterned in large part upon 28 U.S.C. § 1335 and FRCP 22. While the statute does not expressly supersede the traditional equity suit for interpleader it is believed that in practice the equity procedure will be displaced because of the greater availability, simplicity, and completeness of remedy which the statute affords. Cf. Bell Storage Company v. Harrison, 164 Va. 278, 180 S.E. 320 (1935).

It is to be noted that the statute expressly provides in subsection B "The remedy herein provided is in addition to and in no way supersedes or limits the remedy provided by *any other section of this Code* ." (Emphasis added.) This provision is significant because of the statutory interpleader procedure provided for in the Uniform Commercial Code (§ 8.7-603) for the benefit of bailees as defined in Article 7 of the U.C.C. and which is applicable principally to warehousemen and carriers.

The fact that a rule of the Supreme Court of Virginia has been added to Part Two of the Rules, designed to implement § 8.01-364, should not be interpreted as adding to the statute the restrictions of the traditional equity suit for interpleader which the statute itself does not require.

Cross references. — As to claims of other persons to attached property, see §§ 8.01-567, 8.01-568, 8.01-573.

Law Review. — For survey of Virginia practice and pleading for the year 1977-1978, see 64 Va. L. Rev. 1501 (1978). For comment on interpleader in Virginia, see 13 U. Rich. L. Rev. 331 (1979).

I. DECISIONS UNDER PRIOR LAW.

Editor's note. — The cases cited below were decided under corresponding provisions of former law. The term "this section," as used below, refers to former provisions.

This section does not enlarge the rules governing bills of interpleader nor limit or affect equitable jurisdiction by suit. This section merely furnishes another special, cumulative and concurrent remedy. Runkle v. Runkle, 112 Va. 788, 72 S.E. 695 (1911).

It does not apply where defendant has guaranteed payment to plaintiff. — Where defendants, for whom a building was being erected, agreed with plaintiff, who furnished supplies to a contractor, to retain sufficient funds and pay plaintiff for the materials furnished, defendants were not mere stakeholders of the fund because they guaranteed the debt to plaintiff, and hence were not entitled to have plaintiff and the mechanics' lienors interpleaded and required to litigate their respective claims. Nicholas v. Harrisonburg Bldg. & Supply Co., 181 Va. 207, 24 S.E.2d 452 (1943).

Answer held not interpleader. — See Rinehart & Dennis Co. v. McArthur, 123 Va. 556, 96 S.E. 829 (1918).

Article 2.

Claims of Third Parties to Property Distrained or Levied on.

§ 8.01-365. How claim of third party tried. — When a writ of fieri facias issued from a circuit court, or a warrant of distress, is levied on property, or when a lien is acquired on money or other personal estate by virtue of § 8.01-501, and when some other person than the one against whom the process issued claims the property, money, other personal estate, or some part or the proceeds thereof, then either (i) the claimant, if such suspending bond as is hereinafter mentioned has been given, (ii) the officer having such process, if no indemnifying bond has been given, or (iii) the party who had the process issued, may apply to try the claim, by motion to the adverse party, to the circuit court of the county or city wherein the property, money, or other personal estate is located. (Code 1950, § 8-227; 1962, c. 10; 1977, c. 617.)

REVISERS' NOTE

Although the wording and sequence of former § 8-227 has been altered in § 8.01-365 to conform more closely with § 16.1-119 (Proceedings to try title to property levied on under distress or execution), the substance of former § 8-227 remains unchanged. However, its application has been restricted to circuit courts, leaving to Title 16.1 the appropriate provisions for the district courts.

I. Decisions Under Current Law.
II. Decisions Under Prior Law.

I. DECISIONS UNDER CURRENT LAW.

A motion to quash under § 8.01-477 may not be used by strangers to the underlying judgment as a substitute for the statutory method prescribed in this section or in lieu of a common law action of trespass. The application of § 8.01-477 is limited to attacks on the regularity and validity of a writ of fieri facias. Barbuto v. Southern Bank, 231 Va. 63, 340 S.E.2d 813 (1986).

Third parties who claimed ownership of certain property levied upon improperly sought to prosecute a common law action of trespass and to simultaneously claim ownership of the property seized in the levy. This was an improper use of the statutory motion to quash. Their remedy was under this section, a statute specifically providing strangers to the underlying judgment a swift, direct, and summary method to determine conflicting ownership of property seized in a levy. Barbuto v. Southern Bank, 231 Va. 63, 340 S.E.2d 813 (1986).

Applied in International Fid. Ins. Co. v. Ashland Lumber Co., 250 Va. 507, 463 S.E.2d 664 (1995).

II. DECISIONS UNDER PRIOR LAW.

Editor's note. — The cases cited below were decided under corresponding provisions of former law. The term "this section," as used below, refers to former provisions.

Section is substitute for replevin. — The statutory proceeding by interpleader in Virginia is a substitute for the common-law writ of replevin. Kiser v. Hensley, 123 Va. 536, 96 S.E. 777 (1918). See Allen v. Hart, 59 Va. (18 Gratt.) 722 (1868).

This section and § 8.01-370 are remedial and are to be liberally construed, and are not to be construed in such manner as to make them unconstitutional if it can be avoided. Sauls v. Thomas Andrews & Co., 163 Va. 407, 175 S.E. 760 (1934).

§ 8.01-366. Sale of property when no forthcoming bond is given. — In such case as is mentioned in § 8.01-365, when no bond is given for the forthcoming of the property, the court may, before a decision of the rights of the parties, make an order for the sale of the property, or any part thereof, on such terms as the court may deem advisable, and for the proper application of the proceeds. The court may make such orders and enter such judgment as to costs and all other matters as may be just and proper. (Code 1950, § 8-228; 1977, c. 617.)

REVISERS' NOTE

Section 8.01-366 is former § 8-228 with minor changes. The reference to the "judge thereof in vacation" has been omitted. In addition, the words "in any case before mentioned in this chapter," which appeared in the last sentence of the former statute, have been deleted as unnecessary in view of § 8.01-364 C.

§ 8.01-367. Indemnifying bond to officer. — If any officer levies or is required to levy a fieri facias, an attachment, or a warrant of distress on property, and the officer doubts whether such property is liable to such levy, he may give the plaintiff, his agent or attorney-at-law, notice that an indemnifying bond is required in the case; bond may thereupon be given by any person, with good security, payable to the officer in a penalty equal to the value of the property in the case of a fieri facias or a warrant of distress on property and equal to double the value of the property in case of an attachment, with condition to indemnify him against all damage which he may sustain in consequence of the seizure or sale of such property and to pay to any claimant of such property all damage which he may sustain in consequence of such seizure or sale, and also to warrant and defend to any purchaser of the property such estate or interest therein as is sold.

Provided, however, that when the property claimed to be liable by virtue of the process aforesaid is in the possession of any of the parties against whom such process was issued but is claimed by any other person or is claimed to belong to any other person, the officer having such process in his hands to be executed shall proceed to execute the same notwithstanding such claim unless the claimant of the property or someone for him shall give a suspending bond as provided by § 8.01-370 and shall within thirty days after such bond is given proceed to have the title to the property settled in accordance with the provisions of this chapter. And in case such claimant or someone for him fails to give such suspending bond, or having given such bond fails to have such proceedings instituted to settle the title thereto, the claimant shall be barred from asserting such claim to the property and the officer shall proceed to execute the process, and the officer who executes such process shall not be liable to any such claimant for any damages resulting from the proper execution of such process as is required by this section. If an indemnifying bond be not given within a reasonable time after such notice, the officer may refuse to levy on such property, or may restore it to the person from whose possession it was taken. If such bond be given, the officer shall proceed to levy (i) if he has not already done so, or (ii) if necessary to restore a levy previously released. (Code 1950, § 8-229; 1968, c. 490; 1972, c. 327; 1977, c. 617.)

REVISERS' NOTE

Section 8.01-367 is taken from former § 8-229. The provision in the former section that "the property shall be conclusively presumed to be the property of the party in possession" if the indemnifying bond has not been given, has been removed. But the officer is absolved of liability to the adverse claimant failing to give the bond.

I. Decisions Under Current Law.
II. Decisions Under Prior Law.

I. DECISIONS UNDER CURRENT LAW.

Remedy to prevent levy and stop sale. — A third party who claims ownership of property that has been levied on, or is about to be levied on, has an orderly remedy under this section and § 8.01-370 not only to stop the sale after levy but to prevent the levy from being made in the first place. This is accomplished by giving a suspending bond and by proceeding within 30 days to have title to the property settled. Alternatively, the third party has the option to file an action for common law trespass in a separate proceeding. Barbuto v. Southern Bank, 231 Va. 63, 340 S.E.2d 813 (1986).

II. DECISIONS UNDER PRIOR LAW.

Editor's note. — The cases cited below were decided under corresponding provisions of former law. The term "this section," as used below, refers to former provisions.

Constable may take bond. — See Davis v. Davis, 43 Va. (2 Gratt.) 363 (1845).

One indemnifying bond may be taken on several executions. Davis v. Davis, 43 Va. (2 Gratt.) 363 (1845).

And it is not necessary to set out the executions in the bond. Davis v. Davis, 43 Va. (2 Gratt.) 363 (1845).

Omission of provision for protection of purchaser does not invalidate bond. — A bond under this section may be sufficient for the protection of the sheriff from the action of the claimant of the property, although it does not contain a provision for the protection of the purchaser of the property. Aylett v. Roane, 42 Va. (1 Gratt.) 282 (1844).

Bond executed by one partner in partnership name is sufficient. — Where the plaintiffs in the execution are a firm, a bond executed by one of the firm, in the partnership name, is a good bond of the person so executing it, and the recital in the bond of the names of the plaintiffs in the execution by their partnership name is sufficient. Davis v. Davis, 43 Va. (2 Gratt.) 363 (1845).

This section does not preclude injunction to prevent sale. — A sheriff having doubts as to the title to property taken in execution may demand from the creditor an indemnifying bond, yet this remedy is not in exclusion of a bill of injunction to prevent the sale. Wilson v. Butler, 17 Va. (3 Munf.) 559 (1813).

But the sheriff, having received the bond of indemnity, is bound to sell the property taken in execution, whether it belongs to the debtor or not. Stone v. Pointer, 19 Va. (5 Munf.) 287 (1816).

And he is liable if he releases property instead of requiring bond. — Where an officer released property as to which the debtor wrongfully claimed the benefit of the homestead exemption without demanding an indemnifying bond of the creditor, or even notifying him of the claim of homestead, and the property was subsequently lost to the creditor, the sheriff and his sureties were liable to the creditor for the resulting damages. Sage v. Dickinson, 74 Va. (33 Gratt.) 361 (1880).

But he is excused if creditor fails to give bond on demand. — A deputy was excusable for not levying and selling under the circumstances, where after the one who had issued the fieri facias had failed to give the indemnifying bond demanded of him; and, therefore the creditor could not recover against the sheriff and his sureties, on his official bond, the debt thus lost by the failure to levy. Huffman v. Leffell, 73 Va. (32 Gratt.) 41 (1879).

Action must be brought in the name of the officer. — An action on an indemnifying bond given to a sheriff for sale of property taken in execution must be brought in the name of the sheriff, but it can only be maintained at the relation of the party injured. But though the party injured is not named as relator in the declaration or other pleadings, yet if the breach assigned is that the obligors did not pay the damages sustained by B. by reason of the sale, and if a special verdict in the cause shows that B. was considered the real plaintiff, this is enough to show that B. is the relator; or supposing the pleadings defective in this particular, the defect is cured after verdict by the statute of jeofails. Lewis v. Adams, 33 Va. (6 Leigh) 320 (1835).

By holder of legal title to property. — An indemnifying bond given to a sheriff, under this section, can only be put in suit at the relation of the person having the legal title to the property taken in execution and sold by the sheriff, not at the relation of any person having an equitable right therein. Garland v. Jacobs, 29 Va. (2 Leigh) 651 (1830).

Recovery is value of goods not returned. — Recovery on a replevin bond, when part of the goods only are returned, is the value of the goods not so returned. Kiser v. Hensley, 123 Va. 536, 96 S.E. 777 (1918).

Or value of claimant's interest therein. — In an action on an indemnifying bond, the relator claims title to the property sold, under a sale made by one partner without the knowledge or consent of the other, of partnership property. The relator may recover for the undivided interest of the partner who made the sale, under a general allegation in the declaration of his ownership of the property. Forkner v. Stuart, 47 Va. (6 Gratt.) 197 (1849).

And evidence is admissible to show claimant is only life tenant. — In debt on an indemnifying bond given to a sheriff for seizure and sale of a slave under execution, it is competent to the defendants to prove, that the claimant had only a life estate in the slave, though it appear that he had bona fide purchased of the tenant for life an absolute estate. Stevens v. Bransford, 33 Va. (6 Leigh) 246 (1835).

Plea of bond need not set out judgment. — In an action against a constable, for taking the property of the plaintiff, upon three executions against a third person, the constable filed a special plea, in which he set up an indemnifying bond executed by the plaintiffs in the executions. It was held that it is not necessary to set out the judgments in the plea. Davis v. Davis, 43 Va. (2 Gratt.) 363 (1845).

Defendant must crave oyer to show variance in bond and motion. — A motion on an indemnifying bond in the name of the administrator de bonis non of the high sheriff, sets out the bond as made to himself, and without craving oyer of the bond, the defendants demur. As there is enough in the motion to enable the court to proceed to judgment according to law and the very right of the cause, the demurrer should be overruled. To take advantage by demurrer of a variance between the motion and the bond declared on, the defendant should crave oyer of the bond. Duval v. Malone, 55 Va. (14 Gratt.) 24 (1857). See Kevan v. Branch, 42 Va. (1 Gratt.) 274 (1844); Dickinson v. Smith, 46 Va. (5 Gratt.) 135 (1848).

§ 8.01-368. Return of such bond to clerk's office. — Any indemnifying bond taken by an officer under the preceding section shall be returned by him within twenty-one days to the clerk's office of the circuit court of the county or city wherein the property levied on, or to be levied on, is located. (Code 1950, § 8-230; 1977, c. 617.)

REVISERS' NOTE

Section 8.01-368 is former § 8-230, modified to conform to present practice of the officer's return of an indemnifying bond and to eliminate procedural details felt to be unnecessary; e.g., the time for return of the bond by the officer is changed from twenty to twenty-one days.

§ **8.01-369. Effect of such bond.** — The claimant or purchaser of such property shall, after such bond is so returned, be barred from any action against the officer levying thereon, provided the security therein be good at the time of taking it. (Code 1950, § 8-231; 1977, c. 617.)

I. DECISIONS UNDER PRIOR LAW.

Editor's note. — The cases cited below were decided under corresponding provisions of former law. The term "this section," as used below, refers to former provisions.

Officer has discharged his duty in taking indemnifying bond. — By his act in giving an indemnifying bond under this section, the creditor agrees to save the officer harmless from the claims of any third party, and when the officer takes from an execution creditor the proper indemnifying bond with ample security and then proceeds to sell and pay the money received to the execution creditor, he has discharged his duties to all parties. Wheeler v. City Sav. & Loan Corp., 156 Va. 402, 157 S.E. 726 (1931).

If bond conforms to § 8.01-367. — The constable, sheriff, or other officer who sells property taken under execution is not protected from an action of trespass by the claimant, unless the indemnifying bond taken by him under § 8.01-367 conforms in all respects to that section, and particularly contains the clause inserted for the benefit of the person claiming title to the property. M'Clunn v. Steel, 4 Va. (2 Va. Cas.) 256 (1821).

And obligors thereon are solvent. — If the claimant should bring his action against the officer, it will not be sufficient for him to show that he has established his claim to the property in the action on the indemnifying bond; he must go further, and show that the officer failed in his official duty, in not taking a solvent bond. Stevens v. Bransford, 33 Va. (6 Leigh) 246 (1835).

Claimant's sole remedy is against such obligors. — Claimant was barred by this section from pursuing the property in the possession of a purchaser at an execution sale, and his remedy was not against the officer and his surety but against the obligors on the indemnifying bond. Wheeler v. City Sav. & Loan Corp., 156 Va. 402, 157 S.E. 726 (1931).

§ **8.01-370. Claimant may give suspending bond; proceedings to have title settled; action on indemnifying or suspending bond.** — The sale of any property levied on under a fieri facias or distress warrant shall be suspended at the instance of any claimant thereof who will deliver to the officer a suspending bond, with good security, in a penalty equal to double the value thereof, payable to such officer, with condition to pay to all persons who may be injured by suspending the sale thereof, until the claim thereto is adjudicated or otherwise adjusted, such damage as they may sustain by such suspension. If the property claimed to be liable by virtue of such process is in the possession of any of the parties against whom such process was issued, but is claimed by any other person, or is claimed to belong to any other person, the officer having such process in his hands to be executed shall, whether an indemnifying bond has been given or not, after notice to the claimant, or his agent, proceed to execute the same notwithstanding such claim, unless the claimant of such property or someone for him shall give the suspending bond aforesaid, and shall within thirty days after such bond is given proceed to have the title to such property settled in accordance with the provisions of this chapter. And in case such claimant or someone for him fails to give a suspending bond, or having given such bond fails to have such proceedings instituted to settle the title thereto, the claimant shall be barred from asserting such claim to the property and the sale of the property shall proceed. For the purpose of this section, a person making a claim of ownership of property on behalf of another shall be deemed to be the latter's agent, and the notice required by this section may be verbal or in writing. Upon any such indemnifying or suspending bond as is mentioned in this section or § 8.01-369 an action may be prosecuted in the name of the officer for the benefit of the claimant, creditor, purchaser, or other person injured, and such damages recovered in such action as a jury may assess. The action may be prosecuted and a writ of fieri facias had in the name of such officer when he is dead in like manner as if he were alive. (Code 1950, § 8-232; 1977, c. 617.)

REVISERS' NOTE

Section 8.01-370 is former § 8-232. The provision which appeared in the former section with respect to the conclusiveness of ownership when the required bond was not given, has been eliminated. See Reviser's note to § 8.01-367. Also the word "suspending" has been inserted before "bond" in several places to remove any confusion as to the type of bond addressed by this section.

I. Decisions Under Current Law.
II. Decisions Under Prior Law.

I. DECISIONS UNDER CURRENT LAW.

Remedy to prevent levy and stop sale. — A third party who claims ownership of property that has been levied on, or is about to be levied on, has an orderly remedy under § 8.01-367 and this section not only to stop the sale after levy but to prevent the levy from being made in the first place. This is accomplished by giving a suspending bond and by proceeding within 30 days to have title to the property settled. Alternatively, the third party has the option to file an action for common law trespass in a separate proceeding. Barbuto v. Southern Bank, 231 Va. 63, 340 S.E.2d 813 (1986).

II. DECISIONS UNDER PRIOR LAW.

Editor's note. — The cases cited below were decided under corresponding provisions of former law. The term "this section," as used below, refers to former provisions.

Claimant must give bond and institute proceedings. — Where an execution is levied on property in the possession of the execution debtor, and the property is claimed by another, it is necessary, under the provisions of this section, not only for the claimant to execute a suspending bond, but also, within 30 days after the execution of such bond, to institute proceedings to settle the title to the property so levied on, else it will be conclusively presumed to be the property of the party in possession. Fields-Watkins Co. v. Hensley, 117 Va. 661, 86 S.E. 113 (1915).

Failure to do so within 30 days establishes validity of levy. — Where the sole defense in distress proceedings was that the property levied upon was not that of the defendant therein, but no suspending bond had been given and no effort made to have title settled until more than 30 days had elapsed from the date of service of notice under this section or the time required to give the suspending bond, this section established the conclusive presumption that the property in question was the property of the party in possession, and concluded the question of ownership and established the validity of the levy. Boswell v. Lipscomb, 172 Va. 33, 200 S.E. 756 (1939).

And claimant then holds property at his risk. — Where claimant failed to institute his interpleader proceedings within 30 days from the date of the suspending bond, it was held that from the expiration of the period of 30 days, the possession of the property by the claimant was unlawful, and hence at his risk. Kiser v. Hensley, 123 Va. 536, 96 S.E. 777 (1918).

When bond was given and proceedings instituted is question for court. — When the suspending bond was given and when the proceedings were instituted are questions to be determined by the court as they appear on the record, and it is error to refer them to the jury. Fields-Watkins Co. v. Hensley, 117 Va. 661, 86 S.E. 113 (1915).

When memorandum has been made, process issued and served, and petition filed, there has been such an appeal to the court as to bring the controversy within the purview of this section. Sauls v. Thomas Andrews & Co., 163 Va. 407, 175 S.E. 760 (1934).

§ 8.01-371. How forthcoming bond taken of claimant of property the sale whereof has been suspended.

— The sheriff or other officer levying a writ of fieri facias or distress warrant on property, the sale of which is suspended under this chapter at the instance of a claimant thereof, may, if such claimant desires the property to remain in such possession as it was immediately before the levy, and if the case be one in which a bond for the forthcoming of the property is not prohibited from being taken from the debtor by § 8.01-531, take from the claimant a bond, with sufficient surety, in a penalty equal to double the value of the property, payable to the creditor, with such recital as is required in a forthcoming bond taken from the debtor, and with condition that the property shall be forthcoming at such day and place of sale as may be thereafter lawfully appointed. Such property may then be permitted to remain, at the risk of such claimant, in such possession as it was immediately before the levy; and §§ 8.01-527, 8.01-528, 8.01-530, 8.01-531 and 55-232 shall apply to such forthcoming bond in like manner as to a forthcoming bond taken from the debtor. (Code 1950, § 8-233; 1977, c. 617.)

Cross references. — As to forthcoming bonds generally, see §§ 8.01-526 through 8.01-532.

Law Review. — For survey of Virginia commercial law for the year 1974-1975, see 61 Va. L. Rev. 1668 (1975).

I. DECISIONS UNDER PRIOR LAW.

Editor's note. — The cases cited below were decided under corresponding provisions of former law. The terms "the statute" and "this section," as used below, refer to former provisions.

To be good as statutory bonds, bonds must substantially conform to the statutes authorizing their execution. Under this section, a bond payable to the sheriff and not to the creditor, which does not recite the amount due upon the execution, including the fee for taking the bond, commissions and other charges, and conditioned that the claimant shall have property forthcoming and subject to the order of the court, instead of forthcoming at such time and place of sale as may be thereafter lawfully appointed, as required by the statute, is not good as a statutory forthcoming bond. Kiser v. Hensley, 123 Va. 536, 96 S.E. 777 (1918).

But bond not good under this section may be construed as at common law. — It is proper to construe a bond not valid as a statutory forthcoming bond under this section, but good as a common-law bond, as it would have been construed at common law, if it had been a replevin bond, or a redelivery bond, in an action of replevin. Kiser v. Hensley, 123 Va. 536, 96 S.E. 777 (1918).

Measure of recovery on such bonds is value of property. — The measure of recovery on a bond given by a claimant to sheriff for property levied on under an execution, which bond was not valid as a statutory forthcoming bond under this section, but was good as a common-law bond, for failure to produce for sale the property levied on, was not the execution debts, principal, interest, costs and commissions, but the value of the property levied upon, and it may be doubted whether, even if the bond had conformed strictly to the statute, the measure would have been different. If the value of the property levied on had exceeded the amount of the execution, the measure of recovery would have been the amount of the execution, interest, costs, etc. Kiser v. Hensley, 123 Va. 536, 96 S.E. 777 (1918).

If a sheriff improperly refuses to receive a forthcoming bond he is responsible for damages to those who may be injured. Hamilton v. Shrewsbury, 25 Va. (4 Rand.) 427 (1826). See also, Saunders v. Pate, 25 Va. (4 Rand.) 8 (1826).

§ 8.01-372. Sale despite bond when property perishable, etc.

— In such case as is mentioned in § 8.01-371 and whether a forthcoming bond is given or not, if the property be expensive to keep or perishable, the court in which proceedings in the case under § 8.01-365 are pending or may be had, may, before a decision of the rights of the parties under such proceedings, on the application of such claimant or of the surety in such suspending or forthcoming bond, after reasonable notice of the intended application has been given by such claimant or the surety to the other parties in the case, order a sale of the property, or any part thereof, on such terms as the court may deem advisable. The court shall apply the proceeds according to the rights of the parties when determined. (Code 1950, § 8-234; 1977, c. 617.)

§ 8.01-373. **When property sells for more than claim, how surplus paid.** — When property, the sale of which is indemnified, sells for more than enough to satisfy the execution, attachment, or distress warrant under which it is taken, the surplus shall be paid by the officer into the court where the indemnifying bond is required to be returned, or as such court may direct. The court wherein the surplus is held may make such order for the disposition thereof, either temporarily until the question as to the title of the property sold is determined, or absolutely, as in respect to the rights of those interested may seem to it proper. (Code 1950, § 8-235; 1977, c. 617.)

CHAPTER 13.
CERTAIN INCIDENTS OF TRIAL.

Sec.	
8.01-374.	Procedure when original papers in cause are lost.
8.01-374.1.	Consolidation or bifurcation of issues or claims in certain cases; appeal.
8.01-375.	Exclusion of witnesses in civil cases.
8.01-376.	Views by juries.
8.01-377.	Remedy when variance appears between evidence and allegations.
8.01-377.1.	Summary judgment.
8.01-378.	Trial judge not to direct verdicts.
8.01-379.	Argument before jury.
8.01-379.1.	Informing jury of amounts sued for.
8.01-379.2.	Jury instructions.
8.01-380.	Dismissal of action by nonsuit.
8.01-381.	What jury may carry out.
8.01-382.	Verdict, judgment or decree to fix period at which interest begins; judgment or decree for interest.
8.01-383.	Power to grant new trial; how often.
8.01-383.1.	Appeal when verdict reduced and accepted under protest; new trial for inadequate damages.
8.01-384.	Formal exceptions to rulings or orders of court unnecessary; motion for new trial unnecessary in certain cases.
8.01-384.1.	Interpreters for deaf in civil proceedings.
8.01-384.1:1.	Interpreters for non-English-speaking persons in civil cases.
8.01-384.2.	Waiver of discovery time limitations by parties.

§ 8.01-374. **Procedure when original papers in cause are lost.** — If in any case the original papers therein, or any of them, or the record for or in an appellate court, or any paper filed or connected with such record, be lost or destroyed, any party to such case may present to the court wherein the case is, or in which it would or ought to be, but for such loss or destruction, a petition verified by affidavit stating such loss or destruction, and praying that such case be heard and determined or tried on the reproduction of such record or papers, or satisfactory proof of their contents. Upon such petition and an authenticated copy of what is lost or destroyed, the court may hear and determine the case, or proceed to a trial thereof, if before a jury. The court may also hear and determine the case, or proceed to the trial thereof, if before a jury, upon proof, after reasonable notice to the parties interested, of the contents of such record or papers, or so much thereof, as may be necessary for a decision by the court, or by a jury, and may make such order or decree as if the papers or any of them had not been lost or destroyed.

The court may in its discretion, require new pleadings to be made up in whole or in part.

A plaintiff instead of proceeding under this section may commence and prosecute a new suit for the same matter; and no certified copy of any deed, will, account, or other original paper required by law to be recorded shall be used by any party as evidence for him, in any case when the original deed, will, account, or other original paper or record thereof has been destroyed, until such copy has been properly admitted to record, according to law. This section shall not apply to criminal cases. (Code 1950, § 8-209; 1977, c. 617.)

REVISERS' NOTE

Former § 8-210.2 (Physical or mental examination of party) has been deleted since the subject matter is provided for in Rule 4:10.

Cross references. — As to evidence in establishing lost instruments, see §§ 8.01-392 through 8.01-395. As to method of admitting copy to record where original is lost, see § 55-109.

I. DECISIONS UNDER PRIOR LAW.

Editor's note. — The cases cited below were decided under corresponding provisions of former law. The term "this section," as used below, refers to former provisions.

Sufficient compliance when bill and answer admit destruction. — It is a sufficient compliance with this section where a sworn bill alleges and an answer admits the destruction of the original papers in a cause where there was a decree for sale of certain lands, and there is filed a certified copy of the papers from the Supreme Court, where the cause was on appeal. An injunction will not lie to such sale on the ground that "no affidavit of the destruction was filed." Hudson v. Yost, 88 Va. 347, 13 S.E. 436 (1891).

Reinstatement of cause. — Where the records in a cause which was on the docket of the circuit court at its last session before the Civil War were destroyed, it not appearing that the cause had been legally removed, it was no error to reinstate it on proper motion. Dismal Swamp Land Co. v. McCauley, 85 Va. 16, 6 S.E. 697 (1888).

§ 8.01-374.1. Consolidation or bifurcation of issues or claims in certain cases; appeal.

— A. In any circuit court in which there are pending more than forty civil actions against manufacturers or suppliers of asbestos or products for industrial use that contain asbestos in which recovery is sought for personal injury or wrongful death alleged to have been caused by exposure to asbestos or products for industrial use that contain asbestos, the court may order a joint hearing or trial by jury of any or all common questions of law or fact which are at issue in those actions. The court may order any or all the actions consolidated, unless the court finds consolidation would adversely affect the rights of the parties to a fair trial. The court may submit special interrogatories to the jury to resolve specific issues of fact, and may make such orders concerning proceedings therein consistent with the right of each of the parties to a fair trial as may be appropriate to avoid unnecessary costs, duplicative litigation or delay.

B. To further convenience or avoid prejudice in such consolidated hearings, when separate or bifurcated trials will be conducive to judicial economy, the court may order a separate or bifurcated trial of any claim, or any number of claims, cross-claims, counterclaims, third-party claims, or separate issues, always preserving the right of trial by jury. However, in any such bifurcated proceeding, the entitlement of an individual plaintiff to an award of punitive damages against any defendant shall not be determined unless compensatory damages have been awarded to that individual.

C. Any order entered pursuant to this section shall, for purposes of appeal, be an interlocutory order. Any findings of the court or jury in any bifurcated trial shall not be appealable until a final order adjudicating all issues on a specific claim or consolidated group of claims has been entered.

D. This section shall not apply to actions arising under Article 6 (§ 8.01-57 et seq.) of Chapter 3 of this title or the Federal Employers Liability Act (45 U.S.C. § 51 et seq.). In addition, this section shall not apply to any party defendant unless that defendant was a manufacturer of, or a supplier of, asbestos or products for industrial use that contain asbestos, at any of the times alleged in the motion for judgment. (1992, c. 615.)

Editor's note. — Acts 1992, c. 615, cl. 2, which provided for the expiration of this section on June 30, 1995, was repealed by Acts 1995, c. 14, cl. 1, effective June 30, 1995, and by Acts 1995, c. 138, cl. 1, effective March 9, 1995.

§ 8.01-375. Exclusion of witnesses in civil cases.

— The court trying any civil case may upon its own motion and shall upon the motion of any party, require the exclusion of every witness. However, each named party who is an individual, one officer or agent of each party which is a corporation or association and an attorney alleged in a habeas corpus proceeding to have acted ineffectively shall be exempt from the rule of this section as a matter of right. Where expert witnesses are to testify in the case, the court may, at the request of all parties, allow one expert witness for each party to remain in the courtroom. (Code 1950, § 8-211.1; 1966, c. 268; 1975, c. 652; 1977, c. 617; 1986, c. 36; 1987, c. 70.)

REVISERS' NOTE

Section 8.01-375 alters former § 8-211.1 by removing criminal cases from its application. NOTE: The provisions of former §§ 8-211, 8-212, 8-213, and 8-214 have been amended and incorporated into § 8.01-336. The provisions of former § 8-215 have been incorporated in § 8.01-358.

Cross references. — As to exclusion of persons from trial of criminal case, see § 19.2-266.

Law Review. — For survey of Virginia criminal law for the year 1971-1972, see 58 Va. L. Rev. 1206 (1972). For survey of Virginia law on practice and pleading for the year 1974-1975, see 61 Va. L. Rev. 1799 (1975). As to expert witnesses in the courtroom, see 22 U. Rich. L. Rev. 621 (1988).

I. Decisions Under Current Law.
II. Decisions Under Prior Law.

I. DECISIONS UNDER CURRENT LAW.

The purpose of this section is to discourage and expose fabrication and collusion by witnesses and to minimize the likelihood that witnesses will alter their testimony so that such testimony is consistent with testimony provided by other witnesses. Motley v. Tarmac Am., Inc., 258 Va. 98, 516 S.E.2d 7 (1999).

Exception for agent of corporation. — Former employee, whose negligent acts and omissions were at issue in litigation, was not an agent of the defendant within the intent of this section because he was neither employed by the defendant at the time of trial, nor did he have any other relationship with the defendant at that time. Thus, former employee should not have been allowed to remain in the courtroom to observe the testimony of other witnesses. Motley v. Tarmac Am., Inc., 258 Va. 98, 516 S.E.2d 7 (1999).

II. DECISIONS UNDER PRIOR LAW.

Editor's note. — The cases cited below were decided under corresponding provisions of former law. The term "this section," as used below, refers to former provisions.

Testimony of witness violating order directing his exclusion. — There is nothing in the language of this section to support the argument of counsel for the defendant that the presence of a witness in the courtroom, in disobedience of the order of exclusion, disqualifies such witness from testifying. On the contrary, it is generally held that it is within the sound discretion of the trial court to permit the testimony of a witness who has violated an order directing his exclusion from the courtroom. Brickhouse v. Commonwealth, 208 Va. 533, 159 S.E.2d 611 (1968).

Section gave an accused an absolute right to have all witnesses excluded from the courtroom during his trial. Martin v. Commonwealth, 217 Va. 847, 234 S.E.2d 62 (1977).

While a defendant's right to exclusion under former § 8-211.1 before its amendment in 1975 was qualified, i.e., it extended only to those witnesses whose presence at trial was not necessary, the amendment, which deleted the words "whose presence is not necessary to the proceedings" following "witness," removed that qualification and made a defendant's right absolute. In its amended form, former § 8-211.1 permitted no rational construction but that

§ 8.01-376

"upon the motion of any party" a trial court "shall" exclude "every witness" during the trial of "every case, civil or criminal." Johnson v. Commonwealth, 217 Va. 682, 232 S.E.2d 741 (1977).

§ **8.01-376. Views by juries.** — The jury may, in any civil case, at the request of either party, be taken to view the premises or place in question, or any property, matter or thing relating to the controversy between the parties, when it shall appear to the court that such view is necessary to a just decision; provided that the expenses of the jury and the officers who attend them in taking the view shall be afterwards taxed like other legal costs. (Code 1950, § 8-216; 1977, c. 617; 1978, c. 367.)

REVISERS' NOTE

The references in former § 8-216 to criminal cases have been deleted and transferred to § 19.2-264.1.

I. DECISIONS UNDER PRIOR LAW.

Editor's note. — The cases cited below were decided under corresponding provisions of former law. The term "this section," as used below, refers to former provisions.

History of section. — This provision in the statute of law of the State first appeared in the Code of 1849 (chapter 162, page 629, § 10), and with the exception of the words "civil or criminal," added by the act of December 10, 1903 (Acts 1902-3-4, page 605) [and changed to "civil" in Acts 1977, c. 617], has remained unchanged. Noell v. Commonwealth, 135 Va. 600, 115 S.E. 679 (1923). See also Litton v. Commonwealth, 101 Va. 833, 44 S.E. 923 (1903).

Scope of section. — In regard to a view of the premises by the jury, this section undertakes to occupy the whole field upon this subject. Noell v. Commonwealth, 135 Va. 600, 115 S.E. 679 (1923).

Object of view. — The view of the grounds at the scene of an accident which is the basis of an action may better enable the jury to apply the testimony disclosed upon the trial, but does not authorize them to base their verdict on such view, nor to become silent witnesses to facts which were not testified to in court. City of Norfolk v. Anthony, 117 Va. 777, 86 S.E. 68 (1915); P. Lorillard Co. v. Clay, 127 Va. 734, 104 S.E. 384 (1920).

A view is not intended to supply evidence. — It has been definitely and repeatedly said by the Supreme Court that a view is not intended to supply evidence, but only to explain and clarify it. Noell v. Commonwealth, 135 Va. 600, 115 S.E. 679 (1923).

But is a source of proof. — A view by a jury is to be considered as constituting a source of proof for or against the accused. Even in those cases in which it has been held as a general proposition that the presence of the prisoner at a view is not essential, it is never questioned that if evidence is taken during the view in the prisoner's absence, he cannot be convicted. Noell v. Commonwealth, 135 Va. 600, 115 S.E. 679 (1923).

Necessity of motion for view by parties. — Under this section, a view ought not to be ordered in any case except upon the motion of one or both parties, or by consent of both parties, which would be tantamount to a joint motion. Although it might be error to order a view over the protest of both parties, where neither party objects, their acquiescence is equivalent to consent. Noell v. Commonwealth, 135 Va. 600, 115 S.E. 679 (1923).

Right to view rests in discretion of court. — The right to a view is not an absolute right of a litigant, but rests in the sound discretion of the trial court, subject to review under proper circumstances. B & O R.R. v. Polly, Woods & Co., 55 Va. (14 Gratt.) 447 (1858); Litton v. Commonwealth, 101 Va. 833, 44 S.E. 923 (1903); In re Cutchin, 113 Va. 452, 74 S.E. 403 (1912); P. Lorillard Co. v. Clay, 127 Va. 734, 104 S.E. 384 (1920); Noell v. Commonwealth, 135 Va. 600, 115 S.E. 679 (1923).

The propriety of ordering a view lies largely in the discretion of the trial court, which should only grant it when it is reasonably certain that it will be of substantial aid to the jury in reaching a correct verdict, and its decision refusing a view will not be reversed unless the record shows that it did appear to the trial court that such view was necessary to a just decision, and that the statutory provision for expenses in a civil case was complied with. C & O Ry. v. Nickel, 157 Va. 382, 161 S.E. 248 (1931); Early v. City of Norfolk, 183 Va. 659, 33 S.E.2d 177 (1945).

When view proper. — A court should only

487

grant a view when it is reasonably certain that it will be of substantial aid to the jury in reaching a correct verdict. In re Cutchin, 113 Va. 452, 74 S.E. 403 (1912); Abernathy v. Emporia Mfg. Co., 122 Va. 406, 95 S.E. 418 (1918); Scott v. Doughty, 124 Va. 358, 97 S.E. 802 (1919); P. Lorillard Co. v. Clay, 127 Va. 734, 104 S.E. 384 (1920).

When properly refused. — A view of the premises was rightly refused where the accident happened some 18 months prior, when conditions may have been different, especially in view of the absence of any evidence that conditions were the same when the view was asked as when the accident happened. P. Lorillard Co. v. Clay, 127 Va. 734, 104 S.E. 384 (1920); Noell v. Commonwealth, 135 Va. 600, 115 S.E. 679 (1923).

Effect of view unauthorized by the court. — Generally a new trial will not be granted where an unauthorized view is casual, incidental, and not reasonably calculated to influence a jury in arriving at a verdict. Crockett v. Commonwealth, 187 Va. 687, 47 S.E.2d 377 (1948).

Where the gist of the action is the character or condition of the locus in quo, or where a better view of it will enable the jurors better to determine the credibility of witnesses and other disputed facts, or where the mere fact of an inspection, in view of the nature of the suit, is calculated to influence the jury to the prejudice of the unsuccessful party, it will be presumed that the knowledge obtained by an unauthorized view was in fact prejudicial, and in the absence of evidence to the contrary, a new trial will be granted. Crockett v. Commonwealth, 187 Va. 687, 47 S.E.2d 377 (1948).

Discretion held not abused. — There was no abuse of discretion by the trial court in permitting a view by the jury of the place on defendant's premises where plaintiff slipped on an allegedly worn stair tread. Evidence was first taken to establish that the condition of the stair was substantially the same as at the time of plaintiff's fall. Culpepper v. Neff, 204 Va. 800, 134 S.E.2d 315 (1964).

§ 8.01-377. Remedy when variance appears between evidence and allegations.

— If, at the trial of any action, there appears to be a variance between the evidence and the allegations or recitals, the court, if it consider that substantial justice will be promoted and that the opposite party cannot be prejudiced thereby, may allow the pleadings to be amended, on such terms as to the payment of costs or postponement of the trial, or both, as it may deem reasonable. Or, instead of the pleadings being amended, the court may direct the jury to find the facts, and, after such finding, if it consider the variance such as could not have prejudiced the opposite party, shall give judgment according to the right of the case. (Code 1950, § 8-217; 1977, c. 617.)

Law Review. — For comment on application of section, see 45 Va. L. Rev. 1443 (1959). For survey of Virginia law on wills, trusts and estates for the year 1973-1974, see 60 Va. L. Rev. 1632 (1974).

I. Decisions Under Current Law.
II. Decisions Under Prior Law.
   A. General Consideration.
   B. Amendment of Immaterial Allegations.

I. DECISIONS UNDER CURRENT LAW.

Purpose is to prevent surprise. — The rule that the proofs must correspond with the allegation is fully recognized, but like every other rule should be reasonably applied. Its purpose is to prevent surprise. Where there is no surprise to the party invoking it, there is no good reason for enforcing the rule. Graves Constr., Inc. v. National Cellulose Corp., 226 Va. 164, 306 S.E.2d 898 (1983).

Party entitled to adversary's ground of complaint. — A court may not base a judgment or decree upon facts not alleged or upon a right, however meritorious, that has not been pleaded and claimed; every litigant is entitled to be told in plain and explicit language the adversary's ground of complaint. Hensley v. Dreyer, 247 Va. 25, 439 S.E.2d 372 (1994).

In a case of variance, this section gives a trial court the discretion to apply principle that it may not base a judgment or decree upon facts not alleged or upon a right, however meritorious, that has not been pleaded or claimed, reasonably either by permitting amendment of the pleadings (and possibly postponing the trial) or, in lieu of amendment, by having the facts determined and rendering judgment, but only on the condition that no prejudice results; while the statute is remedial in purpose and should be liberally construed, it should not be interpreted in a manner inconsistent with its plain language. Hensley v. Dreyer, 247 Va. 25, 439 S.E.2d 372 (1994).

Grounds for divorce. — A trial court is authorized by Sup. Ct. Rule 1:8 and this section to permit a party to amend pleadings to allege a different or dual grounds of divorce from that initially pleaded. Megill v. Megill, No. 1906-96-2 (Ct. of Appeals Apr. 29, 1997).

II. DECISIONS UNDER PRIOR LAW.

A. General Consideration.

Editor's note. — The cases cited below were decided under corresponding provisions of former law. The term "this section," as used below, refers to former provisions.

For judicial history of this section, see Long Pole Lumber Co. v. Gross, 180 F. 5 (4th Cir. 1910).

Purpose is to prevent surprise. — The rule that the proofs must correspond with the allegation is fully recognized, but like every other rule should be reasonably applied. Its purpose is to prevent surprise. Where there is no surprise to the party invoking it, there is no good reason for enforcing the rule. Caputo v. Holt, 217 Va. 302, 228 S.E.2d 134 (1976).

Section liberally construed. — This section and § 8.01-545 allow substantial amendments in the pleadings for the promotion of justice, and they have always been liberally construed by the Supreme Court as remedial in purpose. Langhorne v. Richmond City Ry., 91 Va. 364, 22 S.E. 357 (1895); New River Mineral Co. v. Painter, 100 Va. 507, 42 S.E. 300 (1902); C & O Ry. v. Swartz, 115 Va. 723, 80 S.E. 568 (1914); Norfolk & W. Ry. v. Perdue, 117 Va. 111, 83 S.E. 1058 (1915); Standard Paint Co. v. E.K. Vietor & Co., 120 Va. 595, 91 S.E. 752 (1917); Russell Lumber Co. v. Thompson & Lambert, 137 Va. 386, 119 S.E. 117 (1923); Dillow v. Stafford, 181 Va. 483, 25 S.E.2d 330 (1943); Provident Life & Accident Ins. Co. v. Walker, 190 Va. 1016, 59 S.E.2d 126 (1950).

Liberal construction is especially the case where the amendment will further the ends of justice and permit the controversy to be determined on its merits. McKee v. Bunting, McNeal Real Estate Co., 114 Va. 639, 77 S.E. 515 (1913).

Leave to amend pleadings should be liberally granted in furtherance of the ends of justice. Haymore v. Brizendine, 210 Va. 578, 172 S.E.2d 774 (1970).

This section expressly authorizes a court to impose conditions to the granting of leave to amend pleadings. Haymore v. Brizendine, 210 Va. 578, 172 S.E.2d 774 (1970).

Objection or motion to exclude proper. — In case of variance between the evidence and allegations, the usual and correct practice is to object to the evidence when offered or move to exclude it. Attention is thus called to the discrepancy and an opportunity afforded the trial court to meet the emergency, in a proper case, in one of the modes prescribed by this section. Portsmouth St. R.R. v. Peed's Adm'r, 102 Va. 662, 47 S.E. 850 (1904); Holdsworth v. Anderson Drug Co., 118 Va. 359, 87 S.E. 565 (1916).

The proper method of objecting to a variance between the allegations and proof is by motion to exclude the evidence. Southern Ry. v. Finley & Seymour, 127 Va. 132, 102 S.E. 559 (1920).

Where there is a variance between a contract set out in a plea, and the contract offered in evidence in support of the plea, and no motion is made to amend the plea, as provided by this section then the contract offered in evidence should be excluded. Richmond Standard Steel, Spike & Iron Co. v. Chesapeake Coal Co., 102 Va. 417, 46 S.E. 397 (1904).

Objection may be waived. — No objection having been made to the admission of evidence, and no motion made to exclude it on account of a supposed variance, the objection must be considered as having been waived. Burruss v. Suddith, 187 Va. 473, 47 S.E.2d 546 (1948).

Pursuant to this section, that no objection having been made to the admissibility of evidence, or no motion to exclude it on account of the supposed variance, the objection must be considered as having been waived. Newport News & O.P. Ry. & Elec. Co. v. McCormick, 106 Va. 517, 56 S.E. 281 (1907).

An objection to a variance between proof and pleadings is waived where no objection is made to the admission of evidence, and no motion is made to exclude it because of the supposed variance. If this rule of practice was not adhered to, it would deprive parties of their right to amend their pleadings to conform with the evidence, which is permitted in proper cases under this section. Culmore Realty Co. v. Caputi, 203 Va. 403, 124 S.E.2d 7 (1962).

Effect of failure to invoke statute. — This statute authorizes amendments upon terms fair to both parties, whenever a variance between the pleadings and the proof develops during the trial. It has always been regarded with favor, and construed with liberality by the courts. Having failed to avail himself of the remedy thus provided, or to give the opposite party or the court the opportunity to invoke it, a party cannot take advantage of an irregularity which the statute would have cured. Chandler v. Kelley, 149 Va. 221, 141 S.E. 389 (1928).

The record in a consolidated action is competent evidence in a companion case for the plaintiffs. No objection was made to the record as evidence in the trial court. Furthermore, slight variances between the declaration and the record, which would not prevent the record in the present case from being a bar to another action for the same cause, are not sufficient to exclude it under this section. Forbes v. Hagman, 75 Va. 168 (1881).

Objection cannot be made for the first time in appellate court. — It is elementary law that the proof must correspond to the allegations. But a party wishing to avail himself of this rule is required to make timely objection to the variance in the trial court. Du Pont Eng'r Co. v. Blair, 129 Va. 423, 106 S.E. 328 (1921).

This section was enacted to obviate the difficulties which frequently arise after a trial has been commenced, when it appears that there is a variance between the evidence and the allegations in the pleadings. Such objection cannot be made for the first time in the appellate court. Bertha Zinc Co. v. Martin's Adm'r, 93 Va. 791, 22 S.E. 869 (1895); Virginia & S.W. Ry. v. Bailey, 103 Va. 205, 49 S.E. 33 (1904).

It was urged by the defendant, that as the action was based upon a wrongful discharge, the plaintiff should have declared specially upon the contract and its breach, whereas his allegation contained only the common counts in assumpsit. Conceding that the allegation was defective, it was the duty of the defendant, if it intended to rely upon that point, to then and there call the court's attention to it. This section authorizing amendments, upon terms fair to both parties, whenever a variance between the pleadings and the proof develops during the trial, was expressly designed to meet just such a situation as would have been presented in the trial court if the question first raised on appeal had been raised there. This statute has always, and most properly, been regarded with favor and construed with liberality by the courts of this State; and its terms would have fully met the condition complained of by defendant. Having failed to avail itself of the remedy thus provided, or to give the plaintiff or the court the opportunity to invoke it, the defendant cannot upon appeal take advantage of the irregularity which the statute would have cured. Conrad v. Ellison-Harvey Co., 120 Va. 458, 91 S.E. 763 (1917).

Under this section the trial court is vested with discretion in cases of variance. And even if the court errs in allowing a case to go to the jury without requiring the plaintiff to amend his notice of motion so as to conform more closely to the proof, this is an error of which defendant should not be allowed to take advantage, if the entire record showed that the judgment accomplished substantial justice according to the right of the case. The Supreme Court should correct substantial errors and should not reverse judgments for defects which do not injuriously affect the substantial rights of the parties. Kennedy v. Mullins, 155 Va. 166, 154 S.E. 568 (1930).

Variance cannot be based on immaterial allegations. — Allegations in pleadings which are immaterial to the real issues in the case cannot form the basis of a claim that there is a fatal variance between allegation and proof. Simmers v. DePoy, 212 Va. 447, 184 S.E.2d 776 (1971).

Where the allegation was immaterial, the contradicting testimony merely created a conflict in the evidence and did not constitute a variance requiring the action contemplated by this section. Simmers v. DePoy, 212 Va. 447, 184 S.E.2d 776 (1971).

B. Amendment of Immaterial Allegations.

Date of accident in notice may be amended. — Where an amendment under this section is germane to a material fact in controversy, i.e., the date of the accident which caused the disability of the insured, and where the change in the notice of motion is allowed before the evidence of the plaintiff has been fully submitted and merely prevents a variance of fact between the evidence and an allegation or recital in the pleadings, it is not error to allow the amendment. Provident Life & Accident Ins. Co. v. Walker, 190 Va. 1016, 59 S.E.2d 126 (1950).

Also quantum of damages in notice. — In an action for breach of contract, before plaintiffs had concluded their evidence it was shown that the damages exceeded the amount laid in the notice of motion and they then moved the court to allow them to amend the notice in respect to the quantum of damages, which motion was granted over defendants' objection. It was held that in the absence of a motion for a continuance the court was clearly right in allowing the amendment, authority for which is furnished by this section. Wood v. Quillin, 167 Va. 255, 188 S.E. 216 (1936).

Instances of immaterial amendments. — In an action on a contract against a corporation, plaintiff's declaration purported to set out the contract verbatim, and recited that it was signed by its president and attested by its secretary and corporate seal. In copying the contract into the declaration there was nothing to represent the seal. When the contract was produced in evidence, it was apparent that the corporate seal had been attached as recited in the contract, thereupon leave was granted plaintiff to amend the declaration to conform to the facts. Such amendment was authorized by this section and by Rev. St. § 954 [U.S. Comp. St. 1901, p. 696.] Mathieson Alkali Works v. Mathieson, 150 F. 241 (4th Cir. 1906), cert. denied, 204 U.S. 674, 27 S. Ct. 787, 51 L. Ed. 674 (1907).

The plaintiff sought to recover for injuries while operating a locomotive because of the collapse of a bridge, and alleged that the defendant was negligent in the construction of the bridge. But the evidence showed that the defendant's failure to inspect the bridge after a rain was the cause of the accident. The court held that under this section at the conclusion of the evidence it could properly permit the plaintiff to amend his declaration so as to allege that the stringer of the bridge which broke was insufficient unless properly supported, and that by reason of defendant's failure to make reasonable inspections it was not properly supported at the time of the accident, and caused the injury, there being no demand by the defendant for the imposition of terms or for a continuance by reason of such amendment. Long Pole Lumber Co. v. Gross, 180 F. 5 (4th Cir. 1910).

In an action for damages for fraud and breach of warranty in the sale of defective roofing, the dates of the several sales were each alleged in the declaration under a videlicet. The defendant knew the precise dates of each sale, and after one of its witnesses had supplied those dates the court permitted each count in the declaration to be amended by the insertion of the precise dates. Such amendments were not material, and if they were, were fully authorized by this section. Standard Paint Co. v. E.K. Vietor & Co., 120 Va. 595, 91 S.E. 752 (1917).

Where a motion charges that the slanderous words were uttered in the presence of three named persons, and proof is that one of the three was not present, motion may be amended at the trial, as the variance is immaterial. Harman v. Cundiff, 82 Va. 239 (1886).

If one corporation is sued for a personal injury, and the evidence of the defendants tends to show that the injury was committed by another corporation, the plaintiff, upon request, under this section, should be allowed to amend his motion so as to charge that the two corporations were one and the same corporation, known by both names. Langhorne v. Richmond Ry., 91 Va. 369, 22 S.E. 159 (1895).

A notice is addressed by B. to R., late sheriff, and his surviving sureties by name, survivors of themselves and James Sims. On the trial B. introduces the bond which is signed by R. and all the surviving sureties; but it is objected to as evidence because the name described in the address of the notice as James Sims is written Jos. Sin. This is not a material variance, and is curable under this statute. Beasley v. Robinson, 65 Va. (24 Gratt.) 325 (1874).

The effect of an amendment under this section is to admit new evidence which would not have been admissible before the amendment. Norfolk & W. Ry. v. Perdue, 117 Va. 111, 83 S.E. 1058 (1915).

Continuance after amendment. — Where there is a variance between the allegations of the pleadings and the evidence, it is in conformity with this section to allow the pleadings to be amended and if, need be, continue the case, and the practice is to be commenced as promotive of substantial justice. C & O Ry. v. Swartz, 115 Va. 723, 80 S.E. 568 (1914).

Proceeding with trial after amendment. — In an action on a policy, the motion omitted one of the conditions indorsed upon it. On the trial when the policy was offered in evidence, it was objected to for the variance. The court properly allowed the plaintiff to amend the motion by inserting the omitted condition, and proceeded with the trial. New York Life Ins. Co. v. Hendren, 65 Va. (24 Gratt.) 536 (1874), appeal dismissed, 92 U.S. 286, 22 L. Ed. 709 (1875).

At trial, in case of variance between allegations and evidence, the court may allow the former to be amended by striking out immaterial words without remanding the case to rules. Alexandria & F.R.R. v. Herndon, 87 Va. 193, 12 S.E. 289 (1890).

§ 8.01-377.1. Summary judgment. — In any action at law or equity at the close of all the evidence, any party may move for a summary judgment upon the entire case or upon any severable issue including the issue of liability alone although there is a genuine issue as to damages. (1990, c. 628.)

Cross references. — As to summary judgment in equity and at law, see Rules 2:21 and 3:18.

§ 8.01-378. Trial judge not to direct verdicts. — In no action tried before a jury shall the trial judge give to the jury a peremptory instruction directing what verdict the jury shall render. If the trial judge has granted a motion to strike the evidence of the plaintiff or the defendant, the judge shall enter summary judgment or partial summary judgment in conformity with his ruling on the motion to strike. (Code 1950, § 8-218; 1958, c. 208; 1977, c. 617; 1985, c. 214; 1986, c. 253.)

§ 8.01-378 CODE OF VIRGINIA § 8.01-378

Cross references. — As to summary judgment in equity and at law, see Rules 2:21 and 3:18.

Law Review. — For comment on interpretation of section, see 46 Va. L. Rev. 1652 (1960).

I. Decisions Under Current Law.
II. Decisions Under Prior Law.

I. DECISIONS UNDER CURRENT LAW.

Directed verdicts prohibited. — Directed verdicts were expressly prohibited by statute in Virginia prior to 1958, and are prohibited now. During the interval 1958-1986, directed verdicts were permitted only where the court had sustained a motion to strike the evidence. Kesler v. Allen, 233 Va. 130, 353 S.E.2d 777 (1987).

Applied in Board of Supvrs. v. Southern Cross Coal Corp., 238 Va. 91, 380 S.E.2d 636 (1989).

II. DECISIONS UNDER PRIOR LAW.

Editor's note. — The cases cited below were decided under corresponding provisions of former law. The term "this section," as used below, refers to former provisions.

Validity of statute. — The court declined to pass on the constitutionality of this section in Linkous v. Harris, 134 Va. 63, 113 S.E. 831 (1922).

This section is not in conflict with § 8.01-430, declaring that if a verdict be set aside as contrary to the evidence, etc., the trial court shall render judgment, for this section is intended to prevent errors by the court in the heat of trial, while § 8.01-430 allows the court to act after deliberation. W.S. Forbes & Co. v. Southern Cotton Oil Co., 130 Va. 245, 108 S.E. 15 (1921).

Nor does it affect § 8.01-380 as to nonsuits. — After a motion by defendant for a directed verdict, a plaintiff has no absolute right then to suffer a nonsuit. Section 8.01-380, against taking a nonsuit after the jury retires, does not govern in view of the accepted Virginia practice under this section not to direct verdicts. Pannill v. Roanoke Times Co., 252 F. 910 (W.D. Va. 1918).

Nor is the scintilla doctrine reinstated. — This section applies only to peremptory instructions which direct what verdict the jury shall render. The statute is not to be construed as applying to cases in which the verdict of the jury depends necessarily and exclusively upon a question of law, nor is it to be construed as reinstating the scintilla doctrine formerly prevailing in this State but now rejected. Barksdale v. Southern Ry., 152 Va. 604, 148 S.E. 683 (1929).

Purpose is to prohibit application of doctrine of harmless error. — This section was passed for the express purpose of prohibiting the application of the doctrine of harmless error to the mandatory direction of verdicts. Small v. Virginia Ry. & Power Co., 125 Va. 416, 99 S.E. 525 (1919).

Under this section even in a case where no other verdict could have been properly rendered, and the error might therefore have been regarded as harmless, yet a peremptory instruction directing the verdict must be regarded as prejudicial and reversible error. Small v. Virginia Ry. & Power Co., 125 Va. 416, 99 S.E. 525 (1919).

Distinction between directed verdicts and demurrers to evidence. — Obviously the laws of Virginia recognize a marked distinction between demurrer to evidence and direction of a verdict — the former is permitted; the latter is expressly prohibited. Barrett v. Virginian Ry., 250 U.S. 473, 39 S. Ct. 540, 63 L. Ed. 1092 (1919).

Methods of accomplishing same results as by directed verdict. — This section forbids the trial court to direct a verdict, but under Virginia practice it is still possible by less summary methods to accomplish the same results. A demurrer to evidence may be interposed; evidence may be stricken out; the trial court may set aside the verdict, and in a proper case give final judgment; the trial court may decline to give any instruction where the evidence would not sustain a verdict, and it may in substance direct a verdict by stating in an instruction a hypothetical case and telling the jury if they so believe, to find, etc. Davis v. Rodgers, 139 Va. 618, 124 S.E. 408 (1924).

Section does not apply to criminal cases. — In a prosecution for car breaking, the defendant asked for an instruction that, "There is no evidence in this case to support the charge of car breaking." It was held that while this section, which expressly forbids such an instruction in a civil case, does not apply to criminal cases, the practice of giving such instructions as that in question cannot be approved by the courts, although not forbidden by statute. Myers v. Commonwealth, 132 Va. 746, 111 S.E. 463 (1922).

Even in a criminal case it has been held that "it is not the practice of the courts of this State to give instructions which amount in substance to telling the jury that the evidence is not sufficient to convict a prisoner, and such instructions should not be given." Montgomery v. Commonwealth, 98 Va. 852, 37 S.E. 1 (1900); Mazer v. Commonwealth, 142 Va. 649, 128 S.E.

514 (1925). See Small v. Virginia Ry. & Power Co., 125 Va. 416, 99 S.E. 525 (1919).

Spirit of section to be observed. — An instruction is objectionable which violates the spirit, if not the letter, of this statute against directing verdicts. Norfolk & W. Ry. v. Simmons, 127 Va. 419, 103 S.E. 609 (1920). See also, Norfolk & W. Ry. v. Hardy, 152 Va. 783, 148 S.E. 839 (1929).

Statement tantamount to direction of verdict. — A statement by the court, "Yes, as I have already told you, you cannot recover a verdict against the defendant," taking place as it did in the presence of the jury, was tantamount to a direction by the court of a verdict for the defendant. Small v. Virginia Ry. & Power Co., 125 Va. 416, 99 S.E. 525 (1919).

Directing verdict on probate of will within prohibition. — A soldier wrote his aunt that his war risk insurance was made payable to his mother, but that his mother in case of his death was to give his aunt half of it. This letter was admitted to probate as the soldier's will. On appeal by the mother from the order of probate, the circuit court instructed the jury to find against the proposed will, because the letter designated no beneficiary under the war risk insurance act and under that act the aunt could not be named as beneficiary. It was held that this was error as the jury were not concerned with what, if anything, passed by the will, and the instruction was directly within the prohibition of this section. Reeves v. White, 136 Va. 443, 118 S.E. 103 (1923).

To what instructions applied. — This section is not to be construed as applying to cases in which the verdict of the jury depends necessarily and exclusively upon a question of law, such as the legal effect of a deed or contract. An instruction, therefore, which merely contained the construction of a written contract by the trial judge is not per se in violation of this section, although directing a verdict for one of the parties. Small v. Virginia Ry. & Power Co., 125 Va. 416, 99 S.E. 525 (1919); Realty Co. v. Burcum, 129 Va. 466, 106 S.E. 375 (1921); Harrison v. Gardner Inv. Corp., 132 Va. 238, 111 S.E. 234 (1922); Inter-Ocean Cas. Co. v. Smith, 167 Va. 246, 188 S.E. 210 (1936).

Striking out evidence does not violate section. — Where the court simply strikes out the evidence offered by a party because no verdict could be properly rendered thereon sustaining the contention of the party it does not direct the verdict in violation of this section. Barksdale v. Southern Ry., 152 Va. 604, 148 S.E. 683 (1929).

Directed verdict improper where no motion to strike had been granted. — An instruction directing the jury what verdict to return was contrary to the prohibition contained in this section where no motion to strike had first been granted. Turner v. Burford Buick Corp., 201 Va. 693, 112 S.E.2d 911 (1960).

§ 8.01-379. Argument before jury. — Counsel's right to argument before a jury is preserved. (1977, c. 617.)

REVISERS' NOTE

Section 8.01-379 has altered former § 8-219 to express the right to argument by counsel and to delete the former restriction upon the number of counsel permitted to argue without leave.

§ 8.01-379.1. Informing jury of amounts sued for. — Notwithstanding any other provision of law, any party in any civil action may inform the jury of the amount of damages sought by the plaintiff in the opening statement or closing argument, or both. The plaintiff may request an amount which is less than the ad damnum in the motion for judgment. (1988, c. 321; 1993, c. 615.)

I. DECISIONS UNDER CURRENT LAW.

Applied in Paul v. Gomez, 190 F.R.D. 402 (W.D. Va. 2000).

§ 8.01-379.2. Jury instructions. — A proposed jury instruction submitted by a party, which constitutes an accurate statement of the law applicable to the case, shall not be withheld from the jury solely for its nonconformance with the model jury instructions. (1992, c. 522.)

Editor's note. — Acts 1992, c. 522, which enacted this section, in cl. 2 provides that the provisions of the 1992 act are declaratory of existing law.

§ 8.01-380. Dismissal of action by nonsuit. — A. A party shall not be allowed to suffer a nonsuit as to any cause of action or claim, or any other party to the proceeding, unless he does so before a motion to strike the evidence has been sustained or before the jury retires from the bar or before the action has been submitted to the court for decision. After a nonsuit no new proceeding on the same cause of action or against the same party shall be had in any court other than that in which the nonsuit was taken, unless that court is without jurisdiction, or not a proper venue, or other good cause is shown for proceeding in another court, or when such new proceeding is instituted in a federal court. If after a nonsuit an improper venue is chosen, the court shall not dismiss the matter but shall transfer it to the proper venue upon motion of any party.

B. Only one nonsuit may be taken to a cause of action or against the same party to the proceeding, as a matter of right, although the court may allow additional nonsuits or counsel may stipulate to additional nonsuits. The court, in the event additional nonsuits are allowed, may assess costs and reasonable attorney's fees against the nonsuiting party.

C. A party shall not be allowed to nonsuit a cause of action, without the consent of the adverse party who has filed a counterclaim, cross claim or third-party claim which arises out of the same transaction or occurrence as the claim of the party desiring to nonsuit unless the counterclaim, cross claim, or third-party claim can remain pending for independent adjudication by the court. (Code 1950, §§ 8-220, 8-244; 1954, cc. 333, 611; 1977, c. 617; 1983, c. 404; 1991, c. 19.)

REVISERS' NOTE

Section 8.01-380: (1) adopts the provisions of former § 8-220 but (2) restricts the number of nonsuits which may be taken in an action by a party as a matter of right, and (3) expands the final sentence of former § 8-244.

Subsection A adds to the language of former § 8-220 the phrase "as to any cause of action or any other party to the proceeding." Subsection B adds several provisions to the former section. First, a party is restricted to one nonsuit as a matter of right. After taking the first nonsuit, a party can, with leave of court, or upon stipulation of the other party, be allowed additional nonsuits. The court, in permitting the additional nonsuit, may impose costs and reasonable attorney's fees upon the nonsuiting party. Similarly, a party agreeing to an additional nonsuit may stipulate upon what conditions he will permit the nonsuit.

Subsection C is former § 8-244 expanded to cover cross-claims and third-party claims. Additionally, even if the adverse party who has filed such a claim does not consent to the nonsuit, a nonsuit may be taken if such claim can remain pending for independent adjudication by the court.

Law Review. — For article, "Nonsuit in Virginia," see 52 Va. L. Rev. 751 (1966). For comment, "The Voluntary Nonsuit in Virginia," see 7 Wm. & Mary L. Rev. 357 (1966). For an overview of Virginia Supreme Court decisions on domestic relations, see 15 U. Rich. L. Rev. 321 (1981). For note on venue restrictions on cases which have previously been nonsuited, see 40 Wash. & Lee L. Rev. 534 (1983). For survey on civil procedure and practice in Virginia for 1989, see 23 U. Rich. L. Rev. 511 (1989). For an article, 'Final and Interlocutory Appeals in Virginia,' see 8 Geo. Mason L. Rev. 337 (1999).

I. Decisions Under Current Law.
   A. General Consideration.
   B. Withdrawal of Nonsuit.
II. Decisions Under Prior Law.

I. DECISIONS UNDER CURRENT LAW.

A. General Consideration.

Application of section. — The venue restriction of this section applies only to causes filed and nonsuited in Virginia. Clark v. Clark, 11 Va. App. 286, 398 S.E.2d 82 (1990).

A statutory plea filed pursuant to this section, successor to § former 8-241, is not a counterclaim as that term is used in subsection C of this section, successor to former 8-244. Therefore, the conditions attaching to a nonsuit under subsection C do not apply. Bremer v. Doctor's Bldg. Partnership, 251 Va. 74, 465 S.E.2d 787 (1996).

Plaintiff has absolute right to one nonsuit. — Under this section, a plaintiff has an absolute right to one nonsuit. The election is his and if he insists upon taking the nonsuit within the limitations imposed by this section, neither the trial court nor opposing counsel can prevent him from doing so. Nash v. Jewell, 227 Va. 230, 315 S.E.2d 825 (1984).

The common law considerations of prejudice were codified in this section by prohibiting a nonsuit if a pending counterclaim, cross claim, or third-party claim could not be independently adjudicated. Therefore, a plaintiff is entitled to one nonsuit as a matter of right if the provisions of this section are met without further analysis of prejudice to the defendant. Bremer v. Doctor's Bldg. Partnership, 251 Va. 74, 465 S.E.2d 787 (1996).

This section gives a plaintiff a statutory right to one nonsuit even if a counterclaim or third-party claim is pending, if those claims can be independently adjudicated. Gilbreath v. Brewster, 250 Va. 436, 463 S.E.2d 836 (1995).

"The action" subject to nonsuit request. — Under the language of this section, "the action" subject to a plaintiff's nonsuit request is comprised of the claims and parties remaining in the case after any other claims and parties have been dismissed with prejudice or otherwise eliminated from the case. Dalloul v. Agbey, 255 Va. 511, 499 S.E.2d 279 (1998).

The difference in a FRCP Rule 41 dismissal and a Virginia nonsuit under this section goes more to matters of form than substance. While the Virginia statute does not require the consent of the defendant and can be taken at later stages in the proceeding, both the federal rule and the Virginia statute have as their purpose the voluntary dismissal of an action by a plaintiff without prejudice at some stage of a proceeding. Scoggins v. Douglas, 760 F.2d 535 (4th Cir. 1985).

This section pertains exclusively to limitations on the plaintiff's ability to obtain a nonsuit and the organization of § 8.01-229 E supports the conclusion that § 8.01-229 E 3 applies only where the plaintiff has voluntarily dismissed an action. Ambrose Branch Coal Co. v. Tankersley, 106 Bankr. 462 (W.D. Va. 1989).

Limitations on right of nonsuit. — This section, the nonsuit statute, while giving a party the absolute right to one voluntary nonsuit, contains a number of limitations on that right. McManama v. Plunk, 250 Va. 27, 458 S.E.2d 759 (1995).

This section provides conditions to balance the exercise of a nonsuit. — The right to take a nonsuit on the eve of trial, notwithstanding a defendant's loss of time and expense incurred in preparation, and notwithstanding any disruption which may result to the court's docket, is a powerful tactical weapon in the hands of a plaintiff. The General Assembly has provided, in this section, several conditions to give balance to the exercise of that right. Nonsuit remains, however, distinctly a weapon in the arsenal of a plaintiff. Trout v. Commonwealth Transp. Comm'r, 241 Va. 69, 400 S.E.2d 172 (1991).

Trial court cannot add limitations by judicial fiat. — Trial court erroneously placed limitations on the plaintiff's right to the voluntary nonsuit when it ruled that defendant "must first had to have been served with process, must have been before a court with jurisdiction over the defendant's person, and the defendant must have been given notice of hearing and an opportunity to be heard." None of these requirements is found in the applicable statutes, and a court should not add them by judicial fiat. McManama v. Plunk, 250 Va. 27, 458 S.E.2d 759 (1995).

Reach of nonsuit. — The plain language of this section declares that a nonsuit can be taken for an entire cause of action, which the Virginia Supreme Court defines as all the operative facts which, under the substantive law, may give rise to a right of action. Winchester Homes, Inc. v. Osmose Wood Preserving, Inc., 37 F.3d 1053 (4th Cir. 1994).

When trial court has reached final determination in a proceeding regarding any claims or parties to claims, those claims and parties are excluded by operation of law from any nonsuit request. Dalloul v. Agbey, 255 Va. 511, 499 S.E.2d 279 (1998).

Attorney fees. — This section limits the assessment of attorney's fees to the cause of action being nonsuited. It does not authorize such an assessment in a subsequent action. Nor does this section give the court the right to condition the filing of an amended motion for judgment upon the payment of such fees. Albright v. Burke & Herbert Bank & Trust Co., 249 Va. 463, 457 S.E.2d 776 (1995).

Effect of a nonsuit. — The only effect of a nonsuit is to put an end to the pending litigation without prejudice to either party. Alderman v. Chrysler Corp., 480 F. Supp. 600 (E.D. Va. 1979).

A judgment of nonsuit does not operate as a bar to a subsequent suit between the same parties on the same cause of action. Alderman v. Chrysler Corp., 480 F. Supp. 600 (E.D. Va. 1979).

The entry of nonsuit in the state court was against the three defendants in the instant case, and, therefore, served to nonsuit the entire cause of action as to these defendants, rather than only the particular claims remaining in the suit at the time of nonsuit. Winchester Homes, Inc. v. Osmose Wood Preserving, Inc., 37 F.3d 1053 (4th Cir. 1994).

This section permitted the plaintiff to refile her action in circuit court because the ad damnum clause in her motion for judgment exceeded the general district court's jurisdictional limit of $10,000; therefore the district court was without jurisdiction to adjudicate her claims. Conner v. Rose, 252 Va. 57, 471 S.E.2d 478 (1996).

Nonsuit prior to ruling on motion to strike. — When trial judge analyzes motion to strike, summarizes and discusses the evidence, and then rules on the motion, a plaintiff is free to suffer a nonsuit at any time prior to a ruling by the court. Newton v. Veney, 220 Va. 947, 265 S.E.2d 707 (1980).

On a motion to strike, the court "rules" or "decides" when it sustains or overrules the motion. It is this act that imparts finality to and disposition of the matter, and until it occurs a party is allowed to suffer a nonsuit. Newton v. Veney, 220 Va. 947, 265 S.E.2d 707 (1980).

The "forum shopping" limitation in subsection A is made to apply only where a new proceeding is brought after a nonsuit is taken in an action previously filed. It would not prohibit the prosecution of a proceeding filed before a nonsuit is taken in a pending action covering the same claim. Moore v. Gillis, 239 Va. 239, 389 S.E.2d 453 (1990).

Applicability of section in condemnation proceedings. — An "action" and a "cause of action" are quite different: "action" is defined by § 8.01-2, and "cause of action" is defined as a set of operative facts which, under the substantive law, may give rise to a right of action. Because of that difference, there are no express terms in this section making it specifically applicable to condemnation proceedings. Trout v. Commonwealth Transp. Comm'r, 241 Va. 69, 400 S.E.2d 172 (1991).

Petitioner in condemnation proceeding is not a traditional plaintiff. — The parties to a condemnation proceeding are not in the position of plaintiffs and defendants in traditional actions or suits. Traditional burden-of-proof rules are inapplicable to condemnation cases. The petitioner in a condemnation case is, therefore, not a traditional plaintiff. Although he has the statutory duty to institute the proceeding, he has no ultimate risk of nonpersuasion. Trout v. Commonwealth Transp. Comm'r, 241 Va. 69, 400 S.E.2d 172 (1991).

Indeed, after the condemnor has acquired title and instituted the proceeding for the ascertainment of just compensation, he is in the position of a defendant. The condemnor, therefore, is not entitled to nonsuit the proceeding over the owner's objection because of any traditional advantages inhering in the position of a plaintiff in an action at law. Trout v. Commonwealth Transp. Comm'r, 241 Va. 69, 400 S.E.2d 172 (1991).

A condemnor has no right to a nonsuit or a voluntary dismissal of a condemnation proceeding, without the owners' consent, after any interest in, or possession of, the property has been acquired. Trout v. Commonwealth Transp. Comm'r, 241 Va. 69, 400 S.E.2d 172 (1991).

Actions previously filed and nonsuited in a jurisdiction other than Virginia. — This section does not preclude a party from filing a cognizable cause of action in Virginia courts even though he or she has previously filed and nonsuited the same action in a jurisdiction other than in Virginia. Clark v. Clark, 11 Va. App. 286, 398 S.E.2d 82 (1990).

Notice to defendant who had filed cross-claim. — An order of nonsuit should not have been entered against a defendant without notice to another defendant who had previously filed a cross-claim against the nonsuited defendant. Iliff v. Richards, 221 Va. 644, 272 S.E.2d 645 (1980).

Order of nonsuit appealable. — Where a dispute exists whether the trial court properly granted a motion for nonsuit, that order of nonsuit is a final, appealable order within the meaning of § 8.01-670 A 3. Wells v. Lorcom House Condominiums' Council of Co-Owners, 237 Va. 247, 377 S.E.2d 381 (1989).

Ordinarily, an order of nonsuit is not to be considered a final judgment for purposes of appeal. An order of nonsuit is a final, appealable order within the meaning of § 8.01-670 A 3, only when a dispute exists whether the trial court properly granted a motion for nonsuit. McManama v. Plunk, 250 Va. 27, 458 S.E.2d 759 (1995).

New suit in federal court. — While in general after a nonsuit, a new suit on the same cause of action must be brought in the same court in which the nonsuit was suffered, unless that court is without jurisdiction, is of improper venue, or other good cause is shown for proceeding in another court, this limitation does not apply to a new suit in a federal court having proper jurisdiction. Alderman v. Chrysler Corp., 480 F. Supp. 600 (E.D. Va. 1979).

A federal court sitting in diversity must honor Virginia law restricting the court within which a nonsuited plaintiff may

recommence in order to invoke the saving provision as the Virginia restriction is an integral part of the several policies served by Virginia's statutes of limitations and must be applied in consolidated federal diversity actions. Yarber v. Allstate Ins. Co., 674 F.2d 232 (4th Cir. 1982).

Judgment against plaintiff where property was seized and placed beyond court's jurisdiction. — Where the plaintiff, after seizing property under authority of statute and placing it beyond the jurisdiction of the court, decided to manipulate the statutory scheme by exercising the privilege of nonsuit, the detinue statutes contemplated entry of a specific judgment in the detinue proceedings against the plaintiff for the value of the property. J.I. Case Co. v. United Va. Bank, 232 Va. 210, 349 S.E.2d 120 (1986).

The trial court did not err in ruling that defendants' motion for nonsuit came too late since it would be absurd to hold that a claimant could suffer a nonsuit as a matter of right after a court had decided the claim. Khanna v. Dominion Bank, 237 Va. 242, 377 S.E.2d 378 (1989).

Motion before ruling held timely. — Move to nonsuit during the court's discussion of its proposed ruling, but before it had ruled, was timely. Hilb, Rogal & Hamilton Co. v. DePew, 247 Va. 240, 440 S.E.2d 918 (1994).

A request for a nonsuit was timely where it was made before the court recessed to consider the merits of the defendant's motion for judgment on the pleadings. Kelly v. Carrico, 256 Va. 282, 504 S.E.2d 368 (1998).

Applied in Elliott v. Greater Atl. Mgt. Co., 236 Va. 334, 374 S.E.2d 27 (1988); Price v. Food Lion, Inc., 768 F. Supp. 181 (E.D. Va. 1991); Homeowners Whse., Inc. v. Rawlins, 409 S.E.2d 115 (1991); Lee Gardens Arlington Ltd. Partnership v. Arlington County Bd., 250 Va. 534, 463 S.E.2d 646 (1995).

B. Withdrawal of Nonsuit.

Court may permit withdrawal of nonsuit before order entered. — There is no termination of litigation until the court enters an appropriate order. Therefore, before entry of such an order the plaintiff may reconsider his decision to take a nonsuit. He has no right to withdraw the nonsuit, but he has a right to move the trial court to permit withdrawal. The granting or denial of the motion is a matter for the trial court to determine in the exercise of judicial discretion. Nash v. Jewell, 227 Va. 230, 315 S.E.2d 825 (1984).

II. DECISIONS UNDER PRIOR LAW.

Editor's note. — The cases cited below were decided under corresponding provisions of former law. The term "this section," as used below, refers to former provisions.

Under this section, plaintiff has the absolute right to take a nonsuit. Joseph v. Blair, 488 F.2d 403 (4th Cir. 1973), cert. denied, 416 U.S. 955, 94 S. Ct. 1968, 40 L. Ed. 2d 305 (1974).

That the trial court has indicated how it will decide a case does not preclude plaintiff from taking a nonsuit. Berryman v. Moody, 205 Va. 516, 137 S.E.2d 900 (1964).

The statutory privilege of taking a nonsuit cannot be denied a plaintiff upon the suspicion or surmise that his counsel has correctly divined the intention of the trial court to give a peremptory instruction against him. Such a construction would lead to confusion and render uncertain and precarious a right based upon the compliance with terms which are clearly and plainly defined. Berryman v. Moody, 205 Va. 516, 137 S.E.2d 900 (1964).

The effect of a nonsuit is simply to put an end to the present action, but is no bar to a subsequent action for the same cause. Manifestly, it is unsuited to pure appellate procedure. Thomas Gemmell, Inc. v. Svea Fire & Life Ins. Co., 166 Va. 95, 184 S.E. 457 (1936).

A nonsuit is not a final judgment within the meaning of § 8.01-670. Mallory v. Taylor, 90 Va. 348, 18 S.E. 438 (1893).

Procedure under 1977 version of section. — Under § 8.01-229 E 3 (1978 version) and this section (1977 version) if a plaintiff took a nonsuit, the statute of limitations would be tolled provided that the plaintiff recommenced the action in the same court in which the nonsuit was taken within six months. Thus where plaintiffs filed their actions in federal court in 1980, took voluntary dismissals in 1985, and recommenced their actions within six months, they were entitled to invoke the tolling provision of the 1978 version of § 8.01-229 E 3 to save their cases from the personal injury statute of limitations. Sherman v. Hercules, Inc., 636 F. Supp. 305 (W.D. Va. 1986).

Practice when necessary to substitute entirely new plaintiff. — An entirely new plaintiff cannot be substituted after it has become manifest that the original plaintiff could not maintain the action. The proper practice in such a case would have been for the plaintiff to ask to be allowed to suffer a nonsuit under this section, and to have renewed the suit in the name of the proper plaintiff. Norfolk S.R.R. v. Greenwich Corp., 122 Va. 631, 95 S.E. 389 (1918).

For a "submission" to occur under the procedural circumstances of a suit such as a divorce suit, in which both litigants are represented by counsel who filed pleadings in the cause, it is necessary for the parties, by counsel, to both yield the issues to the court for consideration and decision. This could be accomplished either as the result of oral or written argument, formal notice and motion, or by tendering a jointly endorsed sketch for a decree (or in the case of disagreement over the form, two separate drafts upon notice and motion). Moore v. Moore, 218 Va. 790, 240 S.E.2d 535 (1978).

Unilateral act of the defendant in an action for divorce of forwarding to the court a sketch for a decree is not equivalent to a "submission" of the cause to the trial court for decision. Moore v. Moore, 218 Va. 790, 240 S.E.2d 535 (1978).

Neither is mere filing of commissioner's report. — The mere filing by the commissioner of his report in a divorce case, without more, under Virginia equity practice does not amount to a "submission" of the cause to the trial court for decision. Moore v. Moore, 218 Va. 790, 240 S.E.2d 535 (1978).

New suit in federal court. — This section was intended to regulate procedure and practice in the courts of the State and was not intended to limit the jurisdiction of courts of the United States. Popp v. Archbell, 203 F.2d 287 (4th Cir. 1953).

The effect of this section is merely to limit the venue of any new action brought on the cause of action which has been nonsuited and a State venue statute can have no application to courts of the United States. Popp v. Archbell, 203 F.2d 287 (4th Cir. 1953).

Application in federal practice of directing verdicts. — After a motion by defendant for a directed verdict, a plaintiff has no absolute right then to suffer a nonsuit. This section does not govern in view of the accepted Virginia practice, under § 8.01-378, not to direct verdicts. Pannill v. Roanoke Times Co., 252 F. 910 (W.D. Va. 1918).

Federal intervention not warranted. — Where plaintiff previously found guilty of a violation of a city ordinance, but where his sentencing was postponed pending adjudication in a federal suit of the validity of the ordinance, and where plaintiff had moved for a nonsuit under this section in his civil action in a state court on the validity of the ordinance, there were no proceedings in the state courts, civil or criminal, which would warrant federal intervention. Joseph v. Blair, 488 F.2d 403 (4th Cir. 1973), cert. denied, 416 U.S. 955, 94 S. Ct. 1968, 40 L. Ed. 2d 305 (1974).

§ 8.01-381. What jury may carry out. — No pleadings may be carried from the bar by the jury. Exhibits may, by leave of court, be so carried by the jury. Upon request of any party, the court shall instruct the jury that they may request exhibits for use during deliberations. Exhibits requested by the jury shall be sent to the jury room or may otherwise be made available to the jury. (Code 1950, § 8-221; 1977, c. 617; 1992, c. 495.)

REVISERS' NOTE

Former § 8-221 has been altered to provide that no pleadings may be taken to the jury room but that exhibits may be so taken with the court's approval.

I. Decisions Under Current Law.
II. Decisions Under Prior Law.

I. DECISIONS UNDER CURRENT LAW.

Past recollection recorded may be read into evidence but may not itself be received as an exhibit unless offered by an adverse party. Scott v. Greater Richmond Transit Co., 241 Va. 300, 402 S.E.2d 214 (1991).

Handwriting exemplars. — Once handwriting exemplars were admitted into evidence, the trial judge had the discretion to allow the jury to examine them in the jury room. He did not abuse his discretion by doing so. Lynn v. Commonwealth, No. 0129-93-3 (Ct. of Appeals Jan. 17, 1995).

Defendant's recorded out-of-court statement held an "exhibit." — An out-of-court statement, whether written or recorded, which is introduced into evidence, is an "exhibit." Therefore, the jury was entitled to take murder defendant's recorded statement, which was introduced into evidence as an exhibit, into the jury room. Pugliese v. Commonwealth, 16 Va. App. 82, 428 S.E.2d 16 (1993).

Applied in Fisher v. Commonwealth, 236 Va. 403, 374 S.E.2d 46 (1988).

II. DECISIONS UNDER PRIOR LAW.

Editor's note. — The cases cited below were decided under corresponding provisions of former law. The term "this section," as used below, refers to former provisions.

The documents or statements must have been introduced in evidence. — The inference from the evidence that the statements carried to the jury room were introduced in evidence was irresistible, and it followed that there could be no valid objection to the jury carrying them into the jury room. Ballard v. Commonwealth, 156 Va. 980, 159 S.E. 222 (1931).

The plaintiff has no right under this section to demand that papers shown to a witness for the purpose of identifying the signature of a defendant thereto but which were never introduced in evidence, shall be allowed to go to the jury for their inspection after the conclusion of the evidence and arguments. Wilson v. Wooldridge, 118 Va. 209, 86 S.E. 872 (1915).

Depositions. — A deposition which has been read to the jury may be taken with them in their retirement if what is objectionable in it has been erased. Hansbrough v. Stinnett, 66 Va. (25 Gratt.) 495 (1874).

§ 8.01-382. Verdict, judgment or decree to fix period at which interest begins; judgment or decree for interest.

— In any action at law or suit in equity, the verdict of the jury, or if no jury the judgment or decree of the court, may provide for interest on any principal sum awarded, or any part thereof, and fix the period at which the interest shall commence. The judgment or decree entered shall provide for such interest until such principal sum be paid. If a judgment or decree be rendered which does not provide for interest, the judgment or decree awarded shall bear interest from its date of entry, at the rate as provided in § 6.1-330.54, and judgment or decree entered accordingly; provided, if the judgment entered in accordance with the verdict of a jury does not provide for interest, interest shall commence from the date that the verdict was rendered. Notwithstanding the provisions of this section, any judgment entered for a sum due under a negotiable instrument, as defined by § 8.3A-104, shall provide for interest on the principal sum in accordance with § 8.3A-112 at the rate specified in the instrument. If no such rate is specified, interest on the principal sum shall be at the rate provided in § 6.1-330.54. (Code 1950, § 8-223; 1964, c. 219; 1974, c. 172; 1975, c. 448; 1977, c. 617; 1979, c. 501; 1997, c. 551.)

REVISERS' NOTE

Former § 8-223 has been rewritten to place the court and the jury on the same footing when it comes to providing for interest on the principal sum awarded in the judgment or decree. Also, § 8.01-382 applies to all actions and suits, and thereby expands the former section's application which was limited to actions on contract, tort, and suits in equity. Finally, this section provides that the interest awarded shall become part of the judgment or decree.

Law Review. — For survey of Virginia commercial law for the year 1972-1973, see 59 Va. L. Rev. 1426 (1973). For comment, "Insurer's liability for prejudgment interest: A modern approach," see 17 U. Rich. L. Rev. 617 (1983).

I. Decisions Under Current Law.
II. Decisions Under Prior Law.

I. DECISIONS UNDER CURRENT LAW.

"Judgment" defined. — The word "judgment," when used in the context of this section, contemplates a debt that is presently due and owing, not a debt due and payable in the future. Pledger v. Pledger, 6 Va. App. 627, 371 S.E.2d 43 (1988).

General comment. — This section states that if a judgment be rendered which does not provide for interest, then the interest shall commence from the date of entry. It also permits the court to provide for interest and fix the period at which the interest shall commence. Hayes v. Hayes, No. 2038-96-4 (Ct. of Appeals June 3, 1997).

Construction with other law. — Section 15.1-549 (see now § 15.2-1244) prohibits a county from paying interest on a judgment. This section simply had no application here. The supreme court had to apply former § 15.1-549 in this appeal because it was a statute of specific application which took precedence over this section, a statute of general application. County of Fairfax v. Century Concrete Servs.,

§ 8.01-382　　　　　　　　CODE OF VIRGINIA　　　　　　　　§ 8.01-382

Inc., 254 Va. 423, 492 S.E.2d 648 (1997).

Virginia law governs award of prejudgment interest in diversity case. — See Hitachi Credit Am. Corp. v. Signet Bank, 166 F.3d 614 (4th. Cir. 1999).

Prejudgment interest is permitted by statute, and is designed to compensate the plaintiff who has been without relief for an extended period of time. Gill v. Rollins Protective Servs. Co., 836 F.2d 194 (4th Cir. 1987).

Postjudgment interest is not an element of damages, but is a statutory award for the delay in the payment of money actually due. Ragsdale v. Ragsdale, 30 Va. App. 283, 516 S.E.2d 698 (1999).

Distinction between prejudgment and postjudgment interest. — By its express language, this section draws an important distinction between prejudgment and postjudgment interest. This section provides for the discretionary award of prejudgment interest by the trier of fact, who may provide for such interest and fix the time of its commencement. The accrual of postjudgment interest, however, is mandatory; the entire amount of a judgment or decree shall bear interest from its date of entry. Dairyland Ins. Co. v. Douthat, 248 Va. 627, 449 S.E.2d 799 (1994).

Postjudgment interest is extra-contractual obligation. — Although the insurer's duty to pay damages is a contractual liability, enforced by the insurance statutes, the duty to pay postjudgment interest is an extra-contractual obligation that is imposed as a statutory penalty for failure to pay a liquidated debt when due. Dairyland Ins. Co. v. Douthat, 248 Va. 627, 449 S.E.2d 799 (1994).

No prejudgment interest duty. — Because no such obligation is imposed by this section or any other statute, an insurer has no duty to pay prejudgment interest in excess of policy limits, absent a contractual provision to the contrary. Dairyland Ins. Co. v. Douthat, 248 Va. 627, 449 S.E.2d 799 (1994).

Complete discretion with trial court. — Whether prejudgment interest should be awarded under this section is a matter within the sound discretion of the district court. Hitachi Credit Am. Corp. v. Signet Bank, 166 F.3d 614 (4th. Cir. 1999).

Trial court did not abuse its discretion in refusing to award prejudgment interest to truck driver in his suit against driver of automobile for contribution, for while the amount of the contribution owed by automobile driver was ascertainable from the date of the verdict in the wrongful death litigation, a legitimate controversy existed as to whether driver's negligence had been resolved in that litigation, and furthermore, as recognized by the trial court, the delay in resolving that issue was not attributable to the parties, but involved, among other things, the necessity of reassigning the case due to the death of the original trial judge. Reid v. Ayscue, 246 Va. 454, 436 S.E.2d 439 (1993).

Complete discretion with trial court. — This statute has been interpreted as granting courts complete discretion in awarding prejudgment interest. Continental Ins. Co. v. City of Va. Beach, 908 F. Supp. 341 (E.D. Va. 1995).

No exception for bona fide legal disputes. — There is no language in the statute which provides that cases containing bona fide legal disputes are beyond the reach of the statute, and no Virginia cases mention a bona fide legal dispute exception to the statute. Gill v. Rollins Protective Servs. Co., 836 F.2d 194 (4th Cir. 1987).

Interest on permanent financing commitment fee. — In a suit brought by a developer against a lender alleging that the lender breached an oral commitment to provide construction financing for construction of a condominium project, the federal district court, which included as an element of damages for the lender's breach the fee which the developer paid to the lender for the permanent financing commitment, did not abuse its discretion in not awarding interest on the permanent financing commitment fee. Coastland Corp. v. Third Nat'l Mtg. Co., 611 F.2d 969 (4th Cir. 1979).

Accrual of interest on property settlement. — Where a property settlement agreement specified that the wife's portion of the husband's retirement would be entered as a "judgment" and no money was due until the husband either retired or received a lump sum payment, interest did not begin to accrue from the date of final decree of the divorce judgment, but rather, from the date money due was not paid. Pledger v. Pledger, 6 Va. App. 627, 371 S.E.2d 43 (1988).

Interest permitted where claim is unliquidated. — An award of interest is permissible, even if the claim is unliquidated, so long as there is a rational basis in the evidence upon which to fix the date when interest should begin to run. Nor is there an exception in the language of the statute placing beyond its reach cases in which there exist bona fide legal disputes. McClung v. Smith, 870 F. Supp. 1384 (E.D. Va. 1994), modified, 89 F.3d 829 (4th Cir. 1996).

Court did not abuse its discretion in failing to award prejudgment interest to wife on her share of husband's medical practice before the entry of the court's amended final decree of divorce. Husband had no obligation to pay wife her share of the practice until the court made its equitable distribution award and ordered him to make payments in accordance with it. Ragsdale v. Ragsdale, 30 Va. App. 283, 516 S.E.2d 698 (1999).

Applied in Commonwealth v. United Airlines, 219 Va. 374, 248 S.E.2d 124 (1978); Board of Supvrs. v. Safeco Ins. Co. of Am., 226 Va. 329, 310 S.E.2d 445 (1983); Pierce v. Martin, 230 Va. 94, 334 S.E.2d 576 (1985); Marks v. Sanzo, 231 Va. 350, 345 S.E.2d 263 (1986); Rush v. Hartford Mut. Ins. Co., 652 F. Supp. 1432 (W.D. Va. 1987); Insurance Co. of N. Am. v. United States Gypsum Co., 870 F.2d 148 (4th Cir. 1989); Skretvedt v. Kouri, 248 Va. 26, 445 S.E.2d 481 (1994); City of Winchester v. American Woodmark Corp., 250 Va. 451, 464 S.E.2d 148 (1995).

II. DECISIONS UNDER PRIOR LAW.

Editor's note. — The cases cited below were decided under corresponding provisions of former law. The term "this section," as used below, refers to former provisions.

The purpose of this section is that interest may be allowed when its allowance appears necessary to compensate the plaintiff adequately, i.e., to make him whole; or withheld when its allowance is not necessary to accomplish such purpose. City of Danville v. C & O Ry., 34 F. Supp. 620 (W.D. Va. 1940).

This section changes the common law and permits the jury or the court to allow interest on the verdict or judgment. Doyle & Russell, Inc. v. Welch Pile Driving Corp., 213 Va. 698, 194 S.E.2d 719 (1973).

Its language is permissive. Whether to allow interest is left to the sound discretion of the jury or trial court. Doyle & Russell, Inc. v. Welch Pile Driving Corp., 213 Va. 698, 194 S.E.2d 719 (1973); Hewitt v. Hutter, 432 F. Supp. 795 (W.D. Va. 1977), aff'd, 574 F.2d 182 (4th Cir. 1978).

Discretion of trial court. — The allowance of interest is in the sound discretion of the trial court (and now the jury). Wolford v. Williams, 195 Va. 489, 78 S.E.2d 660 (1953); Safway Steel Scaffolds of Va., Inc. v. Coulter, 198 Va. 469, 94 S.E.2d 541 (1956); Columbia Heights Section 3, Inc. v. Griffith-Consumers Co., 205 Va. 43, 135 S.E.2d 116 (1964).

Awards of prejudgment interest are sometimes inappropriate in cases involving a bona fide dispute on the merits. Hewitt v. Hutter, 432 F. Supp. 795 (W.D. Va. 1977), aff'd, 574 F.2d 182 (4th Cir. 1978).

This section gives legislative recognition that interest "is a legal incident of the debt" and follows the principal after maturity as "the shadow follows the substance." Parsons v. Parsons, 167 Va. 374, 189 S.E. 448 (1937).

A jury may not allow a rate of interest greater than the maximum rate permitted by state law. Marsteller Corp. v. Ranger Constr. Co., 530 F.2d 608 (4th Cir. 1976).

Maximum rate of interest which a jury may impose under this section is the maximum allowed under former § 6.1-330.11 when no exceptions are applicable. Marsteller Corp. v. Ranger Constr. Co., 530 F.2d 608 (4th Cir. 1976).

When the right to interest arises from the power conferred on a jury by this section and not from an express or implied contract to pay interest, the maximum rate a jury may allow is that allowed under former § 6.1-330.11. Marsteller Corp. v. Ranger Constr. Co., 530 F.2d 608 (4th Cir. 1976).

This section does not stipulate the rate a jury may allow, and an award of less than six percent is proper. Marsteller Corp. v. Ranger Constr. Co., 530 F.2d 608 (4th Cir. 1976).

Interest on judgments not element of "damages". — Interest the law allows on judgments is not an element of "damages" but a statutory award for delay in the payment of money due. Nationwide Mut. Ins. Co. v. Finley, 215 Va. 700, 214 S.E.2d 129 (1975).

Interest is allowable on all contracts and assurances made directly, or indirectly for the loan, or forbearance of money, or other things. And the obligation to pay interest, when not expressly waived, is implied and begins when the debt is due and payable. Beale v. Moore, 183 Va. 519, 32 S.E.2d 696 (1945); Columbia Heights Section 3, Inc. v. Griffith-Consumers Co., 205 Va. 43, 135 S.E.2d 116 (1964).

Section does not permit allowance of interest contrary to terms of contract. — This section does not contemplate or permit the allowance of interest in the decree or judgment contrary to the terms of the contract between the parties. Pittston Co. v. O'Hara, 191 Va. 886, 63 S.E.2d 34, appeal dismissed, 342 U.S. 803, 72 S. Ct. 38, 96 L. Ed. 608 (1951).

This section gives the jury, or the judge in a nonjury trial, discretionary power to provide for interest on any principal sum awarded, and to fix the period at which the interest shall commence. But this section does not permit the allowance of interest in a decree or judgment for specific performance by the purchasers under a contract for the purchase of land contrary to the terms of the contract. Eascalco, Inc. v. Caulfield, 220 Va. 475, 259 S.E.2d 821 (1979).

Purpose of amendment adding exception as to commercial paper. — The 1964 amendment, which added the exception at the beginning of the section, was designed to remove from the jury or the court the discretionary power to set the time from which interest would run in the case of commercial paper. Schwab v. Norris, 217 Va. 582, 231 S.E.2d 222 (1977).

Time from which interest would run on a negotiable promissory note held governed by former § 8.3-122 (see now § 8.3A-118) and not former § 8-223 (now § 8.01-382). Schwab v. Norris, 217 Va. 582, 231 S.E.2d 222 (1977).

In action for damages for failure to com-

ply with order of Interstate Commerce Commission awarding reparation for unreasonable freight charges, it was held that the allowance of interest was proper. City of Danville v. C & O Ry., 34 F. Supp. 620 (W.D. Va. 1940).

Confirmation of erroneous date was not exercise of discretion. — The special master, through obvious error as to dates, found that interest on plaintiff's claim should run from January 15, 1962, rather than from the date of January 15, 1961, indicated by the record. The chancellor's confirmation of this date did not, under the circumstances, represent an exercise of his discretion under this section to set the date for the running of interest; hence, the decree was modified on appeal to give interest from the correct date. Globe Iron Constr. Co. v. First Nat'l Bank, 205 Va. 841, 140 S.E.2d 629 (1965).

Instructions as to interest held erroneous. — The allegation contained the common counts in assumpsit and also a special count upon the contract. The evidence was such as to have made it possible for the jury to find for the plaintiff, either upon the special contract, or upon the general assumpsit. Under all the circumstances of the case the section applied, and the jury had the right, in their discretion, to fix the date from which the interest should begin to run. Consequently, a peremptory instruction of the lower court to the jury that if they found for the plaintiff they should allow interest from the time the plaintiff's demand accrued, under the terms of the contract, was in conflict with this section and was such an invasion of the province of the jury as to constitute reversible error. Washington & Old Dominion Ry. v. Westinghouse Elec. & Mfg. Co., 120 Va. 620, 89 S.E. 131 (1916).

Under this section, it is error to instruct the jury as a matter of law that they should allow interest. Riverside & Dan River Cotton Mills, Inc. v. Thomas Branch & Co., 147 Va. 509, 137 S.E. 620 (1927); Thomas Branch & Co. v. Riverside & Dan River Cotton Mills, Inc., 147 Va. 522, 137 S.E. 614 (1927); Jones v. Foster, 70 F.2d 200 (4th Cir.), cert. denied, 293 U.S. 558, 55 S. Ct. 70, 79 L. Ed. 659 (1934).

In an action by seller of cattle against buyer for balance of purchase price, the court instructed the jury that if they should find for the plaintiff they should allow interest from the time of delivery of the cattle. It was held that this instruction was erroneous under this section, which permits the jury in actions on contract to allow interest and fix the period at which such interest shall commence. Latham v. Powell, 127 Va. 382, 103 S.E. 638 (1920).

Instructions held proper. — Instructions to the jury that the damages were "with interest from September 28, 1898," did not take from the jury the discretion, given by this section, of determining from what period, if at all, their verdict should bear interest. The appellate court divided equally upon this question. Kimball v. Borden, 97 Va. 477, 34 S.E. 45 (1899).

Effect in appellate court when jury erroneously instructed. — Where the lower court erred in peremptorily directing the jury to allow interest to plaintiff from the time the plaintiff's demand accrued, where under this section such allowance of interest was discretionary with the jury, the appellate court may affirm the judgment on condition that plaintiff relinquish the interest upon the principal sum found by the jury. Washington & Old Dominion Ry. v. Westinghouse Elec. & Mfg. Co., 120 Va. 620, 89 S.E. 131 (1916).

Judgment when verdict does not allow interest. — The statute is express and imperative that "if a verdict be rendered which does not allow interest, the sum thereby found shall bear interest from its date, and judgment shall be entered accordingly." Fry v. Leslie, 87 Va. 269, 12 S.E. 671 (1891).

In an action of debt on a decree for an amount of interest found due the plaintiff from the defendant, it was held that interest on the amount of the decree may be recovered in the shape of damages for its detention though the decree makes no provision for the payment of interest thereon. Stuart v. Hurt, 88 Va. 343, 13 S.E. 438 (1891).

If the trial court has failed to enter judgment for the interest, its judgment will be amended in this respect on cross error assigned by the plaintiff in the appellate court. Atlantic C.L.R.R. v. Grubbs, 113 Va. 214, 74 S.E. 144 (1912).

A judgment which did not bear interest was not a complete and final adjudication, because it did not meet the requirements of this section, and until the court ascertained and adjudicated when interest should begin there was no final judgment. Amalgamated Clothing Workers of Am. v. Kiser, 174 Va. 229, 6 S.E.2d 562 (1940).

Unliquidated claims. — There is nothing in the language used in this section to indicate that the discretion of a jury to award interest and fix the time thereof shall not be exercised in the case of an unliquidated claim. The fact that the provisions of the statute are to be applied in a tort action which is usually on an unliquidated claim, clearly indicates a legislative intent that an unliquidated claim is within its purview. Beale v. King, 204 Va. 443, 132 S.E.2d 476 (1963).

§ 8.01-383. Power to grant new trial; how often.

— In any civil case or proceeding, the court before which a trial by jury is had, may grant a new trial, unless it be otherwise specially provided. A new trial may be granted as well where the damages awarded are too small as where they are excessive. Not more than two new trials shall be granted to the same party in the same cause on the ground that the verdict is contrary to the evidence, either by the trial court or the appellate court, or both. (Code 1950, § 8-224; 1977, c. 617.)

Cross references. — As to allowing appeal when verdict reduced and accepted under protest, see § 8.01-383.1. As to when final judgment to be entered after verdict is set aside, see § 8.01-430. As to payment of costs when new trial is granted, see § 17.1-610.

I. Decisions Under Current Law.
   A. General Consideration.
   B. Excessive Damages.
   C. Inadequate Damages.
II. Decisions Under Prior Law.

I. DECISIONS UNDER CURRENT LAW.

A. General Consideration.

Discretion of court. — In awarding a new trial, it is within the trial judge's discretion to decide whether a new trial should be on all issues or solely on the issue of damages. Sampson v. Sampson, 221 Va. 896, 275 S.E.2d 597 (1981).

In determining whether an excessive damage award requires a new trial on all issues, a new trial limited to damages, an order of remittitur, or a judgment confirming the award, a trial judge is vested with broad discretion, and the Supreme Court will not reverse his ruling unless the record plainly shows an abuse of discretion. Ford Motor Co. v. Bartholomew, 224 Va. 421, 297 S.E.2d 675 (1982).

Before a new trial should be limited to the amount of damages, it should be reasonably clear that the misconception of the jury has not extended to its determination of the question of liability as well as to its determination of the amount of damages. Rutherford v. Zearfoss, 221 Va. 685, 272 S.E.2d 225 (1980).

Amount of damages in personal injury cases. — In personal injury cases, where the action merely sounds in damages, and there is no rule for measuring such damages, the amount to be awarded is left largely to the discretion of the jury. The verdict of the jury, arrived at upon competent evidence and controlled by proper instructions, has always been held to be inviolate against disturbance by the courts. Taylor v. Maritime Overseas Corp., 224 Va. 562, 299 S.E.2d 340 (1983).

After-discovered evidence. — One of the criteria for determining whether a new trial should be ordered for after-discovered evidence is whether the evidence could have been discovered before trial by the exercise of due diligence. Taylor v. Maritime Overseas Corp., 224 Va. 562, 299 S.E.2d 340 (1983).

B. Excessive Damages.

Remittitur discretionary. — The power to order remittitur lies within the sound discretion of the trial court. Robinson v. Old Dominion Freight Line, 236 Va. 125, 372 S.E.2d 142 (1988).

When court will correct award. — Where the attack upon a verdict is based upon its alleged excessiveness, if the amount awarded is so great as to shock the conscience of the court and to create the impression that the jury has been motivated by passion, corruption or prejudice, or has misconceived or misconstrued the facts or the law, or if the award is so out of proportion to the injuries suffered as to suggest that it is not the product of a fair and impartial decision, the court is empowered, and in fact obligated, to step in and correct the injustice. Rutherford v. Zearfoss, 221 Va. 685, 272 S.E.2d 225 (1980).

Trial de novo not mandatory where award not based on sympathy or bias. — A trial de novo is not mandatory, when the monetary award, though out of proportion to the injuries suffered, is not so excessive as to compel the conclusion that the liability verdict was the product of sympathy for the plaintiff or bias against the defendant. In such case, if the evidence before the jury clearly supports its finding of liability, a trial judge has two options. He may put the plaintiff on terms to accept a remittitur in lieu of a new trial, § 8.01-383.1, or he may grant the defendant a new trial limited to damages, under this section. Ford Motor Co. v. Bartholomew, 224 Va. 421, 297 S.E.2d 675 (1982).

Court may require part of award be remitted or order new trial. — Although the amount to award the wronged party is a matter within the discretion of the jury, if the trial court concludes that a verdict is excessive, it also has the authority under this section and

§ 8.01-383.1 to require plaintiff to remit a portion of the award or to submit to a new trial. If a new trial is ordered, it is within the trial court's discretion to grant a new trial on all issues or solely on the issue of damages. LaVay Corp. v. Dominion Fed. Sav. & Loan Ass'n, 645 F. Supp. 612 (E.D. Va. 1986), modified on other grounds, 830 F.2d 522 (4th Cir. 1987), cert. denied, 484 U.S. 1065, 108 S. Ct. 1027, 98 L. Ed. 2d 991 (1988).

C. Inadequate Damages.

In cases in which the evidence is insufficient to sustain a verdict finding defendant not liable, the court will set aside a verdict in favor of the plaintiff on the ground of inadequacy and grant a new trial, whether the verdict be for merely a nominal amount or for a substantial but inadequate sum. And the new trial should be limited to the question of the amount of the damages. Sampson v. Sampson, 221 Va. 896, 275 S.E.2d 597 (1981).

Error in refusal to set aside verdict in wrongful death action. — In a wrongful death action where the decedent's widow and children were awarded nothing for sorrow, mental anguish and solace, and the children were awarded nothing for lost services and protection, the award by the jury rendered the entire verdict suspect and lead to the conclusion that the jury must have misconceived or misunderstood the facts or the law; hence, the trial court erred in refusing to set aside the verdict. Johnson v. Smith, 241 Va. 396, 403 S.E.2d 685 (1991).

II. DECISIONS UNDER PRIOR LAW.

Editor's note. — The cases cited below were decided under corresponding provisions of former law. The term "this section," as used below, refers to former provisions.

Purpose. — The General Assembly intended, in enacting this section, that trial judges be empowered in their sound discretion to exercise supervision over the verdicts of juries. Clatterbuck v. Miller, 215 Va. 359, 209 S.E.2d 904 (1974).

Litigant entitled to one fair trial. — Under a sound public policy, the law accords to every litigant one fair and regular trial, but only one. Vaughan v. Mayo Milling Co., 127 Va. 148, 102 S.E. 597 (1920).

A motion for a new trial is addressed to the sound discretion of the trial court. Citizens Bank v. Taylor & Co., 104 Va. 164, 51 S.E. 159 (1905).

A sound discretion is vested in the trial court as to whether the ends of justice will be better served by setting aside, or refusing to set aside, an inadequate verdict. Rawle v. McIlhenny, 163 Va. 735, 177 S.E. 214 (1934).

Greater latitude is allowed the trial court in granting than in refusing a new trial on the ground that the verdict is contrary to the evidence. Cardwell v. Norfolk & W. Ry., 114 Va. 500, 77 S.E. 612 (1913).

Remittitur discretionary. — This section and § 8.01-383.1 tacitly recognize and implicitly ratify the common-law rule that the power to order remittitur lies within the sound discretion of the trial court. Bassett Furn. Indus., Inc. v. McReynolds, 216 Va. 897, 224 S.E.2d 323 (1976); Bunch v. State Hwy. & Transp. Comm'r, 217 Va. 627, 231 S.E.2d 324 (1977).

Review of discretion. — The appellate court will not reverse the action of the trial court setting aside a verdict as inadequate unless it plainly appears from the record that its action in so doing is plainly wrong. Rawle v. McIlhenny, 163 Va. 735, 177 S.E. 214 (1934).

If the verdict is supported by sufficient evidence and is reached in a fair and impartial trial, it cannot be disturbed. Edmiston v. Kupsenel, 205 Va. 198, 135 S.E.2d 777 (1964).

When court will set verdict aside for excessive or inadequate damages. — While the law wisely leaves the assessment of damages, as a rule, to juries, nevertheless, judges have the power and are clearly charged with the duty of setting aside verdicts, where the damages are either so excessive or so small as to shock the conscience and to create the impression that the jury has been influenced by passion or prejudice, or has in some way misconceived or misinterpreted the facts or the law which should guide them to a just conclusion. C & O Ry. v. Arrington, 126 Va. 194, 101 S.E. 415 (1919), cert. denied, 255 U.S. 573, 41 S. Ct. 376, 65 L. Ed. 792 (1921).

The verdict will not be disturbed on the ground that the damages awarded are too large or too small unless it shows the jury were actuated by passion, prejudice, or undue influence. Borland v. Barrett, 76 Va. 128 (1882); Bertha Zinc Co. v. Black's Adm'r, 88 Va. 303, 13 S.E. 452 (1891). See also, Rawle v. McIlhenny, 163 Va. 735, 177 S.E. 214 (1934).

Since the enactment of this section, courts have had the power and been charged with the duty of setting aside, in proper cases, the verdict in an action for a personal tort, such as a physical injury to the body or slander, where the damages are either inadequate or excessive. But the rule has been, and still is, that a court will not disturb the verdict in such a case either because of its smallness or because of its largeness, unless, in the light of all the evidence, it is manifestly so inadequate or so excessive as to show very plainly that the verdict has resulted from one or both of two causes: (A) The misconduct of the jury; (B) The jury's misconception of the merits of the case insofar as they relate to the amount of damages, if any, recoverable. Rawle v. McIlhenny,

163 Va. 735, 177 S.E. 214 (1934).

Where the attack upon a verdict is based upon its alleged excessiveness, if the amount awarded is so great as to shock the conscience of the court and to create the impression that the jury has been motivated by passion, corruption or prejudice, or has misconceived or misconstrued the facts or the law, or if the award is so out of proportion to the injuries suffered as to suggest that it is not the product of a fair and impartial decision, the court is empowered, and in fact obligated, to step in and correct the injustice. Edmiston v. Kupsenel, 205 Va. 198, 135 S.E.2d 777 (1964); Campbell v. Hankins, 217 Va. 800, 232 S.E.2d 794 (1977).

Issues in new trial. — In cases in which the evidence is insufficient to sustain a verdict finding the defendant not liable, the court will set aside a verdict in favor of the plaintiff on the ground of inadequacy and grant a new trial, whether the verdict be for merely a nominal amount or for a substantial but inadequate sum. And the new trial should be limited to the question of the amount of the damages. But where the amount of damages recoverable is not distinctly separable from the matters involved in the issue as to liability, the new trial should be granted on all issues. Rawle v. McIlhenny, 163 Va. 735, 177 S.E. 214 (1934).

Alternatives where court determines that verdict is excessive. — Under the law as it now exists, taking into consideration the practice at common law, as supplemented by this section and § 8.01-383.1, in a case where the quantum of damages is the sole issue, if a court determines that a verdict is excessive, it may put the successful party on terms to accept a reduced amount, deemed reasonable to compensate the injured party, as an alternative to awarding a new trial, or it may order a new trial as to the whole amount of damages. Smithey v. Sinclair Ref. Co., 203 Va. 142, 122 S.E.2d 872 (1961); Edmiston v. Kupsenel, 205 Va. 198, 135 S.E.2d 777 (1964).

It appears that the action of the court should be the same in libel and slander cases as in personal injury cases where the motion is to set aside the verdict of the jury, or a part thereof, on the ground that the damages awarded are inadequate. Taylor v. Virginia Metal Prods. Corp., 111 F. Supp. 321 (E.D. Va. 1952), aff'd, 204 F.2d 457 (4th Cir.), cert. denied, 346 U.S. 865, 74 S. Ct. 104, 98 L. Ed. 375 (1953).

A **remittitur or new trial is not warranted if the verdict merely appears to be large** and more than the trial judge would have awarded had he been a member of the jury. Edmiston v. Kupsenel, 205 Va. 198, 135 S.E.2d 777 (1964).

Remittitur held proper. — Although the evidence was devoid of even a suggestion that the jury was actuated by passion, prejudice or corruption, the size of the verdict, so out of proportion as it was to the plaintiff's injuries and his medical expenses and loss of wages was sufficient, standing alone, to shock the conscience of the court and to cast upon it the stamp of unfairness. Therefore it was proper to order remittitur. Smithey v. Sinclair Ref. Co., 203 Va. 142, 122 S.E.2d 872 (1961).

When verdict for plaintiff but preponderance of evidence against him. — In cases in which clearly the decided preponderance of the evidence is against the right of the plaintiff to recover, though there is sufficient evidence to support a finding by the jury that the defendant is liable, the court will refuse to set aside a verdict for the plaintiff for inadequacy. Rawle v. McIlhenny, 163 Va. 735, 177 S.E. 214 (1934).

In cases of conflicting evidence, in which there is sufficient evidence to support a verdict in favor of either the plaintiff or the defendant, but in which there is no clear preponderance of the evidence in favor of either, where a verdict in favor of the plaintiff is for substantial though inadequate damages, it cannot upon any reasonable theory be considered a finding for the defendant, and it should be set aside, and a new trial granted, which ordinarily should be limited to the question of the amount of damages. Rawle v. McIlhenny, 163 Va. 735, 177 S.E. 214 (1934).

Plaintiff not moving for new trial waives objection on appeal. — Where a judgment has been entered on a verdict for the plaintiff, subject to the court's opinion on demurrer to the evidence, the plaintiff, not moving in court below for a new trial, cannot insist in the appellate court that the damages allowed him by the verdict are too small. Without such motion below, the appellate court cannot award a new trial. Western Union Tel. Co. v. Virginia Paper Co., 87 Va. 418, 12 S.E. 755 (1891).

Effect of setting aside judgment on demurrer to evidence on third trial. — Where two verdicts are rendered in succession, giving the plaintiff damages for an injury received by him through negligence of the defendant, and each, in turn, is set aside on defendant's motion, that is all that can be set aside under this section. Where a third verdict is rendered, giving the plaintiff a larger amount of damages, subject, however, to a demurrer to the evidence, which is erroneously decided by the court below against the plaintiff, he is entitled to judgment on last verdict, when the judgment on the demurrer is set aside on appeal. Jones v. Old Dominion Cotton Mills, 82 Va. 140 (1886).

New judge should not set aside verdict because he did not preside at trial. — Where trial judge dies or becomes permanently incapacitated to act by reason of sickness, after the jurors have rendered a verdict in a case, and pending a motion to set aside the verdict on the ground that it is contrary to the evidence, his successor in office, or the judge appointed to hold his court, is not bound to set the verdict aside simply because he did not preside at the trial before the jury. Southall v. Evans, 114 Va. 461, 76 S.E. 929 (1913).

Equity has no power to order new trial in law action. — A bill was brought to obtain a new trial of an issue in an action at law, in which there was a verdict and judgment for the defendant. At the hearing the court annulled the judgment, set aside the verdict, and ordered a new trial in the action at law. A court of chancery, under our system of jurisprudence, is invested with no such power as this. It may act on the parties, but not directly on the judgment, nor on the court which rendered it. Wynne v. Newman, 75 Va. 811 (1881).

§ 8.01-383.1. Appeal when verdict reduced and accepted under protest; new trial for inadequate damages.

— A. In any action at law in which the trial court shall require a plaintiff to remit a part of his recovery, as ascertained by the verdict of a jury, or else submit to a new trial, such plaintiff may remit and accept judgment of the court thereon for the reduced sum under protest, but, notwithstanding such remittitur and acceptance, if under protest, the judgment of the court in requiring him to remit may be reviewed by the Supreme Court upon an appeal awarded the plaintiff as in other actions at law; and in any such case in which an appeal is awarded the defendant, the judgment of the court in requiring such remittitur may be the subject of review by the Supreme Court, regardless of the amount.

B. In any action at law when the court finds as a matter of law that the damages awarded by the jury are inadequate, the trial court may (i) award a new trial or (ii) require the defendant to pay an amount in excess of the recovery of the plaintiff found in the verdict. If either the plaintiff or the defendant declines to accept such additional award, the trial court shall award a new trial.

If additur pursuant to this subsection is accepted by either party under protest, it may be reviewed on appeal. (Code 1950, § 8-350; 1977, c. 617; 1994, c. 807; 1998, c. 861.)

Law Review. — For an article, "Civil Practice and Procedure," see 32 U. Rich. L. Rev. 1009 (1998).

I. Decisions Under Current Law.
　A. General Consideration.
　B. Appellate Review.
II. Decisions Under Prior Law.

I. DECISIONS UNDER CURRENT LAW.

A. General Consideration.

Statute unconstitutional in unliquidated damages cases. — In cases involving unliquidated damages, statute giving trial court post-verdict option to award a new trial or impose additur violates the right to jury trial provided by Article I, § 11 of the Virginia Constitution because it fails to provide plaintiff an option either to consent to the use of additur or to have a new trial. Supinger v. Stakes, 255 Va. 198, 495 S.E.2d 813 (1998).

Power of court. — While a trial judge may not arbitrarily substitute his opinion for that of the jury, he has both the power and the duty to correct a verdict which he finds so excessive as to shock the conscience of the court or to compel the conclusion that the verdict was the product of passion or prejudice or some misunderstanding of the facts or the law. When the judge makes such a finding, it is the sole function of the Supreme Court to determine whether he has abused the discretion accorded him by the statutes and the common law. Hogan v. Carter, 226 Va. 361, 310 S.E.2d 666 (1983).

Discretion of court as to handling of excessive award. — In determining whether an excessive damage award requires a new trial on all issues, a new trial limited to damages, an order of remittitur, or a judgment confirming the award, a trial judge is vested with broad discretion, and the Supreme Court will not reverse his ruling unless the record plainly shows an abuse of discretion. Ford Motor Co. v. Bartholomew, 224 Va. 421, 297 S.E.2d 675 (1982).

When plaintiff may be put upon terms. — If the trial court concludes that a verdict is excessive, it has the authority under this section to require the plaintiff to remit a portion of the award or submit to a new trial. Sampson v. Sampson, 221 Va. 896, 275 S.E.2d 597 (1981).

If the monetary award is out of proportion to the injuries suffered but not so large that the jury's verdict as to liability is impeached, the court may put the plaintiff to the choice of accepting a remittur or facing a new trial. Freeman v. Case Corp., 924 F. Supp. 1456 (W.D. Va. 1996), rev'd on other grounds, 118 F.3d 1011 (4th Cir. 1997), cert. denied, 522 U.S. 1069, 118 S. Ct. 739, 139 L. Ed. 2d 676 (1998).

Trial de novo not mandatory where award not based on sympathy or bias. — A trial de novo is not mandatory, when the monetary award, though out of proportion to the injuries suffered, is not so excessive as to compel the conclusion that the liability verdict was the product of sympathy for the plaintiff or bias against the defendant. In such case, if the evidence before the jury clearly supports its finding of liability, a trial judge has two options. He may put the plaintiff on terms to accept a remittitur in lieu of a new trial, under this section, or he may grant the defendant a new trial limited to damages, under § 8.01-383. Ford Motor Co. v. Bartholomew, 224 Va. 421, 297 S.E.2d 675 (1982).

The trial court is required to state its reasons for granting a remittitur. Reel v. Ramirez, 243 Va. 463, 416 S.E.2d 226 (1992).

Court may require part of award be remitted or order new trial. — Although the amount to award the wronged party is a matter within the discretion of the jury, if the trial court concludes that a verdict is excessive, it also has the authority under § 8.01-383 and this section to require plaintiff to remit a portion of the award or to submit to a new trial. If a new trial is ordered, it is within the trial court's discretion to grant a new trial on all issues or solely on the issue of damages. LaVay Corp. v. Dominion Fed. Sav. & Loan Ass'n, 645 F. Supp. 612 (E.D. Va. 1986), modified on other grounds, 830 F.2d 522 (4th Cir. 1987), cert. denied, 484 U.S. 1065, 108 S. Ct. 1027, 98 L. Ed. 2d 991 (1988).

Verdict not set aside or remitted where evidence sufficient and absent proof of jury misunderstanding, passion, corruption, or prejudice. — In a medical malpractice action, where the award was not out of proportion to the grievous physical injury suffered by the infant or the devastating emotional trauma and financial difficulty suffered by her parents, there was no reason to believe that the jury misconceived or misunderstood the facts or the law, there was nothing to indicate passion, corruption, or prejudice on the part of the jury, and the verdicts were supported by sufficient evidence and reached by a fair and impartial jury, the court could not set aside the verdicts or put plaintiffs on terms to remit part of their recovery pursuant to provisions of this section. Boyd v. Bulala, 647 F. Supp. 781 (W.D. Va. 1986), aff'd in part, rev'd in part, 877 F.2d 1191 (4th Cir. 1989).

Applied in Gazette, Inc. v. Harris, 229 Va. 1, 325 S.E.2d 713 (1985); Lawrence Chrysler Plymouth Corp. v. Brooks, 251 Va. 94, 465 S.E.2d 806 (1996); Walker v. Mason, 257 Va. 65, 510 S.E.2d 734 (1999).

B. Appellate Review.

Scope of review of remittitur. — On appeal of an order of remittitur, the Supreme Court does not sit to determine whether a damage award is excessive as a matter of law. Hogan v. Carter, 226 Va. 361, 310 S.E.2d 666 (1983).

Standard of review of exercise of discretion. — When it appears from the record that the trial judge made a finding that the verdict was plainly excessive and remittitur should be ordered and that, in reaching his conclusion, he considered factors in evidence relevant to a reasoned evaluation of the damages incurred and to be incurred, his order will not be disturbed on appeal if the recovery after remittitur bears a reasonable relation to the damages disclosed by the evidence. "Reasonableness" in this context is the standard by which the exercise of discretion must be tested in the Supreme Court. Ford Motor Co. v. Bartholomew, 224 Va. 421, 297 S.E.2d 675 (1982).

If the judge's statement shows that in reaching his conclusion, he considered factors in evidence relevant to a reasoned evaluation of the damages incurred and to be incurred, his order will not be disturbed on appeal if the recovery after remittitur bears a reasonable relation to the damages disclosed by the evidence. Hogan v. Carter, 226 Va. 361, 310 S.E.2d 666 (1983).

Remittitur will be reversed if reasons not stated. — The Supreme Court can determine whether the trial judge abused his discretion only when the judge states the reasons underlying his decision. If the record on appeal contains no such statement, the Supreme Court will reverse the order of remittitur, reinstate the damage award, and, absent reversible error on the issue of liability, enter final judgment on the verdict. Hogan v. Carter, 226 Va. 361, 310 S.E.2d 666 (1983).

II. DECISIONS UNDER PRIOR LAW.

Editor's note. — The cases cited below were decided under corresponding provisions of former law. The term "this section," as used below, refers to former provisions.

Purpose. — The General Assembly intended, in enacting this section, that trial judges be empowered in their sound discretion to exercise supervision over the verdicts of juries. Clatterbuck v. Miller, 215 Va. 359, 209 S.E.2d 904 (1974).

This section recognizes the right of the trial court to direct a remittitur, and allows the party against whom it is ordered to accept under protest and to appeal from the judgment on the reduced verdict. Plant Lipford, Inc. v. E.W. Gates & Son Co., 141 Va. 325, 127 S.E. 183 (1925).

Appellate court may also direct remittitur. — Appellate and trial courts, in cases in which excessive damages have been awarded, and in which the plaintiff is entitled to substantial damages, may indicate the excess and give plaintiff the option to remit and take judgment for the residue or be awarded a new trial. Plant Lipford, Inc. v. E.W. Gates & Son Co., 141 Va. 325, 127 S.E. 183 (1925).

Remittitur discretionary. — Section 8.01-383 and this section tacitly recognize and implicitly ratify the common-law rule that the power to order remittitur lies within the sound discretion of the trial court. Bassett Furn. Indus., Inc. v. McReynolds, 216 Va. 897, 224 S.E.2d 323 (1976); Bunch v. State Hwy. & Transp. Comm'r, 217 Va. 627, 231 S.E.2d 324 (1977).

Court has authority and duty to correct unfair verdict. — The courts are clothed with the authority, and charged with the duty, to correct what plainly appears to be an unfair verdict in a personal injury case. The use of this authority is but the exercise of the inherent discretion of the trial courts, limited by the admonitory principle that it is the jury's function, ordinarily, to assess damages. Edmiston v. Kupsenel, 205 Va. 198, 135 S.E.2d 777 (1964).

Where the attack upon a verdict is based upon its alleged excessiveness, if the amount awarded is so great as to shock the conscience of the court and to create the impression that the jury has been motivated by passion, corruption or prejudice, or has misconceived or misconstrued the facts or the law, or if the award is so out of proportion to the injuries suffered as to suggest that it is not the product of a fair and impartial decision, the court is empowered, and in fact obligated, to step in and correct the injustice. Edmiston v. Kupsenel, 205 Va. 198, 135 S.E.2d 777 (1964).

Where the jury verdict in a personal injury case appears to be the result of passion, prejudice or corruption, or misconception of facts or law, or where the disproportion between the plaintiff's injuries and the award is so great as to suggest that the decision was not fair and impartial, it is the duty of the trial court to set aside the verdict and grant a new trial as to damages or to put the successful party on terms to accept a reduced amount. But where the jury's verdict is supported by sufficient evidence and reached by a fair and impartial jury, it cannot be disturbed merely because the trial judge would have awarded damages in a lesser amount if he had been a member of the jury. Hardy v. Greene, 207 Va. 81, 147 S.E.2d 719 (1966); Davenport v. Aldrich, 207 Va. 271, 148 S.E.2d 768 (1966); Miller v. Vaughn Motor Co., 207 Va. 900, 153 S.E.2d 266 (1967).

Plaintiff has three choices. — Although a plaintiff "may" avail himself of the option to consent under protest to a reduced award, he is not obliged to do so. The permissive language of the statute leaves him with the three choices posited by entry of the order of remittitur, viz., the right to grant unconditional consent to entry of final judgment on the reduced award, the right to grant conditional consent and seek immediate appellate review of the intermediate order, or the right to withhold consent altogether and submit to a new trial. Campbell v. Hankins, 217 Va. 800, 232 S.E.2d 794 (1977).

When plaintiff may be put upon terms. — If the verdict may be set aside as excessive, but is not so excessive as to evidence passion, prejudice or corruption, the plaintiff may be put upon terms to accept a reduced amount, although there is no measure of the damages, and if he accepts it, the defendant cannot complain. But it is only in such a case that the reduction can be made. E.I. Du Pont de Nemours & Co. v. Taylor, 124 Va. 750, 98 S.E. 866 (1919).

If the court has no right to set aside verdict as excessive — there being no measure of damages — it has no right to put a party upon terms to accept a less amount than that fixed by the verdict. Boyd v. Boyd, 116 Va. 326, 82 S.E. 110 (1914).

In cases (such as personal injury cases) where there is no legal measure of damages, as well as in those in which such legal measure exists, where the verdict is plainly excessive the court may put the successful party on terms to release what it regards as excessive. Smithey v. Sinclair Ref. Co., 203 Va. 142, 122 S.E.2d 872 (1961).

If the verdict is determined to be excessive, the court may put the successful party on terms to accept a reduced amount, deemed reasonable compensation for his injuries, as an alternative to awarding a new trial, or it may order a new trial as to the whole amount of damages. Edmiston v. Kupsenel, 205 Va. 198, 135 S.E.2d 777 (1964).

Final judgment where plaintiff consents under protest. — If a plaintiff consents under protest to entry of judgment for a reduced award, judgment entered on the reduced award becomes a final judgment to which a writ of error may lie. Thus, the statute affords a protesting plaintiff the option of immediate appellate review of an intermediate ruling of the trial court, i.e., the order of remittitur. Campbell v. Hankins, 217 Va. 800, 232 S.E.2d 794 (1977).

Final judgment where plaintiff with-

holds consent. — Where a plaintiff chooses to withhold all consent to entry of a judgment for a reduced award and no such judgment was entered, the order of remittitur is an intermediate order subject to review upon appeal from the final judgment order entered after a new trial. Campbell v. Hankins, 217 Va. 800, 232 S.E.2d 794 (1977).

Defendant need not consent. — It is not necessary in this State that the losing party should consent to the remitter. E.I. Du Pont de Nemours & Co. v. Taylor, 124 Va. 750, 98 S.E. 866 (1919).

Plaintiff is not deprived of right of appeal. — By this section the plaintiff is no longer deprived of his right of appeal. He does not surrender his right of appeal by accepting a judgment for the reduced amount, provided it is done under protest, but retains the right to insist on the verdict of the jury and to contest the correctness of the judgment of the trial court in reducing it. When the case reaches the Supreme Court, it will affirm the judgment, upon the presumption of its correctness, in the absence of evidence to the contrary; but when the evidence is certified, and it appears that the verdict is not so excessive as to warrant the belief that the jury were influenced by partiality, prejudice, or corruption, or have been misled by some mistaken view of the merits of the case, and no standard is disclosed by which the trial court could have measured the reduction, the Supreme Court will uphold the verdict of the jury, because the jury is the tribunal appointed by law to ascertain the damages sustained. E.I. Du Pont de Nemours & Co. v. Taylor, 124 Va. 750, 98 S.E. 866 (1919).

Judgment must be final. — Though this section authorizes the review upon a writ of error of the judgment of the court in requiring plaintiff to remit a part of the verdict returned in his favor, it does not authorize such review until final judgment has been entered for him. Wade v. Peebles, 162 Va. 479, 174 S.E. 769 (1934).

And records must show grounds relied on. — The practice which permits the trial court to reduce a verdict to an amount deemed reasonable and proper is a wise one, and should not be lightly interfered with. The court, however, cannot in this matter act arbitrarily. Generally, the record must show the grounds relied on in support of such action, otherwise it cannot be upheld. The assessment of damages is peculiarly within the province of the jury, and when the question before the jury is merely as to the quantum of damages to which the plaintiff is entitled, and there is evidence to sustain the verdict found by the jury, no mere difference of opinion, however decided, justifies an interference with the verdict for that cause. Hoffman v. Shartle, 113 Va. 262, 74 S.E. 171 (1912).

The record must show the grounds relied on in support of remittitur, otherwise it cannot be upheld. Bassett Furn. Indus., Inc. v. McReynolds, 216 Va. 897, 224 S.E.2d 323 (1976).

Appellate court may fix amount of judgment. — In an action for personal injuries, the Supreme Court having determined that no error was committed in fixing liability upon defendant for plaintiff's injury, but that the verdict was excessive, if the case were remanded to the trial court it would be solely for the purpose of assessing the damages. But when the Supreme Court is in as good position to do that as a jury would be, the remand is unnecessary. P. Lorillard Co. v. Clay, 127 Va. 734, 104 S.E. 384 (1920).

Discretion reviewed on appeal for abuse. — The ultimate test in determining whether the order of remittitur should stand on appeal is whether or not the trial court abused its discretion. Bassett Furn. Indus., Inc. v. McReynolds, 216 Va. 897, 224 S.E.2d 323 (1976).

In determining whether the trial court abused its discretion, "reasonableness" is the standard by which the exercise of discretion must be tested in the Supreme Court. Bassett Furn. Indus., Inc. v. McReynolds, 216 Va. 897, 224 S.E.2d 323 (1976); Bunch v. State Hwy. & Transp. Comm'r, 217 Va. 627, 231 S.E.2d 324 (1977).

When it appears from the record before the Supreme Court that the trial judge made a finding that the verdict was plainly excessive and remittitur should be ordered and that, in reaching his conclusion, he considered factors in evidence relevant to a reasoned evaluation of the damages incurred and to be incurred, his order will not be disturbed on appeal if the recovery after remittitur bears a reasonable relation to the damages disclosed by the evidence. Bassett Furn. Indus., Inc. v. McReynolds, 216 Va. 897, 224 S.E.2d 323 (1976); Bunch v. State Hwy. & Transp. Comm'r, 217 Va. 627, 231 S.E.2d 324 (1977).

But verdict supported by sufficient evidence may not be disturbed. — If the verdict is supported by sufficient evidence and is reached in a fair and impartial trial, it cannot be disturbed. Edmiston v. Kupsenel, 205 Va. 198, 135 S.E.2d 777 (1964).

A remittitur or new trial is not warranted if the verdict merely appears to be large and more than the trial judge would have awarded had he been a member of the jury. Edmiston v. Kupsenel, 205 Va. 198, 135 S.E.2d 777 (1964); Miller v. Vaughan Motor Co., 207 Va. 900, 153 S.E.2d 266 (1967).

Remand for new trial on question of damages only. — Where, although the record contained no evidence that the jury was actuated by passion, corruption or prejudice, the verdict was so excessive as to shock the conscience of the court and create the impression that the jury misconceived or misunderstood the facts or the law and that the verdict was not the product of a fair and impartial decision, the case was a proper one for the trial court to have exercised the power vested in it by this section and put the plaintiff on terms to accept a lesser sum, or face a new trial on the issue of damages. In the absence of such action, and being of opinion that the verdict was excessive, the Supreme Court reversed the judgment of the trial court and remanded the cause for a new trial limited to the question of damages only.

National Cab Co. v. Thompson, 208 Va. 731, 160 S.E.2d 769 (1968).

Affirmance of judgment in part when defense goes to whole. — Where the defendant in ejectment obtains a writ of error to the judgment of the trial court awarding the entire premises to the plaintiff, the plaintiff cannot ask to have the judgment affirmed in part, where the defense goes to the entire action. To grant this prayer would be putting not the successful but the unsuccessful litigant on terms. Grizzle v. Davis, 119 Va. 567, 89 S.E. 870 (1916).

§ 8.01-384. Formal exceptions to rulings or orders of court unnecessary; motion for new trial unnecessary in certain cases. — A. Formal exceptions to rulings or orders of the court shall be unnecessary; but for all purposes for which an exception has heretofore been necessary, it shall be sufficient that a party, at the time the ruling or order of the court is made or sought, makes known to the court the action which he desires the court to take or his objections to the action of the court and his grounds therefor; and, if a party has no opportunity to object to a ruling or order at the time it is made, the absence of an objection shall not thereafter prejudice him on motion for a new trial or on appeal. No party, after having made an objection or motion known to the court, shall be required to make such objection or motion again in order to preserve his right to appeal, challenge, or move for reconsideration of, a ruling, order, or action of the court. No party shall be deemed to have agreed to, or acquiesced in, any written order of a trial court so as to forfeit his right to contest such order on appeal except by express written agreement in his endorsement of the order. Arguments made at trial via written pleading, memorandum, recital of objections in a final order, oral argument reduced to transcript, or agreed written statements of facts shall, unless expressly withdrawn or waived, be deemed preserved therein for assertion on appeal.

B. The failure to make a motion for a new trial in any case in which an appeal, writ of error, or supersedeas lies to or from a higher court shall not be deemed a waiver of any objection made during the trial if such objection be properly made a part of the record. (Code 1950, §§ 8-225, 8-225.1; 1970, c. 558; 1977, c. 617; 1992, c. 564.)

Cross references. — As to questions considered on appeal, see Rules 5:25 and 5A:18.

Editor's note. — Acts 1992, c. 564, which amended this section, in cl. 2 provides that the provisions of the 1992 act are declaratory of existing law.

Law Review. — For survey of Virginia law on practice and pleading for the year 1969-1970, see 56 Va. L. Rev. 1500 (1970).

I. Decisions Under Current Law.
II. Decisions Under Prior Law.

I. DECISIONS UNDER CURRENT LAW.

The primary function of the contemporaneous objection rule is to alert the trial judge to possible error so that the judge may consider the issue intelligently and take any corrective actions necessary to avoid unnecessary appeals, reversals and mistrials. Johnson v. Commonwealth, 20 Va. App. 547, 458 S.E.2d 599 (1995).

Both this section and Rule 5A:18 are not limited to evidentiary rule or other rulings relating to incidents of the trial. This section is applicable to any "rulings or order of the court." Rule 5A:18 includes the phrase that "[a] mere statement that the judgment or award is contrary to the law and the evidence is not sufficient." Both provisions negated appellant's contention that Rule 5A:18 was applicable only to evidentiary and similar rulings and not legal decisions and findings. The myriad of cases interpreting Rule 5:25, Rule 5A:18's counterpart for the Supreme Court, also belied that contention. Lee v. Lee, 12 Va. App. 512, 404 S.E.2d 736 (1991).

Procedure to preserve on appeal issue objected to at trial court. — Neither this section nor Rule 5A:18 mandate a specific procedure to preserve for appeal an issue objected to in the trial court. A simple statement that embodies the objection and reason therefor suffices. However, neither this section nor Rule 5A:18 is complied with merely by objecting generally to an order. Lee v. Lee, 12 Va. App. 512, 404 S.E.2d 736 (1991).

Where trial court on its own motion instructed jury to ignore parts of an instruction, without previous consultation with counsel, defense counsel did not have an opportunity to object to the trial court's ruling, and was not precluded from raising the issue on appeal. Mason v. Commonwealth, 7 Va. App. 339, 373 S.E.2d 603 (1988).

Court has affirmative duty to instruct on principles of law. — When a principle of law is vital to a defendant in a criminal case, a trial court has an affirmative duty to properly instruct a jury about the matter. That principle applies even when an objection has not been stated. Johnson v. Commonwealth, 20 Va. App. 547, 458 S.E.2d 599 (1995).

Motion to set aside verdict did not save failure to object to instructions. — Where the defendant did make a motion to set aside the verdict, this does not save him from his failure to object to the instructions which submitted the issues of contributory negligence and proximate cause to the jury. Spitzli v. Minson, 231 Va. 12, 341 S.E.2d 170 (1986).

Failure to indicate or seek action of trial court. — Merely stating an objection to "the irregularity of the jury" failed to indicate what action the defendant wanted the trial court to take; thus, defendant's failure to seek a mistrial or other action by the trial court prevented consideration of the error as a basis for a reversal. Parker v. Commonwealth, 14 Va. App. 592, 421 S.E.2d 450 (1992).

Counsel's statement held to raise issue of sufficiency of evidence. — Where an issue of sufficiency of evidence was presented to a trial court, sitting without a jury, in a motion to strike at the conclusion of the Commonwealth's evidence, and upon its denial and upon conclusion of the defendant's evidence, the same issue was presented in the defendant's final argument to the court, the defendant had preserved his right to appeal this issue, even though he did not make a motion to strike at the conclusion of his own evidence. Campbell v. Commonwealth, 12 Va. App. 476, 405 S.E.2d 1 (1991).

The requirement for noting an exception to a final adverse ruling of the trial judge has been eliminated. Johnson v. Commonwealth, 20 Va. App. 547, 458 S.E.2d 599 (1995).

Where court was aware of plaintiff's objections to order sustaining defendant's plea asserting statute of limitations defense, she was not required to make formal exception. Ward v. Insurance Co. of N. Am., 253 Va. 232, 482 S.E.2d 795 (1997).

Sufficient to make objection at trial. — Once a party has made an objection at trial it is not required to make it again to preserve the issue for appellate review. Richmond Dep't of Soc. Servs. v. Carter, 28 Va. App. 494, 507 S.E.2d 87 (1998).

Sufficient actions to preserve issue for appeal. — Defendant's endorsement of the final order as "seen," accompanied by her repeated oral and written arguments challenging the sufficiency of the evidence to support a cause of action for negligent entrustment, clearly afforded the trial court the opportunity to consider the merits of those arguments and adequately preserved the issue for appeal. Kingrey v. Hill, 245 Va. 76, 425 S.E.2d 798 (1993).

Although appellant did not note on the final order specific grounds of objection relating to the trial court's ruling, his presentation to the trial court of a memorandum of points and authorities that discussed, among other things, the reasons why his motion for judgment sufficiently alleged injury to his business combined with his objection to the trial court's ruling noted on the final order was sufficient to preserve the issue for appeal. Luckett v. Jennings, 246 Va. 303, 435 S.E.2d 400 (1993).

Where appellant did not list specific objections to the trial court's order on the order itself, although no transcripts were provided on appeal, the trial record showed that the parties submitted memoranda addressing the issue, and the trial judge noted in his order that he based his decision on review of the pleadings, memoranda, and arguments of counsel, the appellant afforded the trial court an opportunity to rule intelligently on the issues presented prior to entry of the decree; therefore, the issue raised was properly preserved for appeal. Griffin v. Sprouse, 18 Va. App. 859, 448 S.E.2d 152 (1994), rev'd on other grounds, 458 S.E.2d 770 (1995).

Where before and in its pretrial motion for summary judgment, the buyer noted that a failure to investigate the truth of a warranty is no defense to an action predicated on that breach, this objection need not have been repeated when the issue was submitted to the jury. Stuarts Draft Shopping Ctr., L.P. v. S-D Assocs., 251 Va. 483, 468 S.E.2d 885 (1996).

Where defendant's counsel consistently maintained that testimony was admissible, and where this section has eliminated the requirement that counsel make formal exceptions to rulings or orders of the trial judge, requiring defendant to "object" after the judge's refusal to admit testimony would, in effect, have recreated the requirement of noting an exception to a final adverse ruling of the trial judge. Counsel's argument therefore was sufficient as an objection to preserve the issue for appeal. Brown v. Commonwealth, 23 Va. App. 225, 475 S.E.2d 836 (1996), aff'd on reh'g en banc, 25 Va. App. 171, 487 S.E.2d 248 (1997).

Applied in McGee v. Commonwealth, 4 Va. App. 317, 357 S.E.2d 738 (1987); Zipf v. Zipf, 8 Va. App. 387, 382 S.E.2d 263 (1989); Rodriguez v. Commonwealth, 18 Va. App. 277, 443 S.E.2d 419 (1994); Chawla v. BurgerBusters, Inc., 255 Va. 616, 499 S.E.2d 829 (1998); Coleman v. Commonwealth, 27 Va. App. 768, 501 S.E.2d 461 (1998); Bennett v. Commonwealth, 29 Va. App. 261, 511 S.E.2d 439 (1999).

II. DECISIONS UNDER PRIOR LAW.

Editor's note. — The cases cited below were decided under corresponding provisions of former law. The term "this section, " as used below, refers to former provisions.

Complete record sufficient to make error apparent. — Where a record consists of a joint petition for a declaratory judgment together with exhibits, and the judgment of the trial court, error, if there be error, is apparent upon the face of the record, as it stands. There is nothing which can be added to it by a bill of exceptions nor is a motion for a new trial necessary to give the appellate court jurisdiction of an appeal from the declaratory judgment. American Nat'l Bank & Trust Co. v. Kushner, 162 Va. 378, 174 S.E. 777 (1934).

When plaintiff waives right to assign cross-error. — While subsection B provides that a failure to make a motion for a new trial shall not be deemed a waiver of any objection made during the trial, if such objection be properly made a part of the record, when a plaintiff fails to renew its motion, fails to object to the instructions submitting the entire case to the jury, and fails to move the court to set aside the verdict and enter judgment for it, he waives his right to assign cross-error. Shenandoah Milling Co. v. Phosphate Prods. Corp., 161 Va. 642, 171 S.E. 681 (1933).

§ 8.01-384.1. Interpreters for deaf in civil proceedings. — In any civil proceeding in which a speech-impaired or hearing-impaired person is a party or witness, the court may appoint a qualified interpreter to assist such person in the proceeding. The court shall appoint an interpreter for any speech-impaired or hearing-impaired person who requests this assistance.

Interpreters for the deaf in these proceedings shall be procured through the Department for the Deaf and Hard-of-Hearing.

Any person who is eligible for an interpreter pursuant to this section may waive the use of an interpreter appointed by the court for all or a portion of the proceedings. A person who waives his right to an interpreter may provide his own interpreter at his own expense without regard to whether the interpreter is qualified under this section.

The compensation of interpreters appointed pursuant to this section shall be fixed by the court and paid from the general fund of the state treasury or may, in the discretion of the court, be assessed as a part of the cost of the proceedings.

The provisions of this section shall apply in both circuit courts and district courts. (1982, c. 444.)

Cross references. — As to interpreters for the deaf in criminal cases in which a deaf person is the accused, see § 19.2-164.1.

§ 8.01-384.1:1. Interpreters for non-English-speaking persons in civil cases. — A. In any trial, hearing or other proceeding before a judge in a civil case in which a non-English-speaking person is a party or witness, an interpreter for the non-English-speaking person may be appointed by the court. A qualified English-speaking person fluent in the language of the non-English-speaking person may be appointed by the judge of the court in which the case is to be heard unless the non-English-speaking person shall obtain a qualified interpreter of his own choosing who is approved by the court as being competent.

B. To the extent of available appropriations, the compensation of such interpreter shall be fixed by the court and shall be paid from the general fund of the state treasury as part of the expense of trial. The amount allowed by the court to the interpreter may, in the discretion of the court, be assessed against either party as a part of the cost of the case and, if collected, the same shall be paid to the Commonwealth.

C. Whenever a person communicates through an interpreter to any person under such circumstances that the communications would be privileged, and such persons could not be compelled to testify as to the communications, this privilege shall also apply to the interpreter. The provisions of this section shall apply in circuit, family and district courts. (1996, c. 559.)

Editor's note. — Acts 2000, c.1073, items 30, 31, 32 and 33 provide that funds appropriated for General District Courts, Circuit Courts, Juvenile and Domestic Relations Courts, and the Combined District Courts shall be used to provide interpreters for non-English-speaking persons in civil cases.

§ 8.01-384.2. Waiver of discovery time limitations by parties. — Parties involved in any civil litigation may, without court order and upon agreement of all of them or their counsel, waive any time limitations established by the Rules of the Virginia Supreme Court relating to any response to a motion or request for discovery or the scheduling of any discovery proceedings. The court shall allow any such waiver unless an order establishing discovery or filing deadlines has been entered previously by the court in the action. (1991, c. 75.)

CHAPTER 14.

Evidence.

Article 1.

Judicial Notice.

Sec.
8.01-385. Definitions.
8.01-386. Judicial notice of laws.
8.01-387. Notice by courts and officers of signatures of judges and Governor.
8.01-388. Judicial notice of official publications.

Article 2.

Laws, Public Records, and Copies of Original Records as Evidence.

8.01-389. Judicial records as evidence; full faith and credit; recitals in deeds, deeds of trust, and mortgages; "records" defined.
8.01-390. Nonjudicial records as evidence.
8.01-390.1. School records as evidence.
8.01-391. Copies of originals as evidence.

Article 3.

Establishing Lost Records, etc.

Sec.
8.01-392. When court order book or equivalent is lost or illegible, what matters may be reentered.
8.01-393. When book or paper or equivalent in clerk's office lost, destroyed, or illegible to be again recorded.
8.01-394. How contents of any such lost record, etc., proved.
8.01-395. Validating certain proceedings under § 8.01-394.

Article 4.

Witnesses Generally.

8.01-396. No person incompetent to testify by reason of interest, or because a party.
8.01-396.1. Competency of witness.
8.01-397. Corroboration required and evidence receivable when one party incapable of testifying.

513

Sec.
8.01-397.1. Evidence of habit or routine practice; defined.
8.01-398. Competency of husband and wife to testify; privileged communications and exceptions thereto.
8.01-399. Communications between physicians and patients.
8.01-400. Communications between ministers of religion and persons they counsel or advise.
8.01-400.1. Privileged communications by interpreters for the deaf.
8.01-400.2. Communications between counselors, social workers and psychologists and clients.
8.01-401. How adverse party may be examined; effect of refusal to testify.
8.01-401.1. Opinion testimony by experts; hearsay exception.
8.01-401.2. Chiropractor as expert witness.
8.01-401.3. Opinion testimony and conclusions as to facts critical to civil case resolution.
8.01-402. Members of Department of Motor Vehicles' Crash Investigation Team not to be required to give evidence in certain cases.
8.01-403. Witness proving adverse; contradiction; prior inconsistent statement.
8.01-404. Contradiction by prior inconsistent writing.
8.01-405. Who may administer oath to witness.
8.01-406. Interpreters; recording testimony of deaf witness.

Article 5.

Compelling Attendance of Witnesses, etc.

8.01-407. (Contingent expiration date — See note) How summons for witness issued, and to whom directed; prior permission of court to summon certain officials and judges; attendance before commissioner of other state; attorney-issued summons.
8.01-407. (Contingent effective date — See note) How summons for witness issued, and to whom directed; prior permission of court to summon certain officials and judges; attendance before commissioner of other state.
8.01-408. Recognizance taken upon continuance of case.
8.01-409. When court may have process for witness executed by its own officer in another county or city.
8.01-410. Convicts as witnesses in civil actions.

Article 6.

Uniform Foreign Depositions Act.

Sec.
8.01-411. Compelling attendance of witnesses for taking depositions and production of documents to be used in foreign jurisdiction.
8.01-412. Uniformity of interpretation; reciprocal privileges.
8.01-412.1. Short title.

Article 6.1.

Uniform Audio-Visual Deposition Act.

8.01-412.2. Authorization of audio-visual deposition; official record; uses.
8.01-412.3. Notice of audio-visual deposition.
8.01-412.4. Procedure.
8.01-412.5. Costs.
8.01-412.6. Promulgation of rules for standards and guidelines.
8.01-412.7. Short title.

Article 7.

Medical Evidence.

8.01-413. (Contingent expiration date — See note) Certain copies of health care provider's records or papers of patient admissible; right of patient or his attorney to copies of such records or papers; subpoena; damages, costs and attorney's fees.
8.01-413. (Contingent effective date — See note) Certain copies of health care provider's records or papers of patient admissible; right of patient or his attorney to copies of such records or papers; subpoena; damages, costs and attorney's fees.
8.01-413.01. Authenticity and reasonableness of medical bills; presumption.

Article 7.1.

Employment Evidence.

8.01-413.1. Certain copies of employment records or papers admissible; right of employee or his attorney to copies of such records or papers; subpoena; damages, costs and attorney's fees.

Article 8.

Certain Affidavits.

8.01-414. Affidavit prima facie evidence of nonresidence.
8.01-415. Affidavit evidence of publication.
8.01-416. Affidavit re damages to motor vehicle.

Article 9.
Miscellaneous Provisions.

Sec.
8.01-417. Copies of written statements or transcriptions of verbal statements by injured person to be delivered to him.
8.01-417.1. Use of portions of documents in evidence.
8.01-418. When plea of guilty or nolo contendere or forfeiture in criminal prosecution or traffic case admissible in civil action; proof of such plea.
8.01-418.1. Evidence of subsequent measures taken not admissible to prove negligence.
8.01-418.2. Evidence of polygraph examination inadmissible in any proceeding.
8.01-418.3. Year 2000 assessments and documents not actionable.

Sec.
8.01-419. Table of life expectancy.
8.01-419.1. Motor vehicle value.
8.01-420. Depositions as basis for motion for summary judgment or to strike evidence.
8.01-420.01. Limiting further disclosure of discoverable materials and information; protective order.
8.01-420.1. Abolition of common-law perpetuation of testimony.
8.01-420.2. Limitation on use of recorded conversations as evidence.
8.01-420.3. Court reporters to provide transcripts; when recording may be stopped; use of transcript as evidence.
8.01-420.4. Taking of depositions.
8.01-420.5. Estoppel effect of judicial determination of employment status.

REVISERS' NOTE

The statutory provisions in the evidence chapter of Title 8 relating to discovery have been omitted from Title 8.01. This has been done since a revised part four of the Rules of Court has been promulgated, effective October 1, 1977, containing the substance of the repealed statutes. The sections involved are former §§ 8-111.1, 8-301 through 8-315, 8-316, and 8-317 through 8-327.2.

The first three articles of the former evidence chapter (chapter sixteen, §§ 8-263 through 8-279.2) pertain generally to the evidentiary status of laws and records of this Commonwealth, other states, the United States, and other countries. A review of these 21 statutes revealed many out-dated provisions.

Sections 8.01-385 through 8.01-391 address the same substantive matters formerly covered in those articles. While these sections preserve the substance of the former provisions, they also make several substantive amendments.

Article 1.

Judicial Notice.

§ 8.01-385. Definitions. — As used in this chapter:

1. The term *"United States"* shall be deemed to refer to the United States of America and to include any of its territories, commonwealths, insular possessions, the District of Columbia, and any of its other political subdivisions other than states.

2. The term *"court"* shall be deemed to include the courts of this Commonwealth, any other person or body appointed by it or acting under its process or authority in a judicial or quasi-judicial capacity, and any other judicial, quasi-judicial, or fact-finding body acting pursuant to the laws of the Commonwealth, including without limitation, the State Corporation Commission and the Virginia Workers' Compensation Commission.

3. The term *"political subdivision"* shall: (i) as applied to the United States, include any other political subdivision other than states and including without limitation the District of Columbia and the Commonwealth of Puerto Rico; (ii) as applied to other countries, include without limitation states, counties, cities, towns, boroughs, and any division thereof recognized and vested with the authority to enact or promulgate ordinances, rules, and regulations having the force or effect of law; (iii) as applied to this Commonwealth and other states of

the United States, include without limitation counties, cities, towns, boroughs, and any other division thereof recognized and vested with the authority to enact or promulgate ordinances, rules, and regulations having the force or effect of law.

4. The term *"agency"* shall be deemed to include without limitation any department, division, commission, association, board, or other administrative body established pursuant to the laws of a jurisdiction. (1977, c. 617.)

REVISERS' NOTE

Definitions have been added.
Former § 8-263 (This Code ... to be evidence) has been deleted.

Law Review. — For survey of Virginia law on evidence for the year 1976-77, see 63 Va. L. Rev. 1428 (1977).

§ 8.01-386. Judicial notice of laws.

— A. Whenever, in any civil action it becomes necessary to ascertain what the law, statutory or otherwise, of this Commonwealth, of another state, of the United States, of another country, or of any political subdivision or agency of the same is, or was, at any time, the court shall take judicial notice thereof whether specially pleaded or not.

B. The court, in taking such notice, may consult any book, record, register, journal, or other official document or publication purporting to contain, state, or explain such law, and may consider any evidence or other information or argument that is offered on the subject. (Code 1950, §§ 8-264, 8-270, 8-273; 1960, c. 504; 1977, c. 617.)

REVISERS' NOTE

Under subsection A of § 8.01-386 all laws of the named jurisdictions are given equal status and courts of the Commonwealth shall take judicial notice thereof.

The word "law," as used in this section, includes statutes, ordinances, resolutions, judicial decisions, and administrative rulings and regulations of the respective jurisdictions. It is no longer necessary, for example, to prove ordinances of local cities or counties.

Subsection B adopts the provision found in former § 8-273, which recognizes the right of the court to have the law researched and to hear any evidence with respect thereto.

Law Review. — For survey of Virginia law on evidence for the year 1976-77, see 63 Va. L. Rev. 1428 (1977). For survey of Virginia law on evidence for the year 1977-1978, see 64 Va. L. Rev. 1451 (1978). For article on the admissibility of written health care standards in medical and hospital negligence actions in Virginia, see 18 U. Rich. L. Rev. 725 (1984).

I. Decisions Under Current Law.
II. Decisions Under Prior Law.

I. DECISIONS UNDER CURRENT LAW.

When compliance with section not required. — In a proceeding under the Habitual Traffic Offender Act wherein a licensee who has been convicted of driving while intoxicated in two other states did not raise any challenge with respect to the similarity between the Virginia statute and the laws under which he had been convicted, it was unnecessary for the trial court to comply with this section. Davis v. Commonwealth, 219 Va. 808, 252 S.E.2d 299 (1979).

Zoning ordinances. — Even though a part of an amendment to a zoning ordinance was not introduced or marked as an exhibit as required and, therefore, was not part of the record, the court could take judicial notice of the contents of the original and amended zoning ordinances. Hardy v. Board of Zoning Appeals, 257 Va. 232, 508 S.E.2d 886 (1999).

Appellate court limitation on judicial notice. — An appellate court may not take judicial notice of such documents when they were not relied upon before the court or commission below. Commonwealth v. Woodward, 249 Va. 21, 452 S.E.2d 656 (1995).

II. DECISIONS UNDER PRIOR LAW.

Editor's note. — The cases cited below were decided under corresponding provisions of former law. The term "this section," as used below, refers to former provisions.

Decisions of courts. — This section, in effect, requires Virginia courts to take judicial notice of all of the decisions of all of the courts everywhere. In re Reid, 198 F. Supp. 689 (W.D. Va. 1961), aff'd, 304 F.2d 351 (4th Cir. 1962).

Judicial notice of municipal ordinances. — Municipal and trial justice courts will take judicial notice of the existence of ordinances of the municipalities and counties within their own territorial jurisdiction. Sisk v. Town of Shenandoah, 200 Va. 277, 105 S.E.2d 169 (1958).

The Supreme Court will not take judicial notice of a statute invoked there for the first time. It is required to take judicial notice only of statutes relied on in the trial court. Stevens v. Mirakian, 177 Va. 123, 12 S.E.2d 780 (1941).

The Supreme Court will not take judicial notice of the existence or contents of legislative charters of private corporations which were not relied on in the court below. Commonwealth v. Castner, Curran & Bullitt, Inc., 138 Va. 81, 121 S.E. 894 (1924).

§ 8.01-387. Notice by courts and officers of signatures of judges and Governor. — All courts and officers shall take notice of the signature of any of the judges, or of the Governor of this Commonwealth, to any judicial or official document. (Code 1950, § 8-274; 1977, c. 617.)

Law Review. — For survey of Virginia law on evidence for the year 1976-77, see 63 Va. L. Rev. 1428 (1977).

§ 8.01-388. Judicial notice of official publications. — The court shall take judicial notice of the contents of all official publications of this Commonwealth and its political subdivisions and agencies required to be published pursuant to the laws thereof, and of all such official publications of other states, of the United States, of other countries, and of the political subdivisions and agencies of each published within those jurisdictions pursuant to the laws thereof. (1977, c. 617.)

REVISERS' NOTE

Section 8.01-388, based upon former § 8-272, provides for judicial notice generally of official publications required to be published by the laws of the respective jurisdictions.

Law Review. — For survey of Virginia law on evidence for the year 1976-77, see 63 Va. L. Rev. 1428 (1977).

I. DECISIONS UNDER PRIOR LAW.

Editor's note. — The cases cited below were decided under corresponding provisions of former law. The term "this section," as used below, refers to former provisions.

Purpose of section. — This section and § 8.01-389 were intended to make competent evidence which had been theretofore incompetent. Proof at common law remained as it had theretofore been. P.R. Smith Motor Sales v. Lay, 173 Va. 117, 3 S.E.2d 190 (1939).

This section is not exclusive and there may be an authentication under the common-law rule. McGuire v. Atlantic C.L.R.R., 136 Va. 382, 118 S.E. 225 (1923); Southern Ry. v. Wilcox & DeJarnette, 99 Va. 394, 39 S.E. 144 (1901).

A certificate of title to an automobile, purporting to have been issued by another state, which did not meet the requirements of this section, was properly refused as evidence. Hague v. Valentine, 182 Va. 256, 28 S.E.2d 720 (1944).

ARTICLE 2.

Laws, Public Records, and Copies of Original Records as Evidence.

§ 8.01-389. Judicial records as evidence; full faith and credit; recitals in deeds, deeds of trust, and mortgages; "records" defined. — A. The records of any judicial proceeding and any other official records of any court of this Commonwealth shall be received as prima facie evidence provided that such records are authenticated and certified by the clerk of the court where preserved to be a true record.

A1. The records of any judicial proceeding and any other official record of any court of another state or country, or of the United States, shall be received as prima facie evidence provided that such records are authenticated by the clerk of the court where preserved to be a true record.

B. Every court of this Commonwealth shall give such records of courts not of this Commonwealth the full faith and credit given to them in the courts of the jurisdiction from whence they come.

B1. In any instance in which a court not of this Commonwealth shall have entered an order of injunction limiting or preventing access by any person to the courts of this Commonwealth without that person having had notice and an opportunity for a hearing prior to the entry of such foreign order, that foreign order is not required to be given full faith and credit in any Virginia court. The Virginia court may, in its discretion, hold a hearing to determine the adequacy of notice and opportunity for hearing in the foreign court.

C. Specifically, recitals of any fact in a deed or deed of trust of record conveying any interest in real property shall be prima facie evidence of that fact.

D. "Records" as used in this article, shall be deemed to include any memorandum, report, paper, data compilation, or other record in any form, or any combination thereof. (Code 1950, §§ 8-271, 8-275, 8-276, 8-276.1; 1977, c. 617; 1980, c. 453; 1995, c. 594; 1996, c. 417.)

REVISERS' NOTE

Section 8.01-389, based upon former §§ 8-271, 8-275, and 8-276.1 preserves the provisions of those sections; e.g., making recitals in a deed or deed of trust prima facie evidence of facts recited.

Cross references. — As to authority of the Secretary of the Commonwealth to certify records for use in other states, see § 2.1-69. As to officer of another state or country taking affidavit, see § 49-5.

Law Review. — For survey of Virginia law on domestic relations for the year 1974-1975, see 61 Va. L. Rev. 1732 (1975). For survey of Virginia law on evidence for the year 1976-77, see 63 Va. L. Rev. 1428 (1977). For an overview of Virginia Supreme Court decisions on domestic relations, see 15 U. Rich. L. Rev. 321 (1981). For survey on evidence in Virginia for 1989, see 23 U. Rich. L. Rev. 647 (1989).

I. Decisions Under Current Law.
II. Decisions Under Prior Law.

I. DECISIONS UNDER CURRENT LAW.

Authentication is merely the process of showing that a document is genuine and that it is what its proponent claims it to be. Owens v. Commonwealth, 10 Va. App. 309, 391 S.E.2d 605 (1990).

The terms "authenticated" and "certified" are basically synonymous, and the court of appeals is unwilling to place undue significance on the fact they are used in the conjunctive in the statute. Owens v. Commonwealth, 10 Va. App. 309, 391 S.E.2d 605 (1990); Taylor v. Commonwealth, 28 Va. App. 1, 502 S.E.2d 113 (1998).

No requirement of certificate stating clerk's independent knowledge of facts. — The words "authenticated and certified" do not require the attesting clerk to attach to the copy of the official document an additional certificate stating that he or she is aware of and/or has independent knowledge of the facts stated or offered therein; where the document was a certified copy properly attested to by a deputy clerk, and where the conviction order was stamped and undersigned by the deputy clerk, this was sufficient to "authenticate and certify" the document within the meaning of this section. Owens v. Commonwealth, 10 Va. App. 309, 391 S.E.2d 605 (1990).

This section codifies as part of the written records exception to the hearsay rule judicial "records" which are properly authenticated. Taylor v. Commonwealth, 28 Va. App. 1, 502 S.E.2d 113 (1998).

Blood alcohol analysis photocopy admissible. — Where the Commonwealth introduced into evidence a certified photocopy of the defendant's original certificate of analysis, previously identified by a Commonwealth witness as a "xeroxed copy of the original certificate for analysis," it was proper under the statute, and defendant's contention that the photocopy was hearsay and that only the original could be admitted was without merit. Ingram v. Commonwealth, Nos. 0721-95-4, 0722-95-4 (Ct. of Appeals Jan. 23, 1996).

Authenticated court order reliable evidence of juvenile status. — The recommended and customary practice of circuit courts in determining and recording in the authenticated conviction order a criminal defendant's age or date of birth gives the recorded fact sufficient reliability and trustworthiness to render the order competent to prove accomplice's age in prosecution under § 18.2-255. Parker v. Commonwealth, No. 0406-93-1 (Ct. of Appeals Aug. 16, 1994).

Sister state must have had jurisdiction. — A judgment entered in one state must be respected in another provided that the first state had jurisdiction over the parties and the subject matter. Nero v. Ferris, 222 Va. 807, 284 S.E.2d 828 (1981).

Jurisdiction of the sister state's court is presumed unless disproved by extrinsic evidence or the record itself. Bloodworth v. Ellis, 221 Va. 18, 267 S.E.2d 96 (1980).

And judgment is prima facie evidence. — The judgment of a court of general jurisdiction of a sister state duly authenticated is prima facie evidence of the jurisdiction of the court to render it. Bloodworth v. Ellis, 221 Va. 18, 267 S.E.2d 96 (1980).

Party challenging the jurisdiction of a sister state's court is under a heavy burden when attempting to establish the absence of that court's jurisdiction. Bloodworth v. Ellis, 221 Va. 18, 267 S.E.2d 96 (1980).

Court may inquire into sister state's court's jurisdiction. — As a general rule, a court, when asked to give effect to the judgment of a court in another state, may inquire into that court's jurisdiction without offending the Full Faith and Credit Clause, notwithstanding the averments contained in the record of the judgment itself. Bloodworth v. Ellis, 221 Va. 18, 267 S.E.2d 96 (1980).

A court being asked to domesticate a foreign judgment may inquire into the foreign court's jurisdiction without offending the Full Faith and Credit Clause. This rule has special force when the jurisdictional question has not been fully and fairly litigated and finally determined in the court which rendered the original judgment. Nero v. Ferris, 222 Va. 807, 284 S.E.2d 828 (1981).

Inquiry into credit given by originating state to judgment. — The language of this section makes it clear that it is appropriate to determine what credit the originating state would give its own judgment when that state is advised of the full circumstances surrounding the entry of the particular judgment. Bennett v. Commonwealth, 236 Va. 448, 374 S.E.2d 303 (1988), cert. denied, 490 U.S. 1028, 109 S. Ct. 1765, 104 L. Ed. 2d 200 (1989).

Enforcement of gambling debts. — The mandate of the Full Faith and Credit statute prevails over Virginia's strongly-expressed policy which prohibits the enforcement of gambling debts. Coghill v. Boardwalk Regency Corp., 240 Va. 230, 396 S.E.2d 838 (1990).

When relitigation barred. — A litigant is barred from relitigating in Virginia issues that were properly before and decided by a sister state's court, even when the issues concern jurisdictional matters. Bloodworth v. Ellis, 221 Va. 18, 267 S.E.2d 96 (1980).

Credit given to foreign state's most recent order. — At defendant's request, a California court entered a final order of divorce nunc pro tunc, dissolving wife's first marriage and validating her subsequent marriage to defendant; upon subsequent proceedings on behalf of wife and the former husband, that court set aside the nunc pro tunc judgment; therefore, wife's first marriage was still in effect, precluding husband from objecting to her testimony under § 19.2-271.2, and giving effect to the California court's most recent order was proper under subsection B of this section. Bennett v. Commonwealth, 236 Va. 448, 374 S.E.2d 303 (1988), cert. denied, 490 U.S. 1028, 109 S. Ct. 1765, 104 L. Ed. 2d 200 (1989).

County civil service commission proceeding was not a "court" for purposes of full faith and credit. Rao v. County of Fairfax, 108 F.3d 42 (4th Cir. 1997).

Trial court correctly sustained defendant's plea of res judicata. — Where the administratrix's failure to assert her counterclaim would have barred any later assertion of the same cause of action in any federal court, the trial court correctly sustained defendant's plea of res judicata and dismissed the administratrix's claim she later asserted in state court. Nottingham v. Weld, 237 Va. 416, 377 S.E.2d 621 (1989).

Support judgment established paternity. — Pennsylvania support judgment was sufficient to establish paternity in a manner that was controlling for purposes of Virginia intestate succession. Hupp v. Hupp, 239 Va. 494, 391 S.E.2d 329 (1990).

Order held not properly authenticated. — Where there was no evidence that signature on a county court order was by person authorized to act in place of the court clerk, the order was not properly authenticated and certified as required by this section and therefore should not have been admitted into evidence by the trial court. Carroll v. Commonwealth, 10 Va. App. 686, 396 S.E.2d 137 (1990).

Authentication of date stamp on certificate of analysis. — As evidence of the date a certificate of analysis was filed with the clerk of the court, a court may take judicial notice of the identity of the date stamp employed by its clerk and such notice satisfies the authentication requirement of the statute and is sufficient to permit admission of the date stamp on the certificate as a judicial record. Taylor v. Commonwealth, 28 Va. App. 1, 502 S.E.2d 113 (1998).

Applied in Patterson, Jr. v. Commonwealth, No. 2676-96-2 (Ct. of Appeals March 3, 1998).

II. DECISIONS UNDER PRIOR LAW.

Editor's note. — The cases cited below were decided under corresponding provisions of former law. The term "this section," as used below, refers to former provisions.

Policy of State as to foreign decrees. — A divorce decree rendered in Nevada against defendant in this State where constructive notice was relied upon will entitle the decree to be given full faith and credit under the policy of this State as declared by this section. Humphreys v. Humphreys, 139 Va. 146, 123 S.E. 554 (1924).

The requirements of full faith and credit bar a defendant from collaterally attacking a divorce decree on jurisdictional grounds in the court of a sister state where there has been participation by the defendant in the divorce proceedings, where the defendant has been accorded full opportunity to contest the jurisdictional issues, and where the decree is not susceptible to such collateral attack in the courts of the state which rendered the decree. Evans v. Asphalt Rds. & Materials Co., 194 Va. 165, 72 S.E.2d 321 (1952).

This section declares the policy of the State as to foreign decrees, and the records and judicial proceedings of the courts of the United States and its states, and provides that the same shall have faith and credit given to them in Virginia as they have in the courts of the state from whence such records came. Falco v. Grills, 209 Va. 115, 161 S.E.2d 713 (1968).

Res judicata effect to be given foreign judgment. — The federal constitutional mandate, as implemented by Congress, requires every state to give a foreign judgment at least the res judicata effect which the judgment would be accorded in the state which entered it. Osborne v. Osborne, 215 Va. 205, 207 S.E.2d 875 (1974).

Full faith and credit given though judgment reflects hostile policies. — Subject to rare exceptions, the full faith and credit rule applies even though the sister state's judgment reflects policies hostile to those of the forum state. Osborne v. Osborne, 215 Va. 205, 207 S.E.2d 875 (1974).

Full faith and credit in divorce cases. — Full faith and credit will be accorded a foreign divorce decree as to property and support rights, as well as to marital status, where the divorce court had personal jurisdiction over the parties. Osborne v. Osborne, 215 Va. 205, 207 S.E.2d 875 (1974).

When "divisible divorce" concept applicable. — The "divisible divorce" concept, under which full faith and credit is given to a foreign divorce decree as to dissolution of the marriage but not as to property or support rights when the decree is inconsistent with separate maintenance orders entered in the forum state, is applicable when the foreign divorce has been obtained in ex parte proceedings. Osborne v. Osborne, 215 Va. 205, 207 S.E.2d 875 (1974).

Full faith and credit will not be given to a child support order entered in another state in uncontested proceedings. Osborne v. Osborne, 215 Va. 205, 207 S.E.2d 875 (1974).

A Virginia court, having jurisdiction of the parties and of their minor children, may make a child support award without being bound by any previous award that may have been made in another state, and are not required to give full faith and credit to child custody decrees of another state. Osborne v. Osborne, 215 Va. 205, 207 S.E.2d 875 (1974).

No proof of change of circumstances is required before a Virginia court may make a child support award that differs from the award made in another state. Osborne v. Osborne, 215 Va. 205, 207 S.E.2d 875 (1974).

Full faith and credit in custody cases. — It can be stated as a general proposition that the courts throughout this country have been most reluctant to apply full faith and credit to custody cases. Falco v. Grills, 209 Va. 115, 161 S.E.2d 713 (1968).

While it can be stated as a general proposition that the courts throughout this country have been most reluctant to apply full faith and credit to custody cases, the Supreme Court has never held that it would not apply full faith and credit in such a case. Addison v. Addison, 210 Va. 104, 168 S.E.2d 281 (1969).

The prior ex parte appointment of a guardian in New York was not a judicial decree and not entitled, under either full faith and credit or comity, to control a later judicial proceeding in Virginia over the custody of a minor child. Falco v. Grills, 209 Va. 115, 161 S.E.2d 713 (1968).

Plaintiff barred from relitigation. — Under Article IV, § 1 of the United States Constitution, 28 U.S.C. § 1738, and this section, plaintiff was barred from relitigating in Virginia matters properly adjudicated by court in another state. Osborne v. Osborne, 215 Va. 205, 207 S.E.2d 875 (1974).

Proof of foreign deed of trust. — Where a foreign deed of trust, which was relied upon by defendant in answer to an attachment, was not filed with the answer, but was subsequently offered in evidence, it is so far a compliance with the policy of § 8.01-279 as to render it competent evidence for the defendant, without further proof, under this section, especially in the absence of any affidavit from the plaintiff denying its due execution. F.D. Cummer & Son Co. v. R.M. Hudson Co., 141 Va. 271, 127 S.E. 171 (1925).

Proof when not properly acknowledged. — A deed of trust not recorded in Virginia, nor acknowledged so that it could be recorded in Virginia, is receivable in evidence upon proper proof of the original under the common-law rule, and two affidavits showing that the deed was properly executed is such proper proof, where the affidavits were not objected to as being secondary evidence. F.D. Cummer & Son Co. v. R.M. Hudson Co., 141 Va. 271, 127 S.E. 171 (1925).

Effect of recitals made. — If the recitals in a deed from a commissioner of a court are sufficient to show that the sale was regularly made in accordance with the decrees of the court directing it, then by express terms of this section, the deed is prima facie evidence that such sale was regularly made and that the other recitals of the deed are true, and it is unnecessary to introduce any portion of the record in support of such recitals until such presumption has been overcome. Howard v. Landsberg's Comm., 108 Va. 161, 60 S.E. 769 (1908).

A deed containing all the essential recitals to bring it directly within the purview of this section, is prima facie evidence that the sale therein referred to was regularly made, and that the other recitals therein are true. Saunders v. Terry, 116 Va. 495, 82 S.E. 68 (1914); Ashworth v. Cole, 180 Va. 108, 21 S.E.2d 778 (1942).

Under this section a deed given by the trustee in a deed of trust to a purchaser at a sale under the deed of trust is prima facie evidence that the sale was regularly made and that the other recitals in such deed or conveyance are true. National Valley Bank v. Kanawha Banking & Trust Co., 151 Va. 446, 145 S.E. 432 (1928).

Recital in a deed from a trustee that the creditor requested execution of trust is prima facie true and must stand unless the contrary is proved by competent evidence. Wills v. Chesapeake W. Ry., 178 Va. 314, 16 S.E.2d 649 (1941).

When a decree authorized the court commissioner to make a conveyance, if the defendant in a chancery suit did not himself make the conveyance by a certain date, a recital in the commissioner's deed that the defendant had not made the conveyance, as the commissioner was informed by complainant, should, especially after the lapse of many years, be treated as a recital merely that the defendant had not made the conveyance. By this section this recital is prima facie true. Virginia & W. Va. Coal Co. v. Charles, 251 F. 83 (W.D. Va. 1917), aff'd, 254 F. 379 (4th Cir. 1918), appeal dismissed, 252 U.S. 569, 40 S. Ct. 345, 64 L. Ed. 720 (1920).

Recital in trustee's deed that notice given deemed prima facie correct. — The recital in a deed from a trustee to a purchaser under a deed of trust that due and legal notice was given of the time, place and terms of sale is to be taken as prima facie correct under this section. Hopkins v. Givens, 119 Va. 578, 89 S.E. 871 (1916).

But validity of deed not affected by failure to so recite. — Where a deed executed by a trustee under a deed of trust does not recite that there was any notice of the terms of sale, as required by the deed of trust, the validity of the trustee's deed is not affected by this section. Preston v. Johnson, 105 Va. 238, 53 S.E. 1 (1906).

Recital is sufficient proof of identity of heirs until overcome by other evidence. — A deed of conveyance in the chain of title stating that the grantors therein are all the heirs at law of an intestate decedent shall be prima facie evidence of that fact, which means that such a statement suffices for the proof of the identity of the heirs until the truth of the statement is contradicted and overcome by other evidence. The introduction of such a statement shifts the burden of going forward with the evidence to the litigant contending to the contrary. Hyson v. Dodge, 198 Va. 792, 96 S.E.2d 792 (1957).

This section does not apply to conveyances by "power" or "power of attorney." Virginia & W. Va. Coal Co. v. Charles, 251 F. 83

(W.D. Va. 1917), aff'd, 254 F. 379 (4th Cir. 1918), appeal dismissed, 252 U.S. 569, 40 S. Ct. 345, 64 L. Ed. 720 (1920).

§ 8.01-390. Nonjudicial records as evidence. — A. Copies of records of this Commonwealth, of another state, of the United States, of another country, or of any political subdivision or agency of the same, other than those located in a clerk's office of a court, shall be received as prima facie evidence provided that such copies are authenticated to be true copies either by the custodian thereof or by the person to whom the custodian reports, if they are different.

B. An affidavit signed by an officer deemed to have custody of such an official record, or by his deputy, stating that after a diligent search, no record or entry of such record is found to exist among the records in his office is admissible as evidence that his office has no such record or entry. (1977, c. 617; 1996, c. 668; 2000, c. 334.)

REVISERS' NOTE

Section 8.01-390 refers to those official records of a public entity that are neither published nor maintained in the office of a clerk of a court. Such official records are to be received as prima facie evidence provided they are doubly authenticated.

The 2000 amendments. — The 2000 amendment by c. 334, in subsection A, substituted "either by the custodian thereof or by" for "both by the custodian thereof and" and added "if they are different."

Law Review. — For survey of Virginia law on evidence for the year 1976-77, see 63 Va. L. Rev. 1428 (1977). For survey on evidence in Virginia for 1989, see 23 U. Rich. L. Rev. 647 (1989).

I. Decisions Under Current Law.
II. Decisions Under Prior Law.

I. DECISIONS UNDER CURRENT LAW.

This section creates the "official written statements" exception to the hearsay rule. Under this exception, records and reports prepared by public officials pursuant to a duty imposed by statute, or required by the nature of their offices, are admissible as proof of the facts stated therein. Taylor v. Maritime Overseas Corp., 224 Va. 562, 299 S.E.2d 340 (1983).

This section has codified the official written documents exception recognized in Virginia for documents or copies of documents that are properly authenticated in accordance with its requirements. Ingram v. Commonwealth, 1 Va. App. 335, 338 S.E.2d 657 (1986).

Documents must relate facts within personal knowledge and observation of recording official. — Although a record or report may qualify as a public document, the hearsay objection is overcome only if the document relates facts or events within the personal knowledge and observation of the recording official to which he could testify should he be called as a witness. Taylor v. Maritime Overseas Corp., 224 Va. 562, 299 S.E.2d 340 (1983).

And must be properly authenticated. — While a document qualified as an official document and thus would have been admissible under the exception to the hearsay rule created by this section, it still would be inadmissible where not authenticated properly pursuant to it. This section fixes a simple, easy way to authenticate an official document, and no reason suggests itself for excusing a failure to follow the prescribed course. Taylor v. Maritime Overseas Corp., 224 Va. 562, 299 S.E.2d 340 (1983).

Double authentication necessary. — To comply with this section double authentication is necessary to prove genuineness as a prerequisite to admission of a copy. Proper authentication under this section requires not only certification of the copy as a true copy by the custodian of the record and the person to whom he reports, but also a showing that the persons certifying are indeed the custodian and the person to whom he reports. Ingram v. Commonwealth, 1 Va. App. 335, 338 S.E.2d 657 (1986) (decided prior to 2000 amendment.)

Proper authentication under this statute requires not only certification of the copy as a true copy by the custodian of the record and the person to whom he reports, but also a showing that the persons certifying are indeed the custodian and the person to whom he reports. Zubricki v. Motter, 12 Va. App. 999, 406 S.E.2d 672 (1991) (decided prior to 2000 amendment.)

Section avoids inconvenience of requiring officials to be present. — The inconvenience of requiring public officials to appear in court and testify concerning the subject matter of their statements would be suffered not only by a declarant whose statements are sought to be introduced into evidence but also by the officials whose authentication is required by this section, viz., the custodian of the records containing the statements and the person to whom the custodian reports. Hence, the court appearance of none of these officials is required, provided the records are authenticated properly. Taylor v. Maritime Overseas Corp., 224 Va. 562, 299 S.E.2d 340 (1983).

The official records exception allows the admission of certain official public documents, without the necessity of producing the record keeper, so long as the keeper or entrant had personal knowledge contained in those records and could be called to testify regarding them. Hooker v. Commonwealth, 14 Va. App. 454, 418 S.E.2d 343 (1992).

Records of Department of Motor Vehicles. — In light of the established "official written statements" exception to hearsay recognized in Virginia, one of the obvious purposes of the single authentication provision in former § 46.1-34.1 (now see § 46.2-215), rather than double authentication as required by this section, is to ease the burden on the Commissioner of Motor Vehicles in certifying records that are frequently utilized at trial. Ingram v. Commonwealth, 1 Va. App. 335, 338 S.E.2d 657 (1986).

Transcript of driving record authenticated under former § 46.1-34.1. — Former § 46.1-34.1 (now § 46.2-215) is the controlling statute on the issue of authentication of a transcript of defendant's driving record. A statute of specific or particular application is not controlled or nullified by the statute of general application unless the Legislature clearly intended such a result. There is no such intent apparent between this section and former § 46.1-34.1 (now § 46.2-215). Ingram v. Commonwealth, 1 Va. App. 335, 338 S.E.2d 657 (1986).

Tax assessor's strip file showing value of property was not admissible in evidence under official documents exception to hearsay rule, since this exception does not extend to statements not within the personal knowledge and observation of the recording official, nor does the exception permit the introduction of opinion evidence contained in any such records, and complainants did not establish that the commissioner of revenue had personal knowledge of the value of the property; in any event, that knowledge would only have been his opinion; therefore, the commissioner and trial court correctly excluded the evidence of the tax assessor's strip file. Smith v. Woodlawn Constr. Co., 235 Va. 424, 368 S.E.2d 699 (1988).

Duplicate originals of certificates of fingerprint analysis. — Since the duplicate originals of certificates of fingerprint analysis were as reliable and trustworthy as the originals, and the prosecution properly filed them with the clerk, they were admissible under § 19.2-187. Compliance with this section was unnecessary. Lovak v. Commonwealth, No. 2001-93-4 (Ct. of Appeals March 14, 1995).

II. DECISIONS UNDER PRIOR LAW.

Editor's note. — The cases cited below were decided under corresponding provisions of former law. The term "this section," as used below, refers to former provisions.

What Auditor's certificate signifies. — A certificate purporting to be made by the Auditor of the State, of land forfeited for nonpayment of taxes, being in the usual form in which he certifies papers from his office, is evidence of the execution of such certificate, and of the official character of the paper, and also of the facts therein contained. Usher v. Pride, 56 Va. (15 Gratt.) 190 (1858).

Paper certified must be from officer's records. — This section does not authorize the Auditor of Public Accounts to give an ex parte certificate. A paper which does not purport to be a copy of any paper on file in his office is not admissible. Virginia & W. Va. Coal Co. v. Charles, 251 F. 83 (W.D. Va. 1917), aff'd, 254 F. 379 (4th Cir. 1918), appeal dismissed, 252 U.S. 569, 40 S. Ct. 345, 64 L. Ed. 720 (1920).

§ 8.01-390.1. School records as evidence. — In a proceeding where a minor's school records relating to attendance, transcripts or grades are material, copies of school records solely relating thereto shall be received as evidence in any matter involving the custody of that minor or the termination of parental rights of that minor's parents, provided that such copies are authenticated to be true copies by the custodian thereof. An affidavit signed by the custodian of such records, stating that such records are true and accurate copies of such records shall be valid authentication for the purposes of this section. Except for copies of report cards and letters previously sent to parents, subjective information, including observations, comments or opinions shall be redacted, by the court, from any records prior to admittance of the records into evidence pursuant to this section. (2000, c. 558.)

§ 8.01-391. Copies of originals as evidence. — A. Whenever the original of any official publication or other record has been filed in an action or introduced as evidence, the court may order the original to be returned to its custodian, retaining in its stead a copy thereof. The court may make any order to prevent the improper use of the original.

B. If any department, division, institution, agency, board, or commission of this Commonwealth, of another state or country, or of the United States, or of any political subdivision or agency of the same, acting pursuant to the law of the respective jurisdiction or other proper authority, has copied any record made in the performance of its official duties, such copy shall be as admissible into evidence as the original, whether the original is in existence or not, provided that such copy is authenticated as a true copy either by the custodian of said record or by the person to whom said custodian reports, if they are different, and is accompanied by a certificate that such person does in fact have the custody.

C. If any court or clerk's office of a court of this Commonwealth, of another state or country, or of the United States, or of any political subdivision or agency of the same, has copied any record made in the performance of its official duties, such copy shall be admissible into evidence as the original, whether the original is in existence or not, provided that such copy is authenticated as a true copy by a clerk or deputy clerk of such court.

D. If any business or member of a profession or calling in the regular course of business or activity has made any record or received or transmitted any document, and again in the regular course of business has caused any or all of such record or document to be copied, the copy shall be as admissible in evidence as the original, whether the original exists or not, provided that such copy is satisfactorily identified and authenticated as a true copy by a custodian of such record or by the person to whom said custodian reports, if they be different, and is accompanied by a certificate that said person does in fact have the custody. Copies in the regular course of business shall be deemed to include reproduction at a later time, if done in good faith and without intent to defraud. Copies in the regular course of business shall include items such as checks which are regularly copied before transmission to another person or bank, or records which are acted upon without receipt of the original when the original is retained by another party.

The original of which a copy has been made may be destroyed in the regular course of business unless its preservation is required by law, or its validity has been questioned.

E. The introduction in an action of a copy under this section neither precludes the introduction or admission of the original nor the introduction of a copy or the original in another action.

F. Copy, as used in this section, shall include photographs, microphotographs, photostats, microfilm, microcard, printouts or other reproductions of electronically stored data, or copies from optical disks, electronically transmitted facsimiles, or any other reproduction of an original from a process which forms a durable medium for its recording, storing, and reproducing. (Code 1950, §§ 8-266, 8-267, 8-268, 8-278, 8-279, 8-279.1, 8-279.2; 1950, pp. 604, 640; 1954, c. 333; 1968, c. 723; 1972, cc. 441, 549, 645, 786; 1973, c. 177; 1977, cc. 532, 617; 1978, c. 75; 1979, c. 447; 1989, c. 212; 1990, c. 355; 1991, c. 145; 1992, c. 393; 2000, c. 334.)

REVISERS' NOTE

Section 8.01-391 addresses the evidentiary status of copies of publications and records. Subsection A recognizes the authority of the court to exchange the original for a copy. Subsections B and C (now subsections B and D), respectively, place copies of official records covered by §§ 8.01-388 and 8.01-389 and business records on the same evidentiary footing as the original provided such copy is doubly authenticated.

Cross references. — As to admissibility in evidence of reproductions of checks or drafts drawn by the Treasurer of Virginia, see § 2.1-190.1.

Editor's note. — Former § 8-266, one of the sections from which this § 8.01-391 derives, was amended by Acts 1977, c. 532. Since the substance of the amendment was already incorporated in § 8.01-391 as enacted by Acts 1977, c. 617, the Code Commission did not make any change in the above section pursuant to the amendatory act.

The 2000 amendments. — The 2000 amendment by c. 334, in subsection B, substituted "either by the custodian of said record or" for "both by the custodian of said record and" and "such person" for "such officer."

Law Review. — For survey of Virginia law on evidence for the year 1976-77, see 63 Va. L. Rev. 1428 (1977).

I. Decisions Under Current Law.
II. Decisions Under Prior Law.

I. DECISIONS UNDER CURRENT LAW.

In order to admit a business record into evidence, it must be verified by testimony of the entrant of the record or of a superior who testifies to the regular course of business. Sparks v. Commonwealth, 24 Va. App. 279, 482 S.E.2d 69 (1997).

"True copy" construed. — The legislature intended for the term "true copy" as it appears in § 46.2-882 to be controlled by the requirements for authenticating a true copy found in subsection B of this section. Statutes must be construed consistently with each other so as to reasonably and logically effectuate their intended purpose. There is no conflict between this section and § 46.2-882; the former defines the requirements for authenticating a true copy, and the latter uses that term in a consistent manner. Untiedt v. Commonwealth, 18 Va. App. 836, 447 S.E.2d 537 (1994).

Photocopy lacking proper attestation inadmissible. — While certificate admitted as evidence of the accuracy of the tuning forks used to calibrate the radar device contained a notary public's attestation, that attestation did not aver that the notary was the custodian of the original nor that she had (or had at the time) the original in her custody. Accordingly, the photocopy of the certificate was not a "true copy" within the meaning of the Code, but was, rather, inadmissible hearsay. Untiedt v. Commonwealth, 18 Va. App. 836, 447 S.E.2d 537 (1994).

Attested blood alcohol analysis photocopy admissible. — Where the Commonwealth introduced into evidence a certified photocopy of the defendant's original certificate of analysis, previously identified by a Commonwealth witness as a "xeroxed copy of the original certificate for analysis," it was proper under the statute, and defendant's contention that the photocopy was hearsay and that only the original could be admitted was without merit. Ingram v. Commonwealth, Nos. 0721-95-4, 0722-95-4 (Ct. of Appeals Jan. 23, 1996).

Subsection D was not applicable to carbon copies where the routine practice was that the carbon copies of the petty cash vouchers were made simultaneously with the original ink copies and were not as part of two separate events procedure which subsection D encompasses. Jackson v. Commonwealth, 13 Va. App. 599, 413 S.E.2d 662 (1992).

Continuance to permit authentication. — There was no abuse of discretion in the trial court's granting the Commonwealth a continuance from 12:25 p.m. on October 20, to the start of trial on October 21, in order to allow the authentication of important papers. Bennett v. Commonwealth, 236 Va. 448, 374 S.E.2d 303 (1988), cert. denied, 490 U.S. 1028, 109 S. Ct. 1765, 104 L. Ed. 2d 200 (1989).

Bank vice-president, who had general supervisory authority over bank personnel but no direct supervision over the persons responsible for preparing or maintaining the bank's records, was a person who could authenticate the bank's records. She demonstrated knowledge of how the bank's records were maintained in the regular course of its business and her testimony that she had access to the records established the trustworthiness and reliability of the bank's records. Sparks v. Commonwealth, 24 Va. App. 279, 482 S.E.2d 69 (1997).

II. DECISIONS UNDER PRIOR LAW.

Editor's note. — The cases cited below were decided under corresponding provisions of former law. The term "this section," as used below, refers to former provisions.

Records and copies equally admissible. — Records furnishing evidence of title, and copies therefrom, equally with the originals, are admissible in evidence. Kelly v. Lehigh Mining & Mfg. Co., 98 Va. 405, 36 S.E. 511 (1900).

Duly certified copies of survey and plat for patent which are copies of records in the register's office are made admissible under this section. Virginia & W. Va. Coal Co. v. Charles, 251 F. 83 (W.D. Va. 1917), aff'd, 254 F. 379 (4th Cir. 1918), appeal dismissed, 252 U.S. 569, 40 S. Ct. 345, 64 L. Ed. 720 (1920).

The mere fact that a record or report qualifies as a public document does not automatically overcome the hearsay objection unless the document relates facts or events within the personal knowledge and observation of the recording official to which he could testify should he be called as a witness. Williams v. Commonwealth, 213 Va. 45, 189 S.E.2d 378 (1972).

Section applies only to authorized records. — An original grant from the Commonwealth was not then authorized to be recorded in the clerk's office of any court so as to become a record in such clerk's office. Accordingly, a certified copy from the clerk's office could not be regarded as evidence of the original under this section. Matney v. Yates, 131 Va. 208, 108 S.E. 578 (1921).

Paper must be from official records and duly authenticated. — In a prosecution for statutory rape, the Commonwealth introduced a paper, allegedly signed by Federal officers in West Virginia, stating that prosecutrix was born on a certain date. The paper did not purport to be a copy of statistics from the official files of the Bureau of Census in Washington or the official records of West Virginia. It had the appearance of an official document but was not duly authenticated. It was held that, under the circumstances, the admission of the certificate as evidence constituted prejudicial error. Dotson v. Commonwealth, 170 Va. 630, 196 S.E. 623 (1938).

Admissibility of copy where original lost with other suit papers. — A copy of an original contract, the original being lost, made by counsel and filed with the bill of one of the parties to the contract, which bill alleged that the original had been filed with the answer of the party in another suit, although not authenticated by the certificate of the clerk of the court among the records of which the original was filed at the time such copy was made, is admissible in evidence. The fact that at the time such copy was filed it was not the best evidence and valid objection might have been made in that suit to its introduction in evidence, is immaterial, after the original has been lost, and this section has no application. Baber v. Baber, 121 Va. 740, 94 S.E. 209 (1917).

Effect of copy of recorded copy where original destroyed. — An original will and will-book having been destroyed, and a copy previously made from said will-book, and exhibited in a suit, having been withdrawn by leave and recorded, a copy from the copy thus recorded must be taken, prima facie, as a true copy of the will. Effinger v. Hall, 81 Va. 94 (1885).

Form of attestation certificate not prescribed by this section. — Where the copy of a will is attested by "A. B. Buchanan, D. Clerk," without saying for whom or for what county he is deputy clerk, but this is immediately followed by a copy of the order of probate which is attested by "A. B. Buchanan, deputy clerk for S. M. Graham, clerk of the circuit court of Tazewell County, Virginia," it plainly appears that A. B. Buchanan is the deputy clerk of Tazewell County, authorized by law to act in place of his principal, and the copy of the will so authenticated is admissible in evidence under this section. The form of the attestation certificate is not prescribed by this section. Hurley v. Charles, 112 Va. 706, 72 S.E. 689 (1911).

Copy of arrest report as evidence. — The fact that this section provides that a copy of an arrest report filed with the Central Criminal Records Exchange may be admitted in evidence does not mean that all items in the report may be admitted for any purpose. Williams v. Commonwealth, 213 Va. 45, 189 S.E.2d 378 (1972).

ARTICLE 3.

Establishing Lost Records, etc.

§ 8.01-392. When court order book or equivalent is lost or illegible, what matters may be reentered. — When any book, microfilm record, or record in other form containing judgments, decrees, orders or proceedings of a court is lost, destroyed, or illegible, and there can be again entered correctly, by means of any writing, any matters which were in such book, such court may cause its clerk to have such matters reentered, and such reentries shall have the same effect as the original entries. (Code 1950, § 8-280; 1977, c. 617.)

REVISERS' NOTE

Section 8.01-392 is derived from former § 8-280, and anticipates future forms of records as well as present forms. The final sentence of former § 8-280 pertaining to the clerk's compensation for such re-recording has been transferred to Title 14.1.

Editor's note. — Title 14.1, referred to in the Revisers' note above, was repealed by Acts 1998, c. 872. For location of comparable new sections, the comparable sections table in Volume 10 may be consulted.

§ 8.01-393. When book or paper or equivalent in clerk's office lost, destroyed, or illegible to be again recorded.

— When any such book, or any book, microfilm record, or record in other form containing the record of wills, deeds, or other papers, or any other paper filed in a clerk's office, is lost, destroyed, or is illegible, the clerk in whose office such book or paper was, upon the production to him of any original paper which was recorded in such book, or of an attested copy of the record thereof, or of anything else in such book, or of any paper so filed, shall, on application, record the same anew. The record shall show whether it is made from an original or a copy, and how the paper from which it was made was authenticated or attested. Such record shall have, as far as may be, the same effect that the record or paper for which it is substituted would have had. (Code 1950, § 8-281; 1977, c. 617.)

REVISERS' NOTE

Section 8.01-393 derived from former § 8-281, also takes care of future forms of recording.

I. DECISIONS UNDER PRIOR LAW.

Editor's note. — The cases cited below were decided under corresponding provisions of former law. The term "this section," as used below, refers to former provisions.

Effect of recording. — The act of the clerk admitting a paper to record is conclusive upon the question whether the paper is what it purports to be and evidence to prove that the copy was not certified by the clerk whose name is affixed to the certificate but by another person, who was not authorized to make the certificate, is inadmissible in a collateral action. Taliaferro v. Pryor, 53 Va. (12 Gratt.) 277 (1855).

When copy of a copy admissible. — A paper offered in evidence was a certified copy taken from a county deed book which was made from an attested copy in 1894, by which paper it was shown that the original deed was recorded in 1874, that a certified copy was made in 1883, and that this copy was recorded in 1894. The testimony of the clerk and custodian of the county deed books was that the book in which the original deed was recorded was not in existence. The copy was admissible under this section. Virginia & W. Va. Coal Co. v. Charles, 251 F. 83 (W.D. Va. 1917), aff'd, 254 F. 379 (4th Cir. 1918), appeal dismissed, 252 U.S. 569, 40 S. Ct. 345, 64 L. Ed. 720 (1920).

Original will and will-book having been destroyed, and a copy previously made from said will-book, and exhibited in a suit, having been withdrawn by leave and recorded, a copy from the copy thus recorded must be taken, prima facie, as a true copy of the will. Effinger v. Hall, 81 Va. 94 (1885).

Copy from another county is inadmissible. — When a copy of a deed taken from the deed book of one county which shows that the record was made from the attested copy of the deed taken from the deed book of another county, this section does not apply, and as evidence of the transfer of title the copy was inadmissible. Virginia & W. Va. Coal Co. v. Charles, 251 F. 83 (W.D. Va. 1917), aff'd, 254 F. 379 (4th Cir. 1918), appeal dismissed, 252 U.S. 569, 40 S. Ct. 345, 64 L. Ed. 720 (1920).

When a copy of a deed was taken from a deed book of a certain county and it appeared from the county clerk's certificate of admission to record that the paper presented to him was not the original deed, but was a copy, and no evidence was offered to show that any of the land conveyed lay in such county, the case did not come under the terms of either § 55-109 or this section and the copy was inadmissible. Virginia & W. Va. Coal Co. v. Charles, 251 F. 83 (W.D. Va. 1917), aff'd, 254 F. 379 (4th Cir. 1918), appeal dismissed, 252 U.S. 569, 40 S. Ct. 345, 64 L. Ed. 720 (1920).

§ 8.01-394. How contents of any such lost record, etc., proved. — A. Any person desirous of proving the contents of any such book, record, or other paper as is mentioned in either § 8.01-392 or § 8.01-393, may file before the circuit court of the county or city in which such record, book, or other paper was a petition in writing, stating the nature of the record, book, or paper, the contents of which he desires to prove, and what persons may be affected by such proof. Thereupon the court shall appoint a time and place for proceeding on such petition, of which reasonable notice shall be given by him to all parties named in such petition, or interested in the proceedings, and to any others who shall be known to the court, or who shall claim to be so interested. If any party interested other than the petitioner, or who may be affected by the proof, be a person under a disability, the court shall appoint a guardian ad litem to represent his interest in the proceeding.

B. The evidence upon said petition shall be in writing and filed, and the court shall make such order in respect to such record, book, or other paper, or anything therein, as may be necessary to secure the benefits thereof to the parties interested, or such other order as may be proper in the case.

Before such court shall make such order, the petitioner shall cause to be served on the persons interested a notice in writing that he will apply for such order, in the manner provided by § 8.01-296, at least ten days before such order is to be made; but if such persons, or any of them, do not reside in this Commonwealth, or after due diligence cannot be found therein, an order of publication may be issued as provided by §§ 8.01-316 and 8.01-317. (Code 1950, §§ 8-282, 8-283; 1977, c. 617.)

REVISERS' NOTE

Former §§ 8-282 and 8-283 are combined in § 8.01-394. The only significant change is the removal of the requirement that the petition be referred to a commissioner.

I. DECISIONS UNDER PRIOR LAW.

Editor's note. — The cases cited below were decided under corresponding provisions of former law. The terms "this statute" and "this section," as used below, refer to former provisions.

Nature of statute. — This statute is only cumulative, and does not deprive the party of his remedy at common law. Smith v. Carter, 24 Va. (3 Rand.) 167 (1825).

A party is under no obligation to avail himself of the provisions of this section. It gives only a cumulative remedy. Smith v. Carter, 24 Va. (3 Rand.) 167 (1825); Newcomb v. Drummond, 31 Va. (4 Leigh) 57 (1832); Corbett v. Nutt, 59 Va. (18 Gratt.) 624 (1868), aff'd, 77 U.S. 464, 19 L. Ed. 976 (1870).

After proof of loss of record of will, its contents may be established by parol and secondary evidence, such being the best proof the nature of the case admits of under this statute. Apperson v. Dowdy, 82 Va. 776, 1 S.E. 105 (1887).

Description of property and persons affected is jurisdictional. — Compliance with respect to naming the persons and describing the property which might be affected is necessary to give the court jurisdiction with regard to the subject matter, and the parties affected thereby. Mountain Mission School, Inc. v. White, 204 Va. 256, 130 S.E.2d 452 (1963).

Notice to interested parties. — The statute, in order to be valid must be construed as being intended to meet the requirements for due process of law under the Constitutions of the Commonwealth of Virginia and the United States. It is elementary that every man is entitled to a day in court to defend his rights, and that a decree rendered against him when he has had no opportunity for defense, is a nullity and may be so pronounced by any court wherein it may be drawn into controversy. Mountain Mission School, Inc. v. White, 204 Va.

256, 130 S.E.2d 452 (1963).

Effect of lapse of time. — Where 10 years after the destruction of a record, an effort is made to assail for the first time a title and possession long enjoyed, by proceedings to set up a lost will upon evidence of its contents, by a witness then 85 years old testifying that 68 years before she had heard the will read and stating the testamentary disposition of the testator's property, the testimony, though admissible, is insufficient. Apperson v. Dowdy, 82 Va. 776, 1 S.E. 105 (1887).

§ 8.01-395. Validating certain proceedings under § 8.01-394.

— All proceedings had in any case, under the provisions of § 8.01-394, wherein a final judgment or decree has stood unimpeached for more than twenty years are declared to be valid and binding in all respects. (Code 1950, § 8-284; 1977, c. 617.)

REVISERS' NOTE

Former § 8-284 has been changed to a general validating statute.

I. DECISIONS UNDER PRIOR LAW.

Editor's note. — The case cited below was decided under corresponding provisions of former law. The term "this section," as used below, refers to former provisions.

Section only cures irregularities. — This section is a curative statute only created to provide a remedy in addition to that afforded by the common law. It applies where there have been irregularities in the set up proceeding, but not to a null and void proceeding. It was not intended to breathe life into a proceeding which never had any validity. Mountain Mission School, Inc. v. White, 204 Va. 256, 130 S.E.2d 452 (1963).

And cannot validate void proceedings. — This section cannot give validity to a proceeding which was void because necessary parties were not joined and because the land description was not adequate. Not even the legislature may take property without due process of law. Mountain Mission School, Inc. v. White, 204 Va. 256, 130 S.E.2d 452 (1963).

ARTICLE 4.

Witnesses Generally.

§ 8.01-396. No person incompetent to testify by reason of interest, or because a party.

— No person shall be incompetent to testify because of interest, or because of his being a party to any civil action; but he shall, if otherwise competent to testify, and subject to the rules of evidence and practice applicable to other witnesses, be competent to give evidence in his own behalf and be competent and compellable to attend and give evidence on behalf of any other party to such action; but, in any case, the court, for good cause shown, may require any such person to attend and testify ore tenus and, upon his failure to so attend and testify, may exclude his deposition. (Code 1950, § 8-285; 1977, c. 617.)

Cross references. — As to persons with interest in will or estate being competent as witnesses in will cases, see § 64.1-51.

I. DECISIONS UNDER PRIOR LAW.

Editor's note. — The cases cited below were decided under corresponding provisions of former law. The terms "this statute" and "this section," as used below, refer to former provisions.

Scope of section. — This statute was made to widen, and not to narrow the field of competency. Radford v. Fowlkes, 85 Va. 820, 8 S.E. 817 (1889).

This section removed common law disqualifications as to witnesses on account of interest or because a party. Robertson's Ex'r v. Atlantic Coast Realty Co., 129 Va. 494, 106 S.E. 521 (1921).

Applicable to parties as witnesses. — Under this section it is very clear the rule in respect to objections for incompetency on the ground of interest is equally applicable to parties examined as a witness as to those who are not parties. Hord v. Colbert, 69 Va. (28 Gratt.) 49 (1877). See Alspaugh v. Diggs, 195 Va. 1, 77 S.E.2d 362 (1953).

Volunteer to pay bond as competent witness. — One not a party to a bond, but who has agreed with the obligor to pay it, and has received from him money for that purpose, is a competent witness to prove payment, though he is interested. Wager v. Barbour, 84 Va. 419, 4 S.E. 842 (1888).

Where plaintiff doctor was injured in a motor vehicle collision, and he had been qualified as a medical expert, even though he was a party in interest and he was not to perform the surgery, he was competent to express an opinion about his future medical needs. State Farm Mut. Auto. Ins. Co. v. Kendrick, 254 Va. 206, 491 S.E.2d 286 (1997).

§ 8.01-396.1. Competency of witness. — No child shall be deemed incompetent to testify solely because of age. (1993, cc. 441, 605.)

Cross references. — As to applicability of §§ 8.01-396.1, 8.01-402, 8.01-405, and 8.01-407 through 8.01-410 to criminal cases, see § 19.2-267.

§ 8.01-397. Corroboration required and evidence receivable when one party incapable of testifying. — In an action by or against a person who, from any cause, is incapable of testifying, or by or against the committee, trustee, executor, administrator, heir, or other representative of the person so incapable of testifying, no judgment or decree shall be rendered in favor of an adverse or interested party founded on his uncorroborated testimony. In any such action, whether such adverse party testifies or not, all entries, memoranda, and declarations by the party so incapable of testifying made while he was capable, relevant to the matter in issue, may be received as evidence in all proceedings including without limitation those to which a person under a disability is a party. The phrase "from any cause" as used in this section shall not include situations in which the party who is incapable of testifying has rendered himself unable to testify by an intentional self-inflicted injury. (Code 1950, § 8-286; 1977, c. 617; 1988, c. 426.)

REVISERS' NOTE

Former § 8-286 has been amended to provide that it applies to proceedings in which a person under a disability is a party. Also, the receiving as evidence of the entries, etc., of the person incapable of testifying shall no longer be contingent on the adverse party's testifying.

Cross references. — As to witnesses to mode of executing will, see § 64.1-49. As to persons with interest in will or estate being competent as witnesses in will cases, see § 64.1-51.

Law Review. — For note on this section, see 39 Va. L. Rev. 396 (1953). For note on nature and degree of corroboration required, see 39 Va. L. Rev. 397 (1953). For note, "Erosion of the Hearsay Rule," see 3 U. Rich. L. Rev. 91 (1968). For survey of Virginia law on evidence for the year 1976-77, see 63 Va. L. Rev. 1428 (1977). For 1995 survey of civil practice and procedure, see 29 U. Rich. L. Rev. 897 (1995). For an article, "Civil Practice and Procedure," see 32 U. Rich. L. Rev. 1009 (1998).

I. Decisions Under Current Law.
  A. General Consideration.
  B. Corroboration.
II. Decisions Under Prior Law.
  A. General Consideration.
  B. Construction.
    1. In General.
    2. Object of Section.
    3. Definitions.

  4. Memoranda and Declarations.
 C. Corroboration.
  1. In General.
  2. Illustrations.
 D. Procedure.

I. DECISIONS UNDER CURRENT LAW.

A. General Consideration.

Purpose. — One of the purposes of this section is to prevent a surviving party from having the benefit of his own testimony where, by reason of the death of his adversary, the latter's personal representative is deprived of the decedent's version of the transaction. Hereford v. Paytes, 226 Va. 604, 311 S.E.2d 790 (1984).

The statute was designed to prevent an opportunity for the survivor to prevail by relying on his own unsupported credibility, while his opponent, who alone might have contradicted him, is silenced by death. Hereford v. Paytes, 226 Va. 604, 311 S.E.2d 790 (1984).

The statute substitutes a requirement that testimony be corroborated in place of the harsher common law rule which disqualified the surviving witness for interest. Diehl v. Butts, 255 Va. 482, 499 S.E.2d 833 (1998).

The deadman's statute (this section) is inapplicable in instances where a plaintiff offers an adverse party's testimony in his case and that testimony is not contradicted or inherently improbable. Brown v. Metz, 240 Va. 127, 393 S.E.2d 402 (1990).

Argument that dead man's statute (this section) was not applicable because the jury ultimately returned a verdict in favor of the plaintiff and, thus, no judgment was "rendered in favor of an adverse or interested party" was without merit because under this analysis, a trial court would be required to wait until after the jury rendered a verdict before determining whether a party's testimony must be corroborated. Certainly this section does not mandate this illogical procedure. Diehl v. Butts, 255 Va. 482, 499 S.E.2d 833 (1998).

The deadman's statute (this section) is an evidentiary rule inapplicable to hearings before the Industrial (now Workers' Compensation) Commission. Armada, Inc. v. Lucas, 2 Va. App. 414, 345 S.E.2d 14 (1986).

This section does not apply to hearings before Industrial (now Workers' Compensation) Commission, and Rule 1 (see now Rule 2.2) of the Commission, enacted pursuant to former § 65.1-18 (now § 65.2-201), correctly permits the use of hearsay evidence without corroboration. Franklin Mtg. Corp. v. Walker, 5 Va. App. 95, 360 S.E.2d 861 (1987), aff'd, 6 Va. App. 108, 367 S.E.2d 191 (1988).

This section's application will not be extended to criminal proceedings arising out of the alleged forgery of checks on an account once held by a decedent since the person incapable of testifying is not a party to such proceedings. Bowman v. Commonwealth, 28 Va. App. 204, 503 S.E.2d 241 (1998).

In an action for specific performance of the decedent's oral promise to devise his property, this section made the decedent a witness in any action by or against his personal representative as to any relevant evidence which he could have given had he been alive at the time of trial. Adams v. Adams, 233 Va. 422, 357 S.E.2d 491 (1987).

B. Corroboration.

What constitutes corroboration. — Corroborating evidence is such evidence as tends to confirm and strengthen the testimony of the witness sought to be corroborated — that is, such as tends to show the truth, or the probability of its truth. Penn v. Manns, 221 Va. 88, 267 S.E.2d 126 (1980).

Corroboration depends on facts of each case. — In considering whether the testimony of an adverse or interested party has been corroborated, it is not possible to formulate any hard and fast rule, and each case must be decided upon its own facts and circumstances. Penn v. Manns, 221 Va. 88, 267 S.E.2d 126 (1980).

When confidential relationship existed between parties at time of transaction which gave rise to the cause of action, a higher degree of corroboration is necessary to satisfy the requirements of this section. Diehl v. Butts, 255 Va. 482, 499 S.E.2d 833 (1998).

Confirmation is not necessary, for that removes all doubt, while corroboration only gives more strength than was had before. Penn v. Manns, 221 Va. 88, 267 S.E.2d 126 (1980).

Not needed as to all material points. — It is not essential that an adverse or interested party's testimony be corroborated on all material points. Penn v. Manns, 221 Va. 88, 267 S.E.2d 126 (1980).

Corroboration may be established by circumstantial evidence. This corroboration need not independently establish the fact but must itself tend in some degree to support an issue essential to the case which, if unsupported, would be fatal to the case. Cooper v. Cooper, 249 Va. 511, 457 S.E.2d 88 (1995).

Corroborating evidence need not emanate from other witnesses but may be furnished by surrounding circumstances adequately established. Penn v. Manns, 221 Va.

88, 267 S.E.2d 126 (1980).

Need not itself be sufficient to support verdict. — It is not necessary that the corroborative evidence should of itself be sufficient to support a verdict, for then there would be no need for the adverse or interested party's testimony to be corroborated. Penn v. Manns, 221 Va. 88, 267 S.E.2d 126 (1980).

Corroboration held necessary. — Where the only survivor of a two-car automobile accident testified that before he left the northbound lane, the car driven by the decedent crossed the centerline, entered his lane, and confronted him with a sudden emergency in which the trier of fact might find that he was justified in crossing into the southbound lane, which testimony furnished him with the explanation required for his driving on the wrong side of the road, but which rested upon his credibility alone, and received no support from the evidence of surrounding circumstances, or from any other source, it presented an allegation which the fact-finder must believe if he was to prevail; therefore its absence would be "fatal to the case." This is precisely the kind of issue upon which the "dead man" statute wisely requires corroboration. Hereford v. Paytes, 226 Va. 604, 311 S.E.2d 790 (1984).

II. DECISIONS UNDER PRIOR LAW.

A. General Consideration.

Editor's note. — The cases cited below were decided under corresponding provisions of former law. The term "this section," as used below, refers to former provisions.

Origin of section. — This section was taken, in part at least, from the statute of New Mexico. Burton v. Manson, 142 Va. 500, 129 S.E. 356 (1925).

Section does not deny equal protection of the law. — The construction given to this section, by which corroboration is not required of a contracting agent of a corporation, upon the death of the other party, does not deny the equal protection of the law to private persons. The agent of a private person stands on the same footing, as to competency, as the agent of a corporation. The right of an agent to testify existed at common law, and he required no more corroboration than any other witness. Robertson's Ex'r v. Atlantic Coast Realty Co., 129 Va. 494, 106 S.E. 521 (1921).

Under this section the interest of a witness is no longer a disqualification. Ratliff v. Jewell, 153 Va. 315, 149 S.E. 409 (1929).

Applied in Varner v. White, 149 Va. 177, 140 S.E. 128 (1927); Grace v. Virginia Trust Co., 150 Va. 56, 142 S.E. 378 (1928); Southwest Motor Co. v. Kendrick, 157 Va. 251, 160 S.E. 31 (1931); Hamrick v. Fahrney, 157 Va. 396, 161 S.E. 43 (1931); Hendrickson v. Meredith, 161 Va. 193, 170 S.E. 602 (1933); McNelis v. Colonial-American Nat'l Bank, 163 Va. 284, 176 S.E. 176 (1934); Gudebrod v. Ward, 165 Va. 444, 182 S.E. 118 (1935); Gillespie v. Somers, 177 Va. 231, 13 S.E.2d 330 (1941); Purcell v. Purcell, 188 Va. 91, 49 S.E.2d 335 (1948); Roane v. Roane, 193 Va. 18, 67 S.E.2d 906 (1951); Taylor v. Hopkins, 196 Va. 571, 84 S.E.2d 430 (1954); Grove v. Metropolitan Life Ins. Co., 271 F.2d 918 (4th Cir. 1959); Hackett v. Emmett, 215 Va. 726, 214 S.E.2d 139 (1975); Muth v. Gamble, 216 Va. 436, 219 S.E.2d 894 (1975); Salyer v. Salyer, 216 Va. 521, 219 S.E.2d 889 (1975).

B. Construction.

1. In General.

Scope of statute. — By the Code of 1919, practically all disqualifications of witnesses for interest have been removed. The revisors, however, recognized that in removing such disqualifications, and especially in the case of a survivor of a transaction, there should be some compensating advantages. Hence, to meet the difficulties that might arise in consequence of the removal of the disqualifications which had been effected by the repeal of various sections of the then existing statutes, this section was added. But by this section corroboration is required only of those witnesses who have been rendered competent to testify by the repeals aforesaid, and not of witnesses already competent. The purpose of the section was to remove disqualifications, not to create them in any case, nor to impose burdens on witnesses already competent. Robertson's Ex'r v. Atlantic Coast Realty Co., 129 Va. 494, 106 S.E. 521 (1921); Epes' Adm'r v. Hardaway, 135 Va. 80, 115 S.E. 712 (1923).

This section is broad in its scope and is not limited in time. Wrenn v. Daniels, 200 Va. 419, 106 S.E.2d 126 (1958).

This section is highly remedial in its nature. Epes' Adm'r v. Hardaway, 135 Va. 80, 115 S.E. 712 (1923).

It does not undertake to prescribe the source from which the corroborating evidence shall come. It may come from the mouth of any competent witness, or any other legal source. Arwood v. Hill's Adm'r, 135 Va. 235, 117 S.E. 603 (1923).

It deals with evidence necessary to establish a contract and not with the contract itself. Timberlake v. Pugh, 158 Va. 397, 163 S.E. 402 (1932); Brooks v. Worthington, 206 Va. 352, 143 S.E.2d 841 (1965).

Section does not change traditional objection to hearsay. — This section has been interpreted as making no attempt to change the traditional objection to evidence which is purely hearsay and which would be inadmissible under any circumstances. In re Cherokee Trawler Corp., 157 F. Supp. 414 (E.D. Va. 1957).

2. Object of Section.

Purpose of section. — The revisors of the Code of 1919 made material changes in the law governing the competency of witnesses to testify. They removed practically all disqualifications except to safeguard confidential communications. It was deemed necessary in order to meet difficulties that might result from the removal of disqualifications to add a new section, which is now this section. The revisors deemed this section, coupled with the safeguard of cross-examination, to be sufficient protection for estates of persons under disability or who are incapable of testifying. Hoge v. Anderson, 200 Va. 364, 106 S.E.2d 121 (1958).

One of the purposes of this section is to prevent a surviving party from having the benefit of his own testimony where, by reason of the death of his adversary, the latter's personal representative is deprived of the decedent's version of the transaction. Seaboard Citizens Nat'l Bank v. Revere, 209 Va. 684, 166 S.E.2d 258 (1969).

The object of this section is twofold: first, that there shall be no judgment in favor of an adverse or interested party founded on his uncorroborated testimony; and second, in case an adverse party testifies, then to admit as evidence the memoranda and declarations of the opposite party, incapable of testifying. Atlantic Coast Realty Co. v. Robertson's Ex'r, 135 Va. 247, 116 S.E. 476 (1923); Ratliff v. Jewell, 153 Va. 315, 149 S.E. 409 (1929).

The purpose of this section was to remove disqualifications, not to create them in any case, nor to impose burdens on witnesses already competent. Union Trust Corp. v. Fugate, 172 Va. 82, 200 S.E. 624 (1939).

This section was intended to require corroboration of those witnesses who are financially interested in the result as well as of the adverse parties of the suit or action. Atlantic Coast Realty Co. v. Robertson's Ex'r, 135 Va. 247, 116 S.E. 476 (1923).

One of the purposes of this section is to prevent a surviving party from having the benefit of his own testimony where, by reason of the death of his adversary, the latter's personal representative is deprived of the decedent's version of the transaction. Haynes v. Glenn, 197 Va. 746, 91 S.E.2d 433 (1956).

Sufficient protection afforded. — This section is new and was intended to remove all disqualifications affecting the competency of witnesses in suits by or against the estates of persons laboring under disability or who are from any cause incapable of testifying. It was believed by the revisors that the provision requiring the testimony of such witnesses to be corroborated, together with the right of cross-examination, would be a sufficient protection to the estates of persons so incapable of testifying. The object of the statute was to remove disqualifications, not create them. And in the instant case the court erred in excluding the testimony of witnesses on the ground that they were interested or adverse parties and that their testimony had not been corroborated as required by law. Arwood v. Hill's Adm'r, 135 Va. 235, 117 S.E. 603 (1923).

Section for protection of decedent's estates. — The relevancy of evidence offered to corroborate a witness is not always obvious when the evidence is offered, or it may be relevant to a limited extent only, and, hence, much latitude must be allowed to the wisdom and discretion of the trial court. But the feature of this section which requires corroboration, in the class of cases to which it applies, is a wise one, and its observance is necessary for the protection of the estates of decedents. Varner v. White, 149 Va. 177, 140 S.E. 128 (1927).

This section is designed to prevent fraud, and for that reason may not be whittled away. Timberlake v. Pugh, 158 Va. 397, 163 S.E. 402 (1932).

3. Definitions.

"Adverse or interested party" defined. — An adverse party, within the meaning of this section, is one who is a party to the record, against whom or in whose favor a judgment is sought. An interested party is one, not a party to the record, who is pecuniarily interested in the result of the suit. Merchants Supply Co. v. Hughes' Ex'rs, 139 Va. 212, 123 S.E. 355 (1924).

To hold that the words used in this section, "adverse" or "interested" party whose testimony requires corroboration, are synonymous and refer only to the parties of the suit, is to hold that the word "interested" in that connection is superfluous. If any effective meaning is to be attached to this word (interested) it must be held that one who has a pecuniary interest in the recovery, although not a party to the record, is a witness requiring corroboration. Ratliff v. Jewell, 153 Va. 315, 149 S.E. 409 (1929).

A disqualifying interest, which requires corroboration of the witness under this section, may result from the witness being liable for the debt therefor, liable to reimburse the party for whom his testimony is offered in case the decision is against such party, or subject to liability from which the success of the party in whose favor he would testify would relieve him, an interest in the property concerned in the litigation which may be beneficial or adversely affected by the result of the suit, a beneficial interest in the fund sought to be recovered, or a liability for costs of the action. Ratliff v. Jewell, 153 Va. 315, 149 S.E. 409 (1929).

4. Memoranda and Declarations.

**The entries, memoranda, and declarations mentioned in this section are only admissible "if such adverse party testifies," but as the agent of the real estate company who testified in the instant case is no such party, a statement of decedent of the matter in controversy and a sworn bill to perpetuate his testimony were not admissible under this section. Robertson's Ex'r v. Atlantic Coast Realty Co., 129 Va. 494, 106 S.E. 521 (1921).

Where the only witnesses who testified that deceased had not paid an insurance premium were agents of the insurer, the depositions of members of the family of the deceased stating that he had told them he paid the premium were not rendered admissible by this section to refute the testimony of the agents. Johnson v. Nationwide Mut. Ins. Co., 276 F.2d 574 (4th Cir. 1960).

The word "may" as used near the end of this section is mandatory and not permissive. Hoge v. Anderson, 200 Va. 364, 106 S.E.2d 121 (1958).

Provision applies when adverse party testifies concerning any phase of his case. — When an adverse party testifies concerning any phase of his case, then "all entries, memoranda, and declarations by the party so incapable of testifying made while he was capable, relevant to the matter in issue, may be received as evidence." Hoge v. Anderson, 200 Va. 364, 106 S.E.2d 121 (1958).

In an action against a decedent's estate to recover for personal injuries received in an automobile accident, plaintiff testified as to his injuries and earnings, but did not testify as to the circumstances surrounding the accident, as he was rendered unconscious as a result of the accident and did not remember events prior to, during or after the collision. It was held that a written signed statement made by decedent five days after the accident, in which he related his version of the accident, was admissible in evidence, because plaintiff, an adverse party, had testified. Hoge v. Anderson, 200 Va. 364, 106 S.E.2d 121 (1958).

But not where surviving party's only testimony is stricken. — Where the only testimony of the surviving party was stricken from the case on her own motion, the trial court properly ruled that this section was not applicable to cause the declarations of decedent to become admissible. Carter v. Nelms, 204 Va. 338, 131 S.E.2d 401 (1963).

Decedent's declaration against his interest admissible. — The declaration of a decedent made in connection with the matter in litigation, and against his interest, are admissible as evidence to go before the jury. Lackey v. Price, 142 Va. 789, 128 S.E. 268 (1925).

Declarations that decedent had no donative intent in opening joint bank accounts. — Where a father had opened bank accounts in names of himself and his son "as joint tenants with right of survivorship and not as tenants in common," and also caused various shares of stock owned by him to be similarly re-registered in the joint names, and after his death the son claimed the stock and funds, it was held that testimony as to declarations of the father indicating he had no donative intent was admissible under this section, for the son's interest was adverse to that of his father and his estate and the son had testified. Wrenn v. Daniels, 200 Va. 419, 106 S.E.2d 126 (1958).

Competent to prove instructions of deceased members of board of trustees. — Where the defendant contracted to furnish certain building materials with a board of trustees but was afterwards instructed by two members of such board to dispose of materials because the building would not be constructed, in an action of assumpsit against him after the death of the two members of the board, to prove, under this section, the instructions given by such deceased members. Lackey v. Price, 142 Va. 789, 128 S.E. 268 (1925).

C. Corroboration.

1. In General.

How much corroboration is required depends on no hard and fast rule but upon the facts in each case. Trevillian v. Bullock, 185 Va. 958, 40 S.E.2d 920 (1947); Leckie v. Lynchburg Trust & Sav. Bank, 191 Va. 360, 60 S.E.2d 923 (1950).

Whether corroboration exists and the degree and quality required are to be determined by the facts and circumstances of the particular case. Clay v. Clay, 196 Va. 997, 86 S.E.2d 812 (1955); Everton v. Askew, 199 Va. 778, 102 S.E.2d 156 (1958); Seaboard Citizens Nat'l Bank v. Revere, 209 Va. 684, 166 S.E.2d 258 (1969).

In considering whether the testimony of an adverse or interested party has been corroborated, it is not possible to formulate any hard and fast rule, and each case must be decided upon its own facts and circumstances. Brooks v. Worthington, 206 Va. 352, 143 S.E.2d 841 (1965); Seaboard Citizens Nat'l Bank v. Revere, 209 Va. 684, 166 S.E.2d 258 (1969).

In order to require corroboration, there must be a witness who testifies in the cause, and he must be seeking a judgment or decree in his favor, and thus be "an adverse or interested party." He must in some way be beneficially interested in the judgment or decree which is sought to be obtained on his testimony against a party who is incapable of testifying, or some representative of such a party. Robertson's Ex'r v. Atlantic Coast Realty Co., 129 Va. 494, 106 S.E. 521 (1921).

Corroboration not limited to "adverse party". — It is significant that in the clause of the statute which requires corroboration, the descriptive language is "adverse or interested party," whereas in that which permits the admission as evidence of the memoranda and declarations of the person then incapable of testifying, who or whose representative is a party to the suit, the language used is "adverse party"; so that, if an adverse party — that is, a party to the record, against whom or in whose favor a judgment is sought — testifies, then such memoranda and declarations of his adversary in the litigation if relevant are admissible. On the other hand, when referring to the corroboration required, this is not limited to the adverse party, but includes both the adverse party and the interested party. This language must have been chosen designedly. Atlantic Coast Realty Co. v. Robertson's Ex'r, 135 Va. 247, 116 S.E. 476 (1923).

It does not require the testimony of an adverse witness to be corroborated in every particular. The statute only requires that there should be such corroboration as would confirm and strengthen the testimony of such adverse witness. Cannon v. Cannon, 158 Va. 12, 163 S.E. 405 (1932); Morrison v. Morrison, 174 Va. 58, 4 S.E.2d 776 (1939); Heath v. Valentine, 177 Va. 731, 15 S.E.2d 98 (1941); Rorer v. Taylor, 182 Va. 49, 27 S.E.2d 923 (1943).

It is not essential that an adverse or interested party's testimony be corroborated on all material points. Brooks v. Worthington, 206 Va. 352, 143 S.E.2d 841 (1965).

This section only requires that there should be such corroboration as would confirm and strengthen the belief of the jury in the testimony of such adverse witnesses. Krikorian v. Dailey, 171 Va. 16, 197 S.E. 442 (1938); Shenandoah Valley Nat'l Bank v. Lineburg, 179 Va. 734, 20 S.E.2d 541 (1942).

It is not necessary that the corroborating evidence should be of itself sufficient to support a verdict, but it must, of its own strength, tend to support some essential allegation. Krikorian v. Dailey, 171 Va. 16, 197 S.E. 442 (1938); Shenandoah Valley Nat'l Bank v. Lineburg, 179 Va. 734, 20 S.E.2d 541 (1942); Leckie v. Lynchburg Trust & Sav. Bank, 191 Va. 360, 60 S.E.2d 923 (1950); Hancock v. Smith, 90 F. Supp. 45 (W.D. Va. 1950).

It is not necessary that the corroborative evidence should of itself be sufficient to support a verdict, for then there would be no need for the adverse or interested party's testimony to be corroborated. Brooks v. Worthington, 206 Va. 352, 143 S.E.2d 841 (1965).

Depends upon the facts of each particular case. — There seems to be no obscurity in the language of this section, but its application to particular cases may be sometimes difficult. That a judgment cannot be founded upon the uncorroborated testimony of one who is either a party to the action, or of one who though not a party to the action is interested in its result, is certainly true, but as the facts and circumstances attending each case are always different from the precise facts of another case, it is impossible to frame a general rule which could be universally applied. Corroboration in such cases there must be. The precise nature of the required corroboration or the weight to be given to the corroborating evidence depends upon the facts of each particular case. Noland Co. v. Wagner, 153 Va. 254, 149 S.E. 478 (1929).

What constitutes corroboration. — The facts and circumstances attending one case are so entirely different from those of another, that the statement of a general rule of universal application as to what constitutes a sufficiency of corroborating evidence would be unwise. The cases must be dealt with as they arise. But it is clear that the witness to be corroborated need not be corroborated on all material points. Merchants Supply Co. v. Executors of Estate of Hughes, 139 Va. 212, 123 S.E. 355 (1924), is not authority to the contrary, nor is it necessary that the corroborative evidence should of itself be sufficient to support a verdict, for then there would be no need for the testimony sought to be corroborated. Burton v. Manson, 142 Va. 500, 129 S.E. 356 (1925); Davies v. Silvey, 148 Va. 132, 138 S.E. 513 (1927).

However, it may be stated as an abstract rule, that corroborative evidence, under this section, is such evidence as tends in some degree, of its own strength and independency, to support some essential allegation or issue raised by the pleadings testified to by the witness whose evidence is sought to be corroborated, which allegation or issue, if unsupported, would be fatal to the case; and such corroborating evidence must, of itself without the aid of any other evidence, exhibit its corroborative character by pointing with reasonable certainty to the allegation or issue which it supports, and such evidence will not be material unless the evidence sought to be corroborated itself supports the allegations or the point in issue. Burton v. Manson, 142 Va. 500, 129 S.E. 356 (1925); Davies v. Silvey, 148 Va. 132, 138 S.E. 513 (1927).

Corroborative evidence, under this section, is such evidence as tends in some degree, of its own strength and independence, to support some essential allegation or issue raised by the pleadings testified to by the witness, whose evidence is sought to be corroborated, which allegation if unsupported would be fatal to the case. White v. Pacific Mut. Life Ins. Co., 150 Va. 849, 143 S.E. 340 (1928).

Corroborating evidence is such evidence as tends to confirm and strengthen the testimony of the witness sought to be corroborated — that is, such as tends to show the truth, or the probability of its truth. Brooks v. Worthington, 206 Va. 352, 143 S.E.2d 841 (1965).

The character and sufficiency of the cor-

roboration should be gauged and appraised by the fact sought to be proved. Just what is necessary to be corroborated (i.e., delivery of a deed) must not be overlooked. Crump v. Gilliam, 190 Va. 935, 59 S.E.2d 72 (1950); Everton v. Askew, 199 Va. 778, 102 S.E.2d 156 (1958).

Confirmation is not necessary, for that removes all doubt, while corroboration only gives more strength than was had before. Brooks v. Worthington, 206 Va. 352, 143 S.E.2d 841 (1965).

No corroboration of inconsistent and contradictory testimony. — The instruction that "the law does not require the testimony of such an adverse witness to be corroborated in every particular, but that what the law requires is that there should be such corroboration as would confirm and strengthen the belief of the jury in the testimony of the witness" probably would be a sufficiently accurate statement if the testimony of the witness to be corroborated had been consistent and harmonious throughout. The belief of the jury in inconsistent and contradictory testimony could not be strengthened by evidence corroborating it. Burton v. Manson, 142 Va. 500, 129 S.E. 356 (1925).

No hard and fast rule can define satisfactorily what is sufficient corroboration. The witness need not be corroborated on all material points but must be supported on some essential fact whose establishment is necessary to sustain the judgment. If the testimony to be corroborated is inconsistent and contradictory then to speak of corroboration at all would be a solecism. Ratliff v. Jewell, 153 Va. 315, 149 S.E. 409 (1929).

Where the narrative to be corroborated runs counter to common experience, more is required to corroborate it than where it is in line with common experience. Trevillian v. Bullock, 185 Va. 958, 40 S.E.2d 920 (1947). See also, Ingles v. Greear, 181 Va. 838, 27 S.E.2d 222 (1943).

Where a confidential relationship existed between the parties a higher degree of corroboration is required by this section than in ordinary transactions. Nicholson v. Shockey, 192 Va. 270, 64 S.E.2d 813 (1951); Clay v. Clay, 196 Va. 997, 86 S.E.2d 812 (1955); Everton v. Askew, 199 Va. 778, 102 S.E.2d 156 (1958).

Where a confidential relation existed between the parties at the time of the transaction relied on, a higher degree of corroboration is required than in ordinary transactions. Seaboard Citizens Nat'l Bank v. Revere, 209 Va. 684, 166 S.E.2d 258 (1969).

The close and confidential relationship of the parties emphasizes the necessity of subjecting the transaction to a close scrutiny and of requiring more than ordinary corroboration. Seaboard Citizens Nat'l Bank v. Revere, 209 Va. 684, 166 S.E.2d 258 (1969).

This section was not applicable where plaintiff called defendant as an adverse witness. The usual rule was applied, and, accordingly, the plaintiff was bound by the testimony of the defendant insofar as it was uncontradicted and not inherently improbable. Balderson v. Robertson, 203 Va. 484, 125 S.E.2d 180 (1962).

Source of corroboration. — Corroboration of an adverse or interested party may not emanate from him or depend upon his credibility, but it may come from any other competent witness or other legal source. Leckie v. Lynchburg Trust & Sav. Bank, 191 Va. 360, 60 S.E.2d 923 (1950).

Corroborating evidence need not emanate from other witnesses but may be furnished by surrounding circumstances adequately established. Brooks v. Worthington, 206 Va. 352, 143 S.E.2d 841 (1965).

This section is not applicable to evidence plainly inadmissible as hearsay. Carter Coal Co. v. Litz, 54 F. Supp. 115 (W.D. Va. 1943), aff'd, 140 F.2d 934 (4th Cir. 1944).

2. Illustrations.

What evidence needed to establish a contract with a decedent. — In order to establish a contract with a deceased person, under this section, there must be disinterested testimony pointing with reasonable certainty to, and corroboration of, the material evidence given by an interested witness or witnesses. White v. Pacific Mut. Life Ins. Co., 150 Va. 849, 143 S.E. 340 (1928).

Under the provisions of this section there must be corroborative evidence of the agreement, when it appears that one of the parties is dead. Truslow v. Ball, 166 Va. 608, 186 S.E. 71 (1936).

A deed as evidence of a debt does not have to be corroborated. — A deed, evidencing the debt and carrying the provision which created the lien, was in evidence. It was held sufficient proof of the debt and the lien, and it, as evidence, did not have to be corroborated under this section. Harper v. Harper, 159 Va. 210, 165 S.E. 490 (1932).

Application to deed from wife to husband. — In an effort to establish the validity of an unacknowledged deed from his deceased wife to himself, the plaintiff was able to present only his own uncorroborated testimony that his wife had several years previously given him the deed in question but that he had given it back to her to keep with their other important papers. Since such testimony emanated from an adverse and interested party and since the wife, who was the other party to the transaction, was dead, such testimony, even though uncontradicted, standing alone could not sustain a decree in favor of the plaintiff under the provisions of this section. Crump v. Gilliam, 190 Va. 935, 59 S.E.2d 72 (1950).

Section not applicable to agent's testimony. — The instant case was an action by a broker to recover commissions for the sale of standing timber. The contract was made between an agent of the landowner, acting for his principal, and the broker. The action was brought in the lifetime of the landowner, but upon her death the action was revived and the broker testified as a witness in his own behalf. It was held that prior to the Code of 1919 plaintiff was a competent witness and required no corroboration of any kind, and that notwithstanding this section, providing that no judgment shall be rendered in favor of an adverse or interested party founded on his uncorroborated testimony where the other party is incapable of testifying, plaintiff still required no corroboration. Epes' Adm'r v. Hardaway, 135 Va. 80, 115 S.E. 712 (1923).

Plaintiff, a real estate broker, was asking for a judgment against the administrator of a landowner. Defendant's intestate had placed his property in the hands of one K., a real estate broker, for sale, and K. had asked plaintiff to obtain a customer, agreeing to share the commissions. K. refused to join the plaintiff in his action against the administrator and declined to make any charge for his services against the estate. It was held that while the plaintiff was an adverse or interested party, K. was not and was a competent witness, and that the jury should have been allowed to consider K.'s testimony in corroboration of the plaintiff and for other purposes. Arwood v. Hill's Adm'r, 135 Va. 235, 117 S.E. 603 (1923).

In an action by a real estate company to recover damages against an executor for breach of an alleged parol contract, whereby plaintiff was to have the exclusive right of selling a tract of land of executor's decedent for a stipulated compensation, the agent of the plaintiff who was not a party to the action, was not an officer of the plaintiff, and had no pecuniary interest in the result of the litigation, is not "an adverse or interested party," as that term is used in this section. Competent at common law, he is not rendered incompetent by the statute, although he was plaintiff's contracting agent in making the contract in litigation. Robertson's Ex'r v. Atlantic Coast Realty Co., 129 Va. 494, 106 S.E. 521 (1921).

This section was inapplicable to a suit attacking a decedent's will, where the suit was between living persons capable of testifying. Croft v. Snidow, 183 Va. 649, 33 S.E.2d 208 (1945).

Inapplicable to testimony of beneficiary of surety bond where principal dead. — Where H. and G. entered into contract and G. gave bond to H. for its faithful performance with A. signing as surety, there is no merit in the contention that, in an action on the bond by H. against A. after G.'s death, H. cannot testify concerning such bond under this section, because even under section 3346 of the Code of 1887, which was superseded by the Code of 1919, H. would have been a competent witness in view of the fact that the agent of the corporation who represented the corporation in making the bond is living and capable of testifying. American Sur. Co. v. Hannah, 143 Va. 291, 130 S.E. 411 (1925).

Nor when corporation is a party and officer unable to testify. — This section does not provide that if an officer of a corporation, which is a party to an action, is dead, and such officer made the contract for the corporation with the opposite party to the litigation, the testimony of such opposite party cannot be received unless corroborated. The section does not create a disqualification when a corporation is a party, nor impose additional burdens upon an opposite party, because of the inability of an officer of a corporation to testify. Union Trust Corp. v. Fugate, 172 Va. 82, 200 S.E. 624 (1939).

This section is not applicable to an action against John Doe under the Uninsured Motorist Law, former § 38.1-381. The fictitious John Doe is not a person incapable of testifying in the sense intended by this section. John Doe v. Faulkner, 203 Va. 522, 125 S.E.2d 169 (1962).

Section held not applicable. — Where, a husband having exercised his statutory right to renounce his wife's will and take the interest in her property given him by law, the proponent of the will introduced a release of all interest in the wife's tangible personal estate, signed by the husband but not under seal and not purporting to be for any consideration, whereupon the husband testified that there was no consideration for the release, this section did not apply, for the burden was on the proponent to prove that the husband had no right to renounce the will, and, proponent having failed to do so, the decree in favor of the husband was based not upon the husband's testimony, but upon the right given him by statute, independent of the supposed release. Ballard v. Cox, 191 Va. 654, 62 S.E.2d 1 (1950).

The provisions of this section requiring corroboration where one party to a transaction is dead are not applicable where, at a first trial of the action, the original defendant was living and had full opportunity to controvert the plaintiff's testimony. Haynes v. Glenn, 197 Va. 746, 91 S.E.2d 433 (1956).

In an action arising out of an automobile accident, if it had been shown that the defendant suffered retrograde amnesia and so could not remember how the accident occurred, it was, nonetheless, unnecessary that the plaintiff's testimony be corroborated. The Dead

Man's Statute simply does not apply to this type of case. The defendant was not incapable of testifying. He was merely unable, supposedly, to recall the actual details of the accident. That is not such an incapability as is envisioned by the statute. Sturman v. Johnson, 209 Va. 227, 163 S.E.2d 170 (1968).

But is applicable to stockholder as witness for corporation. — A stockholder in a corporation is one who has a pecuniary interest in the result when such corporation is a party to the litigation in which a judgment is sought by or against it and as such must, under this section, be corroborated, or a judgment in favor of the corporation cannot be founded on his testimony in an action against an incapable party or his representative. Atlantic Coast Realty Co. v. Robertson's Ex'r, 135 Va. 247, 116 S.E. 476 (1923).

To creditor in suit to set aside deed in trustee's sale. — In a suit to set aside a deed from a trustee, the deed recited that the creditor requested the execution of the trust, but the creditor testified that he did not request the trustee to make the sale. It was held that the creditor was not entitled to a decree based upon his testimony, unless such testimony was corroborated, since the provisions of this section applied squarely to the situation. Willis v. Chesapeake W. Ry., 178 Va. 314, 16 S.E.2d 649 (1941).

To debtor in action by executor against decedent's debtors. — Where defendants, in an action by an executor to recover on a bond made by defendants, payable to the executor's decedent, alleged that the bond has been paid and the chief witness for the defense was one of the defendants, such witness falls within the designation of this section as an adverse and interested party, and must be corroborated. Burton v. Manson, 142 Va. 500, 129 S.E. 356 (1921).

To testimony of beneficiary of alleged parol trust in realty. — The claims of the alleged beneficiaries under an alleged parol trust bore the stamp of inconsistency and was contrary to human experience and it followed, as a corollary, that since the alleged grantor was dead the evidence of the beneficiary must be corroborated. Ingles v. Greear, 181 Va. 838, 27 S.E.2d 222 (1943).

And to plaintiff in action against administrator for services rendered decedent. — In action against administrator to recover for services rendered decedent during his lifetime, based on an oral agreement to devise and bequeath to plaintiff all of decedent's property, this section required corroboration of plaintiff's testimony with respect to her claim. Ricks v. Sumler, 179 Va. 571, 19 S.E.2d 889 (1942).

Section held applicable. — Where plaintiffs brought suit against their brother to determine the ownership of funds received by their deceased mother in a land transaction in which defendant represented her as attorney, and deposited by her in joint bank accounts to the credit of herself and defendant and of defendant and his father, technically there was not a suit by defendant against his mother's estate or personal representative, but there was in effect such a proceeding, defendant was an adverse or interested party who sought a decree against his mother's estate sustaining a gift of the funds to him, and the presumption of fraud arising from the fiduciary relationship between defendant and his mother could not be overcome by defendant's uncorroborated testimony. Nicholson v. Shockey, 192 Va. 270, 64 S.E.2d 813 (1951).

Corroborative evidence held sufficient. — In an action against the heirs of a decedent based on an alleged oral contract made by decedent with plaintiff to leave plaintiff decedent's business and all he had if plaintiff would learn the business, the testimony of nine witnesses, most of whom were not interested or related to the parties, that decedent had stated to them on various occasions that he expected to leave his business to plaintiff, afforded sufficient corroboration of the contract to supply the essentials required by the provisions of this section. Clark v. Atkins, 188 Va. 668, 51 S.E.2d 222 (1949).

In an action against an executor on a note given by his decedent, defendant objected to a judgment for plaintiff upon the ground that it was founded on the uncorroborated testimony of the plaintiff, contrary to the provisions of this section. It was held that there was no merit in this objection, as the note itself and the presumption arising from it aided the plaintiff in carrying the burden of proof. Moreover, the testimony for the defendant as to the soundness of mind of the decedent further corroborated the testimony of the plaintiff. Good v. Dyer, 137 Va. 114, 119 S.E. 277 (1923).

In a suit against the estate of a deceased vendor for specific performance of a contract for the sale of real estate, plaintiff's testimony that a noninterest-bearing bond had been executed for the purchase price was sufficiently corroborated by the verbal and documentary evidence. Leckie v. Lynchburg Trust & Sav. Bank, 191 Va. 360, 60 S.E.2d 923 (1950).

In an action against the committee of an incompetent to recover damages for the incompetent's fraud in "selling" to the plaintiff a piece of land which he did not own, the deed with special warranty of title, the admission of defendant's counsel that the incompetent did not own the property, and the other circumstances constituted sufficient corroboration of plaintiff's testimony under this section. Grimes v. Peoples Nat'l Bank, 191 Va. 505, 62 S.E.2d 22 (1950).

Testimony of wife as to loans to husband,

since deceased, was held sufficiently corroborated to comply with this section. Morrison v. Morrison, 174 Va. 58, 4 S.E.2d 776 (1939).

As to sufficient corroboration of testimony of claimant against estate, see Rorer v. Taylor, 182 Va. 49, 27 S.E.2d 923 (1943).

Possession of bond and relation of parties held sufficient corroboration of gift. Shenandoah Valley Nat'l Bank v. Lineburg, 179 Va. 734, 20 S.E.2d 541 (1942).

In a widow's suit to determine the validity of an antenuptial contract a decree finding the contract invalid was not based on the uncorroborated testimony of the widow where she proved, without the aid of her own testimony, that: (1) While she was engaged to her deceased husband they executed an antenuptial contract; (2) thereafter they were married; (3) the consideration stated in the antenuptial contract was unreasonably small in proportion to the value of the property then owned by the intended husband. Batleman v. Rubin, 199 Va. 156, 98 S.E.2d 519 (1957).

Corroboration of a deceased father's indebtedness to his daughter was substantial and ample. Bickers v. Pinnell, 199 Va. 444, 100 S.E.2d 20 (1957).

Parol agreement of wife to devise property to husband held sufficiently corroborated. Everton v. Askew, 199 Va. 778, 102 S.E.2d 156 (1903).

Where a woman testified to an alleged marriage ceremony with a deceased person, ample corroboration of her testimony was to be found in the testimony of others that they considered the decedent and the woman to be married, and in the decedent's letters, in which he repeatedly addressed her as his wife. Grove v. Metropolitan Life Ins. Co., 271 F.2d 918 (4th Cir. 1959).

Corroborative evidence held insufficient. — Corroborative evidence of promise by wife to devise property to husband held insufficient. Clay v. Clay, 196 Va. 997, 86 S.E.2d 812 (1955).

Evidence of close relationship between mother and son held insufficient corroboration under this section. Nicholson v. Shockey, 192 Va. 270, 64 S.E.2d 813 (1951).

D. Procedure.

Whether the requirement of corroboration under this section has been satisfied is usually an issue for the jury. Whitmer v. Marcum, 214 Va. 64, 196 S.E.2d 907 (1973).

But corroboration need not always present a jury issue; a trial judge is not precluded from a determination that the witness's testimony has been corroborated as a matter of law. Whitmer v. Marcum, 214 Va. 64, 196 S.E.2d 907 (1973).

Where the trial court found as a matter of law that testimony was corroborated, the issue of corroboration was erroneously submitted to the jury. Whitmer v. Marcum, 214 Va. 64, 196 S.E.2d 907 (1973).

Jury to be instructed. — This section provides that, in an action or suit by or against a person who, from any cause, is incapable of testifying, or by or against his representative, no judgment or decree shall be rendered in favor of an adverse or interested party founded on his uncorroborated testimony. It was held that the proper practice under the statute is not to exclude the testimony of such interested or adverse party but to properly instruct the jury on that subject. Arwood v. Hill's Adm'r, 135 Va. 237, 117 S.E. 603 (1923).

When litigant should offer instructions. — It is the duty of a litigant, who thinks the instructions given as to corroboration under this section do not fairly present the case from the standpoint of the evidence which is favorable to him, to prepare and offer such instructions as will accomplish this purpose. Whitmer v. Marcum, 214 Va. 64, 197 S.E.2d 907 (1973).

Instruction need not set forth every judicial statement on legal principles involved. — It is not necessary that an instruction on corroboration which fully and fairly apprises the jury according to its purpose set forth every judicial statement on the principles of law involved. Whitmer v. Marcum, 214 Va. 64, 196 S.E.2d 907 (1973).

Motion for judgment or new trial when jury disregards instruction. — If the jury disregard the instructions to the effect that they are not to return a verdict against an incapable person or his representative upon the uncorroborated testimony of an interested or adverse party, the remedy of the other party is a motion to set aside the verdict and grant a new trial, or for the court to enter a final judgment, as shall seem right and proper. Arwood v. Hill's Adm'r, 135 Va. 235, 117 S.E. 603 (1923).

Party in interest enforces section. — Where witness is rendered generally competent by § 8.01-396, objection to his testimony on account of qualifications made by this section must come from some party who is interested in the transaction which is the subject of investigation. McClanahan's Adm'r v. Norfolk & W. Ry, 122 Va. 705, 96 S.E. 453 (1918).

§ 8.01-397.1. Evidence of habit or routine practice; defined. —
A. Admissibility. Evidence of the habit of a person or of the routine practice of an organization, whether corroborated or not and regardless of the presence of eye witnesses, is relevant to prove that the conduct of the person or organiza-

tion on a particular occasion was in conformity with the habit or routine practice. Evidence of prior conduct may be relevant to rebut evidence of habit or routine practice.

B. Habit and routine practice defined. A "habit" is a person's regular response to repeated specific situations. A "routine practice" is a regular course of conduct of a group of persons or an organization in response to repeated specific situations.

C. The provisions of this section are applicable only in civil proceedings. (2000, c. 1026.)

Effective date. — This section is effective April 19, 2000.

§ 8.01-398. Competency of husband and wife to testify; privileged communications and exceptions thereto.

— A. Husband and wife shall be competent witnesses to testify for or against each other in all civil actions; provided that neither husband nor wife shall, without the consent of the other, be examined in any action as to any communication privately made by one to the other while married, nor shall either be permitted, without such consent, to reveal in testimony after the marriage relation ceases any such communication made while the marriage subsisted.

B. The proviso in subsection A of this section shall not apply in those instances where the law of this Commonwealth confers upon a spouse a right of action against the other spouse. (Code 1950, §§ 8-287, 8-289; 1977, c. 617.)

REVISERS' NOTE

Subsection A of § 8.01-398 is a combination of former §§ 8-287 and 8-289.

The common-law rule that neither husband nor wife could sue the other has been eliminated by statute and case law except with respect to personal injury actions (other than those arising out of an automobile accident).

However, a change in the law of evidence has not accompanied this expansion of the spouses' rights of action. Subsection B of this section therefore provides that if by the laws of this Commonwealth one spouse is permitted to sue the other, the privileged status of communications between the two made while married is abrogated as to such proceedings.

Former § 8-288 (Testimony of husband and wife in criminal cases) was transferred to § 19.2-271.2.

Cross references. — As to testimony of husband and wife in criminal cases, see § 19.2-271.2.

Law Review. — For survey of Virginia law on evidence for the year 1969-1970, see 56 Va. L. Rev. 1325 (1970). For survey of Virginia law on evidence for the year 1971-1972, see 58 Va. L. Rev. 1268 (1972). For survey of Virginia law on evidence for the year 1973-1974, see 60 Va. L. Rev. 1543 (1974). For survey of Virginia law on evidence for the year 1976-77, see 63 Va. L. Rev. 1428 (1977). For comment on confidential communication privileges under federal and Virginia law, see 13 U. Rich. L. Rev. 593 (1979).

I. Decisions Under Current Law.
II. Decisions Under Prior Law.

I. DECISIONS UNDER CURRENT LAW.

Applicability in criminal cases. — The phrase in § 19.2-271.2, "subject to the exception stated in § 8.01-398" is construed as a cross-reference which embodies the proviso in this section concerning confidential communications. This has the effect of retaining, as a part of the law of criminal procedure, the historic interspousal confidential communication privilege which was formerly contained in § 8-289, notwithstanding the apparent confinement of its successor statute, the present § 8.01-398, to "civil actions." In the absence of an express enactment to that effect, the Supreme Court will not assume that the General Assembly intended to abrogate this long-standing rule. Church v. Commonwealth, 230 Va.

208, 335 S.E.2d 823 (1985).

Admissibility of observations about attire. — There is no per se rule allowing the admission of spouse's observations of other's attire. Some acts, such as cross-dressing, or wearing bloody clothing, might be considered confidential communications. Edwards v. Commonwealth, 20 Va. App. 470, 457 S.E.2d 797 (1995).

Communication made during now-dissolved marriage. — The interspousal confidential communication privilege survived the dissolution of marriage. The confidential communications made by the defendant to his wife during their marriage must be treated as privileged if the case is tried again. Church v. Commonwealth, 230 Va. 208, 335 S.E.2d 823 (1985).

Permissible testimony. — Wife's description of the defendant's clothing, which he displayed in public when he left the home, was not a confidential communication. Further, it is reasonable to infer that clothing worn in public was not intended to be kept private or confidential. Therefore, the wife's testimony about the defendant's attire on the evening of the offense was properly admitted. Edwards v. Commonwealth, 20 Va. App. 470, 457 S.E.2d 797 (1995).

The wife's testimony about the defendant's interest in purchasing a car and his intent to test-drive a car with an older couple was also not the sort of communication a spouse would reasonably consider of a secret nature between husband and wife. The information was not conveyed with an expression of confidentiality, nor did its content imply that it should be kept confidential. In fact, the defendant not only expressed his intent to the victim and his wife, but also arranged to meet them in a public place, further supporting a finding that this communication was not a marital secret. Edwards v. Commonwealth, 20 Va. App. 470, 457 S.E.2d 797 (1995).

Defendant's wife's testimony that the defendant instructed her over the phone to meet him at his relative's house was not disclosure of a secret communication because it lacked any objective indicia of confidential intent. If anything, the defendant's actions indicate the opposite, since he instructed her to meet him at a place where other people would be present to witness the meeting. Edwards v. Commonwealth, 20 Va. App. 470, 457 S.E.2d 797 (1995).

When the wife testified that she looked through the defendant's belongings, which he had deposited in their bedroom outside of her presence, and found a wallet containing the victim's driver's license and credit card, she was not describing a communication. While a spouse's conduct may convey information to the other spouse and would, therefore, be privileged, a spouse's conduct which does not convey information to the other spouse is not privileged. The former wife's discovery of the contents of the wallet conveyed information to her, as did the fact that she discovered it among the defendant's belongings. However, the defendant's conduct—leaving the wallet among his belongings—was not observed by the former wife and did not convey information to her. Edwards v. Commonwealth, 20 Va. App. 470, 457 S.E.2d 797 (1995).

II. DECISIONS UNDER PRIOR LAW.

Editor's note. — The cases cited below were decided under corresponding provisions of former law. The term "this section," as used below, refers to former provisions.

Section removed common-law disqualification, except in specified instances. Menefee v. Commonwealth, 189 Va. 900, 55 S.E.2d 9 (1949).

Basis of rule. — Communications between husband and wife are privileged, and neither can be made to testify as to them. This rule is independent of any consideration of interest or indemnity, and is upheld on the ground of public policy. The fact that they were living apart from each other, at the time when the communications were made, though not divorced, is immaterial. Murphy v. Commonwealth, 64 Va. (23 Gratt.) 960 (1873).

A person is not incompetent to testify against his spouse under Virginia law. Shiflett v. Virginia, 447 F.2d 50 (4th Cir. 1971), cert. denied, 405 U.S. 994, 92 S. Ct. 1267, 31 L. Ed. 2d 462 (1972).

And he can testify freely unless the spouse objects. Shiflett v. Virginia, 447 F.2d 50 (4th Cir. 1971), cert. denied, 405 U.S. 994, 92 S. Ct. 1267, 31 L. Ed. 2d 462 (1972).

In which event the spouse is privileged to prevent any testimony. — See Shiflett v. Virginia, 447 F.2d 50 (4th Cir. 1971), cert. denied, 405 U.S. 994, 92 S. Ct. 1267, 31 L. Ed. 2d 462 (1972).

This section's application is limited to judicial testimony and, therefore, it is not pertinent where wife did not testify at trial, but provides evidence leading to conviction. Wood v. Hodnett, 377 F. Supp. 740 (W.D. Va. 1974).

To what communications applicable. — Under the provisions of this section, neither husband nor wife can without the consent of the other be examined in any case as to any communication made by the one to the other while married, nor can such communication be revealed, without such consent, after the marriage relation ceases. The statute is founded on public policy and applies to any communication between them, of any nature, whether confidential or not, and it is immaterial by whom or for what purpose the husband or wife may be called as a witness, or whether for or against each other. Conversations, therefore, between a husband and his wife as to the making of his will cannot be given in evidence by his widow, no matter by whom she is called as a witness. Wilkes v. Wilkes, 115 Va. 886, 80 S.E. 745 (1914).

Supreme Court has adopted the liberal view that privileged communications between husband and wife include all information or knowledge privately imparted and made known by one spouse to the other by virtue of and in consequence of the marital relation through conduct, acts, signs and spoken or written words. Osborne v. Commonwealth, 214 Va. 691, 204 S.E.2d 289 (1974).

Effect of "privately". — But note the effect of the insertion, in this section by the revisors of 1919, of the word "privately," which seems to make statutory the holding that communications between husband and wife made in the presence of third persons are in no just sense either confidential or privileged. Pilcher v. Pilcher, 117 Va. 356, 84 S.E. 667 (1915).

The word "privately" as used in this section is intended to be synonymous with confidential. In other words, the communications referred to were intended to mean those of a secret nature between husband and wife. Thomas v. First Nat'l Bank, 166 Va. 497, 186 S.E. 77 (1936).

Admissibility does not depend upon presence of third person. — The admissibility of communications between husband and wife was not intended to depend upon whether the communication was made in the presence of some third person, but upon the nature of the communication — that is, whether it was intended to be secret or confidential, or a communication to which those attributes do not attach. Thomas v. First Nat'l Bank, 166 Va. 497, 186 S.E. 77 (1936).

Communications between husband and wife as to business matters admissible. — Under this section, neither husband nor wife can, without consent of the other, testify (either during the coverture or afterwards) as to any communication made by one to the other while married, but this rule of privilege does not apply to communications between husband and wife with regard to a business matter in which he is acting as her agent. Lurty v. Lurty, 107 Va. 466, 59 S.E. 405 (1907).

Communications include acts. — The immunity and ban of this section applies to and includes all information or knowledge privately imparted and made known by one spouse to the other by virtue of and in consequence of the marital relation through conduct, acts, signs and spoken or written words. Menefee v. Commonwealth, 189 Va. 900, 55 S.E.2d 9 (1949).

But a beating was not a communication within the meaning of this section for it did not impart knowledge or information made privileged. Osborne v. Commonwealth, 214 Va. 691, 204 S.E.2d 289 (1974).

This rule operates only where there is a valid marriage. United States v. Neeley, 475 F.2d 1136 (4th Cir. 1973).

When the defendant has never legally divorced his third wife he cannot rely on any exclusionary rules based on the existence of subsequent valid marriages. United States v. Neeley, 475 F.2d 1136 (4th Cir. 1973).

Adoption of wife's words by accused made them his own. — Where a defendant in a confession agreed with his wife's statement concerning what happened in the incident in which the defendant was involved, it was necessary to give content to his indication of acquiescence. His adoption of her words made them his own, and did not constitute testimony by the wife over the defendant's objection. Shiflett v. Virginia, 447 F.2d 50 (4th Cir. 1971), cert. denied, 405 U.S. 994, 92 S. Ct. 1267, 31 L. Ed. 2d 462 (1972).

Effect on burden of proof as to conveyances from husband to wife. — The doctrine in Virginia which places the burden upon those attempting to support a conveyance from a husband to the wife as against existing creditors of the husband is well settled, and while the section has made the testimony of either consort competent in controversies of this character, it has in no sense changed the burden or shifted the recognized presumptions in such cases. Davis v. Southern Distrib. Co., 148 Va. 779, 139 S.E. 495 (1927).

Both spouses have right to object. — The object of this section was to give to both spouses the right to object to the other testifying in violation of the section. Daniels v. Morris, 199 Va. 205, 98 S.E.2d 694 (1957).

Claim of privilege waived. — Wife's answer which was responsive to question asked by her husband's attorney waived his claim of privilege. Osborne v. Commonwealth, 214 Va. 691, 204 S.E.2d 289 (1974).

To allow a widow to testify as to privileged communication constitutes reversible error. Edmundson v. Edmundson, 11 Va. L. Reg. (n.s.) 30 (1925).

Section held not violated. — The examination of plaintiff's wife by plaintiff's counsel in an action for alienation of affection and criminal conversation did not violate the provisions of this section, where the record failed to show that any questions concerning private communications between husband and wife were involved, and no objections or exceptions were interposed by defendant's counsel to any question propounded. Daniels v. Morris, 199 Va. 205, 98 S.E.2d 694 (1957).

§ 8.01-399. Communications between physicians and patients. —
A. Except at the request or with the consent of the patient, no duly licensed practitioner of any branch of the healing arts shall be required to testify in any civil action, respecting any information which he may have acquired in attending, examining or treating the patient in a professional capacity.

B. Notwithstanding subsection A, when the physical or mental condition of the patient is at issue in a civil action, facts communicated to, or otherwise learned by, such practitioner in connection with such attendance, examination or treatment shall be disclosed but only in discovery pursuant to the Rules of Court or through testimony at the trial of the action. In addition, disclosure may be ordered when a court, in the exercise of sound discretion, deems it necessary to the proper administration of justice. However, no disclosure of facts communicated to, or otherwise learned by, such practitioner shall occur if the court determines, upon the request of the patient, that such facts are not relevant to the subject matter involved in the pending action or do not appear to be reasonably calculated to lead to the discovery of admissible evidence.

C. This section shall not (i) be construed to repeal or otherwise affect the provisions of § 65.2-607 relating to privileged communications between physicians and surgeons and employees under the Workers' Compensation Act or (ii) apply to information communicated to any such practitioner in an effort unlawfully to procure a narcotic drug, or unlawfully to procure the administration of any such drug.

D. Neither a lawyer, nor anyone acting on the lawyer's behalf, shall obtain, in connection with pending or threatened litigation, information from a practitioner of any branch of the healing arts without the consent of the patient, except through discovery pursuant to the Rules of the Court as herein provided. However, the prohibition of this subsection shall not apply to:

1. Communication between a lawyer retained to represent a practitioner of the healing arts, or that lawyer's agent, and that practitioner's employers, partners, agents, servants, employees, co-employees or others for whom, at law, the practitioner is or may be liable or who, at law, are or may be liable for the practitioner's acts or omissions;

2. Information about a patient provided to a lawyer or his agent by a practitioner of the healing arts employed by that lawyer to examine or evaluate the patient in accordance with Rule 4:10 of the Rules of the Supreme Court; or

3. Contact between a lawyer or his agent and a nonphysician employee or agent of a practitioner of healing arts for any of the following purposes: (i) scheduling appearances, (ii) requesting a written recitation by the practitioner of handwritten records obtained by the lawyer or his agent from the practitioner, provided the request is made in writing and, if litigation is pending, a copy of the request and the practitioner's response is provided simultaneously to the patient or his attorney, (iii) obtaining information necessary to obtain service upon the practitioner in pending litigation, (iv) determining when records summoned will be provided by the practitioner or his agent, (v) determining what patient records the practitioner possesses in order to summons records in pending litigation, (vi) explaining any summons which the lawyer or his agent caused to be issued and served on the practitioner, (vii) verifying dates the practitioner treated the patient, provided that if litigation is pending the information obtained by the lawyer or his agent is promptly given, in writing, to the patient or his attorney, (viii) determining charges by the practitioner for appearance at a deposition or to testify before any tribunal or administrative body, or (ix) providing to or obtaining from the practitioner directions to a place to which he is or will be summoned to give testimony.

E. A clinical psychologist duly licensed under the provisions of Chapter 36 (§ 54.1-3600 et seq.) of Title 54.1 shall be considered a practitioner of a branch of the healing arts within the meaning of this section.

§ 8.01-399 CODE OF VIRGINIA § 8.01-399

F. Nothing herein shall prevent a duly licensed practitioner of the healing arts from disclosing any information which he may have acquired in attending, examining or treating a patient in a professional capacity where such disclosure is necessary in connection with the care of the patient, the protection or enforcement of the practitioner's legal rights including such rights with respect to medical malpractice actions, or the operations of a health care facility or health maintenance organization or in order to comply with state or federal law. (Code 1950, § 8-289.1; 1956, c. 446; 1966, c. 673; 1977, c. 617; 1993, c. 556; 1996, cc. 937, 980; 1998, c. 314.)

REVISERS' NOTE

The only change in substance to former § 8-289.1 is to make § 8.01-399 applicable to all courts and not circuit courts only.

Cross references. — As to physicians permitting State Department of Health to examine records relating to diseases and death of patients, see §§ 32.1-40 and 32.1-41. As to the exemption from liability of physicians reporting disabilities to aircraft pilot licensing authorities, see § 54.1-2966.

Editor's note. — Legal Ethics Opinion Nos. 1042, 1158, and 1235 were overruled by subsection D of this section, as amended in 1993, the Virginia State Bar Standing Committee on Legal Ethics has determined. The subsection precludes a lawyer or anyone acting on the lawyer's behalf from obtaining, in connection with pending or threatened litigation, information from a practitioner of any branch of the healing arts without the consent of the patient except through discovery pursuant to the Rules of the Court.

Law Review. — For comment on confidential communication privileges under federal and Virginia law, see 13 U. Rich. L. Rev. 593 (1979). For a review of Fourth Circuit cases on criminal procedure, see 36 Wash. & Lee L. Rev. 485 (1979). For an article, "Civil Practice and Procedure," see 32 U. Rich. L. Rev. 1009 (1998).

I. Decisions Under Current Law.
II. Decisions Under Prior Law.

I. DECISIONS UNDER CURRENT LAW.

The "legal rights" referred to in subsection F include, but are not limited to, such rights "with respect to medical malpractice actions" and, thus, include such rights with respect to being deposed. Subsection F does not require that the physician be an actual or potential party to a medical malpractice action. Archambault v. Roller, 254 Va. 210, 491 S.E.2d 729 (1997).

Where insurance company presented no rationale for disclosure of life insurance beneficiary's medical records, other than to "see what information, if any, those medical records contained relating to the murder of the beneficiary's husband and her involvement therein," the trial court did not abuse its discretion in granting the beneficiary's motion to quash the insurance company's subpoena of those medical records. Peoples Sec. Life Ins. Co. v. Arrington, 243 Va. 89, 412 S.E.2d 705 (1992).

Applied in Seidman v. Fishburne-Hudgins Educ. Found., Inc., 724 F.2d 413 (4th Cir. 1984).

II. DECISIONS UNDER PRIOR LAW.

Editor's note. — The cases cited below were decided under corresponding provisions of former law. The term "this section," as used below, refers to former provisions.

Common law recognized no such privilege in either civil or criminal proceedings. Gibson v. Commonwealth, 216 Va. 412, 219 S.E.2d 845 (1975).

There exists no physician-patient privilege in a criminal prosecution in Virginia., Gibson v. Commonwealth, 216 Va. 412, 219 S.E.2d 845 (1975), cert. denied, 425 U.S. 994, 96 S. Ct. 2207, 48 L. Ed. 2d 819 (1976).

There exists no physician-patient privilege in a criminal prosecution in Virginia. In re Times-World Corp., 25 Va. App. 405, 488 S.E.2d 677 (1997).

Privilege confined to civil proceedings. — While Virginia has enacted a statutory privilege, it is expressly confined to civil proceedings. Gibson v. Commonwealth, 216 Va. 412, 219 S.E.2d 845 (1975), cert. denied, 425 U.S.

994, 96 S. Ct. 2207, 48 L. Ed. 2d 819 (1976).

Where physical condition of patient at issue. — The contents of a medical report, though arising out of the physician-patient relationship are not privileged if the physical condition of the patient is at issue in a legal proceeding. City of Portsmouth v. Cilumbrello, 204 Va. 11, 129 S.E.2d 31 (1963); In re Trinidad Corp., 238 F. Supp. 928 (E.D. Va. 1965).

Medical reports of a plaintiff in a civil action are not protected by the physician-patient privilege if the plaintiff's physical or mental condition is in issue. Wiggins v. Fairfax Park Ltd. Partnership, 22 Va. App. 432, 470 S.E.2d 591 (1996).

Physician required to testify. — The exception in this section was properly applied and a physician was required to testify where he had previously treated plaintiff and subsequently examined plaintiff for defendant's attorney. De Foe v. Duhl, 286 F.2d 205 (4th Cir. 1961).

§ 8.01-400. Communications between ministers of religion and persons they counsel or advise.

— No regular minister, priest, rabbi, or accredited practitioner over the age of eighteen years, of any religious organization or denomination usually referred to as a church, shall be required to give testimony as a witness or to relinquish notes, records or any written documentation made by such person, or disclose the contents of any such notes, records or written documentation, in discovery proceedings in any civil action which would disclose any information communicated to him in a confidential manner, properly entrusted to him in his professional capacity and necessary to enable him to discharge the functions of his office according to the usual course of his practice or discipline, wherein such person so communicating such information about himself or another is seeking spiritual counsel and advice relative to and growing out of the information so imparted. (Code 1950, § 8-289.2; 1962, c. 466; 1977, c. 617; 1979, c. 3; 1994, c. 198.)

REVISERS' NOTE

Former § 8-289.2 has been preserved except to change the age to 18.

Law Review. — For comment on confidential communication privileges under federal and Virginia law, see 13 U. Rich. L. Rev. 593 (1979). For survey on evidence in Virginia for 1989, see 23 U. Rich. L. Rev. 647 (1989).

I. DECISIONS UNDER CURRENT LAW.

To whom privilege granted. — The plain meaning of this section grants the privilege only to the minister, priest or rabbi, not to the penitent or lay communicant. Seidman v. Fishburne-Hudgins Educ. Found., Inc., 724 F.2d 413 (4th Cir. 1984).

Consent of penitent not required for disclosure. — Most penitent-priest statutes have a common feature: they explicitly prohibit the clergyman from disclosing the contents of a confidential communication "without the consent of the person making the communication." Significantly, this section contains no such prohibition; it simply says that "no regular minister, priest, rabbi or accredited practitioner . . . shall be required to disclose any information" entrusted to him in a confidential conversation. This language plainly invests the priest with the privilege and leaves it to his conscience to decide when disclosure is appropriate. Seidman v. Fishburne-Hudgins Educ. Found., Inc., 724 F.2d 413 (4th Cir. 1984).

Penitent's disclosures treated differently from disclosures to doctor or psychologist. — The legislature included provisions in §§ 8.01-399 and 8.01-400.2 which allow communicants to require doctors or psychologists to give testimony concerning confidential disclosures. The legislature's omission of a similar provision from the priest-penitent statute strongly indicates that the clergyman's privilege cannot be affected by the communicant. Seidman v. Fishburne-Hudgins Educ. Found., Inc., 724 F.2d 413 (4th Cir. 1984).

§ 8.01-400.1. Privileged communications by interpreters for the deaf.

— Whenever a deaf person communicates through an interpreter to any person under such circumstances that the communication would be privileged,

§ 8.01-400.2 CODE OF VIRGINIA § 8.01-401

and such person could not be compelled to testify as to the communications, this privilege shall also apply to the interpreter. (1978, c. 601.)

Cross references. — As to the visual electronic recording of the testimony of a deaf individual and the interpretation thereof for use in verification of the official transcript of civil proceedings, see § 8.01-406. As to privileged communications by interpreters for the deaf in criminal cases, see § 19.2-164.1.

Law Review. — For survey of Virginia law on evidence for the year 1977-1978, see 64 Va. L. Rev. 1451 (1978).

§ 8.01-400.2. Communications between counselors, social workers and psychologists and clients.

— Except at the request of or with the consent of the client, no licensed professional counselor, as defined in § 54.1-3500, licensed clinical social worker, as defined in § 54.1-3700, or licensed psychologist, as defined in § 54.1-3600, shall be required in giving testimony as a witness in any civil action to disclose any information communicated to him in a confidential manner, properly entrusted to him in his professional capacity and necessary to enable him to discharge his professional or occupational services according to the usual course of his practice or discipline, wherein such person so communicating such information about himself or another is seeking professional counseling or treatment and advice relative to and growing out of the information so imparted; provided, however, that when the physical or mental condition of the client is at issue in such action, or when a court, in the exercise of sound discretion, deems such disclosure necessary to the proper administration of justice, no fact communicated to, or otherwise learned by, such practitioner in connection with such counseling, treatment or advice shall be privileged, and disclosure may be required. The privileges conferred by this section shall not extend to testimony in matters relating to child abuse and neglect nor serve to relieve any person from the reporting requirements set forth in § 63.1-248.3. (1982, c. 537.)

I. DECISIONS UNDER CURRENT LAW.

Applied in Seidman v. Fishburne-Hudgins Educ. Found., Inc., 724 F.2d 413 (4th Cir. 1984).

§ 8.01-401. How adverse party may be examined; effect of refusal to testify.

— A. A party called to testify for another, having an adverse interest, may be examined by such other party according to the rules applicable to cross-examination.

B. If any party, required by another to testify on his behalf, refuses to testify, the court, officer, or person before whom the proceeding is pending, may, in addition to punishing said party as for contempt, dismiss the action, or other proceeding of the party so refusing, as to the whole or any part thereof, or may strike out and disregard the plea, answer, or other defense of such party, or any part thereof, as justice may require. (Code 1950, §§ 8-290, 8-291; 1977, c. 617.)

REVISERS' NOTE

Section 8.01-401 combines former §§ 8-290 and 8-291 and changes former § 8-290 to provide that the sanctions listed are cumulative, the court still being empowered to hold the refusing party in contempt.

Law Review. — For comment, "Expert Opinion from the Defendant-Physician," see 25 Wash. & Lee L. Rev. 115 (1968). For article reviewing recent developments and changes in legislation, case law, and Virginia Supreme Court Rules affecting civil litigation, see "Civil

Practice and Procedure," 26 U. Rich. L. Rev. 679 (1992).

I. Decisions Under Current Law.
II. Decisions Under Prior Law.

I. DECISIONS UNDER CURRENT LAW.

Applicability of subsection A. — Subsection A has been held applicable to criminal cases, and in that subsection, the word "party" is not limited to litigants. Sluss v. Commonwealth, No. 1252-93-3 (Ct. of Appeals Jan. 10, 1995).

Refusal to answer questions pertinent to the issues involved. — Implicit in subsection B of this section is the requirement that the party who is seeking affirmative relief and who has exercised the privilege against self-incrimination must have refused to answer questions pertinent to the issues involved; such party asserting the privilege must have frustrated an attempt by the other party to obtain information relevant to the cause of action alleged and to possible defenses to the claim. Davis v. Davis, 233 Va. 452, 357 S.E.2d 495 (1987).

Where the plaintiff's claims dealt with recovery of one-half of the proceeds of a cashier's check, the assertion by the defendant of his constitutional right against self-incrimination bore on issues relevant to those claims; however, the claims of the defendant set forth in the crossbill and counterclaim dealt with demands for debts allegedly due him by his former wife based on credit card charges and other advances made on her behalf, and his refusal to answer questions about the negotiation of the check was not pertinent to the issues involved in the claims which he sought to prosecute, nor did such conduct frustrate any attempt by the plaintiff to obtain information relevant to his claims against her or possible defenses to those claims; consequently, the trial court erred in striking the cross-bill and counterclaim pursuant to subsection B of this section. Davis v. Davis, 233 Va. 452, 357 S.E.2d 495 (1987).

Scope of examination of adverse witness. — This section, which applies in both criminal and civil actions, provides that a party may call to the stand a witness "having an adverse interest" and may examine the witness "according to the rules applicable to cross-examination." Weller v. Commonwealth, 16 Va. App. 886, 434 S.E.2d 330 (1993).

An employee of a party litigant is not per se an adverse witness. Hegwood v. Virginia Natural Gas, Inc., 256 Va. 362, 505 S.E.2d 372 (1998).

Witness must be hostile or adverse for this rule to apply. — The application of this rule is limited to instances when it is clear that the witness is in fact hostile or adverse at trial. The determination of whether a witness is "unwilling or hostile" is a matter that rests with the discretion of the trial court. Weller v. Commonwealth, 16 Va. App. 886, 434 S.E.2d 330 (1993).

This section also applies "where the witness has no adverse interest, but is shown to be adverse or hostile to the party introducing him." Weller v. Commonwealth, 16 Va. App. 886, 434 S.E.2d 330 (1993).

Adverse interest is more than testimony being adverse to calling party. — A nonparty witness does not have an "adverse interest" simply because his or her testimony is adverse to the calling party. The test is not whether the witness's testimony would necessarily be adverse, but whether the witness has an adverse interest. Weller v. Commonwealth, 16 Va. App. 886, 434 S.E.2d 330 (1993).

Adverse party may be impeached by prior inconsistent statements. — Where driver hit victim in a car accident, and the trial court permitted driver to call victim to the stand as a part of his case in rebuttal, solely to impeach her credibility, trial court did not err in permitting such impeachment on rebuttal even though it could have been done earlier in the cross-examination of victim, subsection A and § 8.01-403 do not preclude impeachment of an adverse party by prior inconsistent statements. Mastin v. Theirjung, 238 Va. 434, 384 S.E.2d 86 (1989).

Refusal to allow cross-examination as adverse witness proper. — The trial court properly refused to allow the defendant to cross-examine a defense witness who testified that he was at home at the time of the crimes at issue as an adverse witness, since the witness had been totally exonerated of the crimes by DNA testing, especially as the court allowed the defendant to thoroughly question the witness regarding his conflicting statements to the police. Painter v. Commonwealth, No. 1502-97-1 (Ct. of Appeals April 7, 1998).

II. DECISIONS UNDER PRIOR LAW.

Editor's note. — The cases cited below were decided under corresponding provisions of former law. The term "this section," as used below, refers to former provisions.

Strict construction required. — Subsection B of this section is in derogation of the common law, and, therefore, must be strictly construed. VEPCO v. Bowers, 181 Va. 542, 25 S.E.2d 361 (1943).

§ 8.01-401.1   CODE OF VIRGINIA   § 8.01-401.1

Section applies to criminal cases as well as civil cases. — The Supreme Court held in McCue v. Commonwealth, 103 Va. 870, 49 S.E. 623 (1905), that this section applies to criminal cases as well as civil cases. Trout v. Commonwealth, 167 Va. 511, 188 S.E. 219 (1936); Moore v. Commonwealth, 202 Va. 667, 119 S.E.2d 324 (1961).

What constitutes "adverse interest" defined. — By the use of the words "having an adverse interest," in this section, the legislature intended to include, first, a party to the litigation, and, second, a person, though not a party, who had a financial or other personal interest in the outcome. The legislature did not mean to include a party merely because his testimony was or would be adverse to the party calling him. "Adverse interest" was used in its common and accepted meaning and was not used synonymously with "adverse testimony." Butler v. Parrocha, 186 Va. 426, 43 S.E.2d 1 (1947); Matthews v. Hicks, 197 Va. 112, 87 S.E.2d 629 (1955); Daniels v. Morris, 199 Va. 205, 98 S.E.2d 694 (1957).

A contention that this section does not apply where a witness was not shown to have an adverse interest cannot be maintained. The section has expressly been held to apply where the witness has no adverse interest, but is shown to be adverse or hostile to the party introducing him. Nelson v. Commonwealth, 153 Va. 909, 150 S.E. 407 (1929). See Trout v. Commonwealth, 167 Va. 511, 188 S.E. 219 (1936).

"A party" means a litigant and not a mere witness. This is emphasized by subsection B authorizing the court to dismiss the suit "of the party so refusing," or to strike out the plea, answer, or other defense "of such party." VEPCO v. Bowers, 181 Va. 542, 25 S.E.2d 361 (1943).

Subsection B does not apply when attorney for defendant refuses to produce evidence. — Where attorney for defendant corporation refused to produce a statement of the operator of defendant's street car which had been involved in an accident, the court was not authorized to strike out defendant's plea of not guilty and order that the case proceed as on a writ of inquiry to assess the damages against defendant corporation. VEPCO v. Bowers, 181 Va. 542, 25 S.E.2d 361 (1943).

Effect of testimony. — In an action for personal injuries, plaintiff called the defendant as a witness in order that he might cross-examine him, a right accorded by this section. While plaintiff might not be bound by such of defendant's statements as might be in conflict with the evidence introduced on behalf of the plaintiff, plaintiff, the court, and the jury are bound by so much of the clear, logical testimony of the defendant as is reasonable and uncontradicted. Saunders v. Temple, 154 Va. 714, 153 S.E. 691 (1930).

Where defendant was called as an adverse witness by plaintiffs, plaintiffs were bound by so much of his testimony as was reasonable and uncontradicted. Crabtree v. Dingus, 194 Va. 615, 74 S.E.2d 54 (1953).

A litigant is bound by the uncontradicted evidence of his opponent when not inherently improbable and counter to no reasonable inference and this is especially true where the evidence is elicited from the opponent when called as an adverse witness. Hailey v. Johnson, 201 Va. 775, 113 S.E.2d 664 (1960).

Adverse party may not be impeached by evidence of bad character. — Where defendant's only testimony was given in response to questions asked by plaintiff's counsel when defendant was called as an adverse witness, and where there was a direct conflict in the pleadings and in the evidence as to the essential facts of the controversy, it was prejudicial error for the trial court to permit plaintiff to recall defendant at the conclusion of all the evidence for the sole purpose of asking him whether or not he had been convicted of a felony. Smith v. Lohr, 204 Va. 331, 130 S.E.2d 433 (1963).

§ 8.01-401.1. Opinion testimony by experts; hearsay exception. — In any civil action any expert witness may give testimony and render an opinion or draw inferences from facts, circumstances or data made known to or perceived by such witness at or before the hearing or trial during which he is called upon to testify. The facts, circumstances or data relied upon by such witness in forming an opinion or drawing inferences, if of a type normally relied upon by others in the particular field of expertise in forming opinions and drawing inferences, need not be admissible in evidence.

The expert may testify in terms of opinion or inference and give his reasons therefor without prior disclosure of the underlying facts or data, unless the court requires otherwise. The expert may in any event be required to disclose the underlying facts or data on cross-examination.

To the extent called to the attention of an expert witness upon cross-examination or relied upon by the expert witness in direct examination, statements contained in published treatises, periodicals or pamphlets on a subject of history, medicine or other science or art, established as a reliable authority by testimony or by stipulation shall not be excluded as hearsay. If admitted, the statements may be read into evidence but may not be received as exhibits. If the statements are to be introduced through an expert witness upon direct examination, copies of the statements shall be provided to opposing parties thirty days prior to trial unless otherwise ordered by the court. (1982, c. 392; 1994, c. 328.)

Law Review. — For article on the admissibility of written health care standards in medical and hospital negligence actions in Virginia, see 18 U. Rich. L. Rev. 725 (1984). For article, "Improving Expert Testimony," see 20 U. Rich. L. Rev. 473 (1986).

I. DECISIONS UNDER CURRENT LAW.

The text of this section gives it no broader scope than that of the parent federal rules, and the court would not attribute to the General Assembly any purpose beyond that which motivated the federal drafters; the admission of hearsay expert opinion without the testing safeguard of cross-examination is fraught with overwhelming unfairness to the opposing party. McMunn v. Tatum, 237 Va. 558, 379 S.E.2d 908 (1989).

Section limited to civil actions. — This section, which essentially adopts the view of the Federal Rules of Evidence 703 and 705, is expressly limited to "any civil action." This limitation is a clear expression of legislative intent to retain the historic restrictions upon expert testimony in criminal cases in Virginia. Simpson v. Commonwealth, 227 Va. 557, 318 S.E.2d 386 (1984).

Effect of 1994 amendment. — The 1994 amendment to this section made a substantive change in the statute. The statute as amended permits, in certain limited instances, the hearsay content of statements contained in published treatises, periodicals or pamphlets on a subject of history, medicine or other science or art, established as a reliable authority by testimony or by stipulation, to be read into the record as substantive evidence, provided no other evidentiary rule prohibits such admission. Weinberg v. Given, 252 Va. 221, 476 S.E.2d 502 (1996).

No litigant in our judicial system is required to contend with the opinions of absent experts whose qualifications have not been established to the satisfaction of the court, whose demeanor cannot be observed by the trier of fact, and whose pronouncements are immune from cross-examination. McMunn v. Tatum, 237 Va. 558, 379 S.E.2d 908 (1989).

Hypothetical questions are unnecessary where an expert testifies from his own knowledge of the facts disclosed in his testimony, or since 1982, where he renders an opinion from facts, circumstances or data made known to or perceived by such witness at or before the hearing or trial. Cantrell v. Commonwealth, 229 Va. 387, 329 S.E.2d 22 (1985), cert. denied, 496 U.S. 911, 110 S. Ct. 2600, 110 L. Ed. 2d 280 (1990).

Proof of similarity of conditions existing at time of tests and facts. — The trial court should refuse to admit expert testimony unless there is proof of a similarity of conditions existing at the time of the expert's tests and at the time relevant to the facts at issue. Tarmac Mid-Atlantic, Inc. v. Smiley Block Co., 250 Va. 161, 458 S.E.2d 462 (1995).

Expert may express opinion and draw inferences from inadmissible sources. — The language of the statute clearly allows the expert to express an opinion or draw inferences from inadmissible sources, such as hearsay. M.E.D. v. J.P.M., 3 Va. App. 391, 350 S.E.2d 215 (1986).

Ordinarily inadmissible facts and data may be revealed in the context of expert opinion. — The sources of such ordinarily inadmissible "facts and data" may be revealed to the fact finder in the context of expert opinion, and disclosure of the information itself "may in any event be required on cross-examination." Cox v. Oakwood Mining, Inc., 16 Va. App. 965, 434 S.E.2d 904 (1993).

Qualification of an expert witness does not insure admission of his every statement and opinion since this section allows an expert to express an opinion without initially disclosing the basis for the opinion and to base the opinion on hearsay evidence otherwise inadmissible but it does not, however, relieve the court from its responsibility, when proper objection is made, to determine whether the factors required to be included in formulating the opinion were actually utilized. Swiney v. Overby, 237 Va. 231, 377 S.E.2d 372 (1989).

Expert's reliance upon hearsay is a matter affecting weight to be given to his conclusions. M.E.D. v. J.P.M., 3 Va. App. 391, 350 S.E.2d 215 (1986).

Although appellant argued that in various respects expert's conclusions were open to challenge, any such weaknesses in his testimony were not grounds for its exclusion, but were matters properly to be considered by the jury in determining the weight to be given the evidence. Tarmac Mid-Atlantic, Inc. v. Smiley Block Co., 250 Va. 161, 458 S.E.2d 462 (1995).

§ 8.01-401.1 CODE OF VIRGINIA § 8.01-401.1

This section does not authorize the admission in evidence, upon the direct examination of an expert witness, of hearsay matters of opinion upon which the expert relied in reaching his own opinion, notwithstanding the fact that the opinion of the expert witness is itself admitted, and not withstanding the fact that the hearsay is of a type normally relied upon by others in the witness' particular field of expertise. McMunn v. Tatum, 237 Va. 558, 379 S.E.2d 908 (1989).

Expert opinion testimony based on hearsay factual information. — Expert opinion testimony is frequently based on hearsay factual information, and that is no bar to admission of the expert opinion in a civil case. Bowers v. Huddleston, 241 Va. 83, 399 S.E.2d 811 (1991).

A medical expert's recital of the confirming opinion of an absent physician is inadmissible hearsay. CSX Transp., Inv. v. Casale, 247 Va. 180, 441 S.E.2d 212 (1994).

Testimony based on mere assumption with no evidentiary support. — This section does not sanction the admission of expert testimony based upon a mere assumption which has no evidentiary support. Lawson v. Doe, 239 Va. 477, 391 S.E.2d 333 (1990).

Expert testimony is inadmissible if it is speculative or founded on assumptions that have no basis in fact. Tarmac Mid-Atlantic, Inc. v. Smiley Block Co., 250 Va. 161, 458 S.E.2d 462 (1995).

Opinion may not be based on facts not in evidence. — Generally, an expert witness in Virginia has not been permitted to base his opinion on facts not in evidence. Simpson v. Commonwealth, 227 Va. 557, 318 S.E.2d 386 (1984).

Consideration of all variables bearing on inferences drawn from facts. — Expert testimony should not be admitted unless the trial court is satisfied that the expert has considered all the variables bearing on the inferences to be drawn from the facts observed. Tarmac Mid-Atlantic, Inc. v. Smiley Block Co., 250 Va. 161, 458 S.E.2d 462 (1995).

An opponent of expert evidence need not wait until after the evidence has been admitted to assert a challenge, but may raise a challenge prior to trial by a motion to exclude the evidence or at trial by examining the expert, out of the presence of the jury, prior to a ruling on the admissibility of the test results; furthermore, the proponent of the evidence may be required to make a prior disclosure of the underlying facts or data relied on by the expert if the opponent of the evidence objects to admissibility of the test results or the expert's opinion. Commonwealth ex rel. Evans v. Harrison, 5 Va. App. 8, 360 S.E.2d 212 (1987).

When read together, this section and § 20-61.2 (see now § 20-49.3) allow the admission of the results of human leukocyte antigen blood tests and a properly qualified expert's opinion concerning the results; once the expert has testified that the blood samples tested were those of the parties involved, that his conclusion is based upon facts, circumstances, or data made known to or perceived by him and normally relied upon by others in his field of expertise, the test results and his expert opinion are prima facie admissible. Commonwealth ex rel. Evans v. Harrison, 5 Va. App. 8, 360 S.E.2d 212 (1987).

Unnecessarily narrow construction of § 65.2-504. — By declining to permit consideration of the autopsy evidence in conjunction with the several conflicting opinions from the radiographic evidence, through both direct and cross-examination of the experts, the commission adopted an unnecessarily narrow construction of § 65.2-504 (former § 65.1-56.1). Cox v. Oakwood Mining, Inc., 16 Va. App. 965, 434 S.E.2d 904 (1993).

Admission of hearsay testimony held reversible error. — In an action by an employee against a railroad company under the Federal Employer's Liability Act, 45 U.S.C. § 51 et seq., alleging personal injury, admission of hearsay consisting of testimony by one physician regarding a new and different diagnosis by another physician was material and prejudicial to the railroad's defense on the issue of damages, and therefore, constituted reversible error. CSX Transp., Inv. v. Casale, 247 Va. 180, 441 S.E.2d 212 (1994).

Expert's testimony failed to meet the fundamental requirements. There was no showing that the crash tests relied upon were conducted under conditions similar to those existing at the accident scene. More importantly, the expert never examined the vehicles involved in the collision; rather, he relied solely upon the photographs of the vehicles to determine the permanent crash damage thereto. Tittsworth v. Robinson, 252 Va. 151, 475 S.E.2d 261 (1996).

"Rental Rate Blue Book for Construction Equipment" was inadmissible hearsay where no expert witness tendered an opinion based on reference to that book and, instead, the book itself was tendered as authoritative evidence of its contents. Commonwealth v. Asphalt Roads & Materials, Inc., No. 1665-97-1 (Ct. of Appeals March 3, 1998).

Applied in Gaalaas ex rel. Gaalaas v. Morrison, 233 Va. 148, 353 S.E.2d 898 (1987); CSX Transp., Inc. v. Casale, 250 Va. 359, 463 S.E.2d 445 (1995).

§ **8.01-401.2. Chiropractor as expert witness.** — A doctor of chiropractic, when properly qualified, may testify as an expert witness in a court of law as to etiology, diagnosis, prognosis, and disability, including anatomical, physiological, and pathological considerations within the scope of the practice of chiropractic as defined in § 54.1-2900. (1984, c. 569.)

§ **8.01-401.3. Opinion testimony and conclusions as to facts critical to civil case resolution.** — A. In a civil proceeding, if scientific, technical, or other specialized knowledge will assist the trier of fact to understand the evidence or to determine a fact in issue, a witness qualified as an expert by knowledge, skill, experience, training, or education may testify thereto in the form of an opinion or otherwise.

B. No expert or lay witness while testifying in a civil proceeding shall be prohibited from expressing an otherwise admissible opinion or conclusion as to any matter of fact solely because that fact is the ultimate issue or critical to the resolution of the case. However, in no event shall such witness be permitted to express any opinion which constitutes a conclusion of law.

C. Except as provided by the provisions of this section, the exceptions to the "ultimate fact in issue" rule recognized in the Commonwealth prior to enactment of this section shall remain in full force. (1993, c. 909.)

I. DECISIONS UNDER CURRENT LAW.

Expert testimony is inadmissible if it is speculative or founded on assumptions that have no basis in fact. Tarmac Mid-Atlantic, Inc. v. Smiley Block Co., 250 Va. 161, 458 S.E.2d 462 (1995).

When expert testimony admissible. — Expert testimony is admissible where the jury is confronted with issues that require scientific or specialized knowledge or experience in order to be properly understood and which cannot be determined intelligently merely from the deductions made and inferences drawn on the basis of ordinary knowledge, common sense and practical experience gained in the ordinary affairs of life. Holmes v. Doe, 257 Va. 573, 515 S.E.2d 117 (1999).

When expert evidence inadmissible. — When the issue to be decided involves matters of common knowledge or those as to which the jury are as competent to form an intelligent and accurate opinion as the expert witness, expert evidence is inadmissible. Holcombe v. Nationsbank Fin. Servs. Corp., 248 Va. 445, 450 S.E.2d 158 (1994).

Proof of similarity of conditions existing at time of tests and facts. — The trial court should refuse to admit expert testimony unless there is proof of a similarity of conditions existing at the time of the expert's tests and at the time relevant to the facts at issue. Tarmac Mid-Atlantic, Inc. v. Smiley Block Co., 250 Va. 161, 458 S.E.2d 462 (1995).

Expert testimony should not be admitted unless the trial court is satisfied that the expert has considered all the variables bearing on the inferences to be drawn from the facts observed. Tarmac Mid-Atlantic, Inc. v. Smiley Block Co., 250 Va. 161, 458 S.E.2d 462 (1995).

An expert may give opinions either based upon his own knowledge of facts disclosed in his testimony or he may give an opinion based upon facts in evidence assumed in a hypothetical question. Davison v. Commonwealth, 18 Va. App. 496, 445 S.E.2d 683 (1994).

Expert's testimony failed to meet fundamental requirements, where there was no showing that crash tests relied upon were conducted under conditions similar to those existing at the accident scene. More importantly, the expert never examined the vehicles involved in the collision; rather, he relied solely upon the photographs of the vehicles to determine the permanent crash damage thereto. Tittsworth v. Robinson, 252 Va. 151, 475 S.E.2d 261 (1996).

It was error to prohibit expert accountant from expressing his opinion regarding the cause of plaintiff's losses, where he had analyzed plaintiff's financial statements and had considered the records of other dealerships in the area and the industry in general, since he had corrected laid a proper foundation for the formation of his opinion. R.K. Chevrolet, Inc. v. Hayden, 480 S.E.2d 477 (1997).

Expert testimony in automobile accident case about average driver reaction times lacked the required foundation where there was no evidence that the defendant driver's physical and mental characteristics relevant to his perception and reaction times placed him within the average range of persons tested for reaction times. Keesee v. Donigan, 259 Va. 157, 524 S.E.2d 645 (2000).

Matters properly considered by jury. — Although appellant argued that in various respects expert's conclusions were open to chal-

§ 8.01-402

lenge, any such weaknesses in his testimony were not grounds for its exclusion, but were matters properly to be considered by the jury in determining the weight to be given the evidence. Tarmac Mid-Atlantic, Inc. v. Smiley

Block Co., 250 Va. 161, 458 S.E.2d 462 (1995).

Applied in Franconia Assocs. v. Clark, 250 Va. 444, 463 S.E.2d 670 (1995); Price v. Taylor, 251 Va. 82, 466 S.E.2d 87 (1996).

§ **8.01-402. Members of Department of Motor Vehicles' Crash Investigation Team not to be required to give evidence in certain cases.** — No member of the Department of Motor Vehicles' Crash Investigation Team shall be required to give evidence concerning any statements made to him in the course of such investigation before any court or grand jury in any case involving a motor vehicle crash on the highways of the Commonwealth in which any member or members of such Crash Investigation Team made or took part in any investigation pursuant to a directive from the Commissioner of the Department of Motor Vehicles for purposes of research and evaluation of the Commonwealth's highway safety program. (Code 1950, § 8-296.1; 1974, c. 390; 1977, c. 617; 1992, c. 108.)

Cross references. — As to applicability of §§ 8.01-396.1, 8.01-402, 8.01-405, and 8.01-407 through 8.01-410 to criminal cases, see § 19.2-267.

§ **8.01-403. Witness proving adverse; contradiction; prior inconsistent statement.** — A party producing a witness shall not be allowed to impeach his credit by general evidence of bad character, but he may, in case the witness shall in the opinion of the court prove adverse, by leave of the court, prove that he has made at other times a statement inconsistent with his present testimony; but before such last mentioned proof can be given the circumstances of the supposed statement, sufficient to designate the particular occasion, must be mentioned to the witness, and he must be asked whether or not he has made such statement. In every such case the court, if requested by either party, shall instruct the jury not to consider the evidence of such inconsistent statements, except for the purpose of contradicting the witness. (Code 1950, § 8-292; 1977, c. 617.)

Law Review. — For comment on a comparison of Uniform Rules of Evidence 63 (1) and (4) and Virginia law, see 18 Wash. & Lee L. Rev. 358 (1961). For survey of Virginia law on evidence for the year 1977-1978, see 64 Va. L. Rev. 1451 (1978). As to prior inconsistent statements of a party's own witness, see 22 U. Rich. L. Rev. 621 (1988).

I. Decisions Under Current Law.
II. Decisions Under Prior Law.

I. DECISIONS UNDER CURRENT LAW.

This section applies to criminal as well as civil cases. Brown v. Commonwealth, 6 Va. App. 82, 366 S.E.2d 716 (1988).

"Adverse" construed. — This section refers only to a witness who "proves adverse," namely, "a witness whom the party expected to testify favorably has suddenly turned sour and testified unfavorably." The determination whether a witness has proved to be "adverse" rests within the sound discretion of the trial court. Sluss v. Commonwealth, No. 1252-93-3 (Ct. of Appeals Jan. 10, 1995).

Prior inconsistent statements are admitted solely to attack credibility of witness who has told different stories at different times. They are not evidence of the truth of the content of the statements, and the court must so instruct the jury. Hall v. Commonwealth, 233 Va. 369, 355 S.E.2d 591 (1987).

Adverse party may be impeached by prior inconsistent statements. — Where driver hit victim in a car accident, and the trial court permitted driver to call victim to the stand as a part of his case in rebuttal, solely to impeach her credibility, trial court did not err in permitting such impeachment on rebuttal even though it could have been done earlier in the cross-examination of victim, § 8.01-401 A and this section do not preclude impeachment of an adverse party by prior inconsistent statements. Mastin v. Theirjung, 238 Va. 434, 384 S.E.2d 86 (1989).

Foundation must be laid. — The statute clearly requires that a foundation be laid by confronting the witness with the specific statements he allegedly made. Underwood v. Brown, 1 Va. App. 318, 338 S.E.2d 854 (1986).

Impeachment is not allowed if testimony simply fails to meet litigant's expectations. Underwood v. Brown, 1 Va. App. 318, 338 S.E.2d 854 (1986).

If testimony is negative in character and of no probative value to the fact finder, there is no statutory basis for impeachment. Underwood v. Brown, 1 Va. App. 318, 338 S.E.2d 854 (1986).

Impeachment improper where testimony conformed with affidavit. — Where trial counsel testified at the plenary hearing on the habeas corpus petition in conformance with his affidavit, which was filed over five months prior to the hearing, the habeas court should not have allowed petitioner's counsel at the hearing to impeach trial counsel's testimony at the hearing with evidence of alleged prior inconsistent statements, since counsel at the hearing could not reasonably claim surprise. The fact that the trial counsel did not recall the alleged inconsistent statements made during an earlier telephone conversation carried no probative value. Underwood v. Brown, 1 Va. App. 318, 338 S.E.2d 854 (1986).

Impeachment not erroneously allowed where questions were for purpose of resolving inconsistency. — The court did not erroneously permit the Commonwealth to impeach one of its witnesses, the local medical examiner, whose testimony allegedly proved adverse to the Commonwealth, where the questions put to the local medical examiner were simply to resolve an apparent inconsistency in his testimony and introduce his best recollection. Williams v. Commonwealth, 234 Va. 168, 360 S.E.2d 361 (1987), cert. denied, 484 U.S. 1020, 108 S. Ct. 733, 98 L. Ed. 2d 681 (1988), cert. denied, 484 U.S. 1020, 108 S. Ct. 733, 98 L. Ed. 2d 681 (1988).

Refusal to allow impeachment held proper. — The trial court properly refused to allow the defendant to impeach a defense witness under this section, since the witness had been totally exonerated of the crimes by DNA testing and his testimony was not damaging or injurious to the defendant's case, especially as the court allowed the defendant to thoroughly question the witness regarding his conflicting statements to the police. Painter v. Commonwealth, No. 1502-97-1 (Ct. of Appeals April 7, 1998).

Use of preliminary hearing transcript to impeach. — Where the Commonwealth's attorney asked an evasive witness whether he remembered testifying at the preliminary hearing of the case and, receiving an affirmative reply, the prosecutor read from a transcript of the preliminary hearing and called his attention to several statements that were inconsistent with his testimony at trial, and the trial court told the jury in an oral instruction that the witness' prior statements were not substantive evidence and could not be considered on the question of the defendant's guilt or innocence but solely for the purpose of affecting his credibility, the procedure followed by the trial court was sanctioned by this section. Roberts v. Commonwealth, 230 Va. 264, 337 S.E.2d 255 (1985).

Testimony must be injurious or damaging to the case for grounds of impeachment. — In order to impeach one's own witness it is not sufficient merely that the witness gave a contradictory statement on a prior occasion, rather, the testimony offered must be injurious or damaging to the case of the party who called the witness. Ragland v. Commonwealth, 16 Va. App. 913, 434 S.E.2d 675 (1993).

Testimony having no probative value not subject of impeachment. — Commonwealth's witness' testimony that he did not know either defendant or murder victim and did not see stabbing had no probative value, as it could not have assisted the trier of fact in determining defendant's guilt or innocence, and thus was neither damaging nor injurious to the Commonwealth's case. Therefore, this witness's testimony was not subject to impeachment, and the trial court erred when it allowed police officer to testify that witness gave a statement to him that he saw defendant stab fellow inmate. Brown v. Commonwealth, 6 Va. App. 82, 366 S.E.2d 716 (1988).

If the testimony is of a negative character and has no probative value, there is no statutory basis for impeachment. Ragland v. Commonwealth, 16 Va. App. 913, 434 S.E.2d 675 (1993).

Applied in Smallwood v. Commonwealth, No. 1616-96-1 (Ct. of Appeals February 17, 1998).

II. DECISIONS UNDER PRIOR LAW.

Editor's note. — The cases cited below were decided under corresponding provisions of former law. The term "this section," as used below, refers to former provisions.

Section applies to criminal as well as civil cases. — This section allowing a party whose witness has unexpectedly proved adverse, with leave of the court, to prove his prior inconsistent statements, applies to criminal as well as civil cases. Its language is broad and general, and there is no suggestion on its face to limit its operation to civil cases. While it is true that the statute is found in the Code under the title "proceedings in civil cases," yet, in the same chapter with that section, there are other sections applicable alike, by their terms, to criminal and civil cases, and the mere collocation of that section cannot be permitted to override every other consideration, and require the courts to confine it to civil cases, when it is a remedy for an evil as great in criminal cases as in civil, and the consequences of which may be even more serious. McCue v. Commonwealth, 103 Va. 870, 49 S.E. 623 (1905).

This section, as to proof of inconsistent statements where a witness in the opinion of the court proves adverse to the party introducing him, applies to criminal as well as civil cases. Tate v. Commonwealth, 155 Va. 1016, 154 S.E. 508 (1930).

Application within discretion of court. — The ruling of the trial court permitting the Commonwealth's attorney to cross-examine three witnesses for the Commonwealth relative to alleged prior inconsistent statements, was held to be within his sound judicial discretion, and there was nothing to show that it had been abused. Trout v. Commonwealth, 167 Va. 511, 188 S.E. 219 (1936).

"Adverse interest" and "adverse testimony" distinguished. — It is to be noted that the words "adverse interest" are not used in this section, but the language is "in case the witness shall in the opinion of the court prove adverse." Here "adverse" is also used as an adjective to describe the word "witness," meaning his testimony. The distinction between "adverse interest" and "adverse testimony" has not always been observed in the cases construing this section and § 8.01-401. Butler v. Parrocha, 186 Va. 426, 43 S.E.2d 1 (1947).

Proof that witness is not adverse. — In the instant case the prosecution claimed that a witness introduced by it had turned adverse, which contention was supported by the trial court. There was no suggestion that the witness had ever made any inconsistent statements, and no effort was made to prove that he had ever done so. Nor did it appear from the record that the witness was adverse or had made inconsistent statements on former occasions. Some of his testimony supported the theory of the prosecution, and some of it the theory of the defense. It was held that the claim that the witness had proved adverse could not be maintained. Tate v. Commonwealth, 155 Va. 1016, 154 S.E. 508 (1930).

Testimony to be adverse must be injurious or damaging. — One is not permitted to impeach his own witness merely because the latter does not come up to his expectation. It is only when the testimony of the witness is injurious or damaging to the case of the party introducing him that the witness can be said to be adverse so as to justify his impeachment. If the testimony is of a negative character and has no probative value, there is no need to discredit the witness. VEPCO v. Hall, 184 Va. 102, 34 S.E.2d 382 (1945).

Limitations on right of contradiction of own witness. — The right of contradiction of one's own witness under this section is subject to these limitations: (1) The trial court, and not counsel, is the judge as to whether a witness has proven adverse or hostile to the party introducing him; (2) the purpose of such contradiction is merely to impeach the credit of the witness and show that he is unworthy of belief. His prior inconsistent statements are not substantive evidence of the matters therein contained. VEPCO v. Hall, 184 Va. 102, 34 S.E.2d 382 (1945).

Adverse witness may not be impeached by evidence of bad character. — A reading of the Code nowhere indicates that it was the intention of the legislature to permit a litigant to call an adverse witness for the purpose of helping his case and later impeach his credibility by evidence of bad character. Such a rule would permit one to call a witness known to be unworthy of belief for the purpose of proving his case. Smith v. Lohr, 204 Va. 331, 130 S.E.2d 433 (1963).

Witness' character cannot be discredited by opinions of prosecuting attorney. — As a witness cannot under this section be impeached by general evidence of his bad character; a fortiori he should not be discredited before the jury by opinions of the prosecuting attorney with respect to his character. Tate v. Commonwealth, 155 Va. 1016, 154 S.E. 508 (1930); Green v. Commonwealth, 122 Va. 862, 94 S.E. 940 (1918).

Place not material in laying foundation for contradictory statement. — A party may contradict his own witness who appears to be adverse by other testimony, provided foundation is laid for such contradictory evidence by first calling to the attention of the witness the circumstances of the supposed contradictory statement sufficiently to designate the particular occasion. This should usually embrace the time, place and person to whom the statement was made, but the omission of place will not be material where it is evident the witness fully understood the occasion referred to. Gordon v. Funkhouser, 100 Va. 675, 42 S.E. 677 (1902).

Details of prior inconsistent statements may be given. — In proving the prior inconsistent statements of a witness who has unexpectedly proven adverse to the party calling, the party is not restricted by the provisions of this section to proof of the fact that such statements were made, but may give in evidence the details of such statements. McCue v. Commonwealth, 103 Va. 870, 49 S.E. 623 (1905).

Effect of statements made by adverse witnesses. — A party is not bound by all the statements of a witness called by him, if adverse, even though no other witnesses are called against him. The witness may, on a material point, be contradicted by the physical facts proved by any other competent evidence introduced in the case. Washington & Old Dominion Ry. v. Jackson's Adm'r, 117 Va. 636, 85 S.E. 496 (1915).

Inconsistent statements only for purpose of contradicting witness. — An instruction that the jury could consider alleged inconsistent statements of adverse witness only for the purpose of contradicting him was held in accord with this section. Yellow Cab Co. v. Eden, 178 Va. 325, 16 S.E.2d 625 (1941).

And jury should be so instructed. — Where a State witness turns out to be adverse, and his evidence takes the prosecution by surprise, it is proper under this section to impeach, by proof of his prior inconsistent statements, the witness' credibility, and to so instruct the jury. Hardy v. Commonwealth, 110 Va. 910, 67 S.E. 522 (1910).

Review. — The trial court sees and hears a witness on the stand and observes his demeanor, and hence is in a much better position to determine whether he is in fact adverse or hostile, within the meaning of this section than is an appellate court which must rely on the printed record. VEPCO v. Hall, 184 Va. 102, 34 S.E.2d 382 (1945).

§ 8.01-404. Contradiction by prior inconsistent writing. — A witness may be cross-examined as to previous statements made by him in writing or reduced into writing, relative to the subject matter of the civil action, without such writing being shown to him; but if it is intended to contradict such witness by the writing, his attention must, before such contradictory proof can be given, be called to the particular occasion on which the writing is supposed to have been made, and he may be asked if he did not make a writing of the purport of the one to be offered to contradict him, and if he denies making it, or does not admit its execution, it shall then be shown to him, and if he admits its genuineness, he shall be allowed to make his own explanation of it; but it shall be competent for the court at any time during the trial to require the production of the writing for its inspection, and the court may thereupon make such use of it for the purpose of the trial as it may think best. This section is subject to the qualification, that in an action to recover for a personal injury or death by wrongful act or neglect, no ex parte affidavit or statement in writing other than a deposition, after due notice, of a witness and no extrajudicial recording of the voice of such witness, or reproduction or transcript thereof, as to the facts or circumstances attending the wrongful act or neglect complained of, shall be used to contradict him as a witness in the case. Nothing in this section shall be construed to prohibit the use of any such ex parte affidavit or statement in an action on an insurance policy based upon a judgment recovered in a personal injury or death by wrongful act case. (Code 1950, § 8-293; 1958, c. 380; 1960, c. 114; 1964, c. 356; 1977, c. 617.)

REVISERS' NOTE

The sentence in former § 8-293 applying its provisions to criminal cases has been deleted. Also, the phrase "civil action" has been inserted in the first sentence to provide that § 8.01-404 applies to all civil proceedings.

Law Review. — For survey of Virginia law on evidence for the year 1969-1970, see 56 Va. L. Rev. 1325 (1970).

I. Decisions Under Current Law.
II. Decisions Under Prior Law.
  A. General Consideration.
  B. Personal Injury and Wrongful Death Actions.

I. DECISIONS UNDER CURRENT LAW.

Exclusionary sentence did not apply to document. — Where investigator for bus company wrote out a statement from plaintiff who was in a car accident, and where investigator testified as to the writing, exclusionary sentence (second sentence) of this section did not

§ 8.01-404 CODE OF VIRGINIA § 8.01-404

prohibit bus company's use of bus company investigator's document to contradict plaintiff, whether in her cross-examination or by its use as part of the bus company's case in chief, as the written document was neither signed by the plaintiff nor in the handwriting of the plaintiff. However, the document should not have been made an exhibit. Scott v. Greater Richmond Transit Co., 241 Va. 300, 402 S.E.2d 214 (1991).

II. DECISIONS UNDER PRIOR LAW.

A. General Consideration.

Editor's note. — The cases cited below were decided under corresponding provisions of former law. The term "this section," as used below, refers to former provisions.

Writings not per se admissible under section. — This section does not per se render admissible in evidence a writing which independently of the statute would be inadmissible. The use herein referred to means legitimate use. Ellison v. Commonwealth, 130 Va. 748, 107 S.E. 697 (1921).

This section is confined to the contradiction of a witness by the introduction of a prior inconsistent statement in writing. Harris v. Harrington, 180 Va. 210, 22 S.E.2d 13 (1942); Alspaugh v. Diggs, 195 Va. 1, 77 S.E.2d 362 (1953).

Motion to suppress deposition for violation of this section made too late. — See Ketchmark v. Lindauer, 198 Va. 42, 92 S.E.2d 286 (1956).

Contradictory evidence must be introduced by leave of court and after the witness has been fully put on guard with respect to it. Green v. Commonwealth, 122 Va. 862, 94 S.E. 940 (1918).

And proper foundation must be laid. — This section was intended to permit the introduction of a prior inconsistent statement only after a proper foundation is laid. Saunders v. Hall, 176 Va. 526, 11 S.E.2d 592 (1940).

Error to force defendant to produce statement when foundation not laid. — In the instant case while a witness was being examined in chief by counsel for the plaintiff, he stated that "they claim I heard the whistle blow and the gong was sounded, but I did not hear either one, I didn't see the train even." To this counsel for defendant objected. Thereupon counsel for plaintiff called on defendant's counsel "to produce any statement they have now," and the court compelled counsel for defendant, over their objection, to produce a statement in their possession which the witness had previously made to an agent of the company as to the blowing of the whistle and sounding of the gong. The statement of the witness had in no way been mentioned or referred to by counsel for the defendant. It had not been produced in court and made use of in the examination of the witness. This was held error. Norfolk & W. Ry. v. Wilkes' Adm'r, 137 Va. 302, 119 S.E. 122 (1923).

Cross-examination as to the contents of paper. — After a witness has been put on his guard and questioned as to the contents of a paper which he said he had rewritten, he may, on cross-examination, be further asked if he had not on a former occasion (fixing time and place) made statements contradictory of his testimony as to the contents of the paper, for the purpose of testing the witness as to his recollection and credibility, and of contradicting him, if he denies it. Lester v. Simpkins, 117 Va. 55, 83 S.E. 1062 (1915).

No necessity of introducing writing when admitted by witness. — Where in a prosecution for larceny, witness's attention was called to statements made by him in a prior affidavit relating to the same matter which were in conflict with his present testimony, and he was asked to explain the conflict, the defendant was not obliged to show the affidavit to the witness at this stage of his examination, and, as witness admitted making the affidavit, was under no obligation to show it to him or offer it in evidence. Ellison v. Commonwealth, 130 Va. 748, 107 S.E. 697 (1921).

First part of section applies only to cross-examination of a witness. — The first part of this section, as to the contradiction of a witness by a prior inconsistent writing, applies only to the cross-examination of a witness, "as to previous statements made by him in writing or reduced into writing," and not to an examination in chief of one's own witness. Norfolk & W. Ry. v. Wilkes' Adm'r, 137 Va. 302, 119 S.E. 122 (1923).

"Witness" as including real parties. — It was held unnecessary to decide whether the words, "a witness," as used in this section include real parties. VEPCO v. Mitchell, 159 Va. 855, 164 S.E. 800 (1933).

B. Personal Injury and Wrongful Death Actions.

Effect of second sentence of section. — The trial judge was right in refusing to allow a witness, in an action for personal injuries, to be questioned as to contradictory statements made by him on the day of the accident when it became manifest that it was the intention of the defendant to contradict the witness by a prior inconsistent written statement. Any other ruling would have annulled this section. Washington & Old Dominion Ry. v. Weakley, 140 Va. 796, 125 S.E. 672 (1924).

Under the first sentence of this section, a prior inconsistent statement of a witness is admissible to impeach him if the terms of the statute are met. However, under the second sentence of this section, a prior written statement of a witness may not be used to contradict the witness where the action is one to recover for a personal injury or to recover for death by wrongful act or neglect unless it be in the form of a deposition taken after due notice. Saunders v. Hall, 176 Va. 526, 11 S.E.2d 592 (1940).

The introduction in evidence of a prior ex parte written statement signed by an interested party is within the purview of the second sentence of this section and cannot be used for the purpose of contradicting him. Alspaugh v. Diggs, 195 Va. 1, 77 S.E.2d 362 (1953).

The second sentence was intended to correct abuses of taking statements shortly after accident. — The purpose of the second sentence of this section was to correct the unfair practice of contradicting a witness by a written statement taken shortly after an accident, resulting in death or personal injury, when such witness may not have fully recovered from the shock and may not be in full possession of his faculties. Harris v. Harrington, 180 Va. 210, 22 S.E.2d 13 (1942); Robertson v. Commonwealth, 181 Va. 520, 25 S.E.2d 352 (1943). See Liberty Mut. Ins. Co. v. Venable, 194 Va. 357, 73 S.E.2d 366 (1952); Alspaugh v. Diggs, 195 Va. 1, 77 S.E.2d 362 (1953).

But it does not prohibit oral proof of prior inconsistent statements. — To the extent that the second sentence of this section was intended to correct abuses, it is a modification of the rule as to best evidence, but it was never intended to prohibit the proof of prior inconsistent statements by oral testimony. Harris v. Harrington, 180 Va. 210, 22 S.E.2d 13 (1942). See Alspaugh v. Diggs, 195 Va. 1, 77 S.E.2d 362 (1953).

It was the intention of the 1919 Code Revisors, in adding the second sentence to this section, to permit the jury to determine the truth of the matter under investigation from an oral examination of the witnesses on the stand, uninfluenced by an ex parte written statement prepared by an interested party for the purpose of introducing it in evidence. Harris v. Harrington, 180 Va. 210, 22 S.E.2d 13 (1942).

Impeachment of a witness by the testimony of a former attorney for defendants who had interviewed this witness a few days after the accident, was not inadmissible under the second sentence of this section, notwithstanding that the substance of the interview had been reduced to writing, where counsel who attempted to impeach the witness made no reference to a written statement but confined his questions to oral statements made by the witness, and signified his intention to contradict the witness by the oral testimony of the attorney who had interviewed her. Harris v. Harrington, 180 Va. 210, 22 S.E.2d 13 (1942).

This section, before its amendment by Acts 1958, c. 380, unconditionally declared "that in an action to recover for a personal injury or death by wrongful act or neglect, no ex parte affidavit or statement in writing other than a deposition, . . . shall be used to contradict him as a witness in the case." Though the ex parte statement was voluntarily made by the injured party, yet it could not be thereafter used though affiant's adversary might be dependent upon it to establish his nonliability on an asserted claim. This section did not, however, prohibit the admission in evidence of a prior inconsistent oral statement. Public Fin. Corp. v. Londeree, 200 Va. 607, 106 S.E.2d 760 (1959).

Only deposition taken on notice may be used. — This section prohibits the introduction in evidence of a statement of a witness to an accident involving personal injury unless it is a deposition taken on notice. Krizak v. W.C. Brooks & Sons, 320 F.2d 37 (4th Cir. 1963).

Second sentence applies only to tort actions for personal injury or death. — The qualification appearing in the second sentence of this section is specifically made applicable only to actions to recover for personal injury or death by wrongful act. While the "unfair practice" referred to in Harris v. Harrington, 180 Va. 210, 22 S.E.2d 13 (1942), might well be prevalent in other types of actions, the statutory qualification, as written, applies only to tort actions for personal injury or death by wrongful act. Liberty Mut. Ins. Co. v. Venable, 194 Va. 357, 73 S.E.2d 366 (1952).

Where plaintiff obtained judgment against insured's employee for injuries sustained in accident while riding in insured's truck driven by employee, action by plaintiff against insurance carrier under "omnibus clause" of policy on truck issued to insured was based on a contract, the policy of insurance, and was not an action to recover for personal injury or death by wrongful act. Thus, the qualification of the second sentence of this section was not applicable to such suit. Liberty Mut. Ins. Co. v. Venable, 194 Va. 357, 73 S.E.2d 366 (1952).

But applies to litigant called as a witness as well as to disinterested party. — The second sentence of this section makes no distinction between a witness who is a party to the action and a witness who is not. The same reasons which led to the adoption of the statute would seem to apply to a party litigant, if called as a witness, as well as to a disinterested party. Alspaugh v. Diggs, 195 Va. 1, 77 S.E.2d 362 (1953).

Report by motorman to employer of accident cannot be used to contradict motorman. — Written statement or report of accident made by streetcar motorman to his employer, which was not in the form of a deposition taken after due notice, under the express terms of this section was not admissible for the purpose of contradicting the motorman. Robertson v. Commonwealth, 181 Va. 520, 25 S.E.2d 352 (1943).

§ **8.01-405. Who may administer oath to witness.** — Any person before whom a witness is to be examined may administer an oath to such witness. In addition, a clerk or deputy clerk may administer an oath to a witness in the presence and at the direction of a judge before whom the witness is to be examined. (Code 1950, § 8-294; 1977, c. 617; 1984, c. 536.)

Cross references. — As to applicability of §§ 8.01-396.1, 8.01-402, 8.01-405, and 8.01-407 through 8.01-410 to criminal cases, see § 19.2-267.

§ **8.01-406. Interpreters; recording testimony of deaf witness.** — Interpreters shall be sworn truly so to do. In any judicial proceeding, the judge on his own motion or on the motion of a party to the proceeding may order all of the testimony of a deaf individual and the interpretation thereof to be visually electronically recorded for use in verification of the official transcript of the proceedings. (Code 1950, § 8-295; 1977, c. 617; 1978, c. 601.)

Cross references. — As to privileged communications by interpreters for the deaf, see § 8.01-400.1. As to the visual electronic recording of the testimony of a deaf individual and the interpretation thereof for use in verification of the official transcript of criminal proceedings, see § 19.2-164.1.

ARTICLE 5.

Compelling Attendance of Witnesses, etc.

§ **8.01-407. (Contingent expiration date — See note) How summons for witness issued, and to whom directed; prior permission of court to summon certain officials and judges; attendance before commissioner of other state; attorney-issued summons.** — A. A summons may be issued, directed as prescribed in § 8.01-292, commanding the officer to summon any person to attend on the day and at the place that such attendance is desired, to give evidence before a court, grand jury, arbitrators, magistrate, notary, or any commissioner or other person appointed by a court or acting under its process or authority in a judicial or quasi-judicial capacity. The summons may be issued by the clerk of the court if the attendance is desired at a court or in a proceeding pending in a court. The clerk shall not impose any time restrictions limiting the right to properly request a summons up to and including the date of the proceeding:

If attendance is desired before a commissioner in chancery or other commissioner of a court, the summons may be issued by the clerk of the court in which the matter is pending, or by such commissioner in chancery or other commissioner;

If attendance is desired before a notary or other officer taking a deposition, the summons may be issued by such notary or other officer at the instance of the attorney desiring the attendance of the person sought;

If attendance is sought before a grand jury, the summons may be issued by the attorney for the Commonwealth, or the clerk of the court, at the instance of the attorney for the Commonwealth.

Except as otherwise provided in this subsection, if attendance is desired in a civil proceeding pending in a court or at a deposition in connection with such proceeding, a summons may be issued by an attorney-at-law who is an active member of the Virginia State Bar at the time of issuance, as an officer of the court. An attorney-issued summons shall be on a form approved by the

§ 8.01-407 CIVIL REMEDIES AND PROCEDURE § 8.01-407

Supreme Court, signed by the attorney and shall include the attorney's address. The summons shall be deemed to be a pleading to which the provisions of § 8.01-271.1 shall apply. A copy of the summons, together with payment of all clerk's fees, if applicable, and, if served by a sheriff, all service of process fees, shall be mailed or delivered to the clerk's office of the court in which the case is pending on the day of issuance by the attorney. The law governing summonses issued by a clerk shall apply mutatis mutandis. When an attorney-at-law transmits one or more attorney-issued subpoenas to a sheriff to be served in his jurisdiction, such subpoenas shall be accompanied by a transmittal sheet. The transmittal sheet, which may be in the form of a letter, shall contain for each subpoena: (i) the person to be served, (ii) the name of the city or county in which the subpoena is to be served, in parentheses, (iii) the style of the case in which the subpoena was issued, (iv) the court in which the case is pending, and (v) the amount of fees tendered or paid to each clerk in whose court the case is pending together with a photocopy of the payment instrument or clerk's receipt. If copies of the same transmittal sheet are used to send subpoenas to more than one sheriff for service of process, then subpoenas shall be grouped by the jurisdiction in which they are to be served. Such transmittal sheet shall be signed by the transmitting attorney under penalty of perjury. For each person to be served, an original subpoena and copy thereof shall be included. If the attorney desires a return copy of the transmittal sheet as proof of receipt, he shall also enclose an additional copy of the transmittal sheet together with an envelope addressed to the attorney with sufficient first class postage affixed. Upon receipt of such transmittal, the transmittal sheet shall be date-stamped and, if the extra copy and above-described envelope are provided, the copy shall also be date-stamped and returned to the attorney-at-law in the above-described envelope.

However, when such transmittal does not comply with the provisions of this section, the sheriff may promptly return such transmittal if accompanied by a short description of such noncompliance. An attorney may not issue a summons in any of the following civil proceedings: (i) habeas corpus under Article 3 (§ 8.01-654 et seq.) of Chapter 25 of this title, (ii) delinquency or abuse and neglect proceedings under Article 3 (§ 16.1-241 et seq.) of Chapter 11 of Title 16.1, (iii) issuance of a protective order pursuant to Article 4 (§ 16.1-246 et seq.) or Article 9 (§ 16.1-278 et seq.) of Chapter 11 of Title 16.1, or Chapter 9.1 (§ 19.2-152.8 et seq.) of Title 19.2, (iv) civil forfeiture proceedings, (v) habitual offender proceedings under Article 9 (§ 46.2-351 et seq.) of Chapter 3 of Title 46.2, (vi) administrative license suspension pursuant to § 46.2-391.2 and (vii) petition for writs of mandamus or prohibition in connection with criminal proceedings. A subpoena issued by an attorney shall not be issued less than five business days prior to the date that attendance is desired.

In other cases, if attendance is desired, the summons may be issued by the clerk of the circuit court of the county or city in which the attendance is desired.

A summons shall express on whose behalf, and in what case or about what matter, the witness is to attend. Failure to respond to any such summons shall be punishable by the court in which the proceeding is pending as for contempt. When any subpoena is served less than five calendar days before appearance is required, the court may, after considering all of the circumstances, refuse to enforce the subpoena for lack of adequate notice.

B. No subpoena shall, without permission of the court first obtained, issue for the attendance of the Governor, Lieutenant Governor, or Attorney General of this Commonwealth, or a judge of any court thereof; the President or Vice President of the United States; any member of the President's Cabinet; any ambassador or consul; or any military officer on active duty holding the rank of admiral or general.

C. This section shall be deemed to authorize a summons to compel attendance of a citizen of the Commonwealth before commissioners or other persons appointed by authority of another state when the summons requires the attendance of such witness at a place not out of his county or city. (Code 1950, §§ 8-296, 8-297; 1952, c. 122; 1977, c. 617; 1992, c. 506; 2000, c. 813.)

REVISERS' NOTE

The scope of former § 8-296 is extended to include persons acting in a judicial or quasi-judicial capacity, and altered to delete umpires, justices, coroners, and surveyors. The court's power to punish as for contempt (see § 18.2-456(5)) is expressly included so as to permit such punishment for disobedience of any summons authorized. Subsection B, requiring prior court order to summon certain officials and judges, is new. Former § 8-297 has been made subsection C without substantive change.

Section set out twice. — The section above is effective until July 1, 2001, unless the provisions of Acts 2000, c. 813 are reenacted by the 2001 General Assembly. For the version of this section effective July 1, 2001 if Acts 2000, c. 813 is not reenacted by the 2001 General Assembly, see the following section, also numbered 8.01-407.

Cross references. — As to compliance with subpoena by the State Treasurer or an employee of the Department of Treasury, see § 2.1-190.1. As to applicability of §§ 8.01-396.1, 8.01-402, 8.01-405, and 8.01-407 through 8.01-410 to criminal cases, see § 19.2-267.

Editor's note. — Acts 2000, c. 813, cl. 2 provides: "That the provisions of this act shall expire on July 1, 2001, unless reenacted by the 2001 General Assembly. Any subpoena or subpoena duces tecum issued by an attorney in compliance with this act shall remain valid notwithstanding the expiration of this act."

Acts 2000, c. 813, cl. 3 provides: "That the Virginia Bar Association, with the support of the Virginia Sheriffs Association and such other organizations from which it may request assistance, shall conduct a study of the effectiveness of this act and report its findings to the General Assembly no later than January 1, 2001."

The 2000 amendments. — The 2000 amendment by c. 813 rewrote subsection A.

I. DECIDED UNDER PRIOR LAW.

Editor's note. — The cases cited below were decided under corresponding provisions of former law. The term "this section," as used below, refers to former provisions.

This section is applicable alike by its terms to both criminal and civil actions. McCue v. Commonwealth, 103 Va. 870, 49 S.E. 623 (1905).

Witness in court may be called upon to testify though not served with subpoena. — A litigant's attendance upon the trial may be compelled by the issuance and service upon him of a subpoena under this section, as is the case with any other witness, but a party to a civil suit, as well as any other witness, who is present in court may be called upon to testify although he may not have been served with a subpoena. Robertson v. Commonwealth, 181 Va. 520, 25 S.E.2d 352 (1943).

§ 8.01-407. (Contingent effective date — See note) How summons for witness issued, and to whom directed; prior permission of court to summon certain officials and judges; attendance before commissioner of other state; attorney-issued summons. — A. A summons may be issued, directed as prescribed in § 8.01-292, commanding the officer to summon any person to attend on the day and at the place that such attendance is desired, to give evidence before a court, grand jury, arbitrators, magistrate, notary, or any commissioner or other person appointed by a court or acting under its process or authority in a judicial or quasi-judicial capacity. The summons may be issued, if the attendance be desired at a court or in a proceeding pending in a court, by the clerk thereof, and the clerk shall not impose any time restrictions limiting the right to properly request a summons up to and including the date of the proceeding; if before a commissioner in chancery or other commissioner of a court, by the clerk of the court in which the matter is pending, or by such commissioner in chancery or other commissioner; if before a notary or other officer taking a deposition, by such notary or other officer at the instance of the attorney desiring the attendance of the person sought; if before a grand jury, by the attorney for the Commonwealth, or the clerk of the court, at the instance of the attorney for the Commonwealth; and in other cases, by the clerk of the circuit court of the county or city in which the attendance is desired. It shall express on whose behalf, and in what case or about what matter, the witness is to attend. Failure to respond to any such summons shall be punishable by the court in which the proceeding is pending as for contempt.

B. No subpoena shall, without permission of the court first obtained, issue for the attendance of the Governor, Lieutenant Governor, or Attorney General of this Commonwealth, or a judge of any court thereof; the President or Vice-President of the United States; any member of the President's Cabinet; any ambassador or consul; or any military officer on active duty holding the rank of admiral or general.

C. This section shall be deemed to authorize a summons to compel attendance of a citizen of the Commonwealth before commissioners or other persons appointed by authority of another state when the summons requires the attendance of such witness at a place not out of his county or city. (Code 1950, §§ 8-296, 8-297; 1952, c. 122; 1977, c. 617; 1992, c. 506.)

Section set out twice. — The section above is effective July 1, 2001, unless the provisions of Acts 2000, c. 813 are reenacted by the 2001 General Assembly. For the version of this section effective until and after July 1, 2001 if Acts 2000, c. 813 is reenacted by the 2001 General Assembly, see the preceding section, also numbered 8.01-407.

§ 8.01-408. Recognizance taken upon continuance of case.

— Upon the continuance of any civil case in a court, the court shall at the request of any party litigant require such party's witnesses then present to enter into recognizance in such penalty as the court may deem proper, either with or without security, for their appearance to give evidence in such case on such day as may then be fixed for the trial thereof, such recognizance to be taken, conditioned, and entered of record in the same manner provided in §§ 19.2-135 to 19.2-137, for taking recognizance. (Code 1950, § 8-298; 1977, c. 617.)

REVISERS' NOTE

The application of former § 8-298 to criminal cases has been deleted in § 8.01-408 and the provisions of this section have been made applicable to all courts.

Cross references. — As to applicability of §§ 8.01-396.1, 8.01-402, 8.01-405, and 8.01-407 through 8.01-410 to criminal cases, see § 19.2-267.

§ 8.01-409. When court may have process for witness executed by its own officer in another county or city.

— Whenever on the calling or during the trial of a civil case in any court it appears to the court that it is necessary to have a witness from a county or city other than that of trial, the summons, rule, or attachment issued for such witness from the trial court may, when the court so orders, be executed by its officers in any county or city of the Commonwealth, for which services the officer shall be allowed a reasonable compensation by the court. (Code 1950, § 8-299; 1977, c. 617.)

REVISERS' NOTE

As in § 8.01-408, the application of former § 8-299 to criminal cases has been deleted. Also the provisions of this section have been made applicable to all courts.

Cross references. — As to applicability of §§ 8.01-396.1, 8.01-402, 8.01-405, and 8.01-407 through 8.01-410 to criminal cases, see § 19.2-267.

§ 8.01-410. Convicts as witnesses in civil actions.

— Whenever any party in a civil action in any circuit court in this Commonwealth shall require as a witness in his behalf, a convict or prisoner in a correctional or penal institution as defined in § 53.1-1, the court, on the application of such party or his attorney may, in its discretion and upon consideration of the importance of the personal appearance of the witness and the nature of the offense for which he is imprisoned, issue an order to the Director of the Department of Corrections to deliver such witness to the sheriff of the county or the city, as the case may be, who shall go where such witness may then be. Under such conditions as shall be prescribed by the superintendent of the institution, such officer shall carry the convict to the court to testify as such witness, and after he shall have so testified and been released as such witness, carry him back to the place whence he came.

If necessary the sheriff may confine the convict for the night in any convenient city or county correctional institution.

Under such rules and regulations as the superintendent of such an institution may prescribe, any party to a civil action in any circuit court in this Commonwealth may take the deposition of a convict or prisoner in the institution, which deposition, when taken, may be admissible in evidence as other depositions in civil actions.

The party seeking the testimony of such prisoner shall advance a sum sufficient to defray the expenses and compensation of the officers, which the court shall tax as other costs. (Code 1950, § 8-300.1; 1952, c. 487; 1966, c. 227; 1974, cc. 44, 45; 1977, c. 617; 1998, c. 596.)

REVISERS' NOTE

Several minor language changes have been made in former § 8-300.1 without changing its substance — e.g., the adoption by reference of the definition of correctional and penal institutions in § 53.1-1. Also the final phrase in the first paragraph of the former section pertaining to expenses of the sheriff is relocated in Title 14.1.

Former § 8-300, convicts as witnesses in criminal cases, was transferred to § 19.2-271.1.

Cross references. — As to applicability of §§ 8.01-396.1, 8.01-402, 8.01-405, and 8.01-407 through 8.01-410 to criminal cases, see § 19.2-267.

Editor's note. — Title 14.1, referred to in the Revisers' note above, was repealed by Acts 1998, c. 872. For location of comparable new sections, the comparable table in Volume 10 may be consulted.

Article 6.

Uniform Foreign Depositions Act.

§ 8.01-411. Compelling attendance of witnesses for taking depositions and production of documents to be used in foreign jurisdiction.

— Whenever any mandate, writ or commission is issued out of any court of record in any other state, territory, district or foreign jurisdiction, or whenever upon notice or agreement it is required to take the testimony of a witness or witnesses or produce or inspect designated documents in this Commonwealth, witnesses may be compelled to appear and testify and to produce and permit inspection or copying of documents in the same manner and by the same process and proceeding as may be employed for the purpose of taking testimony or producing documents in proceedings pending in this Commonwealth. (Code 1950, § 8-316.1; 1958, c. 58; 1977, c. 617; 1986, c. 599.)

I. DECISIONS UNDER CURRENT LAW.

Applied in Smith v. Givens, 223 Va. 455, 290 S.E.2d 844 (1982).

§ 8.01-412. Uniformity of interpretation; reciprocal privileges. — This article shall be so interpreted and construed as to effectuate its general purposes to make uniform the law of those states which enact it. The privilege extended to persons in other states by § 8.01-411 shall only apply to those states which extended the same privilege to persons in this Commonwealth. (Code 1950, § 8-316.2; 1958, c. 58; 1977, c. 617.)

§ 8.01-412.1. Short title. — This article may be cited as the Uniform Foreign Depositions Act. (Code 1950, § 8-316.3; 1958, c. 58; 1977, c. 617.)

ARTICLE 6.1.

Uniform Audio-Visual Deposition Act.

§ 8.01-412.2. Authorization of audio-visual deposition; official record; uses. — Any deposition may be recorded by audio-visual means without a stenographic record. Any party may make, at his own expense, a simultaneous stenographic or audio record of the deposition. Upon request and at his own expense, any party is entitled to an audio or audio-visual copy of the audio-visual recording.

The audio-visual recording is an official record of the deposition. A transcript prepared by a court reporter shall also be deemed an official record of the deposition. An audio-visual deposition may be used for any purpose and under any circumstances in which a stenographic deposition may be used.

For purposes of this article, "audio-visual" shall include video conferencing and teleconferencing. (1983, c. 305; 2000, c. 821.)

The 2000 amendments. — The 2000 amendment by c. 821 added the third undesignated paragraph.

Law Review. — For article, "Admissibility of Day in the Life Films in Virginia," see 18 U. Rich. L. Rev. 751 (1984). For 1985 survey of Virginia civil procedure and practice, see 19 U. Rich. L. Rev. 679 (1985).

§ 8.01-412.3. Notice of audio-visual deposition. — The notice for taking an audio-visual deposition and the subpoena for attendance at that deposition shall state that the deposition will be recorded by audio-visual means. (1983, c. 305.)

§ 8.01-412.4. Procedure. — The taking of audio-visual depositions shall be in accordance with the rules of the Supreme Court generally applicable to depositions. However, the following procedure shall be observed in recording an audio-visual deposition:

The deposition must begin with an oral or written statement on camera which includes (i) each operator's name and business address or, if applicable, the identity of the video conferencing or teleconferencing proprietor and locations participating in the video conference or teleconference; (ii) the name and business address of the operator's employer; (iii) the date, time and place of the deposition; (iv) the caption of the case; (v) the name of the witness; (vi) the party on whose behalf the deposition is being taken; (vii) with respect to video conferencing or teleconferencing, the identities of persons present at the deposition and the location of each such person; and (viii) any stipulations by the parties.

In addition, all counsel present on behalf of any party or witness shall identify themselves on camera. The oath for witnesses shall be administered on camera. If the length of a deposition requires the use of more than one recording unit, the end of each unit and the beginning of each succeeding unit shall be announced on camera. At the conclusion of a deposition, a statement shall be made on camera that the deposition is concluded. A statement may be made on camera setting forth any stipulations made by counsel concerning the custody of the audio-visual recording and exhibits or other pertinent matters.

All objections must be made as in the case of stenographic depositions. In any case where the court orders the audio-visual recording to be edited prior to its use, the original recording shall not be altered but shall be maintained as is.

Unless otherwise stipulated by the parties, the original audio-visual recording of a deposition, any copy edited pursuant to an order of the court, and exhibits shall be filed with the clerk of the court in accordance with the rules of the Supreme Court. (1983, c. 305; 1993, c. 208; 2000, c. 821.)

The 2000 amendments. — The 2000 amendment by c. 821, in the second undesignated paragraph, substituted "each" for "the" at the beginning of clause (i), added "or, if applicable, the identity of the video conferencing or teleconferencing proprietor and locations participating in the video conference or teleconference" at the end of clause (i); added present clause (vii); and redesignated former clause (vii) as present clause (viii).

§ 8.01-412.5. Costs. — In any case where a deposition taken pursuant to this article doe not conform to the requirements for use of such deposition as provided in the rules of the Supreme Court, the expense of conforming the recording shall be borne by the proponent of the deposition. (1983, c. 305; 1984, c. 95.)

§ 8.01-412.6. Promulgation of rules for standards and guidelines. — The Supreme Court may promulgate rules establishing standards for audio-visual equipment and guidelines for taking and using audio-visual depositions. (1983, c. 305.)

§ 8.01-412.7. Short title. — This article may be cited as the "Uniform Audio-Visual Deposition Act." (1983, c. 305.)

ARTICLE 7.

Medical Evidence.

§ 8.01-413. (Contingent expiration date — See note) Certain copies of health care provider's records or papers of patient admissible; right of patient or his attorney to copies of such records or papers; subpoena; damages, costs and attorney's fees. — A. In any case where the hospital, nursing facility, physician's, or other health care provider's original records or papers of any patient in a hospital or institution for the treatment of physical or mental illness are admissible or would be admissible as evidence, any typewritten copy, photograph, photostatted copy, or microphotograph or printout or other hard copy generated from computerized or other electronic storage, microfilm, or other photographic, mechanical, electronic or chemical storage process thereof shall be admissible as evidence in any court of this Commonwealth in like manner as the original, if the printout or hard copy or microphotograph or photograph is properly authenticated by the employees having authority to release or produce the original records.

564

Any hospital, nursing facility, physician, or other health care provider whose records or papers relating to any such patient are subpoenaed for production as provided by law may comply with the subpoena by a timely mailing to the clerk issuing the subpoena or in whose court the action is pending properly authenticated copies, photographs or microphotographs in lieu of the originals. The court whose clerk issued the subpoena or, in the case of an attorney-issued subpoena, in which the action is pending, may, after notice to such hospital, nursing facility, physician, or other health care provider, enter an order requiring production of the originals, if available, of any stored records or papers whose copies, photographs or microphotographs are not sufficiently legible. The party requesting the subpoena duces tecum or on whose behalf an attorney-issued subpoena duces tecum was issued shall be liable for the reasonable charges of the hospital, nursing facility, physician, or other health care provider for the service of maintaining, retrieving, reviewing, preparing, copying and mailing the items produced. Except for copies of X-ray photographs, however, such charges shall not exceed fifty cents for each page up to fifty pages and twenty-five cents a page thereafter for copies from paper and one dollar per page for copies from microfilm or other micrographic process, plus all postage and shipping costs and a search and handling fee not to exceed ten dollars.

B. Copies of hospital, nursing facility, physician's, or other health care provider's records or papers shall be furnished within fifteen days of such request to the patient or his attorney upon such patient's or attorney's written request, which request shall comply with the requirements of subsection E of § 32.1-127.1:03. However, copies of a patient's records shall not be furnished to such patient where the patient's treating physician has made a part of the patient's records a written statement that in his opinion the furnishing to or review by the patient of such records would be injurious to the patient's health or well-being, but in any such case such records shall be furnished to the patient's attorney within fifteen days of the date of such request. A reasonable charge may be made for the service of maintaining, retrieving, reviewing and preparing such copies. Except for copies of X-ray photographs, however, such charges shall not exceed fifty cents per page for up to fifty pages and twenty-five cents a page thereafter for copies from paper and one dollar per page for copies from microfilm or other micrographic process, plus all postage and shipping costs and a search and handling fee not to exceed ten dollars. Any hospital, nursing facility, physician, or other health care provider receiving such a request from a patient's attorney shall require a writing signed by the patient confirming the attorney's authority to make the request and shall accept a photocopy, facsimile, or other copy of the original signed by the patient as if it were an original.

C. Upon the failure of any hospital, nursing facility, physician, or other health care provider to comply with any written request made in accordance with subsection B within the period of time specified in that subsection and within the manner specified in subsections E and F of § 32.1-127.1:03, the patient or his attorney may cause a subpoena duces tecum to be issued. The subpoena may be issued (i) upon filing a request therefor with the clerk of the circuit court wherein any eventual suit, would be required to be filed, and payment of the fees required by subdivision A 18 of § 17.1-275, and fees for service or (ii) by the patient's attorney in a pending civil case in accordance with § 8.01-407 if issued by such attorney at least five business days prior to the date that production of the record is desired upon payment of the fees required by subdivision A 23 of § 17.1-275 at the time of filing of a copy of the subpoena duces tecum with the clerk. The subpoena shall be returnable within twenty days of proper service, directing the hospital, nursing facility, physician, or other health care provider to produce and furnish copies of the reports

§ 8.01-413   CODE OF VIRGINIA   § 8.01-413

and papers to the clerk who shall then make the same available to the patient or his attorney. If the court finds that a hospital, nursing facility, physician, or other health care provider willfully refused to comply with a written request made in accordance with subsection B, either by willfully or arbitrarily refusing or by imposing a charge in excess of the reasonable expense of making the copies and processing the request for records, the court may award damages for all expenses incurred by the patient to obtain such copies, including court costs and reasonable attorney's fees.

D. The provisions of subsections A, B, and C hereof shall apply to any health care provider whose office is located within or without the Commonwealth if the records pertain to any patient who is a party to a cause of action in any court in the Commonwealth of Virginia, and shall apply only to requests made by an attorney, or his client, in anticipation of litigation or in the course of litigation.

E. Health care provider, as used in this section, shall have the same meaning as provided in § 32.1-127.1:03 and shall also include an independent medical copy retrieval service contracted to provide the service of retrieving, reviewing, and preparing such copies for distribution.

F. Notwithstanding the authorization to admit as evidence patient records in the form of microphotographs, prescription dispensing records maintained in or on behalf of any pharmacy registered or permitted in Virginia shall only be stored in compliance with §§ 54.1-3410, 54.1-3411 and 54.1-3412. (Code 1950, § 8-277.1; 1954, c. 329; 1976, c. 50; 1977, cc. 208, 617; 1981, c. 457; 1982, c. 378; 1990, cc. 99, 320; 1992, c. 696; 1994, cc. 390, 572; 1995, c. 586; 1997, c. 682; 1998, c. 470; 2000, cc. 813, 923.)

REVISERS' NOTE

Former § 8-277.1 has been amended to require that copies of physicians' as well as hospital records be furnished to the patient, with some limitations; that such copies be furnished in 15 days; that a reasonable charge may be made for the same; and that sanctions may be imposed for failure to comply.

Former § 8-329.1 was transferred to § 20-61.2.

Section set out twice. — The section above is effective until July 1, 2001, unless the provisions of Acts 2000, c. 813 are reenacted by the 2001 General Assembly. For the version of this section effective July 1, 2001 if Acts 2000, c. 813 is not reenacted by the 2001 General Assembly, see the following section, also numbered 8.01-413.

Editor's note. — Former § 8-277.1, corresponding to this section, was amended by Acts 1977, c. 208. This section as enacted by Acts 1977, c. 617, incorporated in substance most of the changes made in the original former § 8-277.1 by c. 208. There were certain minor discrepancies, and, pursuant to § 9-77.11 and Acts 1977, c. 617, cl. 4, the Code Commission, in such instances, used the language of c. 208.

Section 20-61.2, referred to in the second paragraph of the Revisers' note, was repealed by Acts 1988, cc. 866 and 878.

The 2000 amendments. — The 2000 amendment by c. 813, in the first sentence of the first undesignated paragraph of subsection A, substituted "as provided by law" for "under this section or the Rules of the Supreme Court of Virginia", and inserted "or in whose court the action is pending"; inserted "or, in the case of an attorney-issued subpoena, in which the action is pending," in the second sentence of the first undesignated paragraph of subsection A; inserted "duces tecum or on whose behalf an attorney-issued subpoena duces tecum was issued" in the third sentence of the first undesignated paragraph of subsection A; in subsection B, inserted "subsection E of" preceding "§ 32.1-127.1:03" at the end of the first sentence; and rewrote subsection C.

The 2000 amendment by c. 923 added "and shall accept a photocopy, facsimile, or other copy of the original signed by the patient as if it were an original" at the end of subsection B.

Law Review. — For survey on evidence in Virginia for 1989, see 23 U. Rich. L. Rev. 647 (1989).

§ 8.01-413. **(Contingent effective date — See note) Certain copies of health care provider's records or papers of patient admissible; right of patient or his attorney to copies of such records or papers; subpoena; damages, costs and attorney's fees.** — A. In any case where the hospital, nursing facility, physician's, or other health care provider's original records or papers of any patient in a hospital or institution for the treatment of physical or mental illness are admissible or would be admissible as evidence, any typewritten copy, photograph, photostatted copy, or microphotograph or printout or other hard copy generated from computerized or other electronic storage, microfilm, or other photographic, mechanical, electronic or chemical storage process thereof shall be admissible as evidence in any court of this Commonwealth in like manner as the original, if the printout or hard copy or microphotograph or photograph is properly authenticated by the employees having authority to release or produce the original records.

Any hospital, nursing facility, physician, or other health care provider whose records or papers relating to any such patient are subpoenaed for production under this section or the Rules of the Supreme Court of Virginia may comply with the subpoena by a timely mailing to the clerk issuing the subpoena properly authenticated copies, photographs or microphotographs in lieu of the originals. The court whose clerk issued the subpoena may, after notice to such hospital, nursing facility, physician, or other health care provider, enter an order requiring production of the originals, if available, of any stored records or papers whose copies, photographs or microphotographs are not sufficiently legible. The party requesting the subpoena shall be liable for the reasonable charges of the hospital, nursing facility, physician, or other health care provider for the service of maintaining, retrieving, reviewing, preparing, copying and mailing the items produced. Except for copies of X-ray photographs, however, such charges shall not exceed fifty cents for each page up to fifty pages and twenty-five cents a page thereafter for copies from paper and one dollar per page for copies from microfilm or other micrographic process, plus all postage and shipping costs and a search and handling fee not to exceed ten dollars.

B. Copies of hospital, nursing facility, physician's, or other health care provider's records or papers shall be furnished within fifteen days of such request to the patient or his attorney upon such patient's or attorney's written request, which request shall comply with the requirements of § 32.1-127.1:03. However, copies of a patient's records shall not be furnished to such patient where the patient's treating physician has made a part of the patient's records a written statement that in his opinion the furnishing to or review by the patient of such records would be injurious to the patient's health or well-being, but in any such case such records shall be furnished to the patient's attorney within fifteen days of the date of such request. A reasonable charge may be made for the service of maintaining, retrieving, reviewing and preparing such copies. Except for copies of X-ray photographs, however, such charges shall not exceed fifty cents per page for up to fifty pages and twenty-five cents a page thereafter for copies from paper and one dollar per page for copies from microfilm or other micrographic process, plus all postage and shipping costs and a search and handling fee not to exceed ten dollars. Any hospital, nursing facility, physician, or other health care provider receiving such a request from a patient's attorney shall require a writing signed by the patient confirming the attorney's authority to make the request and shall accept a photocopy, facsimile, or other copy of the original signed by the patient as if it were an original.

C. Upon the failure of any hospital, nursing facility, physician, or other health care provider to comply with any written request made in accordance with subsection B within the period of time specified in that subsection and

§ 8.01-413.01   CODE OF VIRGINIA   § 8.01-413.01

within the manner specified in § 32.1-127.1:03, the patient or his attorney may by affidavit filed with the clerk of the circuit court wherein any eventual suit, if any, would be required to be filed, upon payment of the fees required by subdivision A 18 of § 17.1-275, and fees for service, request that the clerk subpoena such records or papers. The clerk shall thereupon issue a subpoena, returnable within twenty days of proper service, directing the hospital, nursing facility, physician, or other health care provider to produce and furnish copies of the reports and papers to him, whereupon, the clerk shall make the same available to the patient or his attorney. If the court finds that a hospital, nursing facility, physician, or other health care provider willfully refused to comply with a written request made in accordance with subsection B, either by willfully or arbitrarily refusing or by imposing a charge in excess of the reasonable expense of making the copies and processing the request for records, the court may award damages for all expenses incurred by the patient to obtain such copies, including court costs and reasonable attorney's fees.

D. The provisions of subsections A, B, and C hereof shall apply to any health care provider whose office is located within or without the Commonwealth if the records pertain to any patient who is a party to a cause of action in any court in the Commonwealth of Virginia, and shall apply only to requests made by an attorney, or his client, in anticipation of litigation or in the course of litigation.

E. Health care provider, as used in this section, shall have the same meaning as provided in § 32.1-127.1:03 and shall also include an independent medical copy retrieval service contracted to provide the service of retrieving, reviewing, and preparing such copies for distribution.

F. Notwithstanding the authorization to admit as evidence patient records in the form of microphotographs, prescription dispensing records maintained in or on behalf of any pharmacy registered or permitted in Virginia shall only be stored in compliance with §§ 54.1-3410, 54.1-3411 and 54.1-3412. (Code 1950, § 8-277.1; 1954, c. 329; 1976, c. 50; 1977, cc. 208, 617; 1981, c. 457; 1982, c. 378; 1990, cc. 99, 320; 1992, c. 696; 1994, cc. 390, 572; 1995, c. 586; 1997, c. 682; 1998, c. 470; 2000, c. 923.)

Section set out twice. — The section above is effective July 1, 2001, unless the provisions of Acts 2000, c. 813 are reenacted by the 2001 General Assembly. For the version of this section effective until and after July 1, 2001 if Acts 2000, c. 813, is reenacted by the 2001 General Assembly, see the preceding section, also numbered 8.01-413.

The 2000 amendments. — The 2000 amendment by c. 923 added "and shall accept a photocopy, facsimile, or other copy of the original signed by the patient as if it were an original" at the end of subsection B.

§ 8.01-413.01. Authenticity and reasonableness of medical bills; presumption. — A. In any action for personal injuries, wrongful death, or for medical expense benefits payable under a motor vehicle insurance policy issued pursuant to § 38.2-124 or § 38.2-2201, the authenticity of bills for medical services provided and the reasonableness of the charges of the health care provider shall be rebuttably presumed upon identification by the plaintiff of the original bill or a duly authenticated copy and the plaintiff's testimony (i) identifying the health care provider, (ii) explaining the circumstances surrounding his receipt of the bill, (iii) describing the services rendered and (iv) stating that the services were rendered in connection with treatment for the injuries received in the event giving rise to the action. The presumption herein shall not apply unless the opposing party or his attorney has been furnished such medical records at least twenty-one days prior to the trial.

B. Where no medical bill is rendered or specific charge made by a health care provider to the insured, an insurer, or any other person, the usual and customary fee charged for the service rendered may be established by the testimony or the affidavit of an expert having knowledge of the usual and customary fees charged for the services rendered. If the fee is to be established by affidavit, the affidavit shall be submitted to the opposing party or his attorney at least twenty-one days prior to trial. The testimony or the affidavit is subject to rebuttal and may be admitted in the same manner as an original bill or authenticated copy described in subsection A of this section. (1993, c. 610; 1996, c. 516; 1997, c. 503.)

ARTICLE 7.1.

Employment Evidence.

§ 8.01-413.1. Certain copies of employment records or papers admissible; right of employee or his attorney to copies of such records or papers; subpoena; damages, costs and attorney's fees. — In any case where the original wage or salary records or papers of any employee are admissible or would be admissible as evidence, any typewritten copy, photograph, photostatic copy, or microphotograph thereof shall be admissible as evidence in any court of this Commonwealth in like manner as the original, provided the typewritten copy, photograph, photostatic copy or microphotograph is properly authenticated by the individual who would have authority to release or produce in court the original records. Any employer whose records or papers relating to any such employee are subpoenaed for production may comply with the subpoena by a timely mailing to the clerk issuing the subpoena properly authenticated copies, photographs or microphotographs in lieu of the originals. The court whose clerk issued the subpoena may, after notice to such employer, enter an order requiring production of the originals, if available, of any records or papers whose copies, photographs or microphotographs are not sufficiently legible. The party requesting the subpoena shall be liable for the reasonable charges of the employer for copying and mailing the items produced. (1987, c. 503.)

Law Review. — As to copies of employment records, see 22 U. Rich. L. Rev. 621 (1988).

ARTICLE 8.

Certain Affidavits.

§ 8.01-414. Affidavit prima facie evidence of nonresidence. — In any action, an affidavit that a witness or party resides out of this Commonwealth, or is out of it, shall be prima facie evidence of the fact, although such affidavit be made by a party, and without previous notice. (Code 1950, § 8-328; 1977, c. 617.)

§ 8.01-415. Affidavit evidence of publication. — When anything is authorized or required by law to be published in a newspaper, the certificate of the editor, publisher, business manager or assistant business manager, or the affidavit of any other person, shall be admitted as evidence of what is stated herein as to the publication. (Code 1950, § 8-329; 1977, c. 617.)

§ 8.01-416. Affidavit re damages to motor vehicle. — A. In a civil action in any court, whether sounding in contract or tort, to recover for damages to a motor vehicle in excess of $1,000, evidence as to such damages may be presented by an itemized estimate or appraisal sworn to by a person who also makes oath (i) that he is a motor vehicle repairman, estimator or appraiser qualified to determine the amount of such damage or diminution in value; (ii) as to the approximate length of time that he has engaged in such work; and (iii) as to the trade name and address of his business and employer. Such estimate shall not be admitted unless by consent of the adverse party or his counsel, or unless a true copy thereof is mailed or delivered to the adverse party or his counsel not less than seven days prior to the date fixed for trial.

B. In a civil action in any court, whether sounding in contract or tort, to recover for damages to a motor vehicle of $1,000 or less, evidence as to such damages may be presented by an itemized estimate or appraisal sworn to by a person who also makes oath (i) that he is a motor vehicle repairman, estimator or appraiser qualified to determine the amount of such damage or diminution in value; (ii) as to the approximate length of time that he has engaged in such work; and (iii) as to the trade name and address of his business and employer. (1977, c. 617; 1980, c. 183; 1990, c. 724.)

REVISERS' NOTE

The admission into evidence of an ex parte estimate of the damages to a motor vehicle, now applicable pursuant to § 16.1-88.1 only to general district courts, is made applicable by this section to all courts.

Editor's note. — Section 16.1-88.1, referred to in the Revisers' note, was repealed by Acts 1980, c. 183.

ARTICLE 9.
Miscellaneous Provisions.

§ 8.01-417. Copies of written statements or transcriptions of verbal statements by injured person to be delivered to him. — Any person who takes from a person who has sustained a personal injury a signed written statement or voice recording of any statement relative to such injury shall deliver to such injured person a copy of such written statement forthwith or a verified typed transcription of such recording within thirty days from the date such statement was given or recording made, when and if the statement or recording is transcribed or in all cases when requested by the injured person or his attorney. (Code 1950, § 8-628.2; 1954, c. 390; 1977, c. 617.)

§ 8.01-417.1. Use of portions of documents in evidence. — To expedite trial proceedings in civil cases, upon appropriate and timely motion by counsel, the court may permit the reading to the jury, or the introduction into evidence, of relevant portions of lengthy and complex documents without the necessity of having the jury read or receive the entire document. The court, in its discretion, may permit the entire document to be received by the jury, or may order the parties to edit from any such document admitted into evidence information that is irrelevant to the proceedings. (1992, c. 720.)

§ 8.01-418. When plea of guilty or nolo contendere or forfeiture in criminal prosecution or traffic case admissible in civil action; proof of such plea. — Whenever, in any civil action, it is contended that any party thereto pled guilty or nolo contendere or suffered a forfeiture in a prosecution for a criminal offense or traffic infraction which arose out of the same occurrence upon which the civil action is based, evidence of said plea or forfeiture as shown by the records of the criminal court shall be admissible. Where the records of the court in which such prosecution was had are silent or ambiguous as to whether or not such plea was made or forfeiture occurred the court hearing the civil case shall admit such evidence on the question of such plea or forfeiture as may be relevant, and the question of whether such plea was made or forfeiture suffered shall be a question for the court to determine. (Code 1950, § 8-267.1; 1970, c. 354; 1977, c. 617; 1986, c. 46.)

REVISERS' NOTE

Former § 8-267.1 is amended to include the party's having pled nolo contendere or suffered a forfeiture, as well as having pled guilty. It has been changed to provide that in the event of a dispute about such plea or forfeiture, the question is to be decided by the court.

Law Review. — For survey of recent legislation on civil procedure — evidence of guilty plea admissible in civil action arising out of same occurrence, see 5 U. Rich. L. Rev. 185 (1970). For survey of Virginia law on evidence for the year 1976-77, see 63 Va. L. Rev. 1428 (1977). For article, "Preclusion of Evidence of Criminal Conviction in Civil Action Arising from the Same Incident," see 10 Geo. Mason L. Rev. 107 (1988).

I. DECISIONS UNDER CURRENT LAW.

This statute deals with evidentiary question of admissions and apparently was enacted to change the rule enunciated in Fulcher v. Whitlow, 208 Va. 34, 155 S.E.2d 362 (1967). Selected Risks Ins. Co. v. Dean, 233 Va. 260, 355 S.E.2d 579 (1987).

Failure to appear in court and pay fines does not constitute forfeiture. — The mere failure to appear in general district court to contest a traffic offense and the subsequent payment of a fine and costs do not constitute a forfeiture within the meaning of this section. Yeager v. Adkins, 250 Va. 1, 458 S.E.2d 467 (1995).

Trial court erred in granting motion in limine which precluded the plaintiff from adducing evidence of the defendant's guilty plea to a charge of reckless driving stemming from his falling asleep at the wheel and of the chain of events beginning with defendant's negligently falling asleep and ending with collision. Koutsounadis v. England, 238 Va. 128, 380 S.E.2d 644 (1989).

§ 8.01-418.1. Evidence of subsequent measures taken not admissible to prove negligence. — When, after the occurrence of an event, measures are taken which, if taken prior to the event would have made the event less likely to occur, evidence of such subsequently taken measures is not admissible to prove negligence or culpable conduct as a cause of the occurrence of the event; provided, that evidence of subsequent measures taken shall not be required to be excluded when offered for another purpose for which it may be admissible, including, but not limited to, proof of ownership, control, feasibility of precautionary measures if controverted, or for impeachment. (1978, c. 165.)

Law Review. — For survey of Virginia law on evidence for the year 1977-1978, see 64 Va. L. Rev. 1451 (1978).

I. DECISIONS UNDER CURRENT LAW.

Feasibility became controverted in instant case when the plaintiff raised the issue of precautionary measures with a defense witness and the witness stated there was no place at all to store partitions other than the bathroom in the defendant's office. Therefore, on retrial, the trial court should permit the plaintiff to show that, on the day after the plaintiff was injured, the defendant moved the partitions from the bathroom where they had been stored to an unoccupied office suite used by the defendant to store repossessed furniture. Holcombe v. Nationsbank Fin. Servs. Corp., 248 Va. 445, 450 S.E.2d 158 (1994).

§ 8.01-418.2. Evidence of polygraph examination inadmissible in any proceeding. — The analysis of any polygraph test charts produced during any polygraph examination administered to a party or witness shall not be admissible in any proceeding conducted pursuant to Chapter 10.01 (§ 2.1-116.01 et seq.) of Title 2.1 or conducted by any county, city or town over the objection of any party except as to disciplinary or other actions taken against a polygrapher. (1993, c. 570; 1995, cc. 770, 818.)

§ 8.01-418.3. Year 2000 assessments and documents not actionable.
— A. For purposes of this section, unless the context requires a different meaning:

"Document" means information collected, generated, or developed in the course of, and in the planning for, a Year 2000 assessment, which is clearly marked as such on the face of the document, and includes, but is not limited to, interview notes, audits, records of inspections, findings, opinions, suggestions, conclusions, drafts, memoranda, electronic mail messages, charts, test data, drawings, electronic data, photographs, videotape, computer-generated or electronically recorded information, and surveys. "Document" shall not include information generated or developed prior to the commencement or after the conclusion of a Year 2000 assessment.

"Year 2000 assessment" means a voluntary evaluation of the Year 2000 processing capabilities of the technology systems any person owns or uses. The assessment shall be or have been performed between January 1, 1996, and July 1, 2000; designed to solve a Year 2000 problem or avert a Year 2000 failure; and conducted at the person's request by the person's employees or an independent contractor.

"Year 2000 problem" or *"Year 2000 failure"* means any computing, physical, enterprise, or distribution system complication that has occurred or may occur as a result of the change of the year from 1999 to 2000 in any person's technology system, including, without limitation, computer hardware, programs, software, or systems; embedded chip calculations or embedded systems; firmware; microprocessors; or management systems, business processes, or computing applications that govern, utilize, drive, or depend on the Year 2000 processing capabilities of the person's technology systems. Such complications may include the common computer programming practice of using a two-digit field to represent a year, resulting in erroneous date calculations; an ambiguous interpretation of the term or field "00"; the failure to recognize 2000 as a leap year; algorithms that use "99" or "00" to activate another function; or the use of any other applications, software, or hardware that are date-sensitive.

"Year 2000 processing" means the processing, calculating, comparing, sequencing, displaying, storing, transmitting, or receiving of date or date-sensitive data from, into, and between the twentieth and twenty-first centuries, during the years 1999 and 2000, and leap year calculations.

B. No Year 2000 assessment or document shall be discoverable or admissible in evidence, except that the court, following in camera review and for good cause shown, may order the discovery or admission of such assessments or documents. (1999, c. 17.)

Cross references. — For other Y2K provisions enacted in 1999, see § 8.01-226.6 and §§ 8.01-227.1 through 8.01-227.3.

§ 8.01-419. Table of life expectancy.
— Whenever, in any case not otherwise specifically provided for, it is necessary to establish the expectancy of continued life of any person from any period of such person's life, whether he be living at the time or not, the following table shall be received in all courts and by all persons having power to determine litigation as evidence, with other

§ 8.01-419   CIVIL REMEDIES AND PROCEDURE   § 8.01-419

evidence as to the health, constitution and habits of such person, of such expectancy represented by the figures in the following columns:

AGE	BOTH SEXES	MALE	FEMALE
0	75.4	71.8	78.8
1	75.1	71.6	78.4
2	74.1	70.6	77.5
3	73.1	69.7	76.5
4	72.2	68.7	75.5
5	71.2	67.7	74.5
6	70.2	66.8	73.6
7	69.2	65.8	72.6
8	68.2	64.8	71.6
9	67.3	63.8	70.6
10	66.3	62.8	69.6
11	65.3	61.8	68.6
12	64.3	60.8	67.6
13	63.3	59.8	66.6
14	62.3	58.9	65.7
15	61.3	57.9	64.7
16	60.4	57.0	63.7
17	59.4	56.0	62.7
18	58.5	55.1	61.8
19	57.5	54.2	60.8
20	56.6	53.3	59.8
21	55.7	52.3	58.8
22	54.7	51.4	57.9
23	53.8	50.5	56.9
24	52.8	49.6	55.9
25	51.9	48.7	55.0
26	51.0	47.8	54.0
27	50.0	46.9	53.0
28	49.1	45.9	52.1
29	48.1	45.0	51.1
30	47.2	44.1	50.0
31	46.3	43.2	49.2
32	45.3	42.3	48.2
33	44.4	41.4	47.2
34	43.5	40.5	46.3
35	42.6	39.6	45.3
36	41.6	38.7	44.4
37	40.7	37.8	43.4
38	39.8	36.9	42.5
39	38.9	36.0	41.5
40	38.0	35.1	40.6
41	37.0	34.2	39.6
42	36.1	33.3	38.7
43	35.2	32.4	37.8
44	34.3	31.5	36.8
45	33.4	30.7	35.9
46	32.5	29.8	35.0
47	31.6	28.9	34.1
48	30.7	28.1	33.1
49	29.9	27.2	32.2
50	29.1	26.4	31.3
51	28.1	25.5	30.5
52	27.3	24.7	29.6
53	26.4	23.9	28.7
54	25.6	23.1	27.8
55	24.8	22.3	27.0
56	24.0	21.5	26.1

AGE	BOTH SEXES	MALE	FEMALE
57	23.2	20.7	25.3
58	22.4	20.0	24.4
59	21.6	19.2	23.6
60	20.8	18.5	22.8
61	20.1	17.8	22.4
62	19.4	17.1	21.2
63	18.6	16.4	20.4
64	17.9	15.8	19.7
65	17.2	15.1	18.9
66	16.5	14.5	18.2
67	15.9	13.8	17.4
68	15.2	13.2	16.7
69	14.5	12.6	16.0
70	13.9	12.0	15.3
71	13.3	11.5	14.6
72	12.7	10.9	13.9
73	12.1	10.4	13.3
74	11.5	9.9	12.6
75	10.9	9.4	12.0
76	10.4	8.9	11.3
77	9.8	8.4	10.7
78	9.3	7.9	10.1
79	8.8	7.5	9.5
80	8.3	7.1	9.0
81	7.8	6.7	8.4
82	7.4	6.3	7.9
83	6.9	5.9	7.4
84	6.5	5.6	6.9
85	6.1	5.2	6.4

(Code 1950, § 8-263.1; 1966, c. 472; 1977, c. 617; 1986, c. 317; 1996, c. 394.)

REVISERS' NOTE

Former § 8-263.1 has been updated to 1973 figures of the United States Department of Health, Education, and Welfare.

I. Decisions Under Current Law.
II. Decisions Under Prior Law.

I. DECISIONS UNDER CURRENT LAW.

Wrongful death action. — The expectancy of continued life of the decedent is relevant and necessary to establish the extent of loss for the decedent's society, companionship, comfort, guidance, advice, services, protection, care, and assistance set out in § 8.01-52. The expectancy table in this section therefore, is admissible if such items of loss are supported by the evidence. Graddy v. Hatchett, 233 Va. 65, 353 S.E.2d 741 (1987).

Personal injury action. — In an action for damages arising out of an automobile accident, where there was evidence that the injury to the plaintiff was not only permanent in nature, but was of a type and character from which the jury could have reasonably inferred the plaintiff would suffer a lessening of his earning capacity, it was proper for the court to have permitted evidence of plaintiff's life expectancy. Exxon Corp. v. Fulgham, 224 Va. 235, 294 S.E.2d 894 (1982).

Applied in Wingo v. Norfolk & W. Ry., 638 F. Supp. 107 (W.D. Va. 1986).

II. DECISIONS UNDER PRIOR LAW.

Editor's note. — The cases cited below were decided under corresponding provisions of former law. The term "this section," as used below, refers to former provisions.

The table is to be considered as evidence. Edwards v. Syrkes, 211 Va. 600, 179 S.E.2d 902 (1971).

But it is not conclusive or binding. Edwards v. Syrkes, 211 Va. 600, 179 S.E.2d 902 (1971).

And should be considered with other evidence. — It is the duty of the court, when so requested in an action for wrongful death, to tell the jury that a mortality table introduced into evidence is to be considered by them, but it is not conclusive or binding. It shall be considered along with all the other evidence relating to the health, habits, and other circumstances of the person which may tend to influence his life expectancy. Edwards v. Syrkes, 211 Va. 600, 179 S.E.2d 902 (1971).

Reading section to jury. — The objection now made to the action of the trial court in permitting counsel for the plaintiff to read to the jury from this section, it being the table of life expectancy, does not appear to have been voiced in the court below. While this method of introducing the life expectancy table in evidence is unusual, and not an approved procedure, it does not here constitute reversible error. State Farm Mut. Auto. Ins. Co. v. Futrell, 209 Va. 266, 163 S.E.2d 181 (1968).

Instruction in wrongful death action. — In a wrongful death action, the jury should be instructed, if requested, substantially as follows: "The court instructs the jury that the life expectancy table introduced in evidence is to be considered by you as an aid in determining life expectancy, but it is not in any way conclusive or binding. You should consider it along with all the other evidence relating to the health, constitution, and habits of the decedent in your determination of his life expectancy." Edwards v. Syrkes, 211 Va. 600, 179 S.E.2d 902 (1971).

§ 8.01-419.1. Motor vehicle value. — Whenever in any case not otherwise specifically provided for the value of an automobile is in issue, either civilly or criminally, the tabulated retail values set forth in the National Automobile Dealers' Association (NADA) "yellow" or "black" books, in effect on the relevant date, shall be admissible as evidence of fair market value on the relevant date.

The determination of value shall be subject to such other creditable evidence as any party may offer to demonstrate that the value as set forth in the NADA publication fails to reflect the actual condition of the vehicle and that therefore the value may be greater or less than that shown by the NADA publication. (1993, c. 759.)

§ 8.01-420. Depositions as basis for motion for summary judgment or to strike evidence. — No motion for summary judgment or to strike the evidence shall be sustained when based in whole or in part upon any discovery depositions under Rule 4:5, unless all parties to the suit or action shall agree that such deposition may be so used. (Code 1950, § 8-315.1; 1973, c. 483; 1977, c. 617; 1978, c. 417.)

Law Review. — For survey of Virginia law on practice and pleading for the year 1974-1975, see 61 Va. L. Rev. 1799 (1975). For article on libel and slander in Virginia, see 17 U. Rich. L. Rev. 769 (1983).

§ 8.01-420.01. Limiting further disclosure of discoverable materials and information; protective order. — A. A protective order issued to prevent disclosure of materials or information related to a personal injury action or action for wrongful death produced in discovery in any cause shall not prohibit an attorney from voluntarily sharing such materials or information with an attorney involved in a similar or related matter, with the permission of the court, after notice and an opportunity to be heard to any party or person protected by the protective order, and provided the attorney who receives the material or information agrees, in writing, to be bound by the terms of the protective order.

B. The provisions of this section shall apply only to protective orders issued on or after July 1, 1989. (1989, c. 702.)

Law Review. — For essay on protective orders, see 24 U. Rich. L. Rev. 109 (1989). For essay, "Protective Orders in Products Liability Litigation: Striking the Proper Balance," see 48 Wash. & Lee L. Rev. 1503 (1991).

§ **8.01-420.1. Abolition of common-law perpetuation of testimony.** — The common-law proceeding to perpetuate testimony is abolished. (1977, c. 617.)

REVISERS' NOTE

This is a new section in Title 8.01, enacted in view of the revision of Part Four of the Rules of Court, to make the proceeding provided in Rule 4:2 the exclusive proceeding to perpetuate testimony.

§ **8.01-420.2. Limitation on use of recorded conversations as evidence.** — No mechanical recording, electronic or otherwise, of a telephone conversation shall be admitted into evidence in any civil proceeding unless (i) all parties to the conversation were aware the conversation was being recorded or (ii) the portion of the recording to be admitted contains admissions that, if true, would constitute criminal conduct which is the basis for the civil action, and one of the parties was aware of the recording and the proceeding is not one for divorce, separate maintenance or annulment of a marriage. The parties' knowledge of the recording pursuant to clause (i) shall be demonstrated by a declaration at the beginning of the recorded portion of the conversation to be admitted into evidence that the conversation is being recorded. This section shall not apply to emergency reporting systems operated by police and fire departments and by rescue squads, nor to any communications common carrier utilizing service observing or random monitoring pursuant to § 19.2-62. (1983, c. 503; 1992, c. 567.)

I. DECISIONS UNDER CURRENT LAW.

A state evidentiary rule does not control admissibility of evidence in federal proceedings. Leitman v. McAusland, 934 F.2d 46 (4th Cir. 1991).

§ **8.01-420.3. Court reporters to provide transcripts; when recording may be stopped; use of transcript as evidence.** — Upon the request of any counsel of record, or of any party not represented by counsel, and upon payment of the reasonable cost thereof, the court reporter covering any proceeding shall provide the requesting party with a copy of the transcript of such proceeding or any requested portion thereof.

The court shall not direct the court reporter to cease recording any portion of the proceeding without the consent of all parties or of their counsel of record.

Whenever a party seeks to introduce the transcript or record of the testimony of a witness at an earlier trial, hearing or deposition, it shall not be necessary for the reporter to be present to prove the transcript or record, provided the reporter duly certifies, in writing, the accuracy of the transcript or record. (1983, c. 505; 1990, c. 77.)

The number of this section was assigned by the Virginia Code Commission, the number in the 1983 act having been 8.01-420.2.

I. DECISIONS UNDER CURRENT LAW.

The value of a transcript of a prior mistrial can ordinarily be assumed because it can be used as a discovery device, for trial preparation, or for impeachment purposes at the new trial. Anderson v. Commonwealth, 19 Va. App. 208, 450 S.E.2d 394 (1994).

Establishing need for free transcript. — A defendant who claims the right to a free transcript does not bear the burden of proving inadequate such alternatives as may be suggested by the state or conjured up by a court in hindsight. Anderson v. Commonwealth, 19 Va. App. 208, 450 S.E.2d 394 (1994).

In determining whether a defendant needs a free transcript, two factors are relevant: (1) the value of the transcript to the defendant in connection with the appeal or trial for which it is sought, and (2) the availability of alternative devices that would fulfill the same functions as a transcript. Anderson v. Commonwealth, 19 Va. App. 208, 450 S.E.2d 394 (1994).

No party-to-party duty. — One party is under no duty to provide a transcript at its own expense for the other's benefit. White v. Morano, 249 Va. 27, 452 S.E.2d 856 (1995).

§ 8.01-420.4. Taking of depositions. — Depositions shall be taken in the county or city in which suit is pending, in an adjacent county or city or in the county or city of the Commonwealth of Virginia where a nonparty witness resides, is employed, or has his principal place of business, except that depositions may be taken at a place upon which the parties agree or at a place that the court in such suit may, for good cause, designate. If a nonparty witness is not a resident of the Commonwealth, his deposition may be taken in the locality where he resides or is employed, or at any other location agreed upon by the parties. Additionally, the restrictions, as to parties within the Commonwealth, set forth in this section shall not apply where no responsive pleading has been filed or an appearance otherwise made. (1989, c. 209; 1991, c. 81; 1993, cc. 428, 940.)

Law Review. — For survey on civil procedure and practice in Virginia for 1989, see 23 U. Rich. L. Rev. 511 (1989).

§ 8.01-420.5. Estoppel effect of judicial determination of employment status. — A final, unappealed order entered by a circuit court of this Commonwealth that a person is or is not an employee of another for the purpose of obtaining jurisdiction shall estop either of said parties from asserting otherwise in any subsequent action between such parties upon the same claim or cause of action before a court of this Commonwealth or the Virginia Workers' Compensation Commission. (1997, c. 333.)

CHAPTER 15.

PAYMENT AND SETOFF.

Sec.
8.01-421. Payment may be pleaded; payment into court of part of claim; procedure upon such payment.

Sec.
8.01-422. Pleading equitable defenses.
8.01-423. When plaintiff claims as assignee or transferee.

§ 8.01-421. Payment may be pleaded; payment into court of part of claim; procedure upon such payment. — A. In any action for recovery of a debt the defendant may plead payment of the debt or any part thereof prior to the commencement of the action.

B. In any personal action, the defendant may pay into court a sum of money on account of what is claimed, or by way of compensation or amends, and plead that he is not indebted to the plaintiff, or that the plaintiff has not sustained damages, to a greater amount than such sum. The plaintiff may accept such sum either in full satisfaction, and then have judgment for his costs, or in part satisfaction, and reply to the allegations of the defendant's pleadings, and, if issue thereon be found for the defendant, judgment shall be given for the defendant, and he shall recover his costs. The payment of such sum into court shall not be admissible in evidence. (Code 1950, §§ 8-236, 8-237, 8-238; 1954, c. 333; 1977, c. 617; 1978, c. 416.)

REVISERS' NOTE

Former § 8-236 has been rewritten to modernize the language and is subsection A of § 8.01-421. Subsection A is, like the former statute, limited to actions for the recovery of a debt.

Former §§ 8-237 and 8-238 are subsection B with minor changes. The clerk is no longer designated to receive payment into court, as this was felt to be unnecessary. As in the former statute, subsection B applies to all personal actions, whether sounding in contract or in tort. The last sentence of subsection B has been added.

I. DECIDED UNDER PRIOR LAW.

Editor's note. — The cases cited below were decided under corresponding provisions of former law. The term "this section," as used below, refers to former provisions.

A plea of payment is a plea in confession and avoidance. Colley v. Sheppard, 72 Va. (31 Gratt.) 312 (1879); Norvell v. Little, 79 Va. 141 (1884).

This section has reference to the effect of tender after maturity, and not to the character of the tender. The statute was not designed to affect the law as it applies to the question of a legal tender is pais. Therefore, it does not alter the right of a vendor to demand payment of purchase money in legal tender. Vick v. Howard, 136 Va. 101, 116 S.E. 465 (1923).

§ 8.01-422. Pleading equitable defenses. — In any action on a contract, the defendant may file a pleading, alleging any matter which would entitle him to relief in equity, in whole or in part, against the obligation of the contract; or, if the contract be by deed, alleging any such matter arising under the contract, existing before its execution, or any such mistake therein, or in the execution thereof, or any such other matter as would entitle him to such relief in equity; and in either case alleging the amount to which he is entitled by reason of the matters contained in the pleading. If the amount claimed by the defendant exceed the amount of the plaintiff's claim the court may, in a proper case, give judgment in favor of the defendant for such excess. (Code 1950, § 8-241; 1954, c. 617; 1977, c. 617.)

REVISERS' NOTE

Section 8.01-422 is former § 8-241. Rule 3:8 covers nearly any defense to an action or claim, but upon close examination, the rule in its present form does not appear to include equitable defenses to an action on contract such as estoppel or unconscionability. It was therefore decided to retain, without change, this section, which has been in the Code for many years.

Cross references. — As to period of limitation for counterclaims, see § 8.01-233. For rule of court allowing counterclaims in actions in personam for money, and certain other actions at law, see Rule 3:8.

I. Decisions Under Current Law.
II. Decisions Under Prior Law.
   A. General Consideration.
      1. In General.
      2. Nature of Defendant's Demand.
      3. Necessity That Defendant's Demand Arise Out of Contract in Suit.
      4. In What Actions Plea May Be Filed.
      5. By Whom Plea May Be Filed.
   B. Grounds for Plea.
      1. Fraud in Procurement of Contract.
      2. Failure of Consideration.
      3. Breach of Warranty.

4. Other Matters Entitling Defendant to Equitable Relief.
C. Procedure.
 1. In General.
 2. Plea.
  a. In General.
  b. Setting Out Grounds of Defense.
 3. Appeal and Error.

I. DECISIONS UNDER CURRENT LAW.

A statutory plea filed pursuant to this section, successor to § 8-241, is not a counterclaim as that term is used in § 8.01-380C, successor to § 8-244. Therefore, the conditions attaching to a nonsuit under subsection C of § 8.01-380 do not apply. Bremer v. Doctor's Bldg. Partnership, 251 Va. 74, 465 S.E.2d 787 (1996).

Defenses asserted in response to a motion for judgment, such as filed under this section seeking affirmative relief, are not barred or otherwise lost. They may be reasserted if the motion for judgment is subsequently refiled. Bremer v. Doctor's Bldg. Partnership, 251 Va. 74, 465 S.E.2d 787 (1996).

II. DECISIONS UNDER PRIOR LAW.

A. General Consideration.

1. In General.

Editor's note. — The cases cited below were decided under corresponding provisions of former law. The term "this section," as used below, refers to former provisions.

The object of this section was to remedy the defects of the common law, and to enable a defendant both to make such defenses as fraud, failure of consideration, and the like to a suit at law on specialties, and also to recover against the plaintiff any excess of damages he may have sustained, in order to settle in one suit all the rights of the parties arising under the contract, and to prevent circuity of action and a multiplicity of suits. Hamilton v. Goodridge, 164 Va. 123, 178 S.E. 874 (1935).

And to allow certain equitable defenses to be made at law. — This section was enacted for the purpose of allowing certain equitable defenses to be made at law, and the defendant, on the issue tendered by the plea, has the right to make the same defense as in equity. Guarantee Co. of N. Am. v. First Nat'l Bank, 95 Va. 480, 28 S.E. 909 (1898).

And to dispose of all matters in controversy in one action. — The purpose of this section plainly is to allow all matters in controversy between the plaintiff and the defendant arising out of the same cause of action — i.e., all matters of recoupment — to be disposed of in one action at law, so as to avoid the necessity of the defendant's bringing a separate suit, whether at law or in equity, to determine any such matter. Cox v. Hagan, 125 Va. 656, 100 S.E. 666 (1919). See Watkins v. West Wytheville Land & Imp. Co., 92 Va. 1, 22 S.E. 554 (1895); Newport News & Old Point Ry. & Elec. Co. v. Bickford, 105 Va. 182, 52 S.E. 1011 (1906).

Plea under this section is not true plea of setoff. — The plea provided for by this section, often miscalled "plea in the nature of a plea of setoff," bears no resemblance whatever to a setoff, but is a mere enlargement of the common-law right of recoupment. It arises out of the contract sued on; never out of a transaction dehors the contract, as in the case of setoff. The amount need not be liquidated, and it may not only repel plaintiff's claim, as in common-law recoupment, but defendant may recover over against plaintiff for the excess. It must be specially pleaded and cannot be availed of under the general issue, and it may be used though plaintiff's action is on a sealed instrument. It may be based on equitable grounds. Dexter-Portland Cement Co. v. Acme Supply Co., 147 Va. 758, 133 S.E. 788 (1926).

The section embodies the law of statutory recoupment. — Neely v. White, 177 Va. 358, 14 S.E.2d 337 (1941).

A special plea of setoff in Virginia is in effect a statutory plea of recoupment, and an enlargement of the common-law right of recoupment. Odessky v. Monterey Wine Co., 188 Va. 184, 49 S.E.2d 330 (1948).

It enlarges the common-law right of recoupment. — The provisions of this section were intended to enlarge the right of recoupment theretofore existing at common law. They were intended, not to impair any previous right or take away any defenses previously allowed by the common law, but, in addition thereto, to permit the defendant to recover any legal damages he can prove in excess of the damages claimed by the plaintiff. Davis v. Baxter, 2 Pat. & H. 133 (1856); Columbia Accident Ass'n v. Rockey, 93 Va. 678, 25 S.E. 1009 (1896); Leterman v. Charlottesville Lumber Co., 110 Va. 769, 67 S.E. 281 (1910).

This section applies to proceedings to recover unpaid stock subscriptions. — Dickens v. Radford-Willis Southern Ry., 121 Va. 353, 93 S.E. 625 (1917).

2. Nature of Defendant's Demand.

Claim may be in tort or for unliquidated damages. — The fact that the defendant's claim is in tort or for unliquidated damages is immaterial. If it is based upon matters directly connected with, and injuries growing out of, the contract sued on by plaintiff, it can be asserted as a setoff under this section. Newport News & Old Point Ry. & Elec. Co. v. Bickford, 105 Va. 182, 52 S.E. 1011 (1906). See Leterman v. Charlottesville Lumber Co., 110 Va. 769, 67 S.E. 281 (1910).

If damages are not too speculative. — Where plaintiff brought an action to recover for a carload of potatoes and defendant pleaded damages to two other carloads previously brought by way of setoff, the damages were too speculative, as the claim was based upon such items as: "labor account of rots and frosts," "loss account frosted and number two potatoes," when number one was bought, "profit on car," "never sold," etc. Baker & Co. v. Hartman, 139 Va. 612, 124 S.E. 425 (1924).

3. Necessity That Defendant's Demand Arise Out of Contract in Suit.

Words "or any other matter" are restricted by enumerated defenses. — The meaning of the words "or any other matter" used in this section is restricted by the enumerated defenses which precede them. American Manganese Co. v. Virginia Manganese Co., 91 Va. 272, 21 S.E. 466 (1895). See Huff v. Broyles, 67 Va. (26 Gratt.) 283 (1875); Gates & Son Co. v. City of Richmond, 103 Va. 702, 49 S.E. 965 (1905).

Hence, defendant's claim must grow out of contract in suit. — No setoff can be pleaded by a defendant under this section which does not grow out of the contract in suit. American Manganese Co. v. Virginia Manganese Co., 91 Va. 272, 21 S.E. 466 (1895). See Huff v. Broyles, 67 Va. (26 Gratt.) 283 (1875); Gates & Son Co. v. City of Richmond, 103 Va. 702, 49 S.E. 965 (1905).

Under this section defendant cannot avail himself of a plea of setoff and counterclaim unless his claim grows out of the contract sued on. Bunting v. Cochran, 99 Va. 558, 39 S.E. 229 (1901); Richmond College v. Scott-Nuckols Co., 124 Va. 333, 98 S.E. 1 (1919); Cox v. Hagan, 125 Va. 656, 100 S.E. 666 (1919); Baker & Co. v. Hartman, 139 Va. 612, 124 S.E. 425 (1924).

A special plea of setoff is available under this section only when the claim sought to be set off grows out of the contract sued on. Odessky v. Monterey Wine Co., 188 Va. 184, 49 S.E.2d 330 (1948).

And not out of independent agreement. — Where plaintiff, a contractor, sued defendant for a balance due for work done under two contracts, defendant could not set off damages suffered by it under an independent third contract with plaintiff, which had been fully and completely performed. Richmond College v. Scott-Nuckols Co., 124 Va. 333, 98 S.E. 1 (1919).

4. In What Actions Plea May Be Filed.

Plea may be filed in proceedings by notice of motion. — The proceeding by notice of motion for a judgment for money is an action, and the defendant may file a plea under this section to such notice. Newport News & Old Point Ry. & Elec. Co. v. Bickford, 105 Va. 182, 52 S.E. 1011 (1906).

And in actions on sealed instruments. — This section changes the common-law rule that no damages are to be allowed the defendant by way of recoupment against the plaintiff's demand, when that demand is based on an instrument under seal. Columbia Accident Ass'n v. Rockey, 93 Va. 678, 25 S.E. 1009 (1896); Kinzie v. Riely, 100 Va. 709, 42 S.E. 872 (1902).

And on contracts relating to realty. — There is nothing in the terms of this section to restrict the plea of equitable setoff to contracts in relation to personalty, and there can be no reason for excluding all contracts relating to the sale and purchase of real property from the operation of the section. Watkins v. Hopkins, 54 Va. (13 Gratt.) 743 (1857).

Unless equitable relief is necessary. — Where the equitable grounds relied on require a rescission of the contract, and a reinvestment of the vendor with the title, a special plea under this section is not available; because in such a case a court of law is incompetent to do complete justice between the parties, and recourse must, in the nature of things, be had to a court of equity. Shiflett v. Orange Humane Soc'y, 48 Va. (7 Gratt.) 297 (1851); Watkins v. Hopkins, 54 Va. (13 Gratt.) 743 (1857); Watkins v. West Wytheville Land & Imp. Co., 92 Va. 1, 22 S.E. 554 (1895); Mangus v. McClelland, 93 Va. 786, 22 S.E. 364 (1895); Tyson v. Williamson, 96 Va. 636, 32 S.E. 42 (1899); Mundy v. Garland, 116 Va. 922, 83 S.E. 491 (1914).

But plea of failure of consideration is waiver of right to specific performance. — Where the defendant in an action at law on a purchase-money bond, given pursuant to a contract for the sale of land, pleads failure of consideration by reason of the refusal of the plaintiff to make title, he thereby waives his right to have specific performance of the contract in equity. Watkins v. Hopkins, 54 Va. (13 Gratt.) 743 (1857).

5. By Whom Plea May Be Filed.

Defense is personal to principal debtor. — The defense allowed by this section is personal to the principal, though if successfully made it would redound to the benefit of the surety. Kinzie v. Riely, 100 Va. 709, 42 S.E. 872 (1902).

It does not pass to transferee of stock. —

Although, in a suit to collect assessments to corporate stock from a subscriber, the subscriber may set up any defense allowed by this section, these defenses are personal to him, and do not pass to the transferee of the stock. Lewis v. Berryville Land & Imp. Co., 90 Va. 693, 19 S.E. 781 (1894).

But agent of undisclosed principal may plead. — If the agent of an undisclosed principal, when sued upon a contract by the other party thereto, defends under this section, it is no ground of objection to the plea that the beneficial interest in the recovery, if any, is in another, or that the agent will have to account to another. Leterman v. Charlottesville Lumber Co., 110 Va. 769, 67 S.E. 281 (1910).

B. Grounds for Plea.

1. Fraud in Procurement of Contract.

Section changes the common law. — Fraud in the procurement of a bond was not available at common law in an action on the bond, but is so available under this section. Tyson v. Williamson, 96 Va. 636, 32 S.E. 42 (1899). See also Taylor v. King, 20 Va. (6 Munf.) 358 (1819); Wyche v. Macklin, 23 Va. (2 Rand.) 426 (1824); Burtners v. Keran, 65 Va. (24 Gratt.) 42 (1873); Hayes v. Virginia Mut. Protection Ass'n, 76 Va. 225 (1882); Guarantee Co. of N. Am. v. First Nat'l Bank, 95 Va. 480, 28 S.E. 909 (1898).

Defendant may show fraud in sale of real estate. — A party claiming to have been damaged by fraud or misrepresentation in the procurement of a contract for the sale or purchase of real estate may elect to rescind the contract, or may proceed at law to recover damages. If he is sued at law on bonds given for deferred payment of purchase money, he may file a special plea under this section, and have set off against the plaintiff's demand the amount of damages sustained by him in consequence of such fraud or misrepresentation. Watkins v. West Wytheville Land & Imp. Co., 92 Va. 1, 22 S.E. 554 (1895).

And fraud in procurement of notes. — Where a person is sued on notes he may make defense under this section, that the notes were procured by fraudulent representations. Strickland v. Graybill, 97 Va. 602, 34 S.E. 475 (1899).

The defense of a misrepresentation of law may be made at law by a special plea under the statute, setting out the facts. Brown v. Rice, 67 Va. (26 Gratt.) 467 (1875); Brown v. Rice, 76 Va. 629 (1882).

2. Failure of Consideration.

Defendant may plead failure of consideration in action on note. — In an action upon a note the defendant pleaded failure of consideration and sought by a special plea of setoff to be compensated in damages for breach of the contract on the part of the payee which was the main consideration for the note. It was held that under this section defendant had a right to do this. Wallinger v. Kelly, 136 Va. 547, 117 S.E. 850 (1923).

And on bond. — While failure of consideration could not be shown in defense of an action on a bond at common law, this defense may now be made by a sworn plea under this section. See Isbell v. Norvell, 45 Va. (4 Gratt.) 176 (1847); Watkins v. Hopkins, 54 Va. (13 Gratt.) 743 (1857); Watkins v. West Wytheville Land & Imp. Co., 92 Va. 1, 22 S.E. 554 (1895).

But want of consideration for bond is no defense. — A defense to an action on a bond showing that the bond was originally without consideration cannot be made at common law, nor can such defense be made by special plea under this section allowing equitable defenses to be made at law. The words "failure in the consideration," as used herein, refer to contracts originally founded on a valuable consideration, which has failed, and not to contracts originally voluntary. Harris v. Harris, 64 Va. (23 Gratt.) 737 (1873).

Failure to deliver personalty hired may be shown. — In an action on a bond given for the hire of property, the obligor is entitled, under a special plea filed under this section, to show a failure of the consideration of the bond, in that part of the property was never in his possession but always remained in the possession of the obligee. Isbell v. Norvell, 45 Va. (4 Gratt.) 176 (1847).

And so may failure to deliver land at time and in condition agreed. — A plea under this section setting up a failure to deliver land at the time and in the condition stipulated for in the contract sued on is a good plea, as setting up a partial failure of the consideration. Watkins v. Hopkins, 54 Va. (13 Gratt.) 743 (1857).

And lessor's failure to make repairs. — A lessor covenanted to put certain repairs upon the demised premises, which he failed to do. In an action of replevin upon a distress for rent, the tenant may set off the damages accrued by the failure of the lessor to make the repairs. Caldwell & Co. v. Pennington, 44 Va. (3 Gratt.) 91 (1846).

3. Breach of Warranty.

Section allows recoupment for breach of warranty in sealed instrument. — Damages for breach of warranty in a sealed instrument can only be claimed under this section, and in the manner prescribed therein. Such damages cannot be claimed at common law by way of recoupment against a sealed instrument. Kinzie v. Riely, 100 Va. 709, 42 S.E. 872 (1902).

And for breach of warranty of title to realty. — A grantee of real estate, when sued at law by his grantor for the purchase price, may under this section file a special plea claiming damages for a breach of warranty or covenant of title by his grantor, unless the defense would require the contract to be rescinded and the grantor to be reinvested with the title conveyed. Kinzie v. Riely, 100 Va. 709, 42 S.E. 872 (1902). See Pence v. Huston, 47 Va. (6 Gratt.) 304 (1849); Watkins v. Hopkins, 54 Va. (13 Gratt.) 743 (1857); Tyson v. Williamson, 96 Va. 636, 32 S.E. 42 (1899).

4. Other Matters Entitling Defendant to Equitable Relief.

Equitable damages may be asserted in a plea of statutory recoupment under this section. Odessky v. Monterey Wine Co., 188 Va. 184, 49 S.E.2d 330 (1948).

Special plea may set up defense of mistake of fact. — A plea averred that the note in suit was made for the balance of a note given for the aggregate of sundry notes, and that in the aggregate there was by mistake included a note which had been paid, and that the mistake had been continued on into the note in suit, and was only recently discovered by defendant. It was held that, if such was a defense, it should have been made by a sworn plea under this section, or in a court of equity. Keckley v. Union Bank, 79 Va. 458 (1884).

Or defense that attorney's fee is unreasonable or unconscionable. — The defense in an action by an indorser, who has taken up and paid the note at maturity against the makers, that the amount claimed by plaintiff as attorney's fee under the obligation sued on, and provided for therein, is unreasonable in amount or unconscionable, can be made by special plea under this section, although there is no necessity therefor. Cox v. Hagan, 125 Va. 656, 100 S.E. 666 (1919).

But plea based on defendant's own fraud will not be allowed. — In an action on a bond the defendant filed a special plea alleging that he voluntarily executed the bond for the express purpose of defeating certain claimants who had sued him for damages, because in the excitement prevailing just after the war the court and the jury would not have done him justice in those suits. He attempted to sustain this plea on the ground that it alleged such matter existing before the execution of the bond as entitled him to relief in equity against the obligation thereof. It was held that he was, in effect, asking the court to relieve him from the consequences of his own fraud and that the court must presume that no injustice would have been perpetrated in the regular course of legal proceedings. Harris v. Harris, 64 Va. (23 Gratt.) 737 (1873).

C. Procedure.

1. In General.

Equitable rules apply. — Where the plaintiff sues the defendant at law on a bond given for the purchase money of land, and the defendant sets up the defense of equitable setoff, under this section, for the value of a deficiency in the quantity of the land sold, the rules governing in an equitable forum are applicable, and the plaintiff may rebut the claim of the defendant by any evidence which would have been appropriate to his defense had the defendant elected to proceed by bill in equity. Caldwell v. Craig, 62 Va. (21 Gratt.) 132 (1871). See Grayson v. Buchanan, 88 Va. 251, 13 S.E. 457 (1891).

And this should be recognized in instructions. — When in a court of law the defendant makes an equitable defense under the statute, the rules of equity prevail, and he is entitled to the same relief as in a court of equity. Hence, an instruction that ignorance or mistake of law cannot be considered as a defense because the suit is in a court of law, is erroneous. Brown v. Rice, 76 Va. 629 (1882). See also, Brown v. Rice, 67 Va. (26 Gratt.) 467 (1875).

Instructions may not ignore special plea. — Where a defendant has filed a special plea of setoff and has introduced evidence tending to support it, it is error to ignore entirely the defendant's case and instruct the jury to find for the plaintiff if they believe he has established the items of his account sued for. The jury should be instructed that the amount found to be due the plaintiff was to be off-set by whatever sum, if any, they might believe from the evidence was due from the plaintiff to the defendant, and that the verdict should be for the party to whom the balance was found due. Carlin v. Fraser, 105 Va. 216, 53 S.E. 145 (1906). See King & Co. v. Hancock & Sons, 114 Va. 596, 77 S.E. 510 (1913).

Finding of jury on issue of fraud is conclusive. — Where the jury found for the plaintiff on an issue of fraud in the procurement of a contract made by a special plea, the finding could not be disturbed on an appeal, as the jury were the judges of the weight and credibility of the testimony. Rausch & Co. v. Graham Mfg. Corp., 140 Va. 445, 124 S.E. 427, 126 S.E. 2 (1924).

Verdict on motion to strike defendant's evidence. — Where the only defense set up to the plaintiff's cause of action is for damages by way of a special setoff under this section, and the plaintiff demurs (now moves to strike) to the defendant's evidence, the verdict should be for the defendant, assessing his damages at a stated sum, subject to the opinion of the court upon the plaintiff's demurrer to the evidence (now motion to strike), and if upon the demurrer to the evidence (now motion to strike), the law be with the plaintiff, then for the plaintiff, whatever sum the jury ascertain to be due. South Roanoke Land Co. v. Roberts, 99 Va. 487, 39 S.E. 133 (1901).

2. Plea.

a. In General.

Certain matters of recoupment are provable under general issue. — The defense of recoupment as to unsealed instruments, to the extent that it does not exceed the plaintiff's demand, can be made under the general issue, and, in such a case, a special plea under this section is unnecessary. Winn Bros. & Baker v. Lipscomb, 127 Va. 554, 103 S.E. 623 (1920). See Davis v. Baxter, 2 Pat. & H. 133 (1856); Columbia Accident Ass'n v. Rockey, 93 Va. 678, 25 S.E. 1009 (1895); Keckley v. Union Bank, 79 Va. 458 (1884).

Time of making plea is in discretion of court. — A plea of special setoff was filed nearly two months before the trial, giving the opposite party ample time to prepare for trial. It was held that the determination of the question as to whether the plea was tendered in time rested in the sound discretion of the trial court, and that in allowing the plea there was no abuse of this discretion. Wallinger v. Kelly, 136 Va. 547, 117 S.E. 850 (1923).

Inconsistent pleas are allowed. — In an action of assumpsit brought by the seller of goods against the buyer for failure to accept and pay for the goods ordered, defendant pleaded non-assumpsit, and a special plea of recoupment under this section to recover damages of plaintiff for failure to deliver the goods to the defendant. It was insisted on behalf of plaintiff that when the defendant filed its special plea it forever waived its right to defend on the ground that it had rescinded the contract because of the failure of the plaintiff to begin deliveries at the time agreed upon. It was held that this position was not tenable. Norfolk Hosiery & Underwear Mills v. Aetna Hosiery Co., 124 Va. 221, 98 S.E. 43 (1919).

Plea must show compliance with section. — A plea of equitable offset must show that the offset is such as may be set up under this section. Watkins v. Hopkins, 54 Va. (13 Gratt.) 743 (1857).

It should state amount of defendant's claim. — A special plea under this section must allege the amount to which the defendant is entitled by reason of the matters contained in the plea. Tyson v. Williamson, 96 Va. 636, 32 S.E. 42 (1899); Richmond Ice Co. v. Crystal Ice Co., 99 Va. 239, 37 S.E. 851 (1901); Cox v. Hagan, 125 Va. 656, 100 S.E. 666 (1902).

Or extent to which plaintiff's claim is unreasonable or unconscionable. — If in an action by an indorser against the maker of a note, defense by way of special plea under this section is adopted to plaintiff's claim for attorney's fee, the plea should allege the amount to the extent of which the defendant claims the attorney's fee in question is unreasonable or unconscionable. Cox v. Hagan, 125 Va. 656, 100 S.E. 666 (1902).

b. Setting Out Grounds of Defense.

Grounds of defense should be set forth with certainty. — The defendant, in order to avail himself of the defenses provided by this section, should file a special plea averring the fraud or special circumstances which entitle him to relief in equity. And the facts should be set forth with sufficient precision and certainty to apprise the plaintiff of the character of the defense intended to be made, and to enable the court to decide whether the matter relied on constitutes a valid claim to equitable relief. Burtners v. Keran, 65 Va. (24 Gratt.) 42 (1873); Richardson v. Insurance Co., 68 Va. (27 Gratt.) 749 (1876); Cox v. Hagan, 125 Va. 656, 100 S.E. 666 (1902).

Neither fraud nor breach of warranty can be left to inference. — In an action of debt on a bond for the hire of personalty, if the obligor files a special plea under the statute, and relies on the contract of hiring as furnishing him with an equitable defense, he should set forth the contract of hiring according to its terms or legal effect, and he must allege distinctly any fraud or warranty in regard to it, upon which he founds his defense. Neither fraud nor a breach of warranty can properly be left by the plea to conjecture or inference. Howell v. Cowles, 47 Va. (6 Gratt.) 393 (1849).

Facts showing fraud or existence of warranty must be averred. — In an action of debt on a bond, a special plea was defective and was properly rejected which alleged that the bond was given for the price of goods which defendant bought of plaintiff, who represented that they were sound and marketable, when in fact they were unsound and damaged, and by reason thereof unsalable; but which did not aver a warranty of the quality of the goods, or that the plaintiff knew that the said representations made by him were untrue, or that he used any fraud or art to disguise or conceal their true condition or quality. But in such case a plea would be good which averred that the representations were untrue, and that the plaintiff at the time of making them knew them to be untrue, and knowingly made them with the intent to defraud the defendant, and which proceeded to set out the unsoundness of numerous articles purchased, and to detail particulars in which the representations had turned out to be untrue. Cunningham v. Smith, 51 Va. (10 Gratt.) 255, 60 Am. Dec. 333 (1853). But see

Guarantee Co. of N. Am. v. First Nat'l Bank, 95 Va. 480, 28 S.E. 909 (1898).

But plea need not allege scienter. — A plea under this section is sufficient which avers that the statements of facts were falsely and fraudulently made for the purpose of procuring the contract, that they were material, that they were untrue, and that the defendant to whom they were made relied upon them, and was by them induced to enter into the contract, although it does not in its terms aver scienter. Strickland v. Graybill, 97 Va. 602, 34 S.E. 475 (1899).

It is immaterial that a plea under this section does not allege that the misrepresentations relied on were known by the plaintiff to be false. If a party innocently misrepresents a material fact by mistake, the effect is the same on the party who is misled by it as if he who innocently made the misrepresentation knew it to be positively false. Guarantee Co. of N. Am. v. First Nat'l Bank, 95 Va. 480, 28 S.E. 909 (1898). But see Cunningham v. Smith, 51 Va. (10 Gratt.) 255, 60 Am. Dec. 333 (1853).

It must allege worthlessness of property at time contract made. — A plea of special set-off under this section which sets up the worthlessness of property which formed the consideration of the contract in suit, must aver worthlessness at the time of the contract, and not at the date of the plea. South Roanoke Land Co. v. Roberts, 99 Va. 487, 39 S.E. 133 (1901); Tyson v. Williamson, 96 Va. 636, 32 S.E. 42 (1901).

Allegation of unsoundness in general terms is sufficient. — In an action on a bond given for the price of personalty a special plea was good, which averred in general terms that the property was unsound at the time of the sale, and that the plaintiff knew the fact, and fraudulently concealed it from the defendant, and that upon discovering the fact the defendant offered to return the property and demanded a rescission of the contract, which plaintiff refused, laying the damages to the whole amount of the price, or not laying any damages, and praying for judgment in bar of the action. And if such a plea averred in general terms the unsoundness of the property, and then added a specific unsoundness, the defendant might under the plea prove any unsoundness, and he would not be confined to the specific unsoundness mentioned in the plea. Fleming v. Toler, 48 Va. (7 Gratt.) 310 (1851).

Plea held sufficiently certain and precise. — In an action upon a note the defendant pleaded failure of consideration, and sought by a special plea of setoff to be compensated in damages for breach of the contract on the part of the payee which was the main consideration for the note. It was objected that the plea did not set out the things alleged with sufficient precision and certainty. It was held that though there should be such precision and certainty, and the plea alleged both failure of consideration and fraud, yet in view of the circumstance that the plea was not filed after the first trial of the case, in which the defendant had fully developed in evidence all the details of the matters alleged in the plea, it was plain that the allegations were sufficiently precise. Wallinger v. Kelly, 136 Va. 547, 117 S.E. 850 (1923).

3. Appeal and Error.

Surety alone cannot prosecute writ of error. — If in an action by a grantor against the grantee and his surety on a bond given for the purchase price of real estate, a joint plea is filed by principal and surety under this section, claiming damages for a breach of warranty of title, and the plea be found against the defendants, the surety cannot alone prosecute a writ of error. Kinzie v. Riely, 100 Va. 709, 42 S.E. 872 (1902).

Amount in controversy. — Where the full amount of a setoff allowed exceeds the jurisdictional amount, an appeal lies to the Supreme Court on behalf of the complainant, although the amount decreed against him is less than that sum. Bunting v. Cochran, 99 Va. 558, 39 S.E. 229 (1901).

§ 8.01-423. When plaintiff claims as assignee or transferee. — If the plaintiff claims as assignee or transferee under a person with whom the contract sued on was originally made, and the defendant's claim exceeds the plaintiff's demand, the defendant:

1. In his counterclaim, may waive the benefit of his claim as to any excess beyond the plaintiff's claim, whereupon, the further proceedings shall be upon the plaintiff's claim and the defendant's counterclaim as a defense thereto; or

2. Instead of such waiver such defendant may, by rule issued by the court, to which rule shall be attached a copy of the counterclaim and served on the person, under whom plaintiff claims as aforesaid, make such person a party to the action; and, on the trial of the case, the jury shall ascertain and apply, the amount and interest to which the defendant is entitled; and, for any excess beyond the plaintiff's demand for which such person under whom the plaintiff claims as aforesaid is liable, with such interest as the court or jury allows,

judgment shall be rendered for the defendant against such person. (Code 1950, § 8-246; 1954, c. 619; 1977, c. 617.)

REVISERS' NOTE

Section 8.01-423 is former § 8-246 from which the phrase "or, on his application, issued by the clerk of the court in vacation" has been deleted from subsection 2 as being unnecessary.

Other language changes have been made but the substance of this seldom-used statute has not been changed.

CHAPTER 16.

COMPROMISES.

Sec.
8.01-424. Approval of compromises on behalf of persons under a disability in suits or actions to which they are parties.

Sec.
8.01-425. How fiduciaries may compromise liabilities due to or from them.
8.01-425.1. Release of liability; right of rescission.

§ 8.01-424. Approval of compromises on behalf of persons under a disability in suits or actions to which they are parties. — A. In any action or suit wherein a person under a disability is a party, the court in which the matter is pending shall have the power to approve and confirm a compromise of the matters in controversy on behalf of such party, including claims under the provisions of any liability insurance policy, if such compromise is deemed to be to the interest of the party. Any order or decree approving and confirming the compromise shall be binding upon such party, except that the same may be set aside for fraud.

B. In case of damage to the person or property of a person under a disability, caused by the wrongful act, neglect or default of any person, when death did not ensue therefrom, any person or insurer interested in compromise of any claim for such damages, including any claim under the provisions of any liability insurance policy, may, upon motion to the court in which the action is pending for the recovery of damages on account of such injury, or if no such action is pending, then to any circuit court, move the court to approve the compromise. The court shall require the movant to give reasonable notice of such motion to all parties and to any person found by the court to be interested in the compromise.

C. A compromise action involving a claim for wrongful death shall be in accordance with the applicable provisions of § 8.01-55. Nothing in this section shall be construed to affect the provisions of § 8.01-76.

D. In any compromise action the court shall direct the payment of the proceeds of the compromise agreement, when approved, as follows:

1. Payment of the sum into court as provided by § 8.01-600 or to the general receiver of such court;

2. To a duly qualified fiduciary of the person under a disability, after due inquiry as to the adequacy of the bond of such fiduciary;

3. As provided in § 8.01-606; or

4. Where the agreement of settlement provides for payments to be made over a period of time in the future, whether such payments are lump sum, periodic, or a combination of both, the court shall approve the settlement only if it finds that all payments which are due to be made are (i) secured by a bond issued by an insurance company authorized to write such bonds in this Commonwealth or (ii) to be made by an insurance company or companies

§ 8.01-424 CODE OF VIRGINIA § 8.01-424

authorized to do business in this Commonwealth and which is rated "A plus" (A+) or better by Best's Insurance Reports. Payments made under this subdivision totaling not more than $4,000 in any calendar year may be paid in accordance with § 8.01-606. Payments made under this subdivision, totaling more than $4,000 in any calendar year while the recipient is under a disability, shall be paid to a duly qualified fiduciary after due inquiry as to adequacy of the bond of such fiduciary.

E. Payments made under this section, in the case of damage to the person or property of a minor, may be made payable in the discretion of the court to the parent or guardian of the minor to be held in trust for the benefit of the minor. Any such trust shall be subject to court approval and the court may provide for the termination of such trust at any time following attainment of majority which the court deems to be in the best interest of the minor. In an order authorizing the trust or additions to an existing trust the court may order that the trustee thereof be subject to the same duty to qualify in the clerk's office and to file an inventory and annual accountings with the commissioner of accounts as would apply to a testamentary trustee. (Code 1950, §§ 8-169, 8-170; 1956, c. 575; 1960, cc. 301, 302; 1964, c. 500; 1970, c. 10; 1977, c. 617; 1985, c. 499; 1988, c. 409; 1991, cc. 97, 257; 1993, c. 945; 1994, c. 39; 1998, cc. 584, 607, 610.)

REVISERS' NOTE

Section 8.01-424 is a combination of former §§ 8-169 and 8-170.

In the revision of former Title 8, the new phrase "person under a disability" has been adopted in most instances in lieu of such terms as "incompetent," "incapacitated," "insane," or "infant"; this term, as defined, includes all persons unable to protect their property or legal rights regardless of the particular impairment.

A substantial change in the new statute is the elimination of the right of an infant to attack an order of compromise within six months after reaching his majority. With the deletion of that provision, distinctions between infancy and other types of disabilities are no longer relevant.

Former § 8-170 has been completely rewritten to simplify the procedure for compromising personal injury and property claims of persons under a disability. The provisions pertaining to the court wherein a motion for such a compromise is to be made have been changed. Section 8.01-424 provides that if an action to recover damages for injury to a person under a disability has been filed, the motion seeking approval of a compromise must be presented to the court in which that action is pending. However, if no such action has been brought, the motion may be made to any circuit court within the Commonwealth. Former § 8-170 required that such approval be obtained by the "court wherein an action might be brought." The change thus reflected in § 8.01-424 is in conformity with the broadened venue provisions of chapter 5, and is premised on the likelihood that parties agreeing to a compromise will be able to agree upon a mutually convenient circuit court for approval of that compromise.

In addition to the greater flexibility of the present section, the deletion of the provision making it unnecessary to make any person whose whereabouts are unknown a party to such proceedings affords increased protection to the interests of such person.

The provisions incorporated in former § 8-170 dealing with procedures set forth in other sections of the Code have been retained in § 8.01-424. See §§ 8.01-55 (Wrongful death compromise), 8.01-76 (Disposition of proceeds from sales of lands of persons under disabilities), 8.01-600 (Deposit of money under court's control), 8.01-606 (Payment of small amounts to infants, etc.).

Cross references. — For provision as to rights of fiduciaries to compromise claims generally, see § 8.01-425.

Law Review. — For comment, "The Covenant Not to Sue: Virginia's Effort to Bury the Common Law Rule Regarding the Release of Joint Tortfeasors," see 14 U. Rich. L. Rev. 809 (1980). For article, "The Duty to Settle," see 76 Va. L. Rev. 1113 (1990). For 1991 survey on wills, trusts, and estates, see 25 U. Rich. L. Rev. 925 (1991).

I. Decisions Under Current Law.
II. Decisions Under Prior Law.

I. DECISIONS UNDER CURRENT LAW.

Power of court. — Explicitly, the statute gives the court power to approve a compromise. Implicitly, the court has the power under the statute to disapprove a compromise. However, neither the statute nor any "inherent" power the court may possess permits the court to create a settlement and then to impose such a settlement upon a guardian, and the trial court erred in forcing the guardian to accept hospital's offer of settlement. Gunn v. Richmond Community Hosp., 235 Va. 282, 367 S.E.2d 480 (1988).

Court's duty not ended by settlement and stipulation of dismissal. — An incompetent person's suit cannot be ended upon settlement followed by the filing of a stipulation of dismissal. It is only when a settlement occurs that the court's duty to oversee the settlement arises. If that duty could be aborted by the filing of a stipulation, the role of the court would be effectively avoided. Neither law nor logic sanction such a result. Crawford v. Loving, 84 F.R.D. 80 (E.D. Va. 1979).

The court's duty to oversee the settlement of claims asserted on behalf of incompetent persons cannot be abandoned simply because the parties assert, following a purported settlement, that they "no longer wish to litigate the matter further." Crawford v. Loving, 84 F.R.D. 80 (E.D. Va. 1979).

The federal district court did not lose jurisdiction over a civil rights action on behalf of an incompetent against prison officials simply because the parties agreed to a settlement. Indeed, it was because there was a settlement that the matter was properly before the court for its approval. Crawford v. Loving, 84 F.R.D. 80 (E.D. Va. 1979).

Applied in Potomac Hosp. Corp. v. Dillon, 229 Va. 335, 329 S.E.2d 41 (1985); Cauthorn v. British Leyland, U.K., Ltd., 233 Va. 202, 355 S.E.2d 306 (1987); Parrish v. Jessee, 250 Va. 514, 464 S.E.2d 141 (1995).

II. DECISIONS UNDER PRIOR LAW.

Editor's note. — The case cited below was decided under corresponding provisions of former law. The term "this section," as used below, refers to former provisions.

A divorced mother with sole custody of a minor child has the right to compromise the child's claim for damages tortiously inflicted. Sims v. VEPCO, 550 F.2d 929 (4th Cir.), cert. denied, 431 U.S. 925, 97 S. Ct. 2199, 53 L. Ed. 2d 239 (1977).

§ 8.01-425. How fiduciaries may compromise liabilities due to or from them.

— Any fiduciary may compromise any liability due to or from him, provided that such compromise be ratified and approved by a court of competent jurisdiction, all parties in interest being before such court by proper process. When such compromise shall have been so ratified and approved, it shall be binding on all parties in interest before such court. Nothing contained in this section shall affect the right of indemnity or of contribution among the parties. (Code 1950, §§ 8-171, 8-173; 1977, c. 617.)

REVISERS' NOTE

Section 8.01-425 is former § 8-171, without substantive change. The cautionary provision that nothing in the statute shall affect the right of indemnity or contribution is former § 8-173.

Because joint stock companies are an enigma under current Virginia law, former § 8-172, the only section in the Code dealing with such organizations, has been deleted.

Cross references. — As to power of fiduciaries to submit to arbitration, see § 8.01-581.

I. DECISIONS UNDER CURRENT LAW.

This section does not require that, to be valid, compromises made by a fiduciary must be approved by a court; rather, the provisions of this section are permissive. Subsequent litigation of a compromise executed by a fiduciary without court approval may void the compromise as to some or all of the affected parties in interest; however, the compromise is not void at its inception, merely voidable under appropriate circumstances. Kelly v. R.S. Jones & Assocs., 242 Va. 79, 406 S.E.2d 34 (1991).

§ 8.01-425.1. **Release of liability; right of rescission.** — When a claimant or plaintiff executes a release of liability as a condition of settlement in a claim or action for personal injury within thirty days of the incident giving rise to such claim, such claimant or plaintiff shall have a right of rescission until midnight of the third business day after the day on which the release was executed, provided that he was not represented by counsel when the release was executed, the rescission was made in writing to the person or persons being released, their representative or insurance carrier, and the claimant returns to the person or persons being released any check or settlement proceeds received by the claimant prior to the rescission. A release of liability executed within thirty days of the incident giving rise to the claim for personal injury by a person who is not represented by counsel shall contain a notice of the claimant's or the plaintiff's right to rescind conspicuously and separately stated on the release. (1999, c. 326; 2000, c. 839.)

The 2000 amendments. — The 2000 amendment by c. 839 added the second sentence.

CHAPTER 17.

Judgments and Decrees Generally.

Article 1.

In General.

Sec.
8.01-426. "Judgment" includes decree.
8.01-427. Persons entitled under decree deemed judgment creditors; execution on decree.
8.01-427.1. [Repealed.]
8.01-428. Setting aside default judgments; clerical mistakes; independent actions to relieve party from judgment or proceedings; grounds and time limitations.
8.01-429. Action of appellate court when there might be redress under § 8.01-428.
8.01-430. When final judgment to be entered after verdict set aside.

Article 2.

Judgments by Confession.

8.01-431. Judgment or decree by confession in pending suit.
8.01-432. Confession of judgment irrespective of suit pending.
8.01-433. Setting aside judgments confessed under § 8.01-432.
8.01-433.1. Notice of confession of judgment provision.
8.01-434. Lien of such judgments.
8.01-435. Who may confess judgment.
8.01-436. Form of confession of judgment.
8.01-437. Endorsement of clerk thereon.

Sec.
8.01-438. When judgment confessed by attorney-in-fact copy to be served on judgment debtor.
8.01-439. Filing of records by clerk.
8.01-440. Docketing and execution.
8.01-441. When judgment confessed by virtue of power of attorney invalid.

Article 3.

When There Are Several Defendants.

8.01-442. In joint actions on contract plaintiff, though barred as to some, may have judgment against others.
8.01-443. Joint wrongdoers; effect of judgment against one.
8.01-444. Where new parties added; if some not liable, how judgment entered.

Article 4.

Distinction Between Term and Vacation Abolished.

8.01-445. Distinction between term and vacation abolished; effect of time.

Article 5.

Keeping of Docket Books; Execution Thereon; Disposal of Exhibits.

8.01-446. Clerks to keep judgment dockets; what judgments to be docketed therein.
8.01-446.1. Keeping of docket books by clerk of

Sec.		Sec.	
	court using micrographic process; form.	8.01-456.	Satisfaction of judgment when judgment creditor cannot be located.
8.01-447.	Docketing of judgments and decrees of United States courts.	8.01-457.	Marking satisfied judgments for Commonwealth; payment by third parties releasing recognizances.
8.01-448.	Attorney General, etc., to have judgments in favor of Commonwealth docketed.		
8.01-449.	How judgments are docketed.		**Article 7.**
8.01-450.	How indexed.		**Lien and Enforcement Thereof.**
8.01-451.	Judgments to be docketed and indexed in new names of judgment debtors; how execution may thereafter issue.	8.01-458.	From what time judgment to be a lien on real estate; docketing revived judgment.
8.01-452.	Entry of assignment of judgment on judgment lien docket.	8.01-459.	Priority of judgments.
		8.01-460.	Decree for support and maintenance of spouse or infant children of parties as lien on real estate.
8.01-452.1.	Disposal of exhibits in civil cases.		
	Article 6.	8.01-461.	Abstracts of judgments.
	Satisfaction.	8.01-462.	Jurisdiction of equity to enforce lien of judgment; when it may decree sale.
8.01-453.	When and how payment or discharge entered on judgment docket.	8.01-463.	Enforcement of lien when judgment does not exceed twenty dollars.
8.01-454.	Judgment, when paid, to be so noted by creditor.	8.01-464.	Order of liability between alienees of different parts of estate.
8.01-455.	Court, on motion of defendant, etc., may have payment of judgment entered.	8.01-465.	Chapter embraces recognizances and bonds having force of judgment.

Article 1.

In General.

§ 8.01-426. "Judgment" includes decree. — A decree for land or specific personal property, and a decree or order requiring the payment of money, shall have the effect of a judgment for such land, property, or money, and be embraced by the word "judgment," where used in this chapter or in Chapters 18, 19 or 20 of this title or in Title 43; but a party may proceed to carry into execution a decree or order in chancery other than for the payment of money, as he might have done if this and the following section had not been enacted. (Code 1950, § 8-343; 1977, c. 617.)

Cross references. — As to actions by the Commonwealth, see §§ 8.01-196 through 8.01-216. As to confession of judgment, see § 8.01-431 et seq. As to executions of judgement, see § 8.01-466 et seq. As to records, recordation and indexing, see § 17.1-223 et seq. As to homestead exemptions as affecting this chapter, see §§ 34-24, 34-25. As to recordation, of decrees affecting title to land, see § 55-138.

I. Decisions Under Current Law.
II. Decisions Under Prior Law.

I. DECISIONS UNDER CURRENT LAW.

Satisfaction of monetary award granted under § 20-107.3 is governed by this section. Brown v. Brown, 5 Va. App. 238, 361 S.E.2d 364 (1987).

Award of monetary sum under § 20-107.3 D equivalent to money judgment. — To the extent a decree awards a monetary sum pursuant to subsection D of § 20-107.3, it is the equivalent of a money judgment and must be satisfied as such. The trial court may provide, however, that a monetary award be payable as a lump sum or in periodic fixed amounts. In either instance, the trial court may exercise its discretion in determining when the lump sum award or the periodic fixed amounts are due and payable. If no due date is specified in the

§ 8.01-427

decree, or if the award (or any portion thereof) is not satisfied by the payment date set forth in the decree, that award (or portion thereof) becomes the equivalent of a money judgment. Brown v. Brown, 5 Va. App. 238, 361 S.E.2d 364 (1987).

Order pursuant to § 20-107.3 held to exceed courts authority. — The trial court exceeded its authority in ordering mandatory payment of the monetary award under subsection D of § 20-107.3 within 120 days. While it was authorized to fix a date upon which the award was due and payable, the trial court lacked authority to order mandatory payment subject to enforcement by its contempt powers. Brown v. Brown, 5 Va. App. 238, 361 S.E.2d 364 (1987).

II. DECISIONS UNDER PRIOR LAW.

Editor's note. — The cases cited below were decided under corresponding provisions of former law. The term "this section," as used below, refers to former provisions.

Only by force of our statute law can process of execution be sued out upon decrees in chancery. Windrum v. Parker, 29 Va. (2 Leigh) 361 (1830); Shackelford v. Apperson, 47 Va. (6 Gratt.) 451 (1849); Snavely v. Harkrader, 71 Va. (30 Gratt.) 487 (1878).

Decree in equity and order in mandamus are equally "judgments". — A decree in an equity cause ordering the clerk to pay over money, and an order in a mandamus proceeding to compel the clerk to do so, were held to be "judgments" against the clerk within this section, and it was the clerk's duty to issue execution thereon as required by § 8.01-466. Rinehart & Dennis Co. v. McArthur, 123 Va. 556, 96 S.E. 829 (1918).

Person entitled to property or money is judgment creditor. — A decree for specific property, or requiring the payment of money, has the effect of a judgment, and persons entitled thereto are judgment creditors. Hutchison v. Grubbs, 80 Va. 251 (1885).

Statute fixing lien of judgment applies to decrees. — Since a decree for money, by express enactment, is embraced by the word "judgment," the statute fixing the lien of a judgment applies equally to such decrees. Hockman v. Hockman, 93 Va. 455, 25 S.E. 534 (1896).

And decree creates lien on lands. — A decree in chancery, equally with a judgment at law, creates a lien on lands. Haley v. Williams, 28 Va. (1 Leigh) 140 (1829); Withers v. Carter, 45 Va. (4 Gratt.) 407 (1848); Burbridge v. Higgins, 47 Va. (6 Gratt.) 119 (1849); Buchanan v. Clark, 51 Va. (10 Gratt.) 164 (1853); Lee v. Swepson, 75 Va. 173 (1881).

This rule applies to decree for alimony. — A decree for alimony payable in monthly installments during the life of the beneficiary constitutes a lien in her favor upon the husband's real estate from the date of the decree, not only for the installments presently due but for those that shall fall due under such decree in the future. Isaacs v. Isaacs, 117 Va. 730, 86 S.E. 105 (1915). See Morris v. Henry, 193 Va. 631, 70 S.E.2d 417 (1952).

To decree for support of infant child. — See Morris v. Henry, 193 Va. 631, 70 S.E.2d 417 (1952).

And to decree directing commissioner to pay money out of funds in his hands. — A commissioner made a sale under a decree, and received one-third of the purchase money, without giving bond as required. The sale was confirmed, and a decree entered and docketed, directing the commissioner, out of funds reported in his hands, to pay certain creditors therein. Five days later the commissioner conveyed in trust his own real estate to secure his own creditor. It was held that the decree against the commissioner had the effect of a judgment, and, the decree being docketed, the commissioner's creditor was affected with notice thereof, though the purchaser paid the commissioner in his own wrong. Lee v. Swepson, 76 Va. 173 (1882).

An alimony decree is not a mere money decree within the meaning of this section and § 8.01-427, under which courts of equity do not have power to enforce decrees for the payment of money by process of contempt, and the same principles apply to an award for counsel fees and suit money. Eddens v. Eddens, 188 Va. 511, 50 S.E.2d 397 (1948).

Any execution which may be taken upon a judgment may be taken upon a decree. Tate v. Liggat, 29 Va. (2 Leigh) 84 (1830).

This section gives courts of chancery the power to superintend the issuing of executions on their own decrees, and the power to correct irregularities and abuses therein, to the same extent, and by the same means, as courts of law. Windrum v. Parker, 29 Va. (2 Leigh) 361 (1830); Snavely v. Harkrader, 71 Va. (30 Gratt.) 487 (1878).

And to quash executions irregularly sued out. — Courts of chancery may quash executions irregularly sued out on their decrees. Windrum v. Parker, 29 Va. (2 Leigh) 361 (1830).

§ 8.01-427. Persons entitled under decree deemed judgment creditors; execution on decree. — The persons entitled to the benefit of any decree or order requiring the payment of money shall be deemed judgment creditors, although the money be required to be paid into a court, or a bank, or other place of deposit. In such case, an execution on the decree or order shall make such recital thereof, and of the parties to it, as may be necessary to identify the case; and if a time be specified in the decree or order within which the payment is to be made, the execution shall not issue until the expiration of that time. (Code 1950, § 8-344; 1977, c. 617.)

REVISERS' NOTE

Former § 8-347 (When judgment by default on scire facias to become final) has been deleted. See § 8.01-251.

I. DECISIONS UNDER PRIOR LAW.

Editor's note. — The case cited below was decided under corresponding provisions of former law. The term "this section," as used below, refers to former provisions.

Every execution should conform accurately to the judgment or decree which it is used to enforce. Beale's Adm'r v. Botetourt Justices, 51 Va. (10 Gratt.) 278 (1853); O'Bannon v. Saunders, 65 Va. (24 Gratt.) 138 (1873); Snavely v. Harkrader, 71 Va. (30 Gratt.) 487 (1878).

§ 8.01-427.1: Repealed by Acts 1978, c. 426, effective March 31, 1978.

§ 8.01-428. Setting aside default judgments; clerical mistakes; independent actions to relieve party from judgment or proceedings; grounds and time limitations. — A. *Default judgments and decrees pro confesso; summary procedure.* — Upon motion of the plaintiff or judgment debtor and after reasonable notice to the opposite party, his attorney of record or other agent, the court may set aside a judgment by default or a decree pro confesso upon the following grounds: (i) fraud on the court, (ii) a void judgment, (iii) on proof of an accord and satisfaction. Such motion on the ground of fraud on the court shall be made within two years from the date of the judgment or decree.

B. *Clerical mistakes.* — Clerical mistakes in all judgments or other parts of the record and errors therein arising from oversight or from an inadvertent omission may be corrected by the court at any time on its own initiative or upon the motion of any party and after such notice, as the court may order. During the pendency of an appeal, such mistakes may be corrected before the appeal is docketed in the appellate court, and thereafter while the appeal is pending such mistakes may be corrected with leave of the appellate court.

C. *Failure to notify party or counsel of final order.* — If counsel, or a party not represented by counsel, who is not in default in a circuit court is not notified by any means of the entry of a final order and the circuit court is satisfied that such lack of notice (i) did not result from a failure to exercise due diligence on the part of that party and (ii) denied that party an opportunity to file an appeal therefrom, the circuit court may, within sixty days of the entry of such order, grant the party leave to appeal. The computation of time for noting and perfecting an appeal shall run from the entry of such order, and such order shall have no other effect.

D. *Other judgments or proceedings.* — This section does not limit the power of the court to entertain at any time an independent action to relieve a party from any judgment or proceeding, or to grant relief to a defendant not served with process as provided in § 8.01-322, or to set aside a judgment or decree for fraud upon the court. (1977, c. 617; 1991, c. 39; 1993, c. 951.)

REVISERS' NOTE

Section 8.01-428 is an adaptation of FRCP 55 and 60 and replaces former § 8-348, which has been deemed unclear (Federal Realty v. Litterio & Co., 213 Va. 3, 189 S.E.2d 314 (1972)). The time limitation for setting aside a default judgment or decree pro confesso on the ground of fraud on the court has been reduced from three to two years. No limitation period is provided when the ground is a void judgment or an accord and satisfaction. (See § 8.01-428 A.) In addition, no time limitation is proposed for the grounds set forth in § 8.01-428 B and C.

A court's inherent equity power to entertain an independent action to relieve a party from any judgment has been preserved.

Cross references. — As to grant of new trial from judgment of general district court, see § 16.1-97.1.

Law Review. — For survey of Virginia law on practice and pleading for the year 1974-1975, see 61 Va. L. Rev. 1799 (1975).

I. Decisions Under Current Law.
  A. General Consideration.
  B. Procedure.
  C. Relief.
  D. Other Judgments or Proceedings.
II. Decisions Under Prior Law.
  A. General Consideration.
  B. Procedure.
  C. Relief.

I. DECISIONS UNDER CURRENT LAW.

A. General Consideration.

Purpose of subsection A. — The object of subsection A, apparent on its face, is to grant a summary procedure for relief from judgments which are subject to one of the three specific defects mentioned in the statute. McEwen Lumber Co. v. Lipscomb Bros. Lumber Co., 234 Va. 243, 360 S.E.2d 845 (1987).

Section narrowly construed. — This section and its predecessors, which create exceptions to the finality of judgments, is narrowly construed. McEwen Lumber Co. v. Lipscomb Bros. Lumber Co., 234 Va. 243, 360 S.E.2d 845 (1987).

Section not limited to civil proceedings. — While predecessor statutes may have been intended to apply only in civil proceedings, the language of this section evidences no such restrictive intent. Lamb v. Commonwealth, 222 Va. 161, 279 S.E.2d 389 (1981).

Authority of court. — This section covers more than errors committed by court clerks; it authorizes a court to correct its own errors and omissions. Hunter v. Commonwealth, 23 Va. App. 306, 477 S.E.2d 1 (1996).

Effect of Rule 1:1. — Supreme Court Rule 1:1 was not intended to limit, and in fact could not limit, the trial court's statutory authority to correct clerical errors in the judgment or errors therein arising from oversight or from an inadvertent omission at any time. Dorn v. Dorn, 222 Va. 288, 279 S.E.2d 393 (1981).

The power conferred by this section is not limited by Rule 1:1, but is confined to "the rare situation where the evidence clearly supports the conclusion that an error covered by this Code section has been made." Dixon v. Pugh, No. 1647-90-2 (Ct. of Appeals Aug. 13, 1991).

The order in which the trial judge ruled that the husband was entitled to a credit was entered more than two years after entry of the final decree. In the absence of an exception to Rule 1:1, the trial judge lost jurisdiction over the case twenty-one days after the initial judgment, and he could not issue a valid modification order. Decker v. Decker, 22 Va. App. 486, 471 S.E.2d 775 (1996).

Scope of subsection B. — Although subsection B of this section is entitled "Clerical mistakes," the text includes other errors in the record "arising from oversight or from an inadvertent omission." Thus, the language of this section clearly is broad enough to cover more than errors committed by the clerk or one of the clerk's employees. Lamb v. Commonwealth, 222 Va. 161, 279 S.E.2d 389 (1981).

The word "clerical" in subsection B is not limited by the identity of the person who made the mistake. Lamb v. Commonwealth, 222 Va. 161, 279 S.E.2d 389 (1981).

This section is sufficiently comprehensive to authorize the correction of an inadvertent error in a transcript made by a court reporter. Lamb v. Commonwealth, 222 Va. 161, 279 S.E.2d 389 (1981).

Subsection B confers upon a court the power to correct on its own initiative clerical mistakes

§ 8.01-428

in judgments which arise from oversight or inadvertent omission. However, to invoke such authority the evidence must clearly support the conclusion that an error of oversight or inadvertence has been made. Cass v. Lassiter, 2 Va. App. 273, 343 S.E.2d 470 (1986).

The trial court has the inherent power, independent of statutory authority, to correct errors in the record so as to cause its acts and proceedings to be set forth correctly. Davis v. Mullins, 251 Va. 141, 466 S.E.2d 90 (1996).

While there may have been mistakes made by client's counsel in suggesting a modification which worked to client's disadvantage, it was not the kind of clerical mistake which may be corrected under subsection B of this section. This was not a scrivener's error, or an error which is demonstrably contradicted by all other written documents. In fact, the evidence demonstrated that the modification to the consent decree was not an act of oversight or inadvertent omission as required in the statute, but was instead a deliberate revision. Keough v. Pelletieri, No. 0914-95-4 (Ct. of Appeals Oct. 31, 1995).

Subsection B has no application to errors in the reasoning and conclusions of the court about contested matters. Therefore, where the error that defendant alleged to exist concerned the trial judge's conclusion that a sentence of 30 years imprisonment with 15 years suspended was consistent with the plea agreement recitation of a "sentence not to exceed 15 years," the alleged error concerned the trial judge's reasoning about a contested matter and was not remedied by application of subsection B. D'Alessandro v. Commonwealth, 15 Va. App. 163, 423 S.E.2d 199 (1992).

Court may presume inconsistencies to be unintentional absent reasonable explanation. — In the absence of any reasonable explanation as to why the parties might have intentionally altered the language of the in-court stipulation, the trial court may presume that any inconsistencies are unintentional and are within its authority to amend. Artis v. Artis, 10 Va. App. 356, 392 S.E.2d 504 (1990).

Subsection C does not create any new rights or remedies, but merely preserves a court's inherent equity power to entertain an independent action. Charles v. Precision Tune, Inc., 243 Va. 313, 414 S.E.2d 831 (1992).

Subsection C of this section must be given a narrow construction. This is so because judicial proceedings must have a certainty of result, and a high degree of finality must attach to judgments. Byrum v. Lowe & Gordon, Ltd., 225 Va. 362, 302 S.E.2d 46, cert. denied, 464 U.S. 961, 104 S. Ct. 394, 78 L. Ed. 2d 337 (1983).

Subsection C specifically preserves the long-recognized right to bring an independent action in equity to relieve a party from the detrimental consequences flowing from an earlier judgment which allegedly resulted from fraud on the court. Gulfstream Bldg. Ass'n v. Britt, 239 Va. 178, 387 S.E.2d 488 (1990).

It is a fundamental principle of equity jurisprudence that a litigant who files an independent action in equity to set aside a judgment must be free of fault or neglect. Charles v. Precision Tune, Inc., 243 Va. 313, 414 S.E.2d 831 (1992).

Independent action under subsection C. — Defendant may invoke the provision in subsection C, which provides that the section "does not limit the power of the court to entertain at any time an independent action to relieve a party from any judgment or proceeding," and seek relief from the default judgment only by instituting an "independent action," not by a motion filed as part of the cause in which the judgment order was entered. Basile v. American Filter Serv., Inc., 231 Va. 34, 340 S.E.2d 800 (1986).

The trial court's inherent equity power to set aside the default judgment is properly exercised only in an independent proceeding initiated by a party seeking relief from a judgment. Basile v. American Filter Serv., Inc., 231 Va. 34, 340 S.E.2d 800 (1986).

A party who suffers a default judgment and files an independent action may obtain relief only by proving all of the necessary elements, including fraud, accident, or mistake which prevented him from obtaining the benefit of his defense. Therefore, where evidence failed to establish any of those elements, trial court erred by setting aside the default judgment. Charles v. Precision Tune, Inc., 243 Va. 313, 414 S.E.2d 831 (1992).

Subsection (c) (now subsection D) does not provide a court unlimited authority to set aside a judgment procured by fraud; it does not override the rule of finality of judgments or grant a court the authority to set aside what is, at most, a voidable judgment. Warren v. Pham, No. 0479-98-4 (Ct. of Appeals July 28, 1998).

Challenge to foreign judgment precluded by default. — Once a valid default judgment has been entered in a Virginia court in a proceeding to domesticate a foreign judgment, general rules applicable to challenges permitted in the domestication proceeding no longer apply. By suffering a default, the defendant in the domestication proceeding loses the opportunity to attack the foreign judgment upon which the Virginia proceeding is based. Washington v. Anderson, 236 Va. 316, 373 S.E.2d 712 (1988).

Judge's misstatement regarding length of sentence. — Trial judge's misstatement regarding the length of time defendant was ordered to serve in the penitentiary was an error covered by this section; therefore, she had the authority to correct her misstatement and resentence defendant in accordance with her original intention. Nelson v. Commonwealth, 12 Va. App. 835, 407 S.E.2d 326 (1991).

Erroneous information given to counsel by the clerk's staff over the telephone did not constitute a "clerical mistake" within the meaning of this section. School Bd. v. Caudill Rowlett Scott, Inc., 237 Va. 550, 379 S.E.2d 319 (1989).

Court did not err in refusal to amend where counsel endorsed order. — Where order of November 1, 1985 did not conform to the stipulation that "'wife did all the duties ... as a mother and as a wife' and instead held that wife 'had made an equal contribution to the marriage, well being of the family, and to the acquisition, care and maintenance of the marital property,'" counsel's endorsement of the order, and his stated reasons for so endorsing, sufficiently corroborated the wife's explanation that the November 1 order reflected the intent of the stipulation; accordingly, the trial court did not err in refusing to amend. Artis v. Artis, 10 Va. App. 356, 392 S.E.2d 504 (1990).

Sufficient prima facie evidence of extrinsic fraud. — Where core of the husband's claim was that his wife told him that the attorney she hired would represent both of their interests in divorce, and further, he alleged that because of the special relationship of trust between him and his wife, he relied on this statement and did not obtain his own legal counsel, the husband's allegation that the wife's misrepresentation precluded him from presenting his true case and rights to the court stated a prima facie claim of extrinsic fraud sufficient to withstand a demurrer. Zdanis v. Deely, Nos. 1078-94-4, 1689-94-4 (Ct. of Appeals May 9, 1995).

Applied in Cutshaw v. Cutshaw, 220 Va. 638, 261 S.E.2d 52 (1979); Forrest v. Forrest, 3 Va. App. 236, 349 S.E.2d 157 (1986); M.E.D. v. J.P.M., 3 Va. App. 391, 350 S.E.2d 215 (1986); Dennis v. Jones, 240 Va. 12, 393 S.E.2d 390 (1990); Francis v. Francis, 30 Va. App. 584, 518 S.E.2d 842 (1999).

B. Procedure.

Procedure under subsections A and B differs from that under C. — Subsections A and B of this section speak of a motion, while subsection C of this section speaks of an independent action. Clearly, by using different terminology in different paragraphs of the same Code section, the General Assembly meant to provide for a different procedure under C than under A and B. This view is reinforced by the Revisers' Note to this section which states that subsection C is meant to preserve "[a] court's inherent equity power to entertain an independent action to relieve a party from any judgment ...." This view is further reinforced by an examination of the predecessor section of this section, former § 8-348, which provided for relief from a default judgment only upon motion. Byrum v. Lowe & Gordon, Ltd., 225 Va. 362, 302 S.E.2d 46 (1983), cert. denied, 464 U.S. 961, 104 S. Ct. 394, 78 L. Ed. 2d 337 (1983).

Subsection A affords a summary procedure for relief from judgments which are subject to three specific, gross defects. Subsection B contains a more liberal rule for the correction of clerical errors, matters of oversight, and inadvertent omissions. Subsection C applies to cases not mentioned in the two preceding subsections, in which the right to relief is less clear, or where the interests of third parties may be affected, and which therefore require the full opportunities for pleading, discovery, and presentation of evidence afforded by a plenary suit in equity. McEwen Lumber Co. v. Lipscomb Bros. Lumber Co., 234 Va. 243, 360 S.E.2d 845 (1987).

Supreme Court Rule 5:11 does not provide the exclusive procedure for correcting errors. Lamb v. Commonwealth, 222 Va. 161, 279 S.E.2d 389 (1981).

But it provides the preferred procedure that should be used in all cases to correct transcripts. Lamb v. Commonwealth, 222 Va. 161, 279 S.E.2d 389 (1981).

Circuit court empowered to correct mistake of district court records. — Once the district court records became part of the circuit court record, the circuit court was empowered to correct a clerical mistake in the district court proceedings on its own initiative, so long as the evidence clearly supported the court's conclusion that an error of oversight or inadvertence had been made; moreover, the court was empowered to hold an evidentiary hearing in order to make this determination. Loving v. Commonwealth, No. 1563-88-4 (Ct. of Appeals May 22, 1990).

There is no time limit prescribed for making the correction under subsection B of this section. Lamb v. Commonwealth, 222 Va. 161, 279 S.E.2d 389 (1981).

Correction after docketing of appeal. — Where a criminal appeal was docketed before an error in the trial transcript was discovered, correction could be made only with leave of the Supreme Court. Lamb v. Commonwealth, 222 Va. 161, 279 S.E.2d 389 (1981).

C. Relief.

Court may enter order nunc pro tunc. — Supreme Court Rule 1:1 or Richardson v. Moore, 217 Va. 422, 229 S.E.2d 864 (1976), does not preclude a trial court, under subsection B of this section, from correcting, nunc pro tunc, a mutually unintended drafting error contained in a divorce decree. Dorn v. Dorn, 222 Va. 288, 279 S.E.2d 393 (1981).

Subsection B of this section, unlike § 20-108, gives courts the authority to enter nunc pro tunc orders modifying support obligations in the rare situation where the evidence clearly supports the conclusion that an error covered by subsection B has been made. Dorn v. Dorn, 222 Va. 288, 279 S.E.2d 393 (1981).

Nunc pro tunc order may not remediate court error. — An order nunc pro tunc may not be created to remediate an error of the court or to reflect what the court should have done as distinguished from what actually occurred. Blackburn v. Commonwealth, No. 2166-96-3 (Ct. of Appeals Oct. 14, 1997).

An order entered nunc pro tunc cannot create a fiction that an act not yet performed has already occurred. Rather, the power of the trial court to amend by nunc pro tunc order is restricted to placing upon the record evidence of judicial action which has already been taken, but was earlier omitted or misstated in the record. Taylor v. Taylor, No. 2694-96-2 (Ct. of Appeals June 3, 1997).

No authority to amend decree with nunc pro tunc order. — Trial court had no authority to amend decree by entering a nunc pro tunc order. A court's statutory and inherent power to amend the record nunc pro tunc could not be used to acquire subject matter jurisdiction where the decree of spousal support failed to contain a clear and explicit reservation of jurisdiction. Dixon v. Pugh, 244 Va. 539, 423 S.E.2d 169 (1992).

Nunc pro tunc order invalid. — Where neither defendant nor Commonwealth requested a continuance, and trial judge did not grant a continuance, rather the parties and trial judge agreed upon a date on which they would convene in order to schedule the case for trial, the trial judge's entry of an order nunc pro tunc stating that the appellant moved for and was granted a continuance did not establish that a continuance was granted. The trial court attempted, after the fact, to establish that it had granted a continuance, when, in fact, the parties and the court merely agreed to a date on which they would schedule trial. Thus, the trial court's order nunc pro tunc was invalid, and the Commonwealth failed to bring the appellant to trial within the period prescribed by § 19.2-243. Blackburn v. Commonwealth, No. 2166-96-3 (Ct. of Appeals Oct. 14, 1997).

Where case had been continued by agreement but no court entry upon the record reflected such a continuance, because trial court never considered a motion for a continuance and never ordered a continuance, there was no defect or omission in the record. Therefore, the trial court lacked authority to issue an order nunc pro tunc reciting that a continuance had been granted when in fact the court had not granted a motion for a continuance on the motion of or with the concurrence of the defendant. The nunc pro tunc order was thus invalid and could not bar appellant's speedy trial claim. Blevins v. Commonwealth, No. 1264-96-3 (Ct. of Appeals Sept. 30, 1997).

Default judgment obtained by misleading defendant into thinking a continuance had been agreed upon is fraudulent and should be set aside. National Airlines v. Shea, 223 Va. 578, 292 S.E.2d 308 (1982).

A writ of prohibition will not lie where the proper resolution of the disputed issue depends upon matters of statutory interpretation that are not clear-cut, or upon a review of contested factual issues. In re McCarthy, No. 1116-87-4 (Ct. of Appeals Oct. 16, 1987).

Garnishment not set aside on basis of accord and satisfaction between principal defendant and garnishee. — Subsection A was not basis for setting aside judgment in garnishment on grounds that an accord and satisfaction had been entered into, where no contention was made that the plaintiff and garnishee had entered into an accord and satisfaction. Although principal defendant's judgment against garnishee may have been the subject of an accord and satisfaction, plaintiff's judgment alone was the subject of the proceeding below, and it was unimpaired by any of the defects mentioned in subsection A. McEwen Lumber Co. v. Lipscomb Bros. Lumber Co., 234 Va. 243, 360 S.E.2d 845 (1987).

Post-appeal conviction, sentencing order change not authorized. — Trial court's power to correct clerical mistakes did not authorize it to enter post-appeal order changing conviction and sentencing orders entered 5 years before to reflect that defendant had been convicted under different section; those orders became final 21 days after their entry. The trial court's order being a nullity, it was not an order from which an appeal to challenge defendant's conviction could be brought anew. Myers v. Commonwealth, 26 Va. App. 544, 496 S.E.2d 80 (1998).

D. Other Judgments or Proceedings.

Motion filed as part of case is not "independent" action. — The revisor's note appended to this section indicates that it was enacted to preserve the court's inherent equity power to grant relief from the enforcement of a judgment in a proper case. However, a motion filed as a part of the case in which the judgment order was entered is not an "independent action" to relieve a party from a judgment under subsection C. McEwen Lumber Co. v. Lipscomb Bros. Lumber Co., 234 Va. 243, 360 S.E.2d 845 (1987).

Defense to a contempt proceeding in a divorce case is not an independent action as contemplated by subsection C. Rook v. Rook, 233 Va. 92, 353 S.E.2d 756 (1987).

Non-party may maintain suit if interest jeopardized by enforcement of judgment. — A non-party may maintain a suit to set aside an allegedly damaging judgment if he has an interest which is jeopardized by enforcement of the judgment and the circumstances support a present grant of relief. The right of the non-party must have existed at the time the judgment was rendered. Gulfstream Bldg. Ass'n v. Britt, 239 Va. 178, 387 S.E.2d 488 (1990).

In a suit to set aside a judgment involving title to land, the prejudiced right or interest must have been in existence at the time of the judgment and have belonged either to the present claimant or to his predecessor in interest. Gulfstream Bldg. Ass'n v. Britt, 239 Va. 178, 387 S.E.2d 488 (1990).

Fundamental unfairness of Virginia court's child support order should have been challenged by defendant at entry and on direct appeal. Nonetheless, due process did require allowance of this subsequent challenge in federal court. United States v. Johnson, 114 F.3d 476 (4th Cir. 1997), cert. denied, 522 U.S. 904, 118 S. Ct. 258, 139 L. Ed. 2d 185 (1997).

II. DECISIONS UNDER PRIOR LAW.

A. General Consideration.

Editor's note. — The cases cited below were decided under corresponding provisions of former law. The term "this section," as used below, refers to former provisions.

Former section constitutional. — The predecessor to this section was constitutional, being a statute passed in aid of judicial proceedings and which tended to their support by precluding parties from taking advantage of errors, apparent on the face of the proceedings, which did not affect their substantial rights. Such statutes are not regarded as an interference with judicial authority, but only in aid of judicial proceedings for the purpose of correcting errors, such as are mentioned in the statute. Ratcliffe v. Anderson, 72 Va. (31 Gratt.) 105 (1878).

The object of the legislature was to save the parties the delay and loss of an appeal to correct irregularities and formal errors, errors which seldom affect the merits of the controversy, and which would have been corrected at once by the court if pointed out. Davis v. Commonwealth, 57 Va. (16 Gratt.) 134 (1861).

Remedy is cumulative. — This statutory remedy is cumulative and has not superseded or abolished petitions for rehearing which may still be had according to the course of equity, in the same manner as before the enactment of the statute. Kendrick v. Whitney, 69 Va. (28 Gratt.) 646 (1877).

B. Procedure.

Motion must be after notice to opposite party. — Every motion under this section must be after reasonable notice to the opposite party, his agent or attorney in fact or at law. Hill v. Bowyer, 59 Va. (18 Gratt.) 364 (1868); Goolsby v. Strother, 62 Va. (21 Gratt.) 107 (1871).

But only reasonable notice is required. — The notice of the motion to reverse or correct is required to be only reasonable notice. This section does not contemplate the more formal, expensive, and dilatory proceedings, by bill and regular process. Ballard v. Whitlock, 59 Va. (18 Gratt.) 235 (1867); Hill v. Bowyer, 59 Va. (18 Gratt.) 364 (1868); Dillard v. Thornton, 70 Va. (29 Gratt.) 392 (1877).

It need not specify errors relied on. — The notice under this section need not specify the errors for which the court is asked to correct or reverse its judgment by default, or decree in a bill taken for confessed. Saunders v. Grigg, 81 Va. 506 (1886).

Record must show error. — No motion to amend was made under this section, and if it had been it would not have availed the appellant, because there was nothing in the record to show that the trial court committed an error. Owen v. Owen, 157 Va. 580, 162 S.E. 46 (1932).

Method of seeking appellate review may be material. — In considering questions arising under this section, it would seem to be important to bear in mind whether review by the appellate court would be upon writ of error or upon an appeal. Craddock v. Craddock, 158 Va. 58, 163 S.E. 387 (1932).

C. Relief.

This section provides for the correction of errors generally, on a judgment by default or bill taken for confessed, and for misprisions of the clerk, or clerical misprisions of the judge where the judgment may be safely corrected in the manner prescribed. Thompson v. Carpenter, 88 Va. 702, 14 S.E. 181 (1892); Shipman v. Fletcher, 91 Va. 473, 22 S.E. 458 (1895).

It has no application to errors in the reasoning and conclusions of the court about contested matters. Thompson v. Carpenter, 88 Va. 702, 14 S.E. 181 (1892); Shipman v. Fletcher, 91 Va. 473, 22 S.E. 458 (1895); Safety Motor Transit Corp. v. Cunningham, 161 Va. 356, 171 S.E. 432 (1933).

It applies to all judgments when there has been no appearance. — All judgments of every character whether in common-law actions or on motions under some statute, when there has been no appearance by the defendant, are judgments by default within the meaning of this section. Brown v. Chapman, 90 Va. 174, 17 S.E. 855 (1893); Staunton Perpetual Bldg. & Loan v. Haden, 92 Va. 201, 23 S.E. 285 (1895).

But if, the record shows appearance,

§ 8.01-428 CIVIL REMEDIES AND PROCEDURE § 8.01-428

judgment is not by default. — If the record merely shows an appearance by the party complaining, the judgment will not be treated as being by default, although he may neither demur nor plead, or it may appear that he withdrew all his pleas and defenses. Compton v. Cline, 46 Va. (5 Gratt.) 137 (1848); Richardson v. Jones, 53 Va. (12 Gratt.) 53 (1855); Goolsby v. Strother, 62 Va. (21 Gratt.) 107 (1871).

Trial court may correct clerical errors in decree. — Under this section as it formerly read, upon notice to the opposite party, his agent, or attorney-at-law or in-fact, the court wherein the decree is rendered, may on motion correct such decree as to any clerical error therein where there is sufficient in the record to enable the court to safely amend the same. Dillard v. Dillard, 77 Va. 820 (1883).

Court may set aside judgment prematurely entered. — A judgment and award of execution upon a forfeited forthcoming bond having been entered by default upon a day prior to that to which notice was given, the court in which the judgment and award of execution was rendered has jurisdiction on the motion of the plaintiff to set aside the judgment and quash the execution, upon reasonable notice to the defendants. Ballard v. Whitlock, 59 Va. (18 Gratt.) 235 (1867).

Or judgment against a party not served with process. — A judgment against a party who was not served with process and against whom the suit had abated is void as to her but not as to her codefendants, as it is an error that can and should be corrected under this section. Manor v. Hindman, 123 Va. 767, 97 S.E. 332 (1918).

It may allow amendment of return to show proper service. — Where, under this section, defendant moves the judge in vacation to reverse a judgment by default upon a defective return of substituted service of the summons, and to remand the case for trial, the court may then allow the sheriff to amend his return so as to show a proper service, and dismiss the defendant's motion. Stotz v. Collins & Co., 83 Va. 423, 2 S.E. 737 (1887).

Verdict may be put in approved form. — It is the duty of the trial courts to require the verdicts of juries to be put in approved form in order to effectuate their true intent and meaning, and hence, where the jury reported a verdict written upon a piece of paper in the following words: "We, the jury, find for the plaintiff and fix the damages due by the defendant to be twelve hundred dollars," there was no error where the verdict was in open court, written upon the declaration and signed by the foreman in these words: "We, the jury, find for the plaintiff on the issues joined, and fix his damages at twelve hundred dollars." Manor v. Hindman, 123 Va. 767, 97 S.E. 332 (1918).

And may reverse decree on bill not stating case for relief in equity. — Where a bill in equity does not state a case proper for relief in that forum, the court should dismiss it upon the hearing, and it was, therefore, error to dismiss the motion made under this section, where a decree on such a bill was taken for confessed. Graveley v. Graveley, 84 Va. 145, 4 S.E. 218 (1887).

Or where record does not show notice to take depositions given. — In a suit for divorce, in which the defendant did not appear until after the decree was rendered, the decree was properly set aside on the motion of the defendant, where the record failed to show that notices to take depositions were duly given. Craddock v. Craddock, 158 Va. 58, 163 S.E. 387 (1932). But see Hill v. Bowyer, 59 Va. (18 Gratt.) 364 (1868).

When default judgment valid. — As a general proposition, a default judgment is valid if the trial court had territorial jurisdiction, subject-matter jurisdiction and if adequate notice has been given to the defaulting party. Landcraft Co. v. Kincaid, 220 Va. 865, 263 S.E.2d 419 (1980).

Default judgment may be invalidated when the motion for judgment fails to state a cause of action; under such circumstances, that failure is held to disable the court from entering a valid default judgment. Landcraft Co. v. Kincaid, 220 Va. 865, 263 S.E.2d 419 (1980).

Default judgment may be reversed. — A judgment by default obtained on substituted service may, under this section, be reversed by the trial court for any error for which an appellate court might reverse it. Such a judgment does not import a verity which cannot be attacked. Brame v. Nolen, 139 Va. 413, 124 S.E. 299 (1924).

Entry of default judgment as judgment by confession cannot be corrected. — A judgment by confession entered by mistake of the clerk instead of a judgment upon nil dicit, cannot be corrected at the next term of the court, under either this section or § 8.01-677. Richardson v. Jones, 53 Va. (12 Gratt.) 53 (1855).

Nor can it be vacated. — If a court has no power to change a judgment by confession to one nil dicit, plainly it has no power to wipe it away. Nor is such power given by this section. New York Life Ins. Co. v. Barton, 166 Va. 426, 186 S.E. 65 (1936).

Error in amount of decree released. — Where an error in the amount of a decree is released according to this section, the appellate court will not reverse the decree on that account. Dickinson v. Clement, 87 Va. 41, 12 S.E. 105 (1890).

Court may enter order nunc pro tunc. — On an application to a trial court to correct a judgment by default, under the provisions of this section, it appeared that no order was entered by the court on the day to which a notice of a motion for a judgment was returnable, but that judgment by default was entered at a subsequent term. It was held that it was within the power and discretion of the court to enter an order nunc pro tunc docketing the motion and continuing it to the next term, and validating the judgment, as between the original parties and annexing a condition thereto that the judgment should not affect the rights of innocent third persons whose rights had accrued since the original judgment and before the nunc pro tunc order. Such an order, when made, is an entirety, and is not valid as to the judgment and void as to the condition. The two provisions are dependent on each other. Powers v. Carter Coal & Iron Co., 100 Va. 450, 41 S.E. 867 (1902).

Corrected judgment is valid. — Where the petition alleged that a note had been returned for taxation but, due to an omission of the clerk, the judgment did not show it, but the error was corrected under this section, after due notice, there was no merit in the contention that the judgment was void. Jayne v. Kane, 140 Va. 27, 124 S.E. 247 (1924).

Decree may be corrected on bill of review. — In a suit for the removal of a guardian and the settlement of his accounts, a final decree can be reheard after the term at which it is entered only upon motion under this section where the decree was on a bill taken for confessed, or on a bill of review. But as the practice in Virginia is liberal, touching mere forms of pleading, the court will regard petitions of a guardian and his surety, praying that such decree be reheard, vacated and set aside, as bills of review. Gills v. Gills, 126 Va. 526, 101 S.E. 900 (1920).

And original bill may be treated as motion under this section. — An original bill which seeks to correct errors in a decree by default apparent on its face, and also to set it aside on the ground of mistake and surprise, having been filed without leave, cannot be treated as a bill of review. But a copy of the original record being filed with the bill, the court may consider and correct any errors apparent in the face of the decree which may be corrected by the court under this section. Hill v. Bowyer, 59 Va. (18 Gratt.) 364 (1868).

But injunction will not issue where this section provides remedy. — An injunction will not be awarded to a judgment by default upon summons directed to sheriff of a county other than the one in which the action is brought; for although the summons was issued contrary to law, the judgment, though erroneous, is not void, and the defendant has a complete remedy at law under this section. Brown v. Chapman, 90 Va. 174, 17 S.E. 855 (1893). See Goolsby v. St. John, 66 Va. (25 Gratt.) 146 (1874).

When the court exceeds its jurisdiction in rendering a personal decree, injunction will not lie as the error may be corrected under this section. Preston v. Kindrick, 94 Va. 760, 27 S.E. 588 (1897).

Section gives no power to validate vacation judgments. — The object and purpose of this section is to correct errors of mistake, miscalculation or recital in judgments and decrees where matter appears in the record by which the correction may be safely made. It confers no power to give validity and force to vacation judgments and decrees which are void for want of power in the judge to render them. Wingfield v. McGhee, 108 Va. 120, 60 S.E. 755 (1908).

Correction of errors in commissioner's report. — Where a final decree has been entered in a litigated case confirming the report of a commissioner, without exception or objection, the court will not reverse the decree, on motion under this section, for errors alleged in said report and not appearing on the face of it. Shipman v. Fletcher, 91 Va. 473, 22 S.E. 458 (1895).

In the absence of objection in the court below, that the commissioner had not regularly adjourned from time to time the taking of the accounts, an appellate court would presume that they were regular; and the objection is not therefore available under this statute. Hill v. Bowyer, 59 Va. (18 Gratt.) 364 (1868).

Trial court cannot correct its own order vacating judgment. — The court below having vacated a judgment upon a motion of the defendant, where all parties appeared by their counsel, it had no jurisdiction to correct its action in that regard under this section; the proper remedy was by appeal. Dillard v. Thornton, 70 Va. (29 Gratt.) 392 (1877).

The Supreme Court is without power to correct a clerical error in its own decrees when the application for relief is made after the expiration of the term at which the decree was rendered, or after the expiration of the period within which a petition for rehearing may be filed. Southern Ry. v. Glenn's Adm'r, 7 Va. L. Reg. 532 (1900).

Statement that no exceptions had been filed was neither a finding of fact nor a conclusion of law, but was merely an erroneous recital of what took place during the proceedings, and correction was properly made under this section. State Hwy. Comm'r v. Easley, 215 Va. 197, 207 S.E.2d 870 (1974).

§ 8.01-429. Action of appellate court when there might be redress under § 8.01-428. — No appeal shall be allowed by the Court of Appeals or the Supreme Court or any judge or justice thereof for any matter for which a judgment or decree is liable to be reversed or amended, on motion as aforesaid, by the court which rendered it, or the judge thereof, until such motion is made and overruled in whole or in part. And when the Court of Appeals or the Supreme Court hears a case on appeal, if it appears that, either before or since the appeal, the judgment or decree has been so amended, the Court of Appeals or the Supreme Court shall affirm the judgment or decree, unless there is other error. If it appears that the amendment ought to be, and has not been made, the Court of Appeals or the Supreme Court may make such amendment, and affirm in like manner the judgment or decree, unless there is other error. (Code 1950, § 8-349; 1977, c. 617; 1984, c. 703.)

REVISERS' NOTE

Former § 8-350 has been transferred to § 8.01-383.1.

I. DECISIONS UNDER PRIOR LAW.

Editor's note. — The cases cited below were decided under corresponding provisions of former law. The term "this section," as used below, refers to former provisions.

Appeal is not allowed unless relief is sought in trial court. — Pursuant to this section, the Supreme Court has no jurisdiction of an appeal from a decree by default until relief has been sought under § 8.01-428, by motion to the court in which the decree was rendered. When the time allowed by § 8.01-428 has expired, the decree becomes final and irreversible. Smith v. Powell, 98 Va. 431, 36 S.E. 522 (1900).

Hence supersedeas would be dismissed. — If a party obtains a supersedeas to a judgment by default, before applying to the court in which the judgment was rendered, or the judge thereof, to correct the errors of which he complains, his supersedeas will be dismissed as improvidently awarded. Davis v. Commonwealth, 57 Va. (16 Gratt.) 134 (1861).

A mistake of the trial court in rendering judgments for damages after the verdict may be corrected by appellate court under the provisions of this section. Powers v. Hamilton, 117 Va. 810, 86 S.E. 98 (1915).

Trial court erred in vacating default judgment. — Where defendant had been personally served and plaintiff had strictly complied with all the formalities of rules of pleading and the motion for judgment stated a cause of action, the trial court erred in vacating a default judgment, there being no errors on which an appellate court might reverse and no cognizable mistake. Landcraft Co. v. Kincaid, 220 Va. 865, 263 S.E.2d 419 (1980).

§ 8.01-430. When final judgment to be entered after verdict set aside. — When the verdict of a jury in a civil action is set aside by a trial court upon the ground that it is contrary to the evidence, or without evidence to support it, a new trial shall not be granted if there is sufficient evidence before the court to enable it to decide the case upon its merits, but such final judgment shall be entered as the court shall seem right and proper. If necessary to assess damages which have not been assessed, the court may empanel a jury at its bar to make such assessment, and then enter such final judgment.

Nothing in this section contained shall be construed to give to trial courts any greater power over verdicts than they now have under existing rules of procedure, nor to impair the right to move for a new trial on the ground of after-discovered evidence. (Code 1950, § 8-352; 1977, c. 617.)

REVISERS' NOTE

Former § 8-353 (How judgment entered on bond for payment of money) has been deleted, since this section was merely declaratory of long-standing and clear principles of substantive law.

Former § 8-354 (Right of infant to show cause against decree) has also been deleted. The infant is protected by the tolling statute found in § 8.01-229.

Cross references. — As to power of trial court to grant a new trial on the grounds of inadequate or excessive damages, see § 8.01-383 and note. As to rule of decision on appeal from order granting or overruling motion to set aside a verdict as contrary to the evidence, see § 8.01-680 and note.

Law Review. — For note, "New Trial on the Issue of Damages in Virginia," see 41 Va. L. Rev. 269 (1955). For article reviewing recent developments and changes in legislation, case law, and Virginia Supreme Court Rules affecting civil litigation, see "Civil Practice and Procedure," 26 U. Rich. L. Rev. 679 (1992).

I. Decisions Under Current Law.
II. Decisions Under Prior Law.
   A. General Consideration.
   B. When Verdict Should Be Set Aside.
   C. Power of Court to Enter Final Judgment.
   D. Power of Court to Impanel Jury to Assess Damages.
   E. When New Trial Should Be Granted.
   F. Effect of Section on Appeal.

I. DECISIONS UNDER CURRENT LAW.

Criteria for setting verdict aside. — The power conferred on the trial judge under this section to set aside a jury verdict and enter judgment thereon can only be exercised where the verdict is plainly wrong or without credible evidence to support it. If there is a conflict in the testimony on a material point, or if reasonable men may differ in their conclusions of fact to be drawn from the evidence, or if the conclusion is dependent on the weight to be given the testimony, the trial judge cannot substitute his conclusion for that of the jury merely because he would have voted for a different verdict if he had been on the jury. The weight of a jury's verdict, when there is credible evidence upon which it can be based, is not overborne by the trial judge's disapproval. Lane v. Scott, 220 Va. 578, 260 S.E.2d 238 (1979), cert. denied, 446 U.S. 986, 100 S. Ct. 2969, 64 L. Ed. 2d 843 (1980); Dutton v. Locker, 224 Va. 535, 297 S.E.2d 814 (1982).

Under this section, a verdict may be set aside only where it is contrary to the evidence or without evidence to support it and the trial court may then enter final judgment rather than grant a new trial if there is sufficient evidence to enable the court to decide the case upon its merits. Sampson v. Sampson, 221 Va. 896, 275 S.E.2d 597 (1981).

When conflicting inferences have been resolved by a jury and those necessarily underlying the conclusion reflected in the verdict are reasonably deducible from the evidence, a trial judge should not set the verdict aside. Lane v. Scott, 220 Va. 578, 260 S.E.2d 238 (1979), cert. denied, 446 U.S. 986, 100 S. Ct. 2969, 64 L. Ed. 2d 843 (1980); Coleman v. Blankenship Oil Corp., 221 Va. 124, 267 S.E.2d 143 (1980); Sampson v. Sampson, 221 Va. 896, 275 S.E.2d 597 (1981).

Reviewing court must reinstate jury verdict if there is credible evidence to support it. — If there is credible evidence in the record which supports the jury's verdict, the reviewing court must reinstate that verdict and enter judgment thereon. Rogers v. Marrow ex rel. Marrow, 243 Va. 162, 413 S.E.2d 344 (1992).

Reviewing court accords verdict recipient benefit of all conflict in evidence. — In analyzing the evidence, even where the trial court has set aside the verdict, the reviewing court accords the recipient of the verdict the benefit of all substantial conflict in the evidence, as well as all inferences which may be reasonably drawn from the evidence. Rogers v. Marrow ex rel. Marrow, 243 Va. 162, 413 S.E.2d 344 (1992).

Trial court erred in setting aside jury verdict based on defendant's evidence where the defendant had no obligation to produce any evidence; the burden of proof in a negligence case rests solely on the plaintiff and does not shift. Rogers v. Marrow ex rel. Marrow, 243 Va. 162, 413 S.E.2d 344 (1992).

Applied in Board of Supvrs. v. Safeco Ins. Co. of Am., 226 Va. 329, 310 S.E.2d 445 (1983); Brown v. Koulizakis, 229 Va. 524, 331 S.E.2d

440 (1985); Carter v. Lambert, 246 Va. 309, 435 S.E.2d 403 (1993); Allstate Ins. Co. v. White, 257 Va. 73, 510 S.E.2d 461 (1999).

II. DECISIONS UNDER PRIOR LAW.

A. General Consideration.

Editor's note. — The cases cited below were decided under corresponding provisions of former law. The term "this section," as used below, refers to former provisions.

The object of this section is to put an end to litigation, to obviate repeated trials and the delay and expense of litigation, and to remove the temptation to perjury by patching up the weak places disclosed at a former trial, not by after-discovered evidence, but by the same witnesses relied upon at the former trial. W.S. Forbes & Co. v. Southern Cotton Oil Co., 130 Va. 245, 108 S.E. 15 (1921).

The object of this section is to end the action at once and put the losing party to his writ of error, thus avoiding the temptation to perjury, and in many cases the unnecessary expense of a second trial. Clark v. Hugo, 130 Va. 99, 107 S.E. 730 (1921). See Sykes v. Brown, 156 Va. 881, 159 S.E. 202 (1931).

The policy and purpose of this section and § 8.01-681 is a speedy determination of litigation and the rendition of a final judgment where it is clear, that upon the facts before it, the court can by such order attain the ends of justice. Morris & Co. v. Alvis, 130 Va. 434, 107 S.E. 664 (1921); Standard Dredging Co. v. Barnalla, 158 Va. 367, 163 S.E. 367 (1932).

It does not deny constitutional guaranty of jury trial. — When a verdict is properly set aside as contrary to the evidence, or without evidence to support it, the power to enter a final judgment conferred upon the court by this section is not the power to determine any disputed fact in a controversy touching property, or a suit between man and man, and is not forbidden by the Constitution. W.S. Forbes & Co. v. Southern Cotton Oil Co., 130 Va. 245, 108 S.E. 15 (1921).

Which does not apply where case depends on question of law. — If no evidence is offered, or none that would warrant a jury in finding a verdict in accordance therewith, then the rights of the parties become a question of law, and there is no controversy to be determined by a jury, and the constitutional guaranty does not apply. W.S. Forbes & Co. v. Southern Cotton Oil Co., 130 Va. 245, 108 S.E. 15 (1921).

Limitation of scope of new trial does not violate Federal Constitution. — The practice that the scope of a new trial may be limited to less than all the issues of fact, when they are separable, does not violate the requirements of the Seventh Amendment to the Federal Constitution. The legislature and courts of Virginia have recognized the propriety of this practice. Schuerholz v. Roach, 58 F.2d 32 (4th Cir.), cert. denied, 287 U.S. 623, 53 S. Ct. 78, 77 L. Ed. 541 (1932).

Federal court cannot enter final judgment. — Even though this section allows the court to decide cases on their merits when the verdict is set aside, without granting a new trial, it does not permit the exercise of such power by a judge of a federal court, because the Seventh Amendment of the Federal Constitution, as interpreted by the U.S. Supreme Court, denies any such powers to a judge in a federal court. Norton v. City Bank & Trust Co., 294 F. 839 (4th Cir. 1923).

The section applies only to civil cases. — This section, with reference to the order to be entered by a trial court upon setting aside a verdict, and § 8.01-681, with reference to the order of reversal to be entered in the Supreme Court, do not apply to criminal cases. As to such cases the practice remains unchanged and is controlled by § 19.2-324. Henderson v. Commonwealth, 130 Va. 761, 107 S.E. 700 (1921).

Prior motion to strike evidence not required. — Whether or not there has been a prior motion to strike the evidence, the motion to set aside the verdict may be used as an appropriate method of testing the sufficiency of the evidence. Gabbard v. Knight, 202 Va. 40, 116 S.E.2d 73 (1960).

Where verdict set aside as contrary to or unsupported by evidence. — Neither this section nor § 8.01-681 has any application except where there has been a motion to set aside the verdict because it is contrary to the evidence, or is without evidence to support it. If the verdict is set aside for some other reason, these sections do not apply. Hogg v. Plant, 145 Va. 175, 133 S.E. 759 (1926).

It does not apply to proceedings to remove public officer. — From the use of the technical term "civil action" in this section it is apparent that the section means to embrace only private personal actions, and not such a quasi-criminal statutory proceeding as a proceeding to remove a public officer under former §§ 15.1-63 through 15.1-66, which is not a private or personal action — is not purely private or civil — but is an action primarily public in its nature, which, although not criminal, is highly penal, and in which the Commonwealth is a party. Warren v. Commonwealth, 136 Va. 573, 118 S.E. 125 (1923). See Commonwealth ex rel. Davis v. Malbon, 195 Va. 368, 78 S.E.2d 683 (1953).

It is not in conflict with § 8.01-378. — There is no difficulty in harmonizing § 8.01-378, forbidding peremptory instructions directing a verdict, with this section, providing for final judgment where a verdict is set aside as without evidence or contrary to the evidence. W.S. Forbes & Co. v. Southern Cotton Oil Co.,

130 Va. 245, 108 S.E. 15 (1921).

Although it reaches same result as directed verdict. — Under the federal practice it is the duty of the judge to direct a verdict in favor of one of the parties when the testimony and all the inferences which the jury could justifiably draw therefrom would be insufficient to support a different finding. Under the practice in Virginia the same results are reached if the necessities of the case require it, by virtue of this section and § 8.01-680, which provide when final judgment is to be entered by the appellate court after a verdict is set aside, and the rule of decision where the evidence and not the facts are certified. Southern Ry. v. Wilmouth, 154 Va. 582, 153 S.E. 874, cert. denied, 282 U.S. 878, 51 S. Ct. 81, 75 L. Ed. 775 (1930).

While § 8.01-378 forbids the trial court to direct a verdict, it is still possible to accomplish the same results by less summary methods. Evidence may be stricken out; the trial court may set aside the verdict, and in a proper case give final judgment under this section; the trial court may decline to give any instruction where the evidence would not sustain a verdict, and it may in substance direct a verdict by stating in an instruction a hypothetical case and telling the jury if they so believe, to find, etc. Davis v. Rodgers, 139 Va. 618, 124 S.E. 408 (1924).

It provides a substitute for new trial or remittitur. — If the evidence, in an action to recover unliquidated damages, showed that the amount of damages fixed by the jury was grossly inadequate or grossly excessive, trial courts, at common law, have, with due caution, exercised the power to set aside such verdicts and grant new trials, or, in the event the amount of the verdict was grossly excessive, have put the plaintiff on terms and entered judgment for a smaller sum. Under this section the practice, in such cases, is for the trial court to set aside the verdict and impanel a jury to assess proper damages. Isenhour v. McGranighan, 178 Va. 365, 17 S.E.2d 383 (1941).

B. When Verdict Should Be Set Aside.

Criteria for not setting aside verdict. — If there is conflict of testimony on a material point, or if reasonably fair-minded men may differ as to the conclusions of fact to be drawn from the evidence, or if the conclusion is dependent upon the weight to be given the testimony, in all such cases the verdict of the jury is final and conclusive, and cannot be disturbed either by the trial court or by the Supreme Court, and if improperly set aside by the trial court, it will be reinstated by the Supreme Court. It is not sufficient that the judge, if on the jury, would have rendered a different verdict. It is not sufficient that there is a great preponderance of the evidence against it. But with all the respect that is justly due to the verdict of a jury, if there has been "a plain deviation from right and justice," even a court of law will not make itself a party to such a wrong by entering up judgment on it. W.S. Forbes & Co. v. Southern Cotton Oil Co., 130 Va. 245, 108 S.E. 15 (1921). See also, Peninsula Produce Exch., Inc. v. Upshur, 149 Va. 639, 140 S.E. 651 (1927); Meade v. Saunders, 151 Va. 636, 144 S.E. 711 (1928); Hoover v. J.P. Neff & Son, 183 Va. 56, 31 S.E.2d 265 (1944).

The power conferred on the trial judge under this section to set aside a jury verdict and enter judgment thereon can only be exercised where the verdict is plainly wrong or without credible evidence to support it. If there is a conflict in the testimony on a material point, or if reasonable men may differ in their conclusions of fact to be drawn from the evidence, or if the conclusion is dependent on the weight to be given the testimony, the trial judge cannot substitute his conclusion for that of the jury merely because he would have voted for a different verdict if he had been on the jury. The weight of a jury's verdict, when there is credible evidence upon which it can be based, is not overborne by the trial judge's disapproval. Commonwealth v. McNeely, 204 Va. 218, 129 S.E.2d 687 (1963); Tyree v. Lariew, 208 Va. 382, 158 S.E.2d 140 (1967).

Section does not enlarge power of trial court over verdict. — While it is true that this section conferred enlarged powers upon the trial courts, it is well settled by the decisions of the Supreme Court that trial courts have no greater power over verdicts than they had before the enactment of the section. Sykes v. Brown, 156 Va. 881, 159 S.E. 202 (1931).

Nor power of Supreme Court. — Trial courts have no greater power over verdicts now than they had before the enactment of this section, nor has the Supreme Court. The Supreme Court has always exercised the power and duty, when not hampered by statute, of setting aside a judgment that was plainly wrong or without evidence to support it. Norfolk & W. Ry. v. T.W. Thayer Co., 137 Va. 294, 119 S.E. 107 (1923).

Its only office is to test sufficiency of evidence. — This section is a highly useful statute, but its only office is to test the sufficiency of the evidence. In this respect it is a desirable substitute for a demurrer to the evidence or a peremptory instruction. But it was not designed to materially change or affect the control of trial courts over verdicts of the jury in cases where there is any material conflict of testimony. Flowers v. Virginian Ry., 135 Va. 367, 116 S.E. 672 (1923). See also, Drake v. Norfolk Steam Laundry Corp., 135 Va. 354, 116 S.E. 668 (1923); Alessandrini v. Mullins, 178 Va. 69, 16 S.E.2d 323 (1941).

Court must to some extent pass on weight of evidence. — The very fact that the trial court is given the power to set aside a verdict as contrary to the evidence necessarily means that it must, to some extent at least, pass upon the weight of the evidence. It would, indeed, be a futile and idle thing for the law to give a court a supervisory authority over the proceedings and the manner of conducting a cause before the jury, and the right to set aside the verdict of the jury therein because contrary to the evidence, unless the judge vested with such power could consider, to some extent at least, the evidence in the cause. Cardwell v. Norfolk & W. Ry., 114 Va. 500, 77 S.E. 612 (1913); Braswell v. VEPCO, 162 Va. 27, 173 S.E. 365 (1934); Cloutier v. Virginia Gas Distribution Corp., 202 Va. 646, 119 S.E.2d 234 (1961).

But it does not sit as a jury. — In setting aside a verdict under this section, the trial judge must, to some extent at least, pass upon the weight of the evidence, but he does not sit as a jury, it is not his duty to pass upon the preponderance of evidence, and he should not set aside a verdict supported by testimony which there is no reason to discredit. McQuown v. Phaup, 172 Va. 419, 2 S.E.2d 330 (1939).

And may not substitute its view for that of jury. — In a collision action, where the evidence was conflicting as to whether the truck involved was the one which defendant's employee was authorized to operate, and there was nothing inherently incredible in the testimony, it was error for the trial court to substitute its view of the case for that of the jury and render judgment for the defendant notwithstanding the verdict. Hoover v. J.P. Neff & Son, 183 Va. 56, 31 S.E.2d 265 (1944).

Verdict must be plainly contrary to or unsupported by evidence. — It is well settled law in Virginia that the trial court cannot set aside the verdict of the jury as contrary to the evidence, unless it is plainly contrary to the evidence. Norfolk & W. Ry. v. T.W. Thayer Co., 137 Va. 294, 119 S.E. 107 (1923). See Stallard v. Atlantic Greyhound Lines, 169 Va. 223, 192 S.E. 800 (1937); Alessandrini v. Mullins, 178 Va. 69, 16 S.E.2d 323 (1941).

Under this section the trial court is without power to set aside a verdict unless it is contrary to the evidence, or without evidence to support it. There is not a great deal of difference between a verdict which is contrary to the evidence, or without evidence to support it. In either event, the verdict lacks the necessary support for approval. Burch v. Grace St. Bldg. Corp., 168 Va. 329, 191 S.E. 672 (1937).

When evidence incredible. — To be incredible, evidence must be either so manifestly false that reasonable men ought not to believe it, or it must be shown to be false by objects or things as to the existence and meaning of which reasonable men should not differ. Commonwealth v. McNeely, 204 Va. 218, 129 S.E.2d 687 (1963).

Action of court must proceed from firm conviction. — A trial court is not warranted in setting aside a verdict merely because the court, if upon the jury, would have rendered a different verdict. The action of the trial court must proceed from a firm conviction that the verdict is plainly wrong or without evidence to support it. Sykes v. Brown, 156 Va. 881, 159 S.E. 202 (1931).

If fair-minded men might differ, verdict should stand. — The verdict must be set aside before judgment is entered, and this cannot be done if there is a conflict of testimony on a material point over which fair-minded men might differ. But if there has been a "plain deviation from right and justice," even a court of law will not make itself a party to the wrong by entering judgment on the verdict. Gregory v. Seaboard Air Line Ry., 142 Va. 750, 128 S.E. 272 (1920).

A verdict founded on conflicting evidence may not be set aside and final judgment entered against the verdict, as to do this would in effect deprive a litigant of a jury trial. He is entitled to have controverted issues passed upon by a jury. Gable v. Bingler, 177 Va. 641, 15 S.E.2d 33 (1941).

But court should set aside verdict that is plainly wrong. — Where it can be seen from the evidence as a whole that the verdict has recorded a finding in plain deviation from right and justice, the court may, indeed should, set it aside. Meade v. Saunders, 151 Va. 636, 144 S.E. 711 (1928). See also, Kendricks v. City of Norfolk, 139 Va. 702, 124 S.E. 210 (1924); Flannagan v. Northwestern Mut. Life Ins. Co., 152 Va. 38, 146 S.E. 353 (1929); Tabb v. Willis, 155 Va. 836, 156 S.E. 556 (1931); Clark v. Parker, 161 Va. 480, 171 S.E. 600 (1933).

If the trial judge overrules a motion to strike and submits the case to the jury, and a verdict is returned, he then may set aside the verdict on the ground that it is contrary to the evidence, or without evidence to support it. If upon review the appellate court reaches a different conclusion, the record includes the verdict, and final judgment may be entered by the appellate court. This was the purpose of this section. Leath v. Richmond, F. & P.R.R., 162 Va. 705, 174 S.E. 678 (1934).

Court may reconsider instructions. — It is well settled in this State that on a motion for a new trial involving the correctness of the instructions, the court may reconsider the instructions, although not objected to, and if they are found to be incorrect and calculated to mislead the jury, may set aside the verdict. Smith v. Combined Ins. Co. of Am., 202 Va. 758, 120 S.E.2d 267 (1961).

Facts justifying setting aside verdict. — In an action to recover on an insurance policy for loss from fire, defendant claimed that the loss was caused by order of civil authority, which was excepted by the policy. The trial court had instructed that if the fire was set to the building by order of the mayor it was by order of civil authority, and as defendant had not objected to this instruction it was the law of the case. It was held that under the evidence, it was clear that the fire was set by policemen in consequence and as a result of an order of the mayor, and accordingly the verdict for plaintiff was without evidence to support it, and was contrary to the law laid down in the instructions, and should have been set aside under this section. Queen Ins. Co. v. Perkinson, 129 Va. 216, 105 S.E. 580 (1921).

C. Power of Court to Enter Final Judgment.

Court is not required to impanel jury to fix damages. — A verdict was set aside only because it was contrary to the evidence as to the amount of damages sustained by plaintiff. It was held that this section does not mean that when a verdict is set aside a new trial can be ordered only on the whole case, both as to liability and damages, or that the court must necessarily impanel a jury to fix damages which have not been properly assessed. Therefore, the action of the trial court in entering judgment for the amount of damages admitted by the defendant to have been suffered by the plaintiff was not error. Apperson-Lee Motor Co. v. Ring, 150 Va. 283, 143 S.E. 694 (1928).

But may enter judgment for amount warranted by evidence. — Where liability has been fixed by the jury and there is in the evidence no conflict in regard to the damages suffered by the plaintiff, under this section the trial court can set aside the verdict of the jury and enter judgment in an amount warranted by the evidence. Bass v. Peterson, 168 Va. 273, 191 S.E. 519 (1937).

And should not hesitate to do so. — This section was intended to secure speedy determination of litigation, and the court should not hesitate to enter final judgment in cases where it is clear upon the facts that the ends of justice can thereby be attained. Gable v. Bingler, 177 Va. 641, 15 S.E.2d 33 (1941).

Unless evidence is conflicting. — This section unquestionably empowers the court, when the evidence is clear, to render final judgment upon setting aside the verdict, but if there is a conflict on a material point, or if reasonably fair-minded men may differ as to the conclusions of fact to be drawn from the evidence, then a question of fact is presented and the safe rule to follow is to submit the matter to the determination of the jury. Standard Dredging Co. v. Barnalla, 158 Va. 367, 163 S.E. 367 (1932).

Where facts show contributory negligence, defendant should have judgment. — Where, in an action for negligence, plaintiff's admissions in his pleadings and evidence in the first trial, in which he took a nonsuit, showed that he was guilty of contributory negligence as a matter of law, the trial court, in setting aside a verdict for the plaintiff in the second trial as contrary to the law and the evidence, was able to decide the case on its merits, and rightly entered final judgment for the defendant. Burch v. Grace St. Bldg. Corp., 168 Va. 329, 191 S.E. 672 (1931).

Although instructions submitting the case to the jury have not been objected to, the trial court is not thereby precluded from setting aside the verdict and entering final judgment. Smith v. Combined Ins. Co. of Am., 202 Va. 758, 120 S.E.2d 267 (1961).

Judgment is res judicata. — Where a verdict was set aside and judgment entered for defendant, under this section, in an action for damages to a truck which collided with a streetcar, it was conclusively determined that the plaintiff's negligence was the proximate cause, and the judgment is res judicata of plaintiff's negligence in an action for personal injury received in the same collision. Virginia Ry. & Power Co. v. Leland, 143 Va. 920, 129 S.E. 700 (1925).

Action against master and servant. — In an action to recover damages for injuries inflicted by an alleged servant of a filling station operator, the jury found a verdict in favor of plaintiff against the operator of the station, but was silent as to the alleged servant, although the uncontested evidence disclosed the liability of the servant beyond any doubt, and the court had instructed the jury that if plaintiff's injuries were the result of the servant's negligence, then they should find a verdict against him. The court, under this section, entered a judgment against the servant. The sole controverted issue was the existence or nonexistence of the relation of master and servant. It was held that, the liability of the servant not being an issue but an uncontroverted established fact, and the jury having, through inadvertence or otherwise, failed to fix liability against him, the court was clearly within its power when it pronounced judgment against him. Gable v. Bingler, 177 Va. 641, 15 S.E.2d 33 (1941).

D. Power of Court to Impanel Jury to Assess Damages.

Court may confine issue to quantum of damages. — The power of the trial court to set aside a verdict and confine the issue to be tried to the quantum of damages, in a proper case, is conferred in express terms by this section. Kirn v. Bembury, 163 Va. 891, 178 S.E. 53 (1935).

E. When New Trial Should Be Granted.

New trial is proper if evidence imperfectly developed at first trial. — Where there is insufficient evidence before the trial court to enable it, under this section, to decide the case upon its merits, because the evidence was imperfectly developed at the trial, this section should not be invoked, and a new trial should be granted. Branning Mfg. Co. v. Norfolk-Southern R.R., 138 Va. 43, 121 S.E. 74 (1924).

When the record shows that because of an inadvertent failure of a party to comply with some technical rule of procedure he has been estopped from fully developing the question of his liability, there is not sufficient evidence, within the meaning of this section, before the court to enable it to pass upon the "merits of the case." Under such circumstances, the court, if it determines to set aside the verdict, should not restrict the issue to be submitted to another jury to the question of damages. Kirn v. Bembury, 163 Va. 891, 178 S.E. 53 (1935).

Effect of failure to request final judgment. — While failure to request final judgment would not prevent the lower court or the appellate court from entering a final order in a proper case, it is perhaps a circumstance indicating that the merits of the case ought to be finally determined by a jury. Morris & Co. v. Alvis, 130 Va. 434, 107 S.E. 664 (1921).

F. Effect of Section on Appeal.

If the trial court improperly sets aside a verdict it will be reinstated by the appellate court. Gregory v. Seaboard Air Line Ry., 142 Va. 750, 128 S.E. 272 (1925).

Under the well established rule the appellate court must first look to the record of the first trial and if the court erred in setting aside the verdict rendered in that trial, the first verdict will be reinstated and all proceedings subsequent thereto will be annulled. Eubank v. Hayden, 202 Va. 634, 119 S.E.2d 328 (1961).

Effect of trial court's disapproval of verdict. — A verdict which has been disapproved by the trial judge is not entitled to the same weight on appeal as one that has been approved by him. Braswell v. VEPCO, 162 Va. 27, 173 S.E. 365 (1934); Maurer v. City of Norfolk, 147 Va. 900, 133 S.E. 484 (1926); Cloutier v. Virginia Gas Distribution Corp., 202 Va. 646, 119 S.E.2d 234 (1961).

Effect of approval of verdict. — Where the case was one for the jury, and its verdict of guilty has been approved by the trial court, under this section and § 8.01-680, the judgment must be affirmed. Holloman v. Commonwealth, 138 Va. 758, 120 S.E. 852 (1924).

Supreme Court may enter final judgment. — If on review the Supreme Court does not agree with the judge of the trial court in its action in setting aside the verdict, the verdict is in the record, and final judgment may be entered by the appellate court. This procedure eliminates the delay and expense of a second trial, speeds final determination of litigation, and removes possible temptation for the commission of perjury on the second trial. These were the main objects contemplated by this section and § 8.01-681. Walton v. Walton, 168 Va. 418, 191 S.E. 768 (1937).

Effect of failure to ask reformation of verdict in court below. — If there was error in the amount allowed by the jury the court below might have reformed the verdict under the provisions of this section, but it was not asked to do so. Defendant did not complain in the court below and hence cannot be heard on appeal. National Fire Proofing Co. v. Bickford, 141 Va. 706, 126 S.E. 668 (1925).

ARTICLE 2.

Judgments by Confession.

§ 8.01-431. Judgment or decree by confession in pending suit. — In any suit a defendant may, whether the suit be on the court docket or not, confess a judgment in the clerk's office for so much principal and interest as the plaintiff may be willing to accept a judgment or decree for. The same shall be entered of record by the clerk in the order book and be as final and as valid as if entered in court on the day of such confession. And the clerk shall enter upon the margin of such book opposite where such judgment or decree is entered, the date and time of the day at which the same was confessed, and the lien of such judgment or decree shall run from the time such judgment is recorded on the judgment lien docket of the clerk's office of the county or city in which land of the defendant lies. (Code 1955, § 8-355; 1962, c. 388; 1977, c. 617.)

§ 8.01-431

Cross references. — As to docketing of judgments by confession, see § 8.01-449. As to priority of liens, see § 8.01-459. As to confession of judgment by surety, see § 49-28.

Law Review. — For survey of Virginia law on practice and pleading for the year 1973-1974, see 60 Va. L. Rev. 1572 (1974).

I. Decisions Under Current Law.
II. Decisions Under Prior Law.

I. DECISIONS UNDER CURRENT LAW.

An underinsured motorist carrier has the right to file pleadings and take other actions allowable by law for injuries when the tortfeasor confesses judgment in an amount exceeding the applicable liability coverage. State Farm Mut. Auto. Ins. Co. v. Beng, 249 Va. 165, 455 S.E.2d 2 (1995).

Section not applicable. — Where petitioner, an adult who was adopted as a child, appealed the denial of her petition to set aside the adoption, where the petition contained a signature purporting to be that of the adoptive father, and where the record also contained an affidavit, received by the trial court, after it had denied the petition, in which the adoptive father purported to consent to "annulling the adoptive order," while this section allows a judgment to be entered upon confession, the provisions were not applicable to this case. In re Dwyer, 18 Va. App. 437, 445 S.E.2d 157 (1994).

II. DECISIONS UNDER PRIOR LAW.

Editor's note. — The cases cited below were decided under corresponding provisions of former law. The term "this section," as used below, refers to former provisions.

This and the following section expressly authorize the confession of a judgment in the clerk's office in a pending suit or action. Deeds v. Gilmer, 162 Va. 157, 174 S.E. 37 (1934).

Judgment by confession has all attributes of other judgments. — Although no adjudication is in fact required in entering a judgment of confession without action, yet it has all the qualities, incidents and attributes of other judgments and it cannot be valid unless entered in a court which might lawfully have pronounced the same judgment in a contested action. Beazley v. Sims, 81 Va. 644 (1886).

It is valid from the moment of the acceptance. Beazley v. Sims, 81 Va. 644 (1886).

Substantial compliance with section is sufficient. — The provisions of this section with reference to judgments confessed in the clerk's office are, for the most part, merely declaratory of the common law, and such judgments will be declared valid where there has been substantial compliance with this section. Saunders v. Lipscomb, 90 Va. 647, 19 S.E. 450 (1894); Manson v. Rawlings, 112 Va. 384, 71 S.E. 564 (1911). See American Bank & Trust Co. v. National Bank, 170 Va. 169, 196 S.E. 693 (1938).

No suit need be pending. — An office judgment confessed may be valid though no suit is pending against the defendant. Brockenbrough v. Brockenbrough, 72 Va. (31 Gratt.) 580 (1879).

And no process need have been issued or served. Shadrack v. Woolfolk, 73 Va. (32 Gratt.) 707 (1880); Saunders v. Lipscomb, 90 Va. 647, 19 S.E. 450 (1894).

Lien begins at time of confession. — The holding that the lien of a judgment by confession begins on the first moment of the day on which it was confessed is expressly overruled by this section, and the lien begins at the time of confession. Hockman v. Hockman, 93 Va. 455, 25 S.E. 534 (1896).

Entry on order book may be made at any time. — If the entry of a judgment confessed in the office upon the order or minute book has not been made at the time of its confession, the clerk may make the entry at any time, and if he fails to do it, the court may at any time direct him to make the entry. Shadrack v. Woolfolk, 73 Va. (32 Gratt.) 707 (1880).

Failure to make entry does not invalidate judgment. — Judgment confessed in the clerk's office, though no process appears to have been issued or served, and though the clerk has failed to enter it upon the order book or any other book in his office, and the only evidence of it is an unsigned memorandum endorsed on a declaration which seems to have been filed and the bond enclosed in the declaration, is a valid judgment and entitled to rank as such as against other creditors of the debtor. Shadrack v. Woolfolk, 73 Va. (32 Gratt.) 707 (1880); Saunders v. Lipscomb, 90 Va. 647, 19 S.E. 450 (1894).

For provision as to entry is directory only. — The provision for entry of the judgment on the order book of the clerk is directory only, and, if in fact confessed, the judgment will be upheld though not entered on that or any other book in his office, but evidenced merely by authenticated memoranda of the clerk taking the confession. Manson v. Rawlings, 112 Va. 384, 71 S.E. 564 (1911).

Clerk may enter his own confession. — In entering a confession of judgment under this section, the clerk acts purely as a ministerial officer, and he may enter his own confession of judgment in favor of his creditor, and it will be valid. Smith v. Mayo, 83 Va. 910, 5 S.E. 276 (1887).

A person of weak understanding may confess judgment, in person or by attorney. Mason v. Williams, 17 Va. (3 Munf.) 126 (1811).

One of joint defendants may confess. — One of several joint defendants in ejectment, from whom the others purchased, may confess judgment. Virginia & Tenn. Coal & Iron Co. v. Fields, 94 Va. 102, 26 S.E. 426 (1896).

Judgment may be confessed by attorney in fact. — A judgment may be confessed either in court or in the clerk's office, by attorney-in-fact, though the attorney is not a lawyer. Insurance Co. v. Barley's Adm'r, 57 Va. (16 Gratt.) 363 (1863).

Power of attorney executed in name of partnership. — In the absence of proof of nonassent on the part of some of the members of a firm, a power of attorney to confess judgment executed by one partner in the firm name must be held when assailed collaterally; although the power is under seal, the seal being unnecessary. Alexander v. Alexander, 85 Va. 353, 7 S.E. 335 (1888).

Power authorizing confession "in any court," "at any time," is valid. — Where a power of attorney authorized confession of judgment "in any court" and "at any time," a confession before a clerk under this warrant is valid; and as all the clerk's proceedings in vacation are subject to the control of the court at the next term, the obligors are afforded all the protection they could have gotten from a confession in court. Walker v. Temple, 130 Va. 567, 107 S.E. 720 (1921).

§ 8.01-432. Confession of judgment irrespective of suit pending.

— Any person being indebted to another person, or any attorney-in-fact pursuant to a power of attorney, may at any time confess judgment in the clerk's office of any circuit court in this Commonwealth, whether a suit, motion or action be pending therefor or not, for only such principal and interest as his creditor may be willing to accept a judgment for, which judgment, when so confessed, shall be forthwith entered of record by the clerk in whose office it is confessed, in the proper order book of his court. Such judgment shall be as final and as binding as though confessed in open court or rendered by the court, subject to the control of the court in the clerk's office of which the same shall have been confessed. (Code 1950, § 8-356; 1977, c. 617.)

REVISERS' NOTE

The language "or any attorney-in-fact pursuant to a power of attorney," has been inserted in former § 8-356.

I. DECISIONS UNDER PRIOR LAW.

Editor's note. — The cases cited below were decided under corresponding provisions of former law. The term "this section," as used below, refers to former provisions.

Judgment may be confessed on contingent obligation. — A director of a bank executed a note to create a reserve out of which any loss to the assets of the bank might be made good during a period of three years, and authorized a confession of judgment upon it. It was held that upon the happening of the contingency anticipated at the time of the execution of the note, that is, when the assets of the bank were found insufficient to cover its total obligation, the director's obligation became definite and certain in such form that the holder had a right to maintain an action of debt thereon, and the director was therefore "indebted to another" within the meaning of this section, and judgment could be confessed upon the note. Spady v. Farmers & Merchants Trust Bank, 168 Va. 143, 190 S.E. 173 (1937).

Entry in common law order book is not essential to validity of judgment. — It was contended that the "proper order book" designated in this section meant the "Common Law Order Book," that the duty of the clerk to enter the judgment in the "Common Law Order Book" was mandatory and essential to the validity of the judgment, and that a confessed judgment which was entered by the clerk in a book labeled "Common Law Order Book — Confession of Judgment — No. 1," was void. It was held that there was no merit in this contention, since, if the legislature had intended that the failure of the clerk to make the entry should render the confessed judgment void, this section would have said so plainly, in view of prior decisions of the Supreme Court that a similar provision in § 8.01-431 relating to judgments confessed in vacation was merely directory. The failure of this section to invalidate the judgment by reason of the clerk's not making the required entry becomes all the more significant when we consider that in § 8.01-441 the legislature has expressly said that a judgment confessed by virtue of a warrant or power of attorney which does not comply with this article shall be invalid. American Bank & Trust Co. v. National Bank, 170 Va. 169, 196 S.E. 693 (1938).

A defendant confessing judgment is estopped, in the absence of fraud, to question its validity on account of irregularities to which he did not object, or to dispute any facts set forth in the confession, and if, after the entry of the judgment, he ratifies or accepts it, or acquiesces in it, he is estopped to deny the authority on which it was confessed or otherwise to impeach its validity. Johnson v. Alvis, 159 Va. 229, 165 S.E. 489 (1932).

And defendant's creditor or trustee in bankruptcy may be estopped. — A creditor of the judgment debtor, having recognized the validity of a judgment by confession by seeking, in interpleader proceedings, to obtain the balance of the proceeds derived from the sale of the debtor's property under execution of the judgment, was estopped to attack the judgment on the grounds that it was not obtained in compliance with this section. Likewise, the judgment debtor's trustee in bankruptcy, having been a party to the interpleader proceedings and acquiesced in and agreed to a disbursement of the fund by the court, was estopped to set aside the judgment. Smith v. Litton, 167 Va. 263, 188 S.E. 214 (1936).

But decision is not res adjudicata in bankruptcy court. — The decision of the Supreme Court that a trustee in bankruptcy was estopped to attack a judgment confessed by an officer of the bankrupt corporation under this section, on the ground that the judgment was irregular and void on its face, was not res adjudicata so as to prevent the federal district court from examining the judgment and disallowing or subordinating it as a claim in bankruptcy proceedings. Pepper v. Litton, 308 U.S. 295, 60 S. Ct. 238, 84 L. Ed. 281 (1939).

§ 8.01-433. Setting aside judgments confessed under § 8.01-432. — Any judgment confessed under the provisions of § 8.01-432 may be set aside or reduced upon motion of the judgment debtor made within twenty-one days following notice to him that such judgment has been entered against him, and after twenty-one days notice to the judgment creditor or creditors for whom the judgment was confessed, on any ground which would have been an adequate defense or setoff in an action at law instituted upon the judgment creditor's note, bond or other evidence of debt upon which such judgment was confessed. Whenever any such judgment is set aside or modified the case shall be placed on the trial docket of the court, and the proceedings thereon shall thereafter be the same as if an action at law had been instituted upon the bond, note or other evidence of debt upon which judgment was confessed. After such case is so docketed the court shall make such order as to the pleadings, future proceedings and costs as to the court may seem just. (Code 1950, § 8-357; 1977, c. 617.)

REVISERS' NOTE

The language "creditor or creditors for whom the judgment was confessed" has been inserted in former § 8-357 for clarification. The judgment debtor must give the judgment creditors 21 days' notice that he will file a motion to set aside or reduce the confessed judgment.

Law Review. — For survey of Virginia law on practice and pleading for the year 1973-1974, see 60 Va. L. Rev. 1572 (1974).

I. DECISIONS UNDER CURRENT LAW.

Applied in Harris & Harris v. Tabler, 232 Va. 75, 348 S.E.2d 241 (1986).

§ 8.01-433.1. Notice of confession of judgment provision. — No judgment shall be confessed upon a note, bond, or other evidence of debt pursuant to a confession of judgment provision contained therein which does not contain a statement typed in boldface print of not less than eight point type on its face:

IMPORTANT NOTICE

THIS INSTRUMENT CONTAINS A CONFESSION OF JUDGMENT PROVISION WHICH CONSTITUTES A WAIVER OF IMPORTANT RIGHTS YOU MAY HAVE AS A DEBTOR AND ALLOWS THE CREDITOR TO OBTAIN A JUDGMENT AGAINST YOU WITHOUT ANY FURTHER NOTICE.

This section shall only apply to notes, bonds, or other evidences of debt containing confession of judgment provisions entered into after January 1, 1993. (1992, c. 396.)

Law Review. — For article reviewing recent developments and changes in legislation, case law, and Virginia Supreme Court Rules affecting civil litigation, see "Civil Practice and Procedure," 26 U. Rich. L. Rev. 679 (1992).

§ 8.01-434. Lien of such judgments. — The clerk shall enter on the margin of the record of any judgment confessed under the provisions of § 8.01-432, the day and hour when the same was confessed and the lien thereof shall attach and be binding from the time such judgment is recorded on the judgment lien docket of the clerk's office of the county or city in which land of the defendant lies. If the credit was extended for personal, family or household purposes, the judgment shall not be a lien against the real estate of the obligor or the basis of obtaining execution against his personal property until the expiration of the twenty-one-day period allowed the judgment debtor as set forth in § 8.01-433. In the event the judgment debtor files a motion or other pleading within such twenty-one-day period, the judgment shall not be a lien against such real estate or its basis of execution against personal property until an order to that effect is entered by the court. It will be presumed that the obligation is for personal, family or household purposes if the debtor is a natural person, unless the plaintiff or someone on his behalf makes oath or makes out and files an affidavit that the obligation was not for such purposes, or the obligation for which judgment is confessed recites that it is for other purposes. (Code 1950, § 8-358; 1962, c. 388; 1970, c. 395; 1977, c. 617; 1986, c. 523.)

REVISERS' NOTE

The phrases "allowed the judgment debtor as . . ." and ". . . other evidence of debt . . ." have been inserted in former § 8-358.

Law Review. — For survey of recent legislation on liens — confession of judgment, see 5 U. Rich. L. Rev. 197 (1970). For survey of Virginia commercial law for the year 1969-1970, see 56 Va. L. Rev. 1387 (1970).

I. DECISIONS UNDER PRIOR LAW.

Editor's note. — The case cited below was decided under corresponding provisions of former law. The term "this section," as used below, refers to former provisions.

Lien runs from time of confession. — It will be observed that under the language of § 8.01-431 "the lien of the said judgment or decree shall run only from the time of day of the confession." The language in this section is to the same effect when it provides that "the lien thereof shall attach and be binding from the time of such confession so entered." In the latter instance the lien runs "from the time of such confession," and the words "so entered" are merely descriptive of the clerk's ministerial duties with reference to recording the judgment. American Bank & Trust Co. v. National Bank, 170 Va. 169, 196 S.E. 693 (1938).

§ 8.01-435. Who may confess judgment. — Confession of judgment under the provisions of § 8.01-432 may be made either by the debtor himself or by his duly constituted attorney-in-fact, acting under and by virtue of a power of attorney duly executed and acknowledged by him as deeds are required to be acknowledged, before any officer or person authorized to take acknowledgments of writings to be recorded in this Commonwealth, provided, however, that any power of attorney incorporated in, and made part of, any note or bond authorizing the confession of judgment thereon against the makers and endorsers in the event of default in the payment thereof at maturity need not be acknowledged, but shall specifically name therein the attorney or attorneys or other person or persons authorized to confess such judgment and the clerk's office in which the judgment is to be confessed. (Code 1950, § 8-359; 1977, c. 617.)

REVISERS' NOTE

The phrase "power of attorney" has been substituted for the word "warrant" in former § 8-359.

I. Decisions Under Current Law.
II. Decisions Under Prior Law.

I. DECISIONS UNDER CURRENT LAW.

Strict construction of section. — Given the considerable authority that is created by the power to confess judgment, this section should be strictly construed to prevent abuse. Benton Land Fund v. Nvmercure Ltd. Partnership, 849 F. Supp. 1123 (E.D. Va. 1994).

II. DECISIONS UNDER PRIOR LAW.

Editor's note. — The cases cited below were decided under corresponding provisions of former law. The term "this section, "as used below, refers to former provisions.

Power of attorney need not be under seal. — A warrant or power of attorney to confess judgment embodied in a note and made a part of the note is not required by this section to be executed under seal. Johnson v. Alvis, 159 Va. 229, 165 S.E. 489 (1932). See Bank of Chatham v. Arendall, 178 Va. 183, 16 S.E.2d 352 (1941).

Authority to confess judgment in the clerk's office must be strictly pursued, but in absence of proof to the contrary the presumption is that the agent performed his duty in the authorized manner. Bank of Chatham v. Arendall, 178 Va. 183, 16 S.E.2d 352 (1941).

Warrant of authority in note evidencing contingent obligation. — Where the obligation of the maker of a note was contingent, the ancient, accepted and regular procedure, by one of the common-law actions or by notice of motion, would have been preferable to the confession of judgment on the note by virtue of a warrant of authority made of part thereof. However, in view of this section, and the fact that the final result of the litigation on the note in question would have been the same regardless of what form of action the holder had instituted against the maker, the confession of judgment did not constitute reversible error. Spady v. Farmers & Merchants Trust Bank, 168 Va. 143, 190 S.E. 173 (1937).

§ 8.01-436. Form of confession of judgment. — On the presentation of any such power of attorney as is mentioned in § 8.01-435 by any of the persons therein named as attorney-in-fact, or on the personal appearance of the debtor and the expression by him of his desire to confess such judgment, the clerk of the court mentioned in such power of attorney, or before whom such debtor shall so appear, shall draw and require the attorney-in-fact so appearing, or the debtor, as the case may be, to sign a confession of judgment, which shall be in form substantially as follows:

"Virginia: In the clerk's office of the .... court of the .... of ...., I, (or we) A.B., (or A.B. and C.D., etc.) hereby acknowledged myself (or ourselves) to be justly indebted to, and do hereby confess judgment in favor of (name of creditor) in the sum of .... dollars ($.......) with interest thereon from the .... day of ...., two thousand ...., until paid, and the cost of this proceeding (including the attorney's fees and collection fees provided for in the instrument on which the proceeding is based) hereby waiving the benefit of my (or our) homestead exemptions as to the same, provided the instrument on which the proceeding is based carries such homestead waiver.

Given under my (or our) hand, this .... day of ...., two thousand and ....

(Signatures)

or, if by an attorney-in-fact, signatures and seals of debtors,

By ....

his (or their) attorney-in-fact."

(Code 1950, § 8-360; 1977, c. 617.)

REVISERS' NOTE

The word "warrant" has been replaced with the phrase "power of attorney" in former § 8-360.

Law Review. — For survey of Virginia law on torts for the year 1972-1973, see 59 Va. L. Rev. 1590 (1973).

I. DECISIONS UNDER PRIOR LAW.

Editor's note. — The case cited below was decided under corresponding provisions of former law. The term "this section," as used below, refers to former provisions.

Substantial compliance with section is sufficient. — The form of a confession of judgment failed to comply with the form set out in this section in the following particulars: (1) The name of the clerk's office wherein the confession was made was not stated; (2) it failed to "acknowledge" that the debtors were "justly indebted to" the named creditors; and (3) the seals following the debtors' signatures were omitted. It was held that the form of confession was substantially the same as that set out in this section and the variations therefrom did not invalidate the confession. Bank of Chatham v. Arendall, 178 Va. 183, 16 S.E.2d 352 (1941).

§ 8.01-437. Endorsement of clerk thereon. — When a judgment is so confessed, the clerk shall endorse upon such confession, or attach thereto, his certificate in manner and form substantially as follows:

"Virginia: In the clerk's office of the .... court of the ....of ....

The foregoing (or attached) judgment was duly confessed before me in my said office on the .... day of ...., two thousand and ...., at .... o'clock ....a.m., p.m. and has been duly entered of record in common-law order book number ...., page ....

Teste:

.... clerk."

(Code 1950, § 8-361; 1977, c. 617.)

I. DECISIONS UNDER PRIOR LAW.

Editor's note. — The case cited below was decided under corresponding provisions of former law. The term "this section," as used below, refers to former provisions.

Failure of clerk to sign certificate does not invalidate judgment. — Failure of the clerk to sign a certificate of confession of judgment does not invalidate the judgment, since the duties of the clerk in connection with the entry and recordation of a confessed judgment are directory only and not mandatory. Bank of Chatham v. Arendall, 178 Va. 183, 16 S.E.2d 352 (1941).

§ 8.01-438. When judgment confessed by attorney-in-fact copy to be served on judgment debtor. — If a judgment is confessed by an attorney-in-fact, it shall be the duty of the clerk within ten days from the entry thereof to cause to be served upon the judgment debtor a certified copy of the order so entered in the common-law order book, to which order shall be appended a notice setting forth the provisions of § 8.01-433. The officer who serves the order shall make return thereof within ten days after service to the clerk. The clerk shall promptly file the order with the papers in the case. The failure to serve a copy of the order within sixty days from the date of entry thereof shall render the judgment void as to any debtor not so served.

Service of a copy of the order on a nonresident judgment debtor by an officer of the county or city of his residence, authorized by law to serve processes therein, or by the clerk of the court sending a copy of the order by registered or certified mail to such nonresident judgment debtor at his last known post-office address and the filing of a certificate with the papers in the case showing that such has been done or of a receipt showing the receipt of such letter by such nonresident judgment debtor, shall be deemed sufficient service thereof for the purposes of this section. (Code 1950, § 8-362; 1972, c. 611; 1976, c. 617; 1988, c. 420.)

REVISERS' NOTE

The phrase "registered mail" in former § 8-362 has been changed to "certified mail" with respect to service on the nonresident judgment debtor.

I. DECISIONS UNDER PRIOR LAW.

Editor's note. — The case cited below was decided under corresponding provisions of former law. The term "this section," as used below, refers to former provisions.

This section clearly contemplates a valid signature on the note or bond appointing an attorney-in-fact and authorizing the confession. Pate v. Southern Bank & Trust Co., 214 Va. 596, 203 S.E.2d 126 (1974).

The entire procedure for confession of judgment by an attorney-in-fact is predicated upon, and presupposes, a valid authorization in a note or bond containing the cognovit clause. Without such authorization the attorney-in-fact is without authority to act and the court is without jurisdiction to enter judgment. Pate v. Southern Bank & Trust Co., 214 Va. 596, 203 S.E.2d 126 (1974).

A person cannot be held accountable for a consent judgment which was obtained by virtue of a forged signature to a power of attorney. Pate v. Southern Bank & Trust Co., 214 Va. 596, 203 S.E.2d 126 (1974).

§ 8.01-439. Filing of records by clerk. — Such confession and clerk's certificate, together with the power of attorney if the confession be by an attorney-in-fact, and the note, bond or other obligation, if there be such, on which the judgment is based, shall be securely attached together by the clerk and filed by him among the records in his office. (Code 1950, § 8-363; 1977, c. 617.)

§ 8.01-440. Docketing and execution. — The clerk shall forthwith docket such judgment in the current judgment lien docket in his office and shall issue execution thereon as he may be directed by the creditor therein named, or his assigns, in the manner prescribed by law. (Code 1950, § 8-364; 1977, c. 617.)

REVISERS' NOTE

Former § 8-365 (Fees and costs) has been transferred to § 14.1-178.1.

I. DECISIONS UNDER PRIOR LAW.

Editor's note. — The case cited below was decided under corresponding provisions of former law. The term "this section," as used below, refers to former provisions.

The object and purpose of docketing judgments is to give notice to purchasers for value and without notice of the real estate of the judgment debtor. It was not designed to protect other judgment creditors. American Bank & Trust Co. v. National Bank, 170 Va. 169, 196 S.E. 693 (1938).

And failure of clerk to "forthwith docket" does not invalidate judgment. — The failure of the clerk to "forthwith docket such judgment," as required by this section, does not invalidate the judgment. American Bank & Trust Co. v. National Bank, 170 Va. 169, 196 S.E. 693 (1938).

§ 8.01-441. When judgment confessed by virtue of power of attorney invalid. — No judgment confessed in the office of the clerk of any circuit court in this Commonwealth, by virtue of a power of attorney, shall be valid, unless such power of attorney be in conformity with the provisions of this article. (Code 1950, § 8-366; 1977, c. 617.)

ARTICLE 3.

When There Are Several Defendants.

§ 8.01-442. In joint actions on contract plaintiff, though barred as to some, may have judgment against others. — In an action or motion, founded on contract, against two or more defendants, although the plaintiff may be barred as to one or more of them, yet he may have judgment against any other or others of the defendants, against whom he is not so barred. (Code 1950, § 8-367; 1977, c. 617.)

Cross references. — As to procedure in actions on contracts made by several persons, see § 8.01-30.

I. DECISIONS UNDER PRIOR LAW.

Editor's note. — The cases cited below were decided under corresponding provisions of former law. The term "this section," as used below, refers to former provisions.

This section modifies the common-law rule that in all actions of contract the plaintiff must prove his contract against as many persons as he alleged it against, and that he must recover against all or none. New York, P. & N.R.R. v. Cromwell, 98 Va. 227, 35 S.E. 444 (1900); Cahoon v. McCullock, 92 Va. 177, 23 S.E. 225 (1895).

It applies where defense is personal to some defendants. — This section applies to an action on a contract against two or more defendants, when the defense of some is personal to themselves, though the defense is that they never were parties to the contract sued on, as non est factum. Bush v. Campbell, 67 Va. (26 Gratt.) 403 (1875); McIntyre v. Smyth, 108 Va. 736, 62 S.E. 930 (1908).

But not defense going to right of recovery. — This section does not apply where one of several joint defendants alone pleads matter which is not merely personal to himself, but which goes to the plaintiff's right of recovery against all the defendants. In such a case, if the plea is good, judgment cannot be rendered against any of the defendants. Schofield v. Palmer, 134 F. 753 (C.C.W.D. Va. 1904).

Nor where nothing in record shows that defense is personal. — This section has no application in an action against two who file a joint plea of non assumpsit, where the plaintiff has the action dismissed as to one, and asks leave to amend his declaration as to the other, and there is nothing to show that the defense relied on is personal to the former. Hence, it is not error to refuse such leave. Gibson v. Beveridge, 90 Va. 696, 19 S.E. 785 (1894).

There may be judgments against different defendants at different times. — Under this section there may be a judgment in favor of some of the defendants at one time, and against others at another. Bush v. Campbell, 67 Va. (26 Gratt.) 403 (1875); McIntyre v. Smyth, 108 Va. 736, 62 S.E. 930 (1908).

And default judgment against some defendants after discontinuance as to others. — Plaintiff brought an action of debt against F. and M. as late partners and makers of a negotiable note, and against C. and G. as indorsers. The case stood on the office judgment docket at the next term of the court, when F. filed his plea of nil debet, which was sworn to. On the motion of plaintiff, the cause was discontinued as to F. The other parties not appearing, there was a judgment by default against them. It was held that the judgment was a valid judgment against M., C. and G. Muse v. Farmers Bank, 68 Va. (27 Gratt.) 252 (1876).

And judgment barred against principal is not barred against surety. — Under this section and § 8.01-251, where judgment has been recovered against a principal and his surety, no length of time short of the period prescribed by the act of limitations will bar the right of the creditor to enforce his judgment against the surety, or his estate, even though an action is barred as to the principal. Manson v. Rawlings, 112 Va. 384, 71 S.E. 564 (1911).

§ 8.01-443. Joint wrongdoers; effect of judgment against one. — A judgment against one of several joint wrongdoers shall not bar the prosecution of an action against any or all the others, but the injured party may bring separate actions against the wrongdoers and proceed to judgment in each, or, if sued jointly, he may proceed to judgment against them successively until judgment has been rendered against, or the cause has been otherwise disposed of as to, all of the defendants, and no bar shall arise as to any of them by reason of a judgment against another, or others, until the judgment has been satisfied. If there be a judgment against one or more joint wrongdoers, the full satisfaction of such judgment accepted as such by the plaintiff shall be a discharge of all joint wrongdoers, except as to the costs; provided, however, this section shall have no effect on the right of contribution between joint wrongdoers as set out in § 8.01-34. (Code 1950, § 8-368; 1977, c. 617.)

REVISERS' NOTE

Section 8.01-443 changes the former law so that discharge of all joint tort-feasors, except as to costs, occurs only when one of multiple judgments has been fully satisfied and has been accepted as such by the plaintiff. "Satisfaction" is determined by case law and in an appropriate situation would include, besides full payment, an accord and satisfaction or a covenant not to sue supported by consideration. (See Shortt v. Hudson Supply Co., 191 Va. 306, 60 S.E.2d 900 (1950). See also Dickenson v. Tabb, 208 Va. 184, 156 S.E.2d 795 (1967) and Harris v. City of Roanoke, 179 Va. 1, 18 S.E.2d 303 (1942). Right of contribution is preserved.

Cross references. — As to effect of release or covenant not to sue upon liability and contribution among joint tort-feasors, see § 8.01-35.1.

Law Review. — For article, "Effect of Virginia Workmen's Compensation Act Upon the Right of a Third-Party Tortfeasor to Obtain Contribution From an Employer Whose Concurrent Negligence Causes Employee's Death or Injury," see 13 U. Rich. L. Rev. 117 (1978). For comment "The Covenant Not to Sue: Virginia's Effort to Bury the Common Law Rule Regarding the Release of Joint Tortfeasors," see 14 U. Rich. L. Rev. 809 (1980).

I. Decisions Under Current Law.
II. Decisions Under Prior Law.

I. DECISIONS UNDER CURRENT LAW.

Plaintiff may elect which joint tortfeasor he will seek to satisfy judgment against. — The effect of this section is that once a plaintiff in a personal injury action has obtained a judgment against several joint tortfeasors, the plaintiff has the right to elect against which tortfeasor he will seek to satisfy his judgment. Harleysville Mut. Ins. Co. v. Nationwide Mut. Ins. Co., 789 F.2d 272 (4th Cir. 1986).

II. DECISIONS UNDER PRIOR LAW.

Editor's note. — The cases cited below were decided under corresponding provisions of former law. The term "this section," as used below, refers to former provisions.

Section changes the common law. — In England, and formerly in this jurisdiction, a judgment without satisfaction, against one tortfeasor operated as a release of all other tortfeasors liable for the same wrong. This rule was strictly applied from 1802, when Wilkes v.

Jackson, 12 Va. (2 Hen. & M.) 355 (1808), was decided, until the adoption in 1919 of this section. McLaughlin v. Siegel, 166 Va. 374, 185 S.E. 873 (1936).

Plaintiff may elect whether he will prosecute judgment against joint tortfeasor. — Under this section plaintiff has the right to elect whether he will or will not prosecute a judgment against several joint tortfeasors, and has the right to await the trial and result of an action against another joint tortfeasor before deciding whether he will prosecute the first judgment by suing out execution thereon. Fitzgerald v. Campbell, 131 Va. 486, 109 S.E. 308 (1921). See Town of Waynesboro v. Wiseman, 163 Va. 778, 177 S.E. 224 (1934).

But release of one joint tortfeasor releases all. — A release of one jointly liable for a wrong will operate as a release of all other wrongdoers liable for the same injury, and this is true even if the release itself contains a statement reserving the right of action against other wrongdoers. McLaughlin v. Siegel, 166 Va. 374, 185 S.E. 873 (1936).

The legislature did not intend to change this rule. — The fact that the General Assembly changed the general rule respecting the release of joint obligors, and left unimpaired the rule respecting joint wrongdoers, is persuasive that it was satisfied with and approved the law applicable to the release of joint wrongdoers. First & Merchants Nat'l Bank v. Bank of Waverly, 170 Va. 496, 197 S.E. 462 (1938).

§ 8.01-444. Where new parties added; if some not liable, how judgment entered. — If it shall appear at the trial that all the original defendants are liable, but that one or more of the other persons added under the provisions of § 8.01-5 are not liable, the plaintiff shall be entitled to judgment, or to verdict and judgment, as the case may be, against the defendants who appear liable, and such as are not liable shall have judgment and recover costs as against the plaintiff, who shall be allowed the same as costs against the defendants who cause them to be made parties. (Code 1950, § 8-369; 1977, c. 617.)

ARTICLE 4.

Distinction Between Term and Vacation Abolished.

§ 8.01-445. Distinction between term and vacation abolished; effect of time. — The distinction of what a court may do in term as opposed to vacation is hereby abolished. The period of time provided for the doing of any act or the taking of any proceeding is not affected or limited by the continued existence or expiration of a term of court. The continued existence or expiration of a term of court in no way affects the power of a court to do any act or take any proceeding in any civil action which has been pending before it. (1977, c. 617.)

REVISERS' NOTE

Section 8.01-445 rewrites former §§ 8-370 through 8-372 to empower a court to operate in vacation as it does in term. Conforming amendments, eliminating references to "vacation," have been made in various sections of Title 8.01.

ARTICLE 5.

Keeping of Docket Books; Execution Thereon; Disposal of Exhibits.

§ 8.01-446. Clerks to keep judgment dockets; what judgments to be docketed therein. — The clerk of each court of every circuit shall keep in his office, in a well-bound book, a judgment docket, in which he shall docket, without delay, any judgment for a specific amount of money rendered in his court, and shall likewise docket without delay any judgment for a specific amount of money rendered in this Commonwealth by any other court of this Commonwealth or federal court, when he shall be required so to do by any person interested, on such person delivering to him an authenticated legible abstract of it and also upon the request of any person interested therein, any such judgment rendered by a district court judge whose book has been filed in his office under the provisions of Title 16.1 or of which a legible abstract is delivered to him certified by the district court judge who rendered it; provided, that judgments docketed in the clerk's office of the Circuit Court of the City of Williamsburg and the County of James City shall be docketed and indexed in one book. A specific judgment for money shall state that it is a judgment for money in a specific amount in favor of a named party, against a named party, with that party's address, if known, and it shall further state the time from which the judgment bears interest. An order of restitution docketed pursuant to § 19.2-305.2 shall have the same force and effect as a specific judgment for money and shall state that it is an order of restitution in a specific amount in favor of a named party, against a named party, with that party's address, if known, and it shall further state the time from which the judgment bears interest. If the clerk determines that an abstract is not legible, the clerk shall refuse to record it and shall return it to the person who tendered the abstract for recording. (Code 1950, § 8-373; 1952, c. 438; 1962, c. 568; 1973, c. 544; 1975, cc. 182, 575; 1977, c. 617; 1993, c. 412; 1994, c. 538; 1995, c. 434; 1997, c. 579.)

REVISERS' NOTE

Former § 8-374 (Certification of judgment by clerks of other courts) has been deleted as unnecessary.

Law Review. — For article on title examination in Virginia, see 17 U. Rich. L. Rev. 229 (1983).

I. DECISIONS UNDER CURRENT LAW.

Docketing of restitution order as judgment against person does not improperly modify sentence by enhancing punishment, and requirement that restitution order be docketed "without delay" does not relate to entry of docketing order by circuit court. Frazier v. Commonwealth, 20 Va. App. 719, 460 S.E.2d 608 (1995).

§ 8.01-446.1. Keeping of docket books by clerk of court using micrographic process; form.
— Whenever judgments are docketed in the judgment lien book in the office of the clerk of the circuit court and are recorded by a procedural micrographic process as provided in § 17.1-240, or by any other method or process which renders impractical or impossible the subsequent entry of notations upon the docketed judgment, an appropriate certificate of assignment, release, partial release, certified copy of any order, or other separate instrument setting forth the necessary information as provided in this section shall be recorded and indexed according to law. Such instrument shall conform substantially with the following form:

TYPE OF FILING (Check One)
  ( ) Assignment   ORIGINAL BOOK # ..... PAGE ....
  ( ) Release
  ( ) Partial Release   ORIGINAL DATE DOCKETED: ......
  ( ) Credit(s)
  ( ) Additional Debtor(s)
  ( ) New Name of Debtor

Date of Judgment:
Amount of Judgment:
Plaintiff(s):

Defendant(s):

Assignee (If assignment): ....

Payments (If credits): AMOUNT .... DATE PAID ......

(Complete below if additional debtor or change of name of debtor)
Debtor:
Social Security Number of Debtor (If known):

Given under my hand this ...... day of ...., ...

....
(Plaintiff) (Attorney for Plaintiff)
(Authorized Agent for Plaintiff)

Any judgment creditor who knowingly gives false information upon such certificate made under this section shall be guilty of a Class 1 misdemeanor. (1985, c. 48.)

Cross references. — As to punishment for Class 1 misdemeanors, see § 18.2-11.

§ 8.01-447. Docketing of judgments and decrees of United States courts.
— Judgments and decrees rendered in the circuit court of appeals or a district court of the United States within this Commonwealth may be docketed and indexed in the clerks' offices of courts of this Commonwealth in the same manner and under the same rules and requirements of law as judgments and decrees of courts in this Commonwealth. (Code 1950, § 8-375; 1977, c. 617.)

Law Review. — For article on title examination in Virginia, see 17 U. Rich. L. Rev. 229 (1983).

I. DECISIONS UNDER PRIOR LAW.

Editor's note. — The case cited below was decided under corresponding provisions of former law. The term "this section," as used below, refers to former provisions.

Innocent purchaser protection where judgment not properly docketed. — A judgment of a federal court in this State which is not docketed in the county where the land lies is not notice to and does not bind an innocent purchaser who acquires title for value after such judgment is rendered. King v. Davis, 137 F. 222 (C.C.W.D. Va. 1905), aff'd sub nom. Blankenship v. King, 157 F. 676 (4th Cir. 1906).

§ 8.01-448. Attorney General, etc., to have judgments in favor of Commonwealth docketed.
— Whenever a judgment is recovered in favor of the Commonwealth, it shall be the duty of the Attorney General or other attorney representing the Commonwealth, to cause such judgment to be docketed in all counties and cities wherein there is any real estate owned by any person against whom the judgment is recovered. (Code 1950, § 8-376; 1977, c. 617.)

Cross references. — As to actions by the Commonwealth, see §§ 8.01-196 through 8.01-216.

§ 8.01-449. How judgments are docketed.
— The judgment docket required by § 8.01-446 may be kept in a well-bound book, or any other media

§ 8.01-450

permitted by § 17.1-240. The date and time of docketing shall be recorded with each judgment docketed. The clerk of the circuit court of any county using card files on July 1, 1975, may continue to use the card file system. The docketing may be done by copying the wording of the judgment order verbatim or by abstracting the information therefrom into fixed columns of a book or into fixed fields of an electronic data storage system. Where a procedural microphotographic system is used, the docketing may be done by recording and storing a retrievable image of the judgment order, judgment abstract, or other source document such as a certificate of assignment or release. Where an electronic imaging system is used, the document image shall be stored in a data format which permits recall of the image.

Where a well-bound book is used for the judgment docket there shall be stated in separate columns (i) the date and amount of the judgment, (ii) the time from which it bears interest, (iii) the costs, (iv) the full names of all the parties thereto, including the address, date of birth and social security number, if known, of each party against whom judgment is rendered, (v) the alternative value of any specific property recovered by it, (vi) the date and the time of docketing it, (vii) the amount and date of any credits thereon, (viii) the court by which it was rendered and the case number, and (ix) when paid off or discharged in whole or in part, the time of payment or discharge and by whom made when there is more than one defendant. And in case of a judgment or decree by confession, the clerk shall also enter in such docket the time of day at which the same was confessed, or at which the same was received in his office to be entered of record. There shall also be shown on such book the name of the plaintiff's attorney, if any.

Error or omission in the entry of the address or addresses or the social security number or numbers of each party against whom judgment is rendered shall in no way affect the validity, finality or priority of the judgment docketed. (Code 1950, § 8-377; 1973, c. 544; 1977, c. 617; 1982, c. 405; 1985, c. 171; 1988, c. 420; 1996, c. 427; 1997, c. 579.)

Cross references. — As to confession of judgment, see § 8.01-431. As to recording satisfaction of judgment, see §§ 8.01-453, 8.01-454.

Editor's note. — Acts 1996, c. 427, cl. 2, provides: "[t]hat the provisions of this act shall apply to judgments docketed on or after July 1, 1996."

I. DECISIONS UNDER PRIOR LAW.

Editor's note. — The case cited below was decided under corresponding provisions of former law. The term "this section," as used below, refers to former provisions.

Omission of Christian name of party is fatal to lien. — This section requires that the docket show the names of all the parties to the judgment. These names must be set out, and the omission of the Christian name is fatal to the judgment lien. Richardson v. Gardner, 128 Va. 676, 105 S.E. 225 (1920).

Commissioner's report of judgment as lien should show docketing. — A commissioner's report that reports a judgment as a subsisting lien against land held by a purchaser, without showing, or even stating, that the judgment has ever been docketed, reports a conclusion of law that a court should not be content to accept. Richardson v. Gardner, 128 Va. 676, 105 S.E. 225 (1920).

§ 8.01-450. How indexed. — Every judgment shall, as soon as it is docketed, be indexed by the clerk in the name of each defendant, as required by § 17.1-249, and shall not be regarded as docketed as to any defendant in whose name it is not so indexed. The clerk may maintain such index on computer, word processor, microfilm, microfiche, or other micrographic process. (Code 1950, § 8-378; 1977, c. 617; 1985, c. 171.)

Cross references. — As to records, recordation and indexing, see § 17.1-223 et seq.

Law Review. — For article on title examination in Virginia, see 17 U. Rich. L. Rev. 229 (1983).

I. Decisions Under Current Law.
I. Decisions Under Prior Law.

I. DECISIONS UNDER CURRENT LAW.

Federal law governs the filing of a notice of a federal tax lien, and the states may not prescribe the form or contents of that notice. The sufficiency of the notice is a question of federal law, and is determined without regard to the precise recording requirements of a particular state. Hudgins v. IRS, 132 Bankr. 115 (E.D. Va. 1991), modified, 967 F.2d 973 (4th Cir. 1992).

I. DECISIONS UNDER PRIOR LAW.

Editor's note. — The cases cited below were decided under corresponding provisions of former law. The term "this section, "as used below, refers to former provisions.

The object of this section is to apprise third persons who exercise ordinary care and prudence of the existence and character of the judgment. Fulkerson v. Taylor, 102 Va. 314, 46 S.E. 309 (1904).

It requires that a docketed judgment shall be indexed in the name of each defendant, and shall not be regarded as docketed as to any defendant in whose name it is not indexed. Richardson v. Gardner, 128 Va. 676, 105 S.E. 225 (1920).

Omission of Christian name of party is fatal. — The index must show the names of all the parties to the judgment. These names must be set out, and the omission of the Christian name is fatal to the judgment. Richardson v. Gardner, 128 Va. 676, 105 S.E. 225 (1920).

Christian name of married woman should be shown. — Docketing and indexing a judgment in the name of "Mrs. John Smith" is no notice of a judgment against Mary Smith, who is in fact the wife of John Smith. Bankers Loan & Inv. Co. v. Blair, 99 Va. 606, 39 S.E. 231 (1901).

"Same" may be used. — Where the name of a judgment debtor is entered in the index of the judgment lien docket, giving reference to a page of the docket, and immediately under his name the word "same" is written, also giving reference to a page of docket, this is a sufficient compliance with the provisions of this section as to the second-named judgment. Fulkerson v. Taylor, 102 Va. 314, 46 S.E. 309 (1904).

Allegation and proof of indexing required. — An allegation in a bill that a judgment sought to be enforced was duly docketed is a sufficient allegation of the indexing of the judgment as required by this section, but if the fact of indexing be put in issue it must be proved, and it would seem that this is not sufficiently done by the mere production of an abstract of the judgment which does not certify that it was duly docketed, and makes no reference to the indexing. Fulkerson v. Taylor, 100 Va. 426, 41 S.E. 863 (1902).

§ 8.01-451. Judgments to be docketed and indexed in new names of judgment debtors; how execution may thereafter issue. — Whenever there is a judgment docketed and indexed, as required by § 17.1-249, and thereafter a judgment debtor whose name is so recorded changes his name, whether by marriage, court order, by a voluntary assumption of a new name or otherwise, the clerk of the court in which the judgment was obtained, upon satisfactory proof that the judgment debtor has acquired a new name, shall docket and index the judgment in the new name. Execution may thereafter issue against the judgment debtor in the prior name, the new name, or both. The clerk may require the submission by any party interested in the judgment or by his duly authorized attorney or agent of a form similar to that set out in § 8.01-446.1 indicating that the judgment debtor has acquired a new name, and stating the new name. Such form shall constitute satisfactory proof of the new name. This section shall apply to all judgments obtained prior or subsequent to the enactment hereof. (Code 1950, § 8-378.1; 1950, p. 440; 1977, c. 617; 1998, c. 639.)

Cross references. — As to fees collected by clerks of circuit courts, see § 17.1-275.

§ 8.01-452. Entry of assignment of judgment on judgment lien docket. — Whenever there shall be an assignment of a judgment, there may be a notation of the assignment made upon the judgment docket, where the same is recorded, by the clerk. An assignment, in order to be so noted, must be in writing, showing the date thereof, the name of the assignor and assignee, the amount of the judgment, and when and by what court granted, and either acknowledged as are deeds for recordation in the clerks' offices of circuit courts in this Commonwealth, or signed by the assignor, attested by two witnesses; or such judgment may be assigned by notation on the margin of the judgment lien docket on the page of the book where same is docketed, by the judgment creditor or his attorney of record, and attested by the clerk. The assignment, after the same is noted upon the judgment docket as is herein provided, shall be filed by the clerk with the other papers in the case in his office. When such assignment is made and noted as herein provided further executions shall be issued in the name of the assignee as the plaintiff in the case. (Code 1950, § 8-379; 1977, c. 617.)

Cross references. — As to fees collected by clerks of circuit courts, see § 17.1-275.

§ 8.01-452.1. Disposal of exhibits in civil cases. — A clerk of court, after sixty days have elapsed from the entry of judgment in a civil case or, if the civil case is appealed or notice of appeal is pending or the case is being reheard, when the appeal or rehearing is concluded, may dispose of or donate any exhibits filed in the case and in his possession after notifying the owner or his attorney by first-class mail and after twenty-one days from the mailing of the notice to the owner or attorney unless the owner or attorney requests the return of the exhibits. (1981, c. 312; 1992, c. 57; 1995, c. 13; 1997, c. 135; 1998, c. 886.)

Law Review. — For 1995 survey of civil practice and procedure, see 29 U. Rich. L. Rev. 897 (1995).

ARTICLE 6.

Satisfaction.

§ 8.01-453. When and how payment or discharge entered on judgment docket. — The fact of payment or discharge, either in whole or in part, of any judgment so docketed, and if there is more than one defendant, by which defendant it was paid or discharged, shall be entered by the clerk in whose office the judgment is docketed whenever it appears from a certificate of the clerk of the court in which the judgment was rendered, that the judgment has been satisfied, in whole or in part, or upon the direction, in writing, of the judgment creditor or his duly authorized attorney or other agent. (Code 1950, § 8-380; 1977, c. 617; 1979, c. 192; 1986, c. 276; 1988, c. 420.)

REVISERS' NOTE

The phrase "..., his duly authorized attorney or other agent ..." has been added to former § 8-380.

Former § 8-381 (When clerk to certify satisfaction of judgment) has been deleted. Sections 8.01-453, 8.01-454, and 8.01-455 are adequate to cover the import of this statute.

Cross references. — As to executions of judgments and other means of recovery generally, see §§ 8.01-466 through 8.01-525.

§ 8.01-454. Judgment, when paid, to be so noted by creditor. — In all cases in which payment or satisfaction of any judgment so docketed is made, which is not required to be certified to the clerk under § 8.01-455, it shall be the duty of the judgment creditor, himself, or by his agent or attorney, to cause such payment or satisfaction by the defendant, whether in whole or in part, and if there is more than one defendant, by which defendant it was paid or discharged, to be entered within thirty days after the same is made, on such judgment docket. If the judgment has not been docketed, then the entry shall be made on the execution book in the office of the clerk from which the execution issued. For any failure to do so, after ten days' notice to do so by the judgment debtor, his agent or attorney, the judgment creditor shall be liable to a fine of up to fifty dollars. The entry of payment or satisfaction shall be signed by the creditor, his duly authorized attorney or other agent, and be attested by the clerk in whose office the judgment is docketed, or, when not docketed, by the clerk from whose office the execution issued; however, the cost of the release shall be paid by the judgment debtor. (Code 1950, § 8-382; 1977, c. 617; 1988, c. 420.)

REVISERS' NOTE

The 90-day period of former § 8-382 has been reduced to 30 days. The fine has been increased from $20 to a maximum of $50. Other minor changes have been made.

Cross references. — As to release of other liens, see §§ 43-67 through 43-71.

I. DECISIONS UNDER PRIOR LAW.

Editor's note. — The case cited below was decided under corresponding provisions of former law. The term "this section," as used below, refers to former provisions.

Ratification of act of attorney in indorsing judgment as satisfied. — The holder of a note sent it to attorneys with instructions to renew if possible, but otherwise to sue. After judgment was obtained, the holder received from the attorneys a new note and money, with the intimation that if a small balance was paid they would receive it in satisfaction of the judgment. The holder accepted the new note and money, and announced the balance due, and the attorneys indorsed the judgment on the lien docket as "satisfied." The holder did nothing further for five years, when an attempt was made to cancel the indorsement on the ground of fraud or mistake. It was held that the holder had ratified the indorsement by the attorneys. Higginbotham v. May, 90 Va. 233, 17 S.E. 941 (1893).

§ 8.01-455. Court, on motion of defendant, etc., may have payment of judgment entered. — A. A defendant in any judgment, his heirs or personal representatives, may, on motion, after ten days' notice thereof to the plaintiff in such judgment, or his assignee, or if he be dead, to his personal representative, or if he be a nonresident, to his attorney, if he have one, apply to the court in which the judgment was rendered, to have the same marked satisfied, and upon proof that the judgment has been paid off or discharged, such court shall order such satisfaction to be entered on the margin of the page in the book wherein such judgment was entered, and a certificate of such order to be made to the clerk of the court in which such judgment is required by § 8.01-446 to be docketed, and the clerk of such court shall immediately, upon the receipt of such certificate, enter the same in the proper column of the judgment docket opposite the place where such judgment is docketed. If the plaintiff be a nonresident and have no attorney of record residing in this Commonwealth, the notice may be published and posted as an order of publication is required to be published and posted under §§ 8.01-316 and 8.01-317. Upon a like motion and similar proceeding, the court may order to be marked "discharged in bankruptcy," any judgment which may be shown to have been so discharged.

B. The cost of such proceedings, including reasonable attorney's fees, may be ordered to be paid by the plaintiff. (Code 1950, § 8-383; 1977, c. 617.)

REVISERS' NOTE

Subsection B, providing that the cost of such a proceeding be borne by the plaintiff, is new in Title 8.01.

Cross references. — As to entry of order of publication, see §§ 8.01-316, 8.01-317. As to place where judgment is docketed, see § 8.01-446.

I. Decisions Under Current Law.
II. Decisions Under Prior Law.

I. DECISIONS UNDER CURRENT LAW.

Discharge in bankruptcy would not prevent enforcement of lien acquired before bankruptcy proceedings. — A debtor's discharge in bankruptcy would not prevent a judgment creditor from a post-discharge enforcement of its lien upon debtor's real property interests that were acquired before the commencement of the bankruptcy proceedings. Where the creditor's judgment was recorded before the debtor filed his bankruptcy petition, the judgment continued to be a lien on any interest the debtor may have had in land despite debtor's bankruptcy discharge from personal liability for payment of the judgement. Therefore, the judgment lien was not "paid off or discharged" in the debtor's bankruptcy proceedings. And the trial court erred in ordering that the lien be released. Leasing Serv. Corp. v. Justice, 243 Va. 441, 416 S.E.2d 439 (1992).

Discharge in bankruptcy made lien ineffective against real property acquired after commencement of bankruptcy proceedings. — Although lien was imposed on all of debtor's real property interests in the county that were acquired after judgment creditor's judgment was recorded, debtor's discharge in bankruptcy made the lien ineffective as to any real property interests in the county that debtor acquired after the commencement of his bankruptcy proceedings. Leasing Serv. Corp. v. Justice, 243 Va. 441, 416 S.E.2d 439 (1992).

Incorrect order of "satisfied in bankruptcy." — Trial court incorrectly ordered a judgment creditor's recorded judgment marked "satisfied in bankruptcy"; the trial court could only order the release of judgment creditor's lien in a proceeding under this section upon proof that the lien had been discharged in bankruptcy; furthermore, debtor had the burden of proof as to his entitlement to relief under this section; thus, the trial court also erred in imposing the burden on judgment creditor to show that debtor had property in county that was subject to its lien. Leasing Serv. Corp. v. Justice, 243 Va. 441, 416 S.E.2d 439 (1992).

Applied in Groh v. B.F. Saul Real Estate Inv. Trust, 224 Va. 156, 294 S.E.2d 859 (1982); In re Woolard, 190 Bankr. 70 (Bankr. E.D. Va. 1995).

II. DECISIONS UNDER PRIOR LAW.

Editor's note. — The cases cited below were decided under corresponding provisions of former law. The term "this section," as used below, refers to former provisions.

The object of this section is to afford a summary remedy for having marked satisfied the liens mentioned therein upon proof that the judgment has been actually paid or discharged. The section was not intended to enable persons to have such liens marked satisfied because liable to be defeated by presumption of payment, or because barred by the statute of limitations. Turnbull v. Mann, 94 Va. 182, 26 S.E. 510 (1897).

Court may direct jury to try facts. — If, on a motion to enter a judgment satisfied, the relief of the party depends on matters of fact, the court has discretion to direct a jury to try the facts. Smock v. Dade, 26 Va. (5 Rand.) 639 (1826).

A suit in equity is the proper remedy to vacate an entry of satisfaction. Such a suit may be maintained where there has been fraud or mistake. And it may be maintained by the attorneys who obtained the judgment. Higginbotham v. May, 90 Va. 233, 17 S.E. 941 (1893). See also, Bradshaw v. Bratton, 96 Va. 577, 32 S.E. 56 (1899).

§ 8.01-456. Satisfaction of judgment when judgment creditor cannot be located.

— Whenever a judgment debtor or anyone for him or any party liable on the judgment wishes to pay off and discharge a judgment, of record in any clerk's office in this Commonwealth, when the judgment creditor cannot be located, he may do so by paying into the court having jurisdiction over such judgment an amount sufficient to pay the principal, interest, and all costs due thereupon, together with the cost of entering necessary orders, and other service attendant upon the proceeding herein provided for, and satisfaction upon such judgment. Upon such payment, the court, by an order entered of record shall direct the clerk to deposit the same at interest in any bank which is a member of the Federal Deposit Insurance Corporation and is designated in such order; to file evidence of such deposit in the office of the clerk in an appropriate file and shall be payable to the court entering the order for the benefit of the judgment creditor; and to enter upon the judgment docket, where the judgment is docketed, the date of such deposit, the date of the entry of the order of the court receiving same, referring to the number and page of the order book in which it is entered.

The judgment creditor or his attorney may have the money, so paid, to which he is entitled, upon application to the court therefor whenever it may appear to the court that it should be paid to him.

From and after the time of such payment, into the court, as aforesaid, the property of the defendant shall be free and clear of any lien created by any such judgment, or any execution issued thereupon. (Code 1950, § 8-384; 1977, c. 617.)

REVISERS' NOTE

Former § 8-384 has been changed by substituting for "any interested party..." the language "a judgment debtor or anyone for him or any party liable on the judgment" before the word "wishes." The language "any bank which is a member of the Federal Deposit Insurance Corporation..." has been inserted in place of the former language "some solvent bank...." The words "at interest" have been inserted after the language "deposit the same." The language "to take an interest bearing certificate therefor which shall be filed..." has been replaced with "to file evidence of such deposit...."

I. DECISIONS UNDER CURRENT LAW.

Lis pendens is not a lien or a judgment. It is merely notice that an action is pending, seeking to obtain a judgment. Cavalier Serv. Corp. v. Wise, 645 F. Supp. 31 (E.D. Va. 1986).

§ 8.01-457. Marking satisfied judgments for Commonwealth; payment by third parties releasing recognizances.

— It shall be the duty of the clerks of the circuit courts of this Commonwealth, upon the payment of any judgment in favor of the Commonwealth by any person or upon the release of any recognizance by court order, to mark the same satisfied upon the judgment lien docket at every place such judgment or recognizance, as the case may be, shall have been recorded upon such lien docket. In marking such recognizance satisfied it shall be the duty of such clerk to refer by marginal reference to the court order, if any, releasing or discharging such recognizance. (Code 1950, § 8-385; 1977, c. 617; 1986, c. 132.)

Article 7.
Lien and Enforcement Thereof.

§ 8.01-458. From what time judgment to be a lien on real estate; docketing revived judgment. — Every judgment for money rendered in this Commonwealth by any state or federal court or by confession of judgment, as provided by law, shall be a lien on all the real estate of or to which the defendant in the judgment is or becomes possessed or entitled, from the time such judgment is recorded on the judgment lien docket of the clerk's office of the county or city where such land is situated; provided, however, when a judgment is revived under the provisions of § 8.01-251, that such revived judgment shall not be a lien as prescribed in this section unless and until such judgment is again docketed as provided herein. In such event the lien shall be effective from the date of the original docketing. Any judgment or decree properly docketed under the provisions of this section shall, if the real estate subject to the lien of such judgment has been annexed to or merged with an adjoining city subsequent to such docketing, be deemed to have been docketed in the proper clerk's office of such city. (Code 1950, § 8-386; 1954, c. 333; 1960, c. 466; 1964, c. 309; 1977, c. 617.)

Cross references. — As to decrees being considered as judgments, see § 8.01-426. As to lien of judgment by confession, see § 8.01-431. As to homestead, exemption see § 34-4 et seq. As to necessity of certain contracts being in writing, see § 11-1. As to form and effect of deeds and leases, see § 55-48 et seq. As to necessity for recordation of contracts, etc., see § 55-96 et seq.

Law Review. — For article on fraudulent conveyances and preferences in Virginia, see 36 Wash. & Lee L. Rev. 51 (1979). For article on title examination in Virginia, see 17 U. Rich. L. Rev. 229 (1983).

I. Decisions Under Current Law.
  A. General Consideration.
  B. When Lien Attaches.
  C. Property Subject to Lien.
II. Decisions Under Prior Law.
  A. General Consideration.
  B. When Lien Attaches.
  C. Property Subject to Lien.

I. DECISIONS UNDER CURRENT LAW.

A. General Consideration.

Section 8.01-268 must be read in conjunction with this section, which states that "[e]very judgment for money rendered in this Commonwealth by any state or federal court ... shall be a lien on all the real estate of ... the defendant...." Thus, any suit in which the defendant is an individual has the potential to affect the title to real estate. Hart v. United Va. Bank, 24 Bankr. 821 (Bankr. E.D. Va. 1982).

This section must be read in conjunction with § 55-96. Leake v. Finance One Mtg., Inc. (In re Snyder), 57 Bankr. 438 (Bankr. W.D. Va. 1985).

Procedure available to any party seeking money judgment. — Under § 8.01-268 and this section, the recording of a memorandum of lis pendens is open to any litigating party seeking a money judgment against an individual property owner in Virginia. Hart v. United Va. Bank, 24 Bankr. 821 (Bankr. E.D. Va. 1982).

A judgment lien is a right given the judgment creditor to have his claim satisfied by the seizure of the land of his judgment debtor. In re Washington, 6 Bankr. 226 (Bankr. E.D. Va. 1980).

Effect of discharge in bankruptcy. — A discharge in bankruptcy does not necessarily affect a specific lien, but only releases the bankrupt from personal liability. Turshen v. Bennett Heating & Air Conditioning, Inc. (In re Brisbane), 2 Bankr. 636 (Bankr. E.D. Va. 1980).

Monetary award in equitable distribution proceedings. — A party who is granted a monetary award in an equitable distribution proceeding is in the same position as any other judgment creditor and has the same enforcement remedies available. Booth v. Booth, 7 Va. App. 22, 371 S.E.2d 569 (1988).

Applied in In re Morrissey, 37 Bankr. 571 (Bankr. E.D. Va. 1984); In re Trent, 42 Bankr.

279 (Bankr. W.D. Va. 1984); Barzee v. Trammel, 63 Bankr. 878 (Bankr. E.D. Va. 1986); Massie v. Yamrose, 169 Bankr. 585 (W.D. Va. 1994).

B. When Lien Attaches.

Docketing is a necessary prerequisite to the validity of a judgment lien. Turshen v. Bennett Heating & Air Conditioning, Inc. (In re Brisbane), 2 Bankr. 636 (Bankr. E.D. Va. 1980); Bartl v. G. Weinberger & Co. (In re Claxton), 32 Bankr. 215 (Bankr. E.D. Va. 1983).

The ultimate statutory effect of this section has been to maintain the peculiar relationship between the rendition of a judgment and the docketing of such judgment from which a lien obtains. Turshen v. Bennett Heating & Air Conditioning, Inc. (In re Brisbane), 2 Bankr. 636 (Bankr. E.D. Va. 1980).

A judgment may not be a lien on real property ex proprio vigore until it becomes such, as by docketing in a register's office, and further, the Virginia courts and legislature have long acknowledged the unique relationship between docketing of a judgment lien and the rendition of such judgment. Turshen v. Bennett Heating & Air Conditioning, Inc. (In re Brisbane), 2 Bankr. 636 (Bankr. E.D. Va. 1980).

Discharge in bankruptcy would not prevent enforcement of lien acquired before bankruptcy proceedings. — A debtor's discharge in bankruptcy would not prevent a judgment creditor from a post-discharge enforcement of its lien upon debtor's real property interests that were acquired before the commencement of the bankruptcy proceedings. Where the creditor's judgment was recorded before the debtor filed his bankruptcy petition, the judgment continued to be a lien on any interest the debtor may have had in land despite his bankruptcy discharge from personal liability for payment of the judgment. Therefore, the judgment lien was not "paid off or discharged" in the debtor's bankruptcy proceedings. And the trial court erred in ordering that the lien be released. Leasing Serv. Corp. v. Justice, 243 Va. 441, 416 S.E.2d 439 (1992).

C. Property Subject to Lien.

Property fraudulently conveyed. — A properly docketed judgment lien attaches also to property which the judgment debtor has conveyed away in fraud of the judgment creditor. Bartl v. G. Weinberger & Co. (In re Claxton), 32 Bankr. 215 (Bankr. E.D. Va. 1983).

Lien attaches to after-acquired property. — This section does not restrict operation of a judgment lien to property held by the judgment debtor at the time the lien arises. Rather, a properly docketed judgment lien will attach to after-acquired real estate as well. Bartl v. G. Weinberger & Co. (In re Claxton), 32 Bankr. 215 (Bankr. E.D. Va. 1983).

Discharge in bankruptcy made lien ineffective against real property acquired after commencement of bankruptcy proceedings. — Although lien was imposed on all of debtor's real property interests in the county that were acquired after judgment creditor's judgment was recorded, debtor's discharge in bankruptcy made the lien ineffective as to any real property interests in the county that debtor acquired after the commencement of his bankruptcy proceedings. Leasing Serv. Corp. v. Justice, 243 Va. 441, 416 S.E.2d 439 (1992).

Property held by the entirety where one spouse files for bankruptcy. — The interest of one spouse in tenants by the entirety property is not subject to execution by the creditor of that one spouse only. Creditors holding joint debts, however, may subject entireties property to satisfy their claims and can obtain relief to enforce such a joint debt when one of the spouses seeks relief in a liquidation under Chapter 7 of Title 11 of the United States Code. Stern Shoe Repair Co. v. Menefee, 22 Bankr. 425 (Bankr. E.D. Va. 1982).

Where a husband has filed a wage earner plan under Chapter 13 of the Bankruptcy Reform Act of 1978, the creditor on a joint debt of the husband and wife is entitled to relief from the automatic stay granted under 11 U.S.C. § 362 so as to enable it to obtain a lien on real property held by the entirety. However, should the plan be confirmed, the creditor would be enjoined from foreclosing or otherwise enforcing the lien during the life of the plan. Stern Shoe Repair Co. v. Menefee, 22 Bankr. 425 (Bankr. E.D. Va. 1982).

II. DECISIONS UNDER PRIOR LAW.

A. General Consideration.

Editor's note. — The cases cited below were decided under corresponding provisions of former law. The term "this section," as used below, refers to former provisions.

Section applies to decrees. — Since a decree for money, by express enactment, is embraced by the word "judgment," the statute fixing the lien of a judgment applies equally to such decrees. Hockman v. Hockman, 93 Va. 455, 25 S.E. 534 (1896).

Lien is a legal one. — The lien of a judgment given by this section is a legal lien, and the judgment creditor can enforce it in a court of equity without pursuing his debtor's personalty. The lien, being a plain legal one, expressly created by statute, cannot be judicially modified to soften the supposed hardship of secret encumbrances. Gurnee v. Johnson, 77 Va. 712 (1883); Hutchison v. Grubbs, 80 Va. 251 (1885); Blakemore v. Wise, 95 Va. 269, 28 S.E. 332 (1897); Flanary v. Kane, 102 Va. 547, 46 S.E. 312 (1904).

It may be enforced immediately. — The

debt evidenced by a judgment, unlike many obligations described in mortgages or deeds of trust, is past due. There is nothing to prevent its immediate enforcement. Jones v. Hall, 177 Va. 658, 15 S.E.2d 108 (1941).

Judgment cannot be impaired by any act of the debtor. — When a judgment creditor has obtained his judgment and caused it to be docketed, his lien is perfect and complete, and cannot be defeated or impaired by any act of his debtor in which he did not participate. Strayer v. Long, 93 Va. 695, 26 S.E. 409 (1896).

But it is lost if third person acquires title by adverse possession. — It is true that the lien of a judgment may be indefinitely continued against the land of the judgment debtor in his possession, or of others holding titles derived from and in privity with him. But obviously the same rule cannot be applied to strangers who have acquired a perfect legal title not in privity with but adversely to the title of the judgment debtor. In other words, the life of a judgment may be indefinitely prolonged as to any property upon which it can operate, but whenever the right of the judgment debtor to make an entry on or bring an action to recover any land held adversely is tolled by § 8.01-236, the right of his judgment creditor to subject land to the satisfaction of his judgment also ceases. The lien is a vested right, but not more so than the title to which the lien attaches, and when the statute of limitations destroys the latter it necessarily destroys the former. McClanahan's Adm'r v. Norfolk & W. Ry., 122 Va. 705, 96 S.E. 453 (1918). But see Flanary v. Kane, 102 Va. 547, 46 S.E. 312 (1904), wherein it was held that § 8.01-236 did not apply to a suit to enforce a judgment lien.

Judgment creditor has no interest in the land of his debtor. He has neither a jus in re nor a jus ad rem. He has no right to the possession. He has simply a lien upon the land, and the right to subject it to the discharge of that lien. McClanahan's Adm'r v. Norfolk & W. Ry., 122 Va. 705, 96 S.E. 453 (1918).

He has no proprietary right, merely a right to levy. — A judgment lien is a right given the judgment creditor to have his claim satisfied by the seizure of the land of his judgment debtor. It is not a proprietary right in the lands of the judgment debtor, but merely a right to levy on any such lands for the purpose of satisfying the judgment to the exclusion or destruction of any right which may have accrued to others since the attachment of the lien. Jones v. Hall, 177 Va. 658, 15 S.E.2d 108 (1941).

Title of debtor is not divested by entry of judgment. — When levy on real property is actually made by a judgment creditor under a judgment lien, the title of the creditor, for this purpose, relates back to the time of his judgment, so as to cut out intermediate incumbrances. But subject to this, the debtor has full power to sell or otherwise dispose of the land. His title to it is not divested or transferred, by the judgment, to the judgment creditor. Jones v. Hall, 177 Va. 658, 15 S.E.2d 108 (1941).

Court may restrain acts tending to lessen value of lien. — If, in a suit to enforce a judgment lien on real property, it is shown that the owner of the land, or his assignee in possession, is doing any act that tends to lessen its value and to jeopardize the full satisfaction of the judgment, the act may be restrained until the land is, in due course, offered for sale. Jones v. Hall, 177 Va. 658, 15 S.E.2d 108 (1941).

A decree for alimony constitutes a lien under this section upon all of the husband's real estate from the date of such decree, not only for the installments presently due, but for those that shall fall due under such decree in the future; and where a temporary decree for alimony is subsequently made permanent, the lien for the whole amount dates from the date of the temporary decree. Issacs v. Issacs, 117 Va. 730, 86 S.E. 105 (1915); Morris v. Henry, 193 Va. 631, 70 S.E.2d 417 (1952).

Lien of decree for support of infant held to continue after father's death. — Divorce decree directing defendant father to pay a certain sum monthly for alimony and support of his infant daughter, became a lien upon the land he then owned and which he conveyed less than two months later to his father, and the lien so created, to the extent that the amount thereof was for the benefit of the infant daughter, was intended to and did by said decree continue in effect after the death of her father, and until she became 21 (now 18) years old or self-supporting. Morris v. Henry, 193 Va. 631, 70 S.E.2d 417 (1952).

A judgment rendered on a void process constitutes no lien. Lavell v. McCurdy, 77 Va. 763 (1883).

Judgment liens were not affected by separation of West Virginia. — The lien of a judgment which had attached to land in either Virginia or West Virginia prior to the separation was not lost upon the division of these two states, whereby the county in which the judgment lien originally attached fell either within the one state or the other. Gatewood v. Goode, 64 Va. (23 Gratt.) 880 (1873).

B. When Lien Attaches.

Suit to set aside fraudulent conveyance does not postpone lien. — A judgment creditor's bringing a suit to set aside as fraudulent a deed executed and recorded prior to the time the judgment was rendered does not postpone the lien of the judgment to the time of the bringing of the suit, or operate as an abandonment or waiver of the existing lien of the judgment against the property in the hands of the fraudulent grantee. Tucker v. Foster, 154 Va. 182, 152 S.E. 376 (1930).

Judgment against contingent remainderman becomes lien when remainder vests. — Under this section a judgment against a contingent remainderman is a lien on the after-acquired vested remainder in possession. Wilson v. Langhorne, 102 Va. 631, 47 S.E. 871 (1904).

C. Property Subject to Lien.

The lien of a judgment reaches far. It reaches every interest of the judgment debtor in land which the record of the title shows that he had, either before or after the judgment was docketed, unless the record itself shows a previous transfer by deed duly recorded. It is always necessary, however, to show the judgment debtor's present or former title to the specific land before the lien attaches. Miller v. Kemp, 157 Va. 178, 160 S.E. 203 (1931).

In equity judgments are liens on the whole of the debtor's equitable estate. Haleys v. Williams, 28 Va. (1 Leigh) 140 (1829). See Withers v. Carter, 45 Va. (4 Gratt.) 407 (1848); Buchanan v. Clark, 51 Va. (10 Gratt.) 164 (1853).

A judgment creditor has a lien in equity on the equitable estate of the debtor, in like manner as he has a lien at law on his legal estate. Coutts v. Walker, 29 Va. (2 Leigh) 268 (1830); Michaux v. Brown, 51 Va. (10 Gratt.) 612 (1854).

A judgment is a lien on an equity of redemption. Michaux v. Brown, 51 Va. (10 Gratt.) 612 (1854); Hale v. Horne, 62 Va. (21 Gratt.) 112 (1871); McClanahan's Adm'r v. Norfolk & W. Ry., 122 Va. 705, 96 S.E. 453 (1918).

But lien is subject to prior deed of trust. — A creditor, whose judgment is subsequent to a deed of trust on the debtor's land, has a lien only on the equity of redemption, and cannot have the deed of trust enforced, and the land sold to pay the debts thereby secured, until default. Wytheville Crystal Ice & Dairy Co. v. Frick Co., 96 Va. 141, 30 S.E. 491 (1898); Shurtz v. Johnson, 69 Va. (28 Gratt.) 657 (1877).

For creditor gets only rights of debtor. — Where the recording acts do not interfere, the judgment creditor can acquire no better right to the estate than the debtor himself had at the date of the recovery of the judgment. Coldiron v. Asheville Shoe Co., 93 Va. 364, 25 S.E. 238 (1896); McClanahan's Adm'r v. Norfolk & W. Ry., 122 Va. 705, 96 S.E. 453 (1918); Van Nostrand & Co. v. Virginia Zinc & Chem. Corp., 126 Va. 131, 101 S.E. 65 (1919).

Judgment against partnership is lien on real estate of partner. — A judgment against partners for a firm liability is a lien against the real estate of each partner, and has preference over an unsecured debt of a deceased partner in the administration of his assets. Pitts v. Spotts, 86 Va. 71, 9 S.E. 501 (1889).

Lien remains though judgment is suspended by injunction. — Though at the time of the conveyance, execution upon the judgment was suspended by an injunction, yet the judgment is a lien upon land in the hands of a purchaser. Craig v. Sebrell, 50 Va. (9 Gratt.) 131 (1852). See also, Michaux v. Brown, 51 Va. (10 Gratt.) 612 (1854).

It binds subsequent improvements by grantee with notice. — The lien of a judgment against the grantor of lands binds improvements made on the land by a grantee who, at the date of his purchase, had constructive and actual notice of the judgment, and of a lis pendens to enforce it. Nixdorf v. Blount, 111 Va. 127, 68 S.E. 258 (1910).

Debtor must own some beneficial interest in land. — Before the lien of the judgment can attach, the judgment debtor must own, or have owned, some beneficial interest in the specific land involved. Miller v. Kemp, 157 Va. 178, 160 S.E. 203 (1931).

A judgment creditor cannot subject to the lien of his judgment real estate or any interest therein not owned by the debtor at or after the recovery of the judgment. Powell v. Bell, 81 Va. 222 (1885).

Lien does not attach to interest of mortgagee. — A creditor whose debt is secured by deed of trust or mortgage on real estate has no such interest in the land conveyed as amounts to a right of property therein, or as would be bound by judgment against the creditor. Augusta Nat'l Bank v. Beard, 100 Va. 687, 42 S.E. 694 (1902).

Or to land held by debtor in constructive trust. — Where the purchase price of land is paid by one person while the legal title is conveyed to another, the latter has no beneficial interest in the land, and it is not bound by a judgment against him, as only the debtor's beneficial interest in land can be subjected by his creditors. The debtor in such a case is a mere trustee, and has no beneficial interest. Straley v. Esser, 117 Va. 135, 83 S.E. 1075 (1915). See also, Coldiron v. Asheville Shoe Co., 93 Va. 364, 25 S.E. 238 (1896).

Or to land of which he has had only transitory seisin. — Transitory seisin is not such an interest as becomes subject to a lien of a judgment. Hence, where land is conveyed to judgment debtor, and eo instante reconveyed by him to trustee to secure the purchase money, he has no interest subject to the judgment lien as against the trust deed. Straus v. Bodeker, 86 Va. 543, 10 S.E. 570 (1889); Charlottesville Hdwe. Co. v. Perkins, 118 Va. 34, 86 S.E. 869 (1915); Moomaw v. Jordan, 118 Va. 414, 87 S.E. 569 (1916).

Facts insufficient to show equitable title

in third person. — Where land was conveyed to a land company by an unconditional deed without reservation of lien or any right of any other sort, and the deed showed on its face that the land was bought from the grantor by three of the directors of the company, and that it was conveyed to the company at the instance and request of these directors, who had assigned the benefit of their purchase to the company, and the company caused the land to be platted, and sold various lots to different purchasers, and conveyed the same to them, in some of which conveyances the directors united, stating that the conveyance to the company had been made at their instance and request, and there was no evidence that the directors had any equity whatsoever in the land, the land was bound by judgments against the company. Overstreet v. Griffin, 119 Va. 678, 89 S.E. 879 (1916).

Lands aliened before judgment are not subject to lien. — Aside from any question of recordation, judgments acquired after lands have been aliened to a purchaser in good faith and for value do not attach as liens to such land. Bowman v. Hicks, 80 Va. 806 (1885).

Unless conveyed in fraud of creditor. — If a judgment has been duly rendered and docketed, it is a lien both upon the real estate then held by the judgment debtor and also upon any real estate, which he may have conveyed in fraud of such judgment creditor, after the debt was contracted and before judgment was rendered. Matney v. Combs, 171 Va. 244, 198 S.E. 469 (1938).

And lien on land fraudulently conveyed is subject to superior equities. — When a judgment has been rendered and duly docketed the effect thereof is to impose a lien both upon the real estate then held by the judgment debtor and also upon any that he may have theretofore conveyed away in fraud of the judgment creditor after his debt was contracted and before judgment was rendered, subject of course in the latter case to the superior equities of bona fide purchasers for value and without notice. Tucker v. Foster, 154 Va. 182, 152 S.E. 376 (1930).

No lien attaches to personal property. — Under this section a decree for alimony and suit money constitutes a lien on the real estate of the husband. There is no suggestion that such a lien attaches to the personal property of the husband. This omission in the statute is fatal to the contention that a court of equity has the inherent power to impound the personal property of the husband to secure the payment of alimony and support money. Ring v. Ring, 185 Va. 269, 38 S.E.2d 471 (1946).

Timber severed from the debtor's land is not subject to the general lien of a judgment, since the judgment lien confers no right on the creditor before levy to sue for waste. The same is true of rents and profits from real estate. Jones v. Hall, 177 Va. 658, 15 S.E.2d 108 (1941).

For a judgment debtor has a right to cut fire wood and timber upon his land previous to a levy, and it follows that such wood and timber cut, but not removed, becomes his personal property, and do not pass by a levy upon, and sale of, the land. Jones v. Hall, 177 Va. 658, 15 S.E.2d 108 (1941).

Creditor cannot follow proceeds of sale. — If a judgment debtor should sell his estate, he judgment creditor has no right to follow the proceeds of the sale into the hands of vendor or vendee, or to claim the purchase money in the hands of the vendee. The creditor's remedy is against the thing itself. Jones v. Hall, 177 Va. 658, 15 S.E.2d 108 (1941).

The lien of a judgment did not extend to the proceeds of part of the land sold by a purchaser with notice to purchasers without notice. The lien of a judgment attaches to the debtor's land, but not to the proceeds of the sale thereof. And the judgment creditor's contention that the proceeds should have been considered held in constructive trust came too late because raised for the first time in her brief on appeal, and furthermore was not within the purview of her assignment of error. Orphanoudakis v. Orphanoudakis, 199 Va. 142, 98 S.E.2d 676 (1957).

§ 8.01-459. Priority of judgments. — Judgments against the same person shall, as among themselves, attach to his real estate, and be payable thereout in the order of the priority of the lien of such judgments, respectively. (Code 1950, § 8-387; 1977, c. 617.)

REVISERS' NOTE

The language "the lien of" has been inserted in former § 8-387.

§ 8.01-460. CIVIL REMEDIES AND PROCEDURE § 8.01-460

Law Review. — For article on fraudulent conveyances and preferences in Virginia, see 36 Wash. & Lee L. Rev. 51 (1979).

I. Decisions Under Current Law.
II. Decisions Under Prior Law.

I. DECISIONS UNDER CURRENT LAW.

Lis pendens is not a lien or a judgment. It is merely notice that an action is pending, seeking to obtain a judgment. Cavalier Serv. Corp. v. Wise, 645 F. Supp. 31 (E.D. Va. 1986).

II. DECISIONS UNDER PRIOR LAW.

Editor's note. — The cases cited below were decided under corresponding provisions of former law. The term "this section," as used below, refers to former provisions.

In equity, whole estate must be applied first to elder judgment. — In equity, judgments are liens on the whole of the debtor's equitable estate, and the whole is first to be applied to the elder judgment, then the whole of the residue to the junior judgment, and in neither case is only a moiety to be applied to their satisfaction. Haleys v. Williams, 28 Va. (1 Leigh) 140 (1829). See Withers v. Carter, 45 Va. (4 Gratt.) 407 (1848); Buchanan v. Clark, 51 Va. (10 Gratt.) 164 (1853).

§ 8.01-460. Decree for support and maintenance of spouse or infant children of parties as lien on real estate.

— A decree, order or judgment for support and maintenance of a spouse or of infant children of the parties payable in future installments or a monetary award for future installments as provided for in § 20-107.3, shall be a lien upon such real estate of the obligor as the court shall, from time to time, designate by order or decree. An order after reasonable notice to the obligor adjudicating that the obligor is delinquent, shall be a lien on the obligor's real estate. Liens under this section shall arise when duly docketed in the manner prescribed for the docketing of other judgments for money; however, no such decree, order or judgment for support and maintenance or for a monetary award in accordance with § 20-107.3 shall be docketed unless so ordered by the court in such decree, order or judgment. On petition by any interested person and after reasonable notice to the obligee, the court in which the obligor was adjudicated delinquent may order the release or other modification of such lien.

The lien may also be released upon agreement of all persons for whom support and maintenance is ordered under the decree, order or judgment, provided all such persons are sui juris. The clerk shall note the release on the record upon receipt of an affidavit from all the obligees stating that (i) all the obligees are sui juris and (ii) they agreed to the release of the lien on specified real property. Any lien created pursuant to this section shall expire upon the support obligation being paid in full by the obligor. The clerk may release such liens upon receipt of an affidavit of all the obligees that such support obligation has been paid in full, or upon an order or decree of a court of competent jurisdiction. (Code 1950, § 8-388; 1977, c. 617; 1979, c. 496; 1985, c. 529; 1989, c. 8.)

REVISERS' NOTE

A change has been made in former § 8-388 so that the lien for maintenance and support of a spouse or infant children arises only after the order adjudicating the obligor delinquent and creating the lien has been docketed as other money judgments are docketed. The lien shall attach to such real estate of the obligor as the court shall designate and shall be subject to modification by the court upon petition.

Cross references. — For statutes on decrees for maintenance and support of spouses and custody and support of children, see §§ 20-107.1 and 20-107.2.

I. Decisions Under Current Law.
II. Decisions Under Prior Law.

I. DECISIONS UNDER CURRENT LAW.

Monetary award in equitable distribution proceedings. — A party who is granted a monetary award in an equitable distribution proceeding is in the same position as any other judgment creditor and has the same enforcement remedies available. Booth v. Booth, 7 Va. App. 22, 371 S.E.2d 569 (1988).

II. DECISIONS UNDER PRIOR LAW.

Editor's note. — The cases cited below were decided unde corresponding provisions of former law. The term "this section," as used below, refers to former provisions.

Chancellor may provide that payments shall not be a lien. — It is within the sound discretion of the chancellor to provide that alimony and support (now maintenance and support) payments should not be a lien upon the real estate of the party required to make such payments. Canavos v. Canavos, 205 Va. 744, 139 S.E.2d 825 (1965).

A decree for payments in lieu of alimony (now maintenance and support), approving a contract between the parties, is not a lien on the realty of the husband. Durrett v. Durrett, 204 Va. 59, 129 S.E.2d 50 (1963).

§ 8.01-461. Abstracts of judgments.

— An abstract of any judgment shall, upon request to the clerk of the court wherein the judgment is rendered, be granted to any person interested immediately upon its rendition, subject to the future action of the court rendering the same. (Code 1950, § 8-389; 1977, c. 617; 1982, c. 105.)

§ 8.01-462. Jurisdiction of equity to enforce lien of judgment; when it may decree sale.

— Jurisdiction to enforce the lien of a judgment shall be in equity. If it appear to the court that the rents and profits of all real estate subject to the lien will not satisfy the judgment in five years, the court may decree such real estate, or any part thereof, to be sold, and the proceeds applied to the discharge of the judgment. (Code 1950, § 8-391; 1977, c. 617.)

Cross references. — As to enforcement of judgment lien by Commonwealth, see §§ 8.01-211 through 8.01-215. As to limitations on enforcement of judgments, see § 8.01-251.

I. Decisions Under Prior Law.
  A. General Consideration.
  B. Judicial Sale or Renting.

I. DECISIONS UNDER PRIOR LAW.

A. General Consideration.

Editor's note. — The cases cited below were decided under corresponding provisions of former law. The term "this section," as used below, refers to former provisions.

This section applies only to suits for the enforcement of judgment liens. Neff v. Wooding, 83 Va. 432, 2 S.E. 731 (1887).

It does not apply to suits to enforce vendor's lien. — The court may decree a sale of land to satisfy a vendor's lien, as distinguished from a judgment lien, without ascertaining whether the rents and profits would be sufficient to pay within five years. Neff v. Wooding, 83 Va. 432, 2 S.E. 731 (1887).

Or deeds of trust. — In a suit to enforce a trust deed the value of the rents and profits of the land is immaterial, as the deed is not a judgment within the meaning of this section. Kyger v. Sipe, 89 Va. 507, 16 S.E. 627 (1892).

Or to suits to subject decedents' lands to payment of debts. — This section limits the jurisdiction of the court in the sale of real estate to enforce a judgment lien, and applies to a suit in equity brought to subject the lands of a living debtor to the "lien of a judgment" thereon. It has no application to an equity suit to subject the lands of a decedent to the payment of his debts. Morrison v. Morrison, 177 Va. 417, 14 S.E.2d 322 (1941).

Suit is not one to recover land. — The suit of a judgment creditor to enforce his lien against land is not a suit to recover the land itself. McClanahan's Adm'r v. Norfolk & W. Ry., 122 Va. 705, 96 S.E. 453 (1918).

§ 8.01-462   CIVIL REMEDIES AND PROCEDURE   § 8.01-462

Jurisdiction extends only as far as is necessary to enforce lien. — Jurisdiction in equity to enforce the lien of a judgment against real estate is conferred by this section, but such jurisdiction extends only so far as may be necessary to satisfy the judgment lien. Tacklett v. Bolling, 172 Va. 326, 1 S.E.2d 285 (1939).

But court may do complete justice between parties. — Equity has jurisdiction of a bill to enforce a judgment lien under this section, and having acquired jurisdiction for this purpose, it will go on and do complete justice between the parties, even to the extent of enforcing purely legal demands of which it would not otherwise have jurisdiction. Steinman v. Clinchfield Coal Corp., 121 Va. 611, 93 S.E. 684 (1917); Moorman v. Board, 121 Va. 112, 92 S.E. 833 (1917).

Doctrine of laches has no application. — The equitable doctrine of laches has no application to a suit in equity to enforce against the lands of a defendant the lien of a judgment which has been kept alive and is not barred by the statute of limitations. The creditor is seeking to enforce a legal, and not an equitable right, expressly conferred by statute and not subject to terms or conditions. Motley v. Carstairs, McCall & Co., 114 Va. 429, 76 S.E. 948 (1913); McClanahan's Adm'r v. Norfolk & W. Ry., 118 Va. 388, 87 S.E. 731 (1916).

Nor has rule that one seeking equity must do equity. — A judgment creditor who comes into a court of equity to enforce his lien upon the debtor's land is not asserting an equitable right or seeking relief which it is in the courts' equitable discretion to grant or deny. His judgment is a legal lien created expressly by statute. Hence, while it is an ordinary rule of the courts of chancery that he who seeks equity must do equity, this principle has no application here because the judgment creditor's right to resort to the court of equity to enforce his lien is a legal right, without terms and conditions imposed. Motley v. Carstairs, McCall & Co., 114 Va. 429, 76 S.E. 948 (1913).

Remedies available to judgment creditor. — In Morrison v. Morrison, 177 Va. 417, 14 S.E.2d 322 (1941), a suit brought under the predecessor to § 64.1-181, the court merely stated that an instance in which the ancestor to former § 8-391 may be applied is to a suit in equity brought to subject the lands of a living debtor to the lien of a judgment thereon. The Morrison court then recognized the two different remedies with separate rules of law available to a judgment creditor, one a general creditors' suit, and another the judgment-lien creditor's suit brought either while the judgment debtor is living or after such debtor dies. Maness v. Tidewater Sand Co., 220 Va. 1042, 266 S.E.2d 438 (1980).

Creditor need not have exhausted remedy at law. — Equity now has jurisdiction to enforce a judgment lien against the land of the debtor, notwithstanding the judgment creditor has not exhausted his remedy at law. Price v. Thrash, 71 Va. (30 Gratt.) 515 (1878); Gordon v. Rixey, 76 Va. 694 (1882); Stovall v. Border Grange Bank, 78 Va. 188 (1883); Hutchison v. Grubbs, 80 Va. 251 (1885); Moore v. Bruce, 85 Va. 139, 7 S.E. 195 (1888).

He need not proceed first against personalty. — A judgment creditor, if he so elects, may resort to a court of equity to enforce the lien of his judgment against the real estate of his debtor, without first proceeding by execution at law to subject the personal estate, or assigning any reason for not doing so. Stovall v. Border Grange Bank, 78 Va. 188 (1883).

A judgment creditor having established his debt against the judgment debtor during the debtor's lifetime has the right to look to the deceased debtor's estate, real and personal, as equally liable. This is a right the creditor may properly exercise, unless some equitable reason demands he proceed first against the personal estate, and the creditor is not compelled to look to the realty merely as a secondary fund for payment. Maness v. Tidewater Sand Co., 220 Va. 1042, 266 S.E.2d 438 (1980).

Or show want of personal assets, or issue of fi. fa. — A judgment creditor may file a bill to subject real estate of his debtor to the satisfaction of his judgment lien without alleging or proving want of personal assets, and without issuing a fi. fa. Moore v. Bruce, 85 Va. 139, 7 S.E. 195 (1888).

Judgment need not be revived against personal representative of debtor. — A bill in equity may be maintained against the personal representative of a decedent and his devisees or heirs at law, to subject the real estate of the decedent to the payment of a judgment recovered against him in his lifetime, without first reviving the judgment at law. James v. Life, 92 Va. 702, 24 S.E. 275 (1896).

Proceeding by judgment creditor held general creditors' suit under § 64.1-181. — See Peatross v. Gray, 181 Va. 847, 27 S.E.2d 203 (1943).

B. Judicial Sale or Renting.

All other liens on land should be ascertained. — Where there are various liens on the land of a debtor, it is premature and erroneous to decree a sale of the land to satisfy certain liens, without first ascertaining all the liens existing against the land, and determining and definitely fixing their respective amounts and priorities. Daingerfield v. Smith, 83 Va. 81, 1 S.E. 599 (1887); Adkins v. Edwards, 83 Va. 300, 2 S.E. 435 (1887); Alexander v. Howe, 85 Va. 198, 7 S.E. 248 (1888); Houck v. Dunham, 92 Va. 211, 23 S.E. 238 (1895); Fidelity Loan &

Trust Co. v. Dennis, 93 Va. 504, 25 S.E. 546 (1896).

And all impediments to fair sale removed. — Before a sale is decreed, any cloud on the title or other impediment of any kind to a fair sale ought to be removed, as far as it is practicable to do so, in order that the land may be sold to the best advantage. Alexander v. Howe, 85 Va. 198, 7 S.E. 248 (1888); Brown v. Lawson, 86 Va. 284, 9 S.E. 1014 (1889); Thomas v. Farmers' Nat'l Bank, 86 Va. 291, 9 S.E. 1122 (1889).

Inquiry should be held as to rents and profits. — Where the insufficiency of the rents and profits is not alleged, or is alleged and denied, there must be an inquiry, and the court must ascertain the annual value of the rents and profits with a reasonable certainty before decreeing a sale. Ewart v. Saunders, 66 Va. (25 Gratt.) 203 (1874); Muse v. Friedenwald, 77 Va. 57 (1883); Neff v. Wooding, 83 Va. 432, 2 S.E. 731 (1887).

And rents and profits compared with debt. — Before a sale of realty can be decreed to pay judgment liens, the court must, in some way, be convinced that the rents and profits will not in five years satisfy those liens. Preston v. Aston, 85 Va. 104, 7 S.E. 344 (1888); Cooper v. Daugherty, 85 Va. 343, 7 S.E. 387 (1888); Dillard v. Krise, 86 Va. 410, 10 S.E. 430 (1889); Mustain v. Pannill, 86 Va. 33, 9 S.E. 419 (1889); Kyger v. Sipe, 89 Va. 507, 16 S.E. 627 (1892); Etter v. Scott, 90 Va. 762, 19 S.E. 776 (1894); Kane v. Mann, 93 Va. 239, 24 S.E. 938 (1896).

But inquiry may be waived. — If none of the parties ask for an inquiry to ascertain whether the rents and profits will pay the debt in the requisite period, they are presumed to have waived it, and there may be a decree for the sale of the property. M'Clung v. Beirne, 37 Va. (10 Leigh) 394 (1839); Brengle v. Richardson, 78 Va. 406 (1884).

Section prescribes no particular method of comparison. — This section prescribes no particular mode by which it shall be made to appear that the rents and profits will not pay the judgment in five years. Ewart v. Saunders, 66 Va. (25 Gratt.) 203 (1874); Horton v. Bond, 69 Va. (28 Gratt.) 815 (1877); Muse v. Friedenwald, 77 Va. 57 (1883); Brengle v. Richardson, 78 Va. 406 (1884); Neff v. Wooding, 83 Va. 432, 2 S.E. 731 (1887).

Inadequacy of rents and profits may be shown by pleadings or admissions. — The fact that the rents and profits of the lands will not discharge the judgment in five years, may be shown by the pleadings or by the admissions of the parties. Effinger v. Kenney, 79 Va. 551 (1884); Etter v. Scott, 90 Va. 762, 19 S.E. 776 (1894).

Or court may direct commissioner to report. — When there is a doubt whether or not the rents and profits will pay the judgments in five years, or an inquiry is demanded by either of the parties, the court will generally direct one of its commissioners to ascertain and report the annual rents and profits of the land. But this is not necessary in every case. Ewart v. Saunders, 66 Va. (25 Gratt.) 203 (1874); Muse v. Friedenwald, 77 Va. 57 (1883); Cooper v. Daugherty, 85 Va. 343, 7 S.E. 387 (1888).

Commissioner should report on all lands of debtor. — Where there has been a reference to ascertain whether the property would rent for a sufficient sum in five years to pay the indebtedness, the commissioner should consider and report the rental value of all lands owned by defendant, including those in counties other than the one in which the suit was brought. Kane v. Mann, 93 Va. 239, 24 S.E. 938 (1896).

But lands of debtor's wife are not to be considered. — Upon the creditor's bill to subject lands of a debtor to the payment of the lien of judgments thereon, the debtor cannot, by any agreement with his wife, who is not a party to the suit, and is in no wise bound for the judgments, have the rents and profits of her lands considered in an estimate to ascertain whether the rents and profits of his lands for five years will pay and satisfy the judgments. Kane v. Mann, 93 Va. 239, 24 S.E. 938 (1896).

Terms of renting are in discretion of court. — The terms of renting, whether the rents shall be payable annually or at shorter periods, must be determined by the court before whom the cause is pending, in the exercise of a sound discretion and in the light of all the circumstances, such as the character of the property, its locality, the usage of the country, etc. Compton v. Tabor, 73 Va. (32 Gratt.) 121 (1879).

Land should generally be offered first for one year. — In general, to ascertain whether the rents will pay the debts in five years, the commissioner should be directed to offer the land first for one year and so on, if necessary, up to five years, closing the contract whenever the rents will pay the debt. Compton v. Tabor, 73 Va. (32 Gratt.) 121 (1879).

§ 8.01-463. Enforcement of lien when judgment does not exceed twenty dollars. — If the amount of the judgment does not exceed twenty dollars, exclusive of interest and costs, no bill to enforce the lien thereof shall be entertained, unless it appear that thirty days before the institution of the suit, the judgment debtor or his personal representative, and the owner of the real estate on which the judgment is a lien, or, in case of a nonresident, his agent or attorney, if he had one in this Commonwealth, had notice that the suit would be instituted, if the judgment was not paid within that time. (Code 1950, § 8-392; 1977, c. 617.)

REVISERS' NOTE

The provisions of former §§ 8-393 (When suit to enforce lien of judgment barred in equity), 8-394 (When right of subrogation enforced ...), 8-396 (Limitation of proceedings to enforce judgment) and 8-397 (Provision construing and qualifying § 8-396) have been transferred to § 8.01-251.

Cross references. — For similar provision as to suits in equity, see § 64.1-186.

I. DECISIONS UNDER PRIOR LAW.

Editor's note. — The cases cited below were decided under corresponding provisions of former law. The term "this section," as used below, refers to former provisions.

The evident purpose of this section is to spare a judgment debtor the expense of a suit brought to enforce the lien of a judgment in such a small amount until he shall have been given a final opportunity of paying the claim. Sutherland v. Rasnake, 169 Va. 257, 192 S.E. 695 (1937).

The requirement of notice is mandatory. Sutherland v. Rasnake, 169 Va. 257, 192 S.E. 695 (1937).

For it is jurisdictional. — The requirement of the notice is jurisdictional. The language is, "... no bill to enforce the lien thereof shall be entertained" — that is, no suit shall be brought — unless it appear that 30 days before the institution of the suit the required notice has been given. Sutherland v. Rasnake, 169 Va. 257, 192 S.E. 695 (1937). See Chaney v. Kibler, 171 Va. 194, 198 S.E. 877 (1938).

§ 8.01-464. Order of liability between alienees of different parts of estate. — When the real estate liable to the lien of a judgment is more than sufficient to satisfy the same, and it, or any part of it, has been aliened, as among the alienees for value, that which was aliened last, shall, in equity, be first liable, and so on with other successive alienations, until the whole judgment is satisfied. And as among alienees who are volunteers under such judgment debtor, the same rule as to the order of liability shall prevail; but as among alienees for value and volunteers, the lands aliened to the latter shall be subjected before the lands aliened to the former are resorted to; and, in either case, any part of such real estate retained by the debtor shall be first liable to the satisfaction of the judgment. An alienee for value, however, from a volunteer shall occupy the same position that he would have occupied had he purchased from the debtor at the time he purchased from the voluntary donee. (Code 1950, § 8-395; 1977, c. 617.)

Cross references. — As to limitations on enforcement of judgments, see § 8.01-251 et seq.

I. DECISIONS UNDER PRIOR LAW.

Editor's note. — The cases cited below were decided under corresponding provisions of former law. The terms "this section," as used below, refers to former provisions.

Land retained by debtor should be first subjected. — If the judgment debtor retains sufficient lands to pay the judgment, they should be first subjected. Dickerson v. Clement, 87 Va. 41, 12 S.E. 105 (1890); Blakemore v. Wise, 95 Va. 269, 28 S.E. 332 (1897).

For aliened land is only secondarily liable. — Lands being liable for judgments in the inverse order of alienation, those primarily liable should be first subjected before proceeding against the purchaser, whose land is only secondarily liable. Nelson v. Turner, 97 Va. 54, 33 S.E. 390 (1899).

Land is chargeable in inverse order of alienation. — The law is now well settled that where land which is subject to the lien of a judgment or other incumbrance is sold in parcels to different persons by successive alienations, it is chargeable in the hands of the purchaser in the inverse order of such alienations. This rule is not only established by the decisions of courts of equity, but in Virginia it is prescribed by this section. Harman v. Oberdorfer, 74 Va. (33 Gratt.) 497 (1880); Whitten v. Saunders, 75 Va. 563 (1881). See also, Schultz v. Hansbrough, 74 Va. (33 Gratt.) 567 (1880); Miller v. Holland, 84 Va. 652, 5 S.E. 701 (1888).

And lands sold contemporaneously must contribute pro rata. — But where the different parcels of land are sold contemporaneously they must contribute pro rata to the satisfaction of the judgment. Harman v. Oberdorfer, 74 Va. (33 Gratt.) 497 (1880).

Date of deed is presumed to be time of alienation. — Without evidence of any preceding executory agreements between the parties, or any evidence of the time of the delivery of deeds, except what may be inferred from their duties, it will be presumed that the dates on the deeds are the dates of their delivery, and the land conveyed by the last dated deed will be first liable. Harman v. Oberdorfer, 74 Va. (33 Gratt.) 497 (1880).

But lands sold under contemporaneous identical contracts are sold contemporaneously. — Where several lots of land are sold on the same day, on the same terms of several parties, all of whom are immediately put in possession under the same agreement as to the deeds conveying the lots, and the trust deed to secure the purchase money, although the deeds conveying them are really delivered and recorded at different times, they will all be regarded as "alienations" as of the day of sale, and, in subjecting them to the payment of a judgment docketed against a vendor at the time of the sale, each lot must bear its proportion, according to their relative values on the day of sale. Alley v. Rogers, 60 Va. (19 Gratt.) 366 (1869); Harman v. Oberdorfer, 74 Va. (33 Gratt.) 497 (1880).

Alienee must allege or prove that land is more than sufficient. — Where it nowhere appears, and it has not been suggested as a fact, that real estate to liens is more than sufficient to satisfy the same, a person intending to rely upon the land's being more than sufficient should allege the fact by answer or establish it by proof. Preston v. National Exch. Bank, 97 Va. 222, 33 S.E. 546 (1899).

§ 8.01-465. Chapter embraces recognizances and bonds having force of judgment. — The foregoing sections of this chapter, so far as they relate to the docketing of judgments, the entering of satisfaction thereof, and the liens of judgments and enforcement of such liens, shall be construed as embracing recognizances, and bonds having the force of a judgment. (Code 1950, § 8-398; 1977, c. 617.)

I. DECISIONS UNDER CURRENT LAW.

Enforcement of gambling debts. — The mandate of the Full Faith and Credit clause prevails over Virginia's strongly-expressed policy which prohibits the enforcement of gambling debts. Coghill v. Boardwalk Regency Corp., 240 Va. 230, 396 S.E.2d 838 (1990).

CHAPTER 17.1.

UNIFORM ENFORCEMENT OF FOREIGN JUDGMENTS ACT.

Sec.
8.01-465.1. Application of chapter.
8.01-465.2. Filing and status of foreign judgments.

Sec.
8.01-465.3. Notice of filing.
8.01-465.4. Stay of enforcement.
8.01-465.5. Optional procedure.

§ 8.01-465.1. Application of chapter. — As used in this chapter "foreign judgment" means any judgment, decree, or order of a court of the United States or of any other court which is entitled to full faith and credit in this state. (1988, c. 539.)

Law Review. — As to recent legislation in domestication of foreign judgments, see 22 U. Rich. L. Rev. 517 (1988).

I. DECISIONS UNDER CURRENT LAW.

Under the Uniform Enforcement of Foreign Judgments Act, the trial judge correctly ruled that "community interest" involved here is determined by Arizona law; the foreign judgment alone is before the Virginia court, not the underlying transaction on which it is based. Bullis v. Bullis, 22 Va. App. 24, 467 S.E.2d 830 (1996).

Applied in Bullis v. Bullis, 21 Va. App. 394, 464 S.E.2d 538 (1995).

§ **8.01-465.2. Filing and status of foreign judgments.** — A copy of any foreign judgment authenticated in accordance with the act of Congress or the statutes of this Commonwealth may be filed in the office of the clerk of any circuit court of any city or county of this Commonwealth upon payment of the fee prescribed in subdivision A 17 of § 17.1-275. The clerk shall treat the foreign judgment in the same manner as a judgment of the circuit court of any city or county of this Commonwealth. A judgment so filed has the same effect and is subject to the same procedures, defenses and proceedings for reopening, vacating, or staying as a judgment of a circuit court of any city or county of this Commonwealth and may be enforced or satisfied in like manner. (1988, c. 539; 1990, c. 738.)

I. DECISIONS UNDER CURRENT LAW.

When recognition required. — Even if the courts of Virginia were not compelled to do so under the full faith and credit clause of the federal constitution, "upon principles of comity they may establish as their own decree a foreign decree . . ., with the same force and effect as if it had been entered in Virginia, provided, of course, the foreign decree violates no public policy of Virginia." Moreover, such a result now seems required by the Uniform Interstate Family Support Act, Code § 20-88.32, et seq. Sheppard v. Sheppard, No. 0571-95-2 (Ct. of Appeals April 9, 1996).

§ **8.01-465.3. Notice of filing.** — At the time of the filing of the foreign judgment, the judgment creditor or his lawyer shall make and file with the clerk of court an affidavit setting forth the name and last known post office address of the judgment debtor, and the judgment creditor.

Promptly upon the filing of the foreign judgment and the affidavit, the clerk shall mail notice of the filing of the foreign judgment to the judgment debtor at the address given and shall make a note of the mailing in the docket. The notice shall include the name and post office address of the judgment creditor and the judgment creditor's lawyer, if any, in the Commonwealth. In addition, the judgment creditor may mail a notice of the filing of the judgment to the judgment debtor and may file proof of mailing with the clerk. Lack of mailing notice of filing by the clerk shall not affect the enforcement proceedings if proof of mailing by the judgment creditor has been filed. (1988, c. 539.)

§ **8.01-465.4. Stay of enforcement.** — If the judgment debtor shows the circuit court that an appeal from the foreign judgment is pending or will be taken, or that a stay of execution has been granted, the court shall stay enforcement of the foreign judgment until the appeal is concluded, the time for appeal expires, or the stay of execution expires or is vacated, upon proof that the judgment debtor has furnished the security for the satisfaction of the judgment required by the state in which it was rendered.

If the judgment debtor shows the circuit court any ground upon which enforcement of a judgment of any court of this Commonwealth would be stayed, including the ground that an appeal from the foreign judgment is pending or will be taken, or that the time for taking such an appeal has not expired, the court shall stay enforcement of the foreign judgment for an appropriate period until all available appeals are concluded or the time for taking all appeals has expired, upon requiring the same security for satisfaction of the judgment which is required in this Commonwealth, subject to the provisions of subsections J and K of § 8.01-676.1. (1988, c. 539; 2000, c. 100.)

The 2000 amendments. — The 2000 amendment by c. 100, effective March 10, 2000, and applicable to any action which is pending on or which is filed after that date, in the second paragraph inserted "including the ground that an appeal from the foreign judgment is pending or will be taken, or that the time for taking such an appeal has not expired," following "Commonwealth would be stayed," inserted "until all available appeals are concluded or the time for taking all appeals has expired," and added "subject to the provisions of subsections J and K of § 8.01-676.1."

§ 8.01-465.5. Optional procedure. — The right of a judgment creditor to bring an action to enforce his judgment instead of proceeding under this chapter remains unimpaired. (1988, c. 539.)

CHAPTER 17.2.

UNIFORM FOREIGN COUNTRY MONEY-JUDGMENTS RECOGNITION ACT.

Sec.
8.01-465.6. Title.
8.01-465.7. Definitions.
8.01-465.8. Application.
8.01-465.9. Enforceability of a foreign country money judgment.
8.01-465.10. Judgment not conclusive; not to be recognized.

Sec.
8.01-465.11. Lack of personal jurisdiction.
8.01-465.12. Stay of the proceedings.
8.01-465.13. Situations not covered by this chapter.

§ 8.01-465.6. Title. — This chapter may be cited as the "Foreign Country Money-Judgments Recognition Act." (1990, c. 276.)

§ 8.01-465.7. Definitions. — As used in this chapter:
"Foreign country" means any governmental unit other than the United States or any state, district, commonwealth, territory, or insular possession thereof;
"Foreign country money judgment" means any judgment of a foreign country granting or denying recovery of a sum of money, other than a judgment for taxes, a fine or other penalty, or a judgment for support in matrimonial or family matters. (1990, c. 276.)

§ 8.01-465.8. Application. — The provisions of this chapter apply to any foreign country money judgment that is final and conclusive and enforceable where rendered even though an appeal therefrom is pending or is subject to appeal. (1990, c. 276.)

§ 8.01-465.9. Enforceability of a foreign country money judgment. — Except as provided in § 8.01-465.10, a foreign country money judgment meeting the requirements of § 8.01-465.8 is conclusive between the parties to the extent that it grants or denies recovery of a sum of money. The foreign country money judgment is enforceable in the same manner as the judgment of a sister state which is entitled to full faith and credit. (1990, c. 276.)

§ 8.01-465.10. **Judgment not conclusive; not to be recognized.** — A. A foreign country money judgment is not conclusive if:
1. The judgment was rendered under a system which does not provide impartial tribunals or procedures compatible with the requirements of due process of law;
2. The foreign court did not have personal jurisdiction over the defendant; or
3. The foreign court did not have jurisdiction over the subject matter.
B. A foreign country money judgment need not be recognized if:
1. The defendant in the proceedings in the foreign court did not receive notice of the proceedings in sufficient time to enable him to defend;
2. The judgment was obtained by fraud;
3. The claim for relief on which the judgment is based is repugnant to the public policy of this Commonwealth;
4. The judgment conflicts with another final and conclusive judgment;
5. The proceeding in the foreign court was contrary to an agreement between the parties under which the dispute in question was to be settled otherwise than by proceedings in that court; or
6. In the case of jurisdiction based only on personal service, the foreign court was a seriously inconvenient forum for the trial of the action. (1990, c. 276.)

§ 8.01-465.11. **Lack of personal jurisdiction.** — A. The foreign country money judgment shall not be refused recognition for lack of personal jurisdiction if:
1. The defendant was served personally in the foreign country;
2. The defendant voluntarily appeared in the proceedings, other than for the purpose of protecting property seized or threatened with seizure in the proceedings or of contesting the jurisdiction of the court over him;
3. The defendant, prior to the commencement of the proceedings, had agreed to submit to the jurisdiction of the foreign court with respect to the subject matter involved;
4. The defendant was domiciled in the foreign country when the proceedings were instituted, or, being a body corporate had its principal place of business, was incorporated, or had otherwise acquired corporate status, in the foreign country;
5. The defendant had a business office in the foreign country and the proceedings in the foreign court involved a claim for relief arising out of business done by the defendant through that office in the foreign country; or
6. The defendant operated a motor vehicle or airplane in the foreign country and the proceedings involved a claim for relief arising out of such operation.
B. The courts of this Commonwealth may recognize other bases of jurisdiction consistent with fairness and substantial justice in the context of international commerce or relations. (1990, c. 276.)

§ 8.01-465.12. **Stay of the proceedings.** — If the defendant satisfies the court either that an appeal is pending or that he is entitled and intends to appeal from the foreign country judgment, the court may stay the proceedings until the appeal has been determined or until the expiration of a period of time sufficient to enable the defendant to prosecute the appeal. (1990, c. 276.)

§ 8.01-465.13. **Situations not covered by this chapter.** — The provisions of this article shall not prevent the recognition of a foreign country money judgment in situations not covered by this chapter. (1990, c. 276.)

CHAPTER 17.3.

UNIFORM FOREIGN-MONEY CLAIMS ACT.

Sec.
8.01-465.14. Definitions.
8.01-465.15. Scope.
8.01-465.16. Variation by agreement.
8.01-465.17. Determining money of the claim.
8.01-465.18. Determining amount of the money of certain contract claims.
8.01-465.19. Asserting and defending foreign-money claim.
8.01-465.20. Judgments and awards on foreign-money claims; times of money conversion; form of judgment.

Sec.
8.01-465.21. Conversions of foreign money in distribution proceeding.
8.01-465.22. Prejudgment and judgment interest.
8.01-465.23. Enforcement of foreign judgments.
8.01-465.24. Determining United States dollar value of foreign-money claims for limited purposes.
8.01-465.25. Effect of substitution of currency by issuing authority.

§ 8.01-465.14. Definitions. — As used in this chapter:

"Action" means a judicial proceeding or arbitration in which a payment in money may be awarded or enforced with respect to a foreign-money claim.

"Bank-offered spot rate" means the spot rate of exchange at which a bank will sell foreign money at a spot rate.

"Conversion date" means the banking day next preceding the date on which money, in accordance with this chapter, is (i) paid to a claimant in an action or distribution proceeding; (ii) paid to the official designated by law to enforce a judgment or award on behalf of a claimant; or (iii) used to recoup, set off, or counterclaim in different moneys in an action or distribution proceeding.

"Distribution proceeding" means a judicial or nonjudicial proceeding for the distribution of a fund in which one or more foreign-money claims are asserted and includes an accounting, an assignment for the benefit of creditors, a foreclosure, the liquidation or rehabilitation of a corporation or other entity, and the distribution of an estate, trust, or other fund.

"Foreign money" means money other than money of the United States of America.

"Foreign-money claim" means a claim upon an obligation to pay, or a claim for recovery of a loss, expressed in or measured by a foreign money.

"Money" means a medium of exchange for the payment of obligations or a store of value authorized or adopted by a government or by intergovernmental agreement.

"Money of the claim" means the money determined as proper pursuant to § 8.01-465.17.

"Person" means an individual, a corporation, government or governmental subdivision or agency, business trust, estate, trust, joint venture, partnership, association, two or more persons having a joint or common interest, or any other legal or commercial entity.

"Rate of exchange" means the rate at which money of one country may be converted into money of another country in a free financial market convenient to or reasonably usable by a person obligated to pay or to state a rate of conversion. If separate rates of exchange apply to different kinds of transactions, the term means the rate applicable to the particular transaction giving rise to the foreign-money claim.

"Spot rate" means the rate of exchange at which foreign money is sold by a bank or other dealer in foreign exchange for immediate or next day availability or for settlement by immediate payment in cash or equivalent, by charge to an account, or by an agreed delayed settlement not exceeding two days.

"State" means a state of the United States, the District of Columbia, the Commonwealth of Puerto Rico, or a territory or insular possession subject to the jurisdiction of the United States. (1991, c. 24.)

§ 8.01-465.15. Scope. — This chapter applies only to a foreign-money claim in an action or distribution proceeding and applies to foreign-money issues even if other law under the conflict-of-laws rules of the Commonwealth applies to other issues in the action or distribution proceeding. (1991, c. 24.)

§ 8.01-465.16. Variation by agreement. — The effect of this chapter may be varied by agreement of the parties made before or after commencement of an action or distribution proceeding or the entry of judgment.

Parties to a transaction may agree upon the money to be used in a transaction giving rise to a foreign-money claim and may agree to use different moneys for different aspects of the transaction. Stating the price in a foreign money for one aspect of a transaction does not alone require the use of that money for other aspects of the transaction. (1991, c. 24.)

§ 8.01-465.17. Determining money of the claim. — The money in which the parties to a transaction have agreed that payment is to be made is the proper money of the claim for payment. If the parties to a transaction have not otherwise agreed, the proper money of the claim is the money (i) regularly used between the parties as a matter of usage or course of dealing; (ii) used at the time of a transaction in international trade, by trade usage or common practice, for valuing or settling transactions in the particular commodity or service involved; or (iii) in which the loss was ultimately felt or will be incurred by the party claimant. (1991, c. 24.)

§ 8.01-465.18. Determining amount of the money of certain contract claims. — A. If an amount contracted to be paid in a foreign money is measured by a specified amount of a different money, the amount to be paid is determined on the conversion date.

B. If an amount contracted to be paid in a foreign money is to be measured by a different money at the rate of exchange prevailing on a date before default, that rate of exchange applies only to payments made within a reasonable time after default, not exceeding thirty days. Thereafter, conversion is made at the bank-offered spot rate on the conversion date.

C. A monetary claim is neither usurious nor unconscionable because the agreement on which it is based provides that the amount of the debtor's obligation to be paid in the debtor's money, when received by the creditor, must equal a special amount of the foreign money of the country of the creditor. If, because of unexcused delay in payment of a judgment or award, the amount received by the creditor does not equal the amount of the foreign money specified in the agreement, the court or arbitrator shall amend the judgment or award accordingly. (1991, c. 24.)

§ 8.01-465.19. Asserting and defending foreign-money claim. — A person may assert a claim in a specified foreign money. If a foreign-money claim is not asserted, the claimant makes the claim in United States dollars.

An opposing party may allege and shall prove that all or part of a claim is in a different money than that asserted by the claimant. A person may assert a defense, setoff, recoupment, or counterclaim in any money without regard to the money of other claims.

The determination of the proper money of the claim is a question of law. (1991, c. 24.)

§ 8.01-465.20. Judgments and awards on foreign-money claims; times of money conversion; form of judgment. — A. A judgment or award on a foreign-money claim must be stated in an amount of the money of the claim. However, assessed costs must be entered in United States dollars. A judgment in substantially the following form complies with this subsection: [IT IS ADJUDGED AND ORDERED, that Defendant (insert name) pay to Plaintiff (insert name) the sum of (insert amount in the foreign money) plus interest on that sum at the rate of (insert rate — see § 8.01-465.22) percent a year or, at the option of the judgment debtor, the number of United States dollars which will purchase the (insert name of foreign money) with interest due, at a bank-offered spot rate at or near the close of business on the banking day next before the day of payment, together with assessed costs of (insert amount) United States dollars.]

B. A judgment or award on a foreign-money claim is payable in that foreign money or, at the option of the debtor, in the amount of United States dollars which will purchase that foreign money on the conversion date at a bank-offered spot rate.

Each payment in United States dollars must be accepted and credited on a judgment or award on a foreign-money claim in the amount of the foreign money that could be purchased by the dollars at a bank-offered spot rate of exchange at or near the close of business on the conversion date for that payment.

C. A judgment or award made in an action or distribution proceeding on both a defense, setoff, recoupment, or counterclaim and the adverse party's claim, must be netted by converting the money of the smaller into the money of the larger, and by subtracting the smaller from the larger, and shall specify the rates of exchange used.

D. If a contract claim is of the type covered by § 8.01-465.18 A or B, the judgment or award must be entered for the amount of money stated to measure the obligation to be paid in the money specified for payment or, at the option of the debtor, the number of United States dollars which will purchase the computed amount of the money of payment on the conversion date at a bank-offered spot rate.

E. A judgment shall be docketed and indexed in foreign money in the same manner, and has the same effect as a lien, as other judgments. It may be discharged by payment. (1991, c. 24.)

§ 8.01-465.21. **Conversions of foreign money in distribution proceeding.** — The rate of exchange prevailing at or near the close of business on the day the distribution proceeding is initiated governs all exchanges of foreign money in a distribution proceeding. A foreign-money claimant in a distribution proceeding shall assert its claim in the named foreign money and show the amount of United States dollars resulting from a conversion as of the date the proceeding was initiated. (1991, c. 24.)

§ 8.01-465.22. **Prejudgment and judgment interest.** — With respect to a foreign-money claim, recovery of prejudgment or preaward interest and the rate of interest to be applied in the action or distribution proceeding are matters of the substantive law governing the right to recovery under the conflict-of-laws rules of the Commonwealth.

However, the court or arbitrator shall increase or decrease the amount of prejudgment or preaward interest otherwise payable in a judgment or award in foreign money to the extent required by the law of the Commonwealth.

A judgment or award on a foreign-money claim bears interest at the rate applicable to judgments of the Commonwealth. (1991, c. 24.)

§ 8.01-465.23. **Enforcement of foreign judgments.** — If an action is brought to enforce a judgment of another jurisdiction expressed in a foreign money and the judgment is enforceable in the Commonwealth, the enforcing judgment must be entered as provided in § 8.01-465.20, whether or not the foreign judgment confers an option to pay in an equivalent amount of United States dollars.

A foreign judgment may be filed in accordance with Chapter 17.1 (§ 8.01-465.1 et seq.) and Chapter 17.2 (§ 8.01-465.6 et seq.) of this title.

A satisfaction or partial payment made upon the foreign judgment, on proof thereof, must be credited against the amount of foreign money specified in the judgment, notwithstanding the entry of judgment in the Commonwealth.

A judgment entered on a foreign-money claim only in United States dollars in another state shall be enforced in United States dollars only. (1991, c. 24.)

§ 8.01-465.24. Determining United States dollar value of foreign-money claims for limited purposes. — For the limited purpose of facilitating the enforcement of provisional remedies in an action, (i) the value in United States dollars of assets to be seized or restrained pursuant to a writ of attachment, garnishment, execution, or other legal process, (ii) the amount of United States dollars at issue for assessing costs, or (iii) the amount of United States dollars involved for a surety bond or other court-required undertaking shall be ascertained by a party seeking the process, costs, bond or other undertaking as follows:

1. The amount of the foreign money claimed shall be computed from a bank-offered spot rate prevailing at or near the close of business on the banking day next preceding the filing of (i) a request or application for the issuance of process or for the determination of costs, or (ii) an application for a bond or other court-required undertaking.

2. An affidavit or certificate executed in good faith by the party's counsel or a bank officer shall be filed with each request or application, stating the market quotation used and how it was obtained, and setting forth the calculation. Affected court officials incur no liability, after a filing of the affidavit or certificate, for acting as if the judgment were in the amount of United States dollars stated in the affidavit or certificate.

Computations under this section are for the limited purposes of the section and do not affect computation of the United States dollar equivalent of the money of the judgment for the purpose of payment. (1991, c. 24.)

§ 8.01-465.25. Effect of substitution of currency by issuing authority. — If, after an obligation is expressed or a loss is incurred in a foreign money, the country issuing or adopting that money substitutes a new money in place of that money, the obligation or the loss is treated as if expressed or incurred in the new money at the rate of conversion the issuing country establishes for the payment of like obligations or losses denominated in the former money. If such substitution occurs after a judgment or award is entered on a foreign-money claim, the court or arbitrator shall amend the judgment or award by a like conversion of the former money. (1991, c. 24.)

CHAPTER 18.

Executions and Other Means of Recovery.

Article 1.

Issue and Form; Motion to Quash.

Sec.
8.01-466. Clerk to issue fieri facias on judgment for money.
8.01-467. What writs may not issue.
8.01-468. Executions against corporations.
8.01-469. Executions on joint judgments.
8.01-470. Writs on judgments for specific property.

Sec.
8.01-471. Time period for issuing writs of possession in unlawful entry and detainer; when returnable.
8.01-472. Writs on judgments for personal property.
8.01-473. Judgment for benefit of other person than plaintiff; remedies of such person.
8.01-474. What writ of fieri facias to command.
8.01-475. Subsequent executions.
8.01-476. New execution after loss of property sold under indemnifying bond.
8.01-477. When executions may be quashed; how proceedings thereon stayed.
8.01-477.1. Claims of exemption from execution.

Article 2.
Lien in General.

8.01-478. On what property writ of fieri facias levied; when lien commences.
8.01-479. Time for enforcement.
8.01-480. Prior security interest on property levied on.
8.01-481. Territorial extent of lien.
8.01-482. If levy be on coin or currency, how accounted for.

Article 3.
Return and Venditioni Exponas.

8.01-483. Return of officer on fieri facias; statement filed therewith.
8.01-484. When writ may be destroyed.
8.01-485. When venditioni exponas may issue; proceedings thereon.
8.01-486. Procedure when officer taking property under execution dies before sale.

Article 4.
Enforcement Generally.

8.01-487. Officer to endorse on fieri facias time of receiving it.
8.01-487.1. Officer to leave copy of writ where levy made.
8.01-488. When several writs of fieri facias, how satisfied.
8.01-489. Growing crops, not severed, not liable to distress or levy.
8.01-490. No unreasonable distress or levy; sustenance provided for livestock; removal of property.
8.01-491. Officer may break open dwelling house and levy on property in personal possession of debtor.
8.01-492. Sale of property.
8.01-493. Adjournment of sale.
8.01-494. Resale of property if purchaser fails

Sec.
to comply; remedy against such purchaser.
8.01-495. When money received by officer under execution to be repaid to debtor.
8.01-496. Officer not required to go out of his jurisdiction to pay over money.
8.01-497. Suit by officer to recover estate on which fieri facias is lien.
8.01-498. Selling officers and employees not to bid or to purchase.
8.01-499. Officer receiving money to make return thereof and pay net proceeds; commission, etc.
8.01-500. Officer receiving money to notify person entitled to receive it.

Article 5.
Lien on Property Not Capable of Being Levied on.

8.01-501. Lien of fieri facias on estate of debtor not capable of being levied on.
8.01-502. Person paying debtor not affected by lien unless notice given.
8.01-502.1. Serving notice of lien on financial institution.
8.01-503. Withholding of wages or salary not required by preceding sections unless garnishment process served.
8.01-504. Penalty for service of notice of lien when no judgment exists.
8.01-505. When lien acquired on intangibles under § 8.01-501 ceases.

Article 6.
Interrogatories.

8.01-506. Proceedings by interrogatories to ascertain estate of debtor; summons; proviso; objections by judgment debtor.
8.01-506.1. Production of book accounts or other writing compelled.
8.01-507. Conveyance or delivery of property disclosed by interrogatories.
8.01-507.1. Interrogatories, answers, etc., to be returned to court.
8.01-508. How debtor may be arrested and held to answer.
8.01-509. Order for sale and application of debtor's estate.
8.01-510. Sale, collection and disposition of debtor's estate by officer.

Article 7.
Garnishment.

8.01-511. Institution of garnishment proceedings.
8.01-512, 8.01-512.1. [Repealed.]

Sec.
8.01-512.2. Fee for garnishee-employers.
8.01-512.3. Form of garnishment summons.
8.01-512.4. Notice of exemptions from garnishment.
8.01-512.5. Hearing on claim of exemption from garnishment.
8.01-513. Service upon corporation.
8.01-514. When garnishment summons returnable.
8.01-515. How garnishee examined; determining exemption from employee's withholding certificate; amount due pursuant to exemptions in § 34-29 (a).
8.01-516. [Repealed.]
8.01-516.1. Garnishment dispositions.
8.01-517. Exemption of portion of wages; payment of excess into court.

Sec.
8.01-518. When garnishee is personal representative of decedent.
8.01-519. Proceedings where garnishee fails to appear or answer, or to disclose his liability.
8.01-520. Payment, etc., by garnishee before return of summons.
8.01-521. Judgments as to costs.
8.01-522. Wages and salaries of State employees.
8.01-523. Service upon federal government.
8.01-524. Wages and salaries of city, town and county officials, clerks and employees.
8.01-525. Who are officers and employees of cities, towns and counties.

ARTICLE 1.

Issue and Form; Motion to Quash.

§ 8.01-466. Clerk to issue fieri facias on judgment for money. — On a judgment for money, it shall be the duty of the clerk of the court in which such judgment was rendered, upon request of the judgment creditor, his assignee or his attorney, to issue a writ of fieri facias at the expiration of twenty-one days from the date of the entry of the judgment and place the same in the hands of a proper person to be executed and take his receipt therefor. The writ shall be issued together with the form for requesting a hearing on a claim of exemption from levy as provided in § 8.01-546.1. For good cause the court may order an execution to issue on judgments and decrees at an earlier period. (Code 1950, § 8-399; 1954, c. 620; 1976, c. 354; 1977, c. 617; 1986, c. 341; 1996, cc. 501, 608.)

REVISERS' NOTE

Section 8.01-466 is former § 8-399. The principal change is the substitution of the language "... upon request of the judgment creditor, his assignee or his attorney" for the former language "... only if so requested by a party in interest...." It was felt that the language of the former statute was too broad, and that the request to issue the writ should be restricted as provided in the present statute.

Conforming changes to § 16.1-98 governing general district courts have been made.

Law Review. — For survey of Virginia practice and pleading for the year 1975-1976, see 62 Va. L. Rev. 1460 (1976). For article on the effect of delay on a surety's obligations in Virginia, see 18 U. Rich. L. Rev. 781 (1984).

I. DECISIONS UNDER CURRENT LAW.

Execution is not to be issued within 21 days absent court order. — Bank's alleged lien was defective and was not secured on the vehicle because the writ of fieri facias was issued only eight days after the judgment was rendered and one day after docketing in Virginia and because there was no order of the court permitting the issuance of the writ of fieri facias before the expiration of 21 days; an execution is not to be issued within the 21 days unless "good cause" is shown to the court. Wick v. IRS (In re Bhatti), 126 Bankr. 229 (Bankr. W.D. Va. 1991).

Execution issued before expiration of 21 days was void since this section states that "it shall be the duty of the clerk ... to issue a writ of fieri facias at the expiration of twenty-one days from the date of entry of the judgment"; if an execution is voidable, it is valid until avoided, and its invalidity cannot be set up in a suit to enforce the judgment; but if it is void, it is a nullity, and that fact, may be shown by anybody, anywhere and at any time. Wick v. IRS (In re Bhatti), 126 Bankr. 229 (Bankr. W.D. Va. 1991).

§ **8.01-467. What writs may not issue.** — No writ of levari facias, writ of extendi facias, writ of elegit, writ of capias ad satisfaciendum, or writ of distringas shall be issued hereafter. (Code 1950, § 8-400; 1977, c. 617; 1984, c. 94.)

Law Review. — For article, "Body Attachment and Body Execution," see 17 Wm. & Mary L. Rev. 543 (1976).

I. DECISIONS UNDER CURRENT LAW.

Applied in Dorer v. Arel, 60 F. Supp. 2d 558 (E.D. Va. 1999).

§ **8.01-468. Executions against corporations.** — Such executions as may issue against a natural person may issue against a corporation. (Code 1950, § 8-401; 1977, c. 617.)

REVISERS' NOTE

Section 8.01-468 is the first sentence of former § 8-401 without change.

§ **8.01-469. Executions on joint judgments.** — When a judgment is against several persons jointly, executions thereon may be joint against all of them. (Code 1950, § 8-401; 1977, c. 617.)

REVISERS' NOTE

Section 8.01-469 is the last sentence of former § 8-401. The word "shall" has been replaced by "may" in the belief that the execution creditor should be permitted to request execution against less than all the joint judgment debtors.

I. DECISIONS UNDER PRIOR LAW.

Editor's note. — The case cited below was decided under corresponding provisions of former law. The term "this section," as used below, refers to former provisions.

One execution even though judgments not entered at same time. — Where in a proceeding at law against several parties, judgments against one or more are entered at one time, and against others at another time, one execution may issue against all. Walker v. Commonwealth, 59 Va. (18 Gratt.) 13 (1867).

§ **8.01-470. Writs on judgments for specific property.** — On a judgment for the recovery of specific property, real or personal, a writ of possession may issue for the specific property, which shall conform to the judgment as to the description of the property and the estate, title and interest recovered, and there may also be issued a writ of fieri facias for the damages or profits and costs. In cases of unlawful entry and detainer and of ejectment, the officer to whom a writ of possession has been delivered to be executed shall, at least seventy-two hours before execution, serve notice of intent to execute, including the date and time of execution, on the defendant in accordance with § 8.01-296, with a copy of the writ attached. The execution of the writ of possession by the sheriff should occur within fifteen calendar days from the date the writ of possession is received by the sheriff, or as soon as practicable thereafter, but in no event later than thirty days from the date the writ of possession is issued. In cases of unlawful entry and detainer and of ejectment, whenever the officer to whom a writ of possession has been delivered to be executed finds the premises locked, he may, after declaring at the door the cause of his coming and demanding to have the door opened, employ reasonable and necessary force to break and enter the door and put the plaintiff in possession. And an officer having a writ of possession for specific personal property, if he finds locked or fastened the building or place wherein he has reasonable cause to believe the property specified in the writ is located, may in the daytime, after notice to the defendant, his agent or bailee, break and enter such building or place for the purpose of executing such writ. (Code 1950, § 8-402; 1977, c. 617; 1991, c. 503; 2000, c. 640.)

Cross references. — As to direction and execution of process, see § 8.01-292. As to fieri facias, see §§ 8.01-474, 8.01-478, 8.01-479. As to other "breaking and entry" provisions, see § 8.01-491.

The 2000 amendments. — The 2000 amendment by c. 640 added the present third sentence.

I. DECISIONS UNDER PRIOR LAW.

Editor's note. — The cases cited below were decided under corresponding provisions of former law. The term "this section," as used below, refers to former provisions.

It is an established rule that writs of possession must follow the judgment for the recovery of specific property. King v. Davis, 137 F. 222 (C.C.W.D. Va. 1905), aff'd sub nom., Blankenship v. King, 157 F. 676 (4th Cir. 1906).

Writs of possession issued only in favor of prevailing plaintiff. — Since a judgment in favor of a plaintiff in an action of ejectment is not self-executing, a prevailing plaintiff needs a writ of possession to enforce his right to possession. But a prevailing defendant, being already in possession, needs no writ to enforce his right to possession. So this section provides for the issuance of a writ of possession only in favor of a plaintiff who has prevailed. Page v. Luhring, 211 Va. 503, 178 S.E.2d 527 (1971).

§ 8.01-471. Time period for issuing writs of possession in unlawful entry and detainer; when returnable.

— Writs of possession, in case of unlawful entry and detainer, shall be issued within one year from the date of judgment for possession and shall be made returnable within thirty days from the date of issuing the writ. No writ shall issue, however, if, following the entry of judgment, the landlord has accepted rent payments without reservation, as described in § 55-248.34. (Code 1950, § 8-403; 1977, c. 617; 1999, c. 683.)

REVISERS' NOTE

Section 8.01-471 is former § 8-403. The statute has made 30 days uniform for returns of writs of possession irrespective of the location of the property.

The 1999 amendment inserted "shall be issued within one year from the date of judgments for possession and" in the first sentence, and added the second sentence.

§ 8.01-472. Writs on judgments for personal property.

— When the judgment is for personal property, the plaintiff may, at his option, have a fieri facias for the alternative value, instead of a writ of possession, and the damages and costs. (Code 1950, § 8-404; 1977, c. 617.)

I. DECISIONS UNDER PRIOR LAW.

Editor's note. — The case cited below was decided under corresponding provisions of former law. The term "this section," as used below, refers to former provisions.

This section establishes a general rule. McClure Grocery Co. v. Watson, 148 Va. 601, 139 S.E. 288 (1927).

§ 8.01-473. Judgment for benefit of other person than plaintiff; remedies of such person.

— When an execution issues on a judgment, for the benefit, in whole or in part, of any person other than the plaintiff, if the fact appears by the record, the clerk shall, in the execution, or by an endorsement thereon, state the extent of the interest therein of such person; and such person, either in his own name or that of the plaintiff, may, as a party injured, prosecute a suit or motion against the officer. (Code 1950, § 8-405; 1977, c. 617.)

I. DECISIONS UNDER PRIOR LAW.

Editor's note. — The case cited below was decided under corresponding provisions of former law. The term "this section," as used below, refers to former provisions.

Motion by debtor against sheriff for failure to return execution. — An execution debtor who has paid the amount of the execution cannot maintain a motion in the name of the execution creditor against the sheriff for failing to return the execution. Fletcher v. Chapman, 29 Va. (2 Leigh) 560 (1831).

§ 8.01-474. What writ of fieri facias to command. — By a writ of fieri facias, the officer shall be commanded to make the money therein mentioned out of the goods and chattels of the person against whom the judgment is. (Code 1950, § 8-406; 1977, c. 617.)

Cross references. — As to what writ levied on, see § 8.01-478. As to time for enforcement of lien, see § 8.01-479.

I. DECISIONS UNDER CURRENT LAW.

Applied in Barbuto v. Southern Bank, 231 Va. 63, 340 S.E.2d 813 (1986).

§ 8.01-475. Subsequent executions. — Subject to the limitations prescribed by Chapter 17 (§ 8.01-426 et seq.) of this title, a party obtaining an execution may sue out other executions at his own costs, though the return day of a former execution has not arrived; and may sue out other executions at the defendant's costs, when on a former execution there is a return by which it appears that the writ has not been executed, or that it or any part of the amount thereof is not levied, or that property levied on has been discharged by legal process which does not prevent a new execution on the judgment. In no case shall there be more than one satisfaction for the same money or thing.

And the fact that a judgment creditor may have availed himself of the benefit of any other remedies under this chapter, shall not prevent him from issuing, from time to time, without impairing his lien under it, other executions upon his judgment until the same is satisfied. (Code 1950, § 8-407; 1977, c. 617.)

Cross references. — As to limitations on enforcement of judgments, see § 8.01-251.

I. DECISIONS UNDER PRIOR LAW.

Editor's note. — The cases cited below were decided under corresponding provisions of former law. The term "this section," as used below, refers to former provisions.

Executions issued until judgment satisfied. — If, by a misunderstanding of the directions of the plaintiff by the sheriff and the defendants, the property is released by the sheriff to them, the plaintiff may have a new execution. Walker v. Commonwealth, 59 Va. (18 Gratt.) 13 (1867).

Where an execution was issued and sale of the property was made under it, but none of the purchase price was paid, the judgment was not satisfied and another execution could be issued. Richardson v. Wymer, 104 Va. 236, 51 S.E. 219 (1905).

But debtor will not be unnecessarily oppressed by numerous executions. — The right of issuing numerous executions will not be permitted to be used for the purpose of unnecessarily oppressing or injuring the debtor. Hence, where it appears by the record that the first execution was returned executed by an ample levy, and there being no return thereunder by which it appears that it was not fully and completely executed, there is no ground for the issuance of a new execution. Sutton v. Marye, 81 Va. 329 (1886).

Until the plaintiff "has gotten to the end of his suit"; in other words, until he has gotten satisfaction of his demand, or what is equivalent thereto, he may continue to prosecute his remedy to judgment and sue out execution after execution thereon, taking care not to oppress or injure the defendant or his sureties, if there be any. Puryear v. Taylor, 53 Va. (12 Gratt.) 401 (1855); Walker v. Commonwealth, 59 Va. (18 Gratt.) 13 (1867).

§ 8.01-476. New execution after loss of property sold under indemnifying bond. — When property sold under an execution, or its value, is recovered from an obligor on an indemnifying bond given before such sale, or from a purchaser having a right of action on such bond, the person having such execution, or his personal representative, may, by motion, after reasonable notice to the person, or the personal representative of the person, against whom the execution was, obtain a new execution against him, without credit for the amount for which the property was sold under the former execution. Such motion shall be made within the period of time prescribed by § 8.01-255.2. (Code 1950, § 8-408; 1977, c. 617.)

§ 8.01-477. When executions may be quashed; how proceedings thereon stayed. — A motion to quash an execution may, after reasonable notice to the adverse party, be heard and decided by the court which issued the execution. Such court, on the application of the plaintiff in the motion, may make an order staying the proceedings on the execution until the motion be heard and determined, the order not to be effectual until bond be given in such penalty and with such condition, and either with or without surety, as the court may prescribe. The clerk from whose office the execution issued, shall take the bond and make as many copies of the order as may be necessary and endorse thereon that the bond required has been given; and a copy shall be served on the plaintiff in the execution and on the officer in whose hands the execution is placed. (Code 1950, § 8-410; 1977, c. 617.)

I. Decisions Under Current Law.
II. Decisions Under Prior Law.

I. DECISIONS UNDER CURRENT LAW.

A motion to quash under this section may not be used by strangers to underlying judgment as substitute for statutory method prescribed in § 8.01-365 or in lieu of a common law action of trespass. The application of this section is limited to attacks on the regularity and validity of a writ of fieri facias. Barbuto v. Southern Bank, 231 Va. 63, 340 S.E.2d 813 (1986).

A motion to quash was improperly used where third parties who claimed ownership of certain property levied upon, improperly sought to prosecute a common law action of trespass and to simultaneously claim ownership of the property seized in the levy. This was an improper use of the statutory motion to quash. Their remedy was under § 8.01-365, a statute specifically providing strangers to the underlying judgment a swift, direct, and summary method to determine conflicting ownership of property seized in a levy. Barbuto v. Southern Bank, 231 Va. 63, 340 S.E.2d 813 (1986).

Applied in Harris v. Bailey, 574 F. Supp. 966 (W.D. Va. 1983).

II. DECISIONS UNDER PRIOR LAW.

Editor's note. — The cases cited below were decided under corresponding provisions of former law. The term "this section," as used below, refers to former provisions.

Notice must be reasonable. — It is necessary that notice be given to the opposite party when a motion to quash is to be made. But all that is required is that it must be a "reasonable notice." Ballard v. Whitlock, 59 Va. (18 Gratt.) 235 (1867); Dillard v. Thornton, 70 Va. (29 Gratt.) 392 (1877); Snavely v. Harkrader, 71 Va. (30 Gratt.) 487 (1878).

But it is not required to be in writing. — The notice of a motion to quash an execution is not required to be in writing. Dillard v. Thornton, 70 Va. (29 Gratt.) 392 (1877).

A void execution can be attacked collaterally or directly by anybody, anywhere and at any time. Johnston v. Pearson, 121 Va. 453, 93 S.E. 640 (1917).

There is no limitation on the time within which a motion must be made to quash a fieri facias. Lowenbach v. Kelly, 111 Va. 439, 69 S.E. 352 (1910).

Irregular execution is ground for motion. — It is well settled that a motion to quash is the proper remedy where an execution is irregular and has been issued without authority of law. Snavely v. Harkrader, 71 Va. (30 Gratt.) 487 (1878); Sutton v. Marye, 81 Va. 329 (1886). See Broyhill v. Dawson, 168 Va. 321, 191 S.E. 779 (1937).

Second execution after sufficient execution also grounds. — A second execution will be quashed, if issued after a former execution has been satisfied or levied on property sufficient to satisfy it. Sutton v. Marye, 81 Va. 329 (1886).

Effect of quashing. — After a voidable execution has been quashed it is as void as if it had been a nullity ab initio. Riely v. Solenberger, 18 Va. L. Reg. 352 (1912).

§ 8.01-477.1. Claims of exemption from execution. — The procedures specified in § 8.01-546.2 shall govern further proceedings regarding claims of exemption from levy. (1986, c. 341.)

ARTICLE 2.

Lien in General.

§ 8.01-478. On what property writ of fieri facias levied; when lien commences. — The writ of fieri facias may be levied as well on the current money and bank notes, as on the goods and chattels of the judgment debtor, except such as are exempt from levy under Title 34, and shall bind what is capable of being levied on only from the time it is actually levied by the officer to whom it has been delivered to be executed. (Code 1950, § 8-411; 1977, c. 617.)

REVISERS' NOTE

Section 8.01-478 is former § 8-411. The time at which the execution lien becomes effective is changed from that of its delivery to the officer to the time of actual levy. This change in the common law will prevent the injustice which results when a bona fide purchaser takes tangible property from the judgment debtor and later discovers an officer with a writ in his pocket which he had failed to execute.

Cross references. — As to judgment lien against real estate, see § 8.01-458. As to failure of officer to endorse the date and time of levy on the writ, see § 8.01-487. As to satisfaction of multiple writs of fieri facias, see § 8.01-488. As to suit by officer to recover estate on which fieri facias is lien, § 8.01-497. As to lien of fieri facias on property not capable of being levied on, see §§ 8.01-501 through 8.01-505. As to homestead and other exemptions, see §§ 34-1 et seq. As to levy by execution, fieri facias, etc., upon motion vehicles, trailers or semitrailers, see § 46.2-644.

Law Review. — For article on fraudulent conveyances and preferences in Virginia, see 36 Wash. & Lee L. Rev. 51 (1979). For article on the effect of delay on a surety's obligations in Virginia, see 18 U. Rich. L. Rev. 781 (1984).

I. Decisions Under Current Law.
II. Decisions Under Prior Law.
   A. General Consideration.
   B. Lien.

I. DECISIONS UNDER CURRENT LAW.

Under Virginia law, the officer is not required to seize the property levied on, but only to have it in his power and note it on the execution. The lien acquired by the levy of the execution is both substantial and enduring, as much so as a mortgage or a pledge. In re Lamm, 47 Bankr. 364 (E.D. Va. 1984).

Applied in Lubman v. J.B. Eurell Co. (In re Fregosi), 23 Bankr. 641 (Bankr. E.D. Va. 1982); In re Hess, 40 Bankr. 491 (Bankr. W.D. Va. 1984).

II. DECISIONS UNDER PRIOR LAW.

A. General Consideration.

Editor's note. — The cases cited below were decided under corresponding provisions of former law. The term "this section," as used below, refers to former provisions.

The second step after the issuance of the execution is to levy the same on specific tangible property, by which such property is set apart from the general property of the defendant and placed in the custody of the law until it can be sold and applied to the payment of the execution. Walker v. Commonwealth, 59 Va. (18 Gratt.) 13 (1867).

What constitutes levy. — Under the law of Virginia, actual seizure of the goods levied upon is not necessary. If the officer has the goods in his view and power and notes on the writ the fact of his levy thereon, this will in general suffice. Palais v. DeJarnette, 145 F.2d 953 (4th Cir. 1944).

By levying an execution is meant the setting aside of specific property from the general property of the defendant and placing the same in the custody of the law until it can be sold and applied to the payment of the execution. Walker v. Commonwealth, 59 Va. (18 Gratt.) 13 (1867).

To constitute an effectual levy, it is not essential that the officer should make an actual seizure. If he has the goods in his power and view, this may suffice. Dorrier v. Masters, 83 Va. 459, 2 S.E. 927 (1887).

Failure to remove property from debtor's premises does not, of itself, invalidate the levy. The practice in Virginia has been to permit it to remain on the premises of the debtor until the day of sale, in order to save expenses. Officers are not without "power" to levy because they are physically incapable of carrying away household goods levied on. Palais v. DeJarnette, 145 F.2d 953 (4th Cir. 1944).

No notice need be given debtor. — A valid levy may be made on household goods in the owner's absence and where he had no formal notice. As to notice to the debtor, the rule in Virginia is that while notice is advisable, it is not essential. Palais v. DeJarnette, 145 F.2d 953 (4th Cir. 1944).

Plaintiff has right of control. — In executing a writ of fieri facias the sheriff is the agent of the beneficial plaintiff, and he and his attorney have the right to control the execution of the writ and to say whether the sheriff shall levy it, or return it without doing so. Rowe v. Hardy, 97 Va. 674, 34 S.E. 625 (1899).

A plaintiff may always, with the consent of the defendants, abandon a levy upon the property of all or any of them, retaining the right to sue out a new execution against all the defendants. Walker v. Commonwealth, 59 Va. (18 Gratt.) 13 (1867).

If the defendants in an execution be a principal and his sureties, and the property levied on be that of the sureties, the plaintiff may, with the consent of the sureties only, abandon the levy, and afterwards sue out executions against all the defendants. Walker v. Commonwealth, 59 Va. (18 Gratt.) 13 (1867).

Property fraudulently conveyed may be levied on. — If property subject to execution be conveyed and such conveyance be either with intent to hinder, delay or defraud creditors, or be upon consideration deemed voluntary in law, execution may still be enforced. For where the conveyance is fraudulent it is void as to both existing creditors, and subsequent purchasers, and where the conveyance is voluntary only, it is void as to antecedent creditors, though it may be sustained as against subsequent purchasers. Lucas v. Claffin & Co., 76 Va. 269 (1882); Fishburne v. Ferguson, 84 Va. 87, 4 S.E. 575 (1887); Roanoke Nat'l Bank v. Farmers' Nat'l Bank, 84 Va. 603, 5 S.E. 682 (1888); Rucker v. Moss, 84 Va. 634, 5 S.E. 527 (1888); Beecher v. Wilson, 84 Va. 813, 6 S.E. 209 (1888); Rixey v. Detrick, 85 Va. 42, 6 S.E. 615 (1888).

Execution cannot be levied on real estate. — Congress gave judgment creditors in federal causes the remedies provided by the state law. This section does not provide for levy of execution on real estate, and a federal court has no power to order it. Clark v. Allen, 117 F. 699 (W.D. Va. 1902); Allen v. Clark, 126 F. 738 (4th Cir. 1903).

Execution cannot be levied on real estate. Davis v. National Grange Ins. Co., 281 F. Supp. 998 (E.D. Va. 1968).

A levy was not abandoned though creditors postponed sale at the request of debtor, where no relinquishment of the lien was found. As the court said in Walker v. Commonwealth, 59 Va. (18 Gratt.) 13, 98 Am. Dec. 631 (1867): "A mere suspension of proceedings on a levied execution does not release the levy." Palais v. DeJarnette, 145 F.2d 953 (4th Cir. 1944).

B. Lien.

Lien exists on things capable of being levied on. Such things are goods and chattels corporeal, as distinguished from incorporeal personalty, or, in other words, goods and chattels in possession as distinguished from choses in action. For example, horses, household and kitchen furniture, etc., are leviable; bonds, notes, and stocks are not. But while goods and chattels corporeal are in their nature leviable, they will cease to be so while in the hands of a receiver. For to levy execution upon them would be to interfere with the possession and control of the court. Davis v. Bonney, 89 Va. 755, 17 S.E. 229 (1893).

Nature of the lien. — The lien acquired by placing a writ of execution in the hands of the sheriff is of so imperfect a nature as that the plaintiff may abandon it at pleasure by withdrawing his execution from the hands of the sheriff or by directing him not to levy it, without discharging the judgment or even affecting the liability of a surety who may be one of several defendants. Humphrey v. Hitt, 47 Va. (6 Gratt.) 509 (1850); Walker v. Commonwealth, 59 Va. (18 Gratt.) 13 (1867). See also, Rhea v. Preston, 75 Va. 757 (1881).

The lien which a creditor acquires by a levy of his execution upon personal property is, if not enforced by a sale thereof, only temporary. Carr

v. Glasscock, 44 Va. (3 Gratt.) 343 (1846).

The lien acquired by the levying of a fieri facias "is substantial and enduring, as much so as a mortgage or a pledge." Humphrey v. Hitt, 47 Va. (6 Gratt.) 509 (1850).

The general lien of a fieri facias was intended as a substitute for the writ of capias ad satisfaciendum by which the judgment creditor could reach the unleviable property of an insolvent debtor. In re Acorn Elec. Supply, Inc., 348 F. Supp. 277 (E.D. Va. 1972).

The remedy afforded by garnishment was designed simply to enforce this lien of execution. The lien itself is as complete and perfect without it as with it. It continues in full force, although the creditor should never resort to that remedy. In re Acorn Elec. Supply, Inc., 348 F. Supp. 277 (E.D. Va. 1972).

And prior execution lien is superior to garnishment attachment. — A prior lien by writ of fieri facias is superior to a garnishment attachment even though the garnishment attachment was served on the garnishee first. In re Acorn Elec. Supply, Inc., 348 F. Supp. 277 (E.D. Va. 1972).

When lien commences. — A fieri facias constitutes a lien from the time it is delivered to the officer to be executed. Charron & Co. v. Boswell, 59 Va. (18 Gratt.) 216 (1868); Crump v. Commonwealth, 75 Va. 922 (1882); Frayser v. Richmond & A.R.R., 81 Va. 388 (1886); Boisseau v. Bass, 100 Va. 207, 40 S.E. 647 (1902).

A creditor's judgments do not become liens on a third party's indebtedness to the debtor until the garnishment summonses are issued. First Nat'l Bank v. Norfolk & W. Ry., 327 F. Supp. 196 (E.D. Va. 1971).

Validity of lien for purposes of bankruptcy. — Since attachment liens are valid in Virginia for the purposes of bankruptcy, then liens by writ of fieri facias must also be valid, because a prior existing fieri facias lien will defeat a subsequent attachment lien. In re Acorn Elec. Supply, Inc., 348 F. Supp. 277 (E.D. Va. 1972).

When lien on intangibles perfected for bankruptcy. — The Virginia execution lien on intangibles is perfected for bankruptcy when the writ of fieri facias is delivered to the officer to be executed. In re Acorn Elec. Supply, Inc., 348 F. Supp. 277 (E.D. Va. 1972).

Satisfaction of preexisting execution lien within four months of bankruptcy not a preference. — The satisfaction of a preexisting execution lien, during the four-month period preceding the filing of a bankruptcy petition, is not a preference. In re Acorn Elec. Supply, Inc., 348 F. Supp. 277 (E.D. Va. 1972).

Instructions not to levy do not necessarily forfeit lien. — A creditor delivers a fieri facias to a deputy sheriff acting in a different district of the county from that in which the debtor resides, in order by such delivery to bind the debtor's property, but with directions to the deputy to hold it till a future day, and then to transfer it to the deputy of the district in which the debtor resides, to be by him levied, unless the debt should be paid in the meantime, or unless the debtor should bring his property to the district of the first deputy to be sold, in which case the first deputy was to levy the execution upon it. It was held, that the writ became a lien from the time it was delivered to the officer notwithstanding the fact that the officer was instructed not to levy unless the conditions should be carried out. Pegram v. May, 36 Va. (9 Leigh) 176 (1838).

§ 8.01-479. Time for enforcement. — Property levied on, on or before the return day, may be advertised and sold within a reasonable time thereafter, and the lien given by this section may also be enforced after the return day of the writ by proceedings under § 8.01-506 and following of this chapter, if such proceedings be commenced before that day. (Code 1950, § 8-412; 1977, c. 617; 1984, c. 557.)

Cross references. — As to return of writ, see §§ 8.01-483, 8.01-484.

I. DECISIONS UNDER PRIOR LAW.

Editor's note. — The cases cited below were decided under corresponding provisions of former law. The term "this section," as used below, refers to former provisions.

No levy after return day. — An execution may not be levied after the date upon which it is returnable, and the imperative duty to return does not arise until it is no longer possible to levy it. The life of the execution ends upon the date to which it is returnable, and the duty to return it then arises. That duty should be promptly performed. Moorman v. Board, 121 Va. 112, 92 S.E. 833 (1917).

Levy necessary to sale. — Before there can be a sale of corporeal personal property under execution there must be an actual levy of the writ of fieri facias and the mere delivery of the writ to the sheriff without a levy creates no security for the debt. Humphrey v. Hitt, 47 Va. (6 Gratt.) 509 (1850); Walker v. Commonwealth, 59 Va. (18 Gratt.) 13 (1867); Charron & Co. v. Boswell, 59 Va. (18 Gratt.) 216 (1868).

Right to levy is source of authority of officer. — The authority of an officer to collect money in discharge of an execution does not result from the lien, but is a consequence of the right to levy and sell the debtor's property under the execution. So long as the right to sell continues, the right to receive remains; but no longer. Grandstaff v. Ridgely, 71 Va. (30 Gratt.) 1 (1878).

In the case of a sheriff's sale, the sheriff derives his authority to sell from the writ of a fieri facias. Turnbull v. Clairborne, 30 Va. (3 Leigh) 392 (1831).

Duration of power to sell. — If the officer levies before the return day of the writ, he continues to have the power to sell, even after the return day has passed, and this power continues for a reasonable time. Reasonable time is a question of fact, dependent on the circumstances of each case. The test, of course, is whether an intention to abandon was manifest from the acts of the creditors. Palais v. DeJarnette, 145 F.2d 953 (4th Cir. 1944).

If the officer levies before the return day of the writ he may sell after the return day has passed; but if he fails to levy before the return day his authority to sell afterward ceases. Grandstaff v. Ridgely, 71 Va. (30 Gratt.) 1 (1878).

Necessity for sale. — The third and last step after the issuance of the execution, is the sale of the property. Then and not until then, the plaintiff may be said to have gotten to the end of his suit, at least as far as the defendant is concerned, and to the extent of the value of the property. Walker v. Commonwealth, 59 Va. (18 Gratt.) 13 (1867); Rhea v. Preston, 75 Va. 757 (1881).

A mere levy of an execution is not a satisfaction. There must be a sale or some other act divesting the debtor of his title or depriving him of his property. Rhea v. Preston, 75 Va. 757 (1881).

Officer may fix details. — Sheriffs, being clothed with the power of the Commonwealth, may fix the time and place of sale. Carter v. Harris, 25 Va. (4 Rand.) 199 (1826).

§ **8.01-480. Prior security interest on property levied on.** — Tangible personal property subject to a prior security interest, or in which the execution debtor has only an equitable interest, may nevertheless be levied on for the satisfaction of a fieri facias. If the prior security interest is due and payable, the officer levying the fieri facias may sell the property free of such security interest, and apply the proceeds first to the payment of such security interest, and the residue, so far as necessary, to the satisfaction of the fieri facias. In the event the property is to be sold free of such prior security interest, the judgment creditor shall give written notice by certified mail to each secured party of record as hereafter specified, as his name and address shall appear on record, of the proposed sale, or to any secured party of whom the judgment creditor shall have actual knowledge. Such notice shall be given to each secured party who is of record at the State Corporation Commission, at the Department of Motor Vehicles, at the Department of Game and Inland Fisheries, or in the clerk's office in the city or county in Virginia, where the debtor has resided to the knowledge of the judgment creditor at any time during a one-year period prior to the sale. Certification of such notice shall be delivered to the sheriff or other officer conducting the sale pursuant to execution of the judgment, who shall announce that except as to such person so notified, the sale is subject to any prior security interest of record, other than one of record at a place where the debtor may have resided more than one year previously. If such prior security interest is not due and payable at the time of sale, such officer shall sell the property levied on subject to such security interest. (Code 1950, § 8-413; 1977, c. 617; 1979, c. 491; 1990, c. 553.)

§ **8.01-481. Territorial extent of lien.** — The lien given by this chapter on personal property by levy shall, as to property capable of being levied on, be restricted to the bailiwick of the officer into whose hands the execution is placed to be executed, but as to property not capable of being levied on the lien shall extend throughout the limits of the Commonwealth. (Code 1950, § 8-414; 1977, c. 617.)

REVISERS' NOTE

Section 8.01-481 is former § 8-414. The language "... placing an execution in the hands of an officer to be executed shall ..." has been deleted and the words "levy shall" have been inserted in its place. This change comports with the language in § 8.01-478.

Cross references. — As to lien on property not capable of being levied on, see § 8.01-501 et seq.

I. DECISIONS UNDER CURRENT LAW.

State law clearly provides that a lien of fieri facias on intangible property extends throughout the Commonwealth. The manner in which the statute is worded indicates that a limitation to the coverage of the lien was not intended but rather that the lien was to be effective over as large a territory as possible. The fact remains, however, that the lien would not cover any property of the debtor located outside the Commonwealth. Homeowner's Fin. Corp. v. Pennington, 47 Bankr. 322 (Bankr. E.D. Va. 1985).

§ 8.01-482. If levy be on coin or currency, how accounted for. — If the levy be on coin or currency (including notes) made a legal tender for the payment of debts, the same shall be accounted for at its par value as so much money made under the execution. If it be upon coin or currency (including notes) not a legal tender for the payment of debts, and the creditor will not take them at their nominal value, they shall be sold and accounted for as any other property taken under execution. (Code 1950, § 8-415; 1977, c. 617.)

ARTICLE 3.

Return and Venditioni Exponas.

§ 8.01-483. Return of officer on fieri facias; statement filed therewith. — Upon a writ of fieri facias, the officer shall return whether the money therein mentioned has been or cannot be made. If there is only part thereof which is or cannot be made, he shall return the amount of such part. With every execution under which money is recovered, he shall return a statement of the amount received, including his fees and other charges, and shall pay such amount, except such fees and charges, to the person entitled. In his return upon every execution, the officer shall also state in what manner a copy of the writ was served in accordance with § 8.01-487.1, whether or not he made a levy of the same, the date and time of such levy, the date when he received such payment or obtained such satisfaction upon such execution and, if there is more than one defendant, from which defendant he received the same. (Code 1950, § 8-416; 1977, c. 617; 1986, c. 341.)

REVISERS' NOTE

Section 8.01-483 is former § 8-416. The language "... date and time ..." has been inserted before the words "of such levy." This language comports with the changes made in §§ 8.01-478 and 8.01-487.

Cross references. — As to amendment of return, see § 8.01-277. For return of summonses in garnishment, see § 8.01-514.

I. DECISIONS UNDER PRIOR LAW.

Editor's note. — The cases cited below were decided under corresponding provisions of former law. The term "this section," as used below, refers to former provisions.

A return on a writ of process is the short official statement of the officer indorsed thereon of what he has done in obedience to the mandate of the writ, or why he has done nothing. Rowe v. Hardy, 97 Va. 674, 34 S.E. 625 (1899).

A valid return may be made after the day to which the execution is returnable. In the present case, the executions were returned "no effects" two days after the return day. This was clearly within a reasonable time, and, therefore, the returns were made in the lawful performance of a delayed duty. Moorman v. Board of Supvrs., 121 Va. 112, 92 S.E. 838 (1917).

Amendment of return. — A sheriff cannot amend his return upon an execution after it has been filed, except by motion to the court, upon notice to the creditor. Hammen v. Minnick, 73 Va. (32 Gratt.) 249 (1879).

A return on a former execution is, generally, very material evidence on the hearing of a motion to quash an execution and it is often important, in the course of the proceedings, to permit the sheriff to make or amend his return according to the truth of the case, and with a view to its effect upon the decision of the motion. Such permission has always been given by our courts. Walker v. Commonwealth, 59 Va. (18 Gratt.) 13 (1867).

Where the truth of a return on an execution is not questioned, and no good reason to the contrary is shown, the officer making it should be allowed to amend by signing it, and thus make valid that which before had no appearance of official authenticity. Courts are liberal in allowing amendments of returns in proper cases, so as to conform to the truth, and the amendment when made has the same effect as though it were the original return, where the rights of third persons have not intervened, and it does not appear that injustice can result to anyone. There is no specific time within which a return must be amended, but, after a great lapse of time, an amendment should be permitted with caution, and in no case should it be allowed unless the court can see that it is in furtherance of justice. Slingluff v. Collins, 109 Va. 717, 64 S.E. 1055 (1909).

No amendment after decree entered against officer on return. — Having made return on an execution and on that return, in part, a decree having been entered, in subsequent proceedings against him and his sureties, the sheriff will not be permitted to amend his return, so as to explain it away and enable his sureties to escape liability for his default. Carr v. Meade, 77 Va. 142 (1883).

But may amend after notice of motion against officer. — A sheriff may have leave to amend his return upon an execution, after notice of a motion against him founded on the original return. And the amended return may be made by a deputy who did not make the first return. Stone v. Wilson, 51 Va. (10 Gratt.) 529 (1853).

Presumption that officer did his duty. — In the absence of a date, or other evidence showing when the return of an officer on a writ was made, it is presumed to have been made at a time when he had the right to make it, and in due time, as the prima facie presumption is that the officer has done his duty. Rowe v. Hardy, 97 Va. 674, 34 S.E. 625 (1899).

Sufficiency of return. — It is required that the officer shall return upon a writ of fieri facias, "whether the money is or cannot be made." A return of "Not levied by reason of the stay law" is a return substantially that the money "cannot be made," and sufficient. Hamilton v. McConkey, 83 Va. 533, 2 S.E. 724 (1887).

A return on an execution "no effects known to me" is not vitiated by the fact that it is made before the return day of the writ, where, as in the case at bar, it is an agreed fact that, at the time the writ was placed in the hands of the officer, the defendants were notoriously insolvent. Slingluff v. Collins, 109 Va. 717, 64 S.E. 1055 (1909).

§ 8.01-484. When writ may be destroyed. — A writ of fieri facias returned by the officer to the clerk's office with a notation that the money cannot be made may be destroyed after two years from the date of the return. (Code 1950, § 8-417; 1962, c. 110; 1977, c. 617; 1988, c. 420.)

§ 8.01-485. When venditioni exponas may issue; proceedings thereon. — When it appears by the return on an execution that property taken to satisfy it remains unsold, a writ of venditioni exponas may issue, whereupon the like proceedings shall be had as might have been had on the first execution; except, that if it issue upon a return of no sale for want of bidders, or of a sufficient bid, the advertisement shall state the fact, and that the sale will be made peremptorily. (Code 1950, § 8-418; 1977, c. 617.)

Cross references. — As to proceedings at sales generally, see § 8.01-96 et seq. and § 8.01-492 et seq. As to issuance of writ of venditioni exponas for property levied on for debts due the Commonwealth, see § 8.01-211 et seq. As to issuance and levy of fieri facias, see § 8.01-466 et seq. and § 8.01-478 et seq. As to return of and sale under distress warrants, see § 55-237.

§ 8.01-486. Procedure when officer taking property under execution dies before sale. — If an officer taking property under execution die before the sale thereof, and there be no deputies of such officer acting in the case, upon a suggestion of the fact a writ of venditioni exponas may be directed to the sheriff or other officer of the county or city wherein the property was taken. Whereupon the officer to whom the writ is directed shall take possession of the property previously levied upon, whether the same be in possession of the representatives of the deceased officer or the execution debtor, and proceed to advertise and sell it and account for the proceeds thereof in like manner as if the levy had been made by himself. (Code 1950, § 8-419; 1977, c. 617.)

ARTICLE 4.

Enforcement Generally.

§ 8.01-487. Officer to endorse on fieri facias time of receiving it. — Every officer shall endorse on each writ of fieri facias the date and time he receives the same and also when he levies upon tangible personal property of the debtor. If he fail to do so, the judgment creditor may, by motion, recover against him and his sureties, jointly and severally, in the court in which the judgment was rendered, a sum not exceeding fifteen percent upon the amount of the execution. (Code 1950, § 8-420; 1977, c. 617.)

REVISERS' NOTE

Section 8.01-487 is former § 8-420 rewritten to require every officer to endorse on each writ of fi. fa. the "date and time" when he receives the writ and also when he levies. This comports with § 8.01-478.

Cross references. — As to time from which lien binds property levied on, see § 8.01-478. As to penalty for service of notice of lien of a writ when no judgment exists, see § 8.01-504.

§ 8.01-487.1. Officer to leave copy of writ where levy made. — An officer into whose hands a writ of fieri facias is placed to be levied, when making a levy shall serve a copy of the writ and any attachments thereto on the judgment debtor or other responsible person at the premises where the levy is made. If no such person is present, a copy of the writ and any attachments thereto shall be posted on the front door of such premises. (1986, c. 341.)

§ 8.01-488. When several writs of fieri facias, how satisfied. — Of writs of fieri facias, that which was first delivered to the officer, though two or more be delivered on the same day, shall be first levied and satisfied, and when several such executions are delivered to the officer at the same time they shall be satisfied ratably. But if an indemnifying bond be required by the officer as a prerequisite to a sale, and the same to be given by some of the creditors and not by others, and the officer sells under the protection of such bond, the proceeds of the sale shall be paid to the creditors giving the bond in the order in which their liens attached. (Code 1950, § 8-421; 1977, c. 617.)

Law Review. — For article on fraudulent conveyances and preferences in Virginia, see 36 Wash. & Lee L. Rev. 51 (1979).

§ 8.01-489. Growing crops, not severed, not liable to distress or levy.
— No growing crop of any kind, not severed, shall be liable to distress or levy. (Code 1950, § 8-421.1; 1977, c. 617.)

REVISERS' NOTE

The outdated exceptions in former § 8-421.1 of crops that may be taken by a writ of fi. fa. have been deleted from § 8.01-489.

Law Review. — For note on crops as personalty or realty, see 39 Va. L. Rev. 1115 (1953).

I. DECISIONS UNDER PRIOR LAW.

Editor's note. — The case cited below was decided under corresponding provisions of former law. The term "this section," as used below, refers to former provisions.

Crops raised on homestead land are exempt. — Crops raised in the ordinary course of husbandry upon land previously set apart as a homestead are exempt from levy to the same extent as the land itself. Neblett v. Shackleton, 111 Va. 707, 69 S.E. 946 (1911).

§ 8.01-490. No unreasonable distress or levy; sustenance provided for livestock; removal of property.
— Officers shall in no case make an unreasonable distress or levy. For horses, or any livestock distrained or levied on, the officer shall provide sufficient sustenance while they remain in his possession. Nothing distrained or levied on shall be removed by him out of his county or city, unless when it is otherwise specially provided. (Code 1950, § 8-421.2; 1977, c. 617.)

I. DECISIONS UNDER PRIOR LAW.

Editor's note. — The case cited below was decided under corresponding provisions of former law. The term "this section," as used below, refers to former provisions.

Acceptance of excess by debtor waiver of any rights against officer for sale. — If an officer levies on and sells more goods than are necessary to pay a distress warrant in his hands, and pays over the excess to the tenant, who accepts the same, the receipt of the excess is a ratification of the officer's act in selling more than he ought to have sold, and is a waiver of any wrongdoing on his part in making the sale. The tenant cannot affirm in part and disaffirm as to the residue. Manchester Home Bldg. & Loan Ass'n v. Porter, 106 Va. 528, 56 S.E. 337 (1907).

§ 8.01-491. Officer may break open dwelling house and levy on property in personal possession of debtor.
— An officer into whose hands an execution is placed to be levied, may, if need be, break open the outer doors of a dwelling house in the daytime, after having first demanded admittance of the occupant, in order to make a levy, and may also levy on property in the personal possession of the debtor if the same be open to observation. (Code 1950, § 8-422; 1977, c. 617.)

REVISERS' NOTE

Section 8.01-491 is former § 8-422 without change. The demand provision of this statute parallels § 8.01-470.

Cross references. — As to use of force in levying writ for specific property, see § 8.01-470. As to what writ may be levied on, see § 8.01-478. As to unreasonable levy, see § 8.01-490. As to use of force in levying distress warrant, see § 55-235.

§ 8.01-492. Sale of property. — In any case of goods and chattels which an officer shall distrain or levy on, otherwise than under an attachment, or which he may be directed to sell by an order of a court, unless such order prescribe a different course, the officer shall fix upon a time and place for the sale thereof and post notice of the same at least ten days before the day of sale at some place near the residence of the owner if he reside in the county or city and at two or more public places in the officer's county or city. If the goods and chattels be expensive to keep or perishable, the court from whose clerk's office the writ of fieri facias or the distress warrant was issued under which the seizure is made, or if the distress warrant was issued by a clerk, the court of which he is a clerk, may order a sale of the property seized under fieri facias or distress warrant to be made upon such notice less than ten days as to such court may seem proper. At the time and place so appointed, such officer shall sell to the highest bidder, for cash, such goods and chattels, or so much thereof as may be necessary. (Code 1950, § 8-422.1; 1962, c. 10; 1977, c. 617.)

Cross references. — As to judicial sales, see § 8.01-96 et seq. As to terms of sale of real estate on executions for debts due the Commonwealth, see § 8.01-206.

I. DECISIONS UNDER CURRENT LAW.

Private versus public sale. — Although an execution sale need not be advertised, where sheriff's notice of execution sale of hotel furnishings was posted at two court houses advertising "public sale" yet sale itself was held in a private room in the hotel, and the parties agreed to a predetermined sale price, these circumstances effectively limited the number of bidders and resulted in a private sale. Manufacturers Hanover Trust Co. v. Koubek, 240 Va. 276, 396 S.E.2d 669 (1990).

§ 8.01-493. Adjournment of sale. — When there is not time, on the day appointed for any such sale, to complete the same, the sale may be adjourned from day to day until completed. (Code 1950, § 8-422.2; 1977, c. 617.)

§ 8.01-494. Resale of property if purchaser fails to comply; remedy against such purchaser. — If, at any sale by an officer, the purchaser does not comply with the terms of sale, the officer may sell the property, either forthwith or under a new advertisement, or return that the property was not sold for want of bidders. If, on a resale, the property be sold for less than it sold for before, the first purchaser shall be liable for the difference to the creditor, so far as is required to satisfy him, and to the debtor for the balance. This section shall not prevent the creditor from proceeding as he might have done if it had not been enacted. (Code 1950, § 8-423; 1977, c. 617.)

Cross references. — As to purchasers at judicial sales, see §§ 8.01-101 and 8.01-102.

I. DECISIONS UNDER PRIOR LAW.

Editor's note. — The cases cited below were decided under corresponding provisions of former law. The term "this section," as used below, refers to former provisions.

Resale is at purchaser's risk. — When a resale is ordered, upon default of the purchaser to comply with his contract by paying the purchase money, the former sale is not set aside, but the property is sold as the property of the purchaser and at his risk. Clarkson v. Read, 56 Va. (15 Gratt.) 288 (1858); Tyler v. Toms, 75 Va. 116 (1880); Hurt v. Jones, 75 Va. 341 (1881); Virginia Fire & Marine Ins. Co. v. Cottrell, 85 Va. 857, 9 S.E. 132 (1889); Whitehead v. Bradley, 87 Va. 676, 13 S.E. 195 (1891).

By bidding, the purchaser subjects himself to the jurisdiction of the court, and in effect becomes a party to the proceedings in which the sale is made, and may be compelled to complete his purchase by the process of the court. Brent v. Green, 33 Va. (6 Leigh) 16 (1835); Robertson v. Smith, 94 Va. 250, 26 S.E. 579 (1897).

The purchaser is responsible for any

difference between the sum at which he agreed to buy, i.e., the unpaid purchase money of the former sale together with the costs and expenses of the resale, and the amount which the property brings on resale. Clarkson v. Read, 56 Va. (15 Gratt.) 288 (1858); Tyler v. Toms, 75 Va. 116 (1880); Hurt v. Jones, 75 Va. 341 (1881); Virginia Fire & Marine Ins. Co. v. Cottrell, 85 Va. 857, 9 S.E. 132 (1889); Whitehead v. Bradley, 87 Va. 676, 13 S.E. 195 (1891).

And he is entitled to any surplus. — If, upon a resale of the property to compel the purchaser to comply with his contract, the property brings more than his liability he is entitled to the surplus. Tyler v. Toms, 75 Va. 116 (1880); Hurt v. Jones, 75 Va. 341 (1881); Virginia Fire & Marine Ins. Co. v. Cottrell, 85 Va. 857, 9 S.E. 132 (1889); Whitehead v. Bradley, 87 Va. 676, 13 S.E. 195 (1891).

§ 8.01-495. When money received by officer under execution to be repaid to debtor. — When an officer has received money under execution, if any surplus remain in his hands after satisfying the execution, such surplus shall be repaid to the debtor; and if the debtor, or his personal representative, obtain an injunction or supersedeas to an execution, in whole or in part, before money received under it, or any part of it, is paid over to the creditor, the officer shall repay such debtor the money so received and not so paid over, or so much thereof as the injunction or supersedeas may extend to, unless such process otherwise direct. (Code 1950, § 8-424; 1977, c. 617.)

Cross references. — As to officer receiving money making return thereof and paying net proceeds, see § 8.01-499.

§ 8.01-496. Officer not required to go out of his jurisdiction to pay over money. — No officer receiving money under execution, when the person to whom it is payable resides in a different county or city from that in which the officer resides, shall be liable to have any judgment rendered against him or his sureties for the nonpayment thereof, until a demand of payment be made of such officer in his county or city, by such creditor or his attorney-at-law, or some person having a written order from the creditor. (Code 1950, § 8-425; 1977, c. 617.)

I. DECISIONS UNDER PRIOR LAW.

Editor's note. — The cases cited below were decided under corresponding provisions of former law. The term "this section," as used below, refers to former provisions.

Necessity for demand. — Where the plaintiff in an action against a sheriff to recover money received under an execution lives in the county no demand of the money is necessary before proceeding to subject the sheriff. Tyree v. Donnally, 50 Va. (9 Gratt.) 64 (1852); Grandstaff v. Ridgely, 71 Va. (30 Gratt.) 1 (1878).

County creditor provided for in the county levy is not bound to apply to the sheriff or to his deputies for payment before he proceeds to enforce payment of his debt by the sheriff and his sureties. Ballard v. Thomas, 60 Va. (19 Gratt.) 14 (1868).

But when the plaintiff in execution does not reside in the same county with the sheriff, there must be a demand of payment before an action can be maintained on the sheriff's official bond. Grandstaff v. Ridgely, 71 Va. (30 Gratt.) 1 (1878).

Demand by attorney sufficient. — Where an execution is delivered to the sheriff of a county other than that in which the creditor resides, and the creditor employs an attorney practicing in the sheriff's county, to collect the money without giving the attorney a written order and the attorney makes a demand on the sheriff, such demand, if no objection be made at the time to the surety of the attorney, is sufficient to justify a judgment against the sheriff. Chapman v. Chevis, 36 Va. (9 Leigh) 297 (1838).

A demand by an attorney at law who prosecuted the suit and obtained judgment was sufficient to authorize a motion against the sheriff for nonpayment. Wilson v. Stokes, 18 Va. (4 Munf.) 455 (1815).

Procedure. — In an action by an execution creditor against the sheriff and his sureties upon his official bond for the failure to pay over the money he had collected on the execution, the motion not stating that the plaintiff did not reside in the county of the sheriff, it is not necessary to aver that a demand had been made upon the sheriff, as prescribed by the statute before the action was instituted. But if it appears upon the trial that the plaintiff did

§ 8.01-497. Suit by officer to recover estate on which fieri facias is lien.

not reside in the same county with the sheriff, the plaintiff must prove the demand in accordance with this section or his action will fail.

Grandstaff v. Ridgely, 71 Va. (30 Gratt.) 1 (1878).

§ **8.01-497. Suit by officer to recover estate on which fieri facias is lien.** — For the recovery of any estate on which a writ of fieri facias is a lien under this chapter, or on which the judgment on which such writ issues is a lien under Chapter 17 (§ 8.01-426 et seq.) of this title, or for the enforcement of any liability in respect to any such estate, a suit may be maintained, at law or in equity, as the case may require, in the name of the officer to whom such writ was delivered, or in the name of any other officer who may be designated for the purpose by an order of the court in which the judgment is entered. No officer shall be bound to bring such suit unless bond, with sufficient surety, be given him to indemnify him against all expenses and costs which he may incur or become liable for by reason thereof. But any person interested may bring such suit at his own costs in the officer's name. (Code 1950, § 8-426; 1977, c. 617.)

Cross references. — As to property on which writ of fieri facias may be levied, see § 8.01-478. As to lien on property not capable of being levied on, see §§ 8.01-501 through 8.01-505.

§ **8.01-498. Selling officers and employees not to bid or to purchase.** — No officer of any city, town, county or constitutional officer or employee of any such city, town, county or constitutional office shall, directly or indirectly, bid on or purchase effects sold under a writ by such officer. Anyone violating this section shall be guilty of a Class 1 misdemeanor. (Code 1950, § 8-427; 1975, c. 84; 1977, c. 617; 1988, c. 674.)

REVISERS' NOTE

Section 8.01-498 is former § 8-427, the application of which has been changed. The statute applies to any officer or employee of a city, town or county.

Cross references. — As to punishment for Class 1 misdemeanors, see § 18.2-11.

§ **8.01-499. Officer receiving money to make return thereof and pay net proceeds; commission, etc.** — An officer receiving money under this chapter shall make return thereof forthwith to the court or the clerk's office of the court in which the judgment is entered. For failing to do so, the officer shall be liable as if he had acted under an order of such court. After deducting from such money a commission of five per centum and his necessary expenses and costs, including reasonable fees to sheriff's counsel, he shall pay the net proceeds, and he and his sureties and their representatives shall be liable therefor, in like manner as if the same had been made under a writ of fieri facias on the judgment. (Code 1950, § 8-429; 1977, c. 617.)

REVISERS' NOTE

Section 8.01-499 is former § 8-429, rewritten to require the officer receiving money to return it "forthwith" instead of within thirty days. Antiquated language has been deleted to allow the statute to comport with modern practice.

Cross references. — As to disposition of surplus from sale, see § 8.01-373. As to disposition of proceeds from sale of realty, see § 8.01-462. As to fee for officer who after distraining or levying on property neither sells nor receives payment, etc., see § 15.2-1609.3. As to fee when no levy is made, see § 17.1-272.

§ 8.01-500. Officer receiving money to notify person entitled to receive it.

— Every officer collecting or receiving money to be applied on any execution or other legal process, or on any claim, whether judgment has been rendered thereon or not, shall notify in writing by mail or otherwise, within thirty days after such money is received, the person entitled to receive such money, if known. Any officer failing without good cause to comply with this section within the time prescribed shall be fined not less than twenty dollars nor more than fifty dollars for each offense. (Code 1950, § 8-430; 1977, c. 617.)

REVISERS' NOTE

Section 8.01-500 is former § 8-430. The dollar limits on the fine have been increased from $5 and $20, to $20 and $50, respectively.

ARTICLE 5.

Lien on Property Not Capable of Being Levied on.

§ 8.01-501. Lien of fieri facias on estate of debtor not capable of being levied on.

— Every writ of fieri facias shall, in addition to the lien it has under §§ 8.01-478 and 8.01-479 on what is capable of being levied on under those sections, be a lien from the time it is delivered to a sheriff or other officer, or any person authorized to serve process pursuant to § 8.01-293, to be executed, on all the personal estate of or to which the judgment debtor is, or may afterwards and on or before the return day of such writ become, possessed or entitled, in which, from its nature is not capable of being levied on under such sections, except such as is exempt under the provisions of Title 34, and except that, as against an assignee of any such estate for valuable consideration, the lien by virtue of this section shall not affect him unless he had notice thereof at the time of the assignment. (Code 1950, § 8-431; 1977, c. 617; 1996, c. 1002.)

Cross references. — As to issuance of other executions, see § 8.01-475. As to lien of writ, see §§ 8.01-478, 8.01-479. As to territorial extent of lien of execution, see § 8.01-481. As to homestead and other exemptions, see § 34-1 et seq.

Law Review. — For article on fraudulent conveyances and preferences in Virginia, see 36 Wash. & Lee L. Rev. 51 (1979). For article on the effect of delay on a surety's obligations in Virginia, see 18 U. Rich. L. Rev. 781 (1984). As to scope of assets subject to lien, see 22 U. Rich. L. Rev. 517 (1988).

I. Decisions Under Current Law.
II. Decisions Under Prior Law.

I. DECISIONS UNDER CURRENT LAW.

Execution lien dates from time writ is delivered to the sheriff. — Such lien on intangibles is perfected in that it has priority over all subsequent execution liens. In re Dulaney, 29 Bankr. 79 (Bankr. W.D. Va. 1982).

The execution of a writ of fieri facias establishes a lien on intangibles from the time the writ is delivered to the sheriff. Pischke v. Murray, 11 Bankr. 913 (Bankr. E.D. Va. 1981); Hughson v. Dressler Motors, Inc., 74 Bankr. 438 (Bankr. W.D. Va. 1987).

The lien is created when execution is delivered to the officer. The lien exists from that date. The issuance and service of the garnishment is the means of enforcing the lien. In re Lamm, 47 Bankr. 364 (E.D. Va. 1984).

§ 8.01-501

Where plaintiff had no possessory interest in funds retained by VDOT on August 29, 1994, no lien was established and no garnishment of funds could result. International Fid. Ins. Co. v. Ashland Lumber Co., 250 Va. 507, 463 S.E.2d 664 (1995).

Under Virginia law, the officer is not required to seize the property levied on, but only to have it in his power and note it on the execution. The lien acquired by the levy of the execution is both substantial and enduring, as much so as a mortgage or a pledge. In re Lamm, 47 Bankr. 364 (E.D. Va. 1984).

Execution on intangible property. — In Virginia, a creditor who has obtained a money judgment may enforce that judgment against his debtor's personal property by execution. Execution on intangible personalty, including a chose in action owned by the debtor, is carried out by means of a writ of fieri facias which is issued and placed in the hands of the sheriff. In re Dulaney, 29 Bankr. 79 (Bankr. W.D. Va. 1982).

A writ of fieri facias shall be a lien on all the personal estate of the judgment debtor including intangible, unleviable property. Homeowner's Fin. Corp. v. Pennington, 47 Bankr. 322 (Bankr. E.D. Va. 1985).

The lien of fieri facias extends to all the personal estate of the judgment debtor which is not capable of being levied on, which includes bonds, notes, stocks, debts of all kinds, including a debt payable in the future and includes all choses in action to which a debtor may be entitled. In re Lamm, 47 Bankr. 364 (E.D. Va. 1984).

Execution lien is not effective as against a bona fide assignee or purchaser for value who is without notice of such lien. In re Dulaney, 29 Bankr. 79 (Bankr. W.D. Va. 1982).

Under this section, "the only person who can defeat the fieri facias lien is a bona fide purchaser or assignee for value without notice," and "the satisfaction of ... (the) preexisting execution lien, during the four-month period preceding the filing of the bankruptcy petition, was not a preference." This "means that the Virginia execution lien on intangibles is perfected for bankruptcy when the writ of fieri facias is delivered to the officer to be executed." In re Lamm, 47 Bankr. 364 (E.D. Va. 1984).

The mere issuance of an execution constitutes no notice to a bona fide assignee for valuable consideration, since this section expressly excepts such an execution from the operation of the section. Virginia Mach. & Well Co. v. Hungerford Coal Co., 182 Va. 550, 29 S.E.2d 359 (1944).

Priority of charging order. — Plaintiff did not cause a writ of execution to issue. Instead, it merely sought the entry of a charging order armed only with what may be best described as a "naked" final judgment. Therefore, until a charging order entered, the judgment debtor virtually was free, as against the instant plaintiff, to encumber intangible property, including her interests to discretionary distributions of limited partnerships. A charging order, without more, does not take priority over a security interest perfected after judgment but before the entry date of the charging order. First Union Nat'l Bank v. Craun, 853 F. Supp. 209 (W.D. Va. 1994).

Debts of garnishee subject to this section. — Construing §§ 8.01-511 and 8.01-512.3 together against the background of this section, a garnishment subjects to the execution lien of this section, not only those debts already due the judgment debtor when the summons in garnishment is served upon the garnishee, but also any indebtedness of the garnishee to the judgment debtor which arises between the date of service of such summons on the garnishee and the return date of the summons. Virginia Nat'l Bank v. Blofeld, 234 Va. 395, 362 S.E.2d 692 (1987).

Priority in bankruptcy proceeding determined by sequence of charging orders. — In a proceeding under Chapter XI of the Bankruptcy Act, in which the debtor in possession, a limited partner, filed a complaint seeking a determination of the validity, priority or extent of various liens upon its property, the judgment lien holders obtained priority, if at all, in the sequence in which they were granted charging orders under former § 50-65 by a court of competent jurisdiction, rather than in the order of the dates on which the writs of fieri facias were delivered to the sheriff for execution, in the absence of any evidence that any of the defendants holding judgment liens were precluded from seeking charging orders pursuant to former § 50-65. Pischke v. Murray, 11 Bankr. 913 (Bankr. E.D. Va. 1981).

Trustee's interest in debtor's property. — Although the creditor has an interest superior to that of the trustee with respect to the debtor's property covered by the judicial lien obtained through the execution of the writ of fieri facias, the trustee's interest in debtor's property not properly covered by the lien as of the petition filing date is superior to that of the creditor. Homeowner's Fin. Corp. v. Pennington, 47 Bankr. 322 (Bankr. E.D. Va. 1985).

When lien perfected. — The lien described in this section is perfected against unleviable, intangible personal property which the judgment debtor possesses (or is entitled to possess) at the time the fieri facias writ is delivered to the sheriff or acquires possession of (or entitlement thereto) at any time up to, and including, the return date of the writ. In re Hess, 40 Bankr. 491 (Bankr. W.D. Va. 1984).

When lien ceases. — The execution of a writ of fieri facias establishes a lien on intangibles from the time it is delivered to the officer. The lien, once established, only ceases when the right of the judgment creditor to enforce the judgment by execution or by action, or to extend the right by motion, ceases. Further, as to intangibles, the lien shall cease one year from the return date of the execution pursuant to which the lien arose, or where the intangible is a debt due from or a claim upon a third person in favor of the judgment debtor or the estate of such person, one year from the final determination of the amount owed to the judgment debtor. In re Lamm, 47 Bankr. 364 (E.D. Va. 1984).

If creditor's lien is extant under state law prior to commencement of bankruptcy, the lien remains viable even if under the terms of the law creating the lien it would expire absent some action of the creditor. For example, the creditor would not be obliged to seek relief from the stay in order to seek a new writ of fieri facias to keep the lien in effect. Thus, the lien of fieri facias remains viable during the pendency of the bankruptcy proceedings. Homeowner's Fin. Corp. v. Pennington, 47 Bankr. 322 (Bankr. E.D. Va. 1985).

Applied in Johnston Mem. Hosp. v. Hess, 44 Bankr. 598 (W.D. Va. 1984); Canfield v. Simpson (In re Jones), 47 Bankr. 786 (Bankr. E.D. Va. 1985); Official Comm. of Unsecured Creditors ex rel. S. Galeski Optical Co. v. Estate of Galeski, 169 Bankr. 360 (Bankr. E.D. Va. 1994); In re Andrews, 210 Bankr. 719 (Bankr. E.D. Va. 1997).

II. DECISIONS UNDER PRIOR LAW.

Editor's note. — The cases cited below were decided under corresponding provisions of former law. The term "this section," as used below, refers to former provisions.

The general lien of fieri facias was intended as a substitute for the writ of capias ad satisfaciendum by which the judgment creditor could reach the unleviable property of an insolvent debtor. In re Acorn Elec. Supply, Inc., 348 F. Supp. 277 (E.D. Va. 1972).

Validity of lien. — Since attachment liens are valid in Virginia for the purposes of bankruptcy, then liens by writ of fieri facias must also be valid because a prior existing fieri facias lien will defeat a subsequent attachment lien. In re Acorn Elec. Supply, Inc., 348 F. Supp. 277 (E.D. Va. 1972).

Lien begins from the time the writ is delivered to the sheriff for execution, the same as the lien under § 8.01-478. Charron & Co. v. Boswell, 59 Va. (18 Gratt.) 216 (1868); Frayser v. Richmond & A.R.R., 81 Va. 388 (1886).

The Virginia execution lien on intangibles is perfected for bankruptcy when the writ of fieri facias is delivered to the officer to be executed. In re Acorn Elec. Supply, Inc., 348 F. Supp. 277 (E.D. Va. 1972).

Fieri facias lien and attachment lien take effect at different times. — The two Code chapters dealing with garnishment in aid of the fieri facias lien on unleviable property and garnishment by attachment lien provide for their taking effect at different times. In re Acorn Elec. Supply, Inc., 348 F. Supp. 277 (E.D. Va. 1972).

The remedy afforded by garnishment was designed simply to enforce this lien of execution. The lien itself is as complete and perfect without it and with it. It continues in full force, although the creditor should never resort to that remedy. In re Acorn Elec. Supply, Inc., 348 F. Supp. 277 (E.D. Va. 1972).

Property subject to lien. — Speaking generally, this lien extends to such things as are not affected by the lien under §§ 8.01-478 and 8.01-479. Hence, it extends to all the personal estate of the judgment debtor which is not capable of being levied on. This includes incorporeal personalty, such as bonds, notes, stocks, debts of all kinds, etc. A debt which has a present existence, although payable in the future, may be subjected to the lien of a fieri facias, but not a debt which rests upon a contingency which may or may not happen, and over which the court has no control. Boisseau v. Bass, 100 Va. 207, 40 S.E. 647 (1902).

The lien of a fieri facias includes all choses in action to which the debtor is entitled. Evans v. Greenhow, 56 Va. (15 Gratt.) 153 (1859).

Lien on amount due for work done. — Under this section a writ of fieri facias against a contractor, is a lien upon the amount due him by a city for work done between the date the writ was placed in the hands of an officer to be executed and the return day of the writ, although the amount be a percent of the contract price reserved as security for the completion of the work, and is not payable until the work is completed. If the work is subsequently completed, the lien may be enforced. Hicks v. Roanoke Brick Co., 94 Va. 741, 27 S.E. 596 (1897). But see Boisseau v. Bass, 100 Va. 207, 40 S.E. 647 (1902), questioning this decision.

And on a legacy. — Under this section, a lien may be acquired upon a legacy. Baer v. Ingram, 99 Va. 200, 37 S.E. 905 (1901).

But not on interest in a life insurance policy. — The interest of an assured in a policy on his life which has no present market value, but is dependent for its continued existence on voluntary payments to be made in the future by the assured, is not such an interest or estate as can be reached by a fieri facias. Boisseau v. Bass, 100 Va. 207, 40 S.E. 647 (1902).

Nor on wages payable in advance. — If, after service of notice on the employer of a judgment debtor under this section such debtor and garnishee enter into a new agreement of employment by the terms of which the employer is to pay the daily wage agreed upon to the employee each day in advance, such wages paid by the employer after notice of the fieri facias and before its return day are not such debts due the judgment debtor by the garnishee as are subject to the lien of the fieri facias. South Boston Bank v. Johnston, 16 Va. L. Reg. 911 (1911).

Bona fide assignees for value not affected by lien. — The lien of an execution is held not to affect a bona fide assignee of intangible property, for value and without notice of such lien. Evans v. Greenhow, 56 Va. (15 Gratt.) 153 (1859); Charron & Co. v. Boswell, 59 Va. (18 Gratt.) 216 (1868); Trevillian v. Guerrant, 72 Va. (31 Gratt.) 525 (1879).

The trustees and beneficiaries in a deed to secure bona fide debts, without notice, are purchasers for valuable consideration and will be preferred to an execution creditor of the grantor in the deed as to a chose in action thereby conveyed. Evans v. Greenhow, 56 Va. (15 Gratt.) 153 (1859).

Under this section an insolvent debtor may, notwithstanding his insolvency, make a valid assignment of a chose in action owned by him, and the bona fide assignee for value of such chose in action takes title thereto superior to the lien of a fieri facias against such debtor. It is immaterial whether the debtor intended to commit a fraud in making the assignment or not, if the assignee has no notice of such intent or of the existence of the fieri facias, and pays value. Shields v. Mahoney, 94 Va. 487, 27 S.E. 23 (1897).

The mere issuance of an execution constitutes no notice to a bona fide assignee for valuable consideration, since this section expressly excepts such an execution from the operation of the section. Virginia Mach. & Well Co. v. Hungerford Coal Co., 182 Va. 550, 29 S.E.2d 359 (1944).

The lien of a fieri facias has priority over a subsequent attachment. Puryear v. Taylor, 53 Va. (12 Gratt.) 401 (1855).

A prior lien by writ of fieri facias is superior to a garnishment attachment even though the garnishment attachment was served on the garnishee first. In re Acorn Elec. Supply, Inc., 348 F. Supp. 277 (E.D. Va. 1972).

And over a subsequent execution lien. — It has priority over a subsequent execution lien under the same law, even though there has been a proceeding by suggestion sooner than under the senior execution, and this though the executions issued from different courts. Charron & Co. v. Boswell, 59 Va. (18 Gratt.) 216 (1868).

Satisfaction of preexisting lien within four months of bankruptcy not a preference. — The satisfaction of a preexisting execution lien, during the four-month period preceding the filing of a bankruptcy petition, is not a preference. In re Acorn Elec. Supply, Inc., 348 F. Supp. 277 (E.D. Va. 1972).

§ 8.01-502. Person paying debtor not affected by lien unless notice given. — As against a person making a payment to the judgment debtor, the lien referred to in § 8.01-501 shall not affect him, unless and until he be given written notice thereof setting forth (i) the name of the person against whom obtained, (ii) by whom obtained, (iii) the amount and costs of the judgment, (iv) the date recovered, (v) the date of the issuance or renewal of execution thereon, (vi) the return day of execution, and (vii) the date of placing of the execution in the hands of the officer or other person authorized to serve process pursuant to § 8.01-293, and unless such notice shall be personally signed by the plaintiff or his attorney and shall have been duly served upon the person making payment and the judgment debtor by an officer authorized to serve civil process. (Code 1950, § 8-432; 1954, c. 615; 1977, c. 617; 1996, c. 1002.)

I. DECISIONS UNDER PRIOR LAW.

Editor's note. — The case cited below was decided under corresponding provisions of former law. The term "this section," as used below, refers to former provisions.

Payment by sub-debtor without notice is good. — A payment to the execution debtor by his debtor in good faith without notice is good against the execution creditor. See Evans v. Greenhow, 56 Va. (15 Gratt.) 153 (1859).

§ 8.01-502.1. Serving notice of lien on financial institution. — No judgment creditor or attorney for a judgment creditor shall have a notice of lien served on a financial institution under § 8.01-502 unless such judgment creditor or attorney has a reasonable basis for believing that the judgment debtor is entitled to a payment from such institution. The fact that a financial institution is doing business in a geographic area where the judgment debtor resides, works or has a place of business is not, by itself, a reasonable basis for believing that the judgment debtor is entitled to a payment from a financial institution. Any person violating this section shall be liable to a financial institution for the sum of $100 for each notice of lien wrongfully served on such institution. In any action at law to recover an amount due hereunder, the judgment creditor or attorney for the judgment creditor causing the notice of lien to be served on the financial institution shall have the burden of showing a reasonable basis for believing that the judgment debtor was entitled to a payment from such institution.

A financial institution served with a valid notice of lien shall provide a written response to the judgment creditor or attorney for the judgment creditor within twenty-one days after being served with such notice of lien indicating the amount of money held by the financial institution pursuant to the notice of lien. (1997, c. 750; 1999, c. 48.)

The 1999 amendment inserted the second paragraph.

§ 8.01-503. **Withholding of wages or salary not required by preceding sections unless garnishment process served.** — Nothing contained in §§ 8.01-501 and 8.01-502 shall have the effect of requiring any employer paying wages or salary to an employee to withhold any part of such wages or salary unless and until such employer is duly served with process in garnishment. (Code 1950, § 8-432.1; 1954, c. 379; 1977, c. 617.)

§ 8.01-504. **Penalty for service of notice of lien when no judgment exists.** — Whoever causes to be served a notice of lien of a writ of fieri facias without there being a judgment against the defendant named therein, shall pay to him the sum of $100, and whoever serves a notice of lien of a writ of fieri facias before the issuance of a writ of fieri facias, or after the return day thereof, or serves or in any way gives a notice of a lien of fieri facias by means other than by service by an officer authorized to serve civil process, shall pay to the named defendant the sum of $100, to be recoverable as damages in an action at law, in addition to whatever damages may be alleged and proven. (Code 1950, § 8-433; 1977, c. 617.)

REVISERS' NOTE

Section 8.01-504 is former § 8-433, the last sentence of which has been deleted as unnecessary. The language "causes to be" has been inserted after the word "Whoever" to clarify the intent of the statute.

Also, the fine has been increased from $50 to $100.

§ 8.01-505. **When lien acquired on intangibles under § 8.01-501 ceases.** — The lien acquired under § 8.01-501 on intangibles shall cease whenever the right of the judgment creditor to enforce the judgment by execution or by action, or to extend the right by motion, ceases or is suspended by a forthcoming bond being given and forfeited or by other legal process. Furthermore, as to all such intangibles the lien shall cease upon the expiration of the following periods whichever is the longer: (i) one year from the return day of the execution pursuant to which the lien arose, or (ii) if the intangible is a debt due from, or a claim upon, a third person in favor of the judgment debtor or the estate of such third person, one year from the final determination of the amount owed to the judgment debtor. (Code 1950, § 8-434; 1977, c. 617.)

REVISERS' NOTE

Section 8.01-505 is former § 8-434 which has been rewritten for clarity. No change in substance is intended. The changes made in the section are in accordance with the case law interpreting its meaning and applicability. (See Baer v. Ingram, 99 Va. 200, 37 S.E. 905 (1901).)

Cross references. — As to issuing other executions, see § 8.01-475. As to quashing execution, see § 8.01-477.

I. Decisions Under Current Law.
II. Decisions Under Prior Law.

I. DECISIONS UNDER CURRENT LAW.

The lien of fieri facias extends to all the personal estate of the judgment debtor which is not capable of being levied on, which includes bonds, notes, stocks, debts of all kinds, including a debt payable in the future and includes all choses in action to which a debtor may be entitled. In re Lamm, 47 Bankr. 364 (E.D. Va. 1984).

Lien ceases when judgment creditor's enforcement rights cease. — The execution of a writ of fieri facias establishes a lien on intangibles from the time it is delivered to the officer. The lien, once established, only ceases when the right of the judgment creditor to enforce the judgment by execution or by action, or to extend the right by motion, ceases. Further, as to intangibles, the lien shall cease one year from the return date of the execution pursuant to which the lien arose, or where the intangible is a debt due from or a claim upon, a third person in favor of the judgment debtor or the estate of such person, one year from the final determination of the amount owed to the judgment debtor. In re Lamm, 47 Bankr. 364 (E.D. Va. 1984).

Effect of bankruptcy on one-year period. — One-year perfection of lien under this section held not converted into permanent perfection by bankruptcy of debtor. See Pischke v. Murray, 11 Bankr. 913 (Bankr. E.D. Va. 1981).

If creditor's lien is extant under state law prior to commencement of bankruptcy, the lien remains viable even if under the terms of the law creating the lien it would expire absent some action of the creditor. For example, the creditor would not be obliged to seek relief from the stay in order to seek a new writ of fieri facias to keep the lien in effect. Thus, the lien of fieri facias remains viable during the pendency of the bankruptcy proceedings. Homeowner's Fin. Corp. v. Pennington, 47 Bankr. 322 (Bankr. E.D. Va. 1985).

Applied in Johnston Mem. Hosp. v. Hess, 44 Bankr. 598 (W.D. Va. 1984); In re Andrews, 210 Bankr. 719 (Bankr. E.D. Va. 1997).

II. DECISIONS UNDER PRIOR LAW.

Editor's note. — The cases cited below were decided under corresponding provisions of former law. The term "this section," as used below, refers to former provisions.

The lien of a writ of fieri facias continues so long as the judgment can be enforced. Hicks v. Roanoke Brick Co., 94 Va. 741, 27 S.E. 596 (1897), overruled on another point, 100 Va. 207, 40 S.E. 647 (1902); Boisseau v. Bass, 100 Va. 207, 40 S.E. 647 (1902).

Quashing of second execution does not suspend lien of first. — A second execution was quashed on a petition alleging that it was issued contrary to an agreement by the creditor before entry of judgment that no execution should issue until a certain time, and was also in disregard of a payment made on the judgment. The first execution was held to be a lien on legacies left to the debtor, and other creditors objected, claiming that the first execution was suspended by virtue of the judgment quashing the second. The agreement not to issue execution being a personal one and there being no mention whatever of the first execution in the proceedings to quash the second, the first was held not suspended under this section. Baer v. Ingram, 99 Va. 200, 37 S.E. 905 (1901).

Death of either debtor or creditor does not affect lien. — The lien of a writ of fieri facias upon the debtor's choses in action, although not asserted in the lifetime of the debtor or creditor is not defeated or impaired by the death of either or both, and this lien may be enforced in a suit for the administration of the assets or by other remedies. Trevillian v. Guerrant, 72 Va. (31 Gratt.) 525 (1879). See also, Frayser v. Richmond & A.R.R., 81 Va. 388 (1886); Allan v. Hoffman, 83 Va. 129, 2 S.E. 602 (1887).

Article 6.

Interrogatories.

§ 8.01-506. Proceedings by interrogatories to ascertain estate of debtor; summons; proviso; objections by judgment debtor. — A. To ascertain the personal estate of a judgment debtor, and to ascertain any real estate, in or out of this Commonwealth, to which the debtor named in a judgment and fieri facias is entitled, upon the application of the execution creditor, the clerk of the court from which such fieri facias issued shall issue a summons against (i) the execution debtor, (ii) any officer of the corporation if such execution debtor is a corporation having an office in this Commonwealth, (iii) any employee of a corporation if such execution debtor is a corporation having an office but no officers in the Commonwealth provided that a copy of the summons shall also be served upon the registered agent of the corporation, or (iv) any debtor to, or bailee of, the execution debtor.

B. The summons shall require him to appear before the court from which the fieri facias issued or a commissioner of the county or city in which such court is located, or a like court or a commissioner of a county or city contiguous thereto, or upon request of the execution creditor, before a like court or a commissioner of the county or city in which the execution debtor resides, or of a county or city contiguous thereto, to answer such interrogatories as may be propounded to him by the execution creditor or his attorney, or the court, or the commissioner, as the case may be.

C. Provided, however, that as a condition precedent to proceeding under this section, the execution creditor has furnished to the court a certificate setting forth that he has not proceeded against the execution debtor under this section within the six months last preceding the date of such certificate. Except that for good cause shown, the court may, on motion of the execution creditor, issue an order allowing further proceedings before a commissioner by interrogatories during the six-month period. Any judgment creditor who knowingly gives false information upon any such certificate made under this article shall be guilty of a Class 1 misdemeanor.

D. The debtor or other person served with such summons shall appear at the time and place mentioned and make answer to such interrogatories. The commissioner shall, at the request of either of the parties, enter in his proceedings and report to the court mentioned in § 8.01-507.1, any and all objections taken by such debtor against answering such interrogatories, or any or either of them, and if the court afterwards sustains any one or more of such objections, the answers given to such interrogatories as to which objections are sustained shall be held for naught in that or any other case.

E. Notwithstanding the foregoing provisions of this section, the court from which a writ of fieri facias issued, upon motion by the execution debtor and for good cause shown, shall transfer debtor interrogatory proceedings to a forum more convenient to the execution debtor. (Code 1950, § 8-435; 1952, c. 699; 1968, c. 599; 1977, c. 617; 1978, c. 66; 1979, c. 225; 1985, c. 433; 1987, c. 182; 1991, c. 463.)

REVISERS' NOTE

Section 8.01-506 is former § 8-435 with minor language changes. The restriction against commissioners causing process to be served outside or contiguous to the county or city for which they were appointed has been deleted. This change is compatible with the issuance (statewide) of process found in chapter 8, Process. General district courts are also authorized to employ similar procedure to compel a judgment debtor to reveal his assets to the judgment creditor. See § 16.1-103.

Cross references. — As to punishment for Class 1 misdemeanors, see § 18.2-11.

Law Review. — For article, "Body Attachment and Body Execution," see 17 Wm. & Mary L. Rev. 543 (1976). For an article on the need for reform of and a proposed revision of Virginia's exemption statutes, see 37 Wash. & Lee L. Rev. 127 (1980).

I. Decisions Under Current Law.
II. Decisions Under Prior Law.

I. DECISIONS UNDER CURRENT LAW.

This section provides statutory authority for trial court to order judgment debtor to deliver stock certificates in his possession or control, including those in a professional legal corporation, so that his interest could be liquidated according to law. Sa'ad El-Amin v. Adams, No. 0282-94-2 (Ct. of Appeals May 16, 1995).

II. DECISIONS UNDER PRIOR LAW.

Editor's note. — The cases cited below were decided under corresponding provisions of former law. The term "this section," as used below, refers to former provisions.

Object of section. — This section enables the creditor to compel the debtor to surrender his estate and to compel any other person on whom there is a liability by reason of such lien, to discharge such liability. By resorting to these means the creditor is generally able to prevent an evasion of his execution lien. Evans v. Greenhow, 56 Va. (15 Gratt.) 153 (1859).

This section is by its terms limited to questions the object of which is to disclose the property of the debtor which can be made subject to the execution or judgment by appropriate orders in that proceeding, to which the debtor and creditor are the sole parties, whose rights are directly involved. Thompson v. Commonwealth, 156 Va. 1032, 159 S.E. 98 (1931).

Section 8.01-612 inapplicable to proceeding to ascertain assets of judgment debtor. — Section 8.01-612, providing that a commissioner in chancery could compel attendance of witnesses, was inapplicable to the special proceeding authorized by this section to ascertain the assets of a judgment debtor. Early Used Cars, Inc. v. Province, 218 Va. 605, 239 S.E.2d 98 (1977).

§ 8.01-506.1. Production of book accounts or other writing compelled. — In any proceeding under the provisions of § 8.01-506, a subpoena duces tecum may be issued for a book of accounts or other writing containing material evidence pursuant to Rule 4:9 of the Rules of the Supreme Court. However, notwithstanding the provisions of Rule 4:9, a subpoena duces tecum issued pursuant to this section may (i) be directed to a party to the case and (ii) be issued by a commissioner and may direct that evidence and any custodians subpoenaed be produced before the commissioner. If the subpoena duces tecum is against a party who is not a resident of the Commonwealth, but who has appeared in the case or been served with process in this Commonwealth, the service may be on his attorney of record.

The provisions of Rule 4:1 (c) of the Supreme Court as to protective orders shall be applicable to proceedings under this section. (1978, c. 339; 1986, c. 249; 1993, c. 267.)

Law Review. — For survey of Virginia practice and pleading for the year 1977-1978, see 64 Va. L. Rev. 1501 (1978).

§ 8.01-507. Conveyance or delivery of property disclosed by interrogatories. — Any real estate out of this Commonwealth to which it may appear by such answer that the debtor is entitled shall, upon order of the court or commissioner, be forthwith conveyed by him to the officer to whom was delivered such fieri facias, and any money, bank notes, securities, evidences of debt, or other personal estate, tangible or intangible, which it may appear by such answers are in possession of or under the control of the debtor or his debtor or bailee, shall be delivered by him or them, as far as practicable, to such officer, or to some other, or in such manner as may be ordered by the commissioner or court. (Code 1950, § 8-436; 1977, c. 617.)

Cross references. — As to method of enforcing judgments on realty, see §§ 8.01-458 through 8.01-465.

§ 8.01-507.1. Interrogatories, answers, etc., to be returned to court.

— The commissioner shall, at the request of either of the parties, return the interrogatories and answers filed with him, and a report of the proceedings under §§ 8.01-506 and 8.01-507, to the court in which the judgment is rendered. (Code 1950, § 8-437; 1954, c. 624; 1977, c. 617.)

REVISERS' NOTE

Section 8.01-507.1 is former § 8-437 with no substantial change. However, the return will not be made by the commissioner unless requested by either party. The proviso which restricts the commissioner's duty to report to the court where only personal property is involved has been deleted.

§ 8.01-508. How debtor may be arrested and held to answer.

— If any person summoned under § 8.01-506 fails to appear and answer, or makes any answers which are deemed by the commissioner or court to be evasive, or if, having answered, fails to make such conveyance and delivery as is required by § 8.01-507, the commissioner or court shall issue (i) a capias directed to any sheriff requiring such sheriff to take the person in default and deliver him to the commissioner or court so that he may be compelled to make proper answers, or such conveyance or delivery, as the case may be or (ii) a rule to show cause why the person summoned should not appear and make proper answer or make conveyance and delivery. If the person in default fails to answer or convey and deliver he may be incarcerated until he makes such answers or conveyance and delivery. Where a capias is issued, the person in default shall be admitted to bail as provided in Article 1 (§ 19.2-119 et seq.) of Chapter 9 of Title 19.2 if he cannot be brought promptly before the commissioner or court in the county or city to which the capias is returnable. Upon making such answers, or such conveyance and delivery, he shall be discharged by the commissioner or the court. He may also be discharged by the court from whose clerk's office the capias issued in any case where the court is of the opinion that he was improperly committed or is improperly or unlawfully detained in custody. If the person in default appeals the decision of the commissioner or court, he shall be admitted to bail as provided in Article 1 (§ 19.2-119 et seq.) of Chapter 9 of Title 19.2.

If the person held for failure to appear and answer interrogatories is detained in a jurisdiction other than that where the summons is issued, the sheriff in the requesting jurisdiction shall have the duty to transport such person to the place where interrogatories are to be taken. (Code 1950, § 8-438; 1977, c. 617; 1983, c. 278; 1985, c. 290; 1986, c. 326; 1999, cc. 829, 846.)

The 1999 amendments. — The 1999 amendments by cc. 829 and 846 are identical, and substituted "admitted to bail as provided in Article 1 (§ 19.2-119 et seq.) of Chapter 9 of Title 19.2" for "entitled to bail pursuant to § 19.2-120" in the third and sixth sentences in the first paragraph.

Law Review. — For article, "Body Attachment and Body Execution," see 17 Wm. & Mary L. Rev. 543 (1976).

I. DECISIONS UNDER PRIOR LAW.

Editor's note. — The cases cited below were decided under corresponding provisions of former law. The term "this section," as used below, refers to former provisions.

The language of this section is mandatory. Early Used Cars, Inc. v. Province, 218 Va. 605, 239 S.E.2d 98 (1977).

Section applies when defendant merely

fails to appear. — While this section is worded in the conjunctive rather than the disjunctive, the contention that the provisions of this section apply only when a judgment debtor fails to appear and answer, and not when he merely fails to appear, is without merit. Early Used Cars, Inc. v. Province, 218 Va. 605, 239 S.E.2d 98 (1977).

This section does not require that notice be given to the debtor that his failure to appear might result in his arrest. Early Used Cars, Inc. v. Province, 218 Va. 605, 239 S.E.2d 98 (1977).

Nor does it require that a rule issue requiring the debtor to show cause why he should not be imprisoned. Early Used Cars, Inc. v. Province, 218 Va. 605, 239 S.E.2d 98 (1977).

A writ stating, as an alternative not provided in this section, that the debtor could end the proceedings summarily by paying the debt, with interest and costs, in the amount specified, did not make payment a condition for avoiding imprisonment, and although the commissioner had the discretionary power to revise the writ to conform more closely to this section, his refusal to issue the writ at all was error. Early Used Cars, Inc. v. Province, 218 Va. 605, 239 S.E.2d 98 (1977).

§ **8.01-509. Order for sale and application of debtor's estate.** — The court to which the commissioner returns his report may make any order it may deem right, as to the sale and proper application of the estate conveyed and delivered under §§ 8.01-506 and 8.01-507. (Code 1950, § 8-439; 1977, c. 617.)

Cross references. — As to rule in absence of specific directions by court, see § 8.01-510.

§ **8.01-510. Sale, collection and disposition of debtor's estate by officer.** — Real estate, conveyed to an officer under this chapter, shall, unless the court otherwise direct, be sold as other property levied on is required to be sold under § 8.01-492 and be conveyed to the purchaser by the officer. An officer to whom there is delivery under this chapter, when the delivery is of money, bank notes, or any goods or chattels, shall dispose of the same as if levied on by him under a fieri facias; and when the delivery is of evidences of debts, other than such bank notes, may receive payment of such debts within sixty days after such delivery. Any evidence of debt or other security, remaining in his hands at the end of such sixty days, shall be returned by him to the clerk's office of such court, and collection thereof may be enforced as prescribed by § 8.01-497. For a failure to make such return, he may be proceeded against as if an express order of the court for such return had been disobeyed. (Code 1950, § 8-440; 1977, c. 617.)

Cross references. — As to sale of real estate on executions of debts due the Commonwealth, see §§ 8.01-201 et seq. As to disposition of money, see §§ 8.01-373, 8.01-482, 8.01-499. As to conveyance of property disclosed by interrogatories, see § 8.01-507.

ARTICLE 7.

Garnishment.

§ **8.01-511. Institution of garnishment proceedings.** — On a suggestion by the judgment creditor that, by reason of the lien of his writ of fieri facias, there is a liability on any person other than the judgment debtor or that there is in the hands of some person in his capacity as personal representative of some decedent a sum of money to which a judgment debtor is or may be entitled as creditor or distributee of such decedent, upon which sum when determined such writ of fieri facias is a lien, a summons in the form prescribed by § 8.01-512.3 may (i) be sued out of the clerk's office of the court from which an execution on the judgment is issued so long as the judgment shall remain enforceable as provided in § 8.01-251, (ii) be sued out of the clerk's office to which an execution issued thereon has been returned as provided in § 16.1-99 against such person, or (iii) be sued out of the clerk's office from which an execution issued as provided in § 16.1-278.18. The summons and the notice and claim for exemption form required pursuant to § 8.01-512.4 shall be served on the garnishee, and shall be served on the judgment debtor promptly after service on the garnishee. Service on the judgment debtor and the garnishee shall be made pursuant to subdivision 1 or 2 of § 8.01-296. When making an application for garnishment, the judgment creditor shall set forth on the suggestion for summons in garnishment the last known address of the judgment debtor, and shall furnish the clerk, if service is to be made by the sheriff, or shall furnish any other person making service with an envelope, with first-class postage attached, addressed to such address. A copy of the summons and the notice and claim for exemptions form required under § 8.01-512.4 shall be sent by the clerk to the sheriff or provided by the judgment creditor to the person making service, with the process to be served. Promptly after service on the garnishee, the person making service shall mail such envelope by first-class mail to the judgment debtor at his last known address. If the person making service is unable to serve the judgment debtor pursuant to subdivision 1 of § 8.01-296, such mailing shall satisfy the mailing requirements of subdivision 2 b of § 8.01-296. The person making service shall note on his return the date of such mailing which, with the notation "copy mailed to judgment debtor" shall be sufficient proof of the mailing of such envelope with the required copy of the summons and the notice and claim for exemption form with no examination of such contents being required nor separate certification by the clerk or judgment creditor that the appropriate documents have been so inserted. If the person making service is unable to serve the judgment debtor pursuant to subdivision 1 or 2 of § 8.01-296, such mailing shall constitute service of process on the judgment debtor. The judgment creditor shall furnish the social security number of the judgment debtor to the clerk, except as hereinafter provided.

The judgment creditor may require the judgment debtor to furnish his correct social security number by the use of interrogatories. However, use of such interrogatories shall not be a required condition of a judgment creditor's diligent good faith effort to secure the judgment debtor's social security number. Such remedy shall be in addition to all other lawful remedies available to the judgment creditor.

Except as hereinafter provided, no summons shall be issued pursuant to this section for the garnishment of wages, salaries, commissions or other earnings unless it: (i) is in the form prescribed by § 8.01-512.3, (ii) is directed to only one garnishee for the garnishment of only one judgment debtor and (iii) contains both the "TOTAL BALANCE DUE" and the social security number of the judgment debtor in the proper places as provided on the summons. Upon receipt of a summons not in compliance with this provision, the garnishee shall file a written answer to that effect and shall have no liability to the judgment creditor, such summons being void upon transmission of the answer.

However, if the judgment which the judgment creditor seeks to enforce (i) does not involve a business, trade or professional credit transaction entered into on or after January 1, 1984, or (ii) is based on any transaction entered into prior to January 1, 1984, then upon a representation by the judgment creditor, or his agent or attorney, that he has made a diligent good faith effort to secure the social security number of the judgment debtor and has been unable to do so, the garnishment shall be issued without the necessity for such number. In such cases, if the judgment debtor's correct social security number is not shown in the place provided on the summons, and the judgment debtor's name and address as shown on the garnishment summons do not match the name and current address of any employee as shown on the current payroll records of the garnishee, the garnishee shall file a written answer to that effect and shall have no liability to the judgment creditor, such summons being void upon transmission of the answer.

The judgment creditor shall, in the suggestion, specify the amount of interest, if any, that is claimed to be due upon the judgment, calculated to the return day of the summons. He shall also set out such credits as may have been made upon the judgment.

No summons shall be issued pursuant to this section at the suggestion of the judgment creditor or his assignee against the wages of a judgment debtor unless the judgment creditor, or his agent or attorney, shall allege in his suggestion that the judgment for which enforcement is sought either (i) involves a business, trade or professional credit transaction entered into on or after January 1, 1984, or (ii) does not involve a business, trade or professional credit transaction entered into on or after January 1, 1984, and a diligent good faith effort has been made by the judgment creditor, or his agent or attorney, to secure the social security number of the judgment debtor.

In addition, the suggestion shall contain an allegation that:

1. The summons is based upon a judgment upon which a prior summons has been issued but not fully satisfied; or

2. No summons has been issued upon his suggestion against the same judgment debtor within a period of eighteen months, other than under the provisions of subdivision 1; or

3. The summons is based upon a judgment granted against a debtor upon a debt due or made for necessary food, rent or shelter, public utilities including telephone service, drugs, or medical care supplied the debtor by the judgment creditor or to one of his lawful dependents, and that it was not for luxuries or nonessentials; or

4. The summons is based upon a judgment for a debt due the judgment creditor to refinance a lawful loan made by an authorized lending institution; or

5. The summons is based upon a judgment on an obligation incurred as an endorser or comaker upon a lawful note; or

6. The summons is based upon a judgment for a debt or debts reaffirmed after bankruptcy.

Any judgment creditor who knowingly gives false information upon any such suggestion or certificate made under this chapter shall be guilty of a Class 1 misdemeanor. (Code 1950, § 8-441; 1960, c. 502; 1966, c. 212; 1972, c. 104; 1976, c. 659; 1977, cc. 454, 617; 1978, cc. 321, 506; 1979, cc. 242, 345; 1980, c. 537; 1983, cc. 399, 468; 1984, c. 1; 1985, c. 524; 1991, c. 534; 1996, cc. 501, 608.)

REVISERS' NOTE

Section 8.01-511 is former § 8-441. Notice to the judgment debtor is still required, but such notice may be given by certified mail sent by the clerk pursuant to affidavit of the judgment creditor stating the last known post-office address of the judgment debtor. Notice by publication is no longer permitted.

Cross references. — As to garnishment of joint accounts and trust accounts, see § 6.1-125.3. As to lien on property not capable of being levied on, see §§ 8.01-501 et seq. As to proceedings by interrogatories, see §§ 8.01-506 through 8.01-510. As to garnishment or execution upon wages and salaries of State, city, town and county officials and employees, see §§ 8.01-522, 8.01-524, and 8.01-525. As to punishment for Class 1 misdemeanor, see § 18.2-11. As to exemption of unemployment benefits from garnishment generally and procedure where funds claimed to be exempt have been deposited with financial institution, etc., see § 60.2-600. As to exemption of workers' compensation funds from garnishment generally and procedure where funds claimed to be exempt have been deposited with financial institution, etc., see § 65.2-531.

Editor's note. — Acts 1977, c. 454, amended

§ 8.01-511

former § 8-441, corresponding to this section. Pursuant to § 9-77.11 and Acts 1977, c. 617, cl. 4, that amendment was deemed to have amended this section.

Law Review. — For survey of Virginia practice and pleading for the year 1975-1976, see 62 Va. L. Rev. 1460 (1976). For article on the need for reform of and a proposed revision of Virginia's exemption statutes, see 37 Wash. & Lee L. Rev. 127 (1980). For note on bank's right of setoff in Virginia, see 41 Wash. & Lee L. Rev. 1603 (1984). For comment "Adequate Protection — The Equitable Yardstick of Chapter 11," see 22 U. Rich. L. Rev. 455 (1988). For survey of creditor's rights, see 22 U. Rich. L. Rev. 517 (1988).

I. Decisions Under Current Law.
II. Decisions Under Prior Law.

I. DECISIONS UNDER CURRENT LAW.

Garnishment is the process by which a judgment creditor enforces the lien of his execution against a debt or property due his judgment debtor in the hands of a third person, garnishee. In re Lamm, 47 Bankr. 364 (E.D. Va. 1984).

Under Virginia law, a garnishment proceeding is a separate proceeding in which the judgment creditor enforces the lien of his execution against property or contractual rights of the judgment debtor which are in the hands of a third person, the garnishee. United States ex rel. Global Bldg. Supply, Inc. v. Harkins Bldrs., Inc., 45 F.3d 830 (4th Cir. 1995).

Debts of garnishee subject to § 8.01-501. — Construing this section and § 8.01-512.3 together against the background of § 8.01-501, a garnishment subjects to the execution lien of § 8.01-501, not only those debts already due the judgment debtor when the summons in garnishment is served upon the garnishee, but also any indebtedness of the garnishee to the judgment debtor which arises between the date of service of such summons on the garnishee and the return date of the summons. Virginia Nat'l Bank v. Blofeld, 234 Va. 395, 362 S.E.2d 692 (1987).

Timely notice requirements of due process. — In order to meet the timely notice requirements of due process, the creditor should be required to provide the debtor with notice simultaneously with or within a reasonable time after the garnishment. Harris v. Bailey, 574 F. Supp. 966 (W.D. Va. 1983).

Due process mandates hearing within reasonable time. — Along with timely and adequate notice, due process mandates a hearing within a meaningful time. Harris v. Bailey, 574 F. Supp. 966 (W.D. Va. 1983).

Garnishment is regarded, not as a process of execution to enforce a judgment, but as an independent suit by the judgment-debtor in the name of the judgment-creditor against the garnishee. Butler v. Butler, 219 Va. 164, 247 S.E.2d 353 (1978).

Issue adjudicated. — Ordinarily, the only adjudicable issue in a garnishment is whether the garnishee is liable to the judgment-debtor, and if so, the amount due. Butler v. Butler, 219 Va. 164, 247 S.E.2d 353 (1978).

The garnishment statute plainly contemplates only a personal judgment against the garnishee. Butler v. Butler, 219 Va. 164, 247 S.E.2d 353 (1978).

Notice of exemptions from garnishment. — The summons served on the debtor is required to contain a list of those essential federal and state exemptions that provide the basic necessities of life for someone in the position of a widow whose social security benefits are her sole source of income. The social security exemption certainly should be included; such benefits provide the bare necessities for many in the society. Beyond this list of absolutely essential exemptions such as social security benefits, the debtor should be informed simply that other possible exemptions from garnishment exist under the law. Harris v. Bailey, 574 F. Supp. 966 (W.D. Va. 1983).

The fieri facias issued on the judgment became a lien when the garnishment summons was issued and served. In re Lamm, 47 Bankr. 364 (E.D. Va. 1984).

The lien is created when execution is delivered to the officer. The lien exists from that date. The issuance and service of the garnishment is the means of enforcing the lien. In re Lamm, 47 Bankr. 364 (E.D. Va. 1984).

Summons in garnishment under Virginia statute is warning to garnishee not to pay the money or deliver the property of judgment debtor in his hands, upon penalty that if he does, he may subject himself to personal judgment. In re Lamm, 47 Bankr. 364 (E.D. Va. 1984).

There being a lien against the funds in the hands of the garnishee, he is merely a stakeholder, and may escape all liability by surrendering the funds to the court for its proper disposition. The garnishment summons itself does not create a lien, but the lien is created by the fieri facias, and dates from the date of the delivery of the fieri facias to the officer. The garnishment is the notice of the lien. For the purposes of bankruptcy, the judgment lien need not be absolute, unequivocal or irrevocable, but need only be superior to the rights of a subsequent judgment lien creditor, and in Virginia, the lien by writ of fieri facias is such a lien. In re Lamm, 47 Bankr. 364 (E.D. Va. 1984).

Social security payments are exempt from garnishment under 42 U.S.C. § 407. A garnishment procedure which permitted a judgment creditor to freeze a social security recipient's bank account without regard to whether it contained social security funds would stand as an obstacle to the accomplishment and execution of the full purposes and objectives of Congress and consequently be invalid under the supremacy clause, U.S. Const., Art. VI, cl. 2. Harris v. Bailey, 574 F. Supp. 966 (W.D. Va. 1983).

Response to summons. — The garnishee is required to respond to the garnishment summons by confessing the amount owed to the judgment debtor or by denying it has any property of the judgment debtor. It may also pay such monies into court as it confesses. If liability or the amount confessed is disputed, the court determines whether the garnishee holds property belonging to the judgment debtor and the property's value. United States ex rel. Global Bldg. Supply, Inc. v. Harkins Bldrs., Inc., 45 F.3d 830 (4th Cir. 1995).

Garnishee not to pay judgment debtor directly. — The summons issued in a garnishment proceeding warns the garnishee not to pay the judgment debtor's money to the judgment debtor, with the sanction that if the garnishee were to do so, it would become personally liable for the amount paid. United States ex rel. Global Bldg. Supply, Inc. v. Harkins Bldrs., Inc., 45 F.3d 830 (4th Cir. 1995).

Judgment creditor not in shoes of judgment debtor. — By act of garnishment, the judgment creditor does not replace the judgment debtor as owner of the property, but merely has the right to hold the garnishee liable for the value of that property. So too in the instant case, where the property is in the form of a contract right, the judgment creditor does not step into the shoes of the judgment debtor and become a party to the contract, but merely has the right to hold the garnishee liable for the value of that contract right. United States ex rel. Global Bldg. Supply, Inc. v. Harkins Bldrs., Inc., 45 F.3d 830 (4th Cir. 1995).

No provision for direct transfer of debtor's property to creditor. — There appears to be no statutory provision for the direct transfer of the judgment debtor's property to the judgment creditor, and where a third party controls the property subject to the writ, a judgment creditor typically must follow garnishment procedures. Dorer v. Arel, 60 F. Supp. 2d 558 (E.D. Va. 1999).

The garnishee can escape all garnishment liability by surrendering the funds to the court for its proper disposition. United States ex rel. Global Bldg. Supply, Inc. v. Harkins Bldrs., Inc., 45 F.3d 830 (4th Cir. 1995).

Motion to quash is not adequate relief for invalid garnishment summons. — A judgment debtor in the position of a widow whose social security benefits are her sole source of income must have an opportunity to assert and adjudicate claims of exemption as promptly as possible after the garnishment. The relief available to the debtor by way of a motion to quash the garnishment summons is not adequate. A few days delay in the adjudication of the exemption claim of a debtor in such a position may well cause severe harm. Too much uncertainty is inherent in such relief. Harris v. Bailey, 574 F. Supp. 966 (W.D. Va. 1983).

Joinder of third-party claimant. — The trial court did not err in a garnishment proceeding by joining a third-party claimant and by adjudicating in that proceeding the validity of the third-party's claim to the fund which was the subject of the garnishment. Holston Int'l, Inc. v. Coulthard, 241 Va. 219, 401 S.E.2d 865 (1991).

II. DECISIONS UNDER PRIOR LAW.

Editor's note. — The cases cited below were decided under corresponding provisions of former law. The terms "this article" and "this section," as used below, refer to former provisions.

Garnishment is a proceeding which exists only by virtue of statutory enactment. Under this article, garnishment is the process by which a judgment creditor enforces the lien of his execution against any debt or property due his judgment debtor in the hands of a third person, garnishee. Lynch v. Johnson, 196 Va. 516, 84 S.E.2d 419 (1954).

Garnishment and attachment by levy distinguished. — The proceeding of garnishment is in many respects similar to attachment by levy, but differs in at least one particular, that is, the creditor does not acquire a clear and full lien upon the specific property in the garnishee's possession, but only such a lien as gives him the right to hold the garnishee personally liable for it or its value. Lynch v. Johnson, 196 Va. 516, 84 S.E.2d 419 (1954).

A summons of garnishment under our statutes is a warning to the garnishee not to pay the money or deliver the property of the judgment debtor in his hands, upon penalty that if he does he may subject himself to personal judgment. Lynch v. Johnson, 196 Va. 516, 84 S.E.2d 419 (1954).

When judgments become liens. — A creditor's judgments do not become liens on a third party's indebtedness to the debtor until the garnishment summonses are issued. First Nat'l Bank v. Norfolk & W. Ry., 327 F. Supp. 196 (E.D. Va. 1971).

The remedy afforded by garnishment was designed simply to enforce the lien of execution. — The lien itself is as complete and perfect without it and with it. It continues in full force, although the creditor should never resort to this remedy. In re Acorn Elec. Supply, Inc., 348 F. Supp. 277 (E.D. Va. 1972).

And garnishment summons itself creates no lien. — A summons in garnishment creates no lien. It is a means of enforcing the lien of an execution placed in the hands of an officer to be levied. In re Acorn Elec. Supply, Inc., 348 F. Supp. 277 (E.D. Va. 1972).

The garnishment summons itself cannot fix a lien on the particular property held by the garnishee. In re Acorn Elec. Supply, Inc., 348 F. Supp. 277 (E.D. Va. 1972).

The writ of garnishment cannot create a lien where a judgment debtor had no right to the property in the first place. In re Acorn Elec. Supply, Inc., 348 F. Supp. 277 (E.D. Va. 1972).

Garnishment merely affords the judgment creditor a remedy against another party, thus further making sure that the right will be effectively enforced. In re Acorn Elec. Supply, Inc., 348 F. Supp. 277 (E.D. Va. 1972).

Section does not operate when garnishee has title. — Personal property fraudulently transferred to a wife by her husband cannot be reached by a summons in garnishment on the wife upon an execution against her husband. The garnishment statute does not contemplate or operate upon an estate in the possession of the garnishee to which he has title. Section 8.01-497 furnishes an efficient remedy, by action at law or suit in equity, for reaching such property; or the execution creditor of the husband may levy on the property as that of the husband, and, upon proper proceedings had, have it sold, or the title thereto tried. Freitas v. Griffith, 112 Va. 343, 71 S.E. 531 (1911).

Property subject to garnishment. — An order from a person to whom money is due or to become due, on the person in whose hands or under whose control it may be, to pay to the payee, constitutes an equitable assignment, and the fund cannot be garnished at suit of the assignor's creditors. Mack Mfg. Co. v. Smoot & Co., 102 Va. 724, 47 S.E. 859 (1904).

Claim of judgment debtor against garnishee must be certain and absolute. — In a garnishment proceeding the claim of the judgment debtor against the garnishee must be certain and absolute, because our statutes do not authorize a court of law, in a mere side issue growing out of a garnishment proceeding, to exercise the intricate and complicated duties of a chancellor. Lynch v. Johnson, 196 Va. 516, 84 S.E.2d 419 (1954).

Judgment creditor can acquire no greater right against garnishee than debtor himself possesses. — A proceeding in garnishment is substantially an action at law by the judgment debtor in the name of the judgment creditor against the garnishee, and therefore the judgment creditor stands upon no higher ground than the judgment debtor and can acquire no greater right than such debtor himself possesses. Lynch v. Johnson, 196 Va. 516, 84 S.E.2d 419 (1954).

No liability on insurance company to judgment creditor, where debtor's policy contained no action clause. — Where a judgment against a defendant for damages caused by an automobile accident was returned "no effects," the judgment creditor could not collect from an insurance company by garnishment under this section on an alias execution, where the insurance contract contained the usual "no action clause." Combs v. Hunt, 140 Va. 627, 125 S.E. 661 (1924).

Setoff proper. — The note of an employee payable to a partnership is a valid setoff against any claim against it for his services, whether asserted by the employee or his creditors. Beale v. Hall, 97 Va. 383, 34 S.E. 53 (1899).

Applied in Union Indem. Co. v. Small, 153 Va. 458, 163 S.E. 685 (1930).

§§ 8.01-512, 8.01-512.1: Repealed by Acts 1983, c. 399.

Cross references. — For present provisions as to the form of a garnishment summons, see § 8.01-512.3.

§ 8.01-512.2. Fee for garnishee-employers.

— Garnishee-employers may charge and collect a fee of up to ten dollars from a judgment-debtor employee on account of such employers' expense in processing each garnishment summons served on such employers on account of the judgment-debtor employee. (1980, c. 537; 1994, c. 664.)

§ 8.01-512.3. **Form of garnishment summons.** — Any garnishment issued pursuant to § 8.01-511 shall be in the following form:
(a) Front side of summons:
GARNISHMENT SUMMONS
(Court Name)
(Name, address and telephone number of judgment creditor except that when the judgment creditor's attorney's name, address and telephone number appear on the summons, only the creditor's name shall be used.)
(Name, address and telephone number of judgment creditor's attorney)
(Name, street address and social security number of judgment debtor)
(Name and street address of garnishee)
.... Hearing Date and Time

MAXIMUM PORTION OF DISPOSABLE EARNINGS SUBJECT TO GARNISHMENT	STATEMENT	
	Judgment Principal	$...
	Credits	$...
	Interest	$...
☐ Support	Judgment Costs	$...
☐ 50% ☐ 55% ☐ 60% ☐ 65%	Attorney's Fees	$...
(if not specified, then 50%)	Garnishment Costs	$...
☐ state taxes, 100%		
If none of the above is checked, then § 34-29 (a) applies.	TOTAL BALANCE DUE The garnishee shall rely on this amount.	$...

....
Date of Judgment

TO ANY AUTHORIZED OFFICER: You are hereby commanded to serve this summons on the judgment debtor and the garnishee.

TO THE GARNISHEE: You are hereby commanded to
(1) File a written answer with this court, or
(2) Deliver payment to this court, or
(3) Appear before this court on the return date and time shown on this summons to answer the Suggestion for Summons in Garnishment of the judgment creditor that, by reason of the lien of writ of fieri facias, there is a liability as shown in the statement upon the garnishee.

As garnishee, you shall withhold from the judgment debtor any sums of money to which the judgment debtor is or may be entitled from you during the period between the date of service of this summons on you and the date for your appearance in court, subject to the following limitations:

(1) The maximum amount which may be garnished is the "TOTAL BALANCE DUE" as shown on this summons.

(2) If the sums of money being garnished are earnings of the judgment debtor, then the provision of "MAXIMUM PORTION OF DISPOSABLE EARNINGS SUBJECT TO GARNISHMENT" shall apply.

If a garnishment summons is served on an employer having 1,000 or more employees, then money to which the judgment debtor is or may be entitled from his or her employer shall be considered those wages, salaries, commissions or other earnings which, following service on the garnishee-employer, are determined and are payable to the judgment debtor under the garnishee-employer's normal payroll procedure with a reasonable time allowance for making a timely return by mail to this court.

....
Date of Issuance of Summons   Clerk
....
Date of delivery of writ of fieri facias to sheriff if different from date of issuance of this summons.

(b) A plain language interpretation of § 34-29 shall appear on the reverse side of the summons as follows:

"The following statement is not the law but is an interpretation of the law which is intended to assist those who must respond to this garnishment. You may rely on this only for general guidance because the law itself is the final word. (Read the law, § 34-29 of the Code of Virginia, for a full explanation. A copy of § 34-29 is available at the clerk's office. If you do not understand the law, call a lawyer for help.)

An employer may take as much as 25 percent of an employee's disposable earnings to satisfy this garnishment. But if an employee makes the minimum wage or less for his week's earnings, the employee will ordinarily get to keep 30 times the minimum hourly wage."

But an employer may withhold a different amount of money from that above if:

(1) The employee must pay child support or spousal support and was ordered to do so by a court procedure or other legal procedure. No more than 65 percent of an employee's earnings may be withheld for support;

(2) Money is withheld by order of a bankruptcy court; or

(3) Money is withheld for a tax debt.

"Disposable earnings" means the money an employee makes after taxes and after other amounts required by law to be withheld are satisfied. Earnings can be salary, hourly wages, commissions, bonuses or otherwise, whether paid directly to the employee or not. After those earnings are in the bank for 30 days, they are not considered earnings any more.

If an employee tries to transfer, assign or in any way give his earnings to another person to avoid the garnishment, it will not be legal; earnings are still earnings.

An employee cannot be fired because he is garnished for one debt.

Financial institutions that receive an employee's paycheck by direct deposit do not have to determine what part of a person's earnings can be garnished. (1983, c. 399; 1994, c. 40; 1995, c. 379; 1996, c. 1051.)

Editor's note. — The plain language interpretation of § 34-29 set out in subsection (b) of this section does not reflect changes made by Acts 1996, c. 330 to current subdivision (d) (1) of § 34-29. That act inserted "payments to an independent contractor" in the definition of "earnings," and deleted "provided, that in no event shall funds that have been deposited by or for an individual for more than thirty days be considered earnings" from that definition. While Acts 1996, c. 330 eliminated language which excepted "funds that have been deposited by or for an individual for more than thirty days" from the term "earnings" under the plain language interpretation in § 34-29, the term "disposable earnings" as used in the form provided for in this section and as defined in subsection (b) thereof does not reflect the change made by Acts 1996, c. 330 to the substantive law in § 34-29.

Law Review. — As to scope of assets subject to lien, see 22 U. Rich. L. Rev. 517 (1988).

I. DECISIONS UNDER CURRENT LAW.

Debts of garnishee subject to § 8.01-501. — Construing § 8.01-511 and this section together against the background of § 8.01-501, a garnishment subjects to the execution lien of § 8.01-501, not only those debts already due the judgment debtor when the summons in garnishment is served upon the garnishee, but also any indebtedness of the garnishee to the judgment debtor which arises between the date of service of such summons on the garnishee and the return date of the summons. Virginia Nat'l Bank v. Blofeld, 234 Va. 395, 362 S.E.2d 692 (1987).

Information on possible exemptions required by due process. — Due process requires that the garnishment summons include some information on possible exemptions as well as the process for contesting the garnishment. Harris v. Bailey, 574 F. Supp. 966 (W.D. Va. 1983).

But all possible exemptions need not be listed. — Actual notice of all available exemptions is not likely to increase the probability of the debtor's correcting an erroneous deprivation. Such a potentially confusing laundry list is not required by due process. The complex myriad of state and federal exemptions therefore is not required to be set out on the summons. Rather, what is required is that the summons served on the debtor contain a list of those essential federal and state exemptions that provide the basic necessities of life for someone in the position of a widow whose social security benefits are her sole source of income. The social security exemption certainly should be included; such benefits provide the bare necessities for many in the society. Beyond this list of absolutely essential exemptions such as social security benefits, the debtor should be informed simply that other possible exemptions from garnishment exist under the law. Harris v. Bailey, 574 F. Supp. 966 (W.D. Va. 1983).

Validity of lien. — A garnishment of funds or other intangible property cannot proceed without a valid lien on that property by writ of fieri facias. International Fid. Ins. Co. v. Ashland Lumber Co., 250 Va. 507, 463 S.E.2d 664 (1995).

Lien not established. — Where plaintiff had no possessory interest in funds retained by VDOT on August 29, 1994, no lien was established and no garnishment of funds could result. International Fid. Ins. Co. v. Ashland Lumber Co., 250 Va. 507, 463 S.E.2d 664 (1995).

§ **8.01-512.4. Notice of exemptions from garnishment.** — No summons in garnishment shall be issued or served unless a notice of exemptions and claim for exemption form are attached. The notice shall contain the following statement:

NOTICE TO JUDGMENT DEBTOR
HOW TO CLAIM EXEMPTIONS FROM GARNISHMENT

The attached Summons in Garnishment has been issued on request of a creditor who holds a judgment against you. The Summons may cause your property or wages to be held or taken to pay the judgment.

The law provides that certain property and wages cannot be taken in garnishment. Such property is said to be exempted. A summary of some of the major exemptions is set forth in the request for hearing form. There is no exemption solely because you are having difficulty paying your debts.

If you claim an exemption, you should (i) fill out the claim for exemption form and (ii) deliver or mail the form to the clerk's office of this court. You have a right to a hearing within seven business days from the date you file your claim with the court. If the creditor is asking that your wages be withheld, the method of computing the amount of wages which are exempt from garnishment by law is indicated on the Summons in Garnishment attached. You do not need to file a claim for exemption to receive this exemption, but if you believe the wrong amount is being withheld you may file a claim for exemption.

On the day of the hearing you should come to court ready to explain why your property is exempted, and you should bring any documents which may help you prove your case. If you do not come to court at the designated time and prove that your property is exempt, you may lose some of your rights.

It may be helpful to you to seek the advice of an attorney in this matter.
REQUEST FOR HEARING-GARNISHMENT EXEMPTION CLAIM
I claim that the exemption(s) from garnishment which are checked below apply in this case:
MAJOR EXEMPTIONS UNDER FEDERAL AND STATE LAW
 . . . . 1. Social Security benefits and Supplemental Security Income (SSI) (42 U.S.C. § 407).
 . . . . 2. Veterans' benefits (38 U.S.C. § 3101).
 . . . . 3. Federal civil service retirement benefits (5 U.S.C. § 8346).
 . . . . 4. Annuities to survivors of federal judges (28 U.S.C. § 376(n)).
 . . . . 5. Longshoremen and Harborworkers Compensation Act (33 U.S.C. § 916).
 . . . . 6. Black lung benefits.
Exemptions listed under 1 through 6 above may not be applicable in child support and alimony cases (42 U.S.C. § 659).
 . . . . 7. Seaman's, master's or fisherman's wages, except for child support or spousal support and maintenance (46 U.S.C. § 1109).

.... 8. Unemployment compensation benefits (§ 60.2-600, Code of Virginia).
This exemption may not be applicable in child support cases (§ 60.2-608, Code of Virginia).
.... 9. Portions or amounts of wages subject to garnishment (§ 34-29, Code of Virginia).
.... 10. Public assistance payments (§ 63.1-88, Code of Virginia).
.... 11. Homestead exemption of $5,000 in cash (§ 34-4, Code of Virginia). This exemption may not be available in certain cases, such as payment of rent or services of a laborer or mechanic (§ 34-5, Code of Virginia).
.... 12. Property of disabled veterans — additional $2,000 cash (§ 34-4.1, Code of Virginia).
.... 13. Workers' Compensation benefits (§ 65.2-531, Code of Virginia).
.... 14. Growing crops (§ 8.01-489, Code of Virginia).
.... 15. Benefits from group life insurance policies (§ 38.2-3339, Code of Virginia).
.... 16. Proceeds from industrial sick benefits insurance (§ 38.2-3549, Code of Virginia).
.... 17. Assignments of certain salary and wages (§ 55-165, Code of Virginia).
.... 18. Benefits for victims of crime (§ 19.2-368.12, Code of Virginia).
.... 19. Preneed funeral trusts (§ 54.1-2823, Code of Virginia).
.... 20. Certain retirement benefits (§ 34-34, Code of Virginia).
.... 21. Other (describe exemption): $ ....
I request a court hearing to decide the validity of my claim. Notice of the hearing should be given me at:

....
(address)   (telephone no.)

The statements made in this request are true to the best of my knowledge and belief.

....
(date)   (signature of judgment debtor)

(1984, c. 1; 1986, c. 489; 1989, c. 684; 1994, c. 40.)

§ 8.01-512.5. **Hearing on claim of exemption from garnishment.** — A judgment debtor shall have the right to a hearing on his claim of exemption from garnishment no later than seven business days from the date that the claim is filed with the court.

The clerk shall notify the parties of the date, time and place of the hearing and the exemption being claimed. The garnishee shall comply with the garnishment summons unless and until ordered otherwise in writing by the court. The order shall take effect upon receipt by the garnishee. The clerk is required to provide a copy of the order or other hearing disposition to the garnishee only if the garnishment summons is dismissed or is modified by the judge. (1984, c. 1.)

§ 8.01-513. **Service upon corporation.** — If the person upon whom there is a suggestion of liability as provided in § 8.01-511 is a corporation, the summons shall be served upon an officer, an employee designated by the corporation other than an officer of the corporation, or, if there is no designated employee or the designated employee cannot be found, upon a managing employee of the corporation other than an officer of the corporation. If the judgment creditor or his attorney files with the court a certificate that he has used due diligence and that (i) no such officer or employee or other person authorized to accept such service can be found within the Commonwealth or (ii) such designated or managing employee found is also the judgment debtor, then such summons shall be served on the registered agent of the corporation or upon the clerk of the State Corporation Commission as provided in §§ 13.1-637, 13.1-766, 13.1-836 and 13.1-928. However, service on the corporation shall not be made upon a designated or managing employee who is also the judgment debtor. If the corporation intends to designate an employee for service, the corporation shall file a designation with the State Corporation Commission. (Code 1950, § 8-441.2; 1974, c. 561; 1977, c. 617; 1980, c. 514; 1997, c. 395; 1998, cc. 723, 737.)

The 1997 amendment rewrote this section.

§ 8.01-514. When garnishment summons returnable.

— The summons in garnishment shall be returnable to the general district court from which it issued not more than ninety days after the date thereof and to the circuit court from which it issued, not more than ninety days after the date thereof. When issued by a district court, such summons may be directed to a sheriff of any county or city wherein the judgment debtor resides or where the garnishment defendant resides or where either may be found and made returnable before the general district court, and shall be made returnable within ninety days at some certain place within such county or city named in such summons. (Code 1950, § 8-442; 1976, c. 659; 1977, cc. 454, 617; 1979, c. 36.)

REVISERS' NOTE

Section 8.01-514 is former § 8-442. The first sentence was rewritten so that the summons in garnishment is returnable to the general district court not more than sixty days after the date thereof and to the circuit court not more than ninety days from the date thereof. This change comports with the return date of executions found in § 16.1-99 and the return period for writs specified in Rule 3:2.

Editor's note. — Acts 1977, c. 454, amended former § 8-442, corresponding to this section. Pursuant to § 9-77.11 and Acts 1977, c. 617, cl. 4, that amendment was deemed to have amended this section.

The Reviser's note under this section accompanied the original enactment of Title 8.01 in 1977. The reference therein to a 60-day period for return of the summons in garnishment to the general district court does not reflect the subsequent amendment of this section in 1979.

I. DECISIONS UNDER CURRENT LAW.

The life of the garnishment summons is 90 days under Virginia law. Thus, if funds are deposited into the debtor's bank account subsequent to the service of the garnishment summons but prior to the return date of the writ, such funds would be subject to the reach of the creditor in garnishment. Canfield v. Simpson (In re Jones), 47 Bankr. 786 (Bankr. E.D. Va. 1985).

A garnishment lien of the type acquired by creditors in Virginia is a transfer by virtue of being an involuntary disposing or parting with an interest in property. Canfield v. Simpson (In re Jones), 47 Bankr. 786 (Bankr. E.D. Va. 1985).

A "transfer" under a garnishment lien on a bank account cannot occur until funds are actually deposited into the debtor's account. Consequently, only those funds present in the debtor's bank account on the date the garnishment summons was served coupled with all other funds likewise deposited more than 90 days prior to the date of the filing of the petition in bankruptcy constitute valid transfers not avoidable by the trustee in bankruptcy as a preference pursuant to 11 U.S.C. § 547(b). To the extent that funds were deposited into the debtor's garnished bank account within 90 days prior to bankruptcy, those funds would be a preference and may be recovered by the trustee for the benefit of the creditors of the estate. Canfield v. Simpson (In re Jones), 47 Bankr. 786 (Bankr. E.D. Va. 1985).

§ 8.01-515. How garnishee examined; determining exemption from employee's withholding certificate; amount due pursuant to exemp-

tions in § 34-29 (a). — A person so summoned shall appear in person and be examined on oath or he may file a statement. A corporation so summoned shall appear by an authorized agent who shall be examined on oath or may file a statement, not under seal of such authorized agent. Such statement shall show the amount the garnishee is indebted to the judgment debtor, if any, or what property or effects, if any, the garnishee has or holds which belongs to the judgment debtor, or in which he has an interest. Payment to the court of any amount by the garnishee shall have the same force and effect as a statement which contains the information required by this section. If the judgment debtor or judgment creditor disputes the verity or accuracy of such statement or amount and so desires, then summons shall issue requiring the appearance of such person or authorized agent for examination on oath, and requiring him to produce such books and papers as may be necessary to determine the fact.

In determining the exemption to which the employee is entitled, the employer may until otherwise ordered by the court rely upon the information contained in the employee's withholding exemption certificate filed by the employee for federal income tax purposes, and any person showing more than one exemption thereon shall be considered by him to be a householder or head of a family.

The employer may apply the exemptions provided in § 34-29 (a) unless otherwise specified on the summons, or unless otherwise ordered by the court. (Code 1950, § 8-443; 1954, c. 379; 1977, c. 617; 1979, c. 242; 1983, c. 399.)

I. DECISIONS UNDER PRIOR LAW.

Editor's note. — The cases cited below were decided under corresponding provisions of former law. The term "the statute," as used below, refers to former provisions.

Statute contemplates personal judgment against garnishee. — Under our statutes garnishment is simply the process by which a creditor enforces the lien of his execution against the effects of his debtor in the hands of the garnishee, and the statute plainly contemplates only a personal judgment in such case based upon proof or rather upon the confession of the garnishee that he has effects in his hands belonging to the debtor. Bickle v. Chrisman, 76 Va. 678 (1822).

When order can be made. — On a summons on suggestion the court can make no order against the garnishee unless he owes a debt to the defendant in the execution or has in his hands personal estate of such defendant for which debt or estate the defendant could maintain an action at law. Freitas v. Griffith, 112 Va. 343, 71 S.E. 531 (1911).

§ **8.01-516:** Repealed by Acts 1983, c. 399.

§ **8.01-516.1. Garnishment dispositions.** — A. If the amount of liability is not disputed and the garnishee admits liability to the court either by (i) examination on the return date of the summons, or (ii) written statement as provided by § 8.01-515 on or before the return date of the summons, the court shall order the delivery of such estate or payment of the value of such estate into court without entering judgment against the garnishee. Should a garnishee fail to comply with the order within thirty days after service of such order on the garnishee, then judgment may be entered against the garnishee.

B. Upon certification by the judgment creditor, its bona fide employee, or its attorney that its claim has been satisfied or that it desires its action against the garnishee to be dismissed for any other reason, the court, or clerk thereof, where the action has been filed, shall, by written order, which may be served by the sheriff, notify the garnishee to cease withholding assets of the judgment debtor, and to treat any funds previously withheld as if the original garnishment action had not been filed. The court in which the garnishment action was filed shall then dismiss the action on or before the return date. (1983, c. 399; 1993, c. 385.)

I. DECISIONS UNDER CURRENT LAW.

Applied in Virginia Nat'l Bank v. Blofeld, 234 Va. 395, 362 S.E.2d 692 (1987).

§ 8.01-517. Exemption of portion of wages; payment of excess into court.

— Notwithstanding the provisions of §§ 8.01-515 and 8.01-516.1, any employer against whom any garnishment is served in connection with an action or judgment against an employee may pay to such employee when due wages or salary not exceeding the amount exempted by § 34-29 unless such exemptions shall have been specifically disallowed by the court and shall answer such garnishment summons by a written statement verified by affidavit, showing the amount of wages or salary due on the return date of the garnishment summons and the amount of wages or salary so exempted, and if there shall be an excess of wages or salary so due over the amount of the exemptions, the employer may pay the amount of such excess into the court where the garnishment summons is returnable, which payment when determined by the court to be correct will constitute a discharge of any liability of the employer to the employee for the wages or salary so withheld. (Code 1950, § 8-445; 1952, c. 377; 1954, c. 379; 1977, c. 617.)

REVISERS' NOTE

Section 8.01-517 is former § 8-445 without substantive change. The language that states the affidavit need not be under seal has been deleted.

§ 8.01-518. When garnishee is personal representative of decedent.

— If the person so summoned be the personal representative of a decedent, he shall answer in writing whether or not there is in his hands in his fiduciary capacity, any sum of money owing to the judgment debtor, and if so, the amount thereof, if the same has been definitely determined, and when it will be payable by him; and if such amount has not been definitely ascertained, the court shall continue the case, with direction to him to thereafter, and as soon as such amount has been definitely determined, report the same to the court, and say when it will be payable by him. In either event, and when the amount so owing to the judgment debtor has been definitely fixed and determined, the court shall direct the disposition of such fund to the creditor of such other person or persons according as their rights may be determined. (Code 1950, § 8-446; 1977, c. 617.)

§ 8.01-519. Proceedings where garnishee fails to appear or answer, or to disclose his liability.

— If the garnishee, after being served with the summons, fail to appear or answer personally, or if it be suggested that he has not fully disclosed his liability, the proceedings shall be according to §§ 8.01-564 and 8.01-565, mutatis mutandis, except that when the summons is before a general district court, the court shall proceed without a jury. (Code 1950, § 8-447; 1977, c. 617.)

REVISERS' NOTE

Section 8.01-519 is former § 8-447. The only change is the insertion of the phrase "or answer personally" which a garnishee may do instead of a physical appearance.

I. DECISIONS UNDER CURRENT LAW.

Entry of judgment. — Upon proof of any debt owed by the garnishee to the judgment debtor, the court may enter judgment in favor of the judgment creditor against the garnishee in the amount of such debt. Virginia Bldrs' Supply, Inc. v. Brooks & Co., 250 Va. 209, 462 S.E.2d 85 (1995).

§ 8.01-520. Payment, etc., by garnishee before return of summons.

— Any person, summoned under § 8.01-511, before the return day of the summons, may pay what he is liable for to the clerk of the court issuing the summons and such clerk shall give a receipt, upon request, for what is so paid. (Code 1950, § 8-448; 1977, c. 617; 1983, c. 399.)

I. DECISIONS UNDER CURRENT LAW.

Applied in In re Lamm, 47 Bankr. 364 (E.D. Va. 1984).

§ 8.01-521. Judgments as to costs.

— Unless the garnishee appear to be liable for more than is so delivered and paid, there shall be no judgment against him for costs. In other cases, judgment under §§ 8.01-516.1 and 8.01-519 may be for such costs, and against such party, as the court may deem just. (Code 1950, § 8-449; 1977, c. 617.)

§ 8.01-522. Wages and salaries of State employees.

— Unless otherwise exempted, the wages and salaries of all employees of this Commonwealth, other than State officers, shall be subject to garnishment or execution upon any judgment rendered against them. Whenever the salary or wages of such employees as above mentioned shall be garnished under this section, the process shall be such as is usual in other cases of garnishment and shall be served on the judgment debtor and on the officer or supervisor who is head of the department, agency, or institution where the employee is employed, or other officer through whom the judgment debtor's salary or wages is paid, provided that process shall not be served upon the State Treasurer or the State Comptroller except as to employees of their respective departments, and upon such service the officer or supervisor shall, on or before the return day of process, transmit to the clerk of the court issuing the process a certificate showing the amount due from the Commonwealth to such judgment debtor, up to the return day of the process, which amount the officer or supervisor shall hold subject to order of the court issuing the process. Such certificate shall be evidence of all facts therein stated, unless the court direct that the deposition of the officer or supervisor, or such other officer through whom the judgment debtor's salary or wages be paid, be taken, in which event the deposition of the officer or supervisor shall be taken in his office and returned to the clerk of the court in which the garnishment is, just as other depositions are returned, and in no such case shall the officer or supervisor be required to leave his office to testify. In all proceedings under this section, if the judgment be for the plaintiff, the amount found to be due the judgment debtor by the Commonwealth shall be paid as directed by the court. (Code 1950, § 8-449.1; 1958, c. 430; 1973, c. 236; 1977, c. 617.)

Cross references. — As to exemption from garnishment of pensions and insurance of certain public officers and employees, see §§ 51.1-124.4, 51.1-510, and 51.1-802.

Law Review. — For survey of Virginia law on municipal corporations for the year 1972-1973, see 59 Va. L. Rev. 1548 (1973). For an article on the need for reform of and a proposed revision of Virginia's Exemption Statutes, see 37 Wash. & Lee L. Rev. 127 (1980).

I. DECISIONS UNDER PRIOR LAW.

Editor's note. — The cases cited below were decided under corresponding provisions of former law. The term "this section," as used below, refers to former provisions.

The object of this section and §§ 8.01-524 and 8.01-525 was to place the wages and salaries of municipal employees and all employees of the State, except State officials, on the same basis as the wages and salaries of employees of persons engaged in ordinary business enterprises. Knight v. Peoples Nat'l Bank, 182 Va. 380, 29 S.E.2d 364 (1944).

Wages, etc., earned between date of fieri facias and return day are bound by it. — This section and §§ 8.01-524 and 8.01-525, authorizing certain salaries, wages or compensation to be garnished, include not only the amount of such wages, salaries or other compensation due at the time the fieri facias is issued, but bind all of such unearned wages, salaries or compensation as may be earned between the date of the fieri facias and its return day. Knight v. Peoples Nat'l Bank, 182 Va. 380, 29 S.E.2d 364 (1944).

Salaries of constitutional officers are exempt. — The Supreme Court has consistently held that the salary of a constitutional officer is exempt from garnishment or attachment. This rule has not been changed by the passage of this section. Hilton v. Amburgey, 198 Va. 727, 96 S.E.2d 151 (1957).

Salary of Attorney General not liable to attachment. — The salary of the Attorney General is of constitutional grant, and of public official right. It is not liable to attachment, to garnishment and upon principles of public policy, it has absolute immunity from detention for debt or counterclaim. Blair v. Marye, 80 Va. 485 (1885).

§ 8.01-523. Service upon federal government. — A. If the suggestion of liability as provided in § 8.01-511 is against the United States of America, the summons shall be served upon the managing employee of the agency of the federal government which is alleged to be liable, or, if the judgment debtor is a member of the armed forces of the United States, upon the chief fiscal officer of the military post to which the judgment debtor was last assigned.

B. If service on the agents identified in subsection A for service of process on the United States cannot be made, then service may be made on a United States attorney or other agent in the manner set forth in Rule 4 (d) (4) of the Federal Rules of Civil Procedure, as from time to time amended. (Code 1950, § 8-441.3; 1976, c. 659; 1977, c. 617.)

REVISERS' NOTE

Section 8.01-523 is identical with former § 8-441.3 except for the addition of the provision specifying the method of service on the federal government which appears as subsection B.

Law Review. — For survey of Virginia practice and pleading for the year 1975-1976, see 62 Va. L. Rev. 1460 (1976).

§ 8.01-524. Wages and salaries of city, town and county officials, clerks and employees. — Unless otherwise exempt, the wages and salaries of all officials, clerks and employees of any city, town or county shall be subject to garnishment or execution upon any judgment rendered against them. (Code 1950, § 8-449.2; 1977, c. 617.)

Cross references. — As to exemption from garnishment of pensions and insurance of certain public officers and employees, see §§ 51.1-124.4, 51.1-510, and 51.1-802.

Law Review. — For survey of Virginia law on municipal corporations for the year 1972-1973, see 59 Va. L. Rev. 1548 (1973).

I. DECISIONS UNDER PRIOR LAW.

Editor's note. — The cases cited below were decided under corresponding provisions of former law. The term "this section," as used below, refers to former provisions.

A municipal corporation may be garnisheed or attached for a debt due to one of its creditors just as a natural person may be. Such a proceeding is not contrary to the public policy of this State. Portsmouth Gas Co. v. Sanford, 97 Va. 124, 33 S.E. 516 (1899).

Salary of sheriff is exempt. — The salary of a sheriff as a constitutional officer is not

§ 8.01-525. Who are officers and employees of cities, towns and counties.

— All officers, clerks and employees who hold their office by virtue of authority from the General Assembly or by virtue of city, town or county authority whether by election or appointment and who receive compensation for their services from the moneys of such city, town or county shall, for the purposes of garnishment, be deemed to be, and are, officers, clerks or employees of such city, town or county. (Code 1950, § 8-449.3; 1977, c. 617.)

I. DECISIONS UNDER PRIOR LAW.

Editor's note. — The case cited below was decided under corresponding provisions of former law. The term "this section," as used below, refers to former provisions.

Sheriffs, clerks of court, treasurers, Commonwealth's attorneys and commissioners of revenue do not hold their offices by virtue of authority of the General Assembly or by virtue of authority of a municipality or county. Such officers hold their offices by virtue of Va. Const., Art. VII, § 4. Hilton v. Amburgey, 198 Va. 727, 96 S.E.2d 151 (1957).

The fact that the county pays one third of the salary of a sheriff does not make him an officer or employee of the county within the definition of such officers stated in this section. Hilton v. Amburgey, 198 Va. 727, 96 S.E.2d 151 (1957).

CHAPTER 19.
FORTHCOMING BONDS.

Sec.
8.01-526. When forthcoming bond taken; property remains in debtor's possession.
8.01-527. If bond forfeited, where returned; its effect; clerk to endorse time of return.
8.01-528. Liability of obligors; how recovery on bond is had.
8.01-529. When bond returned, how endorsed and recorded by clerk; lien.
8.01-530. Remedy of creditor if bond quashed.
8.01-531. In what cases forthcoming bond not to be taken.
8.01-532. How bond withdrawn from clerk's office.

§ 8.01-526. When forthcoming bond taken; property remains in debtor's possession.

— The sheriff or other officer levying a writ of fieri facias, or distress warrant, may take from the debtor a bond, with sufficient surety, payable to the creditor, reciting the service of such writ or warrant, and the amount due thereon, including the officer's fee for taking the bond, commissions, and other lawful charges, if any, with condition that the property shall be forthcoming at the day and place of sale; whereupon, such property may be permitted to remain in the possession and at the risk of the debtor. (Code 1950, § 8-450; 1977, c. 617.)

Cross references. — As to forthcoming bond in interpleader, see § 8.01-371. As to forthcoming bond in attachment, see §§ 8.01-553, 8.01-562, 8.01-566. As to forthcoming bond on award of injunction, see § 8.01-630 et seq. As to distress warrants, see § 55-230 et seq.

I. DECISIONS UNDER PRIOR LAW.

Editor's note. — The cases cited below were decided under corresponding provisions of former law. The term "this section," as used below, refers to former provisions.

The law relating to forthcoming bonds was passed for the benefit of the owner of the goods taken, to enable him, at his risk, to retain the possession and use of the goods, and to avoid the expense of their safekeeping until the day of sale. Garland v. Lynch, 40 Va. (1 Rob.) 545 (1843).

Bonds not conforming to statute may be good as common-law bonds. — To be good as to a statutory bond, bonds must substantially conform to the statutes authorizing their execution. Unless they do so conform, while they may be good as common-law bonds, they are not valid as statutory bonds. Kiser v. Hensley, 123 Va. 536, 96 S.E. 777 (1918).

A forthcoming bond taken under this section and made payable to the sheriff, instead of the execution creditor, as required by that section, does not have the force of a judgment against the obligors herein, under § 8.01-527. The lien given by § 8.01-527 being statutory, the steps which lead up to it must be substantially in accordance with the provisions of the statute which create it. The bond is inoperative as a statutory bond and creates no lien, though it may be a good common-law bond and the sheriff may sue upon it. In the absence of a statute to that effect, a bond payable to one person cannot operate as a lien in favor of another. Lynchburg Trust & Sav. Bank v. Elliott & Co., 94 Va. 700, 27 S.E. 467 (1897).

§ 8.01-527. If bond forfeited, where returned; its effect; clerk to endorse time of return.

— If the condition of such forthcoming bond be not performed, the officer, unless payment be made of the amount due on the execution or warrant, including his fee, commission, and charges as aforesaid, shall, after the bond is forfeited, return it forthwith, with the execution or warrant, to such court, or the clerk's office of such court as is prescribed by § 15.1-80. The clerk shall endorse on the bond the date of its return; and against such of the obligors therein as may be alive when it is forfeited and so returned, it shall have the force of a judgment. But no execution shall issue thereon under this section. (Code 1950, § 8-451; 1977, c. 617.)

REVISERS' NOTE

Section 8.01-527 is former § 8-451. The only substantial change is the requirement that the return of the bond be made "forthwith" instead of the former provision that it be made within thirty days. A corresponding change has been made in § 15.1-80 relating to the duty of officers of cities, counties and towns.

Cross references. — As to where bonds in attachment proceedings may be returned and filed, see § 8.01-554.

I. DECISIONS UNDER PRIOR LAW.

Editor's note. — The cases cited below were decided under corresponding provisions of former law. The term "this section," as used below, refers to former provisions.

Principal may forfeit bond. — It is well settled that the principal in a delivery bond has the legal right of forfeiting his bond by failing to have the property forthcoming on the day appointed for its delivery and sale, which right no court can obstruct. Lusk v. Ramsay, 17 Va. (3 Munf.) 417 (1811).

Equity will treat as a nullity a forfeited forthcoming bond on the execution issued on the judgment whereon there has been a return of "nulla bona," and regard the lien of the original judgment as still subsisting for the benefit of the creditor. Cooper v. Daugherty, 85 Va. 343, 7 S.E. 387 (1888).

Bond not according to § 8.01-526 creates no lien. — A forthcoming bond taken under § 8.01-526 and made payable to the sheriff, instead of to the creditor as required by that section, does not have the force of a judgment against the obligors therein under this section. Lynchburg Trust & Sav. Bank v. Elliott & Co., 94 Va. 700, 27 S.E. 467 (1897).

§ 8.01-528. Liability of obligors; how recovery on bond is had.

— The obligors in such forfeited bond shall be liable for the money therein mentioned, with interest thereon from the date of the bond till paid, and the costs. The obligee or his personal representative shall be entitled to recover the same by action or motion. (Code 1950, § 8-452; 1977, c. 617.)

I. DECISIONS UNDER PRIOR LAW.

Editor's note. — The cases cited below were decided under corresponding provisions of former law. The term "this section," as used below, refers to former provisions.

A judgment can be obtained on a forthcoming bond only by action or motion. Allen v. Hart, 59 Va. (18 Gratt.) 722 (1868).

When action on bond accrues. — No right of action accrues upon a forthcoming bond until the forfeiture thereon has been incurred. Lusk v. Ramsay, 17 Va. (3 Munf.) 417 (1811).

Necessity for filing bond on motion. — On a motion on a forthcoming bond, it is not essential that the bond shall have been filed in the clerk's office previous to the motion, but the bond must be so filed when the judgment is given. Lipscomb v. Davis, 31 Va. (4 Leigh) 303 (1833).

No formal issue need be joined on a motion on a forthcoming bond, as the pleadings may be ore tenus, and the court may pronounce judgment on the evidence. M'Kinster v. Garrott, 24 Va. (3 Rand.) 554 (1825).

§ 8.01-529. When bond returned, how endorsed and recorded by clerk; lien.

Upon the return of a forthcoming bond to the clerk's office in the manner prescribed by § 8.01-527, it shall be the duty of the clerk to endorse thereon the date of such return, and his fee as provided by law for recordation of items specified herein, and to record in a book to be kept by him for the purpose, the date of such bond and of the return endorsed thereon, the amount of the penalty thereof, the amount, the payment whereof will discharge such penalty, and the names of the obligee and obligor to such bond. Such bond, when so returned to the clerk's office aforesaid, shall constitute a lien on the real estate of the obligor. (Code 1950, § 8-458; 1977, c. 617.)

Cross references. — As to fee for endorsing and recording returned forthcoming bond, see § 17.1-275.

I. Decisions Under Prior Law.
I. Decisions Under Prior Law.

I. DECISIONS UNDER PRIOR LAW.

Editor's note. — The case cited below was decided under corresponding provisions of former law. The term "this section," as used below, refers to former provisions.

I. DECISIONS UNDER PRIOR LAW.

Presumption as to return. — There being no evidence that a forthcoming bond was returned to the clerk's office before the day on which there was an award of execution thereon by the court, it will be regarded as having been returned to the office on that day. Jones v. Myrick, 49 Va. (8 Gratt.) 179 (1851).

§ 8.01-530. Remedy of creditor if bond quashed.

If any forthcoming bond be at any time quashed, the obligee, besides his remedy against the officer, may have such execution on his judgment, or issue such distress warrant, as would have been lawful if such bond had not been taken. (Code 1950, § 8-454; 1977, c. 617.)

§ 8.01-531. In what cases forthcoming bond not to be taken.

No bond for the forthcoming of property shall be taken:
1. On an execution on a forthcoming bond;
2. On an execution on a judgment against (i) a treasurer, sheriff, or a deputy of either of them, or a surety or personal representative of either such officer or deputy, for money received by any such officer or deputy, by virtue of his office, (ii) any such officer or his personal representative, in favor of a surety of such officer for money paid or a judgment rendered for a default in office, or (iii) a deputy of any such officer, or his surety or personal representative, in favor of his principal or the personal representative of such principal, for money paid or a judgment rendered for a default in office; or

3. On any other execution on which the clerk is required by law or by order of court to endorse that "no security is to be taken." (Code 1950, § 8-455; 1954, c. 333; 1977, c. 617.)

REVISERS' NOTE

Section 8.01-531 is former § 8-455. References to sergeant, constable and coroner have been deleted. The latter office has been abolished and the former two are embraced by the term "sheriff" as defined in § 8.01-2.

§ 8.01-532. How bond withdrawn from clerk's office. — The obligee in a forthcoming bond, or his agent, may, at any time after the record of such bond is made by the clerk, required by § 8.01-529, withdraw the same from the clerk's office, leaving a copy thereof attested by the clerk. (Code 1950, § 8-459; 1977, c. 617.)

CHAPTER 20.

ATTACHMENTS AND BAIL IN CIVIL CASES.

Article 1.

Attachments Generally.

Sec.
8.01-533. Who may sue out attachment.
8.01-534. Grounds of action for pretrial levy or seizure of attachment.
8.01-535. Jurisdiction of attachments; trial or hearing of issues.
8.01-536. Pleadings in attachment.
8.01-537. Petition for attachment; costs, fees and taxes.
8.01-537.1. Plaintiff to file bond.
8.01-538. Attachment of ships, boats and other vessels of more than twenty tons.
8.01-539. Who made defendants.
8.01-540. Issuance of attachment; against what attachment to issue.
8.01-541. To whom attachments directed; when and where returned.
8.01-542. Issue and execution of attachment on any day.
8.01-543. Issue of other attachments on original petition.
8.01-544. When attachment not served other attachments may issue; order of publication.
8.01-545. Amendments; formal defects.

Article 2.

Summons; Levy; Lien; Bonds, etc.

8.01-546. What attachment to command; summons.
8.01-546.1. Exemption claims form.
8.01-546.2. Hearing on claim of exemption from levy or seizure.

Sec.
8.01-547. Attachment against remainders.
8.01-548. Who may levy attachment and on what.
8.01-549. Restraining order or receiver.
8.01-550. How attachment levied.
8.01-551. When officer to take possession of property.
8.01-552. [Repealed.]
8.01-553. Bonds for retention of property or release of attachment; revising bonds mentioned in this and § 8.01-551.
8.01-554. Where bond returned and filed; exceptions to bond.
8.01-555. When appeal bond given property to be delivered to owner.
8.01-556. Bonds may be given by any person.
8.01-557. Lien of attachment; priority of holder in due course.
8.01-558. Attachment lien on effects already in hands of officer.
8.01-559. Return by officer.

Article 3.

Subsequent Proceedings Generally.

8.01-560. How interest and profits of property applied in certain cases.
8.01-561. How property to be kept; how sold, when expensive to keep or perishable.
8.01-562. Examination on oath of codefendant; order and bond.
8.01-563. Principal defendant may claim exemption.
8.01-564. Procedure when codefendant fails to appear.

§ 8.01-533　　　　CIVIL REMEDIES AND PROCEDURE　　　　§ 8.01-533

Sec.		Sec.	
8.01-565.	Suggestion that codefendant has not made full disclosure.	8.01-571.	When defendant not served fails to appear plaintiff required to give bond.
8.01-566.	Who may make defense to attachment.	8.01-572.	Sale of real estate attached.
8.01-567.	What defense may be made to attachments.	8.01-573.	How and when claims of other persons to property tried.
8.01-568.	Quashing attachment or rendering judgment for defendant.	8.01-574.	Attachments in connection with pending suits or actions.
8.01-569.	When petition dismissed; when retained and cause tried.	8.01-575.	Rehearing permitted when judgment rendered on publication.
8.01-570.	Judgment, etc., of court when claim of plaintiff established.	8.01-576.	Order of court on rehearing or new trial; restitution to defendant.

Article 1.

Attachments Generally.

§ 8.01-533. Who may sue out attachment. — If any person has a claim, legal or equitable, to (i) any specific personal property, (ii) any debt, including rent, whether the debt is due and payable or not, (iii) damages for breach of any contract, express or implied, or (iv) damages for a wrong, or for a judgment for which no supersedeas or other appeal bond has been posted, he may sue out an attachment therefor on any one or more of the grounds stated in § 8.01-534. However, if the claim is for a debt not due and payable, no attachment shall be sued out when the only ground for the attachment is that the defendant or one of the defendants is a foreign corporation, or is not a resident of this Commonwealth, and has estate or debts owing to him within this Commonwealth. (Code 1950, § 8-519; 1954, c. 333; 1977, c. 617; 1986, c. 341; 1993, c. 841.)

REVISERS' NOTE

Section 8.01-533 is former § 8-519. The significant change is expressed in the addition of "rent" to the enumerated claims for which attachment will lie. The legislative decision was made to include rent, whether due or to become due, among the claims amenable to the attachment process, and to eliminate the former special provisions allowing attachment for future rent contained in former §§ 8-566 to 8-568, which have been deleted.

Cross references. — As to necessity of recording attachments as to purchasers, see §§ 8.01-268, 8.01-269. As to attachments of persons, see §§ 8.01-284, 19.2-190. For provision as to indemnifying bonds on attachment proceedings, see §§ 8.01-367 through 8.01-369. As to bail in criminal cases, see §§ 19.2-119 et seq. As to attachments on crops to recover advancements, see § 43-29.

Law Review. — For comment on cumulative remedies under article 9 of the U.C.C., see 14 Wm. & Mary L. Rev. 213 (1972). For survey of Virginia law on domestic relations for the year 1975-1976, see 62 Va. L. Rev. 1431 (1976). For article discussing the constitutionality of Virginia's detinue and attachment statutes, see 12 U. Rich. L. Rev. 157 (1977).

I. Decisions Under Current Law.
II. Decisions Under Prior Law.

I. DECISIONS UNDER CURRENT LAW.

Constitutionality. — Fuller v. Hurley, 559 F. Supp. 313 (W.D. Va. 1983).
Constitutional requirements of due process apply to garnishment and prejudgment attachment procedures whenever officers of the State act jointly with a creditor in securing the property in dispute. Lugar v. Edmondson Oil Co., 457 U.S. 922, 102 S. Ct.

2744, 73 L. Ed. 2d 482 (1982).

Procedural scheme created by statute is product of state action. — While private misuse of a state statute does not describe conduct that can be attributed to the State, the procedural scheme created by the statute is the product of state action. This is subject to constitutional restraints and properly may be addressed in a 42 U.S.C. § 1983 action, if the private parties may be characterized as "state actors." Lugar v. Edmondson Oil Co., 457 U.S. 922, 102 S. Ct. 2744, 73 L. Ed. 2d 482 (1982).

A person acts under color of state law in using attachment procedure set forth in this section. Fuller v. Hurley, 559 F. Supp. 313 (W.D. Va. 1983).

When private party is "state actor" under Fourteenth Amendment. — A private party's joint participation with state officials in the seizure of disputed property is sufficient to characterize that party as a "state actor" for purposes of U.S. Const., Amend. XIV. Lugar v. Edmondson Oil Co., 457 U.S. 922, 102 S. Ct. 2744, 73 L. Ed. 2d 482 (1982).

Attachment statute is not ambiguous. — Virginia attachment statute is as firm and unambiguous as it is constitutionally required to be, given the extensive protection it offers against the prospect of erroneous deprivation. Keystone Bldrs., Inc. v. Floor Fashions of Va., Inc., 829 F. Supp. 181 (W.D. Va. 1993).

Requirements for 42 U.S.C. § 1983 action based on this section. — Where the invoking of this section without the grounds to do so could in no way be attributed to a state rule or a state decision, a cause of action under 42 U.S.C. § 1983 is not stated. Lugar v. Edmondson Oil Co., 457 U.S. 922, 102 S. Ct. 2744, 73 L. Ed. 2d 482 (1982).

Applied in Lugar v. Edmondson Oil Co., 639 F.2d 1058 (4th Cir. 1981); Unidyne Corp. v. Government of Iran, 512 F. Supp. 705 (E.D. Va. 1981).

II. DECISIONS UNDER PRIOR LAW.

Editor's note. — The cases cited below were decided under corresponding provisions of former law. The terms "this article" and "this section," as used below, refer to former provisions.

The chief purpose of attachment proceedings is to secure a contingent lien on the defendant's property until the plaintiff can, by appropriate proceedings, obtain a judgment and have such property applied to its satisfaction. Ross v. Peck Iron & Metal Co., 264 F.2d 262 (4th Cir. 1959).

The procedure under this article is a hybrid. It is neither a formal action at law nor a bill in equity, but a new statutory procedure. It is in the nature of a proceeding at law, but with equity powers where necessary to attain the ends of justice. Winfree v. Mann, 154 Va. 683, 153 S.E. 837 (1930).

Compliance with requirements must be shown. — The remedy by attachment against the estate of a nonresident is wholly statutory, and is harsh in its operation towards the debtor and his creditors, and the proceeding must show on its face that the requirements of this article have been substantially complied with. McAllister v. Guggenheimer, 91 Va. 317, 21 S.E. 475 (1895).

And debt on which action based must be within statute. — In a suit by foreign attachment to subject property of a nonresident, it must be shown that the debt on which the proceeding is based is such a one as comes within the meaning of this section, and not merely such a one as might be established, by a suit for the specific performance of a contract, out of which, if enforced, the debt would arise. Barksdale v. Hendree, 2 Pat. & H. 43 (1856).

Under this section it is only necessary for the attaching party to have a legal or equitable claim to specific personal property, based upon a debt which is due, as well as one or more of the grounds for an attachment provided in § 8.01-534. Ross v. Peck Iron & Metal Co., 264 F.2d 262 (4th Cir. 1959).

Attachment may be had to set aside fraudulent conveyance. — A creditor at large may maintain an attachment suit to set aside as fraudulent a deed conveying real estate, made by his debtor, where both the debtor and his grantee are living out of the State. Peay v. Morrison, 51 Va. (10 Gratt.) 149 (1853).

Attachment lies for claim on contract made out of State. — A claim against a nonresident arising out of a contract of bailment made in the District of Columbia is a claim for a debt for which attachment lies. Peter v. Butler, 28 Va. (1 Leigh) 285 (1829).

Nonresident creditor may maintain attachment suit. — A creditor residing in another state may sue out an attachment in Virginia against his debtor, also residing in the other state, and others residing in Virginia, indebted to, or having in their hands effects of, the debtor. Williamson v. Bowie, 20 Va. (6 Munf.) 176 (1818).

Partner may sue out attachment for partnership debt. — One member of a mercantile house to which a debt has been contracted but has not yet fallen due is competent to make complaint on oath and to sue out an attachment against the debtor. Kyle & Co. v. Connelly, 30 Va. (3 Leigh) 719 (1832).

A guarantor of a debt may maintain a foreign attachment against his principal, before he has paid the debt. Moore v. Holt, 51 Va. (10 Gratt.) 284 (1853).

Claim must be due to support foreign attachment. — A suit in the nature of a foreign attachment cannot be maintained unless the claim asserted is actually due. Unless the bill avers that a debt is due the plaintiff from one who is nonresident of this State, and who has estate and effects in this State, it is demurrable. Cirode v. Buchanan, 63 Va. (22 Gratt.) 205 (1872); Batchelder v. White, 80 Va. 103 (1885).

Unless debtor has made, or is about to make, fraudulent conveyance. — Attachments cannot be maintained on undue debts, on ground that the debtors are nonresidents, unless they have disposed or are about to dispose, fraudulently, of their effects. Wingo v. Purdy & Co., 87 Va. 472, 12 S.E. 970 (1891).

Effect of personal decree on right to attachment. — An attachment was sued out under this section by plaintiff in error, and it was insisted by defendant in error that as the party suing out the attachment had a decree for the amount of his debt upon which he could issue an execution at any time, the trial court had no jurisdiction of the attachment. The affidavit for the attachment stated that the amount of affiant's debt was as shown by a decree in a certain chancery suit pending in the circuit court. The decree was simply referred to as showing the amount due, and no copy of the decree was filed, and no evidence was offered to show that the plaintiff in error could subject the property in any way save by the attachment. It was held that it could not be presumed from this mere reference that the plaintiff in error had a personal decree against the debtor for the amount of his debt. Deitz v. Whyte, 131 Va. 19, 109 S.E. 212 (1921).

Effect of removal to federal court. — Where a judgment at law, rendered by a federal court in another state, was released as a result of fraudulent misrepresentations, and suit was brought in a State court of Virginia, to cancel the release and attach real estate of the debtor to satisfy the judgment, removal of the suit to the federal court by the defendant could not deprive plaintiff of his rights under this section. Miller v. Williams, 258 F. 216 (4th Cir. 1919).

§ 8.01-534. Grounds of action for pretrial levy or seizure of attachment. — A. It shall be sufficient ground for an action for pretrial levy or seizure or an attachment that the principal defendant or one of the principal defendants:

1. Is a foreign corporation, or is not a resident of this Commonwealth, and has estate or has debts owing to such defendant within the county or city in which the attachment is, or that such defendant being a nonresident of this Commonwealth, is entitled to the benefit of any lien, legal or equitable, on property, real or personal, within the county or city in which the attachment is. The word "estate," as herein used, includes all rights or interests of a pecuniary nature which can be protected, enforced, or proceeded against in courts of law or equity;

2. Is removing or is about to remove himself out of this Commonwealth with intent to change his domicile;

3. Intends to remove, or is removing, or has removed the specific property sued for, or his own estate, or the proceeds of the sale of his property, or a material part of such estate or proceeds, out of this Commonwealth so that there will probably not be therein effects of such debtor sufficient to satisfy the claim when judgment is obtained therefor should only the ordinary process of law be used to obtain the judgment;

4. Is converting, is about to convert or has converted his property of whatever kind, or some part thereof, into money, securities or evidences of debt with intent to hinder, delay, or defraud his creditors;

5. Has assigned or disposed of or is about to assign or dispose of his estate, or some part thereof, with intent to hinder, delay or defraud his creditors;

6. Has absconded or is about to abscond or has concealed or is about to conceal himself or his property to the injury of his creditors, or is a fugitive from justice.

The intent mentioned in subdivisions 4 and 5 above may be stated either in the alternative or conjunctive.

B. It shall be sufficient ground for an action for pretrial levy or seizure or an attachment if the specific personal property sought to be levied or seized:

1. Will be sold, removed, secreted or otherwise disposed of by the defendant, in violation of an obligation to the plaintiff, so as not to be forthcoming to answer the final judgment of the court respecting the same; or

2. Will be destroyed, or materially damaged or injured if permitted to remain in the possession of the principal defendant or one of the principal defendants or other person or persons claiming under them.

C. In an action for rent, it also shall be a sufficient ground if there is an immediate danger that the property subject to the landlord's lien for rent will be destroyed or concealed. (Code 1950, § 8-520; 1954, c. 333; 1977, c. 617; 1993, c. 841.)

Law Review. — For note discussing prejudgment attachment in the context of consumer due process, see 14 Wm. & Mary L. Rev. 337 (1972). For note on bank's right of setoff in Virginia, see 41 Wash. & Lee L. Rev. 1603 (1984).

I. Decisions Under Current Law.
II. Decisions Under Prior Law.
   A. General Consideration.
   B. Foreign Corporations and Nonresident Debtors.
      1. Foreign Corporations.
      2. Nonresident Debtors.
   C. Removal With Intent to Change Domicile.
   D. Removal of Property.
   E. Fraudulent Assignment or Disposition of Property.

I. DECISIONS UNDER CURRENT LAW.

Severability. — Were court to find the provision which permits attachment on basis that defendant is a foreign corporation or not being a resident of Virginia is unconstitutional, such provision stands independent of the remaining provisions and severing it would in no way thwart the overall intent of the Virginia legislature in enacting the legislation; all other grounds upon which an attachment could issue in Virginia clearly call for exigent circumstances. Keystone Bldrs., Inc. v. Floor Fashions of Va., Inc., 829 F. Supp. 181 (W.D. Va. 1993).

Applied in Richmond, F. & P.R.R. v. Virginia Cent. Ry., 222 Va. 167, 279 S.E.2d 146 (1981); Hart v. United Va. Bank, 24 Bankr. 821 (Bankr. E.D. Va. 1982); Fuller v. Hurley, 559 F. Supp. 313 (W.D. Va. 1983).

II. DECISIONS UNDER PRIOR LAW.

A. General Consideration.

Editor's note. — The cases cited below were decided under corresponding provisions of former law. The term "this section," as used below, refers to former provisions.

Attachment must be regular on its face. — An attachment against an absconding debtor must be regular on its face, and a defect appearing thereon cannot be supplied by averment. Jones v. Anderson, 34 Va. (7 Leigh) 308 (1836).

Grounds must be stated conjunctively. — Where separate and distinct grounds of attachment are stated, and all are relied on, they must be stated conjunctively. They cannot be stated in the alternative. An affidavit which states that either one or another of three separate and distinct grounds of attachment exists does not state the existence of any one of them, and hence is not sufficient basis for an attachment. Northern Neck State Bank v. Gilbert Packing Co., 114 Va. 658, 77 S.E. 451 (1913).

B. Foreign Corporations and Nonresident Debtors.

1. Foreign Corporations.

Foreign insurance company doing business in State is liable to attachment. — An insurance company, incorporated by the laws of another state and having its principal place of business in that state, which has complied with the laws of Virginia in relation to foreign insurance companies doing business in this State, is not a resident of this State, within the meaning of the foreign attachment laws, and its property is liable to attachment as a nonresident. Cowardin v. Universal Life Ins. Co., 73 Va. (32 Gratt.) 445 (1879).

Lessee of railroad in State does not become domestic corporation. — A Maryland corporation, by leasing a railroad in Virginia from a Virginia corporation with the assent of this State did not thereby make itself a corporation of Virginia. Railroad Co. v. Koontz, 104 U.S. 5, 26 L. Ed. 643 (1881).

Nor does foreign corporation appointing local agent. — A corporation chartered and organized under the laws of another state, and holding no charter from this State, is a foreign corporation, although it has an agent, appointed under the statutes of this State, upon whom process may be served, and the fact that it is a foreign corporation is all that is required by this section to justify the issuing of an attachment against its property. Cook & Son Mining Co. v. Thompson, 110 Va. 369, 66 S.E. 79 (1909).

2. Nonresident Debtors.

Section should be strictly construed. — This section, allowing attachments against absent debtors, is an innovation on the common law, and should be carefully watched and strictly confined to the ground covered by it. Kelso v. Blackburn, 30 Va. (3 Leigh) 299 (1831); Bank of United States, Inc. v. Merchants Bank, 40 Va. (1 Rob.) 573 (1843).

Debtor must be actual nonresident. — A party cannot be proceeded against by foreign attachment unless he is actually a nonresident of the State at the time the attachment is sued out. Kelso v. Blackburn, 30 Va. (3 Leigh) 299 (1831); Long v. Ryan, 71 Va. (30 Gratt.) 718 (1877).

And must have debts or estate where attachment is issued. — The words "in which the attachment is" mean "in which the attachment proceeding is instituted," and not "in which the writ of attachment is levied." Therefore, attachment against a nonresident will not lie where the nonresident has neither debts nor estate within the city or county in which the attachment is issued. Winfree v. Mann, 154 Va. 683, 153 S.E. 837 (1930).

"Residence" defined. — The word "residence" as used in this section is to be construed as meaning the act of abiding or dwelling in a place for some continuance of time. Long v. Ryan, 71 Va. (30 Gratt.) 718 (1877).

There is a wide distinction between domicile and residence. To constitute a domicile two things must concur: first, residence; second, the intention to remain for an unlimited time. Residence is to have a permanent abode for the time being, as contradistinguished from a mere temporary locality of existence. Long v. Ryan, 71 Va. (30 Gratt.) 718 (1877).

Intention to remain permanently is not essential to residence. — While on the one hand the casual or temporary sojourn of a person in the State, whether on business or pleasure, does not make him a resident of the State within the meaning of this section, especially if his personal domicile is elsewhere, so, on the other hand, it is not essential that he should come into the State with the intention to remain here permanently, to constitute him a resident. Long v. Ryan, 71 Va. (30 Gratt.) 718 (1877).

Dwelling in State for indefinite period is sufficient. — One who is dwelling in Virginia with no intention of leaving, being engaged in constructing public improvements under a contract that will occupy him for an indefinite period, is not a nonresident within the attachment laws, although his family lives out of the State. Didier v. Patterson, 93 Va. 534, 25 S.E. 661 (1896).

One who was domiciled in Washington obtained a contract to construct three sections of a railroad in Virginia. He rented out his house in Washington, removed his family to a place on the route of the road, and kept house. Before the work was finished or the time for completing it had arrived, an attachment was sued out against his effects. It was held that he was a resident of the State, and the attachment was quashed. Long v. Ryan, 71 Va. (30 Gratt.) 718 (1877).

Residence once established is presumed to continue until proved to have been changed, and the burden of proving the change is on him that asserts it. Starke v. Scott, 78 Va. 180 (1883).

When residence ceases. — A person living in Virginia, determined to remove to another state, and, in pursuance of that purpose, left the place where he had resided, and proceeded directly to the place where he intended to reside. He was held to be a nonresident of the State in the sense of the attachment law. Clark v. Ward, 53 Va. (12 Gratt.) 440 (1855).

Soldier stationed on federal property does not acquire residence. — A person born and domiciled in another state, who comes to Fortress Monroe, which is within the territorial limits of this State, but under the (then) exclusive jurisdiction of the United States, and remains there as an enlisted soldier of the United States, does not thereby acquire a residence in this State so as to defeat the right of a creditor to attach his property in this State on the ground that he is a nonresident. The mere fact that the State has the right to serve process, civil and criminal, in that territory does not affect the personal status of one resident there. The power to serve process on the defendant is not the test of the right to issue an attachment against him as a nonresident. Bank of Phoebus v. Byrum, 110 Va. 708, 67 S.E. 349 (1910).

The property of a fugitive from justice cannot be attached as that of a nonresident, since he, as a wanderer and fugitive, though outside the State can acquire no residence which would make him a nonresident under the attachment laws. Kelso v. Blackburn, 30 Va. (3 Leigh) 299 (1831); Starke v. Scott, 78 Va. 180 (1883).

Residence of committee controls attachment against lunatic. — In determining the right to sue out an attachment on the ground of the nonresidence of a lunatic, the residence of the committee and not that of the lunatic governs. Sheltman v. Taylor's Comm., 116 Va. 762, 82 S.E. 698 (1914).

Creditor may proceed against nonresident surety. — Where the surety to a bond has removed from the country leaving the principal within it, the obligee may proceed against him as an absent defendant and attach any effects or debts he may have in the State. Loop v. Summers, 24 Va. (3 Rand.) 511 (1825).

Petition for foreign attachment held good. — A petition stating as grounds of attachment that the defendant was a nonresident of the State, and that sums of money of the defendant were in the possession of named codefendants in the city in which the attachment was instituted, measured up to the requirements of this section. International Bhd. of Elec. Workers v. Bridgeman, 179 Va. 533, 19 S.E.2d 667 (1942).

C. Removal With Intent to Change Domicile.

Circumstances showing removal with intent to change domicile. — The circumstances were sufficient to show that the debtor had gone beyond the limits of the State without an intention to return when the process issued in a foreign attachment was served. Moore v. Holt, 51 Va. (10 Gratt.) 284 (1853).

Declarations of intention after date of attachment are inadmissible. — Upon a motion by the defendant to abate an attachment which has been sued out against his property by the plaintiff, the defendant's intention and declarations as to leaving the State after the date of the attachment are not admissible as evidence. Wright v. Rambo, 62 Va. (21 Gratt.) 158 (1871).

D. Removal of Property.

Removal in due course of trade is not ground for attachment. — The shipment of the products of an enterprise out of the State in the due course of trade, where the removal is not permanent and the proceeds are brought back for reinvestment, is not sufficient ground for an attachment. Clinch River Mineral Co. v. Harrison, 91 Va. 122, 21 S.E. 660 (1895).

E. Fraudulent Assignment or Disposition of Property.

Every assignment by a debtor of his property must of necessity work some de- lay as to other creditors in the collection of their claim, but this is not such delay as is meant by this section. Breeden v. Peale, 106 Va. 39, 55 S.E. 2 (1906).

Intent to hinder, delay or defraud is controlling factor. — However difficult the proof may be, even against a purchaser for full value, and although a debtor has a right to sell his property and the creditor the right to resort to the substituted property, if it can be made to appear that a conveyance by a debtor was made by him with an intent to hinder, delay and defraud his creditors and this intent was participated in by the grantee, the transaction comes within the purview of this section relating to attachments, and is void as to creditors. Breeden v. Peale, 106 Va. 39, 55 S.E. 2 (1906).

Intent must be proved. — It is not enough that creditors believe and allege the existence of fraudulent intent. They must prove its existence. Wingo v. Purdy & Co., 87 Va. 472, 12 S.E. 970 (1891).

Failure to record deed of trust is not fraudulent. — The mere failure of a bank to record a deed of trust given by a defendant to secure a note, in the absence of evidence of a request or desire on the part of the defendant that the deed should not be recorded, cannot be construed as an attempt on the part of the defendant to hinder or defraud creditors, and is no ground for an attachment. Burruss v. Trant, 88 Va. 980, 14 S.E. 845 (1892).

Facts not justifying attachment. — When a debtor promised to secure his debt, and violated his promise, and appropriated the proceeds of the property, sold at a fair price, to the satisfaction of claims of other creditors, and his purpose to make that sale was not concealed, the facts did not make out the case stated in the affidavit for an attachment — that the defendant had disposed of, or was about to dispose of, his estate, or some part thereof, with intent to hinder, delay or defraud his creditors. Breeden v. Peale, 106 Va. 39, 55 S.E. 2 (1906).

§ 8.01-535. Jurisdiction of attachments; trial or hearing of issues. — Except as provided in § 16.1-77 the jurisdiction of attachments under this chapter shall be in the circuit courts. The trial or hearing of the issues, except as otherwise provided, shall be the same, as near as may be, as in actions in personam. (Code 1950, § 8-521; 1954, c. 333; 1977, c. 617.)

I. DECISIONS UNDER PRIOR LAW.

Editor's note. — The cases cited below were decided under corresponding provisions of former law. The term "this section," as used below, refers to former provisions.

By this section the legislature undertook to simplify the procedure and practice in attachment, and § 8.01-549 shows that it never intended to exclude the equity practice from the proceedings. The plain purpose was to simplify the form of procedure, and allow the courts to use their equitable or legal modes of practice as would best promote a fair trial and justice. Rust v. Indiana Flooring Co., 151 Va. 845, 145 S.E. 321 (1928).

Court's jurisdiction is limited and special. — An attachment is purely a statutory remedy. The jurisdiction thereof is a special and limited jurisdiction, and a court, even of general jurisdiction, cannot proceed by attachment unless the power rests upon express statutory authority. In order that a court may have jurisdiction to issue any particular attachment, it is not enough that it be a court upon which the statute has conferred the power to use the process of attachment, but, conceding its power to use the process of attachment, the court must have before it a case in which the use of such process is authorized by the statute. Winfree v. Mann, 154 Va. 683, 153 S.E. 837 (1930); Fauquier Nat'l Bank v. Hazelwood Sav. & Trust Co., 165 Va. 259, 182 S.E. 566 (1935).

§ 8.01-536. Pleadings in attachment. — No pleading on behalf of the plaintiff shall be necessary except the petition mentioned in § 8.01-537. The principal defendant, and any other defendant who seeks to defeat the petitioner's attachment, may demur to the petition, issue on which demurrer shall be deemed to be joined; but if such demurrer be overruled, such defendant shall answer the petition in writing. No replication shall be necessary to such answer. The answer shall be sworn to by such defendant, or his agent. Any other defendant may answer the petition, under oath, and the cause shall be deemed at issue as to him, if he denies any of the allegations of the petition, without any replication. Answers under this section shall not have the effect of evidence for the defendant. (Code 1950, § 8-523; 1977, c. 617.)

Cross references. — As to amendment of pleadings in attachment, see §§ 8.01-543, 8.01-545.

§ 8.01-537. Petition for attachment; costs, fees and taxes. — A. Every attachment shall be commenced by a petition filed before a judge, magistrate or clerk of a circuit or general district court of the county or city in which venue is given by subdivision 11 of § 8.01-261. If it is sought to recover specific personal property, the petition shall state (i) the kind, quantity, and estimated fair market value thereof, (ii) the character of estate therein claimed by the plaintiff, (iii) the plaintiff's claim with such certainty as will give the adverse party reasonable notice of the true nature of the claim and the particulars thereof and (iv) what sum, if any, the plaintiff claims he is entitled to recover for its detention. If it is sought to recover a debt or damages for a breach of contract, express or implied, or damages for a wrong, the petition shall set forth (i) the plaintiff's claim with such certainty as will give the adverse party reasonable notice of the true nature of the claim and the particulars thereof, (ii) a sum certain which, at the least, the plaintiff is entitled to, or ought to recover, and (iii) if based on a contract and if the claim is for a debt not then due and payable, at what time or times the same will become due and payable. The petition shall also allege the existence of one or more of the grounds mentioned in § 8.01-534, and shall set forth specific facts in support of the allegation. The petition shall ask for an attachment against the specific personal property mentioned in the petition, or against the estate, real and personal, of one or more of the principal defendants, or against the estate, real and personal, of one or more of the principal defendants, or against both the specific personal property and the estate of such defendants, real or personal. The petition shall state whether the officer is requested to take possession of the attached tangible personal property. The petition shall be sworn to by the plaintiff or his agent, or some other person cognizant of the facts therein stated.

B. The plaintiff praying for an attachment shall, at the time that he files his petition, pay to the clerk of the court to which the return is made the proper costs, fees and taxes, and in the event of his failure to do so, the attachment shall not be issued. (Code 1950, §§ 8-524, 8-528; 1954, cc. 333, 622; 1973, c. 545; 1977, c. 617; 1978, c. 418; 1984, c. 646; 1993, c. 841.)

§ 8.01-537.1   CODE OF VIRGINIA   § 8.01-537.1

REVISERS' NOTE

Section 8.01-537 has made certain changes of language in order to clarify the provisions of former § 8-524, and former § 8-528 has been added as a subsection, changing the reference to "justice of the peace" to that of "magistrate."

Cross references. — As to amendment of petition, see §§ 8.01-543, 8.01-545. As to affidavits by corporations and agents generally, see § 49-7.

Law Review. — For note on bank's right of setoff in Virginia, see 41 Wash. & Lee L. Rev. 1603 (1984).

I. Decisions Under Current Law.
II. Decisions Under Prior Law.

I. DECISIONS UNDER CURRENT LAW.

Constitutionality. — Fuller v. Hurley, 559 F. Supp. 313 (W.D. Va. 1983).

Petition dismissed where debtor was not owner or transferred property before debt arose. — The allegation that the debtor transferred the property to a purchaser "with intent to hinder, delay or defraud its creditor" was groundless where the debtor did not own the property, since the debtor could not transfer that which it never owned. Moreover, even if there had been a transfer from the debtor to the purchaser concerning the property, where it occurred before any indebtedness to the creditor, there could not exist any intent to defraud the creditor. Thus, there was no error in the trial court's dismissal of the petition to attach the property. Allsbrook v. Azalea Radiator Serv., Inc., 227 Va. 600, 316 S.E.2d 743 (1984).

II. DECISIONS UNDER PRIOR LAW.

Editor's note. — The cases cited below were decided under corresponding provisions of former law. The term "this section," as used below, refers to former provisions.

The requirements of this section and § 8.01-539 are plain and unambiguous, and until it appears that its mandatory provisions have been met the court is without jurisdiction to exercise any power over the property sought to be attached. Fauquier Nat'l Bank v. Hazelwood Sav. & Trust Co., 165 Va. 259, 182 S.E. 566 (1935).

And they are mandatory. — This section and § 8.01-539 recognize certain rights of the debtor and enjoin upon the creditor certain procedural requirements which are essentially mandatory for the purpose of safeguarding these rights. Unless it affirmatively appears that such steps were taken, a valid lien cannot be acquired. Fauquier Nat'l Bank v. Hazelwood Sav. & Trust Co., 165 Va. 259, 182 S.E. 566 (1935).

Purpose of subsection B is to insure payment of tax. — The purpose of subsection B is to insure promptly and certainly the payment of the tax, and it has no relation to the right or procedure of the action. Jenkins v. Faulkner, 174 Va. 43, 4 S.E.2d 788 (1939).

Subsection B is not intended to penalize a litigant. Jenkins v. Faulkner, 174 Va. 43, 4 S.E.2d 788 (1939).

Dismissal is in nature of nonsuit. — When an attachment is dismissed ipso facto for failure to pay the writ tax as required by subsection B, the dismissal is in the nature of a nonsuit. Jenkins v. Faulkner, 174 Va. 43, 4 S.E.2d 788 (1939).

It does not extinguish right of action. — The dismissal of an attachment under this section for failure to pay the writ tax within the time prescribed only bars proceedings on that attachment, and does not extinguish the right of action. Senter v. Lively, 160 Va. 417, 168 S.E. 328 (1933).

The word "thereon" can only refer to the attachment, not to the right of action. The latter remains as if no proceedings of any kind had been instituted. Senter v. Lively, 160 Va. 417, 168 S.E. 328 (1933).

Court may allow payment to clerk in open court. — Upon a motion to dismiss an attachment proceeding for the failure of the plaintiff to comply with the provisions of subsection B, it was not error for the court to allow the plaintiff to pay the writ tax to the clerk in open court and to overrule the motion to dismiss. Jenkins v. Faulkner, 174 Va. 43, 4 S.E.2d 788 (1939).

§ 8.01-537.1. Plaintiff to file bond. — A. The plaintiff or someone for him shall, at the time of suing out an attachment or other pretrial levy or seizure, give bond. The fact that bond has been given shall be endorsed on the process, or certified by the clerk to the serving officer. If certified by the clerk, the serving officer shall return the certificate with the process. The bond shall be a bond with approved surety, a cash bond or a property bond.

B. If the plaintiff seeks only pretrial levy on property and a bond with approved surety or cash bond is posted, the amount of the bond shall be at least the estimated fair market value of the property to be levied. If a property bond is posted, the amount of the bond shall be at least double the estimated fair market value of the property to be levied.

C. If the plaintiff seeks pretrial seizure of property, the amount of the bond shall be at least double the estimated fair market value of the property to be seized.

D. The bond shall contain a condition to pay all costs and damages which may be awarded against the plaintiff, or sustained by any person, by reason of a wrongful levy or seizure. (1984, c. 646; 1993, c. 841.)

§ 8.01-538. Attachment of ships, boats and other vessels of more than twenty tons. — No attachment against any ship, boat, or other vessel of more than twenty tons, shall issue unless the plaintiff or someone in his behalf, shall first establish, to the satisfaction of the court in which he files his petition for attachment that he has a reasonable expectation of recovering an amount exclusive of all costs, equal to at least one-half the damages demanded in the petition for attachment. Reasonable notice of appearance before the court shall be given the owner, agent or master of said vessel, and at the time of the appearance the court shall determine the amount of such reasonable expectation of recovery and the amount of bond necessary to secure the release of the vessel if and when a writ be levied in accordance with this section.

No attachment issued in violation of the provisions of this section shall create a valid lien upon the property sought to be attached, and no levy made under authority thereof shall be of any effect. (Code 1950, § 8-524.1; 1954, c. 254; 1977, c. 617.)

§ 8.01-539. Who made defendants. — A person against whom the plaintiff is asserting the claim shall be made a defendant to the petition, and shall be known as a principal defendant. There shall also be made a defendant any person indebted to or having in his possession property, real or personal, belonging to a principal defendant, which is sought to be attached. There may also be made a defendant any person claiming title to, and interest in, or a lien upon the property sought to be attached. A defendant, other than a principal defendant, shall be known as a codefendant. (Code 1950, § 8-525; 1977, c. 617.)

I. DECISIONS UNDER CURRENT LAW.

This section on joining lienholders is permissive. Eastern Indem. Co. v. J.D. Conti Elec. Co., 573 F. Supp. 1036 (E.D. Va. 1983).

§ 8.01-540. Issuance of attachment; against what attachment to issue. — A judge or magistrate of the court in which a petition for attachment is filed shall make an ex parte review of the petition. The judge or magistrate shall issue an attachment in accordance with the prayer of the petition only upon a determination that (i) there is reasonable cause to believe that grounds for attachment may exist and (ii) the petition complies with §§ 8.01-534, 8.01-537 and 8.01-538. The judge or magistrate may receive evidence only in the form of a sworn petition which shall be filed in the office of the clerk of the court. If the plaintiff seeks the recovery of specific personal property, the attachment may be (i) against such property and against the principal defendant's estate for so much as is sufficient to satisfy the probable damages for its detention or (ii) at the option of the plaintiff, against the principal defendant's estate for the value of the specific property and the damages for its detention. If the plaintiff seeks to recover a debt or damages for the breach of a contract, express or implied, or damages for a wrong, the attachment shall be against the principal defendant's estate for the amount specified in the petition as that which the plaintiff at the least is entitled to or ought to recover.

If the attachment is issued by a magistrate, it shall be returnable as prescribed by § 8.01-541. The magistrate shall promptly return to the clerk's office of the court to which the attachment is returnable the petition and the bond, if any, filed before him. The proceedings thereafter shall be the same as if the attachment had been issued by a judge. (Code 1950, § 8.526; 1954, c. 254; 1977, c. 617; 1984, c. 646; 1993, c. 841.)

I. Decisions Under Current Law.
II. Decisions Under Prior Law.

I. DECISIONS UNDER CURRENT LAW.

Constitutionality. — Fuller v. Hurley, 559 F. Supp. 313 (W.D. Va. 1983).

II. DECISIONS UNDER PRIOR LAW.

Editor's note. — The case cited below was decided under corresponding provisions of former law. The term "this and the following sections," as used below, refers to former provisions.

Mere issuance of attachment creates no lien. — The mere issuance of an attachment under this and the following sections creates no lien on the real estate, since, in order to create a lien, it is necessary for the officer to cause his return to show that he has made a levy, and for the return to mention and describe the real property with such substantial accuracy as to cause it to be readily identified. Harris v. Lipson, 167 Va. 365, 189 S.E. 349 (1937).

§ 8.01-541. To whom attachments directed; when and where returned. — Any attachment issued under this chapter may be directed to the sheriff of any county or city. Except when otherwise provided, it shall be returnable to the office of the clerk of court wherein the petition has been filed not more than thirty days from its date of issuance. (Code 1950, § 8-527; 1954, c. 333; 1977, c. 617; 1993, c. 841.)

REVISERS' NOTE

Section 8.01-541 is based on former § 8-527. References to "terms of court" have been eliminated, and appropriate directions for the return have been added.

§ 8.01-542. Issue and execution of attachment on any day. — Such attachment may be issued or executed on any day, including a Sunday or holiday. (Code 1950, § 8-529; 1977, c. 617.)

REVISERS' NOTE

Section 8.01-542 extends the provisions of former § 8-529 to permit the issuance of an attachment not only on a Sunday, but on any holiday, and upon any of the grounds specified in § 8.01-534.

§ 8.01-543. Issue of other attachments on original petition. — Upon the written application of the plaintiff, his agent or attorney, other attachments founded on the original petition may be issued from time to time by the clerk of the court in which the original attachment is pending, and the same may be directed, executed, and returned in like manner as an original attachment. However, the clerk shall not issue an attachment where new or additional grounds of attachment are relied upon or where any ship, boat or vessel of more than twenty tons is sought to be attached.

If new or additional grounds of attachment are relied on, the plaintiff may amend his petition in accordance with Rule of Court 1:8 according to the facts and swear to the same. Except as otherwise provided in this section, an additional attachment as prayed for shall be issued by a judge or magistrate only upon his determination that (i) there is reasonable cause to believe that the grounds for attachment may exist and (ii) that the amended petition complies with §§ 8.01-534 and 8.01-537. Where any ship, boat, or other vessel of more than twenty tons is sought to be attached, a judge or magistrate shall issue the additional attachment only on his determination that § 8.01-538 has been complied with. The cause shall proceed, under the provisions of this chapter, upon the petition as amended.

The court shall adjudge the costs of such attachments as it deems proper.

The following, or its equivalent, shall be a sufficient form of application for an additional attachment:

To A.B., clerk of the .... court of .... county (or city): In the case of .... v. ...., on an attachment, an additional attachment and summons is requested to be issued against .................X.Y. (or X.Y. by H., attorney or agent, as the case may be). (Code 1950, § 8-530; 1977, c. 617; 1984, c. 646.)

§ 8.01-544. When attachment not served other attachments may issue; order of publication.

— When an attachment is returned not served on a principal defendant, whether levied on property or not, further attachments and summonses may be issued until service is obtained on him, if he be a resident of the Commonwealth. If for any cause service cannot be had in the Commonwealth, upon affidavit of that fact, an order of publication shall be made against him. (Code 1950, § 8-531; 1977, c. 617.)

I. DECISIONS UNDER PRIOR LAW.

Editor's note. — The case cited below was decided under corresponding provisions of former law. The term "this section," as used below, refers to former provisions.

Jurisdiction is not acquired by service on garnishee. — Jurisdiction cannot be acquired of the fund attached by service of process on the garnishee, where no legal service of notice is had on the nonresident defendant. Dorr v. Rohr, 82 Va. 359 (1886).

Or by seizure of property attached. — A garnishee in a foreign attachment is not the agent and representative of his creditor, the principal defendant; hence a seizure of the res, or attached fund, is not notice to the nonresident defendant, and cannot give jurisdiction. Dorr v. Rohr, 82 Va. 359 (1886).

§ 8.01-545. Amendments; formal defects.

— Such amendments shall be allowed of the petition, answer and of any of the other proceedings in the attachment as shall be conducive to the attainment of the ends of substantial justice, and upon such terms as to continuance and costs as may seem proper. An amendment when made shall as against the principal defendant and as to claims against him existing at the time the attachment was issued relate back to the time of the levy of the attachment, unless otherwise directed. No attachment shall be quashed or dismissed for mere formal defects. (Code 1950, § 8-532; 1977, c. 617.)

Cross references. — As to amendment of pleadings generally, see § 8.01-273. As to amendment when variance appears between evidence and allegations, see § 8.01-377. For rule of court as to amendment of pleadings after filing, see Rule 1:8.

I. Decisions Under Current Law.
II. Decisions Under Prior Law.

I. DECISIONS UNDER CURRENT LAW.

Applied in Lugar v. Edmondson Oil Co., 639 F.2d 1058 (4th Cir. 1981).

II. DECISIONS UNDER PRIOR LAW.

Editor's note. — The cases cited below were decided under corresponding provisions of former law. The term "this section," as used below, refers to former provisions.

Section is to be liberally construed. — Section 8.01-377 and this section allow substantial amendments in the pleadings for the promotion of justice, and they have always been liberally construed, as remedial in purpose. Russell Lumber Co. v. Thompson, 137 Va. 386, 119 S.E. 117 (1923). See Dillow v. Stafford, 181 Va. 483, 25 S.E.2d 330 (1943); Provident Life & Accident Ins. Co. v. Walker, 190 Va. 1016, 59 S.E.2d 126 (1950).

But it does not destroy effect of §§ 8.01-537 and 8.01-539. — The General Assembly, by the provisions of this section, did not intend to wipe away and destroy the mandatory procedural requirements of §§ 8.01-537 and 8.01-539. If it had been the legislative intent to abrogate the requirements of those sections, and especially the requirement in § 8.01-539 that a party in possession of real estate must be made a party defendant, then surely the legislature would have done so by some express language free from doubt as to its meaning. Fauquier Nat'l Bank v. Hazelwood Sav. & Trust Co., 165 Va. 259, 182 S.E. 566 (1935).

ARTICLE 2.

Summons; Levy; Lien; Bonds, etc.

§ 8.01-546. What attachment to command; summons. — Every attachment sued out against specific personal property shall command the sheriff or other officer to whom it may be directed to attach the specific property claimed in the petition, and so much more of the real and personal property of the principal defendant as shall be necessary to cover the damages for the detention of the specific property sued for and the costs of the attachment. Every other attachment shall command the sheriff or other officer to whom it may be directed to attach the property mentioned and sought to be attached in the petition, if any, and so much of the lands, tenements, goods, chattels, moneys and effects of the principal defendant not exempt from execution as will be sufficient to satisfy the plaintiff's demand, and, in case of tangible personal property, taken possession of under § 8.01-551, to keep the same safely in his possession to satisfy any judgment that may be recovered by the plaintiff in such attachment.

Every attachment sued out under this section shall also command the sheriff or other officer to summon the defendant or defendants, if he or they are found within his county or city, or any county or city wherein he may have seized property under and by virtue of such writ, to appear and answer the petition for the attachment.

Each copy of the summons shall be issued together with a form for requesting a hearing on a claim of exemption from levy or seizure as provided in § 8.01-546.1. Both documents shall be served on each defendant. (Code 1950, § 8-533; 1977, c. 617; 1986, c. 341.)

I. DECISIONS UNDER PRIOR LAW.

Editor's note. — The case cited below was decided under corresponding provisions of former law. The term "this section," as used below, refers to former provisions.

Effect of defendant's appearance where not summoned. — The only purpose of the command to the officer to summon a defendant, required by this section, is to bring the defendant into court and allow and require him to make his defense, if he has any. By voluntarily coming into the cause, contesting the plaintiff's claim and pleading counterclaim and setoff, without reservation, the defendant does for himself all that this section requires that the plaintiff do for him. Montague Mfg. Co. v. Ten Weeges, 297 F. 221 (4th Cir. 1924).

§ 8.01-546.1. Exemption claims form. — The form for requesting a hearing or a claim for exemption from levy or seizure shall be designed by the

Supreme Court and provided to all courts which may issue attachments and to all magistrates. (1986, c. 341.)

§ 8.01-546.2. Hearing on claim of exemption from levy or seizure. — A judgment debtor shall have the right to a hearing on his claim of exemption from levy or seizure. If a defendant files a request for a hearing, the clerk shall (i) schedule a hearing no later than ten business days from the date that the request is filed with the court, and (ii) notify the parties of the date, time and place of hearing and the exemption being claimed. This hearing may be combined with a hearing pursuant to § 8.01-119 or § 8.01-568 or with a trial on the merits if held within the ten-business day limitation.

The clerk shall notify the parties and the sheriff of the date, time and place of hearing and the exemption being claimed. The court may stay the sale pending this hearing by interlocutory order. The sheriff shall comply with the writ unless and until ordered otherwise in writing by the court. The order shall take effect upon receipt by the sheriff. The clerk is required to provide a copy of the order or the hearing disposition to the sheriff only if the writ or levy is dismissed or is modified by the judge. The court shall release all exempt property from the judgment creditor's lien and order the sheriff to return such exempt property to the judgment debtor. (1986, c. 341.)

§ 8.01-547. Attachment against remainders. — If the attachment be against a principal defendant who is a nonresident or an absconding debtor, the attachment may also direct the sheriff or other officer to levy the same on any remainder, vested or contingent, of the principal defendant, or so much thereof as may be sufficient to pay the amount for which it issues. But no such remainder shall be sold until it becomes vested. A judgment, however, ascertaining the amount due the plaintiff may be docketed as other judgments are docketed, but unless it be a personal judgment, it shall be a lien only on the property levied on. (Code 1950, § 8-534; 1977, c. 617.)

§ 8.01-548. Who may levy attachment and on what. — An attachment may be levied upon any estate of the defendant, whether the same be in the county or city in which the attachment issued, or in any other, either by the officer of the county or city wherein the attachment issued, or by the officer of the county or city where the estate is. (Code 1950, § 8-535; 1977, c. 617.)

Law Review. — For article on fraudulent conveyances and preferences in Virginia, see 36 Wash. & Lee L. Rev. 51 (1979).

I. DECISIONS UNDER PRIOR LAW.

Editor's note. — The cases cited below were decided under corresponding provisions of former law. The term "this section," as used below, refers to former provisions.

Attachment may be levied on any visible and tangible effects of a nonresident debtor in his actual or constructive possession, in the common-law mode, as in the case of an execution. Dorrier v. Masters, 83 Va. 459, 2 S.E. 927 (1887).

But only property within State may be attached. — An attachment against a nonresident can be levied only upon his estate and effects within this State. Batchelder v. White, 80 Va. 103 (1885).

Creditor of decedent may attach against nonresident heirs. — A creditor of a deceased debtor may proceed by foreign attachment against heirs residing abroad to subject land or its proceeds, in the State, descended to them from the debtor. Carrington v. Didier, 49 Va. (8 Gratt.) 260 (1851).

And a legatee's interest in the hands of an executor could be attached. Anderson v. DeSoer, 47 Va. (6 Gratt.) 363 (1849); Vance v. McLaughlin, 49 Va. (8 Gratt.) 289 (1851). See also Moores v. White, 44 Va. (3 Gratt.) 139 (1846).

Money on special deposit may be attached. — Money was left with a person who was a member of a firm, on a special deposit, and in his absence it was entered on the books of the firm to the credit of the depositor, and paid out by the firm for their own uses, they paying the depositor's checks upon it, by checks in their name upon the bank. An attachment was served upon the firm as garnishees in a suit against the depositor, the summons being served on the other member of the firm. It was held that the attachment bound the money in the hands of the firm. Pulliam v. Aler, 56 Va. (15 Gratt.) 54 (1859).

As may debts due by open account. — Debts due a nonresident debtor by an open account may be attached in the hands of resident garnishees. Porter v. Young, 85 Va. 49, 6 S.E. 803 (1888).

Shares in joint stock company are liable to attachment. — The shares of a stockholder in a joint stock company, incorporated by and conducting its operations, in whole or in part, in the State, are such estate as is liable to be attached. C & O R.R. v. Paine & Co., 70 Va. (29 Gratt.) 502 (1877); Shenandoah Valley R.R. v. Griffith, 76 Va. 913 (1882).

Private creditor of partner may attach interest in partnership. — Under this section a private creditor of one member of a firm may ordinarily attach the interest of the debtor partner in the partnership. Kern v. Wyatt, 89 Va. 885, 17 S.E. 549 (1893).

Vendor's creditor cannot attach realty in possession of purchaser. — A house sold by parol contract to a purchaser who has paid the purchase money and taken possession of the property cannot be taken by an attachment against the vendor as an absent debtor and subjected to the payment of his debt. Hicks v. Riddick, 69 Va. (28 Gratt.) 418 (1877).

Or goods transferred by indorsement of bill of lading. — Goods transferred by indorsement of a bill of lading to a bank, which pays the draft of the shipper for the value of the goods, are not attachable by creditors of the shipper. Buckeye Nat'l Bank v. Huff, 114 Va. 1, 75 S.E. 769 (1912).

Property held by debtor as trustee cannot be attached. — Where crops are produced on the lands of another under an agreement that the landowner is to have a certain share and the producer is to have the residue, and the whole crop is shipped to market in the name of the landowner, who is to pay over to the producer his share of the proceeds thereof, and the crops are marked in the name of the producer and are capable of identification, the landowner is a mere trustee, and the proceeds of the crops are not subject to attachment by creditors of the landowner. Jones v. Crumpler, 119 Va. 143, 89 S.E. 232 (1916).

Nor may property held by trustee under deed of trust. — An attachment was served upon trustees in a deed of trust given for the payment of certain debts, among them the debts due to the plaintiff in the attachment. It was held that there could be no surplus in the hands of the trustees until the debts secured by the deed were paid, and consequently there was nothing in their hands liable to the attachment. Clark v. Ward, 53 Va. (12 Gratt.) 440 (1855).

Funds in hands of public officer are not liable to attachment. — Funds in the hands of the State Treasurer, which he holds by law in pursuance of a trust, are not liable to attachment at the suit of an individual. Rollo v. Andes Ins. Co., 64 Va. (23 Gratt.) 509 (1873); Buck v. Guarantors' Liab. Indem. Co., 97 Va. 719, 34 S.E. 950 (1900).

But attachment lies against municipal corporation. — A municipal corporation may be attached for a debt due to one of its creditors just as a natural person may be. Such a proceeding is not contrary to the public policy of this State. Portsmouth Gas Co. v. Sanford, 97 Va. 124, 33 S.E. 516 (1899).

§ 8.01-549. Restraining order or receiver. — The court may interpose by a restraining order, or the appointment of a receiver, or otherwise, to secure the forthcoming of the specific property sued for, and so much other estate as will probably be required to satisfy any further order that may be made in the proceedings. (Code 1950, § 8-536; 1977, c. 617.)

§ 8.01-550. How attachment levied. — An attachment may be levied as follows:

On tangible personal property in possession of a principal defendant, whether such possession be actual or constructive, it may be levied as at common law or by delivering a copy of the attachment to such principal defendant or, if possession is requested in the petition, then by taking possession of such personal property;

On choses in action or on tangible personal property in possession of any defendant other than the principal defendant, it may be levied by delivering a copy of the attachment to the person indebted to the principal defendant or having possession of the property belonging to him; and

On real estate, it may be levied by such estate being mentioned and described in an endorsement on the attachment by the officer to whom it is delivered for service to the following effect:

"Levied on the following real estate of the defendant A. (or defendants A. and B.), to-wit: (here describe the real estate) this the .... day of .... at .... o'clock. E.F., sheriff (or other officer)," and by service of the attachment on the person, if any, in possession of such real estate.

Wherever a copy of an attachment is required or allowed to be served on any person, natural or artificial, it may be served as a notice is served under §§ 8.01-296, 8.01-299, 8.01-300 or 8.01-301, as the case may be. (Code 1950, § 8-537; 1977, c. 617; 1984, c. 646.)

Cross references. — As to levy on property held under process, see § 8.01-558.

I. DECISIONS UNDER PRIOR LAW.

Editor's note. — The cases cited below were decided under corresponding provisions of former law. The term "this section," as used below, refers to former provisions.

The levy of the attachment is the foundation of the suit. If the property attached is not the defendant's property, the court is without jurisdiction. Culbertson v. Stevens, 82 Va. 406, 4 S.E. 607 (1886).

Actual seizure is not essential. — To constitute an effectual levy, it is not essential that the officer make an actual seizure. If he have the goods in his view and power, and note on the writ the fact of his levy thereon, this will in general suffice. Bullitt v. Winstons, 15 Va. (1 Munf.) 269 (1810); Dorrier v. Masters, 83 Va. 459, 2 S.E. 927 (1887).

Inventory need not be made at time of levy. — If an officer, without committing a trespass, enters the premises and announces his levy by acts and words, the goods are then in his control, even though an inventory is not made at the time. First Nat'l Bank v. Johnson, 183 Va. 227, 31 S.E.2d 581 (1944).

Officer may levy on personalty in possession of third person. — An officer has a right to levy upon tangible personal property even though the possession of such property is in the hands of a third person not a party to the suit. First Nat'l Bank v. Johnson, 183 Va. 227, 31 S.E.2d 581 (1944).

Return must show realty levied on as property of defendant. — The return must show that the attachment was levied upon the property as the property of the defendant, in order to make a valid levy on real estate. Robertson v. Hoge, 83 Va. 124, 1 S.E. 667 (1887).

And must contain general description of land. — The levy of an attachment on real estate must contain such general description of the land, and describe it with such substantial accuracy, that it may be easily identified when conveyed, by looking alone to the levy without the aid of extrinsic evidence. Raub v. Otterback, 92 Va. 517, 23 S.E. 883 (1896).

Description held adequate. — A return on an attachment that it was levied on a tract of land of the defendant company containing about three hundred and sixty acres, located in the county of M., in the magisterial district of P., of said county, "being the same land conveyed to said company by L. C. Garnett, Esq., special commissioner of Mathews county circuit court, by deed recorded in deed book No. 15, pp. 58-59," is a substantial, if not a literal, compliance with this section. Richardson v. Hoskins Lumber Co., 111 Va. 755, 69 S.E. 935 (1911).

Description held insufficient. — Where the return of the sheriff was: "executed upon the tract of land within mentioned," the levy was too vague and uncertain. Raub v. Otterback, 92 Va. 517, 23 S.E. 883 (1896). See Robertson v. Hoge, 83 Va. 124, 1 S.E. 667 (1887).

"Any person" includes corporation. — The words "any person," used in this section, include corporations as well as natural persons. Portsmouth Gas Co. v. Sanford, 97 Va. 124, 33 S.E. 516 (1899); B & O R.R. v. Gallahue's Adm'rs, 53 Va. (12 Gratt.) 655 (1855).

§ 8.01-551. When officer to take possession of property. — If so requested by the plaintiff in his petition, the officer to whom the attachment is directed shall take possession of the property specified in the attachment, or when no such property is specified, of any estate or effects of the defendant, or so much thereof as is sufficient to pay the plaintiff's claim. But the officer levying the attachment shall, before taking possession of any property as aforesaid, make his certificate of the estimated fair market value of the property on which the attachment is levied, and he shall not take possession of the same unless and until bond in conformance with § 8.01-537.1 based on the estimated fair market value of the property as so stated in his certificate is posted. The certificate shall be filed in the clerk's office of the court to which the attachment is returnable and the value so certified shall be subject to review by the court to which the attachment is returnable. (Code 1950, § 8-538; 1973, c. 545; 1977, c. 617; 1984, c. 646; 1993, c. 841.)

Cross references. — As to who may give bond, see §§ 8.01-4.2, 8.01-556. As to giving of indemnifying bond to officer, see §§ 8.01-367 through 8.01-369. As to bond given upon suing out attachment, see § 8.01-537.1. As to bonds on appeal for restoration of property, see § 8.01-555.

I. DECISIONS UNDER PRIOR LAW.

Editor's note. — The cases cited below were decided under corresponding provisions of former law. The terms "this article" and "this section," as used below, refer to former provisions.

Property cannot be seized and taken possession of unless the creditor has given a bond. Dorrier v. Masters, 83 Va. 459, 2 S.E. 927 (1887).

Under the attachment statutes, the officer is not required to take possession of the property unless the plaintiff in the attachment suit gives bond as required by this section. First Nat'l Bank v. Johnson, 183 Va. 227, 31 S.E.2d 581 (1944).

Partner may give bond in attachment by firm. — The bond of a partner suing out an attachment, with surety, conditioned that that partner should pay all costs, in case the house should be cast in the suit, and all damages that should be adjudged against him for suing out the attachment, was a good bond. Kyle & Co. v. Connelly, 30 Va. (3 Leigh) 719 (1832).

But bond should show partnership as plaintiff in attachment. — An attachment being sued out by one member of a firm, for a debt due to the firm, and in the name of the firm, it was proper that the bond executed by the partner who sued out the attachment and his surety should bind the obligors to be answerable for the failure of the firm to prosecute their attachment with success. M'Clung & Co. v. Jackson, 47 Va. (6 Gratt.) 96 (1849).

An attachment against an absconding debtor was sued out in the name of a partnership, for a debt due the partnership; the bond taken was the bond of F., one of the partners, with surety, reciting that F. had obtained the attachment, and conditioned that if he should be cast in the suit, he should pay all costs and damages which should be recovered against him. It was held that the bond was void, and the attachment was therefore illegal and void. Jones v. Anderson, 34 Va. (7 Leigh) 308 (1836).

No action lies if attachment sued out with good cause. — The sureties in the attachment bond, when the attachment has been sued out with good cause, are not responsible for the failure of the officer to discharge his duty, or for a trespass committed by him. Offtendinger v. Ford, 92 Va. 636, 24 S.E. 246 (1896).

What is probable cause. — Probable cause for suing out an attachment is a belief by the attaching creditor in the existence of the facts essential to the prosecution of his attachment, founded upon facts which might induce such a belief on the part of a man of ordinary caution, prudence and judgment. Spengler v. Davy, 56 Va. (15 Gratt.) 381 (1858).

Only defendant or owner of specific property attached may sue. — Where the attachment issues against the effects of the defendant generally, he alone can sue upon the bond, and where the attachment is issued against specific property, only the defendant or the owner of the specific property can sue. Davis v. Commonwealth, 54 Va. (13 Gratt.) 139 (1856).

If property belonging to a third person is seized under an attachment issued against the general estate of a debtor, the remedy of the owner of the property is an action of trespass against the sheriff who made the levy, or an action on the sheriff's bond. Davis v. Commonwealth, 54 Va. (13 Gratt.) 139 (1856). See also, James v. M'Cubbin, 6 Va. (2 Call) 273 (1800); Mosby v. Mosby, 50 Va. (9 Gratt.) 584 (1853); Sangster v. Commonwealth, 58 Va. (17 Gratt.) 124 (1866).

Damages need not be assessed in some prior action. — If any damages have been sustained, it is not necessary that they should be previously assessed in some other action to justify an action on an attachment bond. Dickinson v. M'Craw, 25 Va. (4 Rand.) 158 (1826); Offtendinger v. Ford, 92 Va. 636, 24 S.E. 246 (1896).

Costs and damages must be alleged. — In an action on an attachment bond, it is not sufficient to allege in the declaration, that the defendant "did not pay all such costs and damages as have accrued, etc.," but it must be expressly averred that costs and damages had been actually sustained. Dickinson v. M'Craw, 25 Va. (4 Rand.) 158 (1826).

Variance between attachment and bond. — If the claim of the plaintiff in an attachment against an absconding debtor is stated as for a certain sum, due by negotiable note, with interest from the day when the note should have been paid, and the bond for prosecuting the attachment describes it as sued out for the sum of money mentioned therein, saying nothing of interest, the variance is not material. Smith v. Pearce, 20 Va. (6 Munf.) 585 (1820).

§ 8.01-552: Repealed by Acts 1984, c. 646.

§ 8.01-553. Bonds for retention of property or release of attachment; revising bonds mentioned in this and § 8.01-551. — Any property levied on or seized as aforesaid, under any attachment, may be retained by or returned to the defendant or other person in whose possession it was on his giving bond, with condition to have the same forthcoming at such time and place as the court may require. In the alternative, the principal defendant may, by giving bond with condition to perform the judgment of the court, release from any attachment the whole of any estate attached. The bond in either case shall be taken by the officer serving the attachment, with surety, payable to the plaintiff, and in a penalty in the latter case either double the amount or value for which the attachment issued or double the value of the property on which the attachment was levied, at the option of the person giving it, and in the former, either double the amount of value for which the attachment issued or double the value of the property retained or returned, at the option of the person giving it. However, in the event the court shall consider that the amount of any bond required by this section or § 8.01-551 is excessive or inadequate, such court may, upon motion of any party in interest after reasonable notice to the opposite party if he can be found in the jurisdiction of the court or to his attorney of record, if any, fix the amount of such bond to conform to the equities of the case. (Code 1950, § 8-540; 1977, c. 617; 1984, c. 646.)

Cross references. — As to who may give bond, see §§ 8.01-4.2, 8.01-556. As to bond given by codefendant indebted to, or having in possession property belonging to, principal defendant, see § 8.01-562.

I. DECISIONS UNDER PRIOR LAW.

Editor's note. — The cases cited below were decided under corresponding provisions of former law. The term "this section," as used below, refers to former provisions.

Forthcoming bond is not necessary where no attachment bond given. — Under the terms of § 8.01-551 the officer levying an attachment is not required to take possession of the property unless the plaintiff has given bond, and where no such attachment bond is given there is no necessity for the defendant in the attachment to execute a forthcoming bond in order that the possession of the property may be "retained by or returned to" him. Foster v. Wilson, 139 Va. 82, 123 S.E. 527 (1924).

Bond is security in lieu of property attached. — Where an attachment is sustained, the bond stands as a security in lieu of the property on which the attachment was levied. Hilton & Allen v. Consumers' Can Co., 103 Va. 255, 48 S.E. 899 (1904).

Giving of bond does not bar other attachments. — The giving of a bond under this section does not debar the plaintiff from suing out other attachments for the same debt and having them levied on other property of the defendant. Kaylor v. Davy Pocahontas Coal Co., 118 Va. 369, 87 S.E. 551 (1916).

Nor does it give court personal jurisdiction of defendant. — The execution of a forthcoming bond does not give the court in which the attachment was sued out jurisdiction to enter a personal decree against the defendant. Hilton & Allen v. Consumers' Can Co., 103 Va. 255, 48 S.E. 899 (1904).

And bond loses vitality when attachment dismissed. — If a bond is given by the defendant in attachment in pursuance of this section, conditioned to have the property forthcoming at such time and place as the court may require, or to perform the judgment of the court, there is no question but that the bond loses its vitality when the attachment is dismissed. Maryland Cas. Co. v. Parrish, 150 Va. 473, 143 S.E. 750 (1928).

Bond with condition to perform judgment releases whole estate attached. — The effect of a bond given by the defendant under this section with condition to perform the judgment of the court is to release from any attachment the whole of the estate attached. Kaylor v. Davy Pocahontas Coal Co., 118 Va. 369, 87 S.E. 551 (1916).

The words "perform the judgment of the court" have acquired a definite legal meaning, to wit, to pay such money judgment as may be rendered against the defendant in attachment. Foster v. Wilson, 139 Va. 82, 123 S.E. 527 (1924).

Bond not complying with this section may yet be enforceable. — A bond which recited attachment proceedings and the desire of the debtor to retain the property attached,

703

conditioned to produce the property attached at such time and place as the court might require and to perform the judgment of the court, taken by the clerk of court without the knowledge or consent of the sheriff or the attaching creditor, and filed with the papers in the attachment proceeding, did not comply with the provisions of this section, but was a valid common-law obligation, enforceable according to its terms. Foster v. Wilson, 139 Va. 82, 123 S.E. 527 (1924).

Thus sheriff may sue on bond made payable to him. — If a forthcoming bond be made payable to the sheriff instead of to the creditor, the sheriff may maintain an action thereon. Beale v. Downman, 5 Va. (1 Call) 249 (1798).

Bond prepared without notice to obligee construed against obligors. — Where a release bond in attachment proceedings was prepared by counsel for the obligors without notice to opposing counsel or opportunity on their part to suggest its form or object to its terms, if there is doubt or ambiguity the words of the instrument should be construed most strongly against the obligors. Foster v. Wilson, 139 Va. 82, 123 S.E. 527 (1924).

§ 8.01-554. Where bond returned and filed; exceptions to bond. — Every such bond shall be returned by the officer to and filed by the clerk of the court in which the attachment is pending, or to which the attachment is returnable, and the plaintiff may, within thirty days after the return thereof, file exceptions to the same, or to the sufficiency of the surety therein. If such exception be sustained, the court shall order the officer to file a good bond, with sufficient surety, to be approved by it, on or before a certain day to be fixed by the court. If he fail to do so, he and his sureties in his official bond shall be liable to the plaintiff as for a breach of such bond; but the officer shall have the same rights and remedies against the parties to any bonds so adjudged bad as if he were a surety for them. (Code 1950, § 8-541; 1977, c. 617.)

§ 8.01-555. When appeal bond given property to be delivered to owner. — When judgment in favor of the plaintiff is rendered by a general district court in any case in which an attachment is issued and on appeal therefrom to a circuit court an appeal bond is given, with condition to prosecute the appeal with effect or pay the debt, interest, costs and damages, as well as the costs of the appeal, the officer, in whose custody any attached property is, shall deliver the same to the owner thereof. When an appeal is from a circuit court to the Supreme Court and an appeal bond is given pursuant to § 8.01-676.1, the officer having custody shall proceed in like manner. (Code 1950, § 8-543; 1977, c. 617.)

REVISERS' NOTE

Section 8.01-555 is former § 8-543. The language "...by a general district court..." has been inserted after the word "rendered," and "...to a circuit court..." after the word "therefrom." A sentence as to how the officer in custody shall proceed when an appeal is taken from a circuit court to the Supreme Court has been added. (See § 8.01-676.1.)

I. DECISIONS UNDER PRIOR LAW.

Editor's note. — The case cited below was decided under corresponding provisions of former law. The term "this section," as used below, refers to former provisions.

An appeal bond given by the defendant does not release the general attachment lien. Magill v. Sauer, 61 Va. (20 Gratt.) 540 (1871).

§ 8.01-556. Bonds may be given by any person. — Any bond authorized or required by any section of this chapter may be given either by the party himself or by any other person. (Code 1950, § 8-544; 1977, c. 617.)

§ 8.01-557 CIVIL REMEDIES AND PROCEDURE § 8.01-557

Cross references. — As to bond for obtaining writ of order in civil cases generally, see § 8.01-4.2.

I. DECISIONS UNDER PRIOR LAW.

Editor's note. — The case cited below was decided under corresponding provisions of former law. The term "this section," as used below, refers to former provisions.

It is not necessary that the plaintiff in attachment should be a party to an attachment bond. Offtendinger v. Ford, 92 Va. 636, 24 S.E. 246 (1896).

§ 8.01-557. Lien of attachment; priority of holder in due course.

— The plaintiff shall have a lien from the time of the levying of such attachment, or serving a copy thereof as aforesaid, upon the personal property of the principal defendant, when the same is in his possession, actual or constructive, and upon the personal property, choses in action, and other securities of such defendant in the hands of, or owing by a codefendant on whom it is so served; and on any real estate mentioned in such an endorsement by the officer on the attachment or summons as is prescribed by § 8.01-550, from the time of levy and service pursuant to such section. But a holder in due course of negotiable paper shall have priority over an attachment levied thereon. (Code 1950, § 8-545; 1977, c. 617.)

REVISERS' NOTE

Section 8.01-557 is former § 8-545. The language "... the suing out of the same" has been deleted and the language "... from the time of levy and service pursuant to such section" has been substituted therefor. This change abolishes the distinction between real and personal property regarding the time when the lien arises. See § 8.01-268 requiring a memorandum of lis pendens in order to bind the attached property, real or personal, against the claim of a bona fide purchaser for value.

Cross references. — As to recordation of attachments, see §§ 8.01-268, 8.01-269. As to lien of attachment on property held under process, see § 8.01-558. As to who is a holder in due course and the rights thereof, see § 8.3A-302. As to priority of lien in attachment of crops for advances to tenants, see § 43-29.

I. Decisions Under Current Law.
II. Decisions Under Prior Law.
   A. General Consideration.
   B. Property Subject to Lien.
   C. Priorities.

I. DECISIONS UNDER CURRENT LAW.

Lien of an attachment is perfected by the levy of the officer. S.W. Rawls, Inc. v. Forrest, 224 Va. 264, 295 S.E.2d 791 (1982).

II. DECISIONS UNDER PRIOR LAW.

A. General Consideration.

Editor's note. — The cases cited below were decided under corresponding provisions of former law. The term "this section," as used below, refers to former provisions.

Court has no inherent jurisdiction over property to be attached. — Under this section a lien is not acquired by virtue of the inherent jurisdiction of the court over the property; on the contrary, the court's power over the property does not exist and cannot be exercised until a substantial compliance with the statutory prerequisites appears. These, and only these, procedural prerequisites give the creditor the right to a lien, and when this right is established the court is clothed with jurisdiction over the attached property. Fauquier Nat'l Bank v. Hazelwood Sav. & Trust Co., 165 Va. 259, 182 S.E. 566 (1935).

It must acquire jurisdiction through statutory proceedings. — The court must acquire jurisdiction over the property to be attached through the proceedings prescribed by this and the preceding sections before there can exist a valid lien on such property. Fauquier Nat'l Bank v. Hazelwood Sav. & Trust Co., 165 Va. 259, 182 S.E. 566 (1935).

Lien commences at time of levy. — The

705

lien of the attachment in Virginia commences from the time of its levy or service. Williamson v. Bowie, 20 Va. (6 Munf.) 176 (1818); Allan v. Hoffman, 83 Va. 129, 2 S.E. 602 (1887); First Nat'l Bank v. Johnson, 183 Va. 227, 31 S.E.2d 581 (1944).

It is perfected by levy. — The lien of the attachment is perfected by the levy thereof, and the subsequent judgment or decree is simply the enforcement of a valid preexisting lien. It is the creation of the lien, and not its enforcement, that is denounced by the Bankruptcy Act. Jackson v. Valley Tie & Lumber Co., 108 Va. 714, 62 S.E. 964 (1908).

And final judgment relates back. — The levy of an attachment creates an inchoate lien upon the property attached, and when final judgment is rendered for the plaintiff it relates back to the levy, but it cannot by relation render a transaction unlawful which was not unlawful at the time it took place. Trimble v. Covington Grocery Co., 112 Va. 826, 72 S.E. 724 (1911).

Fieri facias lien and attachment lien take effect at different times. — The two Code chapters dealing with garnishment in aid of the fieri facias lien on unleviable property and garnishment by attachment lien provide for their taking effect at different times. In re Acorn Elec. Supply, Inc., 348 F. Supp. 277 (E.D. Va. 1972).

A judgment or decree in enforcement of a valid preexisting lien is not the judgment or decree denounced by the Bankruptcy Act, which was plainly confined to judgments creating liens. In re Acorn Elec. Supply, Inc., 348 F. Supp. 277 (E.D. Va. 1972).

The service of the attachment operates to inhibit a transfer of the debtor's property from the defendants to any other person. M'Kim v. Fulton, 10 Va. (6 Call) 106 (1806); Smith v. Henny, 14 Va. (4 Hen. & M.) 440 (1809); Williamson v. Bowie, 20 Va. (6 Munf.) 176 (1818).

B. Property Subject to Lien.

Lien affects only debts owed and property held by person served. — The attachment operates as a lien only upon the debts and effects of the absent debtor, in the hands of the home defendants against whom, and upon whom, it is served. Farmers Bank v. Day, 47 Va. (6 Gratt.) 360 (1849).

And only debts due and property held at time of service. — Where a codefendant in an attachment is named as a person who is indebted to or has in his possession property belonging to the principal defendant, by the service of a copy of the attachment upon the codefendant the plaintiff acquires an inchoate lien upon any debt then owed to the principal defendant by the codefendant, and upon any property of the principal defendant then in the possession of the codefendant. But he acquires no lien whatever upon any indebtedness of the codefendant to the principal defendant which accrues after the service of the attachment, or upon any property of the principal defendant which comes into the possession of the codefendant after the service of the attachment. Deeds v. Gilmer, 162 Va. 157, 174 S.E. 37 (1934).

Creditor acquires no right superior to that of debtor. — By attachment, a creditor acquires in the proceeds of property claimed by his debtor no right or interest superior to that possessed by the latter therein at the time of the levy or service of the writ. Seward & Co. v. Miller, 106 Va. 309, 55 S.E. 681 (1906).

Lien does not attach to funds subject to forfeiture. — The estimates of work done by a contractor for a railroad company are made up to the 20th of each month, when they are considered due, though not paid for some days afterwards. As the price of the work done by the contractor after the 20th may be forfeited to the company for several causes before the 20th of the next month, no debt is due from the company to the contractor until the 20th arrives, and therefore an attachment served on the company on the 14th of the month creates no lien, as there is nothing then in his hands due to the contractor which may be attached, though in fact no forfeiture occurs. B & O R.R. v. Gallahue's Adm'rs, 55 Va. (14 Gratt.) 563 (1858).

Service on lessee binds only rents due at time of service. — Where, in a foreign attachment, the home defendant holds lands of the absent debtor upon a lease, the service of the attachment upon the lessee binds only the rents due to the absent defendant at the time the attachment was served, and does not bind the rents accruing subsequently. Haffey v. Miller, 47 Va. (6 Gratt.) 454 (1849).

Service on executor creates lien on legacy. — Service of process of foreign attachment on an executor before qualification creates a lien in favor of the attaching creditor on a legacy to an absent debtor. Sandridge v. Graves, 1 Pat. & H. 101 (1855).

No lien is acquired on realty not described in endorsement on process. — If the endorsement on the process of attachment does not mention or describe real estate, the attachment does not operate upon any real estate. Clark v. Ward, 53 Va. (12 Gratt.) 440 (1855).

C. Priorities.

Lien of attachment is subject to bona fide earlier lien. — If property, when attached, is subject to a lien placed thereon by the defendant in good faith, that lien must be respected and the attachment postponed to it.

Seward & Co. v. Miller, 106 Va. 309, 55 S.E. 681 (1906).

And to prior assignment to chose in action. — Since the Virginia recording acts do not embrace choses in action, an assignment of a chose in action to a trustee to pay the debts of the assignor is valid against a subsequent attaching creditor of the assignor. Kirkland v. Brune, 72 Va. (31 Gratt.) 126 (1878); Gregg v. Sloan, 76 Va. 497 (1882). See also, Tazewell's Ex'r v. Barrett & Co., 14 Va. (4 Hen. & M.) 259 (1809); Wilson v. Davisson, 19 Va. (5 Munf.) 178 (1816); Schofield v. Cox, 49 Va. (8 Gratt.) 533 (1852).

And prior deed of trust. — A subpoena was sued out against an absent debtor and home defendants. The subpoena was returned executed on the home defendants, but the date of its service upon them was not stated. After the issue of the subpoena, but before the return day thereof, the debtor executed a deed to secure certain creditors, which was duly filed. It was held that the attachment was postponed to the deed. Richeson v. Richeson, 43 Va. (2 Gratt.) 497 (1846).

Priority of holder in due course of negotiable paper. — While this section gives a holder in due course of negotiable paper a priority over an attachment levied upon the seized property, this in no sense grants a right of action in tort to a party secondarily liable on the negotiable instrument. Ross v. Peck Iron & Metal Co., 264 F.2d 262 (4th Cir. 1959).

Priority over unrecorded deed to chattels. — An attachment has priority over a deed of trust conveying goods and chattels, recorded in another state but not in Virginia. Smith v. Smith, 60 Va. (19 Gratt.) 545 (1869).

A prior lien by writ of fieri facias is superior to a garnishment attachment even though the garnishment attachment was served on the garnishee first. In re Acorn Elec. Supply, Inc., 348 F. Supp. 277 (E.D. Va. 1972).

Fieri facias is superior to subsequent attachment. — A fieri facias placed in the hands of an officer for execution is a legal lien under § 8.01-479 and continues in effect after the return day. Such lien has priority over an attachment subsequently levied. Puryear v. Taylor, 53 Va. (12 Gratt.) 401 (1855); Charron & Co. v. Boswell, 59 Va. (18 Gratt.) 216 (1868).

Attachment first sued out and served has priority. — Among attaching creditors proceeding by foreign attachment, the creditor whose subpoena is first sued out and served is entitled to priority of satisfaction. Farmers Bank v. Day, 47 Va. (6 Gratt.) 360 (1849).

Two attachments against an absconding debtor were levied on the same property. The first levied was quashed, but upon appeal this judgment was reversed. Pending the appeal an order was made in the second attachment case for a sale of the property, and it was sold and the proceeds paid over to the creditor in the second attachment. It was held that an action for money had and received would lie by the first attaching creditor against the creditor in the second attachment for the proceeds of the sale. Caperton v. M'Corkle, 46 Va. (5 Gratt.) 177 (1848).

Subsequent purchaser without notice takes land free of lien. — A purchaser of land without notice of an attachment which had been previously levied upon it, but which had not been recorded or docketed as required by § 8.01-268, is entitled to hold the land free from the lien of the attachment. Cammack v. Soran, 71 Va. (30 Gratt.) 292 (1878).

Unless lis pendens has been filed. — A lis pendens in attachment proceedings filed in the clerk's office of the proper county, as provided by § 8.01-268, operates to give constructive notice of the lien of the attachment to a subsequent grantee of the defendant, and such grantee stands upon no better footing as to the attaching creditor than his grantor. Breeden v. Peale, 106 Va. 39, 55 S.E. 2 (1906).

Lien is superior to claim of wife in subsequent divorce suit. — An attachment against the effects of the husband as an absconding debtor, levied before the institution of a suit by the wife for a divorce, entitles the attaching creditor to be satisfied out of the attached effects, in preference to the claim of the wife. Jennings v. Montague, 43 Va. (2 Gratt.) 350 (1845).

Attachment and distress for rent. — Distress for rent cannot be made off the demised premises, and, therefore, an attachment served upon property found off the premises was preferred to it. Mosby v. Leeds, 7 Va. (3 Call) 439 (1803).

Priority between partnership creditors where partners are bankrupt. — Where partners have been declared bankrupts, one creditor of the partnership cannot attach the partnership effects so as to obtain a preference over the other partnership creditors. Lindsey v. Corkery, 70 Va. (29 Gratt.) 650 (1878).

§ 8.01-558. Attachment lien on effects already in hands of officer. — When an officer has in his possession or custody money or effects of the defendant held under an attachment executed, or other legal process, a delivery to such officer of an attachment under this chapter shall be deemed a levy thereof as to such money or effects, and constitute a lien thereon from the time of such delivery. (Code 1950, § 8-546; 1977, c. 617.)

§ 8.01-559 CODE OF VIRGINIA § 8.01-562

§ **8.01-559. Return by officer.** — The officer levying the attachment shall show in his return the time, date and manner of the service, or execution thereof, on each person and parcel of property, and also give a list and description of the property, if any, levied on under the attachment. (Code 1950, § 8-547; 1954, c. 333; 1977, c. 617.)

I. DECISIONS UNDER PRIOR LAW.

Editor's note. — The cases cited below were decided under corresponding provisions of former law. The term "this section," as used below, refers to former provisions.

The return must show that the attachment was levied on the property of the defendant in order to make it valid. Robertson v. Hodge, 83 Va. 124, 1 S.E. 667 (1887); Offtendinger v. Ford, 86 Va. 917, 12 S.E. 1 (1890).

Attachment presumed legally executed. — If the return is regular on its face, it will be presumed, in the absence of evidence to the contrary, that the attachment was legally executed. Guarantee Co. of N. Am. v. First Nat'l Bank, 95 Va. 480, 28 S.E. 909 (1898).

The officer's return may be amended if defective. Pulliam v. Aler, 56 Va. (15 Gratt.) 54 (1859).

ARTICLE 3.

Subsequent Proceedings Generally.

§ **8.01-560. How interest and profits of property applied in certain cases.** — When any attachment is sued out, although the property or estate attached be not seized, the interest and profits thereof pending the attachment and before judgment may be paid to the defendant, if the court deem it proper. (Code 1950, § 8-548; 1977, c. 617.)

§ **8.01-561. How property to be kept; how sold, when expensive to keep or perishable.** — Any property seized under any attachment and not sold before judgment shall be kept in the same manner as similar property taken under execution. But such as is expensive to keep or perishable may be sold by order of the court upon such terms as the court may direct. If the court directs that the sale may be made on credit, the court may order the sheriff to take a bond with sufficient surety, payable to the sheriff, for the benefit of the party entitled. Such bond shall be returned forthwith by the officer to the court. (Code 1950, § 8-549; 1977, c. 617.)

REVISERS' NOTE

Section 8.01-561 is former § 8-549 without material change. In order to simplify the procedure, however, all of the language of the former statute following the phrase "...by order of the court..." has been rewritten. The words "replevied or" have been deleted. The action of replevin has been abolished since the enactment of the Code of 1919.

Cross references. — As to disposition of surplus proceeds on sale of property, see § 8.01-373. As to judgment and directing of sale thereon in attachment proceedings, see §§ 8.01-570, 8.01-572. As to protection of purchaser of property sold under attachment, see § 8.01-575.

§ **8.01-562. Examination on oath of codefendant; order and bond.** — A defendant who at the time of service of the attachment was alleged to be indebted to a principal defendant, or had in his possession personal property belonging to such principal defendant, shall appear in person and submit to an examination on oath touching such debt or personal property, or he may, with the consent of the court, after reasonable notice to the plaintiff, file an answer in writing under oath, stating whether or not he was so indebted, and if so, the amount thereof and the time of maturity, or whether he had in his possession any personal property belonging to such principal defendant and, if so, the nature and value thereof. If it appear on such examination or by his answer that at the time of the service of the attachment, he was indebted to the principal defendant, or had in his possession or control any goods, chattels, money, securities or other effects belonging to such defendant, the court may order him to pay the amount so owing by him, or to deliver such effects to the sheriff, or other person designated by the court to receive the same; or such defendant may, with the leave of the court, give bond with sufficient security, payable to such person and in such penalty as the court shall prescribe, with condition to pay the amount owing by him, and have such effects forthcoming, at such time and place as the court may thereafter require. An answer under oath under this section shall be deemed prima facie to be true. (Code 1950, § 8-550; 1977, c. 617.)

REVISERS' NOTE

Section 8.01-562 is former § 8-550. The language "after reasonable notice to the plaintiff" has been inserted after the language "consent of the court."

Cross references. — As to garnishment in connection with executions on judgments, see §§ 8.01-511 et seq.

I. Decisions Under Current Law.
II. Decisions Under Prior Law.
   A. General Consideration.
   B. Who May Be Garnished.
   C. What May Be Garnished.
   D. Practice and Procedure.

I. DECISIONS UNDER CURRENT LAW.

Applied in Greene v. Warrenton Prod. Credit Ass'n, 223 Va. 462, 291 S.E.2d 209 (1982).

II. DECISIONS UNDER PRIOR LAW.

A. General Consideration.

Editor's note. — The cases cited below were decided under corresponding provisions of former law. The term "this section," as used below, refers to former provisions.

Service of notice of attachment gives plaintiff a lien upon a debt owing by the garnishee to defendant. Trimble v. Covington Grocery Co., 112 Va. 826, 72 S.E. 724 (1911).

Contingent debt cannot be collected. — The contract between a railroad company and one of the contractors on its line of improvement provided that the contractor should not receive the amount of final estimate of his work until he should release, under seal, all claims or demands upon the company arising out of the contract. The contractor could not recover the amount of the final estimate until he had executed the release, and an attaching creditor at law had no greater rights against the company in respect to this final estimate than the contractor had, and therefore could not recover the amount unless the contractor had executed the release. B & O R.R. v. McCullough & Co., 53 Va. (12 Gratt.) 595 (1855).

Plaintiff cannot acquire greater right than principal defendant. — Garnishment is substantially a suit by the principal defendant in the attachment, in the name of the plaintiff against the garnishee. The plaintiff stands upon no higher ground than the defendant, and can acquire no greater right than the defendant himself possesses. Rollo v. Andes Ins. Co., 64 Va. (23 Gratt.) 509 (1873).

Lien is enforced by judgment against garnishee. — The lien of the attachment cannot be enforced without rendering a judgment against the garnishee. B & O R.R. v. McCullough & Co., 53 Va. (12 Gratt.) 595 (1855).

Plaintiff must first establish his debt against principal defendant. — As the whole object of garnishment is to reach effects or credits in the garnishee's hands so as to subject them to the payment of such judgment as the plaintiff may recover against the principal defendant, it follows necessarily that there can be no judgment against the garnishee until judgment against the principal defendant has been recovered. And the judgment against the defendant must be a final one. If it is appealed from by the defendant there can be no judgment against the garnishee while the appeal is pending. George v. Blue, 7 Va. (3 Call) 455 (1803); Withers v. Fuller, 71 Va. (30 Gratt.) 547 (1878). See Gibson v. White & Co., 17 Va. (3 Munf.) 94 (1812).

Garnishee is liable only for consuming or appropriating property. — If the defendant appears not to be a debtor of the absentee, but holds effects belonging to him, by a title not effectual against creditors, or without any title at all, he should be considered personally responsible only for so much as he may have consumed, or appropriated to his own use so that it is not forthcoming, or for the profits he may have received. Gibson v. White & Co., 17 Va. (3 Munf.) 94 (1812).

Garnishee's claim for keeping property should be satisfied. — In a proceeding by foreign attachment, a home defendant having property of the absent defendant in his possession, for the keeping of which the absent defendant is indebted to him, is entitled, as against the attaching creditor, to have his claim first satisfied out of the property. Williamson v. Gayle, 48 Va. (7 Gratt.) 152 (1850).

Judgment should be only for amount of plaintiff's demand. — An attaching creditor should be decreed only so much of the debt garnished as is equal to his demand. Watts Ex'rs v. Robertson, 14 Va. (4 Hen. & M.) 442 (1809).

For the attaching creditor has no interest in the subject beyond his demand. — If the garnishee admits funds to that amount, or the jury finds them, he looks no further but takes his judgment accordingly. He is not concerned to contest whether his debtor has no further demands against the garnishee, and the judgment against the latter ascertains that there is so much at least in his hands, but not, as against the debtor, that there may not be more. B & O R.R. v. McCullough & Co., 53 Va. (12 Gratt.) 595 (1855).

Judgment for residue may be given in favor of principal defendant. — Where a foreign attachment is sued out against an absent debtor and a resident garnishee, in a case equitable in its nature, it is competent to the court to decree between the debtor and the garnishee what may be due from the latter to the former, after satisfying the claims of the plaintiff. But the evidence, in such a case, must arise from the pleadings and proofs between the plaintiff and defendant. Templeman v. Fauntleroy, 24 Va. (3 Rand.) 434 (1825).

B. Who May Be Garnished.

A corporation may be summoned and proceeded against as a garnishee, upon proceedings under this section. B & O R.R. v. Gallahue's Adm'rs, 53 Va. (12 Gratt.) 655 (1855).

A municipal corporation may be garnished or attached for a debt due to one of its creditors just as a natural person may be. Such a proceeding is not contrary to the public policy of this State. Portsmouth Gas Co. v. Sanford, 97 Va. 124, 33 S.E. 516 (1899).

State Treasurer cannot be garnished in attachment against foreign insurance company. — The treasurer of the State, who holds bonds of a foreign insurance company doing business in the State, is not liable to be summoned as garnishee by a foreign creditor of the insurance company. Rollo v. Andes Ins. Co., 64 Va. (23 Gratt.) 509 (1873).

C. What May Be Garnished.

Money on deposit is subject to garnishment. — Money was left with a person who was a member of a firm, on a special deposit, and in his absence it was entered on the books of the firm to the credit of the depositor, and paid out by the firm for their own uses, they paying the depositor's checks upon it, by checks in their own name upon the bank. An attachment was served upon the firm as garnishees in a suit against the depositor, the summons being served on the other member of the firm. It was held that the attachment bound the money in the hands of the firm. Pulliam v. Aler, 56 Va. (15 Gratt.) 54 (1859).

Trust funds in hands of public officer are not. — No lien can be obtained by attachment upon funds charged with a trust in the hands of a public officer. Rollo v. Andes Ins. Co., 64 Va. (23 Gratt.) 509 (1873); Foley v. Shriver, 81 Va. 568 (1886); Buck v. Guarantors' Liab. Indem. Co., 97 Va. 719, 34 S.E. 950 (1900).

Land in possession of garnishee. — In a proceeding by foreign attachment, the home defendant denied that he had any effects of the absent debtor in his hands. He said that a tract of land which had belonged to the absent debtor, had been purchased by himself and paid for, and he in fact held the receipt of the absent debtor for the amount of the purchase money. As, however, he did not pretend he had paid the amount in money, and as the accounts which he endeavored to establish were not proved to the satisfaction of the commissioner and the court, the land was held liable. Kelly v. Linkenhoger, 49 Va. (8 Gratt.) 104 (1851).

The shares of a stockholder in a joint stock company may properly be considered, for the purpose of attachment proceedings, as in the possession of the corporation in which the shares are held and the corporation may properly be summoned as garnishee in the case. C & O R.R. v. Paine & Co., 70 Va. (29 Gratt.) 502 (1877).

D. Practice and Procedure.

Garnishee may be compelled to pay interest. — A home defendant decreed to pay money to a creditor of an absent defendant will be compelled to pay interest, unless he makes a legal tender, or brings the money into court. Ross v. Austin, 14 Va. (4 Hen. & M.) 502 (1810).

Garnishee may set up equitable defense. — The garnishee may set up any equitable defense which shows that in equity he owes no debt to the defendant. Glassell v. Thomas, 30 Va. (3 Leigh) 113 (1831).

He may interplead third person claiming property. — Where, along with the answer of the garnishee, an affidavit is filed, alleging that some third person claims the property to be attached, and that the garnishee claims no interest therein, nor does it collude with the claimant, but is ready to dispose of the property as the court shall direct, the court should require the third person to appear and state the nature of his claim, and maintain or relinquish the same. C & O R.R. v. Paine & Co., 70 Va. (29 Gratt.) 792 (1878).

He may waive irregularity of service and return. — Though the service of an attachment upon a garnishee, and the return thereon, are irregular, yet if the garnishee appears to the action and defends it, without objecting to the irregularity, he cannot afterwards make the objection in the appellate court. Pulliam v. Aler, 56 Va. (15 Gratt.) 54 (1859).

Court may order payment to receiver. — A garnishee having admitted his indebtedness to the debtor, the court may order him to pay his debt to a receiver appointed by the court, and a payment to the receiver by the garnishee is a valid payment, and a discharge of his indebtedness as to the attaching creditor. Withers v. Fuller, 71 Va. (30 Gratt.) 547 (1878).

§ 8.01-563. Principal defendant may claim exemption. — The principal defendant, if a householder or head of a family, may claim that the amount so found owing from his codefendant, or the personal property in his possession, shall be exempt from liability for the plaintiff's claim; and if it shall appear that the principal defendant is entitled to such exemption, then the court shall render a judgment against the defendant only for the excess, if any, beyond the exemption to which the principal defendant is entitled. (Code 1950, § 8-551; 1977, c. 617.)

Cross references. — As to homestead and other exemptions, § 34-1 et seq.

§ 8.01-564. Procedure when codefendant fails to appear. — If the attachment be served on a defendant who the petition alleges is indebted to, or has in his possession effects of, the principal defendant, and he fail to appear, the court may either compel him to appear, or hear proof of any debt owing by him, or of effects in his hands belonging to a principal defendant in such attachment, and make such orders in relation thereto as if what is so proved had appeared on his examination. (Code 1950, § 8-552; 1977, c. 617.)

Cross references. — As to application of this and following section in garnishment proceedings to enforce execution lien, see § 8.01-519.

§ 8.01-565. Suggestion that codefendant has not made full disclosure. — When it is suggested by the plaintiff in any attachment that a codefendant has not fully disclosed the debts owing by him, or effects in his hands belonging to the principal defendant in such attachment, the court, without any formal pleading, shall inquire as to such debts and effects, or, if either party demand, it shall cause a jury to be impaneled for that purpose, and proceed in respect to any such debts or effects found by the court or the jury in the same manner as if they had been confessed by such codefendant. If the judgment of the court or verdict of the jury be in favor of such codefendant, he shall have judgment for his costs against the plaintiff. (Code 1950, § 8-553; 1977, c. 617.)

§ 8.01-566. Who may make defense to attachment. — Any of the defendants in any such attachment, or any party to any forthcoming bond given as aforesaid, or the officer who may be liable to the plaintiff by reason of such bond being adjudged bad, or any person authorized by § 8.01-573 to file a petition, may make defense to such attachment, but the attachment shall not thereby be discharged, or the property levied on released. (Code 1950, § 8-554; 1973, c. 545; 1977, c. 617.)

§ 8.01-567. What defense may be made to attachments. — Any party in interest may show that the court is without jurisdiction to hear and determine the controversy.

The principal defendant, if not served with process, may appear specially and show that the attachment was issued on false suggestion or without sufficient cause, in which event the attachment shall be quashed.

Any person claiming title to, an interest in, or a lien upon the property attached, or any part thereof, after being admitted as a party defendant, if not already a defendant, and the principal defendant, may contest the liability of the principal defendant for the plaintiff's claim, in whole or in part, by proof of any manner which would constitute a good defense by the principal defendant to an action at law on such claim, and may also show that the attachment was not issued on any of the grounds set forth in § 8.01-534, or that the plaintiff is not likely to succeed on the merits of his underlying claim. The principal defendant may also file counterclaims or defenses available under § 8.01-422 as in an action at law.

Other defendants shall be limited to defenses personal to themselves, or which may prevent a liability upon them or their property. (Code 1950, § 8-555; 1977, c. 617.)

REVISERS' NOTE

Section 8.01-567 is former § 8-555. The word "defendant" in the first sentence has been replaced by the phrase "... party in interest...." The language "...on false suggestion or without sufficient cause" has been replaced with the language "...on any of the grounds set forth in § 8.01-534, or that the plaintiff is not likely to succeed on the merits of the underlying claim." In place of the word "set-offs," the language "...counterclaims or defenses available under § 8.01-422..." has been substituted in order to comport with the applicable rules of court and the statute relating to equitable defenses.

Cross references. — As to jurisdiction of attachments, see § 8.01-535.

§ 8.01-568. Quashing attachment or rendering judgment for defendant. — The court in which an attachment is pending shall, on motion of the principal defendant, or any defendant claiming title to, an interest in, or a lien upon the property attached, or any part thereof, after reasonable notice to the plaintiff, hear testimony and quash the attachment, if of opinion that (i) the attachment is invalid on its face, (ii) none of the grounds for attachment in § 8.01-534 exist, or (iii) the plaintiff is not likely to succeed on the merits of his underlying claim. The hearing shall be held not later than ten business days following the defendant's motion. When the attachment is properly sued out, and the case is heard upon its merits, if the court is of opinion that the claim of the plaintiff is not established, final judgment shall be given for the

§ 8.01-568

defendant. In either case, he shall recover his costs, and damages for loss of the use of his property, and there shall be an order for the restoration of the attached effects. The plaintiff shall have the burden of proof in proceedings pursuant to this section. (Code 1950, § 8-556; 1977, c. 617; 1984, c. 646.)

REVISERS' NOTE

Section 8.01-568 is former § 8-556. The language "...was issued on false suggestion, or without sufficient cause" has been replaced with the language "... that none of the grounds for attachment in § 8.01-534 exist, or that the plaintiff is not likely to succeed on the merits of his underlying claim." The words "attaching creditor" have been replaced with the word "plaintiff." Following the word "costs," the language "...and damages for loss of the use of his property..." has been added. A final sentence has been added specifying that the plaintiff is to have the burden of proof in proceedings under this section. This codifies case law on former § 8-556. (See Wright v. Rambo, 62 Va. (21 Gratt.) 158 (1871); see also, Burruss v. Trant, 88 Va. 980, 14 S.E. 845 (1892)).

I. Decisions Under Current Law.
II. Decisions Under Prior Law.

I. DECISIONS UNDER CURRENT LAW.

Applied in Fuller v. Hurley, 559 F. Supp. 313 (W.D. Va. 1983).

II. DECISIONS UNDER PRIOR LAW.

Editor's note. — The cases cited below were decided under corresponding provisions of former law. The term "this section," as used below, refers to former provisions.

If an affidavit (now petition) is defective, the remedy is by motion to quash the attachment. Anderson v. Johnson, 73 Va. (32 Gratt.) 558 (1879).

Appearance on motion to quash is not waiver of defects. — An appearance on a motion to quash an attachment because of irregular execution is not an appearance to the action whereby alleged defects are waived. Petty v. Frick Co., 86 Va. 501, 10 S.E. 886 (1890).

Attachment may be abated at any time before final judgment. — The authority given the court under this section to enter judgment abating the attachment may be exercised at any time before a final judgment has been entered disposing of the property attached. Northern Neck State Bank, Inc. v. Gilbert Packing Co., 114 Va. 658, 77 S.E. 451 (1913).

Former order overruling motion does not bind court. — The court is not precluded from abating the attachment because at a former stage of the proceeding a motion to abate was overruled, if upon further consideration it is satisfied that the writ was issued upon an insufficient affidavit. Northern Neck State Bank, Inc. v. Gilbert Packing Co., 114 Va. 658, 77 S.E. 451 (1913).

An attachment irregularly issued ought to be quashed ex officio by the court to which it is returned, though bail is not given, nor any plea filed by the defendant. Mantz v. Hendley, 12 Va. (2 Hen. & M.) 308 (1808).

Irregular attachment may be dismissed on appeal. — Objections to the regularity of attachment proceedings may be taken advantage of, not only in the trial court, but in an appellate court, although not raised in the trial court, and the court may, of its own motion, dismiss an irregular attachment, and ought to do so when there has been no appearance by the nonresident debtor, and no personal service upon him. McAllister v. Guggenheimer, 91 Va. 317, 21 S.E. 475 (1895). But see Sims v. Tyrer, 96 Va. 5, 26 S.E. 508 (1898).

Validity of plaintiff's demand is not involved. — The question of the validity of the debt or demand of the plaintiff, i.e., whether it is or is not established, does not arise upon a preliminary motion to quash the attachment, but only when the case is heard upon its merits. Consequently, the question of the liability of a partnership for torts of one of the partners is not within the scope of a motion to quash an attachment, but must be determined when the case comes up for trial on its merits. Henry Myers & Co. v. Lewis, 121 Va. 50, 92 S.E. 988 (1917).

But actual existence of sufficient cause must be shown. — The question is whether, upon all the evidence, there was probable cause to believe the defendant was doing the act which would authorize the attachment, and not whether the facts as they appeared to the affiant, though only a small part perhaps of the facts of the case, afforded him reasonable grounds for such a belief. Claflin & Co. v.

Steenbock & Co., 59 Va. (18 Gratt.) 842 (1868).

And mere belief of plaintiff is insufficient. — The remedy is justified, not by the belief of the affiant, however honestly entertained upon reasonable grounds that the fact sworn to in the petition exists, but by the existence of that fact. Sublett v. Wood, 76 Va. 318 (1882).

Proceeding must be good on its face. — The remedy by attachment against the estate of a nonresident is wholly statutory, harsh in its operation towards the debtor and his creditors, and the proceeding must show on its face that the requirements of this section have been substantially complied with. McAllister v. Guggenheimer, 91 Va. 317, 21 S.E. 475 (1895).

The return must show that the attachment was levied on the property of the defendant in order to make it valid. Robertson v. Hoge, 83 Va. 124, 1 S.E. 667 (1887); Offtendinger v. Ford, 86 Va. 917, 12 S.E. 1 (1890).

Burden of proving sufficient cause is on plaintiff. — Upon a motion to abate an attachment, the burden of proof is on the plaintiff to show that the attachment was issued on sufficient cause, and he may therefore be required to introduce his evidence first. Wright v. Rambo, 62 Va. (21 Gratt.) 158 (1871); Sublett v. Wood, 76 Va. 318 (1882); Burruss v. Trant, 88 Va. 980, 14 S.E. 845 (1892).

§ 8.01-569. When petition dismissed; when retained and cause tried.

— If the principal defendant has not appeared generally, nor been served with process, and the sole ground of jurisdiction of the court is the right to sue out the attachment, and this right be decided against the plaintiff, the petition shall be dismissed at the cost of the plaintiff; but if the plaintiff's claim be due at the hearing, and the court would otherwise have jurisdiction of an action against such defendant for the cause set forth in the petition, and such defendant has appeared generally, or been served with process, it shall retain the cause and proceed to final judgment as in other actions at law. (Code 1950, § 8-557; 1977, c. 617.)

Cross references. — As to failure to pay writ tax, see § 8.01-537.

I. DECISIONS UNDER PRIOR LAW.

Editor's note. — The cases cited below were decided under corresponding provisions of former law. The term "this section," as used below, refers to former provisions.

If defendant appears generally, court may enter personal judgment. — Under this section, where the defendant in attachment was properly before the court, the court undoubtedly had jurisdiction to enter a personal judgment against the defendant, even though the attachment was dismissed. Maryland Cas. Co. v. Parrish, 150 Va. 473, 143 S.E. 750 (1928).

Jury may be impaneled to try issue. — It is not error for the trial court to impanel a jury in an attachment case to try the issue, as § 8.01-336 provides that where an issue of fact is joined on motion, a jury may be impaneled, when in the opinion of the court it is proper. Jayne v. Kane, 140 Va. 27, 124 S.E. 247 (1924).

Failure to dismiss attachment held not error. — Where the principal defendant assigned as error the failure to dismiss the attachment because the executor of an estate who was indebted to, and had in his possession property belonging to the principal defendant, was made a party defendant before there had been an ascertainment of whether there were any prior liens on the principal defendant's share of the estate, as there had been a general appearance by the principal defendant under this section, there was no issue before the Supreme Court with regard to the attachment. Continental Trust Co. v. Witt, 139 Va. 458, 124 S.E. 265 (1924).

§ 8.01-570. Judgment, etc., of court when claim of plaintiff established.

— If the claim of the plaintiff be established, judgment shall be rendered for him, and the court shall dispose of the specific property levied on, as may be right, and order the sale of any other effects or real estate which shall not have been previously released or sold under this chapter, and direct the proceeds of sale, and whatever else is subject to the attachment, including what is embraced by such forthcoming bond, to be applied in satisfaction of the judgment. (Code 1950, § 8-558; 1977, c. 617.)

I. Decisions Under Current Law.
II. Decisions Under Prior Law.

I. DECISIONS UNDER CURRENT LAW.

Attachment proceedings include both establishment of a lien on the property attached and execution of the lien through a judicial sale, after adjudication of the petitioner's right thereto. Hence, the attachment proceeding in effect incorporates an action to foreclose on the lien that is created by the attachment. Eastern Indem. Co. v. J.D. Conti Elec. Co., 573 F. Supp. 1036 (E.D. Va. 1983).

II. DECISIONS UNDER PRIOR LAW.

Editor's note. — The cases cited below were decided under corresponding provisions of former law. The term "this section," as used below, refers to former provisions.

Plaintiff is entitled to personal judgment. — The attaching creditor, having established his debt, is entitled to a personal decree against the absent debtor though the whole property attached is exhausted in paying the debt of the home defendant. Williamson v. Gayle, 48 Va. (7 Gratt.) 152 (1850). See also, Hairston v. Medley, 42 Va. (1 Gratt.) 96 (1844); Schofield v. Cox, 49 Va. (8 Gratt.) 533 (1852).

Order of sale is not personal judgment. — An order in an attachment case which recites that it appears to the satisfaction of the court that the defendant is indebted to the plaintiff in a stated sum, and directs a sale of the attached effects, or so much thereof as may be necessary to pay the sum so stated, is not a personal judgment against the defendant, but reaches only the goods attached. Bernard v. McClanahan, 115 Va. 453, 79 S.E. 1059 (1913).

The judgment must require plaintiff to give security as provided in § 8.01-571. Watts Ex'rs v. Robertson, 14 Va. (4 Hen. & M.) 442 (1809).

Judgment for interest. — If the attachment demands only principal and costs, the court cannot give judgment for interest. George v. Blue, 7 Va. (3 Call) 455 (1803).

§ 8.01-571. When defendant not served fails to appear plaintiff required to give bond. — If the principal defendant has not appeared or been served with a copy of the attachment ten days before the judgment therein mentioned, the plaintiff shall not have the benefit of § 8.01-570 unless and until he shall have given bond with sufficient surety in such penalty as the court shall approve, with condition to perform such future order as may be made upon the appearance of such defendant and his making defense. If the plaintiff fail to give such bond in a reasonable time, the court shall dispose of the estate attached, or the proceeds thereof, as to it shall seem just. (Code 1950, § 8-542; 1977, c. 617.)

I. DECISIONS UNDER PRIOR LAW.

Editor's note. — The cases cited below were decided under corresponding provisions of former law. The term "this section," as used below, refers to former provisions.

Bond is not necessary if defendant has been served. — If it appears that a copy of the attachment was served on the defendant 60 (now 10) days before a decree (now a judgment) for the sale of land attached, the order for the sale may be made without requiring the bond provided for in this section. Anderson v. Johnson, 73 Va. (32 Gratt.) 558 (1879).

Or if time for rehearing case has expired. — The time allowed by § 8.01-575, within which a case may be reheard, having expired, a plaintiff is entitled to the benefit of a decree without giving the security originally required. Ross v. Austin, 14 Va. (4 Hen. & M.) 502 (1810).

§ 8.01-572. Sale of real estate attached. — No real estate shall be sold until all other property and money subject to the attachment have been exhausted, and then only so much thereof as is necessary to pay the judgment. Upon a sale of real estate, under an attachment the court shall have the same powers and jurisdiction, and like proceedings thereon may be had, as if it were a sale of real estate by a court of equity exercising general equity powers. (Code 1950, § 8-559; 1977, c. 617.)

§ 8.01-573. How and when claims of other persons to property tried. — Any person may file his petition at any time before the property attached as the estate of a defendant is sold or the proceeds of sale paid to the plaintiff under the judgment, disputing the validity of the plaintiff's attachment thereon, or stating a claim thereto, or an interest in or lien on the same, under any other attachment or otherwise, and its nature, and upon giving security for cost, the court, without any other pleading, shall inquire into such claim, or, if either party demand it, impanel a jury for that purpose. If it be found that the petitioner has title to, or a lien on, or any interest in, such property, or its proceeds, the court shall make such order as may be necessary to protect his rights. The costs of such inquiry shall be paid by either party, at the discretion of the court. (Code 1950, § 8-560; 1977, c. 617.)

I. Decisions Under Current Law.
II. Decisions Under Prior Law.

I. DECISIONS UNDER CURRENT LAW.

Applied in Eastern Indem. Co. v. J.D. Conti Elec. Co., 573 F. Supp. 1036 (E.D. Va. 1983).

II. DECISIONS UNDER PRIOR LAW.

Editor's note. — The cases cited below were decided under corresponding provisions of former law. The term "this section," as used below, refers to former provisions.

This section was intended for the protection of the rights of third parties, and not of the plaintiff in the attachment. Littell v. Lansburg Furn. & Carpet Co., 96 Va. 540, 32 S.E. 63 (1899).

It protects equitable as well as legal rights. — The evident purpose of this section was to protect the equitable as well as the legal rights and interests of third persons in the attachment proceedings, and that the lien of the attaching creditor should be subordinated to all such rights and interests as exist at the time the attachment is levied. Barnes v. American Fertilizer Co., 144 Va. 692, 130 S.E. 902 (1925).

Wife's interest in divorce settlement will be protected. — A decree in a divorce suit approving an agreement between the parties to transfer the husband's real estate to the wife and children, in the absence of fraud or collusion, under this section vests the wife and children with an equitable interest which is superior to a subsequent attachment against the husband and which will be protected under this section. Barnes v. American Fertilizer Co., 144 Va. 692, 130 S.E. 902 (1925).

Plaintiff in attachment cannot unite with trustees in deed of trust. — A plaintiff in attachment, who has a deed of trust on the property attached, cannot unite with the trustees in the deed and come into the attachment suit by petition under this section and ask to have the attached property delivered to the trustees. Littell v. Lansburg Furn. & Carpet Co., 96 Va. 540, 32 S.E. 63 (1899).

Proper issue. — Where a petitioner claims the attached property under this section, the proper issue to be tried is "whether or not petitioner has any title to, lien on or interest in the attached property or its proceeds." Starke v. Scott, 78 Va. 180 (1883).

Hearing by consent. — Where, in attachment against property of nonresident debtors, who had not been served with process personally or by publication, complainants consented to the hearing of a motion by a claimant of the property to abate the attachment, a decree abating the attachment, and declaring the estate not to belong to the debtors, was not premature or erroneous. Kern v. Wyatt, 89 Va. 885, 17 S.E. 549 (1893).

§ 8.01-574. Attachments in connection with pending suits or actions. — If an attachment be desired in connection with a pending suit or action, a petition for an attachment may be filed in the same court in which such suit or action is pending, and the procedure thereon shall be the same as if no suit or action were pending; but the attachment may be heard along with any suit in equity relating to the same subject so far as may be necessary for the convenient administration of justice. The suing out of an attachment in connection with a pending suit or action shall not be deemed the prosecution of a second action for the same cause. (Code 1950, § 8-561; 1977, c. 617.)

I. DECISIONS UNDER CURRENT LAW.

Applied in First Charter Land Corp. v. Fitzgerald, 643 F.2d 1011 (4th Cir. 1981).

§ 8.01-575. Rehearing permitted when judgment rendered on publication.

— If a defendant, against whom, on publication, judgment is rendered under any attachment, or his personal representative, shall return to or appear openly in this Commonwealth, he may, within one year after a copy of such judgment shall be served on him at the instance of the plaintiff, or within two years from the date of the judgment, if he be not so served, petition to have the proceedings reheard. On giving security for costs he shall be admitted to make defense against such judgment, as if he had appeared in the case before the same was rendered, except that the title of any bona fide purchaser to any property, real or personal, sold under such attachment, shall not be brought in question or impeached. But this section shall not apply to any case in which the petitioner, or his decedent, was served with a copy of the attachment more than ten days before the date of the judgment, or to any case in which he appeared and made defense. (Code 1950, § 8-562; 1977, c. 617.)

REVISERS' NOTE

Section 8.01-575 is former § 8-562. The present five-year period of limitation has been reduced to two years in order to comport with § 8.01-322, relating to orders of publication generally.

Former Article 4, which consisted of one section, § 8-564, dealing with attachment for a claim not exceeding twenty dollars, has been deleted since such a claim is de minimis and would not likely merit the attachment remedy.

Former Article 5, dealing with the attachment of rent and consisting of §§ 8-566 through 8-568, has been deleted as rent is no longer to be accorded separate treatment for attachment purposes.

Former Article 6, comprised of §§ 8-569 through 8-577, dealing with capias ad respondendum, has been deleted as obsolete and unnecessary.

I. DECISIONS UNDER PRIOR LAW.

Editor's note. — The cases cited below were decided under corresponding provisions of former law. The term "this section," as used below, refers to former provisions.

Section limits rights of nonresidents. — Nonresidents labor under no disability with respect to the right to institute or prosecute suit at any time to assert or preserve any right of action they may have, and no such right is reserved to them by statute. On the contrary when proceeded against by order of publication, etc., their rights in this respect are restricted and limited by this section and § 8.01-322. Baber v. Baber, 121 Va. 740, 94 S.E. 209 (1917).

Absent defendant may appear while suit is pending. — Under this section a defendant in a foreign attachment may appear at any time pending the suit, and have the cause reheard, tendering security for costs. Anderson v. Johnson, 73 Va. (32 Gratt.) 558 (1879).

After judgment, sole remedy is under this section. — An absent defendant, against whom a decree (now judgment) has been made, cannot appeal from the decree. His only remedy is that provided by this section. Platt v. Howland, 37 Va. (10 Leigh) 507 (1839); Barbee & Co. v. Pannill, 47 Va. (6 Gratt.) 442 (1849).

Effect on judgment upon filing petition. — Where nonresident defendants filed a petition in strict conformity with this section, and were never at any time prior to filing their petition served with process or a copy of the attachment, nor did they appear or make any defense, the judgment granted by the court against the defendants fixing a personal liability upon them lost that effect upon the filing of defendants' petition, for this section allowed them to make defense against the judgment as if they had appeared in the case before the same was rendered. This could only mean that they were to be in no wise prejudiced by the judgment, but should occupy the same position as if no such judgment had been rendered. Wessel, Duval & Co. v. Winborn & Co., 125 Va. 502, 99 S.E. 719 (1919).

Service out of State does not affect right to rehearing. — Under this section, defendants in foreign attachment may appear pending the suit, tender security for costs and have it reheard. The exception of a defendant served with a copy of the attachment, or with process in the suit, does not refer to a service thereof outside the proceedings in the suit or outside the State; such service can have no greater effect than an order of publication duly posted and published. This rule applies also to acknowledgments of such services made outside the State. Anderson v. Johnson, 73 Va. (32 Gratt.) 558 (1879); Smith & Winnsatt v.

Chilton, 77 Va. 535 (1883).
This section applies to attachment against a foreign corporation not doing business in the State, for breach of a contract made out of the State. Smith v. Life Ass'n of Am., 76 Va. 380 (1882).

§ 8.01-576. Order of court on rehearing or new trial; restitution to defendant. — On any rehearing or new trial had under § 8.01-575, the court may order the plaintiff in the original attachment to restore any money paid to him under such judgment to such defendant if living, or if dead to the heir or personal representative of such defendant, as the same may be, the proceeds of real or personal estate, and enter a judgment therefor against him; or it may confirm the former judgment. In either case it shall adjudge the costs of the prevailing party. (Code 1950, § 8-563; 1977, c. 617.)

Law Review. — For article, "Explaining Restitution," see 71 Va. L. Rev. 65 (1985).

CHAPTER 20.1.
Summary Jury Trial.

Sec.
8.01-576.1. Election by parties; order of court.
8.01-576.2. Summary jury trial; selection of jury; fees.

Sec.
8.01-576.3. Procedures; verdict not binding unless otherwise agreed.

§ 8.01-576.1. Election by parties; order of court. — In any civil action pending before a circuit court, the parties may, by agreement in writing submitted to the court at any time prior to trial, elect to have a summary jury trial of the issues in the case in accordance with this chapter. However, where the court determines that the election is made for the purpose of delaying a trial on the merits, a summary jury trial shall not be had. (1988, c. 759.)

§ 8.01-576.2. Summary jury trial; selection of jury; fees. — Upon election of the parties, the court shall schedule a summary jury trial to be held as soon as convenient. Notice shall be given to the parties by means adequate to ensure their presence at the time and place of the trial. Seven jurors shall be randomly selected in accordance with the procedures specified in Chapter 11 (§ 8.01-336 et seq.). Fees shall be allowed to jurors selected for a summary jury trial as provided in § 17.1-618. (1988, c. 759.)

§ 8.01-576.3. Procedures; verdict not binding unless otherwise agreed. — A judge of the court having jurisdiction over the case shall preside over a summary jury trial. Counsel for the parties or, if a party is not represented by counsel, a party shall verbally present a summary of the issues in the case and the evidence on behalf of each party. Evidence for the plaintiff shall be presented first. Each party shall be given the opportunity to rebut the evidence of another party upon request. The testimony of witnesses and the submission of documentary evidence shall not be allowed except as stipulated or agreed to by the parties.

Upon conclusion of the presentations of the summary evidence, the court shall instruct the jury on the law applicable to the cause. The jury shall advise the court of its verdict upon conclusion of the deliberations.

Unless otherwise agreed by the parties in writing submitted to the court prior to a jury being impanelled pursuant to this chapter, the verdict of a summary jury shall not be binding on either party and shall not be admissible on any subsequent trial of the case. If the parties have agreed to be bound by the verdict, judgment shall be entered by the court in accordance with the verdict. (1988, c. 759.)

CHAPTER 20.2.
Dispute Resolution Proceedings.

Sec.
8.01-576.4. Definitions.
8.01-576.5. Referral of disputes to dispute resolution proceedings.
8.01-576.6. Notice and opportunity to object.
8.01-576.7. Costs.
8.01-576.8. Qualifications of neutrals; referral.

Sec.
8.01-576.9. Standards and duties of neutrals; confidentiality; liability.
8.01-576.10. Confidentiality of dispute resolution proceeding.
8.01-576.11. Effect of written settlement agreement.
8.01-576.12. Vacating orders and agreements.

§ **8.01-576.4. Definitions.** — As used in this chapter:
"Conciliation" means a process in which a neutral facilitates settlement by clarifying issues and serving as an intermediary for negotiations in a manner which is generally more informal and less structured than mediation.

"Court" means any juvenile and domestic relations district court, general district court, circuit court, or appellate court, and includes the judges and any intake specialist to whom the judge has delegated specific authority under this chapter.

"Dispute resolution proceeding" means any structured process in which a neutral assists disputants in reaching a voluntary settlement by means of dispute resolution techniques such as mediation, conciliation, early neutral evaluation, nonjudicial settlement conferences or any other proceeding leading to a voluntary settlement conducted consistent with the requirements of this chapter. The term includes the evaluation session.

"Dispute resolution program" means a program that offers dispute resolution services to the public which is run by the Commonwealth or any private for-profit or not-for-profit organization, political subdivision, or public corporation, or a combination of these.

"Dispute resolution services" includes screening and intake of disputants, conducting dispute resolution proceedings, drafting agreements and providing information or referral services.

"Evaluation session" means a preliminary meeting during which the parties and the neutral assess the case and decide whether to continue with a dispute resolution proceeding or with adjudication.

"Intake specialist" means an individual who is trained in analyzing and screening cases to assist in determining whether a case is appropriate for referral to a dispute resolution proceeding.

"Mediation" means a process in which a neutral facilitates communication between the parties and, without deciding the issues or imposing a solution on the parties, enables them to understand and resolve their dispute.

"Neutral" means an individual who is trained or experienced in conducting dispute resolution proceedings and in providing dispute resolution services. (1993, c. 905.)

§ **8.01-576.5. Referral of disputes to dispute resolution proceedings.** — While protecting the right to trial by jury, a court, on its own motion or on motion of one of the parties, may refer any contested civil matter, or selected issues in a civil matter, to a dispute resolution evaluation session in order to encourage the early settlement of disputes through the use of procedures that facilitate (i) open communication between the parties about the issues in the dispute, (ii) full exploration of the range of options to resolve the dispute, (iii) improvement in the relationship between the parties, and (iv) control by the parties over the outcome of the dispute. The court shall set a date for the parties to return to court in accordance with its regular docket and procedure, irrespective of the referral to an evaluation session. The parties shall notify the court, in writing, if the dispute is resolved prior to the return date.

Upon such referral, the parties shall attend one evaluation session unless excused pursuant to § 8.01-576.6. Further participation in a dispute resolution proceeding shall be by consent of all parties. Attorneys for any party may be present during a dispute resolution proceeding. (1993, c. 905.)

§ **8.01-576.6. Notice and opportunity to object.** — When a court has determined that referral to a dispute resolution evaluation session is appropriate, an order of referral to a neutral or to a dispute resolution program shall be entered and the parties shall be so notified as expeditiously as possible. The court shall excuse the parties from participation in a dispute resolution evaluation session if, within fourteen days after entry of the order, a written statement signed by any party is filed with the court, stating that the dispute resolution process has been explained to the party and he objects to the referral. (1993, c. 905.)

§ **8.01-576.7. Costs.** — The evaluation session shall be conducted at no cost to the parties. Unless otherwise provided by statute or agreed to by the parties and the neutral, the court may set a reasonable fee for the services of any neutral to whom a case is referred by the court as provided in § 8.01-576.8. Prior to setting the rate and method of payment pursuant to this chapter, the court shall determine whether any of the parties is indigent. If it is determined that one or more of the parties is indigent and no agreement as to payment is reached between the parties, the court shall refer the case to a dispute resolution program that offers services at no charge to the parties or to a neutral who has agreed to accept cases on a pro bono or volunteer basis. If it is determined that neither of the parties is indigent, and the parties have not selected a dispute resolution program that offers services at no cost nor agreed with the neutral as to another method of payment, the judge may assess the fees of the neutral as costs of suit. (1993, c. 905.)

§ **8.01-576.8. Qualifications of neutrals; referral.** — A neutral who provides dispute resolution services other than mediation pursuant to this chapter shall provide the court with a written statement of qualifications, describing the neutral's background and relevant training and experience in the field. A mediator who desires to receive referrals from the court shall be certified pursuant to guidelines promulgated by the Judicial Council of Virginia. A dispute resolution program may satisfy the requirements of this section on behalf of its neutrals by providing the court with a written statement of the background, training, experience and certification, as appropriate, of any neutral who participates in its program.

The court shall maintain a list of neutrals and dispute resolution programs which have met the requirements of this section. The list may be divided among the areas of specialization or expertise maintained by the neutrals. At the conclusion of the evaluation session, or no later than ten days thereafter, parties electing to continue with the dispute resolution proceeding may: (i) continue with the neutral who conducted the evaluation session, (ii) select any neutral or dispute resolution program from the list maintained by the court to conduct such proceedings, or (iii) pursue any other alternative for voluntarily resolving the dispute to which the parties agree. If the parties choose to proceed with the dispute resolution proceeding but are unable to agree on a neutral or dispute resolution program during that period, the court shall refer the case to a neutral or dispute resolution program on the list maintained by the court on the basis of a fair and equitable rotation, taking into account the subject matter of the dispute and the expertise of the neutral, as appropriate. (1993, c. 905.)

§ 8.01-576.9. **Standards and duties of neutrals; confidentiality; liability.** — A neutral selected to conduct a dispute resolution proceeding under this chapter may encourage and assist the parties in reaching a resolution of their dispute, but may not compel or coerce the parties into entering into a settlement agreement. A neutral has an obligation to remain impartial and free from conflict of interests in each case, and to decline to participate further in a case should such partiality or conflict arise. Unless expressly authorized by the disclosing party, the neutral may not disclose to either party information relating to the subject matter of the dispute resolution proceeding provided to him in confidence by the other. In reporting on the outcome of the dispute resolution proceeding to the referring court, the neutral shall indicate only the terms of any agreement reached or the fact that no agreement was reached. The neutral shall not disclose information exchanged or observations regarding the conduct and demeanor of the parties and their counsel during the dispute resolution proceeding, unless the parties otherwise agree.

However, where the dispute involves the support of minor children of the parties, the parties shall disclose between themselves and to the neutral the information to be used in completing the child support guidelines worksheet required by § 20-108.2. The guidelines computations and any reasons for deviation shall be incorporated in any written agreement between the parties.

With respect to liability, the provisions of § 8.01-581.23 shall apply in claims arising out of services rendered by any neutral. (1993, c. 905; 1994, c. 687.)

§ 8.01-576.10. **Confidentiality of dispute resolution proceeding.** — All memoranda, work products or other materials contained in the case files of a neutral or dispute resolution program are confidential. Any communication made in or in connection with the dispute resolution proceeding which relates to the controversy, whether made to the neutral or dispute resolution program or to a party, or to any other person if made at a dispute resolution proceeding, is confidential. However, a written settlement agreement shall not be confidential, unless the parties otherwise agree in writing.

Confidential materials and communications are not subject to disclosure in any judicial or administrative proceeding except (i) where all parties to the dispute resolution proceeding agree, in writing, to waive the confidentiality, (ii) in a subsequent action between the neutral or dispute resolution program and a party to the dispute resolution proceeding for damages arising out of the dispute resolution proceeding, or (iii) statements, memoranda, materials and other tangible evidence, otherwise subject to discovery, which were not prepared specifically for use in and actually used in the dispute resolution proceeding. The use of attorney work product in a dispute resolution proceeding shall not result in a waiver of the attorney work product privilege.

Notwithstanding the provisions of this section, in any case where the dispute involves support of the minor children of the parties, financial information, including information contained in the child support guidelines worksheet, and written reasons for any deviation from the guidelines shall be disclosed to each party and the court for the purpose of computing a basic child support amount pursuant to § 20-108.2. (1993, c. 905; 1994, c. 687.)

I. DECISIONS UNDER CURRENT LAW.

Objection to use at trial. — Although admission of the evidence challenged in the two assignments of error relying on this section was the subject of several objections by plaintiff's counsel during the hearing, not once did counsel cite to the trial judge or rely on this section, or any other statute dealing with dispute resolution proceedings. Thus, the trial court was never afforded the opportunity to address and rule on the issues that the plaintiff now raises, and the state supreme court will not consider them for the first time on appeal. Snyder-Falkinham v. Stockburger, 249 Va. 376, 457 S.E.2d 36 (1995).

§ 8.01-576.11. Effect of written settlement agreement. — If the parties reach a settlement and execute a written agreement disposing of the dispute, the agreement is enforceable in the same manner as any other written contract. Upon request of all parties and consistent with law and public policy, the court shall incorporate the written agreement into the terms of its final decree disposing of a case. In cases in which the dispute involves support for the minor children of the parties, an order incorporating a written agreement shall also include the child support guidelines worksheet and, if applicable, the written reasons for any deviation from the guidelines. The child support guidelines worksheet shall be attached to the order. (1993, c. 905; 1994, c. 687.)

§ 8.01-576.12. Vacating orders and agreements. — Upon the filing of an independent action by a party, the court shall vacate a mediated agreement reached in a dispute resolution proceeding pursuant to this chapter, or vacate an order incorporating or resulting from such agreement, where:

1. The agreement was procured by fraud or duress, or is unconscionable;
2. If property or financial matters are in dispute, the parties failed to provide substantial full disclosure of all relevant property and financial information; or
3. There was evident partiality or misconduct by the neutral, prejudicing the rights of any party.

For purposes of this section, "misconduct" includes failure of the neutral to inform the parties in writing at the commencement of the mediation process that: (i) the neutral does not provide legal advice, (ii) any mediated agreement will affect the legal rights of the parties, (iii) each party to the mediation has the opportunity to consult with independent legal counsel at any time and is encouraged to do so, and (iv) each party to the mediation should have any draft agreement reviewed by independent counsel prior to signing the agreement or should waive his opportunity to do so.

The fact that any provisions of a mediated agreement were such that they could not or would not be granted by a court of law or equity is not, in and of itself, grounds for vacating an agreement.

A motion to vacate under this section shall be made within two years after the mediated agreement is entered into, except that, if predicated upon fraud, it shall be made within two years after these grounds are discovered or reasonably should have been discovered. (1993, c. 905.)

CHAPTER 21.

ARBITRATION AND AWARD.

Article 1.

General Provisions.

Sec.
8.01-577. Submission of controversy; agreement to arbitrate; condition precedent to action.
8.01-578 through 8.01-580. [Repealed.]
8.01-581. Fiduciary may submit to arbitration.

Article 2.
Uniform Arbitration Act

Sec.
8.01-581.01. Validity of arbitration agreement.
8.01-581.02. Proceedings to compel or stay arbitration.
8.01-581.03. Appointment of arbitrators by court; powers of arbitrators.
8.01-581.04. Hearing.
8.01-581.05. Representation by attorney.
8.01-581.06. Witnesses, subpoenas, depositions.

Sec.
8.01-581.07. Award; fees and expenses to be fixed.
8.01-581.08. Change of award by arbitrators.
8.01-581.09. Confirmation of an award.
8.01-581.010. Vacating an award.
8.01-581.011. Modification or correction of award.
8.01-581.012. Judgment or decree on award.
8.01-581.013. Applications to court.
8.01-581.014. Court; jurisdiction.
8.01-581.015. Venue.
8.01-581.016. Appeals.

Article 1.

General Provisions.

§ 8.01-577. Submission of controversy; agreement to arbitrate; condition precedent to action. — A. Persons desiring to end any controversy, whether there is a suit pending therefor or not, may submit the same to arbitration, and agree that such submission may be entered of record in any court. Upon proof of such agreement out of court, or by consent of the parties given in court in person or by counsel, it shall be entered in the proceedings of such court. Thereupon a rule shall be made, that the parties shall submit to the award which shall be made in accordance with such agreement and the provisions of this chapter.

B. Neither party shall have the right to revoke an agreement to arbitrate except on a ground which would be good for revoking or annulling other agreements. Submission of any claim or controversy to arbitration pursuant to such agreement shall be a condition precedent to institution of suit or action thereon, and the agreement to arbitrate shall be enforceable, unless the agreement also provides that submission to arbitration shall not be a condition precedent to suit or action. (Code 1950, § 8-503; 1968, c. 244; 1977, c. 617; 1983, c. 485; 1986, c. 614.)

REVISERS' NOTE

Section 8.01-577 B has been changed to require that arbitration agreements be in writing.

Cross references. — As to compromise of wrongful death claim, see § 8.01-55. As to approval of compromises on behalf of persons under a disability, see § 8.01-424. As to compromise by fiduciaries, see § 8.01-425. As to the Uniform Arbitration Act, see § 8.01-581.01 et seq. As to arbitration of medical malpractice claims, see § 8.01-581.12. As to compromise and satisfaction in general, see §§ 11-10 through 11-13. As to bribery of arbitrators, see § 18.2-441.

Law Review. — For survey of Virginia commercial law for the year 1972-1973, see 59 Va. L. Rev. 1426 (1973). For comment, "Toward a Uniform State Product Liability Law — Virginia and the Uniform Product Liability Act," see 36 Wash. & Lee L. Rev. 1145 (1979). For comment, "The Enforceability of Arbitration Clauses in Virginia Marital Separation Agreements," see 19 U. Rich. L. Rev. 333 (1985). For 1985 survey of Virginia civil procedure and practice, see 19 U. Rich. L. Rev. 679 (1985).

I. Decisions Under Current Law.
  A. General Consideration.
  B. Submission.
II. Decisions Under Prior Law.
  A. General Consideration.
  B. Submission.
    1. Who May Make.
    2. What May Be Submitted.
    3. Operation and Effect.

I. DECISIONS UNDER CURRENT LAW.

A. General Consideration.

Applicability of federal law. — Though state law might in some cases be applied in a diversity action to determine whether a right to arbitrate exists, federal law will preempt state law if the contract underlying a potentially arbitrable dispute evidences a transaction involving interstate commerce. Maxum Founds., Inc. v. Salus Corp., 779 F.2d 974 (4th Cir. 1985).

Where owner confessed error on issue of whether arbitration agreement with contractor was mandatory and irrevocable, but nevertheless, the owner argued waiver on appeal, a proposition never decided by the trial court and never preserved for appellate review by an assignment of cross-error, judgment below was reversed and the case was remanded with direction that the trial court stay the proceedings in the civil action to permit the controversy to be submitted to arbitration, according to the provisions of the contract and the provisions of this section. Maynard Constr. Co. v. Driver, 230 Va. 79, 334 S.E.2d 567 (1985).

The Commonwealth is not estopped to deny the validity of an ultra vires contract containing an arbitration clause because its agents executed the document nor is it estopped to deny the validity of the arbitrator's award because its agents performed the contract by participating in the arbitration proceedings. An ultra vires contract is void ab initio — not voidable only, but wholly void, and of no legal effect, and no performance on either side can give the unlawful contract any validity, or be the foundation of any right of action upon it. When the contract is once declared ultra vires, the fact that it is executed does not validate it, nor can it be ratified so as to make it the basis of suit or action, nor does the doctrine of estoppel apply. Richard L. Deal & Assocs. v. Commonwealth, 224 Va. 618, 299 S.E.2d 346 (1983).

Waiver. — A judgment creditor did not waive its rights by failing to intervene in arbitration, when the garnishee refused the judgment creditor's request to be allowed to participate; once the garnishee withheld consent, the judgment creditor was not obligated to seek intervention through the defaulting judgment debtor or to seek a court order allowing intervention; nothing in the garnishment statutes, or in the statutes dealing with arbitration, requires such action by a judgment creditor. Virginia Bldrs' Supply, Inc. v. Brooks & Co., 250 Va. 209, 462 S.E.2d 85 (1995).

B. Submission.

The Commonwealth is not a "person" or "party" authorized by this section to enter into a written agreement to arbitrate which will be as binding as any other agreement. Richard L. Deal & Assocs. v. Commonwealth, 224 Va. 618, 299 S.E.2d 346 (1983).

The General Assembly did not intend to include the Commonwealth as a person or party within the contemplation of the arbitration statutes, and its agents have no authority to bind it to an arbitration agreement. Richard L. Deal & Assocs. v. Commonwealth, 224 Va. 618, 299 S.E.2d 346 (1983).

While the word "person" may extend and be applied to bodies politic and corporate as well as individuals, and the word may apply to counties and cities under certain circumstances, the sovereign is a person or party within the intendment of a statute only when the General Assembly names it expressly or by necessary implication. Nothing in the legislative history of the arbitration statutes supports the implication that the Commonwealth is a "person" or "party" within the meaning of this section. Richard L. Deal & Assocs. v. Commonwealth, 224 Va. 618, 299 S.E.2d 346 (1983).

II. DECISIONS UNDER PRIOR LAW.

A. General Consideration.

Editor's note. — The cases cited below were decided under corresponding provisions of former law. The term "this section," as used below, refers to former provisions.

Section enlarges common-law arbitration. — At common law two kinds of submission and award were known. The first was upon a submission in pais, or in the country, and was where, in the absence of any pending suit, parties agreed to submit their then existing controversies to arbitration. The second was a submission made in a pending suit, in which case the award was returnable to the court, and was enforced by a rule after notice to show cause against it. There is in Virginia, by virtue of this section, an additional or statutory submission or award, which arises when parties to an actual controversy then existing agree to submit their differences to arbitration, with the provision that the award so made may be returned to and entered as a judgment of the court. Edge Hill Stock Farm, Inc. v. Morris, 155 Va. 103, 154 S.E. 473 (1930). See Glovier v. Dingus, 173 Va. 268, 4 S.E.2d 551 (1939); John W. Daniel & Co. v. Janaf, Inc., 169 F. Supp. 219 (E.D. Va. 1958), aff'd, 262 F.2d 958 (4th Cir. 1959).

This section, wherever applicable, must be applied in light of the terms of the arbitration agreement sought to be enforced. Doyle & Russell, Inc. v. Roanoke Hosp. Ass'n, 213 Va. 489, 193 S.E.2d 662 (1973).

This section may prohibit revocation of an arbitration agreement. Doyle & Russell, Inc. v. Roanoke Hosp. Ass'n, 213 Va. 489, 193 S.E.2d 662 (1973).

A party cannot be compelled to submit to arbitration unless he has first agreed to arbitrate. Doyle & Russell, Inc. v. Roanoke Hosp. Ass'n, 213 Va. 489, 193 S.E.2d 662 (1973).

By the same token, he cannot be compelled to arbitrate a question which, under his agreement, is not arbitrable. And the resisting party is entitled to a presubmission judicial determination of arbitrability. Doyle & Russell, Inc. v. Roanoke Hosp. Ass'n, 213 Va. 489, 193 S.E.2d 662 (1973).

It is the province of the courts to determine the threshold question of arbitrability, given the terms of the contract between the parties. This is so because the extent of the duty to arbitrate, just as the initial duty to arbitrate at all, arises from contractual undertakings. Doyle & Russell, Inc. v. Roanoke Hosp. Ass'n, 213 Va. 489, 193 S.E.2d 662 (1973).

Provision for arbitration in contract is no bar to action. — It cannot be doubted that a mere provision in a contract that all differences arising under it shall be submitted to arbitrators, thereafter to be chosen, will not prevent a party from maintaining a suit in the first instance in a court to enforce his rights under the contract. Condon v. South Side R.R., 55 Va. (14 Gratt.) 302 (1858); Corbin v. Adams, 76 Va. 58 (1881); Rison v. Moon, 91 Va. 384, 22 S.E. 165 (1895).

An agreement to arbitrate not consummated by an award is held to be no bar to a suit at law or equity; nor can it be the foundation of a decree for specific execution. Parties litigant cannot by such agreements oust the jurisdiction of the courts or deprive themselves of the right to resort to the legal tribunals for the settlement of their controversies. United States ex rel. Air-Con, Inc. v. Al-Con Dev. Corp., 271 F.2d 904 (4th Cir. 1959).

The authority of arbitrators, where they are required to pass upon the ultimate liability of the parties, may be revoked at any time before the award is made, and the agreement to arbitrate will be no bar to an action on the original contract, because such a course is supposed to oust the courts of their jurisdiction. United States ex rel. Air-Con, Inc. v. Al-Con Dev. Corp., 271 F.2d 904 (4th Cir. 1959).

But arbitration may be made condition precedent to action. — In order for an agreement to arbitrate to be a bar to action it must appear by the agreement that the parties intended that the arbitration should be a condition precedent to action. Condon v. South Side R.R., 55 Va. (14 Gratt.) 302 (1858); Corbin v. Adams, 76 Va. 58 (1881); Rison v. Moon, 91 Va. 384, 22 S.E. 165 (1895).

The general rule that an agreement for arbitration not consummated by an award is no bar to a suit at law or in equity is subject to an exception, namely, that the parties may, by contract, lawfully make the decision of the arbitrators a condition precedent to a right of action on the contract. In such case, until the decision is made, the courts have no jurisdiction of the case. United States ex rel. Air-Con, Inc. v. Al-Con Dev. Corp., 271 F.2d 904 (4th Cir. 1959).

Agreement to arbitrate does not lack consideration. — A dispute between a city and a streetcar company, as to the car company's liabilities under its charter and under a contract, furnishes valuable consideration to support their agreement to arbitrate. McKennie v. Charlottesville & A. Ry., 110 Va. 70, 65 S.E. 503 (1909).

It may be by parol. — An agreement to arbitrate may be by parol, and where the submission does not require that the award be in writing, a parol award is binding, even though the controversy relates to the boundaries of land. Miller v. Miller, 99 Va. 125, 37 S.E. 792 (1901); Cox v. Heuseman, 124 Va. 159, 97 S.E. 778 (1919).

Right to make motion for arbitration and petition for stay of proceedings. — In an action by one party to an arbitration agreement providing that an award should be a condition precedent to suit, the other party had the right to raise the issue of lack of jurisdiction of the district court over the subject matter by motion for arbitration and petition for stay of proceedings, and such right was not waived by the subsequent filing of an answer in the action. United States ex rel. Air-Con, Inc. v. Al-Con Dev. Corp., 271 F.2d 904 (4th Cir. 1959).

Where there was nothing to arbitrate, the court did right in annulling an agreement for arbitration in order to terminate the litigation. Corbin v. Adams, 76 Va. 58 (1881).

B. Submission.

1. Who May Make.

Some of several heirs or distributees may make submission. — Where some of several heirs or distributees submit their interests to arbitration, the submission and the award made in pursuance thereof are binding on them, so far as their interests are concerned. Smith v. Smith, 25 Va. (4 Rand.) 95 (1826); Boyd's Heirs v. Magruder's Heirs, 41 Va. (2 Rob.) 761 (1844).

A municipal corporation may submit disputed claims made against it, or made by it against others, to arbitration. McKennie v. Charlottesville & A. Ry., 110 Va. 70, 65 S.E. 503 (1909).

Submission by infant is not binding. — A submission by an infant, even though with an adult, is not binding on either party, even though the submission is by rule of court, and the award in his favor. Britton v. Williams' Devisees, 20 Va. (6 Munf.) 453 (1819).

Partner cannot bind his copartner. — One partner has no authority by virtue of the partnership relation to bind his copartner by an agreement to submit claims or transactions growing out of the partnership business to arbitration, but the partner who makes the agreement is bound thereby, and the agreement is valid and binding between the parties thereto. Fletcher v. Pollard, 12 Va. (2 Hen. & M.) 544 (1808); Wood v. Shepherd, 2 Pat. & H. 442 (1857); Forrer v. Coffman, 64 Va. (23 Gratt.) 871 (1873).

Nor purchaser his vendor. — Where a dispute arises between a purchaser of property and a third party as to the ownership of the property, the purchaser cannot submit the matter to arbitration without authority from the vendor to do so; and if he does make the submission without authority, he has no remedy against the vendor where the award is made against him. Dust v. Conrod, 19 Va. (5 Munf.) 411 (1817).

Nor tenant his landlord. — In an action of ejectment, brought against the person in possession, the landlord of such person may come in and be allowed to defend the action whether the actual relation of lessor and lessee exists between them or not, and this will be permitted even where the plaintiff and defendant in possession have submitted the matters between them to arbitration. Hanks v. Price, 73 Va. (32 Gratt.) 107 (1879).

2. What May Be Submitted.

Parties may agree to settle boundaries by arbitration. — Parties may agree by parol to settle by arbitration the dividing line between their lots of land, and an award made in pursuance of submission for that purpose will bind the parties, although the arbitrators make a parol award, where the submission does not require the award to be in writing. Miller v. Miller, 99 Va. 125, 37 S.E. 792 (1901); Cox v. Heuseman, 124 Va. 159, 97 S.E. 778 (1919).

Land established as public road cannot be affected. — No easement in land which has been established as a public road can be acquired by arbitration proceedings, to which the public is no party, between the original owner and the mover of prior proceedings to establish the road. Norfolk & W.R.R. v. Rasnake, 90 Va. 170, 17 S.E. 879 (1893).

Controversy may be submitted after default judgment. — After judgment by default has gone against the defendant and a writ of inquiry of damages has been awarded, a submission to arbitration may be made by the parties to the action without setting aside the judgment by default, and the submission is valid. Sutton v. Dickinson, 36 Va. (9 Leigh) 142 (1837).

3. Operation and Effect.

The submission to arbitration of a pending suit operates as a release of all errors up to the time the submission was made. Ligon v. Ford, 19 Va. (5 Munf.) 10 (1816).

Death of plaintiff does not avoid submission. — After submission to arbitration by rule of court, the plaintiff died, and the suit was revived by his administrator. The administrator of the plaintiff and the defendant proceeded in the arbitration, without any new submission, and an award was made. It was held that the death of the plaintiff did not avoid the submission, and the award under it was good. Wheatley v. Martin's Adm'r, 33 Va. (6 Leigh) 62 (1835).

§§ 8.01-578 through 8.01-580: Repealed by Acts 1986, c. 614.

Cross references. — As to the Uniform Arbitration Act, see § 8.01-581.01 et seq.

§ 8.01-581. Fiduciary may submit to arbitration. — Any personal representative of a decedent, fiduciary of a person under a disability, or other fiduciary may submit to arbitration any suit or matter of controversy touching the estate or property of such decedent, or person under a disability or in respect to which he is trustee. And any submission so made in good faith, and the award made thereupon, shall be binding and entered as the judgment of a court, if so required by the agreement, in the same manner as other submissions and awards. No such fiduciary shall be responsible for any loss sustained by an award adverse to the interests of the person under a disability or beneficiary under any such trust, unless it was caused by his fault or neglect. (Code 1950, § 8-507; 1977, c. 617.)

REVISERS' NOTE

The terms "fiduciary" and "person under a disability," as defined in § 8.01-2 have been used in § 8.01-581.

Cross references. — As to compromise by fiduciary, see §§ 8.01-55, 8.01-424, 8.01-425.

I. DECISIONS UNDER PRIOR LAW.

Editor's note. — The case cited below was decided under corresponding provisions of former law. The term "this section," as used below, refers to former provisions.

Where an executor declines to oppose the confirmation of an award, the next of kin may maintain the suit for the protection of infant heirs. Moore v. Luckess Next of Kin, 64 Va. (23 Gratt.) 160 (1873).

ARTICLE 2.

Uniform Arbitration Act.

§ **8.01-581.01. Validity of arbitration agreement.** — A written agreement to submit any existing controversy to arbitration or a provision in a written contract to submit to arbitration any controversy thereafter arising between the parties is valid, enforceable and irrevocable, except upon such grounds as exist at law or in equity for the revocation of any contract. This article also applies to arbitration agreements between employers and employees or between their respective representatives unless otherwise provided in the agreement; provided, however, that nothing in this chapter shall be construed to create any right to arbitration with respect to any controversy regarding the employment or terms and conditions of employment of any officer or employee of the Commonwealth. (1986, c. 614.)

I. DECISIONS UNDER CURRENT LAW.

Standard of review involving arbitration agreements. — Nowhere in the Uniform Arbitration Act, as adopted by Virginia, are courts required to review an arbitration agreement in a domestic relations context with more scrutiny than other disputes; the standard of review involving arbitration agreements in domestic relations should conform to the standard set forth in this section. Bandas v. Bandas, 16 Va. App. 427, 430 S.E.2d 706 (1993).

Applied in Waterfront Marine Constr., Inc. v. North End 49ers Sandbridge Bulkhead Groups A, B & C, 251 Va. 417, 468 S.E.2d 894 (1996).

§ **8.01-581.02. Proceedings to compel or stay arbitration.** — A. On application of a party showing an agreement described in § 8.01-581.01, and the opposing party's refusal to arbitrate, the court shall order the parties to proceed with arbitration. However, if the opposing party denies the existence of the agreement to arbitrate, the court shall proceed summarily to the determination of the issue of the existence of an agreement and shall order arbitration only if found for the moving party.

B. On application, the court may stay an arbitration proceeding commenced or threatened on a showing that there is no agreement to arbitrate. Such an issue, when in substantial and bona fide dispute, shall be forthwith and summarily tried and the stay ordered if found for the moving party. If found for the opposing party, the court shall order the parties to proceed to arbitration.

C. If an issue referable to arbitration under the alleged agreement is involved in an action or proceeding pending in a court having jurisdiction to hear applications under subsection A of this section, the application shall be made therein. Otherwise, subject to § 8.01-581.015, the application may be made in any court of competent jurisdiction.

D. Any action or proceeding involving an issue subject to arbitration shall be stayed if an order for arbitration or an application therefor has been made under this section. However, if the issue is severable, the stay may be with respect thereto only. When the application is made in such action or proceeding, the order for arbitration shall include the stay.

E. An order for arbitration shall not be refused on the ground that the claim in issue lacks merit or bona fides or because any fault or grounds for the claim sought to be arbitrated have not been shown. (1986, c. 614.)

Law Review. — For 1995 survey of civil practice and procedure, see 29 U. Rich. L. Rev. 897 (1995).

I. DECISIONS UNDER CURRENT LAW.

Trial court erred in denying defendant's request for arbitration and a stay since although there was nothing to arbitrate with respect to plaintiff's $25,300 claim, because defendant admitted it, defendant was entitled to arbitration of its counterclaim for back charges and delay damages. Piland Corp. v. League Constr. Co., 238 Va. 187, 380 S.E.2d 652 (1989).

Applied in McMullin v. Union Land & Mgt. Co., 242 Va. 337, 410 S.E.2d 636 (1991); Food Lion, Inc. v. Cox, 257 Va. 449, 513 S.E.2d 860 (1999).

§ 8.01-581.03. Appointment of arbitrators by court; powers of arbitrators. — If the arbitration agreement provides a method of appointment of arbitrators, this method shall be followed. In the absence thereof, or if the agreed method fails or for any reason cannot be followed, or when an arbitrator appointed fails or is unable to act and his successor has not been duly appointed, the court on application of a party shall appoint one or more arbitrators. An arbitrator so appointed has all the powers of one specifically named in the agreement.

The powers of the arbitrators may be exercised by a majority, unless otherwise provided by the agreement or by this article. (1986, c. 614.)

§ 8.01-581.04. Hearing. — Unless otherwise provided by the agreement:

1. The arbitrators shall appoint a time and place for the hearing and cause notification to the parties to be served personally or by registered mail not less than five days before the hearing. Appearance at the hearing waives such notice. The arbitrators may adjourn the hearing from time to time as necessary and, on request of a party for good cause, or upon their own motion may postpone the hearing to a time not later than the date fixed by the agreement for making the award unless the parties consent to a later date. The arbitrators may hear and determine the controversy upon the evidence produced notwithstanding the failure of a party duly notified to appear. The court on application may direct the arbitrators to proceed promptly with the hearing and determination of the controversy.

2. The parties are entitled to be heard, to present evidence material to the controversy and to cross-examine witnesses appearing at the hearing.

3. The hearing shall be conducted by all the arbitrators, but a majority may determine any question and render a final award. If, during the course of the hearing, an arbitrator for any reason ceases to act, the remaining arbitrator or arbitrators appointed to act as neutrals may continue with the hearing and determination of the controversy. (1986, c. 614.)

§ **8.01-581.05. Representation by attorney.** — A party has the right to be represented by an attorney at any proceeding or hearing under this article. A waiver thereof prior to the proceeding or hearing is ineffective. (1986, c. 614.)

§ **8.01-581.06. Witnesses, subpoenas, depositions.** — The arbitrators may issue subpoenas for the attendance of witnesses and for the production of books, records, documents and other evidence, and shall have the power to administer oaths. Subpoenas so issued shall be served, and upon application to the court by a party or the arbitrators, enforced, in the manner provided by law for the service and enforcement of subpoenas in a civil action. All provisions of law compelling a person under subpoena to testify are applicable.

On application of a party and for use as evidence, the arbitrators may permit a deposition to be taken of a witness who cannot be subpoenaed or is unable to attend the hearing, in the manner and upon the terms designated by the arbitrators.

Fees for attendance as a witness shall be the same as for a witness in the circuit court. (1986, c. 614.)

§ **8.01-581.07. Award; fees and expenses to be fixed.** — The award shall be in writing and signed by the arbitrators joining in the award. The arbitrators shall deliver a copy to each party personally or by registered mail, or as provided in the agreement.

An award shall be made within the time fixed therefor by the agreement or, if not so fixed, within such time as the court orders on application of a party. The parties may extend the time in writing either before or after the expiration thereof. A party waives the objection that an award was not made within the time required unless he notifies the arbitrators of his objection prior to the delivery of the award to him. Unless otherwise provided in the agreement to arbitrate, the arbitrators' expenses and fees incurred in the conduct of the arbitration, and all other expenses, not including counsel fees, shall be paid as provided in the award. (1986, c. 614.)

§ **8.01-581.08. Change of award by arbitrators.** — On application of a party or, if an application to the court is pending under §§ 8.01-581.09, 8.01-581.010 or § 8.01-581.011, on submission to the arbitrators by the court under such conditions as the court may order, the arbitrators may modify or correct the award upon the grounds stated in subdivisions 1 and 3 of § 8.01-581.011, or for the purpose of clarifying the award. The application shall be made within twenty days after delivery of the award to the applicant. Written notice thereof shall be given forthwith to the opposing party, stating that he must serve his objections thereto, if any, within ten days from the notice. The award as modified or corrected is subject to the provisions of §§ 8.01-581.09, 8.01-581.010 or § 8.01-581.011. (1986, c. 614.)

I. DECISIONS UNDER CURRENT LAW.

Time limitations. — This statute provides a limited time within which the parties may ask an arbitrator to reconsider or modify an award; after that time the arbitrator has no further authority over an award. Waterfront Marine Constr., Inc. v. North End 49ers Sandbridge Bulkhead Groups A, B & C, 251 Va. 417, 468 S.E.2d 894 (1996).

§ **8.01-581.09. Confirmation of an award.** — Upon application of a party any time after an award is made, the court shall confirm an award, unless within the time limits hereinafter imposed grounds are urged for vacating or modifying or correcting the award, in which case the court shall proceed as provided in §§ 8.01-581.010 and 8.01-581.011. (1986, c. 614; 1998, c. 303.)

§ 8.01-581.010　　　　　　CODE OF VIRGINIA　　　　　　§ 8.01-581.010

I. DECISIONS UNDER PRIOR LAW.

Editor's note. — The case cited below was decided under corresponding provisions of former law. The term "this section," as used below, refers to former provisions.

Awards are to be liberally construed to the end that they may be upheld if possible. An award, being the judgment of a judge of the parties' own choosing, ought to be favorably viewed by the courts; and effect ought to be given to it by them, whenever it can be done consistently with the rules of law. Virginia Beach Bd. of Realtors, Inc. v. Goodman Segar Hogan, Inc., 224 Va. 659, 299 S.E.2d 360 (1983) (decided under former § 8.01-579).

§ 8.01-581.010. Vacating an award. — Upon application of a party, the court shall vacate an award where:

1. The award was procured by corruption, fraud or other undue means;
2. There was evident partiality by an arbitrator appointed as a neutral, corruption in any of the arbitrators, or misconduct prejudicing the rights of any party;
3. The arbitrators exceeded their powers;
4. The arbitrators refused to postpone the hearing upon sufficient cause being shown therefor or refused to hear evidence material to the controversy or otherwise so conducted the hearing, contrary to the provisions of § 8.01-581.04, in such a way as to substantially prejudice the rights of a party; or
5. There was no arbitration agreement and the issue was not adversely determined in proceedings under § 8.01-581.02 and the party did not participate in the arbitration hearing without raising the objection.

The fact that the relief was such that it could not or would not be granted by a court of law or equity is not grounds for vacating or refusing to confirm the award.

An application under this section shall be made within ninety days after delivery of a copy of the award to the applicant, except that, if predicated upon corruption, fraud or other undue means, it shall be made within ninety days after such grounds are known or reasonably should have been known. An application shall be made by filing a petition with the appropriate court within the prescribed time limits of this section, or by raising reasons supporting vacation in response to another party's petition to confirm the award, provided that such response is filed within the prescribed time limits of this section.

In vacating the award on grounds other than that stated in subdivision 5, the court may order a rehearing before new arbitrators chosen as provided in the agreement, or in the absence thereof, by the court in accordance with § 8.01-581.03. If the award is vacated on grounds set forth in subdivisions 3 and 4 the court may order a rehearing before the arbitrators who made the award or their successors appointed in accordance with § 8.01-581.03. The time within which the agreement requires the award to be made is applicable to the rehearing and commences from the date of the order.

If the application to vacate is denied and no motion to modify or correct the award is pending, the court shall confirm the award. (1986, c. 614; 1998, c. 303.)

I. Decisions Under Current Law.
II. Decisions Under Prior Law.
　A. General Consideration.
　B. Decisions Under Former § 8.01-580.
　　1. In General.
　　2. Grounds.
　C. Decisions Prior to Enactment of Title 8.01.
　　1. In General.
　　2. Grounds.
　　　a. Fraud or Mistake.
　　　b. Misconduct of Arbitrators.
　　3. Jurisdiction and Procedure.

I. DECISIONS UNDER CURRENT LAW.

Federal labor action. — In action under § 301 of the Labor Management Relations Act, 29 U.S.C. § 185, to vacate an arbitration award, the most closely analogous statute of limitation under Virginia law as former § 8.01-579 (see now subdivision 5 of this section), rather than § 8.01-246 or § 8.01-248. Local Union 8181, UMW v. Westmoreland Coal Co., 649 F. Supp. 603 (W.D. Va. 1986).

Hearsay evidence. — Arbitrators do not exceed their powers by admitting or considering hearsay evidence. Farkas v. Receivable Fin. Corp., 806 F. Supp. 84 (E.D. Va. 1992).

Arbitrators did not exceed their powers by deciding what the contract meant. To the contrary, that was one of the issues which the parties submitted for decision in the arbitration. The arbitrators did not exceed their powers by misinterpreting the contract or by committing an error of law. As a matter of law, neither reason constituted a ground on which an award could be vacated. Farkas v. Receivable Fin. Corp., 806 F. Supp. 84 (E.D. Va. 1992).

II. DECISIONS UNDER PRIOR LAW.

A. General Consideration.

Editor's note. — The cases cited below were decided under corresponding provisions of former law. The term "this section," as used below, refers to former provisions.

B. Decisions Under Former § 8.01-580.

1. In General.

Nothing is considered to be apparent on the face of the award but what forms a part of it; no calculations, nor any of the grounds of it, unless incorporated with it or annexed to it at the time of delivery, are to be regarded or received as reasons or grounds to avoid it. Wyatt Realty Enters., Ltd. v. Bob Jones Realty Co., 222 Va. 365, 282 S.E.2d 8 (1981).

Awards are to be liberally construed to the end that they may be upheld if possible. An award, being the judgment of a judge of the parties' own choosing, ought to be favorably viewed by the courts; and effect ought to be given to it by them, whenever it can be done consistently with the rules of law. Virginia Beach Bd. of Realtors, Inc. v. Goodman Segar Hogan, Inc., 224 Va. 659, 299 S.E.2d 360 (1983).

This section is not applicable to the state employee grievance procedure. Detweiler v. Virginia Dep't of Rehabilitative Servs., 705 F.2d 557 (4th Cir. 1983).

2. Grounds.

A **"palpable" error** is one that is obvious and easily perceptible. United Paperworkers Int'l Union v. Chase Bag Co., 222 Va. 324, 281 S.E.2d 807 (1981).

Palpable errors are those of such a nature, as to induce a belief that they must have proceeded from some improper bias in the minds of the arbitrators, or from some gross misbehavior or inattention. United Paperworkers Int'l Union v. Chase Bag Co., 222 Va. 324, 281 S.E.2d 807 (1981).

The rule as to palpable mistakes does not comprehend errors of judgment in its fair exercise upon the matter. United Paperworkers Int'l Union v. Chase Bag Co., 222 Va. 324, 281 S.E.2d 807 (1981).

Procedural errors. — A court may modify or set aside an arbitrator's award for errors in procedural, as well as substantive, matters. United Paperworkers Int'l Union v. Chase Bag Co., 222 Va. 324, 281 S.E.2d 807 (1981).

Lack of signature of each arbitrator. — When an otherwise valid award contains the signature of the chairman of the arbitration panel, it should not be invalidated merely because it lacks the signature of each arbitrator. To do so would elevate form over substance. The fact that the arbitrators other than the chairman failed to sign is a procedural omission which should not abrogate the substance of the arbitration award. Their signatures serve no other function than to memorialize concurrence in the award. Virginia Beach Bd. of Realtors, Inc. v. Goodman Segar Hogan, Inc., 224 Va. 659, 299 S.E.2d 360 (1983).

C. Decisions Prior to Enactment of Title 8.01.

1. In General.

Reason must appear on face of award. — It is equally the rule of equity as of law that the reasons for setting aside an award must appear on its face, or there must be misbehavior in the arbitrators, or some palpable mistake. Shermer v. Beale, 1 Va. (1 Wash.) 11 (1791); Head v. Muir, 24 Va. (3 Rand.) 122 (1825); Wheatley v. Martin's Adm'r, 33 Va. (6 Leigh) 62 (1835); Moore v. Luckess Next of Kin, 64 Va. (23 Gratt.) 160 (1873); McKennie v. Charlottesville & A. Ry., 110 Va. 70, 65 S.E. 503 (1909).

Nothing is considered to be apparent on the face of the award but what forms a part of it; no calculations, nor any of the grounds of it, unless incorporated with it or annexed to it at the time of delivery, are to be regarded or received as reasons or grounds to avoid it. Taylor's Adm'r v. Nicolson, 11 Va. (1 Hen. & M.) 67 (1806); Wheatley v. Martin's Adm'r, 33 Va. (6 Leigh) 62 (1835).

Awards which do not conform to the submission are void. Taylor's Adm'r v. Nicolson, 11 Va. (1 Hen. & M.) 67 (1806); Martin v. Martin, 39 Va. (12 Leigh) 495 (1842); Wood v. Shepherd, 2 Pat. & H. 442 (1857); Moore v. Luckess Next of Kin, 64 Va. (23 Gratt.) 160

(1873); Pollock's Adm'r v. Sutherlin, 66 Va. (25 Gratt.) 78 (1874); Lynchburg Female Orphan Asylum v. Ford, 66 Va. (25 Gratt.) 566 (1874); Shipman v. Fletcher, 82 Va. 601 (1886).

Unless afterwards confirmed by parties. — An award which does not conform to the submission is of no effect unless the parties confirmed it afterwards. Pollock's Adm'r v. Sutherlin, 66 Va. (25 Gratt.) 78 (1874).

But submission will be construed favorably to award. — In determining whether the award is within the scope of the submission, both the submission and award will be construed favorably to the award. Pollock's Adm'r v. Sutherlin, 66 Va. (25 Gratt.) 78 (1874).

If, on any fair presumption, the award may be brought within the submission, it should be sustained. Ross v. Overton, 7 Va. (3 Call) 309 (1802); Morris v. Ross, 12 Va. (2 Hen. & M.) 408 (1808); Richards v. Brockenbrough's Adm'r, 22 Va. (1 Rand.) 449 (1823); Head v. Muir, 24 Va. (3 Rand.) 122 (1825); Armstrong v. Armstrong, 28 Va. (1 Leigh) 491 (1829); Bassett's Adm'r v. Cunningham's Adm'r, 50 Va. (9 Gratt.) 684 (1853); Pollock's Adm'r v. Sutherlin, 66 Va. (25 Gratt.) 78 (1874); Coons v. Coons, 95 Va. 434, 28 S.E. 885 (1897).

And as much of award as is within submission will be enforced. — Where an award settles matters which are, and other matters which are not, within the submission, the court may reject the excess, and render judgment on so much of the award as is within the submission if it can be separated. Taylor's Adm'r v. Nicolson, 11 Va. (1 Hen. & M.) 67 (1806); Horrel v. M'Alexander, 24 Va. (3 Rand.) 94 (1824); Martin v. Martin, 39 Va. (12 Leigh) 495 (1842); Morris v. Morris, 50 Va. (9 Gratt.) 637 (1853); Moore v. Luckess Next of Kin, 64 Va. (23 Gratt.) 160 (1873); Pollock's Adm'r v. Sutherlin, 66 Va. (25 Gratt.) 78 (1874); Lynchburg Female Orphan Asylum v. Ford, 66 Va. (25 Gratt.) 566 (1874); McKennie v. Charlottesville & A. Ry., 110 Va. 70, 65 S.E. 503 (1909).

Award is not vitiated by signature of stranger. — If a third person who signed an award were a mere stranger, this would not vitiate the award. Rison v. Berry, 25 Va. (4 Rand.) 275 (1826).

Award uncertain on its face is void. — An award which is uncertain on its face, and does not refer to something else by which it may be made certain, is void. Thus an award that one of the parties should refund the sum which the other had paid for certain corn, without stating the amount, or referring to anything to make the amount certain, was held void. Cauthorn v. Courtney, 47 Va. (6 Gratt.) 381 (1849).

2. Grounds.

a. Fraud or Mistake.

Award procured by fraud will be set aside. — An award procured through the fraud of one of the parties to the submission will be set aside for that cause by a court of equity in a proper case. Bierly v. Williams, 32 Va. (5 Leigh) 700 (1834); Kidwell v. B & O R.R., 52 Va. (11 Gratt.) 676 (1854); Condon v. South Side R.R., 55 Va. (14 Gratt.) 302 (1858); B & O R.R. v. Polly, 55 Va. (14 Gratt.) 447 (1858); B & O R.R. v. Laffertys, 55 Va. (14 Gratt.) 478 (1858); Mills v. Norfolk & W.R.R., 90 Va. 523, 19 S.E. 171 (1894).

Clerical errors may be corrected. Byars v. Thompson, 39 Va. (12 Leigh) 550 (1841); Forrer v. Coffman, 64 Va. (23 Gratt.) 871 (1873).

Mistake must appear upon face of award. — To authorize the setting aside of an award for a mistake of the arbitrators, either as to law or fact, the mistake must appear on the face of the award. Pleasants v. Ross, 1 Va. (1 Wash.) 156 (1793). See Scott v. Trents, 14 Va. (4 Hen. & M.) 356 (1809).

Unless arbitrators certify principles on which they decided. — If the arbitrators will certify the principles on which they decided, the court will set aside the award if they appear to have acted under a mistake. Affidavits may be introduced, but they must go to prove partiality or misbehavior in the arbitrators. Pleasants v. Ross, 1 Va. (1 Wash.) 156 (1793). See Scott v. Trents, 14 Va. (4 Hen. & M.) 356 (1809).

The award ought not to be set aside unless the mistake is very palpable. Morris v. Ross, 12 Va. (2 Hen. & M.) 408 (1808).

The mere fact that one of the arbitrators, after the award, may think that he made a mistake is insufficient to set it aside. Pollard v. Lumpkin, 47 Va. (6 Gratt.) 398 (1849).

Award may be set aside for material mistake of law. — Where arbitrators mean to decide according to law, and they mistake the law in a palpable material point, the award will be set aside. But their decision, upon a doubtful point of law, or in a case where the question of law is designedly left to their judgment, will generally be held conclusive. It must appear that they grossly mistook the law; and the court will not interfere merely because it would have given a different decision in the particular case. Ross v. Overton, 7 Va. (3 Call) 309 (1802); Smith v. Smith, 25 Va. (4 Rand.) 95 (1826); Moore v. Luckess Next of Kin, 64 Va. (23 Gratt.) 160 (1873); Portsmouth v. Norfolk County, 72 Va. (31 Gratt.) 727 (1879).

But when parties submit a question of law alone, the award is binding, though contrary to law. Smith v. Smith, 25 Va. (4 Rand.) 95 (1826).

If arbitrators intended to decide according to law, error will be corrected. — Where it appeared in the award of the arbitrators that they had taken the institution of the action, instead of the filing of the plea of setoff, as the date from which the statute of limitations would cease to run against the setoff, the court corrected the error, it appearing that the arbitrators had intended to decide according to law. Moore v. Luckess Next of Kin, 64 Va. (23 Gratt.) 160 (1873).

But arbitrators may disregard the law entirely, and decide upon principles of equity and good conscience exclusively. Moore v. Luckess Next of Kin, 64 Va. (23 Gratt.) 160 (1873).

Presumption is that award is based on correct proposition of law. — If an arbitrator, intending to decide the questions submitted to him according to law, states in his award two propositions of law, one of which is erroneous, and the other correct upon the facts as he considers them to be, a court in passing upon the validity of the award will presume that it is based upon the latter proposition, and cannot inquire whether the arbitrator took a correct view of the facts. Willoughby v. Thomas, 65 Va. (24 Gratt.) 521 (1874).

b. Misconduct of Arbitrators.

Award is vitiated by misbehavior resulting in injustice. — An award of arbitrators will be set aside on the ground of circumstances in their conduct amounting to misbehavior, though not to corruption, and resulting in injustice to one of the parties. Head v. Muir, 24 Va. (3 Rand.) 122 (1825); Graham's Adm'rs v. Pence, 27 Va. (6 Rand.) 529 (1828); May v. Yancey, 31 Va. (4 Leigh) 362 (1833); Lee v. Patillo, 31 Va. (4 Leigh) 436 (1833); City of Portsmouth v. Norfolk County, 72 Va. (31 Gratt.) 727 (1879); Shipman v. Fletcher, 82 Va. 601 (1886).

Such as hearing cause in absence of parties and without notice. — Hearing and deciding the cause in the absence of the parties and without notice to them of the time and place of the hearing is such misconduct on the part of the arbitrators as will vitiate their award. McCormick v. Blackford & Son, 45 Va. (4 Gratt.) 133 (1847); Jenkins v. Liston, 54 Va. (13 Gratt.) 535 (1856); Tate v. Vance, 68 Va. (27 Gratt.) 571 (1876); Shipman v. Fletcher, 82 Va. 601 (1886). But see Miller v. Kennedy, 24 Va. (3 Rand.) 2 (1825).

But partition of land by arbitrators in the absence of the parties is binding. Miller v. Miller, 99 Va. 125, 37 S.E. 792 (1901).

Parties should have notice of appointment of umpire. — Where the submission empowers the arbitrators named therein to appoint an umpire or third arbitrator to decide any matter that they might not be able to agree upon, and the arbitrators fail to notify a party of the appointment of a third arbitrator, and of their readiness to proceed with the case, thus affording him the opportunity to introduce evidence in support of his contentions, the award should be vacated and annulled. Coons v. Coons, 95 Va. 434, 28 S.E. 885 (1897).

Joint award of arbitrators and umpire is good. — Where a submission was made to two persons and "such umpire as they shall choose," and the arbitrators and umpire acted together and made a joint award, the award was good. Rison v. Berry, 25 Va. (4 Rand.) 275 (1826).

The court can look into the testimony which was before the arbitrators, for the purpose of determining from it and from other circumstances whether the errors were so gross or palpable as to show fraud, corruption or gross misconduct in the arbitrators, and where these are shown the court will set aside the award. Moore v. Luckess Next of Kin, 64 Va. (23 Gratt.) 160 (1873).

An award made on ex parte evidence is invalid. Thus where the defendant refused to submit his case or his evidence, because the arbitrators had refused to act and had only been induced to act upon the request of the plaintiff, and the arbitrators rendered an award in the plaintiff's favor upon his ex parte evidence, this was held sufficient to invalidate the award. Graham's Adm'rs v. Pence, 27 Va. (6 Rand.) 529 (1828).

Receiving evidence of one party without the knowledge of the other is erroneous, and will invalidate the award. Jenkins v. Liston, 54 Va. (13 Gratt.) 535 (1856); Tate v. Vance, 68 Va. (27 Gratt.) 571 (1876).

Arbitrators should not admit improper evidence, and if they do their award is thereby invalidated, and this is true even though they say that their opinions were formed before such evidence was received. M'Alister v. M'Alister, 1 Va. (1 Wash.) 193 (1793); Jenkins v. Liston, 54 Va. (13 Gratt.) 535 (1856).

But it may be presumed that improper testimony was disregarded. — Where arbitrators are selected in part because of their high legal attainments, it will be presumed by the court that all improper testimony was discarded from their consideration in making their decisions. Bassett's Adm'r v. Cunningham's Adm'r, 50 Va. (9 Gratt.) 684 (1853).

Refusal to hear proper evidence vitiates award. — Where arbitrators unreasonably refuse to hear competent witnesses offered by either party this will vitiate their award. Ligon v. Ford, 19 Va. (5 Munf.) 10 (1816).

Excessive damages alone are ground for relief in equity, as proving the arbitrators to have acted in an unjustifiable manner. Beverley v. Rennolds, Wythe 121 (1791).

3. Jurisdiction and Procedure.

The power of the court of equity to revise awards is concurrent with that of the courts of common law; but if the court of law first gets possession of the subject, its decision is binding on the court of equity, unless new circumstances are shown to authorize the interposition of the latter. Flournoy's Ex'rs v. Halcomb, 16 Va. (2 Munf.) 34 (1811).

Rules governing new trials for after-discovered evidence apply. — The rules governing courts of equity in awarding new trials in actions at law, on the ground of after-discovered evidence, apply equally to motions to set aside an award on that ground. Adams v. Hubbard, 66 Va. (25 Gratt.) 129 (1874).

Relief against bond given under invalid award is in equity. — An award condemning a party to pay damages for refusing to ratify an illegal and fraudulent contract is not binding, and relief against a bond given in conformity with it is properly sought in equity. Beverley v. Rennolds, Wythe 121 (1791).

Equity court may decide whole controversy. — Where all the parties are before the court upon a bill to set aside an award upon grounds which unquestionably give a court of equity jurisdiction, the jurisdiction having once attached for the purpose of injunction, the court may decide the whole controversy, and render a final decree, though all the issues are legal in their nature and capable of being tried by a court of law, and the legal remedies therefor are adequate. Coons v. Coons, 95 Va. 434, 28 S.E. 885 (1897).

It will not set aside award for objections available at law. — A court of equity will not set aside an award for objections, which, if available at all, were available at law, but which the party did not avail himself of at law, surprise having been alleged but not proved, and no fraud having been alleged or proved. Head v. Muir, 24 Va. (3 Rand.) 122 (1825); Wheatley v. Martin's Adm'r, 33 Va. (6 Leigh) 62 (1835).

Lapse of time is defense to bill to impeach award. — Unless the fund is such a fund as a court of equity will pursue regardless of the statute of limitations, lapse of time is a good defense to a bill brought to impeach an award. Lesslie v. Brown, 1 Pat. & H. 216 (1855).

All evidence before arbitrators must be before court. — Where all evidence before the arbitrators is not before the court on the motion to set aside the award, the motion must fail. Adams v. Hubbard, 66 Va. (25 Gratt.) 129 (1874).

Extrinsic evidence admissible to show appointment of umpire. — Although the award does not state that a third person, who signed it, has been chosen by the arbitrators as umpire, that fact may be proved by other evidence. Rison v. Berry, 25 Va. (4 Rand.) 275 (1826).

Time of making award. — An award made by an umpire before the expiration of the time within which the arbitrators themselves might, according to the terms of the original submission, have made an award is nevertheless good. Richards v. Brockenbrough's Adm'r, 22 Va. (1 Rand.) 449 (1823).

Nothing is considered to be apparent on the face of the award but what forms a part of it; no calculations, nor any of the grounds of it, unless incorporated with it or annexed to it at the time of delivery, are to be regarded or received as reasons or grounds to avoid it. Wyatt Realty Enters., Ltd. v. Bob Jones Realty Co., 222 Va. 365, 282 S.E.2d 8 (1981).

§ 8.01-581.011. Modification or correction of award. — Upon application made within ninety days after delivery of a copy of the award to the applicant, the court shall modify or correct the award where:

1. There was an evident miscalculation of figures or an evident mistake in the description of any person, thing or property referred to in the award;

2. The arbitrators have awarded upon a matter not submitted to them and the award may be corrected without affecting the merits of the decision upon the issues submitted; or

3. The award is imperfect in a matter of form, not affecting the merits of the controversy.

If the application is granted, the court shall modify and correct the award so as to effect its intent and shall confirm the award as so modified and corrected. Otherwise, the court shall confirm the award as made.

An application to modify or correct an award may be joined in the alternative with an application to vacate the award. (1986, c. 614.)

§ 8.01-581.012. Judgment or decree on award. — Upon granting an order confirming, modifying or correcting an award, a judgment or decree shall be entered in conformity therewith and be docketed and enforced as any other judgment or decree. Costs of the application and of the proceedings subsequent thereto, and disbursements may be awarded by the court. (1986, c. 614.)

§ 8.01-581.013. Applications to court. — An application to the court under this article shall be by motion and shall be heard in the manner and upon the notice provided by law or rule of court for the making and hearing of motions. Unless the parties have agreed otherwise, notice of an initial application for an order shall be served in the manner provided by law for the service of a summons in an action. (1986, c. 614.)

§ 8.01-581.014. Court; jurisdiction. — The term *"court"* means a court of this Commonwealth having jurisdiction over the subject matter of the controversy. (1986, c. 614; 1995, c. 342.)

§ 8.01-581.015. Venue. — Except as provided in subsection B of § 8.01-262.1, an initial application shall be made to the court of the county or city in which the agreement provides the arbitration hearing shall be held or, if the hearing has been held, in the county or city in which it was held. Otherwise, venue of the application shall be as provided in Chapter 5 (§ 8.01-257 et seq.) of this title. All subsequent applications shall be made to the court hearing the initial application unless the court otherwise directs. (1986, c. 614; 1991, c. 489.)

§ 8.01-581.016. Appeals. — An appeal may be taken from:
1. An order denying an application to compel arbitration made under § 8.01-581.02;
2. An order granting an application to stay arbitration made under subsection B of § 8.01-581.02;
3. An order confirming or denying an award;
4. An order modifying or correcting an award;
5. An order vacating an award without directing a rehearing; or
6. A judgment or decree entered pursuant to the provisions of this article.

The appeal shall be taken in the manner and to the same extent as from orders or judgments in a civil action. (1986, c. 614.)

REVISERS' NOTE

The terms "fiduciary" and "person under a disability," as defined in § 8.01-2 have been used in § 8.01-581.

Cross references. — As to compromise by fiduciary, see §§ 8.01-55, 8.01-424, 8.01-425.

I. DECISIONS UNDER PRIOR LAW.

Editor's note. — The case cited below was decided under corresponding provisions of former law. The term "this section," as used below, refers to former provisions.

Where an executor declines to oppose the confirmation of an award, the next of kin may maintain the suit for the protection of infant heirs. Moore v. Luckess Next of Kin, 64 Va. (23 Gratt.) 160 (1873).

CHAPTER 21.1.

MEDICAL MALPRACTICE.

Article 1.

Medical Malpractice Review Panels; Arbitration of Malpractice Claims.

Sec.
8.01-581.1. Definitions.
8.01-581.2. Request for review by medical malpractice review panel; rescission of request; determination on request.
8.01-581.2:1. Additional parties.
8.01-581.3. Composition, selection, etc., of panel.
8.01-581.3:1. Completion of discovery; hearing date; notification to parties and panel members; oath of panel members.
8.01-581.4. Submission of evidence to panel; depositions and discovery; duties of chairman; access to material.
8.01-581.4:1. Assembly of record.
8.01-581.4:2. Removal of record for inspection and copying; notice.
8.01-581.5. When hearing to be held; notice to parties.
8.01-581.6. Conduct of proceedings.
8.01-581.7. Opinion of panel.
8.01-581.7:1. Limitation on panel opinion.
8.01-581.8. Admissibility of opinion as evidence; appearance of panel members as witnesses; immunity from civil liability.
8.01-581.9. [Repealed.]
8.01-581.10. Per diem and expenses of panel.
8.01-581.11. Rules and regulations.
8.01-581.11:1. Objections not waived by participation.
8.01-581.12. Arbitration of medical malpractice claims.

Sec.
8.01-581.12:1. [Repealed.]
8.01-581.12:2. Article not applicable to actions arising prior to July 1, 1976.

Article 2.

Miscellaneous Provisions.

8.01-581.13. Civil immunity for certain health professionals and health profession students serving as members of certain entities.
8.01-581.14. Immunity of members of rate review board established by Virginia Hospital Association.
8.01-581.15. Limitation on recovery in certain medical malpractice actions.
8.01-581.16. Civil immunity for members of or consultants to certain boards or committees.
8.01-581.17. Privileged communications of certain committees and entities.
8.01-581.18. Delivery of results of laboratory tests and other examinations not authorized by physician; immunity of physician.
8.01-581.19. Civil immunity for physicians, psychologists, podiatrists, optometrists, veterinarians and nursing home administrators while members of certain committees.
8.01-581.19:1. Civil immunity for persons providing information to certain committees.
8.01-581.20. Standard of care in proceeding before medical malpractice review panel; expert testimony; determination of standard in action for damages.

ARTICLE 1.

Medical Malpractice Review Panels; Arbitration of Malpractice Claims.

§ 8.01-581.1. Definitions. — As used in this chapter:

"Health care" means any act, or treatment performed or furnished, or which should have been performed or furnished, by any health care provider for, to, or on behalf of a patient during the patient's medical diagnosis, care, treatment or confinement.

"Health care provider" means (i) a person, corporation, facility or institution licensed by this Commonwealth to provide health care or professional services as a physician or hospital, dentist, pharmacist, registered nurse or licensed practical nurse, optometrist, podiatrist, chiropractor, physical therapist, physical therapy assistant, clinical psychologist, clinical social worker, professional counselor, licensed dental hygienist or health maintenance organization, (ii) a professional corporation, all of whose shareholders or members are so licensed,

§ 8.01-581.1   CIVIL REMEDIES AND PROCEDURE   § 8.01-581.1

(iii) a partnership, all of whose partners are so licensed, (iv) a nursing home as defined in § 54.1-3100 except those nursing institutions conducted by and for those who rely upon treatment by spiritual means alone through prayer in accordance with a recognized church or religious denomination, (v) a professional limited liability company comprised of members as described in § 13.1-1102 A 2, or an officer, employee or agent thereof acting in the course and scope of his employment, or (vi) a corporation, partnership, limited liability company or any other entity, except a state-operated facility, which employs or engages a licensed health care provider and which primarily renders health care services.

"Health maintenance organization" means any person licensed pursuant to Chapter 43 (§ 38.2-4300 et seq.) of Title 38.2 who undertakes to provide or arrange for one or more health care plans.

"Hospital" means a public or private institution licensed pursuant to Chapter 5 (§ 32.1-123 et seq.) of Title 32.1 or Chapter 8 (§ 37.1-179 et seq.) of Title 37.1.

"Impartial attorney" means an attorney who has not represented (i) the claimant, his family, his partners, co-proprietors or his other business interests; or (ii) the health care provider, his family, his partners, co-proprietors or his other business interests.

"Impartial health care provider" means a health care provider who (i) has not examined, treated or been consulted regarding the claimant or his family; (ii) does not anticipate examining, treating, or being consulted regarding the claimant or his family; or (iii) has not been an employee, partner or co-proprietor of the health care provider against whom the claim is asserted.

"Malpractice" means any tort based on health care or professional services rendered, or which should have been rendered, by a health care provider, to a patient.

"Physician" means a person licensed to practice medicine or osteopathy in this Commonwealth pursuant to Chapter 29 (§ 54.1-2900 et seq.) of Title 54.1.

"Patient" means any natural person who receives or should have received health care from a licensed health care provider except those persons who are given health care in an emergency situation which exempts the health care provider from liability for his emergency services in accordance with § 8.01-225. (Code 1950, § 8-911; 1976, c. 611; 1977, c. 617; 1981, c. 305; 1986, cc. 227, 511; 1989, cc. 146, 730; 1991, cc. 455, 464; 1993, c. 268; 1994, cc. 114, 616, 651.)

Cross references. — As to tort liability of hospitals, see § 8.01-38. As to limitation on recovery of punitive damages in actions, including medical malpractice actions, see § 8.01-38.1. As to notice of claims against the Commonwealth involving medical malpractice, see § 8.0-195.6. As to statute of limitations for claims against the Commonwealth involving medical malpractice, see § 8.01-195.7. As to practitioner's disclosure of information when necessary for the protection or enforcement of the practitioner's legal rights including such rights with respect to medical malpractice actions, see § 8.01-399. As to limitation on recovery in certain medical malpractice actions, see § 8.01-581.15. As to the Medical Malpractice Joint Underwriting Association, see § 38.2-2800. For the Medical Malpractice Rules of Practice, see Volume 11 of the Code of Virginia.

Law Review. — For article on Virginia's Medical Malpractice Review Panel, see 11 U. Rich. L. Rev. 51 (1976). For note, "Medical Malpractice Arbitration: A Comparative Analysis," see 62 Va. L. Rev. 1285 (1976). For survey of Virginia insurance law for the year 1975-1976, see 62 Va. L. Rev. 1446 (1976). For survey of Virginia tort law for the year 1975-1976, see 62 Va. L. Rev. 1489 (1976). For note on a constitutional analysis of Virginia's Medical Malpractice Act, see 37 Wash. & Lee L. Rev. 1192 (1980). For article on the limitation on recovery in medical negligence cases in Virginia, see 16 U. Rich. L. Rev. 799 (1982). For article, "Medical Malpractice Review Panels in Operation in Virginia," see 19 U. Rich. L. Rev. 273 (1985). For comment, "Scope of Permissible Pretrial Discovery of Medical Malpractice Review Panel Deliberations in Virginia: Klarfeld v. Salsbury," see 10 Geo. Mason L. Rev. 577 (1988). For survey on medical malpractice in Virginia for 1989, see 23 U. Rich. L. Rev. 731 (1989). For article, "Recent Developments in Medical Malpractice and Health Care Law," see 24 U. Rich. L. Rev. 655 (1990). For article,

"Autonomy and Informed Consent in Medical Decisionmaking: Toward a New Self-Fulfilling Prophecy," see 47 Wash. & Lee L. Rev. 379 (1990). For a review of damages in medical malpractice in Virginia, see 33 U. Rich. L. Rev. 919 (1999).

I. DECISIONS UNDER CURRENT LAW.

Editor's note. — Some of the cases cited below were decided under this article as it read prior to later amendments thereto.

Constitutionality. — Virginia Medical Malpractice Act does not violate Va. Const., Art. IV, § 14, which prohibits the enactment of any local, special or private law regulating the practice in or changing the rules of evidence in any judicial proceedings or inquiry before the courts or other tribunals but constitutes a valid legislative classification, since a law may apply to a small class so long as the classification is reasonable and the law applies equally to all persons within the class. DiAntonio v. Northampton-Accomack Mem. Hosp., 628 F.2d 287 (4th Cir. 1980).

The different treatment of medical malpractice plaintiffs from other tort plaintiffs is not a denial of equal protection, when the special problems posed by soaring insurance costs are considered. DiAntonio v. Northampton-Accomack Mem. Hosp., 628 F.2d 287 (4th Cir. 1980).

Purpose of 1994 amendments. — The General Assembly intended the 1994 amendments adding new entities to the definition of "health care provider" to serve the same purpose as the original enactment of the medical malpractice cap, i.e., to provide a remedy for a perceived social problem, the unavailability of medical malpractice insurance at affordable rates. Thus, the Virginia Supreme Court rejected the argument that the 1994 amendment contained no statement of purpose and therefore failed the test that a statutory scheme must bear a reasonable and substantial relationship to the object sought to be accomplished by the legislation. Pulliam v. Coastal Emergency Servs. of Richmond, Inc., 257 Va. 1, 509 S.E.2d 307 (1999).

Actions constituting "torts" under the act. — Assault and battery as well as intentional infliction of emotional distress are "torts," and qualify as "any" tort under the act. Hagan v. Antonio, 240 Va. 347, 397 S.E.2d 810 (1990).

"Health care provider." — Corporation which provides emergency physicians to staff emergency departments of hospitals was an entity which primarily renders health care services within the meaning of the definition of "health care provider." Pulliam v. Coastal Emergency Servs. of Richmond, Inc., 257 Va. 1, 509 S.E.2d 307 (1999).

Alleged breach of duty of confidentiality sounded in tort and not in contract; because the alleged breach of duty of confidentiality sounded in tort, it was "malpractice" for the reason that it was "any tort based on health care" under the act. It followed that the trial court properly sustained the motion to dismiss because notice of claim was not given before suit was filed in violation of § 8.01-581.2(A). Pierce v. Caday, 244 Va. 285, 422 S.E.2d 371 (1992).

Breast examination within the meaning of health care. — A breast examination, including the touching, is an inseparable part of a typical, complete physical examination of a woman, and therefore the defendant's conduct during a breast examination was "based on health care" within the meaning of the act. Hagan v. Antonio, 240 Va. 347, 397 S.E.2d 810 (1990).

Availability of review provisions in federal court. — Even if federal courts are required to apply the provisions of the Virginia Medical Malpractice Act under the *Erie* doctrine, the malpractice review provisions otherwise available to a defendant in state court litigation are not available when the action is commenced in federal court. Adkins v. Commonwealth ex rel. UVA Medical Ctr., 154 F.R.D. 139 (W.D. Va. 1994).

Exhaustion of remedies under chapter as prerequisite to action in federal court. — The Virginia Medical Malpractice Act is applicable in a diversity action. Thus, exhaustion of this available remedy is required before bringing a medical malpractice action in a federal court sitting in diversity in Virginia. Herer v. Burns, 577 F. Supp. 762 (W.D. Va. 1984).

However, exhaustion of state remedies is not a prerequisite to an action under 42 U.S.C. § 1983. Therefore, plaintiffs, who did not rely solely on diversity jurisdiction, were not required to avail themselves of the Virginia Medical Malpractice Act before a federal court had jurisdiction to consider constitutional and pendent wrongful death claims. Herer v. Burns, 577 F. Supp. 762 (W.D. Va. 1984).

Cap applies to recoveries under the Emergency Medical Treatment and Active Labor Act. — The statutory cap of $1,000,000 (now $1,500,000) imposed by § 8.01-581.15 applies to medical malpractice recoveries under the Emergency Medical Treatment and Active Labor Act, 42 U.S.C. § 1395dd. Lee ex rel. Wetzel v. Alleghany Regional Hosp. Corp., 778 F. Supp. 900 (W.D. Va. 1991).

Virginia's medical malpractice damages cap applied to claim under Emergency Medical Treatment and Active Labor Act (42 U.S.C. 1395dd) for failure to provide an appropriate medical screening. Power v. Arlington Hosp. Ass'n, 42 F.3d 851 (4th Cir. 1994).

Child has statutory cap separate from cap on mother's claims. — A mother and her newborn child are separate "patients," and thus, each may recover a maximum of $1,500,000. Lee ex rel. Wetzel v. Alleghany Regional Hosp. Corp., 778 F. Supp. 900 (W.D. Va. 1991).

A father seeking damages for emotional harm and medical expenses, resulting from the malpractice to the mother and child, may not recover separately. Lee ex rel. Wetzel v. Alleghany Regional Hosp. Corp., 778 F. Supp. 900 (W.D. Va. 1991).

The father's claims for emotional distress and medical expenses are derivative of the child's, and thus fall within the child's statutory cap. Lee ex rel. Wetzel v. Alleghany Regional Hosp. Corp., 778 F. Supp. 900 (W.D. Va. 1991).

The Virginia Medical Malpractice Act contains no provision for vicarious liability, and the breadth of the statutory scheme suggests that none is intended; for example, because a physician, a nurse, or a hospital each may be held liable in their own right, there is no basis or reason for holding a physician liable for the conduct of another physician, a hospital nurse, or any other hospital employee. Peck v. Tegtmeyer, 834 F. Supp. 903 (W.D. Va. 1992), aff'd, 4 F.3d 985 (4th Cir. 1993).

Adult homes not held to same standard of care as health care providers. — Although hospitals and nursing homes are included within the definition of "health care provider" in this section, adult homes are not so included; the omission is significant, and adult homes, where residents are provided room and board but there are no medically-trained personnel on the staff and residents are free to come and go at will, are not held to the standard of care which applies to health care providers. Furthermore, subject to the provisions of § 63.1-182.1, such homes do not have a duty to care for the health, welfare, and safety of their residents when such residents are absent from the home's premises. Commercial Distribs., Inc. v. Blankenship, 240 Va. 382, 397 S.E.2d 840 (1990).

Adult homes are neither hospitals, nursing homes, nor custodial institutions; they exist pursuant to statutes intended to provide a residence for persons under disabilities, offering those persons the greatest degree of freedom and participation in normal life consistent with their conditions. Commercial Distribs., Inc. v. Blankenship, 240 Va. 382, 397 S.E.2d 840 (1990).

Breach of contract action not malpractice. — Had the General Assembly meant to include breach of contract actions within the definition of "malpractice," surely it would have so provided. Glisson v. Loxley, 235 Va. 62, 366 S.E.2d 68 (1988).

The legislature was directing its attention to torts and not breaches of contract in the enactment which established the medical malpractice review system. Glisson v. Loxley, 235 Va. 62, 366 S.E.2d 68 (1988).

Unlicensed physician not health care provider. — Since the doctor who performed the service was not licensed in the Commonwealth when he rendered the services to the deceased, he was not a health care provider within the purview of the statute. Taylor v. Mobil Corp., 248 Va. 101, 444 S.E.2d 705 (1994).

Clinical laboratory not health care provider. — A clinical laboratory which provided erroneous test results to a physician was not a health care provider under the Virginia Medical Malpractice Act. Richman v. National Health Labs., Inc., 235 Va. 353, 367 S.E.2d 508 (1988).

Clinical laboratory was not an agent or employee of doctors and thus was not a health care provider. Consequently, this act did not apply to the lab, and filing the notice of claim under the act did not toll the statute of limitations as to the claim of negligence against the lab. Richman v. National Health Labs., Inc., 235 Va. 353, 367 S.E.2d 508 (1988).

When infant is obstetrician's patient. — At the moment of live birth, and until the pediatrician assumes responsibility for the care of the newborn, the infant is the obstetrician's "patient." Bulala v. Boyd, 239 Va. 218, 389 S.E.2d 670 (1990).

Refusal to provide ventilator treatment for infant with an encephaly. — Where hospital sought a declaration that its refusal to provide infant born with anencephaly with ventilator treatment did not constitute malpractice under the Virginia Medical Malpractice Act, the federal district court declined to "elbow its way" into Virginia medical malpractice standards by addressing the issue because of the significant state interest manifested by the review process as well as the Commonwealth's interest in resolving contentious and unsettled social issue for itself. In re Baby "K", 832 F. Supp. 1022 (E.D. Va. 1993), aff'd, 16 F.3d 590 (4th Cir.), cert. denied, 513 U.S. 825, 115 S. Ct. 91, 130 L. Ed. 2d 42 (1994).

Applied in Lawrence v. Wirth, 226 Va. 408, 309 S.E.2d 315 (1983); Edwards v. City of Portsmouth, 237 Va. 167, 375 S.E.2d 747 (1989); Gonzalez v. Fairfax Hosp. Sys., 239 Va. 307, 389 S.E.2d 458 (1990); Turner v. Wexler, 244 Va. 124, 418 S.E.2d 886 (1992).

§ 8.01-581.2. Request for review by medical malpractice review panel; rescission of request; determination on request. — A. At any time within thirty days from the filing of the responsive pleading in any action brought for malpractice against a health care provider, the plaintiff or defendant may request a review by a medical malpractice review panel established as provided in § 8.01-581.3. The request shall be forwarded by the party making the request to the Clerk of the Supreme Court of Virginia with a copy of the Motion for Judgment and a copy of all responsive pleadings. A copy of the request shall be filed with the clerk of the circuit court, and a copy shall be sent to all counsel of record. The request shall include the name of the judge to whom the case is assigned, if any. Upon receipt of such request, the Supreme Court shall select the panel members as provided in § 8.01-581.3:1 and shall designate a panel within sixty days after receipt of the request. If a panel is requested, proceedings on the action based on the alleged malpractice shall be stayed during the period of review by the medical review panel, except that the judge may rule on any motions, demurrers, or pleas that can be disposed of as a matter of law and, prior to the designation of the panel, shall rule on any motions to transfer venue.

B. After the selection of the members of the review panel, the requesting party may rescind a request for review by the panel only with the consent of all parties or with leave of the judge presiding over the panel.

C. Any health care provider named as a defendant shall have the right to request a panel and, in that event, shall give notice of its request to the other health care providers named in the motion for judgment as well as to the plaintiff and his counsel of record. When a request for a medical review panel is made by any party, a single panel shall be designated and all health care providers against whom a claim is asserted shall be subject to the jurisdiction of such panel. The provisions of this subsection shall not prohibit the addition of parties pursuant to § 8.01-581.2:1. (Code 1950, § 8-912; 1976, c. 611; 1977, c. 617; 1982, c. 151; 1984, cc. 443, 777; 1986, c. 227; 1989, c. 561; 1993, c. 928; 1994, c. 38; 1995, c. 367; 2000, c. 213.)

The 2000 amendments. — The 2000 amendment by c. 213, in subsection A, substituted "party making the request to" for "clerk of the circuit court" and added "with a copy of the Motion for Judgment and a copy of all responsive pleadings" in the second sentence, added a third and a fourth sentence, and added "and shall designate a panel within sixty days after receipt of the request" at the end of the fifth sentence.

Law Review. — For survey of Virginia tort law for the year 1975-1976, see 62 Va. L. Rev. 1489 (1976). For note on constitutional analysis of Virginia's Medical Malpractice Act, see 37 Wash. & Lee L. Rev. 1192 (1980). For a re-examination of sovereign tort immunity in Virginia, see 15 U. Rich. L. Rev. 247 (1981). For comment, "A Frivolous Lawsuit May Destroy the Career of a Professional: Is There No Remedy?", see 17 U. Rich. L. Rev. 421 (1983). For article, "Medical Malpractice Review Panels in Operation in Virginia," see 19 U. Rich. L. Rev. 273 (1985). For comment, "Scope of Permissible Pretrial Discovery of Medical Malpractice Review Panel Deliberations in Virginia: Klarfeld v. Salsbury," see 10 Geo. Mason L. Rev. 577 (1988). For survey on medical malpractice in Virginia for 1989, see 23 U. Rich. L. Rev. 731 (1989).

I. DECISIONS UNDER CURRENT LAW.

Editor's note. — Some of the cases below were decided under this article as it read prior to later amendments.

The statutory language is clear and unambiguous; thus, the court will apply the plain meaning of the act's language to the facts of each case. Hagan v. Antonio, 240 Va. 347, 397 S.E.2d 810 (1990).

Non-adversarial procedure for developing medical records. — This unique prelitigation procedure gives a Virginia health care provider an opportunity to develop the medical record in a non-adversarial fashion. Gardner v. Aetna Cas. & Sur. Co., 841 F.2d 82 (4th Cir. 1988).

Virginia's procedural requirements not applicable to EMTALA claims. — The notice of claim provisions of this section conflict with the requirements of the federal Emergency Medical Treatment and Women in Active Labor provisions, 42 U.S.C. § 1395 dd, of the Consolidated Omnibus Budget Reconciliation Act (COBRA), and therefore, are inapplicable to such causes of action. Smith v. Richmond Mem. Hosp., 243 Va. 445, 416 S.E.2d 689, cert. denied, 506 U.S. 967, 113 S. Ct. 442, 121 L. Ed. 2d 361 (1992).

Because Virginia's procedural requirements

under this section are potentially in direct conflict with, and therefore inconsistent with the Emergency Medical Treatment and Active Labor Act (EMTALA), 42 U.S.C. § 1395dd, they are not applicable to an EMTALA claim. Power v. Arlington Hosp. Ass'n, 42 F.3d 851 (4th Cir. 1994).

Or to actions commenced in federal court. — Even if federal courts are required to apply the provisions of the Virginia Medical Malpractice Act under the *Erie* doctrine, the malpractice review provisions otherwise available to a defendant in state court litigation are not available when the action is commenced in federal court. Adkins v. Commonwealth ex rel. UVA Medical Ctr., 154 F.R.D. 139 (W.D. Va. 1994); Swaim v. Fogle, 68 F. Supp. 2d 703 (E.D. Va. 1999).

Treatment of Filing Procedure in Medical Malpractice Rules. — The provisions of Rule Two(c) (see now Rule 2(a)) of the Medical Malpractice Rules stating that the request for a panel shall be deemed to be filed when delivered or mailed be registered or certified mail, do not conflict with the provisions of the Medical Malpractice Act, in violation of Va. Const., Art. VII, § 5. The authors of the act expressly empowered the Chief Justice to promulgate rules necessary to carry out its provisions. Rule Two(c)(see now Rule 2(a)) merely particularizes the mechanics of the filing requirements of this section and former § 8.01-581.9. Horn v. Abernathy, 231 Va. 228, 343 S.E.2d 318 (1986).

A battery arising from health care is malpractice within the clear meaning of the malpractice statutes and the required notice should have been given. Glisson v. Loxley, 235 Va. 62, 366 S.E.2d 68 (1988).

Clinical laboratory not health care provider. — A clinical laboratory, which provided erroneous test results to a physician, was not a health care provider under the Virginia Medical Malpractice Act. Richman v. National Health Labs., Inc., 235 Va. 353, 367 S.E.2d 508 (1988).

Clinical laboratory was not an agent or employee of doctors and thus was not a health care provider. Consequently, this act did not apply to the lab, and filing the notice of claim under the act did not toll the statute of limitations as to the claim of negligence against the lab. Richman v. National Health Labs., Inc., 235 Va. 353, 367 S.E.2d 508 (1988).

The method of service of a claim specified in this section is a procedural requirement which is deemed waived if an objection is not timely raised. Hewitt v. Virginia Health Servs. Corp., 239 Va. 643, 391 S.E.2d 59 (1990).

The notice required by this section is neither a bill of particulars nor a pleading of any other kind. It is not required to contain a summary of the plaintiff's evidence or an exposition of the plaintiff's theories of the case; rather, its purpose is simply to call the defendant's attention to the identity of the patient, the time of the alleged malpractice, and a description of the alleged acts of malpractice sufficient to enable the defendant to identify the case to which the plaintiff is referring. Hudson v. Surgical Specialists, Inc., 239 Va. 101, 387 S.E.2d 750 (1990).

This section calls for reasonable notice. However, a notice of claims by its nature is not meant to be a particularized statement of claims. A notice calls the recipient's attention to the general time, place, and character of the events complained of in the malpractice suit. Grubbs v. Rawls, 235 Va. 607, 369 S.E.2d 683 (1988).

Notice does not need to contain particularized statement of claims. — This section does not intent that the notice contain a particularized statement of claims; trial court erred in restricting plaintiff's evidence in malpractice case to the specific facts alleged in her notice of claim. Hudson v. Surgical Specialists, Inc., 239 Va. 101, 387 S.E.2d 750 (1990).

The giving of notice to an adverse party is not a filing. Horn v. Abernathy, 231 Va. 228, 343 S.E.2d 318 (1986).

Notice letters held sufficient to encompass negligent post-operative treatment as well as failure to obtain informed consent and negligent surgery. Grubbs v. Rawls, 235 Va. 607, 369 S.E.2d 683 (1988).

Application of notice and panel review provisions in federal court. — The notice requirement set forth in this section and the provision for panel review set forth in this section at the instance of either party to a medical malpractice action are so intimately bound up with the rights and obligations being asserted as to require their application in federal courts under the doctrine of Erie R.R. v. Tompkins, 304 U.S. 64, 58 S. Ct. 817, 82 L. Ed. 1188 (1938). DiAntonio v. Northampton-Accomack Mem. Hosp., 628 F.2d 287 (4th Cir. 1980).

Reasonable compliance required for defective notice. — When faced with an allegedly defective notice of claim, as opposed to the failure to file any such notice, reasonable compliance with the notice requirements is all that is mandated. Dolwick v. Leech, 800 F. Supp. 321 (E.D. Va. 1992).

Second notice and failure to seek leave to amend first notice. — Despite plaintiff's failure to seek any leave to amend its June 18 notice of claim, the October 25 notice operated independently to reasonably comply with the requirements of the Virginia Medical Malpractice Act and tolled the running of the statute of limitations; further, the procedural requirements of the act were deemed waived since no timely objection was made. Dolwick v. Leech, 800 F. Supp. 321 (E.D. Va. 1992).

Former § 8.01-581.9 compensated for this section's restrictions upon free access to courts. — As a result of this section as it read prior to amendment in 1993, a medical malpractice claimant was absolutely forbidden from filing an action until 90 days after notification to the health care provider and then, if a review panel was requested, for the entire period the matter was under review by the panel. In an obvious effort to compensate for these restrictions upon a claimant's usual free access to the courts and to provide relief from an otherwise harsh application of the statute of limitations, the General Assembly enacted former § 8.01-581.9, providing for tolling of the statute of limitations upon the giving of notice of a claim, etc. Baker v. Zirkle, 226 Va. 7, 307 S.E.2d 234 (1983); Dye v. Staley, 226 Va. 15, 307 S.E.2d 237 (1983).

Prohibition against filing suit prior to 90 days after notice. — The prohibition contained in this section prior to its amendment in 1993 against filing suit prior to 90 days after giving notice of a medical malpractice claim was a mandatory procedural requirement; failure to comply with this provision did not divest the court of subject matter jurisdiction. Morrison v. Bestler, 239 Va. 166, 387 S.E.2d 753 (1990).

The Medical Malpractice Act itself gave plaintiff fair notice affecting the right to file suit, where under this section as it read prior to amendment in 1993 the notice of claim foreclosed that right for 90 days, but the running of the two-year statute of limitations, which otherwise would have expired, was suspended for 120 days with 10 days of the two-year period remaining. Thus, plaintiff was on notice that the act authorized suit to be filed any time after the 90-day period expired and before the running of the limitations period. Horn v. Abernathy, 231 Va. 228, 343 S.E.2d 318 (1986).

Effect on substantive rights. — Where plaintiff could have filed a motion for judgment instead of a notice of claim in a timely manner, pursuant to the 1993 amendment to this section, her substantive right to seek damages for the alleged medical malpractice was not materially curtailed. Harris v. DiMattina, 250 Va. 306, 462 S.E.2d 338 (1995).

Where the tolling provisions of former Code § 8.01-581.9 provided necessary statutory relief from the running of the statute of limitations, since this section as it read prior to 1993 amendment prohibited plaintiffs from filing a motion for judgment until 90 days after they had given notice of claim, and after the review panel process had been completed, delays imposed by the statute when plaintiff filed his notice of claim and refrained from filing suit, would result in a miscarriage of justice if he was denied benefit of the tolling provisions. Harris v. DiMattina, 250 Va. 306, 462 S.E.2d 338 (1995).

Sanction for noncompliance with prohibition. — The proper sanction for noncompliance with the provision in this section as it read prior to amendment in 1993, prohibiting filing suit prior to 90 days after giving notice, would depend on the circumstances of each case; other courts which have considered the issue have seen fit to dismiss the suit without prejudice, stay the proceedings, or abate the proceedings. Morrison v. Bestler, 239 Va. 166, 387 S.E.2d 753 (1990).

Sovereign immunity not extended to faculty members of medical school. — In an action to recover damages for personal injuries resulting from alleged negligent acts of defendant doctors, the defendants, who were fully licensed to practice medicine, and were full-time members of the faculty of the Medical School of the University of Virginia and attending staff physicians of the University of Virginia Hospital, were not entitled to invoke the doctrine of sovereign immunity. James v. Jane, 221 Va. 43, 267 S.E.2d 108 (1980).

Applied in Edwards v. City of Portsmouth, 237 Va. 167, 375 S.E.2d 747 (1989); Cowan v. Psychiatric Assoc., 239 Va. 59, 387 S.E.2d 747 (1990); Gonzalez v. Fairfax Hosp. Sys., 239 Va. 307, 389 S.E.2d 458 (1990); Pierce v. Caday, 244 Va. 285, 422 S.E.2d 371 (1992).

§ 8.01-581.2:1. Additional parties. — The judge of the circuit court hearing the case may grant leave to amend the request for a review panel to add additional parties or causes of action in furtherance of the ends of justice except where (i) the request for leave to amend is made less than ten days before the date set for the review panel to convene or for the hearing or (ii) the judge finds that the request for leave to amend is without merit. If leave to amend is granted, the judge may, upon motion of either party, stay the review panel proceedings or continue the trial, extend the time for completion of discovery, filing of pleadings and other procedural limitations periods, or enter such other orders as are appropriate to avoid prejudice to the parties and to avoid unnecessary delay and duplication in the proceedings.

The statute of limitations as to any party added shall be tolled from the date of the request until completion of the panel proceedings. Leave to add additional parties to the review panel proceeding shall not be granted if the judge finds that the applicable statute of limitations has expired with respect to the new or additional parties or causes of action. (1986, c. 227; 1993, c. 928.)

Law Review. — For survey on medical malpractice in Virginia for 1989, see 23 U. Rich. L. Rev. 731 (1989).

I. DECISIONS UNDER CURRENT LAW.

Editor's note. — Some of the cases cited under the sections of this article were decided under the article as it read prior to later amendments thereto.

Reasonable compliance required for defective notice. — When faced with an allegedly defective notice of claim, as opposed to the failure to file any such notice, reasonable compliance with the notice requirements is all that is mandated. Dolwick v. Leech, 800 F. Supp. 321 (E.D. Va. 1992).

Second notice and failure to seek leave to amend first notice. — Despite plaintiff's failure to seek any leave to amend its June 18 notice of claim, the October 25 notice operated independently to reasonably comply with the requirements of the Virginia Medical Malpractice Act and tolled the running of the statute of limitations; further, the procedural requirements of the act were deemed waived since no timely objection was made. Dolwick v. Leech, 800 F. Supp. 321 (E.D. Va. 1992).

§ 8.01-581.3. Composition, selection, etc., of panel. — The medical review panel shall consist of (i) two impartial attorneys and two impartial health care providers, licensed and actively practicing their professions in the Commonwealth and (ii) the judge of a circuit court in which the action was filed, who shall preside over the panel. The judge shall have no vote and need not attend or participate in the deliberations. The medical review panel shall be selected by the Supreme Court from a list of health care providers submitted by the Board of Medicine and a list of attorneys submitted by the Virginia State Bar. In the selection of the health care provider members, the Court shall give due regard to the nature of the claim and the nature of the practice of the health care provider. (Code 1950, § 8-913; 1976, c. 611; 1977, cc. 202, 617; 1983, c. 208; 1984, c. 777; 1986, c. 227; 1993, c. 928; 1994, c. 384.)

Editor's note. — Acts 1977, c. 202, amended former § 8-913, corresponding to this section. This section, as enacted by Acts 1977, c. 617, already incorporated the changes made in former § 8-913 by the amendment, and therefore no change was made in the wording of this section pursuant to the amendment.

Law Review. — For article discussing possibly unconstitutional usurpation of judicial power by the legislature, see 11 U. Rich. L. Rev. 51 (1976). For survey of Virginia tort law for the year 1975-1976, see 62 Va. L. Rev. 1489 (1976). For article, "Medical Malpractice Review Panels in Operation in Virginia," see 19 U. Rich. L. Rev. 273 (1985). For comment, "Scope of Permissible Pretrial Discovery of Medical Malpractice Review Panel Deliberations in Virginia: Klarfeld v. Salsbury," see 10 Geo. Mason L. Rev. 577 (1988). For survey on medical malpractice in Virginia for 1989, see 23 U. Rich. L. Rev. 731 (1989).

I. DECISIONS UNDER CURRENT LAW.

Editor's note. — Some of the cases cited under the sections of this article were decided under the article as it read prior to later amendments thereto.

Application of notice and panel review provisions in federal court. — The notice requirement set forth in § 8.01-581.2 and the provision for panel review set forth in this section at the instance of either party to a medical malpractice action are so intimately bound up with the rights and obligations being asserted as to require their application in federal courts under the doctrine of Erie R.R. v. Tompkins, 304 U.S. 64, 58 S. Ct. 817, 82 L. Ed. 1188 (1938). DiAntonio v. Northampton-Accomack Mem. Hosp., 628 F.2d 287 (4th Cir. 1980).

Review provisions not applicable to action commenced in federal court. — Even if federal courts are required to apply the provisions of the Virginia Medical Malpractice Act under the *Erie* doctrine, the malpractice review provisions otherwise available to a defendant in state court litigation are not available when the action is commenced in federal court. Adkins v. Commonwealth ex rel. UVA Medical Ctr., 154 F.R.D. 139 (W.D. Va. 1994).

Decision of chairman of medical malpractice panel was a judicial act. — Although decision of judge who was appointed chairman of medical malpractice panel to impose sanctions was subject to later judicial

§ 8.01-581.3:1   CODE OF VIRGINIA   § 8.01-581.4

consideration, it was nonetheless a judicial act that could not be enjoined. Power v. Kendrick, 247 Va. 59, 439 S.E.2d 345 (1994).

Applied in Klarfeld v. Salsbury, 233 Va. 277, 355 S.E.2d 319 (1987); Deasy v. Hill, 833 F.2d 38 (4th Cir. 1987).

§ 8.01-581.3:1. Completion of discovery; hearing date; notification to parties and panel members; oath of panel members. — At the time that the panel is designated, the Supreme Court shall advise the clerk of the circuit court in which the matter was filed of the names of the panel members.

Except for good cause shown, the date for completion of discovery shall not be set beyond 120 days from the date on which the panel was requested. Within the period set for the taking of discovery and upon consultation with the panel members, the judge shall notify the parties of the date set for a hearing by the review panel, if any, or the date on which the panel will convene. Such date shall not be set sooner than ten days after the date for completion of discovery. Upon completion of discovery, the clerk of the circuit court shall notify the parties of the name, address and professional practice of each panel member and shall also notify the panel members, in writing, of their appointment.

The written notification to the panel members shall include the definitions of "impartial attorney" and "impartial health care provider" as contained in § 8.01-581.1 and a copy of the oath to which the panel members will be required to subscribe when the panel convenes. The oath shall be as follows:

"I do solemnly swear (or affirm) that I have no past or present relationship with the parties nor am I aware of anything that would prevent me from being impartial in my deliberations. I further swear (or affirm) that I will render an opinion faithfully and fairly on the basis of the evidence presented, applying any professional expertise I may have, giving due regard to the nature of the claim and the nature of the practice of the health care provider." A panel member who, for any reason, could not take the oath of impartiality shall promptly notify the judge presiding over the panel, in writing, of such inability. The judge shall notify the Supreme Court, which shall then select and notify another panel member in place of and practicing the same profession as the disqualified member. (1986, c. 227; 1993, c. 928.)

Law Review. — For comment, "Scope of Permissible Pretrial Discovery of Medical Malpractice Review Panel Deliberations in Virginia: Klarfeld v. Salsbury," see 10 Geo. Mason L. Rev. 577 (1988).

§ 8.01-581.4. Submission of evidence to panel; depositions and discovery; duties of chairman; access to material. — The evidence to be considered by the medical review panel shall be promptly submitted by the respective parties, upon appointment of the panel, to each member of the panel in written form. Either party, upon request, shall be granted a hearing before the panel. The evidence may consist of medical charts, X-rays, laboratory tests, excerpts of treatises, and depositions of witnesses, including parties, and, when a hearing is held, oral testimony before the panel. The parties shall submit to the panel members only those portions of deposition transcripts, medical records, treatises and other documents which are relevant to the claim. However, upon request of the judge, a party shall produce all or part of any such document submitted. At the discretion of the judge, additional depositions of parties and witnesses may be taken, or other additional discovery may be had, at any time prior to hearing by any party. The judge shall rule on the admissibility of all or any part of a deposition offered as evidence at the hearing. Either party may have discovery pursuant to procedures set out in Part Four of the Rules of the Supreme Court of Virginia prior to appointment of the panel or thereafter in the discretion of the judge.

Process shall be returnable to the office of the clerk where the action was filed and shall issue under the style of the case as filed. Process for discovery shall issue upon application to the clerk. Any such discovery and any depositions taken for purposes of discovery or otherwise, under this section, may be used in the action filed for any purpose otherwise proper under Part Four of the Rules of Court. The judge of the panel shall advise the panel relative to any legal question involved in the review proceeding and shall prepare the opinion of the panel as provided in § 8.01-581.7. All parties shall have full access to any material submitted to the panel. (Code 1950, § 8-914; 1976, c. 611; 1977, c. 617; 1979, c. 261; 1984, c. 777; 1986, c. 227; 1993, c. 928.)

Law Review. — For survey of Virginia law on practice and pleading for the year 1978-1979, see 66 Va. L. Rev. 343 (1980). For article, "Medical Malpractice Review Panels in Operation in Virginia," see 19 U. Rich. L. Rev. 273 (1985). For comment, "Scope of Permissible Pretrial Discovery of Medical Malpractice Review Panel Deliberations in Virginia: Klarfeld v. Salsbury," see 10 Geo. Mason L. Rev. 577 (1988).

I. DECISIONS UNDER CURRENT LAW.

Applied in Deasy v. Hill, 833 F.2d 38 (4th Cir. 1987).

§ 8.01-581.4:1. Assembly of record. — Upon conclusion of deliberations and rendering of an opinion by the panel, all documentary evidence submitted to the panel, a transcript of the ore tenus hearing, if any, and a copy of the written opinion of the panel shall be filed in the office of the clerk. The record shall be maintained until the action is completed in the circuit court. Upon completion of the action, the clerk of the trial court shall include a copy of the panel record along with the record of the case. (1986, c. 227; 1993, c. 928.)

§ 8.01-581.4:2. Removal of record for inspection and copying; notice. — Any party may, upon notice to all other parties or their counsel, remove any book, record or document which has been filed with the clerk or has become a part of the permanent record filed with the Executive Secretary for purposes of inspection and copying. The party removing the documents shall give an appropriate receipt to the clerk or Executive Secretary and shall be responsible for the return of the materials within ten days. (1986, c. 227.)

§ 8.01-581.5. When hearing to be held; notice to parties. — The plaintiff or defendant may request the medical review panel to hold a hearing on any claim referred to the medical review panel, in which case the medical review panel shall conduct a hearing thereon in accordance with § 8.01-581.6 after notice to the parties by means adequate to ensure their presence at the time and place of the hearing. (Code 1950, § 8-915; 1976, c. 611; 1977, c. 617; 1979, c. 261; 1984, c. 777; 1993, c. 928.)

§ 8.01-581.6. Conduct of proceedings. — In the conduct of its proceedings:
1. The testimony of the witnesses shall be given under oath. Members of the medical review panel, once sworn, shall have the power to administer oaths.
2. In the event a hearing is held, the parties are entitled to be heard, to present relevant evidence, and to cross-examine witnesses to the extent necessary to enable the panel to render an opinion as specified in § 8.01-581.7. The rules of evidence need not be observed. The medical review panel may proceed with the hearing and shall render an opinion upon the evidence produced, notwithstanding the failure of a party duly notified to appear.
3. The medical review panel may issue or cause to be issued, on its own motion or on application of any party, subpoenas for the attendance of witnesses and for the production of books, records, documents, and other evidence. Subpoenas so issued shall be served and, upon application by a party or the panel to a court of proper venue having jurisdiction over a motion for

judgment based on such claim, enforced in the manner provided for the service and enforcement of subpoenas in a civil action. All provisions of law compelling a person under subpoena to testify are applicable.

4. [Repealed.]

5. The hearing shall be conducted by all members of the medical review panel unless the parties otherwise agree. A majority of the members present may determine any question and may render an opinion.

6. The medical review panel members may apply their expertise in evaluating the evidence giving due regard to the nature of the claim and the nature of the practice of the health care provider, whether expert medical opinions are presented by the parties or not. (Code 1950, § 8-916; 1976, c. 611; 1977, c. 617; 1979, c. 261; 1984, c. 777; 1986, c. 227.)

Law Review. — For note, "Medical Malpractice Arbitration: A Comparative Analysis," see 62 Va. L. Rev. 1285 (1976). For survey of Virginia insurance law for the year 1975-1976, see 62 Va. L. Rev. 1446 (1976). For article, "Medical Malpractice Review Panels in Operation in Virginia," see 19 U. Rich. L. Rev. 273 (1985). For comment, "Scope of Permissible Pretrial Discovery of Medical Malpractice Review Panel Deliberations in Virginia: Klarfeld v. Salsbury," see 10 Geo. Mason L. Rev. 577 (1988).

I. DECISIONS UNDER CURRENT LAW.

Applied in DiAntonio v. Northampton-Accomack Mem. Hosp., 628 F.2d 287 (4th Cir. 1980).

§ 8.01-581.7. Opinion of panel. — A. Within thirty days, after receiving all the evidence, the panel shall have the duty, after joint deliberation, to render one or more of the following opinions:

1. The evidence does not support a conclusion that the health care provider failed to comply with the appropriate standard of care;

2. The evidence supports a conclusion that the health care provider failed to comply with the appropriate standard of care and that such failure is a proximate cause in the alleged damages;

3. The evidence supports a conclusion that the health care provider failed to comply with the appropriate standard of care and that such failure is not a proximate cause in the alleged damages; or

4. The evidence indicates that there is a material issue of fact, not requiring an expert opinion, bearing on liability for consideration by a court or jury.

B. If the review panel's finding is that set forth in subdivision 2 of subsection A of this section, the panel may determine whether the plaintiff suffered any disability or impairment and the degree and extent thereof.

C. The opinion shall be in writing and shall be signed by all panelists who agree therewith. Any member of the panel may note his dissent. All such opinions shall be filed with the clerk of the court in which the action is pending and mailed to the plaintiff and the defendant within five days of the date of their rendering. However, this subsection shall not be construed to preclude the panel from announcing the opinion in the presence of the parties or their counsel, provided a signed written opinion is subsequently mailed as provided in this subsection. (Code 1950, § 8-917; 1976, c. 611; 1977, c. 617; 1986, c. 227; 1993, c. 928.)

Law Review. — For survey of Virginia tort law for the year 1975-1976, see 62 Va. L. Rev. 1489 (1976). For article, "Medical Malpractice Review Panels in Operation in Virginia," see 19 U. Rich. L. Rev. 273 (1985). For comment, "Scope of Permissible Pretrial Discovery of Medical Malpractice Review Panel Deliberations in Virginia: Klarfeld v. Salsbury," see 10 Geo. Mason L. Rev. 577 (1988).

I. DECISIONS UNDER CURRENT LAW.

Editor's note. — Some of the cases cited under the sections of this article were decided under the article as it read prior to later amendments thereto.

Written opinion of review panel not sufficient as expert testimony. — Expert testimony is ordinarily required in malpractice cases on (1) the standard of care, (2) a deviation from the standard, and (3) causation. The written opinion of the medical malpractice review panel is not in itself sufficient to fulfill those requirements. Raines v. Lutz, 231 Va. 110, 341 S.E.2d 194 (1986).

Applied in DiAntonio v. Northampton-Accomack Mem. Hosp., 628 F.2d 287 (4th Cir. 1980); Deasy v. Hill, 833 F.2d 38 (4th Cir. 1987).

§ 8.01-581.7:1. **Limitation on panel opinion.** — Unless the parties otherwise agree, any opinion of the panel shall be rendered no later than six months from the designation of the panel unless the judge shall extend the period one time, not to exceed ninety days, upon a showing of extraordinary circumstances. If the opinion of the panel is not rendered within the time provided, any panel opinion rendered subsequently shall be inadmissible as evidence unless the failure of the panel to render a decision within the time provided was caused by delay on the plaintiff's part. (1981, c. 327; 1993, c. 928.)

Law Review. — For article, "Medical Malpractice Review Panels in Operation in Virginia," see 19 U. Rich. L. Rev. 273 (1985).

I. DECISIONS UNDER CURRENT LAW.

Applied in Fairfax Hosp. Sys. v. Curtis, 249 Va. 531, 457 S.E.2d 66 (1995).

§ 8.01-581.8. **Admissibility of opinion as evidence; appearance of panel members as witnesses; immunity from civil liability.** — An opinion of the medical review panel shall be admissible as evidence in the action brought by the plaintiff, but shall not be conclusive. Either party shall have the right to call, at his cost, any member of the panel, except the judge, as a witness. If called, each witness shall be required to appear and testify. The panelist shall have absolute immunity from civil liability for all communications, findings, opinions and conclusions made in the course and scope of duties prescribed by this chapter. (Code 1950, § 8-918; 1976, c. 611; 1977, c. 617; 1978, c. 406; 1993, c. 928.)

Law Review. — For a discussion of various problems relating to the admissibility into evidence of the opinion of the panel, see 11 U. Rich. L. Rev. 51 (1976). For survey of Virginia law on evidence for the year 1977-1978, see 64 Va. L. Rev. 1451 (1978). For article, "Medical Malpractice Review Panels in Operation in Virginia," see 19 U. Rich. L. Rev. 273 (1985). For comment, "Scope of Permissible Pretrial Discovery of Medical Malpractice Review Panel Deliberations in Virginia: Klarfeld v. Salsbury," see 10 Geo. Mason L. Rev. 577 (1988).

I. DECISIONS UNDER CURRENT LAW.

Editor's note. — Some of the cases cited under the sections of this article were decided under the article as it read prior to later amendments thereto.

Constitutionality. — The Virginia Medical Malpractice Act does not violate Va. Const., Art. IV, § 14, vesting the judicial power in the Supreme Court and other courts established by the General Assembly, since the essence of judicial power is the final authority to render and enforce a judgment, and the medical malpractice review panel's opinion is binding upon no one. DiAntonio v. Northampton-Accomack Mem. Hosp., 628 F.2d 287 (4th Cir. 1980).

The admitting of the opinions of the medical review board into evidence is not an unconstitutional infringement on plaintiff's right to a jury trial as guaranteed by Va. Const., Art. I, § 11. Speet v. Bacaj, 237 Va. 290, 377 S.E.2d 397 (1989).

Panel's opinion is item of evidence. — Unlike a jury's verdict, a malpractice panel's decision is only an opinion that becomes an item of evidence at the trial but is not conclusive. And such item of evidence should be subject to scrutiny, just as any other piece of evidence, in order to test its probative value and credibility. Klarfeld v. Salsbury, 233 Va. 277, 355 S.E.2d 319 (1987).

Written opinion of review panel not sufficient as expert testimony. — Expert testimony is ordinarily required in malpractice cases on (1) the standard of care, (2) a deviation from the standard, and (3) causation. The written opinion of the medical malpractice review panel is not in itself sufficient to fulfill those requirements. Raines v. Lutz, 231 Va. 110, 341 S.E.2d 194 (1986).

The General Assembly, in enacting the medical malpractice laws, did not decide to make the review panel's opinion a sufficient substitute for expert testimony, or indeed, conclusive upon the jury. Raines v. Lutz, 231 Va. 110, 341 S.E.2d 194 (1986).

Applicability in diversity cases. — The provision for admission into evidence of the panel opinion set forth in this section is intimately related to Virginia's alteration of the substantive cause of action and it is intimately related to Virginia's strong policy of encouraging and promoting pretrial mediation, and because it enforces and implements those interests, the admission provision is applicable in diversity cases. DiAntonio v. Northampton-Accomack Mem. Hosp., 628 F.2d 287 (4th Cir. 1980).

Scope of pretrial questioning of panel member. — A party during pretrial deposition should be permitted to ask a panelist any question designed to test the probative value or credibility of the panel's opinion. Klarfeld v. Salsbury, 233 Va. 277, 355 S.E.2d 319 (1987).

A panelist may be questioned during discovery about, for example, the procedures followed by the panel in executive session, the testimonial and documentary evidence considered, the extent of deliberation, the professional qualifications of the deponent with reference to the issues involved in the claim, the reasoning employed by the deponent and the basis for his conclusion reached during deliberations, whether there were preliminary votes prior to the final vote, and the voting tally at each stage of deliberations. Klarfeld v. Salsbury, 233 Va. 277, 355 S.E.2d 319 (1987).

Excluding interrogation about panel's deliberations was error. — The trial court erred in limiting the scope of the plaintiffs' questioning of a physician panel member pretrial by excluding interrogation about the panel's deliberative process. Klarfeld v. Salsbury, 233 Va. 277, 355 S.E.2d 319 (1987).

Report by private hospital not "state action." — A private hospital's action, pursuant to former § 54-325.1 (now see § 54.1-2906) and this section, in reporting the revocation of a physician's clinical staff privileges to Commonwealth medical licensing authorities in no way constitutes "state action" for purposes of the Fourteenth Amendment to the United States Constitution. Modaber v. Culpeper Mem. Hosp., 674 F.2d 1023 (4th Cir. 1982).

Applied in Deasy v. Hill, 833 F.2d 38 (4th Cir. 1987).

§ 8.01-581.9: Repealed by Acts 1993, c. 928.

§ 8.01-581.10. Per diem and expenses of panel. — Each member of the medical review panel shall be reimbursed for his actual and necessary expenses and shall be paid at a rate of fifty dollars per diem for work performed as a member of the panel exclusive of time involved if called as a witness to testify in court. Per diem and expenses of the panel shall be borne by the parties in such proportions as may be determined by the chairman in his discretion. (Code 1950, § 8-920; 1976, c. 611; 1977, c. 617; 1984, c. 777.)

I. DECISIONS UNDER CURRENT LAW.

Applied in DiAntonio v. Northampton-Accomack Mem. Hosp., 628 F.2d 287 (4th Cir. 1980).

§ 8.01-581.11. Rules and regulations. — The Chief Justice of the Supreme Court of Virginia shall promulgate all necessary rules and regulations to carry out the provisions of this chapter. (Code 1950, § 8-921; 1976, c. 611; 1977, c. 617.)

Cross references. — For the Medical Malpractice Rules of Practice, see Volume 11 of the Code of Virginia.

Law Review. — For comment, "Scope of Permissible Pretrial Discovery of Medical Malpractice Review Panel Deliberations in Virginia: Klarfeld v. Salsbury," see 10 Geo. Mason L. Rev. 577 (1988).

I. DECISIONS UNDER CURRENT LAW.

Editor's note. — Some of the cases cited under the sections of this article were decided under the article as it read prior to later amendments thereto.

Treatment of Filing Procedure in Medical Malpractice Rules. — The provisions of

Rule Two(c)(see now Rule 26)) of the Medical Malpractice Rules, stating that the request for a panel shall be deemed to be filed when delivered or mailed by registered or certified mail, do not conflict with the provisions of the Medical Malpractice Act, in violation of Va. Const., Art. VII, § 5. The authors of the act expressly empowered the Chief Justice to promulgate rules necessary to carry out its provisions. Rule Two(c)(see now Rule 2(a)) merely particularizes the mechanics of the filing requirements of § 8.01-581.2 and former § 8.01-581.9. Horn v. Abernathy, 231 Va. 228, 343 S.E.2d 318 (1986).

Applied in DiAntonio v. Northampton-Accomack Mem. Hosp., 628 F.2d 287 (4th Cir. 1980); Klarfeld v. Salsbury, 233 Va. 277, 355 S.E.2d 319 (1987).

§ **8.01-581.11:1. Objections not waived by participation.** — Participation in any medical malpractice review panel proceeding pursuant to this article shall not constitute a waiver by a party to the proceedings of any objections to the review panel procedure. (1986, c. 227.)

§ **8.01-581.12. Arbitration of medical malpractice claims.** — A. Persons desiring to enter into an agreement to arbitrate medical malpractice claims which have then arisen or may thereafter arise may submit such matters to arbitration under the provisions of Chapter 21 (§ 8.01-577 et seq.) of this title and an agreement to submit such matters shall be binding upon the parties if the patient or claimant or his guardian, conservator, committee or personal representative is allowed by the terms of the agreement to withdraw therefrom, and to decline to submit any matter then or thereafter in controversy, within a period of at least sixty days after the termination of health care or, if the patient is under disability by reason of age and at the time of termination without a guardian who could take such action for him, or if he is incapacitated and without a guardian or conservator who could take such action for him, or if such termination is by death or if death occurs within sixty days after termination, then within a period of at least sixty days after the appointment and qualification of the guardian, conservator or committee or personal representative.

B. Proof of agreement to arbitrate and submission of a medical malpractice claim pursuant thereto shall be in accordance with Chapter 21 of this title, and a medical malpractice panel appointed under this article may be designated to arbitrate the matter, either by the arbitration agreement or by the parties to the agreement.

C. An insurer of a health care provider shall be bound by the award of an arbitration panel or arbitrators acting pursuant to a good faith submission hereunder to the extent to which it would have been obligated by a judgment entered in an action at law with respect to the matter submitted; provided, that such insurer has agreed prior to the submission to be bound by the award of such arbitration panel or arbitrators. (Code 1950, § 8-922; 1976, c. 611; 1977, c. 617; 1997, c. 801.)

Editor's note. — Acts 1997, c. 801, cl. 2, provides: "That the provisions of this act shall become effective on January 1, 1998. The powers granted and duties imposed pursuant to this act shall apply prospectively to guardians and conservators appointed by court order entered on or after that date, or modified on or after that date if the court so directs, without regard to when the petition was filed. The procedures specified in this act governing proceedings for appointment of a guardian or conservator or termination or other modification of a guardianship shall apply on and after that date without regard to when the petition therefor was filed or the guardianship or conservatorship created."

Law Review. — For survey of Virginia insurance law for the year 1975-1976, see 62 Va. L. Rev. 1446 (1976).

§ 8.01-581.12:1: Repealed by Acts 1979, c. 325.

Cross references. — For a new section relating to similar subject matter, see § 8.01-581.20.

§ 8.01-581.12:2. Article not applicable to actions arising prior to July 1, 1976. — (a) The provisions of this article shall not apply to any cause of action which arose prior to July 1, 1976, and as to which the statute of limitations had not run prior to that date, regardless of the date any suit brought thereon is filed. Notwithstanding the foregoing, in actions which accrued prior to July 1, 1976, if a claimant has filed notice under § 8.01-581.2 of this article, his cause of action and any defense thereto shall be governed by this article.

(b) The term "has filed," as used in this section, is deemed to include the filing of notice under § 8.01-581.2 (or under repealed § 8-912) of this article where such filing occurred prior to the expiration of any applicable statute of limitation when the cause of action arose prior to July 1, 1976. This subsection (b) shall be applied retroactively to such causes of action. (Code 1950, § 8-924; 1977, c. 422; 1978, c. 262.)

The number of this section was assigned by the Virginia Code Commission, the number in the 1977 act having been 8-923.

I. DECISIONS UNDER PRIOR LAW.

Editor's note. — The cases cited below were decided under corresponding provisions of former law. The term "this section," as used below, refers to former provisions.

This section was intended to have retrospective effect. Fletcher v. Tarasidis, 219 Va. 658, 250 S.E.2d 739 (1979).

This section is purely procedural and by its very wording clearly implies a legislative intent that it be applied retroactively. Chapman v. Edgerton, 529 F. Supp. 519 (W.D. Va. 1982).

Even as to judgments entered before its enactment. — Where a patient's medical malpractice action accrued prior to the effective date of this article, and the statute of limitations had not run against his action on that date, this section would apply so as to render the article inapplicable. This is so, even though at the time judgment was entered by the trial court, the exemption statute had not been enacted, and the judgment was correct when entered. Fletcher v. Tarasidis, 219 Va. 658, 250 S.E.2d 739 (1979).

Notice given after effective date of section. — By giving notice under § 8.01-581.2 subsequent to March 25, 1977, the effective date of this section, but prior to the expiration of the two-year statute of limitations, plaintiffs invoked § 8.01-581.9 so as to prevent the claims from being time-barred. Armstrong v. Erasmo, 220 Va. 883, 263 S.E.2d 655 (1980).

ARTICLE 2.

Miscellaneous Provisions.

§ 8.01-581.13. Civil immunity for certain health professionals and health profession students serving as members of certain entities. — A. For the purposes of this subsection, "health professional" means any certified substance abuse counselor, clinical psychologist, applied psychologist, school psychologist, dentist, licensed professional counselor, licensed substance abuse treatment practitioner, marriage and family therapist, nurse, optometrist, pharmacist, physician, chiropractor, podiatrist, or veterinarian who is actively engaged in the practice of his profession or any member of the Intervention Program Committee pursuant to Chapter 25.1 (§ 54.1-2515 et seq.) of Title 54.1.

Unless such act, decision, or omission resulted from such health professional's bad faith or malicious intent, any health professional, as defined in this subsection, shall be immune from civil liability for any act, decision or omission resulting from his duties as a member or agent of any entity which functions primarily (i) to investigate any complaint that a physical or mental impairment, including alcoholism or drug addiction, has impaired the ability of any such health professional to practice his profession and (ii) to encourage, recommend and arrange for a course of treatment or intervention, if deemed appropriate, or (iii) to review the duration of patient stays in health facilities or delivery of professional services for the purpose of promoting the most efficient use of available health facilities and services, the adequacy and quality of professional services, or the reasonableness or appropriateness of charges made by or on behalf of such health professionals. Such entity shall have been established pursuant to a federal or state law, or by one or more public or licensed private hospitals, or a relevant health professional society, academy or association affiliated with the American Medical Association, the American Dental Association, the American Pharmaceutical Association, the American Psychological Association, the American Podiatric Medical Association, the American Society of Hospitals and Pharmacies, the American Veterinary Medical Association, the American Association for Counseling and Development, the American Optometric Association, International Chiropractic Association, the American Chiropractic Association, the National Association of Alcoholism and Drug Abuse Counselors, the American Association for Marriage and Family Therapy or a governmental agency.

B. For the purposes of this subsection, "health profession student" means a student in good standing who is enrolled in an accredited school, program, or curriculum in clinical psychology, counseling, dentistry, medicine, nursing, pharmacy, chiropractic, marriage and family therapy, substance abuse treatment, or veterinary medicine and has received training relating to substance abuse.

Unless such act, decision, or omission resulted from such health profession student's bad faith or malicious intent, any health profession student, as defined in this subsection, shall be immune from civil liability for any act, decision, or omission resulting from his duties as a member of an entity established by the institution of higher education in which he is enrolled or a professional student's organization affiliated with such institution which functions primarily (i) to investigate any complaint of a physical or mental impairment, including alcoholism or drug addiction, of any health profession student and (ii) to encourage, recommend, and arrange for a course of treatment, if deemed appropriate.

C. The immunity provided hereunder shall not extend to any person with respect to actions, decisions or omissions, liability for which is limited under the provisions of the federal Social Security Act or amendments thereto. (Code 1950, § 8-654.6; 1975, c. 418; 1977, c. 617; 1983, c. 567; 1984, c. 494; 1987, c. 713; 1989, c. 729; 1992, c. 590; 1993, c. 702; 1995, c. 636; 1996, cc. 937, 980; 1997, cc. 439, 901.)

Cross references. — As to immunity from civil liability of members of certain groups authorizing, etc., certain programs or research protocols, see § 8.01-44.1. For provisions exempting from liability persons rendering emergency care, see § 8.01-225. As to immunity for team physicians, see § 8.01-225.1. As to immunity for those rendering care to animals, see § 8.01-225.2. For other statutes conferring immunity upon physicians and others in certain cases, see § 54.1-2900 et seq.

Law Review. — For survey of Virginia law on torts for the year 1974-1975, see 61 Va. L. Rev. 1856 (1975).

§ 8.01-581.14. Immunity of members of rate review board established by Virginia Hospital Association. — Each member of the rate review board established by the Virginia Hospital Association pursuant to Senate Joint Resolution No. 17 of the 1972 Session of the General Assembly shall be immune from civil liability for any act, decision or omission done or made in performance of his duties while serving as a member of such board

§ 8.01-581.15 CODE OF VIRGINIA § 8.01-581.15

provided that such act, decision or omission is not done or made in bad faith or with malicious intent. (Code 1950, § 8-654.7; 1975, c. 435; 1977, c. 617.)

§ 8.01-581.15. Limitation on recovery in certain medical malpractice actions. — In any verdict returned against a health care provider in an action for malpractice where the act or acts of malpractice occurred on or after August 1, 1999, which is tried by a jury or in any judgment entered against a health care provider in such an action which is tried without a jury, the total amount recoverable for any injury to, or death of, a patient shall not exceed $1.5 million. The maximum recovery limit of $1.5 million shall increase on July 1, 2000, and each July 1 thereafter by $50,000 per year; however, the annual increase on July 1, 2007, and the annual increase on July 1, 2008, shall be $75,000 per year. Each annual increase shall apply to the act or acts of malpractice occurring on or after the effective date of the increase. The July 1, 2008, increase shall be the final annual increase.

In interpreting this section, the definitions found in § 8.01-581.1 shall be applicable. (Code 1950, §§ 8-654.8; 1976, c. 611; 1977, c. 617; 1983, c. 496; 1999, c. 711.)

The 1999 amendment, effective August 1, 1999, in the first paragraph, substituted "August 1, 1999" for "October 1, 1983," substituted "$1.5 million" for "one million dollars," and added the last three sentences.

Law Review. — For discussion of the constitutional implications of the recovery limit in this section, see 11 U. Rich. L. Rev. 51 (1976). For survey of Virginia insurance law for the year 1975-1976, see 62 Va. L. Rev. 1446 (1976). For survey of Virginia tort law for the year 1975-1976, see 62 Va. L. Rev. 1489 (1976). For article on the limitation on recovery in medical negligence cases in Virginia, see 16 U. Rich. L. Rev. 799 (1982). For comment, "The Constitutional Attack on Virginia's Medical Malpractice Cap: Equal Protection and the Right to Jury Trial," see 22 U. Rich. L. Rev. 95 (1987). For comment on Virginia's Birth-Related Neurological Injury Compensation Act, 22 U. Rich. L. Rev. 431 (1988). For note, "Will Tort Reform Combat the Medical Malpractice Insurance Availability and Affordability Problems That Virginia's Physicians Are Facing," see 44 Wash. & Lee L. Rev. 1463 (1988). For survey on medical malpractice in Virginia for 1989, see 23 U. Rich. L. Rev. 731 (1989). For comment, "Interpretations of Virginia's Medical Malpractice Act: Boyd v. Bulala," see 12 Geo. Mason L. Rev. 361 (1990). For an article, "Civil Practice and Procedure," see 31 U. Rich. L. Rev. 991 (1997). For a review of damages in medical malpractice in Virginia, see 33 U. Rich. L. Rev. 919 (1999).

I. DECISIONS UNDER CURRENT LAW.

Editor's note. — Some of the cases cited below were decided under corresponding provisions of former law, or under this section prior to later amendments.

Section not violative of prohibition against special legislation. — This section applies to all persons belonging to the class in question without distinction and, therefore, is not special in effect; accordingly, this section does not violate the prohibition against special legislation. Etheridge v. Medical Center Hosps., 237 Va. 87, 376 S.E.2d 525 (1989).

The medical malpractice cap bears a reasonable and substantial relation to the General Assembly's objective to protect the public's health, safety and welfare by insuring the availability of health care providers in the Commonwealth; accordingly, the medical malpractice cap does not constitute special legislation. Pulliam v. Coastal Emergency Servs. of Richmond, Inc., 257 Va. 1, 509 S.E.2d 307 (1999).

This section does not deny the right of trial by jury nor violate the separation of powers, anti-discrimination, and special legislation clauses of the Virginia Constitution. 877 F.2d 1191 (4th Cir. 1989).

This section does not violate the right of trial by jury under the Seventh Amendment. 877 F.2d 1191 (4th Cir. 1989).

This section, which limits the amount of recoverable damages in a medical malpractice action, does not infringe upon the right to a jury trial, because the section does not apply until after a jury has completed its assigned function in the judicial process, and because although a party has the right to have a jury assess his damages, he has no right to have a jury dictate through an award the legal consequences of its assessment. Etheridge v. Medical Center Hosps., 237 Va. 87, 376 S.E.2d 525 (1989).

The jury trial guarantee secures no rights other than those that existed at common law and the common law never recognized a right to full recovery in tort. It follows, therefore, that the medical malpractice cap does not impinge

752

§ 8.01-581.15   CIVIL REMEDIES AND PROCEDURE   § 8.01-581.15

upon the right to trial by jury. Pulliam v. Coastal Emergency Servs. of Richmond, Inc., 257 Va. 1, 509 S.E.2d 307 (1999).

Section not violative of equal protection or due process. — Since the medical malpractice cap is clearly a rational means to achieve the legislative goal of securing the provision of health care services by maintaining the availability of malpractice insurance at affordable rates, this section meets the requirements of the equal protection and due process clauses, and must be upheld on those grounds. Boyd v. Bulala, 647 F. Supp. 781 (W.D. Va. 1986), aff'd in part, rev'd in part, 877 F.2d 1191 (4th Cir. 1989).

Assertion that this section violates procedural due process by creating an irrebuttable presumption was without merit, because this section creates no presumptions whatsoever regarding the individual merits of a medical malpractice claim, but merely affects the parameters of the remedy available after the merits of a claim have been decided. Etheridge v. Medical Center Hosps., 237 Va. 87, 376 S.E.2d 525 (1989).

The purpose of this section, which limits the amount of recoverable damages in a medical malpractice action — to maintain adequate health care services in this Commonwealth — bears a reasonable relation to the legislative cap, i.e., ensuring that health care providers can obtain affordable medical malpractice insurance; therefore, it does not violate substantive due process. Etheridge v. Medical Center Hosps., 237 Va. 87, 376 S.E.2d 525 (1989).

The classification in this section does not violate the Equal Protection Clause. Etheridge v. Medical Center Hosps., 237 Va. 87, 376 S.E.2d 525 (1989).

This section does not violate the Fourteenth Amendment's guarantees of due process or equal protection, since the cap on liability bears a reasonable relation to a valid legislative purpose—the maintenance of adequate health care services in the Commonwealth of Virginia. 877 F.2d 1191 (4th Cir. 1989).

The medical malpractice cap passes the test of constitutionality when judged against the rational basis standard; therefore, plaintiff had suffered no denial of due process or equal protection from application of the cap to the jury verdict. Pulliam v. Coastal Emergency Servs. of Richmond, Inc., 257 Va. 1, 509 S.E.2d 307 (1999).

The Virginia cap cannot violate federal separation of powers principles for the simple reason that those principles are inapplicable. 877 F.2d 1191 (4th Cir. 1989).

The medical malpractice cap does not violate the separation of powers doctrine or invade the province of the judiciary. Pulliam v. Coastal Emergency Servs. of Richmond, Inc., 257 Va. 1, 509 S.E.2d 307 (1999).

Virginia medical malpractice cap legislation clearly does not create suspect classification. Certainly, the law treats victims of medical malpractice differently from the victims of other torts, and within the class of medical malpractice plaintiffs, the law further discriminates between those whose losses exceed the cap and those whose losses do not. Such classifications, while facially unfair, do not violate the equal protection clause according to current interpretation. Boyd v. Bulala, 647 F. Supp. 781 (W.D. Va. 1986), aff'd in part, rev'd in part, 877 F.2d 1191 (4th Cir. 1989).

The purpose of this section, to maintain an adequate level of health care services in the Commonwealth by ensuring that health care providers can obtain affordable insurance, is sufficient justification under the Constitution for treating those injured through medical malpractice differently from those injured in other torts. Boyd v. Bulala, 647 F. Supp. 781 (W.D. Va. 1986), aff'd in part, rev'd in part, 877 F.2d 1191 (4th Cir. 1989).

The rationality of this section justifies the distinction it draws between medical malpractice plaintiffs whose damages are less than the cap amount, who may be completely compensated for their injuries, and those whose damages exceed the cap, who will not be completely compensated. Boyd v. Bulala, 647 F. Supp. 781 (W.D. Va. 1986), aff'd in part, rev'd in part, 877 F.2d 1191 (4th Cir. 1989).

The mandate of this section is that in any judgment entered against a health care provider, the quantum of the recovery for a medical malpractice injury cannot exceed the aggregate amount capable of recovery. Fairfax Hosp. Sys. v. Nevitt, 249 Va. 591, 457 S.E.2d 10 (1995).

The General Assembly enacted medical malpractice cap for the purpose of enabling licensed health care providers to secure medical malpractice insurance at affordable rates. Schwartz v. Brownlee, 253 Va. 159, 482 S.E.2d 827 (1997).

Cap applies to recoveries under the Emergency Medical Treatment and Active Labor Act. — The statutory cap of $1,000,000 (now $1,500,000) imposed by this section applies to medical malpractice recoveries under the Emergency Medical Treatment and Active Labor Act, 42 U.S.C. § 1395dd. Lee ex rel. Wetzel v. Alleghany Regional Hosp. Corp., 778 F. Supp. 900 (W.D. Va. 1991).

A patient who recovers $1,000,000 (now $1,500,000) in a negligence suit against one health care provider cannot recover more damages for the same injury from a second, even more culpable health care provider. Plaintiff, having recovered $1,000,000 (now $1,500,000) from the hospital under the Emergency Medical Treatment and Active Labor Act cannot recover further malpractice damages from other parties. Power v. Alexandria Physicians

Group, 887 F. Supp. 845 (E.D. Va. 1995), aff'd, 91 F.3d 132 (4th Cir. 1996), cert. denied, 519 U.S. 1010, 117 S. Ct. 514, 136 L. Ed. 2d 403 (1996).

The plain meaning of the statute fixes the "total" amount recoverable at the statutory cap. Thus, application of the $750,000 (now $1,500,000) cap serves to extinguish awards of punitive damages on claims which have exhausted the statutory amount. Bulala v. Boyd, 239 Va. 218, 389 S.E.2d 670 (1990) (decided under former § 8-654.8).

Award in excess of permitted amount would invade province of legislature. — Whether the remedy prescribed in this section, which limits the amount of recoverable damages in a medical malpractice action, is viewed as a modification of the common law or as establishing the jurisdiction of the courts in specific cases, it was a proper exercise of legislative power. Indeed, were a court to ignore the legislatively determined remedy and enter an award in excess of the permitted amount, the court would invade the province of the legislature. Etheridge v. Medical Center Hosps., 237 Va. 87, 376 S.E.2d 525 (1989).

This section is a classic example of an economic regulation. — A legislative effort to structure and accommodate the burdens and benefits of economic life and as such, it is subject only to limited rational basis review; plaintiffs have the burden of demonstrating that in enacting the cap the Virginia legislature had acted in an arbitrary and irrational way. 877 F.2d 1191 (4th Cir. 1989).

The statutory cap sets a separate limit on the total damages recoverable for "any injury" to a single "patient," regardless of the number of claims and claimants and theories of recovery related to that injury. Accordingly, the cap applicable to any single patient's injury covers both compensatory and punitive damage claims of the patient and any claims by others that, by substantive law, are "derivative" of the patient's claims. Boyd v. Bulala, 905 F.2d 764 (4th Cir. 1990).

Having suffered one indivisible set of injuries all stemming from the same malpractice event, plaintiff was entitled to no more than $1,000,000 (now $1,500,000) under the statute. Power v. Alexandria Physicians Group, 887 F. Supp. 845 (E.D. Va. 1995), aff'd, 91 F.3d 132 (4th Cir. 1996), cert. denied, 519 U.S. 1010, 117 S. Ct. 514, 136 L. Ed. 2d 403 (1996).

The statute does not apply a separate $1,000,000 (now $1,500,000) cap to each individual negligent act by health care providers, or to each visit and telephone call between a patient and her doctors. Rather, the statute only allows $1,000,000 (now $1,500,000) per injury, even if the jury arises from several wrongful acts during the course of treatment. Power v. Alexandria Physicians Group, 887 F. Supp. 845 (E.D. Va. 1995), aff'd, 91 F.3d 132 (4th Cir. 1996), cert. denied, 519 U.S. 1010, 117 S. Ct. 514, 136 L. Ed. 2d 403 (1996).

Cap covers both compensatory and punitive damage claims. — The malpractice cap applicable to any single patient's injury covers both compensatory and punitive damage claims of the patient and any claims by others that, by substantive law, are derivative of the patient's claim. Claims of emotional distress caused by injury to a single patient and claims for medical expenses of a single patient are derivative. Starns v. United States, 923 F.2d 34 (4th Cir.), cert. denied, 502 U.S. 809, 112 S. Ct. 54, 116 L. Ed. 2d 31 (1991).

Damages limited to statutory amount regardless of number of legal theories. — In a medical malpractice action, the total damages recoverable for injury to a "patient" are limited to the statutory amount, regardless of the number of legal theories upon which the claims are based. Bulala v. Boyd, 239 Va. 218, 389 S.E.2d 670 (1990).

This section provides that a single $1,000,000 (now $1,500,000) cap applies to all of a patient's "malpractice" claims, regardless of the particular theory or body of law on which they are based. Power v. Alexandria Physicians Group, 887 F. Supp. 845 (E.D. Va. 1995), aff'd, 91 F.3d 132 (4th Cir. 1996), cert. denied, 519 U.S. 1010, 117 S. Ct. 514, 136 L. Ed. 2d 403 (1996).

Patient cannot avoid cap by characterizing each mistake as separate instance. — An injured patient may recover no more than $1,000,000 (now $1,500,000) for injuries arising from one malpractice event. This principle holds whether the patient sues one defendant or many, whether she cites one action or several separate ones, or whether she proceeds under more than one legal theory or cause of action constituting "an action for malpractice" under the statute. Moreover, a patient cannot avoid the $1,000,000 (now $1,500,000) cap by characterizing each of the health care provider's mistakes that contribute to her injury as a separate instance of malpractice. Power v. Alexandria Physicians Group, 887 F. Supp. 845 (E.D. Va. 1995), aff'd, 91 F.3d 132 (4th Cir. 1996), cert. denied, 519 U.S. 1010, 117 S. Ct. 514, 136 L. Ed. 2d 403 (1996).

A parent's cause of action for medical and incidental expenses is derivative of the child's action. Lee v. Adrales, 778 F. Supp. 904 (W.D. Va. 1991).

Child has statutory cap separate from cap on mother's claims. — At the moment of live birth, and until the pediatrician assumes responsibility for the care of the newborn, the infant is the obstetrician's "patient." Hence, a separate statutory cap for compensatory damages applies to the child's case. Bulala v. Boyd, 239 Va. 218, 389 S.E.2d 670 (1990).

A mother and her newborn child are separate

"patients," and thus, each may recover a maximum of $1,000,000 (now $1,500,000). Lee ex rel. Wetzel v. Alleghany Regional Hosp. Corp., 778 F. Supp. 900 (W.D. Va. 1991).

The child's medical expenses must be included in her own damage award. Lee v. Adrales, 778 F. Supp. 904 (W.D. Va. 1991).

Father's emotional distress claim was covered by the Medical Malpractice Act where it was wholly derivative of his child's claim. However, the total damages recoverable for injury to the child, including derivative claims, were limited to the statutory amount. Bulala v. Boyd, 239 Va. 218, 389 S.E.2d 670 (1990).

Since the damages awarded for the value of the mother's past services, for lost wages of the father, and for hospital and travel expenses incurred on behalf of the baby are derivative, they must be included within the injured baby's cap. Starns v. United States, 923 F.2d 34 (4th Cir.), cert. denied, 502 U.S. 809, 112 S. Ct. 54, 116 L. Ed. 2d 31 (1991).

A father seeking damages for emotional harm and medical expenses, resulting from the malpractice to the mother and child, may not recover separately. Lee ex rel. Wetzel v. Alleghany Regional Hosp. Corp., 778 F. Supp. 900 (W.D. Va. 1991).

The father's claims for emotional distress and medical expenses are derivative of the child's, and thus fall within the child's statutory cap. Lee ex rel. Wetzel v. Alleghany Regional Hosp. Corp., 778 F. Supp. 900 (W.D. Va. 1991).

Damages limited. — Where plaintiff's claim was for an indivisible injury, caused by the concurring negligence of each defendant, her damages were limited to a total of $750,000(now $1,500,000 under this section. Etheridge v. Medical Center Hosps., 237 Va. 87, 376 S.E.2d 525 (1989).

Damages limited to $1,000,000 (now $1,500,000) in death of two babies. — Jury award of $2,000,000 based on preterm birth and subsequent loss of two infants because of defendants' failure to adequately treat preterm labor was reduced to $1,000,000 under this section. Daniel v. Jones, 39 F. Supp. 2d 635 (E.D. Va. 1999).

Error in credit calculation. — Where trial court reduced the $2,000,000 jury verdict rendered against the hospital by $600,000 (the amount of the health care group's settlement) and then reduced the remainder ($1,400,000) to the medical malpractice cap of $1,000,000 (now $1,500,000), the plain meaning of § 8.01-35.1 and this section, read together, is that where there is a verdict by a jury or a judgment by a court against a health care provider for "injury to ... a patient" and the total amount recovered in that action and in all settlements related to the medical malpractice injury exceeds $1,000,000 (now $1,500,000), the total amount the plaintiff can recover for that injury is $1,000,000 (now $1,500,000). Accordingly, the trial court erred when it failed to apply the $600,000 credit for the statutory recovery cap in determining the quantum of plaintiff's judgment. Fairfax Hosp. Sys. v. Nevitt, 249 Va. 591, 457 S.E.2d 10 (1995).

Award of statutory maximum not abuse of discretion. — Award of statutory maximum for mental and physical injuries to mother who gave birth to stillborn child due to defendant's negligence held not abuse of discretion. Modaber v. Kelley, 233 Va. 60, 348 S.E.2d 233 (1986).

Physician's corporation liable for excess of jury award. — Where physician-defendant was also president and sole shareholder in S corporation, which was not licensed as a health care provider, physician was entitled to protection of statutory $1,000,000 (now $1,500,000) medical malpractice cap, but corporation was liable for excess when jury award of $1.85 million was rendered jointly and severally. Schwartz v. Brownlee, 253 Va. 159, 482 S.E.2d 827 (1997).

Applied in Boyd v. Bulala, 678 F. Supp. 612 (W.D. Va. 1988); Jenkins v. Payne, 251 Va. 122, 465 S.E.2d 795 (1996); Paul v. Gomez, 190 F.R.D. 402 (W.D. Va. 2000).

§ 8.01-581.16. Civil immunity for members of or consultants to certain boards or committees. — Every member of, or health care professional consultant to, any committee, board, group, commission or other entity shall be immune from civil liability for any act, decision, omission, or utterance done or made in performance of his duties while serving as a member of or consultant to such committee, board, group, commission or other entity, with functions primarily to review, evaluate, or make recommendations on (i) the duration of patient stays in health care facilities, (ii) the professional services furnished with respect to the medical, dental, psychological, podiatric, chiropractic, veterinary or optometric necessity for such services, (iii) the purpose of promoting the most efficient use of available health care facilities and services, (iv) the adequacy or quality of professional services, (v) the competency and qualifications for professional staff privileges, or (vi) the reasonableness or appropriateness of charges made by or on behalf of health care facilities;

provided that such entity has been established pursuant to federal or state law or regulation, or pursuant to Joint Commission on Accreditation of Hospitals requirements, or established and duly constituted by one or more public or licensed private hospitals, or with a governmental agency and provided further that such act, decision, omission, or utterance is not done or made in bad faith or with malicious intent. (Code 1950, § 8-654.9; 1976, c. 611; 1977, c. 617; 1981, c. 174; 1987, c. 713; 1989, c. 729; 1993, c. 702.)

Law Review. — For comment, "Scope of Permissible Pretrial Discovery of Medical Malpractice Review Panel Deliberations in Virginia: Klarfeld v. Salsbury," see 10 Geo. Mason L. Rev. 577 (1988). For survey on evidence in Virginia for 1989, see 23 U. Rich. L. Rev. 647 (1989). For survey on medical malpractice in Virginia for 1989, see 23 U. Rich. L. Rev. 731 (1989).

I. DECISIONS UNDER CURRENT LAW.

Scope of immunity of panel members. — Members of medical malpractice panels arguably may be within the scope of this section and entitled to civil immunity because of the reference to "other entity." Nevertheless, the scope of § 8.01-581.17 is more limited. That statute is restricted to certain specified "committees," including by cross-reference those "committees" performing the functions set forth in this section. Stated differently, § 8.01-581.17 does not include an "other entity" referred to in this section which is not a "committee." Klarfeld v. Salsbury, 233 Va. 277, 355 S.E.2d 319 (1987).

Injury under this section refers collectively to a constellation of harms arising from a particular act or treatment. Power v. Alexandria Physicians Group, 887 F. Supp. 845 (E.D. Va. 1995), aff'd, 91 F.3d 132 (4th Cir. 1996), cert. denied, 519 U.S. 1010, 117 S. Ct. 514, 136 L. Ed. 2d 403 (1996).

§ 8.01-581.17. Privileged communications of certain committees and entities. — The proceedings, minutes, records, and reports of any (i) medical staff committee, utilization review committee, or other committee as specified in § 8.01-581.16 and (ii) nonprofit entity that provides a centralized credentialing service, together with all communications, both oral and written, originating in or provided to such committees or entities, are privileged communications which may not be disclosed or obtained by legal discovery proceedings unless a circuit court, after a hearing and for good cause arising from extraordinary circumstances being shown, orders the disclosure of such proceedings, minutes, records, reports, or communications. Nothing in this section shall be construed as providing any privilege to hospital medical records kept with respect to any patient in the ordinary course of business of operating a hospital nor to any facts or information contained in such records nor shall this section preclude or affect discovery of or production of evidence relating to hospitalization or treatment of any patient in the ordinary course of hospitalization of such patient.

For purposes of this section *"centralized credentialing service"* means (i) gathering information relating to applications for professional staff privileges at any public or licensed private hospital or for participation as a provider in any health maintenance organization, preferred provider organization or any similar organization and (ii) providing such information to those hospitals and organizations that utilize the service. Additionally, for the purposes of this section, accreditation and peer review records of the American College of Radiology and the Medical Society of Virginia are considered privileged communications. (Code 1950, § 8-654.10; 1976, c. 611; 1977, c. 617; 1995, c. 500; 1997, c. 292.)

Law Review. — For survey on medical malpractice in Virginia for 1989, see 23 U. Rich. L. Rev. 731 (1989).

I. DECISIONS UNDER CURRENT LAW.

Scope of immunity of panel members. — Members of medical malpractice panels arguably may be within the scope of § 8.01-581.16 and entitled to civil immunity because of the reference to "other entity." Nevertheless, the scope of this section is more limited. That statute is restricted to certain specified "committees," including by cross-reference those "committees" performing the functions set forth in § 8.01-581.16. Stated differently, this section does not include an "other entity" referred to in § 8.01-581.16 which is not a "committee." Klarfeld v. Salsbury, 233 Va. 277, 355 S.E.2d 319 (1987).

§ 8.01-581.18. Delivery of results of laboratory tests and other examinations not authorized by physician; immunity of physician. — A. Whenever a laboratory test or other examination of the physical or mental condition of any person is conducted by or under the supervision of a person other than a physician and not at the request or with the written authorization of a physician, any report of the results of such test or examination shall be provided by the person conducting such test or examination to the person who was the subject of such test or examination. Such report shall state in bold type that it is the responsibility of the recipient to arrange with his physician for consultation and interpretation of the results of such test or examination. The provisions of this subsection shall not apply to any test or examination conducted under the auspices of the State Department of Health.

B. Any physician shall be immune from civil liability for any failure to review, or to take any action in response to the receipt of, any report of the results of any laboratory test or other examination of the physical or mental condition of any person, which test or examination such physician neither requested nor authorized in writing, unless such report is provided directly to the physician by the person so examined or tested with a request for consultation or by the State Department of Health.

C. As used in this section, *"physician"* means a person licensed to practice medicine, chiropractic or osteopathy in this Commonwealth pursuant to Chapter 29 (§ 54.1-2900 et seq.) of Title 54.1. (Code 1950, § 8-654.11; 1977, c. 527; 1993, c. 702.)

The number of this section was assigned by the Virginia Code Commission, the number in the 1977 act having been 8-654.11.

Law Review. — For survey of Virginia law on torts for the year 1976-77, see 63 Va. L. Rev. 1491 (1977).

§ 8.01-581.19. Civil immunity for physicians, psychologists, podiatrists, optometrists, veterinarians and nursing home administrators while members of certain committees. — A. Any physician, chiropractor, psychologist, podiatrist, veterinarian or optometrist licensed to practice in this Commonwealth shall be immune from civil liability for any communication, finding, opinion or conclusion made in performance of his duties while serving as a member of any committee, board, group, commission or other entity that is responsible for resolving questions concerning the admission of any physician, psychologist, podiatrist, veterinarian or optometrist to, or the taking of disciplinary action against any member of, any medical society, academy or association affiliated with the American Medical Association, the Virginia Academy of Clinical Psychologists, the American Psychological Association, the Virginia Applied Psychology Academy, the Virginia Academy of School Psychologists, the American Podiatric Medical Association, the American Veterinary Medical Association, the International Chiropractic Association, the American Chiropractic Association, the Virginia Chiropractic Association, or the American Optometric Association; provided that such communication, finding, opinion or conclusion is not made in bad faith or with malicious intent.

B. Any nursing home administrator licensed under the laws of this Commonwealth shall be immune from civil liability for any communication, finding, opinion, decision or conclusion made in performance of his duties while serving as a member of any committee, board, group, commission or other entity that is responsible for resolving questions concerning the admission of any health care facility to, or the taking of disciplinary action against any member of, the Virginia Health Care Association, provided that such communication, finding, opinion, decision or conclusion is not made in bad faith or with malicious intent. (1978, c. 541; 1987, c. 713; 1989, c. 729; 1993, c. 702; 1996, cc. 937, 980.)

§ 8.01-581.19:1. Civil immunity for persons providing information to certain committees. — Any person who provides information to any committee, board, group, commission, or other entity which is authorized to investigate any complaint of physical or mental impairment, that may show that any practitioner of medicine, osteopathy, optometry, chiropractic, podiatry, clinical psychology, physical therapy, veterinary medicine or any physical therapist assistant is unable to practice his profession with reasonable skill and safety, by reason of the use of alcohol, drugs, or other substances, or as a result of any mental or physical condition, shall be immune from civil liability for any act done for, or any utterance or communication made to, such entity in the course of providing such information. However, this section shall not apply if the act, utterance, or communication is done or made in bad faith or with malicious intent or if such disclosure is prohibited by federal law or regulations promulgated thereunder.

The provisions of this section shall apply only to such entities described in this section as are (i) established pursuant to a federal or state law, (ii) established and duly constituted by one or more public or licensed private hospitals, (iii) a medical or chiropractic society that is operating its health care provider impairment program in cooperation with the Board of Medicine, or another governmental agency, (iv) an optometric society or association that is operating its optometric impairment program in cooperation with the Virginia Board of Optometry, (v) a veterinary medical association that is operating its veterinarian impairment program in cooperation with the Virginia Board of Veterinary Medicine, or (vi) a clinical psychology academy that is operating its clinical psychology impairment program in cooperation with the Board of Psychology. (1986, c. 604; 1987, c. 713; 1989, c. 729; 1993, c. 702; 1996, cc. 937, 980.)

§ 8.01-581.20. Standard of care in proceeding before medical malpractice review panel; expert testimony; determination of standard in action for damages. — A. In any proceeding before a medical malpractice review panel or in any action against a physician, clinical psychologist, podiatrist, dentist, nurse, hospital or other health care provider to recover damages alleged to have been caused by medical malpractice where the acts or omissions so complained of are alleged to have occurred in this Commonwealth, the standard of care by which the acts or omissions are to be judged shall be that degree of skill and diligence practiced by a reasonably prudent practitioner in the field of practice or specialty in this Commonwealth and the testimony of an expert witness, otherwise qualified, as to such standard of care, shall be admitted; provided, however, that the standard of care in the locality or in similar localities in which the alleged act or omission occurred shall be applied if any party shall prove by a preponderance of the evidence that the health care services and health care facilities available in the locality and the customary practices in such locality or similar localities give rise to a standard of care which is more appropriate than a statewide standard. Any physician who is licensed to practice in Virginia shall be presumed to know the statewide standard of care in the specialty or field of medicine in which he is qualified and certified. This presumption shall also apply to any physician who is licensed in some other state of the United States and meets the educational and examination requirements for licensure in Virginia. An expert witness who is familiar with the statewide standard of care shall not have his testimony excluded on the ground that he does not practice in this Commonwealth. A witness shall be qualified to testify as an expert on the standard of care if he demonstrates expert knowledge of the standards of the defendant's specialty and of what conduct conforms or fails to conform to those standards and if he has had active clinical practice in either the defendant's specialty or a related field of medicine within one year of the date of the alleged act or omission forming the basis of the action.

B. In any action for damages resulting from medical malpractice, any issue as to the standard of care to be applied shall be determined by the jury, or the court trying the case without a jury. (1979, c. 325; 1980, c. 164; 1989, cc. 146, 729; 1992, c. 240.)

Law Review. — For comment on the abolition in Virginia of the locality rule in medical malpractice, see 13 U. Rich. L. Rev. 927 (1979). For survey of Virginia law on torts for the year 1978-1979, see 66 Va. L. Rev. 375 (1980). For note on the erosion of the locality rule and the qualification of experts testifying in medical malpractice suits in Virginia, see 4 Geo. Mason L. Rev. 99 (1981). For article on statewide standard of care in medical malpractice cases, see 18 U. Rich. L. Rev. 361 (1984). For article on the admissibility of written health care standards in medical and hospital negligence actions in Virginia, see 18 U. Rich. L. Rev. 725 (1984). For survey on medical malpractice in Virginia for 1989, see 23 U. Rich. L. Rev. 731 (1989). For an article, "Civil Practice and Procedure," see 31 U. Rich. L. Rev. 991 (1997).

I. Decisions Under Current Law.
  A. General Consideration.
  B. Standard of Care.
II. Decisions Under Prior Law.

I. DECISIONS UNDER CURRENT LAW.

A. General Consideration.

This section does not require a plaintiff to present expert testimony in all medical malpractice actions. Dickerson v. Fatehi, 253 Va. 324, 484 S.E.2d 880 (1997).

Retroactivity of witness qualification provisions. — The current provisions of this section regarding the admissibility of the testimony of expert witnesses from outside of Virginia are procedural, rather than substantive, and, therefore, were applicable to a pending action rather than the version of the statute in effect in 1979, when the alleged malpractice occurred. Gaynor v. OG/GYN Specialists, Ltd., 51 F. Supp. 2d 718 (W.D. Va. 1999).

Most significant element about this section is that expertise in a medical malpractice case does not have to come from an individual practicing in the same specialty which is the subject matter of the cause of action. Daniel v. Jones, 39 F. Supp. 2d 635 (E.D. Va. 1999).

Neonatologist who established his knowledge of the Virginia standard of care in dealing with a pregnant woman in a high-risk pregnancy was qualified to testify in obstetrical case, when issue was how to prevent preterm labor and extend the pregnancy in order to assure the more complete development of the fetus. Daniel v. Jones, 39 F. Supp. 2d 635 (E.D. Va. 1999).

A medical opinion based on a "possibility" is irrelevant, purely speculative and, hence, inadmissible. In order for such testimony to become relevant, it must be brought out of the realm of speculation and into the realm of reasonable probability; the law in this area deals in "probabilities" and not "possibilities." Fairfax Hosp. Sys. v. Curtis, 249 Va. 531, 457 S.E.2d 66 (1995).

Completion of licensure requirements sufficient to testify as expert. — Where, the applicable standard is that of the entire Commonwealth, where the proffered witness has lived, worked, taught, and practiced, and the doctor went so far as to complete the requirements for licensure as a general practitioner of medicine in Virginia, the field with which his familiarity must be demonstrated if he is to testify as an expert, this is a sufficient factual showing to establish, prima facie, that he possessed the necessary knowledge, skill, and experience to testify as an expert to the appropriate standard of care in his field when he was admitted to practice in it. Grubb v. Hocker, 229 Va. 172, 326 S.E.2d 698 (1985).

Lack of current practice no basis for excluding testimony. — Because of the 1980 amendment to this section, it was clear that the doctor's lack of current practice in Virginia formed no basis, in itself, for the exclusion of his testimony. The lapse of his Virginia license and his absence from the State did not serve to negate the familiarity with the applicable standard which he demonstrated by qualifying for admission to practice in Virginia. Indeed, he testified to continuing contacts, visits and study which would only serve to maintain the familiarity with professional standards which he had previously acquired. Grubb v. Hocker, 229 Va. 172, 326 S.E.2d 698 (1985).

Written opinion of review panel not sufficient as expert testimony. — Expert testimony is ordinarily required in malpractice cases on (1) the standard of care, (2) a deviation from the standard, and (3) causation. The written opinion of the medical malpractice review panel is not in itself sufficient to fulfill those requirements. Raines v. Lutz, 231 Va. 110, 341 S.E.2d 194 (1986).

Health care providers are required by law to possess and exercise only that degree of skill and diligence practiced by a reasonably prudent practitioner in the same field of practice or specialty in Virginia. Expert testimony is ordinarily necessary to establish the appropriate standard of care, to establish a deviation from the standard, and to establish that such a deviation was the proximate cause of the claimed damages. Raines v. Lutz, 231 Va. 110, 341 S.E.2d 194 (1986).

As to actions for "wrongful pregnancy," see Miller v. Johnson, 231 Va. 177, 343 S.E.2d 301 (1986).

District judge may reverse the magistrate judge's order with respect to plaintiff's expert if the factual findings are clearly erroneous or legal conclusions are contrary to law. Peck v. Tegtmeyer, 834 F. Supp. 903 (W.D. Va. 1992), aff'd, 4 F.3d 985 (4th Cir. 1993).

Applied in Henning v. Thomas, 235 Va. 181, 366 S.E.2d 109 (1988); Black v. Bladergroen, 258 Va. 438, 521 S.E.2d 168 (1999).

B. Standard of Care.

Only one standard of care. — The Virginia Medical Malpractice Act makes no distinction between a mechanical standard of care and a general professional standard of care; clearly there is only one standard of care: that degree of skill and diligence practiced by a reasonably prudent practitioner in the field of practice or specialty in the Commonwealth. Peck v. Tegtmeyer, 834 F. Supp. 903 (W.D. Va. 1992), aff'd, 4 F.3d 985 (4th Cir. 1993).

"Reasonably prudent practitioner" standard. — A physician must demonstrate that degree of skill and diligence in the diagnosis and treatment of the patient employed by a reasonably prudent practitioner in his field of practice or specialty. Brown v. Koulizakis, 229 Va. 524, 331 S.E.2d 440 (1985).

Expert testimony not always necessary. — Nothing in this section requires a plaintiff to present in all medical malpractice actions expert testimony to establish that degree of skill and diligence practiced by a reasonably prudent practitioner. Beverly Enterprises-Virginia, Inc. v. Nichols, 247 Va. 264, 441 S.E.2d 1 (1994).

Physician is not an insurer of the success of his diagnosis and treatment nor is he held to the highest degree of care known to his profession. The mere fact that he has failed to effect a cure or that his diagnosis and treatment have been detrimental to the patient's health does not raise a presumption of negligence. Brown v. Koulizakis, 229 Va. 524, 331 S.E.2d 440 (1985).

Applicability in diversity proceeding. — Qualification requirements for a standard of care expert as set forth in this section are applicable to experts' qualifications in a diversity case. Peck v. Tegtmeyer, 834 F. Supp. 903 (W.D. Va. 1992), aff'd, 4 F.3d 985 (4th Cir. 1993).

Error in instructing the jury that it could apply the local standard of care was not harmless, where the defendant had observed or should have observed the patient's jaundice when he first examined him, and the jury had heard evidence that, under such circumstances, the statewide standard of care required a bilirubin test while the local standard did not; notwithstanding the absence of evidence that the local standard was the more appropriate measure of the doctor's duty to his or her patient, the jury could have been led by the erroneous instruction to conclude that, because the defendant's expert witnesses had testified that he had complied with the local standard, he was not guilty of actionable negligence. Rhoades v. Painter, 234 Va. 20, 360 S.E.2d 174 (1987).

Qualifications for radiology expert. — Because radiation physicist had never had a clinical practice of any kind, he did not meet the statutory requirements for qualification as an expert on the standard of care in radiology. Peck v. Tegtmeyer, 834 F. Supp. 903 (W.D. Va. 1992), aff'd, 4 F.3d 985 (4th Cir. 1993).

Active clinical practice not found. — Doctor's employment as director of a helicopter transport service which transported sick and injured patients could not be deemed an active clinical practice within the contemplation of this section. Fairfax Hosp. Sys. v. Curtis, 249 Va. 531, 457 S.E.2d 66 (1995).

Expert testimony properly excluded. —

Trial court properly excluded certain expert testimony because the hospital's expert witnesses could not say within a reasonable degree of medical probability that certain factors associated with a near-sudden infant death syndrome event specifically caused infant's cardiopulmonary arrest. Fairfax Hosp. Sys. v. Curtis, 249 Va. 531, 457 S.E.2d 66 (1995).

The trial court did not abuse its discretion by refusing to permit the physician to qualify as an expert witness on the defendant's specialty, orthopaedic surgery as it involves the procedure of chemonucleolysis. The physician had never performed the procedure nor had he observed an actual procedure being performed. Even though the physician had received a certificate for participating in a seminar on chemonucleolysis, such limited instruction was not sufficient to conclude the physician was qualified to render opinions on the subject. Lawson v. Elkins, 252 Va. 352, 477 S.E.2d 510 (1996).

Question within experience of jury. — The question of whether a reasonably prudent nursing home would permit its employees to leave a tray of food with an unattended patient who had a history of choking and who was unable to eat without assistance was certainly within the common knowledge and experience of a jury. Beverly Enterprises-Virginia, Inc. v. Nichols, 247 Va. 264, 441 S.E.2d 1 (1994).

II. DECISIONS UNDER PRIOR LAW.

Editor's note. — The cases cited below were decided under corresponding provisions of former law. The term "this section," as used below, refers to former provisions.

The standard of care in a medical malpractice action is a matter of substantive law and thus federal courts are bound to apply the law of the Commonwealth. Chapman v. Edgerton, 529 F. Supp. 519 (W.D. Va. 1982).

Statutory standard of care not retroactive. — As the standard of care in medical malpractice actions is substantive and not procedural, there is no statutory standard of care applicable to actions which arose prior to the enactment of section setting forth same. Chapman v. Edgerton, 529 F. Supp. 519 (W.D. Va. 1982).

The standard of care required of a plastic surgeon is that of other like specialists in good standing, in the same or similar localities as the defendant. Chapman v. Edgerton, 529 F. Supp. 519 (W.D. Va. 1982).

CHAPTER 21.2.

MEDIATION.

Sec.
8.01-581.21. Definitions.
8.01-581.22. Confidentiality; exceptions.
8.01-581.23. Civil immunity.

§ 8.01-581.21. Definitions. — As used in this chapter:

"Mediation" means the process by which a mediator assists and facilitates two or more parties to a controversy in reaching a mutually acceptable resolution of the controversy and includes all contacts between the mediator and any party or parties, until such time as a resolution is agreed to by the parties or the parties discharge the mediator.

"Mediation program" means a program through which mediators or mediation is made available and includes the director, agents and employees of the program.

"Mediator" means an impartial third party selected by agreement of the parties to a controversy to assist them in mediation. (1988, cc. 623, 857.)

I. DECISIONS UNDER CURRENT LAW.

Applied in Anderson v. Anderson, 29 Va. App. 673, 514 S.E.2d 369 (1999).

§ 8.01-581.22. Confidentiality; exceptions. — All memoranda, work products and other materials contained in the case files of a mediator or mediation program are confidential. Any communication made in or in connection with the mediation which relates to the controversy being mediated, whether made to the mediator or a party, or to any other person if made at a mediation session, is confidential. However, a mediated agreement shall not be confidential, unless the parties otherwise agree in writing.

Confidential materials and communications are not subject to disclosure in any judicial or administrative proceeding except (i) where all parties to the mediation agree, in writing, to waive the confidentiality, (ii) in a subsequent action between the mediator and a party to the mediation for damages arising out of the mediation, or (iii) statements, memoranda, materials and other tangible evidence, otherwise subject to discovery, which were not prepared specifically for use in and actually used in the mediation. (1988, cc. 623, 857.)

I. DECISIONS UNDER CURRENT LAW.

Where doctor's relationship with parties was that of therapist, not mediator, the trial court erred in excluding his testimony pursuant to this section. Anderson v. Anderson, 29 Va. App. 673, 514 S.E.2d 369 (1999).

§ 8.01-581.23. Civil immunity. — Mediators and mediation programs shall be immune from civil liability for, or resulting from, any act or omission done or made while engaged in efforts to assist or facilitate a mediation, unless the act or omission was made or done in bad faith, with malicious intent or in a manner exhibiting a willful, wanton disregard of the rights, safety or property of another. (1988, cc. 623, 857.)

CHAPTER 22.

Receivers, General and Special.

Article 1.

General Receivers.

Sec.
8.01-582. Appointment of general receivers; their duties; audit of funds.
8.01-583. How securities taken and kept; power of receivers over same.
8.01-584. How dividends and interest collected and invested.
8.01-585. How accounts kept by receivers.
8.01-586. Inquiry as to unknown owners of funds.
8.01-587. Liability of general receivers.
8.01-588. Bonds generally.
8.01-588.1. Bonds apportioned to funds under control; annual reports.
8.01-589. Compensation and fees; when none allowed.
8.01-590. Penalty for failure of duty.

Article 2.

Special Receivers.

8.01-591. Notice required prior to appointment of receiver.
8.01-592. Notice not required in emergencies.
8.01-593. Subsequent proceedings after emergency appointment.
8.01-594. Notice not required to parties served with process.

Sec.
8.01-595. Preparation of list of creditors; notice to them.
8.01-596. No sale prior to such notification; exceptions.
8.01-597. Suits against receivers in certain cases.
8.01-598. Effect of judgment against receiver.
8.01-599. Warrant or motion for judgment against receiver in general district court, when to be tried.

Article 3.

General Provisions for Moneys Under Control of Court.

8.01-600. How money under control of court deposited; record kept; liability of clerk.
8.01-600.1. [Repealed.]
8.01-601. Deposit with general receiver of certain funds under supervision of fiduciary and belonging to person under disability.
8.01-602. Proceedings when owner of money under control of court unknown.
8.01-603. [Repealed.]
8.01-604. How State Treasurer to keep account of such money.
8.01-605. How person entitled to money paid into state treasury may recover it.

Sec.
8.01-606. Payment of small amounts to certain persons through court without intervention of fiduciary; authority of commissioners of accounts.

ARTICLE 1.

General Receivers.

§ 8.01-582. Appointment of general receivers; their duties; audit of funds. — Any circuit court may appoint a general receiver of the court, who may be the clerk of the court, and who shall hold his office at its pleasure. The general receiver's duty shall be, unless it is otherwise specially ordered, to receive, take charge of and hold all moneys paid under any judgment, order or decree of the court, and also to pay out or dispose of same as the court orders or decrees. Moneys held pursuant to this section shall be deemed public deposits as set forth in Chapter 23 (§ 2.1-359 et seq.) of Title 2.1 and shall be invested in certificates of deposit or time deposits, and in accordance with the provisions of Chapter 18 (§ 2.1-327 et seq.) of Title 2.1, as ordered by the court. Orders creating funds pursuant to this section shall include information necessary to make prudent investment and disbursement decisions. The order shall include, except when it is unreasonable, (i) the beneficiary's social security number and date of birth and (ii) the proposed dates of final and periodic disbursements.

Unless otherwise ordered by the court, the provisions of this section shall not apply to:

1. Cash or other money received in lieu of surety on any bond posted in any civil or criminal case, including but not limited to, bail bonds, appeal bonds in appeals from a district court or circuit court, bonds posted in connection with the filing of an attachment, detinue seizure or distress, suspending bonds, and performance bonds;

2. Cash or other money paid or deposited in the clerk's office prior to final disposition of the case, including but not limited to interpleaders or eminent domain; or

3. Cash or other money deposits in lieu of surety on any bond posted in the clerk's office which is not posted in connection with any civil or criminal case, including bonds posted by executors or administrators.

To this end, the general receiver is authorized to verify, receive, and give acquittances for all such moneys, as the court may direct. Any interest which accrues on the funds, minus allowable fees and bond costs, shall be credited and payable to the person or persons entitled to receive such funds.

All moneys received under this section are subject to audit by the Auditor of Public Accounts. The Auditor of Public Accounts shall prescribe mandatory record keeping and accounting standards for general receivers. (Code 1950, § 8-725; 1973, c. 354; 1977, c. 617; 1979, c. 498; 1988, c. 553; 1990, c. 414; 1991, c. 635; 1999, c. 198.)

Cross references. — As to deposit of money under control of court, see § 8.01-600.

The 1999 amendment inserted "shall be deemed public deposits as set forth in Chapter 23 (§ 2.1-359 et seq.) of Title 2.1 and" in the third sentence in the first paragraph.

I. DECISIONS UNDER CURRENT LAW.

Applied in In re Williamsburg Suites, Ltd., 117 Bankr. 216 (Bankr. E.D. Va. 1990).

§ 8.01-583. How securities taken and kept; power of receivers over same. — The securities in which under the orders of the court such investments may be made shall be taken in the name of the general receiver and be kept by him, unless otherwise specially ordered. He shall have power to sell, transfer or collect the same, only upon order of the court; and in case of his death, resignation or removal his successor, or any person specially appointed by the court for that purpose, shall have like power.

Notwithstanding the foregoing paragraph, when a general receiver places funds in a security or investment which is insured by the Federal Deposit Insurance Corporation or other federal insurance agency, the general receiver shall to the extent practicable invest these funds so that insurance coverage is provided by the Federal Deposit Insurance Corporation or other federal insurance agency. (Code 1950, § 8-726; 1977, c. 617; 1988, c. 553; 1990, c. 3.)

§ 8.01-584. How dividends and interest collected and invested. — The general receiver shall collect the dividends and interest on all the securities in which investments have been or may be made, under the orders or decrees of his court, or under the provisions of § 8.01-582, when and as often as the same may become due and payable thereon, and shall invest the same in like securities, unless the court has ordered or decreed some other investment or disposition to be made thereof; and in such case he shall invest or dispose of the same as the court shall have ordered or decreed. (Code 1950, § 8-727; 1977, c. 617.)

§ 8.01-585. How accounts kept by receivers. — Each such general receiver shall keep an accurate and particular account of all moneys received, invested and paid out by him, showing the respective amounts to the credit of each case in the court and designating in the items the judgments, orders or decrees of court under which the respective sums have been received, invested or paid out. No later than October 1 of each year, he shall make a report to his court showing the balance to the credit of each case in the court in which money has been received by him, the manner of each case in the court in which money has been received by him, the manner in which it is invested, the amounts received, invested or paid out during the year ending June 30 of the current year, the approximate date on which the moneys held for the beneficiaries will become payable, and the whole amount then invested and subject to the future order of the court. A copy of the annual report shall be recorded in the trust fund order book. He shall, at any time when required by the court or the Auditor of Public Accounts so to do, furnish a statement of the amount subject to the order of the court in any case pending therein and any other information required by the court or the Auditor of Public Accounts as to any money or other property under his control. He shall annually make formal settlement of his accounts before the court or before the commissioner mentioned in § 8.01-617 which settlement shall be recorded as provided in § 8.01-619. (Code 1950, § 8-728; 1977, c. 617; 1988, c. 553; 1989, c. 69.)

Cross references. — As to penalty for failure to perform duty required by this section, see § 8.01-590.

§ 8.01-586. Inquiry as to unknown owners of funds. — When funds are held because of inability to find the person to whom payable, such receiver may be ordered by the court to make inquiry and due diligence to ascertain such person in order that payment may be made; and for this purpose, and to secure any other relevant information, he shall have power to summon witnesses and take evidence; and he shall report specifically to the court in each annual report, and at any other time when so ordered by the court, the details and results of his efforts. (Code 1950, § 8-729; 1977, c. 617; 1988, c. 553.)

§ 8.01-587. Liability of general receivers. — Except as otherwise ordered by the court, for good cause shown, a general receiver shall be liable for any loss of income which results from his (i) failure to invest any money held by him pursuant to §§ 8.01-582 through 8.01-586 within sixty days of his receipt of the funds or (ii) failure to pay out any money so ordered by the court within sixty days of the court order. He shall be charged with interest from the date of the court order until such investment or payment is made. (Code 1950, § 8-730; 1977, c. 617; 1988, c. 841.)

§ 8.01-588. Bonds generally. — A general receiver shall annually give before the court a bond with surety to be approved by it, in such penalty as the court directs, sufficient at least to cover the probable amount under his control in any one year.

This section shall apply to the clerk if the clerk is appointed such receiver, and his official bond as clerk shall not cover money or property under his control as general receiver. (Code 1950, § 8-731; 1977, c. 617; 1988, c. 841.)

§ 8.01-588.1. Bonds apportioned to funds under control; annual reports. — The general receiver shall obtain bond through the Department of the Treasury's Division of Risk Management. No later than October 1 of each year, he shall report to the Division the amount of moneys under his control pursuant to § 8.01-582 as of June 30 of the current year and shall report the amount he expects to come under his control for the year ending on June 30 of the following year. He shall also report any other information reasonably required by the Division concerning bond coverage of moneys under his control. The cost of the bond shall be apportioned among the funds under his control as of the billing date based on the amount of each owner's or beneficiary's moneys. This section shall not apply to any financial institution fulfilling the requirements set out in § 6.1-18 or § 6.1-195.82. (1988, c. 841; 2000, cc. 618, 632.)

The 2000 amendments. — The 2000 amendments by cc. 618 and 632 are identical, and substituted "the Treasury's" for "General Services" in the first sentence.

§ 8.01-589. Compensation and fees; when none allowed. — A. A general receiver may receive as compensation for his services such amount as the court deems reasonable, but not exceeding:

1. Ten dollars at receipt of the originating court order to receive funds, deposit funds, and establish files and accounting records with respect to those funds;

2. Ten dollars when all funds held for a beneficiary or beneficiaries are disbursed;

3. Ten dollars per draft or check for periodic and final disbursements;

4. Five percent of the interest income earned; and

5. Ten dollars for remitting funds to the State Treasurer and up to ten dollars per draft for remitting those funds.

B. Notwithstanding the foregoing subsections, general receivers shall not deduct fees or otherwise be compensated for services with respect to those funds which should have been reported and then remitted to the State Treasurer in accordance with § 8.01-602 or § 55-210.9:1.

A general receiver shall promptly report to the court the execution of the bond or bonds required in § 8.01-588 and make the reports and perform the duties required of him. No compensation shall be allowed him until he has performed the duties aforesaid.

If such receiver is the clerk of court and if compensation is allowed, it shall be fee and commission income to the office of such clerk in accordance with § 17.1-287. (Code 1950, § 8-732; 1977, c. 617; 1979, c. 498; 1988, c. 841.)

§ 8.01-590. Penalty for failure of duty. — If a general receiver fail to keep the account, or to make out and return the statements required by § 8.01-585, he shall be subject to a fine of not less than $100 nor more than $1,000 to be imposed by the court at its discretion; and the condition of his official bond shall be taken to embrace the liability of himself and his sureties for any such fine. (Code 1950, § 8-733; 1977, c. 617.)

REVISERS' NOTE

Former § 8-734 (When interest payable) was deleted as obsolete.

ARTICLE 2.

Special Receivers.

§ 8.01-591. Notice required prior to appointment of receiver. — Whenever the pleadings in any suit make out a proper case for the appointment of a receiver and application is made therefor to any court, such court shall designate the time and place for hearing such application, and shall require reasonable notice thereof to be given to the defendant and to all other parties having a substantial interest, either as owners of or lienors of record and lienors known to the plaintiff, in the subject matter. The court to whom such application is made shall inquire particularly of the applicant as to the parties so substantially interested in the subject matter, and such applicant, for any intentional or wilful failure to disclose fully all material information relating to such inquiry, may be adjudged in contempt of court. (Code 1950, § 8-735; 1977, c. 617.)

Cross references. — As to settlement of accounts of special receivers, see §§ 8.01-617 through 8.01-619. As to contempt proceedings, see § 18.2-456 et seq.

ing liens. S.W. Rawls, Inc. v. Forrest, 224 Va. 264, 295 S.E.2d 791 (1982).

I. DECISIONS UNDER CURRENT LAW.

Appointment of receiver does not affect vested rights or order of priority of exist-

§ 8.01-592. Notice not required in emergencies. — Section 8.01-591 shall not apply to those cases in which an emergency exists and it is necessary that a receiver be immediately appointed to preserve the subject matter. In such emergency cases a receiver may be appointed and the order of appointment shall state the emergency and necessity for immediate action, and shall require bond in proper amount of the applicant or someone for him with sufficient surety conditioned to protect and save harmless the owners, lienors and creditors, lien or general, in the subject matter taken over by the receiver, from all damages and injury properly and naturally flowing from such emergency appointment of a receiver. (Code 1950, § 8-736; 1977, c. 617.)

I. DECISIONS UNDER CURRENT LAW.

Applied in S.W. Rawls, Inc. v. Forrest, 224 Va. 264, 295 S.E.2d 791 (1982).

§ 8.01-593. Subsequent proceedings after emergency appointment. — Such emergency appointment shall be limited to a period of not longer than thirty days, during which period notice shall be given by the applicant to all parties having a substantial interest, either as owner of or lienor in the subject matter, of any motion to extend such receivership; and upon the hearing on such motion, the court shall hear the matter de novo, and shall discharge such receiver, or shall appoint the same receiver, or other receivers to act with him, or new receivers as to the court may seem right. Unless such receivership shall be so extended, all the rights and powers of such emergency receiver over the subject matter, at the end of such period for which he shall have been appointed, shall cease and determine, and such receiver shall forthwith file with such court an account of his dealing with such estate. The notices required to be given under this section and §§ 8.01-591 and 8.01-592 shall be served, as to residents of this Commonwealth, in any of the modes prescribed by § 8.01-296, and as to nonresidents of this Commonwealth, or persons unknown, or in any case in which the number of persons to be given notice exceeds thirty, in the manner prescribed by § 8.01-319. (Code 1950, § 8-737; 1977, c. 617.)

REVISERS' NOTE

Section 8.01-593 provides for two weeks' notice by publication; therefore the exception in former § 8-737 has been deleted.

§ 8.01-594. Notice not required to parties served with process. — In any suit matured and docketed in which the bill or petition prays for the appointment of a receiver, no notice shall be required under this article to be given to any defendant upon whom process to answer such bill or petition shall have been served. (Code 1950, § 8-738; 1977, c. 617.)

§ 8.01-595. Preparation of list of creditors; notice to them. — When a receiver has been appointed he shall immediately prepare or cause to be prepared a list of all creditors, lien and general, of the person, firm, corporation or of any other legal or commercial entity for which he is a receiver; and the court may by proper order compel any defendant for whom a receiver is appointed, or any officer of the corporation or of any other legal or commercial entity for whom the receiver is appointed, to furnish or deliver to the receiver a list, duly sworn to, of all creditors, lien or general, together with their addresses if known. The receiver shall then promptly notify by mail each creditor whose name and address has been ascertained of the appointment of the receiver.

When a permanent receiver is appointed he shall not be required to make a new list of creditors if a temporary receiver or a prior receiver appointed in the same proceedings has already prepared one which is adequate, nor shall he be required to mail other notices to creditors if the prior receiver has given proper notice to the parties entitled thereto. (Code 1950, § 8-739; 1977, c. 617.)

REVISERS' NOTE

Added after "... of the person, firm, (or) corporation ..." is the language "... or any other legal or commercial entity ..." The language is an adaptation of the "Long Arm Statute" definition of "person." See § 8.01-328. In the second paragraph, language has been added with respect to the list and notice given by a prior receiver so as not to relieve the permanent receiver of these duties if they have not been adequately or properly discharged by his predecessor.

§ 8.01-596. **No sale prior to such notification; exceptions.** — No court shall order the sale of any assets of the receivership until a receiver has reported to the court in writing that he has mailed such notices to such creditors at least five days prior to the filing of such report, except that the court may at any time permit the sale of perishable or seasonable goods when necessary to preserve the estate, or may permit the receiver to conduct the business for which he is a receiver as a going business and to sell in the usual course of such business. (Code 1950, § 8-740; 1977, c. 617.)

§ 8.01-597. **Suits against receivers in certain cases.** — Any receiver of any property appointed by the courts of this Commonwealth may be sued in respect of any act or transaction of his in carrying on the business connected with such property, without the previous leave of the court in which such receiver was appointed; but the institution or pendency of such suit shall not interfere with or delay a sale by trustees under a deed of trust or a decree of sale for foreclosure of any mortgage upon such property. (Code 1950, § 8-741; 1977, c. 617.)

REVISERS' NOTE

The language after the word "delay," "... a sale by trustees under a deed of trust or ...," has been added to clarify the last sentence of former § 8-741.

I. DECISIONS UNDER PRIOR LAW.

Editor's note. — The case cited below was decided under corresponding provisions of former law. The term "this section," as used below, refers to former provisions.

This section permits suits against court receivers without express permission of the appointing court. Ellis v. Cates, 178 F.2d 791 (4th Cir. 1949), cert. denied, 339 U.S. 964, 70 S. Ct. 999, 94 L. Ed. 1373 (1950), 342 U.S. 870, 72 S. Ct. 113, 96 L. Ed. 655 (1951).

§ 8.01-598. **Effect of judgment against receiver.** — A judgment against a receiver under § 8.01-597 shall not be a lien on the property or funds under the control of the court, nor shall any execution issue thereon, but upon filing a certified copy of such judgment in the cause in which the receiver was appointed, the court shall direct payment of such judgment in the same manner as if the claim upon which the judgment is based had been proved and allowed in such cause. (Code 1950, § 8-742; 1977, c. 617.)

§ 8.01-599. **Warrant or motion for judgment against receiver in general district court, when to be tried.** — A warrant or motion for judgment before a general district court under §§ 8.01-597 and 8.01-598 may be tried not less than ten days after service of process. (Code 1950, § 8-743; 1977, c. 617.)

REVISERS' NOTE

Since § 16.1-81 ff. permits use of a motion for judgment in the general district courts, the motion for judgment is included in § 8.01-599.

ARTICLE 3.

General Provisions for Moneys Under Control of Court.

§ 8.01-600. How money under control of court deposited; record kept; liability of clerk. — A. This section pertains only to money held by the clerk of the circuit court, when the court orders moneys to be held by the clerk pursuant to this section. The clerk shall have the duty, unless it is otherwise specially ordered, to receive, take charge of, hold or invest in such manner as the court orders and also to pay out or dispose of these moneys as the court orders or decrees. To this end, the clerk is authorized to verify, receive, and give acquittances for all such moneys as the court may direct.

B. Orders creating funds pursuant to this section or § 8.01-582 shall include information necessary to make prudent investment and disbursement decisions. The orders shall include, except when it is unreasonable, (i) the beneficiary's social security number and date of birth and (ii) the proposed dates of periodic and final disbursements.

Unless otherwise ordered by the court, the provisions of this section shall not apply to:

1. Cash or other money received in lieu of surety on any bond posted in any civil or criminal case, including but not limited to bail bonds, appeal bonds in appeals from a district court or circuit court, bonds posted in connection with the filing of an attachment, detinue seizure or distress, suspending bonds, and performance bonds;

2. Cash or other money paid or deposited in the clerk's office prior to final disposition of the case, including but not limited to interpleaders or eminent domain; or

3. Cash or other money deposited in lieu of surety on any bond posted in the clerk's office which is not posted in connection with any civil or criminal case, including bonds posted by executors or administrators.

C. All deposits under this section shall be secured in accordance with the Virginia Security for Public Deposits Act (§ 2.1-359 et seq.).

D. Moneys held pursuant to this section shall be invested in certificates of deposit and time deposits, and in accordance with the provisions of Chapter 18 (§ 2.1-327 et seq.) of Title 2.1 as ordered by the court.

E. Any interest which accrues on the funds, minus allowable fees and bond costs, shall be credited and payable to the person or persons entitled to receive such funds. The court may order the clerk to consolidate for investment purposes money received under this section, with income received hereunder to be apportioned among the several accounts.

F. Except as otherwise ordered by the court, for good cause shown, the clerk shall be liable for any loss of income which results from his (i) failure to invest the money within sixty days of the court order creating the fund or (ii) failure to pay out any money so ordered by the court within sixty days of the court order. He shall be charged with interest from the date of the court order until such investment or payment is made.

G. The clerk shall keep an accurate and particular account of all moneys received, invested, and paid out by him, showing the respective amounts to the credit of each case in the court and designating in the items the judgments, orders or decrees of court under which the respective sums have been received, invested or paid out. At least annually and no later than October 1 of each year, the clerk shall make a report to the court showing the balance to the credit of each case in the court in which money has been received by him, the manner in which money has been received by him, the manner in which it is invested, the amounts received, invested or paid out during the year ending June 30 of the current year, the approximate date on which the moneys held for the beneficiaries will become payable, and the whole amount then invested and subject to the future order of the court. A copy of this report shall be recorded in the trust fund order book. The clerk shall, at any time when required by the court or the Auditor of Public Accounts to do so, furnish a statement of the amount subject to the order of the court in any case pending therein and any other information required by the court or the Auditor of Public Accounts as to any money or other property under his control before the court. When the clerk receives funds under this section, he shall be entitled to receive fees in accordance with § 17.1-287 in the amounts as specified for general receivers in § 8.01-589.

H. All moneys received under this section are subject to audit by the Auditor of Public Accounts. (Code 1950, § 8-744; 1977, c. 617; 1986, c. 644; 1988, c. 841; 1990, cc. 3, 414; 1991, c. 635.)

REVISERS' NOTE

The reference in former § 8-744 to a court order which stated that the fund will be promptly paid out has been deleted as unnecessary.

Law Review. — For note, "Virginia's Acquisition of Unclaimed and Abandoned Personal Property," see 27 Wm. & Mary L. Rev. 409 (1986).

§ **8.01-600.1:** Repealed by Acts 1993, c. 939.

§ **8.01-601. Deposit with general receiver of certain funds under supervision of fiduciary and belonging to person under disability.** — Whenever it appears to any fiduciary as defined in § 8.01-2 that a person under a disability as defined in § 8.01-2 is not represented by a fiduciary as defined above and is entitled to funds not exceeding $3,000 under the supervision and control of the fiduciary in charge of such funds, he may report such fact to the commissioner of accounts of the court in which he was admitted to qualify. With the approval of such commissioner of accounts, the fiduciary in charge of such funds may deposit such funds with the general receiver of the court in which he was admitted to qualify. The general receiver shall issue a receipt to such fiduciary which shall show the source of such fund, the amount and to whom it belongs and shall enter the amount and such facts in his accounts. (Code 1950, § 8-744.1; 1970, c. 352; 1977, c. 617.)

REVISERS' NOTE

Section 8.01-601 uses the terms "a person under a disability" and "fiduciary" as those terms are defined in § 8.01-2. See also §§ 8.01-606 and 64.1-124.

Former § 8-745 (Reports and collection of taxes thereon) was deleted as unnecessary since there is no longer a tax on intangibles.

§ **8.01-602. Proceedings when owner of money under control of court unknown.** — Whenever any money has remained payable or distributable for one year in the custody or under the control of any court of this Commonwealth without anyone known to the court claiming the same, except funds deposited as compensation and damages in condemnation proceedings pursuant to § 25-46.24 pending a final order or pursuant to § 33.1-120, the court shall cause such money to be reported and then remitted to the State Treasurer pursuant to §§ 55-210.9:1, 55-210.12 and 55-210.14.

The general receiver, if one has been appointed, and the clerk of the circuit court shall be responsible for identifying such money held by them in their respective control pursuant to §§ 8.01-582 and 8.01-600 and for petitioning the court to remit as provided in this section. (Code 1950, § 8-746; 1966, c. 210; 1977, c. 617; 1982, c. 155; 1984, c. 121; 1987, c. 708; 1988, c. 841.)

REVISERS' NOTE

A minor change with respect to the requirement of newspaper publication has been made. See § 8.01-586.

Editor's note. — Section 55-210.14, referred to in this section, was repealed by Acts 1988, c. 378.

§ **8.01-603:** Repealed by Acts 1982, c. 155.

Cross references. — As to disposition of unclaimed property, see § 55-210.1 et seq.

§ **8.01-604. How State Treasurer to keep account of such money.** — The State Treasurer shall keep an account of all money thus paid to him, showing the amount thereof, when, by whom, and under what order it was paid, and the name of the court, and, as far as practicable, a description of the suit or proceeding in which the order was made, and, as far as known, the names of the parties thereto. (Code 1950, § 8-748; 1977, c. 617; 1981, c. 514; 1982, c. 155.)

§ **8.01-605. How person entitled to money paid into state treasury may recover it.** — Money paid into the state treasury under the provisions of this article shall be accounted for and disbursed under the procedures provided for in Article 4 of Chapter 11.1 of Title 55 (§ 55-210.12 et seq.). (Code 1950, § 8-749; 1962, c. 607; 1977, c. 617; 1981, c. 514; 1982, c. 155.)

REVISERS' NOTE

Section 8.01-605 is former § 8-749 with several changes. A reference to this "article" has been inserted in order to point out that the application of this statute is limited to money paid into the State treasury under the conditions outlined in this article. The limitation on the amount which the Comptroller may allow upon satisfactory proof has been eliminated. The former requirement of venue in the Circuit Court of the city of Richmond when the Comptroller disallows a claim has been eliminated;

§ 8.01-605 permits the claimant to apply to an appropriate circuit court. The reference to the statute of limitations on claims against the State has been replaced by the provision that no statute of limitations shall bar any claim presented under this section; this change has been made in order that an unknown person will not be barred of his rights to funds held by the Commonwealth when he has a proper claim thereto.

§ **8.01-606. Payment of small amounts to certain persons through court without intervention of fiduciary; authority of commissioners of accounts.** — A. Whenever there is due to any person, any sum of money from any source, not exceeding $10,000, the fund may be paid into the circuit court of the county or city in which the fund became due or such person resides. The court may, by an order entered of record, (i) pay the fund to the person to whom it is due, if the person is considered by the court competent to expend and use the same in his behalf, or (ii) pay the fund to some other person who is considered competent to administer it, for the benefit of the person entitled to the fund, without the intervention of a fiduciary, whether the other person resides within or without this Commonwealth. The clerk of the court shall take a receipt from the person to whom the money is paid, which shall show the source from which it was derived, the amount, to whom it belongs, and when and to whom it was paid. The receipt shall be signed and acknowledged by the person receiving the money, and entered of record in the book in the clerk's office in which the current fiduciary accounts are entered and indexed.

Upon the payment into court the person owing the money shall be discharged of such obligation.

No bond shall be required of the party to whom the money is paid by the court.

B. Whenever (i) it appears to the court having control of a fund, tangible personal property or intangible personal property or supervision of its administration, whether a suit is pending therefor or not, that a person under a disability who has no fiduciary, is entitled to a fund arising from the sale of lands for a division or otherwise, or a fund, tangible personal property or intangible personal property as distributee of any estate, or from any other source, (ii) a judgment, decree, or order for the payment of a sum of money or for delivery of tangible personal property or intangible personal property to a person under a disability who has no fiduciary is rendered by any court, and the amount to which such person is entitled or the value of the tangible personal property or intangible personal property is not more than $10,000, or (iii) a person under a disability is entitled to receive payments of income, tangible personal property or intangible personal property and the amount of the income payments is not more than $10,000 in any one year, or the value of the tangible personal property is not more than $10,000, or the current market value of the intangible personal property is not more than $10,000, the court may, without the intervention of a fiduciary, cause such fund, property or income to be paid or delivered to any person deemed by the court capable of properly handling it, to be used solely for the education, maintenance and support of the person under a disability. In any case in which an infant is entitled to such fund, property or income, the court may, upon its being made to appear that the infant is of sufficient age and discretion to use the fund, property or income judiciously, cause the fund to be paid or delivered directly to the infant.

Whenever a person is entitled to a fund or such property distributable by a fiduciary settling his accounts before the commissioner of accounts of the court in which the fiduciary qualified, and the amount or value of the fund or property, or the value of any combination thereof, is not more than $10,000, the commissioner of accounts may approve distribution thereof in the same manner and to the extent of the authority herein conferred upon a court including exemption from filing further accounts where the value of the fund being administered is less than $10,000.

Whenever an incapacitated person or infant is entitled to a fund or such property distributable by a fiduciary settling accounts before the commissioner of accounts of the court in which the fiduciary qualified and the will or trust instrument under which the fiduciary serves, authorizes the fiduciary to distribute the property or fund to the incapacitated person or infant without the intervention of a guardian, conservator or committee, and the amount or value of such fund or property, or the value of any combination thereof, is not more than $10,000, the commissioner of accounts may approve distribution thereof in the same manner and to the extent of the authority hereinabove conferred upon a court or judge thereof.

§ 8.01-606

Whenever a fiduciary is administering funds not exceeding $10,000, the circuit court of the county or city in which the fund is being administered by order entered of record may authorize the fiduciary, when considered competent to administer the funds, to continue to administer the funds for the benefit of the person entitled to the fund without the necessity of filing any further accounts, whether such person resides within or without this Commonwealth. The clerk of the court shall take a receipt from the fiduciary, which shall show the amount of the fund remaining, to whom it belongs, and the date the court entered the order exempting the filing of further accounts. The receipt shall be signed and acknowledged by the fiduciary, and entered of record in the book in the clerk's office in which the current fiduciary accounts are entered and indexed.

No bond shall be required of a fiduciary granted an exemption from filing any further accounts. (Code 1950, §§ 8-750, 8-751; 1952, c. 103; 1954, cc. 238, 526; 1962, c. 465; 1966, cc. 332, 339; 1970, c. 566; 1977, cc. 462, 617; 1978, c. 525; 1980, c. 544; 1985, c. 216; 1987, c. 378; 1995, c. 405; 1997, c. 801.)

REVISERS' NOTE

Former §§ 8-750 and 8-751 have been combined in § 8.01-606. Certain of the monetary limits of these sections have been changed. The term "person under a disability" has replaced the phrase "incompetent person or infant" in all but one place, the last sentence of the first paragraph of subsection B. Also, the term "fiduciary" has been used instead of "administrator," etc. Other clarifying language changes have been made.

Former § 8-750.1 (Personal representatives for recipients of welfare funds) was transferred to § 63.1-88.1.

Editor's note. — Pursuant to § 9-77.11 and Acts 1977, c. 617, cl. 4, the amendment to former § 8-751, corresponding to this section, in Acts 1977, c. 462, was deemed to have amended this section.

Acts 1997, c. 801, cl. 2, provides: "That the provisions of this act shall become effective on January 1, 1998. The powers granted and duties imposed pursuant to this act shall apply prospectively to guardians and conservators appointed by court order entered on or after that date, or modified on or after that date if the court so directs, without regard to when the petition was filed. The procedures specified in this act governing proceedings for appointment of a guardian or conservator or termination or other modification of a guardianship shall apply on and after that date without regard to when the petition therefor was filed or the guardianship or conservatorship created."

Law Review. — For article, "Updating Virginia's Probate Law," see 4 U. Rich. L. Rev. 223 (1970). For survey of Virginia law on trusts and estates for the year 1976-77, see 63 Va. L. Rev. 1503 (1977). For 1995 survey of wills, trusts, and estates, see 29 U. Rich. L. Rev. 1175 (1995).

I. DECISIONS UNDER PRIOR LAW.

Editor's note. — The case cited below was decided under corresponding provisions of former law. The term "this section," as used below, refers to former provisions.

Section ineffective to transform merely benevolent trust into charitable trust. — The possibility of administering under this section proceeds from a testamentary trust for the education of school children was ineffective to transform it into a charitable trust where the basic intent of testator was construed to be merely benevolent and not charitable. Shenandoah Valley Nat'l Bank v. Taylor, 192 Va. 135, 63 S.E.2d 786 (1951).

CHAPTER 23.

COMMISSIONERS IN CHANCERY.

Sec.
8.01-607. Appointment and removal.
8.01-608. How accounts referred.

Sec.
8.01-609. Duties; procedure generally.
8.01-609.1. Commissioners in chancery.

Sec.		Sec.	
8.01-610.	Weight to be given commissioner's report.	8.01-616.	Delivery of original papers of suit by clerk to commissioner.
8.01-611.	Notice of time and place of taking account.	8.01-617.	Settlement of accounts of special receivers and special commissioners.
8.01-612.	Commissioner may summons witnesses.	8.01-618.	Reports of such settlements; when new bond required.
8.01-613.	Commissioner may ask instructions of court.	8.01-618.1.	Fees of special receivers and commissioners for reports.
8.01-614.	His power to adjourn his proceedings.	8.01-619.	Recordation of reports of such settlements.
8.01-615.	When cause heard on report; time for filing exceptions.		

§ **8.01-607. Appointment and removal.** — Each circuit court shall, from time to time, appoint such commissioners in chancery as may be deemed necessary for the convenient dispatch of the business of such court. Such commissioners shall be removable at pleasure. (Code 1950, § 8-248; 1977, c. 617.)

REVISERS' NOTE

Former § 8-248 has been updated to reflect, inter alia, 1973 amendments to Title 17 (Courts of Record).

I. Decisions Under Current Law.
II. Decisions Under Prior Law.

I. DECISIONS UNDER CURRENT LAW.

Appointment of commissioner within court's discretion. — The question of when it is proper, or may be useful, to resort to the aid of a commissioner is one which addresses itself to the sound discretion of the court. Klein v. Klein, 11 Va. App. 155, 396 S.E.2d 866 (1990).

It is entirely compatible with the practice and statutory law of the Commonwealth for a court to refer questions regarding the circumstances and factors which contributed to the dissolution of the marriage to a commissioner in chancery. Klein v. Klein, 11 Va. App. 155, 396 S.E.2d 866 (1990).

II. DECISIONS UNDER PRIOR LAW.

Editor's note. — The case cited below was decided under corresponding provisions of former law. The term "this chapter," as used below, refers to former provisions.

Chapter does not restrict court as to class of case that may be referred. — This chapter deals with the procedure before the commissioner and the weight to be given his findings. It does not limit or restrict the court as to the class of case that it may refer to a commissioner. The court, acting within its sound discretion, must determine when the convenient dispatch of business requires an order of reference. Raiford v. Raiford, 193 Va. 221, 68 S.E.2d 888 (1952).

§ **8.01-608. How accounts referred.** — Accounts to be taken in any case shall be referred to a commissioner appointed pursuant to § 8.01-607, unless the parties interested agree, or the court shall deem it proper, that they be referred to some other person. (Code 1950, § 8-249; 1977, c. 617.)

§ 8.01-609   CIVIL REMEDIES AND PROCEDURE   § 8.01-609

REVISERS' NOTE

The first sentence of former § 8-249 has been retained without change. The second sentence has been modified and is set forth in § 8.01-609.

Cross references. — As to proceedings before commissioner in chancery, see Rule 2:18.

I. DECISIONS UNDER PRIOR LAW.

Editor's note. — The cases cited below were decided under corresponding provisions of former law. The term "this section," as used below, refers to former provisions.

For what cases may be referred by the court to a commissioner, see Kraker v. Shields, 61 Va. (20 Gratt.) 377 (1871).

Discretion of court. — The question when it is proper, or may be useful, to resort to the aid of the commissioner is one which addresses itself to the sound discretion of the court. Of course the court ought to exercise such discretion soundly to prevent unnecessary expense or delay. Raiford v. Raiford, 193 Va. 221, 68 S.E.2d 888 (1952).

Appointment of commissioner in suit to subject land to payment of judgment authorized. — In a suit to subject land to payment of a judgment, an order of reference was entered and a special commissioner appointed to ascertain and report what amount complainant was entitled to recover. It was held that such an appointment was authorized by this section. Woodhouse v. Burke & Herbert Bank & Trust Co., 166 Va. 706, 185 S.E. 876 (1936).

Account will not be ordered to reopen previously settled accounts. — An order for an account will not be awarded merely to enable a party to make out his case, or to reopen the investigation of the account of an indebtedness which has been previously settled by the parties with the aid of their counsel, and the integrity and correctness of which has not been impugned. Hamilton v. Stephenson, 106 Va. 77, 55 S.E. 577 (1906).

When party guilty of laches. — After the funds in a cause have passed beyond the control of the court, and the cause is practically ready for a final decree, a court of equity will not, at the instance of the counsel for some of the parties (who has paid no attention to the case for years, and whose clients have been, in the meantime represented by other counsel) order an account to ascertain what is due to him from his clients for services rendered in the cause. Miller v. Penniman & Bro., 110 Va. 780, 67 S.E. 516 (1910).

No account ordered when there is no proof to support pleadings. — No account shall be ordered when the answer denies all the material allegations of the bill and there is no proof to sustain them. Lee County Justice v. Fulkerson, 62 Va. (21 Gratt.) 182 (1871); Sadler v. Whitehurst, 83 Va. 46, 1 S.E. 410 (1887).

§ 8.01-609. Duties; procedure generally. — Every commissioner shall examine, and report upon, any matters as may be referred to him by any court. The proceedings before a commissioner in chancery shall be conducted as set forth in this chapter and the Rules of Court. (Code 1950, § 8-249; 1977, c. 617; 1981, c. 613; 1992, c. 297.)

REVISERS' NOTE

Section 8.01-609 sets forth the second sentence of former § 8-249 with minor modifications and with the addition of language referring to the provisions of this chapter and the Rules of Court for the conduct of proceedings before commissioners in chancery.

Cross references. — As to proceedings before commissioner in chancery, see Rule 2:18.

I. DECISIONS UNDER PRIOR LAW.

Editor's note. — The cases cited below were decided under corresponding provisions of former law. The term "this section," as used below, refers to former provisions.

A chancellor does not delegate his judicial functions to a commissioner in chancery when he refers a cause to him. Raiford v. Raiford, 193 Va. 221, 68 S.E.2d 888 (1952).

The court is responsible for the correct decision of the cause, and cannot shift such responsibility from its own shoulders to those of a commissioner. But it can avail itself of the assistance of a commissioner to prepare the cause and place it in the best possible state to enable the court to decide it correctly. Raiford v.

Raiford, 193 Va. 221, 68 S.E.2d 888 (1952).

Competency of commissioners. — An attorney employed in a cause is not a competent commissioner to take an account ordered in the cause. Bowers v. Bowers, 70 Va. (29 Gratt.) 697 (1878).

A commissioner, who is a creditor and a party to suit to subject debtor's land to pay his lien debts, is incompetent to take an account ordered therein. Dillard v. Krise, 86 Va. 410, 10 S.E. 430 (1889); Etter v. Scott, 90 Va. 762, 19 S.E. 776 (1894).

§ 8.01-609.1. Commissioners in chancery.

— A commissioner in chancery may, for services rendered by virtue of his office, charge the following fees, to wit:

For services which might be performed by notaries, the fees for such services and for any other service such fees as the court by which the commissioner is appointed may from time to time prescribe.

A commissioner shall not be compelled to make out or return a report until his fees therefor are paid or security given him to pay so much as may be adjudged appropriate by the court to which the report is to be returned or by the judge thereof in vacation, unless the court finds cause to order it to be made out and returned without such payment or security. (Code 1950, § 14-142; 1964, c. 386, § 14.1-133; 1998, c. 872.)

I. DECISIONS UNDER PRIOR LAW.

Editor's note. — The case cited below was decided under corresponding provisions of former law. The term "this section," as used below, refers to former provisions.

Time to object to fees. — Unless exception be made in the court below to the amount charged by the commissioner for his fees which are allowed by that court, it is too late to make exception thereto in the appellate court. Shipman v. Fletcher, 83 Va. 349, 2 S.E. 198 (1887).

§ 8.01-610. Weight to be given commissioner's report.

— The report of a commissioner in chancery shall not have the weight given to the verdict of a jury on conflicting evidence, but the court shall confirm or reject such report in whole or in part, according to the view which it entertains of the law and the evidence. (Code 1950, § 8-250; 1977, c. 617.)

I. Decisions Under Current Law.
II. Decisions Under Prior Law.

I. DECISIONS UNDER CURRENT LAW.

Weight of commissioner's report. — While the report of a commissioner in chancery does not carry the weight of a jury's verdict, it should be sustained unless the trial court concludes that the commissioner's findings are not supported by the evidence. This rule applies with particular force to a commissioner's findings of fact based upon evidence taken in his presence, but is not applicable to pure conclusions of law contained in the report. Jamison v. Jamison, 3 Va. App. 644, 352 S.E.2d 719 (1987).

This section clearly gives the trial court substantial discretion in the manner in which it reviews the report of a commissioner; however, it does not allow the trial judge simply to ignore the report or portions thereof. Gulfstream Bldg. Ass'n v. Britt, 239 Va. 178, 387 S.E.2d 488 (1990).

The court erred in placing the burden upon the claimant to justify the commissioner's report and in rejecting the commissioner's factual findings where the chancellor made no finding that the commissioner's report was unsupported by the evidence since the commissioner's report came to the court armed with a presumption of correctness which the additional evidence heard in court did nothing to overcome. Morris v. United Va. Bank, 237 Va. 331, 377 S.E.2d 611 (1989).

Report should be sustained where findings are supported by evidence. — While the report of a commissioner in chancery does not carry the weight of a jury's verdict, it should be sustained unless the trial court concludes that the commissioner's findings are not supported by the evidence. This rule applies with particular force to a commissioner's findings of fact based upon evidence taken in his presence, but is not applicable to pure conclusions of law contained in the report. Hill v. Hill, 227 Va. 569, 318 S.E.2d 292 (1984); Dodge v. Dodge, 2 Va. App. 238, 343 S.E.2d 363 (1986).

Appellate review where chancellor disapproves commissioner's findings. — On appeal, a decree which approves a commissioner's report will be affirmed unless plainly wrong, but where the chancellor has disapproved the commissioner's findings, the Supreme Court must review the evidence and ascertain whether, under a correct application of the law, the evidence supports the findings of the commissioner or the conclusions of the trial court. Hill v. Hill, 227 Va. 569, 318 S.E.2d 292 (1984).

On appeal when the chancellor has disapproved the commissioner's findings, the appellate court must review the evidence and ascertain whether, under a correct application of law, the evidence supports the findings of the commissioner or the conclusions of the trial court. Hodges v. Hodges, 2 Va. App. 508, 347 S.E.2d 134 (1986).

Where the trial judge disagreed with the commissioner not upon the facts but upon the conclusions of law, the Court of Appeals must review the evidence and ascertain whether, under the correct application of the law, the evidence supports the findings of the commissioner or the conclusions of the trial court. Jamison v. Jamison, 3 Va. App. 644, 352 S.E.2d 719 (1987).

Where report of a commissioner in chancery recommended that a deed be set aside based upon the commissioner's finding that clear and convincing evidence established that the deed had been procured by fraud, where a final order overruling the report of the commissioner was entered, where the chancellor's basis for disapproving the commissioner's finding depended upon "facts" not in the record of this case, where even if evidence of mother's mental condition from the separate and unrelated hearing was a permissible subject of judicial notice, the chancellor's opinion letter clearly indicated that she was not judicially declared "incompetent" until more than eight months after the commissioner's hearing, and where the evidence before the commissioner was entirely unrebutted, upon the record, the commissioner's findings were supported by the evidence, and the supreme court reversed the judgment of the circuit court. Branham v. Branham, 254 Va. 320, 491 S.E.2d 715 (1997).

Trial court improperly modified chancery commissioner's ruling in custody case where there was nothing in the record showing that it found insufficient evidence to support the commissioner's recommendation for joint custody and payment by husband of $2500 attorney's fees. Jones v. Jones, 26 Va. App. 689, 496 S.E.2d 150 (1998).

Chancellor abused his discretion in rejecting commissioner in chancery's recommendation that property be publicly marketed and instead ordering sale at public action, in the absence of any evidence that the parties' interests would be promoted by this method of sale or that the parties were unable to agree on terms for listing the property through a licensed real estate broker. Orgain v. Butler, 255 Va. 129, 496 S.E.2d 433 (1998).

Applied in Burks Bros. v. Jones, 232 Va. 238, 349 S.E.2d 134 (1986); Graves v. Graves, 4 Va. App. 326, 357 S.E.2d 554 (1987); Wagner v. Wagner, 4 Va. App. 397, 358 S.E.2d 407 (1987); Chesapeake Bldrs., Inc. v. Lee, 254 Va. 294, 492 S.E.2d 141 (1997); Far East Bank/Vien Dong Ngan Hang v. Dang, 257 Va. 524, 514 S.E.2d 337 (1999).

II. DECISIONS UNDER PRIOR LAW.

Editor's note. — The cases cited below were decided under corresponding provisions of former law. The term "this section," as used below, refers to former provisions.

Commissioner appointed to assist, not replace court. — When a cause is referred to a commissioner in chancery, the chancellor does not delegate his judicial function to him. He is appointed for the purpose of assisting the chancellor and not to supplant or replace him. It is the duty of the chancellor to weigh the evidence according to correct principles of law and arrive at his own conclusions. Hoffecker v. Hoffecker, 200 Va. 119, 104 S.E.2d 771 (1958); Plattner v. Plattner, 202 Va. 263, 117 S.E.2d 128 (1960); Kullgren v. Sletter, 202 Va. 507, 118 S.E.2d 514 (1961); Higgins v. Higgins, 205 Va. 324, 136 S.E.2d 793 (1964).

Report entitled to respect. — While the report of a commissioner does not have the weight given to the verdict of a jury on conflicting evidence, it is entitled to respect, if his judgment is supported by the testimony, and unless it is clear that he has erred. Parksley Nat'l Bank v. Parks, 172 Va. 169, 200 S.E. 629 (1939).

Report has great weight when evidence taken in his presence. — The report of a commissioner, when the evidence has been taken in his presence, is entitled to great weight, and should not be disturbed unless its conclusions are clearly unsupported by the evidence, and such report on the value of property, based upon conflicting testimony, and sustained by the trial court, will not be overruled on appeal. Ingram v. Ingram, 130 Va. 329, 107 S.E. 653 (1921). See Kraker v. Shields, 61 Va. (20 Gratt.) 377 (1871); Bowers v. Bowers, 70 Va. (29 Gratt.) 697 (1878); Stuart, Palmer & Co. v. Hendricks, 80 Va. 601 (1885); Dermott v. Carter, 151 Va. 81, 144 S.E. 602 (1928); Mitchell v. Cox, 189 Va. 236, 52 S.E.2d 105 (1949); Henderson v. Henderson, 190 Va. 805, 58 S.E.2d 77 (1950); Kramer Bros. Co. v. Powers, 195 Va. 131, 77 S.E.2d 468 (1953).

The report of a commissioner in chancery is entitled to respect and to a greater weight where the evidence has been taken in his presence. However, it is the duty of the court to review and weigh the evidence, and if in its opinion such report is unsupported by the evidence, to reject it. Jacobs v. Jacobs, 184 Va. 281, 35 S.E.2d 119 (1945).

It is established in Virginia that the conclusions of a commissioner, where the evidence has been taken in his presence, should be sustained unless it plainly appears, upon a fair and full review, that the weight of the evidence is contrary to his findings. Although the trial court is given power of review over his findings, it cannot arbitrarily disturb the report, if it is supported by sufficient proof. Hudson v. Clark, 200 Va. 325, 106 S.E.2d 133 (1958); Newton v. Newton, 202 Va. 96, 116 S.E.2d 94 (1960); McGrue v. Brownfield, 202 Va. 418, 117 S.E.2d 701 (1961); Thrasher v. Thrasher, 202 Va. 594, 118 S.E.2d 820 (1961).

The practice is to accept the report as prima facie correct. Raiford v. Raiford, 193 Va. 221, 68 S.E.2d 888 (1952).

A report of a commissioner in chancery, on questions of fact, is deemed to be prima facie correct and entitled to great weight, although it does not bind the court like the verdict of a jury. Eppes v. Eppes, 181 Va. 970, 27 S.E.2d 164 (1943).

The report of a master in chancery, except as to errors appearing on its face, is prima facie correct when the evidence is conflicting. Buckle v. Marshall, 176 Va. 139, 10 S.E.2d 506 (1940).

Commissioner's conclusions may not be arbitrarily disturbed. — Though the court is by this section given broad power of review over the findings of the commissioner, in so doing it is required to apply correct principles of law in evaluating the evidence and may not arbitrarily disturb the report if supported by competent and preponderating proof. The conclusion of the commissioner should not be upset unless upon a fair and full review according to correct principles of law it appears that the weight of the evidence is contrary to his finding. Leckie v. Lynchburg Trust & Sav. Bank, 191 Va. 360, 60 S.E.2d 923 (1950); Shepheard v. Boggs, 198 Va. 299, 94 S.E.2d 300 (1956).

And Commissioner's report should not be disturbed unless not supported by evidence. — Commissioner's report is entitled to great weight and should not be disturbed unless its conclusions are unsupported by the evidence; and this rule applies with special force when the findings of the commissioner have been approved by the trial court. Surf Realty Corp. v. Standing, 195 Va. 431, 78 S.E.2d 901 (1953); Pavlock v. Gallop, 207 Va. 989, 154 S.E.2d 153 (1967).

While the report of a commissioner in chancery does not carry the weight of a jury's verdict, it should be sustained unless it plainly appears, upon a fair and full review, that his findings are not supported by the evidence. Strauss v. Princess Anne Marine & Bulkheading Co., 209 Va. 217, 163 S.E.2d 198 (1968).

Though a commissioner's report is not entitled to the weight of a jury verdict, yet where it has been confirmed the judgment confirming it should be set aside only because contrary to the evidence or the result of applying wrong principles of law. Hodge v. Kennedy, 198 Va. 416, 94 S.E.2d 274 (1956); Hoffecker v. Hoffecker, 200 Va. 119, 104 S.E.2d 771 (1958).

The conclusions of the chancellor should not be upset unless, upon a fair and full review according to correct principles of law, it appears that the weight of the evidence is contrary to his finding. Higgins v. Higgins, 205 Va. 324, 136 S.E.2d 793 (1964).

But courts should review the report if fairly challenged. — Under the influence of this section, the court has said that a report of a commissioner approved by the trial court is prima facie correct, or is entitled to great weight, or should not be disturbed unless its conclusions are at variance with the evidence. It is fundamental that, notwithstanding the weight due a commissioner's report and the respect which is accorded his findings, neither the trial court nor this court should avoid the duty of weighing the evidence when its sufficiency is fairly challenged. Gilmer v. Brown, 186 Va. 630, 44 S.E.2d 16 (1947); Hoffecker v. Hoffecker, 200 Va. 119, 104 S.E.2d 771 (1958).

And court has duty to review evidence and examine conclusions when report objected to. — When reports of commissioners in chancery are objected to, it is the duty of the court to examine the evidence returned by the commissioner, and upon which his conclusions are based, and review his conclusions. If the evidence consists of depositions which have been taken by the commissioner, or in his presence, and is conflicting, and his conclusions are clearly supported by competent and unimpeached witnesses, his report will not be disturbed, unless it is clear that the weight of the testimony is contrary to his conclusions. But, even in such case, the court will review and weigh the evidence, and, if not satisfied with the findings of the commissioner, will overrule them. The report will only be accepted as conclusive when the testimony, though conflicting, is evenly balanced, and the report is supported by the testimony of competent and unimpeached witnesses. Diebold & Sons' Stone Co. v. Tatteson, 115 Va. 766, 80 S.E. 585 (1914). See also, Hall v. Hall, 104 Va. 773, 52 S.E. 557 (1906); Herrell v. Board, 113 Va. 594, 75 S.E. 87 (1912).

And when report is overturned, appellate court should review evidence. — In view of this section, the Supreme Court, when the report of the commissioner is overturned by the trial court, must review the evidence and ascertain whether it supports the holding of the commissioner or that of the trial court. Parkes v. Gunter, 168 Va. 94, 190 S.E. 159 (1937).

Individual and extrajudicial knowledge on the part of a judge will not dispense with proof of facts not judicially cognizable, and cannot be resorted to for the purpose of supplementing the record. Newton v. Newton, 202 Va. 96, 116 S.E.2d 94 (1960).

Decree based on commissioner's report is not given weight of jury verdict. — Where the evidence adduced was heard by a commissioner in chancery and not ore tenus by the chancellor the decree of the trial court, while presumed to be correct, is not given the same weight on appeal as a jury verdict. Hoffecker v. Hoffecker, 200 Va. 119, 104 S.E.2d 771 (1958).

§ 8.01-611. Notice of time and place of taking account. — The court, ordering an account to be taken, may direct that notice of the time and place of taking it be published once a week for two successive weeks in a newspaper meeting the requirements of § 8.01-324, and may also require notice to be served on the parties in the manner set forth in the Rules of Court for the taking of depositions. (Code 1950, § 8-251; 1977, c. 617.)

REVISERS' NOTE

Former § 8-251 has been updated. The clause stating that publication shall be equivalent to personal service has been removed as being constitutionally suspect; to insure more adequate notice, a provision has been added to permit mailing or delivering the notice of the time and place of taking the account to counsel of record and to a party having no counsel.

Cross references. — For general sections on orders of publication, see § 8.01-316 et seq. As to notice requirements for depositions, see Rules 4:2, 4:5, 4:6, and 4:7.

I. DECISIONS UNDER PRIOR LAW.

Editor's note. — The cases cited below were decided under corresponding provisions of former law. The term "this section," as used below, refers to former provisions.

Class of cases to which this section applies not limited. — This section does not limit the class of cases in which a court of equity may direct that notice be given for hearings before its commissioners. Hill v. Bowyer, 59 Va. (18 Gratt.) 364 (1868); Goins v. Garber, 131 Va. 59, 108 S.E. 868 (1921).

Guardian ad litem must have notice. — It is erroneous to proceed to the taking of accounts where the notice was served on minors by publication, the guardian ad litem not being named therein, nor otherwise served with notice. Strayer v. Long, 83 Va. 715, 3 S.E. 372 (1887).

Time required between publication and hearing. — When notice of taking an account is ordered to be given by publication in a newspaper under this section, there must be at least twenty-eight days (now fourteen days) between the first insertion and the day of taking the account. Dillard v. Krise, 86 Va. 410, 10 S.E. 430 (1889).

§ 8.01-612. Commissioner may summons witnesses. — A commissioner in chancery, to whom has been referred any matter, may compel the attendance of all needed witnesses by summons. A summonsed witness who fails to attend shall be reported to the court for appropriate contempt proceedings. (Code 1950, § 8-252; 1977, c. 617.)

REVISERS' NOTE

Section 8.01-612 changes former § 8-252 by making the court solely responsible for the punishment of witnesses who fail to respond to a summons initiated by a commissioner in chancery.

I. DECISIONS UNDER PRIOR LAW.

Editor's note. — The case cited below was decided under corresponding provisions of former law. The term "this section," as used below, refers to former provisions.

Section inapplicable to proceeding under § 8.01-506. — This section was inapplicable to the special proceeding authorized by former § 8.01-506 to ascertain the assets of a judgment debtor. Early Used Cars, Inc. v. Province, 218 Va. 605, 239 S.E.2d 98 (1977).

§ **8.01-613. Commissioner may ask instructions of court.** — A commissioner, who has doubts as to any point which arises before him, may, in writing, submit the point to the court, who may instruct him thereon. (Code 1950, § 8-253; 1977, c. 617.)

§ **8.01-614. His power to adjourn his proceedings.** — A commissioner in chancery may adjourn his proceedings from time to time, after the day to which notice was given, without any new notice, until his report is completed; and, when it is completed, it may be filed in the clerk's office at any time thereafter. The commissioner may, if it shall appear to him necessary, adjourn such proceedings, to any place within the Commonwealth, and there continue such proceedings and take depositions and other evidence in like manner and with like force and effect as if the same were done in the place where he was appointed, and the commissioner shall have the power to compel the attendance of witnesses before him in the manner prescribed by § 8.01-612. (Code 1950, §§ 8-254, 8-255; 1977, c. 617.)

REVISERS' NOTE

This section combines and condenses former §§ 8-254 and 8-255 without substantive change.

Former § 8-256 (How report to be made out ...) is to be deleted as the matters set forth are largely addressed by the Rules of Court. (See Rule 2:18). Costs are currently provided under chapter 3 in Title 14.1 (Costs, Etc.).

§ **8.01-615. When cause heard on report; time for filing exceptions.** — A cause may be heard by the court upon a commissioner's report. Subject to the Rules of Court regarding dispensing with notice of taking proofs and other proceedings, reasonable notice of such hearing shall be given to counsel of record and to parties not represented by counsel. Exceptions to the commissioner's report shall be filed within ten days after the report has been filed with the court, or for good cause shown, at a later time specified by the court.

This section shall not apply to the report of a commissioner appointed to sell property; in such cases the report of such commissioner, when filed in the clerk's office, shall be either confirmed, modified, or rejected forthwith. (Code 1950, § 8-257; 1958, c. 67; 1977, c. 617; 1978, c. 237; 1981, c. 500; 1982, c. 339.)

REVISERS' NOTE

Section 8.01-615 eliminates the requirement in former § 8-257 that the commissioner's report generally must lie in the clerk's office for ten days before there can be a hearing. This requirement is no longer considered necessary.

The court can provide for reasonable notice of a hearing. The second paragraph permits the confirmation, without notice, of a commissioner's report regarding the sale of property.

I. Decisions Under Current Law.
II. Decisions Under Prior Law.

I. DECISIONS UNDER CURRENT LAW.

Report of commissioner in chancery prima facie correct. — Except as to error which appears on the face of the report of the commissioner or on the face of the decree of the trial court, a report of a commissioner in chancery is prima facie correct. Dodge v. Dodge, 2 Va. App. 238, 343 S.E.2d 363 (1986).

The trial court's decree is presumed correct; however, where the evidence is heard by a commissioner and not ore tenus by the trial court, the decree is not given the same weight as a jury verdict. If such decrees are supported by substantial, competent and credible evidence in depositions, they will not be overturned on appeal. Dodge v. Dodge, 2 Va. App. 238, 343 S.E.2d 363 (1986).

II. DECISIONS UNDER PRIOR LAW.

Editor's note. — The case cited below was decided under corresponding provisions of former law. The term "this provision," as used below, refers to former provisions.

The purpose of this provision is to prevent vexatious delays and to facilitate the placing and decision of chancery causes. Hughes v. Harvey, 75 Va. 200 (1881).

§ 8.01-616. Delivery of original papers of suit by clerk to commissioner. — The clerk of a court shall, upon the request of any commissioner in chancery who has before him for execution an order made in such action, deliver to him the original papers thereof; and it shall not be necessary for the clerk to copy such papers, nor shall he charge any fee for copies of any of them, unless the same be specially ordered. The commissioner to whom such papers may be delivered, shall give his receipt therefor, and return the papers as speedily as possible to the office of the clerk of the court. (Code 1950, § 8-258; 1977, c. 617.)

§ 8.01-617. Settlement of accounts of special receivers and special commissioners. — Every circuit court, by an order entered of record, shall appoint one of its commissioners in chancery, who shall hold office at its pleasure, to state and settle the accounts of all special receivers and of all special commissioners holding funds or evidences of debt subject to the order of the court.

All special receivers and special commissioners shall, unless their accounts have been previously verified and approved by the court, and ordered to be recorded, with reasonable promptness, and not longer than four months after any money in their hands should be distributed or at other intervals specified by the court, present to such commissioner in chancery an accurate statement of all receipts and disbursements, duly signed and supported by proper vouchers; and the commissioner in chancery shall examine and verify the same, and attach his certificate thereto approving it, if it is correct, or stating any errors or inaccuracies therein, and file same in the cause in which the special receiver or special commissioner was appointed, and present the same to the court.

The court may at any time appoint any of its other commissioners in chancery to perform the duties herein required in any case in which the regular commissioner in chancery appointed hereunder is himself the special receiver or special commissioner whose accounts are to be settled.

For his services performed hereunder the commissioner in chancery shall receive such compensation as the court allows, to be paid out of the fund in the hands of the special receiver or special commissioner.

If any special receiver or special commissioner fails to make settlement as herein required within the time herein provided, he shall forfeit his compensation, or so much thereof as the court orders.

The court may order its general receiver also to state and settle his accounts in the manner herein provided. When a general receiver settles his accounts before a commissioner of accounts or commissioner in chancery, fees charged by the commissioner are to be reasonable but may not exceed $100 per general receiver settlement or $1 per disbursement made by the general receiver as reflected in the settlement, whichever is greater. (Code 1950, § 8-259; 1977, c. 617; 1988, c. 553.)

I. DECISIONS UNDER PRIOR LAW.

Editor's note. — The case cited below was decided under corresponding provisions of former law.

Failure to comply with court order requiring payment of money is contempt. — A failure without legal excuse on the part of a special commissioner of the court to comply with a court order requiring the payment of money is a contempt and a commitment for failure to obey such an order is not imprisonment for debt. French v. Pobst, 203 Va. 704, 127 S.E.2d 137 (1962).

§ 8.01-618. Reports of such settlements; when new bond required. — The court shall examine the reports required by § 8.01-617, when the same are made to it; and, if satisfied of the correctness thereof, shall order them to be recorded. If it appears from the report of the commissioner that any bond of a receiver, or any bond or other security given by any person to whom money has been loaned under its order, is insufficient, the court shall order additional security to be given, or a new bond to be executed before it, in such penalty as may seem right, and with sufficient sureties. But the execution of such new bond shall not discharge the sureties in any prior bond for their liability for acts of the principal obligor done previous to the execution of such new bond. (Code 1950, § 8-260; 1977, c. 617.)

§ 8.01-618.1. Fees of special receivers and commissioners for reports. — Special receivers and commissioners may charge, for the reports made under § 8.01-617, the same fees allowed by law to commissioners in chancery for other reports, to be paid out of the fund in court, and charged to the respective cases therein, in such proportions as the court deems appropriate. (Code 1950, § 8-262; 1977, c. 624, § 14.1-133.1; 1998, c. 872.)

§ 8.01-619. Recordation of reports of such settlements. — The circuit court clerk shall record reports of receivers and commissioners when approved by the court, in a fiduciary book and properly index same to show the name of the receiver or commissioner and also the style of the suit in which the report is made; and such book shall be kept as a public record in the office of the clerk. (Code 1950, § 8-261; 1977, c. 617.)

REVISERS' NOTE

Section 8.01-619 alters former § 8-261 by providing that the clerk shall file the commissioner's reports after approval by the court in "a fiduciary" book (some clerk's offices apparently do not maintain the "Settlement of Receivers and Commissioners" books called for under the former statute).

Former § 8-262 (Fees of clerks and Commissioners) was transferred to Title 14.1.

CHAPTER 24.

INJUNCTIONS.

Sec.	
8.01-620.	General jurisdiction of circuit court to award injunctions.
8.01-621.	[Repealed.]
8.01-622.	Injunction to protect plaintiff in suit for specific property.
8.01-622.1.	Injunction against assisted suicide; damages; professional sanctions.
8.01-623.	Injunction against decree subject to bill of review; limitations to bill of review.

Sec.		Sec.	
8.01-624.	Duration of temporary injunctions to be fixed therein.	8.01-629.	Notice required.
8.01-625.	Dissolution of injunctions.	8.01-630.	Forthcoming bond in connection with injunction against removal of property.
8.01-626.	When court grants or refuses injunction, justice of Supreme Court or judge of Court of Appeals may review it.	8.01-631.	Injunction bond.
		8.01-631.1.	Environmental injunction; financial capacity.
8.01-627.	To what clerk order for injunction directed.	8.01-632.	How surety in forthcoming bond may obtain additional security.
8.01-628.	Equity of prayer for temporary injunction to be shown by affidavit or otherwise.	8.01-633.	Damages on dissolution.
		8.01-634.	Dismissal of injunction bill.

§ 8.01-620. General jurisdiction of circuit court to award injunctions.

— Every circuit court shall have jurisdiction to award injunctions, including cases involving violations of the Uniform Statewide Building Code, whether the judgment or proceeding enjoined be in or out of the circuit, or the party against whose proceedings the injunction be asked resides in or out of the circuit. (Code 1950, § 8-610; 1977, c. 617; 1995, c. 310.)

Cross references. — See also § 8.01-40 (unauthorized use of person's name or picture); § 8.01-495 (executions); § 8.01-123 (damages to property detained under injunction to judgment for specific property); § 8.01-549 (attachments); § 8.01-495 (executions on judgments); As to jurisdiction of circuit courts generally, see § 17.1-513. § 38.2-1507 (liquidation of insurance companies); §§ 48-7 through 48-15 (houses of prostitution); § 56-6 (against public service corporation). For rules of court governing equity practice and procedure, in general, see Rules 2:1 through 2:21.

I. Decisions Under Current Law.
II. Decisions Under Prior Law.

I. DECISIONS UNDER CURRENT LAW.

Ripeness required. — Where a suit attempted to mount a collateral attack on state court judgments, which the federal district court lacked jurisdiction to hear, and, further, assumed that the Virginia courts would not follow the Constitution, an assumption that raised issues not yet ripe for decision, such claims would be dismissed for lack of subject matter and supplemental jurisdiction, respectively. Jordahl v. Democratic Party, 947 F. Supp. 236 (W.D. Va. 1996), aff'd, 122 F.3d 192 (4th Cir. 1997).

Claims in federal district court properly dismissed. — Claims under 42 U.S.C. § 1983 for alleged injuries caused by state court injunctions enjoining plaintiffs from distributing voters guides were properly dismissed by the federal district court under the Rooker-Feldman doctrine, which prohibits United States district courts from sitting in direct review of state court decisions, except for habeas corpus actions. Jordahl v. Democratic Party, 122 F.3d 192 (4th Cir. 1997).

II. DECISIONS UNDER PRIOR LAW.

Editor's note. — The cases cited below were decided under corresponding provisions of former law. The term "this section," as used below, refers to former provisions.

This section gives the judge jurisdiction only to award the injunction, not to hear and determine the cause. Randolph v. Tucker, 37 Va. (10 Leigh) 655 (1840).

Applied in Fralin & Waldron, Inc. v. City of Martinsville, 493 F.2d 481 (4th Cir. 1974).

§ 8.01-621: Repealed by Acts 1987, c. 567.

Cross references. — As to venue in proceedings to award an injunction, see subdivision 15 of § 8.01-261.

§ 8.01-622. Injunction to protect plaintiff in suit for specific property.

— An injunction may be awarded to protect any plaintiff in a suit for specific property, pending either at law or in equity, against injury from the sale, removal, or concealment of such property. (Code 1950, § 8-612; 1977, c. 617.)

Cross references. — As to recovery of damages upon dissolution of injunction, see § 8.01-123.

§ 8.01-622.1. Injunction against assisted suicide; damages; professional sanctions. — A. Any person who knowingly and intentionally, with the purpose of assisting another person to commit or attempt to commit suicide, (i) provides the physical means by which another person commits or attempts to commit suicide or (ii) participates in a physical act by which another person commits or attempts to commit suicide shall be liable for damages as provided in this section and may be enjoined from such acts.

B. A cause of action for injunctive relief against any person who is reasonably expected to assist or attempt to assist a suicide may be maintained by any person who is the spouse, parent, child, sibling or guardian of, or a current or former licensed health care provider of, the person who would commit suicide; by a Commonwealth's attorney with appropriate jurisdiction; or by the Attorney General. The injunction shall prevent the person from assisting any suicide in the Commonwealth.

C. A spouse, parent, child or sibling of a person who commits or attempts to commit suicide may recover compensatory and exemplary damages in a civil action from any person who provided the physical means for the suicide or attempted suicide or who participated in a physical act by which the other person committed or attempted to commit suicide.

D. A licensed health care provider who assists or attempts to assist a suicide shall be considered to have engaged in unprofessional conduct for which his certificate or license to provide health care services in the Commonwealth shall be suspended or revoked by the licensing authority.

E. Nothing in this section shall be construed to limit or conflict with § 54.1-2971.01 or the Health Care Decisions Act (§ 54.1-2981 et seq.). This section shall not apply to a licensed health care provider who (i) administers, prescribes or dispenses medications or procedures to relieve another person's pain or discomfort and without intent to cause death, even if the medication or procedure may hasten or increase the risk of death, or (ii) withholds or withdraws life-prolonging procedures as defined in § 54.1-2982. This section shall not apply to any person who properly administers a legally prescribed medication without intent to cause death, even if the medication may hasten or increase the risk of death.

F. For purposes of this section:

"Licensed health care provider" means a physician, surgeon, podiatrist, osteopath, osteopathic physician and surgeon, physician assistant, nurse, dentist or pharmacist licensed under the laws of this Commonwealth.

"Suicide" means the act or instance of taking one's own life voluntarily and intentionally. (1998, c. 624.)

Cross references. — For provisions authorizing a physician to prescribe a dosage of a pain-relieving agent in excess of the recommended dosage in certain cases, see §§ 54.1-2971.01, 54.1-3408.1. For the Health Care Decisions Act, see § 54.1-2981 et seq. For provision that the witholding or withdrawal of life-prolonging procedures in accordance with the provisions of the Health Care Decisions Act shall not, for any purpose, constitute a suicide, see § 54.1-2991.

§ 8.01-623. Injunction against decree subject to bill of review; limitations to bill of review.

— A court allowing a bill of review may award an injunction to the decree to be reviewed. But no bill of review shall be allowed to a final decree, unless it be exhibited within six months next after such decree, except that a person under a disability as defined in § 8.01-2 may exhibit the same within six months after the removal of his or her disability. In no case shall such a bill be filed without the leave of court first obtained, unless it be for error of law apparent upon the face of the record. (Code 1950, § 8-613; 1977, c. 617.)

REVISERS' NOTE

The language "... an infant or insane person ..." in former § 8-613 has been replaced with the language "... a person under a disability as defined in § 8.01-2."

I. Decisions Under Current Law.
II. Decisions Under Prior Law.

I. DECISIONS UNDER CURRENT LAW.

A bill of review is limited in scope and is rarely utilized in Virginia procedure. Indeed, in modern appellate practice wherein most litigants have a statutory right to appeal from judgments of trial courts, use of a bill of review is discouraged. Nonetheless, it remains an available procedural device until abolished by the General Assembly. Blunt v. Lentz, 241 Va. 547, 404 S.E.2d 62 (1991).

Trial court was required to examine both record and decree. — Where bill of review identified, with the requisite degree of accuracy and definiteness, errors of law which allegedly were in the record and in the decree, the trial court was required to examine both the record and the decree to determine whether errors of law existed. By limiting its examination to whether errors of law existed upon face of the decree, the trial court erred because it failed to examine both the decree and the record. Blunt v. Lentz, 241 Va. 547, 404 S.E.2d 62 (1991).

II. DECISIONS UNDER PRIOR LAW.

Editor's note. — The cases cited below were decided under corresponding provisions of former law. The terms "the statute" and "this section," as used below, refer to former provisions.

"Bill of review" defined. — A bill of review is a bill filed to reverse or modify a decree that has been signed and enrolled for error in law apparent upon the face of such decree or on account of new facts discovered since publication was passed in the original cause, and which could not by the exercise of due diligence have been discovered or used before the decree was made. Phipps v. Wise Hotel Co., 116 Va. 739, 82 S.E. 681 (1914).

The office of a bill of review is to have the trial court reexamine a previous final decree in the cause and to accomplish a reversal, modification or nullification of the decree. Rice v. Standard Prods. Co., 199 Va. 380, 99 S.E.2d 529 (1901).

Courts are reluctant to reverse decrees on such bills. — Unless parties can be placed in status quo, courts are properly reluctant to reverse decrees on bill of review unless the errors complained of are clear and have been specifically excepted to and pointed out in the original proceedings. Powers v. Howard, 131 Va. 275, 108 S.E. 687 (1921).

A bill of review lies only to a final decree. Roanoke Nat'l Bank v. Farmers' Nat'l Bank, 84 Va. 603, 5 S.E. 682 (1888); Diffendal v. Virginia Midland R.R., 86 Va. 459, 10 S.E. 536 (1890); Epes v. Williams, 89 Va. 794, 17 S.E. 235 (1893); Diamond State Iron Co. v. Rarig & Co., 93 Va. 595, 25 S.E. 894 (1896); Dellinger v. Foltz, 93 Va. 729, 25 S.E. 998 (1896).

What is a final decree. — A decree which disposes of the whole subject and gives all the relief that was contemplated, so that nothing remains to be done in the cause, is a final decree. Vanmeter v. Vanmeter, 44 Va. (3 Gratt.) 148 (1846); Jones v. Turner, 81 Va. 709 (1886); Parker v. Logan Bros. & Co., 82 Va. 376, 4 S.E. 613 (1886); Yates v. Wilson, 86 Va. 625, 10 S.E. 976 (1890).

Exception when there is clerical error in consent decree. — A decree or order made by consent of the counsel for the parties cannot be set aside by bill of review, unless by clerical error something was inserted in the order to which the party had not consented, in which case a bill of review might lie. Prince v. McLemore, 108 Va. 269, 61 S.E. 802 (1908).

A bill of review must be filed within the time prescribed by this section and the limitation there prescribed is not subject to any exceptions not contained in the statute. No inherent equity can create an exception where the statute makes none, and a mere want of knowledge of a creditor is insufficient to suspend the operation of the statute. Matthews & Co. v. Progress Distilling Co., 108 Va. 777, 62 S.E. 924 (1908); Searles v. Gordon, 156 Va. 289, 157 S.E. 759 (1931).

It is not necessary to plead the statutory limitations against a bill of review. It ought to appear in the bill itself that it is exhibited within the time prescribed by law, or that the complainant is protected by some of the savings in the statute. Otherwise it ought not to be received. And if the fact alleged to prevent the operation of the decree be not true, it may be denied by the answer of the other party. On the proofs, if it is shown not to be true, the bill of review should be rejected. Shepherd v. Larue, 20 Va. (6 Munf.) 529 (1820).

Who may file. — A bill of review can only be filed by a person who was a party or privy to the former suit. Even persons having an interest in the cause, if not aggrieved by the particular errors assigned in the decree, cannot maintain a bill of review, however injuriously the decree may affect the rights of third parties. Armstead v. Bailey, 83 Va. 242, 2 S.E. 38 (1887); Heermans v. Montague, 2 Va. Dec. 6, 20 S.E. 899 (1890); Gibson v. Green, 89 Va. 524, 16 S.E. 661 (1893).

A bill of review does not lie for assignees. Armstead v. Bailey, 83 Va. 242, 2 S.E. 38 (1887); Gibson v. Green, 89 Va. 524, 16 S.E. 661 (1893).

On a bill of review by an infant, the infant is entitled to show any good cause existing, at date of rendition, against the original decree against him. Pracht & Co. v. Lange, 81 Va. 711 (1886). See also, Zirkle v. McCue, 67 Va. (26 Gratt.) 517 (1875); Morriss v. Virginia Ins. Co., 85 Va. 588, 8 S.E. 383 (1888).

This section extends the time in which infants may file a bill of review, but it does not authorize them to attack decrees as a general rule upon any grounds except those which would be available to other parties. Powers v. Howard, 131 Va. 275, 108 S.E. 687 (1921).

Grounds for review in general. — In Virginia, as elsewhere, the general rule is that a final decree cannot be reheard except upon two grounds: (1) error apparent on the face of the record, or (2) after-discovered evidence. Gills v. Gills, 126 Va. 526, 101 S.E. 900 (1920).

Only two grounds are available for a bill of review, viz.: (1) for error of law apparent on the face of the record, or (2) newly discovered evidence. Rice v. Standard Prods. Co., 199 Va. 380, 99 S.E.2d 529 (1957).

Error apparent on record as ground. — Error apparent upon the face of the record is not restricted to error in the decree. To determine on bill of review whether or not error of law exists, the court will examine the bill and answer filed in the cause, all orders and decrees made and entered therein, and all other proceedings, to ascertain whether upon the whole case error of law has been committed. Hancock v. Hutcherson, 76 Va. 609 (1882); Pracht & Co. v. Lange, 81 Va. 711 (1886); Valz v. Coiner, 110 Va. 467, 66 S.E. 730 (1909); Gills v. Gills, 126 Va. 526, 101 S.E. 900 (1920); Powers v. Howard, 131 Va. 275, 108 S.E. 687 (1921).

If error of law be apparent from an inspection of the record in the cause, and a final decree has been entered, a proper case for a bill of review is presented. Powers v. Howard, 131 Va. 275, 108 S.E. 687 (1921). See also, Gray v. Francis, 139 Va. 350, 124 S.E. 446 (1924).

On a bill of review attacking a final decree for error of law on the face of the record the court cannot consider the sufficiency or insufficiency of the proofs beyond the evidence of statement of facts recited in the decree. Rice v. Standard Prods. Co., 199 Va. 380, 99 S.E.2d 529 (1957).

In a suit to determine riparian boundaries, no error was apparent from the face of the record which could be reached by bill of review. Rice v. Standard Prods. Co., 199 Va. 380, 99 S.E.2d 529 (1957).

The action of the court in overruling a motion to force production of further evidence, made after both parties had rested and counsel had argued, should have been questioned by petition to rehear or appeal rather than by bill of review. Rice v. Standard Prods. Co., 199 Va. 380, 99 S.E.2d 529 (1957).

Bill should be denied when errors not apparent. — A bill of review ought to specify with some degree of accuracy and definiteness the errors relied upon. Thus, where it nowhere appears that the action of the court relied upon as ground for the bill of review was excepted to, and there was nothing upon the face of the record to show that such action was erroneous, the bill cannot be entertained on that ground. Phipps v. Wise Hotel Co., 116 Va. 739, 82 S.E. 681 (1914); Powers v. Howard, 131 Va. 275, 108 S.E. 687 (1921).

Also, for errors of judgment. — When the errors sought to be corrected by a bill of review are not errors of law but errors of judgment in the determination of facts the bill should be denied. The only remedy in such case is by appeal. Rawlings v. Rawlings, 75 Va. 76 (1880); Hancock v. Hutcherson, 76 Va. 609 (1882); Kern v. Wyatt, 89 Va. 885, 17 S.E. 549 (1893); Rice v. Standard Prods. Co., 199 Va. 380, 99 S.E.2d 529 (1957).

Newly discovered evidence as ground. — A bill of review for newly discovered evidence will not lie where the evidence is simply confirmatory or cumulative. It must be decisive in its character, and such as would, if true, produce a different decree upon rehearing, and must be evidence of which the party was ignorant at the time of the decree, and could not have learned by the exercise of reasonable diligence. Harman v. McMullin, 85 Va. 187, 7 S.E. 349 (1888); Reynolds v. Reynolds, 88 Va. 149, 13 S.E. 395 (1891); Kern v. Wyatt, 89 Va. 885, 17 S.E. 549 (1893); Durbin v. Roanoke Bldg. Co., 108 Va. 468, 62 S.E. 339 (1908); Becker v. Johnson, 111 Va. 245, 68 S.E. 986 (1910); Sutherland v. Gent, 111 Va. 511, 69 S.E. 340 (1910); Phipps v. Wise Hotel Co., 116 Va. 739, 82 S.E. 681 (1914); Goode v. Bryant, 118 Va. 314, 87 S.E. 588 (1916); Gills v. Gills, 126 Va. 526, 101 S.E. 900 (1920).

Leave of court necessary when bill based on newly discovered facts. — There need be no leave of court to file a bill of review based on error of law, but such leave is necessary when the bill of review is based on newly discovered facts. Hatcher v. Hatcher, 77 Va. 600 (1883); Heermans v. Montague, 2 Va. Dec. 6, 20 S.E. 899 (1890).

Illustrative cases. — A deposition was excepted to on the ground that the witness making it was incapable of testifying, and the commissioner, without specifically passing upon the objection, plainly indicated that he gave no weight or effect to the deposition. The decree expressly mentioned the deposition and exception, and in terms clearly sustained the latter. It was held that this action clearly appeared upon the face of the record, and if it is error and material, it is not a conclusion of fact depending upon the evidence, but is an error of law, which may be taken advantage of by bill of review. Powers v. Howard, 131 Va. 275, 108 S.E. 687 (1921).

It is not ground for a bill of review that the party was prevented from proving important facts by the wrong advice of counsel; nor that counsel was prevented by illness from attending the trial. Franklin v. Wilkinson, 17 Va. (3 Munf.) 112 (1812).

That certain documentary evidence intended to be used in the original cause was lost or mislaid by the complainant's counsel, and could not be found till after the hearing is no ground for a bill of review. Jones v. Pilcher, 20 Va. (6 Munf.) 425 (1819).

An error in determining the ownership of attached property is one in fact, and not one of law and cannot be a subject of a bill of review. Kern v. Wyatt, 89 Va. 885, 17 S.E. 549 (1893).

Effect of injunction. — When upon filing a bill of review, an injunction against the decree to be reversed has been granted, and all that was done in the suit has been set aside, the effect is to leave all the issues presented in that record undetermined to await the final decree of the court upon the bill of review. The former decree cannot be pleaded anywhere as a final adjudication of the controversy. Sutherland v. Gent, 111 Va. 511, 69 S.E. 340 (1910).

§ 8.01-624. Duration of temporary injunctions to be fixed therein. — When any court authorized to award injunctions shall grant a temporary injunction, either with or without notice to the adverse party, such court shall prescribe in the injunction order the time during which such injunction shall be effective and at the expiration of that time such injunction shall stand dissolved unless, before the expiration thereof, it be enlarged. Such injunction may be enlarged or a further injunction granted by the court in which the cause is pending or by the court to whom the bill is addressed in the event the cause be not matured, after reasonable notice to the adverse party, or to his attorney of record of the time and place of moving for the same. (Code 1950, § 8-614; 1977, c. 617.)

REVISERS' NOTE

The words "at law or in fact" following "attorney" in former § 8-614 have been replaced with "of record."

§ 8.01-625. Dissolution of injunctions. — Any court wherein an injunction has been awarded may at any time when such injunction is in force dissolve the same after reasonable notice to the adverse party, or to his attorney of record, in which notice shall be set forth the grounds upon which such dissolution will be asked, unless such grounds be set forth in an answer previously filed in the case by the party giving such notice. (Code 1950, § 8-615; 1977, c. 617.)

REVISERS' NOTE

The reference in former § 8-615 to the adverse party's attorney-in-fact has been deleted. Other minor language changes have been made.

Former § 8-616 (Records of certain orders in vacation) has been deleted in conformity with the elimination of the distinction between what a court may or may not do in term and vacation.

(See § 8.01-445.) Moreover, it is assumed that the clerk will handle the papers and orders of the case as he does in all other cases.

Former § 8-617 (No appeal from certain orders) has also been deleted, since it is inconsistent with § 8.01-670 which permits an appeal from an interlocutory or a final order granting or dissolving an injunction.

I. DECISIONS UNDER PRIOR LAW.

Editor's note. — The case cited below was decided under corresponding provisions of former law. The term "this section," as used below, refers to former provisions.

Dissolution by circuit court judge when issued by appellate justice. — While an injunction awarded by one of the judges (now justices) of the Supreme Court, after due hearing upon notice, will not be precipitately dissolved under the authority granted by this section, the circuit court, or the judge thereof in vacation, after reasonable notice, has the unquestioned power to dissolve an injunction granted by one of the judges (now justices) of the Supreme Court, who acts, not in an appellate capacity, but as a judge of another court of coordinate jurisdiction. To the extent that the cases of Toll Bridge v. Free Bridge, 22 Va (1 Rand.) 206 (1822), and Wilder v. Kelley, 88 Va. 274, 13 S.E. 483 (1891), are in conflict with this view, they are overruled. Nichols v. Central Va. Power Co., 143 Va. 405, 130 S.E. 764 (1925).

§ 8.01-626. When court grants or refuses injunction, justice of Supreme Court or judge of Court of Appeals may review it. — Wherein a circuit court (i) grants an injunction or (ii) refuses an injunction or (iii) having granted an injunction, dissolves or refuses to enlarge it, an aggrieved party may, within fifteen days of the court's order, present a petition for review to a justice of the Supreme Court; however, if the issue concerning the injunction arose in a case over which the Court of Appeals would have appellate jurisdiction under § 17.1-405 or § 17.1-406, the petition for review shall be initially presented to a judge of the Court of Appeals within fifteen days of the court's order. The petition shall be accompanied by a copy of the proceedings, including the original papers and the court's order respecting the injunction. The justice or judge may take such action thereon as he considers appropriate under the circumstances of the case.

When a judge of the Court of Appeals has initially acted upon a petition for review of an order of a circuit court respecting an injunction, a party aggrieved by such action of the judge of the Court of Appeals may, within fifteen days of the order of the judge of the Court of Appeals, present a petition for review of such order to a justice of the Supreme Court if the case would otherwise be appealable to the Supreme Court in accordance with § 17.1-410. The petition shall be accompanied by a copy of the proceedings before the circuit court, including the original papers and the circuit court's order respecting the injunction, and a copy of the order of the judge of the Court of Appeals from which review is sought. The justice may take such action thereon as he considers appropriate under the circumstances of the case. (Code 1950, § 8-618; 1977, c. 617; 1984, c. 703.)

REVISERS' NOTE

Former § 8-618 provided an extraordinary procedure for review by a single Supreme Court justice of the trial court's action respecting an injunction. Section 8.01-626 alters former § 8-618 in two respects: (1) The presentation of a petition to a single justice shall be within 15 days of the circuit court's order respecting an injunction; (2) The petition may be with respect to an injunction granted by the circuit court as well as an order refusing to grant an injunction or an order dissolving or refusing to enlarge a temporary injunction.

Future development of the interrelationship of the extraordinary procedure of this section and the appeals from granting or dissolution of an injunction under § 8.01-670 et seq. is left to the courts.

Cross references. — For a petition for review pursuant to this section, see Supreme Court Rule 5:17A.

Law Review. — For note discussing the Virginia Judicial Council's intermediate appellate court proposal, see 16 U. Rich. L. Rev. 209 (1982). For an article, "Final and Interlocutory Appeals in Virginia," see 8 Geo. Mason L. Rev. 337 (1999).

I. Decisions Under Current Law.
II. Decisions Under Prior Law.

I. DECISIONS UNDER CURRENT LAW.

Section not substitute for appeal under § 8.01-670. — The summary procedure for review of orders regarding injunctions under this section may not be employed as a substitute for an appeal under § 8.01-670 when a final judgment within the meaning of § 8.01-670 has been entered in the circuit court. Omega Corp. v. Cobb, 222 Va. 875, 292 S.E.2d 44 (1981).

Applied in Omega Corp. v. Malloy, 228 Va. 12, 319 S.E.2d 728 (1984); Reid v. Gholson, 229 Va. 179, 327 S.E.2d 107 (1985).

II. DECISIONS UNDER PRIOR LAW.

Editor's note. — The cases cited below were decided under corresponding provisions of former law. The terms "this statute" and "this section," as used below, refer to former provisions.

Original jurisdiction only when injunction refused by lower court. — This statute confers no original jurisdiction upon one of the judges (now justices) of the Supreme Court to award an injunction, except in the case where the application has been made, first to a judge of an inferior court and has been refused. Mayo v. Haines, 16 Va. (2 Munf.) 423 (1811); Gilliam v. Allen, 22 Va. (1 Rand.) 414 (1823); Randolph v. Randolph, 27 Va. (6 Rand.) 194 (1828); Fredenheim v. Rohr, 87 Va. 764, 13 S.E. 193 (1891).

Procedure. — Where a circuit court judge refuses to award an injunction, the remedy is by application, accompanied by the original papers and the order of refusal, to a judge (now justice) of the Supreme Court, who may review and reverse the action of the circuit court judge, and award the injunction. Wilder v. Kelley, 88 Va. 274, 13 S.E. 483 (1891), overruled in Nichols v. Central Va. Power Co., 143 Va. 405, 130 S.E. 764 (1925), on another point. See also, Fredenheim v. Rohr, 87 Va. 764, 13 S.E. 193 (1891).

Who may grant. — The judges (now justices) of the Supreme Court, or any one of them out of court, have power to award such injunctions, but this power is not possessed by the court itself. Mayo v. Haines, 16 Va. (2 Munf.) 423 (1811).

When an injunction, refused by a judge of a circuit court, is presented to a judge (now justice) of the Supreme Court who also refuses it, the injunction may be awarded by another judge of that court. Jaynes v. Brock, 51 Va. (10 Gratt.) 211 (1853).

Does not affect § 8.01-670. — This section does not take away the right of appeal under § 8.01-670 in a case of equitable relief by injunction. French v. Chapin-Sacks Mfg. Co., 118 Va. 117, 86 S.E. 842 (1915).

§ 8.01-627. To what clerk order for injunction directed. — Every order, awarding an injunction made under § 8.01-620 or § 8.01-626, shall be directed to the clerk of the court which has venue under § 8.01-261 and the proceedings thereupon shall be as if the order has been made by such court. (Code 1950, § 8-619; 1977, c. 617.)

Cross references. — As to venue, see § 8.01-261. As to jurisdiction of circuit courts generally, see § 17.1-513.

§ 8.01-628. Equity of prayer for temporary injunction to be shown by affidavit or otherwise.
— No temporary injunction shall be awarded unless the court shall be satisfied of the plaintiff's equity. (Code 1950, § 8-620; 1977, c. 617.)

I. Decisions Under Current Law.
II. Decisions Under Prior Law.

I. DECISIONS UNDER CURRENT LAW.

Federal standard compared. — There is no great difference between federal and Virginia standards for preliminary injunctions. Both draw upon the same equitable principles. Capital Tool & Mfg. Co. v. Maschinenfabrik Herkules, 837 F.2d 171 (4th Cir. 1988).

Applied in Vardell v. Vardell, 225 Va. 351, 302 S.E.2d 41 (1983).

II. DECISIONS UNDER PRIOR LAW.

Editor's note. — The cases cited below were decided under corresponding provisions of former law. The term "this section," as used below, refers to former provisions.

Affidavit held sufficient. — The affidavit of the president of a corporation that the allegations of the bill of which he has knowledge are true, and that he believes that all other matters stated therein are true, is a sufficient compliance with this section. Southern Ry. v. Washington, A. & M.V. Ry., 102 Va. 483, 46 S.E. 784 (1904).

Error for perpetual injunction to be granted on affidavits. — It is sometimes necessary, from force of circumstances, for preliminary applications for injunctions to be heard upon affidavits only, but the general rule is that, where a case made on a bill for injunction is heard upon the merits, the hearing should be had on depositions regularly taken. It is error for the issues in an injunction suit to be heard and determined upon affidavits and a perpetual injunction granted thereon. Virginian Ry. v. Echols, 117 Va. 182, 83 S.E. 1082 (1915).

§ 8.01-629. Notice required.
— Any court may require that reasonable notice be given to the adverse party, or to his attorney of record, of the time and place of moving for it, before the injunction is granted, if, in the opinion of the court, it be proper that such notice be given. (Code 1950, § 8-621; 1977, c. 617.)

REVISERS' NOTE

Former § 8-621 has been changed by (1) deleting reference to the attorney-in-fact of an adverse party, (2) replacing "attorney-at-law" with the language "attorney of record," and (3) deleting the last sentence as surplusage.

I. DECISIONS UNDER PRIOR LAW.

Editor's note. — The cases cited below were decided under corresponding provisions of former law. The term "this section," as used below, refers to former provisions.

Discretion of court as to notice. — It is obvious from this section that the requirement for notice to defendant before the award of a preliminary injunction rests largely in the discretion of the trial court, and this has always been the approved practice. The cases are rare indeed which justify the awarding of a preliminary injunction without notice to those affected thereby. The ex parte statement of the bill and affidavits usually presented for the complainant in such cases, should not be accepted as justifying the issuance of a preliminary injunction unless necessary to prevent threatened and irreparable damage. Frequently the application is so delayed by the complainant that there is little time for notice, but this delay should impel the judge to whom application is made to scrutinize the alleged reasons therefor with greater care, so as to avoid abuse of the power. Cohen v. Rosen, 157 Va. 71, 160 S.E. 36 (1931).

Notice should usually be given. — Notice of an application for an injunction should always be given to the adverse party except in case of most obvious necessity for prompt action. Bristow v. Catlin, 91 Va. 18, 20 S.E. 946 (1895).

§ 8.01-630. **Forthcoming bond in connection with injunction against removal of property.** — A court awarding an injunction to restrain the removal of property out of this Commonwealth may require bond with security to be given before such officer and in such penalty as the court may direct, with condition to have the property forthcoming to abide the future order or decree of the court and, unless such bond be given, may order the officer serving its process to take possession of the property and keep it until the bond be given or until further order of the court. (Code 1950, § 8-622; 1977, c. 617.)

Cross references. — For general provisions as to forthcoming bonds, see §§ 8.01-526 through 8.01-532. As to bonds taken by courts and officers, generally, see §§ 49-12 through 49-21.

I. DECISIONS UNDER PRIOR LAW.

Editor's note. — The case cited below was decided under corresponding provisions of former law. The term "this section," as used below, refers to former provisions.

Power to require in discretion of court. — The power to require bond is to be exercised, not as a matter of course, but of sound discretion, according to circumstances. Holliday v. Coleman, 16 Va. (2 Munf.) 162 (1811).

§ 8.01-631. **Injunction bond.** — Except in the case of a fiduciary or any other person from whom in the opinion of the court awarding an injunction it may be improper or unnecessary to require bond, no injunction shall take effect until bond be given in such penalty as the court awarding it may direct, with condition either to pay the judgment or decree, proceedings on which are enjoined, or to pay the value of the property levied on by the officer, when there has been a levy, or to have the property forthcoming to abide the future order or decree of court, and, in either case, to pay all such costs as may be awarded against the party obtaining the injunction, and all such damages as may be incurred, in case the injunction shall be dissolved, and with a further condition, if a forthcoming bond has been given under such judgment or decree, to indemnify and save harmless the sureties in such forthcoming bond and their representatives against all loss or damage in consequence of such suretyship, or, if the injunction be not to proceedings on a judgment or decree, with such condition as the court or judge may prescribe. The bond shall be given before the clerk of the court in which the judgment or decree is, and, in other cases, before the clerk of the court in which the suit is, wherein the injunction is awarded.

For any temporary or permanent injunction sought by, or awarded to, the Commonwealth, or any of its officers or agencies, no bond shall be required. (Code 1950, § 8-623; 1976, c. 238; 1977, c. 617.)

REVISERS' NOTE

The last two sentences of former § 8-623 have been deleted since they have no modern utility. Minor language changes have been made.

Cross references. — For provisions as to bonds taken by courts and officers, in general, see §§ 49-12 through 49-21.

I. DECISIONS UNDER PRIOR LAW.

Editor's note. — The cases cited below were decided under corresponding provisions of former law. The terms "the statute" and "this section," as used below, refer to former provisions.

Injunction granted without board only in exceptional cases. — It is a very exceptional case in which a court can, without abusing its discretion, grant an injunction to a person, other than a personal representative or some other person suing in a similar representative capacity, without requiring bond. Deeds v. Gilmer, 162 Va. 157, 174 S.E. 37 (1934).

Executors and administrators usually need not give security. — Executors and administrators having given security for their administration are not generally required to give security upon obtaining injunctions. Wilson v. Wilson, 11 Va. (1 Hen. & M.) 16 (1806); Shearman v. Christian, 22 Va. (1 Rand.) 393 (1823); Lomax v. Picot, 23 Va. (2 Rand.) 247 (1824).

Form and conditions of bonds. — An injunction order requiring an injunction bond to be given with condition "according to law" is sufficient authority to the clerk to make the condition "to answer all costs and damages that may be incurred by reason of the suing out the injunction in case the same shall be dissolved," and is a substantial compliance with the provisions of this section directing the court to prescribe the condition of the bond. It is the usual, if not almost the universal, practice of the courts of original jurisdiction to prescribe the conditions of such bonds in this manner when the circumstances are not such as to render special conditions necessary. Columbia Amusement Co. v. Pine Beach Inv. Corp., 109 Va. 325, 63 S.E. 1002 (1909).

Although the condition of an injunction bond is not so extensive, as the statute requires, yet if it contains a material part of the conditions required, the bond is not void, but binds the obligors to the extent of such condition or conditions. When the bond contains some conditions or provisions not required by the statute, and some of those which are required, it is valid and binding to the extent of the latter. Fox v. Mountjoy, 20 Va. (6 Munf.) 36 (1817); White v. Clay, 34 Va. (7 Leigh) 68 (1836); Gillespie v. Thompson, 46 Va. (5 Gratt.) 132 (1848); Pratt v. Wright, 54 Va. (13 Gratt.) 175 (1856); Gibson v. Beckham, 57 Va. (16 Gratt.) 321 (1862).

Estoppel to deny effective bond. — Where an injunction bond has been signed, sealed and acknowledged by the obligors in the presence of the court and has been accepted and acted on as their bond, the obligors are estopped to deny that the penalty of the bond conforms to the direction of the judge who awarded the injunction. Harman v. Howe, 68 Va. (27 Gratt.) 676 (1876). See Wray v. Davenport, 79 Va. 19 (1884).

It is error to order an increase of an injunction bond where the claim of the adverse party is fully protected by collateral security. Ruffin v. Commercial Bank, 90 Va. 708, 19 S.E. 790 (1894).

If an injunction be dissolved, the debt should be collected by suit on the injunction bond. Fauber v. Gentry, 89 Va. 312, 15 S.E. 899 (1892).

Extent of liability. — The liability of the obligors in an injunction bond is determined by the bond alone. Damages recoverable in an action for breach thereof must be such as are the natural and proximate result of the issuance of the writ. Virginia Beach Dev. Co. v. Commonwealth, 115 Va. 280, 78 S.E. 617 (1913).

§ **8.01-631.1. Environmental injunction; financial capacity.** — A court awarding a temporary or permanent injunction to the Commonwealth, or any of its officers or agencies, requiring any party to (i) abate, control, prevent, remove, or contain any substantial or imminent threat to public health or the environment, or (ii) develop a closure plan to address any substantial or imminent threat to public health or the environment that may result when a business ceases operation, shall require the defendant to demonstrate its financial capability to comply with the injunction. Financial capability may be demonstrated, at the court's discretion, by the establishment of an escrow account, the creation of a trust fund, the submission of a bond, or such other instruments as the court may deem appropriate.

For the purposes of this section *"ceases operation"* means to cease conducting the normal operation of a business in the Commonwealth where it would be reasonable to expect that such operation will not be resumed by the owner. The term shall not include the ordinary sale or transfer of a business. (1991, c. 236.)

§ **8.01-632. How surety in forthcoming bond may obtain additional security.** — Any surety in the forthcoming bond described in §§ 8.01-630 and 8.01-631, or his personal representative, may move for and obtain an order for other or additional security, in the same manner as the defendant in an injunction. (Code 1950, § 8-624; 1977, c. 617.)

§ **8.01-633. Damages on dissolution.** — When an injunction to stay proceedings on a judgment or decree for money is dissolved wholly or in part there shall be paid to the party having such judgment or decree damages at the rate of ten per centum per annum from the time the injunction took effect until the dissolution, on such sum as appears to be due, including the costs; but the court wherein the injunction is may direct that no such damages be paid, or that there be paid only such portion thereof as it may deem just. In a case wherein a forthcoming bond was forfeited, and no execution was had thereon before the injunction took effect, a court awarding such execution shall include in its judgment or decree damages as aforesaid. In other cases damages may be included in the execution on the judgment or decree to which the injunction was awarded. (Code 1950, § 8-625; 1977, c. 617.)

REVISERS' NOTE

The last sentence of former § 8-625 has been deleted as unnecessary.

Cross references. — As to recovery of damages sustained for property withheld during appeal, see § 8.01-123.

I. DECISIONS UNDER PRIOR LAW.

Editor's note. — The cases cited below were decided under corresponding provisions of former law. The term "the statute," as used below, refers to former provisions.

The condition of an injunction bond is broken by a dissolution of the injunction in part, as well as by a total dissolution. An action lies on the bond whether the injunction be partly or wholly dissolved. White v. Clay, 34 Va. (7 Leigh) 68 (1836).

Who is liable for damages. — If a person, not a party to a judgment, enjoins it, and the injunction is dissolved, he is liable to pay the ten percent damages prescribed by the statute. Claytor v. Anthony, 56 Va. (15 Gratt.) 518 (1860).

Computation of damages. — Upon the dissolution of an injunction on a judgment, the damages for retarding execution by the injunction should be computed on the aggregate of principal, interest and costs, appearing due on the judgment at the date of the injunction. And the damages should be ascertained, and the precept to levy them inserted, in the body of the execution. Washington v. Parks, 33 Va. (6 Leigh) 581 (1835).

The damages are to be computed not upon the amount of judgment at the time it was first granted on the original bill but on the amount of the judgment at the time it was granted on the bill of review. Claytor v. Anthony, 56 Va. (15 Gratt.) 518 (1860).

An injunction was dissolved, and on appeal the decree was affirmed. Ten percent damages was to be computed from the time when the injunction was granted to the date of the dissolution thereof in the court below, but not for the time it was pending in the appellate court. Jeter v. Langhorne, 46 Va. (5 Gratt.) 193 (1848).

Statutory rate of interest implied unless remitted. — Where an injunction bond provides in terms for the payment of such damages on dissolution as may be awarded by the court, the ten percent damages given by statute are to be deemed awarded unless expressly remitted by the court. Claytor v. Anthony, 56 Va. (15 Gratt.) 518 (1860). See also, Fox v. Mountjoy, 20 Va. (6 Munf.) 36 (1817).

Damages part of judgment lien. — The damages on the dissolution of an injunction to a judgment become, as to the party obtaining it, a part of the judgment, and are embraced in the lien of the judgment upon the equity of redemption. Michaux v. Brown, 51 Va. (10 Gratt.) 612 (1854).

Damages may be recovered under bond after principal paid. — If the judgment, principal, interest, costs and damages on an injunction amount to more than the penalty of the injunction bond, and the plaintiff in the judgment sued out execution on the judgment and made the money, principal, interest and costs, he may also recover the damages by suit upon the bond. Claytor v. Anthony, 56 Va. (15 Gratt.) 518 (1860).

Suit on injunction bond. — Where an administrator recovered judgment for a debt due the estate, but was enjoined by the judgment debtor from collecting the same, if the injunction should be dissolved, and the administrator permitted to collect the debt, it should be done by a suit on the injunction bond. Fauber v. Gentry, 89 Va. 312, 15 S.E. 899 (1892).

§ 8.01-634. Dismissal of injunction bill. — When an injunction is wholly dissolved the bill shall stand dismissed with costs, unless sufficient cause be shown against such dismissal. (Code 1950, § 8-626; 1977, c. 617.)

REVISERS' NOTE

The following requirements in former § 8-626 have been deleted: (1) that a showing not to dismiss the injunction be carried over to the next term and (2) that the clerk shall enter the dismissal on the last day of term. These requirements are inconsistent with modern practice.

Cross references. — As to costs and damages, see §§ 8.01-631, 8.01-633. As to appeal upon dissolution, see §§ 8.01-670 through 8.01-672.

I. DECISIONS UNDER PRIOR LAW.

Editor's note. — The cases cited below were decided under corresponding provisions of former law. The term "this section," as used below, refers to former provisions.

After an injunction has been wholly dissolved, if the cause be set for hearing on motion of the defendant in equity, he cannot take advantage of the circumstance that the bill should have been dismissed under this section. Franklin v. Wilkinson, 17 Va. (3 Munf.) 112 (1812).

This section applies only to a pure bill of injunction, and not to a case where the bill prays for other relief besides the injunction. Pending the litigation for the subjection of the land to sale for the purchase money, it is not error to appoint a receiver to rent the land, and, if necessary, to collect the bond given by the vendee for the rent, as was done in the case at bar. Adkins v. Edwards, 83 Va. 300, 2 S.E. 435 (1887).

This section does not apply to a bill which is not merely a bill of injunction, but has the further object in view of obtaining a decree for a conveyance. Hough v. Shreeve, 18 Va. (4 Munf.) 490 (1815); Singleton v. Lewis, 20 Va. (6 Munf.) 397 (1819). See also Pulliam v. Winston, 32 Va. (5 Leigh) 324 (1834).

CHAPTER 25.
Extraordinary Writs.

Article 1.
Writ of Quo Warranto.

Sec.
8.01-635. Common-law writ of quo warranto and information in the nature of writ of quo warranto abolished; statutory writ of quo warranto established.
8.01-636. In what cases writ issued.
8.01-637. By whom filed; when leave granted and writ issued.
8.01-638. [Repealed.]
8.01-639. How summons directed and served.
8.01-640. Judgment when defendant fails to appear.
8.01-641. Reopening same when made on service by publication.
8.01-642. Pleading when defendant appears.
8.01-643. Trial; verdict; judgment; costs; attorney's fee.

Article 2.
Mandamus and Prohibition.

8.01-644. Application for mandamus or prohibition.
8.01-644.1. Limitations of actions for petition for mandamus.

Sec.
8.01-645. What petition to state; where presented.
8.01-646. When writ awarded if no defense made.
8.01-647. Defense; how made.
8.01-648. What judgment to be rendered.
8.01-649. Proceedings when application is to Supreme Court or Court of Appeals.
8.01-650. Suspension of proceedings, where prohibition applied for.
8.01-651. Suspension of proceedings by justice of Supreme Court or judge of Court of Appeals.
8.01-652. Service of writ; how obedience enforced.
8.01-653. Mandamus to secure construction of act directing payment out of treasury of the Commonwealth.
8.01-653.1. Mandamus to secure construction of act granting power to incur certain obligations for transportation needs.

Article 3.
Habeas Corpus.

8.01-654. When and by whom writ granted; what petition to contain.

Sec.		Sec.	
8.01-654.1.	Limitation on consideration of petition filed by prisoner sentenced to death.	8.01-663.	Judgment conclusive.
		8.01-664.	How and when Supreme Court summoned to try appeal therefrom.
8.01-655.	Form and contents of petition filed by prisoner.	8.01-665.	When execution of judgment suspended; when prisoner admitted to bail.
8.01-656.	Bond may be required of petitioner.		
8.01-657.	How directed and returnable.		
8.01-658.	How writ served.	8.01-666.	When and by whom writs of habeas corpus ad testificandum granted.
8.01-659.	Penalty for disobeying it.		
8.01-660.	When affidavits may be read.		
8.01-661.	Facts proved may be made part of record.	8.01-667.	Transmission of records to federal court.
8.01-662.	Judgment of court or judge trying it; payment of costs and expenses when petition denied.	8.01-668.	Writ de homine abolished.

ARTICLE 1.

Writ of Quo Warranto.

§ 8.01-635. Common-law writ of quo warranto and information in the nature of writ of quo warranto abolished; statutory writ of quo warranto established. — The common-law writ of quo warranto and information in the nature of writ of quo warranto is hereby abolished and superseded by the statutory writ of quo warranto. (1977, c. 617.)

REVISERS' NOTE

Since neither proceedings by the common-law writ of quo warranto nor information in the nature of a writ of quo warranto seems to have been understood and have fallen into disuse, § 8.01-635 abolishes them. Instead, a single procedure, a statutory writ of quo warranto, is created and provides the same relief as possible under the former writs.

Law Review. — For an article, "Final and Interlocutory Appeals in Virginia," see 8 Geo. Mason L. Rev. 337 (1999).

I. DECISIONS UNDER PRIOR LAW.

Editor's note. — The case cited below was decided under corresponding provisions of former law. The term "this article," as used below, refers to former provisions.

The object of this article is to simplify the procedure in quo warranto cases, and to define the cases in which it may be used. Watkins v. Venable, 99 Va. 440, 39 S.E. 147 (1901).

§ 8.01-636. In what cases writ issued. — A writ of quo warranto may be issued and prosecuted in the name of the Commonwealth in any of the following cases:

1. Against a domestic corporation, other than a municipal corporation, for the misuse or nonuse of its corporate privileges and franchises, or for the exercise of a privilege or franchise not conferred upon it by law, or when a charter of incorporation has been obtained by it for a fraudulent purpose, or for a purpose not authorized by law;

2. Against a person for the misuse or nonuse of any privilege conferred upon him by law;

2a. Against a person engaged in the practice of any profession without being duly authorized or licensed to do so;

3. Against any person or persons acting as a corporation, other than a municipal corporation, without authority of law; and

4. Against any person who intrudes into or usurps any public office. But no writ shall be issued or prosecuted against any person now in office for any cause which would have been available in support of a proceeding to contest his election.

Provided that nothing herein shall be construed to give jurisdiction to any court to judge the election, qualifications, or returns of the members of either house of the General Assembly. (Code 1950, § 8-857; 1977, c. 617; 1980, c. 705.)

REVISERS' NOTE

Section 8.01-636 adds to former § 8-857 the proviso preserving to the General Assembly the authority to judge the elections, qualifications, and/or returns of its members. See Constitution of Virginia, 1971, Article IV, § 7.

Law Review. — For article, "Virginia: The Unauthorized Practice of Law Experience," see 19 U. Rich. L. Rev. 499 (1985).

I. DECISIONS UNDER PRIOR LAW.

Editor's note. — The cases cited below were decided under corresponding provisions of former law. The term "this section," as used below, refers to former provisions.

This section is broad enough to embrace all corporations other than municipal corporations. South & W. Ry. v. Commonwealth, 104 Va. 314, 51 S.E. 824 (1905).

Quo warranto lies to try title to a public office. Sinclair v. Young, 100 Va. 284, 40 S.E. 907 (1902), cited in City of Roanoke v. Elliott, 123 Va. 393, 96 S.E. 819 (1918). See Dotson v. Commonwealth, 192 Va. 565, 66 S.E.2d 490 (1951).

But such remedy is not exclusive, and is not the usual remedy resorted to by a successor in office to try the title of his predecessor and to recover the property belonging to the office. Sinclair v. Young, 100 Va. 284, 40 S.E. 907 (1902).

And mandamus also lies. — This article does not abolish by implication the established procedure of trying title to office by mandamus. Sinclair v. Young, 100 Va. 284, 40 S.E. 907 (1902).

Mandamus is an appropriate remedy to compel one not entitled to public office to refrain from exercising its functions, and to deliver the rightful claimant property belonging to the office. Neither detinue nor quo warranto is an adequate remedy, even if detinue would lie in such a case to recover the property. Sinclair v. Young, 100 Va. 284, 40 S.E. 907 (1902).

Common law as to trying title to public office compared. — Chapter 145 of the Code of 1887, similar to this chapter, did not narrow the writ of quo warranto, or make it less comprehensive in trying the title to an office than it was at common law, where title to an office could be tested if the incumbent were not in possession de jure, although he might be a full de facto officer. The provisions of that chapter were not restricted to cases in which the incumbent was a mere intruder or usurper without color or pretense of title. Watkins v. Venable, 99 Va. 440, 39 S.E. 147 (1901). See Dotson v. Commonwealth, 192 Va. 565, 66 S.E.2d 490 (1951).

Where the term of an officer expires pending a quo warranto proceeding to test his right to hold it, the proceeding will be dismissed. Commonwealth v. Gleason, 111 Va. 383, 69 S.E. 448 (1910).

§ 8.01-637. By whom filed; when leave granted and writ issued. — A. The Attorney General or attorney for the Commonwealth of any county or city of which the circuit court has jurisdiction of the proceeding, at his own instance or at the relation of any interested person, or any interested person, may apply to such court by petition verified by oath for a writ of quo warranto. In case of an application under § 8.01-636 2a the term "any interested person" shall include any attorney licensed to practice law in this Commonwealth and qualified to practice before the Supreme Court of Virginia, or the circuit court in which the petition is filed.

B. If, in the opinion of the court, the matters stated in the petition are sufficient in law to authorize the issuance of such writ, a writ shall issue

§ 8.01-637   CIVIL REMEDIES AND PROCEDURE   § 8.01-637

thereon, commanding the sheriff to summon the defendant to appear at a date set forth in the writ.

C. If the petition is filed on the relation of any person or by any person at his own instance, before the clerk shall issue the writ the court shall require the relator or person to give bond with sufficient surety, to be approved by the clerk, to indemnify the Commonwealth against all costs and expenses of the proceedings, in case the same shall not be recovered from and paid by the defendant. (Code 1950, §§ 8-858, 8-859, 8-860; 1977, c. 617; 1980, c. 705.)

REVISERS' NOTE

Section 8.01-637 is a consolidation of former §§ 8-858 to 8-860. Subsection A adopts the substance of former §§ 8-859 and 8-860 regarding who may file the writ. Subsection B also adopts the substance of these two sections granting to the court the discretion to decide the sufficiency/insufficiency of the matters stated in the petition. However, instead of making the summons returnable to the next term of court, subsection B requires the defendant to appear at a date set forth in the writ. Subsection C has combined and rewritten the last sentences of former §§ 8-859 and 8-860; however, no change in substance is intended.

Cross references. — As to jurisdiction of circuit courts generally, see § 17.1-513.

I. DECISIONS UNDER PRIOR LAW.

Editor's note. — The cases cited below were decided under corresponding provisions of former law. The term "this section," as used below, refers to former provisions.

This section is substantially the same as the old practice developed under common-law rules. Hammer v. Commonwealth, 169 Va. 355, 193 S.E. 496 (1937).

Private persons may institute proceedings. — Under this section a quo warranto proceeding may be instituted in the name of the Commonwealth against a corporation, for a nonuse or misuse of its corporate franchise, not only by the attorney for the Commonwealth for the proper county, but also by private persons under certain conditions. South & W. Ry. v. Commonwealth, 104 Va. 314, 51 S.E. 824 (1905).

A "person interested". — A court should be satisfied that the person seeking its permission to file the information is a "person interested" before such permission is granted. Hammer v. Commonwealth, 169 Va. 355, 193 S.E. 496 (1937).

A relator, having shown himself to be a bona fide claimant to a public office and having made out a prima facie case, is a "person interested" within this section. Hammer v. Commonwealth, 169 Va. 355, 193 S.E. 496 (1937).

Need not request Attorney General or Commonwealth's attorney to apply for writ. — This section does not require "any person interested" to request the Attorney General or the Commonwealth's attorney to apply for the writ as a condition precedent for such a person to institute proceedings under this section. Hammer v. Commonwealth, 169 Va. 355, 193 S.E. 496 (1937).

An applicant is not entitled to the writ as a matter of absolute right, but whether it shall be awarded or not is within the exercise of judicial discretion. Watkins v. Venable, 99 Va. 440, 39 S.E. 147 (1901), cited in Albemarle Oil & Gas Co. v. Morris, 138 Va. 1, 121 S.E. 60 (1924).

However fundamental may be the irregularities in the organization of a municipal government, the writ of quo warranto does not issue as a matter of course. The court, in determining the question, will consider the public interest involved, and the extent of the injury complained of, and, where little practical benefit would result to the relator, and injury and inconvenience would result to the public, will deny the writ. Albemarle Oil & Gas Co. v. Morris, 138 Va. 1, 121 S.E. 60 (1924).

The first notice to the defendant of a quo warranto proceeding is the writ itself. Watkins v. Venable, 99 Va. 440, 39 S.E. 147 (1901).

Defendant as party. — The defendant does not become a party to a quo warranto proceeding until the writ is awarded. If a circuit court refuses to award the writ the defendant is no party to the proceeding in that court, and cannot be made a party on a writ of error from the Supreme Court, and process against him in the appellate court, if awarded, will be quashed. Watkins v. Venable, 99 Va. 440, 39 S.E. 147 (1901).

The Supreme Court has no original jurisdiction in cases of quo warranto, nor has any judge (now justice) thereof jurisdiction to issue the writ and send the case to the circuit court to be proceeded with, as in cases of injunction. Watkins v. Venable, 99 Va. 440, 39 S.E. 147 (1901).

A writ of error lies from the Supreme Court to a judgment of a circuit court refusing to entertain a petition for writ of quo warranto tendered by a bona fide claimant of an office to test the title thereto. Watkins v. Venable, 99 Va. 440, 39 S.E. 147 (1901).

In a proceeding to determine the validity of a city government, the interests of the relator were slight and the interest of the public was great. The granting and successful prosecution of the writ would have resulted in the suspension of all municipal government. It was held that the lower court did not err in vacating the writ and dismissing the petition. Albemarle Oil & Gas Co. v. Morris, 138 Va. 1, 121 S.E. 60 (1924).

§ **8.01-638:** Repealed by Acts 1987, c. 567.

Cross references. — As to venue in proceedings by writ of quo warranto, see subdivision 14 of § 8.01-261.

§ **8.01-639. How summons directed and served.** — The writ and a copy of the petition attached thereto may be directed to the sheriff of any county or city and shall be served as in other actions. (Code 1950, § 8-861; 1977, c. 617.)

REVISERS' NOTE

Section 8.01-639 alters former § 8-861 by requiring that a copy of the petition be attached to the writ.

§ **8.01-640. Judgment when defendant fails to appear.** — If the defendant fails to appear in accordance with the writ, the court may hear proof of the allegations of the petition, and if the allegations are sustained, shall give judgment accordingly. (Code 1950, § 8-862; 1977, c. 617.)

§ **8.01-641. Reopening same when made on service by publication.** — But if service is made by publication, the defendant against whom the judgment is rendered may file a motion within thirty days from the rendition of judgment to have such judgment set aside, upon giving bond with good security as prescribed by the court, with condition to pay all such costs as shall be awarded in the cause against the defendant. The defendant may then make such defense to the petition as he might have made, and in the same manner, before the judgment was rendered. (Code 1950, § 8-863; 1977, c. 617.)

REVISERS' NOTE

Section 8.01-641 alters former § 8-863 by replacing the period provided by "at the next term of the court" with the uniform period of "thirty days from the rendition of judgment."

§ **8.01-642. Pleading when defendant appears.** — The defendant against whom the writ was issued may plead, demur or answer the petition within the time set forth in the writ for his appearance. (Code 1950, § 8-864; 1977, c. 617.)

REVISERS' NOTE

Section 8.01-642 condenses and simplifies former § 8-864. The reference to pleading "not guilty" and to allegations not denied by the answer has been eliminated as no longer necessary in view of Rule 3:5. Also, the reference to the next term of court is deleted and replaced by the time provision of § 8.01-637 B; the references to the abolished writ and information are eliminated.

§ 8.01-643. Trial; verdict; judgment; costs; attorney's fee.

— Unless the defendant shall ask for a trial by jury, the court shall hear the same. If the case is tried by jury and the defendant is found guilty as to only a part of the charges, the verdict shall be guilty as to such part and shall particularly specify the same. As to the residue of such charges, the verdict shall be not guilty.

If the defendant appears and is found guilty the court shall give such judgment as is appropriate and authorized by law and for costs incurred in the prosecution of the information, including a reasonable attorney's fee to be prescribed by the court. (Code 1950, § 8-865; 1977, c. 617.)

REVISERS' NOTE

Section 8.01-643 rewrites former § 8-865 and alters case law by requiring a trial by jury of proceedings by writ of quo warranto only when the defendant so requests. See Dotson v. Commonwealth, 192 Va. 565, 66 S.E.2d 490 (1951). Also, the specific monetary limits on recovery of attorney's fees is replaced with a reasonableness standard.

ARTICLE 2.
Mandamus and Prohibition.

§ 8.01-644. Application for mandamus or prohibition.

— Application for a writ of mandamus or a writ of prohibition shall be on petition verified by oath, after the party against whom the writ is prayed has been served with a copy of the petition and notice of the intended application a reasonable time before such application is made. (Code 1950, § 8-704; 1977, c. 617.)

Cross references. — As to original jurisdiction of the Supreme Court over writs of mandamus and prohibition, see Va. Const., Art. VI, § 1. As to jurisdiction over writs of mandamus and prohibition generally, see §§ 17.1-309, 17.1-513.

Law Review. — For note on use of mandamus in judicial proceedings, see 40 Va. L. Rev. 817 (1954). For survey of Virginia practice and pleading for the year 1975-1976, see 62 Va. L. Rev. 1460 (1976). For comment, "Prohibition: The Elusive and Misunderstood Writ," see 16 U. Rich. L. Rev. 693 (1982).

I. Decisions Under Current Law.
  A. General Consideration.
  B. Mandamus.
  C. Prohibition.
II. Decisions Under Prior Law.
  A. General Consideration.
  B. Mandamus.
  C. Prohibition.

I. DECISIONS UNDER CURRENT LAW.

A. General Consideration.

Applied in Jones v. Willard, 224 Va. 602, 299 S.E.2d 504 (1983); Town of Narrows v. ClearView Cable TV, Inc., 227 Va. 272, 315 S.E.2d 835 (1984).

B. Mandamus.

Compelling performance of ministerial act. — Mandamus is an extraordinary remedy employed to compel a public official to perform a purely ministerial duty imposed upon him by law. A ministerial act is one which a person performs in a given state of facts and prescribed manner in obedience to the mandate of legal authority without regard to, or the exercise of his own judgment upon the propriety of the act being done. Richlands Medical Ass'n v. Commonwealth ex rel. State Health Comm'r, 230 Va. 384, 337 S.E.2d 737 (1985).

Public official's discretion not subject to review by mandamus. — When a public official is vested with discretion or judgment, his actions are not subject to review by mandamus. Richlands Medical Ass'n v. Commonwealth ex rel. State Health Comm'r, 230 Va. 384, 337 S.E.2d 737 (1985).

And trial court exceeds function in so doing. — A trial court exceeds its function and usurps the authority granted to a public official when it undertakes in a mandamus proceeding to review the discretion of the official. Richlands Medical Ass'n v. Commonwealth ex rel. State Health Comm'r, 230 Va. 384, 337 S.E.2d 737 (1985).

Function of a trial court in a mandamus proceeding is to command and execute, and not to inquire and adjudicate. Richlands Medical Ass'n v. Commonwealth ex rel. State Health Comm'r, 230 Va. 384, 337 S.E.2d 737 (1985).

Writ does not lie to prohibit erroneous adjudication. — Circuit court erred by issuing a writ of prohibition against a general district court judge in connection with action taken by the judge in the course of adjudicating civil cases, because a writ of prohibition does not lie to prevent a lower court from adjudicating erroneously. Elliott v. Greater Atl. Mgt. Co., 236 Va. 334, 374 S.E.2d 27 (1988).

Mandamus is applied prospectively only; it will not be granted to undo an act already done. Richlands Medical Ass'n v. Commonwealth ex rel. State Health Comm'r, 230 Va. 384, 337 S.E.2d 737 (1985).

Mandamus not a substitute for appeal. — The extraordinary remedy of mandamus may not be used as a substitute for an appeal. Mandamus lies to compel, not to revise or correct action, however erroneous it may have been and is not like a writ of error or appeal, which is a remedy for erroneous decisions. Richlands Medical Ass'n v. Commonwealth ex rel. State Health Comm'r, 230 Va. 384, 337 S.E.2d 737 (1985).

Where the controversy was over the legal correctness of judge's supervision of attorney's fees collected from tenants, issuance of a writ of prohibition was error. Elliott v. Greater Atl. Mgt. Co., 236 Va. 334, 374 S.E.2d 27 (1988).

C. Prohibition.

Function of the Court of Appeals in considering the application for a writ of prohibition is not to pass judgment upon individual evidentiary rulings as it would do on direct appeal. In re Fox, No. 0116-85 (Ct. of Appeals Mar. 19, 1985).

Discretion of court. — The issuance of the writ of prohibition is a matter that is within the sound discretion of the Court of Appeals, to be granted or denied considering the particular circumstances of this case. In re Fox, No. 0116-85 (Ct. of Appeals Mar. 19, 1985).

Writ of prohibition is to be issued with great caution and forbearance. In re Fox, No. 0116-85 (Ct. of Appeals Mar. 19, 1985).

Writ of prohibition may not be used as a substitute for appeal. It is not a vehicle for simply correcting errors of the trial court. In re Fox, No. 0116-85 (Ct. of Appeals Mar. 19, 1985).

Prohibition lies where error would deprive court of jurisdiction. — If the ruling complained of is mere error (e.g., evidentiary ruling), then appeal is the proper route for the aggrieved party to pursue; however, if it is alleged that the ruling of the trial court is erroneous and would deprive it of jurisdiction to retry the defendant, then prohibition lies where the facts are not in dispute. In re Fox, No. 0116-85 (Ct. of Appeals Mar. 19, 1985).

II. DECISIONS UNDER PRIOR LAW.

A. General Consideration.

Editor's note. — The cases cited below were decided under corresponding provisions of former law. The term "this section," as used below, refers to former provisions.

B. Mandamus.

Mandamus was a common-law writ, but the proceedings are now largely statutory. State Bd. of Educ. v. Carwile, 169 Va. 663, 194 S.E. 855 (1938).

A writ of mandamus is an extraordinary remedial process. It lies to compel performance of a ministerial act by a public official only when there is a clear and unequivocal duty imposed by law upon the officer to perform the act. The absence of another adequate remedy at law is essential to its application. May v. Whitlow, 201 Va. 533, 111 S.E.2d 804 (1960).

The function of a writ of mandamus is to enforce the performance of duties growing out of the discharge of public functions, or imposed by statute, or in some respect involving a trust or official duty. Richmond Ry. & Elec. Co. v. Brown, 97 Va. 26, 32 S.E. 775 (1899); Carolina, C & O Ry. v. Board of Supvrs., 109 Va. 34, 63 S.E. 412 (1909).

It should be issued only where there is a clear and specific legal right. — The writ of mandamus should be issued only where there is a clear and specific legal right to be enforced or a duty which ought to be and can be performed, and where there is no other specific and adequate legal remedy, and it is never granted in doubtful cases. Gilliam v. Harris, 203 Va. 316, 124 S.E.2d 188 (1962).

Mandamus will never issue in doubtful cases and therefore was denied where petitioner failed to prove his allegations. Legum v. Harris, 205 Va. 99, 135 S.E.2d 125 (1964).

Mandamus should be reserved to discharge its principal purpose, i.e., to enforce a clearly established right and to enforce a corresponding imperative duty created or imposed by law. Stroobants v. Fugate, 209 Va. 275, 163 S.E.2d 192 (1968).

Mandamus will never be allowed to

usurp the functions of a writ of error, appeal or certiorari. Thus the writ was refused where it was sought to compel a judge to allow a certain person to become a party to a suit, appeal being the proper remedy. Moon v. Wellford, 84 Va. 34, 4 S.E. 572 (1887).

It will not issue to require exercise of discretionary legislative function. — Mandamus will not issue to require a local political unit to exercise its discretionary, legislative function in levying taxes and appropriating funds for the maintenance of public schools. Griffin v. Board of Supvrs., 203 Va. 321, 124 S.E.2d 227 (1962).

Mandamus cannot be used to enforce mere contractual obligation. — Mandamus is an extraordinary legal remedy, designed to meet emergencies, and to prevent failure of justice. It cannot be used to enforce a mere contractual obligation nor, generally, to enforce collection of a mere money demand from public officer, if the creditor has an adequate remedy by action at law. Rinehart & Dennis Co. v. McArthur, 123 Va. 556, 96 S.E. 829 (1918).

Mandamus is proper remedy of stockholder denied his right of inspection. — The writ of mandamus is a proper remedy both under the statute and at common law, available to a stockholder who has been improperly denied his right of inspection, but the petition must state "plainly and concisely the grounds of the application." It is fundamental that in order to secure the enforcement of such right, by mandamus or any other remedy, the complainant must satisfy the court that a right of inspection exists in the particular instance. Bank of Giles County v. Mason, 199 Va. 176, 98 S.E.2d 905 (1957).

It lies to compel city official to promulgate regulations as required by ordinance. — Mandamus is a proper remedy to compel a city official to promulgate regulations which a city ordinance requires that he promulgate, even though he cannot be controlled in the exercise of discretion which the ordinance may give him as to the content of the regulations. Richmond Funeral Dirs. Ass'n v. Groth, 202 Va. 792, 120 S.E.2d 467 (1961).

And to determine right of former city official to payment of salary. — Mandamus was held to be a proper procedure for determination by a former city sergeant of his right to payment of salary after termination of his regular term in office as a result of the consolidation of two cities. Walker v. Massie, 202 Va. 886, 121 S.E.2d 448 (1961).

Mandamus is not technically and strictly a proper remedy to require commencement of condemnation proceedings. But its use was not error in view of particular facts and circumstances. May v. Whitlow, 201 Va. 533, 111 S.E.2d 804 (1960).

Mandamus will not lie to compel the Highway Commissioner (now Commonwealth Transportation Commissioner) to institute condemnation proceedings in the proper court to ascertain what compensation is due petitioners for the damages which, they allege, have been done to their property by the acts of the respondent, since, under § 8.01-187, the cause of action asserted by the petitioners can be resolved in a declaratory judgment proceeding in a lower court. Stroobants v. Fugate, 209 Va. 275, 163 S.E.2d 192 (1968).

The original jurisdiction of the Supreme Court could not be invoked to issue a writ of mandamus to require the State Highway Commissioner (now Commonwealth Transportation Commissioner) to condemn land which he believed already to be property of the State. A declaratory judgment proceeding is an adequate means for determining the ownership of such land. Gilliam v. Harris, 203 Va. 316, 124 S.E.2d 188 (1962).

Mandamus to compel condemnation by the State Highway Commissioner (now Commonwealth Transportation Commissioner) was properly denied where petitioner's proof left in doubt his allegation that highway construction had caused damage to his building. Legum v. Harris, 205 Va. 99, 135 S.E.2d 125 (1964).

A court has jurisdiction by mandamus to compel its clerk to do a ministerial act concerning which he had no discretion. Rinehart & Dennis Co. v. McArthur, 123 Va. 556, 96 S.E. 829 (1918).

And judge may be compelled to sign bill of exceptions. — The Supreme Court has power, by mandamus, to compel a judge of an inferior court to sign a proper bill of exceptions. Collins v. Christian, 92 Va. 731, 93 Va. 1, 24 S.E. 472, 24 S.E. 472 (1896).

C. Prohibition.

Plea to jurisdiction of lower court as prerequisite to issuance of prohibition. — As a general rule a writ of prohibition will not be issued to an inferior court unless a plea to the jurisdiction has been filed in the court whose proceeding it seeks to arrest, but the rule is to be applied in the discretion of the superior court on the principle that the matter of judicial courtesy to a lower court should yield to substantial rights of litigants, particularly where the case involves matters of public interest and convenience. King v. Hening, 203 Va. 582, 125 S.E.2d 827 (1962).

Function of writ of prohibition. — The writ of prohibition lies to prevent the exercise of the jurisdiction of the court by the judge to whom it is directed, either where he has no jurisdiction at all or is exceeding his jurisdiction. Grief v. Kegley, 115 Va. 552, 79 S.E. 1062 (1913).

Prohibition is the appropriate remedy to prevent a justice of the peace, or police justice, from exceeding his jurisdiction. Martin v. City of Richmond, 108 Va. 765, 62 S.E. 800 (1908).

§ 8.01-644.1. Limitations of actions for petition for mandamus. — A petition for extraordinary writ of mandamus, filed by or on behalf of a person confined in a state correctional facility, shall be brought within one year after the cause of action accrues. (1998, c. 596.)

§ 8.01-645. What petition to state; where presented. — The petition shall state plainly and concisely the grounds of the application, concluding with a prayer for the writ, and shall be presented to the court having jurisdiction, unless the application is to the Court of Appeals or the Supreme Court. (Code 1950, § 8-705; 1977, c. 617; 1984, c. 703.)

I. DECISIONS UNDER PRIOR LAW.

Editor's note. — The case cited below was decided under corresponding provisions of former law. The term "this section," as used below, refers to former provisions.

Jurisdiction to compel maintenance of bridge between adjacent counties. — A circuit judge has jurisdiction to compel a county by mandamus to contribute to maintain a bridge over a place between it and an adjacent county. Gloucester County v. Middlesex County, 88 Va. 843, 14 S.E. 660 (1892).

§ 8.01-646. When writ awarded if no defense made. — When the application is made, on proof of notice and service of the copy of the petition as aforesaid, if the defendant fails to appear, or appearing fails to make defense, and the petition states a proper case for the writ, a peremptory writ shall be awarded with costs. (Code 1950, § 8-706; 1977, c. 617.)

§ 8.01-647. Defense; how made. — The defendant may file a demurrer or answer on oath to the petition, or both. The court may permit amendments of the pleadings as in other cases. (Code 1950, § 8-707; 1977, c. 617.)

Law Review. — For survey of Virginia practice and pleading for the year 1975-1976, see 62 Va. L. Rev. 1460 (1976).

I. DECISIONS UNDER PRIOR LAW.

Editor's note. — The cases cited below were decided under corresponding provisions of former law. The term "this section," as used below, refers to former provisions.

Allegations in petition for mandamus are not admitted as true by failure of the answer to traverse them. Board of Supvrs. v. Randolph, 89 Va. 614, 16 S.E. 722 (1893).

What defenses may be made. — In a mandamus proceeding, under this chapter, it would seem that any defense may be made which shows that the petitioner is not entitled to the writ prayed for. Rinehart & Dennis Co. v. McArthur, 123 Va. 556, 96 S.E. 829 (1918).

Admission of third-party claimants as parties. — If the defendant is the mere custodian of a fund, in which he claims no interest, but which is in good faith claimed by another, there is no good reason, under the liberal provisions of the new procedure, why the claimant should not be admitted as a party, and the rights of the parties thus speedily determined in the mandamus proceeding. Rinehart & Dennis Co. v. McArthur, 123 Va. 556, 96 S.E. 829 (1918).

Waiver of objection to procedure. — Defendant waived his objection to mandamus procedure when he answered the petition without filing objections to the procedure, or to the jurisdiction, and joined in the issue, thereby submitting himself to the jurisdiction of the court, permitting it to promptly determine the merits of the principal question in controversy. May v. Whitlow, 201 Va. 533, 111 S.E.2d 804 (1960).

§ 8.01-648. What judgment to be rendered. — The court shall award or deny the writ according to the law and facts of the case, with or without costs. (Code 1950, § 8-709; 1977, c. 617.)

§ 8.01-649. Proceedings when application is to Supreme Court or Court of Appeals. — If the application is to the Court of Appeals or the Supreme Court, the procedure shall be in accordance with the provisions of Rules of Court. (Code 1950, § 8-710; 1977, c. 617; 1984, c. 703.)

REVISERS' NOTE

Section 8.01-649 conforms former § 8-710 with Rule 5:5.

§ 8.01-650. Suspension of proceedings, where prohibition applied for. — On petition for a writ of prohibition, the court may, at any time before or after the application for the writ is made, make an order, a copy of which shall be served on the defendant, suspending the proceedings sought to be prohibited until the final decision of the cause. (Code 1950, § 8-711; 1977, c. 617.)

§ 8.01-651. Suspension of proceedings by justice of Supreme Court or judge of Court of Appeals. — Whenever a court having jurisdiction refuses to suspend proceedings as provided in § 8.01-650 of this chapter, a copy of the proceedings in court, with any orders entered in the proceedings, may be presented to a judge of the Court of Appeals, if an application for a writ of prohibition is pending in that court, or to a justice of the Supreme Court if the application for a writ is pending there. Such judge or justice may thereupon award a suspension of the proceedings sought to be prohibited until the final decision of the cause. (Code 1950, § 8-711.1; 1972, c. 673; 1977, c. 617; 1984, c. 703.)

REVISERS' NOTE

Former § 8-712 (How proceedings in vacation certified...) is deleted as unnecessary.

§ 8.01-652. Service of writ; how obedience enforced. — Service of a copy of the order awarding the writ shall be equivalent to service of the writ, and obedience to the writ or order may be enforced by process of contempt. (Code 1950, § 8-713; 1977, c. 617.)

§ 8.01-653. Mandamus to secure construction of act directing payment out of treasury of the Commonwealth. — Whenever the Comptroller or the Treasurer of the Commonwealth shall notify the Attorney General, in writing, that they, or either of them, entertain such doubt respecting the proper construction or interpretation of any act of the General Assembly which appropriates or directs the payment of money out of the treasury of the Commonwealth, or respecting the constitutionality of any such act, that they, or either of them, do not feel that it would be proper or safe to pay such money until there has been a final adjudication by the Supreme Court determining any and all such questions, and that, for such reason, they will not make payments pursuant to such act until such adjudication has been made, the Attorney General may file in such court a petition for a writ of mandamus directing or requiring the Comptroller or Treasurer of the Commonwealth, or both, to pay such money as provided by any such act at such time in the future as may be proper. In order to avoid delays in payments after the time for making them has arrived, any such petition may be filed at any time after the passage of any such act although the time for making such payments has not arrived and no demand for such payments has been made. In any such proceeding the court shall consider and determine all questions raised by the Attorney General's petition pertaining to the constitutionality or interpretation of any such act, even though some of such questions may not be necessary to the decision of the question of the duty of such Comptroller and Treasurer of the Commonwealth to make payment of the moneys appropriated or directed to be paid.

The Comptroller and the Treasurer of the Commonwealth, or either of them, as the case may be, shall be made a party or parties defendant to any such petition and the court may, in its discretion, cause such other officers or persons to be made parties defendant as it may deem proper, and may make such order respecting the employment of an attorney or attorneys for any officer of the Commonwealth who is a party defendant as may be appropriate. The compensation of any such attorney shall be fixed by such court and upon its order paid out of the appropriation to the office or department of any such public officer represented by any such attorney in such proceeding. (Code 1950, § 8-714; 1977, c. 617.)

Law Review. — For a review of civil practice and procedure in Virginia for year 1999, see 33 U. Rich. L. Rev. 801 (1999).

I. Decisions Under Current Law.
II. Decisions Under Prior Law.

I. DECISIONS UNDER CURRENT LAW.

This section does not permit the Attorney General to challenge the constitutionality of an act by adding parties in the role of petitioners whom he expects will defend that act and seek payment under it. Earley v. Landsdle, 257 Va. 365, 514 S.E.2d 153 (1999).

Subject matter jurisdiction exceeded. — Where the Attorney General assumed the role of party defendant by asking the court to direct the Comptroller not to pay money under challenged items until the next session of the Virginia General Assembly, the petition exceeded the subject matter jurisdiction granted to the Virginia Supreme Court under this section, as the statute only permits the Attorney General to petition the court to seek payment of money that he believes the Comptroller is improperly withholding. Earley v. Landsdle, 257 Va. 365, 514 S.E.2d 153 (1999).

Applied in Coleman v. Pross, 219 Va. 143, 246 S.E.2d 613 (1978).

II. DECISIONS UNDER PRIOR LAW.

Editor's note. — The case cited below was decided under corresponding provisions of former law. The term "this section," as used below, refers to former provisions. Baliles v. Mazur, 224 Va. 462, 297 S.E.2d 695 (1982).

The Supreme Court is not limited to the questions raised by the Attorney General's petition for mandamus, but may consider all constitutional questions presented. Almond v. Day, 197 Va. 419, 89 S.E.2d 851 (1955).

§ 8.01-653.1. Mandamus to secure construction of act granting power to incur certain obligations for transportation needs. — Whenever the Comptroller notifies the Attorney General in writing that he entertains doubt respecting the constitutionality of any act of the General Assembly granting an agency of the Commonwealth or other governmental board or entity of the Commonwealth general powers to incur obligations for transportation needs where such obligations are subject to authorization by the General Assembly, the Attorney General shall file in the Supreme Court a petition for a writ of mandamus directing or requiring the Comptroller to pay the money as provided by any such act at such time in the future as may be proper. In order to expedite long-term planning by such an agency of the Commonwealth or other governmental board or entity of the Commonwealth and expedite its advice to the Governor and the General Assembly on possible alternative means of financing Virginia's transportation needs, the petition may be filed after the enactment date of any such act, although (i) the General

Assembly may not have enacted legislation specifically authorizing such an agency of the Commonwealth or other governmental board or entity of the Commonwealth to enter into specific obligations under its general authority or (ii) if such specific obligations have been authorized, the time for making payments has not arrived and no demand for payment has been made. The court shall consider and determine all questions raised by the Attorney General's petition pertaining to the constitutionality or interpretation of any such act, even though some of the questions may not be necessary to the decision regarding the duty of the Comptroller to make payment of the moneys appropriated or directed to be paid.

The Comptroller shall be made a party defendant to the petition. The court may, in its discretion, cause other officers or persons to be made parties defendant as it may deem proper, and may make such order respecting the employment of an attorney or attorneys for any officer of the Commonwealth who is a party defendant as may be appropriate. The compensation of any attorney so employed shall be fixed by the court and upon its order paid out of the appropriation to the office or department of the public officer represented by the attorney in the proceeding. (1986, Sp. Sess., cc. 14, 16.)

I. DECISIONS UNDER CURRENT LAW.

Applied in Terry v. Mazur, 234 Va. 442, 362 S.E.2d 904 (1987).

ARTICLE 3.

Habeas Corpus.

§ 8.01-654. When and by whom writ granted; what petition to contain. — A. 1. The writ of habeas corpus ad subjiciendum shall be granted forthwith by the Supreme Court or any circuit court, to any person who shall apply for the same by petition, showing by affidavits or other evidence probable cause to believe that he is detained without lawful authority.

2. A petition for writ of habeas corpus ad subjiciendum, other than a petition challenging a criminal conviction or sentence, shall be brought within one year after the cause of action accrues. A habeas corpus petition attacking a criminal conviction or sentence, except as provided in § 8.01-654.1 for cases in which a death sentence has been imposed, shall be filed within two years from the date of final judgment in the trial court or within one year from either final disposition of the direct appeal in state court or the time for filing such appeal has expired, whichever is later.

B. 1. With respect to any such petition filed by a petitioner held under criminal process, and subject to the provisions of subsection C of this section and of § 17.1-310, only the circuit court which entered the original judgment order of conviction or convictions complained of in the petition shall have authority to issue writs of habeas corpus. If a district court entered the original judgment order of conviction or convictions complained of in the petition, only the circuit court for the city or county wherein the district court sits shall have authority to issue writs of habeas corpus. Hearings on such petition, where granted in the circuit court, may be held at any circuit court within the same circuit as the circuit court in which the petition was filed, as designated by the judge thereof.

2. Such petition shall contain all allegations the facts of which are known to petitioner at the time of filing and such petition shall enumerate all previous applications and their disposition. No writ shall be granted on the basis of any allegation the facts of which petitioner had knowledge at the time of filing any previous petition.

3. Such petition may allege detention without lawful authority through challenge to a conviction, although the sentence imposed for such conviction is suspended or is to be served subsequently to the sentence currently being served by petitioner.

4. In the event the allegations of illegality of the petitioner's detention can be fully determined on the basis of recorded matters, the court may make its determination whether such writ should issue on the basis of the record.

5. The court shall give findings of fact and conclusions of law following a determination on the record or after hearing, to be made a part of the record and transcribed.

6. If petitioner alleges as a ground for illegality of his detention the inadequacy of counsel, he shall be deemed to waive his privilege with respect to communications between such counsel and himself to the extent necessary to permit a full and fair hearing for the alleged ground.

C. 1. With respect to any such petition filed by a petitioner held under the sentence of death, and subject to the provisions of this subsection, the Supreme Court shall have exclusive jurisdiction to consider and award writs of habeas corpus. The circuit court which entered the judgment order setting the sentence of death shall have authority to conduct an evidentiary hearing on such a petition only if directed to do so by order of the Supreme Court.

2. Hearings conducted in a circuit court pursuant to an order issued under the provisions of subdivision 1 of this subsection shall be limited in subject matter to the issues enumerated in the order.

3. The circuit court shall conduct such a hearing within ninety days after the order of the Supreme Court has been received and shall report its findings of fact and recommend conclusions of law to the Supreme Court within sixty days after the conclusion of the hearing. Any objection to the report of the circuit court must be filed in the Supreme Court within thirty days after the report is filed. (Code 1950, § 8-596; 1958, c. 215; 1968, c. 487; 1977, c. 617; 1978, c. 124; 1995, c. 503; 1998, c. 577.)

Cross references. — For constitutional provisions, see VA. Const., Art. I, § 9, Art. VI, § 1. As to jurisdiction of habeas corpus, see § 17.1-310. For provision that members of the General Assembly must obey the writ, see § 30-8. As to use of writ to test legality of detention of persons held in custody as mentally ill, see §§ 37.1-103 et seq.

Law Review. — For article, "Federal Habeas Corpus: State Prisoners and the Concept of Custody," see 4 U. Rich. L. Rev. 1 (1969). For note, "The Attorney-Client Privilege," see 19 U. Rich. L. Rev. 559 (1985).

I. Decisions Under Current Law.
   A. General Consideration.
   B. Petitioners Held Under Criminal Process.
II. Decisions Under Prior Law.
   A. General Consideration.
   B. Petitioners Held Under Criminal Process.

I. DECISIONS UNDER CURRENT LAW.

A. General Consideration.

Virginia's pro se procedures are in no sense futile or arcane. The form contained in § 8.01-655 is a simple one. Mallory v. Smith, 27 F.3d 991 (4th Cir. 1994), cert. denied, 513 U.S. 1047, 115 S. Ct. 644, 130 L. Ed. 2d 549 (1994).

Scope of jurisdiction of Court of Appeals. — The Court of Appeals has original jurisdiction to issue writs of habeas corpus. However, only the circuit court which entered the original judgment order of conviction may issue a writ for one held under criminal process. The Supreme Court's grant of original jurisdiction in habeas corpus matters is not subject to this limitation. However, the Court of Appeal's grant of jurisdiction in these matters is limited. Bullock v. Director of Dep't of Cors., 1 Va. App. 70, 334 S.E.2d 150, cert. denied, 474 U.S. 1023, 106 S. Ct. 576, 88 L. Ed. 559 (1985).

Writ of habeas corpus not to determine guilt or innocence of prisoner. — The only issue which it presents is whether or not the prisoner is restrained of his liberty by due process of law. Further, it is well settled that habeas corpus cannot be used to perform the function of an appeal or writ of error, to review errors, or to modify or revise a judgment of conviction pronounced by a court of competent jurisdiction. It cannot be used to secure a judicial determination of any question which, even if determined in the prisoner's favor, could not affect the lawfulness of his immediate custody and detention. Fitzgerald v. Bass, 6 Va. App. 38, 366 S.E.2d 615 (1988), cert. denied, 493 U.S. 945, 110 S. Ct. 354, 107 L. Ed. 2d 342 (1989).

Interests served by habeas filing requirements. — Requiring a petitioner to assert all his known claims at one time in a single document obviously serves a valid state interest in assuring finality of decisions. Moreover, requiring parties to refrain from filing any document after the initial pleadings without permission of the state supreme court serves a valid interest in assuring the orderly processing of petitions. Taylor v. Murray, 855 F. Supp. 124 (E.D. Va. 1994).

Court of Appeals should not consider original petition for writ of habeas corpus when adequate remedy may be had in circuit courts under this section. White v. Garraghty, 2 Va. App. 117, 341 S.E.2d 402 (1986).

Federal court won't determine if state court should have seen additional claims in pleading. — Where prisoner identified three grounds in his pleadings under § 8.01-655, and the Virginia Supreme Court disposed of each of those three grounds in its order, the federal appellate court will not go further and determine whether the Virginia Supreme Court should have seen another claim in his filings. To have the federal court scan the information contained in prisoner's brief for further facts that conceivably might make out other federal claims would send a strong signal to state courts that their procedures will not be respected by their federal counterparts and would also signal litigants that they may ignore state procedures and still expect the federal courts to hear claims that state courts would have had to stitch together from stray references in order to review. Mallory v. Smith, 27 F.3d 991 (4th Cir. 1994), cert. denied, 513 U.S. 1047, 115 S. Ct. 644, 130 L. Ed. 2d 549 (1994).

Defendant must address reason for not raising known grounds in earlier petition to receive federal consideration. — In Virginia, a writ of habeas corpus may be granted on the basis of any allegation the facts of which defendant had knowledge at the time of filing any previous petition; thus where defendant knew of the grounds of his present Brady claim when he filed his first petition, this section precluded review of his claim in any future state habeas corpus proceeding. Because defendant made no attempt to demonstrate cause or prejudice for his default in state habeas corpus proceedings, it could not then be raised in his federal suit for such writ. Gray v. Netherland, 518 U.S. 152, 116 S. Ct. 2074, 135 L. Ed. 2d 457 (1996).

Habeas corpus petitions must allege sufficient facts which, if true, would support the conclusion of law advanced; mere conclusions or opinions of the pleader will not suffice to make out a case. Fitzgerald v. Bass, 6 Va. App. 38, 366 S.E.2d 615 (1988), cert. denied, 493 U.S. 945, 110 S. Ct. 354, 107 L. Ed. 2d 342 (1989).

Limitation on basis for relief. — Under this section, no writ of habeas corpus will be granted on the basis of any factual or legal claim which petitioner did not previously make but could have. Satcher v. Netherland, 944 F. Supp. 1222 (E.D. Va. 1996), aff'd in part and rev'd in part on other grounds sub nom. Satcher v. Pruett, 126 F.3d 561 (4th Cir.), cert. denied, 522 U.S. 1010, 118 S. Ct. 595, 139 L. Ed. 2d 431 (1997).

Limitation on procedural default bar. — The dismissal of an inmate's state petition on the grounds of a procedural default under subdivision (B)(2) ordinarily bars federal review in that this section is an independent and adequate ground for denying relief; however, even where an inmate's state petition has been dismissed there is no bar to federal review if a miscarriage of justice would result from lack of federal review. Jennings v. Parole Bd., 34 F. Supp. 2d 375 (E.D. Va. 1999).

A default determination under subdivision B 2, reflects a finding that indeed the petitioner either knew or had available all of the facts on which the current petition was based. While this finding is often implicit, it is a finding nonetheless, and must be accorded presumptive validity. Barnes v. Thompson, 58 F.3d 971 (4th Cir. 1995), cert. denied, 516 U.S. 972, 116 S. Ct. 435, 133 L. Ed. 2d 350 (1995).

The subdivision B 2 default determination by the Commonwealth's highest court reflects a finding that all of the facts on which the current petition was based were either known or available to the petitioner. Barnes v. Thompson, 58 F.3d 971 (4th Cir. 1995), cert. denied, 516 U.S. 972, 116 S. Ct. 435, 133 L. Ed. 2d 350 (1995).

And this factual finding is entitled to a presumption of correctness on federal habeas review, and may be rebutted only if the finding is not fairly supported by the record. Barnes v. Thompson, 58 F.3d 971 (4th Cir. 1995), cert. denied, 516 U.S. 972, 116 S. Ct. 435, 133 L. Ed. 2d 350 (1995).

Defendant must be sentenced to term of incarceration to file valid writ. — Defendants writ of habeas corpus could not test the legality of any incarceration because he was not sentenced to any term of incarceration, but only fined and placed on supervised probation. McClenny v. Murray, 246 Va. 132, 431 S.E.2d 330 (1993).

Petitioner failed to present his claim of ineffective assistance of counsel in his first state habeas petition, where what petitioner presented suggested only his disagreement with his counsel's advice. Accordingly the Virginia Supreme Court's application of subdivision B 2 of this section to bar review was justified and presents a procedural bar to a federal district court's review of his claim absent a showing of "cause" and "prejudice." Smith v. Baker, 624 F. Supp. 1075 (E.D. Va. 1985).

The Virginia Supreme Court's finding of a procedural bar was barred because petitioner failed to adequately present it in his first state habeas petition, constitutes an adequate and independent state ground which prohibits the federal district court from considering the merits of petitioner's claim. Smith v. Baker, 624 F. Supp. 1075 (E.D. Va. 1985).

Deferral of parole review without reason not grounds for habeas corpus jurisdiction. — Trial court had no jurisdiction to grant habeas corpus writ on the basis that defendant was denied due process when the Virginia Parole Board deferred his annual parole review without providing a reason, because the court's determination did not affect the lawfulness of defendant's immediate custody and detention and his release from his immediate detention would not have followed as a result of the court's order. Virginia Parole Bd. v. Wilkins, 255 Va. 419, 498 S.E.2d 695 (1998).

New factual allegations present state court matter precluding federal review of ineffective assistance of counsel claim. — Petitioner's mere presentation to the state court with the theory of ineffective assistance of counsel was insufficient to encompass the new factual allegations contained in one of the claims of his federal habeas corpus petition. Petitioner's failure to give the state court an opportunity to resolve the claim precluded the federal court from addressing the merits, and the claim was dismissed. Banks v. Powell, 917 F. Supp. 414 (E.D. Va. 1996).

When evidence required to resolve issues. — When a factual dispute remains, evidence from witnesses examined ore tenus or by depositions is required to resolve the issue. Collison v. Underwood, No. 0204-85 (Ct. of Appeals Feb. 5, 1986).

Subdivision B 4 clearly envisions that there may be some cases in which the trial record will be sufficient for a determination whether counsel was ineffective and further testimony would not be necessary to resolve the issue. Hill v. Commonwealth, 8 Va. App. 60, 379 S.E.2d 134 (1989).

Where the state court found that the incompetency claim was defaulted because defendant knew of the facts underlying the claim at the time of his prior state petition was a factual finding with regard to prior knowledge, and it was entitled to a presumption of correctness from the federal district court. Clanton v. Muncy, 845 F.2d 1238 (4th Cir.), cert. denied, 485 U.S. 1000, 108 S. Ct. 1459, 99 L. Ed. 2d 690 (1988).

Defendant's challenge to sufficiency of evidence was properly exhausted in state courts. — Defendant's challenge to the sufficiency of the evidence under the federal due process clause to convict him had been properly exhausted in the state courts; the Commonwealth's contention that it has not been properly exhausted in the state courts rested on the erroneous premise that it involved a constitutional challenge to the facial validity of the permissive inference; it was not that, but was a straightforward due process challenge to the sufficiency of the evidence (in this case consisting solely of the basic facts of the inference) to convict; the fact that defendant did not couch his objections and challenges in state court in specific constitutional terms was of no consequence; it was not necessary to cite "book and verse on the federal Constitution" so long as the constitutional substance of the claim was evident. West v. Wright, 931 F.2d 262 (4th Cir. 1991), rev'd on other grounds, 502 U.S. 917, 112 S. Ct. 2482, 120 L. Ed. 2d 225 (1992).

Applied in Rivers v. Martin, 484 F. Supp. 162 (W.D. Va. 1980); Grooms v. Mitchell, 500 F. Supp. 137 (E.D. Va. 1980); Fitzgerald v. Commonwealth, 223 Va. 615, 292 S.E.2d 798 (1982); Clanton v. Blair, 619 F. Supp. 1491 (E.D. Va. 1985); Smith v. Thompson, 1 Va. App. 407, 339 S.E.2d 556 (1986); Dodson v. Director of Dep't of Cors., 233 Va. 303, 355 S.E.2d 573 (1987); Bowles v. Nance, 236 Va. 310, 374 S.E.2d 19 (1988); Coleman v. Thompson, 798 F. Supp. 1209 (W.D. Va. 1992); Turner v. Williams, 812 F. Supp. 1400 (E.D. Va. 1993); Townes v. Murray, 68 F.3d 840 (4th Cir. 1995); Hoke v. Netherland, 92 F.3d 1350 (4th Cir. 1996); Brown v. Angelone, 938 F. Supp. 340 (W.D. Va. 1996); Royal v. Netherland, 4 F. Supp. 2d 540 (E.D. Va. 1998); Fisher v. Angelone, 163 F.3d 835 (4th Cir. 1998); Goins v. Angelone, 52 F. Supp. 2d 638 (E.D. Va. 1999).

B. Petitioners Held Under Criminal Process.

Deprivation of a constitutional right of a prisoner may be raised by habeas corpus. But this principle is inapplicable when a prisoner has been afforded a full and fair opportunity to raise his constitutional claim at trial and on appeal. Cartera v. Mitchell, 553 F. Supp. 866 (E.D. Va. 1982).

Determination upon trial record alone. — If the record of the criminal trial is sufficient itself to show the merit or lack of merit of a habeas petition, the case may be determined upon that record alone. Walker v. Mitchell, 224 Va. 568, 299 S.E.2d 698 (1983).

Court not bound by omission in record in determining validity of waiver. — While the question of whether there is a proper waiver should be clearly determined by the trial court, and it would be fitting and appropriate for that determination to appear upon the record, a habeas court considering the validity of a waiver is not bound by an omission in the trial record. Superintendent of Powhatan Correctional Center v. Barnes, 221 Va. 780, 273 S.E.2d 558 (1981).

Prima facie showing by affidavit or other evidence of facts which, if true, show that petitioner is illegally detained entitles petitioner to hearing on his petition. Subdivision B 4 provides, however, that where a writ petitioner's allegations "can be fully determined on the basis of recorded matters, the court may make its determination whether such writ should issue on the basis of the record." Collison v. Underwood, No. 0204-85 (Ct. of Appeals Feb. 5, 1986).

Affidavits not prohibited. — This section permits the habeas court to adjudicate a petitioner's claims based upon the trial record; it does not prohibit the use of affidavits in the habeas proceeding. Yeatts v. Murray, 249 Va. 285, 455 S.E.2d 18 (1995).

Findings presumed correct on appeal. — The factual findings of the trial court in a habeas corpus hearing are presumed to be correct and will be upheld on appeal unless plainly wrong or unsupported by credible evidence. Moreover, in reviewing the sufficiency of evidence on appeal, all evidence will be considered in the light most favorable to the appellee. Lee v. Neff, No. 0120-85 (Ct. of Appeals Nov. 8, 1985).

Knowledge of facts alleged at time of previous petition. — Where the facts alleged in the petition are those which the petitioner must have had knowledge of at the time he filed his previous petitions, a writ may not be granted on the basis of the facts alleged in this petition. Bonner v. Sielaff, No. 0580-85 (Ct. of Appeals Dec. 13, 1985).

Dismissal of petition where filing long delayed. — Where the filing of a petition for habeas corpus claiming ineffective assistance of counsel is so long delayed that the Commonwealth is prejudiced in its defense of the claim, the petition may be dismissed unless the petitioner shows that, in the exercise of reasonable diligence, he could not have known of the grounds for the petition before the prejudice occurred. Walker v. Mitchell, 224 Va. 568, 299 S.E.2d 698 (1983).

Lack of effective assistance of counsel. — Ordinarily, a claim of ineffective assistance of counsel would not be raised at the trial itself, so that such a claim would not be cognizable on direct appeal to the Supreme Court, under Supreme Court Rule 5:21 (see now Rule 5:25). Thus, a prisoner could not receive a full and fair opportunity to litigate the issue on appeal, and a state habeas action would lie on the ineffective assistance issue. Cartera v. Mitchell, 553 F. Supp. 866 (E.D. Va. 1982).

Exhaustion of remedies where parole date miscalculated. — Although a Virginia prisoner in United States District Court claimed a denial of equal protection and due process on the ground that the Virginia Parole Board miscalculated his mandatory parole release date, this action was properly one in habeas corpus, requiring exhaustion of state remedies, where the prisoner sought declaratory relief to compel his release as well as punitive and compensatory damages, notwithstanding the fact that the prisoner styled his action as one under the Civil Rights Act. Derrow v. Shields, 482 F. Supp. 1144 (W.D. Va. 1980).

After-discovered perjury of government witness. — Such a claim may support a timely motion for a new trial, but unless the commonwealth knew of the perjury, or the court prevented effective cross-examination of the witness, no denial of due process has occurred and no basis for habeas relief exists. Fitzgerald v. Bass, 6 Va. App. 38, 366 S.E.2d 615 (1988), cert. denied, 493 U.S. 945, 110 S. Ct. 354, 107 L. Ed. 2d 342 (1989).

Request for correction of sentence. — Where the petitioner sought no appeal from the order denying his correction of sentence motion, to consider petitioner's request after the time of appeal had expired would allow him to substitute habeas corpus and/or mandamus for the appeal which he failed to pursue. In re Brown, No. 0320-85 (Ct. of Appeals Nov. 22, 1985).

Revocation of suspended sentence. — Defendant lacked standing to raise the issue of the validity of the revocation of a suspended misdemeanor sentence for the first time in a habeas corpus proceeding. The function of a writ of habeas corpus is to inquire into jurisdictional defects amounting to want of legal authority for the detention of a person on whose behalf it is asked. Smith v. Underwood, 1 Va. App. 237, 337 S.E.2d 305 (1985).

Hearing not held where petitioner offered no explanation of previous denial of promise of leniency. — The trial court correctly applied the law when it denied and dismissed the habeas petition without ordering a plenary hearing, where the petition alleged an unkept promise of leniency, given to induce his guilty pleas, but petitioner therein failed to offer any reason why he denied having been promised leniency in response to the trial court's questions as to such promises, and therefore failed to offer any reason why he should be permitted to controvert these statements. Brady v. Garraghty, No. 0126-85 (Ct. of Appeals Oct. 10, 1985).

Appellate claim of foreign national barred. — A reasonably diligent attorney would have discovered the applicability of the Vienna Convention to a foreign national defendant; thus the foreign national defendant's failure to raise his Vienna Convention claim in state court barred his claim at the appellate level. Breard v. Pruett, 134 F.3d 615 (4th Cir. 1998).

II. DECISIONS UNDER PRIOR LAW.

A. General Consideration.

Editor's note. — The cases cited below were decided under corresponding provisions of former law. The term "this section," as used below, refers to former provisions.

Nature and purpose of writ. — The office of the writ of habeas corpus is not to determine the guilt or innocence of the prisoner. The only issue which it presents is whether or not the prisoner is restrained of his liberty by due process of law. Lacey v. Palmer, 93 Va. 159, 24 S.E. 930 (1896).

Habeas corpus is a writ of inquiry granted to determine whether a person is detained without lawful authority. Peyton v. Williams, 206 Va. 595, 145 S.E.2d 147 (1965).

Void proceedings are reviewable. — Where the proceedings, whether civil or criminal, under which a party is detained in custody are void the same are reviewable on habeas corpus, and the party may be discharged. Ex parte Rollins, 80 Va. 314 (1885); Ex parte Marx, 86 Va. 40, 9 S.E. 475 (1889); Ex parte Henry, 14 Va. L. Reg. 596 (1908).

But not merely voidable judgments. — It will not lie to attack a judgment of conviction that is merely voidable by reason of error of law or of fact, omissions or other irregularities. Smyth v. Bunch, 202 Va. 126, 116 S.E.2d 33 (1960), cert. denied, 364 U.S. 935, 81 S. Ct. 382, 5 L. Ed. 2d 366 (1961).

Habeas cannot be used to perform function of appeal or writ of error. — Habeas corpus is a writ of inquiry granted to determine whether a person is illegally detained. It cannot be used to perform the function of an appeal or writ of error, to review errors, or to modify or revise a judgment of conviction pronounced by a court of competent jurisdiction. Smyth v. Midgett, 199 Va. 727, 101 S.E.2d 575 (1958).

The writ of habeas corpus does not lie as a substitute for an appeal or writ of error. Council v. Smyth, 201 Va. 135, 109 S.E.2d 116 (1959).

Section refers to detention in Virginia. — Habeas corpus is available in Virginia whenever a person is "detained without lawful authority." This obviously refers to detention in the State of Virginia. United States ex rel. Smith v. Jackson, 234 F.2d 742 (2d Cir. 1956).

Section 8.01-677 does not supplant this section. — Section 8.01-677 is in simple, clear and unambiguous language, and the Supreme Court reads it to mean what it says. It does not provide that it may be used to obtain a writ or error, or an appeal, or for any purpose other than to correct a "clerical error or error in fact." It does not supplant the writ of habeas corpus. If its provisions should be widened, the enlargement should be effected by the legislature. Blowe v. Peyton, 208 Va. 68, 155 S.E.2d 351 (1967).

The doctrine of res judicata does not limit the availability of habeas corpus in Virginia. Ferguson v. Cox, 464 F.2d 461 (4th Cir. 1972).

Discharge is relief provided. — The Virginia habeas corpus statutes are designed to provide relief in the form of discharge from the person in whose custody a petitioner is detained without lawful authority. Morgan v. Juvenile & Domestic Relations Court, 491 F.2d 456 (4th Cir. 1974).

Providing for custody of person released. — The proper office of the writ of habeas corpus is to release from illegal restraint. Where the party is of years of discretion and sui juris, nothing more is done than to discharge him. But if he be not of an age to determine for himself, the court or judge must decide for him, and make an order for his being placed in the proper custody, and to enable it to do so, must determine to whom the right to the custody belongs. Armstrong v. Stone, 50 Va. (9 Gratt.) 102 (1852).

Allegations and prima facie showing. — This section gives to one in confinement the right to the writ, if he alleges facts which show that he is illegally restrained of his liberty and supports his allegations by affidavits or other evidence. Such a prima facie showing entitles the petitioner to a hearing of his complaint. The court is not confined to a consideration of affidavits if an issue of fact arises but is free to receive the evidence of witnesses in open court and to make its determination as in any other controverted case. Davis v. Smyth, 155 F.2d 3 (4th Cir. 1946).

Broad conclusory allegations are not sufficient for habeas consideration. — A habeas corpus petition must allege facts and mere conclusions or opinions of the petitioner will not suffice to make out a case. Kelly v. Cox, 353 F. Supp. 1050 (W.D. Va. 1972).

Right to counsel in habeas corpus proceedings. — It is generally held that the constitutional requirement that a defendant in a criminal prosecution is entitled to the assistance of counsel does not apply to a habeas corpus proceeding because it is a civil and not a criminal proceeding. Darnell v. Peyton, 208 Va. 675, 160 S.E.2d 749 (1968).

The rule adopted by the majority of the courts is that while a petitioner is not in every instance entitled to the assistance of counsel in the prosecution of his petition for a writ of habeas corpus, the nature and contents of the relief sought and the basis of the error or defect charged may require that such appointment be made. If it appears from a reading of the petition that the points raised are frivolous and plainly do not justify a judicial inquiry, as is frequently the case, the appointment of counsel is not required. On the other hand, where a petition presents a triable issue of fact the clear presentation of which requires an ability to organize factual data or to call witnesses and elicit testimony in a logical fashion, it is much the better practice to assign counsel. Darnell v. Peyton, 208 Va. 675, 160 S.E.2d 749 (1968).

The petition for a writ of habeas corpus to obtain possession of a child may be in the name of the infant by his next friend, or in the name of the person claiming possession. And where it is the mother of the child who is claiming the possession, and she is a married woman, it may be in the names of her husband and herself. Armstrong v. Stone, 50 Va. (9 Gratt.) 102 (1852).

Under this section a person adjudged to be insane and committed to an institution under former § 37.1-67 (see §§ 37.1-67.1 through 37.1-67.5) may apply for a writ of habeas corpus to contest the validity of such statutes and the procedure thereunder. But the federal district court refused to grant a writ of habeas corpus where petitioner had failed to exhaust his remedies in the state court. Hall v. Verdel, 40 F. Supp. 941 (W.D. Va. 1941).

B. Petitioners Held Under Criminal Process.

Application of subsection B. — Subsection B applies only to those cases involving petitioners held under criminal process. The authority of any circuit court, or any judge thereof, to issue writs of habeas corpus in child custody cases, and to make such writs returnable to any circuit court, or the judges thereof, is left unimpaired. Walker v. Brooks, 203 Va. 417, 124 S.E.2d 195 (1962).

Habeas corpus is available only where the release of the prisoner from his immediate detention will follow as a result of an order in his favor. It is not available to secure a judicial determination of any question which, even if determined in the prisoner's favor, could not affect the lawfulness of his immediate custody and detention. It cannot be used to modify or revise a judgment of conviction. McDorman v. Smyth, 187 Va. 522, 47 S.E.2d 441 (1948).

Not applicable to sentence not begun. — A sentence which a prisoner has not begun to serve cannot be the cause of restraint which is made the subject of inquiry in a habeas corpus proceeding. McDorman v. Smyth, 187 Va. 522, 47 S.E.2d 441 (1948).

Nor where petitioner no longer detained. — Where a petitioner is no longer detained and there is no custody from which to discharge him, the state court is without jurisdiction to entertain the case. Morgan v. Juvenile & Domestic Relations Court, 491 F.2d 456 (4th Cir. 1974).

Nor to determine validity of sentence fully served. — While subsection B extends jurisdiction to permit a petitioner to challenge the validity of a sentence to be served subsequently, it does not extend jurisdiction to the courts of Virginia to permit a determination of the validity of a sentence fully served before the proceeding for a writ of habeas corpus is instituted. Moore v. Peyton, 211 Va. 119, 176 S.E.2d 427 (1970).

There is no available state procedure to attack a conviction when the sentence complained of has been fully served and a judgment for the petitioner could not affect the lawfulness of his immediate custody, nor grant him relief from that detention. Eldridge v. Peyton, 295 F. Supp. 621 (W.D. Va. 1968).

Time served under completed void sentence may not be credited against present valid sentence. — A court does not have jurisdiction to determine the validity of a sentence under which the prisoner is not being detained. It follows that where a prisoner is being detained under a valid sentence he is not entitled to credit for time served on a void sentence fully served before the proceeding for writ of habeas corpus is instituted. Smyth v. Midgett, 199 Va. 727, 101 S.E.2d 575 (1958).

The jurisdiction of the court upon a petition for habeas corpus was limited to a consideration of the validity of the conviction under which the petitioner was being detained at the time of the hearing. The court had no jurisdiction to review the validity of a conviction under which the petitioner had already served the sentence imposed prior to the institution of the proceeding, or to order the time served under the prior conviction to be credited against a valid sentence to be served by him pursuant to a conviction in a different court, at a different time, upon a charge involving a wholly unrelated offense. Smyth v. Holland, 199 Va. 92, 97 S.E.2d 745 (1957), cert. denied, 357 U.S. 944, 78 S. Ct. 1394, 2 L. Ed. 2d 1556 (1958).

But prisoner presently detained under void sentence is entitled to credit against valid sentence. — If a prisoner is being detained under a void sentence, he is entitled to credit for the time served under such sentence on a valid sentence, or sentences entered against him prior to the time he began serving the void sentence. Smyth v. Midgett, 199 Va. 727, 101 S.E.2d 575 (1958).

And one detained as repeater may attack validity of sentence he has completely served. — One may attack in a habeas corpus proceeding the validity of a sentence he has completely served when he is detained under former § 53-296 as a repeater. Smyth v. Midgett, 199 Va. 727, 101 S.E.2d 575 (1958).

The usual rule limiting Virginia habeas corpus to the term of the sentence of the conviction under attack does not apply in this instance, where the prisoner has finished serving his sentence for burglary but is still in state custody because of an additional sentence under former § 53-296, because a recidivist sentence does not constitute a separate conviction. Ferguson v. Cox, 464 F.2d 461 (4th Cir. 1972).

Exhaustion of state remedies before seeking federal habeas corpus. — One seeking habeas relief must initially allow the highest state tribunal to consider each of his allegations before a federal court will rule on the merits of his petition. Alley v. Paderick, 373 F. Supp. 918 (W.D. Va. 1974).

A petitioner is required to exhaust his state remedies as a prerequisite to seeking habeas corpus in a federal court to avoid extradition. Tickle v. Summers, 270 F.2d 848 (4th Cir. 1959).

Where the well-pleaded allegations of the petition are not denied they must be accepted as true. Morris v. Smyth, 202 Va. 832, 120 S.E.2d 465 (1961), cert. denied, 371 U.S. 849, 83 S. Ct. 83, 9 L. Ed. 83 (1962).

Requirement that petition enumerate previous applications is not jurisdictional. — The failure of the petition for habeas corpus to state that there had been no previous applications of like nature did not warrant the lower court in dismissing the petition. This requirement is not jurisdictional. Morris v. Smyth, 202 Va. 832, 120 S.E.2d 465 (1961), cert. denied, 371 U.S. 849, 83 S. Ct. 83, 9 L. Ed. 2d 83 (1962).

Judicial inquiry not required where allegations frivolous. — In some cases the allegations of a petition for habeas corpus are patently frivolous and plainly do not justify judicial inquiry. Arey v. Peyton, 209 Va. 370, 164 S.E.2d 691 (1968); Younger v. Cox, 323 F. Supp. 412 (W.D. Va. 1971).

Or, in other cases, the merits of the allegations may be determined by reference to records of previous judicial proceedings. Arey v. Peyton, 209 Va. 370, 164 S.E.2d 691 (1968).

And, in such cases, a full evidentiary hearing may not be required. Arey v. Peyton, 209 Va. 370, 164 S.E.2d 691 (1968); Younger v. Cox, 323 F. Supp. 412 (W.D. Va. 1971).

Refusal to allow petitioner's evidence where trial records sufficient to refute petition. — If the records of a petitioner's criminal trials contain matter sufficient to refute the essential factual allegations of his habeas corpus petition, the court does not err in not allowing him to present evidence concerning those allegations at the habeas corpus proceeding. Younger v. Cox, 323 F. Supp. 412 (W.D. Va. 1971).

Person in custody of federal authorities. — If a person is in the actual custody of the United States for a violation of its laws, no state can by habeas corpus, or any other process, take such person from the custody of the federal tribunal or officer. So, on the other hand, a person in custody under the process or authority of a state, is, by express enactment, beyond the reach of the federal courts or judges. Judiciary act, § 14; act March 2, 1833, § 7; 4 Stat. at Large, 634; 28 U.S.C.A. § 453. Bowling v. Commonwealth, 123 Va. 340, 96 S.E. 739 (1918).

Defective indictment. — The underlying question in habeas corpus proceedings where the sufficiency of an indictment is challenged is directed to whether the indictment is so fatally defective and void that the court in which the petitioner was convicted did not have jurisdiction of the person and crime charged and to whether the court had jurisdiction to render the particular judgment. If the court had jurisdiction of the person and the crime charged, and if the punishment imposed is of the character prescribed by law, a writ of habeas corpus does not lie to release the prisoner from custody for mere irregularities or insufficiency of an indictment no matter how vulnerable to direct attack on motion to quash. Council v. Smyth, 201 Va. 135, 109 S.E.2d 116 (1959).

An indictment or information charging an offense substantially in the language of the statute is not subject to attack on habeas corpus. A mere inartificiality in pleading, or mere defects and irregularities in, or insufficiency of, and indictment constitute no ground for release by habeas corpus where the court has jurisdiction over the offense charged. McDorman v. Smyth, 187 Va. 522, 47 S.E.2d 441 (1948).

Sentence for murder under indictment for manslaughter held not subject to attack. — Where it was clear from the record that defendant, the attorneys and the trial court regarded the trial as one for murder, even though the indictment was for manslaughter only, there was no jurisdictional flaw in the proceeding, and therefore defendant could not successfully utilize habeas corpus to attack the life sentence which he received. Cunningham v. Hayes, 204 Va. 851, 134 S.E.2d 271, cert. denied, 376 U.S. 973, 84 S. Ct. 1140, 12 L. Ed. 2d 86 (1964).

Defective verdict. — Where in a murder case the jury in its verdict used the word "recommend" rather than a more proper term such as "fix" with regard to the ascertainment of punishment, the defect was of the kind that could have been amended before the jury was discharged, and the judgment entered on the verdict was not void and could not be successfully attacked by means of habeas corpus. Smyth v. Bunch, 202 Va. 126, 116 S.E.2d 33 (1960), cert. denied, 364 U.S. 935, 81 S. Ct. 382, 5 L. Ed. 2d 366 (1961).

Lack of effective representation by counsel. — A federal court cannot order the release of a state prisoner, grounded upon the lack of effective counsel in the state court proceeding, unless the incompetence and ineffectiveness of the attorney is so obvious that it becomes the duty of the trial judge or prosecutor (both state officers) to intervene and protect the rights of the accused. An appropriate exception to the general rule exists where an attorney, furnished to an indigent defendant, candidly admits that his conscience prevented him from effectively representing his client according to the customary standards prescribed by attorneys and the courts, and this was not apparent to the trial judge or prosecutor. Johns v. Smyth, 176 F. Supp. 949 (E.D. Va. 1949).

To support a claim of inadequate representation, habeas corpus petitioner must show that his trial was nothing more than a farce or a sham. Mistakes in trial tactics during a trial do not deprive an individual of his constitutional rights even when it concerns whether or not the defendant should plead guilty. Davis v. Slayton, 353 F. Supp. 571 (W.D. Va. 1973).

Hearing held not required where petitioner utterly fails to substantiate allegations. — Where defendant has pleaded guilty with full knowledge of the nature and the consequences of his action and he later seeks to cast responsibility for his predicament on his attorney, no hearing on petition for writ of habeas corpus is required where the record shows that defendant was completely represented and he utterly fails to substantiate his general allegations. Brown v. Smyth, 271 F.2d 227 (4th Cir. 1959).

Mere allegation that counsel suggested to defendant that if he stood trial he was in jeopardy of a death sentence does not show such coercion as to make the plea of guilty an involuntary act, requiring a hearing upon a petition for writ of habeas corpus. Brown v. Smyth, 271 F.2d 227 (4th Cir. 1959).

Where counsel privately retained by petitioner. — An individual cannot claim in a habeas corpus petition that he was denied his right to effective counsel where counsel was privately retained by the petitioner and the situation, if true, was itself created by the petitioner. Davis v. Slayton, 353 F. Supp. 571 (W.D. Va. 1973).

§ 8.01-654.1. Limitation on consideration of petition filed by prisoner sentenced to death. — No petition for a writ of habeas corpus filed by a prisoner held under a sentence of death shall be considered unless it is filed within sixty days after the earliest of: (i) denial by the United States Supreme Court of a petition for a writ of certiorari to the judgment of the Supreme Court of Virginia on direct appeal, (ii) a decision by the United States Supreme Court affirming imposition of the sentence of death when such decision is in a case resulting from a granted writ of certiorari to the judgment of the Supreme Court of Virginia on direct appeal, or(iii) the expiration of the period for filing a timely petition for certiorari without a petition being filed.

However, notwithstanding the time restrictions otherwise applicable to the filing of a petition for a writ of habeas corpus, an indigent prisoner may file such a petition within 120 days following appointment, made under § 19.2-163.7, of counsel to represent him. (1995, c. 503; 1998, c. 199.)

I. DECISIONS UNDER CURRENT LAW.

Applied in George v. Angelone, 901 F. Supp. 1070 (E.D. Va. 1995); Weeks v. Angelone, 4 F. Supp. 2d 497 (E.D. Va. 1998); Royal v. Netherland, 4 F. Supp. 2d 540 (E.D. Va. 1998).

§ 8.01-655. Form and contents of petition filed by prisoner. — A. Every petition filed by a prisoner seeking a writ of habeas corpus must be filed on the form set forth in subsection B. The failure to use such form and to comply substantially with such form shall entitle the court to which such petition is directed to return such petition to the prisoner pending the use of and substantial compliance with such form. The petitioner shall be responsible for all statements contained in the petition and any false statement contained

§ 8.01-655   CODE OF VIRGINIA   § 8.01-655

therein, if the same be knowingly or wilfully made, shall be a ground for prosecution and conviction of perjury as provided for in § 18.2-434.

B. Every petition filed by a prisoner seeking a writ of habeas corpus shall be filed on a form to be approved and provided by the office of the Attorney General, the contents of which shall be substantially as follows:

IN THE .... COURT
....
Full name and prisoner   Case No. ....
number (if any) of   (To be supplied by
Petitioner   the Clerk of the
-vs-   Court)
....
....
Name and Title of Respondent

PETITION FOR WRIT OF HABEAS CORPUS

Instructions—Read Carefully

In order for this petition to receive consideration by the Court, it must be legibly handwritten or typewritten, signed by the petitioner and verified before a notary or other officer authorized to administer oaths. It must set forth in concise form the answers to each applicable question. If necessary, petitioner may finish his answer to a particular question on an additional page. Petitioner must make it clear to which question any such continued answer refers. The petitioner may also submit exhibits.

Since every petition for habeas corpus must be sworn to under oath, any false statement of a material fact therein may serve as the basis of prosecution and conviction for perjury under § 18.2-434. Petitioners should, therefore, exercise care to assure that all answers are true and correct.

When the petition is completed, the original and two copies (total of three) should be mailed to the clerk of the court. The petitioner shall keep one copy.

NOTICE

The granting of a writ of habeas corpus does not entitle the petitioner to dismissal of the charges for conviction of which he is being detained, but may gain him no more than a new trial.

....
Place of detention: ....

A. Criminal Trial

1. Name and location of court which imposed the sentence from which you seek relief:
   ....
   ....

2. The offense or offenses for which sentence was imposed (include indictment number or numbers if known):
   a. ....
   b. ....
   c. ....

3. The date upon which sentence was imposed and the terms of the sentence:
   a. ....
   b. ....
   c. ....

4. Check which plea you made and whether trial by jury: Plea of guilty: ....; Plea of not guilty: ....; Trial by jury: ....; Trial by judge without jury: ....

5. The name and address of each attorney, if any, who represented you at your criminal trial:
....

6. Did you appeal the conviction? ....

7. If you answered "yes" to 6, state: the result and the date in your appeal or petition for certiorari:
  a. ....
  b. ....
  citations of the appellate court opinions or orders:
  a. ....
  b. ....

8. List the name and address of each attorney, if any, who represented you on your appeal:
....
....

B. Habeas Corpus

9. Before this petition did you file with respect to this conviction any other petition for habeas corpus in either a State or federal court? ....

10. If you answered "yes" to 9, list with respect to each petition: the name and location of the court in which each was filed:
  a. ....
  b. ....
  the disposition and the date:
  a. ....
  b. ....
  the name and address of each attorney, if any, who represented you on your habeas corpus:
  a. ....
  b. ....

11. Did you appeal from the disposition of your petition for habeas corpus?

12. If you answered "yes" to 11, state: the result and the date of each petition:
  a. ....
  b. ....
  citations of court opinions or orders on your habeas corpus petition:
  a. ....
  b. ....
  the name and address of each attorney, if any, who represented you on appeal of your habeas corpus:
  a. ....
  b. ....

C. Other Petitions, Motions or Applications

13. List all other petitions, motions or applications filed with any court following a final order of conviction and not set out in A or B. Include the nature of the motion, the name and location of the court, the result, the date, and citations to opinions or orders. Give the name and address of each attorney, if any, who represented you.
  a. ....
  b. ....

c. ....

D. Present Petition

14. State the grounds which make your detention unlawful, including the facts on which you intend to rely:
   a. ....
   b. ....
   c. ....

15. List each ground set forth in 14, which has been presented in any other proceeding:
   a. ....
   b. ....
   c. ....
   List the proceedings in which each ground was raised:
   a. ....
   b. ....
   c. ....

16. If any ground set forth in 14 has not been presented to a court, list each ground and the reason why it was not:
   a. ....
   b. ....
   c. ....

....
Signature of Petitioner
....
Address of Petitioner

STATE OF VIRGINIA
CITY/COUNTY OF ....
   The petitioner being first duly sworn, says:
   1. He signed the foregoing petition;
   2. The facts stated in the petition are true to the best of his information and belief.

....
Signature of Petitioner

Subscribed and sworn to before me
this .... day of ...., 20.......
....
Notary Public
My commission expires: ....
   The petition will not be filed without payment of court costs unless the petitioner is entitled to proceed in forma pauperis and has executed the affidavit in forma pauperis.
   The petitioner who proceeds in forma pauperis shall be furnished, without cost, certified copies of the arrest warrants, indictment and order of his conviction at his criminal trial in order to comply with the instructions of this petition.

AFFIDAVIT IN FORMA PAUPERIS

STATE OF VIRGINIA
CITY/COUNTY OF ....
   The petitioner being duly sworn, says:
   1. He is unable to pay the costs of this action or give security therefor;
   2. His assets amount to a total of $ ....

....
Signature of Petitioner

Subscribed and sworn to before me this .... day of ...., 20 ....
....
        Notary Public
My commission expires: ....
(Code 1950, § 8-596.1; 1968, c. 359; 1977, c. 617.)

REVISERS' NOTE

Section 8.01-655 changes former § 8-596.1 by adding the last sentence preceding "Affidavit in Forma Pauperis." This addition represents a codification of McCoy v. Lankford, 210 Va. 264, 170 S.E.2d 11 (1969).

Law Review. — For survey of Virginia criminal law and procedure for the year 1969-1970, see 56 Va. L. Rev. 1572 (1970).

I. Decisions Under Current Law.
II. Decisions Under Prior Law.

I. DECISIONS UNDER CURRENT LAW.

Virginia's pro se procedures are in no sense futile or arcane. The form contained in this section is a simple one. Mallory v. Smith, 27 F.3d 991 (4th Cir. 1994), cert. denied, 513 U.S. 1047, 115 S. Ct. 644, 130 L. Ed. 2d 549 (1994).

Federal court won't determine if state court should have seen additional claims in pleading. — Where prisoner identified three grounds in his pleadings under this section, and the Virginia Supreme Court disposed of each of those three grounds in its order, the federal appellate court will not go further and determine whether the Virginia Supreme Court should have seen another claim in his filings. To have the federal court scan the information contained in prisoner's form for further facts that conceivably might make out other federal claims would send a strong signal to state courts that their procedures will not be respected by their federal counterparts and would also signal litigants that they may ignore state procedures and still expect the federal courts to hear claims that state courts would have had to stitch together from stray references in order to review. Mallory v. Smith, 27 F.3d 991 (4th Cir. 1994), cert. denied, 513 U.S. 1047, 115 S. Ct. 644, 130 L. Ed. 2d 549 (1994).

II. DECISIONS UNDER PRIOR LAW.

Editor's note. — The case cited below was decided under corresponding provisions of former law. The term "this section," as used below, refers to former provisions.

Copies of indictment and order of conviction needed. — In order to comply with the instructions incorporated in this section and answer the specified questions a petitioner needs copies of the indictment and order of conviction. McCoy v. Lankford, 210 Va. 264, 170 S.E.2d 11 (1969).

Court records or transcript need not be appended. — This section, which prescribes the form of a petition for a writ of habeas corpus, does not require that court records or transcript be appended to the same. McCoy v. Lankford, 210 Va. 264, 170 S.E.2d 11 (1969).

Petitioner was furnished, without cost, certified copies of the arrest warrants, indictment and the order of conviction at his criminal trial. McCoy v. Lankford, 210 Va. 264, 170 S.E.2d 11 (1969).

§ 8.01-656. Bond may be required of petitioner. — Before granting the writ, the court may require the petitioner to give bond with surety in a reasonable amount for the payment of such costs and charges as may be awarded against him.

Such bond shall be made payable to the person to whom the writ is directed, with condition that the petitioner will not escape, and shall be filed with the other proceedings on the writ, and may be sued on for the benefit of any person injured by the breach of its condition. (Code 1950, § 8-597; 1977, c. 617.)

I. DECISIONS UNDER PRIOR LAW.

Editor's note. — The case cited below was decided under corresponding provisions of former law. The term "this section," as used below, refers to former provisions.

Where the person alleged to be unlawfully detained labors under disabilities, the petitioner is the person from whom the bond provided for by this section may be required, and who is liable for the costs, whether the writ is issued upon the petition of the person asserting the claim to the custody or upon the petition of the person detained by his next friend. Armstrong v. Stone, 50 Va. (9 Gratt.) 102 (1852).

§ 8.01-657. How directed and returnable. — The writ shall be directed to the person in whose custody the petitioner is detained and shall be made returnable as soon as may be before the court ordering the same, or any other of such courts.

Provided that in the event the allegations of illegality of the petitioner's detention present a case for the determination of unrecorded matters of fact relating to any previous judicial proceeding, such writ shall be made returnable before the court in which such judicial proceeding occurred. (Code 1950, § 8-598; 1958, c. 215; 1977, c. 617.)

I. DECISIONS UNDER PRIOR LAW.

Editor's note. — The cases cited below were decided under corresponding provisions of former law. The term "this section," as used below, refers to former provisions.

Applicability of second paragraph. — The second paragraph applies only to cases involving petitioners held under criminal process. Walker v. Brooks, 203 Va. 417, 124 S.E.2d 195 (1962).

The second paragraph of this section was applicable to a petition alleging an inconsistency between indictment and sentence, incompetency of court-appointed counsel, and improper inducement of a guilty plea, since these allegations presented a case for the determination of unrecorded matters of fact relating to petitioner's trial. Cunningham v. Frye, 203 Va. 539, 125 S.E.2d 846 (1962).

§ 8.01-658. How writ served. — The writ shall be served on the person to whom it is directed, or, in his absence from the place where the petitioner is confined, on the person having the immediate custody of him. (Code 1950, § 8-599; 1977, c. 617.)

§ 8.01-659. Penalty for disobeying it. — If the person on whom such writ is served shall, in disobedience to the writ, fail to bring the petitioner, with a return of the cause of his detention, before a court before which the writ is returnable, he shall forfeit to the petitioner $300. (Code 1950, § 8-600; 1977, c. 617.)

REVISERS' NOTE

Section 8.01-659 changes former § 8-600 by deleting the obsolete reference to a three-day period for compliance.

§ 8.01-660. When affidavits may be read. — In the discretion of the court or judge before whom the petitioner is brought, the affidavits of witnesses taken by either party, on reasonable notice to the other, may be read as evidence. (Code 1950, § 8-601; 1977, c. 617.)

I. Decisions Under Current Law.
II. Decisions Under Prior Law.

I. DECISIONS UNDER CURRENT LAW.

This section permits a habeas court to consider affidavits when deciding a motion to dismiss. Yeatts v. Murray, 249 Va. 285, 455 S.E.2d 18 (1995).

Applied in Walker v. Mitchell, 224 Va. 568, 299 S.E.2d 698 (1983).

II. DECISIONS UNDER PRIOR LAW.

Editor's note. — The case cited below was decided under corresponding provisions of former law. The term "this section, "as used below, refers to former provisions.

Affidavits to show illegality. — The affidavits referred to in this section are such as are introduced to show illegality, not the mere irregularity, of the prisoner's detention, and do not authorize a review of the judgment under which he is detained. Ex parte Marx, 86 Va. 40, 9 S.E. 475 (1889).

§ 8.01-661. Facts proved may be made part of record. — All the material facts proved shall, when it is required by either party, be made a part of the proceedings and entered by the clerk among the records of the court. (Code 1950, § 8-602; 1977, c. 617.)

§ 8.01-662. Judgment of court or judge trying it; payment of costs and expenses when petition denied. — After hearing the matter both upon the return and any other evidence, the court before whom the petitioner is brought shall either discharge or remand him, or admit him to bail and adjudge the cost of the proceeding, including the charge for transporting the prisoner.

Provided, however, that if the petition is denied, the costs and expenses of the proceeding and the attorney's fees of any attorney appointed to represent the petitioner shall be assessed against the petitioner. If such cost, expenses and fees are collected, they shall be paid to the Commonwealth. (Code 1950, § 8-603; 1968, c. 482; 1977, c. 617.)

I. Decisions Under Current Law.
II. Decisions Under Prior Law.

I. DECISIONS UNDER CURRENT LAW.

Applied in Walker v. Mitchell, 224 Va. 568, 299 S.E.2d 698 (1983).

II. DECISIONS UNDER PRIOR LAW.

Editor's note. — The case cited below was decided under corresponding provisions of former law. The term "this section," as used below, refers to former provisions.

Judgment on habeas corpus held not final disposition of case. — A judgment on habeas corpus that the order under which petitioner was committed to the penitentiary was defective, directing that the prisoner be released from the penitentiary and remanded to the sheriff for further action, was not a final disposition of the case. Teasley v. Commonwealth, 188 Va. 376, 49 S.E.2d 604 (1948).

§ 8.01-663. Judgment conclusive. — Any such judgment entered of record shall be conclusive, unless the same be reversed, except that the petitioner shall not be precluded from bringing the same matter in question in an action for false imprisonment. (Code 1950, § 8-605; 1977, c. 617.)

Law Review. — For survey of Virginia law on criminal law and procedure for the year 1969-1970, see 56 Va. L. Rev. 1572 (1970).

I. Decisions Under Current Law.
II. Decisions Under Prior Law.

I. DECISIONS UNDER CURRENT LAW.

The principle of res judicata does not apply to habeas corpus proceedings. Bland v. Johnson, 495 F. Supp. 735 (E.D. Va. 1980).

Previous determination of issues by either State or federal courts will be conclusive, absent a change of circumstances. Bland v. Johnson, 495 F. Supp. 735 (E.D. Va. 1980).

Repetitious petition. — Pursuant to this section, a Virginia court may dismiss a petition for a writ of habeas corpus summarily if it determines that it is repetitious. Bland v. Johnson, 495 F. Supp. 735 (E.D. Va. 1980).

II. DECISIONS UNDER PRIOR LAW.

Editor's note. — The case cited below was decided under corresponding provisions of former law. The term "this section," as used below, refers to former provisions.

The principle of res judicata does not apply to habeas corpus proceedings. Hawks v. Cox, 211 Va. 91, 175 S.E.2d 271 (1970).

Nevertheless, this section affords relief from the increasing burden of repetitive habeas corpus applications. Hawks v. Cox, 211 Va. 91, 175 S.E.2d 271 (1970).

If a court has determined that a petition for habeas corpus is repetitious then, without appointing counsel, it may deny the writ under this section. Inevitably, there will be instances when the court receiving a petition which appears meritorious on its face will issue a show cause order before finding that all the allegations have previously been resolved against the petitioner. In such cases the Attorney General can only move to dismiss under the same statutory authority. Hawks v. Cox, 211 Va. 91, 175 S.E.2d 271 (1970).

Previous determination of issues by either state or federal courts will be conclusive, absent a change of circumstances. Hawks v. Cox, 211 Va. 91, 175 S.E.2d 271 (1970).

§ 8.01-664. How and when Supreme Court summoned to try appeal therefrom. — If, during the recess of the Supreme Court, the Governor or the Chief Justice of the Court should think the immediate revision of any such judgment to be proper, he may summon the Court for that purpose, to meet on any day to be fixed by him. (Code 1950, § 8-606; 1977, c. 617.)

§ 8.01-665. When execution of judgment suspended; when prisoner admitted to bail. — When the prisoner is remanded, the execution of the judgment shall not be suspended by a petition for appeal or by a writ of error, or for the purpose of applying for such writ. When he is ordered to be discharged, and the execution of the judgment is suspended for the purpose of petitioning for appeal to the Court of Appeals or applying for a writ of error from the Supreme Court, the court making such suspending order may admit the prisoner to bail until the expiration of the time allowed for filing a petition for appeal or applying for the writ of error, or, in case the petition for appeal is filed or the writ of error is allowed, until the decision of the Court of Appeals or the Supreme Court thereon is duly certified. (Code 1950, § 8-607; 1977, c. 617; 1984, c. 703.)

§ 8.01-666. When and by whom writs of habeas corpus ad testificandum granted. — Writs of habeas corpus ad testificandum may be granted by any circuit court in the same manner and under the same conditions and provisions as are prescribed by this chapter as to granting the writ of habeas corpus ad subjiciendum so far as the same are applicable. (Code 1950, § 8-608; 1977, c. 617.)

§ 8.01-667. Transmission of records to federal court. — Whenever any habeas corpus case is pending in a federal court, upon written request of the Attorney General or any assistant attorney general, a court of this Commonwealth shall transmit to such federal court such records as may be requested. (Code 1950, § 8-608.1; 1975, c. 389; 1977, c. 617.)

§ 8.01-668. Writ de homine abolished. — The writ de homine replegiando is abolished. (Code 1950, § 8-609; 1977, c. 617.)

CHAPTER 26.

APPEALS TO THE SUPREME COURT.

Article 1.
Definitions.

Sec.
8.01-669. Definitions.

Article 2.
When Granted.

8.01-670. In what cases awarded.
8.01-671. Time within which petition must be presented.
8.01-672. Jurisdictional amount.

Article 3.
The Record.

8.01-673. Inspection and return of records; certiorari when part of record is omitted; binding or retention of records.

Article 4.
The Petition.

8.01-674. With whom filed; endorsement thereon; reference to justice or justices; when deemed to be filed.
8.01-675. [Repealed.]
8.01-675.1. When dismissal final; when reinstated.
8.01-675.2. Rehearing.

ARTICLE 1.

Definitions.

§ 8.01-669. Definitions. — As used in Chapters 26, 26.1 and 26.2, unless the context otherwise requires, the term:

"Judgment" includes a decree, order, finding, or award.

"Petitioner" means a party who petitions to the Court of Appeals or the Supreme Court for an appeal.

"Appellant" means any aggrieved party who has an appeal of right or who has been granted an appeal by the Court of Appeals or the Supreme Court.

"Appellate court" means either the Court of Appeals or the Supreme Court, or both as the context may indicate. (1977, c. 617; 1984, c. 703.)

REVISERS' NOTE

This section contains definitions for certain terms appearing throughout chapter 26. The terms defined economize the language of various sections which formerly used multiple terms, e.g., "judgment, decree or order."

ARTICLE 2.

When Granted.

§ 8.01-670. In what cases awarded. — A. Except as provided by § 17.1-405, any person may present a petition for an appeal to the Supreme Court if he believes himself aggrieved:

1. By any judgment in a controversy concerning:
   a. The title to or boundaries of land,
   b. The condemnation of property,
   c. The probate of a will,
   d. The appointment or qualification of a personal representative, guardian, conservator, committee, or curator,
   e. A mill, roadway, ferry, wharf, or landing,

f. The right of the Commonwealth, or a county, or municipal corporation to levy tolls or taxes, or

g. The construction of any statute, ordinance, or county proceeding imposing taxes; or

2. By the order of a court refusing a writ of quo warranto or by the final judgment on any such writ; or

3. By a final judgment in any other civil case.

B. Except as provided by § 17.1-405, any party may present a petition for an appeal to the Supreme Court in any case in chancery wherein there is an interlocutory decree or order:

1. Granting, dissolving or denying an injunction; or

2. Requiring money to be paid or the possession or title of property to be changed; or

3. Adjudicating the principles of a cause. (Code 1950, § 8-462; 1977, c. 617; 1984, c. 703; 1997, c. 801.)

REVISERS' NOTE

References to appeals from judgments of the State Corporation Commission and from awards of the Industrial (now Workers' Compensation) Commission have been deleted because §§ 12.1-39 and 65.1-98 (now § 65.2-706), respectively, cover such appeals.

Section 8.01-670 B 1 permits an appeal from an interlocutory order or decree granting, dissolving, or denying an injunction. This expands the former provision which permitted an appeal only from the dissolution of an injunction. Conforming changes have been made in § 8.01-626. (Final orders or decrees affecting an injunction can be appealed under § 8.01-670 A 3.)

Editor's note. — Acts 1997, c. 801, cl. 2, provides: "That the provisions of this act shall become effective on January 1, 1998. The powers granted and duties imposed pursuant to this act shall apply prospectively to guardians and conservators appointed by court order entered on or after that date, or modified on or after that date if the court so directs, without regard to when the petition was filed. The procedures specified in this act governing proceedings for appointment of a guardian or conservator or termination or other modification of a guardianship shall apply on and after that date without regard to when the petition therefor was filed or the guardianship or conservatorship created."

Cross references. — As to appellate jurisdiction of Supreme Court, see Va. Const., Art. VI, § 1 and § 17.1-310. As to recovery of damages sustained for property withheld during appeal, see § 8.01-123. As to appeal bonds, see § 8.01-676.1. As to jurisdiction over appeals from grant or denial of injunctions, see § 8.01-626. For appeals in habeas corpus proceedings, see §§ 8.01-664, 8.01-665. For provisions relating to decisions on appeal, see §§ 8.01-680 et seq. For writs of error in criminal cases, see §§ 19.2-317 et seq. For provisions as to appeals concerning roadways, see §§ 56-16, 56-19, 56-21, 56-28, 56-31. As to appeals from the Virginia Employment Commission, see § 60.2-625. As to appeals from the Workers' Compensation Commission, see § 65.2-706. For rules of court as to appellate proceedings in the Supreme Court, see Rules 5:1 through 5:42. For Rules of Court as to Appellate proceedings in the Court of Appeals, see Rules 5A:1 through 5A:36. For a petition for review pursuant to § 8.01-626, and for final judgments within the meaning of this section not being reviewable by a justice of the Supreme Court under § 8.01-626, see Rule 5:17A.

Law Review. — For article, "Appellate Justice: A Crisis in Virginia?", see 57 Va. L. Rev. 3 (1971). For note discussing the Virginia Judicial Council's intermediate appellate court proposal, see 16 U. Rich. L. Rev. 209 (1982). For an article, "Final and Interlocutory Appeals in Virginia," see 8 Geo. Mason L. Rev. 337 (1999).

I. Decisions Under Current Law.
  A. General Consideration.
  B. Appealable Judgments, Orders and Decrees.
    1. In General.
    2. Interlocutory Decrees.
  C. Who May Appeal.

§ 8.01-670   CIVIL REMEDIES AND PROCEDURE   § 8.01-670

II. Decisions Under Prior Law.
  A. General Consideration.
  B. Jurisdiction.
  C. Appealable Judgments, Orders and Decrees.
    1. In General.
    2. Appealability as Dependent on Finality of Decisions.
      a. In General.
      b. Final Judgments.
      c. Application of Rule in Particular Cases.
        i. Decisions Held Final and Appealable.
        ii. Decisions Held Not Final and Unappealable.
    3. Jurisdiction in Special Matters.
      a. Condemnation Proceedings.
      b. Controversies Touching Probate of a Will.
      c. Controversies Touching Mills, Roadways, Ferries or Landings.
      d. Right to Levy Tolls or Taxes.
      e. Controversies Touching Constitutionality of a Law.
      f. Writs.
    4. Interlocutory Decrees.
      a. In General.
      b. Decree or Order as to Dissolution of Injunction.
      c. Decree or Order Requiring Possession or Title of Property to Be Changed.
      d. Decree or Order Adjudicating Principles of Cause.
  D. Who May Appeal.
    1. In General.
    2. Must Be Aggrieved.
      a. General Rule.
      b. Application of Rule.
    3. The Commonwealth.
    4. Counties and Cities.
    5. Joint Appeals.
    6. Estoppel to Appeal.

I. DECISIONS UNDER CURRENT LAW.

A. General Consideration.

Constitutionality. — The right to appellate review is a statutory right and is not a necessary element of due process; thus, no due process violation occurs if an appeal is barred. Payne v. Commonwealth, 233 Va. 460, 357 S.E.2d 500, cert. denied, 484 U.S. 933, 108 S. Ct. 308, 98 L. Ed. 2d 267 (1987).

The statutes which limit review of a death penalty case to the Supreme Court do not violate equal protection rights, as it is rational for the General Assembly, given the gravity of cases involving a sentence to death, to provide death-penalty defendants an automatic, plenary review in the Commonwealth's highest court. Payne v. Commonwealth, 233 Va. 460, 357 S.E.2d 500, cert. denied, 484 U.S. 933, 108 S. Ct. 308, 98 L. Ed. 2d 267 (1987).

Section controls over § 8.01-626 in final judgments. — The summary procedure for review of orders regarding injunctions under § 8.01-626 may not be employed as a substitute for an appeal under this section when a final judgment within the meaning of this section has been entered in the circuit court. Omega Corp. v. Cobb, 222 Va. 875, 292 S.E.2d 44 (1981).

Appellate jurisdiction in child guardian matters. — Subdivision 3 e of former § 17-166.05 gives jurisdiction to the Court of Appeals in "[a]ny final judgment, order, or decree of a circuit court involving ... [t]he control or disposition of a child." Because this section clearly contemplates the Court of Appeals having initial appellate jurisdiction over at least some of the judgments listed in that section, and because guardianship is a matter commonly involving the control or disposition of a child, these two jurisdictional statutes when read together evince a legislative intent to grant the Court of Appeals initial appellate jurisdiction in matters involving the appointment or qualification of guardians for a minor child. In re O'Neil, 18 Va. App. 674, 446 S.E.2d 475 (1994).

The Court of Appeals does not have jurisdiction of final decisions of circuit courts on appeal from decisions of boards of zoning appeals. Appellate jurisdiction of such cases lies in the Supreme Court under subdivision A 3, assuming, but not deciding, that a petition for certiorari under former § 15.1-497 (see now § 15.2-2314) is an "appeal" from a decision of a board of zoning appeals within the meaning of former § 17-116.05(1). Virginia Beach Beautification Comm'n v. Board

823

of Zoning Appeals, 231 Va. 415, 344 S.E.2d 899 (1986), cert. denied, 484 U.S. 933, 108 S. Ct. 308, 98 L. Ed. 2d 267 (1987).

Supreme Court had jurisdiction in refusal to submit to alcohol test case. — Although former § 18.2-268 V (now § 18.2-268.4) regulated the procedure on appeal, a defendant's substantive right of appeal is regulated by this section, which authorizes an appeal to the Supreme Court by any person aggrieved by a final judgment in any other civil case. Thus, the Supreme Court had jurisdiction in a refusal to submit to a blood or breath alcohol test case. Commonwealth v. Rafferty, 241 Va. 319, 402 S.E.2d 17 (1991).

For an action protesting the decision to award a contract brought under § 11-70 of the Virginia Public Procurement Act and not under the administrative appeals procedure authorized by § 11-71, appellate jurisdiction lies with the Supreme Court and not the Court of Appeals. Allstar Towing, Inc. v. City of Alexandria, 231 Va. 421, 344 S.E.2d 903 (1986).

Applied in VEC v. A.I.M. Corp., 225 Va. 338, 302 S.E.2d 534 (1983); Smith v. Woodlawn Constr. Co., 235 Va. 424, 368 S.E.2d 699 (1988); County of Fairfax v. Fleet Indus. Park Ltd. Partnership, 242 Va. 426, 410 S.E.2d 669 (1991); Sovran Bank v. Creative Indus., Inc., 245 Va. 93, 425 S.E.2d 504 (1993); Black v. Eagle, 248 Va. 48, 445 S.E.2d 662 (1994).

B. Appealable Judgments, Orders and Decrees.

1. In General.

Nonsuit against defendant against whom cross-claim filed. — When an order of nonsuit improperly dismisses a party defendant against whom a valid cross-claim has been duly filed, effectively time-barring the cause of action set forth in the cross-claim, such order is a final, appealable judgment as to the cross-claimant within the meaning of this statute. Iliff v. Richards, 221 Va. 644, 272 S.E.2d 645 (1980).

Ordinarily, an order of nonsuit is not to be considered a final judgment for purposes of appeal. An order of nonsuit is a final, appealable order within the meaning of subdivision A 3, only when a dispute exists whether the trial court properly granted a motion for nonsuit. McManama v. Plunk, 250 Va. 27, 458 S.E.2d 759 (1995).

Absent an appealable order in an adoption proceeding the Supreme Court may not determine whether any of the requirements for adoption have been met. Where the order in a case was not a final or even an interlocutory order of adoption nor was it appealable as an order adjudicating the principles of a cause, any finding made in the adoption proceeding is not yet appealable. Shortridge v. Deel, 224 Va. 589, 299 S.E.2d 500 (1983).

Where a dispute exists whether the trial court properly granted a motion for nonsuit, that order of nonsuit is a final, appealable order within the meaning of subdivision A 3. Wells v. Lorcom House Condominiums' Council of Co-Owners, 237 Va. 247, 377 S.E.2d 381 (1989).

2. Interlocutory Decrees.

Foreign divorce decree held appealable. — In an appeal by a husband of a foreign court's divorce decree where the wife challenged the Virginia court's jurisdiction to entertain the appeal, the decree was appealable since it denied the husband an injunction, and since it adjudicated the principles of the cause. Ceyte v. Ceyte, 222 Va. 11, 278 S.E.2d 791 (1981).

C. Who May Appeal.

Elimination of codefendant who could be held jointly liable. — The defendant manifestly was aggrieved, within the contemplation of this section, by the court's action in erroneously eliminating a codefendant who could be held jointly liable with defendant to the plaintiff. Government Employees Ins. Co. v. Gallop, 224 Va. 720, 299 S.E.2d 525 (1983).

Virginia Employment Commission held not an aggrieved person, with the right of appeal under this section, where circuit court reversed Commission's decisions with respect to entitlement of benefits. See VEC v. City of Virginia Beach, 222 Va. 728, 284 S.E.2d 595 (1981).

II. DECISIONS UNDER PRIOR LAW.

A. General Consideration.

Editor's note. — The cases cited below were decided under corresponding provisions of former law. The term "this section," as used below, refers to former provisions.

Section conforms to the provision of the Constitution relating to the jurisdiction of the Supreme Court. The 1928 amendment to the section of the Constitution, which eliminated the limitations on the jurisdiction of the Supreme Court, in no way impaired the provision of this section. Unemployment Comp. Comm'n v. Harvey, 179 Va. 202, 18 S.E.2d 390 (1942).

The legislature has the power to deny to litigants any review of the proceedings by the Supreme Court. Town of Falls Church v. County Bd., 166 Va. 192, 184 S.E. 459 (1936).

Liberal construction. — This section being remedial should be construed liberally so as to effectuate the purpose of its enactment. Southern Ry. v. Hill, 106 Va. 501, 56 S.E. 278 (1907); Hampton Rds. San. Dist. Comm'n v. Smith, 193 Va. 371, 68 S.E.2d 497 (1952).

This section does not deal with the completion of the record in the trial court. — This and other sections regulating appeals and applications for writs of error do not purport to deal with the time or the manner in which the record shall be completed in the trial court. Nethers v. Nethers, 160 Va. 335, 168 S.E. 428 (1933).

Appeals and writs of error are not allowed for the purpose of settling abstract questions, however interesting and important to the public they may be, but only to correct errors injuriously affecting the appellant or plaintiff in error. Nicholas v. Lawrence, 161 Va. 589, 171 S.E. 673 (1933).

Real controversy must exist. — Whenever it appears, or is made to appear by extrinsic evidence, that there is no actual controversy, or that if one existed, it has ceased, the appeal or writ of error should be dismissed. Courts of justice sit to decide actual controversies by a judgment which can be enforced, and not to give opinions upon moot questions or abstract propositions of law. Hamer v. Commonwealth, 107 Va. 636, 59 S.E. 400 (1907); Levy v. Kosmo, 129 Va. 446, 106 S.E. 228 (1921).

Appeal dismissed if controversy settled. — Where, after a writ of error was granted to the judgment of the circuit court refusing to grant the plaintiff in error a mandamus to compel the clerk of the board of election commissioners to give him a certificate of election, it appeared that the controversy had been decided in a proper proceeding, the writ of error was dismissed. Franklin v. Peers, 95 Va. 602, 29 S.E. 321 (1898).

Whether a party has a right to appeal is not a question for the lower but for the appellate court. Todd v. Gallego Mills Mfg. Co., 84 Va. 586, 5 S.E. 676 (1888).

Appellate court has no power when decree not appealable. — Where the Supreme Court has reached the conclusion that the decree under review is not an appealable decree, that court is without jurisdiction to decide any other question in the case. Lee v. Lee, 142 Va. 244, 128 S.E. 524 (1925).

B. Jurisdiction.

An appeal from the decision of an inferior court does not lie, unless jurisdiction to entertain such appeal is conferred by Constitution or statute. Richmond Cedar Works & Liberty Mut. Ins. Co. v. Harper, 129 Va. 481, 106 S.E. 516 (1921).

The Virginia Constitution does not, proprio vigore, confer jurisdiction upon the Supreme Court. Therefore, whatever jurisdiction it exercises must be by virtue of statutory authority given in pursuance of the Constitution. The provisions of the Constitution in this particular are carried into effect by §§ 8.01-670 and 8.01-672. Barnett v. Meredith, 51 Va. (10 Gratt.) 650 (1854); Page v. Clopton, 71 Va. (30 Gratt.) 417 (1878); Prison Ass'n v. Ashby, 93 Va. 667, 25 S.E. 893 (1896). See also, Rudacille v. State Comm'n of Conservation & Dev., 155 Va. 808, 156 S.E. 829 (1931).

Legislature has right to extend or deny remedy. — Where the Constitution does not expressly give the right of an appeal the legislature has the right to extend or deny this remedy to the litigant. Hulvey v. Roberts, 106 Va. 189, 55 S.E. 585 (1906).

The burden is upon him who invokes the authority of the Supreme Court to establish its jurisdiction over the matter in controversy. Harman v. City of Lynchburg, 74 Va. (33 Gratt.) 37 (1880); Forbes v. State Council, 107 Va. 853, 60 S.E. 81 (1908), appeal dismissed, 216 U.S. 396, 30 S. Ct. 295, 54 L. Ed. 534 (1909); Lamb v. Thompson, 112 Va. 134, 70 S.E. 507 (1911); C.L. Ritter Lumber Co. v. Coal Mt. Mining Co., 115 Va. 370, 79 S.E. 322 (1913); Jones v. Buckingham Slate Co., 116 Va. 120, 81 S.E. 28 (1914).

The burden of showing the existence of jurisdiction to hear the appeal is on the plaintiff in error, and such jurisdiction must affirmatively appear from the record. Williamson v. Payne, 103 Va. 551, 49 S.E. 600 (1905); C.L. Ritter Lumber Co. v. Coal Mt. Mining Co., 115 Va. 370, 79 S.E. 322 (1913). See also, Jones v. Buckingham Slate Co., 116 Va. 120, 81 S.E. 28 (1914); J.A. Heisler & Bro. v. Merchants Cold Storage & Ice Mfg. Co., 139 Va. 114, 123 S.E. 505 (1924).

When jurisdiction affirmatively appears. — The jurisdiction of the Supreme Court affirmatively appears from the record, when the court can see that the judgment of the lower court necessarily involved the constitutionality of some statute or ordinance, or drew in question some right under the federal or State Constitution. Ward Lumber Co. v. Henderson-White Mfg. Co., 107 Va. 626, 59 S.E. 476 (1907).

C. Appealable Judgments, Orders and Decrees.

1. In General.

Jurisdiction limited to the issue. — The jurisdiction of the court below was limited to the issue made by the pleadings and the same is true of the jurisdiction of the Supreme Court. Reynolds v. Adams, 125 Va. 295, 99 S.E. 695 (1919).

Appeal will lie to a void decree. — A writ of error or appeal will lie to or from a judgment, decree or order of a court, although the same may be void for want of jurisdiction or for other cause. Crane v. Crane, 62 Va. (21 Gratt.) 579 (1871).

An order of a court of record affirming a

§ 8.01-670

decision of a board of zoning appeals is a final order in a "civil case," and is appealable under subdivision A 3 of this section. Burkhardt v. Board of Zoning Appeals, 192 Va. 606, 66 S.E.2d 565 (1951).

And from order overruling exceptions to report of commissioner of accounts. — An appeal lies to the Supreme Court from an order of an inferior court overruling exceptions to and confirming a commissioner of account's report upon the accounts of a county treasurer, which disallowed credits claimed by the treasurer of $893.78 and awarded costs against him. The judgment of the lower court was, in effect, a judgment against the treasurer for upwards of $900, and was a final judgment and appealable under the provisions of this section. Leachman v. Board of Supvrs., 124 Va. 616, 98 S.E. 656 (1919).

Also from final order in county bond election controversy. — In a proceeding to determine the regularity and validity of an election to determine whether or not county bonds shall be issued for permanent road improvements in the magisterial districts of a county, an appeal lies to the court of appeals from the final order of the circuit court in such controversy. Board of Supvrs. v. Spilman, 113 Va. 391, 74 S.E. 151 (1912).

But not from default judgments and decrees. — The Supreme Court has no jurisdiction of an appeal from a decree by default until relief has been sought under § 8.01-428, by motion to the court in which the decree was rendered. When the time allowed by that section expires the decree becomes final and irreversible. Smith v. Powell, 98 Va. 431, 36 S.E. 522 (1900).

Nor from judgments by confession. — Where the defendant relinquishes his plea, and agrees to the plaintiff's damages, there is a judgment by confession, amounting to a release of errors and defendant cannot appeal even by consent of plaintiff. Cooke v. Pope, 17 Va. (3 Munf.) 167 (1812). See also, Edmonds v. Green, 22 Va. (1 Rand.) 44 (1822).

Under this section specifying in what cases appeals may be awarded, there is no denial of the right of appeal by a defendant from a decree taken for confessed as to him. Shocket v. Silberman, 209 Va. 490, 165 S.E.2d 414 (1969).

Nor from consent decree. — No appeal lies from a consent decree, as the consent cures all errors. Hinton v. Bland, 81 Va. 588 (1886); Hounshell v. Hounshell, 116 Va. 675, 82 S.E. 689 (1914).

2. Appealability as Dependent on Finality of Decisions.

a. In General.

Under this section in an action at law a writ of error does not lie until a final judgment has been entered in the case by the court below, even though the court may have entered an order which indicates clearly what its final judgment would have been had it entered a final judgment. Salem Loan & Trust Co. v. Kelsey, 115 Va. 382, 79 S.E. 329 (1913); Brown v. Carolina, C & O Ry., 116 Va. 597, 83 S.E. 981 (1914); Wade v. Peebles, 162 Va. 479, 174 S.E. 769 (1934).

Under this section and § 8.01-671, which must be considered together, no writ of error may be granted unless the judgment is final. Hatke v. Globe Indem. Co., 167 Va. 184, 188 S.E. 164 (1936).

In the absence of special statutory provision to the contrary, the jurisdiction of the trial court must cease before the jurisdiction of the appellate court accrues. Allison v. Wood, 104 Va. 765, 52 S.E. 559 (1906).

Under this section a decree in equity is not appealable unless it be final or one that adjudicates principles of the cause. Lee v. Lee, 142 Va. 244, 128 S.E. 524 (1925).

Although a decree adjudicating the principles of the cause is appealable, still if it leaves any vital questions unsettled it is not final in the sense of § 8.01-671, providing that no appeal or writ of error to any final judgment or decree shall lie where the judgment or decree was rendered more than six (now four) months before the petition was presented. Allen v. Parkey, 154 Va. 739, 149 S.E. 615 (1929).

b. Final Judgments.

Definition. — A final order is one that disposes of the whole subject, gives all of the relief contemplated, provides with reasonable completeness for giving effect to the sentence, and leaves nothing to be done in the cause save to superintend ministerially the execution of the order. Burch v. Hardwicke, 64 Va. (23 Gratt.) 51 (1873); Alexander v. Byrd, 85 Va. 690, 8 S.E. 577 (1889); Postal Tel. Cable Co. v. Norfolk & W. Ry., 87 Va. 349, 12 S.E. 613 (1891), appeal dismissed, 163 U.S. 700, 16 S. Ct. 1205, 41 L. Ed. 315 (1896); Salem Loan & Trust Co. v. Kelsey, 115 Va. 382, 79 S.E. 329 (1913); Gills v. Gills, 126 Va. 526, 101 S.E. 900 (1920); Richardson v. Gardner, 128 Va. 676, 105 S.E. 225 (1920); Lee v. Lee, 142 Va. 244, 128 S.E. 524 (1925). See also, Brown v. Carolina, C & O Ry., 116 Va. 597, 83 S.E. 981 (1914); Ashworth v. Hagan Estates, Inc., 165 Va. 151, 181 S.E. 381 (1935); Dearing v. Walter, 175 Va. 555, 9 S.E.2d 336 (1940).

A decree which settles the principles of a cause, determines the rights of creditors, the validity of stock subscriptions, and the liability of stockholders to pay the same as far as necessary to satisfy the demands of creditors, and leaves nothing to be done except to execute and give effect to it, is a final decree on the

§ 8.01-670   CIVIL REMEDIES AND PROCEDURE   § 8.01-670

merits. Martin v. South Salem Land Co., 97 Va. 349, 33 S.E. 600 (1899).

A decree that ends the cause, so that no further action of the court in the cause is necessary is a final decree. Battaile v. Maryland Hosp. for Insane, 76 Va. 63 (1881).

A decree may be final as to one party and not to another in the same cause, but it cannot be final as to any party who is not put out of the cause. As to any party remaining in the court, it can, in the nature of things, be only interlocutory. Lee v. Lee, 142 Va. 244, 128 S.E. 524 (1925). See Dearing v. Walter, 175 Va. 555, 9 S.E.2d 336 (1940).

Decree dismissing one of two joint causes is final. — Where two causes are heard together and one of them is dismissed and the other continued, the decree is final as to the one dismissed, and unless an appeal is taken within a year (now four months) as provided by statute, the right of appeal is lost. The same rule applies to a so-called amended and supplemental bill which makes an entirely new case and which is dismissed. Smith v. Pyrites Mining & Chem. Co., 101 Va. 301, 43 S.E. 564 (1903).

As is one refusing or granting relief sought. — A decree is final so as to be appealable when it either refuses or grants the relief sought by the party complaining. Jones v. Buckingham Slate Co., 116 Va. 120, 81 S.E. 28 (1914).

A judgment may be final although it is not a final determination of rights of parties. — A judgment in an action is final within the meaning of this section when it is a termination of the particular action or suit, although it is not a final determination of the right of the parties. Brown v. Carolina, C & O Ry., 116 Va. 597, 83 S.E. 981 (1914).

But if further action is necessary it is not final. — If it appears upon the face of the judgment that further action in the cause is necessary to give completely the relief contemplated by the court, then the judgment is not final. Salem Loan & Trust Co. v. Kelsey, 115 Va. 382, 79 S.E. 329 (1913); Johnson v. Merrit, 125 Va. 162, 99 S.E. 785 (1919); Gills v. Gills, 126 Va. 526, 101 S.E. 900 (1920).

c. Application of Rule in Particular Cases.

i. Decisions Held Final and Appealable.

A decree dismissing a bill is a final decree, which can only be set aside by appeal, or by bill of review, within the periods limited by statute. Battaile v. Maryland Hosp. for Insane, 76 Va. 63 (1881); Pace v. Ficklin's Ex'r, 76 Va. 292 (1882); Jones v. Turner, 81 Va. 709 (1886).

And an order refusing to admit to probate a paper offered as a will is a final judgment to which a writ of error lies, although no provision is made for the costs of the proceedings in which the will is offered. Wallen v. Wallen, 107 Va. 131, 57 S.E. 596 (1907).

Order refusing to allow bill of review to be filed. — The refusal of the lower court to allow a bill of review to be filed is a proper subject of appeal. Ambrouse v. Keller, 63 Va. (22 Gratt.) 769 (1872); Connolly v. Connolly, 73 Va. (32 Gratt.) 657 (1880).

Decree refusing injunction. — In an injunction suit in which the case was submitted for a decree on the merits, an appeal from a decree refusing the injunction will not be dismissed on the ground that such decree is not appealable under this section. Clintwood Coal Corp. v. Turner, 133 Va. 464, 114 S.E. 117 (1922).

Decree dissolving injunction. — The appellants had the right to appeal because the decree dissolved the injunction and also adjudicated the principles of the case. Good v. Board of Supvrs., 140 Va. 399, 125 S.E. 321 (1924).

And judgment as to setoffs. — In an action by the plaintiff against two defendants, one of the defendants filed a plea of setoff in excess of the plaintiff's demand, and other defendant filed no plea. The court without the intervention of a jury gave judgment in favor of the defendant pleading for the excess of his setoffs over and above the plaintiff's demand and for his costs. This was a final judgment, disposing of the case as to both defendants, and to it a writ of error lies. Stimmel v. Benthall, 108 Va. 141, 60 S.E. 765 (1908).

ii. Decisions Held Not Final and Unappealable.

A decree overruling a motion to dismiss the bill and granting leave to the plaintiff to file an amended bill is not appealable. Commercial Bank v. Rucker, 2 Va. Dec. 350, 24 S.E. 388 (1896); London-Virginia Mining Co. v. Moore, 98 Va. 256, 35 S.E. 722 (1900).

Decree fixing liability for rent. — A decree fixing upon a party liability for rent is interlocutory until the amount of rent is ascertained. The amount may not be sufficient to give the court jurisdiction. Goodloe v. Woods, 115 Va. 540, 80 S.E. 108 (1913).

A decree ordering sale of land, but not directing application of proceeds held interlocutory and not final, though it adjudicated the principles of the cause. Richardson v. Gardner, 128 Va. 676, 105 S.E. 225 (1920).

Order upholding right to condemn. — An order adjudicating the Highway Commissioner's right to condemn was not a final order since it did not finally dispose of the case. Dove v. May, 201 Va. 761, 113 S.E.2d 840 (1960).

Nonsuit. — A nonsuit is not a final judgment within the meaning of this section, since a nonsuit must be suffered, if at all, before the jury retire from the bar. Mallory v. Taylor, 90

Va. 348, 18 S.E. 438 (1893).

Order appointing commissioner to assess damages. — There must be a degree of finality about every judgment taken up to be reviewed by appellate courts. Judgment appointing commissioners to fix a just compensation for land proposed to be taken in condemnation proceedings, is not final and not appealable. Ludlow v. City of Norfolk, 87 Va. 319, 12 S.E. 612 (1891); Postal Tel. Cable Co. v. Norfolk & W. Ry., 87 Va. 349, 12 S.E. 613 (1891), appeal dismissed, 163 U.S. 700, 16 S. Ct. 1205, 41 L. Ed. 315 (1896).

Order granting or refusing amendments to pleadings. — No appeal lies to an interlocutory order, granting or refusing amendments to pleadings until there has been a final decree, except as otherwise provided by statute. The case in judgment is not within any of the exceptions provided for by this section. Hobson v. Hobson, 100 Va. 216, 40 S.E. 899 (1902).

Order overruling motion to quash process. — In an action against an uninsured motorist under former § 38.1-381, an order which overruled the insurance company's motion to quash process was not a final order. Rodgers v. Danko, 204 Va. 140, 129 S.E.2d 828 (1963).

Order refusing or allowing filing of supplemental bill. — There can be no appeal from a decree or order refusing to allow, or allowing, an amended and supplemental bill to be filed, unless and until there is an appeal from a decree which is final, or is appealable under this section. Smith v. Pyrites Mining & Chem. Co., 101 Va. 301, 43 S.E. 564 (1903).

Order touching process. — An order declaring a summons void as an alias summons, but good as an original summons, is not appealable under this section, as being a final judgment. Roger's Adm'r v. Bertha Zinc Co., 1 Va. Dec. 827, 19 S.E. 782 (1894).

An order overruling exceptions to an answer for insufficiency is not a final decree or order, as that term is used in this section. Johnson v. Mundy, 123 Va. 730, 97 S.E. 564 (1918).

Judgment awarding new trial. — A judgment awarding a new trial is not a final judgment within the meaning of this section. Smiley v. Provident Life & Trust Co., 106 Va. 787, 56 S.E. 728 (1907).

Judgment as to two of three notes. — An order made by the trial court setting aside the verdict as to two of the notes where an action was brought on three notes, and awarding a new trial as to them, but refusing to set it aside as to the other note, and directing that the plaintiff take nothing by his action as to that note, is not a final order or judgment to which a writ of error will lie. Salem Loan & Trust Co. v. Kelsey, 115 Va. 382, 79 S.E. 329 (1913).

Decree refusing relief until further legislation. — A decree which declines to grant the relief prayed until the legislature enacts a further law on the subject, is not a final decree, nor does it adjudicate the principles of the cause. From it no appeal lies. If a decision is desired, the proper remedy is by mandamus to compel the trial court to hear and determine the cause. Board of Supvrs. v. City Council, 95 Va. 469, 28 S.E. 882 (1898).

Order directing an issue out of chancery. — No appeal will lie from a decree in a chancery cause directing an issue to be tried at the bar of the court to ascertain what amount of money, if any, was due from the appellee to the appellant. The appeal does not fall within the provisions of this section, and must be dismissed as having improvidently awarded. Moore v. Lipscombe, 82 Va. 546 (1886).

A decree disallowing and rejecting defendant's plea of a prior suit pending and requiring defendant to answer does not make any disposition of the prior suit. Nor is it in any sense a decree adjudicating the principles of the cause. The finality of such a decree must be tested by its effect upon the rights of the parties in the instant case, and not in the other suit pending. Lee v. Lee, 142 Va. 244, 128 S.E. 524 (1925).

Action of trial court in setting aside a default judgment and ordering defendant to file its grounds of defense within three weeks, was not a final order, so that the writ of error was improvidently awarded and must be dismissed. Hatke v. Globe Indem. Co., 167 Va. 184, 188 S.E. 164 (1936). See Massanutten Bank v. Glaize, 177 Va. 519, 14 S.E.2d 285 (1941).

3. Jurisdiction in Special Matters.

a. Condemnation Proceedings.

Claim for interest allowed in condemnation proceedings. — It is manifest that where interest is allowed it constitutes a part of the just compensation which must be paid by the condemnor, in order to secure the property desired, and involves a matter concerning the condemnation of property within the meaning of this section. City of Richmond v. Goodwyn, 132 Va. 442, 112 S.E. 787 (1922).

b. Controversies Touching Probate of a Will.

Degree of finality required. — It is not every order of a court in a cause, however incidental such order may be, that will in good sense and wise policy, warrant an appellate proceeding, in order to correct an apprehended error therein, and such proceeding must probably be confined to those orders which have about them a certain character of finality and conclusiveness, either in respect to the general merits of the cause, or in respect to some

§ 8.01-670

branch thereof, or of some matter collateral thereto, and yet of great interest to the parties, or to one of them. Tucker v. Sandridge, 82 Va. 532 (1886).

Order setting aside verdict and ordering new trial not appealable. — This section is to be considered along with § 64.1-83, so that an appeal will not be allowed from any order, but only from a final order or sentence, so that an appeal allowed to the order of a circuit court setting aside the verdict of a jury against a will and awarding a new trial will be dismissed as improvidently awarded. Tucker v. Sandridge, 82 Va. 532 (1886).

c. Controversies Touching Mills, Roadways, Ferries or Landings.

Legislature has right to limit appeals under the general road law. — While it is true that under the general road law there is an unrestricted appeal to the Supreme Court, it is within the power of the legislature, by special enactment, to limit that right to judicial questions only. Wilburn v. Raines, 111 Va. 334, 68 S.E. 993 (1910).

Action for damages by mill limited by § 8.01-672 on appeal. — In an action on the case for consequential damages, occasioned by the erection of a mill, if the damages recovered be less than one hundred dollars (now $500) the defendant cannot appeal to the Supreme Court, notwithstanding it appears from the record that the right to erect the mill was drawn in question. Skipwith v. Young, 19 Va. (5 Munf.) 276 (1816).

d. Right to Levy Tolls or Taxes.

Reason for subdivision A 1 f. — The dominating reason which impelled the adoption of the provision conferring jurisdiction upon the Supreme Court to review any judgment involving the right of the State or any of its subdivisions to levy a tax, etc., was to insure uniform construction of such laws to serve as a guide to officers collecting taxes as well as to property owners. City of Richmond v. Eubank, 179 Va. 70, 18 S.E.2d 397 (1942).

Liberal interpretation of subdivision A 1 f requires an expansion of the meaning of this jurisdictional provision to meet those cases which are clearly within the spirit or reason of the law, provided such an interpretation is not inconsistent with the language used. Hampton Rds. San. Dist. Comm'n v. Smith, 193 Va. 371, 68 S.E.2d 497 (1952).

Subdivision authorizes appeal by sanitation district. — A sanitation district has the general and usual attributes of a municipal corporation, and hence is within the sphere of the legislative intent as expressed in subdivision A 1 f of this section. Hampton Rds. San. Dist. Comm'n v. Smith, 193 Va. 371, 68 S.E.2d 497 (1952). See Farquhar v. Board of Supvrs., 196 Va. 54, 82 S.E.2d 577 (1954).

Right of city to tax bonds is appealable. — A question involving the right of a city to tax certain bonds is within the jurisdiction of the Supreme Court, regardless of the amount of the tax. City of Staunton v. Stout's Ex'r, 86 Va. 321, 10 S.E. 5 (1889).

As is motion to recover payroll taxes. — A motion for judgment by the Unemployment Compensation Commission to recover payroll taxes was a controversy concerning the right of the State to levy tolls or taxes, or was one involving the construction of a statute imposing taxes, and came squarely within the jurisdiction of the Supreme Court as defined in this section. Unemployment Comp. Comm'n v. Harvey, 179 Va. 202, 18 S.E.2d 390 (1942).

But judgment against town for shutting off water is not. — In a suit for damages caused by the action of a town in shutting off the water from the plaintiff's hotel for nonpayment of a water bill, it was held that the record presented no controversy concerning the right of the town to levy toll or taxes, and since the judgment was for less than $300 (now $500) the Supreme Court had no jurisdiction of the cause. Town of Colonial Beach v. De Atley, 154 Va. 451, 153 S.E. 734 (1930).

Nor judgment where ordinance has been declared void. — Where ordinance imposing sewer tax had been declared void, there was no ordinance in force within the purview of this section to be construed, and the Supreme Court had no jurisdiction of an action for the refund of $109.32 paid as sewer taxes under such ordinance. City of Richmond v. Eubank, 179 Va. 70, 18 S.E.2d 397 (1942).

e. Controversies Touching Constitutionality of a Law.

The appellate jurisdiction of the Supreme Court is not determined by the value of the subject matter in controversy, in cases "involving the constitutionality of law." Ward Lumber Co. v. Henderson-White Mfg. Co., 107 Va. 626, 59 S.E. 476 (1907); Norfolk & W.R.R. v. Pendleton, 86 Va. 1004, 11 S.E. 1062 (1890), aff'd, 156 U.S. 667, 15 S. Ct. 413, 39 L. Ed. 574 (1895).

Any proceeding which necessarily puts the validity of a law in issue, whether it be by plea, instruction, or otherwise, is sufficient to give the Supreme Court jurisdiction of the case. Adkins & Co. v. City of Richmond, 98 Va. 91, 34 S.E. 967 (1900).

When constitutionality is already established, there is no jurisdiction. — Where the only ground of jurisdiction of the Supreme Court is the constitutionality of a statute, the validity of which has been established by former decisions, the writ of error will be dismissed for want of jurisdiction. Western Union Tel. Co. v. White, 113 Va. 421, 74 S.E. 174 (1912).

Error committed in the construction and interpretation of a statute will not of itself confer jurisdiction, but the constitutionality of the statute, as distinguished from its interpretation, is the source of appellate jurisdiction. Hulvey v. Roberts, 106 Va. 189, 55 S.E. 585 (1906); Ward Lumber Co. v. Henderson-White Mfg. Co., 107 Va. 626, 59 S.E. 476 (1907).

No direct appeal from justice's judgment. — No appeal lies directly to the Supreme Court from a judgment of a justice of the peace involving the constitutionality of a law. Southern Ry. v. Hill, 106 Va. 501, 56 S.E. 278 (1907).

But there were means for an indirect appeal to the Supreme Court from the judgment of a justice involving the constitutionality of a statute. Southern Ry. v. Hill, 106 Va. 501, 56 S.E. 278 (1907).

f. Writs.

Controversy involving title to office appealable. — When the subject matter of a controversy is title to an office, not matter merely pecuniary, an order of a judge of the circuit court is final, and, under the provisions of this section and § 8.01-671, a writ of error will lie. Watkins v. Venable, 99 Va. 440, 39 S.E. 147 (1901).

Writs of error in mandamus proceedings. — The Supreme Court has jurisdiction under Va. Const., Art. VI, § 1, and the laws passed in pursuance thereof, of writs of error in proceedings by mandamus, although the amount involved is less than the jurisdictional amount. A mandamus, in a proper case, always involves some matter not merely pecuniary. The Constitution does not proprio vigore confer the jurisdiction, but this section and §§ 8.01-671 and 8.01-672 carry into effect the constitutional provision. Price v. Smith, 93 Va. 14, 24 S.E. 474 (1896).

Action compellable by mandamus not appealable. — An action which can certainly be compelled by mandamus cannot be appealed from. Richmond Cedar Works & Liberty Mut. Ins. Co. v. Harper, 129 Va. 481, 106 S.E. 516 (1921).

4. Interlocutory Decrees.

a. In General.

Interlocutory decrees are sometimes appealable. Armstrong v. Bryant, 189 Va. 760, 55 S.E.2d 5 (1949).

Jurisdiction purely statutory. — The jurisdiction of the Supreme Court in relation to appeals from interlocutory decrees is purely statutory. Lancaster v. Lancaster, 86 Va. 201, 9 S.E. 988 (1889).

The appellate court in the absence of statute has no jurisdiction of an appeal from an interlocutory decree. Hobson v. Hobson, 105 Va. 394, 53 S.E. 964 (1906); Smiley v. Provident Life & Trust Co., 106 Va. 787, 56 S.E. 728 (1907).

Every decree which leaves anything in the cause to be done by the court is interlocutory as between the parties remaining in the court. Dearing v. Walter, 175 Va. 555, 9 S.E.2d 336 (1940).

Right of appeal optional. — By virtue of this section a party is given the right to appeal from certain interlocutory decrees if he desires to do so. Hess v. Hess, 108 Va. 483, 62 S.E. 273 (1908). See also, Southern Ry. v. Glenn's Adm'r, 98 Va. 309, 36 S.E. 395 (1900).

In chancery only. — Only in a case in chancery is a party authorized to appeal from a decree or order which is not final, and then only from such decree or order as the law prescribes. Elder v. Harris, 75 Va. 68 (1880).

Orders as to joinder or substitution of parties generally not appealable. — As a general rule interlocutory decrees or orders overruling motions as to joinder of parties, or a substitution of parties, are not appealable. Thrasher v. Lustig, 204 Va. 399, 131 S.E.2d 286 (1963).

b. Decree or Order as to Dissolution of Injunction.

Appeal or rehearing. — Where complainants were dissatisfied or aggrieved by an order of the chancellor dissolving the injunction, their plain remedy, as prescribed by this section, was by appeal, or by application to the chancellor for a rehearing and reinstatement of the injunction, upon notice to the defendant; and, if that had been denied, they could have appealed from that denial. Fredenheim v. Rohr, 87 Va. 764, 13 S.E. 193 (1891). See also, Randolph v. Randolph, 27 Va. (6 Rand.) 194 (1828).

The right of appeal from an order refusing to dissolve an injunction seems to be settled in this State, and is placed on the ground that it adjudicates the principles of the cause. Lynch v. Clinch Motor Co., 131 Va. 202, 108 S.E. 641 (1921).

Jurisdictional amount must be involved. — No appeal lies from a decree dissolving an injunction where the subject involved is pecuniary, and is of less amount than $350 (now $500). The right of appeal given by this section is limited by § 8.01-672. Shoemaker v. Bowman, 98 Va. 688, 37 S.E. 278 (1900).

Refusal to reinstate injunction. — An appeal lies from the refusal of a chancellor to reinstate an injunction. Webster v. Couch, 27 Va. (6 Rand.) 519 (1828).

Effect of § 8.01-626. — The right of appeal given by this section is the same in a case for equitable relief by injunction as in other equity cases, and this right is not taken away by § 8.01-626. French v. Chapin-Sacks Mfg. Co., 118 Va. 117, 86 S.E. 842 (1915).

c. Decree or Order Requiring Possession or Title of Property to Be Changed.

Decree appointing a receiver is appealable. — A decree appointing a receiver to take charge of the assets of an insolvent association is appealable under this section, as it requires the possession of property to be changed. Deckert v. Chesapeake W. Co., 101 Va. 804, 45 S.E. 799 (1903).

Where property is in the hands of receivers of another court, a direction to the local receiver to intervene in that court and apply for the possession, and to take and receive the property from the receivers of that court is a sufficient change in possession and control to warrant an appeal to this court. Virginia Passenger & Power Co. v. Fisher, 104 Va. 121, 51 S.E. 198 (1905).

Decree for sale of land in partition is appealable. — A decree for the sale of land in a partition suit, though interlocutory, is appealable under this section, as it requires change of title and possession. This is especially true where the decree settles the principles of the cause. Stevens v. McCormick, 90 Va. 735, 19 S.E. 742 (1894).

Decree or order requiring money to be paid. — See Elder v. Harris, 75 Va. 68 (1880); Lancaster v. Lancaster, 86 Va. 201, 9 S.E. 988 (1889); Smith v. Pyrites Mining & Chem. Co., 101 Va. 301, 43 S.E. 564 (1903).

d. Decree or Order Adjudicating Principles of Cause.

"The principles of the cause" defined. — It must refer to principles which affect the subject of the litigation and the rules by which the court will determine the rights of the parties in the particular suit. It must mean that the rules or methods by which the rights of the parties are to be finally worked out have been so far determined that it is only necessary to apply those rules or methods to the facts of the case, in order to ascertain the relative rights of the parties with regard to the subject matter of the suit. Lancaster v. Lancaster, 86 Va. 201, 9 S.E. 988 (1889); Lee v. Lee, 142 Va. 244, 128 S.E. 524 (1925).

The phrase refers to principles which affect the subject matter of the litigation and the rules by which the rights of the parties to the suit are to be finally determined. Thrasher v. Lustig, 204 Va. 399, 131 S.E.2d 286 (1963).

This clause is not applicable to judgments at law. — This section, providing for an appeal from an interlocutory decree in equity "adjudicating the principles of a cause" does not apply to judgments at law, which, under the plain terms of the section, must be final to be appealable. Baber v. Page, 137 Va. 489, 120 S.E. 137 (1923).

Under this clause it is immaterial whether a decree is technically a final decree. — An appeal will lie to the Supreme Court from a decree adjudicating the principles of a cause, although the same may not be a final decree, and an appeal also lies from a final decree. So that a party may appeal at once from a decree settling the principles in a cause against him, or he may, at his option, await the final decree in the cause and then appeal. Harper v. Vaughan, 87 Va. 426, 12 S.E. 785 (1891).

Decree as to validity of deed is appealable. — Where a decree decides that the deed attacked by the bill as fraudulent per se is not so, thus overruling one of the grounds on which relief is prayed for in the bill, it adjudicates, to a certain extent, the principles of the cause, and is therefore an appealable order. Norris v. Lake, 89 Va. 513, 16 S.E. 663 (1893).

Also an order overruling exceptions to answer. — In a suit to determine whether certain gifts from a parent to a child and her husband were gifts or advancements, an order overruling plaintiff's exceptions to defendants' answer, which decided against the plaintiff a very important question to him, namely, the right to the relief sought by his bill of a discovery by the defendants of all sums of money or property received by them or either of them from the decedent, determined a rule of evidence by which the rights of the parties were to be finally worked out and adjudicated a "principle of the cause," and, hence, is appealable. Johnson v. Mundy, 123 Va. 730, 97 S.E. 564 (1918).

And decree denying injunction. — Where the court and the parties understood that the case was submitted for a decree upon the merits, no further proof being contemplated, and the court took the case "for final determination" pursuant to an agreed decree formerly entered in the cause, a decree that the complainant was not entitled to the injunction prayed for necessarily adjudicated the principles of the cause, and was clearly appealable under this section, notwithstanding that through inadvertence or otherwise the decree failed to dismiss the bill at complainant's cost. Clintwood Coal Corp. v. Turner, 133 Va. 464, 114 S.E. 117 (1922).

Decree overruling plea that plaintiff was not real party in interest is not appealable. — A decree overruling defendant's plea that plaintiff was not the real party in interest did not adjudicate the principles of the cause and hence was not appealable. Thrasher v. Lustig, 204 Va. 399, 131 S.E.2d 286 (1963).

Nor is a decree as to sufficiency of supplemental pleading. — A decree which merely passed upon the sufficiency of a supplemental pleading, and dismissed it, is not an interlocutory decree adjudicating the principles of the cause from which an appeal lies, under this section. Smith v. Pyrites Mining & Chem. Co., 101 Va. 301, 43 S.E. 564 (1903).

D. Who May Appeal.

1. In General.

The "person" referred to in this section is the person who was a party to the suit in the court below, and who was aggrieved by the decree therein rendered. In order to render one a proper party to an appeal these two circumstances must concur. Southern Ry. v. Glenn's Adm'r, 102 Va. 529, 46 S.E. 776 (1904).

A person who is not a party to the proceeding in which the judgment of the court below complained of was rendered cannot obtain a supersedeas to such judgment. Board of Supvrs. v. Gorrell, 61 Va. (20 Gratt.) 484 (1871); Ex parte Lester, 77 Va. 663 (1883).

The "person" granted the right to appeal from a decree is one who is "aggrieved" thereby. Shocket v. Silberman, 209 Va. 490, 165 S.E.2d 414 (1969).

Or one entitled to be party, but rejected when he attempts to intervene. — A litigant who seeks to become a party, and is entitled to become a party to proceedings in which he is interested, and is erroneously rejected, should not be required to seek relief in a roundabout fashion by a distinct and separate suit, but should be regarded, for the purposes of appeal, as possessing the status of one who is a formal party to the proceedings in which his rights and interests are being litigated. Jones v. Rhea, 130 Va. 345, 107 S.E. 814 (1921).

Where a person was not a party to the proceeding, did not ask that he be made a party, or assert any interest therein, he is not a "person interested" or a "party in interest" in, or a "party aggrieved" by, an order. Young v. SCC, 205 Va. 111, 135 S.E.2d 129 (1964).

A writ of error cannot be awarded to a person who is dead, and, if inadvertently done, the writ will be dismissed, but a new writ may be applied for by his representative. Jackson v. Wickham, 112 Va. 128, 70 S.E. 539 (1911).

But personal representative of deceased party may appeal. Jackson v. Wickham, 112 Va. 128, 70 S.E. 539 (1911); Poff v. Poff, 128 Va. 62, 104 S.E. 719 (1920).

And purchaser, but not bidder, at judicial sale is party. — There is a wide distinction between a bidder at a judicial sale and a purchaser. Until confirmed by the court the sale confers no rights. A bid is a mere offer. The purchaser becomes a quasi-party. Roberts v. Roberts, 54 Va. (13 Gratt.) 639 (1857); Hildreth v. Turner, 89 Va. 858, 17 S.E. 471 (1893).

Assignee has rights of the assignor to appeal. — Where land subject to a mechanics' lien is conveyed to a third party, such assignee has a right to prosecute an appeal in the name of his assignor from a decree holding the land subject to the lien. Hendricks v. Fields, 67 Va. (26 Gratt.) 447 (1875).

Infants appeal by guardian ad litem or next friend. — A guardian ad litem may appeal in the names of the infants, by himself as such guardian, from a decree adverse to their interests, but if he fails to do so, the infants may appeal by someone as their next friend. Givens v. Clem, 107 Va. 435, 59 S.E. 413 (1907).

Because one party cannot appeal does not prevent others. — The fact that a receiver appointed by a court cannot appeal from the judgment of that court, will not prevent the other party or parties to the action from appealing. Melendy v. Barbour, 78 Va. 544 (1884).

An amicus curiae cannot appeal. Dunlop v. Commonwealth, 6 Va. (2 Call) 284 (1800); Board of Supvrs. v. Gorrell, 61 Va. (20 Gratt.) 484 (1871).

2. Must Be Aggrieved.

a. General Rule.

In order that an appeal may be successfully prosecuted, it must be shown that the appellant has been aggrieved. Rowland v. Rowland, 104 Va. 673, 52 S.E. 366 (1905); Brown v. Howard, 106 Va. 262, 55 S.E. 682 (1906).

An appellant must have been aggrieved by the decree appealed from or he has no standing in the Supreme Court. Stone v. Henderson, 182 Va. 648, 29 S.E.2d 845 (1944).

Under this section there can be no appeal, unless the party seeking same is a party to the suit and has been aggrieved by the decree entered. These two circumstances must be made to appear. Snavely v. Snavely, 151 Va. 270, 144 S.E. 422 (1928).

In order to entitle any person to a writ of error, or an appeal, he must be aggrieved by the judgment or decree. Edmunds v. Scott, 78 Va. 720 (1884); Osborne v. Kammer, 96 Va. 228, 31 S.E. 19 (1898). See also, Ex parte Lester, 77 Va. 663 (1883).

Petitioner must be aggrieved in some particular manner. — In an action against a municipal body or officer, in order that the petitioners may be aggrieved by a judgment in contemplation of this section it must affirmatively appear that they had some direct interest in the subject matter of such proceeding. Any indirect interest they may have had solely as residents and taxpayers is not sufficient to make them proper parties to such proceeding, and they could not be aggrieved by the judgment rendered therein. It is not sufficient that the interest of such petitioner is merely that of any other taxpayer or resident, but it must be shown that the petitioner is aggrieved in some manner peculiar unto himself, aside and apart from that of other taxpayers and residents. Nicholas v. Lawrence, 161 Va. 589, 171 S.E. 673 (1933).

b. Application of Rule.

Special commissioner not aggrieved. — A special commissioner appointed to make sale of land, cannot appeal from a decree setting aside the decree of sale. So far as it affects him in his capacity of commissioner, the setting aside of a decree of sale is not an appealable grievance within the contemplation of this section. Brown v. Howard, 106 Va. 262, 55 S.E. 682 (1906).

Nor is a party secondarily liable. — Under this section, a grantee of the timber on certain land, decreed only secondarily liable for a deficiency occurring on a sale of the land to satisfy a vendor's lien, could not appeal prior to such sale and showing that a deficiency in excess of three hundred dollars (now $500) existed. C.L. Ritter Lumber Co. v. Coal Mt. Mining Co., 115 Va. 370, 79 S.E. 322 (1913).

A personal representative cannot appeal from a decree of sale of testator's lands, not being interested therein. Edmunds v. Scott, 78 Va. 720 (1884).

One joint tort-feasor cannot appeal judgment against others. — If judgment be against one joint tort-feasor, the other cannot have a writ of error to review it. Walton v. Miller, 109 Va. 210, 63 S.E. 458 (1909).

But creditor of decedent's estate may appeal. — The fact that, after a report of debts against a decedent's estate has been confirmed, other creditors come in by petition and are asserting debts against decedent's estate does not prevent a party, whose rights have been prejudiced by the decree confirming the report of indebtedness, from appealing. Reid v. Windsor, 111 Va. 825, 69 S.E. 1101 (1911).

School board in tax levy proceedings. — In a proceeding by petition asking for relief from certain levies for local taxes, an order granting the relief prayed for was entered and a writ of error was granted. Defendant in error moved to dismiss the writ of error on the ground that the county school board was not a party to the proceeding within the meaning of this section, and therefore, had no right to apply for the writ. It was held that the county school board had the right to become a party defendant in the proceedings in the lower court as it did, and, being aggrieved by the judgment entered therein, was entitled to apply for the writ of error. School Bd. v. Shockley, 160 Va. 405, 168 S.E. 419 (1933).

Person active in proceedings to open highway. — Persons who were the most active parties throughout proceedings to open a highway, and the parties at whose cost the proceedings were dismissed, and at whose wharf the proposed road was to terminate, were such parties as had a sufficient interest to come within the meaning of the words "any person who thinks himself aggrieved by any judgment" granting an appeal in road controversies, and it was not necessary that any other persons who were petitioners or parties otherwise should assist in the prosecution of the appeal. In such cases an appeal by one inures to the benefit of all. Marchant & Taylor v. Mathews County, 139 Va. 723, 124 S.E. 420 (1924).

Appeal by successful party. — A writ of error may be brought by the plaintiff to reverse his own judgment, if erroneous or given for a less sum than he has a right to demand, in order to enable him to bring another action. Ballard v. Whitlock, 59 Va. (18 Gratt.) 235 (1867).

An executor or administrator as such is not an aggrieved party where the judgment affects only the rights of beneficiaries among themselves. An executor cannot litigate the claims of one set of legatees against the others at the expense of the estate. Shocket v. Silberman, 209 Va. 490, 165 S.E.2d 414 (1969).

3. The Commonwealth.

May appeal from petition for proceeds of sale of forfeited vessels. — Where vessels have been forfeited to the Commonwealth for violation of the oyster laws and sold under order of the court, and parties entitled to the proceeds petition therefor, the proceedings are not criminal but civil, and the Commonwealth is entitled to an appeal from a judgment in favor of petitioners if the amount in controversy exceeds the minimum jurisdictional amount. Commonwealth v. Mister, 79 Va. 5 (1884).

4. Counties and Cities.

Counties and cities may sue and be sued and have the right of appeal from an adverse decision both at law and in equity. Commonwealth v. Schmelz, 116 Va. 62, 81 S.E. 45 (1914).

5. Joint Appeals.

Cases involving different issues between same parties require separate writs of error. — Three several judgments rendered in three different proceedings, commenced at different times in which different defenses were made, and never consolidated before the judgments were rendered, though between the same parties, cannot be brought to the Supreme Court by a single writ of error. Commonwealth v. Round Mt. Mining & Mfg. Co., 117 Va. 30, 83 S.E. 1061 (1915).

6. Estoppel to Appeal.

Mere statement no basis of estoppel. — The mere statement of an appellant to an appellee that he did not intend to or would not appeal, does not prevent an appeal, unless there was a consideration for the statement, or the appellee has acted on it to his prejudice. Southern Ry. v. Glenn's Adm'r, 98 Va. 309, 36 S.E. 395 (1900).

Receiving amount less than claimed no waiver of appeal. — Where a decree is entered for a less sum than the party claims, receiving payment of the sum so decreed is not a waiver of errors, nor does it estop him from appealing from the decree as to sums not allowed. Southern Ry. v. Glenn's Adm'r, 98 Va. 309, 36 S.E. 395 (1900).

§ 8.01-671. Time within which petition must be presented. — A. In cases where an appeal is permitted from the trial court to the Supreme Court, no petition shall be presented for an appeal to the Supreme Court from any final judgment whether the Commonwealth be a party or not, (i) which shall have been rendered more than three months before the petition is presented, provided, that in criminal cases, a thirty-day extension may be granted, in the discretion of the court, in order to attain the ends of justice, or (ii) if it be an appeal from a final decree refusing a bill of review to a decree rendered more than four months prior thereto, unless the petition is presented within three months from the date of such decree.

B. When an appeal from an interlocutory decree or order is permitted, the petition for appeal shall be presented within the appropriate time limitation set forth in subsection A hereof.

C. No appeal to the Supreme Court from a decision of the Court of Appeals shall be granted unless a petition for appeal is filed within thirty days after the date of the decision appealed from. (Code 1950, § 8-463; 1977, cc. 2, 617; 1984, c. 703.)

REVISERS' NOTE

Former § 8-463 has been changed by the insertion of subsection B regarding time within which petitions for appeal from interlocutory orders must be presented. References to the State Corporation Commission and Industrial Commission were deleted; see §§ 12.1-39.

Cross references. — As to failure of trial court clerk to deliver record to Supreme Court, see § 8.01-679. For rules as to time and place of filing briefs, see Rule 5:26.

Editor's note. — Pursuant to § 9-77.11 and Acts 1977, c. 617, cl. 4, the amendment by Acts 1977, c. 2, to former § 8-643, corresponding to this section, was deemed to have amended this section.

Law Review. — For survey of Virginia law on practice and pleading for the year 1969-1970, see 56 Va. L. Rev. 1500 (1970).

I. Decisions Under Current Law.
II. Decisions Under Prior Law.
  A. General Consideration.
  B. Period of Limitation.
    1. Final Judgments and Decrees.
    2. Interlocutory Decrees.
    3. Calculation of Period.

I. DECISIONS UNDER CURRENT LAW.

Legislature did not intend to require losing party to note interlocutory appeal or otherwise forfeit his right to later appeal the issue after a final adjudication. Smith v.

Woodlawn Constr. Co., 235 Va. 424, 368 S.E.2d 699 (1988).

II. DECISIONS UNDER PRIOR LAW.

A. General Consideration.

Editor's note. — The cases cited below were decided under corresponding provisions of former law. The term "this section," as used below, refers to former provisions.

This section conforms to the Va. Const., Art. IV, § 1, relating to the jurisdiction of the Supreme Court. The 1928 amendment to that section of the Constitution, which eliminated the limitations on the jurisdiction of the Supreme Court, in no way impaired the provision of this section providing certain limitations on such jurisdiction. Unemployment Comp. Comm'n v. Harvey, 179 Va. 202, 18 S.E.2d 390 (1942).

A limitation on appeal is not unconstitutional. — A statute placing a limitation on the right of appeal even from existing judgments is not unconstitutional. Gaskins v. Commonwealth, 5 Va. (1 Call) 194 (1797).

This section does not regulate the time in which the record shall be completed in the trial court. Nethers v. Nethers, 160 Va. 335, 168 S.E. 428 (1933); Avery v. County School Bd., 192 Va. 329, 64 S.E.2d 767 (1951).

It has no bearing on proceedings in trial court. — This section prohibits litigants from presenting to the Supreme Court an appeal from a final decree after the lapse of six (now four) months from the time it is rendered, but this section has no bearing whatever on what constitutes the record, or the time in which the record must be completed in the trial court. Usually all the proceedings in a chancery cause are in writing and the record is complete on the rendition of the final decree. Owen v. Owen, 157 Va. 580, 162 S.E. 46 (1932).

The jurisdiction of the Supreme Court in relation to appeals is purely statutory. Francis v. Francis, 181 Va. 373, 25 S.E.2d 253 (1943).

The time limit set by this section is jurisdictional. If that time is permitted to elapse before a petition for appeal is presented, the petitioner is without remedy. The situation is not different where a remedy is barred by a statute of limitation. Johnson v. Merritt, 125 Va. 162, 99 S.E. 785 (1919); Cousins v. Commonwealth, 187 Va. 506, 47 S.E.2d 391 (1948). See Avery v. County School Bd., 192 Va. 329, 64 S.E.2d 767 (1951).

The time limit fixed by this section is jurisdictional, and writs of error improvidently awarded by the Supreme Court will be dismissed. Tharp v. Commonwealth, 211 Va. 1, 175 S.E.2d 277 (1970).

This rule is jurisdictional. Vaughn v. Vaughn, 215 Va. 328, 210 S.E.2d 140 (1974).

Statutes of limitation are deemed statutes of repose, and this conception of such statutes applies with peculiar force to limitations upon the right of appeal. Tyson v. Scott, 116 Va. 243, 81 S.E. 57 (1914).

The law in force at the time an appeal is allowed governs. Sexton v. Crocket, 64 Va. (23 Gratt.) 857 (1873); Allison v. Wood, 104 Va. 765, 52 S.E. 559 (1906).

A petition presented two days before an amendment became effective was governed by the prior law as to the time. New York, P. & N.R.R. v. Bundick, Taylor, Corbin-Handy Co., 138 Va. 535, 122 S.E. 261 (1924).

B. Period of Limitation.

1. Final Judgments and Decrees.

Decrees refusing bill of review. — Pursuant to this section, no appeal lies from a final decree dismissing a bill of review to a decree rendered more than six (now four) months prior to such final decree, unless the petition for such appeal be presented within six (now three) months from the date of such final decree. Mason v. Mason, 97 Va. 108, 33 S.E. 1015 (1899).

Filing or granting prayer of bill makes no difference. — Under this section it matters not whether decree of refusal is to filing of, or to granting prayer of bill of review to, final decree rendered more than twelve months (now four months) before, petitions from such decree of refusal must be presented within six months (now three months) from the date of refusal. Jordan v. Cunningham, 85 Va. 418, 7 S.E. 540 (1888).

A letter opinion which requested counsel to "prepare and submit a sketch of an appropriate decree" is not a final judgment. Commonwealth v. Forbes, 214 Va. 109, 197 S.E.2d 195 (1973).

2. Interlocutory Decrees.

Right of appeal optional. — While it is permissible, it is not necessary to appeal from certain interlocutory decrees at the time they are rendered. The party may appeal at any time within a year (now four months) after a final decree has been rendered in the cause, if all other requisites for appeal exist. Hess v. Hess, 108 Va. 483, 62 S.E. 273 (1908).

Limitation inapplicable to interlocutory decrees. — To a decree that adjudicates the principles of the case, though interlocutory because it leaves something in the cause to be done by the court, an appeal lies under this section, and to such decree the statutory period of limitation is inapplicable. Jameson v. Jameson, 86 Va. 51, 9 S.E. 480 (1889).

But limitation applies after final decree allowed. — The right given by this section to appeal from certain interlocutory decrees must be exercised within one year (now four months) from the rendition of a final decree in the cause, and all other requisites of an appeal must exist. Southern Ry. v. Glenn's Adm'r, 98 Va. 309, 36 S.E. 395 (1900).

3. Calculation of Period.

The trial judge is allowed time to examine a transcript of oral testimony presented to him. Avery v. County School Bd., 192 Va. 329, 64 S.E.2d 767 (1951).

Length of time held by judge not computed. — If the petition is presented within the time prescribed by law, it is immaterial how long the judge or court holds the petition and record, that time is not taken into account, and the time fixed by the statute within which the petition and record are to be received by the clerk is regulated by the receipt of the petition and record by the judge or court. New York, P. & N.R.R. v. Bundick, Taylor, Corbin-Handy, 138 Va. 535, 122 S.E. 261 (1924).

The time taken by the reporter to transcribe the testimony is often included in the four months' period. Avery v. County School Bd., 192 Va. 329, 64 S.E.2d 767 (1951).

Actual date of decree refusing bill of review controls. — Under the terms of this section, the petition for an appeal from a decree refusing a bill of review to a decree rendered more than six (now four) months prior thereto must be presented within six months (now three months) from the actual date of the decree appealed from, and not from the beginning or the end of the term at which it was rendered. Buford v. North Roanoke Land Co., 94 Va. 616, 27 S.E. 509 (1897). See also, Mason v. Mason, 97 Va. 108, 33 S.E. 1015 (1899).

First day excluded in computing time. — The final judgment to which a writ of error was obtained was rendered July 22, 1947. It was held that the four-month period began with the advent of July 23, and expired with the departure of November 22, that is, at midnight on November 22. Cousins v. Commonwealth, 187 Va. 506, 47 S.E.2d 391 (1948). See School Bd. v. Alexander, 126 Va. 407, 101 S.E. 349 (1919).

If last day falls on Sunday, time is extended. — If the last day for filing a petition for a writ of error falls on a Sunday the time limit is extended to the following Monday under § 1-13.27. Cousins v. Commonwealth, 187 Va. 506, 47 S.E.2d 391 (1948).

§ 8.01-672. Jurisdictional amount. — No petition shall be presented for an appeal from any judgment of a circuit court except in cases in which the controversy is for a matter of $500 or more in value or amount, and except in cases in which it is otherwise expressly provided; nor to a judgment of any circuit court when the controversy is for a matter less in value or amount than $500, exclusive of costs, unless there be drawn in question a freehold or franchise or the title or bounds of land, or some other matter not merely pecuniary. (Code 1950, § 8-464; 1977, c. 617.)

REVISERS' NOTE

Former § 8-464 has been changed by substituting $500 for $300 and deleting provisions relating to appeals from the State Corporation Commission (see § 12.1-39).

Former § 8-465 has been combined in § 8.01-676.

Former § 8-468.1 has been transferred to Title 14.1.

Former § 8-471 (Supreme Court of Appeals may make or change rules for making out and printing records) has been deleted since covered in Rules of Court.

Editor's note. — Section 8.01-676, referred to in the second paragraph of the Revisers' note, was repealed by Acts 1984, c. 703.

Title 14.1, referred to in the third paragraph of the Revisers' note, has been repealed.

I. Decisions Under Prior Law.
   A. General Consideration.
   B. Construction and Application.
      1. In General.
      2. Matter Not Merely Pecuniary.
      3. Question of Title or Bounds of Land.
      4. Question of Franchise.
      5. Matter in Controversy.
      6. Costs Not Considered.

7. Inclusion of Interest.
8. Debt and Expenses.
9. Effect of Assignment.
10. Test When Plaintiff Appeals.
11. Test When Defendant Appeals.
12. Appeals in Representative Capacity.
C. Application of Rule in Particular Cases.
  1. Suits to Subject Property to Lien of Judgment.
  2. Suits to Set Aside Fraudulent Conveyances.
  3. Consolidated Claims.
  4. Miscellaneous Instances.

I. DECISIONS UNDER PRIOR LAW.

A. General Consideration.

Editor's note. — The cases cited below were decided under corresponding provisions of former law. The term "this section," as used below, refers to former provisions.

Controversy of jurisdictional amount must be continued in appellate court. — The matter in controversy in the lower court must not only equal the jurisdictional amount, but the controversy in relation to matters of that value must be continued by the appeal. Ross v. Gordon, 16 Va. (2 Munf.) 289 (1811); Ashby v. Kiger, 24 Va. (3 Rand.) 165 (1825); Duffy v. Figgat, 80 Va. 664 (1885); Hawkins v. Gresham, 85 Va. 34, 6 S.E. 472 (1888); Hartsook v. Crawford, 85 Va. 413, 7 S.E. 538 (1888).

Amount in controversy must be shown on appeal. — On an appeal, the amount in controversy must, as a general rule, be made to appear affirmatively. If, however, the record is silent on the subject, affidavits may be filed in the appellate court to show the real amount in controversy. Lamb v. Thompson, 112 Va. 134, 70 S.E. 507 (1911).

But appellee alleging reduction below that amount has burden of showing reduction. — When the original demand is pecuniary and in excess of the jurisdictional amount, but is alleged by the appellee to have been reduced below that amount by payment, the onus rests upon him to make that fact appear. Fink, Bro. & Co. v. Denny, 75 Va. 663 (1881); Filler v. Tyler, 91 Va. 458, 22 S.E. 235 (1895); C.L. Ritter Lumber Co. v. Coal Mt. Mining Co., 115 Va. 370, 79 S.E. 322 (1913).

B. Construction and Application.

1. In General.

The amount in controversy in this section refers to the amount in controversy which is before the appellate court and not to the amount in controversy in the lower court. This amount is measured by the difference between what was claimed by the party in a trial court and the amount allowed him in that court. In ascertaining the amount claimed in the trial court, the appellate court should look, in case of the plaintiff, to the amount claimed by him in the body of the declaration and not merely to the ad damnum clause. Madison v. Kroger Grocery & Bakery Co., 160 Va. 303, 168 S.E. 353 (1933). See Davidson v. Jackson, 193 Va. 330, 68 S.E.2d 524 (1952).

The Supreme Court cannot enter a money judgment for less than the jurisdictional amount, namely, $500. Madison v. Kroger Grocery & Bakery Co., 160 Va. 303, 168 S.E. 353 (1933).

Extent of liability must first be ascertained. — Where the amount of defendant's liability cannot be determined until a tract of land has been sold and applied to the payment of his debt, and where his liability is merely pecuniary, he has no right of appeal until the extent of his liability has been ascertained. C.L. Ritter Lumber Co. v. Coal Mt. Mining Co., 115 Va. 370, 79 S.E. 322 (1913).

Writ allowed when larger amount drawn into question. — Where the effect of a judgment is to draw in question the validity of a claim to an amount of greater value than the jurisdictional sum of the appellate court, although the amount involved in the present action is not as large as the minimum required, a writ of error will lie, if it appears that judgment conclusively settles the rights of the parties to the larger amount. But this principle will not be extended further than the adjudged cases have gone. International Harvester Co. v. Smith, 105 Va. 683, 54 S.E. 859 (1906); Jones v. Buckingham Slate Co., 116 Va. 120, 81 S.E. 28 (1914).

2. Matter Not Merely Pecuniary.

Meaning of term. — The words "or some other matter not merely pecuniary" used in this section, have the same meaning as the words "matters not merely pecuniary" used in the Constitution. Price v. Smith, 93 Va. 14, 24 S.E. 474 (1896).

If matter is not merely pecuniary it must be directly the subject of controversy. — If jurisdiction is invoked on the ground that the litigation draws in question a freeholder or franchise, or the title or bounds of land, or some matter not merely pecuniary, these jurisdictional matters must be directly the subject of controversy, and not merely incidentally and collaterally involved. Hutchinson v. Kellam, 17 Va. (3 Munf.) 202 (1811); Cook v. Daugherty, 99 Va. 590, 39 S.E. 223 (1901); Thomas v. State Hwy. Comm'r, 166 Va. 512, 186 S.E. 172 (1936).

Appeal from decree denying alimony not dependent upon pecuniary amount. — On an appeal from a decree denying alimony, appellee moved to dismiss the appeal on the ground that the Supreme Court did not have jurisdiction since the controversy was not one involving $500 exclusive of costs and was not otherwise appealable. It was held that the power of a court of equity to allow alimony is not dependent upon the pecuniary amount involved, but is derived by virtue of its elastic power to deal with a matter of public interest regardless of the amount involved, and since a court of equity has inherent jurisdiction to award alimony, either within or without the provisions of §§ 20-107.1 to 20-113, the contention of appellee was without merit. Wilson v. Wilson, 178 Va. 427, 17 S.E.2d 397 (1941).

An appeal from an order of a court of record affirming the decision of a board of zoning appeals granting a variance from the terms of a zoning ordinance involves "some matter not merely pecuniary," and the Supreme Court is not concerned with the requirements as to jurisdictional amount. Burkhardt v. Board of Zoning Appeals, 192 Va. 606, 66 S.E.2d 565 (1951).

3. Question of Title or Bounds of Land.

This section gives appellate jurisdiction in controversies concerning the title or boundaries of land, whatever the amount and whatever the element of title involved in the controversy. Pannill v. Coles, 81 Va. 380 (1886); Steinman v. Clinchfield Coal Corp., 121 Va. 611, 93 S.E. 684 (1917).

What cases concern title to land. — A decree for sale of land in a partition suit, or for the appointment of a receiver, whereby change is made in possession or control of property, judgments in actions of unlawful entry and detainer, and decrees in suits relating to trust deeds upon real estate securing less than the minimum pecuniary jurisdiction of the court, all concern the title of land. Steinman v. Clinchfield Coal Corp., 121 Va. 611, 93 S.E. 684 (1917).

Action of unlawful detainer. — An appeal lies in an action of unlawful detainer which is an element of title. Pannill v. Coles, 81 Va. 380 (1886).

Controversy as to estate taken under a will. — Where a trust deed to secure a debt less than the jurisdictional amount was executed by a legatee on his interest in realty and personalty under a will, and the question in the court below was whether his interest was vested or contingent, the controversy was one concerning the title to land, from which an appeal lay under this section. Seller v. Reed, 88 Va. 377, 13 S.E. 754 (1891).

Claim for rent. — It was contended that since the amount of rent claimed was only $50 the Supreme Court was without jurisdiction. The annual rental, however, was $1,536 and the parties had selected an agent to collect and hold the monthly rents subject to the decision of the case, and one of the petitioners questioned the correctness of the court's action in declaring her deed invalid and transferring the property to the grantor. Since the court not only entered a judgment on a money demand but solemnly declared that the two instruments under seal were void, the adjudication, on the face of the judgment, drew in question a freehold or the title or bounds of land and was appealable under this section. Parks v. Wiltbank, 177 Va. 461, 14 S.E.2d 281 (1941).

Decree allowing widow's homestead. — An appeal lies to a decree allowing widow homestead for her lifetime in the realty of her deceased husband, though the appellant's interest therein be less than the minimum jurisdictional sum, as the controversy concerns the title to land. Barker v. Jenkins, 84 Va. 895, 6 S.E. 459 (1888).

Suit to set aside deeds as fraudulent is not "controversy ...". — In Virginia, a suit to set aside deeds as fraudulent and subject the land conveyed is not a "controversy concerning the title or boundaries of land" so as to give the Supreme Court appellate jurisdiction irrespective of pecuniary value, but the "matter in controversy" is pecuniary in such case and is the amount of the debt, to satisfy which the suit is brought, so that the debt must not be less than the jurisdictional amount. Fink v. Denny, 75 Va. 663 (1881).

Nor is a decree ordering sale of land. — The fact that land is decreed to be sold unless the sum decreed against the defendant is paid, does not make it a controversy, touching the "title or boundaries of land"; the pecuniary demand is "the matter in controversy." Cook v. Bondurant, 85 Va. 47, 6 S.E. 618 (1888).

4. Question of Franchise.

Where there is drawn in question a franchise, or the rights of a corporation to levy taxes, the case is within the jurisdiction of the Supreme Court, though the matter in controversy is less than the jurisdictional amount. City of Staunton v. Stout's Ex'rs, 86 Va. 321, 10 S.E. 5 (1889).

Suit involving licenses for duck blinds within section. — In a suit involving licenses for duck blinds, defendant filed a motion to dismiss the appeal on the ground that the case did not involve $500 in value and was not otherwise appealable. It was held that, regardless of the value and the amount involved, there was drawn into controversy the right of a franchise as defined in this section, and, hence, the case was appealable. Brumley v. Grimstead, 170 Va. 340, 196 S.E. 668 (1938).

Also a suit as to right of board of supervisors to levy a tax to pay a claim, concerns a franchise, and the Supreme Court has jurisdiction irrespective of amount involved. Board of Supvrs. v. Catlett, 86 Va. 158, 9 S.E. 999 (1889); City of Staunton v. Stout's Ex'rs, 86 Va. 321, 10 S.E. 5 (1889).

5. Matter in Controversy.

The term "matter in controversy" as used in this section means the subject of litigation, the matter for which suit is brought and upon which issue is joined, and in relation to which jurors are called, and witnesses examined. Gage v. Crockett, 68 Va. (27 Gratt.) 735 (1876); Harman v. City of Lynchburg, 74 Va. (33 Gratt.) 37 (1880); Norfolk & W.R.R. v. Clark, 92 Va. 118, 22 S.E. 867 (1895).

The real matter in controversy is that for which the suit is brought and judgment is rendered, and not that which may or may not come in question. In other words, the sole test of jurisdiction is the amount which the defendant may pay and thereby discharge himself, and if that sum be less than the minimum jurisdiction of the court, the appeal or writ of error should be dismissed. Elliott v. Ashby, 104 Va. 716, 52 S.E. 383 (1905). See also, Duncan v. State Hwy. Comm'n, 142 Va. 135, 128 S.E. 546 (1925).

6. Costs Not Considered.

In determining the right of appeal, costs are never to be considered any part of the "matter in controversy," even in absence of legislative prohibition. Cox v. Carr, 79 Va. 28 (1884); Hartsook v. Crawford, 85 Va. 413, 7 S.E. 538 (1888).

Appeal from decree for costs. — But the Supreme Court is not deprived of jurisdiction of an appeal on the ground that it is from a decree for costs only, where it appears that it was for costs of an entirely different proceeding, and the amount exceeds $500. Shipman v. Fletcher, 95 Va. 585, 29 S.E. 325 (1898).

7. Inclusion of Interest.

Interest upon the judgment or decree is to be included in determining whether the court of appeals has jurisdiction. Stratton v. Mutual Assurance Soc'y, 27 Va. (6 Rand.) 22 (1827).

Estimated to date of decree only. — In calculating the amount in controversy interest is never to be estimated beyond the date of the decree. Duffy v. Figgat, 80 Va. 664 (1885); Hawkins v. Gresham, 85 Va. 34, 6 S.E. 472 (1888); Hartsook v. Crawford, 85 Va. 413, 7 S.E. 538 (1888).

Interest may be waived. — In an action of assumpsit to recover excess freight charges, it was entirely competent for the plaintiffs to claim interest or not as they chose. The trial court was powerless to make them claim it on demand of defendant, there being no evidence of a purpose to defeat the jurisdiction of a court of record by the release of a part of a demand previously asserted. Consequently, where the amount in controversy, without interest, was beneath the jurisdictional limit of the Supreme Court, a writ of error must be dismissed as improvidently awarded, unless jurisdiction can be shown on some other ground than the amount in controversy. C & O Ry. v. Williams, 122 Va. 502, 95 S.E. 417 (1918).

8. Debt and Expenses.

Expense of drawing and recording deed of trust included. — Where a debt is secured by a deed of trust on personal property, which also secured the expenses of executing the trust and of drawing and recording the deed, and the validity of the deed is assailed, such expenses are proper to be considered in arriving at the amount in controversy on appeal. Williamson v. Payne, 103 Va. 551, 49 S.E. 660 (1905).

9. Effect of Assignment.

Assignment may bring claim up to jurisdictional amount. — One party plaintiff may acquire the claim of another by assignment, and if his claim is thereby brought up to the jurisdictional amount, the Supreme Court will have jurisdiction, even though the assignment took place after suit brought, if before decree, provided such assignment was bona fide and not merely colorable in order to give the appellate court jurisdiction. In the absence of proof to the contrary it will be presumed to have been bona fide. Fink v. Denny, 75 Va. 663 (1881).

10. Test When Plaintiff Appeals.

Amount of recovery not determinative. — When the plaintiff seeks a revision of the judgment below, if he claims in his declaration money or property of the value of not less than the jurisdictional amount, the court of appeals has jurisdiction, although the judgment may be for less, or for the defendant. Gage v. Crockett, 68 Va. (27 Gratt.) 735 (1876); Cox v. Carr, 79 Va. 28 (1884); Duffy v. Figgat, 80 Va. 664 (1885); Hawkins v. Gresham, 85 Va. 34, 6 S.E. 472 (1888); Hartsook v. Crawford, 85 Va. 413, 7 S.E. 538 (1888); Kendrick v. Spotts, 90 Va. 148, 17 S.E. 853 (1893). See also, Madison v. Kroger Grocery & Bakery, 160 Va. 330, 168 S.E. 353 (1933).

11. Test When Defendant Appeals.

Amount of judgment determines. — Where the revision is sought by the defendant, the amount or value of the judgment at its date determines the jurisdiction. This is the general rule, and the onus is upon the party seeking the revision, to establish the jurisdiction of the appellate court. Gage v. Crockett, 27 Gratt. (68 Va.) 735 (1876); Harman v. City of Lynchburg, 74 Va. (33 Gratt.) 37 (1880); Duffy v. Figgat, 80 Va. 664 (1885); Hawkins v. Gresham, 85 Va. 34, 6 S.E. 472 (1888); Cook v. Bondurant, 85 Va. 47, 6 S.E. 618 (1888); Hartsook v. Crawford, 85 Va. 413, 7 S.E. 538 (1888); Kendrick v. Spotts, 90 Va. 148, 17 S.E. 853 (1893).

12. Appeals in Representative Capacity.

Executor. — Where the claim of several persons to take as legatees under a particular clause of a will is resisted by the executor, and there are separate decrees in their favor, the amount in controversy in the Supreme Court, as to the executor, is the aggregate amount of the decrees against him, although no one of them would be sufficient to give the court jurisdiction. Ginter v. Shelton, 102 Va. 185, 45 S.E. 892 (1903).

Administrator. — Where the amount decreed against administrator is within the jurisdictional limit, the Supreme Court has jurisdiction of his appeal, though the amount decreed to each ward or distributee falls below that limit; the aggregate being the amount in controversy. Updike v. Lane, 78 Va. 132 (1883); Martin v. Fielder, 82 Va. 455, 4 S.E. 602 (1886).

A trustee in an assignment for benefit of creditors, as representative of whole fund, may appeal from a decree, if aggrieved thereby, though none of the debts secured separately amount to the minimum jurisdictional amount. Saunders v. Waggoner & Co., 82 Va. 316 (1886). See also, Cabell v. Southern Mut. Ins. Co., 1 Va. Dec. 610 (1886).

C. Application of Rule in Particular Cases.

1. Suits to Subject Property to Lien of Judgment.

Amount of the judgment controlling. — In a suit to subject land to the payment of a judgment, the amount in controversy is to be determined by the amount of the judgment, and the title or boundary of land is not involved. The jurisdiction of the court on an appeal by the defendant is regulated by the amount decreed against him, or declared to be a lien on the land. Buckner v. Metz, 77 Va. 107 (1883); Steinman v. Clinchfield Coal Corp., 121 Va. 611, 93 S.E. 684 (1917).

Value of the property does not determine. — It is the amount of the judgment, not the value of the land sought to be subjected, that determines the jurisdiction in the appellate court, in a suit to subject land to a judgment. Smith v. Rosenheim, 79 Va. 540 (1884); Pitts v. Spotts, 86 Va. 71, 9 S.E. 501 (1889); Showalter v. Rupe, 2 Va. Dec. 553, 27 S.E. 840 (1897); Cook v. Daugherty, 99 Va. 590, 39 S.E. 223 (1901).

2. Suits to Set Aside Fraudulent Conveyances.

Property covered by deed determines. — In a suit to set aside a fraudulent deed, conveying property worth $1500, or more than the jurisdictional amount, as stated in the deed, although the amount of the debts secured is less than the jurisdictional amount, still the "amount in controversy" is the property covered by the deed; hence, an appeal may be granted. Kahn v. Kergood, 80 Va. 342 (1885).

Where, in a suit to set aside a conveyance as fraudulent as to creditors, the various sums decreed against the purchaser in favor of several creditors exceed in the aggregate the amount necessary to confer jurisdiction on the Supreme Court, the appeal by the purchaser will not be dismissed because the sum due to the parties summoned as appellees is less than $500, where there is a general appearance by counsel for appellees. In the absence of such general appearance, the court will direct process to issue against the parties not served. Wheby v. Moir, 102 Va. 875, 47 S.E. 1005 (1904).

3. Consolidated Claims.

Several claims cannot be consolidated so as to give appellate jurisdiction, even though they be of like nature and against the same defendant. Blankenship v. Virginia Unemployment Comp. Comm'n, 177 Va. 250, 13 S.E.2d 409 (1941); Bolling v. Old Dominion Power Co., 181 Va. 368, 25 S.E.2d 266 (1943).

Several appellants cannot unite claims. — Where the amount involved in each case is less than $500, the appeals in several cases cannot be united so as to give the Supreme Court jurisdiction. Lawson v. Bransford, 87 Va. 75, 12 S.E. 108 (1890), appeal dismissed, 139 U.S. 197, 11 S. Ct. 519, 35 L. Ed. 144 (1891); 149 U.S. 778, 13 S. Ct. 1049, 37 L. Ed. 962 (1893); Gregory v. Bransford, 87 Va. 77, 12 S.E. 109 (1890), appeal dismissed, 139 U.S. 197, 11 S. Ct. 519, 35 L. Ed. 144 (1891).

As when claims based on independent contracts. — Where several parties unite in an appeal, and it appears that there is no joint interest or community among them; that their respective claims each had for its foundation an independent contract which each had the right to enforce without regard to the other, and the interest of no one of them amounts to as much as $500, the appeal will be dismissed as improvidently awarded. White v. Valley Bldg. & Inv. Co., 96 Va. 270, 31 S.E. 20 (1898).

Or when judgment creditors seek to enforce lien on debtor's land. — Where several judgment creditors with judgments each below the jurisdictional amount unite in one suit to enforce their liens on the judgment debtor's land, and their bill is dismissed by the court below, the Supreme Court has no jurisdiction to entertain their appeal. Thompson v. Adams, 82 Va. 672 (1886).

Mechanic's lien claims. — In a proceeding in rem to enforce six separate mechanics' liens against six separate parcels of real estate, six items of $160 each could not be consolidated for the purpose of meeting the jurisdictional amount of $500 required by this section. Shelton v. Ogus, 201 Va. 417, 111 S.E.2d 408 (1959).

4. Miscellaneous Instances.

A set-off is equivalent to an action, and where the amount of a set-off disallowed by the trial court exceeds $500, the amount in controversy is within the jurisdiction of the Supreme Court. Norfolk & W. Ry. v. Potter, 110 Va. 427, 66 S.E. 34 (1909).

Taxes. — A tax is nothing more than a debt due by the citizen to the taxing power, and unless the right to impose the tax or the construction of the statute under which it is imposed is called in question, or necessarily passed upon in the trial court, no appeal lies to the Supreme Court from the judgment of the trial court imposing a tax, if the aggregate amount of the tax imposed is less than $500. Schermerhorn's Ex'x v. Commonwealth, 107 Va. 707, 60 S.E. 65 (1908). See Cohen v. Walford, 111 Va. 812, 70 S.E. 850 (1911).

Validity of stock subscription. — Where the validity of a stock subscription for more than $500 is drawn in question by a judgment for an assessment upon said stock for less than $500, the appellate court has jurisdiction of a writ of error to said judgment. Elliott v. Ashby, 104 Va. 716, 52 S.E. 383 (1905); International Harvester Co. v. Smith, 105 Va. 683, 54 S.E. 859 (1906).

Action on one of a series of notes. — Where a suit on a note for less than $500 involves the plaintiff's right to recover also on two other notes given for parts of the same debt as the note sued on, and together with it amounting to more than $500, so that judgment in the suit would be decisive as to the plaintiff's rights with respect to a sum greater than $500, the amount in controversy is sufficient to give the Virginia appellate court jurisdiction on writ of error. International Harvester Co. v. Smith, 105 Va. 683, 54 S.E. 859 (1906).

Actions for trespass. — For discussion of amount in controversy with reference to jurisdiction on an appeal, in an action of trespass quaere clausum fregit, see Douglas Land Co. v. T.W. Thayer Co., 113 Va. 239, 74 S.E. 215 (1912).

Where the boundary between two tracts of land is incidental to the ownership of the royalties on slate taken from the land, the Supreme Court has no jurisdiction of an appeal from a decree determining the ownership of such royalties where they amount to less than $500. Jones v. Buckingham Slate Co., 116 Va. 120, 81 S.E. 28 (1914).

Loss occasioned by failure to present check when bank fails. — Where the decree of the trial court decides that the holder of a certified check on a suspended bank had accepted it as a payment on a debt, and that, by reason of failure to present it in a reasonable time, he must sustain any loss occasioned by the failure of the bank to pay in full, the amount in controversy in the Supreme Court by such holder, is the amount of such loss, which is measured by the amount of the check less any dividends which may be declared out of the assets of the bank. Lamb v. Thompson, 112 Va. 134, 7 S.E. 507 (1911).

Suit to recover overcharges from power company. — While the claims for overcharges were of like nature, the consumers had no common interest in the fund sought to be recovered, and should they prevail each would be entitled to a separate judgment, each under the jurisdictional amount. Bolling v. Old Dominion Power Co., 181 Va. 368, 25 S.E.2d 266 (1943).

ARTICLE 3.

The Record.

§ 8.01-673. Inspection and return of records; certiorari when part of record is omitted; binding or retention of records. — A. The Supreme Court may, when a case has before been in an appellate court, inspect the record upon the former appeal; and the court may, in any case, after reasonable notice to counsel in the appellate court, award a writ of certiorari to the clerk of the court below, and have brought before it, when part of a record is omitted, the whole or any part of such record.

§ 8.01-673   CODE OF VIRGINIA   § 8.01-673

B. When an appeal is refused or after it has been allowed and decided, the Clerk of the Supreme Court shall return the record to the clerk of the circuit court or other tribunal. The clerk of such court or tribunal shall return the record upon the request of the Clerk of the Supreme Court. As soon as a case is decided, the Clerk of the Supreme Court shall cause the appendix and the briefs of counsel to be recorded and preserved in any manner which meets archival standards as recommended by the Archives and Records Division of The Library of Virginia.

The manuscript of the record in a case in which an opinion was delivered prior to 1950 by the Supreme Court upon refusal of an appeal shall not be destroyed and shall be retained by the clerk of such court in his files. (Code 1950, §§ 8-473, 8-501; 1974, c. 532; 1977, cc. 449, 617; 1984, c. 703; 1988, c. 324; 1994, c. 64.)

REVISERS' NOTE

Former §§ 8-473 and 8-501 have been combined into subsections A and B without material change.

Cross references. — For rule providing for return of original record to trial court, see Rule 5:13(d).

Editor's note. — Former § 8-501, corresponding to subsection B of this section, was amended by Acts 1977, c. 449. Pursuant to § 9-77.11 and Acts 1977, c. 617, cl. 4, that amendment was deemed to have amended this section.

I. Decisions Under Current Law.
II. Decisions Under Prior Law.

I. DECISIONS UNDER CURRENT LAW.

Enlarging record on appeal. — When the record on appeal has been transmitted in compliance with Supreme Court Rule 5:13 by the clerk of the trial court to the Clerk of the Supreme Court and an appeal has been awarded, the record on appeal cannot be enlarged except upon a grant by the Supreme Court of a writ of certiorari under this section. Town of Narrows v. Clear-View Cable TV, Inc., 227 Va. 272, 315 S.E.2d 835, appeal dismissed and cert. denied, 469 U.S. 925, 105 S. Ct. 315, 83 L. Ed. 2d 253 (1984); Godfrey v. Commonwealth, 227 Va. 460, 317 S.E.2d 781 (1984).

II. DECISIONS UNDER PRIOR LAW.

Editor's note. — The cases cited below were decided under corresponding provisions of former law. The term "this section," as used below, refers to former provisions.

Authorization of section. — This section authorizes the court in any case to award certiorari by which the clerk of the court below is directed to send to the appeals court any and all parts of the record which have been omitted from the record transmitted. Washington v. Commonwealth, 216 Va. 185, 217 S.E.2d 815 (1975).

Enlarging record on appeal. — When the record has been transmitted in compliance with Rule 5:15 by the clerk of the trial court to the clerk of the Supreme Court, and a writ of error or appeal has been granted, the record on appeal cannot be enlarged, except upon award of a writ of certiorari as provided in this section. Old Dominion Iron & Steel Corp. v. VEPCO, 215 Va. 658, 212 S.E.2d 715 (1975).

Either party may have portions of record brought up by certiorari. — If parts of the record not required by statute to be certified upon appeal are material to the issue, either party may have a certiorari to bring them up. Craddock v. Craddock, 158 Va. 58, 163 S.E. 387 (1932).

Section cures defect in record. — Where a motion to dismiss a writ of error was based upon the fact that the petition, when presented to the judge awarding the writ, was not accompanied by a complete transcript of the record, but before the motion was presented to the court the record was completed in the manner prescribed by this section, the motion to dismiss the writ was properly overruled. Bowen v. Bowen, 122 Va. 1, 94 S.E. 166 (1917).

Presumption that entire record before appellate court. — Where the record is certified and there is no suggestion that all the

§ 8.01-674   CIVIL REMEDIES AND PROCEDURE   § 8.01-675.1

record is not before the court and no application for certiorari is made under this section, it is presumed that the whole record is before the court. Craddock v. Craddock, 158 Va. 58, 163 S.E. 387 (1932).

Power exercised. — See Shreck v. Virginia Hot Springs Co., 140 Va. 429, 125 S.E. 316 (1924).

Article 4.

The Petition.

§ 8.01-674. With whom filed; endorsement thereon; reference to justice or justices; when deemed to be filed. — The petition for appeal to the Supreme Court shall be filed with the Clerk of the Supreme Court. The Clerk shall endorse thereon the day and year he received it and shall refer it to one or more justices of the Supreme Court as the Court shall direct. A petition shall, for the purposes of § 8.01-671, be deemed to be timely filed if it is mailed postage prepaid to the Clerk by registered or certified mail and if the official postal receipt therefor is exhibited upon the demand of the Clerk or any party and it shows mailing within the prescribed time limits. (Code 1950, § 8-475; 1976, c. 615; 1977, c. 617; 1984, c. 703.)

Cross references. — For rule on transmission of record, see Rule 5:13. For rule of court as to time and place of filing petitions, see Rule 5:17.

Law Review. — For survey of Virginia practice and pleading for the year 1975-1976, see 62 Va. L. Rev. 1460 (1976).

I. DECISIONS UNDER CURRENT LAW.

Appeal from Industrial Commission (now Workers' Compensation Commission) decision. — Where plaintiff's petition for appeal from a decision of the Commission was timely forwarded by certified mail, postage prepaid, to the clerk of the court, the petition was deemed timely filed since there is no reason for a distinction in the manner in which petitions for appeal from the Commission are physically filed as compared to those in civil and criminal litigation. Reese v. Wampler Foods, Inc., 222 Va. 249, 278 S.E.2d 870 (1981).

§ 8.01-675: Repealed by Acts 1984, c. 703, effective Oct. 1, 1984.

§ 8.01-675.1. When dismissal final; when reinstated. — After the dismissal of an appeal by the Supreme Court, no other appeal shall be allowed to or from the same judgment. When an appeal is dismissed by reason of the nonpayment of the writ tax within the time required by law, the Court at its first session after such dismissal may on motion of any party for good cause shown and upon payment of such tax set aside the dismissal; and thereupon the appeal may be perfected as though no such dismissal had taken place. A motion under this section shall be made only after reasonable notice to the adverse party or his counsel. (1984, c. 703.)

Cross references. — For application of this section to criminal cases, see § 19.2-325.

I. DECISIONS UNDER PRIOR LAW.

Editor's note. — The cases cited below was decided under corresponding provisions of former law. The term "this section," as used below, refers to former provisions.

Dismissal serves to affirm judgment. — By virtue of this section, the dismissal of a writ of error or appeal has the effect of affirming the judgment or decree appealed from. While the dismissal of a writ of error is in a sense an affirmance of the judgment appealed from, it is an affirmance in a limited sense only. Aetna Cas. & Sur. Co. v. Board of Supvrs., 160 Va. 11, 168 S.E. 617 (1933).

An order dismissing an appeal or writ of error for failure to print the record effects the same purpose as an affirmance. Cobbs v. Gilchrist, 80 Va. 503 (1885); Woodson v. Leyburn, 83 Va. 843, 3 S.E. 873 (1887); Beecher v. Lewis, 84 Va. 630, 6 S.E. 367 (1888).

Under this section the dismissal of an appeal for failure to give the appeal bond operates an affirmance of the decree of the lower court, without any consideration of it by this court.

Hicks v. Roanoke Brick Co., 94 Va. 741, 27 S.E. 596 (1897), overruled on another point, 100 Va. 207, 40 S.E. 647 (1902).

But dismissal does not impart validity to void judgment, when dismissal is upon a ground which does not bring into issue whether judgment void or not. The dismissal does not give to the judgment any validity which it would not have had before the appeal. Aetna Cas. & Sur. Co. v. Board of Supvrs., 160 Va. 11, 168 S.E. 617 (1933).

Finality of decree. — The case made for the Supreme Court by an appeal from a decree of the court below, whether final or interlocutory, is as to the Supreme Court a complete case in itself, and the decree of that court therein is final and conclusive between the parties, as well upon the court itself as upon the court below. The Supreme Court can do nothing more in the course of the same litigation, until a new and different appeal is brought up to it from some decree of the court below, rendered in the cause upon subsequent proceedings in that court, and the Supreme Court can only review and revise the decree without interfering with its own former decree. Campbell v. Campbell, 63 Va. (22 Gratt.) 649 (1872); Cobbs v. Gilchrist, 80 Va. 503 (1885).

The Supreme Court affirmed an interlocutory decree of a circuit court. Afterwards in the circuit court a petition was filed to rehear said decree, and was dismissed, and the petitioners appealed. It was held that such a decree, under the circumstances cannot be reheard. Woodson v. Leyburn, 83 Va. 843, 3 S.E. 873 (1887).

Only matters involved in appeal can be inquired into. — Where three successive decrees are allowed from three decrees in a cause and the first two are dismissed, it seems that on the last appeal which relates only to the last decree, matters involved in the former appeals can not be inquired into, under the spirit of this section. Barksdale v. Fitzgerald, 76 Va. 892 (1881).

§ 8.01-675.2. Rehearing.

— The Supreme Court, on the petition of a party, shall rehear and review any case decided by such court if one of the justices who decides the case adversely to the petitioner certifies that in his opinion there is good cause for such rehearing. However, a notice of a petition for rehearing shall be filed as provided by the Rules of Court and the petition for rehearing shall be filed within thirty days after the entry of the judgment with the clerk, who shall note the date of such filing on the order book. The judgment resulting from any such rehearing shall be entered forthwith by the clerk who shall transmit a certified copy thereof to the clerk of the court below, to be entered by him as provided by § 8.01-685. (1984, c. 703.)

Cross references. — For application of this section to criminal cases, see § 19.2-325.

I. DECISIONS UNDER PRIOR LAW.

Editor's note. — The case cited below was decided under corresponding provisions of former law. The term "this section," as used below, refers to former provisions.

Rehearing not granted where party failed to file additional briefs. — Where a cause has been submitted with leave to file additional briefs before a certain day, and such briefs are not filed, the court will decide the case upon the arguments made. The failure of counsel to file additional briefs within the time given by the court was not occasioned by the fault of the court, and a petition to rehear will not be granted where the case was decided after the briefs should have been filed. Nicholas v. Nicholas, 100 Va. 660, 42 S.E. 669 (1902) (decided under former § 8.01-687).

CHAPTER 26.1.

APPEALS TO THE COURT OF APPEALS.

Sec.
8.01-675.3. Time within which appeal must be taken; notice.
8.01-675.4. Inspection and return of records; certiorari when part of record is omitted; retention of records.

§ 8.01-675.3. Time within which appeal must be taken; notice.

— Except as provided in § 19.2-400 for appeals by the Commonwealth in criminal cases and in § 19.2-401 for cross appeals by the defendant in such

§ 8.01-675.4

cases a notice of appeal to the Court of Appeals in any case within the jurisdiction of the court shall be filed within thirty days from the date of any final judgment order, decree or conviction. When an appeal from an interlocutory decree or order is permitted, the appeal shall be filed within thirty days from the date of such decree or order, except for appeals pursuant to § 19.2-398.

For purposes of this section, § 17.1-408, and an appeal pursuant to § 19.2-398, a petition for appeal in a criminal case or a notice of appeal to the Court of Appeals, shall be deemed to be timely filed if (i) it is mailed postage prepaid by registered or certified mail and (ii) the official postal receipt, showing mailing within the prescribed time limits, is exhibited upon demand of the clerk or any party. (1984, c. 703; 1987, c. 710.)

Cross references. — For application of this section to criminal cases, see § 19.2-325.

I. DECISIONS UNDER CURRENT LAW.

Effect of clear error in reference. — A notice of appeal that is timely filed and correctly styled, but potentially misleading due to a clear error of reference, does not automatically fail on procedural grounds. Carlton v. Paxton, 14 Va. App. 105, 415 S.E.2d 600, aff'd, 15 Va. App. 265, 422 S.E.2d 423 (1992).

The time requirement for filing is mandatory, and failure of the appellant to file timely the notice of appeal requires dismissal of the appeal. Zion Church Designers & Bldrs. v. McDonald, 18 Va. App. 580, 445 S.E.2d 704 (1994).

Tolling of time limit. — In order to toll the 30-day time limit for filing a notice of appeal once a final order has been entered, it is not sufficient for the aggrieved party to file a post-judgment motion to set aside or reconsider the order or for the trial judge to express a desire to consider action or take an issue under advisement; rather, the trial judge must issue an order modifying, vacating or suspending the order within 21 days of the entry of the order. Vokes v. Vokes, 28 Va. App. 349, 504 S.E.2d 865 (1998).

Time for filing appeal in bifurcated proceeding is not extended. — To preserve the desertion issue for appellate review, the husband should have filed a timely appeal from the divorce decree; the time for filing an appeal in a bifurcated proceeding is not extended. Hall v. Hall, 9 Va. App. 426, 388 S.E.2d 669 (1990).

§ 8.01-675.4. Inspection and return of records; certiorari when part of record is omitted; retention of records. — When a case has previously been in an appellate court, the Court of Appeals may inspect the record of the former appeal. The court may, in any case, after reasonable notice to counsel in the appellate court, award a writ of certiorari to the clerk of the trial court and have brought before it, when part of a record is omitted, the whole or any part of such record. As soon as a case is decided, the clerk of the Court of Appeals shall cause the appendix, if any, and briefs of counsel to be recorded and preserved in any manner which meets archival standards as recommended by the Archives and Records Division of The Library of Virginia. (1984, c. 703; 1988, c. 197; 1994, c. 64.)

I. DECISIONS UNDER CURRENT LAW.

This section does not restrict the Court of Appeals to ordering only those portions of the appellate record as defined by the Rules of Court. Watkins v. Commonwealth, 26 Va. App. 335, 494 S.E.2d 859 (1998).

Burden of producing transcript. — Although the defendant, acting pro se, failed to make the missing transcript of the trial below part of the record on appeal, the issue of voluntary waiver of counsel is so fundamental that the onus of producing the missing transcript was on the Commonwealth in that situation. Watkins v. Commonwealth, 26 Va. App. 335, 494 S.E.2d 859 (1998).

Applied in Crumble v. Commonwealth, 2 Va. App. 231, 343 S.E.2d 359 (1986).

CHAPTER 26.2.

APPEALS GENERALLY.

Article 1.

Appeal Bond.

Sec.
8.01-676. [Repealed.]
8.01-676.1. Security for appeal.

Article 2.

Errors Insufficient in the Appellate Court.

8.01-677. Errors corrected on motion instead of writ of error coram vobis.
8.01-677.1. Appeals filed in inappropriate appellate court.
8.01-678. For what a judgment not to be reversed.

Article 3.

Limitations; Hearing and Decision.

8.01-679. Failure of trial court clerk to deliver record to appellate court.

Sec.
8.01-679.1. Arguments made on brief not waived by oral argument.
8.01-680. When judgment of trial court not to be set aside unless plainly wrong, etc.
8.01-681. Decision of appellate court.
8.01-682. What damages awarded appellee.
8.01-683. When Clerk of Supreme Court to transmit its decisions.
8.01-684. Copies of Court's opinions to be furnished to counsel.
8.01-685. Entry of decision in lower court; issue of execution thereon.
8.01-686, 8.01-687. [Repealed.]

Article 4.

Miscellaneous Provisions.

8.01-688. Order books, etc., of former district courts in custody of Clerk of Supreme Court, etc.

ARTICLE 1.

Appeal Bond.

§ 8.01-676: Repealed by Acts 1984, c. 703.

§ 8.01-676.1. Security for appeal. — A. *Security for costs of appeal of right to Court of Appeals.* — A party filing a notice of an appeal of right to the Court of Appeals shall simultaneously file an appeal bond or irrevocable letter of credit in the penalty of $500, or such sum as the trial court may require, subject to subsection E, conditioned upon paying all costs and fees incurred in the Court of Appeals and the Supreme Court if it takes cognizance of the claim. If the appellant wishes suspension of execution, the security shall also be conditioned as provided in subsection C and shall be in such sum as the trial court may require.

B. *Security for costs on petition for appeal to Court of Appeals or Supreme Court.* — An appellant whose petition for appeal is granted by the Court of Appeals or the Supreme Court shall (if he has not done so) within fifteen days from the date of the Certificate of Appeal file an appeal bond or irrevocable letter of credit in the same penalty as provided in subsection A, conditioned on the payment of all damages, costs, and fees incurred in the Court of Appeals and in the Supreme Court.

C. *Security for suspension of execution.* — An appellant who wishes execution of the judgment or award from which an appeal is sought to be suspended during the appeal shall, subject to the provisions of subsection J, file an appeal bond or irrevocable letter of credit conditioned upon the performance or satisfaction of the judgment and payment of all damages incurred in consequence of such suspension, and except as provided in subsection D, execution shall be suspended upon the filing of such security and the timely prosecution of such appeal. Such security shall be continuing and additional security shall not be necessary except as to any additional amount which may be added by the courts.

D. *Suspension of execution in decrees for support and custody; injunctions.* — The court from which an appeal is sought may refuse to suspend the execution of decrees for support and custody, and may also refuse suspension when a judgment refuses, grants, modifies, or dissolves an injunction.

E. *Increase or decrease in penalty of security.* — The Court of Appeals or the Supreme Court, when it considers a petition for appeal, may order that the penalty of the security for the appeal be decreased or increased if such request is made in the brief of any party filed in the Court of Appeals, or in the Petition for Appeal or the appellee's Brief in Opposition filed in the Supreme Court or the Court of Appeals. Affidavits and counter-affidavits may be filed by the parties containing facts pertinent to such request. Any increase or decrease in the amount of the security so ordered shall be effected in the clerk's office of the trial court within fifteen days of the order of the Court of Appeals or the Supreme Court. If an increase so ordered is not effected within fifteen days, the appeal shall be dismissed. Such increase or decrease in the penalty of the security may also be considered and ordered by the trial court, on motion of either party, at any time until the Court of Appeals or the Supreme Court acts upon the amount of penalty, and failure to increase such penalty as hereinabove provided shall also cause the appeal to be dismissed.

F. *By whom executed.* — Each bond filed shall be executed by a party or another on his behalf, and by surety approved by the clerk of the court from which appeal is sought, or by the clerk of the Supreme Court or the clerk of the Court of Appeals if the bond is ordered by such Court. Any letter of credit posted as security for an appeal shall be in a form acceptable to the clerk of the court from which appeal is sought, or by the clerk of the Supreme Court or the Court of Appeals if the security is ordered by such court. The letter of credit shall be from a bank incorporated or authorized to conduct banking business under the laws of this Commonwealth or authorized to do business in this Commonwealth under the banking laws of the United States, or a federally insured savings institution located in this Commonwealth.

G. *Appeal from State Corporation Commission; security for costs.* — When an appeal of right is entered from the State Corporation Commission to the Supreme Court, and no suspension of the order, judgment, or decree appealed from is requested, such appeal bond or letter of credit shall be filed when and in the amount required by the clerk of the Supreme Court, whose action shall be subject to review by the Supreme Court.

H. *Appeal from State Corporation Commission; suspension.* — Any judgment, order, or decree of the State Corporation Commission subject to appeal to the Supreme Court may be suspended by the Commission or by the Supreme Court pending decision of the appeal if the Commission or the Supreme Court deems such suspension necessary for the proper administration of justice but only upon the written application of an appellant after reasonable notice to all other parties in interest and the filing of a suspending bond or irrevocable letter of credit with such conditions, in such penalty, and with such surety thereon as the Commission or the Supreme Court may deem sufficient. But no surety shall be required if the appellant is any county, city or town of this Commonwealth, or the Commonwealth.

I. *Forms of bonds; letters of credit; where filed.* — The Clerk of the Supreme Court shall prescribe separate forms for appeal bonds, one for costs alone, one for suspension of execution, and one for both and a form for irrevocable letters of credit, to which the bond or bonds or irrevocable letters of credit given shall substantially conform. The forms for each bond and the letter of credit shall be published in the Rules of Court. It shall be sufficient if the bond or letter of credit, when executed as required, is filed with the trial court, clerk of the

Virginia Workers' Compensation Commission, or the clerk of the State Corporation Commission, whichever is applicable, and no personal appearance in the trial court, Virginia Workers' Compensation Commission, or State Corporation Commission by the principal, the surety on the bond or the bank issuing the letter of credit shall be required as a condition precedent to its filing.

J. *Limit on security for suspension of execution.* — If the appellee in a civil action obtains a judgment for damages other than compensatory damages, or in excess of the compensatory damages, and the appellant seeks a stay of execution of the judgment in order to obtain review in the Court of Appeals or Supreme Court, the appeal bond or irrevocable letter of credit for the portion of the damages, other than the compensatory damages, or in excess of the compensatory damages, shall not exceed $25,000,000.

K. *Dissipation of assets.* — If the appellee proves by a preponderance of the evidence that a party bringing an appeal, for whom the appeal bond or irrevocable letter of credit requirement has been limited or waived pursuant to subsection J, is purposefully dissipating its assets or diverting assets outside the jurisdiction of the United States courts for the purpose of evading the judgment, the limitation or waiver granted pursuant to subsection J shall be rescinded and the bond requirement shall be reinstated for the full amount of the judgment. Dissipation of assets shall not include those ongoing expenditures made from assets of the kind that the appellant made in the regular course of business prior to the judgment being appealed, such as the payment of stock dividends and other financial incentives to the shareholders of publicly owned companies, continued participation in charitable and civic activities, and other expenditures consistent with the exercise of good business judgment.

L. For good cause shown, a court may otherwise waive the filing of an appeal bond or irrevocable letter of credit as to the damages in excess of, or other than, the compensatory damages.

M. *Exemption.* — When an appeal is proper to protect the estate of a decedent or person under disability, or to protect the interest of the Commonwealth or any county, city, or town of this Commonwealth, no security for appeal shall be required.

N. *Indigents.* — No person who is an indigent shall be required to post security for an appeal bond.

O. *Virginia Workers' Compensation Commission.* — No claimant who files an appeal from a final decision of the Virginia Workers' Compensation Commission with the Court of Appeals shall be required to post security for costs as provided in subsection A or B of this section if such claimant has not returned to his employment or by reason of his disability is unemployed. Such claimant shall file an affidavit describing his disability and employment status with the Court of Appeals together with a motion to waive the filing of the security under subsection A or B of this section.

P. *Time for filing security for appeal.* — The appeal bond or letter of credit prescribed in subsections A and B is not jurisdictional and the time for filing such security in cases before the Court of Appeals or the Supreme Court may be extended by a judge or justice of the court before which the case is pending on motion for good cause shown and to attain the ends of justice.

Q. *Consideration of appeal bond or letter of credit by Court of Appeals.* — A determination on an issue affecting an appeal bond or letter of credit in a case before the Court of Appeals may be considered by an individual judge of such court rather than by a panel of judges. (1984, c. 703; 1986, c. 89; 1987, cc. 460, 684; 1988, c. 883; 1996, c. 77; 2000, c. 100.)

Cross references. — As to who may give bond for writ or order, see § 8.01-4.2. As to security for appeal in Supreme Court, see Rule 5:24. As to security for appeal in Court of Appeals, see Rule 5A:17.

Editor's note. — Acts 1986, c. 89, cl. 4 provides: "That subsection L [now subsection P] of this act shall apply to all appeals filed here-

§ 8.01-676.1

tofore in the Court of Appeals except that this provision shall not revive appeals in which there can be no further proceedings in any court." The act became effective March 16, 1986.

The 2000 amendments. — The 2000 amendment by c. 100, effective March 10, 2000, and applicable to any action which is pending on or which is filed after that date, inserted "subject to the provisions of subsection J" in subsection C, added subsections J, K and L, and redesignated former subsections J, K, K1, L, and M as present subsections M, N, O, P and Q.

Law Review. — For survey of Virginia practice and pleading for the year 1977-1978, see 64 Va. L. Rev. 1501 (1978).

I. Decisions Under Current Law.
II. Decisions Under Prior Law.
  A. General Consideration.
  B. Necessity for Appeal Bond.
    1. General Rule.
    2. Exceptions.
    3. Waiver of Bond.
  C. Nature and Effect of Bond.
  D. Effect of Failure to Give Bond.
  E. Execution of Bond.
  F. By Whom Bond Given.
  G. Penalty of Bond.
  H. Conditions of Bond.
  I. Sureties.
  J. Defective Bond.
  K. Action on Bond.

I. DECISIONS UNDER CURRENT LAW.

Court of Appeals and Supreme Court have substantially same requirements. — The appeal bond required by statute and the rules applicable to their filing are substantially the same in the Court of Appeals and the Supreme Court. Duckett v. Duckett, 1 Va. App. 279, 337 S.E.2d 759 (1986).

Suspension of spousal support pending appeal. — A trial court may, but is not required to, refuse to suspend an award of spousal support pending appeal. Margoupis v. Margoupis, No. 1168-98-4 (Ct. of Appeals Feb. 23, 1999).

Where case dealt with request to modify, not execute upon, support order, subsection D of this section was not applicable. Decker v. Decker, 17 Va. App. 562, 440 S.E.2d 411 (1994).

II. DECISIONS UNDER PRIOR LAW.

A. General Consideration.

Editor's note. — The cases cited below were decided under corresponding provisions of former law, and under former versions of this section. The terms "the statute" and "this section," as used below, refer to former provisions.

Legislative intent. — It appears to have been clearly the legislative intent under this section and § 8.01-251, to require the appellant, if he desires to delay the plaintiff in exercising the right established by his judgment, to give bond to protect the judgment creditor against loss on account of the delay. Seal v. Puckett, 159 Va. 297, 165 S.E. 496 (1932).

The purpose of subsection A in requiring a suspending bond is to protect the plaintiff against any loss or damage he may sustain by reason of the suspension of his right to proceed with the collection of his judgment against the defendant. Jacob v. Commonwealth ex rel. Myers, 148 Va. 236, 138 S.E. 574 (1927).

Timely bond is jurisdictional. — The requirement of a timely appeal bond under this section is jurisdictional, and is not a defect which may be cured pursuant to Rule 5A:17. Lipscomb v. Rosenthal Chevrolet, No. 0404-85 (Ct. of Appeals Dec. 10, 1985); O'Brien v. O'Brien, No. 0335-85 (Ct. of Appeals Dec. 23, 1985).

Failure to post the appeal bond by the last day on which appellant could file his notice of appeal is a defect which cannot be cured under Rule 5A:17. That rule is applicable when there is a defect in the bond that has been filed, not when no bond is posted at all. Adams v. Adams, Nos. 0064-84 and 0347-85 (Ct. of Appeals Feb. 28, 1986).

Failure to post a bond is a jurisdictional and not a mere defect. Adams v. Adams, Nos. 0064-84 and 0347-85 (Ct. of Appeals Feb. 28, 1986).

Time to file appeal bond may not be extended under Rule 5A:3(b), as that rule allows for the extension of time limits prescribed "in these Rules" and the bond is required by a statute. Lipscomb v. Rosenthal Chevrolet, No. 0404-85 (Ct. of Appeals Dec. 10, 1985); O'Brien v. O'Brien, No. 0335-85 (Ct. of Appeals Dec. 23, 1985).

Dismissal required where bond not

§ 8.01-676.1

filed. — Failure to file an appeal bond as required by this section requires that an appeal be dismissed and neither Rule 5A:3(b) nor 5A:17(b) can be used to extend the time for filing of bonds when none has been given. Burns v. C.W. Wright Constr. Co., 1 Va. App. 256, 336 S.E.2d 908 (1985).

The failure to file an appeal bond within the 15-day period prescribed by subsection B of this section is not such a defect as may be corrected under Rule 5:24 but is a jurisdictional defect requiring dismissal of an appeal either upon the appellee's motion or the Court's own motion. E.B. Rudiger & Sons v. Hanckel-Smith Sales Co., 230 Va. 255, 335 S.E.2d 257 (1985).

Where wife failed to file the required bond within the 30-day appeal period prescribed by subsection A and Rule 5A:16(a), which period expired long before subsection L ever became effective, that appeal was dead, and any effort to keep it alive by way of a petition for rehearing, or otherwise, was unavailing. Foster v. Foster, 237 Va. 484, 378 S.E.2d 826 (1989).

What obligations valid. — A suspension bond under this section being a statutory bond, no obligation which is not provided by the statute can be written in it. Branch v. Richmond Cold Storage, 146 Va. 680, 132 S.E. 848 (1926), overruled on other grounds, Hopkins v. Griffin, 241 Va. 307, 402 S.E.2d 11 (1991).

A supersedeas bond made payable to the Commonwealth is sufficient. Acker v. Alexandria & F.R.R., 84 Va. 648, 5 S.E. 688 (1888).

B. Necessity for Appeal Bond.

1. General Rule.

Bond expressly required. — It is expressly provided by this section that, with certain exceptions, an appeal, writ of error, or supersedeas shall not take effect until a sufficient bond with prescribed conditions is given. Morris v. Deshazo, 25 Va. (4 Rand.) 460 (1826); Cardwell v. Allen, 69 Va. (28 Gratt.) 184 (1877); Forrest v. Hawkins, 169 Va. 470, 194 S.E. 721 (1938).

2. Exceptions.

Where an appeal is "proper to protect the estate of a decedent," no appeal bond is required. Poff v. Poff, 128 Va. 62, 104 S.E. 719 (1920).

The estate of a decedent to be protected, within the meaning of this section, is any claim or right which a personal representative as such must protect or defend because this is his bounden duty and because he is appointed for that very purpose. Richardson v. Shank, 155 Va. 240, 154 S.E. 542 (1930).

Effect of death pending appeal. — After an appeal has been taken by a party himself, in due time so far as the appeal is concerned, and he thereafter dies before the expiration of the statutory period within which an appeal bond would have had to have been given had he lived, leaving the appeal pending and unaffected by the mere fact of his death, the continued pendency of the appeal being in such case unquestionably necessary to protect his estate after his death, the case falls within the first exception of this section. Poff v. Poff, 128 Va. 62, 104 S.E. 719 (1920).

Executors and administrators may appeal without bond. — An executor or administrator who, on his qualification gives bond and security according to law, for the faithful performance of the duties of his office, is allowed to prosecute an appeal without giving an appeal bond, in all cases where the object of the appeal is to assert the rights, or protect the interests of the estate which he represents. Wilson v. Wilson, 11 Va. (1 Hen. & M.) 15 (1806); Linney v. Holliday, 24 Va. (3 Rand.) 1 (1825); M'Cauley v. Griffin, 45 Va. (4 Gratt.) 9 (1846).

No bond was required by the judge who allowed the writ of error. It was claimed that under this section a bond was imperative. The plaintiff in error was suing as an administrator and this section has long been construed to relieve every administrator from giving such a bond. This exception of administrators applies to actions for wrongful death under § 8.01-50. Richardson v. Shank, 155 Va. 240, 154 S.E. 542 (1930).

Even when no security required of them on qualification. — Where an executor or administrator with the will annexed, has been allowed by the direction of the testator, and the order of the court of probate, to qualify without giving security, he ought not to be required to give security for the prosecution of an appeal, where the appeal is for the protection of the estate. M'Cauley v. Griffin, 45 Va. (4 Gratt.) 9 (1846).

But bond required when judgments against them personally. — In an action against an executor, judgment was entered against him personally, instead of de bonis testatoris. Though the judgment was plainly erroneous, an appeal or supersedeas could only be allowed him upon his giving an appeal bond with surety. Pugh v. Jones, 33 Va. (6 Leigh) 299 (1835).

Where in suit in equity against defendant as executor and in his own right as legatee, a decree is rendered against him personally, on appeal allowed him from the decree, an appeal bond with surety shall be required of him. Erskine v. Henry, 33 Va. (6 Leigh) 378 (1835).

Bond and security for prosecuting appeals is required where the decree is partly against an executor, as such, and partly against him in his own right. Dunton v. Robins, 16 Va. (2 Munf.) 341 (1811).

Where an executor is sued in chancery, for a

subject which is in part personal to himself, and in part touching his executorial character, he ought not to be compelled to give an appeal bond for the latter, as the subject is covered by his official bond. Shearman v. Christian, 22 Va. (1 Rand.) 393 (1823).

Legatees required to give bond. — Where executors and legatees jointly appeal, the legatees, being in possession of the property in dispute, may be ruled to give security for the prosecution of the appeal. Sadler v. Green, 11 Va. (1 Hen. & M.) 26 (1806).

On an appeal by executors, from a decree in favor of distributees or legatees, for their proportions of the estate, the executors ought to give bond and security. Porter v. Arnold, 24 Va. (3 Rand.) 479 (1825).

Assignee in bankruptcy not within exception. — An assignee in bankruptcy filed a bill in the State court, which was dismissed with costs. The assignee dying, the appellant was appointed his successor and presented a petition for appeal. It was insisted that no bond was required, as the appeal was partly to protect decedent's estate. It was held that the bond was necessary, the second assignee had nothing, as such, to do with his predecessor's estate. Pace v. Ficklin, 76 Va. 292 (1882).

3. Waiver of Bond.

Marking of counsel's name on docket no waiver. — The mere marking of his name by the counsel of the defendant in error on the docket of the court as counsel for defendant in error will not amount to a release of the plaintiff in error from his obligation to give the bond required by law. Otterback v. Alexandria & F.R.R., 67 Va. (26 Gratt.) 940 (1875).

Objection should be made. — A supersedeas is allowed by the appellate court, without requiring a supersedeas bond, when one ought to have been required, and the cause is docketed without objection. This is not good cause to dismiss the supersedeas, on motion made after lapse of six years from the time of awarding it. Pugh v. Jones, 33 Va. (6 Leigh) 299 (1835).

Delay in moving to dismiss, until after time for giving bond has expired, held not to constitute waiver. — The failure to give the required bond was not discovered by appellees until after the expiration of the time for perfecting the appeal. At the next term of the Supreme Court, and before the record was printed, they moved to dismiss the appeal. It was held that appellees had not waived the failure to give the proper bond. Clinch Valley Lumber Corp. v. Hagan Estates, Inc., 167 Va. 1, 187 S.E. 440 (1936).

C. Nature and Effect of Bond.

Purpose of bond. — A supersedeas bond is one of indemnity, the object of which is to secure to a successful litigant the ultimate fruits of his recovery, in whole or in part, and to insure him against loss from the possible insolvency of his debtor, or from other cause, pending appeal. National Sur. Co. v. Commonwealth, 125 Va. 223, 99 S.E. 657, cert. denied, 250 U.S. 665, 40 S. Ct. 13, 63 L. Ed. 1197 (1919).

Giving of bond does not release attachment. — Upon a decree in favor of an attaching creditor, and an appeal therefrom, the appellant gives an appeal bond. The giving of this bond does not release the attachment. Magill v. Sauer, 61 Va. (20 Gratt.) 540 (1871).

Effect of suspension. — The provision in this section authorizing the court, or judge, to enter an order suspending the execution of a judgment, at any time within 30 days after the end of the term at which the judgment was rendered, has the effect of extending the power of the court over the judgment for that purpose for that length of time, and of giving to an order of suspension, entered within 30 days after the end of the term, the same force and effect as if it had been entered during the term. Aetna Cas. & Sur. Co. v. Board of Supvrs., 160 Va. 11, 168 S.E. 617 (1933).

Suspension does not affect finality of judgment. — The fact that the execution of a judgment was suspended under the provisions of this section, did not affect the finality of the judgment in the lower court. Harley v. Commonwealth, 131 Va. 664, 108 S.E. 648 (1921); Bridges v. Commonwealth, 190 Va. 691, 58 S.E.2d 8 (1950). See Hirschkop v. Commonwealth, 209 Va. 678, 166 S.E.2d 322, cert. denied, 396 U.S. 845, 90 S. Ct. 72, 24 L. Ed. 2d 94 (1969).

Self-executing judgment may be stayed or suspended. — Under this section the trial court in a civil proceeding is empowered to suspend or refuse to suspend the execution of judgment, decree or order to permit an appeal therefrom as it may deem proper. The execution of a self-executing judgment, decree, or order, as well as one which is not self-executing, may be stayed or suspended by the court rendering it. The power to suspend execution of its judgments, decrees and orders is not limited under this section to staying further proceedings for the enforcement thereof, but extends to the suspension of the execution of the judgment, decree, or order however it may be executed, including its execution ex proprio vigore. Aetna Cas. & Sur. Co. v. Board of Supvrs., 160 Va. 11, 168 S.E. 617 (1933). See Sutherland v. Swannanoa Corp., 189 Va. 149, 52 S.E.2d 92 (1949).

D. Effect of Failure to Give Bond.

Dismissal of appeal. — If an appeal bond is not given within the statutory period, the appeal must be dismissed. Pace v. Ficklin, 76 Va.

292 (1882); Clinch Valley Lumber Corp. v. Hagan Estates, Inc., 167 Va. 1, 187 S.E. 440 (1936); Forrest v. Hawkins, 169 Va. 470, 194 S.E. 721 (1938).

Stay of proceedings below. — Until the appeal bond is given, the appellee may proceed to enforce the judgment or decree of the court below. Williamson v. Gayle, 45 Va. (4 Gratt.) 180 (1847).

Does not of itself avoid appeal. — The appeals being allowed, the cause is pending in the Supreme Court. The failure of the appellant to execute the bond directed by the court to be given, on granting the appeal, does not avoid the appeal, but the appeal must be disposed of according to statute. Williamson v. Gayle, 45 Va. (4 Gratt.) 180 (1847).

Appellant may be compelled to give bond. — If the appellant fails to give the bond directed to be given by the court, or the judge allowing the appeal or supersedeas, the appellee may have a rule upon him to compel him to give it. Williamson v. Gayle, 45 Va. (4 Gratt.) 180 (1847).

E. Execution of Bond.

Bond is to be given before clerk of court in which case was tried. — It is not within the intendment of this section that the bond be given in a court or before the clerk of a court different from the court in which the case was tried. Smith v. Jewell Ridge Coal Corp., 203 Va. 499, 125 S.E.2d 175 (1962).

An appeal bond can be taken only after a writ of error has been granted. Branch v. Richmond Cold Storage, 146 Va. 680, 132 S.E. 848 (1926), overruled on other grounds, Hopkins v. Griffin, 241 Va. 307, 402 S.E.2d 11 (1991).

A supersedeas bond may be given before writ of error is issued or even awarded. — This section provides that a judgment debtor may, in lieu of a suspending bond, file in the clerk's office below a supersedeas bond, thereby expressly recognizing that a supersedeas bond may be given before the writ of error is issued or even awarded. Hackley v. Robey, 170 Va. 55, 195 S.E. 689 (1938).

The filing of an appeal bond with the clerk must be in pursuance of an allowance of the appeal, entered on the record. Burch v. White, 24 Va. (3 Rand.) 104 (1824).

This section is in line with the provision of § 8.01-679 that the time the petition is in the hands of the Supreme Court is not to be taken into account in computing the time after final judgment when the petition must be presented. If the petition is presented within the time prescribed by law, it is then immaterial how long the court holds it. Sutherland v. Swannanoa Corp., 189 Va. 149, 52 S.E.2d 92 (1949).

Sufficient execution. — A bond executed by defendant corporation by its attorney and not under its corporate seal, and by defendant's attorney in his individual capacity and with his seal, as joint principals, and by a bonding company as surety, satisfied the requirements of this section. State Farm Mut. Auto. Ins. Co. v. Cook, 186 Va. 658, 43 S.E.2d 863 (1947).

Under this section a bond was not defective because, while it purported to be a joint and several bond and was properly signed and sealed by one of the defendants, and was signed by the other defendant, a corporation, the seal of the corporation was not affixed thereto, since the bond showed on its face that it was executed for the benefit of both petitioners. Brickell v. Shawn, 175 Va. 373, 9 S.E.2d 330 (1940).

F. By Whom Bond Given.

Who may be principal. — The language of this section implies that, except in certain instances, before an appeal or writ of error or supersedeas shall become effective, there must be given or filed in the clerk's office a "bond"; that is a sealed instrument, not merely a written instrument, which must be signed by (1) a principal, who may be either the "appellants or petitioners, or one or more of them, or some other person," and (2) an approved surety. Forrest v. Hawkins, 169 Va. 470, 194 S.E. 721 (1938).

Under this section an attorney could give the bond in his own name for, on behalf of, or in the place and stead of the plaintiffs. Brumley v. Grimstead, 170 Va. 340, 196 S.E. 668 (1938).

But must be authorized by sealed power of attorney to execute for appellant as principal. — See Ness v. Manuel, 187 Va. 209, 46 S.E.2d 331 (1948).

A bond executed by a surety only, without any principal obligor, is insufficient, and a supersedeas issued thereon ought to be quashed. Day v. Pickett, 18 Va. (4 Munf.) 104 (1813); Miller v. Blannerhassett, 19 Va. (5 Munf.) 197 (1816).

G. Penalty of Bond.

Sufficiency. — The penalty of the appeal and supersedeas bond should be sufficient to indemnify and save harmless the surety in the injunction bond. Braxton v. Morris, 1 Va. (1 Wash.) 380 (1794); Cardwell v. Allen, 69 Va. (28 Gratt.) 184 (1877). See also, Smock v. Dade, 26 Va. (5 Rand.) 639 (1826).

Judge may reduce the penalty of the bond without impairing or annulling the appellant's right to a supersedeas. Effinger v. Kenney, 65 Va. (24 Gratt.) 116 (1873), rev'd on other grounds, 115 U.S. 566, 6 S. Ct. 179, 29 L. Ed. 495 (1885).

H. Conditions of Bond.

An appeal bond being a statutory bond, no obligation which is not provided by statute can be written in it. Branch v. Richmond Cold Storage, 146 Va. 680, 132 S.E. 848 (1926), overruled on other grounds, Hopkins v. Griffin, 241 Va. 307, 402 S.E.2d 11 (1991).

Statutory conditions may be read into supersedeas bonds. — The conditions which this section prescribes for a supersedeas bond is to be read into every statutory supersedeas bond which has been taken since its enactment. Thus, where the bond omits to specify and provide for "all actual damages incurred in consequence of the supersedeas," the court will read the statutory condition into the bond. Northern Neck Mut. Fire Ass'n v. Turlington, 136 Va. 44, 116 S.E. 363 (1923).

How condition construed. — The condition of the bond, as prescribed by the judge awarding the supersedeas, was to pay all "costs and damages according to law, and also any deficiency in the funds arising from the land sales decreed in meeting and discharging the sums decreed against the parties, respectively, in case the decree complained of be affirmed, or the appeal or supersedeas dismissed." The condition inserted in the bond by the clerk, was to "pay the judgment," in addition to that prescribed by the judge. On a suit on the appeal bond, it was held that the stipulations in the bond to "pay the judgment," and "also the deficiency" on the resale of the lands, should be regarded as alternative provisions, intended to accomplish but one and the same object, namely, the satisfaction of the decree and the payment of costs and damages according to law. Harnsberger v. Yancey, 74 Va. (33 Gratt.) 527 (1880).

Condition construed to include loss due to depreciation of state bonds. — The language of this section, declaring the condition of every supersedeas bond, is to be read into every statutory supersedeas bond taken, since its enactment, whether inserted in the bond or not. It is broad enough to cover the depreciation in the value of the state bonds between the date when they were directed to be delivered by the decree appealed from and the date of their actual delivery, upon the affirmance of said decree by the appellate court. Bemiss v. Commonwealth, 113 Va. 489, 75 S.E. 115 (1912).

Meaning of words "awarded" and "incurred". — The word "awarded," in this section, refers to the words "damages and costs"; and the word "incurred" to the word "fees" therein, so as to make the meaning the same as if the sentence had been written: "and also to pay all damages and costs which may be awarded against, and all fees which may be incurred by the appellants or petitioners." Cardwell v. Allen, 69 Va. (28 Gratt.) 184 (1877).

Appeal from order dissolving injunction. — On the dissolution of an injunction against a judgment, and an appeal taken, the appellant was not bound to give security for the amount of the judgment, but only for costs which might be awarded against him. Eppes v. Thurman, 25 Va. (4 Rand.) 384 (1826).

A party appealing from an order dissolving an injunction can only be required to give security to perform the decree of the inferior court, and to pay the costs and damages awarded in the appellate court, if the decree shall be affirmed. M'Kay v. Hite, 25 Va. (4 Rand.) 564 (1826).

I. Sureties.

Approved surety required. — Bonds given on appeal to the Supreme Court must be with approved surety. Brooks v. Epperson, 164 Va. 37, 178 S.E. 787 (1935); Clinch Valley Lumber Corp. v. Hagan Estates, Inc., 167 Va. 1, 187 S.E. 440 (1936).

A bond accompanied by a certified check is not a substantial compliance with this section. Clinch Valley Lumber Corp. v. Hagan Estates, Inc., 167 Va. 1, 187 S.E. 440 (1936).

Same surety to appeal and injunction bond not objectionable. — It is not a valid objection to a surety to an appeal bond, that he was surety to the injunction bond also. Johnston v. Syme, 7 Va. (3 Call) 523 (1790).

Clerk liable on official bond for injury. — A party injured by the insufficiency of an appeal bond has his remedy by action on the official bond of the clerk of the court. Chase v. Miller, 88 Va. 791, 14 S.E. 545 (1892).

J. Defective Bond.

Effect of penalties in excess of authority. — Penalties in a suspension bond under this section, in excess of the authority of the court to exact, such as a promise to pay or satisfy the judgment in case the judgment shall be affirmed, will be treated as surplusage. The bond with such penalties eliminated will be enforced as a suspending bond. Branch v. Richmond Cold Storage, 146 Va. 680, 132 S.E. 848 (1926), overruled on other grounds, Hopkins v. Griffin, 241 Va. 307, 402 S.E.2d 11 (1991).

Bond signed by attorney without authority does not satisfy section. — An instrument, purporting on its face to be the bond of plaintiff, was filed, but it was signed and sealed, not by plaintiff, but in his name by his attorney. It was argued that if the attorney acted without authority, then he was personally bound to the obligee in the bond, and that this satisfied the requirement of this section. It was held that the mere fact that the attorney might be liable in damages to the obligee in the instrument did not convert it into a bond and satisfy the statute. Forrest v. Hawkins, 169 Va. 470, 194 S.E. 721 (1938); Ness v. Manuel, 187 Va. 209, 46 S.E.2d 331 (1948).

But invalid supersedeas bond may support appeal. — Where a supersedeas bond failed to conform to the statute in that it failed to specify and provide for "all actual damages incurred in consequence of the supersedeas," in case of affirmance, even if the bond ought to be held invalid as a supersedeas bond, it is sufficient to support a writ of error and to sustain the jurisdiction of the Supreme Court. Northern Neck Mut. Fire Ass'n v. Turlington, 136 Va. 44, 116 S.E. 363 (1923).

Instead of dismissing appeal court could modify order. — On motion to dismiss an appeal for failure to give a proper bond as required by this section, the court could, instead of dismissing the appeal, on motion of the appellants, make an order modifying its order allowing the appeal and supersedeas so as to allow an appeal only, not to operate as a supersedeas to, or in any manner hinder or delay the execution of the decree appealed from. Reid Bros. & Co. v. Norfolk City R.R., 94 Va. 117, 26 S.E. 428 (1896).

Second invalid supersedeas bond did not affect first bond. — Under this section, the appellant was not required to give a second supersedeas bond, and the second supersedeas bond, which did not comply with the statute, did not affect or supersede the former bond which fully complied with the statute. Harrington v. Sencindiver, 173 Va. 33, 3 S.E.2d 381 (1939).

Misrecital does not invalidate. — Bonds reciting the judgment as that of "the circuit court of Alexandria," omitting the words "the city of," are not vitiated by such omission. Acker v. Alexandria & F.R.R., 84 Va. 648, 5 S.E. 688 (1888).

Nor will error of clerk. — Where a supersedeas bond clearly failed to conform to the statute, but there was no doubt that the obligors thereto intended to execute a bond in strict conformity therewith, and the mistake was a mere misprision of the clerk, a motion to dismiss the writ of error therefor will be overruled. Northern Neck Mut. Fire Ass'n v. Turlington, 136 Va. 44, 116 S.E. 363 (1923).

Failure of bond to waive homestead may render it insufficient, but it is not void. — A bond not containing the waiver of homestead exemption required by § 49-12 may be insufficient, and may be made sufficient at any time on the motion of the defendant in error, but it is not a void bond. Acker v. Alexandria & F.R.R., 84 Va. 648, 5 S.E. 688 (1888).

When objection to defective bond deemed waived. — Where the condition of a supersedeas bond does not conform to this section, good faith requires that the defendant in error or appellee should make a motion for the dismissal of the writ of error or appeal before the expiration of the time within which a new bond can be given, so that it can be amended or corrected, and the failure to do so will be deemed a waiver of the objection to the supersedeas bond. Northern Neck Mut. Fire Ass'n v. Turlington, 136 Va. 44, 116 S.E. 363 (1923).

Where a party has a reasonable time to object to an appeal bond as defective, but fails to do so until it is too late for the other party to give a new bond or have another appeal allowed, the appeal will not be dismissed. Johnson v. Syme, 7 Va. (3 Call) 523 (1790); Virginia Fire & Marine Ins. Co. v. New York Carousal Mfg. Co., 95 Va. 515, 28 S.E. 888 (1898). See also, Jackson v. Henderson, 30 Va. (3 Leigh) 196 (1831); Pugh v. Jones, 33 Va. (6 Leigh) 299 (1835); Harris v. Harrington, 180 Va. 210, 22 S.E.2d 13 (1942); Ness v. Manuel, 187 Va. 209, 46 S.E.2d 331 (1948).

Appellee should move to dismiss as soon as defect discovered. — When a case was called for argument in the Supreme Court, defendants in error moved to dismiss the writ of error upon the ground that the condition of the supersedeas bond did not conform to the statute. The bond was not executed until October 20, 1921, and the year within which it could have been given expired on the next day, October 21. It was held that while this would have doubtless excused the failure to make the motion to dismiss the writ of error within the year upon the ground that the condition of the supersedeas bond did not conform to the statute, it did not relieve defendant in error from the obligation to make it promptly just as soon as the error was discovered, so that it could be cured by the tender of a better bond, before the case was called in the Supreme Court. Northern Neck Mut. Fire Ass'n v. Turlington, 136 Va. 44, 116 S.E. 363 (1923).

K. Action on Bond.

No consideration of errors in original suit. — In actions on appeal bonds, the Supreme Court will not consider either judicial errors, or clerical misprisions, in the court below, occurring in the original suit, and in which there has been an acquiescence by the parties not appealing to correct them. Miller v. M'Luer, 21 Va. (Gilmer) 338 (1820).

Appellee can recover depreciation on bonds sued for. — In an action on a supersedeas bond to recover damages by reason of the suspension of a decree, subsequently affirmed, for the delivery of State bonds in kind, the plaintiff is entitled to recover the depreciation in the market value of the bonds between the date of suspension and the date of delivery, together with the difference between the interest (less taxes) he could have made on the money and that actually received on bonds. The fact that he received the bonds in kind makes no difference, as he had to take them in a depreciated condition. Bemiss v. Commonwealth, 113 Va. 489, 75 S.E. 115 (1912).

Action on suspending bond under this section. — For a case involving various questions of pleading, practice, and evidence in such a case, see Budowitz v. Commonwealth, 136 Va. 227, 118 S.E. 238 (1923).

What plaintiff has to prove. — In an action on a suspending bond given under this section, the burden is on the plaintiff to prove, by a preponderance of the evidence, that but for the bond he could have collected his judgment. Jacob v. Commonwealth, 148 Va. 236, 138 S.E. 574 (1927).

ARTICLE 2.

Errors Insufficient in the Appellate Court.

§ 8.01-677. Errors corrected on motion instead of writ of error coram vobis.

— For any clerical error or error in fact for which a judgment may be reversed or corrected on writ of error coram vobis, the same may be reversed or corrected on motion, after reasonable notice, by the court. (Code 1950, § 8-485; 1977, c. 617.)

REVISERS' NOTE

Former § 8-486 (Judgment on confession, a release of errors) has been deleted since it has no modern utility.

Cross references. — As to correction of certain errors in the trial court, see § 8.01-428.

I. Decisions Under Current Law.
II. Decisions Under Prior Law.

I. DECISIONS UNDER CURRENT LAW.

Nunc pro tunc order invalid. — Where case had been continued by agreement but no court entry upon the record reflected such a continuance, because trial court never considered a motion for a continuance and never ordered a continuance, there was no defect or omission in the record. Therefore, the trial court lacked authority to issue an order nunc pro tunc reciting that a continuance had been granted when in fact the court had not granted a motion for a continuance on the motion of or with the concurrence of the defendant. The nunc pro tunc order was thus invalid and could not bar appellant's speedy trial claim. Blevins v. Commonwealth, No. 1264-96-3 (Ct. of Appeals Sept. 30, 1997).

II. DECISIONS UNDER PRIOR LAW.

Editor's note. — The cases cited below were decided under corresponding provisions of former law. The term "this section," as used below, refers to former provisions.

For a full general discussion of the purpose and use of the writ of coram vobis, see Dobie v. Commonwealth, 198 Va. 762, 96 S.E.2d 747 (1957).

This section is in simple, clear and unambiguous language, and the Supreme Court reads it to mean what it says. It does not provide that it may be used to obtain a writ of error, or an appeal, or for any purpose other than to correct a "clerical error or error in fact." It does not supplant the writ of habeas corpus. If its provisions should be widened, the enlargement should be effected by the legislature. Blowe v. Peyton, 208 Va. 68, 155 S.E.2d 351 (1967).

The writ of coram vobis is analogous to a motion for a new trial but on a ground not known in the original trial and hence not reviewable by appeal or motion to set aside the verdict. Dobie v. Commonwealth, 198 Va. 762, 96 S.E.2d 747 (1957).

It does not have function of writ of error. — Defendant's assignment of error that there was a reasonable doubt of his guilt on the original trial, was one not properly to be considered under a motion under this section, for the writ of coram vobis does not have the function of a writ of error to bring that judgment under review. Dobie v. Commonwealth, 198 Va. 762, 96 S.E.2d 747 (1957).

When writ lies for error of fact not apparent on record. — The writ of coram vobis lies for an error of fact not apparent on the record, not attributable to the applicant's negligence, and which if known by the court would have prevented rendition of the judgment. It does not lie for newly-discovered evidence or for facts newly arising or adjudicated at the trial. Dobie v. Commonwealth, 198 Va. 762, 96 S.E.2d 747 (1957).

Conviction on plea of guilty. — Writ of error coram vobis or motion under this section cannot serve to gain a new trial for a defendant after a conviction on a plea of guilty merely because he might have fared better on a plea of not guilty. Dobie v. Commonwealth, 198 Va. 762, 96 S.E.2d 747 (1957).

Change of plea not clerical error. — The change of a plea of not guilty of robbery to a plea of guilty of grand larceny was a matter of judgment, and not a "clerical error or error in fact." Blowe v. Peyton, 208 Va. 68, 155 S.E.2d 351 (1967).

A writ of error coram vobis did not lie in the Supreme Court. Reid v. Strider, 48 Va. (7 Gratt.) 76 (1850).

§ 8.01-677.1. Appeals filed in inappropriate appellate court. — Notwithstanding any other provisions of this Code, no appeal which was otherwise properly and timely filed shall be dismissed for want of jurisdiction solely because it was filed in either the Supreme Court or the Court of Appeals and the appellate court in which it was filed thereafter rules that it should have been filed in the other court. In such event, the appellate court so ruling shall transfer the appeal to the appellate court having appropriate jurisdiction for further proceedings in accordance with the rules of the latter court. The parties shall be allowed a reasonable time to file such additional or amended pleadings as may be appropriate to proceed with the appeal in the appellate court to which the appeal is transferred. (1988, c. 382.)

I. DECISIONS UNDER CURRENT LAW.

Proper transfer of appeal. — Where the grievance panel's decision was "final and binding," only its implementation could be granted or denied by the circuit court. Therefore, proceeding before circuit court was not an appeal of the grievance panel's decision, thus, the Court of Appeals lacked jurisdiction and properly ordered the appeal transferred to the Supreme Court. Virginia Dep't of Taxation v. Daughtry, 19 Va. App. 135, 449 S.E.2d 57 (1994).

§ 8.01-678. For what a judgment not to be reversed. — When it plainly appears from the record and the evidence given at the trial that the parties have had a fair trial on the merits and substantial justice has been reached, no judgment shall be arrested or reversed:

1. For the appearance of either party, being under the age of eighteen years, by attorney, if the verdict, where there is one, or the judgment be for him and not to his prejudice; or

2. For any other defect, imperfection, or omission in the record, or for any error committed on the trial. (Code 1950, § 8-487; 1954, c. 333; 1977, c. 617.)

REVISERS' NOTE

Former § 8-487, part of the old English statute of jeofails, has been rewritten. The age requirement of subdivision (1) has been reduced to 18; subdivisions (2), (3), (4) and (5) have been deleted as no longer necessary.

Cross references. — As to what defects in pleadings not to be regarded, see § 8.01-275.

Law Review. — For survey of Virginia law on evidence for the year 1978-1979, see 66 Va. L. Rev. 293 (1980).

§ 8.01-678   CIVIL REMEDIES AND PROCEDURE   § 8.01-678

I. Decisions Under Current Law.
II. Decisions Under Prior Law.
   A. General Consideration.
   B. Substantial Justice.
   C. Doctrine of Harmless Error.
      1. Construction and Application.
      2. Illustrations.
   D. Incurable Defects.

I. DECISIONS UNDER CURRENT LAW.

Applicability. — This section applies to both civil and criminal cases. Lavinder v. Commonwealth, 12 Va. App. 1003, 407 S.E.2d 910 (1991).

The defendant may not seek to relitigate the truth of a fact on appeal he chose not to contest at trial. Ferguson v. Commonwealth, 16 Va. App. 9, 427 S.E.2d 442 (1993).

Judgment reversed only if merits of case affected. — Where the trial court has committed error, an appellate court will not reverse the judgment on the ground of error unless it affirmatively appears that the error affected the merits of the case. Sargent v. Commonwealth, 5 Va. App. 143, 360 S.E.2d 895 (1987).

A fair trial on the merits and substantial justice are not achieved if an error at trial has affected the verdict. An error does not affect a verdict if a reviewing court can conclude, without usurping the jury's fact-finding function, that, had the error not occurred, the verdict would have been the same. Taylor v. Commonwealth, No. 0566-93-2 (Ct. of Appeals Jan. 17, 1995).

In Virginia, non-constitutional error is harmless when it plainly appears from the record and the evidence given at trial that the parties have had a fair trial on the merits and substantial justice has been reached. A fair trial on the merits and substantial justice are reached if an error at trial has not affected the verdict. Benson v. Commonwealth, No. 1937-93-3 (Ct. of Appeals Dec. 13, 1994).

A criminal conviction shall not be reversed for an error committed at trial when it plainly appears from the record and the evidence given at the trial that the parties have had a fair trial on the merits and substantial justice has been reached. Taylor v. Commonwealth, No. 0566-93-2 (Ct. of Appeals Jan. 17, 1995).

Error presumed prejudicial and burden shifts to Commonwealth. — While an error committed in the trial of a criminal case does not automatically require reversal, once error is established it is presumed to be prejudicial; the burden then shifts to the Commonwealth to show that it was non-prejudicial, and the case will be reversed if it is not shown that the error is harmless beyond a reasonable doubt. Pavlick v. Commonwealth, 25 Va. App. 538, 489 S.E.2d 720 (1997).

Error in admission of evidence presumed prejudicial. — While not every erroneous ruling on the admissibility of evidence will constitute reversible error, once error is established it will be presumed to be prejudicial. In such case, the burden shifts to the opposing party to prove that the error was non-prejudicial. Taylor v. Commonwealth, No. 0566-93-2 (Ct. of Appeals Jan. 17, 1995).

Whether an error is harmless in a particular case depends upon a host of factors, all readily accessible to reviewing courts. These factors include the importance of the witness' testimony in the prosecution's case, whether the testimony was cumulative, the presence or absence of evidence corroborating or contradicting the testimony of the witness on material points, the extent of cross-examination otherwise permitted, and, of course, the overall strength of the prosecution's case. Sargent v. Commonwealth, 5 Va. App. 143, 360 S.E.2d 895 (1987).

An error does not affect a verdict if a reviewing court can conclude, without usurping the jury's fact finding function, that, had the error not occurred, the verdict would have been the same. Lavinder v. Commonwealth, 12 Va. App. 1003, 407 S.E.2d 910 (1991).

If a nonconstitutional error did not affect the verdict, the error is harmless. If it plainly appears from the facts and circumstances of a particular case that a nonconstitutional error did not affect the verdict, the error is harmless. Lavinder v. Commonwealth, 12 Va. App. 1003, 407 S.E.2d 910 (1991).

Court must consider burden of proof applied at trial. — Even though the burden of proof at trial is not part of the test for measuring whether nonconstitutional error is harmless, a reviewing court must take into account the burden of proof applied at trial when evaluating the impact of an error upon a verdict. Lavinder v. Commonwealth, 12 Va. App. 1003, 407 S.E.2d 910 (1991).

To the extent that the impact of an error on a verdict is affected by the burden of proof in a criminal case, the reviewing court must consider that the fact finder was required to reach its verdict "beyond a reasonable doubt." Lavinder v. Commonwealth, 12 Va. App. 1003, 407 S.E.2d 910 (1991).

Judgment will be affirmed where no er-

ror in excluding evidence. — If, upon consideration of all the evidence, including evidence excluded erroneously, the court can conclude that there was no error in the judgment appealed from, the court will affirm it. Pace v. Richmond, 231 Va. 216, 343 S.E.2d 59 (1986).

Reversal required where evidence erroneously admitted. — Reversal was required where two-to-four week old rib fracture evidence as to victim was erroneously admitted, since malice, required for a second degree murder conviction, may have been inferred by jury from that admission. Pavlick v. Commonwealth, 25 Va. App. 538, 489 S.E.2d 720 (1997).

Applied in Rozier v. Commonwealth, 219 Va. 525, 248 S.E.2d 789 (1978); Yager v. Commonwealth, 220 Va. 608, 260 S.E.2d 251 (1979); Hopkins v. Commonwealth, 230 Va. 280, 337 S.E.2d 264 (1985); Lavinder v. Commonwealth, 395 S.E.2d 211 (1990); Conway v. Commonwealth, 12 Va. App. 711, 407 S.E.2d 310 (1991); Knick v. Commonwealth, 15 Va. App. 103, 421 S.E.2d 479 (1992); Galbraith v. Commonwealth, 18 Va. App. 734, 446 S.E.2d 633 (1994); Singleton v. Commonwealth, 19 Va. App. 728, 453 S.E.2d 921 (1995); Cudjoe v. Commonwealth, 23 Va. App. 193, 475 S.E.2d 821 (1996); Castelow v. Commonwealth, 29 Va. App. 305, 512 S.E.2d 137 (1999); Boney v. Commonwealth, 29 Va. App. 795, 514 S.E.2d 810 (1999); Newman v. Commonwealth, No. 2483-97-4, Ct. of Appeals Oct. 27, 1998.

II. DECISIONS UNDER PRIOR LAW.

A. General Consideration.

Editor's note. — The cases cited below were decided under corresponding provisions of former law. The terms "this statute" and "this section," as used below, refer to former provisions.

When section applicable. — This section is only applicable where it plainly appears from the record that there has been a fair trial on the merits, and that substantial justice has been reached. Rinehart & Dennis Co. v. Brown, 137 Va. 670, 120 S.E. 269 (1923); White v. Lee, 144 Va. 523, 132 S.E. 307 (1926); Dozier v. Morrisette, 198 Va. 37, 92 S.E.2d 366 (1956).

This statute is intended to cure a defective statement of a cause of action, but not a statement which makes no case. Orange A. & M.R.R. v. Miles, 76 Va. 773 (1882).

Where a declaration contains a defective statement of a good cause of action, this is the class of error that this section is designed to cure. City of Richmond v. McCormack, 120 Va. 552, 91 S.E. 767 (1917).

Equally applicable to decree in chancery. — This section, while most often invoked to sustain a judgment rendered in an action at law, is equally applicable to a decree in chancery and should always be invoked where it is possible to do so. Morris v. Scruggs, 147 Va. 166, 136 S.E. 655 (1927).

This section and § 8.01-681 are closely related. Kearns v. Hall, 197 Va. 736, 91 S.E.2d 648 (1956).

B. Substantial Justice.

Meaning of substantial justice. — In causes triable and tried by juries "substantial justice" in a legal sense has been attained when litigants have had one fair trial on the merits. Virginia Ry. & Power Co. v. Smith, 129 Va. 269, 105 S.E. 532 (1921); Virginia Ry. & Power Co. v. Wellons, 133 Va. 350, 112 S.E. 843 (1922); Kennedy v. Mullins, 155 Va. 166, 154 S.E. 568 (1930).

Effect when substantial justice done. — "Substantial justice," as used in this section, providing that there shall be no reversal where it appears that the parties have had a fair trial on the merits and substantial justice has been done, has been attained when litigants have had one fair trial on the merits, and although the language of instructions might be the subject of criticism, yet when the instructions read together fairly submitted the conflicting contentions of the parties arising under the evidence, there can be no reversal. Virginia Ry. & Power Co. v. Smith, 129 Va. 269, 105 S.E. 532 (1921); Bryant v. Fox, 135 Va. 296, 116 S.E. 459 (1923). See also, Northwestern Nat'l Ins. Co. v. Cohen, 138 Va. 177, 121 S.E. 507 (1924); McNamara v. Rainey Luggage Corp., 139 Va. 197, 123 S.E. 515 (1924).

Where the Supreme Court decides that a case has been correctly decided on the merits, a discussion of whether or not there was error in giving and refusing instructions is unnecessary under this section. Adam-Christian Co. v. McGavock, 147 Va. 252, 137 S.E. 374 (1927).

Duty of court where error not assigned. — While error in the giving of an instruction on the last clear chance doctrine was not assigned in terms in the petition or brief of counsel, yet it was the duty of the Supreme Court under this section, in order to vitalize said section, to consider the entire record of the law and the evidence, and, if the parties have had one fair trial on the merits, affirm the judgment, if not remand the same for a new trial. Green v. Ruffin, 141 Va. 628, 125 S.E. 742, 127 S.E. 486 (1925).

C. Doctrine of Harmless Error.

1. Construction and Application.

When applied. — The doctrine of harmless error is favored by the Supreme Court, and it will not interfere with a verdict when it can be said that a case has been fairly tried upon its merits. But the doctrine cannot be applied where there would be serious risk of requiring defendant to pay heavy damages in the case, if, where upon correct instructions, the jury might have found a contrary verdict. Director Gen. of R.R.'s v. Pence's Adm'x, 135 Va. 329, 116 S.E. 351 (1923).

Where a fair trial has been had on the merits and substantial justice has been done, this section prevents interference with the judgment of the lower court for harmless error. Mullins v. Mingo Lime & Lumber Co., 176 Va. 44, 10 S.E.2d 492 (1940).

This section is only applicable where it plainly appears from the record that there has been a fair trial on the merits and substantial justice has been reached. If the record shows this, then the formal errors are to be ignored. Irvine v. Carr, 163 Va. 662, 177 S.E. 208 (1934).

Error must be material and prejudicial. — In order to constitute reversible error the ruling of the trial court must be material and prejudicial to the interests of the party complaining of it. Taylor v. Turner, 205 Va. 828, 140 S.E.2d 641 (1965).

Effect when no other verdict could have been reached. — Where no other proper verdict or judgment could have been reached in the trial court, an error in procedure must be regarded as harmless, since, under this section, an error is harmless when a party does not suffer prejudice thereby. Quick v. Southern Churchman Co., 171 Va. 403, 199 S.E. 489 (1938).

No reversal when substantial rights of litigants have not been prejudiced. — Courts are liberal in the allowance of amendments of pleadings in furtherance of justice, and will not reverse a cause for formal defects in procedure if the substantial rights of litigants have not been prejudiced thereby. Rinehart & Dennis Co. v. Brown, 137 Va. 670, 120 S.E. 269 (1923); Rausch & Co. v. Graham Mfg. Corp., 140 Va. 445, 124 S.E. 427, 126 S.E. 2 (1924).

Error is harmless which does not injuriously affect the interest of the party complaining, and such injury is not presumed but must affirmatively appear from the record. Bryant v. Fox, 135 Va. 296, 116 S.E. 459 (1923).

This section goes to the limit of harmless error. Dozier v. Morrisette, 198 Va. 37, 92 S.E.2d 366 (1956).

In criminal case, proof must be also conclusive of defendant's guilt. — In a criminal prosecution the doctrine of harmless error obtains only when it clearly appears that the accused has had a fair trial according to law and the proof is conclusive of his guilt. If either of these elements be lacking, then an accused has not been accorded the right guaranteed him under the provisions of the statute and organic law. Elliott v. Commonwealth, 172 Va. 595, 1 S.E.2d 273 (1939).

However, there is no presumption that an error is harmless. White v. Lee, 144 Va. 523, 132 S.E. 307 (1926); Dozier v. Morrisette, 198 Va. 37, 92 S.E.2d 366 (1956).

Before a federal constitutional error can be held harmless, the court must be able to declare a belief that it was harmless beyond a reasonable doubt. Cardwell v. Commonwealth, 209 Va. 412, 164 S.E.2d 699 (1968).

2. Illustrations.

Failure of infant to sue by next friend. — Where infant, who did not sue by next friend, recovered a verdict which fairly compensated him for his injuries, the verdict was "for him and not to his prejudice" within the meaning of subdivision (1) of this section and was not void because infant did not sue by next friend. Riddle v. Barksdale, 194 Va. 766, 75 S.E.2d 507 (1953).

It is harmless error merely to mention that defendant has casualty insurance. — The provisions of this section inhibit the adoption of the rule that in personal injury actions the mere mention of the fact to the jury that the defendant carries casualty insurance is sufficient to warrant the trial court directing a mistrial. Irvine v. Carr, 163 Va. 662, 177 S.E. 208 (1934).

In the course of the trial of an action for personal injuries the specialist who had treated plaintiff was asked by counsel for defendant whether the doctor who had referred the case wished him to see her from time to time. To answer this the specialist read the letter of referral, which included the statement "This is an insurance case." This was held to be, under the facts of the case and in view of the provisions of this section, harmless error. Simmons v. Boyd, 199 Va. 806, 102 S.E.2d 292 (1958).

As is failure to file motion in time as to other defendants. — Appellant offered to prove an entry in the clerk's rule book was erroneous and that no motion was filed until after more than one month from the time process was returned executed as to one or more defendants, not the appellant. It was held that this was not error affecting the substantial rights of the appellant and that it would fall under the intendment of this section. Whitten v. McClelland, 137 Va. 726, 120 S.E. 146 (1923).

Indirect reference of prosecuting attorney to failure of defendant's husband to testify held harmless error. Mitchell v. Commonwealth, 192 Va. 205, 64 S.E.2d 713 (1951).

Informal entry of judgment. — The informal entry of a judgment is not a ground for reversing it, the informality being a harmless error. Long v. Pence, 93 Va. 584, 25 S.E. 593 (1896).

Any informality in the entry by the clerk

must be corrected by the court below, and is no ground for reversal in the appellate court. Roach v. Blakey, 89 Va. 767, 17 S.E. 228 (1893).

Rulings as to instructions when there could be no other verdict. — The rulings of the trial court in granting and refusing instructions are immaterial, where the jury could properly have found no other verdict. New York P. & N.R.R. v. Bundick, Taylor, Corbin-Handy Co., 138 Va. 535, 122 S.E. 261 (1924).

Under this section, a judgment will not be reversed for error in rulings on the instructions where it plainly appeared from the record and the evidence given at the trial that the parties had had a fair trial on the merits and substantial justice had been reached. New York P. & N.R.R. v. Bundick, Taylor, Corbin-Handy Co., 138 Va. 535, 122 S.E. 261 (1924).

When another instruction gives correct ruling. — Complaint was made of an instruction because it directed a verdict for the plaintiff without making any reference to the defense based on the alleged failure to give as prompt notice of the theft as the policy required. The instruction would have been clearly free from any criticism if it had referred to that defense, and it is equally clear that the lack of such reference rendered it defective, but the error was rendered harmless by another instruction in the case, which fully set forth the defense in question. Northwestern Nat'l Ins. Co. v. Cohen, 138 Va. 177, 121 S.E. 507 (1924).

Entering a judgment against two defendants in the singular number, "defendant," instead of the plural, "defendants" does not affect its validity. Roach v. Blakey, 89 Va. 767, 17 S.E. 228 (1893).

And refusal to require filing of bill of particulars. — Where a full and clear statement of the plaintiff's case is made in the declaration, the defendant is not prejudiced by the refusal of the court to require a bill of particulars to be filed. Blue Ridge Light & Power Co. v. Tutwiler, 106 Va. 54, 55 S.E. 539 (1906).

Where it can be seen from the record that no injury could have resulted to the defendant from the failure to file a bill of particulars earlier, in view of this section a reversal will not be granted on that ground. Clinchfield Coal Corp. v. Hayter, 130 Va. 711, 108 S.E. 854 (1921).

Doctrine held applicable. — In an action against the driver of a car for the death of an occupant of the car, reckless driving was alleged against the driver. The record shows that the jury was fairly instructed, that the parties have had a fair trial upon the merits of the case and that substantial justice has been done. That is enough, under this section. Poole v. Kelley, 162 Va. 279, 173 S.E. 537 (1934).

Doctrine held inapplicable. — Where accused did not testify and the attorney for the Commonwealth, in his closing argument, pointed his finger at accused and said that accused had not denied what a witness for the Commonwealth had stated, the doctrine of harmless error was inapplicable. Elliott v. Commonwealth, 172 Va. 595, 1 S.E.2d 273 (1939).

D. Incurable Defects.

Where a bill fails to state a case proper for relief in equity, the court will dismiss it at the hearing, though no objection has been made in the pleadings. Green v. Massie, 62 Va. (21 Gratt.) 356 (1871).

But a defective bill may be aided by the answer and the evidence. Salamore v. Keiley, 80 Va. 86 (1885).

Defect in order correctible on appeal. — Where the final order in a condemnation suit inadvertently failed to specify the duration of the condemned easements, this defect could be corrected on appeal and did not justify reversal. Brown v. May, 202 Va. 300, 117 S.E.2d 101 (1960).

When failure to appoint guardian ad litem not cured. — The omission to appoint a guardian ad litem for an infant defendant is reversible error in all cases, unless it appears that the judgment or decree is for the infant and not to his prejudice. Weaver v. Glenn, 104 Va. 443, 51 S.E. 835 (1905). See also, Langston v. Bassette, 104 Va. 47, 51 S.E. 218 (1905).

Article 3.

Limitations; Hearing and Decision.

§ 8.01-679. Failure of trial court clerk to deliver record to appellate court. — Notwithstanding any provision of law to the contrary, no appeal shall be refused or dismissed for failure to deliver the record within the required time if it shall appear from evidence satisfactory to the appellate court that the clerk of the court below failed to deliver to the clerk of the appellate court the record on appeal within the required time. (Code 1950, § 8-489; 1964, c. 7; 1976, c. 615; 1977, c. 617; 1984, c. 703.)

REVISERS' NOTE

"Process" is not utilized under modern practice in the granting of an appeal since the procedure under Rule 5:30 is used. Thus, the first two paragraphs in former § 8-489 have been deleted. Since the appeal bond provisions of § 8.01-676.1 contemplate such bonds being set initially by the trial court, there is no need for the limitations of former § 8-489 and the third paragraph thereof has been deleted.

Cross references. — As to time within which petition must be presented, see § 8.01-671. For rules as to time and place of filing briefs, see Rule 5:26.

I. DECISIONS UNDER PRIOR LAW.

Editor's note. — The case cited below was decided under corresponding provisions of former law. The term "this section," as used below, refers to former provisions.

Erroneous refusal of clerk of trial court to transmit record. — Defendant contended he should be released because the clerk of the trial court had erroneously refused to transmit the record on the ground the time for appeal had expired. But since mandamus had been issued pursuant to which the record had been transmitted and the case had been reviewed, there had been no denial of due process and defendant's imprisonment was not illegal. Carter v. Commonwealth, 199 Va. 466, 100 S.E.2d 681 (1957).

§ 8.01-679.1. Arguments made on brief not waived by oral argument.
— It shall not be necessary for any party to expressly reserve in oral argument any argument made on brief before an appellate court and failure to raise any such argument on oral argument shall not constitute a waiver. (1986, c. 268.)

§ 8.01-680. When judgment of trial court not to be set aside unless plainly wrong, etc.
— When a case, civil or criminal, is tried by a jury and a party objects to the judgment or action of the court in granting or refusing to grant a new trial on a motion to set aside the verdict of a jury on the ground that it is contrary to the evidence, or when a case is decided by a court without the intervention of a jury and a party objects to the decision on the ground that it is contrary to the evidence, the judgment of the trial court shall not be set aside unless it appears from the evidence that such judgment is plainly wrong or without evidence to support it. (Code 1950, § 8-491; 1977, c. 617.)

REVISERS' NOTE

The limitation in former § 8-491 that this section applied to a "case at law" was removed and the section made applicable to civil and criminal cases generally. There are instances where a jury is provided in equity cases. See § 8.01-336.

Former § 8-490 (Issuance of process and supersedeas ...) has been deleted, since its subject matter is covered by Rule 5:30.

Former § 8-490.1 (Notice to interveners ...) has been deleted, since its subject matter is covered by Rule 5:11(b).

Cross references. — As to when final judgment to be entered by trial court after verdict is set aside, see § 8.01-430.

Law Review. — For survey of Virginia criminal law for the year 1975-1976, see 62 Va. L. Rev. 1400 (1976).

I. Decisions Under Current Law.
  A. General Consideration.
  B. When Judgment Set Aside.
  C. Weight Given Decision of Court.
II. Decisions Under Prior Law.
  A. General Consideration.

B. When Judgment Set Aside.
  1. In General.
  2. When Evidence Incredible.
C. Verdict Approved or Disapproved.
D. Weight Given Decision of Court.

I. DECISIONS UNDER CURRENT LAW.

A. General Consideration.

A court may not base its findings on a suspicion which is contrary to the undisputed positive testimony. Hankerson v. Moody, 229 Va. 270, 329 S.E.2d 791 (1985).

The burden is on the party alleging trial court error to show by the record that the judgment was erroneous or that the finding was plainly wrong and without evidence to support it by a preponderance of the evidence. Carter v. Thornhill, 19 Va. App. 501, 453 S.E.2d 295 (1995).

On the issue of compensatory damages in libel cases when New York Times malice need not be proven, Virginia will continue to follow the established standard of review mandated by this section, that is, "the judgment of the trial court shall not be set aside unless it appears from the evidence that such judgment is plainly wrong or without evidence to support it." Gazette, Inc. v. Harris, 229 Va. 1, 325 S.E.2d 713, cert. denied sub nom, Fleming v. Moore, 472 U.S. 1032, 105 S. Ct. 3513, 87 L. Ed. 2d 643, cert. denied sub nom Port Packet Corp. v. Lewis, 473 U.S. 905, 105 S. Ct. 3528, 87 L. Ed. 2d 653 (1985).

Applied in Brantley v. Karas, 220 Va. 489, 260 S.E.2d 189 (1979); Green v. Commonwealth, 223 Va. 706, 292 S.E.2d 605 (1982); Dwyer v. Yurgaitis, 224 Va. 176, 294 S.E.2d 792 (1982); Rochelle v. Rochelle, 225 Va. 387, 302 S.E.2d 59 (1983); Stockton v. Commonwealth, 227 Va. 124, 314 S.E.2d 371 (1984); Allsbrook v. Azalea Radiator Serv., Inc., 227 Va. 600, 316 S.E.2d 743 (1984); Commonwealth, Dep't of Taxation v. Wellmore Coal Corp., 228 Va. 149, 320 S.E.2d 509 (1984); Fisher v. Commonwealth, 228 Va. 296, 321 S.E.2d 202 (1984); McGinnis v. McGinnis, 1 Va. App. 272, 338 S.E.2d 159 (1985); Royal v. Commonwealth, 2 Va. App. 59, 341 S.E.2d 660 (1986); Dodge v. Dodge, 2 Va. App. 238, 343 S.E.2d 363 (1986); McLaughlin v. McLaughlin, 2 Va. App. 463, 346 S.E.2d 535 (1986); Walls v. Commonwealth, 2 Va. App. 639, 347 S.E.2d 175 (1986); Albert v. Commonwealth, 2 Va. App. 734, 347 S.E.2d 534 (1986); Mullis v. Commonwealth, 3 Va. App. 564, 351 S.E.2d 919 (1987); Bright v. Commonwealth, 4 Va. App. 248, 356 S.E.2d 443 (1987); O'Brien v. Commonwealth, 4 Va. App. 261, 356 S.E.2d 449 (1987); Martin v. Commonwealth, 4 Va. App. 438, 358 S.E.2d 415 (1987); Surbey v. Surbey, 5 Va. App. 119, 360 S.E.2d 873 (1987); Seehorn v. Seehorn, 7 Va. App. 375, 375 S.E.2d 7 (1988); Kaufman v. Kaufman, 7 Va. App. 488, 375 S.E.2d 374 (1988); Spain v. Commonwealth, 7 Va. App. 385, 373 S.E.2d 728 (1988); Furrow v. State Farm Mut. Auto. Ins. Co., 237 Va. 77, 375 S.E.2d 738 (1989); School Bd. v. Beasley, 238 Va. 44, 380 S.E.2d 884 (1989); Harris v. Commonwealth, 8 Va. App. 424, 382 S.E.2d 292 (1989); Giannotti v. Hamway, 239 Va. 14, 387 S.E.2d 725 (1990); Farley v. Farley, 9 Va. App. 326, 387 S.E.2d 794 (1990); Linkous v. Kingery, 10 Va. App. 45, 390 S.E.2d 188 (1990); City of Hopewell v. County of Prince George, 239 Va. 287, 389 S.E.2d 685 (1990); Bland v. Commonwealth, No. 1733-91-4 (Ct. of Appeals March 16, 1993); Thompson v. Bacon, 245 Va. 107, 425 S.E.2d 512 (1993); Beavers v. Commonwealth, 245 Va. 268, 427 S.E.2d 411; Carter v. Commonwealth, 16 Va. App. 42, 427 S.E.2d 736 (1993); Breard v. Commonwealth, 248 Va. 68, 445 S.E.2d 670 (1994); Hudson v. Hudson, 249 Va. 335, 455 S.E.2d 14 (1995); Williams v. Garraghty, 249 Va. 224, 455 S.E.2d 209 (1995); Nicholson v. Nicholson, 21 Va. App. 231, 463 S.E.2d 334 (1995); Sackadorf v. JLM Group Ltd. Partnership, 250 Va. 321, 462 S.E.2d 64 (1995); Norfolk & W. Ry. v. Johnson, 251 Va. 37, 465 S.E.2d 800 (1996); Richmond, F. & P.R.R. v. Metropolitan Wash. Airports Auth., 251 Va. 201, 468 S.E.2d 90 (1996); Commonwealth v. Jenkins, 255 Va. 516, 499 S.E.2d 263 (1998); Ash v. All Star Lawn & Pest Control, Inc., 256 Va. 520, 506 S.E.2d 540 (1998); Ward v. NationsBank, 256 Va. 427, 507 S.E.2d 616 (1998); Siquina v. Commonwealth, 28 Va. App. 694, 508 S.E.2d 350 (1998); Moody v. Commonwealth, 28 Va. App. 702, 508 S.E.2d 354 (1998); Ramadan v. Commonwealth, 28 Va. App. 708, 508 S.E.2d 357 (1998); Sears v. Commonwealth, 29 Va. App. 158, 510 S.E.2d 274 (1999); Atkins v. Commonwealth, 257 Va. 160, 510 S.E.2d 445 (1999); Hedrick v. Commonwealth, 257 Va. 328, 513 S.E.2d 634 (1999); Richardson v. Richardson, 30 Va. App. 341, 516 S.E.2d 726 (1999).

B. When Judgment Set Aside.

Where the sufficiency of the evidence is challenged after conviction, it is the duty of the trial court to consider it in the light most favorable to the Commonwealth and give it all reasonable inferences fairly deducible therefrom. Black v. Commonwealth, 222 Va. 838, 284 S.E.2d 608 (1981).

Where the sufficiency of the evidence is challenged on appeal, that evidence must be construed in the light most favorable to the Commonwealth, giving it all reasonable inferences fairly deducible therefrom. Norman v. Commonwealth, 2 Va. App. 518, 346 S.E.2d 44 (1986).

When conflicting inferences flow from the undisputed evidence, principles of appellate procedure require the Supreme Court to adopt those conclusions most favorable to the Commonwealth if fairly deducible from the proven facts. Pugh v. Commonwealth, 223 Va. 663, 292 S.E.2d 339 (1982).

Findings not supported by evidence. — The findings of the commissioner and affirmed by the chancellor that wife deserted husband were not supported by substantial, competent and credible evidence. Dexter v. Dexter, 7 Va. App. 36, 371 S.E.2d 816 (1988).

C. Weight Given Decision of Court.

Judgment of court sitting without jury. — When sufficiency of the evidence is attacked, the judgment of the trial court sitting without a jury is entitled to the same weight as a jury verdict, and will not be disturbed on appeal unless plainly wrong or without evidence to support it. Pugh v. Commonwealth, 223 Va. 663, 292 S.E.2d 339 (1982); Beck v. Commonwealth, 2 Va. App. 170, 342 S.E.2d 642 (1986); Hambury v. Commonwealth, 3 Va. App. 435, 350 S.E.2d 524 (1986).

While the judgment of the court sitting without a jury will not be set aside unless it is plainly wrong or without evidence to support it, a trial court's conclusion based on evidence that is not in material conflict does not have this binding effect on appeal. Hankerson v. Moody, 229 Va. 270, 329 S.E.2d 791 (1985).

The judgment of a trial court sitting without a jury is entitled to the same weight as a jury verdict and will not be disturbed on appeal unless plainly wrong or without evidence to support it. Crumble v. Commonwealth, 2 Va. App. 231, 343 S.E.2d 359 (1986).

Basis for setting aside of jury's verdict. — On review, the court of appeals does not substitute its judgment for the trier of fact; instead, the jury's verdict will not be set aside unless it appears that it is plainly wrong or without supporting evidence. Waldrop v. Commonwealth, 23 Va. App. 614, 478 S.E.2d 723 (1996).

Trial court will not be disturbed unless plainly wrong. — As the fact finder, the trial court determines the credibility of the witnesses and the weight of their testimony; its findings, therefore, will not be disturbed on appeal unless plainly wrong or without evidence to support them. Bankers Credit Serv. of Vermont, Inc. v. Dorsch, 231 Va. 273, 343 S.E.2d 339 (1986).

The judgment should be affirmed unless it appears from the evidence that it is plainly wrong or without evidence to support it. Henry v. Commonwealth, 2 Va. App. 194, 342 S.E.2d 655 (1986).

Unless the finding of the trial court is plainly wrong or without evidence to support it, the Court of Appeals will not disturb its findings. Davison v. Commonwealth, 18 Va. App. 496, 445 S.E.2d 683 (1994).

On review by an appellate court, the evidence must be viewed in the light most favorable to the prevailing party, and the trial court's judgment will not be disturbed unless it is plainly wrong or there is no evidence to support it; here the Commonwealth's evidence was overwhelming as to the guilt of the defendant and there was no evidence indicating that anyone but the defendant shot the murder victims. Goins v. Commonwealth, 251 Va. 442, 470 S.E.2d 114 (1996), cert. denied, 519 U.S. 887, 117 S. Ct. 222, 136 L. Ed. 2d 154 (1996).

A trial court's judgment will not be set aside unless it appears that the judgment is plainly wrong or without supporting evidence. Bell v. Commonwealth, 21 Va. App. 693, 467 S.E.2d 289 (1996).

Decree of chancellor in equity. — When a chancellor hears evidence, ore tenus, his decree acquires the same weight as a jury's verdict and the Supreme Court may only reverse the decree if it is plainly wrong or without evidence to support it, after examining the record in the light most favorable to the prevailing parties and determining whether substantial credible evidence supports the chancellor's decision. Carter v. Carter, 223 Va. 505, 291 S.E.2d 218 (1982).

The judgment of a trial court sitting in equity, when based upon an ore tenus hearing, will not be disturbed on appeal unless plainly wrong or without evidence to support it. Box v. Talley, 1 Va. App. 289, 338 S.E.2d 349 (1986).

When the chancellor hears the evidence ore tenus, his decree is entitled to the same weight as the verdict of a jury. Thus, the chancellors' decree will not be disturbed unless it is clearly wrong or without evidence to support it. Bowers v. Westvaco Corp., 244 Va. 139, 419 S.E.2d 661 (1992).

Trial court's factual findings given same weight as jury findings. — The trial court's factual findings in making its admissibility determination are to be given the same weight as is accorded a finding of fact by the jury. Rabeiro v. Commonwealth, 10 Va. App. 61, 389 S.E.2d 731 (1990).

Findings of chancellor in equity. — A chancellor's finding on conflicting evidence, heard ore tenus, will not be disturbed on appeal unless it is plainly wrong or without evidence to support it. Ivy Constr. Co. v. Booth, 226 Va. 299, 309 S.E.2d 300 (1983).

Evidence supported trial court's finding that airport authority worker was fired because he joined the union where authority's executive director stated unequivocally that employee was fired because he joined the union. Norfolk Airport Auth. v. Nordwall, 246 Va. 391, 436 S.E.2d 436 (1993).

Judgment approving jury's verdict. — A trial court's judgment approving a jury's verdict is entitled to great weight on appeal and will not be disturbed unless it is contrary to law or plainly wrong. Gray v. Commonwealth, 233 Va. 313, 356 S.E.2d 157 (1987), cert. denied, 484 U.S. 873, 108 S. Ct. 207, 98 L. Ed. 2d 158 (1987).

Custody decision based on ore tenus hearing. — A trial court's custody decision, when based on an ore tenus hearing, is entitled to great weight and will not be disturbed on appeal unless it is plainly wrong or there is no evidence to support it. Cousins v. Cousins, 5 Va. App. 156, 360 S.E.2d 882 (1987).

II. DECISIONS UNDER PRIOR LAW.

A. General Consideration.

Editor's note. — The cases cited below were decided under corresponding provisions of former law. The term "this section," as used below, refers to former provisions.

This section was intended to secure speedy determination of litigation, and the court should not hesitate to enter final judgment in cases where it is clear upon the facts that the ends of justice can thereby be attained. Gable v. Bingler, 177 Va. 641, 15 S.E.2d 33 (1941).

When section does not apply. — Neither this section nor § 8.01-430 has any application except where there has been a motion to set aside the verdict because it is contrary to the evidence, or is without evidence to support it. If the verdict is set aside for some other reason, or if no final judgment has been entered under § 8.01-430, and, in either case, a new trial has been awarded, the Supreme Court will adopt as a rule of practice that when there have been two trials in the lower court the appellate court will look first to the evidence and proceedings on the first trial, and if it discovers that the court erred in setting aside the verdict on that trial, it will set aside and annul all proceedings subsequent to the first verdict and enter judgment thereon. Hogg v. Plant, 145 Va. 175, 133 S.E. 759 (1926).

Power of courts over verdicts not changed by statute. — Trial courts have no greater power over verdicts now than they had before the enactment of this section and § 8.01-430, nor has the Supreme Court. The Supreme Court has always exercised the power and duty, when not hampered by statute, of setting aside a judgment that was plainly wrong or without evidence to support it. Norfolk & W. Ry. v. T.W. Thayer Co., 137 Va. 294, 119 S.E. 107 (1923).

Case may be heard on certificate of facts or evidence. — Since the Code of 1887 went into effect, a case at law, heard and determined by the court, as well as a case tried by a jury, may be heard in the Supreme Court either upon a certificate of facts, or of the evidence. In either case the court should certify the facts when it can do so, but, if it be unable or unwilling to certify the facts because the evidence is conflicting or complicated, or of doubtful credibility, it should certify the evidence. Western Union Tel. Co. v. Powell, 94 Va. 268, 26 S.E. 828 (1897). And now, as to certificates of evidence or of facts, see § 8.01-678.

Illustrative cases collected. — Davis v. McCall, 133 Va. 487, 113 S.E. 835 (1922), contains the following footnote: "The following cases illustrate the application that has been made of this section: Lorillard Co. v. Clay, 127 Va. 734, 164 S.E. 384 (1920); Rootes v. Holliday, 18 Va. (4 Munf.) 323 (1814); Bird v. Wilkinson, 31 Va. (4 Leigh) 266 (1833); Creigh's Heirs v. Henson, 51 Va. (10 Gratt.) 231 (1853); Clarke v. McClure, 51 Va. (10 Gratt.) 305 (1853); Lucado v. Tutwiler's Adm'x, 69 Va. (28 Gratt.) 39 (1877); Mercantile Coop. Bank v. Brown, 96 Va. 614, 32 S.E. 64 (1899); McClanahan's Adm'r v. Norfolk & W. Ry., 122 Va. 705, 96 S.E. 453 (1918); Faison v. Union Camp Corp., 224 Va. 54, 294 S.E.2d 821 (1982), and cases cited."

B. When Judgment Set Aside.

1. In General.

Judgment referred to is a judgment in support of verdict. — This section must be read in connection with § 8.01-430, relative to setting aside the verdict. When so read, it is fairly plain that the judgment referred to in this section is a judgment in support of the verdict. Davis v. McCall, 133 Va. 487, 113 S.E. 835 (1922); Norfolk & W. Ry. v. T.W. Thayer Co., 137 Va. 294, 119 S.E. 107 (1923); McQuown v. Phaup, 172 Va. 419, 2 S.E.2d 330 (1939).

Evidence viewed in light most favorable to prevailing party. — The respondent, having prevailed in the trial court, is entitled to have the evidence viewed in its most favorable light from his standpoint, and the judgment of the trial court in such circumstances shall not be set aside unless plainly wrong or without evidence to support it. Hern v. Cox, 212 Va. 644, 186 S.E.2d 85 (1972); Slayton v. Weinberger, 213 Va. 690, 194 S.E.2d 703 (1973).

The evidence is not reviewed with respect to what action the court might have taken as members of the jury. Miles v. Commonwealth, 205 Va. 462, 138 S.E.2d 22 (1964).

Court cannot set aside judgment unless plainly wrong or without evidence to support it. — Whatever may be the views of the Supreme Court as to the preponderance of evidence, if it is unable to say that the judgment of the trial court supporting the verdict is plainly wrong or without any evidence to support it, it cannot set aside the judgment of the trial court. Varner v. White, 149 Va. 177, 140 S.E. 128 (1927). See Norfolk S. Ry. v. Harris, 190 Va. 966, 59 S.E.2d 110 (1950).

Upon a motion to set aside the verdict of a jury, the Supreme Court considers the case very much as upon a demurrer to the evidence, and the verdict of the jury will not be set aside unless it appears from the evidence that such verdict is plainly wrong or without evidence to support it. Amos v. Franklin, 159 Va. 19, 165 S.E. 510 (1932). See Planters Nat'l Bank v. Heflin Co., 166 Va. 166, 184 S.E. 216 (1936); Redford v. Booker, 166 Va. 561, 185 S.E. 879 (1936); Wyckoff Pipe & Creosoting Co. v. Saunders, 175 Va. 512, 9 S.E.2d 318 (1940).

Where the conclusion depends on the weight to be given credible testimony, the verdict cannot be disturbed by the Supreme Court or by the trial court. Norfolk S. Ry. v. Harris, 190 Va. 966, 59 S.E.2d 110 (1950).

Where, after a fair trial, the jury has found a verdict of guilty and the circumstances proven are of such character as to warrant that finding, a motion to set aside the verdict on the ground that it is contrary to the evidence should be granted only when it appears from the evidence that such judgment is plainly wrong or without evidence to support it. Orange v. Commonwealth, 191 Va. 423, 61 S.E.2d 267 (1950).

When the sufficiency of the evidence is assailed, it is the Supreme Court's duty to view the evidence which tends to support the verdict and to uphold the verdict unless it is plainly wrong. Miles v. Commonwealth, 205 Va. 462, 138 S.E.2d 22 (1964).

Where, after a fair trial, a verdict of guilty is returned and judgment is entered thereon, such judgment should only be disturbed when it appears that it is plainly wrong or without evidence to support it. Miles v. Commonwealth, 205 Va. 462, 138 S.E.2d 22 (1964).

In view of the judgment of the court in favor of the plaintiff, the evidence and all reasonable inferences therefrom, under settled principles, must be viewed by the Supreme Court in the light most advantageous to the plaintiff. The judgment cannot be set aside unless it appears from the evidence that it is plainly wrong or without evidence to support it. The question is not whether the evidence would have supported a finding of fact for the losing party; but whether the record contains substantial credible evidence which will support the finding of the trial judge. Barnes v. Moore, 199 Va. 227, 98 S.E.2d 683 (1957).

When a case is submitted to the court without the intervention of a jury, on appeal the Supreme Court has no authority under this section to interfere with the judgment of the court below unless it appears from the evidence to support it. Mitchell v. Kennedy, 166 Va. 346, 186 S.E. 40 (1936); Richmond Oil Equip. Co. v. W.T. Holt, Inc., 189 Va. 334, 53 S.E.2d 11 (1949).

Even when in doubt as to correctness of decision. — Under this section, the Supreme Court, even if it has a doubt as to the correctness of the conclusion of the trial judge, will not set the judgment aside, unless it appears that it is plainly wrong or without supporting evidence. Standard Accident Ins. Co. v. Walker, 127 Va. 140, 102 S.E. 585 (1920); Graham v. Commonwealth, 127 Va. 808, 103 S.E. 565 (1920); Bragg v. Commonwealth, 133 Va. 645, 112 S.E. 609 (1922).

Verdict not disturbed where conclusion depends on weight given credible testimony. — Although it is the duty of the court to set aside a verdict that is plainly wrong or without evidence to support it, under this section, where the conclusion depends on the weight to be given credible testimony, the verdict cannot be disturbed. Walrod v. Matthews, 210 Va. 382, 171 S.E.2d 180 (1969).

May set aside when plainly wrong or without evidence to support. — The jury's verdict may be set aside when "it appears from the evidence that such judgment is plainly wrong or without evidence to support it." That is to say, it may be set aside for either of two reasons; it may be set aside when it is without evidence to support it, and it may be set aside when it is plainly wrong even if it is supported by some evidence. Du Pont de Nemours & Co. v. Brown, 129 Va. 112, 105 S.E. 660 (1921); Braswell v. VEPCO, 162 Va. 27, 173 S.E. 365 (1934); Yanago v. Aetna Life Ins. Co., 164 Va. 258, 178 S.E. 904 (1935). See also, Hall v. Commonwealth, 145 Va. 818, 133 S.E. 683 (1926); Peoples v. Commonwealth, 147 Va. 692, 137 S.E. 603 (1927).

A judgment that is plainly wrong or without evidence to support it should not be allowed to stand. Gillespie v. Somers, 177 Va. 231, 13 S.E.2d 330 (1941); Douglas v. United Co., 183 Va. 263, 31 S.E.2d 889 (1944); City of Virginia Beach v. Roman, 201 Va. 879, 114 S.E.2d 749 (1960).

Under this section the Supreme Court will set aside a verdict on the ground that it is contrary to the evidence only in a case where the jury have plainly decided against the evidence, or without evidence. Davis v. Commonwealth, 132 Va. 525, 110 S.E. 252 (1922).

The primary question presented is whether or not the evidence is sufficient to sustain the verdict. Though the verdict was approved by the judgment of the trial court, it is the duty of the appellate court to set aside if it is without evidence to support it or plainly wrong. Esso Standard Oil Co. v. Stewart, 190 Va. 949, 59 S.E.2d 67 (1950); Thalhimer Bros. v. Buckner,

194 Va. 1011, 76 S.E.2d 215 (1953); Shelton v. Detamore, 198 Va. 220, 93 S.E.2d 314 (1956).

Where a litigant is fortified by a jury's verdict and the judgment of the trial court, he occupies a highly favored position; but when a judgment is plainly wrong or without evidence to support it, it becomes duty of Supreme Court to set it aside. Whichard v. Nee, 194 Va. 83, 72 S.E.2d 365 (1953). See Holloway v. Smith, 197 Va. 334, 88 S.E.2d 909 (1955).

It is the duty of the Supreme Court to set aside a judgment that is either plainly wrong or without evidence to support it. Simmons v. Craig, 199 Va. 338, 99 S.E.2d 641 (1957).

Challenging sufficiency of evidence after conviction. — When the sufficiency of the evidence is challenged after conviction, it is the duty of the Supreme Court to view it in the light most favorable to the Commonwealth, granting all reasonable inferences fairly deducible therefrom. Corbett v. Commonwealth, 210 Va. 304, 171 S.E.2d 251 (1969); Boykins v. Commonwealth, 210 Va. 309, 170 S.E.2d 771 (1969); Patler v. Commonwealth, 211 Va. 448, 177 S.E.2d 618 (1970), cert. denied, 407 U.S. 909, 92 S. Ct. 2445, 32 L. Ed. 2d 682 (1972).

Burden is on appellant to show verdict is contrary to evidence. — On an assignment of error to the refusal of the trial court to set aside the verdict of the jury because "contrary to the evidence," the plaintiff in error, under this section, is before the Supreme Court practically as on a demurrer to the evidence and the burden is on him to show that the verdict is contrary to the evidence, or without evidence to support it. Updike v. Texas Co., 147 Va. 208, 136 S.E. 591 (1927).

Court accepts as true all facts favorable to plaintiff, when verdict is for him. — After a verdict has been found in favor of a plaintiff the appellate court must accept as true all of the facts favorable to the plaintiff which the evidence tends to establish. VEPCO v. Blunt's Adm'r, 158 Va. 421, 163 S.E. 329 (1932); Nosay v. Owens, 193 Va. 343, 68 S.E.2d 531 (1952); McDowell v. Dye, 193 Va. 390, 69 S.E.2d 459 (1952).

Setting aside judgment where evidence shows contributory negligence. — If the fact that decedent was guilty of contributory negligence which caused or efficiently contributed to his death is so conclusively established by the evidence that fair-minded men could not differ, then any judgment rendered in plaintiff's favor is plainly wrong and it becomes the duty of the Supreme Court to so decide. Hooker v. Hancock, 188 Va. 345, 49 S.E.2d 711 (1948).

Effect of circumstantial proof. — If the proof relied upon by the Commonwealth is wholly circumstantial, then to establish guilt beyond a reasonable doubt all necessary circumstances proved must be consistent with guilt and inconsistent with innocence. They must overcome the presumption of innocence and exclude all reasonable conclusions inconsistent with that of guilt. To accomplish that, the chain of necessary circumstances must be unbroken and the evidence as a whole must satisfy the guarded judgment that both the corpus delicti and the criminal agency of the accused have been proved to the exclusion of any other rational hypothesis and to a moral certainty. Yet what inferences are to be drawn from proved facts is within the province of the jury and not the court so long as the inferences are reasonable and justified. Boykins v. Commonwealth, 210 Va. 309, 170 S.E.2d 771 (1969).

2. When Evidence Incredible.

Court not required to accept incredible evidence. — Under this section the Supreme Court cannot be compelled to accept as true what in the nature of things could not have occurred in the manner and under the circumstances narrated. VEPCO v. Walker, 152 Va. 883, 148 S.E. 694 (1929).

The statutory rule, under which the Supreme Court must consider the evidence when certified, cannot compel the court to accept as true what in the nature of things could not have occurred in the manner and under the circumstances narrated. Norfolk & W.R.R. v. Strickler, 118 Va. 153, 86 S.E. 824 (1915); Virginian Ry. v. Bell, 118 Va. 492, 87 S.E. 570 (1916); Virginia Ry. & Power Co. v. Bailey, 123 Va. 250, 96 S.E. 275 (1918).

The evidence relied upon to support the verdict must not strain the credulity of the court, but it must fairly sustain the verdict. Langford v. Commonwealth, 154 Va. 879, 153 S.E. 821 (1930); Ramey v. Ramey, 181 Va. 377, 25 S.E.2d 264 (1943).

Rule applies when defendant demurs to plaintiff's evidence. — While the court might be compelled to accept evidence given by the plaintiff on a demurrer to the evidence by the defendant, yet, under this section and § 8.01-430, such evidence need not be accepted, when to do so would strain the credulity of the court, and require the entry of a judgment contradicted by every other fact and circumstance of the case. It was extreme cases of this sort that this section was enacted to meet. Tabb v. Willis, 155 Va. 836, 156 S.E. 556 (1931).

C. Verdict Approved or Disapproved.

A distinction must be made between a verdict approved by the trial court and a verdict disapproved by that court. When the verdict has been approved it is the duty of the Supreme Court to uphold it save in exceptional cases and when it appears to be plainly necessary to prevent injustice. The appellate court cannot undertake to interfere merely because, in its judgment, the jury ought to have reached a different conclusion. Tabb v. Willis, 155 Va. 836, 156 S.E. 556 (1931).

Effect when trial court approves verdict. — Under this section where the question of fact involved is complicated by peculiar conditions, as well as by conflicting evidence, and the trial court has refused to set aside the verdict, the Supreme Court must affirm the judgment of the trial court, except when the judgment is plainly wrong or without evidence to support it. Eastern Coal & Export Corp. v. Norfolk & W. Ry., 133 Va. 525, 113 S.E. 857 (1922).

While the verdict of a jury, approved by the trial court, is entitled to great weight, the language of the revisers in this section, "unless it appears from the evidence that such judgment is plainly wrong," should not be held to be meaningless. Tabb v. Willis, 155 Va. 836, 156 S.E. 556 (1931).

The Supreme Court having under this section carefully considered all of the evidence in the case, and upon giving the weight to the decision of the jury upon the matters of fact dependent upon the evidence which was conflicting, and which involved the credibility of the witnesses, and upon giving due weight to the action of the trial judge in refusing to set aside the verdict, was of opinion that it did not appear from the evidence that the judgment under review was plainly wrong, or without evidence to support it, and hence the judgment was affirmed. Graham v. Commonwealth, 127 Va. 808, 103 S.E. 565 (1920).

Where a conflict of evidence has been passed upon by a jury, whose findings have been approved by the trial court, the judgment will not be disturbed on appeal. Alsop Motor Corp. v. Barker, 138 Va. 598, 123 S.E. 350 (1924); Holloman v. Commonwealth, 138 Va. 758, 120 S.E. 852 (1924); Kilgore v. Commonwealth, 139 Va. 581, 123 S.E. 534 (1924).

A verdict of a jury, approved by the trial judge, brings the case to the Supreme Court practically as upon a demurrer to the evidence, and plaintiff's evidence and all fair inferences which may be drawn therefrom must be accepted as true and evidence in conflict therewith is waived. McDowell v. Dye, 193 Va. 390, 69 S.E.2d 459 (1952).

Verdicts approved by the trial court are entitled to more weight than if they had been set aside by that court. Unless it appears from the evidence that such a judgment is plainly wrong or without evidence to support it, the judgment of the trial court shall not be vacated. Richardson v. Lovvorn, 199 Va. 688, 101 S.E.2d 511 (1958).

A verdict which has been disapproved by the trial judge is not entitled to the same weight on appeal as one that has been approved by him. Maurer v. City of Norfolk, 147 Va. 900, 133 S.E. 484 (1926); Clark v. Parker, 161 Va. 480, 171 S.E. 600 (1933).

Distinction between order granting and order denying new trial. — In setting aside a verdict the trial court must to some extent, pass upon the weight of the evidence before the jury, and a stronger case must be made in order to justify an appellate court in disturbing an order granting a new trial than one refusing it, because the refusal operates as a final adjudication of the rights of the parties while the granting of the new trial simply invites further investigation, and affords an opportunity for showing the truth without concluding either party. Chapman v. Virginia Real Estate Inv. Co., 96 Va. 177, 31 S.E. 74 (1898), cited in Davis v. McCall, 133 Va. 487, 113 S.E. 835 (1922).

New trial not to be granted merely because court differs with decision of jury. — Where the evidence consists of circumstances and presumptions, a new trial will not be granted merely because the court, if upon the jury, would have given a different verdict. To warrant a new trial in such cases the evidence should be plainly insufficient to warrant the finding of the jury. This restriction applies a fortiori to an appellate court. For in the appellate court there is superadded to the weight which must be given to the verdict of a jury fairly rendered, that of the opinion of the judge who presided at the trial, which is always entitled to peculiar respect upon the question of a new trial. Kimball v. Friend, 95 Va. 125, 27 S.E. 901 (1897); Southern Ry. v. Bryant, 95 Va. 212, 28 S.E. 183 (1897); Davis v. Commonwealth, 132 Va. 525, 110 S.E. 252 (1922).

D. Weight Given Decision of Court.

Supreme Court must give to the judgment of the lower court the weight to which it is entitled. Royal Indem. Co. v. Hook, 155 Va. 956, 157 S.E. 414 (1931).

Judgment of a trial court on questions of fact is entitled to great weight and will not be disturbed unless it is plainly wrong or without evidence to support it. Smith v. Board of Supvrs., 201 Va. 87, 109 S.E.2d 501 (1959); Furr v. Arnold, 202 Va. 684, 119 S.E.2d 242 (1961).

Same weight given to decision of court as if it were a verdict of a jury. — When a case at law is decided by the court, without the intervention of a jury, and the judgment is excepted to because contrary to the evidence and the evidence, and not the facts, is certified, the rule of decision in the appellate court is to give the judgment of the trial court the same effect as the verdict of a jury. The judgment will not be disturbed, unless it is contrary to the evidence, or the evidence is plainly insufficient to support it. If the evidence is conflicting on material points the judgment will be affirmed. Martin v. Richmond F. & P.R.R., 101 Va. 406, 44

S.E. 695 (1903); Bristol Belt Line Ry. v. Bullock Elec. Mfg. Co., 101 Va. 652, 44 S.E. 892 (1903); Hamman v. Miller, 116 Va. 873, 83 S.E. 382 (1914); First Nat'l Bank v. Roanoke Oil Co., 169 Va. 99, 192 S.E. 764 (1937).

Where the conclusion depends on the weight to be given credible testimony, the decree based thereon has the same effect as the verdict of a jury, and the decree will be affirmed, although there may be a conflict in the evidence. Trayer v. Bristol Parking, Inc., 198 Va. 595, 95 S.E.2d 224 (1956); Pond v. Fisher, 201 Va. 542, 112 S.E.2d 147 (1960).

The finding of facts by the trial judge has the weight of a jury verdict. McClung v. Henrico County, 200 Va. 870, 108 S.E.2d 513 (1959).

Where the conclusion depends upon the weight to be given credible evidence, the decree or order of the trial court based thereon has the same effect as the verdict of a jury and will be affirmed although there may be conflicts in the evidence. Smith v. Board of Supvrs., 201 Va. 87, 109 S.E.2d 501 (1959).

Where the trial court heard the evidence ore tenus, its finding on questions of fact carries the same weight as that of a jury, and consequently all conflicts in the evidence should be resolved in favor of the prevailing party in the court below. Hawthorne v. Hannowell, 202 Va. 70, 115 S.E.2d 889 (1960).

When a case at law is decided by the court without the intervention of a jury, and the judgment is excepted to on the ground that it is not supported by the evidence, on review to the Supreme Court, the judgment of the trial court is presumed to be correct, even though the evidence is in sharp conflict, and it is to be given the same effect as the verdict of a jury settling all conflicts in the evidence. Reiber v. James M. Duncan, Jr. & Assocs., 206 Va. 657, 145 S.E.2d 157 (1965).

A trial court's finding will not be set aside unless it is plainly wrong or without evidence to support it. Such a finding is presumed to be correct and is given the same effect as a jury verdict, settling all conflicts in the evidence in favor of the prevailing party. Under these well-established rules, the prevailing parties in the trial court are entitled to have the evidence viewed in the light most favorable to them. City of Richmond v. Beltway Properties, Inc., 217 Va. 376, 228 S.E.2d 569 (1976).

Findings of trial judge are conclusive on conflicting evidence. Smith-Gordon Co. v. Snellings, 130 Va. 528, 107 S.E. 651 (1921).

Under this section, when a case is tried by the judge without a jury, and conflicts arise in the testimony, or inferences to be drawn therefrom, the judgment of the trial court should not be set aside, unless it appears from the evidence that it is plainly wrong, or without evidence to support it. Citizens & Marine Bank v. McMurran, 138 Va. 657, 123 S.E. 507 (1924); Eastern Shore of Va. Produce v. Belote, 138 Va. 707, 123 S.E. 372 (1924); Duncan v. State Hwy. Comm'n, 142 Va. 135, 128 S.E. 546 (1925).

Where the question presented was a factual one which the trial judge decided adversely to the defendant on conflicting evidence, his findings will not be disturbed by the Supreme Court. Reiber v. James M. Duncan, Jr. & Assocs., 206 Va. 657, 145 S.E.2d 157 (1965).

But finding that is plainly wrong cannot stand. — While great weight attaches to the finding of the trial court, based on an oral hearing of the testimony, yet if it is plainly wrong or without evidence to support it, it cannot stand. Parker v. Harcum, 201 Va. 441, 111 S.E.2d 449 (1959).

Findings of chancellor in equity. — Under the established rule in Virginia, a finding of the chancellor on conflicting evidence, heard ore tenus, will not be disturbed on appeal unless it is against the clear preponderance of the evidence or without evidence to support it. Flippo v. Broome, 202 Va. 919, 121 S.E.2d 490 (1961).

Great weight must be given to the judgment of a chancellor who has heard the evidence in open court, and his finding will not be set aside unless it be clearly shown to be erroneous. Barnes v. Craig, 202 Va. 229, 117 S.E.2d 63 (1960); Oliver v. Oliver, 202 Va. 268, 117 S.E.2d 59 (1960).

A finding of fact by the chancellor hearing evidence ore tenus carries the weight of a jury verdict, and cannot be disturbed by the Supreme Court unless plainly wrong or without evidence to support it. White v. Perkins, 213 Va. 129, 189 S.E.2d 315 (1972).

The question presented is not whether the evidence would have supported a contrary finding and decree, but whether the record contains substantial credible evidence which, upon application of correct principles of law, supports the finding and decree of the court. Todd v. Todd, 202 Va. 133, 115 S.E.2d 905 (1960).

Effect of submission by consent. — When a case is submitted by consent without the intervention of a jury, on appeal the appellate court has no authority under this section to interfere with the judgment of the court below unless it appears from the evidence to be plainly wrong, or without evidence to support it. It cannot undertake to discuss conflicts in testimony or the impeachment of witnesses. But this does not mean that in such a case every conflict is settled by the judgment of the trial court, for it does not come to the appellate court as on a demurrer to the evidence. Royal Indem. Co. v. Hook, 155 Va. 956, 157 S.E. 414 (1931).

Where all evidence having probative value consists of letters and documents. — The rule that the conclusion of a trial judge

§ 8.01-681　　　　　CIVIL REMEDIES AND PROCEDURE　　　　　§ 8.01-681

after ore tenus hearing on questions of fact is entitled to great weight is of less effect where all evidence having probative value consists of letters and documents. Raney v. Barnes Lumber Corp., 195 Va. 956, 81 S.E.2d 578 (1954).

§ 8.01-681. Decision of appellate court.

— The appellate court shall affirm the judgment if there is no error therein, and reverse the same, in whole or in part, if erroneous, and enter such judgment as to the court shall seem right and proper and shall render final judgment upon the merits whenever, in the opinion of the court, the facts before it are such as to enable the court to attain the ends of justice. A civil case shall not be remanded for a trial de novo except when the ends of justice require it, but the appellate court shall, in the order remanding the case, if it be remanded, designate upon what questions or points a new trial is to be had. (Code 1950, § 8-493; 1977, c. 617; 1984, c. 703.)

Cross references. — As to constitutional provisions concerning opinions, decisions and judgments of Supreme Court of Appeals, see Va. Const., Art. VI, §§ 1 and 6. As to decision of appellate court where judgment or decree is amended pending the appeal, see § 8.01-429. As to decision of appellate court in criminal proceedings, see § 19.2-324.

I. Decisions Under Current Law.
　A. General Consideration.
　B. Remand.
II. Decisions Under Prior Law.
　A. General Consideration.
　B. Affirmance.
　　1. In General.
　　2. Sufficient Evidence to Support Verdict or Findings.
　　3. Where Evidence Conflicting.
　　4. Partial Affirmance.
　C. Reversal.
　　1. In General.
　　2. Entry of Such Judgment as to the Court Shall Seem Right and Proper.
　　　a. Final Judgment.
　　　b. Dismissal.
　　3. Remand.
　　　a. In General.
　　　b. Questions or Points on Which New Trial Is Had.

I. DECISIONS UNDER CURRENT LAW.

A. General Consideration.

The Supreme Court is required by this section to render final judgment upon the merits where the facts before the court are such as to enable the court to "attain the ends of justice." In addition, this section admonishes this court not to remand for a trial de novo except where the ends of justice require it. Powell v. Sears, Roebuck & Co., 231 Va. 464, 344 S.E.2d 916 (1986).

When Court of Appeals should render final judgment on merits in reversing case. — Where the error requires reversal, it does not follow that the Court of Appeals must remand the case in order for further litigation. This section requires the Court of Appeals when reversing a case on appeal, to render final judgment upon the merits whenever, in the opinion of the court, the facts before it are such as to enable the court to attain the ends of justice. Smith v. Board of Supvrs., 234 Va. 250, 361 S.E.2d 351 (1987).

Modification of damages where evidence did not support amount awarded. — The amount of damages supported by the evidence was well below the amount of the verdict returned by the jury and was attributable to another count, under which there was a failure of proof. Therefore, the court modified the judgment to reflect the amount of damages supported by the evidence advanced under count II. Lee Bldrs. Supply Corp. v. Cohen, 229 Va. 621, 331 S.E.2d 803 (1985).

Where trial court has decided a case correctly, but has assigned the wrong reason, the Supreme Court will assign the correct reason and affirm. State Farm Mut. Auto. Ins. Co. v. Seay, 236 Va. 275, 373 S.E.2d 910 (1988); Virginia Farm Bureau Mut. Ins. Co. v. Jerrell, 236 Va. 261, 373 S.E.2d 913 (1988).

Applied in Erie Ins. Exch. v. Meeks, 223 Va. 287, 288 S.E.2d 454 (1982); Benderson Dev. Co. v. Sciortino, 236 Va. 136, 372 S.E.2d 751 (1988).

B. Remand.

Determining damages. — Where decree was required to be reversed for failure to award a judgment for proved damages, but the facts before the Supreme Court did not enable the court to enter a final decree that would "attain the ends of justice," the cause was remanded to the trial court for a new trial limited to the issue of damages, and with directions to order an issue out of chancery and impanel a jury to determine the question of damages. Sampson v. Sampson, 221 Va. 896, 275 S.E.2d 597 (1981).

II. DECISIONS UNDER PRIOR LAW.

A. General Consideration.

Editor's note. — The cases cited below were decided under corresponding provisions of former law. The term "this section," as used below, refers to former provisions.

The policy and purpose of § 8.01-430 and this section is a speedy determination of litigation, and the rendition of a final judgment where it is clear that, upon the facts before it, the court can by such order attain the ends of justice. Morris & Co. v. Alvis, 130 Va. 434, 107 S.E. 664 (1921); Gable v. Bingler, 177 Va. 641, 15 S.E.2d 33 (1941).

Not applicable to criminal cases. — Section 8.01-430, with reference to the order to be entered by a trial court upon setting aside a verdict, and this section in reference to the order of reversal to be entered in the Supreme Court, do not apply to criminal cases. As to such cases the practice remains unchanged and is controlled by § 19.2-324. Henderson v. Commonwealth, 130 Va. 761, 107 S.E. 700 (1921).

This section and § 8.01-678 are closely related. Kearns v. Hall, 197 Va. 736, 91 S.E.2d 648 (1956).

This section relates entirely to appellate procedure in the Supreme Court. It does not confer any original jurisdiction upon the court, and none was exercised by the court in the instant case. Its enactment was clearly within the legislative power. Duncan v. Carson, 127 Va. 306, 103 S.E. 665 (1920).

This relates to procedure in the appellate court, and does not confer original jurisdiction on the court in violation of Va. Const., Art. VI, § 1. Duncan v. Carson, 127 Va. 306, 103 S.E. 665 (1920); Harriss, Magill & Co. v. Rodgers & Co., 143 Va. 815, 129 S.E. 513 (1925).

It requires the appellate court to pass upon the weight of the evidence in appropriate cases, in order to attain the ends of justice. Lough v. Price, 161 Va. 811, 172 S.E. 269 (1934).

The Supreme Court does not consider the evidence as on demurrer. On the other hand, the Supreme Court should not undertake to pass upon matters which clearly and properly fall within the province of the jury. Where it is plain that the ends of justice can be attained, however, the Supreme Court should act. In such a case the court should render final judgment upon the merits. Metropolitan Life Ins. Co. v. Hart, 162 Va. 88, 173 S.E. 769 (1934).

The section does not authorize the appellate court to make a case different from the plaintiff's pleadings, and then try and decide the same upon an issue never suggested or considered by the trial court and jury. Harriss, Magill & Co. v. Rodgers & Co., 143 Va. 815, 129 S.E. 513 (1925).

How case to be stated. — Formerly a plaintiff in error stood in the Supreme Court in the position of a demurrant to the evidence, but this has been changed. Now, under this section, in stating a case in that court which has been tried by a jury, it must be stated as the jury may have viewed it, remembering always that the jury are the sole judges of the weight to be given to the testimony of the witnesses, and also bearing in mind the weight attached to the verdict of a jury which has received the approval of the trial judge. Lorillard Co. v. Clay, 127 Va. 734, 104 S.E. 384 (1920); Queen Ins. Co. v. Perkinson, 129 Va. 216, 105 S.E. 580 (1921).

Cause remanded by United States Supreme Court for return to lower court. — The Supreme Court of the United States vacated the decree of the court of appeals which affirmed a decision of a lower court annulling a miscegenetic marriage, and remanded the cause for return to the lower court so that the record might be made to show more fully the relationship of the parties to Virginia at the time of the marriage. The court of appeals, being without power under the statutes or rules of practice of Virginia to return the cause to the lower court for the purpose directed, and being of opinion that the record was adequate for decision of the issues presented, adhered to its prior decision. Naim v. Naim, 197 Va. 734, 90 S.E.2d 849 (1956).

Attorney's fee allowed. — Under this provision, the Supreme Court has, in cases where it was not necessary to remand the case for the trial court to determine any other issue, allowed counsel an attorney's fee for appearance in the Supreme Court. Hughes v. Hughes, 173 Va. 293, 4 S.E.2d 402 (1939).

Counsel is entitled to compensation to be paid by the husband for his appearance both in the trial court, and in the Supreme Court. Hughes v. Hughes, 173 Va. 293, 4 S.E.2d 402 (1939).

B. Affirmance.

1. In General.

When is judgment "affirmed". — A judgment is "affirmed" within a supersedeas bond conditioned to satisfy it in such event to the extent that it remains unchanged by an amended judgment on appeal, authorized by this section. National Sur. Co. v. Commonwealth, 125 Va. 223, 99 S.E. 657, cert. denied, 250 U.S. 665, 40 S. Ct. 13, 63 L. Ed. 1197 (1919).

Affirmance by equal division of court. — The affirmance of the judgment of a trial court by an equal division of the judges of this court results from necessity, and independently of statute. The former statute in this State on that subject was simply declaratory of a well settled pre-existing rule of necessity which is not changed by the omission from the present statute of anything on the subject. Charlottesville & A. Ry. v. Rubin, 107 Va. 751, 60 S.E. 101 (1908).

For example of affirmation of lower court decision, when judges of Supreme Court divide equally on question, see Kimball v. Borden, 97 Va. 477, 34 S.E. 45 (1899).

Amending and affirming judgment. — Where in an action for personal injuries the jury were told to disregard a release executed by the plaintiff when a minor, the Supreme Court will not remand the case when they do not believe that the interests of justice require it, but render final judgment upon the merits, crediting the judgment of the lower court with the amount received by the plaintiff by way of compromise, and affirming the judgment thus amended. Clinchfield Coal Corp. v. Couch, 127 Va. 634, 104 S.E. 802 (1920).

Affirmance on condition. — Where the lower court erred in peremptorily directing the jury to allow interest to plaintiff from the time the demand accrued where under § 8.01-382 the allowance of such interest was discretionary with the jury, the appellate court may affirm the judgment on condition that plaintiff relinquish the interest upon the principal sum found by the jury. Washington & Old Dominion Ry. v. Westinghouse Elec. & Mfg. Co., 120 Va. 620, 89 S.E. 131 (1916).

2. Sufficient Evidence to Support Verdict or Findings.

Rule stated. — A verdict must stand "unless there is a plain deviation from the evidence or it is palpable the jury have not drawn a correct inference from these facts as certified." Nothing in this section affects this rule. Filer v. McNair, 158 Va. 88, 163 S.E. 335 (1932).

Where a case has been fairly submitted to a jury, their verdict will not be disturbed where there is evidence sufficient to support the verdict. Virginia Ry. & Power Co. v. Meyer, 117 Va. 409, 84 S.E. 742 (1915); McClung v. Folkes, 122 Va. 48, 94 S.E. 156 (1917); Webb v. Commonwealth, 122 Va. 899, 94 S.E. 773 (1918).

When there has been a trial upon the merits of the case, conducted by able and astute counsel, and upon adequate proof the jury have found a verdict in favor of the plaintiff, the case of plaintiff falls within the beneficent provisions of this section. City of Richmond v. Best, 180 Va. 429, 23 S.E.2d 224 (1942).

The decree of the lower court is entitled to great weight upon appeal and ought not to be reversed unless the appellate court is satisfied that it is wrong. Wood v. Lester, 126 Va. 169, 101 S.E. 52 (1919).

3. Where Evidence Conflicting.

Verdict not disturbed unless plainly wrong or against weight of evidence. — Where the evidence in the trial court was conflicting, a verdict fairly rendered, under proper instructions of the court, will not be disturbed in appellate court unless plainly wrong or manifestly against the weight of the evidence. Truckers' Mfg. & Supply Co. v. White, 108 Va. 147, 60 S.E. 630 (1908); Osborne v. Gillenwaters, 128 Va. 21, 104 S.E. 578 (1920); Tucker Sanatorium v. Cohen, 129 Va. 576, 106 S.E. 355 (1921).

4. Partial Affirmance.

The statute in terms authorizes a partial reversal and the entry by the appellate court of a judgment, the effect of which must be to affirm in part and reverse in part the original judgment. It must follow that to the extent to which the judgment is affirmed, it is still valid and binding upon the original judgment debtor, and also upon the sureties in the supersedeas bond, who will be held to have entered into their contract with knowledge that their liability under it was to be controlled by the provisions of this section. National Sur. Co. v. Commonwealth, 125 Va. 223, 99 S.E. 657, cert. denied, 250 U.S. 665, 40 S. Ct. 13, 63 L. Ed. 1197 (1919).

When finding on part of action conclusive. — In an action of assumpsit by purchasers against seller for breach of contract, the evidence on the subject of fraud in the procurement of the contract being conflicting, the finding of the jury on that subject is final and conclusive on appeal, and, even if the case had to be reversed on other grounds, this finding would not be disturbed under the provisions of this section. Upton v. Holloway & Co., 126 Va. 657, 102 S.E. 54 (1920).

Effect as to liens. — A decree was held against an administrator and his sureties. On appeal by plaintiffs the decree was reversed, and the administrator was held liable for a larger amount than was decreed against him, though the decree was also reversed in favor of a purchaser of land from the administrator. The appellate court reversed the decree so far as it was erroneous, but it affirmed it so as to continue the lien of the decree for the security pro tanto of the amounts which were found due by the parties respectively, against whom the said decree was rendered. Moss v. Moorman, 65 Va. (24 Gratt.) 97 (1873).

Where a decree is reversed in part, and affirmed as to the residue, such reversal does not destroy the lien of so much of the decree as is affirmed. Moss v. Moorman, 65 Va. (24 Gratt.) 97 (1873); Shepherd v. Chapman, 83 Va. 215, 2 S.E. 273 (1887).

C. Reversal.

1. In General.

When conclusively shown that appellee not entitled to recover. — Where in an action by a shipper against a carrier it was conclusively shown that the carrier did not receive the goods, the Supreme Court will not remand the cause for a new trial, but will reverse a judgment for plaintiff pursuant to this section. Director-General v. Chandler, 129 Va. 418, 106 S.E. 226 (1921).

Conflict in instructions. — Where there is an irreconcilable conflict in the instructions, the judgment must be reversed. Director-General v. Chandler, 129 Va. 418, 106 S.E. 226 (1921).

Court must find that error is reversible. — The Supreme Court must find, under § 8.01-678, that the error complained of is reversible error before it may reverse the judgment under this section as erroneous; for otherwise there is no error in the judgment, and the same must be affirmed. Kearns v. Hall, 197 Va. 736, 91 S.E.2d 648 (1956).

2. Entry of Such Judgment as to the Court Shall Seem Right and Proper.

a. Final Judgment.

Where there is no new or different evidence. — Where there is no reason to believe that, upon another trial, any new or different evidence would be introduced which ought to affect the result, and the facts before the Supreme Court are such as to enable the court to attain the ends of justice, it should proceed to dispose of the case under this section and enter final judgment upon the merits. Fourth Nat'l Bank v. Bragg, 127 Va. 47, 102 S.E. 649 (1920); Duncan v. Carson, 127 Va. 306, 103 S.E. 665 (1920); Queen Ins. Co. v. Perkinson, 129 Va. 216, 105 S.E. 580 (1921); Atlantic C.L.R.R. v. A.M. Walkup Co., 132 Va. 386, 112 S.E. 663 (1922); Crews v. Sullivan, 133 Va. 478, 113 S.E. 865 (1922); Blenner v. Vim Motor Truck Co., 136 Va. 189, 117 S.E. 834 (1923). See also, Atlantic Life Ins. Co. v. Worley, 161 Va. 951, 172 S.E. 168 (1934).

Before entering final judgment, it should be reasonably apparent that the case has been fully developed in the trial court or, at least, that the parties had a fair opportunity of so developing the case, and the Supreme Court must be of the opinion that, upon the facts before it, the parties have had a fair trial on the merits of the case, and that substantial justice has been reached. Kearns v. Hall, 197 Va. 736, 91 S.E.2d 648 (1956).

Where there is no reason to believe that upon another trial any new or additional evidence of any weight will, or can, be introduced, it becomes the duty of the Supreme Court, under the provisions of this section to enter final judgment. Butler v. Parrocha, 186 Va. 426, 43 S.E.2d 1 (1947).

Even where the trial court would have been warranted in sustaining a motion to strike out all the evidence of the plaintiff made at the conclusion of his evidence in chief, it does not follow that a judgment for the plaintiff will be reversed, if the court overrules the motion. If the cause is thereafter proceeded with to what appears to be a fair development of the evidence for both parties, and upon a consideration of the whole evidence the verdict of the jury in favor of the plaintiff is plainly right, the Supreme Court will not reverse a judgment for the plaintiff and order a new trial. Rawle v. McIlhenny, 163 Va. 735, 177 S.E. 214 (1934).

Correction of decree erroneous in part. — In the instant case, a suit to enjoin the threatened sale by the lessors in a mining lease of the surface and minerals to various persons, the decree of the lower court was in part erroneous, and therefore the Supreme Court reversed the decree and rendered a decree correcting such erroneous part under this section. Hagan Co. v. Norton Coal Co., 137 Va. 140, 119 S.E. 153 (1923).

Amount of judgment. — Where the facts enabled the Supreme Court to attain the ends of justice it was their duty, under this section, to set aside the verdict of the jury, and the judgment thereon, as to the amount awarded the plaintiff, and enter final judgment for him for the full amount claimed. Glascock v. James, 183 Va. 561, 32 S.E.2d 734 (1945).

Where the amount of the judgment entered for plaintiff in lower court, if there can be a recovery at all, is not in dispute, then under authority of this section judgment must be entered for him in said sum. White v. Bott, 158 Va. 442, 158 S.E. 880 (1932).

When Supreme Court will reduce amount of damages. — In an action for personal injuries the Supreme Court having determined that no error was committed in fixing liability upon defendant for plaintiff's injury, but that the verdict was excessive, if the case were remanded to the trial court it would be solely for the purpose of assessing the damages. But when the Supreme Court is in as good condition to do that as a jury would be, the remand is unnecessary. Lorillard Co. v. Clay, 127 Va. 734, 104 S.E. 384 (1920).

When wrong measure as to damages adopted. — A broker's contract of employment definitely fixed his compensation at $2,000 in case of a sale. The jury found a verdict for the broker and fixed his damages at $1,000. The finding was based upon the theory that plaintiff had complied with his contract, and had produced to the defendant a purchaser ready, able, and willing to purchase. It was held that as the contract definitely fixed the measure of the plaintiff's recovery, and there was nothing speculative or uncertain about it, the jury had no right to set up their judgment as to what was fair compensation, against the express terms of the contract, and that under this section, the Supreme Court would set aside the verdict as to the amount of the damages, and enter final judgment for the plaintiff for $2,000. Wilson v. Brown, 136 Va. 634, 118 S.E. 88 (1923).

Final judgment when case decided on agreed facts. — Where the judgment of the trial court is set aside because the law applicable to the "facts agreed" was in favor of the plaintiff in error, the Supreme Court will render final judgment in favor of the plaintiff in error in pursuance of this section. North Shore Imp. Co. v. N.Y.P. & N.R.R., 130 Va. 464, 108 S.E. 11 (1921).

Where case heard by court without jury. — Where a case is heard by the trial court, without the intervention of a jury, the Supreme Court, on reversing the judgment of the trial court, will enter up judgment for the adverse party. United Moderns v. Rathbun, 104 Va. 736, 52 S.E. 552 (1906); City of Danville v. Danville Ry. & Elec. Co., 114 Va. 382, 76 S.E. 913 (1913).

Where verdict and judgment for plaintiff not reversed, though motion to strike sustained by trial court. — If, after the trial court sustains a motion to strike out all the evidence of the plaintiff, the cause is thereafter proceeded with what appears to be a fair development of the evidence for both parties, and upon a consideration of the whole evidence the verdict of the jury in favor of the plaintiff is plainly right, the Supreme Court will not reverse a judgment for the plaintiff and order a new trial. Jones v. Hanbury, 158 Va. 842, 164 S.E. 545 (1932).

The practice of partial new trial ought not to be followed unless it is clear that no injustice will result. Schuerholz v. Roach, 58 F.2d 32 (4th Cir.), cert. denied, 287 U.S. 623, 53 S. Ct. 78, 77 L. Ed. 541 (1932).

Must not violate § 8.01-672. — Final judgment cannot be entered by Supreme Court, under this section, if to do so would violate § 8.01-672 as to jurisdictional amount. Madison v. Kroger Grocery & Bakery Co., 160 Va. 303, 168 S.E. 353 (1933).

When entry of judgment for defendant deemed proper. — When the evidence is examined, otherwise than on a demurrer to the evidence, and it is plain that a verdict of the jury predicated upon their finding was plainly wrong, judgment should be entered for defendant. Taylor v. Mason, 158 Va. 870, 164 S.E. 652 (1932).

Effect of failure to request final judgment. — While failure to request final judgment would not prevent the lower court or the appellate court from entering a final order in a proper case, it is perhaps a circumstance indicating that the merits of the case ought to finally be determined by a jury. Morris & Co. v. Alvis, 130 Va. 434, 107 S.E. 664 (1921).

Cases in which final judgment entered. — See National Bank v. Farmers Bank, 139 Va. 227, 123 S.E. 522 (1924); Continental Trust Co. v. Witt, 139 Va. 458, 124 S.E. 265 (1924); Dalby v. Shannon, 139 Va. 488, 124 S.E. 186 (1924); Davis Bakery, Inc. v. Dozier, 139 Va. 628, 124 S.E. 411 (1924); School Bd. v. Buford, 140 Va. 173, 124 S.E. 286 (1924); Smith v. Commonwealth, 141 Va. 490, 126 S.E. 236 (1925); Clover Creamery Co. v. Kanode, 142 Va. 542, 129 S.E. 222 (1925); Galax v. Waugh, 143 Va. 213, 129 S.E. 504 (1925); Palmetto Fire Ins. Co. v. Fansler, 143 Va. 884, 129 S.E. 727 (1925).

b. Dismissal.

Effect of motion to dismiss. — Where an action was brought by an administratrix against a railroad company and the director general of railroads, for the killing of her decedent by a train, while the system was being operated by the director general, the court should have entertained the motion of the railroad company to dismiss the action against it, yet under this section, this does not affect the liability of the director general. Norfolk & W. Ry. v. Arrington, 131 Va. 564, 109 S.E. 303 (1921).

When action barred by statute of limitations. — Where it was manifest from the evidence that the action was barred by the statute of limitations, the court set aside the verdict because the jury had not passed upon that issue, and being of opinion that the evidence did not support either of the counts in the declaration did not send the case back for a new trial in order to supply the deficiency in the verdict, but reversed the judgment in favor of the plaintiff and entered a nonsuit. Calvert v. Bowdoin, 8 Va. (4 Call) 217 (1791); White & Co. v. Ryan, 131 Va. 619, 109 S.E. 426 (1921).

When dismissal as to one defendant. — Where the facts proved do not establish any liability upon one of the defendants, and the evidence was as full as the circumstances of the case admitted of, and as could be reasonably expected on another trial, and full opportunity was afforded the plaintiff to introduce evidence, the Supreme Court on reversal will, under this section, render judgment of dismissal as to that defendant. Virginia Iron, Coal & Coke Co. v. Odle, 128 Va. 280, 105 S.E. 107 (1920).

When lack of proof of negligence. — Under the former practice of the Supreme Court, the sufficiency of the evidence to sustain the verdict, where the case had to be reversed on other grounds, was not passed upon, but in view of this section, if there had been no proof at all of negligence on the part of the defendant in the instant case, it would have been the duty of the Supreme Court to enter a final judgment and dismiss the case. The court, therefore, had to go into the question of negligence far enough to show that it could not dismiss the case for insufficient evidence of negligence, but with the caution that nothing it said was to be used before the jury at another trial as indicating that it had expressed an opinion upon the weight of the evidence. Director Gen. of R.R.'s v. Pence's Adm'x, 135 Va. 329, 116 S.E. 351 (1923).

When action on illegal contract of carriage. — Under this section, if the facts before it are such as to enable the court to attain the ends of justice, when the Supreme Court reverses a judgment in favor of a plaintiff against a carrier on the ground that the contract of carriage was illegal, it will order that the case be dismissed. Norfolk & W. Ry. v. Dehart Distilling Co., 127 Va. 415, 103 S.E. 594 (1920).

3. Remand.

a. In General.

When facts are insufficient. — Where a case must be reversed, and the facts before the Supreme Court are not sufficient for it to dispose of the case under this section, the case will be remanded to the court below for a trial de novo, to be had if the defendant in error is so advised. Latham v. Powell, 127 Va. 382, 103 S.E. 638 (1920).

When final judgment cannot be rendered. — When, with the objectionable testimony admitted by the lower court stricken out, the case is not left in such condition that final judgment can be entered in the Supreme Court under the provisions of this section, it will be remanded for a new trial to be had in conformity with the opinion of the court. Gallion v. Winfree, 129 Va. 122, 105 S.E. 539 (1921).

When the record is such that the Supreme Court cannot, in justice, determine the judgment that should be finally rendered, the case should be remanded for further development. Kearns v. Hall, 197 Va. 736, 91 S.E.2d 648 (1956).

When testimony obscure. — Where the testimony was obscure and was not developed with sufficient definiteness to enable the Supreme Court to feel satisfied that it would attain the ends of justice if it were to enter judgment under this section, the court awarded a new trial. Greer v. Doriot, 137 Va. 589, 120 S.E. 291 (1923).

When suit in equity and remedy is at law. — Under this section it is the duty of the Supreme Court to enter such judgment, decree or order as to the court shall seem right and proper. Therefore, when a complainant brings a suit in equity when his remedy is at law, the Supreme Court in reversing the decree will remand the cause to the lower court, with instructions to transfer the same to the law side for the appropriate amendment of pleadings and other proceedings in conformity with the provisions of § 8.01-270, notwithstanding the case was disposed of in the lower court before § 8.01-270 became effective. Pence v. Tidewater Townsite Corp., 127 Va. 447, 103 S.E. 694 (1920).

But this section does not authorize the Supreme Court to change the decree of the lower court, except where such decree is reversed in whole or in part. Hence, the Supreme Court in affirming a decree dismissing a bill for lack of equitable jurisdiction cannot remand with direction to to transfer the case to the law side of the court. Ewing v. Dutrow, 128 Va. 416, 104 S.E. 791 (1920).

Case remanded upon sole question of whether required notice was given within reasonable time. — Judgment of the trial court was reversed, a verdict of the jury in plaintiff's favor set aside and the case remanded, under the provisions of this section, for a new trial upon the sole question of whether the notice required by the insurance policy was given within a reasonable time from the date of the accident. Glenns Falls Indem. Co. v. Harris, 168 Va. 438, 191 S.E. 644 (1937).

Change of position. — The law of the case as fixed by the instructions of the trial court, to which there were no exceptions, being with the defendant, and the verdict for the plaintiff being without evidence to support it, the Supreme Court, in pursuance of this section, will enter such judgment as is warranted by the undisputed facts of the case. The case could not be remanded to enable the plaintiff to change her position with reference to the law. Queen Ins. Co. v. Perkinson, 129 Va. 216, 105 S.E. 580 (1921).

When party put on terms. — A party may be in effect put on terms in the appellate court as well as in the trial court. When a party is put on terms in appellate court because a judgment in his favor is excessive, it may reverse the judgment of the trial court and remand the cause, with direction to the trial court to put the successful party upon terms to release the excess, or else submit to a new trial, and if the release is made, to overrule the motion for a new trial, and render judgment for the correct amount with interest and costs. If the error be one of mere calculation, readily corrected from the record, or if the verdict and judgment of the trial court is excessive and the record affords plain and certain proof of the amount of the excess so that it may with safety be corrected, in either event the appellate court will amend and affirm the judgment of the trial court, and will not remand the case for such amendment. National Sur. Co. v. Commonwealth, 125 Va. 223, 99 S.E. 657, cert. denied, 250 U.S. 665, 40 S. Ct. 13, 63 L. Ed. 1197 (1919).

b. Questions or Points on Which New Trial Is Had.

Case remanded for retrial generally. — It was contended that the appellate court should direct that the amount of damages be not again submitted to the jury on the further trial of the case, but that the issue be confined to a finding upon the question of liability of the defendant. But the court, upon consideration of the entire record, was of the opinion that the ends of justice did not require that the court should do otherwise than remand the case generally for a trial de novo. Virginia-Tennessee Motor Truck Corp. v. Wilson, 140 Va. 260, 124 S.E. 231 (1924); Green v. Ruffin, 141 Va. 628, 125 S.E. 742, 127 S.E. 486 (1925).

Remand for new trial on one cause of action only. — Where the evidence was insufficient to justify a finding for alleged negligent blasting but sufficient to find for alleged negligent construction of drainage facilities, the judgment was reversed, the verdict set aside, and a new trial ordered limited to the cause of action based on negligent construction and installation of the drainage facilities. B.G. Young & Sons v. Kirk, 202 Va. 176, 116 S.E.2d 38 (1960).

To determine amount of damages. — A verdict for the plaintiff having determined the question of liability, the case was remanded for a new trial, but only upon the amount of damages the plaintiff was entitled to recover under authority of this section. Baker v. Carrington, 138 Va. 22, 120 S.E. 856 (1924); Certified T.V. & Appliance Co. v. Harrington, 201 Va. 109, 109 S.E.2d 126 (1959).

Where decree was required to be reversed for failure to award a judgment for proved damages, but the facts before the Supreme Court did not enable the court to enter a final decree that would "attain the ends of justice," the cause was remanded to the trial court for a new trial limited to the issue of damages, and with directions to order an issue out of chancery and impanel a jury to determine the question of damages. Washington Golf & Country Club, Inc. v. Briggs & Brennan Developers, Inc., 198 Va. 586, 95 S.E.2d 233 (1956).

Where liability had been admitted by defendant, but certain errors were committed in instructing the jury as to damages, the case was remanded for trial on the issue of damages only. Eubank v. Spencer, 203 Va. 923, 128 S.E.2d 299 (1962).

Remanded when evidence imperfectly developed. — When the evidence was imperfectly developed on the trial, and for that reason there was not sufficient evidence before the Supreme Court to enable it to feel that it would attain the ends of justice by entering a final order under this section, the case will be remanded for a new trial. Branning Mfg. Co. v. Norfolk-Southern R.R., 138 Va. 43, 121 S.E. 74 (1924).

The question whether the plaintiff used reasonable diligence in the resale of the goods after the breach of contract by buyer was manifestly not considered by the jury, or the court, nor put in issue by the parties on the trial below. The Supreme Court did not feel that the facts before it bearing on that question had been sufficiently developed to enable it to feel that it would attain the ends of justice by passing thereon and entering final judgment. Mayflower Mills v. Hardy, 138 Va. 138, 120 S.E. 861 (1924).

When evidence as to plaintiff's insurance admitted. — In an action to recover damages for injuries sustained by plaintiff in a collision between the automobiles of plaintiff and defendant, the judgment of the trial court is reversed for the sole reason that the court admitted evidence regarding the insurance plaintiff carried and the amount he received thereunder by reason of his injuries. The issues of the negligence of defendant and the alleged contributory negligence of plaintiff having been concluded by the verdict adversely to defendant, he is not entitled to a new trial upon them, but, inasmuch as the prejudicial error in admitting the improper evidence in all probability influenced the jury in fixing the amount to be awarded plaintiff, the Supreme Court, in the exercise of its discretion under this section, will remand the case for a new trial, which shall be limited to the sole question of the proper amount of damages to be awarded. Johnson v. Kellam, 162 Va. 757, 175 S.E. 634 (1934).

Effect when amount of damages settled on first trial. — In an action for damages for personal injuries where the judgment is reversed and the cause remanded for error in admitting evidence, where as to the amount of damages the case was fully developed, and the parties had a fair trial, pursuant to this section, the Supreme Court directed that the question of the amount of damages should not be tried again, but that if upon another trial the verdict should be for the plaintiff, the court should enter a judgment thereon in favor of the plaintiff for the amount of damages awarded in the first trial. Whitten v. McClelland, 137 Va. 726, 120 S.E. 146 (1923).

In accordance with the provisions of this section, the order entered in the instant case upon reversal and remand for a new trial directed that the case should not be retried as to the amount of damages, as that question was fairly developed at the present trial, and there was no error assigned as to the instructions thereon, or as to the amount of the verdict. Director Gen. of R.R.'s v. Pence's Adm'x, 135 Va. 329, 116 S.E. 351 (1923).

When only question of liability for negligence remanded. — Where a judgment must be reversed because the case was submitted to the jury on the erroneous theory that plaintiff was a passenger at the time of her injury, the verdict established plaintiff's freedom from contributory negligence and the amount of damages, so that, under this section the case will be remanded, with directions to submit only question of negligence on part of defendant. Virginia Ry. & Power Co. v. Dressler, 132 Va. 342, 111 S.E. 243 (1922).

When remanded as to whether passenger exercised a voluntary choice in leaving train between stations. — Where in an action by a passenger against a carrier for injury from assault the parties have had a fair trial upon all questions, including the amount of damages, except the question of whether the plaintiff exercised a free and voluntary choice in leaving the train after being carried beyond her station, the Supreme Court remanded the cause solely for the determination of that one question pursuant to this section. Hines v. Garrett, 131 Va. 125, 108 S.E. 690 (1921).

§ 8.01-682. What damages awarded appellee. — When any judgment is affirmed, damages shall be awarded to the appellee. Such damages, when the judgment is for the payment of money, shall be the interest to which the parties are legally entitled, from the time the appeal took effect, until the affirmance. Such interest shall be computed upon the whole amount of the recovery, including interest and costs, and such damages shall be in satisfaction of all interest during such period of time. When the judgment is not for the payment of any money, except costs, the damages shall be such specific sum as the appellate court may deem reasonable, not being more than $100 nor less than $30. (Code 1950, § 8-495; 1977, c. 617; 1984, c. 703.)

Cross references. — As to recovery of damages sustained for property with held during appeal, § 8.01-123.

I. Decisions Under Current Law.
II. Decisions Under Prior Law.

I. DECISIONS UNDER CURRENT LAW.

Interest to be paid on original award of sum that includes attorney's fees. — Because attorney's fees are not court "costs," the trial court's original award of a sum that included attorney's fees was, in fact, a judgment for the payment of money and not merely an order to pay "costs"; thus, the trial court did not err in ordering that interest be paid on the original award of attorney's fees in accordance with the second sentence of this section. Jacob v. Jacob, No. 1502-90-4 (Ct. of Appeals, March 17, 1992).

II. DECISIONS UNDER PRIOR LAW.

Editor's note. — The cases cited below were decided under corresponding provisions of former law. The term "this section," as used below, refers to former provisions.

The words "appellant" and "appellee" as used in this section and § 8.01-676 are not used in a technical sense, but in a broader sense by which they include the plaintiffs and defendants in a writ of error as well as in an appeal. Widgins v. Norfolk & W. Ry., 142 Va. 419, 128 S.E. 516 (1925).

This section does not apply to the affirmance of a judgment imposing an amercement or fine. Abrahams v. Commonwealth, 40 Va. (1 Rob.) 675 (1842).

Damages included in lien. — There was an appeal from a judgment for money which was a lien on land, and the judgment was affirmed. It was held that the lien, after such affirmance was not only for the damages, interest and costs recovered by the original judgment, but also for the damages and costs to which the creditor became entitled by the judgment of affirmance. M'Clung v. Beirne, 37 Va. (10 Leigh) 394 (1839).

§ 8.01-683. When Clerk of Supreme Court to transmit its decisions.
— When any term of the Supreme Court is ended, or sooner if the court so direct, the Clerk thereof shall certify and transmit its decision to the clerk of the court or tribunal below, as the case may be, except that it shall not be his duty to certify or transmit a copy of a judgment of affirmance unless the appellee shall have paid all fees due from him in the case, or shall endorse on such copy so much of the judgment, for the benefit of the clerk, as the unpaid fees shall amount to. If any clerk fail to comply with this section for twenty days, except as aforesaid, he shall forfeit fifty dollars to any person aggrieved thereby. (Code 1950, § 8-496; 1977, c. 617.)

REVISERS' NOTE

Former § 8-497 (Postage to be paid by clerk ...) has been deleted as unnecessary.

§ 8.01-684. Copies of Court's opinions to be furnished to counsel.
— When a case is decided by an appellate court the clerk shall furnish a copy of the opinion rendered by the court thereon to each counsel of record without making any charge therefor. (Code 1950, § 8-497.1; 1977, c. 617; 1984, c. 703.)

REVISERS' NOTE

Former § 8-497.1 has been rewritten to ensure that each counsel of record is furnished a copy of the court's opinion without charge.

Cross references. — For application of this section to criminal cases, see § 19.2-325.

§ 8.01-685. Entry of decision in lower court; issue of execution thereon.
— The court or other tribunal from which any case may have come to an appellate court shall enter the decision of the appellate court as its own, and execution or other appropriate process may issue thereon accordingly. When that decision is received by the clerk or secretary of the court or tribunal below, he shall enter it of record in his order book, and thereupon such execution may issue and such proceedings be had in the case as would have been proper if the decision had been entered in court or by such tribunal.

If the judgment of the lower court or tribunal is affirmed, in whole or in part, by the decision of an appellate court, execution or other appropriate process may issue thereon against the principal and surety on any appeal bond which may have been given, for the amount of such judgment, including the interest and cost and the damages awarded by the appellate court, not exceeding, however, the penalty of such bond. (Code 1950, § 8-498; 1977, c. 617; 1984, c. 703.)

REVISERS' NOTE

"Other tribunal" has been inserted in the first line of former § 8-498 to include the State Corporation Commission and the Industrial (now Workers' Compensation) Commission.

I. DECISIONS UNDER PRIOR LAW.

Editor's note. — The case cited below was decided under corresponding provisions of former law. The term "this section," as used below, refers to former provisions.

This section does not apply where the executions were issued upon the original judgments of the circuit court and were not issued under this section. Seal v. Puckett, 159 Va. 297, 165 S.E. 496 (1932).

§§ 8.01-686, 8.01-687: Repealed by Acts 1984, c. 703.

Cross references. — For provisions as to finality of dismissals, see § 8.01-675.1.

Article 4.

Miscellaneous Provisions.

§ 8.01-688. Order books, etc., of former district courts in custody of Clerk of Supreme Court, etc. — The order books, dockets and other office books formerly belonging to the several former district courts shall remain in the custody of the Clerk of the Supreme Court. Said Clerk shall furnish transcripts of the records and proceedings of such district courts when required, and perform all other duties in respect to records and proceedings of such district courts as might have been performed by the clerks of such district courts if such courts had continued to exist. All printed and manuscript orders, and other papers pertaining to cases decided in such district courts, shall remain in the custody of the clerks of the circuit courts at the several places where such district courts held their sessions, who shall be charged with the same duties in respect to such records and papers as might have been performed by the clerks of such district courts respectively, if such courts had continued to exist, and who shall receive for any such service fees similar to those charged by the clerks of district courts for such services. (Code 1950, § 8-502; 1977, c. 617.)

CODE OF VIRGINIA

1950

2001 Supplement

ANNOTATED

Prepared under the Supervision of
The Virginia Code Commission

BY

The Editorial Staff of the Publishers

VOLUME 2
2000 REPLACEMENT

Includes acts adopted at the 2001 Regular Session, Acts 2001, cc. 1 to 875, and at the 2001 Special Session I, Acts 2001, cc. 1 to 4, of the General Assembly

Place in Pocket of Corresponding Volume of Main Set.

MICHIE

LEXIS, NEXIS, *Shepard's* and Martindale-Hubbell are registered trademarks, LEXIS Publishing and MICHIE are trademarks, and *lexis.com* is a service mark of Reed Elsevier Properties Inc., used under license. Matthew Bender is a registered trademark of Matthew Bender Properties Inc.

© 2001 by Matthew Bender & Company, Inc.,
one of the LEXIS Publishing™ companies.
All rights reserved.

P.O. Box 7587, Charlottesville, VA 22906-7587

5044418

ISBN 0-327-11171-2 (set)
ISBN 0-327-13074-1 (Vol. 2)

www.lexis.com

Customer Service: 1-800-833-9844

Preface

A complete explanation of the supplements to the Code of Virginia is contained in the Foreword appearing in 1995 Replacement Volume 1.

Under Article IV, § 13, of the Constitution, the acts adopted at the 2001 Regular Session of the General Assembly are effective July 1, 2001, except where an act has an emergency clause or specifies some other effective date. Effective dates other than the constitutional effective date are stated in notes.

Scope of Legislation

This 2001 Cumulative Supplement includes all acts adopted at the 2001 Regular Session and at the 2001 Special Session of the General Assembly, Acts 2001, cc. 1 to 875, and Acts 2001, Special Session I, cc. 1 to 4.

Scope of Annotations

To better serve our customers, by making our annotations more current, LEXIS Publishing has changed the sources that are read to create annotations for this publication. Rather than waiting for cases to appear in printed reporters, we now read court decisions as they are released by the courts. A consequence of this more current reading of cases, as they are posted online on LEXIS, is that the most recent cases annotated may not yet have print reporter citations. These will be provided, as they become available, through later publications.

This publication contains annotations taken from decisions of the Virginia Supreme Court posted on LEXIS through April 10, 2001, decisions of the Virginia Court of Appeals posted as of April 3, 2001, and decisions of the appropriate federal courts posted as of April 10, 2001. These cases will be printed in the following reports:

South Eastern Reporter, Second Series.
Supreme Court Reporter.
Federal Reporter, Third Series.
Federal Supplement, Second Series.
Federal Rules Decisions.
Bankruptcy Reporter.

Additionally, annotations have been taken from the following sources:

Virginia Law Review, through Volume 86, p. 1575.
Washington and Lee Law Review, through Volume 57, p. 657.
William and Mary Law Review, through Volume 42, p. 350.
University of Richmond Law Review, through Volume 34, p. 1213.
George Mason University Law Review, through Volume 9, p. 235.

Unpublished Opinions of Court of Appeals

Some of the annotations contained in this supplement are derived from unpublished opinions of the Court of Appeals of Virginia. These opinions will not appear in the Court of Appeals Reports or any other court reporter. The unpublished opinions can be identified by their citation, which gives the parties' names, a case number, "Ct. of Appeals," and a date.

The Court of Appeals has placed the following footnote on all unpublished opinions: "Pursuant to Code § 17.1-413, recodifying § 17-116.010, this opinion is not designated for publication."

"Although an unpublished opinion of the Court has no precedential value, a court or commission does not err by considering the rationale and adopting it to the extent it is persuasive." Fairfax County School Board v. Rose, 29 Va. 32, 509 S.E.2d 525 (Va. App. 1999).

A copy of the full text of any unpublished opinion can be obtained by contacting: Court of Appeals of Virginia, Attention: Clerk's Assistant (Opinions), 109 North Eighth Street, Richmond, Virginia 23219.

User's Guide

In order to assist both the legal profession and the lay person in obtaining the maximum benefit from the Code of Virginia, a User's Guide has been included in Volume 1. This guide contains comments and information on the many features found within the Code of Virginia intended to increase the usefulness of this set of laws to the user. See Volume 1 for the complete User's Guide.

Suggestions, comments, or questions about the Code of Virginia or this Cumulative Supplement are welcome. You may call us toll free at (800) 833-9844, fax us toll free at (800) 643-1280, email us at Customer.Support@Bender.com, or write Code of Virginia Editor, Lexis Publishing, P.O. Box 7587, Charlottesville, Virginia 22906-7587.

For an online bookstore, technical and customer support, and other company information, visit Lexis Publishing's Internet home page at http://www.lexis.com.

Table of Titles

TITLE
1. General Provisions.
2. Administration of the Government Generally [Repealed].
2.1. Administration of the Government Generally [Repealed effective October 1, 2001].
2.2. Administration of Government [Effective October 1, 2001].
3. Agriculture, Horticulture and Food [Repealed].
3.1. Agriculture, Horticulture and Food.
4. Alcoholic Beverages and Industrial Alcohol [Repealed].
4.1. Alcoholic Beverage Control Act.
5. Aviation [Repealed].
5.1. Aviation.
6. Banking and Finance [Repealed].
6.1. Banking and Finance.
7. Boundaries, Jurisdiction and Emblems of the Commonwealth [Repealed].
7.1. Boundaries, Jurisdiction and Emblems of the Commonwealth.
8. Civil Remedies and Procedure; Evidence Generally [Repealed].
8.01. Civil Remedies and Procedure.
8.1. Commercial Code — General Provisions.
8.2. Commercial Code — Sales.
8.2A. Commercial Code — Leases.
8.3. Commercial Code — Commercial Paper [Repealed].
8.3A. Commercial Code — Negotiable Instruments.
8.4. Commercial Code — Bank Deposits and Collections.
8.4A. Commercial Code — Funds Transfers.
8.5. Commercial Code — Letters of Credit [Repealed].
8.5A. Commercial Code — Letters of Credit.
8.6. Commercial Code — Bulk Transfers [Repealed].
8.6A. Commercial Code — Bulk Transfers.
8.7. Commercial Code — Warehouse Receipts, Bills of Lading and Other Documents of Title.
8.8. Commercial Code — Investment Securities [Repealed].
8.8A. Commercial Code — Investment Securities.
8.9. Commercial Code — Secured Transactions; Sales of Accounts, Contract Rights and Chattel Paper [Repealed].
8.9A. Secured Transactions.
8.10. Commercial Code — Effective Date — Transitional Provisions.
8.11. 1973 Amendatory Act — Effective Date and Transition Provisions.
9. Commissions, Boards and Institutions Generally [Repealed effective October 1, 2001].
9.1. Commonwealth Public Safety [Effective October 1, 2001.]
10. Conservation Generally [Repealed].
10.1. Conservation.
11. Contracts.
12. Corporation Commission [Repealed].
12.1. State Corporation Commission.
13. Corporations Generally [Repealed].
13.1. Corporations.
14. Costs, Fees, Salaries and Allowances [Repealed].
14.1. Costs, Fees, Salaries and Allowances [Repealed].
15. Counties, Cities and Towns [Repealed].
15.1. Counties, Cities and Towns [Repealed].

TITLE
15.2. COUNTIES, CITIES AND TOWNS.
16. COURTS NOT OF RECORD [Repealed].
16.1. COURTS NOT OF RECORD.
17. COURTS OF RECORD [Repealed].
17.1. COURTS OF RECORD.
18. CRIMES AND OFFENSES GENERALLY [Repealed].
18.1. CRIMES AND OFFENSES GENERALLY [Repealed].
18.2. CRIMES AND OFFENSES GENERALLY.
19. CRIMINAL PROCEDURE [Repealed].
19.1. CRIMINAL PROCEDURE [Repealed].
19.2. CRIMINAL PROCEDURE.
20. DOMESTIC RELATIONS.
21. DRAINAGE, SOIL CONSERVATION, SANITATION AND PUBLIC FACILITIES DISTRICTS.
22. EDUCATION [Repealed].
22.1. EDUCATION.
23. EDUCATIONAL INSTITUTIONS.
24. ELECTIONS [Repealed].
24.1. ELECTIONS [Repealed].
24.2. ELECTIONS.
25. EMINENT DOMAIN.
26. FIDUCIARIES GENERALLY.
27. FIRE PROTECTION.
28. FISH, OYSTERS AND SHELLFISH [Repealed].
28.1. FISH, OYSTERS, SHELLFISH AND OTHER MARINE LIFE [Repealed].
28.2. FISHERIES AND HABITAT OF THE TIDAL WATERS.
29. GAME, INLAND FISHERIES AND DOGS [Repealed].
29.1. GAME, INLAND FISHERIES AND BOATING.
30. GENERAL ASSEMBLY.
31. GUARDIAN AND WARD.
32. HEALTH [Repealed].
32.1. HEALTH.
33. HIGHWAYS, BRIDGES AND FERRIES [Repealed].
33.1. HIGHWAYS, BRIDGES AND FERRIES.
34. HOMESTEAD AND OTHER EXEMPTIONS.
35. HOTELS, RESTAURANTS AND CAMPS [Repealed].
35.1. HOTELS, RESTAURANTS, SUMMER CAMPS, AND CAMPGROUNDS.
36. HOUSING.
37. INSANE, EPILEPTIC, FEEBLE-MINDED AND INEBRIATE PERSONS [Repealed].
37.1. INSTITUTIONS FOR THE MENTALLY ILL; MENTAL HEALTH GENERALLY.
38. INSURANCE [Repealed].
38.1. INSURANCE [Repealed].
38.2. INSURANCE.
39. JUSTICES OF THE PEACE [Repealed].
39.1. JUSTICES OF THE PEACE [Repealed].
40. LABOR AND EMPLOYMENT [Repealed].
40.1. LABOR AND EMPLOYMENT.
41. LAND OFFICE [Repealed].
41.1. LAND OFFICE.
42. LIBRARIES [Repealed].
42.1. LIBRARIES.
43. MECHANICS' AND CERTAIN OTHER LIENS.
44. MILITARY AND EMERGENCY LAWS.
45. MINES AND MINING [Repealed].
45.1. MINES AND MINING.
46. MOTOR VEHICLES [Repealed].
46.1. MOTOR VEHICLES [Repealed].
46.2. MOTOR VEHICLES.
47. NOTARIES AND OUT-OF-STATE COMMISSIONERS [Repealed].

TABLE OF TITLES

TITLE
47.1. Notaries and Out-of-State Commissioners.
48. Nuisances.
49. Oaths, Affirmations and Bonds.
50. Partnerships.
51. Pensions and Retirement [Repealed].
51.01. Persons With Disabilities [Recodified].
51.1. Pensions, Benefits, and Retirement.
51.5. Persons With Disabilities.
52. Police (State).
53. Prisons and Other Methods of Correction [Repealed].
53.1. Prisons and Other Methods of Correction.
54. Professions and Occupations [Repealed].
54.1. Professions and Occupations.
55. Property and Conveyances.
56. Public Service Companies.
57. Religious and Charitable Matters; Cemeteries.
58. Taxation [Repealed].
58.1. Taxation.
59. Trade and Commerce [Repealed].
59.1. Trade and Commerce.
60. Unemployment Compensation [Repealed].
60.1. Unemployment Compensation [Repealed].
60.2. Unemployment Compensation.
61. Warehouses, Cold Storage and Refrigerated Locker Plants [Repealed].
61.1. Warehouses, Cold Storage and Refrigerated Locker Plants.
62. Waters of the State, Ports and Harbors [Repealed].
62.1. Waters of the State, Ports and Harbors.
63. Welfare [Repealed].
63.1. Welfare (Social Services).
64. Wills and Decedents' Estates [Repealed].
64.1. Wills and Decedents' Estates.
65. Workmen's Compensation [Repealed].
65.1. Workers' Compensation [Repealed].
65.2. Workers' Compensation.
66. Juvenile Justice.

In addition, this publication contains

Constitution of the United States of America.
Constitution of Virginia.
Rules of Supreme Court of Virginia.
Legal Ethics Opinions.
Unauthorized Practice of Law Opinions.
Table of Comparative Sections.
Table of Tax Code Sections.
Table of Reorganization Provisions of 1948.
Table of Acts Through 1948 Not Previously Codified.
Table of Acts Codified Subsequent to 1948.
Table of Sections Amended or Repealed.
Tables of Comparable Sections for Certain Repealed and Revised Titles.

CODE OF VIRGINIA

2001 Cumulative Supplement

Title 8.01.

Civil Remedies and Procedure.

Chap. 14. Evidence, §§ 8.01-385 through 8.01-420.6.

CHAPTER 1.

GENERAL PROVISIONS AS TO CIVIL CASES.

§ 8.01-3. Supreme Court may prescribe rules; effective date thereof; rules to be printed and distributed; rules to be published, indexed, and annotated; effect of subsequent enactments of General Assembly.

Cross references. — As to the Virginia Code Commission's responsibility for drafting rules of evidence for introduction into the General Assembly in accordance with the recommendations of the Supreme Court, see § 30-153.

I. DECISIONS UNDER CURRENT LAW.

Applied in Waterman v. Halverson, 261 Va. 203, 540 S.E.2d 867 (2001).

§ 8.01-4. District courts and circuit courts may prescribe certain rules.

I. DECISIONS UNDER CURRENT LAW.

The practice of allowing any circuit judge to handle any probation violation does not violate § 17.1-503 as it pertains to this section. Gurley v. Commonwealth, 34 Va. App. 166, 538 S.E.2d 361 (2000).

CHAPTER 2.

PARTIES.

Article 2.

Special Provisions.

Sec.
8.01-9. Guardian ad litem for persons under disability; when guardian ad litem need not be appointed for person under disability.

Article 1.

General Provisions.

§ 8.01-5. Effect of nonjoinder or misjoinder; limitation on joinder of insurance company.

I. DECISIONS UNDER CURRENT LAW.

Ward's suit in own name not subject to amendment. — Under § 37.1-141, any action on behalf of a ward must be brought by the ward's guardian and this section did not permit amendment of a pleading to comply with the statute where a ward had attempted to bring suit in her own name. Cook v. Radford Community Hosp., Inc., 260 Va. 443, 536 S.E.2d 906 (2000).

Applied in Sullivan v. Sullivan, 33 Va. App. 743, 536 S.E.2d 925 (2000).

§ 8.01-6. Amending pleading; relation back to original pleading.

I. DECISIONS UNDER CURRENT LAW.

Misnomer arises, etc.
This section was not applicable where a ward had attempted to bring suit in her own name as this was not a case in which the right person, that being the ward's guardian, was incorrectly named but one in which the wrong person, that being the ward, was named. Cook v. Radford Community Hosp., Inc., 260 Va. 443, 536 S.E.2d 906 (2000).

Article 2.

Special Provisions.

§ 8.01-9. Guardian ad litem for persons under disability; when guardian ad litem need not be appointed for person under disability.
— A. A suit wherein a person under a disability is a party defendant shall not be stayed because of such disability, but the court in which the suit is pending, or the clerk thereof, shall appoint a discreet and competent attorney-at-law as guardian ad litem to such defendant, whether the defendant has been served with process or not. If no such attorney is found willing to act, the court shall appoint some other discreet and proper person as guardian ad litem. Any guardian ad litem so appointed shall not be liable for costs. Every guardian ad litem shall faithfully represent the estate or other interest of the person under a disability for whom he is appointed, and it shall be the duty of the court to see that the interest of the defendant is so represented and protected. Whenever the court is of the opinion that the interest of the defendant so requires, it shall remove any guardian ad litem and appoint another in his stead. When, in any case, the court is satisfied that the guardian ad litem has rendered substantial service in representing the interest of the person under a disability, it may allow the guardian reasonable compensation therefor, and his actual expenses, if any, to be paid out of the estate of the defendant. However, if the defendant's estate is inadequate for the purpose of paying compensation and expenses, all, or any part thereof, may be taxed as costs in the proceeding or, in the case of proceedings to adjudicate a person under a disability as an habitual offender pursuant to former § 46.2-351.2 or former § 46.2-352, shall be paid by the Commonwealth out of the state treasury from the appropriation for criminal charges. In a civil action against an incarcerated felon for damages arising out of a criminal act, the compensation and expenses of the guardian ad litem shall be paid by the Commonwealth out of the state treasury from the appropriation for criminal charges. If judgment is against the incarcerated felon, the amount allowed by the court to the guardian ad litem shall be taxed against the incarcerated felon as part of the costs of the proceeding, and if collected, the same shall be paid to the Commonwealth.

B. Notwithstanding the provisions of subsection A or the provisions of any other law to the contrary, in any suit wherein a person under a disability is a party and is represented by an attorney-at-law duly licensed to practice in this Commonwealth, who shall have entered of record an appearance for such person, no guardian ad litem need be appointed for such person unless the court determines that the interests of justice require such appointment; or unless a statute applicable to such suit expressly requires that the person under a disability be represented by a guardian ad litem. The court may, in its discretion, appoint the attorney of record for the person under a disability as his guardian ad litem, in which event the attorney shall perform all the duties and functions of guardian ad litem.

Any judgment or decree rendered by any court against a person under a disability without a guardian ad litem, but in compliance with the provisions of this subsection B, shall be as valid as if the guardian ad litem had been appointed. (Code 1950, §§ 8-88, 8-88.1; 1972, c. 720; 1977, c. 617; 1996, c. 887; 1999, cc. 945, 955, 987; 2001, c. 127.)

Editor's note. — The Reviser's note for this section, as set out in the bound volume, was written prior to subsequent amendments, including those made in 2001.

The 2001 amendments. — The 2001 amendment by c. 127, in subsection B, deleted "defendant" following "a party," and substituted "that the person under a disability be represented" for "an answer to be filed."

I. DECISIONS UNDER CURRENT LAW.

Statute irrelevant to suits by persons under disabilities. — This section recognizes that persons under disabilities may be sued in their own names and is concerned with the protection of such persons by appointment of a guardian ad litem but nothing in the statute provides any basis for concluding that, in the converse situation, a suit in his own name by a person under a disability who has a duly appointed fiduciary is valid. Cook v. Radford Community Hosp., Inc., 260 Va. 443, 536 S.E.2d 906 (2000).

Applied in Peters v. Hagerman, No. 2901-98-4 (Ct. of Appeals June 22, 1999); McElroy v. McElroy, No. 0777-99-4 (Ct. of Appeals June 22, 1999); Dishman v. Dishman, No. 1965-99-3 (Ct. of Appeals May 16, 2000).

CHAPTER 3.

ACTIONS.

Article 3.

Injury to Person or Property.

Sec.
8.01-42.3. Civil action for stalking.

Article 4.

Defamation.

Sec.
8.01-47. Immunity of school personnel investigating or reporting certain incidents.

§ 8.01-31. Accounting in equity.

I. DECISIONS UNDER CURRENT LAW.

Former spouse not entitled to rental value where not co-owner. — An accounting occurs and a party is entitled to the fair market rental value of property only when that party has joint ownership of the property; where the owner's former wife conceded that the property was titled solely in her former husband's name, she was not entitled to an award based on the property's rental value because she was not an owner of the property. Snider v. Snider, No. 1539-99-3 (Ct. of Appeals Jan. 16, 2001).

Article 3.

Injury to Person or Property.

§ 8.01-34. When contribution among wrongdoers enforced.

Law Review.
For an article, "A Model for Enhanced Risk Recovery in Tort," see 56 Wash. & Lee L. Rev. 1173 (1999).

For a note, "A Duty Not to Become a Victim: Assessing the Plaintiff's Fault in Negligent Security Actions," see 57 Wash. & Lee L. Rev. 611 (2000).

§ 8.01-38.1. Limitation on recovery of punitive damages.

Cross references. — As to award of punitive damages for stalking, see § 8.01-42.3.

Law Review.
For a note, "The Supreme Court's Backwards Proportionality Jurisprudence: Comparing Judicial Review of Excessive Criminal Punishments and Excessive Punitive Damages Awards," see 86 Va. L. Rev. 1249 (2000).

I. DECISIONS UNDER CURRENT LAW.

Cap applies to action as a whole. — The plain meaning of this section dictates that the cap on punitive damage awards applies to the action as a whole and not to each defendant. Al-Abood v. El-Shamari, 217 F.3d 225 (4th Cir. 2000).

§ 8.01-42.3. Civil action for stalking.

— A. A victim has a civil cause of action against an individual who engaged in conduct that is prohibited under § 18.2-60.3, whether or not the individual has been charged or convicted for the alleged violation, for the compensatory damages incurred by the victim as a result of that conduct, in addition to the costs for bringing the action. If compensatory damages are awarded, a victim may also be awarded punitive damages.

B. As used in this section:

"Compensatory damages" includes damages for all of the defendant's acts prohibited by § 18.2-60.3.

"Victim" means a person who, because of the conduct of the defendant that is prohibited under § 18.2-60.3, was placed in reasonable fear of death, criminal sexual assault, or bodily injury to himself or to a minor child of whom the person is a parent or legal guardian.

C. No action shall be commenced under this section more than two years after the most recent conduct prohibited under § 18.2-60.3. (2001, c. 444.)

Cross references. — As to the statutory limitation on the recovery of punitive damages, see § 8.01-38.1.

§ 8.01-44.5. Exemplary damages for persons injured by intoxicated drivers.

I. DECISIONS UNDER CURRENT LAW.

Proof of "unreasonable refusal." — A plaintiff's failure to incorporate in the factual allegations of his complaint the final sentence of this section relating to the effect of providing a certified copy of a court's determination that the defendant unreasonably refused to submit to a breath test is not fatal to a claim for punitive damages in that compliance with this final sentence merely is but one way to prove an "unreasonable refusal," not the only way. Ritinski v. McGarity, 112 F. Supp. 2d 509 (E.D. Va. 2000).

Article 4.
Defamation.

§ 8.01-45. Action for insulting words.

I. Decisions Under Current Law.
  A. General Consideration.
  C. Illustrations of Actionable Words.
  E. Pleading and Practice.

I. DECISIONS UNDER CURRENT LAW.

A. General Consideration.

Must be danger of violent reaction. — This section only penalizes words used in a verbal attack directed at a particular individual in a face to face confrontation that presents a clear and present danger of a violent physical reaction. Thompson v. Town of Front Royal, — F. Supp. 2d —, 2000 U.S. Dist. LEXIS 3876 (W.D. Va. Mar. 16, 2000).

C. Illustrations of Actionable Words.

Words "nigger" and "niggers" not fighting words. — The words "nigger" and "niggers," allegedly spoken by the African-American plaintiff's supervisor, without more specific allegations of how, when and to whom they were spoken, were not enough to rise to the level of fighting words under this section. The plaintiff did not allege facts in his complaint to prove that any supposed fighting words referred to him and the allegations in the complaint could not be construed as having been directed at a particular individual in a face to face confrontation and as presenting a clear and present danger of a violent physical reaction. Thompson v. Town of Front Royal, — F. Supp. 2d —, 2000 U.S. Dist. LEXIS 3876 (W.D. Va. Mar. 16, 2000).

E. Pleading and Practice.

Exact words must be alleged. — The exact words charged to have been used by the defendant must be alleged in order to state a cause of action for insulting words under this section. Thompson v. Town of Front Royal, — F. Supp. 2d —, 2000 U.S. Dist. LEXIS 3876 (W.D. Va. Mar. 16, 2000).

§ 8.01-46.1. Disclosure of employment-related information; presumptions; causes of action; definitions.

Law Review. — For 2000 survey of Virginia labor and employment law, see 34 U. Rich. L. Rev. 907 (2000).

§ 8.01-47. Immunity of school personnel investigating or reporting certain incidents.
— In addition to any other immunity he may have, any teacher, instructor, principal, school administrator, school coordinator, guidance counselor or any other professional, administrative or clerical staff member or other personnel of any elementary or secondary school, or institution of higher learning who, in good faith with reasonable cause and without malice, acts to report, investigate or cause any investigation to be made into the activities of any student or students or any other person or persons as they relate to conduct involving bomb threats, firebombs, explosive materials or other similar devices as described in clauses (v) and (vi) of § 22.1-279.3:1 A, or alcohol or drug use or abuse in or related to the school or institution or in connection with any school or institution activity, shall be immune from all civil liability that might otherwise be incurred or imposed as the result of the making of such a report, investigation or disclosure. (Code 1950, § 8-631.1; 1972, c. 762; 1977, c. 617; 1982, c. 259; 1988, c. 159; 1995, c. 759; 2000, c. 79; 2001, cc. 688, 820.)

The 2001 amendments. — The 2001 amendments by c. 688 and c. 820 are identical, and substituted "§ 22.1-279.3:1" for "§ 22.1-280.1."

§ 8.01-49.1. Liability for defamatory material on the Internet.

Law Review. — For 2000 survey of Virginia technology law, see 34 U. Rich. L. Rev. 1051. (2000).

ARTICLE 5.

Death by Wrongful Act.

§ 8.01-50. Action for death by wrongful act; how and when to be brought.

I. Decisions Under Current Law.
  A. General Consideration.

I. DECISIONS UNDER CURRENT LAW.

  A. General Consideration.

Applied in Rice v. Charles, 260 Va. 157, 532 S.E.2d 318 (2000).

§ 8.01-52. Amount of damages.

Law Review.
For a note, "The Supreme Court's Backwards Proportionality Jurisprudence: Comparing Judicial Review of Excessive Criminal Punishments and Excessive Punitive Damages Awards," see 86 Va. L. Rev. 1249 (2000).

I. Decisions Under Current Law.
  A. General Consideration.

I. DECISIONS UNDER CURRENT LAW.

  A. General Consideration.

Error to limit damages to funeral expenses. — A jury verdict for the exact amount of a decedent's funeral expenses was inadequate as a matter of law because it failed to compensate her statutory beneficiaries for any other items of damage; by returning a verdict for only the amount of the funeral expenses, the jury demonstrated a misunderstanding of either the law or the facts or both in that the evidence at trial clearly supported the conclusion that the decedent's statutory beneficiaries experienced sorrow, mental anguish and loss of solace as a result of the decedent's death. Rice v. Charles, 260 Va. 157, 532 S.E.2d 318 (2000).

ARTICLE 7.

Motor Vehicle Accidents.

§ 8.01-66. Recovery of damages for loss of use of vehicle.

Cross references. — As to the insurance of state motor vehicles, see § 2.2-1838.

§ 8.01-66.1. Remedy for arbitrary refusal of motor vehicle insurance claim.

Law Review.
For 2000 survey of Virginia insurance law, see 34 U. Rich. L. Rev. 883 (2000).

Article 11.

General Provisions for Judicial Sales.

§ 8.01-109. Commission for selling, collecting, etc.; each piece of property to constitute separate sale.

I. DECISIONS UNDER CURRENT LAW.

Priority of commissioner's claim for fees. — By fixing the amount of the commission in a judicial sale, the general assembly intended that such commission be paid from the proceeds of that sale and a circuit court thus properly directed payment of the fees of a special ommissioner from the sale proceeds before any distribution of the funds to the holder of the first deed of trust. Homeside Lending, Inc. v. Unit Owners Ass'n of Antietam Square Condominium, 261 Va. 161, 540 S.E.2d 894 (2001).

Article 17.

Declaratory Judgments.

§ 8.01-184. Power to issue declaratory judgments.

I. Decisions Under Current Law.
  A. General Consideration.
  B. Actual Controversy.

I. DECISIONS UNDER CURRENT LAW.

A. General Consideration.

Circuit court's authority. — Under the declaratory judgment act, circuit courts have the authority to make binding adjudications of right in cases of actual controversy when there is antagonistic assertion and denial of right. Hoffman Family, L.L.C. v. Mill Two Assocs. Partnership, 259 Va. 685, 529 S.E.2d 318 (2000).

Circuit court's discretion. — The authority to enter a declaratory judgment is discretionary and must be exercised with great care and caution. Hoffman Family, L.L.C. v. Mill Two Assocs. Partnership, 259 Va. 685, 529 S.E.2d 318 (2000).

B. Actual Controversy.

Construction of covenant restricting development of property. — It is not always required that a party establish a vested right, in the form of governmental approval to proceed with development, before obtaining a declaratory judgment on the issue of whether some private right would bar that development. While in some cases the proposed development would be so speculative and indefinite as to not rise to the level of a justiciable controversy, where the developer has taken substantial steps, with significant financial expense, in developing specific plans for the development and where, without a determination as to the effect of a covenant affecting the property, the developer would be required to expend additional sums without relief from the uncertainty and insecurity attendant upon the continuing controversy of its legal rights with regard to the covenant, a justiciable controversy exists. Hoffman Family, L.L.C. v. Mill Two Assocs. Partnership, 259 Va. 685, 529 S.E.2d 318 (2000).

§ 8.01-191. Construction of article.

I. DECISIONS UNDER CURRENT LAW.

Applied in Hoffman Family, L.L.C. v. Mill Two Assocs. Partnership, 259 Va. 685, 529 S.E.2d 318 (2000).

Article 18.

Recovery of Claims Against the Commonwealth of Virginia.

§ 8.01-192. How claims to be prosecuted.

Cross references. — As to the liability of the salary of an officer for a debt he owes the Commonwealth, see § 2.2-2816.

I. DECISIONS UNDER CURRENT LAW.

Construction with other laws. — The procurement act, § 11-35, et seq., is a specific statute relating to the acquisition of services by public bodies and prevails over the more general statutes relating to the presentation of pecuniary claims against the commonwealth, such as those found in this section and § 2.1-223.1. Dr. William E.S. Flory Small Bus. Dev. Ctr., Inc. v. Commonwealth, 261 Va. 230, 541 S.E.2d 915 (2001).

Article 18.1.

Tort Claims Against the Commonwealth of Virginia.

§ 8.01-195.1. Short title.

Cross references. — As to sovereign immunity and the Division of Risk Management, see § 2.2-1842.
Law Review.
For a note, "A Duty Not to Become a Victim: Assessing the Plaintiff's Fault in Negligent Security Actions," see 57 Wash. & Lee L. Rev. 611 (2000).

§ 8.01-195.3. Commonwealth, transportation district or locality liable for damages in certain cases.

Law Review.
For a note, "A Duty Not to Become a Victim: Assessing the Plaintiff's Fault in Negligent Security Actions," see 57 Wash. & Lee L. Rev. 611 (2000).

I. DECISIONS UNDER CURRENT LAW.

Exception for execution of court order. — The exception in subsection (4) which precludes any claim "based upon an act or omission of an officer, agent or employee of any agency of government in the execution of a lawful order of any court" did not bar a claim based on the negligence of government employees in treating an incarcerated prisoner in that the plaintiff's claim did not involve employees who were implementing the directives of a court order to provide medical evaluation and care but, rather, employees at a correctional facility who were providing medical care to the plaintiff's decedent because he was an inmate of that facility. Whitley v. Commonwealth, 260 Va. 482, 538 S.E.2d 296 (2000).

Inmate exception. — The exception in subsection (7) requiring the filing of an affidavit with respect to "any claim by an inmate of a state correctional facility," did not apply to a wrongful death action by a deceased inmate's administrator in that the administrator was not an inmate of a correctional facility and there was nothing in the statutory language indicating that a claim filed by an administrator of the estate of a deceased inmate was subject to the affidavit requirement. Whitley v. Commonwealth, 260 Va. 482, 538 S.E.2d 296 (2000).

§ 8.01-195.6. Notice of claim.

I. DECISIONS UNDER CURRENT LAW.

Certified mail exclusive method of giving notice. — Mailing a notice of claim by certified mail, return receipt requested, is the exclusive method of filing a notice of claim against the commonwealth under the Virginia Tort Claims Act and, accordingly, a plaintiff's claim was untimely where the date on the return receipt was more than one year from the date of her injury even though the commonwealth may have had actual notice of the plaintiff's claim and the plaintiff's attorney had hand-delivered a copy of the claim to the appropriate agency within one year. Melanson v. Commonwealth, 261 Va. 178, 539 S.E.2d 433 (2001).

ARTICLE 20.

Change of Name.

§ 8.01-217. How name of person may be changed.

I. Decisions Under Current Law.
  A. General Consideration.
  B. Minors.

I. DECISIONS UNDER CURRENT LAW.

A. General Consideration.

Burden of proving change in children's best interest. — Under this section, where a parent seeks to change the surname of a child, the burden is upon the petitioning parent, under the circumstances, to prove by satisfactory evidence that the change is in the child's best interests. Rowland v. Shurbutt, 259 Va. 305, 525 S.E.2d 917 (2000).

B. Minors.

Mother's petition to change child's name over father's objection. — This section requires that a parent, who seeks to change a child's surname over the objection of the other parent, demonstrate with satisfactory evidence that the requested name change is in the child's best interest. Generally, a change will be ordered only if (1) the father has abandoned the natural ties ordinarily existing between parent and child, (2) the father has engaged in misconduct sufficient to embarrass the child in the continued use of the father's name, (3) the child otherwise will suffer substantial detriment by continuing to bear the father's name or (4) the child is of sufficient age and discretion to make an intelligent choice and he desires that his name be changed. But, a change of name will not be authorized against the father's objection merely to save the mother and child minor inconvenience or embarrassment. May v. Grandy, 259 Va. 629, 528 S.E.2d 105 (2000).

ARTICLE 21.

Miscellaneous Provisions.

§ 8.01-220. Action for alienation of affection, breach of promise, criminal conversation and seduction abolished.

I. DECISIONS UNDER CURRENT LAW.

Name assigned to conduct not dispositive. — When the general assembly enacted this section, it manifested its intent to abolish common law actions seeking damages for a particular type of conduct, regardless of the name that a plaintiff assigns to that conduct. McDermott v. Reynolds, 260 Va. 98, 530 S.E.2d 902 (2000).

Emotional distress claim based on adultery barred. — Where the essential basis of the plaintiff's claim was that the defendant had an adulterous relationship with the plaintiff's wife, which he continued in an open and notorious manner after being confronted by the plaintiff, this alleged conduct was precisely the type of conduct that the general assembly intended to exclude from civil liability when it enacted this section and the fact that the plaintiff labeled his claim as intentional infliction of emotional distress and recited the elements of that tort in support of his action did not shield the action from the statutory bar. McDermott v. Reynolds, 260 Va. 98, 530 S.E.2d 902 (2000).

§ 8.01-225. Persons rendering emergency care, obstetrical services exempt from liability.

Cross references. — As to the Attorney General's duty to provide all legal service in civil matters for the Commonwealth and its entities, see § 2.2-507.

§ 8.01-226.7. Owner and agent compliance with residential lead-based paint notification; maintenance immunity.

Law Review. — For 2000 survey of Virginia property law, see 34 U. Rich. L. Rev. 981 (2000).

CHAPTER 4.

LIMITATIONS OF ACTIONS.

Article 1.

In General.

Sec.
8.01-229. Suspension or tolling of statute of limitations; effect of disabilities; death; injunction; prevention of service by defendant; dismissal,

Sec.
nonsuit or abatement; devise for payment of debts; new promises; debts proved in creditors' suits.
8.01-250. Limitation on certain actions for damages arising out of defective or unsafe condition of improvements to real property.

ARTICLE 1.

In General.

§ 8.01-229. Suspension or tolling of statute of limitations; effect of disabilities; death; injunction; prevention of service by defendant; dismissal, nonsuit or abatement; devise for payment of debts; new promises; debts proved in creditors' suits. — A. Disabilities which toll the statute of limitations. — Except as otherwise specifically provided in §§ 8.01-237, 8.01-241, 8.01-242, 8.01-243, 8.01-243.1 and other provisions of this Code,

1. If a person entitled to bring any action is at the time the cause of action accrues an infant, except if such infant has been emancipated pursuant to Article 15 (§ 16.1-331 et seq.) of Chapter 11 of Title 16.1, or incapacitated, such person may bring it within the prescribed limitation period after such disability is removed; or

2. After a cause of action accrues,

a. If an infant becomes entitled to bring such action, the time during which he is within the age of minority shall not be counted as any part of the period within which the action must be brought except as to any such period during which the infant has been judicially declared emancipated; or

b. If a person entitled to bring such action becomes incapacitated, the time during which he is incapacitated shall not be computed as any part of the period within which the action must be brought, except where a conservator, guardian or committee is appointed for such person in which case an action may be commenced by such conservator, committee or guardian before the expiration of the applicable period of limitation or within one year after his qualification as such, whichever occurs later.

For the purposes of subdivisions 1 and 2 of this subsection, a person shall be deemed incapacitated if he is so adjudged by a court of competent jurisdiction, or if it shall otherwise appear to the court or jury determining the issue that such person is or was incapacitated within the prescribed limitation period.

3. If a convict is or becomes entitled to bring an action against his committee, the time during which he is incarcerated shall not be counted as any part of the period within which the action must be brought.

B. Effect of death of a party. — The death of a person entitled to bring an action or of a person against whom an action may be brought shall toll the statute of limitations as follows:

1. Death of person entitled to bring a personal action. — If a person entitled to bring a personal action dies with no such action pending before the expiration of the limitation period for commencement thereof, then an action may be commenced by the decedent's personal representative before the expiration of the limitation period including the limitation period as provided by subdivision E 3 or within one year after his qualification as personal representative, whichever occurs later.

2. Death of person against whom personal action may be brought. — a. If a person against whom a personal action may be brought dies before the commencement of such action and before the expiration of the limitation period for commencement thereof then a claim may be filed against the decedent's estate or an action may be commenced against the decedent's personal representative before the expiration of the applicable limitation period or within one year after the qualification of such personal representative, whichever occurs later.

b. If a person against whom a personal action may be brought dies before suit papers naming such person as defendant have been filed with the court, then such suit papers may be amended to substitute the decedent's personal representative as party defendant before the expiration of the applicable limitation period or within two years after the date such suit papers were filed with the court, whichever occurs later, and such suit papers shall be taken as properly filed.

3. Effect of death on actions for recovery of realty, or a proceeding for enforcement of certain liens relating to realty. — Upon the death of any person in whose favor or against whom an action for recovery of realty, or a proceeding for enforcement of certain liens relating to realty, may be brought, such right of action shall accrue to or against his successors in interest as provided in Article 2 (§ 8.01-236 et seq.) of this chapter.

4. Accrual of a personal cause of action against the estate of any person subsequent to such person's death. — If a personal cause of action against a decedent accrues subsequent to his death, an action may be brought against the decedent's personal representative or a claim thereon may be filed against the estate of such decedent before the expiration of the applicable limitation period or within two years after the qualification of the decedent's personal representative, whichever occurs later.

5. Accrual of a personal cause of action in favor of decedent. — If a person dies before a personal cause of action which survives would have accrued to him, if he had continued to live, then an action may be commenced by such decedent's personal representative before the expiration of the applicable limitation period or within one year after the qualification of such personal representative, whichever occurs later.

6. Delayed qualification of personal representative. — If there is an interval of more than two years between the death of any person in whose favor or against whom a cause of action has accrued or shall subsequently accrue and the qualification of such person's personal representative, such personal representative shall, for the purposes of this chapter, be deemed to have qualified on the last day of such two-year period.

C. Suspension during injunctions. — When the commencement of any action is stayed by injunction, the time of the continuance of the injunction shall not be computed as any part of the period within which the action must be brought.

D. Obstruction of filing by defendant. — When the filing of an action is obstructed by a defendant's (i) filing a petition in bankruptcy or filing a petition for an extension or arrangement under the United States Bankruptcy Act or (ii) using any other direct or indirect means to obstruct the filing of an action, then the time that such obstruction has continued shall not be counted as any part of the period within which the action must be brought.

E. Dismissal, abatement, or nonsuit.

1. Except as provided in subdivision 3 of this subsection, if any action is commenced within the prescribed limitation period and for any cause abates or is dismissed without determining the merits, the time such action is pending shall not be computed as part of the period within which such action may be brought, and another action may be brought within the remaining period.

2. If a judgment or decree is rendered for the plaintiff in any action commenced within the prescribed limitation period and such judgment or decree is arrested or reversed upon a ground which does not preclude a new action for the same cause, or if there is occasion to bring a new action by reason of the loss or destruction of any of the papers or records in a former action which was commenced within the prescribed limitation period, then a new action may be brought within one year after such arrest or reversal or such loss or destruction, but not after.

3. If a plaintiff suffers a voluntary nonsuit as prescribed in § 8.01-380, the statute of limitations with respect to such action shall be tolled by the commencement of the nonsuited action, and the plaintiff may recommence his action within six months from the date of the order entered by the court, or within the original period of limitation, or within the limitation period as provided by subdivision B 1, whichever period is longer. This tolling provision shall apply irrespective of whether the action is originally filed in a federal or a state court and recommenced in any other court, and shall apply to all actions irrespective of whether they arise under common law or statute.

F. Effect of devise for payment of debts. — No provision in the will of any testator devising his real estate, or any part thereof, subject to the payment of his debts or charging the same therewith, or containing any other provision for the payment of debts, shall prevent this chapter from operating against such debts, unless it plainly appears to be the testator's intent that it shall not so operate.

G. Effect of new promise in writing.

1. If any person against whom a right of action has accrued on any contract, other than a judgment or recognizance, promises, by writing signed by him or his agent, payment of money on such contract, the person to whom the right has accrued may maintain an action for the money so promised, within such number of years after such promise as it might be maintained if such promise were the original cause of action. An acknowledgment in writing, from which a promise of payment may be implied, shall be deemed to be such promise within the meaning of this subsection.

2. The plaintiff may sue on the new promise described in subdivision 1 of this subsection or on the original cause of action, except that when the new promise is of such a nature as to merge the original cause of action then the action shall be only on the new promise.

H. Suspension of limitations in creditors' suits. — When an action is commenced as a general creditors' action, or as a general lien creditors' action, or as an action to enforce a mechanics' lien, the running of the statute of limitations shall be suspended as to debts provable in such action from the commencement of the action, provided they are brought in before the commissioner in chancery under the first reference for an account of debts; but as to claims not so brought in the statute shall continue to run, without interruption by reason either of the commencement of the action or of the order for an account, until a later order for an account, under which they do come in, or they are asserted by petition or independent action.

In actions not instituted originally either as general creditors' actions, or as general lien creditors' actions, but which become such by subsequent proceedings, the statute of limitations shall be suspended by an order of reference for an account of debts or of liens only as to those creditors who come in and prove their claims under the order. As to creditors who come in afterwards by petition or under an order of recommittal, or a later order of reference for an account, the statute shall continue to run without interruption by reason of previous orders until filing of the petition, or until the date of the reference under which they prove their claims, as the case may be.

I. When an action is commenced within a period of thirty days prior to the expiration of the limitation period for commencement thereof and the defending party or parties desire to institute an action as third-party plaintiff against one or more persons not party to the original action, the running of the period of limitation against such action shall be suspended as to such new party for a period of sixty days from the expiration of the applicable limitation period.

J. If any award of compensation by the Workers' Compensation Commission pursuant to Chapter 5 (§ 65.2-500 et seq.) of Title 65.2 is subsequently found void ab initio, other than an award voided for fraudulent procurement of the award by the claimant, the statute of limitations applicable to any civil action upon the same claim or cause of action in a court of this Commonwealth shall be tolled for that period of time during which compensation payments were made.

K. Suspension of limitations during criminal proceedings. In any personal action for damages, if a criminal prosecution arising out of the same facts is commenced, the time such prosecution is pending shall not be computed as part of the period within which such a civil action may be brought. For purposes of this subsection, the time during which a prosecution is pending shall be calculated from the date of the issuance of a warrant, summons or capias, the return or filing of an indictment or information, or the defendant's first appearance in any court as an accused in such a prosecution, whichever date occurs first, until the date of the final judgment or order in the trial court, the date of the final disposition of any direct appeal in state court, or the date on which the time for noting an appeal has expired, whichever date occurs last. Thereafter, the civil action may be brought within the remaining period of the statute or within one year, whichever is longer.

If a criminal prosecution is commenced and a grand jury indictment is returned or a grand jury indictment is waived after the period within which a civil action arising out of the same set of facts may be brought, a civil action may be brought within one year of the date of the final judgment or order in the trial court, the date of the final disposition of any direct appeal in state court, or the date on which the time for noting an appeal has expired, whichever date occurs last, but no more than ten years after the date of the crime or two years after the cause of action shall have accrued under § 8.01-249, whichever date occurs last. (Code 1950, §§ 8-8, 8-13, 8-15, 8-20, 8-21, 8-25, 8-26, 8-29 through 8-34; 1964, c. 219; 1966, c. 118; 1972, c. 825; 1977, c. 617; 1978, cc. 65, 767; 1983, cc. 404, 437; 1986, c. 506; 1987, cc. 294, 645; 1988, c. 711; 1989, c. 588; 1990, c. 280; 1991, cc. 693, 722; 1993, c. 844; 1997, c. 801; 2000, c. 531; 2001, cc. 773, 781.)

The 2001 amendments. — The 2001 amendments by cc. 773 and 781 are identical and added subsection K.

§ 8.01-230

I. Decisions Under Current Law.
   A. General Consideration.
   B. Dismissal, Abatement or Nonsuit.
   C. Effect of New Promise in Writing.
   E. Effect of Disability.

I. DECISIONS UNDER CURRENT LAW.

A. General Consideration.

Applicability to workers' compensation proceedings. — Subdivision A 1 of this section could not be applied to toll limitation period in workers' compensation proceeding. Whetzel v. Waste Management of Virginia, No. 0352-99-3 (Ct. of Appeals Aug. 10, 1999).
In accordance with the provisions of subsection D, the time consumed while the automatic stay afforded by the bankruptcy laws is operative does not count toward the time limits for enforcing a mechanic's lien. Concrete Structures, Inc. v. Tidewater Crane & Rigging Co., — F. Supp. 2d —, 2001 U.S. Dist. LEXIS 3675 (E.D. Va. Mar. 30, 2001).

B. Dismissal, Abatement or Nonsuit.

Subsection E applies to actions filed in federal court, as well as to actions filed in state court, and the time a case is pending in federal court is, accordingly, not computed as part of the statutory period within which suit must be brought. Welding, Inc. v. Bland County Serv. Auth., 261 Va. 218, 541 S.E.2d 909 (2001).
Tolling of time to bring contract action against public body. — There is no conflict between this section and § 11-69 (see § 2.2-4363), establishing the time limit for filing a contract action against a public body, because § 11-69 does not address the tolling of actions, which is the subject of this section; the time limit for filing suit established by § 11-69 thus may be extended due to application of this statutory tolling provision. Welding, Inc. v. Bland County Serv. Auth., 261 Va. 218, 541 S.E.2d 909 (2001).

C. Effect of New Promise in Writing.

Statute of limitations revived. — Subsection G. provides that if a person who is liable for a debt on a contract makes a new written promise to pay the debt on that contract, then the person owed the debt may maintain an action for the money so promised within a revived statute of limitations running from the date of the new promise. Cadle Co. v. Berkeley Plaza Assocs., No. 99-1908 (4th Cir. May 17, 2000).
Intent of parties may be question of fact. — The question of whether the terms of a writing constituted a new promise to pay turns upon the intent of the alleged promisor and, if there is more than one permissible inference as to intent to be drawn from the language employed, the question of the parties' actual intention is a triable issue of fact. Cadle Co. v. Berkeley Plaza Assocs., No. 99-1908 (4th Cir. May 17, 2000).

E. Effect of Disability.

Infancy. — An infant may bring an action by a next friend at any time during the continuance of his infancy or, after the disability is removed, in his own name within such time as allowed under this section and the prescribed limitation period. Rivera v. Nedrich, 259 Va. 1, 529 S.E.2d 310 (2000).

§ 8.01-230. Accrual of right of action.

I. Decisions Under Current Law.
   A. General Consideration.
   B. Torts.
      1. In General.
   C. Contracts.

I. DECISIONS UNDER CURRENT LAW.

A. General Consideration.

Accrual of cause of action. — Under Virginia law, a claim of injury to person or property accrues when the injury is sustained and a cause of action for breach of contract occurs at the time of the breach. Al-Abood v. El-Shamari, 217 F.3d 225 (4th Cir. 2000).

B. Torts.

1. In General.

Continuing torts. — In arguing for application of the rule that the statute of limitations runs separately where there are discrete instances of wrongdoing, the plaintiff seeking to recover in trespass for damage to its property caused by the migration of petroleum hydrocarbons from the defendant's property overlooked the fact that the migration did not occur in distinct episodes; rather, the migration occurred continuously throughout the decade and, under these circumstances, the plaintiff's cause of action accrued when the hydrocarbons first migrated onto its land and was barred five years later. First Va. Banks, Inc. v. BP Exploration & Oil Co., 206 F.3d 404 (4th Cir. 2000).

C. Contracts.

Promissory notes. — A cause of action on a note accrues when the obligation to pay is breached and, accordingly, where a note contains a due date and the promisor fails to make payment on that date, the cause of action accrues at that time. Rivera v. Nedrich, 259 Va. 1, 529 S.E.2d 310 (2000).

§ 8.01-231. Commonwealth not within statute of limitations.

I. DECISIONS UNDER CURRENT LAW.

Time does not run against the State. No statute of limitations applies to the commonwealth unless the statute expressly so provides. Barr v. S.W. Rodgers Co., 33 Va. App. 273, 532 S.E.2d 920 (2000).

ARTICLE 2.

Limitations on Recovery of Realty and Enforcement of Certain Liens Relating to Realty.

§ 8.01-236. Limitation of entry on or action for land.

I. Decisions Under Current Law.
  C. Requisites for Adverse Possession.

I. DECISIONS UNDER CURRENT LAW.

  C. Requisites for Adverse Possession.

Burden of proof. — The claimant bears the burden of proving the elements of adverse possession by clear and convincing evidence. Kim v. Douval Corp., 259 Va. 752, 529 S.E.2d 92 (2000).

It is well established that a claimant's possession is "hostile" if it is under a claim of right and adverse to the right of the true owner. Kim v. Douval Corp., 259 Va. 752, 529 S.E.2d 92 (2000).

A claim of right can be inferred from unequivocal conduct that is inconsistent with any other reasonable inference. Kim v. Douval Corp., 259 Va. 752, 529 S.E.2d 92 (2000).

Inference of claim of right question for jury. — Whether the conduct relied upon to support an inference of a claim of right is sufficient to establish such a claim is generally a question for the jury. Kim v. Douval Corp., 259 Va. 752, 529 S.E.2d 92 (2000).

Intent to use land to exclusion of others. — The phrase "claim of right," when used in the context of adverse possession, refers to the intent of a claimant to use land as the claimant's own to the exclusion of all others; the existence of a claim of right does not depend on the claimant having any actual title or right to the property. Kim v. Douval Corp., 259 Va. 752, 529 S.E.2d 92 (2000).

Entry with permission of owner. — Where the original entry on another's land was by agreement or permission, possession regardless of its duration presumptively continues as it began, in the absence of an explicit disclaimer. Kim v. Douval Corp., 259 Va. 752, 529 S.E.2d 92 (2000).

ARTICLE 3.

Personal Actions Generally.

§ 8.01-243. Personal action for injury to person or property generally; extension in actions for malpractice against health care provider.

I. Decisions Under Current Law.
  B. Proceedings to Which Section Applicable.
    1. In General.
    3. Civil Rights Actions.
    4. Wrongs Affecting Property and Property Rights.

I. DECISIONS UNDER CURRENT LAW.
B. Proceedings to Which Section Applicable.
1. In General.

Trademark infringement. — The two-year statute of limitations under this section applies to claims of trademark infringement. Teaching Co. Ltd. Partnership v. Unapix Entertainment, Inc., 87 F. Supp. 2d 567 (E.D. Va. 2000).

3. Civil Rights Actions.

Consequences of failure to promote not continuing violation. — Because the plaintiff's failure-to-promote claim was based on events that occurred more than two years before suit was filed, the plaintiff's claim was barred by this section even though the plaintiff alleged repeated assignment to menial tasks following the alleged wrongful conduct. The consequences of a failure to promote do not rise to the standards of a continuing violation of § 1981 for purposes of the statute of limitations. Thompson v. Town of Front Royal, — F. Supp. 2d —, 2000 U.S. Dist. LEXIS 3876 (W.D. Va. Mar. 16, 2000).

4. Wrongs Affecting Property and Property Rights.

Migration of petroleum hydrocarbons onto property was continuous. — The five-year statute of limitations barred the plaintiff's trespass action for damage to its property caused by the migration of petroleum hydrocarbons from property formerly owned by the defendant where the cause of action accrued, at the latest, when the hydrocarbons were discovered on the plaintiff's property and, since the migration did not occur in distinct episodes but was continuous over a decade, there was no basis for applying later, separate accrual dates. First Va. Banks, Inc. v. BP Exploration & Oil Co., 206 F.3d 404 (4th Cir. 2000).

§ 8.01-246. Personal actions based on contracts.

I. Decisions Under Current Law.
B. Proceedings to Which Section Applicable.
1. Actions on Written Contracts.

I. DECISIONS UNDER CURRENT LAW.
B. Proceedings to Which Section Applicable.
1. Actions on Written Contracts.

This section applies to a promissory note. Rivera v. Nedrich, 259 Va. 1, 529 S.E.2d 310 (2000).

§ 8.01-249. When cause of action shall be deemed to accrue in certain personal actions.

I. Decisions Under Current Law.
A. General Consideration.

I. DECISIONS UNDER CURRENT LAW.
A. General Consideration.

Discovery rule in fraud cases. — Generally, actions in Virginia do not accrue when the resulting damage is discovered but there is an exception for actions for fraud; a claim for fraud accrues when the fraud is or should have been discovered in the exercise of due diligence. Al-Abood v. El-Shamari, 217 F.3d 225 (4th Cir. 2000).

Trademark infringement. — Under trademark law, a cause of action is complete and the statute of limitations begins to run when, on all the facts and circumstances, a plaintiff concludes or should conclude that a likelihood of confusion is present, not merely when a confusingly similar use is uncovered. The plaintiff has no obligation to sue until the likelihood of confusion looms large. Teaching Co. Ltd. Partnership v. Unapix Entertainment, Inc., 87 F. Supp. 2d 567 (E.D. Va. 2000).

§ 8.01-250. Limitation on certain actions for damages arising out of defective or unsafe condition of improvements to real property. — No action to recover for any injury to property, real or personal, or for bodily injury

or wrongful death, arising out of the defective and unsafe condition of an improvement to real property, nor any action for contribution or indemnity for damages sustained as a result of such injury, shall be brought against any person performing or furnishing the design, planning, surveying, supervision of construction, or construction of such improvement to real property more than five years after the performance or furnishing of such services and construction.

The limitation prescribed in this section shall not apply to the manufacturer or supplier of any equipment or machinery or other articles installed in a structure upon real property, nor to any person in actual possession and in control of the improvement as owner, tenant or otherwise at the time the defective or unsafe condition of such improvement constitutes the proximate cause of the injury or damage for which the action is brought; rather each such action shall be brought within the time next after such injury occurs as provided in §§ 8.01-243 and 8.01-246. (Code 1950, § 8-24.2; 1964, c. 333; 1968, c. 103; 1973, c. 247; 1977, c. 617.)

Editor's note. — The section above is set out to correct an error in the bound volume.

I. Decisions Under Current Law.
 B. Manufacturers and Suppliers of Equipment and Machinery.

I. DECISIONS UNDER CURRENT LAW.

B. Manufacturers and Suppliers of Equipment and Machinery.

Circuit breaker on pier was equipment. — A plaintiff's action arising out of the explosion of a circuit breaker the plaintiff was installing in a switchgear was not barred in that the switchgear and circuit breaker were "equipment" and not building materials where the switchgear and circuit breaker were not part of the electrical system of the pier on which they were installed but, instead, comprised the electrical system for submarines docked at the pier, the switchgear and circuit breakers were each self-contained and fully assembled by their respective manufacturers and the switchgear and circuit breakers were not fungible or generic materials. Cooper Indus., Inc. v. Melendez, 260 Va. 578, 537 S.E.2d 580 (2000).

Article 5.

Miscellaneous Limitations Provisions.

§ 8.01-255. Time for presenting claim against Commonwealth.

Cross references. — As to referral of time-barred claims to Governor for such payment as he directs, see § 2.2-816. As to the liability of the salary of an officer for a debt he owes the Commonwealth, see § 2.2-2816.

CHAPTER 5.

Venue.

§ 8.01-258. Venue not jurisdictional.

I. DECISIONS UNDER CURRENT LAW.

Collateral proceeding. — Even if it was assumed that a defendant was a non-resident of Virginia at the time he was adjudicated an habitual offender, where the habitual offender proceeding was brought was a matter of venue, not jurisdiction, and since the court had subject matter jurisdiction over the habitual offender proceeding, the defendant could not collaterally attack the adjudication in a later proceeding. Tyson v. Commonwealth, No. 2965-98-3 (Ct. of Appeals Mar. 28, 2000).

Applied in Tyson v. Commonwealth, No. 2965-98-3 (Ct. of Appeals Mar. 28, 2000).

§ 8.01-261. Category A or preferred venue.

Cross references. — As to the venue for proceedings under the Administrative Process Act, see § 2.2-4003.

§ 8.01-264. Venue improperly laid; objection.

I. DECISIONS UNDER CURRENT LAW.

Waiver. — An objection to venue is waived if not raised in a timely manner. Tyson v. Commonwealth, No. 2965-98-3 (Ct. of Appeals Mar. 28, 2000).

CHAPTER 7.

CIVIL ACTIONS; COMMENCEMENT, PLEADINGS, AND MOTIONS.

ARTICLE 2.

Pleadings Generally.

§ 8.01-271.1. Signing of pleadings, motions, and other papers; oral motions; sanctions.

I. DECISIONS UNDER CURRENT LAW.

Policy considerations. — The possibility of a sanction can protect litigants from the mental anguish and expense of frivolous assertions of unfounded factual and legal claims and against the assertions of valid claims for improper purposes but the threat of a sanction should not be used to stifle counsel in advancing novel legal theories or asserting a client's rights in a doubtful case. Gilmore v. Finn, 259 Va. 448, 527 S.E.2d 426 (2000).

An objective standard of "reasonableness" is applied, etc.

The Supreme Court applies an objective standard of reasonableness in order to determine whether a litigant and his attorney, after reasonable inquiry, could have formed a reasonable belief that a pleading was warranted by existing law or a good faith argument for the extension, modification, or reversal of existing law. Gilmore v. Finn, 259 Va. 448, 527 S.E.2d 426 (2000).

The statutory standard does not require that the court decide that the challenged pleading was actually warranted by existing law but, rather, whether the party filing such pleading could have formed a reasonable belief that his action was warranted by existing law or a good faith argument for the extension, modification, or reversal of existing law; the wisdom of hindsight should be avoided in applying the appropriate objectively-reasonable standard of review. Gilmore v. Finn, 259 Va. 448, 527 S.E.2d 426 (2000).

Separate claims considered separately. — The factual and legal viability of separate claims are individually assessed for sanction purposes and the fact that one claim may not have been well grounded in fact may not justify an award of sanctions where this claim was an inessential part of a unitary claim on which the party could, if correct on another part of the claim, obtain the relief sought. Gilmore v. Finn, 259 Va. 448, 527 S.E.2d 426 (2000).

Sanctions upheld. — Trial court did not err in sanctioning father in amount of $ 300 for his repeated attempts to have case referred to mediation. Summers v. Summers, No. 1968-98-4 (Ct. of Appeals Aug. 3, 1999).

Court may award sanctions sua sponte.
— A trial court is authorized to impose sanctions against a party based upon evidence that he filed a motion in order to harass the otherparty and make him expend attorney's fees regardless of whether the other party requests sanctions in his pleadings. Gallahan v. Flood, No. 0479-00-4 (Ct. of Appeals Aug. 8, 2000).

The Governor is not above the law and, where appropriate, is fully subject to the imposition of sanctions under this section. Gilmore v. Finn, 259 Va. 448, 527 S.E.2d 426 (2000).

Actions filed by Governor. — While the Governor's action in filing a suit is not clothed with a dispositive presumption of reasonableness or good faith, when the governor asserts a legal contention in the context of fulfilling the duty to protect the welfare of one or all the citizens of the commonwealth acting in the capacity as parens patriae, any doubts about the good faith of that action should be resolved in favor of the governor's contention; it is only when the governor's legal contention is totally without merit that his action is appropriately sanctioned. Gilmore v. Finn, 259 Va. 448, 527 S.E.2d 426 (2000).

The Governor's legal assertion that § 54.1-2990 prohibited the withdrawal of artificially administered hydration and nutrition from an individual in a persistent vegetative state because such withdrawal would initiate the dying process rather than merely permit the natural process of dying, while ultimately incorrect, was nevertheless not totally without merit; it could not be said that this interpretation had no reasonable possibility of being judicially adopted at the time this assertion was made in the trial court or that the Governor's assertion that a conflict existed between the provisions of § 54.1-2990 and § 54.1-2986 lacked any objectively reasonable basis and the trial court erred, therefore, in awarding sanctions. Gilmore v. Finn, 259 Va. 448, 527 S.E.2d 426 (2000).

§ 8.01-275.1. When service of process is timely.

I. DECISIONS UNDER CURRENT LAW.

No variance between rule and statute. — There is no variance between Rule 3:3(c) and this section in that both of these provisions seek to promote a policy of timely prosecution of law suits and to avoid abuse of the judicial system; the statute, but not the rule, defines timely service as one year while the rule implies that timely service means service within one year. Both the rule and the statute allow a plaintiff to establish the exercise of due diligence to perfect service within the one year period. Waterman v. Halverson, 261 Va. 203, 540 S.E.2d 867 (2001).

Rule permitting nonsuit prior to service not nullified or invalidated. — There is no basis to conclude that the enactment of this section nullified or invalidated the cases construing Rule 3:3(c) and holding that the failure to comply with the one-year service provision of the rule does not preclude a trial court from granting a plaintiff's motion for nonsuit and that the refiled action is entitled to the tolling provisions of § 8.01-229(E)(3). Waterman v. Halverson, 261 Va. 203, 540 S.E.2d 867 (2001).

CHAPTER 8.

Process.

Article 3.

Who and Where to Serve Process.

§ 8.01-293. Who to serve process.

Cross references. — As to the establishment of compulsory minimum entry level, in-service and advanced training standards for deputy sheriffs designated to serve process pursuant to the provisions of this section, see § 9.1-102.

Article 4.

Who to Be Served.

§ 8.01-296. Manner of serving process upon natural persons.

I. Decisions Under Current Law.
A. General Consideration.

I. DECISIONS UNDER CURRENT LAW.

A. General Consideration.

Presumption of proper service. — Court could presume that officer personally served defendant in compliance with subdivision (1) of this section, where adjudication order reflected that defendant had been served. Tyson v. Commonwealth, No. 2965-98-3 (Ct. of Appeals Mar. 28, 2000).

Presumption that order properly served. — A show cause order would have been served by a public officer and, where the adjudication order reflected that the party was served, the court in a collateral proceeding could presume that the officer personally served the party in compliance with this section. Tyson v. Commonwealth, No. 2965-98-3 (Ct. of Appeals Mar. 28, 2000).

Applied in Fredriksen v. Commonwealth, No. 0732-98-4 (Ct. of Appeals June 22, 1999).

§ 8.01-299. How process served on domestic corporations generally.

I. DECISIONS UNDER CURRENT LAW.

Applicability. — The thrust of this section concerns the initial service of process on a domestic corporation rather than interim service of notice for subsequent hearings and other proceedings, such as the filing of a praecipe, after the parties are properly before the court. Fredericksburg Constr. Co. v. J.W. Wyne Excavating, Inc., 260 Va. 137, 530 S.E.2d 148 (2000).

§ 8.01-301. How process served on foreign corporations generally.

C. PERSONS WHO MAY BE SERVED.

Service on registered agent not required. — The fact that the person on whom service was effected is not the registered agent of a foreign corporation is not dispositive as an agent's authority to accept service may be implied in fact. Davies v. Jobs & Adverts Online, GmbH, 94 F. Supp. 2d 719 (E.D. Va. 2000).

Service on attorney insufficient. — Where the plaintiff presented no evidence to establish that the defendant, a foreign corporation, either explicitly or implicitly authorized its local counsel to accept service of process or that the attorney ever represented to anyone that he had such authority, service on the attorney was insufficient. Davies v. Jobs & Adverts Online, GmbH, 94 F. Supp. 2d 719 (E.D. Va. 2000).

§ 8.01-314. *Service* on attorney after entry of general appearance by such *attorney.*

I. DECISIONS UNDER CURRENT LAW.

Applied in Owens v. Commonwealth, No. 1060-98-2 (Ct. of Appeals May 4, 1999).

§ 8.01-319. Publication of interim notice.

I. DECISIONS UNDER CURRENT LAW.

Applies to corporations. — An unrepresented litigant who wishes to be informed of the proceedings must either keep the court advised of where service may be accomplished or retain counsel upon whom service may be had. We see no reason why this rule should not apply to corporations as well as natural persons. Fredericksburg Constr. Co. v. J.W. Wyne Excavating, Inc., 260 Va. 137, 530 S.E.2d 148 (2000).

CHAPTER 9.

PERSONAL JURISDICTION IN CERTAIN ACTIONS.

Sec.
8.01-328.1. When personal jurisdiction over person may be exercised.

Sec.
8.01-329. Service of process or notice; service on Secretary of Commonwealth.

§ 8.01-328. Person defined.

I. DECISIONS UNDER CURRENT LAW.

Applied in Glumiha Bank v. D.C. Diamond Corp., 259 Va. 312, 527 S.E.2d 775 (2000).

§ 8.01-328.1. When personal jurisdiction over person may be exercised. — A. A court may exercise personal jurisdiction over a person, who acts directly or by an agent, as to a cause of action arising from the person's:

1. Transacting any business in this Commonwealth;
2. Contracting to supply services or things in this Commonwealth;
3. Causing tortious injury by an act or omission in this Commonwealth;
4. Causing tortious injury in this Commonwealth by an act or omission outside this Commonwealth if he regularly does or solicits business, or engages in any other persistent course of conduct, or derives substantial revenue from goods used or consumed or services rendered, in this Commonwealth;
5. Causing injury in this Commonwealth to any person by breach of warranty expressly or impliedly made in the sale of goods outside this Commonwealth when he might reasonably have expected such person to use, consume, or be affected by the goods in this Commonwealth, provided that he also regularly does or solicits business, or engages in any other persistent course of conduct, or derives substantial revenue from goods used or consumed or services rendered in this Commonwealth;
6. Having an interest in, using, or possessing real property in this Commonwealth;
7. Contracting to insure any person, property, or risk located within this Commonwealth at the time of contracting;
8. Having (i) executed an agreement in this Commonwealth which obligates the person to pay spousal support or child support to a domiciliary of this Commonwealth, or to a person who has satisfied the residency requirements in suits for annulments or divorce for members of the armed forces pursuant to § 20-97 provided proof of service of process on a nonresident party is made by a law-enforcement officer or other person authorized to serve process in the jurisdiction where the nonresident party is located, (ii) been ordered to pay spousal support or child support pursuant to an order entered by any court of competent jurisdiction in this Commonwealth having in personam jurisdiction over such person, or (iii) shown by personal conduct in this Commonwealth, as alleged by affidavit, that the person conceived or fathered a child in this Commonwealth;
9. Having maintained within this Commonwealth a matrimonial domicile at the time of separation of the parties upon which grounds for divorce or separate maintenance is based, or at the time a cause of action arose for divorce or separate maintenance or at the time of commencement of such suit, if the other party to the matrimonial relationship resides herein; or
10. Having incurred a tangible personal property tax liability to any political subdivision of the Commonwealth.

Jurisdiction in subdivision 9 is valid only upon proof of service of process pursuant to § 8.01-296 on the nonresident party by a person authorized under the provisions of § 8.01-320. Jurisdiction under subdivision 8 (iii) of this subsection is valid only upon proof of personal service on a nonresident pursuant to § 8.01-320.

B. Using a computer or computer network located in the Commonwealth shall constitute an act in the Commonwealth. For purposes of this subsection, "use" and "computer network" shall have the same meanings as those contained in § 18.2-152.2.

C. When jurisdiction over a person is based solely upon this section, only a cause of action arising from acts enumerated in this section may be asserted against him; however, nothing contained in this chapter shall limit, restrict or otherwise affect the jurisdiction of any court of this Commonwealth over foreign corporations which are subject to service of process pursuant to the provisions of any other statute. (Code 1950, § 8-81.2; 1964, c. 331; 1977, c. 617; 1978, c. 132; 1981, c. 6; 1982, c. 313; 1983, c. 428; 1984, c. 609; 1986, c. 275; 1987, c. 594; 1988, cc. 866, 878; 1992, c. 571; 1999, cc. 886, 904, 905; 2001, c. 221.)

The 2001 amendments. — The 2001 amendment by c. 221, in subsection A, deleted "or" at the end of subdivision 8, added "or" at the end of subdivision 9, added subdivision 10, and deleted "of this subsection" following "subdivision 9" in the last paragraph of subsection A.

I. Decisions Under Current Law.
　A. General Consideration.
　B. Transacting Business.
　　2. Minimum Contacts.
　　3. What Constitutes Transacting Business.
　C. Tortious Injury.
　　1. In General.
　　4. Acts or Omissions Outside the Commonwealth.

I. DECISIONS UNDER CURRENT LAW.

　A. General Consideration.

Personal jurisdiction categorized as specific or general. — Specific personal jurisdiction is exercised where the matter before the court arises out of or relates to the nonresident defendant's contacts with the forum whereas general personal jurisdiction is exercised where the matter is not one arising out of or related to the nonresident defendant's contacts with the forum; the former may be based on less significant contacts, while the latter requires more substantial contacts. Heathmount A.E. Corp. v. Technodome.com, 106 F. Supp. 2d 860 (E.D. Va. 2000).

When jurisdiction is sought pursuant to a long-arm statute, a dual analysis is normally required — It is well-settled that the resolution of a challenge to in personam jurisdiction involves a two-step inquiry. First, a court must determine whether the particular facts and circumstances of the case fall within the reach of this section and second, a court must decide whether the long-arm statute's reach in the case exceeds its constitutional grasp, namely, whether the exercise of personal jurisdiction in the matter is consistent with traditional notions of fair play and substantial justice under the due process clause. Alitalia-Linee Aeree Italiane S.p.A. v. Casinoalitalia.com, 128 F. Supp. 2d 340 (E.D. Va. 2001).

Burden of proof.

A plaintiff must disprove the presence of personal jurisdiction in order to proceed in rem, and bears the burden to demonstrate some indicia of due diligence in trying to establish personal jurisdiction over an individual who has been identified as a potential defendant but is not subject to jurisdiction. Alitalia-Linee Aeree Italiane S.p.A. v. Casinoalitalia.com, 128 F. Supp. 2d 340 (E.D. Va. 2001).

Foreseeability.

As a corollary to the "purposeful availment" requirement, courts consider whether the putative nonresident defendant could reasonably have anticipated being haled into court in the forum state. These requirements protect a defendant from being subjected to personal jurisdiction as a result of fortuitous, attenuated or random contacts, or as a result of the unilateral activity of another party. Heathmount A.E. Corp. v. Technodome.com, 106 F. Supp. 2d 860 (E.D. Va. 2000).

Default may constitute admission of jurisdictional facts. — Where a defendant is in default under the Virginia rules of procedure, the trial court properly can find the factual allegations of the motion for judgment accurate as those allegations relate to personal jurisdiction under this section. Glumina Bank v. D.C. Diamond Corp., 259 Va. 312, 527 S.E.2d 775 (2000).

Jurisdiction in federal question cases. — In federal question cases in which there is no provision for nationwide service of process, a federal court in Virginia is required to apply an in personam jurisdiction test very similar to that used in diversity cases which, under the long-arm statute, extends jurisdiction over nonresidents who engage in some purposeful activity in Virginia to the extent permissible under the due process clause of the constitution. Weinstein v. Todd Marine Enters., Inc., 115 F. Supp. 2d 668 (E.D. Va. 2000).

Applied in Masselli & Lane, PC v. Miller & Schuh, PA, No. 99-2440 (4th Cir. May 30, 2000).

B. Transacting Business.

2. Minimum Contacts.

General and specific jurisdiction. — When a defendant's contacts with the forum state are continuous and systematic, a court may exercise general personal jurisdiction over the defendant. In the absence of continuous and systematic contacts, a court may still exercise specific personal jurisdiction when the contacts relate to the cause of action and create a substantial connection with the forum state. Diamond Healthcare of Ohio, Inc. v. Humility of Mary Health Partners, 229 F.3d 448 (4th Cir. 2000).

When a suit does not arise out of the defendant's activities in the forum state, the requisite minimum contacts between the defendant and the forum state must be continuous and systematic, whereas when a suit arises out of the defendant's activities within the forum state, then a court may exercise specific jurisdiction, and the contacts need not be so extensive, but the fair-warning requirement inherent in due process still demands that the defendant purposely directed its activities at the forum. Weinstein v. Todd Marine Enters., Inc., 115 F. Supp. 2d 668 (E.D. Va. 2000).

Due process requirements for specific jurisdiction. — To satisfy due process in the exercise of specific personal jurisdiction, the nature and quality of the nonresident defendant's contacts with the forum must be significant in relation to the specific cause of action and this requires a showing that the defendant purposefully directed his activities at residents of the forum thereby availing himself of the privilege of conducting activities therein and invoking the benefits and protections of the forum's laws. Heathmount A.E. Corp. v. Technodome.com, 106 F. Supp. 2d 860 (E.D. Va. 2000).

Defendant must purposefully avail itself of privilege of conducting activities in forum state.

To establish minimum contacts with the forum state, the actions initiated by the defendant must be purposefully directed at the forum state, creating a substantial connection with that state. Weinstein v. Todd Marine Enters., Inc., 115 F. Supp. 2d 668 (E.D. Va. 2000).

Although lack of physical presence in the forum is not dispositive as to the existence of minimum contacts, jurisdiction is only appropriate where a defendant has purposefully directed his activities at residents of the forum and the litigation results from alleged injuries that arise out of or relate to those activities. America Online, Inc. v. Huang, 106 F. Supp. 2d 848 (E.D. Va. 2000).

A defendant must have purposefully availed itself of the privilege of conducting activities within the forum state to ensure that a defendant will not be haled into a jurisdiction solely as a result of random, fortuitous or attenuated contacts. America Online, Inc. v. Huang, 106 F. Supp. 2d 848 (E.D. Va. 2000).

Contract with resident insufficient. — It is settled that a contract between a resident of the forum state and a nonresident defendant does not, by itself, provide sufficient minimum contacts for personal jurisdiction and that the jurisdictional analysis must focus on the circumstances of the contract negotiations, the contract's execution and the relationship the contract has to the forum state. America Online, Inc. v. Huang, 106 F. Supp. 2d 848 (E.D. Va. 2000).

Minimum contacts held not present.

The plaintiff failed to establish that the defendant had sufficient contacts with Virginia to support personal jurisdiction in an action for breach of contract where the plaintiff, a Virginia corporation, had initiated the contractual relationship in Ohio, the resulting agreement contemplated the bulk of the contract's performance in Ohio and, although there were frequent communications and management activities between the plaintiff's Virginia office and the site of the work in Ohio, most of these were between the plaintiff's employees in Virginia and its own employees in Ohio. Diamond Healthcare of Ohio, Inc. v. Humility of Mary Health Partners, 229 F.3d 448 (4th Cir. 2000).

The fact that a seller of yachts advertised in several national magazines that were distributed in Virginia, that advertisements for boats sold by the seller could be accessed via the Internet from a computer located within Virginia and that the seller mailed product information directly into Virginia was insufficient to establish sufficient contacts with Virginia to give the court general jurisdiction over the seller. Weinstein v. Todd Marine Enters., Inc., 115 F. Supp. 2d 668 (E.D. Va. 2000).

Registration of internet domain name sufficient. — Where it was undisputed that the registrant of an internet domain name was a California resident and that he had registered the name with a corporation that had its principal place of business in Virginia, this minimum contact was sufficient to satisfy due process as well as to support in personam jurisdiction pursuant to this section. Lucent Technologies, Inc. v. Lucentsucks.Com, 95 F. Supp. 2d 528 (E.D. Va. 2000).

Registration of internet domain name insufficient. — The defendant's two domain name registration agreements with a registrar located in Virginia were not sufficient contacts with Virginia for purposes of personal jurisdiction over the defendant in an action arising from the registration of those domain names. America Online, Inc. v. Huang, 106 F. Supp. 2d 848 (E.D. Va. 2000).

A nonresident's mere registration of an Internet domain name with a Virginia registrar was insufficient, standing alone, to create personal jurisdiction over the nonresident. Heathmount A.E. Corp. v. Technodome.com, 106 F. Supp. 2d 860 (E.D. Va. 2000).

3. What Constitutes Transacting Business.

Common factors. — If personal jurisdiction is allegedly based on a single contact, the factors commonly examined by courts to determine whether business has indeed been transacted within the state include: (1) where the contracting and negotiations occurred; (2) who initiated the contact; (3) the extent of the communication; and (4) where the contractual obligations were to be performed. Masselli & Lane, PC v. Miller & Schuh, PA, No. 99-2440 (4th Cir. May 30, 2000).

Legal representation and initiation of contact. — When a case involves legal representation by an out-of-state law firm, courts emphasize the importance of the second factor, namely, who initiated the contact. Masselli & Lane, PC v. Miller & Schuh, PA, No. 99-2440 (4th Cir. May 30, 2000).

Advertising and solicitation of the defendant's products was not a sufficient basis to assert general jurisdiction over the defendant. Chiapua Components Ltd. v. West Bend Co., 95 F. Supp. 2d 505 (E.D. Va. 2000).

Contract to transfer funds. — The plaintiffs' cause of action for breach of contract clearly arose from the defendant bank's "contracting to supply services or things in this Commonwealth," in the language of this section, where the bank, in accord with a prior course of dealing, had contracted to transfer funds deposited by one of the plaintiffs to the plaintiffs in Virginia on a certain date and failed to honor this obligation. Glumina Bank v. D.C. Diamond Corp., 259 Va. 312, 527 S.E.2d 775 (2000).

Contracting for local firm to perform work in state. — It is settled that a nonresident transacts business in Virginia where the nonresident establishes an ongoing contractual relationship with a Virginia firm that requires the latter to perform work in Virginia. America Online, Inc. v. Huang, 106 F. Supp. 2d 848 (E.D. Va. 2000).

C. Tortious Injury.

1. In General.

Sufficiency of contacts over internet. — A plaintiff failed to establish that the court had personal jurisdiction over the nonresident defendants where the defendants appeared to have done nothing more than place information on a pornographic web site with knowledge of the possibility that someone in Virginia might access the site. There was no evidence that the defendants sold products in Virginia, had employees in Virginia, held meetings in Virginia or conducted advertising or other promotional activity directed specifically to Virginia and, even taking the plaintiff's allegations of e-mail and credit card solicitation on the web site as true, the record was abundantly void of evidence that the defendants, through their web site, purposely availed themselves of the benefits of Virginia law or purposely directed their activities at the plaintiff. Roche v. Worldwide Media, Inc., 90 F. Supp. 2d 714 (E.D. Va. 2000).

4. Acts or Omissions Outside the Commonwealth.

Online gambling operation. — The operator of an online gambling site was subject to personal jurisdiction in a Virginia trademark action, even though all of its operations were conducted in the Dominican Republic, where the defendant's use of the domain name at issue constituted a tort, the tort was committed outside of Virginia, the tort caused injury in Virginia in that it was likely to cause confusion, mistake, and deception of Virginia consumers, and the defendant engaged in a persistent course of conduct in Virginia through its maintenance of an interactive web site accessible to Virginia consumers 24 hours a day. Alitalia-Linee Aeree Italiane S.p.A. v. Casinoalitalia.com, 128 F. Supp. 2d 340 (E.D. Va. 2001).

§ 8.01-329. Service of process or notice; service on Secretary of Commonwealth. — A. When the exercise of personal jurisdiction is authorized by this chapter, service of process or notice may be made in the same manner as is provided for in Chapter 8 (§ 8.01-285 et seq.) of this title in any other case in which personal jurisdiction is exercised over such a party, or process or notice may be served on any agent of such person in the county or city in this Commonwealth in which that agent resides or on the Secretary of the Commonwealth of Virginia, hereinafter referred to in this section as the "Secretary," who, for this purpose, shall be deemed to be the statutory agent of such person.

B. When service is to be made on the Secretary, the party or his agent or attorney seeking service shall file an affidavit with the court, stating either (i) that the person to be served is a nonresident or (ii) that, after exercising due diligence, the party seeking service has been unable to locate the person to be served. In either case, such affidavit shall set forth the last known address of the person to be served. For the mailing, by the clerk to the party or his agent or attorney, in accordance with subsection C, of verification of the effective date of service of process, the person filing an affidavit may leave a self-addressed, stamped envelope with the clerk.

When the person to be served is a resident, the signature of an attorney, party or agent of the person seeking service on such affidavit shall constitute a certificate by him that process has been delivered to the sheriff or to a disinterested person as permitted by § 8.01-293 for execution and, if the sheriff or disinterested person was unable to execute such service, that the person seeking service has made a bona fide attempt to determine the actual place of abode or location of the person to be served.

C. Service of such process or notice on the Secretary shall be made by the plaintiff's, his agent's or the sheriff's leaving a copy of the process or notice, together with a copy of the affidavit called for in subsection B hereof and the fee prescribed in § 2.2-409 in the office of the Secretary in the City of Richmond, Virginia. Service of process or notice on the Secretary may be made by mail if such service otherwise meets the requirements of this section. Such service shall be sufficient upon the person to be served, provided that notice of such service, a copy of the process or notice, and a copy of the affidavit are forthwith mailed by certified mail, return receipt requested, by the Secretary to the person or persons to be served at the last known post-office address of such person, and a certificate of compliance herewith by the Secretary or someone designated by him for that purpose and having knowledge of such compliance, shall be forthwith filed with the papers in the action. Service of process or notice on the Secretary shall be effective on the date the certificate of compliance is filed with the court in which the action is pending. Upon receipt of the certificate of compliance, the clerk of the court shall mail verification of the date the certificate of compliance was filed with the court to the person who filed the affidavit required by subsection B hereof, in the self-addressed, stamped envelope, if any, provided to the clerk at the time of filing of the affidavit. The clerk shall not be required to mail verification unless the self-addressed, stamped envelope has been provided.

D. Service of process in actions brought on a warrant or motion for judgment pursuant to § 16.1-79 or § 16.1-81 shall be void and of no effect when such service of process is received by the Secretary within ten days of any return day set by the warrant. In such cases, the Secretary shall return the process or notice, the copy of the affidavit, and the prescribed fee to the plaintiff or his agent. A copy of the notice of the rejection shall be sent to the clerk of the court in which the action was filed.

E. The Secretary shall maintain a record of each notice of service sent to a person for a period of two years. The record maintained by the Secretary shall include the name of the plaintiff or the person seeking service, the name of the person to be served, the date service was received by the Secretary, the date notice of service was forwarded to the person to be served, and the date the certificate of compliance was sent by the Secretary to the appropriate court. The Secretary shall not be required to maintain any other records pursuant to this section. (Code 1950, § 8-813; 1977, c. 617; 1979, c. 31; 1986, c. 388; 1987, cc. 449, 450, 459; 1990, c. 741; 1998, c. 259; 2001, c. 29.)

The 2001 amendments. — The 2001 amendment by c. 29 added the last sentence in the first paragraph of subsection B, and added the last two sentences in subsection C.

I. DECISIONS UNDER CURRENT LAW.

Default. — A defendant's contention that service of a notice of motion for judgment and a praecipe through the secretary of the commonwealth was improper because none of the bases for personal jurisdiction under this section had been alleged or proven was without merit in that this section plainly provides for service of process to be made upon the secretary of the commonwealth as statutory agent of a person against whom the exercise of personal jurisdiction is authorized under § 8.01-328.1 and the nonresident defendant, by defaulting, was deemed to have admitted the facts alleged by the plaintiffs establishing personal jurisdiction under that statute. Glumina Bank v. D.C. Diamond Corp., 259 Va. 312, 527 S.E.2d 775 (2000).

CHAPTER 11.

JURIES.

ARTICLE 1.

When Jury Trial May Be Had.

§ 8.01-336. Jury trial of right; waiver of jury trial; court-ordered jury trial; trial by jury of plea in equity; issue out of chancery.

I. Decisions Under Current Law.
   A. General Consideration.
   C. Issue Out of Chancery.

I. DECISIONS UNDER CURRENT LAW.

A. General Consideration.

Waiver of right to jury trial.
When a defendant executes a waiver of his right to a trial by jury, the court must determine whether the defendant's consent was voluntarily and intelligently given and, in the absence of such a determination, the waiver is not valid and the defendant has the absolute right to be tried by a jury. Williams v. Commonwealth, 33 Va. App. 506, 534 S.E.2d 369 (2000).

C. Issue Out of Chancery.

Discretion of chancellor.
Trial court directed only one factual issue — existence of an agreement — to be determined as an issue out of chancery, and court did not abuse its discretion in denying appellant's further request to refer legal determination of estoppel. Zampolin v. Barnum, No. 0419-99-2 (Ct. of Appeals Dec. 28, 1999).

ARTICLE 3.

Selection of Jurors.

§ 8.01-352. Objections to irregularities in jury lists or for legal disability; effect thereof.

I. DECISIONS UNDER CURRENT LAW.

Applied in Salmon v. Commonwealth, 32 Va. App. 586, 529 S.E.2d 815 (2000).

Article 4.

Jury Service.

§ 8.01-353. Notice to jurors; making copy of jury panel available to counsel; objection to notice.

I. DECISIONS UNDER CURRENT LAW.

Failure to provide timely information concerning panel members not reversible error. — The statutory scheme does not contemplate that a full and accurate jury panel list will always be available for counsel forty-eight hours before the trial but recognizes that, under certain circumstances, the members of the actual jury panel necessarily will vary from those persons listed on a jury panel list provided forty-eight hours before trial. A trial court thus did not err in reconstituting a jury panel due to the limited number of potential jurors available where there was no dispute as to the need to reconstitute the panel and where there was no claim that the resulting jury was not impartial or that the complaining party was otherwise prejudiced. Norfolk S. Ry. v. Bowles, 261 Va. 21, 539 S.E.2d 727 (2001).

§ 8.01-357. Selection of jury panel.

I. DECISIONS UNDER CURRENT LAW.

Doubts as to impartiality resolved in favor of accused. — Any reasonable doubt regarding a prospective juror's ability to give the accused a fair and impartial trial must be resolved in favor of the accused. Shanklin v. Commonwealth, No. 1320-98-4 (Ct. of Appeals Apr. 18, 2000).

The trial court did not err in refusing to strike potential juror for cause. — The prospective juror acknowledged awareness of accounts of the crime in the media but his awareness was coextensive with the brief summary of allegations provided by the trial judge at the commencement of voir dire. Although he characterized the media's account as "prejudging" the accused, the prospective juror repeatedly stated that he would base his decision upon the evidence presented at trial. The trial judge did not err by refusing to strike this prospective juror for cause. DeLaurencio v. Commonwealth, No. 2497-98-1 (Ct. of Appeals June 20, 2000).

Jurors to be removed for cause before peremptory challenges. — An accused is entitled to a panel of jurors free from exception before exercising peremptory challenges. Cressell v. Commonwealth, 32 Va. App. 744, 531 S.E.2d 1 (2000).

Error to force use of peremptory strike.
Trial court erred in disallowing inquiry into prospective juror's previous employment as a law enforcement officer, and in denying defendant's motion to strike prospective juror for cause, which forced defendant to use a peremptory strike to remove prospective juror. Childress v. Commonwealth, No. 1890-98-4 (Ct. of Appeals Feb. 15, 2000).

§ 8.01-358. Voir dire examination of persons called as jurors.

I. Decisions Under Current Law.
 A. General Consideration.
 C. Illustrative Cases.

I. DECISIONS UNDER CURRENT LAW.

A. General Consideration.

Discretion of court in jury selection.
Trial court's decision whether to retain or exclude an individual venireman is given deference on appeal, since it is in a position to see and hear the juror. Caprio v. Commonwealth, No. 2225-98-1 (Ct. of Appeals Mar. 14, 2000).

Error to force use of peremptory strike.
— Trial court erred in disallowing inquiry into prospective juror's previous employment as a law enforcement officer, and in denying defendant's motion to strike prospective juror for cause, which forced defendant to use a peremptory strike to remove prospective juror. Childress v. Commonwealth, No. 1890-98-4 (Ct. of Appeals Feb. 15, 2000).

Error to force use of peremptory challenge.
As a matter of state law, an accused is entitled to a panel of jurors free from exception

before exercising peremptory challenges. Cressell v. Commonwealth, 32 Va. App. 744, 531 S.E.2d 1 (2000).

Reasonable doubt as to impartiality.

Any reasonable doubt regarding a prospective juror's ability to give the accused a fair and impartial trial must be resolved in favor of the accused. Shanklin v. Commonwealth, No. 1320-98-4 (Ct. of Appeals Apr. 18, 2000).

C. Illustrative Cases.

Questions as to weight jurors would give to police testimony.

An indication on the part of a potential juror that he will give unqualified credence to the testimony of a law enforcement officer based solely on the officer's official status constitutes impermissible bias. Shanklin v. Commonwealth, No. 1320-98-4 (Ct. of Appeals Apr. 18, 2000).

Rehabilitative evidence based on assent to leading questions.

Evidence of the requisite qualifications for impartial service must emanate from the juror, unsuggested by leading questions; mere assent to a trial judge's questions or statements is not enough to rehabilitate a prospective juror who has initially demonstrated a prejudice or partial predisposition. Shanklin v. Commonwealth, No. 1320-98-4 (Ct. of Appeals Apr. 18, 2000).

CHAPTER 13.

CERTAIN INCIDENTS OF TRIAL.

Sec.
8.01-375. Exclusion of witnesses in civil cases.
8.01-380. Dismissal of action by nonsuit; fees and costs.

§ 8.01-375. Exclusion of witnesses in civil cases. — The court trying any civil case may upon its own motion and shall upon the motion of any party, require the exclusion of every witness. However, each named party who is an individual, one officer or agent of each party which is a corporation or association and an attorney alleged in a habeas corpus proceeding to have acted ineffectively shall be exempt from the rule of this section as a matter of right.

Where expert witnesses are to testify in the case, the court may, at the request of all parties, allow one expert witness for each party to remain in the courtroom, provided that in cases pertaining to the distribution of marital property pursuant to § 20-107.3, the court may allow one expert witness for each party to remain in the courtroom throughout the hearing. (Code 1950, § 8-211.1; 1966, c. 268; 1975, c. 652; 1977, c. 617; 1986, c. 36; 1987, c. 70; 2001, c. 348.)

The 2001 amendments. — The 2001 amendment by c. 348 inserted "provided that in cases pertaining to the distribution of marital property pursuant to § 20-107.3, the court may allow one expert witness for each party to remain in the courtroom throughout the hearing" at the end of the second paragraph.

§ 8.01-379.2. Jury instructions.

Law Review. — For an article, "The Transformation of the American Civil Trial: The Silent Judge," see 42 Wm. & Mary L. Rev. 195 (2000).

§ 8.01-380. Dismissal of action by nonsuit; fees and costs. — A. A party shall not be allowed to suffer a nonsuit as to any cause of action or claim, or any other party to the proceeding, unless he does so before a motion to strike the evidence has been submitted to the court for decision. After a nonsuit no new proceeding on the same cause of action or against the same party shall be had in any court other than that in which the nonsuit was taken, unless that court is without jurisdiction, or not a proper venue, or other good cause is shown for proceeding in another court, or when such new proceeding is

§ 8.01-381 CERTAIN INCIDENTS OF TRIAL § 8.01-382

instituted in a federal court. If after a nonsuit an improper venue is chosen, the court shall not dismiss the matter but shall transfer it to the proper venue upon motion of any party.

B. Only one nonsuit may be taken to a cause of action or against the same party to the proceeding, as a matter of right, although the court may allow additional nonsuits or counsel may stipulate to additional nonsuits. The court, in the event additional nonsuits are allowed, may assess costs and reasonable attorneys' fees against the nonsuiting party.

C. If notice to take a nonsuit of right is given to the opposing party within five days of trial, the court in its discretion may assess against the nonsuiting party reasonable witness fees and travel costs of expert witnesses scheduled to appear at trial, which are actually incurred by the opposing party solely by reason of the failure to give notice at least five days prior to trial. The court shall have the authority to determine the reasonableness of expert witness fees and travel costs.

D. A party shall not be allowed to nonsuit a cause of action, without the consent of the adverse party who has filed a counterclaim, cross claim or third-party claim which arises out of the same transaction or occurrence as the claim of the party desiring to nonsuit unless the counterclaim, cross claim or third-party claim can remain pending for independent adjudication by the court. (Code 1950, §§ 8-220, 8-244; 1954, cc. 333, 611; 1977, c. 617; 1983, c. 404; 1991, c. 19; 2001, c. 825.)

The 2001 amendments. — The 2001 amendment by c. 825 inserted present subsection C and redesignated former subsection C as present subsection D.

I. Decisions Under Current Law.
  A. General Consideration.

I. DECISIONS UNDER CURRENT LAW.

A. General Consideration.

Service of process on defendant not required for nonsuit. — A plaintiff can secure a valid voluntary nonsuit pursuant to this section even though there has been no service of process on the defendants. Waterman v. Halverson, 261 Va. 203, 540 S.E.2d 867 (2001).

§ 8.01-381. What jury may carry out.

I. DECISIONS UNDER CURRENT LAW.

Defendant's recorded out-of-court statement held an "exhibit."
Trial court did not err by making defendant's videotaped confession, previously shown to jury at trial, available to jury during deliberations. Cull v. Commonwealth, No. 2202-98-2 (Ct. of Appeals Mar. 28, 2000).

Possible overemphasis by jury not grounds for withholding evidence. — The risk that a jury may overemphasize a videotaped statement by the accused if permitted to view such statement in the jury room exists when a jury peruses any exhibit; nothing in the Virginia statutes or case law requires the trial judge to supervise the jury's review of evidence to prevent overemphasis and the fact that a jury may dwell upon or emphasize any evidence, whether testimony or exhibits, is within the jury's purview in weighing and considering the evidence. Cull v. Commonwealth, No. 2202-98-2 (Ct. of Appeals Mar. 28, 2000).

§ 8.01-382. Verdict, judgment or decree to fix period at which interest begins; judgment or decree for interest.

I. DECISIONS UNDER CURRENT LAW.

Construction with other law.
Version of § 20-107.3 in effect at time divorce matter was commenced did not expressly authorize or prohibit application of this section requiring interest on judgments to monetary awards. Therefore husband was precluded from

recovering interest on equitable distribution award. Hird v. Gaynor, No. 0892-99-4 (Ct. of Appeals Mar. 21, 2000).

Purpose of prejudgment interest. — The award of prejudgment interest is to compensate a plaintiff for the loss sustained by not receiving the amount to which he was entitled at the time he was entitled to receive it, and such award is considered necessary to place the plaintiff in the position he would have occupied if the party in default had fulfilled his obligated duty. Walker v. Pfeiffer, No. 1872-99-2 (Ct. of Appeals July 11, 2000).

Discretion of jury. — Under Virginia law, the award of prejudgment interest is a matter within the discretion of the jury. Al-Abood v. El-Shamari, 217 F.3d 225 (4th Cir. 2000).

§ 8.01-384. Formal exceptions to rulings or orders of court unnecessary; motion for new trial unnecessary in certain cases.

I. DECISIONS UNDER CURRENT LAW.

The primary function of the contemporaneous objection rule, etc.
The purpose of this rule is to avoid unnecessary appeals, reversals and mistrials by allowing the trial judge to intelligently consider an issue and, if necessary, to take corrective action. Gurley v. Commonwealth, 34 Va. App. 166, 538 S.E.2d 361 (2000).

CHAPTER 14.

EVIDENCE.

Article 5.

Compelling Attendance of Witnesses, etc.

Sec.
8.01-407. How summons for witness issued, and to whom directed; prior permission of court to summon certain officials and judges; attendance before commissioner of other state; attorney-issued summons.
8.01-410. Convicts as witnesses in civil actions.

Article 7.

Medical Evidence.

Sec.
8.01-413. Certain copies of health care provider's records or papers of patient admissible; right of patient or his attorney to copies of such records or papers; subpoena; damages, costs and attorney's fees.

Article 9.

Miscellaneous Provisions.

8.01-420.6. Number of witnesses whose depositions may be taken.

ARTICLE 2.

Laws, Public Records, and Copies of Original Records as Evidence.

§ 8.01-389. Judicial records as evidence; full faith and credit; recitals in deeds, deeds of trust, and mortgages; "records" defined.

I. DECISIONS UNDER CURRENT LAW.

Foreign order properly certified. — A prior convictions order reflecting a defendant's convictions in California complied with the requirements of this section and was properly admitted into evidence where the order was marked on the back with a stamp reading, "Allen Slater, Executive Officer and Clerk of the Superior Court of the State of California, in and for the County of Orange," contained the seal of the Orange County Superior Court and was signed by "Flor L. Perez," whose signature appeared next to the word, "Deputy." Medici v. Commonwealth, 260 Va. 223, 532 S.E.2d 28 (2000).

Applied in Johnson v. Commonwealth, No. 0348-98-4 (Ct. of Appeals June 22, 1999).

§ 8.01-390. Nonjudicial records as evidence.

I. DECISIONS UNDER CURRENT LAW.

Letter from Division of Purchases and Supplies approving radar device for use by law enforcement authorities was inadmissible as an exception to hearsay rule, since no evidence was presented as to regularity of preparation of letter, and letter was not shown to be an official public document. White v. Commonwealth, No. 2991-98-3 (Ct. of Appeals Feb. 15, 2000).

Document filed with public agency not admissible. — Where it was abundantly clear that the exhibit at issue, which was prepared by a representative of the defendant's predecessor and filed with a state agency, was not prepared by a public official and did not reflect facts or events within the personal knowledge and observation of the recording official, the exhibit was not admissible under this section. Frank Shop, Inc. v. Crown Cent. Petroleum Corp., 261 Va. 169, 540 S.E.2d 897 (2001).

§ 8.01-391. Copies of originals as evidence.

I. DECISIONS UNDER CURRENT LAW.

Applied in Johnson v. Commonwealth, No. 0348-98-4 (Ct. of Appeals June 22, 1999).

ARTICLE 3.
Establishing Lost Records, etc.

§ 8.01-392. When court order book or equivalent is lost or illegible, what matters may be reentered.

I. DECISIONS UNDER CURRENT LAW.

Applicability. — Absent authentication and/or certification of exhibit, Commonwealth was required to follow either this section or § 8.01-394 to replace lost original conviction order. Johnson v. Commonwealth, No. 0348-98-4 (Ct. of Appeals June 22, 1999).

§ 8.01-394. How contents of any such lost record, etc., proved.

I. DECISIONS UNDER CURRENT LAW.

Applicability. — Absent authentication and/or certification of exhibit, Commonwealth was required to follow § 8.01-392 or this section to replace lost original conviction order. Johnson v. Commonwealth, No. 0348-98-4 (Ct. of Appeals June 22, 1999).

ARTICLE 4.
Witnesses Generally.

§ 8.01-397. Corroboration required and evidence receivable when one party incapable of testifying.

I. Decisions Under Current Law.
  A. General Consideration.
  B. Corroboration.

I. DECISIONS UNDER CURRENT LAW.

A. General Consideration.

Adverse party and interested party distinguished. — The phrase "adverse or interested party" refers to two, distinct categories of persons, namely "adverse" parties and "interested" parties; an "adverse party" is one who is a party to the record while an "interested party" is one, not a party to the record, who is pecuniarily interested in the result of the suit. Stephens v. Caruthers, 97 F. Supp. 2d 698 (E.D. Va. 2000).

Interested party. — A person is an "interested party" when that person is in some way beneficially interested in the judgment or decree which is sought to be obtained. In that regard, a person has a beneficial interest in litigation where, inter alia, that person has an interest in the property concerned in the litigation which may be benefited or adversely affected by the result of the suit or a beneficial interest in the fund sought to be recovered. Stephens v. Caruthers, 97 F. Supp. 2d 698 (E.D. Va. 2000).

Exception to defend against testimony of other interested party. — An exception to the bar of testimony by an interested party against a deceased party allows such testimony where some person, having an interest in or under a contract or transaction derived from the party so incapable of testifying, has testified in behalf of the latter or of himself, as to such contract or transaction. Paul v. Gomez, 118 F. Supp. 2d 694 (W.D. Va. 2000).

The Virginia dead man's statute did not apply to prevent a defendant physician from testifying to his version of the treatment he gave his patient where the patient was deceased but where the patient's wife was present at the meetings between her husband and the physician and would testify as to the alleged negligent treatment. Paul v. Gomez, 118 F. Supp. 2d 694 (W.D. Va. 2000).

Spouse who will benefit financially an "interested party." — Where the party to the record in a will contest asserts that she is entitled to recover from a testator's estate on the grounds that the testator had previously executed a joint and reciprocal will and declares that her spouse will share in the inheritance should the contest succeed, the spouse is an "interested party" whose testimony may not serve as corroborating evidence under the dead man's statute. Stephens v. Caruthers, 97 F. Supp. 2d 698 (E.D. Va. 2000).

Statute does not disqualify previously competent witnesses. — No corroboration is required of those witnesses who were competent before the Code of 1919 became operative, adopting the present version of the dead man's statute, and who did not then require corroboration. Paul v. Gomez, 118 F. Supp. 2d 694 (W.D. Va. 2000).

B. Corroboration.

Corroboration depends on facts of each case.

It is impossible to formulate a fixed rule as to the corroboration necessary in every situation because each case must be decided on its particular facts. Rice v. Charles, 260 Va. 157, 532 S.E.2d 318 (2000).

Not needed as to all material points.

It is not essential that a survivor's testimony be corroborated on all material points. Rice v. Charles, 260 Va. 157, 532 S.E.2d 318 (2000).

Corroboration held necessary.

The defense of contributory negligence was properly stricken in a wrongful death case arising out of an accident which occurred after the defendant driver had been consuming alcoholic beverages where the defendant offered no evidence corroborating his own testimony regarding whether the deceased passenger knew or should have known that the defendant's ability to drive was impaired and that she, nevertheless, chose to continue to ride with him. Rice v. Charles, 260 Va. 157, 532 S.E.2d 318 (2000).

Corroborating evidence tends to confirm and strengthen the testimony of the witness and it may come from other witnesses as well as from circumstantial evidence. Rice v. Charles, 260 Va. 157, 532 S.E.2d 318 (2000).

§ 8.01-398. Competency of husband and wife to testify; privileged communications and exceptions thereto.

I. DECISIONS UNDER CURRENT LAW.

The privilege embodied in this statute has been construed broadly to include all information or knowledge privately imparted and made known by one spouse to the other by virtue of and in consequence of the marital relation through conduct, acts, signs, and spoken or written words. Burns v. Commonwealth, 261 Va. 307, 541 S.E.2d 872 (2001).

Privilege inapplicable to testimony by third party. — The plain words utilized in this statutory provision limit the privilege to situations where a spouse is being examined in an action or is revealing a private communication through testimony. The statute does not prevent a third party who is in possession of letters written by one spouse to the other, and who has gained that possession lawfully, from testifying. Burns v. Commonwealth, 261 Va. 307, 541 S.E.2d 872 (2001).

§ 8.01-401.1. Opinion testimony by experts; hearsay exception.

I. DECISIONS UNDER CURRENT LAW.

Expert's testimony based on facts, not hearsay opinions. — Trial court properly allowed expert in parental rights termination proceeding to testify that children were alleged to have engaged in panhandling, despite mother's denial, since expert's opinion was based on events amply demonstrated by other sources. Expert's opinion was based upon facts, not hearsay opinions, and thus fell within scope of this section. Patterson v. Nottoway County Dep't of Social Servs., No. 2528-99-2 (Ct. of Appeals Mar. 28, 2000).

Expert opinion testimony based on hearsay factual information.
Where a psychologist interviewed a mother's children to determine whether the mother told blatant mistruths or whether her perception of things was radically different from that of others, it was proper to permit the psychologist to testify concerning factual information reported to her by the children. The psychologist's opinion was based upon facts, not hearsay opinions, and fell within the scope of this section. Patterson v. Nottoway County Dep't of Social Servs., No. 2528-99-2 (Ct. of Appeals Mar. 28, 2000).

§ 8.01-401.3. Opinion testimony and conclusions as to facts critical to civil case resolution.

I. DECISIONS UNDER CURRENT LAW.

Impeachment of one expert witness by another. — Nothing in subsection B of this section barred wife's introduction of expert testimony designed to impeach valuation testimony of husband's expert. Thompson v. Thompson, No. 1779-99-2 (Ct. of Appeals Feb. 8, 2000).

Testimony concerning workplace safety admissible. — While common knowledge alone may be sufficient to decide whether a task is physically easy or difficult to perform, determining whether the task itself is safe is not solely a function of logic. Whether easy or difficult, a task's safety for the purpose of imposing liability on an employer is determined by its effect on the body and whether there is a need for alternative means of performing the task. Thus, the opinions of an expert in ergonomics analysis and vocational assessment were admissible because those opinions, informed by his acknowledged expertise in the area, could assist the jury in determining the fact in issue, which was whether the employer provided a safe workplace. Norfolk S. Ry. v. Bowles, 261 Va. 21, 539 S.E.2d 727 (2001).

§ 8.01-403. Witness proving adverse; contradiction; prior inconsistent statement.

I. DECISIONS UNDER CURRENT LAW.

"Adverse" construed.
Testimony of witness did not "prove adverse" within meaning of this section, but only failed to meet defendant's expectations, and defense counsel was therefore not entitled to impeach witness under this section. Fetty v. Commonwealth, No. 0176-99-2 (Ct. of Appeals Feb. 1, 2000).

A party's own witness proves adverse if the witness surprises the party by changing stories or becoming hostile on the stand. Wells v. Commonwealth, 32 Va. App. 775, 531 S.E.2d 16 (2000).

Impeachment properly allowed. — In a prosecution for possession of marijuana with intent to distribute, the commonwealth was properly allowed to impeach its witness where the record supported a finding that the witness surprised the commonwealth when she testified inconsistently with her prior statement to a police officer and the inconsistent testimony was on issues relevant to the commonwealth's case, including questions about the defendant's connection to the residence in which the drugs were found, how often he was there, whether he paid rent and whether the defendant and another individual used drugs or sold drugs from the house. Wells v. Commonwealth, 32 Va. App. 775, 531 S.E.2d 16 (2000).

ARTICLE 5.

Compelling Attendance of Witnesses, etc.

§ 8.01-407. How summons for witness issued, and to whom directed; prior permission of court to summon certain officials and judges; attendance before commissioner of other state; attorney-issued sum-

mons. — A. A summons may be issued, directed as prescribed in § 8.01-292, commanding the officer to summon any person to attend on the day and at the place that such attendance is desired, to give evidence before a court, grand jury, arbitrators, magistrate, notary, or any commissioner or other person appointed by a court or acting under its process or authority in a judicial or quasi-judicial capacity. The summons may be issued by the clerk of the court if the attendance is desired at a court or in a proceeding pending in a court. The clerk shall not impose any time restrictions limiting the right to properly request a summons up to and including the date of the proceeding:

If attendance is desired before a commissioner in chancery or other commissioner of a court, the summons may be issued by the clerk of the court in which the matter is pending, or by such commissioner in chancery or other commissioner;

If attendance is desired before a notary or other officer taking a deposition, the summons may be issued by such notary or other officer at the instance of the attorney desiring the attendance of the person sought;

If attendance is sought before a grand jury, the summons may be issued by the attorney for the Commonwealth, or the clerk of the court, at the instance of the attorney for the Commonwealth.

Except as otherwise provided in this subsection, if attendance is desired in a civil proceeding pending in a court or at a deposition in connection with such proceeding, a summons may be issued by an attorney-at-law who is an active member of the Virginia State Bar at the time of issuance, as an officer of the court. An attorney-issued summons shall be on a form approved by the Supreme Court, signed by the attorney and shall include the attorney's address. The summons shall be deemed to be a pleading to which the provisions of § 8.01-271.1 shall apply. A copy of the summons, together with payment of all clerk's fees, if applicable, and, if served by a sheriff, all service of process fees, shall be mailed or delivered to the clerk's office of the court in which the case is pending on the day of issuance by the attorney. The law governing summonses issued by a clerk shall apply mutatis mutandis. When an attorney-at-law transmits one or more attorney-issued subpoenas to a sheriff to be served in his jurisdiction, such subpoenas shall be accompanied by a transmittal sheet. The transmittal sheet, which may be in the form of a letter, shall contain for each subpoena: (i) the person to be served, (ii) the name of the city or county in which the subpoena is to be served, in parentheses, (iii) the style of the case in which the subpoena was issued, (iv) the court in which the case is pending, and (v) the amount of fees tendered or paid to each clerk in whose court the case is pending together with a photocopy of the payment instrument or clerk's receipt. If copies of the same transmittal sheet are used to send subpoenas to more than one sheriff for service of process, then subpoenas shall be grouped by the jurisdiction in which they are to be served. Such transmittal sheet shall be signed by the transmitting attorney under penalty of perjury. For each person to be served, an original subpoena and copy thereof shall be included. If the attorney desires a return copy of the transmittal sheet as proof of receipt, he shall also enclose an additional copy of the transmittal sheet together with an envelope addressed to the attorney with sufficient first class postage affixed. Upon receipt of such transmittal, the transmittal sheet shall be date-stamped and, if the extra copy and above-described envelope are provided, the copy shall also be date-stamped and returned to the attorney-at-law in the above-described envelope.

However, when such transmittal does not comply with the provisions of this section, the sheriff may promptly return such transmittal if accompanied by a short description of such noncompliance. An attorney may not issue a summons in any of the following civil proceedings: (i) habeas corpus under Article 3 (§ 8.01-654 et seq.) of Chapter 25 of this title, (ii) delinquency or abuse and neglect proceedings under Article 3 (§ 16.1-241 et seq.) of Chapter 11 of Title 16.1, (iii) issuance of a protective order pursuant to Article 4 (§ 16.1-246 et seq.) or Article 9 (§ 16.1-278 et seq.) of Chapter 11 of Title 16.1, or Chapter 9.1 (§ 19.2-152.8 et seq.) of Title 19.2, (iv) civil forfeiture proceedings, (v) habitual offender proceedings under Article 9 (§ 46.2-351 et seq.) of Chapter 3 of Title 46.2, (vi) administrative license suspension pursuant to § 46.2-391.2 and (vii) petition for writs of mandamus or prohibition in connection with criminal proceedings. A subpoena issued by an attorney shall not be issued less than five business days prior to the date that attendance is desired.

In other cases, if attendance is desired, the summons may be issued by the clerk of the circuit court of the county or city in which the attendance is desired.

A summons shall express on whose behalf, and in what case or about what matter, the witness is to attend. Failure to respond to any such summons shall be punishable by the court in which the proceeding is pending as for contempt. When any subpoena is served less than five calendar days before appearance is required, the court may, after considering all of the circumstances, refuse to enforce the subpoena for lack of adequate notice.

B. No subpoena shall, without permission of the court first obtained, issue for the attendance of the Governor, Lieutenant Governor, or Attorney General of this Commonwealth, or a judge of any court thereof; the President or Vice President of the United States; any member of the President's Cabinet; any ambassador or consul; or any military officer on active duty holding the rank of admiral or general.

C. This section shall be deemed to authorize a summons to compel attendance of a citizen of the Commonwealth before commissioners or other persons appointed by authority of another state when the summons requires the attendance of such witness at a place not out of his county or city. (Code 1950, §§ 8-296, 8-297; 1952, c. 122; 1977, c. 617; 1992, c. 506; 2000, c. 813.)

Editor's note. — Acts 2001, cc. 514 and 551, repealed Acts 2000, c. 813, cl. 2, which had provided: "That the provisions of this act shall expire on July 1, 2001, unless reenacted by the 2001 General Assembly. Any subpoena or subpoena duces tecum issued by an attorney in compliance with this act shall remain valid notwithstanding the expiration of this act." Therefore, the 2000 amendment to this section by c. 813 will not expire.

Acts 2000, c. 813, cl. 3 provides: "That the Virginia Bar Association, with the support of the Virginia Sheriffs Association and such other organizations from which it may request assistance, shall conduct a study of the effectiveness of this act and report its findings to the General Assembly no later than January 1, 2001."

§ 8.01-410. Convicts as witnesses in civil actions. — Whenever any party in a civil action in any circuit court in this Commonwealth shall require as a witness in his behalf, a convict or prisoner in a correctional or penal institution as defined in § 53.1-1, the court, on the application of such party or his attorney may, in its discretion and upon consideration of the importance of the personal appearance of the witness and the nature of the offense for which he is imprisoned, issue an order to the Director of the Department of Corrections to deliver such witness to the sheriff of the jurisdiction of the court issuing the order. The sheriff shall transport the convict to the court to testify as such witness, and after he shall have so testified and been released as such witness, the sheriff shall return the witness to the custody of the Department.

If necessary the sheriff may confine the convict for the night in any convenient city or county correctional institution.

§ 8.01-411 CIVIL REMEDIES AND PROCEDURE § 8.01-411

Under such rules and regulations as the superintendent of such an institution may prescribe, any party to a civil action in any circuit court in this Commonwealth may take the deposition of a convict or prisoner in the institution, which deposition, when taken, may be admissible in evidence as other depositions in civil actions.

The party seeking the testimony of such prisoner shall advance a sum sufficient to defray the expenses and compensation of the correctional officers and sheriff, which the court shall tax as other costs.

For the purposes of this section, "correctional officers" shall have the same meaning as provided in § 53.1-1. (Code 1950, § 8-300.1; 1952, c. 487; 1966, c. 227; 1974, cc. 44, 45; 1977, c. 617; 1998, c. 596; 2001, c. 513.)

The 2001 amendments. — The 2001 amendment by c. 513, in the first paragraph, substituted "of the jurisdiction of the court issuing the order. The sheriff shall transport" for "of the county or the city, as the case may be, who shall go where such witness may then be. Under such conditions as shall be prescribed by the superintendent of the institution, such officer shall carry," and substituted "the sheriff shall return the witness to the custody of the Department" for "carry him back to the place whence he came"; substituted "correctional officers and sheriff" for "officers" in the fourth paragraph; and added the last paragraph.

I. DECISIONS UNDER CURRENT LAW.

District courts have no authority to order transportation in civil cases. — The authority to issue prisoner transportation orders in civil cases granted by this section is vested solely in the circuit courts. By expressly granting the specific authority to issue prisoner transportation orders in civil cases in this statute only to the circuit courts, the general assembly intended to exclude the general district courts from the authority to issue prisoner transportation orders in civil cases. Commonwealth ex rel. Virginia Dep't of Cors. v. Brown, 259 Va. 697, 529 S.E.2d 96 (2000).

Conflict between right to conduct civil litigation and incarceration. — This section, in clear and unambiguous terms, provides the judicial authority and the mechanism by which the patent conflict between prisoners' incarceration and their ability to exercise the right to conduct civil litigation is appropriately resolved and expressly grants to the circuit courts the authority to issue prisoner transportation orders in civil cases. Commonwealth ex rel. Virginia Dep't of Cors. v. Brown, 259 Va. 697, 529 S.E.2d 96 (2000).

§ 8.01-411. Compelling attendance of witnesses for taking depositions and production of documents to be used in foreign jurisdiction.

I. DECISIONS UNDER CURRENT LAW.

Discovery denied to anonymous plaintiff. — The circumstances did not present a situation where comity should have been granted to an Indiana court's order permitting a plaintiff to proceed anonymously and the plaintiff thus could not pursue discovery in Virginia under the Uniform Foreign Depositions Act where it was uncertain whether personal jurisdiction might be obtained over any of the anonymous defendants and where, although the Indiana court permitted the plaintiff to proceed anonymously, it was clear that no hearing was held concerning the question; no evidence was received by the court, no reasons for the decision were given, and the order permitting anonymous maintenance of the action was granted in a non-adversarial, ex parte proceeding. Significantly, because no evidence was received and no reasons for the decision were given by the Indiana court, it could not be determined whether the procedural and substantive law applied by the Indiana court was reasonably comparable to that of Virginia. America Online, Inc. v. Anonymous Publicly Traded Co., 261 Va. 350, 542 S.E.2d 377 (2001).

The Uniform Foreign Depositions Act is rooted in principles of comity and provides a mechanism for discovery of evidence in aid of actions pending in foreign jurisdictions. America Online, Inc. v. Anonymous Publicly Traded Co., 261 Va. 350, 542 S.E.2d 377 (2001).

An action under the Uniform Foreign Depositions Act is a separate action, distinct from, although ancillary to, the underlying cause of action in the foreign jurisdiction. America Online, Inc. v. Anonymous Publicly Traded Co., 261 Va. 350, 542 S.E.2d 377 (2001).

Article 7.

Medical Evidence.

§ 8.01-413. Certain copies of health care provider's records or papers of patient admissible; right of patient or his attorney to copies of such records or papers; subpoena; damages, costs and attorney's fees.
— A. In any case where the hospital, nursing facility, physician's, or other health care provider's original records or papers of any patient in a hospital or institution for the treatment of physical or mental illness are admissible or would be admissible as evidence, any typewritten copy, photograph, photostatted copy, or microphotograph or printout or other hard copy generated from computerized or other electronic storage, microfilm, or other photographic, mechanical, electronic or chemical storage process thereof shall be admissible as evidence in any court of this Commonwealth in like manner as the original, if the printout or hard copy or microphotograph or photograph is properly authenticated by the employees having authority to release or produce the original records.

Any hospital, nursing facility, physician, or other health care provider whose records or papers relating to any such patient are subpoenaed for production as provided by law may comply with the subpoena by a timely mailing to the clerk issuing the subpoena or in whose court the action is pending properly authenticated copies, photographs or microphotographs in lieu of the originals. The court whose clerk issued the subpoena or, in the case of an attorney-issued subpoena, in which the action is pending, may, after notice to such hospital, nursing facility, physician, or other health care provider, enter an order requiring production of the originals, if available, of any stored records or papers whose copies, photographs or microphotographs are not sufficiently legible. The party requesting the subpoena duces tecum or on whose behalf an attorney-issued subpoena duces tecum was issued shall be liable for the reasonable charges of the hospital, nursing facility, physician, or other health care provider for the service of maintaining, retrieving, reviewing, preparing, copying and mailing the items produced. Except for copies of X-ray photographs, however, such charges shall not exceed fifty cents for each page up to fifty pages and twenty-five cents a page thereafter for copies from paper or other hard copy generated from computerized or other electronic storage, or other photographic, mechanical, electronic, imaging or chemical storage process and one dollar per page for copies from microfilm or other micrographic process, plus all postage and shipping costs and a search and handling fee not to exceed ten dollars.

B. Copies of hospital, nursing facility, physician's, or other health care provider's records or papers shall be furnished within fifteen days of such request to the patient or his attorney upon such patient's or attorney's written request, which request shall comply with the requirements of subsection E of § 32.1-127.1:03. However, copies of a patient's records shall not be furnished to such patient where the patient's treating physician has made a part of the patient's records a written statement that in his opinion the furnishing to or review by the patient of such records would be injurious to the patient's health or well-being, but in any such case such records shall be furnished to the patient's attorney within fifteen days of the date of such request. A reasonable charge may be made for the service of maintaining, retrieving, reviewing and preparing such copies. Except for copies of X-ray photographs, however, such charges shall not exceed fifty cents per page for up to fifty pages and twenty-five cents a page thereafter for copies from paper or other hard copy generated from computerized or other electronic storage, or other photographic, mechanical, electronic, imaging or chemical storage process and one dollar per page for copies from microfilm or other micrographic process, plus all postage and shipping costs and a search and handling fee not to exceed ten dollars. Any hospital, nursing facility, physician, or other health care provider receiving such a request from a patient's attorney shall require a writing signed by the patient confirming the attorney's authority to make the request and shall accept a photocopy, facsimile, or other copy of the original signed by the patient as if it were an original.

C. Upon the failure of any hospital, nursing facility, physician, or other health care provider to comply with any written request made in accordance with subsection B within the period of time specified in that subsection and within the manner specified in subsections E and F of § 32.1-127.1:03, the patient or his attorney may cause a subpoena duces tecum to be issued. The subpoena may be issued (i) upon filing a request therefor with the clerk of the circuit court wherein any eventual suit, would be required to be filed, and payment of the fees required by subdivision A 18 of § 17.1-275, and fees for service or (ii) by the patient's attorney in a pending civil case in accordance with § 8.01-407 if issued by such attorney at least five business days prior to the date that production of the record is desired upon payment of the fees required by subdivision A 23 of § 17.1-275 at the time of filing of a copy of the subpoena duces tecum with the clerk. The subpoena shall be returnable within twenty days of proper service, directing the hospital, nursing facility, physician, or other health care provider to produce and furnish copies of the reports and papers to the clerk who shall then make the same available to the patient or his attorney. If the court finds that a hospital, nursing facility, physician, or other health care provider willfully refused to comply with a written request made in accordance with subsection B, either by willfully or arbitrarily refusing or by imposing a charge in excess of the reasonable expense of making the copies and processing the request for records, the court may award damages for all expenses incurred by the patient to obtain such copies, including court costs and reasonable attorney's fees.

D. The provisions of subsections A, B, and C hereof shall apply to any health care provider whose office is located within or without the Commonwealth if the records pertain to any patient who is a party to a cause of action in any court in the Commonwealth of Virginia, and shall apply only to requests made by an attorney, or his client, in anticipation of litigation or in the course of litigation.

E. Health care provider, as used in this section, shall have the same meaning as provided in § 32.1-127.1:03 and shall also include an independent medical copy retrieval service contracted to provide the service of retrieving, reviewing, and preparing such copies for distribution.

F. Notwithstanding the authorization to admit as evidence patient records in the form of microphotographs, prescription dispensing records maintained in or on behalf of any pharmacy registered or permitted in Virginia shall only be stored in compliance with §§ 54.1-3410, 54.1-3411 and 54.1-3412. (Code 1950, § 8-277.1; 1954, c. 329; 1976, c. 50; 1977, cc. 208, 617; 1981, c. 457; 1982, c. 378; 1990, cc. 99, 320; 1992, c. 696; 1994, cc. 390, 572; 1995, c. 586; 1997, c. 682; 1998, c. 470; 2000, cc. 813, 923; 2001, c. 567.)

Editor's note. — Acts 2001, cc. 514 and 551, repealed Acts 2000, c. 813, cl. 2, which had provided: "That the provisions of this act shall expire on July 1, 2001, unless reenacted by the 2001 General Assembly. Any subpoena or subpoena duces tecum issued by an attorney in compliance with this act shall remain valid notwithstanding the expiration of this act." Therefore, the 2000 amendment to this section by c. 813 will not expire.

Acts 2000, c. 813, cl. 3 provides: "That the Virginia Bar Association, with the support of the Virginia Sheriffs Association and such other organizations from which it may request assistance, shall conduct a study of the effectiveness of this act and report its findings to the General Assembly no later than January 1, 2001."

The 2001 amendments. — The 2001

Article 9.

Miscellaneous Provisions.

§ 8.01-420.3. Court reporters to provide transcripts; when recording may be stopped; use of transcript as evidence.

I. DECISIONS UNDER CURRENT LAW.

Statute inapplicable to request to listen to audio tapes. — This section specifically addresses transcripts of proceedings and the circumstances under which copies may be obtained and does not apply to audio tape recordings, which are not transcripts of proceedings, or to a petition which is concerned only with the listening to the tapes and is not a request to obtain copies of them. Smith v. Richmond Newspapers, Inc., 261 Va. 113, 540 S.E.2d 878 (2001).

§ 8.01-420.6. Number of witnesses whose depositions may be taken.

— Notwithstanding any other provision of law or rule of court, there shall be no limit on the number of witnesses whose depositions may be taken by a party except by order of the court for good cause shown. (2001, c. 595.)

CHAPTER 15.

PAYMENT AND SETOFF.

§ 8.01-422. Pleading equitable defenses.

I. DECISIONS UNDER CURRENT LAW.

Legal defenses inapplicable. — The language of this section is clear and unambiguous and, unlike the language in the predecessor statute, does not contain any provisions subjecting equitable pleas of statutory recoupment to defenses available in an action at law such as the statute of limitations. Cummings v. Fulghum, 261 Va. 73, 540 S.E.2d 494 (2001).

Statute of limitations inapplicable to plea of recoupment. — A plea of recoupment under this section is not subject to a statute of limitations defense. Cummings v. Fulghum, 261 Va. 73, 540 S.E.2d 494 (2001).

CHAPTER 17.

JUDGMENTS AND DECREES GENERALLY.

ARTICLE 1.

In General.

§ 8.01-428. Setting aside default judgments; clerical mistakes; independent actions to relieve party from judgment or proceedings; grounds and time limitations.

I. Decisions Under Current Law.
  A. General Consideration.
  C. Relief.

I. DECISIONS UNDER CURRENT LAW.

A. General Consideration.

Amendment of record only to reflect action actually taken. — The power to amend should not be confounded with the power to create; while the power to amend is inherent in the court, it is restricted to placing upon the record evidence of judicial action which has actually been taken and presupposes action taken at the proper time. Patterson v. Fauquier County Dep't of Social Servs., No. 1232-00-4 (Ct. of Appeals Mar. 20, 2001).

Subsection B authorizes a trial judge to correct the judge's own errors and omissions. Coleman v. Commonwealth ex rel. Hutcherson, No. 1441-99-3 (Ct. of Appeals Apr. 25, 2000).

Order failing to set forth grounds for changes ineffective. — An order apparently intended to correct an error in a prior order that sets forth no basis for concluding that the changes resulted from previous inadvertence or oversight, as distinguished from a change of mind or a perceived adjudicatory error, is ineffective to modify the prior order. Thompson v. Commonwealth, No. 0330-99-3 (Ct. of Appeals Mar. 28, 2000).

Effect of Rule 1:1.

A nunc pro tunc order correcting a clerical error can be entered after twenty-one days from entry of the final order without violating Rule 1:1. A trial court may enter an order nunc pro tunc to reflect judicial action that was, in fact, taken or to correct defects or omissions in the record so as to make the record conform to actual prior events. Coleman v. Commonwealth ex rel. Hutcherson, No. 1441-99-3 (Ct. of Appeals Apr. 25, 2000).

Scope of subsection B.

A clerical mistake or error as contemplated by subsection (B) must be apparent from the record; this subsection does not give the court the authority to hear new evidence or to elaborate on its original decree. Hart v. Hart, 35 Va. App. 221, 544 S.E.2d 366 (2001).

Section B has no application to errors in the reasoning and conclusions of the court about contested matters. Patterson v. Fauquier County Dep't of Social Servs., No. 1232-00-4 (Ct. of Appeals Mar. 20, 2001).

Wife failed to establish fraud by husband sufficient to warrant setting aside final divorce decree. Cossu v. Cossu, No. 2932-98-2 (Ct. of Appeals June 15, 1999).

Defendant provided no evidence that it was free from fault or negligence. — Defendant argued that, although it did not know what happened to the amended motion for judgment, it had a system for handling such matters in place, and, consequently, its lack of knowledge as to why its system apparently did not work properly did not rise to the level of negligence or fault on its part. However, defendant had the burden to produce evidence showing that it was neither at fault nor negligent. Instead, the evidence recited above showed only that a system failed. It did not provide any showing as to how or why the system failed and thus provided no evidence that it was free from fault or negligence when it did not respond to plaintiff's motion for judgment. Media Gen., Inc. v. Smith, 260 Va. 287, 534 S.E.2d 733 (2000).

Applied in Terrell v. Commonwealth, No. 1669-99-2 (Ct. of Appeals Apr. 11, 2000); Deane v. Deane, No. 2347-98-2 (Ct. of Appeals July 20, 1999); Michael v. Commonwealth, No. 2451-98-1 (Ct. of Appeals June 6, 2000); Hickson v. Hickson, 34 Va. App. 246, 540 S.E.2d 508 (2001).

C. Relief.

Court may enter order nunc pro tunc.

Where the failure to enter a timely order was due to attorney error and, without the order, the record did not fully or accurately set forth the appropriate rulings of the trial court, the attorney's omission qualified as a "clerical error" that could be rectified by the court nunc pro tunc. Patterson v. Fauquier County Dep't of Social Servs., No. 1232-00-4 (Ct. of Appeals Mar. 20, 2001).

Nunc pro tunc order invalid.

Trial court's nunc pro tunc order provided no basis for concluding that changes made to earlier order resulted from previous inadvertence or oversight, as distinguished from a change of mind or perceived adjudicatory error, and therefore nunc pro tunc order was ineffective to modify earlier order. Thompson v. Commonwealth, No. 0330-99-3 (Ct. of Appeals Mar. 28, 2000).

§ 8.01-430. When final judgment to be entered after verdict set aside.

I. DECISIONS UNDER CURRENT LAW.

Applied in Kim v. Douval Corp., 259 Va. 752, 529 S.E.2d 92 (2000).

Article 4.

Distinction Between Term and Vacation Abolished.

§ 8.01-445. Distinction between term and vacation abolished; effect of time.

Applied in Trustees of Zion Baptist Church v. Conservators of Estate of Peay, 259 Va. 546, 525 S.E.2d 291 (2000).

CHAPTER 18.

EXECUTIONS AND OTHER MEANS OF RECOVERY.

Article 1.

Issue and Form; Motion to Quash.

Sec.
8.01-470. Writs on judgments for specific property.

ARTICLE 1.

Issue and Form; Motion to Quash.

§ 8.01-470. Writs on judgments for specific property.

— On a judgment for the recovery of specific property, real or personal, a writ of possession may issue for the specific property, which shall conform to the judgment as to the description of the property and the estate, title and interest recovered, and there may also be issued a writ of fieri facias for the damages or profits and costs. In cases of unlawful entry and detainer and of ejectment, the officer to whom a writ of possession has been delivered to be executed shall, at least seventy-two hours before execution, serve notice of intent to execute, including the date and time of execution, as well as the rights afforded to tenants in §§ 55-237.1 and 55-248.38:2, on the defendant in accordance with § 8.01-296, with a copy of the writ attached. The execution of the writ of possession by the sheriff should occur within fifteen calendar days from the date the writ of possession is received by the sheriff, or as soon as practicable thereafter, but in no event later than thirty days from the date the writ of possession is issued. In cases of unlawful entry and detainer and of ejectment, whenever the officer to whom a writ of possession has been delivered to be executed finds the premises locked, he may, after declaring at the door the cause of his coming and demanding to have the door opened, employ reasonable and necessary force to break and enter the door and put the plaintiff in possession. And an officer having a writ of possession for specific personal property, if he finds locked or fastened the building or place wherein he has reasonable cause to believe the property specified in the writ is located, may in the daytime, after notice to the defendant, his agent or bailee, break and enter such building or place for the purpose of executing such writ. (Code 1950, § 8-402; 1977, c. 617; 1991, c. 503; 2000, c. 640; 2001, c. 222.)

The 2001 amendments. — The 2001 amendment by c. 222 inserted "as well as the rights afforded to tenants in §§ 55-237.1 and 55-248.38:2" in the second sentence.

ARTICLE 5.

Lien on Property Not Capable of Being Levied on.

§ 8.01-501. Lien of fieri facias on estate of debtor not capable of being levied on.

I. DECISIONS UNDER CURRENT LAW.

Execution on intangible property. When property of a judgment debtor is not capable of being levied on, as in the case of intangible personal property, such property is nevertheless subject to the execution lien upon delivery of the writ to a sheriff or other officer. Network Solutions, Inc. v. Umbro Int'l, Inc., 259 Va. 759, 529 S.E.2d 80 (2000).

ARTICLE 7.

Garnishment.

§ 8.01-511. Institution of garnishment proceedings.

I. DECISIONS UNDER CURRENT LAW.

Garnishment does not create lien. — A garnishment summons does not create a lien itself, but, instead, is a means of enforcing the lien of an execution placed in the hands of an officer to be levied. Network Solutions, Inc. v. Umbro Int'l, Inc., 259 Va. 759, 529 S.E.2d 80 (2000).

Statute must be strictly satisfied. — Garnishment, like other lien enforcement remedies authorizing seizure of property, is a creature of statute unknown to the common law and hence the provisions of the statute must be strictly satisfied. Network Solutions, Inc. v. Umbro Int'l, Inc., 259 Va. 759, 529 S.E.2d 80 (2000).

Liability defined. — A "liability," that may be subject to garnishment under this section means a legal obligation, enforceable by civil remedy, a financial or pecuniary obligation, or a debt. Network Solutions, Inc. v. Umbro Int'l, Inc., 259 Va. 759, 529 S.E.2d 80 (2000).

Contract for services not subject to garnishment. — A contract for services is not "a liability" as that term is used in this section and hence is not subject to garnishment. Network Solutions, Inc. v. Umbro Int'l, Inc., 259 Va. 759, 529 S.E.2d 80 (2000).

Internet domain names not subject to garnishment. — Whatever contractual rights a judgment debtor has in an internet domain name, those rights do not exist separate and apart from the registrar's services that make the domain name an operational internet address and, since a domain name registration is the product of a contract for services between the registrar and the registrant, it is not subject to garnishment. Network Solutions, Inc. v. Umbro Int'l, Inc., 259 Va. 759, 529 S.E.2d 80 (2000).

Judgment creditor's rights no greater than debtor's. — A proceeding in garnishment is substantially an action at law by the judgment debtor in the name of the judgment creditor against the garnishee, and therefore the judgment creditor stands upon no higher ground than the judgment debtor and can acquire no greater right than such debtor possesses. Network Solutions, Inc. v. Umbro Int'l, Inc., 259 Va. 759, 529 S.E.2d 80 (2000).

§ 8.01-512.3. Form of garnishment summons.

Cross references. — As to limitations of this section applying to the use of administrative offset in the recovery of certain improper payments to state employees, see § 2.2-804.

CHAPTER 21.
Arbitration and Award.

Article 1.
General Provisions.

§ 8.01-577. Submission of controversy; agreement to arbitrate; condition precedent to action.

Law Review. For an article, "As Mandatory Binding Arbitration Meets the Class Action, Will the Class Action Survive?," see 42 Wm. & Mary L. Rev. 1 (2000).

Article 2.
Uniform Arbitration Act.

§ 8.01-581.01. Validity of arbitration agreement.

Law Review. — For an article, "As Mandatory Binding Arbitration Meets the Class Action, Will the Class Action Survive?," see 42 Wm. & Mary L. Rev. 1 (2000).

CHAPTER 21.1.
Medical Malpractice.

Article 1.
Medical Malpractice Review Panels; Arbitration of Malpractice Claims.

Sec.
8.01-581.1. Definitions.
8.01-581.2. Request for review by medical malpractice review panel; rescission of request; determination on request.

Article 2.
Miscellaneous Provisions.

8.01-581.13. Civil immunity for certain health professionals and health profession students serving as members of certain entities.
8.01-581.15. Limitation on recovery in certain medical malpractice actions.
8.01-581.16. Civil immunity for members of or consultants to certain boards or committees.
8.01-581.17. Privileged communications of certain committees and entities.

Article 1.
Medical Malpractice Review Panels; Arbitration of Malpractice Claims.

§ 8.01-581.1. Definitions. — As used in this chapter:
"*Health care*" means any act, or treatment performed or furnished, or which should have been performed or furnished, by any health care provider for, to, or on behalf of a patient during the patient's medical diagnosis, care, treatment or confinement.

"*Health care provider*" means (i) a person, corporation, facility or institution licensed by this Commonwealth to provide health care or professional services as a physician or hospital, dentist, pharmacist, registered nurse or licensed

§ 8.01-581.1 CIVIL REMEDIES AND PROCEDURE § 8.01-581.1

practical nurse, optometrist, podiatrist, chiropractor, physical therapist, physical therapy assistant, clinical psychologist, clinical social worker, professional counselor, licensed dental hygienist or health maintenance organization, (ii) a professional corporation, all of whose shareholders or members are so licensed, (iii) a partnership, all of whose partners are so licensed, (iv) a nursing home as defined in § 54.1-3100 except those nursing institutions conducted by and for those who rely upon treatment by spiritual means alone through prayer in accordance with a recognized church or religious denomination, (v) a professional limited liability company comprised of members as described in § 13.1-1102 A. 2., (vi) a corporation, partnership, limited liability company or any other entity, except a state-operated facility, which employs or engages a licensed health care provider and which primarily renders health care services, or (vii) a director, officer, employee or agent of the persons or entities referenced herein, acting within the course and scope of his employment as related to health care or professional services.

"*Health maintenance organization*" means any person licensed pursuant to Chapter 43 (§ 38.2-4300 et seq.) of Title 38.2 who undertakes to provide or arrange for one or more health care plans.

"*Hospital*" means a public or private institution licensed pursuant to Chapter 5 (§ 32.1-123 et seq.) of Title 32.1 or Chapter 8 (§ 37.1-179 et seq.) of Title 37.1.

"*Impartial attorney*" means an attorney who has not represented (i) the claimant, his family, his partners, co-proprietors or his other business interests; or (ii) the health care provider, his family, his partners, co-proprietors or his other business interests.

"*Impartial health care provider*" means a health care provider who (i) has not examined, treated or been consulted regarding the claimant or his family; (ii) does not anticipate examining, treating, or being consulted regarding the claimant or his family; or (iii) has not been an employee, partner or co-proprietor of the health care provider against whom the claim is asserted.

"*Malpractice*" means any tort based on health care or professional services rendered, or which should have been rendered, by a health care provider, to a patient.

"*Patient*" means any natural person who receives or should have received health care from a licensed health care provider except those persons who are given health care in an emergency situation which exempts the health care provider from liability for his emergency services in accordance with § 8.01-225.

"*Physician*" means a person licensed to practice medicine or osteopathy in this Commonwealth pursuant to Chapter 29 (§ 54.1-2900 et seq.) of Title 54.1. (Code 1950, § 8-911; 1976, c. 611; 1977, c. 617; 1981, c. 305; 1986, cc. 227, 511; 1989, cc. 146, 730; 1991, cc. 455, 464; 1993, c. 268; 1994, cc. 114, 616, 651; 2001, c. 98.)

The 2001 amendments. — The 2001 amendment by c. 98, in the paragraph defining "Health care provider," deleted "or an officer, employee or agent thereof acting in the course and scope of his employment, or" from the end of clause (v), inserted "or" at the end of clause (vi), and added clause (vii); and transferred the paragraph defining "Physician" from next-to-last paragraph to last paragraph.

Law Review.

For a note, "Pulliam v. Coastal Emergency Services of Richmond, Inc.: Reconsidering the Standard of Review and Constitutionality of Virginia's Medical Malpractice Cap," see 8 Geo. Mason L. Rev. 587 (2000).

For an article, "The Quiet Demise of Deference to Custom: Malpractice Law at the Millenium," see 57 Wash. & Lee L. Rev. 163 (2000).

§ 8.01-581.2. Request for review by medical malpractice review panel; rescission of request; determination on request. — A. At any time within thirty days from the filing of the responsive pleading in any action brought for malpractice against a health care provider, the plaintiff or defendant may request a review by a medical malpractice review panel established as provided in § 8.01-581.3. The request shall be forwarded by the party making the request to the Clerk of the Supreme Court of Virginia with a copy of the Motion for Judgment and a copy of all responsive pleadings. A copy of the request shall be filed with the clerk of the circuit court, and a copy shall be sent to all counsel of record. The request shall include the name of the judge to whom the case is assigned, if any. Upon receipt of such request, the Supreme Court shall select the panel members as provided in § 8.01-581.3:1 and shall designate a panel within sixty days after receipt of the request. If a panel is requested, proceedings on the action based on the alleged malpractice shall be stayed during the period of review by the medical review panel, except that the judge may rule on any motions, demurrers, or pleas that can be disposed of as a matter of law, set the trial date after the panel has been designated and, prior to the designation of the panel, shall rule on any motions to transfer venue.

B. After the selection of the members of the review panel, the requesting party may rescind a request for review by the panel only with the consent of all parties or with leave of the judge presiding over the panel.

C. Any health care provider named as a defendant shall have the right to request a panel and, in that event, shall give notice of its request to the other health care providers named in the motion for judgment as well as to the plaintiff and his counsel of record. When a request for a medical review panel is made by any party, a single panel shall be designated and all health care providers against whom a claim is asserted shall be subject to the jurisdiction of such panel. The provisions of this subsection shall not prohibit the addition of parties pursuant to § 8.01-581.2:1. (Code 1950, § 8-912; 1976, c. 611; 1977, c. 617; 1982, c. 151; 1984, cc. 443, 777; 1986, c. 227; 1989, c. 561; 1993, c. 928; 1994, c. 38; 1995, c. 367; 2000, c. 213; 2001, c. 252.)

The 2001 amendments. — The 2001 amendment by c. 252 inserted "set the trial date after the panel has been designated" near the end of subsection A.

Article 2.

Miscellaneous Provisions.

§ 8.01-581.13. Civil immunity for certain health professionals and health profession students serving as members of certain entities. — A. For the purposes of this subsection, *"health professional"* means any clinical psychologist, applied psychologist, school psychologist, dentist, licensed professional counselor, licensed substance abuse treatment practitioner, certified substance abuse counselor, certified substance abuse counseling assistant, marriage and family therapist, nurse, optometrist, pharmacist, physician, chiropractor, podiatrist, or veterinarian who is actively engaged in the practice of his profession or any member of the Intervention Program Committee pursuant to Chapter 25.1 (§ 54.1-2515 et seq.) of Title 54.1.

Unless such act, decision, or omission resulted from such health professional's bad faith or malicious intent, any health professional, as defined in this subsection, shall be immune from civil liability for any act, decision or omission resulting from his duties as a member or agent of any entity which functions primarily (i) to investigate any complaint that a physical or mental impairment, including alcoholism or drug addiction, has impaired the ability of any such health professional to practice his profession and (ii) to encourage, recommend and arrange for a course of treatment or intervention, if deemed appropriate, or (iii) to review the duration of patient stays in health facilities or delivery of professional services for the purpose of promoting the most efficient use of available health facilities and services, the adequacy and quality of professional services, or the reasonableness or appropriateness of charges made by or on behalf of such health professionals. Such entity shall have been established pursuant to a federal or state law, or by one or more public or licensed private hospitals, or a relevant health professional society, academy or association affiliated with the American Medical Association, the American Dental Association, the American Pharmaceutical Association, the American Psychological Association, the American Podiatric Medical Association, the American Society of Hospitals and Pharmacies, the American Veterinary Medical Association, the American Association for Counseling and Development, the American Optometric Association, International Chiropractic Association, the American Chiropractic Association, the NAADAC: the Association for Addiction Professionals, the American Association for Marriage and Family Therapy or a governmental agency.

B. For the purposes of this subsection, *"health profession student"* means a student in good standing who is enrolled in an accredited school, program, or curriculum in clinical psychology, counseling, dentistry, medicine, nursing, pharmacy, chiropractic, marriage and family therapy, substance abuse treatment, or veterinary medicine and has received training relating to substance abuse.

Unless such act, decision, or omission resulted from such health profession student's bad faith or malicious intent, any health profession student, as defined in this subsection, shall be immune from civil liability for any act, decision, or omission resulting from his duties as a member of an entity established by the institution of higher education in which he is enrolled or a professional student's organization affiliated with such institution which functions primarily (i) to investigate any complaint of a physical or mental impairment, including alcoholism or drug addiction, of any health profession student and (ii) to encourage, recommend, and arrange for a course of treatment, if deemed appropriate.

C. The immunity provided hereunder shall not extend to any person with respect to actions, decisions or omissions, liability for which is limited under the provisions of the federal Social Security Act or amendments thereto. (Code 1950, § 8-654.6; 1975, c. 418; 1977, c. 617; 1983, c. 567; 1984, c. 494; 1987, c. 713; 1989, c. 729; 1992, c. 590; 1993, c. 702; 1995, c. 636; 1996, cc. 937, 980; 1997, cc. 439, 901; 2001, c. 460.)

Editor's note. — Acts 2001, c. 460, cl. 2, provides: "That, notwithstanding the provisions of this act, the Board shall certify as a certified substance abuse counselor any person who files an application with the Board after July 1, 2001, but before the effective date of the new certification regulations to be promulgated by the Board pursuant to § 54.1-3505 if such person meets the certification requirements for certified substance abuse counselors in effect prior to July 1, 2001. Unless such certification later is suspended or revoked by the Board, such certification shall remain in effect until the effective date of the new certification regulations to be promulgated by the Board pursuant to § 54.1-3505, at which time the person shall be deemed to hold certification at the appropriate level under § 54.1-3507.1 or § 54.1-3507.2, as determined by the Board."

Acts 2001, c. 460, cl. 3, provides: "That, notwithstanding the provisions of this act, the Board shall approve as a supervisor for individuals seeking certifications as a certified substance abuse counselor or a certified substance abuse counseling assistant any individual who has been approved by the Board as a registered supervisor prior to July 1, 2001."

The 2001 amendments. — The 2001 amendment by c. 460, in subsection A, in the first paragraph, deleted "certified substance abuse counselor" preceding "clinical psychologist," inserted "certified substance abuse counselor, certified substance abuse counseling assistant," and substituted "NAADAC: the Association for Addiction Professionals" for "National Association of Alcoholism and Drug

Abuse Counselors" near the end of the second paragraph.

§ 8.01-581.15. Limitation on recovery in certain medical malpractice actions.
— In any verdict returned against a health care provider in an action for malpractice where the act or acts of malpractice occurred on or after August 1, 1999, which is tried by a jury or in any judgment entered against a health care provider in such an action which is tried without a jury, the total amount recoverable for any injury to, or death of, a patient shall not exceed $1.5 million. The maximum recovery limit of $1.5 million shall increase on July 1, 2000, and each July 1 thereafter by $50,000 per year; however, the annual increase on July 1, 2007, and the annual increase on July 1, 2008, shall be $75,000 per year. Each annual increase shall apply to the act or acts of malpractice occurring on or after the effective date of the increase. The July 1, 2008, increase shall be the final annual increase.

Where the act or acts of malpractice occurred prior to August 1, 1999, the total amount recoverable for any injury to, or death of, a patient shall not exceed the limitation on recovery set forth in this statute as it was in effect when the act or acts of malpractice occurred.

In interpreting this section, the definitions found in § 8.01-581.1 shall be applicable. (Code 1950, §§ 8-654.8; 1976, c. 611; 1977, c. 617; 1983, c. 496; 1999, c. 711; 2001, c. 211.)

Editor's note. — Acts 2001, c. 211, cl. 2 provides: "That the provisions of this act are declaratory of existing law."

The 2001 amendments. — The 2001 amendment by c. 211 added the next to last paragraph.

Law Review.
For a comment, "Slowing Union Corruption: Reforming the Landrum-Griffin Act to Better Combat Union Embezzlement," see 8 Geo. Mason L. Rev. 527 (2000).

§ 8.01-581.16. Civil immunity for members of or consultants to certain boards or committees.
— Every member of, or health care professional consultant to, any committee, board, group, commission or other entity shall be immune from civil liability for any act, decision, omission, or utterance done or made in performance of his duties while serving as a member of or consultant to such committee, board, group, commission or other entity, with functions primarily to review, evaluate, or make recommendations on (i) the duration of patient stays in health care facilities, (ii) the professional services furnished with respect to the medical, dental, psychological, podiatric, chiropractic, veterinary or optometric necessity for such services, (iii) the purpose of promoting the most efficient use of available health care facilities and services, (iv) the adequacy or quality of professional services, (v) the competency and qualifications for professional staff privileges, or (vi) the reasonableness or appropriateness of charges made by or on behalf of health care facilities; provided that such entity has been established pursuant to federal or state law or regulation, or pursuant to Joint Commission on Accreditation of Hospitals requirements, or established and duly constituted by one or more public or licensed private hospitals, community services boards, or behavioral health authorities, or with a governmental agency and provided further that such act, decision, omission, or utterance is not done or made in bad faith or with malicious intent. (Code 1950, § 8-654.9; 1976, c. 611; 1977, c. 617; 1981, c. 174; 1987, c. 713; 1989, c. 729; 1993, c. 702; 2001, c. 381.)

The 2001 amendments. — The 2001 amendment by c. 381 inserted "community services boards, or behavioral health authorities" near the end of the section.

§ 8.01-581.17. Privileged communications of certain committees and entities.

— The proceedings, minutes, records, and reports of any (i) medical staff committee, utilization review committee, or other committee as specified in § 8.01-581.16 and (ii) nonprofit entity that provides a centralized credentialing service, together with all communications, both oral and written, originating in or provided to such committees or entities, are privileged communications which may not be disclosed or obtained by legal discovery proceedings unless a circuit court, after a hearing and for good cause arising from extraordinary circumstances being shown, orders the disclosure of such proceedings, minutes, records, reports, or communications. Nothing in this section shall be construed as providing any privilege to hospital, community services board, or behavioral health authority medical records kept with respect to any patient in the ordinary course of business of operating a hospital, community services board, or behavioral health authority nor to any facts or information contained in such records nor shall this section preclude or affect discovery of or production of evidence relating to hospitalization or treatment of any patient in the ordinary course of hospitalization of such patient.

For purposes of this section *"centralized credentialing service"* means (i) gathering information relating to applications for professional staff privileges at any public or licensed private hospital or for participation as a provider in any health maintenance organization, preferred provider organization or any similar organization and (ii) providing such information to those hospitals and organizations that utilize the service. Additionally, for the purposes of this section, accreditation and peer review records of the American College of Radiology and the Medical Society of Virginia are considered privileged communications. (Code 1950, § 8-654.10; 1976, c. 611; 1977, c. 617; 1995, c. 500; 1997, c. 292; 2001, c. 381.)

The 2001 amendments. — The 2001 amendment by c. 381 inserted "community services board, or behavioral health authority" in the first paragraph, in two places.

I. DECISIONS UNDER CURRENT LAW.

Editor's note. — The cases below were decided prior to later amendments to this section.

Privilege applies to all kinds of litigation. — The privilege established by this section applies to all kinds of litigation, not just to medical malpractice actions. HCA Health Servs. of Va., Inc. v. Levin, 260 Va. 215, 530 S.E.2d 417 (2000).

Subject of review may not waive privilege. — The statutory privilege does not belong to the physician who is the subject of peer review and may not be unilaterally waived by the physician. HCA Health Servs. of Va., Inc. v. Levin, 260 Va. 215, 530 S.E.2d 417 (2000).

Extraordinary circumstances not shown. — There is a vast difference between the legal principle of "relevance" and the term "extraordinary circumstances" used in this section. While peer review documents held by a hospital might be relevant to a physician's defamation suit, there is nothing "extraordinary" about the mere need to defend such suit that would justify ordering the disclosure of such documents; the need to establish a defense, which must be made in all civil actions, is the essence of usual and ordinary and is not "extraordinary." HCA Health Servs. of Va., Inc. v. Levin, 260 Va. 215, 530 S.E.2d 417 (2000).

§ 8.01-581.20. Standard of care in proceeding before medical malpractice review panel; expert testimony; determination of standard in action for damages.

Law Review.
For an article, "The Quiet Demise of Deference to Custom: Malpractice Law at the Millenium," see 57 Wash. & Lee L. Rev. 163 (2000).

I. Decisions Under Current Law.
A. General Consideration.

I. DECISIONS UNDER CURRENT LAW.

A. General Consideration.

Most significant element about this section is that expertise, etc.
Where nothing in the record contradicted testimony of defense medical expert, an obstetrician-gynecologist, that the standards applicable to the performance of a pelvic examination by an obstetrician-gynecologist and an emergency room physician are the same; that expert's lack of knowledge regarding certain procedures of emergency medicine might disqualify him from rendering expert testimony as to those procedures, but that lack of knowledge does not preclude him from giving expert testimony on procedures which are common to both emergency medicine and the field of obstetrics-gynecology and are performed according to the same standard of care. Sami v. Varn, 260 Va. 280, 535 S.E.2d 172 (2000).

CHAPTER 22.

Receivers, General and Special.

Article 1.

General Receivers.

§ 8.01-582. Appointment of general receivers; their duties; audit of funds.

Cross references. — As to a blanket surety bond plan for state and local employees, see § 2.2-1840. As to a blanket surety bond plan for moneys under control of court, see § 2.2-1841.

Article 3.

General Provisions for Moneys Under Control of Court.

§ 8.01-600. How money under control of court deposited; record kept; liability of clerk.

Cross references. — As to a blanket surety bond plan for moneys under control of court, see § 2.2-1841.

CHAPTER 23.

Commissioners in Chancery.

§ 8.01-610. Weight to be given commissioner's report.

I. DECISIONS UNDER CURRENT LAW.

Appellate review where chancellor approves commissioner's findings. — A commissioner's findings of fact which have been accepted by the trial court are presumed to be correct when reviewed on appeal and are to be given great weight by the appellate court; the findings will not be reversed on appeal unless plainly wrong. Gilman v. Gilman, 32 Va. App. 104, 526 S.E.2d 763 (2000).

Commissioner's ability to see, hear and evaluate witnesses. — Although the report of a commissioner in chancery does not carry the weight of a jury's verdict, an appellate court must give due regard to the commissioner's

§ 8.01-623 CIVIL REMEDIES AND PROCEDURE § 8.01-670

ability, not shared by the chancellor, to see, hear and evaluate the witnesses at first hand. Gilman v. Gilman, 32 Va. App. 104, 526 S.E.2d 763 (2000).

Applied in Roberts v. Roberts, 260 Va. 660, 536 S.E.2d 714 (2000); Snyder Plaza Props., Inc. v. Adams Outdoor Adver., Inc., 259 Va. 635, 528 S.E.2d 452 (2000).

CHAPTER 24.

INJUNCTIONS.

§ 8.01-623. Injunction against decree subject to bill of review; limitations to bill of review.

I. DECISIONS UNDER CURRENT LAW.

Bill of review available to correct error of law, not fact. — Bill of review was properly granted where error which wife sought to correct was one of law, not judgment in the determination of facts, and underlying divorce decree was facially erroneous and void. Napert v. Napert, No. 1173-99-4 (Ct. of Appeals Feb. 8, 2000).

Applied in Hickson v. Hickson, 34 Va. App. 246, 540 S.E.2d 508 (2001).

CHAPTER 26.

APPEALS TO THE SUPREME COURT.

ARTICLE 2.

When Granted.

§ 8.01-670. In what cases awarded.

I. Decisions Under Current Law.
  B. Appealable Judgments, Orders and Decrees.
    1. In General.

I. DECISIONS UNDER CURRENT LAW.

  B. Appealable Judgments, Orders and Decrees.

    1. In General.

Discovery orders under Uniform Foreign Depositions Act subject to review. — Ordinarily, a trial court's discovery orders are not subject to review on direct appeal because they are not final within the contemplation of this section but an order granting or refusing a motion to quash or issue a protective order, in a proceeding brought in a court of the commonwealth pursuant to the Uniform Foreign Depositions Act, is a final order subject to appellate review. America Online, Inc. v. Anonymous Publicly Traded Co., 261 Va. 350, 542 S.E.2d 377 (2001).

Discovery orders under Uniform foreign depositions act subject to appeal. — Under the Uniform Foreign Depositions Act, an order of the trial court disposing of all discovery issues before it and concluding the entirety of the proceedings in a Virginia court, is a final order subject to appeal under this section. America Online, Inc. v. Anonymous Publicly Traded Co., 261 Va. 350, 542 S.E.2d 377 (2001).

Order changing child's name. — An order in an independent civil action changing a name, including that of child, is a final judgment in a civil case within the meaning of this section and is, therefore, properly appealable to the Supreme Court. Rowland v. Shurbutt, 259 Va. 305, 525 S.E.2d 917 (2000).

Under the severable-interests rule, a final adjudication of a collateral matter that addresses separate and severable interests can be appealed only when the appeal cannot affect the determination of the remaining issues in the case, even if the adjudication is reversed. The order may be appealed either at the time of its entry or when the trial court enters a final order disposing of the remainder of the case. Thompson v. Skate Am., Inc., 261 Va. 121, 540 S.E.2d 123 (2001).

CHAPTER 26.1.

APPEALS TO THE COURT OF APPEALS.

§ 8.01-675.3. Time within which appeal must be taken; notice.

I. DECISIONS UNDER CURRENT LAW.

Applied in Burgan v. Zein, No. 0720-98-4 (Ct. of Appeals May 4, 1999).

CHAPTER 26.2.

APPEALS GENERALLY.

ARTICLE 2.

Errors Insufficient in the Appellate Court.

§ 8.01-678. For what a judgment not to be reversed.

I. DECISIONS UNDER CURRENT LAW.

Curtailment of presentation of defense. — A defendant's conviction was to be reversed where the trial court, sitting as the fact finder, suggested its disposition of the case before the completion of all incidents of trial and improperly proposed to dismiss the charges after a specified period if certain conditions were met and, in reliance upon that proposal, the defendant curtailed or abandoned the opportunity to present witnesses, to testify in his own defense and to make a closing argument. Powell v. Commonwealth, 34 Va. App. 13, 537 S.E.2d 602 (2000).

A fair trial on the merits and substantial justice are not achieved, etc.

If error at trial has affected the verdict, then "a fair trial on the merits and substantial justice" have not been reached. Shaw v. Commonwealth, No. 0357-98-2 (Ct. of Appeals July 20, 1999).

Effect of curative instruction. — Although an error is generally presumed to have been prejudicial unless it plainly appears that it could not have affected the result, if a curative instruction is given to the jury, the usual presumption of prejudice is replaced by a presumption that the jury followed the instruction and disregarded the improper evidence; in such a case, a conviction is not subject to reversal unless the error suggests a manifest probability that it was prejudicial to the defendant. Newton v. Commonwealth, No. 2009-99-3 (Ct. of Appeals Aug. 15, 2000).

Whether an error is harmless, etc.

An error is harmless (1) if other evidence of guilt is so overwhelming and the error so insignificant by comparison that the error could not have affected the verdict or, even if the evidence of the defendant's guilt is not overwhelming, (2) if the evidence admitted in error was merely cumulative of other, undisputed evidence. McLean v. Commonwealth, 32 Va. App. 200, 527 S.E.2d 443 (2000).

Question of whether verdict would have been the same. — A criminal conviction must be reversed unless it plainly appears from the record and the evidence given at the trial that the error did not affect the verdict. An error does not affect a verdict if a reviewing court can conclude, without usurping the jury's fact finding function, that, had the error not occurred, the verdict would have been the same. McLean v. Commonwealth, 32 Va. App. 200, 527 S.E.2d 443 (2000).

Reversal required where evidence erroneously admitted.

Where a jury had to determine whether or not the defendant was guilty of two counts of distribution of cocaine and the trial court improperly permitted the introduction of evidence that the defendant had been convicted of the identical offense within the past six months and also had a total of five drug convictions, there was a manifest probability that the improperly admitted convictions were prejudicial to the defendant; a cautionary instruction could not undo the damage done by the introduction of such evidence. Newton v. Commonwealth, No. 2009-99-3 (Ct. of Appeals Aug. 15, 2000).

Applied in Laidler v. Commonwealth, No. 0161-99-4 (Ct. of Appeals Mar. 28, 2000); Stockdale v. Stockdale, 33 Va. App. 179, 532 S.E.2d 332 (2000); Burns v. Commonwealth, No. 1459-99-4 (Ct. of Appeals May 30, 2000).

Article 3.

Limitations; Hearing and Decision.

§ 8.01-680. When judgment of trial court not to be set aside unless plainly wrong, etc.

I. Decisions Under Current Law.
  A. General Consideration.

I. DECISIONS UNDER CURRENT LAW.

A. General Consideration.

Applied in Medici v. Commonwealth, No. 0527-98-4 (Ct. of Appeals May 25, 1999); Cline v. Cline, No. 0766-98-3 (Ct. of Appeals June 29, 1999); Iverson v. Iverson, No. 0314-99-2 (Ct. of Appeals Apr. 25, 2000); Newton v. Commonwealth, No. 1586-99-1 (Ct. of Appeals May 16, 2000).